The Sporting News

BASEBALL GUIDE

2002 EDITION

Editors

CRAIG CARTER

DAVE SLOAN

EXPLANATION OF STATISTICAL ABBREVIATIONS

A: assists. **AB:** at-bats. **Avg.:** batting average (hits divided by at-bats). **BB:** bases on balls. **Bk.:** balks. **CG:** complete games. **CS:** caught stealing. **E:** errors. **ER:** earned runs. **ERA:** earned-run average (earned runs times nine divided by innings pitched). **G:** games. **GB:** games behind. **GF:** games finished. **GDP:** grounding into double plays. **GS:** games started. **H:** hits. **HB:** hit batsmen. **HP:** hit by pitches. **HR:** home runs. **IBB:** intentional bases on balls. **IP:** innings pitched. **L:** losses. **OBP:** on-base percentage (hits plus bases on balls plus hit by pitches divided by at-bats plus bases on balls plus hit by pitches plus sacrifice flies). **Pct.:** winning percentage. **PO:** putouts. **Pos.:** position. **R:** runs. **RBI:** runs batted in. **SB:** stolen bases. **SF:** sacrifice flies (run-scoring flyouts). **SH:** sacrifice hits (bunts that advance one or more runners but result in the batter being retired at first base or reaching first on an error). **ShO:** shutouts. **Slg.:** slugging percentage (total bases divided by at-bats). **SO:** strikeouts. **Sv.:** saves. **TB:** total bases (hits plus doubles plus two times the number of triples plus three times the number of home runs). **TBF:** total batters faced. **TC:** total chances (putouts plus assists plus errors). **TPA:** total plate appearances (at-bats plus bases on balls plus sacrifice hits plus sacrifice flies plus hit by pitches plus times reaching base on catcher's interference). **W:** wins. **WP:** wild pitches. **2B:** doubles. **3B:** triples.

World Series, A.L. Championship Series, N.L. Championship Series, A.L. Division Series, N.L. Division Series and All-Star Game highlights written by Jared Hoffman, Jeff Paur and David Walton of THE SPORTING NEWS.

Major league statistics compiled by STATS, Inc., Lincolnwood, Ill.

Minor league statistics compiled by SportsTicker Enterprises, L.P., Boston.

ISBN: 0-89204-669-4

10 9 8 7 6 5 4 3 2 1

CONTENTS

ON THE COVER: Ichiro Suzuki. (Both photos by Albert Dickson/THE SPORTING NEWS.)

Spine photo of Randy Johnson by Bob Leverone/THE SPORTING NEWS.

Back photo of the Arizona Diamondbacks by Albert Dickson/THE SPORTING NEWS.

2002 SEASON

Major League Baseball directories

Team by team

MAJOR LEAGUE BASEBALL

Address
245 Park Avenue
New York, NY 10167
Telephone
212-931-7800
FAX
212-949-5654
Website
www.mlb.com
Commissioner of baseball
Allan H. "Bud" Selig
President & chief operating officer
Paul Beeston
Executive v.p., baseball operations
Richard "Sandy" Alderson
Executive v.p., administration
Robert DuPuy
Executive vice president, labor relations and human resources
Robert Manfred
Executive vice president, business
Timothy Brosnan
Sr. vice president, public relations
Rich Levin

Sr. vice president, security and facilities
Kevin Hallinan
Sr. vice president and general counsel
Tom Ostertag
Sr. vice president, licensing
Howard Smith
Sr. vice president, baseball operations
Jimmie Lee Solomon
Sr. v.p. and chief financial officer
Jeffrey White
V.p., club relations and scheduling
Katy Feeney
Vice president, club relations
Phyllis Merhige
Vice president, on field operations
Frank Robinson
Vice president, umpiring
Ralph Nelson
V.p., international baseball operations
Lou Melendez
Vice president, human resources and office services
Wendy Lewis

V.p. & general counsel, labor relations
Frank Coonelly
Vice president & general counsel
Ethan Orlinsky
V.p., accounting and treasurer
Bob Clark
V.p., international business operations
Paul Archey
Vice president, business affairs domestic & international
Chris Tully
Vice president, special events
Marla Miller
Vice president, programming & sales
James Scott
Vice president, executive producer
Dave Gavant
Vice president, productions operations
Pat Power

OTHER ORGANIZATIONS

LABOR RELATIONS COMMITTEE
Address
245 Park Avenue
New York, NY 10167
Telephone
212-931-7401
212-949-5690 (FAX)
Exec. vice president, labor relations and human resources
Robert D. Manfred Jr.
V.p. & general counsel, labor relations
Francis Coonelly
Associate counsels
Derek Jackson
Paul Mifsud
System administration
John Ricco
Deputy general counsel
Jennifer Gefsky

NATIONAL ASSOCIATION OF PROFESSIONAL BASEBALL LEAGUES
Address
P.O. Box A
St. Petersburg, FL 33731
Telephone
727-822-6937
727-821-5819 (FAX)
President
Mike Moore
Vice president/administration
Pat O'Conner
Exec. director of business operations
Misann Ellmaker

General counsel
Scott Poley
Director/licensing
Brian Earle
Director/media relations
Jim Ferguson
Director of baseball operations
Tim Brunswick
Director of marketing
Rod Meadows
Director of business/finance
Eric Krupa
Director of Professional Baseball Umpire Corporation
Mike Fitzpatrick
Director of Professional Baseball Employment Opportunities
Ann Perkins

BASEBALL ASSISTANCE TEAM INC.
Address
245 Park Avenue
New York, NY 10167
Telephone
212-931-7821
Chairman
Ralph Branca
President
Earl Wilson
Vice presidents
Joe Black
Bob Gibson
Ed Stack
Frank Torre
Executive director
James J. Martin

Secretary
Thomas J. Ostertag
Treasurer
Jeffrey White

ASSOCIATION OF PROFESSIONAL BASEBALL PLAYERS OF AMERICA
Address
1820 W. Orangewood Ave., Suite 206
Orange, CA 92868
Telephone
714-935-9993
714-935-0431 (FAX)
President
John J. McHale
Vice presidents
Roland Hemond
Robert Kennedy
Secretary/treasurer
Dick Beverage

NATIONAL BASEBALL HALL OF FAME AND MUSEUM
Address
P.O. Box 590
Cooperstown, NY 13326
Telephone
607-547-7200
607-547-2044 (FAX)
Hall of Fame board of directors chairman
Jane Forbes Clark
President
Dale Petroskey
V.p. of business and administration
Bill Haase

V.p. and chief curator
William T. Spencer Jr.
Curator of collections
Peter P. Clark
Executive director of retail marketing
Barbara Shinn
Controller
Frances L. Althiser
Librarian
James L. Gates
V.p. of communications and education
Jeff Idelson

MAJOR LEAGUE
SCOUTING BUREAU
Address
3500 Porsche Way, Suite 100
Ontario, CA 91764
Telephone
909-980-1881
909-980-7794 (FAX)
Director
Frank Marcos

MAJOR LEAGUE BASEBALL
PLAYERS ASSOCIATION
Address
12 E. 49th St., 24th Floor
New York, NY 10017
Telephone
212-826-0808
212-752-3649 (FAX)
Executive director and general counsel
Donald M. Fehr
Special assistants
Tony Bernazard
Phil Bradley
Steve Rogers
Associate general counsel
Eugene D. Orza
Assistant general counsel
Jeff Fannell
Doyle R. Pryor
Michael Weiner

Counsel
Robert Leneghan
Director of licensing
Judy Heeter
Director of communications
Greg Bouris

MAJOR LEAGUE BASEBALL
PLAYERS ALUMNI ASSOC.
Address
1631 Mesa Ave., Suite B
Colorado Springs, CO 80906
Telephone
719-477-1870
719-477-1875 (FAX)
President
Brooks Robinson
Vice presidents
Bob Boone
George Brett
Mike Hegan
Chuck Hinton
Al Kaline
Carl Erskine
Rusty Staub
Robin Yount
Vice chairman
Fred Valentine

WORLD UMPIRES ASSOCIATION
Address
P.O. Box 760
Cocoa, FL 32923-0760
Telephone
321-637-3471
321-633-7018 (FAX)
President
John Hirschbeck
Vice president
Joe Brinkman
Secretary/treasurer
Tim Welke
Labor counsel
Joel Smith

BASEBALL WRITERS'
ASSOCIATION OF AMERICA
President
Bill Center, San Diego Union-Tribune
Vice president
Paul Hagen, Philadelphia Daily News
Secretary/treasurer
Jack O'Connell, Hartford Courant

ELIAS SPORTS BUREAU
Address
500 Fifth Ave.
New York, NY 10110
Telephone
212-869-1530
212-354-0980 (FAX)
General manager
Seymour Siwoff

SPORTSTICKER ENTERPRISES, L.P.
Address
Harborside Financial Center
800 Plaza Two
Jersey City, NJ 07311
Boston office
Boston Fish Pier
West Building No. 1
Boston, MA 02210
Telephone
201-309-1200
201-860-9742 (FAX)
Boston office
617-951-0070
617-737-9960 (FAX)
General manager
Jim Morganthaler
Director, special projects
Jay Virshbo
Director, minor league operations
Jim Keller

ANAHEIM ANGELS
AMERICAN LEAGUE WEST DIVISION

April

SUN	MON	TUE	WED	THU	FRI	SAT
	1 CLE	2 CLE	3 CLE	4	5 D TEX	6 TEX
7 D TEX	8 SEA	9 SEA	10 SEA	11 SEA	12 OAK	13 OAK
14 D OAK	15	16 TEX	17 TEX	18 D OAK	19 OAK	20 D OAK
21 D OAK	22 SEA	23 SEA	24 SEA	25	26 TOR	27 TOR
28 D TOR	29	30 CLE				

May

SUN	MON	TUE	WED	THU	FRI	SAT
		1 CLE	2 CLE	3 D TOR	4 D TOR	
5 D TOR	6	7 DET	8 DET	9 DET	10 CWS	11 CWS
12 D CWS	13	14 DET	15 DET	16 DET	17 CWS	18 CWS
19 D CWS	20 KC	21 KC	22 KC	23	24 MIN	25 MIN
26 D MIN	27	28 KC	29 KC	30 MIN	31 MIN	

June

SUN	MON	TUE	WED	THU	FRI	SAT
						1 MIN
2 D MIN	3 TEX	4 TEX	5 TEX	6 TEX	7 CIN	8 CIN
9 D CIN	10 PIT	11 PIT	12 PIT	13	14 LA	15 LA
16 D LA	17	18 STL	19 STL	20 D STL	21 MIL	22 MIL
23 D MIL	24 TEX	25 TEX	26 TEX	27 TEX	28 LA	29 LA
30 LA						

July

SUN	MON	TUE	WED	THU	FRI	SAT
	1	2 BAL	3 BAL	4 BAL	5 TB	6 TB
7 D TB	8	9 *	10	11 KC	12 KC	13 KC
14 D KC	15 MIN	16 D MIN	17 OAK	18 OAK	19 SEA	20 SEA
21 SEA	22	23 OAK	24 OAK	25 D OAK	26 SEA	27 D SEA
28 D SEA	29 BOS	30 BOS	31 BOS			

August

SUN	MON	TUE	WED	THU	FRI	SAT
				1 NYY	2 NYY	3 NYY
4 NYY	5	6 CWS	7 CWS	8 CWS	9 TOR	10 D TOR
11 D TOR	12 DET	13 DET	14 DET	15	16 CLE	17 CLE
18 D CLE	19	20 NYY	21 NYY	22 NYY	23 BOS	24 BOS
25 D BOS	26 BOS	27 TB	28 TB	29 TB	30 BAL	31 BAL

September

SUN	MON	TUE	WED	THU	FRI	SAT
1 BAL	2	3 TB	4 TB	5 TB	6 BAL	7 BAL
8 D BAL	9 OAK	10 OAK	11 OAK	12 OAK	13 TEX	14 TEX
15 TEX	16 OAK	17 OAK	18 OAK	19 D OAK	20 SEA	21 SEA
22 D SEA	23	24 TEX	25 TEX	26 TEX	27 SEA	28 D SEA
29 D SEA	30					

2002 SEASON
CLUB DIRECTORY

Owner
The Walt Disney Company
Chairman and CEO, The Walt Disney Co.
Michael Eisner
President
To be announced
Vice president and general manager
Bill Stoneman
Vice president of finance/administration
Andy Roundtree
V.p., advertising sales and broadcasting
John Covarrubias
V.p., sales, marketing and operations
Kevin Uhlich
Vice president, communications
Tim Mead
V.p. & asst. g.m., bus. and legal affairs
Rick Schlesinger
Assistant general manager
Ken Forsch
Special assistant to general manager
Preston Gomez
Director, scouting
Donny Rowland
Director, player development
Tony Reagins
Manager, baseball operations
Abe Flores
Equipment manager
Ken Higdon
Visiting clubhouse manager
Brian Harkins
Senior video coordinator
Diego Lopez
Manager, baseball information
Larry Babcock
Manager, media services
Nancy Mazmanian
Manager, publications
Doug Ward
Manager, community relations
Matt Bennett

Media services/travel coordinator
Tom Taylor
Director, marketing
Robert Alvarado
Manager, ticket operations
Sheila Brazelton
Medical director
Dr. Lewis Yocum
Team physician
Dr. Craig Milhouse
Head athletic trainer
Ned Bergert
International supervisor
Clay Daniel
Eastern supervisor
Marc Russo
Western supervisor
Tom Davis
Midwestern supervisor
Ron Marigny
National cross-checkers
Guy Mader, Hank Sargent
Major league scouts
Jay Hankins, Jon Niederer, Rich Schlenker, Moose Stubing, Dale Sutherland, Gary Sutherland, John Van Ornum
Scouts
George Biron, Todd Blyleven, Brian Bridges, John Burden, Tom Burns, Arnold Cochrane, Tim Corcoran, Jeff Crane, David Crowson, Bobby Dejardin, Kevin Ham, Tom Kotchman, Dan Lynch, Chris McAlpin, Jeff Scholzen, Mike Silvestri, Jack Uhey
International scouts
Amador Arias, Luis Cuevas, Juan DeSoto, Felipe Gutierrez, Tak Kawamoto, Alex Messier, Leo Perez, Carlos Porte, Dennys Suarez, Takanori Takeuchi, Ramon Valenzuela, Grant Weir

MINOR LEAGUE AFFILIATES

Class	Team	League	Manager
AAA	Salt Lake	Pacific Coast	Mike Brumley
AA	Arkansas	Texas	Doug Sisson
A	Cedar Rapids	Midwest	Todd Claus
A	Rancho Cucamonga	California	Bobby Meacham
Rookie	Mesa Angels	Arizona	Brian Harper
Rookie	Provo	Pioneer	Tom Kotchman

BROADCAST INFORMATION

Radio: KLAC-AM (570).
TV: KCAL-TV (Channel 9).
Cable TV: Fox Sports West.

SPRING TRAINING

Ballpark (city): Tempe Diablo Stadium (Tempe, Ariz.).
Ticket information: 602-254-3300, 800-326-0331.

Follow the Angels all season at: www.sportingnews.com/baseball/teams/angels/

SPRING TRAINING ROSTER

Manager—Mike Scioscia (14).
Coaches—Bud Black (24), Alfredo Griffin (4), Mickey Hatcher (7), Joe Madden (70), Bobby Ramos (13), Ron Roenicke (12).

No.	PITCHERS	B/T	Ht./Wt.	Born	2001 clubs
17	Appier, Kevin	R/R	6-2/200	12-6-67	New York N.L.
61	Callaway, Mickey	R/R	6-2/196	5-13-75	Durham, Tampa Bay
27	Cook, Dennis	L/L	6-3/190	10-4-62	New York N.L., Philadelphia, Scranton/Wilkes-Barre
	Donnelly, Brendan	R/R	6-3/200	7-4-71	Arkansas, Salt Lake
68	Green, Steve	R/R	6-2/195	1-26-78	Anaheim, Salt Lake
	Lackey, John	R/R	6-6/205	10-23-78	Salt Lake, Arkansas
43	Levine, Al	R/R	6-3/198	5-22-68	Anaheim
33	Lukasiewicz, Mark	L/L	6-7/240	3-8-73	Salt Lake, Anaheim
66	Miadich, Bart	R/R	6-4/205	2-3-76	Salt Lake, Anaheim
59	Nina, Elvin	R/R	6-0/185	11-25-75	Salt Lake
36	Ortiz, Ramon	R/R	6-0/175	3-23-76	Anaheim
40	Percival, Troy	R/R	6-3/236	8-9-69	Anaheim
58	Pote, Lou	R/R	6-3/208	8-27-71	Anaheim
60	Schoeneweis, Scott	L/L	6-0/186	10-2-73	Anaheim
30	Sele, Aaron	R/R	6-5/215	6-25-70	Seattle
62	Shields, Scot	R/R	6-1/175	7-22-75	Anaheim
54	Turnbow, Derrick	R/R	6-3/180	1-25-78	Arkansas
56	Washburn, Jarrod	L/L	6-1/198	8-13-74	Salt Lake, Anaheim
57	Weber, Ben	R/R	6-4/180	11-17-69	Anaheim
32	Wise, Matt	R/R	6-4/190	11-18-75	Anaheim, Salt Lake

No.	CATCHERS	B/T	Ht./Wt.	Born	2001 clubs
6	Fabregas, Jorge	L/R	6-3/215	3-13-70	Anaheim
1	Molina, Bengie	R/R	5-11/207	7-20-74	Anaheim, Rancho Cucamonga, Salt Lake
19	Molina, Jose	R/R	6-1/215	6-3-75	Salt Lake, Anaheim
44	Wooten, Shawn	R/R	5-10/205	7-24-72	Anaheim

No.	INFIELDERS	B/T	Ht./Wt.	Born	2001 clubs
	Amezaga, Alfredo	R/R	5-10/165	1-16-78	Arkansas, Salt Lake
22	Eckstein, David	R/R	5-8/165	1-20-75	Toronto
	Fullmer, Brad	L/R	6-0/215	1-17-75	Toronto
10	Gil, Benji	R/R	6-2/190	10-6-72	Anaheim
25	Glaus, Troy	R/R	6-5/229	8-3-76	Anaheim
2	Kennedy, Adam	L/R	6-1/180	1-10-76	Rancho Cucamonga, Anaheim
11	Nieves, Jose	R/R	6-0/180	6-16-75	Anaheim, Salt Lake
23	Spiezio, Scott	B/R	6-2/225	9-21-72	Anaheim

No.	OUTFIELDERS	B/T	Ht./Wt.	Born	2001 clubs
16	Anderson, Garret	L/L	6-3/220	6-30-72	Anaheim
55	DaVanon, Jeff	B/R	6-0/185	12-8-73	Salt Lake, Anaheim
17	Erstad, Darin	L/L	6-2/212	6-4-74	Anaheim
48	Guzman, Elpidio	L/L	6-0/165	2-24-79	Arkansas
53	Haynes, Nathan	L/L	5-9/170	9-7-79	Arkansas
3	Palmeiro, Orlando	L/L	5-11/175	1-19-69	Anaheim
15	Salmon, Tim	R/R	6-3/231	8-24-68	Anaheim, Rancho Cucamonga

BALLPARK INFORMATION

Ballpark (capacity, surface)
Edison International Field of Anaheim (45,050, grass)
Address
2000 Gene Autry Way
Anaheim, CA 92806
Official website
www.angelsbaseball.com
Business phone
714-940-2000
Ticket information
714-634-2000
Ticket prices
$26 (terrace MVP), $24 (club loge, field box)
$21 (terrace box), $16 (lower view MVP)
$15 (lower view box), $10 (view)
$8 (RF pavilion-adult)
$7 (LF pavilion-adult)
$6 (RF pavilion-child)
$4 (LF pavilion-child)
Field dimensions (from home plate)
To left field at foul line, 330 feet
To center field, 400 feet
To right field at foul line, 330 feet
First game played
April 19, 1966 (White Sox 3, Angels 1)

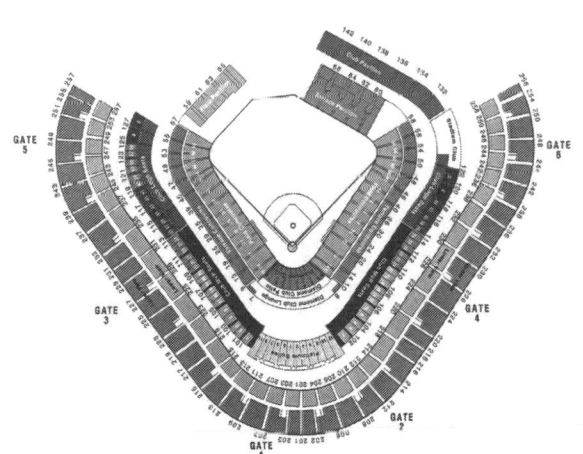

2001 REVIEW
DAY BY DAY

Date	Opp.	Res.	Score	(inn.*)	Hits	Opp. hits	Winning pitcher	Losing pitcher	Save	Record	Pos.	GB
4-3	At Tex.	L	2-3		9	8	Rogers	Schoeneweis	Crabtree	0-1	4th	0.5
4-4	At Tex.	L	3-7		8	8	Oliver	Rapp		0-2	4th	1.5
4-5	At Tex.	W	10-3		13	5	Ortiz	Glynn		1-2	T3rd	1.0
4-6	At Oak.	W	5-4		10	9	Wise	Mulder	Percival	2-2	2nd	1.0
4-7	At Oak.	L	2-4		3	5	Hudson	Levine	Isringhausen	2-3	T2nd	2.0
4-8	At Oak.	W	6-4		12	6	Schoeneweis	Zito	Percival	3-3	2nd	1.0
4-10	Tex.	L	5-7		15	8	Oliver	Rapp	Crabtree	3-4	3rd	2.0
4-11	Tex.	W	7-2		12	7	Ortiz	Glynn		4-4	2nd	2.0
4-12	Tex.	W	13-3		12	11	Pote	Helling		5-4	2nd	2.0
4-13	Sea.	W	4-3		8	10	Hasegawa	Sasaki		6-4	2nd	1.0
4-14	Sea.	L	1-2		2	4	Garcia	Valdes	Sasaki	6-5	2nd	2.0
4-15	Sea.	L	5-7		7	11	Paniagua	Hasegawa	Nelson	6-6	3rd	3.0
4-16	Oak.	L	3-6		6	14	Mulder	Washburn	Isringhausen	6-7	3rd	4.0
4-17	Oak.	L	1-5		6	8	Hudson	Ortiz		6-8	3rd	5.0
4-18	Oak.	W	3-2		8	7	Percival	Mecir		7-8	3rd	4.0
4-19	At Sea.	L	2-3		6	9	Garcia	Valdes	Sasaki	7-9	3rd	5.0
4-20	At Sea.	L	1-4		6	6	Halama	Rapp	Sasaki	7-10	3rd	6.0
4-21	At Sea.	L	2-5		7	8	Moyer	Washburn	Nelson	7-11	3rd	7.0
4-22	At Sea.	L	0-5		6	11	Sele	Ortiz		7-12	3rd	8.0
4-24	At Cle.	W	7-2		9	10	Schoeneweis	Colon		8-12	3rd	8.0
4-25	At Cle.	W	3-1		5	10	Valdes	Sabathia	Percival	9-12	3rd	8.0
4-26	At Cle.	L	5-6		6	9	Shuey	Hasegawa	Wickman	9-13	3rd	9.0
4-27	At Tor.	L	4-12		11	15	Loaiza	Washburn		9-14	3rd	10.0
4-28	At Tor.	W	4-1		7	6	Ortiz	Michalak	Percival	10-14	3rd	10.0
4-29	At Tor.	L	0-2		9	6	Parris	Schoeneweis	Koch	10-15	3rd	10.0
5-1	Chi.	W	6-4		8	7	Rapp	D. Wells	Percival	11-15	T2nd	9.0
5-2	Chi.	W	12-5		16	8	Washburn	Garland		12-15	2nd	9.0
5-3	Chi.	W	3-1		8	6	Valdes	Baldwin	Percival	13-15	2nd	9.0
5-4	Det.	W	7-5		13	10	Weber	Murray	Percival	14-15	2nd	8.0
5-5	Det.	L	2-11		8	15	Weaver	Ortiz		14-16	2nd	9.0
5-6	Det.	W	3-2	(10)	7	6	Levine	Patterson		15-16	2nd	8.0
5-8	At Chi.	L	0-2		9	3	Baldwin	Washburn		15-17	2nd	8.0
5-9	At Chi.	L	5-6		10	12	Howry	Levine		15-18	2nd	9.0
5-10	At Chi.	W	7-6	(10)	12	11	Percival	Foulke		16-18	2nd	9.0
5-11	At Det.	L	6-7	(11)	16	13	Jones	Lukasiewicz		16-19	2nd	10.0
5-12	At Det.	L	1-4		3	8	Anderson	Hasegawa		16-20	2nd	11.0
5-13	At Det.	W	14-2		16	7	Washburn	Holt		17-20	2nd	11.0
5-15	Tor.	L	3-9		7	15	Michalak	Valdes		17-21	2nd	12.0
5-16	Tor.	W	3-1		8	7	Schoeneweis	Parris	Percival	18-21	2nd	12.0
5-17	Tor.	W	4-2		10	4	Hasegawa	Escobar	Percival	19-21	2nd	12.0
5-18	Cle.	L	2-7		6	9	Burba	Rapp		19-22	T2nd	12.0
5-19	Cle.	L	3-4	(10)	11	12	Shuey	Percival	Wickman	19-23	3rd	12.0
5-20	Cle.	W	9-6		14	10	Levine	Rodriguez	Percival	20-23	3rd	12.0
5-23	At Bal.	L	5-12		10	15	Roberts	Schoeneweis		20-24	3rd	12.5
5-24	At Bal.	L	4-6		9	10	Johnson	Ortiz	Ryan	20-25	3rd	13.0
5-25	At T.B.	W	6-4		11	13	Weber	Lopez	Percival	21-25	3rd	13.0
5-26	At T.B.	W	10-4		12	6	Washburn	Wilson		22-25	3rd	13.0
5-27	At T.B.	L	3-4	(10)	8	7	Yan	Levine		22-26	3rd	14.0
5-28	At T.B.	W	3-1		8	5	Schoeneweis	Meacham	Percival	23-26	3rd	14.0
5-29	Min.	L	5-6	(11)	13	9	Cressend	Levine	Carrasco	23-27	3rd	15.0
5-30	Min.	L	0-3		5	7	Mays	Rapp		23-28	3rd	16.0
5-31	Min.	W	5-4	(12)	11	14	Weber	Carrasco		24-28	3rd	16.0
6-1	K.C.	W	7-1		10	6	Valdes	Suppan		25-28	3rd	16.0
6-2	K.C.	W	3-2		5	8	Schoeneweis	Durbin	Percival	26-28	T2nd	16.0
6-3	K.C.	W	7-2		10	7	Ortiz	Suzuki		27-28	T2nd	16.0
6-5	Oak.	W	7-3		11	6	Washburn	Mulder		28-28	2nd	16.5
6-6	Oak.	L	1-4		5	11	Hudson	Rapp	Isringhausen	28-29	T2nd	17.5
6-7	Oak.	W	6-4		7	6	Schoeneweis	Zito	Percival	29-29	2nd	17.0
6-8	At L.A.	W	1-0		6	4	Valdes	Carrara	Percival	30-29	2nd	17.0
6-9	At L.A.	L	1-2		7	9	Shaw	Weber		30-30	2nd	17.0
6-10	At L.A.	W	6-5	(10)	10	12	Levine	Gagne	Percival	31-30	2nd	17.0
6-12	At S.F	L	2-3		10	9	Rueter	Rapp	Nen	31-31	T2nd	18.0
6-13	At S.F	L	0-1		5	6	Ortiz	Schoeneweis	Nen	31-32	3rd	18.5
6-14	At S.F	L	4-10		11	11	Gardner	Valdes		31-33	3rd	19.0
6-15	L.A.	L	2-6		6	17	Park	Ortiz	Fetters	31-34	3rd	20.0
6-16	L.A.	W	6-5		12	7	Percival	Herges		32-34	T2nd	20.0
6-17	L.A.	W	6-4		12	6	Levine	Shaw		33-34	2nd	19.0
6-19	At Tex.	L	5-7		10	11	Moreno	Schoeneweis	Zimmerman	33-35	2nd	19.5
6-20	At Tex.	W	4-3		13	11	Ortiz	Rogers	Percival	34-35	2nd	18.5
6-21	At Tex.	L	3-4		8	7	Helling	Wise	Zimmerman	34-36	2nd	19.5
6-22	At Sea.	W	8-1		10	5	Washburn	Sele		35-36	2nd	18.5
6-23	At Sea.	W	2-1		2	6	Rapp	Moyer	Percival	36-36	2nd	17.5
6-24	At Sea.	L	3-7		8	9	Abbott	Schoeneweis	Sasaki	36-37	2nd	18.5
6-25	Tex.	W	11-7		16	11	Ortiz	Rogers		37-37	2nd	18.0

Date	Opp.	Res.	Score	(inn.*)	Hits	Opp. hits	Winning pitcher	Losing pitcher	Save	Record	Pos.	GB
6-26	Tex.	L	1-8	(11)	8	10	Zimmerman	Lukasiewicz		37-38	2nd	19.0
6-27	Tex.	W	4-2		7	8	Washburn	Davis	Percival	38-38	2nd	18.0
6-28	Tex.	L	3-6		6	12	Oliver	Rapp	Zimmerman	38-39	2nd	18.0
6-29	Sea.	L	5-9		9	12	Moyer	Schoeneweis		38-40	2nd	19.0
6-30	Sea.	L	3-5		11	10	Stark	Ortiz	Sasaki	38-41	T2nd	20.0
7-1	Sea.	L	0-5		8	7	Garcia	Wise		38-42	T2nd	21.0
7-2	At Oak.	L	0-1	(12)	6	9	Tam	Hasegawa		38-43	3rd	22.0
7-3	At Oak.	L	2-5		4	5	Zito	Rapp	Isringhausen	38-44	3rd	23.0
7-4	At Oak.	L	0-2		5	9	Lidle	Schoeneweis	Mecir	38-45	3rd	23.0
7-5	At Oak.	W	5-2		9	5	Valdes	Heredia	Percival	39-45	3rd	22.0
7-6	At Col.	W	6-5		13	9	Ortiz	Hampton	Percival	40-45	3rd	22.0
7-7	At Col.	W	10-3		16	7	Washburn	Suzuki		41-45	3rd	21.0
7-8	At Col.	W	11-3		12	5	Rapp	Chacon	Pote	42-45	3rd	21.0
7-12	Ari.	W	4-1		4	4	Schoeneweis	Anderson	Percival	43-45	3rd	21.0
7-13	Ari.	L	2-6		9	10	Schilling	Valdes		43-46	3rd	21.0
7-14	Ari.	L	5-7		9	15	Prinz	Percival	Kim	43-47	3rd	22.0
7-15	S.D.	L	1-5		7	8	Lawrence	Ortiz		43-48	3rd	23.0
7-16	S.D.	W	7-5		15	10	Weber	Tollberg	Percival	44-48	3rd	22.0
7-17	S.D.	W	8-7		12	10	Levine	Davey	Percival	45-48	3rd	22.0
7-18	At T.B.	W	2-1		11	4	Valdes	Kennedy	Percival	46-48	3rd	22.0
7-19	At T.B.	W	2-1		9	9	Washburn	Wallace	Percival	47-48	3rd	21.0
7-21	At Bal.	W	6-5	(10)	13	9	Hasegawa	Mills		48-48	3rd	21.5
7-22§	At Bal.	W	9-4		11	11	Weber	Roberts	Pote	49-48		
7-22∞	At Bal.	L	1-5		6	9	Johnson	Borland	Groom	49-49	3rd	22.0
7-23	At Bal.	W	9-4		11	14	Valdes	Mercedes		50-49	3rd	22.0
7-24	T.B.	W	9-6		11	11	Washburn	Kennedy	Levine	51-49	3rd	21.0
7-25	T.B.	L	1-3		6	8	Wilson	Wise	Yan	51-50	3rd	21.0
7-26	T.B.	W	5-3		7	6	Ortiz	Rupe	Percival	52-50	3rd	21.0
7-27	Bal.	L	3-4	(10)	6	10	Trombley	Levine	Groom	52-51	3rd	22.0
7-28	Bal.	W	6-4		12	10	Weber	Kohlmeier	Percival	53-51	3rd	22.0
7-29	Bal.	L	0-1		7	5	Mercedes	Valdes	Groom	53-52	3rd	23.0
7-31	At Bos.	W	4-3		6	8	Ortiz	Garces	Percival	54-52	3rd	22.0
8-1	At Bos.	W	4-2		9	5	Schoeneweis	Nomo	Levine	55-52	3rd	22.0
8-2	At Bos.	W	13-4		17	9	Rapp	Saberhagen	Levine	56-52	3rd	22.0
8-3	At N.Y.	L	2-4		7	9	Pettitte	Washburn	Rivera	56-53	3rd	23.0
8-4	At N.Y.	L	4-5		8	6	Rivera	Levine		56-54	3rd	24.0
8-6	At N.Y.	W	4-3		9	11	Ortiz	Mendoza	Percival	57-54	3rd	23.0
8-6	At N.Y.	W	3-1		9	5	Pote	Hitchcock	Percival	58-54	3rd	23.0
8-7	Chi.	W	9-3		15	6	Rapp	K. Wells		59-54	3rd	23.0
8-8	Chi.	L	1-15		4	19	Buehrle	Washburn		59-55	3rd	24.0
8-9	Chi.	W	3-2		7	5	Valdes	Lowe	Percival	60-55	3rd	23.0
8-10	Tor.	W	8-7		11	12	Schoeneweis	Lyon	Percival	61-55	3rd	22.0
8-11	Tor.	L	6-7	(10)	14	17	Plesac	Levine	Koch	61-56	3rd	23.0
8-12	Tor.	W	6-5		11	10	Levine	Plesac	Percival	62-56	3rd	23.0
8-14	At Det.	W	7-1		10	6	Washburn	Cornejo		63-56	3rd	23.0
8-15	At Det.	L	1-5		7	14	Perisho	Holtz		63-57	3rd	24.0
8-16	At Det.	W	4-2		11	6	Schoeneweis	Weaver	Percival	64-57	3rd	23.0
8-17	At Cle.	W	7-2		12	6	Ortiz	Nagy		65-57	3rd	22.0
8-18	At Cle.	L	2-4		3	6	Sabathia	Rapp	Wickman	65-58	3rd	23.0
8-19	At Cle.	W	4-1		7	5	Washburn	Colon	Percival	66-58	3rd	23.0
8-20	Bos.	L	1-6		7	9	Castillo	Valdes		66-59	3rd	23.0
8-21	Bos.	L	5-8		9	10	Cone	Schoeneweis	Urbina	66-60	3rd	24.0
8-22	Bos.	W	4-2		11	6	Levine	Wakefield	Percival	67-60	3rd	24.0
8-23	Bos.	L	6-7		13	10	Garces	Weber	Urbina	67-61	3rd	25.0
8-24	N.Y.	L	6-2		13	12	Hasegawa	Pettitte		68-61	3rd	25.0
8-25	N.Y.	L	5-7		9	9	Clemens	Valdes	Rivera	68-62	3rd	26.0
8-26	N.Y.	W	7-6	(10)	10	9	Percival	Stanton		69-62	3rd	25.0
8-28	At K.C.	L	4-10		7	12	George	Ortiz		69-63	3rd	25.0
8-29	At K.C.	L	3-6		7	9	Suppan	Rapp	Hernandez	69-64	3rd	26.0
8-30	At K.C.	L	1-2		7	8	Grimsley	Levine		69-65	3rd	27.0
8-31	At Min.	L	1-4		8	8	Radke	Valdes	Jones	69-66	3rd	27.0
9-1	At Min.	W	11-9		18	14	Levine	Hawkins	Percival	70-66	3rd	27.0
9-2	At Min.	L	4-5		7	6	Guardado	Levine		70-67	3rd	28.0
9-4	K.C.	L	1-4		3	9	Suppan	Washburn		70-68	3rd	28.5
9-5	K.C.	W	4-1		9	6	Valdes	Durbin	Percival	71-68	3rd	28.5
9-6	K.C.	W	7-6	(10)	13	11	Holtz	Hernandez		72-68	3rd	28.0
9-7	Min.	W	7-3		10	5	Ortiz	Lohse		73-68	3rd	28.0
9-8	Min.	L	4-6		13	10	Reed	Rapp	Guardado	73-69	3rd	29.0
9-9	Min.	L	0-3		4	7	Milton	Washburn	Wells	73-70	3rd	30.0
9-10	Sea.	L	1-5		6	13	Garcia	Valdes		73-71	3rd	31.0
9-18	At Sea.	L	0-4		3	10	Garcia	Ortiz		73-72	3rd	32.0
9-19	At Sea.	L	0-5		5	7	Moyer	Schoeneweis		73-73	3rd	33.0
9-20	At Sea.	W	6-3		12	6	Hasegawa	Halama	Percival	74-73	3rd	32.0
9-21	At Tex.	L	8-9		11	15	Bell	Valdes	Zimmerman	74-74	3rd	32.0
9-22	At Tex.	L	4-5		9	8	Mahomes	Holtz		74-75	3rd	32.0
9-23	At Tex.	L	2-5		10	10	Helling	Ortiz	Zimmerman	74-76	3rd	32.0
9-25	At Oak.	L	3-9		11	11	Hudson	Hasegawa		74-77	3rd	33.5
9-26	At Oak.	L	1-3		4	6	Zito	Washburn	Isringhausen	74-78	3rd	34.5

– 11 –

Date	Opp.	Res.	Score	(inn.*)	Hits	Opp. hits	Winning pitcher	Losing pitcher	Save	Record	Pos.	GB
9-27	At Oak.	L	2-6		5	8	Lidle	Wise		74-79	3rd	35.0
9-28	Tex.	L	2-11		8	15	Myette	Valdes		74-80	3rd	36.0
9-29	Tex.	W	13-2		13	9	Ortiz	Helling		75-80	3rd	35.0
9-30	Tex.	L	6-8		10	13	Davis	Hasegawa	Zimmerman	75-81	3rd	36.0
10-2	Sea.	L	5-14		6	21	Abbott	Washburn		75-82	3rd	37.0
10-3	Sea.	L	3-4		8	13	Charlton	Levine	Sasaki	75-83	3rd	38.0
10-4	Oak.	L	1-5		3	9	Mulder	Valdes		75-84	3rd	39.0
10-5	Oak.	L	2-6		9	11	Hudson	Ortiz		75-85	3rd	40.0
10-6	Oak.	L	3-6		6	11	Magnante	Schoeneweis	Isringhausen	75-86	3rd	41.0
10-7	Oak.	L	2-6		7	7	Zito	Cooper		75-87	3rd	41.0

Monthly records: April (10-15), May (14-13), June (14-13), July (16-11), August (15-14), September (6-15), October (0-6).
*Innings, if other than nine. §Day separate admission. ∞Night separate admission.

HIGHLIGHTS

High point: On August 19, the Angels beat the Indians at Jacobs Field in Cleveland, 4-1, behind the pitching of starter Jarrod Washburn. It completed a road trip in which the Angels won four of six against the Tigers and Indians, and marked their 23rd victory in 33 games.
Low point: The Angels hit rock bottom at the end of the season, finishing the year with seven consecutive losses and 19 losses in their final 21 games. Of those 19 losses, 17 came against A.L. West foes.
Turning point: After a come-from-behind victory over the Yankees on August 26, the Angels were five games behind wild-card leader Oakland and embarked on a six-game trip to Kansas City and Minnesota. But the Angels were swept by the Royals and lost two of three to the Twins.
Most valuable player: Garret Anderson was the club's only consistent player. He hit .289 with 28 homers. His 194 hits and 123 RBIs were career-bests. Anderson never went more than two consecutive games without a hit.
Most valuable pitcher: Troy Percival was about as close to perfect as is possible for a closer. He saved 39 games in 42 opportunities. He gave up only 18 walks and 39 hits in 57 2/3 innings. He did not allow a run in 24 of his first 25 appearances.
Most improved player: IF Benji Gil was a .222 career hitter going into the season, but hit .296 for the season, which was second best on the team and best among those who played in at least 100 games.
Most pleasant surprise: Although a natural second baseman, David Eckstein won the starting job at short. He hit .285 and his .356 on-base percentage was second-best on the team. He struck out once every 11.1 at-bats, second-best in the A.L. to Seattle's Ichiro Suzuki.
Key injuries: Mo Vaughn missed the entire season after he was found to have a ruptured biceps tendon in his left arm in January and needed surgery. ... Gary DiSarcina was expected back in 2001 fol-

lowing shoulder surgery, but reinjured the shoulder during spring training and missed the entire season.
Notable: The Angels were shut out 12 times, the most since they were blanked 15 times in 1992. ... The Angels were 66-0 when leading after eight innings. ... The Angels used 15 players as their designated hitter, who combined to hit .212 with eight homers and 56 RBIs.
—JOE HAAKENSON

RECORDS

2001 regular-season record: 75-87 (3rd in A.L. West); 39-42 at home; 36-45 on road; 24-17 vs. A.L. East; 24-21 vs. A.L. Central; 17-41 vs. A.L. West; 10-8 vs. N.L.; 22-27 vs. lefthanded starters; 53-60 vs. righthanded starters; 68-82 on grass; 7-5 on turf; 20-24 in daytime; 55-63 at night; 24-24 in one-run games; 7-8 in extra-inning games; 0-0-0 in double-headers.
Team record past five years: 396-414 (.489, ranks 9th in league in that span).

TEAM LEADERS

Batting average: Garret Anderson (.289).
At-bats: Garret Anderson (672).
Runs: Troy Glaus (100).
Hits: Garret Anderson (194).
Total Bases: Garret Anderson (321).
Doubles: Garret Anderson (39).
Triples: Benji Gil, Scott Spiezio (4).
Home runs: Troy Glaus (41).
Runs batted in: Garret Anderson (123).
Stolen bases: David Eckstein (29).
Slugging percentage: Troy Glaus (.531).
On-base percentage: Troy Glaus (.367).
Wins: Ramon Ortiz (13).
Earned-run average: Jarrod Washburn (3.77).
Complete games: Ramon Ortiz (2).
Shutouts: None.
Saves: Troy Percival (39).
Innings pitched: Ramon Ortiz (208.2).
Strikeouts: Ramon Ortiz (135).

GAMES BY POSITION

Catcher: Ben Molina 94, Jorge Fabregas 53, Shawn Wooten 25, Jose Molina 15, Jamie Burke 8.
First base: Scott Spiezio 105, Wally Joyner 39, Shawn Wooten 21, Benji Gil 18, Larry Barnes 16, Darin Erstad 12, Jose Fernandez 2, Jose Nieves 1, Jamie Burke 1.
Second base: Adam Kennedy 131, Benji Gil 21, David Eckstein 14, Jose Nieves 11.
Third base: Troy Glaus 159, Scott Spiezio 10, Jose Nieves 2, Jose Fernandez 2, Shawn Wooten 1.
Shortstop: David Eckstein 126, Benji Gil 44, Jose Nieves 10, Troy Glaus 2.
Outfield: Garret Anderson 149, Darin Erstad 146, Tim Salmon 125, Orlando Palmeiro 59, Jeff DaVanon 29, Scott Spiezio 18, Benji Gil 1, Larry Barnes 1.
Designated hitter: Orlando Palmeiro 30, Shawn Wooten 27, Scott Spiezio 20, Glenallen Hill 16, Benji Gil 14, David Eckstein 14, Tim Salmon 12, Garret Anderson 12, Wally Joyner 9, Jose Fernandez 7, Jeff DaVanon 6, Adam Kennedy 5, Darin Erstad 4, Jose Nieves 4, Troy Glaus 2, Ben Molina 1, Jamie Burke 1.

TOP DRAFT CHOICES

1a. **Casey Kotchman,** 1B, Seminole (Fla.) H.S.
1b. **Jeff Mathis,** C, Marianna (Fla.) H.S.
2. **Dallas McPherson,** 3B, The Citadel.
3a. **Steven Shell,** RHP, El Reno (Okla.) H.S.
3b. **Jacob Woods,** LHP, Bakersfield (Calif.) J.C.
4. **Mike Nickoli,** RHP, Birmingham Southern (Fla.) College.
5. **Brad Pinkerton,** LHP, Elon College
6. **Quan Cosby,** OF, Mart (Tex.) H.S.
7. **Rich Hill,** LHP, Univ. of Michigan.
8. **Justin Turner,** 3B, Warner Southern (Fla.) College.
9. **Devin Ivany,** C, Cardinal Gibbons H.S., Fort Lauderdale, Fla.
10. **Matt Brown,** 3B, Coeur d'Alene (Ida.) H.S.

Baltimore Orioles

2002 SEASON

Orioles schedule
Home games shaded
D—Day game (games starting before 5 p.m.)
*All-Star Game at Milwaukee
Subject to changes

April
SUN	MON	TUE	WED	THU	FRI	SAT
	1 D NYY	2	3 NYY	4 NYY	5 D CWS	6 D BOS
7 D BOS	8	9 TB	10 TB	11 TB	12 D CWS	13 D CWS
14 D CWS	15 D CWS	16 NYY	17 NYY	18 NYY	19 TB	20 TB
21 D TB	22	23 BOS	24 BOS	25 D BOS	26 KC	27 KC
28 D KC	29 BOS	30 BOS				

May
SUN	MON	TUE	WED	THU	FRI	SAT
		1 BOS	2 KC	3 KC	4 D KC	
5 D KC	6 CLE	7 CLE	8 CLE	9	10 TB	11 TB
12 D TB	13	14 CLE	15 CLE	16 CLE	17 TB	18 TB
19 TB	20	21 OAK	22 D OAK	23 D OAK	24 SEA	25 SEA
26 D SEA	27	28 OAK	29 OAK	30 SEA	31 SEA	

June
SUN	MON	TUE	WED	THU	FRI	SAT
						1 SEA
2 SEA	3 NYY	4 NYY	5 NYY	6 NYY	7 LA	8 LA
9 LA	10 SD	11 SD	12 D SD	13	14 PHI	15 PHI
16 PHI	17	18 ARI	19 ARI	20 D ARI	21 SF	22 D SF
23 SF	24	25 NYY	26 NYY	27 NYY	28 PHI	29 PHI
30 D PHI						

July
SUN	MON	TUE	WED	THU	FRI	SAT
	1	2 ANA	3 ANA	4 ANA	5 TEX	6 TEX
7 TEX	8	9	10	11 OAK	12 OAK	13 OAK
14 D OAK	15 SEA	16 D SEA	17 TOR	18 TOR	19 CWS	20 CWS
21 D CWS	22 TOR	23 TOR	24 D TOR	25	26 BOS	27 BOS
28 D BOS	29 TB	30 TB	31 TB			

August
SUN	MON	TUE	WED	THU	FRI	SAT
				1 TB	2 TOR	3 D TOR
4 D TOR	5 D TOR	6 MIN	7 MIN	8 D MIN	9 DET	10 DET
11 D DET	12	13 MIN	14 MIN	15 MIN	16 DET	17 DET
18 D DET	19 TB	20 TB	21 TB	22	23 TOR	24 TOR
25 TOR	26	27 TEX	28 TEX	29 TEX	30 ANA	31 ANA

September
SUN	MON	TUE	WED	THU	FRI	SAT
1 ANA	2	3 TEX	4 TEX	5 TEX	6 ANA	7 ANA
8 ANA	9	10 NYY	11 NYY	12 NYY	13 BOS	14 BOS
15 D BOS	16 TOR	17 TOR	18 TOR	19 TOR	20 BOS	21 BOS
22 D BOS	23 BOS	24 TOR	25 TOR	26 TOR	27 NYY	28 NYY
29 D NYY	30					

CLUB DIRECTORY

Chairman of the board/CEO
Peter G. Angelos
Vice chairman/chief operating officer
Joseph E. Foss
Executive vice president
John P. Angelos
Vice president/chief financial officer
Robert A. Ames, CPA
Vice president/baseball operations
Syd Thrift
Special assts. to the v.p., baseball ops.
Ed Kenney Jr., Danny Garcia, Larry
Himes, Mel Didier
Director/minor league operations
Don Buford
Director/scouting
Tony DeMacio
Asst. director/minor league operations
Tripp Norton
Traveling secretary
Philip F. Itzoe
Executive director/communications
Spiro Alafassos
Director/public relations
Bill Stetka
Baseball information manager
Kevin Behan
Director/ballpark operations
Roger Hayden
Director/community relations
Julie Wagner
Director/publishing & creative media
Jessica Fisher
Director/fan & ticket services
Don Grove
Director/sales
Matt Dryer

Director/information systems
James L. Kline
Director/corporate sponsorship & sales
Ron Brown
Head athletic trainer
Richie Bancells
Assistant athletic trainer
Brian Ebel
Strength and conditioning coach
Tim Bishop
Advance scout
Deacon Jones
Professional scouts
Mel Didier, Danny Garcia, Larry Himes,
Bruce Kison, Curt Motton, Tim
Thompson, Fred Uhlman Sr.
National cross-checker
Shawn Pender
Regional cross-checkers
Dean Decillis, Deron Rombach
Full-time scouts
Joe Almaraz, Ralph Garr Jr., John
Gillette, Troy Hoerner, Jim Howard,
Dave Jennings, Ray Krawczyk, Gil
Kubski, Lamar North, Nick Presto,
Harry Shelton, Ed Sprague, Marc
Tramuta, Mike Tullier, Dominic Viola,
Marc Ziegler
Director, Latin American scouting
Carlos Bernhardt
Caribbean & South Amer. supervisor
Jesus Halabi
International scouts
Rob Derkson, Ubaldo Heredia,
Salvador Ramirez, Arturo Sanchez,
Brett Ward

MINOR LEAGUE AFFILIATES

Class	Team	League	Manager
AAA	Rochester	International	Andy Etchebarren
AA	Bowie	Eastern	Dave Cash
A	Frederick	Carolina	Jack Voigt
A	Delmarva	South Atlantic	Joe Ferguson
Rookie	Bluefield	Appalachian	Joe Almaraz
Rookie	Gulf Coast Orioles	Gulf Coast	Jesus Alfaro

BROADCAST INFORMATION

Radio: WBAL-AM (1090).
TV: WJZ (Channel 13), WNUV
(Channel 54), WFTY (Channel 50).
Cable TV: Comcast SportsNet.

SPRING TRAINING

Ballpark (city): Ft. Lauderdale
Stadium (Ft. Lauderdale, Fla.).
Ticket information: 954-776-1921.

Follow the Orioles all season at: www.sportingnews.com/baseball/teams/orioles/

SPRING TRAINING ROSTER

Manager—Mike Hargrove (21).
Coaches—Terry Crowley (48), Rick Dempsey, Elrod Hendricks (44), Sam Perlozzo (2), Tom Trebelhorn (49), Mark Wiley (34).

No.	PITCHERS	B/T	Ht./Wt.	Born	2001 clubs
	Bale, John	L/L	6-4/205	5-22-74	Rochester, Baltimore, Gulf Coast Orioles
	Bauer, Rick	R/R	6-6/215	1-10-77	Bowie, Rochester, Baltimore
	Bechler, Steve	R/R	6-2/207	11-18-79	Frederick, Rochester, Bowie
	Bedard, Erik	L/L	6-1/180	3-6-79	Frederick, Gulf Coast Orioles
	Douglass, Sean	R/R	6-6/200	4-28-79	Rochester, Baltimore
19	Erickson, Scott	R/R	6-4/230	2-2-68	DID NOT PLAY
	Figueroa, Juan	R/R	6-3/150	6-24-79	Bowie, Frederick
67	Foster, Kris	R/R	6-1/200	6-30-74	Jacksonville, Las Vegas, Rochester, Baltimore
27	Groom, Buddy	L/L	6-2/207	7-10-65	Baltimore
	Hentgen, Pat	R/R	6-2/195	11-13-68	Baltimore
41	Johnson, Jason	R/R	6-6/235	10-27-73	Baltimore
	Julio, Jorge	R/R	6-1/190	3-3-79	Rochester, Bowie, Baltimore
60	Maduro, Calvin	R/R	6-0/180	9-5-74	Baltimore, Rochester
	Paradis, Mike	R/R	6-3/190	5-3-78	Bowie
53	Parrish, John	L/L	5-11/180	11-26-77	Rochester, Baltimore
43	Ponson, Sidney	R/R	6-1/225	11-2-76	Baltimore, Bowie
	Riley, Matt	L/L	6-1/201	8-2-79	DID NOT PLAY
60	Rivera, Luis	R/R	6-3/163	6-21-78	DID NOT PLAY
88	Roberts, Willis	R/R	6-3/175	6-19-75	Baltimore
52	Ryan, B.J.	L/L	6-6/230	12-28-75	Baltimore
	Stephens, John	R/R	6-1/200	11-15-79	Bowie, Rochester
	Towers, Josh	R/R	6-1/165	2-26-77	Rochester, Baltimore

No.	CATCHERS	B/T	Ht./Wt.	Born	2001 clubs
26	Fordyce, Brook	R/R	6-0/190	5-7-70	Baltimore
	Gil, Geronimo	R/R	6-2/195	8-7-75	Las Vegas, Rochester, Baltimore
51	Lunar, Fernando	R/R	6-1/190	5-25-77	Baltimore

No.	INFIELDERS	B/T	Ht./Wt.	Born	2001 clubs
7	Batista, Tony	R/R	6-0/205	12-9-73	Toronto, Baltimore
14	Bordick, Mike	R/R	5-11/175	7-21-65	Baltimore, Bowie, Delmarva
18	Conine, Jeff	R/R	6-1/220	6-27-66	Baltimore
	Gibbons, Jay	L/L	6-0/200	3-2-77	Baltimore
15	Hairston, Jerry	R/R	5-10/175	5-29-76	Baltimore
	Harris, Willie	L/R	5-9/175	6-22-78	Bowie, Baltimore
38	Richard, Chris	L/L	6-2/185	6-7-74	Baltimore
	Roberts, Brian	B/R	5-9/170	10-9-77	Bowie, Rochester, Baltimore
	Rogers, Eddie	R/R	6-1/150	8-10-81	Bowie, Frederick
	Segui, David	B/L	6-1/202	7-19-66	Baltimore

No.	OUTFIELDERS	B/T	Ht./Wt.	Born	2001 clubs
	Bigbie, Larry	L/L	6-4/190	11-4-77	Bowie, Rochester, Baltimore
40	Cordova, Marty	R/R	6-0/206	7-10-69	Cleveland
32	Matos, Luis	R/R	6-0/179	10-30-78	Gulf Coast Orioles, Frederick, Bowie, Baltimore
6	Mora, Melvin	R/R	5-10/180	2-2-72	Baltimore
	Raines, Tim Jr.	R/R	5-10/185	8-31-79	Frederick, Bowie, Rochester, Baltimore

BALLPARK INFORMATION

Ballpark (capacity, surface)
Oriole Park at Camden Yards (48,190, grass)
Address
333 W. Camden St.
Baltimore, MD 21201
Official website
www.theorioles.com
Business phone
410-685-9800
Ticket information
410-481-SEAT
Ticket prices
$40 (club box), $35 (field box sec. 20-54)
$32 (field box sec. 14-18, 56-58)
$27 (terrace box sec. 17-55)
$25 (LF club sec. 272-288; lower box sec. 6-12, 60-64)
$23 (terrace box sec. 1-15, 59-65)
$20 (upper box sec. 316-356)
$18 (LF lower box sec. 66-86 & 67-75; upper box sec. 306-312 & 358-372; lower res. sec. 17-55)
$15 (LF upper box sec. 374-388; lower res. sec. 4, 7-15, 59-75, 77-87; upper res. sec. 316-356)
$13 (upper res., sec. 306-312 & 360-364; Eutaw St. res. sec. 90-98)
$9 (upper res. sec. 368-372; LF upper res., sec. 374-388)
$8 (standing room)
Field dimensions (from home plate)
To left field at foul line, 333 feet
To center field, 400 feet
To right field at foul line, 318 feet
First game played
April 6, 1992 (Orioles 2, Indians 0)

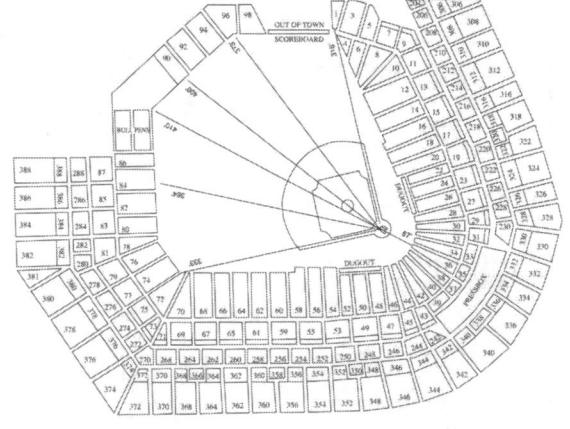

DAY BY DAY

Date	Opp.	Res.	Score	(inn.*)	Hits	Opp. hits	Winning pitcher	Losing pitcher	Save	Record	Pos.	GB
4-2	Bos.	W	2-1	(11)	6	5	Kohlmeier	Lowe		1-0	T1st	...
4-4	Bos.	L	0-3		0	5	Nomo	Ponson		1-1	T3rd	1.0
4-5	Bos.	W	2-1		6	7	Groom	Lowe		2-1	3rd	1.0
4-6	At Cle.	L	3-4		6	5	Rincon	Mercedes	Wickman	2-2	T3rd	1.5
4-7	At Cle.	W	4-2	(11)	10	6	Trombley	Reed	Kohlmeier	3-2	T2nd	1.5
4-8	At Cle.	L	3-4		3	8	Speier	Maduro	Wickman	3-3	4th	1.5
4-10	At Bos.	L	1-10		6	12	Nomo	Ponson	Wakefield	3-4	4th	3.0
4-11	At Bos.	W	5-4		10	10	Roberts	Castillo	Groom	4-4	4th	2.5
4-12	At Bos.	L	2-8		9	11	Ohka	Mercedes	Arrojo	4-5	4th	3.0
4-13	T.B.	L	0-2		3	3	Lopez	Hentgen		4-6	4th	3.5
4-14	T.B.	W	6-5		9	7	Bale	Meacham	Kohlmeier	5-6	4th	3.5
4-15	T.B.	L	4-7		9	13	Creek	Ponson	Yan	5-7	4th	3.5
4-16	T.B.	W	6-2		8	4	Johnson	Rupe		6-7	4th	3.0
4-17	Cle.	L	1-8		4	10	Burba	Mercedes		6-8	4th	4.0
4-18	Cle.	L	1-4		6	6	Colon	Hentgen		6-9	4th	5.0
4-19	Cle.	L	5-11		9	14	Sabathia	McElroy		6-10	4th	6.0
4-20	At T.B.	W	6-3		8	10	Roberts	Rekar	Kohlmeier	7-10	4th	5.0
4-21	At T.B.	L	5-6		11	10	Rupe	Johnson	Yan	7-11	4th	6.0
4-22	At T.B.	W	10-8	(11)	16	10	Paronto	Yan		8-11	4th	5.0
4-24	At Det.	W	8-3		13	8	Hentgen	Weaver		9-11	4th	5.0
4-25	At Det.	W	6-4		6	8	Roberts	Sparks	Kohlmeier	10-11	4th	4.0
4-26	At Det.	L	2-8		9	11	Holt	Johnson		10-12	4th	5.0
4-27	At Min.	L	3-6		6	9	Mays	Mercedes	Hawkins	10-13	4th	6.0
4-28	At Min.	W	5-2		11	8	McElroy	Redman	Trombley	11-13	4th	5.0
4-29	At Min.	L	0-4		5	8	Romero	Hentgen	Hawkins	11-14	4th	5.5
4-30	T.B.	W	5-3		8	5	Roberts	Wilson	Kohlmeier	12-14	4th	4.5
5-1	T.B.	W	3-1		6	4	Johnson	Rekar	Kohlmeier	13-14	4th	4.5
5-2	T.B.	L	1-7		6	15	Rupe	Mercedes	Sturtze	13-15	4th	4.5
5-3	N.Y.	L	5-7		7	8	Mendoza	Paronto	Rivera	13-16	4th	4.5
5-4	N.Y.	L	5-6		10	12	Stanton	Paronto	Rivera	13-17	4th	5.5
5-5	N.Y.	L	2-5		6	8	Pettitte	Roberts	Boehringer	13-18	4th	5.5
5-6	N.Y.	L	1-2		7	7	Mussina	Trombley	Rivera	13-19	4th	6.5
5-8	At T.B.	L	3-4		5	8	Meacham	Mercedes	Yan	13-20	4th	7.5
5-9	At T.B.	W	8-6		10	9	Towers	Rupe	Trombley	14-20	4th	6.5
5-10	At T.B.	W	9-5		9	7	Ryan	Meacham		15-20	4th	5.5
5-11	At N.Y.	L	5-14		11	15	Mussina	Roberts	Mendoza	15-21	4th	6.0
5-12	At N.Y.	L	5-8		11	11	Stanton	Towers	Rivera	15-22	4th	7.0
5-13	At N.Y.	W	10-5	(11)	14	11	Ryan	Rivera		16-22	4th	6.5
5-15	Det.	W	11-3		15	6	Ponson	Mlicki		17-22	4th	6.5
5-16	Det.	W	3-2		3	10	Hentgen	Weaver	Ryan	18-22	4th	5.5
5-17	Det.	L	5-7		10	9	Sparks	Roberts	Jones	18-23	4th	5.5
5-18	Min.	W	7-2		10	6	Johnson	Milton		19-23	4th	5.5
5-19	Min.	L	5-7		6	14	Mays	Ryan	Hawkins	19-24	4th	5.5
5-20	Min.	W	3-2		4	8	Trombley	Wells		20-24	4th	5.5
5-23	Ana.	W	12-5		15	10	Roberts	Schoeneweis		21-24	4th	4.5
5-24	Ana.	W	6-4		10	9	Johnson	Ortiz	Ryan	22-24	4th	4.0
5-25	Tex.	W	7-6		10	12	Mercedes	Mahomes	Trombley	23-24	4th	3.5
5-27	Tex.	W	3-1		8	8	Ponson	Glynn	Trombley	24-24	4th	3.5
5-28	Tex.	L	3-6		7	12	Smart	Paronto		24-25	4th	4.5
5-29	At Sea.	L	2-3		4	9	Garcia	Roberts	Sasaki	24-26	4th	5.0
5-30	At Sea.	L	5-12		13	12	Halama	Johnson		24-27	4th	5.0
5-31	At Sea.	L	1-2		5	6	Sele	Mercedes	Sasaki	24-28	4th	5.5
6-1	At Oak.	W	8-4		10	6	Ponson	Mecir		25-28	4th	5.5
6-2	At Oak.	W	7-0		15	7	Towers	Zito		26-28	3rd	5.5
6-3	At Oak.	L	1-5		9	8	Lidle	Roberts		26-29	3rd	6.5
6-5	At N.Y.	W	10-3		17	5	Johnson	Mussina		27-29	3rd	6.0
6-6	At N.Y.	L	4-7		9	10	Stanton	Groom	Rivera	27-30	3rd	6.0
6-7	At N.Y.	L	0-4		3	12	Clemens	Ponson		27-31	4th	7.0
6-8	Mon.	W	5-0		9	6	Towers	Blank		28-31	4th	7.0
6-9	Mon.	L	2-4		8	9	Lloyd	Ryan	Urbina	28-32	4th	7.0
6-10	Mon.	W	3-2		6	6	Johnson	Vazquez	Groom	29-32	3rd	7.0
6-12	N.Y.	L	3-10		6	14	Reed	Mercedes	White	29-33	4th	8.0
6-13	N.Y.	L	6-7	(10)	13	14	Franco	Groom	Benitez	29-34	4th	8.0
6-14	N.Y.	W	5-2		8	7	Towers	Trachsel	Groom	30-34	4th	8.0
6-15	At Phi.	L	7-15		12	18	Padilla	Roberts		30-35	4th	9.0
6-16	At Phi.	L	6-14		10	15	Brock	Ryan		30-36	4th	9.0
6-17	At Phi.	W	10-7		12	12	Mercedes	Telemaco		31-36	4th	9.0
6-18	Tor.	W	3-2		10	9	Ponson	Borbon	Trombley	32-36	3rd	8.5
6-19	Tor.	W	5-1		11	9	Towers	Hamilton	Groom	33-36	3rd	8.5
6-20	Tor.	L	5-6		10	10	Quantrill	McElroy	Koch	33-37	3rd	9.5
6-21	Chi.	L	0-6		3	13	K. Wells	Johnson		33-38	T3rd	10.5
6-22	Chi.	W	6-4		11	8	Mercedes	D. Wells	Groom	34-38	T3rd	9.5
6-23	Chi.	L	3-8		8	14	Glover	Ponson		34-39	4th	9.5
6-24	Chi.	L	2-8		7	14	Baldwin	Towers	Lowe	34-40	4th	9.5

2002 SEASON Baltimore Orioles

Date	Opp.	Res.	Score	(inn.*)	Hits	Opp. hits	Winning pitcher	Losing pitcher	Save	Record	Pos.	GB
6-25	At Tor.	W	8-2		15	5	Roberts	Hamilton		35-40	4th	9.5
6-26	At Tor.	L	1-3		7	5	Carpenter	Johnson	Koch	35-41	4th	10.5
6-27	At Tor.	W	7-3		12	5	Mercedes	Loaiza		36-41	4th	9.5
6-28	At Chi.	W	5-0		8	2	Ponson	Michalak		37-41	T3rd	8.5
6-29	At Chi.	W	4-0		9	6	Towers	Buehrle	Trombley	38-41	T3rd	7.5
6-30	At Chi.	L	1-4		10	8	Baldwin	Roberts	Foulke	38-42	T3rd	8.5
7-1	At Chi.	W	11-3		15	9	Johnson	Biddle		39-42	3rd	8.5
7-3	N.Y.	L	6-10		7	14	Mendoza	Mercedes		39-43	3rd	9.5
7-4	N.Y.	L	3-4		6	9	Clemens	Maduro	Rivera	39-44	3rd	10.5
7-5	N.Y.	L	3-6		8	12	Lilly	Towers	Rivera	39-45	4th	11.5
7-6	Phi.	L	2-3	(10)	7	8	Cormier	Trombley	Mesa	39-46	4th	12.5
7-7	Phi.	W	4-3		10	6	Johnson	Figueroa	Groom	40-46	4th	11.5
7-8	Phi.	L	4-5		5	11	Wolf	Groom	Mesa	40-47	4th	12.5
7-12	At Atl.	L	5-6		10	11	Maddux	Ryan	Karsay	40-48	4th	12.5
7-13	At Atl.	L	1-7		3	8	Glavine	Towers		40-49	4th	12.5
7-14	At Atl.	W	4-1		8	6	Roberts	Burkett	Groom	41-49	4th	12.5
7-15	At Fla.	L	1-7		5	11	Clement	Johnson		41-50	4th	12.5
7-16	At Fla.	L	0-4		2	7	Sanchez	Mercedes		41-51	4th	13.5
7-17	At Fla.	L	3-8		6	12	Burnett	Ponson	Darensbourg	41-52	4th	14.5
7-18	Tex.	L	4-6		10	11	Helling	Douglass	Zimmerman	41-53	4th	15.0
7-21	Ana.	L	5-6	(10)	9	13	Hasegawa	Mills		41-54	4th	14.0
7-22§	Ana.	L	4-9		11	11	Weber	Roberts	Pote	41-55		
7-22∞	Ana.	W	5-1		9	6	Johnson	Borland	Groom	42-55	4th	14.5
7-23	Ana.	L	4-9		14	11	Valdes	Mercedes		42-56	4th	15.5
7-24	At Tex.	L	7-8		12	10	Venafro	Trombley	Zimmerman	42-57	4th	16.5
7-25†	At Tex.	L	5-6		8	8	Duchscherer	Parrish	Zimmerman	42-58		
7-25‡	At Tex.	L	2-5		4	8	Venafro	Mercedes	Zimmerman	42-59	4th	18.0
7-26	At Tex.	L	7-9		11	13	Oliver	Towers	Venafro	42-60	4th	19.0
7-27	At Ana.	W	4-3	(10)	10	6	Trombley	Levine	Groom	43-60	4th	19.0
7-28	At Ana.	L	4-6		10	12	Weber	Kohlmeier	Percival	43-61	4th	20.0
7-29	At Ana.	W	1-0		5	7	Mercedes	Valdes	Groom	44-61	4th	20.0
7-30	Tex.	L	4-6	(11)	10	13	Moreno	Trombley	Zimmerman	44-62	4th	20.5
7-31	T.B.	L	4-5		9	9	Wilson	Towers	Yan	44-63	4th	20.5
8-1	T.B.	W	6-5		7	10	Mills	Yan		45-63	4th	20.5
8-2	T.B.	L	2-3		8	7	Sturtze	Maduro	Zambrano	45-64	4th	20.5
8-3	At Tor.	L	1-10		4	15	Escobar	Mercedes		45-65	4th	21.5
8-4	At Tor.	L	1-2		4	5	Lyon	Ponson	Koch	45-66	4th	22.5
8-5	At Tor.	L	4-5		11	9	Loaiza	Towers	Koch	45-67	4th	22.5
8-6	At K.C.	W	9-6		14	15	Johnson	George		46-67	4th	21.5
8-7	At K.C.	W	7-3		10	8	Maduro	Suppan	Roberts	47-67	4th	20.5
8-8	At K.C.	W	4-1		8	6	Mercedes	Durbin	Groom	48-67	4th	20.5
8-9	At K.C.	L	4-6		8	12	Wilson	Ponson	Hernandez	48-68	4th	21.5
8-11	Bos.	W	4-2		8	6	Towers	Cone	Roberts	49-68	4th	20.0
8-12	Bos.	L	10-12		8	9	Wakefield	Johnson	Lowe	49-69	4th	20.0
8-14	K.C.	W	5-2		12	4	Maduro	Durbin	Roberts	50-69	4th	20.0
8-15	K.C.	W	5-4		7	5	Mercedes	Wilson	Roberts	51-69	4th	20.0
8-16	K.C.	L	2-9		12	11	Byrd	Ponson		51-70	4th	21.0
8-17	At Bos.	W	11-5		17	12	Towers	Wakefield		52-70	4th	21.0
8-18	At Bos.	L	1-5		4	8	Garces	Johnson		52-71	4th	21.0
8-19	At Bos.	W	13-7		19	11	Wasdin	Pichardo		53-71	4th	20.0
8-21	At T.B.	L	4-8		8	13	Phelps	Mercedes		53-72	4th	20.5
8-22	At T.B.	L	10-11		14	20	Yan	Roberts		53-73	4th	20.5
8-23	At T.B.	W	7-4		15	7	Julio	Zambrano	Roberts	54-73	4th	20.5
8-24	Tor.	L	0-5		7	10	Carpenter	Johnson		54-74	4th	20.5
8-25	Tor.	L	0-9		5	9	Escobar	Maduro		54-75	4th	21.5
8-26	Tor.	L	1-5		3	10	Lyon	Mercedes		54-76	4th	21.5
8-28	Oak.	L	2-6		4	12	Mulder	Ponson		54-77	4th	22.5
8-29	Oak.	L	1-4		3	9	Hudson	Towers		54-78	4th	22.5
8-30	Oak.	L	0-15		5	13	Zito	Johnson		54-79	4th	23.5
8-31	Sea.	W	3-0		7	6	Maduro	Sele		55-79	4th	23.5
9-1	Sea.	L	4-6		7	12	Abbott	Mercedes	Sasaki	55-80	4th	24.5
9-2	Sea.	L	0-1		6	4	Pineiro	Bauer	Sasaki	55-81	4th	25.5
9-3	At Oak.	L	2-4		3	9	Hudson	Towers	Isringhausen	55-82	4th	26.5
9-4	At Oak.	L	2-5		5	6	Zito	Johnson	Isringhausen	55-83	4th	26.5
9-5	At Oak.	L	6-12		13	14	Lidle	Maduro		55-84	4th	27.5
9-7	At Sea.	L	1-10		2	12	Abbott	Mercedes		55-85	4th	28.5
9-8	At Sea.	L	1-6		4	13	Pineiro	Bauer		55-86	4th	29.5
9-9	At Sea.	L	0-6		2	10	Moyer	Towers		55-87	4th	30.5
9-18	At Tor.	L	5-8		9	13	Plesac	Julio	Koch	55-88	4th	31.5
9-19	At Tor.	L	1-4		5	9	Halladay	Maduro	Koch	55-89	4th	32.5
9-20	At Tor.	W	12-6		13	14	Parrish	File		56-89	4th	31.5
9-21	N.Y.	W	7-6		11	9	Roberts	Rivera		57-89	4th	30.5
9-22	N.Y.	W	11-2		16	6	Douglass	Hitchcock		58-89	4th	29.5
9-23	N.Y.	L	4-5	(10)	9	11	Stanton	Parrish	Rivera	58-90	4th	30.5
9-24	At Bos.	W	5-1		14	6	Maduro	Wakefield		59-90	4th	30.0
9-25	At Bos.	W	12-7		14	13	Mercedes	Castillo		60-90	4th	29.0
9-26	At Bos.	L	6-9		7	12	Fossum	Bauer	Urbina	60-91	4th	30.0
9-27	At Bos.	W	4-2		7	4	Douglass	Wakefield	Roberts	61-91	4th	29.5

Date	Opp.	Res.	Score	(inn.*)	Hits	Opp. hits	Winning pitcher	Losing pitcher	Save	Record	Pos.	GB
9-28	At N.Y.	L	0-7		3	9	Mussina	Johnson		61-92	4th	30.5
9-29	At N.Y.	W	7-2		6	7	Maduro	O. Hernandez		62-92	4th	29.5
9-30	At N.Y.	T	1-1	(15)	8	5				62-92	4th	29.5
10-1	Tor.	L	0-1		6	7	Loaiza	Bauer	Koch	62-93	4th	30.5
10-2	Tor.	W	4-3		10	6	Roberts	DeWitt		63-93	4th	30.5
10-3	Tor.	L	6-7		10	13	Eyre	Groom	Koch	63-94	4th	31.5
10-4	Bos.	L	4-5		7	9	Nomo	Wasdin	Urbina	63-95	4th	31.5
10-5§	Bos.	L	0-5		3	10	Castillo	Kohlmeier		63-96		
10-5∞	Bos.	L	5-7	(10)	12	9	Wakefield	Roberts	Garces	63-97	4th	32.0
10-6	Bos.	L	1-5		4	12	Cone	Bauer		63-98	4th	32.0

Monthly records: April (12-14), May (12-14), June (14-14), July (6-21), August (11-16), September (7-13), October (1-6).
*Innings, if other than nine. †First game of a doubleheader. ‡Second game of a doubleheader. §Day separate admission. ∞Night separate admission.

HIGHLIGHTS

High point: The Orioles reached the mid-point of their season, on July 2, just three games below .500 (39-42) and 8 1/2 games off the division lead, giving them outside hopes of a stealth run at a playoff berth.

Low point: In early September, the Orioles lost all six games at Oakland and Seattle, hitting .155 as a team and falling to 32 games below .500. In the final indignity, they were held to three baserunners (two hits and a walk) against two former Orioles—Seattle lefties Jamie Moyer and Arthur Rhodes—plus closer Kazuhiro Sasaki.

Most valuable player: Jeff Conine was going to be the Orioles' utility player, but by the end of the season, he was not only an everyday player, he was the 10th-leading hitter in the American League. With David Segui injured for much of the season, Conine stepped into his role as the veteran anchor of an otherwise underdeveloped lineup.

Most valuable pitcher: Buddy Groom began the season in his usual role of trusted lefthanded setup man, but inherited the closer's job and then returned to his setup role. Groom wound up leading the Orioles with 11 saves, while posting a 3.55 ERA and a 1-4 record.

Most improved player: Jason Johnson reported to spring training camp in 2001 a different pitcher, with better powers of focus and, subsequently, command. Johnson surged to a 10-12 record and dropped his ERA to 4.09.

Most pleasant surprise: The Orioles signed Willis Roberts last winter as a six-year minor-league free agent. By the end of the year, he had become the team's closer and the leading contender to hold that job again in 2002.

Key injuries: The Orioles intended David Segui, Mike Bordick and Pat Hentgen to be the veteran anchors of their offense, defense and pitching staff, respectively. But Bordick (shoulder) and Hentgen (elbow) were lost for the season before the All-Star break, and Segui missed almost half the season with a variety of ailments. ... In addition, rookie first baseman Jay Gibbons had surgery to repair a broken wrist, and right fielder Chris Richard had surgery this offseason on his shoulder.

Notable: The Orioles' record was the worst since the 1988 team (which lost its first 21 games) lost 107 games. ... The Orioles were shut out 14 times in 2001.

—DAVE SHEININ

RECORDS

2001 regular-season record: 63-98 (4th in A.L. East); 30-50 at home; 33-48 on road; 31-44 vs. A.L. East, 16-16 vs. A.L. Central; 10-26 vs. A.L. West; 6-12 vs. N.L.; 13-27 vs. lefthanded starters; 50-71 vs. righthanded starters; 52-84 on grass; 11-14 on turf; 17-30 in daytime, 46-68 at night; 16-27 in one-run games; 5-6 in extra-inning games; 0-1-0 in doubleheaders.

Team record past five years: 392-417 (.485, ranks 10th in league in that span).

TEAM LEADERS

Batting average: Jeff Conine (.311).
At-bats: Jerry Hairston Jr. (532).
Runs: Jeff Conine (75).
Hits: Jeff Conine (163).
Total Bases: Jeff Conine (232).
Doubles: Chris Richard (31).
Triples: Tony Batista, Jerry Hairston Jr. (5).
Home runs: Jay Gibbons, Chris Richard (15).
Runs batted in: Jeff Conine (97).
Stolen bases: Jerry Hairston Jr. (29).
Slugging percentage: Jeff Conine (.443).
On-base percentage: Jeff Conine (.386).
Wins: Jason Johnson (10).
Earned-run average: Jason Johnson (4.09).
Complete games: Sidney Ponson (3).
Shutouts: Sidney Ponson, Josh Towers (1).
Saves: Buddy Groom (11).
Innings pitched: Jason Johnson (196.0).
Strikeouts: Jose Mercedes (123).

GAMES BY POSITION

Catcher: Brook Fordyce 95, Fernando Lunar 64, Geronimo Gil 17, Greg Myers 8, Mike Kinkade 2.
First base: Jeff Conine 80, David Segui 65, Chris Richard 18, Jay Gibbons 7, Casey Blake 5, Mike Kinkade 3.
Second base: Jerry Hairston Jr. 156, Brian Roberts 12, Melvin Mora 1.
Third base: Cal Ripken Jr. 111, Tony Batista 29, Jeff Conine 17, Mike Kinkade 10.
Shortstop: Mike Bordick 58, Brian Roberts 51, Melvin Mora 43, Tony Batista 20.
Outfield: Brady Anderson 120, Chris Richard 96, Melvin Mora 88, Delino DeShields 47, Larry Bigbie 40, Jeff Conine 36, Mike Kinkade 32, Luis Matos 31, Jay Gibbons 28, Willie Harris 8, Tim Raines Jr. 7, Tim Raines Sr. 3, Gene Kingsale 1.
Designated hitter: Tony Batista 33, Jay Gibbons 28, Chris Richard 20, David Segui 16, Cal Ripken Jr. 14, Jeff Conine 12, Greg Myers 11, Mike Kinkade 10, Delino DeShields 8, Brian Roberts 7, Brady Anderson 4, Casey Blake 1, Tim Raines Sr. 1.

TOP DRAFT CHOICES

1a. **Chris Smith**, LHP, Cumberland (Tenn.) Univ.
1b. **Mike Fontenot**, 2B, Louisiana State University.
1c. **Bryan Bass**, SS, Seminole (Fla.) H.S.
3. **Dave Crouthers**, RHP, Southern Illinois University-Edwardsville.
4. **Ronnie Lewis**, LHP, Newport H.S., Bellevue, Wash.
5. **James Johnson**, RHP, Endicott-Union H.S., Endicott, N.Y.
6. **Eli Whiteside**, C, Delta State (Miss.) Univ.
7. **Joe Coppinger**, RHP, Seminole State (Okla.) J.C.
8. **Chris Britton**, RHP, Plantation (Fla.) H.S.
9. **Dustin Yount**, 1B, Chaparral H.S., Phoenix.
10. **Woody Cliffords**, OF, Pepperdine U.

BOSTON RED SOX
AMERICAN LEAGUE EAST DIVISION

Red Sox schedule
Home games shaded
D—Day game (games starting before 5 p.m.)
*All-Star Game at Milwaukee
Subject to changes

April

SUN	MON	TUE	WED	THU	FRI	SAT
	1 D	2		3	4	5	6 D
	TOR		TOR		BAL	BAL
7 D	8	9	10	11	12	13 D
BAL		KC	KC	KC	NYY	NYY
14 D	15 D	16	17	18	19	20
NYY	NYY	TOR	TOR		KC	KC
21 D	22	23	24	25 D	26	27 D
KC		BAL	BAL	BAL	TB	TB
28 D	29	30				
TB	BAL	BAL				

May

SUN	MON	TUE	WED	THU	FRI	SAT
			1	2	3	4
			BAL		TB	TB
5 D	6	7	8	9 D	10	11
TB	TB	OAK	OAK	OAK	SEA	SEA
12 D	13	14	15	16	17	18 D
SEA		OAK	OAK	OAK	SEA	SEA
19 D	20	21	22	23	24	25 D
SEA	CWS	CWS	CWS	NYY	NYY	NYY
26 D	27	28	29	30	31	
NYY	TOR	TOR	TOR		NYY	

June

SUN	MON	TUE	WED	THU	FRI	SAT
						1 D
						NYY
2 D	3	4	5	6 D	7	8 D
NYY	DET	DET	DET	DET	ARI	ARI
9 D	10	11	12	13	14	15 D
ARI	COL	COL	COL		ATL	ATL
16 D	17	18	19	20	21	22 D
ATL		SD	SD	SD	LA	LA
23 D	24	25	26	27	28	29
LA		CLE	CLE	CLE	ATL	ATL
30 D						
ATL						

July

SUN	MON	TUE	WED	THU	FRI	SAT
	1	2	3	4 D	5 D	6
	TOR	TOR	TOR	TOR	DET	DET
7 D	8	9 *	10	11	12	13 D
DET				TOR	TOR	TOR
14 D	15	16	17	18 D	19	20 D
TOR	DET	DET	TB	TB	NYY	NYY
21 D	22	23	24	25	26	27
NYY		TB	TB	TB	BAL	BAL
28 D	29	30	31			
BAL	ANA	ANA	ANA			

August

SUN	MON	TUE	WED	THU	FRI	SAT
				1	2	3
			TEX	TEX	TEX	
4 D	5	6	7	8	9	10
TEX		OAK	OAK	OAK	MIN	MIN
11 D	12	13	14	15	16	17
MIN		SEA	SEA	SEA	MIN	MIN
18 D	19	20	21	22	23	24
MIN		TEX	TEX	TEX	ANA	ANA
25 D	26	27	28	29	30	31
ANA	ANA	NYY	NYY		CLE	CLE

September

SUN	MON	TUE	WED	THU	FRI	SAT
1 D	2	3	4	5 D	6	7
CLE	NYY	NYY	NYY	TOR	TOR	TOR
8 D	9	10	11	12 D	13	14
TOR	TB	TB	TB	TB	BAL	BAL
15 D	16	17	18	19	20	21
BAL	CLE	CLE	CLE		BAL	BAL
22 D	23	24	25	26 D	27	28
BAL	BAL	CWS	CWS	CWS	TB	TB
29 D	30					
TB						

2002 SEASON
CLUB DIRECTORY

Chief executive officer
John L. Harrington
Exec. v.p. and general manager
Daniel F. Duquette
Executive vice president, administration
John S. Buckley
Director of baseball operations
Kent A. Qualls
V.p. and chief financial officer
Robert C. Furbush
Vice president, baseball operations
Michael D. Port
V.p., broadcasting and technology
James P. Healey
Vice president, public affairs
Richard L. Bresciani
Vice president, sales and marketing
Lawrence C. Cancro
Vice president, stadium operations
Joseph F. McDermott
Vice president, assistant g.m. and legal counsel
Elaine W. Steward
Special assistants to the general manager
Lee Thomas, Carlton E. Fisk
Dir. of communications and baseball information
Kevin J. Shea
Dir. of human resources and office management
Michele Julian
Vice president, scouting
W. Wayne Britton
Executive director of int'l baseball operations
R. Ray Poitevint
Director of player development
David P. Jauss
Minor league field coordinator
Gary Jones
Coordinator of Florida operations
Ryan Richeal
Traveling secretary
John F. McCormick
Major league scout
Frank J. Malzone
Major league special assignment scout
G. Edwin Haas
Baseball administration coordinator
Marci S. Blacker
Assistant scouting director
Thomas L. Moore
Director, information technology
Stephen P. Conley
Information technology manager
Clay N. Rendon
Director of sales
Michael D. Schetzel
Group sales manager
Corey Bowdre
Season ticket manager
Joseph F. Matthews
Baseball information coordinator
Glenn Wilburn
Medical director
Arthur M. Pappas, M.D.
Team physician
William J. Morgan, M.D.

Head trainer
James W. Rowe Jr.
Assistant trainer
Christopher T. Correnti
Instructors
Theodore S. Williams, Carl M. Yastrzemski, Jim Rice
Special assignment instructors
John M. Pesky, Edward J. Popowski, Charles T. Wagner
Executive administrative assistant
Lorraine Leong
Equipment manager and clubhouse operations
J. Joseph Cochran
Controller
Stanley H. Tran
Director of advertising and sponsorships
Jeffrey E. Goldenberg
Director of facilities management
Thomas L. Queenan Jr.
Director of 600 Club
Patricia T. Flanagan
Director of ticket operations
Joseph P. Helyar
Executive consultant, public affairs
James "Lou" Gorman
Superintendent, park and maintenance
Joseph P. Mooney
Ticket office manager
Richard J. Beaton Jr.
Broadcasting manager
James E. Shannahan
Community relations manager
Ronald E. Burton Jr.
Customer relations manager
Ann Marie C. Starzyk
Public affairs manager
Fred Seymour Jr.
Ground crew manager
Casey Erven
Promotions and special events manager
Marcita E. Thompson
Publications manager
Debra A. Matson
Coordinator of Latin American scouting
Ben Cherrington
Scouts
Walter Walter "Chet" Atkins, Raymond Boone, Buzz Bowers, Kevin Burrell, Ben Cherrington, Edwin Correa, Ray Crone Jr., George Digby, Johnny DiPuglia, Danny Doyle, Rob English, William Enos, Ray Fagnant, Steve Flores, Danny Haas, Eddie Haas, Matt Haas, Ernie Jacobs, Wally Komatsubara, Chuck Koney, Kenneth "Jack" Lee, Don Lenhardt, Frank Malzone, Joe Mason, Tom Mooney, Gary Rajsich, Eddie Robinson, Jim Robinson, Ed Roebuck, Edward Scott, Mathew Sczesny, Harry Smith, Dick Sorkin, Jerry Stephenson, Joseph Stephenson, Lee Thomas, Fay Thompson, Charles T. Wagner, Jeffrey Zona, Mark Garcia, Jun Kodama, Ray Poitevint, Lee Sigman, Robinson Garcia, Sebastian Martinez, Jose Maza, Carlos Ramirez, Derek Valenzuela, Michael Victoria
International scouts
Mark Garcia, Jun Kodama, Ray Poitevint, Lee Sigman
Latin American scouts
Robinson Garcia, Sebastian Martinez, Jose Maza, Levy Ochoa, Carlos Ramirez, Michael Victoria

MINOR LEAGUE AFFILIATES

Class	Team	League	Manager
AAA	Pawtucket	International	Buddy Bailey
AA	Trenton	Eastern	Ron Johnson
A	Augusta	South Atlantic	Arnie Beyeler
A	Lowell	New York-Pennsylvania	Mike Boulanger
A	Sarasota	Florida State	Billy Gardner
Rookie	Gulf Coast Red Sox	Gulf Coast	John Sanders

BROADCAST INFORMATION

Radio: WEEI-AM (680).
TV: WFXT-TV (Fox 25).
Cable TV: New England Sports Network.

SPRING TRAINING

Ballpark (city): City of Palms Park (Fort Myers, Fla.).
Ticket information: 941-334-4700.

Follow the Red Sox all season at: www.sportingnews.com/baseball/teams/redsox/

SPRING TRAINING ROSTER

Manager—Joe Kerrigan (16).
Coaches—Mike Cubbage, Dwight Evans, Tommy Harper (51), Ralph Treuel.

No.	PITCHERS	B/T	Ht./Wt.	Born	2001 clubs
44	Arrojo, Rolando	R/R	6-4/220	7-18-68	Boston, Sarasota
19	Burkett, John	R/R	6-3/215	11-28-64	Atlanta
	Castillo, Frank	R/R	6-1/200	4-1-69	Boston, Pawtucket
63	Crawford, Paxton	R/R	6-3/205	8-4-77	Boston, Pawtucket
	de la Rosa, Jorge	L/L	6-1/190	4-5-81	Sarasota, Trenton
	Fossum, Casey	R/R	6-1/160	1-9-78	Trenton, Boston
34	Garces, Richard	R/R	6-0/215	5-18-71	Boston, Lowell
	Hancock, Josh	R/R	6-3/220	4-11-78	Trenton
30	Hermanson, Dustin	R/R	6-2/200	12-21-72	St. Louis
62	Kim, Sun-Woo	R/R	6-2/180	9-4-77	Pawtucket, Boston
32	Lowe, Derek	R/R	6-6/200	6-1-73	Boston
	Martinez, Anastacio	R/R	6-2/180	11-3-80	Sarasota
45	Martinez, Pedro	R/R	5-11/170	10-25-71	Boston
28	Oliver, Darren	R/L	6-2/210	10-6-70	Texas, Oklahoma, Tulsa
	Pena, Juan	R/R	6-5/215	6-27-77	Sarasota
41	Urbina, Ugueth	R/R	6-0/205	2-15-74	Montreal, Boston
49	Wakefield, Tim	R/R	6-2/210	8-2-66	Boston

No.	CATCHERS	B/T	Ht./Wt.	Born	2001 clubs
	Lomasney, Steve	R/R	6-0/195	8-29-77	Trenton, Pawtucket
15	Mirabelli, Doug	R/R	6-1/218	10-18-70	Texas, Boston
33	Varitek, Jason	B/R	6-2/220	4-11-72	Boston

No.	INFIELDERS	B/T	Ht./Wt.	Born	2001 clubs
44	Clark, Tony	B/R	6-7/245	6-15-72	Detroit
23	Daubach, Brian	L/R	6-1/201	2-11-72	Boston, Pawtucket, Lowell
	Diaz, Juan	R/R	6-2/228	2-19-76	Pawtucket
5	Garciaparra, Nomar	R/R	6-0/180	7-23-73	Pawtucket, Boston
	Hillenbrand, Shea	R/R	6-1/200	7-27-75	Boston
26	Merloni, Lou	R/R	5-10/195	4-6-71	Pawtucket, Boston
30	Offerman, Jose	B/R	6-0/190	11-8-68	Boston
39	Pickering, Calvin	L/L	6-5/278	9-29-76	Rochester, Louisville, Cincinnati, Boston
	Santos, Angel	B/R	5-11/180	8-14-79	Pawtucket, Trenton, Boston
	Stenson, Dernell	L/L	6-1/230	6-17-78	Pawtucket
	Veras, Wilton	R/R	6-2/198	1-19-78	Pawtucket

No.	OUTFIELDERS	B/T	Ht./Wt.	Born	2001 clubs
4	Coleman, Michael	R/R	5-11/215	8-16-75	New York A.L., Columbus
18	Damon, Johnny	L/L	6-2/190	11-5-73	Oakland
7	Nixon, Trot	L/L	6-2/200	4-11-74	Boston
24	Ramirez, Manny	R/R	6-0/205	5-30-72	Boston

BALLPARK INFORMATION

Ballpark (capacity, surface)
Fenway Park (33,991; grass)

Address
4 Yawkey Way
Boston, MA 02215-3496

Official website
www.redsox.com

Business phone
617-267-9440

Ticket information
617-267-1700, 617-482-4769

Ticket prices
$55 (field box, loge box and infield roof)
$40 (reserved grandstand)
$30 (right-field boxes and right-field roof)
$25 (outfield grandstand)
$20 (lower bleachers)
$18 (upper bleachers)

Field dimensions (from home plate)
To left field at foul line, 310 feet
To center field, 390 feet
To right field at foul line, 302 feet

First game played
April 20, 1912
(Red Sox 7, New York Highlanders 6)

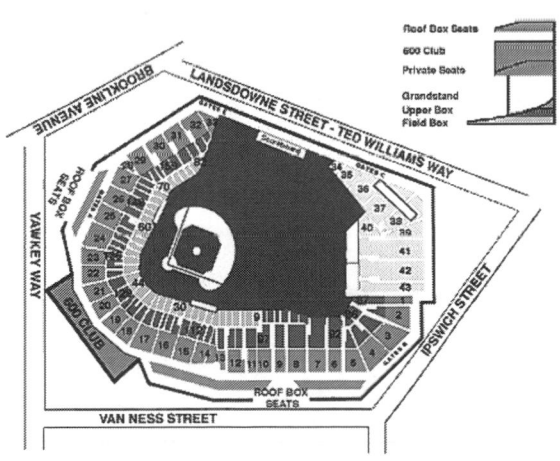

2002 SEASON   *Boston Red Sox*

Date	Opp.	Res.	Score	(inn.*)	Hits	Opp. hits	Winning pitcher	Losing pitcher	Save	Record	Pos.	GB
4-2	At Bal.	L	1-2	(11)	5	6	Kohlmeier	Lowe		0-1	T4th	1.0
4-4	At Bal.	W	3-0		5	0	Nomo	Ponson		1-1	T3rd	1.0
4-5	At Bal.	L	1-2		7	6	Groom	Lowe		1-2	T4th	2.0
4-6	T.B.	W	11-4		11	8	Wakefield	Rupe		2-2	T3rd	1.5
4-7	T.B.	W	6-2		14	4	Crawford	Harper		3-2	T2nd	1.5
4-8	T.B.	W	3-0		7	4	Martinez	Lopez	Lowe	4-2	T2nd	0.5
4-10	Bal.	W	10-1		12	6	Nomo	Ponson	Wakefield	5-2	3rd	1.0
4-11	Bal.	L	4-5		10	10	Roberts	Castillo	Groom	5-3	3rd	1.5
4-12	Bal.	W	8-2		11	9	Ohka	Mercedes	Arrojo	6-3	3rd	1.0
4-13	N.Y.	W	3-2	(10)	8	8	Lowe	Rivera		7-3	T2nd	0.5
4-14	N.Y.	L	2-3		6	8	Stanton	Schourek	Rivera	7-4	3rd	1.5
4-15	N.Y.	W	5-4		15	7	Garces	Pettitte	Arrojo	8-4	T2nd	0.5
4-16	N.Y.	W	4-1		11	5	Castillo	Mussina	Beck	9-4	T1st	...
4-17	At T.B.	W	10-0		11	7	Ohka	Harper		10-4	T1st	...
4-18	At T.B.	W	9-1		15	6	Arrojo	Sturtze		11-4	T1st	...
4-19	At T.B.	W	8-3		8	10	Martinez	Wilson	Lowe	12-4	1st	+1.0
4-20	At N.Y.	L	1-6		6	9	Pettitte	Nomo		12-5	T1st	...
4-21	At N.Y.	W	8-3		9	9	Castillo	Mussina		13-5	1st	+1.0
4-22	At N.Y.	L	3-4	(10)	11	12	Rivera	Lowe		13-6	1st	+1.0
4-24	Min.	W	9-4		14	8	Crawford	Redman	Wakefield	14-6	1st	+1.0
4-25	Min.	L	4-6	(10)	10	10	Wells	Beck	Hawkins	14-7	T1st	...
4-26	Min.	W	2-0		8	2	Nomo	Milton	Lowe	15-7	1st	+0.5
4-27	K.C.	W	9-2		12	7	Castillo	Stein	Arrojo	16-7	1st	+0.5
4-28	K.C.	L	2-8		6	12	Reichert	Ohka		16-8	1st	+0.5
4-29	K.C.	L	8-11	(11)	14	16	Santiago	Lowe	Hernandez	16-9	2nd	0.5
5-1	At Sea.	W	2-0		9	3	Martinez	Halama	Arrojo	17-9	T1st	...
5-2	At Sea.	L	1-5		7	5	Sele	Nomo		17-10	T1st	...
5-3	At Sea.	L	3-10		11	11	Moyer	Castillo		17-11	T1st	...
5-4	At Oak.	L	3-7		8	11	Heredia	Lowe	Tam	17-12	2nd	1.0
5-5	At Oak.	W	7-1		14	6	Crawford	Zito		18-12	T1st	...
5-6	At Oak.	W	5-4		9	6	Martinez	Lidle	Beck	19-12	T1st	...
5-8	Sea.	W	12-4		14	8	Nomo	Moyer		20-12	1st	+0.5
5-9	Sea.	L	5-10		11	14	Nelson	Arrojo	Sasaki	20-13	1st	+0.5
5-10	Sea.	L	2-5		5	8	Halama	Ohka	Sasaki	20-14	1st	+0.5
5-11	Oak.	L	6-7		10	13	Isringhausen	Beck	Tam	20-15	2nd	0.5
5-12	Oak.	W	9-3		19	3	Martinez	Heredia		21-15	2nd	0.5
5-13	Oak.	W	5-4	(11)	9	7	Lowe	Tam		22-15	1st	+0.5
5-15	At Min.	W	5-2		12	7	Castillo	Redman		23-15	1st	+1.5
5-16	At Min.	L	3-4		8	5	Wells	Schourek	Hawkins	23-16	1st	+1.5
5-17	At Min.	L	3-5		6	9	Radke	Arrojo		23-17	1st	+1.5
5-18	At K.C.	W	6-3		10	9	Martinez	Stein		24-17	1st	+1.5
5-19	At K.C.	L	2-6		5	13	Reichert	Nomo		24-18	1st	+1.5
5-20	At K.C.	W	10-3		13	8	Castillo	Meadows		25-18	1st	+1.5
5-23	At N.Y.	L	3-7		6	11	Pettitte	Cone		25-19	1st	+0.5
5-24	At N.Y.	L	1-2		6	6	Mussina	Martinez	Rivera	25-20	2nd	0.5
5-25	Tor.	W	4-0		9	1	Nomo	Loaiza		26-20	1st	+0.5
5-26	Tor.	L	0-5		9	9	Michalak	Castillo		26-21	2nd	0.5
5-27	Tor.	W	4-2		10	6	Wakefield	Parris	Lowe	27-21	2nd	0.5
5-28	N.Y.	L	3-4		9	11	Pettitte	Schourek	Rivera	27-22	2nd	1.5
5-30	N.Y.	W	3-0		4	5	Martinez	Mussina	Lowe	28-22	2nd	0.5
5-31	At Tor.	W	11-5		14	8	Beck	Escobar		29-22	T1st	...
6-1	At Tor.	W	6-4	(11)	16	10	Lowe	Koch		30-22	1st	+1.0
6-2	At Tor.	W	2-1		9	5	Schourek	Plesac	Beck	31-22	1st	+1.0
6-3	At Tor.	W	5-4		8	13	Pichardo	Carpenter	Lowe	32-22	1st	+2.0
6-4	At N.Y.	L	6-7		12	10	Rivera	Beck		32-23	1st	+1.0
6-5	Det.	W	4-3	(18)	12	15	Wakefield	Borkowski		33-23	1st	+2.0
6-6	Det.	L	3-7		12	10	Mlicki	Castillo	Anderson	33-24	1st	+1.0
6-7	Det.	W	8-1		10	5	Wakefield	Santos	Arrojo	34-24	1st	+1.0
6-8	Phi.	W	3-2		8	9	Cone	Wolf	Lowe	35-24	1st	+1.0
6-9	Phi.	L	2-5		6	6	Daal	Martinez	Mesa	35-25	1st	+1.0
6-10	Phi.	W	5-4		9	8	Nomo	Cormier	Lowe	36-25	1st	+2.0
6-12	Fla.	W	4-2		7	8	Castillo	Dempster	Lowe	37-25	1st	+3.0
6-13	Fla.	L	2-4		11	10	Clement	Wakefield	Alfonseca	37-26	1st	+2.0
6-14	Fla.	W	6-4		10	5	Cone	Smith	Beck	38-26	1st	+2.0
6-15	At Atl.	W	9-5	(10)	13	8	Beck	Cabrera		39-26	1st	+2.0
6-16	At Atl.	L	0-8		2	11	Burkett	Nomo		39-27	1st	+1.0
6-17	At Atl.	W	4-3		7	9	Castillo	Perez	Lowe	40-27	1st	+2.0
6-19	At T.B.	W	5-4		7	3	Wakefield	Rekar	Lowe	41-27	1st	+2.5
6-20	At T.B.	W	8-2		9	7	Garces	Rupe		42-27	1st	+3.5
6-21	At T.B.	W	7-4		10	10	Beck	Yan	Lowe	43-27	1st	+4.0
6-22	Tor.	L	3-4		7	7	Borbon	Schourek	Koch	43-28	1st	+3.0
6-23	Tor.	L	6-9		16	13	File	Castillo	Koch	43-29	1st	+2.0
6-24	Tor.	L	2-5		8	5	Plesac	Wakefield	Koch	43-30	1st	+2.0
6-25	T.B.	W	12-8		12	9	Cone	Rupe	Lowe	44-30	1st	+2.0

Date	Opp.	Res.	Score	(inn.*)	Hits	Opp. hits	Winning pitcher	Losing pitcher	Save	Record	Pos.	GB
6-26	T.B.	W	7-6		8	8	Beck	Zambrano	Lowe	45-30	1st	+3.0
6-27	T.B.	L	7-9		12	15	Creek	Schourek		45-31	1st	+2.0
6-28	T.B.	L	3-4		8	9	Colome	Lowe		45-32	1st	+1.5
6-29	At Tor.	L	4-8		8	10	Quantrill	Florie		45-33	1st	+0.5
6-30	At Tor.	W	7-5		14	14	Cone	Hamilton		46-33	1st	+0.5
7-1	At Tor.	W	4-0		7	2	Arrojo	Carpenter		47-33	1st	+0.5
7-2	At Tor.	W	16-4		17	10	Nomo	Loaiza		48-33	1st	+0.5
7-3	At Cle.	L	1-9		5	14	Westbrook	Ohka		48-34	2nd	0.5
7-4	At Cle.	W	13-4		19	7	Wakefield	Burba		49-34	2nd	0.5
7-5	At Cle.	W	5-4		7	7	Lowe	Rocker		50-34	2nd	0.5
7-6	Atl.	L	5-6	(10)	10	12	Karsay	Kim	Cabrera	50-35	2nd	1.5
7-7	Atl.	W	3-1		7	9	Nomo	Marquis	Lowe	51-35	2nd	0.5
7-8	Atl.	L	0-8		4	13	Glavine	Ohka		51-36	2nd	1.5
7-12	At N.Y.	L	2-4		7	7	Leiter	Wakefield	Benitez	51-37	2nd	1.5
7-13	At N.Y.	W	3-1		4	5	Cone	Appier	Lowe	52-37	2nd	0.5
7-14	At N.Y.	L	0-2		1	5	Rusch	Arrojo	Benitez	52-38	2nd	1.5
7-15	At Mon.	W	8-5		14	8	Nomo	Thurman	Lowe	53-38	2nd	0.5
7-16	At Mon.	W	6-5		13	9	Pichardo	Lloyd	Lowe	54-38	2nd	0.5
7-17	At Mon.	L	7-11		16	13	Mattes	Wakefield		54-39	2nd	1.5
7-18	At Tor.	W	5-4		9	8	Garces	Koch	Lowe	55-39	2nd	1.0
7-19	At Tor.	L	3-4		7	8	Escobar	Lowe		55-40	2nd	1.0
7-20	At Chi.	W	7-2		9	10	Nomo	Biddle		56-40	T1st	...
7-21	At Chi.	L	3-10		7	14	Baldwin	Ohka		56-41	T1st	...
7-22	At Chi.	L	8-13		12	13	Garland	Wakefield	Howry	56-42	2nd	1.0
7-24	Tor.	W	6-4		14	10	Cone	Hamilton	Lowe	57-42	2nd	1.5
7-25	Tor.	L	3-4	(10)	4	8	Quantrill	Lowe	Koch	57-43	2nd	2.5
7-26	Tor.	W	6-3		10	9	Nomo	File	Beck	58-43	2nd	2.5
7-27	Chi.	W	9-5		11	10	Saberhagen	K. Wells		59-43	2nd	2.5
7-28	Chi.	L	1-3		5	9	Buehrle	Wakefield	Foulke	59-44	2nd	3.5
7-29	Chi.	W	4-3		5	6	Beck	Embree	Lowe	60-44	2nd	3.5
7-31	Ana.	L	3-4		8	6	Ortiz	Garces	Percival	60-45	2nd	3.5
8-1	Ana.	L	2-4		5	9	Schoenewels	Nomo	Levine	60-46	2nd	4.5
8-2	Ana.	L	4-13		9	17	Rapp	Saberhagen		60-47	2nd	4.5
8-4§	Tex.	W	10-4		15	12	Cone	Helling		61-47		
8-4⌒	Tex.	W	6-2		9	4	Wakefield	Davis		62-47	2nd	4.5
8-5	Tex.	W	6-3		11	5	Arrojo	Oliver	Lowe	63-47	2nd	3.5
8-6	Tex.	W	10-7		13	10	Fossum	Moreno	Lowe	64-47	2nd	2.5
8-7	At Oak.	L	2-5		8	12	Mulder	Saberhagen	Isringhausen	64-48	2nd	2.5
8-8	At Oak.	L	1-6		9	9	Hudson	Castillo		64-49	2nd	3.5
8-9	At Oak.	L	0-6		4	8	Zito	Wakefield		64-50	2nd	4.5
8-11	At Bal.	L	2-4		6	8	Towers	Cone	Roberts	64-51	2nd	4.0
8-12	At Bal.	W	12-10		9	8	Wakefield	Johnson	Lowe	65-51	2nd	3.0
8-14	Sea.	L	3-6	(11)	8	15	Paniagua	Beck	Sasaki	65-52	2nd	4.0
8-15	Sea.	L	2-6		3	11	Garcia	Castillo		65-53	2nd	5.0
8-16	Sea.	W	6-4		9	13	Garces	Sele	Urbina	66-53	2nd	5.0
8-17	Bal.	L	5-11		12	17	Towers	Wakefield		66-54	2nd	6.0
8-18	Bal.	W	5-1		8	4	Garces	Johnson		67-54	2nd	5.0
8-19	Bal.	L	7-13		11	19	Wasdin	Pichardo		67-55	2nd	5.0
8-20	At Ana.	W	6-1		9	7	Castillo	Valdes		68-55	2nd	5.0
8-21	At Ana.	W	8-5		10	9	Cone	Schoenewels	Urbina	69-55	2nd	4.0
8-22	At Ana.	L	2-4		6	11	Levine	Wakefield	Percival	69-56	2nd	4.0
8-23	At Ana.	W	7-6		10	13	Garces	Weber	Urbina	70-56	2nd	4.0
8-24	At Tex.	W	7-4		11	7	Beck	Michalak	Urbina	71-56	2nd	3.0
8-25	At Tex.	L	7-8	(18)	16	13	Michalak	Lowe		71-57	2nd	4.0
8-26	At Tex.	L	4-5		9	9	Davis	Wakefield	Zimmerman	71-58	2nd	4.0
8-28	At Cle.	L	3-8		6	11	Burba	Cone		71-59	2nd	5.0
8-29	At Cle.	L	1-2		6	6	Sabathia	Fossum	Wickman	71-60	2nd	5.0
8-30	At Cle.	L	1-3		12	6	Colon	Nomo	Wickman	71-61	2nd	6.0
8-31	N.Y.	L	1-3		9	8	Clemens	Lowe	Rivera	71-62	2nd	7.0
9-1	N.Y.	L	1-2		5	6	O. Hernandez	Urbina	Rivera	71-63	2nd	8.0
9-2	N.Y.	L	0-1		1	6	Mussina	Cone		71-64	2nd	9.0
9-4	Cle.	L	5-8		13	9	Colon	Nomo	Wickman	71-65	2nd	9.5
9-5	Cle.	W	10-7		15	7	Arrojo	Woodard	Urbina	72-65	2nd	9.5
9-6	Cle.	L	4-6		7	13	Finley	Castillo	Rocker	72-66	2nd	10.0
9-7	At N.Y.	L	2-3		4	8	O. Hernandez	Martinez	Rivera	72-67	2nd	11.0
9-8	At N.Y.	L	2-9		5	11	Mussina	Cone		72-68	2nd	12.0
9-9	At N.Y.	L	2-7		5	11	Pettitte	Nomo		72-69	2nd	13.0
9-18	T.B.	W	7-2		11	5	Nomo	Sturtze		73-69	2nd	13.0
9-19	T.B.	L	2-12		5	16	Wilson	Cone		73-70	2nd	14.0
9-20	T.B.	W	2-1		8	8	Arrojo	Creek	Beck	74-70	2nd	13.0
9-21	Det.	W	5-2		11	5	Fossum	Murray	Urbina	75-70	2nd	12.0
9-22	Det.	L	3-4		5	8	Pettyjohn	Arrojo	Anderson	75-71	2nd	12.0
9-23	Det.	L	6-12		9	13	Weaver	Nomo		75-72	2nd	13.0
9-24	Bal.	L	1-5		6	14	Maduro	Wakefield		75-73	2nd	13.5
9-25	Bal.	L	7-12		13	14	Mercedes	Castillo		75-74	2nd	13.5
9-26	Bal.	W	9-6		12	7	Fossum	Bauer	Urbina	76-74	2nd	13.5
9-27	Bal.	L	2-4		4	7	Douglass	Wakefield	Roberts	76-75	2nd	14.0
9-28	At Det.	L	1-4		10	10	Weaver	Nomo	Anderson	76-76	2nd	15.0

Date	Opp.	Res.	Score	(inn.*)	Hits	Opp. hits	Winning pitcher	Losing pitcher	Save	Record	Pos.	GB
9-29	At Det.	L	2-7		8	9	Sparks	Kim		76-77	2nd	15.0
9-30	At Det.	W	8-5		11	11	Castillo	Lima	Urbina	77-77	2nd	14.5
10-1	At T.B.	L	3-10		9	11	Sturtze	Cone		77-78	2nd	15.5
10-2	At T.B.	L	3-10		13	13	Wilson	Fossum		77-79	2nd	16.5
10-3	At T.B.	W	10-3		14	7	Lowe	Rupe	Wakefield	78-79	2nd	16.5
10-4	At Bal.	W	5-4		9	7	Nomo	Wasdin	Urbina	79-79	2nd	15.5
10-5§	At Bal.	W	5-0		10	3	Castillo	Kohlmeier		80-79		
10-5∞	At Bal.	W	7-5	(10)	9	12	Wakefield	Roberts	Garces	81-79	2nd	14.0
10-6	At Bal.	W	5-1		12	4	Cone	Bauer		82-79	2nd	13.0

Monthly records: April (16-9), May (13-13), June (17-11), July (14-12), August (11-17), September (6-15), October (5-2).
*Innings, if other than nine. §Day separate admission. ∞Night separate admission.

HIGHLIGHTS

High point: Pedro Martinez had not notched a victory in his last five tries against the Yankees. History reversed course on May 30. Martinez threw an eight-inning gem which upped his record to 7-1.

Low point: The fractured elbow catcher Jason Varitek sustained on June 7. Varitek broke his elbow on a hard rubber on-deck circle at Fenway Park, diving for a ball, ending his most promising season yet.

Turning point: When general manager Dan Duquette fired manager Jimy Williams on Aug. 16, the team was five games out of first. The team went 17-26 under replacement manager Joe Kerrigan, including a 1-13 stretch from August 25 to September 9.

Most valuable player: Trot Nixon was the most consistent force all season long. He established career highs in home runs and RBIs.

Most valuable pitcher: Hideo Nomo made a splash with his no-hit debut, but after that, he quietly put together a consistently solid season. Nomo wound up with a team-high 13 wins and 198 innings, plus his 220 strikeouts led the league.

Most improved player: David Cone was seeking redemption with Boston from his awful 2000 with the Yankees. He found it. After suffering a spring-training injury, Cone refined his mechanics and regained his effectiveness. The team won a mid-season stretch of 12 consecutive games that Cone started and in early August his record stood at 7-1 with a 4.18 ERA.

Most pleasant surprise: Casey Fossum was pitching in Class AA before being called up because of injuries. It was as a starter that he showed signs of true promise. Fossum finished 3-2 with a 4.87 ERA.

Key injuries: Pedro Martinez, Nomar Garciaparra and Carl Everett all missed significant time with injuries. ... Jason Varitek didn't play again after breaking his elbow. ... John Valentin came back less than a year after blowing out his

knee but his return lasted just 20 games. ... Rod Beck injured his elbow and underwent Tommy John surgery.

Notable: In his first game and on the first pitch he saw at Fenway Park as a Red Sox, Manny Ramirez hit a home run. ... On Aug. 6, Scott Hatteberg became the first player in major league history to hit into a triple play and hit a grand slam in the same game. ... The Red Sox allowed a major league-high 223 stolen bases and they stole a league-low 46.

—MICHAEL SILVERMAN

RECORDS

2001 regular-season record: 82-79 (2nd in A.L. East); 41-40 at home; 41-39 on road; 41-34 vs. A.L. East; 16-20 vs. A.L. Central; 15-17 vs. A.L. West; 10-8 vs. N.L.; 15-23 vs. lefthanded starters; 67-56 vs. righthanded starters; 64-72 on grass; 18-7 on turf; 24-21 in daytime; 58-58 at night; 19-23 in one-run games; 6-8 in extra-inning games; 0-0-0 in doubleheaders.

Team record past five years: 431-378 (.533, ranks 4th in league in that span).

TEAM LEADERS

Batting average: Manny Ramirez (.306).
At-bats: Trot Nixon (535).
Runs: Trot Nixon (100).
Hits: Manny Ramirez (162).
Total Bases: Manny Ramirez (322).
Doubles: Manny Ramirez (33).
Triples: Troy O'Leary (6).
Home runs: Manny Ramirez (41).
Runs batted in: Manny Ramirez (125).
Stolen bases: Carl Everett (9).
Slugging percentage: Manny Ramirez (.609).
On-base percentage: Manny Ramirez (.405).
Wins: Hideo Nomo (13).
Earned-run average: Tim Wakefield (3.90).
Complete games: Hideo Nomo (2).
Shutouts: Hideo Nomo (2).
Saves: Derek Lowe (24).

Innings pitched: Hideo Nomo (198.0).
Strikeouts: Hideo Nomo (220).

GAMES BY POSITION

Catcher: Scott Hatteberg 72, Doug Mirabelli 52, Jason Varitek 50, Joe Oliver 5, Marcus Jensen 1.

First base: Brian Daubach 106, Jose Offerman 43, Calvin Pickering 12, Shea Hillenbrand 6, Morgan Burkhart 5, Israel Alcantara 4.

Second base: Jose Offerman 91, Chris Stynes 43, Mike Lansing 31, Angel Santos 6, Lou Merloni 5.

Third base: Shea Hillenbrand 129, Chris Stynes 46, John Valentin 3, Lou Merloni 1.

Shortstop: Mike Lansing 76, Lou Merloni 45, Craig Grebeck 23, Nomar Garciaparra 21, John Valentin 18, James Lofton 7.

Outfield: Trot Nixon 145, Carl Everett 93, Troy O'Leary 89, Darren Lewis 69, Manny Ramirez 55, Dante Bichette 53, Brian Daubach 14, Israel Alcantara 8, Chris Stynes 3.

Designated hitter: Manny Ramirez 87, Dante Bichette 46, Scott Hatteberg 8, Carl Everett 7, Darren Lewis 6, Morgan Burkhart 6, Troy O'Leary 4, Calvin Pickering 2, Trot Nixon 1, Shea Hillenbrand 1, Doug Mirabelli 1, Israel Alcantara 1.

TOP DRAFT CHOICES

2a. **Kelly Shoppach,** C, Baylor Univ.
2b. **Matt Chico,** LHP, Fallbrook (Calif.) H.S.
3. **Jonathan DeVries,** C, Irvine (Calif.) H.S.
4. **Stefan Bailie,** 1B, Washington State Univ.
5. **Eric West,** SS, Southside H.S., Gadsden, Ala.
6. **Justin James,** RHP, Yukon (Okla.) H.S.
7. **Rolando Viera,** LHP, Cuba.
8. **Kevin Youkilis,** 3B, U. of Cincinnati.
9. **Billy Simon,** RHP, Wellington (Fla.) Community H.S.
10. **Ben Crockett,** RHP, Harvard Univ.

CHICAGO WHITE SOX
AMERICAN LEAGUE CENTRAL DIVISION

White Sox schedule
Home games shaded
D—Day game (games starting before 5 p.m.)
*All-Star Game at Milwaukee
Subject to changes

April
SUN	MON	TUE	WED	THU	FRI	SAT
1	2 SEA	3 SEA	4 SEA	5 KC	6 KC	
7 KC	8 DET	9 DET	10 DET	11	12 D BAL	13 D BAL
14 D BAL	15 BAL	16 CLE	17 CLE	18 CLE	19 DET	20 DET
21 D DET	22 CLE	23 CLE	24 CLE	25 D CLE	26 OAK	27 D OAK
28 D OAK	29	30 SEA				

May
SUN	MON	TUE	WED	THU	FRI	SAT
			1 SEA	2 SEA	3 OAK	4 OAK
5 D OAK	6 TEX	7 TEX	8 TEX	9 TEX	10 ANA	11 ANA
12 D ANA	13	14 TEX	15 TEX	16 TEX	17 ANA	18 ANA
19 D ANA	20 BOS	21 BOS	22 BOS	23	24 DET	25 DET
26 D DET	27 D NYY	28 NYY	29 NYY	30	31 CLE	

June
SUN	MON	TUE	WED	THU	FRI	SAT
						1 D CLE
2 D CLE	3 KC	4 KC	5 KC	6 KC	7 D MON	8 MON
9 D MON	10 NYM	11 NYM	12 NYM	13	14 D CUB	15 D CUB
16 D CUB	17	18 PHI	19 PHI	20 D PHI	21 D ATL	22 ATL
23 D ATL	24 MIN	25 MIN	26 MIN	27 D MIN	28 CUB	29 D CUB
30 D CUB						

July
SUN	MON	TUE	WED	THU	FRI	SAT
	1	2 DET	3 DET	4 DET	5 CLE	6 CLE
7 CLE	8	9 *	10	11 DET	12 DET	13 DET
14 D DET	15 CLE	16 CLE	17 KC	18 D KC	19 BAL	20 BAL
21 D BAL	22 MIN	23 MIN	24 D MIN	25	26 KC	27 KC
28 D KC	29	30 MIN	31 MIN			

August
SUN	MON	TUE	WED	THU	FRI	SAT
				1 MIN	2 TB	3 TB
4 D TB	5 D TB	6 ANA	7 ANA	8 ANA	9 SEA	10 SEA
11 D SEA	12	13 TEX	14 TEX	15	16 OAK	17 D OAK
18 D OAK	19 MIN	20 MIN	21 MIN	22	23 TB	24 TB
25 D TB	26 TOR	27 TOR	28 D TOR	29	30 DET	31 DET

September
SUN	MON	TUE	WED	THU	FRI	SAT
1 DET	2 D TOR	3 D TOR	4 TOR	5 CLE	6 CLE	7 CLE
8 CLE	9 KC	10 KC	11 KC	12 D KC	13 NYY	14 D NYY
15 D NYY	16	17 KC	18 KC	19 KC	20 MIN	21 MIN
22 D MIN	23	24 BOS	25 BOS	26 D BOS	27 MIN	28 MIN
29 D MIN	30					

2002 SEASON
CLUB DIRECTORY

Chairman
Jerry Reinsdorf
Vice chairman
Eddie Einhorn
Executive vice president
Howard Pizer
Senior vice president, general manager
Ken Williams
Sr. v.p., marketing and broadcasting
Rob Gallas
Senior vice president, baseball
Jack Gould
Senior vice president and special advisor to Jerry Reinsdorf
Ron Schueler
V.p., administration and finance
Tim Buzard
Vice president, stadium operations
Terry Savarise
V.p., free agent and major league scouting
Larry Monroe
Special assistant to Jerry Reinsdorf
Dennis Gilbert
Special assistants to Ken Williams
George Bradley
Dave Yoakum
Executive advisor to Ken Williams
Roland Hemond
Special assignment
Bryan Little
Senior director of scouting
Duane Shaffer
Director of scouting
Doug Laumann
Director of player development
Bob Fontaine Jr.
Director of major league administration
Rick Hahn
Director of minor league administration
Grace Guerrero Zwit
Director of baseball operations systems
Daniel Fabian
Director of minor league instruction
Jim Snyder
Manager of team travel
Ed Cassin
Asst. dir. of baseball operations systems
Andrew Pinter

Director of broadcasting and marketing
Bob Grim
Director of community relations
Christine Makowski
Director of sales
Jim Muno
Director of ticket operations
Bob DeVoy
Dir. of management information services
Don Brown
Director of human resources
Moira Foy
Controller
Bill Waters
Director of public relations
Scott Reifert
Trainers
Herm Schneider, Brian Ball
Director of conditioning
Steve Odgers
Team physicians
Dr. James Boscardin, Dr. Hugo Cuadros, Dr. Bernard Feldman, Dr. David Orth, Dr. Scott Price, Dr. Lowell Scott Weil
Scouting national cross-checker
Ed Pebley
Scouting supervisors
Joe Butler, Ken Stauffer
Professional scouts
Rick Ingalls, Larry Massie, Gary Pellant, Bill Young
Full-time scouts
Herman Cortes, Alex Cosmidis, Nathan Durst, Roberto Espinoza, Alex Flaugherty, Denny Gonzalez, Larry Grefer, Matt Hattabaugh, Nick Hostetler, Warren Hughes, Miguel Ibarra, George Kachigian, John Kazanas, Jose Ortega, Paul Provas, Mark Salas, Keith Staab, Alex Slattery, John Tumminia, Adam Virchis
Part-time scouts
Tommy Butler, Javier Centeno, Jaime Correa, Curt Daniels, Mike Davenport, Mariano DeLeon, John Doldoorian, James Ellison, Chuck Fox, Joe Ingalls, Jack Jolly, Robert Jones, Dario Lodigiani, Don Metzger, Glenn Murdock, Paul Murphy, Al Otto, Wuarnner Rincones, Tony Rodriguez, Oswaldo Salazar, Mike Shireley, Keith Staab, Fermin Urbi

MINOR LEAGUE AFFILIATES

Class	Team	League	Manager
AAA	Charlotte	International	Nick Leyva
AA	Birmingham	Southern	Nick Capra
A	Kannapolis	South Atlantic	Razor Shines
A	Winston-Salem	Carolina	Wally Backman
Rookie	Bristol	Appalachian	John Orton
Rookie	Tucson	Arizona	Jerry Hairston

BROADCAST INFORMATION
Radio: ESPN-AM (1000).
TV: WGN-TV (Channel 9).
Cable TV: Fox Sports Chicago.

SPRING TRAINING
Ballpark (city): Tucson Electric Park (Tucson, Ariz.).
Ticket information: 520-434-1111.

Follow the White Sox all season at: www.sportingnews.com/baseball/teams/whitesox/

SPRING TRAINING ROSTER

Manager—Jerry Manuel (7).
Coaches—Nardi Contreras (54), Wallace Johnson (18), Art Kusnyer (53), Man Soo Lee (59), Joe Nossek (23), Gary Pettis (20), Gary Ward (47).

No.	PITCHERS	B/T	Ht./Wt.	Born	2001 clubs
	Almonte, Edwin	R/R	6-3/200	12-17-76	Birmingham
49	Barcelo, Lorenzo	R/R	6-4/220	8-10-77	Charlotte, Chicago A.L.
60	Biddle, Rocky	R/R	6-3/230	5-21-76	Chicago A.L.
56	Buehrle, Mark	L/L	6-2/200	3-23-79	Chicago A.L.
29	Foulke, Keith	R/R	6-0/200	10-19-72	Chicago A.L.
52	Garland, Jon	R/R	6-6/205	9-27-79	Charlotte, Chicago A.L.
70	Ginter, Matt	R/R	6-1/215	12-24-77	Charlotte, Chicago A.L.
	Glover, Gary	R/R	6-5/205	12-3-76	Charlotte, Chicago A.L.
	Guerrier, Matt	R/R	6-3/185	8-2-78	Birmingham, Charlotte
46	Howry, Bobby	L/R	6-5/215	8-4-73	Chicago A.L.
	Jacquez, Tom	L/L	6-2/195	12-29-75	Scranton/Wilkes-Barre
	Kane, Kyle	L/R	6-3/215	2-4-76	Winston-Salem, Charlotte, Birmingham
50	Kohlmeier, Ryan	R/R	6-2/195	6-25-77	Baltimore, Rochester
40	Masaoka, Onan	R/L	6-0/188	10-27-77	Las Vegas, Charlotte
13	Osuna, Antonio	R/R	5-11/206	4-12-73	Chicago A.L.
40	Parque, Jim	L/L	5-11/165	2-8-76	Chicago A.L.
	Rauch, Jon	R/R	6-11/230	11-27-78	Charlotte
48	Ritchie, Todd	R/R	6-3/220	11-7-71	Pittsburgh
	Wright, Dan	R/R	6-5/225	12-14-77	Birmingham, Chicago A.L.
65	Wunsch, Kelly	L/L	6-5/220	7-12-72	Chicago A.L.
	Wylie, Mitch	R/R	6-3/190	1-14-77	Winston-Salem, Birmingham

No.	CATCHERS	B/T	Ht./Wt.	Born	2001 clubs
15	Alomar, Sandy	R/R	6-5/220	6-18-66	Chicago A.L.
10	Johnson, Mark	L/R	6-0/185	9-12-75	Charlotte, Chicago A.L.
	Olivo, Miguel	R/R	6-0/180	7-15-78	Birmingham
15	Paul, Josh	R/R	6-1/185	5-19-75	Chicago A.L., Charlotte

No.	INFIELDERS	B/T	Ht./Wt.	Born	2001 clubs
	Clayton, Royce	R/R	6-0/183	1-2-70	Chicago A.L.
24	Crede, Joe	R/R	6-3/195	4-26-78	Charlotte, Chicago A.L.
34	Dellaero, Jason	B/R	6-2/195	12-17-76	Charlotte
5	Durham, Ray	B/R	5-8/180	11-30-71	Chicago A.L.
47	Graffanino, Tony	R/R	6-1/195	6-6-72	Chicago A.L.
14	Konerko, Paul	R/R	6-3/211	3-5-76	Chicago A.L.
35	Thomas, Frank	R/R	6-5/270	5-27-68	Chicago A.L.
22	Valentin, Jose	L/R	5-10/190	10-12-69	Chicago A.L.

No.	OUTFIELDERS	B/T	Ht./Wt.	Born	2001 clubs
45	Lee, Carlos	R/R	6-2/220	6-20-76	Chicago A.L.
39	Liefer, Jeff	L/R	6-3/195	8-17-74	Charlotte, Chicago A.L.
30	Ordonez, Magglio	R/R	6-0/200	1-28-74	Chicago A.L.
66	Rowand, Aaron	R/R	6-1/200	8-29-77	Charlotte, Chicago A.L.
27	Simmons, Brian	B/R	6-2/190	9-4-73	Toronto, Syracuse
12	Singleton, Chris	L/L	6-2/195	8-15-72	Chicago A.L.

BALLPARK INFORMATION

Ballpark (capacity, surface)
Comiskey Park (45,887, grass)

Address
333 W. 35th St.
Chicago, IL 60616

Official website
www.whitesox.com

Business phone
312-674-1000

Ticket information
312-674-1000

Ticket prices
$26 (lower deck box, club level)
$20 (lower deck reserved)
$18 (upper deck box, bleacher reserved)
$12 (upper deck reserved)

Field dimensions (from home plate)
To left field at foul line, 330 feet
To center field, 400 feet
To right field at foul line, 335 feet

First game played
April 18, 1991 (Tigers 16, White Sox 0)

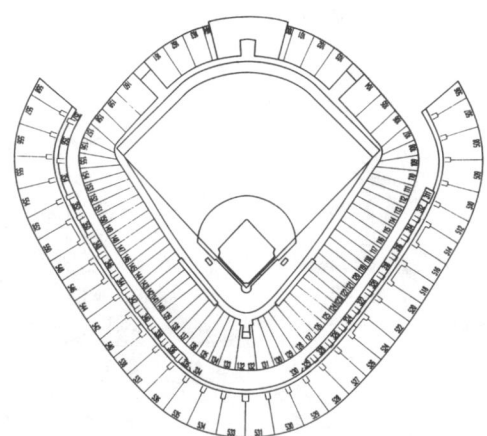

2002 SEASON *Chicago White Sox*

Date	Opp.	Res.	Score	(inn.*)	Hits	Opp. hits	Winning pitcher	Losing pitcher	Save	Record	Pos.	GB
4-2	At Cle.	W	7-4		9	7	D. Wells	Colon	Foulke	1-0	1st	+0.5
4-4	At Cle.	L	4-8		7	11	Finley	Eldred		1-1	T2nd	0.5
4-6	Det.	L	9-10	(10)	14	13	Patterson	Foulke	Jones	1-2	T3rd	2.0
4-7	Det.	L	3-5		8	7	Holt	Buehrle	Jones	1-3	4th	2.0
4-8	Det.	L	3-5		7	11	Weaver	D. Wells	Jones	1-4	5th	2.0
4-9	Cle.	W	9-2		14	11	Biddle	Finley		2-4	4th	2.0
4-10	Cle.	W	8-7		12	7	Glover	Shuey	Foulke	3-4	T2nd	2.0
4-11	Cle.	W	7-6		10	11	Lowe	Burba	Foulke	4-4	2nd	2.0
4-13	At Min.	L	4-7		7	13	Redman	Buehrle	Hawkins	4-5	3rd	3.0
4-14	At Min.	L	4-9		11	12	Radke	D. Wells		4-6	3rd	4.0
4-15	At Min.	L	3-4		8	8	Milton	Parque	Hawkins	4-7	T3rd	5.0
4-17	At Det.	L	4-7		9	13	Anderson	Wunsch	Jones	4-8	4th	5.5
4-18	At Det.	W	6-4		7	7	Buehrle	Holt	Foulke	5-8	3rd	5.5
4-19	At Det.	W	3-1		12	8	D. Wells	Weaver		6-8	3rd	5.0
4-20	Min.	L	1-4		7	7	Radke	Parque		6-9	3rd	6.0
4-21	Min.	L	3-4		7	7	Milton	Glover	Hawkins	6-10	3rd	7.0
4-22	Min.	L	2-4		5	7	Carrasco	Foulke	Hawkins	6-11	3rd	8.0
4-24	Oak.	L	4-6		9	7	Zito	Buehrle	Isringhausen	6-12	3rd	8.0
4-25	Oak.	W	2-1	(11)	8	5	Foulke	Bradford		7-12	3rd	8.0
4-26	Oak.	L	6-16		11	17	Heredia	Parque		7-13	3rd	8.0
4-27	Sea.	L	3-8		9	12	Sele	Baldwin	Sasaki	7-14	T3rd	9.0
4-28	Sea.	L	5-8		7	15	Tomko	Biddle	Sasaki	7-15	T4th	9.0
4-29	Sea.	W	2-1	(14)	7	4	Glover	Franklin		8-15	T4th	9.0
5-1	At Ana.	L	4-6		7	8	Rapp	D. Wells	Percival	8-16	5th	9.5
5-2	At Ana.	L	5-12		8	16	Washburn	Garland		8-17	5th	10.5
5-3	At Ana.	L	1-3		6	8	Valdes	Baldwin	Percival	8-18	5th	11.0
5-5	At Tex.	L	0-2		5	6	Glynn	Biddle	Zimmerman	8-19	5th	11.5
5-6	At Tex.	W	10-5		12	9	D. Wells	Rogers	Foulke	9-19	5th	11.5
5-7	At Tex.	W	7-4		9	10	Garland	Dickey	Foulke	10-19	5th	11.0
5-8	Ana.	W	2-0		3	9	Baldwin	Washburn		11-19	4th	11.0
5-9	Ana.	W	6-5		12	10	Howry	Levine		12-19	4th	10.0
5-10	Ana.	L	0-7	(10)	11	12	Percival	Foulke		12-20	4th	11.0
5-11	Tex.	W	6-5	(10)	9	10	Howry	Venafro		13-20	4th	11.0
5-12	Tex.	L	6-16		8	14	Mahomes	Garland		13-21	4th	11.0
5-13	Tex.	W	6-3		9	5	Baldwin	Helling	Foulke	14-21	4th	11.0
5-15	At Sea.	L	3-4		10	9	Nelson	Howry	Paniagua	14-22	4th	11.5
5-16	At Sea.	L	2-7		5	10	Abbott	Biddle	Paniagua	14-23	4th	12.5
5-17	At Sea.	L	1-5		6	12	Garcia	D. Wells	Nelson	14-24	5th	13.5
5-18	At Oak.	L	2-3		5	7	Heredia	K. Wells	Isringhausen	14-25	5th	13.5
5-19	At Oak.	L	3-4		5	5	Mulder	Baldwin	Isringhausen	14-26	5th	14.5
5-20	At Oak.	L	2-6		5	6	Hudson	Howry		14-27	5th	14.5
5-21	At Tor.	L	3-10		6	15	Parris	Biddle		14-28	5th	15.0
5-23	At Tor.	L	6-9		11	14	Hamilton	D. Wells	Koch	14-29	5th	15.5
5-24	At Tor.	W	3-1		10	7	K. Wells	Carpenter	Foulke	15-29	5th	15.0
5-25	At Det.	W	8-4		8	12	Lowe	Jones		16-29	5th	15.0
5-26	At Det.	W	8-0		12	3	Buehrle	Mlicki		17-29	5th	14.0
5-27	At Det.	W	3-2	(11)	9	4	Barcelo	Patterson	Lowe	18-29	4th	13.5
5-28	Tor.	W	6-3		13	8	Garland	Hamilton	Howry	19-29	4th	13.0
5-29	Tor.	L	0-4		6	9	Carpenter	K. Wells		19-30	4th	14.0
5-30	Tor.	W	4-3		5	6	Wunsch	Escobar	Foulke	20-30	4th	14.0
6-1	Det.	W	3-0		12	4	Buehrle	Mlicki	Foulke	21-30	4th	13.5
6-2	Det.	W	5-3		10	10	D. Wells	Weaver	Foulke	22-30	T3rd	12.5
6-3	Det.	W	9-6	(10)	10	11	Howry	Jones		23-30	3rd	12.5
6-5	At K.C.	W	6-2		11	6	K. Wells	Reichert	Howry	24-30	3rd	12.0
6-6	At K.C.	L	6-12		13	16	Suppan	Baldwin		24-31	3rd	12.5
6-7	At K.C.	W	5-1		13	5	Buehrle	Durbin		25-31	3rd	12.5
6-8	Chi.	W	7-3	(10)	8	8	Foulke	Duncan		26-31	3rd	11.5
6-9	Chi.	L	3-4	(10)	10	9	Van Poppel	Foulke	Fassero	26-32	3rd	12.5
6-10	Chi.	W	3-1		8	6	K. Wells	Lieber	Howry	27-32	3rd	11.5
6-12	Cin.	W	5-0		7	9	D. Wells	Dessens		28-32	3rd	11.0
6-13	Cin.	W	4-2		9	6	Buehrle	Bell	Foulke	29-32	3rd	11.0
6-14	Cin.	W	7-5		9	9	Wunsch	Brower	Foulke	30-32	3rd	10.0
6-15	At St.L.	L	3-10		5	13	An. Benes	Garland		30-33	3rd	10.0
6-16	At St.L.	L	3-8		5	12	Hermanson	K. Wells		30-34	3rd	10.0
6-17	At St.L.	L	3-8		7	10	Smith	D. Wells		30-35	3rd	10.0
6-18	K.C.	W	5-4		9	10	Buehrle	Durbin	Foulke	31-35	3rd	9.5
6-19	K.C.	W	5-3		7	6	Baldwin	Suppan	Foulke	32-35	3rd	9.5
6-20	K.C.	W	2-1		5	5	Garland	Grimsley	Foulke	33-35	3rd	8.5
6-21	At Bal.	W	6-0		13	3	K. Wells	Johnson		34-35	3rd	8.0
6-22	At Bal.	L	4-6		8	11	Mercedes	D. Wells	Groom	34-36	3rd	9.0
6-23	At Bal.	W	8-3		14	8	Glover	Ponson		35-36	3rd	8.0
6-24	At Bal.	W	8-2		14	7	Baldwin	Towers	Lowe	36-36	3rd	8.0
6-26	At Min.	L	6-7		10	11	Miller	Foulke		36-37	3rd	8.5
6-27	At Min.	L	1-4		5	9	Lohse	K. Wells	Hawkins	36-38	3rd	9.0

Date	Opp.	Res.	Score	(inn.*)	Hits	Opp. hits	Winning pitcher	Losing pitcher	Save	Record	Pos.	GB
6-28	At Min.	W	6-3		9	6	Lowe	Radke		37-38	3rd	8.0
6-29	Bal.	L	0-4		6	9	Towers	Buehrle	Trombley	37-39	3rd	9.0
6-30	Bal.	W	4-1		8	10	Baldwin	Roberts	Foulke	38-39	3rd	9.0
7-1	Bal.	L	3-11		9	15	Johnson	Biddle		38-40	3rd	10.0
7-2	Min.	L	5-7		9	9	Lohse	K. Wells	Hawkins	38-41	3rd	11.0
7-3	Min.	L	3-5	12	10		Radke	Lowe	Hawkins	38-42	3rd	12.0
7-4	Min.	W	4-3		9	10	Foulke	Hawkins		39-42	3rd	11.0
7-5	Min.	L	2-12		7	16	Mays	Baldwin		39-43	3rd	12.0
7-6	Pit.	L	6-10		13	11	Manzanillo	Howry		39-44	3rd	13.0
7-7	Pit.	W	4-1		10	4	K. Wells	Schmidt	Foulke	40-44	3rd	13.0
7-8	Pit.	W	9-2		12	7	Lowe	Ritchie		41-44	3rd	13.0
7-12	At Chi.	L	1-5		6	7	Fassero	Garland		41-45	3rd	14.0
7-13	At Chi.	W	7-2		6	9	Buehrle	Wood		42-45	3rd	13.0
7-14	At Chi.	W	3-1		7	4	Lowe	Tavarez	Foulke	43-45	3rd	13.0
7-15	At Mil.	W	3-2		6	5	Biddle	Sheets	Foulke	44-45	3rd	12.0
7-16	At Mil.	W	6-5		7	8	Baldwin	King	Foulke	45-45	3rd	11.0
7-17	At Mil.	W	8-4		12	9	K. Wells	Haynes	Garland	46-45	3rd	10.0
7-18	Cle.	L	4-9		7	10	Sabathia	Buehrle		46-46	3rd	10.0
7-19	Cle.	L	3-10		7	15	Burba	Lowe		46-47	3rd	11.0
7-20	Bos.	L	2-7		10	9	Nomo	Biddle		46-48	3rd	11.0
7-21	Bos.	W	10-3		14	7	Baldwin	Ohka		47-48	3rd	10.0
7-22	Bos.	W	13-8		13	12	Garland	Wakefield	Howry	48-48	3rd	9.0
7-23	At Cle.	L	0-2		4	5	Sabathia	Buehrle	Wickman	48-49	3rd	9.0
7-24	At Cle.	W	4-1		9	7	Lowe	Burba	Foulke	49-49	3rd	8.0
7-25	At Cle.	L	5-7		12	9	Westbrook	Biddle	Wickman	49-50	3rd	9.0
7-26	At Cle.	W	5-4		11	8	Ginter	Nagy	Foulke	50-50	3rd	9.0
7-27	At Bos.	L	5-9		10	11	Saberhagen	K. Wells		50-51	3rd	9.0
7-28	At Bos.	W	3-1		9	5	Buehrle	Wakefield	Foulke	51-51	3rd	8.5
7-29	At Bos.	L	3-4		6	5	Beck	Embree	Lowe	51-52	3rd	8.5
7-31	K.C.	L	1-2	(10)	6	9	Byrd	Foulke	Hernandez	51-53	3rd	8.5
8-1	K.C.	W	7-6		10	12	Wright	George	Foulke	52-53	3rd	8.5
8-2	K.C.	L	3-6		7	8	Suppan	K. Wells	Hernandez	52-54	3rd	8.5
8-3	T.B.	W	4-0		7	1	Buehrle	Bierbrodt		53-54	3rd	8.0
8-4	T.B.	W	8-6		8	15	Biddle	Kennedy	Foulke	54-54	3rd	8.0
8-5	T.B.	L	4-6		9	14	Zambrano	Howry	Yan	54-55	3rd	8.0
8-6	T.B.	W	5-2		7	2	Wright	Wallace	Foulke	55-55	3rd	7.5
8-7	At Ana.	L	3-9		6	15	Rapp	K. Wells		55-56	3rd	7.5
8-8	At Ana.	W	15-1		19	4	Buehrle	Washburn		56-56	3rd	7.5
8-9	At Ana.	L	2-3		5	7	Valdes	Lowe	Percival	56-57	3rd	7.5
8-10	At Sea.	W	8-6		11	6	Biddle	Sasaki	Foulke	57-57	3rd	6.5
8-11	At Sea.	L	3-4		7	8	Franklin	Foulke		57-58	3rd	6.5
8-12	At Sea.	L	1-2		3	7	Rhodes	K. Wells	Sasaki	57-59	3rd	7.5
8-14	Tex.	W	7-4		10	8	Buehrle	Myette	Foulke	58-59	3rd	7.5
8-15	Tex.	W	6-5		8	11	K. Wells	Mahomes	Foulke	59-59	3rd	7.5
8-16	Tex.	W	7-5		12	10	K. Wells	Petkovsek	Foulke	60-59	3rd	7.5
8-17	Oak.	L	2-9		9	12	Hiljus	Wright		60-60	3rd	7.5
8-18	Oak.	L	4-5		9	8	Heredia	Howry	Isringhausen	60-61	3rd	8.5
8-19	Oak.	L	7-8		13	10	Magnante	Biddle	Isringhausen	60-62	3rd	8.5
8-20	At K.C.	L	1-10		5	13	Stein	Lowe		60-63	3rd	8.5
8-21	At K.C.	W	6-1		13	8	Garland	Byrd		61-63	3rd	8.5
8-22	At K.C.	W	13-12		18	18	K. Wells	Henry	Foulke	62-63	3rd	8.5
8-23	At K.C.	W	7-6		13	10	Biddle	Suppan	Foulke	63-63	3rd	8.5
8-24	At T.B.	W	5-4		7	9	Buehrle	Sturtze	Foulke	64-63	3rd	7.5
8-25	At T.B.	L	4-8		9	13	Kennedy	Wright		64-64	3rd	7.5
8-26	At T.B.	W	3-2		7	6	Garland	Seay	Foulke	65-64	3rd	7.5
8-28	At Det.	W	8-6		18	10	Embree	Patterson	Howry	66-64	3rd	7.5
8-29	At Det.	W	8-3		13	7	Glover	Redman		67-64	3rd	7.5
8-30	At Det.	L	1-3		8	6	Cornejo	Buehrle	Anderson	67-65	3rd	8.5
8-31	Cle.	W	11-8		12	13	Howry	Westbrook	Foulke	68-65	3rd	7.5
9-1	Cle.	L	3-4		8	7	Drese	Garland	Wickman	68-66	3rd	8.5
9-2	Cle.	W	19-10		17	12	Biddle	Burba		69-66	3rd	7.5
9-3	Cle.	L	3-6		7	11	Sabathia	Glover	Wickman	69-67	3rd	8.5
9-4†	Det.	W	10-1		15	4	Buehrle	Cornejo		70-67		
9-4‡	Det.	W	4-0		9	4	Lowe	Pettyjohn		71-67	3rd	8.0
9-5	Det.	W	5-3		10	8	Wright	Sparks	Foulke	72-67	3rd	7.0
9-6	Det.	L	2-6		5	12	Weaver	Garland		72-68	3rd	8.0
9-7	At Cle.	W	10-7		18	10	Biddle	Burba	Foulke	73-68	T2nd	7.0
9-8	At Cle.	L	7-8		11	9	Baez	Foulke		73-69	3rd	8.0
9-9	At Cle.	L	8-9		10	11	Wickman	Foulke		73-70	3rd	9.0
9-10	At Cle.	W	7-1		10	6	Wright	Colon		74-70	3rd	8.0
9-18	N.Y.	L	3-11		7	16	O. Hernandez	Buehrle		74-71	3rd	9.0
9-19	N.Y.	L	3-6		7	9	Clemens	Glover	Rivera	74-72	3rd	10.0
9-20	N.Y.	W	7-5		7	8	Lowe	Pettitte	Foulke	75-72	3rd	9.0
9-21	K.C.	W	8-7		11	12	Lowe	Henry		76-72	3rd	8.0
9-22	K.C.	W	5-4	(10)	9	10	Foulke	Stein		77-72	3rd	8.0
9-23	K.C.	W	10-2		8	8	Buehrle	Durbin		78-72	3rd	8.0
9-25	Min.	L	2-4		4	7	Mays	Glover	Guardado	78-73	3rd	8.5
9-26	Min.	W	6-3		8	10	K. Wells	Reed	Foulke	79-73	3rd	8.0

Date	Opp.	Res.	Score	(inn.*)	Hits	Opp. hits	Winning pitcher	Losing pitcher	Save	Record	Pos.	GB
9-27	Min.	W	9-3		11	8	Wright	Radke	Lowe	80-73	T2nd	7.5
9-28	At K.C.	L	2-3		7	8	Durbin	Embree	Hernandez	80-74	3rd	7.5
9-29	At K.C.	W	10-2		16	9	Buehrle	Suppan		81-74	T2nd	7.5
9-30	At K.C.	W	5-2		12	5	Glover	George	Foulke	82-74	2nd	7.5
10-1	At N.Y.	L	1-8		4	8	Hitchcock	K. Wells		82-75	2nd	8.0
10-2	At N.Y.	L	4-6		7	11	Lilly	Wright	Rivera	82-76	3rd	8.0
10-3	At N.Y.	L	1-2		6	6	Mussina	Garland	Rivera	82-77	3rd	9.0
10-5	At Min.	W	7-4		11	12	Buehrle	Reed	Foulke	83-77	T2nd	7.0
10-6	At Min.	L	5-6		10	11	Cressend	Glover	Guardado	83-78	3rd	7.0
10-7	At Min.	L	5-8		7	11	Radke	K. Wells	Guardado	83-79	3rd	8.0

Monthly records: April (8-15), May (12-15), June (18-9), July (13-14), August (17-12), September (14-9), October (1-5).
*Innings, if other than nine. †First game of a doubleheader. ‡Second game of a doubleheader.

HIGHLIGHTS

High point: Trailing the Mariners 6-3 with one out in the ninth inning in an August 10 game at Seattle, the White Sox erupted for five runs off All-Star closer Kazuhiro Sasaki and won 8-6. The victory moved the Sox within 6 1/2 games of first in the A.L. Central.

Low point: On April 27, against the Mariners, Frank Thomas dove for a line drive off the bat of Ichiro Suzuki and landed awkwardly on his right arm. Thomas wound up tearing his right triceps on the play and had season-ending surgery. The injury to Thomas left a huge hole in the middle of the lineup.

Turning point: The team went through the motions in a 9-6 defeat to the Blue Jays on May 23. It was their eighth straight loss and dropped the White Sox 15 games below .500. The Sox regrouped and made a mild run at first place during the second half of the season.

Most valuable player: Magglio Ordonez became the first player in A.L. history to bat .300 and reach 30 home runs, 100 RBIs, 40 doubles and 25 stolen bases in the same season.

Most valuable pitcher: Mark Buehrle seized the job as the No. 5 starter in spring training. The youngster ascended to ace status during the season. He ranked among league leaders with a 3.29 ERA.

Most improved player: Chris Singleton batted .300 in 1999. He hit only .254 in 2000, and when his average dropped to .248 in late May last season, he was buried on the bench. But the smooth-fielding outfielder shortened up his swing and wound up batting .298.

Most pleasant surprise: In 254 at-bats, Jeff Liefer hit 18 home runs while providing some much-needed pop from the left side of the plate. The team desperately needs his bat in the lineup. Liefer can play third and first base and left and right field.

Key injuries: After losing Thomas in the first month of the season, the team also lost starters Cal Eldred, Rocky Biddle and Jim Parque and relievers Antonio Osuna, Kelly Wunsch and Lorenzo Barcelo. ... No. 1 starter David Wells had back surgery in mid-July and missed the rest of the year. ... Injuries also put Harold Baines and Sandy Alomar Jr. on the disabled list.

Notable: The White Sox hit 214 home runs, just two shy of the team record. ... 2B Ray Durham has scored over 100 runs in five straight seasons. ... The White Sox have won 80 or more games nine times over the last 12 seasons.

—SCOT GREGOR

RECORDS

2001 regular-season record: 83-79 (3rd in A.L. Central); 46-35 at home; 37-44 on road; 16-16 vs. A.L. East; 42-34 vs. A.L. Central; 13-23 vs. A.L. West; 12-6 vs. N.L.; 17-18 vs. lefthanded starters; 66-61 vs. righthanded starters; 78-69 on grass; 5-10 on turf; 27-23 in daytime; 56-56 at night; 22-22 in one-run games; 7-4 in extra-inning games; 1-0-0 in doubleheaders.

Team record past five years: 413-395 (.511, ranks 6th in league in that span).

TEAM LEADERS

Batting average: Magglio Ordonez (.305).
At-bats: Ray Durham (611).
Runs: Ray Durham (104).
Hits: Magglio Ordonez (181).
Total Bases: Magglio Ordonez (316).
Doubles: Ray Durham (42).
Triples: Ray Durham (10).
Home runs: Paul Konerko (32).
Runs batted in: Magglio Ordonez (113).
Stolen bases: Magglio Ordonez (25).
Slugging percentage: Magglio Ordonez (.533).
On-base percentage: Magglio Ordonez (.382).
Wins: Mark Buehrle (16).
Earned-run average: Mark Buehrle (3.29).
Complete games: Mark Buehrle (4).
Shutouts: Mark Buehrle (2).

Saves: Keith Foulke (42).
Innings pitched: Mark Buehrle (221.1).
Strikeouts: Mark Buehrle (126).

GAMES BY POSITION

Catcher: Sandy Alomar Jr. 69, Mark L. Johnson 61, Josh Paul 56, Mark Dalesandro 1.

First base: Paul Konerko 144, Jeff Liefer 15, Herbert Perry 12, Frank Thomas 3, Tony Graffanino 1.

Second base: Ray Durham 150, Tony Graffanino 20.

Third base: Herbert Perry 68, Jose Valentin 66, Tony Graffanino 38, Jeff Liefer 15, Joe Crede 15.

Shortstop: Royce Clayton 133, Jose Valentin 43, Tony Graffanino 5.

Outfield: Magglio Ordonez 155, Chris Singleton 133, Carlos Lee 130, Aaron Rowand 61, Jeff Liefer 38, Jose Valentin 24, Julio Ramirez 21, McKay Christensen 6, Tony Graffanino 3, Jose Canseco 2.

Designated hitter: Jose Canseco 68, Harold Baines 22, Carlos Lee 17, Frank Thomas 16, Paul Konerko 11, Herbert Perry 10, Jeff Liefer 10, Magglio Ordonez 3, Tony Graffanino 3, Chris Singleton 2, Ray Durham 1.

TOP DRAFT CHOICES

1a. **Kris Honel**, RHP, Providence Catholic H.S., New Lenox, Ill.
1b. **Wyatt Allen**, RHP, U. of Tennessee.
2. **Ryan Wing**, LHP, Riverside (Calif.) C.C.
3. **Jonathan Zeringue**, C, White H.S., Thibodeaux, La.
4. **Jay Mattox**, OF, Conway (Ark.) H.S.
5. **Andy Gonzalez**, SS, Florida Air Academy, Melbourne, Fla.
6. **Stevie Daniel**, 2B/SS, Univ. of Tennessee.
7. **Brandon Camardese**, LHP, Chaminade-Madonna H.S., Cooper City, Fla.
8. **Andrew Fryson**, RHP, Wallace State (Ala.) J.C.
9. **Jim Bullard**, LHP, UC Santa Barbara.
10. **Tim Bittner**, LHP, Marist University.

CLEVELAND INDIANS
AMERICAN LEAGUE CENTRAL DIVISION

Indians schedule
Home games shaded
D—Day game (games starting before 5 p.m.)
All-Star Game at Milwaukee
Subject to changes

April

SUN	MON	TUE	WED	THU	FRI	SAT
	1 ANA	2 ANA	3 ANA	4	5 D DET	6 D DET
7 DET	8 D MIN	9 MIN	10 MIN	11 MIN	12 KC	13 D KC
14 D KC	15	16 CWS	17 CWS	18 CWS	19 MIN	20 MIN
21 D MIN	22 CWS	23 CWS	24 CWS	25 CWS	26 TEX	27 TEX
28 TEX	29	30 ANA				

May

SUN	MON	TUE	WED	THU	FRI	SAT
			1 ANA	2 ANA	3 TEX	4 D TEX
5 D TEX	6 BAL	7 BAL	8 BAL	9 KC	10 KC	11 KC
12 KC	13 D	14 BAL	15 BAL	16 BAL	17 KC	18 KC
19 KC	20 DET	21 DET	22 DET	23	24 TOR	25 D TOR
26 D TOR	27 D DET	28 DET	29 DET	30 DET	31 CWS	

June

SUN	MON	TUE	WED	THU	FRI	SAT
						1 D CWS
2 CWS	3	4 MIN	5 MIN	6 MIN	7 NYM	8 NYM
9 NYM	10 PHI	11 PHI	12 PHI	13	14 COL	15 COL
16 COL	17	18 FLA	19 FLA	20 FLA	21 MON	22 MON
23 D MON	24	25 BOS	26 BOS	27 BOS	28 ARI	29 ARI
30 D ARI						

July

SUN	MON	TUE	WED	THU	FRI	SAT
	1 NYY	2 NYY	3 NYY	4 D CWS	5 CWS	6 CWS
7 D CWS	8	9 *	10	11 NYY	12 NYY	13 NYY
14 NYY	15 CWS	16 CWS	17 MIN	18 MIN	19 KC	20 KC
21 KC	22	23 NYY	24 NYY	25	26 DET	27 DET
28 DET	29 OAK	30 D OAK	31 D OAK			

August

SUN	MON	TUE	WED	THU	FRI	SAT
				1 SEA	2 SEA	3 D SEA
4 D SEA	5	6 TB	7 TB	8 TB	9 TEX	10 D TEX
11 D TEX	12	13 TB	14 TB	15 TB	16 ANA	17 ANA
18 ANA	19 OAK	20 OAK	21 OAK	22 OAK	23 SEA	24 D SEA
25 D SEA	26 DET	27 DET	28 DET	29	30 BOS	31 BOS

September

SUN	MON	TUE	WED	THU	FRI	SAT
1 D BOS	2 D DET	3 DET	4 DET	5 CWS	6 CWS	7 CWS
8 D CWS	9 TOR	10 TOR	11 TOR	12 MIN	13 MIN	14 MIN
15 MIN	16 BOS	17 BOS	18 BOS	19 KC	20 KC	21 KC
22 KC	23	24 MIN	25 MIN	26 MIN	27 KC	28 KC
29 D KC	30					

2002 SEASON
CLUB DIRECTORY

President and chief executive officer
Lawrence J. Dolan
Executive vice president, general manager
Mark Shapiro
Executive vice president, business
Dennis Lehman
Sr. v.p., finance & chief financial officer
Ken Stefanov
Vice president and general counsel
Paul J. Dolan
Vice president, public relations
Bob DiBiasio
V.p., marketing and broadcasting
Valerie Arcuri
Vice president, sales
Jon Starrett
Vice president, ballpark operations
Jim Folk
V.p., merchandising & licensing
Jayne Churchmack
Assistant g.m., scouting operations
John Mirabelli
Assistant general manager
Neal Huntington
Assistant general manager
Chris Antonetti
Director of player development
John Farrell
Director of player personnel
Steve Lubratich
Assistant director, scouting
Brad Grant
Director of media relations
Bart Swain

Mgr. of media rel., admin. & credentials
Susie Giuliano
Manager, media relations
Curtis Danburg
Coordinator, media relations
Jeff Sibel
Director of team travel
Mike Seghi
Head trainer
Paul Spicuzza
Assistant trainer
Jim Warfield
Clubhouse manager
Ted Walsh
Visiting clubhouse
Cy Buynak
Groundskeeper
Brandon Koehnke
National cross-checker, West Coast supervisor
Jesse Flores
National cross-checker, East Coast supervisor
Jerry Jordan
Midwest supervisor
Bob Mayer
Full-time scouts
Steve Abney, Doug Baker, Keith Boeck, Jim Bretz, Paul Cogan, Henry Cruz, Dan Durst, Jim Gabella, Chris Jefts, Tim Kissner, Chad MacDonald, Scott Meaney, Dave Miller, Les Parari, Chuck Ricci, Phil Rossi, Bill Schudlich, Jason Smith, Shawn Whalen

MINOR LEAGUE AFFILIATES

Class	Team	League	Manager
AAA	Buffalo	International	Eric Wedge
AA	Akron	Eastern	Brad Komminsk
A	Kinston	Carolina	Ted Kubiak
A	Columbus	South Atlantic	Torey Lovullo
A	Mahoning Valley	New York-Pennsylvania	Chris Bando
Rookie	Burlington	Appalachian	Rouglas Odor

BROADCAST INFORMATION
Radio: WTAM-AM (1100).
Cable TV: Fox Sports Net Ohio.

SPRING TRAINING
Ballpark (city): Chain Of Lakes (Winter Haven, Fla.).
Ticket information: 813-287-8844.

Follow the Indians all season at: www.sportingnews.com/baseball/teams/indians/

SPRING TRAINING ROSTER

Manager—Charlie Manuel (32).
Coaches—Luis Isaac (4), Grady Little (38), Dave Miller, Eddie Murray, Joel Skinner (35), Dan Williams (43).

No.	PITCHERS	B/T	Ht./Wt.	Born	2001 clubs
55	Baez, Danys	R/R	6-3/225	9-10-77	Buffalo, Akron, Cleveland
	Vargas, Martin	R/R	6-0/155	2-22-78	Akron, Buffalo
40	Colon, Bartolo	R/R	6-0/230	5-24-75	Cleveland
56	DePaula, Sean	R/R	6-4/215	11-7-73	Buffalo
	Drese, Ryan	R/R	6-3/220	4-5-76	Akron, Buffalo, Cleveland
	Drew, Tim	R/R	6-1/195	8-31-78	Cleveland, Buffalo
73	Rincon, Ricky	L/L	5-10/187	4-13-70	Cleveland
31	Finley, Chuck	L/L	6-6/225	11-26-62	Cleveland, Akron
	Herrera, Alex	L/L	5-11/175	11-5-79	Kinston, Akron
41	Nagy, Charles	L/R	6-3/200	5-5-67	Buffalo, Cleveland
	Paronto, Chad	R/R	6-5/225	7-28-75	Rochester, Baltimore
65	Phillips, Jason	R/R	6-6/225	3-22-74	Altoona, Akron, Buffalo
36	Radinsky, Scott	L/L	6-3/215	3-3-68	Akron, Cleveland, Buffalo
54	Riske, Dave	R/R	6-2/180	10-23-76	Buffalo, Cleveland
	Sabathia, C.C.	L/L	6-7/235	7-21-80	Cleveland
53	Shuey, Paul	R/R	6-3/215	9-16-70	Cleveland, Akron
	Smith, Roy	R/R	6-6/235	5-18-76	Buffalo, Cleveland
78	Westbrook, Jake	R/R	6-3/185	9-29-77	Buffalo, Cleveland
	Wickman, Bob	R/R	6-1/234	2-6-69	Cleveland
	Wohlers, Mark	R/R	6-4/207	1-23-70	Cincinnati, New York A.L.
27	Wright, Jaret	R/R	6-2/230	12-29-75	Buffalo, Akron, Cleveland

No.	CATCHERS	B/T	Ht./Wt.	Born	2001 clubs
2	Diaz, Einar	R/R	5-10/185	12-28-72	Cleveland
36	Laker, Tim	R/R	6-3/225	11-27-69	Buffalo, Cleveland
	Luderer, Brian	R/R	5-11/195	8-19-78	Midland
	Martinez, Victor	B/R	6-2/170	12-23-78	Kinston
10	Taubensee, Eddie	L/R	6-3/230	10-31-68	Cleveland, Buffalo, Akron

No.	INFIELDERS	B/T	Ht./Wt.	Born	2001 clubs
33	Branyan, Russell	L/R	6-3/195	12-19-75	Cleveland
17	Fryman, Travis	R/R	6-1/195	3-25-69	Buffalo, Akron, Cleveland
12	Gutierrez, Ricky	R/R	6-1/195	5-23-70	Chicago N.L.
72	McDonald, John	R/R	5-11/175	9-24-74	Cleveland, Buffalo
25	Thome, Jim	L/R	6-4/240	8-27-70	Cleveland
13	Vizquel, Omar	B/R	5-9/185	4-24-67	Cleveland

No.	OUTFIELDERS	B/T	Ht./Wt.	Born	2001 clubs
9	Anderson, Brady	L/L	6-1/202	1-18-64	Baltimore
24	Bradley, Milton	B/R	6-0/170	4-15-78	Montreal, Ottawa, Buffalo, Cleveland
23	Burks, Ellis	R/R	6-2/205	9-11-64	Cleveland
12	Cordero, Wil	R/R	6-2/200	10-3-71	Cleveland
25	Escobar, Alex	R/R	6-1/180	9-6-78	Norfolk, New York N.L.
24	Garcia, Karim	L/L	6-0/172	10-29-75	Buffalo, Cleveland
50	Lawton, Matt	L/R	5-10/186	11-3-71	Minnesota, New York N.L.

BALLPARK INFORMATION

Ballpark (capacity, surface)
Jacobs Field (43,368, grass)
Address
2401 Ontario St.
Cleveland, OH 44115
Official website
www.indians.com
Business phone
216-420-4200
Ticket information
216-420-4200
Ticket prices
$40 (field box)
$27 (baseline box, IF lower box, view box)
$25 (lower box), $21 (IF upper box)
$20 (lower reserved, mezzanine, upper box)
$19 (field bleachers), $17 (bleachers)
$12 (upper reserved)
$7 (upper reserved general admission)
$6 (standing room)
Field dimensions (from home plate)
To left field at foul line, 325 feet
To center field, 405 feet
To right field at foul line, 325 feet
First game played
April 4, 1994 (Indians 4, Mariners 3, 11 innings)

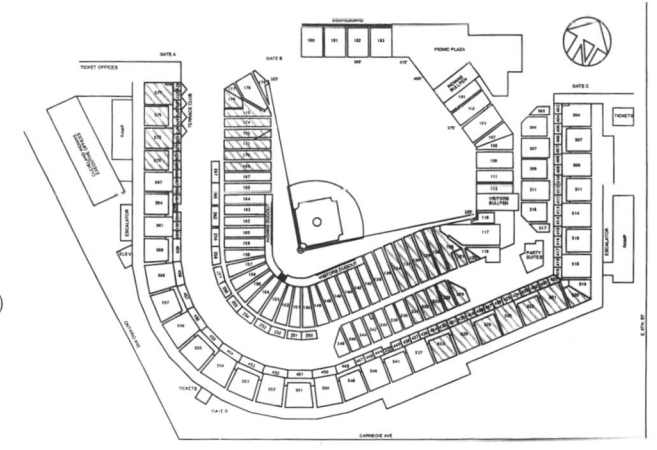

2001 REVIEW
DAY BY DAY

Date	Opp.	Res.	Score	(inn.*)	Hits	Opp. hits	Winning pitcher	Losing pitcher	Save	Record	Pos.	GB
4-2	Chi.	L	4-7		7	9	D. Wells	Colon	Foulke	0-1	T2nd	1.0
4-4	Chi.	W	8-4		11	7	Finley	Eldred		1-1	T2nd	0.5
4-6	Bal.	W	4-3		5	6	Rincon	Mercedes	Wickman	2-1	2nd	1.0
4-7	Bal.	L	2-4	(11)	6	10	Trombley	Reed	Kohlmeier	2-2	T2nd	1.0
4-8	Bal.	W	4-3		8	3	Speier	Maduro	Wickman	3-2	T1st	...
4-9	At Chi.	L	2-9		11	14	Biddle	Finley		3-3	2nd	1.0
4-10	At Chi.	L	7-8		7	12	Glover	Shuey	Foulke	3-4	T2nd	2.0
4-11	At Chi.	L	6-7		11	10	Lowe	Burba	Foulke	3-5	T3rd	3.0
4-12	At Det.	W	5-3		10	9	Colon	Holt	Wickman	4-5	3rd	2.5
4-13	At Det.	W	9-8		15	10	Sabathia	Weaver	Shuey	5-5	2nd	2.5
4-14	At Det.	L	0-1		4	3	Sparks	Finley		5-6	2nd	3.5
4-17	At Bal.	W	8-1		10	4	Burba	Mercedes		6-6	2nd	3.5
4-18	At Bal.	W	4-1		6	6	Colon	Hentgen		7-6	2nd	3.5
4-19	At Bal.	W	11-5		14	9	Sabathia	McElroy		8-6	2nd	3.0
4-20	Det.	W	5-4		12	9	Wickman	Nitkowski		9-6	2nd	3.0
4-21	Det.	W	5-4	(11)	5	7	Reed	Jones		10-6	2nd	3.0
4-22	Det.	W	11-3		19	7	Burba	Mlicki		11-6	2nd	3.0
4-24	Ana.	L	2-7		10	9	Schoeneweis	Colon		11-7	2nd	3.0
4-25	Ana.	L	1-3		10	5	Valdes	Sabathia	Percival	11-8	2nd	4.0
4-26	Ana.	W	6-5		9	6	Shuey	Hasegawa	Wickman	12-8	2nd	3.0
4-27	Tex.	L	9-11		14	10	Mahomes	Drew	Zimmerman	12-9	2nd	4.0
4-28	Tex.	W	7-3		11	8	Burba	Helling		13-9	2nd	3.0
4-29	Tex.	W	9-2		11	5	Colon	Davis		14-9	2nd	3.0
5-1	At K.C.	W	13-2		11	7	Finley	Durbin		15-9	2nd	2.5
5-2	At K.C.	W	8-4		12	9	Sabathia	Suzuki		16-9	2nd	2.5
5-3	At K.C.	W	9-4		13	10	Burba	Reichert		17-9	2nd	2.0
5-4	At T.B.	W	8-6		14	13	Colon	Lopez	Shuey	18-9	2nd	2.0
5-5	At T.B.	W	9-4		12	8	Speier	Wilson	Karsay	19-9	2nd	1.0
5-6	At T.B.	W	10-3		13	9	Finley	Creek		20-9	2nd	1.0
5-8	K.C.	W	8-4		10	10	Burba	Cogan		21-9	2nd	1.0
5-9	K.C.	W	5-1		10	8	Sabathia	Reichert		22-9	T1st	...
5-10	K.C.	L	3-8		8	13	Meadows	Colon		22-10	2nd	1.0
5-11	T.B.	W	10-6		13	12	Rodriguez	Rekar		23-10	2nd	1.0
5-12	T.B.	W	8-0		10	10	Finley	Rose		24-10	T1st	...
5-13	T.B.	L	0-7		8	14	Sturtze	Burba		24-11	2nd	1.0
5-15	At Tex.	W	8-6		16	10	Sabathia	Davis	Wickman	25-11	2nd	0.5
5-16	At Tex.	W	4-3		11	6	Shuey	Crabtree	Wickman	26-11	2nd	0.5
5-17	At Tex.	L	7-12		12	16	Rogers	Finley		26-12	2nd	1.5
5-18	At Ana.	W	7-2		9	6	Burba	Rapp		27-12	2nd	0.5
5-19	At Ana.	W	4-3	(10)	12	11	Shuey	Percival	Wickman	28-12	2nd	0.5
5-20	At Ana.	L	6-9		10	14	Levine	Rodriguez	Percival	28-13	2nd	0.5
5-22	Det.	L	0-3		7	8	Weaver	Colon	Jones	28-14	2nd	1.5
5-23	Det.	W	4-3	(10)	12	8	Wickman	Borkowski		29-14	2nd	0.5
5-24	Det.	W	8-5		10	14	Burba	Santos	Wickman	30-14	T1st	...
5-25	N.Y.	W	6-4		11	9	Rodriguez	O. Hernandez	Wickman	31-14	1st	+1.0
5-26	N.Y.	L	5-12		10	15	Clemens	Sabathia		31-15	1st	+0.5
5-27	N.Y.	L	2-6		9	7	Lilly	Colon	Rivera	31-16	2nd	0.5
5-28	At Det.	L	6-12		10	15	Sparks	Finley		31-17	2nd	1.0
5-29	At Det.	W	6-4		9	9	Shuey	Murray	Wickman	32-17	2nd	1.0
5-30	At Det.	W	8-4		10	13	Wright	Holt	Wickman	33-17	2nd	1.0
6-1	At N.Y.	W	7-4	(6)	10	5	Sabathia	Lilly	Rincon	34-17	2nd	0.5
6-2	At N.Y.	L	4-9		12	13	Clemens	Colon	Rivera	34-18	2nd	0.5
6-3	At N.Y.	W	4-3		10	6	Nagy	Pettitte	Wickman	35-18	2nd	0.5
6-4	At Min.	L	10-11		14	16	Guardado	Shuey		35-19	2nd	1.5
6-5	At Min.	W	5-0		11	6	Wright	Romero		36-19	2nd	0.5
6-6	At Min.	W	5-2		8	5	Shuey	Cressend	Wickman	37-19	1st	+0.5
6-7	At Min.	W	6-2		8	7	Colon	Radke		38-19	1st	+1.5
6-8	Cin.	L	4-7		7	12	Brower	Rodriguez	Graves	38-20	1st	+0.5
6-9	Cin.	W	10-2		14	5	Burba	O. Fernandez		39-20	1st	+0.5
6-10	Cin.	L	3-9		9	13	Reitsma	Wright		39-21	1st	+0.5
6-12	Mil.	L	2-4		9	7	Fox	Shuey	Leskanic	39-22	2nd	0.5
6-13	Mil.	W	5-2	(10)	9	7	Wickman	Fox		40-22	2nd	0.5
6-14	Mil.	L	4-9		10	17	Sheets	Nagy		40-23	2nd	0.5
6-15	At Pit.	L	3-6		6	11	Anderson	Burba	M. Williams	40-24	2nd	0.5
6-16	At Pit.	L	4-6		11	8	Schmidt	Wright	M. Williams	40-25	2nd	0.5
6-17	At Pit.	L	0-1		4	3	Ritchie	Karsay		40-26	2nd	0.5
6-19	Min.	L	9-10	(12)	16	18	Wells	Nagy		40-27	2nd	1.5
6-20	Min.	W	4-2		9	8	Westbrook	Mays	Wickman	41-27	2nd	0.5
6-21	Min.	W	9-6	(7)	11	9	Woodard	Romero	Rincon	42-27	1st	+0.5
6-22	At K.C.	W	6-5		14	7	Sabathia	Stein	Wickman	43-27	1st	+1.5
6-23	At K.C.	L	2-3		9	4	Durbin	Burba	Hernandez	43-28	1st	+1.5
6-24	At K.C.	W	4-2		10	6	Colon	Suppan	Rocker	44-28	1st	+1.5
6-25	At N.Y.	L	7-8		10	13	Witasick	Rincon	Rivera	44-29	1st	+0.5
6-26	At N.Y.	W	5-3		7	10	Nagy	A. Hernandez	Rocker	45-29	1st	+0.5

Date	Opp.	Res.	Score	(inn.*)	Hits	Opp. hits	Winning pitcher	Losing pitcher	Save	Record	Pos.	GB
6-27	At N.Y.	L	5-15		9	17	Mussina	Sabathia		45-30	2nd	0.5
6-29	K.C.	L	3-5		6	9	Suppan	Burba	Hernandez	45-31	2nd	1.0
6-30	K.C.	L	7-11		10	15	Wilson	Colon		45-32	2nd	2.0
7-1	K.C.	L	11-13		13	15	Stein	Nagy	Hernandez	45-33	2nd	3.0
7-2	K.C.	W	2-1		7	6	Rocker	Cogan		46-33	2nd	3.0
7-3	Bos.	W	9-1		14	5	Westbrook	Ohka		47-33	2nd	3.0
7-4	Bos.	L	4-13		7	19	Wakefield	Burba		47-34	2nd	3.0
7-5	Bos.	L	4-5		7	7	Lowe	Rocker		47-35	2nd	4.0
7-6	St.L.	W	14-2		15	10	Nagy	Morris		48-35	2nd	4.0
7-7	St.L.	W	7-6	(10)	8	11	Rocker	Veres		49-35	2nd	4.0
7-8	St.L.	L	3-4		9	9	Timlin	Rocker		49-36	2nd	5.0
7-12	At Cin.	W	7-0		14	7	Colon	Reitsma		50-36	2nd	5.0
7-13	At Cin.	W	5-1		6	4	Sabathia	Dessens		51-36	2nd	4.0
7-14	At Cin.	L	5-6	(13)	12	9	Graves	Rocker		51-37	2nd	5.0
7-15	At Hou.	L	3-5		6	9	Redding	Westbrook	Wagner	51-38	2nd	5.0
7-16	At Hou.	L	8-10		10	15	Villone	Rocker		51-39	2nd	5.0
7-17	At Hou.	W	10-4		13	9	Colon	Reynolds		52-39	2nd	4.0
7-18	At Chi.	W	9-4		10	7	Sabathia	Buehrle		53-39	2nd	3.0
7-19	At Chi.	W	10-3		15	7	Burba	Lowe		54-39	2nd	3.0
7-20	Det.	L	3-7		10	10	Holt	Westbrook		54-40	2nd	3.0
7-21	Det.	W	8-4		12	7	Nagy	Pettyjohn		55-40	2nd	2.0
7-22	Det.	W	6-3		9	9	Colon	Weaver		56-40	2nd	1.0
7-23	Chi.	W	2-0		5	4	Sabathia	Buehrle	Wickman	57-40	1st	...
7-24	Chi.	L	1-4		7	9	Lowe	Burba	Foulke	57-41	1st	...
7-25	Chi.	W	7-5		9	12	Westbrook	Biddle	Wickman	58-41	1st	...
7-26	Chi.	L	4-5		8	11	Ginter	Nagy	Foulke	58-42	2nd	1.0
7-27	At Det.	W	7-4		11	10	Colon	Pettyjohn	Wickman	59-42	1st	...
7-28§	At Det.	W	6-4		12	6	Daez	Murray	Wickman	60-42		
7-28∞	At Det.	L	2-4		6	9	Weaver	Woodard	Anderson	60-43	1st	+0.5
7-29	At Det.	L	3-8		5	12	Sparks	Burba		60-44	1st	+0.5
7-31	Oak.	L	2-11		8	15	Lidle	Westbrook		60-45	1st	+0.5
8-1	Oak.	W	6-5		12	11	Baez	Mecir	Wickman	61-45	1st	+1.5
8-2	Oak.	L	4-17		7	20	Mulder	Sabathia		61-46	1st	+0.5
8-3	Sea.	L	1-2		3	4	Moyer	Colon	Sasaki	61-47	2nd	0.5
8-4	Sea.	L	5-8		13	14	Garcia	Baez	Rhodes	61-48	2nd	1.5
8-5	Sea.	W	16-14	(11)	23	17	Rocker	Paniagua		62-48	2nd	0.5
8-6	Sea.	L	6-8		9	13	Abbott	Nagy	Paniagua	62-49	2nd	1.0
8-7	At Min.	W	7-2		14	7	Sabathia	Reed		63-49	1st	...
8-8	At Min.	W	8-2	(10)	14	11	Baez	Wells		64-49	1st	+1.0
8-9	At Min.	L	4-6		8	5	Milton	Finley	Hawkins	64-50	T1st	...
8-10	At Tex.	L	2-7		6	9	Davis	Woodard		64-51	T1st	...
8-11	At Tex.	L	5-6		9	9	Petkovsek	Rocker	Zimmerman	64-52	T1st	...
8-12	At Tex.	W	13-2		14	4	Sabathia	Bell		65-52	1st	+1.0
8-14	Min.	W	8-7	(11)	16	10	Baez	Wells		66-52	1st	+2.5
8-15	Min.	W	8-2		14	11	Finley	Mays		67-52	1st	+3.5
8-16	Min.	W	6-1		7	7	Woodard	Johnson		68-52	1st	+4.5
8-17	Ana.	L	2-7		6	12	Ortiz	Nagy		68-53	1st	+4.5
8-18	Ana.	W	4-2		6	3	Sabathia	Rapp	Wickman	69-53	1st	+4.5
8-19	Ana.	L	1-4		5	7	Washburn	Colon	Percival	69-54	1st	+4.5
8-20	At Oak.	L	0-9		4	12	Zito	Finley		69-55	1st	+4.5
8-21	At Oak.	W	2-1		5	6	Woodard	Lidle	Wickman	70-55	1st	+5.5
8-22	At Oak.	W	5-4	(11)	9	12	Wickman	Vizcaino	Riske	71-55	1st	+5.5
8-23	At Oak.	W	9-7		15	7	Nagy	Mulder	Wickman	72-55	1st	+6.5
8-24	At Sea.	L	1-4		3	9	Moyer	Colon	Charlton	72-56	1st	+5.5
8-25	At Sea.	L	2-3	(11)	7	7	Halama	Rocker		72-57	1st	+4.5
8-26	At Sea.	W	4-3		8	10	Riske	Nelson	Wickman	73-57	1st	+4.5
8-28	Bos.	W	8-3		11	6	Burba	Cone		74-57	1st	+5.5
8-29	Bos.	W	2-1		6	6	Sabathia	Fossum	Wickman	75-57	1st	+5.5
8-30	Bos.	W	3-1		6	12	Colon	Nomo	Wickman	76-57	1st	+6.5
8-31	At Chi.	L	8-11		13	12	Howry	Westbrook	Foulke	76-58	1st	+5.5
9-1	At Chi.	W	4-3		7	8	Drese	Garland	Wickman	77-58	1st	+6.5
9-2	At Chi.	L	10-19		12	17	Biddle	Burba		77-59	1st	+5.5
9-3	At Chi.	W	6-3		11	7	Sabathia	Glover	Wickman	78-59	1st	+6.0
9-4	At Bos.	W	8-5		9	13	Colon	Nomo	Wickman	79-59	1st	+7.0
9-5	At Bos.	L	7-10		7	15	Arrojo	Woodard	Urbina	79-60	1st	+6.0
9-6	At Bos.	W	6-4		13	7	Finley	Castillo	Rocker	80-60	1st	+7.0
9-7	Chi.	L	7-10		10	18	Biddle	Burba	Foulke	80-61	1st	+7.0
9-8	Chi.	W	8-7		9	11	Baez	Foulke		81-61	1st	+7.0
9-9	Chi.	W	9-8		11	10	Wickman	Foulke		82-61	1st	+7.0
9-10	Chi.	L	1-7		6	10	Wright	Colon		82-62	1st	+6.0
9-18	K.C.	W	11-2		9	6	Finley	Durbin		83-62	1st	+6.0
9-19	K.C.	W	11-3		10	8	Colon	Suppan		84-62	1st	+7.0
9-20	K.C.	L	2-4		6	9	George	Drese	Hernandez	84-63	1st	+6.0
9-21	At Min.	L	2-6		8	7	Reed	Sabathia	Guardado	84-64	1st	+5.0
9-22	At Min.	W	4-2		10	8	Rincon	Radke	Wickman	85-64	1st	+6.0
9-23	At Min.	W	4-2		5	7	Finley	Milton	Wickman	86-64	1st	+7.0
9-24	Tor.	L	2-3	(11)	6	9	File	Baez	Eyre	86-65	1st	+6.5
9-25	Tor.	W	11-7		14	9	Riske	Plesac		87-65	1st	+6.5

Date	Opp.	Res.	Score	(inn.*)	Hits	Opp. hits	Winning pitcher	Losing pitcher	Save	Record	Pos.	GB
9-28	Min.	L	0-1		3	6	Milton	Baez	Guardado	87-66	1st	+6.5
9-29	Min.	W	9-8		9	11	Westbrook	Guardado		88-66	1st	+7.5
9-30	Min.	W	9-1		14	7	Colon	Reed		89-66	1st	+7.5
10-2	At K.C.	L	1-5		7	6	Hernandez	Rocker		89-67	1st	+7.5
10-3	At K.C.	W	4-1		8	7	Sabathia	MacDougal	Wickman	90-67	1st	+8.5
10-4	At K.C.	L	4-8		9	10	Durbin	Colon		90-68	1st	+7.5
10-5†	At Tor.	L	0-5		2	9	Halladay	Finley		90-69		
10-5‡	At Tor.	L	3-4	(11)	11	9	File	Drese		90-70	1st	+7.0
10-6	At Tor.	L	2-5		5	8	Carpenter	Drew	Quantrill	90-71	1st	+6.0
10-7	At Tor.	W	3-2		6	5	Sabathia	Lyon	Rocker	91-71	1st	+6.0

Monthly records: April (14-9), May (19-8), June (12-15), July (15-13), August (16-13), September (13-8), October (2-5).
*Innings, if other than nine. †First game of a doubleheader. ‡Second game of a doubleheader. §Day separate admission. ∞Night separate admission.

HIGHLIGHTS

High point: The Indians clinched their sixth American League Central title in seven years by defeating Minnesota 9-1 on September 30.

Low point: The Indians rolled into Pittsburgh for a three-game series June 15-17 a half-game out of first place and looking to make up ground. It didn't happen. The Indians were swept.

Turning point: The Indians swept a three-game series from the Twins at Jacobs Field August 14-16. After giving up four runs in the ninth, the Indians rallied for an 8-7 win in 11 innings to win the opener. With the Twins on the ropes, the Indians finished them off with 8-2 and 6-1 wins.

Most valuable player: Roberto Alomar had another superb season. He batted .336 with 20 homers, 100 RBIs, 113 runs scored and 30 stolen bases in addition to hitting .424 with runners in scoring position. Alomar only made five errors all season and played in 157 games.

Most valuble pitcher: C.C. Sabathia made the team in spring training despite the fact he was only 20 years old and had never pitched above the Class AA level. Sabathia held opponents to a .228 batting average and finished 17-5 with a 4.39 ERA.

Most improved player: Catcher Einar Diaz progressed well in his first season as an everyday player. He threw out 46 of 130 (35.4 percent) runners trying to steal. Diaz also set career highs in RBIs and doubles.

Most pleasant surprise: Danys Baez was moved to a short relief role at Class AAA Buffalo. Once recalled by the Indians, Baez became one of the key forces in the bullpen. First batters he faced hit .103 (4-for-39), the best mark among all A.L. relievers.

Key injuries: Travis Fryman missed the first two months of the season with an elbow injury. ... Chuck Finley had only 22 starts due to a neck injury. ... Steve Woodard was hit on the right elbow by line drive on April 6 and missed 24 days.

... Paul Shuey missed almost two months because of elbow problems. ... Ellis Burks missed three weeks with a broken thumb.

Notable: The Indians won a season-high 10 straight games from April 28 to May 9, their longest winning streak since 1994. ... The starting pitchers had a 5.26 ERA, the second-worst mark in the league.

—STEVE HERRICK

RECORDS

2001 regular-season record: 91-71 (1st in A.L. Central); 44-36 at home; 47-35 on road; 22-14 vs. A.L. East; 47-29 vs. A.L. Central; 15-17 vs. A.L. West; 7-11 vs. N.L.; 20-20 vs. lefthanded starters; 71-51 vs. righthanded starters; 80-65 on grass; 11-6 on turf; 23-25 in daytime; 68-46 at night; 25-18 in one-run games; 9-6 in extra-inning games; 0-1-0 in doubleheaders.

Team record past five years: 453-356 (.560, ranks 2nd in league in that span).

TEAM LEADERS

Batting average: Roberto Alomar (.336).
At-bats: Omar Vizquel (611).
Runs: Roberto Alomar (113).
Hits: Roberto Alomar (193).
Total Bases: Jim Thome (328).
Doubles: Roberto Alomar, Einar Diaz, Juan Gonzalez (34).
Triples: Roberto Alomar (12).
Home runs: Jim Thome (49).
Runs batted in: Juan Gonzalez (140).
Stolen bases: Roberto Alomar (30).
Slugging percentage: Jim Thome (.624).
On-base percentage: Jim Thome (.416).
Wins: C.C. Sabathia (17).
Earned-run average: Bartolo Colon (4.09).
Complete games: Dave Burba, Bartolo Colon, Chuck Finley (1).
Shutouts: None.
Saves: Bob Wickman (32).
Innings pitched: Bartolo Colon (222.1).
Strikeouts: Bartolo Colon (201).

GAMES BY POSITION

Catcher: Einar Diaz 134, Eddie Taubensee 38, Tim Laker 14.
First base: Jim Thome 148, Wil Cordero 22, Karim Garcia 2.
Second base: Roberto Alomar 157, Jolbert Cabrera 28, John McDonald 3, Mark Lewis 3, Einar Diaz 1, Eddie Taubensee 1.
Third base: Travis Fryman 96, Russell Branyan 72, Jolbert Cabrera 27, Mark Lewis 4, John McDonald 3.
Shortstop: Omar Vizquel 154, Jolbert Cabrera 14, John McDonald 9, Travis Fryman 1.
Outfield: Kenny Lofton 130, Juan Gonzalez 119, Marty Cordova 106, Jolbert Cabrera 83, Wil Cordero 51, Russell Branyan 32, Jacob Cruz 22, Ellis Burks 20, Karim Garcia 18, Dave Roberts 13, Milton Bradley 9.
Designated hitter: Ellis Burks 102, Juan Gonzalez 21, Wil Cordero 12, Russell Branyan 7, Marty Cordova 7, Jim Thome 6, Eddie Taubensee 5, Travis Fryman 2, Dave Hollins 2, Dave Roberts 2, Jolbert Cabrera 1, Milton Bradley 1.

TOP DRAFT CHOICES

1a. **Dan Denham,** RHP, Deer Valley H.S., Antioch, Calif.
1b. **Alan Horne,** RHP, Marianna (Fla.) H.S.
1c. **J.D. Martin,** RHP, Burroughs H.S., Ridgecrest, Calif.
1d. **Michael Conroy,** OF, Boston College H.S., Dorchester, Mass.
2. **Jake Dittler,** RHP, Green Valley H.S., Henderson, Nev.
3. **Nick Moran,** RHP, Fresno State Univ.
4. **Travis Foley,** RHP, Butler H.S., Louisville.
5. **Marcos Mendoza,** LHP, San Diego State University.
6. **Jim Ed Warden,** RHP, Tennessee Tech.
7. **Josh Noviskey,** OF, Newton (N.J.) H.S.
8. **Mike Quintana,** OF, Florida International University.
9. **Luke Scott,** OF, Oklahoma State U.
10. **Brian Harrison,** RHP, Dalton (Ga.) H.S.

DETROIT TIGERS
AMERICAN LEAGUE CENTRAL DIVISION

Tigers schedule
Home games shaded
D—Day game (games starting before 5 p.m.)
All-Star Game at Milwaukee
Subject to changes

April
SUN	MON	TUE	WED	THU	FRI	SAT
	1	2 TB	3 TB	4 TB	5 D CLE	6 D CLE
7 CLE	8 CWS	9 CWS	10 CWS	11	12 MIN	13 MIN
14 D MIN	15	16 TB	17 TB	18 D TB	19 CWS	20 CWS
21 D CWS	22 KC	23 KC	24 D KC	25	26 MIN	27 D MIN
28 MIN	29 KC	30 KC				

May
SUN	MON	TUE	WED	THU	FRI	SAT
			1 KC	2 D	3 MIN	4 MIN
5 D MIN	6 MIN	7 ANA	8 ANA	9 ANA	10 TEX	11 TEX
12 TEX	13	14 ANA	15 ANA	16 ANA	17 TEX	18 TEX
19 D TEX	20 CLE	21 CLE	22 CLE	23	24 CWS	25 CWS
26 D CWS	27 D CLE	28 CLE	29 CLE	30 CLE	31 TOR	

June
SUN	MON	TUE	WED	THU	FRI	SAT
						1 TOR
2 D TOR	3 BOS	4 BOS	5 BOS	6 D BOS	7 PHI	8 PHI
9 PHI	10 MON	11 MON	12 MON	13	14 ARI	15 ARI
16 D ARI	17	18 ATL	19 ATL	20 ATL	21 FLA	22 FLA
23 FLA	24	25 KC	26 KC	27 KC	28 PIT	29 PIT
30 D PIT						

July
SUN	MON	TUE	WED	THU	FRI	SAT
	1	2 CWS	3 CWS	4 CWS	5 BOS	6 BOS
7 D BOS	8	9 *	10	11 CWS	12 D CWS	13 CWS
14 D CWS	15 BOS	16 BOS	17 NYY	18 D NYY	19 MIN	20 MIN
21 D MIN	22 KC	23 KC	24 KC	25 CLE	26 CLE	27 CLE
28 D CLE	29 SEA	30 SEA	31 SEA			

August
SUN	MON	TUE	WED	THU	FRI	SAT
				1 OAK	2 OAK	3 D OAK
4 D OAK	5	6 TEX	7 TEX	8 OAK	9 BAL	10 BAL
11 D BAL	12	13 ANA	14 ANA	15	16 BAL	17 BAL
18 D BAL	19 SEA	20 SEA	21 SEA	22 OAK	23 OAK	24 OAK
25 D OAK	26 CLE	27 CLE	28 CLE	29	30 CWS	31 CWS

September
SUN	MON	TUE	WED	THU	FRI	SAT
1 D CWS	2 D CLE	3 CLE	4 D CLE	5 CLE	6 NYY	7 D NYY
8 D NYY	9 MIN	10 MIN	11 D MIN	12	13 KC	14 D KC
15 KC	16 MIN	17 MIN	18 MIN	19 MIN	20 NYY	21 D NYY
22 D NYY	23	24 KC	25 KC	26 KC	27 TOR	28 D TOR
29 D TOR	30					

2002 SEASON
CLUB DIRECTORY

Owner
Michael Ilitch
President, chief executive officer
David Dombrowski
Special assistants to the president
Al Kaline, Willie Horton
V.p., baseball operations/g.m.
Randy Smith
V.p., marketing and ticket sales
Michael Dietz
Vice president, facility operations
John Pettit
Vice president, chief financial officer
Steve Quinn
Vice president, planning and research
Elaine Lewis
V.p., suite sales and services
Charles P. Jones
V.p., baseball legal counsel
John Westhoff
Assistant general manager
Scott Bream
Assistant director, minor leagues/scouting
Rick Bennett
Assistant, baseball operations
Foreign Affairs, Ramon Pena
Special assistants to the g.m.
Al Hargesheimer, Randy Johnson
Director of scouting
Greg Smith
Director of minor league operations
Dave Miller
Traveling secretary
Bill Brown
Minor league field coordinator
Steve Boros
Senior director of communications
John Hahn
Manager, public relations
Jim Anderson
Coordinator, public relations
Brian Dritten
Coordinator, public relations
Melanie Waters
Director, community relations
Celia Bobrowsky
Manager, community relations
Fred Feliciano

Coordinator, community relations
Masico Brown
Manager, marketing
Ellen Hill
Coordinator, marketing
Kelly Dahlstrom
Senior director, corporate sales
Dan Sinagoga
Senior director, ticket services
Ken Marchetti
Senior director, information technology
Cole Stewart
Director, corporate sales
Kayla French
Director, ticket sales
Bob Raymond
Director, human resources
Lara Juras
Director, fantasy camps
Jerry Lewis
Director, finance
Jennifer Orow
Dir., promo. and in-game entertainment
Joel Scott
Manager, home clubhouse
Jim Schmakel
Assistant manager, visiting clubhouse
John Nelson
Team physicians
David J. Collon, M.D., Terry Lock, M.D., Louis Saco, M.D., Michael Workings, M.D.
Medical director/head athletic trainer
Russ Miller
Assistant athletic trainer
Steve Carter
Strength and conditioning coach
Dennie Taft
Scouts
Bill Buck, Jerome Cochran, Bob Cummings, Tim Grieve, Rob Guzik, Jack Hays, Mike Herbert, Joe Hodges, Lou Laslo, Dennis Lieberthal, Jeff Malinoff, Mark Monahan, Pat Murtaugh, Steve Nichols, Frank Paine, Larry Parrish, Derrick Ross, Steve Taylor, Clyde Weir, Jeff Wetherby, Rob Wilfong, Ellic Williams, Steve Williams, Gary York, Harold Zonder

MINOR LEAGUE AFFILIATES

Class	Team	League	Manager
AAA	Toledo	International	Bruce Fields
AA	Erie	Eastern	Kevin Bradshaw
A	Lakeland	Florida State	Gary Green
A	West Michigan	Midwest	Phil Regan
A	Oneonta	New York-Pennsylvania	Randy Ready
Rookie	Gulf Coast Tigers	Gulf Coast	Howard Bushong

BROADCAST INFORMATION

Radio: WXYT-AM (1270).
TV: WKBD (Channel 50).
Cable TV: FOX Sports Detroit.

SPRING TRAINING

Ballpark (city): Marchant Stadium (Lakeland, Fla.).
Ticket information: 941-603-6278 or 941-603-6279.

Follow the Tigers all season at: www.sportingnews.com/baseball/teams/tigers/

SPRING TRAINING ROSTER

Manager—Phil Garner (33).
Coaches—Doug Mansolino (32), Ed Ott (56), Luis Pujols, Merv Rettenmund, Juan Samuel (10), Dan Warthen (31), Dennie Taft (00).

No.	PITCHERS	B/T	Ht./Wt.	Born	2001 clubs
14	Anderson, Matt	R/R	6-4/200	8-17-76	Detroit
49	Bernero, Adam	R/R	6-4/205	11-28-76	Toledo, Detroit
	Cornejo, Nate	R/R	6-5/200	9-24-79	Erie, Toledo, Detroit
	Farnsworth, Jeff	R/R	6-2/190	10-6-75	San Antonio
	Kalita, Tim	L/R	6-2/220	11-21-78	Erie
	Keller, Kris	R/R	6-2/225	3-1-78	Toledo
42	Lima, Jose	R/R	6-2/205	9-30-72	Houston, Detroit
	Loux, Shane	R/R	6-2/205	8-13-79	Toledo
	Maroth, Mike	L/L	6-0/180	8-17-77	Toledo
38	Moehler, Brian	R/R	6-3/235	12-31-71	Detroit, Toledo
28	Patterson, Danny	R/R	6-0/185	2-17-71	Detroit
	Perisho, Matt	L/L	6-0/205	6-8-75	Detroit, Toledo
	Pettyjohn, Adam	L/R	6-3/190	6-11-77	Toledo, Detroit
55	Redman, Mark	L/L	6-5/220	1-5-74	Minnesota, Edmonton, Toledo, Detroit
	Rodney, Fernando	R/R	5-11/170	3-17-81	Lakeland, Erie, Gulf Coast Tigers
59	Santos, Victor	R/R	6-3/175	10-2-76	Toledo, Detroit
37	Sparks, Steve	R/R	6-0/180	7-2-65	Detroit
	Valentine, Joe	R/R	6-2/195	12-24-79	Kannapolis, Winston-Salem
	VanHekken, Andy	R/L	6-3/175	7-31-79	Lakeland, Erie
36	Weaver, Jeff	R/R	6-5/210	8-22-76	Detroit

No.	CATCHERS	B/T	Ht./Wt.	Born	2001 clubs
53	Cardona, Javier	R/R	6-1/185	9-15-75	Detroit
18	Fick, Robert	L/R	6-1/189	3-15-74	Detroit
	Inge, Brandon	B/R	5-11/185	5-19-77	Detroit, Gulf Coast Tigers, West Michigan, Toledo
	Meluskey, Mitch	B/R	6-0/185	9-18-73	DID NOT PLAY
	Rivera, Mike	R/R	6-0/190	9-8-76	Erie, Detroit

No.	INFIELDERS	B/T	Ht./Wt.	Born	2001 clubs
9	Easley, Damion	R/R	5-11/185	11-11-69	Detroit
17	Halter, Shane	R/R	6-0/180	11-8-69	Detroit
33	Macias, Jose	B/R	5-10/173	1-25-74	Detroit
17	Munson, Eric	L/R	6-3/220	10-3-77	Erie, Detroit
7	Palmer, Dean	R/R	6-1/210	12-27-68	Toledo, Detroit
21	Paquette, Craig	R/R	6-0/190	3-28-69	St. Louis
	Santana, Pedro	R/R	5-11/160	9-21-76	Toledo, Detroit
15	Simon, Randall	L/L	6-0/180	5-26-75	Toledo, Detroit

No.	OUTFIELDERS	B/T	Ht./Wt.	Born	2001 clubs
4	Higginson, Bobby	L/R	5-11/195	8-18-70	Detroit
29	Magee, Wendell	R/R	6-0/220	8-3-72	Detroit, Toledo
	Torres, Andres	B/R	5-10/175	1-26-78	Erie
25	Young, Dmitri	B/R	6-2/235	10-11-73	Cincinnati

BALLPARK INFORMATION

Ballpark (capacity, surface)
  Comerica Park (40,120, grass)
Address
  2100 Woodward
  Detroit, MI 48201
Official website
  www.detroittigers.com
Business phone
  313-471-2000
Ticket information
  313-471-BALL
Ticket prices
  $60 (On-Deck Circle, Tiger Den)
  $35 (terrace), $30 (infield box)
  $25 (outfield box, club seats)
  $20 (upper box), $15 (mezzanine)
  $14 (pavilion), $12 (upper reserved)
  $8 (bleachers), $5 (Skyline)
Field dimensions (from home plate)
  To left field at foul line, 345 feet
  To center field, 420 feet
  To right field at foul line, 330 feet
First game played
  April 11, 2000 (Tigers 5, Mariners 2)

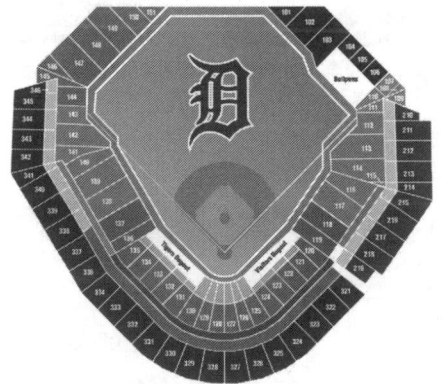

2001 REVIEW
DAY BY DAY

Date	Opp.	Res.	Score	(inn.*)	Hits	Opp. hits	Winning pitcher	Losing pitcher	Save	Record	Pos.	GB
4-3	Min.	L	2-3		7	6	Radke	Weaver	Wells	0-1	T3rd	1.0
4-5	Min.	L	5-9	(10)	10	11	Guardado	Jones		0-2	T4th	2.0
4-6	At Chi.	W	10-9	(10)	13	14	Patterson	Foulke	Jones	1-2	T3rd	2.0
4-7	At Chi.	W	5-3		7	8	Holt	Buehrle	Jones	2-2	T2nd	1.0
4-8	At Chi.	W	5-3		11	7	Weaver	D. Wells	Jones	3-2	T1st	...
4-9	At Min.	L	5-11		13	11	Radke	Sparks		3-3	T2nd	1.0
4-10	At Min.	L	2-8		6	12	Milton	Perisho		3-4	T2nd	2.0
4-11	At Min.	L	1-12		6	15	Mays	Mlicki		3-5	T3rd	3.0
4-12	Cle.	L	3-5		9	10	Colon	Holt	Wickman	3-6	4th	3.5
4-13	Cle.	L	8-9		10	15	Sabathia	Weaver	Shuey	3-7	4th	4.5
4-14	Cle.	W	1-0		3	4	Sparks	Finley		4-7	4th	4.5
4-17	Chi.	W	7-4		13	9	Anderson	Wunsch	Jones	5-7	3rd	4.5
4-18	Chi.	L	4-6		7	7	Buehrle	Holt	Foulke	5-8	T3rd	5.5
4-19	Chi.	L	1-3		8	12	D. Wells	Weaver		5-9	4th	6.0
4-20	At Cle.	L	4-5		9	12	Wickman	Nitkowski		5-10	4th	7.0
4-21	At Cle.	L	4-5	(11)	7	5	Reed	Jones		5-11	4th	8.0
4-22	At Cle.	L	3-11		7	19	Burba	Mlicki		5-12	5th	9.0
4-24	Bal.	L	3-8		8	13	Hentgen	Weaver		5-13	5th	9.0
4-25	Bal.	L	4-6		8	6	Roberts	Sparks	Kohlmeier	5-14	5th	10.0
4-26	Bal.	W	8-2		11	9	Holt	Johnson		6-14	5th	9.0
4-27	T.B.	W	4-2		7	7	Mlicki	Rupe	Jones	7-14	T3rd	9.0
4-28	T.B.	L	3-7		8	8	Judd	Perisho		7-15	T4th	9.0
4-29	T.B.	W	6-1		12	7	Weaver	Lopez		8-15	T4th	9.0
5-1	At Tex.	W	6-3	(10)	10	11	Patterson	Zimmerman	Jones	9-15	4th	8.5
5-2	At Tex.	W	8-4		14	10	Holt	Oliver	Anderson	10-15	3rd	8.5
5-3	At Tex.	W	9-4		12	7	Mlicki	Helling		11-15	3rd	8.0
5-4	At Ana.	L	5-7		10	13	Weber	Murray	Percival	11-16	3rd	9.0
5-5	At Ana.	W	11-2		15	8	Weaver	Ortiz		12-16	3rd	8.0
5-6	At Ana.	L	2-3	(10)	6	7	Levine	Patterson		12-17	3rd	9.0
5-8	Tex.	W	5-4		12	11	Jones	Crabtree		13-17	3rd	9.0
5-9	Tex.	W	3-2		10	8	Mlicki	Davis	Jones	14-17	3rd	8.0
5-10	Tex.	W	6-5		7	9	Patterson	Zimmerman	Jones	15-17	3rd	8.0
5-11	Ana.	W	7-6	(11)	13	16	Jones	Lukasiewicz		16-17	3rd	8.0
5-12	Ana.	W	4-1		8	3	Anderson	Hasegawa		17-17	3rd	7.0
5-13	Ana.	L	2-14		7	16	Washburn	Holt		17-18	3rd	8.0
5-15	At Bal.	L	3-11		6	15	Ponson	Mlicki		17-19	3rd	8.5
5-16	At Bal.	L	2-3		10	3	Hentgen	Weaver	Ryan	17-20	3rd	9.5
5-17	At Bal.	W	7-5		9	10	Sparks	Roberts	Jones	18-20	3rd	9.5
5-18	At T.B.	W	18-2		19	4	Santos	Sturtze		19-20	3rd	8.5
5-19	At T.B.	W	10-5		17	12	Holt	Lopez	Patterson	20-20	3rd	8.5
5-20	At T.B.	L	2-10		6	13	Wilson	Mlicki		20-21	3rd	8.5
5-22	At Cle.	W	3-0		8	7	Weaver	Colon	Jones	21-21	3rd	8.5
5-23	At Cle.	L	3-4	(10)	8	12	Wickman	Borkowski		21-22	3rd	8.5
5-24	At Cle.	L	5-8		14	10	Burba	Santos	Wickman	21-23	3rd	9.0
5-25	Chi.	L	4-8		12	8	Lowe	Jones		21-24	3rd	10.0
5-26	Chi.	L	0-8		3	12	Buehrle	Mlicki		21-25	3rd	10.0
5-27	Chi.	L	2-3	(11)	4	9	Barcelo	Patterson	Lowe	21-26	3rd	10.5
5-28	Cle.	W	12-6		15	10	Sparks	Finley		22-26	3rd	10.0
5-29	Cle.	L	4-6		9	9	Shuey	Murray	Wickman	22-27	3rd	11.0
5-30	Cle.	L	4-8		13	10	Wright	Holt	Wickman	22-28	3rd	12.0
6-1	At Chi.	L	0-3		4	12	Buehrle	Mlicki	Foulke	22-29	3rd	12.5
6-2	At Chi.	L	3-5		10	10	D. Wells	Weaver	Foulke	22-30	T3rd	12.5
6-3	At Chi.	L	6-9	(10)	11	10	Howry	Jones		22-31	4th	13.5
6-5	At Bos.	L	3-4	(18)	15	12	Wakefield	Borkowski		22-32	4th	14.0
6-6	At Bos.	W	7-3		10	12	Mlicki	Castillo	Anderson	23-32	4th	13.5
6-7	At Bos.	L	1-8		5	10	Wakefield	Santos	Arrojo	23-33	4th	14.5
6-8	Mil.	W	9-4		12	13	Weaver	Rigdon		24-33	4th	13.5
6-9	Mil.	W	6-5		11	11	Anderson	Leskanic		25-33	4th	13.5
6-10	Mil.	L	3-8		6	11	Wright	Holt		25-34	4th	13.5
6-12	Pit.	L	3-13		7	15	Ritchie	Mlicki		25-35	4th	14.0
6-13	Pit.	W	6-3		9	11	Weaver	Beimel	Anderson	26-35	4th	14.0
6-14	Pit.	W	6-4		11	12	Sparks	Arroyo	Anderson	27-35	4th	13.0
6-15	At Ari.	W	5-2		7	9	Holt	Brohawn	Anderson	28-35	4th	12.0
6-16	At Ari.	L	1-3		7	7	Ellis	Blair	Prinz	28-36	4th	12.0
6-17	At Ari.	L	3-8		11	12	Schilling	Mlicki		28-37	4th	12.0
6-18	N.Y.	L	1-10		8	11	Clemens	Weaver		28-38	4th	12.5
6-19	N.Y.	W	7-1		14	3	Sparks	Keisler		29-38	4th	12.5
6-20	N.Y.	W	5-2		6	9	Holt	A. Hernandez	Anderson	30-38	4th	11.5
6-22	Min.	W	5-4		12	13	Jones	Wells		31-38	4th	11.5
6-23	Min.	W	10-9		16	17	Patterson	Carrasco	Jones	32-38	4th	10.5
6-24	Min.	L	5-14		9	11	Milton	Sparks		32-39	4th	11.5
6-25	Min.	L	3-6		8	9	Mays	Holt	Hawkins	32-40	4th	11.5
6-26	At K.C.	L	5-12		6	13	Reichert	Blair		32-41	4th	12.5
6-27	At K.C.	L	4-5		10	12	Hernandez	Jones		32-42	4th	13.0

Date	Opp.	Res.	Score	(inn.*)	Hits	Opp. hits	Winning pitcher	Losing pitcher	Save	Record	Pos.	GB
6-28	At K.C.	L	2-9		9	13	Durbin	Weaver		32-43	4th	13.0
6-29	At Min.	L	2-3		7	11	Wells	Murray	Hawkins	32-44	4th	14.0
6-30	At Min.	L	2-3		4	7	Mays	Holt	Guardado	32-45	5th	15.0
7-1	At Min.	L	3-8		7	9	Santana	Blair		32-46	5th	16.0
7-3	K.C.	W	8-4		9	12	Lima	Durbin		33-46	4th	16.5
7-4	K.C.	W	6-4		11	8	Weaver	Bailey	Anderson	34-46	4th	15.5
7-5	K.C.	W	7-1		13	5	Sparks	Wilson		35-46	4th	15.5
7-6	Chi.	L	9-15		13	21	Heredia	Nitkowski		35-47	4th	16.5
7-7	Chi.	L	6-10		11	14	Lieber	Blair		35-48	4th	17.5
7-8	Chi.	W	9-6		13	7	Jones	Heredia	Anderson	36-48	4th	17.5
7-12	At St.L.	W	7-5		11	6	Weaver	Kile	Anderson	37-48	4th	17.5
7-13	At St.L.	W	4-1		10	6	Sparks	Matthews		38-48	4th	16.5
7-14	At St.L.	L	2-3		6	6	Morris	Lima	Kline	38-49	4th	17.5
7-15	At Cin.	W	8-5		15	11	Blair	Nichting	Anderson	39-49	4th	16.5
7-16	At Cin.	L	1-9		5	11	Davis	Pettyjohn		39-50	4th	16.5
7-17	At Cin.	W	3-1		8	6	Weaver	Reitsma	Anderson	40-50	4th	15.5
7-18§	N.Y.	L	5-8		11	13	Clemens	Sparks	Rivera	40-51		
7-18∞	N.Y.	W	12-4		16	14	Santos	Lilly		41-51	4th	15.0
7-19	N.Y.	W	11-2		15	7	Lima	Pettitte		42-51	4th	15.0
7-20	At Cle.	W	7-3		10	10	Holt	Westbrook		43-51	4th	14.0
7-21	At Cle.	L	4-8		7	12	Nagy	Pettyjohn		43-52	4th	14.0
7-22	At Cle.	L	3-6		9	9	Colon	Weaver		43-53	4th	14.0
7-24	At N.Y.	L	5-6		8	13	Pettitte	Sparks	Rivera	43-54	4th	13.5
7-25	At N.Y.	L	2-4		6	7	Witasick	Lima	Rivera	43-55	4th	14.5
7-26	At N.Y.	L	8-14		11	18	Mendoza	Holt		43-56	4th	15.5
7-27	Cle.	L	4-7		10	11	Colon	Pettyjohn	Wickman	43-57	4th	15.5
7-28§	Cle.	L	4-6		6	12	Baez	Murray	Wickman	43-58		
7-28∞	Cle.	W	4-2		9	6	Weaver	Woodard	Anderson	44-58	4th	15.5
7-29	Cle.	W	8-3		12	5	Sparks	Burba		45-58	4th	14.5
7-31	Sea.	W	4-2		10	6	Lima	Sele	Anderson	46-58	4th	13.5
8-1	Sea.	L	1-7		5	14	Abbott	Holt		46-59	4th	14.5
8-2	Sea.	L	1-2		4	8	Pineiro	Pettyjohn	Sasaki	46-60	4th	14.5
8-3	Oak.	L	1-2		9	4	Hudson	Weaver		46-61	4th	15.0
8-4	Oak.	L	1-10		2	10	Zito	Sparks		46-62	4th	16.0
8-5	Oak.	L	1-4		3	8	Lidle	Lima	Isringhausen	46-63	4th	16.0
8-6	Oak.	L	3-6		6	9	Vizcaino	Patterson	Isringhausen	46-64	4th	16.5
8-7	At Tex.	W	7-3		11	7	Perisho	Venafro		47-64	4th	15.5
8-8	At Tex.	W	19-6		21	13	Patterson	Venafro		48-64	4th	15.5
8-9	At Tex.	L	3-7		9	15	Helling	Sparks		48-65	4th	15.5
8-10	At K.C.	L	3-7		7	8	Byrd	Weaver	Stein	48-66	4th	15.5
8-11	At K.C.	L	1-4		5	6	George	Lima	Hernandez	48-67	4th	15.5
8-12	At K.C.	L	4-6		9	10	Suppan	Pettyjohn	Hernandez	48-68	4th	16.5
8-14	Ana.	L	1-7		6	10	Washburn	Cornejo		48-69	4th	17.5
8-15	Ana.	W	5-1		14	7	Perisho	Holtz		49-69	4th	17.5
8-16	Ana.	L	2-4		6	11	Schoeneweis	Weaver	Percival	49-70	4th	18.5
8-17	K.C.	W	4-2		7	5	Lima	George	Anderson	50-70	4th	17.5
8-18	K.C.	L	4-8		7	14	Suppan	Nitkowski		50-71	4th	18.5
8-19	K.C.	W	4-3		7	8	Cornejo	Durbin	Anderson	51-71	4th	17.5
8-20	At Sea.	W	4-1		11	5	Sparks	Garcia		52-71	4th	16.5
8-21	At Sea.	L	1-4		3	11	Sele	Weaver	Sasaki	52-72	4th	17.5
8-22	At Sea.	L	1-16		6	20	Abbott	Lima		52-73	4th	18.5
8-23	At Sea.	L	1-5		3	10	Pineiro	Redman		52-74	4th	19.5
8-24	At Oak.	W	8-4		12	10	Cornejo	Hudson		53-74	4th	18.5
8-25	At Oak.	L	1-6		5	10	Zito	Sparks		53-75	4th	18.5
8-26	At Oak.	L	6-7		12	9	Tam	Perisho	Isringhausen	53-76	4th	19.5
8-28	Chi.	L	6-8		10	18	Embree	Patterson	Howry	53-77	4th	20.5
8-29	Chi.	L	3-8		7	13	Glover	Redman		53-78	4th	21.5
8-30	Chi.	W	3-1		6	8	Cornejo	Buehrle	Anderson	54-78	4th	21.5
8-31	At Tor.	W	4-3		8	8	Sparks	Borbon	Anderson	55-78	4th	20.5
9-1	At Tor.	L	1-3		4	7	Lyon	Weaver	Plesac	55-79	4th	21.5
9-2	At Tor.	L	0-11		5	10	Loaiza	Lima		55-80	4th	21.5
9-4†	At Chi.	L	1-10		4	15	Buehrle	Cornejo		55-81		
9-4‡	At Chi.	L	0-4		4	9	Lowe	Pettyjohn		55-82	5th	23.5
9-5	At Chi.	L	3-5		8	10	Wright	Sparks	Foulke	55-83	5th	23.5
9-6	At Chi.	W	6-2		12	5	Weaver	Garland		56-83	4th	23.5
9-7	Tor.	L	1-2		7	7	Lyon	Lima	Koch	56-84	4th	23.5
9-8	Tor.	W	4-3		9	6	Murray	Halladay	Anderson	57-84	4th	23.5
9-9	Tor.	L	3-6		10	10	Carpenter	Cornejo		57-85	4th	24.5
9-10	Min.	L	2-3		4	8	Mays	Pineda	Guardado	57-86	T4th	24.5
9-18	At Min.	L	3-8		3	18	Radke	Weaver		57-87	4th	25.5
9-19	At Min.	W	6-2		12	6	Sparks	Milton		58-87	4th	25.5
9-20	At Min.	L	0-3		6	6	Mays	Lima		58-88	T4th	25.5
9-21	At Bos.	L	2-5		5	11	Fossum	Murray	Urbina	58-89	T4th	25.5
9-22	At Bos.	W	4-3		8	5	Pettyjohn	Arrojo	Anderson	59-89	4th	25.5
9-23	At Bos.	W	12-6		13	9	Weaver	Nomo		60-89	4th	25.5
9-24	At K.C.	W	4-2		6	8	Sparks	Suppan	Anderson	61-89	4th	24.5
9-25	At K.C.	W	6-4		10	11	Lima	George	Anderson	62-89	4th	24.5
9-26	At K.C.	L	6-8		12	11	Stein	Murray	Hernandez	62-90	4th	25.0

Date	Opp.	Res.	Score	(inn.*)	Hits	Opp. hits	Winning pitcher	Losing pitcher	Save	Record	Pos.	GB
9-27	At K.C.	L	7-8		11	15	MacDougal	Cornejo	Hernandez	62-91	4th	25.5
9-28	Bos.	W	4-1		10	10	Weaver	Nomo	Anderson	63-91	4th	24.5
9-29	Bos.	W	7-2		9	8	Sparks	Kim		64-91	4th	24.5
9-30	Bos.	L	5-8		11	11	Castillo	Lima	Urbina	64-92	4th	25.5
10-2	Min.	L	0-5		3	12	Radke	Murray		64-93	4th	25.5
10-3	Min.	W	9-5		13	11	Cornejo	Fiore		65-93	4th	25.5
10-4	Min.	L	4-5		8	11	Carrasco	Anderson	Guardado	65-94	4th	25.5
10-6†	K.C.	L	3-8		7	11	Suppan	Weaver	Hernandez	65-95		
10-6‡	K.C.	W	2-1		4	10	Sparks	George		66-95	4th	24.0
10-7	K.C.	L	4-10		6	13	Stein	Lima		66-96	4th	25.0

Monthly records: April (8-15), May (14-13), June (10-17), July (14-13), August (9-20), September (9-14), October (2-4).
*Innings, if other than nine. †First game of a doubleheader. ‡Second game of a doubleheader. §Day separate admission. ∞Night separate admission.

HIGHLIGHTS

High point: After a 5-14 start, the Tigers won 12 of their next 15 games and reached the .500 mark with a 4-1 victory over Anaheim at Comerica Park May 12. The victory marked the first time the team had been .500 in May in six years.

Low point: The team tied a major league record by scoring exactly one run in five straight games Aug. 1-5. The club totaled 23 hits in those games.

Turning point: The team was 21-21 before a 4-3 loss at Cleveland. On May 23 the club began a 1-11 skid that dropped it 10 games below .500. An eight-game losing streak in late June then finished any realistic hopes of a competitive season.

Most valuable player: Matt Anderson emerged as one of the game's most promising closers by converting 22 straight save opportunities. Anderson's improved control—walking only 18 batters—was the key to maximizing his 100-mph fastball and devastating slider.

Most valuable pitcher: Steve Sparks (14-9, 3.65) was the team's most consistent starter and led the league with eight complete games. The 36-year-old Sparks, rescued from Class AAA the season before, had excellent control of the flutter pitch, which he throws at two different speeds.

Most improved player: Career backup Shane Halter, taking advantage of a chance to play daily due to a shoulder injury that ended Dean Palmer's season in July, was hitting .335 as late as July 18 before tailing off to a still-respectable .284.

Most pleasant surprise: June call-up Randall Simon was hitting .380 through July before settling at .305 in 81 games. Simon was exciting to watch with his slashing, ultra-aggressive approach to hitting.

Key injuries: It was the Year of the Bum Shoulder. Mitch Meluskey, slated to be the starting catcher after being acquired from Houston, had a recurrence of a shoulder injury during spring training. He had surgery and missed the entire

season. ... Rotation mainstay Brian Moehler made one start before his season ended because of shoulder surgery. ... Dean Palmer underwent shoulder surgery in July.

Notable: An undisciplined offense scored one run in 11 different games in August. ... CF Roger Cedeno overcame a slow start to finish at .293 with 55 stolen bases, and would have led the league in steals had not manager Phil Garner inexplicably benched him for the rest of the season after a shouting match in early September. Cedeno didn't play after September 10.

—REID CREAGER

RECORDS

2001 regular-season record: 66-96 (4th in A.L. Central); 37-44 at home; 29-52 on road; 17-19 vs. A.L. East; 24-52 vs. A.L. Central; 15-17 vs. A.L. West; 10-8 vs. N.L.; 19-27 vs. lefthanded starters; 47-69 vs. righthanded starters; 62-85 on grass; 4-11 on turf; 19-37 in daytime; 47-59 at night; 14-21 in one-run games; 3-7 in extra-inning games; 0-1-1 in doubleheaders.

Team record past five years: 358-451 (.443, ranks 11th in league in that span).

TEAM LEADERS

Batting average: Roger Cedeno (.293).
At-bats: Damion Easley (585).
Runs: Bobby Higginson (84).
Hits: Roger Cedeno (153).
Total Bases: Bobby Higginson (241).
Doubles: Shane Halter (32).
Triples: Roger Cedeno (11).
Home runs: Robert Fick (19).
Runs batted in: Tony Clark (75).
Stolen bases: Roger Cedeno (55).
Slugging percentage: Tony Clark (.481).
On-base percentage: Bobby Higginson (.367).
Wins: Steve W. Sparks (14).
Earned-run average: Steve W. Sparks (3.65).

Complete games: Steve W. Sparks (8).
Shutouts: Steve W. Sparks (1).
Saves: Matt Anderson (22).
Innings pitched: Steve W. Sparks (232.0).
Strikeouts: Jeff Weaver (152).

GAMES BY POSITION

Catcher: Brandon Inge 79, Robert Fick 78, Javier Cardona 44, Mike Rivera 4.
First base: Tony Clark 78, Randall Simon 43, Ryan Jackson 35, Robert Fick 26, Eric Munson 17, Shane Halter 8.
Second base: Damion Easley 153, Jose Macias 18, Pedro Santana 1.
Third base: Jose Macias 80, Shane Halter 74, Jarrod Patterson 13, Deivi Cruz 7.
Shortstop: Deivi Cruz 109, Shane Halter 62.
Outfield: Bobby Higginson 142, Roger Cedeno 120, Juan Encarnacion 116, Wendell Magee 74, Ryan Jackson 34, Jose Macias 29, Chris Wakeland 10, Robert Fick 8, Billy McMillon 7.
Designated hitter: Dean Palmer 57, Tony Clark 42, Randall Simon 29, Wendell Magee 11, Robert Fick 8, Roger Cedeno 7, Bobby Higginson 5, Ryan Jackson 5, Billy McMillon 3, Juan Encarnacion 2, Jermaine Clark 2, Jose Macias 2, Shane Halter 1, Javier Cardona 1.

TOP DRAFT CHOICES

1a. **Kenny Baugh,** RHP, Rice University.
1b. **Michael Woods,** 2B, Southern U.
2a. **Preston Larrison,** RHP, Univ. of Evansville.
2b. **Matt Coenen,** LHP, Charleston Southern University.
3. **Jack Hannahan,** 3B, U. of Minnesota.
4. **Mike Rabelo,** C, Univ. of Tampa.
5. **Ryan Raburn,** 3B, South Florida C.C.
6. **Jason Knoedler,** OF, Miami (O.) Univ.
7. **Tom Farmer,** RHP, U. of Miami (Fla.).
8. **Donald Kelly,** SS, Point Park (Pa.) College.
9. **David Mattle,** OF, Kent State Univ.
10. **Vincent Blue,** OF, Lamar H.S., Houston.

KANSAS CITY ROYALS
AMERICAN LEAGUE CENTRAL DIVISION

Royals schedule
Home games shaded
D—Day game (games starting before 5 p.m.)
*All-Star Game at Milwaukee
Subject to changes

April

SUN	MON	TUE	WED	THU	FRI	SAT
	1 D MIN	2	3 MIN	4	5 CWS	6 D CWS
7 D CWS	8	9 BOS	10 BOS	11 BOS	12 CLE	13 D CLE
14 CLE	15	16 MIN	17 MIN	18 D MIN	19 BOS	20 BOS
21 D BOS	22 DET	23 DET	24 D DET	25	26 BAL	27 BAL
28 D BAL	29 DET	30 DET				

May

SUN	MON	TUE	WED	THU	FRI	SAT
			1 D DET	2 D BAL	3 BAL	4 D BAL
5 D BAL	6	7 MIN	8 MIN	9 CLE	10 CLE	11 CLE
12 D CLE	13 MIN	14 MIN	15 MIN	16 MIN	17 CLE	18 CLE
19 D CLE	20 ANA	21 ANA	22 ANA	23 TEX	24 TEX	25 TEX
26 D TEX	27	28 ANA	29 ANA	30	31 TEX	

June

SUN	MON	TUE	WED	THU	FRI	SAT
						1 TEX
2 TEX	3 CWS	4 CWS	5 CWS	6 D CWS	7 STL	8 STL
9 STL	10 FLA	11 FLA	12 D FLA	13	14 STL	15 D STL
16 D STL	17	18 MON	19 MON	20 MON	21 NYM	22 NYM
23 NYM	24	25 DET	26 DET	27 DET	28 SD	29 SD
30 D SD						

July

SUN	MON	TUE	WED	THU	FRI	SAT
	1 SEA	2 SEA	3 SEA	4 OAK	5 OAK	6 D OAK
7 D OAK	8	9 *	10	11 ANA	12 ANA	13 ANA
14 ANA	15 TEX	16 TEX	17 CWS	18 CWS	19 CLE	20 CLE
21 D CLE	22	23 DET	24 DET	25 DET	26 CWS	27 CWS
28 D CWS	29 TOR	30 TOR	31 TOR			

August

SUN	MON	TUE	WED	THU	FRI	SAT
				1 D TOR	2 D MIN	3 MIN
4 D MIN	5 D MIN	6 NYY	7 NYY	8 D NYY	9 TB	10 TB
11 TB	12	13 NYY	14 NYY	15 NYY	16 TB	17 TB
18 D TB	19 TOR	20 TOR	21 D TOR	22 MIN	23 MIN	24 D SEA
25 D MIN	26 OAK	27 OAK	28 OAK	29	30 SEA	31 SEA

September

SUN	MON	TUE	WED	THU	FRI	SAT
1 D SEA	2 D OAK	3 D OAK	4 OAK	5	6 SEA	7 SEA
8 D SEA	9 CWS	10 CWS	11 CWS	12 D DET	13 DET	14 D DET
15 DET	16 DET	17 CWS	18 CWS	19 CWS	20 CLE	21 CLE
22 D CLE	23	24 DET	25 D DET	26 DET	27 CLE	28 CLE
29 D CLE	30					

2002 SEASON
CLUB DIRECTORY

Board of directors
Ruth Glass, Don Glass, Dayna Martz, Julia Irene Kauffman, Herk Robinson
Chairman/owner
David Glass
President
Dan Glass
Executive v.p. & chief operating officer
Herk Robinson
Sr. v.p. & g.m., baseball operations
Allard Baird
Senior vice president, business operations
Mark Gorris
Vice president, baseball operations
George Brett
V.p., finance & information services
Dale Rohr
Vice president, marketing & communications
Charlie Seraphin
General counsel
Dick Nixon
Asst. general manager, baseball operations
Muzzy Jackson
Assistant to the general manager
Brian Murphy
Senior advisor to the general manager
Art Stewart
Special assistants to the general manager
Pat Jones, Frank White
Manager of Major League operations
Karol Kyte
Senior director, scouting
Deric Ladnier
Senior director, minor league operations
Bob Hegman
Manager, team travel
Jeff Davenport
Director, Lancer program
Rick Amos
Director, season ticket services
Joe Grigoli
Senior director/controller
John Luther
Director, payroll & benefits accounting
Tom Pfannenstiel
Senior director, information systems
Jim Edwards
Senior director, media relations
David Witty
Director, broadcast services & Royals alumni
Fred White
Manager, media relations
Aaron Babcock

Manager, media services
Chris Stathos
Coordinator, media relations
Lora Grosshans
Director, community relations
Shani Tate
Senior director, sales development
Mike Phillips
Director, corporate sponsorship sales
Kevin Battle
Director, group sales
Michele Kammerer
Director, promotions
Kim Hillix
Dir., event operations & revenue development
Chris Richardson
Director, groundskeeping & landscaping
Trevor Vance
Director, stadium operations
Rodney Lewallen
Director, ticket operations
Lance Buckley
Team physician
Dr. Steve Joyce
Athletic trainer
Nick Swartz
Assistant athletic trainer
Lee Kuntz
Strength and conditioning coordinator
Tim Maxey
Equipment manager
Mike Burkhalter
Visiting clubhouse manager
Chuck Hawke
Professional scouts
Rod Fridley, Louie Medina, Earl Winn
Special assignment scouts
Carlos Pascual, John Wathan
Regional cross-checkers
Jeff McKay, Junior Vizcaino, Dennis Woody
Latin American scouting coordinator
Albert Gonzalez
Dominican scouting coordinator
Luis Silverio
Territorial scouts
Bob Bishop, Mike Brown, Jason Bryans, Steve Connolly, Albert Gonzalez, Spencer Graham, Dave Herrera, Keith Hughes, Phil Huttman, Gary Johnson, Cliff Pastornicky, Johnny Ramos, Max Semler, Chet Sergo, Greg Smith, Gerald Turner, Brad Vaughn, Jon Weil, Mark Willoughby

MINOR LEAGUE AFFILIATES

Class	Team	League	Manager
AAA	Omaha	Pacific Coast	Bucky Dent
AA	Wichita	Texas	Keith Bodie
A	Burlington	Midwest	Joe Szekely
A	Spokane	Northwest	Tom Poquette
A	Wilmington	Carolina	Jeff Garber
Rookie	Gulf Coast Royals	Gulf Coast	Lloyd Simmons

BROADCAST INFORMATION

Radio: KMBZ-AM (980).
TV: KMBC (Channel 9), KCWB (Channel 29).
Cable TV: Fox Sports Net.

SPRING TRAINING

Ballpark (city): Baseball City Stadium (Davenport, Fla.).
Ticket information: 863-424-2500.

Follow the Royals all season at: www.sportingnews.com/baseball/teams/royals/

SPRING TRAINING ROSTER

Manager—Tony Muser (40).
Coaches—Rich Dauer (25), Tom Gamboa (10), Lamar Johnson (23), John Mizerock, Al Nipper (35), Bob Schaefer.

No.	PITCHERS	B/T	Ht./Wt.	Born	2001 clubs
	Affeldt, Jeremy	L/L	6-4/185	6-5-79	Wichita
	Asencio, Miguel	R/R	6-2/160	9-29-80	Clearwater
	Austin, Jeff	R/R	6-0/185	10-19-76	Omaha, Kansas City
62	Bailey, Cory	R/R	6-1/210	1-24-71	Omaha, Kansas City
	Cogan, Tony	L/L	6-2/205	12-21-76	Kansas City, Wichita, Omaha
33	Durbin, Chad	R/R	6-2/200	12-3-77	Kansas City, Omaha
	Field, Nate	R/R	6-2/185	12-11-75	Wichita
	George, Chris	L/L	6-2/200	9-16-79	Omaha, Kansas City
38	Grimsley, Jason	R/R	6-3/205	8-7-67	Kansas City
	Henry, Doug	R/R	6-4/205	12-10-63	Kansas City
39	Hernandez, Roberto	R/R	6-4/250	11-11-64	Kansas City
	MacDougal, Mike	B/R	6-4/195	3-5-77	Omaha, Kansas City
22	May, Darrell	L/L	6-2/184	6-13-72	DID NOT PLAY
45	Moreno, Orber	R/R	6-3/200	4-27-77	Wilmington, Wichita, Omaha
41	Reichert, Dan	R/R	6-3/175	7-12-76	Kansas City, Omaha
50	Rosado, Jose	L/L	6-0/185	11-9-74	DID NOT PLAY
	Snyder, Kyle	B/R	6-8/220	9-9-77	DID NOT PLAY
	Sonnier, Shawn	R/R	6-5/210	7-5-76	Omaha
34	Stein, Blake	R/R	6-7/240	8-3-73	Kansas City
37	Suppan, Jeff	R/R	6-2/210	1-2-75	Kansas City
	Voyles, Brad	R/R	6-0/195	12-30-76	Myrtle Beach, Greenville, Wichita, Kansas City
51	Wilson, Kris	R/R	6-3/225	8-6-76	Kansas City, Omaha
No.	CATCHERS	B/T	Ht./Wt.	Born	2001 clubs
8	Mayne, Brent	L/R	6-1/192	4-19-68	Colorado, Kansas City
No.	INFIELDERS	B/T	Ht./Wt.	Born	2001 clubs
10	Alicea, Luis	B/R	5-9/170	7-29-65	Kansas City
3	Febles, Carlos	R/R	5-11/185	5-24-76	Kansas City, Omaha
	Harvey, Ken	R/R	6-2/240	3-1-78	Wilmington, Wichita, Kansas City
6	McCarty, Dave	R/L	6-5/215	11-23-69	Kansas City
5	Perez, Neifi	B/R	6-0/175	6-2-75	Colorado, Kansas City
16	Randa, Joe	R/R	5-11/190	12-18-69	Kansas City
29	Sweeney, Mike	R/R	6-3/225	7-22-73	Kansas City
No.	OUTFIELDERS	B/T	Ht./Wt.	Born	2001 clubs
15	Beltran, Carlos	B/R	6-1/190	4-24-77	Kansas City
27	Brown, Dee	L/R	6-0/215	3-27-78	Kansas City, Omaha
	Gomez, Alexis	L/L	6-2/160	8-6-80	Wilmington, Wichita
23	Ibanez, Raul	L/R	6-2/200	6-2-72	Kansas City, Omaha
11	Knoblauch, Chuck	R/R	5-9/175	7-7-68	New York A.L.
14	Quinn, Mark	R/R	6-1/195	5-21-74	Kansas City, Omaha
34	Tucker, Michael	L/R	6-2/185	6-25-71	Chicago N.L., Cincinnati

BALLPARK INFORMATION

Ballpark (capacity, surface)
Kauffman Stadium (40,529, grass)

Address
P.O. Box 419969
Kansas City, MO 64141-6969

Official website
www.kcroyals.com

Business phone
816-921-8000

Ticket information
816-921-8000

Ticket prices
$22 (club box)
$21 (dugout box)
$18 (field box, dugout plaza)
$16 (field plaza)
$12 (view box)
$10 (OF plaza, view level IF)
$5 (view level)

Field dimensions (from home plate)
To left field at foul line, 330 feet
To center field, 400 feet
To right field at foul line, 330 feet

First game played
April 10, 1973 (Royals 12, Rangers 1)

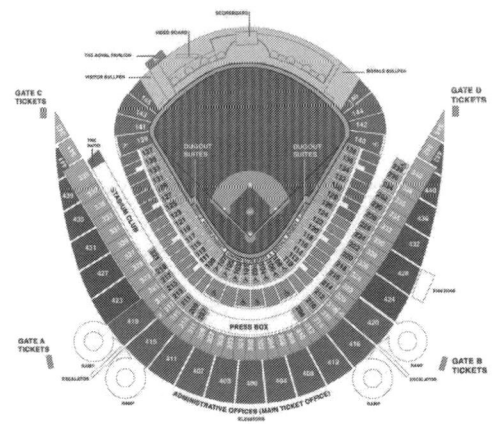

2001 REVIEW
DAY BY DAY

Kansas City Royals · 2002 SEASON

Date	Opp.	Res.	Score	(inn.*)	Hits	Opp. hits	Winning pitcher	Losing pitcher	Save	Record	Pos.	GB
4-2	At N.Y.	L	3-7		7	13	Clemens	Suppan		0-1	T2nd	1.0
4-4	At N.Y.	L	2-8		8	7	Pettitte	Stein		0-2	T4th	1.5
4-5	At N.Y.	L	0-1		5	4	Mussina	Reichert	Rivera	0-3	T4th	2.5
4-6	Min.	L	2-6		5	11	Mays	Meadows		0-4	5th	3.5
4-7	Min.	W	5-3		7	8	Suppan	Redman	Hernandez	1-4	5th	2.5
4-8	Min.	W	15-4		13	9	Suzuki	Romero		2-4	4th	1.5
4-9	N.Y.	L	4-13		12	19	Pettitte	Stein		2-5	5th	2.5
4-10	N.Y.	L	5-9		8	15	Mendoza	Hernandez		2-6	5th	3.5
4-11	N.Y.	L	5-8		10	12	Williams	Meadows	Rivera	2-7	5th	4.5
4-13	At Tor.	L	1-2		4	7	Michalak	Suppan	Koch	2-8	5th	5.5
4-14	At Tor.	L	4-5		9	10	File	Hernandez		2-9	5th	6.5
4-15	At Tor.	W	4-2		8	6	Stein	Carpenter	Hernandez	3-9	5th	6.5
4-16	At Min.	W	5-3		7	11	Reichert	Mays	Hernandez	4-9	5th	5.5
4-17	At Min.	L	5-6		6	11	Wells	Grimsley		4-10	5th	6.5
4-18	At Min.	L	3-5		12	6	Carrasco	Cogan	Hawkins	4-11	5th	7.5
4-20	Tor.	L	4-12		10	13	Carpenter	Suzuki		4-12	5th	8.5
4-21	Tor.	W	5-4	(13)	10	7	Henry	Plesac		5-12	5th	8.5
4-22	Tor.	W	5-1		9	2	Reichert	Loaiza	Hernandez	6-12	4th	8.5
4-24	At T.B.	L	2-4		8	9	Lopez	Meadows	Yan	6-13	4th	8.5
4-25	At T.B.	L	3-5		4	5	Wilson	Suppan	Yan	6-14	4th	9.5
4-26	At T.B.	W	6-0		10	6	Suzuki	Rekar		7-14	4th	8.5
4-27	At Bos.	L	2-9		7	12	Castillo	Stein	Arrojo	7-15	5th	9.5
4-28	At Bos.	W	8-2		12	6	Reichert	Ohka		8-15	3rd	8.5
4-29	At Bos.	W	11-8	(11)	16	14	Santiago	Lowe	Hernandez	9-15	3rd	8.5
4-30	At Tor.	W	6-3		11	9	Suppan	Hamilton	Hernandez	10-15	3rd	8.5
5-1	Cle.	L	2-13		7	11	Finley	Durbin		10-16	3rd	8.5
5-2	Cle.	L	4-8		9	12	Sabathia	Suzuki		10-17	4th	9.5
5-3	Cle.	L	4-9		10	13	Burba	Reichert		10-18	4th	10.0
5-4	Min.	L	2-6		9	13	Redman	Meadows		10-19	4th	11.0
5-5	Min.	W	12-10	(12)	15	16	Bailey	Miller		11-19	4th	10.0
5-6	Min.	L	2-4		7	9	Radke	Durbin	Hawkins	11-20	4th	11.0
5-8	At Cle.	L	4-8		10	10	Burba	Cogan		11-21	5th	12.0
5-9	At Cle.	L	1-5		8	10	Sabathia	Reichert		11-22	5th	12.0
5-10	At Cle.	W	8-3		13	8	Meadows	Colon		12-22	5th	12.0
5-11	At Min.	L	4-5	(11)	9	13	Hawkins	Santiago		12-23	5th	13.0
5-12	At Min.	W	12-4		20	10	Durbin	Radke		13-23	5th	12.0
5-13	At Min.	L	3-7		11	11	Milton	Suzuki		13-24	5th	13.0
5-14	At Min.	L	1-3		6	7	Mays	Reichert	Hawkins	13-25	5th	14.0
5-15	T.B.	W	6-2		14	10	Santiago	Wilson		14-25	5th	13.0
5-16	T.B.	W	9-5		13	11	Hernandez	Yan		15-25	5th	13.0
5-17	T.B.	W	4-2		7	9	Durbin	Rose	Hernandez	16-25	5th	13.0
5-18	Bos.	L	3-6		9	10	Martinez	Stein		16-26	4th	13.0
5-19	Bos.	W	6-2		13	5	Reichert	Nomo		17-26	4th	13.0
5-20	Bos.	L	3-10		8	13	Castillo	Meadows		17-27	4th	13.0
5-22	Oak.	L	1-4		8	11	Mecir	Suppan	Isringhausen	17-28	4th	14.0
5-23	Oak.	W	4-1		10	6	Durbin	Lidle	Hernandez	18-28	4th	13.0
5-25	Sea.	L	6-9		10	14	Franklin	Grimsley	Sasaki	18-29	4th	14.0
5-26	Sea.	L	2-7		10	13	Sele	Meadows		18-30	4th	14.0
5-27	Sea.	L	4-5	(11)	8	9	Charlton	Santiago		18-31	5th	14.5
5-28	Sea.	L	3-13		6	17	Abbott	Durbin		18-32	5th	15.0
5-29	At Tex.	L	2-8		8	7	Helling	Suzuki		18-33	5th	16.0
5-30	At Tex.	W	11-2		19	9	Reichert	Mahomes		19-33	5th	16.0
5-31	At Tex.	W	8-2		15	6	Stein	Davis	Wilson	20-33	5th	15.0
6-1	At Ana.	L	1-7		6	10	Valdes	Suppan		20-34	5th	16.0
6-2	At Ana.	L	2-3		8	5	Schoeneweis	Durbin	Percival	20-35	5th	16.0
6-3	At Ana.	L	2-7		7	10	Ortiz	Suzuki		20-36	5th	17.0
6-5	Chi.	L	2-6		6	11	K. Wells	Reichert	Howry	20-37	5th	17.5
6-6	Chi.	W	12-6		16	13	Suppan	Baldwin		21-37	5th	17.0
6-7	Chi.	L	1-5		5	13	Buehrle	Durbin		21-38	5th	18.0
6-8	Ari.	L	4-11		12	14	Johnson	Byrd		21-39	5th	18.0
6-9	Ari.	W	3-2		9	8	Stein	Reynoso	Hernandez	22-39	5th	18.0
6-10	Ari.	L	5-12		10	14	Ellis	Reichert		22-40	5th	18.0
6-12	St.L.	W	7-4		10	6	Durbin	Kile		23-40	5th	17.5
6-13	St.L.	W	4-1		12	9	Wilson	Morris	Hernandez	24-40	5th	17.5
6-14	St.L.	W	3-2	(13)	10	6	Henry	Stechschulte		25-40	5th	16.5
6-15	At Mil.	W	4-2		9	9	Byrd	Peterson	Hernandez	26-40	5th	16.0
6-16	At Mil.	W	4-1		5	7	Reichert	Haynes	Hernandez	27-40	5th	14.5
6-17	At Mil.	L	2-5		10	8	Wright	Stein	Leskanic	27-41	5th	14.5
6-18	At Chi.	L	4-5		10	9	Buehrle	Durbin	Foulke	27-42	5th	15.0
6-19	At Chi.	L	3-5		6	7	Baldwin	Suppan	Foulke	27-43	5th	16.0
6-20	At Chi.	L	1-2		5	5	Garland	Grimsley	Foulke	27-44	5th	16.0
6-22	Cle.	L	5-6		7	14	Sabathia	Stein	Wickman	27-45	5th	17.0
6-23	Cle.	W	3-2		4	9	Durbin	Burba	Hernandez	28-45	5th	16.0
6-24	Cle.	L	2-4		6	10	Colon	Suppan	Rocker	28-46	5th	17.0

– 40 –

Date	Opp.	Res.	Score	(inn.*)	Hits	Opp. hits	Winning pitcher	Losing pitcher	Save	Record	Pos.	GB
6-26	Det.	W	12-5		13	6	Reichert	Blair		29-46	5th	16.5
6-27	Det.	W	5-4		12	10	Hernandez	Jones		30-46	5th	16.0
6-28	Det.	W	9-2		13	9	Durbin	Weaver		31-46	5th	15.0
6-29	At Cle.	W	5-3		9	6	Suppan	Burba	Hernandez	32-46	5th	15.0
6-30	At Cle.	W	11-7		15	10	Wilson	Colon		33-46	4th	15.0
7-1	At Cle.	W	13-11		15	13	Stein	Nagy	Hernandez	34-46	4th	15.0
7-2	At Cle.	L	1-2		6	7	Rocker	Cogan		34-47	4th	16.0
7-3	At Det.	L	4-8		12	9	Lima	Durbin		34-48	5th	17.0
7-4	At Det.	L	4-6		8	11	Weaver	Bailey	Anderson	34-49	5th	17.0
7-5	At Det.	L	1-7		5	13	Sparks	Wilson		34-50	5th	18.0
7-6	Hou.	L	3-8		11	10	Miller	Reichert	Cruz	34-51	5th	19.0
7-7	Hou.	L	8-10		10	18	Jackson	Byrd	Wagner	34-52	5th	20.0
7-8	Hou.	L	5-14		8	15	Villone	Durbin		34-53	5th	21.0
7-12	At Pit.	L	0-2		6	5	Anderson	Suppan	M. Williams	34-54	5th	22.0
7-13	At Pit.	L	0-1		1	11	Ritchie	Grimsley		34-55	5th	22.0
7-14	At Pit.	W	7-4		12	6	Wilson	D. Williams	Hernandez	35-55	5th	22.0
7-15	At Chi.	L	1-2		7	4	Lieber	Byrd	Gordon	35-56	5th	22.0
7-16	At Chi.	W	4-2		7	5	Reichert	Tapani	Hernandez	36-56	5th	21.0
7-17	At Chi.	L	4-7		9	11	Bere	Cogan	Gordon	36-57	5th	21.0
7-18	Sea.	L	0-2	(10)	5	9	Nelson	Hernandez	Sasaki	36-58	5th	21.0
7-19	Sea.	W	6-3		9	8	Wilson	Garcia		37-58	5th	21.0
7-20	Oak.	L	3-14		10	16	Lidle	Byrd		37-59	5th	21.0
7-21	Oak.	L	1-10		9	11	Heredia	Reichert		37-60	5th	21.0
7-22	Oak.	W	5-4		15	8	Hernandez	Mecir		38-60	5th	20.0
7-23	Oak.	L	2-7		6	9	Hudson	Durbin		38-61	5th	20.0
7-24	At Sea.	W	6-1		11	7	Wilson	Garcia		39-61	5th	19.0
7-25	At Sea.	W	6-1		12	6	Byrd	Sele		40-61	5th	19.0
7-26	At Sea.	L	0-4		2	11	Pineiro	George		40-62	5th	20.0
7-27	At Oak.	L	0-5		4	5	Mulder	Suppan		40-63	5th	20.0
7-28	At Oak.	W	9-3		11	6	Durbin	Hudson		41-63	5th	19.5
7-29	At Oak.	L	4-6		6	7	Isringhausen	Grimsley	Mecir	41-64	5th	19.5
7-31	At Chi.	W	2-1	(10)	9	6	Byrd	Foulke	Hernandez	42-64	5th	18.5
8-1	At Chi.	L	6-7		12	10	Wright	George	Foulke	42-65	5th	19.5
8-2	At Chi.	W	6-3		8	7	Suppan	K. Wells	Hernandez	43-65	5th	18.5
8-3	At Min.	L	7-8	(10)	14	13	Jones	Hernandez		43-66	5th	19.0
8-4	At Min.	L	2-6		9	9	Milton	Wilson		43-67	5th	20.0
8-5	At Min.	W	10-5		20	11	Byrd	Mays		44-67	5th	19.0
8-6	Bal.	L	6-9		15	14	Johnson	George		44-68	5th	19.5
8-7	Bal.	L	3-7		8	10	Maduro	Suppan	Roberts	44-69	5th	19.5
8-8	Bal.	L	1-4		6	8	Mercedes	Durbin	Groom	44-70	5th	20.5
8-9	Bal.	W	6-4		12	8	Wilson	Ponson	Hernandez	45-70	5th	19.5
8-10	Det.	W	7-3		8	7	Byrd	Weaver	Stein	46-70	5th	18.5
8-11	Det.	W	4-1		6	5	George	Lima	Hernandez	47-70	5th	17.5
8-12	Det.	W	6-4		10	9	Suppan	Pettyjohn	Hernandez	48-70	5th	17.5
8-14	At Bal.	L	2-5		4	12	Maduro	Durbin	Roberts	48-71	5th	18.5
8-15	At Bal.	L	4-5		5	7	Mercedes	Wilson	Roberts	48-72	5th	19.5
8-16	At Bal.	W	9-2		11	12	Byrd	Ponson		49-72	5th	19.5
8-17	At Det.	L	2-4		5	7	Lima	George	Anderson	49-73	5th	19.5
8-18	At Det.	W	8-4		14	7	Suppan	Nitkowski		50-73	5th	19.5
8-19	At Det.	L	3-4		8	7	Cornejo	Durbin	Anderson	50-74	5th	19.5
8-20	Chi.	W	10-1		13	5	Stein	Lowe		51-74	5th	18.5
8-21	Chi.	L	1-6		8	13	Garland	Byrd		51-75	5th	19.5
8-22	Chi.	L	12-13		18	18	K. Wells	Henry	Foulke	51-76	5th	20.5
8-23	Chi.	L	6-7		10	13	Biddle	Suppan	Foulke	51-77	5th	21.5
8-24	Min.	L	3-9		12	10	Milton	Durbin	Guardado	51-78	5th	21.5
8-25	Min.	L	1-7		5	14	Mays	Wilson		51-79	5th	21.5
8-26	Min.	L	2-7		3	12	Radke	Stein		51-80	5th	22.5
8-28	Ana.	W	10-4		12	7	George	Ortiz		52-80	5th	22.5
8-29	Ana.	W	6-3		9	7	Suppan	Rapp	Hernandez	53-80	5th	22.5
8-30	Ana.	W	2-1		8	7	Grimsley	Levine		54-80	5th	22.5
8-31	Tex.	L	2-7		6	6	Helling	Byrd		54-81	5th	22.5
9-1	Tex.	W	8-7	(11)	13	10	Hernandez	Mahomes		55-81	5th	22.5
9-2	Tex.	L	6-12		10	17	Michalak	George		55-82	5th	22.5
9-4	At Ana.	W	4-1		9	3	Suppan	Washburn		56-82	4th	23.0
9-5	At Ana.	L	1-4		6	9	Valdes	Durbin	Percival	56-83	4th	23.0
9-6	At Ana.	L	6-7	(10)	11	13	Holtz	Hernandez		56-84	5th	24.0
9-7	At Tex.	L	2-8		6	9	Davis	Wilson		56-85	5th	24.0
9-8	At Tex.	W	8-3		14	8	George	Oliver		57-85	5th	24.0
9-9	At Tex.	L	3-4	(12)	7	12	Zimmerman	Hernandez		57-86	5th	25.0
9-18	At Cle.	L	2-11		6	9	Finley	Durbin		57-87	T4th	25.5
9-19	At Cle.	L	3-11		8	10	Colon	Suppan		57-88	5th	26.5
9-20	At Cle.	W	4-2		9	6	George	Drese	Hernandez	58-88	T4th	25.5
9-21	At Chi.	L	7-8		12	11	Lowe	Henry		58-89	T4th	25.5
9-22	At Chi.	L	4-5	(10)	10	9	Foulke	Stein		58-90	5th	26.5
9-23	At Chi.	L	2-10		8	8	Buehrle	Durbin		58-91	5th	27.5
9-24	Det.	L	2-4		8	6	Sparks	Suppan	Anderson	58-92	5th	27.5
9-25	Det.	L	4-6		11	10	Lima	George	Anderson	58-93	5th	28.5
9-26	Det.	W	8-6		11	12	Stein	Murray	Hernandez	59-93	5th	28.0

Date	Opp.	Res.	Score	(inn.*)	Hits	Opp. hits	Winning pitcher	Losing pitcher	Save	Record	Pos.	GB
9-27	Det.	W	8-7		15	11	MacDougal	Cornejo	Hernandez	60-93	5th	27.5
9-28	Chi.	W	3-2		8	7	Durbin	Embree	Hernandez	61-93	5th	26.5
9-29	Chi.	L	2-10		9	16	Buehrle	Suppan		61-94	5th	27.5
9-30	Chi.	L	2-5		5	12	Glover	George	Foulke	61-95	5th	28.5
10-2	Cle.	W	5-1		6	7	Hernandez	Rocker		62-95	5th	27.5
10-3	Cle.	L	1-4		7	8	Sabathia	MacDougal	Wickman	62-96	5th	28.5
10-4	Cle.	W	8-4		10	9	Durbin	Colon		63-96	5th	27.5
10-6†	At Det.	W	8-3		11	7	Suppan	Weaver	Hernandez	64-96		
10-6‡	At Det.	L	1-2		10	4	Sparks	George		64-97	5th	26.0
10-7	At Det.	W	10-4		13	6	Stein	Lima		65-97	5th	26.0

Monthly records: April (10-15), May (10-18), June (13-13), July (9-18), August (12-17), September (7-14), October (4-2).
*Innings, if other than nine. †First game of a doubleheader. ‡Second game of a doubleheader.

HIGHLIGHTS

High point: The Royals won six straight games from June 26 through July 1, beating the Tigers and the Indians three times each. First baseman Mike Sweeney and center fielder Carlos Beltran each had five homers during the stretch. The team also briefly escaped last place for the first time in more than a month.
Low point: Immediately following that winning streak, the Royals lost nine straight games—one to the Indians, three each to the Tigers and Astros and two to the Pirates. That was their longest skid of the season.
Turning point: That came when the schedule-makers penciled in six games against the Yankees among the Royals' first nine of the season. They lost all six of them and were in last place virtually from the get-go. They never recovered.
Most valuable player: Carlos Beltran led the team's regulars in batting average, runs, hits, RBIs and stolen bases. He also popped 24 homers and 32 doubles.
Most valuable pitcher: Jeff Suppan was seldom spectacular but he didn't miss a start and chewed up 218 1/3 innings while notching a team-high 10 victories. His 4.37 ERA was the lowest of his career.
Most improved player: Designated hitter-outfielder Raul Ibanez was demoted twice to Class AAA Omaha, hitting just .150 when shipped out the second time. Recalled on June 17, Ibanez was mixed into the everyday lineup and batted .301 the rest of the season. He had 51 of his total 54 RBIs after that date.
Most pleasant surprise: Righthander Cory Bailey hadn't pitched in the majors for two years. But he became a valuable setup man, appearing in 53 games with a 3.48 ERA. He had 61 strikeouts in 67 1/3 innings and opponents batted just .234 against him.
Key injuries: Lefthander Jose Rosado sat out the entire season because of a second surgery on his pitching shoulder. ... Catcher Gregg Zaun suffered a torn left calf and played just 39 games. ... Second baseman Carlos Febles was out April 20 to June 7 with a torn ligament in

his right knee. ... A pulled hamstring put left fielder Dee Brown out from June 17 to July 26.
Notable: The 97 losses matched the team record for most in a season (1970, 1999). ... Right fielder Mark Quinn went 241 consecutive plate appearances and 102 games without an unintentional base on balls. He walked just 12 times all season. ... The team was just 14-34 in games against lefthanded starters.
—DICK KAEGEL

RECORDS

2001 regular-season record: 65-97 (5th in A.L. Central); 35-46 at home; 30-51 on road; 13-19 vs. A.L. East; 30-46 vs. A.L. Central; 14-22 vs. A.L. West; 8-10 vs. N.L.; 14-34 vs. lefthanded starters; 51-63 vs. righthanded starters; 59-86 on grass; 6-11 on turf; 19-30 in daytime; 46-67 at night; 11-24 in one-run games; 6-7 in extra-inning games; 0-0-1 in doubleheaders.
Team record past five years: 345-462 (.428, ranks 13th in league in that span).

TEAM LEADERS

Batting average: Carlos Beltran (.306).
At-bats: Carlos Beltran (617).
Runs: Carlos Beltran (106).
Hits: Carlos Beltran (189).
Total Bases: Carlos Beltran (317).
Doubles: Mike Sweeney (46).
Triples: Carlos Beltran (12).
Home runs: Mike Sweeney (29).
Runs batted in: Carlos Beltran (101).
Stolen bases: Carlos Beltran (31).
Slugging percentage: Mike Sweeney (.542).
On-base percentage: Mike Sweeney (.374).
Wins: Jeff Suppan (10).
Earned-run average: Jeff Suppan (4.37).
Complete games: Chad Durbin (2).
Shutouts: None.
Saves: Roberto Hernandez (28).
Innings pitched: Jeff Suppan (218.1).
Strikeouts: Jeff Suppan (120).

GAMES BY POSITION

Catcher: Hector Ortiz 55, Brent Mayne 49, A.J. Hinch 43, Gregg Zaun 35, Sal Fasano 3.
First base: Mike Sweeney 108, Dave McCarty 68, Raul Ibanez 10, Ken Harvey 3.
Second base: Carlos Febles 78, Luis Alicea 67, Luis Ordaz 19, Donnie Sadler 13, Neifi Perez 4, Wilson Delgado 2, Joe Randa 1.
Third base: Joe Randa 137, Luis Alicea 18, Donnie Sadler 15, Wilson Delgado 3, Raul Ibanez 1, Luis Ordaz 1.
Shortstop: Rey Sanchez 100, Neifi Perez 46, Angel Berroa 14, Luis Ordaz 8, Wilson Delgado 6, Donnie Sadler 6.
Outfield: Carlos Beltran 152, Mark Quinn 99, Jermaine Dye 93, Dee Brown 83, Raul Ibanez 42, Endy Chavez 28, Donnie Sadler 16, Dave McCarty 9, Brandon Berger 5, Trenidad Hubbard 3.
Designated hitter: Mike Sweeney 38, Raul Ibanez 33, Luis Alicea 22, Dee Brown 20, Mark Quinn 18, Joe Randa 14, Dave McCarty 7, Jermaine Dye 4, Carlos Beltran 3, A.J. Hinch 2, Gregg Zaun 2, Hector Ortiz 1, Luis Ordaz 1, Donnie Sadler 1, Brandon Berger 1, Ken Harvey 1.

TOP DRAFT CHOICES

1. **Colt Griffin,** RHP, Marshall (Tex.) H.S.
2. **Roscoe Crosby,** OF, Union H.S., Buffalo, S.C.
3. **Matt Ferrara,** 3B, Westminster Christian Acad., Fort Lauderdale, Fla.
4. **John Draper,** C, Cal State Los Angeles.
5. **Chamar McDonald,** 1B, Madison (Miss.) Central H.S.
6. **Clint Frost,** RHP, Jordan H.S., Columbus, Ga.
7. **Chris Tierney,** LHP, Lockport (Ill.) H.S.
8. **Ira Brown,** RHP, Willis (Tex.) H.S.
9. **Justin Nelson,** LHP/OF, Platte Valley H.S., Kersey, Colo.
10. **Danny Tamayo,** RHP, U. of Notre Dame.

MINNESOTA TWINS
AMERICAN LEAGUE CENTRAL DIVISION

Twins schedule
Home games shaded
D—Day game (games starting before 5 p.m.)
*All-Star Game at Milwaukee
Subject to changes

April

SUN	MON	TUE	WED	THU	FRI	SAT
	1 D KC	2	3 KC	4 D TOR	5 TOR	6 D TOR
7 D TOR	8 D CLE	9 CLE	10 CLE	11 CLE	12 DET	13 DET
14 DET	15	16 KC	17 KC	18 D KC	19 CLE	20 CLE
21 D CLE	22	23 TB	24 TB	25 D TB	26 DET	27 D DET
28 D DET	29 TB	30 TB				

May

SUN	MON	TUE	WED	THU	FRI	SAT
			1 TB	2 D TB	3 DET	4 DET
5 D DET	6 DET	7 KC	8 KC	9	10 NYY	11 NYY
12 D NYY	13 KC	14 KC	15 KC	16 D KC	17 NYY	18 D NYY
19 D NYY	20	21 TEX	22 TEX	23	24 ANA	25 ANA
26 D ANA	27 TEX	28 TEX	29 TEX	30 ANA	31 ANA	

June

SUN	MON	TUE	WED	THU	FRI	SAT
						1 ANA
2 D ANA	3	4 CLE	5 CLE	6 CLE	7 FLA	8 FLA
9 D FLA	10 ATL	11 ATL	12 ATL	13	14 MIL	15 MIL
16 D MIL	17	18 NYM	19 NYM	20 NYM	21 PHI	22 PHI
23 D PHI	24 CWS	25 CWS	26 CWS	27 D CWS	28 MIL	29 MIL
30 D MIL						

July

SUN	MON	TUE	WED	THU	FRI	SAT
	1 OAK	2 OAK	3 OAK	4 SEA	5 SEA	6 SEA
7 D SEA	8	9 *	10	11 TEX	12 TEX	13 TEX
14 D TEX	15 ANA	16 D ANA	17 CLE	18 D CLE	19 DET	20 DET
21 D DET	22 CWS	23 CWS	24 D CWS	25	26 TOR	27 TOR
28 D TOR	29	30 CWS	31 CWS			

August

SUN	MON	TUE	WED	THU	FRI	SAT
				1 CWS	2 D KC	3 KC
4 D KC	5 D KC	6 BAL	7 BAL	8 D BAL	9 D BOS	10 BOS
11 D BOS	12	13 BAL	14 BAL	15 BAL	16 BOS	17 BOS
18 D BOS	19 CWS	20 CWS	21 CWS	22 KC	23 KC	24 D KC
25 D KC	26	27 SEA	28 SEA	29 D SEA	30 OAK	31 OAK

September

SUN	MON	TUE	WED	THU	FRI	SAT
1 D OAK	2 D SEA	3	4 D SEA	5	6 D OAK	7 OAK
8 D OAK	9 DET	10 DET	11 D DET	12 CLE	13 CLE	14 CLE
15 D CLE	16	17 DET	18 DET	19 D DET	20 CWS	21 CWS
22 D CWS	23	24 CLE	25 CLE	26 CLE	27 CWS	28 CWS
29 D CWS	30					

2002 SEASON
CLUB DIRECTORY

Owner
Carl R. Pohlad
President
Jerry Bell
Chairman of executive committee
Howard Fox
Directors
Carl R. Pohlad
Eloise Pohlad
James O. Pohlad
Robert C. Pohlad
William M. Pohlad
T. Geron (Jerry) Bell
Kirby Puckett
Chris Clouser
Senior vice president, business affairs
Dave St. Peter
Vice president, general manager
Terry Ryan
Vice president, asst. general manager
Bill Smith
Assistant general manager
Wayne Krivsky
Executive vice president, baseball
Kirby Puckett
Vice president, operations
Matt Hoy
Director of minor leagues
Jim Rantz
Director of scouting
Mike Radcliff
Director of baseball operations
Rob Antony
Traveling secretary
Remzi Kiratli
Director of communications
Brad Ruiter
Manager, media relations
Sean Harlin

Club physicians
Dr. Dan Buss
Dr. VeeJay Eyunni
Dr. John Hallberg
Dr. Tom Jetzer
Dr. John Steubs
Scouts
Kevin Bootay
Ellsworth Brown
Larry Corrigan
Cal Ermer
Marty Esposito
Vern Followell (pro scouting supervisor)
Earl Frishman (east supervisor)
Bill Harford
Deron Johnson (west supervisor)
John Leavitt
Joel Lepel (midwest supervisor)
Bill Lohr
Lee MacPhail
Bill Mele
Gregg Miller
Bill Milos
Tim O'Neil
Hector Otero
Mark Quimuyog
Mike Ruth (midwest supervisor)
Ricky Taylor
Jay Weitzel
Brad Weitzel
John Wilson
Mark Wilson
International scouts
David Kim
Jose Leon
Joe McIlvaine
Howard Norsetter
Yoshi Okamoto
Johnny Sierra
Frank Valdez

MINOR LEAGUE AFFILIATES

Class	Team	League	Manager
AAA	Edmonton	Pacific Coast	John Russell
AA	New Britain	Eastern	Stan Cliburn
A	Fort Myers	Florida State	Jose Marzan
A	Quad City	Midwest	Jeff Carter
Rookie	Elizabethton	Appalachian	Rudy Hernandez
Rookie	Gulf Coast Twins	Gulf Coast	To be announced

BROADCAST INFORMATION

Radio: WCCO-AM (830).
TV: KMSP-TV (Channel 9).
Cable TV: Fox Sports Net North.

SPRING TRAINING

Ballpark (city): Lee County Sports Complex (Fort Myers, Fla.).
Ticket information: 800-33-TWINS.

Follow the Twins all season at: www.sportingnews.com/baseball/teams/twins/

SPRING TRAINING ROSTER

Manager—Ron Gardenhire (35).

Coaches—Rick Anderson, Steve Liddle, Al Newman, Rick Stelmaszek (43), Scott Ullger (45), Jerry White (13).

No.	PITCHERS	B/T	Ht./Wt.	Born	2001 clubs
	Balfour, Grant	R/R	6-2/170	12-30-77	New Britain, Minnesota, Edmonton
59	Cressend, Jack	R/R	6-1/185	5-13-75	Edmonton, Minnesota
47	Duvall, Mike	R/L	6-0/200	10-11-74	Edmonton, Minnesota
62	Fiore, Tony	R/R	6-4/210	10-12-71	Durham, Tampa Bay, Edmonton, Minnesota
	Frederick, Kevin	R/L	6-1/210	11-4-76	Fort Myers, New Britain
18	Guardado, Eddie	R/L	6-0/194	10-2-70	Minnesota
32	Hawkins, LaTroy	R/R	6-5/204	12-21-72	Minnesota
	Johnson, Adam	R/R	6-2/210	7-12-79	New Britain, Minnesota, Edmonton
51	Kinney, Matt	R/R	6-5/220	12-16-76	Edmonton
	Lohse, Kyle	R/R	6-2/190	10-4-78	New Britain, Edmonton, Minnesota
53	Mays, Joe	B/R	6-1/185	12-10-75	Minnesota
20	Miller, Travis	R/L	6-3/215	11-2-72	Minnesota
	Mills, Ryan	L/R	6-5/205	7-21-77	New Britain
21	Milton, Eric	L/L	6-3/220	8-4-75	Minnesota
22	Radke, Brad	R/R	6-2/188	10-27-72	Minnesota
35	Reed, Rick	R/R	6-1/195	8-16-65	New York N.L., Minnesota
	Rincon, Juan	R/R	5-11/190	1-23-79	New Britain, Minnesota
33	Romero, J.C.	B/L	5-11/195	6-4-76	Minnesota, Edmonton
57	Santana, Johan	L/L	6-0/195	3-13-79	Minnesota
	Thomas, Brad	L/L	6-3/205	10-22-77	New Britain, Minnesota
46	Wells, Bob	R/R	6-0/200	11-1-66	Minnesota

No.	CATCHERS	B/T	Ht./Wt.	Born	2001 clubs
24	LeCroy, Matt	R/R	6-2/225	12-13-75	Edmonton, Minnesota
9	Pierzynski, A.J.	L/R	6-3/220	12-30-76	Minnesota
12	Prince, Tom	R/R	5-11/206	8-13-64	Minnesota
17	Valentin, Javier	B/R	5-10/192	9-19-75	Edmonton

No.	INFIELDERS	B/T	Ht./Wt.	Born	2001 clubs
1	Canizaro, Jay	R/R	5-9/178	7-4-73	DID NOT PLAY
	Cuddyer, Mike	R/R	6-2/200	3-27-79	New Britain, Minnesota
15	Guzman, Cristian	B/R	6-0/195	3-21-78	Minnesota, Gulf Coast Twins
7	Hocking, Denny	B/R	5-10/183	4-2-70	Minnesota
47	Koskie, Corey	L/R	6-3/217	6-28-73	Minnesota
25	Mientkiewicz, Doug	L/R	6-2/200	6-19-74	Minnesota
27	Ortiz, David	L/L	6-4/230	11-18-75	Minnesota, Gulf Coast Twins, Fort Myers, New Britain
1	Rivas, Luis	R/R	5-11/175	8-30-79	Minnesota
	Sears, Todd	R/R	6-1/185	10-23-75	Edmonton

No.	OUTFIELDERS	B/T	Ht./Wt.	Born	2001 clubs
30	Buchanan, Brian	R/R	6-4/230	7-21-73	Minnesota
48	Hunter, Torii	R/R	6-2/205	7-18-75	Minnesota
11	Jones, Jacque	L/L	5-10/176	4-25-75	Minnesota
	Mohr, Dustin	R/R	6-0/210	6-19-76	New Britain, Minnesota
	Restovich, Michael	R/R	6-4/235	1-3-79	New Britain

BALLPARK INFORMATION

Ballpark (capacity, surface)
Hubert H. Humphrey Metrodome (48,678, artificial)

Address
34 Kirby Puckett Place
Minneapolis, MN 55415

Official website
www.twinsbaseball.com

Business phone
612-375-1366

Ticket information
1-800-338-9467

Ticket prices
$27 (lower deck club level)
$25 (Diamond View level)
$17 (lower deck reserved)
$11 (upper deck club level; g.a., lower LF)
$5 (g.a., upper deck)

Field dimensions (from home plate)
To left field at foul line, 343 feet
To center field, 408 feet
To right field at foul line, 327 feet

First game played
April 6, 1982 (Mariners 11, Twins 7)

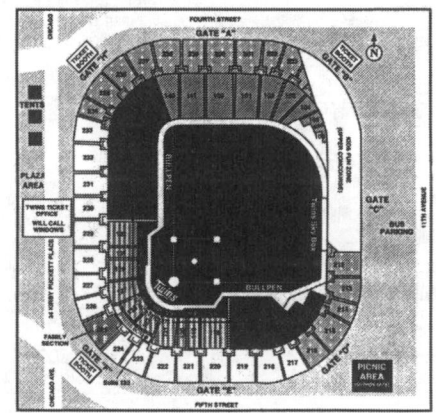

2002 SEASON Minnesota Twins

Date	Opp.	Res.	Score	(inn.*)	Hits	Opp. hits	Winning pitcher	Losing pitcher	Save	Record	Pos.	GB
4-3	At Det.	W	3-2		6	7	Radke	Weaver	Wells	1-0	T1st	...
4-5	At Det.	W	9-5	(10)	11	10	Guardado	Jones		2-0	1st	+1.0
4-6	At K.C.	W	6-2		11	5	Mays	Meadows		3-0	1st	+1.0
4-7	At K.C.	L	3-5		8	7	Suppan	Redman	Hernandez	3-1	1st	+1.0
4-8	At K.C.	L	4-15		9	13	Suzuki	Romero		3-2	T1st	...
4-9	Det.	W	11-5		11	13	Radke	Sparks		4-2	1st	+1.0
4-10	Det.	W	8-2		12	6	Milton	Perisho		5-2	1st	+2.0
4-11	Det.	W	12-1		15	6	Mays	Mlicki		6-2	1st	+2.0
4-13	Chi.	W	7-4		13	7	Redman	Buehrle	Hawkins	7-2	1st	+2.5
4-14	Chi.	W	9-4		12	11	Radke	D. Wells		8-2	1st	+3.5
4-15	Chi.	W	4-3		8	8	Milton	Parque		9-2	1st	+4.0
4-16	K.C.	L	3-5		11	7	Reichert	Mays	Hernandez	9-3	1st	+3.5
4-17	K.C.	W	6-5		11	6	Wells	Grimsley		10-3	1st	+3.5
4-18	K.C.	W	5-3		6	12	Carrasco	Cogan	Hawkins	11-3	1st	+3.5
4-20	At Chi.	W	4-1		7	7	Radke	Parque		12-3	1st	+3.0
4-21	At Chi.	W	4-3		7	7	Milton	Glover	Hawkins	13-3	1st	+3.0
4-22	At Chi.	W	4-2		7	5	Carrasco	Foulke	Hawkins	14-3	1st	+3.0
4-24	At Bos.	L	4-9		8	14	Crawford	Redman	Wakefield	14-4	1st	+3.0
4-25	At Bos.	W	6-4	(10)	10	10	Wells	Beck	Hawkins	15-4	1st	+4.0
4-26	At Bos.	L	0-2		2	8	Nomo	Milton	Lowe	15-5	1st	+3.0
4-27	Bal.	W	6-3		9	6	Mays	Mercedes	Hawkins	16-5	1st	+4.0
4-28	Bal.	L	2-5		8	11	McElroy	Redman	Trombley	16-6	1st	+3.0
4-29	Bal.	W	4-0		8	5	Romero	Hentgen	Hawkins	17-6	1st	+3.0
4-30	N.Y.	W	2-1		3	6	Radke	Pettitte		18-6	1st	+3.5
5-1	N.Y.	L	0-4		3	14	Mussina	Milton		18-7	1st	+2.5
5-2	N.Y.	W	4-2		9	6	Mays	O. Hernandez	Hawkins	19-7	1st	+2.5
5-4	At K.C.	W	6-2		13	9	Redman	Meadows		20-7	1st	+2.0
5-5	At K.C.	L	10-12	(12)	16	15	Bailey	Miller		20-8	1st	+1.0
5-6	At K.C.	W	4-2		9	7	Radke	Durbin	Hawkins	21-8	1st	+1.0
5-8	At N.Y.	W	2-0		8	4	Milton	O. Hernandez		22-8	1st	+1.0
5-9	At N.Y.	L	0-2		4	7	Clemens	Mays	Rivera	22-9	T1st	...
5-10	At N.Y.	W	5-4	(10)	11	5	Guardado	Rivera	Hawkins	23-9	1st	+1.0
5-11	K.C.	W	5-4	(11)	13	9	Hawkins	Santiago		24-9	1st	+1.0
5-12	K.C.	L	4-12		10	20	Durbin	Radke		24-10	T1st	...
5-13	K.C.	W	7-3		11	11	Milton	Suzuki		25-10	1st	+1.0
5-14	K.C.	W	3-1		7	6	Mays	Reichert	Hawkins	26-10	1st	+1.5
5-15	Bos.	L	2-5		7	12	Castillo	Redman		26-11	1st	+0.5
5-16	Bos.	W	4-3		5	8	Wells	Schourek	Hawkins	27-11	1st	+0.5
5-17	Bos.	W	5-3		9	6	Radke	Arrojo		28-11	1st	+1.5
5-18	At Bal.	L	2-7		6	10	Johnson	Milton		28-12	1st	+0.5
5-19	At Bal.	W	7-5		14	6	Mays	Ryan	Hawkins	29-12	1st	+0.5
5-20	At Bal.	L	2-3		8	4	Trombley	Wells		29-13	1st	+0.5
5-22	Sea.	W	12-11		15	15	Wells	Abbott		30-13	1st	+1.5
5-23	Sea.	L	4-5		7	11	Rhodes	Carrasco	Sasaki	30-14	1st	+0.5
5-25	Oak.	L	2-4		9	10	Mulder	Mays	Isringhausen	30-15	2nd	1.0
5-26†	Oak.	L	4-5	(10)	8	9	Mecir	Wells	Guthrie	30-16		
5-26‡	Oak.	W	7-6	(10)	14	10	Guardado	Guthrie		31-16	2nd	0.5
5-27	Oak.	W	9-3		8	12	Guardado	Zito		32-16	1st	+0.5
5-29	At Ana.	W	6-5	(11)	9	13	Cressend	Levine	Carrasco	33-16	1st	+1.0
5-30	At Ana.	W	3-0		7	5	Mays	Rapp		34-16	1st	+1.0
5-31	At Ana.	L	4-5	(12)	14	11	Weber	Carrasco		34-17	1st	+0.5
6-1	At Tex.	W	10-7		12	7	Cressend	Glynn	Guardado	35-17	1st	+0.5
6-2	At Tex.	L	2-3	(10)	8	9	Zimmerman	Hawkins		35-18	1st	+0.5
6-3	At Tex.	W	6-3		15	6	Milton	Helling	Guardado	36-18	1st	+0.5
6-4	Cle.	W	11-10		16	14	Guardado	Shuey		37-18	1st	+1.5
6-5	Cle.	L	0-5		6	11	Wright	Romero		37-19	1st	+0.5
6-6	Cle.	L	2-5		5	8	Shuey	Cressend	Wickman	37-20	2nd	0.5
6-7	Cle.	L	2-6		7	8	Colon	Radke		37-21	2nd	1.5
6-8	Pit.	W	8-6		8	9	Carrasco	Olivares	Hawkins	38-21	2nd	0.5
6-9	Pit.	W	3-2		11	8	Mays	Anderson	Hawkins	39-21	2nd	0.5
6-10	Pit.	L	8-11		12	11	Sauerbeck	Miller	M. Williams	39-22	2nd	0.5
6-12	Hou.	W	7-0		8	4	Radke	Elarton		40-22	1st	+0.5
6-13	Hou.	W	3-1		8	6	Milton	Reynolds		41-22	1st	+0.5
6-14	Hou.	L	3-8		9	16	Oswalt	Mays		41-23	1st	+0.5
6-15	At Chi.	L	3-5		9	7	Tavarez	Romero	Gordon	41-24	1st	+0.5
6-16	At Chi.	L	4-11		10	15	Lieber	Thomas		41-25	1st	+0.5
6-17	At Chi.	L	4-5		7	10	Wood	Radke	Gordon	41-26	1st	+0.5
6-19	At Cle.	W	10-9	(12)	18	16	Wells	Nagy		42-26	1st	+1.5
6-20	At Cle.	L	2-4		8	9	Westbrook	Mays	Wickman	42-27	1st	+0.5
6-21	At Cle.	L	6-9	(7)	9	11	Woodard	Romero	Rincon	42-28	2nd	0.5
6-22	At Det.	L	4-5		13	12	Jones	Wells		42-29	2nd	1.5
6-23	At Det.	L	9-10		17	16	Patterson	Carrasco	Jones	42-30	2nd	1.5
6-24	At Det.	W	14-5		11	9	Milton	Sparks		43-30	2nd	1.5
6-25	At Det.	W	6-3		9	8	Mays	Holt	Hawkins	44-30	2nd	0.5

Date	Opp.	Res.	Score	(inn.*)	Hits	Opp. hits	Winning pitcher	Losing pitcher	Save	Record	Pos.	GB
6-26	Chi.	W	7-6		11	10	Miller	Foulke		45-30	2nd	0.5
6-27	Chi.	W	4-1		9	5	Lohse	K. Wells	Hawkins	46-30	1st	+0.5
6-28	Chi.	L	3-6		6	9	Lowe	Radke		46-31	2nd	...
6-29	Det.	W	3-2		11	7	Wells	Murray	Hawkins	47-31	1st	+1.0
6-30	Det.	W	3-2		7	4	Mays	Holt	Guardado	48-31	1st	+2.0
7-1	Det.	W	8-3		9	7	Santana	Blair		49-31	1st	+3.0
7-2	At Chi.	W	7-5		9	9	Lohse	K. Wells	Hawkins	50-31	1st	+3.0
7-3	At Chi.	W	5-3		10	12	Radke	Lowe	Hawkins	51-31	1st	+3.0
7-4	At Chi.	L	3-4		10	9	Foulke	Hawkins		51-32	1st	+3.0
7-5	At Chi.	W	12-2		16	7	Mays	Baldwin		52-32	1st	+4.0
7-6	Cin.	W	5-4		12	8	Guardado	Nichting	Hawkins	53-32	1st	+4.0
7-7	Cin.	W	7-6		12	10	Wells	Brower	Hawkins	54-32	1st	+4.0
7-8	Cin.	W	7-1		15	3	Radke	Dessens		55-32	1st	+5.0
7-12	At Mil.	W	13-5		15	6	Lohse	Haynes		56-32	1st	+5.0
7-13	At Mil.	L	3-6		6	12	Levrault	Radke		56-33	1st	+4.0
7-14	At Mil.	W	5-3		7	5	Wells	Weathers	Hawkins	57-33	1st	+5.0
7-15	At St.L.	L	1-5		7	14	Hermanson	Mays		57-34	1st	+5.0
7-16	At St.L.	L	3-4		8	10	Kline	Miller	Christiansen	57-35	1st	+5.0
7-17	At St.L.	L	2-4		9	9	Kile	Lohse	Christiansen	57-36	1st	+4.0
7-18	Oak.	L	2-7		6	14	Hudson	Radke		57-37	1st	+3.0
7-19	Oak.	W	12-10		20	11	Milton	Zito	Hawkins	58-37	1st	+3.0
7-20	Sea.	L	0-4		5	10	Sele	Mays		58-38	1st	+3.0
7-21	Sea.	L	3-6		8	6	Halama	Johnson	Sasaki	58-39	1st	+2.0
7-22	Sea.	L	3-6		6	13	Abbott	Lohse		58-40	1st	+1.0
7-23	Sea.	L	2-3		9	9	Moyer	Radke	Sasaki	58-41	2nd	...
7-24	At Oak.	L	6-7		11	11	Isringhausen	Miller		58-42	2nd	...
7-25	At Oak.	W	3-1		11	3	Mays	Lidle	Hawkins	59-42	2nd	...
7-26	At Oak.	W	7-4		13	6	Johnson	Heredia		60-42	1st	+1.0
7-27	At Sea.	L	4-11		7	11	Abbott	Lohse		60-43	2nd	...
7-28	At Sea.	L	1-5		6	11	Moyer	Radke		60-44	2nd	0.5
7-29	At Sea.	L	2-10		5	14	Garcia	Milton		60-45	2nd	0.5
7-31	At Tor.	L	1-3		10	8	Loaiza	Mays	Koch	60-46	2nd	0.5
8-1	At Tor.	L	1-3		7	5	Halladay	Lohse	Koch	60-47	2nd	1.5
8-2	At Tor.	W	9-4		12	16	Reed	Carpenter		61-47	2nd	0.5
8-3	K.C.	W	8-7	(10)	13	14	Jones	Hernandez		62-47	1st	+0.5
8-4	K.C.	W	6-2		9	9	Milton	Wilson		63-47	1st	+1.5
8-5	K.C.	L	5-10		11	20	Byrd	Mays		63-48	1st	+0.5
8-7	Cle.	L	2-7		7	14	Sabathia	Reed		63-49	T1st	...
8-8	Cle.	L	2-8	(10)	11	14	Baez	Wells		63-50	2nd	1.0
8-9	Cle.	W	6-4		5	8	Milton	Finley	Hawkins	64-50	T1st	...
8-10	At T.B.	L	2-4		8	9	Wilson	Mays		64-51	T1st	...
8-11	At T.B.	L	3-4		8	5	Rupe	Thomas	Yan	64-52	T1st	...
8-12	At T.B.	L	3-4	(12)	8	11	Zambrano	Hawkins		64-53	2nd	1.0
8-13	At T.B.	L	1-5		3	13	Bierbrodt	Lohse		64-54	2nd	1.5
8-14	At Cle.	L	7-8	(11)	10	16	Baez	Wells		64-55	2nd	2.5
8-15	At Cle.	L	2-8		11	14	Finley	Mays		64-56	2nd	3.5
8-16	At Cle.	L	1-6		7	7	Woodard	Johnson		64-57	2nd	4.5
8-17	T.B.	L	4-9		8	11	Sturtze	Reed		64-58	2nd	4.5
8-18	T.B.	W	6-4		11	6	Lohse	Bierbrodt	Jones	65-58	2nd	4.5
8-19	T.B.	L	1-5		4	9	Kennedy	Milton		65-59	2nd	4.5
8-20	Tor.	L	2-3		6	5	Escobar	Mays	Koch	65-60	2nd	4.5
8-21	Tor.	L	5-7		11	12	Lyon	Cressend	Koch	65-61	2nd	5.5
8-22	Tor.	W	6-3		11	9	Reed	Loaiza		66-61	2nd	5.5
8-23	Tor.	L	2-6		5	13	Halladay	Lohse		66-62	2nd	6.5
8-24	At K.C.	W	9-3		10	12	Milton	Durbin	Guardado	67-62	2nd	5.5
8-25	At K.C.	W	7-1		14	5	Mays	Wilson		68-62	2nd	4.5
8-26	At K.C.	W	7-2		12	3	Radke	Stein		69-62	2nd	4.5
8-28	Tex.	L	1-10		4	13	Oliver	Reed		69-63	2nd	5.5
8-29	Tex.	W	10-8		10	11	Milton	Bell	Hawkins	70-63	2nd	5.5
8-30	Tex.	L	1-5		5	9	Myette	Mays		70-64	2nd	6.5
8-31	Ana.	W	4-1		8	8	Radke	Valdes	Jones	71-64	2nd	5.5
9-1	Ana.	L	9-11		14	18	Levine	Hawkins	Percival	71-65	2nd	6.5
9-2	Ana.	W	5-4		6	7	Guardado	Levine		72-65	2nd	5.5
9-4	At Tex.	L	5-6		9	9	Venafro	Hawkins		72-66	2nd	7.0
9-5	At Tex.	W	12-2		20	7	Mays	Myette		73-66	2nd	6.0
9-6	At Tex.	L	3-4		8	11	Helling	Radke	Zimmerman	73-67	2nd	7.0
9-7	At Ana.	L	3-7		5	10	Ortiz	Lohse		73-68	T2nd	7.0
9-8	At Ana.	W	6-4		10	13	Reed	Rapp	Guardado	74-68	2nd	7.0
9-9	At Ana.	W	3-0		7	4	Milton	Washburn	Wells	75-68	2nd	7.0
9-10	At Det.	W	3-2		8	4	Mays	Pineda	Guardado	76-68	2nd	6.0
9-18	Det.	W	8-3		18	3	Radke	Weaver		77-68	2nd	6.0
9-19	Det.	L	2-6		6	12	Sparks	Milton		77-69	2nd	7.0
9-20	Det.	W	3-0		6	6	Mays	Lima		78-69	2nd	6.0
9-21	Cle.	W	6-2		7	8	Reed	Sabathia	Guardado	79-69	2nd	5.0
9-22	Cle.	L	2-4		8	10	Rincon	Radke	Wickman	79-70	2nd	6.0
9-23	Cle.	L	2-4		7	5	Finley	Milton	Wickman	79-71	2nd	7.0
9-25	At Chi.	W	4-2		7	4	Mays	Glover	Guardado	80-71	2nd	6.5
9-26	At Chi.	L	3-6		10	8	K. Wells	Reed	Foulke	80-72	2nd	7.0

Date	Opp.	Res.	Score	(inn.*)	Hits	Opp. hits	Winning pitcher	Losing pitcher	Save	Record	Pos.	GB
9-27	At Chi.	L	3-9		8	11	Wright	Radke	Lowe	80-73	T2nd	7.5
9-28	At Cle.	W	1-0		6	3	Milton	Baez	Guardado	81-73	2nd	6.5
9-29	At Cle.	L	8-9		11	9	Westbrook	Guardado		81-74	T2nd	7.5
9-30	At Cle.	L	1-9		7	14	Colon	Reed		81-75	3rd	8.5
10-2	At Det.	W	5-0		12	3	Radke	Murray		82-75	2nd	7.5
10-3	At Det.	L	5-9		11	13	Cornejo	Fiore		82-76	2nd	8.5
10-4	At Det.	W	5-4		11	8	Carrasco	Anderson	Guardado	83-76	2nd	7.5
10-5	Chi.	L	4-7		12	11	Buehrle	Reed	Foulke	83-77	T2nd	7.0
10-6	Chi.	W	6-5		11	10	Cressend	Glover	Guardado	84-77	2nd	6.0
10-7	Chi.	W	8-5		11	7	Radke	K. Wells	Guardado	85-77	2nd	6.0

Monthly records: April (18-6), May (16-11), June (14-14), July (12-15), August (11-18), September (10-11), October (4-2).
*Innings, if other than nine. †First game of a doubleheader. ‡Second game of a doubleheader.

HIGHLIGHTS

High point: The All-Star break. The Twins appeared on course for a magical season when they reached the All-Star break with a 55-32 record and a five-game lead over Cleveland in the A.L. Central.

Low point: The Twins headed to Tampa Bay for a four-game series starting August 10 believing that seven games against the Devil Rays in a 10-game span would provide a cure for their recent woes. Instead, the Twins left Tampa Bay on August 13 having been swept by the Devil Rays. A couple days later Tampa Bay came to the Metrodome and took two of three from the Twins.

Turning point: No one knew just how valuable Cristian Guzman was until July 12, when he left the game with a sore shoulder. Guzman would miss the next 33 games with inflammation around his rotator cuff. The Twins went 8-25 without him, scoring three or fewer runs in 22 of the 33 games.

Most valuable player: Doug Mientkiewicz carried the team with a mixture of timely hits, power and sensational defense at first base. He led the team in batting average and doubles.

Most valuable pitcher: Joe Mays led the Twins in victories and ERA. The key was maturity. Instead of imploding in tight situations as he once did, Mays pitched with confidence and was content to throw strikes and let an excellent defense do the work.

Most improved player: Corey Koskie took the biggest step, improving to 26 homers and 103 RBIs in 2001. Koskie also scored 100 runs.

Most pleasant surprise: Given the chance to start in 2001, A.J. Pierzynski proved that he was a No. 1 catcher, batting .289 and providing solid defense.

Key injuries: The Twins were hit hard by injuries, the most costly being Guzman's. ... The Twins also lost David Ortiz for 10 weeks after he broke his right wrist sliding into home plate. ... The club also had several other key players spend time on

the disabled list, including pitchers Brad Radke and Eddie Guardado and center fielder Torii Hunter.

Notable: After going 55-32 (.632) before the All-Star break, the Twins went 30-45 (.400). The winning percentage differential—.232—afforded the Twins the ignominy of the second greatest collapse in major league history. ... Koskie became the first third baseman in A.L. history to have at least 25 homers, 25 stolen bases and 100 RBI. ... The club had three 15-game winners for the first time since 1991.

—DENNIS BRACKIN

RECORDS

2001 regular-season record: 85-77 (2nd in A.L. Central); 47-34 at home; 38-43 on road; 13-19 vs. A.L. East; 47-29 vs. A.L. Central; 16-20 vs. A.L. West; 9-9 vs. N.L.; 18-21 vs. lefthanded starters; 67-56 vs. righthanded starters; 37-37 on grass; 48-40 on turf; 26-27 in daytime; 59-50 at night; 25-19 in one-run games; 8-7 in extra-inning games; 0-0-1 in doubleheaders.
Team record past five years: 355-453 (.439, ranks 12th in league in that span).

TEAM LEADERS

Batting average: Doug Mientkiewicz (.306).
At-bats: Torii Hunter (564).
Runs: Corey Koskie (100).
Hits: Doug Mientkiewicz (166).
Total Bases: Corey Koskie (274).
Doubles: Doug Mientkiewicz (39).
Triples: Cristian Guzman (14).
Home runs: Torii Hunter (27).
Runs batted in: Corey Koskie (103).
Stolen bases: Luis Rivas (31).
Slugging percentage: Corey Koskie (.488).
On-base percentage: Doug Mientkiewicz (.387).
Wins: Joe Mays (17).
Earned-run average: Joe Mays (3.16).
Complete games: Brad Radke (6).

Shutouts: Joe Mays, Brad Radke (2).
Saves: LaTroy Hawkins (28).
Innings pitched: Joe Mays (233.2).
Strikeouts: Eric Milton (157).

GAMES BY POSITION

Catcher: A.J. Pierzynski 110, Tom Prince 64, Matt LeCroy 3.
First base: Doug Mientkiewicz 148, Denny Hocking 11, David Ortiz 8, Mike Cuddyer 5, Casey Blake 3, Matt LeCroy 2.
Second base: Luis Rivas 150, Denny Hocking 17, Jason Maxwell 9.
Third base: Corey Koskie 150, Jason Maxwell 11, Denny Hocking 6, Casey Blake 5, Mike Cuddyer 2.
Shortstop: Cristian Guzman 118, Denny Hocking 47, Jason Maxwell 12.
Outfield: Torii Hunter 147, Jacque Jones 140, Matt Lawton 94, Brian Buchanan 46, Bobby Kielty 34, Chad Allen 27, Dustan Mohr 19, Denny Hocking 16, Quinton McCracken 10, John Barnes 9.
Designated hitter: David Ortiz 80, Chad Allen 23, Brian Buchanan 19, Denny Hocking 10, Quinton McCracken 9, Matt LeCroy 9, Matt Lawton 7, Jason Maxwell 7, Jacque Jones 5, Casey Blake 4, Corey Koskie 2, Doug Mientkiewicz 2, A.J. Pierzynski 1, Bobby Kielty 1, Dustan Mohr 1, Mike Cuddyer 1.

TOP DRAFT CHOICES

1. **Joe Mauer,** C, Cretin-Derham Hall, St. Paul, Minn.
2. **Scott Tyler,** RHP, Downingtown (Pa.) H.S.
3. **Jose Morales,** SS, Academie la Providencia H.S., Rio Piedras, P.R.
4. **Angel Garcia,** RHP, Nicolas Sevilla H.S., Dorado, P.R.
5. **Jeremy Brown,** RHP, U. of Georgia.
6. **Vince Serafini,** LHP, U. of Evansville.
7. **Matt Vorwald,** RHP, U. of Illinois.
8. **Jared Hemus,** LHP, Grossmont (Calif.) J.C.
9. **Dusty Gomon,** 1B, Terry Parker H.S., Jacksonville, Fla.
10. **Garrett Guzman,** OF, Green Valley H.S., Henderson, Nev.

NEW YORK YANKEES
AMERICAN LEAGUE EAST DIVISION

Yankees schedule
Home games shaded
D—Day game (games starting before 5 p.m.)
*All-Star Game at Milwaukee
Subject to changes

April

SUN	MON	TUE	WED	THU	FRI	SAT
	1 D BAL	2	3 BAL	4 BAL	5 D TB	6 D TB
7 TB	8 TOR	9 TOR	10 TOR	11 D TOR	12 BOS	13 D BOS
14 BOS	15 D BOS	16 BAL	17 BAL	18 BAL	19 TOR	20 D TOR
21 TOR	22	23 OAK	24 OAK	25 D OAK	26 SEA	27 SEA
28 D SEA	29	30 OAK				

May

SUN	MON	TUE	WED	THU	FRI	SAT
		1 OAK	2 OAK	3 SEA	4 D SEA	
5 D SEA	6	7 TB	8 TB	9 TB	10 MIN	11 MIN
12 D MIN	13	14 TB	15 TB	16 TB	17 MIN	18 D MIN
19 D MIN	20 TOR	21 TOR	22 D TOR	23 BOS	24 BOS	25 D BOS
26 BOS	27 D CWS	28 CWS	29 CWS	30	31 BOS	

June

SUN	MON	TUE	WED	THU	FRI	SAT
						1 D BOS
2 BOS	3 BAL	4 BAL	5 BAL	6 BAL	7 SF	8 SF
9 SF	10 ARI	11 ARI	12 D ARI	13	14 NYM	15 NYM
16 NYM	17 COL	18 COL	19 COL	20 D SD	21 SD	22 SD
23 D SD	24 BAL	25 BAL	26 BAL	27 NYM	28 NYM	29 D NYM
30 D NYM						

July

SUN	MON	TUE	WED	THU	FRI	SAT
	1	2 CLE	3 CLE	4 D CLE	5 D TOR	6 D TOR
7 TOR	8	9 *	10	11 CLE	12 CLE	13 CLE
14 CLE	15 TOR	16 DET	17 DET	18 D DET	19 BOS	20 D BOS
21 BOS	22	23 CLE	24 CLE	25	26 TB	27 TB
28 TB	29 TEX	30 TEX	31 TEX			

August

SUN	MON	TUE	WED	THU	FRI	SAT
				1 ANA	2 ANA	3 ANA
4 ANA	5	6 KC	7 KC	8 D KC	9 OAK	10 D OAK
11 OAK	12	13 KC	14 KC	15 KC	16 SEA	17 SEA
18 D SEA	19	20 ANA	21 D ANA	22 D ANA	23 TEX	24 D TEX
25 D TEX	26 D TEX	27 BOS	28 BOS	29 TOR	30 TOR	31 D TOR

September

SUN	MON	TUE	WED	THU	FRI	SAT
1 D TOR	2 D BOS	3 BOS	4 BOS	5 DET	6 DET	7 DET
8 DET	9	10 BAL	11 BAL	12 BAL	13 CWS	14 D CWS
15 CWS	16	17 TB	18 TB	19 TB	20 DET	21 D DET
22 D DET	23 TB	24 TB	25 TB	26 BAL	27 BAL	28 BAL
29 D BAL	30					

2002 SEASON
CLUB DIRECTORY

Principal owner
George M. Steinbrenner III
General partners
Harold Z. Steinbrenner, Henry G. Steinbrenner, Stephen W. Swindal
President
Randy Levine
Chief operating officer
Lonn Trost
Vice president, chief financial officer
Martin Greenspun
Vice president, ticket operations
Frank Swaine
Vice president
Richard Smith
Vice president, marketing
Deborah A. Tymon
Vice president, administration
Sonny Hight
Special advisors
Yogi Berra, Reggie Jackson, Clyde King, Don Mattingly, Al Rosen, Dick Williams
Senior vice president, general manager
Brian Cashman
Senior vice president, baseball operations
Mark Newman
Assistant general manager
Jean Afterman
Vice president, major league scouting
Gene Michael
V.p., international and professional scouting
Gordon Blakeley
Vice president, scouting
Lin Garrett
Vice president, player personnel
Billy Connors
Vice president, corporate and community relations
Brian Smith
Director of player development
Rob Thomson
Director of player personnel
Damon Oppenheimer
Director of baseball operations
Eric Wicks
Assistant directors of baseball operations
John Coppolella, Brian Werner
Traveling secretary
David Szen
Equipment manager
Rob Cucuzza
Visiting clubhouse manager
Lou Cucuzza Jr.
Assistant, video operations
Leo Astacio
Controller
Robert Brown

Senior director of ticket operations
Irfan Kirimca
Director of stadium operations
Kirk Randazzo
Assistant director of stadium operations
Doug Behar
Stadium superintendent
Pete Pullara
Manager, information services
Kris Zocco
Head groundskeeper
Dan Cunningham
Director of media relations & publicity
Rick Cerrone
Assistant director of media relations & publicity
Jason Zillo
Senior advisor
Arthur Richman
Assistants, media relations
Michael Hopper, Joa Martin
Director of concessions & hospitality
Joel White
Director of publications and multimedia
Mark Mandrake
Director of sponsorship services
Michael Tusiani
Scoreboard & broadcasting manager
Mike Bonner
Team physician
Dr. Stuart Hershon
Head trainer
Gene Monahan
Assistant trainer
Steve Donohue
Strength & conditioning coach
Jeff Mangold
Regional cross-checkers
Joe Arnold, Tim Kelly, Greg Orr
Pro scouts
Ron Brand, Joe Caro, Bill Emslie, Ron Hansen, Mick Kelleher, Bob Miske
Scouts
Mike Baker, Brian Barber, Mark Batchko, Steve Boros, Lew Graham, Dick Groch, David Jom, Steve Lemke, Steve McIntosh, Jeff Patterson, Scott Pleis, Cesar Presbott, Gus Quattlebaum, Steve Swail, Leon Wurth
Coordinator of Pacific rim scouting
John Cox
Coordinator of Latin American scouting
Carlos Rios
Foreign scouts
Manny Crespo, Manuel Duran, Ricardo Finol, Karl Heron, Ricardo Heron, Rudy Jabalera, Victor Mata, Jim Patterson, Jose Quintero, Hector Rincones, Edgar Rodriguez, Arquimedes Rojas, Cesar Suarez, Freddy Tiburcio

MINOR LEAGUE AFFILIATES

Class	Team	League	Manager
AAA	Columbus	International	Brian Butterfield
AA	Norwich	Eastern	Stump Merrill
A	Greensboro	South Atlantic	Bill Masse
A	Staten Island	New York-Pennsylvania	Derek Shelton
A	Tampa	Florida State	Mitch Seoane
Rookie	Tampa	Gulf Coast	Manny Crespo

BROADCAST INFORMATION

Radio: WCBS-AM (880).
TV: WCBS-TV (Channel 2).
Cable TV: Yankee Entertainment and Sports Network.

SPRING TRAINING

Ballpark (city): Legends Field (Tampa, Fla.).
Ticket information: 813-879-2244, 813-287-8844.

Follow the Yankees all season at: www.sportingnews.com/baseball/teams/yankees/

Manager—Joe Torre (6).
Coaches—Rick Down, Lee Mazzilli (54), Rich Monteleone, Willie Randolph (30), Mel Stottlemyre (34), Don Zimmer (53).

No.	PITCHERS	B/T	Ht./Wt.	Born	2001 clubs
	Choate, Randy	L/L	6-3/180	9-5-75	New York A.L., Columbus
	Claussen, Brandon	L/L	6-2/175	5-1-79	Tampa, Norwich
22	Clemens, Roger	R/R	6-4/238	8-4-62	New York A.L.
	Graman, Alex	L/L	6-4/200	11-17-77	Norwich
	Hernandez, Adrian	R/R	6-1/185	3-25-75	Columbus, New York A.L.
26	Hernandez, Orlando	R/R	6-2/220	10-11-65	New York A.L., Tampa, Staten Island
41	Hitchcock, Sterling	L/L	6-0/205	4-29-71	Lake Elsinore, Portland, San Diego, New York A.L.
	Jodie, Brett	R/R	6-4/210	3-25-77	Norwich, Columbus, New York A.L., Portland, San Diego
20	Karsay, Steve	R/R	6-3/215	3-24-72	Cleveland, Atlanta
	Keisler, Randy	L/L	6-3/190	2-24-76	Columbus, New York A.L.
	Knight, Brandon	L/R	6-0/170	10-1-75	Columbus, New York A.L.
28	Lilly, Ted	L/L	6-0/185	1-4-76	Columbus, New York A.L.
55	Mendoza, Ramiro	R/R	6-2/195	6-15-72	New York A.L.
35	Mussina, Mike	R/R	6-2/185	12-8-68	New York A.L.
	Parker, Christian	R/R	6-1/200	7-3-75	New York A.L.
46	Pettitte, Andy	L/L	6-5/225	6-15-72	New York A.L.
42	Rivera, Mariano	R/R	6-2/185	11-29-69	New York A.L.
	Rogers, Brian	R/R	6-6/200	2-13-77	Norwich
29	Stanton, Mike	L/L	6-1/215	6-2-67	New York A.L.
27	Watson, Allen	L/L	6-1/224	11-18-70	DID NOT PLAY
	Wells, David	L/L	6-4/235	5-20-63	Chicago A.L.

No.	CATCHERS	B/T	Ht./Wt.	Born	2001 clubs
29	Estalella, Bobby	R/R	6-1/205	8-23-74	San Francisco, Fresno, Columbus, New York A.L.
20	Posada, Jorge	B/R	6-2/200	8-17-71	New York A.L.

No.	INFIELDERS	B/T	Ht./Wt.	Born	2001 clubs
	Almonte, Erick	R/R	6-2/180	2-1-78	Columbus, Norwich, New York A.L.
16	Giambi, Jason	L/R	6-3/235	1-8-71	Oakland
2	Jeter, Derek	R/R	6-3/195	6-26-74	New York A.L.
70	Johnson, Nick	L/L	6-3/224	9-19-78	Columbus, New York A.L.
	Seabol, Scott	R/R	6-4/200	5-17-75	New York A.L., Columbus, Norwich
58	Soriano, Alfonso	R/R	6-1/160	1-7-78	New York A.L.
4	Ventura, Robin	L/R	6-1/198	7-14-67	New York N.L.
25	Wilson, Enrique	B/R	5-11/195	7-27-75	Pittsburgh, New York A.L.

No.	OUTFIELDERS	B/T	Ht./Wt.	Born	2001 clubs
61	Frank, Mike	L/L	6-2/195	1-14-75	Columbus
27	Greene, Todd	R/R	5-10/208	5-8-71	Columbus, New York A.L.
	Rivera, Juan	R/R	6-2/170	7-3-78	Norwich, Columbus, New York A.L.
47	Spencer, Shane	R/R	5-11/225	2-20-72	Columbus, New York A.L.
	Thames, Marcus	R/R	6-2/205	3-6-77	Norwich
28	Vander Wal, John	L/L	6-1/197	4-29-66	Pittsburgh, San Francisco
22	White, Rondell	R/R	6-1/210	2-23-72	Chicago N.L., West Tenn
51	Williams, Bernie	B/R	6-2/205	9-13-68	New York A.L.
4	Williams, Gerald	R/R	6-2/187	8-10-66	Tampa Bay, New York A.L.

Ballpark (capacity, surface)
Yankee Stadium (57,513, grass)
Address
Yankee Stadium
E. 161 St. and River Ave.
Bronx, NY 10451
Official website
www.yankees.com
Business phone
718-293-4300
Ticket information
212-307-1212, 718-293-6013
Ticket prices
$65 (Championship Seat, loge)
$55 (Championship Seat, main box)
$47 (main box MVP)
$42 (field box & loge box MVP)
$37 (main reserved MVP)
$37 (main & loge box)
$33 (tier box), $33 (main reserved)
$17 (tier reserved), $15 (tier reserved value)
$8 (bleachers)
Field dimensions (from home plate)
To left field at foul line, 318 feet
To center field, 408 feet
To right field at foul line, 314 feet
First game played
April 18, 1923 (Yankees 4, Red Sox 1)

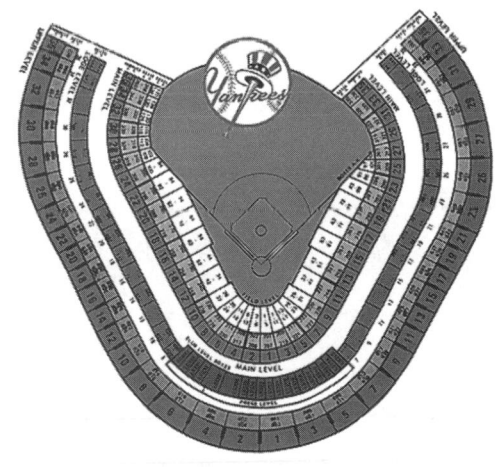

2002 SEASON · New York Yankees

2002 SEASON *New York Yankees*

Date	Opp.	Res.	Score	(inn.*)	Hits	Opp. hits	Winning pitcher	Losing pitcher	Save	Record	Pos.	GB
4-2	K.C.	W	7-3		13	7	Clemens	Suppan		1-0	T1st	...
4-4	K.C.	W	8-2		7	8	Pettitte	Stein		2-0	1st	+0.5
4-5	K.C.	W	1-0		4	5	Mussina	Reichert	Rivera	3-0	1st	+0.5
4-6	Tor.	L	4-13		10	16	Loaiza	Parker		3-1	2nd	0.5
4-7	Tor.	L	2-3		7	7	Michalak	O. Hernandez	Koch	3-2	T2nd	1.5
4-8	Tor.	W	16-5		20	9	Clemens	Parris		4-2	T2nd	0.5
4-9	At K.C.	W	13-4		19	12	Pettitte	Stein		5-2	2nd	0.5
4-10	At K.C.	W	9-5		15	8	Mendoza	Hernandez		6-2	2nd	0.5
4-11	At K.C.	W	8-5		12	10	Williams	Meadows	Rivera	7-2	1st	+0.5
4-13	At Bos.	L	2-3	(10)	8	8	Lowe	Rivera		7-3	T2nd	0.5
4-14	At Bos.	W	3-2		8	6	Stanton	Schourek	Rivera	8-3	2nd	0.5
4-15	At Bos.	L	4-5		7	15	Garces	Pettitte	Arrojo	8-4	T2nd	0.5
4-16	At Bos.	L	1-4		5	11	Castillo	Mussina	Beck	8-5	3rd	1.0
4-17	At Tor.	L	5-6		8	10	Loaiza	Keisler	Koch	8-6	3rd	2.0
4-18	At Tor.	L	2-7		6	13	Michalak	O. Hernandez		8-7	3rd	3.0
4-19	At Tor.	W	6-5	(17)	21	14	Choate	File	Mendoza	9-7	3rd	3.0
4-20	Bos.	W	6-1		9	6	Pettitte	Nomo		10-7	3rd	2.0
4-21	Bos.	L	3-8		9	9	Castillo	Mussina		10-8	3rd	3.0
4-22	Bos.	W	4-3	(10)	12	11	Rivera	Lowe		11-8	3rd	2.0
4-24	Sea.	L	5-7		8	9	Garcia	Stanton	Sasaki	11-9	3rd	3.0
4-25	Sea.	L	5-7		12	10	Charlton	Pettitte	Sasaki	11-10	3rd	3.0
4-26	Sea.	L	3-7		7	14	Moyer	Mussina	Rhodes	11-11	3rd	4.0
4-27	Oak.	W	3-2		8	3	Choate	Mulder	Rivera	12-11	3rd	4.0
4-28	Oak.	W	7-6		14	4	Lilly	Hudson	Rivera	13-11	3rd	3.0
4-29	Oak.	W	3-1		5	7	Clemens	Zito	Rivera	14-11	3rd	2.5
4-30	At Min.	L	1-2		6	3	Radke	Pettitte		14-12	3rd	2.5
5-1	At Min.	W	4-0		14	3	Mussina	Milton		15-12	3rd	2.5
5-2	At Min.	L	2-4		6	9	Mays	O. Hernandez	Hawkins	15-13	3rd	2.5
5-3	At Bal.	W	7-5		8	7	Mendoza	Paronto	Rivera	16-13	3rd	1.5
5-4	At Bal.	W	6-5		12	10	Stanton	Paronto	Rivera	17-13	3rd	1.5
5-5	At Bal.	W	5-2		8	6	Pettitte	Roberts	Boehringer	18-13	3rd	0.5
5-6	At Bal.	W	2-1		7	7	Mussina	Trombley	Rivera	19-13	3rd	0.5
5-8	Min.	L	0-2		4	8	Milton	O. Hernandez		19-14	3rd	1.5
5-9	Min.	W	2-0		7	4	Clemens	Mays	Rivera	20-14	2nd	0.5
5-10	Min.	L	4-5	(10)	5	11	Guardado	Rivera	Hawkins	20-15	2nd	0.5
5-11	Bal.	W	14-5		15	11	Mussina	Roberts	Mendoza	21-15	1st	+0.5
5-12	Bal.	W	8-5		11	11	Stanton	Towers	Rivera	22-15	1st	+0.5
5-13	Bal.	L	5-10	(11)	11	14	Ryan	Rivera		22-16	2nd	0.5
5-15	At Oak.	L	2-3	(12)	15	12	Guthrie	Mendoza		22-17	2nd	1.5
5-16	At Oak.	L	3-4	(10)	7	9	Guthrie	Boehringer		22-18	2nd	1.5
5-17	At Oak.	L	3-8		6	13	Bradford	Mussina		22-19	2nd	1.5
5-18	At Sea.	W	14-10		19	13	Mendoza	Halama		23-19	2nd	1.5
5-19	At Sea.	W	2-1	(10)	4	5	Stanton	Sasaki	Rivera	24-19	2nd	0.5
5-20	At Sea.	L	2-6		9	6	Sele	Clemens		24-20	2nd	1.5
5-23	Bos.	W	7-3		11	6	Pettitte	Cone		25-20	2nd	0.5
5-24	Bos.	W	2-1		6	6	Mussina	Martinez	Rivera	26-20	1st	+0.5
5-25	At Cle.	L	4-6		9	11	Rodriguez	O. Hernandez	Wickman	26-21	2nd	0.5
5-26	At Cle.	W	12-5		15	10	Clemens	Sabathia		27-21	1st	+0.5
5-27	At Cle.	W	6-2		7	9	Lilly	Colon	Rivera	28-21	1st	+0.5
5-28	At Bos.	W	4-3		11	9	Pettitte	Schourek	Rivera	29-21	1st	+1.5
5-30	At Bos.	L	0-3		5	4	Martinez	Mussina	Lowe	29-22	1st	+0.5
6-1	Cle.	L	4-7	(6)	5	10	Sabathia	Lilly	Rincon	29-23	2nd	1.0
6-2	Cle.	W	9-4		13	12	Clemens	Colon	Rivera	30-23	2nd	1.0
6-3	Cle.	L	3-4		6	10	Nagy	Pettitte	Wickman	30-24	2nd	2.0
6-4	Bos.	W	7-6		10	12	Rivera	Beck		31-24	2nd	1.0
6-5	Bal.	L	3-10		5	17	Johnson	Mussina		31-25	2nd	2.0
6-6	Bal.	W	7-4		10	9	Stanton	Groom	Rivera	32-25	2nd	1.0
6-7	Bal.	W	4-0		12	3	Clemens	Ponson		33-25	2nd	1.0
6-8	Atl.	W	7-4		8	8	Pettitte	Glavine	Rivera	34-25	2nd	1.0
6-9	Atl.	L	6-10		8	16	Cabrera	Choate	Rocker	34-26	2nd	1.0
6-10	Atl.	L	1-4		7	7	Maddux	Mussina	Rocker	34-27	2nd	2.0
6-12	Mon.	L	1-2	(12)	6	6	Strickland	Mendoza		34-28	2nd	3.0
6-13	Mon.	W	9-3		11	7	Clemens	Irabu		35-28	2nd	2.0
6-14	Mon.	W	9-6		12	7	Keisler	Yoshii	Rivera	36-28	2nd	2.0
6-15	At N.Y.	W	5-4		9	7	Mendoza	Leiter	Rivera	37-28	2nd	2.0
6-16	At N.Y.	W	2-1		6	7	Mussina	Appier	Rivera	38-28	2nd	1.0
6-17	At N.Y.	L	7-8		9	6	Wendell	Almanzar	Benitez	38-29	2nd	2.0
6-18	At Det.	W	10-1		11	8	Clemens	Weaver		39-29	2nd	1.5
6-19	At Det.	L	1-7		3	14	Sparks	Keisler		39-30	2nd	2.5
6-20	At Det.	L	2-5		9	6	Holt	A. Hernandez	Anderson	39-31	2nd	3.5
6-22	At T.B.	W	6-3		8	10	Mussina	Lopez	Rivera	40-31	2nd	3.0
6-23	At T.B.	W	2-1		6	6	Clemens	Wallace	Rivera	41-31	2nd	2.0
6-24	At T.B.	L	4-5		9	8	Phelps	Stanton		41-32	2nd	2.0
6-25	Cle.	W	8-7		13	10	Witasick	Rincon	Rivera	42-32	2nd	2.0

Date	Opp.	Res.	Score	(inn.*)	Hits	Opp. hits	Winning pitcher	Losing pitcher	Save	Record	Pos.	GB
6-26	Cle.	L	3-5		10	7	Nagy	A. Hernandez	Rocker	42-33	2nd	3.0
6-27	Cle.	W	15-5		17	9	Mussina	Sabathia		43-33	2nd	2.0
6-29	T.B.	W	7-5		11	10	Clemens	Rekar	Rivera	44-33	2nd	0.5
6-30	T.B.	W	5-4		5	11	Stanton	Creek	Rivera	45-33	2nd	0.5
7-1	T.B.	W	6-1		10	6	Pettitte	Sturtze		46-33	2nd	0.5
7-2	T.B.	W	7-1		8	9	Mussina	Lopez		47-33	2nd	0.5
7-3	At Bal.	W	10-6		14	7	Mendoza	Mercedes		48-33	1st	+0.5
7-4	At Bal.	W	4-3		9	6	Clemens	Maduro	Rivera	49-33	1st	+0.5
7-5	At Bal.	W	6-3		12	8	Lilly	Towers	Rivera	50-33	1st	+0.5
7-6	N.Y.	W	8-3		10	8	Pettitte	Leiter	Mendoza	51-33	1st	+1.5
7-7	N.Y.	L	0-3	(10)	4	10	Franco	Rivera	Benitez	51-34	1st	+0.5
7-8	N.Y.	W	4-1		6	7	Mendoza	Wendell	Rivera	52-34	1st	+1.5
7-12	At Fla.	L	3-9		4	13	Burnett	Mussina		52-35	1st	+1.5
7-13	At Fla.	L	1-11		11	15	Smith	Lilly		52-36	1st	+0.5
7-14	At Fla.	W	5-4	(10)	15	11	Rivera	Alfonseca	Mendoza	53-36	1st	+1.5
7-15	At Phi.	L	3-9		7	12	Person	Pettitte		53-37	1st	+0.5
7-16	At Phi.	W	6-3	(13)	7	8	Stanton	Telemaco	Rivera	54-37	1st	+0.5
7-17	At Phi.	W	4-1	(12)	11	13	Choate	Gomes	Rivera	55-37	1st	+1.5
7-18§	At Det.	W	8-5		13	11	Clemens	Sparks	Rivera	56-37		
7-18∞	At Det.	L	4-12		14	16	Santos	Lilly		56-38	1st	+1.0
7-19	At Det.	L	2-11		7	15	Lima	Pettitte		56-39	1st	+1.0
7-20	Tor.	L	4-10		10	13	Loaiza	Jodie		56-40	T1st	...
7-21	Tor.	L	3-5		8	8	Quantrill	Rivera	Koch	56-41	T1st	...
7-22	Tor.	W	7-3		11	6	Mussina	Carpenter		57-41	1st	+1.0
7-23	Tor.	W	7-2		8	9	Clemens	Parris		58-41	1st	+1.5
7-24	Det.	W	6-5		13	8	Pettitte	Sparks	Rivera	59-41	1st	+1.5
7-25	Det.	W	4-2		7	6	Witasick	Lima	Rivera	60-41	1st	+2.5
7-26	Det.	W	14-8		18	11	Mendoza	Holt		61 41	1st	+2.5
7-27	At Tor.	W	9-1		13	5	Mussina	Carpenter		62-41	1st	+2.5
7-28	At Tor.	W	12-1		15	2	Clemens	Escobar		63-41	1st	+3.5
7-29	At Tor.	W	9-3		15	8	Pettitte	Hamilton		64-41	1st	+3.5
7-31	Tex.	L	2-6		8	10	Oliver	Lilly	Zimmerman	64-42	1st	+3.5
8-1	Tex.	W	9-7		13	10	Hitchcock	Bell	Rivera	65-42	1st	+4.5
8-2	Tex.	L	2-12		4	18	Myette	Mussina		65-43	1st	+4.5
8-3	Ana.	W	4-2		9	7	Pettitte	Washburn	Rivera	66-43	1st	+5.0
8 4	Ana.	W	5-4		6	8	Rivera	Levine		67-43	1st	+4.5
8-5	Ana.	L	3-4		11	9	Ortiz	Mendoza	Percival	67 44	1st	+3.5
8-6	Ana.	L	1-3		5	9	Pote	Hitchcock	Percival	67-45	1st	+2.5
8-7	At T.B.	L	2-3		7	9	Sturtze	Mussina	Yan	67-46	1st	+2.5
8-8	At T.B.	W	16-1		17	8	Pettitte	Bierbrodt		68-46	1st	+3.5
8-9	At T.B.	W	4-3		8	7	Mendoza	Yan	Rivera	69-46	1st	+4.5
8-10	At Oak.	L	1-8		4	6	Lidle	Lilly		69-47	1st	+4.0
8-11	At Oak.	L	6-8		13	12	Magnante	Hitchcock	Isringhausen	69-48	1st	+4.0
8-12	At Oak.	L	2-4		7	3	Mulder	Stanton		69-49	1st	+3.0
8-14	T.B.	W	5-3		9	7	Pettitte	Kennedy	Rivera	70-49	1st	+4.0
8-15	T.B.	W	10-3		10	5	Clemens	Wilson		71-49	1st	+5.0
8-16	T.B.	W	12-5		11	11	Hitchcock	Rupe		72-49	1st	+5.0
8-17	Sea.	W	4-0		6	6	Mussina	Abbott	Mendoza	73-49	1st	+6.0
8-18	Sea.	L	6-7		14	10	Rhodes	Lilly	Sasaki	73-50	1st	+5.0
8-19	Sea.	L	2-10		6	15	Moyer	Pettitte		73-51	1st	+5.0
8-20	At Tex.	W	9-5		12	12	Stanton	Moreno		74-51	1st	+5.0
8-21	At Tex.	L	3-13		7	17	Davis	O. Hernandez		74-52	1st	+4.0
8-22	At Tex.	L	1-8		5	10	Oliver	Mussina		74-53	1st	+4.0
8-23	At Tex.	W	5-2		10	10	Hitchcock	Bell	Rivera	75-53	1st	+4.0
8-24	At Ana.	L	2-6		12	13	Hasegawa	Pettitte		75-54	1st	+3.0
8-25	At Ana.	W	7-5		9	9	Clemens	Valdes	Rivera	76-54	1st	+4.0
8-26	At Ana.	L	6-7	(10)	9	10	Percival	Stanton		76-55	1st	+4.0
8-28	Tor.	W	4-0		12	8	Mussina	Loaiza	Rivera	77-55	1st	+5.0
8-29	Tor.	L	2-3		8	8	Halladay	Hitchcock	Koch	77-56	1st	+5.0
8-30	Tor.	W	5-4	(11)	12	10	Witasick	Eyre		78-56	1st	+6.0
8-31	At Bos.	W	3-1		8	9	Clemens	Lowe	Rivera	79-56	1st	+7.0
9-1	At Bos.	W	2-1		6	5	O. Hernandez	Urbina	Rivera	80-56	1st	+8.0
9-2	At Bos.	W	1-0		6	1	Mussina	Cone		81-56	1st	+9.0
9-3	At Tor.	W	7-5		11	12	Wohlers	Koch	Mendoza	82-56	1st	+9.5
9-4	At Tor.	L	0-14		6	17	Carpenter	Pettitte		82-57	1st	+9.5
9-5	At Tor.	W	4-3		7	9	Clemens	Escobar	Rivera	83-57	1st	+9.5
9-7	Bos.	W	3-2		8	4	O. Hernandez	Martinez	Rivera	84-57	1st	+11.0
9-8	Bos.	W	9-2		11	5	Mussina	Cone		85-57	1st	+12.0
9-9	Bos.	W	7-2		11	5	Pettitte	Nomo		86-57	1st	+13.0
9-18	At Chi.	W	11-3		16	7	O. Hernandez	Buehrle		87-57	1st	+13.0
9-19	At Chi.	W	6-3		9	7	Clemens	Glover	Rivera	88-57	1st	+14.0
9-20	At Chi.	L	5-7		8	7	Lowe	Pettitte	Foulke	88-58	1st	+13.0
9-21	At Bal.	L	6-7		9	11	Roberts	Rivera		88-59	1st	+12.0
9-22	At Bal.	L	2-11		6	16	Douglass	Hitchcock		88-60	1st	+12.0
9-23	At Bal.	W	5-4	(10)	11	9	Stanton	Parrish	Rivera	89-60	1st	+13.0
9-25	T.B.	L	0-4		4	12	Sturtze	Clemens		89-61	1st	+13.5
9-26	T.B.	W	5-1		8	9	Lilly	Wilson		90-61	1st	+13.5
9-28	Bal.	W	7-0		9	3	Mussina	Johnson		91-61	1st	+15.0

Date	Opp.	Res.	Score	(inn.*)	Hits	Opp. hits	Winning pitcher	Losing pitcher	Save	Record	Pos.	GB
9-29	Bal.	L	2-7		7	6	Maduro	O. Hernandez		91-62	1st	+15.0
9-30	Bal.	T	1-1	(15)	5	8				91-62	1st	+14.5
10-1	Chi.	W	8-1		8	4	Hitchcock	K. Wells		92-62	1st	+15.5
10-2	Chi.	W	6-4		11	7	Lilly	Wright	Rivera	93-62	1st	+16.5
10-3	Chi.	W	2-1		6	6	Mussina	Garland	Rivera	94-62	1st	+16.5
10-4	At T.B.	L	1-4		3	8	Bierbrodt	A. Hernandez	Yan	94-63	1st	+15.5
10-5	At T.B.	L	4-8		9	8	Kennedy	Clemens	Zambrano	94-64	1st	+14.0
10-6	At T.B.	L	2-5		7	12	Sturtze	Mendoza	Yan	94-65	1st	+13.0
10-7	At T.B.	W	1-0		3	2	O. Hernandez	Colome	Rivera	95-65	1st	+13.5

Monthly records: April (14-12), May (15-10), June (16-11), July (19-9), August (15-14), September (12-6), October (4-3).
*Innings, if other than nine. §Day separate admission. ∞Night separate admission.

HIGHLIGHTS

High point: July 6. The Yankees pounded the Mets, 8-3 at Yankee Stadium, to win their ninth straight game. The team was playing great, and George Steinbrenner always appreciates it when they pound their city rival.

Low point: June 24. To end a road trip in which they didn't play well, the Yankees blew a 4-1 lead to the lowly Devil Rays and lost, 5-4 at Tropicana Field, displaying their lack of bullpen depth.

Turning point: On the weekend of August 31-September 2, the Yankees swept the Red Sox in a three-game series at Fenway Park, boosting their A.L. East lead to nine games and effectively clinching the division.

Most valuable player: Tino Martinez. He provided the life to the team's mediocre offense, delivering myriad clutch hits. He also played his usual superb defense, rescuing his three fellow infielders from several potential throwing errors.

Most valuable pitcher: Roger Clemens. The Rocket, who turned 39 in August, anchored the team's starting rotation for the first five months, firing everyone up with his animated ways and consistently keeping his team in the game.

Most improved player: RHP Ramiro Mendoza. In past years, the Yankees had shifted him between the starting rotation and the bullpen, and it definitely wore on him physically and mentally. This year, the Yankees started him once in June before realizing they should keep him in the pen.

Most pleasant surprise: 2B Alfonso Soriano. He made some rookie mistakes. Yet he came through with numerous big hits, big defensive plays and big efforts while running the bases.

Key injuries: Derek Jeter missed the start of the season with injuries. ... Scott Brosius was hit by a pitch in early August and missed a month and a half with a broken bone in his hand. ... Paul O'Neill was hampered late in the season by a stress fracture in his foot. ... David Justice went on the disabled list twice with an injured groin. ... Shane Spencer needed time at the beginning of the season to recover from a torn ACL. ... Orlando Hernandez missed two and a half months due to an injured left toe. ... Andy Pettitte missed time with a strained groin.

Notable: Mariano Rivera set a career high and a Yankees team record with 50 saves.

—KEN DAVIDOFF

RECORDS

2001 regular-season record: 95-65 (1st in A.L. East); 51-28 at home; 44-37 on road; 50-24 vs. A.L. East; 23-13 vs. A.L. Central; 12-20 vs. A.L. West; 10-8 vs. N.L.; 19-17 vs. lefthanded starters; 76-48 vs. righthanded starters; 81-54 on grass; 14-11 on turf; 38-22 in daytime; 57-43 at night; 30-18 in one-run games; 8-8 in extra-inning games; 0-0-0 in doubleheaders.

Team record past five years: 490-317 (.607, ranks 1st in league in that span).

TEAM LEADERS

Batting average: Derek Jeter (.311).
At-bats: Derek Jeter (614).
Runs: Derek Jeter (110).
Hits: Derek Jeter (191).
Total Bases: Derek Jeter, Tino Martinez (295).
Doubles: Bernie Williams (38).
Triples: Derek Jeter, Chuck Knoblauch, Alfonso Soriano (3).
Home runs: Tino Martinez (34).
Runs batted in: Tino Martinez (113).
Stolen bases: Alfonso Soriano (43).
Slugging percentage: Bernie Williams (.522).
On-base percentage: Bernie Williams (.395).
Wins: Roger Clemens (20).
Earned-run average: Mike Mussina (3.15).
Complete games: Mike Mussina (4).
Shutouts: Mike Mussina (3).
Saves: Mariano Rivera (50).
Innings pitched: Mike Mussina (228.2).
Strikeouts: Mike Mussina (214).

GAMES BY POSITION

Catcher: Jorge Posada 131, Todd Greene 34, Joe Oliver 12, Bobby Estalella 3.
First base: Tino Martinez 149, Nick Johnson 15, Luis Sojo 8, Clay Bellinger 6, Jorge Posada 2, Randy Velarde 1.
Second base: Alfonso Soriano 156, Luis Sojo 7, Enrique Wilson 7.
Third base: Scott Brosius 120, Enrique Wilson 19, Luis Sojo 17, Clay Bellinger 17, Randy Velarde 7.
Shortstop: Derek Jeter 150, Enrique Wilson 20, Luis Sojo 5, Erick Almonte 4, Clay Bellinger 2.
Outfield: Bernie Williams 144, Paul O'Neill 130, Chuck Knoblauch 108, Shane Spencer 68, Gerald Williams 26, David Justice 25, Clay Bellinger 25, Michael Coleman 9, Robert Perez 5, Donzell McDonald 3, Darren Bragg 3, Randy Velarde 3, Juan Rivera 3, Scott Brosius 2.
Designated hitter: David Justice 85, Chuck Knoblauch 24, Shane Spencer 14, Gerald Williams 7, Paul O'Neill 6, Jorge Posada 6, Nick Johnson 6, Randy Velarde 5, Tino Martinez 3, Michael Coleman 3, Erick Almonte 3, Alfonso Soriano 2, Todd Greene 2, Luis Sojo 1, Bernie Williams 1, Clay Bellinger 1, Scott Seabol 1, Robert Perez 1, Henry Rodriguez 1, Enrique Wilson 1.

TOP DRAFT CHOICES

1a. **John-Ford Griffin,** OF, Florida State University.
1b. **Bronson Sardinha,** SS, Kamehameha H.S., Honolulu.
1c. **Jon Skaggs,** RHP, Rice University.
2a. **Shelley Duncan,** OF, U. of Arizona.
2b. **Jason Arnold,** RHP, Univ. of Central Florida.
3. **Chase Wright,** LHP, Iowa Park (Tex.) H.S.
4. **Aaron Rifkin,** 1B, Cal State Fullerton.
5. **Jeff Christensen,** OF, U. of Tennessee.
6. **Rik Currier,** RHP, U. of Southern Cal.
7. **Andy Cannizaro,** SS, Tulane Univ.
8. **Adam Peterson,** RHP, Wichita State U.
9. **Charles Manning,** LHP, U. of Tampa.
10. **Jared Pitney,** 1B, Pepperdine Univ.

OAKLAND ATHLETICS
AMERICAN LEAGUE WEST DIVISION

Athletics schedule
Home games shaded
D—Day game (games starting before 5 p.m.)
All-Star Game at Milwaukee
Subject to changes

April

SUN	MON	TUE	WED	THU	FRI	SAT
	1 TEX	2 TEX	3 TEX	4 D TEX	5 SEA	6 SEA
7 D SEA	8 D	9 TEX	10 TEX	11 D TEX	12 ANA	13 ANA
14 D ANA	15	16 SEA	17 SEA	18 D ANA	19 ANA	20 D ANA
21 D ANA	22	23 D NYY	24 NYY	25 D NYY	26 CWS	27 CWS
28 CWS	29	30 NYY				

May

SUN	MON	TUE	WED	THU	FRI	SAT
		1 NYY	2 NYY	3 CWS	4 CWS	
5 CWS	6	7 BOS	8 BOS	9 D BOS	10 D TOR	11 D TOR
12 D TOR	13	14 BOS	15 BOS	16 BOS	17 TOR	18 D TOR
19 D TOR	20	21 BAL	22 D BAL	23 BAL	24 TB	25 D TB
26 TB	27	28 BAL	29 BAL	30 TB	31 TB	

June

SUN	MON	TUE	WED	THU	FRI	SAT
						1 TB
2 D TB	3 SEA	4 SEA	5 SEA	6 D SEA	7 HOU	8 HOU
9 D HOU	10 MIL	11 MIL	12 D MIL	13	14 SF	15 D SF
16 SF	17	18 PIT	19 PIT	20 PIT	21 CIN	22 CIN
23 CIN	24 SEA	25 SEA	26 SEA	27 D SF	28 SF	29 SF
30 D SF						

July

SUN	MON	TUE	WED	THU	FRI	SAT
	1 MIN	2 MIN	3 MIN	4 KC	5 KC	6 D KC
7 D KC	8	9 *	10	11 BAL	12 BAL	13 BAL
14 D BAL	15 TB	16 TB	17 ANA	18 ANA	19 TEX	20 TEX
21 D TEX	22 ANA	23 ANA	24 ANA	25 D ANA	26 TEX	27 TEX
28 TEX	29 CLE	30 CLE	31 D CLE			

August

SUN	MON	TUE	WED	THU	FRI	SAT
				1 DET	2 DET	3 DET
4 D DET	5	6 BOS	7 BOS	8 BOS	9 NYY	10 D NYY
11 D NYY	12 TOR	13 TOR	14 D TOR	15	16 CWS	17 D CWS
18 D CWS	19 CLE	20 CLE	21 CLE	22 CLE	23 DET	24 DET
25 D DET	26 KC	27 KC	28 KC	29	30 MIN	31 MIN

September

SUN	MON	TUE	WED	THU	FRI	SAT
1 D MIN	2 D KC	3 KC	4	5	6 MIN	7 MIN
8 MIN	9 ANA	10 ANA	11 ANA	12 SEA	13 SEA	14 D SEA
15 SEA	16 ANA	17 ANA	18 D ANA	19 TEX	20 TEX	
22 TEX	23	24 SEA	25 SEA	26 SEA	27 TEX	28 TEX
29 TEX	30					

2002 SEASON
CLUB DIRECTORY

Owners
Stephen C. Schott
Ken Hofmann
President
Michael P. Crowley
Vice president and general manager
Billy Beane
Assistant general manager
Paul DePodesta
Special assistants to general manager
Matt Keough
Ron Hopkins
Director of player development
Keith Lieppman
Director of scouting
Eric Kubota
Director of minor league operations
Ted Polakowski
Director of baseball administration
Pam Pitts
Traveling secretary
Mickey Morabito
Scouting and player dev. coordinator
Danny McCormack
Baseball operations assistant
Dave Forst
V.p., broadcasting and communications
Ken Pries
Director of public relations
Jim Young
Baseball information manager
Mike Selleck
Broadcasting manager
Robert Buan
Vice president, stadium operations
David Rinetti
Vice president, sales and marketing
David Alioto
Director of corporate sales
Franklin Lowe

Dir. of promotions and special events
Susan Weiglein
Director of ticket operations
Steve Fanelli
Director of business services
David Lozow
Executive assistant
Carolyn Jones
Exec. assistant, baseball operations
Betty Shinoda
Team physician
Dr. Allan Pont
Team orthopedist
Dr. Jerrald Goldman
Trainers
Larry Davis
Steven Sayles
Equipment manager
Steve Vucinich
Visiting clubhouse manager
Mike Thalblum
Special assignment scout
Dick Bogard
National field coordinator
Chris Pittaro
Major League advance scout
Bob Johnson
Supervisor of international scouting
Eric Kubota
Scouts
Steve Bowden, Tom Clark, Ruben Escalera, Kelly Heath, Tim Holt, John Kuehl, Rick Magnante, Gary McGraw, Kelsey Mucker, Billy Owens, John Poloni, Jim Pransky, Will Shock, Rich Sparks, Ron Vaughn

MINOR LEAGUE AFFILIATES

Class	Team	League	Manager
AAA	Sacramento	Pacific Coast	Bob Geren
AA	Midland	Texas	Tony DeFrancesco
A	Modesto	California	Greg Sparks
A	Vancouver	Northwest	Orv Franchuk
A	Visalia	California	Webster Garrison
Rookie	Scottsdale A's	Arizona	To be announced

BROADCAST INFORMATION

Radio: KFRC-AM (610).
TV: KICU-TV (Channel 36).
Cable TV: Fox Sports Bay Area.

SPRING TRAINING

Ballpark (city): Phoenix Municipal Stadium (Phoenix, Ariz.).
Ticket information: 602-392-0074.

Follow the Athletics all season at: www.sportingnews.com/baseball/teams/athletics/

SPRING TRAINING ROSTER

Manager—Art Howe (18).
Coaches—Thad Bosley (41), Brad Fischer (35), Ken Macha (39), Rick Peterson (47), Mike Quade (48), Ron Washington (38).

No.	PITCHERS	B/T	Ht./Wt.	Born	2001 clubs
	Bradford, Chad	R/R	6-5/205	9-14-74	Sacramento, Oakland
27	Fyhrie, Michael	R/R	6-2/203	12-9-69	Chicago N.L., Arizona Cubs, Iowa, Oakland
	German, Franklyn	R/R	6-4/170	1-20-80	Visalia
32	Harville, Chad	R/R	5-9/180	9-16-76	Visalia, Modesto, Sacramento, Oakland
35	Hiljus, Erik	R/R	6-5/230	12-25-72	Sacramento, Oakland
15	Hudson, Tim	R/R	6-0/160	7-14-75	Oakland
58	Ireland, Eric	R/R	6-1/170	3-11-77	Sacramento
44	Koch, Billy	R/R	6-3/215	12-14-74	Toronto
27	Lidle, Cory	R/R	5-11/180	3-22-72	Sacramento, Oakland
52	Magnante, Mike	L/L	6-1/185	6-17-65	Oakland
45	Mecir, Jim	B/R	6-1/210	5-16-70	Oakland, Sacramento
20	Mulder, Mark	L/L	6-6/200	8-5-77	Oakland
57	Pena, Juan	L/L	6-3/165	6-4-79	Midland
53	Snow, Bert	R/R	6-1/190	3-23-77	DID NOT PLAY
29	Tam, Jeff	R/R	6-1/202	8-19-70	Oakland
54	Vasquez, Leo	L/L	6-4/193	7-1-73	Sacramento
	Venafro, Mike	L/L	5-10/180	8-2-73	Texas
51	Vizcaino, Luis	R/R	5-11/169	6-1-77	Oakland
75	Zito, Barry	L/L	6-4/205	5-13-78	Oakland

No.	CATCHERS	B/T	Ht./Wt.	Born	2001 clubs
55	Hernandez, Ramon	R/R	6-0/227	5-20-76	Oakland
37	Myers, Greg	L/R	6-2/225	4-14-66	Baltimore, Sacramento, Oakland

No.	INFIELDERS	B/T	Ht./Wt.	Born	2001 clubs
3	Chavez, Eric	L/R	6-0/204	12-7-77	Oakland
	Ellis, Mark	R/R	5-11/180	6-6-77	Sacramento
	German, Esteban	R/R	5-9/165	12-26-78	Midland, Sacramento
7	Giambi, Jeremy	L/L	6-0/200	9-30-74	Oakland, Sacramento
	Grabowski, Jason	L/R	6-3/200	5-24-76	Tacoma
11	Menechino, Frank	R/R	5-9/175	1-7-71	Oakland
	Pena, Carlos	L/L	6-2/210	5-17-78	Oklahoma, Texas
9	Saenz, Olmedo	R/R	6-0/185	10-8-70	Oakland
21	Salazar, Oscar	R/R	6-0/155	6-27-78	Midland, Sacramento
4	Tejada, Miguel	R/R	5-9/188	5-25-76	Oakland
50	Valdez, Mario	L/R	6-1/210	11-19-74	Oakland, Modesto
	Velarde, Randy	R/R	6-0/200	11-24-62	Texas, Tulsa, New York A.L.

No.	OUTFIELDERS	B/T	Ht./Wt.	Born	2001 clubs
22	Byrnes, Eric	R/R	6-2/205	2-16-76	Sacramento, Oakland
60	Colangelo, Mike	R/R	6-1/185	10-22-76	Mobile, Portland, San Diego
24	Dye, Jermaine	R/R	6-5/220	1-28-74	Kansas City, Oakland
28	Justice, David	L/L	6-3/200	4-14-66	New York A.L., Norwich
12	Long, Terrence	L/L	6-1/190	2-29-76	Oakland
5	Piatt, Adam	R/R	6-2/195	2-8-76	Oakland, Sacramento, Modesto
8	Ryan, Rob	L/L	5-11/190	6-24-73	Tucson, Arizona, Sacramento, Oakland

BALLPARK INFORMATION

Ballpark (capacity, surface)
Network Associates Coliseum (43,662, grass)
Address
Oakland Athletics
7000 Coliseum Way
Oakland, CA 94621
Official website
www.oaklandathletics.com
Business phone
510-638-4900
Ticket information
510-638-4627
Ticket prices
$30 (plaza club), $27 (MVP infield)
$22 (field level), $20 (plaza-infield)
$16 (plaza-outfield), $8 (upper reserved)
$7 (bleachers)
Field dimensions (from home plate)
To left field at foul line, 330 feet
To center field, 400 feet
To right field at foul line, 330 feet
First game played
April 17, 1968 (Orioles 4, Athletics 1)

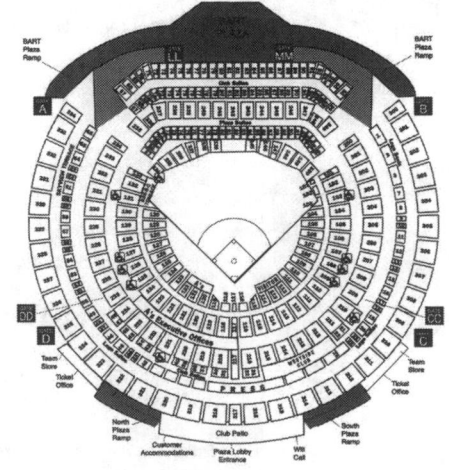

Oakland Athletics — 2002 SEASON

Date	Opp.	Res.	Score	(inn.*)	Hits	Opp. hits	Winning pitcher	Losing pitcher	Save	Record	Pos.	GB
4-2	At Sea.	L	4-5		8	7	Rhodes	Mecir	Sasaki	0-1	T2nd	1.0
4-3	At Sea.	W	5-1		8	6	Zito	Halama		1-1	T1st	...
4-4	At Sea.	L	2-10		8	15	Sele	Heredia		1-2	3rd	1.0
4-6	Ana.	L	4-5		9	10	Wise	Mulder	Percival	1-3	4th	2.0
4-7	Ana.	W	4-2		5	3	Hudson	Levine	Isringhausen	2-3	T2nd	2.0
4-8	Ana.	L	4-6		6	12	Schoeneweis	Zito	Percival	2-4	4th	2.0
4 10	Sea.	L	1-5		5	9	Halama	Heredia	Sasaki	2-5	4th	3.0
4-11	Sea.	L	0-3		4	5	Sele	Mecir	Sasaki	2-6	4th	4.0
4-12	Sea.	L	3-7		10	9	Moyer	Hudson		2-7	4th	5.0
4-13	Tex.	L	1-13		8	18	Davis	Lidle		2-8	4th	5.0
4-14	Tex.	L	8-9		14	11	Zimmerman	Mecir	Crabtree	2-9	4th	6.0
4-15	Tex.	L	8-10		13	15	Oliver	Heredia	Venafro	2-10	4th	7.0
4-16	At Ana.	W	6-3		14	6	Mulder	Washburn	Isringhausen	3-10	4th	7.0
4-17	At Ana.	W	5-1		8	6	Hudson	Ortiz		4-10	4th	7.0
4-18	At Ana.	L	2-3		7	8	Percival	Mecir		4-11	4th	7.0
4-19	At Tex.	W	9-5		15	11	Zito	Rogers	Mathews	5-11	4th	7.0
4-20	At Tex.	L	6-9		9	12	Oliver	Heredia		5-12	4th	8.0
4-21	At Tex.	W	7-6		13	11	Mulder	Mahomes	Isringhausen	6-12	4th	8.0
4-22	At Tex.	L	2-11		6	13	Helling	Hudson		6-13	4th	9.0
4-24	At Chi.	W	6-4		7	9	Zito	Buehrle	Isringhausen	7-13	4th	9.0
4-25	At Chi.	L	1-2	(11)	5	8	Foulke	Bradford		7-14	4th	10.0
4-26	At Chi.	W	16-6		17	11	Heredia	Parque		8-14	4th	10.0
4-27	At N.Y.	L	2-3		3	8	Choate	Mulder	Rivera	8-15	4th	11.0
4-28	At N.Y.	l	6-7		4	14	Lilly	Hudson	Rivera	8-16	4th	12.0
4-29	At N.Y.	L	1-3		7	5	Clemens	Zito	Rivera	8-17	4th	12.0
5-1	Tor.	L	4-5	(10)	9	10	Quantrill	Isringhausen	Koch	8-18	4th	12.0
5-2	Tor.	W	6-0		11	3	Mulder	Loaiza		9-18	4th	12.0
5-3	Tor.	W	3-2	(15)	9	7	Bradford	Borbon		10 18	4th	12.0
5-4	Bos.	W	7-3		11	8	Heredia	Lowe	Tam	11-18	4th	11.0
5-5	Bos.	L	1-7		6	14	Crawford	Zito		11-19	4th	12.0
5-6	Bos.	L	4-5		6	9	Martinez	Lidle	Beck	11-20	4th	12.0
5-8	At Tor.	W	8 6		12	10	Mulder	Loaiza	Mecir	12-20	T3rd	11.0
5-9	At Tor.	W	8-5		9	10	Hudson	Michalak	Isringhausen	13-20	3rd	11.0
5-10	At Tor.	W	14-8		15	13	Guthrie	Painter		14-20	3rd	11.0
5-11	At Bos.	W	7-6		13	10	Isringhausen	Beck	Tam	15-20	3rd	11.0
5-12	At Bos.	L	3-9		3	19	Martinez	Heredia		15-21	3rd	12.0
5-13	At Bos.	L	4-5	(11)	7	9	Lowe	Tam		15-22	3rd	13.0
5-15	N.Y.	W	3-2	(12)	12	15	Guthrie	Mendoza		16-22	3rd	13.0
5-16	N.Y.	W	4-3	(10)	9	7	Guthrie	Boehringer		17-22	3rd	13.0
5-17	N.Y.	W	8-3		13	6	Bradford	Mussina		18-22	3rd	13.0
5-18	Chi.	W	3-2		7	5	Heredia	K. Wells	Isringhausen	19-22	T2nd	12.0
5-19	Chi.	W	4-3		5	5	Mulder	Baldwin	Isringhausen	20-22	2nd	11.0
5-20	Chi.	W	6-2		6	5	Hudson	Howry		21-22	2nd	11.0
5-22	At K.C.	W	4-1		11	8	Mecir	Suppan	Isringhausen	22-22	2nd	10.0
5-23	At K.C.	L	1-4		6	10	Durbin	Lidle	Hernandez	22-23	2nd	11.0
5-25	At Min.	W	4-2		10	9	Mulder	Mays	Isringhausen	23-23	2nd	11.0
5-26†	At Min.	W	5 4	(10)	9	8	Mecir	Wells	Guthrie	24-23		
5-26‡	At Min.	L	6-7	(10)	10	14	Guardado	Guthrie		24-24	2nd	11.5
5-27	At Min.	L	3-9		12	8	Guardado	Zito		24-25	2nd	12.5
5-29	T.B.	L	1-5		6	12	Sturtze	Lidle	Phelps	24-26	2nd	14.0
5-30	T.B.	W	15-2		17	10	Mulder	Lopez		25-26	2nd	14.0
5-31	T.B.	W	10-1		14	4	Hudson	Wilson		26-26	2nd	14.0
6-1	Bal.	L	4-8		6	10	Ponson	Mecir		26-27	2nd	15.0
6-2	Bal.	L	0-7		7	15	Towers	Zito		26-28	T2nd	16.0
6-3	Bal.	W	5-1		8	9	Lidle	Roberts		27-28	T2nd	16.0
6-5	At Ana.	L	3-7		6	11	Washburn	Mulder		27-29	3rd	17.5
6-6	At Ana.	W	4-1		11	5	Hudson	Rapp	Isringhausen	28-29	T2nd	17.5
6-7	At Ana.	L	4-6		6	7	Schoeneweis	Zito	Percival	28-30	3rd	18.0
6-8	S.F	W	4-2		6	7	Heredia	Gardner	Isringhausen	29-30	3rd	18.0
6-9	S.F	L	3-4	(11)	5	9	Rodriguez	Mathews	Nen	29-31	3rd	18.0
6-10	S.F	W	6-2		10	5	Mulder	Hernandez	Bradford	30-31	3rd	18.0
6-12	At S.D.	W	5-2		10	6	Hudson	Williams	Isringhausen	31-31	T2nd	18.0
6-13	At S.D.	W	6-2		9	5	Guthrie	Nunez	Tam	32-31	2nd	17.5
6-14	At S.D.	L	4-6		5	8	Davey	Mecir	Hoffman	32-32	2nd	18.0
6-15	At S.F	L	1-3		5	7	Estes	Mulder	Nen	32-33	2nd	19.0
6-16	At S.F	L	1-2		5	5	Hernandez	Tam	Nen	32-34	T2nd	20.0
6-17	At S.F	L	0-3		5	7	Rueter	Hudson	Nen	32-35	3rd	20.0
6-18	Sea.	W	4-3		4	7	Zito	Charlton	Isringhausen	33-35	3rd	19.0
6-19	Sea.	L	7-8		10	8	Rhodes	Isringhausen	Sasaki	33-36	3rd	20.0
6-20	Sea.	W	6-4		6	9	Guthrie	Sasaki		34-36	3rd	19.0
6-21	Sea.	L	10-12		11	17	Paniagua	Tam	Rhodes	34-37	3rd	20.0
6-22	Tex.	L	1-2		9	5	Davis	Hudson	Zimmerman	34-38	3rd	20.0
6-23	Tex.	W	5-4	(10)	10	6	Isringhausen	Cordero		35-38	3rd	19.0
6-24	Tex.	L	5-9		8	11	Bell	Heredia	Venafro	35-39	3rd	20.0

Date	Opp.	Res.	Score	(inn.*)	Hits	Opp. hits	Winning pitcher	Losing pitcher	Save	Record	Pos.	GB
6-26	At Sea.	L	3-7		9	15	Garcia	Mulder		35-40	3rd	21.0
6-27	At Sea.	W	6-3		10	8	Hudson	Halama	Isringhausen	36-40	3rd	20.0
6-28	At Sea.	W	6-3		9	8	Guthrie	Fuentes	Isringhausen	37-40	3rd	19.0
6-29	At Tex.	L	6-9		7	12	Mahomes	Magnante	Zimmerman	37-41	3rd	20.0
6-30	At Tex.	W	15-4		18	8	Hiljus	Rogers		38-41	T2nd	20.0
7-1	At Tex.	L	1-3		9	6	Venafro	Mulder	Zimmerman	38-42	T2nd	21.0
7-2	Ana.	W	1-0	(12)	9	6	Tam	Hasegawa		39-42	2nd	21.0
7-3	Ana.	W	5-2		5	4	Zito	Rapp	Isringhausen	40-42	2nd	21.0
7-4	Ana.	W	2-0		9	5	Lidle	Schoeneweis	Mecir	41-42	2nd	20.0
7-5	Ana.	L	2-5		5	9	Valdes	Heredia	Percival	41-43	2nd	20.0
7-6	At Ari.	W	3-0		6	1	Mulder	Anderson		42-43	2nd	20.0
7-7	At Ari.	W	5-1		12	8	Hudson	Batista		43-43	2nd	19.0
7-8	At Ari.	W	2-1		5	7	Zito	Schilling	Isringhausen	44-43	2nd	19.0
7-12	L.A.	W	6-0		15	6	Mulder	Adams		45-43	2nd	19.0
7-13	L.A.	W	11-7		14	8	Hudson	Park	Isringhausen	46-43	2nd	18.0
7-14	L.A.	L	3-5	(15)	10	8	Reyes	Guthrie		46-44	2nd	19.0
7-15	Col.	W	6-3		10	5	Lidle	Bohanon	Vizcaino	47-44	2nd	19.0
7-16	Col.	W	5-1		9	7	Heredia	Neagle		48-44	2nd	18.0
7-17	Col.	W	3-2		8	8	Mulder	Astacio	Isringhausen	49-44	2nd	18.0
7-18	At Min.	W	7-2		14	6	Hudson	Radke		50-44	2nd	18.0
7-19	At Min.	L	10-12		11	20	Milton	Zito	Hawkins	50-45	2nd	18.0
7-20	At K.C.	W	14-3		16	10	Lidle	Byrd		51-45	2nd	18.0
7-21	At K.C.	W	10-1		11	9	Heredia	Reichert		52-45	2nd	18.0
7-22	At K.C.	L	4-5		8	15	Hernandez	Mecir		52-46	2nd	19.0
7-23	At K.C.	W	7-2		9	6	Hudson	Durbin		53-46	2nd	19.0
7-24	Min.	W	7-6		11	11	Isringhausen	Miller		54-46	2nd	18.0
7-25	Min.	L	1-3		3	11	Mays	Lidle	Hawkins	54-47	2nd	18.0
7-26	Min.	L	4-7		6	13	Johnson	Heredia		54-48	2nd	19.0
7-27	K.C.	W	5-0		5	4	Mulder	Suppan		55-48	2nd	19.0
7-28	K.C.	L	3-9		6	11	Durbin	Hudson		55-49	2nd	20.0
7-29	K.C.	W	6-4		7	6	Isringhausen	Grimsley	Mecir	56-49	2nd	20.0
7-31	At Cle.	W	11-2		15	8	Lidle	Westbrook		57-49	2nd	19.0
8-1	At Cle.	L	5-6		11	12	Baez	Mecir	Wickman	57-50	2nd	20.0
8-2	At Cle.	W	17-4		20	7	Mulder	Sabathia		58-50	2nd	20.0
8-3	At Det.	W	2-1		4	9	Hudson	Weaver		59-50	2nd	20.0
8-4	At Det.	W	10-1		10	2	Zito	Sparks		60-50	2nd	20.0
8-5	At Det.	W	4-1		8	3	Lidle	Lima	Isringhausen	61-50	2nd	19.0
8-6	At Det.	W	6-3		9	6	Vizcaino	Patterson	Isringhausen	62-50	2nd	19.0
8-7	Bos.	W	5-2		12	8	Mulder	Saberhagen	Isringhausen	63-50	2nd	19.0
8-8	Bos.	W	6-1		9	9	Hudson	Castillo		64-50	2nd	19.0
8-9	Bos.	W	6-0		8	4	Zito	Wakefield		65-50	2nd	18.0
8-10	N.Y.	W	8-1		6	4	Lidle	Lilly		66-50	2nd	17.0
8-11	N.Y.	W	8-6		12	13	Magnante	Hitchcock	Isringhausen	67-50	2nd	17.0
8-12	N.Y.	W	4-2		3	7	Mulder	Stanton		68-50	2nd	17.0
8-14	At Tor.	L	3-6		8	10	Koch	Isringhausen		68-51	2nd	18.0
8-15	At Tor.	L	2-5		6	8	Escobar	Zito	Koch	68-52	2nd	19.0
8-16	At Tor.	W	8-4		12	9	Lidle	Lyon		69-52	2nd	18.0
8-17	At Chi.	W	9-2		12	9	Hiljus	Wright		70-52	2nd	17.0
8-18	At Chi.	W	5-4		8	9	Heredia	Howry	Isringhausen	71-52	2nd	17.0
8-19	At Chi.	W	8-7		10	13	Magnante	Biddle	Isringhausen	72-52	2nd	17.0
8-20	Cle.	W	9-0		12	4	Zito	Finley		73-52	2nd	16.0
8-21	Cle.	L	1-2		6	5	Woodard	Lidle	Wickman	73-53	2nd	17.0
8-22	Cle.	L	4-5	(11)	12	9	Wickman	Vizcaino	Riske	73-54	2nd	18.0
8-23	Cle.	L	7-9		7	15	Nagy	Mulder	Wickman	73-55	2nd	19.0
8-24	Det.	L	4-8		10	12	Cornejo	Hudson		73-56	2nd	20.0
8-25	Det.	W	6-1		10	5	Zito	Sparks		74-56	2nd	20.0
8-26	Det.	W	7-6		9	12	Tam	Perisho	Isringhausen	75-56	2nd	19.0
8-28	At Bal.	W	6-2		12	4	Mulder	Ponson		76-56	2nd	18.0
8-29	At Bal.	W	4-1		9	3	Hudson	Towers		77-56	2nd	18.0
8-30	At Bal.	W	15-0		13	5	Zito	Johnson		78-56	2nd	18.0
8-31	At T.B.	W	9-5		11	9	Lidle	Rekar		79-56	2nd	17.0
9-1	At T.B.	L	6-8		9	12	Seay	Tam	Yan	79-57	2nd	18.0
9-2	At T.B.	W	3-1		9	4	Mulder	Creek		80-57	2nd	18.0
9-3	Bal.	W	4-2		9	3	Hudson	Towers	Isringhausen	81-57	2nd	18.0
9-4	Bal.	W	5-2		6	5	Zito	Johnson	Isringhausen	82-57	2nd	17.0
9-5	Bal.	W	12-6		14	13	Lidle	Maduro		83-57	2nd	17.0
9-7	T.B.	W	9-3		8	8	Hiljus	Rekar		84-57	2nd	17.0
9-8	T.B.	W	10-4		12	10	Mulder	Bierbrodt		85-57	2nd	17.0
9-9	T.B.	W	4-3	(13)	8	10	Vizcaino	Colome		86-57	2nd	17.0
9-10	Tex.	W	7-1		12	4	Zito	Myette		87-57	2nd	17.0
9-18	At Tex.	W	6-5		11	7	Mulder	Venafro	Isringhausen	88-57	2nd	17.0
9-19	At Tex.	L	4-10		10	12	Davis	Hudson	Michalak	88-58	2nd	18.0
9-20	At Tex.	W	7-2		12	8	Zito	Oliver		89-58	2nd	17.0
9-21	Sea.	W	5-1		8	8	Lidle	Abbott	Isringhausen	90-58	2nd	16.0
9-22	Sea.	W	11-2		12	12	Hiljus	Pineiro		91-58	2nd	15.0
9-23	Sea.	W	7-4		7	10	Mulder	Garcia	Isringhausen	92-58	2nd	14.0
9-25	Ana.	W	9-3		11	11	Hudson	Hasegawa		93-58	2nd	14.5
9-26	Ana.	W	3-1		6	4	Zito	Washburn	Isringhausen	94-58	2nd	14.5

Date	Opp.	Res.	Score	(inn.*)	Hits	Opp. hits	Winning pitcher	Losing pitcher	Save	Record	Pos.	GB
9-27	Ana.	W	6-2		8	5	Lidle	Wise		95-58	2nd	14.0
9-28	At Sea.	L	3-5		8	10	Garcia	Mulder	Sasaki	95-59	2nd	15.0
9-29	At Sea.	W	8-4		10	13	Hiljus	Moyer		96-59	2nd	14.0
9-30	At Sea.	L	3-6		7	11	Sele	Hudson		96-60	2nd	15.0
10-2	Tex.	W	9-4		12	10	Zito	Oliver		97-60	2nd	15.0
10-3	Tex.	W	5-4		9	6	Lidle	Michalak	Isringhausen	98-60	2nd	15.0
10-4	At Ana.	W	5-1		9	3	Mulder	Valdes		99-60	2nd	15.0
10-5	At Ana.	W	6-2		11	9	Hudson	Ortiz		100-60	2nd	15.0
10-6	At Ana.	W	6-3		11	6	Magnante	Schoeneweis	Isringhausen	101-60	2nd	15.0
10-7	At Ana.	W	6-2		7	7	Zito	Cooper		102-60	2nd	14.0

Monthly records: April (8-17), May (18-9), June (12-15), July (19-8), August (22-7), September (17-4), October (6-0).
*Innings, if other than nine. †First game of a doubleheader. ‡Second game of a doubleheader.

HIGHLIGHTS

High point: On August 1, the A's were in third place in the wild card race. Eleven games—and 11 wins—later, Oakland had moved out in front in the wild-card hunt, and the A's never relinquished the lead.

Low point: April was cruel to the A's, and on May 1, after being swept at New York and then dropping a home game to the Blue Jays, they found themselves 10 games under .500, at 8-18.

Turning point: On July 25, GM Billy Beane pulled off a two-part deal with two different teams to land Jermaine Dye. Dye provided a big righthanded threat behind Jason Giambi. He had a tremendous month of August, driving in 32 runs in 29 games.

Most valuable player: Jason Giambi does it all: He is a terrific leader and he is among the best hitters in the game, with a keen eye, a powerful bat and great instincts. Even his defense is underrated.

Most valuable pitcher: Mark Mulder surpassed all expectations by leading the league in wins in just his second season. Making the accomplishment all the more remarkable was the fact that his rookie year had been cut short by a back injury.

Most improved player: Eric Chavez leaped from promising youngster to among the elite at his position during a season in which he won a Gold Glove, hit 32 homers (a franchise record for a third baseman) and drove in 114 runs.

Most pleasant surprise: No. 4 starter Cory Lidle, acquired in the Johnny Damon deal, never had spent an entire year in a big league rotation, but he went 13-6 with a 3.59 ERA, terrific numbers for a guy who opened the season in the fifth spot in the rotation.

Key injuries: John Jaha was never able to get back to full health and retired in late June. ... setup man Jim Mecir missed less than a month after having arthroscopic knee surgery in August. ... Adam Piatt contracted viral meningitis in early June. ... Billy McMillon missed the final two months with a shoulder injury.

Notable: The A's were the first team in major league history to win 100 games after falling 10 games under .500. They

went 58-17 after the break, the second-best winning percentage in history (Cleveland went 55-16 in 1974). Oakland is just the seventh team in history to make the playoffs after falling 10 games behind .500. ... The A's were the first team in history to have a third baseman and shortstop hit 30 or more home runs in the same season.

—SUSAN SLUSSER

RECORDS

2001 regular-season record: 102-60 (2nd in A.L. West); 53-28 at home; 49-32 on road; 31-14 vs. A.L. East; 27-14 vs. A.L. Central; 32-26 vs. A.L. West; 12-6 vs. N.L.; 34-22 vs. lefthanded starters; 68-38 vs. righthanded starters; 93-54 on grass; 9-6 on turf; 36-24 in daytime; 66-36 at night; 21-19 in one-run games; 7-7 in extra-inning games; 0-0-1 in doubleheaders.

Team record past five years: 419-390 (.518, ranks 5th in league in that span).

TEAM LEADERS

Batting average: Jason Giambi (.342).
At-bats: Johnny Damon (644).
Runs: Jason Giambi (109).
Hits: Jason Giambi, Terrence Long (178).
Total Bases: Jason Giambi (343).
Doubles: Jason Giambi (47).
Triples: Johnny Damon, Terrence Long (4).
Home runs: Jason Giambi (38).
Runs batted in: Jason Giambi (120).
Stolen bases: Johnny Damon (27).
Slugging percentage: Jason Giambi (.660).
On-base percentage: Jason Giambi (.477).
Wins: Mark Mulder (21).
Earned-run average: Tim Hudson (3.37).
Complete games: Mark Mulder (6).
Shutouts: Mark Mulder (4).
Saves: Jason Isringhausen (34).
Innings pitched: Tim Hudson (235.0).
Strikeouts: Barry Zito (205).

GAMES BY POSITION

Catcher: Ramon Hernandez 135, Greg Myers 28, Sal Fasano 9, Tom Wilson 9.

First base: Jason Giambi 136, Olmedo Saenz 28, Jeremy Giambi 10, Mario Valdez 6, Robin Jennings 6, Ramon Hernandez 2, Johnny Damon 1, Eric Chavez 1, Andy Abad 1.

Second base: Frank Menechino 136, F.P. Santangelo 20, Mark Bellhorn 12, Jose Ortiz 10.

Third base: Eric Chavez 149, Olmedo Saenz 14, Mark Bellhorn 9, F.P. Santangelo 3, Frank Menechino 1.

Shortstop: Miguel Tejada 162, Mark Bellhorn 5, Frank Menechino 3, Eric Chavez 1.

Outfield: Terrence Long 162, Johnny Damon 154, Jermaine Dye 61, Jeremy Giambi 47, Adam Piatt 32, Billy McMillon 16, Robin Jennings 13, Eric Byrnes 12, Ron Gant 11, Mario Valdez 7, F.P. Santangelo 6, Rob Ryan 5, Ryan Christenson 4, Eric Chavez 1, Mark Bellhorn 1.

Designated hitter: Jeremy Giambi 61, Olmedo Saenz 58, Ron Gant 21, Jason Giambi 17, Mario Valdez 12, John Jaha 12, Eric Byrnes 5, Mark Bellhorn 4, Robin Jennings 2, Greg Myers 2, F.P. Santangelo 2, Eric Chavez 1, Adam Piatt 1, Jose Ortiz 1, Ryan Christenson 1, Sal Fasano 1, Frank Menechino 1, Billy McMillon 1, Rob Ryan 1.

TOP DRAFT CHOICES

1a. **Bobby Crosby**, SS, Long Beach State Univ.
1b. **Jeremy Bonderman**, RHP, Pasco (Wash.) H.S.
1c. **John Rheinecker**, LHP, Southwest Missouri State Univ.
2. **Neal Cotts**, LHP, Illinois State Univ.
3. **J.T. Stotts**, SS, Cal State Northridge.
4. **Marcus McBeth**, OF, U. of South Carolina.
5. **Jeff Bruksch**, RHP, Stanford Univ.
6. **Austin Nagle**, OF, Barbe H.S., Lake Charles, La.
7. **Dan Johnson**, 1B, U. of Nebraska.
8. **Mike Frick**, RHP, Cal State Northridge.
9. **Casey Myers**, C, Arizona State Univ.
10. **Mike Wood**, RHP, U. of North Florida.

SEATTLE MARINERS
AMERICAN LEAGUE WEST DIVISION

Mariners schedule
Home games shaded
D—Day game (games starting before 5 p.m.)
All-Star Game at Milwaukee
Subject to changes

April
SUN	MON	TUE	WED	THU	FRI	SAT
	1 CWS	2 CWS	3 CWS	4	5 OAK	6 OAK
7 OAK	8 ANA	9 ANA	10 ANA	11 ANA	12 TEX	13 TEX
14 TEX	15 TEX	16 OAK	17 OAK	18	19 TEX	20 TEX
21 TEX	22 D ANA	23 ANA	24 ANA	25	26 NYY	27 NYY
28 NYY	29	30 CWS				

May
SUN	MON	TUE	WED	THU	FRI	SAT
			1 CWS	2 CWS	3 NYY	4 D NYY
5 D NYY	6	7 TOR	8 TOR	9 BOS	10 BOS	11 BOS
12 D BOS	13	14 TOR	15 TOR	16 TOR	17 BOS	18 D BOS
19 BOS	20	21 TB	22 TB	23 TB	24 BAL	25 BAL
26 D BAL	27	28 TB	29 TB	30 BAL	31 BAL	

June
SUN	MON	TUE	WED	THU	FRI	SAT
						1 BAL
2 D BAL	3 OAK	4 OAK	5 OAK	6 D OAK	7 CUB	8 CUB
9 CUB	10 D STL	11 STL	12 STL	13	14 SD	15 SD
16 SD	17	18 CIN	19 CIN	20 CIN	21 HOU	22 HOU
23 HOU	24 D OAK	25 OAK	26 OAK	27 OAK	28 COL	29 COL
30 D COL						

July
SUN	MON	TUE	WED	THU	FRI	SAT
		2 KC	3 KC	4 MIN	5 MIN	6 MIN
7 D MIN	8	9 *	10	11 TB	12 TB	13 TB
14 D TB	15 BAL	16 D BAL	17 TEX	18 TEX	19 ANA	20 ANA
21 ANA	22	23 TEX	24 TEX	25 TEX	26 ANA	27 D ANA
28 D ANA	29 DET	30 DET	31 DET			

August
SUN	MON	TUE	WED	THU	FRI	SAT
				1 CLE	2 CLE	3 D CLE
4 D CLE	5	6 TOR	7 TOR	8 TOR	9 CWS	10 CWS
11 D CWS	12	13 BOS	14 BOS	15 BOS	16 NYY	17 NYY
18 D NYY	19 DET	20 DET	21 DET	22 DET	23 CLE	24 D CLE
25 CLE	26	27 MIN	28 MIN	29 D MIN	30 KC	31 KC

September
SUN	MON	TUE	WED	THU	FRI	SAT
1 D KC	2 MIN	3	4 MIN	5	6 KC	7 KC
8 KC	9	10 TEX	11 TEX	12 TEX	13 OAK	14 D OAK
15 OAK	16 TEX	17 TEX	18 TEX	19	20 ANA	21 ANA
22 ANA	23	24 OAK	25 OAK	26 D OAK	27 ANA	28 D ANA
29 ANA	30					

2002 SEASON
CLUB DIRECTORY

Chairman & chief executive officer
Howard Lincoln
Board of directors
Howard Lincoln, chairman; John Ellis, chairman emeritus; Minoru Arakawa; Chris Larson; John McCaw; Frank Shrontz; Craig Watjen
President and chief operating officer
Chuck Armstrong
Executive v.p., baseball operations
Pat Gillick
Executive v.p., business operations
Bob Aylward
Exec. v.p., finance and ballpark ops.
Kevin Mather
Vice president, baseball administration
Lee Pelekoudas
V.p., scouting and player development
Roger Jongewaard
Vice president, communications
Randy Adamack
Vice president, ballpark operations
Neil Campbell
Controller
Tim Kornegay
Director, Pacific rim operations
Ted Heid
Director, player development
Benny Looper
Director, professional scouting
Ken Compton
Director, scouting
Frank Mattox
Director, team travel
Ron Spellecy
Director, baseball information
Tim Hevly
Director, public information
Rebecca Hale
Special assignment
Woody Woodward
Baseball, systems coordinator
Jim Na
Coordinator of minor league instruction
Mike Goff
Home clubhouse manager
Scott Gilbert

Visiting clubhouse manager
Henry Genzale
Medical director
Dr. Larry Pedegana
Trainers
Rick Griffin, Tom Newberg, Ken Roll
Team physician
Dr. Mitchel Storey
Team dentist
Dr. Robert Hughes
Video coordinator
Carl Hamilton
Strength and conditioning coach
Allen Wirtala
Head groundskeeper
Bob Christopherson
Assistant groundskeepers
Leo Liebert, Tim Wilson
Senior advisor
Bob Engle
Advance scout
Stan Williams
National cross-checker
Steve Jongewaard
Major League scouts
Bob Harrison, Bill Kearns, Steve Pope
Scouting supervisors
Curtis Dishman, John McMichen, Wayne Norton, Carroll Sembera
Scouts
Dave Alexander, Pedro Avila, Craig Bell, Tom Burgess, Emiliano Carrasquel, Rodney Davis, Stan Eldridge, Luis Fuenmayor, Phil Geisler, Dennis Gonsalves, Pedro Grifol, Patrick Guerrero, Rolando Gutierrez, Ron Hafner, Ron Kaintz, Mark Leavitt, Jae Lee, Jay Lee, Mark Lummus, Les McTavish, Diego Markwell, David May, Mauro Mazziotti, Luis Molina, Robert Mummau, Omer Munoz Sr., Dana Papasedero, Stacey Pettis, Pat Phelan, Myron Pines, Harry Porter, Phil Pote, Carlos Ramirez, Steve Rath, Tim Reynolds, Eric Robinson, Jesus Salazar, Rafael Santo Domingo, Bob Smyth, Fernando Soto, Dennis Springenatic, Jamey Storvick, Kyle Van Hooke, Ray Vince, Curtis Wallace, Karel Williams, Rob Williams

MINOR LEAGUE AFFILIATES

Class	Team	League	Manager
AAA	Tacoma	Pacific Coast	Dan Rohn
AA	San Antonio	Texas	Dave Brundage
A	Everett	Northwest	Terry Pollreisz
A	San Bernardino	California	Daren Brown
A	Wisconsin	Midwest	Gary Thurman
Rookie	Peoria Mariners	Arizona	Darin Garner

BROADCAST INFORMATION
Radio: KIRO-AM (710).
TV: Fox Sports Net Northwest.
Cable TV: Fox Sports Net Northwest.

SPRING TRAINING
Ballpark: Peoria Stadium (Peoria, Ariz.).
Ticket information: 480-784-4444.

Follow the Mariners all season at: www.sportingnews.com/baseball/teams/mariners/

Manager—Lou Piniella (14).
Coaches—John McLaren (7), John Moses (12), Dave Myers (31), Gerald Perry (29), Bryan Price (32), Matt Sinatro (15).

No.	PITCHERS	B/T	Ht./Wt.	Born	2001 clubs
48	Abbott, Paul	R/R	6-3/195	9-15-67	Tacoma, Seattle
	Anderson, Ryan	L/L	6-10/225	7-12-79	DID NOT PLAY
37	Charlton, Norm	B/L	6-3/205	1-6-63	Seattle, Tacoma
	Franklin, Ryan	R/R	6-3/165	3-5-73	Seattle, Tacoma
34	Garcia, Freddy	R/R	6-4/235	10-6-76	Seattle
	Gryboski, Kevin	R/R	6-5/220	11-15-73	Tacoma
54	Halama, John	L/L	6-5/210	2-22-72	Seattle, Tacoma
	Hasegawa, Shigetoshi	R/R	5-11/178	8-1-68	Anaheim
	Heaverlo, Jeff	R/R	6-1/215	1-13-78	San Antonio
	Kaye, Justin	R/R	6-4/185	6-9-76	Tacoma
55	Meche, Gil	R/R	6-3/200	9-8-78	DID NOT PLAY
50	Moyer, Jamie	L/L	6-0/175	11-18-62	Seattle
43	Nelson, Jeff	R/R	6-8/235	11-17-66	Seattle
38	Pineiro, Joel	R/R	6-1/180	9-25-78	Tacoma, Seattle
	Putz, J.J.	R/R	6-5/220	2-22-77	San Antonio
53	Rhodes, Arthur	L/L	6-2/205	10-24-69	Seattle
22	Sasaki, Kazuhiro	R/R	6-4/209	2-22-68	Seattle
64	Serrano, Wascar	R/R	6-2/178	6-2-78	Portland, San Diego
	Simpson, Allan	R/R	6-4/185	8-26-77	San Antonio, San Bernardino
	Soriano, Rafael	R/R	6-1/175	12-19-79	San Bernardino, San Antonio
	Taylor, Aaron	R/R	6-3/205	8-20-77	Wisconsin
	Thornton, Matt	L/L	6-6/220	9-15-76	San Bernardino
	Wooten, Greg	R/R	6-7/210	3-30-74	Tacoma

No.	CATCHERS	B/T	Ht./Wt.	Born	2001 clubs
13	Davis, Ben	B/R	6-4/215	3-10-77	San Diego
6	Wilson, Dan	R/R	6-3/202	3-25-69	Seattle

No.	INFIELDERS	B/T	Ht./Wt.	Born	2001 clubs
9	Arias, Alex	R/R	6-3/202	11-20-67	San Diego
25	Bell, David	R/R	5-10/190	9-14-72	Seattle
	Boone, Bret	R/R	5-10/180	4-6-69	Seattle
	Bloomquist, William	R/R	5-11/185	11-27-77	San Antonio
7	Cirillo, Jeff	R/R	6-1/195	9-23-69	Colorado, Colorado Springs
8	Guillen, Carlos	B/R	6-1/180	9-30-75	Seattle
11	Martinez, Edgar	R/R	5-11/210	1-2-63	Seattle
4	McLemore, Mark	B/R	5-11/207	10-4-64	Seattle
5	Olerud, John	L/L	6-5/220	8-5-68	Seattle
	Perez, Antonio	R/R	5-11/175	7-28-81	San Antonio
	Ugueto, Luis	B/R	5-11/170	2-15-79	Brevard County

No.	OUTFIELDERS	B/T	Ht./Wt.	Born	2001 clubs
9	Cameron, Mike	R/R	6-2/190	1-8-73	Seattle
1	Gipson, Charles	R/R	6-2/180	12-16-72	Seattle
15	Kelly, Kenny	R/R	6-2/180	1-26-79	San Antonio
	Sierra, Ruben	B/R	6-1/200	10-6-65	Oklahoma, Texas
51	Suzuki, Ichiro	L/R	5-9/156	10-22-73	Seattle

Ballpark (capacity, surface)
Safeco Field (47,116, grass)

Address
1250 First Avenue South
Seattle, WA 98104

Official website
www.seattlemariners.com

Business phone
206-346-4000

Ticket information
206-346-4001

Ticket prices
$40 (terrace club infield; lower box)
$35 (terrace club outfield)
$32 (field)
$23 (view box, lower outfield reserved)
$16 (view reserved)
$12 (left field bleachers)
$6 (center field bleachers)

Field dimensions (from home plate)
To left field at foul line, 331 feet
To center field, 405 feet
To right field at foul line, 326 feet

First game played
July 15, 1999 (Padres 3, Mariners 2)

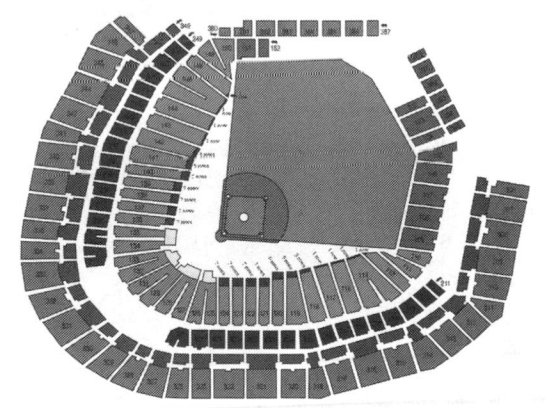

Seattle Mariners **2002 SEASON**

Date	Opp.	Res.	Score	(inn.*)	Hits	Opp. hits	Winning pitcher	Losing pitcher	Save	Record	Pos.	GB
4-2	Oak.	W	5-4		7	8	Rhodes	Mecir	Sasaki	1-0	1st	+0.5
4-3	Oak.	L	1-5		6	8	Zito	Halama		1-1	T1st	...
4-4	Oak.	W	10-2		15	8	Sele	Heredia		2-1	T1st	...
4-6	At Tex.	W	9-7	(10)	12	9	Rhodes	Zimmerman	Sasaki	3-1	1st	+1.0
4-7	At Tex.	W	6-5		12	12	Franklin	Davis	Sasaki	4-1	1st	+2.0
4-8	At Tex.	L	4-5		8	11	Venafro	Paniagua	Crabtree	4-2	1st	+1.0
4-10	At Oak.	W	5-1		9	5	Halama	Heredia	Sasaki	5-2	1st	+1.5
4-11	At Oak.	W	3-0		5	4	Sele	Mecir	Sasaki	6-2	1st	+2.0
4-12	At Oak.	W	7-3		9	10	Moyer	Hudson		7-2	1st	+2.0
4-13	At Ana.	L	3-4		10	8	Hasegawa	Sasaki		7-3	1st	+1.0
4-14	At Ana.	W	2-1		4	2	Garcia	Valdes	Sasaki	8-3	1st	+2.0
4-15	At Ana.	W	7-5		11	7	Paniagua	Hasegawa	Nelson	9-3	1st	+2.5
4-16	Tex.	W	9-7		11	12	Franklin	Glynn		10-3	1st	+3.5
4-17	Tex.	W	6-4		11	7	Moyer	Helling	Sasaki	11-3	1st	+4.5
4-18	Tex.	L	6-8		11	13	Davis	Tomko	Zimmerman	11-4	1st	+3.5
4-19	Ana.	W	3-2		9	6	Garcia	Valdes	Sasaki	12-4	1st	+4.5
4-20	Ana.	W	4-1		6	6	Halama	Rapp	Sasaki	13-4	1st	+4.5
4-21	Ana.	W	5-2		8	7	Moyer	Washburn	Nelson	14-4	1st	+5.5
4-22	Ana.	W	5-0		11	6	Sele	Ortiz		15-4	1st	+5.5
4-24	At N.Y.	W	7-5		9	8	Garcia	Stanton	Sasaki	16-4	1st	+6.5
4-25	At N.Y.	W	7-5		10	12	Charlton	Pettitte	Sasaki	17-4	1st	+7.5
4-26	At N.Y.	W	7-3		14	7	Moyer	Mussina	Rhodes	18-4	1st	+8.0
4-27	At Chi.	W	8-3		12	9	Sele	Baldwin	Sasaki	19-4	1st	+8.0
4-28	At Chi.	W	8-5		15	7	Tomko	Biddle	Sasaki	20-4	1st	+9.0
4-29	At Chi.	L	1-2	(14)	4	7	Glover	Franklin		20-5	1st	+9.0
5-1	Bos.	L	0-2		3	9	Martinez	Halama	Arrojo	20-6	1st	+9.0
5-2	Bos.	W	5-1		5	7	Sele	Nomo		21-6	1st	+9.0
5-3	Bos.	W	10-3		11	11	Moyer	Castillo		22-6	1st	+9.0
5-4	Tor.	L	3-8		6	8	Parris	Abbott		22-7	1st	+8.0
5-5	Tor.	W	7-5		13	9	Rhodes	Borbon	Sasaki	23-7	1st	+9.0
5-6	Tor.	L	3-11		6	14	Carpenter	Halama		23-8	1st	+8.0
5-8	At Bos.	L	4-12		8	14	Nomo	Moyer		23-9	1st	+8.0
5-9	At Bos.	W	10-5		14	11	Nelson	Arrojo	Sasaki	24-9	1st	+9.0
5-10	At Bos.	W	5-2		8	5	Halama	Ohka	Sasaki	25-9	1st	+9.0
5-11	At Tor.	W	7-2		10	5	Abbott	Hamilton		26-9	1st	+10.0
5-12	At Tor.	W	11-7		18	9	Tomko	Escobar		27-9	1st	+11.0
5-13	At Tor.	W	7-5		14	9	Moyer	Loaiza	Sasaki	28-9	1st	+11.0
5-15	Chi.	W	4-3		9	10	Nelson	Howry	Paniagua	29-9	T1st	+12.0
5-16	Chi.	W	7-2		10	5	Abbott	Biddle	Paniagua	30-9	1st	+12.0
5-17	Chi.	W	5-1		12	6	Garcia	D. Wells	Nelson	31-9	1st	+12.0
5-18	N.Y.	L	10-14		13	19	Mendoza	Halama		31-10	1st	+12.0
5-19	N.Y.	L	1-2	(10)	5	4	Stanton	Sasaki	Rivera	31-11	1st	+11.0
5-20	N.Y.	W	6-2		6	9	Sele	Clemens		32-11	1st	+11.0
5-22	At Min.	L	11-12		15	15	Wells	Abbott		32-12	1st	+10.0
5-23	At Min.	W	5-4		11	7	Rhodes	Carrasco	Sasaki	33-12	1st	+11.0
5-25	At K.C.	W	9-6		14	10	Franklin	Grimsley	Sasaki	34-12	1st	+11.0
5-26	At K.C.	W	7-2		13	10	Sele	Meadows		35-12	1st	+11.5
5-27	At K.C.	W	5-4	(11)	9	8	Charlton	Santiago		36-12	1st	+12.5
5-28	At K.C.	W	13-3		17	6	Abbott	Durbin		37-12	1st	+13.0
5-29	Bal.	W	3-2		9	4	Garcia	Roberts	Sasaki	38-12	1st	+14.0
5-30	Bal.	W	12-5		12	13	Halama	Johnson		39-12	1st	+14.0
5-31	Bal.	W	2-1		6	5	Sele	Mercedes	Sasaki	40-12	1st	+14.0
6-1	T.B.	W	8-4		9	5	Moyer	Rekar	Nelson	41-12	1st	+15.0
6-2	T.B.	W	7-4		9	9	Abbott	Rupe	Sasaki	42-12	1st	+16.0
6-3	T.B.	W	8-4		9	8	Garcia	Sturtze	Sasaki	43-12	1st	+16.0
6-4	Tex.	W	11-6		12	7	Franklin	Venafro		44-12	1st	+16.5
6-5	Tex.	W	5-4		6	9	Paniagua	Smart	Sasaki	45-12	1st	+16.5
6-6	Tex.	W	7-3		12	5	Moyer	Oliver		46-12	1st	+17.5
6-8	S.D.	W	7-1		10	5	Abbott	Jarvis		47-12	1st	+17.0
6-9	S.D.	L	3-6		8	8	Jones	Garcia	Hoffman	47-13	1st	+17.0
6-10	S.D.	W	8-1		11	8	Halama	Loewer		48-13	1st	+17.0
6-12	At Col.	W	10-9		13	11	Fuentes	Acevedo	Sasaki	49-13	1st	+18.0
6-14§	At Col.	L	2-8		3	12	Chacon	Moyer		49-14		
6-14∞	At Col.	W	5-1		11	6	Abbott	Astacio		50-14	1st	+18.0
6-15	At S.D.	W	8-4		15	5	Garcia	Jones		51-14	1st	+19.0
6-16	At S.D.	W	9-2		14	11	Halama	Loewer		52-14	1st	+20.0
6-17	At S.D.	L	9-11		9	15	Davey	Nelson	Hoffman	52-15	1st	+19.0
6-18	At Oak.	L	3-4		7	4	Zito	Charlton	Isringhausen	52-16	1st	+18.5
6-19	At Oak.	W	8-7		8	10	Rhodes	Isringhausen	Sasaki	53-16	1st	+19.5
6-20	At Oak.	L	4-6		9	6	Guthrie	Sasaki		53-17	1st	+18.5
6-21	At Oak.	W	12-10		17	11	Paniagua	Tam	Rhodes	54-17	1st	+19.5
6-22	Ana.	L	1-8		5	10	Washburn	Sele		54-18	1st	+18.5
6-23	Ana.	L	1-2		6	2	Rapp	Moyer	Percival	54-19	1st	+17.5
6-24	Ana.	W	7-3		9	8	Abbott	Schoeneweis	Sasaki	55-19	1st	+18.5

Date	Opp.	Res.	Score	(inn.*)	Hits	Opp. hits	Winning pitcher	Losing pitcher	Save	Record	Pos.	GB
6-26	Oak.	W	7-3		15	9	Garcia	Mulder		56-19	1st	+19.0
6-27	Oak.	L	3-6		8	10	Hudson	Halama	Isringhausen	56-20	1st	+18.0
6-28	Oak.	L	3-6		8	9	Guthrie	Fuentes	Isringhausen	56-21	1st	+18.0
6-29	At Ana.	W	9-5		12	9	Moyer	Schoeneweis		57-21	1st	+19.0
6-30	At Ana.	W	5-3		10	11	Stark	Ortiz	Sasaki	58-21	1st	+20.0
7-1	At Ana.	W	5-0		7	8	Garcia	Wise		59-21	1st	+21.0
7-2	At Tex.	W	9-7	(10)	11	12	Nelson	Petkovsek	Sasaki	60-21	1st	+21.0
7-3	At Tex.	W	8-4		13	7	Sele	Oliver		61-21	1st	+21.0
7-4	At Tex.	L	3-6		10	13	Bell	Moyer	Venafro	61-22	1st	+20.0
7-5	At Tex.	L	2-14		7	13	Rogers	Stark		61-23	1st	+20.0
7-6	At L.A.	W	13-0		17	4	Garcia	Brown		62-23	1st	+20.0
7-7	At L.A.	L	1-2		3	5	Herges	Paniagua		62-24	1st	+19.0
7-8	At L.A.	W	9-2		13	5	Sele	Williams		63-24	1st	+19.0
7-12	S.F	W	4-3	(11)	8	8	Rhodes	Boehringer		64-24	1st	+19.0
7-13	S.F	L	3-5		7	10	Ortiz	Moyer	Nen	64-25	1st	+18.0
7-14	S.F	W	3-2		6	3	Garcia	Estes	Sasaki	65-25	1st	+19.0
7-15	Ari.	W	8-0		13	2	Sele	Ellis		66-25	1st	+19.0
7-16	Ari.	L	3-5		5	10	Batista	Halama	Kim	66-26	1st	+18.0
7-17	Ari.	W	6-1		11	8	Abbott	Anderson		67-26	1st	+18.0
7-18	At K.C.	W	2-0	(10)	9	5	Nelson	Hernandez	Sasaki	68-26	1st	+18.0
7-19	At K.C.	L	3-6		8	9	Wilson	Garcia		68-27	1st	+18.0
7-20	At Min.	W	4-0		10	5	Sele	Mays		69-27	1st	+18.0
7-21	At Min.	W	6-3		6	8	Halama	Johnson	Sasaki	70-27	1st	+18.0
7-22	At Min.	W	6-3		13	6	Abbott	Lohse		71-27	1st	+18.0
7-23	At Min.	W	3-2		9	9	Moyer	Radke	Sasaki	72-27	1st	+19.0
7-24	K.C.	L	1-6		7	11	Wilson	Garcia		72-28	1st	+18.0
7-25	K.C.	L	1-5		6	12	Byrd	Sele		72-29	1st	+18.0
7-26	K.C.	W	4-0		11	2	Pineiro	George		73-29	1st	+18.0
7-27	Min.	W	11-4		11	7	Abbott	Lohse		74-29	1st	+19.0
7-28	Min.	W	5-1		11	6	Moyer	Radke		75-29	1st	+20.0
7-29	Min.	W	10-2		14	5	Garcia	Milton		76-29	1st	+19.0
7-31	At Det.	L	2-4		6	10	Lima	Sele	Anderson	76-30	1st	+19.0
8-1	At Det.	W	7-1		14	5	Abbott	Holt		77-30	1st	+20.0
8-2	At Det.	W	2-1		8	4	Pineiro	Pettyjohn	Sasaki	78-30	1st	+20.0
8-3	At Cle.	W	2-1		4	3	Moyer	Colon	Sasaki	79-30	1st	+20.0
8-4	At Cle.	W	8-5		14	13	Garcia	Baez	Rhodes	80-30	1st	+20.0
8-5	At Cle.	L	14-15	(11)	17	23	Rocker	Paniagua		80-31	1st	+19.0
8-6	At Cle.	W	8-6		13	9	Abbott	Nagy	Paniagua	81-31	1st	+19.0
8-7	Tor.	W	5-4	(14)	12	11	Halama	DeWitt		82-31	1st	+19.0
8-8	Tor.	W	12-4		19	8	Moyer	Carpenter		83-31	1st	+19.0
8-9	Tor.	L	5-6		10	14	Quantrill	Garcia	Koch	83-32	1st	+18.0
8-10	Chi.	L	6-8		6	11	Biddle	Sasaki	Foulke	83-33	1st	+17.0
8-11	Chi.	W	4-3		8	7	Franklin	Foulke		84-33	1st	+17.0
8-12	Chi.	W	2-1		9	3	Rhodes	K. Wells	Sasaki	85-33	1st	+17.0
8-14	At Bos.	W	6-3	(11)	15	8	Paniagua	Beck	Sasaki	86-33	1st	+18.0
8-15	At Bos.	W	6-2		11	3	Garcia	Castillo		87-33	1st	+19.0
8-16	At Bos.	L	4-6		13	9	Garces	Sele	Urbina	87-34	1st	+18.0
8-17	At N.Y.	L	0-4		6	6	Mussina	Abbott	Mendoza	87-35	1st	+17.0
8-18	At N.Y.	W	7-6		10	14	Rhodes	Lilly	Sasaki	88-35	1st	+17.0
8-19	At N.Y.	W	10-2		15	6	Moyer	Pettitte		89-35	1st	+17.0
8-20	Det.	L	1-4		5	11	Sparks	Garcia		89-36	1st	+16.0
8-21	Det.	W	4-1		11	3	Sele	Weaver	Sasaki	90-36	1st	+17.0
8-22	Det.	W	16-1		20	6	Abbott	Lima		91-36	1st	+18.0
8-23	Det.	W	5-1		10	3	Pineiro	Redman		92-36	1st	+19.0
8-24	Cle.	W	4-1		9	3	Moyer	Colon	Charlton	93-36	1st	+20.0
8-25	Cle.	W	3-2	(11)	7	7	Halama	Rocker		94-36	1st	+20.0
8-26	Cle.	L	3-4		10	8	Riske	Nelson	Wickman	94-37	1st	+19.0
8-28	At T.B.	L	0-6		6	11	Wilson	Pineiro		94-38	1st	+18.0
8-29	At T.B.	W	5-2		10	5	Moyer	Sturtze		95-38	1st	+18.0
8-30	At T.B.	W	4-0		9	9	Garcia	Rupe		96-38	1st	+18.0
8-31	At Bal.	L	0-3		6	7	Maduro	Sele		96-39	1st	+17.0
9-1	At Bal.	W	6-4		12	7	Abbott	Mercedes	Sasaki	97-39	1st	+18.0
9-2	At Bal.	W	1-0		4	6	Pineiro	Bauer	Sasaki	98-39	1st	+18.0
9-3	T.B.	W	3-2	(11)	13	9	Charlton	Yan		99-39	1st	+18.0
9-4	T.B.	L	3-8	(10)	11	11	Zambrano	Charlton		99-40	1st	+17.0
9-5	T.B.	W	12-6		13	12	Halama	Phelps		100-40	1st	+17.0
9-7	Bal.	W	10-1		12	2	Abbott	Mercedes		101-40	1st	+17.0
9-8	Bal.	W	6-1		13	4	Pineiro	Bauer		102-40	1st	+17.0
9-9	Bal.	W	6-0		10	2	Moyer	Towers		103-40	1st	+17.0
9-10	At Ana.	W	5-1		13	6	Garcia	Valdes		104-40	1st	+17.0
9-18	Ana.	W	4-0		10	3	Garcia	Ortiz		105-40	1st	+17.0
9-19	Ana.	W	5-0		7	5	Moyer	Schoeneweis		106-40	1st	+18.0
9-20	Ana.	L	3-6		6	12	Hasegawa	Halama	Percival	106-41	1st	+17.0
9-21	At Oak.	L	1-5		8	8	Lidle	Abbott	Isringhausen	106-42	1st	+16.0
9-22	At Oak.	L	2-11		12	12	Hiljus	Pineiro		106-43	1st	+15.0
9-23	At Oak.	L	4-7		10	7	Mulder	Garcia	Isringhausen	106-44	1st	+14.0
9-24	At Tex.	W	9-3		13	12	Moyer	Davis		107-44	1st	+14.5
9-25	At Tex.	W	13-2		16	8	Sele	Duchscherer		108-44	1st	+14.5

Date	Opp.	Res.	Score	(inn.*)	Hits	Opp. hits	Winning pitcher	Losing pitcher	Save	Record	Pos.	GB
9-26	At Tex.	W	7-5		10	9	Abbott	Bell	Sasaki	109-44	1st	+14.5
9-28	Oak.	W	5-3		10	8	Garcia	Mulder	Sasaki	110-44	1st	+15.0
9-29	Oak.	L	4-8		13	10	Hiljus	Moyer		110-45	1st	+14.0
9-30	Oak.	W	6-3		11	7	Sele	Hudson		111-45	1st	+15.0
10-2	At Ana.	W	14-5		21	6	Abbott	Washburn		112-45	1st	+15.0
10-3	At Ana.	W	4-3		13	8	Charlton	Levine	Sasaki	113-45	1st	+15.0
10-4	Tex.	W	16-1		19	4	Tomko	Myette		114-45	1st	+15.0
10-5	Tex.	W	6-2		7	4	Moyer	Helling		115-45	1st	+15.0
10-6	Tex.	W	1-0		4	2	Pineiro	Davis	Sasaki	116-45	1st	+15.0
10-7	Tex.	L	3-4		6	12	Mahomes	Nelson	Zimmerman	116-46	1st	+14.0

Monthly records: April (20-5), May (20-7), June (18-9), July (18-9), August (20-9), September (15-6), October (5-1).
*Innings, if other than nine. §Day separate admission. ∞Night separate admission.

HIGHLIGHTS

High point: All spring, manager Lou Piniella talked about the importance of starting fast in a schedule that had the Mariners play their first 19 games of the year against A.L. West teams. At the end of those 19 games, the Mariners were 15-4.

Low point: The Mariners hadn't lost a road series all season until they got to Oakland. There, in a three-game set that began September 21, Seattle was swept. It was the first time all year they'd lost more than two consecutive games.

Turning point: On April 24 the Mariners began a three-game series in New York, facing Roger Clemens, Andy Pettitte and Mike Mussina. The Mariners took all three games.

Most valuable pitcher: Freddy Garcia proved he had the stuff of a No. 1 pitcher. He set career-highs in innings pitched, wins and ERA.

Most valuable player: On the field, it might well have been a tie—2B Bret Boone and Japanese OF Ichiro Suzuki each had dominant offensive seasons. Boone batted .331 with 36 homers and 141 RBIs—all career highs. Where Boone proved to be the MVP was in the clubhouse, where his confidence, sense of humor and leadership helped give the club an identity.

Most improved player: Boone, who entered the season with a career average of .255, exceeded all expectations by batting a career-high .331 and leading the league in RBIs.

Most pleasant suprise: Coming out of spring training, Jamie Moyer was the No. 4 starter in Seattle's rotation. By the All-Star break, Moyer was 9-4. After the break, he was nearly unbeatable: 11-2 with a 2.22 ERA in his last 16 starts, and a 20-game winner for the first time in his career.

Key injuries: Jay Buhner was hurt in spring training and did not play until September. ... Gil Meche and Ryan Anderson were lost for the year to shoulder surgeries. ... Over the course of the year, minor injuries put Paul Abbott, Norm Charlton, Stan Javier and Edgar Martinez on the disabled list.

Notable: Away from home, Seattle went 59-22, setting an American League record. In 26 road series, the Mariners went 21-1-4. ... The Mariners won the "triple crown" by leading the league in batting average (.288), earned-run average (3.54) and fielding percentage (.986)—the first team to do so since the 1948 Indians. ... When Suzuki (56), INF-OF Mark McLemore (39) and OF Mike Cameron (34) all stole more than 30 bases, the Mariners became the first A.L. team since 1992 to have three men steal more than 30 bases.

—LARRY LaRUE

RECORDS

2001 regular-season record: 116-46 (1st in A.L. West); 57-24 at home; 59-22 on road; 33-12 vs. A.L. East; 31-10 vs. A.L. Central; 40-18 vs. A.L. West; 12-6 vs. N.L.; 31-14 vs. lefthanded starters; 85-32 vs. righthanded starters; 106-44 on grass; 10-2 on turf; 37-13 in daytime; 79-33 at night; 26-12 in one-run games; 9-4 in extra-inning games; 0-0-0 in doubleheaders.

Team record past five years: 452-357 (.559, ranks 3rd in league in that span).

TEAM LEADERS

Batting average: Ichiro Suzuki (.350).
At-bats: Ichiro Suzuki (692).
Runs: Ichiro Suzuki (127).
Hits: Ichiro Suzuki (242).
Total Bases: Bret Boone (360).
Doubles: Edgar Martinez (40).
Triples: Mark McLemore (9).
Home runs: Bret Boone (37).
Runs batted in: Bret Boone (141).
Stolen bases: Ichiro Suzuki (56).
Slugging percentage: Bret Boone (.578).
On-base percentage: Edgar Martinez (.423).
Wins: Jamie Moyer (20).
Earned-run average: Freddy Garcia (3.05).
Complete games: Freddy Garcia (4).
Shutouts: Freddy Garcia (3).
Saves: Kazuhiro Sasaki (45).
Innings pitched: Freddy Garcia (238.2).
Strikeouts: Freddy Garcia (163).

GAMES BY POSITION

Catcher: Dan Wilson 122, Tom Lampkin 71, Pat Borders 5, Ed Sprague 1.
First base: John Olerud 158, Ed Sprague 12, Stan Javier 6, Dan Wilson 2, David Bell 2, Edgar Martinez 1.
Second base: Bret Boone 156, Mark McLemore 9, Ramon Vazquez 6, Charles Gipson 1.
Third base: David Bell 134, Mark McLemore 36, Charles Gipson 9, Ed Sprague 8, Ramon Vazquez 2.
Shortstop: Carlos Guillen 137, Mark McLemore 35, Ramon Vazquez 10, Charles Gipson 6.
Outfield: Ichiro Suzuki 152, Mike Cameron 149, Stan Javier 76, Al Martin 73, Mark McLemore 68, Charles Gipson 65, Jay Buhner 12, Anthony Sanders 9, Ed Sprague 9, Gene Kingsale 9, Scott Podsednik 5, Tom Lampkin 1.
Designated hitter: Edgar Martinez 127, Al Martin 16, Charles Gipson 11, Ed Sprague 9, Ichiro Suzuki 4, Jay Buhner 4, Bret Boone 2, Mark McLemore 2, Stan Javier 2, Mike Cameron 1, Carlos Guillen 1, Tom Lampkin 1, Ramon Vazquez 1.

TOP DRAFT CHOICES

1. **Michael Garciaparra**, SS, Don Bosco Tech, La Habra Heights, Calif.
2a. **Rene Rivera**, C, Papa Juan XXIII H.S., Bayamon, P.R.
2b. **Michael Wilson**, OF, Booker T. Washington H.S., Tulsa, Okla.
3a. **Lazaro Abreu**, C, Southridge H.S., Miami.
3b. **Tim Merritt**, SS, Univ. of South Alabama.
4. **Bobby Livingston**, LHP, Trinity Christian H.S., Lubbock, Tex.
5. **John Cole**, 2B/OF, U. of Nebraska.
6. **Justin Ockerman**, RHP, Garden City (Mich.) H.S.
7. **John Axford**, RHP, Assumption College H.S., Brantford, Ontario.
8. **Jeff Ellena**, SS, Cal Poly Pomona.
9. **Justin Blood**, LHP, Franklin Pierce (N.H.) College.
10. **Beau Hintz**, LHP, Fresno State Univ.

TAMPA BAY DEVIL RAYS
AMERICAN LEAGUE EAST DIVISION

Devil Rays schedule
Home games shaded
D—Day game (games starting before 5 p.m.)
*All-Star Game at Milwaukee
Subject to changes

April
SUN	MON	TUE	WED	THU	FRI	SAT
		1	2 DET	3 DET	4 DET D	5 NYY D	6 NYY D
7 NYY D	8	9 BAL	10 BAL	11 BAL	12 TOR	13 TOR
14 TOR D	15	16 DET	17 DET	18 DET D	19 BAL	20 BAL
21 BAL D	22	23 MIN	24 MIN	25 MIN	26 BOS	27 BOS D
28 BOS D	29 MIN	30 MIN				

May
SUN	MON	TUE	WED	THU	FRI	SAT
			1 MIN	2 MIN D	3 BOS	4 BOS
5 BOS D	6 BOS	7 NYY	8 NYY	9 NYY	10 BAL	11 BAL
12 BAL D	13	14 NYY	15 NYY	16 NYY	17 BAL	18 BAL
19 BAL D	20	21 SEA	22 SEA	23 SEA D	24 OAK	25 OAK D
26 OAK D	27	28 SEA	29 SEA	30 OAK	31 OAK	

June
SUN	MON	TUE	WED	THU	FRI	SAT
						1 OAK
2 OAK D	3 TOR	4 TOR	5 TOR	6 TOR D	7 SD	8 SD
9 SD D	10 LA	11 LA	12 LA	13	14 FLA	15 FLA
16 FLA D	17	18 SF	19 SF	20 SF	21 COL	22 COL
23 COL D	24	25 TOR	26 TOR	27 TOR D	28 FLA	29 FLA
30 FLA D						

July
SUN	MON	TUE	WED	THU	FRI	SAT
	1	2 TEX	3 TEX	4 TEX	5 ANA	6 ANA
7 ANA	8	9 *	10	11 SEA	12 SEA	13 SEA
14 SEA D	15 OAK	16 OAK	17 ROS	18 ROS D	19 TOR	20 TOR D
21 TOR D	22	23 BOS	24 BOS	25 BOS	26 NYY	27 NYY
28 NYY D	29 BAL	30 BAL	31 BAL			

August
SUN	MON	TUE	WED	THU	FRI	SAT
				1 BAL	2 CWS	3 CWS
4 CWS D	5 CWS	6 CLE	7 CLE	8 CLE	9 KC	10 KC
11 KC D	12	13 CLE	14 CLE	15 CLE	16 KC	17 KC
18 KC D	19 BAL	20 BAL	21 BAL	22	23 CWS	24 CWS
25 CWS D	26	27 ANA	28 ANA	29 ANA	30 TEX	31 TEX

September
SUN	MON	TUE	WED	THU	FRI	SAT
1 TEX D	2	3 ANA	4 ANA	5 ANA	6 TEX	7 TEX
8 TEX D	9 BOS	10 BOS	11 BOS	12 BOS	13 TOR	14 TOR D
15 TOR D	16	17 NYY	18 NYY	19 NYY	20 TOR	21 TOR
22 TOR D	23 NYY	24 NYY	25 NYY	26 NYY	27 BOS	28 BOS
29 BOS D	30					

2002 SEASON
CLUB DIRECTORY

Managing general partner/CEO
Vincent J. Naimoli
Chief operating officer
John McHale Jr.
Sr. v.p. baseball operations/g.m.
Chuck LaMar
Sr. v.p.-admin/CFO& general counsel
John P. Higgins
Vice president of sales/marketing
John Browne
Vice president of public relations
Rick Vaughn
Vice president of stadium operations
Rick Nafe
Assistant general manager
Bart Braun
Assistant general manager
Scott Proefrock
Special assistant to general manager
Eddie Bane
Director of player personnel
Cam Bonifay
Director of scouting
Dan Jennings
Assistant to player development
Mitch Lukevics
Director of team travel
Jeff Ziegler
Controller
Patrick Smith
Director of human resources
Louis "Jeep" Weber
Director of business administration
Bill Wiener Jr.
Sr. dir. of corporate sales and broadcasting
Larry McCabe
Director of promotions and special events
Allen Jernigan
Managers of sponsorship coordination
Maggie Doran, Kelly Davis, Lauren Miller
Manager of broadcast operations
Kevin Daigle
Coordinator of amateur baseball events
Curt Brooker
Director of ticket operations
Robert Bennett
Assistant director of ticket operations
Ken Mallory
Assistant to the v.p. of public relations
Carmen Molina

Director of media relations
Chris Costello
Assistant media relations manager
Greg Landy
Director of publications
Matt Lorenz
Assistant director of publications
Charles Parker
Manager of community relations
Liz-Beth Lauck
Mascot coordinator
Shawn Christopherson
Director of event productions
John Franzone
Video producer
Jason Rundle
Video coordinator
Chris Fernandez
Head trainer
Jamie Reed
Assistant head trainer
Ken Crenshaw
Strength & conditioning coordinator
Jason Trott
Medical team physician
Dr. Michael Reilly
Orthopedic team physician
Dr. Koco Eaton
Head groundskeeper
Dan Moeller
Clubhouse operations-home
Carlos Ledezma
Clubhouse operations-visitor
Guy Gallagher
Major League scouts
Bart Johnson, Don Williams
Major League consultants
Jerry Gardner, Al LaMacchia
Crosscheckers
R.J. Harrison, Dave Roberts, Mac Seibert
Area scouts
Jonathan Bonifay, James Bonnici, Skip Bundy, Rickey Drexler, Kevin Elfering, Milt Hill, Hank King, Paul Kirsch, Denny Latino, Fred Repke, Joe Robinson Jr., Edwin Rodriguez, Dale Tilleman, Craig Weissmann, Doug Witt, Mike Zimmerman
Part-time scout
Junior Ramirez

MINOR LEAGUE AFFILIATES

Class	Team	League	Manager
AAA	Durham	International	Bill Evers
AA	Orlando	Southern	Mako Oliveras
A	Bakersfield	California	Charlie Montoyo
A	Charleston (S.C.)	South Atlantic	Buddy Biancalana
A	Hudson Valley	New York-Pennsylvania	Dave Howard
Rookie	Princeton	Appalachian	Edwin Rodriguez

BROADCAST INFORMATION
Radio: WFLA-AM (970).
TV: MORE-TV (Channel 32); WTSP (Channel 10).
Cable TV: Fox Sports Net.

SPRING TRAINING
Ballpark (city): Florida Power Park Home of Al Lang Field (St. Petersburg, Fla.).
Ticket information: 727-825-3250.

Follow the Devil Rays all season at: www.sportingnews.com/baseball/teams/devilrays/

SPRING TRAINING ROSTER

Manager—Hal McRae (56).
Coaches—Jackie Brown, Glenn Ezell (55), Tom Foley, Billy Hatcher (22), Lee May (47), Milt May.

No.	PITCHERS	B/T	Ht./Wt.	Born	2001 clubs
40	Alvarez, Wilson	L/L	6-1/245	3-24-70	Orlando, Durham
47	Bierbrodt, Nick	L/L	6-5/185	5-16-78	El Paso, Tucson, Arizona, Tampa Bay
	Colome, Jesus	R/R	6-4/170	6-2-80	Durham, Tampa Bay
38	Creek, Doug	L/L	6-0/200	3-1-69	Tampa Bay
	James, Delvin	R/R	6-4/222	1-3-78	Orlando, Durham
	Kennedy, Joe	R/L	6-4/225	5-24-79	Orlando, Durham, Tampa Bay
	Kent, Steve	B/L	5-11/170	10-3-78	San Bernardino
30	McGlinchy, Kevin	R/R	6-5/220	6-28-77	Gulf Coast Braves
	Phelps, Travis	R/R	6-2/195	7-25-77	Durham, Tampa Bay
24	Rupe, Ryan	R/R	6-5/230	3-31-75	Tampa Bay, Durham
	Seay, Bobby	L/L	6-2/221	6-20-78	Orlando, Tampa Bay
	Standridge, Jason	R/R	6-4/217	11-9-78	Durham, Tampa Bay, Orlando
49	Sturtze, Tanyon	R/R	6-5/205	10-12-70	Tampa Bay
	Veras, Enger	R/R	6-5/230	7-9-81	Bakersfield
	White, Matt	R/R	6-5/230	8-13-78	Durham
41	Wilson, Paul	R/R	6-5/235	3-28-73	Tampa Bay
43	Yan, Esteban	R/R	6-4/230	6-22-74	Tampa Bay, Orlando
	Zambrano, Victor	R/R	6-0/190	8-6-75	Durham, Tampa Bay
No.	**CATCHERS**	**B/T**	**Ht./Wt.**	**Born**	**2001 clubs**
6	Flaherty, John	R/R	6-1/200	10-21-67	Tampa Bay
81	Hall, Toby	R/R	6-3/205	10-21-75	Durham, Tampa Bay
No.	**INFIELDERS**	**B/T**	**Ht./Wt.**	**Born**	**2001 clubs**
	Abernathy, Brent	R/R	6-1/185	9-23-77	Durham, Tampa Bay
	Brewer, Jace	R/R	6-0/170	8-6-79	Charleston, S.C.
38	Caceres, Wilmy	B/R	6-0/165	10-2-78	Salt Lake
28	Cox, Steve	L/L	6-4/222	10-31-74	Tampa Bay, Orlando
10	Gomez, Chris	R/R	6-1/195	6-16-71	San Diego, Portland, Durham, Tampa Bay
21	Huff, Aubrey	L/R	6-4/221	12-20-76	Durham, Tampa Bay
10	Johnson, Russ	R/R	5-10/180	2-22-73	Tampa Bay, Orlando
16	Martinez, Felix	B/R	6-0/180	5-18-74	Tampa Bay, Orlando
71	Rolls, Damian	R/R	6-2/205	9-15-77	Tampa Bay
	Sandberg, Jared	R/R	6-3/212	3-2-78	Orlando, Durham, Tampa Bay
20	Smith, Bobby	R/R	6-3/190	5-10-74	Durham, Tampa Bay
	Smith, Jason	L/R	6-3/190	7-24-77	Iowa, Chicago N.L., Durham
	Soler, Ramon	B/R	6-0/175	7-6-81	Bakersfield
No.	**OUTFIELDERS**	**B/T**	**Ht./Wt.**	**Born**	**2001 clubs**
6	Conti, Jason	L/R	5-11/180	1-27-75	Tucson, Arizona, Durham
14	Grieve, Ben	L/R	6-4/230	5-4-76	Tampa Bay
14	Tyner, Jason	L/L	6-1/170	4-23-77	Durham, Tampa Bay
23	Vaughn, Greg	R/R	6-0/202	7-3-65	Tampa Bay
2	Winn, Randy	B/R	6-2/193	6-9-74	Tampa Bay

BALLPARK INFORMATION

Ballpark (capacity, surface)
Tropicana Field (44,445, artificial)
Address
One Tropicana Drive
St. Petersburg, FL 33705
Official website
www.devilrays.com
Business phone
727-825-3137
Ticket information
727-825-3250
Ticket prices
$195 (home plate box-$125 before May)
$75 (field box)
$40 (lower club box)
$35 (diamond club box, diamond club res.)
$25 (lower box)
$19 (terrace box)
$14 (outfield)
$10 (upper deck reserved)
$5 (the beach-adults)
$2 (the beach-children/seniors)
Field dimensions (from home plate)
To left field at foul line, 315 feet
To center field, 404 feet
To right field at foul line, 322 feet
First game played
March 31, 1998 (Tigers 11, Devil Rays 6)

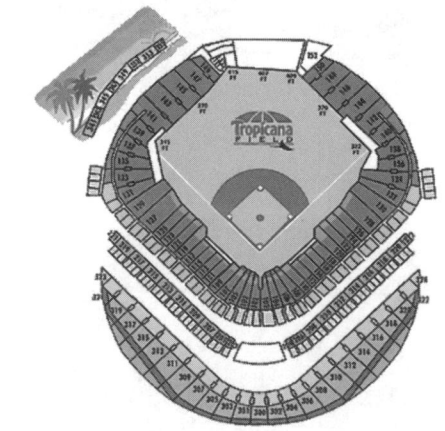

DAY BY DAY

Date	Opp.	Res.	Score	(inn.*)	Hits	Opp. hits	Winning pitcher	Losing pitcher	Save	Record	Pos.	GB
4-3	Tor.	W	8-1		15	7	Lopez	Parris		1-0	T1st	...
4-4	Tor.	L	8-11		13	14	Quantrill	Hill	Koch	1-1	T3rd	1.0
4-5	Tor.	L	0-11		4	13	Carpenter	Rekar		1-2	T4th	2.0
4-6	At Bos.	L	4-11		8	11	Wakefield	Rupe		1-3	5th	2.5
4-7	At Bos.	L	2-6		4	14	Crawford	Harper		1-4	5th	3.5
4-8	At Bos.	L	0-3		4	7	Martinez	Lopez	Lowe	1-5	5th	3.5
4-9	At Tor.	L	1-8		8	9	Hamilton	Wilson		1-6	5th	4.5
4-10	At Tor.	L	2-3	(10)	6	6	Quantrill	Sturtze		1-7	5th	5.5
4-11	At Tor.	W	4-3		8	7	Yan	Koch		2-7	5th	5.0
4-13	At Bal.	W	2-0		3	3	Lopez	Hentgen		3-7	5th	4.5
4-14	At Bal.	L	5-6		7	9	Bale	Meacham	Kohlmeier	3-8	5th	5.5
4-15	At Bal.	W	7-4		13	9	Creek	Ponson	Yan	4-8	5th	4.5
4-16	At Bal.	L	2-6		4	8	Johnson	Rupe		4-9	5th	5.0
4-17	Bos.	L	0-10		7	11	Ohka	Harper		4-10	5th	6.0
4-18	Bos.	L	1-9		6	15	Arrojo	Sturtze		4-11	5th	7.0
4-19	Bos.	L	3-8		10	8	Martinez	Wilson	Lowe	4-12	5th	8.0
4-20	Bal.	L	3-6		10	8	Roberts	Rekar	Kohlmeier	4-13	5th	8.0
4-21	Bal.	W	6-5		10	11	Rupe	Johnson	Yan	5-13	5th	8.0
4-22	Bal.	L	8-10	(11)	10	16	Paronto	Yan		5-14	5th	8.0
4-24	K.C.	W	4-2		9	8	Lopez	Meadows	Yan	6-14	5th	8.0
4-25	K.C.	W	5-3		8	4	Wilson	Suppan	Yan	7-14	5th	7.0
4-26	K.C.	L	0-6		6	10	Suzuki	Rekar		7-15	5th	8.0
4-27	At Det.	L	2-4		7	7	Mlicki	Rupe	Jones	7-16	5th	9.0
4-28	At Det.	W	7-3		8	8	Judd	Perisho		8-16	5th	8.0
4-29	At Det.	L	1-6		7	12	Weaver	Lopez		8-17	5th	8.5
4-30	At Bal.	L	3-5		5	8	Roberts	Wilson	Kohlmeier	8-18	5th	8.5
5-1	At Bal.	L	1-3		4	6	Johnson	Rekar	Kohlmeier	8-19	5th	9.5
5-2	At Bal.	W	7-1		15	6	Rupe	Mercedes	Sturtze	9-19	5th	8.5
5-4	Cle.	L	6-8		13	14	Colon	Lopez	Shuey	9-20	5th	9.0
5-5	Cle.	L	4-9		8	12	Speier	Wilson	Karsay	9-21	5th	9.0
5-6	Cle.	L	3-10		9	13	Finley	Creek		9-22	5th	10.0
5-8	Bal.	W	4-3		8	5	Meacham	Mercedes	Yan	10-22	5th	10.0
5-9	Bal.	L	6-8		9	10	Towers	Rupe	Trombley	10-23	5th	10.0
5-10	Bal.	L	5-9		7	9	Ryan	Meacham		10-24	5th	10.0
5-11	At Cle.	L	6-10		12	13	Rodriguez	Rekar		10-25	5th	10.5
5-12	At Cle.	L	0-8		10	10	Finley	Rose		10-26	5th	11.5
5-13	At Cle.	W	7-0		14	8	Sturtze	Burba		11-26	5th	11.0
5-15	At K.C.	L	2-6		10	14	Santiago	Wilson		11-27	5th	12.0
5-16	At K.C.	L	5-9		11	13	Hernandez	Yan		11-28	5th	12.0
5-17	At K.C.	L	2-4		9	7	Durbin	Rose	Hernandez	11-29	5th	12.0
5-18	Det.	L	2-18		4	19	Santos	Sturtze		11-30	5th	13.0
5-19	Det.	L	5-10		12	17	Holt	Lopez	Patterson	11-31	5th	13.0
5-20	Det.	W	10-2		13	6	Wilson	Mlicki		12-31	5th	13.0
5-22	Tex.	L	2-5		8	9	Rogers	Rekar		12-32	5th	13.5
5-23	Tex.	W	10-6		14	12	Wheeler	Crabtree		13-32	5th	12.5
5-24	Tex.	L	3-9		11	9	Helling	Sturtze		13-33	5th	13.0
5-25	Ana.	L	4-6		13	11	Wobor	Lopez	Percival	13-34	5th	13.5
5-26	Ana.	L	4-10		6	12	Washburn	Wilson		13-35	5th	14.0
5-27	Ana.	W	4-3	(10)	7	8	Yan	Levine		14-35	5th	14.0
5-28	Ana.	L	1-3		5	8	Schoeneweis	Meacham	Percival	14-36	5th	15.0
5-29	At Oak.	W	5-1		12	6	Sturtze	Lidle	Phelps	15-36	5th	14.5
5-30	At Oak.	L	2-15		10	17	Mulder	Lopez		15-37	5th	14.5
5-31	At Oak.	L	1-10		4	14	Hudson	Wilson		15-38	5th	15.0
6-1	At Sea.	L	4-8		5	9	Moyer	Rekar	Nelson	15-39	5th	16.0
6-2	At Sea.	L	4-7		9	9	Abbott	Rupe	Sasaki	15-40	5th	17.0
6-3	At Sea.	L	4-8		8	9	Garcia	Sturtze	Sasaki	15-41	5th	18.0
6-5	At Tor.	L	1-13		8	16	Loaiza	Lopez		15-42	5th	18.5
6-6	At Tor.	W	6-2		8	8	Kennedy	Michalak		16-42	5th	17.5
6-7	At Tor.	L	7-8		13	13	Borbon	Phelps		16-43	5th	18.5
6-8	N.Y.	W	7-5		11	9	Rupe	Trachsel	Yan	17-43	5th	18.5
6-9	N.Y.	W	5-2		6	10	Sturtze	Leiter	Phelps	18-43	T4th	17.5
6-10	N.Y.	L	0-10		4	13	Appier	Lopez		18-44	5th	18.5
6-12	Phi.	W	9-5		11	7	Kennedy	Telemaco		19-44	5th	18.5
6-13	Phi.	W	5-3		8	9	Rekar	Bottalico	Yan	20-44	5th	17.5
6-14	Phi.	W	6-3		11	5	Rupe	Wolf	Yan	21-44	5th	17.5
6-15	At Fla.	L	4-7		7	11	Burnett	Sturtze		21-45	5th	18.5
6-16	At Fla.	L	0-11		1	13	Penny	Lopez		21-46	5th	18.5
6-17	At Fla.	L	4-6		10	9	Dempster	Kennedy	Alfonseca	21-47	5th	19.5
6-19	Bos.	L	4-5		3	7	Wakefield	Rekar	Lowe	21-48	5th	20.5
6-20	Bos.	L	2-8		7	9	Garces	Rupe		21-49	5th	21.5
6-21	Bos.	L	4-7		10	10	Bock	Yan	Lowe	21-50	5th	22.5
6-22	N.Y.	L	3-6		10	8	Mussina	Lopez	Rivera	21-51	5th	22.5
6-23	N.Y.	L	1-2		6	6	Clemens	Wallace	Rivera	21-52	5th	22.5
6-24	N.Y.	W	5-4		8	9	Phelps	Stanton		22-52	5th	21.5

2002 SEASON *Tampa Bay Devil Rays*

Date	Opp.	Res.	Score	(inn.*)	Hits	Opp. hits	Winning pitcher	Losing pitcher	Save	Record	Pos.	GB
6-25	At Bos.	L	8-12		9	12	Cone	Rupe	Lowe	22-53	5th	22.5
6-26	At Bos.	L	6-7		8	8	Beck	Zambrano	Lowe	22-54	5th	23.5
6-27	At Bos.	W	9-7		15	12	Creek	Schourek		23-54	5th	22.5
6-28	At Bos.	W	4-3		9	8	Colome	Lowe		24-54	5th	21.5
6-29	At N.Y.	L	5-7		10	11	Clemens	Rekar	Rivera	24-55	5th	21.5
6-30	At N.Y.	L	4-5		11	5	Stanton	Creek	Rivera	24-56	5th	22.5
7-1	At N.Y.	L	1-6		6	10	Pettitte	Sturtze		24-57	5th	23.5
7-2	At N.Y.	L	1-7		9	8	Mussina	Lopez		24-58	5th	24.5
7-3	Tor.	W	7-2		13	9	Kennedy	Michalak	Phelps	25-58	5th	24.0
7-4	Tor.	L	1-8		7	15	Parris	Rekar		25-59	5th	25.0
7-5	Tor.	L	4-7		10	11	Hamilton	Rupe	Koch	25-60	5th	26.0
7-6	Fla.	W	5-4	(11)	13	10	Zambrano	Bones		26-60	5th	26.0
7-7	Fla.	W	4-3		10	9	Lopez	Penny	Phelps	27-60	5th	25.0
7-8	Fla.	L	1-6		4	10	Dempster	Kennedy		27-61	5th	26.0
7-12	At Mon.	W	10-0		14	6	Sturtze	Mattes		28-61	5th	25.0
7-13	At Mon.	L	2-6		4	9	Vazquez	Kennedy		28-62	5th	25.0
7-14	At Mon.	L	2-10		11	9	Armas	Rekar		28-63	5th	26.0
7-15	At Atl.	W	9-1		13	8	Lopez	Perez		29-63	5th	25.0
7-16	At Atl.	W	6-5		11	10	Zambrano	Karsay	Yan	30-63	5th	25.0
7-17	At Atl.	L	0-4		6	6	Maddux	Sturtze		30-64	5th	26.0
7-18	Ana.	L	1-2		4	11	Valdes	Kennedy	Percival	30-65	5th	26.5
7-19	Ana.	L	1-2		9	9	Washburn	Wallace	Percival	30-66	5th	26.5
7-20	Tex.	L	1-4		11	10	Davis	Lopez	Zimmerman	30-67	5th	26.5
7-21	Tex.	W	2-1		3	7	Zambrano	Oliver	Yan	31-67	5th	25.5
7-22	Tex.	W	7-4		11	9	Sturtze	Moreno	Yan	32-67	5th	25.5
7-24	At Ana.	L	6-9		11	11	Washburn	Kennedy	Levine	32-68	5th	27.0
7-25	At Ana.	W	3-1		6	6	Wilson	Wise	Yan	33-68	5th	27.0
7-26	At Ana.	L	3-5		6	7	Ortiz	Rupe	Percival	33-69	5th	28.0
7-27	At Tex.	L	7-13		9	17	Bell	Sturtze		33-70	5th	29.0
7-28	At Tex.	W	7-3	(10)	11	8	Yan	Foster		34-70	5th	29.0
7-29	At Tex.	L	0-2		4	6	Helling	Kennedy		34-71	5th	30.0
7-31	At Bal.	W	5-4		9	9	Wilson	Towers	Yan	35-71	5th	29.0
8-1	At Bal.	L	5-6		10	7	Mills	Yan		35-72	5th	30.0
8-2	At Bal.	W	3-2		7	8	Sturtze	Maduro	Zambrano	36-72	5th	29.0
8-3	At Chi.	L	0-4		1	7	Buehrle	Bierbrodt		36-73	5th	30.0
8-4	At Chi.	L	6-8		15	8	Biddle	Kennedy	Foulke	36-74	5th	31.0
8-5	At Chi.	W	6-4		14	9	Zambrano	Howry	Yan	37-74	5th	30.0
8-6	At Chi.	L	2-5		2	7	Wright	Wallace	Foulke	37-75	5th	30.0
8-7	N.Y.	W	3-2		9	7	Sturtze	Mussina	Yan	38-75	5th	29.0
8-8	N.Y.	L	1-16		8	17	Pettitte	Bierbrodt		38-76	5th	30.0
8-9	N.Y.	L	3-4		7	8	Mendoza	Yan	Rivera	38-77	5th	31.0
8-10	Min.	W	4-2		9	8	Wilson	Mays		39-77	5th	30.0
8-11	Min.	W	4-3		5	8	Rupe	Thomas	Yan	40-77	5th	29.0
8-12	Min.	W	4-3	(12)	11	8	Zambrano	Hawkins		41-77	5th	28.0
8-13	Min.	W	5-1		13	3	Bierbrodt	Lohse		42-77	5th	27.5
8-14	At N.Y.	L	3-5		7	9	Pettitte	Kennedy	Rivera	42-78	5th	28.5
8-15	At N.Y.	L	3-10		5	10	Clemens	Wilson		42-79	5th	29.5
8-16	At N.Y.	L	5-12		11	11	Hitchcock	Rupe		42-80	5th	30.5
8-17	At Min.	W	9-4		11	8	Sturtze	Reed		43-80	5th	30.5
8-18	At Min.	L	4-6		6	11	Lohse	Bierbrodt	Jones	43-81	5th	30.5
8-19	At Min.	W	5-1		9	4	Kennedy	Milton		44-81	5th	29.5
8-21	Bal.	W	8-4		13	8	Phelps	Mercedes		45-81	5th	29.0
8-22	Bal.	W	11-10		20	14	Yan	Roberts		46-81	5th	28.0
8-23	Bal.	L	4-7		7	15	Julio	Zambrano	Roberts	46-82	5th	29.0
8-24	Chi.	L	4-5		9	7	Buehrle	Sturtze	Foulke	46-83	5th	29.0
8-25	Chi.	W	8-4		13	9	Kennedy	Wright		47-83	5th	29.0
8-26	Chi.	L	2-3		6	7	Garland	Seay	Foulke	47-84	5th	29.0
8-28	Sea.	W	6-0		11	6	Wilson	Pineiro		48-84	5th	29.0
8-29	Sea.	L	2-5		5	10	Moyer	Sturtze		48-85	5th	29.0
8-30	Sea.	L	0-4		9	9	Garcia	Rupe		48-86	5th	30.0
8-31	Oak.	L	5-9		9	11	Lidle	Rekar		48-87	5th	31.0
9-1	Oak.	W	8-6		12	9	Seay	Tam	Yan	49-87	5th	31.0
9-2	Oak.	L	1-3		4	9	Mulder	Creek		49-88	5th	32.0
9-3	At Sea.	L	2-3	(11)	9	13	Charlton	Yan		49-89	5th	33.0
9-4	At Sea.	W	8-3	(10)	11	11	Zambrano	Charlton		50-89	5th	32.0
9-5	At Sea.	L	6-12		12	13	Halama	Phelps		50-90	5th	33.0
9-7	At Oak.	L	3-9		8	8	Hiljus	Rekar		50-91	5th	34.0
9-8	At Oak.	L	4-10		10	12	Mulder	Bierbrodt		50-92	5th	35.0
9-9	At Oak.	L	3-4	(13)	10	8	Vizcaino	Colome		50-93	5th	36.0
9-18	At Bos.	L	2-7		5	11	Nomo	Sturtze		50-94	5th	37.0
9-19	At Bos.	W	12-2		16	5	Wilson	Cone		51-94	5th	37.0
9-20	At Bos.	L	1-2		8	8	Arrojo	Creek	Beck	51-95	5th	37.0
9-21	At Tor.	W	7-4		12	7	Rekar	Lyon	Yan	52-95	5th	36.0
9-22	At Tor.	L	7-8		11	11	Coco	Colome	Koch	52-96	5th	36.0
9-23	At Tor.	W	1-0		4	5	Kennedy	Escobar	Yan	53-96	5th	36.0
9-25	At N.Y.	W	4-0		12	4	Sturtze	Clemens		54-96	5th	35.0
9-26	At N.Y.	L	1-5		9	8	Lilly	Wilson		54-97	5th	36.0
9-27	Tor.	W	5-1		10	5	Colome	Eyre		55-97	5th	35.5

Date	Opp.	Res.	Score	(inn.*)	Hits	Opp. hits	Winning pitcher	Losing pitcher	Save	Record	Pos.	GB
9-28	Tor.	W	6-1		9	6	Rekar	Escobar	Phelps	56-97	5th	35.5
9-29	Tor.	W	5-2		9	9	Bierbrodt	Halladay	Yan	57-97	5th	34.5
9-30	Tor.	L	5-6	(12)	13	13	Quantrill	Creek	Eyre	57-98	5th	35.0
10-1	Bos.	W	10-3		11	9	Sturtze	Cone		58-98	5th	35.0
10-2	Bos.	W	10-3		13	13	Wilson	Fossum		59-98	5th	35.0
10-3	Bos.	L	3-10		7	14	Lowe	Rupe	Wakefield	59-99	5th	36.0
10-4	N.Y.	W	4-1		8	3	Bierbrodt	A. Hernandez	Yan	60-99	5th	35.0
10-5	N.Y.	W	8-4		8	9	Kennedy	Clemens	Zambrano	61-99	5th	34.0
10-6	N.Y.	W	5-2		12	7	Sturtze	Mendoza	Yan	62-99	5th	33.0
10-7	N.Y.	L	0-1		2	3	O. Hernandez	Colome	Rivera	62-100	5th	34.0

Monthly records: April (8-18), May (7-20), June (9-18), July (11-15), August (13-16), September (9-11), October (5-2).
*Innings, if other than nine.

HIGHLIGHTS

High point: April 3. Tampa Bay opened the season with an impressive 8-1 win over Toronto. A crowd of 41,546 turned out at Tropicana Field, the second-largest crowd since 1998. The Rays won their first home opener in four seasons, and it was the only time all season the team was over the .500 mark.

Low point: Larry Rothschild, the first manager in team history, was fired on April 18 after a 4-10 start. By then, the team had clearly lost its competitiveness, and the attitude in the clubhouse was deteriorating rapidly. Many of the veteran players at that point were unhappy.

Turning point: When struggling 3B Vinny Castilla was released on May 10, it was a significant day in franchise history. That was the first real sign that the team's plan to go with high-profile veterans was a mistake. Two months later Fred McGriff was traded to the Cubs.

Most valuable player: Tanyon Sturtze did not have eye-popping numbers, but he had a successful season nonetheless. Sturtze began the season in the bullpen. He did not join the rotation until late May. Once he got settled into a starting role, Sturze was the team's most dependable pitcher.

Most valuable pitcher: Sturtze wins this award with his 11-12 record and 4.42 ERA in 195 1/3 innings.

Most improved player: Randy Winn was a fairly solid player. Offensively, he set career highs in every category except stolen bases and runs scored.

Most pleasant surprise: Victor Zambrano emerged as a big surprise for the Rays. He was called up from Class AAA Durham on June 21. On August 5, Zambrano had a scoreless streak stopped at 17 1/3 innings. Zambrano finished the season with a 6-2 record and a 3.16 ERA.

Key injuries: Greg Vaughn was bothered by nagging leg injuries for most of the second half. ... Also, Wilson Alvarez and Juan Guzman did not pitch in the majors in 2001. Neither recovered from rotator cuff surgery in 2000.

Notables: Tampa Bay became the first A.L. team to lose 100 games since the 1996 Detroit Tigers. ... Tampa Bay was just the second team in history to throw only one complete game in a season. At 152 games, the team has the longest streak ever without one. ... The team's ERA dropped 1.51 from the first half to the second half, the second-best improvement in the majors in the last 10 years. ... The team gave Cy Young winner Roger Clemens two of his three losses.

—CHRIS ANDERSON

RECORDS

2001 regular-season record: 62-100 (5th in A.L. East); 37-44 at home; 25-56 on road; 29-47 vs. A.L. East; 13-19 vs. A.L. Central; 10-26 vs. A.L. West; 10-8 vs. N.L.; 13-23 vs. lefthanded starters; 49-77 vs. righthanded starters; 18-48 on grass; 44-52 on turf; 24-36 in daytime; 38-64 at night; 17-19 in one-run games; 5-5 in extra-inning games; 0-0-0 in doubleheaders.

Team record past five years: 263-384 in four years (.406).

TEAM LEADERS

Batting average: Ben Grieve (.264).
At-bats: Ben Grieve (542).
Runs: Greg Vaughn (74).
Hits: Ben Grieve (143).
Total Bases: Ben Grieve, Greg Vaughn (210).
Doubles: Ben Grieve (30).
Triples: Randy Winn (6).
Home runs: Greg Vaughn (24).
Runs batted in: Greg Vaughn (82).
Stolen bases: Jason Tyner (31).

Slugging percentage: Greg Vaughn (.433).
On-base percentage: Ben Grieve (.372).
Wins: Tanyon Sturtze (11).
Earned-run average: Tanyon Sturtze (4.42).
Complete games: Albie Lopez (1).
Shutouts: Albie Lopez (1).
Saves: Esteban Yan (22).
Innings pitched: Tanyon Sturtze (195.1).
Strikeouts: Ryan Rupe (123).

GAMES BY POSITION

Catcher: John Flaherty 78, Mike DiFelice 48, Toby Hall 46, Paul Hoover 2.
First base: Steve Cox 78, Fred McGriff 74, Aubrey Huff 19, Jared Sandberg 1.
Second base: Brent Abernathy 79, Damian Rolls 42, Russ Johnson 33, Felix Martinez 10, Bobby Smith 6.
Third base: Aubrey Huff 73, Jared Sandberg 38, Russ Johnson 36, Vinny Castilla 24, Damian Rolls 1.
Shortstop: Felix Martinez 67, Chris Gomez 58, Andy Sheets 49, Russ Johnson 6.
Outfield: Ben Grieve 120, Randy Winn 117, Jason Tyner 100, Gerald Williams 59, Greg Vaughn 57, Jose Guillen 36, Damian Rolls 25, Steve Cox 8.
Designated hitter: Greg Vaughn 76, Ben Grieve 32, Aubrey Huff 20, Fred McGriff 17, Damian Rolls 6, Steve Cox 4, Jose Guillen 4, Randy Winn 3, Russ Johnson 2.

TOP DRAFT CHOICES

1. **Dewon Brazelton**, RHP, Middle Tennessee State University.
2. **Jon Switzer**, LHP, Arizona State U.
3. **Chris Flynn**, RHP, U. at Stony Brook.
4. **David Bush**, RHP, Wake Forest Univ.
5. **Chris Seddon**, LHP, Canyon H.S., Santa Clarita, Calif.
6. **Matt Rico**, OF, Fresno (Calif.) C.C.
7. **Tim King**, LHP, Deer Park (Tex.) H.S.
8. **Aaron Clark**, OF, Univ. of Alabama.
9. **Fernando Cortez**, SS, Grossmont (Calif.) C.C.
10. **Jason St. Clair**, SS, Desert Vista H.S., Phoenix.

TEXAS RANGERS
AMERICAN LEAGUE WEST DIVISION

Rangers schedule
Home games shaded
D—Day game (games starting before 5 p.m.)
*All-Star Game at Milwaukee
Subject to changes

April
SUN	MON	TUE	WED	THU	FRI	SAT
	1 OAK	2 OAK	3 OAK	4 OAK D	5 D ANA	6 ANA
7 D ANA	8	9 OAK	10 OAK	11 D OAK	12 SEA	13 SEA
14 SEA	15 SEA	16 ANA	17 ANA	18	19 SEA	20 SEA
21 SEA D	22	23 TOR	24 TOR	25 TOR D	26 CLE	27 CLE
28 CLE	29	30 TOR				

May
SUN	MON	TUE	WED	THU	FRI	SAT
		1 TOR	2 TOR	3 CLE	4 CLE	
5 D CLE	6 CWS	7 CWS	8 CWS	9 CWS	10 DET	11 DET
12 DET	13 CWS	14 CWS	15 CWS	16 DET	17 DET	18 DET
19 D DET	20 MIN	21 MIN	22 D MIN	23 KC	24 KC	25 KC
26 D KC	27 MIN	28 MIN	29 MIN	30	31 KC	

June
SUN	MON	TUE	WED	THU	FRI	SAT
						1 KC
2 KC	3 ANA	4 ANA	5 ANA	6 ANA	7 ATL	8 ATL
9 ATL	10 CIN	11 CIN	12 CIN	13	14 HOU	15 HOU
16 HOU	17	18 CUB	19 D CUB	20 D CUB	21 PIT	22 PIT
23 D PIT	24 ANA	25 ANA	26 ANA	27 ANA	28 HOU	29 HOU
30 HOU						

July
SUN	MON	TUE	WED	THU	FRI	SAT
	1	2 TB	3 TB	4 TB	5 BAL	6 BAL
7 BAL	8	9 *	10	11 MIN	12 MIN	13 MIN
14 D MIN	15 KC	16 KC	17 SEA	18 SEA	19 OAK	20 OAK
21 D OAK	22	23 SEA	24 SEA	25 SEA	26 OAK	27 OAK
28 OAK	29 NYY	30 NYY	31 NYY			

August
SUN	MON	TUE	WED	THU	FRI	SAT
				1 BOS	2 BOS	3 BOS
4 BOS	5	6 DET	7 DET	8 DET	9 CLE	10 CLE D
11 D CLE	12	13 CWS	14 CWS	15	16 TOR	17 TOR
18 TOR	19	20 BOS	21 BOS	22 BOS	23 NYY	24 NYY D
25 D NYY	26 D NYY	27 BAL	28 BAL	29 BAL	30 TB	31 TB

September
SUN	MON	TUE	WED	THU	FRI	SAT
1 D TB	2	3 BAL	4 BAL	5 BAL	6 TB	7 TB
8 D TB	9	10 SEA	11 SEA	12 SEA	13 ANA	14 ANA
15 ANA	16 SEA	17 SEA	18 SEA	19 SEA	20 OAK	21 D OAK
22 D OAK	23	24 ANA	25 ANA	26 D ANA	27 OAK	28 OAK
29 D OAK	30					

2002 SEASON
CLUB DIRECTORY

Chairman of the board and owner
Thomas O. Hicks
CEO, Southwest Sports Group
Michael J. Cramer
President
James R. Lites
Executive vice president, general manager
John Hart
Executive vice president, business operations
Rick McLaughlin
Executive v.p., broadcasting and sales
Bill Strong
Executive vice president, marketing
Jeff Overton
Senior vice president, communications
John Blake
Vice president, finance
Robert Hutson
Vice president, general counsel
Casey Coffman
Vice president, ticket sales
Brian Byrnes
Vice president, advertising sales
Tom Comerford
Vice president, special events & security
John Hardin
Vice president, facilities & construction
Billy Ray Johnson
Vice president, community development
Norman Lyons
Vice president, marketing
Christy Martinez
Vice president, information technology
Steven McNeill
Vice president, business operations
Geoff Moore
Vice president, merchandising
Steve Shilts
Assistant vice president, human resources
Terry Turner
Assistant vice president, new media sales
Brad Alberts
Assistant vice president, sponsorship sales
Tom Fireovid
Assistant vice president, ticket operations
Augie Manfredo
Director, Legends of the Game Museum
Amy Polley
Controller
Kellie Fischer
Asst. g.m., player development & scouting
Grady Fuson
Asst. general manager, baseball operations
Dan O'Brien
Director, player development
Trey Hillman
Director, minor league operations
John Lombardo

Director, travel
Chris Lyngos
Director, Major League administration
Judy Johns
Asst. dir., professional and int'l scouting
Monty Clegg
Assistant to director, amateur scouting
Russ Ardolina
Asst.-baseball operations/statistical analysis
Jon Daniels
Director, grounds
Tom Burns
Equipment and home clubhouse manager
Zack Minasian
Visiting clubhouse manager
Kelly Terrell
Senior director, in-park entertainment
Chuck Morgan
Senior director, graphic design
Rainer Uhlir
Director, marketing
Kelly Calvert
Director, events
Sherry Flow
Director, merchandising
Todd Grizzle
Director, ticket operations
Michael Wood
Director, Rangers ticket operations
Mike Lentz
Director, community relations
Taunee Taylor
Director, publications
Kurt Daniels
Director, customer service
Donnie Pordash
Media relations manager
Rich Rice
Medical director
Dr. John Conway
Team internist
Dr. David Hunter
Head trainer
Danny Wheat
Assistant trainer
Ray Ramirez
Strength & conditioning director
Mike Arndt
Cross-checkers
Tim Hallgren (National), Kip Fagg (West), Doug Harris (East), Dave Klipstein (Central)
Professional scouts
Manny Batista, Dave Birecki, Ted Brzenk, Carl Cassel, Jim Fairey, Tim Fortugno, Mark Geigler, Joel Grampietro, Todd Guggiana, Mark Harris, George Lazerique, Jim Lentine, Dennis Meeks, Gary Neibauer, Mike Puastian, Vince Sagisi, Rick Schroeder, Doug Simmons, Randy Taylor, Aris Tirado, Ron Toenies, Mike Toomey, Greg Whitworth

MINOR LEAGUE AFFILIATES

Class	Team	League	Manager
AAA	Oklahoma	Pacific Coast	Bobby Jones
AA	Tulsa	Texas	Tim Ireland
A	Charlotte	Florida State	Darryl Kennedy
A	Savannah	South Atlantic	Paul Carey
Rookie	Gulf Coast Rangers	Gulf Coast	To be announced
Rookie	Pulaski	Appalachian	To be announced

BROADCAST INFORMATION

Radio: KRLD-AM (1080); KESS (1270), Spanish.
TV: KDFW (Channel 4); KDFI (Channel 27).
Cable TV: Fox Sports Southwest.

SPRING TRAINING

Ballpark (city): Charlotte County Stadium (Port Charlotte, Fla.).
Ticket information: 941-625-9500.

Follow the Rangers all season at: www.sportingnews.com/baseball/teams/rangers/

Manager—Jerry Narron (5).
Coaches—Oscar Acosta, Terry Francona, DeMarlo Hale, Rudy Jaramillo (8), Jamie Quirk, Steve Smith.

No.	PITCHERS	B/T	Ht./Wt.	Born	2001 clubs
29	Bell, Rob	R/R	6-5/225	1-17-77	Cincinnati, Louisville, Texas
34	Burba, Dave	R/R	6-4/240	7-7-66	Cleveland
	Cedeno, Jovanny	R/R	6-0/160	10-25-79	Charlotte
30	Cordero, Francisco	R/R	6-2/200	8-11-77	Oklahoma, Texas
46	Davis, Doug	R/L	6-3/190	9-21-75	Texas, Oklahoma
	Dittfurth, Ryan	R/R	6-6/180	10-18-79	Charlotte
	Duchscherer, Justin	R/R	6-3/165	11-19-77	Trenton, Tulsa, Texas, Oklahoma
	Hughes, Travis	R/R	6-5/215	5-25-78	Tulsa
52	Kolb, Danny	R/R	6-4/215	3-29-75	Charlotte, Tulsa, Oklahoma, Texas
	Lewis, Colby	R/R	6-4/215	8-2-79	Charlotte, Tulsa
66	Moreno, Juan	L/L	6-1/205	2-28-75	Texas
	Myette, Aaron	R/R	6-4/195	9-26-77	Oklahoma, Texas, Tulsa
61	Park, Chan Ho	R/R	6-2/204	6-30-73	Los Angeles
45	Petkovsek, Mark	R/R	6-0/198	11-18-65	Texas
39	Powell, Jay	R/R	6-4/225	1-9-72	Houston, Colorado
	Pratt, Andy	L/L	5-11/160	8-27-79	Tulsa
49	Rocker, John	R/L	6-4/225	10-17-74	Atlanta, Cleveland
37	Rogers, Kenny	L/L	6-1/217	11-10-64	Texas
47	Van Poppel, Todd	R/R	6-5/235	12-9-71	Chicago N.L.
	Woodard, Steve	L/R	6-4/217	5-15-75	Cleveland
59	Zimmerman, Jeff	R/R	6-1/200	8-9-72	Texas

No.	CATCHERS	B/T	Ht./Wt.	Born	2001 clubs
33	Haselman, Bill	R/R	6-3/225	5-25-66	Oklahoma, Texas
7	Rodriguez, Ivan	R/R	5-9/205	11-30-71	Texas

No.	INFIELDERS	B/T	Ht./Wt.	Born	2001 clubs
27	Catalanotto, Frank	L/R	6-0/195	4-27-74	Texas
	Hafner, Travis	L/L	6-3/215	6-3-77	Tulsa
	Hart, Jason	R/R	6-3/225	9-5-77	Sacramento
13	Lamb, Mike	L/R	6-1/195	8-9-75	Oklahoma, Texas
25	Palmeiro, Rafael	L/L	6-0/190	9-24-64	Texas
43	Perry, Herbert	R/R	6-2/220	9-15-69	Chicago A.L.
3	Rodriguez, Alex	R/R	6-3/210	7-27-75	Texas
	Romano, Jason	R/R	6-0/185	6-24-79	Tulsa, Oklahoma, Gulf Coast Rangers, Charlotte
	Teixeira, Mark	B/R	6-3/225	4-11-80	DID NOT PLAY
2	Young, Mike	R/R	6-0/185	10-19-76	Oklahoma, Texas

No.	OUTFIELDERS	B/T	Ht./Wt.	Born	2001 clubs
2	Everett, Carl	B/R	6-0/215	6-3-71	Boston, Sarasota, Gulf Coast Red Sox
	Gonzalez, Juan	R/R	6-3/220	10-16-69	Cleveland
29	Greer, Rusty	L/L	6-0/195	1-21-69	Texas, Tulsa
19	Kapler, Gabe	R/R	6-2/208	8-31-75	Tulsa, Texas
	Ludwick, Ryan	R/L	6-3/205	7-13-78	Midland, Sacramento
	Magruder, Chris	B/R	5-11/200	4-26-77	Fresno, Shreveport, Oklahoma, Texas
	Mench, Kevin	R/R	6-0/215	1-7-78	Tulsa
	Monroe, Craig	R/R	6-1/195	2-27-77	Oklahoma, Texas

Ballpark (capacity, surface)
The Ballpark in Arlington (49,115, grass)
Address
1000 Ballpark Way
Arlington, TX 76011
Official website
www.texasrangers.com
Business phone
817-273-5222
Ticket information
817-273-5100
Ticket prices
$40 (lower box, club box)
$32.50 (club reserved)
$28 (corner box)
$22 (terrace club box)
$20 (left field, lower home run porch)
$16 (upper box)
$13 (upper home run porch)
$12 (upper reserved, bleachers)
$6 (grandstand reserved)
$5 (grandstand)
Field dimensions (from home plate)
To left field at foul line, 332 feet
To center field, 400 feet
To right field at foul line, 325 feet
First game played
April 11, 1994 (Brewers 4, Rangers 3)

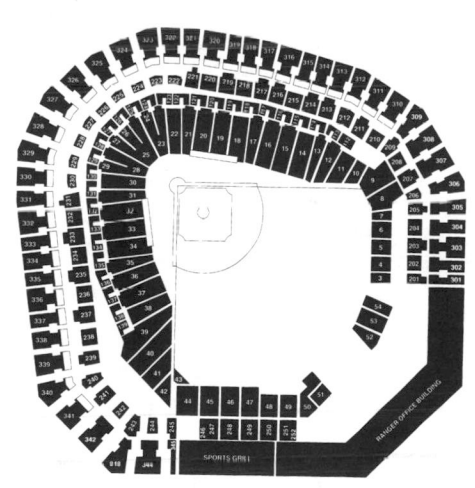

2002 SEASON *Texas Rangers*

2002 SEASON *Texas Rangers*

Date	Opp.	Res.	Score	(inn.*)	Hits	Opp. hits	Winning pitcher	Losing pitcher	Save	Record	Pos.	GB
4-1	At Tor.▲	L	1-8		9	13	Loaiza	Helling		0-1	T1st	0.5
4-3	Ana.	W	3-2		8	9	Rogers	Schoeneweis	Crabtree	1-1	T1st	...
4-4	Ana.	W	7-3		8	8	Oliver	Rapp		2-1	T1st	...
4-5	Ana.	L	3-10		5	13	Ortiz	Glynn		2-2	2nd	0.5
4-6	Sea.	L	7-9	(10)	9	12	Rhodes	Zimmerman	Sasaki	2-3	3rd	1.5
4-7	Sea.	L	5-6		12	12	Franklin	Davis	Sasaki	2-4	4th	2.5
4-8	Sea.	W	5-4		11	8	Venafro	Paniagua	Crabtree	3-4	3rd	1.5
4-10	At Ana.	W	7-5		8	15	Oliver	Rapp	Crabtree	4-4	2nd	1.5
4-11	At Ana.	L	2-7		7	12	Ortiz	Glynn		4-5	3rd	2.5
4-12	At Ana.	L	3-13		11	12	Pote	Helling		4-6	3rd	3.5
4-13	At Oak.	W	13-1		18	8	Davis	Lidle		5-6	3rd	2.5
4-14	At Oak.	W	9-8		11	14	Zimmerman	Mecir	Crabtree	6-6	3rd	2.5
4-15	At Oak.	W	10-8		15	13	Oliver	Heredia	Venafro	7-6	2nd	2.5
4-16	At Sea.	L	7-9		12	11	Franklin	Glynn		7-7	2nd	3.5
4-17	At Sea.	L	4-6		7	11	Moyer	Helling	Sasaki	7-8	2nd	4.5
4-18	At Sea.	W	8-6		13	11	Davis	Tomko	Zimmerman	8-8	2nd	3.5
4-19	Oak.	L	5-9		11	15	Zito	Rogers	Mathews	8-9	2nd	4.5
4-20	Oak.	W	9-6		12	9	Oliver	Heredia		9-9	2nd	4.5
4-21	Oak.	L	6-7		11	13	Mulder	Mahomes	Isringhausen	9-10	2nd	5.5
4-22	Oak.	W	11-2		13	6	Helling	Hudson		10-10	2nd	5.5
4-24	At Tor.	L	5-7		12	10	Frascatore	Mahomes	Koch	10-11	2nd	6.5
4-25	At Tor.	L	5-8		7	9	Quantrill	Rogers	Koch	10-12	2nd	7.5
4-27	At Cle.	W	11-9		10	14	Mahomes	Drew	Zimmerman	11-12	2nd	8.0
4-28	At Cle.	L	3-7		8	11	Burba	Helling		11-13	2nd	9.0
4-29	At Cle.	L	2-9		5	11	Colon	Davis		11-14	2nd	9.0
5-1	Det.	L	3-6	(10)	11	10	Patterson	Zimmerman	Jones	11-15	T2nd	9.0
5-2	Det.	L	4-8		10	14	Holt	Oliver	Anderson	11-16	3rd	10.0
5-3	Det.	L	4-9		7	12	Mlicki	Helling		11-17	3rd	11.0
5-5	Chi.	W	2-0		6	5	Glynn	Biddle	Zimmerman	12-17	3rd	10.5
5-6	Chi.	L	5-10		9	12	D. Wells	Rogers	Foulke	12-18	3rd	10.5
5-7	Chi.	L	4-7		10	9	Garland	Dickey	Foulke	12-19	3rd	11.0
5-8	At Det.	L	4-5		11	12	Jones	Crabtree		12-20	T3rd	11.0
5-9	At Det.	L	2-3		8	10	Mlicki	Davis	Jones	12-21	4th	12.0
5-10	At Det.	L	5-6		9	7	Patterson	Zimmerman	Jones	12-22	4th	13.0
5-11	At Chi.	L	5-6	(10)	10	9	Howry	Venafro		12-23	4th	14.0
5-12	At Chi.	W	16-6		14	8	Mahomes	Garland		13-23	4th	14.0
5-13	At Chi.	L	3-6		5	9	Baldwin	Helling	Foulke	13-24	4th	15.0
5-15	Cle.	L	6-8		10	16	Sabathia	Davis	Wickman	13-25	4th	16.0
5-16	Cle.	L	3-4		6	11	Shuey	Crabtree	Wickman	13-26	4th	17.0
5-17	Cle.	W	12-7		16	12	Rogers	Finley		14-26	4th	17.0
5-18	Tor.	L	3-9		5	11	Carpenter	Myette		14-27	4th	17.0
5-19	Tor.	L	5-6		9	13	Quantrill	Brantley	Koch	14-28	4th	17.0
5-20	Tor.	W	3-2		8	9	Mahomes	Michalak	Zimmerman	15-28	4th	17.0
5-22	At T.B.	W	5-2		9	8	Rogers	Rekar		16-28	4th	16.0
5-23	At T.B.	L	6-10		12	14	Wheeler	Crabtree		16-29	4th	17.0
5-24	At T.B.	W	9-3		9	11	Helling	Sturtze		17-29	4th	16.5
5-25	At Bal.	L	6-7		12	10	Mercedes	Mahomes	Trombley	17-30	4th	17.5
5-27	At Bal.	L	1-3		8	8	Ponson	Glynn	Trombley	17-31	4th	19.0
5-28	At Bal.	W	6-3		12	7	Smart	Paronto		18-31	4th	19.0
5-29	K.C.	W	8-2		7	8	Helling	Suzuki		19-31	4th	19.0
5-30	K.C.	L	2-11		9	19	Reichert	Mahomes		19-32	4th	20.0
5-31	K.C.	L	2-8		6	15	Stein	Davis	Wilson	19-33	4th	21.0
6-1	Min.	L	7-10		7	12	Cressend	Glynn	Guardado	19-34	4th	22.0
6-2	Min.	W	3-2	(10)	9	8	Zimmerman	Hawkins		20-34	4th	22.0
6-3	Min.	L	3-6		6	15	Milton	Helling	Guardado	20-35	4th	23.0
6-4	At Sea.	L	6-11		7	12	Franklin	Venafro		20-36	4th	24.0
6-5	At Sea.	L	4-5		9	6	Paniagua	Smart	Sasaki	20-37	4th	25.0
6-6	At Sea.	L	3-7		5	12	Moyer	Oliver		20-38	4th	26.0
6-8	Hou.	L	4-5	(11)	8	11	Dotel	Crabtree	Jackson	20-39	4th	27.0
6-9	Hou.	W	16-4		17	9	Helling	Bottenfield		21-39	4th	26.0
6-10	Hou.	L	5-6		10	7	J. Powell	Zimmerman	Jackson	21-40	4th	27.0
6-11	At L.A.	W	12-7		16	13	Oliver	Prokopec		22-40	4th	26.5
6-12	At L.A.	L	4-8		6	13	Dreifort	Judd		22-41	4th	27.5
6-13	At L.A.	L	3-5		5	9	Herges	Smart	Shaw	22-42	4th	28.0
6-15	At Hou.	W	12-9		15	13	Mahomes	J. Powell	Zimmerman	23-42	4th	28.0
6-16	At Hou.	L	1-2		6	8	Cruz	Crabtree	Jackson	23-43	4th	29.0
6-17	At Hou.	W	6-2		9	5	Oliver	Elarton		24-43	4th	28.0
6-19	Ana.	W	7-5		11	10	Moreno	Schoeneweis	Zimmerman	25-43	4th	27.5
6-20	Ana.	L	3-4		11	13	Ortiz	Rogers	Percival	25-44	4th	27.5
6-21	Ana.	W	4-3		7	8	Helling	Wise	Zimmerman	26-44	4th	27.5
6-22	At Oak.	W	2-1		5	9	Davis	Hudson	Zimmerman	27-44	4th	26.5
6-23	At Oak.	L	4-5	(10)	6	10	Isringhausen	Cordero		27-45	4th	26.5
6-24	At Oak.	W	9-5		11	8	Bell	Heredia	Venafro	28-45	4th	26.5
6-25	At Ana.	L	7-11		11	16	Ortiz	Rogers		28-46	4th	27.0

Date	Opp.	Res.	Score	(inn.*)	Hits	Opp. hits	Winning pitcher	Losing pitcher	Save	Record	Pos.	GB
6-26	At Ana.	W	8-1	(11)	10	8	Zimmerman	Lukasiewicz		29-46	4th	27.0
6-27	At Ana.	L	2-4		8	7	Washburn	Davis	Percival	29-47	4th	27.0
6-28	At Ana.	W	6-3		12	6	Oliver	Rapp	Zimmerman	30-47	4th	26.0
6-29	Oak.	W	9-6		12	7	Mahomes	Magnante	Zimmerman	31-47	4th	26.0
6-30	Oak.	L	4-15		8	18	Hiljus	Rogers		31-48	4th	27.0
7-1	Oak.	W	3-1		6	9	Venafro	Mulder	Zimmerman	32-48	4th	27.0
7-2	Sea.	L	7-9	(10)	12	11	Nelson	Petkovsek	Sasaki	32-49	4th	28.0
7-3	Sea.	L	4-8		7	13	Sele	Oliver		32-50	4th	29.0
7-4	Sea.	W	6-3		13	10	Bell	Moyer	Venafro	33-50	4th	28.0
7-5	Sea.	W	14-2		13	7	Rogers	Stark		34-50	4th	27.0
7-6	At S.D.	L	3-8		7	13	Jarvis	Holling	Hoffman	34-51	4th	28.0
7-7	At S.D.	W	4-3		11	9	Davis	Jones	Zimmerman	35-51	4th	27.0
7-8	At S.D.	L	2-11		7	12	Williams	Oliver		35-52	4th	28.0
7-12	Col.	W	6-3		11	6	Rogers	Astacio	Zimmerman	36-52	4th	28.0
7-13	Col.	W	10-2		13	4	Helling	Hampton		37-52	4th	27.0
7-14	Col.	L	2-11		7	18	Chacon	Davis		37-53	4th	28.0
7-15	S.F	L	6-7		12	9	Hernandez	Oliver	Nen	37-54	4th	29.0
7-16	S.F	W	2-0		11	6	Bell	Jensen	Zimmerman	38-54	4th	28.0
7-17	S.F	L	2-10		8	12	Rueter	Rogers		38-55	4th	29.0
7-18	At Bal.	W	6-4		11	10	Helling	Douglass	Zimmerman	39-55	4th	29.0
7-20	At T.B.	W	4-1		10	11	Davis	Lopez	Zimmerman	40-55	4th	28.5
7-21	At T.B.	L	1-2		7	3	Zambrano	Oliver	Yan	40-56	4th	29.5
7-22	At T.B.	L	4-7		9	11	Sturtze	Moreno	Yan	40-57	4th	30.5
7-24	Bal.	W	8-7		10	12	Venafro	Trombley	Zimmerman	41-57	4th	30.0
7-25†	Bal.	W	6-5		8	8	Duchscherer	Parrish	Zimmerman	42-57		
7-25‡	Bal.	W	5-2		8	4	Venafro	Mercedes	Zimmerman	43-57	4th	28.5
7-26	Bal.	W	9-7		13	11	Oliver	Towers	Venafro	44-57	4th	28.5
7-27	T.B.	W	13-7		17	9	Bell	Sturtze		45-57	4th	28.5
7-28	T.B.	L	3-7	(10)	8	11	Yan	Foster		45-58	4th	29.5
7-29	T.B.	W	2-0		6	4	Helling	Kennedy		46-58	4th	29.5
7-30	At Bal.	W	6-4	(11)	13	10	Moreno	Trombley	Zimmerman	47-58	4th	29.0
7-31	At N.Y.	W	6-2		10	8	Oliver	Lilly	Zimmerman	48-58	4th	28.0
8-1	At N.Y.	L	7-9		10	13	Hitchcock	Bell	Rivera	48-59	4th	29.0
8-2	At N.Y.	W	12-2		18	4	Myette	Mussina		49-59	4th	29.0
8-4§	At Bos.	L	4-10		12	15	Cone	Helling		49-60		
8-4∞	At Bos.	L	2-6		4	9	Wakefield	Davis		49-61	4th	31.0
8-5	At Bos.	L	3-6		5	11	Arrojo	Oliver	Lowe	49-62	4th	31.0
8-6	At Bos.	L	7-10		10	13	Fossum	Moreno	Lowe	49-63	4th	32.0
8-7	Det.	L	3-7		7	11	Perisho	Venafro		49-64	4th	33.0
8-8	Det.	L	6-19		13	21	Patterson	Venafro		49-65	4th	34.0
8-9	Det.	W	7-3		15	9	Helling	Sparks		50-65	4th	33.0
8-10	Cle.	W	7-2		9	6	Davis	Woodard		51-65	4th	32.0
8-11	Cle.	W	6-5		9	9	Petkovsek	Rocker	Zimmerman	52-65	4th	32.0
8-12	Cle.	L	2-13		4	14	Sabathia	Bell		52-66	4th	33.0
8-14	At Chi.	L	4-7		8	10	Buehrle	Myette	Foulke	52-67	4th	34.0
8-15	At Chi.	L	5-6		11	8	K. Wells	Mahomes	Foulke	52-68	4th	35.0
8-16	At Chi.	L	5-7		10	12	K. Wells	Petkovsek	Foulke	52-69	4th	35.0
8-17	At Tor.	L	3-11		11	16	Loaiza	Oliver		52-70	4th	35.0
8-18	At Tor.	W	12-5		14	7	Moreno	Koch		53-70	4th	35.0
8-19	At Tor.	W	8-4		12	5	Myette	Carpenter		54-70	4th	35.0
8-20	N.Y.	L	5-9		12	12	Stanton	Moreno		54-71	4th	35.0
8-21	N.Y.	W	13-3		17	7	Davis	O. Hernandez		55-71	4th	35.0
8-22	N.Y.	W	8-1		10	5	Oliver	Mussina		56-71	4th	35.0
8-23	N.Y.	L	2-5		10	10	Hitchcock	Bell	Rivera	56-72	4th	36.0
8-24	Bos.	L	4-7		7	11	Beck	Michalak	Urbina	56-73	4th	37.0
8-25	Bos.	W	8-7	(18)	13	16	Michalak	Lowe		57-73	4th	37.0
8-26	Bos.	W	5-4		9	9	Davis	Wakefield	Zimmerman	58-73	4th	36.0
8-28	At Min.	W	10-1		13	4	Oliver	Reed		59-73	4th	35.0
8-29	At Min.	L	8-10		11	10	Milton	Bell	Hawkins	59-74	4th	36.0
8-30	At Min.	W	5-1		9	5	Myette	Mays		60-74	4th	36.0
8-31	At K.C.	W	7-2		6	6	Helling	Byrd		61-74	4th	35.0
9-1	At K.C.	L	7-8	(11)	10	13	Hernandez	Mahomes		61-75	4th	36.0
9-2	At K.C.	W	12-6		17	10	Michalak	George		62-75	4th	36.0
9-4	Min.	W	6-5		9	9	Venafro	Hawkins		63-75	4th	35.5
9-5	Min.	L	2-12		7	20	Mays	Myette		63-76	4th	36.5
9-6	Min.	W	4-3		11	8	Helling	Radke	Zimmerman	64-76	4th	36.0
9-7	K.C.	W	8-2		9	6	Davis	Wilson		65-76	4th	36.0
9-8	K.C.	L	3-8		8	14	George	Oliver		65-77	4th	37.0
9-9	K.C.	W	4-3	(12)	12	7	Zimmerman	Hernandez		66-77	4th	37.0
9-10	At Oak.	L	1-7		4	12	Zito	Myette		66-78	4th	38.0
9-18	Oak.	L	5-6		7	11	Mulder	Venafro	Isringhausen	66-79	4th	39.0
9-19	Oak.	W	10-4		12	10	Davis	Hudson	Michalak	67-79	4th	39.0
9-20	Oak.	L	2-7		8	12	Zito	Oliver		67-80	4th	39.0
9-21	Ana.	W	9-8		15	11	Bell	Valdes	Zimmerman	68-80	4th	38.0
9-22	Ana.	W	5-4		8	9	Mahomes	Holtz		69-80	4th	37.0
9-23	Ana.	W	5-2		10	10	Helling	Ortiz	Zimmerman	70-80	4th	36.0
9-24	Sea.	L	3-9		12	13	Moyer	Davis		70-81	4th	37.0
9-25	Sea.	L	2-13		8	16	Sele	Duchscherer		70-82	4th	38.0

Texas Rangers

2002 SEASON

Date	Opp.	Res.	Score	(inn.*)	Hits	Opp. hits	Winning pitcher	Losing pitcher	Save	Record	Pos.	GB
9-26	Sea.	L	5-7		9	10	Abbott	Bell	Sasaki	70-83	4th	39.0
9-28	At Ana.	W	11-2		15	8	Myette	Valdes		71-83	4th	39.0
9-29	At Ana.	L	2-13		9	13	Ortiz	Helling		71-84	4th	39.0
9-30	At Ana.	W	8-6		13	10	Davis	Hasegawa	Zimmerman	72-84	4th	39.0
10-2	At Oak.	L	4-9		10	12	Zito	Oliver		72-85	4th	40.0
10-3	At Oak.	L	4-5		6	9	Lidle	Michalak	Isringhausen	72-86	4th	41.0
10-4	At Sea.	L	1-16		4	19	Tomko	Myette		72-87	4th	42.0
10-5	At Sea.	L	2-6		4	7	Moyer	Helling		72-88	4th	43.0
10-6	At Sea.	L	0-1		2	4	Pineiro	Davis	Sasaki	72-89	4th	44.0
10-7	At Sea.	W	4-3	12	12	6	Mahomes	Nelson	Zimmerman	73-89	4th	43.0

Monthly records: April (11-14), May (8-19), June (12-15), July (17-10), August (13-16), September (11-10), October (1-5).
*Innings, if other than nine. †First game of a doubleheader. ‡Second game of a doubleheader. §Day separate admission. ∞Night separate admission. ▲Game played in San Juan, Puerto Rico.

HIGHLIGHTS

High point: On April 22, Rick Helling beat Oakland's Tim Hudson 11-2 to push the Rangers to .500 at 10-10. It was the last time during the season that the Rangers saw .500.

Low point: On May 11, reliever Mike Venafro allowed a 10th-inning homer to Jose Valentin to give the Chicago White Sox a 6-5 win. It was the sixth consecutive loss for the Rangers and the second consecutive game in which the bullpen allowed the winning run in the opponents' final at-bat.

Turning point: The Rangers won at Cleveland on April 27, 11-9, but the game really pointed out just how chaotic things were becoming. The Rangers led the game 9-2 at one point, but couldn't hold on to the lead.

Most valuable player: On statistics and work ethic alone, Alex Rodriguez deserved to be A.L. Most Valuable Player. He led the league in homers (52), drove in 135 runs, batted .318 and started every game of the season.

Most valuable pitcher: Jeff Zimmerman got a chance as closer this season. After July 4, Zimmerman converted each of his last 17 save opportunities. He finished the year 4-4 with 28 saves.

Most improved player: In mid-May, the Rangers sent underachieving Doug Davis back to the minors. Out of necessity, they called him back at the end of the month. He recovered to go 9-5 with a 3.77 ERA after June 1.

Most pleasant surprise: Ruben Sierra was named the A.L. Comeback Player of the Year for an unbelievable season at age 36. When the season fell apart, the Rangers called Sierra up. He proved there is still some lightning left in his bat by hitting .291 with 23 home runs and 67 RBIs in 344 at-bats.

Key injuries: Ivan Rodriguez missed the final month of the season after undergoing surgery to repair his left knee. ... Justin Thompson missed his second consecutive year. ... One of Kenny Rogers' ribs was compressing a nerve in his left shoulder and ultimately forced him to have surgery to remove the rib. ... Rusty Greer had a second consecutive season lost to injury.

Notable: Rafael Palmeiro became only the second player in major league history to have at least seven consecutive seasons with 38 or more home runs. The other player to do it: Babe Ruth. ... Palmeiro and Alex Rodriguez teamed to become the fourth pair of teammates to hit 45 or more homers in a season. The others played for the Yankees: Babe Ruth and Lou Gehrig (twice) and Roger Maris and Mickey Mantle.

—EVAN GRANT

RECORDS

2001 regular-season record: 73-89 (4th in A.L. West); 41-41 at home; 32-48 on road; 21-20 vs. A.L. East; 17-28 vs. A.L. Central; 27-31 vs. A.L. West; 8-10 vs. N.L.; 14-28 vs. lefthanded starters; 59-61 vs. righthanded starters; 66-81 on grass; 7-8 on turf; 18-19 in daytime; 55-70 at night; 19-22 in one-run games; 5-8 in extra-inning games; 1-0-0 in doubleheaders.

Team record past five years: 404-406 (.499, ranks 8th in league in that span).

TEAM LEADERS

Batting average: Frank Catalanotto (.330).
At-bats: Alex Rodriguez (632).
Runs: Alex Rodriguez (133).
Hits: Alex Rodriguez (201).
Total Bases: Alex Rodriguez (393).
Doubles: Alex Rodriguez (34).
Triples: Frank Catalanotto (5).
Home runs: Alex Rodriguez (52).
Runs batted in: Alex Rodriguez (135).
Stolen bases: Gabe Kapler (23).
Slugging percentage: Alex Rodriguez (.622).
On-base percentage: Alex Rodriguez (.399).
Wins: Rick Helling (12).
Earned-run average: Doug Davis (4.45).
Complete games: Rick Helling (2).
Shutouts: Rick Helling (1).
Saves: Jeff Zimmerman (28).
Innings pitched: Rick Helling (215.2).
Strikeouts: Rick Helling (154).

GAMES BY POSITION

Catcher: Ivan Rodriguez 106, Bill Haselman 47, Doug Mirabelli 23, Marcus Jensen 11, Mike Hubbard 5, Scott Sheldon 1.
First base: Rafael Palmeiro 113, Andres Galarraga 25, Carlos Pena 16, Randy Velarde 9, Frank Catalanotto 5.
Second base: Michael Young 104, Randy Velarde 52, Frank Catalanotto 13.
Third base: Mike Lamb 74, Ken Caminiti 53, Scott Sheldon 38, Frank Catalanotto 11, Randy Velarde 7, Kelly Dransfeldt 1.
Shortstop: Alex Rodriguez 161, Scott Sheldon 16, Kelly Dransfeldt 3.
Outfield: Gabe Kapler 133, Frank Catalanotto 92, Ricky Ledee 72, Rusty Greer 60, Bo Porter 40, Ruben Mateo 39, Ruben Sierra 36, Chad Curtis 33, Craig Monroe 24, Chris Magruder 12, Cliff Brumbaugh 6, Scott Sheldon 3, Randy Velarde 2.
Designated hitter: Ruben Sierra 50, Rafael Palmeiro 46, Andres Galarraga 39, Randy Velarde 6, Ivan Rodriguez 5, Frank Catalanotto 5, Bo Porter 2, Chad Curtis 2, Rusty Greer 1, Alex Rodriguez 1, Doug Mirabelli 1, Gabe Kapler 1, Craig Monroe 1, Carlos Pena 1.

TOP DRAFT CHOICES

1. **Mark Teixeira,** 3B, Georgia Tech.
4. **Josh Baker,** RHP, Memorial H.S., Houston.
5. **C.J. Wilson,** LHP, Loyola Marymount University.
6. **Ben Keiter,** RHP, Wichita State Univ.
7. **Patrick Boyd,** OF, Clemson Univ.
8. **Masjid Khairy,** OF, Los Angeles C.C.
9. **Gerald Smiley,** RHP, Rainier Beach H.S., Seattle.
10. **Rob Moravek,** RHP, Univ. of Georgia.

TORONTO BLUE JAYS
AMERICAN LEAGUE EAST DIVISION

Blue Jays schedule
Home games shaded
D—Day game (games starting before 5 p.m.)
*All-Star Game at Milwaukee
Subject to changes

April

SUN	MON	TUE	WED	THU	FRI	SAT
	1 D BOS	2	3 BOS	4 D MIN	5 MIN	6 D MIN
7 MIN	8 NYY	9 NYY	10 NYY	11 D NYY	12 TB	13 TB
14 D TB	15	16 BOS	17 BOS	18	19 NYY	20 D NYY
21 NYY	22	23 TEX	24 TEX	25 D TEX	26 ANA	27 ANA
28 ANA	29	30 TEX				

May

SUN	MON	TUE	WED	THU	FRI	SAT
			1 TEX	2 TEX	3 ANA	4 D ANA
5 D ANA	6	7 SEA	8 SEA	9 SEA	10 OAK	11 D OAK
12 D OAK	13	14 SEA	15 SEA	16 SEA	17 OAK	18 D OAK
19 D OAK	20 NYY	21 NYY	22 NYY	23	24 CLE	25 D CLE
26 CLE	27 BOS	28 BOS	29 BOS	30	31 DET	

June

SUN	MON	TUE	WED	THU	FRI	SAT
						1 DET
2 D DET	3 TB	4 TB	5 TB	6 D TB	7 COL	8 D COL
9 D COL	10 CF	11 CF	12 CF	13	14 MON	15 MON
16 D MON	17	18 LA	19 LA	20 LA	21 ARI	22 ARI
23 D ARI	24	25 TB	26 TB	27 D TB	28 MON	29 D MON
30 D MON						

July

SUN	MON	TUE	WED	THU	FRI	SAT
	1 BOS	2 BOS	3 BOS	4 D BOS	5 NYY	6 D NYY
7 D NYY	8	9 *	10	11 BOS	12 BOS	13 D BOS
14 D BOS	15 NYY	16 NYY	17 BAL	18 BAL	19 TB	20 D TB
21 D TB	22 BAL	23 BAL	24 D BAL	25	26 MIN	27 MIN
28 MIN	29 KC	30 KC	31 KC			

August

SUN	MON	TUE	WED	THU	FRI	SAT
				1 D KC	2 BAL	3 D BAL
4 D BAL	5 D BAL	6 SEA	7 SEA	8 D SEA	9 ANA	10 D ANA
11 D ANA	12 OAK	13 OAK	14 D OAK	15	16 TEX	17 TEX
18 TEX	19 KC	20 KC	21 D KC	22	23 BAL	24 BAL
25 D BAL	26 CWS	27 CWS	28 CWS	29 NYY	30 NYY	31 D NYY

September

SUN	MON	TUE	WED	THU	FRI	SAT
1 D NYY	2 D CWS	3 D CWS	4 CWS	5 BOS	6 BOS	7 BOS
8 D BOS	9 CLE	10 CLE	11 CLE	12 TB	13 TB	14 D TB
15 D TB	16 BAL	17 BAL	18 BAL	19 TB	20 TB	21 TB
22 D TB	23	24 BAL	25 BAL	26 BAL	27 DET	28 D DET
29 DET	30					

2002 SEASON
CLUB DIRECTORY

President & CEO
Paul Godfrey
Senior v.p., baseball & general manager
J.P.Ricciardi
Senior vice president, finance
Richard Wong
Sr. vice president, sales and marketing
Paul Allamby
Senior v.p., administration and business
Lisa Novak
Vice president, baseball
Bob Mattick
Vice president, baseball
Tim Wilken
V.p., baseball operations & asst. g.m.
Tim McCleary
Special assistant to general manager
Bill Livesey
Special assistant to president, baseball & g.m./director, international scouting
Wayne Morgan
Vice president, media relations
Howard Starkman
Vice president, ticket sales and service
Steve Smith
V.p., finance and administration
Susan Brioux
V.p., corp. partnerships & business dev.
Mark Lemmon
Vice president, marketing
Peter Cosentino
Director, scouting
Chris Buckley
Assistant director, scouting
Mark Snipp
Director, player development
Dick Scott
Director, minor leagues
Bob Nelson
Director, Florida operations
Ken Carson
Dir., comm., player and alumni relations
Laurel Lindsay

Director, operations
Mario Coutinho
Director, merchandising
Michael Andrejek
Manager, team travel
Bart Given
Trainers
Scott Shannon, George Poulis
Strength and conditioning coordinator
Jeff Krushell
Advance scout
Sal Butera
Team physicians
Dr. Ron Taylor,.Dr. Allan Gross, Dr. Anthony Miniaci, Dr. Steve Mirabello
Special assigment scouts
Chris Bourjos, Pat Kelly, Duane Larson, Ted Lekas, Mel Queen, Gerry Sobeck
Special assign. scout/nat. crosscheckers
Jack Gillis, Mike Mangan
Professional assignment scout
Jeff Taylor
Central regional supervisor
Jeff Cornell
Southeast regional supervisor
Mike Cadahia
Northwest regional supervisor
To be announced
Northeast regional supervisor
Bill Byckowski
Western regional supervisor
Bill Moore
Scouts
Charles Aliano, Tony Arias, Jaymie Bayne, Andy Beene, Armando Cabrera, Rick Cerrone, Joey Davis, Ellis Dungan, Tim Huff, Jim Hughes, Edwin Lawrence, Marty Miller, Ty Nichols, Demerius Pittman, Jorge Rivera, Jim Rooney, Lee Sera, Joe Siers

MINOR LEAGUE AFFILIATES

Class	Team	League	Manager
AAA	Syracuse	International	Omar Malave
AA	Tennessee	Southern	Rocket Wheeler
A	Dunedin	Florida State	Marty Pevey
A	Charleston (WV)	South Atlantic	Paul Elliott
A	Auburn	New York-Penn	Dennis Holmberg
Rookie	Medicine Hat	Pioneer	Rolando Pino

BROADCAST INFORMATION

Radio: The Team (1050).
TV: CBC-TV.
Cable TV: Rogers SportsNet (RSN).

SPRING TRAINING

Ballpark (city): Dunedin Stadium at Grant Field (Dunedin, Fla.).
Ticket information: 800-707-8269; 727-733-0429.

Follow the Blue Jays all season at: www.sportingnews.com/baseball/teams/bluejays/

SPRING TRAINING ROSTER

Manager—Buck Martinez (13).
Coaches—Mark Connor (53), Garth Iorg (16), Gil Patterson (47), Cookie Rojas (4), Carlos Tosca, Mike Barnett.

No.	PITCHERS	B/T	Ht./Wt.	Born	2001 clubs
	Baker, Chris	R/R	6-1/195	8-24-77	Tennessee
51	Borbon, Pedro	L/L	6-1/224	11-15-67	Toronto
	Bowles, Brian	R/R	6-5/220	8-18-76	Syracuse, Toronto
26	Carpenter, Chris	R/R	6-6/225	4-27-75	Toronto
	Cassidy, Scott	R/R	6-2/175	10-3-75	Tennessee, Syracuse
	Chacin, Gustavo	L/L	5-11/185	12-4-80	Tennessee
38	Coco, Pasqual	R/R	6-1/185	9-24-77	Tennessee, Syracuse, Toronto
	Cooper, Brian	R/R	6-1/185	10-22-76	Anaheim
45	Escobar, Kelvim	R/R	6-1/210	4-11-76	Toronto
29	Eyre, Scott	L/L	6-1/200	5-30-72	Syracuse, Toronto
36	File, Bob	R/R	6-4/210	1-28-77	Tennessee, Toronto, Syracuse
32	Halladay, Roy	R/R	6-6/230	5-14-77	Dunedin, Tennessee, Syracuse, Toronto
49	Heredia, Felix	L/L	6-0/180	6-18-76	Chicago N.L.
21	Loaiza, Esteban	R/R	6-3/205	12-31-71	Toronto
	Lyon, Brandon	R/R	6-1/175	8-10-79	Tennessee, Syracuse, Toronto
59	Miller, Justin	R/R	6-2/195	8-27-77	Sacramento
	Orloski, Joe	R/R	6-3/180	5-17-79	Dunedin
39	Parris, Steve	R/R	6-0/195	12-17-67	Toronto, Tennessee, Syracuse
19	Plesac, Dan	L/L	6-5/217	2-4-62	Toronto
	Prokopec, Luke	L/R	5-11/166	2-23-78	Los Angeles, Las Vegas
63	Ricketts, Chad	R/R	6-5/225	2-12-75	Las Vegas
33	Sirotka, Mike	L/L	6-1/200	5-13-71	DID NOT PLAY
	Thurman, Corey	R/R	6-1/240	11-5-78	Wichita, Omaha
No.	**CATCHERS**	**B/T**	**Ht./Wt.**	**Born**	**2001 clubs**
9	Fletcher, Darrin	L/R	6-2/205	10-3-66	Toronto
6	Lawrence, Joe	R/R	6-2/190	2-13-77	Syracuse
17	Phelps, Josh	R/R	6-3/220	5-12-78	Tennessee, Toronto
64	Werth, Jayson	R/R	6-5/190	5-20-79	Tennessee, Dunedin
	Wilson, Tom	R/R	6-3/220	12-19-70	Sacramento, Oakland
No.	**INFIELDERS**	**B/T**	**Ht./Wt.**	**Born**	**2001 clubs**
18	Bush, Homer	R/R	5-10/208	11-12-72	Toronto, Dunedin, Syracuse
25	Delgado, Carlos	L/R	6-3/230	6-25-72	Toronto
	Hinske, Eric	L/R	6-2/225	8-5-77	Sacramento
	Hudson, Orlando	B/R	6-0/185	12-12-77	Tennessee, Syracuse
	Lopez, Felipe	B/R	6-0/175	5-12-80	Tennessee, Syracuse, Toronto
5	Woodward, Chris	R/R	6-0/185	6-27-76	Toronto, Syracuse
No.	**OUTFIELDERS**	**B/T**	**Ht./Wt.**	**Born**	**2001 clubs**
23	Cruz, Jose	B/R	6-0/200	4-19-74	Toronto
	Johnson, Reed	R/R	5-10/180	12-8-76	Tennessee
27	Latham, Chris	B/R	6-0/205	5-26-73	Syracuse, Toronto
43	Mondesi, Raul	R/R	5-11/230	3-12-71	Toronto
24	Stewart, Shannon	R/R	6-1/205	2-25-74	Toronto
10	Wells, Vernon	R/R	6-1/215	12-8-78	Syracuse, Toronto

BALLPARK INFORMATION

Ballpark (capacity, surface)
SkyDome (45,100, artificial)

Address
One Blue Jays Way
Suite 3200
Toronto, Ontario M5V 1J1

Official website
www.bluejays.com

Business phone
416-341-1000

Ticket information
416-341-1234 and 1-888-OK GO JAY

Ticket prices
$44 (premium dugout level)
$41 (field level-infield)
$35 (field level-bases)
$29 (field level-baselines)
$23 (100 & 200 level-outfield; SkyDeck-infield)
$16 (SkyDeck-bases)
$7 (Skydeck-baselines)

Field dimensions (from home plate)
To left field at foul line, 330 feet
To center field, 400 feet
To right field at foul line, 330 feet

First game played
June 5, 1989 (Brewers 5, Blue Jays 3)

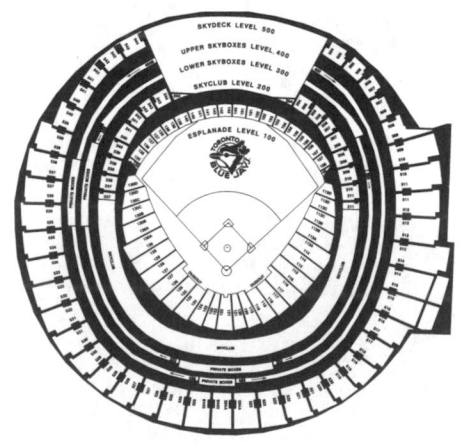

Date	Opp.	Res.	Score	(inn.*)	Hits	Opp. hits	Winning pitcher	Losing pitcher	Save	Record	Pos.	GB
4-1	Tex.▲	W	8-1		13	9	Loaiza	Helling		1-0	1st	+0.5
4-3	At T.B.	L	1-8		7	15	Lopez	Parris		1-1	4th	0.5
4-4	At T.B.	W	11-8		14	13	Quantrill	Hill	Koch	2-1	2nd	0.5
4-5	At T.B.	W	11-0		13	4	Carpenter	Rekar		3-1	2nd	0.5
4-6	At N.Y.	W	13-4		16	10	Loaiza	Parker		4-1	1st	+0.5
4-7	At N.Y.	W	3-2		7	7	Michalak	O. Hernandez	Koch	5-1	1st	+1.5
4-8	At N.Y.	L	5-16		9	20	Clemens	Parris		5-2	1st	+0.5
4-9	T.B.	W	8-1		9	8	Hamilton	Wilson		6-2	1st	+0.5
4-10	T.B.	W	3-2	(10)	6	6	Quantrill	Sturtze		7-2	1st	+0.5
4-11	T.B.	L	3-4		7	8	Yan	Koch		7-3	2nd	0.5
4-13	K.C.	W	2-1		7	4	Michalak	Suppan	Koch	8-3	1st	+0.5
4-14	K.C.	W	5-4		10	9	File	Hernandez		9-3	1st	+0.5
4-15	K.C.	L	2-4		6	8	Stein	Carpenter	Hernandez	9-4	1st	+0.5
4-17	N.Y.	W	6-5		10	8	Loaiza	Keisler	Koch	10-4	T1st	...
4-18	N.Y.	W	7-2		13	6	Michalak	O. Hernandez		11-4	T1st	...
4-19	N.Y.	L	5-6	(17)	14	21	Choate	File	Mendoza	11-5	2nd	1.0
4-20	At K.C.	W	12-4		13	10	Carpenter	Suzuki		12-5	T1st	...
4-21	At K.C.	L	4-5	(13)	7	10	Henry	Plesac		12-6	2nd	1.0
4-22	At K.C.	L	1-5		2	9	Reichert	Loaiza	Hernandez	12-7	2nd	1.0
4-24	Tex.	W	7-5		10	12	Frascatore	Mahomes	Koch	13-7	2nd	1.0
4-25	Tex.	W	8-5		9	7	Quantrill	Rogers	Koch	14-7	T1st	...
4-27	Ana.	W	12-4		15	11	Loaiza	Washburn		15-7	2nd	0.5
4-28	Ana.	L	1-4		6	7	Ortiz	Michalak	Percival	15-8	2nd	0.5
4-29	Ana.	W	2-0		6	9	Parris	Schoeneweis	Koch	16-8	1st	+0.5
4-30	K.C.	L	3-6		9	11	Suppan	Hamilton	Hernandez	16-9	T1st	...
5-1	At Oak.	W	5-4	(10)	10	9	Quantrill	Isringhausen	Koch	17-9	T1st	...
5-2	At Oak.	L	0-6		3	11	Mulder	Loaiza		17-10	T1st	...
5-3	At Oak.	L	2-3	(15)	7	9	Bradford	Borbon		17-11	T1st	...
5-4	At Sea.	W	8-3		8	6	Parris	Abbott		18-11	1st	+1.0
5-5	At Sea.	L	5-7		9	13	Rhodes	Borbon	Sasaki	18-12	T1st	...
5-6	At Sea.	W	11-3		14	6	Carpenter	Halama		19-12	T1st	...
5-8	Oak.	L	5-8		10	12	Mulder	Loaiza	Mecir	19-13	2nd	1.0
5-9	Oak.	L	5-8		10	9	Hudson	Michalak	Isringhausen	19-14	3rd	1.0
5-10	Oak.	L	8-14		13	15	Guthrie	Painter		19-15	3rd	1.0
5-11	Sea.	L	2-7		5	10	Abbott	Hamilton		19-16	3rd	1.5
5-12	Sea.	L	7-11		9	18	Tomko	Escobar		19-17	3rd	2.5
5-13	Sea.	L	5-7		9	14	Moyer	Loaiza	Sasaki	19-18	3rd	3.0
5-15	At Ana.	W	9-3		15	7	Michalak	Valdes		20-18	3rd	3.0
5-16	At Ana.	L	1-3		7	8	Schoeneweis	Parris	Percival	20-19	3rd	3.0
5-17	At Ana.	L	2-4		4	10	Hasegawa	Escobar	Percival	20-20	3rd	3.0
5-18	At Tex.	W	9-3		11	5	Carpenter	Myette		21-20	3rd	3.0
5-19	At Tex.	W	6-5		13	9	Quantrill	Brantley	Koch	22-20	3rd	2.0
5-20	At Tex.	L	2-3		9	8	Mahomes	Michalak	Zimmerman	22-21	3rd	3.0
5-21	Chi.	W	10-3		15	6	Parris	Biddle		23-21	3rd	2.5
5-23	Chi.	W	9-6		14	11	Hamilton	D. Wells	Koch	24-21	3rd	1.5
5-24	Chi.	L	1-3		7	10	K. Wells	Carpenter	Foulke	24-22	3rd	2.0
5-25	At Bos.	L	0-4		1	9	Nomo	Loaiza		24-23	3rd	2.5
5-26	At Bos.	W	5-0		9	9	Michalak	Castillo		25-23	3rd	2.0
5-27	At Bos.	L	2-4		6	10	Wakefield	Parris	Lowe	25-24	3rd	3.0
5-28	At Chi.	L	3-6		8	13	Garland	Hamilton	Howry	25-25	3rd	4.0
5-29	At Chi.	W	4-0		9	6	Carpenter	K. Wells		26-25	3rd	3.5
5-30	At Chi.	L	3-4		6	5	Wunsch	Escobar	Foulke	26-26	3rd	3.5
5-31	Bos.	L	5-11		8	14	Beck	Escobar		26-27	3rd	4.0
6-1	Bos.	L	4-6	(11)	10	16	Lowe	Koch		26-28	3rd	5.0
6-2	Bos.	L	1-2		5	9	Schourek	Plesac	Beck	26-29	4th	6.0
6-3	Bos.	L	4-5		13	8	Pichardo	Carpenter	Lowe	26-30	4th	7.0
6-5	T.B.	W	13-1		16	8	Loaiza	Lopez		27-30	4th	6.5
6-6	T.B.	L	2-6		8	8	Kennedy	Michalak		27-31	4th	6.5
6-7	T.B.	W	8-7		13	13	Borbon	Phelps		28-31	3rd	6.5
6-8	Fla.	W	7-6	(10)	15	12	Koch	Bones		29-31	3rd	6.5
6-9	Fla.	L	1-6		2	9	Burnett	Carpenter		29-32	3rd	6.5
6-10	Fla.	L	2-7		7	8	Penny	Loaiza		29-33	4th	7.5
6-11	Atl.	W	9-4		13	7	File	Burkett		30-33	3rd	7.0
6-12	Atl.	L	0-3		5	7	Perez	Parris	Rocker	30-34	3rd	8.0
6-13	Atl.	W	12-5		15	14	Hamilton	Glavine		31-34	3rd	7.0
6-15	At Mon.	W	9-3		15	13	Carpenter	Vazquez		32-34	3rd	7.5
6-16	At Mon.	L	2-7		10	11	Blank	Loaiza		32-35	3rd	7.5
6-17	At Mon.	L	1-4		9	8	Mota	Quantrill		32-36	3rd	8.5
6-18	At Bal.	L	2-3		9	10	Ponson	Borbon	Trombley	32-37	4th	9.0
6-19	At Bal.	L	1-5		9	11	Towers	Hamilton	Groom	32-38	4th	10.0
6-20	At Bal.	W	6-5		10	10	Quantrill	McElroy	Koch	33-38	4th	10.0
6-22	At Bos.	W	4-3		7	7	Borbon	Schourek	Koch	34-38	T3rd	9.5
6-23	At Bos.	W	9-6		13	16	File	Castillo	Koch	35-38	3rd	8.5
6-24	At Bos.	W	5-2		5	8	Plesac	Wakefield	Koch	36-38	3rd	7.5

Date	Opp.	Res.	Score	(inn.*)	Hits	Opp. hits	Winning pitcher	Losing pitcher	Save	Record	Pos.	GB
6-25	Bal.	L	2-8		5	15	Roberts	Hamilton		36-39	3rd	8.5
6-26	Bal.	W	3-1		5	7	Carpenter	Johnson	Koch	37-39	3rd	8.5
6-27	Bal.	L	3-7		5	12	Mercedes	Loaiza		37-40	3rd	8.5
6-28	Bal.	L	0-5		2	8	Ponson	Michalak		37-41	T3rd	8.5
6-29	Bos.	W	8-4		10	8	Quantrill	Florie		38-41	T3rd	7.5
6-30	Bos.	L	5-7		14	14	Cone	Hamilton		38-42	T3rd	8.5
7-1	Bos.	L	0-4		2	7	Arrojo	Carpenter		38-43	4th	9.5
7-2	Bos.	L	4-16		10	17	Nomo	Loaiza		38-44	4th	10.5
7-3	At T.B.	L	2-7		9	13	Kennedy	Michalak	Phelps	38-45	4th	11.0
7-4	At T.B.	W	8-1		15	7	Parris	Rekar		39-45	4th	11.0
7-5	At T.B.	W	7-4		11	10	Hamilton	Rupe	Koch	40-45	3rd	11.0
7-6	Mon.	L	7-10		8	12	Lloyd	Quantrill	Urbina	40-46	3rd	12.0
7-7	Mon.	W	9-8	(11)	15	17	Plesac	Strickland		41-46	3rd	11.0
7-8	Mon.	W	9-3		12	12	Michalak	Armas	Quantrill	42-46	3rd	11.0
7-12	At Phi.	W	2-1	(11)	8	4	Escobar	Santiago	Koch	43-46	3rd	10.0
7-13	At Phi.	L	2-5		5	8	Daal	Plesac	Mesa	43-47	3rd	10.0
7-14	At Phi.	W	4-2		10	6	Hamilton	Figueroa	Koch	44-47	3rd	10.0
7-15	At N.Y.	L	2-6		7	11	Reed	Michalak		44-48	3rd	10.0
7-16	At N.Y.	L	0-3		4	10	Trachsel	Halladay	Benitez	44-49	3rd	11.0
7-17	At N.Y.	L	0-1		10	4	Leiter	Carpenter	Benitez	44-50	3rd	12.0
7-18	Bos.	L	4-5		8	9	Garces	Koch	Lowe	44-51	3rd	12.5
7-19	Bos.	W	4-3		8	7	Escobar	Lowe		45-51	3rd	11.5
7-20	At N.Y.	W	10-4		13	10	Loaiza	Jodie		46-51	3rd	10.5
7-21	At N.Y.	W	5-3		8	8	Quantrill	Rivera	Koch	47-51	3rd	9.5
7-22	At N.Y.	L	3-7		6	11	Mussina	Carpenter		47-52	3rd	10.5
7-23	At N.Y.	L	2-7		9	8	Clemens	Parris		47-53	3rd	11.5
7-24	At Bos.	L	4-6		10	14	Cone	Hamilton	Lowe	47-54	3rd	12.5
7-25	At Bos.	W	4-3	(10)	8	4	Quantrill	Lowe	Koch	48-54	3rd	12.5
7-26	At Bos.	L	3-6		9	10	Nomo	File	Beck	48-55	3rd	13.5
7-27	N.Y.	L	1-9		5	13	Mussina	Carpenter		48-56	3rd	14.5
7-28	N.Y.	L	1-12		2	15	Clemens	Escobar		48-57	3rd	15.5
7-29	N.Y.	L	3-9		8	15	Pettitte	Hamilton		48-58	3rd	16.5
7-31	Min.	W	3-1		8	10	Loaiza	Mays	Koch	49-58	3rd	15.5
8-1	Min.	W	3-1		5	7	Halladay	Lohse	Koch	50-58	3rd	15.5
8-2	Min.	L	4-9		16	12	Reed	Carpenter		50-59	3rd	15.5
8-3	Bal.	W	10-1		15	4	Escobar	Mercedes		51-59	3rd	15.5
8-4	Bal.	W	2-1		5	4	Lyon	Ponson	Koch	52-59	3rd	15.5
8-5	Bal.	W	5-4		9	11	Loaiza	Towers	Koch	53-59	3rd	14.5
8-7	At Sea.	L	4-5	(14)	11	12	Halama	DeWitt		53-60	3rd	14.0
8-8	At Sea.	L	4-12		8	19	Moyer	Carpenter		53-61	3rd	15.0
8-9	At Sea.	W	6-5		14	10	Quantrill	Garcia	Koch	54-61	3rd	15.0
8-10	At Ana.	L	7-8		12	11	Schoeneweis	Lyon	Percival	54-62	3rd	15.0
8-11	At Ana.	W	7-6	(10)	17	14	Plesac	Levine	Koch	55-62	3rd	14.0
8-12	At Ana.	L	5-6		10	11	Levine	Plesac	Percival	55-63	3rd	14.0
8-14	Oak.	W	6-3		10	8	Koch	Isringhausen		56-63	3rd	14.0
8-15	Oak.	W	5-2		8	6	Escobar	Zito	Koch	57-63	3rd	14.0
8-16	Oak.	L	4-8		9	12	Lidle	Lyon		57-64	3rd	15.0
8-17	Tex.	W	11-3		16	11	Loaiza	Oliver		58-64	3rd	15.0
8-18	Tex.	L	5-12		7	14	Moreno	Koch		58-65	3rd	15.0
8-19	Tex.	L	4-8		5	12	Myette	Carpenter		58-66	3rd	15.0
8-20	At Min.	W	3-2		5	6	Escobar	Mays	Koch	59-66	3rd	15.0
8-21	At Min.	W	7-5		12	11	Lyon	Cressend	Koch	60-66	3rd	14.0
8-22	At Min.	L	3-6		9	11	Reed	Loaiza		60-67	3rd	14.0
8-23	At Min.	W	6-2		13	5	Halladay	Lohse		61-67	3rd	14.0
8-24	At Bal.	W	5-0		10	7	Carpenter	Johnson		62-67	3rd	13.0
8-25	At Bal.	W	9-0		9	5	Escobar	Maduro		63-67	3rd	13.0
8-26	At Bal.	W	5-1		10	3	Lyon	Mercedes		64-67	3rd	12.0
8-28	At N.Y.	L	0-4		8	12	Mussina	Loaiza	Rivera	64-68	3rd	13.0
8-29	At N.Y.	W	3-2		8	8	Halladay	Hitchcock	Koch	65-68	3rd	12.0
8-30	At N.Y.	L	4-5	(11)	10	12	Witasick	Eyre		65-69	3rd	13.0
8-31	Det.	L	3-4		8	8	Sparks	Borbon	Anderson	65-70	3rd	14.0
9-1	Det.	W	3-1		7	4	Lyon	Weaver	Plesac	66-70	3rd	14.0
9-2	Det.	W	11-0		10	5	Loaiza	Lima		67-70	3rd	14.0
9-3	N.Y.	L	5-7		12	11	Wohlers	Koch	Mendoza	67-71	3rd	15.0
9-4	N.Y.	W	14-0		17	6	Carpenter	Pettitte		68-71	3rd	14.0
9-5	N.Y.	L	3-4		9	7	Clemens	Escobar	Rivera	68-72	3rd	15.0
9-7	At Det.	W	2-1		7	7	Lyon	Lima	Koch	69-72	3rd	15.0
9-8	At Det.	L	3-4		6	9	Murray	Halladay	Anderson	69-73	3rd	16.0
9-9	At Det.	W	6-3		10	10	Carpenter	Cornejo		70-73	3rd	16.0
9-18	Bal.	W	8-5		13	9	Plesac	Julio	Koch	71-73	3rd	16.0
9-19	Bal.	W	4-1		9	5	Halladay	Maduro	Koch	72-73	3rd	16.0
9-20	Bal.	L	6-12		14	13	Parrish	File		72-74	3rd	16.0
9-21	T.B.	L	4-7		7	12	Rekar	Lyon	Yan	72-75	3rd	16.0
9-22	T.B.	W	8-7		11	11	Coco	Colome	Koch	73-75	3rd	15.0
9-23	T.B.	L	0-1		5	4	Kennedy	Escobar	Yan	73-76	3rd	16.0
9-24	At Cle.	W	3-2	(11)	9	6	File	Baez	Eyre	74-76	3rd	15.5
9-25	At Cle.	L	7-11		9	14	Riske	Plesac		74-77	3rd	15.5
9-27	At T.B.	L	1-5		5	10	Colome	Eyre		74-78	3rd	16.5

Date	Opp.	Res.	Score	(inn.*)	Hits	Opp. hits	Winning pitcher	Losing pitcher	Save	Record	Pos.	GB
9-28	At T.B.	L	1-6		6	9	Rekar	Escobar	Phelps	74-79	3rd	17.5
9-29	At T.B.	L	2-5		9	9	Bierbrodt	Halladay	Yan	74-80	3rd	17.5
9-30	At T.B.	W	6-5	(12)	13	13	Quantrill	Creek	Eyre	75-80	3rd	17.0
10-1	At Bal.	W	1-0		7	6	Loaiza	Bauer	Koch	76-80	3rd	17.0
10-2	At Bal.	L	3-4		6	10	Roberts	DeWitt		76-81	3rd	18.0
10-3	At Bal.	W	7-6		13	10	Eyre	Groom	Koch	77-81	3rd	18.0
10-5†	Cle.	W	5-0		9	2	Halladay	Finley		78-81		
10-5‡	Cle.	W	4-3	(11)	9	11	File	Drese		79-81	3rd	16.0
10-6	Cle.	W	5-2		8	5	Carpenter	Drew	Quantrill	80-81	3rd	15.0
10-7	Cle.	L	2-3		5	6	Sabathia	Lyon	Rocker	80-82	3rd	16.0

Monthly records: April (16-9), May (10-18), June (12-15), July (11-16), August (16-12), September (10-10), October (5-2).
*Innings, if other than nine. †First game of a doubleheader. ‡Second game of a doubleheader. ▲Game played in San Juan, Puerto Rico.

HIGHLIGHTS

High point: On May 1, a rare victory over Oakland pushed the club's record to 17-9. Alas, the A's and Seattle Mariners administered a reality check by winning nine of the next 11 games from the Blue Jays.

Low point: A three-game sweep by the Yankees July 27-29 immediately preceded the front office neglecting to swing a deal for a starting pitcher at the July 31 trade deadline. Instead, the Jays promoted young players from Class AAA Syracuse.

Turning point: Heading into a four-game set with the Red Sox on May 31 with a 26-26 record, the Jays got swept at home and failed to reach .500 again.

Most valuable player: Jose Cruz Jr. had his best season with the glove and bat since breaking into the majors in 1997. He hit 34 home runs and was successful on 32 of 37 stolen-base attempts.

Most valuable pitcher: Working primarily as the setup man for closer Billy Koch, Paul Quantrill led the A.L. in appearances and shared the club lead with 11 victories.

Most improved player: Roy Halladay started the season at Class AAA Syracuse. After being called up in July, Halladay became the club's most dominant starter, going 5-3 with a 3.16 ERA.

Most pleasant surprise: The major league experience of 30-year-old lefty Chris Michalak consisted of only five relief appearances with Arizona before he made Toronto's rotation in spring training. He started off with a 3-0 record with a 1.62 ERA, but was released in August and picked up by Texas after compiling a 6-7 mark and 4.62 ERA.

Key injuries: Mike Sirotka had shoulder surgery in April and missed the entire season. ... Homer Bush was out twice for extended periods with a pulled right hamstring. ... Steve Parris was placed on the disabled list July 24 with shoulder tendinitis and did not return. ... Jose Cruz Jr. missed 13 games due to a lower back strain.

Notable: Tony Fernandez, serving a fourth stint with his original club, led the A.L. with 15 pinch hits and retired from baseball with the most hits among Dominican-born players (2,276). ... Carlos Delgado surpassed 100 RBIs for the fourth consecutive season, 100 runs for the third straight year, and 100 walks for the second consecutive time. ... Shannon Stewart hit .300 for the third consecutive year and joined Fernandez, Paul Molitor and John Olerud as the only Jays to have achieved 200 hits in a season.

—TOM MALONEY

RECORDS

2001 regular-season record: 80-82 (3rd in A.L. East); 40-42 at home; 40-40 on road; 37-39 vs. A.L. East; 19-13 vs. A.L. Central; 16-20 vs. A.L. West; 8-10 vs. N.L.; 16-20 vs. lefthanded starters; 64-62 vs. righthanded starters; 29-31 on grass; 51-51 on turf; 25-32 in daytime; 55-50 at night; 28-21 in one-run games; 10-6 in extra-inning games; 1-0-0 in doubleheaders.

Team record past five years: 411-399 (.507, ranks 7th in league in that span).

TEAM LEADERS

Batting average: Shannon Stewart (.316).
At-bats: Shannon Stewart (640).
Runs: Shannon Stewart (103).
Hits: Shannon Stewart (202).
Total Bases: Carlos Delgado (310).
Doubles: Shannon Stewart (44).
Triples: Shannon Stewart (7).
Home runs: Carlos Delgado (39).
Runs batted in: Carlos Delgado (102).
Stolen bases: Jose Cruz (32).
Slugging percentage: Carlos Delgado (.540).
On-base percentage: Carlos Delgado (.408).
Wins: Chris Carpenter, Esteban Loaiza, Paul Quantrill (11).

Earned-run average: Chris Carpenter (4.09).
Complete games: Chris Carpenter (3).
Shutouts: Chris Carpenter (2).
Saves: Billy Koch (36).
Innings pitched: Chris Carpenter (215.2).
Strikeouts: Chris Carpenter (157).

GAMES BY POSITION

Catcher: Darrin Fletcher 129, Alberto Castillo 66, Josh Phelps 7.
First base: Carlos Delgado 161, Luis Lopez 5, Chris Woodward 2, Brad Fullmer 1.
Second base: Homer Bush 78, Jeff Frye 47, Cesar Izturis 41, Chris Woodward 17, Ryan Freel 7.
Third base: Tony Batista 72, Felipe Lopez 47, Luis Lopez 28, Jeff Frye 27, Chris Woodward 10.
Shortstop: Alex S. Gonzalez 154, Cesar Izturis 6, Chris Woodward 4, Felipe Lopez 3, Jeff Frye 2.
Outfield: Raul Mondesi 149, Jose Cruz 143, Shannon Stewart 142, Brian Simmons 37, Chris Latham 31, Vernon Wells 30, Ryan Freel 1, Jeff Frye 1.
Designated hitter: Brad Fullmer 135, Shannon Stewart 13, Tony Fernandez 13, Luis Lopez 4, Brian Simmons 2, Darrin Fletcher 1, Jose Cruz 1, Chris Woodward 1.

TOP DRAFT CHOICES

1. **Gabe Gross**, OF, Auburn University.
2. **Brandon League**, RHP, St. Louis H.S., Honolulu.
3. **Tyrell Godwin**, OF, U. of North Carolina.
4. **Chris Sheffield**, RHP, U. of Miami (Fla.).
5. **Michael Rouse**, SS, Cal State Fullerton.
6. **Lee Delfino**, SS, East Carolina Univ.
7. **Jason Colson**, RHP, Winthrop Univ.
8. **Sean Grimes**, LHP, Saunders H.S., London, Ontario.
9. **Luke Hetherington**, OF, Kentwood H.S., Covington, Wash.
10. **Ryan Costello**, LHP, Montclair State (N.J.) University.

ARIZONA DIAMONDBACKS
NATIONAL LEAGUE WEST DIVISION

Diamondbacks schedule
Home games shaded
D—Day game (games starting before 5 p.m.)
*All-Star Game at Milwaukee.
Subject to changes.

April

SUN	MON	TUE	WED	THU	FRI	SAT
	1 D SD	2 SD	3 SD	4	5 MIL	6 MIL
7 D MIL	8 SD	9 D SD	10 SD	11 COL	12 COL	13 D COL
14 D COL	15 STL	16 STL	17 D STL	18	19 COL	20 COL
21 D COL	22	23 ATL	24 ATL	25 ATL	26 FLA	27 FLA
28 D FLA	29	30 NYM				

May

SUN	MON	TUE	WED	THU	FRI	SAT
		1 NYM	2 NYM	3 MON	4 MON	
5 D MON	6 PIT	7 PIT	8 PIT	9	10 PHI	11 PHI
12 D PHI	13 PIT	14 PIT	15 PIT	16 PHI	17 PHI	18 PHI
19 D PHI	20	21 SF	22 SF	23	24 LA	25 LA
26 D LA	27 SF	28 D SF	29 SF	30 SF	31 LA	

June

SUN	MON	TUE	WED	THU	FRI	SAT
						1 D LA
2 D LA	3 HOU	4 HOU	5 HOU	6	7 BOS	8 D BOS
9 D BOS	10 NYY	11 NYY	12 D NYY	13	14 DET	15 DET
16 D DET	17	18 BAL	19 BAL	20 D BAL	21 TOR	22 TOR
23 D TOR	24	25 HOU	26 HOU	27 D HOU	28 CLE	29 CLE
30 D CLE						

July

SUN	MON	TUE	WED	THU	FRI	SAT
	1 LA	2 LA	3 LA	4 D SF	5 SF	6 SF
7 D SF	8	9 *	10	11 LA	12 LA	13 D LA
14 LA	15 D SF	16 SF	17 COL	18 D COL	19 SD	20 SD
21 D SD	22 COL	23 COL	24 COL	25 D SD	26 SD	27 SD
28 D SD	29	30 MON	31 MON			

August

SUN	MON	TUE	WED	THU	FRI	SAT
				1 MON	2 NYM	3 NYM
4 D NYM	5 D NYM	6 ATL	7 ATL	8 ATL	9 D FLA	10 FLA
11 D FLA	12	13 CIN	14 CIN	15 CIN	16 D CUB	17 D CUB
18 D CUB	19	20 CIN	21 CIN	22 CIN	23 CUB	24 CUB
25 D CUB	26 LA	27 LA	28 LA	29	30 SF	31 SF

September

SUN	MON	TUE	WED	THU	FRI	SAT
1 D SF	2 D LA	3 LA	4 D LA	5 D SF	6 D SF	7 SF
8 SF	9 SD	10 SD	11 SD	12	13 MIL	14 MIL
15 D MIL	16	17 SD	18 SD	19 D SD	20 D COL	21 D COL
22 D COL	23 STL	24 STL	25 D COL	26 COL	27 COL	28 COL
29 D COL	30					

2002 SEASON
CLUB DIRECTORY

Managing general partner
Jerry Colangelo
President
Richard Dozer
Vice president and general manager
Joe Garagiola Jr.
Sr. vice president, sales and marketing
Scott Brubaker
Vice president, finance
Thomas Harris
V.p., tickets and special services
Dianne Aguilar
Vice president, corporate sales
Mark Fernandez
Assistant general manager
Sandy Johnson
Director of Hispanic marketing
Richard Saenz
Director of public relations
Mike Swanson
Director of ballpark services
Russ Amaral
Director of suite services
Diney Mahoney
Director of team travel
Roger Riley
Director of player development
Tommy Jones
Director of Pacific Rim operations
Jim Marshall
Director of scouting
Mike Rizzo

Director of baseball operations
Bob Miller
Trainer
Paul Lessard
Assistant trainer
Dave Edwards
Club physician
Dr. Michael Lee
National scouting supervisor
Kendall Carter
Regional supervisors
Mark Baca, Ed Durkin, Kris Kline, Charles Scott
Latin America supervisor
Junior Noboa
Professional scouts
Bill Earnhart, Mike Piatnik
Major League and advance scouts
Mack Babitt, Jim Marshall
Special assignment scouts
Bryan Lambe, Phil Rizzo
Scouts
Ray Blanco, Fred Costello, Mike Daughtry, Doug Gassaway, Ed Gustafson, Scott Jaster, Steve Kmetko, Hal Kurtzman, Greg Lonigro, Steve McAllister, Howard McCullough, Matt Merullo, Mike Valarezo, Luke Wrenn

MINOR LEAGUE AFFILIATES

Class	Team	League	Manager
AAA	Tucson	Pacific Coast	Al Pedrique
AA	El Paso	Texas	Chip Hale
A	Lancaster	California	Steve Scarsone
A	South Bend	Midwest	Dick Schofield
A	Yakima	Northwest	Mike Aldrete
Rookie	Missoula	Pioneer	Bill Plummer

BROADCAST INFORMATION

Radio: KTAR-AM (620).
TV: KTVK (Channel 3).
Cable TV: Fox Sports Net Arizona.

SPRING TRAINING

Ballpark (city): Tucson Electric Park (Tucson, Ariz.).
Ticket information: 520-434-1111.

Follow the Diamondbacks all season at:
www.sportingnews.com/baseball/teams/diamondbacks/

Manager—Bob Brenly (15).
Coaches—Chuck Kniffin, Bob Melvin (3), Dwayne Murphy (21), Eddie Rodriguez (14), Glenn Sherlock (53), Robin Yount.

No.	PITCHERS	B/T	Ht./Wt.	Born	2001 clubs
34	Anderson, Brian	B/L	6-1/183	4-26-72	Arizona, Tucson
43	Batista, Miguel	R/R	6-0/190	2-19-71	Arizona
51	Johnson, Randy	R/L	6-10/230	9-10-63	Arizona
49	Kim, Byung-Hyun	R/R	5-11/176	1-21-79	Arizona
	Koplove, Mike	R/R	6-0/160	8-30-76	El Paso, Tucson, Arizona
31	Mantei, Matt	R/R	6-1/190	7-7-73	Arizona
	Morgan, Mike	R/R	6-2/220	10-8-59	Arizona
	Myers, Mike	L/L	6-4/214	6-26-69	Colorado
24	Patterson, John	R/R	6-5/183	1-30-78	El Paso, Lancaster, Tucson
65	Prinz, Bret	R/R	6-3/185	6-15-77	Tucson, Arizona
27	Reynoso, Armando	R/R	6-0/204	5-1-66	Arizona
66	Sanchez, Duaner	R/R	6-0/160	11-14-79	El Paso, Lancaster
38	Schilling, Curt	R/R	6-4/231	11-14-66	Arizona
30	Stottlemyre, Todd	L/R	6-3/215	5-20-65	DID NOT PLAY
22	Swindell, Greg	L/L	6-3/230	1-2-65	Arizona
	Valverde, Jose	R/R	6-4/220	7-24-79	El Paso
	Ward, Jeremy	R/R	6-3/220	2-24-78	Tucson, El Paso

No.	CATCHERS	B/T	Ht./Wt.	Born	2001 clubs
48	Barajas, Rod	R/R	6-2/220	9-5-75	Arizona, Tucson
26	Miller, Damian	R/R	6-2/212	10-13-69	Arizona
39	Moeller, Chad	R/R	6-3/210	2-18-75	Tucson, Arizona

No.	INFIELDERS	B/T	Ht./Wt.	Born	2001 clubs
33	Bell, Jay	R/R	6-0/184	12-11-65	Arizona
44	Durazo, Erubiel	L/L	6-3/225	1-23-74	Arizona, Tucson
64	Cintron, Alexander	B/R	6-1/170	12-17-78	Tucson, Arizona
28	Colbrunn, Greg	R/R	6-0/205	7-26-69	Arizona, Tucson
4	Counsell, Craig	L/R	6-0/175	8-21-70	Arizona
17	Grace, Mark	L/L	6-2/200	6-28-64	Arizona
	Overbay, Lyle	L/L	6-2/215	1-28-77	El Paso, Arizona
63	Spivey, Junior	R/R	6-0/185	1-28-75	Tucson, Arizona
9	Williams, Matt	R/R	6-2/214	11-28-65	Arizona, Tucson
5	Womack, Tony	L/R	5-9/159	9-25-69	Arizona, Tucson

No.	OUTFIELDERS	B/T	Ht./Wt.	Born	2001 clubs
29	Bautista, Danny	R/R	5-11/170	5-24-72	Arizona
25	Dellucci, David	L/L	5-11/198	10-31-73	Arizona
	Devore, Doug	L/L	6-4/200	12-14-77	El Paso
12	Finley, Steve	L/L	6-2/180	3-12-65	Arizona
20	Gonzalez, Luis	L/R	6-2/190	9-2-67	Arizona
30	Guillen, Jose	R/R	5-11/195	5-17-76	Tampa Bay, Durham
	Gomez, Luis	B/R	6-2/185	5-18-80	El Paso, Yakima, Lancaster

2002 SEASON Arizona Diamondbacks

BALLPARK INFORMATION

Ballpark (capacity, surface)
Bank One Ballpark (49,033, grass)
Address
401 East Jefferson
Phoenix, AZ 85004
Official website
www.azdiamondbacks.com
Business phone
602-462-6500
Ticket information
602-514-8400
Ticket prices
$12 to $28 (lower level)
$1 to $19 (upper level)
$47 to $75 (lower level premium seats)
$30 and $39 (Infiniti Diamond level)
Field dimensions (from home plate)
To left field at foul line, 330 feet
To center field, 407 feet
To right field at foul line, 334 feet
First game played
March 31, 1998 (Rockies 9, Diamondbacks 2)

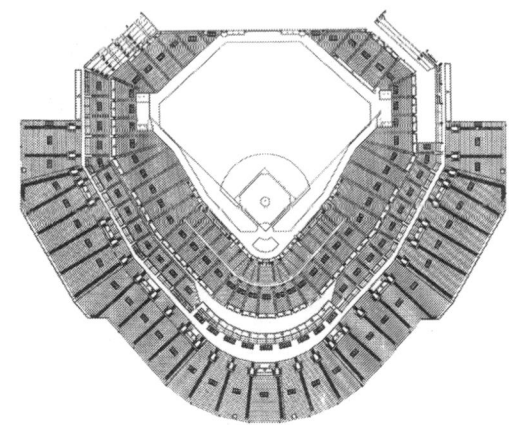

2002 SEASON — *Arizona Diamondbacks*

Date	Opp.	Res.	Score	(inn.*)	Hits	Opp. hits	Winning pitcher	Losing pitcher	Save	Record	Pos.	GB
4-3	At L.A.	W	3-2		12	5	Johnson	Nunez	Mantei	1-0	T1st	...
4-4	At L.A.	W	7-2		14	5	Schilling	Dreifort		2-0	T1st	...
4-5	At L.A.	L	5-7		9	8	Ashby	Anderson	Shaw	2-1	3rd	1.0
4-6	St.L.	L	9-12		12	18	Hermanson	Reynoso		2-2	4th	1.0
4-7	St.L.	L	4-8		11	11	Kile	Witt		2-3	T4th	1.5
4-8	St.L.	L	4-9		7	13	Ankiel	Johnson	Timlin	2-4	5th	2.0
4-10	L.A.	W	2-0		3	2	Schilling	Brown		3-4	T3rd	2.0
4-11	L.A.	L	5-11		5	11	Dreifort	Anderson		3-5	T3rd	3.0
4-12	L.A.	L	4-5		11	12	Ashby	Reynoso	Shaw	3-6	5th	3.0
4-13	At Col.	W	7-3		8	7	Johnson	Bohanon		4-6	T4th	3.0
4-14	At Col.	L	8-9		13	14	Myers	Kim	Jimenez	4-7	5th	3.0
4-15	At Col.	L	7-10	(10)	11	13	Estrada	Brohawn		4-8	5th	3.0
4-16	At St.L.	W	2-1		5	6	Ellis	Morris	Mantei	5-8	5th	2.5
4-17	At St.L.	W	17-4		18	4	Reynoso	Hermanson		6-8	5th	2.5
4-18	At St.L.	L	1-3		6	5	Kile	Johnson	Kline	6-9	5th	3.5
4-20	Col.	W	3-2		6	7	Kim	White		7-9	4th	3.0
4-21	Col.	W	10-5		8	11	Ellis	Villone		8-9	4th	2.0
4-22	Col.	L	1-2		3	6	Astacio	Reynoso	Jimenez	8-10	4th	3.0
4-23	Fla.	W	9-0		7	6	Johnson	Dempster		9-10	4th	2.5
4-24	Fla.	W	9-8		10	13	Prinz	Almanza	Springer	10-10	T3rd	1.5
4-25	Fla.	W	10-7		12	13	Schilling	Grilli	Prinz	11-10	T3rd	1.5
4-26	Atl.	W	13-6		15	8	Ellis	Maddux		12-10	T2nd	0.5
4-27	Atl.	L	0-9		3	14	Burkett	Reynoso		12-11	3rd	1.0
4-28	Atl.	L	1-3		6	7	Glavine	Johnson	Rocker	12-12	4th	2.0
4-29	Atl.	W	7-5		10	7	Sabel	Perez	Brohawn	13-12	3rd	2.0
5-1	At Mon.	W	8-3		10	9	Schilling	Reames		14-12	2nd	1.0
5-2	At Mon.	L	3-4		5	4	Armas	Anderson	Lloyd	14-13	4th	2.0
5-3	At Mon.	W	2-1		6	3	Kim	Lloyd	Prinz	15-13	2nd	2.0
5-4	At N.Y.	L	2-4		8	8	Reed	Batista	Franco	15-14	4th	2.0
5-5	At N.Y.	L	1-8		6	12	Rusch	Ellis		15-15	4th	2.0
5-6	At N.Y.	W	8-2		12	8	Schilling	Trachsel		16-15	2nd	1.0
5-7	Cin.	L	4-5	(10)	10	14	Graves	Swindell		16-16	3rd	2.0
5-8	Cin.	W	4-3	(11)	10	3	Brohawn	Graves		17-16	3rd	1.0
5-9	Cin.	W	5-2		11	5	Batista	Mercado	Prinz	18-16	2nd	1.0
5-11	Phi.	L	1-5		6	12	Wolf	Schilling		18-17	T4th	1.5
5-12	Phi.	L	5-6	(10)	9	14	Bottalico	Batista	Mesa	18-18	T4th	2.5
5-13	Phi.	W	6-1		7	4	Johnson	Person		19-18	T3rd	2.5
5-15	At Cin.	W	5-1		13	5	Sabel	Wohlers	Kim	20-18	3rd	2.0
5-16	At Cin.	W	2-1		7	5	Schilling	Reith	Kim	21-18	3rd	1.5
5-17	At Cin.	W	7-2		9	4	Anderson	Brower		22-18	T2nd	0.5
5-18	At Chi.	W	4-0		10	1	Johnson	Lieber		23-18	1st	+0.5
5-19	At Chi.	L	2-6		6	10	Wood	Batista		23-19	T2nd	0.5
5-20	At Chi.	L	5-6		6	15	Tapani	Ellis	Fassero	23-20	T2nd	0.5
5-21	S.F	W	4-2		7	6	Schilling	Rueter		24-20	1st	+0.5
5-22	S.F	W	12-8		15	13	Anderson	Ortiz		25-20	1st	+1.0
5-23	S.F	L	1-5		3	9	Gardner	Johnson		25-21	T1st	...
5-24	At S.D.	L	1-3		7	5	Serrano	Brohawn	Hoffman	25-22	T2nd	1.0
5-25	At S.D.	W	7-1		11	7	Sabel	Jones		26-22	T1st	...
5-26	At S.D.	W	3-1		7	3	Schilling	Eaton		27-22	T1st	...
5-27	At S.D.	W	6-4		8	7	Swindell	Hoffman	Prinz	28-22	T1st	...
5-28	At S.F	W	2-1	(12)	9	9	Batista	Worrell		29-22	T1st	...
5-29	At S.F	W	1-0	(18)	10	9	Batista	Vogelsong	Swindell	30-22	1st	+1.0
5-30	At S.F	W	4-3		14	8	Ellis	Hernandez	Prinz	31-22	1st	+1.0
6-1	S.D.	W	4-2		13	9	Schilling	Williams	Kim	32-22	1st	+2.0
6-2	S.D.	W	2-1		7	6	Prinz	Davey		33-22	1st	+3.0
6-3	S.D.	W	8-4		10	10	Johnson	Jarvis		34-22	1st	+3.0
6-4	L.A.	L	4-8		6	13	Park	Reynoso		34-23	1st	+2.0
6-5	L.A.	L	5-6		8	9	Herges	Kim	Shaw	34-24	1st	+1.0
6-6	L.A.	W	4-1		10	6	Schilling	Prokopec		35-24	1st	+2.0
6-7	L.A.	W	13-9		12	14	Batista	Dreifort		36-24	1st	+3.0
6-8	At K.C.	W	11-4		14	12	Johnson	Byrd		37-24	1st	+4.0
6-9	At K.C.	L	2-3		8	9	Stein	Reynoso	Hernandez	37-25	1st	+4.0
6-10	At K.C.	W	12-5		14	10	Ellis	Reichert		38-25	1st	+4.0
6-12	Chi.	L	2-6		7	10	Wood	Schilling		38-26	1st	+3.5
6-13	Chi.	W	13-3		19	6	Bierbrodt	Tapani		39-26	1st	+4.5
6-14	Chi.	W	3-2		9	6	Johnson	Bere	Swindell	40-26	1st	+4.0
6-15	Det.	L	2-5		9	7	Holt	Brohawn	Anderson	40-27	1st	+3.0
6-16	Det.	W	3-1		7	7	Ellis	Blair	Prinz	41-27	1st	+4.0
6-17	Det.	W	8-3		12	11	Schilling	Mlicki		42-27	1st	+5.0
6-19	At L.A.	W	9-2		13	7	Johnson	Dreifort		43-27	1st	+6.0
6-20	At L.A.	L	3-4		4	7	Shaw	Sabel		43-28	1st	+5.0
6-21	At Col.	W	14-5		16	11	Bierbrodt	Hampton		44-28	1st	+5.0
6-22	At Col.	W	5-4	(10)	10	15	Swindell	Jimenez	Prinz	45-28	1st	+5.0
6-23	At Col.	W	9-5		13	7	Kim	White		46-28	1st	+6.0

Date	Opp.	Res.	Score	(inn.*)	Hits	Opp. hits	Winning pitcher	Losing pitcher	Save	Record	Pos.	GB
6-24	At Col.	L	6-7		12	9	Neagle	Johnson	Jimenez	46-29	1st	+6.0
6-25	Hou.	L	0-6		6	11	Miller	Batista		46-30	1st	+5.0
6-26	Hou.	L	7-10		14	14	Dotel	Bierbrodt	Wagner	46-31	1st	+5.0
6-27	Hou.	W	7-5		8	7	Schilling	Elarton		47-31	1st	+6.0
6-29	Col.	W	5-3		10	7	Johnson	Astacio	Kim	48-31	1st	+6.0
6-30	Col.	W	6-5		10	9	Brohawn	Davis	Prinz	49-31	1st	+6.0
7-1	Col.	W	5-4	(13)	11	9	Prinz	White		50-31	1st	+6.0
7-3	At Hou.	L	5-6		9	13	Mlicki	Schilling	Wagner	50-32	1st	+4.5
7-4	At Hou.	W	3-2		7	4	Johnson	Reynolds	Kim	51-32	1st	+4.5
7-5	At Hou.	L	1-5		7	5	Oswalt	Ellis		51-33	1st	+4.5
7-6	Oak.	L	0-3		1	6	Mulder	Anderson		51-34	1st	+4.5
7-7	Oak.	L	1-5		8	12	Hudson	Batista		51-35	1st	+3.5
7-8	Oak.	L	1-2		7	5	Zito	Schilling	Isringhausen	51-36	1st	+3.5
7-12	At Ana.	L	1-4		4	4	Schoeneweis	Anderson	Percival	51-37	1st	+3.5
7-13	At Ana.	W	6-2		10	9	Schilling	Valdes		52-37	1st	+4.5
7-14	At Ana.	W	7-5		15	9	Prinz	Percival	Kim	53-37	1st	+4.5
7-15	At Sea.	L	0-8		2	13	Sele	Ellis		53-38	1st	+3.5
7-16	At Sea.	W	5-3		10	5	Batista	Halama	Kim	54-38	1st	+3.5
7-17	At Sea.	L	1-6		8	11	Abbott	Anderson		54-39	1st	+2.5
7-18	At S.D.	W	3-0		7	1	Johnson	Williams		55-39	1st	+2.0
7-19	At S.D.	L	4-8		5	8	Jarvis	Ellis	Hoffman	55-40	1st	+1.5
7-20	At S.F	L	0-1		3	4	Hernandez	Batista	Nen	55-41	1st	+1.5
7-21	At S.F	W	9-2		11	4	Schilling	Jensen		56-41	1st	+1.5
7-22	At S.F	W	12-4		14	6	Anderson	Rueter		57-41	1st	+1.5
7-23	S.D.	L	2-4		8	9	Williams	Bierbrodt	Hoffman	57-42	1st	+0.5
7-24	S.D.	W	11-0		14	1	Johnson	Jarvis		58-42	1st	+0.5
7-25	S.D.	W	9-6		13	9	Batista	Hitchcock	Kim	59-42	1st	+1.5
7-26	S.F	L	3-11		10	13	Hernandez	Schilling		59-43	1st	+0.5
7-27	S.F	L	5-9		14	14	Rueter	Anderson		59-44	2nd	0.5
7-28	S.F	L	4-11		9	18	Ortiz	Lopez		59-45	2nd	1.5
7-29	S.F	L	3-4		5	8	Estes	Kim	Nen	59-46	2nd	1.5
7-31	Mon.	W	3-1		7	8	Schilling	Munoz		60-46	2nd	0.5
8-1	Mon.	L	5-8		11	11	Thurman	Anderson	Stewart	60-47	2nd	0.5
8-2	Mon.	L	0-1		3	5	Vazquez	Lopez	Stewart	60-48	2nd	0.5
8-3	N.Y.	W	7-0		14	2	Johnson	Leiter		61-48	1st	+0.5
8-4	N.Y.	L	2-4		9	7	Appier	Batista	Benitez	61-49	2nd	0.5
8-5	N.Y.	W	2-1		7	6	Schilling	White	Kim	62-49	2nd	0.5
8-7	At Fla.	L	4-10		5	14	Clement	Lopez		62-50	3rd	1.5
8-8	At Fla.	W	7-1		12	6	Johnson	Sanchez		63-50	2nd	1.5
8-9	At Fla.	L	1-3		4	12	Darensbourg	Swindell	Alfonseca	63-51	3rd	1.5
8-10	At Atl.	W	7-0		9	6	Schilling	Millwood		64-51	2nd	0.5
8-11	At Atl.	W	3-1		9	5	Batista	Marquis	Kim	65-51	1st	+0.5
8-12	At Atl.	W	9-1		16	5	Lopez	Maddux		66-51	1st	+0.5
8-13	Pit.	W	3-0		5	5	Johnson	Anderson		67-51	1st	+1.0
8-14	Pit.	W	4-3	(10)	10	10	Batista	Marte		68-51	1st	+1.0
8-15	Pit.	W	5-2		7	8	Schilling	D. Williams		69-51	1st	+1.0
8-17	Chi.	W	7-2		13	8	Lopez	Tapani	Kim	70-51	1st	+1.5
8-18	Chi.	W	5-3		8	9	Johnson	Bere	Kim	71-51	1st	+2.5
8-19	Chi.	W	13-6		13	12	Witt	Ohman		72-51	1st	+2.5
8-21	At Pit.	L	2-4		2	9	Olivares	Schilling	Fetters	72-52	1st	+1.5
8-22	At Pit.	W	6-0		11	4	Lopez	Bolmol		73-52	1st	+2.5
8-23	At Pit.	L	1-5		6	6	McKnight	Johnson	Fetters	73-53	1st	+1.5
8-24	At Phi.	L	5-6		9	9	Daal	Anderson	Mesa	73-54	1st	+1.5
8-25	At Phi.	W	4-3		7	7	Batista	Coggin	Kim	74-54	1st	+2.5
8-26	At Phi.	W	4-3	(10)	11	6	Kim	Politte		75-54	1st	+3.5
8-27	At Phi.	L	1-3		6	5	Person	Lopez	Mesa	75-55	1st	+2.5
8-28	S.F	W	4-1		8	6	Johnson	Hernandez	Kim	76-55	1st	+3.5
8-29	S.F	W	2-0		10	4	Witt	Rueter	Kim	77-55	1st	+4.5
8-30	S.F	L	5-13		11	17	Schmidt	Batista		77-56	1st	+3.5
8-31†	At S.D.	W	4-1		5	6	Schilling	Jodie	Prinz	78-56		
8-31‡	At S.D.	L	5-6		9	13	Nunez	Prinz	Hoffman	78-57	1st	+4.0
9-1	At S.D.	L	5-7		10	11	Lee	Kim	Hoffman	78-58	1st	+3.0
9-2	At S.D.	L	0-1	(13)	7	4	Serrano	Kim		78-59	1st	+2.0
9-4	At S.F	L	2-5		7	7	Schmidt	Swindell	Nen	78-60	1st	+1.5
9-5	At S.F	W	7-2		16	7	Schilling	Ortiz		79-60	1st	+2.5
9-6	At S.F	L	5-9		10	13	Fultz	Lopez		79-61	1st	+1.5
9-7	S.D.	L	3-4		11	10	Fikac	Swindell	Hoffman	79-62	1st	+1.0
9-8	S.D.	W	8-6	(10)	12	6	Kim	Serrano		80-62	1st	+1.5
9-9	S.D.	W	8-2		13	4	Witt	Jones	Kim	81-62	1st	+1.5
9-17	At Col.	W	7-3		7	9	Johnson	Davis		82-62	1st	+2.0
9-18	At Col.	L	9-10		8	16	Myers	Kim		82-63	1st	+2.0
9-19	At Col.	L	2-8		5	14	Hampton	Lopez		82-64	1st	+2.0
9-20	At L.A.	L	2-3	(13)	9	10	Prokopec	Swindell		82-65	1st	+2.0
9-21	At L.A.	W	10-0		10	5	Batista	Mulholland		83-65	1st	+2.0
9-22	At L.A.	L	5-6	(11)	11	7	Gagne	Koplove		83-66	1st	+2.0
9-23	At L.A.	W	6-1		9	6	Schilling	Adams		84-66	1st	+2.0
9-25	Mil.	L	4-9		9	12	D'Amico	Lopez		84-67	1st	+1.5
9-26	Mil.	W	15-9		18	9	Witt	Buddie		85-67	1st	+1.5

Date	Opp.	Res.	Score	(inn.*)	Hits	Opp. hits	Winning pitcher	Losing pitcher	Save	Record	Pos.	GB
9-27	Mil.	W	13-11		16	14	Johnson	Quevedo	Kim	86-67	1st	+2.0
9-28	L.A.	W	4-3	(11)	14	8	Morgan	Trombley		87-67	1st	+2.0
9-29	L.A.	W	8-1		9	5	Batista	Baldwin		88-67	1st	+2.0
9-30	L.A.	L	1-2		6	4	Park	Swindell	Shaw	88-68	1st	+2.0
10-2	Col.	W	10-1		14	8	Johnson	Hampton		89-68	1st	+2.0
10-3	Col.	W	4-3		6	9	Schilling	Chacon	Kim	90-68	1st	+2.0
10-4	Col.	W	5-4		9	8	Anderson	Neagle	Kim	91-68	1st	+2.0
10-5	At Mil.	W	5-0		10	3	Lopez	Levrault		92-68	1st	+3.0
10-6	At Mil.	L	4-5		10	9	Fox	Sabel		92-69	1st	+3.0
10-7	At Mil.	L	5-15		11	16	Sheets	Knott		92-70	1st	+2.0

Monthly records: April (13-12), May (18-10), June (18-9), July (11-15), August (18-11), September (10-11), October (4-2).
*Innings, if other than nine. †First game of a doubleheader. ‡Second game of a doubleheader.

HIGHLIGHTS

High point: In the wee hours after an October 5 victory at Milwaukee, the Diamondbacks watched the Giants lose to the Dodgers and thus were able to celebrate clinching the N.L. West.

Low point: A four-game sweep at the hands of San Francisco at Bank One Ballpark, July 26-29, turned a 1 1/2-game lead in the N.L. West (over the Dodgers) into a 1 1/2-game deficit.

Turning point: In August, the Diamondbacks won nine straight to go from third to first in the N.L. West. They remained in first for the rest of the season.

Most valuable player: Luis Gonzalez hit 57 homers, became the 13th different player to collect 100 extra-base hits in a season and set team records for on-base percentage (.429), slugging percentage (.688), total bases (419), walks (100) and intentional walks (24).

Most valuable pitcher: Curt Schilling and Randy Johnson each had seasons worthy of the Cy Young Award. Schilling was a remarkable 13-1 with a 1.72 ERA in starts following an Arizona loss and 11-1 with a 2.55 ERA against division teams.

Most improved player: Miguel Batista barely made the roster after losing the battle for the No. 5 starter spot. But he learned to harness his hard stuff and was the team's third-winningest pitcher, working in relief and in the rotation.

Most pleasant surprise: Craig Counsell filled in at third base and shortstop before settling in as the regular second baseman, hitting .275 with 76 runs scored in 141 games.

Key injuries: Closer Matt Mantei missed almost the entire season with an elbow injury. ... Nerve damage in RHP Todd Stottlemyre's shoulder cost him the whole year and RHP Bobby Witt missed four months with elbow and shoulder trouble. ... 3B Matt Williams (leg) missed the eight weeks prior to the All-Star break. ... Russ Springer did not pitch after May 22 because of a torn rotator cuff.

Notable: Johnson and Schilling set the record for strikeouts by teammates (665), breaking a record held by Nolan Ryan and Bill Singer (624 with the 1973 Angels). ... Johnson's 372 strikeouts were third-most all-time. ... Arizona became the seventh N.L. team to have nine players with at least 100 hits, first since the 1979 Cardinals. ... The Diamondbacks set a team record and led the N.L. with just 84 errors. ... Erubiel Durazo and David Dellucci each had five pinch homers as Arizona, along with San Francisco, set a record with 14 pinch home runs.

—ED PRICE

RECORDS

2001 regular-season record: 92-70 (1st in N.L. West); 48-33 at home; 44-37 on road; 18-14 vs. N.L. East; 22-17 vs. N.L. Central; 45-31 vs. N.L. West; 7-8 vs. A.L.; 25-16 vs. lefthanded starters; 67-54 vs. righthanded starters; 88-67 on grass; 4-3 on turf; 26-21 in daytime; 66-49 at night; 23-25 in one-run games; 9-6 in extra-inning games; 0-0-1 in doubleheaders.

Team record past five years: 342-306 in four years (.528, ranks 5th in league in that span).

TEAM LEADERS

Batting average: Luis Gonzalez (.325).
At-bats: Luis Gonzalez (609).
Runs: Luis Gonzalez (128).
Hits: Luis Gonzalez (198).
Total Bases: Luis Gonzalez (419).
Doubles: Luis Gonzalez (36).
Triples: Luis Gonzalez (7).
Home runs: Luis Gonzalez (57).
Runs batted in: Luis Gonzalez (142).
Stolen bases: Tony Womack (28).
Slugging percentage: Luis Gonzalez (.688).
On-base percentage: Luis Gonzalez (.429).

Wins: Curt Schilling (22).
Earned-run average: Randy Johnson (2.49).
Complete games: Curt Schilling (6).
Shutouts: Randy Johnson, Albie Lopez (2).
Saves: Byung-Hyun Kim (19).
Innings pitched: Curt Schilling (256.2).
Strikeouts: Randy Johnson (372).

GAMES BY POSITION

Catcher: Damian Miller 121, Rod Barajas 50, Chad Moeller 25, Mike DiFelice 12, Ken Huckaby 1.
First base: Mark Grace 135, Erubiel Durazo 38, Greg Colbrunn 14, Craig Counsell 2.
Second base: Jay Bell 80, Junior Spivey 66, Craig Counsell 55.
Third base: Matt Williams 102, Jay Bell 40, Craig Counsell 38, Greg Colbrunn 10, Juan Sosa 1.
Shortstop: Tony Womack 118, Craig Counsell 58, Alex Cintron 7, Matt Williams 2, Junior Spivey 1.
Outfield: Luis Gonzalez 161, Steve Finley 131, Reggie Sanders 119, Danny Bautista 61, David Dellucci 58, Ryan Christenson 5, Midre Cummings 4, Erubiel Durazo 2, Tony Womack 1, Jason Conti 1, Jack Cust 1.
Designated hitter: Erubiel Durazo 7, Jay Bell 3.

TOP DRAFT CHOICES

1. **Jason Bulger,** RHP, Valdosta State U.
2. **Mike Gosling,** LHP, Stanford Univ.
3. **Scott Hairston,** 2B, Central Arizona J.C.
4. **Justin Wechsler,** RHP, Ball State U.
5. **Rich Barrett,** OF, Ursinas (Pa.) College.
6. **Matt Fox,** RHP, Stoneman Douglas H.S., Coral Springs, Fla.
7. **Chad Tracy,** 3B, East Carolina Univ.
8. **Brandon Medders,** RHP, Mississippi State University.
9. **Jared Ball,** OF, Tomball (Tex.) H.S.
10. **Matt Durkin,** RHP, Willow Glen H.S., San Jose, Calif.

ATLANTA BRAVES
NATIONAL LEAGUE EAST DIVISION

Braves schedule
Home games shaded
D—Day game (games starting before 5 p.m.)
*All-Star Game at Milwaukee
Subject to change

April
SUN	MON	TUE	WED	THU	FRI	SAT
	1 D PHI	2	3 PHI	4 PHI	5 D NYM	6 NYM
7 NYM	8 PHI	9 PHI	10 PHI	11 PHI	12 FLA	13 FLA
14 D FLA	15 NYM	16 NYM	17 D NYM	18	19 FLA	20 FLA
21 FLA	22 FLA	23 ARI	24 ARI	25 ARI	26 HOU	27 HOU
28 HOU	29	30 MIL				

May
SUN	MON	TUE	WED	THU	FRI	SAT
			1 MIL	2 D MIL	3 STL	4 D STL
5 D STL	6	7 LA	8 LA	9 LA	10 SD	11 SD
12 SD	13 SF	14 SF	15 SF	16 SF	17 COL	18 D COL
19 COL	20	21 MON	22 MON	23	24 CIN	25 CIN
26 CIN	27 D MON	28 MON	29 MON	30 MON	31 CIN	

June
SUN	MON	TUE	WED	THU	FRI	SAT
						1 CIN
2 D CIN	3 NYM	4 NYM	5 NYM	6 NYM	7 TEX	8 TEX
9 TEX	10 MIN	11 MIN	12 MIN	13	14 BOS	15 D BOS
16 BOS	17	18 DET	19 DET	20 DET	21 CWS	22 CWS
23 CWS	24 NYM	25 NYM	26 NYM	27 NYM	28 BOS	29 BOS
30 D BOS						

July
SUN	MON	TUE	WED	THU	FRI	SAT
	1 MON	2 MON	3 MON	4 CUB	5 D CUB	6 CUB
7 D CUB	8	9 *	10	11 D MON	12 MON	13 MON
14 D MON	15 CUB	16 D CUB	17 FLA	18 D FLA	19 PHI	20 PHI
21 PHI	22 FLA	23 FLA	24 D FLA	25	26 PHI	27 PHI
28 PHI	29	30 MIL	31 MIL			

August
SUN	MON	TUE	WED	THU	FRI	SAT
				1 MIL	2 STL	3 D STL
4 STL	5	6 ARI	7 ARI	8 ARI	9 HOU	10 HOU
11 D HOU	12 SF	13 SF	14 SF	15 SF	16 COL	17 COL
18 COL	19 D COL	20 SD	21 SD	22 SD	23 LA	24 D LA
25 LA	26	27 PIT	28 PIT	29 D PIT	30 MON	31 MON

September
SUN	MON	TUE	WED	THU	FRI	SAT
1 D MON	2 D PIT	3 D PIT	4 PIT	5	6 D MON	7 MON
8 MON	9	10 NYM	11 NYM	12	13 FLA	14 FLA
15 D FLA	16 PHI	17 PHI	18 PHI	19 PHI	20 FLA	21 FLA
22 D FLA	23	24 PHI	25 PHI	26 PHI	27 NYM	28 NYM
29 D NYM	30					

2002 SEASON
CLUB DIRECTORY

Chairman of the board of directors
William C. Bartholomay
President
Stanley H. Kasten
Executive vice president and general manager
John Schuerholz
Senior v.p. and assistant to the president
Henry L. Aaron
Senior vice president, administration
Bob Wolfe
Vice president, assistant general manager
Frank Wren
Vice president
Lee Douglas
Special assistants to general manager
Jim Fregosi, Paul Snyder, Scott Nethery, Chuck McMichael
Special assistant to g.m./player development
Jose Martinez
Director of team travel, equipment manager
Bill Acree
Director of player development
Dick Balderson
Director of scouting
Roy Clark
Dir. of international and professional scouting
Dayton Moore
Senior director of promotions and civic affairs
Miles McRea
Vice president/Controller
Chip Moore
Director of ticket sales
Paul Adams
Director of minor league business operations
Bruce Baldwin
Director of stadium operations and security
Larry Bowman
Field director
Ed Mangan
Director of ticket operations
Ed Newman
Team counsel
John Cooper
Director of community relations
Cara Maglione
Director of audio video operations
Jennifer Berger
Director of corporate sales
Jim Allen
Director of public relations
Jim Schultz
Director of strategic development, Turner Sports Teams and Venues
David Lee

Director of human resources
Michele Golden
Director of advertising and publicity
Joe Clemente
Director of special events
Sabrina Jenkins
Director of customer service, Turner Sports Teams and Venues
Jason Parker
Media relations manager
Glen Serra
Public relations assistants
Adam Lieberman, Meagan Swingle
Head trainer
Dave Pursley
Assistant trainer
Jeff Porter
Director of medical services
Dr. Joe Chandler
Associate physicians
Dr. William Barber, Dr. John Cantwell, Dr. Xavier Duralde, Dr. Norman Elliott, Dr. Marvin Royster
Major league scout
Bobby Wine
National supervisors
Tim Conroy, John Flannery
Regional supervisors
Harold Cronin, Paul Faulk, "J" Harrison, Kurt Kemp
Area supervisors
Mike Baker, Daniel Bates, Billy Best, Tyrone Brooks, Stu Cann, Sherrod Clinkscales, Ralph Garr, Al Goetz, Marco Paddy, J.J. Picollo, Willie Powell, John Ramey, Charlie Smith, John Stewart, Don Thomas, Terry Tripp
Scouts
Nez Balelo, Joe Caputo, Matt Dodd, Bill Fischer, James Kane, DeWayne Kitts, Al Kubski, Robert Lucas, Rip Tutor
International supervisors
Phil Dale, Rene Francisco, Courtland Hall, Julian Perez
International scouts
Roberto Aquino, Neil Burke, Richard Castro, Jeremy Chou, Edgar Fernandez, Jose Figueroa, Pedro Flores, Bill Froberg, Carlos Garcia, Ruben Garcia, David Latham, Jason Lee, Jose Leon, Andres Lopez, Hiroyuki Oya, Rolando Petit, Elvis Pineda, Miguel Teran, Raymond Tew, Marvin Throneberry, Carlos Torres, Thomas Vasquez
Professional scouts
Rod Gilbreath, Chet Montgomery, Bob Wadsworth, Gene Watson

MINOR LEAGUE AFFILIATES

Class	Team	League	Manager
AAA	Richmond	International	Fredi Gonzalez
AA	Greenville	Southern	Brian Snitker
A	Myrtle Beach	Carolina	Randy Ingle
A	Macon	South Atlantic	Lynn Jones
A	Jamestown	New York-Pennsylvania	Jim Saul
Rookie	Danville	Appalachian	Ralph Henriquez
Rookie	Gulf Coast Braves	Gulf Coast	Rick Albert

BROADCAST INFORMATION

Radio: WSB-AM (750).
TV: TBS-TV.
Cable TV: FOX Sports Net South, Turner South.

SPRING TRAINING

Ballpark (city): Disney's Wide World of Sports Baseball Stadium (Kissimmee, Fla.).
Ticket information: 407-839-3900, 407-939-4263.

Follow the Braves all season at: www.sportingnews.com/baseball/teams/braves/

SPRING TRAINING ROSTER

Manager—Bobby Cox (6).
Coaches—Pat Corrales (39), Bobby Dews (52), Frank Fultz, Glenn Hubbard (16), Leo Mazzone (54), Ned Yost (5).

No.	PITCHERS	B/T	Ht./Wt.	Born	2001 clubs
	Bong, Jung	L/L	6-3/175	7-15-80	Myrtle Beach
51	Cabrera, Jose	R/R	6-0/180	3-24-72	Atlanta
	Ennis, John	R/R	6-5/220	10-17-79	Myrtle Beach
	Foster, John	L/L	6-0/200	5-17-78	Greenville
47	Glavine, Tom	L/L	6-0/185	3-25-66	Atlanta
	Lewis, Derrick	R/R	6-5/215	5-7-76	Richmond
46	Ligtenberg, Kerry	R/R	6-2/215	5-11-71	Atlanta, Richmond
32	Lopez, Albie	R/R	6-2/240	8-18-71	Tampa Bay, Arizona
31	Maddux, Greg	R/R	6-0/185	4-14-66	Atlanta
51	Marquis, Jason	L/R	6-1/185	8-21-78	Atlanta
34	Millwood, Kevin	R/R	6-4/220	12-24-74	Atlanta, Macon, Greenville
61	Moss, Damian	R/L	6-0/187	11-24-76	Richmond, Atlanta, Greenville
	Nelson, Joe	R/R	6-2/185	10-25-74	Richmond, Atlanta
	Ramirez, Horacio	L/L	6-1/170	11-24-79	Greenville
37	Remlinger, Mike	L/L	6-1/210	3-23-66	Atlanta
29	Smoltz, John	R/R	6-3/220	5-15-67	Greenville, Macon, Atlanta
	Sobkowiak, Scott	R/R	6-5/230	10-26-77	Gulf Coast Braves, Greenville, Atlanta
	Spooneybarger, Tim	R/R	6-3/190	10-21-79	Richmond, Greenville, Atlanta
	Sylvester, Billy	R/R	6-5/220	10-1-76	Greenville, Richmond

No.	CATCHERS	B/T	Ht./Wt.	Born	2001 clubs
9	Bako, Paul	L/R	6-2/205	6-20-72	Atlanta
8	Lopez, Javy	R/R	6-3/200	11-5-70	Atlanta
	Torrealba, Steve	R/R	6-0/175	2-24-78	Greenville, Atlanta

No.	INFIELDERS	B/T	Ht./Wt.	Born	2001 clubs
	Betemit, Wilson	B/R	6-2/155	11-2-81	Myrtle Beach, Greenville, Atlanta
9	Castilla, Vinny	R/R	6-1/205	7-4-67	Tampa Bay, Houston
2	DeRosa, Mark	R/R	6-1/195	2-2-75	Richmond, Atlanta
4	Franco, Julio	R/R	6-0/200	8-23-61	Mexico City Tigers, Atlanta
1	Furcal, Rafael	B/R	5-10/165	8-24-80	Atlanta
	Garcia, Jesse	R/R	5-10/171	9-24-73	Richmond, Atlanta
	Giles, Marcus	R/R	5-8/180	5-18-78	Richmond, Atlanta
	Green, Nick	R/R	6-0/180	9-10-78	Myrtle Beach, Richmond
18	Helms, Wes	R/R	6-4/230	5-12-76	Atlanta
10	Jones, Chipper	B/R	6-4/210	4-24-72	Atlanta

No.	OUTFIELDERS	B/T	Ht./Wt.	Born	2001 clubs
	Aldridge, Cory	L/R	6-0/210	6-13-79	Greenville, Atlanta
25	Jones, Andruw	R/R	6-1/210	4-23-77	Atlanta
	Langerhans, Ryan	L/L	6-3/195	2-20-80	Myrtle Beach
	Martinez, Dave	L/L	5-10/190	9-26-64	Atlanta
	Sheffield, Gary	R/R	5-11/205	11-18-68	Los Angeles
15	Surhoff, B.J.	L/R	6-1/200	8-4-64	Atlanta

BALLPARK INFORMATION

Ballpark (capacity, surface)
Turner Field (50,091, grass)
Address
P.O. Box 4064
Atlanta, GA 30302
Official website
www.atlantabraves.com
Business phone
404-522-7630
Ticket information
404-249-6400 or 800-326-4000
Ticket prices
$40 (dugout level)
$32 (club level)
$27 (field level, terrace level)
$18 (field pavilion, terrace pavilion)
$12 (upper level)
$8 (upper level reserved)
$5 (upper pavilion)
$1 (skyline)
Field dimensions (from home plate)
To left field at foul line, 335 feet
To center field, 401 feet
To right field at foul line, 330 feet
First game played
April 4, 1997 (Braves 5, Cubs 4)

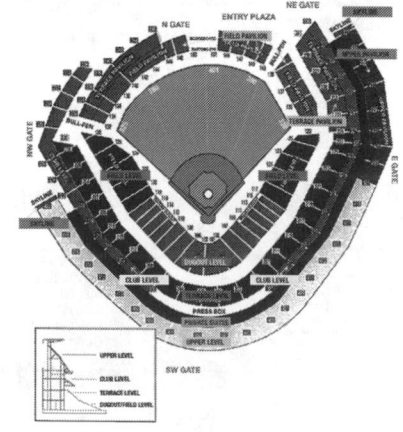

Date	Opp.	Res.	Score	(inn.*)	Hits	Opp. hits	Winning pitcher	Losing pitcher	Save	Record	Pos.	GB
4-2	At Cin.	W	10-4		14	8	Valdes	Reyes		1-0	T1st	...
4-3	N.Y.	L	4-6	(10)	9	7	Cook	Ligtenberg	Benitez	1-1	4th	1.0
4-4	N.Y.	W	3-2		6	6	Rocker	Wall		2-1	3rd	1.0
4-5	N.Y.	L	1-7		3	13	Reed	Perez		2-2	4th	1.5
4-6	At Fla.	W	7-5		11	7	Maddux	Grilli	Rocker	3-2	3rd	0.5
4-7	At Fla.	L	0-8		6	11	Dempster	Burkett		3-3	3rd	1.5
4-8	At Fla.	L	1-6		4	8	Clement	Glavine		3-4	3rd	2.5
4-9	At N.Y.	L	4-9		8	10	Appier	Millwood		3-5	4th	3.5
4-11	At N.Y.	W	2-0		4	1	Maddux	Reed	Rocker	4-5	3rd	2.5
4-12	At N.Y.	L	0-1	(10)	6	6	Benitez	Ligtenberg		4-6	4th	3.0
4-13	Phi.	W	4-2		11	6	Glavine	Wolf	Rocker	5-6	3rd	2.0
4-14	Phi.	L	1-2		8	6	Daal	Millwood	Mesa	5-7	3rd	3.0
4-15	Phi.	W	3-0		5	6	Perez	Person	Rocker	6-7	3rd	2.0
4-16	Fla.	W	4-3		9	7	Rocker	Miceli		7-7	3rd	1.5
4-17	Fla.	L	2-3		5	7	Nunez	Burkett	Alfonseca	7-8	3rd	2.5
4-18	Fla.	W	1-0		5	3	Glavine	Dempster	Rocker	8-8	3rd	1.0
4-20	At Phi.	L	3-8		8	12	Gomes	Perez		8-9	T2nd	2.0
4-21	At Phi.	L	1-4		9	7	Person	Maddux		8-10	T3rd	3.0
4-22	At Phi.	L	2-3		6	4	Telemaco	Burkett	Gomes	8-11	5th	4.0
4-23	At Hou.	W	9-7		11	14	Glavine	Dotel		9-11	3rd	4.0
4-24	At Hou.	L	6-11		8	12	Reynolds	Perez	Bottenfield	9-12	3rd	5.0
4-25	At Hou.	W	11-3		12	8	Millwood	Elarton		10-12	2nd	5.0
4-26	At Ari.	L	6-13		8	15	Ellis	Maddux		10-13	3rd	5.0
4-27	At Ari.	W	9-0		14	3	Burkett	Reynoso		11-13	3rd	4.0
4-28	At Ari.	W	3-1		7	6	Glavine	Johnson	Rocker	12-13	2nd	3.0
4-29	At Ari.	L	5-7		7	10	Sabel	Perez	Brohawn	12-14	2nd	3.0
5-1	Mil.	L	3-5		7	9	Haynes	Millwood	Leskanic	12-15	2nd	4.0
5-2	Mil.	W	1-0		5	2	Maddux	Rigdon		13-15	2nd	3.0
5-3	Mil.	L	0-5		9	10	Sheets	Burkett		13-16	2nd	4.0
5-4	St.L.	L	2-4		7	8	Hermanson	Glavine	Veres	13-17	3rd	4.0
5-5	St.L.	W	6-5		13	9	Remlinger	Timlin	Rocker	14-17	2nd	4.0
5-6	St.L.	W	7-5		15	7	Cabrera	Stechschulte	Rocker	15-17	2nd	4.0
5-8	At S.D.	L	1-7		6	16	Jarvis	Maddux		15-18	2nd	5.5
5-9	At S.D.	W	3-0		6	9	Burkett	Jones	Rocker	16-18	2nd	4.5
5-10	At S.D.	L	5-6		11	6	Myers	Remlinger	Hoffman	16-19	2nd	5.0
5-11	At L.A.	W	5-1		12	8	Perez	Gagne		17-19	2nd	5.0
5-12	At L.A.	L	0-1		3	5	Shaw	Whiteside		17-20	2nd	6.0
5-13	At L.A.	L	1-3		3	7	Prokopec	Maddux	Shaw	17-21	2nd	6.0
5-15	Col.	W	5-3		13	9	Remlinger	Hampton	Rocker	18-21	2nd	5.0
5-16	Col.	W	6-4		11	11	Cabrera	Wasdin	Rocker	19-21	2nd	4.0
5-17	Col.	L	3-8		10	12	Neagle	Smoltz		19-22	2nd	5.0
5-18	S.F	W	6-5		7	7	Cabrera	Nen		20-22	2nd	5.0
5-19	S.F	L	3-6		7	17	Worrell	Cabrera	Nen	20-23	3rd	6.0
5-20	S.F	W	11-6		14	11	Ligtenberg	Hernandez		21-23	2nd	5.0
5-21	At Fla.	W	5-3		7	7	Glavine	Clement	Rocker	22-23	2nd	4.5
5-22	At Fla.	L	2-3		8	10	Smith	Smoltz	Alfonseca	22-24	2nd	5.0
5-25	Pit.	W	1-0		5	7	Maddux	Ritchie		23-24	2nd	6.5
5-26	Pit.	W	9-3		14	8	Burkett	Wengert		24-24	2nd	6.0
5-27	Pit.	L	3-6		11	12	Arroyo	Glavine	M. Williams	24-25	2nd	6.5
5-28	Mon.	W	5-3	(8)	8	10	Smoltz	Yoshii	Rocker	25-25	2nd	6.5
5-29	Mon.	W	7-4		8	7	Perez	Blank	Rocker	26-25	2nd	6.5
5-30	Mon.	L	3-4		7	10	Vazquez	Maddux	Urbina	26-26	2nd	7.5
6-1	At Pit.	W	5-1		10	4	Burkett	Ritchie		27-26	2nd	8.0
6-3†	At Pit.	W	11-7		18	13	Glavine	Olivares		28-26		
6-3‡	At Pit.	W	8-3		12	6	Smoltz	Anderson		29-26	2nd	6.0
6-5	At Mon.	W	3-1		9	7	Maddux	Vazquez	Rocker	30-26	2nd	5.0
6-6	At Mon.	W	2-0		9	3	Burkett	Irabu	Rocker	31-26	2nd	5.0
6-7	At Mon.	W	4-3	(11)	11	8	Marquis	Strickland	Ligtenberg	32-26	2nd	4.0
6-8	At N.Y.	L	4-7		8	8	Pettitte	Glavine	Rivera	32-27	2nd	4.0
6-9	At N.Y.	W	10-6		16	8	Cabrera	Choate	Rocker	33-27	2nd	4.0
6-10	At N.Y.	W	4-1		7	7	Maddux	Mussina	Rocker	34-27	2nd	3.0
6-11	At Tor.	L	4-9		7	13	File	Burkett		34-28	2nd	3.5
6-12	At Tor.	W	3-0		7	5	Perez	Parris	Rocker	35-28	2nd	2.5
6-13	At Tor.	L	5-12		14	15	Hamilton	Glavine		35-29	2nd	2.5
6-15	Bos.	L	5-9	(10)	8	13	Beck	Cabrera		35-30	2nd	3.0
6-16	Bos.	W	8-0		11	2	Burkett	Nomo		36-30	2nd	3.0
6-17	Bos.	L	3-4		9	7	Castillo	Perez	Lowe	36-31	2nd	3.0
6-18	Fla.	L	6-7		9	12	Looper	Rocker	Alfonseca	36-32	2nd	3.5
6-19	Fla.	L	2-12		8	16	Smith	Marquis		36-33	T2nd	3.5
6-20	Fla.	W	7-2		10	4	Maddux	Burnett		37-33	2nd	3.5
6-21	Fla.	L	2-3		6	8	Looper	Rocker	Alfonseca	37-34	2nd	4.5
6-22	At N.Y.	W	10-1		12	7	Perez	Reed		38-34	T2nd	3.5
6-23	At N.Y.	W	9-3	(11)	16	11	Reed	White		39-34	T2nd	2.5
6-24	At N.Y.	W	8-4		15	9	Marquis	Trachsel		40-34	2nd	2.5

– 85 –

Date	Opp.	Res.	Score	(inn.*)	Hits	Opp. hits	Winning pitcher	Losing pitcher	Save	Record	Pos.	GB
6-25	At Phi.	W	9-4		12	11	Maddux	Daal		41-34	2nd	1.5
6-26	At Phi.	W	4-1	(11)	10	4	Remlinger	Gomes	Cabrera	42-34	2nd	0.5
6-27	At Phi.	W	10-4		12	7	Perez	Wolf		43-34	1st	+0.5
6-28	N.Y.	W	6-2	(10)	9	10	Reed	Benitez		44-34	T1st	...
6-29	N.Y.	L	1-3		7	6	Trachsel	Marquis	Benitez	44-35	2nd	1.0
6-30	N.Y.	W	5-2		10	9	Maddux	Leiter	Karsay	45-35	2nd	1.0
7-1	N.Y.	L	1-2		4	6	Appier	Burkett	Benitez	45-36	2nd	2.0
7-3	Phi.	W	14-7		15	11	Cabrera	Santiago		46-36	2nd	1.0
7-4	Phi.	L	1-4		4	10	Coggin	Perez	Mesa	46-37	2nd	2.0
7-5	Phi.	W	9-5		12	10	Maddux	Chen		47-37	2nd	1.0
7-6	At Bos.	W	6-5	(10)	12	10	Karsay	Kim	Cabrera	48-37	2nd	1.0
7-7	At Bos.	L	1-3		9	7	Nomo	Marquis	Lowe	48-38	2nd	1.0
7-8	At Bos.	W	8-0		13	4	Glavine	Ohka		49-38	2nd	1.0
7-12	Bal.	W	6-5		11	10	Maddux	Ryan	Karsay	50-38	T1st	...
7-13	Bal.	W	7-1		8	3	Glavine	Towers		51-38	T1st	...
7-14	Bal.	L	1-4		6	8	Roberts	Burkett	Groom	51-39	T1st	...
7-15	T.B.	L	1-9		8	13	Lopez	Perez		51-40	2nd	1.0
7-16	T.B.	L	5-6		10	11	Zambrano	Karsay	Yan	51-41	2nd	1.0
7-17	T.B.	W	4-0		6	6	Maddux	Sturtze		52-41	T1st	...
7-18	At Cin.	W	3-1	(8)	3	10	Glavine	Dessens	Reed	53-41	1st	+1.0
7-19	At Cin.	W	2-1		8	7	Burkett	Brower	Karsay	54-41	1st	+2.0
7-20	Mon.	L	3-6		8	12	Thurman	Millwood	Urbina	54-42	1st	+1.0
7-21	Mon.	W	2-1	(10)	9	6	Cabrera	Lloyd		55-42	1st	+2.0
7-22	Mon.	W	8-2		14	9	Maddux	Mattes		56-42	1st	+2.0
7-23	Cin.	L	4-5		12	12	Sullivan	Remlinger	Graves	56-43	1st	+2.0
7-24	Cin.	L	3-11		8	12	Brower	Burkett		56-44	1st	+1.0
7-25	Cin.	W	11-3		15	6	Millwood	Acevedo		57-44	1st	+1.0
7-26	At Mon.	L	2-3	(10)	6	10	Urbina	Reed		57-45	T1st	...
7-27	At Mon.	W	7-3		11	7	Maddux	Mattes		58-45	1st	+1.0
7-28	At Mon.	W	10-5		13	7	Glavine	Vazquez		59-45	1st	+2.0
7-29	At Mon.	W	8-1		5	5	Burkett	Armas		60-45	1st	+3.0
7-31	At St.L.	L	2-6		4	13	Hermanson	Reed		60-46	1st	+3.0
8-1	At St.L.	L	0-4		8	8	Kile	Maddux		60-47	1st	+2.0
8-2	At St.L.	W	2-1		8	5	Glavine	Smith	Karsay	61-47	1st	+2.0
8-3	At Mil.	L	2-3	(11)	9	5	Painter	Cabrera		61-48	1st	+2.0
8-4	At Mil.	W	14-2		12	4	Burkett	Quevedo		62-48	1st	+2.0
8-5	At Mil.	W	12-8		14	9	Cabrera	Sheets		63-48	1st	+3.0
8-7	Hou.	W	6-5		6	11	Maddux	Cruz	Karsay	64-48	1st	+3.0
8-8	Hou.	L	1-2	(12)	12	10	Jackson	Cabrera	Wagner	64-49	1st	+2.0
8-9	Hou.	L	5-6		11	12	Dotel	Ligtenberg		64-50	1st	+2.0
8-10	Ari.	L	0-7		6	9	Schilling	Millwood		64-51	1st	+1.0
8-11	Ari.	L	1-3		5	9	Batista	Marquis	Kim	64-52	T1st	...
8-12	Ari.	L	1-9		5	16	Lopez	Maddux		64-53	2nd	1.0
8-14	At Col.	L	4-5	(10)	10	15	Jimenez	Karsay		64-54	2nd	2.0
8-15	At Col.	W	7-2		8	7	Burkett	Hampton		65-54	2nd	2.0
8-16	At Col.	W	4-1		6	10	Millwood	Chacon	Karsay	66-54	2nd	1.0
8-17	At S.F	W	2-1		2	6	Maddux	Hernandez	Smoltz	67-54	T1st	...
8-18	At S.F	W	3-1		8	9	Marquis	Rueter	Karsay	68-54	1st	+1.0
8-19	At S.F	L	1-4		5	9	Schmidt	Glavine	Nen	68-55	1st	+1.0
8-21	S.D.	L	1-3	(10)	4	10	Nunez	Karsay	Hoffman	68-56	1st	+1.0
8-22	S.D.	W	6-3		12	3	Maddux	Tollberg	Remlinger	69-56	1st	+1.0
8-23	S.D.	W	3-2		6	6	Millwood	Lawrence	Smoltz	70-56	1st	+2.0
8-24	L.A.	L	1-4		5	7	Park	Glavine		70-57	1st	+1.0
8-25	L.A.	L	7-8		12	10	Prokopec	Marquis	Shaw	70-58	1st	+1.0
8-26	L.A.	W	9-2		15	9	Burkett	Gagne		71-58	1st	+2.0
8-27	L.A.	L	2-4		9	7	Adams	Remlinger	Shaw	71-59	1st	+1.0
8-28	Mon.	L	0-7		5	9	Vazquez	Millwood		71-60	T1st	...
8-29	Mon.	W	5-3		7	8	Glavine	Armas	Smoltz	72-60	1st	+1.0
8-30	Mon.	L	2-4		7	8	Ohka	Marquis	Strickland	72-61	1st	+1.0
8-31	Chi.	L	2-8		6	12	Cruz	Burkett		72-62	1st	+1.0
9-1	Chi.	L	3-5		9	9	Tavarez	Maddux	Gordon	72-63	T1st	...
9-2	Chi.	W	7-4		12	6	Millwood	Tapani	Smoltz	73-63	1st	+1.0
9-3	At Mon.	W	5-0		10	7	Glavine	Ohka		74-63	1st	+2.0
9-4	At Mon.	W	3-2		7	6	Karsay	Strickland	Smoltz	75-63	1st	+3.0
9-5	At Mon.	L	4-10		9	16	Thurman	Burkett		75-64	1st	+3.0
9-7	At Chi.	W	3-2		8	4	Karsay	Farnsworth	Smoltz	76-64	1st	+3.5
9-8	At Chi.	W	5-3		11	7	Glavine	Tapani	Smoltz	77-64	1st	+3.5
9-9	At Chi.	W	9-5		16	10	Ligtenberg	Bere		78-64	1st	+3.5
9-17	At Phi.	L	2-5		7	6	Person	Maddux	Mesa	78-65	1st	+2.5
9-18	At Phi.	L	3-4		8	7	Bottalico	Smoltz		78-66	1st	+1.5
9-19	At Phi.	L	2-5		6	7	Coggin	Burkett	Mesa	78-67	1st	+0.5
9-20	At Phi.	W	5-1		11	4	Millwood	Wolf		79-67	1st	+1.5
9-21	At N.Y.	L	2-3		9	8	Benitez	Karsay		79-68	1st	+0.5
9-22	At N.Y.	L	3-7		9	13	Trachsel	Perez	Benitez	79-69	1st	+0.5
9-23	At N.Y.	W	5-4	(11)	8	10	Smoltz	Riggan		80-69	1st	+0.5
9-24	At Fla.	L	0-1		7	3	Penny	Burkett	Alfonseca	80-70	T1st	...
9-25	At Fla.	W	5-2	(11)	11	12	Ligtenberg	Darensbourg	Smoltz	81-70	1st	+1.0
9-26	At Fla.	W	4-1		7	5	Marquis	Burnett	Smoltz	82-70	1st	+1.0

Date	Opp.	Res.	Score	(inn.*)	Hits	Opp. hits	Winning pitcher	Losing pitcher	Save	Record	Pos.	GB
9-27	At Fla.	L	1-7		8	11	Acevedo	Maddux		82-71	1st	+1.0
9-28	N.Y.	W	5-3		7	9	Glavine	Trachsel	Smoltz	83-71	1st	+2.0
9-29	N.Y.	W	8-5		8	7	Perez	Benitez		84-71	1st	+2.0
9-30	N.Y.	L	6-9		9	11	Appier	Millwood	Benitez	84-72	1st	+2.0
10-2	Phi.	L	1-3		3	7	Wolf	Maddux	Mesa	84-73	1st	+1.0
10-3	Phi.	W	8-3		13	12	Glavine	Person		85-73	1st	+2.0
10-4	Phi.	W	6-2		9	8	Burkett	Duckworth		86-73	1st	+3.0
10-5	Fla.	W	20-3		14	6	Millwood	Dempster		87-73	1st	+3.5
10-6	Fla.	W	7-3		9	8	Marquis	Beckett		88-73	1st	+3.0
10-7	Fla.	L	2-4		7	6	Burnett	Spooneybarger	Looper	88-74	1st	+2.0

Monthly records: April (12-14), May (14-12), June (19-9), July (15-11), August (12-16), September (12-10), October (4-2).
*Innings, if other than nine. †First game of a doubleheader. ‡Second game of a doubleheader.

HIGHLIGHTS

High point: The Braves became the first pro sports team to win 10 consecutive division championships when they trounced the Marlins 20-3 on October 5. The victory capped a scintillating pennant race in which no more than 3 1/2 games separated the Braves and Phillies from June 22 through the end of the season.
Low point: On the verge of winning three games in a row for the first time, the Braves lost to the Expos on May 30 and dropped 7 1/2 games behind the first-place Phillies.
Turning point: John Smoltz worked two innings for his first save, a 2-1 win over the Giants on August 17, and the Braves didn't fall out of first place during the remainder of the season. With Smoltz as the closer, Steve Karsay was shifted into a setup role, which strengthened the bullpen.
Most valuable player: Chipper Jones posted a career-high .330 batting average and became the first third baseman in major league history to knock in 100 runs in six consecutive seasons. Jones finished among the league's top 10 in nine other offensive categories.
Most valuable pitcher: John Smoltz. After 13 years as a starter, he moved to the bullpen, then into the closer's role, and became one of the league's dominant stoppers. He had a 1.59 ERA out of the bullpen and converted 10 of 11 save opportunities.
Most improved player: Mark DeRosa took over at shortstop after Rafael Furcal went down, and played solid defense while contributing significantly with his bat. He shifted into a backup role when Rey Sanchez was acquired.
Most pleasant surprise: Marcus Giles took over as the regular second baseman when Quilvio Veras was released on July 31, and made the most of his opportunity, hitting .262 and driving in 31 runs in 68 games. He was thrust into the leadoff role and sparked the offense.
Key injuries: Rafael Furcal was lost for the season in July with a dislocated shoulder. ... Kevin Millwood missed two and a half months because of shoulder problems. ... Odalis Perez missed six weeks in the second half after suffering a cut on his left hand.
Notable: Bobby Cox, the winningest manager in Braves history, moved into 12th place on the all-time managerial wins list with 1,704. ... Greg Maddux became just the second pitcher in major league history to win 15 games in at least 14 straight seasons.

—BILL ZACK

RECORDS

2001 regular-season record: 88-74 (1st in N.L. East); 40-41 at home; 48-33 on road; 42-34 vs. N.L. East; 22-14 vs. N.L. Central; 15-17 vs. N.L. West; 9-9 vs. A.L.; 18-9 vs. lefthanded starters; 70-65 vs. righthanded starters; 75-64 on grass; 13-10 on turf; 29-17 in daytime; 59-57 at night; 19-23 in one-run games; 8-8 in extra-inning games; 1-0-0 in double-headers.
Team record past five years: 493-317 (.609, ranks 1st in league in that span).

TEAM LEADERS

Batting average: Chipper Jones (.330).
At-bats: Andruw Jones (625).
Runs: Chipper Jones (113).
Hits: Chipper Jones (189).
Total Bases: Chipper Jones (346).
Doubles: Chipper Jones, B.J. Surhoff (33).
Triples: Chipper Jones (5).
Home runs: Chipper Jones (38).
Runs batted in: Andruw Jones (104).
Stolen bases: Rafael Furcal (22).
Slugging percentage: Chipper Jones (.605).
On-base percentage: Chipper Jones (.427).
Wins: Greg Maddux (17).
Earned-run average: John Burkett (3.04).
Complete games: Greg Maddux (3).
Shutouts: Greg Maddux (3).

Saves: John Rocker (19).
Innings pitched: Greg Maddux (233.0).
Strikeouts: John Burkett (187).

GAMES BY POSITION

Catcher: Javy Lopez 127, Paul Bako 60, Eddie Perez 5, Steve Torrealba 2.
First base: Wes Helms 77, Rico Brogna 67, Ken Caminiti 33, Julio Franco 23, Dave Martinez 10.
Second base: Quilvio Veras 67, Marcus Giles 62, Keith Lockhart 47, Mark DeRosa 5, Jesse Garcia 4, Kurt Abbott 1.
Third base: Chipper Jones 149, Wes Helms 17, Ken Caminiti 13, Keith Lockhart 4, Mark DeRosa 1.
Shortstop: Rafael Furcal 79, Mark DeRosa 48, Rey Sanchez 48, Jesse Garcia 2, Kurt Abbott 1, Wilson Betemit 1.
Outfield: Andruw Jones 161, Brian Jordan 144, B.J. Surhoff 129, Dave Martinez 52, Bernard Gilkey 36, Chipper Jones 8, Cory Aldridge 4, Wes Helms 1, Mark DeRosa 1.
Designated hitter: B.J. Surhoff 3, Mark DeRosa 3, Brian Jordan 2, Dave Martinez 1, Chipper Jones 1, Bernard Gilkey 1, Ken Caminiti 1.

TOP DRAFT CHOICES

1a. **Macay McBride,** LHP, Screven County H.S., Sylvania, Ga.
1b. **Josh Burrus, SS,** Wheeler H.S., Marietta, Ga.
1c. **Richard Lewis,** 2B, Georgia Tech.
2. **J.P. Howell,** LHP, Jesuit H.S., Sacramento.
2. **Cole Barthel,** 3B, Decatur (Ala.) H.S.
3. **Adam Stern,** OF, Univ. of Nebraska.
4. **Kyle Davies,** RHP, Stockbridge (Ga.) H.S.
5. **Matt Esquivel,** OF, McArthur H.S., San Antonio.
6. **Billy McCarthy,** OF, Rutgers Univ.
7. **Roberto Nieves,** RHP, Ileana de Gracia H.S., Vega Alta, P.R.
8. **Alonzo Ruelas,** C, Grayson County (Tex.) C.C.
9. **Donald Furnald,** RHP/3B, Cal Poly Pomona.
10. **Willie Collazo,** LHP, Florida International University.

CHICAGO CUBS
NATIONAL LEAGUE CENTRAL DIVISION

2002 SEASON *Chicago Cubs*

Cubs schedule
Home games shaded
D—Day game (games starting before 5 p.m.)
*All-Star Game at Milwaukee
Subject to changes

April

SUN	MON	TUE	WED	THU	FRI	SAT
	1 D CIN	2	3 CIN	4 CIN	5 D PIT	6 D PIT
7 D PIT	8	9 D NYM	10 D NYM	11 D NYM	12 PIT	13 D PIT
14 D PIT	15 D MON	16 MON	17 MON	18	19 D CIN	20 D CIN
21 D CIN	22	23 SF	24 SF	25 D SF	26 D LA	27 D LA
28 D LA	29	30 SD				

May

SUN	MON	TUE	WED	THU	FRI	SAT
			1 SD	2 D SD	3 D LA	4 LA
5 LA	6 STL	7 STL	8 D STL	9 MIL	10 D MIL	11 D MIL
12 MIL	13 STL	14 D STL	15 STL	16	17 MIL	18 MIL
19 D MIL	20	21 PIT	22 PIT	23 D PIT	24 HOU	25 HOU
26 HOU	27 PIT	28 PIT	29 PIT	30 D PIT	31 D HOU	

June

SUN	MON	TUE	WED	THU	FRI	SAT
						1 D HOU
2 D HOU	3 MIL	4 MIL	5 MIL	6	7 SEA	8 SEA
9 D SEA	10 HOU	11 HOU	12 D HOU	13	14 D CWS	15 D CWS
16 D CWS	17	18 D TEX	19 D TEX	20 D TEX	21 D STL	22 D STL
23 STL	24 CIN	25 CIN	26 CIN	27 CWS	28 CWS	29 D CWS
30 D CWS						

July

SUN	MON	TUE	WED	THU	FRI	SAT
	1 FLA	2 FLA	3 FLA	4 ATL	5 ATL	6 ATL
7 ATL	8	9 *	10	11	12 D FLA	13 D FLA
14 D FLA	15 ATL	16 D ATL	17 PHI	18 PHI	19 D HOU	20 D HOU
21 HOU	22 PHI	23 PHI	24 PHI	25 D PHI	26 STL	27 D STL
28 STL	29	30 SD	31 SD			

August

SUN	MON	TUE	WED	THU	FRI	SAT
				1 SD	2 D COL	3 D COL
4 D COL	5	6 SF	7 SF	8 SF	9 D COL	10 COL
11 D COL	12 HOU	13 HOU	14 D HOU	15 D HOU	16 D ARI	17 D ARI
18 D ARI	19	20 HOU	21 HOU	22 HOU	23 ARI	24 ARI
25 ARI	26 MIL	27 MIL	28 MIL	29 D MIL	30 D STL	31 STL

September

SUN	MON	TUE	WED	THU	FRI	SAT
1 STL	2 MIL	3 MIL	4 MIL	5	6 STL	7 D STL
8 STL	9 MON	10 MON	11 MON	12 CIN	13 CIN	14 CIN
15 CIN	16	17 NYM	18 NYM	19 NYM	20 PIT	21 PIT
22 PIT	23	24 CIN	25 CIN	26 D PIT	27 PIT	28 PIT
29 PIT	30					

2002 SEASON
CLUB DIRECTORY

Board of directors
Dennis FitzSimons
Andrew B. MacPhail
Andrew McKenna

President and chief executive officer
Andrew B. MacPhail

Vice president, player personnel
Jim Hendry

Director, baseball operations
Scott Nelson

Special assistants to the g.m.
Keith Champion, Ken Kravec, Ed Lynch, Billy Williams

Director of scouting
John Stockstill

Dir of player dev./Latin American ops.
Oneri Fleita

Traveling secretary
Jimmy Bank

Executive v.p., business operations
Mark McGuire

Dir., info. services & special projects
Carl Rice

Sr. legal counsel/corporate secretary
Crane Kenney

Controller
Jodi Rieschl

Director, human resources
Jenifer Surma

V.p., marketing and broadcasting
John McDonough

Director, promotions and advertising
Jay Blunk

Director, publications
Lena McDonagh

Manager, publications
Jim McArdle

Director, stadium operations
Paul Rathje

Manager, event operations/security
Mike Hill

Head groundskeeper
Roger Baird

Director, ticket operations
Frank Maloney

Director, media relations
Sharon Pannozzo

Manager, media information
Chuck Wasserstrom

Team physician
Michael Schafer, M.D.

Head athletic trainer
David Tumbas

Assistant athletic trainer
Sandy Krum

Strength and conditioning coordinator
Tim Buss

Home clubhouse manager, emeritus
Yosh Kawano

Home clubhouse manager
Tom Hellmann

Visiting clubhouse manager
Dana Noeltner

Pacific Rim coordinator
Leon Lee

Regional scouting supervisors
Brad Kelley, Mike Soper

Roving crosschecker
Joe Housey

Special assignment scouts
Jim Olander, Glen Van Proyen

Scouts
Mark Adair, Billy Blitzer, Jim Crawford, Steve Fuller, Al Geddes, John Gracio, Bob Hale, Gene Handley, Bill Harford, Steve Hinton, Sam Hughes, Spider Jorgensen, Scott May, Brian Milner, Hector Ortega, Fred Peterson, Tad Powers, Steve Riha, Jose Serra, Mark Servais, Tom Shafer, Billy Swoope, Jose Trujillo

---

MINOR LEAGUE AFFILIATES

Class	Team	League	Manager
AAA	Iowa	Pacific Coast	Bruce Kimm
AA	West Tenn	Southern	Bobby Dickerson
A	Daytona	Florida State	Dave Trembley
A	Lansing	Midwest	Julio Garcia
A	Boise	Northwest	Steve McFarland
Rookie	Mesa Cubs	Arizona	Carmelo Martinez

BROADCAST INFORMATION

Radio: WGN-AM (720).
TV: WGN-TV (Channel 9); WCIU-TV (Channel 26).
Cable TV: Fox Sports Net Chicago.

SPRING TRAINING

Ballpark (city): HoHoKam Park (Mesa, Ariz.).
Ticket information: 800-638-4253.

Follow the Cubs all season at: www.sportingnews.com/baseball/teams/cubs/

Manager—Don Baylor (25).
Coaches—Sandy Alomar Sr. (2), Gene Glynn (3), Rick Kranitz, Rene Lachemann (5), Jeff Pentland (4), Larry Rothschild.

No.	PITCHERS	B/T	Ht./Wt.	Born	2001 clubs
	Beltran, Francis	R/R	6-5/220	7-25-80	Daytona
	Bere, Jason	R/R	6-3/215	5-26-71	Chicago N.L.
	Chiasson, Scott	R/R	6-2/185	8-14-77	West Tenn, Iowa, Chicago N.L.
	Christensen, Ben	R/R	6-4/205	2-7-78	West Tenn
	Cruz, Juan	R/R	6-2/155	10-15-80	West Tenn, Chicago N.L.
59	Duncan, Courtney	L/R	6-0/180	10-9-74	Chicago N.L., Iowa
44	Farnsworth, Kyle	R/R	6-4/215	4-14-76	Chicago N.L.
13	Fassero, Jeff	L/L	6-1/195	1-5-63	Chicago N.L.
45	Gordon, Tom	R/R	5-9/190	11-18-67	Daytona, Iowa, Chicago N.L.
32	Lieber, Jon	L/R	6-3/225	4-2-70	Chicago N.L.
17	Mahay, Ron	L/L	6-2/190	6-28-71	Portland, Iowa, Chicago N.L.
43	Meyers, Mike	R/R	6-2/210	10-18-77	Iowa
50	Norton, Phil	R/L	6-1/190	2-1-76	Iowa
35	Ohman, Will	L/L	6-2/195	8-13-77	Iowa, Chicago N.L.
21	Sanchez, Jesus	L/L	5-10/155	10-11-74	Calgary, Florida
	Smyth, Steve	L/L	6-1/220	6-3-78	West Tenn
50	Tavarez, Julian	L/R	6-2/195	5-22-73	Chicago N.L.
34	Wood, Kerry	R/R	6-5/230	6-16-77	Chicago N.L.
	Zambrano, Carlos	B/R	6-4/250	6-1-81	Iowa, Chicago N.L.

No.	CATCHERS	B/T	Ht./Wt.	Born	2001 clubs
27	Girardi, Joe	R/R	5-11/200	10-14-64	Chicago N.L.
	Hundley, Todd	R/R	5-11/199	5-27-69	Chicago N.L., West Tenn, Iowa
39	Machado, Robert	R/R	6-1/205	6-3-73	Iowa, Chicago N.L.

No.	INFIELDERS	B/T	Ht./Wt.	Born	2001 clubs
49	Bellhorn, Mark	B/R	6-4/214	8-23-74	Sacramento, Oakland
	Choi, Hee Seop	L/L	6-5/235	3-16-79	Iowa
13	Coffie, Ivanon	L/R	6-1/192	5-16-77	Rochester, Gulf Coast Orioles
11	DeShields, Delino	L/R	6-1/175	1-15-69	Baltimore, Chicago N.L.
56	Frese, Nate	R/R	6-3/200	7-10-77	West Tenn
8	Gonzalez, Alex	R/R	6-0/195	4-8-73	Toronto
	Hill, Bobby	B/R	5-10/165	4-3-78	West Tenn, Arizona Cubs
	Kelton, Dave	R/R	6-3/205	12-17-79	West Tenn
29	McGriff, Fred	L/L	6-3/215	10-31-63	Tampa Bay, Chicago N.L.
33	Mueller, Bill	B/R	5-10/180	3-17-71	Chicago N.L., Iowa
57	Ojeda, Augie	B/R	5-9/170	12-20-74	Chicago N.L.
	Stynes, Chris	R/R	5-10/185	1-19-73	Boston, Pawtucket
15	Zuleta, Julio	R/R	6-5/235	3-28-75	Chicago N.L., Iowa

No.	OUTFIELDERS	B/T	Ht./Wt.	Born	2001 clubs
18	Alou, Moises	R/R	6-3/195	7-3-66	Houston
28	Brown, Roosevelt	L/R	5-11/195	8-3-75	Chicago N.L., Iowa
	Lewis, Darren	R/R	6-0/190	8-28-67	Boston
20	Patterson, Corey	L/R	5-10/180	8-13-79	Iowa, Chicago N.L.
21	Sosa, Sammy	R/R	6-0/220	11-12-68	Chicago N.L.

BALLPARK INFORMATION

Ballpark (capacity, surface)
Wrigley Field (39,059, grass)
Address
1060 W. Addison St.
Chicago, IL 60613-4397
Official website
www.cubs.com
Business phone
773-404-2827
Ticket Information
773-404-2827
Ticket prices
$36 (club box-infield)
$32 (club box-outfield, field box-infield)
$30 (field box-outfield)
$26 (upper deck box, terrace box, family section)
$24 (bleachers)
$20 (terrace reserved)
$12 (upper deck reserved)
Field dimensions (from home plate)
To left field at foul line, 355 feet
To center field, 400 feet
To right field at foul line, 353 feet
First game played
April 20, 1916 (Cubs 7, Reds 6)

2002 SEASON *Chicago Cubs*

Date	Opp.	Res.	Score	(inn.*)	Hits	Opp. hits	Winning pitcher	Losing pitcher	Save	Record	Pos.	GB
4-2	Mon.	L	4-5	(10)	9	10	Lloyd	Fyhrie	Urbina	0-1	T1st	0.5
4-4	Mon.	L	2-3		8	9	Reames	Wood	Urbina	0-2	T4th	2.0
4-5	Mon.	W	2-1		4	3	Tapani	Armas	Fassero	1-2	T3rd	2.0
4-6	At Phi.	W	3-2		7	7	Tavarez	Wolf	Fassero	2-2	2nd	2.0
4-7	At Phi.	W	8-4		11	7	Bere	Padilla		3-2	2nd	1.0
4-8	At Phi.	L	1-3		5	4	Person	Lieber	Mesa	3-3	2nd	1.0
4-9	At Mon.	L	5-7		9	8	Lloyd	Aybar	Urbina	3-4	T3rd	1.5
4-10	At Mon.	W	4-2		5	9	Tapani	Armas	Fassero	4-4	3rd	1.5
4-11	At Mon.	W	4-2		8	7	Tavarez	Thurman	Fassero	5-4	3rd	1.5
4-13	Pit.	W	4-2		5	6	Bere	Arroyo	Fassero	6-4	2nd	1.0
4-14	Pit.	W	7-6		13	11	Aybar	Silva	Fassero	7-4	2nd	1.0
4-15	Pit.	W	5-1		11	5	Duncan	Sauerbeck		8-4	T1st	...
4-17	Phi.	L	3-6		12	10	Padilla	Fassero	Mesa	8-5	T1st	...
4-18†	Phi.	W	4-3		5	13	Tapani	Chen	Fassero	9-5		
4-18‡	Phi.	W	5-3		9	6	– Bere	Wolf	Fassero	10-5	1st	+1.5
4-20	At Pit.	W	8-2		7	6	Lieber	Martinez		11-5	1st	+1.5
4-21	At Pit.	W	4-3		7	9	Heredia	M. Williams	Fassero	12-5	1st	+2.5
4-22	At Pit.	L	3-4	(10)	9	12	M. Williams	Fassero		12-6	1st	+1.5
4-24	At Col.	L	1-14		5	19	Hampton	Tapani		12-7	1st	+1.0
4-25	At Col.	L	5-6		8	10	Jimenez	Duncan		12-8	1st	+1.0
4-26	At Col.	W	7-2		10	9	Lieber	Bohanon		13-8	1st	+1.0
4-27	At S.F	W	7-3		8	3	Wood	Gardner		14-8	1st	+1.0
4-28	At S.F	L	0-5		5	9	Estes	Tavarez		14-9	T1st	...
4-29	At S.F	W	11-2		13	6	Aybar	Hernandez		15-9	1st	+1.0
5-1	S.D.	L	3-10		9	8	Tollberg	Bere		15-10	T1st	...
5-2	S.D.	W	8-3		9	6	Lieber	Jarvis		16-10	1st	+1.0
5-3	S.D.	L	3-5		6	6	Jones	Wood	Hoffman	16-11	1st	+1.0
5-4	L.A.	W	4-0		8	4	Tapani	Park		17-11	1st	+2.0
5-5	L.A.	W	20-1		18	6	Tavarez	Dreifort		18-11	1st	+2.0
5-6	L.A.	W	3-2		4	5	Gordon	Herges		19-11	1st	+2.5
5-7	At Mil.	W	7-6		12	9	Van Poppel	Weathers	Gordon	20-11	1st	+3.5
5-8	At Mil.	L	1-4		5	3	Sheets	Wood	Leskanic	20-12	1st	+3.0
5-9	At Mil.	W	6-3		8	6	Tapani	Wright	Gordon	21-12	1st	+3.5
5-10	At Mil.	L	1-11		7	11	Levrault	Tavarez	DeJean	21-13	1st	+2.5
5-11	At St.L.	L	2-7		8	7	Kile	Bere		21-14	1st	+1.5
5-12	At St.L.	L	2-5		6	13	Morris	Lieber	Veres	21-15	1st	+0.5
5-13	At St.L.	L	4-13		9	10	An. Benes	Wood		21-16	2nd	0.5
5-15	Hou.	L	7-9	(12)	9	17	Jackson	Van Poppel	Cruz	21-17	4th	1.5
5-16	Hou.	L	2-6		6	9	Reynolds	Tavarez		21-18	4th	2.5
5-17	Hou.	L	2-4		9	8	Oswalt	Farnsworth	Wagner	21-19	4th	3.5
5-18	Ari.	L	0-4		1	10	Johnson	Lieber		21-20	4th	3.5
5-19	Ari.	W	6-2		10	6	Wood	Batista		22-20	4th	2.5
5-20	Ari.	W	6-5		15	6	Tapani	Ellis	Fassero	23-20	T3rd	2.5
5-22	Cin.	W	5-3		9	4	Duncan	Brower	Gordon	24-20	T2nd	1.5
5-23	Cin.	W	4-2		7	5	Van Poppel	Bell	Gordon	25-20	T2nd	0.5
5-24	Cin.	W	3-0		10	1	Lieber	O. Fernandez		26-20	2nd	0.5
5-25	Mil.	W	1-0		4	1	Wood	Levrault		27-20	2nd	0.5
5-27	Mil.	W	4-1		6	6	Tapani	Haynes	Gordon	28-20	T1st	...
5-28	At Cin.	W	9-6	(13)	15	10	Duncan	Winchester		29-20	T1st	...
5-29	At Cin.	W	10-5		10	10	Bere	O. Fernandez		30-20	1st	+1.0
5-30	At Cin.	W	3-1		9	5	Lieber	Reitsma	Gordon	31-20	1st	+2.0
6-1	At Mil.	W	4-3		10	6	Wood	Haynes	Gordon	32-20	1st	+3.5
6-2	At Mil.	W	10-4		9	16	Tapani	Rigdon		33-20	1st	+3.5
6-3	At Mil.	L	2-4		7	8	Sheets	Tavarez	Leskanic	33-21	1st	+2.5
6-5	St.L.	W	12-6		13	9	Lieber	Hermanson		34-21	1st	+3.0
6-6	St.L.	W	4-1		10	3	Wood	Kile	Gordon	35-21	1st	+4.0
6-7	St.L.	W	4-3	(10)	10	8	Fassero	Timlin		36-21	1st	+5.0
6-8	At Chi.	L	3-7	(10)	8	8	Foulke	Duncan		36-22	1st	+5.0
6-9	At Chi.	W	4-3	(10)	9	10	Van Poppel	Foulke	Fassero	37-22	1st	+5.0
6-10	At Chi.	L	1-3		6	8	K. Wells	Lieber	Howry	37-23	1st	+5.0
6-12	At Ari.	W	6-2		10	7	Wood	Schilling		38-23	1st	+6.0
6-13	At Ari.	L	3-13		6	19	Bierbrodt	Tapani		38-24	1st	+6.0
6-14	At Ari.	L	2-3		6	9	Johnson	Bere	Swindell	38-25	1st	+6.0
6-15	Min.	W	5-3		7	9	Tavarez	Romero	Gordon	39-25	1st	+6.0
6-16	Min.	W	11-4		15	10	Lieber	Thomas		40-25	1st	+6.0
6-17	Min.	W	5-4		10	7	Wood	Radke	Gordon	41-25	1st	+6.0
6-18	At St.L.	L	2-6		5	11	Kile	Tapani		41-26	1st	+5.0
6-19	At St.L.	L	2-3		11	9	Morris	Farnsworth	Veres	41-27	1st	+4.0
6-20	At St.L.	W	9-4		13	11	Tavarez	Matthews		42-27	1st	+5.0
6-21	At St.L.	W	5-2		9	8	Lieber	An. Benes	Gordon	43-27	1st	+6.0
6-22	Mil.	L	1-2		5	5	Weathers	Wood	Leskanic	43-28	1st	+6.0
6-23	Mil.	L	0-4		5	9	Wright	Tapani		43-29	1st	+5.0
6-24	Mil.	L	3-6		8	8	Sheets	Bere	Leskanic	43-30	1st	+4.0
6-25	N.Y.	W	2-1		7	3	Tavarez	Leiter	Gordon	44-30	1st	+4.5

Date	Opp.	Res.	Score	(inn.*)	Hits	Opp. hits	Winning pitcher	Losing pitcher	Save	Record	Pos.	GB
6-26	N.Y.	W	4-2		7	6	Lieber	Appier	Gordon	45-30	1st	+5.0
6-27	N.Y.	L	4-5		9	8	White	Farnsworth	Benitez	45-31	1st	+4.5
6-28	At Cin.	L	2-5		5	16	Dessens	Tapani		45-32	1st	+4.5
6-29	At Cin.	W	7-1		12	8	Bere	Reith		46-32	1st	+5.5
6-30	At Cin.	L	1-7		7	10	Acevedo	Tavarez		46-33	1st	+4.5
7-1	At Cin.	W	2-1		7	6	Lieber	Reitsma	Gordon	47-33	1st	+4.5
7-3	At N.Y.	W	3-0		6	5	Wood	Reed	Gordon	48-33	1st	+4.0
7-4	At N.Y.	L	1-2		6	8	Rusch	Tapani	Benitez	48-34	1st	+4.0
7-5	At N.Y.	W	13-4		15	6	Bere	Trachsel		49-34	1st	+4.0
7-6	At Det.	W	15-9		21	13	Heredia	Nitkowski		50-34	1st	+4.0
7-7	At Det.	W	10-0		11	11	Lieber	Blair		51-34	1st	+4.0
7-8	At Det.	L	6-9		7	13	Jones	Heredia	Anderson	51-35	1st	+3.0
7-12	Chi.	W	5-1		7	6	Fassero	Garland		52-35	1st	+4.0
7-13	Chi.	L	2-7		9	6	Buehrle	Wood		52-36	1st	+3.0
7-14	Chi.	L	1-3		4	7	Lowe	Tavarez	Foulke	52-37	1st	+3.0
7-15	K.C.	W	2-1		4	7	Lieber	Byrd	Gordon	53-37	1st	+3.0
7-16	K.C.	L	2-4		5	7	Reichert	Tapani	Hernandez	53-38	1st	+2.0
7-17	K.C.	W	7-4		11	9	Bere	Cogan	Gordon	54-38	1st	+3.0
7-18	At Pit.	W	6-5		10	6	Fassero	M. Williams	Gordon	55-38	1st	+3.0
7-19	At Pit.	L	2-3		5	11	Olivares	Duncan	M. Williams	55-39	1st	+3.0
7-20	At Hou.	L	2-5		7	10	Redding	Lieber	Wagner	55-40	1st	+2.0
7-21	At Hou.	W	5-4		13	7	Farnsworth	Villone	Gordon	56-40	1st	+3.0
7-22	At Hou.	L	0-3		5	4	Reynolds	Bere	Wagner	56-41	1st	+2.0
7-23	At Hou.	W	6-2		10	10	Wood	Oswalt		57-41	1st	+3.0
7-24	Pit.	W	10-2		17	10	Tavarez	Ritchie		58-41	1st	+3.0
7-25	Pit.	W	6-5		8	11	Lieber	D. Williams		59-41	1st	+4.0
7-26	St.L.	L	1-3		5	6	Smith	Tapani	Kline	59-42	1st	+3.0
7-27	St.L.	W	4-3		7	4	Fassero	Christiansen	Gordon	60-42	1st	+4.0
7-28	St.L.	L	4-7		5	16	Veres	Fyhrie	Kline	60-43	1st	+3.5
7-29	St.L.	W	7-5		9	8	Tavarez	Morris	Gordon	61-43	1st	+4.5
7-31	At S.D.	W	7-3		13	7	Lieber	Lawrence		62-43	1st	+4.5
8-1	At S.D.	L	3-4		9	7	Jones	Heredia	Hoffman	62-44	1st	+4.5
8-2	At S.D.	L	3-4		5	6	McElroy	Fassero	Hoffman	62-45	1st	+3.5
8-3	At L.A.	W	2-1		5	3	Wood	Park	Gordon	63-45	1st	+3.5
8-4	At L.A.	L	1-3		4	8	Baldwin	Tavarez	Shaw	63-46	1st	+2.5
8-5	At L.A.	L	2-3	(10)	9	10	Mulholland	Gordon		63-47	1st	+1.5
8-7	Col.	W	5-4		11	9	Farnsworth	Speier		64-47	1st	+2.5
8-8	Col.	W	2-1		7	7	Bere	Thomson	Gordon	65-47	1st	+2.5
8-9	Col.	L	5-14		11	12	Hampton	Tavarez		65-48	1st	+1.5
8-10	S.F.	W	9-3		9	8	Lieber	Estes		66-48	1st	+1.5
8-11	S.F.	L	4-9		7	15	Hernandez	Borowski		66-49	1st	+1.5
8-12	S.F.	L	6-7		13	10	Rueter	Tapani	Nen	66-50	1st	+0.5
8-13	At Hou.	L	5-9		8	13	Reynolds	Bere		66-51	2nd	0.5
8-14	At Hou.	W	3-1		7	5	Weathers	Villone	Gordon	67-51	2nd	+0.5
8-15	At Hou.	W	5-1		11	3	Lieber	Astacio		68-51	1st	+1.5
8-17	At Ari.	L	2-7		8	13	Lopez	Tapani	Kim	68-52	1st	...
8-18	At Ari.	L	3-5		9	8	Johnson	Bere	Kim	68-53	2nd	1.0
8-19	At Ari.	L	6-13		12	13	Witt	Ohman		68-54	2nd	2.0
8-20†	Mil.	W	7-4		11	9	Farnsworth	King	Gordon	69-54		
8-20‡	Mil.	L	2-10		5	7	Wright	Zambrano		69-55	2nd	2.0
8-21	Mil.	L	1-3		5	6	Quevedo	Cruz	Leskanic	69-56	T2nd	3.0
8-22	Mil.	W	16-3		17	6	Tapani	Suzuki		70-56	2nd	2.0
8-23	Mil.	L	1-8		5	15	Suzuki	Tavarez		70-57	2nd	3.0
8-24	St.L.	L	8-10		12	15	Morris	Bere	Hackman	70-58	T2nd	4.0
8-25	St.L.	W	6-4		8	6	Lieber	Williams	Gordon	71-58	2nd	3.0
8-26	St.L.	W	6-1		11	9	Cruz	Hermanson		72-58	2nd	3.0
8-28	Fla.	L	3-4	(14)	11	14	Nunez	Fassero		72-59	2nd	4.0
8-29	Fla.	W	5-1		9	3	Bere	Clement		73-59	2nd	4.0
8-30	Fla.	W	5-4		7	12	Farnsworth	Bones		74-59	2nd	4.0
8-31	At Atl.	W	8-2		12	6	Cruz	Burkett		75-59	2nd	4.0
9-1	At Atl.	W	5-3		9	9	Tavarez	Maddux	Gordon	76-59	2nd	3.0
9-2	At Atl.	L	4-7		6	12	Millwood	Tapani	Smoltz	76-60	2nd	4.0
9-3	At Fla.	W	10-2		13	7	Bere	Clement		77-60	2nd	3.0
9-4	At Fla.	L	1-8		6	8	Beckett	Lieber		77-61	2nd	4.0
9-5	At Fla.	L	6-7		11	11	Almanza	Gordon		77-62	2nd	5.0
9-7	Atl.	L	2-3		4	8	Karsay	Farnsworth	Smoltz	77-63	2nd	5.5
9-8	Atl.	L	3-5		7	11	Glavine	Tapani	Smoltz	77-64	T2nd	5.5
9-9	Atl.	L	5-9		10	16	Ligtenberg	Bere		77-65	3rd	6.5
9-10	Cin.	W	8-2		11	6	Lieber	Reitsma		78-65	3rd	6.0
9-18	At Cin.	L	5-6		13	11	Graves	Farnsworth		78-66	3rd	7.0
9-19	At Cin.	W	10-0		11	3	Wood	Hamilton		79-66	3rd	7.0
9-20	At Cin.	W	6-5		8	9	Bere	Brower	Fassero	80-66	3rd	7.0
9-21	At Hou.	W	12-4		13	10	Zambrano	Villone		81-66	3rd	6.0
9-22	At Hou.	L	4-8		7	9	Reynolds	Tapani		81-67	3rd	7.0
9-23	At Hou.	L	6-7		8	12	Williams	Weathers	Wagner	81-68	3rd	8.0
9-24	At Pit.	L	6-7		10	10	Lincoln	Chiasson	Loiselle	81-69	3rd	9.0
9-25	At Pit.	L	1-13		6	15	Anderson	Bere		81-70	3rd	9.0
9-26	At Pit.	W	8-4		13	10	Cruz	Arroyo		82-70	3rd	8.0

Date	Opp.	Res.	Score	(inn.*)	Hits	Opp. hits	Winning pitcher	Losing pitcher	Save	Record	Pos.	GB
9-27	Hou.	L	5-6		8	7	Reynolds	Tapani	Wagner	82-71	3rd	9.0
9-28	Hou.	W	6-2		14	6	Lieber	Oswalt		83-71	3rd	8.0
9-29	Hou.	W	6-2		7	4	Wood	Mlicki		84-71	3rd	7.0
9-30	Hou.	W	7-6		6	10	Chiasson	Villone	Farnsworth	85-71	3rd	6.0
10-2	Cin.	L	4-5		7	10	Sullivan	Farnsworth	Graves	85-72	3rd	6.0
10-3	Cin.	W	13-7		15	12	Lieber	MacRae		86-72	3rd	5.0
10-4	Cin.	W	2-0	(8)	6	7	Van Poppel	Acevedo	Farnsworth	87-72	3rd	5.0
10-5	Pit.	L	2-3		6	4	Beimel	Bere	Fetters	87-73	3rd	5.0
10-6	Pit.	W	13-2		16	2	Tavarez	McKnight		88-73	3rd	5.0
10-7	Pit.	L	3-4		9	7	Beimel	Zambrano	Fetters	88-74	3rd	5.0

Monthly records: April (15-9), May (16-11), June (15-13), July (16-10), August (13-16), September (10-12), October (3-3).
*Innings, if other than nine. †First game of a doubleheader. ‡Second game of a doubleheader.

HIGHLIGHTS

High point: The Cubs salvaged a four-game split at St. Louis on June 21 with a 5-2 victory, restoring the six-game division lead they had over the Cardinals at the start of the series.

Low point: The Cubs fell five games behind Houston on September 5 when closer Tom Gordon allowed a game-winning, three-run homer in the ninth inning to Florida's Preston Wilson at Pro Player Stadium.

Turning point: Kerry Wood pitched eight innings in a 2-1 victory at Los Angeles on August 3, but missed the next month because of tendinitis in his right shoulder. The Cubs led the N.L. Central by 3 1/2 games at the time. When he returned on September 7, the Cubs trailed Houston by 4 1/2 games.

Most valuable player: Sammy Sosa hit 64 home runs and and led the majors 160 RBIs. He became the first major league player since Ted Williams in 1949 to have a combined 300 runs scored-RBIs in one season. Sosa's 425 total bases represented the highest total in Cubs history, surpassing the 423 amassed by Hack Wilson in 1930.

Most valuable pitcher: Jon Lieber became the first Cubs pitcher since Greg Maddux in 1992 to post a 20-win season. In 232 1/3 innings, Lieber struck out 148 batters while walking just 41.

Most improved player: Kyle Farnsworth found his niche as a late-inning setup man. Farnsworth worked in 76 games, going 4-6 with a 2.74 ERA and two saves. In 82 innings, he struck out 107 batters.

Most pleasant surprise: When the Cubs signed Jeff Fassero, they hoped to get a middle- to late-inning guy and occasional spot starter. What they got was their leader in appearances with 82.

Key injuries: Bill Mueller missed three months after fracturing his left kneecap May 13. ... Rondell White played only 95 games because of a strained left groin. ... Tom Gordon missed all of April because of a sore right triceps muscle. He did not pitch after September 5 because of tendinitis in his right elbow. ... Todd Hundley missed time because of a strained back.

Notable: The Cubs pitching staff set a major league record for strikeouts with 1,344, breaking the mark of 1,245 set by the 1996 Braves. ... The Cubs' 12-game winning streak, from late May through early June, was the club's longest since 1936. ... The Cubs had the best record in the National League at the All-Star break. It was only the third time since World War II that had happened. The other years were 1969 and 1977. The Cubs didn't make the playoffs in any of those seasons.

—BRUCE MILES

RECORDS

2001 regular-season record: 88-74 (3rd in N.L. Central); 48-33 at home; 40-41 on road; 16-14 vs. N.L. East; 48-36 vs. N.L. Central; 15-18 vs. N.L. West; 9-6 vs. A.L.; 14-22 vs. lefthanded starters; 74-52 vs. righthanded starters; 84-72 on grass; 4-2 on turf; 51-43 in daytime; 37-31 at night; 26-24 in one-run games; 3-6 in extra-inning games; 1-0-1 in doubleheaders.

Team record past five years: 378-433 (.466, ranks 11th in league in that span).

TEAM LEADERS

Batting average: Sammy Sosa (.328).
At-bats: Eric Young (603).
Runs: Sammy Sosa (146).
Hits: Sammy Sosa (189).
Total Bases: Sammy Sosa (425).
Doubles: Eric Young (43).
Triples: Michael Tucker (7).
Home runs: Sammy Sosa (64).
Runs batted in: Sammy Sosa (160).
Stolen bases: Eric Young (31).
Slugging percentage: Sammy Sosa (.737).
On-base percentage: Sammy Sosa (.437).

Wins: Jon Lieber (20).
Earned-run average: Kerry Wood (3.36).
Complete games: Jon Lieber (5).
Shutouts: Jon Lieber, Kerry Wood (1).
Saves: Tom Gordon (27).
Innings pitched: Jon Lieber (232.1).
Strikeouts: Kerry Wood (217).

GAMES BY POSITION

Catcher: Joe Girardi 71, Todd Hundley 70, Robert Machado 47.
First base: Matt Stairs 89, Fred McGriff 49, Ron Coomer 36, Julio Zuleta 35, Michael Tucker 4, Delino DeShields 1.
Second base: Eric Young 147, Delino DeShields 16, Miguel Cairo 11, Augie Ojeda 10, Chad Meyers 4, Matt Stairs 1, Bill Mueller 1.
Third base: Ron Coomer 76, Bill Mueller 64, Miguel Cairo 40, Augie Ojeda 35, Delino DeShields 5, Chad Meyers 1.
Shortstop: Ricky Gutierrez 144, Augie Ojeda 31, Miguel Cairo 1, Jason Smith 1.
Outfield: Sammy Sosa 160, Gary Matthews Jr. 100, Rondell White 90, Michael Tucker 57, Corey Patterson 54, Damon Buford 34, Delino DeShields 33, Todd Dunwoody 26, Matt Stairs 22, Roosevelt Brown 22, Chad Meyers 4.
Designated hitter: Roosevelt Brown 3, Matt Stairs 2, Ron Coomer 1.

TOP DRAFT CHOICES

1. **Mark Prior,** RHP, U. of Southern Cal.
2. **Andy Sisco,** LHP, Eastlake H.S., Sammamish, Wash.
3. **Ryan Theriot,** SS, Louisiana State U.
4. **Ricky Nolasco,** RHP, Rialto (Calif.) H.S.
5. **Brendan Harris,** SS, College of William & Mary.
6. **Adam Wynegar,** LHP, James Madison University.
7. **Sergio Mitre,** RHP, San Diego C.C.
8. **Warren Hanna,** C, U. of South Alabama.
9. **Alan Bomer,** RHP, Iowa State Univ.
10. **Corey Slavik,** 3B, Wake Forest Univ.

CINCINNATI REDS
NATIONAL LEAGUE CENTRAL DIVISION

Reds schedule
Home games shaded
D—Day game (games starting before 5 p.m.)
*All-Star Game at Milwaukee
Subject to changes

April

SUN	MON	TUE	WED	THU	FRI	SAT
	1 D CUB	2	3 CUB	4 CUB	5 MON	6 MON
7 D MON	8 D PIT	9	10 PIT	11 PIT	12 PHI	13 PHI
14 D PHI	15	16 HOU	17 HOU	18 D HOU	19 D CUB	20 D CUB
21 CUB	22	23 COL	24 COL	25 COL	26 SF	27 D SF
26 SF	29	30 LA				

May

SUN	MON	TUE	WED	THU	FRI	SAT
		1 LA	2 LA	3 SF	4 SF
5 D SF	6 MIL	7 D MIL	8 MIL	9	10 STL	11 D STL
12 D STL	13 MIL	14 MIL	15 MIL	16 D STL	17 STL	18 D STL
19 D STL	20 STL	21 FLA	22 FLA	23 FLA	24 ATL	25 ATL
26 D ATL	27 FLA	28 FLA	29 FLA	30 FLA	31 ATL

June

SUN	MON	TUE	WED	THU	FRI	SAT
						1 ATL
2 D ATL	3	4 STL	5 STL	6 D STL	7 ANA	8 ANA
9 D ANA	10 TEX	11 TEX	12 TEX	13	14 PIT	15 PIT
16 D PIT	17	18 SEA	19 SEA	20 SEA	21 OAK	22 OAK
23 D OAK	24 CUB	25 D CUB	26 D CUB	27 CUB	28 STL	29 STL
30 D STL						

July

SUN	MON	TUE	WED	THU	FRI	SAT
	1 HOU	2 HOU	3 HOU	4 D MIL	5 MIL	6 MIL
7 D MIL	8	9 *	10 HOU	11 HOU	12 HOU	13 HOU
14 HOU	15 MIL	16 MIL	17 PIT	18 PIT	19 NYM	20 NYM
21 NYM	22 PIT	23 PIT	24 PIT	25	26 NYM	27 NYM
28 NYM	29	30 LA	31 LA			

August

SUN	MON	TUE	WED	THU	FRI	SAT
				1 LA	2 D SD	3 SD
4 D SD	5	6 COL	7 COL	8 D COL	9 SD	10 SD
11 D SD	12	13 ARI	14 ARI	15 ARI	16 HOU	17 HOU
18 D HOU	19 D HOU	20 ARI	21 ARI	22 ARI	23 HOU	24 HOU
25 D HOU	26	27 STL	28 STL	29 STL	30 MIL	31 MIL

September

SUN	MON	TUE	WED	THU	FRI	SAT
1 D MIL	2 D STL	3 STL	4 STL	5	6 MIL	7 MIL
8 D MIL	9 PIT	10 PIT	11 D PIT	12 CUB	13 CUB	14 D CUB
15 CUB	16 PIT	17 PIT	18 PIT	19 PIT	20 PHI	21 PHI
22 D PHI	23	24 CUB	25 CUB	26 D CUB	27 MON	28 MON
29 D MON	30					

2002 SEASON
CLUB DIRECTORY

Chief executive officer
Carl H. Lindner
Chief operating officer
John Allen
General manager
Jim Bowden
Assistant general manager
Darrell "Doc" Rodgers
Director of player personnel
Leland Maddox
Director of baseball administration
Brad Kullman
Sr. asst. to the general manager/advance scout
Gene Bennett
Special assistants to the general manager
Larry Barton Jr., Al Goldis
Special asst. to the g.m. and dir. of pro scouting
Gary Hughes
Executive assistant to the general manager
Lois Schneider
Consultant to the general manager
Johnny Bench
Director of scouting
Kasey McKeon
Assistant director of scouting
Johnny Almaraz
Director, player development
Tim Naehring
Senior advisor, player development
Sheldon "Chief" Bender
Senior advisor, scouting
Bob Zuk
Director, scouting administration
Wilma Mann
Traveling secretary
Gary Wahoff
Director of media relations
Rob Butcher
Assistant director of media relations
Michael Vassallo
Media relations coordinator
Larry Herms
Controller
Anthony Ward
Director, stadium operations
Declan Mullin
Director, ticket operations
John O'Brien
Director of season and group sales
Pat McCaffrey
Dir. of communications and community relations
Michael Ringering

Assistant director of communications
Ralph Mitchell
Director of new stadium development
Jenny Gardner
Director of marketing
Cal Levy
Director of corporate marketing
Brad Blettner
Executive assistant to chief operating officer
Joyce Pfarr
Business and broadcast manager
Ginny Kamp
Head trainer
Greg Lynn
Assistant trainer
Mark Mann
Medical director
Tim Kremchek, M.D.
Physical therapist
Lonnie Soloff
Video coordinator
Joe Harkins
Senior clubhouse & equipment manager
Bernie Stowe
Reds clubhouse & equipment manager
Rick Stowe
Visiting clubhouse & equipment manager
Mark Stowe
Major League scouts
Jeff Barton, De Jon Watson, Bill Scherrer (East), Butch Baccala (West), Alvin Rittman (Central), John Castleberry (Central)
Director of international scouting
Jorge Oquendo
Scouting supervisors
Terry Abbott, Howard Bowens, John Brickley, Mark Corey, Rex De La Nuez, Robert Filotei, Jerry Flowers, Jimmy Gonzales, Mike Keenan, Craig Kornfeld, Steve Kring, Tom LeVasseur, Brian Mejia, Steve Mondile, Tom Severtson, Perry Smith, Brian Wilson, Greg Zunino
Scouts
Oswaldo Alvarez, John Bellino, George Blackburn, Fred Blair, Kevin Carcamo, Keith Chapman, Edwin Daub, Felix Delgado, Orlando Granda, Jim Grief, Don Gust, Frank Henderson, Don Hill, Thomas Herrera, Juan Linares, Victor Mateo, Denny Nagel, Rafael Nava, Everett Renteria, Glenn Serviente, Marlon Styles, Lee Toole, Ruben Vargas, Mike Wallace, John Walsh, Nathan Ware, Roger Weberg

---

MINOR LEAGUE AFFILIATES

Class	Team	League	Manager
AAA	Louisville	International	Dave Miley
AA	Chattanooga	Southern	Phil Wellman
A	Dayton	Midwest	Donnie Scott
A	Stockton	California	Jayhawk Owens
Rookie	Billings	Pioneer	Rick Burleson
Rookie	Gulf Coast Reds	Gulf Coast	Edgar Caceres

BROADCAST INFORMATION

Radio: WLW-AM (700).
Cable TV: Fox Sports Net.

SPRING TRAINING

Ballpark (city): Ed Smith Stadium (Sarasota, Fla.).
Ticket information: 941-954-4101.

Follow the Reds all season at: www.sportingnews.com/baseball/teams/reds/

SPRING TRAINING ROSTER

Manager—Bob Boone (9).
Coaches—Bill Doran (19), Tim Foli (10), Ken Griffey Sr. (33), Don Gullett (35), Tom Hume (47), Ron Oester (16).

No.	PITCHERS	B/T	Ht./Wt.	Born	2001 clubs
	Acevedo, Jose	R/R	6-0/185	12-18-77	Cincinnati, Chattanooga
	Aramboles, Ricardo	R/R	6-2/170	12-4-81	Tampa, Columbus, Chattanooga, Dayton
	Bohanon, Brian	L/L	6-2/240	8-1-68	Colorado, Colorado Springs
	Booker, Chris	R/R	6-3/230	12-9-76	West Tenn, Chattanooga
52	Brower, Jim	R/R	6-2/205	12-29-72	Louisville, Cincinnati
	Davis, Lance	L/R	6-0/170	9-1-76	Louisville, Cincinnati
40	Etherton, Seth	R/R	6-1/200	10-17-76	DID NOT PLAY
32	Graves, Danny	R/R	5-11/185	8-7-73	Cincinnati
	Hamilton, Joey	R/R	6-4/240	9-9-70	Toronto, Louisville, Cincinnati
38	Harnisch, Pete	R/R	6-0/228	9-23-66	Cincinnati, Louisville
	Haynes, Jimmy	R/R	6-4/214	9-5-72	Milwaukee
74	Hudson, Luke	R/R	6-3/195	5-2-77	Carolina
45	Dessens, Elmer	R/R	6-0/187	1-13-72	Cincinnati
39	Mercado, Hector	L/L	6-3/235	4-29-74	Louisville, Cincinnati
	Piersoll, Chris	R/R	6-4/195	9-25-77	Chattanooga, Cincinnati
	Pineda, Luis	R/R	6-1/160	6-10-78	Erie, Toledo, Detroit
54	Reith, Brian	R/R	6-5/190	2-28-78	Chattanooga, Cincinnati, Louisville
53	Reitsma, Chris	R/R	6-5/214	12-31-77	Cincinnati
46	Riedling, John	R/R	5-11/190	8-29-75	Cincinnati, Louisville
27	Rijo, Jose	R/R	6-3/200	5-13-65	Dayton, Chattanooga, Louisville, Cincinnati
56	Sullivan, Scott	R/R	6-3/210	3-13-71	Cincinnati
36	White, Gabe	L/L	6-2/200	11-20-71	Colorado
48	Williamson, Scott	R/R	6-0/185	2-17-76	Cincinnati

No.	CATCHERS	B/T	Ht./Wt.	Born	2001 clubs
2	LaRue, Jason	R/R	5-11/200	3-19-74	Cincinnati
	Miller, Corky	R/R	6-1/225	3-18-76	Chattanooga, Louisville, Cincinnati
50	Sardinha, Dane	R/R	5-11/205	4-8-79	Mudville
35	Stinnett, Kelly	R/R	5-11/225	2-4-70	Cincinnati

No.	INFIELDERS	B/T	Ht./Wt.	Born	2001 clubs
17	Boone, Aaron	R/R	6-2/200	3-9-73	Cincinnati, Louisville
21	Casey, Sean	L/R	6-4/225	7-2-74	Cincinnati
12	Castro, Juan	R/R	5-10/187	6-20-72	Cincinnati
6	Dawkins, Gookie	R/R	6-1/180	5-12-79	Chattanooga
79	Espinosa, David	B/R	6-1/170	12-16-81	Dayton
11	Larkin, Barry	R/R	6-0/185	4-28-64	Cincinnati
14	Walker, Todd	L/R	6-0/181	5-25-73	Colorado, Cincinnati

No.	OUTFIELDERS	B/T	Ht./Wt.	Born	2001 clubs
	Broussard, Ben	L/L	6-2/220	9-24-76	Mudville, Chattanooga
22	Clark, Brady	R/R	6-2/195	4-18-73	Louisville, Cincinnati
77	Dunn, Adam	L/R	6-6/235	11-9-79	Chattanooga, Louisville, Cincinnati
34	Encarnacion, Juan	R/R	6-3/187	3-8-76	Detroit
30	Griffey, Ken	L/L	6-3/205	11-21-69	Cincinnati
4	Guerrero, Wilton	B/R	6-0/175	10-24-74	Cincinnati, Louisville
56	Jennings, Robin	L/L	6-2/210	4-11-72	Oakland, Sacramento, Colorado Springs, Colorado, Cincinnati, Louisville
	Kearns, Austin	R/R	6-3/220	5-20-80	Chattanooga, Gulf Coast Reds
21	Mateo, Ruben	R/R	6-0/185	2-10-78	Texas, Oklahoma, Louisville
76	Melian, Jackson	R/R	6-2/190	1-7-80	Chattanooga
81	Pena, Wily	R/R	6-3/215	1-23-82	Dayton

BALLPARK INFORMATION

Ballpark (capacity, surface)
Cinergy Field (39,000, grass)
Address
100 Cinergy Field
Cincinnati, OH 45202
Official website
www.cincinnatireds.com
Business phone
513-421-4510
Ticket information
513-421-7337, 1-800-829-5353
Ticket prices
$32 (Blue Box Zone A)
$24 (Blue Box Zone B, Green Box Zone A)
$16 (Green Box Zone B)
$15 (Yellow Box), $14 (Red Box)
$9 (Red Reserve), $5 (Top Six)
Field dimensions (from home plate)
To left field at foul line, 325 feet
To center field, 404 feet
To right field at foul line, 325 feet
First game played
June 30, 1970 (Braves 8, Reds 2)

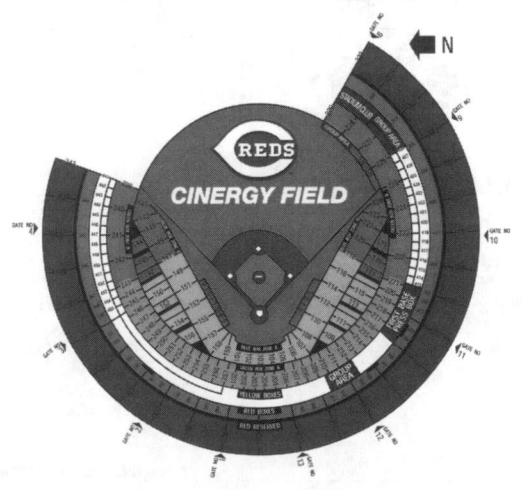

2002 SEASON *Cincinnati Reds*

Date	Opp.	Res.	Score	(inn.*)	Hits	Opp. hits	Winning pitcher	Losing pitcher	Save	Record	Pos.	GB
4-2	Atl.	L	4-10		8	14	Valdes	Reyes		0-1	T1st	0.5
4-3	Pit.	W	3-2		4	7	O. Fernandez	Ritchie	Graves	1-1	2nd	0.5
4-4	Pit.	L	5-6	(10)	18	7	M. Williams	Sullivan		1-2	3rd	1.5
4-5	Pit.	W	4-1		5	7	Dessens	Anderson	Riedling	2-2	2nd	1.5
4-6	At Mil.	L	4-5		7	6	Weathers	Reyes		2-3	3rd	2.5
4-7	At Mil.	L	1-6		3	10	Wright	Harnisch		2-4	T5th	2.5
4-8	At Mil.	L	4-8		9	9	Haynes	O. Fernandez		2-5	6th	2.5
4-9	At Pit.	W	8-2		12	6	Reitsma	Ritchie		3-5	6th	2.0
4-11	At Pit.	L	5-6		15	10	Silva	Riedling	M. Williams	3-6	T5th	3.5
4-12	At Pit.	W	11-6		12	7	Harnisch	Olivares		4-6	T5th	2.5
4-13	At N.Y.	W	3-2		5	10	O. Fernandez	Trachsel	Graves	5-6	4th	2.5
4-14	At N.Y.	W	1-0		6	5	Reitsma	Leiter	Graves	6-6	3rd	2.5
4-15	At N.Y.	W	3-1		13	7	Brower	Appier	Graves	7-6	3rd	1.5
4-17	Mil.	W	3-2		6	5	Sullivan	Cunnane	Graves	8-6	3rd	0.5
4-18	Mil.	L	4-7		9	11	Wright	Harnisch	Weathers	8-7	3rd	2.0
4-20	N.Y.	W	9-5		11	9	O. Fernandez	Leiter	Brower	9-7	3rd	2.0
4-21	N.Y.	L	2-5		8	6	Appier	Reitsma	Benitez	9-8	3rd	3.0
4-22	N.Y.	L	1-5		7	11	Reed	Dessens		9-9	3rd	3.0
4-24	At S.F	W	9-5		17	7	Brower	Hernandez		10-9	3rd	2.0
4-25	At S.F	W	7-5		15	12	O. Fernandez	Rueter	Graves	11-9	T2nd	1.0
4-26	At S.F	W	7-5		13	13	Reyes	Embree	Graves	12-9	2nd	1.0
4-27	At Col.	W	12-9		17	14	Mercado	Myers	Graves	13-9	2nd	1.0
4-28	At Col.	W	9-4		14	8	Dessens	Davis		14-9	T1st	...
4-29	At Col.	L	7-14		14	18	Wasdin	Mercado	Jimenez	14-10	2nd	1.0
5-1	L.A.	W	7-6		9	11	Wohlers	Herges	Graves	15-10	T1st	...
5-2	L.A.	L	3-7		5	13	Brown	Harnisch		15-11	2nd	1.0
5-3	L.A.	L	6-8		7	12	Prokopec	Reitsma	Shaw	15-12	T2nd	1.0
5-4	S.D.	L	5-11		12	15	Eaton	Dessens		15-13	T2nd	2.0
5-5	S.D.	L	2-5		9	11	Williams	Bell	Hoffman	15-14	4th	3.0
5-6	S.D.	L	2-8		4	13	Tollberg	O. Fernandez		15-15	4th	4.0
5-7	At Ari.	W	5-4	(10)	14	10	Graves	Swindell		16-15	T3rd	4.0
5-8	At Ari.	L	3-4	(11)	3	10	Brohawn	Graves		16-16	5th	4.0
5-9	At Ari.	L	2-5		5	11	Batista	Mercado	Prinz	16-17	5th	5.0
5-12†	Hou.	L	1-2		7	8	Reynolds	Bell	Wagner	16-18		
5-12‡	Hou.	W	5-4		12	6	Graves	Dotel		17-18	5th	3.5
5-13	Hou.	L	3-4		7	8	Bottenfield	Brower	Wagner	17-19	5th	4.0
5-14	Hou.	L	4-6		10	10	Oswalt	Reitsma	Wagner	17-20	5th	4.5
5-15	Ari.	L	1-5		5	13	Sabel	Wohlers	Kim	17-21	5th	5.5
5-16	Ari.	L	1-2		5	7	Schilling	Reith	Kim	17-22	5th	6.5
5-17	Ari.	L	2-7		4	9	Anderson	Brower		17-23	5th	7.5
5-18	At Hou.	W	7-4		10	7	O. Fernandez	Bottenfield	Graves	18-23	5th	6.5
5-19	At Hou.	L	3-6		8	10	Miller	Reitsma	Wagner	18-24	5th	6.5
5-20	At Hou.	W	6-5		10	12	Dessens	Lima	Graves	19-24	5th	6.5
5-22	At Chi.	L	3-5		4	9	Duncan	Brower	Gordon	19-25	5th	6.5
5-23	At Chi.	L	2-4		5	7	Van Poppel	Bell	Gordon	19-26	5th	6.5
5-24	At Chi.	L	0-3		1	10	Lieber	O. Fernandez		19-27	5th	7.5
5-25	St.L.	L	4-5		8	8	Al. Benes	Graves	Veres	19-28	5th	8.5
5-26	St.L.	W	7-2		9	6	Dessens	Hermanson		20-28	5th	7.5
5-27	St.L.	L	0-2		8	11	Kile	Reith	Veres	20-29	5th	8.5
5-28	Chi.	L	6-9	(13)	10	15	Duncan	Winchester		20-30	5th	9.5
5-29	Chi.	L	5-10		10	10	Bere	O. Fernandez		20-31	5th	10.5
5-30	Chi.	L	1-3		5	9	Lieber	Reitsma	Gordon	20-32	5th	11.5
6-1	At St.L.	W	5-1		10	4	Mercado	Kile	Graves	21-32	5th	11.5
6-2	At St.L.	L	5-8		7	11	Morris	Reith	Stechschulte	21-33	5th	12.5
6-3	At St.L.	L	3-4		7	7	Timlin	Bell	Veres	21-34	5th	12.5
6-4	At St.L.	L	2-5		7	12	An. Benes	O. Fernandez	Veres	21-35	5th	13.0
6-5	At Mil.	W	4-3	(13)	16	8	Wohlers	Cunnane	Nichting	22-35	5th	13.0
6-6	At Mil.	W	6-3		11	10	Dessens	Haynes	Graves	23-35	5th	13.0
6-8	At Cle.	W	7-4		12	7	Brower	Rodriguez	Graves	24-35	5th	12.5
6-9	At Cle.	L	2-10		5	14	Burba	O. Fernandez		24-36	5th	13.5
6-10	At Cle.	W	9-3		13	9	Reitsma	Wright		25-36	5th	12.5
6-12	At Chi.	L	0-5		9	7	D. Wells	Dessens		25-37	5th	13.5
6-13	At Chi.	L	2-4		6	9	Buehrle	Bell	Foulke	25-38	5th	13.5
6-14	At Chi.	L	5-7		9	9	Wunsch	Brower	Foulke	25-39	5th	13.5
6-15	Col.	L	4-8		8	11	Villone	Reitsma		25-40	5th	14.5
6-16	Col.	L	7-8	(12)	11	15	Jimenez	Brower	Dingman	25-41	5th	15.5
6-17	Col.	L	3-4		6	8	Bohanon	Dessens	Jimenez	25-42	5th	16.5
6-18	Mil.	L	4-6		11	9	Levrault	Reith	Leskanic	25-43	5th	16.5
6-19	Mil.	L	8-10		11	11	Sheets	Acevedo	King	25-44	5th	16.5
6-20	Mil.	W	11-3		14	8	Reitsma	Cunnane		26-44	5th	16.5
6-21	At Hou.	W	8-7	(11)	13	13	Brower	Slusarski		27-44	5th	16.5
6-22	At Hou.	W	7-5	(10)	10	9	Wohlers	Wagner		28-44	5th	15.5
6-23	At Hou.	L	3-9		7	12	Reynolds	Reith		28-45	5th	15.5
6-24	At Hou.	L	5-7		8	10	Dotel	Nichting	Wagner	28-46	5th	15.5

– 95 –

Date	Opp.	Res.	Score	(inn.*)	Hits	Opp. hits	Winning pitcher	Losing pitcher	Save	Record	Pos.	GB
6-26	At St.L.	W	10-9		14	15	Sullivan	Stechschulte	Graves	29-46	5th	16.0
6-27	At St.L.	W	3-1		9	4	Davis	Hermanson	Graves	30-46	5th	15.0
6-28	Chi.	W	5-2		16	5	Dessens	Tapani		31-46	5th	14.0
6-29	Chi.	L	1-7		8	12	Bere	Reith		31-47	5th	15.0
6-30	Chi.	W	7-1		10	7	Acevedo	Tavarez		32-47	5th	14.0
7-1	Chi.	L	1-2		6	7	Lieber	Reitsma	Gordon	32-48	5th	15.0
7-2	Pit.	L	5-10		10	13	Schmidt	Davis		32-49	5th	15.5
7-3	Pit.	L	2-3		5	9	Ritchie	Dessens	M. Williams	32-50	5th	16.5
7-4	Pit.	L	3-14		9	19	Beimel	Reith		32-51	6th	16.5
7-5	Pit.	W	7-1		7	8	Acevedo	D. Williams		33-51	5th	16.5
7-6	At Min.	L	4-5		8	12	Guardado	Nichting	Hawkins	33-52	6th	17.5
7-7	At Min.	L	6-7		10	12	Wells	Brower	Hawkins	33-53	6th	18.5
7-8	At Min.	L	1-7		3	15	Radke	Dessens		33-54	6th	18.5
7-12	Cle.	L	0-7		7	14	Colon	Reitsma		33-55	6th	19.5
7-13	Cle.	L	1-5		4	6	Sabathia	Dessens		33-56	6th	19.5
7-14	Cle.	W	6-5	(13)	9	12	Graves	Rocker		34-56	6th	18.5
7-15	Det.	L	5-8		11	15	Blair	Nichting	Anderson	34-57	6th	19.5
7-16	Det.	W	9-1		11	5	Davis	Pettyjohn		35-57	6th	18.5
7-17	Det.	L	1-3		6	8	Weaver	Reitsma	Anderson	35-58	6th	19.5
7-18	Atl.	L	1-3	(8)	10	3	Glavine	Dessens	Reed	35-59	6th	20.5
7-19	Atl.	L	1-2		7	8	Burkett	Brower	Karsay	35-60	6th	20.5
7-20	At Fla.	L	3-5		10	8	Clement	Acevedo	Alfonseca	35-61	6th	20.5
7-21	At Fla.	W	8-4		9	8	Davis	Penny		36-61	6th	20.5
7-22	At Fla.	L	7-11		13	15	Burnett	Reitsma		36-62	6th	20.5
7-23	At Atl.	W	5-4		12	12	Sullivan	Remlinger	Graves	37-62	6th	20.5
7-24	At Atl.	W	11-3		12	8	Brower	Burkett		38-62	6th	20.5
7-25	At Atl.	L	3-11		6	15	Millwood	Acevedo		38-63	6th	21.5
7-27	Fla.	W	10-5		10	12	Davis	Clement	Graves	39-63	6th	21.0
7-28	Fla.	W	5-0		4	6	Dessens	Penny		40-63	T5th	20.0
7-29	Fla.	W	8-4		11	9	Reitsma	Burnett		41-63	T5th	20.0
7-31	At L.A.	W	3-1	(11)	8	4	Graves	Orosco		42-63	5th	20.0
8-1	At L.A.	W	10-5		20	10	Davis	Adams		43-63	5th	19.0
8-2	At L.A.	W	7-4		9	9	Dessens	Prokopec	Graves	44-63	5th	18.0
8-3	At S.D.	W	9-2		11	6	Brower	Jarvis		45-63	5th	18.0
8-4	At S.D.	L	0-2		4	6	Tollberg	Reitsma	Hoffman	45-64	5th	18.0
8-5	At S.D.	W	10-9		8	15	Graves	Seanez		46-64	5th	17.0
8-7	S.F	L	3-9	(11)	10	16	Christiansen	Graves		46-65	5th	18.0
8-8	S.F	W	11-9		13	15	Mercado	Schmidt	Graves	47-65	5th	18.0
8-9	S.F	L	4-6		9	11	Ortiz	Winchester	Nen	47-66	5th	18.0
8-10	Col.	L	7-16		9	15	Miceli	Reitsma		47-67	5th	19.0
8-11	Col.	W	7-3		12	9	Acevedo	Bohanon		48-67	5th	18.0
8-12	Col.	L	6-7		14	12	Powell	Graves	Jimenez	48-68	5th	18.0
8-13	At St.L.	L	2-3		9	8	An. Benes	Dessens	Veres	48-69	5th	18.5
8-14	At St.L.	L	1-7		4	8	Morris	Reyes		48-70	5th	19.0
8-15	At St.L.	L	4-8		7	11	Williams	Reitsma		48-71	5th	20.0
8-16	At St.L.	L	3-8		6	10	Hermanson	Acevedo		48-72	5th	20.5
8-17	Mil.	L	1-5		8	12	Suzuki	Davis		48-73	5th	20.5
8-18	Mil.	L	5-6		8	9	Haynes	Dessens		48-74	5th	21.5
8-19	Mil.	L	4-6		8	10	Neugebauer	Reyes	DeJean	48-75	5th	22.5
8-20	St.L.	W	5-4	(11)	13	8	Riedling	An. Benes		49-75	5th	22.0
8-21	St.L.	L	6-11		13	14	Hermanson	Acevedo		49-76	5th	23.0
8-22	St.L.	W	3-1		8	5	Davis	Kile	Graves	50-76	5th	22.0
8-23	St.L.	W	12-2		18	9	Dessens	Smith		51-76	5th	22.0
8-24	At Mon.	L	4-6		10	8	Stewart	Brower	Strickland	51-77	5th	23.0
8-25	At Mon.	W	4-2		11	7	Reitsma	Thurman	Graves	52-77	5th	22.0
8-26	At Mon.	W	17-4		20	8	Acevedo	Munoz		53-77	5th	22.0
8-28	At Hou.	L	4-6		8	9	Miller	Brower	Wagner	53-78	5th	23.0
8-29	At Hou.	L	2-6		6	12	Cruz	Dessens		53-79	5th	24.0
8-30	At Hou.	L	1-6		3	7	Oswalt	Reyes		53-80	5th	25.0
8-31	Pit.	W	11-3		12	7	Reitsma	Ritchie		54-80	5th	25.0
9-1	Pit.	L	0-7		5	8	D. Williams	Acevedo		54-81	5th	25.0
9-2	Pit.	W	8-6		14	11	Sullivan	Lincoln	Graves	55-81	5th	25.0
9-3	Hou.	W	3-2		9	4	Sullivan	Dotel	Graves	56-81	5th	24.0
9-4	Hou.	L	1-7		7	14	Oswalt	Reyes		56-82	5th	25.0
9-5	Hou.	L	3-10		10	13	Mlicki	Reitsma		56-83	5th	26.0
9-6	At Pit.	W	8-6		10	10	Brower	Loiselle	Graves	57-83	5th	25.0
9-7	At Pit.	L	1-3		7	6	McKnight	Davis	Olivares	57-84	5th	26.0
9-8	At Pit.	L	2-5		9	10	Anderson	Dessens		57-85	5th	26.0
9-9	At Pit.	W	5-3		8	13	Reyes	Vogelsong	Graves	58-85	5th	26.0
9-10	At Chi.	L	2-8		6	11	Lieber	Reitsma		58-86	5th	26.5
9-18	Chi.	W	6-5		11	13	Graves	Farnsworth		59-86	5th	26.5
9-19	Chi.	L	0-10		3	11	Wood	Hamilton		59-87	5th	27.5
9-20	Chi.	L	5-6		9	8	Bere	Brower	Fassero	59-88	5th	28.5
9-21	At Mil.	W	5-2		6	8	Davis	Suzuki	Graves	60-88	5th	27.5
9-22	At Mil.	W	3-1		5	6	Acevedo	Quevedo	Graves	61-88	5th	27.5
9-23	At Mil.	L	3-6		7	8	Wright	Dessens	Leskanic	61-89	5th	28.5
9-25	At Phi.	W	8-1		10	7	Hamilton	Coggin		62-89	5th	28.0
9-26	At Phi.	L	0-8		1	7	Wolf	J. Fernandez		62-90	5th	28.0

Date	Opp.	Res.	Score	(inn.*)	Hits	Opp. hits	Winning pitcher	Losing pitcher	Save	Record	Pos.	GB
9-27	At Phi.	W	2-1		8	2	Davis	Daal	Graves	63-90	5th	28.0
9-28	Mon.	L	6-7		14	12	Stewart	Strickland	Graves	63-91	5th	28.0
9-29	Mon.	W	7-4		15	11	Dessens	Yoshii	Graves	64-91	5th	27.0
9-30	Mon.	W	5-4		9	13	Sullivan	Eischen	Graves	65-91	T4th	26.0
10-2	At Chi.	W	5-4		10	7	Sullivan	Farnsworth	Graves	66-91	4th	25.0
10-3	At Chi.	L	7-13		12	15	Lieber	MacRae		66-92	T4th	25.0
10-4	At Chi.	L	0-2	(8)	7	6	Van Poppel	Acevedo	Farnsworth	66-93	T4th	26.0
10-6†	Phi.	L	1-2		4	10	Daal	Dessens	Mesa	66-94		
10-6‡	Phi.	L	1-5		10	12	Coggin	Hamilton		66-95	5th	27.0
10-7	Phi.	L	1-4		7	11	Wolf	Davis	Mesa	66-96	5th	27.0

Monthly records: April (14-10), May (6-22), June (12-15), July (10-16), August (12-17), September (11-11), October (1-5).
*Innings, if other than nine. †First game of a doubleheader. ‡Second game of a doubleheader.

HIGHLIGHTS

High point: May 1. The Reds forged a tie for first place in the division with a 7-6 win over Los Angeles in Deion Sanders' return to the major leagues after an absence of more than three years. Sanders singled on his first swing of the bat and hit a three-run homer with his second.

Low point: July 13. The Reds' ninth loss in 10 games left them buried in last place, 19 1/2 games out of first.

Turning point: May 3. An 8-6 loss to Los Angeles was the second of 13 in the next 15 games for the Reds, who fell from a tie for first place to fifth, 7 1/2 games behind the leader, by May 17.

Most valuable player: Switch-hitting Dmitri Young now has four seasons of playing in more than 126 games and four seasons of hitting .300 or better. Young also set a career-high with 21 homers.

Most valuable pitcher: Scott Sullivan made exactly 79 appearances for the third consecutive season and led major-league relievers in innings for a record fourth consecutive season. He was as effective as he was durable, finishing 7-1 with a 3.31 ERA .

Most improved player: The Reds' most improved player was Jason LaRue. LaRue was solid defensively in his first full season as a starter. LaRue led all N.L. catchers and was second in the majors only to the Rangers' Ivan Rodriguez with a 60-percent (27-of-41) success rate of throwing out would-be basestealers.

Most pleasant surprise: Nothing was more heartwarming than the comeback of Jose Rijo. After more than six years of inactivity caused by elbow problems that had required five surgical procedures, Rijo, 36, didn't return for simply sentimental reasons. Pitching in relief, he posted a 2.12 ERA in 13 games and hopes to be back in the rotation for 2002.

Key injuries: Ken Griffey Jr. tried to play with his torn left hamstring, but he was completely ineffective and spent 1 1/2 months on the disabled list. Coupled with

the losses of Barry Larkin and Aaron Boone, the lineup had little punch. ... The starting rotation was thin even before veteran Pete Harnisch went on the disabled list for good on May 11.

Notable: How much did injuries affect the Reds? GM Jim Bowden made 101 roster moves. ... Reds batters struck out a club-record 1,172 times. ... Jose Rijo became the first player to appear in a major league game after receiving a Hall of Fame vote since OF Minnie Minoso played for the White Sox in 1976 and 1980 after receiving six votes in 1969.
—MARK SCHMETZER

RECORDS

2001 regular-season record: 66-96 (5th in N.L. Central); 27-54 at home; 39-42 on road; 16-14 vs. N.L. East; 32-52 vs. N.L. Central; 14-19 vs. N.L. West; 4-11 vs. A.L.; 14-23 vs. lefthanded starters; 52-73 vs. righthanded starters; 62-91 on grass; 4-5 on turf; 21-33 in daytime; 45-63 at night; 20-22 in one-run games; 7-5 in extra-inning games; 0-1-1 in doubleheaders.

Team record past five years: 400-411 (.493, ranks 9th in league in that span).

TEAM LEADERS

Batting average: Sean Casey (.310).
At-bats: Dmitri Young (540).
Runs: Sean Casey (69).
Hits: Sean Casey (165).
Total Bases: Dmitri Young (260).
Doubles: Sean Casey (40).
Triples: Alex Ochoa (4).
Home runs: Ken Griffey Jr. (22).
Runs batted in: Sean Casey (89).
Stolen bases: Pokey Reese (25).
Slugging percentage: Dmitri Young (.481).
On-base percentage: Sean Casey (.369).
Wins: Elmer Dessens (10).
Earned-run average: Elmer Dessens (4.48).
Complete games: Lance Davis, Elmer Dessens (1).

Shutouts: Elmer Dessens (1).
Saves: Danny Graves (32).
Innings pitched: Elmer Dessens (205.0).
Strikeouts: Elmer Dessens (128).

GAMES BY POSITION

Catcher: Jason LaRue 107, Kelly Stinnett 59, Corky Miller 17.
First base: Sean Casey 136, Dmitri Young 38, D.T. Cromer 8, Robin Jennings 8, Bill Selby 2, Jason LaRue 1, Juan Castro 1.
Second base: Todd Walker 65, Pokey Reese 51, Juan Castro 37, Bill Selby 21, Donnie Sadler 15, Wilton Guerrero 11.
Third base: Aaron Boone 103, Dmitri Young 36, Juan Castro 19, Brandon Larson 9, Bill Selby 8, Wilton Guerrero 4, Jason LaRue 3.
Shortstop: Pokey Reese 78, Juan Castro 46, Barry Larkin 44, Wilton Guerrero 16, Donnie Sadler 12, Todd Walker 1.
Outfield: Ruben Rivera 99, Ken Griffey Jr. 90, Dmitri Young 87, Alex Ochoa 85, Michael Tucker 70, Adam Dunn 63, Brady Clark 43, Deion Sanders 16, Robin Jennings 15, Donnie Sadler 8, Wilton Guerrero 6, Jason LaRue 2, Raul Gonzalez 2.
Designated hitter: Sean Casey 3, Ken Griffey Jr. 2, Deion Sanders 2, Alex Ochoa 1, Wilton Guerrero 1, Kelly Stinnett 1, Donnie Sadler 1, D.T. Cromer 1, Brady Clark 1.

TOP DRAFT CHOICES

1. **Jeremy Sowers,** LHP, Ballard H.S., Louisville.
2. **Justin Gillman,** RHP, Mosley H.S., Panama City, Fla.
3. **Alan Moye,** OF, Pine Tree H.S., Longview, Tex.
4. **Steve Kelly,** RHP, Georgia Tech.
5. **Daylan Childress,** RHP, McLennan (Tex.) C.C.
6. **Scott Light,** RHP, Elon College.
7. **Bobby Basham,** RHP, U. of Richmond.
8. **Jose Rodriguez,** C, Warren H.S., Downey, Calif.
9. **Junior Ruiz,** OF/2B, San Jose State University.
10. **Bryan Prince,** C, Georgia Tech.

COLORADO ROCKIES
NATIONAL LEAGUE WEST DIVISION

Rockies schedule
Home games shaded
D—Day game (games starting before 5 p.m.)
*All-Star Game at Milwaukee
Subject to changes

April
SUN	MON	TUE	WED	THU	FRI	SAT
	1 D STL	2	3 STL	4 D STL	5 LA	6 LA
7 D LA	8 D HOU	9 D HOU	10 D HOU	11 ARI	12 ARI	13 D ARI
14 D ARI	15 LA	16 LA	17 D LA	18	19 ARI	20 ARI
21 ARI	22	23 CIN	24 CIN	25 CIN	26 PHI	27 D PHI
28 D PHI	29	30 PIT				

May
SUN	MON	TUE	WED	THU	FRI	SAT
			1 PIT	2 D PIT	3 PHI	4 PHI
5 D PHI	6	7 MON	8 MON	9 MON	10 NYM	11 D NYM
12 D NYM	13 FLA	14 FLA	15 FLA	16 D FLA	17 ATL	18 D ATL
19 D ATL	20	21 SD	22 SD	23 D SD	24 SF	25 D SF
26 D SF	27 SD	28 SD	29 SD	30 D SD	31 D SF	

June
SUN	MON	TUE	WED	THU	FRI	SAT
						1 SF
2 SF	3 LA	4 LA	5 D LA	6	7 TOR	8 D TOR
9 D TOR	10 BOS	11 BOS	12 BOS	13	14 CLE	15 CLE
16 D CLE	17	18 NYY	19 NYY	20 D NYY	21 TB	22 TB
23 D TB	24 LA	25 LA	26 LA	27 LA	28 SEA	29 SEA
30 D SEA						

July
SUN	MON	TUE	WED	THU	FRI	SAT
	1 SF	2 SF	3 SF	4	5 D SD	6 SD
7 D SD	8	9 *	10	11 SF	12 SF	13 SF
14 SF	15 SD	16 SD	17 ARI	18 D ARI	19 MIL	20 MIL
21 MIL	22 ARI	23 ARI	24 ARI	25	26 MIL	27 MIL
28 D MIL	29	30 PIT	31 PIT			

August
SUN	MON	TUE	WED	THU	FRI	SAT
				1 PIT	2 D CUB	3 D CUB
4 D CUB	5	6 CIN	7 CIN	8 D CIN	9 CUB	10 CUB
11 CUB	12 FLA	13 FLA	14 FLA	15	16 ATL	17 ATL
18 D ATL	19 D ATL	20 MON	21 MON	22 D MON	23 NYM	24 NYM
25 NYM	26 SF	27 SF	28 SF	29 SF	30 SD	31 SD

September
SUN	MON	TUE	WED	THU	FRI	SAT
1 D SD	2 SD	3 SF	4 SF	5 D	6 SD	7 D SD
8 D SD	9 HOU	10 HOU	11 HOU	12 LA	13 LA	14 D LA
15 D LA	16	17 STL	18 STL	19 D STL	20 ARI	21 D ARI
22 ARI	23	24 LA	25 LA	26 ARI	27 ARI	28 ARI
29 D ARI	30					

2002 SEASON
CLUB DIRECTORY

Chairman and chief executive officer
Jerry D. McMorris
Vice chairman
Charles K. Monfort
Vice chairman
Richard L. Monfort
President
Keli S. McGregor
Executive vice president, g.m.
Daniel J. O'Dowd
Sr. v.p., business operations
Gregory D. Feasel
Sr. v.p., chief financial officer
Harold R. Roth
Vice president, ballpark operations
Kevin Kahn
Vice president, finance
Michael J. Kent
V.p., ticket operations and sales
Sue Ann McClaren
Sr. dir., communications/p.r.
Jay Alves
Senior director, baseball operations, assistant general manager
Josh Byrnes
Sr. dir., ticket ops. & development
Kevin G. Fenton
Senior director, corporate sales
Marcy English Glasser
Sr. dir., personnel & administration
Elizabeth Stecklein
Director, player development
Michael Hill
Director, player personnel
Bill Geivett
Director, major league operations
Paul Egins
Director, scouting
Bill Schmidt
Director, merchandising
Jim Kellogg

Director, information systems
Bill Stephani
Director, promotions & broadcasting
Alan Bossart
Director, season tickets
Jeff Benner
Director, ticket operations & finances
Kent Hakes
Dir., ticket services & spring training business operations
Chuck Javernick
Dir., community affairs & exec. dir. of the Colorado Rockies Foundation
Roger Kinney
Director, ticket sales
Jill Roberts
Head groundskeeper
Mark Razum
Coordinator of instruction
Rick Mathews
Special assignment scout
Dave Holliday, Terry Wetzel
Regional supervisors
Ty Coslow, Bo Hughes, Danny Montgomery
Major league scouts
Pat Daugherty, Will George
Professional scouts
Joe McDonald, Art Pontarelli, Steve Schryver
Scouts
John Cedarburg, Scott Corman, Dar Cox, Mike Day, Jeff Edwards, Billy Eppler, Mike Ericson, Mike Garlatti, Orsino Hill, Bert Holt, Greg Hopkins, Damon Iannelli, Jay Matthews, Sean O'Connor, Ed Santa, Gary Wilson
International scouts
Phil Allen, Dario Arias, Kent Blasingame, Francisco Cartaya, Felix Feliz, Cristobal A. Giron, Jorge Moreno

MINOR LEAGUE AFFILIATES

Class	Team	League	Manager
AAA	Colorado Springs	Pacific Coast	Chris Cron
AA	Carolina	Southern	To be announced
A	Asheville	South Atlantic	Joe Mikulik
A	Salem	Carolina	Stu Cole
A	Tri-City	Northwest	Ron Gideon
Rookie	Casper	Pioneer	P.J. Carey

BROADCAST INFORMATION

Radio: KOA-AM (850), KCUV-AM (1150).
TV: KWGN-TV (Channel 2).
Cable TV: Fox Sports Rocky Mountain.

SPRING TRAINING

Ballpark (city): Hi Corbett Field (Tucson, Ariz.).
Ticket information: 1-800-388-ROCK.

Follow the Rockies all season at: www.sportingnews.com/baseball/teams/rockies/

2002 SEASON Colorado Rockies

Manager—Buddy Bell (25).
Coaches—Rich Donnelly (26), Toby Harrah (11), Clint Hurdle (13), Fred Kendall (16), Dallas Williams (20), Jim Wright.

No.	PITCHERS	B/T	Ht./Wt.	Born	2001 clubs
36	Belitz, Todd	L/L	6-3/200	10-23-75	Sacramento, Colorado Springs, Colorado
56	Chacon, Shawn	R/R	6-3/212	12-23-77	Colorado Springs, Colorado
70	Cook, Aaron	R/R	6-3/175	2-8-79	Salem
37	Davis, Kane	R/R	6-3/194	6-25-75	Colorado, Colorado Springs
50	Elarton, Scott	R/R	6-7/240	2-23-76	Houston, Colorado, Colorado Springs
	Esslinger, Cam	R/R	5-11/170	12-28-76	Carolina
	Fuentes, Brian	L/L	6-4/220	8-9-75	Tacoma, Seattle
10	Hampton, Mike	R/L	5-10/180	9-9-72	Colorado
48	House, Craig	R/R	6-2/210	7-8-77	Colorado Springs
	Jennings, Jason	R/R	6-2/245	7-17-78	Carolina, Colorado Springs, Colorado
49	Jimenez, Jose	R/R	6-3/228	7-7-73	Colorado
	Jones, Todd	R/R	6-3/230	4-24-68	Detroit, Minnesota
60	Kalinowski, Josh	L/L	6-2/190	12-12-76	Carolina
15	Neagle, Denny	L/L	6-3/225	9-13-68	Colorado
36	Paniagua, Jose	R/R	6-2/190	8-20-73	Seattle
49	Reyes, Dennys	R/L	6-3/246	4-19-77	Cincinnati, Louisville
46	Speier, Justin	R/R	6-4/205	11-6-73	Cleveland, Colorado, Colorado Springs
	Stark, Dennis	R/R	6-2/210	10-27-74	Tacoma, Seattle, San Antonio
52	Thomson, John	R/R	6-3/187	10-1-73	Colorado Springs, Colorado
	White, Rick	R/R	6-4/230	12-23-68	New York N.L.
	Young, Colin	L/L	6-0/185	8-1-77	Salem

No.	CATCHERS	B/T	Ht./Wt.	Born	2001 clubs
29	Bennett, Gary	R/R	6-0/208	4-17-72	Philadelphia, New York N.L., Norfolk, Colorado
	Eusebio, Tony	R/R	6-2/210	4-27-67	Houston
15	Petrick, Ben	R/R	6-0/205	4-7-77	Colorado, Colorado Springs

No.	INFIELDERS	B/T	Ht./Wt.	Born	2001 clubs
2	Butler, Brent	R/R	6-0/180	2-11-78	Colorado Springs, Colorado
	Gload, Ross	L/L	6-0/185	4-5-76	Iowa
17	Helton, Todd	L/L	6-2/206	8-20-73	Colorado
31	Norton, Greg	B/R	6-1/205	7-6-72	Colorado
2	Ortiz, Jose	R/R	5-9/177	6-13-77	Oakland, Sacramento, Colorado
	Reyes, Rene	B/R	5-11/215	2-21-78	Asheville
22	Shumpert, Terry	R/R	6-0/200	8-16-66	Colorado
51	Uribe, Juan	R/R	5-11/175	7-22-80	Carolina, Colorado, Colorado Springs

No.	OUTFIELDERS	B/T	Ht./Wt.	Born	2001 clubs
40	Barnes, John	R/R	6-2/205	4-24-76	Edmonton, Minnesota
	Cust, Jack	L/R	6-1/205	1-16-79	Tucson, Arizona
24	Encarnacion, Mario	R/R	6-2/205	9-24-77	Sacramento, Colorado Springs, Colorado
27	Hollandsworth, Todd	L/L	6-2/215	4-20-73	Colorado
58	Little, Mark	R/R	6-0/195	7-11-72	Colorado, Colorado Springs
7	Ochoa, Alex	R/R	6-0/195	3-29-72	Cincinnati, Colorado
9	Pierre, Juan	L/L	6-0/170	8-14-77	Colorado
33	Walker, Larry	L/R	6-3/237	12-1-66	Colorado

2002 SEASON Colorado Rockies

BALLPARK INFORMATION

Ballpark (capacity, surface)
Coors Field (50,445, grass)
Address
2001 Blake St.
Denver, CO 80205 2000
Official website
www.coloradorockies.com
Business phone
303-292-0200
Ticket information
800-388-7625
Ticket prices
$32 (club level, infield), $30 (club level, outfield)
$27 (infield box), $21.50 (outfield box)
$16 (lower reserved, infield)
$13 (lower reserved, outfield)
$12 (upper reserved infield, RF box)
$11 (lower reserved corner)
$10 (RF mezzanine)
$9 (upper reserved, outfield; lower pavilion)
$8 (lower pavilion)
$7 (upper reserved corner)
$6 (lower RF reserved), $5 (upper RF reserved)
$4 (rockpile), $1 (rockpile)
Field dimensions (from home plate)
To left field at foul line, 347 feet
To center field, 415 feet
To right field at foul line, 350
First game played
April 26, 1995 (Rockies 11, Mets 9, 14 innings)

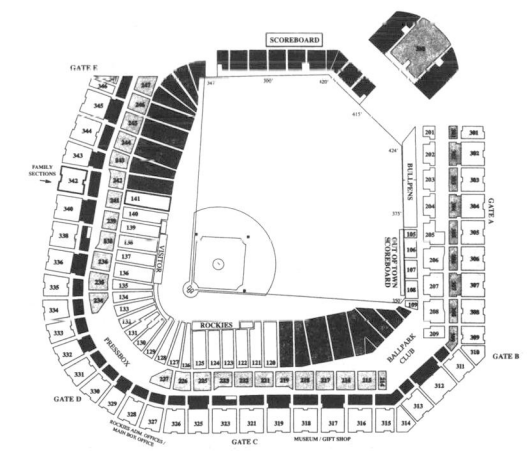

2002 SEASON *Colorado Rockies*

Date	Opp.	Res.	Score	(inn.*)	Hits	Opp. hits	Winning pitcher	Losing pitcher	Save	Record	Pos.	GB
4-2	St.L.	W	8-0		15	5	Hampton	Kile		1-0	T1st	...
4-4	St.L.	W	13-9		13	14	Neagle	An. Benes	Jimenez	2-0	T1st	...
4-5	St.L.	W	11-2		15	7	Astacio	Morris		3-0	T1st	...
4-6	S.D.	L	6-10		10	13	Eaton	Bohanon		3-1	T1st	...
4-7	S.D.	L	10-14		14	16	Williams	Myers	Hoffman	3-2	T2nd	0.5
4-8	S.D.	L	3-11		7	16	Tollberg	Estrada		3-3	T3rd	1.0
4-9	At St.L.	L	2-3		5	6	Timlin	White		3-4	4th	1.5
4-11	At St.L.	L	1-3		7	5	Morris	Astacio	Veres	3-5	T3rd	3.0
4-12	At St.L.	W	6-4		5	8	Wasdin	Kline	Jimenez	4-5	T3rd	2.0
4-13	Ari.	L	3-7		7	8	Johnson	Bohanon		4-6	T4th	3.0
4-14	Ari.	W	9-8		14	13	Myers	Kim	Jimenez	5-6	4th	2.0
4-15	Ari.	W	10-7	(10)	13	11	Estrada	Brohawn		6-6	T3rd	1.0
4-17	At S.D.	W	9-5		13	7	Astacio	Jones	Jimenez	7-6	2nd	1.0
4-18	At S.D.	W	8-0		8	5	Hampton	Eaton		8-6	2nd	1.0
4-19	At S.D.	W	4-0		12	6	Neagle	Williams		9-6	T1st	...
4-20	At Ari.	L	2-3		7	6	Kim	White		9-7	2nd	1.0
4-21	At Ari.	L	5-10		11	8	Ellis	Villone		9-8	3rd	1.0
4-22	At Ari.	W	2-1		6	3	Astacio	Reynoso	Jimenez	10-8	2nd	1.0
4-24	Chi.	W	14-1		19	5	Hampton	Tapani		11-8	T1st	
4-25	Chi.	W	6-5		10	8	Jimenez	Duncan		12-8	1st	+1.0
4-26	Chi.	L	2-7		9	10	Lieber	Bohanon		12-9	1st	+0.5
4-27	Cin.	L	9-12		14	17	Mercado	Myers	Graves	12-10	2nd	0.5
4-28	Cin.	L	4-9		8	14	Dessens	Davis		12-11	T2nd	1.5
4-29	Cin.	W	14-7		18	14	Wasdin	Mercado	Jimenez	13-11	2nd	1.5
5-1	At Phi.	L	1-7		4	8	Daal	Neagle		13-12	T3rd	1.5
5-2	At Phi.	W	6-2		12	7	Bohanon	Person	Jimenez	14-12	T2nd	1.5
5-3	At Phi.	L	5-7		10	11	Telemaco	Astacio		14-13	T3rd	2.5
5-4	At Pit.	W	9-3		13	6	Hampton	Arroyo		15-13	T2nd	1.5
5-5	At Pit.	L	3-11		3	12	Olivares	Chacon		15-14	T2nd	1.5
5-6	At Pit.	L	3-4	(11)	12	9	Beimel	White		15-15	T3rd	1.5
5-7	N.Y.	L	9-10		17	14	Gonzalez	Bohanon		15-16	T4th	2.5
5-8	N.Y.	W	12-4		18	8	Astacio	Appier		16-16	T4th	1.5
5-9	N.Y.	W	6-0		11	7	Hampton	Reed		17-16	T3rd	1.5
5-10	N.Y.	W	8-2		13	6	Chacon	Rusch		18-16	T2nd	1.5
5-11	Mon.	W	13-4		16	7	Neagle	Peters		19-16	T2nd	0.5
5-12	Mon.	L	4-8		6	11	Armas	Thomson		19-17	3rd	1.5
5-13	Mon.	L	10-14		15	15	Lloyd	Astacio		19-18	T3rd	2.5
5-15	At Atl.	L	3-5		9	13	Remlinger	Hampton	Rocker	19-19	4th	3.0
5-16	At Atl.	L	4-6		11	11	Cabrera	Wasdin	Rocker	19-20	T4th	3.5
5-17	At Atl.	W	8-3		12	10	Neagle	Smoltz		20-20	T4th	2.5
5-18	At Fla.	L	1-2		10	4	Burnett	Astacio	Alfonseca	20-21	T4th	3.0
5-19	At Fla.	L	0-1		3	4	Penny	Thomson	Alfonseca	20-22	5th	3.5
5-20	At Fla.	W	7-2		9	11	Hampton	Dempster		21-22	5th	2.5
5-21	L.A.	W	6-3		8	5	Chacon	Dreifort	Jimenez	22-22	5th	2.0
5-22	L.A.	W	11-8		14	12	White	Herges	Jimenez	23-22	5th	2.0
5-23	L.A.	L	4-6		10	7	Brown	Astacio	Shaw	23-23	5th	2.0
5-24	At S.F	L	1-5		2	7	Estes	Thomson		23-24	5th	3.0
5-25	At S.F	W	6-1		9	7	Hampton	Hernandez		24-24	5th	2.0
5-26	At S.F	W	10-4		11	10	Chacon	Rueter		25-24	T4th	2.0
5-27	At S.F	L	4-5		12	6	Ortiz	Neagle	Nen	25-25	5th	3.0
5-28	At L.A.	L	10-11	(11)	11	18	Herges	Villone		25-26	5th	4.0
5-29	At L.A.	W	7-2		10	6	Bohanon	Brown		26-26	T4th	4.0
5-30	At L.A.	L	1-4		4	4	Park	Hampton	Shaw	26-27	T4th	5.0
6-1	S.F	L	7-11		10	11	Rueter	Chacon		26-28	5th	6.0
6-2	S.F	W	7-5		12	13	Jimenez	Nen		27-28	T3rd	6.0
6-3	S.F	W	11-2		19	3	Astacio	Gardner		28-28	3rd	6.0
6-5	Hou.	W	9-4		12	9	Hampton	Miller		29-28	3rd	4.5
6-6	Hou.	W	9-8		16	13	Bohanon	Elarton	Jimenez	30-28	3rd	4.5
6-7	Hou.	L	1-2		7	5	Reynolds	Chacon	Jackson	30-29	3rd	5.5
6-8	St.L.	W	9-1		14	4	Neagle	Matthews		31-29	3rd	5.5
6-9	St.L.	L	2-8		5	15	An. Benes	Astacio		31-30	3rd	5.5
6-10	St.L.	W	12-3		14	7	Hampton	Hermanson		32-30	3rd	5.5
6-12	Sea.	L	9-10		11	13	Fuentes	Acevedo	Sasaki	32-31	3rd	5.5
6-14§	Sea.	W	8-2		12	3	Chacon	Moyer		33-31		
6-14∞	Sea.	L	1-5		6	11	Abbott	Astacio		33-32	4th	6.5
6-15	At Cin.	W	8-4		11	8	Villone	Reitsma		34-32	4th	5.5
6-16	At Cin.	W	8-7	(12)	15	11	Jimenez	Brower	Dingman	35-32	4th	5.5
6-17	At Cin.	W	4-3		8	6	Bohanon	Dessens	Jimenez	36-32	4th	5.5
6-18	At Hou.	L	5-13		14	12	Reynolds	Astacio		36-33	4th	6.0
6-19	At Hou.	L	4-6		6	9	Oswalt	Chacon	Wagner	36-34	4th	7.0
6-20	At Hou.	L	2-7		4	12	Miller	Villone	Dotel	36-35	4th	7.0
6-21	Ari.	L	5-14		11	16	Bierbrodt	Hampton		36-36	4th	8.0
6-22	Ari.	L	4-5	(10)	15	10	Swindell	Jimenez	Prinz	36-37	4th	9.0
6-23	Ari.	L	5-9		7	13	Kim	White		36-38	4th	10.0

Date	Opp.	Res.	Score	(inn.*)	Hits	Opp. hits	Winning pitcher	Losing pitcher	Save	Record	Pos.	GB
6-24	Ari.	W	7-6		9	12	Neagle	Johnson	Jimenez	37-38	4th	9.0
6-25	S.D.	L	4-6		8	7	Jarvis	White	Hoffman	37-39	4th	9.0
6-26	S.D.	L	3-11		9	13	Jones	Hampton		37-40	T4th	9.0
6-27	S.D.	W	10-9	15	15	14	Jimenez	Davey		38-40	4th	9.0
6-29	At Ari.	L	3-5		7	10	Johnson	Astacio	Kim	38-41	4th	10.0
6-30	At Ari.	L	5-6		9	10	Brohawn	Davis	Prinz	38-42	4th	11.0
7-1	At Ari.	L	4-5	(13)	9	11	Prinz	White		38-43	4th	12.0
7-3	At S.D.	L	5-6		14	9	Nunez	Davis	Hoffman	38-44	4th	12.0
7-4	At S.D.	L	3-8		5	8	Hitchcock	Suzuki		38-45	5th	13.0
7-5	At S.D.	W	4-0		8	3	Astacio	Eaton		39-45	4th	12.0
7-6	Ana.	L	5-6		9	13	Ortiz	Hampton	Percival	39-46	5th	12.0
7-7	Ana.	L	3-10		7	16	Washburn	Suzuki		39-47	5th	12.0
7-8	Ana.	L	3-11		5	12	Rapp	Chacon	Pote	39-48	5th	12.0
7-12	At Tex.	L	3-6		6	11	Rogers	Astacio	Zimmerman	39-49	5th	12.0
7-13	At Tex.	L	2-10		4	13	Helling	Hampton		39-50	5th	13.0
7-14	At Tex.	W	11-2		18	7	Chacon	Davis		40-50	5th	13.0
7-15	At Oak.	L	3-6		5	10	Lidle	Bohanon	Vizcaino	40-51	5th	13.0
7-16	At Oak.	L	1-5		7	9	Heredia	Neagle		40-52	5th	14.0
7-17	At Oak.	L	2-3		8	8	Mulder	Astacio	Isringhausen	40-53	5th	14.0
7-18	At S.F	L	0-10		5	12	Ortiz	Hampton		40-54	5th	14.5
7-19	At S.F	L	1-2		5	9	Rodriguez	Acevedo		40-55	5th	15.0
7-20	L.A.	W	11-3		14	6	Bohanon	Prokopec		41-55	5th	14.0
7-21	L.A.	L	7-22		12	23	Gagne	Neagle		41-56	5th	15.0
7-22	L.A.	L	8-9		16	16	Adams	Astacio	Shaw	41-57	5th	16.0
7-23	S.F	W	8-2		11	5	Hampton	Ortiz		42-57	5th	15.0
7-24	S.F	W	6-4		10	7	Chacon	Estes	Jimenez	43-57	5th	15.0
7-25	S.F	L	3-9		10	15	Jensen	Bohanon		43-58	5th	16.0
7-26	At L.A.	L	1-3		5	6	Gagne	Neagle	Shaw	43-59	5th	16.0
7-27	At L.A.	L	2-4		7	10	Adams	Astacio	Shaw	43-60	5th	16.5
7-28	At L.A.	L	6-10		12	13	Park	Hampton	Shaw	43-61	5th	17.5
7-29	At L.A.	W	3-2		9	5	Powell	Herges	Jimenez	44-61	5th	16.5
7-31	Phi.	W	7-6		10	15	Jimenez	Cormier		45-61	5th	15.5
8-1	Phi.	L	1-8	(7)	4	11	Wolf	Neagle		45-62	5th	15.5
8-2	Phi.	L	2-4		11	7	Coggin	Thomson	Mesa	45-63	5th	15.5
8-3	Pit.	W	12-7		15	11	Hampton	Anderson		46-63	5th	15.0
8-4	Pit.	L	3-6		10	9	Ritchie	Chacon		46-64	5th	15.5
8-5	Pit.	L	4-5		10	9	Lincoln	Bohanon	Fetters	46-65	5th	16.5
8-7	At Chi.	L	4-5		9	11	Farnsworth	Speier		46-66	5th	17.5
8-8	At Chi.	L	1-2		7	7	Bere	Thomson	Gordon	46-67	5th	18.5
8-9	At Chi.	W	14-5		12	11	Hampton	Tavarez		47-67	5th	17.5
8-10	At Cin.	W	16-7		15	9	Miceli	Reitsma		48-67	5th	16.5
8-11	At Cin.	L	3-7		9	12	Acevedo	Bohanon		48-68	5th	17.0
8-12	At Cin.	W	7-6		12	14	Powell	Graves	Jimenez	49-68	5th	17.0
8-14	Atl.	W	5-4	(10)	15	10	Jimenez	Karsay		50-68	5th	17.5
8-15	Atl.	L	2-7		7	8	Burkett	Hampton		50-69	5th	18.5
8-16	Atl.	L	1-4		10	6	Millwood	Chacon	Karsay	50-70	5th	19.0
8-17	Fla.	W	12-5		13	13	Speier	Dempster		51-70	5th	19.0
8-18	Fla.	W	8-3		13	6	Neagle	Almanza	Powell	52-70	5th	19.0
8-19	Fla.	W	6-5		15	10	Thomson	Sanchez	Miceli	53-70	5th	19.0
8-21	At N.Y.	L	2-5		9	7	Leiter	Hampton	Benitez	53-71	5th	19.0
8-22	At N.Y.	L	1-2		2	7	Appier	Chacon	Benitez	53-72	5th	20.0
8-23	At N.Y.	W	10-0		17	5	Jennings	Rusch		54-72	5th	19.0
8-24	At Mil.	W	12-6		12	11	Neagle	Neugebauer		55-72	5th	18.0
8-25	At Mil.	L	4-5		8	11	DeJean	White	Leskanic	55-73	5th	19.0
8-26	At Mil.	W	3-2		8	6	Hampton	Quevedo	Powell	56-73	5th	19.0
8-28	At L.A.	W	4-3		11	11	Davis	Shaw	Powell	57-73	5th	18.5
8-29	At L.A.	W	5-3		13	10	Jennings	Baldwin	Powell	58-73	5th	18.5
8-30	At L.A.	L	4-5		9	6	Park	Neagle	Shaw	58-74	5th	18.5
8-31	At S.F	W	5-2		5	9	Thomson	Ortiz	Powell	59-74	5th	18.0
9-1	At S.F	L	1-2		3	5	Nen	Speier		59-75	5th	18.0
9-2	At S.F	L	1-3		8	5	Hernandez	Chacon	Nen	59-76	5th	18.0
9-3	At S.F	W	4-1		9	4	Jennings	Rueter	Powell	60-76	5th	17.5
9-4	L.A.	W	5-2		8	6	Neagle	Baldwin	Powell	61-76	5th	16.5
9-5	L.A.	L	2-7		7	6	Herges	Myers		61-77	5th	17.5
9-6	L.A.	L	5-9		13	11	Adams	Hampton		61-78	5th	17.5
9-7	S.F	W	3-2	(12)	10	10	Miceli	Worrell		62-78	5th	16.5
9-8	S.F	L	3-7		7	12	Rueter	Jennings		62-79	5th	17.5
9-9	S.F	L	4-9	(11)	8	13	Gomes	Belitz		62-80	5th	18.5
9-17	Ari.	L	3-7		9	7	Johnson	Davis		62-81	5th	19.5
9-18	Ari.	W	10-9		16	8	Myers	Kim		63-81	5th	18.5
9-19	Ari.	W	8-2		14	5	Hampton	Lopez		64-81	5th	17.5
9-20	At Mon.	L	3-8		8	11	Lloyd	Powell		64-82	5th	17.5
9-21	At Mon.	W	11-9	(11)	14	13	Davis	Mota		65-82	5th	17.5
9-22	At Mon.	L	1-3		6	3	Yoshii	Elarton	Strickland	65-83	5th	17.5
9-23	At Mon.	W	5-3		11	8	Speier	Stewart	Jimenez	66-83	5th	17.5
9-24	S.D.	W	15-11		20	16	Speier	Lundquist		67-83	5th	17.0
9-25	S.D.	L	7-8		14	10	Tollberg	Hampton	Hoffman	67-84	5th	17.0
9-26	S.D.	L	1-3		8	6	Lawrence	Speier	Hoffman	67-85	5th	18.0

Date	Opp.	Res.	Score	(inn.*)	Hits	Opp. hits	Winning pitcher	Losing pitcher	Save	Record	Pos.	GB
9-27	S.D.	W	13-9	18	14	Belitz	Herndon			68-85	5th	18.0
9-28	Mil.	W	6-5	12	8	Powell	Leskanic			69-85	5th	18.0
9-29	Mil.	W	14-12	16	14	Speier	Haynes	Jimenez		70-85	5th	18.0
9-30	Mil.	W	10-0	15	5	Thomson	D'Amico			71-85	5th	17.0
10-2	At Ari.	L	1-10	8	14	Johnson	Hampton			71-86	5th	18.0
10-3	At Ari.	L	3-4	9	6	Schilling	Chacon	Kim		71-87	5th	19.0
10-4	At Ari.	L	4-5	8	9	Anderson	Neagle	Kim		71-88	5th	20.0
10-5	At S.D.	W	4-0	6	4	Jennings	Jarvis			72-88	5th	20.0
10-6	At S.D.	L	4-10	11	10	Tollberg	Elarton			72-89	5th	20.0
10-7	At S.D.	W	14-5	14	9	Thomson	Lawrence			73-89	5th	19.0

Monthly records: April (13-11), May (13-16), June (12-15), July (7-19), August (14-13), September (12-11), October (2-4).
*Innings, if other than nine. §Day separate admission. ∞Night separate admission.

HIGHLIGHTS

High point: April 2. Freshly signed Mike Hampton pitched eight shutout innings and the Rockies pounded National League pennant-favorite St. Louis, 8-0. After completing a season-opening, three-game sweep, it looked like the Rockies had what it takes.

Low point: The Brent Mayne trade. After snapping a six-game losing streak with a win June 24 against Arizona's Randy Johnson, the Rockies returned to the clubhouse only to find their veteran catcher had been traded to Kansas City. The team wound up losing 19 of its next 23 games.

Turning point: After finishing off a three-game sweep at Cincinnati on June 17, the Rockies were four games over .500 (36-32) and a half-game off the wild-card lead. They went to Enron Field, where the 33-33 Astros awaited. Houston won all three and the Rockies disintegrated.

Most valuable player: It was difficult to separate Todd Helton from Larry Walker for team MVP. Helton gets the nod, however, because he played in 160 games—missing just two games to a hamstring injury. Helton had a team-high 49 homers and 146 RBIs. He also won his first Gold Glove.

Most valuable pitcher: Through June 10, Mike Hampton was 9-2 with a 2.98 ERA. A groin injury limited his effectiveness, however, and he finished the season with a 14-13 record and a Coors Field-like 5.41 ERA.

Most improved player: Juan Pierre batted .327 and showed great improvement with his defense in center field, bunting, basestealing and hitting the ball with authority. He led the N.L. with 163 singles and tied for the league lead with 46 stolen bases.

Most pleasant surprise: Shawn Chacon. Nearly released from the organization in 1999, he had a solid season at Class AA Carolina in 2000 and became a mainstay in the rotation.

Key injuries: Todd Hollandsworth was off to a terrific start until he fouled a ball off his shin while pinch-hitting on May 12 and never returned.

Notable: Reliever Gabe White was 11-2 with a 2.17 ERA and 82 strikeouts and 14 walks in 67 games in 2000; 1-7 with a 6.25 ERA and 47 strikeouts against 26 walks in 69 games this year. … Rookie Jason Jennings had arguably one of the greatest major league debuts in history when he pitched a complete-game shutout and hit a home run in a 10-0 win against the Mets. … Jeff Cirillo finished the season with an 85-game errorless streak that shattered the old N.L. record for third basemen.

—MIKE KLIS

RECORDS

2001 regular-season record: 73-89 (5th in N.L. West); 41-40 at home; 32-49 on road; 15-17 vs. N.L. East; 24-18 vs. N.L. Central; 32-44 vs. N.L. West; 2-10 vs. A.L.; 15-19 vs. lefthanded starters; 58-70 vs. righthanded starters; 70-85 on grass; 3-4 on turf; 28-30 in daytime; 45-59 at night; 18-28 in one-run games; 5-5 in extra-inning games; 0-0-0 in doubleheaders.

Team record past five years: 387-423 (.478, ranks 10th in league in that span).

TEAM LEADERS

Batting average: Larry Walker (.350).
At-bats: Juan Pierre (617).
Runs: Todd Helton (132).
Hits: Juan Pierre (202).
Total Bases: Todd Helton (402).
Doubles: Todd Helton (54).
Triples: Juan Pierre, Juan Uribe (11).
Home runs: Todd Helton (49).
Runs batted in: Todd Helton (146).
Stolen bases: Juan Pierre (46).
Slugging percentage: Todd Helton (.685).

On-base percentage: Larry Walker (.449).
Wins: Mike Hampton (14).
Earned-run average: Denny Neagle (5.38).
Complete games: Pedro Astacio (4).
Shutouts: Pedro Astacio, Mike Hampton, Jason Jennings, John Thomson (1).
Saves: Jose Jimenez (17).
Innings pitched: Mike Hampton (203.0).
Strikeouts: Denny Neagle (139).

GAMES BY POSITION

Catcher: Ben Petrick 77, Brent Mayne 44, Sal Fasano 25, Adam Melhuse 23, Gary Bennett 19.
First base: Todd Helton 157, Greg Norton 13, Ben Petrick 2, Brent Mayne 1, Brooks Kieschnick 1, Adam Melhuse 1.
Second base: Todd Walker 77, Jose Ortiz 51, Terry Shumpert 41, Brent Butler 23.
Third base: Jeff Cirillo 137, Greg Norton 24, Terry Shumpert 12, Brent Butler 9.
Shortstop: Neifi Perez 87, Juan Uribe 69, Brent Butler 10, Terry Shumpert 4.
Outfield: Juan Pierre 154, Larry Walker 129, Alex Ochoa 52, Ron Gant 51, Todd Hollandsworth 31, Mark Little 29, Greg Norton 25, Terry Shumpert 24, Jacob Cruz 24, Mario Encarnacion 20, Brooks Kieschnick 12, Cliff Brumbaugh 11, Kimera Bartee 10, Robin Jennings 1.
Designated hitter: Larry Walker 5, Greg Norton 1.

TOP DRAFT CHOICES

1. **Jayson Nix,** SS, Midland (Tex.) H.S.
2. **Trey Taylor,** LHP, Mansfield (Tex.) H.S.
3. **Jason Frome,** OF, Indiana State Univ.
4. **Jay Mitchell,** RHP, LaGrange (Ga.) H.S.
5. **Gerrit Simpson,** RHP, U. of Texas.
6. **Jamie Tricoglou,** RHP, Kennesaw State University.
7. **Cory Sullivan,** OF, Wake Forest Univ.
8. **Scott Nicholson,** LHP, Oregon State University.
9. **James Sweeney,** C, Bellaire (Tex.) H.S.
10. **Tony Miller,** OF, Univ. of Toledo.

FLORIDA MARLINS
NATIONAL LEAGUE EAST DIVISION

Marlins schedule
Home games shaded
D—Day game (games starting before 5 p.m.)
*All-Star Game at Milwaukee
Subject to changes

April
SUN	MON	TUE	WED	THU	FRI	SAT
	1	2 MON	3 MON	4 MON	5 PHI	6 D PHI
7 D PHI	8 MON	9	10 MON	11 MON	12 ATL	13 ATL
14 D ATL	15	16 PHI	17 PHI	18 PHI	19 ATL	20 ATL
21 D ATL	22 ATL	23 HOU	24 HOU	25 HOU	26 ARI	27 ARI
26 D ARI	29	30 STL				

May
SUN	MON	TUE	WED	THU	FRI	SAT
		1 STL	2 D STL	3 MIL	4 D MIL
5 D MIL	6	7 SD	8 SD	9 SD	10 LA	11 LA
12 D LA	13 COL	14 COL	15 COL	16 COL	17 SF	18 D SF
19 CF	20	21 CIN	22 CIN	23 D CIN	24 NYM	25 D NYM
26 D NYM	27 D NYM	28 CIN	29 CIN	30 CIN	31 NYM	

June
SUN	MON	TUE	WED	THU	FRI	SAT
						1 NYM
2 D NYM	3	4 PHI	5 PHI	6 PHI	7 MIN	8 MIN
9 D MIN	10 KC	11 KC	12 KC	13	14 TB	15 TB
16 D TB	17	18 CLE	19 CLE	20 CLE	21 DET	22 DET
23 D DET	24 PHI	25 PHI	26 PHI	27 PHI	28 TB	29 TB
30 D TB						

July
SUN	MON	TUE	WED	THU	FRI	SAT
	1 CUB	2 CUB	3 CUB	4 NYM	5 NYM	6 NYM
7 D NYM	8	9 *	10	11	12 D CUB	13 D CUB
14 D CUB	15 NYM	16 D NYM	17 ATL	18 ATL	19 D MON	20 MON
21 D MON	22 ATL	23 ATL	24 ATL	25 MON	26 MON	27 MON
28 D MON	29	30 STL	31 STL			

August
SUN	MON	TUE	WED	THU	FRI	SAT
				1 STL	2 MIL	3 MIL
4 D MIL	5	6 HOU	7 HOU	8 D HOU	9 ARI	10 ARI
11 D ARI	12 COL	13 COL	14 COL	15	16 SF	17 SF
18 D SF	19 D SF	20 LA	21 LA	22 D LA	23 SD	24 SD
25 D SD	26	27 NYM	28 NYM	29	30 PIT	31 PIT

September
SUN	MON	TUE	WED	THU	FRI	SAT
1 D PIT	2 D NYM	3 NYM	4 NYM	5 NYM	6 PIT	7 PIT
8 D PIT	9	10 PHI	11 PHI	12 PHI	13 ATL	14 ATL
15 D ATL	16 MON	17 MON	18 MON	19 MON	20 ATL	21 ATL
22 D ATL	23	24 MON	25 MON	26 MON	27 PHI	28 PHI
29 D PHI	30					

2002 SEASON
CLUB DIRECTORY

Owner/chairman
John W. Henry
Vice chairman
David Ginsberg
Vice president and assistant general manager
Al Avila
V.p. and assistant to the general manager
Scott Reid
Exec. v.p., sales, marketing & communication
Julio G. Rebull Jr.
V.p., communications & broadcasting
Ron Colangelo
V.p., sales & marketing
Andy Dunn
Vice president, finance
Susan Jaison
Vice president, legal affairs/ballpark
Lucinda Treat
Director of team travel
Bill Beck
Director, scouting
David Chadd
Director, Latin-American operations
Louie Eljaua
Sr. advisor & special asst. to general manager
Whitey Lockman
Special assistants to the g m
Andre Dawson, Orrin Freeman, Tony Perez
Director, Major League operations
Dan Lunetta
Director, minor league operations
Rick Williams
Director Space Coast operations
Mike Parkinson
Manager, minor league administration
Kim-Lee Carkeek Luchs
Manager, scouting administration
Cheryl Evans
Director of media relations
Steve Copses
Media information coordinator
Andrew Feirstein
Administrative assistant, media relations
Maria Armella
Manager, broadcasting
Sandra van Meek
Manager, community affairs
Israel Negron
Director, marketing
Susan Budd
Director, advertising
Maria Meilan
Manager, Marlins en Miami store
Juan Martinez

Director, marketing partnerships
Kevin Farlow
Dir., creative services & in-game entertainment
Leslie Riguero
Director, season & group sales
Pat McNamara
Manager, customer service
Jeff Tanzer
Director, team security
Dan Vaniman
Employee relations manager
Ana Hernandez
Exec. dir., Florida Marlins Community Foundation
Nancy Olson
Manager, baseball information systems
David Kuan
MLB advanced media site editor
Lindsay Reid
Team physician
Dr. Dan Kanell
Head athletic trainer
Larry Starr
Strength and conditioning director
Rick Slate
Asst. strength and conditioning coach
Kazu Tamooka
Equipment manager
Mike Wallace
Visiting clubhouse manager
Matt Rosenthal
Cross-checkers
Murray Cook, Curtis Dishman, David Finley, Bob Laurie, Mike Russell, Tim Schmidt, Doug Strange
Director, Latin-American development
Rafael Bournigal
Director, Dominican Republic operations
Jesus Alou
Scouts
Ed Bockman, Kelvin Bowles, Al Diez, Lou Fitzgerald, Dr. Demi Mainieri, Charlie Silvera, John Booher, Ty Brown, Brad DelBarba, Jon Deeble, Sean Johnson, Larry Keller, Cucho Rodriguez, Doug Rogalski, Jim Rough, Dennis Sheehan, Keith Snider, Mike Tosar, Stan Zielinski, Tom Evans, Fred Long, Dave McQueen, Dave Mumper, John Nilmeyer, James Orr, Terry Sullivan, Dick Wilson, Pedro Cintron, Dick Smith, Pablo Lantigua, Cesar Santiago, Ramon Webster, Alvaro Blanco, Hubert Silva, Miguel Angel Garcia, Ernesto Gomez, Jesus Laya, Jorge Rangel, German Robles, Oscar Sarmiento, James Woodward, Alejandro Rodriguez, Jesus Garces, Jovel Jimenez

MINOR LEAGUE AFFILIATES

Class	Team	League	Manager
AAA	Calgary	Pacific Coast	Rick Renteria
AA	Portland	Eastern	Dave Huppert
A	Brevard County	Florida State	To be announced
A	Kane County	Midwest	Russ Morman
A	Utica	New York-Pennsylvania	To be announced
Rookie	Gulf Coast Marlins	Gulf Coast	Jon Deeble

BROADCAST INFORMATION
Radio: WQAM-AM (560); WQBA-AM (1140, Spanish language).
TV: WAMI-TV (Channel 69).
Cable TV: Fox Sports Net.

SPRING TRAINING
Ballpark (city): Space Coast Stadium (Melbourne, Fla.).
Ticket information: 321-633-9200.

Follow the Marlins all season at: www.sportingnews.com/baseball/teams/marlins/

SPRING TRAINING ROSTER

Manager—To be announced.
Coaches—To be announced.

No.	PITCHERS	B/T	Ht./Wt.	Born	2001 clubs
57	Alfonseca, Antonio	R/R	6-5/235	4-16-72	Florida
55	Almanza, Armando	L/L	6-3/220	10-26-72	Florida
64	Anderson, Wes	R/R	6-4/175	9-10-79	Brevard County, Gulf Coast Marlins
	Baez, Benito	L/L	6-0/160	5-6-77	Calgary, Florida
61	Beckett, Josh	R/R	6-4/190	5-15-80	Brevard County, Portland, Florida
43	Burnett, A.J.	R/R	6-5/205	1-3-77	Brevard County, Florida
21	Clement, Matt	R/R	6-3/195	8-12-74	Florida
22	Darensbourg, Vic	L/L	5-10/165	11-13-70	Florida
46	Dempster, Ryan	R/R	6-1/201	5-3-77	Florida
54	Goetz, Geoff	L/L	5-11/165	3-3-79	Portland
37	Grilli, Jason	R/R	6-4/185	11-11-76	Florida, Calgary, Gulf Coast Marlins, Brevard County, Portland
	Izquierdo, Hansel	R/R	6-2/205	1-2-77	Kane County, Brevard County, Portland
56	Knotts, Gary	R/R	6-4/200	2-12-77	Calgary, Florida
41	Looper, Braden	R/R	6-5/225	10-28-74	Florida
53	Neal, Blaine	R/L	6-5/205	4-6-78	Portland, Florida
36	Nunez, Vladimir	R/R	6-4/224	3-15-75	Florida, Kane County
	Olsen, Kevin	R/R	6-2/200	7-26-76	Portland, Florida
28	Penny, Brad	R/R	6-4/200	5-24-78	Florida
45	Smith, Chuck	R/R	6-1/185	10-21-69	Brevard County, Calgary, Florida
58	Tejera, Michael	L/L	5-9/175	10-18-76	Portland
	Teut, Nathan	R/L	6-7/215	3-11-76	Iowa
47	Vargas, Claudio	R/R	6-3/210	5-19-79	Portland

No.	CATCHERS	B/T	Ht./Wt.	Born	2001 clubs
17	Castro, Ramon	R/R	6-3/225	3-1-76	Florida, Calgary
23	Johnson, Charles	R/R	6-2/220	7-20-71	Florida
52	Redmond, Mike	R/R	6-1/185	5-5-71	Florida

No.	INFIELDERS	B/T	Ht./Wt.	Born	2001 clubs
1	Castillo, Luis	B/R	5-11/196	9-12-75	Florida
6	Fox, Andy	L/R	6-4/202	1-12-71	Florida, Calgary
11	Gonzalez, Alex	R/R	6-0/170	2-15-77	Florida
25	Lee, Derrek	R/R	6-5/242	9-6-75	Florida
19	Lowell, Mike	R/R	6-4/205	2-24-74	Florida
15	Millar, Kevin	R/R	6-0/210	9-24-71	Florida
3	Ozuna, Pablo	R/R	6-0/160	8-25-78	DID NOT PLAY
26	Rolison, Nate	L/R	6-6/240	3-27-77	Gulf Coast Marlins, Brevard County, Portland, Calgary

No.	OUTFIELDERS	B/T	Ht./Wt.	Born	2001 clubs
	Ambres, Chip	R/R	6-1/190	12-19-78	Kane County
30	Floyd, Cliff	L/R	6-4/240	12-5-72	Florida
14	Nunez, Abraham	R/R	6-2/185	2-5-80	Portland
8	Owens, Eric	R/R	6-0/198	2-3-71	Florida, Calgary
44	Wilson, Preston	R/R	6-2/208	7-19-74	Florida, Calgary

BALLPARK INFORMATION

Ballpark (capacity, surface)
Pro Player Stadium (36,331, grass)
Address
2267 Dan Marino Blvd.
Miami, Fla. 33056
Official website
www.floridamarlins.com
Business phone
305-626-7400
Ticket information
305-350-5050
Ticket prices
$55 (founders club), $32 (club level section A)
$25 (infield box), $24 (club level section B)
$18 (power alley section C)
$15 (terrace box, mezzanine box)
$12 (club level sections B & C-senior citizens)
$10 (OF reserved, adult), $9 (mezzanine reserved, adult)
$5 (OF reserved, children), $4 (fish tank-last three rows, adult)
$3 (mezzanine reserved, children)
$2 (fish tank-last three rows, children)
Field dimensions (from home plate)
To left field at foul line, 330 feet
To center field, 434 feet
To right field at foul line, 345 feet
First game played
April 5, 1993 (Marlins 6, Dodgers 3)

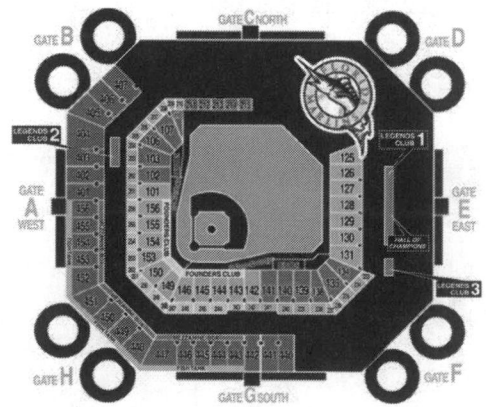

Date	Opp.	Res.	Score	(inn.*)	Hits	Opp. hits	Winning pitcher	Losing pitcher	Save	Record	Pos.	GB
4-2	Phi.	L	5-6	(13)	8	12	Telemaco	Nunez		0-1	T4th	1.0
4-3	Phi.	L	3-4		6	9	Brock	Looper	Mesa	0-2	5th	2.0
4-4	Phi.	L	3-7		13	10	Cormier	Miceli		0-3	5th	3.0
4-6	Atl.	L	5-7		7	11	Maddux	Grilli	Rocker	0-4	5th	3.0
4-7	Atl.	W	8-0		11	6	Dempster	Burkett		1-4	5th	3.0
4-8	Atl.	W	6-1		8	4	Clement	Glavine		2-4	T4th	3.0
4-9	At Phi.	L	4-5		5	10	Bottalico	Bones		2-5	5th	4.0
4-10	At Phi.	L	6-7		9	12	Gomes	Alfonseca	Mesa	2-6	5th	4.0
4-13	At Mon.	W	9-3		13	6	Dempster	Vazquez		3-6	5th	3.0
4-14	At Mon.	L	2-8		8	14	Reames	Clement		3-7	5th	4.0
4-15	At Mon.	W	6-3		9	7	Grilli	Armas	Alfonseca	4-7	4th	3.0
4-16	At Atl.	L	3-4		7	5	Rocker	Miceli		4-8	5th	3.5
4-17	At Atl.	W	3-2		7	5	Nunez	Burkett	Alfonseca	5-8	5th	3.5
4-18	At Atl.	L	0-1		3	5	Glavine	Dempster	Rocker	5-9	5th	3.0
4-19	Mon.	W	5-2		8	3	Looper	Strickland	Alfonseca	6-9	T4th	2.5
4-20	Mon.	W	5-1		8	5	Grilli	Armas		7-9	4th	2.5
4-21	Mon.	W	5-0		7	4	Penny	Thurman		8-9	2nd	2.5
4-22	Mon.	L	2-6		7	9	Peters	Nunez		8-10	T3rd	3.5
4-23	At Ari.	L	0-9		6	7	Johnson	Dempster		8-11	5th	4.5
4-24	At Ari.	L	8-9		13	10	Prinz	Almanza	Springer	8-12	5th	5.5
4-25	At Ari.	L	7-10		13	12	Schilling	Grilli	Prinz	8-13	5th	6.5
4-27	At Hou.	W	9-8	(10)	13	10	Alfonseca	Wagner		9-13	4th	5.0
4-28	At Hou.	L	4-6		8	11	Miller	Dempster		9-14	T4th	5.0
4-29	At Hou.	W	11-5		19	12	Bones	Reynolds		10-14	4th	4.0
5-1	St.L.	W	4-3		10	9	Nunez	An. Benes	Alfonseca	11-14	3rd	4.0
5-2	St.L.	L	2-4	(11)	12	13	Kline	Alfonseca	Veres	11-15	4th	4.0
5-4	Mil.	W	9-6		11	10	Dempster	Wright	Alfonseca	12-15	2nd	3.5
5-5	Mil.	L	2-8		5	8	Leiter	Clement		12-16	4th	4.5
5-6	Mil.	W	5-1		9	3	Smith	Haynes		13-16	3rd	4.5
5-7	At L.A.	L	0-1		2	3	Brown	Burnett	Shaw	13-17	4th	5.5
5-8	At L.A.	W	7-6		11	10	Penny	Prokopec	Alfonseca	14-17	3rd	5.5
5-9	At L.A.	L	2-3		5	8	Park	Dempster	Shaw	14-18	3rd	5.5
5-10	At L.A.	L	3-4		9	9	Dreifort	Clement	Shaw	14-19	3rd	6.0
5-11	At S.D.	L	6-7	(10)	11	9	Witasick	Looper		14-20	3rd	7.0
5-12	At S.D.	W	3-0		7	0	Burnett	Serrano		15-20	3rd	7.0
5-13	At S.D.	W	10-4		11	7	Penny	Witasick		16-20	3rd	6.0
5-15	S.F.	L	4-7		10	9	Hernandez	Dempster	Nen	16-21	3rd	6.0
5-16	S.F.	W	4-3		10	5	Clement	Rueter	Alfonseca	17-21	3rd	5.0
5-17	S.F.	W	8-3		10	4	Smith	Ortiz		18-21	3rd	5.0
5-18	Col.	W	2-1		4	10	Burnett	Astacio	Alfonseca	19-21	3rd	5.0
5-19	Col.	W	1-0		4	3	Penny	Thomson	Alfonseca	20-21	2nd	5.0
5-20	Col.	L	2-7		11	9	Hampton	Dempster		20-22	3rd	5.0
5-21	Atl.	L	3-5		7	7	Glavine	Clement	Rocker	20-23	3rd	5.5
5-22	Atl.	W	3-2		10	8	Smith	Smoltz	Alfonseca	21-23	3rd	5.0
5-24	At N.Y.	L	3-11		6	10	Appier	Burnett		21-24	3rd	7.0
5-25	At N.Y.	L	3-4	(10)	8	8	Franco	Miceli		21-25	3rd	8.0
5-26	At N.Y.	W	7-3		18	6	Dempster	Rusch		22-25	3rd	7.5
5-27	At N.Y.	L	4-5		13	8	Wendell	Miceli	Benitez	22-26	3rd	8.0
5-28	At Pit.	L	5-8		10	12	Silva	Miceli	M. Williams	22-27	3rd	9.0
5-29	At Pit.	W	5-0		9	8	Burnett	Anderson		23-27	3rd	9.0
5-30	At Pit.	W	9-7	(10)	12	12	Alfonseca	M. Williams	Looper	24-27	3rd	9.0
5-31	N.Y.	W	5-3		7	7	Dempster	Wendell	Alfonseca	25-27	3rd	9.0
6-1	N.Y.	L	5-11		7	13	Gonzalez	Clement		25-28	3rd	10.0
6-2	N.Y.	L	1-7		6	11	Leiter	Smith		25-29	3rd	10.0
6-3	N.Y.	W	1-0		4	4	Alfonseca	Wendell		26-29	3rd	9.0
6-5	Pit.	L	2-5		6	8	Schmidt	Penny	M. Williams	26-30	3rd	9.0
6-6	Pit.	W	7-2		10	8	Dempster	Ritchie		27-30	3rd	9.0
6-7	Pit.	W	5-3		8	7	Bones	Manzanillo	Alfonseca	28-30	3rd	8.0
6-8	At Tor.	L	6-7	(10)	12	15	Koch	Bones		28-31	3rd	8.0
6-9	At Tor.	W	6-1		9	2	Burnett	Carpenter		29-31	3rd	8.0
6-10	At Tor.	W	7-2		8	7	Penny	Loaiza		30-31	3rd	7.0
6-12	At Bos.	L	2-4		8	7	Castillo	Dempster	Lowe	30-32	3rd	7.0
6-13	At Bos.	W	4-2		10	11	Clement	Wakefield	Alfonseca	31-32	3rd	6.0
6-14	At Bos.	L	4-6		5	10	Cone	Smith	Beck	31-33	3rd	6.0
6-15	T.B.	W	7-4		11	7	Burnett	Sturtze		32-33	3rd	6.0
6-16	T.B.	W	11-0		13	1	Penny	Lopez		33-33	3rd	6.0
6-17	T.B.	W	6-4		9	10	Dempster	Kennedy	Alfonseca	34-33	3rd	5.0
6-18	At Atl.	W	7-6		12	9	Looper	Rocker	Alfonseca	35-33	3rd	4.5
6-19	At Atl.	W	12-2		16	8	Smith	Marquis		36-33	T2nd	3.5
6-20	At Atl.	L	2-7		4	10	Maddux	Burnett		36-34	3rd	4.5
6-21	At Atl.	W	3-2		8	6	Looper	Rocker	Alfonseca	37-34	T2nd	4.5
6-22	Phi.	W	8-1		13	7	Dempster	Wolf		38-34	T2nd	3.5
6-23	Phi.	W	12-1		14	6	Clement	Telemaco		39-34	T2nd	2.5
6-24	Phi.	L	3-9		6	14	Chen	Smith		39-35	3rd	3.5

Date	Opp.	Res.	Score	(inn.*)	Hits	Opp. hits	Winning pitcher	Losing pitcher	Save	Record	Pos.	GB
6-25	Mon.	L	1-3		6	7	Vazquez	Burnett	Urbina	39-36	3rd	3.5
6-26	Mon.	W	3-0		10	1	Penny	Thurman	Alfonseca	40-36	3rd	2.5
6-27	Mon.	W	9-1		7	4	Sanchez	Armas		41-36	3rd	2.0
6-28†	At Phi.	L	5-6		8	12	Person	Dempster	Mesa	41-37		
6-28‡	At Phi.	L	7-8		11	10	Cormier	Looper	Mesa	41-38	3rd	3.5
6-29	At Phi.	L	0-5		8	8	Chen	Smith		41-39	3rd	4.5
6-30	Bal.	L	4-6		7	11	Daal	Burnett	Mesa	41-40	3rd	5.5
7-1	At Phi.	L	1-8		7	14	Figueroa	Penny		41-41	3rd	6.5
7-3	At Mon.	W	7-0		10	4	Dempster	Armas		42-41	3rd	5.5
7-4	At Mon.	L	6-9		12	15	Lloyd	Clement	Urbina	42-42	3rd	6.5
7-5	At Mon.	L	6-9		12	15	Vazquez	Smith	Urbina	42-43	3rd	6.5
7-6	At T.B.	L	4-5	(11)	10	13	Zambrano	Bones		42-44	3rd	7.5
7-7	At T.B.	L	3-4		9	10	Lopez	Penny	Phelps	42-45	3rd	7.5
7-8	At T.B.	W	6-1		10	4	Dempster	Kennedy		43-45	3rd	7.5
7-12	N.Y.	W	9-3		13	4	Burnett	Mussina		44-45	3rd	6.5
7-13	N.Y.	W	11-1		15	11	Smith	Lilly		45-45	3rd	6.5
7-14	N.Y.	L	4-5	(10)	11	15	Rivera	Alfonseca	Mendoza	45-46	3rd	6.5
7-15	Bal.	W	7-1		11	5	Clement	Johnson		46-46	3rd	6.5
7-16	Bal.	W	4-0		7	2	Sanchez	Mercedes		47-46	3rd	5.5
7-17	Bal.	W	8-3		12	6	Burnett	Ponson	Darensbourg	48-46	3rd	4.5
7-18	At N.Y.	L	3-4	(11)	7	10	Wendell	Nunez		48-47	3rd	5.5
7-19	At N.Y.	W	8-3		12	7	Dempster	Rusch		49-47	3rd	5.5
7-20	Cin.	W	5-3		8	10	Clement	Acevedo	Alfonseca	50-47	3rd	4.5
7-21	Cin.	L	4-8		8	9	Davis	Penny		50-48	3rd	5.5
7-22	Cin.	W	11-7		15	13	Burnett	Reitsma		51-48	3rd	5.5
7-24	N.Y.	W	4-3		9	6	Bones	Appier	Alfonseca	52-48	3rd	4.0
7-25	N.Y.	L	2-5		8	12	Rusch	Dempster	Benitez	52-49	3rd	5.0
7-27	At Cin.	L	5-10		12	10	Davis	Clement	Graves	52-50	3rd	5.5
7-28	At Cin.	L	0-5		6	4	Dessens	Penny		52-51	3rd	6.5
7-29	At Cin.	L	4-8		9	11	Reitsma	Burnett		52-52	3rd	7.5
7-31	At Mil.	W	5-1		9	3	Dempster	Sheets		53-52	3rd	6.5
8-1	At Mil.	W	5-4	(10)	13	11	Almanza	King	Alfonseca	54-52	3rd	5.5
8-2	At Mil.	L	3-4		7	7	Levrault	Knotts	Leskanic	54-53	3rd	6.5
8-3†	At St.L.	L	5-9		11	15	Morris	Penny	Kline	54-54		
8-3‡	At St.L.	W	6-4		7	8	Nunez	Veres	Alfonseca	55-54	3rd	6.0
8-4	At St.L.	L	0-3		8	7	Williams	Burnett	Stechschulte	55-55	3rd	7.0
8-5	At St.L.	W	5-3		8	10	Dempster	Hermanson	Alfonseca	56-55	3rd	7.0
8-7	Ari.	W	10-4		14	5	Clement	Lopez		57-55	3rd	7.0
8-8	Ari.	L	1-7		6	12	Johnson	Sanchez		57-56	3rd	7.0
8-9	Ari.	W	3-1		12	4	Darensbourg	Swindell	Alfonseca	58-56	3rd	6.0
8-10	Hou.	L	2-7		5	15	Astacio	Burnett		58-57	3rd	6.0
8-11	Hou.	W	13-5		18	6	Dempster	B. Powell		59-57	3rd	5.0
8-12	Hou.	L	5-10		7	13	Mlicki	Clement		59-58	3rd	6.0
8-14	At S.F	L	7-13		13	20	Schmidt	Sanchez		59-59	3rd	7.0
8-15	At S.F	L	1-2		5	3	Nen	Darensbourg		59-60	3rd	8.0
8-16	At S.F	L	3-5		8	7	Worrell	Burnett	Nen	59-61	3rd	8.0
8-17	At Col.	L	5-12		13	13	Speier	Dempster		59-62	3rd	8.0
8-18	At Col.	L	3-8		6	13	Neagle	Almanza	Powell	59-63	3rd	9.0
8-19	At Col.	L	5-6		10	15	Thomson	Sanchez	Miceli	59-64	3rd	9.0
8-21	L.A.	L	4-5		9	9	Carrara	Nunez	Shaw	59-65	3rd	9.0
8-22	L.A.	W	8-6		14	9	Burnett	Adams		60-65	3rd	9.0
8-23	L.A.	L	2-6		5	10	Baldwin	Dempster		60-66	3rd	10.0
8-24	S.D.	W	6-3		8	8	Clement	Jones	Alfonseca	61-66	3rd	9.0
8-25	S.D.	L	1-7		8	8	Herndon	Sanchez		61-67	3rd	9.0
8-26	S.D.	L	0-10		8	15	Jarvis	Penny		61-68	3rd	10.0
8-27	S.D.	L	3-8		7	10	Tollberg	Burnett		61-69	3rd	10.0
8-28	At Chi.	W	4-3	(14)	14	11	Nunez	Fassero		62-69	3rd	9.0
8-29	At Chi.	L	1-5		3	9	Bere	Clement		62-70	3rd	10.0
8-30	At Chi.	L	4-5		12	7	Farnsworth	Bones		62-71	4th	10.0
8-31	At N.Y.	L	1-6		5	9	Leiter	Penny		62-72	4th	10.0
9-1	At N.Y.	L	2-3	(11)	6	8	Roberts	Acevedo		62-73	4th	10.0
9-2	At N.Y.	W	5-1		10	5	Dempster	Rusch		63-73	4th	10.0
9-3	Chi.	L	2-10		7	13	Bere	Clement		63-74	4th	11.0
9-4	Chi.	W	8-1		8	6	Beckett	Lieber		64-74	4th	11.0
9-5	Chi.	W	7-6		11	11	Almanza	Gordon		65-74	4th	10.0
9-6	N.Y.	L	2-5		10	10	Appier	Penny	Benitez	65-75	4th	10.5
9-7	N.Y.	L	1-6		8	9	Rusch	Burnett		65-76	4th	11.5
9-8	N.Y.	L	7-9		11	17	Franco	Alfonseca	Benitez	65-77	4th	12.5
9-9	N.Y.	W	4-2		9	6	Acevedo	Trachsel	Alfonseca	66-77	4th	12.5
9-17	At Mon.	W	10-6		18	9	Bones	Mota		67-77	4th	11.5
9-18	At Mon.	W	3-1		7	10	Penny	Thurman	Alfonseca	68-77	4th	10.5
9-19	At Mon.	L	2-5		7	7	Pavano	Beckett	Strickland	68-78	4th	10.5
9-21	At Phi.	L	0-1		6	6	Mesa	Nunez		68-79	4th	11.0
9-22	At Phi.	W	3-2		8	8	Clement	Santiago	Alfonseca	69-79	4th	10.0
9-23	At Phi.	L	4-5	(10)	6	10	Mesa	Acevedo		69-80	4th	11.0
9-24	Atl.	W	1-0		3	7	Penny	Burkett	Alfonseca	70-80	4th	10.0
9-25	Atl.	L	2-5	(11)	12	11	Ligtenberg	Darensbourg	Smoltz	70-81	4th	11.0
9-26	Atl.	L	1-4		5	7	Marquis	Burnett	Smoltz	70-82	4th	12.0

Date	Opp.	Res.	Score	(inn.*)	Hits	Opp. hits	Winning pitcher	Losing pitcher	Save	Record	Pos.	GB
9-27	Atl.	W	7-1		11	8	Acevedo	Maddux		71-82	4th	11.0
9-28	Phi.	W	6-5	(10)	11	10	Alfonseca	Politte		72-82	4th	11.0
9-29	Phi.	L	4-5		7	8	Duckworth	Penny	Mesa	72-83	4th	12.0
9-30	Phi.	W	8-3		7	6	Beckett	Coggin		73-83	4th	11.0
10-2	Mon.	W	4-3		7	6	Burnett	Armas	Looper	74-83	4th	10.0
10-3	Mon.	L	0-2		4	9	Stewart	Acevedo	Strickland	74-84	4th	11.0
10-4	Mon.	W	6-2		12	6	Penny	Yoshii		75-84	4th	11.0
10-5	At Atl.	L	3-20		6	14	Millwood	Dempster		75-85	4th	12.0
10-6	At Atl.	L	3-7		8	9	Marquis	Beckett		75-86	4th	13.0
10-7	At Atl.	W	4-2		6	7	Burnett	Spooneybarger	Looper	76-86	4th	12.0

Monthly records: April (10-14), May (15-13), June (16-13), July (12-12), August (9-20), September (11-11), October (3-3).
*Innings, if other than nine. †First game of a doubleheader. ‡Second game of a doubleheader.

HIGHLIGHTS

High point: Inspired by Tony Perez, who replaced fired manager John Boles on May 28, the Marlins began by winning 15 of Perez's first 22 games. The apex came on June 27, when the Marlins—having won two of three at home against Philadelphia—beat Montreal to go five games above .500 and within two games of first place.

Low point: The Marlins hit bottom on August 19 when they lost to Colorado, 6-5, to cap an 0-6 road trip that started in San Francisco. Although it was mid-August, the road trip signaled the end of the season. Perez said his players "look like they quit."

Turning point: The turning point of the season came on a road trip to Philadelphia, Montreal and Tampa Bay from June 28-July 8. The Phillies were the only tough team they played, but the Marlins still managed to lose nine of the 11 games, starting with a doubleheader sweep in Philadelphia, the first two of five games they would lose at the Vet.

Most valuable player: For most of his career, the book on Cliff Floyd said he could be one of the league's best hitters—if he stayed healthy. Floyd wasn't 100 percent healthy in 2001, but he stayed off the disabled list and played nearly every day. As a result, he posted a great season by putting up single-season club records with 123 runs and 79 extra-base hits.

Most valuable pitcher: He wasn't as sharp as he was in 2000, but Ryan Dempster battled through slumps and still posted the best numbers of any Marlins starter. He posted a 15-12 record and led the team with 171 strikeouts.

Most improved player: Under Perez, Kevin Millar played every day and flourished. He batted .314 and hit a career-high 20 homers with 85 RBIs.

Most pleasant surprise: Vladimir Nunez found his niche as a middle reliever. He went 4-5, but posted a 2.74 ERA in 92 innings pitched over 52 games, the lowest ERA among regular staff pitchers.

Key injuries: Preston Wilson missed significant action with a bad back and thumb. ... Chuck Smith hurt his elbow in late July and missed the rest of the season. ... Luis Castillo missed the last two weeks of the season with a severe ankle sprain. ... Antonio Alfonseca underwent surgery to repair a herniated disc.

Notable: The Marlins set team records with 166 home runs and a .983 fielding percentage, committing a franchise-low 103 errors. The team led the N.L. with 325 doubles. ... The Marlins led the majors in losses in their opponents' last at-bat (24).

—JOE CAPOZZI

RECORDS

2001 regular-season record: 76-86 (4th in N.L. East); 46-34 at home; 30-52 on road; 34-42 vs. N.L. East; 19-17 vs. N.L. Central; 11-21 vs. N.L. West; 12-6 vs. A.L.; 15-23 vs. lefthanded starters; 61-63 vs. righthanded starters; 67-70 on grass; 9-16 on turf; 23-21 in daytime; 53-65 at night; 19-29 in one-run games; 5-11 in extra-inning games; 0-1-1 in doubleheaders.

Team record past five years: 365-444 (.451, ranks 14th in league in that span).

TEAM LEADERS

Batting average: Cliff Floyd (.317).
At-bats: Derrek Lee (561).
Runs: Cliff Floyd (123).
Hits: Cliff Floyd (176).
Total Bases: Cliff Floyd (321).
Doubles: Cliff Floyd (44).
Triples: Luis Castillo (10).
Home runs: Cliff Floyd (31).
Runs batted in: Cliff Floyd (103).
Stolen bases: Luis Castillo (33).
Slugging percentage: Cliff Floyd (.578).
On-base percentage: Cliff Floyd (.390).

Wins: Ryan Dempster (15).
Earned-run average: Brad Penny (3.69).
Complete games: A.J. Burnett, Ryan Dempster (2).
Shutouts: A.J. Burnett, Ryan Dempster, Brad Penny (1).
Saves: Antonio Alfonseca (28).
Innings pitched: Ryan Dempster (211.1).
Strikeouts: Ryan Dempster (171).

GAMES BY POSITION

Catcher: Charles Johnson 125, Mike Redmond 47, Ramon Castro 4, Alex Gonzalez 1.
First base: Derrek Lee 156, Kevin Millar 15, Ryan McGuire 4, John Mabry 1.
Second base: Luis Castillo 133, Dave Berg 34, Andy Fox 2.
Third base: Mike Lowell 144, Dave Berg 10, Kevin Millar 10, Andy Fox 9, Mike Gulan 1.
Shortstop: Alex Gonzalez 142, Dave Berg 19, Andy Fox 12.
Outfield: Cliff Floyd 142, Preston Wilson 121, Eric Owens 106, Kevin Millar 86, John Mabry 39, Jeff Abbott 17, Ryan Thompson 16, Lyle Mouton 11, Ryan McGuire 9, Chad Mottola 5, Andy Fox 2.
Designated hitter: Kevin Millar 6, Cliff Floyd 3, Eric Owens 1, John Mabry 1.

TOP DRAFT CHOICES

2. **Garrett Berger,** RHP, Carmel (Ind.) H.S.
3. **Allen Baxter,** RHP, Varina H.S., Sandston, Va.
4. **Chris Resop,** RHP/OF, Barron Collier H.S., Naples, Fla.
5. **Tyler Lumsden,** LHP, Cave Spring H.S., Roanoke, Va.
6. **Adam Bostick,** LHP, Greensburg-Salem H.S., Greensburg, Pa.
7. **Lincoln Holdzkom,** RHP, Arizona Western C.C.
8. **Jeff Fulchino,** RHP, U. of Connecticut.
9. **Dustin Kupper,** RHP, Pima (Ariz.) C.C.
10. **Kody Naylor,** RHP, Western Michigan University.

HOUSTON ASTROS
NATIONAL LEAGUE CENTRAL DIVISION

Astros schedule
Home games shaded
D—Day game (games starting before 5 p.m.)
*All-Star Game at Milwaukee
Subject to changes

April

SUN	MON	TUE	WED	THU	FRI	SAT
	1	2 D MIL	3 MIL	4 D MIL	5 D STL	6 STL
7 D STL	8 D COL	9 COL	10 D COL	11 D	12 STL	13 D STL
14 STL	15	16 CIN	17 CIN	18 D CIN	19 SF	20 SF
21 D SF	22	23 FLA	24 FLA	25 FLA	26 ATL	27 ATL
28 D ATL	29	30 MON				

May

SUN	MON	TUE	WED	THU	FRI	SAT
			MON	2 D MON	3 NYM	4 NYM
5 D NYM	6	7 PHI	8 PHI	9 PHI	10 PIT	11 PIT
12 D PIT	13 PHI	14 PHI	15 PHI	16 PIT	17 PIT	18 PIT
19 D PIT	20	21 STL	22 STL	23 STL	24 D CUB	25 CUB
26 CUB	27 D STL	28 STL	29 STL	30	31 D CUB	

June

SUN	MON	TUE	WED	THU	FRI	SAT
						1 D CUB
2 D CUB	3 D ARI	4 ARI	5 ARI	6	7 OAK	8 OAK
9 D OAK	10 CUB	11 CUB	12 D CUB	13	14 TEX	15 TEX
16 D TEX	17 MIL	18 MIL	19 MIL	20 D MIL	21 D SEA	22 SEA
23 SEA	24	25 ARI	26 ARI	27 D ARI	28 TEX	29 TEX
30 TEX						

July

SUN	MON	TUE	WED	THU	FRI	SAT
	1 CIN	2 CIN	3 CIN	4 D PIT	5 D PIT	6 PIT
7 D PIT	8	9 *	10	11 CIN	12 CIN	13 CIN
14 D CIN	15 PIT	16 D PIT	17 MIL	18 D MIL	19 D CUB	20 D CUB
21 CUB	22 MIL	23 MIL	24 MIL	25 D PIT	26 PIT	27 PIT
28 D PIT	29	30 NYM	31 NYM			

August

SUN	MON	TUE	WED	THU	FRI	SAT
				1 NYM	2 MON	3 MON
4 D MON	5	6 FLA	7 FLA	8 D FLA	9 D ATL	10 ATL
11 D ATL	12 CUB	13 CUB	14 D CUB	15 D CIN	16 CIN	17 CIN
18 D CIN	19 D CIN	20 CUB	21 CUB	22 CUB	23 CIN	24 CIN
25 D CIN	26	27 SD	28 SD	29 D LA	30 LA	31 LA

September

SUN	MON	TUE	WED	THU	FRI	SAT
1 D LA	2	3 SD	4 SD	5 D SD	6 D LA	7 D LA
8 D LA	9 COL	10 COL	11 COL	12 STL	13 STL	14 STL
15 D STL	16	17 MIL	18 MIL	19 D MIL	20 STL	21 D STL
22 D STL	23 MIL	24 MIL	25 MIL	26	27 SF	28 SF
29 D SF	30					

2002 SEASON
CLUB DIRECTORY

Chairman and chief executive officer
Drayton McLane Jr.

President, baseball operations
Tal Smith

President, business operations
Pam Gardner

General manager
Gerry Hunsicker

Assistant general manager
Tim Purpura

Director of baseball administration
Barry Waters

Director of scouting
David Lakey

Special asst. to the g.m. for international scouting and development
Andres Reiner

Sr. v.p., ops. and communications
Rob Matwick

Sr. v.p., finance and administration
Teresa Pelanne

Vice president, human resources
Mike Anders

V.p., security and traffic operations
Don Collins

V.p., community development
Marian Harper

Vice president, market development
Rosi Hernandez

Vice president, sales and broadcasting
Jamie Hildreth

Vice president, engineering
Bert Pope

Vice president, marketing
Garry Sawka

Vice president, special events
Kala Sorenson

V.p., ticket sales and services
John Sorrentino

Director of media relations
Warren Miller

Assistant director of media relations
Todd Fedewa

Professional scouts
Kimball Crossley, Gene DeBoer, Leo Labossiere, Joe Pittman, Tom Romenesko, Scipio Spinks

Major league scouts
Stan Benjamin, Bill Kelso, Jack Lind, Walt Matthews, Paul Weaver

Full-time scouts
Bob Blair, Joe Bogar, Ralph Bratton, Chuck Carlson, Andrew Cotner, Gerry Craft, Doug Deutsch, James Farrar, David Henderson, Dan Huston, Marc Johnson, Brian Keegan, Mike Maggart, Jerry Marik, Tom McCormack, Mel Nelson, Rusty Pendergrass, Bob Poole, Joe Robinson, Tad Slowik, Frankie Thon, Tim Tolman, Nick Venuto, Danny Watkins, Gene Wellman

Foreign scouts
Ricardo Aponte, Jesus Aristimuno, Sergio A. Beltre, Rafael Cariel, Arnold Elles, Orlando Fernandez, Mario Gonzalez, Julio Linares, Rodney Linares, Omar Lopez, Carlos Maldonado, Ramon Morales, Oscar Padron, Guillermo Ramirez, Rafael Ramirez, Wolfgang Ramos, Anibal Reluz, Adriano Rodriguez, Dr. Lester Storey, Alejandro Tavares, Pablo Torrealba, Calixto Vargas, Mark Van Zanten

MINOR LEAGUE AFFILIATES

Class	Team	League	Manager
AAA	New Orleans	Pacific Coast	Chris Maloney
AA	Round Rock	Texas	Jackie Moore
A	Lexington	South Atlantic	J.J. Cannon
A	Michigan	Midwest	John Massarelli
A	Tri-City	New York-Pennsylvania	Ivan DeJesus
Rookie	Martinsville	Appalachian	Jorge Orta

BROADCAST INFORMATION

Radio: KTRH-AM (740); KRTX-AM (980, Spanish language).
TV: KNWS-TV (Channel 51).
Cable TV: Fox Sports Southwest.

SPRING TRAINING

Ballpark (city): Osceola County Stadium (Kissimmee, Fla.).
Ticket information: 407-839-3900.

Follow the Astros all season at: www.sportingnews.com/baseball/teams/astros/

SPRING TRAINING ROSTER

Manager—Jimy Williams.
Coaches—Jose Cruz (25), Harry Spilman (12), Burt Hooton (48), Gene Lamont, Tony Pena, John Tamargo (30).

No.	PITCHERS	B/T	Ht./Wt.	Born	2001 clubs
	Brocail, Doug	L/R	6-5/235	5-16-67	New Orleans, Round Rock
	Cruz, Nelson	R/R	6-1/185	9-13-72	Houston
41	Dotel, Octavio	R/R	6-0/175	11-25-75	Houston
53	Franklin, Wayne	L/L	6-2/195	3-9-74	Houston, New Orleans
	Hernandez, Carlos	L/L	5-10/145	4-22-80	Round Rock, Houston
	Jamison, Ryan	R/R	6-3/185	1-5-78	Round Rock, Lexington
	Lidge, Brad	R/R	6-5/200	12-23-76	Round Rock
36	Linebrink, Scott	R/R	6-3/185	8-4-76	Houston, New Orleans
73	Mann, Jim	R/R	6-3/225	11-17-74	New Orleans, Houston
	Mathews, T.J.	R/R	6-1/225	1-19-70	Oakland, Memphis, St. Louis
	Miller, Greg	L/L	6-5/215	9-30-79	Round Rock
52	Miller, Wade	R/R	6-2/185	9-13-76	Houston
30	Mlicki, Dave	R/R	6-4/205	6-8-68	Detroit, Houston
	Nitkowski, C.J.	L/L	6-3/205	3-9-73	Detroit, Toledo, New York N.L.
	Oswalt, Roy	R/R	6-0/170	8-29-77	New Orleans, Houston
	Puffer, Brandon	R/R	6-3/190	10-5-75	Round Rock
	Redding, Tim	R/R	6-0/180	2-12-78	Round Rock, New Orleans, Houston
37	Reynolds, Shane	R/R	6-3/210	3-26-68	Round Rock, New Orleans, Houston
66	Rodriguez, Wilfredo	L/L	6-3/180	3-20-79	Round Rock, Houston
	Rosario, Rodrigo	R/R	6-2/165	12-14-79	Lexington
	Shearn, Tom	R/R	6-4/200	8-28-77	Round Rock
	Stone, Ricky	R/R	6-1/168	2-28-75	Houston, New Orleans
13	Wagner, Billy	L/L	5-11/180	7-25-71	Houston, Round Rock

No.	CATCHERS	B/T	Ht./Wt.	Born	2001 clubs
	Ausmus, Brad	R/R	5-11/195	4-14-69	Houston
	Buck, John	R/R	6-3/210	7-7-80	Lexington
71	Chavez, Raul	R/R	5-11/210	3-18-73	New Orleans
44	Zaun, Gregg	B/R	5-10/190	4-14-71	Gulf Coast Royals, Omaha, Kansas City

No.	INFIELDERS	B/T	Ht./Wt.	Born	2001 clubs
5	Bagwell, Jeff	R/R	6-0/195	5-27-68	Houston
7	Biggio, Craig	R/R	5-11/180	12-14-65	Houston
2	Ensberg, Morgan	R/R	6-2/210	8-26-75	New Orleans
3	Everett, Adam	R/R	6-0/156	2-2-77	New Orleans, Houston
1	Ginter, Keith	R/R	5-10/190	5-5-76	New Orleans, Houston
4	Lugo, Julio	R/R	6-2/165	11-16-75	Houston
6	Truby, Chris	R/R	6-2/190	12-9-73	Houston, New Orleans
	Vizcaino, Jose	B/R	6-1/180	3-26-68	Houston

No.	OUTFIELDERS	B/T	Ht./Wt.	Born	2001 clubs
17	Berkman, Lance	B/L	6-1/205	2-10-76	Houston
15	Hidalgo, Richard	R/R	6-3/190	7-2-75	Houston
	Lane, Jason	R/L	6-2/215	12-22-76	Round Rock
9	Merced, Orlando	L/R	6-1/195	11-2-66	Houston
31	Ward, Daryle	L/L	6-2/230	6-27-75	Houston

BALLPARK INFORMATION

Ballpark (capacity, surface)
Enron Field (40,950, grass)

Address
P.O. Box 288
Houston, TX 77001-0288

Official website
www.astros.com

Business phone
713-259-8000

Ticket information
713-259-8500; 1-877-9-ASTROS

Ticket prices
$39 (club I), $36 (dugout)
$33 (club II), $30 (field box)
$24 (Crawford box), $20 (bullpen box)
$15 (mezzanine, terrace deck)
$12 (view deck), $5-$1 (outfield deck)

Field dimensions (from home plate)
To left field at foul line, 315 feet
To center field, 435 feet
To right field at foul line, 326 feet

First game played
April 7, 2000 (Phillies 4, Astros 1)

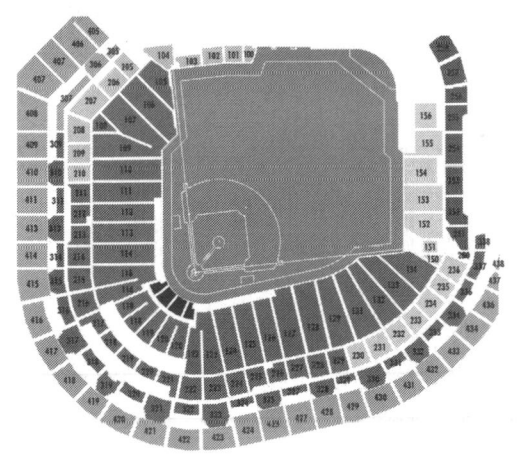

2002 SEASON *Houston Astros*

Date	Opp.	Res.	Score	(inn.*)	Hits	Opp. hits	Winning pitcher	Losing pitcher	Save	Record	Pos.	GB
4-3	Mil.	W	11-3		11	9	Elarton	Haynes		1-0	1st	+0.5
4-4	Mil.	W	8-6	(12)	16	13	J. Powell	Leskanic		2-0	1st	+1.0
4-5	Mil.	W	8-2		11	7	Miller	Sheets		3-0	1st	+1.5
4-6	Pit.	W	4-1		7	5	Dotel	Olivares	Wagner	4-0	1st	+2.0
4-7	Pit.	L	3-5		6	13	Arroyo	Bottenfield	M. Williams	4-1	1st	+1.0
4-8	Pit.	L	3-9		7	12	Beimel	Elarton		4-2	1st	+1.0
4-10	At Mil.	W	3-0		6	6	Lima	Leskanic	Wagner	5-2	1st	+1.0
4-11	At Mil.	W	7-1		13	3	Miller	Sheets		6-2	1st	+1.0
4-12	At Mil.	L	4-12		7	14	D'Amico	Dotel		6-3	1st	+1.0
4-13	At St.L.	W	4-2		10	9	Bottenfield	Kile	Wagner	7-3	1st	+1.0
4-14	At St.L.	W	7-4		7	5	Elarton	Ankiel	Wagner	8-3	1st	+1.0
4-15	At St.L.	L	5-6		9	12	James	J. Powell	Kline	8-4	T1st	...
4-16	At Pit.	L	0-3		8	5	Anderson	Miller	M. Williams	8-5	2nd	0.5
4-18	At Pit.	L	4-8		6	12	Arroyo	Reynolds		8-6	2nd	1.5
4-20	St.L.	W	10-1		10	3	Elarton	Ankiel		9-6	2nd	1.5
4-21	St.L.	L	2-9		8	9	Morris	Lima		9-7	2nd	2.5
4-22	St.L.	W	4-3		8	6	Miller	Stechschulte	Wagner	10-7	2nd	1.5
4-23	Atl.	L	7-9		14	11	Glavine	Dotel		10-8	2nd	2.0
4-24	Atl.	W	11-6		12	8	Reynolds	Perez	Bottenfield	11-8	2nd	1.0
4-25	Atl.	L	3-11		8	12	Millwood	Elarton		11-9	T2nd	1.0
4-27	Fla.	L	8-9	(10)	10	13	Alfonseca	Wagner		11-10	3rd	2.5
4-28	Fla.	W	6-4		11	8	Miller	Dempster		12-10	3rd	1.5
4-29	Fla.	L	5-11		12	19	Bones	Reynolds		12-11	4th	2.5
4-30	At N.Y.	L	2-8		8	11	Trachsel	Elarton		12-12	T4th	3.0
5-1	At N.Y.	L	5-7		10	11	Martin	Cruz	Benitez	12-13	T4th	3.0
5-2	At N.Y.	W	6-5	(10)	9	11	Wagner	Benitez		13-13	T4th	3.0
5-4	At Mon.	W	8-4		12	6	Miller	Vazquez		14-13	T4th	2.5
5-5	At Mon.	W	4-3		3	8	Reynolds	Reames	Wagner	15-13	3rd	2.5
5-6	At Mon.	W	13-7		18	16	Elarton	Telford		16-13	2nd	2.5
5-7	Phi.	L	0-5		2	9	Person	Bottenfield		16-14	2nd	3.5
5-8	Phi.	L	2-3		4	6	Telemaco	Jackson	Mesa	16-15	T3rd	3.5
5-9	Phi.	W	7-6		11	11	Wagner	Bottalico		17-15	T2nd	3.5
5-12†	At Cin.	W	2-1		8	7	Reynolds	Bell	Wagner	18-15		
5-12‡	At Cin.	L	4-5		6	12	Graves	Dotel		18-16	3rd	2.0
5-13	At Cin.	W	4-3		8	7	Bottenfield	Brower	Wagner	19-16	3rd	1.5
5-14	At Cin.	W	6-4		10	10	Oswalt	Reitsma	Wagner	20-16	3rd	1.0
5-15	At Chi.	W	9-7	(12)	17	15	Jackson	Van Poppel	Cruz	21-16	2nd	1.0
5-16	At Chi.	W	6-2		9	6	Reynolds	Tavarez		22-16	2nd	1.0
5-17	At Chi.	W	4-2		8	9	Oswalt	Farnsworth	Wagner	23-16	2nd	1.0
5-18	Cin.	L	4-7		7	10	O. Fernandez	Bottenfield	Graves	23-17	2nd	1.0
5-19	Cin.	W	6-3		10	8	Miller	Reitsma	Wagner	24-17	T1st	...
5-20	Cin.	L	5-6		12	10	Dessens	Lima	Graves	24-18	2nd	1.0
5-21	S.D.	L	6-7		11	10	Eaton	Reynolds	Hoffman	24-19	2nd	1.5
5-22	S.D.	L	2-6		7	8	Williams	Elarton	Witasick	24-20	T2nd	1.5
5-23	S.D.	L	6-7		10	12	Witasick	Wagner	Hoffman	24-21	4th	1.5
5-25	At L.A.	L	1-4		7	9	Park	Miller	Shaw	24-22	4th	3.0
5-26	At L.A.	L	2-7		6	10	Prokopec	Reynolds		24-23	4th	3.0
5-27	At L.A.	L	4-5	(12)	6	9	Fetters	Oswalt		24-24	4th	4.0
5-29	At S.D.	L	4-5		6	8	Jarvis	Bottenfield	Hoffman	24-25	4th	5.5
5-30	At S.D.	W	7-4		15	9	Miller	Jones	Wagner	25-25	4th	5.5
5-31	At S.D.	W	8-4		13	7	Reynolds	Serrano		26-25	4th	5.0
6-1	L.A.	W	10-9		16	11	Dotel	Fetters		27-25	4th	5.0
6-2	L.A.	W	2-1		7	5	Oswalt	Dreifort	Wagner	28-25	3rd	5.0
6-3	L.A.	L	8-9	(10)	11	16	Fetters	Dotel	Shaw	28-26	4th	5.0
6-5	At Col.	L	4-9		9	12	Hampton	Miller		28-27	4th	6.0
6-6	At Col.	L	8-9		13	16	Bohanon	Elarton	Jimenez	28-28	4th	7.0
6-7	At Col.	W	2-1		5	7	Reynolds	Chacon	Jackson	29-28	T3rd	7.0
6-8	At Tex.	W	5-4	(11)	11	8	Dotel	Crabtree	Jackson	30-28	3rd	6.0
6-9	At Tex.	L	4-16		9	17	Helling	Bottenfield		30-29	3rd	7.0
6-10	At Tex.	W	6-5		7	10	J. Powell	Zimmerman	Jackson	31-29	3rd	6.0
6-12	At Min.	L	0-7		4	8	Radke	Elarton		31-30	T3rd	7.0
6-13	At Min.	L	1-3		6	8	Milton	Reynolds		31-31	T3rd	7.0
6-14	At Min.	W	8-3		16	9	Oswalt	Mays		32-31	T2nd	6.0
6-15	Tex.	L	9-12		13	15	Mahomes	J. Powell	Zimmerman	32-32	4th	7.0
6-16	Tex.	W	2-1		8	6	Cruz	Crabtree	Jackson	33-32	3rd	7.0
6-17	Tex.	L	2-6		5	9	Oliver	Elarton		33-33	T3rd	8.0
6-18	Col.	W	13-5		12	14	Reynolds	Astacio		34-33	T3rd	7.0
6-19	Col.	W	6-4		9	6	Oswalt	Chacon	Wagner	35-33	T3rd	6.0
6-20	Col.	W	7-2		12	4	Miller	Villone	Dotel	36-33	3rd	6.0
6-21	Cin.	L	7-8	(11)	13	13	Brower	Slusarski		36-34	3rd	7.0
6-22	Cin.	L	5-7	(10)	9	10	Wohlers	Wagner		36-35	4th	7.0
6-23	Cin.	W	9-3		12	7	Reynolds	Reith		37-35	4th	6.0
6-24	Cin.	W	7-5		10	8	Dotel	Nichting	Wagner	38-35	4th	5.0
6-25	At Ari.	W	6-0		11	6	Miller	Batista		39-35	3rd	5.0

Date	Opp.	Res.	Score	(inn.*)	Hits	Opp. hits	Winning pitcher	Losing pitcher	Save	Record	Pos.	GB
6-26	At Ari.	W	10-7		14	14	Dotel	Bierbrodt	Wagner	40-35	2nd	5.0
6-27	At Ari.	L	5-7		7	8	Schilling	Elarton		40-36	2nd	5.0
6-29	At Mil.	L	1-6		6	9	Sheets	Reynolds		40-37	2nd	5.5
6-30	At Mil.	W	7-4		13	9	Oswalt	Levrault		41-37	2nd	4.5
7-1	At Mil.	W	6-1		10	7	Miller	Rigdon		42-37	2nd	4.5
7-2	At Mil.	W	6-4		11	8	Redding	Haynes	Wagner	43-37	2nd	4.0
7-3	Ari.	W	6-5		13	9	Mlicki	Schilling	Wagner	44-37	2nd	4.0
7-4	Ari.	L	2-3		4	7	Johnson	Reynolds	Kim	44-38	2nd	4.0
7-5	Ari.	W	5-1		5	7	Oswalt	Ellis		45-38	2nd	4.0
7-6	At K.C.	W	8-3		10	11	Miller	Reichert	Cruz	46-38	2nd	4.0
7-7	At K.C.	W	10-8		18	10	Jackson	Byrd	Wagner	47-38	2nd	4.0
7-8	At K.C.	W	14-5		15	8	Villone	Durbin		48-38	2nd	3.0
7-12	S.D.	L	4-7		9	14	Jones	Reynolds	Hoffman	48-39	2nd	4.0
7-13	S.D.	W	11-3		17	8	Oswalt	Williams		49-39	2nd	3.0
7-14	S.D.	L	6-8		9	7	Jarvis	Miller	Hoffman	49-40	2nd	3.0
7-15	Cle.	W	5-3		9	6	Redding	Westbrook	Wagner	50-40	2nd	3.0
7-16	Cle.	W	10-8		15	10	Villone	Rocker		51-40	2nd	2.0
7-17	Cle.	L	4-10		9	13	Colon	Reynolds		51-41	2nd	3.0
7-18	St.L.	W	17-11		16	18	Villone	Hackman		52-41	2nd	3.0
7-19	St.L.	L	1-4		5	5	Morris	Miller	Timlin	52-42	2nd	3.0
7-20	Chi.	W	5-2		10	7	Redding	Lieber	Wagner	53-42	2nd	2.0
7-21	Chi.	L	4-5		7	13	Farnsworth	Villone	Gordon	53-43	2nd	3.0
7-22	Chi.	W	3-0		4	5	Reynolds	Bere	Wagner	54-43	2nd	2.0
7-23	Chi.	L	2-6		10	10	Wood	Oswalt		54-44	2nd	3.0
7-24	At St.L.	W	2-1		7	2	Miller	Morris	Wagner	55-44	2nd	3.0
7-25	At St.L.	L	2-10		6	13	Hermanson	Redding		55-45	2nd	4.0
7-26	At Pit.	W	3-2		6	6	Mlicki	Schmidt	Wagner	56-45	2nd	3.0
7-27	At Pit.	L	2-3		9	10	Beimel	Reynolds	M. Williams	56-46	2nd	4.0
7-28§	At Pit.	L	8-9		12	12	Olivares	Wagner		56-47		
7-28∞	At Pit.	W	12-3		15	11	McKnight	Anderson		57-47	2nd	3.5
7-29	At Pit.	L	1-4		6	7	Ritchie	Miller	M. Williams	57-48	2nd	4.5
7-31	N.Y.	W	3-2	(10)	8	6	Cruz	Riggan		58-48	2nd	4.5
8-1	N.Y.	L	2-8	(10)	4	12	White	Jackson		58-49	2nd	4.5
8-2	N.Y.	W	4-3	(10)	8	10	Williams	Riggan		59-49	2nd	3.5
8-3	Mon.	W	6-2		13	7	Reynolds	Armas		60-49	2nd	3.5
8-4	Mon.	W	4-1		6	3	Oswalt	Ohka		61-49	2nd	2.5
8-5	Mon.	W	4-1		12	7	Villone	Munoz	Wagner	62-49	2nd	1.5
8-7	At Atl.	L	5-6		11	6	Maddux	Cruz	Karsay	62-50	2nd	2.5
8-8	At Atl.	W	2-1	(12)	10	12	Jackson	Cabrera	Wagner	63-50	2nd	2.5
8-9	At Atl.	W	6-5		12	11	Dotel	Ligtenberg		64-50	2nd	1.5
8-10	At Fla.	W	7-2		15	5	Astacio	Burnett		65-50	2nd	1.5
8-11	At Fla.	L	5-13		6	18	Dempster	B. Powell		65-51	2nd	1.5
8-12	At Fla.	W	10-5		13	7	Mlicki	Clement		66-51	2nd	0.5
8-13	Chi.	W	9-5		13	8	Reynolds	Bere		67-51	1st	+0.5
8-14	Chi.	L	1-3		5	7	Weathers	Villone	Gordon	67-52	2nd	0.5
8-15	Chi.	L	1-5		3	11	Lieber	Astacio		67-53	2nd	1.5
8-16	Pit.	W	4-3		10	10	Miller	Beimel	Wagner	68-53	2nd	1.0
8-17	Pit.	W	6-5		12	8	Mlicki	McKnight	Wagner	69-53	2nd	...
8-18	Pit.	W	3-0		6	2	Hernandez	Anderson	Dotel	70-53	1st	+1.0
8-19	Pit.	W	12-2		13	7	Oswalt	Ritchie		71-53	1st	+2.0
8-21	At Phi	W	8-2		10	8	Astacio	Figueroa		72-53	1st	+2.0
8-22	At Phi.	L	1-2		3	7	Person	Miller	Mesa	72-54	1st	+2.0
8-23	At Phi.	W	2-1	(11)	6	11	Jackson	Santiago	Wagner	73-54	1st	+3.0
8-24	At Pit.	W	5-1		7	7	Oswalt	Anderson		74-54	1st	+4.0
8-25	At Pit.	L	2-8		10	7	Ritchie	Mlicki		74-55	1st	+3.0
8-26	At Pit.	W	3-1		6	7	Villone	D. Williams	Wagner	75-55	1st	+3.0
8-28	Cin.	W	6-4		9	8	Miller	Brower	Wagner	76-55	1st	+4.0
8-29	Cin.	W	6-2		12	6	Cruz	Dessens		77-55	1st	+4.0
8-30	Cin.	W	6-1		7	3	Oswalt	Reyes		78-55	1st	+4.0
8-31	At Mil.	W	3-2		9	8	Williams	Wright	Wagner	79-55	1st	+4.0
9-1	At Mil.	L	3-4		6	6	Fox	Jackson		79-56	1st	+3.0
9-2	At Mil.	W	1-0		7	6	Miller	Suzuki	Wagner	80-56	1st	+4.0
9-3	At Cin.	L	2-3		4	9	Sullivan	Dotel	Graves	80-57	1st	+3.0
9-4	At Cin.	W	7-1		14	7	Oswalt	Reyes		81-57	1st	+4.0
9-5	At Cin.	W	10-3		13	10	Mlicki	Reitsma		82-57	1st	+5.0
9-6	Mil.	L	3-4	(10)	7	8	Fox	Wagner	Leskanic	82-58	1st	+4.5
9-7	Mil.	W	5-3		5	11	Miller	Suzuki	Wagner	83-58	1st	+5.5
9-8	Mil.	L	2-7		6	12	Quevedo	Villone		83-59	1st	+5.5
9-9	Mil.	W	8-0		11	7	Oswalt	D'Amico		84-59	1st	+5.5
9-18	At S.F	W	3-2		5	6	Williams	Nen	Wagner	85-59	1st	+4.5
9-19	At S.F	W	10-3		14	6	Mlicki	Hernandez		86-59	1st	+4.5
9-20	At S.F	W	5-4	(10)	8	7	Dotel	Nen	Wagner	87-59	1st	+4.5
9-21	Chi.	L	4-12		10	13	Zambrano	Villone		87-60	1st	+3.5
9-22	Chi.	W	8-4		9	7	Reynolds	Tapani		88-60	1st	+3.5
9-23	Chi.	W	7-6		12	8	Williams	Weathers	Wagner	89-60	1st	+4.5
9-24	St.L.	W	9-3		12	6	Mlicki	Morris		90-60	1st	+5.5
9-25	St.L.	L	2-3		3	7	Williams	Miller		90-61	1st	+4.5
9-26	St.L.	L	1-5		5	8	Kile	Villone		90-62	1st	+3.5

Date	Opp.	Res.	Score	(inn.*)	Hits	Opp. hits	Winning pitcher	Losing pitcher	Save	Record	Pos.	GB
9-27	At Chi.	W	6-5		7	8	Reynolds	Tapani	Wagner	91-62	1st	+4.0
9-28	At Chi.	L	2-6		6	14	Lieber	Oswalt		91-63	1st	+3.0
9-29	At Chi.	L	2-6		4	7	Wood	Mlicki		91-64	1st	+2.0
9-30	At Chi.	L	6-7		10	6	Chiasson	Villone	Farnsworth	91-65	1st	+1.0
10-2	S.F	L	1-4		8	10	Rueter	Reynolds	Nen	91-66	T1st	...
10-3	S.F	L	8-11		12	15	Schmidt	Cruz		91-67	T1st	...
10-4	S.F	L	2-10		8	11	Ortiz	Mlicki	Boehringer	91-68	2nd	1.0
10-5	At St.L.	W	2-1		9	4	Jackson	Stechschulte	Wagner	92-68	T1st	...
10-6	At St.L.	L	6-10		8	13	Timlin	Villone	Kline	92-69	2nd	1.0
10-7	At St.L.	W	9-2		13	10	Reynolds	Kile		93-69	T1st	...

Monthly records: April (12-12), May (14-13), June (15-12), July (17-11), August (21-7), September (12-10), October (2-4).
*Innings, if other than nine. †First game of a doubleheader. ‡Second game of a doubleheader. §Day separate admission. ∞Night separate admission.

HIGHLIGHTS

High point: The 9-2 win over the Cardinals in St. Louis that wrapped up the Central Division title, their fourth in five years, on the last day of the season. It was the first day in more than a month the players could actually sit back and enjoy themselves. It followed a near-total collapse the last two weeks of the season.

Low point: A 5-4 loss at San Diego on May 29 that was the team's eighth in a row and saw the Astros go from one game out of first to fourth place in the division. It triggered a three-week free-fall that saw the team drop eight games out of first before starting a slow comeback.

Turning point: A 4-3 win over the Pirates at Enron Field August 16. Moises Alou broke out of an 0-for-11 slump with two RBI-singles as the Astros began a five-game winning streak that vaulted them back into first place for the first time since mid-April.

Most valuable player: Despite having the third-lowest batting average of his career, Jeff Bagwell still led the team in homers, RBIs, runs and walks.

Most valuable pitcher: Wade Miller was 16-8 to narrowly edge Roy Oswalt. Miller led the team in wins, strikeouts and was second in ERA. Miller was an ironman, pitching six or more innings in 28 of his 32 starts.

Most improved player: Craig Biggio's .292 average that included 118 runs scored, 20 home runs and 35 doubles was a big comeback from his .268 season cut short by major surgery in 2000.

Most pleasant surprise: Oswalt, not counted on to pitch higher than Class AAA, won his first six games and went on to post a 14-3 mark. Oswalt led all major league rookies in ERA and winning percentage.

Key injuries: Reliever Doug Brocail missed the entire season, and utility player Bill Spiers had back surgery and missed 156 games before retiring. ... Kent Bottenfield missed 100 games with shoulder surgery and Pedro Astacio missed the final 36 games with a partially torn labrum in his right shoulder.

Notable: Miller and Shane Reynolds became the first pitchers to go 5-0 in one season against one team (vs. the Brewers and Cubs respectively) since Orel Hershiser did it in 1989 vs. the Braves. ... After averaging more than 37 home runs per month the first five months of the season, the Astros managed just 17 in September and five in the six regular-season games in October. ... Brad Ausmus became the first Astros catcher ever to win a Gold Glove.

—JIM CARLEY

RECORDS

2001 regular-season record: 93-69 (1st in N.L. Central); 44-37 at home; 49-32 on road; 18-12 vs. N.L. East; 50-34 vs. N.L. Central; 16-17 vs. N.L. West; 9-6 vs. A.L.; 22-12 vs. lefthanded starters; 71-57 vs. righthanded starters; 87-66 on grass; 6-3 on turf; 24-21 in daytime; 69-48 at night; 29-23 in one-run games; 9-7 in extra-inning games; 0-0-1 in doubleheaders.

Team record past five years: 448-362 (.553, ranks 4th in league in that span).

TEAM LEADERS

Batting average: Moises Alou (.331).
At-bats: Craig Biggio (617).
Runs: Jeff Bagwell (126).
Hits: Lance Berkman (191).
Total Bases: Lance Berkman (358).
Doubles: Lance Berkman (55).
Triples: Lance Berkman (5).
Home runs: Jeff Bagwell (39).
Runs batted in: Jeff Bagwell (130).
Stolen bases: Julio Lugo (12).
Slugging percentage: Lance Berkman (.620).

On-base percentage: Lance Berkman (.430).
Wins: Wade Miller (16).
Earned-run average: Wade Miller (3.40).
Complete games: Roy Oswalt, Shane Reynolds (3).
Shutouts: Roy Oswalt (1).
Saves: Billy Wagner (39).
Innings pitched: Wade Miller (212.0).
Strikeouts: Wade Miller (183).

GAMES BY POSITION

Catcher: Brad Ausmus 127, Tony Eusebio 48, Scott Servais 9.
First base: Jeff Bagwell 160, Daryle Ward 9, Charlie Hayes 2, Chris Truby 1, Orlando Merced 1.
Second base: Craig Biggio 154, Jose Vizcaino 18, Mendy Lopez 3, Julio Lugo 2.
Third base: Vinny Castilla 121, Chris Truby 35, Charlie Hayes 11, Jose Vizcaino 7, Orlando Merced 2, Mendy Lopez 2.
Shortstop: Julio Lugo 133, Jose Vizcaino 53, Adam Everett 6, Vinny Castilla 3.
Outfield: Lance Berkman 155, Richard Hidalgo 144, Moises Alou 130, Glen Barker 60, Daryle Ward 42, Orlando Merced 31, Julio Lugo 8.
Designated hitter: Moises Alou 4, Daryle Ward 3, Craig Biggio 1, Charlie Hayes 1.

TOP DRAFT CHOICES

1. **Chris Burke,** 2B/SS, U. of Tennessee.
2. **Mike Rodriguez,** OF, U. of Miami (Fla.).
3. **Kirk Saarloos,** RHP, Cal State Fullerton University.
4. **Phillip Barzilla,** LHP, Rice University.
5. **Charlton Jimerson,** OF, U. of Miami (Fla.).
6. **Russell Rohlicek,** LHP, Long Beach State University.
7. **Ryan Stegall,** SS, Univ. of Missouri.
8. **Brooks Conrad,** 2B, Arizona State U.
9. **Kerry Hodges,** OF, Texas Tech.
10. **Lance Cormier,** RHP, U. of Alabama.

LOS ANGELES DODGERS
NATIONAL LEAGUE WEST DIVISION

Dodgers schedule
Home games shaded
D—Day game (games starting before 5 p.m.)
All-Star Game at Milwaukee
Subject to changes

April
SUN	MON	TUE	WED	THU	FRI	SAT
	1	2 SF	3 D SF	4 SF	5 COL	6 COL
7 COL	8 SF	9 SF	10 D SF	11 SF	12 D SD	13 SD
14 D SD	15 COL	16 COL	17 D COL	18 SD	19 SD	20 SD
21 D SD	22	23 PIT	24 PIT	25 D PIT	26 D CUB	27 D CUB
28 CUB	29	30 CIN				

May
SUN	MON	TUE	WED	THU	FRI	SAT
			1 CIN	2 CIN	3 CUB	4 CUB
5 CUB	6	7 ATL	8 ATL	9 ATL	10 FLA	11 FLA
12 D FLA	13 NYM	14 NYM	15 NYM	16 MON	17 MON	18 MON
19 D MON	20	21 MIL	22 MIL	23 MIL	24 ARI	25 ARI
26 ARI	27 D MIL	28 MIL	29 D MIL	30	31 ARI	

June
SUN	MON	TUE	WED	THU	FRI	SAT
						1 D ARI
2 D ARI	3 COL	4 COL	5 D COL	6	7 BAL	8 BAL
9 D BAL	10 TB	11 TB	12 TB	13	14 ANA	15 ANA
16 D ANA	17	18 TOR	19 TOR	20 TOR	21 BOS	22 D BOS
23 D BOS	24 COL	25 COL	26 COL	27 COL	28 ANA	29 ANA
30 ANA						

July
SUN	MON	TUE	WED	THU	FRI	SAT
	1 ARI	2 ARI	3 ARI	4 STL	5 STL	6 D STL
7 D STL	8	9 *	10	11 ARI	12 ARI	13 D ARI
14 ARI	15 STL	16 D STL	17 STL	18 SD	19 SF	20 D SF
21 SF	22 SD	23 SD	24 D SD	25	26 D CF	27 CF
28 SF	29	30 CIN	31 CIN			

August
SUN	MON	TUE	WED	THU	FRI	SAT
				1 D CIN	2 PHI	3 PHI
4 D PHI	5 D PHI	6 D PIT	7 PIT	8 PIT	9 PHI	10 PHI
11 PHI	12	13 MON	14 MON	15 MON	16 NYM	17 NYM
18 D NYM	19	20 FLA	21 FLA	22 D FLA	23 ATL	24 D ATL
25 ATL	26 ARI	27 ARI	28 ARI	29	30 HOU	31 HOU

September
SUN	MON	TUE	WED	THU	FRI	SAT
1 D HOU	2 ARI	3 ARI	4 D ARI	5	6 D HOU	7 D HOU
8 D HOU	9 SF	10 SF	11 D SF	12 COL	13 COL	14 D COL
15 COL	16 SF	17 SF	18 SF	19 SF	20 SD	21 SD
22 D SD	23	24 COL	25 COL	26 SD	27 SD	28 SD
29 D SD	30					

2002 SEASON
CLUB DIRECTORY

President and CEO
Robert Daly
Board of directors
Chase Carey, Peter Chernin, Peter O'Malley, Bob Graziano, Sam Fernandez
Executive vice president and g.m.
Dan Evans
Vice president, assistant g.m.
Kim Ng
Executive vice president and CMO
Kris Rone
Senior vice president, communications
Derrick Hall
Senior v.p., baseball operations
Dave Wallace
Senior vice president
Tommy Lasorda
Vice president, external affairs
Tommy Hawkins
Advisor, team travel
Billy DeLury
Sr. vice president and general counsel
Sam Fernandez
Vice president, human resources & admin.
David Walkley
V.p., spring training/minor league facilities
Craig Callan
Director of player development
Bill Bavasi
Vice president and CFO
Cristine Hurley
Director, chief information officer
Mike Mularky
Director of sales and marketing
Sergio Del Prado
Director, public relations
John Olguin
Director, team travel
Shaun Rachau
Director, community affairs
Erikk Aldridge
Asst. to the president & dir., Asian operations
Acey Kohrogi
Director, Dominican operations
Pablo Peguero
Director, community relations
Don Newcombe
Vice president, stadium operations
Doug Duennes

Director, ticket operations
Billy Hunter
Director, professional scouting
Matt Slater
Director, amateur scouting
Logan White
Head athletic trainer
Stan Johnston
Assistant athletic trainer
Matt Wilson
Physical therapist
Pat Screnar
Strength and conditioning coach
Todd Clausen
Club physicians
Dr. Ralph Gambardella, Dr. Herndon Harding, Dr. Frank Jobe, Dr. Michael Mellman
Senior advisor, baseball operations
John Boles
Senior advisor, baseball operations
Joe Amalfitano
Special asst. to the general manager, director, international scouting
Jeff Schugal
Senior scouting advisor
Don Welke
Minor league field coordinator
Terry Collins
Advance scout
Mark Weidemaier
Major league scouts
Carl Loewenstine, Claude Osteen
Coordinator, minor league scouting
Terry Reynolds
Professional scouts
Dan Freed, Vance Lovelace, Ron Rizzi
National crosscheckers
Jimmy Lester, Gib Bodet
Regional supervisors
Joe Ferrone, Mike Hankins, John Barr
Area scouts
Doug Carpenter, Jim Chapman, Bobby Darwin, Scott Groot, Clarence Johns, Hank Jones, Lon Joyce, John Kosciak, Marty Lamb, Mike Leuzinger, James Merriweather, Bill Pleis, Scott Sharp, Mark Sheehy, Chris Smith, Bob Szymkowski, Tom Thomas, Mitch Webster
International scouts
Mike Brito, Pat Kelly, Camilo Pascual

MINOR LEAGUE AFFILIATES

Class	Team	League	Manager
AAA	Las Vegas	Pacific Coast	Brad Mills
AA	Jacksonville	Southern	Dino Ebel
A	Vero Beach	Florida State	Juan Bustabad
A	Wilmington	South Atlantic	Scott Little
Rookie	Great Falls	Pioneer	Dann Bilardello
Rookie	Gulf Coast Dodgers	Gulf Coast	Luis Salazar

BROADCAST INFORMATION

Radio: XTRA-AM (1150); KWKW-AM (1330, Spanish language).
TV: KCOP-TV (Channel 13)
Cable TV: Fox Sports Net 2.

SPRING TRAINING

Ballpark (city): Holman Stadium (Vero Beach, Fla.).
Ticket information: 561-569-6858.
General number: 561-569-4900

Follow the Dodgers all season at: www.sportingnews.com/baseball/teams/dodgers/

SPRING TRAINING ROSTER

Manager—Jim Tracy (12).
Coaches—Jack Clark (44), Jim Colborn (45), Glenn Hoffman (35), Jim Lett (17), Manny Mota (11), Jim Riggleman (5), John Shelby (31).

No.	PITCHERS	B/T	Ht./Wt.	Born	2001 clubs
	Alvarez, Victor	L/L	5-10/150	11-8-76	Jacksonville, Las Vegas
43	Ashby, Andy	R/R	6-1/202	7-11-67	Los Angeles
27	Brown, Kevin	R/R	6-4/200	3-14-65	Los Angeles
77	Carrara, Giovanni	R/R	6-2/210	3-4-68	Las Vegas, Los Angeles
	Colyer, Steve	L/L	6-4/205	2-22-79	Vero Beach
37	Daal, Omar	L/L	6-3/195	3-1-72	Philadelphia
37	Dreifort, Darren	R/R	6-2/211	5-3-72	Los Angeles
48	Gagne, Eric	R/R	6-2/195	1-7-76	Los Angeles, Las Vegas
	Garcia, Carlos	R/R	6-3/232	9-23-78	DID NOT PLAY
49	Herges, Matt	L/R	6-0/200	4-1-70	Los Angeles
52	Mota, Danny	R/R	6-0/170	10-9-75	Edmonton, Las Vegas
45	Mulholland, Terry	R/L	6-3/220	3-9-63	Pittsburgh, Altoona, Los Angeles
	Nomo, Hideo	R/R	6-2/230	8-31-68	Boston
	Perez, Odalis	L/L	6-0/150	6-7-78	Atlanta, Richmond
48	Quantrill, Paul	L/R	6-1/195	11-3-68	Toronto
	Rodriguez, Ricardo	R/R	6-3/165	5-21-79	Vero Beach
28	Trombley, Mike	R/R	6-2/204	4-14-67	Baltimore, Los Angeles
54	Williams, Jeff	R/L	6-0/185	6-6-72	Las Vegas, Los Angeles

No.	CATCHERS	B/T	Ht./Wt.	Born	2001 clubs
	Diaz, Jose	R/R	6-0/175	4-13-80	Wilmington, Great Falls
21	Kreuter, Chad	B/R	6-2/200	8-26-64	Los Angeles
16	Lo Duca, Paul	R/R	5-10/185	4-12-72	Los Angeles, Las Vegas

No.	INFIELDERS	B/T	Ht./Wt.	Born	2001 clubs
	Allen, Luke	L/R	6-2/208	8-4-78	Jacksonville, Las Vegas
29	Beltre, Adrian	R/R	5-11/170	4-7-79	Vero Beach, Las Vegas, Los Angeles
66	Bocachica, Hiram	R/R	5-11/165	3-4-76	Los Angeles
3	Cora, Alex	L/R	6-0/180	10-18-75	Los Angeles
8	Grudzielanek, Mark	R/R	6-1/185	6-30-70	Los Angeles
25	Hansen, Dave	L/R	6-0/195	11-24-68	Vero Beach, Los Angeles
68	Hiatt, Phil	R/R	6-3/200	5-1-69	Las Vegas, Los Angeles
3	Izturis, Cesar	B/R	5-9/175	2-10-80	Syracuse, Toronto
23	Karros, Eric	R/R	6-4/226	11-4-67	Los Angeles
62	Nunez, Jorge	R/R	5-10/158	3-1-78	Jacksonville
12	Reboulet, Jeff	R/R	6-0/175	4-30-64	Los Angeles
	Thurston, Joe	L/R	5-11/175	9-29-79	Jacksonville

No.	OUTFIELDERS	B/T	Ht./Wt.	Born	2001 clubs
78	Chen, Chin-Feng	R/R	6-1/189	10-28-77	Vero Beach, Jacksonville
26	Christensen, McKay	L/L	5-11/180	8-14-75	Charlotte, Chicago A.L., Las Vegas, Los Angeles
24	Goodwin, Tom	L/R	6-1/175	7-27-68	Los Angeles, Wilmington
15	Green, Shawn	L/L	6-4/200	11-10-72	Los Angeles
9	Grissom, Marquis	R/R	5-11/190	4-17-67	Los Angeles
	Jordan, Brian	R/R	6-1/205	3-29-67	Atlanta

BALLPARK INFORMATION

Ballpark (capacity, surface)
Dodger Stadium (56,000, grass)
Address
1000 Elysian Park Ave.
Los Angeles, CA 90012
Official website
www.dodgers.com
Business phone
323-224-1500
Ticket information
323-224-1448
Ticket prices
$21 (outer field)
$17 (inner reserve)
$16 (outer loge)
$10 (outer reserve)
$6 (top deck, left and right pavilion)
Field dimensions (from home plate)
To left field at foul line, 330 feet
To center field, 395 feet
To right field at foul line, 330 feet
First game played
April 10, 1962 (Reds 6, Dodgers 3)

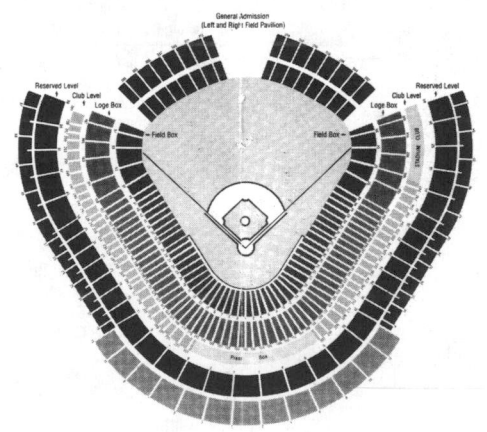

Date	Opp.	Res.	Score	(inn.*)	Hits	Opp. hits	Winning pitcher	Losing pitcher	Save	Record	Pos.	GB
4-2	Mil.	W	1-0		5	6	Park	Wright	Shaw	1-0	T1st	...
4-3	Ari.	L	2-3		5	12	Johnson	Nunez	Mantei	1-1	4th	0.5
4-4	Ari.	L	2-7		5	14	Schilling	Dreifort		1-2	4th	1.5
4-5	Ari.	W	7-5		8	9	Ashby	Anderson	Shaw	2-2	4th	1.5
4-6	S.F	W	10-1		12	4	Prokopec	Estes		3-2	3rd	0.5
4-7	S.F	W	10-4		10	6	Park	Hernandez		4-2	1st	+0.5
4-8	S.F	L	3-8		8	11	Rueter	Gagne		4-3	2nd	0.5
4-10	At Ari.	L	0-2		2	3	Schilling	Brown		4-4	2nd	1.5
4-11	At Ari.	W	11-5		11	5	Dreifort	Anderson		5-4	2nd	1.5
4-12	At Ari.	W	5-4		12	11	Ashby	Reynoso	Shaw	6-4	2nd	0.5
4-13	At S.D.	L	4-5	(10)	5	7	Hoffman	Herges		6-5	2nd	1.5
4-14	At S.D.	L	4-5		7	4	Hoffman	Olson		6-6	3rd	1.5
4-15	At S.D.	W	5-4		6	5	Brown	Myers	Shaw	7-6	2nd	0.5
4-17	At S.F	L	2-3		9	7	Rodriguez	Adams	Nen	7-7	3rd	1.5
4-18	At S.F	L	4-5		11	7	Fultz	Park	Nen	7-8	3rd	2.5
4-19	At S.F	W	10-1		15	7	Gagne	Rueter		8-8	3rd	1.5
4-20	S.D.	W	3-1		6	6	Brown	Tollberg	Shaw	9-8	3rd	1.5
4-21	S.D.	W	4-2		9	7	Prokopec	Jarvis	Shaw	10-8	2nd	0.5
4-22	S.D.	L	6-7	(11)	12	8	Witasick	Shaw	Myers	10-9	3rd	1.5
4-24	Pit.	L	1-5		4	7	Olivares	Park		10-10	T3rd	1.5
4-25	Pit.	W	6-5		5	10	Adams	Manzanillo		11-10	T3rd	1.5
4-26	Pit.	W	6-3		8	6	Brown	Ritchie		12-10	T2nd	0.5
4-27	Phi.	W	4-0		0	6	Adams	Gomes		13-10	1st	+0.5
4-28	Phi.	W	7-6		13	8	Herges	Bottalico	Shaw	14-10	1st	+1.5
4-29	Phl.	W	4-1		8	3	Park	Wolf	Shaw	15-10	1st	+1.5
5-1	At Cin.	L	6-7		11	9	Wohlers	Herges	Graves	15-11	1st	+1.0
5-2	At Cin.	W	7-3		13	5	Brown	Harnisch		16-11	1st	+1.5
5-3	At Cin.	W	8-6		12	7	Prokopec	Reitsma	Shaw	17-11	1st	+2.0
5-4	At Chi.	L	0-4		4	8	Tapani	Park		17-12	1st	+1.5
5-5	At Chi.	L	1-20		6	18	Tavarez	Dreifort		17-13	1st	+1.5
5-6	At Chi.	L	2-3		5	4	Gordon	Herges		17-14	1st	+1.0
5-7	Fla.	W	1-0		3	2	Brown	Burnett	Shaw	18-14	1st	+1.5
5-8	Fla.	L	6-7		10	11	Penny	Prokopec	Alfonseca	18-15	1st	+0.5
5-9	Fla.	W	3-2		8	5	Park	Dempster	Shaw	19-15	1st	+1.0
5-10	Fla.	W	4-3		9	9	Dreifort	Clement	Shaw	20-15	1st	+1.5
5-11	Atl.	L	1-5		8	12	Perez	Gagne		20-16	1st	+0.5
5-12	Atl.	W	1-0		5	3	Shaw	Whiteside		21-16	1st	+0.5
5-13	Atl.	W	3-1		7	3	Prokopec	Maddux	Shaw	22-16	1st	+0.5
5-15	At Mon.	L	0-2		2	6	Vazquez	Park		22-17	2nd	0.5
5-16	At Mon.	W	7-2		11	6	Dreifort	Reames		23-17	1st	+0.5
5-17	At Mon.	L	1-3		7	5	Armas	Gagne	Urbina	23-18	1st	+0.5
5-18	At N.Y.	L	0-8		5	11	Leiter	Brown	Wendell	23-19	2nd	0.5
5-19	At N.Y.	W	10-2		13	6	Prokopec	Appier		24-19	1st	+0.5
5-20	At N.Y.	L	5-6		7	11	Benitez	Adams		24-20	1st	+0.5
5-21	At Col.	L	3-6		5	8	Chacon	Dreifort	Jimenez	24-21	2nd	0.5
5-22	At Col.	L	8-11		12	14	White	Herges	Jimenez	24-22	3rd	1.5
5-23	At Col.	W	6-4		7	10	Brown	Astacio	Shaw	25-22	3rd	0.5
5-25	Hou.	W	4-1		9	7	Park	Miller	Shaw	26-22	T1st	...
5-26	Hou.	W	7-2		10	6	Prokopec	Reynolds		27-22	T1st	...
5-27	Hou.	W	5-4	(12)	9	6	Fetters	Oswalt		28-22	T1st	...
5-28	Col.	W	11-10	(11)	18	11	Herges	Villone		29-22	T1st	...
5-29	Col.	L	2-7		6	10	Bohanon	Brown		29-23	2nd	1.0
5-30	Col.	W	4-1		4	4	Park	Hampton	Shaw	30-23	2nd	1.0
6-1	At Hou.	L	9-10		11	16	Dotel	Fetters		30-24	2nd	2.0
6-2	At Hou.	L	1-2		5	7	Oswalt	Dreifort	Wagner	30-25	2nd	3.0
6-3	At Hou.	W	9-8	(10)	16	11	Fetters	Dotel	Shaw	31-25	2nd	3.0
6-4	At Ari.	W	8-4		13	6	Park	Reynoso		32-25	2nd	2.0
6-5	At Ari.	W	6-5		9	8	Herges	Kim	Shaw	33-25	2nd	1.0
6-6	At Ari.	L	1-4		6	10	Schilling	Prokopec		33-26	2nd	2.0
6-7	At Ari.	L	9-13		14	12	Batista	Dreifort		33-27	2nd	3.0
6-8	Ana.	L	0-1		4	6	Valdes	Carrara	Percival	33-28	2nd	4.0
6-9	Ana.	W	2-1		9	7	Shaw	Weber		34-28	2nd	3.0
6-10	Ana.	L	5-6	(10)	12	10	Levine	Gagne	Percival	34-29	2nd	4.0
6-11	Tex.	L	7-12		13	16	Oliver	Prokopec		34-30	2nd	4.5
6-12	Tex.	W	8-4		13	6	Dreifort	Judd		35-30	2nd	3.5
6-13	Tex.	W	5-3		9	5	Herges	Smart	Shaw	36-30	2nd	3.5
6-15	At Ana.	W	6-2		17	6	Park	Ortiz	Fetters	37-30	2nd	3.0
6-16	At Ana.	L	5-6		7	12	Percival	Herges		37-31	2nd	4.0
6-17	At Ana.	L	4-6		6	12	Levine	Shaw		37-32	T2nd	5.0
6-19	Ari.	L	2-9		7	13	Johnson	Dreifort		37-33	T2nd	6.0
6-20	Ari.	W	4-3		7	4	Shaw	Sabel		38-33	T2nd	5.0
6-22	S.D.	L	6-9		13	12	Witasick	Herges	Hoffman	38-34	3rd	6.5
6-23	S.D.	L	2-6		5	8	Lawrence	Prokopec	Seanez	38-35	3rd	7.5
6-24	S.D.	L	1-6		3	10	Eaton	Dreifort		38-36	3rd	7.5

Date	Opp.	Res.	Score	(inn.*)	Hits	Opp. hits	Winning pitcher	Losing pitcher	Save	Record	Pos.	GB
6-25	At S.F	L	2-5		5	6	Gardner	Park	Nen	38-37	3rd	7.5
6-26	At S.F	W	14-8		18	14	Reyes	Worrell		39-37	3rd	6.5
6-27	At S.F	W	7-3		12	8	Adams	Hernandez		40-37	3rd	6.5
6-28	At S.D.	W	7-4		10	8	Carrara	Seanez	Shaw	41-37	T2nd	6.0
6-29	At S.D.	W	7-5		11	8	Williams	Eaton	Shaw	42-37	T2nd	6.0
6-30	At S.D.	W	7-3		13	5	Herges	Hoffman		43-37	T2nd	6.0
7-1	At S.D.	W	8-0		11	4	Brown	Jones	Reyes	44-37	T2nd	6.0
7-2	S.F	W	8-6		16	8	Adams	Vogelsong	Shaw	45-37	2nd	5.5
7-3	S.F	W	4-3		6	10	Williams	Hernandez	Shaw	46-37	2nd	4.5
7-4	S.F	W	4-3		9	12	Herges	Rodriguez	Shaw	47-37	2nd	4.5
7-5	S.F	L	2-3		4	7	Ortiz	Reyes	Nen	47-38	2nd	4.5
7-6	Sea.	L	0-13		4	17	Garcia	Brown		47-39	2nd	4.5
7-7	Sea.	W	2-1		5	3	Herges	Paniagua		48-39	2nd	3.5
7-8	Sea.	L	2-9		5	13	Sele	Williams		48-40	2nd	3.5
7-12	At Oak.	L	0-6		6	15	Mulder	Adams		48-41	2nd	3.5
7-13	At Oak.	L	7-11		8	14	Hudson	Park	Isringhausen	48-42	2nd	4.5
7-14	At Oak.	W	5-3	(15)	8	10	Reyes	Guthrie		49-42	2nd	4.5
7-15	At Pit.	W	4-2		7	7	Brown	Schmidt	Shaw	50-42	2nd	3.5
7-16	At Pit.	W	6-4		8	7	Gagne	Beimel	Shaw	51-42	2nd	3.5
7-17	At Pit.	W	4-1		8	5	Adams	Anderson	Herges	52-42	2nd	2.5
7-18	Mil.	W	5-0		7	2	Park	Levrault		53-42	2nd	2.0
7-19	Mil.	W	8-6		7	12	Herges	Weathers	Shaw	54-42	2nd	1.5
7-20	At Col.	L	3-11		6	14	Bohanon	Prokopec		54-43	2nd	1.5
7-21	At Col.	W	22-7		23	12	Gagne	Neagle		55-43	2nd	1.5
7-22	At Col.	W	9-8		16	16	Adams	Astacio	Shaw	56-43	2nd	1.5
7-23	At Mil.	W	3-1		11	5	Park	Levrault	Shaw	57-43	2nd	0.5
7-24	At Mil.	W	7-2		12	6	Springer	Wright		58-43	2nd	0.5
7-25	At Mil.	L	3-4		5	9	Weathers	Herges		58-44	2nd	1.5
7-26	Col.	W	3-1		6	5	Gagne	Neagle	Shaw	59-44	2nd	0.5
7-27	Col.	W	4-2		10	7	Adams	Astacio	Shaw	60-44	1st	+0.5
7-28	Col.	W	10-6		13	12	Park	Hampton	Shaw	61-44	1st	+1.5
7-29	Col.	L	2-3		5	9	Powell	Herges	Jimenez	61-45	1st	+1.5
7-31	Cin.	L	1-3	(11)	4	8	Graves	Orosco		61-46	1st	+0.5
8-1	Cin.	L	5-10		10	20	Davis	Adams		61-47	1st	+0.5
8-2	Cin.	L	4-7		9	9	Dessens	Prokopec	Graves	61-48	1st	+0.5
8-3	Chi.	L	1-2		3	5	Wood	Park	Gordon	61-49	T2nd	0.5
8-4	Chi.	W	3-1		8	4	Baldwin	Tavarez	Shaw	62-49	1st	+0.5
8-5	Chi.	W	3-2	(10)	10	9	Mulholland	Gordon		63-49	1st	+0.5
8-7	At Pit.	W	2-1		9	7	Adams	McKnight	Shaw	64-49	1st	+1.0
8-8	At Pit.	W	9-4		13	11	Carrara	Anderson		65-49	1st	+1.5
8-9	At Pit.	L	5-8		11	11	Ritchie	Park	Fetters	65-50	1st	+1.0
8-10	At Phi.	L	5-10		10	10	Figueroa	Baldwin		65-51	1st	+0.5
8-11	At Phi.	L	3-7		5	8	Person	Gagne		65-52	T2nd	0.5
8-12	At Phi.	L	2-3		5	8	Duckworth	Adams	Mesa	65-53	3rd	1.5
8-14	Mon.	L	1-4		5	7	Lloyd	Shaw		65-54	3rd	3.0
8-15	Mon.	W	13-1		20	7	Carrara	Pavano		66-54	3rd	3.0
8-16	Mon.	L	3-7		9	10	Reames	Trombley		66-55	3rd	3.5
8-17	N.Y.	W	8-3		10	6	Adams	Rusch		67-55	3rd	3.5
8-18	N.Y.	L	4-5		8	7	Riggan	Trombley	Benitez	67-56	3rd	4.5
8-19	N.Y.	L	5-6		10	11	Trachsel	Park	Benitez	67-57	3rd	5.5
8-21	At Fla.	W	5-4		9	9	Carrara	Nunez	Shaw	68-57	3rd	4.5
8-22	At Fla.	L	6-8		9	14	Burnett	Adams		68-58	3rd	5.5
8-23	At Fla.	W	6-2		10	5	Baldwin	Dempster		69-58	3rd	4.5
8-24	At Atl.	W	4-1		7	5	Park	Glavine		70-58	3rd	3.5
8-25	At Atl.	W	8-7		10	12	Prokopec	Marquis	Shaw	71-58	3rd	3.5
8-26	At Atl.	L	2-9		9	15	Burkett	Gagne		71-59	3rd	4.5
8-27	At Atl.	W	4-2		7	9	Adams	Remlinger	Shaw	72-59	3rd	3.5
8-28	Col.	L	3-4		11	11	Davis	Shaw	Powell	72-60	3rd	4.5
8-29	Col.	L	3-5		10	13	Jennings	Baldwin	Powell	72-61	3rd	5.5
8-30	Col.	W	5-4		6	9	Park	Neagle	Shaw	73-61	3rd	4.5
8-31	St.L.	L	1-5		4	8	Williams	Gagne		73-62	3rd	5.0
9-1	St.L.	W	3-1		8	4	Adams	Hermanson	Shaw	74-62	3rd	4.0
9-2	St.L.	W	7-3		12	7	Brown	Kile		75-62	3rd	3.0
9-4	At Col.	L	2-5		6	8	Neagle	Baldwin	Powell	75-63	3rd	3.0
9-5	At Col.	W	7-2		6	7	Herges	Myers		76-63	3rd	3.0
9-6	At Col.	W	9-5		11	13	Adams	Hampton		77-63	3rd	2.0
9-7	At St.L.	W	7-1		12	4	Brown	Hermanson		78-63	2nd	1.0
9-8	At St.L.	L	5-6		7	13	Al. Benes	Baldwin	Stechschulte	78-64	3rd	2.0
9-9	At St.L.	L	1-8		4	11	Mathews	Park		78-65	3rd	3.0
9-17	S.D.	L	4-6		8	9	Middlebrook	Park	Hoffman	78-66	3rd	4.0
9-18	S.D.	L	2-3		5	4	Jarvis	Adams	Hoffman	78-67	3rd	4.0
9-19	S.D.	L	3-4	(10)	9	9	Nunez	Trombley	Hoffman	78-68	3rd	4.0
9-20	Ari.	W	3-2	(13)	10	9	Prokopec	Swindell		79-68	3rd	3.0
9-21	Ari.	L	0-10		5	10	Batista	Mulholland		79-69	3rd	4.0
9-22	Ari.	W	6-5	(11)	7	11	Gagne	Koplove		80-69	3rd	3.0
9-23	Ari.	L	1-6		6	9	Schilling	Adams		80-70	3rd	4.0
9-24	S.F	L	1-2		4	11	Hernandez	Baldwin	Nen	80-71	3rd	4.5
9-25	S.F	W	9-5		13	9	Park	Rueter		81-71	3rd	3.5

Date	Opp.	Res.	Score	(inn.*)	Hits	Opp. hits	Winning pitcher	Losing pitcher	Save	Record	Pos.	GB
9-26	S.F	L	4-6		6	13	Rodriguez	Shaw	Nen	81-72	3rd	4.5
9-28	At Ari.	L	3-4	(11)	8	14	Morgan	Trombley		81-73	3rd	6.0
9-29	At Ari.	L	1-8		5	9	Batista	Baldwin		81-74	3rd	7.0
9-30	At Ari.	W	2-1		4	6	Park	Swindell	Shaw	82-74	3rd	6.0
10-2	At S.D.	W	5-2		11	5	Carrara	Hoffman	Shaw	83-74	3rd	6.0
10-3	At S.D.	W	12-5		16	6	Gagne	Jones		84-74	3rd	6.0
10-4	At S.D.	L	3-6		11	11	Middlebrook	Prokopec	Hoffman	84-75	3rd	7.0
10-5	At S.F	W	11-10		15	10	Carrara	Worrell	Shaw	85-75	3rd	7.0
10-6	At S.F	W	6-2		10	5	Baldwin	Hernandez	Shaw	86-75	3rd	6.0
10-7	At S.F	L	1-2		4	9	Gardner	Springer	Nen	86-76	3rd	6.0

Monthly records: April (15-10), May (15-13), June (13-14), July (18-9), August (12-16), September (9-12), October (4-2).
*Innings, if other than nine.

HIGHLIGHTS

High point: The Dodgers came from behind twice in a pivotal September 22 game against Arizona to win 6-5 in 11 innings. Paul Lo Duca belted a two-run homer with no outs in the ninth off Randy Johnson to tie it, and Lo Duca scored the game-winning run two innings later on Adrian Beltre's single.

Low point: On April 19, an organization mired in chaos was greeted with more controversy, uncertainty and distraction when general manager Kevin Malone resigned under extreme pressure. Less than a week before that, Malone engaged in a shouting match with a fan in San Diego during a Dodgers game.

Turning point: The Dodgers had a chance to sweep a three-game series in Pittsburgh on August 9, and they had Chan Ho Park on the mound. Park got hammered, allowing seven runs in five innings of an 8-5 loss. The Dodgers, in first place at the time, went on to get swept by Philadelphia in a three-game series.

Most valuable player: Paul Lo Duca caught four of every five games and by the end of the season was starting at first base on the fifth day. He batted first through seventh in the lineup, hitting .320 with 25 homers and 90 RBIs despite missing a month with injuries.

Most valuable pitcher: Chan Ho Park finished 15-11 with a 3.50 ERA, but of his 35 starts, 26 were quality starts. Park led the staff in wins, innings pitched and strikeouts.

Most improved player: Terry Adams went from career setup man to reliable starter in 2001 and went 12-8 with a 4.33 ERA.

Most pleasant surprise: Entering spring training there were questions whether Lo Duca could handle a major league staff and hit on the major league level. Lo Duca had no problem with either.

Key injuries: A week into the season Andy Ashby was out with elbow problems, and by the end of the season start-ing pitchers Darren Dreifort and Kevin Brown also had surgery on their elbows. ... Gary Sheffield played much of the season with a torn ligament in his left index finger and first baseman Eric Karros battled back problems the first four months of the season.

Notable: Giovanni Carrara became the Matt Herges of 2001 by coming out of nowhere to make a huge contribution. Carrara went 6-1 with a 3.16 ERA to bolster the bullpen. ... Jeff Shaw set the franchise record with 129 career saves.

—JASON REID

RECORDS

2001 regular-season record: 86-76 (3rd in N.L. West); 44-37 at home; 42-39 on road; 17-15 vs. N.L. East; 23-16 vs. N.L. Central; 40-36 vs. N.L. West; 6-9 vs. A.L.; 25-18 vs. lefthanded starters; 61-58 vs. righthanded starters; 85-71 on grass; 1-5 on turf; 22-23 in daytime; 64-53 at night; 29-29 in one-run games; 7-6 in extra-inning games; 0-0-0 in doubleheaders.

Team record past five years: 420-300 (.519, ranks 6th in league in that span).

TEAM LEADERS

Batting average: Paul Lo Duca (.320).
At-bats: Shawn Green (619).
Runs: Shawn Green (121).
Hits: Shawn Green (184).
Total Bases: Shawn Green (370).
Doubles: Shawn Green (31).
Triples: Tom Goodwin (5).
Home runs: Shawn Green (49).
Runs batted in: Shawn Green (125).
Stolen bases: Tom Goodwin (22).
Slugging percentage: Shawn Green (.598).
On-base percentage: Gary Sheffield (.417).
Wins: Chan Ho Park (15).
Earned-run average: Chan Ho Park (3.50).
Complete games: Chan Ho Park (2).

Shutouts: Chan Ho Park (1).
Saves: Jeff Shaw (43).
Innings pitched: Chan Ho Park (234.0).
Strikeouts: Chan Ho Park (218).

GAMES BY POSITION

Catcher: Paul Lo Duca 99, Chad Kreuter 70, Angel Pena 15, Brian Johnson 2.
First base: Eric Karros 119, Paul Lo Duca 33, Dave Hansen 25, Chris Donnels 7, Phil Hiatt 6, Tim Bogar 3, Shawn Green 1.
Second base: Mark Grudzielanek 133, Jeff Reboulet 22, Hiram Bocachica 19, Jeff Branson 6, Alex Cora 1.
Third base: Adrian Beltre 124, Dave Hansen 21, Phil Hiatt 17, Chris Donnels 14, Hiram Bocachica 8, Jeff Reboulet 7, Tim Bogar 1, Jeff Branson 1.
Shortstop: Alex Cora 132, Jeff Reboulet 56, Tim Bogar 2, Adrian Beltre 2, Jeff Branson 2, Dave Hansen 1.
Outfield: Shawn Green 159, Gary Sheffield 141, Marquis Grissom 123, Tom Goodwin 78, McKay Christensen 14, Hiram Bocachica 13, Bruce Aven 9, Paul Lo Duca 5, Jeff Reboulet 2.
Designated hitter: Gary Sheffield 2, Marquis Grissom 2, Chad Kreuter 1, Paul Lo Duca 1, Dave Hansen 1.

TOP DRAFT CHOICES

2. **Brian Pilkington,** RHP, Santiago H.S., Garden Grove, Calif.
3. **David Taylor,** RHP, Southlake H.S., Clermont, Fla.
4. **Kole Strayhorn,** RHP, Shawnee H.S., Seminole, Okla.
5. **Steve Nelson,** RHP, Cole Harbour District H.S., Dartmouth, Nova Scotia.
6. **Edwin Jackson,** OF, Shaw H.S., Columbus, Ga.
7. **David Cuen,** LHP, Cibola H.S., Somerton, Ariz.
8. **David Cardona,** OF, San Jose de Calasanza H.S., Trujillo Alta, P.R.
9. **Sean Pierce,** OF, San Diego State U.
10. **Thom Ott,** RHP, U. of Nebraska.

MILWAUKEE BREWERS
NATIONAL LEAGUE CENTRAL DIVISION

Brewers schedule
Home games shaded
D—Day game (games starting before 5 p.m.)
*All-Star Game at Milwaukee
Subject to changes

April

SUN	MON	TUE	WED	THU	FRI	SAT
	1	2 D HOU	3 HOU	4 D HOU	5 ARI	6 ARI
7 ARI	8	9 STL	10 STL	11 D STL	12 SF	13 SF
14 D SF	15 PIT	16 PIT	17 D PIT	18 STL	19 STL	20 STL
21 STL	22	23 MON	24 MON	25 MON	26 NYM	27 D NYM
28 D NYM	29	30 ATL				

May

SUN	MON	TUE	WED	THU	FRI	SAT
		1 ATL	2 D ATL	3 FLA	4 D FLA
5 FLA	6 CIN	7 CIN	8 CIN	9 D CUB	10 D CUB	11 D CUB
12 CUB	13 CIN	14 CIN	15 CIN	16 D CUB	17 CUB	18 CUB
19 CUB	20	21 LA	22 LA	23 D LA	24 SD	25 SD
26 D SD	27 D LA	28 LA	29 D LA	30	31 SD	

June

SUN	MON	TUE	WED	THU	FRI	SAT
						1 SD
2 SD	3 CUB	4 CUB	5 CUB	6	7 PIT	8 PIT
9 PIT	10 OAK	11 OAK	12 D OAK	13	14 MIN	15 MIN
16 MIN	17 HOU	18 HOU	19 HOU	20 D HOU	21 ANA	22 ANA
23 ANA	24	25 STL	26 STL	27 STL	28 MIN	29 MIN
30 D MIN						

July

SUN	MON	TUE	WED	THU	FRI	SAT
	1 PIT	2 PIT	3 PIT	4 D CIN	5 CIN	6 CIN
7 CIN	8	9 *	10	11 PIT	12 PIT	13 PIT
14 D PIT	15 CIN	16 CIN	17 HOU	18 HOU	19 COL	20 COL
21 COL	22 HOU	23 HOU	24 HOU	25	26 COL	27 COL
28 COL	29	30 ATL	31 ATL			

August

SUN	MON	TUE	WED	THU	FRI	SAT
				1 ATL	2 FLA	3 FLA
4 D FLA	5	6 NYM	7 NYM	8 D NYM	9 D MON	10 MON
11 MON	12	13 PHI	14 PHI	15 PHI	16 PIT	17 PIT
18 D PIT	19	20 PHI	21 PHI	22 D PHI	23 PIT	24 PIT
25 D PIT	26 CUB	27 CUB	28 CUB	29 CUB	30 CIN	31 CIN

September

SUN	MON	TUE	WED	THU	FRI	SAT
1 D CIN	2 D CUB	3 D CUB	4 CUB	5 D	6 CIN	7 CIN
8 CIN	9 STL	10 STL	11 STL	12	13 ARI	14 ARI
15 D ARI	16	17 HOU	18 HOU	19 D HOU	20 SF	21 SF
22 D SF	23 HOU	24 HOU	25 HOU	26 STL	27 STL	28 D STL
29 STL	30					

2002 SEASON
CLUB DIRECTORY

President and chief executive officer
Wendy Selig-Prieb
Sr. vice president and general manager
Dean Taylor
Vice president & general counsel
Tom Gausden
Assistant general counsel
Eugene (Pepi) Randolph
Special assistant to the president
Sal Bando
Vice president, community and governmental affairs
Lynn Sprangers
Vice president, tickets and advertising
Dean Rennicke
Vice president, finance
Paul Baniel
Vice president, marketing
Laurel Prieb
Vice president, player personnel
David Wilder
Vice president, stadium operations
Scott Jenkins
Director, community relations
Michael Downs
Director, event services
Steve Ethier
Director, grounds
Gary Vanden Berg
Director, media relations
Jon Greenberg
Director, player development
Greg Riddoch
Director, Brewers Gold Club & Baseball for Wisconsin
Mike Harlan
Director of publications
Mario Ziino
Director of ticket operations
John Barnes
Director, scouting
Jack Zduriencik

Director, clubhouse operations
Tony Migliaccio
Director of team travel
Dan Larrea
Trainers
Roger Caplinger
Dan Wright
Strength and conditioning coach
Phil Falco
Team physician
Dr. William Raasch
National cross-checker
Larry Doughty
West coast supervisor
Ric Wilson
Midwest supervisor
Tom Allison
Latin America supervisor
Epy Guerrero
East coast supervisor
Bobby Heck
Professional scouts
Hank Allen, Carl Blando, Dick Hager, Alan Regier, Daraka Shaheed
Major League scouts
Russ Bove, Ken Califano, Larry Haney, Bill Lajoie, Al Monchak, Chuck Tanner, Elanis Westbrooks, Dick Wiencek
Scouts
Larry Aaron, Jeff Brookens, Mike Farrell, Edward Fastaia, Dick Foster, Mike Gibbons, Manolo Hernandez, Brian Johnson, Chris Knabenshue, Harvey Kuenn Jr., John Logan, Justin McCray, Tom McNamara, Chris Miller, Brandon Newell, Larry Pardo, Douglas Reynolds, Corey Rodriguez, Bruce Seid, Jim Stevenson, Tom Tanous, Andy Tomberlin, John Viney, Walter Youse

MINOR LEAGUE AFFILIATES

Class	Team	League	Manager
AAA	Indianapolis	International	Ed Romero
AA	Huntsville	Southern	Frank Kremblas
A	Beloit	Midwest	Don Money
A	High Desert	California	Mike Caldwell
Rookie	Maryvale	Arizona	Carlos Lezcano
Rookie	Ogden	Pioneer	Wendell Kim

BROADCAST INFORMATION

Radio: WTMJ-AM (620).
TV: WCGV-TV (Channel 24).
Cable TV: Fox Sports North.

SPRING TRAINING

Ballpark (city): Maryvale Baseball Park (Phoenix, Ariz.).
Ticket information: 623-245-5500.

Follow the Brewers all season at: www.sportingnews.com/baseball/teams/brewers/

Manager—Davey Lopes (30).
Coaches—Gary Allenson (45), Bill Castro (35), Dave Collins (29), Gary Matthews (36), Jerry Royster (3), Dave Stewart (43).

No.	PITCHERS	B/T	Ht./Wt.	Born	2001 clubs
47	Buddie, Mike	R/R	6-3/219	12-12-70	Indianapolis, Milwaukee
60	Childers, Matt	R/R	6-5/195	12-3-78	High Desert, Huntsville
13	D'Amico, Jeff	R/R	6-7/250	12-27-75	Milwaukee, Beloit, Huntsville
28	De Los Santos, Valerio	L/L	6-2/206	10-6-75	Milwaukee
18	DeJean, Mike	R/R	6-2/212	9-28-70	Milwaukee
40	Fox, Chad	R/R	6-3/190	9-3-70	Indianapolis, Milwaukee
56	Garcia, Jose	R/R	6-3/195	4-29-78	Huntsville
	Gold, J.M.	R/R	6-5/220	4-18-80	Arizona Brewers, Ogden
46	King, Ray	L/L	6-1/240	1-15-74	Milwaukee
39	Leskanic, Curtis	R/R	6-0/196	4-2-68	Milwaukee
55	Levrault, Allen	R/R	6-3/230	8-15-77	Indianapolis, Milwaukee
	Mallette, Brian	R/R	6-0/185	1-19-75	Huntsville, Indianapolis
	Martinez, Luis	R/R	6-1/185	1-20-80	High Desert, Huntsville
	Mieses, Jose	R/R	6-1/165	10-14-79	Huntsville, Indianapolis, Arizona Brewers, Ogden
	Neugebauer, Nick	R/R	6-3/235	7-15-80	Huntsville, Indianapolis, Milwaukee
	Perez, George	R/R	6-4/220	3-20-79	Dunedin
48	Quevedo, Ruben	R/R	6-1/230	1-5-79	Iowa, Milwaukee
31	Rigdon, Paul	R/R	6-5/242	11-2-75	Milwaukee
	Sheets, Ben	R/R	6-1/195	7-18-78	Indianapolis, Milwaukee
	Sosa, Jorge	B/R	6-2/180	4-28-78	Everett, Wisconsin
21	Wright, Jamey	R/R	6-5/236	12-24-74	Milwaukee

No.	CATCHERS	B/T	Ht./Wt.	Born	2001 clubs
12	Blanco, Henry	R/R	5-11/224	8-29-71	Milwaukee
25	Casanova, Raul	B/R	6-0/221	8-23-72	Milwaukee

No.	INFIELDERS	B/T	Ht./Wt.	Born	2001 clubs
10	Belliard, Ron	R/R	5-8/190	7-4-76	Milwaukee
16	Collier, Lou	R/R	5-10/182	8-21-73	Indianapolis, Milwaukee
	Deardorff, Jeff	R/R	6-3/220	8-14-78	High Desert, Huntsville
	Hall, Bill	R/R	6-0/175	12-28-79	High Desert, Huntsville
18	Hernandez, Jose	R/R	6-1/186	7-14-69	Milwaukee
2	Houston, Tyler	L/R	6-1/218	1-17-71	Milwaukee, Beloit
1	Lopez, Luis	B/R	5-11/170	9-4-70	Milwaukee
8	Loretta, Mark	R/R	6-0/189	8-14-71	Indianapolis, Milwaukee
23	Pena, Elvis	B/R	5-11/155	9-15-76	Indianapolis, Milwaukee
11	Sexson, Richie	R/R	6-8/215	12-29-74	Milwaukee
	Young, Eric	R/R	5-8/175	5-18-67	Chicago N.L.

No.	OUTFIELDERS	B/T	Ht./Wt.	Born	2001 clubs
20	Burnitz, Jeromy	L/R	6-0/213	4-15-69	Milwaukee
28	Christenson, Ryan	R/R	6-0/210	3-28-74	Oakland, Sacramento, Arizona, Tucson
	Guerrero, Cristian	R/R	6-5/175	4-12-81	High Desert
6	Hammonds, Jeffrey	R/R	6-0/200	3-5-71	Milwaukee, Arizona Brewers
5	Jenkins, Geoff	L/R	6-1/206	7-21-74	Milwaukee, Beloit
	Sanchez, Alex	L/L	5-10/180	8-26-76	Indianapolis, Milwaukee
23	Sweeney, Mark	L/L	6-1/215	10-26-69	Indianapolis, Milwaukee

BALLPARK INFORMATION

Ballpark (capacity, surface)
Miller Park (41,900, grass)

Address
One Brewers Way
Milwaukee, WI 53214-3652

Official website
www.milwaukeebrewers.com

Business phone
414-902-4400

Ticket information
414-902-4000

Ticket prices
$35 (field IF box, club IF box)
$28 (field OF box), $30 (loge diamond box)
$26 (club OF box), $26 (loge IF box)
$21 (loge OF box), $17 (terrace box)
$12 (terrace reserved), $10 (field bleachers)
$6 (loge bleachers)
$5 (Bernie's Terrace)
$1 (Uecker seats)

Field dimensions (from home plate)
To left field at foul line, 342 feet
To center field, 400 feet
To right field at foul line, 345 feet

First game played
April 6, 2001 (Brewers 5, Reds 4)

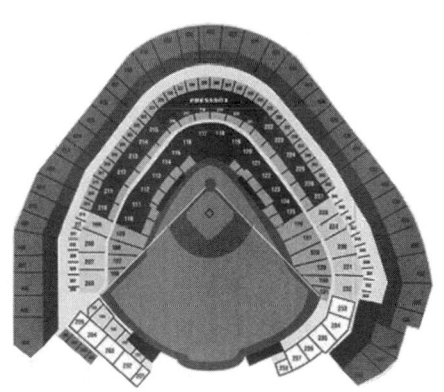

2002 SEASON *Milwaukee Brewers*

Date	Opp.	Res.	Score	(inn.*)	Hits	Opp. hits	Winning pitcher	Losing pitcher	Save	Record	Pos.	GB
4-2	At L.A.	L	0-1		6	5	Park	Wright	Shaw	0-1	T1st	0.5
4-3	At Hou.	L	3-11		9	11	Elarton	Haynes		0-2	T3rd	1.5
4-4	At Hou.	L	6-8	(12)	13	16	J. Powell	Leskanic		0-3	T4th	2.5
4-5	At Hou.	L	2-8		7	11	Miller	Sheets		0-4	T5th	3.5
4-6	Cin.	W	5-4		6	7	Weathers	Reyes		1-4	6th	3.5
4-7	Cin.	W	6-1		10	3	Wright	Harnisch		2-4	T5th	2.5
4-8	Cin.	W	8-4		9	9	Haynes	O. Fernandez		3-4	5th	1.5
4-10	Hou.	L	0-3		6	6	Lima	Leskanic	Wagner	3-5	T5th	2.5
4-11	Hou.	L	1-7		3	13	Miller	Sheets		3-6	T5th	3.5
4-12	Hou.	W	12-4		14	7	D'Amico	Dotel		4-6	T5th	2.5
4-13	S.F	L	3-7		3	12	Rueter	Wright		4-7	6th	3.5
4-14	S.F	W	11-6		14	9	DeJean	Gardner		5-7	5th	3.5
4-15	S.F	W	7-4		6	7	Rigdon	Ortiz	Leskanic	6-7	5th	2.5
4-17	At Cin.	L	2-3		5	6	Sullivan	Cunnane	Graves	6-8	T4th	2.5
4-18	At Cin.	W	7-4		11	9	Wright	Harnisch	Weathers	7-8	T4th	3.0
4-20	At S.F	L	1-3		2	3	Ortiz	Haynes	Nen	7-9	T4th	4.0
4-21	At S.F	W	6-3		14	9	Rigdon	Gardner	Weathers	8-9	T4th	4.0
4-22	At S.F	L	4-6		8	8	Estes	D'Amico	Nen	8-10	T4th	4.0
4-24	N.Y.	W	6-4		12	9	DeJean	Wall	Leskanic	9-10	T4th	3.0
4-25	N.Y.	W	7-2		13	9	Haynes	Trachsel	Weathers	10-10	T4th	2.0
4-26	N.Y.	W	12-8		19	13	Fox	Hinchliffe		11-10	4th	2.0
4-27	Mon.	L	1-6		5	8	Thurman	Leiter		11-11	T4th	3.0
4-28	Mon.	W	8-4		9	9	Sheets	Peters		12-11	4th	2.0
4-29	Mon.	W	10-0		14	2	Wright	Vazquez		13-11	3rd	2.0
5-1	At Atl.	W	5-3		9	7	Haynes	Millwood	Leskanic	14-11	3rd	1.0
5-2	At Atl.	L	0-1		2	5	Maddux	Rigdon		14-12	3rd	2.0
5-3	At Atl.	W	5-0		10	9	Sheets	Burkett		15-12	T2nd	1.0
5-4	At Fla.	L	6-9		10	11	Dempster	Wright	Alfonseca	15-13	T2nd	2.0
5-5	At Fla.	W	8-2		8	5	Leiter	Clement		16-13	2nd	2.0
5-6	At Fla.	L	1-5		3	9	Smith	Haynes		16-14	3rd	3.0
5-7	Chi.	L	6-7		9	12	Van Poppel	Weathers	Gordon	16-15	T3rd	4.0
5-8	Chi.	W	4-1		3	5	Sheets	Wood	Leskanic	17-15	2nd	3.0
5-9	Chi.	L	3-6		6	8	Tapani	Wright	Gordon	17-16	4th	4.0
5-10	Chi.	W	11-1		11	7	Levrault	Tavarez	DeJean	18-16	4th	3.0
5-11	Pit.	L	0-3		4	6	Schmidt	Haynes	M. Williams	18-17	4th	3.0
5-12	Pit.	W	5-4	(12)	9	13	Leskanic	Beimel		19-17	4th	2.0
5-13	Pit.	W	4-1		8	5	Sheets	Anderson		20-17	4th	1.5
5-14	Pit.	W	11-8		13	13	Wright	Wengert	Leskanic	21-17	3rd	1.0
5-15	At Phi.	W	14-10	(10)	22	12	Leskanic	Bottalico		22-17	3rd	1.0
5-16	At Phi.	W	6-1		10	9	Haynes	Chen		23-17	3rd	1.0
5-17	At Phi.	L	1-2	(12)	6	9	Gomes	DeJean		23-18	3rd	2.0
5-19	At Pit.	L	1-6		5	9	Anderson	Sheets		23-19	3rd	1.5
5-20	At Pit.	L	7-8		10	12	Manzanillo	Weathers	M. Williams	23-20	T3rd	2.5
5-22	St.L.	W	5-0		9	6	Haynes	Kile		24-20	T2nd	1.5
5-23	St.L.	W	7-3		9	8	Rigdon	Morris		25-20	T2nd	0.5
5-24	St.L.	L	4-7		4	10	Matthews	Sheets		25-21	3rd	1.5
5-25	At Chi.	L	0-1		1	4	Wood	Levrault		25-22	3rd	2.5
5-27	At Chi.	L	1-4		6	6	Tapani	Haynes	Gordon	25-23	3rd	3.0
5-28	At St.L.	L	2-6		8	10	Morris	Rigdon	Christiansen	25-24	3rd	4.0
5-29	At St.L.	W	7-0		12	5	Sheets	Matthews		26-24	3rd	4.0
5-30	At St.L.	W	11-1	(6)	13	5	Levrault	An. Benes		27-24	3rd	4.0
5-31	At St.L.	W	6-2		9	6	Peterson	Hermanson		28-24	3rd	3.5
6-1	Chi.	L	3-4		6	10	Wood	Haynes	Gordon	28-25	3rd	4.5
6-2	Chi.	L	4-10		16	9	Tapani	Rigdon		28-26	4th	5.5
6-3	Chi.	W	4-2		8	7	Sheets	Tavarez	Leskanic	29-26	3rd	4.5
6-5	Cin.	L	3-4	(13)	8	16	Wohlers	Cunnane	Nichting	29-27	3rd	5.5
6-6	Cin.	L	3-6		10	11	Dessens	Haynes	Graves	29-28	3rd	6.5
6-8	At Det.	L	4-9		13	12	Weaver	Rigdon		29-29	4th	7.0
6-9	At Det.	L	5-6		11	11	Anderson	Leskanic		29-30	4th	8.0
6-10	At Det.	W	8-3		11	6	Wright	Holt		30-30	4th	7.0
6-12	At Cle.	W	4-2		7	9	Fox	Shuey	Leskanic	31-30	T3rd	7.0
6-13	At Cle.	L	2-5	(10)	7	9	Wickman	Fox		31-31	T3rd	7.0
6-14	At Cle.	W	9-4		17	10	Sheets	Nagy		32-31	T2nd	6.0
6-15	K.C.	L	2-4		9	9	Byrd	Peterson	Hernandez	32-32	3rd	6.5
6-16	K.C.	L	1-4		7	5	Reichert	Haynes	Hernandez	32-33	4th	8.0
6-17	K.C.	W	5-2		8	10	Wright	Stein	Leskanic	33-33	T3rd	8.0
6-18	At Cin.	W	6-4		9	11	Levrault	Reith	Leskanic	34-33	T3rd	7.0
6-19	At Cin.	W	10-8		11	11	Sheets	Acevedo	King	35-33	T3rd	6.0
6-20	At Cin.	L	3-11		8	14	Reitsma	Cunnane		35-34	4th	7.0
6-22	At Chi.	W	2-1		5	5	Weathers	Wood	Leskanic	36-34	3rd	6.5
6-23	At Chi.	W	4-0		9	5	Wright	Tapani		37-34	3rd	5.5
6-24	At Chi.	W	6-3		8	8	Sheets	Bere	Leskanic	38-34	3rd	4.5
6-25	At Pit.	L	4-6		7	10	D. Williams	Levrault	M. Williams	38-35	4th	5.5
6-26	At Pit.	L	6-7	(12)	12	10	Olivares	King		38-36	4th	6.5

Date	Opp.	Res.	Score	(inn.*)	Hits	Opp. hits	Winning pitcher	Losing pitcher	Save	Record	Pos.	GB
6-27	At Pit.	L	2-6		4	10	Schmidt	Haynes		38-37	4th	6.5
6-28	At Pit.	L	0-1		6	7	Ritchie	Wright	M. Williams	38-38	4th	6.5
6-29	Hou.	W	6-1		9	6	Sheets	Reynolds		39-38	4th	6.5
6-30	Hou.	L	4-7		9	13	Oswalt	Levrault		39-39	4th	6.5
7-1	Hou.	L	1-6		7	10	Miller	Rigdon		39-40	4th	7.5
7-2	Hou.	L	4-6		8	11	Redding	Haynes	Wagner	39-41	4th	8.0
7-3	St.L.	W	2-0		9	3	Wright	Kline	Weathers	40-41	T3rd	8.0
7-4	St.L.	L	2-7		7	11	Matthews	Sheets		40-42	4th	8.0
7-5	St.L.	L	2-5		6	13	Kile	Peterson	Timlin	40-43	4th	9.0
7-6	At S.F	L	2-3	(11)	4	11	Zerbe	Leskanic		40-44	4th	10.0
7-7	At S.F	W	13-3		15	5	Haynes	Estes	Buddie	41-44	4th	10.0
7-8	At S.F	W	6-4	(13)	13	12	DeJean	Boehringer		42-44	4th	9.0
7-12	Min.	L	5-13		6	15	Lohse	Haynes		42-45	4th	10.0
7-13	Min.	W	6-3		12	6	Levrault	Radke		43-45	T3rd	9.0
7-14	Min.	L	3-5		5	7	Wells	Weathers	Hawkins	43-46	4th	9.0
7-15	Chi.	L	2-3		5	6	Biddle	Sheets	Foulke	43-47	4th	10.0
7-16	Chi.	L	5-6		8	7	Baldwin	King	Foulke	43-48	4th	10.0
7-17	Chi.	L	4-8		9	12	K. Wells	Haynes	Garland	43-49	4th	11.0
7-18	At L.A.	L	0-5		2	7	Park	Levrault		43-50	4th	12.0
7-19	At L.A.	L	6-8		12	7	Herges	Weathers	Shaw	43-51	4th	12.0
7-20	At S.D.	L	2-11		10	14	Hitchcock	Sheets		43-52	4th	12.0
7-21	At S.D.	L	3-5		8	5	Tollberg	Suzuki	Hoffman	43-53	4th	13.0
7-22	At S.D.	L	0-4		5	7	Jones	Haynes		43-54	4th	13.0
7-23	L.A.	L	1-3		5	11	Park	Levrault	Shaw	43-55	4th	14.0
7-24	L.A.	L	2-7		6	12	Springer	Wright		43-56	4th	15.0
7-25	L.A.	W	4-3		9	5	Weathers	Herges		44-56	4th	15.0
7-27	S.D.	W	8-0		15	6	Haynes	Jones		45-56	4th	14.5
7-28	S.D.	L	2-6		6	9	Williams	Levrault	Hoffman	45-57	4th	14.5
7-29	S.D.	L	5-12		10	14	Jarvis	Wright		45-58	4th	15.5
7-31	Fla.	L	1-5		3	9	Dempster	Sheets		45-59	4th	16.5
8-1	Fla.	L	4-5	(10)	11	13	Almanza	King	Alfonseca	45-60	4th	16.5
8-2	Fla.	W	4-3		7	7	Levrault	Knotts	Leskanic	46-60	4th	15.5
8-3	Atl.	W	3-2	(11)	5	9	Painter	Cabrera		47-60	4th	15.5
8-4	Atl.	L	2-14		4	12	Burkett	Quevedo		47-61	4th	15.5
8-5	Atl.	L	8-12		9	14	Cabrera	Sheets		47-62	4th	15.5
8-7	At N.Y.	L	0-3		2	6	Chen	Haynes	Benitez	47-63	4th	16.5
8-8	At N.Y.	L	4-5		6	6	Trachsel	Levrault	Benitez	47-64	4th	17.5
8-9	At N.Y.	L	3-4		5	8	Leiter	DeJean	White	47-65	4th	17.5
8-10	At Mon.	W	5-1		11	10	Quevedo	Thurman		48-65	4th	17.5
8-11	At Mon.	W	6-0		10	3	Suzuki	Munoz		49-65	4th	16.5
8-12	At Mon.	L	0-5		6	9	Vazquez	Haynes		49-66	4th	16.5
8-14	Phi.	L	4-10		10	10	Coggin	Levrault		49-67	4th	17.0
8-15	Phi.	L	6-8		11	13	Daal	Wright	Mesa	49-68	4th	18.0
8-16	Phi.	W	5-4		7	8	Quevedo	Figueroa	Leskanic	50-68	4th	17.5
8-17	At Cin.	W	5-1		12	8	Suzuki	Davis		51-68	4th	16.5
8-18	At Cin.	W	6-5		9	8	Haynes	Dessens		52-68	4th	16.5
8-19	At Cin.	W	6-4		10	8	Neugebauer	Reyes	DeJean	53-68	4th	16.5
8-20†	At Chi.	L	4-7		9	11	Farnsworth	King	Gordon	53-69		
8-20‡	At Chi.	W	10-2		7	5	Wright	Zambrano		54-69	4th	16.5
8-21	At Chi.	W	3-1		6	5	Quevedo	Cruz	Leskanic	55-69	4th	16.5
8-22	At Chi.	L	3-16		6	17	Tapani	Suzuki		55-70	4th	16.5
8-23	At Chi.	W	8-1		15	5	Suzuki	Tavarez		56-70	4th	16.5
8-24	Col.	L	6-12		11	12	Neagle	Neugebauer		56-71	4th	17.5
8-25	Col.	W	5-4		11	8	DeJean	White	Leskanic	57-71	4th	16.5
8-26	Col.	L	2-3		6	8	Hampton	Quevedo	Powell	57-72	4th	17.5
8-27	Pit.	W	12-5		12	9	Coppinger	Beimel	Buddie	58-72	4th	17.0
8-28	Pit.	L	5-6		11	10	Sauerbeck	Leskanic	Fetters	58-73	4th	18.0
8-29	Pit.	W	9-8		11	12	Levrault	Anderson	Fox	59-73	4th	18.0
8-31	Hou.	L	2-3		8	9	Williams	Wright	Wagner	59-74	4th	19.5
9-1	Hou.	W	4-3		6	6	Fox	Jackson		60-74	4th	18.5
9-2	Hou.	L	0-1		6	7	Miller	Suzuki	Wagner	60-75	4th	19.5
9-3†	At Pit.	W	12-7		11	12	Leiter	Vogelsong		61-75		
9-3‡	At Pit.	L	2-3		6	6	Fetters	Fox		61-76	4th	19.0
9-4	At Pit.	L	2-5		6	6	Arroyo	Levrault	Fetters	61-77	4th	20.0
9-5	At Pit.	L	1-5		3	8	Ritchie	Wright		61-78	4th	21.0
9-6	At Hou.	W	4-3	(10)	8	7	Fox	Wagner	Leskanic	62-78	4th	20.0
9-7	At Hou.	L	3-5		11	5	Miller	Suzuki	Wagner	62-79	4th	21.0
9-8	At Hou.	W	7-2		12	6	Quevedo	Villone		63-79	4th	20.0
9-9	At Hou.	L	0-8		7	11	Oswalt	D'Amico		63-80	4th	21.0
9-10	St.L.	L	0-8		9	9	Kile	Wright	Matthews	63-81	4th	21.5
9-17	At St.L.	L	1-2		4	6	Smith	Quevedo	Kline	63-82	4th	22.0
9-18	At St.L.	L	4-9		8	10	Hermanson	Wright		63-83	4th	23.0
9-19	At St.L.	L	2-8		9	10	Morris	D'Amico		63-84	4th	24.0
9-21	Cin.	L	2-5		8	6	Davis	Suzuki	Graves	63-85	4th	24.5
9-22	Cin.	L	1-3		6	5	Acevedo	Quevedo	Graves	63-86	4th	25.5
9-23	Cin.	W	6-3		8	7	Wright	Dessens	Leskanic	64-86	4th	25.5
9-25	At Ari.	W	9-4		12	9	D'Amico	Lopez		65-86	4th	25.0
9-26	At Ari.	L	9-15		9	18	Witt	Buddie		65-87	4th	25.0

Date	Opp.	Res.	Score	(inn.*)	Hits	Opp. hits	Winning pitcher	Losing pitcher	Save	Record	Pos.	GB
9-27	At Ari.	L	11-13		14	16	Johnson	Quevedo	Kim	65-88	4th	26.0
9-28	At Col.	L	5-6		8	12	Powell	Leskanic		65-89	4th	26.0
9-29	At Col.	L	12-14		14	16	Speier	Haynes	Jimenez	65-90	4th	26.0
9-30	At Col.	L	0-10		5	15	Thomson	D'Amico		65-91	T4th	26.0
10-2	St.L.	L	1-5		4	13	Kile	Sheets		65-92	5th	26.0
10-3	St.L.	W	9-7		15	15	Wright	Smith	Fox	66-92	T4th	25.0
10-4	St.L.	L	3-10		6	11	Morris	Haynes		66-93	T4th	26.0
10-5	Ari.	L	0-5		3	10	Lopez	Levrault		66-94	5th	26.0
10-6	Ari.	W	5-4		9	10	Fox	Sabel		67-94	4th	26.0
10-7	Ari.	W	15-5		16	11	Sheets	Knott		68-94	4th	25.0

Monthly records: April (13-11), May (15-13), June (11-15), July (6-20), August (14-15), September (6-17), October (3-3).
*Innings, if other than nine. †First game of a doubleheader. ‡Second game of a doubleheader.

HIGHLIGHTS

High point: The Brewers swept a three-game series against the first-place Cubs at Wrigley Field June 22-24, which put them just two games out of first place. The Brewers' pitching staff gave up just four runs in three games.

Low point: Fading in late June and early July, the season began to collapse on July 14, when the Brewers dropped the first of 11 straight games and fell completely out of the race.

Turning point: After sweeping the Cubs at Wrigley Field, the Brewers had a golden chance to get closer to first place with a four-game set in Pittsburgh, but instead of pounding the hapless Pirates, the Brewers dropped all four games.

Most valuable player: Richie Sexson showed the Brewers that the 2000 season wasn't a fluke. Sexson hit .271 with 125 RBIs and tied a franchise record held by Gorman Thomas with 45 home runs.

Most valuable pitcher: Ben Sheets went 10-5 with a 3.59 ERA in the first half of the season and pitched in the All-Star Game. A sore shoulder later caused Sheets to miss more than a month.

Most improved player: Jose Hernandez. The move from third base to shortstop really helped him. Only Rich Aurilia had more home runs among N.L. shortstops, and Hernandez was excellent on the defensive end.

Most pleasant surprise: Chad Fox. After missing two seasons with arm and elbow problems, Fox joined the club in late April and quickly became one of the top setup men in the N.L. He was 5-2 with a 1.89 ERA and 20 holds.

Key injuries: None of the Brewers' top five starters were able to make all their starts. Injuries to Jeff D'Amico, Paul Rigdon, Jimmy Haynes, Ben Sheets and Nick Neugebauer hurt the rotation. ... The biggest injury disappointment was Jeffrey Hammonds, who played in only 49 games. ... Geoff Jenkins missed significant time with a variety of injuries and

Tyler Houston hardly played after the All-Star Game because of a stress fracture in his foot. ... Mark Loretta missed the first month of the season with torn ligaments in his thumb.

Notable: The free-swinging Brewers set a Major League record for strikeouts with 1,399. As a team, they had more strikeouts than hits (1,378). ... The bullpen led the league in ERA for much of the season but tired in the second half when the arms were overworked.

—EMMETT PROSSER

RECORDS

2001 regular-season record: 68-94 (4th in N.L. Central); 36-45 at home; 32-49 on road; 15-15 vs. N.L. East; 37-47 vs. N.L. Central; 11-22 vs. N.L. West; 5-10 vs. A.L.; 14-20 vs. lefthanded starters; 54-74 vs. righthanded starters; 64-92 on grass; 4-2 on turf; 29-31 in daytime; 39-63 at night; 13-25 in one-run games; 5-7 in extra-inning games; 0-0-2 in doubleheaders.

Team record past five years: 367-441 (.454, ranks 13th in league in that span).

TEAM LEADERS

Batting average: Richie Sexson (.271).
At-bats: Richie Sexson (598).
Runs: Jeromy Burnitz (104).
Hits: Richie Sexson (162).
Total Bases: Richie Sexson (327).
Doubles: Jeromy Burnitz (32).
Triples: Jeromy Burnitz (4).
Home runs: Richie Sexson (45).
Runs batted in: Richie Sexson (125).
Stolen bases: Devon White (18).
Slugging percentage: Richie Sexson (.547).
On-base percentage: Jeromy Burnitz (.347).
Wins: Ben Sheets, Jamey Wright (11).
Earned-run average: Jimmy Haynes (4.85).

Complete games: Allen Levrault, Ben Sheets, Jamey Wright (1).
Shutouts: Ben Sheets, Jamey Wright (1).
Saves: Curtis Leskanic (17).
Innings pitched: Jamey Wright (194.2).
Strikeouts: Jamey Wright (129).

GAMES BY POSITION

Catcher: Henry Blanco 102, Raul Casanova 56, Kevin L. Brown 16, Jesse Levis 11.
First base: Richie Sexson 158, Angel Echevarria 10, Tyler Houston 3, Mark Sweeney 2.
Second base: Ronnie Belliard 96, Mark Loretta 52, Luis Lopez 15, Elvis Pena 11.
Third base: Tyler Houston 62, Luis Lopez 46, Mark Loretta 39, Mike Coolbaugh 27, Lou Collier 16, Tony Fernandez 13.
Shortstop: Jose Hernandez 150, Luis Lopez 17, Mark Loretta 9, Mike Coolbaugh 3.
Outfield: Jeromy Burnitz 153, Geoff Jenkins 104, Devon White 100, James Mouton 53, Jeffrey Hammonds 46, Angel Echevarria 23, Lou Collier 23, Mark Sweeney 20, Alex Sanchez 19, Jose Hernandez 2, Robert Perez 1.
Designated hitter: Mark Loretta 4, Raul Casanova 2, James Mouton 1, Angel Echevarria 1, Lou Collier 1.

TOP DRAFT CHOICES

1. **Mike Jones,** RHP, Thunderbird H.S., Phoenix.
2. **J.J. Hardy,** SS, Sabino H.S., Tucson.
3. **Jon Steitz,** RHP, Yale University.
4. **Brad Nelson,** 1B, Bishop Garrigan H.S., Algona, Iowa.
5. **Judd Richardson,** RHP, Miami (O.) U.
6. **Calvin Carpenter,** RHP, Natchitoches (La.) Central H.S.
7. **Taylor McCormack,** 3B, Dunedin (Fla.) H.S.
8. **Brandon Gemoll,** 1B, Fresno State U.
9. **Dennis Sarfate,** RHP, Chandler-Gilbert (Ariz.) C.C.
10. **Greg Moreira,** RHP, Lake Brantley H.S., Apopka, Fla.

MONTREAL EXPOS
NATIONAL LEAGUE EAST DIVISION

2002 SEASON Montreal Expos

Expos schedule
Home games shaded
D—Day game (games starting before 5 p.m.)
All-Star Game at Milwaukee
Subject to changes.

April

SUN	MON	TUE	WED	THU	FRI	SAT
	1	2 FLA	3 FLA	4 FLA	5 CIN	6 D CIN
7 CIN	8 D FLA	9	10 FLA	11 FLA	12 NYM	13 D NYM
14 D NYM	15 CUB	16 CUB	17 CUB	18 NYM	19 NYM	20 D NYM
21 NYM	22	23 MIL	24 MIL	25 MIL	26 STL	27 D STL
28 STL	29	30 HOU				

May

SUN	MON	TUE	WED	THU	FRI	SAT
			1 HOU	2 D HOU	3 ARI	4 ARI
5 ARI	6 D	7 COL	8 COL	9 COL	10 SF	11 SF
12 SF	13	14 SF	15 SD	16 SD	17 LA	18 LA
19 D LA	20	21 ATL	22 ATL	23	24 PHI	25 PHI
26 D PHI	27 D ATL	28 ATL	29 ATL	30 ATL	31 PHI	

June

SUN	MON	TUE	WED	THU	FRI	SAT
						1 PHI
2 D PHI	3 PIT	4 PIT	5 PIT	6	7 CWS	8 D CWS
9 D CWS	10 DET	11 DET	12 DET	13	14 TOR	15 TOR
16 D TOR	17	18 KC	19 KC	20 KC	21 CLE	22 CLE
23 D CLE	24	25 PIT	26 PIT	27 PIT	28 TOR	29 D TOR
30 D TOR						

July

SUN	MON	TUE	WED	THU	FRI	SAT
	1 ATL	2 ATL	3 ATL	4 PHI	5 PHI	6 PHI
7 D PHI	8	9 *	10	11 ATL	12 ATL	13 ATL
14 ATL	15 PHI	16 PHI	17 NYM	18 NYM	19 FLA	20 FLA
21 D FLA	22 NYM	23 NYM	24 NYM	25 FLA	26 FLA	27 FLA
28 D FLA	29	30 ARI	31 ARI			

August

SUN	MON	TUE	WED	THU	FRI	SAT
				1 ARI	2 HOU	3 HOU
4 D HOU	5	6 STL	7 STL	8 STL	9 MIL	10 MIL
11 MIL	12	13 LA	14 LA	15 LA	16 SD	17 SD
18 D SD	19 D SD	20 COL	21 COL	22 COL	23 SF	24 D SF
25 SF	26	27 PHI	28 PHI	29 PHI	30 ATL	31 ATL

September

SUN	MON	TUE	WED	THU	FRI	SAT
1 ATL	2 D PHI	3 PHI	4 PHI	5 PHI	6 D ATL	7 ATL
8 D ATL	9 CUB	10 CUB	11 D CUB	12 NYM	13 NYM	14 NYM
15 D NYM	16	17 FLA	18 FLA	19 FLA	20 NYM	21 D NYM
22 D NYM	23	24 FLA	25 FLA	26 FLA	27 CIN	28 CIN
29 D CIN	30					

CLUB DIRECTORY

Chairman, CEO & managing general partner
Jeffrey H. Loria
Executive vice president
David P. Samson
V.p., dir. of international operations
Fred Ferreira
Interim general manager
Larry Beinfest
Director, scouting
Jim Fleming
Director, player development
Tony LaCava
Assistant director, scouting
Gregg Leonard
Assistant director, player development
Adam Wogan
Assistant dir., international scouting
Randy Kierce
Coord., conditioning & team travel
Sean Cunningham
Vice president & CFO
Michel Bussiere
V.p., dev. & stadium operations
Claude Delorme
Director, media & community relations
P.J. Loyello
Director, media services
Monique Giroux

Director, broadcast activities & web site editor
Marc Griffin
Director, promotions & special events
Gina Hackl
Director, ticket sales
John Di Terlizzi
Dir., administration, sales & marketing
Chantal Dalpe
Dir., management information systems
Yves Poulin
Team orthopedist
Dr. Larry Coughlin
Team physician
Dr. Mike Thomassin
Minor league training & rehab coord.
Paul Fournier
Major League advance scout
Joe Moeller
Major League scout
Tommy Thompson
Scouts
Alex Agostino, Matt Anderson, Carlos Berroa, Darrell Brown, Dennis Cardoza, Enrique Constante, Robby Corsaro, Dave Dangler, Hal DeBerry, Scot Engler, John Hughes, John Martin, Joel Matthews, Bob Oldis, Steve Payne, Rene Picota, Pat Puccinelli, Joel Smith, Scott Stanley

MINOR LEAGUE AFFILIATES

Class	Team	League	Manager
AAA	Ottawa	International	Tim Leiper
AA	Harrisburg	Eastern	Eric Fox
A	Clinton	Midwest	Steve Phillips
A	Jupiter	Florida State	Luis Dorante
A	Vermont	New York-Pennsylvania	Johnny Rodriguez
Rookie	Gulf Coast Expos	Gulf Coast	Jesus Campos

BROADCAST INFORMATION

Radio: KCAC and Team 990.
Cable TV: TSN, RDS (French).

SPRING TRAINING

Ballpark (city): Roger Dean Stadium (Jupiter, Fla.).
Ticket information: 561-775-1818.

Follow the Expos all season at: www.sportingnews.com/baseball/teams/expos/

SPRING TRAINING ROSTER

Manager—Jeff Torborg (1).
Coaches—Brad Arnsberg (38), Pierre Arsenault (67), Jeff Cox (26), Ozzie Guillen (13), Perry Hill (7), Rick Renick (44), Pat Roessler (6).

No.	PITCHERS	B/T	Ht./Wt.	Born	2001 clubs
36	Armas, Tony	R/R	6-4/205	4-29-78	Montreal
	Bridges, Donnie	R/R	6-4/195	12-10-78	Jupiter, Harrisburg, Ottawa
	Chiavacci, Ron	R/R	6-2/220	9-5-77	Harrisburg
41	Cubillan, Darwin	R/R	6-2/170	11-15-74	Oklahoma, Ottawa, Montreal
	Day, Zach	R/R	6-4/185	6-15-78	Akron, Buffalo, Ottawa
48	Downs, Scott	L/L	6-2/190	3-17-76	DID NOT PLAY
	Good, Eric	R/L	6-3/185	4-10-80	Jupiter
37	Lloyd, Graeme	L/L	6-7/225	4-9-67	Montreal
	Mattes, Troy	R/R	6-7/185	8-26-75	Ottawa, Montreal
40	Mota, Guillermo	R/R	6-4/205	7-25-73	Montreal, Ottawa
53	Ohka, Tomo	R/R	6-1/179	3-18-76	Boston, Pawtucket, Montreal
45	Pavano, Carl	R/R	6-5/230	1-8-76	Jupiter, Ottawa, Montreal
68	Reames, Britt	R/R	5-11/170	8-19-73	Montreal, Ottawa
	Stewart, Scott	R/L	6-2/225	8-14-75	Montreal, Ottawa
20	Strickland, Scott	R/R	5-11/180	4-26-76	Montreal
52	Tucker, T.J.	R/R	6-3/245	8-20-78	Harrisburg, Ottawa
23	Vazquez, Javier	R/R	6-2/195	7-25-76	Montreal
21	Yoshii, Masato	R/R	6-2/210	4-20-65	Montreal

No.	CATCHERS	B/T	Ht./Wt.	Born	2001 clubs
39	Schneider, Brian	L/R	6-1/180	11-26-76	Ottawa, Montreal

No.	INFIELDERS	B/T	Ht./Wt.	Born	2001 clubs
5	Barrett, Michael	R/R	6-2/200	10-22-76	Montreal
11	Blum, Geoff	B/R	6-3/195	4-26-73	Montreal
18	Cabrera, Orlando	R/R	5-10/175	11-2-74	Montreal
2	De La Rosa, Tomas	R/R	5-10/165	1-28-78	Ottawa, Montreal
	Hodges, Scott	L/R	6-0/185	12-26-78	Harrisburg
	Mateo, Henry	B/R	5-11/170	10-14-76	Ottawa, Montreal
12	Mordecai, Mike	R/R	5-10/185	12-13-67	Montreal
9	Stevens, Lee	L/L	6-4/219	7-10-67	Montreal
23	Tatis, Fernando	R/R	5-10/180	1-1-75	Montreal
46	Tracy, Andy	L/L	6-3/220	12-11-73	Montreal, Ottawa
	Valdez, Wilson	R/R	5-11/160	5-20-80	Jupiter
3	Vidro, Jose	B/R	5-11/190	8-27-74	Montreal

No.	OUTFIELDERS	B/T	Ht./Wt.	Born	2001 clubs
33	Bergeron, Peter	L/R	6-0/185	11-9-77	Ottawa, Montreal
	Calloway, Ron	L/L	6-0/190	9-4-76	Harrisburg, Ottawa
	Cepicky, Matt	L/R	6-2/215	11-10-77	Harrisburg
27	Guerrero, Vladimir	R/R	6-3/205	2-9-76	Montreal
	Pascucci, Val	R/R	6-6/235	11-17-78	Harrisburg
	Ruan, Wilken	R/R	6-0/170	11-18-79	Jupiter, Harrisburg
	Wilkerson, Brad	L/L	6-0/200	6-1-77	Montreal, Ottawa, Jupiter

BALLPARK INFORMATION

Ballpark (capacity, surface)
Olympic Stadium (46,620, artificial)
Address
P.O. Box 500, Station M
Montreal, Que. H1V 3P2
Official website
www.montrealexpos.com
Business phone
514-253-3434
Ticket information
800-GO-EXPOS
Ticket prices
$36 (VIP box seats)
$26 (box seats)
$16 (terrace)
$8 (general admission)
Field dimensions (from home plate)
To left field at foul line, 325 feet
To center field, 404 feet
To right field at foul line, 325 feet
First game played
April 15, 1977 (Phillies 7, Expos 2)

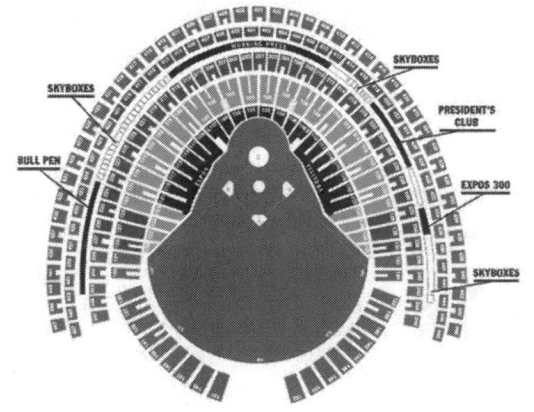

2002 SEASON *Montreal Expos*

Date	Opp.	Res.	Score	(inn.*)	Hits	Opp. hits	Winning pitcher	Losing pitcher	Save	Record	Pos.	GB
4-2	At Chi.	W	5-4	(10)	10	9	Lloyd	Fyhrie	Urbina	1-0	T1st	...
4-4	At Chi.	W	3-2		9	8	Reames	Wood	Urbina	2-0	T1st	0.5
4-5	At Chi.	L	1-2		3	4	Tapani	Armas	Fassero	2-1	T2nd	1.0
4-6	N.Y.	W	10-6		13	9	Thurman	Rose		3-1	T1st	...
4-7	N.Y.	W	10-0		10	4	Vazquez	Trachsel		4-1	1st	+1.0
4-8	N.Y.	W	5-2		10	10	Peters	Leiter	Urbina	5-1	1st	+1.0
4-9	Chi.	W	7-5		8	9	Lloyd	Aybar	Urbina	6-1	1st	+1.0
4-10	Chi.	L	2-4		9	5	Tapani	Armas	Fassero	6-2	T1st	...
4-11	Chi.	L	2-4		7	8	Tavarez	Thurman	Fassero	6-3	2nd	0.5
4-13	Fla.	L	3-9		6	13	Dempster	Vazquez		6-4	2nd	0.5
4-14	Fla.	W	8-2		14	8	Reames	Clement		7-4	2nd	0.5
4-15	Fla.	L	3-6		7	9	Grilli	Armas	Alfonseca	7-5	2nd	0.5
4-16	At N.Y.	L	3-4		7	7	Reed	Thurman	Benitez	7-6	2nd	1.0
4-17	At N.Y.	L	0-4		6	10	Rusch	Peters		7-7	2nd	2.0
4-18	At N.Y.	W	7-1		12	2	Vazquez	Trachsel		8-7	2nd	0.5
4-19	At Fla.	L	2-5		3	8	Looper	Strickland	Alfonseca	8-8	T2nd	1.0
4-20	At Fla.	L	1-5		5	8	Grilli	Armas		8-9	T2nd	2.0
4-21	At Fla.	L	0-5		4	7	Penny	Thurman		8-10	T3rd	3.0
4-22	At Fla.	W	6-2		9	7	Peters	Nunez		9-10	2nd	3.0
4-24	At St.L.	L	2-7		8	14	Kile	Vazquez		9-11	2nd	4.5
4-25	At St.L.	L	2-5		5	8	An. Benes	Reames	Stechschulte	9-12	3rd	5.5
4-26	At St.L.	W	4-3	(15)	14	16	Yoshii	James		10-12	2nd	4.5
4-27	At Mil.	W	6-1		8	5	Thurman	Leiter		11-12	2nd	3.5
4-28	At Mil.	L	4-8		9	9	Sheets	Peters		11-13	3rd	3.5
4-29	At Mil.	L	0-10		2	14	Wright	Vazquez		11-14	3rd	3.5
5-1	Ari.	L	3-8		9	10	Schilling	Reames		11-15	T4th	4.5
5-2	Ari.	W	4-3		4	5	Armas	Anderson	Lloyd	12-15	3rd	3.5
5-3	Ari.	L	1-2		3	6	Kim	Lloyd	Prinz	12-16	3rd	4.5
5-4	Hou.	L	4-8		6	12	Miller	Vazquez		12-17	5th	4.5
5-5	Hou.	L	3-4		8	3	Reynolds	Reames	Wagner	12-18	5th	5.5
5-6	Hou.	L	7-13		16	18	Elarton	Telford		12-19	5th	6.5
5-7	At S.F	L	2-6		7	5	Ortiz	Armas	Fultz	12-20	5th	7.5
5-8	At S.F	L	1-9		6	12	Estes	Thurman		12-21	5th	8.5
5-9	At S.F	W	8-0		11	7	Vazquez	Hernandez		13-21	5th	7.5
5-10	At S.F	L	0-13		6	18	Rueter	Reames		13-22	5th	8.0
5-11	At Col.	L	4-13		7	16	Neagle	Peters		13-23	5th	9.0
5-12	At Col.	W	8-4		11	6	Armas	Thomson		14-23	5th	9.0
5-13	At Col.	W	14-10		15	15	Lloyd	Astacio		15-23	4th	8.0
5-15	L.A.	W	2-0		6	2	Vazquez	Park		16-23	4th	7.0
5-16	L.A.	L	2-7		6	11	Dreifort	Reames		16-24	4th	7.0
5-17	L.A.	W	3-1		5	7	Armas	Gagne	Urbina	17-24	4th	7.0
5-18	S.D.	W	3-1		7	5	Thurman	Jarvis	Urbina	18-24	4th	7.0
5-19	S.D.	L	7-20		13	20	Serrano	Yoshii		18-25	4th	8.0
5-20	S.D.	L	3-5		6	7	Jones	Vazquez	Hoffman	18-26	4th	8.0
5-21	N.Y.	L	3-6		9	10	Rusch	Reames	Benitez	18-27	5th	8.5
5-22	N.Y.	W	3-0		10	9	Armas	Gonzalez	Urbina	19-27	4th	8.0
5-23	N.Y.	L	2-4		8	9	Leiter	Peters	Benitez	19-28	5th	9.5
5-25	At Phi.	L	8-10		13	9	Oropesa	Urbina		19-29	5th	11.0
5-27†	At Phi.	L	5-7		9	12	Brock	Reames	Mesa	19-30		
5-27‡	At Phi.	W	7-3		8	6	Armas	Byrd		20-30	5th	11.0
5-28	At Atl.	L	3-5	(8)	10	8	Smoltz	Yoshii	Rocker	20-31	5th	12.0
5-29	At Atl.	L	4-7		7	8	Perez	Blank	Rocker	20-32	5th	13.0
5-30	At Atl.	W	4-3		10	7	Vazquez	Maddux	Urbina	21-32	5th	13.0
5-31	Phi.	L	2-5		5	12	Cormier	Strickland	Mesa	21-33	5th	14.0
6-1	Phi.	L	2-13		6	13	Chen	Reames		21-34	5th	15.0
6-2	Phi.	W	12-5		14	7	Armas	Wolf		22-34	5th	14.0
6-3	Phi.	W	10-3		16	6	Yoshii	Daal		23-34	5th	13.0
6-5	Atl.	L	1-3		7	9	Maddux	Vazquez	Rocker	23-35	5th	13.0
6-6	Atl.	L	0-2		3	9	Burkett	Irabu	Rocker	23-36	5th	14.0
6-7	Atl.	L	3-4	(11)	8	11	Marquis	Strickland	Ligtenberg	23-37	5th	14.0
6-8	At Bal.	L	0-5		6	9	Towers	Blank		23-38	5th	14.0
6-9	At Bal.	W	4-2		9	8	Lloyd	Ryan	Urbina	24-38	5th	14.0
6-10	At Bal.	L	2-3		6	6	Johnson	Vazquez	Groom	24-39	5th	14.0
6-12	At N.Y.	W	2-1	(12)	6	6	Strickland	Mendoza		25-39	5th	13.0
6-13	At N.Y.	L	3-9		7	11	Clemens	Irabu		25-40	5th	13.0
6-14	At N.Y.	L	6-9		7	12	Keisler	Yoshii	Rivera	25-41	5th	13.0
6-15	Tor.	L	3-9		13	15	Carpenter	Vazquez		25-42	5th	14.0
6-16	Tor.	W	7-2		11	10	Blank	Loaiza		26-42	5th	14.0
6-17	Tor.	W	4-1		8	9	Mota	Quantrill		27-42	5th	13.0
6-18	At N.Y.	L	1-2		6	9	Wendell	Yoshii	Benitez	27-43	5th	13.5
6-19	At N.Y.	L	1-4		5	5	White	Mota	Franco	27-44	5th	13.5
6-20	At N.Y.	L	3-4		5	11	Leiter	Vazquez	Benitez	27-45	5th	14.5
6-21	At N.Y.	W	10-3		14	7	Blank	Appier		28-45	5th	14.5
6-22	At Pit.	W	11-5		10	7	Armas	Schmidt		29-45	5th	13.5

Date	Opp.	Res.	Score	(inn.*)	Hits	Opp. hits	Winning pitcher	Losing pitcher	Save	Record	Pos.	GB
6-23	At Pit.	L	4-7		9	13	Ritchie	Yoshii	M. Williams	29-46	5th	13.5
6-24	At Pit.	W	11-4		16	8	Mattes	Beimel		30-46	5th	13.5
6-25	At Fla.	W	3-1		7	6	Vazquez	Burnett	Urbina	31-46	5th	12.5
6-26	At Fla.	L	0-3		1	10	Penny	Thurman	Alfonseca	31-47	5th	12.5
6-27	At Fla.	L	1-9		4	7	Sanchez	Armas		31-48	5th	13.0
6-29	Pit.	W	12-3		14	5	Mattes	Beimel		32-48	5th	13.5
6-30	Pit.	W	7-6		12	11	Lloyd	M. Williams		33-48	5th	13.5
7-1	Pit.	W	9-3		10	7	Thurman	Anderson		34-48	5th	13.5
7-3	Fla.	L	0-7		4	10	Dempster	Armas		34-49	5th	13.5
7-4	Fla.	W	9-6		15	12	Lloyd	Clement	Urbina	35-49	5th	13.5
7-5	Fla.	W	9-6		15	12	Vazquez	Smith	Urbina	36-49	5th	12.5
7-6	At Tor.	W	10-7		12	8	Lloyd	Quantrill	Urbina	37-49	4th	12.5
7-7	At Tor.	L	8-9	(11)	17	15	Plesac	Strickland		37-50	5th	12.5
7-8	At Tor.	L	3-9		12	12	Michalak	Armas	Quantrill	37-51	5th	13.5
7-12	T.B.	L	0-10		6	14	Sturtze	Mattes		37-52	5th	13.5
7-13	T.B.	W	6-2		9	4	Vazquez	Kennedy		38-52	5th	13.5
7-14	T.B.	W	10-2		9	11	Armas	Rekar		39-52	5th	12.5
7-15	Bos.	L	5-8		8	14	Nomo	Thurman	Lowe	39-53	5th	13.5
7-16	Bos.	L	5-6		9	13	Pichardo	Lloyd	Lowe	39-54	5th	13.5
7-17	Bos.	W	11-7		13	16	Mattes	Wakefield		40-54	5th	12.5
7-18	Phi.	W	7-6		12	8	Urbina	Cormier		41-54	5th	12.5
7-19	Phi.	W	5-2		9	7	Strickland	Cormier	Urbina	42-54	5th	12.5
7-20	At Atl.	W	6-3		12	8	Thurman	Millwood	Urbina	43-54	5th	11.5
7-21	At Atl.	L	1-2	(10)	6	9	Cabrera	Lloyd		43-55	5th	12.5
7-22	At Atl.	L	2-8		9	14	Maddux	Mattes		43-56	5th	13.5
7-23	At Phi.	W	3-0		9	7	Vazquez	Daal		44-56	5th	12.5
7-24	At Phi.	L	2-10		7	14	Figueroa	Armas		44-57	5th	12.5
7-25	At Phi.	L	4-8		8	13	Person	Thurman		44-58	5th	13.5
7-26	Atl.	W	3-2	(10)	10	6	Urbina	Reed		45-58	5th	12.5
7-27	Atl.	L	3-7		7	11	Maddux	Mattes		45-59	5th	13.5
7-28	Atl.	L	5-10		7	13	Glavine	Vazquez		45-60	5th	14.5
7-29	Atl.	L	1-8		5	5	Burkett	Armas		45-61	5th	15.5
7-31	At Ari.	L	1-3		8	7	Schilling	Munoz		45-62	5th	15.5
8-1	At Ari.	W	8-5		11	11	Thurman	Anderson	Stewart	46-62	5th	14.5
8-2	At Ari.	W	1-0		5	3	Vazquez	Lopez	Stewart	47-62	5th	14.5
8-3	At Hou.	L	2-6		7	13	Reynolds	Armas		47-63	5th	14.5
8-4	At Hou.	L	1-4		3	6	Oswalt	Ohka		47-64	5th	15.5
8-5	At Hou.	L	1-4		7	12	Villone	Munoz	Wagner	47-65	5th	16.5
8-7	St.L.	L	1-3		4	6	Kile	Vazquez		47-66	5th	17.5
8-8	St.L.	W	6-5	(11)	10	11	Yoshii	Hackman		48-66	5th	16.5
8-9	St.L.	L	6-9		12	13	Morris	Ohka		48-67	5th	16.5
8-10	Mil.	L	1-5		10	11	Quevedo	Thurman		48-68	5th	16.5
8-11	Mil.	L	0-6		3	10	Suzuki	Munoz		48-69	5th	16.5
8-12	Mil.	W	5-0		9	6	Vazquez	Haynes		49-69	5th	16.5
8-14	At L.A.	W	4-1		7	5	Lloyd	Shaw		50-69	5th	16.5
8-15	At L.A.	L	1-13		7	20	Carrara	Pavano		50-70	5th	17.5
8-16	At L.A.	W	7-3		10	9	Reames	Trombley		51-70	5th	16.5
8-17	At S.D.	W	4-0		9	4	Vazquez	Lawrence		52-70	5th	15.5
8-18	At S.D.	L	3-4		8	8	Jones	Thurman	Hoffman	52-71	5th	16.5
8-19	At S.D.	W	2-1		6	3	Armas	Herndon	Strickland	53-71	5th	15.5
8-21	S.F	L	2-10		4	13	Ortiz	Pavano		53-72	5th	15.5
8-22	S.F	W	7-1		9	5	Vazquez	Estes		54-72	5th	15.5
8-23	S.F	L	5-10		8	16	Rodriguez	Lloyd		54-73	5th	16.5
8-24	Cin.	W	6-4		8	10	Stewart	Brower	Strickland	55-73	5th	15.5
8-25	Cin.	L	2-4		7	11	Reitsma	Thurman	Graves	55-74	5th	15.5
8-26	Cin.	L	4-17		8	20	Acevedo	Munoz		55-75	5th	16.5
8-28	At Atl.	W	7-0		9	5	Vazquez	Millwood		56-75	5th	15.0
8-29	At Atl.	L	3-5		8	7	Glavine	Armas	Smoltz	56-76	5th	16.0
8-30	At Atl.	W	4-2		8	7	Ohka	Marquis	Strickland	57-76	5th	15.0
8-31	At Phi.	W	5-1		14	3	Thurman	Figueroa	Strickland	58-76	5th	14.0
9-1	At Phi.	L	1-4		4	10	Person	Pavano	Mesa	58-77	5th	14.0
9-2	At Phi.	W	6-2		12	5	Vazquez	Mesa		59-77	5th	14.0
9-3	Atl.	L	0-5		7	10	Glavine	Ohka		59-78	5th	15.0
9-4	Atl.	L	2-3		6	7	Karsay	Strickland	Smoltz	59-79	5th	16.0
9-5	Atl.	W	10-4		16	9	Thurman	Burkett		60-79	5th	15.0
9-6	Phi.	L	0-3		4	4	Person	Pavano	Mesa	60-80	5th	15.5
9-7	Phi.	W	4-2		6	4	Vazquez	Duckworth	Stewart	61-80	5th	15.5
9-8	Phi.	L	0-6		6	18	Wolf	Ohka		61-81	5th	16.5
9-9	Phi.	L	4-12		7	10	Politte	Lloyd		61-82	5th	17.5
9-17	Fla.	L	6-10		9	18	Bones	Mota		61-83	5th	17.5
9-18	Fla.	L	1-3		10	7	Penny	Thurman	Alfonseca	61-84	5th	17.5
9-19	Fla.	W	5-2		7	7	Pavano	Beckett	Strickland	62-84	5th	16.5
9-20	Col.	W	8-3		11	8	Lloyd	Powell		63-84	5th	16.5
9-21	Col.	L	9-11	(11)	13	14	Davis	Mota		63-85	5th	16.5
9-22	Col.	W	3-1		3	6	Yoshii	Elarton	Strickland	64-85	5th	15.5
9-23	Col.	L	3-5		8	11	Speier	Stewart	Jimenez	64-86	5th	16.5
9-25	N.Y.	L	0-2		4	5	Appier	Pavano	Benitez	64-87	5th	17.0
9-26	N.Y.	L	2-5		9	7	Rusch	Armas	Benitez	64-88	5th	18.0

Date	Opp.	Res.	Score	(inn.*)	Hits	Opp. hits	Winning pitcher	Losing pitcher	Save	Record	Pos.	GB
9-27	N.Y.	L	6-12		10	19	White	Strickland		64-89	5th	18.0
9-28	At Cin.	W	7-6		12	14	Stewart	Graves	Strickland	65-89	5th	18.0
9-29	At Cin.	L	4-7		11	15	Dessens	Yoshii	Graves	65-90	5th	19.0
9-30	At Cin.	L	4-5		13	9	Sullivan	Eischen	Graves	65-91	5th	19.0
10-2	At Fla.	L	3-4		6	7	Burnett	Armas	Looper	65-92	5th	19.0
10-3	At Fla.	W	2-0		9	4	Stewart	Acevedo	Strickland	66-92	5th	19.0
10-4	At Fla.	L	2-6		6	12	Penny	Yoshii		66-93	5th	20.0
10-5	At N.Y.	W	8-6		11	11	Thurman	Leiter	Strickland	67-93	5th	20.0
10-6	At N.Y.	L	0-4		6	11	Appier	Pavano		67-94	5th	21.0
10-7	At N.Y.	W	5-0		7	3	Reames	Rusch		68-94	5th	20.0

Monthly records: April (11-14), May (10-19), June (12-15), July (12-14), August (13-14), September (7-15), October (3-3).
*Innings, if other than nine. †First game of a doubleheader. ‡Second game of a doubleheader.

HIGHLIGHTS

High point: April 6. A crowd of 45,183 was on hand for one of the most emotional moments in recent Expos history: the dramatic introduction of longtime Expos star Tim Raines Sr.—back again at age 41—as the starting left fielder. The Expos trailed at one point, 4-0, but ended up winning 10-6.

Low point: The last week of spring training, when Scott Downs underwent Tommy John surgery, and it was announced that both Carl Pavano and Hideki Irabu would stay behind in extended spring, both having had setbacks in their recovery from elbow surgery. Three-fifths of the expected starting rotation went out of commission in one fell swoop.

Turning point: After manager Felipe Alou was fired on May 31 and replaced by Jeff Torborg. There was no doubt the clubhouse atmosphere was more upbeat. The players said they loved playing for Torborg.

Most valuable player: Vladimir Guerrero didn't have the best year of his career, but he was still the best player on the team. He ended up with 34 homers, 108 RBIs, a .307 average and 37 stolen bases.

Most valuable pitcher: Javier Vazquez struggled with his command in the first half. After the All-Star break, he was one of the best pitchers in baseball with a 9-2 record and an ERA of 1.60.

Most improved player: Everyone knew Orlando Cabrera was going to be a decent player, but he posted career highs in every offensive category and drove in 95 runs as a surprisingly effective cleanup hitter.

Most pleasant surprise: Scott Stewart made the club out of spring training as the third lefty in the bullpen. A May ERA of 15.19 put him on the disabled list, for his head more than his sore thumb, and earned him a stern talking-to from pitching coach Brad Arnsberg. Stewart listened. He didn't allow a run in August and his post All-Star ERA was 2.08.

Key injuries: Losing Fernando Tatis hurt a lot. ... Jose Vidro missed nearly 40 games with a forearm muscle tear and a concussion. ... Pavano came back at the end of the season and showed just how much he was missed.

Notable: Vladimir Guerrero had 24 intentional walks, but grounded into 24 double plays ... Lee Stevens struck out 157 times, nearly twice as often as anyone else on the team.

—STEPHANIE MYLES

RECORDS

2001 regular-season record: 68-94 (5th in N.L. East); 34-47 at home; 34-47 on road; 30-46 vs. N.L. East; 14-22 vs. N.L. Central; 16-16 vs. N.L. West; 8-10 vs. A.L.; 21-25 vs. lefthanded starters; 47-69 vs. righthanded starters; 29-40 on grass; 39-54 on turf; 23-23 in daytime; 45-71 at night; 13-15 in one-run games; 5-4 in extra-inning games; 0-0-1 in doubleheaders.

Team record past five years: 346-464 (.427, ranks 16th in league in that span).

TEAM LEADERS

Batting average: Jose Vidro (.319).
At-bats: Orlando Cabrera (626).
Runs: Vladimir Guerrero (107).
Hits: Vladimir Guerrero (184).
Total Bases: Vladimir Guerrero (339).
Doubles: Vladimir Guerrero (45).
Triples: Orlando Cabrera (6).
Home runs: Vladimir Guerrero (34).
Runs batted in: Vladimir Guerrero (108).
Stolen bases: Vladimir Guerrero (37).
Slugging percentage: Vladimir Guerrero (.566).
On-base percentage: Vladimir Guerrero (.377).
Wins: Javier Vazquez (16).
Earned-run average: Javier Vazquez (3.42).
Complete games: Javier Vazquez (5).

Shutouts: Javier Vazquez (3).
Saves: Ugueth Urbina (15).
Innings pitched: Javier Vazquez (223.2).
Strikeouts: Javier Vazquez (208).

GAMES BY POSITION

Catcher: Michael Barrett 131, Randy Knorr 27, Brian Schneider 14, Mike Mordecai 1, Sandy Martinez 1.
First base: Lee Stevens 152, Geoff Blum 14, Fernando Seguignol 7, Andy Tracy 3, Mike Mordecai 1, Ryan Minor 1, Mark Smith 1.
Second base: Jose Vidro 121, Mike Mordecai 32, Geoff Blum 25, Henry Mateo 2.
Third base: Geoff Blum 72, Mike Mordecai 42, Fernando Tatis 41, Ryan Minor 24, Andy Tracy 11.
Shortstop: Orlando Cabrera 162, Mike Mordecai 4, Geoff Blum 4.
Outfield: Vladimir Guerrero 158, Peter Bergeron 101, Milton Bradley 65, Mark Smith 60, Brad Wilkerson 38, Geoff Blum 35, Curtis Pride 23, Terry Jones 22, Tim Raines 20, Rob Ducey 14, Fernando Seguignol 13, Ryan Minor 2, Mike Mordecai 1.
Designated hitter: Ryan Minor 3, Rob Ducey 3, Jose Vidro 2, Andy Tracy 2, Curtis Pride 2, Mike Mordecai 1.

TOP DRAFT CHOICES

1. **Josh Karp,** RHP, UCLA.
2. **Donald Levinski,** RHP, Weimar (Tex.) H.S.
3. **Mike Hinckley,** LHP, Moore (Okla.) H.S.
4. **Nick Long,** RHP, Shaw H.S., Columbus, Ga.
5. **Reggie Fitzpatrick,** OF, McNair H.S., Atlanta.
6. **Josh Labandiera,** SS, Fresno State U.
7. **Chad Bentz,** LHP, Long Beach State University.
8. **Greg Thissen,** 3B, Triton (Ill.) J.C.
9. **Shawn Norris,** 3B, Cal State Fullerton.
10. **Eddie Diaz,** RHP, Colonial H.S., Orlando.

NEW YORK METS
NATIONAL LEAGUE EAST DIVISION

Mets schedule
Home games shaded
D—Day game (games starting before 5 p.m.)
All-Star Game at Milwaukee
Subject to changes

April

SUN	MON	TUE	WED	THU	FRI	SAT
	1 D PIT	2	3 D PIT	4 D PIT	5 ATL	6 ATL
7 ATL	8	9 D CUB	10 D CUB	11 D CUB	12 MON	13 D MON
14 MON	15 ATL	16 ATL	17 ATL	18 MON	19 MON	20 D MON
21 MON	22	23 STL	24 STL	25 STL	26 MIL	27 D MIL
28 D MIL	29	30 ARI				

May

SUN	MON	TUE	WED	THU	FRI	SAT
		1 ARI	2 ARI	3 HOU	4 HOU	
5 D HOU	6	7 SF	8 SF	9 SF	10 COL	11 D COL
12 D COL	13 LA	14 LA	15 LA	16 SD	17 SD	18 SD
19 D SD	20	21 PHI	22 PHI	23 D PHI	24 FLA	25 D FLA
26 FLA	27 D PHI	28 PHI	29 PHI	30	31 FLA	

June

SUN	MON	TUE	WED	THU	FRI	SAT
						1 FLA
2 D FLA	3 ATL	4 ATL	5 ATL	6 ATL	7 D CLE	8 CLE
9 D CLE	10 CWS	11 CWS	12 CWS	13	14 NYY	15 NYY
16 NYY	17	18 MIN	19 MIN	20 MIN	21 KC	22 KC
23 KC	24 ATL	25 ATL	26 ATL	27 ATL	28 NYY	29 D NYY
30 D NYY						

July

SUN	MON	TUE	WED	THU	FRI	SAT
	1 PHI	2 PHI	3 PHI	4 FLA	5 FLA	6 FLA
7 D FLA	8	9 *	10	11 MON	12 PHI	13 PHI
14 PHI	15 D FLA	16 D FLA	17 MON	18 D MON	19 CIN	20 CIN
21 CIN	22 MON	23 MON	24 MON	25	26 CIN	27 CIN
28 D CIN	29	30 HOU	31 HOU			

August

SUN	MON	TUE	WED	THU	FRI	SAT
				1 HOU	2 ARI	3 ARI
4 D ARI	5 D ARI	6 MIL	7 MIL	8 MIL	9 STL	10 STL
11 D STL	12	13 SD	14 SD	15 D SD	16 LA	17 LA
18 D LA	19	20 SF	21 SF	22 SF	23 COL	24 COL
25 D COL	26	27 FLA	28 FLA	29	30 PHI	31 PHI

September

SUN	MON	TUE	WED	THU	FRI	SAT
1 D PHI	2 D FLA	3 FLA	4 FLA	5 FLA	6 PHI	7 PHI
8 D PHI	9 PHI	10 ATL	11 ATL	12 MON	13 MON	14 MON
15 D MON	16	17 CUB	18 CUB	19 CUB	20 MON	21 D MON
22 D MON	23	24 PIT	25 PIT	26 PIT	27 ATL	28 ATL
29 D ATL	30					

2002 SEASON
CLUB DIRECTORY

Chairman of the board
Nelson Doubleday
President and chief executive officer
Fred Wilpon
Directors
Nelson Doubleday, Fred Wilpon, Saul B. Katz, Steve Phillips, Marvin B. Tepper
Special advisor to the board of directors
Richard Cummins
Senior v.p., general manager
Steve Phillips
Special assistant to the g.m.
Fred Wright
Sr. asst. g.m./international scouting dir.
Omar Minaya
Sr. assistant g.m./player personnel
Jim Duquette
Assistant general manager/scouting
Gary LaRocque
Assistant general manager
Carmen Fusco
Assistant director of amateur scouting
Jack Bowen
Assistant director of player personnel
Kevin Morgan
Senior v.p. and treasurer
Harold W. O'Shaughnessy
Senior v.p. of business & legal affairs
David Howard
Vice president, marketing
To be announced
Vice president and consultant
Bob Mandt
V.p., ticket sales and services
Bill Ianniciello
Senior v.p. and consultant
J. Frank Cashen
Director of marketing
Tina Bucciarelli
Director of marketing production
Tim Gunkel
Director of human resources
Shez Jackson
Vice president, general counsel
David Cohen

Director, information services
Dorothy Pope
Director, community outreach
Jill Knee
Vice president of corporate sales
Paul Danforth
Controller
Lennie Labita
Vice president of media relations
Jay Horwitz
Director, ticket operations
Dan DeMato
Manager, customer relations
Joann Galardy
Director of stadium operations
Kevin McCarthy
Director of minor league operations
Kevin Morgan
Club physician
Dr. Andrew Rokito
Club psychologist/E.A.P.
Dr. Allan Lans
Team trainers
Michael Herbst, Scott Lawrenson
Advance scouts
Bruce Benedict, Mike Toomey
Professional scouts
Bruce Benedict, Edwin Bryant, Joe DelliCarri, Dick Gernert, Roland Johnson, Buddy Kerr, Bill Latham, Harry Minor, John Stearns, Fred Wright
Regional scouting supervisors
Gene Kerns, Bob Minor
Scouting supervisors
Quincy Boyd, Jon Bunnell, Larry Chase, Rodney Henderson, Chuck Hensley Jr., Marlin Jones, Dave Lottsfeldt, Fred Mazuca, Marlin McPhail, Randy Milligan, Greg Morhardt, Joe Morlan, Joe Nigro, Jim Reeves, Junior Roman, Bob Rossi, Joe Salermo
National crosscheckers
Paul Fryer, Terry Tripp

MINOR LEAGUE AFFILIATES

Class	Team	League	Manager
AAA	Norfolk	International	Bobby Floyd
AA	Binghamton	Eastern	Howie Freiling
A	Brooklyn	New York-Pennsylvania	Howard Johnson
A	Capital City	South Atlantic	Tony Tijerina
A	St. Lucie	Florida State	Ken Oberkfell
Rookie	Kingsport	Appalachian	Joey Cora

BROADCAST INFORMATION

Radio: WFAN-AM (660).
TV: WPIX-TV (Channel 11).
Cable TV: Fox Sports New York.

SPRING TRAINING

Ballpark (city): Thomas J. White Stadium (Port St. Lucie, Fla.).
Ticket information: 561-871-2115.

Follow the Mets all season at: www.sportingnews.com/baseball/teams/mets/

SPRING TRAINING ROSTER

Manager—Bobby Valentine (2).
Coaches—Dave Engle (53), Matt Galante, Charlie Hough (54), Randy Niemann (52), Tom Robson, Mookie Wilson (1).

No.	PITCHERS	B/T	Ht./Wt.	Born	2001 clubs
	Astacio, Pedro	R/R	6-2/210	11-28-69	Colorado, Houston
	Bacsik, Mike	L/L	6-3/190	11-11-77	Buffalo, Akron, Cleveland
49	Benitez, Armando	R/R	6-4/229	11-3-72	New York N.L.
26	Cammack, Eric	R/R	6-1/180	8-14-75	DID NOT PLAY
	Cerda, Jaime	L/L	6-0/175	10-26-78	St. Lucie, Binghamton, Norfolk
39	Chen, Bruce	L/L	6-2/210	6-19-77	Philadelphia, Reading, Scran./Wilkes-Barre, New York N.L.
	Corey, Mark	R/R	6-3/210	11-16-74	Binghamton, Norfolk, New York N.L.
55	Estes, Shawn	R/L	6-2/195	2-18-73	San Francisco
45	Franco, John	L/L	5-10/185	9-17-60	New York N.L.
66	Gonzalez, Dicky	R/R	5-11/170	10-21-78	Norfolk, New York N.L.
30	Guthrie, Mark	R/L	6-4/215	9-22-65	Oakland
	Komiyama, Saturo	R/R	6-2/195	9-15-65	Yokohama (Japan)
22	Leiter, Al	L/L	6-3/220	10-23-65	New York N.L.
61	Maness, Nick	R/R	6-4/210	10-17-78	Binghamton
	Roberts, Grant	R/R	6-3/205	9-13-77	Norfolk, New York N.L.
48	Rusch, Glendon	L/L	6-1/200	11-7-74	New York N.L.
63	Seo, Jae	R/R	6-1/215	5-24-77	Binghamton, St. Lucie, Norfolk
	Strange, Pat	R/R	6-5/245	8-23-80	Binghamton, Norfolk
29	Trachsel, Steve	R/R	6-4/205	10-31-70	New York N.L., Norfolk
	Walker, Adam	L/L	6-7/205	5-28-76	Reading, Binghamton
	Walker, Tyler	R/R	6-3/255	5-15-76	Norfolk, St. Lucie, Binghamton
49	Weathers, Dave	R/R	6-3/233	9-25-69	Milwaukee, Chicago N.L.
	Yates, Tyler	R/R	6-4/220	8-7-77	Midland, Sacramento

No.	CATCHERS	B/T	Ht./Wt.	Born	2001 clubs
	Phillips, Jason	R/R	6-1/180	9-27-76	Binghamton, New York N.L., Norfolk
31	Piazza, Mike	R/R	6-3/215	9-4-68	New York N.L.
3	Wilson, Vance	R/R	5-11/190	3-17-73	Norfolk, New York N.L.

No.	INFIELDERS	B/T	Ht./Wt.	Born	2001 clubs
13	Alfonzo, Edgardo	R/R	5-11/187	11-8-73	New York N.L., Norfolk
12	Alomar, Roberto	B/R	6-0/185	2-5-68	Cleveland
19	Harris, Lenny	L/R	5-10/220	10-28-64	New York N.L.
10	Ordonez, Rey	R/R	5-9/159	11-11-72	New York N.L.
30	Toca, Jorge	R/R	6-3/220	1-7-75	Norfolk, New York N.L.
42	Vaughn, Mo	L/R	6-1/268	12-15-67	DID NOT PLAY
9	Zeile, Todd	R/R	6-1/200	9-9-65	New York N.L.

No.	OUTFIELDERS	B/T	Ht./Wt.	Born	2001 clubs
50	Agbayani, Benny	R/R	6-0/225	12-28-71	New York N.L., Norfolk
	Cedeno, Roger	B/R	6-1/205	8-16-74	Detroit
	Matthews, Gary Jr.	B/R	6-3/200	8-25-74	Chicago N.L., Pittsburgh
47	McEwing, Joe	R/R	5-11/170	10-19-72	New York N.L.
44	Payton, Jay	R/R	5-10/185	11-22-72	New York N.L., St. Lucie
65	Peoples, Danny	R/R	6-1/207	1-20-75	Buffalo
6	Perez, Timo	L/L	5-9/165	4-8-77	New York N.L., Norfolk
	Snead, Esix	B/R	5-10/175	6-7-76	New Haven

BALLPARK INFORMATION

Ballpark (capacity, surface)
Shea Stadium (56,749, grass)

Address
123-01 Roosevelt Ave.
Flushing, NY 11368

Official website
www.mets.com

Business phone
718-507-METS

Ticket information
718-507-TIXX

Ticket prices
$64 (Metropolitan Club gold, inner baseline box)
$60 (Metropolitan Club)
$43 (inner field box, inner loge box, outer baseline box)
$38 (middle field box)
$33 (outer field box, outer loge box, mezzanine box)
$29 (loge reserved)
$23 (mezzanine reserved, upper box)
$12 (upper reserved, back rows loge and mezzanine)

Field dimensions (from home plate)
To left field at foul line, 338 feet
To center field, 410 feet
To right field at foul line, 338 feet

First game played
April 17, 1964 (Pirates 4, Mets 3)

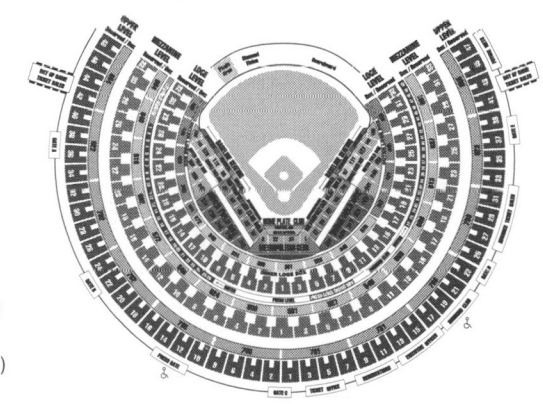

2002 SEASON *New York Mets*

Date	Opp.	Res.	Score	(inn.*)	Hits	Opp. hits	Winning pitcher	Losing pitcher	Save	Record	Pos.	GB
4-3	At Atl.	W	6-4	(10)	7	9	Cook	Ligtenberg	Benitez	1-0	T1st	0.5
4-4	At Atl.	L	2-3		6	6	Rocker	Wall		1-1	4th	1.5
4-5	At Atl.	W	7-1		13	3	Reed	Perez		2-1	T2nd	1.0
4-6	At Mon.	L	6-10		9	13	Thurman	Rose		2-2	4th	1.0
4-7	At Mon.	L	0-10		4	10	Vazquez	Trachsel		2-3	4th	2.0
4-8	At Mon.	L	2-5		10	10	Peters	Leiter	Urbina	2-4	T4th	3.0
4-9	Atl.	W	9-4		10	8	Appier	Millwood		3-4	3rd	3.0
4-11	Atl.	L	0-2		1	4	Maddux	Reed	Rocker	3-5	4th	3.0
4-12	Atl.	W	1-0	(10)	6	6	Benitez	Ligtenberg		4-5	3rd	2.5
4-13	Cin.	L	2-3		10	5	O. Fernandez	Trachsel	Graves	4-6	4th	2.5
4-14	Cin.	L	0-1		5	6	Reitsma	Leiter	Graves	4-7	4th	3.5
4-15	Cin.	L	1-3		7	13	Brower	Appier	Graves	4-8	5th	3.5
4-16	Mon.	W	4-3		7	7	Reed	Thurman	Benitez	5-8	4th	3.0
4-17	Mon.	W	4-0		10	6	Rusch	Peters		6-8	4th	3.0
4-18	Mon.	L	1-7		2	12	Vazquez	Trachsel		6-9	4th	2.5
4-20	At Cin.	L	5-9		9	11	O. Fernandez	Leiter	Brower	6-10	5th	3.5
4-21	At Cin.	W	5-2		6	8	Appier	Reitsma	Benitez	7-10	5th	3.5
4-22	At Cin.	W	5-1		11	7	Reed	Dessens		8-10	T3rd	3.5
4-24	At Mil.	L	4-6		9	12	DeJean	Wall	Leskanic	8-11	4th	5.0
4-25	At Mil.	L	2-7		9	13	Haynes	Trachsel	Weathers	8-12	4th	6.0
4-26	At Mil.	L	8-12		13	19	Fox	Hinchliffe		8-13	T4th	6.0
4-27	At St.L.	L	0-9		6	16	Morris	Appier		8-14	5th	6.0
4-28	At St.L.	W	6-5	(11)	15	8	Benitez	James		9-14	T4th	5.0
4-29	At St.L.	L	1-12		6	18	Kile	Rusch		9-15	5th	5.0
4-30	Hou.	W	8-2		11	8	Trachsel	Elarton		10-15	5th	4.5
5-1	Hou.	W	7-5		11	10	Martin	Cruz	Benitez	11-15	T4th	4.5
5-2	Hou.	L	5-6	(10)	11	9	Wagner	Benitez		11-16	5th	4.5
5-4	Ari.	W	4-2		8	8	Reed	Batista	Franco	12-16	4th	4.0
5-5	Ari.	W	8-1		12	6	Rusch	Ellis		13-16	3rd	4.0
5-6	Ari.	L	2-8		8	12	Schilling	Trachsel		13-17	4th	5.0
5-7	At Col.	W	10-9		14	17	Gonzalez	Bohanon		14-17	3rd	5.0
5-8	At Col.	L	4-12		8	18	Astacio	Appier		14-18	4th	6.0
5-9	At Col.	L	0-6		7	11	Hampton	Reed		14-19	4th	6.0
5-10	At Col.	L	2-8		6	13	Chacon	Rusch		14-20	4th	6.5
5-11	At S.F	L	2-3	(10)	5	12	Nen	Wall		14-21	4th	7.5
5-12	At S.F	L	3-10		10	10	Ortiz	Gonzalez		14-22	4th	8.5
5-13	At S.F	L	3-6		4	7	Zerbe	Appier		14-23	4th	8.5
5-15	S.D.	W	1-0		6	6	Reed	Jones	Benitez	15-23	5th	7.5
5-16	S.D.	L	2-5		5	9	Eaton	Rusch	Hoffman	15-24	5th	7.5
5-17	S.D.	L	3-15		8	17	Williams	Trachsel		15-25	5th	8.5
5-18	L.A.	W	8-0		11	5	Leiter	Brown	Wendell	16-25	5th	8.5
5-19	L.A.	L	2-10		6	13	Prokopec	Appier		16-26	5th	9.5
5-20	L.A.	W	6-5		11	7	Benitez	Adams		17-26	5th	8.5
5-21	At Mon.	W	6-3		10	9	Rusch	Reames	Benitez	18-26	4th	8.0
5-22	At Mon.	L	0-3		9	10	Armas	Gonzalez	Urbina	18-27	5th	8.5
5-23	At Mon.	W	4-2		9	8	Leiter	Peters	Benitez	19-27	4th	9.0
5-24	Fla.	W	11-3		10	6	Appier	Burnett		20-27	4th	9.0
5-25	Fla.	W	4-3	(10)	8	8	Franco	Miceli		21-27	4th	9.0
5-26	Fla.	L	3-7		6	18	Dempster	Rusch		21-28	4th	9.5
5-27	Fla.	W	5-4		8	13	Wendell	Miceli	Benitez	22-28	4th	9.0
5-28	Phi.	L	3-5	(10)	8	12	Mesa	Benitez	Cormier	22-29	4th	10.0
5-29	Phi.	L	3-7		5	8	Gomes	Cook		22-30	4th	11.0
5-30	Phi.	L	3-6		7	13	Padilla	Franco	Mesa	22-31	4th	12.0
5-31	At Fla.	L	3-5		7	7	Dempster	Wendell	Alfonseca	22-32	4th	13.0
6-1	At Fla.	W	11-5		13	7	Gonzalez	Clement		23-32	4th	13.0
6-2	At Fla.	W	7-1		11	6	Leiter	Smith		24-32	4th	12.0
6-3	At Fla.	L	0-1		4	4	Alfonseca	Wendell		24-33	4th	12.0
6-5	At Phi.	W	9-0		15	4	Reed	Person		25-33	4th	11.0
6-6	At Phi.	L	1-6		6	10	Telemaco	Rusch		25-34	4th	12.0
6-7	At Phi.	W	6-5		13	6	Franco	Mesa	Benitez	26-34	4th	11.0
6-8	At T.B.	L	5-7		9	11	Rupe	Trachsel	Yan	26-35	4th	11.0
6-9	At T.B.	L	2-5		10	6	Sturtze	Leiter	Phelps	26-36	4th	12.0
6-10	At T.B.	W	10-0		13	4	Appier	Lopez		27-36	4th	11.0
6-12	At Bal.	W	10-3		14	6	Reed	Mercedes	White	28-36	4th	10.0
6-13	At Bal.	W	7-6	(10)	14	13	Franco	Groom	Benitez	29-36	4th	9.0
6-14	At Bal.	L	2-5		7	8	Towers	Trachsel	Groom	29-37	4th	9.0
6-15	N.Y.	L	4-5		7	9	Mendoza	Leiter	Rivera	29-38	4th	10.0
6-16	N.Y.	L	1-2		7	6	Mussina	Appier	Rivera	29-39	4th	11.0
6-17	N.Y.	W	8-7		6	9	Wendell	Almanzar	Benitez	30-39	4th	10.0
6-18	Mon.	W	2-1		9	6	Wendell	Yoshii	Benitez	31-39	4th	9.5
6-19	Mon.	W	4-1		5	5	White	Mota	Franco	32-39	4th	8.5
6-20	Mon.	W	4-3		11	5	Leiter	Vazquez	Benitez	33-39	4th	8.5
6-21	Mon.	L	3-10		7	14	Blank	Appier		33-40	4th	9.5
6-22	Atl.	L	1-10		7	12	Perez	Reed		33-41	4th	9.5

Date	Opp.	Res.	Score	(inn.*)	Hits	Opp. hits	Winning pitcher	Losing pitcher	Save	Record	Pos.	GB
6-23	Atl.	L	3-9	(11)	11	16	Reed	White		33-42	4th	9.5
6-24	Atl.	L	4-8		9	15	Marquis	Trachsel		33-43	4th	10.5
6-25	At Chi.	L	1-2		3	7	Tavarez	Leiter	Gordon	33-44	4th	10.5
6-26	At Chi.	L	2-4		6	7	Lieber	Appier	Gordon	33-45	4th	10.5
6-27	At Chi.	W	5-4		8	9	White	Farnsworth	Benitez	34-45	4th	10.0
6-28	At Atl.	L	2-6	(10)	10	9	Reed	Benitez		34-46	4th	11.0
6-29	At Atl.	W	3-1		6	7	Trachsel	Marquis	Benitez	35-46	4th	11.0
6-30	At Atl.	L	2-5		9	10	Maddux	Leiter	Karsay	35-47	4th	12.0
7-1	At Atl.	W	2-1		6	4	Appier	Burkett	Benitez	36-47	4th	12.0
7-3	Chi.	L	0-3		5	6	Wood	Reed	Gordon	36-48	4th	12.0
7-4	Chi.	W	2-1		8	6	Rusch	Tapani	Benitez	37-48	4th	12.0
7-5	Chi.	L	4-13		6	15	Bere	Trachsel		37-49	4th	12.0
7-6	At N.Y.	L	3-8		8	10	Pettitte	Leiter	Mendoza	37-50	5th	13.0
7-7	At N.Y.	W	3-0	(10)	10	4	Franco	Rivera	Benitez	38-50	4th	12.0
7-8	At N.Y.	L	1-4		7	6	Mendoza	Wendell	Rivera	38-51	4th	13.0
7-12	Bos.	W	4-2		7	7	Leiter	Wakefield	Benitez	39-51	4th	12.0
7-13	Bos.	L	1-3		5	4	Cone	Appier	Lowe	39-52	4th	13.0
7-14	Bos.	W	2-0		5	1	Rusch	Arrojo	Benitez	40-52	4th	12.0
7-15	Tor.	W	6-2		11	7	Reed	Michalak		41-52	4th	12.0
7-16	Tor.	W	3-0		10	4	Trachsel	Halladay	Benitez	42-52	4th	11.0
7-17	Tor.	W	1-0		4	10	Leiter	Carpenter	Benitez	43-52	4th	10.0
7-18	Fla.	W	4-3	(11)	10	7	Wendell	Nunez		44-52	4th	11.0
7-19	Fla.	L	3-8		7	12	Dempster	Rusch		44-53	4th	11.0
7-20	At Phi.	L	1-10		5	12	Person	Reed		44-54	4th	11.0
7-21	At Phi.	W	6-3		12	6	Trachsel	Wolf	Benitez	45-54	4th	11.0
7-22	At Phi.	L	2-3		11	7	Santiago	Franco	Mesa	45-55	4th	12.0
7-24	At Fla.	L	3-4		6	9	Bones	Appier	Alfonseca	45-56	4th	11.5
7-25	At Fla.	W	5-2		12	8	Rusch	Dempster	Benitez	46-56	4th	11.5
7-26	Phi.	L	2-3		6	11	Santiago	Reed	Mesa	46-57	4th	11.5
7-27	Phi.	W	6-1		10	7	Trachsel	Coggin		47-57	4th	11.5
7-28	Phi.	W	4-3		9	12	Benitez	Wendell		48-57	4th	11.5
7-29	Phi.	W	6-5		13	9	Benitez	Cormier		49-57	4th	11.5
7-31	At Hou.	L	2-3	(10)	6	8	Cruz	Riggan		49-58	4th	11.5
8-1	At Hou.	W	8-2	(10)	12	4	White	Jackson		50-58	4th	10.5
8-2	At Hou.	L	3-4	(10)	10	8	Williams	Riggan		50-59	4th	11.5
8-3	At Ari.	L	0-7		2	14	Johnson	Leiter		50-60	4th	11.5
8-4	At Ari.	W	4-2		7	9	Appier	Batista	Benitez	51-60	4th	11.5
8-5	At Ari.	L	1-2		6	7	Schilling	White	Kim	51-61	4th	12.5
8-7	Mil.	W	3-0		6	2	Chen	Haynes	Benitez	52-61	4th	12.5
8-8	Mil.	W	5-4		6	6	Trachsel	Levrault	Benitez	53-61	4th	11.5
8-9	Mil.	W	4-3		8	5	Leiter	DeJean	White	54-61	4th	10.5
8-10	St.L.	L	6-7	(10)	9	12	Veres	White	Kline	54-62	4th	10.5
8-11	St.L.	L	3-6		11	10	Hermanson	Rusch	Veres	54-63	4th	10.5
8-12	St.L.	L	1-4		5	8	Kile	Chen	Veres	54-64	4th	11.5
8-14	At S.D.	L	0-6		8	8	Herndon	Trachsel		54-65	4th	12.5
8-15	At S.D.	L	1-2		2	9	Jarvis	Leiter	Hoffman	54-66	4th	13.5
8-16	At S.D.	L	5-6		10	10	Fikac	White	Hoffman	54-67	4th	13.5
8-17	At L.A.	L	3-8		6	10	Adams	Rusch		54-68	4th	13.5
8-18	At L.A.	W	5-4		7	8	Riggan	Trombley	Benitez	55-68	4th	13.5
8-19	At L.A.	W	6-5		11	10	Trachsel	Park	Benitez	56-68	4th	12.5
8-21	Col.	W	5-2		7	9	Leiter	Hampton	Benitez	57-68	4th	11.5
8-22	Col.	W	2-1		7	2	Appier	Chacon	Benitez	58-68	4th	11.5
8-23	Col.	L	0-10		5	17	Jennings	Rusch		58-69	4th	12.5
8-24	S.F	W	4-3		11	4	Chen	Rueter	Benitez	59-69	4th	11.5
8-25	S.F	W	3-2	(11)	12	9	Riggan	Nen		60-69	4th	10.5
8-26	S.F	W	6-5		7	7	Leiter	Ortiz	Benitez	61-69	4th	10.5
8-27	S.F	L	5-6		6	12	Rodriguez	White	Nen	61-70	4th	10.5
8-28	Phi.	L	6-9	(11)	12	14	Politte	Wall	Bottalico	61-71	4th	10.5
8-29	Phi.	W	7-5		11	7	Chen	Daal	Benitez	62-71	4th	10.5
8-30	Phi.	W	6-2		11	5	Trachsel	Coggin		63-71	3rd	9.5
8-31	Fla.	W	6-1		9	5	Leiter	Penny		64-71	3rd	8.5
9-1	Fla.	W	3-2	(11)	8	6	Roberts	Acevedo		65-71	3rd	7.5
9-2	Fla.	L	1-5		5	10	Dempster	Rusch		65-72	3rd	8.5
9-3	At Phi.	W	10-7		16	10	Nitkowski	Mesa	Benitez	66-72	3rd	8.5
9-4	At Phi.	W	5-3		8	8	Trachsel	Daal	Benitez	67-72	3rd	8.5
9-5	At Phi.	W	7-4		9	5	Leiter	Coggin		68-72	3rd	7.5
9-6	At Fla.	W	5-2		10	10	Appier	Penny	Benitez	69-72	3rd	7.0
9-7	At Fla.	W	6-1		9	8	Rusch	Burnett		70-72	3rd	7.0
9-8	At Fla.	W	9-7		17	11	Franco	Alfonseca	Benitez	71-72	3rd	7.0
9-9	At Fla.	L	2-4		6	9	Acevedo	Trachsel	Alfonseca	71-73	3rd	8.0
9-17	At Pit.	W	4-1		6	5	Franco	Fetters	Benitez	72-73	3rd	7.0
9-18	At Pit.	W	7-5		10	6	Riggan	Olivares	Benitez	73-73	3rd	6.0
9-19	At Pit.	W	9-2		15	11	Gonzalez	McKnight		74-73	3rd	5.0
9-21	Atl.	W	3-2		8	9	Benitez	Karsay		75-73	3rd	4.5
9-22	Atl.	W	7-3		13	9	Trachsel	Perez	Benitez	76-73	3rd	3.5
9-23	Atl.	L	4-5	(11)	10	8	Smoltz	Riggan		76-74	3rd	4.5
9-25	At Mon.	W	2-0		5	4	Appier	Pavano		77-74	3rd	4.0
9-26	At Mon.	W	5-2		7	9	Rusch	Armas	Benitez	78-74	3rd	4.0

Date	Opp.	Res.	Score	(inn.*)	Hits	Opp. hits	Winning pitcher	Losing pitcher	Save	Record	Pos.	GB
9-27	At Mon.	W	12-6		19	10	White	Strickland		79-74	3rd	3.0
9-28	At Atl.	L	3-5		9	7	Glavine	Trachsel	Smoltz	79-75	3rd	4.0
9-29	At Atl.	L	5-8		7	8	Perez	Benitez		79-76	3rd	5.0
9-30	At Atl.	W	9-6		11	9	Appier	Millwood	Benitez	80-76	3rd	4.0
10-1	Pit.	L	1-5		5	11	Anderson	Rusch	Sauerbeck	80-77	3rd	4.5
10-2	Pit.	L	1-10		5	15	Arroyo	Chen		80-78	3rd	4.5
10-3	Pit.	W	3-0		5	2	Trachsel	Ritchie		81-78	3rd	4.5
10-5	Mon.	L	6-8		11	11	Thurman	Leiter	Strickland	81-79	3rd	6.0
10-6	Mon.	W	4-0		11	6	Appier	Pavano		82-79	3rd	6.0
10-7	Mon.	L	0-5		3	7	Reames	Rusch		82-80	3rd	6.0

Monthly records: April (10-15), May (12-17), June (13-15), July (14-11), August (15-13), September (16-5), October (2-4).
*Innings, if other than nine.

HIGHLIGHTS

High point: September 27 at Montreal. The Mets completed a three-game sweep at Olympic Stadium and went into Atlanta just three games behind the first-place Braves with nine games to play.

Low point: August 16 at San Diego. Mike Daar's first homer in a full year carried San Diego to a three-game sweep, spoiling a late Mets comeback. The next night, the Mets lost at Los Angeles to fall to 54-68.

Turning point: April 24-May 18. That's the period when both Al Leiter and Jay Payton were injured. In that span, the club posted an 8-15 mark, and went from 2 1/2 games out to 8 1/2 games back. The club did not have the pitching reserves or the outfield depth to recover.

Most valuable player: Mike Piazza was the club's sole dynamic offensive presence. For the ninth straight season, Piazza batted .300 or better.

Most valuable pitcher: Kevin Appier was charged with replacing free agent Mike Hampton. Appier led the club in starts, innings and strikeouts. Three seasons removed from major shoulder surgery, Appier displayed durability and a stand-up nature.

Most improved player: Snatched off waivers in October 2000, Desi Relaford became one of manager Bobby Valentine's favorites for his ready versatility. Relaford had 301 at-bats and hit for surprising power at key moments, and was much improved at shortstop and second base.

Most pleasant surprise: Tsuyoshi Shinjo began the year as a complete mystery and became one of the club's most indispensable players. A seven-time Gold Glove winner in Japan, with a history as a clutch hitter, Shinjo excelled in both departments. He kept making adjustments and displayed speed, a strong arm, occasional power and a selective eye at the plate.

Key injuries: Leiter missed 4-5 starts with a strained left elbow and Payton missed nearly two months with a pulled right hamstring. … Shinjo was plagued by a strained quadriceps muscle in the first half. … Benny Agbayani missed two weeks in April and most of the last two months with broken bones in each hand. … Edgardo Alfonzo was bothered by back problems and went on the disabled list twice.

Notable: After a 1-9 start, Steve Trachsel recovered after a three-week minor-league stint and went 10-4 after June 29. … Lenny Harris led the majors with 21 pinch hits. With his last, he broke Manny Mota's all-time record of 150 pinch hits.

—PETE CALDERA

RECORDS

2001 regular-season record: 82-80 (3rd in N.L. East); 44-37 at home; 38-43 on road; 43-33 vs. N.L. East; 15-21 vs. N.L. Central; 14-17 vs. N.L. West; 10-8 vs. A.L.; 15-17 vs. lefthanded starters; 67-63 vs. righthanded starters; 70-71 on grass; 12-9 on turf; 22-34 in daytime; 60-46 at night; 30-20 in one-run games; 10-10 in extra-inning games; 0-0-0 in doubleheaders.

Team record past five years: 449-362 (.554, ranks 3rd in league in that span).

TEAM LEADERS

Batting average: Mike Piazza (.300).
At-bats: Todd Zeile (531).
Runs: Mike Piazza (81).
Hits: Mike Piazza (151).
Total Bases: Mike Piazza (288).
Doubles: Mike Piazza (29).
Triples: Rey Ordonez (4).
Home runs: Mike Piazza (36).
Runs batted in: Mike Piazza (94).
Stolen bases: Desi Relaford (13).
Slugging percentage: Mike Piazza (.573).
On-base percentage: Mike Piazza (.384).
Wins: Kevin Appier, Al Leiter, Steve Trachsel (11).
Earned-run average: Al Leiter (3.31).

Complete games: Rick Reed (3).
Shutouts: Kevin Appier, Rick Reed, Steve Trachsel (1).
Saves: Armando Benitez (43).
Innings pitched: Kevin Appier (206.2).
Strikeouts: Kevin Appier (172).

GAMES BY POSITION

Catcher: Mike Piazza 131, Todd Pratt 31, Vance Wilson 27, Jason Phillips 5.
First base: Todd Zeile 149, Mark P. Johnson 21, Lenny Harris 7, Joe McEwing 3, Jorge Toca 3.
Second base: Edgardo Alfonzo 122, Desi Relaford 54, Joe McEwing 5, Lenny Harris 1.
Third base: Robin Ventura 139, Joe McEwing 25, Desi Relaford 20, Lenny Harris 11, Jorge Velandia 1.
Shortstop: Rey Ordonez 148, Desi Relaford 25, Joe McEwing 12, Jorge Velandia 8.
Outfield: Tsuyoshi Shinjo 119, Jay Payton 103, Benny Agbayani 84, Timo Perez 73, Joe McEwing 62, Matt Lawton 48, Darryl Hamilton 37, Mark P. Johnson 19, Darren Bragg 16, Alex Escobar 15, Lenny Harris 8, Jorge Toca 2.
Designated hitter: Mike Piazza 5, Mark P. Johnson 3, Lenny Harris 2, Joe McEwing 1.

TOP DRAFT CHOICES

1a. **Aaron Heilman,** RHP, U. of Notre Dame.
1b. **David Wright,** 3B, Hickory H.S., Chesapeake, Va.
2a. **Alhaji Turay,** OF, Auburn (Wash.) H.S.
2b. **Corey Ragsdale,** SS, Nettleton H.S., Jonesboro, Ark.
3. **Lenny DiNardo,** LHP, Stetson Univ.
4. **Brian Walker,** LHP, U. of Miami (Fla.).
5. **Danny Garcia,** 2B, Pepperdine, Univ.
6. **Jason Weintraub,** RHP, Jefferson H.S., Tampa.
7. **Tyler Beuerlein,** C, Grand Canyon (Ariz.) University.
8. **Brett Kay,** C, Cal State Fullerton.
9. **Jayson Weir,** LHP, Boone H.S., Orlando.
10. **Ryan Olson,** LHP, UNLV.

PHILADELPHIA PHILLIES
NATIONAL LEAGUE EAST DIVISION

Phillies schedule
Home games shaded
D—Day game (games starting before 5 p.m.)
All-Star Game at Milwaukee
Subject to changes

April
SUN	MON	TUE	WED	THU	FRI	SAT
	1 D ATL	2	3 ATL	4 ATL	5 FLA	6 D FLA
7 D FLA	8 ATL	9 ATL	10 ATL	11 ATL	12 CIN	13 CIN
14 D CIN	15	16 FLA	17 FLA	18 FLA	19 PIT	20 D PIT
21 D PIT	22	23 SD	24 SD	25 D SD	26 COL	27 D COL
28 COL	29 SF	30 SF				

May
SUN	MON	TUE	WED	THU	FRI	SAT
			1 SF	2	3 COL	4 COL
5 D COL	6	7 HOU	8 HOU	9 HOU	10 ARI	11 ARI
12 D ARI	13 HOU	14 HOU	15 HOU	16 ARI	17 ARI	18 ARI
19 D ARI	20	21 NYM	22 NYM	23 NYM	24 MON	25 MON
26 D MON	27	28 NYM	29 NYM	30	31 MON	

June
SUN	MON	TUE	WED	THU	FRI	SAT
						1 MON
2 D MON	3	4 FLA	5 FLA	6 FLA	7 DET	8 DET
9 D DET	10 CLE	11 CLE	12 CLE	13 BAL	14 BAL	15 BAL
16 D BAL	17	18 CWS	19 CWS	20 CWS	21 MIN	22 MIN
23 D MIN	24 FLA	25 FLA	26 FLA	27 FLA	28 BAL	29 BAL
30 D BAL						

July
SUN	MON	TUE	WED	THU	FRI	SAT
	1 NYM	2 NYM	3 NYM	4 MON	5 MON	6 MON
7 D MON	8	9	* 10	11 NYM	12 NYM	13 NYM
14 D NYM	15	16 MON	17 CUB	18 CUB	19 ATL	20 ATL
21 D ATL	22 CUB	23 D CUB	24 D CUB	25 D CUB	26 ATL	27 ATL
28 D ATL	29	30 SF	31 SF			

August
SUN	MON	TUE	WED	THU	FRI	SAT
				1 SF	2 LA	3 LA
4 D LA	5 D LA	6 SD	7 SD	8 D SD	9 LA	10 D LA
11 LA	12	13 MIL	14 MIL	15 MIL	16 STL	17 STL
18 D STL	19	20 MIL	21 MIL	22 D MIL	23 STL	24 STL
25 D STL	26	27 MON	28 MON	29 MON	30 NYM	31 NYM

September
SUN	MON	TUE	WED	THU	FRI	SAT
1 D NYM	2 D MON	3 D MON	4 MON	5 D NYM	6 D NYM	7 NYM
8 D NYM	9 D NYM	10 NYM	11 FLA	12 FLA	13 PIT	14 PIT
15 D PIT	16	17 ATL	18 ATL	19 ATL	20 CIN	21 CIN
22 D CIN	23	24 ATL	25 ATL	26 ATL	27 FLA	28 FLA
29 D FLA	30					

2002 SEASON
CLUB DIRECTORY

General partner, president, CEO
David Montgomery
Chairman
Bill Giles
Senior vice president, CFO
Jerry Clothier
Vice president & general manager
Ed Wade
Vice president, public relations
Larry Shenk
Vice president, ticket operations
Richard Deats
Vice president, advertising sales
David Buck
V.p., general counsel and secretary
Bill Webb
V.p., operations and administration
Michael Stiles
Assistant general manager
Ruben Amaro Jr.
Asst. g.m., scouting & player dev.
Mike Arbuckle
Chief communications officer
Sharon Swainson
Director, business development
Joe Giles
Director, baseball administration
Susan Ingersoll
Director, minor league operations
Steve Noworyta
Controller
John Fusco
Director, information systems
Brian Lamoreaux
Director, media relations
Leigh Tobin
Director, community relations
Gene Dias
Director, events
Kurt Funk
Director, entertainment
Chris Long
Director, broadcasting & video services
Rory McNeil

Director, ticket department
Dan Goroff
Director, sales
John Weber
Director, group sales
Kathy Killian
Director, facility management
Mike DiMuzio
Director, event operations
Eric Tobin
Club physician
Dr. Michael Ciccotti
Club trainers
Jeff Cooper, Mark Andersen
Mgr., equipment and team travel
Frank Coppenbarger
Manager, visiting clubhouse
Kevin Steinhour
Director, scouting
Marti Wolever
Coordinators, scouting
Jim Fregosi Jr., Mike Ledna
Director, Florida operations
John Timberlake
Director, Latin American operations
Sal Artiaga
Director, Major League scouts
Gordon Lakey
Major League scout
Jimmy Stewart
Advance scout, Major Leagues
Hank King
Special assignment scout
Dean Jongewaard
Coordinator, professional coverage
Dick Lawlor
Regional supervisors
Brian Kohlscheen, Mitch Sokol
Area supervisors
Sal Agostinelli, Darrell Connor, Ken
Hultzapple, Tim Kissner, Jerry Lafferty,
Matt Lundin, Miguel Machado, Lloyd
Merritt, Venice Murray, Dave Owen,
Scott Ramsay, Paul Scott, Mike
Stauffer, Doug Takaragawa, Roy
Tanner, Jeff Wren

MINOR LEAGUE AFFILIATES

Class	Team	League	Manager
AAA	Scranton/Wilkes-Barre	International	Marc Bombard
AA	Reading	Eastern	Greg Legg
A	Clearwater	Florida State	John Morris
A	Lakewood	South Atlantic	Jeff Manto
A	Batavia	New York-Pennsylvania	Ronnie Ortegon
Rookie	Gulf Coast Phillies	Gulf Coast	Roly de Armas

BROADCAST INFORMATION

Radio: WPEN-AM (950).
TV: UPN 57.
Cable TV: Comcast SportsNet.

SPRING TRAINING

Ballpark (city): Jack Russell Stadium
(Clearwater, Fla.).
Ticket information: 215-463-1000 or
727-442-8496.

Follow the Phillies all season at: www.sportingnews.com/baseball/teams/phillies/

SPRING TRAINING ROSTER

Manager—Larry Bowa (10).
Coaches—Greg Gross (21), Ramon Henderson (59), Vern Ruhle (46), Tony Scott (30), Gary Varsho, John Vukovich (18).

No.	PITCHERS	B/T	Ht./Wt.	Born	2001 clubs
	Adams, Terry	R/R	6-3/215	3-6-73	Los Angeles
	Baisley, Brad	R/R	6-9/205	8-24-79	Clearwater, Reading
	Bottalico, Ricky	L/R	6-1/215	8-26-69	Philadelphia, Reading
48	Coggin, Dave	R/R	6-4/205	10-30-76	Scranton/Wilkes-Barre, Philadelphia
	Cordero, Jesus	R/R	6-1/170	5-5-79	Wilmington, Vero Beach
33	Cormier, Rheal	L/L	5-10/187	4-23-67	Philadelphia, Reading
62	Duckworth, Brandon	B/R	6-2/185	1-23-76	Scranton/Wilkes-Barre, Philadelphia
57	Figueroa, Nelson	B/R	6-1/155	5-18-74	Scranton/Wilkes-Barre, Philadelphia
	Junge, Eric	R/R	6-5/215	1-5-77	Jacksonville
49	Mesa, Jose	R/R	6-3/225	5-22-66	Philadelphia
51	Nickle, Doug	R/R	6-4/210	10-2-74	Scranton/Wilkes-Barre, Philadelphia
73	Nunez, Franklin	R/R	6-0/175	1-18-77	Reading
44	Padilla, Vicente	R/R	6-2/200	9-27-77	Philadelphia, Scranton/Wilkes-Barre
31	Person, Robert	R/R	6-0/194	10-6-69	Philadelphia
35	Politte, Cliff	R/R	5-11/185	2-27-74	Clearwater, Philadelphia
46	Santiago, Jose	R/R	6-3/215	11-5-74	Kansas City, Philadelphia
	Serrano, Elio	R/R	6-3/215	12-4-78	Clearwater, Reading
68	Silva, Carlos	R/R	6-4/225	4-23-79	Reading
70	Thomas, Evan	R/R	5-10/170	6-14-74	Scranton/Wilkes-Barre
99	Wendell, Turk	L/R	6-2/205	5-19-67	New York N.L., Philadelphia
43	Wolf, Randy	L/L	6-0/194	8-22-76	Philadelphia, Scranton/Wilkes-Barre, Reading
	Zamora, Pete	L/L	6-3/185	8-13-75	Scranton/Wilkes-Barre

No.	CATCHERS	B/T	Ht./Wt.	Born	2001 clubs
76	Estrada, Johnny	B/R	5-11/210	6-27-76	Scranton/Wilkes-Barre, Philadelphia
24	Lieberthal, Mike	R/R	6-0/190	1-18-72	Philadelphia

No.	INFIELDERS	B/T	Ht./Wt.	Born	2001 clubs
8	Anderson, Marlon	L/R	5-11/198	1-6-74	Philadelphia
52	Crespo, Felipe	B/R	5-11/200	3-5-73	San Francisco, Fresno, Philadelphia
	Lee, Travis	L/L	6-3/210	5-26-75	Philadelphia
	Machado, Anderson	B/R	5-11/165	1-25-81	Clearwater, Reading
13	Perez, Tomas	B/R	5-11/177	12-29-73	Philadelphia
75	Punto, Nick	R/R	5-9/170	11-8-77	Scranton/Wilkes-Barre, Philadelphia
17	Rolen, Scott	R/R	6-4/226	4-4-75	Philadelphia
29	Rollins, Jimmy	B/R	5-8/165	11-27-78	Philadelphia

No.	OUTFIELDERS	B/T	Ht./Wt.	Born	2001 clubs
53	Abreu, Bobby	L/R	6-0/197	3-11-74	Philadelphia
5	Burrell, Pat	R/R	6-4/225	10-10-76	Philadelphia
	Byrd, Marlon	R/R	6-0/225	8-30-77	Reading
6	Glanville, Doug	R/R	6-2/172	8-25-70	Philadelphia
16	Lee, Travis	L/L	6-3/214	5-26-75	Philadelphia
67	Michaels, Jason	R/R	6-0/205	5-4-76	Scranton/Wilkes-Barre, Philadelphia
	Padilla, Jorge	R/R	6-2/200	8-11-79	Clearwater
28	Taylor, Reggie	L/R	6-1/178	1-12-77	Scranton/Wilkes-Barre, Philadelphia
71	Valent, Eric	L/L	6-0/190	4-4-77	Scranton/Wilkes-Barre, Philadelphia

BALLPARK INFORMATION

Ballpark (capacity, surface)
Veterans Stadium (62,418, artificial)
Address
P.O. Box 7575
Philadelphia, PA 19101
Official website
www.phillies.com
Business phone
215-463-6000
Ticket information
215-463-1000
Ticket prices
$26 (field box)
$22 (sections 258-201, terrace box)
$20 (loge box)
$15 (reserved, 600 level)
$8 (reserved, 700 level, adult gen. admission)
$5 (children's general admission)
Field dimensions (from home plate)
To left field at foul line, 330 feet
To center field, 408 feet
To right field at foul line, 330 feet
First game played
April 10, 1971 (Phillies 4, Expos 1)

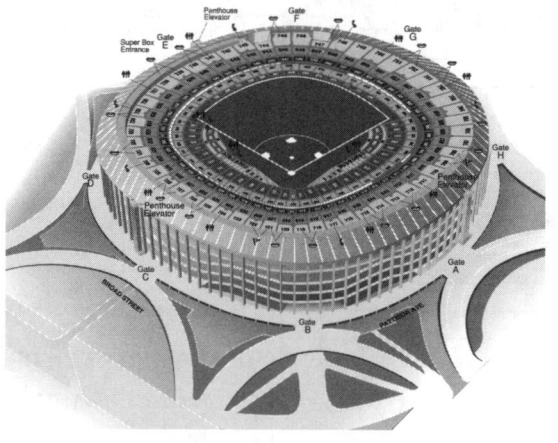

DAY BY DAY

Date	Opp.	Res.	Score	(inn.*)	Hits	Opp. hits	Winning pitcher	Losing pitcher	Save	Record	Pos.	GB
4-2	At Fla.	W	6-5	(13)	12	8	Telemaco	Nunez		1-0	T1st	...
4-3	At Fla.	W	4-3		9	6	Brock	Looper	Mesa	2-0	T1st	+0.5
4-4	At Fla.	W	7-3		10	13	Cormier	Miceli		3-0	T1st	+0.5
4-6	Chi.	L	2-3		7	7	Tavarez	Wolf	Fassero	3-1	T1st	...
4-7	Chi.	L	4-8		7	11	Bere	Padilla		3-2	2nd	1.0
4-8	Chi.	W	3-1		4	5	Person	Lieber	Mesa	4-2	2nd	1.0
4-9	Fla.	W	5-4		10	5	Bottalico	Bones		5-2	2nd	1.0
4-10	Fla.	W	7-6		12	9	Gomes	Alfonseca	Mesa	6-2	T1st	...
4-13	At Atl.	L	2-4		6	11	Glavine	Wolf	Rocker	6-3	1st	+0.5
4-14	At Atl.	W	2-1		6	8	Daal	Millwood	Mesa	7-3	1st	+0.5
4-15	At Atl.	L	0-3		6	5	Perez	Person	Rocker	7-4	1st	+0.5
4-17	At Chi.	W	6-3		10	12	Padilla	Fassero	Mesa	8-4	1st	+2.0
4-18†	At Chi.	L	3-4		13	5	Tapani	Chen	Fassero	8-5		
4-18‡	At Chi.	L	3-5		6	9	Bere	Wolf	Fassero	8-6	1st	+0.5
4-20	Atl.	W	8-3		12	8	Gomes	Perez		9-6	1st	+2.0
4-21	Atl.	W	4-1		7	9	Person	Maddux		10-6	1st	+2.5
4-22	Atl.	W	3-2		4	6	Telemaco	Burkett	Gomes	11-6	1st	+3.0
4-23	At S.D.	W	5-3		7	7	Chen	Eaton	Bottalico	12-6	1st	+3.5
4-24	At S.D.	W	12-7		17	8	Wolf	Williams		13-6	1st	+4.5
4-25	At S.D.	W	5-3		7	11	Daal	Tollberg	Mesa	14-6	1st	+5.0
4-26	At S.D.	L	0-11		7	13	Jarvis	Person		14-7	1st	+4.5
4-27	At L.A.	L	3-4		6	9	Adams	Gomes		14-8	1st	+3.5
4-28	At L.A.	L	6-7		8	13	Herges	Bottalico	Shaw	14-9	1st	+3.0
4-29	At L.A.	L	1-4		3	8	Park	Wolf	Shaw	14-10	1st	+3.0
5-1	Col.	W	7-1		8	4	Daal	Neagle		15-10	1st	+4.0
5-2	Col.	L	2-6		7	12	Bohanon	Person	Jimenez	15-11	1st	+3.0
5-3	Col.	W	7-5		11	10	Telemaco	Astacio		16-11	1st	+4.0
5-4	S.F.	L	2-4		8	5	Hernandez	Chen	Nen	16-12	1st	+3.5
5-5	S.F.	W	4-2		7	8	Wolf	Fultz	Mesa	17-12	1st	+4.0
5-6	S.F.	W	10-8		12	14	Daal	Rueter	Mesa	18-12	1st	+4.0
5-7	At Hou.	W	5-0		9	2	Person	Bottenfield		19-12	1st	+4.5
5-8	At Hou.	W	3-2		6	4	Telemaco	Jackson	Mesa	20-12	1st	+5.5
5-9	At Hou.	L	6-7		11	11	Wagner	Bottalico		20-13	1st	+4.5
5-11	At Ari.	W	5-1		12	6	Wolf	Schilling		21-13	1st	+5.0
5-12	At Ari.	W	6-5	(10)	14	9	Bottalico	Batista	Mesa	22-13	1st	+6.0
5-13	At Ari.	L	1-6		4	7	Johnson	Person		22-14	1st	+6.0
5-15	Mil.	L	10-14	(10)	12	22	Leskanic	Bottalico		22-15	1st	+5.0
5-16	Mil.	L	1-6		9	10	Haynes	Chen		22-16	1st	+4.0
5-17	Mil.	W	2-1	(12)	9	6	Gomes	DeJean		23-16	1st	+5.0
5-18	St.L.	W	5-4		7	7	Daal	Timlin	Mesa	24-16	1st	+5.0
5-19	St.L.	W	3-2		8	4	Person	An. Benes		25-16	1st	+5.0
5-20	St.L.	L	1-3		5	12	Hermanson	Telemaco	Veres	25-17	1st	+5.0
5-23†	Pit.	W	4-0		10	3	Wolf	Schmidt	Bottalico	26-17		
5-23‡	Pit.	W	5-2		9	10	Daal	Olivares	Mesa	27-17	1st	+6.0
5-24	Pit.	W	6-5		12	8	Cormier	Sauerbeck	Mesa	28-17	1st	+6.5
5-25	Mon.	W	10-8		9	13	Oropesa	Urbina		29-17	1st	+6.5
5-27†	Mon.	W	7-5		12	9	Brock	Reames	Mesa	30-17		
5-27‡	Mon.	L	3-7		6	8	Armas	Byrd		30-18	1st	+6.5
5-28	At N.Y.	W	5-3	(10)	12	8	Mesa	Benitez	Cormier	31-18	1st	+6.5
5-29	At N.Y.	W	7-3		8	5	Gomes	Cook		32-18	1st	+6.5
5-30	At N.Y.	W	6-3		13	7	Padilla	Franco	Mesa	33-18	1st	+7.5
5-31	At Mon.	W	5-2		12	5	Cormier	Strickland	Mesa	34-18	1st	+8.0
6-1	At Mon.	W	13-2		13	6	Chen	Reames		35-18	1st	+8.0
6-2	At Mon.	L	5-12		7	14	Armas	Wolf		35-19	1st	+7.5
6-3	At Mon.	L	3-10		6	16	Yoshii	Daal		35-20	1st	+6.0
6-5	N.Y.	L	0-9		4	15	Reed	Person		35-21	1st	+5.0
6-6	N.Y.	W	6-1		10	6	Telemaco	Rusch		36-21	1st	+5.0
6-7	N.Y.	L	5-6		6	13	Franco	Mesa	Benitez	36-22	1st	+4.0
6-8	At Bos.	L	2-3		9	8	Cone	Wolf	Lowe	36-23	1st	+4.0
6-9	At Bos.	W	5-2		6	6	Daal	Martinez	Mesa	37-23	1st	+4.0
6-10	At Bos.	L	4-5		8	9	Nomo	Cormier	Lowe	37-24	1st	+3.0
6-12	At T.B.	L	5-9		7	11	Kennedy	Telemaco		37-25	1st	+2.5
6-13	At T.B.	L	3-5		9	8	Rekar	Bottalico	Yan	37-26	1st	+2.5
6-14	At T.B.	L	3-6		5	11	Rupe	Wolf	Yan	37-27	1st	+2.0
6-15	Bal.	W	15-7		18	12	Padilla	Roberts		38-27	1st	+3.0
6-16	Bal.	W	14-6		15	10	Brock	Ryan		39-27	1st	+3.0
6-17	Bal.	L	7-10		12	12	Mercedes	Telemaco		39-28	1st	+3.0
6-19	At Pit.	L	5-8		8	17	Beimel	Chen	Sauerbeck	39-29	1st	+3.5
6-20	At Pit.	W	9-5		14	8	Daal	Arroyo		40-29	1st	+3.5
6-21	At Pit.	W	6-3		8	5	Person	Anderson	Mesa	41-29	1st	+4.5
6-22	At Fla.	L	1-8		7	13	Dempster	Wolf		41-30	1st	+3.5
6-23	At Fla.	L	1-12		6	14	Clement	Telemaco		41-31	1st	+2.5
6-24	At Fla.	W	9-3		14	6	Chen	Smith		42-31	1st	+2.5
6-25	Atl.	L	4-9		11	12	Maddux	Daal		42-32	1st	+1.5

Date	Opp.	Res.	Score	(inn.*)	Hits	Opp. hits	Winning pitcher	Losing pitcher	Save	Record	Pos.	GB
6-26	Atl.	L	1-4	(11)	4	10	Remlinger	Gomes	Cabrera	42-33	1st	+0.5
6-27	Atl.	L	4-10		7	12	Perez	Wolf		42-34	2nd	0.5
6-28†	Fla.	W	6-5		12	8	Person	Dempster	Mesa	43-34		
6-28‡	Fla.	W	8-7		10	11	Cormier	Looper	Mesa	44-34	T1st	
6-29	Fla.	W	5-0		8	8	Chen	Smith		45-34	1st	+1.0
6-30	Fla.	W	6-4		11	7	Daal	Burnett	Mesa	46-34	1st	+1.0
7-1	Fla.	W	8-1		14	7	Figueroa	Penny		47-34	1st	+2.0
7-3	At Atl.	L	7-14		11	15	Cabrera	Santiago		47-35	1st	+1.0
7-4	At Atl.	W	4-1		10	4	Coggin	Perez	Mesa	48-35	1st	+2.0
7-5	At Atl.	L	5-9		10	12	Maddux	Chen		48-36	1st	+1.0
7-6	At Bal.	W	3-2	(10)	8	7	Cormier	Trombley	Mesa	49-36	1st	+1.0
7-7	At Bal.	L	3-4		6	10	Johnson	Figueroa	Groom	49-37	1st	+1.0
7-8	At Bal.	W	5-4		11	5	Wolf	Groom	Mesa	50-37	1st	+1.0
7-12	Tor.	L	1-2	(11)	4	8	Escobar	Santiago	Koch	50-38	T1st	...
7-13	Tor.	W	5-2		8	5	Daal	Plesac	Mesa	51-38	T1st	...
7-14	Tor.	L	2-4		6	10	Hamilton	Figueroa	Koch	51-39	T1st	...
7-15	N.Y.	W	9-3		12	7	Person	Pettitte		52-39	1st	+1.0
7-16	N.Y.	L	3-6	(13)	8	7	Stanton	Telemaco	Rivera	52-40	1st	+1.0
7-17	N.Y.	L	1-4	(12)	13	11	Choate	Gomes	Rivera	52-41	T1st	...
7-18	At Mon.	L	6-7		8	12	Urbina	Cormier		52-42	2nd	1.0
7-19	At Mon.	L	2-5		7	9	Strickland	Cormier	Urbina	52-43	2nd	2.0
7-20	N.Y.	W	10-1		12	5	Person	Reed		53-43	2nd	1.0
7-21	N.Y.	L	3-6		6	12	Trachsel	Wolf	Benitez	53-44	2nd	2.0
7-22	N.Y.	W	3-2		7	11	Santiago	Franco	Mesa	54-44	2nd	2.0
7-23	Mon.	L	0-3		7	9	Vazquez	Daal		54-45	2nd	2.0
7-24	Mon.	W	10-2		14	7	Figueroa	Armas		55-45	2nd	1.0
7-25	Mon.	W	8-4		13	8	Person	Thurman		56-45	2nd	1.0
7-26	At N.Y.	W	3-2		11	6	Santiago	Reed	Mesa	57-45	T1st	...
7-27	At N.Y.	L	1-6		7	10	Trachsel	Coggin		57-46	2nd	1.0
7-28	At N.Y.	L	3-4		12	9	Benitez	Wendell		57-47	2nd	2.0
7-29	At N.Y.	L	5-6		9	13	Benitez	Cormier		57-48	2nd	3.0
7-31	At Col.	L	6-7		15	10	Jimenez	Cormier		57-49	2nd	3.0
8-1	At Col.	W	8-1	(7)	11	4	Wolf	Neagle		58-49	2nd	2.0
8-2	At Col.	W	4-2		7	11	Coggin	Thomson	Mesa	59-49	2nd	2.0
8-3	At S.F	L	2-4		6	5	Rodriguez	Cormier		59-50	2nd	2.0
8-4	At S.F	W	12-2		17	7	Figueroa	Estes		60-50	2nd	2.0
8-5	At S.F	L	4-8		10	14	Hernandez	Person		60-51	2nd	3.0
8-7	S.D.	W	7-3		13	6	Duckworth	Jones		61-51	2nd	3.0
8-8	S.D.	W	4-3		11	7	Coggin	Herndon	Mesa	62-51	2nd	2.0
8-9	S.D.	L	2-6		5	11	Jarvis	Daal		62-52	2nd	2.0
8-10	L.A.	W	10-5		10	10	Figueroa	Baldwin		63-52	2nd	1.0
8-11	L.A.	W	7-3		8	5	Person	Gagne		64-52	T1st	...
8-12	L.A.	W	3-2		8	5	Duckworth	Adams	Mesa	65-52	1st	+1.0
8-14	At Mil.	W	10-4		10	10	Coggin	Levrault		66-52	1st	+2.0
8-15	At Mil.	W	8-6		13	11	Daal	Wright	Mesa	67-52	1st	+2.0
8-16	At Mil.	L	4-5		8	7	Quevedo	Figueroa	Leskanic	67-53	1st	+1.0
8-17	At St.L.	L	3-4		10	13	Veres	Wendell		67-54	T1st	...
8-18	At St.L.	L	3-6		11	11	Kline	Politte	Veres	67-55	2nd	1.0
8-19	At St.L.	L	0-9		7	14	Morris	Coggin		67-56	2nd	1.0
8-21	Hou.	L	2-8		8	10	Astacio	Figueroa		67-57	2nd	1.0
8-22	Hou.	W	2-1		7	3	Person	Miller	Mesa	68-57	2nd	1.0
8-23	Hou.	L	1-2	(11)	11	6	Jackson	Santiago	Wagner	68-58	2nd	2.0
8-24	Ari.	W	6-5		9	9	Daal	Anderson	Mesa	69-58	2nd	1.0
8-25	Ari.	L	3-4		7	7	Batista	Coggin	Kim	69-59	2nd	1.0
8-26	Ari.	L	3-4	(10)	6	11	Kim	Politte		69-60	2nd	2.0
8-27	Ari.	W	3-1		5	6	Person	Lopez	Mesa	70-60	2nd	1.0
8-28	At N.Y.	W	9-6	(11)	14	12	Politte	Wall	Bottalico	71-60	T1st	...
8-29	At N.Y.	L	5-7		7	11	Chen	Daal	Benitez	71-61	2nd	1.0
8-30	At N.Y.	L	2-6		5	11	Trachsel	Coggin		71-62	2nd	1.0
8-31	Mon.	L	1-5		3	14	Thurman	Figueroa	Strickland	71-63	2nd	1.0
9-1	Mon.	W	4-1		10	4	Person	Pavano	Mesa	72-63	T1st	...
9-2	Mon.	L	2-6		5	12	Vazquez	Mesa		72-64	2nd	1.0
9-3	N.Y.	L	7-10		10	16	Nitkowski	Mesa	Benitez	72-65	2nd	2.0
9-4	N.Y.	L	3-5		8	8	Trachsel	Daal	Benitez	72-66	2nd	3.0
9-5	N.Y.	L	4-7		5	9	Leiter	Coggin		72-67	2nd	3.0
9-6	At Mon.	W	3-0		4	5	Person	Pavano	Mesa	73-67	2nd	2.5
9-7	At Mon.	L	2-4		4	6	Vazquez	Duckworth	Stewart	73-68	2nd	3.5
9-8	At Mon.	W	6-0		18	6	Wolf	Ohka		74-68	2nd	3.5
9-9	At Mon.	W	12-4		10	7	Politte	Lloyd		75-68	2nd	3.5
9-17	Atl.	W	5-2		6	7	Person	Maddux	Mesa	76-68	2nd	2.5
9-18	Atl.	W	4-3		7	8	Bottalico	Smoltz		77-68	2nd	1.5
9-19	Atl.	W	5-2		7	6	Coggin	Burkett	Mesa	78-68	2nd	0.5
9-20	Atl.	L	1-5		4	11	Millwood	Wolf		78-69	2nd	1.5
9-21	Fla.	W	1-0		6	6	Mesa	Nunez		79-69	2nd	0.5
9-22	Fla.	L	2-3		8	8	Clement	Santiago	Alfonseca	79-70	2nd	0.5
9-23	Fla.	W	5-4	(10)	10	6	Mesa	Acevedo		80-70	2nd	0.5
9-25	Cin.	L	1-8		7	10	Hamilton	Coggin		80-71	2nd	1.0
9-26	Cin.	W	8-0		7	1	Wolf	J. Fernandez		81-71	2nd	1.0

Date	Opp.	Res.	Score	(inn.*)	Hits	Opp. hits	Winning pitcher	Losing pitcher	Save	Record	Pos.	GB
9-27	Cin.	L	1-2		2	8	Davis	Daal	Graves	81-72	2nd	1.0
9-28	At Fla.	L	5-6	(10)	10	11	Alfonseca	Politte		81-73	2nd	2.0
9-29	At Fla.	W	5-4		8	7	Duckworth	Penny	Mesa	82-73	2nd	2.0
9-30	At Fla.	L	3-8		6	7	Beckett	Coggin		82-74	2nd	2.0
10-2	At Atl.	W	3-1		7	3	Wolf	Maddux	Mesa	83-74	2nd	1.0
10-3	At Atl.	L	3-8		12	13	Glavine	Person		83-75	2nd	2.0
10-4	At Atl.	L	2-6		8	9	Burkett	Duckworth		83-76	2nd	3.0
10-6†	At Cin.	W	2-1		10	4	Daal	Dessens	Mesa	84-76		
10-6‡	At Cin.	W	5-1		12	10	Coggin	Hamilton		85-76	2nd	3.0
10-7	At Cin.	W	4-1		11	7	Wolf	Davis	Mesa	86-76	2nd	2.0

Monthly records: April (14-10), May (20-8), June (12-16), July (11-15), August (14-14), September (11-11), October (4-2).
*Innings, if other than nine. †First game of a doubleheader. ‡Second game of a doubleheader.

HIGHLIGHTS

High point: On June 1, following a 13-2 drubbing of Montreal at Olympic Stadium, the Phillies had a commanding eight-game lead over Atlanta. With a 35-18 record, the team's 17 games over the .500 mark also represented the high-water point of the season.

Low point: The Phillies were one game behind Atlanta with five to play. Staff ace Robert Person had a chance to draw the team even on October 3 at Turner Field, but he was tagged for seven runs in 4 1/3 innings. The Braves essentially secured their 10th straight division crown with a 6-2 win the following night.

Turning point: The entire month of June was a disaster for the team, as it posted a 12-16 record that included a 5.79 ERA. The pitching staff wound up allowing 288 hits in 244 innings in June.

Most valuable player: Jimmy Rollins' enthusiasm and athleticism clearly was a major factor for the Phillies. Rollins led the league in triples while batting .274. He played spectacular defense alongside Scott Rolen.

Most valuable pitcher: Jose Mesa converted 42 of 46 save opportunities while solidifying the back end of manager Larry Bowa's bullpen. His 2.34 ERA was a defiant answer to the critics who insisted his two-year, $6.8 million free agent contract was a mistake.

Most improved player: One year after losing his job during spring training, second baseman Marlon Anderson rebounded to hit .293 with 30 doubles, 11 home runs and 61 RBIs.

Most pleasant surprise: Bobby Abreu became the first player in the franchise's 119-year history to amass 30 home runs (31) and steal 30 bases (36). Abreu also tied his career-high with 118 runs scored.

Key injuries: With the exception of Mike Lieberthal, the team enjoyed a largely injury-free campaign. Randy Wolf suffered a sprained ankle during early August and missed several starts, and Turk Wendell was shut down in September by elbow tendinitis.

Notable: The Phillies' 21-game improvement represented just the seventh time since 1995 that an N.L. team advanced 20 or more games the following season. The team struck out 1,125 times, or almost seven per game. ... The team set a franchise record with 91 errors, eclipsing the previous mark of 100.

—CHRIS EDWARDS

RECORDS

2001 regular-season record: 86-76 (2nd in N.L. East); 47-34 at home; 39-42 on road; 41-35 vs. N.L. East; 19-17 vs. N.L. Central; 19-13 vs. N.L. West; 7-11 vs. A.L.; 17-18 vs. lefthanded starters; 69-58 vs. righthanded starters; 34-34 on grass; 52-42 on turf; 25-27 in daytime; 61-49 at night; 27-22 in one-run games; 7-8 in extra-inning games; 3-1-1 in doubleheaders.

Team record past five years: 371-439 (.458, ranks 12th in league in that span).

TEAM LEADERS

Batting average: Marlon Anderson (.293).
At-bats: Jimmy Rollins (656).
Runs: Bobby Abreu (118).
Hits: Jimmy Rollins (180).
Total Bases: Bobby Abreu (319).
Doubles: Bobby Abreu (48).
Triples: Jimmy Rollins (12).
Home runs: Bobby Abreu (31).
Runs batted in: Bobby Abreu (110).
Stolen bases: Jimmy Rollins (46).
Slugging percentage: Bobby Abreu (.543).
On-base percentage: Bobby Abreu (.393).
Wins: Robert Person (15).
Earned-run average: Randy Wolf (3.70).
Complete games: Randy Wolf (4).
Shutouts: Randy Wolf (2).
Saves: Jose Mesa (42).
Innings pitched: Robert Person (208.1).
Strikeouts: Robert Person (183).

GAMES BY POSITION

Catcher: Johnny Estrada 89, Todd Pratt 34, Mike Lieberthal 33, Gary Bennett 24.
First base: Travis Lee 156, Kevin Jordan 10, Felipe Crespo 2, Todd Pratt 1.
Second base: Marlon Anderson 140, Tomas Perez 29, Kevin Jordan 10, David Newhan 1, Felipe Crespo 1, P.J. Forbes 1.
Third base: Scott Rolen 151, Kevin Jordan 10, Tomas Perez 9.
Shortstop: Jimmy Rollins 157, Tomas Perez 8, Nick Punto 1.
Outfield: Bobby Abreu 162, Doug Glanville 150, Pat Burrell 146, Brian L. Hunter 41, Eric Valent 8, Felipe Crespo 4, Rob Ducey 3, Reggie Taylor 2, Tomas Perez 1, Jason Michaels 1.
Designated hitter: Pat Burrell 5, Eric Valent 4, Brian L. Hunter 1.

TOP DRAFT CHOICES

1. **Gavin Floyd,** RHP, Mount St. Joseph H.S., Baltimore.
4. **Terry Jones,** SS, Upland (Calif.) H.S.
5. **Ryan Howard,** 1B, Southwest Missouri State University.
6. **Bryan Hansen,** OF, Longwood H.S., Coram, N.Y.
7. **Vinny DeChristofaro,** LHP, Richmond Hill (Ga.) H.S.
8. **Taft Cable,** RHP, UNC Greensboro.
9. **Chris Roberson,** OF, Feather River (Calif.) J.C.
10. **Rocky Cherry,** RHP, U. of Oklahoma.

PITTSBURGH PIRATES
NATIONAL LEAGUE CENTRAL DIVISION

Pirates schedule
Home games shaded
D—Day game (games starting before 5 p.m.)
*All-Star Game at Milwaukee
Subject to changes

April
SUN	MON	TUE	WED	THU	FRI	SAT
	1 D NYM	2	3 D NYM	4 D NYM	5 D CUB	6 D CUB
7 CUB	8 CIN	9	10 CIN	11 CIN	12 CUB	13 D CUB
14 CUB	15 MIL	16 MIL	17 MIL	18	19 PHI	20 D PHI
21 PHI	22	23 LA	24 LA	25 D LA	26 SD	27 SD
28 D SD	29	30 COL				

May
SUN	MON	TUE	WED	THU	FRI	SAT
		1 COL	2 D COL	3 SD	4 SD	
5 D SD	6 ARI	7 ARI	8 ARI	9	10 HOU	11 HOU
12 HOU	13 ARI	14 ARI	15 ARI	16 HOU	17 HOU	18 HOU
19 D HOU	20	21 CUB	22 CUB	23 D CUB	24 STL	25 STL
26 D STL	27 CUB	28 CUB	29 CUB	30 D CUB	31 STL	

June
SUN	MON	TUE	WED	THU	FRI	SAT
						1 STL
2 D STL	3 MON	4 MON	5 MON	6	7 MIL	8 MIL
9 D MIL	10 ANA	11 ANA	12 ANA	13	14 CIN	15 CIN
16 D CIN	17	18 OAK	19 OAK	20 OAK	21 TEX	22 TEX
23 D TEX	24	25 MON	26 MON	27 D MON	28 DET	29 DET
30 D DET						

July
SUN	MON	TUE	WED	THU	FRI	SAT
	1 MIL	2 MIL	3 MIL	4 D HOU	5 HOU	6 HOU
7 D HOU	8	9 *	10	11 MIL	12 MIL	13 MIL
14 MIL	15 D HOU	16 D HOU	17 CIN	18 CIN	19 STL	20 STL
21 D STL	22 CIN	23 CIN	24 CIN	25 D HOU	26 HOU	27 HOU
28 D HOU	29	30 COL	31 COL			

August
SUN	MON	TUE	WED	THU	FRI	SAT
				1 COL	2 SF	3 SF
4 D SF	5	6 LA	7 LA	8 LA	9 SF	10 D SF
11 SF	12 STL	13 STL	14 STL	15 STL	16 MIL	17 MIL
18 D MIL	19 STL	20 STL	21 STL	22 STL	23 MIL	24 MIL
25 D MIL	26	27 ATL	28 ATL	29 ATL	30 FLA	31 FLA

September
SUN	MON	TUE	WED	THU	FRI	SAT
1 D FLA	2 D ATL	3 ATL	4 ATL	5	6 D FLA	7 FLA
8 D FLA	9 CIN	10 CIN	11 D CIN	12	13 PHI	14 PHI
15 D PHI	16 CIN	17 CIN	18 CIN	19 CIN	20 CUB	21 CUB
22 D CUB	23	24 NYM	25 NYM	26 NYM	27 D CUB	28 D CUB
29 CUB	30					

2002 SEASON
CLUB DIRECTORY

General partner
Kevin S. McClatchy
Board of directors
William B. Allen, Donald Beaver, Frank Brenner, Chip Ganassi, Kevin S. McClatchy, Mayor Tom Murphy, G. Ogden Nutting, William E. Springer
Chief operating officer
Dick Freeman
Sr. v.p. and general manager
Dave Littlefield
Assistant g.m./baseball operations
To be announced
Assistant g.m./player personnel
Roy Smith
Sr. advisor/player personnel
Lenny Yochim
Special assistants to the g.m.
John Flores, John Green, Ken Parker, Pete Vuckovich
V.p., finance and administration
Jim Plake
V.p., broadcasting and marketing
Vic Gregovits
V.p., communications and ballpark dev.
Steven N. Greenberg
Vice president, operations
Dennis DaPra
Vice president, corporate projects
Nellie Briles
Assistant vice president, communications and ballpark development
Patty Paytas
Controller
David Bowman
Director of office services
Patti Mistick
Traveling secretary
Greg Johnson
Coordinator of baseball operations
Jon Mercurio
Dir. of corporate sales
Mike Berry
Director of community development
Rod Scott
Director of Florida baseball operations
Mike Kennedy

Director of community development
To be announced
Director of information systems
Terry Zeigler
Director of media relations
Jim Trdinich
Director of merchandising
Joe Billetdeaux
Director of operations
Chris Hunter
Director of player development
Brian Graham
Dir. of community & player relations
Kathy Guy
Dir. of promotions and advertising
Rick Orienza
Director of sales
Jim Alexander
Director of security & contract services
Jeff Podobnik
Director of ticket operations
Glen Davis
Head trainer
Kent Biggerstaff
Assistant trainers
Mark Rogow, Mike Sandoval
Equipment manager
Roger Wilson
Director of scouting
Ed Creech
Scouting coordinators
Steve Fleming, Mark McKnight
Special assignment scout
Brannon Bonifay, Chris Lein, Mickey White
Latin America coordinator
Jose Luna
Scouting supervisors
Tom Barnard, Russell Bowen, Dana Brown, Kevin Clouser, Mark Germann, Duane Gustavson, Mike Kendall, Jose Luna, Greg McClain, Jack Powell, Everett Russell, Delvy Santiago, Rob Sidwell, Charlie Sullivan, Mike Williams, Ted Williams

MINOR LEAGUE AFFILIATES

Class	Team	League	Manager
AAA	Nashville	Pacific Coast	Marty Brown
AA	Altoona	Eastern	Dale Sveum
A	Hickory	South Atlantic	Tony Beasley
A	Lynchburg	Carolina	Pete Mackanin
A	Williamsport	New York-Pennsylvania	To be announced
Rookie	Gulf Coast Pirates	Gulf Coast	Woody Huyke

BROADCAST INFORMATION
Radio: KDKA-AM (1020).
Cable TV: Fox Sports Pittsburgh.

SPRING TRAINING
Ballpark (city): McKechnie Field (Bradenton, Fla.).
Ticket information: 941-748-4610.

Follow the Pirates all season at: www.sportingnews.com/baseball/teams/pirates/

Manager—Lloyd McClendon (23).
Coaches—Dave Clark (35), Trent Jewett (44), Tommy Sandt (37), Bruce Tanner (52), Bill Virdon (19), Spin Williams (54).

No.	PITCHERS	B/T	Ht./Wt.	Born	2001 clubs
55	Anderson, Jimmy	L/L	6-1/215	1-22-76	Pittsburgh
69	Arroyo, Bronson	R/R	6-5/181	2-24-77	Pittsburgh, Nashville
53	Beimel, Joe	L/L	6-2/200	4-19-77	Pittsburgh
34	Benson, Kris	R/R	6-4/195	11-7-74	Pittsburgh
60	Burnside, Adrian	R/L	6-3/168	3-15-77	Jacksonville, Altoona
56	Fetters, Mike	R/R	6-4/226	12-19-64	Los Angeles, Pittsburgh
	Fogg, Josh	R/R	6-2/205	12-13-76	Charlotte, Chicago A.L.
	Gonzalez, Mike	R/L	6-2/215	5-23-78	Lynchburg, Altoona
39	Grabow, John	L/L	6-2/190	11-4-78	Altoona, Gulf Coast Pirates, Lynchburg
46	Guzman, Wilson	L/L	5-9/200	7-14-77	DID NOT PLAY
	Lincoln, Mike	R/R	6-2/210	4-10-75	Nashville, Pittsburgh
50	Lowe, Sean	R/R	6-2/205	3-29-71	Chicago A.L., Charlotte
28	Marte, Damaso	L/L	6-0/170	2-14-75	Norwich, Nashville, Pittsburgh
59	McKnight, Tony	R/R	6-5/205	6-29-77	New Orleans, Houston, Pittsburgh
47	Sauerbeck, Scott	R/L	6-3/197	11-9-71	Pittsburgh
14	Vogelsong, Ryan	R/R	6-3/195	7-22-77	Fresno, San Francisco, Nashville, Pittsburgh
32	Wells, Kip	R/R	6-3/196	4-21-77	Charlotte, Chicago A.L.
58	Williams, David	L/L	6-2/205	3-12-79	Pittsburgh, Nashville, Altoona
	Williams, Mike	R/R	6-2/200	7-29-68	Pittsburgh, Houston

No.	CATCHERS	B/T	Ht./Wt.	Born	2001 clubs
11	Cota, Humberto	R/R	6-0/175	2-7-79	Nashville, Pittsburgh
	House, J.R.	R/R	6-1/202	11-11-79	Altoona
18	Kendall, Jason	R/R	6-0/195	6-26-74	Pittsburgh
15	Osik, Keith	R/R	6-0/195	10-22-68	Pittsburgh
36	Wilson, Craig	R/R	6-2/217	11-30-76	Nashville, Pittsburgh

No.	INFIELDERS	B/T	Ht./Wt.	Born	2001 clubs
6	Benjamin, Mike	R/R	6-0/175	11-22-65	Pittsburgh
	Mackowiak, Rob	L/R	5-10/170	6-20-76	Nashville, Pittsburgh
2	Meares, Pat	R/R	6-0/187	9-6-68	Pittsburgh
30	Morris, Warren	L/R	5-11/180	1-11-74	Nashville, Pittsburgh
10	Nunez, Abraham	B/R	5-11/185	3-16-76	Pittsburgh
16	Ramirez, Aramis	R/R	6-1/219	6-25-78	Pittsburgh
12	Wilson, Jack	R/R	6-0/175	12-29-77	Pittsburgh, Nashville
29	Young, Kevin	R/R	6-3/225	6-16-69	Pittsburgh

No.	OUTFIELDERS	B/T	Ht./Wt.	Born	2001 clubs
	Alvarez, Tony	R/R	6-1/200	5-10-79	Lynchburg, Altoona
14	Bell, Derek	R/R	6-2/215	12-11-68	Pittsburgh, Nashville
13	Brown, Adrian	B/R	6-0/185	2-7-74	Pittsburgh, Altoona, Lynchburg, Williamsport
26	Davis, J.J.	R/R	6-4/250	10-25-78	Altoona, Gulf Coast Pirates
24	Giles, Brian	L/L	5-10/200	1-20-71	Pittsburgh
3	Hermansen, Chad	R/R	6-2/185	9-10-77	Nashville, Pittsburgh
5	Redman, Tike	L/L	5-11/166	3-10-77	Nashville, Pittsburgh
1	Rios, Armando	L/L	5-9/185	9-13-71	San Francisco, Pittsburgh

BALLPARK INFORMATION

Ballpark (capacity, surface)
PNC Park (37,898, grass)

Address
PNC Park at North Shore
115 Federal Street
Pittsburgh, PA 15212

Official website
www.pittsburghpirates.com

Business phone
412-323-5000

Ticket information
800-BUY-BUCS

Ticket prices
$35 (dugout boxes)
$27 (infield boxes)
$26 (baseline boxes)
$24 (LF/RF boxes)
$18 (OF reserved)
$16 (deck seating, grandstand)
$14 (bleachers)
$11 (LF/RF grandstand)
$9 (LF terrace)

Field dimensions (from home plate)
To left field at foul line, 325 feet
To center field, 399 feet
To right field at foul line, 320 feet

First game played
April 9, 2001 (Reds 8, Pirates 2)

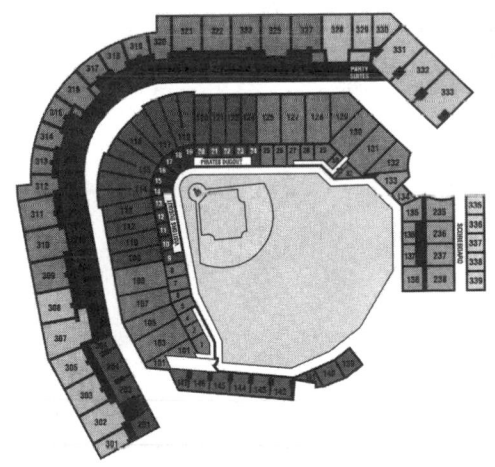

2002 SEASON *Pittsburgh Pirates*

Date	Opp.	Res.	Score	(inn.*)	Hits	Opp. hits	Winning pitcher	Losing pitcher	Save	Record	Pos.	GB
4-3	At Cin.	L	2-3		7	4	O. Fernandez	Ritchie	Graves	0-1	T3rd	1.0
4-4	At Cin.	W	6-5	(10)	7	18	M. Williams	Sullivan		1-1	2nd	1.0
4-5	At Cin.	L	1-4		7	5	Dessens	Anderson	Riedling	1-2	T3rd	2.0
4-6	At Hou.	L	1-4		5	7	Dotel	Olivares	Wagner	1-3	T4th	3.0
4-7	At Hou.	W	5-3		13	6	Arroyo	Bottenfield	M. Williams	2-3	T3rd	2.0
4-8	At Hou.	W	9-3		12	7	Beimel	Elarton		3-3	T2nd	1.0
4-9	Cin.	L	2-8		6	12	Reitsma	Ritchie		3-4	T3rd	1.5
4-11	Cin.	W	6-5		10	15	Silva	Riedling	M. Williams	4-4	4th	2.0
4-12	Cin.	L	6-11		7	12	Harnisch	Olivares		4-5	4th	2.0
4-13	At Chi.	L	2-4		6	5	Bere	Arroyo	Fassero	4-6	5th	3.0
4-14	At Chi.	L	6-7		11	13	Aybar	Silva	Fassero	4-7	6th	4.0
4-15	At Chi.	L	1-5		5	11	Duncan	Sauerbeck		4-8	6th	4.0
4-16	Hou.	W	3-0		5	8	Anderson	Miller	M. Williams	5-8	6th	3.5
4-18	Hou.	W	8-4		12	6	Arroyo	Reynolds		6-8	6th	3.5
4-20	Chi.	L	2-8		6	7	Lieber	Martinez		6-9	6th	4.5
4-21	Chi.	L	3-4		9	7	Heredia	M. Williams	Fassero	6-10	6th	5.5
4-22	Chi.	W	4-3	(10)	12	9	M. Williams	Fassero		7-10	6th	4.5
4-24	At L.A.	W	5-1		7	4	Olivares	Park		8-10	6th	3.5
4-25	At L.A.	L	5-6		10	5	Adams	Manzanillo		8-11	6th	3.5
4-26	At L.A.	L	3-6		6	8	Brown	Ritchie		8-12	6th	4.5
4-27	At S.D.	W	3-0		6	8	Anderson	Jones	M. Williams	9-12	6th	4.5
4-28	At S.D.	L	1-8		5	14	Eaton	Arroyo		9-13	6th	4.5
4-29	At S.D.	L	1-6		6	9	Williams	Olivares	Hoffman	9-14	6th	5.5
5-1	S.F	L	6-11		7	14	Rueter	Martinez		9-15	6th	5.5
5-2	S.F	L	6-7		7	9	Ortiz	Silva	Nen	9-16	6th	6.5
5-3	S.F	W	4-3		6	9	Silva	Estes	M. Williams	10-16	6th	5.5
5-4	Col.	L	3-9		6	13	Hampton	Arroyo		10-17	6th	6.5
5-5	Col.	W	11-3		12	3	Olivares	Chacon		11-17	6th	6.5
5-6	Col.	W	4-3	(11)	9	12	Beimel	White		12-17	6th	6.5
5-7	At St.L.	L	0-7		4	10	Morris	Ritchie		12-18	6th	7.5
5-8	At St.L.	L	2-8		4	8	An. Benes	Anderson		12-19	6th	7.5
5-9	At St.L.	L	2-6		5	10	Hermanson	Arroyo		12-20	6th	8.5
5-10	At St.L.	L	5-11		4	17	Matthews	Silva		12-21	6th	8.5
5-11	At Mil.	W	3-0		6	4	Schmidt	Haynes	M. Williams	13-21	6th	7.5
5-12	At Mil.	L	4-5	(12)	13	9	Leskanic	Beimel		13-22	6th	7.5
5-13	At Mil.	L	1-4		5	8	Sheets	Anderson		13-23	6th	8.0
5-14	At Mil.	L	8-11		13	13	Wright	Wengert	Leskanic	13-24	6th	8.5
5-15	St.L.	L	3-8		9	14	Hermanson	Olivares		13-25	6th	9.5
5-16	St.L.	L	0-3		7	5	Kile	Schmidt		13-26	6th	10.5
5-17	St.L.	L	2-12		8	13	Morris	Ritchie		13-27	6th	11.5
5-19	Mil.	W	6-1		9	5	Anderson	Sheets		14-27	6th	10.0
5-20	Mil.	W	8-7		12	10	Manzanillo	Weathers	M. Williams	15-27	6th	10.0
5-23†	At Phi.	L	0-4		3	10	Wolf	Schmidt	Bottalico	15-28		
5-23‡	At Phi.	L	2-5		10	9	Daal	Olivares	Mesa	15-29	6th	10.0
5-24	At Phi.	L	5-6		8	12	Cormier	Sauerbeck	Mesa	15-30	6th	11.0
5-25	At Atl.	L	0-1		7	5	Maddux	Ritchie		15-31	6th	12.0
5-26	At Atl.	L	3-9		8	14	Burkett	Wengert		15-32	6th	12.0
5-27	At Atl.	W	6-3		12	11	Arroyo	Glavine	M. Williams	16-32	6th	12.0
5-28	Fla.	W	8-5		12	10	Silva	Miceli	M. Williams	17-32	6th	12.0
5-29	Fla.	L	0-5		8	9	Burnett	Anderson		17-33	6th	13.0
5-30	Fla.	L	7-9	(10)	12	12	Alfonseca	M. Williams	Looper	17-34	6th	14.0
6-1	Atl.	L	1-5		4	10	Burkett	Ritchie		17-35	6th	15.0
6-3†	Atl.	L	7-11		13	18	Glavine	Olivares		17-36		
6-3‡	Atl.	L	3-8		6	12	Smoltz	Anderson		17-37	6th	16.0
6-5	At Fla.	W	5-2		8	6	Schmidt	Penny	M. Williams	18-37	6th	16.0
6-6	At Fla.	L	2-7		8	10	Dempster	Ritchie		18-38	6th	17.0
6-7	At Fla.	L	3-5		7	8	Bones	Manzanillo	Alfonseca	18-39	6th	18.0
6-8	At Min.	L	6-8		9	8	Carrasco	Olivares	Hawkins	18-40	6th	18.0
6-9	At Min.	L	2-3		8	11	Mays	Anderson	Hawkins	18-41	6th	19.0
6-10	At Min.	W	11-8		11	12	Sauerbeck	Miller	M. Williams	19-41	6th	18.0
6-12	At Det.	W	13-3		15	7	Ritchie	Mlicki		20-41	6th	18.0
6-13	At Det.	L	3-6		11	9	Weaver	Beimel	Anderson	20-42	6th	18.0
6-14	At Det.	L	4-6		12	11	Sparks	Arroyo	Anderson	20-43	6th	18.0
6-15	Cle.	W	6-3		11	6	Anderson	Burba	M. Williams	21-43	6th	18.0
6-16	Cle.	W	6-4		8	11	Schmidt	Wright	M. Williams	22-43	6th	18.0
6-17	Cle.	W	1-0		3	4	Ritchie	Karsay		23-43	6th	18.0
6-19	Phi.	W	8-5		17	8	Beimel	Chen	Sauerbeck	24-43	6th	16.5
6-20	Phi.	L	5-9		8	14	Daal	Arroyo		24-44	6th	17.5
6-21	Phi.	L	3-6		5	8	Person	Anderson	Mesa	24-45	6th	18.5
6-22	Mon.	L	5-11		7	10	Armas	Schmidt		24-46	6th	18.5
6-23	Mon.	W	7-4		13	9	Ritchie	Yoshii	M. Williams	25-46	6th	17.5
6-24	Mon.	L	4-11		8	16	Mattes	Beimel		25-47	6th	17.5
6-25	Mil.	W	6-4		10	7	D. Williams	Levrault	M. Williams	26-47	6th	17.5
6-26	Mil.	W	7-6	(12)	10	12	Olivares	King		27-47	6th	17.5

Date	Opp.	Res.	Score	(inn.*)	Hits	Opp. hits	Winning pitcher	Losing pitcher	Save	Record	Pos.	GB
6-27	Mil.	W	6-2		10	4	Schmidt	Haynes		28-47	6th	16.5
6-28	Mil.	W	1-0		7	6	Ritchie	Wright	M. Williams	29-47	6th	15.5
6-29	At Mon.	L	3-12		5	14	Mattes	Beimel		29-48	6th	16.5
6-30	At Mon.	L	6-7		11	12	Lloyd	M. Williams		29-49	6th	16.5
7-1	At Mon.	L	3-9		7	10	Thurman	Anderson		29-50	6th	17.5
7-2	At Cin.	W	10-5		13	10	Schmidt	Davis		30-50	6th	17.0
7-3	At Cin.	W	3-2		9	5	Ritchie	Dessens	M. Williams	31-50	6th	17.0
7-4	At Cin.	W	14-3		19	9	Beimel	Reith		32-50	5th	16.0
7-5	At Cin.	L	1-7		8	7	Acevedo	D. Williams		32-51	6th	17.0
7-6	At Chi.	W	10-6		11	13	Manzanillo	Howry		33-51	5th	17.0
7-7	At Chi.	L	1-4		4	10	K. Wells	Schmidt	Foulke	33-52	5th	18.0
7-8	At Chi.	L	2-9		7	12	Lowe	Ritchie		33-53	5th	18.0
7-12	K.C.	W	2-0		5	6	Anderson	Suppan	M. Williams	34-53	5th	18.0
7-13	K.C.	W	1-0		11	1	Ritchie	Grimsley		35-53	5th	18.0
7-14	K.C.	L	4-7		6	12	Wilson	D. Williams	Hernandez	35-54	5th	17.0
7-15	L.A.	L	2-4		7	7	Brown	Schmidt	Shaw	35-55	5th	18.0
7-16	L.A.	L	4-6		7	8	Gagne	Beimel	Shaw	35-56	5th	18.0
7-17	L.A.	L	1-4		5	8	Adams	Anderson	Herges	35-57	5th	19.0
7-18	Chi.	L	5-6		6	10	Fassero	M. Williams	Gordon	35-58	5th	20.0
7-19	Chi.	W	3-2		11	5	Olivares	Duncan	M. Williams	36-58	5th	19.0
7-20	At St.L.	W	4-1		4	2	Schmidt	Hermanson	Manzanillo	37-58	5th	18.0
7-21	At St.L.	L	2-9		9	7	Smith	Beimel		37-59	5th	19.0
7-22	At St.L.	W	2-0		9	6	Anderson	Timlin	M. Williams	38-59	5th	18.0
7-24	At Chi.	L	2-10		10	17	Tavarez	Ritchie		38-60	5th	19.5
7-25	At Chi.	L	5-6		11	8	Lieber	D. Williams		38-61	5th	20.5
7-26	Hou.	L	2-3		6	6	Mlicki	Schmidt	Wagner	38-62	5th	20.5
7-27	Hou.	W	3-2		10	9	Beimel	Reynolds	M. Williams	39-62	5th	20.5
7-28§	Hou.	W	9-8		12	12	Olivares	Wagner		40-62		
7-28∞	Hou.	L	3-12		11	15	McKnight	Anderson		40-63	T5th	20.0
7-29	Hou.	W	4-1		7	6	Ritchie	Miller	M. Williams	41-63	T5th	20.0
7-31	At S.F	L	7-8	(11)	13	16	Gomes	Wilkins		41-64	6th	21.0
8-1	At S.F	L	1-3		2	7	Schmidt	Beimel	Nen	41-65	6th	21.0
8-2	At S.F	L	0-3		3	9	Rueter	McKnight	Nen	41-66	6th	21.0
8-3	At Col.	L	7-12		11	15	Hampton	Anderson		41-67	6th	22.0
8-4	At Col.	W	6-3		9	10	Ritchie	Chacon		42-67	6th	21.0
8-5	At Col.	W	5-4		9	10	Lincoln	Bohanon	Fetters	43-67	6th	20.0
8-7	L.A.	L	1-2		7	9	Adams	McKnight	Shaw	43-68	6th	21.0
8-8	L.A.	L	4-9		11	13	Carrara	Anderson		43-69	6th	22.0
8-9	L.A.	W	8-5		11	11	Ritchie	Park	Fetters	44-69	6th	21.0
8-10	S.D.	L	2-3		7	7	Tollberg	D. Williams	Hoffman	44-70	6th	22.0
8-11	S.D.	L	2-6		7	12	Lawrence	Beimel		44-71	6th	22.0
8-12	S.D.	W	7-6		13	11	Manzanillo	Myers		45-71	6th	21.0
8-13	At Ari.	L	0-3		5	5	Johnson	Anderson		45-72	6th	21.5
8-14	At Ari.	L	3-4	(10)	10	10	Batista	Marte		45-73	6th	22.0
8-15	At Ari.	L	2-5		8	7	Schilling	D. Williams		45-74	6th	23.0
8-16	At Hou.	L	3-4		10	10	Miller	Beimel	Wagner	45-75	6th	23.5
8-17	At Hou.	L	5-6		8	12	Mlicki	McKnight	Wagner	45-76	6th	23.5
8-18	At Hou.	L	0-3		2	6	Hernandez	Anderson	Dotel	45-77	6th	24.5
8-19	At Hou.	L	2-12		7	13	Oswalt	Ritchie		45-78	6th	25.5
8-21	Ari.	W	4-2		9	2	Olivares	Schilling	Fetters	46-78	6th	25.5
8-22	Ari.	L	0-6		4	11	Lopez	Beimel		46-79	6th	25.5
8-23	Ari.	W	5-1		6	6	McKnight	Johnson	Fetters	47-79	6th	25.5
8-24	Hou.	L	1-5		7	7	Oswalt	Anderson		47-80	6th	26.5
8-25	Hou.	W	8-2		7	10	Ritchie	Mlicki		48-80	6th	25.5
8-26	Hou.	L	1-3		7	6	Villone	D. Williams	Wagner	48-81	6th	26.5
8-27	At Mil.	L	5-12		9	12	Coppinger	Beimel	Buddie	48-82	6th	27.0
8-28	At Mil.	W	6-5		10	11	Sauerbeck	Leskanic	Fetters	49-82	6th	27.0
8-29	Al Mil.	L	8-9		12	11	Levrault	Anderson	Fox	49-83	6th	28.0
8-31	At Cin.	L	3-11		7	12	Reitsma	Ritchie		49-84	6th	29.5
9-1	At Cin.	W	7-0		8	5	D. Williams	Acevedo		50-84	6th	28.5
9-2	At Cin.	L	6-8		11	14	Sullivan	Lincoln	Graves	50-85	6th	29.5
9-3†	Mil.	L	7-12		12	11	Leiter	Vogelsong		50-86		
9-3‡	Mil.	W	3-2		6	6	Fetters	Fox		51-86	6th	29.0
9-4	Mil.	W	5-2		6	6	Arroyo	Levrault	Fetters	52-86	6th	29.0
9-5	Mil.	W	5-1		8	3	Ritchie	Wright		53-86	6th	29.0
9-6	Cin.	L	6-8		10	10	Brower	Loiselle	Graves	53-87	6th	29.0
9-7	Cin.	W	3-1		6	7	McKnight	Davis	Olivares	54-87	6th	29.0
9-8	Cin.	W	5-2		10	9	Anderson	Dessens		55-87	6th	28.0
9-9	Cin.	L	3-5		13	8	Reyes	Vogelsong	Graves	55-88	6th	29.0
9-17	N.Y.	L	1-4		5	6	Franco	Fetters	Benitez	55-89	6th	29.5
9-18	N.Y.	L	5-7		6	10	Riggan	Olivares	Benitez	55-90	6th	30.5
9-19	N.Y.	L	2-9		11	15	Gonzalez	McKnight		55-91	6th	31.5
9-20	St.L.	L	1-9		4	11	Williams	Anderson		55-92	6th	32.5
9-21	St.L.	L	5-9		8	13	Hackman	Olivares		55-93	6th	32.5
9-22	St.L.	L	1-4		5	10	Smith	Ritchie	Stechschulte	55-94	6th	33.5
9-23	St.L.	W	2-1		7	4	D. Williams	Hermanson	Manzanillo	56-94	6th	33.5
9-24	Chi.	W	7-6		10	10	Lincoln	Chiasson	Loiselle	57-94	6th	33.5
9-25	Chi.	W	13-1		15	6	Anderson	Bere		58-94	6th	32.5

Date	Opp.	Res.	Score	(inn.*)	Hits	Opp. hits	Winning pitcher	Losing pitcher	Save	Record	Pos.	GB
9-26	Chi.	L	4-8		10	13	Cruz	Arroyo		58-95	6th	32.5
9-28	At St.L.	L	3-14		6	15	Hermanson	Ritchie		58-96	6th	33.0
9-29	At St.L.	L	0-2		5	3	Morris	D. Williams	Stechschulte	58-97	6th	33.0
9-30	At St.L.	L	3-7		3	9	Williams	McKnight		58-98	6th	33.0
10-1	At N.Y.	W	5-1		11	5	Anderson	Rusch	Sauerbeck	59-98	6th	32.5
10-2	At N.Y.	W	10-1		15	5	Arroyo	Chen		60-98	6th	31.5
10-3	At N.Y.	L	0-3		2	5	Trachsel	Ritchie		60-99	6th	31.5
10-5	At Chi.	W	3-2		4	6	Beimel	Bere	Fetters	61-99	6th	31.0
10-6	At Chi.	L	2-13		2	16	Tavarez	McKnight		61-100	6th	32.0
10-7	At Chi.	W	4-3		7	9	Beimel	Zambrano	Fetters	62-100	6th	31.0

Monthly records: April (9-14), May (8-20), June (12-15), July (12-15), August (8-20), September (9-14), October (4-2).
*Innings, if other than nine. †First game of a doubleheader. ‡Second game of a doubleheader. §Day separate admission. ∞Night separate admission.

HIGHLIGHTS

High point: A three-game sweep of the Indians from June 15-17 represented some of the Pirates' best baseball, and showed how electric the atmosphere at PNC Park might be if the Pirates ever put a contender on the field.

Low point: The Pirates were blown out in both ends of a Sunday doubleheader against the Braves on June 3. The sight of disgruntled fans streaming across the Roberto Clemente Bridge after leaving the park early probably sealed the fate of GM Cam Bonifay, who was fired a week later.

Turning point: It came in spring training when Kris Benson reported pain in his elbow. It turned out he needed reconstructive surgery, and he joined starters Jason Schmidt and Francisco Cordova on the sidelines, dooming the Pirates to a bad season with inexperienced starting pitching.

Most valuable player: Brian Giles gets the nod over Aramis Ramirez, who is still prone to defensive mishaps. Giles started slowly, then settled into his usual level of production.

Most valuable pitcher: Todd Ritchie was forced into the No. 1 spot by the injuries to Benson, Cordova and Schmidt. He endured through a tough start that was often a product of poor offensive and defensive support.

Most improved player: Ramirez elevated his game and became a dependable run producer. He welcomed opportunities with the game on the line and frequently delivered.

Most pleasant surprise: Injuries brought C/1B/OF Craig Wilson to the majors and his pinch hitting success kept him on the roster. Wilson went from marginal prospect to a player who could get 500 at-bats this season.

Key injuries: Adrian Brown missed most of the season with a shoulder injury that required surgery. ... Jose Silva didn't pitch again after a batted ball broke his leg on June 3. ... Armando Rios, acquired from the Giants, had a season-ending knee injury in his second game with the Pirates. Ryan Vogelsong, who came in the same deal, blew out his elbow in his second Pittsburgh start.

Notable: The Pirates had their seventh 100-loss season in 115 years and first since 1985. ... The club had its ninth consecutive losing season, the longest streak since the Pirates had nine losing years from 1949-57.

—JOHN MEHNO

RECORDS

2001 regular-season record: 62-100 (6th in N.L. Central); 38-43 at home; 24-57 on road; 7-23 vs. N.L. East; 36-48 vs. N.L. Central; 11-22 vs. N.L. West; 8-7 vs. A.L.; 12-20 vs. lefthanded starters; 50-80 vs. righthanded starters; 61-92 on grass; 1-8 on turf; 18-30 in daytime; 44-70 at night; 22-20 in one-run games; 4-4 in extra-inning games; 0-2-1 in doubleheaders.

Team record past five years: 357-452 (.441, ranks 15th in league in that span).

TEAM LEADERS

Batting average: Brian Giles (.309).
At-bats: Jason Kendall (606).
Runs: Brian Giles (116).
Hits: Aramis Ramirez (181).
Total Bases: Brian Giles (340).
Doubles: Aramis Ramirez (40).
Triples: Brian Giles (7).
Home runs: Brian Giles (37).
Runs batted in: Aramis Ramirez (112).
Stolen bases: Kevin Young (15).
Slugging percentage: Brian Giles (.590).
On-base percentage: Brian Giles (.404).
Wins: Todd Ritchie (11).
Earned-run average: Todd Ritchie (4.47).
Complete games: Todd Ritchie (4).
Shutouts: Todd Ritchie (2).
Saves: Mike Williams (22).
Innings pitched: Todd Ritchie (207.1).
Strikeouts: Todd Ritchie (124).

GAMES BY POSITION

Catcher: Jason Kendall 133, Keith Osik 39, Craig A. Wilson 10, Humberto Cota 3, John Wehner 1.

First base: Kevin Young 137, Craig A. Wilson 26, John Vander Wal 13, John Wehner 11, Keith Osik 5, Andy Barkett 4, Adam Hyzdu 4, Alex Hernandez 2, Rob Mackowiak 1.

Second base: Pat Meares 85, Abraham Nunez 48, Warren Morris 29, Rob Mackowiak 21, Enrique Wilson 10, Mendy Lopez 9, Luis Figueroa 3, Keith Osik 2, John Wehner 1.

Third base: Aramis Ramirez 157, John Wehner 6, Mendy Lopez 4, Keith Osik 3, Enrique Wilson 2, Rob Mackowiak 2, Abraham Nunez 1, Warren Morris 1.

Shortstop: Jack Wilson 107, Abraham Nunez 48, Enrique Wilson 28, Mendy Lopez 6.

Outfield: Brian Giles 159, John Vander Wal 73, Emil Brown 54, Derek Bell 46, Rob Mackowiak 46, Gary Matthews Jr. 44, Tike Redman 35, Jason Kendall 27, Adam Hyzdu 27, Chad Hermansen 20, Craig A. Wilson 14, Andy Barkett 10, John Wehner 8, Adrian Brown 7, Alex Hernandez 4, Armando Rios 2, Abraham Nunez 1, Keith Osik 1.

Designated hitter: John Vander Wal 7, Craig A. Wilson 2, Andy Barkett 1.

TOP DRAFT CHOICES

1. **John VanBenschoten,** RHP/1B, Kent State University.
3. **Jeremy Guthrie,** RHP, Stanford Univ.
4. **Jeff Keppinger,** SS, U. of Georgia.
5. **Travis Chapman,** 1B, Indian River (Fla.) C.C.
6. **Drew Friedberg,** LHP, Arizona State U.
7. **Michael McCuistion,** C Yucaipa (Calif.) H.S.
8. **Chris Duffy,** OF, Arizona State Univ.
9. **Jason Fellows,** 1B, Berkmar H.S., Lawrenceville, Ga.
10. **Aaron Bulkley,** SS, Port Byron (N.Y.) H.S.

ST. LOUIS CARDINALS
NATIONAL LEAGUE CENTRAL DIVISION

Cardinals schedule
Home games shaded
D—Day game (games starting before 5 p.m.)
*All-Star Game at Milwaukee
Subject to change

April
SUN	MON	TUE	WED	THU	FRI	SAT
	1 D COL	2	3 COL	4 D COL	5 HOU	6 HOU
7 D HOU	8	9 MIL	10 MIL	11 D MIL	12 HOU	13 D HOU
14 D HOU	15 ARI	16 ARI	17 D ARI	18 MIL	19 MIL	20 MIL
21 D MIL	22	23 NYM	24 NYM	25 NYM	26 MON	27 D MON
28 MON	29	30 FLA				

May
SUN	MON	TUE	WED	THU	FRI	SAT
		1 FLA	2 D FLA	3 ATL	4 D ATL
5 ATL	6 CUB	7 CUB	8 D CUB	9 CIN	10 CIN	11 D CIN
12 CIN	13 CUB	14 D CUB	15 CUB	16	17 CIN	18 D CIN
19 D CIN	20 CIN	21 HOU	22 HOU	23 HOU	24 PIT	25 PIT
26 D PIT	27 D HOU	28 HOU	29 HOU	30	31 PIT	

June
SUN	MON	TUE	WED	THU	FRI	SAT
						1 PIT
2 D PIT	3	4 CIN	5 CIN	6 D CIN	7 KC	8 KC
9 D KC	10 SEA	11 SEA	12 SEA	13	14 KC	15 D KC
16 D KC	17	18 ANA	19 ANA	20 D ANA	21 D CUB	22 D CUB
23 CUB	24	25 MIL	26 MIL	27 MIL	28 CIN	29 CIN
30 CIN						

July
SUN	MON	TUE	WED	THU	FRI	SAT
	1 SD	2 SD	3 SD	4 LA	5 LA	6 D LA
7 D LA	8	9	*10	11	12 SD	13 SD
14 D SD	15 LA	16 D LA	17 SF	18 SF	19 PIT	20 PIT
21 D PIT	22 SF	23 SF	24 SF	25 SF	26 CUB	27 D CUB
28 D CUB	29	30 FLA	31 FLA			

August
SUN	MON	TUE	WED	THU	FRI	SAT
				1 FLA	2 ATL	3 D ATL
4 D ATL	5	6 MON	7 MON	8 MON	9 NYM	10 D NYM
11 D NYM	12 PIT	13 PIT	14 PIT	15 PIT	16 PHI	17 PHI
18 D PHI	19 PIT	20 PIT	21 PIT	22 PIT	23 PHI	24 PHI
25 D PHI	26	27 CIN	28 CIN	29 D CIN	30 D CUB	31 D CUB

September
SUN	MON	TUE	WED	THU	FRI	SAT
1 D CUB	2 D CIN	3 D CIN	4 CIN	5	6 CUB	7 D CUB
8 CUB	9 MIL	10 MIL	11 MIL	12 HOU	13 HOU	14 HOU
15 HOU	16 COL	17 COL	18 COL	19 D HOU	20 HOU	21 D HOU
22 HOU	23 ARI	24 ARI	25 D ARI	26 MIL	27 MIL	28 MIL
29 MIL	30					

2002 SEASON
CLUB DIRECTORY

Chairman of the board/general partner
William O. DeWitt Jr.
Chairman
Frederick O. Hanser
Secretary-treasurer
Andrew N. Baur
President
Mark C. Lamping
Vice president, general manager
Walt Jocketty
Admin. assistant to the president
Julie Laningham
Sr. exec. asst. to v.p., general manager
Judy Carpenter-Barada
Vice president/player personnel
Jerry Walker
V.p., special asst. to the g.m.
Bob Gebhard
Special assistant to the general manager
Mike Jorgensen
Senior v.p., sales and marketing
Dan Farrell
Vice president, controller
Brad Wood
Vice president, community relations
Marty Hendin
Vice president, business development
Bill DeWitt III
Vice president, stadium operations
Joe Abernathy
Vice president, ticket operations
Josie Arnold
Vice president, ticket sales
Kevin Wade
Director, group sales
Joe Strohm
Manager, ticket sales
Mark Murray
Director, corporate sales/marketing
Thane van Breusegen
V.p., group dir., community outreach/ Cardinals Care
Tim Hanser
Director, target marketing
Ted Savage
Director, media relations
Brian Bartow
Mgr., media relations & publications
Steve Zesch

Assistant to director, media relations
Brad Hainje
Traveling secretary
C.J. Cherre
Director, player development
Bruce Manno
Director, baseball operations
John Mozeliak
Director, professional scouting
Marteese Robinson
Director, amateur scouting
Marty Maier
Director, international scouting
Jeff Scott
Director, minor league operations
Scott Smulczenski
Mgr., baseball info./player dev.
John Vuch
Major league trainer
Barry Weinberg
Assistant major league trainer
Brad Henderson
Medical/rehabilitation coordinator
Mark O'Neal
Equipment manager
Buddy Bates
Assistant equipment manager
Rip Rowan
Video coordinator
Chad Blair
Special assignment scouts
Bing Devine, Jim Leyland, Joe Sparks, Mike Squires
Special instructor
Boots Day
Professional scouts
Clark Crist, Marty Keough
Cross-checkers
Chuck Fick, Fred McAlister, Mike Roberts, Roger Smith
Scouts
Randy Benson, Ben Galante, Steve Gossett, Manny Guerra, Dave Karaff, Scott Melvin, Scott Nichols, Jay North, Dan Ontiveros, Joe Rigoli, Tommy Shields, Steve Turco, Dane Walker
International scouts
Jorge Brito, Domingo Carrasquel, Bobby Diaz

MINOR LEAGUE AFFILIATES

Class	Team	League	Manager
AAA	Memphis	Pacific Coast	Gaylen Pitts
AA	New Haven	Eastern	Mark DeJohn
A	Potomac	Carolina	Joe Cunningham
A	Peoria	Midwest	Danny Sheaffer
A	New Jersey	New York-Pennsylvania	Tommy Shields
Rookie	Johnson City	Appalachian	Brian Rupp

BROADCAST INFORMATION

Radio: KMOX-AM (1120).
TV: KPLR-TV (Channel 11).
Cable TV: Fox Sports Midwest.

SPRING TRAINING

Ballpark (city): Roger Dean Stadium (Jupiter, Fla.).
Ticket information: 561-966-3309.

Follow the Cardinals all season at: www.sportingnews.com/baseball/teams/cardinals/

SPRING TRAINING ROSTER

Manager—Tony La Russa (10).
Coaches—Dave Duncan (18), Marty Mason (38), Dave McKay (39), Jose Oquendo (11), Mitchell Page (12), Joe Pettini.

No.	PITCHERS	B/T	Ht./Wt.	Born	2001 clubs
66	Ankiel, Rick	L/L	6-1/210	7-19-79	St. Louis, Memphis, Johnson City
40	Benes, Andy	R/R	6-6/245	8-20-67	St. Louis
	Caple, Chance	R/R	6-6/215	8-9-78	DID NOT PLAY
	Crudale, Mike	R/R	6-0/205	1-3-77	New Haven
63	Hackman, Luther	R/R	6-4/195	10-10-74	New Haven, Memphis, St. Louis
65	Hutchinson, Chad	R/R	6-5/230	2-21-77	St. Louis, Memphis
44	Isringhausen, Jason	R/R	6-3/210	9-7-72	Oakland
50	Joseph, Kevin	R/R	6-4/200	8-1-76	Shreveport, San Jose, Fresno, Memphis
	Journell, Jimmy	R/R	6-4/205	12-29-77	Potomac, New Haven
57	Kile, Darryl	R/R	6-5/212	12-2-68	St. Louis
44	Kline, Steve	B/L	6-1/215	8-22-72	St. Louis
	Lambert, Jeremy	R/R	6-1/195	1-10-79	New Haven, Memphis
	Layfield, Scotty	R/R	6-2/205	9-13-76	Potomac
50	Matthews, Mike	L/L	6-2/180	10-24-73	St. Louis
35	Morris, Matt	R/R	6-5/210	8-9-74	St. Louis
	Pearce, Josh	R/R	6-3/215	8-20-77	New Haven, Memphis
52	Smith, Bud	L/L	6-0/170	10-23-79	St. Louis, Memphis
67	Stechschulte, Gene	R/R	6-5/210	8-12-73	St. Louis
55	Stephenson, Garrett	R/R	6-5/208	1-2-72	Memphis
50	Timlin, Mike	R/R	6-4/210	3-10-66	St. Louis
43	Veres, Dave	R/R	6-2/220	10-19-66	St. Louis
	Walrond, Les	L/L	6-0/195	11-7-76	New Haven
18	Williams, Woody	R/R	6-0/195	8-19-66	San Diego, St. Louis

No.	CATCHERS	B/T	Ht./Wt.	Born	2001 clubs
8	Difelice, Mike	R/R	6-2/205	5-28-69	Tampa Bay, Arizona, Tucson
26	Marrero, Eli	R/R	6-1/180	11-17-73	St. Louis
44	Matheny, Mike	R/R	6-3/205	9-22-70	St. Louis
32	McDonald, Keith	R/R	6-2/215	2-8-73	Memphis, St. Louis

No.	INFIELDERS	B/T	Ht./Wt.	Born	2001 clubs
41	Cairo, Miguel	R/R	6-1/200	5-4-74	Iowa, Chicago N.L., St. Louis
	Garcia, Luis	R/R	6-4/185	11-5-78	Sarasota, Trenton
24	Martinez, Tino	L/R	6-2/210	12-7-67	New York A.L.
27	Polanco, Placido	R/R	5-10/168	10-10-75	St. Louis
5	Pujols, Albert	R/R	6-3/210	1-16-80	St. Louis
3	Renteria, Edgar	R/R	6-1/180	8-7-75	St. Louis
4	Vina, Fernando	L/R	5-9/174	4-16-69	St. Louis

No.	OUTFIELDERS	B/T	Ht./Wt.	Born	2001 clubs
7	Drew, J.D.	L/R	6-1/195	11-20-75	St. Louis, Peoria
15	Edmonds, Jim	L/L	6-1/212	6-27-70	St. Louis
	Ortega, Bill	R/R	6-4/205	7-24-75	Memphis, St. Louis
13	Robinson, Kerry	L/L	6-0/175	10-3-73	St. Louis, Memphis
99	Taguchi, So	R/R	5-10/163	7-2-69	Orix (Japan)

BALLPARK INFORMATION

Ballpark (capacity, surface)
Busch Stadium (49,814, grass)
Address
250 Stadium Plaza
St. Louis, MO 63102
Official website
www.stlcardinals.com
Business phone
314-421-3060
Ticket information
314-421-2400
Ticket prices
$37 (field boxes-IF), $34 (loge boxes-IF)
$32 (field boxes-OF), $28 (loge boxes-OF)
$25 (loge reserved-IF), $23 (terrace boxes-IF)
$21 (terrace boxes-OF, loge reserved-OF)
$18 (terrace reserved-adults), $10 (bleachers)
$9 (upper terrace-OF-adults)
$8 (terrace reserved-children)
$4 (upper terrace reserved-children)
Field dimensions (from home plate)
To left field at foul line, 330 feet
To center field, 402 feet
To right field at foul line, 330 feet
First game played
May 12, 1966 (Cardinals 4, Braves 3)

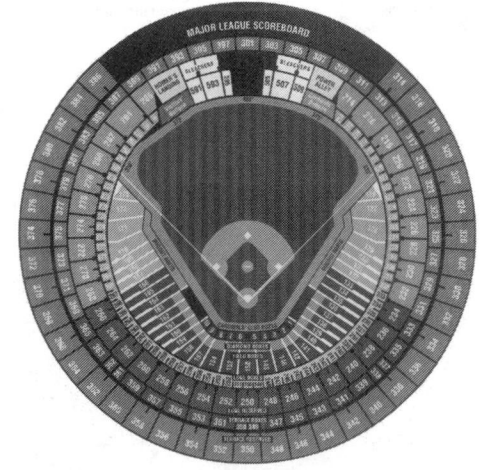

Date	Opp.	Res.	Score	(inn.*)	Hits	Opp. hits	Winning pitcher	Losing pitcher	Save	Record	Pos.	GB
4-2	At Col.	L	0-8		5	15	Hampton	Kile		0-1	T1st	0.5
4-4	At Col.	L	9-13		14	13	Neagle	An. Benes	Jimenez	0-2	T4th	2.0
4-5	At Col.	L	2-11		7	15	Astacio	Morris		0-3	T5th	3.0
4-6	At Ari.	W	12-9		18	12	Hermanson	Reynoso		1-3	T4th	3.0
4-7	At Ari.	W	8-4		11	11	Kile	Witt		2-3	T3rd	2.0
4-8	At Ari.	W	9-4		13	7	Ankiel	Johnson	Timlin	3-3	T2nd	1.0
4-9	Col.	W	3-2		6	5	Timlin	White		4-3	2nd	0.5
4-11	Col.	W	3-1		5	7	Morris	Astacio	Veres	5-3	2nd	1.0
4-12	Col.	L	4-6		8	5	Wasdin	Kline	Jimenez	5-4	T2nd	1.0
4-13	Hou.	L	2-4		9	10	Bottenfield	Kile	Wagner	5-5	3rd	2.0
4-14	Hou.	L	4-7		5	7	Elarton	Ankiel	Wagner	5-6	4th	3.0
4-15	Hou.	W	6-5		12	9	James	J. Powell	Kline	6-6	4th	2.0
4-16	Ari.	L	1-2		6	5	Ellis	Morris	Mantei	6-7	T4th	2.5
4-17	Ari.	L	4-17		4	18	Reynoso	Hermanson		6-8	T4th	2.5
4-18	Ari.	W	3-1		5	6	Kile	Johnson	Kline	7-8	T4th	3.0
4-20	At Hou.	L	1-10		3	10	Elarton	Ankiel		7-9	T4th	4.0
4-21	At Hou.	W	9-2		9	8	Morris	Lima		8-9	T4th	4.0
4-22	At Hou.	L	3-4		6	8	Miller	Stechschulte	Wagner	8-10	T4th	4.0
4-24	Mon.	W	7-2		14	8	Kile	Vazquez		9-10	T4th	3.0
4-25	Mon.	W	5-2		8	5	An. Benes	Reames	Stechschulte	10-10	T4th	2.0
4-26	Mon.	L	3-4	(15)	16	14	Yoshii	James		10-11	5th	3.0
4-27	N.Y.	W	9-0		16	6	Morris	Appier		11-11	5th	3.0
4-28	N.Y.	L	5-6	(11)	8	15	Benitez	James		11-12	5th	3.0
4-29	N.Y.	W	12-1		18	6	Kile	Rusch		12-12	5th	3.0
5-1	At Fla.	L	3-4		9	10	Nunez	An. Benes	Alfonseca	12-13	T4th	3.0
5-2	At Fla.	W	4-2	(11)	13	12	Kline	Alfonseca	Veres	13-13	T4th	3.0
5-4	At Atl.	W	4-2		8	7	Hermanson	Glavine	Veres	14-13	14th	2.5
5-5	At Atl.	L	5-6		9	13	Remlinger	Timlin	Rocker	14-14	5th	3.5
5-6	At Atl.	L	5-7		7	15	Cabrera	Stechschulte	Rocker	14-15	5th	4.5
5-7	Pit.	W	7-0		10	4	Morris	Ritchie		15-15	5th	4.5
5-8	Pit.	W	8-2		8	4	An. Benes	Anderson		16-15	T3rd	3.5
5-9	Pit.	W	6-2		10	5	Hermanson	Arroyo		17-15	T2nd	3.5
5-10	Pit.	W	11-5		17	4	Matthews	Silva		18-15	2nd	2.5
5-11	Chi.	W	7-2		7	8	Kile	Bere		19-15	2nd	1.5
5-12	Chi.	W	5-2		13	6	Morris	Lieber	Veres	20-15	2nd	0.5
5-13	Chi.	W	13-4		10	9	An. Benes	Wood		21-15	1st	+0.5
5-15	At Pit.	W	8-3		14	9	Hermanson	Olivares		22-15	1st	+1.0
5-16	At Pit.	W	3-0		5	7	Kile	Schmidt		23-15	1st	+1.0
5-17	At Pit.	W	12-2		13	8	Morris	Ritchie		24-15	1st	+1.0
5-18	At Phi.	L	4-5		7	7	Daal	Timlin	Mesa	24-16	1st	+1.0
5-19	At Phi.	L	2-3		4	8	Person	An. Benes		24-17	T1st	...
5-20	At Phi.	W	3-1		12	5	Hermanson	Telemaco	Veres	25-17	1st	+1.0
5-22	At Mil.	L	0-5		6	9	Haynes	Kile		25-18	1st	+1.5
5-23	At Mil.	L	3-7		8	9	Rigdon	Morris		25-19	1st	+0.5
5-24	At Mil.	W	7-4		10	4	Matthews	Sheets		26-19	1st	+0.5
5-25	At Cin.	W	5-4		8	8	Al. Benes	Graves	Veres	27-19	1st	+0.5
5-26	At Cin.	L	2-7		6	9	Dessens	Hermanson		27-20	T1st	...
5-27	At Cin.	W	2-0		11	8	Kile	Reith	Veres	28-20	T1st	...
5-28	Mil.	W	6-2		10	8	Morris	Rigdon	Christiansen	29-20	T1st	...
5-29	Mil.	L	0-7		5	12	Sheets	Matthews		29-21	2nd	1.0
5-30	Mil.	L	1-11	(6)	5	13	Levrault	An. Benes		29-22	2nd	2.0
5-31	Mil.	L	2-6		6	9	Peterson	Hermanson		29-23	2nd	2.5
6-1	Cin.	L	1-5		4	10	Mercado	Kile	Graves	29-24	2nd	3.5
6-2	Cin.	W	8-5		11	7	Morris	Reith	Stechschulte	30-24	2nd	3.5
6-3	Cin.	W	4-3		7	7	Timlin	Bell	Veres	31-24	2nd	2.5
6-4	Cin.	W	5-2		12	7	An. Benes	O. Fernandez	Veres	32-24	2nd	2.0
6-5	At Chi.	L	6-12		9	13	Lieber	Hermanson		32-25	2nd	3.0
6-6	At Chi.	L	1-4		3	10	Wood	Kile	Gordon	32-26	2nd	4.0
6-7	At Chi.	L	3-4	(10)	8	10	Fassero	Timlin		32-27	2nd	5.0
6-8	At Col.	L	1-9		4	14	Neagle	Matthews		32-28	2nd	5.0
6-9	At Col.	W	8-2		15	5	An. Benes	Astacio		33-28	2nd	5.0
6-10	At Col.	L	3-12		7	14	Hampton	Hermanson		33-29	2nd	5.0
6-12	At K.C.	L	4-7		6	10	Durbin	Kile		33-30	2nd	6.0
6-13	At K.C.	L	1-4		9	12	Wilson	Morris	Hernandez	33-31	2nd	6.0
6-14	At K.C.	L	2-3	(13)	6	10	Henry	Stechschulte		33-32	4th	6.0
6-15	Chi.	W	10-3		13	5	An. Benes	Garland		34-32	2nd	6.0
6-16	Chi.	W	8-3		12	5	Hermanson	K. Wells		35-32	2nd	6.0
6-17	Chi.	W	8-3		10	7	Smith	D. Wells		36-32	2nd	6.0
6-18	Chi.	W	6-2		11	5	Kile	Tapani		37-32	2nd	5.0
6-19	Chi.	W	3-2		9	11	Morris	Farnsworth	Veres	38-32	2nd	4.0
6-20	Chi.	L	4-9		11	13	Tavarez	Matthews		38-33	2nd	5.0
6-21	Chi.	L	2-5		8	9	Lieber	An. Benes	Gordon	38-34	2nd	6.0
6-22	S.F	L	5-10		7	13	Hernandez	Hermanson		38-35	2nd	6.0
6-23	S.F	W	6-5		10	12	Christiansen	Embree		39-35	2nd	5.0

Date	Opp.	Res.	Score	(inn.*)	Hits	Opp. hits	Winning pitcher	Losing pitcher	Save	Record	Pos.	GB
6-24	S.F	W	7-3		11	8	Morris	Ortiz	Veres	40-35	2nd	4.0
6-26	Cin.	L	9-10		15	14	Sullivan	Stechschulte	Graves	40-36	3rd	5.5
6-27	Cin.	L	1-3		4	9	Davis	Hermanson	Graves	40-37	3rd	5.5
6-29	At S.F	L	2-3		4	8	Rodriguez	Kline	Nen	40-38	3rd	6.0
6-30	At S.F	L	2-5		7	11	Rodriguez	Timlin	Nen	40-39	3rd	6.0
7-1	At S.F	L	4-5		8	10	Zerbe	An. Benes	Nen	40-40	3rd	7.0
7-3	At Mil.	L	0-2		3	9	Wright	Kline	Weathers	40-41	T3rd	8.0
7-4	At Mil.	W	7-2		11	7	Matthews	Sheets		41-41	3rd	7.0
7-5	At Mil.	W	5-2		13	6	Kile	Peterson	Timlin	42-41	3rd	7.0
7-6	At Cle.	L	2-14		10	15	Nagy	Morris		42-42	3rd	8.0
7-7	At Cle.	L	6-7	(10)	11	8	Rocker	Veres		42-43	3rd	9.0
7-8	At Cle.	W	4-3		9	9	Timlin	Rocker		43-43	3rd	8.0
7-12	Det.	L	5-7		6	11	Weaver	Kile	Anderson	43-44	3rd	9.0
7-13	Det.	L	1-4		6	10	Sparks	Matthews		43-45	T3rd	9.0
7-14	Det.	W	3-2		6	6	Morris	Lima	Kline	44-45	3rd	8.0
7-15	Min.	W	5-1		14	7	Hermanson	Mays		45-45	3rd	8.0
7-16	Min.	W	4-3		10	8	Kline	Miller	Christiansen	46-45	3rd	7.0
7-17	Min.	W	4-2		9	9	Kile	Lohse	Christiansen	47-45	3rd	7.0
7-18	At Hou.	L	11-17		18	16	Villone	Hackman		47-46	3rd	8.0
7-19	At Hou.	W	4-1		5	5	Morris	Miller	Timlin	48-46	3rd	7.0
7-20	Pit.	L	1-4		2	4	Schmidt	Hermanson	Manzanillo	48-47	3rd	7.0
7-21	Pit.	W	9-2		7	9	Smith	Beimel		49-47	3rd	7.0
7-22	Pit.	L	0-2		6	9	Anderson	Timlin	M. Williams	49-48	3rd	7.0
7-24	Hou.	L	1-2		2	7	Miller	Morris	Wagner	49-49	3rd	8.5
7-25	Hou.	W	10-2		13	6	Hermanson	Redding		50-49	3rd	8.5
7-26	At Chi.	W	3-1		6	5	Smith	Tapani	Kline	51-49	3rd	7.5
7-27	At Chi.	L	3-4		4	7	Fassero	Christiansen	Gordon	51-50	3rd	8.5
7-28	At Chi.	W	7-4		16	5	Veres	Fyhrie	Kline	52-50	3rd	7.5
7-29	At Chi.	L	5-7		8	9	Tavarez	Morris	Gordon	52-51	3rd	8.5
7-31	Atl.	W	6-2		13	4	Hermanson	Reed		53-51	3rd	8.5
8-1	Atl.	W	4-0		8	8	Kile	Maddux		54-51	3rd	7.5
8-2	Atl.	L	1-2		5	8	Glavine	Smith	Karsay	54-52	3rd	7.5
8-3†	Fla.	W	9-5		15	11	Morris	Penny	Kline	55-52		
8-3‡	Fla.	L	4-6		8	7	Nunez	Veres	Alfonseca	55-53	3rd	8.0
8-4	Fla.	W	3-0		7	8	Williams	Burnett	Stechschulte	56-53	3rd	7.0
8-5	Fla.	L	3-5		10	8	Dempster	Hermanson	Alfonseca	56-54	3rd	7.0
8-7	At Mon.	W	3-1		6	4	Kile	Vazquez		57-54	3rd	7.0
8-8	At Mon.	L	5-6	(11)	11	10	Yoshii	Hackman		57-55	3rd	8.0
8-9	At Mon.	W	9-6		13	12	Morris	Ohka		58-55	3rd	7.0
8-10	At N.Y.	W	7-6	(10)	12	9	Veres	White	Kline	59-55	3rd	7.0
8-11	At N.Y.	W	6-3		10	11	Hermanson	Rusch	Veres	60-55	3rd	6.0
8-12	At N.Y.	W	4-1		8	5	Kile	Chen	Veres	61-55	3rd	5.0
8-13	Cin.	W	3-2		8	9	An. Benes	Dessens	Veres	62-55	3rd	4.5
8-14	Cin.	W	7-1		8	4	Morris	Reyes		63-55	3rd	4.0
8-15	Cin.	W	8-4		11	7	Williams	Reitsma		64-55	3rd	4.0
8-16	Cin.	W	8-3		10	6	Hermanson	Acevedo		65-55	3rd	3.5
8-17	Phi.	W	4-3		13	10	Veres	Wendell		66-55	3rd	2.5
8-18	Phi.	W	6-3		11	11	Kline	Politte	Veres	67-55	3rd	2.5
8-19	Phi.	W	9-0		14	7	Morris	Coggin		68-55	3rd	2.5
8-20	At Cin.	L	4-5	(11)	8	13	Riedling	An. Benes		68-56	3rd	3.0
8-21	At Cin.	W	11-6		14	13	Hermanson	Acevedo		69-56	T2nd	3.0
8-22	At Cin.	L	1-3		5	8	Davis	Kile	Graves	69-57	3rd	3.0
8-23	At Cin.	L	2-12		9	18	Dessens	Smith		69-58	3rd	4.0
8-24	At Chi.	W	10-8		15	12	Morris	Bere	Hackman	70-58	T2nd	4.0
8-25	At Chi.	L	4-6		6	8	Lieber	Williams	Gordon	70-59	3rd	4.0
8-26	At Chi.	L	1-6		9	11	Cruz	Hermanson		70-60	3rd	5.0
8-28	S.D.	L	2-5		5	11	Lawrence	Kile	Hoffman	70-61	3rd	6.0
8-29	S.D.	W	16-14		15	15	Stechschulte	Jones		71-61	3rd	6.0
8-30	S.D.	W	13-3		13	10	Morris	Herndon		72-61	3rd	6.0
8-31	At L.A.	W	5-1		8	4	Williams	Gagne		73-61	3rd	6.0
9-1	At L.A.	L	1-3		4	8	Adams	Hermanson	Shaw	73-62	3rd	6.0
9-2	At L.A.	L	3-7		7	12	Brown	Kile		73-63	3rd	7.0
9-3	At S.D.	W	4-0		8	0	Smith	Jones		74-63	3rd	6.0
9-4	At S.D.	W	6-1		9	8	Morris	Herndon		75-63	3rd	6.0
9-5	At S.D.	W	2-0		5	2	Williams	Jarvis		76-63	3rd	6.0
9-7	L.A.	L	1-7		4	12	Brown	Hermanson		76-64	3rd	6.5
9-8	L.A.	W	6-5		13	7	Al. Benes	Baldwin	Stechschulte	77-64	T2nd	5.5
9-9	L.A.	W	8-1		11	4	Mathews	Park		78-64	2nd	5.5
9-10	At Mil.	W	8-0		9	9	Kile	Wright	Matthews	79-64	2nd	5.0
9-17	Mil.	W	2-1		6	4	Smith	Quevedo	Kline	80-64	2nd	4.5
9-18	Mil.	W	9-4		10	8	Hermanson	Wright		81-64	2nd	4.5
9-19	Mil.	W	8-2		10	9	Morris	D'Amico		82-64	2nd	4.5
9-20	At Pit.	W	9-1		11	4	Williams	Anderson		83-64	2nd	4.5
9-21	At Pit.	W	9-5		13	8	Hackman	Olivares		84-64	2nd	3.5
9-22	At Pit.	W	4-1		10	5	Smith	Ritchie	Stechschulte	85-64	2nd	3.5
9-23	At Pit.	L	1-2		4	7	D. Williams	Hermanson	Manzanillo	85-65	2nd	4.5
9-24	At Hou.	L	3-9		6	12	Mlicki	Morris		85-66	3rd	5.5
9-25	At Hou.	W	3-2		7	3	Williams	Miller		86-66	2nd	4.5

Date	Opp.	Res.	Score	(inn.*)	Hits	Opp. hits	Winning pitcher	Losing pitcher	Save	Record	Pos.	GB
9-26	At Hou.	W	5-1		8	5	Kile	Villone		87-66	2nd	3.5
9-28	Pit.	W	14-3		15	6	Hermanson	Ritchie		88-66	2nd	3.0
9-29	Pit.	W	2-0		3	5	Morris	D. Williams	Stechschulte	89-66	2nd	2.0
9-30	Pit.	W	7-3		9	3	Williams	McKnight		90-66	2nd	1.0
10-2	At Mil.	W	5-1		13	4	Kile	Sheets		91-66	T1st	...
10-3	At Mil.	L	7-9		15	15	Wright	Smith	Fox	91-67	T1st	...
10-4	At Mil.	W	10-3		11	6	Morris	Haynes		92-67	1st	+1.0
10-5	Hou.	L	1-2		4	9	Jackson	Stechschulte	Wagner	92-68	1st	...
10-6	Hou.	W	10-6		13	8	Timlin	Villone	Kline	93-68	1st	+1.0
10-7	Hou.	L	2-9		10	13	Reynolds	Kile		93-69	T1st	...

Monthly records: April (12-12), May (17-11), June (11-16), July (13-12), August (20-10), September (17-5), October (3-3).
*Innings, if other than nine. †First game of a doubleheader. ‡Second game of a doubleheader.

HIGHLIGHTS

High point: Rookie lefthander Bud Smith pitched a no-hitter at San Diego on September 3 in just his 11th career start. This game was the start of a stretch in which the Cardinals won 12 of 13 games and surged into contention in the N.L. Central.

Low point: After stumbling to the All-Star break at 43-43, the Cardinals lost the first two games after the break to the lowly Detroit Tigers.

Turning point: The acqusition of righthander Woody Williams from San Diego on August 2. On that day, the Cardinals were two games over .500. They finished 24 over as Williams won seven of his eight decisions.

Most valuable player: Albert Pujols became not only the Rookie of the Year, but one of the most valuable players in the league. Besides the fact that Pujols hit .329 with 37 homers and 130 RBIs, he started 30 or more games at four different positions—third base, first base, left field and right field.

Most valuable pitcher: Matt Morris, who won three games in relief in 2000, his first year after Tommy John elbow surgery, won 22 games, tying Arizona's Curt Schilling for the major league high.

Most improved player: Pujols hadn't even played a game in Class AA before this year and only a few in Class AAA as a playoff call-up in 2000.

Most pleasant surprise: Pujols wins this category, too, since nobody expected him to be a regular player, let alone a star, in his first big league season. Honorable mentions go to Craig Paquette, who hit a club-high .372 with men in scoring position, and Placido Polanco, who hit above .300 for the second straight year.

Key injuries: Mark McGwire never did shake a knee ailment even though he had undergone offseason surgery. ... J.D. Drew missed six-weeks with a broken bone in his right hand. ... Garrett

Stephenson never threw a ball in a major league game and was out all year after Tommy John surgery.

Notable: Reliever Steve Kline went two months and one day without allowing a run in a span that covered 28 2/3 innings. ... The Cardinals had winning streaks of 11, 10 and nine games, falling one game short of the Milwaukee Braves' mark of three double-figure winning streaks in 1953. ... The Cardinals tied for the division title without anybody having 20 saves or 20 stolen bases.

—RICK HUMMEL

RECORDS

2001 regular-season record: 93-69 (1st in N.L. Central); 54-28 at home; 39-41 on road; 19-11 vs. N.L. East; 49-35 vs. N.L. Central; 17-16 vs. N.L. West; 8-7 vs. A.L.; 16-15 vs. lefthanded starters; 77-54 vs. righthanded starters; 90-66 on grass; 3-3 on turf; 37-23 in daytime; 56-46 at night; 15-21 in one-run games; 2-7 in extra-inning games; 0-0-1 in doubleheaders.

Team record past five years: 419-390 (.518, ranks 7th in league in that span).

TEAM LEADERS

Batting average: Albert Pujols (.329).
At-bats: Fernando Vina (631).
Runs: Albert Pujols (112).
Hits: Albert Pujols (194).
Total Bases: Albert Pujols (360).
Doubles: Albert Pujols (47).
Triples: Fernando Vina (8).
Home runs: Albert Pujols (37).
Runs batted in: Albert Pujols (130).
Stolen bases: Edgar Renteria, Fernando Vina (17).
Slugging percentage: Albert Pujols (.610).
On-base percentage: Jim Edmonds (.410).
Wins: Matt Morris (22).
Earned-run average: Darryl Kile (3.09).

Complete games: Woody Williams (3).
Shutouts: Darryl Kile, Matt Morris, Bud Smith, Woody Williams (1).
Saves: Dave Veres (15).
Innings pitched: Darryl Kile (227.1).
Strikeouts: Matt Morris (185).

GAMES BY POSITION

Catcher: Mike Matheny 121, Eli Marrero 65, Keith McDonald 2.
First base: Mark McGwire 90, Albert Pujols 42, Bobby Bonilla 33, Craig Paquette 23, Larry Sutton 11, Eli Marrero 6, Jim Edmonds 2, Mike Matheny 2, John Mabry 2, Edgar Renteria 1, Miguel Cairo 1.
Second base: Fernando Vina 151, Placido Polanco 15, Miguel Cairo 5, Craig Paquette 4, Stubby Clapp 4.
Third base: Placido Polanco 103, Albert Pujols 55, Craig Paquette 33, Miguel Cairo 3.
Shortstop: Edgar Renteria 137, Placido Polanco 42, Miguel Cairo 1.
Outfield: Jim Edmonds 147, J.D. Drew 107, Ray Lankford 85, Albert Pujols 78, Kerry Robinson 74, Craig Paquette 56, Eli Marrero 15, Bobby Bonilla 10, Luis Saturria 9, Miguel Cairo 6, Stubby Clapp 4, Larry Sutton 3, John Mabry 2.
Designated hitter: Albert Pujols 2, Bobby Bonilla 2, Edgar Renteria 1, Placido Polanco 1.

TOP DRAFT CHOICES

1. **Justin Pope,** RHP, Univ. of Central Florida.
2. **Dan Haren,** RHP, Pepperdine Univ.
3. **Joe Mather,** SS, Mountain Pointe H.S., Phoenix.
4. **Josh Brey,** LHP, Liberty University.
5. **Skip Schumaker,** OF, UC Santa Barbara.
6. **John Killalea,** LHP, Seminole (Fla.) H.S.
7. **Tyler Adamczyk,** RHP, Westlake H.S., Westlake Village, Calif.
8. **John Nelson,** SS, U. of Kansas.
9. **Rhett Parrott,** RHP, Georgia Tech.
10. **Seth Davidson,** SS, U. of Southern Cal.

SAN DIEGO PADRES
NATIONAL LEAGUE WEST DIVISION

Padres schedule
Home games shaded
D—Day game (games starting before 5 p.m.)
All-Star Game at Milwaukee
Subject to changes

April

SUN	MON	TUE	WED	THU	FRI	SAT
	1 D ARI	2 ARI	3 ARI	4	5 D SF	6 D SF
7 SF	8 D ARI	9 ARI	10 ARI	11	12 LA	13 LA
14 D LA	15 SF	16 SF	17 SF	18 LA	19 LA	20 LA
21 D LA	22	23 PHI	24 PHI	25 D PHI	26 PIT	27 PIT
28 D PIT	29	30 CUB				

May

SUN	MON	TUE	WED	THU	FRI	SAT
			1 D CUB	2 CUB	3 PIT	4 PIT
5 D PIT	6	7 FLA	8 FLA	9 FLA	10 ATL	11 ATL
12 D ATL	13 MON	14 MON	15 D MON	16 NYM	17 NYM	18 NYM
19 D NYM	20	21 COL	22 COL	23 COL	24 D MIL	25 MIL
26 D MIL	27 COL	28 COL	29 COL	30 D MIL	31 MIL	

June

SUN	MON	TUE	WED	THU	FRI	SAT
						1 MIL
2 D MIL	3 SF	4 SF	5 SF	6	7 TB	8 TB
9 D TB	10 BAL	11 BAL	12 D BAL	13	14 SEA	15 SEA
16 D SEA	17	18 BOS	19 BOS	20 BOS	21 NYY	22 NYY
23 D NYY	24 SF	25 SF	26 SF	27 SF	28 KC	29 KC
30 D KC						

July

SUN	MON	TUE	WED	THU	FRI	SAT
	1 STL	2 STL	3 STL	4	5 D COL	6 COL
7 COL	8	9 *	10	11	12 STL	13 STL
14 D STL	15 COL	16 COL	17 LA	18 LA	19 ARI	20 ARI
21 D ARI	22 LA	23 LA	24 LA	25 D ARI	26 ARI	27 ARI
28 D ARI	29	30 D CUB	31 D CUB			

August

SUN	MON	TUE	WED	THU	FRI	SAT
				1 D CUB	2 CIN	3 CIN
4 D CIN	5	6 PHI	7 PHI	8 D PHI	9 CIN	10 CIN
11 D CIN	12	13 NYM	14 NYM	15 D NYM	16 MON	17 MON
18 D MON	19 D MON	20 ATL	21 ATL	22 D ATL	23 FLA	24 FLA
25 D FLA	26	27 HOU	28 HOU	29 D HOU	30 COL	31 COL

September

SUN	MON	TUE	WED	THU	FRI	SAT
1 D COL	2 COL	3 HOU	4 HOU	5 D HOU	6 COL	7 D COL
8 D COL	9 ARI	10 ARI	11 ARI	12 D SF	13 SF	14 SF
15 D SF	16	17 ARI	18 ARI	19 ARI	20 LA	21 LA
22 D LA	23	24 SF	25 D SF	26 LA	27 LA	28 LA
29 D LA	30					

2002 SEASON
CLUB DIRECTORY

Chairman
John Moores

President and chief executive officer
Bob Vizas

Executive vice president, public affairs
Charles Steinberg

Exec. v.p., baseball ops. and g.m.
Kevin Towers

Senior vice president, finance
Fred Gerson

Vice president, community relations
Michele Anderson

Vice president, stadium operations
Mark Guglielmo

V.p., scouting and player development
Ted Simmons

Assistant general manager
Fred Uhlman Jr.

Executive director, merchandising
Michael Babida

Executive director, finance
Steve Fitch

Exec. dir., human resources/admin.
Lucy Freeman

Executive director, communications
Glenn Geffner

Executive director, Friartix
Chandra George

Executive director, new ballpark ticketing
Dave Gilmore

Executive director, ballpark planning
Erik Judson

Executive director, corporate partnerships & broadcasting
Sam Kennedy

Executive director, ticket sales
Mark Tilson

Director, Padres Foundation
Sue Botos

Director, Padres Productions
Tom Catlin

Director, military marketing
Captain Jack Ensch (Ret.)

Director, baseball operations
Theo Epstein

Director, scouting
Bill "Chief" Gayton

Director, stadium operations
Ken Kanwachi

Director, corporate communications
Tim Katzman

Director, ticketing
Jim Kiersnowski

Director, information systems
Joe Lewis

Director, minor league operations
Priscilla Oppenheimer

Director, team travel
Brian Prilaman

Director, player development
Tye Waller

Trainer
Todd Hutcheson

Assistant trainer
Jim Daniel

Strength and conditioning coordinator
Bill Henry

Club physicians
Cliff Colwell, Jan Fronek, Paul Hirshman, Blaine Phillips

Major league scouts
Ken Bracey, Moose Johnson, Brad Sloan

Director of professional scouting
Gary Nickels

Advance scout
Mike Basso

Director of international scouting
Bill Clark

National cross-checker
Jay Darnell

Cross-checker
Tim McWilliam

Professional scouts
Ray Crone, Steve Demeter, Gail Henley, Ron King, Ben McLure, Craig Shipley, Van Smith

Full-time scouts
Joe Bochy, Rich Bordi, Jim Bretz, Lane Decker, Jimmy Dreyer, Leroy Dreyer, Mal Fichman, Ronquito Garcia, Chris Gwynn, Don "Trip" Keister, Jason McLeod, Billy Merkel, Darryl Milne, Mike Rickard, Gene Thompson, Scott Trcka, Mark Wasinger

MINOR LEAGUE AFFILIATES

Class	Team	League	Manager
AAA	Portland	Pacific Coast	Rick Sweet
AA	Mobile	Southern	Craig Colbert
A	Eugene	Northwest	Jeff Gardner
A	Fort Wayne	Midwest	Tracy Woodson
A	Lake Elsinore	California	George Hendrick
Rookie	Idaho Falls	Pioneer	Don Werner

BROADCAST INFORMATION

Radio: KOGO-AM (600), KURS-AM (1040, Spanish)
TV: KUSI (Channel 9).
Cable TV: Channel 4 Padres.

SPRING TRAINING

Ballpark (city): Peoria Stadium (Peoria, Ariz.).
Ticket information: 623-878-4337, 800-409-1511.

Follow the Padres all season at: www.sportingnews.com/baseball/teams/padres/

SPRING TRAINING ROSTER

Manager—Bruce Bochy (15).
Coaches—Darrel Akerfelds, Greg Booker (38), Duane Espy (52), Tim Flannery (11), Rob Picciolo (5), Alan Trammell (3).

No.	PITCHERS	B/T	Ht./Wt.	Born	2001 clubs
74	Abreu, Winston	R/R	6-2/155	4-5-77	Greenville
	Baerlocher, Ryan	R/R	6-5/220	8-6-77	Wichita
	Bartosh, Cliff	L/L	6-2/175	9-5-79	Lake Elsinore, Mobile
	Boyd, Jason	R/R	6-3/173	2-23-73	Scranton/Wilkes-Barre
	Bynum, Mike	L/L	6-4/200	3-20-78	Mobile
	Cyr, Eric	L/R	6-4/200	2-11-79	Lake Elsinore
44	Davey, Tom	R/R	6-7/230	9-11-73	San Diego
53	Eaton, Adam	R/R	6-2/190	11-23-77	San Diego
56	Embree, Alan	L/L	6-2/190	1-23-70	San Francisco, Fresno, Chicago A.L.
	Fikac, Jeremy	R/R	6-2/185	4-8-75	Mobile, Portland, San Diego
51	Hoffman, Trevor	R/R	6-0/205	10-13-67	San Diego
	Howard, Ben	R/R	6-2/190	1-15-79	Lake Elsinore, Mobile
65	Jarvis, Kevin	L/R	6-2/190	8-1-69	San Diego
28	Jones, Bobby	R/R	6-4/225	2-10-70	San Diego
57	Lawrence, Brian	R/R	6-0/195	5-14-76	Portland, San Diego
54	Middlebrook, Jason	R/R	6-3/215	6-26-75	Mobile, Portland, San Diego
	Nunez, Jose	L/L	6-2/175	3-14-79	Los Angeles, San Diego
37	Ramsay, Robert	L/L	6-5/215	12-3-73	Tacoma
	Shibilo, Andy	R/R	6-7/220	9-16-76	Lake Elsinore
	Tankersley, Dennis	R/R	6-2/185	2-24-79	Lake Elsinore, Mobile, Portland
55	Tollberg, Brian	R/R	6-3/195	9-16-72	San Diego, Portland, Lake Elsinore
40	Tomko, Brett	R/R	6-4/215	4-7-73	Seattle, Tacoma
56	Walker, Kevin	L/L	6-4/190	9-20-76	San Diego
40	Watkins, Steve	R/R	6-4/190	7-19-78	Mobile, Lake Elsinore

No.	CATCHERS	B/T	Ht./Wt.	Born	2001 clubs
7	Gonzalez, Wiki	R/R	5-11/203	5-17-74	San Diego, Lake Elsinore
17	Lampkin, Tom	L/R	5-11/195	3-4-64	Seattle

No.	INFIELDERS	B/T	Ht./Wt.	Born	2001 clubs
	Burroughs, Sean	L/R	6-2/200	9-12-80	Portland
63	Eberwein, Kevin	R/R	6-4/200	3-30-77	Portland, Lake Elsinore
2	Jackson, Damian	R/R	5-11/185	8-6-73	San Diego, Portland
68	Jimenez, D'Angelo	B/R	6-0/194	12-21-77	Columbus, San Diego
30	Klesko, Ryan	L/L	6-3/220	6-12-71	San Diego
17	Mendez, Donaldo	R/R	6-1/155	6-7-78	San Diego
22	Nady, Xavier	R/R	6-2/205	11-14-78	Lake Elsinore
23	Nevin, Phil	R/R	6-2/231	1-19-71	San Diego
	Vazquez, Ramon	L/R	5-11/170	8-21-76	Tacoma, Seattle

No.	OUTFIELDERS	B/T	Ht./Wt.	Born	2001 clubs
	Crespo, Cesar	B/R	5-11/170	5-23-79	Portland, San Diego
26	Darr, Mike	L/R	6-3/205	3-21-76	San Diego, Mobile
25	DeHaan, Kory	L/R	6-2/187	7-16-76	Portland, Mobile
	Donovan, Todd	R/R	6-1/175	8-12-78	Lake Elsinore
7	Kotsay, Mark	L/L	6-0/201	12-2-75	San Diego
16	Lankford, Ray	L/L	5-11/200	6-5-67	St. Louis, San Diego
61	Owens, Jeremy	R/R	6-1/200	12-9-76	Mobile, Lake Elsinore
27	Trammell, Bubba	R/R	6-2/220	11-6-71	San Diego

BALLPARK INFORMATION

Ballpark (capacity, surface)
Qualcomm Stadium (66,307, grass)
Address
P.O. Box 2000
San Diego, CA 92112-2000
Official website
www.padres.com
Business phone
619-881-6500
Ticket information
888-697-2373
Ticket prices
$28 (field level/IF), $26 (club level/IF)
$24 (field level/OF, plaza level/IF, club level/OF)
$22 (plaza level/OF), $20 (loge level/IF)
$16 (loge level/OF), $15 (press level)
$10 (grandstand/plaza level, view level/lower IF)
$10 (grandstand/club level)
$9 (view level/IF)
$8 (view level/OF), $6 (outfield bleachers)
Field dimensions (from home plate)
To left field at foul line, 327 feet
To center field, 405 feet
To right field at foul line, 330 feet
First game played
April 8, 1969 (Padres 2, Astros 1)

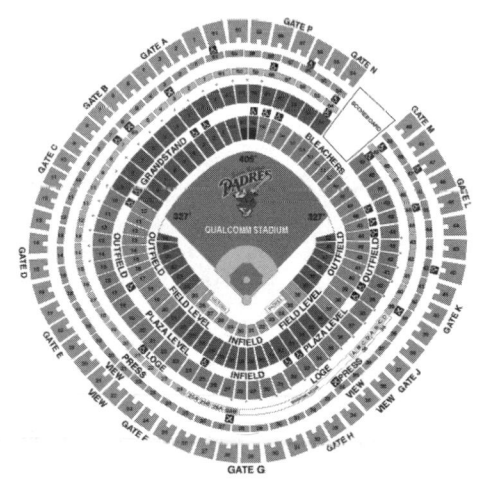

2002 SEASON *San Diego Padres*

Date	Opp.	Res.	Score	(inn.*)	Hits	Opp. hits	Winning pitcher	Losing pitcher	Save	Record	Pos.	GB
4-2	At S.F	L	2-3		7	10	Hernandez	Williams	Nen	0-1	T4th	1.0
4-4	At S.F	L	7-8		14	11	Nen	Witasick		0-2	5th	2.0
4-5	At S.F	L	2-8		10	11	Ortiz	Jones		0-3	5th	3.0
4-6	At Col.	W	10-6		13	10	Eaton	Bohanon		1-3	5th	2.0
4-7	At Col.	W	14-10		16	14	Williams	Myers	Hoffman	2-3	T4th	1.5
4-8	At Col.	W	11-3		16	7	Tollberg	Estrada		3-3	T3rd	1.0
4-10	S.F	L	6-11		10	11	Ortiz	Jarvis		3-4	T3rd	2.0
4-11	S.F	L	1-2		3	5	Fultz	Hoffman	Nen	3-5	T3rd	3.0
4-12	S.F	W	8-3		11	8	Eaton	Hernandez		4-5	T3rd	2.0
4-13	L.A.	W	5-4	(10)	7	5	Hoffman	Herges		5-5	3rd	2.0
4-14	L.A.	W	5-4		4	7	Hoffman	Olson		6-5	2nd	1.0
4-15	L.A.	L	4-5		5	6	Brown	Myers	Shaw	6-6	T3rd	1.0
4-17	Col.	L	5-9		7	13	Astacio	Jones	Jimenez	6-7	4th	2.0
4-18	Col.	L	0-8		5	8	Hampton	Eaton		6-8	4th	3.0
4-19	Col.	L	0-4		6	12	Neagle	Williams		6-9	T4th	3.0
4-20	At L.A.	L	1-3		6	6	Brown	Tollberg	Shaw	6-10	5th	4.0
4-21	At L.A.	L	2-4		7	9	Prokopec	Jarvis	Shaw	6-11	5th	4.0
4-22	At L.A.	W	7-6	(11)	8	12	Witasick	Shaw	Myers	7-11	5th	4.0
4-23	Phi.	L	3-5		7	7	Chen	Eaton	Bottalico	7-12	5th	4.5
4-24	Phi.	L	7-12		8	17	Wolf	Williams		7-13	5th	4.5
4-25	Phi.	L	3-5		11	7	Daal	Tollberg	Mesa	7-14	5th	5.5
4-26	Phi.	W	11-0		13	7	Jarvis	Person		8-14	5th	4.5
4-27	Pit.	L	0-3		8	6	Anderson	Jones	M. Williams	8-15	5th	5.0
4-28	Pit.	W	8-1		14	5	Eaton	Arroyo		9-15	5th	5.0
4-29	Pit.	W	6-1		9	6	Williams	Olivares	Hoffman	10-15	5th	5.0
5-1	At Chi.	W	10-3		8	9	Tollberg	Bere		11-15	5th	4.0
5-2	At Chi.	L	3-8		6	9	Lieber	Jarvis		11-16	5th	5.0
5-3	At Chi.	W	5-3		6	6	Jones	Wood	Hoffman	12-16	5th	5.0
5-4	At Cin.	W	11-5		15	12	Eaton	Dessens		13-16	5th	4.0
5-5	At Cin.	W	5-2		11	9	Williams	Bell	Hoffman	14-16	5th	3.0
5-6	At Cin.	W	8-2		13	4	Tollberg	O. Fernandez		15-16	5th	2.0
5-8	Atl.	W	7-1		16	6	Jarvis	Maddux		16-16	T4th	1.5
5-9	Atl.	L	0-3		9	6	Burkett	Jones	Rocker	16-17	5th	2.5
5-10	Atl.	W	6-5		6	11	Myers	Remlinger	Hoffman	17-17	5th	2.5
5-11	Fla.	W	7-6	(10)	9	11	Witasick	Looper		18-17	T4th	1.5
5-12	Fla.	L	0-3		0	7	Burnett	Serrano		18-18	T4th	2.5
5-13	Fla.	L	4-10		7	11	Penny	Witasick		18-19	5th	3.5
5-15	At N.Y.	L	0-1		6	6	Reed	Jones	Benitez	18-20	5th	4.0
5-16	At N.Y.	W	5-2		9	5	Eaton	Rusch	Hoffman	19-20	T4th	3.5
5-17	At N.Y.	W	15-3		17	8	Williams	Trachsel		20-20	T4th	2.5
5-18	At Mon.	L	1-3		5	7	Thurman	Jarvis	Urbina	20-21	T4th	3.0
5-19	At Mon.	W	20-7		20	13	Serrano	Yoshii		21-21	4th	2.5
5-20	At Mon.	W	5-3		7	6	Jones	Vazquez	Hoffman	22-21	4th	1.5
5-21	At Hou.	W	7-6		10	11	Eaton	Reynolds	Hoffman	23-21	T3rd	1.0
5-22	At Hou.	W	6-2		8	7	Williams	Elarton	Witasick	24-21	2nd	1.0
5-23	At Hou.	W	7-6		12	10	Witasick	Wagner	Hoffman	25-21	T1st	...
5-24	Ari.	W	3-1		5	7	Serrano	Brohawn	Hoffman	26-21	1st	+1.0
5-25	Ari.	L	1-7		7	11	Sabel	Jones		26-22	T1st	...
5-26	Ari.	L	1-3		3	7	Schilling	Eaton		26-23	3rd	1.0
5-27	Ari.	L	4-6		7	8	Swindell	Hoffman	Prinz	26-24	T3rd	2.0
5-29	Hou.	W	5-4		8	6	Jarvis	Bottenfield	Hoffman	27-24	3rd	2.5
5-30	Hou.	L	4-7		9	15	Miller	Jones	Wagner	27-25	3rd	3.5
5-31	Hou.	L	4-8		7	13	Reynolds	Serrano		27-26	3rd	4.0
6-1	At Ari.	L	2-4		9	13	Schilling	Williams	Kim	27-27	T3rd	5.0
6-2	At Ari.	L	1-2		6	7	Prinz	Davey		27-28	T3rd	6.0
6-3	At Ari.	L	4-8		10	10	Johnson	Jarvis		27-29	T4th	7.0
6-4	At S.F	L	1-3		4	12	Estes	Jones	Nen	27-30	5th	7.0
6-5	At S.F	L	6-7		9	12	Hernandez	Davey	Nen	27-31	5th	7.0
6-6	At S.F	L	4-6		8	11	Rueter	Williams	Nen	27-32	5th	8.0
6-7	At S.F	W	10-7		12	8	Eaton	Ortiz		28-32	5th	8.0
6-8	At Sea.	L	1-7		5	10	Abbott	Jarvis		28-33	5th	9.0
6-9	At Sea.	W	6-3		8	8	Jones	Garcia	Hoffman	29-33	5th	8.0
6-10	At Sea.	L	1-8		8	11	Halama	Loewer		29-34	5th	9.0
6-12	Oak.	L	2-5		6	10	Hudson	Williams	Isringhausen	29-35	5th	9.0
6-13	Oak.	L	2-6		5	9	Guthrie	Nunez	Tam	29-36	5th	10.0
6-14	Oak.	W	6-4		8	5	Davey	Mecir	Hoffman	30-36	5th	10.0
6-15	Sea.	L	4-8		5	15	Garcia	Jones		30-37	5th	10.0
6-16	Sea.	L	2-9		11	14	Halama	Loewer		30-38	5th	11.0
6-17	Sea.	W	11-9		15	9	Davey	Nelson	Hoffman	31-38	5th	11.0
6-19	S.F	W	4-3	(15)	10	12	Witasick	Vogelsong		32-38	5th	11.0
6-20	S.F	L	6-8		12	13	Gardner	Jarvis	Nen	32-39	5th	11.0
6-21	S.F	L	3-8		9	14	Estes	Jones		32-40	5th	12.0
6-22	At L.A.	W	9-6		12	13	Witasick	Herges	Hoffman	33-40	5th	12.0
6-23	At L.A.	W	6-2		8	5	Lawrence	Prokopec	Seanez	34-40	5th	12.0

Date	Opp.	Res.	Score	(inn.*)	Hits	Opp. hits	Winning pitcher	Losing pitcher	Save	Record	Pos.	GB
6-24	At L.A.	W	6-1		10	3	Eaton	Dreifort		35-40	5th	11.0
6-25	At Col.	W	6-4		7	8	Jarvis	White	Hoffman	36-40	5th	10.0
6-26	At Col.	W	11-3		13	9	Jones	Hampton		37-40	T4th	9.0
6-27	At Col.	L	9-10		14	15	Jimenez	Davey		37-41	5th	10.0
6-28	L.A.	L	4-7		8	10	Carrara	Seanez	Shaw	37-42	5th	10.5
6-29	L.A.	L	5-7		8	11	Williams	Eaton	Shaw	37-43	5th	11.5
6-30	L.A.	L	3-7		5	13	Herges	Hoffman		37-44	5th	12.5
7-1	L.A.	L	0-8		4	11	Brown	Jones	Reyes	37-45	5th	13.5
7-3	Col.	W	6-5		9	14	Nunez	Davis	Hoffman	38-45	5th	12.5
7-4	Col.	W	8-3		8	5	Hitchcock	Suzuki		39-45	4th	12.5
7-5	Col.	L	0-4		3	8	Astacio	Eaton		39-46	5th	12.5
7-6	Tex.	W	8-3		13	7	Jarvis	Helling	Hoffman	40-46	4th	11.5
7-7	Tex.	L	3-4		9	11	Davis	Jones	Zimmerman	40-47	4th	11.5
7-8	Tex.	W	11-2		12	7	Williams	Oliver		41-47	4th	10.5
7-12	At Hou.	W	7-4		14	9	Jones	Reynolds	Hoffman	42-47	4th	9.5
7-13	At Hou.	L	3-11		8	17	Oswalt	Williams		42-48	4th	10.5
7-14	At Hou.	W	8-6		7	9	Jarvis	Miller	Hoffman	43-48	4th	10.5
7-15	At Ana.	W	5-1		8	7	Lawrence	Ortiz		44-48	4th	9.5
7-16	At Ana.	L	5-7		10	15	Weber	Tollberg	Percival	44-49	4th	10.5
7-17	At Ana.	L	7-8		10	12	Levine	Davey		44-50	4th	10.5
7-18	Ari.	L	0-3		1	7	Johnson	Williams		44-51	4th	10.5
7-19	Ari.	W	8-4		8	5	Jarvis	Ellis	Hoffman	45-51	4th	10.5
7-20	Mil.	W	11-2		14	10	Hitchcock	Sheets		46-51	4th	9.5
7-21	Mil.	W	5-3		5	8	Tollberg	Suzuki	Hoffman	47-51	4th	9.5
7-22	Mil.	W	4-0		7	5	Jones	Haynes		48-51	4th	9.5
7-23	At Ari.	W	4-2		9	8	Williams	Bierbrodt	Hoffman	49-51	4th	8.5
7-24	At Ari.	L	0-11		1	14	Johnson	Jarvis		49-52	4th	9.5
7-25	At Ari.	L	6-9		9	13	Batista	Hitchcock	Kim	49-53	4th	10.5
7-27	At Mil.	L	0-8		6	15	Haynes	Jones		49-54	4th	10.5
7-28	At Mil.	W	6-2		9	6	Williams	Levrault	Hoffman	50-54	4th	10.5
7-29	At Mil.	W	12-5		14	10	Jarvis	Wright		51-54	4th	9.5
7-31	Chi.	L	3-7		7	13	Lieber	Lawrence		51-55	4th	9.5
8-1	Chi.	W	4-3		7	9	Jones	Heredia	Hoffman	52-55	4th	8.5
8-2	Chi.	W	4-3		6	5	McElroy	Fassero	Hoffman	53-55	4th	7.5
8-3	Cin.	L	2-9		8	11	Brower	Jarvis		53-56	4th	8.0
8-4	Cin.	W	2-0		6	4	Tollberg	Reitsma	Hoffman	54-56	4th	7.5
8-5	Cin.	L	9-10		15	8	Graves	Seanez		54-57	4th	8.5
8-7	At Phi.	L	3-7		6	13	Duckworth	Jones		54-58	4th	9.5
8-8	At Phi	L	3-4		7	11	Coggin	Herndon	Mesa	54-59	4th	10.5
8-9	At Phi.	W	6-2		11	5	Jarvis	Daal		55-59	4th	9.5
8-10	At Pit.	W	3-2		7	7	Tollberg	D. Williams	Hoffman	56-59	4th	8.5
8-11	At Pit.	W	6-2		12	7	Lawrence	Beimel		57-59	4th	8.0
8-12	At Pit.	L	6-7		11	13	Manzanillo	Myers		57-60	4th	9.0
8-14	N.Y.	W	6-0		8	8	Herndon	Trachsel		58-60	4th	9.5
8-15	N.Y.	W	2-1		9	2	Jarvis	Leitor	Hoffman	59-60	4th	9.5
8-16	N.Y.	W	6-5		10	10	Fikac	White	Hoffman	60-60	4th	9.0
8-17	Mon.	L	0-4		4	9	Vazquez	Lawrence		60-61	4th	10.0
8-18	Mon.	W	4-3		8	8	Jones	Thurman	Hoffman	61-61	4th	10.0
8-19	Mon.	L	1-2		3	6	Armas	Herndon	Strickland	61-62	4th	11.0
8-21	At Atl.	W	3-1	(10)	10	4	Nunez	Karsay	Hoffman	62-62	4th	10.0
8-22	At Atl.	L	3-6		3	12	Maddux	Tollberg	Remlinger	62-63	4th	11.0
8-23	At Atl.	L	2-3		6	6	Millwood	Lawrence	Smoltz	62-64	4th	11.0
8-24	At Fla.	L	3-6		8	8	Clement	Jones	Alfonseca	62-65	4th	11.0
8-25	At Fla.	W	7-1		8	8	Herndon	Sanchez		63-65	4th	11.0
8-26	At Fla.	W	10-0		15	8	Jarvis	Penny		64-65	4th	11.0
8-27	At Fla.	W	8-3		10	7	Tollberg	Burnett		65-65	4th	10.0
8-28	At St.L.	W	5-2		11	5	Lawrence	Kile	Hoffman	66-65	4th	10.0
8-29	At St.L.	L	14-16		15	15	Stechschulte	Jones		66-66	4th	11.0
8-30	At St.L.	L	3-13		10	13	Morris	Herndon		66-67	4th	11.0
8-31†	Ari.	L	1-4		6	5	Schilling	Jodie	Prinz	66-68		
8-31‡	Ari.	W	6-5		13	9	Nunez	Prinz	Hoffman	67-68	4th	11.0
9-1	Ari.	W	7-5		11	10	Lee	Kim	Hoffman	68-68	4th	10.0
9-2	Ari.	W	1-0	(13)	4	7	Serrano	Kim		69-68	4th	9.0
9-3	St.L.	L	0-4		0	8	Smith	Jones		69-69	4th	9.5
9-4	St.L.	L	1-6		8	9	Morris	Herndon		69-70	4th	9.5
9-5	St.L.	L	0-2		2	5	Williams	Jarvis		69-71	4th	10.5
9-7	At Ari.	W	4-3		10	11	Fikac	Swindell	Hoffman	70-71	4th	9.0
9-8	At Ari.	L	6-8	(10)	6	12	Kim	Serrano		70-72	4th	10.0
9-9	At Ari.	L	2-8		4	13	Witt	Jones	Kim	70-73	4th	11.0
9-17	At L.A.	W	6-4		9	8	Middlebrook	Park	Hoffman	71-73	4th	11.0
9-18	At L.A.	W	3-2		4	5	Jarvis	Adams	Hoffman	72-73	4th	10.0
9-19	At L.A.	W	4-3	(10)	9	9	Nunez	Trombley	Hoffman	73-73	4th	9.0
9-21	S.F	L	0-2		7	7	Schmidt	Lawrence	Nen	73-74	4th	9.5
9-22	S.F	W	4-3	(10)	6	7	Hoffman	Boehringer		74-74	4th	8.5
9-23	S.F	L	2-11		7	17	Ortiz	Herndon		74-75	4th	9.5
9-24	At Col.	L	11-15		16	20	Speier	Lundquist		74-76	4th	10.0
9-25	At Col.	W	8-7		10	14	Tollberg	Hampton	Hoffman	75-76	4th	9.0
9-26	At Col.	W	3-1		6	8	Lawrence	Speier	Hoffman	76-76	4th	9.0

Date	Opp.	Res.	Score	(inn.*)	Hits	Opp. hits	Winning pitcher	Losing pitcher	Save	Record	Pos.	GB
9-27	At Col.	L	9-13		14	18	Belitz	Herndon		76-77	4th	10.0
9-28	At S.F.	L	5-10		11	15	Estes	Middlebrook		76-78	4th	11.0
9-29	At S.F	L	1-3		6	6	Ortiz	McElroy	Nen	76-79	4th	12.0
9-30	At S.F.	W	5-4	12	12	8	Tollberg	Worrell	Hoffman	77-79	4th	11.0
10-2	L.A.	L	2-5		5	11	Carrara	Hoffman	Shaw	77-80	4th	12.0
10-3	L.A.	L	5-12		6	16	Gagne	Jones		77-81	4th	13.0
10-4	L.A.	W	6-3		11	11	Middlebrook	Prokopec	Hoffman	78-81	4th	13.0
10-5	Col.	L	0-4		4	6	Jennings	Jarvis		78-82	4th	14.0
10-6	Col.	W	10-4		10	11	Tollberg	Elarton		79-82	4th	13.0
10-7	Col.	L	5-14		9	14	Thomson	Lawrence		79-83	4th	13.0

Monthly records: April (10-15), May (17-11), June (10-18), July (14-11), August (16-13), September (10-11), October (2-4).
*Innings, if other than nine. †First game of a doubleheader. ‡Second game of a doubleheader.

HIGHLIGHTS

High point: Led by rookie pitcher Wascar Serrano, the club gained full possession of first place with a 3-1 victory over the Diamondbacks on May 24. The victory improved the team's record to 26-21 and dropped Arizona into second place.

Low point: On the first day of summer, Padres infielders made four errors in an 8-3 loss to the Giants. Manager Bruce Bochy termed it an embarrassing performance, and general manager Kevin Towers hinted of personnel shakeups to come. Five days later, Towers traded for SS D'Angelo Jimenez.

Turning point: The Diamondbacks hit a pair of two-run home runs off closer Trevor Hoffman for a 6-4 victory on May 27 that kept Arizona in first place and the Padres in second. The Padres lost eight of their next nine games.

Most valuable player: Phil Nevin again delivered excellent returns as the team's cleanup man. Nevin led the team in home runs and RBIs and earned praise for being a fiery leader. On October 6, Nevin hit three home runs in a game, something no Padre had done in a home game over the franchise's history.

Most valuable pitcher: Trevor Hoffman became the first big leaguer to record at least 40 saves in four consecutive seasons and five 40-save seasons in a career. He also became the 14th pitcher to log 300 career saves.

Most improved player: Damian Jackson evolved into a standout defender one year after his meltdowns in the field cost him the shortstop job. Jackson became perhaps the best defender among N.L. second basemen. He made good use of his exceptional speed and quickness in the field.

Most pleasant surprise: Relief pitcher Jeremy Fikac earned a promotion directly from Class AA Mobile and became the bullpen's top righthanded setup man.

Key injuries: Torn elbow ligaments ended the seasons of LHP Kevin Walker and RHP Adam Eaton. ... Mark Kotsay didn't start after September 9, when he aggravated a sprained right hand. ... Torn knee cartilage limited Tony Gwynn to pinch-hitting duty after July 12.

Notable: The Padres made 145 errors, the highest total in the majors. ... Phil Nevin and Ryan Klesko powered the offense, combining for 239 RBIs, the most by a tandem in franchise history. ... The club set a franchise record for walks received with 678. ... Ten N.L. clubs posted lower ERAs than San Diego's 4.52 total, which was the club's worst ranking since it finished 13th in 1997.

—TOM KRASOVIC

RECORDS

2001 regular-season record: 79-83 (4th in N.L. West); 35-46 at home; 44-37 on road; 17-15 vs. N.L. East; 24-15 vs. N.L. Central; 32-44 vs. N.L. West; 6-9 vs. A.L.; 18-26 vs. lefthanded starters; 61-57 vs. righthanded starters; 76-80 on grass; 3-3 on turf; 28-23 in daytime; 51-60 at night; 24-15 in one-run games; 8-1 in extra-inning games; 0-0-1 in doubleheaders.

Team record past five years: 403-407 (.498, ranks 8th in league in that span).

TEAM LEADERS

Batting average: Phil Nevin (.306).
At-bats: Phil Nevin (546).
Runs: Ryan Klesko (105).
Hits: Phil Nevin (167).
Total Bases: Phil Nevin (321).
Doubles: Ryan Klesko (34).
Triples: Damian Jackson, Ryan Klesko (6).
Home runs: Phil Nevin (41).
Runs batted in: Phil Nevin (126).
Stolen bases: Rickey Henderson (25).
Slugging percentage: Phil Nevin (.588).
On-base percentage: Phil Nevin (.388).
Wins: Kevin Jarvis (12).
Earned-run average: Kevin Jarvis (4.79).

Complete games: Adam Eaton (2).
Shutouts: Kevin Jarvis (1).
Saves: Trevor Hoffman (43).
Innings pitched: Bobby J. Jones (195.0).
Strikeouts: Kevin Jarvis (133).

GAMES BY POSITION

Catcher: Ben Davis 135, Wiki Gonzalez 47, Rick Wilkins 7.
First base: Ryan Klesko 145, Alex Arias 17, Dave Magadan 9, Kevin Witt 9, Ben Davis 2, Rick Wilkins 1.
Second base: Damian Jackson 118, Cesar Crespo 34, Alex Arias 13, Adam Riggs 11, Chris Gomez 8, Santiago Perez 2, Dave Magadan 1.
Third base: Phil Nevin 145, Dave Magadan 22, Alex Arias 18, Cesar Crespo 2, Adam Riggs 1.
Shortstop: D'Angelo Jimenez 85, Donaldo Mendez 46, Chris Gomez 36, Alex Arias 13, Santiago Perez 8, Damian Jackson 3, Dave Magadan 1, Cesar Crespo 1.
Outfield: Bubba Trammell 132, Mark Kotsay 111, Rickey Henderson 104, Mike Darr 93, Mike Colangelo 40, Ray Lankford 38, Santiago Perez 26, Cesar Crespo 18, Tony Gwynn 17, Emil Brown 11, Damian Jackson 2.
Designated hitter: Bubba Trammell 3, Dave Magadan 2, Tony Gwynn 1, Phil Nevin 1, Wiki Gonzalez 1, Rickey Henderson 1.

TOP DRAFT CHOICES

1. **Jake Gautreau**, 3B, Tulane University.
2. **Matt Harrington**, RHP, St. Paul (Northern League).
3. **Taggert Bozeid**, 1B/3B, U. of San Francisco.
4. **Josh Barfield**, 2B, Klein HS, Spring, Tex.
5. **Greg Sain**, C/3B, U. of San Diego.
6. **Jason Weidmeyer**, LHP, U. of Memphis.
7. **Doc Brooks**, OF, U. of Georgia.
8. **David Pauley**, RHP, Longmont (Colo.) H.S.
9. **Jon Benick**, 1B, Univ. of Virginia.
10. **Ben Fox**, LHP, Dixie State (Utah) J.C.

SAN FRANCISCO GIANTS
NATIONAL LEAGUE WEST DIVISION

Giants schedule
Home games shaded
D—Day game (games starting before 5 p.m.)
*All-Star Game at Milwaukee
Subject to changes

April
SUN	MON	TUE	WED	THU	FRI	SAT
	1	2 D LA	3 LA	4 LA	5 D SD	6 SD
7 SD	8	9 LA	10 LA	11 D LA	12 MIL	13 MIL
14 D MIL	15 SD	16 SD	17 SD	18	19 HOU	20 HOU
21 D HOU	22	23 CUB	24 CUB	25 D CUB	26 CIN	27 CIN
28 D CIN	29 PHI	30 PHI				

May
SUN	MON	TUE	WED	THU	FRI	SAT
			1 PHI	2	3 CIN	4 CIN
5 D CIN	6	7 NYM	8 NYM	9 NYM	10 MON	11 MON
12 D MON	13 ATL	14 ATL	15 ATL	16 ATL	17 FLA	18 D FLA
19 FLA	20	21 ARI	22 ARI	23	24 COL	25 D COL
26 D COL	27 ARI	28 D ARI	29 ARI	30 ARI	31 D COL	

June
SUN	MON	TUE	WED	THU	FRI	SAT
						1 COL
2 COL	3 SD	4 SD	5 SD	6	7 NYY	8 NYY
9 NYY	10 TOR	11 TOR	12 TOR	13	14 D OAK	15 OAK
16 OAK	17	18 TB	19 TB	20 TB	21 BAL	22 D BAL
23 BAL	24 SD	25 D SD	26 SD	27 SD	28 OAK	29 OAK
30 D OAK						

July
SUN	MON	TUE	WED	THU	FRI	SAT
	1 COL	2 COL	3 COL	4 D ARI	5 ARI	6 ARI
7 D ARI	8	9 *	10	11 COL	12 COL	13 COL
14 COL	15 D ARI	16 ARI	17 STL	18 D STL	19 LA	20 LA
21 LA	22 STL	23 STL	24 STL	25 D STL	26 D LA	27 LA
28 LA	29	30 PHI	31 PHI			

August
SUN	MON	TUE	WED	THU	FRI	SAT
				1 PHI	2 PIT	3 PIT
4 D PIT	5	6 CUB	7 CUB	8 CUB	9 PIT	10 D PIT
11 PIT	12	13 ATL	14 ATL	15 ATL	16 FLA	17 FLA
18 D FLA	19 D FLA	20 NYM	21 NYM	22 NYM	23 MON	24 D MON
25 MON	26 COL	27 COL	28 COL	29 D COL	30 ARI	31 ARI

September
SUN	MON	TUE	WED	THU	FRI	SAT
1 D ARI	2	3 COL	4 D COL	5 ARI	6 D ARI	7 ARI
8 ARI	9	10 LA	11 LA	12 D LA	13 SD	14 SD
15 D SD	16 LA	17 LA	18 LA	19 MIL	20 MIL	21 MIL
22 D MIL	23	24 SD	25 D SD	26	27 HOU	28 HOU
29 D HOU	30					

2002 SEASON
CLUB DIRECTORY

President and managing general partner
Peter A. Magowan
Executive vice president/COO
Larry Baer
Senior v.p. and general manager
Brian Sabean
Vice president and assistant g.m.
Ned Colletti
Vice president of player personnel
Dick Tidrow
Special assistant to the general manager
Ron Perranoski
Director of player development
Jack Hiatt
Coordinator of international operations
Rick Ragazzo
Sr. v.p. and chief financial officer
John Yee
Sr. v.p., ballpark operations/security
Jorge Costa
Sr. vice president, corporate marketing
Mario Alioto
Sr. v.p., consumer marketing
Tom McDonald
V.p., general manager, retail
Connie Kullberg
Director of ballpark operations
Gene Telucci
Vice president, ticket services
Russ Stanley
Director of travel
Reggie Younger Jr.

Sr. vice president and general counsel
Jack Bair
Media relations manager
Jim Moorehead
Baseball information manager
Blake Rhodes
Mgr., media services and broadcasting
Maria Jacinto
Western regional cross-checker
Doug Mapson
Eastern regional cross-checker
Alan Marr
West Coast cross-checker
Darren Wittcke
East Coast cross-checker
Bobby Myrick
Canadian cross-checker
Steve Arnieri
Major league scouts
Joe DiCarlo, Stan Saleski, Paul Turco, Randy Waddill, Tom Zimmer
Major league advance scout
Pat Dobson
Special assignment scouts
Dick Cole, Bo Osborne
Scouts
Mateo Alou, Jose Cassino, Pedro Chavez, Manuel D'Jesus, John DiCarlo, Lee Elder, Charlie Gonzalez, Tom Korenek, Doug McMillan, Matt Nerland, Luis Pena, John Shafer, Joe Strain, Todd Thomas, Alex Torres, Glenn Tufts, Paul Turco Jr., Ciro Villalobos

MINOR LEAGUE AFFILIATES

Class	Team	League	Manager
AAA	Fresno	Pacific Coast	Shane Turner
AA	Shreveport	Texas	Mario Mendoza
A	Hagerstown	South Atlantic	Bill Hayes
A	San Jose	California	To be announced
Rookie	Salem-Keizer	Northwest	Fred Stanley
Rookie	Giants	Arizona	To be announced

BROADCAST INFORMATION
Radio: KNBR-AM (680).
TV: KTVU-TV (Channel 2).
Cable TV: FOX Sports Net.

SPRING TRAINING
Ballpark (city): Scottsdale Stadium (Scottsdale, Ariz.).
Ticket information: 602-990-7972.

Follow the Giants all season at: www.sportingnews.com/baseball/teams/giants/

SPRING TRAINING ROSTER

Manager—Dusty Baker (12).

Coaches—Gene Clines (20), Sonny Jackson (15), Joe Lefebvre, Juan Lopez (59), Dave Righetti (19), Ron Wotus (10).

No.	PITCHERS	B/T	Ht./Wt.	Born	2001 clubs
32	Ainsworth, Kurt	R/R	6-3/190	9-9-78	Fresno, San Francisco
48	Christiansen, Jason	R/L	6-5/241	9-21-69	Memphis, St. Louis, San Francisco
53	Diaz, Felix	R/R	6-1/180	7-27-81	Hagerstown
38	Fultz, Aaron	L/L	6-0/196	9-4-73	San Francisco
61	Hernandez, Livan	R/R	6-2/222	2-20-75	San Francisco
43	Jensen, Ryan	R/R	6-0/205	9-17-75	Fresno, San Francisco
36	Nathan, Joe	R/R	6-4/195	11-22-74	Fresno, Shreveport
31	Nen, Robb	R/R	6-5/215	11-28-69	San Francisco
48	Ortiz, Russ	R/R	6-1/210	6-5-74	San Francisco
47	Rodriguez, Felix	R/R	6-1/190	12-5-72	San Francisco
46	Rueter, Kirk	L/L	6-3/205	12-1-70	San Francisco
22	Schmidt, Jason	R/R	6-5/220	1-29-73	Altoona, Nashville, Pittsburgh, San Francisco
40	Urban, Jeff	L/R	6-8/215	1-25-77	Shreveport
34	Witasick, Jay	R/R	6-4/235	8-28-72	San Diego, New York A.L.
45	Worrell, Tim	R/R	6-4/231	7-5-67	San Francisco, Arizona Giants
41	Zerbe, Chad	L/L	6-0/190	4-27-72	Fresno, San Francisco

No.	CATCHERS	B/T	Ht./Wt.	Born	2001 clubs
33	Santiago, Benito	R/R	6-1/195	3-9-65	San Francisco
9	Torrealba, Yorvit	R/R	5-11/190	7-19-78	Fresno, San Francisco

No.	INFIELDERS	B/T	Ht./Wt.	Born	2001 clubs
35	Aurilia, Rich	R/R	6-1/185	9-2-71	San Francisco
28	Castro, Nelson	R/R	5-10/190	6-4-76	Fresno, Shreveport
39	Feliz, Pedro	R/R	6-1/195	4-27-77	San Francisco
	Guzman, Edwards	L/R	5-11/205	9-11-76	Fresno, San Francisco
21	Kent, Jeff	R/R	6-1/205	3-7-68	San Francisco
34	Martinez, Ramon	R/R	6-1/187	10-10-72	San Francisco
22	Minor, Damon	L/L	6-7/230	1-9-75	San Francisco, Fresno
23	Ransom, Cody	R/R	6-2/190	2-17-76	Fresno, San Francisco
2	Relaford, Desi	B/R	5-9/174	9-16-73	New York N.L.
50	Santos, Deivis	L/L	6-1/175	2-9-80	Hagerstown
6	Snow, J.T.	L/L	6-2/205	2-26-68	San Francisco, Fresno

No.	OUTFIELDERS	B/T	Ht./Wt.	Born	2001 clubs
7	Benard, Marvin	L/L	5-9/185	1-20-70	San Francisco
25	Bonds, Barry	L/L	6-2/210	7-24-64	San Francisco
23	Dunston, Shawon	R/R	6-1/180	3-21-63	San Francisco
49	McDowell, Arturo	L/L	6-1/175	9-7-79	San Jose
8	Murray, Calvin	R/R	5-11/190	7-30-71	Fresno, San Francisco
	Sanders, Reggie	R/R	6-1/185	12-1-67	Arizona, Tucson
5	Shinjo, Tsuyoshi	R/R	6-1/185	1-28-72	New York N.L., Brooklyn
14	Torcato, Tony	L/R	6-1/195	10-25-79	San Jose, Shreveport, Fresno
53	Valderrama, Carlos	R/R	6-3/186	11-30-77	Shreveport

BALLPARK INFORMATION

Ballpark (capacity, surface)
Pacific Bell Park (41,341, grass)

Address
24 Willie Mays Plaza
San Francisco, CA 94107

Official website
www.sfgiants.com

Business phone
415-972-2000

Ticket information
415-972-2000

Ticket prices
$26 (lower box)
$20 (view box, arcade)
$16 (view reserved)
$10 (bleachers)

Field dimensions (from home plate)
To left field at foul line, 339 feet
To center field, 399 feet
To right field at foul line, 309 feet

First game played
April 11, 2000 (Dodgers 6, Giants 5)

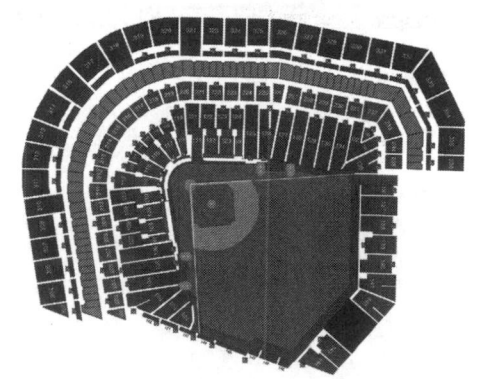

2002 SEASON *San Francisco Giants*

Date	Opp.	Res.	Score	(inn.*)	Hits	Opp. hits	Winning pitcher	Losing pitcher	Save	Record	Pos.	GB
4-2	S.D.	W	3-2		10	7	Hernandez	Williams	Nen	1-0	T1st	...
4-4	S.D.	W	8-7		11	14	Nen	Witasick		2-0	T1st	...
4-5	S.D.	W	8-2		11	10	Ortiz	Jones		3-0	T1st	...
4-6	At L.A.	L	1-10		4	12	Prokopec	Estes		3-1	T1st	...
4-7	At L.A.	L	4-10		6	10	Park	Hernandez		3-2	T2nd	0.5
4-8	At L.A.	W	8-3		11	8	Rueter	Gagne		4-2	1st	+0.5
4-10	At S.D.	W	11-6		11	10	Ortiz	Jarvis		5-2	1st	+1.5
4-11	At S.D.	W	2-1		5	3	Fultz	Hoffman	Nen	6-2	1st	+1.5
4-12	At S.D.	L	3-8		8	11	Eaton	Hernandez		6-3	1st	+0.5
4-13	At Mil.	W	7-3		12	3	Rueter	Wright		7-3	1st	+1.5
4-14	At Mil.	L	6-11		9	14	DeJean	Gardner		7-4	1st	+1.0
4-15	At Mil.	L	4-7		7	6	Rigdon	Ortiz	Leskanic	7-5	1st	+0.5
4-17	L.A.	W	3-2		7	9	Rodriguez	Adams	Nen	8-5	1st	+1.0
4-18	L.A.	W	5-4		7	11	Fultz	Park	Nen	9-5	1st	+1.0
4-19	L.A.	L	1-10		7	15	Gagne	Rueter		9-6	T1st	...
4-20	Mil.	W	3-1		3	2	Ortiz	Haynes	Nen	10-6	1st	+1.0
4-21	Mil.	L	3-6		9	14	Rigdon	Gardner	Weathers	10-7	1st	+0.5
4-22	Mil.	W	6-4		8	8	Estes	D'Amico	Nen	11-7	1st	+1.0
4-24	Cin.	L	5-9		7	17	Brower	Hernandez		11-8	T1st	...
4-25	Cin.	L	5-7		12	15	O. Fernandez	Rueter	Graves	11-9	2nd	1.0
4-26	Cin.	L	5-7		13	13	Reyes	Embree	Graves	11-10	4th	1.0
4-27	Chi.	L	3-7		3	8	Wood	Gardner		11-11	4th	1.5
4-28	Chi.	W	5-0		9	5	Estes	Tavarez		12-11	T2nd	1.5
4-29	Chi.	L	2-11		6	13	Aybar	Hernandez		12-12	4th	2.5
5-1	At Pit.	W	11-6		14	7	Rueter	Martinez		13-12	T3rd	1.5
5-2	At Pit.	W	7-6		9	7	Ortiz	Silva	Nen	14-12	T2nd	1.5
5-3	At Pit.	L	3-4		9	6	Silva	Estes	M. Williams	14-13	T3rd	2.5
5-4	At Phi.	W	4-2		5	8	Hernandez	Chen	Nen	15-13	T2nd	1.5
5-5	At Phi.	L	2-4		8	7	Wolf	Fultz	Mesa	15-14	T2nd	1.5
5-6	At Phi.	L	8-10		14	12	Daal	Rueter	Mesa	15-15	T3rd	1.5
5-7	Mon.	W	6-2		5	7	Ortiz	Armas Jr	Fultz	16-15	2nd	1.5
5-8	Mon.	W	9-1		12	6	Estes	Thurman		17-15	2nd	0.5
5-9	Mon.	L	0-8		7	11	Vazquez	Hernandez		17-16	T3rd	1.5
5-10	Mon.	W	13-0		18	6	Rueter	Reames		18-16	T2nd	1.5
5-11	N.Y.	W	3-2	(10)	12	5	Nen	Wall		19-16	T2nd	0.5
5-12	N.Y.	W	10-3		10	10	Ortiz	Gonzalez		20-16	2nd	0.5
5-13	N.Y.	W	6-3		7	4	Zerbe	Appier		21-16	2nd	0.5
5-15	At Fla.	W	7-4		9	10	Hernandez	Dempster	Nen	22-16	1st	+0.5
5-16	At Fla.	L	3-4		5	10	Clement	Rueter	Alfonseca	22-17	2nd	0.5
5-17	At Fla.	L	3-8		4	10	Smith	Ortiz		22-18	3rd	1.0
5-18	At Atl.	L	5-6		7	7	Cabrera	Nen		22-19	3rd	1.0
5-19	At Atl.	W	6-3		17	7	Worrell	Cabrera	Nen	23-19	T2nd	0.5
5-20	At Atl.	L	6-11		11	14	Ligtenberg	Hernandez		23-20	T2nd	0.5
5-21	At Ari.	L	2-4		6	7	Schilling	Rueter		23-21	T3rd	1.0
5-22	At Ari.	L	8-12		13	15	Anderson	Ortiz		23-22	T4th	2.0
5-23	At Ari.	W	5-1		9	3	Gardner	Johnson		24-22	4th	1.0
5-24	Col.	W	5-1		7	2	Estes	Thomson		25-22	T2nd	1.0
5-25	Col.	L	1-6		7	9	Hampton	Hernandez		25-23	4th	1.0
5-26	Col.	L	4-10		10	11	Chacon	Rueter		25-24	T4th	2.0
5-27	Col.	W	5-4		6	12	Ortiz	Neagle	Nen	26-24	T3rd	2.0
5-28	Ari.	L	1-2	(12)	9	9	Batista	Worrell		26-25	4th	3.0
5-29	Ari.	L	0-1	(18)	9	10	Batista	Vogelsong	Swindell	26-26	T4th	4.0
5-30	Ari.	L	3-4		8	14	Ellis	Hernandez	Prinz	26-27	T4th	5.0
6-1	At Col.	W	11-7		11	10	Rueter	Chacon		27-27	T3rd	5.0
6-2	At Col.	L	5-7		13	12	Jimenez	Nen		27-28	T3rd	6.0
6-3	At Col.	L	2-11		3	19	Astacio	Gardner		27-29	T4th	7.0
6-4	S.D.	W	3-1		12	4	Estes	Jones	Nen	28-29	4th	6.0
6-5	S.D.	W	7-6		12	9	Hernandez	Davey	Nen	29-29	4th	5.0
6-6	S.D.	W	6-4		11	8	Rueter	Williams	Nen	30-29	4th	5.0
6-7	S.D.	L	7-10		8	12	Eaton	Ortiz		30-30	4th	6.0
6-8	At Oak.	L	2-4		7	6	Heredia	Gardner	Isringhausen	30-31	4th	7.0
6-9	At Oak.	W	4-3	(11)	9	5	Rodriguez	Mathews	Nen	31-31	4th	6.0
6-10	At Oak.	L	2-6		5	10	Mulder	Hernandez	Bradford	31-32	4th	7.0
6-12	Ana.	W	3-2		9	10	Rueter	Rapp	Nen	32-32	4th	6.0
6-13	Ana.	W	1-0		6	5	Ortiz	Schoeneweis	Nen	33-32	4th	6.0
6-14	Ana.	W	10-4		11	11	Gardner	Valdes		34-32	3rd	6.0
6-15	Oak.	W	3-1		7	5	Estes	Mulder	Nen	35-32	3rd	5.0
6-16	Oak.	W	2-1		5	5	Hernandez	Tam	Nen	36-32	3rd	5.0
6-17	Oak.	W	3-0		7	5	Rueter	Hudson	Nen	37-32	T2nd	5.0
6-19	At S.D.	L	3-4	(15)	12	10	Witasick	Vogelsong		37-33	T2nd	6.0
6-20	At S.D.	W	8-6		13	12	Gardner	Jarvis	Nen	38-33	T2nd	5.0
6-21	At S.D.	W	8-3		14	9	Estes	Jones		39-33	2nd	5.0
6-22	At St.L.	W	10-5		13	7	Hernandez	Hermanson		40-33	2nd	5.0
6-23	At St.L.	L	5-6		12	10	Christiansen	Embree		40-34	2nd	6.0

Date	Opp.	Res.	Score	(inn.*)	Hits	Opp. hits	Winning pitcher	Losing pitcher	Save	Record	Pos.	GB
6-24	At St.L.	L	3-7		8	11	Morris	Ortiz	Veres	40-35	2nd	6.0
6-25	L.A.	W	5-2		6	5	Gardner	Park	Nen	41-35	2nd	5.0
6-26	L.A.	L	8-14		14	18	Reyes	Worrell		41-36	2nd	5.0
6-27	L.A.	L	3-7		8	12	Adams	Hernandez		41-37	2nd	6.0
6-29	St.L.	W	3-2		8	4	Rodriguez	Kline	Nen	42-37	T2nd	6.0
6-30	St.L.	W	5-2		11	7	Rodriguez	Timlin	Nen	43-37	T2nd	6.0
7-1	St.L.	W	5-4		10	8	Zerbe	An. Benes	Nen	44-37	T2nd	6.0
7-2	At L.A.	L	6-8		8	16	Adams	Vogelsong	Shaw	44-38	3rd	6.5
7-3	At L.A.	L	3-4		10	6	Williams	Hernandez	Shaw	44-39	3rd	6.5
7-4	At L.A.	L	3-4		12	9	Herges	Rodriguez	Shaw	44-40	3rd	7.5
7-5	At L.A.	W	3-2		7	4	Ortiz	Reyes	Nen	45-40	3rd	6.5
7-6	Mil.	W	3-2	(11)	11	4	Zerbe	Leskanic		46-40	3rd	5.5
7-7	Mil.	L	3-13		5	15	Haynes	Estes	Buddie	46-41	3rd	5.5
7-8	Mil.	L	4-6	(13)	12	13	DeJean	Boehringer		46-42	3rd	5.5
7-12	At Sea.	L	3-4	(11)	8	8	Rhodes	Boehringer		46-43	3rd	5.5
7-13	At Sea.	W	5-3		10	7	Ortiz	Moyer	Nen	47-43	3rd	5.5
7-14	At Sea.	L	2-3		3	6	Garcia	Estes	Sasaki	47-44	3rd	6.5
7-15	At Tex.	W	7-6		9	12	Hernandez	Oliver	Nen	48-44	3rd	5.5
7-16	At Tex.	L	0-2		6	11	Bell	Jensen	Zimmerman	48-45	3rd	6.5
7-17	At Tex.	W	10-2		12	8	Rueter	Rogers		49-45	3rd	5.5
7-18	Col.	W	10-0		12	5	Ortiz	Hampton		50-45	3rd	5.0
7-19	Col.	W	2-1		9	5	Rodriguez	Acevedo		51-45	3rd	4.5
7-20	Ari.	W	1-0		4	3	Hernandez	Batista	Nen	52-45	3rd	3.5
7-21	Ari.	L	2-9		4	11	Schilling	Jensen		52-46	3rd	4.5
7-22	Ari.	L	4-12		6	14	Anderson	Rueter		52-47	3rd	5.5
7-23	At Col.	L	2-8		5	11	Hampton	Ortiz		52-48	3rd	5.5
7-24	At Col.	L	4-6		7	10	Chacon	Estes	Jimenez	52-49	3rd	6.5
7-25	At Col.	W	9-3		15	10	Jensen	Bohanon		53-49	3rd	6.5
7-26	At Ari.	W	11-3		13	10	Hernandez	Schilling		54-49	3rd	5.5
7-27	At Ari.	W	9-5		14	14	Rueter	Anderson		55-49	3rd	5.0
7-28	At Ari.	W	11-4		18	9	Ortiz	Lopez		56-49	3rd	5.0
7-29	At Ari.	W	4-3		8	5	Estes	Kim	Nen	57-49	3rd	4.0
7-31	Pit.	W	8-7	(11)	16	13	Gomes	Wilkins		58-49	3rd	3.0
8-1	Pit.	W	3-1		7	2	Schmidt	Beimel	Nen	59-49	3rd	2.0
8-2	Pit.	W	3-0		9	3	Rueter	McKnight	Nen	60-49	3rd	1.0
8-3	Phi.	W	4-2		5	6	Rodriguez	Cormier		61-49	T2nd	0.5
8-4	Phi.	L	2-12		7	17	Figueroa	Estes		61-50	3rd	1.0
8-5	Phi.	W	8-4		14	10	Hernandez	Person		62-50	3rd	1.0
8-7	At Cin.	W	9-3	(11)	16	10	Christiansen	Graves		63-50	2nd	1.0
8-8	At Cin.	L	9-11		15	13	Mercado	Schmidt	Graves	63-51	3rd	2.0
8-9	At Cin.	W	6-4		11	9	Ortiz	Winchester	Nen	64-51	2nd	1.0
8-10	At Chi.	L	3-9		8	9	Lieber	Estes		64-52	3rd	1.0
8-11	At Chi.	W	9-4		15	7	Hernandez	Borowski		65-52	T2nd	0.5
8-12	At Chi.	W	7-6		10	13	Rueter	Tapani	Nen	66-52	2nd	0.5
8-14	Fla.	W	13-7		20	13	Schmidt	Sanchez		67-52	2nd	1.0
8-15	Fla.	W	2-1		3	5	Nen	Darensbourg		68-52	2nd	1.0
8-16	Fla.	W	5-3		7	8	Worrell	Burnett	Nen	69-52	2nd	0.5
8-17	Atl.	L	1-2		6	2	Maddux	Hernandez	Smoltz	69-53	2nd	1.5
8-18	Atl.	L	1-3		9	8	Marquis	Rueter	Karsay	69-54	2nd	2.5
8-19	Atl.	W	4-1		9	5	Schmidt	Glavine	Nen	70-54	2nd	2.5
8-21	At Mon.	W	10-2		13	4	Ortiz	Pavano		71-54	2nd	1.5
8-22	At Mon.	L	1-7		5	9	Vazquez	Estes		71-55	2nd	2.5
8-23	At Mon.	W	10-5		16	8	Rodriguez	Lloyd		72-55	2nd	1.5
8-24	At N.Y.	L	3-4		4	11	Chen	Rueter	Benitez	72-56	2nd	1.5
8-25	At N.Y.	L	2-3	(11)	9	12	Riggan	Nen		72-57	2nd	2.5
8-26	At N.Y.	L	5-6		7	7	Leiter	Ortiz	Benitez	72-58	2nd	3.5
8-27	At N.Y.	W	6-5		12	6	Rodriguez	White	Nen	73-58	2nd	2.5
8-28	At Ari.	L	1-4		6	8	Johnson	Hernandez	Kim	73-59	2nd	3.5
8-29	At Ari.	L	0-2		4	10	Witt	Rueter	Kim	73-60	2nd	4.5
8-30	At Ari.	W	13-5		17	11	Schmidt	Batista		74-60	2nd	3.5
8-31	Col.	L	2-5		9	5	Thomson	Ortiz	Powell	74-61	2nd	4.0
9-1	Col.	W	2-1		5	3	Nen	Speier		75-61	2nd	3.0
9-2	Col.	W	3-1		5	8	Hernandez	Chacon	Nen	76-61	2nd	2.0
9-3	Col.	L	1-4		4	9	Jennings	Rueter	Powell	76-62	2nd	2.5
9-4	Ari.	W	5-2		7	7	Schmidt	Swindell	Nen	77-62	2nd	1.5
9-5	Ari.	L	2-7		7	16	Schilling	Ortiz		77-63	2nd	2.5
9-6	Ari.	W	9-5		13	10	Fultz	Lopez		78-63	2nd	1.5
9-7	At Col.	L	2-3	(12)	10	10	Miceli	Worrell		78-64	3rd	1.5
9-8	At Col.	W	7-3		12	7	Rueter	Jennings		79-64	2nd	1.5
9-9	At Col.	W	9-4	(11)	13	8	Gomes	Belitz		80-64	2nd	1.5
9-18	Hou.	L	2-3		6	5	Williams	Nen	Wagner	80-65	2nd	2.0
9-19	Hou.	L	3-10		6	14	Mlicki	Hernandez		80-66	2nd	2.0
9-20	Hou.	L	4-5	(10)	7	8	Dotel	Nen	Wagner	80-67	2nd	2.0
9-21	At S.D.	W	2-0		7	7	Schmidt	Lawrence	Nen	81-67	2nd	2.0
9-22	At S.D.	L	3-4	(10)	7	6	Hoffman	Boehringer		81-68	2nd	2.0
9-23	At S.D.	W	11-2		17	7	Ortiz	Herndon		82-68	2nd	2.0
9-24	At L.A.	W	2-1		11	4	Hernandez	Baldwin	Nen	83-68	2nd	1.5
9-25	At L.A.	L	5-9		9	13	Park	Rueter		83-69	2nd	1.5

Date	Opp.	Res.	Score	(inn.*)	Hits	Opp. hits	Winning pitcher	Losing pitcher	Save	Record	Pos.	GB
9-26	At L.A.	W	6-4	13		6	Rodriguez	Shaw	Nen	84-69	2nd	1.5
9-28	S.D.	W	10-5		15	11	Estes	Middlebrook		85-69	2nd	2.0
9-29	S.D.	W	3-1		6	6	Ortiz	McElroy	Nen	86-69	2nd	2.0
9-30	S.D.	L	4-5		8	12	Tollberg	Worrell	Hoffman	86-70	2nd	2.0
10-2	At Hou.	W	4-1		10	8	Rueter	Reynolds	Nen	87-70	2nd	2.0
10-3	At Hou.	W	11-8		15	12	Schmidt	Cruz		88-70	2nd	2.0
10-4	At Hou.	W	10-2		11	8	Ortiz	Mlicki	Boehringer	89-70	2nd	2.0
10-5	L.A.	L	10-11		10	15	Carrara	Worrell	Shaw	89-71	2nd	3.0
10-6	L.A.	L	2-6		5	10	Baldwin	Hernandez	Shaw	89-72	2nd	3.0
10-7	L.A.	W	2-1		9	4	Gardner	Springer	Nen	90-72	2nd	2.0

Monthly records: April (12-12), May (14-15), June (17-10), July (15-12), August (16-12), September (12-9), October (4-2).
*Innings, if other than nine.

HIGHLIGHTS

High point: July 29. Marvin Benard's ninth-inning homer off Byung-Hyun Kim gave the Giants a 4-3 victory and a four-game sweep at Arizona, the launching point of a nine-game winning streak that brought the Giants within a half game of first place.

Low point: The Giants ended the first half with a miserable 6-4, 13-inning loss to lowly Milwaukee at Pacific Bell Park. The Giants loaded the bases in the bottom of the 10th, 11th and 12th innings yet couldn't push across the winning run.

Turning point: General manager Brian Sabean's acquisitions of Andres Galarraga and pitchers Jason Schmidt and Jason Christiansen just before the July 31 trading deadline injected incredible life into the team.

Most valuable player: Barry Bonds is the no-brainer choice here. Besides setting the single-season home run record, Bonds also set records for walks and slugging percentage. He reached base in more than half his plate appearances.

Most valuable pitcher: Setup man Felix Rodriguez was incredible out of the bullpen, going 9-1 with a 1.68 ERA in a team-high 80 games.

Most improved player: Rich Aurilia was already a good hitter, one of the best offensive shortstops in baseball. But his performance in 2001 put him in MVP territory. His 37 homers, 97 RBIs and .324 batting average bettered his previous career highs.

Most pleasant surprise: Benito Santiago, signed a week before the regular season began, became an everyday catcher at age 36 and played a remarkable 133 games. Although his hitting waned significantly in the second half, he was a steadying influence behind the plate.

Key injuries: The biggest problem was pitcher Shawn Estes' ankle; it caused him to miss a month down the stretch. ... Eric Davis never could get on track because of a lingering shoulder injury, which he aggravated with a dive the sec-ond day of the season.

Notable: The Giants joined the Diamondbacks in setting a major league record with 14 pinch home runs. Benard and Shawon Dunston led the Giants with three apiece. ... One reason for the Giants' downfall in the N.L. West: They stranded a league-leading 1,242 runners. ... The Giants reached 90 victories for the second straight season, the first time that has happened since 1966-67. ... The Giants set a franchise record by hitting 235 home runs.

—HENRY SCHULMAN

RECORDS

2001 regular-season record: 90-72 (2nd in N.L. West); 49-32 at home; 41-40 on road; 18-14 vs. N.L. East; 21-18 vs. N.L. Central; 41-35 vs. N.L. West; 10-5 vs. A.L.; 21-13 vs. lefthanded starters; 69-59 vs. righthanded starters; 87-69 on grass; 3-3 on turf; 30-26 in daytime; 60-46 at night; 28-22 in one-run games; 6-9 in extra-inning games; 0-0-0 in double-headers.

Team record past five years: 452-359 (.557, ranks 2nd in league in that span).

TEAM LEADERS

Batting average: Barry Bonds (.328).
At-bats: Rich Aurilia (636).
Runs: Barry Bonds (129).
Hits: Rich Aurilia (206).
Total Bases: Barry Bonds (411).
Doubles: Jeff Kent (49).
Triples: Jeff Kent (6).
Home runs: Barry Bonds (73).
Runs batted in: Barry Bonds (137).
Stolen bases: Barry Bonds (13).
Slugging percentage: Barry Bonds (.863).
On-base percentage: Barry Bonds (.515).
Wins: Russ Ortiz (17).
Earned-run average: Russ Ortiz (3.29).
Complete games: Livan Hernandez (2).
Shutouts: Russ Ortiz (1).
Saves: Robb Nen (45).

Innings pitched: Livan Hernandez (226.2).
Strikeouts: Russ Ortiz (169).

GAMES BY POSITION

Catcher: Benito Santiago 130, Bobby Estalella 28, Edwards Guzman 26, Yorvit Torrealba 3.
First base: J.T. Snow 92, Andres Galarraga 41, Jeff Kent 30, Felipe Crespo 16, Damon Minor 11, Edwards Guzman 7, Benito Santiago 2, Shawon Dunston 1, John Vander Wal 1.
Second base: Jeff Kent 140, Ramon E. Martinez 42, Edwards Guzman 3, Felipe Crespo 2.
Third base: Pedro Feliz 86, Ramon E. Martinez 70, Russ Davis 46, Edwards Guzman 7.
Shortstop: Rich Aurilia 149, Ramon E. Martinez 24, Cody Ransom 6.
Outfield: Barry Bonds 143, Marvin Benard 109, Calvin Murray 104, Armando Rios 87, Shawon Dunston 60, Eric Davis 48, John Vander Wal 41, Dante Powell 9, Jalal Leach 3, Edwards Guzman 2, Felipe Crespo 1.
Designated hitter: Barry Bonds 6, Russ Davis 1, Eric Davis 1, Shawon Dunston 1, Felipe Crespo 1, Pedro Feliz 1.

TOP DRAFT CHOICES

1a. **Brad Hennessey,** RHP, Youngstown State University.
1b. **Noah Lowry,** LHP, Pepperdine Univ.
1c. **Todd Linden,** OF, Louisiana State U.
2. **Jesse Foppert,** RHP, U. of San Francisco.
3. **Julian Benevidez,** 3B, Diablo Valley (Calif.) C.C.
4. **Josh Cram,** RHP, Clemson University.
5. **Justin Knoedler,** RHP, Miami (O.) U.
6. **David Cash,** RHP, U. of California.
7. **Jamie Athas,** SS, Wake Forest Univ.
8. **Jason Waddell,** LHP, Riverside (Calif.) C.C.
9. **T.J. Lange,** RHP, Seminole (Fla.) H.S.
10. **Wesley Hutchinson,** RHP, Lewis-Clarke State (Ida.) College.

2001 REVIEW

Year in review

American League Division Series

National League Division Series

American League Championship Series

National League Championship Series

World Series

All-Star Game

Notable Performances

Transactions

Award Winners

Miscellaneous

Necrology

YEAR IN REVIEW

By STEVE GIETSCHIER
TSN Senior Managing Editor

Without all the hoopla that just three seasons before had accompanied the joint assault of Mark McGwire and Sammy Sosa on Roger Maris' record of 61 home runs in a season, major league baseball witnessed in 2001 not just another single-season home run record, but rather one of the greatest individual offensive seasons of all time. Set against the backdrop of several exciting division pennant races and the anticipated retirements of two beloved stars, tempered by the tragic events of September 11 and their legacy and succeeded by a World Series that ranked among the very best, the performance of Barry Bonds, including a once-unthinkable 73 home runs, shone as a beacon of excellence. Bonds was so good in 2001 that some fans, perhaps even a majority, were willing, at least temporarily, to excuse his often surly demeanor and chronic disregard for the part they play in the complexities of the game.

Causes for celebration were, as usual, manifold. The American League, baseball's so-called "junior circuit," played the first season of its second century, and the Seattle Mariners ran away with the A.L. West Division, tying the all-time record for wins with 116. All three National League division races were closely fought and not decided until the season's final weekend. The Arizona Diamondbacks, with financial troubles so severe that just a year before Major League Baseball had to guarantee a loan so the team could pay its bills, won a thrilling seven-game World Series over the New York Yankees. The Diamondbacks, moreover, won their first championship more quickly (in their fourth season) than any previous expansion team, and Bob Brenly became the first rookie manager to win the World Series since Ralph Houk of the Yankees did it, ironically, in Maris' 61-homer season of 1961.

Still, whatever progress baseball made during the season to expand its popularity and recapture the dominant position it once occupied within the American sporting scene, it was severely compromised just two days after the conclusion of the World Series. On November 6, Commissioner Allan H. (Bud) Selig announced that major league owners had voted 28-2 to eliminate two teams prior to the start of the 2002 season. With the collective bargaining agreement between MLB and the Major League Baseball Players Association set to expire, Selig's pronouncement that the game's problems required this radical adjustment, dubbed contraction, and others yet to come cast a pall over what had been an exciting and, in some ways, inspiring season. "This is not a sad day," the commissioner grimly insisted. "Change is necessary." But observers who had hoped for a smooth off-season highlighted by a labor agreement reached without a work stoppage for the first time were less sanguine.

SEPTEMBER 11

In the aftermath of the terrorist attacks that saw hijacked airplanes crash into New York City's World Trade Center, the Pentagon and a field in western Pennsylvania, baseball reacted with dignified dispatch. Almost immediately, Selig cancelled an owners' meeting and the slate of games scheduled for that day. Later in the week, he announced that all games through Sunday, September 16—a total of 91—would be postponed and made up by extending the regular season one week. When play resumed, an air of heightened security and patriotism enveloped every game. Fans endured close scrutiny by stadium guards; players wore American flags on their uniforms; grounds crews painted intertwined red, white and blue ribbons on fields; and "God Bless America" replaced "Take Me Out to the Ball Game" as the song of choice at the seventh inning stretch.

Baseball contributed to funds aiding the victims' families and honored the firefighters, police officers and other emergency personnel whose demonstrations of courage elevated them to the status of national heroes. Teams visited the site known as Ground Zero and spent time at firehouses and police stations. The New York Mets and the Yankees donned T-shirts and caps bearing the logos "FDNY" and "NYPD." The three World Series games played in New York, featuring uniformed personnel singing the National Anthem and a bald eagle swooping in from center field before each game, became part of the nation's catharsis in the wake of this unspeakable horror.

SELIG URGES DRAFT CHANGES

In December 2000, Selig sent all clubs a memo proposing changes in the June free-agent draft. He urged that all players around the world be made subject to the draft, mainly to prevent Cuban defectors and Dominican players from commanding high signing bonuses. He also proposed eliminating eligibility for college juniors, thereby taking away leverage from those who might threaten to return to school if they were displeased with the team that drafted them or their draft position. He also suggested an annual competitive balance draft to be held after the World Series but before the winter meetings. The eight teams with the lowest winning percentages over the previous three years would be allowed to select one player from the rosters of the top eight teams, each of whom could protect just 25 players. On January 17, owners voted to seek the union's approval for these changes, but at year's end, no action had been taken.

CONTRACTION MEETS OBSTACLES

Selig called these proposals part of a complete overhaul of baseball's economic structure, but he made no further public pronouncements until November 6. While the owners' decision to pursue contraction from 30 teams to 28 did not come as a complete surprise, negative reaction to it was swift and vociferous, especially as speculation swirled that the Minnesota Twins and Montreal Expos would be the two clubs eliminated. No one was willing to argue for the continued viability of the Expos, a team that averaged just 7,524 fans per home game in 2001, but support for the Twins and criticism of the whole proposal came from many quarters. Former Commissioner Francis T. (Fay) Vincent took the owners to task for not consulting with the Players Association before making their decision. Former Players Association Executive Director Marvin Miller accused Selig of a conflict of interest because the elimination of the Twins would unduly benefit the Milwaukee Brewers. Selig put his controlling interest in the Brewers in a trust when he became commissioner, and his daughter is the team's CEO. Florida Attorney General Bob Butterworth issued subpoenas designed to compel MLB to turn over all documents on contraction as they pertain to the Florida Marlins and the Tampa Bay Devil Rays, two teams mentioned as alternative candidates for extinction, and Minnesota Attorney General Mike Hatch threatened to file an antitrust lawsuit against MLB in federal court.

The Metropolitan Sports Facilities Commission, owner of the Hubert H. Humphrey Metrodome, immediately filed a lawsuit compelling the Twins to honor their lease and won a temporary restraining order in Hennepin County District Court to block any changes in the team's situation. Judge Harry Crump later granted a temporary injunction ordering the team to play its 2002 schedule in the Metrodome. MLB and the Twins appealed, asking the Minnesota Supreme Court to bypass the Court of Appeals and take the case directly no later than December 7. Hatch and the MSFC opposed this request for the fast track approach. The Supreme Court ruled on November 30 not to take the case but ordered the Court of Appeals to move expeditiously. This put contraction on hold at least until December 27, when the Court of Appeals agreed to hear the case.

The Players Association filed a grievance on November 7 claiming that the owners' vote had violated the collective bargaining agreement, then just hours from expiration. Hearings before arbitrator Shyam Das began December 4. The union took the position that contraction should be part of negotiations for a new labor agreement, while MLB argued that contraction can occur without union approval with only the details subject to negotiation. Affirming Selig's leadership of their cause, owners voted on November 27 to extend his contract through December 2006.

Senator Paul Wellstone of Minnesota and Representative John Conyers of Michigan introduced bills to limit baseball's exemption from federal antitrust laws by making the elimination or relocation of teams subject to antitrust challenges from injured parties, including government entities, stadium authorities or players. Testifying before the House Judiciary Committee on December 6, Selig said baseball's financial system was badly flawed. He claimed owners sustained operating losses totalling $232 million in 2001 ($519 million with interest payments and depreciation added in). He was challenged not only by several members of the committee who criticized his lack of detail but also by Minnesota Governor Jesse Ventura, who said, "I have a hard time believing it, Mr. Selig, that they're losing that kind of money and still paying the salaries they're paying."

One day later, MLB opened talks with the union to discuss ways to approve contraction but delay its implementation for at least a year. These talks put the hearing on the union's grievance on hold, but when negotiations broke down on December 13, the hearing before Das resumed and was then adjourned until January.

UMPIRES AND THE STRIKE ZONE

The fate of the 22 umpires who resigned their positions in 1999 as part of the negotiating strategy of the Major League Umpires Association remained uncertain. Management and the union, subsequently decertified and replaced by the World Umpires Association, had agreed to submit MLUA's grievance over the umpires' termination to arbitrator Alan Symonette. After hearing testimony from December 1999 through August 2000, he decided on May 11 that MLB must rehire, with back pay, two A.L. umps (Drew Coble and Greg Kosc) and five N.L. umps (Gary Darling, Bill Hohn, Larry Poncino, Larry Vanover and Joe West) and take back two others, Frank Pulli and Terry Tata, who had announced their intention to retire. Symonette's decision said that Coble and Kosc had never resigned in writing and that then-N.L. President Leonard Coleman had "abused his discretion" in not explaining clearly why the other five were terminated. Symonette upheld the discharge of the remaining 13.

Although arbitrators' decisions are difficult to overturn, both MLB and the MLUA decided to appeal Symonette's ruling in U.S. District Court in Philadelphia. Judge Harvey Bartle III heard arguments on November 27 and rendered his decision on December 14. Essentially, he upheld the arbitration ruling ordering MLB to take back nine umpires and approved termination for 10 others. But he ordered new arbitration hearings for Paul Nauert, Bruce Dreckman and Sam Holbrook, three of the dismissed 13, saying that Symonette had wrongly concluded that umpires with less than five years' experience could be terminated at will. Both sides could appeal further.

In January, umpires attended a training session in Chandler, Arizona, designed, in part, to encourage calling a consistent strike zone according to the rule book. Specifically, umpires were instructed to call the "high strike" on pitches above the waist and below the midpoint between the top of the shoulders and the top of the pants. The extent to which umpires complied with this directive was a subject of much discussion during the early part of the season. On July 14, the WUA filed a grievance alleging that the Commissioner's Office was violating the collective bargaining agreement by evaluating umpires' judgment of the strike zone based in part on the average number of pitches in games each worked behind the plate. In the letter notifying MLB of the grievance, union attorneys Larry Gibson and Joel Smith wrote, "The union has learned that the office of the commissioner believes the average to be around 285 pitches in a nine-inning game. Umpires are being told that this number is too high." They added that umpires have been urged to "call more strikes," "be aggressive" and "hunt for strikes." Sandy Alderson, MLB's Executive Vice President for Baseball Operations, responded that this issue had been taken way out of context by the union, but Larry Barnett, one of baseball's umpire supervisors and a former A.L. umpire, retired on July 6, saying he was uncomfortable having to counsel umpires to call more strikes. The dispute was resolved on July 18 when the Commissioner's Office announced that pitch counts would not be used as an evaluation technique. In response, the union dropped the grievance. Alderson, though, was still not satisfied. "We're not getting nearly what the strike zone definition requires," he said on July 23.

Whether or not the stricter definition of the strike zone was responsible, offense declined during the season. Overall batting average fell from .270 to .264, runs per game dropped from 10.28 to 9.55 (7.1 percent), and the number of home runs hit decreased from 5,693 to 5,458 (4.2 percent). As a result, overall earned-run average fell from 4.76 to 4.41 (7.4 percent). A dozen players hit 40 or more home runs, down from 44 in 2000, and 46 players drove in 100 or more runs, down from 53 in 2000.

SEASON OPENER IN PUERTO RICO

For the third consecutive season, MLB opened its season with games outside the continental United States and Canada. After sojourns to Monterrey, Mexico in 1999 and Tokyo, Japan in 2000, MLB opened the 2001 season in San Juan, Puerto Rico on Sunday, April 1. The Toronto Blue Jays defeated the Texas Rangers, 8-1, before an announced crowd of 19,891.

TWO BALLPARKS OPEN

The Brewers opened Miller Park on April 6, defeating the Cincinnati Reds, 5-4, before a sellout crowd of 42,024. The opening of this new ballpark, the only facility in North America with a fan-shaped retractable roof, had been delayed for a year following an accident in July, 1999 that took the lives of three workers. The Pittsburgh Pirates opened their new home, PNC Park, on April 9, losing to the Reds, 8-2, before a sellout crowd of 36,954. Located in downtown Pittsburgh, the park features a view of the city's skyline and the Allegheny River. The celebratory atmosphere at the opening was dampened by the death of former Pirates star Willie Stargell earlier in the day.

UNBALANCED SCHEDULE

In an attempt to emphasize the importance of the six division races, the teams played unbalanced schedules, a concept the A.L. had abandoned in 1977 and the N.L. in 1993. Clubs in the four five-team divisions played 19 games against each division opponent, the four A.L. West clubs played 19 or 20 and the six N.L. Central teams played 16 or 17.

INTERLEAGUE PLAY IN FIFTH YEAR

Regular-season games between A.L. and N.L. clubs continued for the fifth consecutive season. The schedule had each team again playing its interleague games against the teams in the corresponding division of the other league, except that the Houston Astros and Rangers played each other for the first time. There were two periods of interleague play: June 8-17 and July 6-17, surrounding the All-Star break. All A.L. teams and teams in the N.L. East played 18 games. All others played 15, except for the Colorado Rockies, who played 12.

Overall, A.L. teams won 132 interleague games

and lost 120, narrowing the N.L.'s margin over five seasons to 597-595. The Chicago White Sox, Oakland Athletics and Mariners compiled the best interleague record among A.L. teams (12-6) while the Baltimore Orioles won only six games. In the N.L., the Marlins finished with the best record (12-6), and the Rockies finished worst (2-10). Attendance at interleague games averaged 33,703, slightly up from 2000's 33,213 and 15.2 percent higher than the average for intraleague games played prior to the interleague periods.

BARRY BONDS' MAGNIFICENT SEASON

The general decrease in offense did not affect Bonds, left fielder for the San Francisco Giants. He batted .328 (tied for seventh in the N.L.), drove in 137 runs (fourth in the league) and smashed McGwire's record for home runs in a season (70) set in 1998. Moreover, he led the league in on-base percentage (.515), set a major league record for slugging percentage (.863, surpassing Babe Ruth's .847 in 1920) and set a major league record for walks in a season (177, surpassing Ruth's 170 in 1923). He was one of four players to hit 50 or more homers, and at age 37 he became the oldest player to lead the majors in home runs.

Entering the season with 494 homers, Bonds became the 17th player to reach 500 on April 17. He hit his 30th homer of the year on June 4 against the San Diego Padres in the Giants' 57th game and his 50th on August 11 against the Chicago Cubs, reaching 50 faster than anyone else. He hit No. 60 on September 6 against the Diamondbacks, becoming the fifth, the fastest and the oldest player to reach that still-hallowed mark. Nos. 61, 62 and 63 all came in the same game against Colorado on September 9, but as the Giants came down the stretch hoping to secure a playoff spot, their opponents, especially the Astros, often refused to give Bonds good pitches to hit. Sitting on 69 homers, he drew three walks against Houston on October 3 to pass Ruth. The next night, the Astros' Wilfredo Rodriguez gave Bonds a pitch to hit in the ninth inning, and Bonds drove it into the second deck at Enron Field to tie McGwire's record. He then hit Nos. 71 and 72 on October 5 versus Chan Ho Park of the Los Angeles Dodgers, and added No. 73 on October 7, the last day of the season, hitting it off the Dodgers' Dennis Springer in the first inning.

The number of records Bonds set boggles the mind: Besides most homers and most walks in a season, he set single-season marks for most home runs hit on the road (36) and most extra bases (255). He also set records for most seasons leading a league in walks (7), most career intentional walks (355), most career homers by a lefthanded batter (567) and most consecutive seasons with 30 or more homers (10).

ATLANTA WINS DIVISION AGAIN

The Braves won the N.L. East title for the seventh year in a row. Leaving aside the incomplete 1994 season, Atlanta won an unprecedented 10th straight division title. The Braves loitered behind the Philadelphia Phillies for the first half and did not reach first place for good until August 17. Thereafter, they held off the stubborn Phillies and the hard-charging Mets, clinching the division on October 5 with a 20-5 romp over the Marlins. Atlanta became the first team to make the playoffs with a losing record at home (40-41).

The Braves' offense was again led by Chipper Jones, who hit .330 (fifth in the N.L.) with 38 home runs and 102 runs batted in, and Andruw Jones, who added 34 homers and 104 RBIs despite batting only .251. Except for Chipper Jones, no other Brave hit over .300, but Brian Jordan had 25 homers and 97 RBIs.

Atlanta's pitching staff led the league in ERA (3.59) and was third in batting-average-against (.250). Greg Maddux won 17 games and finished fourth in the league in ERA (3.05). Tom Glavine won 16, and John Burkett, with 12 wins, finished third in ERA (3.04). John Rocker had 19 saves before being traded to the Cleveland Indians, and John Smoltz, coming back from injury, had 10 after being moved from the starting rotation into the bullpen.

HOUSTON WINS N.L. CENTRAL TITLE

The Astros regained the title they had surrendered to the St. Louis Cardinals in 2000, but their championship did not come easy. As late as August 1, they were 4.5 games behind the surprising Cubs, but then a spurt of nine wins in 11 games pushed them to first place on August 13. Chicago faded, and Houston was pressed to hold off the Cardinals. When the Astros took two of three games in St. Louis on the season's final weekend, the teams wound up with identical records, 93-69. Houston was awarded the division crown by virtue of its 9-7 record in head-to-head competition.

Houston's offense was led by first baseman Jeff Bagwell, who batted .288 with 39 home runs and 130 runs batted in, and switch-hitting outfielder Lance Berkman, who batted .331 with 34 home runs and 126 RBIs. Moises Alou added 27 homers and 108 RBIs while batting .331 (tied with Berkman for third in the league), Vinny Castilla hit 23 homers and Craig Biggio hit 20.

Fourteen Astros pitchers won at least one game for the team, but only three won more than 10. Wade Miller led the way with 16 wins and finished 10th in the N.L. in ERA (3.40). Shane Reynolds and Roy Oswalt, TSN's N.L. Rookie Pitcher of the Year, won 14 games apiece, and Billy Wagner had 39 saves, sixth best in the league.

CARDINALS SETTLE FOR WILD CARD

St. Louis qualified as the N.L. wild card for the first time in team history. After a sluggish first half that saw them reach the All-Star break at 43-43, the Cardinals climbed to second place on September 8 and challenged Houston down the stretch. Both teams clinched playoff spots on October 5, but St. Louis lost an outright division title on a tiebreaker. Albert Pujols, TSN's N.L. Rookie Player of the Year, hit .329 (sixth in the league) with 37 home runs. He set N.L. rookie records for RBIs (130), extra-base hits (88) and total bases (360). J.D. Drew (.323, 27, 73) and Jim Edmonds (.304, 30, 110) augmented the attack. Matt Morris, TSN's N.L. Comeback Player of the Year, tied for the league lead with 22 wins, and Darryl Kile won 16. Dave Veres had 15 saves.

ARIZONA WINS N.L. WEST FLAG

The Diamondbacks won their second division title in just four years of existence. They moved into first place in mid-May and built a six-game lead, only

to see it disappear by late July. Rebounding in August, they held off the Giants and clinched the pennant on October 5, beating Milwaukee, 5-0, and then waiting to see the Dodgers eliminate San Francisco, 11-10.

The Diamondbacks' offense was led by Luis Gonzalez, who batted .325 with 57 home runs (third in the N.L. and 26 more than his previous career high) and 142 RBIs (also third). Reggie Sanders added 33 homers and 90 RBIs.

Arizona's pitching, led by Curt Schilling, TSN's Sportsman of the Year and N.L. Pitcher of the Year, and Randy Johnson, was excellent. Schilling won 22 games (tied for the N.L. lead), led the league with six complete games and finished second in ERA (2.98) and strikeouts (293). Johnson won 21 games and led the league with a 2.49 ERA. He also became the first pitcher to strike out more than 300 batters four seasons in a row. His total, 372, was the third-highest ever. Byung-Hyun Kim, replacing injured closer Matt Mantei, recorded 19 saves.

NEW YORK WINS A.L. EAST

The Yankees won their fourth consecutive A.L. East title and fifth in six seasons. The Yankees trailed the Boston Red Sox for most of the first half before moving into first place for good on July 3. They increased their lead to 4.5 games on August 1, eight games on September 1 and a high of 16.5 games on October 2. New York clinched the division on September 25, as Baltimore beat the Red Sox, and finished 13.5 games ahead of Boston.

Once again, no Yankee put up astounding offensive numbers. Tino Martinez hit 34 home runs and drove in 113 runs but batted only .280. Bernie Williams added 26 homers and 94 RBIs, and Jorge Posada had 95 RBIs. Rookie Alfonso Soriano stole 43 bases, third best in the league.

Roger Clemens, TSN's A.L. Pitcher of the Year, won 16 games in a row and finished with a record of 20-3 and a 3.51 earned-run average. He became a 20-game winner for the sixth time in his career and, at 39, was the oldest 20-game winner since Early Wynn in 1959. He also set the A.L. record for strikeouts in a career. Mike Mussina had 17 wins, and Andy Pettitte added 15. Mariano Rivera led the A.L. with a career-high 50 saves.

CLEVELAND REGAINS CENTRAL CROWN

The Indians won their sixth A.L. Central title in seven years, finishing six games ahead of the surprising Twins. Cleveland was at or near the top of the division for most of the season and took over first place for good on August 7. The Indians clinched the pennant on September 30, beating the Twins, 9-1. The 2000 champions, the White Sox, finished third.

Cleveland had an outstanding year offensively, outshone only by Seattle. The Indians finished second in the league in runs and total bases and third in home runs (212). Jim Thome hit 49 home runs and drove in 124 runs while batting .291. Juan Gonzalez hit .325 with 35 homers and 140 RBIs. Roberto Alomar hit .336 (third in the A.L.) and had 100 RBIs. C.C. Sabathia, TSN's A.L. Rookie Pitcher of the Year, led the Tribe with 17 wins. Bartolo Colon added 14 and 201 strikeouts (fifth in the league). Sixteen pitchers recorded at least one victory for Cleveland,

and Bob Wickman earned 32 saves (seventh in the league).

SEATTLE STORMS TO WEST TITLE

Led by heralded newcomer Ichiro Suzuki, the first Japanese position player to sign with an American major league team, the Mariners romped to the A.L. West title by 14 games over Oakland. Seattle won 116 games, tying the major league record set by the 1906 Cubs, who did it in 154 games compared to the Mariners' 162. Seattle held first place wire-to-wire—the eighth team to perform the feat—and was never seriously challenged. The Mariners led the division nine games at the end of April, 20 at the end of June and 17 at the end of August. They clinched the pennant on September 19 when the A's lost to Texas, 10-4.

Suzuki, a seven-time batting champion with the Orix Blue Wave of the Japan Pacific League, had an outstanding offensive season. He led the A.L. in batting (.350) and stolen bases (56), the first player to lead his league in both categories since Jackie Robinson in 1949. He got 242 hits, breaking the A.L. rookie record, put together 23- and 21-game hitting streaks and had 75 multiple-hit games. TSN named him A.L. Rookie Player of the Year. Bret Boone batted .331 (fourth in the league) with 37 homers and led the league in RBIs with 141. Edgar Martinez (.306, 23, 116) and John Olerud (.302, 21, 95) added to a Seattle attack that led the A.L. in batting average, hits, runs and stolen bases.

The Mariners' pitching was just as effective, leading the league with a 3.54 ERA. Jamie Moyer became the oldest pitcher to win 20 games for the first time. Freddy Garcia won 18 games and led the league in ERA (3.05). Paul Abbott won 17 games, Aaron Sele 15 and John Halama 10. Kazuhiro Sasaki recorded 45 saves, second in the league.

OAKLAND TAKES WILD CARD

The A's won 102 games and finished with baseball's second-best record, but they had to settle for the wild card spot in the playoffs, clinching it on September 23 with a 7-4 win over Seattle. After an 8-18 start in April, Oakland rebounded and played the Mariners even from June 1 on (76-34). They became the first team to win 100 or more games after falling 10 games under .500 and won the wild card by 17 games over Minnesota. The A's were led offensively by Jason Giambi, who hit .342 (second in the league) with 38 homers and 120 RBIs, Eric Chavez (32 homers and 114 RBIs) and Miguel Tejada (31 homers and 113 RBIs). Mark Mulder led the league in wins with 21. Tim Hudson won 18 games, and Barry Zito added 17. Jason Isringhausen recorded a career-high 34 saves.

DIVISION SERIES WINNERS

For the fourth season in a row, the teams qualifying for the best-of-five Division Series were seeded to determine their opponents. In the N.L., the Astros earned home-field advantage only to be swept by the Braves, while the Diamondbacks defeated the Cardinals, three games to two. In the A.L., the top-seeded Mariners dropped two of the first three games to the Indians but came back to win the next two, while the Yankees beat the A's in five, becoming the first team to win a division series after losing the first two games.

D'BACKS OUST BRAVES IN FIVE

In the N.L. Championship Series, the Diamondbacks and the Braves split the first two games in Arizona. In Game 1, Johnson pitched a three-hitter and struck out 11 to defeat Maddux, 2-0. In Game 2, the Braves scored two runs in the seventh inning and five in the eighth to win, 8-1, behind Glavine.

When the series shifted to Atlanta, the home team fumbled away Game 3, 5-1, making two miscues that led to three runs in the fifth inning. For Arizona, Schilling pitched his third complete game of the postseason to put his team ahead, two games to one. Maddux came back on three days' rest to pitch Game 4 for Atlanta, but the D'backs were victorious, 11-4. The Braves got 13 hits, but they committed four errors while Craig Counsell batted in four runs and Gonzalez knocked in three for the winners. Johnson faced Glavine in Game 5 and came away victorious, 3-2. Erubiel Durazo, pinch-hitting for the injured Mark Grace in the fifth inning, hit a two-run homer to break a 1-1 tie. The Braves added a run in the seventh, but it was not enough. The Diamondbacks thus advanced to their first World Series faster than any other expansion team. The Marlins reached and won the World Series in 1997, their fifth year of existence.

YANKEES DEFEAT MARINERS IN FIVE

The Yankees frustrated the Mariners, winning the first two games of the A.L. Championship Series in Seattle. Pettitte, yielding but three hits in eight innings, bested Sele in Game 1, 4-2, with Paul O'Neill contributing a two-run homer. Mussina pitched just as well in Game 2, beating Garcia, 3-2, with Scott Brosius driving in a pair of runs in the second inning.

When the series moved to New York, the Mariners rebounded, 14-3, behind Moyer. Seattle got 15 hits, three by Boone, who knocked in five runs. Moyer held the Yankees to four hits in seven innings. New York won Game 4, 3-1, to take a commanding three games to one lead in the series. Clemens gave up only one hit in five innings but the Yankees trailed, 1-0, going to the bottom of the eighth. Williams hit a homer off Arthur Rhodes to even the score, and then in the ninth, Brosius reached on an infield single, and Soriano hit a 'walk-off' home run to win the game. New York closed out the series the following day with an easy 12-3 victory. Pettitte took a shutout to the seventh inning thanks to home runs by Williams, O'Neill and Martinez. The Yankees thus returned to the World Series for the fourth consecutive season and the fifth time in six years.

ARIZONA WINS STUNNING SERIES

Although baseball fans seldom approach consensus when arguing which World Series should be called the best ever, the events of the 2001 Series will certainly make the seven-game masterpiece between the Yankees and the Diamondbacks a significant part of any such future discussion. The Series opened in Phoenix with Schilling, going for his fourth postseason win, opposing Mussina. The Yankees scored a run in the first on a double by Bernie Williams, but Arizona answered in the same inning with a Counsell home run. In the third, the Diamondbacks added four more runs, two on a

Gonzalez home run and one each on a Matt Williams sacrifice fly and a double by Damian Miller. Arizona scored another four in the fourth to put the game away. Schilling gave up only three hits through seven innings, and Arizona came away with a 9-1 win. The Diamondbacks extended their series lead by winning Game 2, 4-0, behind Johnson's three-hit, 11-strikeout pitching. Arizona tallied one run in the second on a Danny Bautista double off Pettitte and three more in the seventh when Matt Williams hit a three-run homer.

New York was thus put in the position of trying to become the eighth team to win a Series after losing the first two games on the road. In Game 3 at Yankee Stadium, Posada gave the Yankees a 1-0 lead with a home run in the second off Brian Anderson, who hadn't started a game since September 8, but Arizona evened the score in the fourth on another Matt Williams sacrifice fly. Soriano and Shane Spencer made diving catches to preserve the tie before New York scored the decisive run in the sixth. Bernie Williams singled, went to second on a wild pitch and scored on Brosius' two-out single. The following night, Schilling pitched seven strong innings again and staked his team to a 3-1 lead. But Martinez hit a two-run homer with two out in the ninth off Kim, and Jeter hit a homer in the 10th to give New York an improbable 4-3 victory. Not since Game 4 of the 1939 Series had a team come back to win a Series game after being down two runs going into the ninth inning. Yet, incredibly, the Yankees did the same thing in Game 5 (the first World Series game ever played in November), and Kim was again the victim. This time, the Diamondbacks took a 2-0 lead into the ninth when Brosius tied the score with a home run. In the 12th, Chuck Knoblauch singled, Brosius sacrificed him to second, and he scored on a Soriano single to give New York a series lead of three games to two.

Back in Phoenix, the Diamondbacks took quick control of Game 6, scoring 12 runs in the first three innings en route to an easy 15-2 win. That set up a Game 7 showdown between two of the premier pitchers of the 2001 season: Schilling vs. Clemens. Arizona scored first when Bautista doubled home Steve Finley in the sixth, but the Yankees tied the game in the seventh and went ahead in the eighth on a homer by Soriano. In the ninth, batting against the usually impregnable Rivera, Arizona tied the game on a double by Tony Womack and won it on Gonzalez' bloop single over a drawn-in infield that scored pinch-hitter Jay Bell.

The Diamondbacks voted 50 full World Series shares, each worth $279,260.41, 13 partial shares and 17 cash awards. The Yankees voted 35 full shares, each worth $201,014.06, 49 partial shares and four cash awards. Television ratings for the Series rose 26 percent over the 2000 Yankees-Mets series. Game 7 drew a television audience of 40 million people, the largest for a televised baseball game since Game 7 of the 1991 Series.

OTHER FEATS AND EVENTS

Hideo Nomo of the Red Sox pitched the second no-hitter of his career on April 4, defeating the Orioles, 3-0. He struck out 11 and walked three, with only one runner reaching second base. Nomo thus became the fifth pitcher to record no-hitters in two major leagues after Ted Breitenstein, Cy Young, Jim Bunning and Nolan Ryan. Nomo's first no-hitter came in 1996 when as a Dodger he beat the Rockies, 9-0. A.J. Burnett of the Marlins pitched a no-hitter on May 12 defeating the Padres, 3-0. He walked nine, a record for a no-hitter. Bud Smith of the Cardinals no-hit the Padres on September 3, 4-0. He walked four and became the first rookie to pitch a no-hitter since the Cardinals' Jose Jimenez in 1999.

Rickey Henderson of the Padres walked for the 2,063rd time in his career on April 25, thus passing Babe Ruth for most career walks. He tied Ty Cobb's record for career runs, 2,245, on October 3, scoring from first on Ryan Klesko's double against the Dodgers, and broke Cobb's record on October 4 with a home run against the Dodgers. Henderson got a double, the 3,000th hit of his career, on the season's last day, October 7.

Larry Walker of the Rockies led the N.L. in batting for the third time, with a .350 average. He hit .406 at home. Sosa drove in 160 runs to lead the N.L. and hit 64 home runs, thus becoming the first player to hit 60 or more homers three times. Colorado's Juan Pierre and Philadelphia's Jimmy Rollins tied for the league lead in stolen bases with 46. Robb Nen of the Giants led the league in saves with 45. Randy Johnson struck out 20 Reds on May 8 to tie the major league record held by Clemens and Kerry Wood and set a record for lefthanders. He pitched nine innings of a game that went 11. Alex Rodriguez of the Rangers led the A.L. in home runs with 52, a record for a shortstop. He also led the league in runs (133). Jason Giambi of the A's led the league in doubles (47), walks (129), on-base percentage (.477) and slugging percentage (.660). Nomo led the league in strikeouts (220).

The average length of a nine-inning game in the N.L. fell two minutes to 2:53, and the average time in the A.L. fell four minutes to 2:56. The overall average fell four minutes to 2:54, down from 2000's all-time high.

NEW VETERANS COMMITTEE

On August 6, the National Baseball Hall of Fame and Museum's Board of Directors voted to restructure the Committee on Baseball Veterans and to revise the procedure for electing long-retired players, managers, umpires and executives. The existing 15-member Veterans Committee was replaced by a larger group consisting of all living members of the Hall of Fame, recipients of the J.G. Taylor Spink Award and the Ford C. Frick Award and the three members of the former committee whose terms had not expired. Starting in 2003, the new committee will hold elections for players every two years and elections for managers, umpires and executives every four years. A screening committee composed of 60 members of the Baseball Writers' Association of America—two from each major league city and four from cities with two teams—will identify 25 candidates for each Players Ballot and 15 candidates for each Composite Ballot. In addition, an independent screening committee of six Hall of Fame members will identify up to five other candidates for the Players Ballot. Election will still require receiving votes on at least 75 percent of ballots cast.

The Board of Directors also revised the eligibility standard for consideration by the new committee.

All players who played in at least 10 major league seasons, including those from the 19th century, who are not on MLB's ineligible list and who are not being considered for election by the BBWAA, will now be eligible for election. This revision gives new hope to more than 1,700 players whose names had been dropped from consideration for failure to receive a requisite number of votes in past elections. The Hall of Fame has also commissioned a study of African-American baseball, 1860-1960. When this study is complete, a committee will review its results and make a recommendation to the Board of Directors on how best to proceed with respect to Negro Leagues candidates.

ATTENDANCE FALLS SLIGHTLY

Major league baseball drew 72,417,945 fans, down less than one percent from 2000's record attendance. Average attendance, 30,012, topped the 30,000-mark for the second consecutive season. N.L. teams drew 39,634,306 to their home games while A.L. teams attracted 32,783,639 to theirs.

Eight teams drew more than three million fans: Seattle (which led both leagues with 3,507,975), New York, Cleveland and Baltimore in the A.L., and San Francisco, Colorado (over three million for a record ninth consecutive year), St. Louis and Los Angeles in the N.L. Twelve other teams exceeded the two-million mark, and all other clubs except Montreal (609,473) drew at least one million. A measure of baseball's popularity is this: Not until 1998 did the New York Yankees, perhaps baseball's most prosperous team, draw more than 2.7 million fans. In 2001, 14 teams surpassed that mark.

Milwaukee showed the greatest increase, up 1,237,420 to 2,811,041 following the opening of Miller Park. Cincinnati declined the most, 694,619 to 1,882,732.

EIGHT MANAGERIAL CHANGES

For the first time since 1991, four teams fired their managers before one-third of the season had elapsed. The Devil Rays dismissed Larry Rothschild, the first manager in franchise history, on April 18 after the team got off to a 4-10 start. Bench coach Hal McRae replaced him for the balance of the season, but the team still finished last in the A.L. East at 62-100. Johnny Oates resigned as manager of the Rangers on May 4 with Texas in third place in the A.L. West at 11-17. Third base coach Jerry Narron replaced him, but Texas finished last at 73-89. On May 28, Florida, third in the N.L. East with a record of 22-26, fired John Boles and named Tony Perez, special assistant to the general manager, as his interim replacement. Perez took the job permanently on May 31 but returned to his previous position after the season. The Marlins finished in fourth place at 76-86. Montreal fired Felipe Alou on May 31 with the team in last place in the N.L. East at 21-32. Alou's successor was Jeff Torborg, who had previously managed the Indians, White Sox and Mets. The Expos finished last at 68-94.

Boston fired Jimy Williams on August 16 with the team in second place in the A.L. East at 65-53. Boston had held first place from May 31 through July 3, but was 31-43 after the All-Star break. The Red Sox promoted pitching coach Joe Kerrigan, who guided the team to a second-place finish at 82-79.

Tom Kelly, baseball's longest-tenured manager, retired from the Twins on October 12. He compiled a career record of 1,140-1,244 and won two World Series, in 1987 and 1991. Larry Dierker resigned as manager of the Astros on October 18 and was replaced by Jimy Williams on November 1. Dierker had led the team to four division titles in five years, but each time the Astros lost their opening playoff series.

RED SOX SOLD

The limited partners that own the Red Sox announced an agreement on December 20 to sell the franchise and other assets to a group headed by Marlins owner John Henry and former Padres owner Tom Werner for a record $660 million plus $40 million in assumed debt. Henry is simultaneously negotiating to sell the Marlins to Expos owner Jeffrey Loria, who hopes to see the Montreal franchise eliminated. Both transactions could be approved by an owners' vote as early as January.

FOURTEEN ARBITRATION CASES

A total of 101 players filed for salary arbitration, but only 14 cases proceeded through the hearing and decision stage. Teams exchanged figures with 63 players, including Derek Jeter, who asked for a record $18.5 million against the Yankees' offer of $14.25 million, almost double what any player had previously earned via the arbitration process. Jeter avoided a hearing by agreeing to a 10-year contract worth $189 million.

For the first time, three-person panels heard every case. Andruw Jones won his case for $8.2 million versus the Braves' offer of $6.4 million. This award set a record, bettering the $7.25 million given to Mariano Rivera, who lost his case in 2000. Besides Jones, five other players (Terry Adams, Sean Casey, Keith Foulke, Damian Miller and Gregg Zaun) won their cases, and eight (Danny Graves, Osvaldo Fernandez, Chris Holt, Jose Mercedes, Kevin Millwood, John Rocker, Travis Lee and Javier Vasquez) lost theirs. These decisions gave the owners a cumulative record of 250-191 since arbitration began in 1974.

The players who filed earned an average increase of 144 percent, up from 124 percent in 2000. Sixty-one players doubled their salaries, 40 tripled theirs, 22 got fivefold increases and 15 got sixfold increases. Richard Hidalgo made $330,000 in 2000 and $8,000,000 in 2001, a 24-fold hike. None of those who filed took a pay cut, but Eddie Perez, with just 22 at-bats in 2000, wound up with the same salary, $650,000.

SALARIES RISE

According to figures compiled by the Players Association and released by the Associated Press in December, the average major league salary rose 12.8 percent to $2,138,896, topping the two-million-dollar mark for the first time. (Salary figure calculations, it should be noted, can differ, depending on what factors are included.) The Yankees had the highest average salary for the third consecutive year, $3,930,334, and the Expos had the lowest, $926,333.

RETIREMENTS

Cal Ripken announced his retirement on June 18, effective at the end of the season. Ripken is best known for playing in a record 2,632 consecutive games, a streak that began on May 30, 1982 and ended on September 20, 1998. In 21 seasons, all with the Orioles, Ripken batted .276 with 431 home runs and 1,695 RBIs. He is one of only seven players to record 3,000 hits and 400 homers.

Tony Gwynn announced his retirement on June 28, also effective at the end of the season. He played 20 seasons, all with the Padres, and compiled a batting average of .338. He won an N.L.-record-tying eight batting titles and hit over .300 for 19 consecutive years, every one but his first.

On November 4, Mark McGwire faxed an announcement of his retirement to ESPN. In 16 seasons with Oakland and the Cardinals, he hit 583 home runs, good for fifth place on the all-time list.

McGwire will be remembered for hitting 70 home runs in 1998, but he also hit 49 in 1987 (a rookie record), 52 in 1996, 58 in 1997 and 65 in 1999.

CONCLUSION

When Commissioner Selig announced the owners' intention to eliminate two major league teams before the start of next season, he was asked if November 6 would be remembered as a sad day for baseball. He replied, "Is it a sad day after the World Series and the things we've done? No, I don't think so." However accurate his characterization of this event proves to be, here is how the game on the field ended up in 2001:

FINAL STANDINGS

AMERICAN LEAGUE

EAST DIVISION

Team	N.Y.	Bos.	Tor.	Bal.	T.B.	Cle.	Min.	Chi.	Det.	K.C.	Sea.	Oak.	Ana.	Tex.	Atl.	Phi.	N.Y.	Fla.	Mon.	W	L	Pct.	GB
New York	....	13	11	13	13	5	2	5	5	6	3	3	3	3	1-2	2-1	4-2	1-2	2-1	95	65	.594	....
Boston	5	....	12	10	14	3	3	4	3	3	4	3	5	3-3	2-1	1-2	2-1	2-1	82	79	.509	13.5
Toronto	8	7	....	12	10	4	5	3	4	3	3	3	4	6	2-1	2-1	0-3	1-2	3-3	80	82	.494	16.0
Baltimore	5	9	7	....	10	1	3	3	4	5	1	2	5	2	1-2	2-4	1-2	0-3	2-1	63	98	.391	32.5
Tampa Bay	6	5	9	9	....	1	6	2	2	2	2	2	2	4	1-2	3-0	2-1	2-4	1-2	62	100	.383	34.0

CENTRAL DIVISION

Team	Cle.	Min.	Chi.	Det.	K.C.	N.Y.	Bos.	Tor.	Bal.	T.B.	Sea.	Oak.	Ana.	Tex.	Hou.	St.l.	Chi.	Mil.	Cin.	Pit.	Ari.	W	L	Pct.	GB
Cleveland	....	14	9	13	11	4	6	2	5	5	2	4	4	5	1-2	2-1		1-2	3-3	0-3		91	71	.562	....
Minnesota	5	....	14	15	13	4	3	2	3	1	1	5	6	4	2-1	0-3	0-3	2-1	3-0	2-1		85	77	.525	6.0
Chicago	10	5	....	13	14	1	3	5	4	5	2	1	3	7		0-3	4-2	3-0	3-0	2-1		83	79	.512	8.0
Detroit	6	4	6	....	8	4	5	2	2	4	2	1	4	8	2-1	1-2	2-1	2-1	2-1	2-1		66	96	.407	25.0
Kansas City	8	6	5	11	....	0	0	4	2	3	4	3	3	4	0-3	3-0	1-2	2-1		1-2	1-2	65	97	.401	26.0

WEST DIVISION

Team	Sea.	Oak.	Ana.	Tex.	N.Y.	Bos.	Tor.	Bal.	T.B.	Cle.	Min.	Chi.	Det.	K.C.	Ari.	S.F.	L.A.	S.D.	Col.	Hou.	W	L	Pct.	GB
Seattle	....	10	15	15	6	6	6	8	7	5	8	7	5	6	2-1	2-1	2-1	4-2	2-1		116	46	.716	....
Oakland	9	....	14	9	6	5	6	7	7	3	4	8	6	6	3-0	2-4	2-1	2-1	3-0		102	60	.630	14.0
Anaheim	4	6	....	7	4	4	5	4	7	5	3	6	5	5	1-2	0-3	4-2	2-1	3-0		75	87	.463	41.0
Texas	5	10	12	....	4	2	3	7	5	4	5	2	1	5		1-2	1-2	1-2	2-1	3-3	73	89	.451	43.0

NOTE: Read across for wins, down for losses; interleague games are shaded.

Tie game—Baltimore at New York, September 30 (15 innings).

Clinching dates: New York (East)—September 25; Cleveland (Central)—September 30; Seattle (West)—September 19; Oakland (wild card)—September 23.

NATIONAL LEAGUE

EAST DIVISION

Team	Atl.	Phi.	N.Y.	Fla.	Mon.	Hou.	St.L.	Chi.	Mil.	Cin.	Pit.	Ari.	S.F.	L.A.	S.D.	Col.	N.Y.	Bos.	Tor.	Bal.	T.B.	W	L	Pct.	GB
Atlanta	....	10	10	9	13	3	3	4	3	4	5	2	4	2	3	4	2-1	3-3	1-2	2-1	1-2	88	74	.543	....
Philadelphia	9	....	8	14	10	3	2	2	3	4	5	4	3	3	5	4	1-2	1-2	1-2	4-2	0-3	86	76	.531	2.0
New York	9	11	....	12	11	3	1	2	3	2	4	3	3	4	1	3	2-4	2-1	3-0	2-1	1-2	82	80	.506	6.0
Florida	10	5	7	....	12	3	3	3	4	2	4	2	2	2	3	2	2-1	1-2	2-1	3-0	4-2	76	86	.469	12.0
Montreal	6	9	8	7	....	0	2	3	2	2	5	3	2	4	3	4	1-2	1-2	3-3	1-2	2-1	68	94	.420	20.0

CENTRAL DIVISION

Team	Hou.	St.L.	Chi.	Mil.	Cin.	Pit.	Atl.	Phi.	N.Y.	Fla.	Mon.	Ari.	S.F.	L.A.	S.D.	Col.	Tex.	Cle.	Min.	Chi.	Det.	K.C.	W	L	Pct.	GB
Houston	....	9	9	12	11	9	3	3	3	3	6	4	3	2	3	4	3-3	2-1	1-2			3-0	93	69	.574	....
St. Louis	7	....	8	10	10	14	3	4	5	3	4	4	2	3	5	3		1-2	3-0	3-0	1-2	0-3	93	69	.574	....
Chicago	8	9	....	8	13	10	2	4	4	3	3	4	2	3	4	2			3-0	2-4	2-1	2-1	88	74	.543	5.0
Milwaukee	5	7	9	....	10	6	3	3	3	2	4	3	5	1	1	1		2-1	1-2	0-3	1-2	1-2	68	94	.420	25.0
Cincinnati	6	7	4	6	....	9	2	2	4	4	1	4	4	2	3		3-3	0-3	0-3	1-2		66	96	.407	27.0
Pittsburgh	8	3	6	11	8	....	1	1	2	2	1	2	1	2	2	4		3-0	1-2	1-2	2-1		62	100	.383	31.0

WEST DIVISION

Team	Ari.	S.F.	L.A.	S.D.	Col.	Atl.	Phi.	N.Y.	Fla.	Mon.	Hou.	St.L.	Chi.	Mil.	Cin.	Pit.	K.C.	Det.	Sea.	Oak.	Ana.	Tex.	W	L	Pct.	GB
Arizona	....	10	10	12	13	5	3	3	4	3	2	2	6	3	5	4	2-1	2-1	1-2	0-3	2-1		92	70	.568	....
San Fran.	9	....	8	14	10	2	3	4	4	5	3	4	3	4	2	5			1-2	4-2	3-0	2-1	90	72	.556	2.0
Los Ang.	9	11	....	9	11	5	3	2	5	2	4	3	2	5	2	7			1-2	1-2	2-4	2-1	86	76	.531	6.0
San Diego	7	5	10	....	10	3	2	5	4	3	6	1	4	5	4	4			2-4	1-2	1-2	2-1	79	83	.488	13.0
Colorado	6	9	8	9	....	2	2	4	4	3	2	6	3	5	6	2			1-2	0-3	0-3	1-2	73	89	.451	19.0

NOTE: Read across for wins, down for losses; interleague games are shaded.

Clinching dates: Atlanta (East)—October 5; Houston (Central)—October 7; Arizona (West)—October 5; St. Louis (wild card)—October 7.

A.L. DIVISION SERIES

SEATTLE VS. CLEVELAND

The bottom line: With the exception of Games 1 and 3, the Indians struggled to hit or pitch well enough to beat the favored Mariners. Chuck Finley, after battling injuries throughout the regular season, didn't last more than four innings in either of his two playoff starts. Bartolo Colon held the Mariners scoreless over 14 straight innings at one point, but he allowed three runs in Game 4 that the Indians' offense couldn't match. And with the glaring exception of Game 3, the Mariners bullpen held up under the pressure of the postseason. So did Seattle's hitters. The Mariners managed to get enough timely hits to win Games 4 and 5 while facing postseason elimination.

Why the Mariners won: After winning an American League-record 116 games during the regular season, they faced two must-win situations and prevailed both times. They rebounded from an embarrassing 17-2 loss in Game 3 by winning Game 4 in come-from-behind fashion and then dominated the decisive fifth game behind 38-year-old lefthander Jamie Moyer. Right fielder Ichiro Suzuki, whose stellar play during the regular season disproved the theory that Japanese everyday players couldn't succeed in the U.S. major leagues, proved he could play with the best and produced when his team needed him the most.

The turning points:

Game 1: The Indians took a page from the Mariners' regular-season success. Their hitters sprayed the ball all over the field, content to hit singles-eight of Cleveland's 11 hits in Game 1 were singles. They were able to hit the A.L. ERA champion Freddy Garcia well enough to open a 3-0 lead after four innings. After Roberto Alomar doubled into the left-field corner to lead off the inning, Juan Gonzalez singled to right, driving home Alomar with the first run of the game. Jim Thome walked and Ellis Burks hit a shot down the third-base line that Mariners third basemen David Bell couldn't handle, the ball dropping out of his glove. Both Travis Fryman and Marty Cordova followed with run-scoring singles. Given a lead with which to work, Bartolo Colon shut down the Mariners offense, striking out 10 while allowing six hits in eight innings.

Game 2: It was for games like this that the Indians signed Chuck Finley as a free agent in December 1999. They needed a veteran lefthanded pitcher they could count on in the playoffs. Unfortunately for the Tribe, Finley was in trouble after only 14 pitches in the first postseason start of his career. After walking leadoff man Ichiro Suzuki, Finley threw a two-strike

pitch that No. 2 hitter Mike Cameron belted over the left-field fence for a home run. Bret Boone singled up the middle, and cleanup man Edgar Martinez followed with a home run of his own. After facing just four batters, Finley trailed 4-0. His counterpart, Seattle lefty Jamie Moyer, threw six solid innings to get the win. The Mariners had just six hits, but they made them count. David Bell homered off Finley in the fifth. The Indians scored their lone run in the seventh before Arthur Rhodes and Kazuhiro Sasaki teamed up to pitch scoreless eighth and ninth innings to nail down the win.

Game 3: After a shaky first inning in which the Mariners scored the game's first run, Indians lefthander C.C. Sabathia showed why he was the second-best rookie (after the Mariners' Ichiro Suzuki) in the American League in 2001. In six innings of work, Sabathia allowed six hits, two runs and struck out five. While Sabathia was good on the mound, his teammates were even better at the plate. They scored two runs in the bottom of the first and two more in the second inning before exploding for another four runs in the third inning. Righthander Aaron Sele lasted just two innings for Seattle before being replaced by Paul Abbott, who didn't fare much better-Abbott allowed eight runs (all earned) in the three innings he worked. The top four hitters in the Cleveland lineup-Kenny Lofton, Omar Vizquel, Roberto Alomar and Juan Gonzalez-led the offensive onslaught by driving in 14 of the Indians' 17 runs.

Game 4: The Indians, up two games to one in the series, took a 1-0 lead in the second inning and appeared on their way to ending the Mariners' dream season before the roof caved in. In the seventh inning, Cleveland starter Bartolo Colon walked John Olerud, and Stan Javier followed with a single. Colon then tried to pick Olerud off second base but threw the ball into center field instead, Olerud advancing to third. Colon then walked Mike Cameron to load the bases. After Al Martin hit into a fielder's choice at the plate, David Bell fouled a ball down the left-field line that left fielder Marty Cordova caught, but it was deep enough for Javier to tag and score, tying the game. Ichiro and Mark McLemore each then followed with RBI singles to chase Colon from the game.

Game 5: The Mariners led, 2-1, in the third inning before the Indians loaded the bases and threatened to take the lead. Switch-hitter Roberto Alomar, who had grounded into a double play in the first inning while batting righthanded, came to the plate swinging from the right side again against Seattle lefthander Jamie Moyer. Alomar, who had not grounded into a double play all season while batting from the right side, did so for the second time in three innings in this game, swinging at Moyer's first pitch and hitting into a 5-4-3 inning-ending double play. The Mariners bullpen, two days after being hammered in a 17-2 loss, pitched three scoreless innings to close out the game and the series.

Notable:

Indians: Cleveland pitchers had held the Mariners scoreless for 22 consecutive innings before Mike Cameron homered in the first inning of Game 2. The streak began in the 1995 A.L. Championship Series. ... Game 2 starter Chuck Finley had not appeared in a playoff game since pitching in relief for the California Angels in the 1986 American League Championship Series vs. Boston. ... Jim Thome's home run in the sixth inning of Game 3 was the 17th postseason homer of his career, one shy of the record shared by Mickey Mantle and Reggie Jackson. ... C.C. Sabathia (21 years, 85 days) became the second youngest pitcher to win a Division Series game. Only the Dodgers' Fernando Valenzuela (20 years, 339 days in 1981) was younger. ... SS Omar Vizquel's error in the first inning of Game 4 was just his second error in 271 chances in 56 postseason games.

Mariners: The Mariners had been shut out only four times in the regular season prior to being whitewashed 5-0 in Game 1. ... Aaron Sele, who lasted just two innings in his Game 3 start, dropped to 0-4 in five career postseason starts. ... The Mariners committed five errors in the series (three in Game 3) after leading the league in fielding percentage during the regular season. ... Playoff pressure? Ichiro Suzuki batted .600 (12-for-20) in the first postseason series of his career.

Quotable:

Indians: Shortstop Omar Vizquel, on playing the Mariners: "Sometimes it's easier to play when you're not the team to beat." ... Manager Charlie Manuel, assessing Chuck Finley's performance in Game 2: "He got off slow. He was having a hard time throwing strikes and he had trouble with his command and made some mistakes." ... Kenny Lofton, on facing Jamie Moyer in Game 2: "Moyer did what Moyer has done to us. He threw slower, slower and slower." ... Manuel, after his team's 17-2 Game 3 win: "We've still got one more game to win. Do we want to end it? You bet your butt we do. Hopefully, we'll hit like that tomorrow." ... Jim Thome, on C.C. Sabathia's pitching in Game 3: "You sure can't tell he's a 21-year-old kid. He doesn't act his age. He's been special for us all season." ... Chuck Finley, before Game 5: "I'm elated about getting to pitch in a fifth game. I started thinking about that after Game 2. I had the feeling we might be back in Seattle anyway." ... Omar Vizquel, on the Mariners' series win: "They have the look of a 116-win team. They made the plays when they needed to, they got the outs when they needed them, and they got the pitching when they needed it."

Mariners: Shortstop Mark McLemore, on Bart-

olo Colon's Game 1 performance: "He shut down a very potent offense. But it's not like he was some slouch off the street who they called and said, 'Come in and pitch this game for us.' " ... First baseman John Olerud, on the Mariners' four-run first inning in Game 2: "When you get down 4-0, it puts extra pressure on your offense to score some runs. I think it put a lot of pressure on them." ... Center fielder Mike Cameron, on winning Game 2 after losing the opener: "I think we proved how resilient we've been. They had all the emotion going in their direction." ... Manager Lou Piniella on his team's 17-2 loss in Game 3: "This is probably the worst game we've played all year. If we're good enough, we'll win tomorrow. If we're not, we'll congratulate Cleveland and go home." ... Cameron, on the Mariners being nine outs away from elimination: "There was no tension. It was just a matter of swinging the bats, and waiting for that one break."

GAME 1 BOX SCORE

CLEVELAND 5, SEATTLE 0

TUESDAY, OCTOBER 9, AT SEATTLE

Cleveland	AB	R	H	RBI	PO	A
Lofton, cf	4	0	0	0	1	0
Vizquel, ss	5	0	1	0	2	5
Alomar, 2b	5	1	1	0	1	1
Gonzalez, rf	5	1	1	1	0	0
Thome, 1b	3	1	0	0	9	1
Burks, dh	4	1	3	1	0	0
Fryman, 3b	4	1	2	1	0	1
Cordova, lf	4	0	2	1	1	0
Cabrera, lf	0	0	0	0	0	0
Diaz, c	4	0	1	1	13	1
Colon, p	0	0	0	0	0	0
Wickman, p	0	0	0	0	0	0
Totals	38	5	11	5	27	9

Seattle	AB	R	H	RBI	PO	A
Suzuki, rf	4	0	3	0	0	0
McLemore, ss	4	0	0	0	2	1
Boone, 2b	4	0	0	0	2	1
Martinez, dh	3	0	1	0	0	0
Olerud, 1b	4	0	0	0	6	0
Cameron, cf	4	0	0	0	1	0
Javier, lf	3	0	1	0	3	0
Wilson, c	3	0	1	0	12	1
Bell, 3b	2	0	0	0	1	1
Garcia, p	0	0	0	0	0	1
Charlton, p	0	0	0	0	0	0
Paniagua, p	0	0	0	0	0	0
Halama, p	0	0	0	0	0	0
Totals	31	0	6	0	27	5

Cleveland	0	0	0	3	0	1	0	1	0—5
Seattle	0	0	0	0	0	0	0	0	0—0

Cleveland	IP	H	R	ER	BB	SO
Colon (W)	8.0	6	0	0	2	10
Wickman	1.0	0	0	0	0	2

Seattle	IP	H	R	ER	BB	SO
Garcia (L)	5.1	9	4	4	2	8
Charlton	1.2	0	0	0	0	2
Paniagua	1.0	1	1	1	0	1
Halama	1.0	1	0	0	0	2

E—Diaz, Garcia. DP—Cleveland 1. LOB—Cleveland 8, Seattle 6. 2B—Burks, Alomar, Javier, Suzuki. HR—Burks. SB—Martinez. CS—Suzuki. T—3:05. A—48,033. U—Rippley, plate; Barrett, first; Danley, second; Layne, third; Hirschbeck, left field; Kulpa, right field.

GAME 2 BOX SCORE

SEATTLE 5, CLEVELAND 1

THURSDAY, OCTOBER 11, AT SEATTLE

Cleveland	AB	R	H	RBI	PO	A
Lofton, cf	4	0	0	0	4	0
Vizquel, ss	3	0	1	0	0	2
Alomar, 2b	4	0	0	0	1	1
Gonzalez, rf	4	0	1	0	1	0
Burks, dh	4	1	2	0	0	0
Thome, 1b	4	0	1	0	8	1
Fryman, 3b	3	0	0	0	1	4
Cordova, lf	3	0	0	0	1	0
Diaz, c	3	0	1	0	7	1
Finley, p	0	0	0	0	0	1
Riske, p	0	0	0	0	1	0
Shuey, p	0	0	0	0	0	0
Baez, p	0	0	0	0	0	0
Totals	32	1	6	0	24	10
Seattle	AB	R	H	RBI	PO	A
Suzuki, rf	3	1	1	0	6	0
Cameron, cf	4	1	1	2	3	0
Boone, 2b	4	1	1	0	3	2
Martinez, dh	4	1	1	2	0	0
Olerud, 1b	3	0	0	0	5	0
Buhner, lf	1	0	0	0	1	0
Javier, lf	1	0	0	0	0	0
Wilson, c	3	0	0	0	7	0
Bell, 3b	3	1	2	1	0	0
McLemore, ss	3	0	0	0	1	2
Moyer, p	0	0	0	0	1	1
Nelson, p	0	0	0	0	0	0
Rhodes, p	0	0	0	0	0	0
Sasaki, p	0	0	0	0	0	0
Totals	29	5	6	5	27	5

Cleveland	0	0	0	0	0	0	1	0	0—1
Seattle	4	0	0	0	1	0	0	0	x—5

Cleveland	IP	H	R	ER	BB	SO
Finley (L)	4.1	5	5	5	2	3
Riske	1.2	0	0	0	0	3
Shuey	1.0	1	0	0	0	1
Baez	1.0	0	0	0	0	1
Seattle	IP	H	R	ER	BB	SO
Moyer (W)	*6.0	5	1	1	1	4
Nelson	1.0	0	0	0	1	0
Rhodes	1.0	0	0	0	0	1
Sasaki	1.0	1	0	0	0	2

*Pitched to two batters in seventh.

DP—Cleveland 1, Seattle 1. LOB—Cleveland 6, Seattle 2. HR—Cameron, Martinez, Bell. SB—Suzuki. T—2:41. A—48,052. U—Barrett, plate; Danley, first; Layne, second; M. Hirschbeck, third; Kulpa, left field; Rippley, right field.

GAME 3 BOX SCORE

CLEVELAND 17, SEATTLE 2

SATURDAY, OCTOBER 13, AT CLEVELAND

Seattle	AB	R	H	RBI	PO	A
Suzuki, rf	4	1	2	1	1	0
Sprague, ph	1	0	0	0	0	0
Cameron, cf	4	0	2	0	4	0
Boone, 2b	4	0	0	0	1	3
Martinez, dh	3	0	0	0	0	0
Olerud, 1b	3	0	0	1	6	2
Buhner, lf	2	0	0	0	3	1
Martin, ph	1	0	0	0	0	0
Vazquez, ss	0	0	0	0	0	1
Wilson, c	3	0	1	0	5	0
Lampkin, ph-c	1	0	0	0	0	0
Bell, 3b	4	1	2	0	0	1
McLemore, ss-lf	2	0	0	0	3	4

Seattle	AB	R	H	RBI	PO	A
Gipson, ph	1	0	0	0	0	0
Sele, p	0	0	0	0	0	0
Abbott, p	0	0	0	0	0	0
Halama, p	0	0	0	0	0	0
Paniagua, p	0	0	0	0	1	0
Totals	33	2	7	2	24	12
Cleveland	AB	R	H	RBI	PO	A
Lofton, cf	3	2	1	2	1	0
Vizquel, ss	6	2	4	6	1	6
Alomar, 2b	4	2	3	3	1	3
Gonzalez, rf	6	1	4	3	2	1
Thome, 1b	6	1	2	1	12	1
Burks, dh	4	2	1	0	0	0
Fryman, 3b	4	2	0	0	0	0
Branyan, lf	3	1	1	0	0	0
Cabrera, ph-lf	1	1	1	1	0	0
Diaz, c	4	3	2	1	9	0
Sabathia, p	0	0	0	0	0	2
Riske, p	0	0	0	0	0	0
Rincon, p	0	0	0	0	0	0
Burba, p	0	0	0	0	0	1
Rocker, p	0	0	0	0	1	0
Totals	41	17	19	17	27	14

Seattle	1	0	0	0	0	0	1	0	0—2
Cleveland	2	2	4	0	1	3	0	5	x—17

Seattle	IP	H	R	ER	BB	SO
Sele (L)	2.0	5	4	2	0	0
Abbott	*3.0	9	8	8	5	3
Halama	2.0	2	0	0	0	1
Paniagua	1.0	3	5	5	2	0
Cleveland	IP	H	R	ER	BB	SO
Sabathia (W)	†6.0	6	2	2	5	5
Riske	0.2	0	0	0	1	1
Rincon	0.1	0	0	0	0	0
Burba	1.0	0	0	0	0	1
Rocker	1.0	1	0	0	0	1

*Pitched to three batters in sixth.
†Pitched to three batters in seventh.

E—Suzuki, Boone, Buhner. DP—Seattle 1. LOB—Seattle 10, Cleveland 9. 2B—Alomar 2, Gonzalez 2, Vizquel, Cameron 2, Wilson, Bell. 3B—Vizquel. HR—Gonzalez, Lofton, Thome. SF—Lofton. HBP—By Paniagua (Cabrera). T—3:24. A—45,069. U—Schrieber, plate; Reed, first; Rapuano, second; Gibson, third; DeMuth, left field; Nelson, right field.

GAME 4 BOX SCORE

SEATTLE 6, CLEVELAND 2

SUNDAY, OCTOBER 14, AT CLEVELAND

Seattle	AB	R	H	RBI	PO	A
Suzuki, rf	5	1	3	1	1	0
McLemore, ss	5	0	1	1	3	2
Martinez, dh	4	1	2	2	0	0
Boone, 2b	5	0	1	0	4	2
Olerud, 1b	4	0	2	0	6	1
Javier, lf	3	2	1	0	2	0
Cameron, cf	3	1	1	1	2	0
Wilson, c	2	0	0	0	5	0
Martin, ph	1	1	0	0	0	0
Lampkin, c	1	0	0	0	2	0
Bell, 3b	3	0	0	1	0	3
Garcia, p	0	0	0	0	1	2
Nelson, p	0	0	0	0	0	1
Rhodes, p	0	0	0	0	1	0
Sasaki, p	0	0	0	0	0	0
Totals	36	6	11	6	27	11
Cleveland	AB	R	H	RBI	PO	A
Lofton, cf	4	0	0	0	1	0
Vizquel, ss	4	0	2	0	2	5
Alomar, 2b	4	0	0	0	4	3
Gonzalez, rf	4	2	2	1	1	0
Thome, 1b	3	0	0	0	7	1

Cleveland	AB	R	H	RBI	PO	A
Burks, dh	4	0	0	0	0	0
Fryman, 3b	3	0	0	1	0	1
Cordova, lf	2	0	1	0	3	0
Branyan, ph	0	0	0	0	0	0
Cordero, ph-lf	1	0	0	0	1	0
Diaz, c	3	0	0	0	8	0
Colon, p	0	0	0	0	0	0
Baez, p	0	0	0	0	0	0
Rincon, p	0	0	0	0	0	0
Shuey, p	0	0	0	0	0	0
Totals	32	2	5	2	27	10

Seattle	0	0	0	0	0	0	3	1	2—6
Cleveland	0	1	0	0	0	0	1	0	0—2

Seattle	IP	H	R	ER	BB	SO
Garcia (W)	6.1	4	2	1	1	5
Nelson	0.1	0	0	0	0	1
Rhodes	1.1	0	0	0	0	0
Sasaki	1.0	0	0	0	0	2

Cleveland	IP	H	R	ER	BB	SO
Colon (L)	6.2	6	3	3	4	3
Baez	1.0	2	1	1	0	1
Rincon	1.0	1	1	1	0	2
Shuey	0.1	2	1	1	0	1

E—Vizquel, Colon. DP—Seattle 1, Cleveland 2. LOB—Seattle 8, Cleveland 4. 2B—Gonzalez, Martinez, Cameron. HR—Gonzalez, Martinez. SF—Bell. SB—Boone, Vizquel. WP—Rhodes. PB—Lampkin. T—3:06. A—45,025. U—Reed, plate; Rapuano, first; Gibson, second; DeMuth, third; Nelson, left field; Schrieber, right field.

GAME 5 BOX SCORE

SEATTLE 3, CLEVELAND 1

MONDAY, OCTOBER 15, AT SEATTLE

Cleveland	AB	R	H	RBI	PO	A
Lofton, cf	4	0	1	1	2	0
Vizquel, ss	4	0	1	0	1	3
Alomar, 2b	4	0	0	0	2	1
Gonzalez, rf	4	0	0	0	0	0
Burks, dh	3	0	0	0	0	0
Thome, 1b	3	0	0	0	4	1

Cleveland	AB	R	H	RBI	PO	A
Fryman, 3b	3	1	1	0	1	2
Cordova, lf	3	0	0	0	0	0
Diaz, c	2	0	1	0	14	2
Finley, p	0	0	0	0	0	1
Riske, p	0	0	0	0	0	0
Rincon, p	0	0	0	0	0	0
Baez, p	0	0	0	0	0	0
Totals	30	1	4	1	24	10

Seattle	AB	R	H	RBI	PO	A
Suzuki, rf	4	1	3	0	1	0
Javier, lf	1	0	0	0	1	0
Boone, 2b	4	0	0	0	2	4
Martinez, dh	2	1	1	1	0	0
Martin, pr-dh	0	0	0	0	0	0
Olerud, 1b	3	1	1	0	9	1
Cameron, cf	3	0	0	0	1	0
Wilson, c	4	0	1	0	11	0
Bell, 3b	4	0	1	0	0	2
McLemore, ss	4	0	2	2	1	3
Moyer, p	0	0	0	0	1	0
Nelson, p	0	0	0	0	0	0
Rhodes, p	0	0	0	0	0	0
Sasaki, p	0	0	0	0	0	0
Totals	29	3	9	3	27	10

Cleveland	0	0	1	0	0	0	0	0	0—1
Seattle	0	2	0	0	0	0	1	0	x—3

Cleveland	IP	H	R	ER	BB	SO
Finley (L)	4.1	4	2	2	4	7
Riske	1.1	2	0	0	0	1
Rincon	0.2	1	1	1	0	1
Baez	1.2	2	0	0	0	4

Seattle	IP	H	R	ER	BB	SO
Moyer (W)	6.0	3	1	1	1	6
Nelson	1.2	1	0	0	0	4
Rhodes	0.1	0	0	0	0	0
Sasaki (S)	1.0	0	0	0	0	0

E—McLemore. DP—Seattle 2. LOB—Cleveland 3, Seattle 9. 2B—Fryman. SH—Javier 2. CS—Suzuki, Cameron. HBP—By Finley (Cameron). WP—Finley, Rincon. T—3:18. A—47,867. U—M. Hirschbeck, plate; Kulpa, first; Rippley, second; Barrett, third; Danley, left field; Layne, right field.

STATISTICS

SEATTLE MARINERS' BATTING AND FIELDING AVERAGES

Player, position	G	AB	R	H	TB	2B	3B	HR	RBI	BB	IBB	SO	Avg.	PO	A	E	Avg.
Suzuki, rf	5	20	4	12	13	1	0	0	2	1	0	0	.600	9	0	1	.900
Bell, 3b	5	16	2	5	9	1	0	1	2	1	0	6	.313	1	7	0	1.000
Martinez, dh	5	16	3	5	12	1	0	2	5	5	1	2	.313	0	0	0	.000
Javier, lf	4	8	2	2	3	1	0	0	0	2	0	1	.250	6	0	0	1.000
Cameron, cf	5	18	2	4	10	3	0	1	3	2	0	7	.222	11	0	0	1.000
Wilson, c	5	15	0	3	4	1	0	0	0	0	0	5	.200	40	1	0	1.000
Olerud, 1b	5	17	1	3	3	0	0	0	1	3	0	5	.176	32	4	0	1.000
McLemore, ss-lf	5	18	0	3	3	0	0	0	3	1	0	8	.167	10	12	1	.957
Boone, 2b	5	21	1	2	2	0	0	0	0	1	0	11	.095	12	12	1	.960
Abbott, p	1	0	0	0	0	0	0	0	0	0	0	0	.000	0	0	0	.000
Charlton, p	1	0	0	0	0	0	0	0	0	0	0	0	.000	0	0	0	.000
Garcia, p	2	0	0	0	0	0	0	0	0	0	0	0	.000	1	3	1	.800
Halama, p	2	0	0	0	0	0	0	0	0	0	0	0	.000	0	0	0	.000
Moyer, p	2	0	0	0	0	0	0	0	0	0	0	0	.000	2	1	0	1.000
Nelson, p	3	0	0	0	0	0	0	0	0	0	0	0	.000	0	1	0	1.000
Paniagua, p	2	0	0	0	0	0	0	0	0	0	0	0	.000	1	0	0	1.000
Rhodes, p	3	0	0	0	0	0	0	0	0	0	0	0	.000	1	0	0	1.000
Sasaki, p	3	0	0	0	0	0	0	0	0	0	0	0	.000	0	0	0	.000
Sele, p	1	0	0	0	0	0	0	0	0	0	0	0	.000	0	0	0	.000
Vazquez, ss	1	0	0	0	0	0	0	0	0	0	0	0	.000	0	1	0	1.000
Gipson, ph	1	1	0	0	0	0	0	0	0	0	0	0	.000	0	0	0	.000
Sprague, ph	1	1	0	0	0	0	0	0	0	0	0	0	.000	0	0	0	.000
Lampkin, ph-c	2	2	0	0	0	0	0	0	0	0	0	2	.000	2	0	0	1.000

Player, position	G	AB	R	H	TB	2B	3B	HR	RBI	BB	IBB	SO	Avg.	PO	A	E	Avg.
						BATTING									**FIELDING**		
Martin, ph-pr	3	2	1	0	0	0	0	0	0	0	0	0	.000	0	0	0	.000
Buhner, lf	2	3	0	0	0	0	0	0	0	2	0	1	.000	4	1	1	.833
Totals	5	158	16	39	59	8	0	4	16	18	1	48	.247	132	43	5	.972

CLEVELAND INDIANS' BATTING AND FIELDING AVERAGES

Player, position	G	AB	R	H	TB	2B	3B	HR	RBI	BB	IBB	SO	Avg.	PO	A	E	Avg.
						BATTING									**FIELDING**		
Cabrera, lf-ph	2	1	1	1	1	0	0	0	1	0	0	0	1.000	0	0	0	.000
Vizquel, ss	5	22	2	9	12	1	1	0	6	1	0	1	.409	6	21	1	.964
Gonzalez, rf	5	23	4	8	17	3	0	2	5	0	0	7	.348	4	1	0	1.000
Branyan, lf-ph	2	3	1	1	1	0	0	0	0	0	0	1	.333	0	0	0	.000
Burks, dh	5	19	4	6	10	1	0	1	1	1	0	3	.316	0	0	0	.000
Diaz, c	5	16	3	5	5	0	0	0	2	2	0	1	.313	51	4	1	.982
Cordova, lf	4	12	0	3	3	0	0	0	1	0	0	5	.250	5	0	0	1.000
Alomar, 2b	5	21	3	4	7	3	0	0	3	2	0	5	.190	9	9	0	1.000
Fryman, 3b	5	17	4	3	4	1	0	0	2	2	0	7	.176	2	8	0	1.000
Thome, 1b	5	19	2	3	6	0	0	1	1	2	0	8	.158	40	5	0	1.000
Lofton, cf	5	19	2	2	5	0	0	1	3	3	0	5	.105	9	0	0	1.000
Baez, p	3	0	0	0	0	0	0	0	0	0	0	0	.000	0	0	0	.000
Burba, p	1	0	0	0	0	0	0	0	0	0	0	0	.000	0	1	0	1.000
Colon, p	2	0	0	0	0	0	0	0	0	0	0	0	.000	0	0	1	.000
Finley, p	2	0	0	0	0	0	0	0	0	0	0	0	.000	0	2	0	1.000
Rincon, p	3	0	0	0	0	0	0	0	0	0	0	0	.000	0	0	0	.000
Riske, p	3	0	0	0	0	0	0	0	0	0	0	0	.000	1	0	0	1.000
Rocker, p	1	0	0	0	0	0	0	0	0	0	0	0	.000	1	0	0	1.000
Sabathia, p	1	0	0	0	0	0	0	0	0	0	0	0	.000	0	2	0	1.000
Shuey, p	2	0	0	0	0	0	0	0	0	0	0	0	.000	0	0	0	.000
Wickman, p	1	0	0	0	0	0	0	0	0	0	0	0	.000	0	0	0	.000
Cordero, ph-lf	1	1	0	0	0	0	0	0	0	0	0	0	.000	1	0	0	1.000
Totals	5	173	26	45	71	9	1	5	25	13	0	43	.260	129	53	3	.984

SEATTLE MARINERS' PITCHING RECORDS

Pitcher	G	GS	CG	IP	H	R	ER	HR	BB	IBB	SO	HB	WP	W	L	Pct.	ERA
Halama	2	0	0	3.0	3	0	0	0	0	0	3	0	0	0	0	.000	0.00
Sasaki	3	0	0	3.0	1	0	0	0	0	0	5	0	0	0	0	.000	0.00
Nelson	3	0	0	3.0	1	0	0	0	1	0	5	0	0	0	0	.000	0.00
Rhodes	3	0	0	2.2	1	0	0	0	0	0	1	0	1	0	0	.000	0.00
Charlton	1	0	0	1.2	0	0	0	0	0	0	2	0	0	0	0	.000	0.00
Moyer	2	2	0	12.0	8	2	2	0	2	0	10	0	0	2	0	1.000	1.50
Garcia	2	2	0	11.2	13	6	5	1	3	0	13	0	0	1	1	.500	3.86
Sele	1	1	0	2.0	5	4	2	0	0	0	0	0	0	0	1	.000	9.00
Abbott	1	0	0	3.0	9	8	8	3	5	0	3	0	0	0	0	.000	24.00
Paniagua	2	0	0	2.0	4	6	6	1	2	0	1	1	0	0	0	.000	27.00
Totals	5	5	0	44.0	45	26	23	5	13	0	43	1	1	3	2	.600	4.70

No shutouts. Save—Sasaki.

CLEVELAND INDIANS' PITCHING RECORDS

Pitcher	G	GS	CG	IP	H	R	ER	HR	BB	IBB	SO	HB	WP	W	L	Pct.	ERA
Riske	3	0	0	3.1	2	0	0	0	1	0	5	0	0	0	0	.000	0.00
Burba	1	0	0	1.0	0	0	0	0	0	0	1	0	0	0	0	.000	0.00
Rocker	1	0	0	1.0	1	0	0	0	0	0	1	0	0	0	0	.000	0.00
Wickman	1	0	0	1.0	0	0	0	0	0	0	2	0	0	0	0	.000	0.00
Colon	2	2	0	14.2	12	3	3	0	6	0	13	0	0	1	1	.500	1.84
Baez	3	0	0	3.2	4	1	1	0	0	0	6	0	0	0	0	.000	2.45
Sabathia	1	1	0	6.0	6	2	2	0	5	1	5	0	0	1	0	1.000	3.00
Shuey	2	0	0	2.0	3	1	1	1	0	0	2	0	0	0	0	.000	4.50
Finley	2	2	0	8.1	9	7	7	3	6	0	10	1	1	0	2	.000	7.56
Rincon	3	0	0	2.0	2	2	2	0	0	0	3	0	1	0	0	.000	9.00
Totals	5	5	0	43.0	39	16	16	4	18	1	48	1	2	2	3	.400	3.35

Shutout—Colon and Wickman (combined). No saves.

SCORE BY INNINGS

Seattle	5	2	0	0	1	0	5	1	2—16
Cleveland	2	3	5	3	1	4	2	6	0—26

MISCELLANEOUS STATISTICS

Sacrifice hits—Javier 2.
Sacrifice flies—Lofton, Bell.
Stolen bases—Martinez, Suzuki, Boone, Vizquel.

Caught stealing—Suzuki 2, Cameron.
Double plays—Garcia, McLemore and Olerud 2; Alomar, Vizquel and Thome; Bell, Boone and Olerud; Fryman, Alomar and Thome; McLemore, Boone and Olerud; McLemore and Olerud; Thome, Vizquel and Thome; Vizquel and Thome.
Left on bases—Seattle 6, 2, 10, 8, 9—35; Cleveland 8, 6, 9, 4, 3—30.
Hit by pitcher—By Paniagua (Cabrera), by Finley (Cameron).
Passed balls—Lampkin.
Balks—None.
Time of games—First game, 3:05; second game, 2:41; third game, 3:24; fourth game, 3:06; fifth game, 3:18.
Attendance—First game, 48,033; second game, 48,052; third game, 45,069; fourth game, 45,025; fifth game, 47,867.
Umpires—Rippley, Barrett, Danley, Layne, M. Hirschbeck, Kulpa, Schrieber, Reed, Rapuano, Gibson, DeMuth, Nelson.
Official scorers—Hank Kozloski, Terry Mosher.

NEW YORK VS. OAKLAND

HIGHLIGHTS

The bottom line: The Yankees had one thing going for them in this series that the A's didn't: postseason experience. And it was big. After losing the first two games at home, the Yankees were able to somehow turn it on in Game 3 in Oakland, and then rode that momentum through Games 4 and 5. The A's clearly missed right fielder Jermaine Dye, who suffered a broken leg while fouling off a pitch in Game 4 and did not play the remainder of the series. But it's hard to say if Dye's presence would have made a difference in either game. The Yankees were simply better than the A's when the final three games were on the line.

Why the Yankees won: For the second straight year, the A's made miscues in the field that led to Yankee runs in the fifth and deciding game of a postseason series. And while the Yankees didn't get as much out of their starting pitchers as they have been accustomed, they got enough to win three straight elimination games. Two of those wins came in Oakland, a place where New York hadn't won all season.

The turning points:

Game 1: Yankees righthander Roger Clemens, his team trailing 2-0, was pitching to the first batter in the top of the fifth inning when he appeared to be uncomfortable. Yankees manager Joe Torre immediately went to the mound and Clemens went to the dugout. He had strained a hamstring making a play in the field earlier in the game. Now, it would be up to the New York bullpen to keep the defending champions in the game. Unfortunately, it couldn't. Clemens' replacement, Sterling Hitchcock, got hit hard. The A's, with home runs from Terrence Long and Jason Giambi and a masterful pitching performance from starter Mark Mulder, took the first game.

Game 2: For eight innings Oakland righthander Tim Hudson and Yankee hitters engaged in an epic battle. He allowed six hits and one walk over those eight innings, but none of the Yankees ever crossed home plate. Hudson ran into major trouble in the bottom of the sixth when Chuck Knoblauch and Derek Jeter hit back-to-back singles with two outs, bringing Paul O'Neill to the plate. O'Neill worked Hudson to a full count, only to fly out to shallow cen-

ter to end the threat. In the seventh inning, the Yankees put men on first and third with two outs, but Hudson once again worked out of a jam by getting Scott Brosius to ground out to second. As the A's tried to close out the game in the ninth with Jason Isringhausen on the mound, Bernie Williams doubled and Tino Martinez walked with no outs. But Jorge Posada struck out looking and David Justice and Scott Brosius both popped out, putting the A's one win away from sweeping the Yankees out of the 2001 playoffs.

Game 3: In nine career at-bats against A's righthander Barry Zito, Yankees catcher Jorge Posada had no hits. Nada. The trend looked to continue as Posada fell behind in the count, 0-1, in the fifth inning of a scoreless Game 3. But Zito made a mistake, throwing a fastball that didn't tail in on Posada the way it should have, and Posada sent it over the left-field wall to give New York a 1-0 lead. Amazingly, it was the only run the Yankees would need. The A's came close to scoring in the seventh. With Jeremy Giambi on first base and two outs, Terrence Long hit a shot into the right-field corner. Shane Spencer fielded the ball cleanly but overthrew the cutoff man, as Giambi was charging for home. Derek Jeter, however, came all the way over from his shortstop position, scooped the ball up midway between home and first and then flipped it sidearm to Posada, all in one motion. The Yankee catcher swiped the back of Giambi's leg, just before the runner's other foot touched home plate. Giambi was called out and the inning was over. Mike Mussina and Mariano Rivera made the 1-0 lead stand up for the Yankees' first win of the series.

Game 4: Orlando Hernandez was 8-1 in his postseason career prior to his Game 4 start, but it didn't take long for A's to test him. Oakland put runners on first and third with no outs in the first inning with the heart of the lineup coming to bat. But Hernandez managed to get out of it, inducing Jason Giambi and Jermaine Dye to pop out and then, after walking Terrence Long to load the bases, getting Jeremy Giambi to foul out. Meanwhile, Bernie Williams supplied the offense the Yankees were desperately looking for, going 3-for-4 with two doubles and five RBIs. A's starter Cory Lidle, however, had trouble with more hitters than just Williams. He allowed five hits, three walks and six runs in $3^1/_3$

innings. But the crushing blow for Oakland came when right fielder Jermaine Dye fouled a ball off his lower leg while batting and had to leave the game. It later was discovered that the leg was broken and Dye would not play for the rest of the playoffs.

Game 5: Back home at Yankee Stadium, the Yankees fell behind 2-0 before tying the game on a two-run single by Alfonso Soriano in the second inning. New York took the lead an inning when a strikeout by Bernie Williams turned into disaster for the A's. The ball eluded catcher Greg Myers-who had replaced starter Ramon Hernandez-and Myers' throw bounced under the glove of first baseman Jason Giambi and into right field. The next batter, Tino Martinez, was plunked on a hip by a Mark Mulder pitch, and Shane Spencer then walked to load the bases with two outs. Scott Brosius hit what appeared to be a harmless grounder to third. Eric Chavez fielded the ball but appeared to get distracted when the runner, Martinez, crossed in front of him. The ball popped out of Chavez's glove as Williams scored to give the Yankees a 3-2 lead. Another Oakland error in the fourth inning led to another New York run, and another Yankee celebration seemed a foregone conclusion. Mike Stanton, Ramiro Mendoza and Mariano Rivera pitched a scoreless final $4^2/3$ innings to close out the game and the series.

Notable:

A's: Terrence Long's two home runs in Game 1 marked the first time he had ever homered twice in the same game. ... With a home run in Game 2, Ron Gant increased his career postseason homer total to eight. ... Prior to Game 3, the A's had won 17 straight games at Network Associates Coliseum. ... Righthander Cory Lidle, who bombed in his first career playoff start in Game 4, was 11-2 with a 2.96 ERA after the All-Star break.

Yankees: Roger Clemens has never beaten Oakland (0-4) in a postseason game. ... New York lost for the first time in 10 postseason starts by Andy Pettitte. ... The 4 hours, 13 minutes it took to play Game 4 made it the longest Division Series game ever. It was just one minute short of being the longest nine-inning postseason game. ... David Justice hit the 14th postseason homer of his career in Game 5 to move into fifth place on the all-time list. He leads with 55 RBIs.

Quotable:

A's: Manager Art Howe, on Game 1 starter/winner Mark Mulder: "That's why we gave him the ball first. He's a big-time pitcher." ... Third baseman Eric Chavez, on going to back Oakland for Game 3 leading the series 2-0: "Given all this-New York, Roger Clemens, Andy Pettitte, World Champions-no one would have expected us to win two games here." ... First baseman Jason Giambi, on where Oakland's 2-0 win in Game 2 ranks on his all-time list: "This probably has to be Number One. This was one of the greatest games I've ever been involved in." ... Barry Zito, on Jorge Posada's Game 3 home run: "You

make a mistake most times, it's not going to get hit out of the park." ... Jason Giambi, on Jermaine Dye's injury: "It's definitely going to be tough without Jermaine. He'll be missed. He's a big part of why we're here. He's a tough guy, so when he stayed on the ground, we knew he was hurt seriously." ... Howe, on New York shortstop Derek Jeter: "I guess that's the reason he's wearing so many rings. This kid is as good as they come. Whenever they need a big play, he's there to make it. Whenever they need a big hit, he gets it."

Yankees: Manager Joe Torre, on Roger Clemens' subpar performance in Game 1: "We're used to seeing dynamite stuff from Roger, and tonight he didn't have great command. If you're gonna play Oakland, you have to pitch equal to them." ... Torre, on Game 2 starter Andy Pettitte: "He pitched his tail off tonight. But so did (Tim) Hudson." ... Designated hitter Paul O'Neill, on losing the first two games of the best-of-five series: "They've beaten us at our own game. These are the close games we normally win in the postseason." ... Derek Jeter, after the Yankees' win in Game 3: "Everyone thought we were dead, but no one in here thought that. We feel very confident about our abilities." ... Torre, on Jeter's great play in the seventh inning of Game 3: "He's the backup cut-off man in that situation. He was there, and he made a sensational play. The kid has got great instincts, and he holds it together." ... Torre, on what winning the series meant to the city of New York: "There was no question we knew there was a great deal of responsibility on our shoulders."

GAME 1 BOX SCORE

OAKLAND 5, NEW YORK 3

WEDNESDAY, OCTOBER 10, AT NEW YORK

Oakland	AB	R	H	RBI	PO	A
Damon, cf	4	1	4	0	1	0
Tejada, ss	4	0	0	1	2	3
Ja. Giambi, 1b	3	1	1	2	11	0
Dye, rf	4	0	1	0	2	0
Chavez, 3b	5	0	1	0	2	2
Je. Giambi, dh	4	0	1	0	0	0
Gant, ph-dh	1	0	0	0	0	0
Long, lf	4	2	2	2	2	0
R. Hernandez, c	2	0	0	0	7	2
Menechino, 2b	4	1	0	0	0	3
Mulder, p	0	0	0	0	0	1
Mecir, p	0	0	0	0	0	0
Isringhausen, p	0	0	0	0	0	0
Totals	35	5	10	5	27	12

New York	AB	R	H	RBI	PO	A
Knoblauch, lf	4	0	1	1	4	0
Jeter, ss	4	0	3	0	0	3
Williams, cf	4	1	0	0	3	0
Martinez, 1b	4	1	1	2	11	0
Posada, c	4	0	3	0	3	0
O'Neill, dh	4	0	0	0	0	0
Justice, rf	4	0	0	0	3	0
Brosius, 3b	4	0	0	0	1	1
Soriano, 2b	4	1	2	0	2	3
Clemens, p	0	0	0	0	0	2
Hitchcock, p	0	0	0	0	0	0

New York	AB	R	H	RBI	PO	A
Witasick, p	0	0	0	0	0	0
Stanton, p	0	0	0	0	0	0
Totals	36	3	10	3	27	9

Oakland	1	0	0		1	0	0		1	2	0—5
New York	0	0	0		0	1	0		0	2	0—3

Oakland	IP	H	R	ER	BB	SO
Mulder (W)	6.2	7	1	1	0	5
Mecir	1.1	3	2	2	0	0
Isringhausen (S)	1.0	0	0	0	0	2

New York	IP	H	R	ER	BB	SO
Clemens (L)	*4.0	4	2	2	3	1
Hitchcock	†3.0	5	2	2	0	2
Witasick	0.2	1	1	1	1	0
Stanton	1.1	0	0	0	0	0

*Pitched to one batter in fifth.
†Pitched to one batter in eighth.

E—Menechino, Knoblauch. DP—Oakland 1, New York 1. LOB—Oakland 10, New York 6. 2B—Dye, Je. Giambi, Posada. HR—Long 2, Ja. Giambi, Martinez. SF—Ja. Giambi, Tejada. SB—Damon 2, Soriano. CS—Soriano. HBP—By Clemens (R. Hernandez). T—3:45. A—56,697. U—DeMuth, plate; Nelson, first; Schrieber, second; Reed, third; Rapuano, left field; Gibson, right field.

GAME 2 BOX SCORE

OAKLAND 2, NEW YORK 0

THURSDAY, OCTOBER 11, AT NEW YORK

Oakland	AB	R	H	RBI	PO	A
Damon, cf	5	1	2	0	1	0
Tejada, ss	5	0	2	0	1	3
Ja. Giambi, 1b	3	0	0	0	13	0
Dye, rf	3	0	0	0	1	0
Chavez, 3b	4	0	0	0	2	1
Gant, dh	3	1	2	1	0	0
Je. Giambi, ph-dh	1	0	0	0	0	0
Long, lf	4	0	2	0	0	0
R. Hernandez, c	4	0	0	0	4	0
Menechino, 2b	4	0	1	0	4	6
Hudson, p	0	0	0	0	1	4
Isringhausen, p	0	0	0	0	0	0
Totals	36	2	9	1	27	14

New York	AB	R	H	RBI	PO	A
Knoblauch, lf	4	0	2	0	1	0
Jeter, ss	4	0	2	0	1	1
O'Neill, dh	4	0	0	0	0	0
Williams, cf	4	0	1	0	2	0
Martinez, 1b	3	0	1	0	11	1
Bellinger, pr	0	0	0	0	0	0
Posada, c	3	0	0	0	7	0
Justice, rf	4	0	1	0	1	0
Brosius, 3b	4	0	0	0	1	4
Soriano, 2b	3	0	0	0	3	1
Pettitte, p	0	0	0	0	0	1
Mendoza, p	0	0	0	0	0	0
Rivera, p	0	0	0	0	0	0
Totals	33	0	7	0	27	8

Oakland	0	0	0		1	0	0		0	0	1—2
New York	0	0	0		0	0	0		0	0	0—0

Oakland	IP	H	R	ER	BB	SO
Hudson (W)	8.0	6	0	0	1	3
Isringhausen (S)	1.0	1	0	0	1	1

New York	IP	H	R	ER	BB	SO
Pettitte (L)	6.1	7	1	1	2	4
Mendoza	1.2	1	0	0	1	1
Rivera	1.0	1	1	1	0	1

E—Brosius. DP—Oakland 1, New York 1. LOB—Oakland 10, New York 8. 2B—Tejada 2, Damon, Long, Williams. 3B—Damon. HR—Gant. T—3:24. A—56,684. U—Nelson, plate; Schrieber, first; Reed, second; Rapuano, third; Gibson, left field; DeMuth, right field.

GAME 3 BOX SCORE

NEW YORK 1, OAKLAND 0

SATURDAY, OCTOBER 13, AT OAKLAND

New York	AB	R	H	RBI	PO	A
Knoblauch, lf	4	0	0	0	3	0
Soriano, 2b	4	0	0	0	1	4
Jeter, ss	3	0	0	0	3	3
Williams, cf	3	0	0	0	2	0
Martinez, 1b	3	0	0	0	10	1
Posada, c	3	1	1	1	6	0
Spencer, rf	3	0	1	0	1	1
Velarde, dh	3	0	0	0	0	0
Brosius, 3b	3	0	0	0	1	2
Mussina, p	0	0	0	0	0	0
Rivera, p	0	0	0	0	0	0
Totals	29	1	2	1	27	11

Oakland	AB	R	H	RBI	PO	A
Damon, cf	4	0	0	0	7	0
Tejada, ss	4	0	0	0	0	1
Ja. Giambi, 1b	4	0	1	0	8	0
Dye, rf	4	0	2	0	1	0
Chavez, 3b	4	0	0	0	0	2
Je. Giambi, dh	3	0	1	0	0	0
Long, lf	3	0	1	0	2	0
R. Hernandez, c	2	0	0	0	6	0
Saenz, ph	1	0	0	0	0	0
Santangelo, 2b	0	0	0	0	0	0
Menechino, 2b	2	0	0	0	3	1
Myers, ph-c	1	0	1	0	0	1
Zito, p	0	0	0	0	0	0
Guthrie, p	0	0	0	0	0	0
Totals	32	0	6	0	27	5

New York	0	0	0		0	1	0		0	0	0—1
Oakland	0	0	0		0	0	0		0	0	0—0

New York	IP	H	R	ER	BB	SO
Mussina (W)	7.0	4	0	0	1	4
Rivera (S)	2.0	2	0	0	0	1

Oakland	IP	H	R	ER	BB	SO
Zito (L)	8.0	2	1	1	1	6
Guthrie	1.0	0	0	0	0	0

E—Tejada. DP—Oakland 1. LOB—New York 4, Oakland 6. 2B—Spencer, Dye, Long. HR—Posada. HBP—By Zito 2 (Martinez, Jeter). T—2:42. A—55,861. U—Danley, plate; Layne, first; M. Hirschbeck, second; Kulpa, third; Rippley, left field; Barrett, right field.

GAME 4 BOX SCORE

NEW YORK 9, OAKLAND 2

SUNDAY, OCTOBER 14, AT OAKLAND

New York	AB	R	H	RBI	PO	A
Knoblauch, lf	5	0	1	0	1	0
Jeter, ss	4	2	1	0	2	1
Justice, dh	3	2	1	0	0	0
Williams, cf	4	2	3	5	5	0
Martinez, 1b	5	0	0	0	7	1
Posada, c	4	1	2	1	9	0
O'Neill, rf	3	1	1	0	1	0
Spencer, ph-rf	2	0	0	0	0	0
Brosius, 3b	3	0	1	1	1	1
Soriano, 2b	3	1	1	1	0	1
O. Hernandez, p	0	0	0	0	0	0
Stanton, p	0	0	0	0	0	1
Mendoza, p	0	0	0	0	0	1
Totals	36	9	11	8	27	5

Oakland	AB	R	H	RBI	PO	A
Damon, cf	5	0	2	0	0	0
Tejada, ss	5	1	4	0	2	3
Ja. Giambi, 1b	3	1	0	0	13	1

— 175 —

Oakland	AB	R	H	RBI	PO	A
Saenz, ph	1	0	0	0	0	0
Dye, rf	2	0	0	0	1	0
Gant, ph-lf	3	0	0	0	1	0
Long, lf-rf	3	0	1	1	2	1
Je. Giambi, dh	3	0	1	1	0	0
Byrnes, ph-dh	1	0	0	0	0	0
Chavez, 3b	4	0	2	0	0	4
Myers, c	3	0	0	0	3	2
R. Hernandez, ph-c	1	0	0	0	0	0
Santangelo, 2b	3	0	1	0	5	4
Lidle, p	0	0	0	0	0	1
Hiljus, p	0	0	0	0	0	0
Magnante, p	0	0	0	0	0	0
Guthrie, p	0	0	0	0	0	0
Bradford, p	0	0	0	0	0	0
Tam, p	0	0	0	0	0	0
Totals	37	2	11	2	27	16

New York .... 0 2 2   3 0 0   0 0 2—9
Oakland .... 0 0 2   0 0 0   0 0—2

New York	IP	H	R	ER	BB	SO
O. Hernandez (W)	5.2	8	2	2	2	5
Stanton	1.2	2	0	0	0	1
Mendoza	1.2	1	0	0	0	3

Oakland	IP	H	R	ER	BB	SO
Lidle (L)	3.1	5	6	4	3	0
Hiljus	0.1	0	1	1	2	0
Magnante	1.1	3	0	0	1	1
Guthrie	2.0	0	0	0	0	1
Bradford	1.0	0	0	0	0	1
Tam	1.0	3	2	2	0	0

E—Brosius, Santangelo. DP—New York 1. LOB—New York 7, Oakland 11. 2B—Williams 2, O'Neill, Tejada, Chavez, Santangelo. 3B—Justice. SH—Brosius. SB—Soriano. CS—Jeter. HBP—By O. Hernandez (Santangelo). WP—O. Hernandez. T—4:13. A—43,681. U—Layne, plate; M. Hirschbeck, first; Kulpa, second; Rippley, third; Barrett, left field; Danley, right field.

GAME 5 BOX SCORE

NEW YORK 5, OAKLAND 3

MONDAY, OCTOBER 15, AT NEW YORK

Oakland	AB	R	H	RBI	PO	A
Damon, cf	4	1	1	0	1	0
Tejada, ss	3	0	0	0	3	5
Ja. Giambi, 1b	4	0	4	2	8	1
Chavez, 3b	4	0	0	0	0	2

Oakland	AB	R	H	RBI	PO	A
Long, rf	4	1	1	0	1	0
Gant, lf	4	0	0	0	2	0
Je. Giambi, dh	2	0	1	1	0	0
Saenz, ph-dh	2	0	0	0	0	0
R. Hernandez, c	1	0	0	0	0	0
Myers, c	3	0	0	0	6	1
Menechino, 2b	2	1	0	0	3	2
Byrnes, ph	1	0	0	0	0	0
Mulder, p	0	0	0	0	0	2
Hudson, p	0	0	0	0	0	0
Mecir, p	0	0	0	0	0	0
Totals	34	3	7	3	24	13

New York	AB	R	H	RBI	PO	A
Knoblauch, lf	5	1	2	0	3	0
Velarde, dh	2	0	1	0	0	0
Justice, ph-dh	2	1	1	1	0	0
Jeter, ss	3	0	2	1	3	2
Williams, cf	3	1	0	0	1	0
Martinez, 1b	3	0	0	0	8	1
Posada, c	4	1	2	0	8	0
Spencer, rf	3	1	1	0	3	0
Brosius, 3b	3	0	0	0	1	2
Soriano, 2b	4	0	1	2	0	1
Clemens, p	0	0	0	0	0	1
Stanton, p	0	0	0	0	0	1
Mendoza, p	0	0	0	0	0	1
Rivera, p	0	0	0	0	0	0
Totals	32	5	10	4	27	9

Oakland .... 1 1 0   0 1 0   0 0 0—3
New York .... 0 2 1   0 1 1   0 0 x—5

Oakland	IP	H	R	ER	BB	SO
Mulder (L)	4.1	7	4	2	2	2
Hudson	1.2	2	1	1	0	2
Mecir	2.0	1	0	0	0	4

New York	IP	H	R	ER	BB	SO
Clemens	4.1	5	3	3	1	5
Stanton (W)	1.2	1	0	0	0	0
Mendoza	1.0	0	0	0	0	1
Rivera (S)	2.0	1	0	0	0	2

E—Myers, Chavez, Ja. Giambi, Brosius. DP—Oakland 1, New York 1. LOB—Oakland 6, New York 9. 2B—Damon, Long, Knoblauch, Jeter. HR—Justice. SH—Velarde. SF—Jeter. SB—Je. Giambi, Posada, Knoblauch. CS—Knoblauch, Williams. HBP—By Mulder 2 (Brosius, Martinez), by Clemens (Tejada). WP—Clemens. T—3:23. A—56,642. U—Rapuano, plate; Gibson, first; DeMuth, second; Nelson, third; Schrieber, left field; Reed, right field.

STATISTICS

NEW YORK YANKEES' BATTING AND FIELDING AVERAGES

Player, position	G	AB	R	H	TB	2B	3B	HR	RBI	BB	IBB	SO	Avg.	PO	A	E	Avg.
Jeter, ss	5	18	2	8	9	1	0	0	1	1	0	0	.444	9	10	0	1.000
Posada, c	5	18	3	8	12	1	0	1	2	2	0	2	.444	33	0	0	1.000
Knoblauch, lf	5	22	1	6	7	1	0	0	1	0	0	0	.273	12	0	1	.923
Spencer, rf-ph	3	8	1	2	3	1	0	0	0	1	0	4	.250	4	1	0	1.000
Justice, rf-dh-ph	4	13	3	3	8	0	1	1	1	2	0	5	.231	4	0	0	1.000
Soriano, 2b	5	18	2	4	4	0	0	0	3	1	0	5	.222	7	9	0	1.000
Williams, cf	5	18	4	4	7	3	0	0	5	3	0	3	.222	13	0	0	1.000
Velarde, dh	2	5	0	1	1	0	0	0	0	0	0	1	.200	0	0	0	.000
Martinez, 1b	5	18	1	2	5	0	0	1	2	1	0	6	.111	47	4	0	1.000
O'Neill, dh-rf	3	11	1	1	2	1	0	0	0	0	0	0	.091	1	0	0	1.000
Brosius, 3b	5	17	0	1	1	0	0	0	1	0	0	3	.059	5	10	3	.833
Bellinger, pr	1	0	0	0	0	0	0	0	0	0	0	0	.000	0	0	0	.000
Clemens, p	2	0	0	0	0	0	0	0	0	0	0	0	.000	0	3	0	1.000
Hitchcock, p	1	0	0	0	0	0	0	0	0	0	0	0	.000	0	0	0	.000
Mendoza, p	3	0	0	0	0	0	0	0	0	0	0	0	.000	0	2	0	1.000
Mussina, p	1	0	0	0	0	0	0	0	0	0	0	0	.000	0	0	0	.000
O. Hernandez, p	1	0	0	0	0	0	0	0	0	0	0	0	.000	0	0	0	.000
Pettitte, p	1	0	0	0	0	0	0	0	0	0	0	0	.000	0	1	0	1.000

Player, position	G	AB	R	H	TB	2B	3B	HR	RBI	BB	IBB	SO	Avg.	PO	A	E	Avg.
Rivera, p	3	0	0	0	0	0	0	0	0	0	0	0	.000	0	0	0	.000
Stanton, p	3	0	0	0	0	0	0	0	0	0	0	0	.000	0	2	0	1.000
Witasick, p	1	0	0	0	0	0	0	0	0	0	0	0	.000	0	0	0	.000
Totals	5	166	18	40	59	8	1	3	16	11	0	29	.241	135	42	4	.978

OAKLAND ATHLETICS' BATTING AND FIELDING AVERAGES

Player, position	G	AB	R	H	TB	2B	3B	HR	RBI	BB	IBB	SO	Avg.	PO	A	E	Avg.
Damon, cf	5	22	3	9	13	2	1	0	0	1	0	1	.409	10	0	0	1.000
Long, lf-rf	5	18	3	7	16	3	0	2	3	1	0	2	.389	7	1	0	1.000
Ja. Giambi, 1b	5	17	2	6	9	0	0	1	4	4	1	2	.353	53	2	1	.982
Santangelo, 2b	2	3	0	1	2	1	0	0	0	0	0	0	.333	5	4	1	.900
Je. Giambi, dh-ph	5	13	0	4	5	1	0	0	2	1	0	0	.308	0	0	0	.000
Tejada, ss	5	21	1	6	9	3	0	0	1	0	0	3	.286	8	15	1	.958
Dye, rf	4	13	0	3	5	2	0	0	0	2	0	2	.231	5	0	0	1.000
Gant, ph-dh-lf	4	11	1	2	5	0	0	1	1	0	0	3	.182	3	0	0	1.000
Myers, ph-c	3	7	0	1	1	0	0	0	0	0	0	3	.143	9	4	1	.929
Chavez, 3b	5	21	0	3	4	1	0	0	0	0	0	5	.143	4	11	1	.938
Menechino, 2b	4	12	2	1	1	0	0	0	0	1	0	4	.083	10	12	1	.957
Bradford, p	1	0	0	0	0	0	0	0	0	0	0	0	.000	0	0	0	.000
Guthrie, p	2	0	0	0	0	0	0	0	0	0	0	0	.000	0	0	0	.000
Hiljus, p	1	0	0	0	0	0	0	0	0	0	0	0	.000	0	0	0	.000
Hudson, p	2	0	0	0	0	0	0	0	0	0	0	0	.000	1	4	0	1.000
Isringhausen, p	2	0	0	0	0	0	0	0	0	0	0	0	.000	0	0	0	.000
Lidle, p	1	0	0	0	0	0	0	0	0	0	0	0	.000	0	1	0	1.000
Magnante, p	1	0	0	0	0	0	0	0	0	0	0	0	.000	0	0	0	.000
Mecir, p	2	0	0	0	0	0	0	0	0	0	0	0	.000	0	1	0	1.000
Mulder, p	2	0	0	0	0	0	0	0	0	0	0	0	.000	0	3	0	1.000
Tam, p	1	0	0	0	0	0	0	0	0	0	0	0	.000	0	0	0	.000
Zito, p	1	0	0	0	0	0	0	0	0	0	0	0	.000	0	0	0	.000
Byrnes, ph	2	2	0	0	0	0	0	0	0	0	0	1	.000	0	0	0	.000
Saenz, ph-dh	3	4	0	0	0	0	0	0	0	0	0	1	.000	0	0	0	.000
R. Hernandez, c-ph	5	10	0	0	0	0	0	0	0	1	0	4	.000	17	2	0	1.000
Totals	5	174	12	43	70	13	1	4	11	11	1	31	.247	132	60	6	.970

NEW YORK YANKEES' PITCHING RECORDS

Pitcher	G	GS	CG	IP	H	R	ER	HR	BB	IBB	SO	HB	WP	W	L	Pct.	ERA
Mussina	1	1	0	7.0	4	0	0	0	1	0	4	0	0	1	0	1.000	0.00
Rivera	3	0	0	5.0	4	1	0	0	4	0	4	0	0	0	0	.000	0.00
Mendoza	3	0	0	4.1	2	0	0	0	1	1	5	0	0	0	0	.000	0.00
Stanton	3	0	0	4.2	3	0	0	0	0	0	1	0	0	1	0	1.000	0.00
Pettitte	1	1	0	6.1	7	1	1	1	2	0	4	0	0	0	1	.000	1.42
O. Hernandez	1	1	0	5.2	8	2	2	0	2	0	5	1	1	1	0	1.000	3.18
Clemens	2	2	0	8.1	9	5	5	1	4	0	6	2	1	0	1	.000	5.40
Hitchcock	1	0	0	3.0	5	2	2	2	0	0	2	0	0	0	0	.000	6.00
Witasick	1	0	0	0.2	1	1	1	0	1	0	0	0	0	0	0	.000	13.50
Totals	5	5	0	45.0	43	12	11	4	11	1	31	3	2	3	2	.600	2.20

Shutout—Mussina and Rivera (combined). Saves—Rivera 2.

OAKLAND ATHLETICS' PITCHING RECORDS

Pitcher	G	GS	CG	IP	H	R	ER	HR	BB	IBB	SO	HB	WP	W	L	Pct.	ERA
Guthrie	2	0	0	3.0	0	0	0	0	0	0	2	0	0	0	0	.000	0.00
Bradford	1	0	0	1.0	0	0	0	0	0	0	1	0	0	0	0	.000	0.00
Isringhausen	2	0	0	1.0	1	0	0	0	1	0	3	0	0	0	0	.000	0.00
Magnante	1	0	0	1.1	3	0	0	0	1	0	1	0	0	0	0	.000	0.00
Hudson	2	1	0	9.2	8	1	1	1	1	0	5	0	0	1	0	1.000	0.93
Zito	1	1	0	8.0	2	1	1	1	1	0	6	2	0	0	1	.000	1.13
Mulder	2	2	0	11.0	14	5	3	0	2	0	7	2	0	1	1	.500	2.45
Mecir	2	0	0	3.1	4	2	2	1	0	0	4	0	0	0	0	.000	5.40
Lidle	1	1	0	3.1	5	6	4	0	3	0	0	0	0	0	1	.000	10.80
Tam	1	0	0	1.0	3	2	2	0	0	0	0	0	0	0	0	.000	18.00
Hiljus	1	0	0	0.1	0	1	1	0	2	0	0	0	0	0	0	.000	27.00
Totals	5	5	0	43.0	40	18	14	3	11	0	29	4	0	2	3	.400	2.93

Shutout—Hudson and Isringhausen (combined). Saves—Isringhausen 2.

SCORE BY INNINGS

New York	0	4	3	4	2	1	0	2	2—18	
Oakland	2	1	2	2	1	0	1	2	1—12	

MISCELLANEOUS STATISTICS

Sacrifice hits—Brosius, Velarde.

Sacrifice flies—Ja. Giambi, Tejada, Jeter.

Stolen bases—Damon 2, Soriano 2, Je. Giambi, Posada, Knoblauch.

Caught stealing—Soriano, Jeter, Knoblauch, Williams.

Double plays—Martinez, Jeter and Martinez 2; Chavez, Menechino and Ja. Giambi; Jeter and Martinez; Martinez (unassisted); Hudson and Ja. Giambi; Menechino, Tejada and Ja. Giambi; Tejada and Ja. Giambi.

Left on bases—New York 6, 8, 4, 7, 9—34; Oakland 10, 10, 6, 11, 6—43.

Hit by pitcher—By Clemens 2 (R. Hernandez, Tejada), by Zito 2 (Martinez, Jeter), by Mulder 2 (Brosius, Martinez), by O. Hernandez (Santangelo).

Passed balls—None.

Balks—None.

Time of games—First game, 3:45; second game, 3:24; third game, 2:42; fourth game, 4:13; fifth game, 3:23.

Attendance—First game, 56,697; second game, 56,684; third game, 55,861; fourth game, 43,681; fifth game, 56,6420.

Umpires—DeMuth, Nelson, Schrieber, Reed, Rapuano, Gibson, Danley, Layne, M. Hirschbeck, Kulpa, Rippley, Barrett.

Official scorers—Red Foley, Howie Karpin, Art Santo Domingo, Bill Shannon.

2001 REVIEW A.L. Division Series

ATLANTA VS. HOUSTON

The bottom line: The Braves entered the 2001 postseason with the worst record of any playoff team, but regular-season records didn't matter in their first-round sweep of the Astros. Atlanta outscored Houston 14-6 and outhit the Astros 30-19 to advance to the National League Championship Series for the ninth time in 11 years. The Braves, who became the first team in history to reach the playoffs after compiling a losing record at home (40-41), had little trouble dismissing an Astros team that hit only .200 in the series, including .000 with runners in scoring position.

Why the Braves won: Their pitchers were terrific. Starters Tom Glavine, Greg Maddux and John Burkett combined to allow just four earned runs in 20⅓ innings and starter-turned-closer John Smoltz (whose fastball approached 100 mph) finished up all three games. Craig Biggio, Lance Berkman and Moises Alou all went 2-for-12 in the series, and while Jeff Bagwell's 3-for-7 (he walked five times) sounds impressive, he drove in no runs the entire series. Braves hitters, meanwhile, averaged .303 as a team and hit six home runs.

The turning points:

Game 1: The Astros led, 3-2, and had Mike Jackson on the mound when pinch-hitter Keith Lockhart doubled to start the top of the eighth inning. Pinch-hitter Ken Caminiti struck out, but rookie Marcus Giles hit a grounder that glanced off the glove of second baseman Craig Biggio and into center field, scoring Lockhart. With the game tied, Julio Franco hit a sharp ground ball right at shortstop Julio Lugo, a made-to-order double play ball. But Lugo booted it, allowing Chipper Jones to come to the plate with men on base instead of leading off the next inning. Houston manager Larry Dierker yanked Jackson for Billy Wagner, marking the first time all season Dierker summoned his closer prior to the ninth inning. The move made sense, as Wagner had held Jones hitless in eight at-bats with six strikeouts. That didn't matter, however, after Jones took Wagner's first pitch over the left-field wall for a three-run home run to spur the Braves to victory.

Game 2: Misplays again doomed the Astros. B.J. Surhoff led off the Atlanta second with a double into the left-field corner. He advanced to third when Houston shortstop Julio Lugo bounced a throw past first baseman Jeff Bagwell after diving to smother a hard-hit ball by Andruw Jones that was ruled an infield single. The error was Lugo's second of the game and third of the series. Rey Sanchez followed Jones by grounding into a double play, but Surhoff was able to dash home with what proved to be the

winning run. Tom Glavine made the tally stand up by holding the Astros to six hits over eight innings while striking out three and walking two. John Smoltz pitched the ninth to preserve the victory.

Game 3: The Braves gained momentum early in the game from a surprising source, catcher Paul Bako. With two outs in the second inning, Rey Sanchez doubled on an 0-2 pitch from Houston starter Shane Reynolds. Reynolds got ahead of the next batter, Bako, as well, but left a slider over the middle of the plate. Bako took the misguided 1-2 pitch 403 feet over the right-field wall for his first homer since June 1 and the first postseason hit of his major league career. The Braves added two more runs over the next two innings on a Julio Franco homer and a Bako RBI. Bako collected his third RBI of the game on a squeeze play that scored Andruw Jones. That was all the run support John Burkett needed as he allowed two runs in 6⅓ innings to earn the win.

Notable:

Braves: Prior to Game 1, the Braves hadn't won a postseason game since Game 6 of the 1999 National League Championship Series against the New York Mets. ... The Braves hit into four double plays in Game 2 and a combined six in the first two games. ... Andruw Jones tied a playoff record with five straight hits, two at the end of Game 1 and three at the start of Game 2. ... The Braves improved their all-time record against the Astros in postseason play to 9-1.

Astros: Jeff Bagwell ended the season with a .174 career average in postseason play. ... Despite winning four of five N.L. Central titles from 1997-2001, the Astros failed to win a playoff series. ... Houston has a record of 2-12 in four playoff appearances under manager Larry Dierker. The Astros scored two runs or fewer in eight of those 14 games.

Quotable:

Braves: Chipper Jones, after the Game 1 victory at Houston: "As a team coming in on the road in the playoffs ... your worst-case scenario is you want to leave with a split. We've accomplished our worst-case scenario. Now we'll try for the best-case scenario." ... Tom Glavine, on not having lost to the Astros since June 1995: "I think we've been in a situation against these guys where seemingly everything's gone our way. I think in playoff situations, what's happened in the past, you throw out the window. If you believe in the law of averages, then you've got to believe sooner or later things are going to be right for these guys. But you don't know if it's going to be this year or somewhere down the road." ... Brian Jordan, on winning the series: "It all came together at the right time. We're very confident right now." ... John Smoltz, the winningest pitcher in post-season history, on his new role of closer: "It was incredible. My job is to ride the emotion in the ninth. I wanted to make it quick."

Astros: Billy Wagner, on giving up the game-winning home run to Chipper Jones in Game 1: "We should have won that game. To lose that game on one pitch like that, it's tough." ... Larry Dierker, after his club was shut out in Game 2: "I think we would generally expect to get a few runs, more than one. When you face the Braves, you face tough pitching. But those guys are better hitters than that." ... Dierker, on losing yet another playoff series: "Honestly, I thought we had a better team than the Braves." ... Jeff Bagwell, on the Astros' lack of postseason success: "Winning four (division) championships in five years is not too shabby. We just haven't been able to get over this first-round thing." ... Craig Biggio, on the team's poor hitting: "We hit the ball good. Unfortunately, every time we hit the ball on the nose, they had a guy there."

GAME 1 BOX SCORE

ATLANTA 7, HOUSTON 4

TUESDAY, OCTOBER 9, AT HOUSTON

Atlanta	AB	R	H	RBI	PO	A
Giles, 2b	4	2	2	1	3	3
Smoltz, p	1	0	0	0	0	0
Franco, 1b	5	1	2	0	6	0
C. Jones, 3b	4	1	2	3	0	1
Jordan, rf	3	1	1	2	2	0
Surhoff, lf	4	0	1	0	4	0
A. Jones, cf	4	1	2	1	3	0
Sanchez, ss	2	0	0	0	1	4
Martinez, ph	1	0	0	0	0	0
DeRosa, ss	1	0	1	0	0	1
Bako, c	2	0	0	0	7	0
Lockhart, ph-2b	2	1	1	0	0	1
Maddux, p	2	0	0	0	0	0
Seanez, p	0	0	0	0	0	0
Caminiti, ph	1	0	0	0	0	0
Torrealba, c	1	0	1	0	1	0
Totals	37	7	13	7	27	10

Houston	AB	R	H	RBI	PO	A
Biggio, 2b	4	0	1	0	3	2
Lugo, ss	3	1	0	0	4	3
Vizcaino, ph-ss	1	0	0	0	0	1
Bagwell, 1b	3	0	1	0	5	0
Berkman, lf	4	0	1	0	2	0
Alou, rf	4	0	0	1	1	0
Castilla, 3b	4	1	2	1	1	0
Hidalgo, cf	1	1	0	0	2	0
Ausmus, c	4	1	1	2	9	2
Miller, p	2	0	0	0	0	0
Merced, ph	1	0	0	0	0	0
Jackson, p	0	0	0	0	0	0
Wagner, p	0	0	0	0	0	0
Williams, p	0	0	0	0	0	0
Ward, ph	1	0	0	0	0	0
Totals	32	4	6	4	27	8

Atlanta	1	0	0	1	0	0	0	4	1—7
Houston	0	0	0	0	2	1	0	0	1—4

Atlanta	IP	H	R	ER	BB	SO
Maddux	6.0	4	3	2	3	5
Seanez (W)	1.0	0	0	0	1	0
Smoltz (S)	2.0	2	1	1	0	1

Houston	IP	H	R	ER	BB	SO
Miller	7.0	7	2	2	0	6
Jackson (L)	0.1	2	3	2	0	1
Wagner	0.2	1	1	1	0	1
Williams	1.0	3	1	1	0	1

E—Sanchez, Lugo. DP—Atlanta 2, Houston 2. LOB—Atlanta 4, Houston 5. 2B—Lockhart, Torrealba. HR—C. Jones, Jordan, A. Jones, Castilla, Ausmus. SF—Jordan. CS—C. Jones, Franco. T—2:51, A—35,553. U—Froemming, plate; Meriwether, first; Winters, second; Gorman, third; Joyce, left field; Everitt, right field.

GAME 2 BOX SCORE

ATLANTA 1, HOUSTON 0

WEDNESDAY, OCTOBER 10, AT HOUSTON

Atlanta	AB	R	H	RBI	PO	A
Giles, 2b	4	0	1	0	2	7
Franco, 1b	4	0	0	0	10	2
C. Jones, 3b	2	0	0	0	0	0
Jordan, rf	4	0	0	0	4	0
Surhoff, lf	3	1	2	0	0	0
A. Jones, cf	4	0	3	0	1	0
Sanchez, ss	4	0	0	0	6	3
Bako, c	3	0	0	0	3	0
Glavine, p	3	0	1	0	1	3
Smoltz, p	0	0	0	0	0	0
Totals	31	1	7	0	27	15

Houston	AB	R	H	RBI	PO	A
Biggio, 2b	4	0	0	0	3	2
Lugo, ss	4	0	0	0	3	1
Bagwell, 1b	2	0	2	0	8	0
Berkman, lf	4	0	0	0	2	0
Alou, rf	4	0	1	0	2	0
Hidalgo, cf	3	0	1	0	0	0
Castilla, 3b	3	0	1	0	4	5
Ausmus, c	3	0	1	0	5	0
Mlicki, p	1	0	0	0	0	0
Truby, ph	1	0	0	0	0	0
Dotel, p	0	0	0	0	0	1
Jackson, p	0	0	0	0	0	0
Cruz, p	0	0	0	0	0	0
Vizcaino, ph	1	0	1	0	0	0
Wagner, p	0	0	0	0	0	0
Totals	30	0	7	0	27	9

Atlanta	0	1	0	0	0	0	0	0	0—1
Houston	0	0	0	0	0	0	0	0	0—0

Atlanta	IP	H	R	ER	BB	SO
Glavine (W)	8.0	6	0	0	2	3
Smoltz (S)	1.0	1	0	0	0	0

Houston	IP	H	R	ER	BB	SO
Mlicki (L)	5.0	4	1	0	2	0
Dotel	2.0	2	0	0	0	2
Jackson	0.1	1	0	0	0	0
Cruz	0.2	0	0	0	1	1
Wagner	1.0	0	0	0	0	0

E—Lugo 2. DP—Atlanta 3, Houston 4. LOB—Atlanta 7, Houston 5. 2B—Giles, Surhoff. SB—Surhoff. CS—Bagwell. HBP—By Wagner (Surhoff). WP—Wagner. T—2:41. A—35,704. U—Meriwether, plate; Winters, first; Gorman, second; Joyce, third; Everitt, left field; Froemming, right field.

GAME 3 BOX SCORE

ATLANTA 6, HOUSTON 2

FRIDAY, OCTOBER 12, AT ATLANTA

Houston	AB	R	H	RBI	PO	A
Biggio, 2b	4	0	1	0	0	3
Vizcaino, ss	4	0	0	0	3	2
Bagwell, 1b	2	0	0	0	8	2
Berkman, lf	4	0	1	0	2	0
Alou, rf	4	0	1	0	2	0
Castilla, 3b	4	0	0	0	0	2

Houston	AB	R	H	RBI	PO	A
Hidalgo, cf	4	0	0	0	4	0
Eusebio, c	3	1	2	0	4	1
Ausmus, ph	1	0	0	0	0	0
Reynolds, p	1	0	0	0	0	3
Lugo, ph	1	0	0	0	0	0
Cruz, p	0	0	0	0	1	0
Ward, ph	1	1	1	2	0	0
Dotel, p	0	0	0	0	0	0
Villone, p	0	0	0	0	0	0
Totals	33	2	6	2	24	13

Atlanta	AB	R	H	RBI	PO	A
Giles, 2b	4	0	0	0	1	0
Franco, 1b	4	2	2	1	8	0
C. Jones, 3b	3	1	2	2	0	4
Jordan, rf	4	0	1	0	4	0
Surhoff, lf	4	0	0	0	3	0
A. Jones, cf	4	1	1	0	3	0
Sanchez, ss	3	1	2	0	1	2
Bako, c	2	1	2	3	7	0
Burkett, p	2	0	0	0	0	1
Reed, p	0	0	0	0	0	0
Remlinger, p	0	0	0	0	0	0
Caminiti, ph	1	0	0	0	0	0
Karsay, p	0	0	0	0	0	0
Smoltz, p	0	0	0	0	0	0
Totals	31	6	10	6	27	7

Houston	0	0	0		0	0	0		2	0	0—2
Atlanta	0	2	1		1	0	0		0	2	x—6

Houston	IP	H	R	ER	BB	SO
Reynolds (L)	4.0	6	4	4	1	1
Cruz	2.0	1	0	0	0	0
Dotel	1.1	3	2	2	0	3
Villone	0.2	0	0	0	0	0

Atlanta	IP	H	R	ER	BB	SO
Burkett (W)	6.1	6	2	2	2	4
Reed	0.1	0	0	0	0	0
Remlinger	0.1	0	0	0	0	0
Karsay	1.0	0	0	0	0	1
Smoltz	1.0	0	0	0	0	2

DP—Houston 1. LOB—Houston 6, Atlanta 3. 2B—Sanchez, Bako, Alou, Eusebio. HR—Franco, C. Jones, Bako, Ward. SH—Bako. CS—Jordan. T—2:33. A—39,923. U—Young, plate; Tschida, first; Scott, second; Marquez, third; Marsh left field; J. Hirschbeck, right field.

STATISTICS

ATLANTA BRAVES' BATTING AND FIELDING AVERAGES

Player, position	G	AB	R	H	TB	2B	3B	HR	RBI	BB	IBB	SO	Avg.	PO	A	E	Avg.
DeRosa, ss	1	1	0	1	1	0	0	0	0	0	0	0	1.000	0	1	0	1.000
Torrealba, c	1	1	0	1	2	1	0	0	0	0	0	0	1.000	1	0	0	1.000
A. Jones, cf	3	12	2	6	9	0	0	1	1	0	0	3	.500	7	0	0	1.000
Lockhart, ph-2b	1	2	1	1	2	1	0	0	0	0	0	0	.500	0	1	0	1.000
C. Jones, 3b	3	9	2	4	10	0	0	2	5	3	1	1	.444	0	5	0	1.000
Glavine, p	1	3	0	1	1	0	0	0	0	0	0	0	.333	1	3	0	1.000
Franco, 1b	3	13	3	4	7	0	0	1	1	0	0	1	.308	24	2	0	1.000
Bako, c	3	7	1	2	6	1	0	0	3	1	0	0	.286	17	0	0	1.000
Surhoff, lf	3	11	1	3	4	1	0	0	0	0	0	0	.273	7	0	0	1.000
Giles, 2b	3	12	2	3	4	1	0	0	1	0	0	3	.250	6	10	0	1.000
Sanchez, ss	3	9	1	2	3	1	0	0	0	0	0	2	.222	8	9	1	.944
Jordan, rf	3	11	1	2	5	0	0	1	2	0	0	5	.182	10	0	0	1.000
Karsay, p	1	0	0	0	0	0	0	0	0	0	0	0	.000	0	0	0	.000
Reed, p	1	0	0	0	0	0	0	0	0	0	0	0	.000	0	0	0	.000
Remlinger, p	1	0	0	0	0	0	0	0	0	0	0	0	.000	0	0	0	.000
Seanez, p	1	0	0	0	0	0	0	0	0	0	0	0	.000	0	0	0	.000
Martinez, ph	1	1	0	0	0	0	0	0	0	0	0	0	.000	0	0	0	.000
Smoltz, p	3	1	0	0	0	0	0	0	0	0	0	0	.000	0	0	0	.000
Burkett, p	1	2	0	0	0	0	0	0	0	0	0	1	.000	0	1	0	1.000
Caminiti, ph	2	2	0	0	0	0	0	0	0	0	0	1	.000	0	0	0	.000
Maddux, p	1	2	0	0	0	0	0	0	0	0	0	1	.000	0	0	0	.000
Totals	3	99	14	30	54	6	0	6	13	4	1	18	.303	81	32	1	.991

HOUSTON ASTROS' BATTING AND FIELDING AVERAGES

Player, position	G	AB	R	H	TB	2B	3B	HR	RBI	BB	IBB	SO	Avg.	PO	A	E	Avg.
Eusebio, c	1	3	1	2	3	1	0	0	0	0	0	0	.667	4	1	0	1.000
Ward, ph	2	2	1	1	4	0	0	1	2	0	0	0	.500	0	0	0	.000
Bagwell, 1b	3	7	0	3	3	0	0	0	0	5	0	1	.429	21	2	0	1.000
Castilla, 3b	3	11	1	3	6	0	0	1	1	0	0	3	.273	5	7	0	1.000
Ausmus, c-ph	3	8	1	2	5	0	0	1	2	0	0	0	.250	14	2	0	1.000
Alou, rf	3	12	0	2	3	1	0	0	1	0	0	1	.167	5	0	0	1.000
Berkman, lf	3	12	0	2	2	0	0	0	0	0	0	4	.167	6	0	0	1.000
Biggio, 2b	3	12	0	2	2	0	0	0	0	0	0	1	.167	6	7	0	1.000
Vizcaino, ph-ss	3	6	0	1	1	0	0	0	0	0	0	1	.167	3	3	0	1.000
Hidalgo, cf	3	8	1	1	1	0	0	0	0	3	0	2	.125	6	0	0	1.000
Cruz, p	2	0	0	0	0	0	0	0	0	0	0	0	.000	1	0	0	1.000
Dotel, p	2	0	0	0	0	0	0	0	0	0	0	0	.000	0	1	0	1.000
Jackson, p	2	0	0	0	0	0	0	0	0	0	0	0	.000	0	0	0	.000
Villone, p	1	0	0	0	0	0	0	0	0	0	0	0	.000	0	0	0	.000
Wagner, p	2	0	0	0	0	0	0	0	0	0	0	0	.000	0	0	0	.000
Williams, p	1	0	0	0	0	0	0	0	0	0	0	0	.000	0	0	0	.000

Player, position	G	AB	R	H	TB	2B	3B	HR	RBI	BB	IBB	SO	Avg.	PO	A	E	Avg.
Merced, ph	1	1	0	0	0	0	0	0	0	0	0	0	.000	0	0	0	.000
Mlicki, p	1	1	0	0	0	0	0	0	0	0	0	0	.000	0	0	0	.000
Reynolds, p	1	1	0	0	0	0	0	0	0	0	0	0	.000	0	3	0	1.000
Truby, ph	1	1	0	0	0	0	0	0	0	0	0	1	.000	0	0	0	.000
Miller, p	1	2	0	0	0	0	0	0	0	0	0	0	.000	0	0	0	.000
Lugo, ss-ph	3	8	1	0	0	0	0	0	0	0	0	2	.000	7	4	3	.786
Totals	3	95	6	19	30	2	0	3	6	8	0	16	.200	78	30	3	.973

ATLANTA BRAVES' PITCHING RECORDS

Pitcher	G	GS	CG	IP	H	R	ER	HR	BB	IBB	SO	HB	WP	W	L	Pct.	ERA
Glavine	1	1	0	8.0	6	0	0	0	2	0	3	0	0	1	0	1.000	0.00
Karsay	1	0	0	1.0	0	0	0	0	0	0	1	0	0	0	0	.000	0.00
Seanez	1	0	0	1.0	0	0	0	0	1	0	0	0	0	1	0	1.000	0.00
Reed	1	0	0	0.1	0	0	0	0	0	0	0	0	0	0	0	.000	0.00
Remlinger	1	0	0	0.1	0	0	0	0	0	0	0	0	0	0	0	.000	0.00
Smoltz	3	0	0	4.0	3	1	1	1	0	0	3	0	0	0	0	.000	2.25
Burkett	1	1	0	6.1	6	2	2	1	2	0	4	0	0	1	0	1.000	2.84
Maddux	1	1	0	6.0	4	3	2	1	3	0	5	0	0	0	0	.000	3.00
Totals	3	3	0	27.0	19	6	5	3	8	0	16	0	0	3	0	1.000	1.67

Shutout—Glavine and Smoltz (combined). Saves—Smoltz 2.

HOUSTON ASTROS' PITCHING RECORDS

Pitcher	G	GS	CG	IP	H	R	ER	HR	BB	IBB	SO	HB	WP	W	L	Pct.	ERA
Mlicki	1	1	0	5.0	4	1	0	0	2	0	0	0	0	0	1	.000	0.00
Cruz	2	0	0	2.2	1	0	0	0	1	1	1	0	0	0	0	.000	0.00
Villone	1	0	0	0.2	0	0	0	0	0	0	0	0	0	0	0	.000	0.00
Miller	1	1	0	7.0	7	2	2	1	0	0	6	0	0	0	0	.000	2.57
Dotel	2	0	0	3.1	5	2	2	1	0	0	5	0	0	0	0	.000	5.40
Wagner	2	0	0	1.2	1	1	1	1	0	0	3	1	1	0	0	.000	5.40
Reynolds	1	1	0	4.0	6	4	4	2	1	0	1	0	0	0	1	.000	9.00
Williams	1	0	0	1.0	3	1	1	1	0	0	1	0	0	0	0	.000	9.00
Jackson	2	0	0	0.2	3	3	2	0	0	0	1	0	0	0	1	.000	27.00
Totals	3	3	0	26.0	30	14	12	6	4	1	18	1	1	0	3	.000 *	4.15

No shutouts or saves.

SCORE BY INNINGS

Atlanta	1	3	1	2	0	0	0	6	1—14
Houston	0	0	0	0	2	1	2	0	1— 6

MISCELLANEOUS STATISTICS

Sacrifice hit—Bako.
Sacrifice fly—Jordan.
Stolen base—Surhoff.
Caught stealing—C. Jones, Franco, Bagwell, Jordan.
Double plays—Sanchez, Giles and Franco 3; Castilla and Bagwell 2; Lugo, Biggio and Bagwell 2; Ausmus and Lugo; Bagwell, Vizcaino and Cruz; Castilla and Biggio; Franco, Sanchez and Franco; Glavine, Sanchez and Franco.
Left on bases—Atlanta 4, 7, 3—14; Houston 5, 5, 6—16.
Hit by pitcher—By Wagner (Surhoff).
Passed balls—None.
Balks—None.
Time of games—First game, 2:51; second game, 2:41; third game, 2:33.
Attendance—First game, 35,553; second game, 35,704; third game, 39,923.
Umpires—Froemming, Meriwether, Winters, Gorman, Joyce, Everitt, Young, Tschida, Scott, Marquez, Marsh and J. Hirschbeck.
Official scorers—David Matheson, Mike Stamus, Trey Wilkinson.

ARIZONA VS. ST. LOUIS

HIGHLIGHTS

The bottom line: The Diamondbacks advanced to the National League Championship Series for the first time in franchise history by defeating St. Louis, 2-1, in dramatic fashion in Game 5. Second baseman Tony Womack delivered the series-clinching hit, singling with two outs in the ninth inning to drive home pinch-runner Danny Bautista from third base with the winning run. The Diamondbacks and Cardinals split the first four games of the series, with each team winning once in the other's ballpark. In the end, though, Arizona righthander Curt Schilling was too much for the Cardinals, who failed to advance to the NLCS for a second straight year.

Why the Diamondbacks won: Curt Schilling proved to be as dominant in the playoffs as he had been for most of the regular season. Schilling, a 22-game winner in 2001, held St. Louis to just one run while pitching two complete games. As a whole, the

Arizona pitching staff held Cardinal hitters to a .191 average in the series, including an anemic .060 (2-for-33) with runners in scoring position. N.L. Rookie of the Year Albert Pujols went two for 18, J.D. Drew batted .154 and Mark McGwire had just one hit in 11 at-bats. Steve Finley and Reggie Sanders, meanwhile, carried an Arizona offense that collectively hit just .237. Finley hit .421 in the series, Sanders .357.

The turning points:

Game 1: A matchup of the National League's only 22-game winners at Bank One Ballpark proved to be a true duel in the desert. The Diamondbacks' Curt Schilling, however, was a little better than the Cardinals' Matt Morris. Schilling, in his first postseason appearance since 1993, held the Cardinals to three hits in going the distance for a 1-0 victory. Morris, making the first postseason start of his career, was almost as good, holding the Diamondbacks to one run on six hits over seven innings. The game's lone run came in the fifth. After Morris grazed leadoff batter Damian Miller with a pitch, Schilling put down a sacrifice bunt with two strikes to move the runner to second. Tony Womack flied to left for the second out, but Steve Finley lined a shot up the middle to drive in Miller from second base.

Game 2: Righthander Woody Williams, acquired from the Padres in a profitable late-season trade, picked up where he left off in the regular season, limiting the Diamondbacks to four hits and one run in seven innings for a 4-1 St. Louis victory. He also struck out nine to improve his overall record as a Cardinal to 8-1. Rookie Albert Pujols provided all the offense Williams would need with a two-out, two-run, opposite-field homer in the first inning off Arizona ace Randy Johnson, who lost his major league record seventh straight postseason game. Williams pitched into the eighth before being lifted for Steve Kline with Craig Counsell at first and no outs. Pinch-hitter Greg Colbrunn singled off Kline to move Counsell to second base, the first Diamondback to get that far in the game. The runners advanced to second and third on Tony Womack's sacrifice bunt, and Counsell scored when Danny Bautista, pinch-hitting for Steve Finley, grounded out to third. Luis Gonzalez, 0-for-8 in the series at that point, ended the rally by grounding out to first.

Game 3: The Cardinals, in their first home play-off game, saw a 2-1 seventh-inning lead disappear quickly when light-hitting Craig Counsell pounded a three-run homer into the right-field seats at Busch Stadium, the crushing blow in a 5-3 Arizona victory. Cardinals starter Darryl Kile, who allowed two runs, three hits and five walks in six innings, gave way to reliever Mike Matthews after walking leadoff hitter Matt Williams in the seventh. Matthews retired the first batter he faced, Steve Finley, on a sacrifice attempt before Damian Miller singled. Pinch-hitter Greg Colbrunn followed with a broken bat single to left to drive in Williams to tie the score at 2-2. Tony Womack hit a sharp ground ball to second that

Fernando Vina fielded and fired to the plate to get Miller, keeping it a tie game. But Counsell, who had hit only four homers in 458 at-bats during the regular season, connected on a 3-1 pitch from Matthews that easily cleared the right-field wall to give the Diamondbacks a 5-3 lead.

Game 4: The Cardinals broke out of an offensive slump by scoring four runs in the first three innings off Arizona starter Albie Lopez. Fernando Vina led the way with a 3-for-3 performance, including a home run in the third inning that went just inside the foul pole down the right-field line. Along with his three hits, Vina scored two runs, drove in a pair and stole a base. Rookie Bud Smith allowed one run in five innings to get the win, with Dustin Hermanson (three perfect innings) and Steve Kline (the ninth inning) helping out in relief in a game that was delayed at the start by rain for more than 3 1/2 hours.

Game 5: As in Game 1, starters Matt Morris and Curt Schilling were spectacular. Morris allowed one run in eight innings while Schilling allowed one in nine, with both runs coming on home runs. Neither pitcher, however, was on the mound when the game was decided. Cardinals manager Tony La Russa lifted Morris, who had a blister on his right thumb, for Dave Veres in the ninth. The first batter Veres faced, Matt Williams, greeted him with a double down the right-field line. After the next hitter, Damian Miller, advanced pinch-runner Midre Cummings to third with a sacrifice bunt, La Russa lifted Veres in favor of Steve Kline, who intentionally walked pinch-hitter Greg Colbrunn to put runners on first and third with one out. The Diamondbacks gambled at this point with the suicide squeeze, but Tony Womack couldn't make contact with a breaking ball in the dirt and Cummings was tagged out easily. Colbrunn alertly moved to second on the play, where Danny Bautista replaced him as a pinch-runner. Four pitches later, Womack slapped a single to left field on an inside fastball. Kerry Robinson fielded the ball and made a strong throw to the plate but had no chance to get the speedy Bautista, who touched the plate to send the Diamondbacks into their first National League Championship Series.

Notable:

Cardinals: After the Game 1 loss, manager Tony La Russa benched Mark McGwire and J.D. Drew in favor of Miguel Cairo and Craig Paquette. Although Cairo, who had a career .429 average against Randy Johnson (6-for-14), was held hitless in three at-bats, the Cardinals wound up winning Game 2. ... McGwire was 0-for-6, with five strikeouts, against Curt Schilling in the series, dropping his lifetime average against the Arizona righthander to .190 (4-for-21). All four of hits were home runs. ... Mike Matthews, the victim of Craig Counsell's pivotal Game 3 homer, had held lefthanded batters to a .133 average with one homer in 98 at-bats during the regular season.

Diamondbacks: Prior to hitting his leadoff double in the ninth inning of Game 5, Matt Williams had been 0-for-15 in the series and had been booed unmercifully by fans at Bank One Ballpark. ... Arizona went 3-for-7 with runners in scoring position in Game 3 after going 1-for-15 in such situations in the first two games. ... Craig Counsell's go-ahead, three-run homer in Game 3 was the first of his career against a lefthanded pitcher.

Quotable:

Cardinals: Matt Morris, after losing Game 1: "I don't know how many pitches I threw . . . 120 or something. One or two of them decided the ballgame. You know Curt's going to go out there and put up zeros. All I can do is go out there and try to keep stride with him." ... Manager Tony La Russa, after watching Woody Williams outpitch Randy Johnson in Game 2: "One thing our team knew was the guy who was going to take the mound for us has got no fear. Based on what we've seen for two months, we thought he'd give us a chance to win." ... Mike Matthews, on the pitch he threw to Craig Counsell in Game 3: "It wasn't a good pitch. I didn't want to walk him because (Luis) Gonzalez was on deck, so I made a bad pitch to him." ... La Russa, on Morris' two losses: "I'm not a betting man, but 16 innings, two runs, and you would thought he would have won them both. He was great."

Diamondbacks: Center fielder Steve Finley, on Game 1 starter Curt Schilling: "I had a real good feeling we were going to win. I had a good feeling that if we put at least a run on the board, with his stuff it could have a chance to be lights out." ... Randy Johnson, on his postseason problems: "If someone is to blame, I guess I am. I gave up three runs (in Game 2). It seems like I've been in this position behind a microphone in the postseason every year." ... Manager Bob Brenly, on Game 4 starter Bud Smith of the Cardinals: "I thought he pitched a tremendous ballgame, especially after that first inning. He executed his pitches, put balls on the corners and kept it at the knees." ... Schilling, on the dramatic conclusion to Game 5: "It's a hair-pulling, nail-biting, teeth-grinding experience. We gave the fans everything they could want in this series. It was fitting that it would go down to the fifth game and the ninth inning."

GAME 1 BOX SCORE

ARIZONA 1, ST. LOUIS 0

TUESDAY, OCTOBER 9, AT ARIZONA

St. Louis	AB	R	H	RBI	PO	A
Vina, 2b	4	0	0	0	1	0
Polanco, 3b	4	0	0	0	1	1
Drew, rf	3	0	0	0	4	0
Pujols, lf	4	0	0	0	2	0
Edmonds, cf	4	0	1	0	1	0
McGwire, 1b	3	0	0	0	7	2
Renteria, ss	3	0	2	0	0	3
Matheny, c	2	0	0	0	6	0
Cairo, ph	1	0	0	0	0	0
Stechschulte, p	0	0	0	0	0	0
Veres, p	0	0	0	0	0	0
Morris, p	1	0	0	0	1	0
Marrero, ph-c	1	0	0	0	1	0
Totals	30	0	3	0	24	6

Arizona	AB	R	H	RBI	PO	A
Womack, ss	3	0	1	0	0	1
Finley, cf	4	0	3	1	2	0
Gonzalez, lf	4	0	0	0	0	0
Sanders, rf	4	0	2	0	4	0
Grace, 1b	3	0	2	0	10	0
M. Williams, 3b	4	0	0	0	0	2
Counsell, 2b	4	0	0	0	1	4
Miller, c	2	1	0	0	10	0
Schilling, p	3	0	0	0	0	2
Totals	31	1	8	1	27	9

St. Louis	0	0	0	0	0	0	0	0	0—0
Arizona	0	0	0	0	1	0	0	0	x—1

St. Louis	IP	H	R	ER	BB	SO
Morris (L)	7.0	6	1	1	2	6
Stechschulte	0.1	2	0	0	0	0
Veres	0.2	0	0	0	1	1

Arizona	IP	H	R	ER	BB	SO
Schilling (W)	9.0	3	0	0	1	9

E—Pujols, Womack. LOB—St. Louis 5, Arizona 11. 2B—Edmonds, Renteria, Finley, Sanders, Grace. SH—Morris, Schilling. HBP—By Morris (Miller). T—2:36. A—42,251. U—Marsh, plate; J. Hirschbeck, first; Young, second; Tschida, third; Scott, left field; Marquez, right field.

GAME 2 BOX SCORE

ST. LOUIS 4, ARIZONA 1

WEDNESDAY, OCTOBER 10, AT ARIZONA

St. Louis	AB	R	H	RBI	PO	A
Vina, 2b	4	0	1	0	1	1
Polanco, 3b	3	0	2	1	0	3
Renteria, ss	3	1	0	0	2	0
Pujols, 1b	4	1	2	2	8	1
Edmonds, cf	2	1	0	0	1	0
Paquette, rf-lf	4	0	1	0	2	0
Matheny, c	0	0	0	0	0	0
Cairo, lf	3	0	0	0	1	0
Drew, rf	1	0	0	0	1	0
Marrero, c	3	0	0	0	9	0
Robinson, ph-lf	1	0	0	1	0	0
W. Williams, p	3	1	1	0	2	0
Kline, p	0	0	0	0	0	1
Totals	31	4	7	4	27	6

Arizona	AB	R	H	RBI	PO	A
Womack, ss	3	0	0	0	1	2
Finley, cf	3	0	0	0	2	0
Bautista, ph-cf	1	0	0	1	1	0
Gonzalez, lf	4	0	0	0	1	0
Sanders, rf	4	0	1	0	3	0
Grace, 1b	4	0	1	0	6	0
M. Williams, 3b	3	0	0	0	0	2
Bell, 2b	3	0	1	0	3	2
Morgan, p	0	0	0	0	0	0
Swindell, p	0	0	0	0	0	1
Batista, p	0	0	0	0	0	0
Miller, c	2	0	0	0	9	1
Counsell, ph-2b	1	1	1	0	1	0
Johnson, p	2	0	0	0	0	0
Dellucci, ph	0	0	0	0	0	0
Colbrunn, ph	1	0	1	0	0	0
Barajas, c	0	0	0	0	0	0
Totals	31	1	5	1	27	9

St. Louis	2	0	1	0	0	0	0	0	1—4
Arizona	0	0	0	0	0	0	0	1	0—1

St. Louis	IP	H	R	ER	BB	SO
W. Williams (W)	*7.0	4	1	1	1	9
Kline (S)	2.0	1	0	0	0	0

Arizona	IP	H	R	ER	BB	SO
Johnson (L)	8.0	6	3	3	2	9
Morgan	†0.0	1	1	1	1	0
Swindell	0.1	0	0	0	0	0
Batista	0.2	0	0	0	0	0

*Pitched to one batter in eighth.
†Pitched to two batters in ninth.
E—M. Williams, Batista. DP—Arizona 2. LOB—St. Louis 6, Arizona 5. 2B—W. Williams. HR—Pujols. SH—Vina, Kline, Womack. SF—Polanco. T—3:15. A—41,793. U—J. Hirschbeck, plate; Young, first; Tschida, second; Scott, third; Marquez, left field; Marsh, right field.

*Pitched to one batter in seventh.
†Pitched to one batter in ninth.
DP—Arizona 1. LOB—Arizona 8, St. Louis 6. HR—Edmonds, Renteria, Counsell, Gonzalez. SH—Batista, Womack, Drew. SB—Polanco, Cairo. CS—Womack. WP—Kim. T—3:36. A—52,273. U—Winters, plate; Gorman, first; Joyce, second; Everitt, third; Froemming, left field; Meriwether, right field.

GAME 3 BOX SCORE

ARIZONA 5, ST. LOUIS 3

FRIDAY, OCTOBER 12, AT ST. LOUIS

Arizona	AB	R	H	RBI	PO	A
Womack, ss	2	1	0	0	2	1
Counsell, 2b	4	1	1	3	1	2
Gonzalez, lf	5	1	2	1	1	0
Bautista, rf-cf	5	0	0	0	1	0
Grace, 1b	3	0	0	0	10	1
M. Williams, 3b	2	0	0	0	1	7
Finley, cf	4	1	2	0	3	0
Kim, p	0	0	0	0	0	0
Miller, c	4	0	2	0	7	0
Batista, p	1	0	0	0	0	1
Colbrunn, ph	1	0	1	1	0	0
Cummings, pr	0	1	0	0	0	0
Anderson, p	0	0	0	0	0	0
Morgan, p	0	0	0	0	0	0
Sanders, rf	1	0	1	0	1	0
Totals	32	5	9	5	27	12

St. Louis	AB	R	H	RBI	PO	A
Vina, 2b	4	0	1	0	4	1
Polanco, 3b	3	1	1	0	0	3
Stechschulte, p	0	0	0	0	0	0
Kline, p	0	0	0	0	0	0
Drew, rf	2	0	0	0	1	0
Pujols, 1b	3	0	0	0	10	1
Edmonds, cf	4	1	1	2	2	1
Paquette, lf-3b	3	0	0	0	0	1
Robinson, ph	1	0	1	0	0	0
Renteria, ss	3	1	1	1	3	3
Matheny, c	4	0	0	0	7	1
Kile, p	2	0	0	0	0	1
Matthews, p	0	0	0	0	0	0
Timlin, p	0	0	0	0	0	0
Cairo, ph-lf	1	0	1	0	0	0
McGwire, ph	1	0	0	0	0	0
Totals	31	3	6	3	27	12

Arizona	0 0 0	0 0 1	4 0 0—5			
St. Louis	0 0 0	2 0 0	1 0 0—3			

Arizona	IP	H	R	ER	BB	SO
Batista (W)	6.0	3	2	2	1	4
Anderson	1.0	1	1	1	0	1
Morgan	0.2	1	0	0	1	0
Kim (S)	1.1	1	0	0	2	1

St. Louis	IP	H	R	ER	BB	SO
Kile	*6.0	3	2	2	5	5
Matthews (L)	0.2	4	3	3	0	0
Timlin	1.1	1	0	0	0	0
Stechschulte	†0.0	1	0	0	0	0
Kline	1.0	0	0	0	1	0

GAME 4 BOX SCORE

ST. LOUIS 4, ARIZONA 1

SATURDAY, OCTOBER 13, AT ST. LOUIS

Arizona	AB	R	H	RBI	PO	A
Womack, ss	4	0	1	0	1	4
Sanders, rf	3	1	0	0	3	0
Gonzalez, lf	2	0	1	0	1	0
Colbrunn, 1b	4	0	0	0	11	0
Finley, cf	4	0	2	1	1	0
M. Williams, 3b	3	0	0	0	0	3
Counsell, 2b	4	0	1	0	3	2
Miller, c	4	0	1	0	4	1
Lopez, p	1	0	0	0	0	0
Bell, ph	1	0	0	0	0	0
Anderson, p	0	0	0	0	0	3
Durazo, ph	1	0	0	0	0	0
Swindell, p	0	0	0	0	0	1
Morgan, p	0	0	0	0	0	0
Totals	31	1	6	1	24	14

St. Louis	AB	R	H	RBI	PO	A
Vina, 2b	3	2	3	2	5	5
Polanco, 3b	1	0	0	0	0	4
Drew, rf	4	0	1	1	2	0
Pujols, lf-1b	3	0	0	0	4	0
Edmonds, cf	3	1	1	1	4	0
McGwire, 1b	4	0	1	0	10	0
Kline, p	0	0	0	0	0	0
Renteria, ss	4	0	1	0	0	4
Marrero, c	3	0	0	0	2	0
Smith, p	1	1	0	0	0	2
Hermanson, p	1	0	0	0	0	1
Robinson, lf	0	0	0	0	0	0
Totals	27	4	7	4	27	16

Arizona	1	0 0	0 0 0	0 0 0—1		
St. Louis	1	1 2	0 0 0	0 0 x—4		

Arizona	IP	H	R	ER	BB	SO
Lopez (L)	3.0	4	4	4	3	0
Anderson	3.0	2	0	0	0	2
Swindell	1.1	1	0	0	0	2
Morgan	0.2	0	0	0	0	1

St. Louis	IP	H	R	ER	BB	SO
Smith (W)	5.0	4	1	1	4	2
Hermanson	3.0	0	0	0	0	0
Kline (S)	1.0	2	0	0	0	0

F—Polanco. DP—Arizona 1, St. Louis 2. LOB—Arizona 7, St. Louis 6. 2B—Womack. HR—Vina, Edmonds. SH—Polanco 3. SB—Sanders, Vina. HBP—By Anderson (Vina). T—2:47. A—52,194. U—Gorman, plate; Joyce, first; Everitt, second; Froemming, third; Meriwether, left field; Winters, right field.

STATISTICS

ARIZONA DIAMONDBACKS' BATTING AND FIELDING AVERAGES

Player, position	G	AB	R	H	TB	2B	3B	HR	RBI	BB	IBB	SO	Avg.	PO	A	E	Avg.
Finley, cf	5	19	1	8	9	1	0	0	2	0	0	2	.421	11	0	0	1.000
Sanders, rf	5	14	2	5	9	1	0	1	1	3	0	3	.357	12	0	0	1.000
Colbrunn, ph-1b	4	6	0	2	2	0	0	0	1	1	1	0	.333	11	0	0	1.000
Womack, ss	5	17	1	5	6	1	0	0	1	3	0	2	.294	8	11	2	.905
Miller, c	5	15	1	4	4	0	0	0	0	1	1	3	.267	39	3	0	1.000
Gonzalez, lf	5	19	1	5	8	0	0	1	1	2	0	4	.263	3	0	0	1.000

– 185 –

Player, position	G	AB	R	H	TB	2B	3B	HR	RBI	BB	IBB	SO	Avg.	PO	A	E	Avg.
								BATTING							FIELDING		
Bell, 2b-ph	2	4	0	1	1	0	0	0	0	0	0	1	.250	3	2	0	1.000
Grace, 1b	4	14	0	3	4	1	0	0	0	2	0	3	.214	32	2	0	1.000
Counsell, 2b-ph	5	16	2	3	6	0	0	1	3	2	0	2	.188	8	11	0	1.000
M. Williams, 3b	5	16	0	1	2	1	0	0	0	4	0	4	.063	2	15	1	.944
Anderson, p	2	0	0	0	0	0	0	0	0	0	0	0	.000	0	3	0	1.000
Barajas, c	1	0	0	0	0	0	0	0	0	0	0	0	.000	0	0	0	.000
Cummings, pr	2	0	1	0	0	0	0	0	0	0	0	0	.000	0	0	0	.000
Dellucci, ph	2	0	0	0	0	0	0	0	0	0	0	0	.000	0	0	0	.000
Kim, p	1	0	0	0	0	0	0	0	0	0	0	0	.000	0	0	0	.000
Morgan, p	3	0	0	0	0	0	0	0	0	0	0	0	.000	0	0	0	.000
Swindell, p	2	0	0	0	0	0	0	0	0	0	0	0	.000	0	2	0	1.000
Batista, p	2	1	0	0	0	0	0	0	0	0	0	0	.000	0	2	1	.667
Durazo, ph	1	1	0	0	0	0	0	0	0	0	0	0	.000	0	0	0	.000
Lopez, p	1	1	0	0	0	0	0	0	0	0	0	0	.000	0	0	0	.000
Johnson, p	1	2	0	0	0	0	0	0	0	0	0	2	.000	0	0	0	.000
Schilling, p	2	5	0	0	0	0	0	0	0	0	0	2	.000	1	3	0	1.000
Bautista, ph-cf-rf-pr	3	6	1	0	0	0	0	0	1	0	0	1	.000	2	0	0	1.000
Totals	5	156	10	37	51	5	0	3	10	18	2	29	.237	132	54	4	.979

ST. LOUIS CARDINALS' BATTING AND FIELDING AVERAGES

Player, position	G	AB	R	H	TB	2B	3B	HR	RBI	BB	IBB	SO	Avg.	PO	A	E	Avg.
								BATTING							FIELDING		
Robinson, ph-lf	4	2	0	1	1	0	0	0	1	0	0	0	.500	0	0	0	.000
W. Williams, p	1	3	1	1	2	1	0	0	0	0	0	1	.333	2	0	0	1.000
Vina, 2b	5	19	2	6	9	0	0	1	2	0	0	1	.316	14	8	0	1.000
Polanco, 3b	5	15	1	4	4	0	0	0	1	1	0	1	.267	1	15	1	.941
Edmonds, cf	5	17	3	4	11	1	0	2	3	3	0	6	.235	10	1	0	1.000
Renteria, ss	5	17	2	4	8	1	0	1	1	2	0	4	.235	7	14	1	.955
Matheny, c	4	10	0	2	2	0	0	0	0	0	0	0	.200	20	1	0	1.000
Cairo, ph-lf	3	5	0	1	1	0	0	0	0	0	0	1	.200	1	0	0	1.000
Drew, rf	5	13	1	2	5	0	0	1	2	3	0	1	.154	12	0	0	1.000
Paquette, rf-lf-3b	2	7	0	1	1	0	0	0	0	0	0	5	.143	2	1	0	1.000
Pujols, lf-1b	5	18	1	2	5	0	0	1	2	2	0	2	.111	25	2	1	.964
McGwire, 1b-ph	4	11	0	1	1	0	0	0	0	0	0	6	.091	24	2	0	1.000
Kline, p	4	0	0	0	0	0	0	0	0	0	0	0	.000	0	1	0	1.000
Matthews, p	1	0	0	0	0	0	0	0	0	0	0	0	.000	0	0	0	.000
Stechschulte, p	2	0	0	0	0	0	0	0	0	0	0	0	.000	0	0	0	.000
Timlin, p	1	0	0	0	0	0	0	0	0	0	0	0	.000	0	0	0	.000
Veres, p	2	0	0	0	0	0	0	0	0	0	0	0	.000	0	0	0	.000
Hermanson, p	1	1	0	0	0	0	0	0	0	0	0	1	.000	0	1	0	1.000
Smith, p	1	1	1	0	0	0	0	0	0	1	0	1	.000	0	2	0	1.000
Kile, p	1	2	0	0	0	0	0	0	0	0	0	2	.000	0	1	0	1.000
Morris, p	2	4	0	0	0	0	0	0	0	0	0	3	.000	1	1	0	1.000
Marrero, ph-c	3	7	0	0	0	0	0	0	0	0	0	0	.000	12	0	0	1.000
Totals	5	152	12	29	50	3	0	6	12	12	0	38	.191	131	50	3	.984

ARIZONA DIAMONDBACKS' PITCHING RECORDS

Pitcher	G	GS	CG	IP	H	R	ER	HR	BB	IBB	SO	HB	WP	W	L	Pct.	ERA
Swindell	2	0	0	1.2	1	0	0	0	0	0	2	0	0	0	0	.000	0.00
Kim	1	0	0	1.1	1	0	0	0	2	0	1	0	1	0	0	.000	0.00
Schilling	2	2	2	18.0	9	1	1	1	2	0	18	0	0	2	0	1.000	0.50
Anderson	2	0	0	4.0	3	1	1	1	0	0	3	1	0	0	0	.000	2.25
Batista	2	1	0	6.2	3	2	2	1	1	0	4	0	0	1	0	1.000	2.70
Johnson	1	1	0	8.0	6	3	3	1	2	0	9	0	0	0	1	.000	3.38
Morgan	3	0	0	2.0	2	1	1	0	2	0	1	0	0	0	0	.000	6.75
Lopez	1	1	0	3.0	4	4	4	2	3	0	0	0	0	0	1	.000	12.00
Totals	5	5	2	44.0	29	12	12	6	12	0	38	1	1	3	2	.600	2.45

Shutout—Schilling. Save—Kim.

ST. LOUIS CARDINALS' PITCHING RECORDS

Pitcher	G	GS	CG	IP	H	R	ER	HR	BB	IBB	SO	HB	WP	W	L	Pct.	ERA
Hermanson	1	0	0	3.0	0	0	0	0	0	0	0	0	0	0	0	.000	0.00
Timlin	1	0	0	1.1	1	0	0	0	0	0	0	0	0	0	0	.000	0.00
Veres	2	0	0	1.0	1	0	0	0	1	1	1	0	0	0	0	.000	0.00
Stechschulte	2	0	0	0.1	3	0	0	0	0	0	0	0	0	0	0	.000	0.00
Morris	2	2	0	15.0	13	2	2	1	5	0	12	1	0	0	1	.000	1.20
W. Williams	1	1	0	7.0	4	1	1	1	1	0	9	0	0	1	0	1.000	1.29
Smith	1	1	0	5.0	4	1	1	0	4	0	2	0	0	1	0	1.000	1.80
Kline	4	0	0	4.1	4	1	1	0	2	1	0	0	0	0	1	.000	2.08

Pitcher	G	GS	CG	IP	H	R	ER	HR	BB	IBB	SO	HB	WP	W	L	Pct.	ERA
Kile....................................	1	1	0	6.0	3	2	2	1	5	0	5	0	0	0	0	.000	3.00
Matthews	1	0	0	0.2	4	3	3	1	0	0	0	0	0	0	1	.000	40.50
Totals	5	5	0	43.2	37	10	10	3	18	2	29	1	0	2	3	.400	2.06

No shutouts. Saves—Kline 2.

SCORE BY INNINGS

Arizona	1	0	0		1	1	1		4	1	1—10
St. Louis	3	1	3		2	0	0		1	1	1—12

MISCELLANEOUS STATISTICS

Sacrifice hits—Polanco 3, Schilling 2, Womack 2, Batista, Drew, Kline, Miller, Morris, Robinson, Vina.
Sacrifice flies—Polanco.
Stolen bases—Cairo, Polanco, Sanders, Vina.
Caught stealing—Cummings, Womack.
Double plays—Polanco, Renteria and McGwire; Polanco, Vina and McGwire; Renteria, Vina and Pujols; Vina, Renteria and McGwire;
    M. Williams, Bell and Grace; M. Williams, Counsell and Colbrunn; M. Williams and Grace; Womack, Bell and Grace.
Left on bases—Arizona 11, 5, 8, 7, 9—40; St. Louis 5, 6, 6, 6, 7—30.
Hit by pitcher—By Anderson (Vina), by Morris (Miller).
Passed balls—None.
Balks—None.
Time of games—First game, 2:36; second game, 3:15; third game, 3:36; fourth game, 2:47; fifth game, 3:05.
Attendance—First game, 42,251; second game, 41,793; third game, 52,273; fourth game, 52,194; fifth game, 42,810.
Umpires—Marsh, J. Hirschbeck, Young, Tschida, Scott, Marquez, Winters, Gorman, Joyce, Everitt, Froemming, Meriwether.
Official scorers—Bob Eger, Jeff Durbin.

A.L. CHAMPIONSHIP SERIES

HIGHLIGHTS

The bottom line: The Mariners may have won an American League record 116 games during the regular season, but that didn't mean much to the Yankees, whose 1998 record Seattle surpassed. A Seattle offense that scored a major league-high 927 runs in the regular season scored just 22 in five games against New York. Take away the 14 runs the Mariners scored in their only victory, in Game 3, and they scored just eight runs in four games. Seattle's pitchers weren't bad, but they couldn't hold the team close in most games. The bullpen, which had been a strength of the Mariners all season, struggled mightily. The only relievers who didn't allow runs in the series were ex-Yankee Jeff Nelson and veteran lefty Norm Charlton. The Yankees, on the other hand, got clutch hitting and clutch pitching performances. Some came from unexpected sources such as Alfonso Soriano, who belted a game-winning home run in Game 4, and Paul O'Neill, who hit .417 with two home runs and three RBIs in the penultimate postseason series of his career.

Why the Yankees won: Their pitchers were as clutch as their hitters. Lefthander Andy Pettitte pitched two gems, allowing only 11 hits and four runs in 14.1 innings of work, and Mike Mussina showed little postseason rust, earning a win in his first start in an American League Championship Series game since 1997. The Mariners' big hitters during the regular season were little hitters vs. New York. American League MVP Ichiro Suzuki batted .222, Edgar Martinez hit .150 and John Olerud hit .211 with just three RBIs. Meanwhile, five Yankee regulars batted .250 or better.

The turning points:

Game 1: It didn't take long for the Yankees to gain control. They took a 1-0 lead in the second inning of Game 1 when Jorge Posada walked, advanced to second on a single by Alfonso Soriano and came home when Chuck Knoblauch singled off the glove of Seattle third baseman David Bell. Then, in the fourth inning, the Yankees scored two more runs off Mariners starter Aaron Sele, with Posada playing the role of catalyst again. After narrowly beating a perfect throw from right fielder Ichiro Suzuki to the second-base bag for a double, Posada came home when Paul O'Neill drove a Sele pitch over the right-field wall to give the Yankees a 3-0 lead. Although the Mariners threatened in the fifth, Pettitte worked out of it, allowing only one run after Seattle put runners at second and third with no outs.

Game 2: Like in Game 1, the Yankees jumped on top early, scoring all three of their runs in the second inning off righthanded starter Freddy Garcia. Two of the runs came home on a double by Scott Brosius, another on a single by Chuck Knoblauch.

On Brosius' double, left fielder Stan Javier failed to field the ball cleanly in the corner, allowing two runs to score instead of one. Javier later hit a two-run homer that would have tied the score at 2-2, but because of his defensive miscue, his club still trailed by a run. Mike Mussina was solid for the Yankees, allowing two runs on four hits in six innings before being relieved by Ramiro Mendoza and Mariano Rivera, the latter of whom struck out three to pick up his second save of the series.

Game 3: The Mariners got some timely hits and some stellar defensive plays to clobber the Yankees, 14-3, for their first (and what would be only) win in the series. In the third inning, left fielder Stan Javier robbed Alfonso Soriano of a home run with a leaping catch. An inning later, right fielder Ichiro Suzuki snared a Bernie Williams drive to the wall to keep the Yankees' lead at 2-0. The New York defense was not nearly as foolproof. In the fifth inning pitcher Orlando Hernandez fielded what should have been an inning-ending double play ball but threw wide of second baseman Soriano, keeping the inning alive. Hernandez then threw 10 of his next 14 pitches out of the strike zone, walking Ichiro and Mark McLemore to load the bases before Bret Boone flared a base hit to left that escaped the glove of outfielder Chuck Knoblauch to tie the game 2-2. Edgar Martinez struck out to end the inning, but the Mariners picked up right where they left off in the sixth inning. John Olerud led off with a home run and the rout was on. The Mariners sent 11 men to the plate in the sixth inning and seven of them scored.

Game 4: Although Mariners righthander Paul Abbott and Yankees righthander Roger Clemens worked five innings apiece and held the other team scoreless, neither starting pitcher was a deciding factor in the outcome. The bullpens were. Norm Charlton and Jeff Nelson held the Yankees scoreless for two innings, while Ramiro Mendoza pitched three solid innings for New York, allowing only a Bret Boone homer in the eighth. Bernie Williams answered Boone's homer with a round-tripper of his own off of Arthur Rhodes in the bottom of the inning to tie the game. After Rivera threw just three pitches in a 1-2-3 top of the ninth, Alfonso Soriano hammered a Kazuhiro Sasaki pitch over the center-field wall with a runner on base to give the Yankees a 3-1 victory, putting them within a win of their fourth straight American League pennant.

Game 5: Trailing three games to one and facing postseason elimination, the Mariners missed a chance to take an early lead in Game 5 when, after a one-out double by Mike Cameron in the first, New York left fielder Chuck Knoblauch made a great catch of a soft line drive off the bat of Edgar Martinez to save a run. Two innings later, in the Yankees' third, Seattle third baseman David Bell misplayed a Scott Brosius grounder for an error.

Alfonso Soriano then singled to center field. After a sacrifice bunt by Knoblauch, Derek Jeter hit a sacrifice fly to give the Yankees a 1-0 lead. David Justice followed up with an RBI double. Then Bernie Williams homered into the Yankee Stadium monuments in left-center to increase New York's lead to 4-0, a lead too great for the offensively challenged Mariners to overcome.

Notable:

Mariners: Bret Boone, who led the American League with 141 RBIs during the regular season, didn't drive in a run in the ALCS until Game 3, when he drove in five. ... Aaron Sele's career postseason record fell to 0-6, with four of the losses to the Yankees. ... The Mariners had just four runs and 10 hits in the first two games, both losses. ... Paul Abbott's eight walks in Game 4 were one shy of the League Championship Series record set by Baltimore's Mike Cuellar in 1974 against Oakland. ... The Mariners joined baseball's only other 116-win team, the 1906 Cubs, as a postseason dud. The '06 Cubs lost to the crosstown White Sox in six games in the World Series.

Yankees: Series MVP Andy Pettitte was 0-2 with an 8.03 ERA against Seattle during the regular season-and 2-0 with a 2.51 ERA in the playoffs. ... Paul O'Neill's home run in Game 1 was his first in a postseason game since 1998. ... Scott Brosius had been 1-for-20 in the postseason (stretching back to 2000) before his two-run double in the second inning of Game 2. ... Mike Mussina held Seattle's 2-3-4-5 hitters to a 2-for-16 showing in Game 2. ... The 14 runs allowed by the Yankees in Game 3 were the most ever allowed by a Yankee team in a postseason game. ... The Yankees ended the series 40-11 in their last 51 playoff games, a .784 winning percentage. ... Bernie Williams' two-run homer in the third inning of Game 5 was his 16th in postseason play, one better than Babe Ruth on the all-time list. Williams ended the series one homer behind Cleveland's Jim Thome and two back of co-leaders Mickey Mantle and Reggie Jackson.

Quotable:

Mariners: OF Ichiro Suzuki (through a translator), on playing in his first ALCS: "I didn't change my approach toward the game from the way I played all season. I feel I'm just normal. I feel the same as I do all the time. My feet are firmly on the field." ... Bret Boone, on losing Game 1: "The bottom line is we didn't get anything going." ... Manager Lou Piniella, after his team lost the first two games of the series at home: "We're going to be back here to play Game 6, OK? I've got confidence in my baseball club. We've gone to New York and beat this baseball team five out of six times (in the regular season) and we're going to do it again." ... Boone, after Seattle fell behind 2-0 in the series: "I don't think there's any pressure on us right now. It's just good pitching by the Yankees." ... LHP Jamie Moyer, on winning Game 3: "I felt like once I got to the fourth inning, I

got a second wind. Why that is, I have no idea. I just tried to focus on making good pitches." ... Tom Lampkin, on the failure of the Seattle bullpen to nail down the win in Game 4: "I think in that situation again, I would take our pen in a heartbeat. Everybody on our club has confidence in them." ... Piniella, after his club failed to deliver on his guarantee that the series would resume in Seattle for Game 6: "First of all, I won't say it again. You live and learn. I just had confidence in my team. That was it."

Yankees: LHP Andy Pettitte, on Seattle star Ichiro Suzuki: "He causes chaos when he gets on. You've got to worry about him because you realize he can steal." ... Pettitte, on his team's play during the postseason: "I think our whole team just takes it to a different level once we get to the postseason. We have a confidence." ... Mike Mussina, on the first ALCS win of his career, in Game 2: "It was work. It was tough. It was a struggle. It was a fight the whole time." ... Manager Joe Torre, on Chuck Knoblauch: "This postseason has been really big for him because he's been causing problems. I'm happy for him and I'm happy for us. We're a better team when he's leading off because we don't have to mess with our lineup that much." ... Torre, after watching the Mariners score 14 runs in Game 3: "It's just something you dismiss, and you hope they got tired today. Maybe they won't be as spry tomorrow." ... Alfonso Soriano (through an interpreter), on his game-winning home run in Game 4: "It's something very big to be a hero in a game like this. It was a very big moment. It was a very big time for me." ... Torre, on the 2001 Yankees: "I have never been prouder of a group of men in my life. Whatever motivates us, I know the NY on your cap had a lot to do with it. This ballclub will be remembered by me forever."

GAME 1 BOX SCORE

NEW YORK 4, SEATTLE 2

WEDNESDAY, OCTOBER 17, AT SEATTLE

New York	AB	R	H	RBI	PO	A
Knoblauch, lf	5	0	3	1	1	0
Jeter, ss	5	0	0	0	1	3
Justice, dh	4	0	1	1	0	0
Williams, cf	3	0	0	0	1	0
T. Martinez, 1b	4	0	0	0	11	2
Posada, c	3	2	1	0	7	0
O'Neill, rf	3	1	2	2	0	0
Spencer, ph-rf	1	0	0	0	1	0
Brosius, 3b	3	0	0	0	0	3
Soriano, 2b	4	1	2	0	2	6
Pettitte, p	0	0	0	0	1	0
Rivera, p	0	0	0	0	2	1
Totals	35	4	9	4	27	15

Seattle	AB	R	H	RBI	PO	A
Suzuki, rf	4	1	1	0	2	0
Guillen, ss	3	0	0	0	2	3
Javier, ph	1	0	0	0	0	0
Boone, 2b	3	0	1	0	3	2
E. Martinez, dh	4	1	1	0	0	0
Cameron, cf	2	0	1	0	4	0
Olerud, 1b	3	0	0	1	8	1
Buhner, lf	3	0	0	0	3	0
D. Wilson, c	3	0	0	0	5	0

Seattle	AB	R	H	RBI	PO	A
Bell, 3b	2	0	0	0	0	1
McLemore, ph	1	0	0	0	0	0
Sele, p	0	0	0	0	0	0
Charlton, p	0	0	0	0	0	0
Paniagua, p	0	0	0	0	0	0
Totals	29	2	4	1	27	7

New York	0	1	0	2	0	0	0	0	1—4
Seattle	0	0	0	0	1	0	0	0	1—2

New York	IP	H	R	ER	BB	SO
Pettitte (W)	8.0	3	1	1	1	7
Rivera (S)	1.0	1	1	1	1	0

Seattle	IP	H	R	ER	BB	SO
Sele (L)	6.0	7	3	3	3	3
Charlton	1.1	0	0	0	1	2
Paniagua	1.2	2	1	1	0	0

DP—New York 2. LOB—New York 9, Seattle 2. 2B—Knoblauch, Posada, Suzuki, Cameron. HR—O'Neill. SH—Brosius. SB—Soriano. WP—Rivera 2. T—3:06. A—47,644. U—Montague, plate; Bell, first; Cederstrom, second; Reliford, third; Shulock, left field; Welke, right field.

GAME 2 BOX SCORE

NEW YORK 3, SEATTLE 2

THURSDAY, OCTOBER 18, AT SEATTLE

New York	AB	R	H	RBI	PO	A
Knoblauch, lf	3	0	2	1	6	0
Jeter, ss	2	0	1	0	2	0
Justice, dh	3	0	0	0	0	0
Williams, cf	4	0	1	0	2	0
T. Martinez, 1b	4	1	2	0	7	1
Posada, c	3	1	0	0	6	1
O'Neill, rf	3	0	1	0	2	0
Spencer, rf	1	0	1	0	0	0
Brosius, 3b	4	1	1	2	1	2
Soriano, 2b	4	0	0	0	1	2
Mussina, p	0	0	0	0	0	0
Mendoza, p	0	0	0	0	0	0
Rivera, p	0	0	0	0	0	0
Totals	31	3	9	3	27	6

Seattle	AB	R	H	RBI	PO	A
Suzuki, rf	3	0	1	0	1	0
McLemore, ss	4	0	0	0	2	1
Boone, 2b	4	0	1	0	2	2
E. Martinez, dh	4	0	1	0	0	0
Gipson, pr-dh	0	0	0	0	0	0
Olerud, 1b	4	0	0	0	7	0
Cameron, cf	3	1	0	0	3	0
Javier, lf	3	1	1	2	4	0
D. Wilson, c	3	0	2	0	8	2
Martin, ph	1	0	0	0	0	0
Bell, 3b	4	0	0	0	0	1
Garcia, p	0	0	0	0	0	1
Rhodes, p	0	0	0	0	0	0
Nelson, p	0	0	0	0	0	0
Totals	33	2	6	2	27	7

New York	0	3	0	0	0	0	0	0	0—3
Seattle	0	0	0	2	0	0	0	0	0—2

New York	IP	H	R	ER	BB	SO
Mussina (W)	6.0	4	2	2	1	3
Mendoza	1.1	2	0	0	1	0
Rivera (S)	1.2	0	0	0	0	3

Seattle	IP	H	R	ER	BB	SO
Garcia (L)	7.1	7	3	3	4	6
Rhodes	1.0	1	0	0	0	1
Nelson	0.2	1	0	0	0	1

E—Williams. DP—New York 1, Seattle 2. LOB—New York 6, Seattle 7. 2B—Spencer, Brosius. HR—Javier. SH—Jeter. SB—Spencer. CS—Knoblauch, T. Martinez. HBP—By Mussina (Cameron). T—3:25. A—47,791. U—Bell, plate; Cederstrom, first; Reliford, second; Shulock, third; Welke, left field; Montague, right field.

GAME 3 BOX SCORE

SEATTLE 14, NEW YORK 3

SATURDAY, OCTOBER 20, AT NEW YORK

Seattle	AB	R	H	RBI	PO	A
Suzuki, rf	3	2	1	0	2	0
Guillen, ph-ss	1	0	0	0	2	1
McLemore, ss-lf-2b	4	1	1	3	0	0
Boone, 2b	5	1	3	5	2	5
Buhner, ph-rf	1	1	1	1	0	0
E. Martinez, dh	5	0	0	0	0	0
Martin, ph-dh	1	1	1	0	0	0
Olerud, 1b	5	1	2	2	10	1
Javier, lf	5	1	2	0	3	0
Gipson, pr-rf-lf	1	1	0	0	0	0
Cameron, cf	4	2	0	0	1	0
Lampkin, c	2	0	1	0	5	0
D. Wilson, ph-c	3	2	0	0	1	0
Bell, 3b	5	1	2	2	0	3
Moyer, p	0	0	0	0	1	1
Paniagua, p	0	0	0	0	0	0
Halama, p	0	0	0	0	0	0
Totals	45	14	15	13	27	11

New York	AB	R	H	RBI	PO	A
Knoblauch, lf	3	0	0	0	2	0
Bellinger, lf	1	0	0	0	1	0
Jeter, ss	3	0	1	0	1	1
E. Wilson, ss	1	0	1	0	0	0
Justice, dh	2	1	1	1	0	0
Williams, cf	4	1	1	2	2	0
T. Martinez, 1b	3	0	0	0	3	0
Sojo, 1b	1	0	0	0	4	0
Posada, c	3	0	0	0	9	1
Greene, c	1	0	0	0	1	0
O'Neill, rf	2	0	0	0	2	0
Spencer, ph-rf	2	0	1	0	0	0
Brosius, 3b	2	0	0	0	0	0
Velarde, ph-3b	1	0	0	0	0	2
Soriano, 2b	3	1	2	0	2	2
Hernandez, p	0	0	0	0	0	1
Stanton, p	0	0	0	0	0	0
Wohlers, p	0	0	0	0	0	0
Witasick, p	0	0	0	0	0	1
Totals	32	3	7	3	27	8

Seattle	0	0	0	0	2	7	2	1	2—14
New York	2	0	0	0	0	0	0	1	0—3

Seattle	IP	H	R	ER	BB	SO
Moyer (W)	7.0	4	2	2	1	5
Paniagua	1.0	3	1	1	0	0
Halama	1.0	0	0	0	0	0

New York	IP	H	R	ER	BB	SO
Hernandez (L)	*5.0	5	5	4	5	7
Stanton	0.1	1	3	3	1	0
Wohlers	†0.2	3	3	1	1	1
Witasick	3.0	6	3	3	0	2

*Pitched to three batters in sixth.
†Pitched to three batters in seventh.

E—Stanton, Wohlers. DP—Seattle 2. LOB—Seattle 11, New York 4. 2B—E. Martinez. 3B—McLemore, Martin. HR—Boone, Buhner, Olerud, Williams. SB—Suzuki, Javier. HBP—By Moyer (Justice). T—3:49. A—56,517. U—Cederstrom, plate; Reliford, first; Shulock, second; Welke, third; Montague, left field; Bell, right field.

GAME 4 BOX SCORE

NEW YORK 3, SEATTLE 1

SUNDAY, OCTOBER 21, AT NEW YORK

Seattle	AB	R	H	RBI	PO	A
Suzuki, rf	3	0	0	0	1	0
McLemore, ss	4	0	0	0	3	1
Boone, 2b	3	1	1	1	0	2

Seattle	AB	R	H	RBI	PO	A
E. Martinez, dh	3	0	0	0	0	0
Olerud, 1b	4	0	1	0	12	1
Javier, lf	4	0	0	0	2	0
Cameron, cf	3	0	0	0	1	0
Lampkin, c	2	0	0	0	5	2
Bell, 3b	3	0	0	0	0	4
Abbott, p	0	0	0	0	1	2
Charlton, p	0	0	0	0	0	0
Nelson, p	0	0	0	0	0	0
Rhodes, p	0	0	0	0	0	0
Sasaki, p	0	0	0	0	0	0
Totals	29	1	2	1	25	12

New York	AB	R	H	RBI	PO	A
Knoblauch, lf	3	0	0	0	1	0
Jeter, ss	4	0	0	0	1	4
Justice, dh	4	0	0	0	0	0
Williams, cf	2	1	1	1	1	0
T. Martinez, 1b	4	0	1	0	9	1
Posada, c	1	0	0	0	10	1
O'Neill, rf	1	0	0	0	1	0
Spencer, ph-rf	1	0	0	0	0	0
Brosius, 3b	3	1	1	0	1	1
Soriano, 2b	2	1	1	2	1	2
Clemens, p	0	0	0	0	0	1
Mendoza, p	0	0	0	0	1	0
Rivera, p	0	0	0	0	1	0
Totals	25	3	4	3	27	10

```
Seattle ............  0 0 0   0 0 0   0 1  0—1
New York ...........  0 0 0   0 0 0   0 1  2—3
```
One out when winning run scored

Seattle	IP	H	R	ER	BB	SO
Abbott	5.0	0	0	0	8	2
Charlton	0.1	1	0	0	1	0
Nelson	1.2	0	0	0	1	2
Rhodes	1.0	1	1	1	0	1
Sasaki (L)	0.1	2	2	2	0	0

New York	IP	H	R	ER	BB	SO
Clemens	5.0	1	0	0	4	7
Mendoza	3.0	1	1	1	1	3
Rivera (W)	1.0	0	0	0	0	0

DP—Seattle 1. LOB—Seattle 6, New York 8. 2B—T. Martinez. HR—Boone, Williams, Soriano. SH—Brosius. SB—Suzuki, Soriano. CS—Williams. WP—Clemens. T—3:24. A—56,375. U—Reliford, plate; Shulock, first; Welke, second; Montague, third; Bell, left field; Cederstrom, right field.

Seattle	AB	R	H	RBI	PO	A
Suzuki, lf-rf	5	0	1	1	1	0
Cameron, cf	5	0	2	0	4	0
Boone, 2b	4	0	0	0	2	2
E. Martinez, dh	4	0	0	0	0	0
Buhner, rf	2	1	1	0	0	0
Javier, ph-lf	1	0	0	0	0	0
Olerud, 1b	3	1	1	0	9	0
D. Wilson, c	4	0	0	0	8	0
Guillen, ss	4	1	2	0	1	2
Bell, 3b	2	0	1	2	0	3
McLemore, ph	1	0	1	0	0	0
Sele, p	0	0	0	0	0	0
Halama, p	0	0	0	0	0	0
Pineiro, p	0	0	0	0	0	0
Paniagua, p	0	0	0	0	0	1
Totals	35	3	9	3	24	8

New York	AB	R	H	RBI	PO	A
Knoblauch, lf	4	0	1	1	3	0
Jeter, ss	3	0	0	2	1	1
Justice, dh	5	2	3	2	0	0
Williams, cf	4	2	1	2	3	0
T. Martinez, 1b	5	2	2	3	9	1
Posada, c	4	1	2	0	2	0
O'Neill, rf	3	1	2	1	2	0
Spencer, pr-rf	2	1	0	0	1	0
Brosius, 3b	4	1	1	0	3	3
Soriano, 2b	2	2	1	0	2	1
Pettitte, p	0	0	0	0	0	2
Mendoza, p	0	0	0	0	0	0
Stanton, p	0	0	0	0	0	0
Rivera, p	0	0	0	0	1	0
Totals	36	12	13	11	27	8

```
Seattle ............  0 0 0   0 0 0   3 0 0— 3
New York ...........  0 0 4   1 0 4   0 3 x—12
```

Seattle	IP	H	R	ER	BB	SO
Sele (L)	4.0	4	5	1	1	2
Halama	*1.0	3	3	3	0	0
Pineiro	2.0	4	1	1	2	5
Paniagua	1.0	2	3	3	1	1

New York	IP	H	R	ER	BB	SO
Pettitte (W)	6.1	8	3	3	1	1
Mendoza	1.0	0	0	0	0	1
Stanton	0.2	0	0	0	1	0
Rivera	1.0	1	0	0	0	0

*Pitched to three batters in sixth.
E—Bell, Soriano. DP—New York 1. LOB—Seattle 8, New York 7. 2B—Cameron, Justice, Brosius. HR—Williams, T. Martinez, O'Neill. SH—Bell, Knoblauch. SF—Jeter. HBP—By Sele (Soriano). WP—Pineiro, Paniagua. T—3:18. A—56,370. U—Shulock, plate; Welke, first; Montague, second; Bell, third; Cederstrom, left field; Reliford, right field.

STATISTICS

NEW YORK YANKEES' BATTING AND FIELDING AVERAGES

Player, position	G	AB	R	H	TB	2B	3B	HR	RBI	BB	IBB	SO	Avg.	PO	A	E	Avg.
E. Wilson, ss	1	1	0	1	1	0	0	0	0	0	0	0	1.000	0	0	0	.000
O'Neill, rf	5	12	2	5	11	0	0	2	3	1	0	0	.417	7	0	0	1.000
Soriano, 2b	5	15	5	6	9	0	0	1	2	3	0	3	.400	8	13	1	.955
Knoblauch, lf	5	18	0	6	7	1	0	0	3	2	0	3	.333	13	0	0	1.000
Spencer, ph-rf-pr	5	7	1	2	3	1	0	0	0	1	0	1	.286	2	0	0	1.000
Justice, dh	5	18	3	5	6	1	0	0	4	3	0	1	.278	0	0	0	.000
T. Martinez, 1b	5	20	3	5	9	1	0	1	3	0	0	4	.250	39	5	0	1.000
Williams, cf	5	17	4	4	13	0	0	3	5	5	0	4	.235	9	0	1	.900
Posada, c	5	14	2	3	4	1	0	0	0	6	1	7	.214	34	3	0	1.000

A.L. Championship Series

2001 REVIEW

Player, position	G	AB	R	H	TB	2B	3B	HR	RBI	BB	IBB	SO	Avg.	PO	A	E	Avg.
Brosius, 3b	5	16	3	3	5	2	0	0	2	0	0	6	.188	5	9	0	1.000
Jeter, ss	5	17	0	2	2	0	0	0	2	2	0	2	.118	6	9	0	1.000
Clemens, p	1	0	0	0	0	0	0	0	0	0	0	0	.000	0	1	0	1.000
Hernandez, p	1	0	0	0	0	0	0	0	0	0	0	0	.000	0	1	0	1.000
Mendoza, p	3	0	0	0	0	0	0	0	0	0	0	0	.000	1	0	0	1.000
Mussina, p	1	0	0	0	0	0	0	0	0	0	0	0	.000	0	0	0	.000
Pettitte, p	2	0	0	0	0	0	0	0	0	0	0	0	.000	1	2	0	1.000
Rivera, p	4	0	0	0	0	0	0	0	0	0	0	0	.000	4	1	0	1.000
Stanton, p	2	0	0	0	0	0	0	0	0	0	0	0	.000	0	0	1	.000
Witasick, p	1	0	0	0	0	0	0	0	0	0	0	0	.000	0	1	0	1.000
Wohlers, p	1	0	0	0	0	0	0	0	0	0	0	0	.000	0	0	1	.000
Bellinger, lf	1	1	0	0	0	0	0	0	0	0	0	0	.000	1	0	0	1.000
Greene, c	1	1	0	0	0	0	0	0	0	0	0	0	.000	1	0	0	1.000
Sojo, 1b	1	1	0	0	0	0	0	0	0	0	0	0	.000	4	0	0	1.000
Velarde, ph-3b	1	1	0	0	0	0	0	0	0	0	0	0	.000	0	2	0	1.000
Totals	5	159	25	42	70	7	0	7	24	23	1	31	.264	135	47	4	.978

SEATTLE MARINERS' BATTING AND FIELDING AVERAGES

Player, position	G	AB	R	H	TB	2B	3B	HR	RBI	BB	IBB	SO	Avg.	PO	A	E	Avg.
Martin, ph-dh	2	2	1	1	3	0	1	0	0	0	0	0	.500	0	0	0	.000
Buhner, lf-ph-rf	3	6	2	2	5	0	0	1	1	1	0	3	.333	3	0	0	1.000
Boone, 2b	5	19	2	6	12	0	0	2	6	2	0	2	.316	9	13	0	1.000
Guillen, ss-ph	3	8	1	2	2	0	0	0	0	0	0	1	.250	5	6	0	1.000
Lampkin, c	2	4	0	1	1	0	0	0	0	1	0	2	.250	10	2	0	1.000
Suzuki, rf-lf	5	18	3	4	5	1	0	0	1	4	2	4	.222	7	0	0	1.000
Javier, ph-lf	5	14	2	3	6	0	0	1	2	1	0	3	.214	9	0	0	1.000
Olerud, 1b	5	19	2	4	7	0	0	1	3	2	0	4	.211	45	3	0	1.000
Bell, 3b	5	16	1	3	3	0	0	0	4	0	0	3	.188	0	12	1	.923
Cameron, cf	5	17	3	3	5	2	0	0	0	4	0	4	.176	13	0	0	1.000
D. Wilson, c-ph	4	13	2	2	2	0	0	0	0	0	0	1	.154	22	2	0	1.000
E. Martinez, dh	5	20	1	3	4	1	0	0	0	1	0	6	.150	0	0	0	.000
McLemore, ph-ss-lf-2b	5	14	1	2	4	0	1	0	3	2	0	2	.143	5	2	0	1.000
Abbott, p	1	0	0	0	0	0	0	0	0	0	0	0	.000	1	2	0	1.000
Charlton, p	2	0	0	0	0	0	0	0	0	0	0	0	.000	0	1	0	1.000
Garcia, p	1	0	0	0	0	0	0	0	0	0	0	0	.000	0	1	0	1.000
Halama, p	2	0	0	0	0	0	0	0	0	0	0	0	.000	0	0	0	.000
Moyer, p	1	0	0	0	0	0	0	0	0	0	0	0	.000	1	1	0	1.000
Nelson, p	2	0	0	0	0	0	0	0	0	0	0	0	.000	0	0	0	.000
Paniagua, p	3	0	0	0	0	0	0	0	0	0	0	0	.000	0	1	0	1.000
Pineiro, p	1	0	0	0	0	0	0	0	0	0	0	0	.000	0	0	0	.000
Rhodes, p	2	0	0	0	0	0	0	0	0	0	0	0	.000	0	0	0	.000
Sasaki, p	1	0	0	0	0	0	0	0	0	0	0	0	.000	0	0	0	.000
Sele, p	2	0	0	0	0	0	0	0	0	0	0	0	.000	0	0	0	.000
Gipson, pr-dh-rf-lf	2	1	1	0	0	0	0	0	0	0	0	0	.000	0	0	0	.000
Totals	5	171	22	36	59	4	2	5	20	18	2	35	.211	130	45	1	.994

NEW YORK YANKEES' PITCHING RECORDS

Pitcher	G	GS	CG	IP	H	R	ER	HR	BB	IBB	SO	HB	WP	W	L	Pct.	ERA
Clemens	1	1	0	5.0	1	0	0	0	4	0	7	0	1	0	0	.000	0.00
Mendoza	3	0	0	5.1	3	1	1	1	2	1	4	0	0	0	0	.000	1.69
Rivera	4	0	0	4.2	2	1	1	0	1	0	3	0	2	1	0	1.000	1.93
Pettitte	2	2	0	14.1	11	4	4	0	2	0	8	0	0	2	0	1.000	2.51
Mussina	1	1	0	6.0	4	2	2	1	1	0	3	1	0	1	0	1.000	3.00
Hernandez	1	1	0	5.0	5	5	4	1	5	0	7	0	0	0	1	.000	7.20
Witasick	1	0	0	3.0	6	3	3	1	0	0	2	0	0	0	0	.000	9.00
Wohlers	1	0	0	0.2	3	3	1	1	1	0	1	0	0	0	0	.000	13.50
Stanton	2	0	0	1.0	1	3	3	0	2	1	0	0	0	0	0	.000	27.00
Totals	5	5	0	45.0	36	22	19	5	18	2	35	1	3	4	1	.800	3.80

No shutouts. Saves—Rivera 2.

SEATTLE MARINERS' PITCHING RECORDS

Pitcher	G	GS	CG	IP	H	R	ER	HR	BB	IBB	SO	HB	WP	W	L	Pct.	ERA
Abbott	1	1	0	5.0	0	0	0	0	8	0	2	0	0	0	0	.000	0.00
Nelson	2	0	0	2.1	1	0	0	0	1	0	3	0	0	0	0	.000	0.00
Charlton	2	0	0	1.2	1	0	0	0	2	1	2	0	0	0	0	.000	0.00
Moyer	1	1	0	7.0	4	2	2	1	1	0	5	1	0	1	0	1.000	2.57
Sele	2	2	0	10.0	11	8	4	3	4	0	5	1	0	0	2	.000	3.60
Garcia	1	1	0	7.1	7	3	3	0	4	0	6	0	0	0	1	.000	3.68

Pitcher	G	GS	CG	IP	H	R	ER	HR	BB	IBB	SO	HB	WP	W	L	Pct.	ERA
Pineiro	1	0	0	2.0	4	1	1	0	2	0	5	0	1	0	0	.000	4.50
Rhodes..........................	2	0	0	2.0	2	1	1	1	0	0	2	0	0	0	0	.000	4.50
Paniagua	3	0	0	3.2	7	5	5	1	1	0	1	0	1	0	0	.000	12.27
Halama..........................	2	0	0	2.0	3	3	3	0	0	0	0	0	0	0	0	.000	13.50
Sasaki	1	0	0	0.1	2	2	2	1	0	0	0	0	0	0	1	.000	54.00
Totals	5	5	0	43.1	42	25	21	7	23	1	31	2	2	1	4	.200	4.36

No shutouts or saves.

SCORE BY INNINGS

New York...2	4	4		3	0	4		0	5	3—25
Seattle 0	0	0		2	3	7		5	2	3—22

MISCELLANEOUS STATISTICS

Sacrifice hits—Brosius 2, Jeter, Knoblauch, Bell.
Sacrifice fly—Jeter.
Stolen bases—Soriano 2, Suzuki 2, Spencer, Javier.
Caught stealing—Knoblauch, T. Martinez, Williams.
Double plays—Boone, McLemore and Olerud 2; Brosius, Soriano and T. Martinez 2; Bell, Boone and Olerud; Boone, Guillen and Olerud;
    T. Martinez (unassisted); Soriano, Jeter and T. Martinez; D. Wilson and McLemore.
Left on bases—New York 9, 6, 4, 8, 7—34; Seattle 2, 7, 11, 6, 8—34.
Hit by pitcher—By Mussina (Cameron), by Moyer (Justice), by Sele (Soriano).
Passed balls—None.
Balks—None.
Time of games—First game, 3:06; second game, 3:25; third game, 3:49; fourth game, 3:24; fifth game, 3:18.
Attendance—First game, 47,644; second game, 47,791; third game, 56,517; fourth game, 56,375; fifth game, 56,370.
Umpires—Montague, Bell, Cederstrom, Reliford, Shulock and Welke.
Official scorers—Red Foley, Howie Karpin, Terry Mosher, Bill Shannon.

2001 REVIEW A.L. Championship Series

N.L. CHAMPIONSHIP SERIES

The bottom line: The Diamondbacks became the fastest expansion team in Major League Baseball history to reach the World Series with a 4-1 victory in their best-of-seven series with the Atlanta Braves. The Florida Marlins took five years to reach the World Series, but the Diamondbacks made it in four behind the duo of Randy Johnson and Curt Schilling. Johnson picked up two wins over the Braves and Schilling threw a complete-game victory in Game 3 to help the Diamondbacks clinch the series. Johnson allowed no runs in his Game 1 start and allowed only two in Game 5. Atlanta picked up the victory in Game 2 behind the strong pitching of Tom Glavine, but the Diamondbacks took control of the series again in Game 3, when Schilling threw his third complete game of the postseason in a 5-1 victory. The Diamondbacks took advantage of some errors in Games 4 and 5 to wrap up the series. Arizona took the fourth game, 11-4, and squeaked out a one-run victory in Game 5 to clinch the series. Erubiel Durazo delivered the big blow for the Diamondbacks in the finale with a two-run homer that led to Arizona's 3-2 win.

Why the Diamondbacks won: Strong pitching and costly Atlanta errors led to the Diamondbacks' series victory. Randy Johnson and Curt Schilling were dominant in their starts. They allowed only three runs in 25 innings of work while striking out 31 and walking five. They also held the Braves to just 14 hits in their three starts. Byung-Hyun Kim was also solid for the Diamondbacks in relief, picking up two saves and not allowing a hit in five innings of work. Craig Counsell was the hitting star for the Diamondbacks, batting .381 with four RBIs and five runs scored.

The turning points:

Game 1: The Diamondbacks got all the offense they needed in the first inning. They gave starter Randy Johnson the early lead with the help of Craig Counsell, who singled with one out in the first inning. Luis Gonzalez followed and reached safely when his grounder scooted under the glove of second baseman Marcus Giles for an error. If Giles would have fielded the ball cleanly, the Braves likely would have turned a double play and gotten starter Greg Maddux out of the inning. Instead, it was first and third with one out. Reggie Sanders made the Braves pay and lined a single up the middle to score Counsell and make it 1-0. That's all the run support Johnson needed as he shut down the Braves. After allowing a first inning single off the glove of Matt Williams, Johnson retired the next 20 Braves in order before walking Bernard Gilkey in the eighth. Johnson was one out away from pitching a one-hitter when Julio Franco and Chipper Jones singled to put runners at first and third. Johnson finished the game, though, with a strikeout of Brian Jordan to give him 11 strikeouts in the game and the victory.

Game 2: Javy Lopez's two-run homer in the seventh broke open a tie game and propelled Atlanta to an 8-1 win that deadlocked the NLCS at one game apiece. This was Lopez's first start of the postseason since battling an ankle injury that sidelined him in the Braves' opening round matchup against the Astros. After giving up a home run on the first pitch of the game to Marcus Giles, Diamondbacks starter Miguel Batista did not allow another hit until the seventh. Batista walked Andruw Jones with two outs in the seventh. Then Lopez swung at the first pitch and knocked it off the right field foul pole to give the Braves a 3-1 lead and all starter Tom Glavine needed. Glavine was at his best, allowing just one run in his seven innings. The Braves broke the game open with five runs in the eighth to seal the victory.

Game 3: Arizona had a 2-1 lead in the fifth and took command of the game with the help of two Atlanta miscues that led to three runs. Curt Schilling led off with a single to right field. Tony Womack followed with a bunt right back to Braves starter John Burkett, but neither Julio Franco nor second baseman Marcus Giles covered first base. Womack was credited with a single and Counsell followed by bunting the runners into scoring position. After an intentional walk to Luis Gonzalez, Steve Reed relieved and got Matt Williams to hit a grounder to Jones at third base on the first pitch. Jones fielded the chopper and threw home and the ball easily beat Schilling, but Javy Lopez let it skim off his glove. Schilling pushed Lopez in the chest and knocked him on the play and when no one immediately got the ball, Womack scooted home from second base. Mike Remlinger came in for the Braves to face lefty Steve Finley. Finley greeted him with an RBI-single off the glove of a leaping Franco at first. The Diamondbacks had a 5-1 lead and that was all Schilling needed as he threw his third straight complete game of the postseason. Schilling gave up four hits and struck out 12.

Game 4: More Atlanta miscues led to another Diamondbacks victory in Game 4. Chipper Jones got the defense started by bobbling Tony Womack's grounder to third. That error didn't hurt the Braves, though, as Womack was thrown out trying to steal second. But it was a precursor for things to come. Craig Counsell followed with a routine grounder to Rey Sanchez, who sidearmed the throw to first and watched it sail off the screen in front of the Braves dugout for their second straight error. Counsell moved to third on a Luis Gonzalez single. Reggie Sanders hit a grounder back to Braves starter Greg Maddux, who fielded the ball, but instead of wheeling around to start a double play, looked at Counsell on third. Maddux hesitated, waiting for Jones to cover the bag, but even when he got to third, Maddux didn't throw. He then looked to first to get Sanders, but it was too late. The bases were loaded for Steve Finley, who made the Braves pay with a liner up the middle. Maddux got a glove on the ball, scrambled off the mound to get the ball and made an off-balance throw to the plate. The ball sailed past catcher Paul Bako, allowing two runs to score. Matt Williams and Mark Grace followed with consecutive RBI-singles to give the Diamondbacks a 4-2 lead. That lead held up as the Diamondbacks cruised to an 11-4 victory.

Game 5: An unlikely hero helped clinch the series for the Diamondbacks with a clutch pinch home run in the fifth inning. Another error for the Braves led to the game-winning homer. With the score tied at one in the top of the fifth, Marcus Giles booted a grounder by Craig Counsell leading off the inning. Luis Gonzalez grounded into a force play and Reggie Sanders followed with a strikeout. Mark Grace was due to bat next, but he left the game with a tight hamstring. Erubiel Durazo batted in his place. Durazo got to hit in the inning thanks to the Giles error, and made the Braves pay with a fly ball that just carried over the fence a few feet inside the left field foul pole. The Diamondbacks' held on for the win with a strong starting performance by Randy Johnson and two solid innings of relief by Byung-Hyun Kim.

Notable:

Braves: Tom Glavine made his record 29th post-season start in Game 2. … Kevin Millwood, left out of Atlanta's starting rotation in the postseason, relieved in the eighth inning of Game 3. … Greg Maddux dropped to 4-8 in the NLCS and 10-13 overall in playoff games, but is 257-146 in the regular season. … The Braves have reached the postseason 10 consecutive years but have only made it to the World Series once in that time.

Diamondbacks: The Diamondbacks' sellout crowd of 49,334 for Game 2 was the second-largest paid attendance in Bank One Ballpark history and came just one day after the teams played in front of some 11,000 empty seats in the opener. … Curt Schilling became the first pitcher since Orel Hershiser in 1988 to throw three straight complete games in a postseason. … Craig Counsell was named NLCS Most Valuable Player after batting .381 with three doubles, four runs batted in and five runs scored.

Quotable:

Braves: Greg Maddux, on Randy Johnson's performance in Game 1: "Randy pitched great. That was probably the best I've ever seen him change speeds. As a compliment, he was Jamie Moyer with a real good fastball." … Bobby Cox, on the return of Javy Lopez in Game 2: "We couldn't wait to see if he can make some difference in our run support. I just told the coaches we were going to get Javy in there and he might hit a homer, might produce some runs. And

that's exactly what happened." … Tom Glavine, after taking Game 2 of the series: "I always feel like Game 2 is urgent in any series. So much can happen one way or the other. To me, it's a huge swing game. You can either go up two or down two or tie a series up. Any of those situations is vastly different from any of the others." … Chipper Jones, after losing, 3-2, to the Diamondbacks in Game 5: "We had opportunities. We had guys up. We had Julio up with runners in scoring position, and we had (Jordan) up with runners in scoring position, and Johnson got out of it both times. That's why he's paid the big bucks."

Diamondbacks: Craig Counsell, after watching Randy Johnson shut down the Braves in Game 1: "You're kind of sitting out there in awe almost. You're just amazed at what he's doing." … Randy Johnson, after defeating Greg Maddux to give the Diamondbacks a 1-0 series lead: "This kind of game is more mentally draining than it is physically draining because you realize if you make one mistake, that could be the ballgame." … Randy Johnson, after snapping his major league record seven consecutive losses in postseason play: "Assuming someone might say here, 'Is this a monkey off your back?' This is more like a gorilla—King Kong." … Diamondback president Jerry Colangelo, after winning the NLCS and advancing to the World Series for the first time in franchise history: "It's very satisfying to be where we are as quickly as we are. I waited a long time for this to happen in my lifetime. I've been to the NBA Finals a couple of times, but this takes the cake for me: Getting to the World Series in four years."

GAME 1 BOX SCORE

ARIZONA 2, ATLANTA 0

TUESDAY, OCTOBER 16, AT ARIZONA

Atlanta	AB	R	H	RBI	PO	A
Giles, 2b	4	0	0	0	2	2
Franco, 1b	4	0	1	0	9	2
Marquis, pr	0	0	0	0	0	0
C. Jones, 3b	4	0	2	0	0	2
Jordan, rf	4	0	0	0	2	0
A. Jones, cf	3	0	0	0	0	0
Gilkey, lf	2	0	0	0	0	0
Sanchez, ss	3	0	0	0	2	3
Bako, c	2	0	0	0	5	0
J. Lopez, ph-c	1	0	0	0	2	0
Maddux, p	2	0	0	0	2	3
Remlinger, p	0	0	0	0	0	0
Karsay, p	0	0	0	0	0	0
DeRosa, ph	1	0	0	0	0	0
Totals	30	0	3	0	24	12

Arizona	AB	R	H	RBI	PO	A
Womack, ss	4	0	0	0	1	0
Counsell, 2b	4	2	2	0	0	1
Gonzalez, lf	4	0	1	1	0	0
Sanders, rf	3	0	2	1	3	0
Grace, 1b	4	0	1	0	7	0
Williams, 3b	4	0	1	0	1	4
Finley, cf	2	0	0	0	4	0
Miller, c	3	0	1	0	11	0
Johnson, p	3	0	0	0	0	0
Totals	31	2	8	2	27	5

Atlanta.........	0 0 0	0 0 0	0 0	0—0
Arizona.........	1 0 0	0 1 0	0 0	x—2

Atlanta	IP	H	R	ER	BB	SO
Maddux (L)	7.0	6	2	2	2	5
Remlinger................	0.2	0	0	0	0	2
Karsay.....................	0.1	0	0	0	0	0

Arizona	IP	H	R	ER	BB	SO
Johnson (W)	9.0	3	0	0	1	11

E—Giles. DP—Atlanta 2. LOB—Atlanta 4, Arizona 7. 2B—Counsell. T—2:44. A—37,729. U—Crawford, plate; Kellogg, first; Hernandez, second; Reilly, third; Davis, left field; McClelland, right field.

GAME 2 BOX SCORE

ATLANTA 8, ARIZONA 1

WEDNESDAY, OCTOBER 17, AT ARIZONA

Atlanta	AB	R	H	RBI	PO	A
Giles, 2b............................	5	1	1	1	0	3
Franco, 1b..........................	5	1	1	0	12	2
C. Jones, 3b.......................	3	1	0	0	0	0
Jordan, rf...........................	4	1	1	2	2	0
Surhoff, lf...........................	4	1	1	2	2	0
A. Jones, cf........................	3	2	1	0	3	0
J. Lopez, c	4	1	2	2	2	0
Marquis, pr	0	0	0	0	0	0
Bako, c..............................	0	0	0	0	4	0
Sanchez, ss	4	0	1	1	0	4
Glavine, p..........................	2	0	0	0	2	0
Martinez, ph	2	0	0	0	0	0
Karsay, p...........................	0	0	0	0	0	1
Smoltz, p...........................	0	0	0	0	0	1
Totals	36	8	8	8	27	11

Arizona	AB	R	H	RBI	PO	A
Counsell, ss	4	0	0	0	0	4
Bell, 2b.............................	4	0	0	0	1	3
Gonzalez, lf	4	0	0	0	2	0
Sanders, rf.........................	3	1	0	0	4	0
Finley, cf............................	4	0	1	0	1	0
Williams, 3b.......................	3	0	2	1	0	4
Dellucci, ph	1	0	0	0	0	0
Grace, 1b	3	0	2	0	14	2
Durazo, ph	1	0	0	0	0	0
Miller, c	2	0	0	0	3	1
Batista, p...........................	2	0	0	0	2	1
Colbrunn, ph	1	0	0	0	0	0
Morgan, p	0	0	0	0	0	0
Swindell, p	0	0	0	0	0	0
Witt, p	0	0	0	0	0	0
Kim, p	0	0	0	0	0	0
Totals	32	1	5	1	27	15

Atlanta.........	1	0 0	0 0 0	2	5	0—8
Arizona.........	0	0 0	0 0 1	0	0	0—1

Atlanta	IP	H	R	ER	BB	SO
Glavine (W)	7.0	5	1	1	2	2
Karsay	1.0	0	0	0	0	2
Smoltz	1.0	0	0	0	0	1

Arizona	IP	H	R	ER	BB	SO
Batista (L)	7.0	2	3	3	2	3
Morgan................................	0.2	2	3	3	1	0
Swindell..............................	*0.0	1	1	1	0	0
Witt	0.1	3	1	1	0	0
Kim	1.0	0	0	0	0	1

*Pitched to one batter in eighth.
E—Williams. LOB—Atlanta 4, Arizona 6. 2B—Jordan. HR—Giles, Surhoff, J. Lopez. T—2:54. A—49,334. U—Kellogg, plate; Hernandez, first; Reilly, second; Davis, third; McClelland, left field; Crawford, right field.

GAME 3 BOX SCORE

ARIZONA 5, ATLANTA 1

FRIDAY, OCTOBER 19, AT ATLANTA

Arizona	AB	R	H	RBI	PO	A
Womack, ss	5	1	1	0	0	2
Counsell, 2b.......................	4	1	3	0	2	2
Gonzalez, lf	4	1	0	0	1	0
Williams, 3b.......................	3	1	1	0	0	2
Finley, cf............................	3	0	2	3	3	0
Sanders, rf.........................	3	0	0	0	2	0
Grace, 1b	4	0	1	0	6	2
Miller, c	4	0	0	0	12	0
Schilling, p	4	1	1	0	1	2
Totals	34	5	9	3	27	10

Atlanta	AB	R	H	RBI	PO	A
Giles, 2b............................	3	1	1	0	3	2
Franco, 1b..........................	4	0	1	0	4	1
C. Jones, 3b.......................	4	0	1	1	1	4
Jordan, rf...........................	4	0	1	0	6	0
Surhoff, lf...........................	4	0	0	0	1	1
A. Jones, cf........................	3	0	0	0	4	0
J. Lopez, c	2	0	0	0	7	0
Sanchez, ss	2	0	0	0	0	1
Martinez, ph	1	0	0	0	0	0
Millwood, p	0	0	0	0	0	0
Marquis, p..........................	0	0	0	0	1	0
Burkett, p	1	0	0	0	0	0
Reed, p	0	0	0	0	0	0
Remlinger, p.......................	0	0	0	0	0	0
Ligtenberg, p......................	0	0	0	0	0	0
Lockhart, ph	1	0	0	0	0	0
Seanez, p	0	0	0	0	0	0
DeRosa, ss.........................	1	0	0	0	0	1
Totals	30	1	4	1	27	10

Arizona.........	0	0 2	0 3 0	0 0	0—5
Atlanta.........	0	0 0	1 0 0	0 0	0—1

Arizona	IP	H	R	ER	BB	SO
Schilling (W)	9.0	4	1	1	2	12

Atlanta	IP	H	R	ER	BB	SO
Burkett (L)...........................	4.1	7	5	4	2	2
Reed	*0.0	0	0	0	0	0
Remlinger...........................	0.2	1	0	0	1	0
Ligtenberg	1.0	0	0	0	0	1
Seanez...............................	1.0	1	0	0	1	2
Millwood	1.0	0	0	0	0	1
Marquis	1.0	0	0	0	0	1

*Pitched to one batter in fifth.
E—Williams, Lopez. DP—Arizona 1, Atlanta 1. LOB—Arizona 7, Atlanta 4. 2B—Williams, Finley, Giles, Jordan. SH—Counsell. SB—Counsell. CS—Surhoff. T—2:59. A—41,624. U—Hernandez, plate; Reilly, first; Davis, second; McClelland, third; Crawford, left field; Crawford, right field.

GAME 4 BOX SCORE

ARIZONA 11, ATLANTA 4

SATURDAY, OCTOBER 20, AT ATLANTA

Arizona	AB	R	H	RBI	PO	A
Womack, ss	6	3	2	0	1	5
Counsell, 2b.......................	6	2	3	4	3	3
Gonzalez, lf	3	2	2	3	3	0
Sanders, rf.........................	5	1	0	0	2	0
Finley, cf............................	4	1	1	1	3	0
Kim, p	1	0	0	0	0	0
Williams, 3b.......................	5	0	1	1	1	0
Grace, 1b	3	0	1	1	11	0
Miller, c	5	0	1	0	2	0
A. Lopez, p.........................	1	0	0	0	0	0
Dellucci, ph	1	1	1	0	0	0
Anderson, p	1	0	0	0	0	0
Morgan, p	0	0	0	0	0	0

Arizona	AB	R	H	RBI	PO	A
Swindell, p	0	0	0	0	0	0
Cummings, ph	1	0	0	0	0	0
Batista, p	0	0	0	0	0	0
Bautista, cf	0	1	0	0	1	0
Totals	42	11	12	10	27	8

Atlanta	AB	R	H	RBI	PO	A
Giles, 2b	4	2	1	0	5	2
Franco, 1b	5	0	1	0	5	1
C. Jones, 3b	5	0	2	1	1	2
Jordan, rf	5	0	1	1	1	0
Surhoff, lf	4	0	2	0	0	0
A. Jones, cf	4	2	2	1	5	0
Sanchez, ss	4	0	2	0	3	2
Bako, c	1	0	0	0	1	1
Gilkey, ph	0	0	0	0	0	0
Ligtenberg, p	0	0	0	0	0	0
DeRosa, ph	1	0	0	0	0	0
Seanez, p	0	0	0	0	0	0
Karsay, p	0	0	0	0	0	0
Martinez, ph	1	0	1	0	0	0
Marquis, p	0	0	0	0	0	0
Maddux, p	1	0	1	0	0	0
Remlinger, p	0	0	0	0	0	0
J. Lopez, ph-c	3	0	0	0	6	0
Totals	38	4	13	3	27	8

Arizona										
Arizona	0	0	4	2	0	0	0	1	4—11	
Atlanta	1	1	0	0	0	0	1	1	0— 4	

Arizona	IP	H	R	ER	BB	SO
A. Lopez	3.0	5	2	2	1	1
Anderson (W)	3.1	4	1	1	1	0
Morgan	0.1	1	0	0	0	1
Swindell	0.1	0	0	0	0	0
Batista	†0.0	3	1	1	0	0
Kim (3)	2.0	0	0	0	0	0

Atlanta	IP	H	R	ER	BB	SO
Maddux (L)	*3.0	8	6	4	0	2
Remlinger	1.0	0	0	0	1	0
Ligtenberg	2.0	0	0	0	1	1
Seanez	1.0	0	0	0	2	1
Karsay	1.0	2	1	1	1	3
Marquis	1.0	2	4	0	2	2

*Pitched to three batters in fourth.
†Pitched to three batters in eighth.

E—Sanchez 2, C. Jones, Maddux. DP—Arizona 2, Atlanta 2. LOB—Arizona 12, Atlanta 9. Counsell 2, Womack, C. Jones, Sanchez, Maddux. HR—Gonzalez, A. Jones. SB—Sanders, Finley. CS—Womack. HBP— By Maddux (Gonzalez). WP—Karsay. PB—Bako. T—3:47. A—42,291. U—Reilly, plate; Davis, first; McClelland, second; Crawford, third, Kellogg, left field; Hernandez, right field.

Arizona	AB	R	H	RBI	PO	A
Womack, ss	5	0	1	0	0	2
Counsell, 2b	3	0	0	0	3	1
Gonzalez, lf	4	1	1	0	1	0
Sanders, rf	3	0	0	0	3	0
Grace, 1b	2	1	1	0	5	0
Durazo, ph-1b	2	1	1	2	2	0
Williams, 3b	3	0	0	0	1	1
Bautista, cf	4	0	1	1	1	0
Kim, p	0	0	0	0	0	0
Miller, c	3	0	1	0	10	0
Johnson, p	3	0	0	0	0	1
Finley, cf	1	0	0	0	1	0
Totals	33	3	6	3	27	5

Atlanta	AB	R	H	RBI	PO	A
Giles, 2b	4	0	1	0	0	3
Franco, 1b	5	1	2	2	10	1
C. Jones, 3b	3	0	0	0	0	2
Jordan, rf	4	0	1	0	8	0
A. Jones, cf	4	0	0	0	1	0
J. Lopez, c	4	0	0	0	5	0
Gilkey, lf	3	0	1	0	1	0
Martinez, ph-lf	1	0	0	0	1	0
Sanchez, ss	4	1	2	0	1	2
Glavine, p	1	0	0	0	0	3
DeRosa, ph	1	0	0	0	0	0
Karsay, p	0	0	0	0	0	0
Surhoff, ph	1	0	0	0	0	0
Smoltz, p	0	0	0	0	0	1
Lockhart, ph	0	0	0	0	0	0
Totals	35	2	7	2	27	12

Arizona	0	0	0	1	2	0	0	0	0—3	
Atlanta	0	0	0	1	0	0	1	0	0—2	

Arizona	IP	H	R	ER	BB	SO
Johnson (W)	7.0	7	2	2	2	8
Kim (S)	2.0	0	0	0	1	2

Atlanta	IP	H	R	ER	BB	SO
Glavine (L)	5.0	5	3	1	3	3
Karsay	2.0	1	0	0	0	1
Smoltz	2.0	0	0	0	0	0

E—Williams, Giles. LOB—Arizona 7, Atlanta 9. HR—Durazo, Franco. SH—Counsell. WP—Glavine. T—3:13. A—35,652. U—Davis, plate; McClelland, first; Crawford, second; Kellogg, third; Hernandez, left field; Reilly, right field.

STATISTICS

ARIZONA DIAMONDBACKS' BATTING AND FIELDING AVERAGES

Player, position	G	AB	R	H	TB	2B	3B	HR	RBI	BB	IBB	SO	Avg.	PO	A	E	Avg.
Dellucci, ph	2	2	1	1	1	0	0	0	0	0	0	0	.500	0	0	0	.000
Counsell, 2b-ss	5	21	5	8	11	3	0	0	4	0	0	3	.381	8	11	0	1.000
Grace, 1b	5	16	1	6	6	0	0	0	1	2	1	1	.375	43	4	0	1.000
Durazo, ph-1b	2	3	1	1	4	0	0	1	2	0	0	1	.333	2	0	0	1.000
Finley, cf	5	14	1	4	5	1	0	0	4	3	2	1	.286	12	0	0	1.000
Williams, 3b	5	18	1	5	6	1	0	0	2	2	0	3	.278	3	11	3	.824
Bautista, cf	2	4	1	1	1	0	0	0	1	1	0	1	.250	2	0	0	1.000
Schilling, p	1	4	1	1	1	0	0	0	0	0	0	2	.250	1	2	0	1.000
Gonzalez, lf	5	19	4	4	7	0	0	1	4	3	2	3	.211	7	0	0	1.000
Womack, ss	4	20	4	4	5	1	0	0	0	0	0	2	.200	2	9	0	1.000
Miller, c	5	17	0	3	3	0	0	0	0	2	0	5	.176	38	1	0	1.000
Sanders, rf	5	17	2	2	2	0	0	0	1	5	0	5	.118	14	0	0	1.000
Morgan, p	2	0	0	0	0	0	0	0	0	0	0	0	.000	0	0	0	.000
Swindell, p	2	0	0	0	0	0	0	0	0	0	0	0	.000	0	0	0	.000
Witt, p	1	0	0	0	0	0	0	0	0	0	0	0	.000	0	0	0	.000

2001 REVIEW N.L. Championship Series

Player, position	G	AB	R	H	TB	2B	3B	HR	RBI	BB	IBB	SO	Avg.	PO	A	E	Avg.
Anderson, p	1	1	0	0	0	0	0	0	0	0	0	1	.000	0	0	0	.000
Colbrunn, ph	1	1	0	0	0	0	0	0	0	0	0	0	.000	0	0	0	.000
Cummings, ph	1	1	0	0	0	0	0	0	0	0	0	0	.000	0	0	0	.000
Kim, p	3	1	0	0	0	0	0	0	0	0	0	0	.000	0	0	0	.000
A. Lopez, p	1	1	0	0	0	0	0	0	0	0	0	1	.000	0	0	0	.000
Batista, p	2	2	0	0	0	0	0	0	0	0	0	1	.000	2	1	0	1.000
Bell, 2b	1	4	0	0	0	0	0	0	0	0	0	0	.000	1	3	0	1.000
Johnson, p	2	6	0	0	0	0	0	0	0	0	0	2	.000	0	1	0	1.000
Totals	5	172	22	40	52	6	0	2	19	18	5	32	.233	135	43	3	.983

ATLANTA BRAVES' BATTING AND FIELDING AVERAGES

Player, position	G	AB	R	H	TB	2B	3B	HR	RBI	BB	IBB	SO	Avg.	PO	A	E	Avg.
Maddux, p	2	3	0	1	2	1	0	0	0	0	0	2	.333	2	3	1	.833
Sanchez, ss	5	17	1	5	6	1	0	0	1	0	0	4	.294	6	12	2	.900
C. Jones, 3b	5	19	1	5	6	1	0	0	2	3	0	6	.263	2	10	1	.923
Franco, 1b	5	23	2	6	9	0	0	1	2	0	0	2	.261	40	7	0	1.000
Surhoff, lf-ph	4	13	1	3	6	0	0	1	2	0	0	1	.231	3	1	0	1.000
Giles, 2b	5	20	4	4	8	1	0	1	1	3	0	4	.200	10	12	2	.917
Gilkey, lf-ph	3	5	0	1	1	0	0	0	0	2	0	1	.200	1	0	0	1.000
Martinez, ph-lf	4	5	0	1	1	0	0	0	0	0	0	1	.200	1	0	0	1.000
Jordan, rf	5	21	1	4	6	2	0	0	3	0	0	6	.190	19	0	0	1.000
A. Jones, cf	5	17	4	3	6	0	0	1	1	1	0	5	.176	13	0	0	1.000
J. Lopez, ph-c	5	14	1	2	5	0	0	1	2	1	0	4	.143	22	0	1	.957
Karsay, p	4	0	0	0	0	0	0	0	0	0	0	0	.000	0	0	0	.000
Ligtenberg, p	2	0	0	0	0	0	0	0	0	0	0	0	.000	0	0	0	.000
Marquis, pr-p	4	0	0	0	0	0	0	0	0	0	0	0	.000	1	0	0	1.000
Millwood, p	1	0	0	0	0	0	0	0	0	0	0	0	.000	0	0	0	.000
Reed, p	1	0	0	0	0	0	0	0	0	0	0	0	.000	0	0	0	.000
Remlinger, p	3	0	0	0	0	0	0	0	0	0	0	0	.000	0	0	0	.000
Seanez, p	2	0	0	0	0	0	0	0	0	0	0	0	.000	0	0	0	.000
Smoltz, p	2	0	0	0	0	0	0	0	0	0	0	0	.000	0	2	0	1.000
Burkett, p	1	1	0	0	0	0	0	0	0	0	0	1	.000	0	0	0	.000
Lockhart, ph	2	1	0	0	0	0	0	0	0	1	0	0	.000	0	0	0	.000
Bako, c	3	3	0	0	0	0	0	0	0	0	0	0	.000	10	1	0	1.000
Glavine, p	2	3	0	0	0	0	0	0	0	0	0	2	.000	2	3	0	1.000
DeRosa, ph-ss	4	4	0	0	0	0	0	0	0	0	0	0	.000	0	1	0	1.000
Totals	5	169	15	35	56	6	0	5	14	11	0	39	.207	132	52	7	.963

ARIZONA DIAMONDBACKS' PITCHING RECORDS

Pitcher	G	GS	CG	IP	H	R	ER	HR	BB	IBB	SO	HB	WP	W	L	Pct.	ERA
Kim	3	0	0	5.0	0	0	0	0	1	0	3	0	0	0	0	.000	0.00
Schilling	1	1	1	9.0	4	1	1	0	2	0	12	0	0	1	0	1.000	1.00
Johnson	2	2	1	16.0	10	2	2	1	3	0	19	0	0	2	0	1.000	1.13
Anderson	1	0	0	3.1	4	1	1	0	1	0	0	0	0	1	0	1.000	2.70
Batista	2	1	0	7.0	5	4	4	2	2	0	3	0	0	0	1	.000	5.14
A. Lopez	1	1	0	3.0	5	2	2	1	1	0	1	0	0	0	0	.000	6.00
Morgan	2	0	0	1.0	3	3	3	0	1	0	1	0	0	0	0	.000	27.00
Swindell	2	0	0	0.1	1	1	1	1	0	0	0	0	0	0	0	.000	27.00
Witt	1	0	0	0.1	3	1	1	0	0	0	0	0	0	0	0	.000	27.00
Totals	5	5	2	45.0	35	15	15	5	11	0	39	0	0	4	1	.800	3.00

Shutout—Johnson. Saves—Kim 2.

ATLANTA BRAVES' PITCHING RECORDS

Pitcher	G	GS	CG	IP	H	R	ER	HR	BB	IBB	SO	HB	WP	W	L	Pct.	ERA
Ligtenberg	2	0	0	3.0	0	0	0	0	1	0	2	0	0	0	0	.000	0.00
Smoltz	2	0	0	3.0	0	0	0	0	0	0	1	0	0	0	0	.000	0.00
Marquis	2	0	0	2.0	2	4	0	1	2	0	3	0	0	0	0	.000	0.00
Remlinger	3	0	0	2.1	3	0	0	0	2	0	2	0	0	0	0	.000	0.00
Seanez	2	0	0	2.0	1	0	0	0	3	2	3	0	0	0	0	.000	0.00
Millwood	1	0	0	1.0	0	0	0	0	0	0	1	0	0	0	0	.000	0.00
Glavine	2	2	0	12.0	10	4	2	1	5	0	5	0	1	1	1	.500	1.50
Karsay	4	0	0	4.1	3	1	1	0	1	1	6	0	1	0	0	.000	2.08
Maddux	2	2	0	10.0	14	8	6	0	2	1	7	1	0	0	2	.000	5.40
Burkett	1	1	0	4.1	7	5	4	0	2	1	2	0	0	0	1	.000	8.31
Totals	5	5	0	44.0	40	22	13	2	18	5	32	1	2	1	4	.200	2.66

No shutouts or saves.

SCORE BY INNINGS

Arizona	1	0	6	3	6	1	0	1	4—22
Atlanta	2	1	0	2	0	0	4	6	0—15

MISCELLANEOUS STATISTICS

Sacrifice hits—Counsell 2.

Sacrifice flies—None.

Stolen bases—Counsell, Sanders, Finley.

Caught stealing—Surhoff, Womack.

Double plays—Maddux, Sanchez and Franco 2; Counsell, Womack and Grace; Giles, Sanchez and Franco; C. Jones, Giles and Franco; Sanchez, Giles and Franco; Williams, Counsell and Grace; Womack, Counsell and Grace.

Left on bases—Arizona 7, 6, 7, 12, 7—39; Atlanta 4, 4, 4, 9, 9—30.

Hit by pitcher—By Maddux (Gonzalez).

Passed ball—Bako.

Balks—None.

Time of games—First game, 2:44; second game, 2:54; third game, 2:59; fourth game, 3:47; fifth game, 3:13.

Attendance—First game, 37,729; second game, 49,334; third game, 41,624; fourth game, 42,291; fifth game, 35,652.

Umpires—Crawford, Kellogg, Hernandez, Reilly, Davis and McClelland.

Official scorers—Mark Frederickson and Rodney Johnson.

WORLD SERIES

ARIZONA 9, NEW YORK 1

Why the Diamondbacks won: The pitching of Curt Schilling continued to dominate opposing teams, as he shut down the Yankees allowing just three hits in seven innings. He also struck out eight while only walking one. The Diamondbacks jumped on top early with nine runs in the first four innings and Schilling cruised from there. Arizona took advantage of two Yankee errors that led to five unearned runs. The Diamondbacks also pounded out 10 hits that led to nine runs.

Why the Yankees lost: Mike Mussina struggled in his first career World Series start. Mussina lasted just three innings and allowed six hits and five runs. He also wasn't helped out much by the Yankee offense that was held to just three hits and scored only a run. Bernie Williams provided the only offense with a double in the first that scored Derek Jeter who reached when he was hit by a pitch. David Justice was hitless in three at-bats with three strikeouts.

The turning point: The Diamondbacks gave Schilling all the offense he needed with a four-run third inning. Tony Womack was hit by a Mussina pitch to lead off the inning. Craig Counsell laid down a bunt moving Womack to second. Luis Gonzalez followed with a home run into the right field stands that gave the Diamondbacks a 3-1 lead. Reggie Sanders singled up the middle. David Justice then misplayed a fly ball off the bat of Steve Finley that led to two more Diamondback runs. With runners at second and third after the Justice error, Matt Williams hit a sacrifice fly to center scoring Sanders, and Damian Miller doubled down the left field corner to score Finley. The Diamondbacks led 5-1 after three.

Notable: The last time the Yankees were held to three or fewer hits in a World Series game was in 1963 against the Los Angeles Dodgers. Don Drysdale threw a three-hit shutout in a 1-0 victory for the Dodgers. ... Derek Jeter had his 14-game World Series hitting streak stopped three short of the record held by former Yankee Hank Bauer. ... The Yankees' last game played in Arizona was in 1951 when they held spring training in Phoenix. It was Mickey Mantle's rookie year. ... Mike Mussina and Curt Schilling both pitched for Class AAA Rochester in 1990. They were never with Baltimore's top farm team at the same time, though.

Quotable: Bob Brenly, on winning the first game: "Just getting a win in Game 1 was huge. But I don't think there is any carryover effect from the score." ... Curt Schilling, talking about facing the Yankees in Game 1: "I know all about the history of the Yankees. But I wasn't pitching against Babe Ruth or Mickey Mantle today. I was pitching against these Yankees." ... Mike Mussina, after getting roughed up for five runs in three innings: "I was just awful." ... Derek Jeter, talking about the lopsided victory for the Diamondbacks: "Who cares what the score is? A loss is a loss."

BOX SCORE

SATURDAY, OCTOBER 27, AT ARIZONA

New York	AB	R	H	RBI	PO	A
Knoblauch, lf	4	0	0	0	0	0
Stanton, p	0	0	0	0	1	0
Jeter, ss	3	1	0	0	0	2
Justice, rf-lf	3	0	0	0	1	0
∞Spencer, ph	1	0	0	0	0	0
B. Williams, cf	4	0	1	1	2	0
Martinez, 1b	3	0	0	0	7	2
Posada, c	3	0	1	0	11	1
Soriano, 2b	3	0	0	0	1	1
Brosius, 3b	3	0	1	0	0	1
Mussina, p	1	0	0	0	1	0
Choate, p	0	0	0	0	0	1
†Wilson, ph	1	0	0	0	0	0
Hitchcock, p	0	0	0	0	0	0
§O'Neill, ph-rf	1	0	0	0	0	0
Totals	**30**	**1**	**3**	**1**	**24**	**8**

Arizona	AB	R	H	RBI	PO	A
Womack, ss	4	1	0	0	1	4
Counsell, 2b	4	1	1	1	2	2
Gonzalez, lf	5	2	2	2	1	0
Sanders, rf	3	2	2	0	0	0
Finley, cf	4	2	1	1	6	0
M. Williams, 3b	3	1	1	1	0	0
Grace, 1b	3	0	1	2	8	0
Miller, c	4	0	2	1	9	0
Schilling, p	3	0	0	0	0	0
‡Bell, ph	1	0	0	0	0	0
Morgan, p	0	0	0	0	0	0
Swindell, p	0	0	0	0	0	0
Totals	**34**	**9**	**10**	**8**	**27**	**6**

New York	1	0	0	0	0	0	0	0	0—1
Arizona	1	0	4	4	0	0	0	0	x—9

New York	IP	H	R	ER	BB	SO
Mussina (L)	3.0	6	5	3	1	4
Choate	1.0	3	4	1	1	1
Hitchcock	3.0	1	0	0	0	6
Stanton	1.0	0	0	0	0	0

Arizona	IP	H	R	ER	BB	SO
Schilling (W)	7.0	3	1	1	1	8
Morgan	1.0	0	0	0	0	0
Swindell	1.0	0	0	0	1	1

Bases on balls—Off Mussina 1 (Grace), off Choate 1 (Sanders), off Schilling 1 (Posada), off Swindell 1 (Martinez). Intentional bases on balls—Off Mussina (Grace), off Choate (Sanders).

Strikeouts—By Mussina 4 (Womack, Gonzalez, M. Williams, Schilling), by Choate 1 (Counsell), by Hitchcock 6 (Schilling, Counsell, Gonzalez, Finley, Miller, Bell), by Schilling 8 (Justice 3, Posada, Mussina, B. Williams, Soriano, Brosius), by Swindell 1 (B. Williams).

†Grounded out for Choate in fifth. ‡Struck out for Schilling in seventh. §Popped out for Hitchcock in eighth. ∞Popped out for Justice in ninth.

E—Justice, Brosius. LOB—New York 5, Arizona 6. 2B—B. Williams, Brosius, Gonzalez, Grace, Miller. HR—Counsell, Gonzalez. SH—Counsell. SF—M. Williams. HBP—By Mussina (Womack), by Schilling (Jeter). T—2:44. A—49,646. U—Rippley, plate; M. Hirschbeck, first; Scott, second; Rapuano, third; Joyce, left field; DeMuth, right field.

FIRST INNING

Yankees—Knoblauch popped to Counsell. Jeter hit by a pitch. Justice struck out. B. Williams doubled to left, scoring Jeter. Martinez grounded out, Womack to Grace. Yankees 1, Diamondbacks 0.

Diamondbacks—Womack struck out and was thrown out on the dropped third strike, Posada to Martinez. Counsell homered to right. Gonzalez struck out. Sanders singled to right-center. Finley grounded to Martinez, unassisted. Yankees 1, Diamondbacks 1.

SECOND INNING

Yankees—Posada struck out. Soriano flied to Finley. Brosius doubled to center. Mussina struck out.

Diamondbacks—M. Williams struck out. Grace lined to Soriano. Miller singled to left-center. Schilling struck out.

THIRD INNING

Yankees—Knoblauch fouled to Grace. Jeter grounded out, Womack to Grace. Justice struck out.

Diamondbacks—Womack hit by a pitch. Counsell hit a sacrifice bunt, Martinez to Mussina, Womack advanced to second. Gonzalez homered to right, scoring Womack. Sanders singled to center. Finley reached second on a fielding error by Justice as Sanders advanced to third. M. Williams hit a sacrifice fly to B. Williams, scoring Sanders as Finley advanced to third. Grace was intentionally walked. Miller doubled to left, scoring Finley as Grace advanced to third. Schilling grounded out, Jeter to Martinez. Four runs. Diamondbacks 5, Yankees 1.

FOURTH INNING

Yankees—B Williams struck out. Martinez flied to Gonzalez. Posada singled to center. Soriano struck out.

Diamondbacks—Choate now pitching. Womack fouled to Posada. Counsell struck out. Gonzalez doubled to left. Sanders was intentionally walked. Finley singled to right, scoring Gonzalez as Sanders advanced to third. M. Williams reached second on a fielding error by Brosius, scoring Sanders as Finley advanced to third. Grace doubled to right-center, scoring Finley and M. Williams. Miller grounded out, Choate to Martinez. Four runs. Diamondbacks 9, Yankees 1.

FIFTH INNING

Yankees—Brosius flied to Finley. Wilson, pinch-hitting for Choate, grounded out, Counsell to Grace. Knoblauch grounded out, Womack to Grace.

Diamondbacks—Hitchcock now pitching. Schilling struck out. Womack grounded out, Brosius to Martinez. Counsell struck out.

SIXTH INNING

Yankees—Jeter grounded out, Grace, unassisted. Justice struck out. B. Williams grounded out, Counsell to Grace.

Diamondbacks—Gonzalez struck out. Sanders grounded out, Jeter to Martinez. Finley struck out.

SEVENTH INNING

Yankees—Martinez flied to Finley. Posada walked. Soriano flied to Finley. Brosius struck out.

Diamondbacks—M. Williams singled to center. Grace lined to Justice. Miller struck out. Bell, pinch-hitting for Schilling, struck out.

EIGHTH INNING

Yankees—Morgan now pitching. O'Neill, pinch-hitting for Hitchcock, popped to Womack. Knoblauch grounded out, Womack to Grace. Jeter flied to Finley.

Diamondbacks—Justice now in left, O'Neill in right and Stanton pitching. Womack flied to B. Williams. Counsell grounded out, Soriano to Martinez. Gonzalez grounded out, Martinez to Stanton.

NINTH INNING

Yankees—Swindell now pitching. Spencer, pinch-hitting for Justice, popped to Counsell. B. Williams struck out. Martinez walked. Posada flied to Finley. Final score: Diamondbacks 9, Yankees 1.

ARIZONA 4, NEW YORK 0

Why the Diamondbacks won: Randy Johnson. He was almost unhittable as he held the Yankees to just three hits in his shutout. Johnson struck out 11 and walked just one. Over the first three innings, Johnson had struck out seven of his first nine outs.

Why the Yankees lost: The Yankees struggled at the plate again, only mustering three hits for the second consecutive game. They were held hitless until the fifth when Jorge Posada hit a single to right to start the inning. The top four hitters for the Yankees were 0 for 14 against Johnson. The only time the Yankees got two runners on in an inning was the eighth, but Johnson got out of the jam with a strikeout and a double play.

The turning point: With the Diamondbacks hanging on to a one-run lead in the seventh, Matt Williams gave Johnson a bigger cushion with a clutch home run. Yankee starter Andy Pettitte made a mistake to Luis Gonzalez as he hit him with a pitch after getting ahead in the count. Pettitte retired the next hitter before Danny Bautista reached on an infield single. Williams then took a 0-1 Pettitte offering deep into the stands in left for a three-run homer. That is all the insurance that Johnson needed as he shut the door the last two innings to preserve Arizona's 4-0 victory. Pettitte pitched strong as well for the Yankees, allowing just five hits in seven innings.

Notable: Randy Johnson called former teammate Jamie Moyer a week before the game for advice on how to pitch against the Yankees. Moyer suggested a few changeups. ... Johnson threw the first complete-game shutout in the World Series since Curt Schilling did it in 1993 for Philadelphia. ... The Yankees rallied from an 0-2 deficit in the 1996 World Series against the Atlanta Braves. They won that series in six games. ... Matt Williams became the first player to hit World Series home runs for three teams. He has hit homers for San Francisco and Cleveland as well as Arizona.

Quotable: Randy Johnson, after throwing his complete-game shutout: "I got to enjoy the game last night, watching Curt pitch. It was nice, obviously, to take two ballgames, but this is far from over." ... Derek Jeter, on the Diamondbacks: "This was one of those games where we were just dominated. They're not just pitching well against me. They were pitching well against everyone." ... Joe Torre, talking about Randy Johnson: "He was terrific. He lived up to what he's supposed to be. The axiom has never changed, good pitching stops good hitting. And that's what we've seen." ... Bob Brenly, talking about the series moving to New York for Game 3: "It's no trip to the beach going into Yankee Stadium."

BOX SCORE

SUNDAY, OCTOBER 28, AT ARIZONA

New York	AB	R	H	RBI	PO	A
Knoblauch, lf	4	0	0	0	1	0
Velarde, 1b	3	0	0	0	10	0
Jeter, ss	4	0	0	0	0	2
B. Williams, cf	3	0	0	0	0	0
Posada, c	3	0	1	0	9	0
Spencer, rf	3	0	1	0	0	0
Soriano, 2b	3	0	1	0	4	5
Brosius, 3b	3	0	0	0	0	5
Pettitte, p	2	0	0	0	0	1
†Sojo, ph	1	0	0	0	0	0
Stanton, p	0	0	0	0	0	0
Totals	29	0	3	0	24	13

Arizona	AB	R	H	RBI	PO	A
Womack, ss	4	0	0	0	1	3
Counsell, 2b	4	0	0	0	3	1
Gonzalez, lf	2	0	0	0	2	0
Sanders, rf	3	2	1	0	1	0
Bautista, cf	3	1	2	1	0	0
Finley, cf	0	0	0	0	0	0
M. Williams, 3b	3	1	2	3	0	6
Grace, 1b	3	0	0	0	9	0
Miller, c	3	0	0	0	11	0
Johnson, p	3	0	0	0	0	1
Totals	28	4	5	4	27	11

New York	0	0	0	0	0	0	0	0	0—0
Arizona	0	1	0	0	0	0	3	0	x—4

New York	IP	H	R	ER	BB	SO
Pettitte (L)	7.0	5	4	4	0	8
Stanton	1.0	0	0	0	0	0

Arizona	IP	H	R	ER	BB	SO
Johnson (W)	9.0	3	0	0	1	11

Bases on balls—Off Johnson 1 (Velarde).

Strikeouts—By Pettitte 8 (Counsell 2, Gonzalez 2, Womack, Grace, Johnson, Miller), by Johnson 11 (Knoblauch, Jeter, B. Williams, Posada, Soriano 2, Brosius 2, Pettitte, Spencer, Velarde).

†Grounded into double play for Pettitte in eighth.

DP—New York 1, Arizona 1. LOB—New York 3, Arizona 1. 2B—Bautista. HR—M. Williams. HBP—By Pettitte (Gonzalez). T—2:35. A—49,646. U—M. Hirschbeck, plate; Scott, first; Rapuano, second; Joyce, third; DeMuth, left field; Rippley, right field.

PLAY BY PLAY

FIRST INNING

Yankees—Knoblauch struck out. Velarde grounded out, Johnson to Grace. Jeter struck out.

Diamondbacks—Womack grounded out, Pettitte to Velarde. Counsell and Gonzalez struck out.

SECOND INNING

Yankees—B. Williams and Posada struck out. Spencer grounded out, M. Williams to Grace.

Diamondbacks—Sanders singled to short. Bautista doubled to right-center and advanced to third on the throw as Sanders scored. M. Williams grounded out, Brosius to Velarde. Grace reached first on a fielder's choice as Bautista was thrown out at the plate, Soriano to Posada. Miller forced Grace at second, Brosius to Soriano. One run. Diamondbacks 1, Yankees 0.

THIRD INNING

Yankees—Soriano, Brosius and Pettitte struck out.

Diamondbacks—Johnson grounded out, Jeter to Velarde. Womack and Counsell struck out.

FOURTH INNING

Yankees—Knoblauch flied to Gonzalez. Velarde walked. Jeter forced Velarde at second, Womack to Counsell. B. Williams grounded out, Womack to Grace.

Diamondbacks—Gonzalez struck out. Sanders popped to Velarde. Bautista popped to Soriano.

FIFTH INNING

Yankees—Posada singled to right. Spencer and Soriano struck out. Brosius flied to Gonzalez.

Diamondbacks—M. Williams singled to left. Grace struck out. Miller grounded into a double play, Brosius to Soriano to Velarde.

SIXTH INNING

Yankees—Pettitte grounded out, M. Williams to Grace. Knoblauch popped to Womack. Velarde grounded out, M. Williams to Grace.

Diamondbacks—Johnson struck out. Womack grounded out, Brosius to Velarde. Counsell grounded out, Soriano to Velarde.

SEVENTH INNING

Yankees—Jeter and B. Williams grounded out, M. Williams to Grace. Posada grounded out, Womack to Grace.

Diamondbacks—Gonzalez hit by a pitch. Sanders forced Gonzalez at second, Brosius to Soriano. Bautista singled to the mound as Sanders advanced to second. M. Williams homered to left as Sanders and Bautista scored. Grace grounded out, Soriano to Velarde. Miller struck out. Three runs. Diamondbacks 4, Yankees 0.

EIGHTH INNING

Yankees—Finley now in center. Spencer singled to right. Soriano singled to left as Spencer advanced to second. Brosius struck out. Sojo, pinch-hitting for Pettitte, grounded into a double play, M. Williams to Counsell to Grace.

Diamondbacks—Stanton now pitching. Johnson grounded out, Jeter to Velarde. Womack grounded out, Soriano to Velarde. Counsell flied to Knoblauch.

NINTH INNING

Yankees—Knoblauch flied to Sanders. Velarde struck out. Jeter lined to Counsell. Final score: Diamondbacks 4, Yankees 0.

GAME 3

HIGHLIGHTS

NEW YORK 2, ARIZONA 1

Why the Yankees won: Roger Clemens gave the Yankees the pitching performance they needed to win Game 3 and get right back in the series. Clemens allowed three hits in seven innings while fanning nine. The offense still sputtered with only seven hits, but two runs were enough with Clemens on the mound. Mariano Rivera was his dominant self, throwing two perfect innings to close out the game.

Why the Diamondbacks lost: The loss could be summed up with one word: three. That was the number of errors, wild pitches and hits that Arizona collected in the game. Those mistakes and lack of hits led to the Diamondbacks' loss. Clemens dominated Arizona hitters who could only muster a run on a Matt Williams sacrifice fly. The Diamondbacks also uncharacteristically played sloppy defense, with catcher Damian Miller having the most problems as he struggled all night on pop-ups. Three Arizona pitchers uncorked wild pitches as well.

The turning point: The Yankees gave Roger Clemens the lead in the sixth. With the score tied at one, Bernie Williams led off the inning with a single to left off Arizona starter Brian Anderson. Damian Miller and Mark Grace then misplayed a Tino Martinez pop-up but that didn't prove costly as Martinez later flew out to right for the first out.

Williams advanced to second on a wild pitch before Jorge Posada walked on four pitches. Anderson was lifted for reliever Mike Morgan, who struck out pinch-hitter David Justice for the second out of the inning. Scott Brosius was the Yankee hero though as he got a clutch two-out hit with a single to left. Williams scored to give the Yankees a 2-1 lead that held up behind the strong pitching of Clemens and Mariano Rivera.

Notable: A raucous crowd of over 55,000 welcomed President Bush, who threw out the first pitch. ... The Yankees have scored just three runs in the Series and have only 13 hits. ... The game-time temperature was 53 degrees and dropped to 40 degrees cooler than it was in Phoenix for Games 1 and 2. ... The Yankees were glad to come away with a victory in Game 3 as no baseball team has ever rallied from an 0-3 deficit to win a postseason series. ... Roger Clemens improved to 3-0 lifetime in the World Series. ... The Yankees' 19-inning scoreless streak, which was broken in Game 3, was the longest since Oakland had an 18-inning slump against Los Angeles in 1988.

Quotable: Roger Clemens, after winning Game 3: "This is a big win for us. We feel like we've put ourselves back in the series." ... Joe Torre, on Clemens' clutch performance: "Roger was dynamite. He realized what we needed and he gave us every bit of it." ... Bob Brenly, talking about Clemens: "He was as good as advertised. He had a good fastball up in the zone and he threw just enough sliders to give us something to think about." ... Brian Anderson, on the Diamondbacks' task of winning in New York: "It's tough to come here. We knew it was going to be tough trying to beat them on their home field." ... Clemens, talking about the pregame festivities: "I stopped warming up to watch the President throw out the first pitch. I wanted to take it all in. A lot of things happened tonight that I'll remember for a long time."

BOX SCORE

TUESDAY, OCTOBER 30, AT NEW YORK

Arizona	AB	R	H	RBI	PO	A
Counsell, 2b	4	0	0	0	1	4
Finley, cf	2	1	0	0	5	0
Gonzalez, lf	4	0	1	0	1	0
Sanders, rf	3	0	0	0	2	0
Durazo, dh	3	0	2	0	0	0
M. Williams, 3b	3	0	0	1	0	1
Grace, 1b	3	0	0	0	11	0
Miller, c	3	0	0	0	3	0
Womack, ss	3	0	0	0	1	6
Anderson, p	0	0	0	0	0	0
Morgan, p	0	0	0	0	0	0
Swindell, p	0	0	0	0	0	0
Totals	28	1	3	1	24	11

New York	AB	R	H	RBI	PO	A
Knoblauch, dh	4	0	0	0	0	0
Jeter, ss	4	0	1	0	2	1
O'Neill, rf	4	0	2	0	2	0
‡Bellinger, pr-lf	0	0	0	0	0	0
B. Williams, cf	3	1	1	0	1	0
Martinez, 1b	4	0	0	0	7	1
Posada, c	3	1	1	1	13	1
Spencer, lf	1	0	0	0	1	0
†Justice, ph-lf-rf	2	0	0	0	0	0

New York	AB	R	H	RBI	PO	A
Brosius, 3b	3	0	1	1	0	0
Soriano, 2b	3	0	1	0	0	2
Clemens, p	0	0	0	0	0	3
Rivera, p	0	0	0	0	1	0
Totals	31	2	7	2	27	8

Arizona	0	0	0	1	0	0	0	0	0—1
New York	0	1	0	0	0	1	0	0	x—2

Arizona	IP	H	R	ER	BB	SO
Anderson (L)	5.1	5	2	2	3	1
Morgan	1.1	1	0	0	0	1
Swindell	1.1	1	0	0	0	1

New York	IP	H	R	ER	BB	SO
Clemens (W)	7.0	3	1	1	3	9
Rivera (S)	2.0	0	0	0	0	4

Bases on balls—Off Anderson 3 (B. Williams, Spencer, Posada), off Clemens 3 (Finley 2, Durazo).

Strikeouts—By Anderson 1 (Jeter), by Morgan 1 (Justice), by Swindell 1 (Justice), by Clemens 9 (Gonzalez 2, Sanders, M. Williams, Miller 2, Womack 2, Counsell), by Rivera 4 (Finley, Gonzalez, Sanders, Durazo).

†Struck out for Spencer in sixth. ‡Pinch ran for O'Neill in seventh.

E—Womack, Miller, Grace, Soriano. DP—Arizona 1, New York 1. LOB—Arizona 5, New York 8. HR—Posada. SF—M. Williams. SB—Sanders, O'Neill. CS—Finley. HBP—By Clemens (Sanders). WP—Anderson, Morgan, Swindell. T—3:26. A—55,820. U—Scott, plate; Rapuano, first; Joyce, second; DeMuth, third; Rippley, left field; M. Hirschbeck, right field.

PLAY BY PLAY

FIRST INNING

Diamondbacks—Counsell reached first on a fielding error by Soriano. Counsell picked off at first, Clemens to Martinez. Finley walked. Gonzalez struck out into a double play as Finley was caught trying to steal second, Posada to Jeter.

Yankees—Knoblauch popped to Womack. Jeter struck out. O'Neill singled to left. O'Neill stole second. B. Williams walked. Martinez flied to Finley.

SECOND INNING

Diamondbacks—Sanders struck out. Durazo singled to center. M. Williams struck out. Grace forced Durazo at second, Martinez to Jeter.

Yankees—Posada homered to left. Spencer grounded out, Womack to Grace. Brosius grounded out, Counsell to Grace. Soriano singled to center. Knoblauch flied to Finley. One run. Yankees 1, Diamondbacks 0.

THIRD INNING

Diamondbacks—Miller and Womack struck out. Counsell grounded out, Soriano to Martinez.

Yankees—Jeter singled to short. O'Neill grounded into a double play, Counsell to Grace. B. Williams grounded out, M. Williams to Grace.

FOURTH INNING

Diamondbacks—Finley walked. Gonzalez singled to left as Finley advanced to second. Sanders flied to O'Neill as Finley advanced to third. Durazo walked. M. Williams hit a sacrifice fly to O'Neill, scoring Finley as Gonzalez advanced to third. Grace grounded out, Soriano to Martinez. One run. Yankees 1, Diamondbacks 1.

Yankees—Martinez grounded out, Womack to Grace. Posada grounded out, Counsell to Grace. Spencer walked. Brosius reached first on a fielding error by the shortstop as Spencer advanced to second. After Miller made an error dropping a pop fly by Soriano that went foul, Soriano flied to Finley.

FIFTH INNING

Diamondbacks—Miller and Womack grounded out, Clemens to Martinez. Counsell struck out.

Yankees—Knoblauch grounded out, Counsell to Grace. Jeter grounded out, Womack to Grace. O'Neill flied to Gonzalez.

SIXTH INNING

Diamondbacks—Finley popped to Martinez. Gonzalez struck out. Sanders hit by a pitch. Sanders stole second. Durazo singled to second as Sanders advanced to third. M. Williams lined to Spencer.

Yankees—B. Williams singled to short. After Martinez's at-bat was prolonged when Grace made an error dropping a foul pop, Martinez flied to Sanders. B. Williams advanced to second on a wild pitch. Posada walked. Morgan now pitching. Justice, pinch-hitting for Spencer, struck out. Brosius singled to left, scoring B. Williams as Posada advanced to second. Posada advanced to third and Brosius to second on a wild pitch. Soriano grounded out, Womack to Grace. One run. Yankees 2, Diamondbacks 1.

SEVENTH INNING

Diamondbacks—Justice now in left. Grace flied to B. Williams. Miller and Womack struck out.

Yankees—Knoblauch and Jetergrounded out, Womack to Grace. Swindell now pitching. O'Neill singled tto left. Bellinger now pinch-running for O'Neill. Bellinger advanced to second on a wild pitch. B. Williams flied to Sanders.

EIGHTH INNING

Diamondbacks—Bellinger now in left, Justice in right and Rivera pitching. Counsell grounded out, Rivera, unassisted. Finley and Gonzalez struck out.

Yankees—Martinez and Posada flied to Finley. Justice struck out.

NINTH INNING

Diamondbacks—Sanders and Durazo struck out. M. Williams grounded out, Jeter to Martinez. Final score: Yankees 2, Diamondbacks 1.

GAME 4
HIGHLIGHTS

NEW YORK 4, ARIZONA 3 (10 INNINGS)

Why the Yankees won: Clutch hitting, clutch hitting, clutch hitting. Tino Martinez and Derek Jeter clubbed two-out home runs to propel the Yankees to victory. Martinez had the biggest hit for the Yankees, tying the game with two outs in the ninth on a two-run home run off Arizona closer Byung-Hyun Kim. Derek Jeter carried over that momentum into the 10th inning with a two-out home run off Kim that closed out the game and tied the series at two games apiece. Starter Orlando Hernandez pitched well enough for the win, allowing one run on four hits in 6$^{1}/_{3}$ innings. Besides the home runs, though, the Yankees struggled again at the plate collecting just three hits off Arizona starter Curt Schilling. The home runs provided enough offense for the Yankees to even up the series.

Why the Diamondbacks lost: They couldn't close out the game. On just three days rest, Curt Schilling threw a great game as he allowed just one run on three hits in seven innings. He also struck out nine and walked only one. With a 3-1 lead, though, Kim couldn't close out the game and allowed a two-out ninth-inning homer to tie it and then a 10th-inning homer to lose the game.

The turning point: The Yankee offense had been shut down all game and appeared dead in the water in the ninth as Kim was rolling. Kim struck out the

side in the eighth and got two of the first three batters in the ninth. Derek Jeter grounded out to start the ninth. Paul O'Neill then battled Kim before slapping a single to left. Kim then struck out Bernie Williams for the second out of the ninth. Tino Martinez, hitless in the series, launched a drive over the center-field fence to tie it on the first pitch he saw from Kim. The Yankees had all the momentum after the home run and carried that over into extra innings where they won the game. Kim set down the first two batters in the 10th before facing Jeter, who was only 1-for-15 in the Series. Jeter fouled off three two-strike pitches before homering down the right field line for the win.

Notable: Chad Curtis was the last player and last Yankee to end a World Series game with a home run. Curtis hit a game-winner in 1999 against Atlanta to win the game. ... David Justice struck out in his first eight at-bats, breaking the World Series record of five straight strikeouts held by several players. Justice had an infield single in the ninth to break the streak. ... Tony Womack broke an 0-for-11 streak with a hit to lead off the game. That was his first hit of the series. ... Craig Counsell tied a World Series record set by the Cubs' Joe Tinker in 1906 with three sacrifice bunts.

Quotable: Derek Jeter, on his game-winning home run: "When I first hit it, I had no idea whether it was going to go out. But once it goes out, it's a pretty special feeling. I've never hit a walkoff home run before." ... Joe Torre, talking about the thrilling Yankee victory: "It's just got to be at the top. Surprising things happen. And yet, when you really think about it, it doesn't surprise you because this ballclub never quits. I know it's an old cliche, but I've lived it for six years." ... Tino Martinez, hoping his home run sparks his production: "I have struggled in the postseason in the past and tried to press and make up for it. This time, I took it one at-bat at a time. To get a hit like that obviously is a boost for the team. Hopefully, it will get myself going and the rest of the offense." ... Curt Schilling, on manager Bob Brenly's decision to lift him after seven innings: "I told him I had at least another one easy. He felt the decision was to bring BK in. He's done it all year long and it's worked, and tonight it didn't." ... Luis Gonzalez, talking about his club's inability to hold the lead: "We just couldn't close it out. Tomorrow's a new day. This was a tough loss, I'm not going to lie to you, but our team's fine. We'll bounce right back. We seem to play better when our backs are to the wall."

BOX SCORE

WEDNESDAY, OCTOBER 31, AT NEW YORK

Arizona	AB	R	H	RBI	PO	A
Womack, ss	4	0	2	0	2	3
Counsell, 2b	2	0	0	0	0	2
Gonzalez, lf	3	1	1	0	2	0
Durazo, dh	3	0	1	1	0	0
Arizona	**AB**	**R**	**H**	**RBI**	**PO**	**A**

†Cummings, pr dh............	0	1	0	0	0	0
‡Bautista, ph-dh.............	1	0	0	0	0	0
M. Williams, 3b..............	4	0	0	1	0	2
Finley, cf......................	4	0	1	0	0	0
Sanders, rf....................	4	0	0	0	2	0
Grace, 1b	3	1	1	1	8	1
Miller, c	3	0	0	0	14	0
Schilling, p...................	0	0	0	0	1	0
Kim, p..........................	0	0	0	0	0	0
Totals..........................	31	3	6	3	29	8

New York	AB	R	H	RBI	PO	A
Jeter, ss.......................	5	1	1	1	2	5
O'Neill, rf.....................	4	1	1	0	1	0
B. Williams, cf...............	4	0	1	0	1	0
Martinez, 1b..................	3	1	1	2	11	1
Posada, c	3	0	0	0	8	0
Justice, dh	4	0	1	0	0	0
Spencer, lf	4	1	1	1	1	1
Brosius, 3b	4	0	1	0	1	4
Soriano, 2b	4	0	0	0	5	4
Hernandez, p..................	0	0	0	0	0	0
Stanton, p.....................	0	0	0	0	0	0
Mendoza, p....................	0	0	0	0	0	1
Rivera, p.......................	0	0	0	0	0	0
Totals..........................	35	4	7	4	30	16

```
Arizona.................. 0 0 0   1 0 0   0 2 0   0—3
New York................ 0 0 1   0 0 0   0 0 2   1—4
```
Two out when winning run scored.

Arizona	IP	H	R	ER	BB	SO
Schilling	7.0	3	1	1	1	9
Kim (L).........................	2.2	4	3	3	1	5

New York	IP	H	R	ER	BB	SO
Hernandez	6.1	4	1	1	4	5
Stanton........................	1.0	2	2	2	0	0
Mendoza.......................	1.2	0	0	0	0	1
Rivera (W).....................	1.0	0	0	0	0	0

Bases on balls—Off Schilling 1 (Martinez), off Kim 1 (Posada), off Hernandez 4 (Durazo, Womack, Gonzalez, Grace).

Strikeouts—By Schilling 9 (B. Williams, Justice 3, Brosius, O'Neill, Martinez, Posada, Soriano), by Kim 5 (Spencer 2, Brosius, Soriano, B. Williams), by Hernandez 5 (M. Williams, Sanders, Miller, Durazo, Finley), by Mendoza 1 (Miller).

†Pinch ran for Durazo in eighth. ‡Grounded out for Cummings in 10th.

DP—Arizona 1, New York 3. LOB—Arizona 7, New York 4. 2B—Womack, Durazo, Brosius. HR—Grace, Jeter, Martinez, Spencer. SH—Counsell 3. HBP—By Hernandez 2 (Gonzalez, Miller). T—3:31. A—55,863. U—Rapuano, plate; Joyce, first; DeMuth, second; Rippley, third; M. Hirschbeck, left field; Scott, right field.

PLAY BY PLAY

FIRST INNING

Diamondbacks—Womack singled to center. Counsell hit a sacrifice bunt, Brosius to Martinez as Womack advanced to second. Gonzalez hit by a pitch. Durazo walked. M. Williams struck out. Finley popped to Brosius.

Yankees—Jeter lined to Womack. O'Neill grounded out, Womack to Grace. B. Williams struck out.

SECOND INNING

Diamondbacks—Sanders struck out. Grace grounded out, Soriano to Martinez. Miller struck out.

Yankees—Martinez grounded out, Counsell to Grace. Posada flied to Gonzalez. Justice struck out.

THIRD INNING

Diamondbacks—Womack walked. Counsell hit a sacrifice bunt, Brosius to Martinez, as Womack advanced to second. Gonzalez walked. Durazo flied to O'Neill as Womack advanced to third. M. Williams forced Gonzalez at second, Brosius to Soriano.

Yankees—Spencer homered to right. Brosius struck out. Soriano flied to Sanders. Jeter grounded out, Womack to Grace. One run. Yankees 1, Diamondbacks 0.

FOURTH INNING

Diamondbacks—Finley singled to center. Sanders grounded into a double play, Jeter to Soriano to Martinez. Grace homered to right. Miller popped to Soriano. One run. Yankees 1, Diamondbacks 1.

Yankees—O'Neill struck out. B. Williams grounded out, Grace, unassisted. Martinez struck out.

FIFTH INNING

Diamondbacks—Womack doubled to right. Counsell hit a sacrifice bunt, Martinez to Soriano, as Womack advanced to third. Gonzalez flied to Spencer, who threw to Posada to retire Womack on a double play.

Yankees—Posada and Justice struck out. Spencer grounded out, M. Williams to Grace.

SIXTH INNING

Diamondbacks—Durazo struck out. M. Williams fouled to Posada. Finley struck out.

Yankees—Brosius doubled to center. Soriano struck out. Jeter grounded out, Grace, unassisted, as Brosius advanced to third. O'Neill grounded out, Grace to Schilling.

SEVENTH INNING

Diamondbacks—Sanders grounded out, Jeter to Martinez. Grace walked. Miller hit by a pitch. Stanton now pitching. Womack grounded into a double play, Soriano to Jeter to Martinez.

Yankees—B. Williams singled to left. Martinez walked. Posada grounded into a double play, Counsell to Womack to Grace, as B. Williams advanced to third. Justice struck out.

EIGHTH INNING

Diamondbacks—Counsell flied to B. Williams. Gonzalez singled to center. Durazo doubled to center and advanced to third on the throw as Gonzalez scored. Cummings now pinch running for Durazo. Mendoza now pitching. M. Williams reached first on a fielder's choice, Cummings scored. Finley popped to Jeter. Sanders forced M. Williams at second, Brosius to Soriano. Two runs. Diamondbacks 3, Yankees 1.

Yankees—Kim now pitching. Spencer, Brosius and Soriano struck out.

NINTH INNING

Diamondbacks—Grace grounded out, Jeter to Martinez. Miller struck out. Womack grounded out, Mendoza to Martinez.

Yankees—Jeter grounded out, M. Williams to Grace. O'Neill singled to left. B. Williams struck out. Martinez homered to center, scoring O'Neill. Posada walked. Justice singled to second as Posada advanced to second. Spencer struck out. Two runs. Diamondbacks 3, Yankees 3.

10TH INNING

Diamondbacks—Rivera now pitching. Counsell grounded out, Jeter to Martinez. Gonzalez grounded out, Martinez, unassisted. Bautista, pinch-hitting for Cummings, grounded out, Soriano to Martinez.

Yankees—Brosius flied to Sanders. Soriano flied to Gonzalez. Jeter homered to right. One run. Final score: Yankees 4, Diamondbacks 3.

GAME 5
HIGHLIGHTS

NEW YORK 3, ARIZONA 2 (12 INNINGS)

Why the Yankees won: Deja vu was the theme in this game as the Yankees once again tied the game with two outs in the ninth on a two-run home run off Arizona closer Byung-Hyun Kim. This time it was Scott Brosius who provided the heroics by belting a shot into the left field stands. Alfonso Soriano gave the Yankees the win with an RBI single in the 12th. Mike Mussina kept the Yankees in the game with a strong pitching performance as he allowed just two runs on five hits in eight innings of work. Once again, the Yankee offense was non-existent until the game was on the line, but that was enough to give them a 3-2 victory and a 3-2 series lead.

Why the Diamondbacks lost: They left nine men on base in the game and couldn't score with the bases loaded and one out in the 11th. The Diamondbacks also missed an opportunity to extend their two-run lead in the eighth with Tony Womack on third and no outs, but the heart of the Arizona lineup could not get Womack home from third. The bullpen squandered another great pitching performance by a Diamondback starter as Miguel Batista did not allow a run in $7^2/_3$ innings. Steve Finley and catcher Rod Barajas, who was filling in for the injured Damian Miller, provided the runs for the Diamondbacks. Each hit solo home runs to give the Diamondbacks a 2-0 lead.

The turning point: The bottom of the ninth inning proved to be as pivotal as in Game 4. Jorge Posada led off the inning with a double off Kim. Shane Spencer grounded out and Kim struck out Chuck Knoblauch for the second out. Scott Brosius, the 1998 World Series MVP, played hero again and hit a bomb into the left field stands. Upon hitting the pitch, he immediately raised his arm in the air to celebrate the game-tying home run. The Yankees used that momentum once again to earn another victory. Arizona had its chance in the 11th against Mariano Rivera, as they loaded the bases with one out. Rivera got out of it, though, as Alfonso Soriano made a diving catch on Reggie Sanders' liner up the middle and Mark Grace grounded out to Brosius at third. Chuck Knoblauch led off the 12th with his first hit of the series and moved up to second on Brosius' sacrifice bunt. Soriano followed with a single off pitcher Albie Lopez that scored Knoblauch from second just ahead of the throw of right fielder Reggie Sanders.

Notable: Craig Counsell went 0-for-6 and has been in an 0-for-19 slump since homering off Mike Mussina in the opening inning of Game 1. ... Rod Barajas made his first start of the postseason as he replaced catcher Damian Miller, who was injured with a strained right calf. Barajas hit a home run in the game, his first since April 21. ... Chuck Knoblauch ended an 0-for-13 drought with his first hit of the series to open up the 12th. ... According to the Elias Sports Bureau, the Yankees became the first team in postseason history to win two straight games when trailing after eight innings. ...The Yankees won their Series-record 10th straight home game.

Quotable: Scott Brosius, on the Yankee heroics: "It's pretty amazing. You can't draw up two better innings than we had other than maybe trying to score some runs earlier in the game. But to have a

situation two nights in a row and have it happen is pretty unbelievable." ... Joe Torre, talking about the two amazing Yankee wins: "I don't know what's going on. You just shake your head. I said I didn't know last night. You just double that." ... Bob Brenly, on going with Byung-Hyun Kim in the ninth: "He's our closer. I talked to him at length this afternoon. He wanted the ball. I called down to our bullpen coach and asked how he was warming up. He said his stuff was electric." ... Matt Williams, discussing Brenly's decision to go with Kim: "I don't think he should be second-guessed. You turn the ball over to your closer. Miguel hasn't been in the regular rotation pitching every fifth day, so his pitch count is somewhat limited. He made the right decision." ... Byung-Hyun Kim, talking through an interpreter: "I am sorry to my teammates and my manager for giving up the tying run. I want to thank my manager for giving me another chance to pitch." ... Chuck Knoblauch, on the thrilling last two games: "No disrespect to the fans or the Diamondbacks, but you have to sit back and kind of chuckle a little bit because it's so unbelievable."

BOX SCORE

THURSDAY, NOVEMBER 1, AT NEW YORK

Arizona	AB	R	H	RBI	PO	A
Womack, ss	6	0	1	0	1	4
Counsell, 2b	6	0	0	0	3	6
Gonzalez, lf	4	0	0	0	2	0
Bautista, lf	1	0	1	0	2	0
Durazo, dh	4	0	1	0	0	0
M. Williams, 3b	4	0	0	0	1	2
Finley, cf	4	1	3	1	0	0
Sanders, rf	5	0	0	0	3	0
Grace, 1b	3	0	0	0	15	0
Barajas, c	5	1	2	1	7	2
Batista, p	0	0	0	0	0	1
Swindell, p	0	0	0	0	0	0
Kim, p	0	0	0	0	0	0
Morgan, p	0	0	0	0	0	0
Lopez, p	0	0	0	0	0	0
Totals	42	2	8	2	34	15

New York	AB	R	H	RBI	PO	A
Jeter, ss	5	0	1	0	1	1
O'Neill, rf	3	0	0	0	1	0
B. Williams, cf	4	0	1	0	3	0
Martinez, 1b	5	0	1	0	9	1
Posada, c	5	1	1	0	10	0
Spencer, lf	4	0	1	0	3	0
Justice, dh	2	0	0	0	0	0
†Knoblauch, pr-dh	2	1	1	0	0	0
Brosius, 3b	4	1	1	2	2	2
Soriano, 2b	5	0	2	1	6	4
Mussina, p	0	0	0	0	1	0
Mendoza, p	0	0	0	0	0	0
Rivera, p	0	0	0	0	0	1
Hitchcock, p	0	0	0	0	0	0
Totals	39	3	9	3	36	9

Arizona	0	0	0	0	2	0	0	0	0	0 0—2
New York	0	0	0	0	0	0	0	0	2	0 1—3

Arizona	IP	H	R	ER	BB	SO
Batista	7.2	5	0	0	5	6
Swindell	0.1	0	0	0	0	0
Kim	0.2	2	2	2	0	1
Morgan	2.1	0	0	0	0	0
Lopez (L)	0.1	2	1	1	0	0

New York	IP	H	R	ER	BB	SO
Mussina	8.0	5	2	2	3	10
Mendoza	1.0	1	0	0	0	0
Rivera	2.0	2	0	0	1	0
Hitchcock (W)	1.0	0	0	0	0	0

Bases on balls—Off Batista 5 (O'Neill 2, B. Williams, Spencer, Justice), off Mussina 3 (Grace 2, Durazo), off Rivera 1 (Finley). Intentional bases on balls—Off Mussina 2 (Grace, Durazo), off Rivera 1 (Finley).

Strikeouts—By Batista 6 (Posada 2, Spencer, Jeter 2, Justice), by Kim 1 (Knoblauch), by Mussina 10 (Counsell 2, M. Williams, Finley, Sanders 3, Durazo, Womack, Gonzalez).

†Pinch ran for Justice in seventh.

E—Posada. DP—Arizona 2, New York 1. LOB—Arizona 9, New York 8. 2B—Posada. HR—Finley, Barajas, Brosius. SH—M. Williams, Brosius. SB—Womack. CS—Soriano. WP—Batista, Mussina. T—4:15. A—56,018. U—Joyce, plate; DeMuth, first; Rippley, second; M. Hirschbeck, third; Scott, left field; Rapuano, right field.

PLAY BY PLAY

FIRST INNING

Diamondbacks—Womack flied to O'Neill. Counsell struck out. Gonzalez grounded out, Martinez, unassisted.

Yankees—Jeter flied to Sanders. O'Neill walked. B. Williams flied to Gonzalez. Martinez singled to right as O'Neill advanced to third. Posada struck out.

SECOND INNING

Diamondbacks—Durazo flied to B. Williams. M. Williams and Finley struck out.

Yankees—Spencer struck out. Justice grounded out, Womack to Grace. Brosius grounded out, Counsell to Grace.

THIRD INNING

Diamondbacks—Sanders struck out. Grace walked. Barajas singled to center as Grace advanced to second. Womack flied to Spencer. Counsell struck out.

Yankees—Soriano singled to center. Soriano was caught trying to steal second, Barajas to Womack. Jeter struck out. O'Neill grounded out, Womack to Grace.

FOURTH INNING

Diamondbacks—Gonzalez popped to Soriano. Durazo struck out. M. Williams lined to Brosius.

Yankees—B. Williams walked. Martinez fouled to Grace. Posada grounded into a double play, Womack to Counsell to Grace.

FIFTH INNING

Diamondbacks—Finley homered to right. Sanders struck out. Grace grounded out, Martinez, unassisted. Barajas homered to left. Womack struck out. Two runs. Diamondbacks 2, Yankees 0.

Yankees—Spencer singled to second. Spencer advanced to second on a wild pitch. Justice struck out. Brosius flied to Sanders. Soriano grounded out, M. Williams to Grace.

SIXTH INNING

Diamondbacks—Counsell grounded out, Soriano to Martinez. Gonzalez flied to B. Williams. Durazo grounded out, Mussina, unassisted.

Yankees—Jeter singled to center. O'Neill grounded into a double play, Counsell to Grace. B. Williams grounded out, Counsell to Grace.

SEVENTH INNING

Diamondbacks—M. Williams grounded out, Brosius to Martinez. Finley singled to right. Sanders struck out. Finley advanced to second on a wild pitch. Grace was intentionally walked. Barajas lined to Spencer.

Yankees—Martinez grounded out, Batista to Grace. Posada struck out. Spencer and Justice walked. Knoblauch now pinch-running for Justice. Brosius flied to Sanders.

EIGHTH INNING

Diamondbacks—Womack singled to center. Womack stole second and advanced to third on a throwing error by the catcher.

Counsell grounded out, Martinez, unassisted. Gonzalez struck out. Durazo was intentionally walked. M. Williams popped to Soriano.

Yankees—Soriano grounded out, Counsell to Grace. Jeter struck out. O'Neill walked. B. Williams singled to left-center as O'Neill advanced to third. Swindell now pitching. Martinez flied to Gonzalez.

NINTH INNING

Diamondbacks—Mendoza now pitching. Finley singled to left-center. Sanders forced Finley at second, Brosius to Soriano. Grace grounded into a double play, Soriano to Jeter to Martinez.

Yankees—Kim now pitching and Bautista in left. Posada doubled to left. Spencer grounded out, M. Williams to Grace. Knoblauch struck out. Brosius homered to left, scoring Posada. Morgan now pitching. Soriano flied to Bautista. Two runs. Diamondbacks 2, Yankees 2.

10TH INNING

Diamondbacks—Rivera now pitching. Barajas popped to Soriano. Womack grounded out, Soriano to Martinez. Counsell grounded out, Rivera to Martinez.

Yankees—Jeter grounded out, Womack to Grace. O'Neill grounded out, Counsell to Grace. B. Williams grounded out, Barajas to Grace.

11TH INNING

Diamondbacks—Bautista singled to right. Durazo singled to center as Bautista advanced to second. M. Williams hit a sacrifice bunt, Martinez to Soriano, as Bautista advanced to third and Durazo to second. Finley was intentionally walked. Sanders lined to Soriano. Grace forced Durazo at third, Brosius, unassisted.

Yankees—Martinez flied to Bautista. Posada fouled to M. Williams. Spencer popped to Counsell.

12TH INNING

Diamondbacks—Hitchcock now pitching. Barajas grounded out, Soriano to Martinez. Womack flied to Spencer. Counsell flied to B. Williams.

Yankees—Lopez now pitching. Knoblauch singled to center. Brosius hit a sacrifice bunt, Grace, unassisted, as Knoblauch advanced to second. Soriano singled to right, scoring Knoblauch. One run. Final score: Yankees 3, Diamondbacks 2.

GAME 6
HIGHLIGHTS

ARIZONA 15, NEW YORK 2

Why the Diamondbacks won: The offense pounded out 22 hits and collected 15 runs en route to a 15-2 thrashing of the Yankees. Every Diamondback starter including Randy Johnson got a hit. Danny Bautista was the offensive star with a 3-for-4 performance that included five RBIs. Matt Williams also had three hits and Reggie Sanders led the team with four hits. An amazing 23 of the first 30 Arizona hitters reached base. Fifteen runs were plenty for Johnson as he allowed just two runs in seven innings.

Why the Yankees lost: The pitching staff got pounded early and often. Starter Andy Pettitte lasted just two innings and allowed six runs on seven hits. Relief pitcher Jay Witasick wasn't much better as he got knocked around for nine runs and 10 hits in just $1^1/_3$ innings. Before the Yankees could even blink, they were down by 15 after four innings. The offense sputtered again with just seven hits and two runs.

The turning point: Already up 4-0 just two innings into the game, the Diamondbacks exploded for eight runs in the third to open up a 12-0 lead. Arizona scored eight runs on nine hits in the inning. Reggie Sanders, Jay Bell, Johnson and Greg Colbrunn had RBI singles. Luis Gonzalez scored a run on a double and Matt Williams had two doubles and an RBI in the inning. Danny Bautista collected his third and fourth RBIs of the game on a single. Yankee relief pitcher Witasick was roughed up as he allowed eight of the first nine Arizona batters to reach by a hit. The Diamondbacks added three more runs in the fourth.

Notable: The Diamondbacks set a World Series record with 22 hits. ... The 13-run loss was the most lopsided in 293 postseason games for the Yankees. ... Randy Johnson scored two runs for the first time in his career, making him the first pitcher to do it in a Series game since Bob Gibson in 1968. ... Matt Williams became the first player to hit two doubles in an inning in a World Series. He was the 18th player to have two hits in an inning. ... With seven strikeouts, Randy Johnson raised his strikeout total on the year for the regular season and postseason to 412. Sandy Koufax set the old record of 411 in 1965, although that was with only one round of playoffs.

Quotable: Arizona manager Bob Brenly, on how his team rebounded from the last two games: "As heartbreaking as those games were, all three losses in New York, they had no bearing on this game. You can stink up the joint one night and come back and win the next." ... Joe Torre, on the rout his team received: "Nobody likes to get beat up as badly as we got beat up. The only saving grace is that it was only one game. We were in the position to be able to take this." ... Randy Johnson, talking about pitching in a lopsided game: "Everybody came out hitting the ball well tonight. Tip your hat to all of our hitters tonight. It makes your job easier." ... Andy Pettitte, on lasting just two innings: "Obviously, I was expecting a lot more out of myself. It was a shock. To see that inning go on, it was almost as amazing as those home runs we hit."

BOX SCORE

SATURDAY, NOVEMBER 3, AT ARIZONA

New York	AB	R	H	RBI	PO	A
Knoblauch, lf	3	0	0	0	0	1
Stanton, p	0	0	0	0	0	0
Jeter, ss	2	0	0	0	1	2
Wilson, ss	2	0	0	0	0	1
B. Williams, cf	2	1	1	0	3	0
Posada, c	2	0	0	0	5	1
Greene, c	2	1	1	0	4	0
Spencer, rf	4	0	1	1	1	0
Martinez, 1b	2	0	1	0	5	1
Sojo, 1b	2	0	1	1	3	0
Soriano, 2b	4	0	1	0	1	2
Brosius, 3b	4	0	0	0	0	3
Pettitte, p	1	0	1	0	0	0
Witasick, p	0	0	0	0	0	0
Choate, p	1	0	0	0	0	0
§Bellinger, ph-lf	2	0	0	0	1	0
Totals	33	2	7	2	24	11

Arizona	AB	R	H	RBI	PO	A
Womack, ss	6	2	3	2	0	2
Bautista, cf	4	0	3	5	3	0
‡Finley, ph-cf	1	0	0	0	0	0
Gonzalez, lf	4	1	2	2	1	0
†Dellucci, pr-lf	2	0	1	0	1	0
Colbrunn, 1b	5	2	2	1	5	0
M. Williams, 3b	5	1	3	1	0	1
Sanders, rf	5	2	4	1	1	0
Bell, 2b	5	2	1	1	7	1
Miller, c	4	3	2	1	7	0
Barajas, c	0	0	0	0	2	0
Johnson, p	4	2	1	1	0	0
∞Durazo, ph	1	0	0	0	0	0
Witt, p	0	0	0	0	0	0
Brohawn, p	0	0	0	0	0	1
Totals	46	15	22	15	27	5

New York	0	0	0		0	0	2		0 0 0— 2
Arizona	1	3	8		3	0	0		0 0 x—15

New York	IP	H	R	ER	BB	SO
Pettitte (L)	*2.0	7	6	6	2	1
Witasick	1.1	10	9	8	0	4
Choate	2.2	4	0	0	0	1
Stanton	2.0	1	0	0	1	3

Arizona	IP	H	R	ER	BB	SO
Johnson (W)	7.0	6	2	2	2	7
Witt	1.0	0	0	0	1	1
Brohawn	1.0	1	0	0	0	1

*Pitched to two batters in third.

Bases on balls—Off Pettitte 2 (Miller, Colbrunn), off Stanton 1 (Finley), off Johnson 2 (Knoblauch, B. Williams), off Witt 1 (B. Williams). Intentional bases on balls—OffPettitte 1 (Miller).

Strikeouts—By Pettitte 1 (Gonzalez), by Witasick 4 (Womack, Sanders, Bell, Johnson), by Choate 1 (Miller), by Stanton 3 (Miller, Durazo, Colbrunn), by Johnson 7 (Jeter, Brosius, Posada, Spencer, Choate, Soriano, Bellinger), by Witt 1 (Spencer), by Brohawn 1 (Bellinger).

†Pinch ran for Gonzalez in fourth. ‡Flied out for Bautista in sixth. §Struck out for Choate in seventh. ∞Struck out for Johnson in seventh.

E—Soriano. DP—New York 1, Arizona 1. LOB—New York 7, Arizona 10. 2B—Greene, Womack, Gonzalez, M. Williams 2, Sanders, Miller. WP—Witasick. T—3:33. A—49,707. U—DeMuth, plate; Rippley, first; M. Hirschbeck, second; Scott, third; Rapuano, left field; Joyce, right field.

PLAY BY PLAY

FIRST INNING

Yankees—Knoblauch flied to Gonzalez. Jeter struck out. B. Williams fouled to Colbrunn.

Diamondbacks—Womack doubled to right. Bautista singled to center, scoring Womack. Gonzalez grounded into a double play, Soriano to Martinez to Jeter. Colbrunn grounded out, Jeter to Martinez. One run. Diamondbacks 1, Yankees 0.

SECOND INNING

Yankees—Posada and Spencer flied to Bautista. Martinez singled to center. Soriano lined to Bell.

Diamondbacks—M. Williams singled to right. Sanders doubled to center as M. Williams advanced to third. Bell grounded out, Brosius to Martinez. Miller was intentionally walked. Johnson forced M. Williams at the plate, Brosius to Posada as Sanders advanced to third and Miller advanced to second. Womack singled to center, scoring Sanders and Miller as Johnson advanced to second. Bautista singled to left-center, scoring Johnson as Womack advanced to third. Gonzalez struck out. Three runs. Diamondbacks 4, Yankees 0.

THIRD INNING

Yankees—Brosius struck out. Pettitte singled to left. Knoblauch walked. Jeter forced Knoblauch at second, Womack to Bell. B. Williams walked. Posada struck out.

Diamondbacks—Colbrunn walked. M. Williams doubled to right as Colbrunn advanced to third. Witasick now pitching. Sanders singled to left, scoring Colbrunn as M. Williams advanced to third. Bell singled to left, scoring M. Williams as Sanders advanced to second. Miller singled to left as Sanders advanced to third and Bell to second. Johnson singled to right, scoring Sanders as Bell advanced to third and Miller to second. Womack struck out. Bautista singled to center, scoring Bell and Miller as Johnson advanced to second. Gonzalez doubled to left and advanced to third on the throw as Johnson scored and Bautista was thrown out at the plate, Knoblauch to Jeter to Posada. Colbrunn singled to center, scoring Gonzalez. M. Williams doubled to right-center, scoring Colbrunn. Sanders struck out and was thrown out at first after a dropped third strike, Posada to Martinez. Eight runs. Diamondbacks 12, Yankees 0.

FOURTH INNING

Yankees—Spencer struck out. Martinez flied to Bautista. Soriano flied to Sanders.

Diamondbacks—Bell struck out, but was safe at first on a third-strike wild pitch. Miller doubled to center, scoring Bell. Johnson struck out. Womack singled to left as Miller advanced to third. Choate now pitching. Bautista reached first on a fielding error by Soriano, scoring Miller as Womack advanced to second. Gonzalez singled to left, scoring Womack as Bautista advanced to third. Dellucci now pinch-running for Gonzalez. Colbrunn popped to Soriano. M. Williams grounded out, Brosius to Martinez. Four runs. Diamondbacks 15, Yankees 0.

FIFTH INNING

Yankees—Dellucci now in left. Brosius popped to Bell. Choate struck out. Knoblauch grounded out, Womack to Colbrunn.

Diamondbacks—Wilson now at short, Sojo at first and Greene catching. Sanders singled to right. Bell flied to B. Williams. Miller struck out. Johnson flied to Spencer.

SIXTH INNING

Yankees—Wilson popped to Colbrunn. B. Williams singled to center. Greene doubled to left as B. Williams advanced to third. Spencer singled to left, scoring B. Williams as Greene advanced to third. Sojo singled to short, scoring Greene as Spencer advanced to second. Soriano struck out. Brosius popped to Bell. Two runs. Diamondbacks 15, Yankees 2.

Diamondbacks—Womack grounded out, Sojo, unassisted. Finley, pinch-hitting for Bautista, flied to B. Williams. Dellucci singled to right. Colbrunn singled to center as Dellucci advanced to second. M. Williams grounded out, Soriano to Sojo.

SEVENTH INNING

Yankees—Finley now in center. Bellinger, pinch-hitting for Choate, struck out. Knoblauch flied to Dellucci. Wilson popped to Bell.

Diamondbacks—Bellinger now in left and Stanton pitching. Sanders singled to left. Bell flied to Bellinger. Miller struck out. Durazo, pinch-hitting for Johnson, struck out.

EIGHTH INNING

Yankees—Barajas now catching and Witt pitching. B. Williams walked. Greene grounded into a double play, M. Williams to Bell to Colbrunn. Spencer struck out.

Diamondbacks—Womack grounded out, Wilson to Sojo. Finley walked. Dellucci flied to B. Williams. Colbrunn struck out.

NINTH INNING

Yankees—Brohawn now pitching. Sojo grounded out, Brohawn to Colbrunn. Soriano singled to right-center. Brosius popped to Bell. Bellinger struck out. Final score: Diamondbacks 15, Yankees 2.

GAME 7
HIGHLIGHTS

ARIZONA 3, NEW YORK 2

Why the Diamondbacks won: They gave the Yankees a taste of their own medicine with some late-inning heroics off closer Mariano Rivera. The Diamondbacks were able to get two runs off Rivera,

who had converted 23 straight postseason save opportunities, to win the game and the series. Tony Womack and Luis Gonzalez collected RBIs in the ninth to complete the Diamondbacks comeback. Arizona starter Curt Schilling was outstanding on just three days rest. Schilling threw $7^1/3$ innings and allowed two runs and struck out nine. Game 6 starter Randy Johnson picked up the win in relief with $1^1/3$ innings of perfect baseball. Schilling and Johnson were named co-MVPs of the series as they combined to win all four of Arizona's series victories.

Why the Yankees lost: It hadn't happened in a while, but Rivera picked a bad time to blow a postseason save. The normally untouchable righthander allowed two runs in the ninth and blew his first save in postseason play since October 5, 1997 against the Cleveland Indians in the Division Series. Roger Clemens started and threw well. He allowed only a run and struck out 10 in $6^1/3$ innings. The Yankees' struggles at the plate continued, as they had just six hits and struck out 10 times in Game 7. The Yankees hit only .183 as a team in the series. Alfonso Soriano gave the Yankees the lead in the eighth with a home run but that didn't hold up. Tino Martinez provided the other RBI for New York with a single in the seventh.

The turning point: You could not have asked for a better ending to one of the most exciting World Series in recent history. With the Yankees up 2-1 in the bottom of the ninth and the series on the line, Rivera took to the mound for his second inning of work after shutting down the Diamondbacks in the eighth. Mark Grace led off with a single and then Rivera threw away Damian Miller's bunt for an error, putting runners at first and second. Jay Bell tried to bunt the runners up a base but bunted into a force play at third. Tony Womack, who won Game 5 of the Division Series over the Cardinals with an RBI single, lined a game-tying double down the right field line. Craig Counsell was hit by a pitch to load the bases. With the infield in, Luis Gonzalez hit a little blooper that fell behind Derek Jeter at short and in front of Bernie Williams in center field. Bell scored and the Diamondbacks had their first World Series title.

Notable: The Diamondbacks became the fastest team to win a World Series, breaking the mark held by the Florida Marlins of five years. It took the Arizona franchise only four years. ... The Diamondbacks prevented the Yankees from becoming the third team in history to win four titles in a row. Two previous Yankee teams did it in 1936-39 and 1949-53. ... Randy Johnson became the first pitcher to win three Series games since Detroit's Mickey Lolich in 1968. ... The Diamondbacks outscored New York 37-14 in the series. ... The home team won every game for just the third time in World Series history.

... All 50 players on the rosters appeared in at least one game. ... Curt Schilling became the first pitcher to start three games in one Series since Jack Morris did it for Minnesota in 1991.

Quotable: Bob Brenly, on co-MVPs Randy Johnson and Curt Schilling: "I know a lot of comparisons have been made to Sandy Koufax and Don Drysdale and Warren Spahn and Johnny Sain and other great duos, but as a fan watching the game, I don't believe there's ever been two pitchers who are able to maintain their dominance all season long the way these guys have. It's just been phenomenal." ... Mariano Rivera, talking about giving up two runs to lose the game: "That's baseball. There's nothing I can do about it." ... Joe Torre, talking about how the series went: "We're obviously disappointed in the result, but not the effort." ... George Steinbrenner, on his team: "I'm proud of my team. We played our hearts out. It was a very tough loss. I will be a gracious loser. We'll be back. Mark that down. We'll be back." ... New York City Mayor Rudolph Giuliani, after the game: "That was the greatest Game 7 ever. As a Yankees fan, I wish it turned out differently." ... Curt Schilling, on winning his first World Series: "We went through sports' greatest dynasty to win our first World Series."

BOX SCORE

SUNDAY, NOVEMBER 4, AT ARIZONA

New York	AB	R	H	RBI	PO	A
Jeter, ss	4	1	1	0	1	4
O'Neill, rf	3	0	2	0	0	0
‡Knoblauch, ph-lf	1	0	0	0	0	0
B. Williams, cf	4	0	0	0	2	1
Martinez, 1b	4	0	1	1	6	1
Posada, c	4	0	0	0	13	1
Spencer, lf-rf	3	0	0	0	0	0
Soriano, 2b	3	1	1	1	1	2
Brosius, 3b	3	0	0	0	2	0
Clemens, p	2	0	0	0	0	0
Stanton, p	0	0	0	0	0	0
†Justice, ph	1	0	1	0	0	0
Rivera, p	0	0	0	0	0	1
Totals	32	2	6	2	25	10

Arizona	AB	R	H	RBI	PO	A
Womack, ss	5	0	2	1	1	1
Counsell, 2b	4	0	1	0	2	1
Gonzalez, lf	5	0	1	1	2	0
M. Williams, 3b	4	0	1	0	1	1
Finley, cf	4	1	2	0	5	0
Bautista, rf	3	0	1	1	4	1
Grace, 1b	4	0	3	0	2	1
§Dellucci, pr	0	0	0	0	0	0
Miller, c	4	0	0	0	10	0
▲Cummings, pr	0	1	0	0	0	0
Schilling, p	3	0	0	0	0	0
Batista, p	0	0	0	0	0	0
Johnson, p	0	0	0	0	0	0
∞Bell, ph	1	1	0	0	0	0
Totals	37	3	11	3	27	5

New York	0	0 0		0 0 0		1 1	0—2
Arizona	0	0 0		0 0 1		0 0	2—3

One out when winning run scored.

New York	IP	H	R	ER	BB	SO
Clemens	6.1	7	1	1	1	10
Stanton	0.2	0	0	0	0	0
Rivera (L)	1.1	4	2	2	0	3

Arizona	IP	H	R	ER	BB	SO
Schilling	7.1	6	2	2	0	9
Batista	0.1	0	0	0	0	0
Johnson (W)	1.1	0	0	0	0	1

Bases on balls—Off Clemens 1 (Bautista).

Strikeouts—By Clemens 10 (M. Williams, Miller 3, Schilling 3, Womack, Gonzalez, Finley), by Rivera 3 (Gonzalez, M. Williams, Bautista), Schilling 9 (Jeter, Martinez, Clemens, O'Neill, B. Williams, Posada, Soriano, Brosius 2), by Johnson 1 (Posada).

†Singled for Stanton in eighth. ‡Flied out for O'Neill in eighth. §Pinch ran for Grace in ninth. ∞Reached on fielder's choice for Johnson in ninth. ▲Pinch ran for Miller in ninth.

E—Clemens, Soriano, Rivera. LOB—New York 3, Arizona 11. 2B—O'Neill, Womack, Bautista. HR—Soriano. CS—Womack. HBP—By Rivera (Counsell). T—3:20. A—49,589. U—Rippley, plate; M. Hirschbeck, first; Scott, second; Rapuano, third; Joyce, left field; DeMuth, right field.

PLAY BY PLAY

FIRST INNING

Yankees—Jeter struck out. O'Neill doubled to right-center and was out trying for third, Bautista to Counsell to M. Williams. B. Williams flied to Finley.

Diamondbacks—Womack flied to B. Williams. Counsell reached first on a fielding error by Clemens after a toss from Martinez. Gonzalez grounded out, Martinez, unassisted, as Counsell advanced to second. M. Williams struck out.

SECOND INNING

Yankees—Martinez struck out. Posada flied to Gonzalez. Spencer lined to Finley.

Diamondbacks—Finley grounded out, Jeter to Martinez. Bautista walked. Grace singled to left as Bautista advanced to second. Miller and Schilling struck out.

THIRD INNING

Yankees—Soriano flied to Bautista. Brosius fouled to Grace. Clemens struck out.

Diamondbacks—Womack struck out. Counsell singled to center. Gonzalez struck out. M. Williams singled to third as Counsell advanced to second. Finley struck out.

FOURTH INNING

Yankees—Jeter flied to Bautista. O'Neill and B. Williams struck out.

Diamondbacks—Bautista flied to B. Williams. Grace singled to short. Miller and Schilling struck out.

FIFTH INNING

Yankees—Martinez flied to Finley. Posada struck out. Spencer popped to Counsell.

Diamondbacks—Womack grounded out, Soriano to Martinez. Counsell grounded out, Jeter to Martinez. Gonzalez reached first on a fielding error by Soriano. M. Williams forced Gonzalez at second, Jeter to Soriano.

SIXTH INNING

Yankees—Soriano and Brosius struck out. Clemens flied to Bautista.

Diamondbacks—Finley singled to center. Bautista doubled to left-center and was out trying for third, B. Williams to Jeter to Brosius, as Finley scored. Grace grounded out, Soriano to Martinez. Miller struck out. One run. Diamondbacks 1, Yankees 0.

SEVENTH INNING

Yankees—Jeter singled to right. O'Neill singled to center as Jeter advanced to second. B. Williams forced O'Neill at second, Grace to Womack, as Jeter advanced to third. Martinez singled to right, scoring Jeter as B. Williams advanced to second. Posada flied to Gonzalez. Spencer flied to Finley. One run. Diamondbacks 1, Yankees 1.

Diamondbacks—Schilling struck out. Womack singled to right. Stanton now pitching. Womack caught trying to steal second, Posada to Jeter. Counsell fouled to Martinez.

EIGHTH INNING

Yankees—Soriano homered to left. Brosius struck out. Justice, pinch-hitting for Stanton, singled to center. Batista now pitching. Jeter forced Justice at second, M. Williams to Counsell. Johnson now pitching. Knoblauch, pinch-hitting for O'Neill, flied to Bautista. One run. Yankees 2, Diamondbacks 1.

Diamondbacks—Knoblauch now in left, Spencer in right and Rivera pitching. Gonzalez and M. Williams struck out. M. Williams struck out. Finley singled to right. Bautista struck out.

NINTH INNING

Yankees—B. Williams flied to Finley. Martinez grounded out, Womack to Grace. Posada struck out.

Diamondbacks—Grace singled to center. Dellucci now pinch-running for Grace. Miller reached first on a fielder's choice and Dellucci reached second on a throwing error by Rivera. Bell, pinch-hitting for Johnson, forced Dellucci at third, Rivera to Brosius as Miller advanced to second. Cummings now pinch-running for Miller. Womack doubled to right, scoring Cummings as Bell advanced to third. Counsell hit by a pitch. Gonzalez singled to left-center, scoring Bell as Womack advanced to third and Counsell to second. Two runs. Final score: Diamondbacks 3, Yankees 2.

STATISTICS

ARIZONA DIAMONDBACKS' BATTING AND FIELDING AVERAGES

Player, position	G	AB	R	H	TB	2B	3B	HR	RBI	BB	IBB	SO	Avg.	PO	A	E	Avg.
Bautista, cf-ph-dh-lf-rf	5	12	1	7	9	2	0	0	7	1	0	1	.583	9	1	0	1.000
Dellucci, pr-lf..................	2	2	0	1	1	0	0	0	0	0	0	0	.500	1	0	0	1.000
Barajas, c	2	5	1	2	5	0	0	1	1	0	0	0	.400	9	2	0	1.000
Colbrunn, 1b	1	5	2	2	2	0	0	0	1	1	0	1	.400	5	0	0	1.000
Finley, cf-ph	7	19	5	7	10	0	0	1	2	4	1	5	.368	16	0	0	1.000
Durazo, dh-ph	4	11	0	4	5	1	0	0	1	3	1	4	.364	0	0	0	.000
Sanders, rf	6	23	6	7	8	1	0	0	1	1	1	7	.304	9	0	0	1.000
M. Williams, 3b..............	7	26	3	7	12	2	0	1	7	0	0	6	.269	2	13	0	1.000
Grace, 1b	6	19	1	5	9	1	0	1	3	4	2	1	.263	53	2	1	.982
Gonzalez, lf	7	27	4	7	12	2	0	1	5	1	0	11	.259	11	0	0	1.000
Womack, ss	7	32	3	8	11	3	0	0	3	1	0	7	.250	7	23	1	.968
Miller, c	6	21	3	4	6	2	0	0	2	1	1	11	.190	54	0	1	.982
Bell, ph-2b	3	7	3	1	1	0	0	0	1	0	0	2	.143	7	1	0	1.000
Johnson, p	3	7	2	1	1	0	0	0	1	0	0	2	.143	0	1	0	1.000
Counsell, 2b	6	24	1	2	5	0	0	1	1	0	0	7	.083	11	16	0	1.000
Anderson, p	1	0	0	0	0	0	0	0	0	0	0	0	.000	0	0	0	.000
Batista, p	2	0	0	0	0	0	0	0	0	0	0	0	.000	0	1	0	1.000
Brohawn, p	1	0	0	0	0	0	0	0	0	0	0	0	.000	0	1	0	1.000
Cummings, pr-dh............	2	0	2	0	0	0	0	0	0	0	0	0	.000	0	0	0	.000
Kim, p	2	0	0	0	0	0	0	0	0	0	0	0	.000	0	0	0	.000
Lopez, p	1	0	0	0	0	0	0	0	0	0	0	0	.000	0	0	0	.000
Morgan, p	3	0	0	0	0	0	0	0	0	0	0	0	.000	0	0	0	.000
Swindell, p	3	0	0	0	0	0	0	0	0	0	0	0	.000	0	0	0	.000
Witt, p	1	0	0	0	0	0	0	0	0	0	0	0	.000	0	0	0	.000
Schilling, p	3	6	0	0	0	0	0	0	0	0	0	5	.000	1	0	0	1.000
Totals	7	246	37	65	97	14	0	6	36	17	6	70	.264	195	61	3	.988

NEW YORK YANKEES' BATTING AND FIELDING AVERAGES

Player, position	G	AB	R	H	TB	2B	3B	HR	RBI	BB	IBB	SO	Avg.	PO	A	E	Avg.
Greene, c......................	1	2	1	1	2	1	0	0	0	0	0	0	.500	4	0	0	1.000
Pettitte, p	2	3	0	1	1	0	0	0	0	0	0	1	.333	0	1	0	1.000
Sojo, ph-1b	2	3	0	1	1	0	0	0	1	0	0	0	.333	3	0	0	1.000
O'Neill, ph-rf	5	15	1	5	6	1	0	0	0	2	0	2	.333	4	0	0	1.000
Soriano, 2b	7	25	1	6	9	0	0	1	2	0	0	7	.240	18	20	3	.927
B. Williams, cf..............	7	24	2	5	6	1	0	0	1	4	0	6	.208	12	1	0	1.000
Spencer, ph-rf-lf...........	7	20	1	4	7	0	0	1	2	2	0	6	.200	6	1	0	1.000
Martinez, 1b.................	6	21	1	4	7	0	0	1	3	2	0	2	.190	45	7	0	1.000
Posada, c	7	23	2	4	8	1	0	1	1	3	0	8	.174	69	4	1	.986
Justice, rf-lf-ph-dh.........	5	12	0	2	2	0	0	0	0	1	0	9	.167	1	0	1	.500
Brosius, 3b...................	7	24	1	4	9	2	0	1	3	0	0	8	.167	5	15	1	.952
Jeter, ss	7	27	3	4	7	0	0	1	1	0	0	6	.148	7	17	0	1.000
Knoblauch, lf-dh-pr-ph....	6	18	1	1	1	0	0	0	0	1	0	2	.056	1	1	0	1.000
Hernandez, p	1	0	0	0	0	0	0	0	0	0	0	0	.000	0	0	0	.000
Hitchcock, p	2	0	0	0	0	0	0	0	0	0	0	0	.000	0	0	0	.000
Mendoza, p	2	0	0	0	0	0	0	0	0	0	0	0	.000	0	1	0	1.000
Rivera, p	4	0	0	0	0	0	0	0	0	0	0	0	.000	1	2	1	.750
Stanton, p	5	0	0	0	0	0	0	0	0	0	0	0	.000	1	0	0	1.000
Witasick, p	1	0	0	0	0	0	0	0	0	0	0	0	.000	0	0	0	.000
Choate, p......................	2	1	0	0	0	0	0	0	0	0	0	1	.000	0	1	0	1.000
Mussina, p	2	1	0	0	0	0	0	0	0	0	0	1	.000	2	0	0	1.000
Bellinger, pr-lf-ph	2	2	0	0	0	0	0	0	0	0	0	2	.000	1	0	0	1.000

Player, position	G	AB	R	H	TB	2B	3B	HR	RBI	BB	IBB	SO	Avg.	PO	A	E	Avg.
						BATTING										FIELDING	
Clemens, p	2	2	0	0	0	0	0	0	0	0	0	1	.000	0	3	1	.750
Velarde, 1b	1	3	0	0	0	0	0	0	0	1	0	1	.000	10	0	0	1.000
Wilson, ph-ss	2	3	0	0	0	0	0	0	0	0	0	0	.000	0	1	0	1.000
Totals	7	229	14	42	66	6	0	6	14	16	0	63	.183	190	75	8	.971

ARIZONA DIAMONDBACKS' PITCHING RECORDS

Pitcher	G	GS	CG	IP	H	R	ER	HR	BB	IBB	SO	HB	WP	W	L	Pct.	ERA
Batista	2	1	0	8.0	5	0	0	0	5	0	6	0	1	0	0	.000	0.00
Morgan	3	0	0	4.2	1	0	0	0	0	0	1	0	1	0	0	.000	0.00
Swindell	3	0	0	2.2	1	0	0	0	1	0	2	0	1	0	0	.000	0.00
Brohawn	1	0	0	1.0	1	0	0	0	0	0	1	0	0	0	0	.000	0.00
Witt	1	0	0	1.0	0	0	0	0	1	0	1	0	0	0	0	.000	0.00
Johnson	3	2	1	17.1	9	2	2	0	3	0	19	0	0	3	0	1.000	1.04
Schilling	3	3	0	21.1	12	4	4	2	2	0	26	1	0	1	0	1.000	1.69
Anderson	1	1	0	5.1	5	2	2	1	3	0	1	0	1	0	1	.000	3.38
Kim	2	0	0	3.1	6	5	5	3	1	0	6	0	0	0	1	.000	13.50
Lopez	1	0	0	0.1	2	1	1	0	0	0	0	0	0	0	1	.000	27.00
Totals	7	7	1	65.0	42	14	14	6	16	0	63	1	4	4	3	.571	1.94

Shutout—Johnson. No saves.

NEW YORK YANKEES' PITCHING RECORDS

Pitcher	G	GS	CG	IP	H	R	ER	HR	BB	IBB	SO	HB	WP	W	L	Pct.	ERA
Hitchcock	2	0	0	4.0	1	0	0	0	0	0	6	0	0	1	0	1.000	0.00
Mendoza	2	0	0	2.2	1	0	0	0	0	0	1	0	0	0	0	.000	0.00
Clemens	2	2	0	13.1	10	2	2	0	4	0	19	1	0	1	0	1.000	1.35
Hernandez	1	1	0	6.1	4	1	1	1	4	0	5	2	0	0	0	.000	1.42
Rivera	4	0	0	6.1	6	2	1	0	1	1	7	1	0	1	1	.500	1.42
Choate	2	0	0	3.2	7	4	1	0	1	1	2	0	0	0	0	.000	2.45
Stanton	5	0	0	5.2	3	2	2	0	1	0	3	0	0	0	0	.000	3.18
Mussina	2	2	0	11.0	11	7	5	4	4	3	14	1	1	0	1	.000	4.09
Pettitte	2	2	0	9.0	12	10	10	1	2	1	9	1	0	0	2	.000	10.00
Witasick	1	0	0	1.1	10	9	8	0	0	0	4	0	1	0	0	.000	54.00
Totals	7	7	0	63.1	65	37	30	6	17	6	70	6	2	3	4	.429	4.26

No shutouts. Save—Rivera.

SCORE BY INNINGS

Arizona	2	4	12	9	2	1	3	2	2	0	0	0—37
New York	1	1	1	0	0	3	1	1	4	1	0	1—14

MISCELLANEOUS STATISTICS

Sacrifice hits—Counsell 4, Brosius, M. Williams.

Sacrifice flies—M. Williams 2.

Stolen bases—O'Neill, Sanders, Womack.

Caught stealing—Finley, Soriano, Womack.

Double plays—Counsell and Grace 2; Soriano, Jeter and Martinez 2; Brosius, Soriano and Velarde; Counsell, Womack and Grace; Jeter, Soriano and Martinez; Posada and Jeter; Soriano, Martinez and Jeter; Spencer and Posada; M. Williams, Bell and Colbrunn; M. Williams, Counsell and Grace; Womack, Counsell and Grace.

Left on bases—Arizona 6, 1, 5, 7, 9, 10, 11—49; New York 5, 3, 8, 4, 8, 7, 3—38.

Hit by pitcher—By Hernandez 2 (Gonzalez, Miller), by Clemens (Sanders), by Mussina (Womack), by Pettitte (Gonzalez), by Rivera (Counsell), by Schilling (Jeter).

Passed balls—None.

Balks—None.

Time of games—First game, 2:44; second game, 2:35; third game, 3:26; fourth game, 3:31; fifth game, 4:15; sixth game, 3:33; seventh game, 3:20.

Attendance—First game, 49,646; second game, 49,646; third game, 55,820; fourth game, 55,863; fifth game, 56,018; sixth game, 49,707; seventh game, 49,589.

Umpires—Rippley, M. Hirschbeck, Scott, Rapuano, Joyce and DeMuth.

Official scorers—Bob Eger, Red Foley, Howie Karpin, Ian MacDonald, Jack O'Connell, T.J. Quinn, Bill Shannon.

ALL-STAR GAME

AT SAFECO FIELD, SEATTLE, JULY 10, 2001

HIGHLIGHTS

AMERICAN LEAGUE 4, NATIONAL LEAGUE 1

Why the American League won: A combination of great pitching and the long ball helped lead the A.L. to its fifth consecutive All-Star victory and 11th in 14 games. Three of the A.L.'s four runs came on solo homers by Cal Ripken Jr., Derek Jeter and Magglio Ordonez, who was the only player for either team to have two hits. Meanwhile, A.L. pitchers held N.L. batters to just three hits.

Why the National League lost: While their pitchers prevented A.L. hitters from putting together a big inning, three of the eight hits they allowed were homers. And the N.L.'s own offense was anemic. The senior circuit had only three hits-two singles and a double-and didn't have a runner reach base until Luis Gonzalez led off the fourth inning with a single. The 3-4-5 spots in the N.L. lineup went a combined 0 for 12.

The turning points:

1. The A.L. got on the scoreboard in the third inning when Ripken, playing in his 18th and final All-Star Game, hit a solo homer to left field on the first pitch he saw from Chan Ho Park to give the A.L. a lead it would never surrender. Ripken received a thunderous standing ovation from the crowd at Seattle's Safeco Field and eventually was named All-Star Game MVP.

2. Trailing 2-0 in the top of the sixth, the N.L. mounted its best chance for a big inning but scored only one run. Jeff Kent led off the inning with a double to right field off Paul Quantrill. Rich Aurilia then grounded out to third and Kent was unable to advance. Lance Berkman then singled to right, putting N.L. runners on the corners with only one out. A.L. manager Joe Torre brought in one of his own players, Yankees lefthander Mike Stanton, to face Ryan Klesko, who hit a sacrifice fly to center to make it 2-1. Vladimir Guerrero came up with a chance to tie the game or put the N.L. ahead but flied out to left to end the inning.

3. After the N.L. had cut the A.L.'s lead in half with a run in the sixth to make it 2-1, the A.L. came right back with two runs of its own. With Jon Lieber pitching, Jeter led off the inning with a homer to center. Ordonez followed Jeter with another homer to center and the A.L. had a 4-1 lead.

Notable: With his homer in the third, Ripken, 40, became the oldest player to homer in an All-Star Game. It was the second career All-Star homer for Ripken, who also hit a three-run shot in the 1991 game in Toronto. ... Ripken became just the fifth player to be named All-Star Game MVP more than once. The previous multiple winners: Ted Williams, Willie Mays, Steve Garvey and Gary Carter. ... The

consecutive homers by Jeter and Ordonez in the sixth marked the fifth time that had happened in All-Star history. ... Jeter became the first Yankee to hit a home run in an All-Star Game since Yogi Berra in 1959. ... Torre improved his record to 4-0 as an All-Star manager. ... Roger Clemens, the starting pitcher for the American League, and became the sixth pitcher to start an All-Star Game representing two different teams.

Quotable: Ripken, on homering in his final All-Star Game: "I've been able to go to whole lot of them, but this is by far the most special." ... Park, on giving up the dramatic homer to Ripken: "It was an amazing moment. The first pitch I ever threw in an All-Star Game was the last home run for Mr. Ripken. It's a big gift for him. It made him MVP, that's pretty good." ... N.L. manager Bobby Valentine, on why his squad managed only three hits: "When you have one at-bat to adjust, it was a tough thing for the hitters. And their pitchers made really good pitches." ... Johnson, on starting in place of Arizona teammate Curt Schilling (who skipped the start because he started a game two days earlier): "I know Schilling is going to be asking for some favor on the golf course."

BOX SCORE

National League	AB	R	H	RBI	PO	A
L. Gonzalez, cf (D'backs)	2	0	1	0	0	0
Berkman, cf (Astros)	2	0	1	0	2	0
Helton, 1b (Rockies)	2	0	0	0	3	0
Klesko, 1b (Padres)	1	0	0	1	7	0
Bonds, lf (Giants)	2	0	0	0	0	0
†Guerrero, ph-rf (Expos)	1	0	0	0	1	0
◆Giles, ph (Pirates)	1	0	0	0	0	0
Sosa, rf (Cubs)	2	0	0	0	1	0
Alou, rf-lf (Astros)	1	0	0	0	1	0
■Casey, ph (Reds)	1	0	0	0	0	0
Walker, dh (Rockies)	2	0	0	0	0	0
§Floyd, ph-dh (Marlins)	2	0	0	0	0	0
Piazza, c (Mets)	2	0	0	0	5	0
Pujols, 3b-2b (Cardinals)	0	0	0	0	0	1
C. Jones, 3b (Braves)	2	0	0	0	0	1
C. Johnson, c (Marlins)	1	0	0	0	3	0
Kent, 2b (Giants)	2	1	1	0	0	4
▲Nevin, ph-3b (Padres)	1	0	0	0	0	0
Aurilia, ss (Giants)	2	0	0	0	1	3
Rollins, ss (Phillies)	0	0	0	0	0	1
R. Johnson, p (D'backs)	0	0	0	0	0	0
Park, p (Dodgers)	0	0	0	0	0	0
Burkett, p (Braves)	0	0	0	0	0	0
Hampton, p (Rockies)	0	0	0	0	0	0
Lieber, p (Cubs)	0	0	0	0	0	0
Morris, p (Cardinals)	0	0	0	0	0	0
Shaw, p (Dodgers)	0	0	0	0	0	0
Wagner, p (Astros)	0	0	0	0	0	0
Sheets, p (Brewers)	0	0	0	0	0	0
Totals	**29**	**1**	**3**	**1**	**24**	**10**
American League	**AB**	**R**	**H**	**RBI**	**PO**	**A**
Suzuki, cf-rf (Mariners)	3	0	1	0	0	0
Williams, cf (Yankees)	1	0	0	0	2	0
A. R'dr'g'z, ss-3b-ss (Rangers)	2	0	0	0	1	2
Jeter, ss (Yankees)	1	1	1	1	0	0

American League	AB	R	H	RBI	PO	A
∞Guzman, ph-ss (Twins)	1	0	0	0	0	0
Ramirez, lf (Red Sox)	1	0	0	0	3	0
Ordonez, lf (White Sox)	3	1	2	1	4	0
Boone, 2b (Mariners).............	2	0	0	0	1	0
Alomar, 2b (Indians)	2	0	0	0	0	1
J. Gonzalez, rf (Indians).........	1	0	0	0	1	0
Cameron, cf-rf (Mariners)......	3	0	1	0	1	0
Olerud, 1b (Mariners)	2	0	0	0	4	0
*Giambi, pr-1b (Athletics)......	1	1	0	0	1	0
Sweeney, 1b (Royals)	1	0	0	0	2	1
Martinez, dh (Mariners)	2	0	0	0	0	0
‡Clark, ph-dh (Tigers)...........	1	0	0	0	0	0
Ripken, 3b-ss-3b (Orioles)	2	1	1	1	1	2
Glaus, 3b (Angels)	1	0	0	0	0	2
I. Rodriguez, c (Rangers).......	2	0	1	1	2	0
Posada, c (Yankees)	1	0	1	0	3	0
Clemens, p (Yankees)	0	0	0	0	0	1
Garcia, p (Mariners).............	0	0	0	0	0	0
Pettitte, p (Yankees)..............	0	0	0	0	0	0
Mays, p (Twins)	0	0	0	0	0	0
Quantrill, p (Blue Jays)	0	0	0	0	0	0
Stanton, p (Yankees).............	0	0	0	0	0	0
Nelson, p (Mariners)..............	0	0	0	0	0	0
Percival, p (Angels)	0	0	0	0	0	0
Sasaki, p (Mariners)	0	0	0	0	1	0
Totals.................................	33	4	8	4	27	9

National League	0	0	0		0	0	1		0	0	0—1
American League	0	0	1		0	1	2		0	0	x—4

National League	IP	H	R	ER	BB	SO
R. Johnson (Diamondbacks) .	2.0	1	0	0	0	3
Park (Dodgers) (L)................	1.0	1	1	1	0	1
Burkett (Braves)...................	1.0	0	0	0	0	1
Hampton (Rockies)	1.0	1	1	0	0	0
Lieber (Cubs)........................	1.0	3	2	2	0	1
Morris (Cardinals).................	1.0	1	0	0	0	1
Shaw (Dodgers)....................	0.1	1	0	0	0	0
Wagner (Astros)	0.1	0	0	0	0	0
Sheets (Brewers)	0.1	0	0	0	0	0

American League	IP	H	R	ER	BB	SO
Clemens (Yankees)	2.0	0	0	0	0	1
Garcia (Mariners) (W)............	1.0	0	0	0	0	0
Pettitte (Yankees).................	1.0	1	0	0	0	1
Mays (Twins)	1.0	0	0	0	0	0
Quantrill (Blue Jays)	0.1	2	1	1	0	0
Stanton (Yankees)	0.2	0	0	0	0	0
Nelson (Mariners)..................	1.0	0	0	0	1	1
Percival (Angels)	1.0	0	0	0	1	1
Sasaki (Mariners) (S)............	1.0	0	0	0	0	1

Bases on balls—Off Nelson 1 (Pujols), off Percival 1 (Rollins).

Strikeouts—By R. Johnson 3 (A. Rodriguez, Ramirez, Martinez), by Park 1 (A. Rodriguez), by Burkett 1 (Cameron), by Lieber 1 (Clark), by Morris 1 (Guzman), by Clemens 1 (Helton), by Pettitte 1 (Bonds), by Nelson 1 (Alou), by Percival 1 (Klesko), by Sasaki 1 (Casey).

*Ran for Olerud in fifth. †Flied out for Bonds in sixth. ‡Struck out for Martinez in sixth. §Flied out for Walker in seventh. ∞Struck out for Jeter in seventh. sFlied out for Kent in eighth. uGrounded out for Guerrero in ninth. nStruck out for Alou in ninth. E—Kent. LOB—N.L. 4, A.L. 5. 2B—Kent, Cameron, Posada. HR—Ripken, Jeter, Ordonez. SB—Rollins, Suzuki. SF—Klesko. T—2:48. A—47,364. U—DeMuth, plate; Scott, first; Joyce, second; Layne, third; Kulpa, left field; Randazzo, right field. Official scorers—Ian McDonald, Terry Mosher and Bob Sherwin.

Players listed on rosters but not used: N.L.—Reed (Mets); Schilling (Diamondbacks); Milton (Twins), Vaughn (Devil Rays).

PLAY BY PLAY

FIRST INNING

N.L.—A. Rodriguez went to third (as an honorary gesture to Cal Ripken) and Ripken to short. L. Gonzalez popped to A. Rodriguez. Helton struck out. Bonds grounded out, Clemens to Olerud.

A.L.—Suzuki singled to first. A. Rodriguez struck out as Suzuki stole second. Ramirez struck out. Boone popped to Aurilia.

SECOND INNING

N.L.—A. Rodriguez went to short and Ripken to third. Sosa grounded out, A. Rodriguez to Olerud. Walker flied to Ramirez. Piazza flied to J. Gonzalez.

A.L.—J. Gonzalez flied to Sosa. Olerud grounded out, Kent to Helton. Martinez struck out.

THIRD INNING

N.L.—Garcia now pitching. C. Jones and Kent flied to Ramirez. Aurilia grounded out, Ripken to Olerud.

A.L.—Park now pitching. Ripken homered to left. I. Rodriguez and Suzuki grounded out, Kent to Helton. A. Rodriguez struck out. One run. One run. A.L. 1, N.L. 0.

FOURTH INNING

N.L.—Ordonez now in left, Cameron in center, Pettitte pitching and Suzuki moves to right. L. Gonzalez singled to right. Helton popped to Ripken. Bonds struck out. Sosa forced L. Gonzalez at second, A. Rodriguez to Boone.

A.L.—Klesko now at first, Alou in right and Burkett pitching. Ordonez grounded out, Aurilia to Klesko. Boone grounded out, C. Jones to Klesko. Cameron struck out.

FIFTH INNING

N.L.—Mays now pitching. Walker flied to Ordonez. Piazza grounded out, Ripken to Olerud. C. Jones flied to Ordonez.

A.L.—Pujols now at third, Berkman in center, C. Johnson catching and Hampton pitching. Olerud reached second on a throwing error by Kent. Giambi now pinch-running for Olerud. Martinez and Ripken grounded out, Aurilia to Klesko. I. Rodriguez singled to center, scoring Giambi. Suzuki grounded out, Pujols to Klesko. One run. A.L. 2, N.L. 0.

SIXTH INNING

N.L.—Giambi now at first, Alomar at second, Glaus at third, Jeter at short, Williams at center, Posada catching, Quantrill pitching and Cameron moves to right. Game delayed at 7:06 p.m. due to a ceremony to honor Tony Gwynn and Cal Ripken with the Commissioner's Historic Achievement Award. Game restarted at 7:12 p.m. Kent doubled to right. Aurilia grounded out, Glaus to Giambi. Berkman singled to left as Kent advanced to third. Stanton now pitching. Klesko hit a sacrifice fly to Williams, scoring Kent. Guerrero, pinch-hitting for Bonds, flied out to Ordonez. One run. A.L. 2, N.L. 1.

A.L.—Rollins now at short, Guerrero in right, Lieber pitching and Alou moves to left. Jeter homered to center. Ordonez homered to right-center. Alomar lined to Alou. Cameron doubled to left. Giambi grounded out, Rollins to Klesko as Cameron advanced to third. Clark, pinch-hitting for Martinez, struck out. Two runs. A.L. 4, N.L. 1.

SEVENTH INNING

N.L.—Sweeney now at first and Nelson pitching. Alou struck out. Floyd, pinch-hitting for Walker, flied to Williams. Pujols walked. C. Johnson flied to Ordonez.

A.L.—Morris now pitching. Glaus flied to Berkman. Posada doubled to center. Williams grounded out, Kent to Klesko, as Posada advanced to third. Guzman, pinch-hitting for Jeter, struck out.

EIGHTH INNING

N.L.—Guzman now at short and Percival pitching. Nevin, pinch-hitting for Kent, flied to Cameron. Rollins walked. With Berkman batting, Rollins stole second. Berkman grounded out, Glaus to Sweeney. Klesko struck out.

A.L.—Nevin now at third, Shaw pitching and Pujols moves to second. Ordonez singled to center. Alomar flied to Berkman. Wagner now pitching. Cameron fouled to C. Johnson. Sheets now pitching. Sweeney popped to Guerrero.

NINTH INNING

N.L.—Sasaki now pitching. Giles, pinch-hitting for Guerrero, grounded out, Alomar to Sweeney. Casey, pinch-hitting for Alou, struck out. Floyd grounded out, Sweeney to Sasaki. Final score: A.L. 4, N.L. 1.

NOTABLE PERFORMANCES
BOX SCORES OF NO-HIT GAMES

HIDEO NOMO

BOSTON 3, BALTIMORE 0

WEDNESDAY, APRIL 4, AT BALTIMORE

BOSTON	AB	R	H	RBI	BALTIMORE	AB	R	H	RBI
Stynes, 2b	4	0	1	0	Anderson, lf	4	0	0	0
Lansing, pr-2b	0	0	0	0	Bordick, ss	4	0	0	0
Nixon, rf	4	0	1	0	DeShields, dh	2	0	0	0
Everett, cf	3	0	0	0	Segui, 1b	3	0	0	0
Ramirez, dh	3	0	0	0	Richard, rf	2	0	0	0
O'Leary, lf	4	0	0	0	Mora, cf	3	0	0	0
Varitek, c	3	0	0	0	Ripken, 3b	3	0	0	0
Hillenbrand, 3b	4	1	1	0	Fordyce, c	3	0	0	0
Daubach, 1b	4	2	2	3	Hairston, 2b	3	0	0	0
Grebeck, ss	4	0	0	0					
Totals	33	3	5	3	Totals	27	0	0	0

```
Boston ............  0 0 2   0 0 0   0 1 0—3
Baltimore ..........  0 0 0   0 0 0   0 0 0—0
```

BOSTON	IP	H	R	ER	BB	SO
Nomo (W, 1-0)	9.0	0	0	0	3	11

BALTIMORE	IP	H	R	ER	BB	SO
Ponson (L, 0-1)	7.1	4	3	2	1	10
Ryan	0.1	0	0	0	1	1
Trombley	0.1	0	0	0	1	1
Roberts	1.0	1	0	0	0	1

E—Hillenbrand, Ripken, Bordick. DP—Baltimore 1. LOB—Boston 6, Baltimore 3. 2B—Stynes, Hillenbrand. HR—Daubach 2. CS—Nixon, Segui. WP—Nomo. T—2:29. A—35,602. U—Cooper, plate; Gorman, first; Eddings, second; Crawford, third.

A.J. BURNETT

FLORIDA 3, SAN DIEGO 0

SATURDAY, MAY 12, AT SAN DIEGO

FLORIDA	AB	R	H	RBI	SAN DIEGO	AB	R	H	RBI
Castillo, 2b	5	0	1	0	Henderson, lf	3	0	0	0
Owens, rf	3	1	1	0	Kotsay, cf	3	0	0	0
Floyd, lf	3	1	0	0	Klesko, 1b	2	0	0	0
Wilson, cf	4	1	3	0	Magadan, 3b	3	0	0	0
Johnson, c	4	0	1	2	Davis, c	3	0	0	0
Millar, 3b	4	0	0	0	Trammell, rf	2	0	0	0
Berg, 3b	0	0	0	0	Jackson, 2b	1	0	0	0
Lee, 1b	4	0	0	0	Arias, 2b	2	0	0	0
Gonzalez, ss	4	0	0	0	Mendez, ss	2	0	0	0
Burnett, p	3	0	1	0	Perez, p	1	0	0	0
					Serrano, p	2	0	0	0
					Colangelo, ph	1	0	0	0
					Myers, p	0	0	0	0
					Nevin, ph	1	0	0	0
Totals	34	3	7	2	Totals	26	0	0	0

```
Florida ............  0 0 2   0 1 0   0 0 0—3
San Diego ..........  0 0 0   0 0 0   0 0 0—0
```

FLORIDA	IP	H	R	ER	BB	SO
Burnett (W, 1-1)	9.0	0	0	0	9	7

SAN DIEGO	IP	H	R	ER	BB	SO
Serrano (L, 0-1)	7.0	6	3	1	2	6
Myers	2.0	1	0	0	1	1

E—Jackson, Mendez 2. DP—Florida 1, San Diego 1. LOB—Florida 7, San Diego 9. 2B—Johnson, Burnett. SB—Henderson, Klesko, Mendez. CS—Wilson. HBP—By Burnett (Jackson). WP—Burnett. T—2:39. A—41,811. U—Brinkman, plate; Hodges, first; Nelson, second; Cousins, third.

BUD SMITH

ST. LOUIS 4, SAN DIEGO 0

MONDAY, SEPTEMBER 3, AT SAN DIEGO

ST. LOUIS	AB	R	H	RBI	SAN DIEGO	AB	R	H	RBI
Vina, 2b	4	2	1	0	Henderson, lf	2	0	0	0
Polanco, 3b	5	1	3	1	Jimenez, ss	3	0	0	0
Drew, rf	4	0	1	0	Klesko, 1b	4	0	0	0
Pujols, lf-1b	4	1	2	2	Nevin, 3b	4	0	0	0
Edmonds, cf	3	0	0	0	Trammell, rf	3	0	0	0
McGwire, 1b	4	0	0	0	Lankford, cf	2	0	0	0
Robinson, lf	1	0	0	0	Davis, c	3	0	0	0
Renteria, ss	3	0	1	0	Jackson, 2b	2	0	0	0
Marrero, c	4	0	0	0	Gwynn, ph	1	0	0	0
Smith, p	3	0	0	0	Crespo, 2b	0	0	0	0
					Jones, p	2	0	0	0
					Lee, p	0	0	0	0
					Gonzalez, ph	1	0	0	0
					Serrano, p	0	0	0	0
Totals	35	4	8	3	Totals	27	0	0	0

```
St. Louis ............  2 0 0   0 1 0   1 0 0—4
San Diego ..........  0 0 0   0 0 0   0 0 0—0
```

ST. LOUIS	IP	H	R	ER	BB	SO
Smith (W, 4-2)	9.0	0	0	0	4	7

SAN DIEGO	IP	H	R	ER	BB	SO
Jones (L, 8-17)	6.2	7	4	3	3	3
Lee	1.1	0	0	0	2	1
Serrano	1.0	1	0	0	1	1

E—Davis. LOB—St. Louis 11, San Diego 4. 2B—Polanco. HR—Pujols. SB—Polanco, Drew, Henderson. HBP—By Lee (Renteria). T—2:47. A—36,535. U—Cuzzi, plate; Barron, first; Froemming, second; Meals, third.

LOW-HIT GAMES
AMERICAN LEAGUE

ONE-HIT GAMES

Date **Pitcher(s), Team, Opponent, Result—Player with hit**
5-25 Hideo Nomo, Boston vs. Toronto, W 4-0—Shannon Stewart (double in fourth)
7-6 Mark Mulder, Oakland at Arizona N.L., W 3-0—Danny Bautista (single in eighth)
8-3 Mark Buehrle, Chicago vs. Tampa Bay, W 4-0—Damian Rolls (single in seventh)
9-2 Mike Mussina, New York at Boston, W 1-0—Carl Everett (single in ninth)

TWO-HIT GAMES

Date **Pitcher(s), Team, Opponent, Result—Player(s) with hit(s)**
4-14 Freddy Garcia (7.2 inn.), Jeff Nelson (0.2 inn.), Arthur Rhodes (0.1 inn.) and Kazuhiro Sasaki (0.1 inn.), Seattle at Anaheim, W 2-1—Orlando Palmeiro (single in sixth), Adam Kennedy (triple in seventh)
4-22 Dan Reichert (8 inn.) and Roberto Hernandez (1 inn.), Kansas City vs. Toronto, W 5-1—Alex S. Gonzalez (single in first), Jose Cruz (single in fourth)
4-26 Hideo Nomo (7 inn.) and Derek Lowe (2 inn.), Boston vs. Minnesota, W 2-0—Torii Hunter (single in seventh), Doug Mientkiewicz (single in ninth)
6-23 Jamie Moyer (8 inn.) and Brian Fuentes (1 inn.), Seattle vs. Anaheim, L 1-2—Shawn Wooten (single in fifth), David Eckstein (home run in sixth)
6-28 Sidney Ponson, Baltimore at Toronto, W 5-0—Jeff Frye (single in first), Brad Fullmer (double in second)
7-1 Rolando Arrojo (7 inn.), Rod Beck (1 inn.) and Derek Lowe (1 inn.), Boston at Toronto, W 4-0—Alex S. Gonzalez (single in seventh), Shannon Stewart (single in ninth)
7-15 Aaron Sele, Seattle vs. Arizona N.L., W 8-0—Mark Grace (double in first), Erubiel Durazo (single in second)
7-26 Joel Pineiro (6 inn.), Jeff Nelson (1 inn.), Arthur Rhodes (1 inn.) and Kazuhiro Sasaki (1 inn.), Seattle vs. Kansas City, W 4-0—Brent Mayne (singles in third and ninth)
7-28 Roger Clemens (5.2 inn.), Ramiro Mendoza (1.1 inn.) and Mark Wohlers (2 inn.), New York at Toronto, W 12-1—Shannon Stewart (double in fourth), Carlos Delgado (home run in seventh)
8-4 Barry Zito (8 inn.) and Jeff Tam (1 inn.), Oakland at Detroit, W 10-1—Wendell Magee (home run in second), Ryan Jackson (single in ninth)
8-6 Dan Wright (6.1 inn.), Gary Glover (1.2 inn.) and Keith Foulke (1 inn.), Chicago vs. Tampa Bay, W 5-2—Chris Gomez (double in seventh), Randy Winn (single in eighth)
9-7 Paul Abbott (8 inn.) and Jeff Nelson (1 inn.), Seattle vs. Baltimore, W 10-1—Brady Anderson (single in sixth), Brian Roberts (home run in eighth)
9-9 Jamie Moyer (7 inn.), Arthur Rhodes (1 inn.) and Kazuhiro Sasaki (1 inn.), Seattle vs. Baltimore, W 6-0—Jeff Conine (singles in second and fourth)
10-5 Roy Halladay, Toronto vs. Cleveland, W 5-0—Travis Fryman (single in eighth), Wil Cordero (single in ninth)
10-6 Denny Stark (3 inn.), Paul Abbott (2 inn.), Joel Pineiro (2 inn.), Jeff Nelson (1 inn.) and Kazuhiro Sasaki (1 inn.), Seattle vs. Texas, W 1-0—Rafael Palmeiro (double in second), Mike Lamb (single in fifth)
10-7 Mike Mussina (4 inn.), Orlando Hernandez (4 inn.) and Mariano Rivera (1 inn.), New York at Tampa Bay, W 1-0—Jason Tyner (single in first), Randy Winn (double in seventh)

NATIONAL LEAGUE

ONE-HIT GAMES

Date **Pitcher(s), Team, Opponent, Result—Player with hit**
4-11 Greg Maddux (7 inn.), Mike Remlinger (1 inn.) and John Rocker (1 inn.), Atlanta at New York, W 2-0—Todd Zeile (single in second)
5-18 Randy Johnson (5 inn.), Byung-Hyun Kim (3 inn.) and Bret Prinz (1 inn.), Arizona at Chicago, W 4-0—Ron Coomer (single in first)
5-24 Jon Lieber, Chicago vs. Cincinnati, W 3-0—Juan Castro (single in sixth)
5-25 Kerry Wood, Chicago vs. Milwaukee, W 1-0—Mark Loretta (single in seventh)
6-16 Brad Penny (7 inn.) and Ricky Bones (2 inn.), Florida vs. Tampa Bay A.L., W 11-0—John Flaherty (single in fifth)
6-26 Brad Penny (8 inn.) and Antonio Alfonseca (1 inn.), Florida vs. Montreal, W 3-0—Geoff Blum (single in sixth)
7-13 Todd Ritchie, Pittsburgh vs. Kansas City A.L., W 1-0—Luis Alicea (single in ninth)
7-14 Glendon Rusch (8 inn.) and Armando Benitez (1 inn.), New York vs. Boston A.L., W 2-0—Trot Nixon (single in first)
7-18 Curt Schilling (2 inn.) and Randy Johnson (7 inn.), Arizona at San Diego, W 3-0—Wiki Gonzalez (single in eighth)
7-24 Randy Johnson (7.1 inn.), Troy Brohawn (0.2 inn.) and Erik Sabel (1 inn.), Arizona vs. San Diego, W 11-0—Bubba Trammell (single in first)
9-26 Randy Wolf, Philadelphia vs. Cincinnati, W 8-0—Raul Gonzalez (single in first)

TWO-HIT GAMES

Date **Pitcher(s), Team, Opponent, Result—Player(s) with hit(s)**
4-10 Curt Schilling, Arizona vs. Los Angeles, W 2-0—Paul Lo Duca (single in sixth), Eric Karros (single in eighth)
4-18 Javier Vazquez (6 inn.), Scott Stewart (0.2 inn.), Guillermo Mota (1.1 inn.) and Ugueth Urbina (1 inn.), Montreal at New York, W 7-1—Darryl Hamilton (single in second), Todd Zeile (single in third)
4-20 Russ Ortiz (8 inn.) and Robb Nen (1 inn.), San Francisco vs. Milwaukee, W 3-1—Tyler Houston (single in fourth), Richie Sexson (single in fourth)
4-29 Jamey Wright, Milwaukee vs. Montreal, W 10-0—Javier Vazquez (single in third), Michael Barrett (single in eighth)
5-2 Greg Maddux, Atlanta vs. Milwaukee, W 1-0—Devon White (double in fourth), Jose Hernandez (single in fifth)
5-7 Robert Person, Philadelphia at Houston, W 5-0—Craig Biggio (double in first), Brad Ausmus (single in seventh)
5-7 Kevin Brown (8 inn.) and Jeff Shaw (1 inn.), Los Angeles vs. Florida, W 1-0—Luis Castillo (single in sixth), Alex Gonzalez (single in eighth)
5-15 Javier Vazquez, Montreal vs. Los Angeles, W 2-0—Mark Grudzielanek (single in first), Shawn Green (single in fourth)

Date	Pitcher(s), Team, Opponent, Result—Player(s) with hit(s)
5-24	Shawn Estes (8 inn.) and Aaron Fultz (1 inn.), San Francisco vs. Colorado, W 5-1—Ben Petrick (triple in third and double in eighth)
6-9	A.J. Burnett, Florida at Toronto A.L., W 6-1—Jeff Frye (single in third), Chris Woodward (double in third)
6-16	John Burkett (8 inn.) and Jason Marquis (1 inn.), Atlanta vs. Boston A.L., W 8-0—Jose Offerman (single in first), Mike Lansing (single in sixth)
7-16	Jesus Sanchez (7 inn.), Ricky Bones (1 inn.), Vic Darensbourg (0.1 inn.) and Braden Looper (0.2 inn.), Florida vs. Baltimore A.L., W 4-0—Jeff Conine (double in fourth), Mike Kinkade (double in seventh)
7-18	Chan Ho Park, Los Angeles vs. Milwaukee, W 5-0—Mark Loretta (single in third), Richie Sexson (single in fourth)
7-20	Jason Schmidt (7 inn.), Scott Sauerbeck (0.2 inn.) and Josias Manzanillo (1.1 inn.), Pittsburgh at St. Louis, W 4-1—Edgar Renteria (single in fifth), Bobby Bonilla (double in eighth)
7-24	Wade Miller (8 inn.) and Billy Wagner (1 inn.), Houston at St. Louis, W 2-1—Mark McGwire (home run in fourth), Placido Polanco (double in sixth)
8-1	Jason Schmidt (7 inn.), Felix Rodriguez (1 inn.) and Robb Nen (1 inn.), San Francisco vs. Pittsburgh, W 3-1—Jason Kendall (home run in fourth), Aramis Ramirez (single in eighth)
8-3	Randy Johnson (7 inn.) and Troy Brohawn (2 inn.), Arizona vs. New York, W 7-0—Edgardo Alfonzo (single in fourth), Benny Agbayani (triple in fifth)
8-7	Bruce Chen (7 inn.), John Franco (1 inn.) and Armando Benitez (1 inn.), New York vs. Milwaukee, W 3-0—Richie Sexson (single in fourth), Jeromy Burnitz (single in fourth)
8-15	Kevin Jarvis (8 inn.) and Trevor Hoffman (1 inn.), San Diego vs. New York, W 2-1—Mike Piazza (double in fourth), Todd Zeile (single in fourth)
8-17	Livan Hernandez, San Francisco vs. Atlanta, L 1-2—Marcus Giles (single in fourth), Chipper Jones (triple in seventh)
8-18	Carlos Hernandez (7 inn.) and Octavio Dotel (2 inn.), Houston vs. Pittsburgh, W 3-0—Craig A. Wilson (single in second), Brian Giles (single in eighth)
8-21	Dave Williams (6 inn.), Josias Manzanillo (1 inn.), Scott Sauerbeck (0.2 inn.), Omar Olivares (0.1 inn.) and Mike Fetters (1 inn.), Pittsburgh vs. Arizona, W 4-2—Mark Grace (double in fourth), Damian Miller (single in fifth)
8-22	Kevin Appier (7 inn.), Rick White (1 inn.) and Armando Benitez (1 inn.), New York vs. Colorado, W 2-1—Todd Helton (home run in second), Jeff Cirillo (single in ninth)
9-5	Woody Williams, St. Louis at San Diego, W 2-0—D'Angelo Jimenez (single in seventh), Ben Davis (single in ninth)
9-27	Lance Davis (6 inn.), Scott Sullivan (2 inn.) and Danny Graves (1 inn.), Cincinnati at Philadelphia, W 2-1—Johnny Estrada (single in third), Jimmy Rollins (single in sixth)
10-3	Steve Trachsel, New York vs. Pittsburgh, W 3-0—Aramis Ramirez (single in first), Adam Hyzdu (single in eighth)
10-6	Julian Tavarez (7.1 inn.), Ron Mahay (0.2 inn.) and Jeff Fassero (1 inn.), Chicago vs. Pittsburgh, W 13-2—Mendy Lopez (single in eighth), Kevin Young (single in ninth)

15-STRIKEOUT GAMES
AMERICAN LEAGUE

Date	Pitcher, Team, Opponent	IP	H	R	ER	BB	SO	Result
4-8	Pedro Martinez, Boston vs. Tampa Bay	8.0	3	0	0	3	16	W 3-0

NATIONAL LEAGUE

Date	Pitcher, Team, Opponent	IP	H	R	ER	BB	SO	Result
5-8	Randy Johnson, Arizona vs. Cincinnati (11 inn.)	9.0	3	1	1	0	20	W 4-3
7-18	Randy Johnson, Arizona at San Diego	7.0	1	0	0	1	16	W 3-0
8-23	Randy Johnson, Arizona at Pittsburgh	7.0	5	4	4	2	16	L 1-5
9-27	Randy Johnson, Arizona vs. Milwaukee	6.2	7	5	5	2	16	W 13-11

10-STRIKEOUT GAMES

AMERICAN LEAGUE

Team	No.	Pitchers
Boston	14	Pedro Martinez 9, Hideo Nomo 5.
New York	10	Mike Mussina 6, Roger Clemens 2, Andy Pettitte 1, Ted Lilly 1.
Cleveland	9	Bartolo Colon 5, C.C. Sabathia 3, Chuck Finley 1.
Oakland	8	Barry Zito 5, Tim Hudson 2, Erik Hiljus 1.
Toronto	4	Chris Carpenter 2, Roy Halladay 2.
Baltimore	2	Pat Hentgen 1, Sidney Ponson 1.
Seattle	2	Paul Abbott 1, Joel Pineiro 1.
Anaheim	1	Ramon Ortiz 1.
Detroit	1	Jeff Weaver 1.
Kansas City	1	Blake Stein 1.
Minnesota	1	Eric Milton 1.
Chicago	0	None.
Texas	0	None.
Tampa Bay	0	None.

NATIONAL LEAGUE

Team	No.	Pitchers
Arizona	36	Randy Johnson 23, Curt Schilling 13.
Chicago	10	Kerry Wood 8, Jason Bere 2.
Houston	7	Wade Miller 5, Roy Oswalt 2.
St. Louis	7	Matt Morris 4, Darryl Kile 3.
Los Angeles	6	Chan Ho Park 3, Kevin Brown 2, Luke Prokopec 1.
Philadelphia	6	Randy Wolf 3, Robert Person 2, Omar Daal 1.
Florida	5	Ryan Dempster 2, Brad Penny 2, Matt Clement 1.
Milwaukee	4	Ruben Quevedo 2, Jimmy Haynes 1, Jamey Wright 1.
Atlanta	4	John Burkett 2, Greg Maddux 1, Jason Marquis 1.
Montreal	4	Javier Vazquez 3, Tony Armas Jr. 1.
New York	4	Kevin Appier 2, Steve Trachsel 1, Glendon Rusch 1.
Colorado	4	Pedro Astacio 2, John Thomson 1, Shawn Chacon 1.
San Diego	3	Adam Eaton 2, Kevin Jarvis 1.
Pittsburgh	1	Omar Olivares 1.
San Francisco	1	Livan Hernandez 1.
Cincinnati	0	None.

1-0 GAMES
AMERICAN LEAGUE

Date	Winner	Loser	Inn.*	Site
4-5	†Mike Mussina, New York	†Dan Reichert, Kansas City	1	New York
4-14	Steve W. Sparks, Detroit	Chuck Finley, Cleveland	1	Detroit
6-8	†Ismael Valdes, Anaheim	†Giovanni Carrara, Los Angeles N.L.	2	Los Angeles
7-2	†Jeff Tam, Oakland	†Shigetoshi Hasegawa, Anaheim	12	Oakland
7-29	†Jose Mercedes, Baltimore	†Ismael Valdes, Anaheim	6	Anaheim
9-2	†Joel Pineiro, Seattle	†Rick Bauer, Baltimore	7	Baltimore
9-2	Mike Mussina, New York	†David Cone, Boston	9	Boston
9-23	†Joe Kennedy, Tampa Bay	†Kelvim Escobar, Toronto	1	Toronto
9-28	†Eric Milton, Minnesota	†Danys Baez, Cleveland	8	Cleveland
10-1	†Esteban Loaiza, Toronto	†Rick Bauer, Baltimore	6	Baltimore
10-6	†Joel Pineiro, Seattle	Doug Davis, Texas	1	Seattle
10-7	†Orlando Hernandez, New York	†Jesus Colome, Tampa Bay	8	Tampa Bay

PLAYERS HITTING HOME RUNS IN 1-0 GAMES: 4-5—Paul O'Neill, New York; 6-8—Garret Anderson, Anaheim; 9-2—Bret Boone, Seattle; 9-23—Steve Cox, Tampa Bay; 10-1—Jose Cruz, Toronto; 10-6—Bret Boone, Seattle; 10-7—Clay Bellinger, New York.

*Inning in which run scored. †Did not pitch complete game. Note: Interleague 1-0 games are listed in the winning club's league.

NATIONAL LEAGUE

Date	Winner	Loser	Inn.*	Site
4-2	†Chan Ho Park, Los Angeles	†Jamey Wright, Milwaukee	6	Los Angeles
4-12	†Armando Benitez, New York	†Kerry Ligtenberg, Atlanta	10	New York
4-14	†Chris Reitsma, Cincinnati	†Al Leiter, New York	6	New York
4-18	†Tom Glavine, Atlanta	†Ryan Dempster, Florida	1	Atlanta
5-2	Greg Maddux, Atlanta	†Paul Rigdon, Milwaukee	2	Atlanta
5-7	†Kevin Brown, Los Angeles	†A.J. Burnett, Florida	6	Los Angeles
5-12	†Jeff Shaw, Los Angeles	†Matt Whiteside, Atlanta	9	Los Angeles
5-15	†Rick Reed, New York	†Bobby J. Jones, San Diego	5	New York
5-19	†Brad Penny, Florida	†John Thomson, Colorado	7	Florida
5-25	Greg Maddux, Atlanta	Todd Ritchie, Pittsburgh	8	Atlanta
5-25	Kerry Wood, Chicago	†Allen Levrault, Milwaukee	4	Chicago
5-29	†Miguel Batista, Arizona	†Ryan Vogelsong, San Francisco	18	San Francisco
6-3	†Antonio Alfonseca, Florida	†Turk Wendell, New York	9	Florida
6-13	†Russ Ortiz, San Francisco	†Scott Schoeneweis, Anaheim A.L.	7	San Francisco
6-17	Todd Ritchie, Pittsburgh	†Steve Karsay, Cleveland A.L.	9	Pittsburgh
6-28	†Todd Ritchie, Pittsburgh	†Jamey Wright, Milwaukee	2	Pittsburgh
7-13	Todd Ritchie, Pittsburgh	†Jason Grimsley, Kansas City A.L.	9	Pittsburgh
7-17	†Al Leiter, New York	†Chris Carpenter, Toronto A.L.	1	New York
7-20	†Livan Hernandez, San Francisco	†Miguel Batista, Arizona	3	San Francisco
8-2	†Javier Vazquez, Montreal	†Albie Lopez, Arizona	4	Arizona
9-2	†Wade Miller, Houston	†Mac Suzuki, Milwaukee	3	Milwaukee
9-2	†Wascar Serrano, San Diego	†Byung-Hyun Kim, Arizona	13	San Diego
9-21	†Jose Mesa, Philadelphia	†Vladimir Nunez, Florida	9	Philadelphia
9-24	†Brad Penny, Florida	†John Burkett, Atlanta	9	Florida

PLAYERS HITTING HOME RUNS IN 1-0 GAMES: 4-2—Gary Sheffield, Los Angeles; 5-2—B.J. Surhoff, Atlanta; 5-7—Gary Sheffield, Los Angeles; 5-12—Gary Sheffield, Los Angeles; 5-19—Kevin Millar, Florida; 5-25—Rondell White, Chicago; 6-13—Shawon Dunston, San Francisco; 7-20—Ramon E. Martinez, San Francisco; 8-2—Orlando Cabrera, Montreal; 9-2—Ryan Klesko, San Diego.

*Inning in which run scored. †Did not pitch complete game. Note: Interleague 1-0 games are listed in the winning club's league.

FOUR OR MORE HITS IN ONE GAME
AMERICAN LEAGUE

Team	No.	Hitters
Minnesota	18	Corey Koskie 5, Brian Buchanan 3, Cristian Guzman 3, Matt Lawton 2, Doug Mientkiewicz 2, Torii Hunter 1, A.J. Pierzynski 1, Luis Rivas 1.
Boston	17	Chris Stynes 3, Trot Nixon 3, Jose Offerman 2, Scott Hatteberg 2, Lou Merloni 2, Dante Bichette 1, Mike Lansing 1, Manny Ramirez 1, Jason Varitek 1, Shea Hillenbrand 1.
Seattle	17	Ichiro Suzuki 6, Edgar Martinez 2, John Olerud 2, Bret Boone 2, Stan Javier 1, Mark McLemore 1, Dan Wilson 1, David Bell 1, Mike Cameron 1.
New York	15	Derek Jeter 3, Paul O'Neill 2, Tino Martinez 2, Chuck Knoblauch 2, Alfonso Soriano 2, David Justice 1, Bernie Williams 1, Jorge Posada 1, Shane Spencer 1.
Kansas City	14	Rey Sanchez 3, Mike Sweeney 3, Carlos Beltran 3, Joe Randa 2, Mark Quinn 2, Luis Alicea 1.
Anaheim	12	Benji Gil 2, Garret Anderson 2, Ben Molina 2, David Eckstein 2, Wally Joyner 1, Scott Spiezio 1, Troy Glaus 1, Adam Kennedy 1.
Tampa Bay	12	Jason Tyner 3, Brent Abernathy 3, Greg Vaughn 2, John Flaherty 1, Felix Martinez 1, Ben Grieve 1, Damian Rolls 1.
Cleveland	11	Roberto Alomar 3, Kenny Lofton 3, Ellis Burks 1, Omar Vizquel 1, Juan Gonzalez 1, Jim Thome 1, Marty Cordova 1.

Team	No.	Hitters
Detroit	11	Bobby Higginson 4, Damion Easley 3, Roger Cedeno 2, Tony Clark 1, Jose Macias 1.
Texas	11	Frank Catalanotto 4, Alex Rodriguez 2, Ruben Sierra 1, Rafael Palmeiro 1, Randy Velarde 1, Ivan Rodriguez 1, Carlos Pena 1.
Toronto	11	Brad Fullmer 3, Raul Mondesi 2, Jose Cruz 2, Jeff Frye 1, Alex S. Gonzalez 1, Shannon Stewart 1, Homer Bush 1.
Chicago	10	Ray Durham 2, Chris Singleton 2, Jose Valentin 1, Magglio Ordonez 1, Paul Konerko 1, Carlos Lee 1, Josh Paul 1, Aaron Rowand 1.
Oakland	8	Miguel Tejada 2, Eric Chavez 2, Jason Giambi 1, Johnny Damon 1, Jeremy Giambi 1, Terrence Long 1.
Baltimore	7	Jeff Conine 2, Mike Bordick 1, David Segui 1, Brook Fordyce 1, Chris Richard 1, Jay Gibbons 1.

NATIONAL LEAGUE

Team	No.	Hitters
Colorado	25	Todd Helton 6, Juan Pierre 5, Neifi Perez 3, Larry Walker 2, Jeff Cirillo 2, Jose Ortiz 2, Terry Shumpert 1, Todd Hollandsworth 1, Todd Walker 1, Mark Little 1, Juan Uribe 1.
Houston	19	Lance Berkman 5, Jeff Bagwell 3, Vinny Castilla 3, Craig Biggio 2, Moises Alou 2, Julio Lugo 2, Richard Hidalgo 1, Daryle Ward 1.
San Francisco	19	Rich Aurilia 6, Jeff Kent 2, J.T. Snow 2, Barry Bonds 1, Benito Santiago 1, John Vander Wal 1, Russ Davis 1, Marvin Benard 1, Livan Hernandez 1, Ramon E. Martinez 1, Armando Rios 1, Calvin Murray 1.
Cincinnati	18	Alex Ochoa 3, Aaron Boone 3, Barry Larkin 2, Ruben Rivera 2, Dmitri Young 2, Ken Griffey Jr. 1, Robin Jennings 1, Todd Walker 1, Sean Casey 1, Donnie Sadler 1, Adam Dunn 1.
Los Angeles	15	Shawn Green 4, Adrian Beltre 3, Gary Sheffield 2, Paul Lo Duca 2, Marquis Grissom 1, Tom Goodwin 1, Mark Grudzielanek 1, McKay Christensen 1.
San Diego	14	Damian Jackson 3, Mark Kotsay 3, Ryan Klesko 2, Phil Nevin 2, Mike Darr 2, Rickey Henderson 1, Cesar Crespo 1.
Chicago	11	Sammy Sosa 3, Eric Young 2, Ricky Gutierrez 1, Rondell White 1, Ron Coomer 1, Bill Mueller 1, Roosevelt Brown 1, Corey Patterson 1.
Montreal	11	Vladimir Guerrero 4, Geoff Blum 2, Peter Bergeron 2, Mike Mordecai 1, Orlando Cabrera 1, Milton Bradley 1.
St. Louis	10	Fernando Vina 4, Mark McGwire 1, Ray Lankford 1, Craig Paquette 1, Edgar Renteria 1, Placido Polanco 1, Kerry Robinson 1.
Atlanta	9	Chipper Jones 5, Dave Martinez 1, Brian Jordan 1, Rafael Furcal 1, Marcus Giles 1.
Florida	9	Preston Wilson 2, Cliff Floyd 1, Charles Johnson 1, Eric Owens 1, Derrek Lee 1, Kevin Millar 1, Alex Gonzalez 1, Mike Lowell 1.
Arizona	9	Jay Bell 2, Craig Counsell 2, Junior Spivey 2, Luis Gonzalez 1, Greg Colbrunn 1, Damian Miller 1.
Milwaukee	8	Ronnie Belliard 2, Devon White 1, Luis Lopez 1, Tyler Houston 1, Angel Echevarria 1, Richie Sexson 1, Geoff Jenkins 1.
Philadelphia	8	Jimmy Rollins 4, Doug Glanville 2, Travis Lee 1, Marlon Anderson 1.
Pittsburgh	8	Aramis Ramirez 5, John Vander Wal 1, Abraham Nunez 1, Enrique Wilson 1.
New York	6	Desi Relaford 2, Mike Piazza 1, Darren Bragg 1, Timo Perez 1, Tsuyoshi Shinjo 1.

FIVE OR MORE HITS IN ONE GAME
AMERICAN LEAGUE

Date	Player, Team, Opponent	AB	R	H	2B	3B	HR	RBI	Result
5-12	Joe Randa, Kansas City at Minnesota	6	2	5	3	0	0	2	W 12- 4
5-23	Derek Jeter, New York vs. Boston	5	3	5	1	0	1	1	W 7- 3
6-19	Ellis Burks, Cleveland vs. Minnesota (10 inn.)	7	3	5	1	0	3	3	L 9- 10
7-3	Roberto Alomar, Cleveland vs. Boston	5	1	5	1	0	0	1	W 9- 1
8-8	Damion Easley, Detroit at Texas	6	3	6	0	0	1	3	W 19- 6
8-15	Roger Cedeno, Detroit vs. Anaheim	5	0	5	0	0	0	1	W 5- 1
8-19	Jeff Conine, Baltimore at Boston	6	3	5	0	0	0	3	W 13- 7
8-21	Ruben Sierra, Texas vs. New York	5	2	5	1	0	2	3	W 13- 3
8-22	David Bell, Seattle vs. Detroit	5	3	5	1	0	1	1	W 16- 1

NATIONAL LEAGUE

Date	Player, Team, Opponent	AB	R	H	2B	3B	HR	RBI	Result
4-3	Craig Biggio, Houston vs. Milwaukee	5	3	5	0	0	0	0	W 11- 3
4-6	Fernando Vina, St. Louis at Arizona	5	1	5	0	1	0	3	W 12- 9
4-27	Eric Owens, Florida at Houston (10 inn.)	6	4	5	0	0	1	1	W 9- 8
4-27	Chipper Jones, Atlanta at Arizona	5	3	5	1	0	1	1	W 9- 0
5-6	Julio Lugo, Houston at Montreal	5	3	5	2	0	0	0	W 13- 7
5-15	Tyler Houston, Milwaukee at Philadelphia	6	3	5	1	0	0	1	W 14- 10
5-28	Paul Lo Duca, Los Angeles vs. Colorado (11 inn.)	6	3	6	0	0	1	4	W 11- 10
6-3	Tom Goodwin, Los Angeles at Houston (10 inn.)	5	3	5	1	0	0	1	W 9- 8
6-21	Junior Spivey, Arizona at Colorado	6	3	5	0	1	0	3	W 14- 5
6-28	Alex Ochoa, Cincinnati vs. Chicago	5	2	5	0	0	1	1	W 5- 2
7-6	Roosevelt Brown, Chicago at Detroit A.L.	6	3	5	1	0	1	3	W 15- 9
7-28	Marvin Benard, San Francisco at Arizona	6	2	5	1	0	0	1	W 11- 4

Date	Player, Team, Opponent	AB	R	H	2B	3B	HR	RBI	Result
8-10	Jose Ortiz, Colorado at Cincinnati	6	3	5	1	0	1	4	W 16- 7
8-12	Junior Spivey, Arizona at Atlanta	5	3	5	0	0	0	0	W 9- 1
8-29	Ryan Klesko, San Diego at St. Louis	6	4	5	2	0	2	5	L 14- 16
10-6‡	Marlon Anderson, Philadelphia at Cincinnati	5	1	5	3	0	0	2	W 5- 1

‡Second game of doubleheader

HITTING STREAKS OF 15 OR MORE GAMES

AMERICAN LEAGUE

G	Player, Team	Span of streak
23	Ichiro Suzuki, Seattle	Apr. 22-May 18
22	Marty Cordova, Cleveland	Apr. 22-May 18
21	Rey Sanchez, Kansas City	May 11-June 3
	Ichiro Suzuki, Seattle	Aug. 3-Aug. 24
19	Jose Cruz Jr., Toronto	Apr. 4-Apr. 27
17	Cristian Guzman, Minnesota	June 8-June 26
16	Shannon Stewart, Toronto	May 9-May 26
	Cal Ripken Jr., Baltimore	July 21-Aug. 8
	Bernie Williams, New York	Aug. 16-Sept. 1
	Jermaine Dye, Oakland	Aug. 25-Sept. 18
15	Ichiro Suzuki, Seattle	Apr. 4-Apr. 20
	Doug Mientkiewicz, Minnesota	Apr. 16-May 2
	Darin Erstad, Anaheim	May 19-June 5
	Roberto Alomar, Cleveland	May 28-June 13
	Cal Ripken Jr., Baltimore	June 20-July 14
	Brian Roberts, Baltimore	June 22-July 12
	Juan Gonzalez, Cleveland	Aug. 29-Sept. 19

NATIONAL LEAGUE

G	Player, Team	Span of streak
23	Moises Alou, Houston	June 22-July 18
21	Lance Berkman, Houston	June 17-July 8
20	Placido Polanco, St. Louis	July 21-Aug. 11
19	Peter Bergeron, Montreal	July 1-July 23
18	Mark Grace, Arizona	May 18-June 10
	Craig Biggio, Houston	May 29-June 18
	Cliff Floyd, Florida	June 5-June 24
17	Rondell White, Chicago	May 23-June 13
	Neifi Perez, Colorado	June 1-June 19
	Albert Pujols, St. Louis	July 31-Aug. 16
	Adrian Beltre, Los Angeles	Aug. 25-Sept. 18
16	Todd Hollandsworth, Colorado	Apr. 14-May 3
	Mark Loretta, Milwaukee	May 20-June 9
15	Doug Glanville, Philadelphia	May 3-May 19
	Barry Bonds, San Francisco	May 11-May 27
	Doug Glanville, Philadelphia	May 27-June 12
	Edgardo Alfonzo, New York	Aug. 28-Sept. 23

MULTI-HOMER GAMES
AMERICAN LEAGUE

Team	No.	Hitters
Texas	22	Rafael Palmeiro 6, Alex Rodriguez 5, Ruben Sierra 3, Ivan Rodriguez 2, Michael Young 2, Randy Velarde 1, Rusty Greer 1, Gabe Kapler 1, Carlos Pena 1.
Cleveland	18	Jim Thome 6, Juan Gonzalez 4, Marty Cordova 2, Ellis Burks 1, Roberto Alomar 1, Kenny Lofton 1, Wil Cordero 1, Karim Garcia 1, Russell Branyan 1.
Toronto	16	Carlos Delgado 5, Jose Cruz 4, Raul Mondesi 3, Alex S. Gonzalez 2, Darrin Fletcher 1, Felipe Lopez 1.
Boston	14	Manny Ramirez 5, Trot Nixon 2, Brian Daubach 2, Mike Lansing 1, Troy O'Leary 1, Chris Stynes 1, Jason Varitek 1, Lou Merloni 1.
Anaheim	13	Troy Glaus 4, Tim Salmon 2, Benji Gil 2, Garret Anderson 2, Scott Spiezio 2, Darin Erstad 1.
Minnesota	11	Corey Koskie 3, Torii Hunter 2, Tom Prince 1, Matt Lawton 1, David Ortiz 1, Doug Mientkiewicz 1, Chad Allen 1, Jacque Jones 1.
Oakland	11	Eric Chavez 3, Jason Giambi 2, Miguel Tejada 2, Frank Menechino 2, Johnny Damon 1, Ramon Hernandez 1.
Chicago	10	Jose Valentin 3, Jose Canseco 2, Ray Durham 2, Magglio Ordonez 2, Herbert Perry 1.
New York	9	Tino Martinez 2, Bernie Williams 2, David Justice 1, Chuck Knoblauch 1, Derek Jeter 1, Jorge Posada 1, Clay Bellinger 1.
Kansas City	8	Mike Sweeney 3, Carlos Beltran 2, Gregg Zaun 1, Carlos Febles 1, Mark Quinn 1.
Seattle	7	Bret Boone 4, John Olerud 1, David Bell 1, Mike Cameron 1.
Baltimore	5	Cal Ripken Jr. 1, Delino DeShields 1, Mike Bordick 1, David Segui 1, Tony Batista 1.
Detroit	4	Damion Easley 1, Bobby Higginson 1, Roger Cedeno 1, Robert Fick 1.
Tampa Bay	3	Greg Vaughn 2, Fred McGriff 1.

NATIONAL LEAGUE

Team	No.	Hitters
Milwaukee	21	Richie Sexson 6, Jeromy Burnitz 5, Geoff Jenkins 3, Jose Hernandez 2, Devon White 1, Jeffrey Hammonds 1, Angel Echevarria 1, Kevin L. Brown 1, Ronnie Belliard 1.
San Francisco	17	Barry Bonds 10, Rich Aurilia 2, Andres Galarraga 1, Jeff Kent 1, J.T. Snow 1, Felipe Crespo 1, Armando Rios 1.
Chicago	15	Sammy Sosa 10, Todd Hundley 3, Matt Stairs 1, Roosevelt Brown 1.
Los Angeles	15	Shawn Green 6, Gary Sheffield 4, Marquis Grissom 2, Paul Lo Duca 2, Mark Grudzielanek 1.
Arizona	15	Luis Gonzalez 8, Reggie Sanders 5, Steve Finley 1, Danny Bautista 1.
Houston	14	Moises Alou 4, Vinny Castilla 3, Lance Berkman 3, Craig Biggio 1, Jeff Bagwell 1, Richard Hidalgo 1, Chris Truby 1.
Colorado	14	Todd Helton 4, Larry Walker 2, Mike Hampton 1, Todd Hollandsworth 1, Brooks Kieschnick 1, Todd Walker 1, Mark Little 1, Ben Petrick 1, Jose Ortiz 1, Juan Uribe 1.
Atlanta	13	Chipper Jones 5, Brian Jordan 2, Andruw Jones 2, Wes Helms 2, Ken Caminiti 1, Javy Lopez 1.

Team	No.	Hitters
San Diego	11	Ryan Klesko 5, Phil Nevin 4, Bubba Trammell 1, Cesar Crespo 1.
St. Louis	10	Mark McGwire 3, Jim Edmonds 2, J.D. Drew 2, Albert Pujols 2, Ray Lankford 1.
Florida	10	Preston Wilson 4, Cliff Floyd 3, Charles Johnson 2, Alex Gonzalez 1.
New York	9	Mike Piazza 4, Robin Ventura 2, Edgardo Alfonzo 1, Desi Relaford 1, Alex Escobar 1.
Cincinnati	8	Dmitri Young 2, Ken Griffey Jr. 1, Kelly Stinnett 1, Michael Tucker 1, Aaron Boone 1, Jason LaRue 1, Corky Miller 1.
Pittsburgh	8	Aramis Ramirez 4, Brian Giles 3, Adam Hyzdu 1.
Philadelphia	6	Travis Lee 2, Tomas Perez 1, Doug Glanville 1, Scott Rolen 1, Bobby Abreu 1.
Montreal	4	Lee Stevens 1, Randy Knorr 1, Vladimir Guerrero 1, Geoff Blum 1.

THREE-HOMER GAMES

AMERICAN LEAGUE

Date	Player, Team, Opponent	AB	R	H	2B	3B	HR	RBI	Result	
4-4	Carlos Delgado, Toronto at Tampa Bay	5	3	3	0	0	3	4	W	11-8
4-20	Carlos Delgado, Toronto at Kansas City	4	4	3	0	0	3	4	W	12-4
5-20	Jason Varitek, Boston at Kansas City	4	3	4	0	0	3	7	W	10-3
6-19	Ellis Burks, Cleveland vs. Minnesota (12 inn.)	7	3	5	1	0	3	3	L	9-10
6-30	Miguel Tejada, Oakland at Texas	5	4	4	0	0	3	8	W	15-4
7-6	Jim Thome, Cleveland vs. St. Louis N.L.	5	3	3	0	0	3	6	W	14-2

NATIONAL LEAGUE

Date	Player, Team, Opponent	AB	R	H	2B	3B	HR	RBI	Result	
4-8	Aramis Ramirez, Pittsburgh at Houston	3	3	3	0	0	3	6	W	9-3
4-15	Todd Hollandsworth, Colorado vs. Arizona (10 inn.)	5	3	3	0	0	3	7	W	10-7
4-28	Geoff Jenkins, Milwaukee vs. Montreal	4	3	3	0	0	3	6	W	8-4
5-10	Jeromy Burnitz, Milwaukee vs. Chicago	4	3	3	0	0	3	6	W	11-1
5-19	Barry Bonds, San Francisco at Atlanta	5	3	4	1	0	3	3	W	6-3
6-8	Luis Gonzalez, Arizona at Kansas City A.L.	5	3	3	0	0	3	4	W	11-4
7-28 †	Vinny Castilla, Houston at Pittsburgh	5	3	3	0	0	3	5	L	8-9
8-9	Sammy Sosa, Chicago vs. Colorado	4	3	3	0	0	3	3	L	6-11
8-15	Shawn Green, Los Angeles vs. Montreal	5	3	3	0	0	3	7	W	13-1
8-17	Jose Ortiz, Colorado vs. Florida	5	3	3	0	0	3	4	W	12-5
8-22	Sammy Sosa, Chicago vs. Milwaukee	4	3	3	0	0	3	6	W	16-3
9-9	Barry Bonds, San Francisco at Colorado (11 inn.)	5	3	3	0	0	3	5	W	9-4
9-23	Sammy Sosa, Chicago at Houston	4	3	3	0	0	3	4	L	6-7
9-25	Richie Sexson, Milwaukee at Arizona	4	3	3	0	0	3	5	W	9-4
9-25	Jeromy Burnitz, Milwaukee at Arizona	4	3	3	0	0	3	3	W	9-4
10-6	Phil Nevin, San Diego vs. Colorado	4	3	3	0	0	3	6	W	10-4

† First game of doubleheader.

GRAND SLAMS

AMERICAN LEAGUE

Date	Batter, Team	Pitcher, Team	Inn.*	Site
4-3	Miguel Tejada, Oakland	John Halama, Seattle	3	Seattle
4-4	David Justice, New York	Blake Stein, Kansas City	2	New York
4-6	Tony Clark, Detroit	Antonio Osuna, Chicago	6	Chicago
4-6	Rafael Palmeiro, Texas	Norm Charlton, Seattle	7	Texas
4-8	Jorge Posada, New York	Steve Parris, Toronto	1	New York
4-17	Russell Branyan, Cleveland	B.J. Ryan, Baltimore	6	Baltimore
4-20	Raul Mondesi, Toronto	Kris Wilson, Kansas City	7	Kansas City
4-20	Tino Martinez, New York	Hideo Nomo, Boston	1	New York
4-21	Brad Fullmer, Toronto	Blake Stein, Kansas City	3	Kansas City
4-21	John Olerud, Seattle	Jarrod Washburn, Anaheim	3	Seattle
4-24	Carl Everett, Boston	Mark Redman, Minnesota	2	Boston
4-24	Jason Giambi, Oakland	Mark Buehrle, Chicago	3	Chicago
4-27	Carl Everett, Boston	Jose Santiago, Kansas City	6	Boston
4-27	Gabe Kapler, Texas	Justin Speier, Cleveland	4	Cleveland
5-3	Jeff Conine, Baltimore	Ted Lilly, New York	5	Baltimore
5-16	Joe Randa, Kansas City	Esteban Yan, Tampa Bay	9	Kansas City
5-18	Jeff Conine, Baltimore	Eric Milton, Minnesota	3	Baltimore
6-6	Jorge Posada, New York	Mike Trombley, Baltimore	8	New York
6-8	Carlos Lee, Chicago	Courtney Duncan, Chicago N.L.	10	Chicago A.L.
6-8	Torii Hunter, Minnesota	Omar Olivares, Pittsburgh N.L.	5	Minnesota
6-9	Ivan Rodriguez, Texas	Jose Lima, Houston N.L.	3	Texas
6-12	Ben Grieve, Tampa Bay	Eddie Oropesa, Philadelphia N.L.	7	Tampa Bay
6-14	Brian Daubach, Boston	Chuck Smith, Florida N.L.	4	Boston

Date	Batter, Team	Pitcher, Team	Inn.*	Site
6-14	Paul Konerko, Chicago	Osvaldo Fernandez, Cincinnati N.L.	1	Chicago
6-24	Cristian Guzman, Minnesota	Dave Borkowski, Detroit	7	Detroit
6-25	Dante Bichette, Boston	Ryan Rupe, Tampa Bay	3	Boston
6-26	Greg Vaughn, Tampa Bay	Rolando Arrojo, Boston	5	Boston
6-26	Trot Nixon, Boston	Travis Phelps, Tampa Bay	7	Boston
6-27	Ramon Hernandez, Oakland	John Halama, Seattle	2	Seattle
6-29	Raul Mondesi, Toronto	Bryce Florie, Boston	8	Toronto
6-30	Miguel Tejada, Oakland	Kenny Rogers, Texas	1	Texas
7-5	Alex Rodriguez, Texas	Brian Fuentes, Seattle	4	Texas
7-6	Brad Fullmer, Toronto	Mike Thurman, Montreal N.L.	5	Toronto
7-8	Garret Anderson, Anaheim	Shawn Chacon, Colorado N.L.	1	Colorado
7-12	Jacque Jones, Minnesota	Jimmy Haynes, Milwaukee N.L.	2	Milwaukee
7-21	Paul Konerko, Chicago	Tomokazu Ohka, Boston	3	Chicago
7-22	Greg Vaughn, Tampa Bay	Pat Mahomes, Texas	7	Tampa Bay
7-27	Ben Grieve, Tampa Bay	Rob Bell, Texas	3	Texas
8-6	Scott Hatteberg, Boston	Juan Moreno, Texas	6	Boston
8-8	Shane Halter, Detroit	Brandon Villafuerte, Texas	9	Texas
8-10	Edgar Martinez, Seattle	Rocky Biddle, Chicago	6	Seattle
8-16	Paul O'Neill, New York	Ryan Rupe, Tampa Bay	2	New York
8-18	Ivan Rodriguez, Texas	Billy Koch, Toronto	9	Toronto
8-19	Manny Ramirez, Boston	Calvin Maduro, Baltimore	2	Boston
8-19	Mike Cameron, Seattle	Jay Witasick, New York	7	New York
8-21	Doug Mirabelli, Boston	Scott Schoeneweis, Anaheim	3	Anaheim
8-22	Carlos Beltran, Kansas City	Bob Howry, Chicago	7	Kansas City
8-24	Trot Nixon, Boston	Danny Kolb, Texas	8	Texas
8-30	Eric Chavez, Oakland	Alan Mills, Baltimore	8	Baltimore
8-31	Ruben Sierra, Texas	Paul Byrd, Kansas City	1	Kansas City
9-4	Tony Fernandez, Toronto	Ted Lilly, New York	7	Toronto
9-8	Corey Koskie, Minnesota	Pat Rapp, Anaheim	4	Anaheim
9-8	Juan Gonzalez, Cleveland	Gary Glover, Chicago	1	Cleveland
9-18	Jorge Posada, New York	Alan Embree, Chicago	7	Chicago
9-18	Travis Fryman, Cleveland	Jeff Austin, Kansas City	5	Cleveland
9-23	Magglio Ordonez, Chicago	Chad Durbin, Kansas City	3	Chicago
9-25	Tony Batista, Baltimore	Allen McDill, Boston	9	Boston
9-26	Randall Simon, Detroit	Blake Stein, Kansas City	7	Kansas City
9-29	Miguel Tejada, Oakland	Jose Paniagua, Seattle	7	Seattle
10-5 †	Jose Cruz, Toronto	Chuck Finley, Cleveland	3	Toronto
10-7	Carlos Beltran, Kansas City	Adam Bernero, Detroit	9	Detroit

*Inning in which grand slam was hit. †First game of doubleheader.

NATIONAL LEAGUE

Date	Batter, Team	Pitcher, Team	Inn.*	Site
4-3	Daryle Ward, Houston	Jimmy Haynes, Milwaukee	3	Houston
4-6	Mike Lowell, Florida	Marc Valdes, Atlanta	8	Florida
4-12	Jose Hernandez, Milwaukee	Nelson Cruz, Houston	5	Milwaukee
4-20	Barry Larkin, Cincinnati	Al Leiter, New York	2	Cincinnati
4-20	Kevin Jordan, Philadelphia	Marc Valdes, Atlanta	7	Philadelphia
4-20	Sammy Sosa, Chicago	Jose Silva, Pittsburgh	9	Pittsburgh
4-21	Reggie Sanders, Arizona	Ron Villone, Colorado	3	Arizona
4-26	Tyler Houston, Milwaukee	Brett Hinchliffe, New York	3	Milwaukee
4-27	Julio Lugo, Houston	Brad Penny, Florida	4	Houston
5-1	Ben Davis, San Diego	Jason Bere, Chicago	3	Chicago
5-1	Robin Ventura, New York	Jay Powell, Houston	7	New York
5-6	Jeff Bagwell, Houston	Anthony Telford, Montreal	6	Montreal
5-8	Marvin Benard, San Francisco	Anthony Telford, Montreal	5	San Francisco
5-10	Devon White, Milwaukee	Felix Heredia, Chicago	6	Milwaukee
5-13	Charles Johnson, Florida	Jay Witasick, San Diego	7	San Diego
5-13	Mark Grace, Arizona	Ricky Bottalico, Philadelphia	8	Arizona
5-15	Marcus Giles, Atlanta	Mike Hampton, Colorado	8	Atlanta
5-15	Devon White, Milwaukee	Amaury Telemaco, Philadelphia	2	Philadelphia
5-18	Jason LaRue, Cincinnati	Kent Bottenfield, Houston	4	Houston
5-20	Devon White, Milwaukee	Terry Mulholland, Pittsburgh	4	Pittsburgh
5-21	Jeff Bagwell, Houston	Adam Eaton, San Diego	3	Houston
5-28	Todd Helton, Colorado	Eric Gagne, Los Angeles	3	Los Angeles
5-31	Ryan McGuire, Florida	Turk Wendell, New York	7	Florida
6-1	Mark Grudzielanek, Los Angeles	Nelson Cruz, Houston	7	Houston
6-3	Vinny Castilla, Houston	Eric Gagne, Los Angeles	3	Houston
6-5	Julio Zuleta, Chicago	Alan Benes, St. Louis	2	Chicago
6-5	Kevin Young, Pittsburgh	Brad Penny, Florida	6	Florida
6-14	Lance Berkman, Houston	Hector Carrasco, Minnesota A.L.	7	Minnesota

Date	Batter, Team	Pitcher, Team	Inn.*	Site
6-14	Phil Nevin, San Diego	Chad Bradford, Oakland A.L.	8	San Diego
6-15	Bobby Bonilla, St. Louis	Kelly Wunsch, Chicago A.L.	7	St. Louis
6-17	Tony Womack, Arizona	Dave Mlicki, Detroit A.L.	4	Arizona
6-19	Cliff Floyd, Florida	Joe Nelson, Atlanta	6	Atlanta
6-20	Sammy Sosa, Chicago	Jason Christiansen, St. Louis	7	St. Louis
6-21	Luis Gonzalez, Arizona	Gabe White, Colorado	7	Colorado
6-22	Armando Rios, San Francisco	Dustin Hermanson, St. Louis	2	St. Louis
6-23	Kevin Millar, Florida	Amaury Telemaco, Philadelphia	3	Florida
6-27	Jay Bell, Arizona	Scott Elarton, Houston	2	Arizona
6-28	Javy Lopez, Atlanta	Armando Benitez, New York	10	Atlanta
7-1	Vladimir Guerrero, Montreal	Jimmy Anderson, Pittsburgh	3	Montreal
7-3	Luis Gonzalez, Arizona	Scott Elarton, Houston	3	Houston
7-4	Bubba Trammell, San Diego	Juan Acevedo, Colorado	7	San Diego
7-7	Mark McGwire, St. Louis	Steve Woodard, Cleveland A.L.	4	Cleveland
7-12	Ricky Gutierrez, Chicago	Bob Howry, Chicago A.L.	8	Chicago N.L.
7-13	Shawn Green, Los Angeles	Tim Hudson, Oakland A.L.	6	Oakland
7-14	Damian Jackson, San Diego	Wade Miller, Houston	6	Houston
7-20	Orlando Merced, Houston	Jon Lieber, Chicago	5	Houston
7-21	David Dellucci, Arizona	Brian Boehringer, San Francisco	7	San Francisco
7-26	Barry Bonds, San Francisco	Curt Schilling, Arizona	5	Arizona
7-28	Phil Nevin, San Diego	Allen Levrault, Milwaukee	4	Milwaukee
7-28	Dmitri Young, Cincinnati	Brad Penny, Florida	6	Cincinnati
7-28 †	Brian Giles, Pittsburgh	Billy Wagner, Houston	9	Pittsburgh
8-2	Ryan Klesko, San Diego	Jeff Fassero, Chicago	8	San Diego
8-5	Richie Sexson, Milwaukee	Kevin Millwood, Atlanta	1	Milwaukee
8-10	Fred McGriff, Chicago	Aaron Fultz, San Francisco	8	Chicago
8-10	Pat Burrell, Philadelphia	Matt Herges, Los Angeles	7	Philadelphia
8-11	Travis Lee, Philadelphia	Eric Gagne, Los Angeles	1	Philadelphia
8 14	Barry Bonds, San Francisco	Ricky Bones, Florida	6	San Francisco
8-15	Chipper Jones, Atlanta	Mike Hampton, Colorado	5	Colorado
8-25	Aramis Ramirez, Pittsburgh	Dave Mlicki, Houston	1	Pittsburgh
8-25	Bubba Trammell, San Diego	Ricky Bones, Florida	9	Florida
8-31	Robin Jennings, Cincinnati	Damaso Marte, Pittsburgh	4	Cincinnati
9-1	Ray Lankford, San Diego	Byung-Hyun Kim, Arizona	8	San Diego
9-4	Kevin Millar, Florida	Jon Lieber, Chicago	5	Florida
9-9	Jim Edmonds, St. Louis	Chan Ho Park, Los Angeles	4	St. Louis
9-21	Matt Williams, Arizona	Terry Mulholland, Los Angeles	4	Los Angeles
9-21	Albert Pujols, St. Louis	Omar Olivares, Pittsburgh	9	Pittsburgh
9-26	Jeromy Burnitz, Milwaukee	Bobby Witt, Arizona	5	Arizona
9-26	Steve Finley, Arizona	Gus Gandarillas, Milwaukee	7	Arizona
9-27	Phil Nevin, San Diego	Kane Davis, Colorado	2	Colorado
9-29	Brian Jordan, Atlanta	John Franco, New York	9	Atlanta
9-29	Denny Neagle, Colorado	Jimmy Haynes, Milwaukee	4	Colorado
10-5	Chipper Jones, Atlanta	Benito Baez, Florida	1	Atlanta
10-6	Phil Nevin, San Diego	Scott Elarton, Colorado	1	San Diego

*Inning in which grand slam was hit. †First game of doubleheader.

2001 REVIEW *Notable performances*

TRANSACTIONS

JANUARY 1, 2001-DECEMBER 31, 2001

JANUARY 2
Astros organization signed 3B Charlie Hayes.

JANUARY 3
Rockies traded P David Lee to Yankees for P Jay Tessmer and SS Seth Taylor.
Astros signed P Kent Bottenfield.

JANUARY 4
Red Sox organization signed P Brian Williams. Dodgers organization signed P Giovanni Carrara, P Jim Dougherty, P Kip Gross, P Scott Service, C Steve Bieser, 1B Phil Hiatt and IF Andy Stankiewicz.
Phillies organization signed IF Domingo Cedeno and C Chris Turner.

JANUARY 5
Red Sox organization signed P Kent Mercker and P Bryan Ward.
Athletics signed P Mark Guthrie.
Diamondbacks signed OF Reggie Sanders.
Rockies signed IF Greg Norton.
Mets organization signed P Steve Ontiveros and P Vaughn Eshelman.
Cardinals signed OF Bobby Bonilla, 3B Shane Andrews, OF Bernard Gilkey and OF John Mabry.
Padres signed P Kevin Jarvis.

JANUARY 8
Royals traded OF Johnny Damon, IF Mark Ellis and a player to be named to Athletics for C A.J. Hinch, IF Angel Berroa and cash. Athletics traded OF Ben Grieve to Devil Rays, Devil Rays traded P Roberto Hernandez to Royals and Devil Rays traded P Cory Lidle to Athletics. Devil Rays will receive a player to be named or cash from the Athletics.
Astros organization signed P Jim Mann, P Brad Rigby, P Ricky Stone, C Chris Tremie, C-1B Alan Zinter, IF Mendy Lopez and OF Scott Pose.
Brewers organization signed OF Jason McDonald.

JANUARY 9
Indians signed OF Juan Gonzalez.
Cubs organization signed OF Todd Dunwoody.
Reds signed C Kelly Stinnett and IF Wilton Guerrero.
Reds released P Justin Atchley.
Mets organization signed P Mark Leiter and OF Darren Bragg.
Pirates organization signed OF Thomas Howard.

JANUARY 10
Devil Rays organization signed P Jeff Wallace.
Rangers organization signed P Chris Haney.
Cubs signed 3B Ron Coomer.
Expos organization signed P Chris Peters.
Phillies signed OF Brian L. Hunter.

JANUARY 11
Red Sox signed P David Cone.
Indians organization signed IF Jason Hardtke.
Rangers organization signed P Pat Mahomes.
Brewers organization signed IF-OF Brant Brown.
Indians traded P Tom Martin to Mets for C Javier Ochoa.

JANUARY 12
Rangers organization signed P Jeff Brantley.
Reds organization signed P Justin Atchley.
Padres released P Heathcliff Slocumb.

JANUARY 14
Blue Jays traded P David Wells and P Matt DeWitt to White Sox for P Mike Sirotka, P Kevin Beirne, OF Brian Simmons and P Mike Williams.

JANUARY 16
Angels organization signed DH Jose Canseco.
Tigers organization signed C Scott Servais.
Blue Jays traded OF Chad Mottola to Marlins for a player to be named or cash; Marlins sent cash to complete deal (March 22).
Reds organization signed P Frankie Rodriguez.

JANUARY 17
Astros organization signed C Jeff Reed.
Dodgers organization signed IF Tim Bogar and P Doug Linton.

JANUARY 18
Tigers organization signed P Heath Murray, 3B Tom Evans, 1B/OF Ryan Jackson, 1B Randall Simon and OF Jermaine Allensworth.
Braves organization signed P Matt Whiteside.
Dodgers organization signed P Ramon Martinez.
Boston traded P Rick Croushore to Mets for P Frank Graham and a player to be named.

JANUARY 19
Red Sox organization signed IF Craig Grebeck.
Mariners organization signed IF Carlos Baerga.

JANUARY 20
Indians organization signed P Jerry Spradlin and P Scott Radinsky.

JANUARY 24
Mariners organization signed P Brian Falkenborg.
Padres signed OF Mike Colangelo.

JANUARY 25
Angels organization signed 1B Wally Joyner.

JANUARY 26
Indians organization signed OF-1B Butch Huskey.
Royals signed IF Luis Alicea.
Rangers signed OF Bo Porter.
Braves organization signed P Steve Avery.
Padres sold 1B Joe Vitiello to Orix of Japan Pacific League.

JANUARY 29
Padres organization signed C Rick Wilkins.

JANUARY 31
Devil Rays organization signed P Rusty Meacham.

FEBRUARY 1
Red Sox organization signed IF Chris Stynes.
Mets organization signed C Jim Leyritz.

FEBRUARY 6
Mariners signed P Mark Watson and INF Jason Grabowski.
Cardinals organization signed P Heathcliff Slocumb, P Jim Corsi and P Jeff Tabaka.
Giants signed P Jamie Arnold.

FEBRUARY 8
Indians organization signed P Willie Blair.
Devil Rays organization signed P Ken Hill.
Dodgers organization signed P Jesse Orosco.
Brewers organization signed IF Tony Fernandez.

FEBRUARY 9
Reds organization signed C Matt Walbeck.

FEBRUARY 10
Indians organization signed P Ariel Prieto.

FEBRUARY 13

Devil Rays organization signed IF Mike Caruso.

FEBRUARY 14

Padres organization signed P Rudy Seanez.

FEBRUARY 15

Yankees organization signed OF Henry Rodriguez.
Padres signed P Bobby J. Jones.

FEBRUARY 16

Mariners organization signed SS Manny Alexander.

FEBRUARY 20

Royals released P Steve Rain.
Royals organization signed P Mike Villano.

FEBRUARY 22

Devil Rays released IF Mike Metcalfe.

FEBRUARY 24

Rockies organization signed P John Hudek.
Dodgers traded OF Devon White to Brewers for OF Marquis Grissom and a player to be named; Dodgers acquired P Rudy Lugo to complete deal (June 1).
Brewers announced retirement of P Jim Morris.

MARCH 3

Mets organization signed IF Kevin Stocker.

MARCH 5

Mets announced retirement of IF Kevin Stocker.

MARCH 6

Reds organization signed 1B Hal Morris.

MARCH 7

Rockies announced retirement of P Jerry DiPoto.

MARCH 10

Blue Jays released P Jaime Navarro.

MARCH 12

Tigers released P Curtis King.

MARCH 14

Expos released C Bob Henley.
Padres released OF Ruben Rivera and P Scott Karl.

MARCH 16

Devil Rays released P Sean Bergman.

MARCH 17

Blue Jays released OF Trinidad Hubbard.
Rockies organization signed P Sean Bergman.
Dodgers traded P Antonio Osuna and P Carlos Ortega to White Sox for P Gary Majewski, P Andre Simpson and P Orlando Rodriguez.
Mets released C Jim Leyritz.
Giants organization signed C Benito Santiago.

MARCH 19

Red Sox traded P Mike Rupp to White Sox to complete an earlier trade.
Pirates released P Dan Serafini.
Padres signed OF Rickey Henderson.

MARCH 20

Angels released OF Alex Diaz.
Blue Jays traded P Mike Williams to White Sox for P Matt DeWitt.

MARCH 21

Reds traded 3B Drew Henson and OF Michael Coleman to Yankees for OF Wily Pena.

Mariners released P Wes Hoane, P Neil Longo, P Rhett Riviere and P Greg Beaver.
Mariners announced retirement of C Ryan Bundy.
Reds signed OF Ruben Rivera.

MARCH 22

Yankees released P Scott Kamieniecki.

MARCH 23

Tigers released C Scott Servais.
Royals organization signed OF Trenidad Hubbard.
Mariners released IF Harvey Hargrove, IF Brian Hertel, IF Kevin Olkowski and C Kirk Pierce.

MARCH 24

Angels announced retirement of P Tim Belcher.
Yankees traded P David Lee to Padres for P Carlos Almanzar.
Cubs traded OF Jose Nieves to Angels for P Mike Fyhrie and a player to be named.

MARCH 26

Indians released P Scott Aldred.
Rangers released P Mike Munoz.
Cubs organization signed P Scott Kamieniecki.
Mets traded P Mark Leiter to Rockies for P Brian Rose.
Phillies traded OF Kenny Woods to Orioles for a player to be named.

MARCH 27

Indians released P Ariel Prieto and OF-1B Butch Huskey.
Rangers purchased contract of C Doug Mirabelli from Giants.
Marlins claimed LHP Horacio Estrada on waivers from Brewers.
Astros traded 1B Aaron McNeal to Padres for SS Cristian Berroa.

MARCH 28

Angels traded OF Darren Blakely to Yankees for OF-DH Glenallen Hill.
Angels released DH Jose Canseco.
Athletics traded P Omar Olivares to Pirates for player to be named or cash.
Athletics traded 2B Miguel Cairo to Cubs for IF Eric Hinske.
Devil Rays signed P Ariel Prieto.
Blue Jays released C Todd Greene and P Hector Carrasco.
Diamondbacks traded IF Hanley Frias to Twins for C Chad Moeller.
Rockies released P Masato Yoshii.
Astros organization signed C Scott Servais. Astros released C Jeff Reed.
Dodgers released P Ramon Martinez.
Dodgers traded P Mike Judd to Devil Rays for a player to be named.
Pirates released OF Thomas Howard.
Padres traded OF Eric Owens, P Matt Clement and P Omar Ortiz to Marlins for OF Mark Kotsay and OF Cesar Crespo.
Padres released IF Ed Sprague.

MARCH 29

Red Sox released P Kent Mercker.
Indians released P Jerry Spradlin.
Dodgers released IF-OF F.P. Santangelo.
Cardinals released OF Quinton McCracken and 3B Shane Andrews.

MARCH 30

Yankees announced retirement of P Dwight Gooden.
Yankees traded P Craig Dingman to Rockies for a player to be named; Yankees acquired P Julio De Paula to complete deal (April 20).
Mariners released IF Carlos Baerga.
Braves released P Steve Avery.
Cubs claimed 1B Chris Haas on waivers from Cardinals.
Rockies claimed P Horacio Estrada on waivers from Marlins.

Marlins traded P Manny Aybar to Cubs for P Oswaldo Mairena.
Royals traded OF Michael Curry to Mets for OF Endy Chavez.
Phillies released 1B Brian R. Hunter.

MARCH 31

Royals traded IF Ricardo Montas to Diamondbacks for C Melvin Rosario.
Twins organization signed P Hector Carrasco.
Dodgers released P Jesse Orosco and P Yorkis Perez.

APRIL 2

Reds sold P Ed Yarnall to Orix of Japan Pacific League.

APRIL 4

Devil Rays traded OF Kenny Kelly to Mariners for cash.
Rockies claimed P Jimmy Osting on waivers from Phillies.
Brewers traded P Juan Acevedo, P Kane Davis and IF Jose Flores to Rockies for P Mark Leiter, P Mike DeJean and IF Elvis Pena.
Mets claimed P Justin Brunette on waivers from Cardinals.
Giants organization signed P Dan Serafini.

APRIL 5

Mets sold P Jeff Kubenka to Chiba Lotte of Japan Pacific League.

APRIL 6

Marlins organization signed OF Ryan Thompson.
Brewers claimed OF Alex Sanchez on waivers from Devil Rays.

APRIL 8

Indians organization signed P Rich Rodriguez.

APRIL 9

Cardinals traded OF John Mabry to Marlins for cash.

APRIL 10

Indians signed P Willie Blair and P Paul Spoljaric.

APRIL 11

Pirates signed P Ramon Martinez.
Padres claimed P Jimmy Osting on waivers from Rockies.

APRIL 12

Braves claimed P Jose Cabrera on waivers from Astros.
Braves organization signed OF Bernard Gilkey.

APRIL 13

Twins organization signed OF Quinton McCracken.
Expos signed P Masato Yoshii.

APRIL 15

Yankees announced retirement of P Sid Fernandez.

APRIL 16

Indians organization signed IF Mark Lewis.

APRIL 17

Devil Rays released P Denis Pujals.
Devil Rays organization signed OF Terrell Lowery.

APRIL 19

Mariners claimed IF Jermaine Clark on waivers from Tigers.
Devil Rays released P Ken Hill.

APRIL 20

Rockies claimed IF Kevin Nicholson on waivers from Padres.
Rockies organization signed IF Kevin Stocker.
Mets announced retirement of IF David Howard.

APRIL 23

Rockies traded IF Juan Sosa to Diamondbacks for 3B Ryan Owens.

APRIL 24

Devil Rays claimed P Brian Rose on waivers from Mets.
Dodgers organization signed P Jesse Orosco.

APRIL 27

Rangers traded P Jonathan Johnson to Diamondbacks for cash considerations.

APRIL 29

Indians released P Roy Padilla.

MAY 2

Pirates announced retirement of P Ramon Martinez.

MAY 3

Mariners organization signed IF Ed Sprague.

MAY 4

Dodgers released P Carlos Perez.

MAY 7

Blue Jays organization signed P Vince Perkins.

MAY 8

Rangers traded P Darwin Cubillan to Expos for P Mike Johnson.

MAY 9

Rockies organization signed P Kip Gross.

MAY 10

Yankees organization signed P Chad Ogea.
Devil Rays released 3B Vinny Castilla.

MAY 11

Braves released P Joe Slusarski.
Astros organization signed P Joe Slusarski.

MAY 14

Rockies traded P Jay Tessmer to Indians for a player to be named.

MAY 15

Astros signed 3B Vinny Castilla.

MAY 16

Cubs released OF Damon Buford.

MAY 20

Indians traded P Justin Speier to Mets for cash or a player to be named.

MAY 23

Orioles released IF Julio Vinas.

MAY 24

Indians organization signed P Mark Watson.

MAY 25

Reds released P Matt Skrmetta.

MAY 29

Rangers released P Jeff Brantley.
Rangers claimed P Mike Judd on waivers from Devil Rays.
Rockies claimed P Justin Speier on waivers from Mets.
Brewers released IF Tony Fernandez.

MAY 31

Reds organization signed P Matt Skrmetta and P Dave Maurer.

JUNE 1

Angels released OF-DH Glenallen Hill.
Padres organization signed 1B-C Jim Leyritz.

JUNE 5

Royals traded P Jose Santiago to Phillies for P Paul Byrd.

JUNE 6
Phillies released OF Rob Ducey.

JUNE 8
Orioles organization signed OF Damon Buford.

JUNE 10
Indians organization signed OF Kevin Sefcik.

JUNE 12
Yankees claimed OF Darren Bragg on waivers from Mets.
Rangers traded C Doug Mirabelli to Red Sox for P Justin Duchscherer.
Expos signed OF Rob Ducey.

JUNE 13
Athletics claimed OF Billy McMillon on waivers from Tigers.

JUNE 14
Orioles released C Greg Myers.
Indians released P Willie Blair.
Tigers signed P Willie Blair.
Diamondbacks signed P Mike Mohler.
Mets claimed P Leo Estrella on waivers from Reds
Mets claimed 1B Aaron McNeal on waivers from Padres.

JUNE 15
Rangers traded OF Ruben Mateo and 3B Edwin Encarnacion to Reds for P Rob Bell. Rangers claimed C Marcus Jensen on waivers from Red Sox.

JUNE 18
Angels announced retirement of 1B-DH Wally Joyner.

JUNE 19
Orioles announced 3B Cal Ripken will retire at end of season.
Yankees released OF Henry Rodriguez.
Diamondbacks traded OF Rob Ryan to Athletics for OF Ryan Christenson.

JUNE 20
White Sox signed DH Jose Canseco.
Devil Rays signed OF Greg Martinez.
Reds traded IF Donnie Sadler to Royals for P Cary Ammons.

JUNE 22
Braves traded P John Rocker and 3B Troy Cameron to Indians for P Steve Karsay and P Steve Reed.
Reds released OF Deion Sanders.
Padres released SS Chris Gomez.

JUNE 23
Tigers traded P Dave Mlicki to Astros for P Jose Lima.
Padres traded P Jay Witasick to Yankees for IF D'Angelo Jimenez.
Athletics signed C Greg Myers.
Devil Rays released OF Gerald Williams.

JUNE 25
Orioles claimed 3B Tony Batista on waivers from Blue Jays.
Marlins released P Dan Miceli.

JUNE 26
Rangers sold P Brian Sikorski to Chiba Lotte of Japan Pacific League.

JUNE 27
Devil Rays signed SS Chris Gomez.
Blue Jays organization signed OF Deion Sanders.
Astros traded P Jay Powell to Rockies for P Ron Villone.

JUNE 28
Padres announced retirement of OF Tony Gwynn at end of season.

JUNE 29
Giants traded P Alan Embree and cash to White Sox for P Derek Hasselhoff.
Yankees signed OF Gerald Williams.
Reds organization signed IF-OF Pete Rose Jr.

JULY 1
Reds traded P Mark Wohlers to Yankees for P Ricardo Aromboles.
Athletics announced retirement of DH John Jaha.

JULY 2
Rangers released 3B Ken Caminiti.
Reds organization signed P Jose Rijo.
Rockies organization signed P Dan Miceli.

JULY 3
Rockies traded OF Ron Gant to Athletics for OF Robin Jennings.
Brewers signed P Lance Painter.
Cardinals traded 1B-OF Larry Sutton to Twins for IF Hanley Frias.

JULY 4
Yankees traded P Brian Boehringer to Giants for C Bobby Estalella and P Joe Smith.

JULY 5
Braves signed 3B Ken Caminiti.

JULY 6
Cubs signed IF-OF Delino DeShields.

JULY 9
Astros released 3B Charlie Hayes.

JULY 10
Pirates traded OF Emil Brown to Padres for P Shawn Camp and OF Shawn Garrett.

JULY 11
Mets released OF Daryl Hamilton.

JULY 12
Brewers claimed P Mac Suzuki on waivers from Rockies.

JULY 13
Dodgers traded P Wade Parrish to White Sox for OF McKay Christenson.
Angels traded OF Kim Bartee to Rockies for IF Chone Figgins.

JULY 17
Braves announced retirement of 1B Rico Brogna.
Reds claimed P Leo Estrella on waivers from Mets.

JULY 18
Rockies organization signed OF Darryl Hamilton.

JULY 19
Reds traded OF Alex Ochoa to Rockies for 2B Todd Walker and OF Robin Jennings.

JULY 20
Reds traded OF Michael Tucker to Cubs for P Chris Booker and P Ben Shaffar.

JULY 23
Dodgers claimed P Manny Mota on waivers from Twins.
Phillies traded C Gary Bennett to Mets for C Todd Pratt.
Padres signed P Chuck McElroy.

JULY 24
Rangers traded 1B Andres Galarraga to Giants for P Erasma Ramirez, IF Chris Magruder and P Todd Ozias.

JULY 25

Royals traded OF Jermaine Dye to Athletics, who traded OF Mario Encarnacion, IF Jose Ortiz and P Todd Belitz to Rockies, who traded SS Neifi Perez to Royals.

Devil Rays traded P Albie Lopez and C Mike DiFelice to Diamondbacks for OF Jason Conti and P Nick Bierbrodt.

JULY 26

White Sox traded P James Baldwin and cash to Dodgers for P Onan Masaoka, P Gary Majewski and OF Jeff Barry.

JULY 27

Devil Rays traded 1B Fred McGriff to Cubs for P Manny Aybar and a player to be named; Devil Rays acquired IF Jason Smith to complete deal (August 6).

Expos organization signed OF Geronimo Berroa.

Mets traded P Turk Wendell and P Dennis Cook to Phillies for P Bruce Chen and P Adam Walker.

Phillies traded P Wayne Gomes to San Francisco for IF Felipe Crespo.

JULY 28

Tigers traded P Todd Jones to Twins for P Mark Redman.

JULY 30

Red Sox released P Bryce Florie.

Brewers traded P David Weathers and P Roberto Miniel to Cubs for P Ruben Quevedo and OF Peter Zoccolillo.

Mets traded P Rick Reed to Twins for OF Matt Lawton.

Pirates traded P Jason Schmidt and OF John Vander Wal to Giants for OF Armando Rios and P Ryan Vogelsong.

Padres traded P Sterling Hitchcock to Yankees for P Brett Jodie and OF Darren Blakely.

JULY 31

Orioles traded P Mike Trombley to Dodgers for P Kris Foster and C Geronimo Gil.

Red Sox traded P Tomo Ohka and P Rich Rundles to Expos for P Ugueth Urbina.

Royals traded SS Rey Sanchez to Braves for P Brad Voyles and IF Alejandro Machado.

Blue Jays released P John Frascatore.

Rockies traded P Pedro Astacio and cash to Astros for P Scott Elarton and a player to be named.

Dodgers traded P Mike Fetters and P Adrian Burnside to Pirates for P Terry Mulholland.

Expos traded OF Milton Bradley to Indians for P Zach Day.

Pirates traded P Mike Williams to Astros for P Tony McKnight.

Cardinals traded P Jason Christiansen to Giants for P Kevin Joseph and a player to be named or cash.

AUGUST 2

Tigers organization signed P Bryce Florie.

Padres traded P Woody Williams to Cardinals for OF Ray Lankford and cash.

AUGUST 3

Blue Jays released P Joey Hamilton.

AUGUST 5

Braves organization signed P Brad Clontz.

AUGUST 6

Rockies traded P Juan Acevedo to Marlins for IF Josue Espada.

AUGUST 7

Braves released 2B Quilvio Veras.

AUGUST 10

Pirates claimed OF Gary Matthews, Jr. on waivers from Cubs.

Cardinals claimed IF Miguel Cairo on waivers from Cubs.

AUGUST 14

Pirates claimed IF Mendy Lopez on waivers from Astros.

AUGUST 15

Mets claimed IF Luis Figueroa on waivers from Pirates.

AUGUST 17

Reds organization signed P Joey Hamilton.

AUGUST 19

Red Sox organization signed 2B Quilvio Veras.

AUGUST 20

Red Sox announced retirement of P Hipolito Pichardo.

AUGUST 22

Rangers claimed P Chris Michalak on waivers from Blue Jays.

AUGUST 23

White Sox claimed P Bill Pulsipher on waivers from Red Sox.

Mets traded C Gary Bennett to Rockies for a player to be named; Mets acquired OF Ender Chavez to complete deal (December 27).

Mets claimed OF Jaisen Randolph on waivers from Cubs.

AUGUST 27

Mariners purchased contract of C Pat Borders from Devil Rays.

Rangers released P Kevin Foster.

AUGUST 28

Mariners organization signed P Randy Myers.

AUGUST 30

Orioles traded 1B Calvin Pickering to Reds for future considerations.

AUGUST 31

Rangers traded IF Randy Velarde to Yankees for two players to be named; Rangers acquired P Randy Flores and P Rosman Garcia to complete deal (October 12).

Padres traded P Rudy Seanez to Braves for a player to be named; Padres acquired P Winston Abreu to complete deal (September 6).

Braves purchased 1B Julio Franco from Mexico City of Mexican League.

Tigers traded OF Lyle Mouton to Astros for a player to be named.

SEPTEMBER 2

Indians released P Jamie Brown.

Tigers traded P C.J. Nitkowski and cash to Mets for a player to be named; Tigers acquired P Kyle Kessel to complete deal (December 13).

SEPTEMBER 4

Cubs traded P Mike Fyhrie to Athletics for OF Michael Wenner.

SEPTEMBER 6

Red Sox claimed 1B Calvin Pickering off waivers from Reds.

Expos released P Hideki Irabu.

SEPTEMBER 18

Reds released P Chris Nichting.

Rockies claimed OF John Barnes on waivers from Twins.

SEPTEMBER 19

Rockies signed P Chris Nichting.

SEPTEMBER 21

Orioles claimed 3B Casey Blake on waivers from Twins.

SEPTEMBER 26

Red Sox released P Carlos Castillo.

Marlins announced retirement of P Alex Fernandez.

OCTOBER 3

Expos traded OF Tim Raines Sr. to Orioles for a player to be named.

OCTOBER 7

Devil Rays released P Juan Guzman.

OCTOBER 10

Red Sox released IF Morgan Burkhart and SS Craig Grebeck.
Cubs claimed IF Jose Fernandez on waivers from Angels.

OCTOBER 12

Twins claimed 3B Casey Blake on waivers from Orioles.
Brewers released P Mac Suzuki.

OCTOBER 19

Rockies released P Chris Nichting.

OCTOBER 23

Reds organization signed P Jared Fernandez.
Pirates released P Brian O'Connor and IF Mendy Lopez.

OCTOBER 24

Astros announced retirement of IF Bill Spiers.

OCTOBER 26

Indians organization signed IF Greg LaRocca.

NOVEMBER 2

Orioles organization signed C Mike Hubbard.
Cubs traded IF Adam Morrissey to Athletics for IF Mark Bellhorn.

NOVEMBER 6

Indians organization signed OF Todd Dunwoody.

NOVEMBER 7

Tigers released P Dave Borkowski.
Tigers organization signed P Dave Borkowski.
Athletics organization signed P Rocky Coppinger, P Ismael Villegas, IF Jose Flores, IF Chad Meyers and OF Michael Warner.
Rangers organization signed C Brad King, IF Eddy Martinez and IF Juan Silvestre.

NOVEMBER 8

Yankees released OF Richard Brown.

NOVEMBER 9

Phillies traded P Omar Daal to Dodgers for P Eric Junge and P Jesus Cordero.

NOVEMBER 12

Cardinals announced retirement of 1B Mark McGwire.

NOVEMBER 16

Orioles released OF Brady Anderson.
Orioles traded 3B Ivanon Coffie to Cubs for a player to be named.
Orioles organization signed P Travis Driskill and OF Ryan McGuire.
Rangers organization signed IF Jason Maxwell.
Giants claimed OF Ruben Rivera on waivers from Reds.

NOVEMBER 19

White Sox claimed P Ryan Kohlmeier on waivers from Orioles.
Indians claimed P Chad Paronto on waivers from Orioles.
Cubs organization signed 3B Kevin Orie.

NOVEMBER 20

Red Sox claimed 1B Tony Clark.
White Sox claimed OF Brian Simmons on waivers from Blue Jays.
Tigers released P Chris Holt and P Heath Murray.
Athletics released IF-OF F.P. Santangelo and OF Billy McMillon.
Athletics organization signed P Mike Colangelo.
Diamondbacks organization signed P Eddie Oropesa and P Jose Parra.
Mets claimed OF Esix Snead on waivers from Cardinals.

Mets claimed on waivers P Saul Rivera from Twins.
Cardinals signed C Mike DiFelice.
Padres claimed P Rob Ramsay on waivers from Mariners.

NOVEMBER 26

Rangers signed P Todd Van Poppel.

NOVEMBER 27

White Sox traded IF Herbert Perry to Rangers for a player to be named; White Sox acquired P Corey Lee to complete deal (December 17).
Rangers signed OF Julio Ramirez.
Yankees announced retirement of 3B Scott Brosius.
Devil Rays released OF Jose Guillen.
Rangers organization signed IF Santiago Perez and P Fernando Rijo.

NOVEMBER 29

Red Sox claimed P Jeff Wallace on waivers from Devil Rays.

NOVEMBER 30

Rockies released OF Jacob Cruz.

DECEMBER 2

Mets signed P Satoru Komiyama.

DECEMBER 3

Astros signed OF Brian Hunter.
Giants released P Wayne Gomes, OF Jalal Leach and OF Dante Powell.

DECEMBER 4

Orioles signed OF Marty Cordova.
Rangers organization signed P Juan Alvarez.

DECEMBER 6

Indians signed OF Brady Anderson.
Rangers organization signed P Dan Murray.
Padres organization signed OF Scott Morgan, P Jason Kershner, P Jason Boyd and P Brandon Villafuerte.

DECEMBER 7

Yankees traded OF David Justice to Mets for 3B Robin Ventura.
Yankees signed P Steve Karsay.
Blue Jays traded P Billy Koch to Athletics for 3B Eric Hinske and RHP Justin Miller.

DECEMBER 8

Braves signed 3B Vinny Castilla.
Astros signed C Gregg Zaun.

DECEMBER 10

Blue Jays traded SS Alex Gonzalez to Cubs for P Felix Heredia and a player to be named later; Blue Jays acquired INF James Deschaine to complete deal (December 13).
Cardinals signed P Jason Isringhausen.

DECEMBER 11

Indians traded 2B Roberto Alomar, P Mike Bacsik and OF-1B Danny Peoples to Mets for OF Matt Lawton, OF Alex Escobar, P Jerrod Riggan and two players to be named later; Indians acquired P Billy Traber and 1B Earl Snyder to complete deal (December 13).
Mariners traded P Brett Tomko, C Tom Lampkin, SS Ramon Vazquez and cash to Padres for C Ben Davis, P Wascar Serrano and INF Alex Arias.
Rangers signed P Jay Powell.
Marlins traded P Jesus Sanchez to Cubs for P Nate Teut.
Reds traded OF Dmitri Young to Tigers for OF Juan Encarnacion and P Luis Pineda.

DECEMBER 12

Red Sox traded OF Carl Everett to Rangers for P Darren Oliver.
Diamondbacks signed OF Jose Guillen.

DECEMBER 13

Indians released P Steve Woodard.
Expos traded P Joe Valentine to Tigers for cash.
Tigers signed INF Craig Paquette.
Yankees signed 1B Jason Giambi.
Blue Jays released C Alberto Castillo and INF Luis Lopez.
Blue Jays traded P Paul Quantrill and INF Cesar Izturis to Dodgers for P Luke Prokopec and P Chad Ricketts.
Mets signed OF Roger Cedeno and P David Weathers.
Phillies traded P Chris Brock to Orioles for P John Wasdin.
White Sox traded P Kip Wells, P Sean Lowe and P Josh Fogg to Pirates for P Todd Ritchie and C Lee Evans.
Giants traded OF John Vander Wal to Yankees for P Jay Witasick.

DECEMBER 14

Mets traded OF David Justice to Athletics for P Mark Guthrie and P Tyler Yates.
Yankees traded 2B Bernabel Castro to Padres for OF Kevin Reese.

DECEMBER 16

Cardinals traded P Dustin Hermanson to Red Sox for OF Rick Asadoorian, 1B Luis Garcia and 1B Dustin Brisson.
Rockies traded 3B Jeff Cirillo to Mariners for P Jose Paniagua, P Dennis Stark and P Brian Fuentes.
Mets traded OF Tsuyoshi Shinjo and INF Desi Relaford to Giants for P Shawn Estes.

DECEMBER 17

Indians signed INF Ricky Gutierrez.
Yankees signed OF Rondell White.
Angels traded INF Wilmy Caceres to Devil Rays for P Mickey Callaway.

DECEMBER 18

Red Sox signed P Willie Banks.
Red Sox organization signed 2B Carlos Baerga.
Indians traded P John Rocker to Rangers for P Dave Elder.
Indians organization signed INF Bill Selby, P Heath Murray and P Dave Maurer.
Royals signed OF Chuck Knoblauch.
Rangers organization signed P Jeremi Gonzalez.
Rockies traded P Gabe White and P Luke Hudson to Reds for 2B Pokey Reese and P Dennys Reyes.
Cardinals signed 1B Tino Martinez.

DECEMBER 19

Angels signed P Dennis Cook.
Rockies traded 2B Pokey Reese to Red Sox for C Scott Hatteberg.

Red Sox signed P John Burkett.
Tigers signed P Oscar Henriquez, P Brian Powell, P Julio Santana, P Jamie Walker, C Yohanny Valera, INF Adam Riggs, INF Juan Sosa and OF Chad Alexander.
Cubs traded OF Michael Tucker to Royals for a player to be named later.
Mariners announced retirement of OF Jay Buhner.
Rangers signed P Dave Burba.
Cubs signed OF Moises Alou.

DECEMBER 20

Tigers organization signed P Juan Acevedo.
Tigers claimed OF Endy Chavez on waivers from Royals.
Braves signed P Albie Lopez.
Dodgers signed P Hideo Nomo.
Pirates traded P Jose Silva to Reds for P Ben Shaffar.

DECEMBER 22

Red Sox signed OF Johnny Damon to a four-year contract.
Angels traded OF Scott Bikowski and INF Josh Shaffer to White Sox for P Dan Mozingo and P Jim Sweeney.
Tigers organization signed OF Jacob Cruz.
Yankees organization signed C Alberto Castillo and OF F.P. Santangelo.
Astros organization signed P T.J. Mathews and P C.J. Nitkowski.
Indians traded OF Dave Roberts to Dodgers for P Christian Bridenbaugh and P Nial Hughes.

DECEMBER 23

Rangers signed P Chan Ho Park.

DECEMBER 26

Angels signed P Aaron Sele.
Mariners signed OF Ruben Sierra.

DECEMBER 27

Angels traded 1B Mo Vaughn to Mets for P Kevin Appier.
Rangers organization signed P Hideki Irabu and P Bill Pulsipher.
Padres signed P Alan Embree.

DECEMBER 28

Pirates traded OF Gary Matthews, Jr. to Mets for cash considerations.
Mets organization signed P John Frascatore.

DECEMBER 30

Athletics signed C Scott Hatteberg.

AWARD WINNERS

AMERICAN LEAGUE

Pitcher of the Year: Roger Clemens, New York
Rookie Player of the Year: Ichiro Suzuki, Seattle, OF
Rookie Pitcher of the Year: C.C. Sabathia, Cleveland
Fireman of the Year: Mariano Rivera, New York
Comeback Player of the Year: Ruben Sierra, Texas
Manager of the Year: Lou Piniella, Seattle

MAJOR LEAGUE

Player of the Year: Barry Bonds, San Francisco
Executive of the Year: Pat Gillick, Seattle

NATIONAL LEAGUE

Pitcher of the Year: Curt Schilling, Arizona
Rookie Player of the Year: Albert Pujols, St. Louis, OF-3B-1B
Rookie Pitcher of the Year: Roy Oswalt, Houston
Fireman of the Year: Armando Benitez, New York
　　　　　　　　　　　　　　Robb Nen, San Francisco
Comeback Player of the Year: Matt Morris, St. Louis
Manager of the Year: Larry Bowa, Philadelphia

MINOR LEAGUE

Player of the Year: Josh Beckett, Brevard County, Florida State; Portland, Eastern
Manager of the Year: Tony Pena, New Orleans, Pacific Coast
Executive of the Year: Jay Miller, Round Rock, Texas

BASEBALL WRITERS' ASSOCIATION OF AMERICA
AMERICAN LEAGUE

MOST VALUABLE PLAYER

Player, Team	1	2	3	4	5	6	7	8	9	10	Pts.
Ichiro Suzuki, Seattle	11	10	3	1	1	-	2	-	-	-	289
Jason Giambi, Oakland	8	11	7	2	-	-	-	-	-	-	281
Bret Boone, Seattle	7	4	8	7	2	-	-	-	-	-	259
Roberto Alomar, Cleveland	2	2	2	8	1	4	3	2	1	1	165
Juan Gonzalez, Cleveland	-	-	3	4	10	6	1	3	-	1	156
Alex Rodriguez, Texas	-	1	2	4	4	5	8	1	2	-	141
Jim Thome, Cleveland	-	-	2	2	3	5	2	7	2	1	107
Roger Clemens, New York	-	-	-	-	2	4	3	6	-	5	67
Manny Ramirez, Boston	-	-	-	-	2	1	2	4	5	3	50
Derek Jeter, New York	-	-	-	-	1	2	3	1	4	3	42
Mariano Rivera, New York	-	-	1	-	1	-	1	1	2	2	27
Tino Martinez, New York	-	-	-	-	1	-	2	-	2	-	18
Mark Mulder, Oakland	-	-	-	-	-	1	-	1	2	-	12
Rafael Palmeiro, Texas	-	-	-	-	-	-	-	1	-	2	5
Doug Mientkiewicz, Minnesota	-	-	-	-	-	-	-	-	2	1	5
Edgar Martinez, Seattle	-	-	-	-	-	-	1	-	-	-	4
Cristian Guzman, Minnesota	-	-	-	-	-	-	-	1	-	1	4
Mike Cameron, Seattle	-	-	-	-	-	-	-	-	2	-	4
Miguel Tejada, Oakland	-	-	-	-	-	-	-	-	1	1	3
Kazu Sasaki, Seattle	-	-	-	-	-	-	-	-	-	3	3
Torii Hunter, Minnesota	-	-	-	-	-	-	-	-	1	-	2
Mike Sweeney, Kansas City	-	-	-	-	-	-	-	-	1	-	2
Barry Zito, Oakland	-	-	-	-	-	-	-	-	1	-	2
Garret Anderson, Anaheim	-	-	-	-	-	-	-	-	-	2	2
Corey Koskie, Minnesota	-	-	-	-	-	-	-	-	-	1	1
Shannon Stewart, Toronto	-	-	-	-	-	-	-	-	-	1	1

Fourteen points awarded for a first-place vote, nine for second and down to one for 10th.

CY YOUNG AWARD

Pitcher, Team	1	2	3	Pts.
Roger Clemens, New York	21	5	2	122
Mark Mulder, Oakland	2	13	11	60
Freddy Garcia, Seattle	4	8	11	55
Jamie Moyer, Seattle	1	2	1	12
Mike Mussina, New York	-	-	2	2
Tim Hudson, Oakland	-	-	1	1

Five points awarded for a first-place vote, three for second and one for third.

ROOKIE OF THE YEAR

Player, Team	1	2	3	Pts.
Ichiro Suzuki, Seattle	27	1	-	138
C.C. Sabathia, Cleveland	1	21	5	73
Alfonso Soriano, New York	-	6	17	35
David Eckstein, Anaheim	-	-	6	6

Five points awarded for a first-place vote, three for second and one for third.

MANAGER OF THE YEAR

Manager, Team	1	2	3	Pts.
Lou Piniella, Seattle	22	6	-	128
Art Howe, Oakland	5	17	1	77
Tom Kelly, Minnesota	1	4	8	25
Jimy Williams, Boston	-	-	12	12
Joe Torrre, New York	-	1	5	8
Charlie Manuel, Cleveland	-	-	1	1
Mike Scioscia, Anaheim	-	-	1	1

Five points awarded for a first-place vote, three for second and one for third.

MOST VALUABLE PLAYER

Player, Team	1	2	3	4	5	6	7	8	9	10	Pts.
Barry Bonds, San Francisco	30	2	-	-	-	-	-	-	-	-	438
Sammy Sosa, Chicago	2	17	8	4	-	1	-	-	-	-	278
Luis Gonzalez, Arizona	-	8	21	3	-	-	-	-	-	-	261
Albert Pujols, St. Louis	-	5	3	18	3	-	1	1	1	-	222
Lance Berkman, Houston	-	-	-	1	13	5	1	2	1	3	125
Shawn Green, Los Angeles	-	-	-	1	5	5	4	6	7	2	112
Jeff Bagwell, Houston	-	-	-	3	5	5	3	2	7	1	109
Chipper Jones, Atlanta	-	-	-	-	2	5	11	3	5	-	100
Todd Helton, Colorado	-	-	-	1	1	6	5	6	3	3	90
Curt Schilling, Arizona	-	-	-	-	-	2	1	2	1	2	24
Randy Johnson, Arizona	-	-	-	1	-	-	1	3	-	3	23
Rich Aurilia, San Francisco	-	-	-	-	-	-	2	2	1	4	20
Mike Piazza, New York	-	-	-	-	1	1	-	1	-	-	14
Moises Alou, Houston	-	-	-	-	2	-	-	-	-	1	13
Matt Morris, St. Louis	-	-	-	-	-	1	1	1	-	1	13
Bobby Abreu, Philadelphia	-	-	-	-	-	-	-	2	-	3	9
Jimmy Rollins, Philadelphia	-	-	-	-	-	-	-	1	2	1	8
Brian Jordan, Atlanta	-	-	-	-	-	1	-	-	1	-	7
Paul Lo Duca, Los Angeles	-	-	-	-	-	-	1	-	-	2	6
Felix Rodriguez, San Francisco	-	-	-	-	-	-	1	-	-	-	4
Phil Nevin, San Diego	-	-	-	-	-	-	-	-	1	1	3
Cliff Floyd, Florida	-	-	-	-	-	-	-	-	1	-	2
Roy Oswalt, Houston	-	-	-	-	-	-	-	-	1	-	2
Brian Giles, Pittsburgh	-	-	-	-	-	-	-	-	1	1	1
Vladimir Guerrero, Montreal	-	-	-	-	-	-	-	-	-	1	1
Steve Kline, St. Louis	-	-	-	-	-	-	-	-	-	1	1
Scott Rolen, Philadelphia	-	-	-	-	-	-	-	-	-	1	1
Larry Walker, Colorado	-	-	-	-	-	-	-	-	-	1	1

Fourteen points awarded for a first-place vote, nine for second and down to one for 10th.

CY YOUNG AWARD

Pitcher, Team	1	2	3	Pts.
Randy Johnson, Arizona	30	2	-	156
Curt Schilling, Arizona	2	29	1	98
Matt Morris, St. Louis	-	1	28	31
Jon Lieber, Chicago	-	-	2	2
Roy Oswalt, Houston	-	-	1	1

Five points awarded for a first-place vote, three for second and one for third.

ROOKIE OF THE YEAR

Player, Team	1	2	3	Pts.
Albert Pujols, St. Louis	32	-	-	160
Roy Oswalt, Houston	-	25	7	82
Jimmy Rollins, Philadelphia	-	7	23	44
Bud Smith, St. Louis	-	-	1	1
Adam Dunn, Cincinnati	-	-	1	1

Five points awarded for a first-place vote, three for second and one for third.

MANAGER OF THE YEAR

Manager, Team	1	2	3	Pts.
Larry Bowa, Philadelphia	18	6	5	113
Jim Tracy, Los Angeles	4	8	4	48
Tony La Russa, St. Louis	4	5	3	38
Bob Brenly, Arizona	3	4	6	33
Larry Dierker, Houston	1	4	4	21
Don Baylor, Chicago	-	3	4	13
Bobby Cox, Atlanta	2	-	2	12
Dusty Baker, San Francisco	-	2	4	10

Five points awarded for a first-place vote, three for second and one for third.

MISCELLANEOUS

ATTENDANCE

AMERICAN LEAGUE

	Home	Road
Seattle	3,507,975	2,572,882
New York	3,264,777	2,817,798
Cleveland	3,175,523	2,365,421
Baltimore	3,094,841	2,333,664
Texas	2,831,111	2,247,629
Boston	2,625,333	2,695,389
Oakland	2,133,277	2,266,814
Anaheim	2,000,917	2,491,562
Detroit	1,921,305	2,205,142
Toronto	1,915,438	2,197,292
Minnesota	1,782,926	2,274,453
Chicago	1,766,172	2,209,357
Kansas City	1,536,371	2,232,980
Tampa Bay	1,227,673	2,289,235
Totals	32,783,639	33,199,618

NATIONAL LEAGUE

	Home	Road
San Francisco	3,277,244	2,856,363
Colorado	3,159,385	2,487,736
St. Louis	3,113,091	2,710,279
Los Angeles	3,017,502	2,664,554
Houston	2,904,280	2,344,277
Atlanta	2,823,494	2,303,372
Milwaukee	2,811,041	2,328,454
Chicago	2,779,456	2,821,982
Arizona	2,740,554	2,566,082
New York	2,658,279	2,423,211
Pittsburgh	2,436,126	2,204,272
San Diego	2,377,969	2,532,725
Cincinnati	1,882,732	2,663,529
Philadelphia	1,782,460	2,117,822
Florida	1,261,220	2,088,475
Montreal	609,473	2,105,194
Totals	39,634,306	39,218,327

DEBUTS

Player	Pos.	Team	Birth date	Birthplace	Debut
Abad, Fausto Andres	PH	Oakland	8-25-72	West Palm Beach, Florida	9-10
Abernathy, Michael Brent	2B	Tampa Bay	9-23-77	Atlanta, Georgia	6-25
Acevedo, Jose Omar	P	Cincinnati	12-18-77	Santo Domingo, Dominican Republic	6-19
Ainsworth, Kurt Harold	P	San Francisco	9-9-78	Baton Rouge, Louisiana	9-5
Aldridge, Cory Jerome	RF	Atlanta	6-13-79	San Angelo, Texas	9-5
Almonte, Erick	SS	New York A.L.	2-1-78	Santo Domingo, Dominican Republic	9-4
Atchley, Justin Scott	P	Cincinnati	9-5-73	Sedro Woolley, Washington	4-7
Austin, Jeffrey	P	Kansas City	10-19-76	San Bernardino, California	6-26
Bacsik, Michael J.	P	Cleveland	11-11-77	Dallas, Texas	8-5
Baez, Benito	P	Florida	5-6-77	Bonao, Dominican Republic	8-25
Baez, Danys	P	Cleveland	9-10-77	Pinar Del Rio, Cuba	5-13
Balfour, Grant	P	Minnesota	12-30-77	Sydney, Australia	7-22
Barkett, Andrew	LF	Pittsburgh	9-5-74	Miami, Florida	5-28
Barnes, Larry Richard	PH	Anaheim	7-23-74	Bakersfield, California	4-11
Bauer, Richard Edward	P	Baltimore	1-10-77	Garden Grove, California	9-2
Beckett, Josh	P	Florida	5-15-80	Austin, Texas	9-4
Beimel, Joseph Ronald	P	Pittsburgh	4-19-77	St. Marys, Pennsylvania	4-8
Benoit, Joaquin Antonio	P	Texas	7-26-79	Santiago, Dominican Republic	8-8
Berger, Brandon Charles	PR	Kansas City	2-21-75	Covington, Kentucky	9-9
Berroa, Angel	SS	Kansas City	1-27-80	Santo Domingo, Dominican Republic	9-18
Betemit, Wilson	PR	Atlanta	11-2-81	Santo Domingo, Dominican Republic	9-18
Bierbrodt, Nicholas Raymond	P	Arizona	5-16-78	Tarzana, California	6-7
Bigbie, Larry	RF	Baltimore	11-4-77	Hobart, Indiana	6-23
Bowles, Brian Christopher	P	Toronto	8-18-76	Harbor City, California	6-27
Brohawn, Michael Troy	P	Arizona	1-14-73	Cambridge, Maryland	4-14
Brumbaugh, Clifford Michael	LF	Texas	4-21-74	Wilmington, Delaware	5-30
Burke, James Eugene	C	Anaheim	9-24-71	Roseburg, Oregon	5-9
Butler, Justin Brent	2B	Colorado	2-11-78	Laurinburg, North Carolina	7-4
Chacon, Shawn A.	P	Colorado	12-23-77	Anchorage, Alaska	4-29
Chavez, Endy DeJesus	CF	Kansas City	2-7-78	Valencia, Venezuela	5-29
Chiasson, Scott	P	Chicago N.L.	8-14-77	Norwich, Connecticut	9-19
Christman, Timothy Arthur	P	Colorado	3-31-75	Oneonta, New York	4-21
Cintron, Alexander	PR	Arizona	12-17-78	Humacao, Puerto Rico	7-24
Clapp, Richard Keith	PH	St. Louis	2-24-73	Windsor, Canada	6-18
Clark, Jermaine Marcel	PR	Detroit	9-29-76	Berkeley, California	4-3
Cogan, Anthony Michael	P	Kansas City	12-21-76	Chicago, Illinois	4-2
Colome, Jesus	P	Tampa Bay	6-2-80	San Pedro de Macoris, D.R.	6-21
Coolbaugh, Mike	PH	Milwaukee	6-5-72	Binghamton, New York	7-16
Corey, Mark Franklin	P	New York N.L.	11-16-74	Coudersport, Pennsylvania	10-2
Cornejo, Nathan J.	P	Detroit	9-24-79	Wellington, Kansas	8-8
Cota, Humberto Figueroa	PH	Pittsburgh	2-7-79	San Luis Rio Colorado, Mexico	9-9
Crespo, Cesar Antonio	2B	San Diego	5-23-79	Rio Piedras, Puerto Rico	5-29
Cruz, Juan Carlos	P	Chicago N.L.	10-15-80	Banao, Dominican Republic	8-21

Player	Pos.	Team	Birth date	Birthplace	Debut
Cuddyer, Michael Brent	DH	Minnesota	3-27-79	Norfolk, Virginia	9-23
Cust, John Joseph	PH	Arizona	1-16-79	Flemington, New Jersey	9-26
Davis, Johnny Lance	P	Cincinnati	9-1-76	Winter Haven, Florida	6-16
Dickey, Robert Alan	P	Texas	10-29-74	Nashville, Tennessee	4-22
Douglass, Sean	P	Baltimore	4-28-79	Lancaster, California	7-18
Drese, Ryan Thomas	P	Cleveland	4-5-76	San Francisco, California	7-29
Duchscherer, Justin Craig	P	Texas	11-19-77	Aberdeen, South Dakota	7-25
Duckworth, Brandon J.	P	Philadelphia	1-23-76	Salt Lake City, Utah	8-7
Duncan, Courtney	P	Chicago N.L.	10-9-74	Mobile, Alabama	4-2
Dunn, Adam Troy	LF	Cincinnati	11-9-79	Houston, Texas	7-20
Eckstein, David Mark	2B	Anaheim	1-20-75	Sanford, Florida	4-3
Encarnacion, Mario	LF	Colorado	9-24-77	Bani, Dominican Republic	8-26
Escobar, Alexander Jose	CF	New York N.L.	9-6-78	Valencia, Venezuela	5-8
Estrada, Johnny	C	Philadelphia	6-27-76	Hayward, California	5-15
Everett, Jeffrey Adam	SS	Houston	2-2-77	Austell, Georgia	8-30
Fernandez, Jared Wade	P	Cincinnati	2-2-72	Salt Lake City, Utah	9-19
Figueroa, Luis	2B	Pittsburgh	2-16-74	Bayamon, Puerto Rico	6-27
Fikac, Jeremy Joseph	P	San Diego	4-8-75	Shiner, Texas	8-16
File, Robert	P	Toronto	1-28-77	Philadelphia, Pennsylvania	4-14
Fogg, Joshua Smith	P	Chicago A.L.	12-13-76	Lynn, Massachusetts	9-2
Fossum, Casey Paul	P	Boston	1-9-78	Cherry Hill, New Jersey	7-28
Foster, John Kristian	P	Baltimore	8-30-74	Riverdale, New Jersey	8-3
Freel, Ryan Paul	2B	Toronto	3-8-76	Jacksonville, Florida	4-4
Fuentes, Brian Christopher	P	Seattle	8-9-75	Merced, California	6-2
Gandarillas, Gus	P	Milwaukee	7-19-71	Coral Gables, Florida	7-17
George, Christopher Coleman	P	Kansas City	9-16-79	Houston, Texas	7-26
Gibbons, Jay Jonathon	PH	Baltimore	3-2-77	Rochester, Michigan	4-6
Gil, Geronimo	C	Baltimore	8-7-75	Oaxaca, Mexico	9-8
Giles, Marcus William	2B	Atlanta	5-18-78	San Diego, California	4-17
Gonzalez, Dicky Angel	P	New York N.L.	12-21-78	Bayamon, Puerto Rico	5-1
Green, Steve	P	Anaheim	1-26-78	Greenfield Park, Canada	4-7
Harris, William Charles	CF	Baltimore	6-22-78	Cairo, Georgia	9-2
Harvey, Kenneth Eugene	DH	Kansas City	3-1-78	Los Angeles, California	9-18
Hernandez, Adrian	P	New York A.L.	3-25-75	Havana, Cuba	4-21
Hernandez, Carlos E.	P	Houston	4-22-80	Guacara, Venezuela	8-18
Herndon, Harry Francis	P	San Diego	9-11-78	Liberal, Kansas	8-2
Hillenbrand, Shea Matthew	3B	Boston	7-27-75	Mesa, Arizona	4-2
Hoover, Paul Chester	PH	Tampa Bay	4-14-76	Columbus, Ohio	9-8
Huckaby, Ken	C	Arizona	1-27-71	San Leandro, California	10-6
Hutchinson, Chad Martin	P	St. Louis	2-21-77	San Diego, California	4-4
Inge, Charles Brandon	C	Detroit	5-19-77	Lynchburg, Virginia	4-3
Izturis, Cesar D.	SS	Toronto	2-10-80	Lara, Venezuela	6-23
Jennings, Jason	P	Colorado	7-17-78	Dallas, Texas	8-23
Jensen, Larry Ryan	P	San Francisco	9-17-75	Salt Lake City, Utah	5-19
Jodie, Brett	P	New York A.L.	3-25-77	Columbia, South Carolina	7-20
Johnson, Adam Bryant	P	Minnesota	7-12-79	San Jose, California	7-16
Johnson, Nicholas Robert	1B	New York A.L.	9-19-78	Sacramento, California	8-21
Julio, Jorge Dandys	P	Baltimore	3-3-79	Caracas, Venezuela	4-26
Karnuth, Jason Andre	P	St. Louis	5-15-76	LaGrange, Illinois	4-20
Kennedy, Joseph Darley	P	Tampa Bay	5-24-79	La Mesa, California	6-6
Kielty, Robert Michael	CF	Minnesota	8-5-76	Fontana, California	4-10
Kim, Sun-Woo	P	Boston	9-4-77	Inchon, South Korea	6-15
Knight, Brandon Michael	P	New York A.L.	10-1-75	Oxnard, California	6-5
Knott, Eric James	P	Arizona	9-23-74	Harvey, Illinois	9-1
Knotts, Gary Everett	P	Florida	2-12-77	Decatur, Alabama	7-28
Koplove, Michael Paul	P	Arizona	8-30-76	Philadelphia, Pennsylvania	9-6
Larson, Brandon John	PH	Cincinnati	5-24-76	San Angelo, Texas	5-4
Lawrence, Brian	P	San Diego	5-14-76	Fort Collins, Colorado	4-15
Leach, Jalal Donnell	PH	San Francisco	3-14-69	San Francisco, California	9-5
Lofton, James O'Neal	PH	Boston	3-6-74	Los Angeles, California	9-19
Lohse, Kyle M.	P	Minnesota	10-4-78	Chico, California	6-22
Lopez, Felipe	3B	Toronto	5-12-80	Bayamon, Puerto Rico	8-3
Lopez, Luis	PH	Toronto	10-5-73	Brooklyn, New York	4-29
Lukasiewicz, Mark	P	Anaheim	3-8-73	Jersey City, New Jersey	5-11
Lyon, Brandon J.	P	Toronto	8-10-79	Salt Lake City, Utah	8-4
MacDougal, Robert Michael	P	Kansas City	3-5-77	Las Vegas, Nevada	9-22
Mackowiak, Robert William	2B	Pittsburgh	6-20-76	Oak Lawn, Illinois	5-19
MacRae, Scott Patrick	P	Cincinnati	8-13-74	Dearborn, Michigan	7-24
Magruder, Christopher James	PR	Texas	4-26-77	Tacoma, Washington	9-4
Mateo, Henry	2B	Montreal	10-14-76	Santo Domingo, Dominican Republic	7-28
Mattes, Troy Walter	P	Montreal	8-26-75	Champaign, Illinois	6-19

Player	Pos.	Team	Birth date	Birthplace	Debut
McDonald, Donzell	PH	New York A.L.	2-20-75	Long Beach, California	4-19
Mendez, Donaldo	SS	San Diego	6-7-78	Barquisimeto, Venezuela	4-5
Miadich, John Barton	P	Anaheim	2-3-76	Torrence, California	9-2
Michaels, Jason Drew	PH	Philadelphia	5-4-76	Tampa, Florida	4-6
Middlebrook, Jason Douglas	P	San Diego	6-26-75	Jackson, Michigan	9-17
Miller, Corky Abraham Philip	C	Cincinnati	3-18-76	Loma Linda, California	9-4
Miller, Matthew Lincoln	P	Detroit	8-2-74	Lubbock, Texas	5-8
Mohr, Dustan K.	RF	Minnesota	6-19-76	Hattiesburg, Mississippi	8-29
Monroe, Craig Keystone	RF	Texas	2-27-77	Texarkana, Texas	7-28
Moreno, Juan Carlos Vegas	P	Texas	2-28-75	Maiquetia, Venezuela	5-17
Moss, Damian Joseph	P	Atlanta	11-24-76	Darlinghurst, Australia	4-26
Neal, Blaine	P	Florida	4-6-78	Maurelton, New Jersey	9-3
Nelson, Joseph Georrge	P	Atlanta	10-25-74	Alameda, California	6-13
Neugebauer, Nickolas D.	P	Milwaukee	7-15-80	Riverside, California	8-19
Nunez, Jose Antonio	P	Los Angeles	3-14-79	Monte Cristy, Dominican Republic	4-3
Olsen, Kevin	P	Florida	7-26-76	Covina, California	9-7
Oropesa, Edilberto	P	Philadelphia	11-23-71	Colen Matanzas, Cuba	4-2
Ortega, Bill	PH	St. Louis	7-24-75	Havana, Cuba	9-7
Osting, James Michael	P	San Diego	4-7-77	Louisville, Kentucky	5-2
Oswalt, Roy Edward	P	Houston	8-29-77	Kosciusko, Mississippi	5-6
Overbay, Lyle Stefan	PH	Arizona	1-28-77	Centralia, Washington	9-19
Parker, Christian Michael	P	New York A.L.	7-3-75	Albuquerque, New Mexico	4-6
Paronto, Chad	P	Baltimore	7-28-75	Haverhill, New Hampshire	4-18
Patterson, Jarrod Lane	3B	Detroit	9-7-73	Montgomery, Alabama	6-16
Pena, Carlos	1B	Texas	5-17-78	Santo Domingo, Dominican Republic	9-5
Pettyjohn, Adam Christopher	P	Detroit	6-11-77	Phoenix, Arizona	7-16
Phelps, Travis Howard	P	Tampa Bay	7-25-77	Rocky Comfort, Missouri	4-19
Phillips, Jason	C	New York N.L.	9-27-76	La Mesa, California	9-19
Piersoll, Christopher Earl	P	Cincinnati	9-25-77	Van Nuys, California	8-31
Pineda, Luis A.	P	Detroit	6-10-78	San Cristobal, Dominican Republic	8-4
Podsednik, Scott Eric	PR	Seattle	3-18-76	West, Texas	7-6
Prinz, Bret Randolph	P	Arizona	6-15-77	Chicago Heights, Illinois	4-22
Pujols, Jose Albert	LF	St. Louis	1-16-80	Santo Domingo, Dominican Republic	4-2
Punto, Nicholas Paul	PH	Philadelphia	11-8-77	San Diego, California	9-9
Raines Jr., Timothy	CF	Baltimore	8-31-79	Memphis, Tennessee	10-1
Ransom, Bryan Cody	PH	San Francisco	2-17-76	Mesa, Arizona	9-5
Redding, Tim	P	Houston	2-12-78	Rochester, New York	6-24
Reith, Brian Eric	P	Cincinnati	2-20-78	Ft. Wayne, Indiana	5-16
Reitsma, Christopher Michael	P	Cincinnati	12-31-77	Minneapolis, Minnesota	4-4
Rincon, Juan Manuel	P	Minnesota	1-23-79	Maracaibo, Venezuela	6-7
Rivera, Juan Luis	RF	New York A.L.	7-3-78	Guarenas, Venezuela	9-4
Rivera, Michael R.	C	Detroit	9-8-76	Rio Piedras, Puerto Rico	9-18
Roberts, Brian M.	SS	Baltimore	10-9-77	Durham, North Carolina	6-14
Rodriguez, Wilfredo Jose	P	Houston	3-20-79	Bolivar, Venezuela	9-21
Rowand, Aaron Ryan	PH	Chicago A.L.	8-29-77	Portland, Oregon	6-16
Sabathia, Carsten Charles	P	Cleveland	7-21-80	Vallejo, California	4-8
Sanchez, Alexis	CF	Milwaukee	8-26-76	Havana, Cuba	6-15
Sandberg, Jared Lawrence	3B	Tampa Bay	3-2-78	Olympia, Washington	8-7
Santana, Pedro	2B	Detroit	9-21-76	San Pedro de Macoris, D.R.	7-16
Santos, Angel Ramon	PH	Boston	8-14-79	Rio Piedras, Puerto Rico	9-8
Santos, Victor Irving	P	Detroit	10-2-76	San Pedro de Macoris, D.R.	4-9
Seabol, Scott Anthony	PH	New York A.L.	5-17-75	McKeesport, Pennsylvania	4-8
Seay, Robert Michael	P	Tampa Bay	6-20-78	Sarasota, Florida	8-14
Serrano, Wascar Radames	P	San Diego	6-2-78	Santo Domingo, Dominican Republic	5-12
Sheets, Ben M.	P	Milwaukee	7-18-78	St. Amant, Louisiana	4-5
Shields, Robert Scot	P	Anaheim	7-22-75	Ft. Lauderdale, Florida	5-26
Shinjo, Tsuyoshi	PR	New York N.L.	1-28-72	Fukuoka, Japan	4-3
Smith, Jason William	PH	Chicago N.L.	7-24-77	Meridian, Mississippi	6-17
Smith, Robert A.	P	St. Louis	10-23-79	Torrance, California	6-10
Smith, Walter Roy	P	Cleveland	5-18-76	St. Petersburg, Florida	5-26
Sobkowiak, Scott	P	Atlanta	10-26-77	Woodstock, Illinois	10-7
Spivey, Ernest Lee	PR	Arizona	1-28-75	Oklahoma City, Oklahoma	6-2
Spooneybarger, Timothy F.	P	Atlanta	10-21-79	San Diego, California	9-5
Standridge, Jason Wayne	P	Tampa Bay	11-9-78	Birmingham, Alabama	7-29
Stewart, Scott	P	Montreal	8-14-75	Stoughton, Massachusetts	4-5
Stone, Ricky	P	Houston	2-28-75	Hamilton, Ohio	9-21
Suzuki, Ichiro	RF	Seattle	10-22-73	Kasugai, Japan	4-2
Thomas, Bradley Richard	P	Minnesota	10-22-77	Sydney, Australia	5-26
Torrealba, Steve Alexander	PH	Atlanta	2-24-78	Barquisimeto, Venezuela	10-6
Torrealba, Yorvit Adolfo	C	San Francisco	7-19-78	Caracas, Venezuela	9-5
Towers, Joshua Eric	P	Baltimore	2-26-77	Port Hueneme, California	5-2

Player	Pos.	Team	Birth date	Birthplace	Debut
Uribe, Juan C.	PH	Colorado	7-22-80	Bani, Dominican Republic	4-8
Valent, Eric Christian	DH	Philadelphia	4-4-77	La Mirada, California	6-8
Vazquez, Ramon	PH	Seattle	8-21-76	Aibonito, Puerto Rico	9-7
Vining, Kenneth Edward	P	Chicago A.L.	12-5-74	Decatur, Georgia	5-23
Voyles, Bradley Roy	P	Kansas City	12-30-76	Green Bay, Wisconsin	9-8
Wakeland, Christopher Robert	RF	Detroit	6-15-74	Huntington Beach, California	9-4
Wilkerson, Stephen Bradley	LF	Montreal	6-1-77	Daviess, Kentucky	7-12
Williams, David Aaron	P	Pittsburgh	3-12-79	Anchorage, Alaska	6-6
Wilson, Craig Alan	PH	Pittsburgh	11-30-76	Fountain Valley, California	4-22
Wilson, Jack	SS	Pittsburgh	12-29-77	Westlake Village, California	4-3
Wilson, Thomas Leroy	C	Oakland	12-19-70	Fullerton, California	5-19
Wright, Jonathan Daniel	P	Chicago A.L.	12-14-77	Longview, Texas	7-27
Zambrano, Carlos Alberto	P	Chicago N.L.	6-1-81	Carabobo, Venezuela	8-20
Zambrano, Victor Manuel	P	Tampa Bay	8-6-75	Los Teques, Venezuela	6-21

SALARY ARBITRATION RESULTS

WINNERS

Player, Team	Salary awarded	Team's offer
Andruw Jones, Atlanta	$8,200,000	$6,400,000
Keith Foulke, Chicago A.L.	$3,100,000	$2,200,000
Sean Casey, Cincinnati	$3,000,000	$2,600,000
Terry Adams, Los Angeles	$2,600,000	$1,950,000
Damian Miller, Arizona	$1,250,000	$850,000
Gregg Zaun, Kansas City	$1,150,000	$850,000

LOSERS

Player, Team	Salary awarded	Player's request
Kevin Millwood, Atlanta	$3,100,000	$3,900,000
Jose Mercedes, Baltimore	$2,750,000	$3,800,000
Danny Graves, Cincinnati	$2,100,000	$3,075,000
Javier Vasquez, Montreal	$2,000,000	$2,850,000
John Rocker, Atlanta	$1,900,000	$2,980,000
Chris Holt, Detroit	$1,850,000	$2,300,000
Travis Lee, Philadelphia	$800,000	$1,600,000
Osvaldo Fernandez, Cincinnati	$600,000	$1,200,000

2001 FREE-AGENT FILINGS

AMERICAN LEAGUE

Anaheim: Gary DiSarcina, Jorge Fabregas, Pat Rapp, Ismael Valdes.

Baltimore: Jose Mercedes, Alan Mills, Tim Raines Sr., Cal Ripken Jr.

Boston: Rod Beck, Dante Bichette, David Cone, Mike Lansing, Darren Lewis, Hideo Nomo, Troy O'Leary, Joe Oliver, Hipolito Pichardo, Bret Saberhagen, John Valentin.

Chicago: Harold Baines, Jose Canseco, Cal Eldred, Alan Embree, Bill Simas, David Wells.

Cleveland: Dave Burba, Marty Cordova, Juan Gonzalez, Kenny Lofton, Rich Rodriguez.

Detroit: Roger Cedeno.

Kansas City: Luis Alicea, Gregg Zaun.

Minnesota: Todd Jones.

New York: Scott Brosius, Sterling Hitchcock, Chuck Knoblauch, Tino Martinez, Paul O'Neill, Luis Sojo, Randy Velarde, Allen Watson, Mark Wohlers.

Oakland: Johnny Damon, Ron Gant, Jason Giambi, Gil Heredia, Jason Isringhausen.

Seattle: David Bell, Bret Boone, Pat Borders, Jay Buhner, Norm Charlton, Stan Javier, Al Martin, Mark McLemore, Aaron Sele, Ed Sprague.

Tampa Bay: Chris Gomez.

Texas: Tim Crabtree, Chad Curtis, Pat Mahomes, Ruben Sierra.

Toronto: Tony Fernandez, Jeff Frye.

NATIONAL LEAGUE

Arizona: Danny Bautista, Albie Lopez, Mike Morgan, Mike Mohler, Reggie Sanders, Russ Springer, Bobby Witt.

Atlanta: Kurt Abbott, John Burkett, Ken Caminiti, Julio Franco, Bernard Gilkey, Steve Karsay, Keith Lockhart, Javy Lopez, Eduardo Perez, Steve Reed, Rey Sanchez, Rudy Seanez, John Smoltz.

Chicago: Ron Coomer, Delino DeShields, Ricky Gutierrez, Matt Stairs, Kevin Tapani, Todd Van Poppel, David Weathers, Rondell White, Eric Young.

Cincinnati: Joey Hamilton, Pete Harnisch, Jose Rijo.

Colorado: Brian Bohanon, Jerry DiPoto, Dan Miceli, Jay Powell.

Florida: Ricky Bones, Alex Fernandez, Charles Johnson, John Mabry.

Houston: Moises Alou, Pedro Astacio, Kent Bottenfield, Doug Brocail, Vinny Castilla, Tony Eusebio, Mike Jackson, Orlando Merced, Scott Servais, Bill Spiers, Ron Villone, Jose Vizcaino, Mike Williams.

Los Angeles: Terry Adams, James Baldwin, Tim Bogar, Jesse Orosco, Chan Ho Park, Jeff Shaw.

Milwaukee: Mark Leiter, James Mouton, Lance Painter, Devon White.

Montreal: Rob Ducey, Randy Knorr, Bob Scanlon.

New York: None.

Philadelphia: Ricky Bottalico, Dennis Cook, Brian L. Hunter, Todd Pratt.

Pittsburgh: Francisco Cordova, Josias Manzanillo, Ramon J. Martinez, Omar Olivares.

St. Louis: Bobby Bonilla, Carlos Hernandez, Mike James, T.J. Mathews, Craig Paquette.

San Diego: Tony Gwynn, Rickey Henderson, Dave Magadan, Chuck McElroy.

San Francisco: Barry Bonds, Jason Christiansen, Eric Davis, Andres Galarraga, Mark Gardner, Benito Santiago, Jason Schmidt.

MAJOR LEAGUE RULE 5 DRAFT

(Listed in order of selection)

Player	Pos.	Drafted by	Drafted from (major league organization)
Kevin McGlinchy	P	Tampa Bay	Richmond, International League (Braves)
Luis Ugueto	SS	Pittsburgh	Calgary, Pacific Coast League (Marlins)
Miguel Asencio	P	Kansas City	Scranton/Wilkes-Barre, International League (Phillies)
Joseph Valentine	P	Montreal	Charlotte, International League (White Sox)
Jeffrey Farnsworth	P	Detroit	Tacoma, Pacific Coast League (Mariners)
Jorge Sosa	P	Milwaukee	Tacoma, Pacific Coast League (Mariners)
Steven Kent	P	Anaheim	Tacoma, Pacific Coast League (Mariners)
Corey Thurman	P	Toronto	Omaha, Pacific Coast League (Royals)
Ryan Baerlocher	P	San Diego	Omaha, Pacific Coast League (Royals)
Jason Grabowski	3B	Oakland	Tacoma, Pacific Coast League (Mariners)
Felix Escalona	3B	San Francisco	New Orleans, Pacific Coast League (Astros)
Ryan Christenson	OF	Milwaukee	Tucson, Pacific Coast League (Diamondbacks)

NECROLOGY

2001 REVIEW Necrology

Tommie Agee, 58, at New York on January 22. Center fielder Agee was a key player for the Mets' 1969 World Series champions. He hit a career-high 26 home runs in the regular season, then helped the Mets to a stunning Series victory over Baltimore with two sensational catches—and a leadoff homer—in Game 3. Playing for the White Sox three years earlier, he had been voted American League Rookie of the Year.

George Archie, 87, at Nashville on September 20. Archie, a third baseman/first baseman, played for the Tigers, Washington Senators and St. Louis Browns in a three-decade major league career. He batted .269 in 379 at-bats for Washington in 1941, a year in which he was traded to the Browns late in the season.

Johnny Babich, 87, at Richmond, Calif., on January 19. Righthander Babich was 30-45 in five big-league seasons. His best year was 1940, when he compiled a 14-13 record for the Philadelphia Athletics.

Bo Belinsky, 64, at Las Vegas, Nev., on November 23. In his fourth major league start after being drafted out of the Baltimore organization the previous November, Belinsky tossed a no-hitter for the Los Angeles Angels against the Orioles on May 5, 1962. The lefthander won his first five decisions in '62 and finished with a 10-11 record. In 1964, he was 9-8 with a 2.86 ERA for the Angels. Belinsky later pitched for the Phillies, Astros, Pirates and Reds and wound up with a 28-51 mark over eight major league seasons.

Curt Blefary, 57, at Pompano Beach, Fla., on January 28. Outfielder Blefary was voted the A.L. Rookie of the Year in 1965 after hitting 22 home runs for the Orioles. In '66, he smashed 23 homers and started all four games in Baltimore's World Series sweep of the Dodgers. Blefary also played for the Astros, Yankees, A's and Padres in an eight-year major league career.

Lou Boudreau, 84, at Olympia Fields, Ill., on August 10. As Cleveland's player/manager, shortstop Boudreau won the A.L. MVP award in 1948 and led the Indians to the World Series title that year. He batted .355 and drove in 106 runs in the regular season, then turned in one of the great clutch performances in baseball history in a one-game playoff that decided the American League pennant. With the Indians and Red Sox playing a winner-take-all game at Fenway Park after tying for first place, Boudreau hit two home runs and went 4-for-4 in Cleveland's 8-3 victory. A .295 career hitter, Boudreau won the A.L. batting crown in 1944 with a .327 average. He managed in the majors for 16 years, directing the Red Sox, Kansas City A's and Cubs after a nine-year stint with Cleveland. The Hall of Famer remains the youngest man ever to manage a big-league club at the outset of a season—he was 24 when he began his tenure as Indians manager in 1942.

George Bradley, 58, at Tampa on September 14. Bradley, known for his scouting expertise in a three-decades-plus career as an executive in the majors, was a special assistant to White Sox general manager Ken Williams.

Jimmy Bragan, 72, at Westover, Ala., on June 2. Bragan, a former minor league infielder and manager, coached for the Reds, Expos and Brewers and served as Southern League president for 14 years. He was the brother of Bobby Bragan, who managed in the majors in the 1950s and '60s.

Ike Brown, 59, at Memphis, Tenn., on May 17. Brown was a utilityman for the Tigers in the late 1960s and early '70s. In 1971, he had eight home runs in only 110 at-bats.

Bob Buhl, 72, at Titusville, Fla., on February 16. Buhl, who pitched for the Milwaukee Braves, Cubs and Phillies, was a double-figure winner 10 times in the majors and compiled a 166-132 record in a 15-year career. His best season was 1957, when he went 18-7 with a 2.74 ERA for the World Series champion Braves. He also won 18 games for the Braves in '56. A notoriously poor hitter, Buhl went 0 for 70 at the plate in 1962.

Nelson Burbrink, 79, at Largo, Fla., on April 11. Burbrink, a reserve catcher for the Cardinals in 1955, was a scout for the Mets and Brewers after his playing career and also served as the Mets' director of scouting and director of player development.

Tom Cheney, 67, at Rome, Ga., on November 1. Pitching all 16 innings of a September 12, 1962, game against the Orioles, Washington righthander Cheney set the major league record for most strikeouts in a game, 21. Cheney, who had 12 strikeouts after nine innings, was a 2-1 winner in the game played at Baltimore's Memorial Stadium. Cheney was 19-29 in eight seasons in the majors and made three relief appearances for the Pirates in the 1960 World Series.

Bubba Church, 77, at Birmingham, Ala., on September 17. Church, a righthander, compiled an 8-6 record for the Phillies in his rookie season, 1950, a year in which the Phils won the National League pennant. Church pitched four shutouts and won 15 games for the Phillies in 1951, but he fashioned only a cumulative 13-20 mark in the next four seasons while pitching for the Phils, Reds and Cubs and didn't pitch in the majors after 1955.

Brian Cole, 22, in a highway accident near Marianna, Fla., on March 31. Outfielder Cole was selected player of the year in the Mets' organization in 2000. Playing for Class A St. Lucie and then Class AA Binghamton, he posted overall figures of 19 homers, 86 RBIs and 69 stolen bases.

John Corriden Jr., 82, at Indianapolis on June 4. Corriden, an outfielder and son of a former major leaguer, appeared in one big-league game—in 1946, as a pinch runner for the Dodgers.

Tony Criscola, 86, at La Jolla, Calif., on July 10. Criscola, an outfielder, played for the St. Louis Browns in 1942 and 1943 and for the Reds in 1944. In 184 big-league games, he batted .248.

John Dagenhard, 84, at Bolivar, Ohio, on July 16. Dagenhard's major league career consisted of one start and one relief appearance for the 1943 Boston Braves. In 11 innings overall, the righthander did not allow an earned run. His 1-0 record was the result of a complete-game victory in which he allowed two unearned runs.

Lawrence "Crash" Davis, 82, at Greensboro, N.C., on August 31. Davis, primarily a second baseman, jumped directly from the college ranks (Duke) to the majors and spent three seasons, 1940 through 1942, with the Philadelphia Athletics. He batted .230 in 148 big-league games. Davis spent his last seven professional seasons in the low minors—the final five years in the Carolina League. (The slugging Crash Davis character in the movie Bull Durham was not based on the career of the real-life Davis, who hit only 45 homers in 3,246 minor league at-bats and was a middle infielder, not a veteran catcher. Still, director Ron Shelton was so smitten when he saw "Crash Davis" listed in the Carolina League record book that he gave the name to one of the film's key characters.)

Miguel del Toro, 29, in an automobile accident near Obregon, Mexico, on October 6. Del Toro, who pitched in the Japanese Pacific League in 2001, appeared in a total of 23 games for the Giants in 1999 and 2000 and compiled a 2-0 record.

Clem Dreisewerd, 85, at Ocean Springs, Miss., on September 11. Dreisewerd, a lefthander, pitched for the Red Sox, the St. Louis Browns and the New York Giants during a four-year major league career. His best season was 1946, when he went 4-1 for Boston while pitching mainly in relief. He also made a brief appearance in the '46 World Series.

Ferris Fain, 80, at Georgetown, Calif., on October 18. A .279 hitter for the Philadelphia Athletics over his first four years in the big leagues, first baseman Fain won A.L. batting titles in his next two seasons, 1951 and 1952, when he hit .344 and .327 for the A's. Fain, who was named The Sporting News' A.L. Player of the Year in '51, also played for the White Sox, Tigers and Indians in nine seasons in the majors.

Ford Garrison, 85, at Largo, Fla., on June 6. Outfielder Garrison appeared in 185 major league games—134 of them in 1944, when he became a regular in the Philadelphia Athletics' outfield after being acquired from the Red Sox in a May trade. Garrison hit .262 over four big-league seasons.

Lloyd Gearhart, 77, at Dayton, Ohio, on April 2. Appearing in 73 games for the Giants in 1947 (his only season as a major leaguer), Gearhart, an outfielder, hit .246 with six home runs.

Ralph Hamner, 84, at Little Rock, Ark., on May 22. Hamner, a righthander, pitched in 61 major league games—25 for the White Sox in 1946 and 36 for the Cubs over the next three seasons. He compiled an 8-20 record overall.

Sam Harshaney, 90, at San Antonio on February 1. Harshaney saw limited duty as a Browns catcher from 1937 through 1940. He had 145 at-bats and a .241 average in '39.

Mel Hoderlein, 77, at Mount Carmel, Ohio, on May 21. Infielder Hoderlein played briefly for the Red Sox in 1951 and appeared in a total of 109 games for Washington from 1952 through 1954. His most extensive duty came in '52, when he had 208 at-bats for the Senators and batted .269.

Bert Hodge, 83, at Knoxville, Tenn., on January 8. Third baseman Hodge appeared in eight games for the 1942 Phillies.

Elon "Chief" Hogsett, 97, at Hays, Kan., on July 17. Lefthander Hogsett had an 11-year major league career in which he fashioned a 63-87 record. He pitched for the Tigers in nine of those seasons and also saw duty with the St. Louis Browns and Washington. Hogsett won 11 games for the Tigers in 1932 and 13 for the Browns in 1936. He pitched exclusively in relief for Detroit in 1934 and 1935, years in which he appeared in a total of four World Series games.

Wally Hood Jr., 75, at Glendale, Calif., on June 16. The righthander pitched in two games for the 1949 Yankees. His father was a major league outfielder in the early 1920s.

Jim Hughes, 78, at Worth, Ill., on August 13. A righthanded reliever, Hughes led the majors in games pitched in 1954, appearing in 60 games for Brooklyn. He compiled an 8-4 record and a 3.22 ERA that season. Hughes, who relieved in 48 games for the Dodgers in 1953, also pitched for the Cubs and White Sox in a six-season big-league career.

Woody Jensen, 94, at Wichita, Kan., on October 5. Jensen, who played all nine of his major league seasons with Pittsburgh, was a fixture in the Pirates' outfield from 1935 through 1937, averaging more than 600 at-bats over those three years. His 696 at-bats in 1936 stood as the majors' season record for more than three decades. Jensen hit .324 in 1935, and he posted a career batting average of .285.

Sam Jethroe, 83, at Erie, Pa., on June 16. Jethroe, a veteran of the Negro leagues, was N.L. Rookie of the Year in 1950 when, at age 32, he hit .273 for the Boston Braves with 18 home runs and a league-leading 35 stolen bases. He duplicated his stolen base and homer totals in '51, again topping the league in steals, and hit .280. The outfielder slumped badly in 1952 and appeared in only one major league game thereafter.

Bob Keegan, 80, at Rochester, N.Y., on June 20. Pitching for the White Sox, Keegan threw a no-hitter against the Senators in 1957, a year in which he compiled a 10-8 record. The righthander, who spent all six of his big-league seasons with the White Sox, posted a 16-9 record in 1954 and was 40-36 overall.

Bob Keely, 91, at Sarasota, Fla., on May 20. Keely, a catcher, appeared in one game for the Cardinals in both 1944 and 1945. He was a coach for the Boston and Milwaukee Braves for a 12-year period ending with the 1957 season, a year in which Milwaukee won the World Series against the Yankees.

Newt Kimball, 85, at Las Vegas, Nev., on March 22. Primarily a reliever, Kimball pitched for the Cubs, Dodgers, Cardinals and Phillies during a six-season major league career in which he compiled an 11-9 record. The righthander was 4-1 with a 3.02 ERA in 1940, a year in which he pitched for Brooklyn and, briefly, the Cards.

Dick Kimble, 85, at Toledo, Ohio, on May 7. Shortstop Kimble batted .245 in 20 games for the 1945 Senators.

Al Lary, 71, at Northport, Ala., on July 9. Righthander Lary pitched in 16 big-league games, all for the Cubs. He started one game in 1954, then made three starts and 12 relief appearances in 1962. His overall record: 0-1. Al was the brother of Frank Lary, a standout Tigers pitcher in the 1950s and early '60s.

John LeRoy, 26, at Sioux City, Iowa, on June 25. LeRoy, a righthander for Sioux City of the independent Northern League, appeared in one major league game—for the Braves in 1997, and he came away with a victory after pitching two innings of scoreless relief.

Lou Lombardo, 72, at Rock Hill, S.C., on June 11. At age 19, Lombardo made two relief appearances for the 1948 New York Giants.

Joe Lovitto, 50, at Arlington, Texas, on May 19. Lovitto, the starting center fielder for Texas in the Rangers' first-ever game in 1972, played 306 games for Texas over four seasons and batted .216.

Johnny Lucadello, 82, at San Antonio on October 30. Infielder Lucadello had 686 at-bats over six major league seasons. He was most active in 1941, when he had 351 at-bats for the St. Louis Browns and batted .279. After five years with the Browns, he wound up his big-league career with a 12-game stint with the Yankees in 1947.

Jack Maguire, 76, at Kerrville, Texas, on September 28. Maguire saw action in the outfield and at third base, second base and first base despite appearing in only 94 games in a two-season major league career. Maguire, who played for the New York Giants in 1950 and for the Giants, Pirates and St. Louis Browns in 1951, batted .240 in 192 at-bats overall.

Jim Mallory, 82, at Greenville, N.C., on August 6. Mallory, an outfielder, appeared in four games for the Washington Senators in 1940 and in a total of 50 games for the Cardinals and New York Giants in 1945.

Eddie Mathews, 69, at La Jolla, Calif., on February 18. A two-time National League home run champion and longtime Braves star, Hall of Famer Mathews hit 512 career homers. The third baseman teamed with Hank Aaron to give Milwaukee a fearsome 1-2 punch, which contributed mightily to the Braves' powerhouse teams of the mid-to-late 1950s. Mathews, a fierce competitor, is the only man to have played for the Boston Braves (1952), Milwaukee Braves (1953-65) and Atlanta Braves (1966). He also played for the Astros and Tigers and later managed the Braves.

Tom McBride, 87, at Wichita Falls, Texas, on December 26. McBride, an outfielder, played in 61 games for the pennant-winning Red Sox in 1946 and batted .301. He started the first two games of the '46 World Series against the Cardinals and made pinch-hitting appearances in three other games. Over six major league seasons with the Red Sox and Senators, McBride hit .275.

Pat McKernan, 60, at Albuquerque, N.M., on July 10. McKernan was president and general manager of the Albuquerque franchise of the Pacific Coast League for two decades, ending with the 2000 season.

Jerry McQuaig, 89, at Buford, Ga., on February 5. McQuaig, an outfielder, saw his only big-league duty in 1934. In seven games with the Philadelphia Athletics, he had one hit in 16 at-bats.

Frank Messer, 76, at Deerfield Beach, Fla., on November 13. Messer was a member of the Yankees' radio-television team from 1968 through 1985. He also had broadcasting stints with the Orioles and White Sox.

Stuart Meyer, 67, at Flagler County, Fla., on May 21. Meyer was president of the Cardinals from 1992 to 1994.

Joe Moore, 92, at Bryan, Texas, on April 1. Outfielder Moore batted .298 over 12 major league seasons, all spent with the Giants. He best season was 1934, when he hit .331. Moore was a member of the 1933 World Series-winning Giants and played in two other Series.

Bitsy Mott, 82, at Brandon, Fla., on February 25. Mott's lone major league season was 1945, when he played in 90 games (63 at shortstop) for the Phillies and batted .221 in 289 at-bats.

Bill Mueller, 80, at Glenview, Ill., on October 24. Outfielder Mueller played 26 games for the White Sox in 1942 and 13 games for the Sox in 1945.

Hugh Mulcahy, 88, at Aliquippa, Pa., on October 19. Pitching for downtrodden Phillies teams for eight seasons, Mulcahy twice lost 20 or more games and compiled a 45-89 record. In 1947, his ninth and last year in the majors, the righthander made two no-decision appearances with the Pirates.

Tom Poholsky, 71, at Kirkwood, Mo., on January 6. A righthander, Poholsky was 31-52 in a six-year major league career. He was a nine-game winner for the Cardinals in 1955 and again in 1956.

Eddie Popowski, 88, at Sayreville, N.J., on December 4. Popowski served in the Red Sox's organization for more than 60 years as a player, manager, coach, instructor and scout. As an infielder, Popowski never rose above the high minors, but he served nine years as a Red Sox coach and had two brief stints as the club's interim manager. He spent 21 seasons as a minor league manager.

Johnny Powers, 72, at Birmingham, Ala., on September 25. Powers, an outfielder, played for the Pirates, Reds, Orioles and Indians over six major league seasons (1955 through 1960). Appearing in only 151 games, he batted .195 with six home runs.

Forest "Tot" Pressnell, 94, at Findlay, Ohio, on January 6. Pressnell, a righthander, reached the majors in 1938 at age 31 and compiled an 11-14 record for Brooklyn that year. He was a cumulative 21-16 in his four other big-league seasons (1939-40 with the Dodgers, 1941-42 with the Cubs).

Bill Reeder, 79, at Sulphur Springs, Texas, on March 12. Reeder pitched in 21 games for the 1949 Cardinals and compiled a 1-1 record.

Hank Riebe, 79, at Cleveland on April 16. Riebe, a catcher, played in 61 big-league games—all for the Tigers—over four seasons in the 1940s.

Bill Rigney, 83, at Walnut Creek, Calif., on February 20. A versatile infielder for the New York Giants over eight seasons, Rigney spent 18 years as a major league manager. He succeeded Leo Durocher as Giants manager in 1956, served as the first manager of the San Francisco Giants in 1958, led the Angels to a third-place finish in 1962 when they were a second-year expansion team and directed the Twins to a divisional title in 1970.

Alex Sabo, 90, at Tuckerton, N.J., on January 3. Sabo, a catcher, appeared in four games for the Senators in 1936 and one game for the Washington club in 1937.

Ben Sankey, 94, at Washington, Ga., on October 14. Sankey, a shortstop, played 57 games for the Pirates in 1931 and appeared in 72 games for Pittsburgh over three seasons.

Hank Sauer, 84, at Burlingame, Calif., on August 24. In 1952, Sauer became the first member of a club with a non-winning record to be named MVP since baseball writers began selecting the honoree two decades earlier. Playing for a fifth-place Cubs team that went 77-77 in '52, Sauer hit 37 home runs (good for a share of the N.L. title) and drove in 121 runs (high in the majors). It was the fifth consecutive year that the outfielder had hit 30 or more homers. Sauer also hit a decisive home run in the '52 All-Star Game. By career's end, he had amassed 288 homers over 15 years while playing for four N.L. clubs (Cincinnati, Chicago, St. Louis and New York/San Francisco). His season high was 41, attained with the Cubs in 1954.

Hank Schmulbach, 76, at Belleville, Ill., on May 3. Schmulbach appeared in one major league game—at age 18, as a pinch runner for the St. Louis Browns in 1943.

Dick Selma, 57, at Clovis, Calif., on August 29. A righthander, Selma went 42-54 in his 10-year major league career. In 1968, he pitched three shutouts and compiled a 9-10 record for the Mets. Selected by San Diego that fall in the expansion draft, he started the first game in Padres history on April 8, 1969, and struck out 12 batters in a 2-1 victory over the Astros. Traded to the Cubs 2½ weeks later, he won 10 games for a Chicago team that appeared to be pennant-bound before a late collapse. Selma also pitched for the Phillies, Angels and Brewers.

Barry Shetrone, 63, at Bowie, Md., on July 18. Outfielder Shetrone appeared in 60 games over five big-league seasons. He played sparingly for the Orioles from 1959 through 1962 and had a two-game stint with the Washington Senators in 1963.

Hank Soar, 87, at Pawtucket, R.I., on December 24. Soar, a former National Football League player, became an American League umpire in 1950 and served for more than two decades.

Bill Stafford, 62, at Canton, Mich., on September 19. Stafford was a key member of the rotation for World Series-winning Yankees teams in 1961 and 1962, winning 14 games each season and pitching a complete-game four-hitter in Game 3 of the '62 Series. Working almost exclusively in relief in 1964, the righthander was 5-0 for the Yanks. In eight major league seasons (the last two with the Kansas City A's), he was 43-40 with a 3.52 ERA.

Willie Stargell, 61, at Wilmington, N.C., on April 9. The power-hitting Stargell, a leader on and off the field, helped the Pirates to six division titles and two World Series championships in the 1970s. The Hall of Fame outfielder/first baseman won N.L. homer crowns in 1971 and 1973 and was the league's co-MVP in 1979. In the '79 World Series, Stargell hit a decisive home run in Game 7 and batted .400 overall with three homers. In a 21-year major league career spent entirely with Pittsburgh, he hit 475 homers and batted .282.

Joe Stephenson, 80, at Fullerton, Calif., on September 20. Stephenson, who saw brief service as a catcher for the New York Giants in 1943, the Cubs in 1944 and the White Sox in 1947, was a Red Sox scout for nearly a half-century. His son Jerry was a major league pitcher.

Frank Stewart, 94, at Stillwater, Minn., on April 30. Stewart's only major league appearance came on the final day of the 1927 season when, at age 21, the righthander started—and lost—for the White Sox against the St. Louis Browns.

Leo Thomas, 77, at Concord, Calif., on March 5. Third baseman Thomas played in the majors in 1950 and 1952, appearing in a total of 95 games for the St. Louis Browns and White Sox. He batted .212.

Luther "Bud" Thomas, 90, at Charlottesville, Va., on May 20. Righthander Thomas compiled 8-15 and 9-14 records for the Philadelphia Athletics in 1937 and 1938, then went 7-1 in 1939 while pitching chiefly for the Tigers (but also for the Athletics and Senators). Early in '39, while still with the A's, he gave up Ted Williams' first major league home run.

Eric Tipton, 86, at Newport News, Va., on August 29. Tipton was a regular in the Reds' outfield in 1943 and 1944, years in which he batted .288 and .301. He played in a total of 50 games for the Philadelphia Athletics from 1939 through 1941, then saw action in 451 games with Cincinnati from 1942 through 1945.

Sandy Ullrich, 79, at Miami on April 21. Ullrich, a righthander, was 3-3 overall in two seasons (1944, 1945) with Washington.

Gary Vitto, 59, at Detroit on December 9. Vitto was special assistant to Tigers president John McHale Jr.

Butch Wensloff, 85, at San Rafael, Calif., on February 18. Wensloff won 13 games and posted a 2.54 ERA for the 1943 World Series champion Yankees. He pitched in only two other big-league seasons, going 3-1 for the Yanks in 1947 and 0-1 for the Indians in 1948.

Hal White, 82, at Venice, Fla., on April 21. Righthander White was 46-54 over 12 big-league seasons, 10 of which were spent with the Tigers. After breaking into the majors with four appearances for Detroit in 1941, White pitched four shutouts and compiled a 12-12 record for the Tigers in '42.

Gene Woodling, 78, at Barberton, Ohio, on June 2. Woodling was a key player for the Yankees when the A.L. club won a record five consecutive World Series titles from 1949 through 1953. Playing 112 or more games in each of those seasons, the outfielder hit .270, .283, .281, .309 and .306. Woodling batted .318 with three home runs in 26 Series games. He also played for the Indians, Pirates, Orioles, Senators and first-year (1962) Mets. His best season, statistically, was 1957, when Woodling hit .321 with 19 homers for Cleveland.

Joe Zapustas, 93, at Randolph, Mass., on January 14. An outfielder, Zapustas got into two games with the 1933 A's.

2001 A.L. STATISTICS

Batting

Designated hitting

Pinch-hitting

Pitching

Fielding

Miscellaneous

BATTING

TEAM

Team	Avg.	G	TPA	AB	R	H	TB	2B	3B	HR	RBI	SH	SF	HP	BB	IBB	SO	SB	CS	GDP	LOB	ShO	Slg.	OBP
Seattle	.288	162	6474	5680	927	1637	2530	310	38	169	881	48	70	62	614	54	989	174	42	112	1257	4	.445	.360
Cleveland	.278	162	6357	5600	897	1559	2563	294	37	212	868	49	62	69	577	32	1076	79	41	126	1136	7	.458	.350
Texas	.275	162	6388	5685	890	1566	2676	326	23	246	844	25	55	75	548	27	1093	97	32	131	1161	1	.471	.344
Minnesota	.272	162	6182	5560	771	1514	2410	328	38	164	717	25	38	64	495	42	1083	146	67	124	1102	5	.433	.337
Chicago	.268	162	6150	5464	798	1463	2463	300	29	214	770	63	51	52	520	31	998	123	59	128	1054	4	.451	.334
New York	.267	161	6233	5577	804	1488	2426	289	20	203	774	30	43	64	519	38	1035	161	53	119	1123	5	.435	.334
Boston	.266	161	6264	5605	772	1493	2461	316	29	198	739	28	41	70	520	50	1131	46	35	132	1161	6	.439	.334
Kansas City	.266	162	6176	5643	729	1503	2310	277	37	152	691	36	47	44	406	31	898	100	42	134	1086	6	.409	.318
Oakland	.264	162	6385	5573	884	1469	2444	334	22	199	835	25	59	88	640	57	1021	68	29	131	1171	3	.439	.345
Toronto	.263	162	6284	5663	767	1489	2433	287	36	195	728	34	43	74	470	47	1094	156	55	111	1124	9	.430	.325
Anaheim	.261	162	6221	5551	691	1447	2248	275	26	158	662	46	53	77	494	34	1001	116	52	109	1203	12	.405	.327
Detroit	.260	162	6144	5537	724	1439	2267	291	60	139	691	41	49	51	466	26	972	133	61	120	1093	6	.409	.320
Tampa Bay	.258	162	6104	5524	672	1426	2142	311	21	121	645	45	25	54	456	24	1116	115	52	130	1104	12	.388	.320
Baltimore	.248	162	6150	5472	687	1359	2077	262	24	136	663	38	49	77	514	26	989	133	53	121	1106	14	.380	.319
Totals	.267	1133	87512	78134	11013	20852	33450	4200	440	2506	10508	533	685	921	7239	519	14496	1647	673	1728	15881	94	.428	.334

INDIVIDUAL

TOP QUALIFIERS FOR BATTING CHAMPIONSHIP

Minimum 502 plate appearances. *Lefthanded batter. †Switch-hitter.

Player, Team	Avg.	G	TPA	AB	R	H	TB	2B	3B	HR	RBI	SH	SF	HP	BB	IBB	SO	SB	CS	GDP	Slg.	OBP
Suzuki, Ichiro, Sea.*	.350	157	738	692	127	242	316	34	8	8	69	4	4	8	30	10	53	56	14	3	.457	.381
Giambi, Jason, Oak.*	.342	154	671	520	109	178	343	47	2	38	120	0	9	13	129	24	83	2	0	17	.660	.477
Alomar, Roberto, Cle.†	.336	157	677	575	113	193	311	34	12	20	100	9	9	4	80	5	71	30	6	9	.541	.415
Boone, Bret, Sea.	.331	158	690	623	118	206	360	37	3	37	141	5	13	9	40	5	110	5	5	11	.578	.372
Catalanotto, Frank, Tex.*	.330	133	512	463	77	153	227	31	5	11	54	1	1	8	39	3	55	15	5	5	.490	.391
Gonzalez, Juan, Cle.	.325	140	595	532	97	173	314	34	1	35	140	0	16	6	41	5	94	1	0	18	.590	.370
Rodriguez, Alex, Tex.	.318	162	732	632	133	201	393	34	1	52	135	0	9	16	75	6	131	18	3	17	.622	.399
Stewart, Shannon, Tor.	.316	155	698	640	103	202	296	44	7	12	60	0	1	11	46	1	72	27	10	9	.463	.371
Jeter, Derek, N.Y.	.311	150	686	614	110	191	295	35	3	21	74	5	1	10	56	3	99	27	3	13	.480	.377
Conine, Jeff, Bal.	.311	139	601	524	75	163	232	23	2	14	97	0	8	5	64	6	75	12	8	12	.443	.386
Williams, Bernie, N.Y.†	.307	146	633	540	102	166	282	38	0	26	94	0	9	6	78	11	67	11	5	15	.522	.395
Martinez, Edgar, Sea.	.306	132	581	470	80	144	255	40	1	23	116	0	9	9	93	9	90	4	1	11	.543	.423
Beltran, Carlos, K.C.†	.306	155	680	617	106	189	317	32	12	24	101	1	5	5	52	2	120	31	1	7	.514	.362
Ramirez, Manny, Bos.	.306	142	620	529	93	162	322	33	2	41	125	0	2	8	81	25	147	0	1	9	.609	.405
Mientkiewicz, Doug, Min.*	.306	151	626	543	77	166	252	39	1	15	74	0	7	2	92	2	6	10	.464	.387

DEPARTMENTAL LEADERS: G—Delgado, Tor., Long, Oak., A. Rodriguez, Tex., Tejada, Oak., 162; AB—Suzuki, Sea., 692; R—A. Rodriguez, Tex., 133; H—Suzuki, Sea., 242; TB—A. Rodriguez, Tex., 393; 1B—Suzuki, Sea., 192; 2B—Ja. Giambi, Oak., 47; 3B—Guzman, Min., 14; HR—A. Rodriguez, Tex., 52; RBI—Boone, Sea., 141; SH—Eckstein, Ana., 16; SF—Gonzalez, Cle., 16; HP—Eckstein, Ana., 21; BB—Ja. Giambi, Oak., 129; IBB—Ramirez, Bos., 25; SO—Thome, Cle., 185; SB—Suzuki, Sea., 56; CS—Cedeno, Det., 15; GIDP—Olerud, Sea., 21; Slg. Pct.—Ja. Giambi, Oak., .660; OB. Pct.—Ja. Giambi, Oak., .477.

ALL PLAYERS

*Lefthanded batter. †Switch-hitter.

Player, Team	Avg.	G	TPA	AB	R	H	TB	2B	3B	HR	RBI	SH	SF	HP	BB	IBB	SO	SB	CS	GDP	Slg.	OBP
Abad, Andy, Oak.*	.000	1	1	1	0	0	0	0	0	0	0	0	0	0	0	0	0	0	0	0	.000	.000
Abbott, Paul, Sea.	.250	28	5	4	0	1	1	0	0	0	0	1	0	0	0	0	1	0	0	0	.250	.250
Abernathy, Brent, T.B.	.270	79	335	304	43	82	116	17	1	5	33	3	1	0	27	1	35	8	3	3	.382	.328
Alcantara, Izzy, Bos.	.263	14	41	38	3	10	11	1	0	0	3	0	0	0	3	0	13	1	0	3	.289	.317
Alicea, Luis, K.C.†	.274	113	418	387	44	106	142	16	4	4	32	3	1	4	23	0	56	8	6	6	.367	.320
Allen, Chad, Min.	.263	57	195	175	20	46	75	13	2	4	20	0	1	0	19	1	37	1	2	7	.429	.333
Almonte, Erick, N.Y.	.500	8	4	4	0	2	3	1	0	0	0	0	0	0	0	0	1	2	0	0	.750	.500
Alomar, Roberto, Cle.†	.336	157	677	575	113	193	311	34	12	20	100	9	9	4	80	5	71	30	6	9	.541	.415
Alomar, Sandy Jr., Chi.	.245	70	239	220	17	54	76	8	1	4	21	3	2	2	12	1	17	1	2	6	.345	.288
Anderson, Brady, Bal.*	.202	131	501	430	50	87	129	12	3	8	45	2	1	8	60	4	77	12	4	3	.300	.311
Anderson, Garret, Ana.*	.289	161	704	672	83	194	321	39	2	28	123	0	5	0	27	4	100	13	6	12	.478	.314
Arrojo, Rolando, Bos.	.000	41	4	4	0	0	0	0	0	0	0	0	0	0	0	0	3	0	0	0	.000	.000
Baines, Harold, Chi.*	.131	32	94	84	3	11	12	1	0	0	6	0	2	0	8	0	16	0	0	2	.143	.202
Baldwin, James, Chi.	.000	17	2	2	0	0	0	0	0	0	0	0	0	0	0	0	1	0	0	0	.000	.000
Barnes, John, Min.	.048	9	23	21	1	1	1	0	0	0	0	0	0	0	1	1	3	0	0	0	.048	.130
Barnes, Larry, Ana.*	.100	16	41	40	2	4	7	0	0	1	2	0	0	0	1	0	9	0	0	1	.175	.122
Batista, Tony, Tor.-Bal.	.238	156	622	579	70	138	252	27	6	25	87	0	7	4	32	1	113	5	2	9	.435	.280
Beck, Rod, Bos.	.000	68	1	1	0	0	0	0	0	0	0	0	0	0	0	0	0	0	0	0	.000	.000
Bell, David, Sea.	.260	135	510	470	62	122	195	28	0	15	64	5	4	3	28	1	59	2	1	8	.415	.303
Bellhorn, Mark, Oak.†	.135	38	82	74	11	10	18	1	2	1	4	1	0	0	7	0	37	0	0	1	.243	.210
Bellinger, Clay, N.Y.	.160	51	88	81	12	13	31	1	1	5	12	1	1	1	4	0	23	1	2	2	.383	.207
Beltran, Carlos, K.C.†	.306	155	680	617	106	189	317	32	12	24	101	1	5	5	52	2	120	31	1	7	.514	.362
Berger, Brandon, K.C.	.313	6	18	16	4	5	14	1	1	2	2	0	0	0	2	0	2	0	0	0	.875	.389
Berroa, Angel, K.C.	.302	15	56	53	8	16	18	2	0	0	4	0	0	3	0	10	2	0	2	.340	.339
Bichette, Dante, Bos.	.286	107	415	391	45	112	180	30	1	12	49	0	1	3	20	1	76	2	2	13	.460	.325
Biddle, Rocky, Chi.	.000	30	2	1	0	0	0	0	0	0	0	1	0	0	0	0	1	0	0	0	.000	.000
Bigbie, Larry, Bal.*	.229	47	149	131	15	30	42	6	0	2	11	1	0	0	17	1	42	4	1	2	.321	.318
Blair, Willie, Det.	.000	9	2	2	0	0	0	0	0	0	0	0	0	0	0	0	1	0	0	0	.000	.000

Player, Team	Avg.	G	TPA	AB	R	H	TB	2B	3B	HR	RBI	SH	SF	HP	BB	IBB	SO	SB	CS	GDP	Slg.	OBP
Blake, Casey, Min.-Bal.	.243	19	41	37	3	9	13	1	0	1	4	0	0	0	4	1	12	3	0	0	.351	.317
Boone, Bret, Sea.	.331	158	690	623	118	206	360	37	3	37	141	5	13	9	40	5	110	5	5	11	.578	.372
Borders, Pat, Sea.	.500	5	7	6	1	3	3	0	0	0	0	0	0	0	0	0	1	0	0	0	.500	.500
Bordick, Mike, Bal.	.249	58	257	229	32	57	91	13	0	7	30	2	3	6	17	1	36	9	3	4	.397	.314
Bradley, Milton, Cle.†	.222	10	20	18	3	4	5	1	0	0	0	0	0	0	2	0	3	1	1	1	.278	.300
Bragg, Darren, N.Y.*	.250	5	4	4	1	1	2	1	0	0	0	0	0	0	0	0	1	0	0	0	.500	.250
Branyan, Russell, Cle.*	.232	113	361	315	48	73	153	16	2	20	54	0	5	3	38	1	132	1	1	2	.486	.316
Brosius, Scott, N.Y.	.287	120	478	428	57	123	191	25	2	13	49	6	5	5	34	2	83	3	1	10	.446	.343
Brown, Dee, K.C.*	.245	106	406	380	39	93	133	19	0	7	40	1	2	1	22	4	81	5	3	12	.350	.286
Brumbaugh, Cliff, Tex.	.000	7	11	10	1	0	0	0	0	0	0	0	0	0	1	0	5	0	0	0	.000	.091
Buchanan, Brian, Min.	.274	69	219	197	28	54	96	12	0	10	32	0	1	2	19	0	58	1	1	2	.487	.342
Buehrle, Mark, Chi.*	.000	32	4	3	0	0	0	0	0	0	0	0	0	0	1	0	2	0	0	0	.000	.250
Bulmer, Jay, Sea.	.222	19	53	45	4	10	18	2	0	2	5	0	0	0	8	0	9	0	0	3	.400	.340
Burba, Dave, Cle.	.000	32	4	2	1	0	0	0	0	0	0	2	0	0	0	0	1	0	0	0	.000	.000
Burke, Jamie, Ana.	.200	9	5	5	1	1	1	0	0	0	0	0	0	0	0	0	2	0	0	0	.200	.200
Burkhart, Morgan, Bos.†	.182	11	34	33	3	6	10	1	0	1	4	0	0	0	1	0	11	0	0	1	.303	.206
Burks, Ellis, Cle.	.280	124	515	439	83	123	238	29	1	28	74	0	9	5	62	2	85	5	1	16	.542	.369
Bush, Homer, Tor.	.306	78	291	271	32	83	105	11	1	3	27	2	4	6	8	1	50	13	4	2	.387	.336
Byrd, Paul, K.C.	.000	16	5	4	0	0	0	0	0	0	0	1	0	0	0	0	2	0	0	0	.000	.000
Byrnes, Eric, Oak.	.237	19	43	38	9	9	19	1	0	3	5	0	0	1	4	0	6	1	0	0	.500	.326
Cabrera, Jolbert, Cle.	.261	141	312	287	50	75	100	16	3	1	38	1	2	6	16	0	41	10	4	4	.348	.312
Cameron, Mike, Sea.	.267	150	633	540	99	144	259	30	5	25	110	1	13	10	69	3	155	34	5	13	.480	.353
Caminiti, Ken, Tex.†	.232	54	211	185	24	43	80	8	1	9	25	0	2	2	22	2	41	0	0	5	.432	.318
Canseco, Jose, Chi.	.258	76	306	256	46	66	122	8	0	16	49	0	4	1	45	1	75	2	1	4	.477	.366
Cardona, Javier, Det.	.260	46	102	96	10	25	36	8	0	1	10	2	1	1	2	0	12	0	1	2	.375	.280
Carpenter, Chris, Tor.	.167	34	7	6	0	1	1	0	0	0	0	1	0	0	0	0	3	0	0	0	.167	.167
Castilla, Vinny, T.B.	.215	24	97	93	7	20	32	6	0	2	9	0	0	1	3	0	22	0	0	3	.344	.247
Castillo, Alberto, Tor.	.198	66	146	131	9	26	33	4	0	1	4	5	0	3	7	0	30	1	1	2	.252	.255
Castillo, Frank, Bos.	.000	26	3	2	0	0	0	0	0	0	0	1	0	0	0	0	1	0	0	0	.000	.000
Catalanotto, Frank, Tex.*	.330	133	512	463	77	153	227	31	5	11	54	1	1	8	39	3	55	15	5	5	.490	.391
Cedeno, Roger, Det.†	.293	131	572	523	79	153	207	14	11	6	48	6	5	2	36	1	83	55	15	5	.396	.337
Chavez, Endy, K.C.*	.208	29	80	77	4	16	18	2	0	0	5	0	0	0	3	0	8	0	2	3	.234	.238
Chavez, Eric, Oak.*	.288	151	604	552	91	159	298	43	0	32	114	0	7	4	41	9	99	8	2	7	.540	.338
Choate, Randy, N.Y.*	.000	37	3	3	0	0	0	0	0	0	0	0	0	0	0	0	2	0	0	0	.000	.000
Christensen, McKay, Chi.*	.250	7	5	4	0	1	1	0	0	0	0	0	0	0	1	0	2	0	0	0	.250	.400
Christenson, Ryan, Oak.	.000	7	4	4	1	0	0	0	0	0	0	0	0	0	0	0	1	0	0	0	.000	.000
Clark, Jermaine, Det.*	.000	3	0	0	1	0	0	0	0	0	0	0	0	0	0	0	0	0	0	0	.000	.000
Clark, Tony, Det.†	.287	126	497	428	67	123	206	29	3	16	75	0	6	1	62	10	108	0	1	14	.481	.374
Clayton, Royce, Chi.	.263	135	485	433	62	114	170	21	4	9	60	9	7	3	33	2	72	10	7	16	.393	.315
Clemens, Roger, N.Y.	.000	33	2	2	0	0	0	0	0	0	0	0	0	0	0	0	2	0	0	0	.000	.000
Coleman, Michael, N.Y.	.211	12	39	38	5	8	11	0	0	1	7	0	1	0	0	0	15	0	1	0	.289	.205
Colon, Bartolo, Cle.	.143	34	7	7	0	1	1	0	0	0	0	0	0	0	0	0	5	0	0	1	.143	.143
Cone, David, Bos.*	.000	25	2	1	0	0	0	0	0	0	0	0	0	0	0	0	1	0	0	0	.000	.000
Conine, Jeff, Bal.	.311	139	601	524	75	163	232	23	2	14	97	0	8	5	64	6	75	12	8	12	.443	.386
Cordero, Wil, Cle.	.250	89	299	268	30	67	92	11	1	4	21	2	3	4	22	2	50	0	0	8	.343	.313
Cordova, Marty, Cle.	.301	122	442	409	61	123	207	20	2	20	69	0	2	8	23	0	81	0	3	9	.506	.348
Cox, Steve, T.B.*	.257	108	378	342	37	88	146	22	0	12	51	0	2	10	24	0	75	2	2	11	.427	.323
Crede, Joe, Chi.	.220	17	55	50	1	11	14	1	1	0	7	0	1	1	3	0	11	1	0	1	.280	.273
Cruz, Deivi, Det.	.256	110	438	414	39	106	157	28	1	7	52	1	2	4	17	0	46	4	1	13	.379	.291
Cruz, Jacob, Cle.*	.221	28	76	68	12	15	28	4	0	3	11	0	0	3	5	0	23	0	2	3	.412	.303
Cruz, Jose Jr., Tor.†	.274	146	627	577	92	158	306	38	4	34	88	2	2	1	45	4	138	32	5	8	.530	.326
Cuddyer, Michael, Min.	.222	8	20	18	1	4	6	2	0	0	1	0	0	0	2	0	6	1	0	1	.333	.300
Curtis, Chad, Tex.	.252	38	130	115	24	29	41	3	0	3	10	0	0	1	14	0	21	7	1	3	.357	.338
Damon, Johnny, Oak.*	.256	155	719	644	108	165	234	34	4	9	49	5	4	5	61	1	70	27	12	7	.363	.324
Daubach, Brian, Bos.*	.263	122	472	407	54	107	207	28	3	22	71	1	6	5	53	7	108	1	0	10	.509	.350
DaVanon, Jeff, Ana.|	.193	40	100	88	7	17	36	2	1	5	9	0	1	0	11	0	29	1	3	1	.409	.280
Davis, Doug, Tex.	.000	30	4	3	0	0	0	0	0	0	0	1	0	0	0	0	2	0	0	0	.000	.000
Delgado, Carlos, Tor.*	.279	162	704	574	102	160	310	31	1	39	102	0	3	16	111	22	136	3	0	9	.540	.408
Delgado, Wilson, K.C.†	.120	14	28	25	1	3	3	0	0	0	1	0	0	0	3	0	10	0	0	1	.120	.214
DeShields, Delino, Bal.*	.197	58	222	188	29	37	58	8	2	3	21	1	1	1	31	1	42	11	1	3	.309	.311
Diaz, Einar, Cle.	.277	134	478	437	54	121	169	34	1	4	56	8	0	16	17	0	44	1	2	11	.387	.328
DiFelice, Mike, T.B.	.208	48	164	149	13	31	44	5	1	2	9	2	2	3	8	0	39	1	1	3	.295	.259
Dransfeldt, Kelly, Tex.	.000	4	3	3	0	0	0	0	0	0	0	0	0	0	0	0	0	0	0	0	.000	.000
Durbin, Chad, K.C.	.000	29	2	1	0	0	0	0	0	0	0	1	0	0	0	0	0	0	0	0	.000	.000
Durham, Ray, Chi.†	.267	152	691	611	104	163	285	42	10	20	65	6	6	4	64	3	110	23	10	10	.466	.337
Dye, Jermaine, K.C.-Oak.	.282	158	675	599	91	169	280	31	1	26	106	1	11	7	57	6	112	9	1	8	.467	.346
Easley, Damion, Det.	.250	154	658	585	77	146	220	27	7	11	65	4	4	13	52	3	90	10	5	10	.376	.323
Eckstein, David, Ana.	.285	153	664	582	82	166	208	26	2	4	41	16	2	21	43	0	60	29	4	11	.357	.355
Encarnacion, Juan, Det.	.242	120	457	417	52	101	170	19	7	12	52	5	4	6	25	1	93	9	5	9	.408	.292
Erstad, Darin, Ana.*	.258	157	711	631	89	163	227	35	1	9	63	1	7	10	62	7	113	24	10	8	.360	.331
Estalella, Bobby, N.Y.	.000	3	6	4	1	0	0	0	0	0	0	0	1	0	2	0	0	0	0	0	.000	.333
Everett, Carl, Bos.†	.257	102	449	409	61	105	179	24	4	14	58	0	0	13	27	3	104	9	2	3	.438	.323
Fabregas, Jorge, Ana.*	.223	53	157	148	9	33	47	4	2	2	16	4	2	0	3	0	15	0	0	5	.318	.235
Fasano, Sal, Oak.-K.C.	.045	14	24	22	2	1	1	0	0	0	0	0	0	1	1	0	12	0	0	2	.045	.125
Febles, Carlos, K.C.	.236	79	317	292	45	69	106	9	2	8	25	1	1	1	22	0	58	5	2	7	.363	.291
Fernandez, Jose, Ana.	.080	13	27	25	1	2	3	1	0	0	0	0	0	0	2	0	10	0	1	0	.120	.148
Fernandez, Tony, Tor.†	.305	48	62	59	5	18	25	4	0	1	12	0	1	1	1	0	8	0	1	2	.424	.323
Fick, Robert, Det.*	.272	124	448	401	62	109	191	21	2	19	61	0	4	4	39	3	62	0	3	10	.476	.339
Flaherty, John, T.B.	.238	78	265	248	20	59	90	17	1	4	29	5	1	1	10	1	33	1	0	9	.363	.269
Fletcher, Darrin, Tor.*	.226	134	453	416	36	94	147	20	0	11	56	1	6	6	24	4	43	0	1	18	.353	.274
Fordyce, Brook, Bal.	.209	95	320	292	30	61	94	18	0	5	19	3	1	3	21	1	56	1	2	7	.322	.268
Freel, Ryan, Tor.	.273	9	24	22	1	6	7	1	0	0	3	0	0	1	1	0	4	2	1	0	.318	.333

Player, Team	Avg.	G	TPA	AB	R	H	TB	2B	3B	HR	RBI	SH	SF	HP	BB	IBB	SO	SB	CS	GDP	Slg.	OBP
Frye, Jeff, Tor.	.246	74	194	175	24	43	57	6	1	2	15	4	0	3	12	0	18	2	1	2	.326	.305
Fryman, Travis, Cle.	.263	98	370	334	34	88	112	15	0	3	38	0	3	3	30	1	63	1	2	8	.335	.327
Fullmer, Brad, Tor.*	.274	146	573	522	71	143	232	31	2	18	83	0	7	6	38	8	88	5	2	13	.444	.326
Galarraga, Andres, Tex.	.235	72	271	243	33	57	103	16	0	10	34	0	1	9	18	1	68	1	0	9	.424	.310
Gant, Ron, Oak.	.259	34	93	81	15	21	34	5	1	2	13	0	1	0	11	0	24	2	0	0	.420	.344
Garces, Rich, Bos.	.000	62	2	2	0	0	0	0	0	0	0	0	0	0	0	0	1	0	0	1	.000	.000
Garcia, Freddy, Sea.	.143	34	9	7	0	1	1	0	0	0	0	2	0	0	0	0	4	0	0	0	.143	.143
Garcia, Karim, Cle.*	.311	20	50	45	8	14	32	3	0	5	9	0	1	1	3	0	13	0	0	1	.711	.360
Garciaparra, Nomar, Bos.	.289	21	91	83	13	24	39	3	0	4	8	0	0	1	7	0	9	0	1	1	.470	.352
Garland, Jon, Chi.	.000	35	2	2	0	0	0	0	0	0	0	0	0	0	0	0	1	0	0	0	.000	.000
Giambi, Jason, Oak.*	.342	154	671	520	109	178	343	47	2	38	120	0	9	13	129	24	83	2	0	17	.660	.477
Giambi, Jeremy, Oak.*	.283	124	443	371	64	105	167	26	0	12	57	3	2	4	63	1	83	0	1	13	.450	.391
Gibbons, Jay, Bal.*	.236	73	246	225	27	53	108	10	0	15	36	0	0	4	17	0	39	0	1	7	.480	.301
Gil, Geronimo, Bal.	.293	17	66	58	3	17	19	2	0	0	6	1	0	2	5	0	7	0	0	1	.328	.369
Gil, Benji, Ana.	.296	104	278	260	33	77	124	15	4	8	39	2	2	0	14	0	57	3	4	6	.477	.330
Gipson, Charles, Sea.	.219	94	72	64	16	14	20	2	2	0	5	1	1	2	4	0	20	1	1	2	.313	.282
Glaus, Troy, Ana.	.250	161	708	588	100	147	312	38	2	41	108	0	7	6	107	7	158	10	3	16	.531	.367
Gomez, Chris, T.B.	.302	58	206	189	31	57	97	16	0	8	36	4	3	2	8	0	24	3	0	4	.513	.332
Gonzalez, Alex, Tor.	.253	154	703	636	79	161	247	25	5	17	76	7	10	7	43	0	149	18	11	16	.388	.303
Gonzalez, Juan, Cle.	.325	140	595	532	97	173	314	34	1	35	140	0	16	6	41	5	94	1	0	18	.590	.370
Graffanino, Tony, Chi.	.303	74	169	145	23	44	59	9	0	2	15	4	3	1	16	0	29	4	1	4	.407	.370
Grebeck, Craig, Bos.	.049	23	43	41	1	2	3	1	0	0	2	0	0	0	2	0	9	0	0	0	.073	.093
Greene, Todd, N.Y.	.208	35	100	96	9	20	27	4	0	1	11	0	0	1	3	0	21	0	0	3	.281	.240
Greer, Rusty, Tex.*	.273	62	279	245	38	67	111	23	0	7	29	1	5	1	27	1	32	1	2	5	.453	.342
Grieve, Ben, T.B.*	.264	154	639	542	72	143	210	30	2	11	72	0	2	8	87	2	159	7	1	13	.387	.372
Guillen, Carlos, Sea.†	.259	140	523	456	72	118	162	21	4	5	53	7	6	1	53	0	89	4	1	9	.355	.333
Guillen, Jose, T.B.	.274	41	145	135	14	37	51	5	0	3	11	0	1	3	6	2	26	2	3	2	.378	.317
Guzman, Cristian, Min.†	.302	118	527	493	80	149	235	28	14	10	51	8	0	5	21	0	78	25	8	6	.477	.337
Hairston, Jerry Jr., Bal.	.233	159	602	532	63	124	183	25	5	8	47	9	4	13	44	0	73	29	11	12	.344	.305
Halama, John, Sea.*	.000	31	2	1	0	0	0	0	0	0	0	1	0	0	0	0	0	0	0	0	.000	.000
Hall, Toby, T.B.	.298	49	196	188	28	56	84	16	0	4	30	0	1	3	4	0	16	2	2	5	.447	.321
Halladay, Roy, Tor.	.000	17	2	1	0	0	0	0	0	0	0	1	0	0	0	0	0	0	0	0	.000	.000
Halter, Shane, Det.	.284	136	507	450	53	128	210	32	7	12	65	7	6	7	37	2	100	3	3	14	.467	.344
Hamilton, Joey, Tor.	.333	22	3	3	0	1	2	1	0	0	1	0	0	0	0	0	1	0	0	0	.667	.333
Harris, Willie, Bal.*	.125	9	25	24	3	3	4	1	0	0	0	1	0	0	0	0	7	0	0	0	.167	.125
Harvey, Ken, K.C.	.250	4	12	12	1	3	4	1	0	0	2	0	0	0	0	0	4	0	1	1	.333	.250
Haselman, Bill, Tex.	.285	47	140	130	12	37	52	6	0	3	25	1	0	1	8	0	27	0	1	5	.400	.331
Hatteberg, Scott, Bos.*	.245	94	316	278	34	68	96	19	0	3	25	0	1	4	33	0	26	1	1	7	.345	.332
Helling, Rick, Tex.	.000	34	4	4	0	0	0	0	0	0	0	0	0	0	0	0	1	0	0	0	.000	.000
Heredia, Gil, Oak.	.333	24	3	3	0	1	1	0	0	0	0	0	0	0	0	0	0	0	0	0	.333	.333
Hernandez, Ramon, Oak.	.254	136	509	453	55	115	185	25	0	15	60	9	4	6	37	3	68	1	1	10	.408	.316
Higginson, Bobby, Det.*	.277	147	633	541	84	150	241	28	6	17	71	1	9	2	80	3	65	20	12	8	.445	.367
Hill, Glenallen, Ana.	.136	16	66	66	4	9	12	0	0	1	2	0	0	0	0	0	20	0	0	3	.182	.136
Hillenbrand, Shea, Bos.	.263	139	493	468	52	123	183	20	2	12	49	1	4	7	13	3	61	3	4	12	.391	.291
Hinch, A.J., K.C.	.157	45	134	121	10	19	40	3	0	6	15	1	1	3	8	1	26	1	1	5	.331	.226
Hocking, Denny, Min.†	.251	112	363	327	34	82	111	16	2	3	25	4	1	2	29	1	67	6	1	7	.339	.315
Hollins, Dave, Cle.†	.200	2	7	5	0	1	1	0	0	0	0	1	0	0	1	0	2	0	0	0	.200	.333
Holt, Chris, Det.	.250	30	4	4	0	1	2	1	0	0	0	0	0	0	0	0	3	0	0	0	.500	.250
Hoover, Paul, T.B.	.250	3	4	4	1	1	1	0	0	0	0	0	0	0	0	0	1	0	0	0	.250	.250
Hubbard, Mike, Tex.	.273	5	11	11	1	3	7	1	0	1	1	0	0	0	0	0	4	0	0	0	.636	.273
Hubbard, Trenidad, K.C.	.250	5	12	12	2	3	5	0	1	0	0	0	0	0	0	0	2	0	0	0	.417	.250
Hudson, Tim, Oak.	.000	36	8	8	1	0	0	0	0	0	0	0	0	0	0	0	3	0	0	0	.000	.000
Huff, Aubrey, T.B.*	.248	111	434	411	42	102	153	25	1	8	45	0	0	0	23	2	72	1	3	18	.372	.288
Hunter, Torii, Min.	.261	148	603	564	82	147	270	32	5	27	92	1	1	8	29	0	125	9	6	12	.479	.306
Ibanez, Raul, K.C.*	.280	104	312	279	44	78	138	11	5	13	54	0	1	0	32	2	51	0	2	6	.495	.353
Inge, Brandon, Det.	.180	79	202	189	13	34	45	11	0	0	15	2	2	0	9	0	41	1	4	2	.238	.215
Izturis, Cesar, Tor.†	.269	46	140	134	19	36	52	6	2	2	9	4	0	0	2	0	15	8	1	0	.388	.279
Jackson, Ryan, Det.*	.212	79	126	118	19	25	39	4	2	2	11	2	0	1	5	0	26	3	1	1	.331	.250
Jaha, John, Oak.	.089	12	52	45	2	4	7	3	0	0	8	0	1	0	6	0	15	0	0	3	.156	.192
Javier, Stan, Sea.†	.292	89	323	281	44	82	110	14	1	4	33	3	1	2	36	1	47	11	1	8	.391	.375
Jennings, Robin, Oak.*	.250	20	55	52	4	13	16	3	0	0	4	0	1	0	2	0	6	0	0	0	.308	.273
Jensen, Marcus, Bos.-Tex.†	.172	12	29	29	0	5	6	1	0	0	2	0	0	0	0	0	10	0	0	1	.207	.172
Jeter, Derek, N.Y.	.311	150	686	614	110	191	295	35	3	21	74	5	1	10	56	3	99	27	3	13	.480	.377
Johnson, Adam, Min.	.000	7	2	2	0	0	0	0	0	0	0	0	0	0	0	0	0	0	0	1	.000	.000
Johnson, Jason, Bal.	.333	32	4	3	0	1	1	0	0	0	0	0	0	0	1	0	2	0	0	0	.333	.500
Johnson, Mark L., Chi.*	.249	61	211	173	21	43	66	6	1	5	18	10	3	2	23	1	31	2	1	5	.382	.338
Johnson, Nick, N.Y.*	.194	23	78	67	6	13	21	2	0	2	8	0	0	4	7	0	15	0	0	3	.313	.308
Johnson, Russ, T.B.	.294	85	288	248	32	73	108	19	2	4	33	4	1	1	34	0	57	2	2	2	.435	.380
Jones, Jacque, Min.*	.276	149	519	475	57	131	198	25	0	14	49	2	0	3	39	2	92	12	9	10	.417	.335
Joyner, Wally, Ana.*	.243	53	161	148	14	36	52	5	1	3	14	0	0	0	13	0	18	1	1	3	.351	.304
Judd, Mike, T.B.-Tex.	.000	12	1	1	0	0	0	0	0	0	0	0	0	0	0	0	1	0	0	0	.000	.000
Justice, David, N.Y.*	.241	111	439	381	58	92	164	16	1	18	51	0	4	0	54	5	83	1	2	6	.430	.333
Kapler, Gabe, Tex.	.267	134	556	483	77	129	211	29	1	17	72	2	7	3	61	2	70	23	6	10	.437	.348
Keisler, Randy, N.Y.*	.000	10	2	2	0	0	0	0	0	0	0	0	0	0	0	0	0	0	0	0	.000	.000
Kennedy, Adam, Ana.*	.270	137	532	478	48	129	178	25	3	6	40	7	9	11	27	3	71	12	7	7	.372	.318
Kennedy, Joe, T.B.	.250	20	4	4	1	1	1	0	0	0	0	0	0	0	0	0	2	0	0	0	.250	.250
Kielty, Bobby, Min.†	.250	37	118	104	8	26	40	8	0	2	14	0	5	1	8	2	25	3	0	2	.385	.297
Kingsale, Eugene, Bal.-Sea.†	.263	13	22	19	4	5	5	0	0	0	1	0	0	1	2	0	4	3	1	1	.263	.364
Kinkade, Mike, Bal.	.275	61	177	160	19	44	61	5	0	4	16	0	0	3	14	0	31	2	1	8	.381	.345
Knoblauch, Chuck, N.Y.	.250	137	600	521	66	130	183	20	3	9	44	5	2	14	58	1	73	38	9	10	.351	.339
Konerko, Paul, Chi.	.282	156	650	582	92	164	295	35	0	32	99	0	5	9	54	6	89	1	0	17	.507	.349
Koskie, Corey, Min.*	.276	153	649	562	100	155	274	37	2	26	103	0	7	12	68	9	118	27	6	16	.488	.362

Player, Team	Avg.	G	TPA	AB	R	H	TB	2B	3B	HR	RBI	SH	SF	HP	BB	IBB	SO	SB	CS	GDP	Slg.	OBP
Laker, Tim, Cle.	.182	16	40	33	5	6	9	0	0	1	5	1	0	0	6	0	8	0	0	1	.273	.308
Lamb, Mike, Tex.*	.306	76	306	284	42	87	117	18	0	4	35	1	2	5	14	1	27	2	1	6	.412	.348
Lampkin, Tom, Sea.*	.225	79	231	204	28	46	71	10	0	5	22	1	1	7	18	1	41	1	0	4	.348	.309
Lansing, Mike, Bos.	.250	106	382	352	45	88	135	23	0	8	34	4	3	1	22	1	50	3	3	7	.384	.294
Latham, Chris, Tor.†	.274	43	84	73	12	20	31	3	1	2	10	0	0	1	10	1	28	4	1	1	.425	.369
Lawton, Matt, Min.*	.293	103	444	376	71	110	165	25	0	10	51	0	2	3	63	6	46	19	6	14	.439	.396
LeCroy, Matthew, Min.	.425	15	42	40	6	17	31	5	0	3	12	0	1	1	0	0	8	0	1	0	.775	.429
Ledee, Ricky, Tex.*	.231	78	272	242	33	56	85	21	1	2	36	1	3	3	23	0	58	3	3	3	.351	.303
Lee, Carlos, Chi.	.269	150	605	558	75	150	261	33	3	24	84	1	2	6	38	2	85	17	7	15	.468	.321
Lewis, Darren, Bos.	.280	82	180	164	18	46	60	9	1	1	12	5	0	3	8	0	25	5	5	2	.366	.326
Lewis, Mark, Cle.	.077	6	13	13	1	1	1	0	0	0	0	0	0	0	0	0	4	0	0	0	.077	.077
Lidle, Cory, Oak.	.000	29	2	2	0	0	0	0	0	0	0	0	0	0	0	0	2	0	0	0	.000	.000
Liefer, Jeff, Chi.*	.256	83	279	254	36	65	132	13	0	18	39	1	2	2	20	1	69	0	1	6	.520	.313
Lilly, Ted, N.Y.*	.000	26	3	1	0	0	0	0	0	0	0	2	0	0	0	0	1	0	0	0	.000	.000
Lima, Jose, Det.	.000	18	1	1	0	0	0	0	0	0	0	0	0	0	0	0	1	0	0	0	.000	.000
Loaiza, Esteban, Tor.	.000	36	2	2	0	0	0	0	0	0	0	0	0	0	0	0	0	0	0	0	.000	.000
Lofton, James, Bos.*	.192	8	28	26	1	5	6	1	0	0	1	0	1	0	1	0	4	2	1	1	.231	.214
Lofton, Kenny, Cle.*	.261	133	576	517	91	135	206	21	4	14	66	5	5	2	47	1	69	16	8	8	.398	.322
Lohse, Kyle, Min.	.400	19	5	5	0	2	3	1	0	0	1	0	0	0	0	0	2	0	0	0	.600	.400
Long, Terrence, Oak.*	.283	162	687	629	90	178	259	37	4	12	85	0	6	0	52	8	103	9	3	17	.412	.335
Lopez, Albie, T.B.	.000	20	5	5	0	0	0	0	0	0	0	0	0	0	0	0	3	0	0	0	.000	.000
Lopez, Felipe, Tor.†	.260	49	192	177	21	46	74	5	4	5	23	1	2	0	12	1	39	4	3	2	.418	.304
Lopez, Luis, Tor.	.244	41	128	119	10	29	42	4	0	3	10	1	0	0	8	1	16	0	0	10	.353	.291
Lowe, Derek, Bos.	.000	67	1	1	0	0	0	0	0	0	0	0	0	0	0	0	1	0	0	0	.000	.000
Lowe, Sean, Chi.	.333	45	3	3	0	1	1	0	0	0	0	0	0	0	0	0	1	0	0	0	.333	.333
Lunar, Fernando, Bal.	.246	64	180	167	8	41	48	7	0	0	16	2	1	3	7	0	32	0	0	8	.287	.287
Macias, Jose, Det.†	.268	137	534	488	62	131	191	24	6	8	51	8	3	3	32	0	54	21	6	7	.391	.316
Magee, Wendell Jr., Det.	.213	90	233	207	26	44	78	11	4	5	17	1	1	1	23	1	44	3	0	8	.377	.293
Magruder, Chris, Tex.†	.172	17	31	29	3	5	5	0	0	0	1	0	0	1	1	0	5	0	1	1	.172	.226
Mahomes, Pat, Tex.	1.000	56	1	1	1	1	1	0	0	0	0	0	0	0	0	0	0	0	0	0	1.000	1.000
Martin, Al, Sea.*	.240	100	324	283	41	68	100	15	2	7	42	0	2	2	37	1	60	0	3	2	.382	.330
Martinez, Tino, N.Y.*	.280	154	635	589	89	165	295	24	2	34	113	0	2	2	42	2	89	1	2	12	.501	.329
Martinez, Edgar, Sea.	.306	132	581	470	80	144	255	40	1	23	116	0	9	9	93	9	90	4	1	11	.543	.423
Martinez, Felix, T.B.‖	.247	77	230	219	24	54	72	13	1	1	14	3	1	5	10	0	46	6	5	8	.329	.294
Mateo, Ruben, Tex.	.248	40	147	129	18	32	44	5	2	1	13	1	2	6	9	0	28	1	0	4	.341	.322
Matos, Luis, Bal.	.214	31	112	98	10	21	40	7	0	4	12	2	0	1	11	0	30	7	0	1	.408	.300
Maxwell, Jason, Min.	.191	39	78	68	4	13	20	4	0	1	10	1	0	0	9	2	23	2	0	1	.294	.286
Mayne, Brent, K.C.*	.241	51	180	166	13	40	52	4	1	2	20	0	3	1	10	2	17	1	2	8	.313	.283
Mays, Joe, Min.†	.000	34	2	1	0	0	0	0	0	0	0	1	0	0	0	0	1	0	0	0	.000	.000
McCarty, Dave, K.C.	.250	98	230	200	26	50	81	10	0	7	26	1	4	1	24	1	45	0	0	8	.405	.328
McCracken, Quinton, Min.† ..	.219	24	70	64	7	14	20	2	2	0	3	1	0	0	5	0	13	0	1	2	.313	.275
McDonald, Donzell, N.Y.†	.333	5	4	3	0	1	1	0	0	0	0	0	0	0	0	0	2	0	0	0	.333	.333
McDonald, John, Cle.	.091	17	25	22	1	2	3	1	0	0	0	1	0	1	1	0	7	0	0	0	.136	.167
McGriff, Fred, T.B.*	.318	97	385	343	40	109	184	18	0	19	61	0	2	0	40	9	69	1	1	7	.536	.387
McLemore, Mark, Sea.†	.286	125	487	409	78	117	166	16	9	5	57	3	6	0	69	0	84	39	7	6	.406	.384
McMillon, Billy, Det.-Oak.* ..	.217	40	102	92	7	20	33	8	1	1	14	0	1	2	7	0	25	1	0	1	.359	.284
Mendoza, Ramiro, N.Y.	.000	56	2	2	0	0	0	0	0	0	0	0	0	0	0	0	2	0	0	0	.000	.000
Menechino, Frank, Oak.	.242	139	578	471	82	114	176	22	2	12	60	3	6	19	79	0	97	2	3	13	.374	.369
Mercedes, Jose, Bal.	.000	33	5	5	0	0	0	0	0	0	0	0	0	0	0	0	4	0	0	0	.000	.000
Merloni, Lou, Bos.	.267	52	159	146	21	39	58	10	0	3	13	2	2	3	6	0	31	2	1	6	.397	.306
Michalak, Chris, Tor.-Tex.* ..	.333	35	5	3	0	1	3	0	1	0	2	0	0	0	1	0	1	0	0	0	1.000	.500
Mientkiewicz, Doug, Min.* ..	.306	151	626	543	77	166	252	39	1	15	74	0	7	9	67	6	92	2	6	10	.464	.387
Milton, Eric, Min.*	.000	35	2	2	1	0	0	0	0	0	0	0	0	0	0	0	1	0	0	0	.000	.000
Mirabelli, Doug, Bos.-Bos.	.226	77	224	190	20	43	86	10	0	11	29	1	2	4	27	2	57	0	0	3	.453	.332
Mlicki, Dave, Det.	.000	15	1	1	0	0	0	0	0	0	0	0	0	0	0	0	1	0	0	0	.000	.000
Mohr, Dustan, Min.	.235	20	57	51	6	12	14	2	0	0	4	0	1	0	5	0	17	1	1	0	.275	.298
Molina, Bengie, Ana.	.262	96	355	325	31	85	114	11	0	6	40	2	4	8	16	3	61	0	1	8	.351	.309
Molina, Jose, Ana.	.270	15	42	37	8	10	19	3	0	2	4	2	0	3	0	0	8	0	0	2	.514	.325
Mondesi, Raul, Tor.	.252	149	653	572	88	144	259	26	4	27	84	0	2	6	73	3	128	30	11	13	.453	.342
Monroe, Craig, Tex.	.212	27	58	52	8	11	18	1	0	2	5	0	0	0	6	0	18	2	0	1	.346	.293
Mora, Melvin, Bal.	.250	128	503	436	49	109	158	28	0	7	48	5	7	14	41	2	91	11	4	6	.362	.329
Moyer, Jamie, Sea.*	.000	33	2	1	0	0	0	0	0	0	0	1	0	0	0	0	0	0	0	0	.000	.000
Mulder, Mark, Oak.*	.200	34	5	5	0	1	1	0	0	0	0	0	0	0	0	0	1	0	0	0	.200	.200
Munson, Eric, Det.*	.152	17	69	66	4	10	18	3	1	1	6	0	0	3	0	0	21	0	1	2	.273	.188
Mussina, Mike, N.Y.*	.143	34	7	7	0	1	1	0	0	0	0	0	0	0	0	0	2	0	0	0	.143	.143
Myers, Greg, Bal.-Oak.*	.224	58	182	161	24	36	72	3	0	11	31	0	0	0	21	1	38	0	0	5	.447	.313
Nagy, Charles, Cle.*	1.000	15	2	1	1	1	1	0	0	0	0	0	0	0	1	0	0	0	0	0	1.000	1.000
Nieves, Jose, Ana.	.245	29	59	53	5	13	24	3	1	2	3	2	0	2	2	0	20	0	1	1	.453	.298
Nixon, Trot, Bos.*	.280	148	633	535	100	150	270	31	4	27	88	6	6	7	79	1	113	7	4	8	.505	.376
Nomo, Hideo, Bos.	.200	33	5	5	0	1	1	0	0	0	0	0	0	0	0	0	3	0	0	0	.200	.200
Offerman, Jose, Bos.†	.267	128	594	524	76	140	196	23	3	9	49	3	5	1	61	2	97	5	2	9	.374	.342
Ohka, Tomo, Bos.	.000	12	3	3	0	0	0	0	0	0	0	0	0	0	0	0	2	0	0	0	.000	.000
O'Leary, Troy, Bos.*	.240	104	376	341	50	82	149	16	6	13	50	0	5	5	25	2	73	1	3	9	.437	.298
Olerud, John, Sea.*	.302	159	679	572	91	173	270	32	1	21	95	1	7	5	94	19	70	3	1	21	.472	.401
Oliver, Darren, Tex.	.333	28	8	6	0	2	3	1	0	0	2	2	0	0	0	0	2	0	0	0	.500	.333
Oliver, Joe, N.Y.-Bos.	.250	17	53	48	4	12	17	2	0	1	3	2	1	0	2	0	15	0	0	0	.354	.275
O'Neill, Paul, N.Y.*	.267	137	563	510	77	136	234	33	1	21	70	0	3	2	48	4	59	22	3	20	.459	.330
Ordaz, Luis, K.C.	.250	28	63	56	8	14	17	3	0	0	4	2	1	1	3	0	8	0	1	3	.304	.295
Ordonez, Magglio, Chi.	.305	160	671	593	97	181	316	40	1	31	113	0	3	5	70	7	70	25	7	14	.533	.382
Ortiz, David, Min.*	.234	89	347	303	46	71	144	17	1	18	48	1	2	1	40	8	68	1	0	6	.475	.324
Ortiz, Ramon, Ana.	.000	32	7	7	0	0	0	0	0	0	0	0	0	0	0	0	2	0	0	0	.000	.000
Ortiz, Hector, K.C.	.247	56	166	154	12	38	46	6	1	0	11	2	0	1	9	0	24	1	3	5	.299	.293

Player, Team	Avg.	G	TPA	AB	R	H	TB	2B	3B	HR	RBI	SH	SF	HP	BB	IBB	SO	SB	CS	GDP	Slg.	OBP
Ortiz, Jose, Oak.	.167	11	46	42	4	7	7	0	0	0	3	0	1	0	3	0	5	1	0	4	.167	.217
Palmeiro, Orlando, Ana.*	.243	104	270	230	29	56	74	10	1	2	23	7	5	3	25	2	24	6	6	3	.322	.319
Palmeiro, Rafael, Tex.*	.273	160	714	600	98	164	338	33	0	47	123	0	6	7	101	8	90	1	1	8	.563	.381
Palmer, Dean, Det.	.222	57	246	216	34	48	92	11	0	11	40	0	0	3	27	0	59	4	1	3	.426	.317
Paniagua, Jose, Sea.	.000	60	1	1	0	0	0	0	0	0	0	0	0	0	0	0	0	0	0	0	.000	.000
Parris, Steve, Tor.	.000	19	2	1	0	0	0	0	0	0	0	1	0	0	0	0	1	0	0	0	.000	.000
Patterson, Jarrod, Det.*	.268	13	43	41	6	11	20	1	1	2	4	0	0	2	0	0	4	0	1	2	.488	.302
Paul, Josh, Chi.	.266	57	154	139	20	37	57	11	0	3	18	1	1	0	13	0	25	6	2	3	.410	.327
Pena, Carlos, Tex.*	.258	22	72	62	6	16	31	4	1	3	12	0	0	0	10	0	17	0	0	1	.500	.361
Perez, Neifi, K.C.†	.241	49	220	199	18	48	60	7	1	1	12	7	3	1	10	0	19	3	4	2	.302	.277
Perez, Robert, N.Y.	.267	6	16	15	1	4	5	1	0	0	0	0	0	0	1	0	7	0	1	0	.333	.313
Perry, Herbert, Chi.	.256	92	316	285	38	73	117	21	1	7	32	0	1	7	23	1	55	2	2	11	.411	.326
Petkovsek, Mark, Tex.	.000	55	1	1	0	0	0	0	0	0	0	0	0	0	0	0	0	0	0	0	.000	.000
Pettitte, Andy, N.Y.*	.000	31	5	4	0	0	0	0	0	0	0	1	0	0	0	0	1	0	0	0	.000	.000
Pettyjohn, Adam, Det.	.000	16	2	2	0	0	0	0	0	0	0	0	0	0	0	0	2	0	0	0	.000	.000
Phelps, Josh, Tor.	.000	8	14	12	3	0	0	0	0	0	1	0	0	0	2	0	5	1	0	1	.000	.143
Piatt, Adam, Oak.	.211	36	110	95	9	20	27	5	1	0	6	1	2	0	13	0	26	0	0	5	.284	.300
Pickering, Calvin, Bos.*	.280	17	58	50	4	14	24	1	0	3	7	0	0	0	8	0	13	0	0	4	.480	.379
Pierzynski, A.J., Min.*	.289	114	405	381	51	110	168	33	2	7	55	1	3	4	16	4	57	1	7	7	.441	.322
Podsednik, Scott, Sea.*	.167	5	6	6	1	1	3	0	1	0	3	0	0	0	0	0	1	0	0	1	.500	.167
Ponson, Sidney, Bal.	.000	23	3	3	0	0	0	0	0	0	0	0	0	0	0	0	1	0	0	0	.000	.000
Porter, Bo, Tex.	.230	48	98	87	18	20	31	4	2	1	6	0	2	0	9	0	34	3	2	1	.356	.296
Posada, Jorge, N.Y.†	.277	138	557	484	59	134	230	28	1	22	95	0	5	6	62	10	132	2	6	10	.475	.363
Prince, Tom, Min.	.219	64	215	196	19	43	70	4	1	7	23	0	1	6	12	0	39	3	1	5	.357	.284
Quinn, Mark, K.C.	.269	118	473	453	57	122	208	31	2	17	60	0	1	7	12	1	69	9	5	16	.459	.298
Radke, Brad, Min.	.500	33	4	4	0	2	2	0	0	0	0	0	0	0	0	0	0	0	0	0	.500	.500
Raines, Tim Jr., Bal.	.174	7	27	23	6	4	6	2	0	0	0	1	0	0	3	0	8	3	0	0	.261	.259
Raines, Tim Sr., Bal.†	.273	4	12	11	1	3	6	0	0	1	5	0	1	0	0	0	3	0	0	1	.545	.250
Ramirez, Julio, Chi.	.081	22	39	37	2	3	3	0	0	0	1	0	0	0	2	0	15	2	0	0	.081	.128
Ramirez, Manny, Bos.	.306	142	620	529	93	162	322	33	2	41	125	0	2	8	81	25	147	0	1	9	.609	.405
Randa, Joe, K.C.	.253	151	636	581	59	147	224	34	2	13	83	1	6	6	42	2	80	3	2	15	.386	.307
Rapp, Pat, Ana.	.000	31	5	5	0	0	0	0	0	0	0	0	0	0	0	0	2	0	0	0	.000	.000
Reichert, Dan, K.C.	.000	27	5	5	0	0	0	0	0	0	0	0	0	0	0	0	4	0	0	0	.000	.000
Rekar, Bryan, T.B.	.000	25	2	2	0	0	0	0	0	0	0	0	0	0	0	0	1	0	0	0	.000	.000
Rhodes, Arthur, Sea.*	.000	72	1	1	0	0	0	0	0	0	0	0	0	0	0	0	1	0	0	0	.000	.000
Richard, Chris, Bal.*	.265	136	542	483	74	128	210	31	3	15	61	2	4	8	45	4	100	11	9	15	.435	.335
Rincon, Juan, Min.	1.000	4	1	1	0	1	1	0	0	0	0	0	0	0	0	0	0	0	0	0	1.000	1.000
Ripken, Cal, Bal.	.239	128	516	477	43	114	172	16	0	14	68	2	9	2	26	1	63	0	2	15	.361	.276
Rivas, Luis, Min.	.266	153	619	563	70	150	204	21	6	7	47	5	5	6	40	0	99	31	11	15	.362	.319
Rivera, Juan, N.Y.	.000	3	4	4	0	0	0	0	0	0	0	0	0	0	0	0	0	0	0	0	.000	.000
Rivera, Mike, Det.	.333	4	12	12	2	4	6	2	0	0	1	0	0	0	0	0	2	0	0	0	.500	.333
Roberts, Brian, Bal.†	.253	75	292	273	42	69	93	12	3	2	17	3	3	0	13	0	36	12	3	3	.341	.284
Roberts, Dave, Cle.*	.333	15	13	12	3	4	5	1	0	0	2	0	0	0	1	0	2	0	1	0	.417	.385
Roberts, Willis, Bal.	.250	46	5	4	0	1	1	0	0	0	0	1	0	0	0	0	3	0	0	0	.250	.250
Rodriguez, Alex, Tex.	.318	162	732	632	133	201	393	34	1	52	135	0	9	16	75	6	131	18	3	17	.622	.399
Rodriguez, Henry, N.Y.*	.000	5	8	8	0	0	0	0	0	0	0	0	0	0	0	0	6	0	0	0	.000	.000
Rodriguez, Ivan, Tex.	.308	111	470	442	70	136	239	24	2	25	65	0	1	4	23	3	73	10	3	13	.541	.347
Rogers, Kenny, Tex.*	.000	20	2	2	0	0	0	0	0	0	0	0	0	0	0	0	2	0	0	0	.000	.000
Rolls, Damian, T.B.	.262	81	249	237	33	62	81	11	1	2	12	2	0	0	10	0	47	12	4	5	.342	.291
Romero, J.C., Min.†	.500	14	2	2	1	1	2	1	0	0	0	0	0	0	0	0	0	0	0	0	1.000	.500
Rowand, Aaron, Chi.	.293	63	148	123	21	36	53	5	0	4	20	5	1	4	15	0	28	5	1	2	.431	.385
Rupe, Ryan, T.B.	.333	28	3	3	1	1	2	1	0	0	0	0	0	0	0	0	1	0	0	0	.667	.333
Ryan, Rob, Oak.*	.000	7	7	7	0	0	0	0	0	0	0	0	0	0	0	0	5	0	0	0	.000	.000
Ryan, B.J., Bal.*	.000	61	1	1	0	0	0	0	0	0	0	0	0	0	0	0	0	0	0	1	.000	.000
Sabathia, C.C., Cle.*	.000	33	5	4	0	0	0	0	0	0	0	1	0	0	0	0	0	0	0	1	.000	.000
Sadler, Donnie, K.C.	.129	54	116	101	19	13	16	3	0	0	2	3	1	2	9	0	17	4	1	0	.158	.212
Saenz, Olmedo, Oak.	.220	106	341	305	33	67	117	21	1	9	32	1	3	13	19	1	64	0	1	9	.384	.291
Salmon, Tim, Ana.	.227	137	581	475	63	108	182	21	1	17	49	0	2	8	96	4	121	9	3	11	.383	.365
Sanchez, Rey, K.C.	.303	100	416	390	46	118	142	14	5	0	28	9	4	2	11	0	34	9	1	11	.364	.322
Sandberg, Jared, T.B.	.206	39	149	136	13	28	38	7	0	1	15	2	0	1	10	0	45	1	0	2	.279	.265
Sanders, Anthony, Sea.	.176	9	19	17	1	3	5	2	0	0	2	0	0	0	2	0	3	0	0	0	.294	.263
Santangelo, F.P., Oak.†	.197	32	89	71	16	14	18	4	0	0	8	1	1	5	11	0	17	1	1	1	.254	.341
Santos, Angel, Bos.†	.125	9	19	16	2	2	3	1	0	0	1	0	1	0	2	0	7	0	0	2	.188	.211
Schoeneweis, Scott, Ana.* ...	.000	32	2	0	0	0	0	0	0	0	0	2	0	0	0	0	0	0	0	0	.000	1.000
Seabol, Scott, N.Y.	.000	1	1	1	0	0	0	0	0	0	0	0	0	0	0	0	0	0	0	0	.000	.000
Segui, David, Bal.†	.301	82	347	292	48	88	138	18	1	10	46	0	2	4	49	5	61	1	1	4	.473	.406
Sele, Aaron, Sea.	.167	34	8	6	2	1	1	0	0	0	1	2	0	0	0	0	0	0	0	0	.167	.167
Sheets, Andy, T.B.	.196	49	174	153	10	30	41	8	0	1	14	7	2	0	12	0	35	2	0	0	.268	.251
Sheldon, Scott, Tex.	.200	61	127	120	11	24	38	5	0	3	11	2	2	0	3	0	35	1	1	2	.317	.216
Sierra, Ruben, Tex.†	.291	94	369	344	55	100	193	22	1	23	67	0	6	0	19	0	52	2	0	13	.561	.322
Simmons, Brian, Tor.†	.178	60	117	107	8	19	30	5	0	2	8	0	1	1	8	0	26	1	0	0	.280	.239
Simon, Randall, Det.*	.305	81	274	256	28	78	114	14	2	6	37	1	2	0	15	2	28	0	1	9	.445	.341
Singleton, Chris, Chi.*	.298	140	431	392	57	117	169	21	5	7	45	14	4	1	20	2	61	12	11	5	.431	.330
Smith, Bobby, T.B.	.105	6	22	19	1	2	2	0	0	0	1	0	0	0	3	0	10	0	0	1	.105	.227
Sojo, Luis, N.Y.	.165	39	84	79	5	13	15	2	0	0	9	0	0	1	4	0	12	1	0	0	.190	.214
Soriano, Alfonso, N.Y.	.268	158	614	574	77	154	248	34	3	18	73	3	5	3	29	0	125	43	14	7	.432	.304
Sparks, Steve W., Det.	.000	36	4	4	0	0	0	0	0	0	0	0	0	0	0	0	1	0	0	0	.000	.000
Spencer, Shane, N.Y.	.258	80	311	283	40	73	121	14	2	10	46	0	3	4	21	0	58	4	1	4	.428	.315
Spiezio, Scott, Ana.†	.271	139	503	457	57	124	200	29	4	13	54	3	4	5	34	4	65	5	2	6	.438	.326
Sprague, Ed Jr., Sea.	.298	45	107	94	9	28	41	7	0	2	16	0	1	1	11	1	18	0	0	3	.436	.374
Stein, Blake, K.C.	.000	36	2	2	0	0	0	0	0	0	0	0	0	0	0	0	0	0	0	0	.000	.000
Stewart, Shannon, Tor.	.316	155	698	640	103	202	296	44	7	12	60	0	1	11	46	1	72	27	10	9	.463	.371

Player, Team	Avg.	G	TPA	AB	R	H	TB	2B	3B	HR	RBI	SH	SF	HP	BB	IBB	SO	SB	CS	GDP	Slg.	OBP
Sturtze, Tanyon, T.B.	.125	39	8	8	0	1	1	0	0	0	0	0	0	0	0	0	3	0	0	0	.125	.125
Stynes, Chris, Bos.	.280	96	386	361	52	101	148	19	2	8	33	1	1	3	20	0	56	4	5	12	.410	.322
Suppan, Jeff, K.C.	.400	34	5	5	0	2	2	0	0	0	0	0	0	0	0	0	2	0	0	0	.400	.400
Suzuki, Ichiro, Sea.*	.350	157	738	692	127	242	316	34	8	8	69	4	4	8	30	10	53	56	14	3	.457	.381
Sweeney, Mike, K.C.	.304	147	632	559	97	170	303	46	0	29	99	1	6	2	64	13	64	10	3	13	.542	.374
Taubensee, Eddie, Cle.*	.250	52	128	116	16	29	42	2	1	3	11	1	0	1	10	1	19	0	0	3	.362	.315
Tejada, Miguel, Oak.	.267	162	683	622	107	166	296	31	3	31	113	1	4	13	43	5	89	11	5	14	.476	.326
Thomas, Frank, Chi.	.221	20	79	68	8	15	30	3	0	4	10	0	1	0	10	2	12	0	0	0	.441	.316
Thome, Jim, Cle.*	.291	156	644	526	101	153	328	26	1	49	124	0	3	4	111	14	185	0	1	9	.624	.416
Towers, Josh, Bal.	.000	24	2	2	0	0	0	0	0	0	0	0	0	0	0	0	0	0	0	0	.000	.000
Tyner, Jason, T.B.*	.280	105	420	398	51	111	129	8	5	0	21	5	1	3	15	0	42	31	6	6	.326	.311
Valdes, Ismael, Ana.	.200	27	5	5	0	1	1	0	0	0	0	0	0	0	0	0	2	1	0	0	.200	.200
Valdez, Mario, Oak.*	.278	32	67	54	7	15	19	1	0	1	8	0	0	1	12	1	18	0	0	0	.352	.418
Valentin, John, Bos.	.200	20	70	60	8	12	17	2	0	1	5	0	0	1	9	0	8	0	0	4	.283	.314
Valentin, Jose, Chi.†	.258	124	502	438	74	113	223	22	2	28	68	8	3	3	50	2	114	9	6	7	.509	.336
Varitek, Jason, Bos.†	.293	51	198	174	19	51	85	11	1	7	25	1	1	1	21	3	35	0	0	6	.489	.371
Vaughn, Greg, T.B.	.233	136	562	485	74	113	210	25	0	24	82	0	3	3	71	7	130	11	5	10	.433	.333
Vazquez, Ramon, Sea.*	.229	17	37	35	5	8	8	0	0	0	4	1	0	0	0	0	3	0	0	0	.229	.222
Velarde, Randy, Tex.-N.Y.	.278	93	389	342	50	95	145	19	2	9	32	4	1	8	34	0	86	6	2	8	.424	.356
Vizquel, Omar, Cle.†	.255	155	693	611	84	156	204	26	8	2	50	15	4	2	61	0	72	13	9	14	.334	.323
Wakefield, Tim, Bos.	.333	45	4	3	0	1	1	0	0	0	0	0	1	0	0	0	2	0	0	0	.333	.333
Wakeland, Chris, Det.*	.250	10	36	36	5	9	17	2	0	2	6	0	0	0	0	0	13	0	0	0	.472	.250
Washburn, Jarrod, Ana.*	.600	30	6	5	1	3	3	0	0	0	0	0	0	0	1	0	2	0	0	0	.600	.667
Weaver, Jeff, Det.	.000	33	6	5	0	0	0	0	0	0	0	0	1	0	0	0	0	0	0	0	.000	.000
Wells, David, Chi.*	.000	16	2	2	0	0	0	0	0	0	0	0	0	0	0	0	1	0	0	0	.000	.000
Wells, Kip, Chi.	.167	40	6	6	1	1	1	0	0	0	0	0	0	0	0	0	5	1	0	0	.167	.167
Wells, Vernon, Tor.	.313	30	103	96	14	30	41	8	0	1	6	0	1	1	5	0	15	5	0	0	.427	.350
Westbrook, Jake, Cle.	.000	23	2	1	0	0	0	0	0	0	0	0	1	0	0	0	1	0	0	0	.000	.000
Williams, Bernie, N.Y.†	.307	146	633	540	102	166	282	38	0	26	94	0	9	6	78	11	67	11	5	15	.522	.395
Williams, Gerald, T.B.-N.Y.	.201	100	306	279	42	56	86	18	0	4	19	4	0	5	18	0	55	13	5	9	.308	.262
Wilson, Dan, Sea.	.265	123	408	377	44	100	152	20	1	10	42	8	1	2	20	0	69	3	2	6	.403	.305
Wilson, Enrique, N.Y.†	.242	48	108	99	10	24	34	5	1	1	12	2	1	0	6	0	14	0	2	3	.343	.283
Wilson, Kris, K.C.	.333	29	3	3	1	1	1	0	0	0	0	0	0	0	0	0	1	0	0	0	.333	.333
Wilson, Tom, Oak.	.190	9	24	21	4	4	10	0	0	2	4	0	1	1	1	0	5	0	0	1	.476	.250
Winn, Randy, T.B.†	.273	128	480	429	54	117	172	25	6	6	50	5	2	6	38	0	81	12	10	10	.401	.339
Woodard, Steve, Cle.*	.000	29	1	1	0	0	0	0	0	0	0	0	0	0	0	0	0	0	0	0	.000	.000
Woodward, Chris, Tor.	.190	37	66	63	9	12	25	3	2	2	5	2	0	0	1	0	14	0	1	1	.397	.203
Wooton, Shawn, Ana.	.312	79	232	221	24	69	103	8	1	8	32	0	3	3	5	0	42	2	0	5	.466	.332
Wright, Jarot, Clo.	.600	7	2	2	0	1	1	0	0	0	0	0	0	0	0	0	1	0	0	0	.500	.500
Young, Michael, Tex.	.249	106	429	386	57	96	155	18	4	11	49	9	5	3	26	0	91	3	1	9	.402	.298
Zaun, Gregg, K.C.†	.320	39	138	125	15	40	67	9	0	6	18	0	1	0	12	0	16	1	2	2	.536	.377
Zito, Barry, Oak.*	.000	35	5	5	0	0	0	0	0	0	0	0	0	0	0	0	4	0	0	0	.000	.000

PLAYERS WITH TWO OR MORE TEAMS

Player, Team	Avg.	G	TPA	AB	R	H	TB	2B	3B	HR	RBI	SH	SF	HP	BB	IBB	SO	SB	CS	GDP	Slg.	OBP
Batista, Tony, Tor.	.207	72	291	271	29	56	108	11	1	13	45	0	3	4	13	1	66	0	1	2	.399	.251
Batista, Tony, Bal.	.266	84	331	308	41	82	144	16	5	12	42	0	4	0	19	0	47	5	1	7	.468	.305
Blake, Casey, Min.	.318	13	25	22	1	7	8	1	0	0	2	0	0	3	1	8	1	0	0	.364	.400
Blake, Casey, Bal.	.133	6	16	15	2	2	5	0	0	1	2	0	0	1	0	4	2	0	0	.333	.188
Dye, Jermaine, K.C.	.272	97	410	367	50	100	153	14	0	13	47	1	6	6	30	3	68	7	1	2	.417	.333
Dye, Jermaine, Oak.	.297	61	265	232	41	69	127	17	1	13	59	0	5	1	27	3	44	2	0	6	.547	.366
Fasano, Sal, Oak.	.048	11	23	21	2	1	1	0	0	0	0	0	0	1	1	0	12	0	0	1	.048	.130
Fasano, Sal, K.C.	.000	3	1	1	0	0	0	0	0	0	0	0	0	0	0	0	0	0	0	1	.000	.000
Jensen, Marcus, Bos.†	.250	1	4	4	0	1	1	0	0	0	0	0	0	0	0	1	0	0	0	0	.250	.250
Jensen, Marcus, Tex †	.160	11	25	25	0	4	5	1	0	0	2	0	0	0	0	0	9	0	0	1	.200	.160
Judd, Mike, T.B.	.000	8	0	0	0	0	0	0	0	0	0	0	0	0	0	0	0	0	0	0	.000	.000
Judd, Mike, Tex.	.000	4	1	1	0	0	0	0	0	0	0	0	0	0	0	0	0	0	0	0	.000	.000
Kingsale, Eugene, Bal.†	.000	3	4	4	0	0	0	0	0	0	0	0	0	0	0	2	1	1	0	.000	.000
Kingsale, Eugene, Sea.†	.333	10	18	15	4	5	5	0	0	0	1	0	0	1	2	0	2	2	0	1	.333	.444
McMillon, Billy, Det.*	.088	20	37	34	1	3	7	1	0	1	4	0	0	1	2	0	12	0	0	1	.206	.162
McMillon, Billy, Oak.*	.293	20	65	58	6	17	26	7	1	0	10	0	1	1	5	0	13	1	0	0	.448	.354
Michalak, Chris, Tor.*	.333	24	5	3	0	1	3	0	1	0	0	2	0	0	0	1	0	0	0	1.000	.333
Michalak, Chris, Tex.*	.000	11	0	0	0	0	0	0	0	0	0	0	0	0	0	0	0	0	0	.000	.000
Mirabelli, Doug, Tex.	.102	23	59	49	4	5	13	2	0	2	3	0	0	0	10	0	21	0	0	1	.265	.254
Mirabelli, Doug, Bos.	.270	54	165	141	16	38	73	8	0	9	26	1	2	4	17	2	36	0	0	2	.518	.360
Myers, Greg, Bal.*	.270	25	82	74	11	20	34	2	0	4	18	0	0	0	8	0	17	0	0	3	.459	.341
Myers, Greg, Oak.*	.184	33	100	87	13	16	38	1	0	7	13	0	0	0	13	1	21	0	0	2	.437	.290
Oliver, Joe, N.Y.	.250	12	40	36	3	9	13	1	0	1	2	2	1	0	1	0	12	0	0	0	.361	.263
Oliver, Joe, Bos.	.250	5	13	12	1	3	4	1	0	0	1	0	0	0	1	0	3	0	0	0	.333	.308
Velarde, Randy, Tex.	.297	78	334	296	46	88	135	16	2	9	31	3	1	5	29	0	73	4	2	8	.456	.369
Velarde, Randy, N.Y.	.152	15	55	46	4	7	10	3	0	0	1	1	0	3	5	0	13	2	0	0	.217	.278
Williams, Gerald, T.B.	.207	62	252	232	30	48	77	17	0	4	17	3	0	4	13	0	42	10	4	8	.332	.261
Williams, Gerald, N.Y.	.170	38	54	47	12	8	9	1	0	0	2	1	0	1	5	0	13	3	1	1	.191	.264

AWARDED FIRST BASE ON OBSTRUCTION OR CATCHER'S INTERFERENCE—Erstad, Anaheim 5 (Cardona 3, Fordyce, Taubensee); Pierzynski, Minnesota 2 (Casanova, Mayne); Higginston, Detroit (Mirabelli); J. Jones, Minnesota (Zaun); Richard, Baltimore (B. Molina); Singleton, Chicago (LaRue).

2001 A.L. STATISTICS Batting

DESIGNATED HITTING

TEAM

Team	Avg.	G	TPA	AB	R	H	TB	2B	3B	HR	RBI	SH	SF	HP	BB	IBB	SO	SB	CS	GDP	Slg.	OBP
Seattle	.305	153	702	577	104	176	297	47	1	24	131	0	10	9	106	10	106	9	1	15	.515	.415
Boston	.293	152	676	605	93	177	326	35	3	36	126	0	1	11	59	19	142	2	0	13	.539	.365
Cleveland	.288	153	665	570	115	164	311	34	1	37	105	1	10	6	78	6	115	3	2	14	.546	.373
Texas	.272	153	672	611	98	166	327	36	1	41	101	0	4	8	49	2	117	6	0	23	.535	.332
Toronto	.271	153	660	602	81	163	268	35	2	22	95	0	8	7	43	8	100	4	2	15	.445	.323
Kansas City	.265	153	656	596	77	158	257	32	5	19	97	1	8	1	50	2	90	8	5	16	.431	.319
Minnesota	.260	153	654	577	86	150	265	36	5	23	81	3	3	4	67	8	126	4	4	13	.459	.339
Tampa Bay	.260	153	652	581	78	151	237	32	0	18	80	0	8	6	63	7	136	10	4	15	.408	.340
Detroit	.256	153	652	574	83	147	258	34	4	23	103	0	8	4	66	6	125	8	2	13	.449	.333
Baltimore	.252	153	647	567	86	143	229	23	3	19	84	1	7	4	68	1	118	7	6	18	.404	.333
Oakland	.246	153	687	585	85	144	240	42	0	18	81	2	5	16	79	3	145	2	1	15	.410	.349
Chicago	.244	153	650	561	75	137	231	16	0	26	91	0	8	3	78	6	130	6	2	11	.412	.335
New York	.218	152	655	559	82	122	221	24	3	23	81	2	7	11	76	4	127	12	7	8	.395	.320
Anaheim	.212	153	637	572	40	121	163	18	0	8	56	5	6	6	48	5	132	8	7	14	.285	.277
Totals	.260	2427	9265	8137	1183	2119	3630	444	28	337	1312	15	85	98	930	87	1709	89	43	203	.446	.340

TOP DESIGNATED HITTERS

Minimum 100 at-bats. *Lefthanded batter. †Switch-hitter.

Player, Team	Avg.	G	TPA	AB	R	H	TB	2B	3B	HR	RBI	SH	SF	HP	BB	IBB	SO	SB	CS	GDP	Slg.	OBP
Grieve, Ben, Tampa Bay*	.353	32	138	119	18	42	64	7	0	5	24	0	0	5	14	1	28	4	0	2	.538	.442
Ramirez, Manny, Boston	.333	87	378	327	52	109	199	17	2	23	80	0	1	7	43	18	86	0	0	6	.609	.421
Martinez, Edgar, Seattle	.309	127	573	463	79	143	251	40	1	22	115	0	9	9	92	9	88	4	1	11	.542	.426
Simon, Randall, Detroit*	.291	29	110	103	11	30	45	4	1	3	19	0	1	0	6	1	12	0	0	3	.437	.327
Ibanez, Raul, Kansas City*	.288	33	133	118	19	34	55	6	3	3	22	0	1	0	14	0	20	0	0	1	.466	.361
Palmeiro, Rafael, Texas*	.286	46	200	175	29	50	117	13	0	18	38	0	2	3	20	2	22	0	0	3	.669	.365
Batista, Tony, Baltimore	.283	33	135	120	17	34	61	4	1	7	23	0	3	0	12	0	17	1	1	3	.508	.341
Clark, Tony, Detroit†	.280	42	175	150	22	42	73	14	1	5	28	0	2	0	23	5	34	0	0	6	.487	.371
Giambi, Jeremy, Oakland*	.278	61	238	198	36	55	89	16	0	6	33	0	0	3	37	0	42	0	0	4	.449	.399
Burks, Ellis, Cleveland	.278	102	436	371	73	103	199	25	1	23	60	0	7	3	55	2	67	3	1	13	.536	.369
Fullmer, Brad, Toronto*	.276	135	559	508	70	140	227	31	1	18	82	0	7	6	38	8	87	4	2	13	.447	.329
Sierra, Ruben, Texas†	.273	50	219	205	31	56	113	10	1	15	34	0	2	0	12	0	34	2	0	12	.551	.311
Bichette, Dante, Boston	.268	46	187	179	28	48	92	15	1	9	32	0	0	1	7	0	27	1	0	5	.514	.299
Canseco, Jose, Chicago	.257	68	292	245	42	63	115	7	0	15	48	0	4	1	42	1	72	2	1	4	.469	.363
Galarraga, Andres, Texas	.257	39	161	144	23	37	66	11	0	6	24	0	0	5	12	0	37	0	0	5	.458	.335

ALL DESIGNATED HITTERS

*Lefthanded batter. †Switch-hitter.

Player, Team	Avg.	G	TPA	AB	R	H	TB	2B	3B	HR	RBI	SH	SF	HP	BB	IBB	SO	SB	CS	GDP	Slg.	OBP
Alcantara, Israel, Boston	.250	1	4	4	0	1	1	0	0	0	0	0	0	0	0	0	1	0	0	0	.250	.250
Alicea, Luis, Kansas City†	.307	22	81	75	11	23	34	3	1	2	10	0	0	1	5	0	13	2	0	2	.453	.358
Allen, Chad, Minnesota	.254	23	78	67	8	17	25	3	1	1	8	0	1	0	10	1	11	1	1	3	.373	.346
Almonte, Erick, New York	1.000	3	1	1	0	1	2	1	0	0	0	0	0	0	0	0	2	0	0	0	2.000	1.000
Anderson, Brady, Baltimore*	.300	4	14	10	5	3	6	0	0	1	2	0	0	0	4	0	1	1	0	0	.600	.500
Anderson, Garret, Anaheim*	.308	12	52	52	3	16	25	3	0	2	10	0	0	0	0	0	13	0	0	0	.481	.308
Baines, Harold, Chicago*	.145	22	86	76	3	11	12	1	0	0	6	0	2	0	8	0	11	0	0	2	.158	.221
Batista, Tony, Baltimore	.283	33	135	120	17	34	61	4	1	7	23	0	3	0	12	0	17	1	1	3	.508	.341
Bellhorn, Mark, Oakland†	.000	4	3	2	0	0	0	0	0	0	0	0	1	0	0	0	2	0	0	0	.000	.000
Beltran, Carlos, Kansas City†	.231	3	13	13	1	3	3	0	0	0	1	0	0	0	0	0	3	0	0	0	.231	.231
Berger, Brandon, Kansas City	.000	1	1	1	0	0	0	0	0	0	0	0	0	0	0	0	0	0	0	0	.000	.000
Bichette, Dante, Boston	.268	46	187	179	28	48	92	15	1	9	32	0	0	1	7	0	27	1	0	5	.514	.299
Blake, Casey, Min.-Bal.	.300	5	12	10	2	3	4	1	0	0	1	0	0	0	2	0	5	0	0	0	.400	.417
Boone, Bret, Seattle	.125	2	8	8	0	1	1	0	0	0	0	0	0	0	0	0	0	0	0	1	.125	.125
Bradley, Milton, Cleveland†	.000	1	1	1	0	0	0	0	0	0	0	0	0	0	0	0	1	0	0	0	.000	.000
Branyan, Russell, Cleveland*	.143	7	16	14	4	2	2	0	0	0	0	0	0	0	2	0	7	0	0	0	.143	.250
Brown, Dee, Kansas City*	.263	20	83	80	11	21	33	3	0	3	14	0	0	0	3	1	12	0	2	3	.413	.289
Buchanan, Brian, Minnesota	.318	19	75	66	11	21	38	5	0	4	11	0	1	2	6	0	19	1	0	1	.576	.387
Buhner, Jay, Seattle	.000	4	10	9	0	0	0	0	0	0	0	0	0	1	0	0	2	0	0	0	.000	.100
Burke, Jamie, Anaheim	1.000	1	1	1	1	1	1	0	0	0	0	0	0	0	0	0	0	0	0	0	1.000	1.000
Burkhart, Morgan, Boston†	.167	6	18	18	2	3	7	1	0	1	2	0	0	0	0	0	6	0	0	0	.389	.167
Burks, Ellis, Cleveland	.278	102	436	371	73	103	199	25	1	23	60	0	7	3	55	2	67	3	1	13	.536	.369
Byrnes, Eric, Oakland	.000	5	4	4	0	0	0	0	0	0	0	0	0	0	0	0	1	0	0	0	.000	.000
Cabrera, Jolbert, Cleveland	.000	1	0	0	1	0	0	0	0	0	0	0	0	0	0	0	0	0	0	0	.000	.000
Cameron, Mike, Seattle	.250	1	4	4	0	1	1	0	0	0	0	0	0	0	0	0	1	0	0	0	.250	.250
Canseco, Jose, Chicago	.257	68	292	245	42	63	115	7	0	15	48	0	4	1	42	1	72	2	1	4	.469	.363
Cardona, Javier, Detroit	.500	1	2	2	1	1	2	1	0	0	2	0	0	0	0	0	0	0	0	0	1.000	.500
Catalanotto, Frank, Texas*	.444	5	18	18	4	8	8	0	0	0	0	0	0	0	0	0	3	3	0	0	.444	.444
Cedeno, Roger, Detroit†	.250	7	25	24	2	6	6	0	0	0	3	0	1	0	0	0	1	0	0	0	.333	.240
Chavez, Eric, Oakland*	.333	1	3	3	0	1	2	1	0	0	0	0	0	0	0	0	1	0	0	0	.667	.333
Christenson, Ryan, Oakland	.000	1	0	0	1	0	0	0	0	0	0	0	0	0	0	0	0	0	0	0	.000	.000
Clark, Jermaine, Detroit*	.000	2	0	0	1	0	0	0	0	0	0	0	0	0	0	0	0	0	0	0	.000	.000
Clark, Tony, Detroit†	.280	42	175	150	22	42	73	14	1	5	28	0	2	0	23	5	34	0	0	6	.487	.371
Coleman, Michael, New York	.111	3	10	9	0	1	1	0	0	0	2	0	1	0	0	0	6	0	0	0	.111	.100
Conine, Jeff, Baltimore	.154	12	48	39	5	6	6	0	0	0	4	0	1	0	8	0	9	0	1	2	.154	.292
Cordero, Wil, Cleveland	.211	12	44	38	6	8	14	3	0	1	2	0	0	1	5	0	6	0	0	0	.368	.318
Cordova, Marty, Cleveland	.333	7	30	30	5	10	19	0	0	3	8	0	0	0	0	0	9	0	0	1	.633	.333

Player, Team	Avg.	G	TPA	AB	R	H	TB	2B	3B	HR	RBI	SH	SF	HP	BB	IBB	SO	SB	CS	GDP	Slg.	OBP
Cox, Steve, Tampa Bay*	.313	4	17	16	3	5	6	1	0	0	0	0	0	0	1	0	3	0	0	0	.375	.353
Cruz, Jose, Toronto†	.000	1	1	1	0	0	0	0	0	0	0	0	0	0	0	0	0	0	0	0	.000	.000
Cuddyer, Mike, Minnesota	.500	1	3	2	0	1	2	1	0	0	0	0	0	0	1	0	1	0	0	0	1.000	.667
Curtis, Chad, Texas	.167	2	6	6	1	1	1	0	0	0	0	0	0	0	0	0	2	0	0	0	.167	.167
DaVanon, Jeff, Anaheim†	.182	6	12	11	1	2	5	0	0	1	2	0	0	0	1	0	5	0	1	0	.455	.250
DeShields, Delino, Baltimore*.	.160	8	28	25	4	4	8	1	0	1	3	0	0	0	3	0	4	1	0	2	.320	.250
Durham, Ray, Chicago†	.250	1	4	4	1	1	4	0	0	1	1	0	0	0	0	0	0	0	0	0	1.000	.250
Dye, Jermaine, Kansas City....	.214	4	16	14	1	3	6	0	0	1	3	0	1	0	1	0	5	0	0	0	.429	.250
Eckstein, David, Anaheim	.232	14	67	56	2	13	14	1	0	0	5	2	0	3	6	0	8	4	0	2	.250	.338
Encarnacion, Juan, Detroit	.333	2	3	3	1	1	4	0	0	1	2	0	0	0	0	0	0	0	0	0	1.333	.333
Erstad, Darin, Anaheim*	.000	4	18	15	0	0	0	0	0	0	0	0	0	0	3	0	6	1	1	1	.000	.167
Everett, Carl, Boston†	.200	7	36	30	3	6	10	1	0	1	3	0	0	3	3	1	12	0	0	0	.333	.333
Fasano, Sal, Oakland	.000	1	1	1	0	0	0	0	0	0	0	0	0	0	0	0	1	0	0	0	.000	.000
Fernandez, Jose, Anaheim	.095	7	23	21	1	2	3	1	0	0	0	0	0	0	2	0	7	0	1	0	.143	.174
Fernandez, Tony, Toronto†	.185	13	27	27	2	5	10	2	0	1	6	0	0	0	0	0	6	0	0	0	.370	.185
Fick, Robert, Detroit*	.304	8	28	23	2	7	13	0	0	2	4	0	2	0	3	0	3	0	0	0	.565	.357
Fletcher, Darrin, Toronto*	.000	1	2	1	1	0	0	0	0	0	0	0	0	0	1	0	0	0	0	0	.000	.500
Fryman, Travis, Cleveland	.167	2	6	6	0	1	2	1	0	0	0	0	0	0	0	0	2	0	0	0	.333	.167
Fullmer, Brad, Toronto*	.276	135	559	508	70	140	227	31	1	18	82	0	7	6	38	8	87	4	2	13	.447	.329
Galarraga, Andres, Texas	.257	39	161	144	23	37	66	11	0	6	24	0	5	12	0	37	0	0	5	.458	.335
Gant, Ron, Oakland	.277	21	57	47	11	13	19	3	0	1	6	0	1	0	9	0	15	1	0	0	.404	.386
Giambi, Jason, Oakland*	.316	17	70	57	12	18	42	6	0	6	12	0	0	1	12	3	9	0	0	3	.737	.443
Giambi, Jeremy, Oakland*	.278	61	238	198	36	55	89	16	0	6	33	0	0	3	37	0	42	0	0	4	.449	.399
Gibbons, Jay, Baltimore*	.222	28	111	99	11	22	37	3	0	4	11	0	0	2	10	0	21	0	0	5	.374	.306
Gil, Benji, Anaheim	.172	14	33	29	0	5	5	0	0	0	2	0	1	0	3	0	9	0	1	0	.172	.242
Gipson, Charles, Seattle	.000	11	2	2	5	0	0	0	0	0	0	0	0	0	0	0	1	0	0	0	.000	.000
Glaus, Troy, Anaheim	.143	2	9	7	1	1	1	0	0	0	1	0	0	0	2	0	1	1	0	0	.143	.333
Gonzalez, Juan, Cleveland	.392	21	91	79	20	31	59	4	0	8	33	0	3	1	8	2	15	0	0	0	.747	.440
Graffanino, Tony, Chicago	.000	3	2	1	0	0	0	0	0	0	0	0	0	0	1	0	0	0	0	0	.000	.500
Greene, Todd, New York	.200	2	5	5	1	1	2	1	0	0	0	0	0	0	0	0	1	0	0	0	.400	.200
Greer, Rusty, Texas*	.000	1	2	2	0	0	0	0	0	0	0	0	0	0	0	0	0	0	0	1	.000	.000
Grieve, Ben, Tampa Bay*	.353	32	138	119	18	42	64	7	0	5	24	0	0	5	14	1	28	4	0	2	.538	.442
Guillen, Carlos, Seattle†	.250	1	4	4	0	1	1	0	0	0	0	0	0	0	0	0	1	0	0	0	.250	.250
Guillen, Jose, Tampa Bay	.333	4	4	3	0	1	1	0	0	0	0	0	0	0	1	1	1	0	0	0	.333	.500
Halter, Shane, Detroit	.000	1	5	5	1	0	0	0	0	0	0	0	0	0	0	0	2	0	0	0	.000	.000
Harvey, Ken, Kansas City	.000	1	4	4	0	0	0	0	0	0	1	0	0	0	0	0	3	0	0	0	.000	.000
Hatteberg, Scott, Boston*	.240	8	28	25	2	6	7	1	0	0	4	0	0	0	3	0	3	0	0	1	.280	.321
Higginson, Bobby, Detroit*	.176	5	20	17	1	3	6	1	1	0	3	0	2	0	1	0	3	1	1	0	.353	.200
Hill, Glenallen, Anaheim	.136	16	66	66	4	9	12	0	0	1	2	0	0	0	0	0	20	0	0	3	.182	.136
Hillenbrand, Shea, Boston	.000	1	2	2	0	0	0	0	0	0	0	0	0	0	0	0	0	0	0	0	.000	.000
Hinch, A.J., Kansas City	.000	2	2	2	0	0	0	0	0	0	0	0	0	0	0	0	1	0	0	0	.000	.000
Hocking, Denny, Minnesota† .	.310	10	34	29	7	9	15	2	2	0	5	0	0	0	5	0	3	0	0	1	.517	.412
Hollins, Dave, Cleveland†	.200	2	7	5	0	1	1	0	0	0	0	0	1	0	1	0	2	0	0	0	.200	.333
Huff, Aubrey, Tampa Bay*	.273	20	78	77	11	21	32	5	0	2	11	0	0	1	1	1	11	0	0	5	.416	.282
Ibanez, Raul, Kansas City*	.288	33	133	118	19	34	55	6	3	3	22	0	1	0	14	0	20	0	0	1	.466	.361
Jackson, Ryan, Detroit*	.000	5	1	0	1	0	0	0	0	0	0	0	0	0	1	0	0	1	0	0	.000	1.000
Jaha, John, Oakland	.089	12	52	45	2	4	7	3	0	0	8	0	1	0	6	0	15	0	0	3	.156	.192
Javier, Stan, Seattle†	.200	2	6	5	2	1	1	0	0	0	0	0	0	0	1	0	1	0	0	0	.200	.333
Jennings, Robin, Oakland*	.000	2	2	2	0	0	0	0	0	0	0	0	0	0	0	0	0	0	0	0	.000	.000
Johnson, Nick, New York*	.000	6	24	19	2	0	0	0	0	0	0	0	0	1	4	0	3	0	0	1	.000	.208
Johnson, Russ, Tampa Bay	.143	2	7	7	0	1	1	0	0	0	0	0	0	0	0	0	2	0	0	0	.143	.143
Jones, Jacque, Minnesota*	.250	5	5	4	0	1	1	0	0	0	0	0	1	0	0	0	2	0	0	0	.250	.250
Joyner, Wally, Anaheim*	.346	9	31	26	3	9	13	1	0	1	3	0	0	0	5	0	5	0	1	0	.500	.452
Justice, David, New York*	.228	85	344	298	47	68	130	12	1	16	43	0	3	0	43	4	70	0	1	6	.436	.323
Kapler, Gabe, Texas	.000	1	5	3	0	0	0	0	0	0	0	0	0	0	2	0	1	0	0	0	.000	.400
Kennedy, Adam, Anaheim*	.267	5	17	15	0	4	5	1	0	0	1	1	0	0	1	0	5	0	0	0	.333	.313
Kielty, Bobby, Minnesota†	.000	1	1	1	0	0	0	0	0	0	0	0	0	0	0	0	1	0	0	0	.000	.000
Kinkade, Mike, Baltimore	.214	10	29	28	1	6	6	0	0	0	1	0	0	0	1	0	6	0	0	1	.214	.241
Knoblauch, Chuck, New York .	.250	24	113	92	16	23	36	5	1	2	15	1	2	6	12	0	20	6	3	1	.391	.366
Konerko, Paul, Chicago	.293	11	46	41	5	12	17	2	0	1	3	0	0	1	4	1	10	0	0	0	.415	.370
Koskie, Corey, Minnesota*	.000	2	9	8	0	0	0	0	0	0	0	0	0	0	1	0	1	0	0	0	.000	.111
Lampkin, Tom, Seattle*	.000	1	1	1	1	0	0	0	0	0	0	0	0	0	0	0	0	0	0	0	.000	.000
Lawton, Matt, Minnesota*	.241	7	34	29	5	7	9	2	0	0	3	0	0	0	5	0	1	1	1	1	.310	.353
LeCroy, Matt, Minnesota	.455	9	34	33	5	15	29	5	0	3	11	0	0	1	0	0	6	0	1	0	.879	.471
Lee, Carlos, Chicago	.286	17	66	63	8	18	28	1	0	3	14	0	0	0	3	1	10	0	0	3	.444	.318
Lewis, Darren, Boston	.333	6	3	3	2	1	4	0	0	1	2	0	0	0	0	0	1	0	0	0	1.333	.333
Liefer, Jeff, Chicago*	.172	10	37	29	3	5	6	1	0	0	3	0	1	0	7	0	7	0	0	1	.207	.324
Lopez, Luis, Toronto	.091	4	11	11	1	1	4	0	0	1	1	0	0	0	0	0	2	0	0	2	.364	.091
Macias, Jose, Detroit†	1.000	2	2	2	0	2	2	0	0	0	0	0	0	0	0	0	0	0	0	0	1.000	1.000
Magee, Wendell, Detroit	.273	11	27	22	6	6	12	3	0	1	1	0	0	0	5	0	4	0	0	1	.545	.407
Martin, Al, Seattle*	.326	16	51	43	11	14	24	4	0	2	9	0	1	0	7	0	6	1	0	0	.558	.412
Martinez, Edgar, Seattle	.309	127	573	463	79	143	251	40	1	22	115	0	9	9	92	8	88	4	1	11	.542	.426
Martinez, Tino, New York*	.444	3	10	9	2	4	7	0	0	1	3	0	0	1	0	0	3	0	0	0	.778	.500
Maxwell, Jason, Minnesota	.000	7	3	3	1	0	0	0	0	0	0	0	0	0	0	0	1	0	0	0	.000	.000
McCarty, Dave, Kansas City	.222	7	11	9	1	2	3	1	0	0	1	0	1	0	1	0	2	0	0	0	.333	.273
McCracken, Quinton, Min.†	.219	9	35	32	4	7	11	2	1	0	1	1	0	0	2	0	8	0	1	1	.344	.265
McGriff, Fred, Tampa Bay*	.284	17	74	67	7	19	31	6	0	2	8	0	0	0	7	1	15	0	0	2	.463	.351
McLemore, Mark, Seattle†	.400	2	5	5	0	2	2	0	0	0	0	0	0	0	0	0	1	0	0	0	.400	.400
McMillon, Billy, Det.-Oak.*	.182	4	12	11	0	2	2	0	0	0	1	0	0	1	0	0	5	0	0	0	.182	.250
Menechino, Frank, Oakland	.000	1	1	1	0	0	0	0	0	0	0	0	0	0	0	0	1	0	0	0	.000	.000
Mientkiewicz, Doug, Min.*	.333	2	10	9	2	3	4	1	0	0	0	0	0	0	1	0	0	0	0	0	.444	.400
Mirabelli, Doug, Tex.-Bos	.000	2	2	2	0	0	0	0	0	0	0	0	0	0	0	0	1	0	0	0	.000	.000
Mohr, Dustan, Minnesota	.000	1	1	1	0	0	0	0	0	0	0	0	0	0	0	0	0	0	0	0	.000	.000
Molina, Ben, Anaheim	.333	1	3	3	0	1	1	0	0	0	0	0	0	0	0	0	1	0	0	0	.333	.333
Monroe, Craig, Texas	.000	1	1	1	0	0	0	0	0	0	0	0	0	0	0	0	0	0	0	0	.000	.000

Player, Team	Avg.	G	TPA	AB	R	H	TB	2B	3B	HR	RBI	SH	SF	HP	BB	IBB	SO	SB	CS	GDP	Slg.	OBP
Myers, Greg, Bal.-Oak.*	.262	13	49	42	8	11	22	2	0	3	13	0	0	0	7	0	13	0	0	2	.524	.367
Nieves, Jose, Anaheim	.500	4	2	2	0	1	1	0	0	0	0	0	0	0	0	0	0	0	0	1	.500	.500
Nixon, Trot, Boston*	.000	1	0	0	1	0	0	0	0	0	0	0	0	0	0	0	0	0	0	0	.000	.000
O'Leary, Troy, Boston*	.231	4	14	13	3	3	6	0	0	1	2	0	0	0	1	0	4	0	0	0	.462	.286
O'Neill, Paul, New York*	.263	6	22	19	3	5	12	1	0	2	5	0	0	0	3	0	2	0	0	0	.632	.364
Ordaz, Luis, Kansas City	.000	1	1	1	0	0	0	0	0	0	0	0	0	0	0	0	0	0	0	1	.000	.000
Ordonez, Magglio, Chicago	.250	3	13	12	0	3	3	0	0	0	0	0	0	0	1	0	0	1	0	0	.250	.308
Ortiz, David, Minnesota	.230	80	315	278	40	64	125	14	1	15	40	1	1	1	34	7	63	0	0	6	.450	.315
Ortiz, Hector, Kansas City	.000	1	1	1	0	0	0	0	0	0	0	0	0	0	0	0	1	0	0	0	.000	.000
Ortiz, Jose, Oakland	.000	1	3	3	0	0	0	0	0	0	0	0	0	0	0	0	1	0	0	0	.000	.000
Palmeiro, Orlando, Anaheim*.	.208	30	94	77	8	16	18	2	0	0	11	2	3	0	12	1	8	1	2	1	.234	.304
Palmeiro, Rafael, Texas*	.286	46	200	175	29	50	117	13	0	18	38	0	2	3	20	2	22	0	0	3	.669	.365
Palmer, Dean, Detroit	.222	57	246	216	34	48	92	11	0	11	40	0	0	3	27	0	59	4	1	3	.426	.317
Pena, Carlos, Texas*	.000	1	5	5	0	0	0	0	0	0	0	0	0	0	0	0	2	0	0	0	.000	.000
Perez, Robert, New York	.000	1	5	4	1	0	0	0	0	0	0	0	0	0	1	0	1	0	0	0	.000	.200
Perry, Herbert, Chicago	.281	10	36	32	5	9	16	1	0	2	6	0	0	1	3	1	9	1	1	1	.500	.361
Piatt, Adam, Oakland	.333	1	4	3	0	1	1	0	0	0	1	0	0	0	1	0	1	0	0	0	.333	.500
Pickering, Calvin, Boston*	.000	2	5	3	0	0	0	0	0	0	0	0	0	0	2	0	2	0	0	0	.000	.400
Pierzynski, A.J., Minnesota*.	.400	1	5	5	2	2	2	0	0	0	1	0	0	0	0	0	2	0	0	0	.400	.400
Porter, Bo, Texas	.000	2	1	1	2	0	0	0	0	0	0	0	0	0	0	0	1	0	0	0	.000	.000
Posada, Jorge, New York†	.174	6	27	23	1	4	8	1	0	1	5	0	0	1	3	0	8	1	0	0	.348	.296
Quinn, Mark, Kansas City	.320	18	77	75	9	24	38	6	1	2	8	0	1	0	1	0	10	2	3	2	.507	.325
Raines, Tim, Baltimore†	.000	1	2	1	0	0	0	0	0	0	0	1	0	0	0	0	0	0	0	0	.000	.000
Ramirez, Manny, Boston	.333	87	378	327	52	109	199	17	2	23	80	0	1	7	43	18	86	0	0	6	.609	.421
Randa, Joe, Kansas City	.259	14	62	54	7	14	27	4	0	3	15	0	1	0	7	0	5	0	0	1	.500	.339
Richard, Chris, Baltimore*	.280	20	84	75	13	21	36	7	1	2	12	0	1	1	7	1	23	3	1	1	.480	.345
Ripken, Cal Jr., Baltimore	.241	14	58	54	5	13	14	1	0	0	4	0	0	0	4	0	8	0	0	1	.259	.293
Roberts, Brian, Baltimore†	.333	7	28	24	5	8	10	2	0	0	2	1	1	0	2	0	3	1	1	0	.417	.370
Roberts, Dave, Cleveland*	.000	2	0	0	0	0	0	0	0	0	0	0	0	0	0	0	0	0	1	0	.000	.000
Rodriguez, Alex, Texas	.000	1	4	4	0	0	0	0	0	0	0	0	0	0	0	0	2	0	0	0	.000	.000
Rodriguez, Henry, New York*.	.000	1	4	4	0	0	0	0	0	0	0	0	0	0	0	0	3	0	0	0	.000	.000
Rodriguez, Ivan, Texas	.350	5	20	20	5	7	11	1	0	1	2	0	0	0	0	0	4	1	0	1	.550	.350
Rolls, Damian, Tampa Bay	.000	6	1	1	2	0	0	0	0	0	0	0	0	0	0	0	0	0	0	0	.000	.000
Ryan, Rob, Oakland*	.000	1	1	1	0	0	0	0	0	0	0	0	0	0	0	0	1	0	0	0	.000	.000
Saenz, Olmedo, Oakland	.227	58	206	181	21	41	69	13	0	5	16	1	3	11	10	0	43	0	1	5	.381	.302
Salmon, Tim, Anaheim	.222	12	52	45	6	10	21	2	0	3	7	0	0	0	7	3	13	0	0	1	.467	.327
Santangelo, F.P., Oakland†	.500	2	2	2	0	1	1	0	0	0	1	0	0	0	0	0	0	0	0	0	.500	.500
Seabol, Scott, New York	.000	1	1	1	0	0	0	0	0	0	0	0	0	0	0	0	0	0	0	0	.000	.000
Segui, David, Baltimore†	.278	16	65	54	11	15	23	3	1	1	8	0	0	1	10	0	16	0	1	1	.426	.400
Sierra, Ruben, Texas†	.273	50	219	205	31	56	113	10	1	15	34	0	2	0	12	0	34	2	0	12	.551	.311
Simmons, Brian, Toronto†	.400	2	5	5	1	2	2	0	0	0	0	0	0	0	0	0	1	0	0	0	.400	.400
Simon, Randall, Detroit*	.291	29	110	103	11	30	45	4	1	3	19	0	1	0	6	1	12	0	0	3	.437	.327
Singleton, Chris, Chicago*	.000	2	0	0	0	0	0	0	0	0	0	0	0	0	0	0	0	2	0	0	.000	.000
Sojo, Luis, New York	.000	1	4	4	0	0	0	0	0	0	0	0	0	0	0	0	1	0	0	0	.000	.000
Soriano, Alfonso, New York	.400	2	5	5	1	2	3	1	0	0	0	0	0	0	0	0	2	0	0	0	.600	.400
Spencer, Shane, New York	.222	14	54	45	7	10	16	1	1	1	7	0	1	1	7	0	4	1	1	0	.356	.333
Spiezio, Scott, Anaheim†	.164	20	62	55	5	9	11	2	0	0	5	0	1	1	5	1	8	0	0	2	.200	.242
Sprague, Ed, Seattle	.438	9	20	16	2	7	9	2	0	0	6	0	0	0	4	1	3	0	0	3	.563	.550
Stewart, Shannon, Toronto	.306	13	54	49	6	15	25	2	1	2	6	0	1	0	4	0	4	0	0	0	.510	.352
Suzuki, Ichiro, Seattle*	.353	4	18	17	4	6	7	1	0	0	1	0	0	0	1	0	1	3	0	0	.412	.389
Sweeney, Mike, Kansas City	.225	38	163	142	16	32	56	9	0	5	21	1	3	0	17	1	15	4	0	6	.394	.302
Taubensee, Eddie, Cleveland*.	.273	5	12	11	3	3	6	0	0	1	1	0	0	0	1	0	1	0	0	0	.545	.333
Thomas, Frank, Chicago	.259	16	68	58	8	15	30	3	0	4	10	0	1	0	9	2	11	0	0	0	.517	.353
Thome, Jim, Cleveland*	.333	6	22	15	3	5	9	1	0	1	1	0	0	1	6	2	5	0	0	0	.600	.545
Valdez, Mario, Oakland*	.333	12	32	27	2	9	9	0	0	0	4	0	0	1	4	0	8	0	0	0	.333	.438
Vaughn, Greg, Tampa Bay	.216	76	325	283	37	61	101	13	0	9	37	0	0	2	40	3	75	5	4	5	.357	.317
Velarde, Randy, Tex.-N.Y.	.231	11	44	39	3	9	14	2	0	1	3	0	0	0	5	0	12	1	0	1	.359	.318
Williams, Bernie, New York†	.250	1	5	4	0	1	1	0	0	0	0	0	0	0	1	0	0	0	0	1	.250	.400
Williams, Gerald, New York	.000	7	3	1	1	0	0	0	0	0	0	1	1	0	1	0	0	0	1	1	.000	.500
Wilson, Enrique, New York†	.000	1	3	3	0	0	0	0	0	0	0	0	0	0	0	0	1	0	0	0	.000	.000
Winn, Randy, Tampa Bay†	.125	3	8	8	0	1	1	0	0	0	0	0	0	0	0	0	1	1	0	0	.125	.125
Woodward, Chris, Toronto	.000	1	0	0	0	0	0	0	0	0	0	0	0	0	1	0	0	0	0	0	.000	1.000
Wooten, Shawn, Anaheim	.242	27	95	91	5	22	27	5	0	0	7	0	1	2	1	0	23	1	0	3	.297	.263
Zaun, Gregg, Kansas City†	.286	2	8	7	1	2	2	0	0	0	1	0	0	0	1	0	0	0	0	0	.286	.375

DESIGNATED HITTERS WITH TWO OR MORE TEAMS

Player, Team	Avg.	G	TPA	AB	R	H	TB	2B	3B	HR	RBI	SH	SF	HP	BB	IBB	SO	SB	CS	GDP	Slg.	OBP
Blake, Casey, Minnesota	.300	4	12	10	1	3	4	1	0	0	1	0	0	0	2	0	5	0	0	0	.400	.417
Blake, Casey, Baltimore	.000	1	0	0	1	0	0	0	0	0	0	0	0	0	0	0	0	0	0	0	.000	.000
McMillon, Billy, Detroit*	.143	3	8	7	0	1	1	0	0	0	1	0	0	1	0	0	3	0	0	0	.143	.250
McMillon, Billy, Oakland*	.250	1	4	4	0	1	1	0	0	0	0	0	0	0	0	0	2	0	0	0	.250	.250
Mirabelli, Doug, Texas	.000	1	1	1	0	0	0	0	0	0	0	0	0	0	0	0	0	0	0	0	.000	.000
Mirabelli, Doug, Boston	.000	1	1	1	0	0	0	0	0	0	0	0	0	0	0	0	1	0	0	0	.000	.000
Myers, Greg, Baltimore*	.289	11	45	38	8	11	22	2	0	3	13	0	0	0	7	0	10	0	0	2	.579	.400
Myers, Greg, Oakland*	.000	2	4	4	0	0	0	0	0	0	0	0	0	0	0	0	3	0	0	0	.000	.000
Velarde, Randy, Texas	.269	6	29	26	3	7	11	1	0	1	3	0	0	0	3	0	9	0	0	1	.423	.345
Velarde, Randy, New York	.154	5	15	13	0	2	3	1	0	0	0	0	0	0	2	0	3	1	0	0	.231	.267

The following designated hitters, each of whom appeared in at least one game, had no plate appearances, runs scored or stolen base attempts: Bellinger, Clay, New York; Sadler, Donnie, Kansas City; Vazquez, Ramon, Seattle.

PINCH-HITTING

TEAM

Team	Avg.	G	TPA	AB	R	H	TB	2B	3B	HR	RBI	SH	SF	HP	BB	IBB	SO	SB	CS	GDP	Slg.	OBP
Seattle	.320	80	118	100	20	32	56	10	1	4	25	1	2	3	12	2	23	0	0	3	.560	.402
Baltimore	.275	63	81	69	13	19	26	1	0	2	7	0	0	0	12	0	15	3	0	2	.377	.383
Toronto	.268	86	127	112	11	30	44	6	1	2	17	0	2	2	11	1	18	0	1	4	.393	.339
Anaheim	.245	85	113	102	16	25	42	3	1	4	15	1	2	1	7	1	28	1	1	4	.412	.295
Cleveland	.242	68	105	91	10	22	35	1	0	4	14	2	0	1	11	0	24	0	0	1	.385	.330
Minnesota	.236	75	125	106	14	25	45	3	1	5	17	2	2	0	15	3	30	1	1	2	.425	.325
Detroit	.221	73	91	77	8	17	26	4	1	1	11	2	0	0	12	1	23	3	0	5	.338	.326
Texas	.219	71	106	96	9	21	35	6	1	2	18	0	1	0	9	1	25	0	0	2	.365	.283
New York	.217	61	76	60	8	13	23	1	0	3	9	3	0	0	13	3	12	4	0	3	.383	.356
Oakland	.204	91	128	113	10	23	33	4	0	2	18	3	0	1	11	0	39	0	0	1	.292	.280
Tampa Bay	.194	58	80	67	5	13	19	3	0	1	8	1	0	0	12	2	19	0	0	2	.284	.316
Kansas City	.175	79	108	97	10	17	33	1	3	3	8	0	1	0	10	0	30	1	0	2	.340	.250
Chicago	.170	67	98	88	7	15	20	2	0	1	10	0	1	1	8	0	28	1	1	2	.227	.245
Boston	.148	67	98	88	7	13	21	2	0	2	7	0	0	4	6	1	29	0	0	3	.239	.235
Totals	.225	1024	1454	1266	148	285	458	47	9	36	184	15	11	13	149	15	343	14	4	35	.362	.311

TOP PINCH-HITTERS

Minimum 20 at-bats. *Lefthanded batter. †Switch-hitter.

Player, Team	Avg.	G	TPA	AB	R	H	TB	2B	3B	HR	RBI	SH	SF	HP	BB	IBB	SO	SB	CS	GDP	Slg.	OBP
Fernandez, Tony, Toronto†	.381	45	45	42	5	16	22	3	0	1	10	0	1	1	1	0	4	0	1	2	.524	.400
Palmeiro, Orlando, Anaheim*	.269	28	27	26	7	7	12	2	0	1	6	0	0	0	1	0	3	1	0	1	.462	.296
Saenz, Olmedo, Oakland	.240	28	28	25	3	6	10	1	0	1	4	0	0	0	1	0	7	0	0	0	.400	.269
Alicea, Luis, Kansas City†	.200	21	21	20	3	4	10	1	1	1	1	0	0	0	1	0	5	1	0	0	.500	.238
Ibanez, Raul, Kansas City*	.174	26	26	23	2	4	7	0	0	1	4	0	0	0	3	0	7	0	0	0	.304	.269
Hocking, Denny, Minnesota†	.167	29	29	24	1	4	9	0	1	1	6	1	1	0	3	0	8	0	0	1	.375	.250
Simmons, Brian, Toronto†	.167	27	27	24	1	4	7	3	0	0	2	0	1	1	1	0	7	0	0	0	.292	.222
McCarty, Dave, Kansas City	.080	29	29	25	1	2	2	0	0	0	1	0	1	0	3	0	8	0	0	0	.080	.172

ALL PINCH-HITTERS

*Lefthanded batter. †Switch-hitter.

Player, Team	Avg.	G	TPA	AB	R	H	TB	2B	3B	HR	RBI	SH	SF	HP	BB	IBB	SO	SB	CS	GDP	Slg.	OBP
Abad, Andy, Oakland*	.000	1	1	1	0	0	0	0	0	0	0	0	0	0	0	0	0	0	0	0	.000	.000
Alcantara, Israel, Boston	.500	2	2	2	0	1	1	0	0	0	0	0	0	0	0	0	1	0	0	0	.500	.500
Alicea, Luis, Kansas City†	.200	21	21	20	3	4	10	1	1	1	1	0	0	0	1	0	5	1	0	0	.500	.238
Allen, Chad, Minnesota	.167	7	7	6	0	1	1	0	0	0	0	0	0	0	1	0	2	0	0	0	.167	.286
Alomar, Sandy Jr., Chicago	.250	4	4	4	0	1	1	0	0	0	0	0	0	0	0	0	1	0	0	0	.250	.250
Anderson, Brady, Baltimore*	.167	6	6	6	2	1	1	0	0	0	0	0	0	0	0	0	1	0	0	0	.167	.167
Baines, Harold, Chicago*	.000	10	8	8	0	0	0	0	0	0	0	0	0	0	0	0	5	0	0	0	.000	.000
Barnes, Larry, Anaheim*	.000	1	1	1	0	0	0	0	0	0	0	0	0	0	0	0	0	0	0	0	.000	.000
Batista, Tony, Baltimore	.500	3	2	2	1	1	4	0	0	1	3	0	0	0	0	0	0	0	0	0	2.000	.500
Bell, David, Seattle	.000	3	3	2	1	0	0	0	0	0	0	0	0	0	1	1	0	0	0	0	.000	.333
Bellhorn, Mark, Oakland	.000	4	3	3	0	0	0	0	0	0	0	0	0	0	0	0	2	0	0	0	.000	.000
Bellinger, Clay, New York	.500	3	3	2	0	1	1	0	0	0	0	0	0	1	0	0	0	0	0	1	.500	.500
Bichette, Dante, Boston	.091	11	11	11	0	1	1	0	0	0	1	0	0	0	0	0	7	0	0	0	.091	.091
Bigbie, Larry, Baltimore*	.429	8	8	7	2	3	3	0	0	0	1	0	0	0	1	0	3	0	0	0	.429	.500
Blake, Casey, Minnesota	.000	2	2	2	0	0	0	0	0	0	0	0	0	0	0	0	0	0	0	0	.000	.000
Boone, Bret, Seattle	.333	3	3	3	1	1	4	0	0	1	3	0	0	0	0	0	1	0	0	0	1.333	.333
Borders, Pat, Seattle	1.000	1	1	1	0	1	1	0	0	0	0	0	0	0	0	0	0	0	0	0	1.000	1.000
Bradley, Milton, Cleveland†	.000	1	1	1	0	0	0	0	0	0	0	0	0	0	0	0	1	0	0	0	.000	.000
Bragg, Darren, New York*	.000	2	2	2	0	0	0	0	0	0	0	0	0	0	0	0	1	0	0	0	.000	.000
Branyan, Russell, Cleveland*	.091	11	11	11	1	1	1	0	0	0	0	0	0	0	0	0	6	0	0	0	.091	.091
Brown, Dee, Kansas City*	.200	5	5	5	0	1	1	0	0	0	0	0	0	0	0	0	3	0	0	0	.200	.200
Buchanan, Brian, Minnesota	.400	11	11	10	3	4	11	0	0	2	3	0	0	0	1	0	1	0	1	0	1.100	.455
Buhner, Jay, Seattle	.000	5	5	4	0	0	0	0	0	0	0	0	0	0	1	0	2	0	0	1	.000	.200
Burke, Jamie, Anaheim	.333	3	3	3	1	1	1	0	0	0	0	0	0	0	0	0	1	0	0	0	.333	.333
Burkhart, Morgan, Boston†	.000	3	3	3	0	0	0	0	0	0	0	0	0	0	0	0	2	0	0	0	.000	.000
Burks, Ellis, Cleveland	.000	3	3	1	0	0	0	0	0	0	0	0	0	0	2	0	1	0	0	0	.000	.667
Byrnes, Eric, Oakland	.667	3	3	3	0	2	2	0	0	0	0	0	0	0	0	0	0	0	0	0	.667	.667
Cabrera, Jolbert, Cleveland	.143	15	15	14	1	2	2	0	0	0	2	0	0	0	1	0	1	0	0	0	.143	.200
Cameron, Mike, Seattle	1.000	1	1	1	0	1	2	1	0	0	0	0	0	0	0	0	0	0	0	0	2.000	1.000
Caminiti, Ken, Texas†	.000	2	2	2	0	0	0	0	0	0	0	0	0	0	0	0	0	0	0	0	.000	.000
Canseco, Jose, Chicago	.000	6	6	5	0	0	0	0	0	0	0	0	0	0	1	0	2	0	0	0	.000	.167
Cardona, Javier, Detroit	.500	2	2	2	1	1	2	1	0	0	2	0	0	0	0	0	0	0	0	0	1.000	.500
Catalanotto, Frank, Texas*	.316	25	24	19	4	6	10	2	1	0	4	0	0	0	5	1	2	0	0	0	.526	.458
Chavez, Eric, Oakland*	.333	3	3	3	1	1	1	0	0	0	0	0	0	0	0	0	1	0	0	0	.333	.333
Christensen, McKay, Chi.*	.000	1	1	1	0	0	0	0	0	0	0	0	0	0	0	0	0	0	0	0	.000	.000
Christenson, Ryan, Oakland	.000	2	2	2	0	0	0	0	0	0	0	0	0	0	0	0	1	0	0	0	.000	.000
Clark, Tony, Detroit†	.250	10	10	8	0	2	3	1	0	0	1	0	0	0	2	0	3	0	0	0	.375	.400
Clayton, Royce, Chicago	.000	1	1	1	0	0	0	0	0	0	0	0	0	0	0	0	0	0	0	0	.000	.000
Conine, Jeff, Baltimore	.000	2	2	1	1	0	0	0	0	0	0	0	0	0	1	0	0	0	0	0	.000	.500
Cordero, Wil, Cleveland	.400	12	12	10	1	4	4	0	0	0	1	0	0	1	1	0	3	0	0	0	.400	.500
Cordova, Marty, Cleveland	.300	11	11	10	0	3	3	0	0	0	2	0	0	0	1	0	2	0	0	0	.300	.364

Player, Team	Avg.	G	TPA	AB	R	H	TB	2B	3B	HR	RBI	SH	SF	HP	BB	IBB	SO	SB	CS	GDP	Slg.	OBP
Cox, Steve, Tampa Bay*	.083	18	16	12	0	1	2	1	0	0	2	0	0	0	4	0	3	0	0	1	.167	.313
Crede, Joe, Chicago	.250	4	4	4	0	1	1	0	0	0	1	0	0	0	0	0	2	0	0	0	.250	.250
Cruz, Deivi, Detroit	.000	1	1	1	0	0	0	0	0	0	0	0	0	0	0	0	0	0	0	0	.000	.000
Cruz, Jacob, Cleveland*	.125	10	10	8	0	1	1	0	0	0	0	0	0	0	2	0	1	0	0	0	.125	.300
Cruz, Jose, Toronto†	.500	5	5	4	2	2	5	0	0	1	1	0	0	0	1	0	1	0	0	0	1.250	.600
Curtis, Chad, Texas	.000	3	3	2	1	0	0	0	0	0	0	0	0	0	1	0	1	0	0	0	.000	.333
Damon, Johnny, Oakland*	.000	1	1	1	0	0	0	0	0	0	0	0	0	0	0	0	1	0	0	0	.000	.000
Daubach, Brian, Boston*	.200	5	5	5	0	1	2	1	0	0	0	0	0	0	0	0	3	0	0	0	.400	.200
DaVanon, Jeff, Anaheim†	.200	5	5	5	0	1	1	0	0	0	0	0	0	0	0	0	2	0	0	1	.200	.200
Delgado, Carlos, Toronto*	.000	1	1	0	0	0	0	0	0	0	0	0	0	0	1	0	0	0	0	0	.000	1.000
Delgado, Wilson, K.C.†	.250	5	5	4	1	1	1	0	0	0	0	0	0	0	1	0	2	0	0	0	.250	.400
DeShields, Delino, Baltimore*	.500	3	3	2	0	1	1	0	0	0	0	0	0	0	1	1	1	0	0	0	.500	.667
Diaz, Einar, Cleveland	.000	3	3	2	0	0	0	0	0	0	0	0	1	0	0	0	1	0	0	0	.000	.000
Dransfeldt, Kelly, Texas	.000	1	1	1	0	0	0	0	0	0	0	0	0	0	0	0	0	0	0	0	.000	.000
Durham, Ray, Chicago†	.000	3	3	3	0	0	0	0	0	0	0	0	0	0	0	0	0	0	0	0	.000	.000
Eckstein, David, Anaheim	.500	2	2	2	1	1	1	0	0	0	0	0	0	0	0	0	0	0	0	0	.500	.500
Encarnacion, Juan, Detroit	.000	2	2	2	0	0	0	0	0	0	0	0	0	0	0	0	2	0	0	0	.000	.000
Everett, Carl, Boston†	.667	3	3	3	0	2	2	0	0	0	0	0	0	0	0	0	1	0	0	0	.667	.667
Fasano, Sal, Oakland	.000	2	2	2	0	0	0	0	0	0	0	0	0	0	0	0	2	0	0	0	.000	.000
Fernandez, Jose, Anaheim	.000	3	3	3	0	0	0	0	0	0	0	0	0	0	0	0	2	0	0	0	.000	.000
Fernandez, Tony, Toronto†	.381	45	45	42	5	16	22	3	0	1	10	0	1	1	1	0	4	0	1	2	.524	.400
Fick, Robert, Detroit*	.188	20	19	16	0	3	4	1	0	0	3	0	0	3	0	4	0	2	0	0	.250	.316
Fletcher, Darrin, Toronto*	.182	11	11	11	0	2	2	0	0	0	1	0	0	0	0	0	0	0	0	2	.182	.182
Frye, Jeff, Toronto	.000	4	4	3	1	0	0	0	0	0	0	0	0	0	1	0	0	0	0	0	.000	.250
Fryman, Travis, Cleveland	.000	1	1	0	0	0	0	0	0	0	0	0	0	0	1	0	0	0	0	0	.000	1.000
Fullmer, Brad, Toronto*	.200	10	10	10	1	2	4	0	1	0	1	0	0	0	0	0	1	0	0	0	.400	.200
Galarraga, Andres, Texas	.333	9	9	9	0	3	3	0	0	0	2	0	0	0	0	0	2	0	0	2	.333	.333
Gant, Ron, Oakland	.333	13	13	12	2	4	4	0	0	0	1	0	0	0	1	0	3	0	0	0	.333	.385
Giambi, Jason, Oakland*	.000	1	1	1	0	0	0	0	0	0	0	0	0	0	0	0	0	0	0	0	.000	.000
Giambi, Jeremy, Oakland*	.250	20	20	16	1	4	9	2	0	1	6	1	0	0	3	0	3	0	0	1	.563	.368
Gibbons, Jay, Baltimore*	.300	12	12	10	2	3	6	0	0	1	2	0	0	0	2	0	2	0	0	0	.600	.417
Gil, Benji, Anaheim	.083	17	15	12	1	1	1	0	0	0	0	0	0	0	3	0	5	0	0	0	.083	.267
Gipson, Charles, Seattle	.500	5	5	2	2	1	2	1	0	0	2	0	1	1	1	0	1	0	0	0	1.000	.600
Graffanino, Tony, Chicago	.385	18	16	13	2	5	8	0	0	1	4	0	0	0	3	0	1	1	0	0	.615	.500
Greer, Rusty, Texas*	.000	2	2	2	0	0	0	0	0	0	0	0	0	0	0	0	1	0	0	0	.000	.000
Grieve, Ben, Tampa Bay*	.000	2	2	2	0	0	0	0	0	0	0	0	0	0	0	0	2	0	0	0	.000	.000
Guillen, Carlos, Seattle†	.333	6	6	6	1	2	3	1	0	0	0	0	0	0	0	0	2	0	0	0	.500	.333
Guillen, Jose, Tampa Bay	.250	5	5	4	0	1	1	0	0	0	0	0	0	1	1	0	2	0	0	0	.250	.400
Guzman, Cristian, Min.†	.000	2	2	2	0	0	0	0	0	0	0	0	0	0	0	0	2	0	0	0	.000	.000
Hall, Toby, Tampa Bay	.000	3	3	3	0	0	0	0	0	0	0	0	0	0	0	0	0	0	0	0	.000	.000
Harris, Willie, Baltimore*	.000	1	1	1	0	0	0	0	0	0	0	0	0	0	0	0	1	0	0	0	.000	.000
Haselman, Bill, Texas	.000	1	1	1	0	0	0	0	0	0	0	0	0	0	0	0	0	0	0	0	.000	.000
Hatteberg, Scott, Boston*	.000	20	20	17	1	0	0	0	0	0	0	0	0	0	3	0	4	0	0	1	.000	.150
Hernandez, Ramon, Oakland	.333	3	3	3	0	1	1	0	0	0	0	0	0	0	0	0	1	0	0	0	.333	.333
Hillenbrand, Shea, Boston	.000	5	5	4	0	0	0	0	0	0	0	0	0	1	1	0	1	0	0	1	.000	.200
Hinch, A.J., Kansas City	.000	2	2	2	0	0	0	0	0	0	0	0	0	0	0	0	1	0	0	0	.000	.000
Hocking, Denny, Minnesota†	.167	29	29	24	1	4	9	0	1	1	6	1	1	0	3	0	8	0	1	1	.375	.250
Hoover, Paul, Tampa Bay	1.000	1	1	1	1	1	1	0	0	0	0	0	0	0	0	0	0	0	0	0	1.000	1.000
Hubbard, Trenidad, K.C.	.500	2	2	2	1	1	3	0	1	0	0	0	0	0	0	0	1	0	0	0	1.500	.500
Huff, Aubrey, Tampa Bay*	.000	1	1	1	0	0	0	0	0	0	0	0	0	0	0	0	0	0	0	0	.000	.000
Hunter, Torii, Minnesota	.000	1	1	1	0	0	0	0	0	0	0	0	0	0	0	0	0	0	0	0	.000	.000
Ibanez, Raul, Kansas City*	.174	26	26	23	2	4	7	0	0	1	4	0	0	0	3	0	7	0	0	0	.304	.269
Jackson, Ryan, Detroit*	.333	12	12	12	2	4	4	0	0	0	1	0	0	0	0	0	5	1	0	0	.333	.333
Javier, Stan, Seattle†	.294	19	19	17	3	5	6	1	0	0	1	0	0	0	2	0	3	0	0	0	.353	.368
Jennings, Robin, Oakland*	.200	6	5	5	0	1	1	0	0	0	1	0	0	0	0	0	1	0	0	0	.200	.200
Johnson, Nick, New York*	.250	5	5	4	0	1	1	0	0	0	0	0	0	0	1	0	1	0	0	0	.250	.400
Johnson, Russ, Tampa Bay	.333	21	21	15	3	5	7	2	0	0	4	1	0	0	5	0	5	0	0	0	.467	.500
Jones, Jacque, Minnesota*	.294	21	18	17	2	5	8	0	0	1	1	1	0	0	0	0	5	1	0	0	.471	.294
Joyner, Wally, Anaheim*	.556	10	9	9	1	5	7	0	1	0	1	0	0	0	0	0	2	0	1	0	.778	.556
Justice, David, New York*	.000	3	3	2	1	0	0	0	0	0	0	0	0	0	1	0	0	0	0	0	.000	.333
Kapler, Gabe, Texas	.500	2	2	2	0	1	1	0	0	0	1	0	0	0	0	0	0	0	0	0	.500	.500
Kennedy, Adam, Anaheim*	.000	7	7	5	0	0	0	0	0	0	1	1	1	0	0	0	2	0	0	1	.000	.000
Kielty, Bobby, Minnesota†	.200	6	6	5	1	1	1	0	0	0	0	0	0	0	1	0	2	0	0	0	.200	.333
Kinkade, Mike, Baltimore	.364	15	15	11	2	4	4	0	0	0	0	0	0	0	4	0	0	0	0	1	.364	.533
Knoblauch, Chuck, New York	.571	8	8	7	1	4	5	1	0	0	2	0	0	0	1	0	1	3	0	0	.714	.625
Konerko, Paul, Chicago	.000	1	1	1	0	0	0	0	0	0	0	0	0	0	0	0	0	0	0	0	.000	.000
Koskie, Corey, Minnesota*	.000	2	2	1	0	0	0	0	0	0	0	0	0	0	1	1	0	0	0	0	.000	.500
Laker, Tim, Cleveland	.000	3	3	3	0	0	0	0	0	0	0	0	0	0	0	0	2	0	0	0	.000	.000
Lamb, Mike, Texas*	.000	4	4	4	0	0	0	0	0	0	1	0	0	0	0	0	1	0	0	0	.000	.000
Lampkin, Tom, Seattle*	.100	12	12	10	2	1	1	0	0	0	0	0	0	1	1	0	2	0	0	0	.100	.250
Lansing, Mike, Boston	.333	4	4	3	2	1	1	0	0	0	0	0	0	0	1	0	1	0	0	0	.333	.500
Latham, Chris, Toronto†	.200	13	12	10	1	2	2	0	0	0	1	0	0	0	2	0	5	0	0	0	.200	.333
Lawton, Matt, Minnesota*	.500	6	6	4	1	2	2	0	0	0	0	0	0	0	2	0	0	0	0	1	.500	.667
LeCroy, Matt, Minnesota	.333	3	3	3	1	1	1	0	0	0	1	0	0	0	0	0	1	0	0	0	.333	.333
Ledee, Ricky, Texas*	.273	11	11	11	0	3	4	1	0	0	1	0	0	0	0	0	2	0	0	0	.364	.273
Lee, Carlos, Chicago	.167	6	6	6	0	1	1	0	0	0	1	0	0	0	0	0	1	0	0	1	.167	.167
Lewis, Darren, Boston	.667	3	3	3	0	2	3	1	0	0	0	0	0	0	0	0	0	0	0	0	1.000	.667
Lewis, Mark, Cleveland	.000	2	2	2	0	0	0	0	0	0	0	0	0	0	0	0	1	0	0	0	.000	.000
Liefer, Jeff, Chicago*	.100	11	10	10	0	1	2	1	0	0	1	0	0	0	0	0	2	0	0	0	.200	.100
Lofton, James, Boston†	.000	2	2	2	0	0	0	0	0	0	0	0	0	0	0	0	1	0	0	0	.000	.000
Lofton, Kenny, Cleveland*	.500	5	5	4	2	2	6	1	0	1	3	0	0	0	1	0	0	0	0	0	1.500	.600
Long, Terrence, Oakland*	.000	3	3	2	1	0	0	0	0	0	0	0	0	0	1	0	0	0	0	0	.000	.333

Player, Team	Avg.	G	TPA	AB	R	H	TB	2B	3B	HR	RBI	SH	SF	HP	BB	IBB	SO	SB	CS	GDP	Slg.	OBP
Lopez, Luis, Toronto	.333	9	8	6	0	2	2	0	0	0	1	0	0	0	2	1	0	0	0	0	.333	.500
Lunar, Fernando, Baltimore....	.000	1	1	1	0	0	0	0	0	0	0	0	0	0	0	0	0	0	0	0	.000	.000
Macias, Jose, Detroit†	.625	10	10	8	2	5	9	1	0	1	1	2	0	0	0	0	2	1	0	0	1.125	.625
Magee, Wendell, Detroit.........	.125	11	11	8	2	1	1	0	0	0	0	2	0	0	3	1	1	1	0	1	.125	.364
Magruder, Chris, Texas†	.250	4	4	4	0	1	1	0	0	0	0	0	0	0	0	0	2	0	0	0	.250	.250
Martin, Al, Seattle*	.250	10	9	8	1	2	6	1	0	1	2	0	0	0	1	0	2	0	0	0	.750	.333
Martinez, Edgar, Seattle	.000	4	4	4	0	0	0	0	0	0	0	0	0	0	0	0	1	0	0	0	.000	.000
Martinez, Felix, Tampa Bay†...	.000	2	2	2	0	0	0	0	0	0	0	0	0	0	0	0	1	0	0	0	.000	.000
Martinez, Tino, New York*	.600	6	6	5	2	3	9	0	0	2	3	0	0	0	1	1	1	0	0	0	1.800	.667
Mateo, Ruben, Texas	.000	1	1	1	0	0	0	0	0	0	0	0	0	0	0	0	1	0	0	0	.000	.000
Matos, Luis, Baltimore..........	.333	3	3	3	1	1	1	0	0	0	0	0	0	0	0	0	1	0	0	0	.333	.333
Maxwell, Jason, Minnesota....	.500	2	2	2	0	1	2	1	0	0	2	0	0	0	0	0	0	0	0	0	1.000	.500
Mayne, Brent, Kansas City* ...	1.000	2	2	2	1	2	4	0	1	0	0	0	0	0	0	0	0	0	0	0	2.000	1.000
McCarty, Dave, Kansas City ...	.080	29	29	25	1	2	2	0	0	0	1	0	1	0	3	0	8	0	0	0	.080	.172
McCracken, Quinton, Min.† ...	.286	8	8	7	1	2	2	0	0	0	0	0	0	0	1	0	1	0	0	0	.286	.375
McDonald, Donzell, N.Y.†......	.000	2	2	1	0	0	0	0	0	0	0	0	1	0	0	0	0	0	0	0	.000	.000
McDonald, John, Cleveland.....	.000	2	2	1	0	0	0	0	0	0	0	0	1	0	0	0	0	0	0	0	.000	.000
McGriff, Fred, Tampa Bay*.....	.000	6	6	5	0	0	0	0	0	0	0	0	0	0	1	0	2	0	0	0	.000	.167
McLemore, Mark, Seattle†	.500	15	15	12	1	6	11	2	0	1	6	1	1	0	1	0	3	0	0	0	.917	.500
McMillon, Billy, Det.-Oak.*	.071	17	17	14	0	1	2	1	0	0	3	0	0	1	2	0	6	0	0	1	.143	.235
Menechino, Frank, Oakland	.000	2	2	2	0	0	0	0	0	0	0	0	0	0	0	0	2	0	0	0	.000	.000
Merloni, Lou, Boston	.333	3	3	3	1	1	4	0	0	1	1	0	0	0	0	0	1	0	0	1	1.333	.333
Mientkiewicz, Doug, Min.*	.333	5	5	3	1	1	2	1	0	0	0	0	0	0	2	1	0	0	0	0	.667	.600
Mirabelli, Doug, Tex.-Bos.	.000	5	5	5	0	0	0	0	0	0	0	0	0	0	0	0	1	0	0	0	.000	.000
Mohr, Dustan, Minnesota........	.000	1	1	1	0	0	0	0	0	0	0	0	0	0	0	0	0	0	0	0	.000	.000
Molina, Ben, Anaheim	.200	5	5	5	1	1	4	0	0	1	2	0	0	0	0	0	2	0	0	0	.800	.200
Monroe, Craig, Texas	.000	3	2	2	0	0	0	0	0	0	0	0	0	0	1	0	0	0	0	0	.000	.500
Mora, Melvin, Baltimore.........	.500	2	2	2	0	1	1	0	0	0	0	0	0	0	0	0	0	0	0	0	.500	.500
Myers, Greg, Bal.-Oak.*	.125	11	11	8	1	1	1	0	0	0	0	0	0	0	3	0	3	0	0	0	.125	.364
Nieves, Jose, Anaheim	.333	9	9	9	1	3	4	1	0	0	0	0	0	0	0	0	4	0	0	0	.444	.333
Nixon, Trot, Boston*	.000	3	3	1	0	0	0	0	0	0	0	1	0	2	0	0	1	0	0	0	.000	.667
Offerman, Jose, Boston†	.000	2	2	2	0	0	0	0	0	0	0	0	0	0	0	0	0	0	0	0	.000	.000
O'Leary, Troy, Boston*	.182	13	13	11	1	2	2	0	0	0	0	0	0	1	1	0	3	0	0	1	.182	.308
Olerud, John, Seattle*	.200	5	5	5	1	1	2	1	0	0	2	0	0	0	0	0	1	0	0	0	.400	.200
O'Neill, Paul, New York*	.000	4	4	3	0	0	0	0	0	0	0	0	0	0	1	1	0	1	0	1	.000	.250
Ordaz, Luis, Kansas City	.000	1	1	1	0	0	0	0	0	0	0	0	0	0	0	0	0	0	0	0	.000	.000
Ordonez, Magglio, Chicago	.000	4	4	3	0	0	0	0	0	0	1	0	1	0	0	0	0	0	0	0	.000	.000
Ortiz, David, Minnesota*	.200	7	7	5	1	1	4	0	0	1	3	0	0	0	2	1	1	0	0	0	.800	.429
Ortiz, Hector, Kansas City.......	.000	1	1	1	0	0	0	0	0	0	0	0	0	0	0	0	1	0	0	0	.000	.000
Palmeiro, Orlando, Anaheim* .	.269	28	27	26	7	7	12	2	0	1	6	0	0	0	1	0	3	1	0	1	.462	.296
Palmeiro, Rafael, Texas*	.000	1	1	1	0	0	0	0	0	0	0	0	0	0	0	0	1	0	0	0	.000	.000
Patterson, Jarrod, Detroit*	1.000	1	1	1	1	1	3	0	1	0	0	0	0	0	0	0	0	0	0	0	3.000	1.000
Pena, Carlos, Texas*	.500	5	5	4	0	2	4	2	0	0	2	0	0	0	1	0	2	0	0	0	1.000	.600
Perry, Herbert, Chicago..........	.308	16	16	13	4	4	5	1	0	0	2	0	0	1	2	0	2	0	0	1	.385	.438
Phelps, Josh, Toronto	.000	1	1	1	0	0	0	0	0	0	0	0	0	0	0	0	0	0	0	0	.000	.000
Piatt, Adam, Oakland..............	.000	6	5	4	0	0	0	0	0	0	0	0	1	0	0	0	2	0	0	0	.000	.000
Pickering, Calvin, Boston*	.250	4	4	4	1	1	4	0	0	1	4	0	0	0	0	0	1	0	0	0	1.000	.250
Pierzynski, A.J., Minnesota*....	.111	10	10	9	2	1	1	0	0	0	2	0	1	0	0	0	4	0	0	0	.111	.100
Podsednik, Scott, Seattle*	1.000	1	1	1	1	1	3	0	1	0	3	0	0	0	0	0	0	0	0	0	3.000	1.000
Porter, Bo, Texas	.000	5	5	4	0	0	0	0	0	0	0	0	0	0	1	0	2	0	0	0	.000	.200
Posada, Jorge, New York†	.500	5	5	4	1	2	5	0	0	1	4	0	0	0	1	1	1	0	0	1	1.250	.600
Prince, Tom, Minnesota	.000	1	1	1	0	0	0	0	0	0	0	0	0	0	1	0	0	0	0	0	.000	.000
Quinn, Mark, Kansas City.......	.000	4	4	4	0	0	0	0	0	0	0	1	0	0	0	0	0	0	0	0	.000	.000
Raines, Tim, Baltimore†	.000	2	2	2	0	0	0	0	0	0	0	0	0	0	0	0	0	0	0	0	.000	.000
Richard, Chris, Baltimore*	.000	4	4	3	1	0	0	0	0	0	0	0	0	0	1	0	0	0	0	0	.000	.250
Ripken, Cal Jr., Baltimore	.667	3	3	3	0	2	3	1	0	0	0	0	0	0	0	0	0	0	0	0	1.000	.667
Rivas, Luis, Minnesota............	.333	4	4	3	0	1	1	0	0	0	0	0	0	0	1	0	0	0	0	0	.333	.500
Roberts, Brian, Baltimore†.......	.111	10	10	9	1	1	1	0	0	0	0	0	0	0	1	0	4	2	0	0	.111	.200
Roberts, Dave, Cleveland*	.000	2	2	1	1	0	0	0	0	0	0	1	0	0	1	0	0	0	0	0	.000	.500
Rodriguez, Henry, New York* .	.000	4	4	4	0	0	0	0	0	0	0	0	0	0	0	0	3	0	0	0	.000	.000
Rodriguez, Ivan, Texas	.000	2	2	2	0	0	0	0	0	0	0	0	0	0	0	0	2	0	0	0	.000	.000
Rolls, Damian, Tampa Bay	.000	6	6	6	0	0	0	0	0	0	0	0	0	0	0	0	1	0	0	1	.000	.000
Rowand, Aaron, Chicago........	.000	4	4	3	0	0	0	0	0	0	0	0	0	0	1	0	2	0	0	0	.000	.250
Ryan, Rob, Oakland*	.000	5	5	5	0	0	0	0	0	0	0	0	0	0	0	0	3	0	0	0	.000	.000
Sadler, Donnie, Kansas City ...	.000	3	3	3	0	0	0	0	0	0	0	0	0	0	0	0	1	0	0	0	.000	.000
Saenz, Olmedo, Oakland	.240	26	26	25	3	6	10	1	0	1	4	0	0	0	1	0	7	0	0	0	.400	.269
Sanders, Anthony, Seattle	1.000	1	1	1	0	1	2	1	0	0	2	0	0	0	0	0	0	0	0	0	2.000	1.000
Santangelo, F.P., Oakland†	.250	6	6	4	1	1	1	0	0	0	2	1	0	0	1	0	0	0	0	0	.250	.400
Santos, Angel, Boston†	.000	1	1	1	0	0	0	0	0	0	0	0	0	0	0	0	1	0	0	0	.000	.000
Seabol, Scott, New York	.000	1	1	1	0	0	0	0	0	0	0	0	0	0	0	0	0	0	0	0	.000	.000
Segui, David, Baltimore†..........	.000	1	1	1	0	0	0	0	0	0	0	0	0	0	0	0	0	0	0	0	.000	.000
Sheldon, Scott, Texas..............	.000	7	7	6	0	0	0	0	0	0	1	0	1	0	0	0	2	0	0	0	.000	.000
Sierra, Ruben, Texas†	.273	11	11	11	2	3	9	0	0	2	5	0	0	0	0	0	2	0	0	0	.818	.273
Simmons, Brian, Toronto†	.167	27	27	24	1	4	7	3	0	0	2	0	1	1	1	0	7	0	0	0	.292	.222
Simon, Randall, Detroit*	.000	11	10	8	0	0	0	0	0	0	0	0	0	0	2	0	2	0	0	2	.000	.200
Singleton, Chris, Chicago*......	.333	3	3	3	0	1	1	0	0	0	0	0	0	0	0	0	1	0	0	0	.333	.333
Sojo, Luis, New York..............	.250	5	5	4	0	1	1	0	0	0	0	0	0	0	1	0	0	0	0	0	.250	.400
Soriano, Alfonso, New York ...	.000	1	1	1	0	0	0	0	0	0	0	0	0	0	0	0	0	0	0	0	.000	.000
Spencer, Shane, New York	.000	3	3	3	0	0	0	0	0	0	0	0	0	0	0	0	1	0	0	0	.000	.000
Spiezio, Scott, Anaheim†	.143	17	17	14	0	2	2	0	0	0	2	0	1	0	2	1	4	0	0	1	.143	.235
Sprague, Ed, Seattle...............	.500	17	15	10	2	5	6	1	0	0	3	0	0	1	4	1	3	0	0	0	.600	.667
Stewart, Shannon, Toronto	.000	2	2	1	0	0	0	0	0	0	0	0	0	0	1	0	0	0	0	0	.000	.500

2001 A.L. STATISTICS Pinch-hitting

Player, Team	Avg.	G	TPA	AB	R	H	TB	2B	3B	HR	RBI	SH	SF	HP	BB	IBB	SO	SB	CS	GDP	Slg.	OBP
Stynes, Chris, Boston	.167	7	7	6	1	1	1	0	0	0	0	0	0	1	0	0	1	0	0	0	.167	.286
Suzuki, Ichiro, Seattle*	.250	4	4	4	1	1	1	0	0	0	0	0	0	0	0	0	1	0	0	0	.250	.250
Sweeney, Mike, Kansas City...	.000	1	1	1	0	0	0	0	0	0	0	0	0	0	0	0	0	0	0	0	.000	.000
Taubensee, Eddie, Cleveland* .	.429	16	15	14	3	6	12	0	0	2	3	0	0	0	1	0	2	0	0	0	.857	.467
Thomas, Frank, Chicago	.000	1	1	1	0	0	0	0	0	0	0	0	0	0	0	0	0	0	0	0	.000	.000
Thome, Jim, Cleveland*	.429	7	7	7	1	3	6	0	0	1	2	0	0	0	0	0	2	0	0	0	.857	.429
Tyner, Jason, Tampa Bay*	.200	5	5	5	0	1	1	0	0	0	0	0	0	0	0	0	0	0	0	0	.200	.200
Valdez, Mario, Oakland*	.154	15	15	13	0	2	2	0	0	0	3	0	0	0	2	0	8	0	0	0	.154	.267
Valentin, Jose, Chicago†	.111	11	10	9	1	1	1	0	0	0	0	0	0	0	1	0	6	0	1	0	.111	.200
Varitek, Jason, Boston†	.000	3	3	3	0	0	0	0	0	0	0	0	0	0	0	0	1	0	0	0	.000	.000
Vaughn, Greg, Tampa Bay......	.000	3	3	2	0	0	0	0	0	0	0	0	0	0	1	1	1	0	0	0	.000	.333
Vazquez, Ramon, Seattle*	.500	2	2	2	1	1	1	0	0	0	0	0	0	0	0	0	1	0	0	0	.500	.500
Velarde, Randy, Tex.-N.Y.......	.143	9	9	7	1	1	2	1	0	0	1	0	0	0	2	0	1	0	0	0	.286	.333
Vizquel, Omar, Cleveland†	.000	2	2	2	0	0	0	0	0	0	0	0	0	0	0	0	0	0	0	0	.000	.000
Williams, Bernie, New York† ..	.000	1	1	1	0	0	0	0	0	0	0	0	0	0	0	0	0	0	0	0	.000	.000
Williams, Gerald, TB.-N.Y.	.143	11	11	7	3	1	1	0	0	0	0	1	0	0	3	0	1	0	0	0	.143	.400
Wilson, Dan, Seattle..............	.286	7	7	7	2	2	5	0	0	1	1	0	0	0	0	0	0	0	0	2	.714	.286
Wilson, Enrique, New York† ..	.000	11	11	9	0	0	0	0	0	0	0	0	0	0	2	0	1	0	0	1	.000	.182
Winn, Randy, Tampa Bay†	.571	7	7	7	1	4	7	0	0	1	1	0	0	0	0	0	2	0	0	0	1.000	.571
Woodward, Chris, Toronto	.000	1	1	0	0	0	0	0	0	0	0	0	0	0	1	0	0	0	0	0	.000	1.000
Wooten, Shawn, Anaheim......	.375	11	10	8	3	3	9	0	0	2	3	0	0	1	1	0	1	0	0	0	1.125	.500
Young, Michael, Texas	.500	2	2	2	1	1	1	0	0	0	0	0	0	0	0	0	0	0	0	0	.500	.500
Zaun, Gregg, Kansas City†	.500	6	6	4	1	2	5	0	0	1	1	0	0	0	2	0	0	0	0	1	1.250	.667

PINCH-HITTERS WITH TWO OR MORE TEAMS

Player, Team	Avg.	G	TPA	AB	R	H	TB	2B	3B	HR	RBI	SH	SF	HP	BB	IBB	SO	SB	CS	GDP	Slg.	OBP
McMillon, Billy, Detroit*	.000	13	13	11	0	0	0	0	0	0	1	0	0	0	2	0	4	0	0	0	.000	.154
McMillon, Billy, Oakland*	.333	4	4	3	0	1	2	1	0	0	2	0	0	1	0	0	2	0	0	0	.667	.500
Mirabelli, Doug, Texas...........	.000	1	1	1	0	0	0	0	0	0	0	0	0	0	0	0	0	0	0	0	.000	.000
Mirabelli, Doug, Boston	.000	4	4	4	0	0	0	0	0	0	0	0	0	0	0	0	1	0	0	0	.000	.000
Myers, Greg, Baltimore*	.200	6	6	5	0	1	1	0	0	0	0	0	0	0	1	0	1	0	0	0	.200	.333
Myers, Greg, Oakland*	.000	5	5	3	1	0	0	0	0	0	0	0	0	0	2	0	2	0	0	0	.000	.400
Velarde, Randy, Texas	.200	6	6	5	1	1	2	1	0	0	1	0	0	0	1	0	1	0	0	0	.400	.333
Velarde, Randy, New York......	.000	3	3	2	0	0	0	0	0	0	0	0	0	0	1	0	0	0	0	0	.000	.333
Williams, Gerald, Tampa Bay .	.000	2	2	2	0	0	0	0	0	0	0	0	0	0	0	0	0	0	0	0	.000	.000
Williams, Gerald, New York....	.200	9	9	5	3	1	1	0	0	0	0	1	0	0	3	0	1	0	0	0	.200	.500

PITCHING

TEAM

Team	W	L	Pct.	ERA	G	ShO	Rel.	Sv.	IP	H	TBF	R	ER	HR	SH	SF	HB	BB	IBB	SO	WP	Bk.
Seattle	116	46	.716	3.54	162	14	391	56	1465.0	1293	6096	627	576	160	33	44	64	465	28	1051	40	1
Oakland	102	60	.630	3.59	162	9	416	44	1463.1	1384	6115	645	583	153	45	33	46	440	49	1117	42	3
New York	95	65	.594	4.02	161	9	362	57	1451.1	1429	6174	713	649	158	37	47	55	465	29	1266	54	6
Boston	82	79	.509	4.15	161	9	424	48	1448.0	1412	6272	745	667	146	39	45	93	544	50	1259	54	7
Anaheim	75	87	.463	4.20	162	1	384	43	1437.2	1452	6195	730	671	168	37	39	64	525	47	947	46	2
Toronto	80	82	.494	4.28	162	10	471	41	1462.2	1553	6305	753	696	165	47	43	76	490	60	1041	33	8
Minnesota	85	77	.525	4.51	162	8	402	45	1441.1	1494	6187	766	722	192	55	55	56	445	16	965	58	2
Chicago	83	79	.512	4.55	162	7	406	51	1433.1	1465	6200	795	725	181	48	56	88	500	38	921	57	5
Cleveland	91	71	.562	4.64	162	4	483	42	1446.2	1512	6312	821	746	148	48	50	49	573	44	1218	58	11
Baltimore	63	98	.391	4.67	162	6	392	31	1432.1	1504	6273	829	744	194	31	41	74	528	28	938	37	5
Kansas City	65	97	.401	4.87	162	1	396	30	1440.0	1537	6289	858	779	209	33	51	61	576	26	911	73	2
Tampa Bay	62	100	.383	4.94	162	6	370	30	1423.2	1513	6288	887	781	207	36	64	75	569	21	1030	75	7
Detroit	66	96	.407	5.01	162	2	391	34	1429.1	1624	6361	876	795	180	51	52	73	553	56	859	40	4
Texas	73	89	.451	5.71	162	3	410	37	1438.1	1670	6469	968	913	222	30	73	63	596	33	951	70	9
Totals	1138	1126	.503	4.47	1133	89	5698	589	20213.0	20842	87536	11013	10047	2483	570	693	937	7269	525	14474	737	72

NOTE—Totals for earned runs for several clubs do not agree with composite total for all pitchers of each respective club due to instances in which provisions of Section 10.18(i) of the Scoring Rules were applied. The following differences are to be noted: New York pitchers add to 651; Boston pitchers add to 672; Minnesota pitchers add to 723; Cleveland pitchers add to 747; Baltimore pitchers add to 748; Tampa Bay pitchers add to 784.

INDIVIDUAL

TOP QUALIFIERS FOR EARNED-RUN AVERAGE TITLE

Minimum 162 innings. *Throws lefthanded.

Pitcher, Team	W	L	Pct.	ERA	G	GS	CG	ShO	GF	Sv.	IP	H	TBF	R	ER	HR	SH	SF	HB	BB	IBB	SO	WP	Bk.
Garcia, Freddy, Seattle	18	6	.750	3.05	34	34	4	3	0	0	238.2	199	971	88	81	16	8	5	5	69	6	163	3	1
Mussina, Mike, New York	17	11	.607	3.15	34	34	4	3	0	0	228.2	202	909	87	80	20	5	6	4	42	2	214	6	0
Mays, Joe, Minnesota	17	13	.567	3.16	34	34	4	2	0	0	233.2	205	957	87	82	25	8	8	5	64	2	123	11	0
Buehrle, Mark, Chicago*	16	8	.667	3.29	32	32	4	2	0	0	221.1	188	885	89	81	24	9	4	8	48	2	126	1	5
Hudson, Tim, Oakland	18	9	.667	3.37	35	35	3	0	0	0	235.0	216	980	100	88	20	12	8	6	71	5	181	9	1
Moyer, Jamie, Seattle*	20	6	.769	3.43	33	33	1	0	0	0	209.2	187	851	84	80	24	5	11	10	44	4	119	1	0
Mulder, Mark, Oakland*	21	8	.724	3.45	34	34	6	4	0	0	229.1	214	927	92	88	18	8	3	5	51	4	153	4	0
Zito, Barry, Oakland*	17	8	.680	3.49	35	35	3	2	0	0	214.1	184	902	92	83	18	5	4	13	80	0	205	6	1
Clemens, Roger, New York	20	3	.870	3.51	33	33	0	0	0	0	220.1	205	918	94	86	19	4	4	5	72	1	213	14	0
Lidle, Cory, Oakland	13	6	.684	3.59	29	29	1	0	0	0	188.0	170	762	84	75	23	2	1	10	47	7	118	5	0
Sele, Aaron, Seattle	15	5	.750	3.60	34	33	2	1	0	0	215.0	216	899	93	86	25	5	9	7	51	2	114	1	0
Sparks, Steve W., Detroit	14	9	.609	3.65	35	33	8	1	2	0	232.0	244	982	110	94	22	4	9	6	64	1	116	8	2
Washburn, Jarrod, Anaheim*	11	10	.524	3.77	30	30	1	0	0	0	193.1	196	813	89	81	25	4	7	4	54	4	126	3	0
Wakefield, Tim, Boston	9	12	.429	3.90	45	17	0	0	5	3	168.2	156	732	84	73	13	3	9	18	73	5	148	5	1
Radke, Brad, Minnesota	15	11	.577	3.94	33	33	6	2	0	0	226.0	235	919	105	99	24	10	6	10	26	0	137	4	1

DEPARTMENTAL LEADERS: W—Mulder, Oak., 21; L—Mercedes, Bal., 17; G—Quantrill, Tor., 80; GS—Hudson, Oak., Zito, Oak., 35; CG—Sparks, Det., 8; ShO—Mulder, Oak., 4; GF—Foulke, Chi., 69; Sv.—M. Rivera, N.Y., 50; IP—Garcia, 238.2; H—Helling, Tex., 256; TBF—Weaver, Det., 985; R—Helling, Tex., 134; ER—Helling, Tex., 124; HR—Helling, Tex., 38; SH—Hudson, Oak., Weaver, Det., 12; SF—Wilson, T.B., 12; HB—Wakefield, Bos., 18; TBB—Nomo, Bos., 96; IBB—Howry, Chi., Lowe, Bos., Mahomes, Tex., Stanton, N.Y., Tam, Oak., 9; SO—Nomo, Bos., 220; WP—Clemens, N.Y., K. Wells, Chi., 14; BK—Michalak, Tor.-Tex., 6.

ALL PITCHERS

*Throws lefthanded.

Pitcher, Team	W	L	Pct.	ERA	G	GS	CG	ShO	GF	Sv.	IP	H	TBF	R	ER	HR	SH	SF	HB	BB	IBB	SO	WP	Bk.
Abbott, Paul, Sea.	17	4	.810	4.25	28	27	1	0	0	0	163.0	145	710	79	77	21	3	5	7	87	5	118	11	0
Almanzar, Carlos, N.Y.	0	1	.000	3.38	10	0	0	0	7	0	10.2	14	46	4	4	2	1	0	2	1	6	0	0	
Anderson, Matt, Det.	3	1	.750	4.82	62	0	0	0	41	22	56.0	56	239	33	30	2	1	2	0	18	4	52	9	1
Arrojo, Rolando, Bos.	5	4	.556	3.48	41	9	0	0	11	5	103.1	88	438	44	40	8	6	2	12	35	4	78	2	0
Austin, Jeff, K.C.	0	0	.000	5.54	21	0	0	0	9	0	26.0	27	117	17	16	4	1	2	1	14	2	27	3	0
Bacsik, Mike Jr., Cle.*	0	0	.000	9.00	3	0	0	0	1	0	9.0	13	45	10	9	0	0	1	1	3	1	4	0	0
Baez, Danys, Cle.	5	3	.625	2.50	43	0	0	0	8	0	50.1	34	202	22	14	5	0	1	3	20	4	52	3	0
Bailey, Cory, K.C.	1	1	.500	3.48	53	0	0	0	13	0	67.1	57	283	28	26	3	3	3	0	33	2	61	4	0
Baldwin, James, Chi.	7	5	.583	4.61	17	16	2	1	0	0	95.2	109	431	56	49	15	3	5	4	38	0	42	4	0
Bale, John, Bal.*	1	0	1.000	3.04	14	0	0	0	3	0	26.2	18	113	14	9	2	0	2	1	17	0	21	1	0
Balfour, Grant, Min.	0	0	.000	13.50	2	0	0	0	1	0	2.2	3	14	4	4	2	1	1	0	3	0	2	0	0
Banks, Willie, Bos.	0	0	.000	0.84	5	0	0	0	1	0	10.2	5	42	4	1	0	0	0	4	0	10	1	1	
Barcelo, Lorenzo, Chi.	1	0	1.000	4.71	17	0	0	0	3	0	21.0	24	96	13	11	1	1	1	8	2	15	1	0	
Bauer, Rick, Bal.	0	5	.000	4.64	6	6	0	0	0	0	33.0	35	143	22	17	7	0	1	9	0	16	0	0	
Beck, Rod, Bos.	6	4	.600	3.90	68	0	0	0	28	6	80.2	77	342	42	35	15	3	2	3	28	6	63	5	1
Beirne, Kevin, Tor.	0	0	.000	12.86	5	0	0	0	2	0	7.0	13	40	10	10	1	1	0	0	6	1	5	0	0
Bell, Rob, Tex.	5	5	.500	7.18	18	18	0	0	0	0	105.1	130	482	87	84	23	3	8	4	47	0	64	8	0
Benoit, Joaquin, Tex.	0	0	.000	10.80	1	0	0	0	0	0	5.0	8	26	6	6	3	0	1	0	3	0	4	0	0
Bernero, Adam, Det.	0	0	.000	7.30	5	0	0	0	4	0	12.1	13	56	13	10	4	0	1	1	4	0	8	1	0
Biddle, Rocky, Chi.	7	8	.467	5.39	30	21	0	0	1	0	128.2	137	571	87	77	16	4	3	8	52	3	85	6	0
Bierbrodt, Nick, T.B.*	3	4	.429	4.55	11	11	0	0	0	0	61.1	71	281	38	31	11	0	1	4	27	1	56	3	0
Blair, Willie, Bos.	1	4	.200	10.50	9	4	0	0	1	0	24.0	38	121	30	28	3	2	2	3	11	3	15	0	1
Boehringer, Brian, N.Y.	0	1	.000	3.12	22	0	0	0	8	1	34.2	35	155	15	12	3	1	2	3	12	0	33	0	0
Borbon, Pedro Jr., Tor.*	2	4	.333	3.71	71	0	0	0	14	0	53.1	48	217	24	22	8	2	2	4	12	3	45	0	0
Borkowski, Dave, Det.	0	2	.000	6.37	15	0	0	0	7	0	29.2	30	135	21	21	5	0	2	3	15	3	30	0	0

Pitcher, Team	W	L	Pct.	ERA	G	GS	CG	ShO	GF	Sv.	IP	H	TBF	R	ER	HR	SH	SF	HB	BB	IBB	SO	WP	Bk.
Borland, Toby, Ana.	0	1	.000	10.80	2	0	0	0	1	0	3.1	8	19	5	4	1	1	0	0	1	0	0	0	0
Bowles, Brian, Tor.	0	0	.000	0.00	2	0	0	0	0	0	3.2	4	15	0	0	0	0	0	0	1	0	4	1	0
Bradford, Chad, Oak.	2	1	.667	2.70	35	0	0	0	19	1	36.2	41	154	12	11	6	1	0	1	6	0	34	0	0
Brantley, Jeff, Tex.	0	1	.000	5.14	18	0	0	0	7	0	21.0	26	94	12	12	5	0	1	0	9	1	11	1	0
Brea, Leslie, Bal.	0	0	.000	18.00	2	0	0	0	0	0	2.0	6	14	4	4	2	0	0	0	3	0	0	0	0
Buehrle, Mark, Chi.*	16	8	.667	3.29	32	32	4	2	0	0	221.1	188	885	89	81	24	9	4	8	48	2	126	1	5
Burba, Dave, Cle.	10	10	.500	6.21	32	27	1	0	4	0	150.2	188	684	112	104	16	5	7	3	54	2	118	6	0
Byrd, Paul, K.C.	6	6	.500	4.05	16	15	1	0	0	0	93.1	110	399	45	42	11	2	4	1	22	1	49	1	0
Callaway, Mickey, T.B.	0	0	.000	7.20	2	0	0	0	2	0	5.0	3	20	4	4	2	0	0	0	2	0	2	0	0
Carpenter, Chris, Tor.	11	11	.500	4.09	34	34	3	2	0	0	215.2	229	930	112	98	29	3	1	16	75	5	157	5	0
Carrasco, Hector, Min.	4	3	.571	4.64	56	0	0	0	12	1	73.2	77	317	40	38	6	3	0	0	30	3	70	7	1
Castillo, Carlos, Bos.	0	0	.000	6.00	2	0	0	0	1	0	3.0	3	12	2	2	1	0	1	0	0	0	0	0	0
Castillo, Frank, Bos.	10	9	.526	4.21	26	26	0	0	0	0	136.2	138	580	72	64	14	3	6	5	35	2	89	3	1
Charlton, Norm, Sea.*	4	2	.667	3.02	44	0	0	0	10	1	47.2	36	189	19	16	4	3	1	4	11	0	48	4	0
Choate, Randy, N.Y.*	3	1	.750	3.35	37	0	0	0	13	0	48.1	34	207	21	18	0	2	1	9	27	2	35	3	0
Clemens, Roger, N.Y.	20	3	.870	3.51	33	33	0	0	0	0	220.1	205	918	94	86	19	4	4	5	72	1	213	14	0
Coco, Pasqual, Tor.	1	0	1.000	4.40	7	1	0	0	3	0	14.1	12	63	8	7	0	1	1	2	6	0	9	0	0
Cogan, Tony, K.C.*	0	4	.000	5.84	39	0	0	0	7	0	24.2	32	119	17	16	7	0	1	5	13	0	17	1	0
Colome, Jesus, T.B.	2	3	.400	3.33	30	0	0	0	9	0	48.2	37	209	22	18	8	2	2	2	25	4	31	2	0
Colon, Bartolo, Cle.	14	12	.538	4.09	34	34	1	0	0	0	222.1	220	947	106	101	26	8	4	2	90	2	201	4	1
Cone, David, Bos.	9	7	.563	4.31	25	25	0	0	0	0	135.2	148	614	74	65	17	2	6	10	57	4	115	9	0
Cooper, Brian, Ana.	0	1	.000	2.63	7	1	0	0	5	0	13.2	10	55	5	4	2	0	1	0	4	0	7	0	0
Cordero, Francisco, Tex.	0	1	.000	3.86	3	0	0	0	2	0	2.1	3	12	1	1	0	0	0	2	1	1	1	0	0
Cornejo, Nate, Det.	4	4	.500	7.38	10	10	0	0	0	0	42.2	63	217	38	35	10	2	0	3	28	4	22	1	0
Crabtree, Tim, Tex.	0	5	.000	6.56	21	0	0	0	14	4	23.1	37	117	18	17	3	3	3	1	14	2	16	3	0
Crawford, Paxton, Bos.	3	0	1.000	4.75	8	7	0	0	1	0	36.0	40	161	19	19	3	0	1	2	13	0	25	2	0
Creek, Doug, T.B.*	2	5	.286	4.31	66	0	0	0	16	0	62.2	51	279	34	30	7	1	3	4	49	5	66	4	0
Cressend, Jack, Min.	3	2	.600	3.67	44	0	0	0	9	0	56.1	50	232	24	23	6	2	2	1	16	0	40	2	0
Davis, Doug, Tex.*	11	10	.524	4.45	30	30	1	0	0	0	186.0	220	828	103	92	14	4	6	3	69	1	115	7	2
DeWitt, Matt, Tor.	0	2	.000	3.79	16	0	0	0	9	0	19.0	22	87	8	8	2	1	0	1	10	5	13	2	0
Dickey, R.A., Tex.	0	1	.000	6.75	4	0	0	0	1	0	12.0	13	53	9	9	3	0	0	0	7	1	4	1	0
Douglass, Sean, Bal.	2	1	.667	5.31	4	4	0	0	0	0	20.1	21	94	12	12	3	0	1	1	11	0	17	1	1
Drese, Ryan, Cle.	1	2	.333	3.44	9	4	0	0	2	0	36.2	32	149	15	14	2	1	0	1	15	2	24	0	0
Drew, Tim, Cle.	0	2	.000	7.97	8	6	0	0	0	0	35.0	51	173	39	31	9	1	2	4	16	0	15	5	0
Duchscherer, Justin, Tex.	1	1	.500	12.27	5	2	0	0	1	0	14.2	24	76	20	20	5	0	0	4	4	0	11	1	0
Durbin, Chad, K.C.	9	16	.360	4.93	29	29	2	0	0	0	179.0	201	777	109	98	26	2	7	11	58	0	95	6	0
Duvall, Mike, Min.*	0	0	.000	7.71	8	0	0	0	4	0	4.2	7	22	4	4	1	0	2	0	4	1	0	0	0
Eldred, Cal, Chi.	0	1	.000	13.50	2	2	0	0	0	0	6.0	12	34	9	9	1	0	0	3	3	1	6	0	0
Embree, Alan, Chi.*	1	2	.333	5.03	39	0	0	0	10	0	34.0	31	139	21	19	7	0	3	1	7	0	34	2	0
Erdos, Todd, Bos.	0	0	.000	4.96	10	0	0	0	3	0	16.1	15	71	9	9	2	0	3	8	1	7	0	0
Escobar, Kelvim, Tor.	6	8	.429	3.50	59	11	1	1	15	0	126.0	93	517	51	49	8	2	5	3	52	5	121	2	0
Eyre, Scott, Tor.*	1	2	.333	3.45	17	0	0	0	5	2	15.2	15	66	6	6	1	0	1	1	7	2	16	2	0
File, Bob, Tor.	5	3	.625	3.27	60	0	0	0	18	0	74.1	57	299	28	27	6	3	1	7	29	8	38	2	0
Finley, Chuck, Cle.*	8	7	.533	5.54	22	22	1	0	0	0	113.2	131	495	78	70	14	2	5	2	35	0	96	1	0
Fiore, Tony, T.B.-Min.	0	1	.000	5.59	7	0	0	0	5	0	9.2	9	41	6	6	0	0	0	1	3	0	8	1	0
Florie, Bryce, Bos.	0	1	.000	11.42	7	0	0	0	1	0	8.2	12	45	11	11	1	0	0	7	3	7	0	0
Fogg, Josh, Chi.	0	0	.000	2.03	11	0	0	0	4	0	13.1	10	53	3	3	0	0	1	3	1	17	0	0
Fossum, Casey, Bos.*	3	2	.600	4.87	13	7	0	0	3	0	44.1	44	197	26	24	4	0	1	6	20	1	26	1	1
Foster, Kris, Bal.	0	0	.000	2.70	7	0	0	0	0	0	10.0	9	47	4	3	1	0	0	8	0	8	0	0
Foster, Kevin, Tex.	0	1	.000	6.62	9	0	0	0	3	0	17.2	21	82	14	13	2	0	1	3	10	0	16	1	0
Foulke, Keith, Chi.	4	9	.308	2.33	72	0	0	0	69	42	81.0	57	322	21	21	3	4	1	8	22	1	75	1	0
Franklin, Ryan, Sea.	5	1	.833	3.56	38	0	0	0	14	0	78.1	76	335	32	31	13	1	2	4	24	4	60	2	0
Frascatore, John, Tor.	1	0	1.000	2.20	12	0	0	0	2	0	16.1	16	69	4	4	4	0	0	4	0	9	0	0
Fuentes, Brian, Sea.*	1	1	.500	4.63	10	0	0	0	3	0	11.2	6	47	6	6	2	0	1	3	8	0	10	1	0
Fyhrie, Mike, Oak.	0	0	.000	0.00	3	0	0	0	1	0	5.0	2	17	0	0	0	0	0	1	0	5	0	0
Garces, Rich, Bos.	6	1	.857	3.90	62	0	0	0	5	1	67.0	55	284	32	29	6	3	1	4	25	1	51	2	1
Garcia, Freddy, Sea.	18	6	.750	3.05	34	34	4	3	0	0	238.2	199	971	88	81	16	8	5	5	69	6	163	3	1
Garland, Jon, Chi.	6	7	.462	3.69	35	16	0	0	8	1	117.0	123	510	59	48	16	2	5	4	55	2	61	3	0
George, Chris, K.C.*	4	8	.333	5.59	13	13	1	0	0	0	74.0	83	313	48	46	14	3	4	0	18	0	32	3	2
Ginter, Matt, Chi.	1	0	1.000	5.22	20	0	0	0	7	0	39.2	34	167	23	23	2	0	3	7	14	2	24	2	0
Glover, Gary, Chi.	5	5	.500	4.93	46	11	0	0	10	0	100.1	98	429	61	55	16	2	2	4	32	3	63	4	0
Glynn, Ryan, Tex.	1	5	.167	7.04	12	9	0	0	3	0	46.0	59	219	38	36	7	0	2	0	26	1	15	5	0
Green, Steve, Ana.	0	0	.000	3.00	1	1	0	0	0	0	6.0	4	27	2	2	0	0	0	6	0	4	2	0
Grimsley, Jason, K.C.	1	5	.167	3.02	73	0	0	0	24	0	80.1	71	327	32	27	8	2	1	2	28	5	61	4	0
Groom, Buddy, Bal.*	1	4	.200	3.55	70	0	0	0	35	11	66.0	64	265	28	26	4	0	1	9	0	54	2	0
Guardado, Eddie, Min.*	7	1	.875	3.51	67	0	0	0	26	12	66.2	47	270	27	26	5	5	3	1	23	4	67	4	0
Guthrie, Mark, Oak.*	6	2	.750	4.47	54	0	0	0	11	1	52.1	49	225	29	26	7	1	3	4	20	1	52	3	0
Halama, John, Sea.*	10	7	.588	4.73	31	17	0	0	6	0	110.1	132	485	69	58	18	3	4	6	26	0	50	2	0
Halladay, Roy, Tor.	5	3	.625	3.16	17	16	1	1	0	0	105.1	97	432	41	37	3	3	1	1	25	0	96	4	1
Hamilton, Joey, Tor.	5	8	.385	5.89	22	22	0	0	0	0	122.1	170	554	88	80	17	4	8	3	38	1	82	5	0
Harper, Travis, T.B.	0	2	.000	7.71	2	2	0	0	0	0	7.0	15	36	11	6	5	0	0	0	2	1	0	0	0
Harville, Chad, Oak.	0	0	.000	0.00	3	0	0	0	1	0	3.0	2	11	0	0	0	0	0	0	2	1	0	0	0
Hasegawa, Shigetoshi, Ana.	5	6	.455	4.04	46	0	0	0	10	0	55.2	52	235	28	25	5	1	2	2	20	5	41	2	0
Hawkins, LaTroy, Min.	1	5	.167	5.96	62	0	0	0	51	28	51.1	59	248	34	34	3	1	4	1	39	3	36	7	0
Helling, Rick, Tex.	12	11	.522	5.17	34	34	2	1	0	0	215.2	256	941	134	124	38	3	10	4	63	2	154	6	0
Henry, Doug, K.C.	2	2	.500	6.07	53	0	0	0	20	0	75.2	75	342	53	51	14	5	3	45	2	57	5	0
Hentgen, Pat, Bal.	2	3	.400	3.47	9	9	1	0	0	0	62.1	51	252	25	24	7	1	1	0	19	3	33	1	0
Heredia, Gil, Oak.	7	8	.467	5.58	24	18	0	0	2	0	109.2	144	493	75	68	27	3	4	2	29	3	48	1	0
Hernandez, Adrian, N.Y.	0	3	.000	3.68	6	3	0	0	1	0	22.0	15	91	10	9	7	0	0	2	10	1	10	4	0
Hernandez, Orlando, N.Y.	4	7	.364	4.85	17	16	0	0	0	0	94.2	90	414	51	51	19	2	2	5	42	1	77	0	0
Hernandez, Roberto, K.C.	5	6	.455	4.12	63	0	0	0	55	28	67.2	69	287	34	31	7	1	0	1	26	3	46	6	0
Hiljus, Erik, Oak.	5	0	1.000	3.41	16	11	0	0	3	0	66.0	70	290	29	25	7	2	1	0	21	1	67	2	1

Pitcher, Team	W	L	Pct.	ERA	G	GS	CG	ShO	GF	Sv.	IP	H	TBF	R	ER	HR	SH	SF	HB	BB	IBB	SO	WP	Bk.
Hill, Ken, T.B.	0	1	.000	12.27	5	0	0	0	1	0	7.1	10	38	11	10	4	2	0	1	5	2	2	2	0
Hitchcock, Sterling, N.Y.*	4	4	.500	6.49	10	9	1	0	0	0	51.1	67	238	37	37	5	1	4	2	18	0	28	2	1
Holt, Chris, Det.	7	9	.438	5.77	30	22	1	0	3	0	151.1	197	695	102	97	18	8	5	8	57	5	80	3	0
Holtz, Mike, Ana.*	1	2	.333	4.86	63	0	0	0	11	0	37.0	40	167	24	20	5	3	1	2	15	4	38	5	0
Howry, Bob, Chi.	4	5	.444	4.69	69	0	0	0	23	5	78.2	85	346	41	41	11	4	3	4	30	9	64	6	0
Hudson, Tim, Oak.	18	9	.667	3.37	35	35	3	0	0	0	235.0	216	980	100	88	20	12	8	6	71	5	181	9	1
Isringhausen, Jason, Oak.	4	3	.571	2.65	65	0	0	0	54	34	71.1	54	293	24	21	5	3	1	0	23	5	74	2	0
Jodie, Brett, N.Y.	0	1	.000	27.00	1	1	0	0	0	0	2.0	7	13	6	6	3	0	0	0	1	0	0	1	0
Johnson, Adam, Min.	1	2	.333	8.28	7	4	0	0	0	0	25.0	32	119	25	23	6	1	1	5	13	0	17	1	0
Johnson, Jason, Bal.	10	12	.455	4.09	32	32	2	0	0	0	196.0	194	856	109	89	28	6	6	13	77	3	114	9	0
Johnson, Jonathan, Tex.	0	0	.000	9.58	5	0	0	0	2	0	10.1	13	53	11	11	2	1	3	1	7	1	11	0	0
Jones, Todd, Det.-Min.	5	5	.500	4.24	69	0	0	0	36	13	68.0	87	314	39	32	9	3	3	0	29	1	54	3	0
Judd, Mike, T.B.-Tex.	1	1	.500	5.28	12	5	0	0	3	0	29.0	34	137	24	17	4	0	3	1	15	0	16	1	0
Julio, Jorge, Bal.	1	1	.500	3.80	18	0	0	0	8	0	21.1	25	99	13	9	2	2	0	1	9	0	22	1	0
Karsay, Steve, Cle.	0	1	.000	1.25	31	0	0	0	8	1	43.1	29	166	6	6	1	3	1	0	8	2	44	2	0
Keisler, Randy, N.Y.*	1	2	.333	6.22	10	10	0	0	0	0	50.2	52	236	36	35	12	0	1	0	34	0	36	0	0
Kennedy, Joe, T.B.*	7	8	.467	4.44	20	20	0	0	0	0	117.2	122	498	63	58	16	2	5	3	34	0	78	5	1
Kim, Sun-Woo, Bos.*	0	2	.000	5.83	20	2	0	0	7	0	41.2	54	201	27	27	1	3	0	4	21	5	27	5	0
Knight, Brandon, N.Y.	0	0	.000	10.13	4	0	0	0	2	0	10.2	18	52	12	12	5	0	0	0	3	0	7	0	0
Koch, Billy, Tor.	2	5	.286	4.80	69	0	0	0	56	36	69.1	69	308	39	37	7	5	4	6	33	7	55	5	0
Kohlmeier, Ryan, Bal.	1	2	.333	7.30	34	1	0	0	21	6	40.2	48	188	33	33	13	2	0	2	19	2	29	2	0
Kolb, Danny, Tex.	0	0	.000	4.70	17	0	0	0	1	0	15.1	15	70	8	8	2	1	1	0	10	1	15	3	0
Laker, Tim, Cle.	0	0	.000	0.00	1	0	0	0	1	0	1.0	1	5	0	0	0	0	0	0	1	0	1	0	0
Levine, Al, Ana.	8	10	.444	2.38	64	1	0	0	21	2	75.2	71	316	25	20	7	5	5	2	28	4	40	6	0
Lidle, Cory, Oak.	13	6	.684	3.59	29	29	1	0	0	0	188.0	170	762	84	75	23	2	1	10	47	7	118	5	0
Lilly, Ted, N.Y.*	5	6	.455	5.37	26	21	0	0	2	0	120.2	126	537	81	72	20	2	5	7	51	1	112	9	2
Lima, Jose, Det.	5	10	.333	4.71	18	18	2	0	0	0	112.2	120	470	66	59	23	1	5	4	22	2	43	1	0
Loaiza, Esteban, Tor.	11	11	.500	5.02	36	30	1	1	1	0	190.0	239	837	113	106	27	6	4	9	40	1	110	1	1
Lohse, Kyle, Min.	4	7	.364	5.68	19	16	0	0	2	0	90.1	102	402	67	57	16	1	5	8	29	0	64	5	0
Lopez, Albie, T.B.	5	12	.294	5.34	20	20	1	1	0	0	124.2	152	567	87	74	16	5	3	4	51	1	67	1	1
Lowe, Derek, Bos.	5	10	.333	3.53	67	3	0	0	50	24	91.2	103	404	39	36	7	5	1	6	20	0	82	4	0
Lowe, Sean, Chi.	9	4	.692	3.61	45	11	0	0	9	3	127.0	123	529	55	51	12	3	7	7	32	2	71	6	0
Lukasiewicz, Mark, Ana.*	0	2	.000	6.04	24	0	0	0	11	0	22.1	21	98	17	15	6	1	1	2	9	2	25	2	0
Lyon, Brandon, Tor.	5	4	.556	4.29	11	11	0	0	0	0	63.0	63	261	31	30	6	2	6	1	15	0	35	0	1
MacDougal, Mike, K.C.	1	1	.500	4.70	3	3	0	0	0	0	15.1	18	67	10	8	2	0	0	1	4	0	7	3	0
Maduro, Calvin, Bal.	5	6	.455	4.23	22	12	0	0	3	0	93.2	83	386	44	44	10	0	0	4	36	0	51	1	0
Magnante, Mike, Oak.*	3	1	.750	2.77	65	0	0	0	10	0	55.1	50	223	23	17	7	0	4	1	13	3	23	3	0
Mahomes, Pat, Tex.	7	6	.538	5.70	58	4	0	0	14	0	107.1	115	475	71	68	17	2	7	0	55	9	61	3	0
Martinez, Pedro, Bos.	7	3	.700	2.39	18	18	1	0	0	0	116.2	84	456	33	31	5	2	0	6	25	0	163	4	0
Mathews, T.J., Oak.	0	1	.000	5.09	20	0	0	0	4	1	23.0	28	108	14	13	2	2	0	0	11	3	19	1	0
Mays, Joe, Min.	17	13	.567	3.16	34	34	4	2	0	0	233.2	205	957	87	82	25	8	8	5	64	2	123	11	0
McDill, Allen, Bos.*	0	0	.000	5.52	15	0	0	0	8	0	14.2	13	64	9	9	2	0	1	1	7	1	16	0	0
McElroy, Chuck, Bal.*	1	2	.333	5.36	18	5	0	0	0	0	45.1	49	213	29	27	8	0	1	2	28	2	22	3	0
Meacham, Rusty, T.B.	1	3	.250	5.60	24	0	0	0	5	0	35.1	39	158	24	22	3	1	4	2	10	0	13	2	0
Meadows, Brian, K.C.	1	6	.143	6.97	10	10	0	0	0	0	50.1	73	224	41	39	12	1	2	1	12	2	21	1	0
Mecir, Jim, Oak.	2	8	.200	3.43	54	0	0	0	14	3	63.0	54	264	25	24	4	3	0	1	26	7	61	2	0
Mendoza, Ramiro, N.Y.	8	4	.667	3.75	56	2	0	0	11	6	100.2	89	401	44	42	9	4	3	2	23	3	70	2	0
Mercedes, Jose, Bal.	8	17	.320	5.82	31	31	2	0	1	0	184.0	219	828	125	119	20	2	8	10	63	3	123	5	2
Miadich, Bart, Ana.	0	0	.000	4.50	11	0	0	0	4	0	10.0	6	41	5	5	2	0	0	0	8	0	11	1	0
Michalak, Chris, Tor.-Tex.*	8	9	.471	4.41	35	18	0	0	4	1	136.2	157	610	74	67	19	3	4	13	55	5	67	1	6
Miller, Matt, Det.*	0	0	.000	7.45	13	0	0	0	5	0	9.2	16	48	8	8	0	0	1	4	0	6	1	0	
Miller, Travis, Min.*	1	4	.200	4.81	45	0	0	0	14	0	48.2	54	216	30	26	5	0	4	1	20	1	30	1	0
Mills, Alan, Bal.	1	1	.500	9.64	15	0	0	0	8	0	14.0	20	73	15	15	8	0	0	2	11	3	9	0	0
Milton, Eric, Min.*	15	7	.682	4.32	35	34	2	1	0	0	220.2	222	944	109	106	35	8	6	5	61	0	157	2	0
Mlicki, Dave, Det.	4	8	.333	7.33	15	15	0	0	0	0	81.0	118	391	69	66	10	2	3	6	41	2	48	3	0
Moehler, Brian, Det.	0	0	.000	3.38	1	1	0	0	0	0	8.0	6	30	3	3	0	0	0	0	1	0	2	0	0
Moreno, Juan, Tex.*	3	3	.500	3.92	45	0	0	0	6	0	41.1	22	173	21	18	6	1	0	0	28	2	36	5	3
Moyer, Jamie, Sea.*	20	6	.769	3.43	33	33	1	0	0	0	209.2	187	851	84	80	24	5	11	10	44	4	119	1	0
Mulder, Mark, Oak.*	21	8	.724	3.45	34	34	6	4	0	0	229.1	214	927	92	88	16	8	3	5	51	4	153	4	0
Mullen, Scott, K.C.*	0	0	.000	4.50	17	0	0	0	2	0	10.0	13	52	6	5	0	1	0	9	0	3	0	0	
Murray, Heath, Det.*	1	7	.125	6.54	40	4	0	0	10	0	63.1	82	301	48	46	11	2	1	3	40	5	42	1	0
Mussina, Mike, N.Y.	17	11	.607	3.15	34	34	4	3	0	0	228.2	202	909	87	80	20	5	6	4	42	2	214	6	0
Myette, Aaron, Tex.	4	5	.444	7.14	19	15	0	0	1	0	80.2	94	376	65	64	12	3	4	11	37	0	67	2	0
Nagy, Charles, Cle.	5	6	.455	6.40	15	13	0	0	1	0	70.1	102	325	53	50	10	3	4	0	20	1	29	2	0
Nelson, Jeff, Sea.	4	3	.571	2.76	69	0	0	0	16	4	65.1	30	273	21	20	3	2	0	6	44	1	88	2	0
Nitkowski, C.J., Det.*	0	3	.000	5.56	56	0	0	0	12	0	45.1	51	220	30	28	7	3	1	5	31	7	38	1	0
Nomo, Hideo, Bos.	13	10	.565	4.50	33	33	2	2	0	0	198.0	171	849	105	99	26	4	7	3	96	2	220	6	0
Ohka, Tomo, Bos.	2	5	.286	6.19	12	11	0	0	1	0	52.1	69	241	40	36	7	1	1	2	19	0	37	1	1
Oliver, Darren, Tex.*	11	11	.500	6.02	28	28	1	0	0	0	154.0	189	696	109	103	23	1	5	6	65	0	104	8	2
Ortiz, Ramon, Ana.	13	11	.542	4.36	32	32	2	0	0	0	208.2	223	916	114	101	25	9	6	12	76	6	135	7	0
Osuna, Antonio, Chi.	0	0	.000	20.77	4	0	0	0	0	0	4.1	8	23	10	10	2	0	1	1	2	1	6	0	0
Painter, Lance, Tor.*	0	1	.000	7.85	10	0	0	0	3	0	18.1	27	91	17	16	4	0	0	1	11	0	14	0	0
Paniagua, Jose, Sea.	4	3	.571	4.36	60	0	0	0	24	3	66.0	59	296	35	32	7	0	1	4	38	2	46	3	0
Parker, Christian, N.Y.	0	1	.000	21.00	1	1	0	0	0	0	3.0	8	18	7	7	2	0	0	0	1	0	0	0	0
Paronto, Chad, Bal.	1	3	.250	5.00	24	0	0	0	9	0	27.0	33	128	24	15	5	1	1	1	10	0	16	1	0
Parque, Jim, Chi.*	0	0	.000	8.04	5	5	1	0	0	0	28.0	36	132	26	25	7	2	1	2	10	1	15	0	0
Parris, Steve, Tor.	4	6	.400	4.60	19	19	1	0	0	0	105.2	126	471	60	54	18	4	2	2	41	4	49	3	0
Parrish, John, Bal.*	1	2	.333	6.14	16	1	0	0	7	0	22.0	22	107	17	15	5	1	0	3	17	1	20	1	0
Patterson, Danny, Det.	5	4	.556	3.06	60	0	0	0	16	1	64.2	64	258	24	22	4	5	4	12	5	2	27	2	0
Percival, Troy, Ana.	4	2	.667	2.65	57	0	0	0	50	39	57.2	39	230	19	17	3	0	2	18	1	71	2	0	
Perisho, Matt, Det.*	2	3	.400	5.72	30	4	0	0	5	0	39.1	54	186	29	25	5	2	1	4	14	1	19	0	0
Petkovsek, Mark, Tex.	1	3	.333	6.69	55	0	0	0	19	0	76.2	103	362	61	57	14	3	7	5	28	4	42	4	0

Pitcher, Team	W	L	Pct.	ERA	G	GS	CG	ShO	GF	Sv.	IP	H	TBF	R	ER	HR	SH	SF	HB	BB	IBB	SO	WP	Bk.
Pettitte, Andy, N.Y.*	15	10	.600	3.99	31	31	2	0	0	0	200.2	224	858	103	89	14	8	7	6	41	3	164	2	2
Pettyjohn, Adam, Det.*	1	6	.143	5.82	16	9	0	0	1	0	65.0	81	293	48	42	10	3	3	4	21	2	40	2	0
Phelps, Travis, T.B.	2	2	.500	3.48	49	0	0	0	15	5	62.0	53	268	30	24	6	2	4	3	24	1	54	2	1
Pichardo, Hipolito, Bos.	2	1	.667	4.93	30	0	0	0	5	0	34.2	42	159	23	19	3	2	2	5	10	3	17	3	0
Pineda, Luis, Det.	0	1	.000	4.91	16	0	0	0	4	0	18.1	16	82	10	10	2	0	1	0	14	2	13	0	0
Pineiro, Joel, Sea.	6	2	.750	2.03	17	11	0	0	1	0	75.1	50	289	24	17	2	1	2	3	21	0	56	2	0
Plesac, Dan, Tor.*	4	5	.444	3.57	62	0	0	0	5	1	45.1	34	190	18	18	4	0	1	1	24	5	68	1	0
Ponson, Sidney, Bal.	5	10	.333	4.94	23	23	3	1	0	0	138.1	161	605	83	76	21	3	2	6	37	0	84	2	0
Pote, Lou, Ana.	2	0	1.000	4.15	44	1	0	0	15	2	86.2	88	380	41	40	11	1	3	3	32	5	66	3	0
Prieto, Ariel, T.B.	0	0	.000	2.45	3	0	0	0	2	0	3.2	6	19	1	1	0	0	0	1	2	0	2	0	0
Pulsipher, Bill, Bos.-Chi.*	0	0	.000	6.00	37	0	0	0	8	0	30.0	36	146	23	20	5	0	2	3	21	0	20	1	0
Quantrill, Paul, Tor.	11	2	.846	3.04	80	0	0	0	20	2	83.0	86	341	29	28	6	7	2	6	12	7	58	0	0
Radinsky, Scott, Cle.*	0	0	.000	27.00	2	0	0	0	0	0	2.0	4	13	6	6	2	0	0	0	3	0	3	0	0
Radke, Brad, Min.	15	11	.577	3.94	33	33	6	2	0	0	226.0	235	919	105	99	24	10	6	10	26	0	137	4	1
Rapp, Pat, Ana.	5	12	.294	4.76	31	28	1	0	1	0	170.0	169	731	96	90	20	3	7	2	71	2	82	4	0
Redman, Mark, Min.-Det.*	2	6	.250	4.50	11	11	0	0	0	0	58.0	68	261	32	29	7	2	0	1	23	0	33	6	0
Reed, Rick, Min.	4	6	.400	5.19	12	12	0	0	0	0	67.2	92	303	45	39	12	0	2	4	14	0	43	1	0
Reed, Steve, Cle.	1	1	.500	3.62	31	0	0	0	8	0	27.1	22	116	11	11	3	0	0	2	10	2	21	0	0
Reichert, Dan, K.C.	8	8	.500	5.63	27	19	0	0	4	0	123.0	131	554	83	77	14	3	4	8	67	2	77	12	0
Rekar, Bryan, T.B.	3	13	.188	5.89	25	25	0	0	0	0	140.2	167	630	104	92	21	4	7	6	45	2	87	6	1
Rhodes, Arthur, Sea.*	8	0	1.000	1.72	71	0	0	0	16	3	68.0	46	258	14	13	5	1	0	1	12	0	83	3	0
Rincon, Juan, Min.	0	0	.000	6.35	4	0	0	0	1	0	5.2	7	28	5	4	1	1	0	0	5	0	4	0	0
Rincon, Ricardo, Cle.*	2	1	.667	2.83	67	0	0	0	19	2	54.0	44	223	18	17	3	2	3	0	21	5	50	1	0
Riske, David, Cle.	2	0	1.000	1.98	26	0	0	0	6	1	27.1	20	118	7	6	3	0	1	2	18	3	29	1	0
Rivera, Mariano, N.Y.	4	6	.400	2.34	71	0	0	0	66	50	80.2	61	310	24	21	5	4	1	1	12	2	83	1	0
Roberts, Willis, Bal.	9	10	.474	4.91	46	18	1	0	20	6	132.0	142	593	75	72	15	5	4	11	55	1	95	3	2
Rocker, John, Cle.*	3	7	.300	5.45	38	0	0	0	20	4	34.2	33	165	23	21	2	4	1	3	25	3	43	6	2
Rodriguez, Rich, Tex.*	2	2	.500	4.15	53	0	0	0	6	0	39.0	41	174	24	18	2	2	1	2	17	3	31	1	1
Rogers, Kenny, Tex.*	5	7	.417	6.19	20	20	0	0	0	0	120.2	150	552	88	83	18	1	6	8	49	2	74	4	1
Romero, J.C., Min.*	1	4	.200	6.23	14	11	0	0	1	0	65.0	71	286	48	45	10	3	2	1	24	1	39	1	0
Rose, Brian, T.B.	0	2	.000	8.85	7	3	0	0	2	0	20.1	31	101	20	20	4	0	2	0	12	0	11	7	0
Rupe, Ryan, T.B.	5	12	.294	6.59	28	26	0	0	1	0	143.1	161	635	111	105	30	3	5	11	48	0	123	7	1
Ryan, B.J., Bal.*	2	4	.333	4.25	61	0	0	0	9	2	53.0	47	237	31	25	6	1	2	2	30	4	54	0	0
Sabathia, C.C., Cle.*	17	5	.773	4.39	33	33	0	0	0	0	180.1	149	763	93	88	19	3	5	7	95	1	171	7	3
Saberhagen, Bret, Bos.	1	2	.333	6.00	3	3	0	0	0	0	15.0	19	64	11	10	3	0	0	1	0	0	10	0	0
Santana, Johan, Min.*	1	0	1.000	4.74	15	4	0	0	5	0	43.2	50	195	25	23	6	2	3	3	16	0	28	3	0
Santiago, Jose, K.C.	2	2	.500	6.59	20	0	0	0	6	0	29.1	40	136	22	22	2	3	3	1	9	1	15	1	0
Santos, Victor, Det.	2	2	.500	3.30	33	7	0	0	6	0	76.1	62	335	33	28	9	1	3	3	49	4	52	0	0
Sasaki, Kazuhiro, Sea.	0	4	.000	3.24	69	0	0	0	63	45	66.2	48	261	24	24	6	0	4	4	11	2	62	4	0
Schoeneweis, Scott, Ana.*	10	11	.476	5.08	32	32	1	0	0	0	205.1	227	910	122	116	21	3	8	14	77	2	104	4	1
Schourek, Pete, Bos.*	1	5	.167	4.45	33	0	0	0	7	0	30.1	35	137	19	15	4	1	1	1	15	3	20	0	0
Seay, Bobby, T.B.*	1	1	.500	6.23	12	0	0	0	4	0	13.0	13	58	11	9	3	2	0	1	5	1	12	1	0
Sele, Aaron, Sea.	15	5	.750	3.60	34	33	2	1	0	0	215.0	216	899	93	86	25	5	9	7	51	2	114	1	0
Shields, Scot, Ana.	0	0	.000	0.00	8	0	0	0	6	0	11.0	8	48	1	0	0	0	0	1	7	0	7	2	0
Shuey, Paul, Cle.	5	3	.625	2.82	47	0	0	0	11	2	54.1	53	244	25	17	1	4	2	1	26	5	70	6	0
Smart, J.D., Tex.	1	2	.333	6.46	15	0	0	0	4	0	15.1	19	68	11	11	3	0	2	0	4	0	10	1	0
Smith, Mary, Cle.	0	0	.000	6.06	9	0	0	0	2	0	16.1	16	80	14	11	3	0	0	2	13	1	17	0	0
Sparks, Steve W., Det.	14	9	.609	3.65	35	33	8	1	2	0	232.0	244	982	110	94	22	4	9	6	64	1	116	8	2
Speier, Justin, Cle.	2	0	1.000	6.97	12	0	0	0	2	0	20.2	24	96	16	16	5	0	3	3	8	0	15	2	0
Standridge, Jason, T.B.	0	0	.000	4.66	9	1	0	0	6	0	19.1	19	87	10	10	5	0	0	0	14	1	9	0	0
Stanton, Mike, N.Y.*	9	4	.692	2.58	76	0	0	0	16	0	80.1	80	342	25	23	4	2	3	4	29	9	78	3	1
Stark, Dennis, Sea.	1	1	.500	9.20	4	3	0	0	0	0	14.2	21	68	15	15	5	0	1	0	4	0	12	0	0
Stein, Blake, K.C.	7	8	.467	4.74	36	15	0	0	5	1	131.0	112	568	73	69	20	1	4	3	79	2	113	10	0
Sturtze, Tanyon, T.B.	11	12	.478	4.42	39	27	0	0	6	1	195.1	200	837	98	96	23	2	10	9	79	0	110	11	0
Suppan, Jeff, K.C.	10	14	.417	4.37	34	34	1	0	0	0	218.1	227	946	120	106	26	5	6	12	74	3	120	6	0
Suzuki, Mac, K.C.	2	5	.286	5.30	15	9	0	0	3	0	56.0	61	251	38	33	12	0	3	3	25	1	37	6	0
Tam, Jeff, Oak.	2	4	.333	3.01	70	0	0	0	15	3	74.2	68	310	27	25	3	3	3	3	29	9	44	0	0
Thomas, Brad, Min.*	0	2	.000	9.37	5	5	0	0	0	0	16.1	20	82	17	17	6	1	0	1	14	0	6	2	0
Tolar, Kevin, Det.*	0	0	.000	6.75	9	0	0	0	1	0	10.2	7	50	8	8	0	0	0	0	13	1	11	1	0
Tomko, Brett, Sea.	3	1	.750	5.19	11	4	0	0	1	0	34.2	42	164	24	20	9	1	2	0	15	2	22	1	0
Towers, Josh, Bal.	8	10	.444	4.49	24	20	1	1	2	0	140.1	165	586	74	70	21	3	4	6	16	0	58	1	0
Trombley, Mike, Bal.	3	4	.429	3.46	50	0	0	0	21	6	54.2	38	226	23	21	4	4	3	2	27	2	45	1	0
Urbina, Ugueth, Bos.	0	1	.000	2.25	19	0	0	0	13	9	20.0	16	77	5	5	1	1	0	0	3	0	32	0	0
Valdes, Ismael, Ana.	9	13	.409	4.45	27	27	1	0	0	0	163.2	177	699	82	81	20	3	0	8	50	3	100	3	0
Venafro, Mike, Tex.*	5	5	.500	4.80	70	0	0	0	20	4	60.0	54	266	35	32	2	2	4	7	28	4	29	3	0
Villafuerte, Brandon, Tex.	0	0	.000	14.29	6	0	0	0	4	0	5.2	12	35	9	9	3	0	1	1	4	0	4	1	0
Vining, Ken, Chi.*	0	0	.000	17.55	8	0	0	0	2	0	6.2	15	42	14	13	3	0	1	0	7	0	3	0	0
Vizcaino, Luis, Oak.	2	1	.667	4.66	36	0	0	0	15	1	36.2	38	156	19	19	8	0	1	0	12	1	31	3	0
Voyles, Brad, K.C.	0	0	.000	3.86	7	0	0	0	3	0	9.1	5	40	4	4	1	0	0	1	8	0	6	0	0
Wakefield, Tim, Bos.	9	12	.429	3.90	45	17	0	0	5	3	168.2	156	732	84	73	13	3	9	18	73	5	148	5	1
Wallace, Jeff, T.B.*	0	3	.000	3.40	29	1	0	0	9	0	50.1	43	225	26	19	4	2	0	1	37	0	38	3	1
Wasdin, John, Bal.	1	1	.500	4.17	26	0	0	0	5	0	49.2	54	220	25	23	4	0	4	5	16	4	47	2	0
Washburn, Jarrod, Ana.*	11	10	.524	3.77	30	30	1	0	0	0	193.1	196	813	89	81	25	4	4	7	54	4	126	3	0
Weaver, Jeff, Det.	13	16	.448	4.08	33	33	5	0	0	0	229.1	235	985	116	104	19	12	7	14	68	4	152	3	0
Weber, Ben, Ana.	6	2	.750	3.42	56	0	0	0	19	0	68.1	66	299	28	26	4	0	0	5	31	8	40	0	1
Wells, David, Chi.*	5	7	.417	4.47	16	16	1	0	0	0	100.2	120	432	55	50	12	2	2	3	21	1	59	2	0
Wells, Kip, Chi.	10	11	.476	4.79	40	20	0	0	3	0	133.1	145	603	80	71	14	8	6	12	61	5	99	14	0
Wells, Bob, Min.	8	5	.615	5.11	65	0	0	0	18	2	68.2	72	299	39	39	12	3	4	10	18	2	49	0	0
Westbrook, Jake, Cle.	4	4	.500	5.85	23	6	0	0	3	0	64.2	79	290	43	42	6	1	5	4	22	4	48	4	0
Wheeler, Dan, T.B.	1	0	1.000	8.66	13	0	0	0	3	0	17.2	30	87	17	17	3	0	2	0	5	0	12	1	1
Wickman, Bob, Cle.	5	0	1.000	2.39	70	0	0	0	56	32	67.2	61	270	18	18	4	0	0	2	14	2	66	2	0
Williams, Todd, N.Y.	1	0	1.000	4.70	15	0	0	0	6	0	15.1	22	82	9	8	1	0	3	2	9	2	13	0	0

Pitcher, Team	W	L	Pct.	ERA	G	GS	CG	ShO	GF	Sv.	IP	H	TBF	R	ER	HR	SH	SF	HB	BB	IBB	SO	WP	Bk.
Wilson, Kris, K.C.	6	5	.545	5.19	29	15	0	0	6	1	109.1	132	487	78	63	26	1	3	7	32	0	67	1	0
Wilson, Paul, T.B.	8	9	.471	4.88	37	24	0	0	6	0	151.1	165	674	94	82	21	3	12	13	52	2	119	7	0
Wise, Matt, Ana.	1	4	.200	4.38	11	9	0	0	2	0	49.1	47	211	27	24	11	2	1	2	18	1	50	0	0
Witasick, Jay, N.Y.	3	0	1.000	4.69	32	0	0	0	8	0	40.1	47	188	27	21	5	0	2	2	18	1	53	1	0
Wohlers, Mark, N.Y.	1	0	1.000	4.54	31	0	0	0	14	0	35.2	33	159	20	18	3	1	2	1	18	0	33	7	0
Woodard, Steve, Cle.	3	3	.500	5.20	29	10	0	0	2	0	97.0	129	429	60	56	10	7	3	5	17	1	52	4	3
Wright, Jaret, Cle.	2	2	.500	6.52	7	7	0	0	0	0	29.0	36	140	22	21	2	2	1	0	22	0	18	1	1
Wright, Dan, Chi.	5	3	.625	5.70	13	12	0	0	1	0	66.1	78	307	45	42	12	1	5	2	39	1	36	5	0
Wunsch, Kelly, Chi.*	2	1	.667	7.66	33	0	0	0	2	0	22.1	21	105	19	19	4	3	2	6	9	1	16	0	0
Yan, Esteban, T.B.	4	6	.400	3.90	54	0	0	0	51	22	62.1	64	264	34	27	7	3	1	5	11	1	64	5	0
Zambrano, Victor, T.B.	6	2	.750	3.16	36	0	0	0	19	2	51.1	38	212	21	18	6	2	0	3	18	0	58	4	0
Zimmerman, Jeff, Tex.	4	4	.500	2.40	66	0	0	0	53	28	71.1	48	273	19	19	10	2	1	4	16	1	72	0	0
Zito, Barry, Oak.*	17	8	.680	3.49	35	35	3	2	0	0	214.1	184	902	92	83	18	5	4	13	80	0	205	6	1

PITCHERS WITH TWO OR MORE TEAMS

Pitcher, Team	W	L	Pct.	ERA	G	GS	CG	ShO	GF	Sv.	IP	H	TBF	R	ER	HR	SH	SF	HB	BB	IBB	SO	WP	Bk.
Fiore, Tony, T.B.	0	0	.000	5.40	3	0	0	0	3	0	3.1	4	15	2	2	0	0	0	1	1	0	3	1	0
Fiore, Tony, Min.	0	1	.000	5.68	4	0	0	0	2	0	6.1	5	26	4	4	0	0	0	2	0	0	5	0	0
Jones, Todd, Det.	4	5	.444	4.62	45	0	0	0	28	11	48.2	60	225	31	25	6	2	3	0	22	1	39	3	0
Jones, Todd, Min.	1	0	1.000	3.26	24	0	0	0	8	2	19.1	27	89	8	7	3	1	0	0	7	0	15	0	0
Judd, Mike, T.B.	1	0	1.000	4.05	8	2	0	0	2	0	20.0	19	90	14	9	2	0	3	1	10	0	11	0	0
Judd, Mike, Tex.	0	1	.000	8.00	4	1	0	0	1	0	9.0	15	47	10	8	2	0	0	0	5	0	5	1	0
Michalak, Chris, Tor.*	6	7	.462	4.62	24	18	0	0	2	0	115.0	133	517	66	59	14	3	4	12	49	5	57	0	5
Michalak, Chris, Tex.*	2	2	.500	3.32	11	0	0	0	2	1	21.2	24	93	8	8	5	0	0	1	6	0	10	1	1
Pulsipher, Bill, Bos.*	0	0	.000	5.32	23	0	0	0	6	0	22.0	25	102	15	13	3	0	1	2	14	0	16	1	0
Pulsipher, Bill, Chi.*	0	0	.000	7.88	14	0	0	0	2	0	8.0	11	44	8	7	2	0	1	1	7	0	4	0	0
Redman, Mark, Min.*	2	4	.333	4.22	9	9	0	0	0	0	49.0	57	219	26	23	6	1	0	0	19	0	29	6	0
Redman, Mark, Det.*	0	2	.000	6.00	2	2	0	0	0	0	9.0	11	42	6	6	1	1	0	1	4	0	4	0	0

COMBINATION SHUTOUTS: **Anaheim (1)**—Valdes, Levine, Holtz and Percival. **Baltimore (4)**—Towers and Groom; Towers and Trombley, Mercedes, Ryan, Trombley and Groom; Maduro, Groom and W. Roberts. **Boston (7)**—Martinez and Lowe; Ohka and Garces; Nomo and Lowe; Martinez and Arrojo; Martinez and Lowe; Arrojo, Beck and Lowe; F. Castillo and Banks. **Chicago (4)**—Buehrle, Howry and Foulke; D. Wells and Lowe; K. Wells and Glover; Lowe, Embree, K. Wells, Howry and Foulke. **Cleveland (4)**—Finley and Karsay; Wright, Rodriguez, Karsay and Hincon; Colon, Rincon and Baez, Sabathia, Baez, Rocker and Wickman. **Detroit (1)**—Weaver, Nitkowski and Jones. **Kansas City (1)**—Suzuki and Grimsley. **Minnesota (3)**—Romero, Carrasco, Miller, Wells and Hawkins; Milton and Wells; Milton, Cressend and Guardado. **New York (6)**—Clemens and M. Rivera; Mussina and M. Rivera; Clemens and M. Rivera; Mussina, Stanton and Mendoza; Mussina, Stanton and M. Rivera; Mussina, O. Hernandez and M. Rivera. **Oakland (3)**—Hudson, Isringhausen, Magnante and Tam; Lidle, Magnante and Mecir; Zito, Vizcaino and Heredia. **Seattle (10)**—Sele and Sasaki; Sele, Charlton and Paniagua; Moyer, Nelson and Sasaki; Pineiro, Nelson, Rhodes and Sasaki; Sele, Nelson and Rhodes; Garcia, Charlton, Nelson and Rhodes; Pineiro, Paniagua, Rhodes and Sasaki, Moyer, Rhodes and Sasaki; Moyer, Paniagua, Rhodes, Nelson and Sasaki; Clark, Abbott, Pineiro, Nelson and Sasaki. **Tampa Bay (5)**—Sturtze, Meacham and Yan; Sturtze, Phelps and Zambrano; Wilson, Creek and Phelps; Kennedy and Yan; Sturtze and Zambrano. **Texas (2)**—Glynn and Zimmerman; Bell and Zimmerman. **Toronto (5)**—Carpenter and Beirne; Parris, Escobar and Koch; Michalak and Quantrill; Carpenter, Plesac and Quantrill; Loaiza, Quantrill and Koch.

FIELDING

TEAM

Team	Pct.	G	PO	A	E	TC	DP	TP	PB
Seattle	.986	162	4395	1534	83	6012	137	0	6
Toronto	.985	162	4388	1831	97	6316	184	0	10
Anaheim	.983	162	4313	1690	103	6106	142	0	16
New York	.982	161	4354	1529	109	5992	132	0	21
Cleveland	.982	162	4340	1610	107	6057	137	0	12
Minnesota	.982	162	4324	1542	108	5974	118	0	4
Boston	.981	161	4344	1558	113	6015	129	0	23
Chicago	.981	162	4300	1731	118	6149	149	0	13

Team	Pct.	G	PO	A	E	TC	DP	TP	PB
Kansas City	.981	162	4320	1801	117	6238	204	0	10
Texas	.981	162	4315	1638	114	6067	167	1	2
Oakland	.980	162	4390	1756	125	6271	151	0	4
Detroit	.979	162	4288	1775	131	6194	164	1	30
Baltimore	.979	162	4297	1599	125	6021	137	0	15
Tampa Bay	.977	162	4271	1531	139	5941	144	0	8
Totals	.981	1133	60639	23125	1589	85353	2095	2	174

INDIVIDUAL

FIRST BASEMEN

NOTE: All caps denotes fielding-percentage leader based on 81 games for catchers, 108 for all other non-pitchers and 162 innings for pitchers. *Throws lefthanded.

Player, Team	Pct.	G	PO	A	E	TC	DP
Abad, Andy, Oak.*	1.000	1	2	0	0	2	1
Alcantara, Israel, Bos.	.950	4	17	2	1	20	1
Barnes, Larry, Ana.*	1.000	16	86	7	0	93	5
Bell, David, Sea.	1.000	2	6	0	0	6	1
Bellinger, Clay, N.Y.	1.000	6	8	1	0	9	3
Blake, Casey, Min.-Bal.	.979	8	44	2	1	47	4
Burke, Jamie, Ana.	1.000	1	2	0	0	2	0
Burkhart, Morgan, Bos.*	1.000	5	29	2	0	31	4
Catalanotto, Frank, Tex.	1.000	5	6	2	0	8	0
Chavez, Eric, Oak.	.000	1	0	0	0	0	0
Clark, Tony, Det.	.996	78	647	48	3	698	69
Conine, Jeff, Bal.	.994	80	646	45	4	695	61
Cordero, Wil, Cle.	.994	22	161	10	1	172	17
Cox, Steve, TB.*	.998	78	569	48	1	618	64
Cuddyer, Mike, Min.	.975	5	37	2	1	40	4
Daubach, Brian, Bos.	.988	106	839	75	11	925	71
Delgado, Carlos, Tor.	.994	161	1518	103	9	1630	166
Erstad, Darin, Ana.*	1.000	12	64	7	0	71	8
Fernandez, Jose, Ana.	.000	2	0	0	1	1	0
Fick, Robert, Det.	.995	26	169	12	1	182	10
Fullmer, Brad, Tor.	1.000	1	12	1	0	13	1
Galarraga, Andres, Tex.	.995	25	195	16	1	212	26
Garcia, Karim, Cle.*	1.000	2	3	0	0	3	1
Giambi, Jason, Oak.	.992	136	1224	76	11	1311	107
Giambi, Jeremy, Oak.*	.974	10	74	2	2	78	6
Gibbons, Jay, Bal.*	1.000	7	36	1	0	37	3
Gil, Benji, Ana.	1.000	18	69	8	0	77	7
Graffanino, Tony, Chi.	1.000	1	3	0	0	3	1
Halter, Shane, Det.	1.000	8	69	7	0	76	10
Harvey, Ken, K.C.	1.000	3	11	1	0	12	1
Hernandez, Ramon, Oak.	.800	2	4	0	1	5	0
Hillenbrand, Shea, Bos.	1.000	6	50	3	0	53	4
Hocking, Denny, Min.	1.000	11	47	6	0	53	3
Huff, Aubrey, TB.	.966	19	129	15	5	149	13
Ibanez, Raul, K.C.	.971	10	58	8	2	68	11
Jackson, Ryan, Det.*	1.000	35	126	12	0	138	14
Javier, Stan, Sea.	1.000	6	26	3	0	29	4
Jennings, Robin, Oak.*	1.000	6	35	3	0	38	2
Johnson, Nick, N.Y.*	1.000	15	90	5	0	95	4
Joyner, Wally, Ana.*	.997	39	270	18	1	289	27
Kinkade, Mike, Bal.	1.000	3	3	0	0	3	0
Konerko, Paul, Chi.	.994	144	1276	90	8	1374	120
LeCroy, Matt, Min.	1.000	2	4	0	0	4	0
Liefer, Jeff, Chi.	.973	15	100	9	3	112	12
Lopez, Luis, Tor.	1.000	5	10	1	0	11	0
Martinez, Edgar, Sea.	1.000	1	8	0	0	8	0
Martinez, Tino, N.Y.	.996	149	1144	99	5	1248	105
McCarty, Dave, K.C.*	.988	68	441	45	6	492	56
McGriff, Fred, TB.*	.986	74	558	59	9	626	53
MIENTKIEWICZ, Doug, Min.	.997	148	1263	69	4	1336	95
Munson, Eric, Det.	.994	17	142	14	1	157	14
Nieves, Jose, Ana.	1.000	1	2	0	0	2	0
Offerman, Jose, Bos.	.991	43	297	39	3	339	26
Olerud, John, Sea.*	.993	158	1211	121	9	1341	116
Ortiz, David, Min.*	1.000	8	60	2	0	62	2
Palmeiro, Rafael, Tex.*	.992	113	906	83	8	997	112
Pena, Carlos, Tex.*	.987	16	138	15	2	155	13
Perry, Herbert, Chi.	1.000	12	60	3	0	63	8
Pickering, Calvin, Bos.*	1.000	12	90	6	0	96	8
Posada, Jorge, N.Y.	1.000	2	7	0	0	7	1
Richard, Chris, Bal.*	1.000	18	127	9	0	136	10
Saenz, Olmedo, Oak.	.986	28	196	16	3	215	13
Sandberg, Jared, TB.	.000	1	0	0	0	0	0
Segui, David, Bal.*	.983	65	487	33	9	529	49
Simon, Randall, Det.*	.992	43	353	26	3	382	39
Sojo, Luis, N.Y.	1.000	8	32	3	0	35	2
Spiezio, Scott, Ana.	.999	105	819	74	1	894	64
Sprague, Ed, Sea.	.981	12	51	2	1	54	4
Sweeney, Mike, K.C.	.989	108	945	88	12	1045	124
Thomas, Frank, Chi.	.955	3	20	1	1	22	2
Thome, Jim, Cle.	.992	148	1177	78	10	1265	105
Valdez, Mario, Oak.	1.000	6	15	0	0	15	2
Velarde, Randy, Tex.-N.Y.	1.000	10	79	4	0	83	5
Wilson, Dan, Sea.	1.000	2	3	0	0	3	0
Woodward, Chris, Tor.	1.000	2	3	0	0	3	0
Wooten, Shawn, Ana.	.986	21	134	11	2	147	19

TRIPLE PLAY: Halter, Det.

FIRST BASEMEN WITH TWO OR MORE TEAMS

Player, Team	Pct.	G	PO	A	E	TC	DP
Blake, Casey, Min.	1.000	3	15	2	0	17	1
Blake, Casey, Bal.	.967	5	29	0	1	30	3
Velarde, Randy, Tex.	1.000	9	70	2	0	72	5
Velarde, Randy, N.Y.	1.000	1	9	2	0	11	0

SECOND BASEMEN

Player, Team	Pct.	G	PO	A	E	TC	DP
Abernathy, Brent, TB.	.981	79	150	209	7	366	56
Alicea, Luis, K.C.	.958	67	105	194	13	312	47
ALOMAR, Roberto, Cle.	.993	157	268	423	5	696	88
Bellhorn, Mark, Oak.	.953	12	15	26	2	43	4
Boone, Bret, Sea.	.986	156	286	409	10	705	90
Bush, Homer, Tor.	.990	78	153	254	4	411	68
Cabrera, Jolbert, Cle.	.983	28	20	37	1	58	5
Catalanotto, Frank, Tex.	.953	13	18	23	2	43	8
Delgado, Wilson, K.C.	1.000	2	2	4	0	6	0
Diaz, Einar, Cle.	1.000	1	0	1	0	1	0
Durham, Ray, Chi.	.986	150	280	446	10	736	88
Easley, Damion, Det.	.982	153	279	496	14	789	113
Eckstein, David, Ana.	.948	14	21	34	3	58	9
Febles, Carlos, K.C.	.981	78	128	224	7	359	62
Freel, Ryan, Tor.	.969	7	11	20	1	32	4
Frye, Jeff, Tor.	.995	47	83	122	1	206	30
Gil, Benji, Ana.	.965	21	30	53	3	86	14
Gipson, Charles, Sea.	.000	1	0	0	0	0	0
Graffanino, Tony, Chi.	.988	20	32	51	1	84	13
Hairston, Jerry Jr., Bal.	.976	156	326	458	19	803	93
Hocking, Denny, Min.	.979	17	23	24	1	48	6
Izturis, Cesar, Tor.	.988	41	57	110	2	169	23
Johnson, Russ, TB.	1.000	33	60	83	0	143	21
Kennedy, Adam, Ana.	.984	131	236	376	10	622	64
Lansing, Mike, Bos.	.970	31	53	75	4	132	15
Lewis, Mark, Cle.	1.000	3	2	1	0	3	0
Macias, Jose, Det.	1.000	18	25	31	0	56	3
Martinez, Felix, TB.	1.000	10	15	20	0	35	3
Maxwell, Jason, Min.	1.000	9	4	17	0	21	0
McDonald, John, Cle.	1.000	3	2	2	0	4	1
McLemore, Mark, Sea.	.946	9	18	17	2	37	8
Menechino, Frank, Oak.	.978	136	253	406	15	674	90
Merloni, Lou, Bos.	.947	5	10	8	1	19	3

Player, Team	Pct.	G	PO	A	E	TC	DP
Mora, Melvin, Bal.	.500	1	0	1	1	2	0
Nieves, Jose, Ana.	1.000	11	21	31	0	52	10
Offerman, Jose, Bos.	.974	91	161	249	11	421	44
Ordaz, Luis, K.C.	.987	19	21	53	1	75	16
Ortiz, Jose, Oak.	.951	10	16	23	2	41	7
Perez, Neifi, K.C.	1.000	4	9	13	0	22	1
Randa, Joe, K.C.	1.000	1	3	1	0	4	1
Rivas, Luis, Min.	.974	150	230	335	15	580	65
Roberts, Brian, Bal.	.950	12	13	25	2	40	6
Rolls, Damian, TB.	.968	42	69	113	6	188	21
Sadler, Donnie, K.C.	1.000	13	28	38	0	66	12
Santana, Pedro, Det.	1.000	1	1	0	0	1	0
Santangelo, F.P., Oak.	1.000	20	33	40	0	73	7
Santos, Angel, Bos.	.905	6	7	12	2	21	0
Smith, Bobby, TB.	.958	6	12	11	1	24	3
Sojo, Luis, N.Y.	1.000	7	5	8	0	13	0
Soriano, Alfonso, N.Y.	.973	156	318	366	19	703	93
Stynes, Chris, Bos.	.995	43	73	116	1	190	18
Vazquez, Ramon, Sea.	1.000	6	3	7	0	10	0
Velarde, Randy, Tex.	.988	52	111	135	3	249	38
Wilson, Enrique, N.Y.	1.000	7	9	17	0	26	3
Woodward, Chris, Tor.	.959	17	22	49	3	74	10
Young, Michael, Tex.	.984	104	211	284	8	503	79

TRIPLE PLAYS: Easley, Det.; Velarde, Tex.

THIRD BASEMEN

Player, Team	Pct.	G	PO	A	E	TC	DP
Alicea, Luis, K.C.	.973	18	12	24	1	37	3
Batista, Tony, Tor.-Bal.	.948	101	74	198	15	287	20
Bell, David, Sea.	.961	134	92	257	14	363	21
Bellhorn, Mark, Oak.	.900	9	3	15	2	20	0
Bellinger, Clay, N.Y.	.939	17	16	30	3	49	5
Blake, Casey, Min.	.800	5	1	3	1	5	0
Branyan, Russell, Cle.	.930	72	39	108	11	158	8
Brosius, Scott, N.Y.	.935	120	81	238	22	341	21
Cabrera, Jolbert, Cle.	.970	27	9	23	1	33	2
Caminiti, Ken, Tex.	.940	53	42	99	9	150	10
Castilla, Vinny, TB.	.934	24	26	45	5	76	5
Catalanotto, Frank, Tex.	.958	11	6	17	1	24	0
CHAVEZ, Eric, Oak.	.972	149	100	321	12	433	27
Conine, Jeff, Bal.	1.000	17	15	24	0	39	0
Crede, Joe, Chi.	1.000	15	17	18	0	35	3
Cruz, Deivi, Det.	1.000	7	5	7	0	12	0
Cuddyer, Mike, Min.	.000	2	0	0	0	0	0
Delgado, Wilson, K.C.	1.000	3	0	7	0	7	0
Dransfeldt, Kelly, Tex.	.000	1	0	0	0	0	0
Fernandez, Jose, Ana.	.000	1	0	0	0	0	0
Frye, Jeff, Tor.	1.000	27	7	22	0	29	2
Fryman, Travis, Cle.	.944	96	65	137	12	214	14
Gipson, Charles, Sea.	.889	9	2	6	1	9	0
Glaus, Troy, Ana.	.953	159	103	286	19	408	21
Graffanino, Tony, Chi.	.923	38	16	44	5	65	1
Halter, Shane, Det.	.924	74	57	150	17	224	12
Hillenbrand, Shea, Bos.	.941	129	88	200	18	306	16
Hocking, Denny, Min.	.900	6	1	8	1	10	0
Huff, Aubrey, TB.	.918	73	41	126	15	182	13
Ibanez, Raul, K.C.	.000	1	0	0	1	1	0
Johnson, Russ, TB.	.922	36	21	50	6	77	6
Kinkade, Mike, Bal.	1.000	10	8	11	0	19	0
Koskie, Corey, Min.	.964	150	95	306	15	416	19
Lamb, Mike, Tex.	.914	74	52	139	18	209	14
Lewis, Mark, Cle.	.889	4	2	6	1	9	1
Liefer, Jeff, Chi.	.867	15	7	19	4	30	2
Lopez, Felipe, Tor.	.940	47	20	100	8	134	6
Lopez, Luis, Tor.	.936	28	17	56	5	78	4
Macias, Jose, Det.	.955	89	68	187	12	267	23
Maxwell, Jason, Min.	1.000	11	8	17	0	25	1
McDonald, John, Cle.	1.000	3	0	2	0	2	0
McLemore, Mark, Sea.	.913	36	25	48	7	80	3
Menechino, Frank, Oak.	.000	1	0	0	0	0	0
Merloni, Lou, Bos.	.000	1	0	0	0	0	0
Nieves, Jose, Ana.	1.000	2	0	3	0	3	1
Ordaz, Luis, K.C.	.000	1	0	0	0	0	0
Patterson, Jarrod, Det.	.923	13	9	15	2	26	0
Perry, Herbert, Chi.	.940	68	45	112	10	167	5
Randa, Joe, K.C.	.966	137	111	255	13	379	31
Ripken, Cal Jr., Bal.	.956	111	97	209	14	320	23
Rolls, Damian, TB.	1.000	1	3	3	0	6	0
Sadler, Donnie, K.C.	1.000	15	9	27	0	36	5
Saenz, Olmedo, Oak.	.923	14	5	19	2	26	3
Sandberg, Jared, TB.	.944	38	33	68	6	107	7

Player, Team	Pct.	G	PO	A	E	TC	DP
Santangelo, F.P., Oak.	.000	3	0	0	0	0	0
Sheldon, Scott, Tex.	.951	38	37	61	5	103	1
Sojo, Luis, N.Y.	.933	17	7	21	2	30	2
Spiezio, Scott, Ana.	.917	10	2	9	1	12	1
Sprague, Ed, Sea.	.941	8	5	11	1	17	0
Stynes, Chris, Bos.	.949	46	31	63	5	99	5
Valentin, John, Bos.	1.000	3	1	1	0	2	0
Valentin, Jose, Chi.	.926	66	49	113	13	175	9
Vazquez, Ramon, Sea.	.500	2	0	1	1	2	0
Velarde, Randy, Tex.-N.Y.	.943	14	8	25	2	35	3
Wilson, Enrique, N.Y.	1.000	19	7	29	0	36	2
Woodward, Chris, Tor.	.839	10	6	20	5	31	5
Wooten, Shawn, Ana.	.000	1	0	0	0	0	0

THIRD BASEMEN WITH TWO OR MORE TEAMS

Player, Team	Pct.	G	PO	A	E	TC	DP
Batista, Tony, Tor.	.953	72	56	145	10	211	21
Batista, Tony, Bal.	.934	29	18	53	5	76	5
Velarde, Randy, Tex.	.929	7	4	9	1	14	2
Velarde, Randy, N.Y.	.952	7	4	16	1	21	1

SHORTSTOPS

Player, Team	Pct.	G	PO	A	E	TC	DP
Almonte, Erick, N.Y.	.875	4	4	3	1	8	1
Batista, Tony, Bal.	.990	20	33	63	1	97	11
Bellhorn, Mark, Oak.	.900	5	3	6	1	10	0
Bellinger, Clay, N.Y.	1.000	2	0	3	0	3	0
Berroa, Angel, K.C.	.953	14	21	40	3	64	9
Bordick, Mike, Bal.	.977	58	107	146	6	259	28
Cabrera, Jolbert, Cle.	.951	14	11	28	2	41	4
Chavez, Eric, Oak.	.000	1	0	0	0	0	0
Clayton, Royce, Chi.	.988	133	196	367	7	570	74
Cruz, Deivi, Det.	.964	109	157	292	17	466	69
Delgado, Wilson, K.C.	1.000	6	2	10	0	12	2
Dransfeldt, Kelly, Tex.	1.000	3	0	4	0	4	0
Eckstein, David, Ana.	.971	126	178	332	15	525	66
Frye, Jeff, Tor.	1.000	2	0	2	0	2	0
Fryman, Travis, Cle.	1.000	1	1	2	0	3	1
Garciaparra, Nomar, Bos.	.968	21	34	50	3	93	13
Gil, Benji, Ana.	.945	44	78	110	11	199	24
Gipson, Charles, Sea.	.952	6	9	11	1	21	1
Giaus, Troy, Ana.	1.000	2	0	1	0	1	0
Gomez, Chris, TB.	.968	58	80	131	7	218	29
Gonzalez, Alex S., Tor.	.987	154	249	509	10	768	120
Graffanino, Tony, Chi.	.857	5	2	4	1	7	2
Grebeck, Craig, Bos.	1.000	23	16	32	0	48	4
Guillen, Carlos, Sea.	.980	137	187	313	10	510	75
Guzman, Cristian, Min.	.959	118	165	327	21	513	58
Halter, Shane, Det.	.967	62	97	169	9	275	46
Hocking, Denny, Min.	.983	47	65	111	3	179	26
Izturis, Cesar, Tor.	.964	6	16	11	1	28	5
Jeter, Derek, N.Y.	.974	150	212	343	15	570	68
Johnson, Russ, TB.	.857	6	3	3	1	7	0
Lansing, Mike, Bos.	.966	76	108	172	10	290	37
Lofton, James, Bos.	.920	7	9	14	2	25	3
Lopez, Felipe, Tor.	.917	3	6	5	1	12	1
Martinez, Felix, TB.	.944	67	103	148	15	266	38
Maxwell, Jason, Min.	.893	12	8	17	3	28	3
McDonald, John, Cle.	.955	9	8	13	1	22	2
McLemore, Mark, Sea.	.984	35	41	79	2	122	20
Menechino, Frank, Oak.	.500	3	0	1	1	2	0
Merloni, Lou, Bos.	.987	45	54	100	2	156	19
Mora, Melvin, Bal.	.965	43	69	125	7	201	21
Nieves, Jose, Ana.	.957	10	10	12	1	23	2
Ordaz, Luis, K.C.	.905	8	6	13	2	21	1
Perez, Neifi, K.C.	.978	46	96	131	5	232	38
Roberts, Brian, Bal.	.939	51	84	131	14	229	25
Rodriguez, Alex, Tex.	.976	161	280	452	18	750	118
Sadler, Donnie, K.C.	.923	6	7	17	2	26	3
Sanchez, Rey, K.C.	.994	100	155	333	3	491	99
Sheets, Andy, TB.	.990	49	80	121	2	203	29
Sheldon, Scott, Tex.	.960	16	8	16	1	25	3
Sojo, Luis, N.Y.	1.000	5	7	10	0	17	2
Tejada, Miguel, Oak.	.973	162	256	473	20	749	93
Valentin, John, Bos.	.970	18	22	42	2	66	9
Valentin, Jose, Chi.	.953	43	64	118	9	191	34
Vazquez, Ramon, Sea.	1.000	10	11	9	0	20	3
VIZQUEL, Omar, Cle.	.989	154	219	414	7	640	88
Wilson, Enrique, N.Y.	.952	20	13	27	2	42	4
Woodward, Chris, Tor.	1.000	4	3	8	0	11	2

TRIPLE PLAY: Cruz, Det.; Rodriguez, Tex.

OUTFIELDERS

Player, Team	Pct.	G	PO	A	E	TC	DP
Alcantara, Israel, Bos.	.900	8	8	1	1	10	0
Allen, Chad, Min.	.968	27	57	3	2	62	0
Anderson, Brady, Bal.*	.988	120	239	8	3	250	4
Anderson, Garret, Ana.*	.994	149	313	9	2	324	2
Barnes, John, Min.	.895	9	16	1	2	19	0
Barnes, Larry, Ana.*	.000	1	0	0	0	0	0
Bellhorn, Mark, Oak.	.000	1	0	0	0	0	0
Bellinger, Clay, N.Y.	1.000	25	21	0	0	21	0
Beltran, Carlos, K.C.	.988	152	404	14	5	423	6
Berger, Brandon, K.C.	1.000	5	7	0	0	7	0
Bichette, Dante, Bos.	.955	53	80	4	4	88	1
Bigbie, Larry, Bal.	1.000	40	71	2	0	73	1
Bradley, Milton, Cle.	.929	9	12	1	1	14	0
Bragg, Darren, N.Y.	1.000	3	2	0	0	2	0
Branyan, Russell, Cle.	.933	33	39	3	3	45	0
Brosius, Scott, N.Y.	1.000	2	1	0	0	1	0
Brown, Dee, K.C.	.988	83	159	3	2	164	1
Brumbaugh, Cliff, Tex.	1.000	6	6	0	0	6	0
Buchanan, Brian, Min.	.973	46	70	1	2	73	0
Buhner, Jay, Sea.	1.000	12	15	0	0	15	0
Burks, Ellis, Cle.	1.000	20	25	2	0	27	0
Byrnes, Eric, Oak.	.933	12	14	0	1	15	0
Cabrera, Jolbert, Cle.	.978	83	90	1	2	93	1
Cameron, Mike, Sea.	.986	149	410	8	6	424	2
Canseco, Jose, Chi.	1.000	2	1	0	0	1	0
Catalanotto, Frank, Tex.	.995	92	187	2	1	190	0
Cedeno, Roger, Det.	.953	120	236	5	12	253	1
Chavez, Endy, K.C.*	1.000	28	40	2	0	42	0
Christensen, McKay, Chi.*	1.000	6	2	0	0	2	0
Christenson, Ryan, Oak.	1.000	4	1	0	0	1	0
Coleman, Michael, N.Y.	1.000	9	8	0	0	8	0
Conine, Jeff, Bal.	1.000	36	85	2	0	87	0
Cordero, Wil, Cle.	.985	51	64	1	1	66	0
Cordova, Marty, Cle.	.990	106	200	8	2	210	1
Cox, Steve, TB.*	1.000	8	11	1	0	12	0
Cruz, Jacob, Cle.*	.976	22	40	0	1	41	0
Cruz, Jose, Tor.	.990	143	286	5	3	294	1
Curtis, Chad, Tex.	.988	33	80	2	1	83	1
Damon, Johnny, Oak.*	.991	154	345	4	3	352	1
Daubach, Brian, Bos.	1.000	14	22	0	0	22	0
DaVanon, Jeff, Ana.	.980	29	45	3	1	49	1
DeShields, Delino, Bal.	.967	47	87	2	3	92	0
Dye, Jermaine, K.C.-Oak.	.979	154	274	12	6	292	1
Encarnacion, Juan, Det.	.977	116	247	5	6	258	0
ERSTAD, Darin, Ana.*	.998	146	398	10	1	409	3
Everett, Carl, Bos.	.974	93	185	4	5	194	1
Fick, Robert, Det.	1.000	8	15	1	0	16	0
Freel, Ryan, Tor.	.000	1	0	0	0	0	0
Frye, Jeff, Tor.	.000	1	0	0	0	0	0
Gant, Ron, Oak.	1.000	11	4	0	0	4	0
Garcia, Karim, Cle.*	.905	18	15	4	2	21	0
Giambi, Jeremy, Oak.*	.943	47	49	1	3	53	0
Gibbons, Jay, Bal.*	1.000	28	62	3	0	65	0
Gil, Benji, Ana.	.000	1	0	0	0	0	0
Gipson, Charles, Sea.	1.000	65	40	1	0	41	0
Gonzalez, Juan, Cle.	.987	119	214	10	3	227	3
Graffanino, Tony, Chi.	1.000	3	3	0	0	3	0
Greer, Rusty, Tex.*	.962	60	124	2	5	131	0
Grieve, Ben, TB.*	.984	120	240	4	4	248	0
Guillen, Jose, TB.	.969	36	86	7	3	96	3
Harris, Willie, Bal.	1.000	8	16	1	0	17	1
Higginson, Bobby, Det.	.976	142	321	10	8	339	1
Hocking, Denny, Min.	1.000	16	27	1	0	28	1
Hubbard, Trenidad, K.C.	1.000	3	2	0	0	2	0
Hunter, Torii, Min.	.992	147	460	14	4	478	3
Ibanez, Raul, K.C.	.967	42	56	3	2	61	0
Jackson, Ryan, Det.*	.943	34	33	0	2	35	0
Javier, Stan, Sea.	.993	76	139	1	1	141	1
Jennings, Robin, Oak.*	1.000	13	13	1	0	14	0
Jones, Jacque, Min.*	.983	140	278	8	5	291	0
Justice, David, N.Y.*	.981	25	49	4	1	54	1
Kapler, Gabe, Tex.	.997	133	344	8	1	353	3
Kielty, Bobby, Min.	.956	34	63	2	3	68	1
Kingsale, Gene, Bal.-Sea.	1.000	10	13	0	0	13	0
Kinkade, Mike, Oak.	.962	32	50	1	2	53	0
Knoblauch, Chuck, N.Y.	.989	108	171	8	2	181	4
Lampkin, Tom, Sea.	.000	1	0	0	0	0	0
Latham, Chris, Tor.	1.000	31	47	2	0	49	1
Lawton, Matt, Min.	.980	94	193	2	4	199	2
Ledee, Ricky, Tex.*	.979	72	137	1	3	141	0

Player, Team	Pct.	G	PO	A	E	TC	DP
Lee, Carlos, Chi.	.969	130	241	9	8	258	0
Lewis, Darren, Bos.	1.000	69	102	4	0	106	2
Liefer, Jeff, Chi.	1.000	38	52	2	0	54	0
Lofton, Kenny, Cle.*	.981	130	310	3	6	319	0
Long, Terrence, Oak.*	.980	162	332	5	7	344	3
Macias, Jose, Det.	1.000	29	72	1	0	73	0
Magee, Wendell, Det.	.992	74	123	7	1	131	0
Magruder, Chris, Tex.	1.000	12	21	1	0	22	0
Martin, Al, Sea.*	.971	73	132	3	4	139	2
Mateo, Ruben, Tex.	.986	39	70	0	1	71	0
Matos, Luis, Bal.	.985	31	65	2	1	68	2
McCarty, Dave, K.C.*	.750	9	6	0	2	8	0
McCracken, Quinton, Min.	1.000	10	13	0	0	13	0
McDonald, Donzell, N.Y.	1.000	3	2	0	0	2	0
McLemore, Mark, Sea.	.988	68	81	3	1	85	2
McMillon, Billy, Det.-Oak.*	.967	23	28	1	1	30	0
Mohr, Dustan, Min.	1.000	19	45	0	0	45	0
Mondesi, Raul, Tor.	.972	149	263	18	8	289	2
Monroe, Craig, Tex.	1.000	24	42	3	0	45	1
Mora, Melvin, Bal.	.987	88	218	4	3	225	1
Nixon, Trot, Bos.*	.973	145	280	7	8	295	4
O'Leary, Troy, Bos.*	.994	89	163	3	1	167	0
O'Neill, Paul, N.Y.*	.981	130	210	1	4	215	0
Ordonez, Magglio, Chi.	.983	155	286	11	5	302	0
Palmeiro, Orlando, Ana.*	.989	59	87	2	1	90	1
Perez, Robert, N.Y.	1.000	5	7	0	0	7	0
Piatt, Adam, Oak.	.962	32	48	3	2	53	0
Podsednik, Scott, Sea.*	1.000	5	3	0	0	3	0
Porter, Bo, Tex.	.969	40	61	1	2	64	0
Quinn, Mark, K.C.	.976	99	197	8	5	210	1
Raines, Tim Sr., Bal.	1.000	2	7	0	0	7	0
Raines, Tim Jr., Bal.	1.000	7	12	0	0	12	0
Ramirez, Julio, Chi.	.978	21	43	2	1	46	1
Ramirez, Manny, Bos.	1.000	55	98	1	0	99	0
Richard, Chris, Bal.*	1.000	96	228	6	0	234	2
Rivera, Juan, N.Y.	1.000	3	1	0	0	1	0
Roberts, Dave, Cle.*	1.000	13	8	0	0	8	0
Rolls, Damian, TB.	1.000	25	38	2	0	40	0
Rowand, Aaron, Chi.	.991	61	103	3	1	107	0
Ryan, Rob, Oak.*	1.000	5	2	0	0	2	0
Sadler, Donnie, K.C.	1.000	16	27	2	0	29	0
Salmon, Tim, Ana.	.989	125	254	13	3	270	5
Sanders, Anthony, Sea.	1.000	9	13	0	0	13	0
Santangelo, F.P., Oak.	1.000	6	10	0	0	10	0
Sheldon, Scott, Tex.	1.000	3	2	0	0	2	0
Sierra, Ruben, Tex.	.937	36	59	0	4	63	0
Simmons, Brian, Tex.	1.000	37	59	1	0	60	0
Singleton, Chris, Chi.*	.991	133	310	8	3	321	2
Spencer, Shane, N.Y.	.993	68	139	7	1	147	0
Spiezio, Scott, Ana.	1.000	18	19	0	0	19	0
Sprague, Ed, Sea.	1.000	9	11	0	0	11	0
Stewart, Shannon, Tor.	.981	142	257	7	5	269	0
Stynes, Chris, Bos.	1.000	3	5	0	0	5	0
Suzuki, Ichiro, Sea.	.997	152	335	8	1	344	2
Tyner, Jason, TB.*	.978	100	219	8	5	232	1
Valdez, Mario, Oak.	1.000	7	10	1	0	11	1
Valentin, Jose, Chi.	1.000	24	46	3	0	49	1
Vaughn, Greg, TB.	.978	57	127	4	3	134	2
Velarde, Randy, Tex.-N.Y.	1.000	5	7	0	0	7	0
Wakeland, Chris, Det.*	.941	10	32	0	2	34	0
Wells, Vernon, Tor.	.969	30	61	2	2	65	0
Williams, Bernie, N.Y.	.994	144	348	3	2	353	1
Williams, Gerald, TB.-N.Y.	.986	85	208	5	3	216	1
Winn, Randy, TB.	.981	117	245	12	5	262	0

OUTFIELDERS WITH TWO OR MORE TEAMS

Player, Team	Pct.	G	PO	A	E	TC	DP
Dye, Jermaine, K.C.	.984	93	178	5	3	186	0
Dye, Jermaine, Oak.	.972	61	96	7	3	106	1
Kingsale, Gene, Bal.	1.000	1	1	0	0	1	0
Kingsale, Gene, Sea.	1.000	9	12	0	0	12	0
McMillon, Billy, Det.*	1.000	7	10	0	0	10	0
McMillon, Billy, Oak.*	.950	16	18	1	1	20	0
Velarde, Randy, Tex.	1.000	2	2	0	0	2	0
Velarde, Randy, N.Y.	1.000	3	5	0	0	5	0
Williams, Gerald, TB.	.989	59	179	5	2	186	1
Williams, Gerald, N.Y.	.967	26	29	0	1	30	0

CATCHERS

Player, Team	Pct.	G	PO	A	E	TC	DP	PB
Alomar, Sandy Jr., Chi.	.990	69	367	19	4	390	5	5
Borders, Pat, Sea.	.923	5	10	2	1	13	0	0

Player, Team	Pct.	G	PO	A	E	TC	DP	PB
Burke, Jamie, Ana.	1.000	8	10	1	0	11	0	0
Cardona, Javier, Det.	.980	44	132	15	3	150	1	8
Castillo, Alberto, Tor.	.989	66	324	25	4	353	0	2
Dalesandro, Mark, Chi.	.000	1	0	0	0	0	0	0
Diaz, Einar, Cle.	.992	134	959	93	8	1060	11	7
DiFelice, Mike, TB.	.982	48	293	29	6	328	4	2
Estalella, Bobby, N.Y.	1.000	3	14	1	0	15	0	0
Fabregas, Jorge, Ana.	.990	53	267	23	3	293	3	2
Fasano, Sal, Oak.-K.C.	.955	12	39	3	2	44	0	1
Fick, Robert, Det.	.986	78	412	26	6	444	3	12
Flaherty, John, TB.	.986	78	458	28	7	493	4	4
Fletcher, Darrin, Tor.	.995	129	720	41	4	765	8	8
Fordyce, Brook, Bal.	.983	95	541	30	10	581	7	8
Gil, Geronimo, Bal.	.985	17	121	10	2	133	1	5
Greene, Todd, N.Y.	1.000	34	187	14	0	201	2	1
Hall, Toby, TB.	.986	46	328	20	5	353	2	2
Haselman, Bill, Tex.	1.000	47	234	13	0	247	2	0
Hatteberg, Scott, Bos.	.992	72	491	29	4	524	3	13
Hernandez, Ramon, Oak.	.989	135	907	70	11	988	15	4
Hinch, A.J., K.C.	.987	43	220	14	3	237	2	4
Hoover, Paul, TB.	1.000	2	2	1	0	3	0	0
Hubbard, Mike, Tex.	1.000	5	15	2	0	17	0	0
Inge, Brandon, Det.	.989	79	330	40	4	374	3	10
Jensen, Marcus, Bos.-Tex.	1.000	12	47	4	0	51	0	0
Johnson, Mark L., Chi.	.992	61	326	31	3	360	2	4
Kinkade, Mike, Bal.	1.000	2	11	1	0	12	0	0
Laker, Tim, Cle.	.988	14	76	6	1	83	2	0
Lampkin, Tom, Sea.	.995	71	375	23	2	400	2	3
LeCroy, Matt, Min.	1.000	1	0	1	0	7	0	0
Lunar, Fernando, Bal.	.987	64	267	32	4	303	3	2
Mayne, Brent, K.C.	.993	49	269	19	2	290	2	4
Mirabelli, Doug, Tex.-Bos.	.994	75	413	49	3	465	12	6
Molina, Ben, Ana.	.991	94	527	36	5	568	4	4
Molina, Jose, Ana.	1.000	15	78	6	0	84	1	2
Myers, Greg, Bal.-Oak.	1.000	36	193	19	0	212	2	0
Oliver, Joe, N.Y.-Bos.	.986	17	134	5	2	141	0	3
Ortiz, Hector, K.C.	.990	55	280	28	3	311	1	1
Paul, Josh, Chi.	.980	56	266	24	6	296	3	4
Phelps, Josh, Tor.	1.000	7	28	2	0	30	0	0
Pierzynski, A.J., Min.	.985	110	611	44	10	665	7	4
Posada, Jorge, N.Y.	.990	131	996	52	11	1059	11	18
Prince, Tom, Min.	1.000	64	380	41	0	421	3	0
Rivera, Mike, Det.	.929	4	24	2	2	28	0	0
Rodriguez, Ivan, Tex.	.990	106	631	52	7	690	11	2
Sheldon, Scott, Tex.	1.000	1	4	0	0	4	0	0
Sprague, Ed, Sea.	1.000	1	1	0	0	1	0	0
Taubensee, Eddie, Cle.	.986	38	212	3	3	218	0	5
Varitek, Jason, Bos.	.996	50	425	32	2	459	2	3
WILSON, Dan, Sea.	.999	122	711	32	1	744	1	3
Wilson, Tom, Oak.	.974	9	35	3	1	39	0	0
Wooten, Shawn, Ana.	1.000	25	97	11	0	108	0	8
Zaun, Gregg, K.C.	.975	35	181	11	5	197	4	0

CATCHERS WITH TWO OR MORE TEAMS

Player, Team	Pct.	G	PO	A	E	TC	DP	PB
Fasano, Sal, Oak.	.952	9	37	3	2	42	0	0
Fasano, Sal, K.C.	1.000	3	2	0	0	2	0	1
Jensen, Marcus, Bos.	1.000	1	12	1	0	13	0	0
Jensen, Marcus, Tex.	1.000	11	35	3	0	38	0	0
Mirabelli, Doug, Tex.	.990	23	84	16	1	101	4	0
Mirabelli, Doug, Bos.	.995	52	329	33	2	364	8	6
Myers, Greg, Bal.	1.000	8	41	4	0	45	0	0
Myers, Greg, Oak.	1.000	28	152	15	0	167	2	0
Oliver, Joe, N.Y.	.991	12	101	4	1	106	0	2
Oliver, Joe, Bos.	.971	5	33	1	1	35	0	1

PITCHERS

Player, Team	Pct.	G	PO	A	E	TC	DP
Abbott, Paul, Sea.	1.000	28	16	13	0	29	3
Almanzar, Carlos, N.Y.	1.000	10	1	2	0	3	0
Anderson, Matt, Det.	1.000	62	9	5	0	14	0
Arrojo, Rolando, Bos.	1.000	41	12	17	0	29	3
Austin, Jeff, K.C.	.667	21	2	2	2	6	0
Bacsik, Mike, Cle.*	1.000	3	0	1	0	1	0
Baez, Danys, Cle.	.875	43	4	3	1	8	0
Bailey, Cory, K.C.	.909	53	4	6	1	11	1
Baldwin, James, Chi.	1.000	17	7	17	0	24	3
Dale, John, Bal.*	1.000	14	1	2	0	3	0
Balfour, Grant, Min.	1.000	2	0	1	0	1	0
Banks, Willie, Bos.	.000	5	0	0	0	0	0
Barcelo, Lorenzo, Chi.	1.000	17	3	2	0	5	0

Player, Team	Pct.	G	PO	A	E	TC	DP
Bauer, Rick, Bal.	.750	6	1	2	1	4	1
Beck, Rod, Bos.	1.000	68	3	16	0	19	2
Beirne, Kevin, Tor.	1.000	5	1	3	0	4	0
Bell, Rob, Tex.	1.000	18	7	9	0	16	2
Benoit, Joaquin, Tex.	.000	1	0	0	0	0	0
Bernero, Adam, Det.	1.000	5	3	1	0	4	0
Biddle, Rocky, Chi.	.955	30	6	15	1	22	0
Bierbrodt, Nick, TB.*	1.000	11	1	6	0	7	0
Blair, Willie, Det.	1.000	9	3	3	0	6	0
Boehringer, Brian, N.Y.	1.000	22	0	2	0	2	0
Borbon, Pedro, Tor.*	1.000	71	3	6	0	9	0
Borkowski, Dave, Det.	.833	15	1	4	1	6	1
Burland, Toby, Ana.	1.000	2	1	1	0	2	0
Bowles, Brian, Tor.	.000	2	0	0	0	0	0
Bradford, Chad, Oak.	1.000	35	0	8	0	8	0
Brantley, Jeff, Tex.	1.000	18	0	0	0	0	0
Brea, Leslie, Bal.	.000	2	0	0	0	0	0
Buehrle, Mark, Chi.*	.952	32	11	49	3	63	5
Burba, Dave, Cle.	1.000	32	17	18	0	35	1
Byrd, Paul, K.C.	.952	16	5	15	1	21	0
Callaway, Mickey, TB.	.000	2	0	0	0	0	0
Carpenter, Chris, Tor.	1.000	34	11	25	0	36	6
Carrasco, Hector, Min.	.833	56	0	5	1	6	0
Castillo, Carlos, Bos.	1.000	2	1	0	0	1	0
Castillo, Frank, Bos.	1.000	26	16	16	0	32	1
Charlton, Norm, Sea.*	1.000	44	6	6	0	12	0
Choate, Randy, N.Y.*	1.000	37	2	11	0	13	1
Clemens, Roger, N.Y.	.957	33	11	33	2	46	3
Coco, Pasqual, Tor.	1.000	7	1	3	0	4	0
Cogan, Tony, K.C.*	1.000	39	3	3	0	6	1
Colome, Jesus, TB.	.833	30	4	1	1	6	0
Colon, Bartolo, Cle.	.975	34	12	27	1	40	4
Cone, David, Bos.	.920	25	14	9	2	25	0
Cooper, Brian, Ana.	1.000	7	2	0	0	2	0
Cordero, Francisco, Tex.	.000	3	0	0	0	0	0
Cornejo, Nate, Det.	1.000	10	3	5	0	8	1
Crabtree, Tim, Tex.	1.000	21	1	5	0	6	1
Crawford, Paxton, Bos.	1.000	8	3	4	0	7	0
Creek, Doug, TB.*	.700	66	2	5	3	10	1
Cressend, Jack, Min.	1.000	44	5	7	0	12	0
Davis, Doug, Tex.*	.938	30	5	25	2	32	2
DeWitt, Matt, Tor.	1.000	16	2	3	0	5	1
Dickey, R.A., Tex.	1.000	4	1	1	0	2	0
Douglass, Sean, Bal.	1.000	4	0	1	0	1	0
Drese, Ryan, Cle.	.900	9	4	5	1	10	1
Drew, Tim, Cle.	.875	8	3	4	1	8	1
Duchscherer, Justin, Tex.	1.000	5	1	0	0	1	0
Durbin, Chad, K.C.	.976	29	20	20	1	41	3
Duvall, Mike, Min.*	.000	8	0	0	0	0	0
Eldred, Cal, Chi.	1.000	2	0	2	0	2	0
Embree, Alan, Chi.*	1.000	39	2	3	0	5	1
Erdos, Todd, Bos.	1.000	10	1	1	0	2	1
Escobar, Kelvim, Tor.	.933	59	6	8	1	15	0
Eyre, Scott, Tor.*	1.000	17	0	2	0	2	0
File, Bob, Tor.	.947	60	7	11	1	19	1
Finley, Chuck, Cle.*	.813	22	2	11	3	16	0
Fiore, Tony, TB.-Min.	1.000	7	2	1	0	3	0
Florie, Bryce, Bos.	1.000	7	1	1	0	2	0
Fogg, Josh, Chi.	1.000	11	1	1	0	2	0
Fossum, Casey, Bos.*	1.000	13	3	1	0	4	0
Foster, Kevin, Tex.	.000	9	0	0	0	0	0
Foster, Kris, Bal.	1.000	7	0	4	0	4	0
Foulke, Keith, Chi.	1.000	72	7	11	0	18	0
Franklin, Ryan, Sea.	1.000	38	8	6	0	14	0
Frascatore, John, Tor.	1.000	12	1	5	0	6	0
Fuentes, Brian, Sea.*	1.000	10	1	3	0	4	0
Fyhrie, Mike, Oak.	.000	3	0	0	0	0	0
Garces, Rich, Bos.	1.000	62	7	11	0	18	2
Garcia, Freddy, Sea.	.986	34	29	39	1	69	5
Garland, Jon, Chi.	.962	35	8	17	1	26	4
George, Chris, K.C.*	.923	13	7	5	1	13	0
Ginter, Matt, Chi.	1.000	20	3	4	0	7	0
Glover, Gary, Chi.	.960	46	9	15	1	25	0
Glynn, Ryan, Tex.	1.000	12	7	5	0	12	0
Green, Steve, Ana.	1.000	1	0	1	0	1	1
Grimsley, Jason, K.C.	.818	73	6	12	4	22	2
Groom, Buddy, Bal.*	.900	70	4	5	1	10	1
Guardado, Eddie, Min.*	1.000	67	3	6	0	9	0
Guthrie, Mark, Oak.*	1.000	54	0	6	0	6	0
Halama, John, Sea.*	.968	31	9	21	1	31	0
Halladay, Roy, Tor.	1.000	17	7	16	0	23	0
Hamilton, Joey, Tor.	.923	22	8	16	2	26	2

Player, Team	Pct.	G	PO	A	E	TC	DP
Harper, Travis, TB.	1.000	2	0	1	0	1	0
Harville, Chad, Oak.	1.000	3	1	1	0	2	0
Hasegawa, Shigetoshi, Ana.	.900	46	3	6	1	10	1
Hawkins, LaTroy, Min.	1.000	62	3	5	0	8	0
Helling, Rick, Tex.	.969	34	15	16	1	32	1
Henry, Doug, K.C.	1.000	53	4	5	0	9	1
Hentgen, Pat, Bal.	.944	9	7	10	1	18	1
Heredia, Gil, Oak.	.943	24	16	17	2	35	0
Hernandez, Adrian, N.Y.	.800	6	1	3	1	5	0
Hernandez, Orlando, N.Y.	1.000	17	5	12	0	17	0
Hernandez, Roberto, K.C.	1.000	63	3	6	0	9	0
Hiljus, Erik, Oak.	1.000	16	1	4	0	5	0
Hill, Ken, TB.	.800	5	2	2	1	5	0
Hitchcock, Sterling, N.Y.*	1.000	10	3	5	0	8	0
Holt, Chris, Det.	.963	30	9	17	1	27	1
Holtz, Mike, Ana.*	.929	63	4	9	1	14	0
Howry, Bob, Chi.	1.000	69	2	10	0	12	0
Hudson, Tim, Oak.	.928	35	21	43	5	69	3
Isringhausen, Jason, Oak.	.818	65	1	8	2	11	0
Jodie, Brett, N.Y.	.000	1	0	0	0	0	0
Johnson, Adam, Min.	1.000	7	1	3	0	4	0
Johnson, Jason, Bal.	.833	32	4	16	4	24	1
Johnson, Jonathan, Tex.	.000	5	0	0	0	0	0
Jones, Todd, Det.-Min.	.944	69	7	10	1	18	0
Judd, Mike, TB.-Tex.	1.000	12	3	1	0	4	0
Julio, Jorge, Bal.	.667	18	0	2	1	3	0
Karsay, Steve, Cle.	1.000	31	3	10	0	13	1
Keisler, Randy, N.Y.*	.800	10	2	6	2	10	0
Kennedy, Joe, TB.*	1.000	20	8	14	0	22	2
Kim, Sun-Woo, Bos.	1.000	20	2	5	0	7	1
Knight, Brandon, N.Y.	1.000	4	1	0	0	1	0
Koch, Billy, Tor.	.909	69	4	6	1	11	1
Kohlmeier, Ryan, Bal.	1.000	34	0	2	0	2	0
Kolb, Danny, Tex.	.000	17	0	0	0	0	0
Laker, Tim, Cle.	.000	1	0	0	0	0	0
Levine, Al, Ana.	.857	64	3	9	2	14	1
Lidle, Cory, Oak.	.956	29	13	30	2	45	0
Lilly, Ted, N.Y.*	.931	26	5	22	2	29	0
Lima, Jose, Det.	.933	18	3	11	1	15	2
Loaiza, Esteban, Tor.	.923	36	15	21	3	39	0
Lohse, Kyle, Min.	.955	19	9	12	1	22	2
Lopez, Albie, TB.	.960	20	6	18	1	25	1
Lowe, Derek, Bos.	.958	67	6	17	1	24	2
Lowe, Sean, Chi.	1.000	45	8	21	0	29	0
Lukasiewicz, Mark, Ana.*	1.000	24	0	1	0	1	0
Lyon, Brandon, Tor.	1.000	11	3	9	0	12	0
MacDougal, Mike, K.C.	1.000	3	1	0	0	1	0
Maduro, Calvin, Bal.	1.000	22	2	8	0	10	0
Magnante, Mike, Oak.*	.900	65	2	7	1	10	0
Mahomes, Pat, Tex.	.967	56	15	14	1	30	2
Martinez, Pedro, Bos.	1.000	18	5	5	0	10	0
Mathews, T.J., Oak.	1.000	20	1	3	0	4	0
Mays, Joe, Min.	.978	34	17	28	1	46	2
McDill, Allen, Bos.*	.000	15	0	0	0	0	0
McElroy, Chuck, Bal.*	1.000	18	1	15	0	16	1
Meacham, Rusty, TB.	1.000	24	1	7	0	8	0
Meadows, Brian, K.C.	1.000	10	4	8	0	12	1
Mecir, Jim, Oak.	.933	54	3	11	1	15	1
Mendoza, Ramiro, N.Y.	1.000	56	7	14	0	21	1
Mercedes, Jose, Bal.	1.000	33	15	9	0	24	2
Miadich, Bart, Ana.	1.000	11	1	1	0	2	0
Michalak, Chris, Tor.-Tex.*	.978	35	14	30	1	45	2
Miller, Matt, Det.*	1.000	13	3	3	0	6	0
Miller, Travis, Min.*	.600	45	1	2	2	5	0
Mills, Alan, Bal.	.000	15	0	0	0	0	0
Milton, Eric, Min.*	1.000	35	7	13	0	20	1
Mlicki, Dave, Det.	1.000	15	1	11	0	12	2
Moehler, Brian, Det.	1.000	1	0	2	0	2	0
Moreno, Juan, Tex.*	.800	45	4	0	1	5	0
Moyer, Jamie, Sea.*	1.000	33	17	27	0	44	0
Mulder, Mark, Oak.*	.963	34	12	40	2	54	2
Mullen, Scott, K.C.*	1.000	17	1	1	0	2	1
Murray, Heath, Det.*	1.000	40	4	9	0	13	2
Mussina, Mike, N.Y.	.977	34	18	25	1	44	4
Myette, Aaron, Tex.	.923	19	5	7	1	13	0
Nagy, Charles, Cle.	.955	15	9	12	1	22	1
Nelson, Jeff, Sea.	.800	69	2	6	2	10	1
Nitkowski, C.J., Det.*	1.000	56	2	7	0	9	0
Nomo, Hideo, Bos.	.972	33	17	18	1	36	2
Ohka, Tomokazu, Bos.	.917	12	8	3	1	12	2
Oliver, Darren, Tex.*	1.000	28	7	26	0	33	1
Ortiz, Ramon, Ana.	.864	32	18	20	6	44	1

Player, Team	Pct.	G	PO	A	E	TC	DP
Osuna, Antonio, Chi.	.000	4	0	0	0	0	0
Painter, Lance, Tor.*	1.000	10	2	3	0	5	2
Paniagua, Jose, Sea.	.833	60	2	3	1	6	1
Parker, Christian, N.Y.	1.000	1	0	2	0	2	0
Paronto, Chad, Bal.	1.000	24	2	6	0	8	0
Parque, Jim, Chi.*	1.000	5	2	8	0	10	0
Parris, Steve, Tor.	1.000	19	4	11	0	15	0
Parrish, John, Bal.*	.750	16	0	3	1	4	0
Patterson, Danny, Det.	1.000	60	5	10	0	15	0
Percival, Troy, Ana.	1.000	57	3	1	0	4	0
Perisho, Matt, Det.*	1.000	30	1	5	0	6	0
Petkovsek, Mark, Tex.	1.000	55	5	9	0	14	0
PETTITTE, Andy, N.Y.*	1.000	31	9	40	0	49	2
Pettyjohn, Adam, Det.*	1.000	16	3	8	0	11	1
Phelps, Travis, TB.	.941	49	5	11	1	17	1
Pichardo, Hipolito, Bos.	1.000	30	3	10	0	13	1
Pineda, Luis, Det.	1.000	16	0	2	0	2	0
Pineiro, Joel, Sea.	1.000	17	4	4	0	8	0
Plesac, Dan, Tor.*	1.000	62	0	4	0	4	0
Ponson, Sidney, Bal.	1.000	23	14	19	0	33	2
Pote, Lou, Ana.	.931	44	11	16	2	29	2
Prieto, Ariel, TB.	1.000	3	1	0	0	1	0
Pulsipher, Bill, Bos.-Chi.*	.889	37	2	6	1	9	1
Quantrill, Paul, Tor.	.875	80	2	12	2	16	1
Radinsky, Scott, Cle.*	1.000	2	0	2	0	2	0
Radke, Brad, Min.	.983	33	13	44	1	58	4
Rapp, Pat, Ana.	.978	31	19	26	1	46	1
Redman, Mark, Min.-Det.*	1.000	11	1	10	0	11	1
Reed, Rick, Min.	.944	12	6	11	1	18	1
Reed, Steve, Cle.	.875	31	3	4	1	8	0
Reichert, Dan, K.C.	1.000	27	17	14	0	31	3
Rekar, Bryan, TB.	.944	25	18	16	2	36	2
Rhodes, Arthur, Sea.*	1.000	71	4	9	0	13	0
Rincon, Juan, Min.	1.000	4	0	1	0	1	0
Rincon, Ricardo, Cle.*	.909	67	5	5	1	11	0
Riske, David, Cle.	1.000	26	1	5	0	6	2
Rivera, Mariano, N.Y.	.970	71	17	15	1	33	0
Roberts, Willis, Bal.	.931	46	6	21	2	29	0
Rocker, John, Cle.*	.667	38	2	4	3	9	0
Rodriguez, Rich, Cle.*	1.000	53	0	10	0	10	1
Rogers, Kenny, Tex.*	.976	20	6	34	1	41	3
Romero, J.C., Min.*	.909	14	9	11	2	22	0
Rose, Brian, TB.	1.000	7	0	5	0	5	0
Rupe, Ryan, TB.	.895	28	5	12	2	19	0
Ryan, B.J., Bal.*	.667	61	0	4	2	6	0
Sabathia, C.C., Cle.*	.960	33	3	21	1	25	1
Saberhagen, Bret, Bos.	1.000	3	1	3	0	4	0
Santana, Johan, Min.*	.750	15	0	6	2	8	1
Santiago, Jose, K.C.	1.000	20	4	7	0	11	0
Sasaki, Kazuhiro, Sea.	.889	69	6	2	1	9	2
Schoeneweis, Scott, Ana.*	1.000	32	11	36	0	47	5
Schourek, Pete, Bos.*	.900	33	2	7	1	10	3
Seay, Bobby, TB.*	.750	12	1	2	1	4	0
Sele, Aaron, Sea.	.970	34	15	17	1	33	1
Shields, Scot, Ana.	.500	8	1	1	2	4	1
Shuey, Paul, Cle.	.556	47	1	4	4	9	1
Smart, J.D., Tex.	1.000	15	0	1	0	1	0
Smith, Roy, Cle.	.500	9	0	1	1	2	1
Sparks, Steve W., Det.	.984	35	20	43	1	64	1
Speier, Justin, Cle.	1.000	12	0	1	0	1	0
Standridge, Jason, TB.	1.000	9	1	1	0	2	0
Stanton, Mike, N.Y.*	.889	76	6	10	2	18	1
Stark, Denny, Sea.	1.000	4	2	0	0	2	0
Stein, Blake, K.C.	1.000	36	6	8	0	14	0
Sturtze, Tanyon, TB.	1.000	39	12	21	0	33	2
Suppan, Jeff, K.C.	.981	34	18	33	1	52	1
Suzuki, Mac, K.C.	.938	15	5	10	1	16	0
Tam, Jeff, Oak.	1.000	70	3	11	0	14	1
Thomas, Brad, Min.*	1.000	5	0	4	0	4	0
Tolar, Kevin, Det.*	1.000	9	0	2	0	2	0
Tomko, Brett, Sea.	1.000	11	2	3	0	5	1
Towers, Josh, Bal.	.967	24	10	19	1	30	2
Trombley, Mike, Bal.	1.000	50	6	5	0	11	0
Urbina, Ugueth, Bos.	1.000	19	1	2	0	3	0
Valdes, Ismael, Ana.	1.000	27	7	34	0	41	2
Venafro, Mike, Tex.*	.810	70	4	13	4	21	4
Villafuerte, Brandon, Tex.	1.000	6	0	1	0	1	0
Vining, Ken, Chi.*	1.000	8	1	1	0	2	0
Vizcaino, Luis, Oak.	1.000	36	0	3	0	3	0
Voyles, Brad, K.C.	.000	7	0	0	0	0	0
Wakefield, Tim, Bos.	.947	45	14	22	2	38	0

Player, Team	Pct.	G	PO	A	E	TC	DP
Wallace, Jeff, TB.*	1.000	29	0	8	0	8	0
Wasdin, John, Bal.	1.000	26	4	4	0	8	0
Washburn, Jarrod, Ana.*	.941	30	6	26	2	34	0
WEAVER, Jeff, Det.	1.000	33	21	28	0	49	4
Weber, Ben, Ana.	.889	56	2	14	2	18	2
Wells, Bob, Min.	1.000	65	1	8	0	9	1
Wells, David, Chi.*	.778	16	4	10	4	18	1
Wells, Kip, Chi.	.903	40	9	19	3	31	1
Westbrook, Jake, Cle.	.950	23	4	15	1	20	1
Wheeler, Dan, TB.	1.000	13	3	3	0	6	1
Wickman, Bob, Cle.	1.000	70	8	8	0	16	0
Williams, Todd, N.Y.	.667	15	1	3	2	6	0
Wilson, Kris, K.C.	.920	29	12	11	2	25	4
Wilson, Paul, TB.	.944	37	4	13	1	18	2
Wise, Matt, Ana.	1.000	11	1	2	0	3	0
Witasick, Jay, N.Y.	.600	32	0	3	2	5	0
Wohlers, Mark, N.Y.	.875	31	1	6	1	8	0
Woodard, Steve, Cle.	.913	29	7	14	2	23	3
Wright, Dan, Chi.	.882	13	4	11	2	17	1
Wright, Jaret, Cle.	1.000	7	1	5	0	6	0
Wunsch, Kelly, Chi.*	1.000	33	0	5	0	5	0
Yan, Esteban, TB.	1.000	54	9	6	0	15	0
Zambrano, Victor, TB.	1.000	36	8	5	0	13	0
Zimmerman, Jeff, Tex.	1.000	66	5	4	0	9	1
Zito, Barry, Oak.*	.944	35	9	25	2	36	3

PITCHERS WITH TWO OR MORE TEAMS

Player, Team	Pct.	G	PO	A	E	TC	DP
Fiore, Tony, TB.	1.000	3	1	0	0	1	0
Fiore, Tony, Min.	1.000	4	1	1	0	2	0
Jones, Todd, Det.	.933	45	5	9	1	15	0
Jones, Todd, Min.	1.000	24	2	1	0	3	0
Judd, Mike, TB.	1.000	8	1	0	0	1	0
Judd, Mike, Tex.	1.000	4	2	1	0	3	0
Michalak, Chris, Tor.*	.974	24	11	26	1	38	2
Michalak, Chris, Tex.*	1.000	11	3	4	0	7	0
Pulsipher, Bill, Bos.*	.833	23	2	3	1	6	1
Pulsipher, Bill, Chi.*	1.000	14	0	3	0	3	0
Redman, Mark, Min.*	1.000	9	1	9	0	10	1
Redman, Mark, Det.*	1.000	2	0	1	0	1	0

MISCELLANEOUS

SHUTOUT GAMES

Read across for wins, down for losses.

Team	Sea.	Oak.	Tex.	N.Y.	Chi.	Min.	Bos.	Tor.	Cle.	T.B.	Bal.	Det.	K.C.	Ana.	N.L.	W	L	Pct.
Seattle	..	1	1	0	0	1	0	0	0	1	2	0	2	4	2	14	4	.778
Oakland	0	..	0	0	0	0	1	1	1	0	1	0	1	2	2	9	3	.750
Texas	0	0	..	0	1	0	0	0	0	1	0	0	0	0	1	3	1	.750
New York	1	0	0	..	0	2	1	1	0	1	2	0	1	0	0	9	5	.643
Chicago	0	0	0	0	..	0	0	0	0	1	1	3	0	1	1	7	4	.636
Minnesota	0	0	0	1	0	..	0	0	1	0	1	2	0	2	1	8	5	.615
Boston	1	0	0	1	0	1	..	2	0	2	2	0	0	0	0	9	6	.600
Toronto	0	0	0	1	1	0	1	..	1	1	3	1	0	1	0	10	9	.526
Cleveland	0	0	0	0	1	1	0	0	..	1	0	0	0	0	1	4	7	.364
Tampa Bay	1	0	0	1	0	0	0	1	1	..	1	0	0	0	1	6	12	.333
Baltimore	1	1	0	0	1	0	0	1	0	1	..	0	0	1	1	6	14	.300
Detroit	0	0	0	0	0	0	0	0	2	0	0	..	0	0	0	2	6	.250
Kansas City	0	0	0	0	0	0	0	0	0	1	0	0	..	0	1	1	6	.143
Anaheim	0	0	0	0	0	0	0	0	0	0	0	0	0	..	1	1	12	.077
N.L. Clubs	0	1	0	1	0	0	3	3	1	3	1	0	2	1	..	..	..	
Lost	4	3	1	5	4	5	6	9	7	12	14	6	6	12	..	89	94	.486

A.L. shutouts vs. N.L. clubs (11): Oakland vs. Arizona, Oakland vs. Los Angeles, Seattle vs. Arizona, Seattle vs. Los Angeles, Anaheim vs. Los Angeles, Baltimore vs. Montreal, Chicago vs. Cincinnati, Cleveland vs. Cincinnati, Minnesota vs. Houston, Tampa Bay vs. Montreal, Texas vs. San Francisco.

HOME RECORD

Read across for home wins, down for road losses.

Team	Sea.	Oak.	N.Y.	Min.	Chi.	Cle.	Bos.	Tex.	Tor.	Ana.	Det.	T.B.	K.C.	Bal.	N.L.	W	L	Pct.
Seattle	..	5	1	3	5	2	2	8	3	7	3	5	1	6	6	57	24	.704
Oakland	5	..	6	1	3	1	4	4	2	7	2	5	2	4	7	53	28	.654
New York	1	3	..	1	3	3	8	1	5	2	3	8	3	5	5	51	28	.646
Minnesota	1	3	2	..	7	3	2	1	1	2	8	1	7	2	7	47	34	.580
Chicago	1	1	1	3	..	5	2	5	2	2	6	3	7	1	7	46	35	.568
Cleveland	1	1	1	7	5	..	4	2	1	2	7	2	5	2	4	44	36	.550
Boston	2	2	4	2	2	1	..	4	4	0	3	7	1	4	5	41	40	.506
Texas	3	5	2	3	1	3	2	..	1	7	1	2	3	4	4	41	41	.500
Toronto	0	2	3	2	2	3	2	4	..	2	2	5	2	6	5	40	42	.488
Anaheim	1	3	2	2	5	1	1	5	4	..	2	2	5	1	5	39	42	.481
Detroit	1	0	4	3	2	4	2	3	1	3	..	2	6	1	5	37	44	.457
Tampa Bay	1	1	5	4	1	0	2	3	5	1	1	..	2	4	7	37	44	.457
Kansas City	1	2	0	3	3	3	1	1	2	3	8	3	..	1	4	35	46	.432
Baltimore	1	0	2	2	1	0	3	2	3	3	2	5	2	..	4	30	50	.375
N.L. Clubs	3	4	4	7	4	6	4	5	6	4	4	6	5	7	..	..	..	
Lost on Road	22	32	37	43	44	35	39	48	40	45	52	56	51	48	..	598	534	.528

HOME RECORDS IN INTERLEAGUE GAMES

Team	Atl.	Fla.	Mon.	N.Y.	Phi.
Baltimore	..	..	2-1	1-2	1-2
Boston	1-2	2-1	..	..	2-1
New York	1-2	..	2-1	2-1	..
Tampa Bay	..	2-1	..	2-1	3-0
Toronto	2-1	1-2	2-1	..	..

Team	Chi.	Cin.	Hou.	Mil.	Pit.	St.L.	Ari.
Chicago	2-1	3-0	..	..	..	2-1	..
Cleveland	..	1-2	..	1-2	2-1	..	..
Detroit	1-2	..	..	2-1	2-1	..	..
Kansas City	..	..	0-3	..	..	3-0	1-2
Minnesota	..	3-0	2-1	..	2-1	..	..

Team	Ariz.	Col.	L.A.	S.D.	S.F.	Hou.
Anaheim	1-2	..	1-2	2-1	..	..
Oakland	..	3-0	2-1	..	2-1	..
Seattle	2-1	..	..	2-1	2-1	..
Texas	..	2-1	..	..	1-2	1-2

ROAD RECORD

Read across for road wins, down for home losses.

Team	Sea.	Oak.	Cle.	N.Y.	Bos.	Tor.	Min.	Chi.	Ana.	Bal.	Tex.	K.C.	Det.	T.B.	N.L.	W	L	Pct.
Seattle	..	5	3	5	4	3	5	2	8	2	7	5	2	2	6	59	22	.728
Oakland	4	..	2	0	1	4	3	5	7	3	5	4	4	2	5	49	32	.605
Cleveland	1	3	..	3	2	1	7	4	2	3	3	6	6	3	3	47	35	.573
New York	2	0	2	..	5	6	1	2	1	8	2	3	2	5	5	44	37	.543
Boston	1	2	2	1	..	8	1	1	3	6	1	2	1	7	5	41	39	.513
Toronto	3	1	1	5	5	..	3	1	2	6	2	1	2	5	3	40	40	.500
Minnesota	0	2	2	2	1	1	..	7	4	1	3	6	7	0	2	38	43	.469
Chicago	1	0	5	0	1	1	2	..	1	3	2	7	7	2	5	37	44	.457
Anaheim	3	3	4	2	3	1	1	1	..	3	3	2	0	3	5	36	45	.444
Baltimore	0	2	1	3	6	4	1	2	3	..	0	3	2	5	2	33	48	.407
Texas	2	5	1	2	0	2	2	1	5	3	..	2	0	3	4	32	48	.400
Kansas City	2	1	5	0	2	2	3	2	1	1	3	..	3	1	4	30	51	.370
Detroit	1	1	2	0	3	1	1	4	1	1	5	2	..	2	5	29	52	.358
Tampa Bay	1	1	1	1	3	4	2	1	1	5	1	0	1	..	3	25	56	.309
N.L. Clubs	3	2	5	4	4	4	2	4	5	5	5	5	4	2	..	..	..	
Lost at Home	24	28	36	28	40	42	34	35	42	50	41	46	44	44	..	540	592	.477

ANAHEIM—75-87

Pitcher	Bal. W-L	Bos. W-L	Chi. W-L	Cle. W-L	Det. W-L	K.C. W-L	Min. W-L	N.Y. W-L	Oak. W-L	Sea. W-L	T.B. W-L	Tex. W-L	Tor. W-L	N.L. W-L	Total W-L
Borland, Toby	0-1	0-0	0-0	0-0	0-0	0-0	0-0	0-0	0-0	0-0	0-0	0-0	0-0	0-0	0-1
Cooper, Brian	0-0	0-0	0-0	0-0	0-0	0-0	0-0	0-0	0-1	0-0	0-0	0-0	0-0	0-0	0-1
Green, Steve	0-0	0-0	0-0	0-0	0-0	0-0	0-0	0-0	0-0	0-0	0-0	0-0	0-0	0-0	0-0
Hasegawa, Shigetoshi	1-0	0-0	0-0	0-1	0-1	0-0	0-0	1-0	0-2	2-1	0-0	0-1	1-0	0-0	5-6
Holtz, Mike	0-0	0-0	0-0	0-0	0-1	1-0	0-0	0-0	0-0	0-0	0-0	0-1	0-0	0-0	1-2
Levine, Al	0-1	1-0	0-1	1-0	1-0	0-1	1-2	0-1	0-1	0-1	0-1	0-0	1-1	3-0	8-10
Lukasiewicz, Mark	0-0	0-0	0-0	0-0	0-1	0-0	0-0	0-0	0-0	0-0	0-0	0-1	0-0	0-0	0-2
Miadich, Bart	0-0	0-0	0-0	0-0	0-0	0-0	0-0	0-0	0-0	0-0	0-0	0-0	0-0	0-0	0-0
Ortiz, Ramon	0-1	1-0	0-0	1-0	0-0	1-1	1-0	1-0	0-2	0-3	1-0	5-1	1-0	1-2	13-11
Percival, Troy	0-0	0-0	1-0	0-1	0-0	0-0	0-0	1-0	1-0	0-0	0-0	0-0	0-0	1-1	4-2
Pote, Lou	0-0	0-0	0-0	0-0	0-0	0-0	0-0	0-0	0-0	0-0	0-0	1-0	0-0	0-0	2-0
Rapp, Pat	0-0	1-0	2-0	0-2	0-0	0-1	0-2	0-0	0-2	1-1	0-0	0-3	0-0	1-1	5-12
Schoeneweis, Scott	0-1	1-1	0-0	1-0	1-0	1-0	0-0	0-0	2-2	0-3	1-0	0-2	2-1	1-1	10-11
Shields, Scot	0-0	0-0	0-0	0-0	0-0	0-0	0-0	0-0	0-0	0-0	0-0	0-0	0-0	0-0	0-0
Valdes, Ismael	1-1	0-1	2-0	1-0	0-0	2-0	0-1	0-1	1-1	0-3	1-0	0-2	0-1	1-2	9-13
Washburn, Jarrod	0-0	0-0	1-2	1-0	2-0	0-1	0-1	0-1	1-2	1-2	3-0	1-0	0-1	1-0	11-10
Weber, Ben	2-0	0-1	0-0	0-0	1-0	0-0	1-0	0-0	0-0	0-0	0-0	0-0	0-0	1-1	6-2
Wise, Matt	0-0	0-0	0-0	0-0	0-0	0-0	0-0	0-0	1-1	0-1	0-1	0-1	0-0	0-0	1-4
Totals	4-5	4-3	6-3	5-4	5-4	5-4	3-6	4-3	6-14	4-15	7-2	7-12	5-4	10-8	75-87

INTERLEAGUE: Schoeneweis 1-0, Percival 0-1, Valdes 0-1 vs. Diamondbacks; Ortiz 1-0, Washburn 1-0, Rapp 1-0 vs. Rockies; Levine 2-0, Valdes 1-0, Percival 1-0, Ortiz 0-1, Weber 0-1 vs. Dodgers; Weber 1-0, Levine 1-0, Ortiz 0-1 vs. Padres; Rapp 0-1, Schoeneweis 0-1, Valdes 0-1 vs. Giants. Total: 10-8.

BALTIMORE—63-98

Pitcher	Ana. W-L	Bos. W-L	Chi. W-L	Cle. W-L	Det. W-L	K.C. W-L	Min. W-L	N.Y. W-L	Oak. W-L	Sea. W-L	T.B. W-L	Tex. W-L	Tor. W-L	N.L. W-L	Total W-L
Bale, John	0-0	0-0	0-0	0-0	0-0	0-0	0-0	0-0	0-0	0-0	1-0	0-0	0-0	0-0	1-0
Bauer, Rick	0-0	0-2	0-0	0-0	0-0	0-0	0-0	0-0	0-2	0-0	0-0	0-0	0-1	0-0	0-5
Brea, Leslie	0-0	0-0	0-0	0-0	0-0	0-0	0-0	0-0	0-0	0-0	0-0	0-0	0-0	0-0	0-0
Douglass, Sean	0-0	1-0	0-0	0-0	0-0	0-0	0-0	1-0	0-0	0-0	0-0	0-1	0-0	0-0	2-1
Foster, Kris	0-0	0-0	0-0	0-0	0-0	0-0	0-0	0-0	0-0	0-0	0-0	0-0	0-0	0-0	0-0
Groom, Buddy	0-0	1-0	0-0	0-0	0-0	0-0	0-0	0-1	0-0	0-0	0-0	0-0	0-1	0-2	1-4
Hentgen, Pat	0-0	0-0	0-0	0-1	2-0	0-0	0-0	0-1	0-0	0-0	0-1	0-0	0-0	0-0	2-3
Johnson, Jason	2-0	0-2	1-1	0-0	0-1	1-0	1-0	1-1	0-2	0-1	2-1	0-0	0-2	2-1	10-12
Julio, Jorge	0-0	0-0	0-0	0-0	0-0	0-0	0-0	0-0	0-0	0-0	1-0	0-0	0-1	0-0	1-1
Kohlmeier, Ryan	0-1	1-1	0-0	0-0	0-0	0-0	0-0	0-0	0-0	0-0	0-0	0-0	0-0	0-0	1-2
Maduro, Calvin	0-0	1-0	0-0	0-0	0-0	2-0	0-0	1-1	0-1	1-0	0-1	0-0	0-2	0-0	5-6
McElroy, Chuck	0-0	0-0	0-0	0-1	0-0	0-0	1-0	0-0	0-0	0-0	0-0	0-0	0-1	0-0	1-2
Mercedes, Jose	1-1	1-1	1-0	0-2	0-0	2-0	0-1	0-1	0-0	0-3	0-3	1-1	1-2	1-2	8-17
Mills, Alan	0-1	0-0	0-0	0-0	0-0	0-0	0-0	0-0	0-0	0-0	1-0	0-0	0-0	0-0	1-1
Paronto, Chad	0-0	0-0	0-0	0-0	0-0	0-0	0-0	0-2	0-0	0-1	0-0	0-0	0-0	0-0	1-3
Parrish, John	0-0	0-0	0-0	0-0	0-0	0-0	0-0	0-1	0-0	0-0	0-0	0-1	1-0	0-0	1-2
Ponson, Sidney	0-0	0-2	0-1	0-0	1-0	0-2	0-0	0-1	1-1	0-0	0-1	1-0	2-1	0-0	5-10
Roberts, Willis	1-1	1-1	0-1	0-0	1-1	0-0	0-0	1-2	0-1	0-1	2-1	0-0	2-0	1-1	9-10
Ryan, B.J.	0-0	0-0	0-0	0-0	0-0	0-0	0-1	1-0	0-0	0-0	1-0	0-0	0-0	0-3	2-4
Towers, Josh	0-0	2-0	1-1	0-0	0-0	0-0	0-0	0-2	1-2	0-1	1-1	0-1	1-1	2-1	8-10
Trombley, Mike	1-0	0-0	0-0	1-0	0-0	0-0	1-0	0-1	0-0	0-0	0-0	0-2	0-0	0-1	3-4
Wasdin, John	0-0	0-1	0-0	0-0	0-0	0-0	0-0	0-0	0-0	0-0	0-0	0-0	0-0	0-0	1-1
Totals	5-4	9-10	3-4	1-5	4-2	5-2	3-3	5-13	2-7	1-8	10-9	2-7	7-12	6-12	63-98

INTERLEAGUE: Roberts 1-0, Ryan 0-1, Towers 0-1 vs. Braves; Johnson 0-1, Mercedes 0-1, Ponson 0-1 vs. Marlins; Towers 1-0, Johnson 1-0, Ryan 0-1 vs. Expos; Towers 1-0, Mercedes 0-1, Groom 0-1 vs. Mets; Johnson 1-0, Mercedes 1-0, Roberts 0-1, Groom 0-1, Ryan 0-1, Trombley 0-1 vs. Phillies. Total: 6-12.

BOSTON—82-79

Pitcher	Ana. W-L	Bal. W-L	Chi. W-L	Cle. W-L	Det. W-L	K.C. W-L	Min. W-L	N.Y. W-L	Oak. W-L	Sea. W-L	T.B. W-L	Tex. W-L	Tor. W-L	N.L. W-L	Total W-L
Arrojo, Rolando	0-0	0-0	0-0	1-0	0-1	0-0	0-1	0-0	0-0	0-1	2-0	1-0	1-0	0-1	5-4
Banks, Willie	0-0	0-0	0-0	0-0	0-0	0-0	0-0	0-0	0-0	0-0	0-0	0-0	0-0	0-0	0-0
Beck, Rod	0-0	0-0	1-0	0-0	0-0	0-0	0-1	0-1	0-1	0-1	2-0	1-0	1-0	1-0	6-4
Castillo, Carlos	0-0	0-0	0-0	0-0	0-0	0-0	0-0	0-0	0-0	0-0	0-0	0-0	0-0	0-0	0-0
Castillo, Frank	1-0	1-2	0-0	0-1	1-1	2-0	1-0	2-0	0-1	0-2	0-0	0-0	0-2	2-0	10-9
Cone, David	1-0	1-1	0-0	0-1	0-0	0-0	0-0	0-3	0-0	0-0	1-2	1-0	2-0	3-0	9-7
Crawford, Paxton	0-0	0-0	0-0	0-0	0-0	0-0	1-0	0-0	1-0	0-0	1-0	0-0	0-0	0-0	3-0
Erdos, Todd	0-0	0-0	0-0	0-0	0-0	0-0	0-0	0-0	0-0	0-0	0-0	0-0	0-1	0-0	0-1
Florie, Bryce	0-0	0-0	0-0	0-0	0-0	0-0	0-0	0-0	0-0	0-0	0-0	0-0	0-0	0-0	0-0
Fossum, Casey	0-0	1-0	0-0	0-1	1-0	0-0	0-0	0-0	0-0	0-0	0-1	1-0	0-0	0-0	3-2
Garces, Rich	1-1	1-0	1-0	0-0	0-0	0-0	0-0	0-0	0-0	1-0	1-0	0-0	1-0	0-0	6-1
Kim, Sun-Woo	0-0	0-0	0-0	0-0	0-1	0-0	0-0	0-0	0-0	0-0	0-0	0-0	0-0	0-1	0-2
Lowe, Derek	0-0	0-2	0-0	1-0	0-0	0-0	0-1	1-2	1-1	0-0	1-1	0-1	1-2	0-0	5-10
Martinez, Pedro	0-0	0-0	0-0	0-0	0-0	1-0	0-0	1-2	2-0	1-0	2-0	0-0	0-0	0-1	7-3
McDill, Allen	0-0	0-0	0-0	0-0	0-0	0-0	0-0	0-0	0-0	0-0	0-0	0-0	0-0	0-0	0-0
Nomo, Hideo	0-1	3-0	1-0	0-2	0-2	0-1	1-0	0-2	0-0	1-1	1-0	0-0	3-0	3-1	13-10
Ohka, Tomokazu	0-0	1-0	0-1	0-1	0-0	0-0	0-0	0-0	0-1	1-0	0-0	0-0	0-1	0-0	2-5
Pichardo, Hipolito	0-0	0-1	0-0	0-0	0-0	0-0	0-0	0-0	0-0	0-0	0-0	1-0	1-0	0-0	2-1
Pulsipher, Bill	0-0	0-0	0-0	0-0	0-0	0-0	0-0	0-0	0-0	0-0	0-0	0-0	0-0	0-0	0-0
Saberhagen, Bret	0-1	0-0	1-0	0-0	0-0	0-0	0-0	0-1	0-0	0-0	0-0	0-0	0-0	0-0	1-2
Schourek, Pete	0-0	0-0	0-0	0-0	0-0	0-0	0-1	0-2	0-0	0-0	0-1	0-0	1-1	0-0	1-5

Pitcher	Ana. W-L	Bal. W-L	Chi. W-L	Cle. W-L	Det. W-L	K.C. W-L	Min. W-L	N.Y. W-L	Oak. W-L	Sea. W-L	T.B. W-L	Tex. W-L	Tor. W-L	N.L. W-L	Total W-L
Urbina, Ugueth	0-0	0-0	0-0	0-0	0-0	0-0	0-0	0-1	0-0	0-0	0-0	0-0	0-0	0-0	0-1
Wakefield, Tim	0-1	2-3	0-2	1-0	2-0	0-0	0-0	0-0	0-1	0-0	2-0	1-1	1-1	0-3	9-12
Totals	**3-4**	**10-9**	**3-3**	**3-6**	**4-5**	**3-3**	**3-3**	**5-13**	**4-5**	**3-6**	**14-5**	**5-2**	**12-7**	**10-8**	**82-79**

INTERLEAGUE: Nomo 1-1, Beck 1-0, Castillo 1-0, Kim 0-1, Ohka 0-1 vs. Braves; Castillo 1-0, Cone 1-0, Wakefield 0-1 vs. Marlins; Nomo 1-0, Pichardo 1-0, Wakefield 0-1 vs. Expos; Cone 1-0, Wakefield 0-1, Arrojo 0-1 vs. Mets; Cone 1-0, Nomo 1-0, Martinez 0-1 vs. Phillies. Total: 10-8.

CHICAGO—83-79

Pitcher	Ana. W-L	Bal. W-L	Bos. W-L	Cle. W-L	Det. W-L	K.C. W-L	Min. W-L	N.Y. W-L	Oak. W-L	Sea. W-L	T.B. W-L	Tex. W-L	Tor. W-L	N.L. W-L	Total W-L
Baldwin, James	1-1	2-0	1-0	0-0	0-0	1-1	0-1	0-0	0-1	0-1	0-0	1-0	0-0	1-0	7-5
Barcelo, Lorenzo	0-0	0-0	0-0	0-0	1-0	0-0	0-0	0-0	0-0	0-0	0-0	0-0	0-0	0-0	1-0
Biddle, Rocky	0-0	0-1	0-1	3-1	0-0	1-0	0-0	0-0	0-1	1-2	1-0	0-1	0-1	1-0	7-8
Buehrle, Mark	1-0	0-1	1-0	0-2	4-2	4-0	1-1	0-1	0-1	0-0	2-0	1-0	0-0	2-0	16-8
Eldred, Cal	0-0	0-0	0-0	0-1	0-0	0-0	0-0	0-0	0-0	0-0	0-0	0-0	0-0	0-0	0-1
Embree, Alan	0-0	0-0	0-1	0-0	1-0	0-1	0-0	0-0	0-0	0-0	0-0	0-0	0-0	0-0	1-2
Fogg, Josh	0-0	0-0	0-0	0-0	0-0	0-0	0-0	0-0	0-0	0-0	0-0	0-0	0-0	0-0	0-0
Foulke, Keith	0-1	0-0	0-0	0-2	0-1	1-1	1-2	0-0	1-0	0-1	0-0	0-0	0-0	1-1	4-9
Garland, Jon	0-1	0-0	1-0	0-1	0-1	2-0	0-0	0-1	0-0	0-0	1-0	1-1	1-0	0-2	6-7
Ginter, Matt	0-0	0-0	0-0	1-0	0-0	0-0	0-0	0-0	0-0	0-0	0-0	0-0	0-0	0-0	1-0
Glover, Gary	0-0	1-0	0-0	1-1	1-0	1-0	0-3	0-1	0-0	1-0	0-0	0-0	0-0	0-0	5-5
Howry, Bob	1-0	0-0	0-0	1-0	1-0	0-0	0-0	0-2	0-1	0-1	0-1	1-0	0-0	0-1	4-5
Lowe, Sean	0-1	0-0	0-0	2-1	2-0	1-1	1-1	1-0	0-0	0-0	0-0	0-0	0-0	2-0	9-4
Osuna, Antonio	0-0	0-0	0-0	0-0	0-0	0-0	0-0	0-0	0-0	0-0	0-0	0-0	0-0	0-0	0-0
Parque, Jim	0-0	0-0	0-0	0-0	0-0	0-0	0-2	0-0	0-1	0-0	0-0	0-0	0-0	0-0	0-3
Pulsipher, Bill	0-0	0-0	0-0	0-0	0-0	0-0	0-0	0-0	0-0	0-0	0-0	0-0	0-0	0-0	0-0
Vining, Ken	0-0	0-0	0-0	0-0	0-0	0-0	0-0	0-0	0-0	0-0	0-0	0-0	0-0	0-0	0-0
Wells, David	0-1	0-1	0-0	1-0	2-1	0-0	0-1	0-0	0-0	0-1	0-0	1-0	0-1	1-1	5-7
Wells, Kip	0-1	1-0	0-1	0-0	0-0	2-1	1-3	0-1	0-1	0-1	0-0	2-0	1-1	3-1	10-11
Wright, Dan	0-0	0-0	0-0	1-0	1-0	0-0	0-1	0-1	0-0	0-0	1-1	0-0	0-0	0-0	5-3
Wunsch, Kelly	0-0	0-0	0-0	0-0	0-1	0-0	0-0	0-0	0-0	0-0	1-1	0-0	0-0	1-0	2-1
Totals	**3-6**	**4-3**	**3-3**	**10-9**	**13-6**	**14-5**	**5-14**	**1-5**	**1-8**	**2-7**	**5-2**	**7-2**	**3-3**	**12-6**	**83-79**

INTERLEAGUE: Foulke 1-1, Lowe 1-0, Wells 1-0, Buehrle 1-0, Garland 0-1 vs. Cubs; Wells 1-0, Buehrle 1-0, Wunsch 1-0 vs. Reds; Biddle 1-0, Baldwin 1-0, Wells 1-0 vs. Brewers; Wells 1-0, Lowe 1-0, Howry 0-1 vs. Pirates; Garland 0-1, Wells 0-1, Wells 0-1 vs. Cardinals. Total: 12-6.

CLEVELAND—91-71

Pitcher	Ana. W-L	Bal. W-L	Bos. W-L	Chi. W-L	Det. W-L	K.C. W-L	Min. W-L	N.Y. W-L	Oak. W-L	Sea. W-L	T.B. W-L	Tex. W-L	Tor. W-L	N.L. W-L	Total W-L
Bacsik, Mike	0-0	0-0	0-0	0-0	0-0	0-0	0-0	0-0	0-0	0-0	0-0	0-0	0-0	0-0	0-0
Baez, Danys	0-0	0-0	0-0	1-0	1-0	0-0	2-1	0-0	1-0	0-1	0-0	0-0	0-1	0-0	5-3
Burba, Dave	1-0	1-0	1-1	1-4	2-1	2-2	0-0	0-0	0-0	0-1	1-0	0-0	1-1	0-0	10-10
Colon, Bartolo	0-2	1-0	2-0	0-2	3-1	2-3	2-0	0-2	0-2	0-0	1-0	1-0	0-0	2-0	14-12
Drese, Ryan	0-0	0-0	0-0	1-0	0-0	0-1	0-0	0-0	0-0	0-0	0-0	0-1	0-0	0-0	1-2
Drew, Tim	0-0	0-0	0-0	0-0	0-0	0-0	0-0	0-0	0-0	0-0	0-1	0-1	0-0	0-0	0-2
Finley, Chuck	0-0	0-0	1-0	1-1	0-2	2-0	2-1	0-0	0-1	0-0	2-0	0-1	0-0	0-0	8-7
Karsay, Steve	0-0	0-0	0-0	0-0	0-0	0-0	0-0	0-0	0-0	0-0	0-0	0-0	0-0	0-1	0-1
Laker, Tim	0-0	0-0	0-0	0-0	0-0	0-0	0-0	0-0	0-0	0-0	0-0	0-0	0-0	0-0	0-0
Nagy, Charles	0-1	0-0	0-0	0-1	1-0	0-0	0-1	2-0	1-0	0-1	0-0	0-0	0-0	1-1	5-6
Radinsky, Scott	0-0	0-0	0-0	0-0	0-0	0-0	0-0	0-0	0-0	0-0	0-0	0-0	0-0	0-0	0-0
Reed, Steve	0-0	0-1	0-0	0-0	1-0	0-0	0-0	0-0	0-0	0-0	0-0	0-0	0-0	0-0	1-1
Rincon, Ricardo	0-0	1-0	0-0	0-0	0-0	0-0	1-0	0-1	0-0	0-0	0-0	0-0	0-0	0-0	2-1
Riske, David	0-0	0-0	0-0	0-0	0-0	0-0	0-0	0-0	1-0	0-0	0-0	0-0	1-0	0-0	2-0
Rocker, John	0-0	0-0	0-1	0-0	0-0	1-1	0-0	0-0	1-1	0-0	0-1	0-0	0-0	1-3	3-7
Rodriguez, Rich	0-1	0-0	0-0	0-0	0-0	0-0	0-0	1-0	0-0	0-0	1-0	0-0	0-0	0-1	2-2
Sabathia, C.C.	1-1	1-0	1-0	3-0	1-0	4-0	1-1	1-2	0-1	0-0	0-0	2-0	1-0	1-0	17-5
Shuey, Paul	2-0	0-0	0-0	0-1	1-0	0-0	1-1	0-0	0-0	0-0	1-0	0-0	0-1	0-0	5-3
Smith, Roy	0-0	0-0	0-0	0-0	0-0	0-0	0-0	0-0	0-0	0-0	0-0	0-0	0-0	0-0	0-0
Speier, Justin	0-0	1-0	0-0	0-0	0-0	0-0	0-0	0-0	0-0	0-0	1-0	0-0	0-0	0-0	2-0
Westbrook, Jake	0-0	0-0	1-0	1-1	0-1	0-0	2-0	0-0	0-1	0-0	0-0	0-0	0-0	0-1	4-4
Wickman, Bob	0-0	0-0	0-0	1-0	2-0	0-0	0-0	0-0	1-0	0-0	0-0	0-0	1-0	0-0	5-0
Woodard, Steve	0-0	0-0	0-1	0-0	0-1	0-0	2-0	0-0	1-0	0-0	0-0	0-1	0-0	0-0	3-3
Wright, Jaret	0-0	0-0	0-0	0-0	0-0	0-0	1-0	0-0	0-0	0-0	0-0	0-0	0-0	0-2	2-2
Totals	**4-5**	**5-1**	**6-3**	**9-10**	**13-6**	**11-8**	**14-5**	**4-5**	**4-3**	**2-5**	**5-1**	**5-4**	**2-4**	**7-11**	**91-71**

INTERLEAGUE: Burba 1-0, Colon 1-0, Sabathia 1-0, Rodriguez 0-1, Wright 0-1, Rocker 0-1 vs. Reds; Colon 1-0, Westbrook 0-1, Rocker 0-1 vs. Astros; Wickman 1-0, Shuey 0-1, Nagy 0-1 vs. Brewers; Burba 0-1, Wright 0-1, Karsay 0-1 vs. Pirates; Rocker 1-1, Nagy 1-0 vs. Cardinals. Total: 7-11.

DETROIT—66-96

Pitcher	Ana. W-L	Bal. W-L	Bos. W-L	Chi. W-L	Cle. W-L	K.C. W-L	Min. W-L	N.Y. W-L	Oak. W-L	Sea. W-L	T.B. W-L	Tex. W-L	Tor. W-L	N.L. W-L	Total W-L
Anderson, Matt	1-0	0-0	0-0	1-0	0-0	0-0	0-1	0-0	0-0	0-0	0-0	0-0	0-0	1-0	3-1
Bernero, Adam	0-0	0-0	0-0	0-0	0-0	0-0	0-0	0-0	0-0	0-0	0-0	0-0	0-0	0-0	0-0
Blair, Willie	0-0	0-0	0-0	0-0	0-0	0-1	0-1	0-0	0-0	0-0	0-0	0-0	0-0	1-2	1-4
Borkowski, Dave	0-0	0-0	0-1	0-0	0-1	0-0	0-0	0-0	0-0	0-0	0-0	0-0	0-0	0-0	0-2
Cornejo, Nate	0-1	0-0	0-0	1-1	0-0	1-1	1-0	0-0	1-0	0-0	0-0	0-1	0-0	0-0	4-4
Holt, Chris	0-1	1-0	0-0	1-1	1-2	0-0	0-2	1-1	0-0	0-1	1-0	1-0	0-0	1-1	7-9
Jones, Todd	1-0	0-0	0-0	0-2	0-1	0-1	1-1	0-0	0-0	0-0	1-0	0-0	1-0	0-0	4-5
Lima, Jose	0-0	0-0	0-1	0-0	0-0	3-2	0-1	1-1	0-1	1-1	0-0	0-0	0-2	0-1	5-10
Miller, Matt	0-0	0-0	0-0	0-0	0-0	0-0	0-0	0-0	0-0	0-0	0-0	0-0	0-0	0-0	0-0
Mlicki, Dave	0-0	0-1	1-0	0-2	0-1	0-0	0-1	0-0	0-0	0-0	1-1	2-0	0-0	0-2	4-8
Moehler, Brian	0-0	0-0	0-0	0-0	0-0	0-0	0-0	0-0	0-0	0-0	0-0	0-0	0-0	0-0	0-0

Pitcher	Ana. W-L	Bal. W-L	Bos. W-L	Chi. W-L	Cle. W-L	K.C. W-L	Min. W-L	N.Y. W-L	Oak. W-L	Sea. W-L	T.B. W-L	Tex. W-L	Tor. W-L	N.L. W-L	Total W-L
Murray, Heath	0-1	0-0	0-1	0-0	0-2	0-1	0-2	0-0	0-0	0-0	0-0	0-0	1-0	0-0	1-7
Nitkowski, C.J.	0-0	0-0	0-0	0-0	0-1	0-1	0-0	0-0	0-0	0-0	0-0	0-0	0-0	0-1	0-3
Patterson, Danny	0-1	0-0	0-0	1-2	0-0	0-0	1-0	0-0	0-1	0-0	0-0	3-0	0-0	0-0	5-4
Perisho, Matt	1-0	0-0	0-0	0-0	0-0	0-0	0-1	0-0	0-1	0-0	0-1	1-0	0-0	0-0	2-3
Pettyjohn, Adam	0-0	0-0	1-0	0-1	0-2	0-1	0-0	0-0	0-0	0-1	0-0	0-0	0-0	0-1	1-6
Pineda, Luis	0-0	0-0	0-0	0-0	0-0	0-0	0-1	0-0	0-0	0-0	0-0	0-0	0-0	0-0	0-1
Redman, Mark	0-0	0-0	0-0	0-1	0-0	0-0	0-0	0-0	0-0	0-1	0-0	0-0	0-0	0-0	0-2
Santos, Victor	0-0	0-0	0-1	0-0	0-1	0-0	0-0	1-0	0-0	0-0	1-0	0-0	0-0	0-0	2-2
Sparks, Steve W.	0-0	1-1	1-0	0-1	3-0	3-0	1-2	1-2	0-2	1-0	0-0	0-1	1-0	2-0	14-9
Tolar, Kevin	0-0	0-0	0-0	0-0	0-0	0-0	0-0	0-0	0-0	0-0	0-0	0-0	0-0	0-0	0-0
Weaver, Jeff	1-1	0-2	2-0	2-2	2-2	1-3	0-2	0-1	0-1	0-1	1-0	0-0	0-1	4-0	13-16
Totals	4-5	2-4	5-4	6-13	6-13	8-11	4-15	4-5	1-6	2-5	4-2	8-1	2-4	10-8	66-96

INTERLEAGUE: Holt 1-0, Blair 0-1, Mlicki 0-1 vs. Diamondbacks; Jones 1-0, Nitkowski 0-1, Blair 0-1 vs. Cubs; Blair 1-0, Weaver 1-0, Pettyjohn 0-1 vs. Reds; Weaver 1-0, Anderson 1-0, Holt 0-1 vs. Brewers; Weaver 1-0, Sparks 1-0, Mlicki 0-1 vs. Pirates; Weaver 1-0, Sparks 1-0, Lima 0-1 vs. Cardinals. Total: 10-8.

KANSAS CITY—65-97

Pitcher	Ana. W-L	Bal. W-L	Bos. W-L	Chi. W-L	Cle. W-L	Det. W-L	Min. W-L	N.Y. W-L	Oak. W-L	Sea. W-L	T.B. W-L	Tex. W-L	Tor. W-L	N.L. W-L	Total W-L
Austin, Jeff	0-0	0-0	0-0	0-0	0-0	0-0	0-0	0-0	0-0	0-0	0-0	0-0	0-0	0-0	0-0
Bailey, Cory	0-0	0-0	0-0	0-0	0-0	0-1	1-0	0-0	0-0	0-0	0-0	0-0	0-0	0-0	1-1
Byrd, Paul	0-0	1-0	0-0	1-1	0-0	1-0	1-0	0-0	0-1	1-0	0-0	0-1	0-0	1-3	6-6
Cogan, Tony	0-0	0-0	0-0	0-0	0-2	0-0	0-1	0-0	0-0	0-0	0-0	0-0	0-0	0-1	0-4
Durbin, Chad	0-2	0-2	0-0	1-3	2-2	1-2	1-2	0-0	2-1	0-1	1-0	0-0	0-0	1-1	9-16
George, Chris	1-0	0-1	0-0	0-2	1-0	1-3	0-0	0-0	0-0	0-1	0-0	1-1	0-0	0-0	4-8
Grimsley, Jason	1-0	0-0	0-0	0-1	0-0	0-0	0-1	0-0	0-1	0-1	0-0	0-0	0-1	0-0	1-5
Henry, Doug	0-0	0-0	0-0	0-2	0-0	0-0	0-0	0-0	0-0	0-0	0-0	0-0	1-0	1-0	2-2
Hernandez, Roberto	0-1	0-0	0-0	0-0	1-0	1-0	0-1	0-1	1-0	0-1	1-0	1-1	0-1	0-0	5-0
MacDougal, Mike	0-0	0-0	0-0	0-0	0-1	1-0	0-0	0-0	0-0	0-0	0-0	0-0	0-0	0-0	1-1
Meadows, Brian	0-0	0-0	0-1	0-0	1-0	0-0	0-2	0-1	0-0	0-1	0-1	0-0	0-0	0-0	1-6
Mullen, Scott	0-0	0-0	0-0	0-0	0-0	0-0	0-0	0-0	0-0	0-0	0-0	0-0	0-0	0-0	0-0
Reichert, Dan	0-0	0-0	2-0	0-1	0-2	1-0	1-1	0-1	0-1	0-0	0-0	1-0	1-0	2-2	8-8
Santiago, Jose	0-0	0-0	1-0	0-0	0-0	0-0	0-1	0-0	0-0	0-1	1-0	0-0	0-0	0-0	2-2
Stein, Blake	0-0	0-0	0-2	1-1	1-1	2-0	0-1	0-2	0-0	0-0	0-0	1-0	1-0	1-1	7-8
Suppan, Jeff	2-1	0-1	0-0	2-3	1-2	3-1	1-0	0-1	0-2	0-0	0-1	0-0	1-1	0-1	10-14
Suzuki, Mac	0-1	0-0	0-0	0-0	0-1	0-0	1-1	0-0	0-0	0-0	1-0	0-1	0-1	0-0	2-5
Voyles, Brad	0-0	0-0	0-0	0-0	0-0	0-0	0-0	0-0	0-0	0-0	0-0	0-0	0-0	0-0	0-0
Wilson, Kris	0-0	1-1	0-0	0-0	1-0	0-1	0-2	0-0	0-0	2-0	0-0	0-1	0-0	2-0	6-5
Totals	4-5	2-5	3-3	5-14	8-11	11-8	6-13	0-6	3-6	3-6	4-2	4-5	4-3	8-10	65-97

INTERLEAGUE: Stein 1-0, Byrd 0-1, Reichert 0-1 vs. Diamondbacks; Reichert 1-0, Byrd 0-1, Cogan 0-1 vs. Cubs; Reichert 0-1, Byrd 0-1, Durbin 0-1 vs. Astros; Byrd 1-0, Reichert 1-0, Stein 0-1 vs. Brewers; Wilson 1-0, Suppan 0-1, Grimsley 0-1 vs. Pirates; Durbin 1-0, Wilson 1-0, Henry 0-1 vs. Cardinals. Total: 8-10.

MINNESOTA—85-77

Pitcher	Ana. W-L	Bal. W-L	Bos. W-L	Chi. W-L	Cle. W-L	Det. W-L	K.C. W-L	N.Y. W-L	Oak. W-L	Sea. W-L	T.B. W-L	Tex. W-L	Tor. W-L	N.L. W-L	Total W-L
Balfour, Grant	0-0	0-0	0-0	0-0	0-0	0-0	0-0	0-0	0-0	0-0	0-0	0-0	0-0	0-0	0-0
Carrasco, Hector	0-1	0-0	0-0	1-0	0-0	1-1	0-0	0-0	0-0	0-1	0-0	0-0	1-0	1-0	4-3
Cressend, Jack	1-0	0-0	0-0	1-0	0-1	0-0	0-0	0-0	0-0	0-0	1-0	0-1	0-0	3-2
Duvall, Mike	0-0	0-0	0-0	0-0	0-0	0-0	0-0	0-0	0-0	0-0	0-0	0-0	0-0	0-0	0-0
Fiore, Tony	0-0	0-0	0-0	0-0	0-0	0-1	0-0	0-0	0-0	0-0	0-0	0-0	0-0	0-0	0-1
Guardado, Eddie	1-0	0-0	0-0	0-0	1-1	1-0	0-0	1-0	2-0	0-0	0-0	0-0	0-0	0-0	7-1
Hawkins, LaTroy	0-1	0-0	0-0	0-1	0-0	0-0	1-0	0-0	0-0	0-0	0-0	0-0	0-0	0-0	1-5
Johnson, Adam	0-0	0-0	0-0	0-0	0-1	0-0	0-0	0-0	1-0	0-1	0-0	0-0	0-0	0-0	1-2
Jones, Todd	0-0	0-0	0-0	0-0	0-0	0-0	1-0	0-0	0-0	0-0	0-0	0-0	0-0	0-0	1-0
Lohse, Kyle	0-1	0-0	0-0	2-0	0-0	0-0	0-0	0-0	0-0	0-2	1-1	0-0	0-2	1-1	4-7
Mays, Joe	1-0	2-0	0-0	2-0	0-0	5-0	3-2	1-1	1-1	0-1	0-1	1-1	0-2	1-2	17-13
Miller, Travis	0-0	0-0	0-0	1-0	0-0	0-0	0-1	0-0	0-1	0-0	0-0	0-0	0-0	0-0	1-4
Milton, Eric	1-0	0-1	0-1	2-0	2-1	2-1	3-0	1-1	1-0	0-1	0-1	2-0	0-0	0-0	15-7
Radke, Brad	1-0	0-0	1-0	4-2	0-2	4-0	2-1	1-0	0-1	0-2	0-0	0-1	0-0	2-2	15-7
Redman, Mark	0-0	0-1	0-2	1-0	0-0	0-0	1-1	0-0	0-0	0-0	0-0	0-0	0-0	0-0	2-4
Reed, Rick	1-0	0-0	0-0	0-2	1-2	0-0	0-0	0-0	0-0	0-1	0-1	2-0	0-0	0-0	4-6
Rincon, Juan	0-0	0-0	0-0	0-0	0-0	0-0	0-0	0-0	0-0	0-0	0-0	0-0	0-0	0-0	0-0
Romero, J.C.	0-0	1-0	0-0	0-0	0-2	0-0	0-1	0-0	0-0	0-0	0-0	0-0	0-1	1-4
Santana, Johan	0-0	0-0	0-0	0-0	0-0	1-0	0-0	0-0	0-0	0-0	0-0	0-0	0-0	0-0	1-0
Thomas, Brad	0-0	0-0	0-0	0-0	0-0	0-0	0-0	0-0	0-0	0-0	0-1	0-0	0-0	0-1	0-2
Wells, Bob	0-0	0-1	2-0	0-0	1-2	1-1	1-0	0-0	1-0	1-0	0-0	0-0	0-0	2-0	8-5
Totals	6-3	3-3	3-3	14-5	5-14	15-4	13-6	4-2	5-4	1-8	1-6	4-5	2-5	9-9	85-77

INTERLEAGUE: Romero 0-1, Thomas 0-1, Radke 0-1 vs. Cubs; Guardado 1-0, Wells 1-0, Radke 1-0 vs. Reds; Radke 1-0, Milton 1-0, Mays 0-1 vs. Astros; Lohse 1-0, Wells 1-0, Radke 0-1 vs. Brewers; Carrasco 1-0, Mays 1-0, Miller 0-1 vs. Pirates; Mays 1-0, Miller 0-1, Lohse 0-1 vs. Cardinals. Total: 9-9.

NEW YORK—95-65

Pitcher	Ana. W-L	Bal. W-L	Bos. W-L	Chi. W-L	Cle. W-L	Det. W-L	K.C. W-L	Min. W-L	Oak. W-L	Sea. W-L	T.B. W-L	Tex. W-L	Tor. W-L	N.L. W-L	Total W-L
Almanzar, Carlos	0-0	0-0	0-0	0-0	0-0	0-0	0-0	0-0	0-0	0-0	0-0	0-0	0-0	0-1	0-1
Boehringer, Brian	0-0	0-0	0-0	0-0	0-0	0-0	0-0	0-0	0-1	0-0	0-0	0-0	0-0	0-0	0-1
Choate, Randy	0-0	0-0	0-0	0-0	0-0	0-0	0-0	0-0	1-0	0-0	0-0	0-0	1-0	1-1	3-1
Clemens, Roger	1-0	2-0	1-0	1-0	2-0	2-0	1-0	1-0	0-1	3-2	0-0	4-0	1-0	20-3
Hernandez, Adrian	0-0	0-0	0-0	0-0	0-1	0-1	0-0	0-0	0-0	0-1	0-0	0-0	0-0	0-3

Pitcher	Ana. W-L	Bal. W-L	Bos. W-L	Chi. W-L	Cle. W-L	Det. W-L	K.C. W-L	Min. W-L	Oak. W-L	Sea. W-L	T.B. W-L	Tex. W-L	Tor. W-L	N.L. W-L	Total W-L
Hernandez, Orlando	0-0	0-1	2-0	1-0	0-1	0-0	0-0	0-2	0-0	0-0	1-0	0-1	0-2	0-0	4-7
Hitchcock, Sterling	0-1	0-1	0-0	1-0	0-0	0-0	0-0	0-0	0-1	0-0	1-0	2-0	0-1	0-0	4-4
Jodie, Brett	0-0	0-0	0-0	0-0	0-0	0-0	0-0	0-0	0-0	0-0	0-0	0-0	0-1	0-0	0-1
Keisler, Randy	0-0	0-0	0-0	0-0	0-0	0-1	0-0	0-0	0-0	0-0	0-0	0-0	0-1	1-0	1-2
Knight, Brandon	0-0	0-0	0-0	0-0	0-0	0-0	0-0	0-0	0-0	0-0	0-0	0-0	0-0	0-0	0-0
Lilly, Ted	0-0	1-0	0-0	1-0	1-1	0-0	0-0	0-0	1-1	0-1	1-0	0-1	0-0	0-1	5-6
Mendoza, Ramiro	0-1	2-0	0-0	0-0	0-0	1-0	1-0	0-0	0-1	1-0	1-1	0-0	0-0	2-1	8-4
Mussina, Mike	0-0	3-1	3-3	1-0	1-0	0-0	1-0	1-0	0-1	1-1	2-1	0-2	3-0	1-2	17-11
Parker, Christian	0-0	0-0	0-0	0-0	0-0	0-0	0-0	0-0	0-0	0-0	0-0	0-0	0-1	0-0	0-1
Pettitte, Andy	1-1	1-0	4-1	0-1	0-1	1-1	2-0	0-1	0-0	0-2	3-0	0-0	1-1	2-1	15-10
Rivera, Mariano	1-0	0-2	2-1	0-0	0-0	0-0	0-0	0-1	0-0	0-0	0-0	0-0	1-0	1-1	4-6
Stanton, Mike	0-1	4-0	1-0	0-0	0-0	0-0	0-0	0-0	0-1	1-1	1-1	1-0	0-0	1-0	9-4
Williams, Todd	0-0	0-0	0-0	0-0	0-0	0-0	0-0	0-0	0-0	0-0	0-0	0-0	0-0	1-0	1-0
Witasick, Jay	0-0	0-0	0-0	0-0	1-0	1-0	0-0	0-0	0-0	0-0	0-0	0-0	1-0	0-0	3-0
Wohlers, Mark	0-0	0-0	0-0	0-0	0-0	0-0	0-0	0-0	0-0	0-0	0-0	0-0	1-0	0-0	1-0
Totals	3-4	13-5	13-5	5-1	5-4	5-4	6-0	2-4	3-6	3-6	13-6	3-4	11-8	10-8	95-65

INTERLEAGUE: Pettitte 1-0, Choate 0-1, Mussina 0-1 vs. Braves; Rivera 1-0, Mussina 0-1, Lilly 0-1 vs. Marlins; Clemens 1-0, Keisler 1-0, Mendoza 0-1 vs. Expos; Mendoza 2-0, Pettitte 1-0, Mussina 1-0, Rivera 0-1, Almanzar 0-1 vs. Mets; Choate 1-0, Stanton 1-0, Pettitte 0-1 vs. Phillies. Total: 10-8.

OAKLAND—102-60

Pitcher	Ana. W-L	Bal. W-L	Bos. W-L	Chi. W-L	Cle. W-L	Det. W-L	K.C. W-L	Min. W-L	N.Y. W-L	Sea. W-L	T.B. W-L	Tex. W-L	Tor. W-L	N.L. W-L	Total W-L
Bradford, Chad	0-0	0-0	0-0	0-1	0-0	0-0	0-0	0-0	1-0	0-0	0-0	0-0	1-0	0-0	2-1
Fyhrie, Mike	0-0	0-0	0-0	0-0	0-0	0-0	0-0	0-0	0-0	0-0	0-0	0-0	0-0	0-0	0-0
Guthrie, Mark	0-0	0-0	0-0	0-0	0-0	0-0	0-0	0-1	2-0	2-0	0-0	0-0	0-0	1-1	6-2
Harville, Chad	0-0	0-0	0-0	0-0	0-0	0-0	0-0	0-0	0-0	0-0	0-0	0-0	0-0	0-0	0-0
Heredia, Gil	0-1	0-0	1-1	3-0	0-0	0-0	1-0	0-1	0-0	0-2	0-0	0-3	0-0	2-0	7-8
Hiljus, Erik	0-0	0-0	0-0	1-0	0-0	0-0	0-0	0-0	0-0	2-0	1-0	1-0	0-0	0-0	5-0
Hudson, Tim	5-0	2-0	1-0	1-0	0-0	1-1	1-1	1-0	0-1	1-2	1-0	0-3	1-0	3-1	18-9
Isringhausen, Jason	0-0	0-0	1-0	0-0	0-0	0-0	1-0	1-0	0-0	0-1	0-0	1-0	0-2	0-0	4-3
Lidle, Cory	2-0	2-0	0-1	0-0	1-1	1-0	1-1	0-1	1-0	1-0	1-1	1-1	1-0	1-0	13-6
Magnante, Mike	1-0	0-0	0-0	0-0	0-0	0-0	0-0	1-0	0-0	0-0	0-0	0-1	0-0	0-0	3-1
Mathews, T.J.	0-0	0-0	0-0	0-0	0-0	0-0	0-0	0-0	0-0	0-0	0-0	0-0	0-1	0-0	0-1
Mecir, Jim	0-1	0-1	0-0	0-0	0-1	0-0	1-1	1-0	0-0	0-2	0-0	0-1	0-0	0-1	2-8
Mulder, Mark	2-2	1-0	1-0	1-0	1-1	0-0	1-1	1-1	0-0	1-2	3-0	2-1	2-0	4-1	21-8
Tam, Jeff	1-0	0-0	0-0	0-0	0-0	1-0	0-0	0-0	0-0	0-1	0-1	0-0	0-0	0-1	2-4
Vizcaino, Luis	0-0	0-0	0-0	0-0	0-1	1-0	0-0	0-0	0-0	0-0	0-0	0-0	0-0	0-0	2-1
Zito, Barry	3-2	2-1	1-1	1-0	1-0	2-0	0-0	0-2	0-1	2-0	0-0	4-0	0-1	1-0	17-8
Totals	14-6	7-2	5-4	8-1	3-4	6-1	6-3	4-5	6-3	9-10	7-2	9-10	6-3	12-6	102-60

INTERLEAGUE: Mulder 1-0, Hudson 1-0, Zito 1-0 vs. Diamondbacks; Lidle 1-0, Heredia 1-0, Mulder 1-0 vs. Rockies; Mulder 1-0, Hudson 1-0, Guthrie 0-1 vs. Dodgers; Hudson 1-0, Guthrie 1-0, Mecir 0-1 vs. Padres; Mulder 1-1, Heredia 1-0, Tam 0-1, Mathews 0-1, Hudson 0-1 vs. Giants. Total: 12-6.

SEATTLE—116-46

Pitcher	Ana. W-L	Bal. W-L	Bos. W-L	Chi. W-L	Cle. W-L	Det. W-L	K.C. W-L	Min. W-L	N.Y. W-L	Oak. W-L	T.B. W-L	Tex. W-L	Tor. W-L	N.L. W-L	Total W-L
Abbott, Paul	2-0	2-0	0-0	1-0	1-0	2-0	1-0	2-1	0-1	0-1	1-0	1-0	1-1	3-0	17-4
Charlton, Norm	1-0	0-0	0-0	0-0	0-0	0-0	1-0	0-0	1-0	0-1	1-1	0-0	0-0	0-0	4-2
Franklin, Ryan	0-0	0-0	0-0	1-1	0-0	0-0	1-0	0-0	0-0	0-0	3-0	0-0	0-0	0-0	5-1
Fuentes, Brian	0-0	0-0	0-0	0-0	0-0	0-0	0-0	0-0	0-1	0-0	0-0	0-0	0-0	1-0	1-1
Garcia, Freddy	5-0	1-0	1-0	1-0	1-0	0-1	0-2	1-0	1-0	2-1	2-0	0-0	3-1	1-0	18-6
Halama, John	1-1	1-0	1-1	0-0	1-0	0-0	0-0	1-0	0-1	1-2	0-0	0-1	1-1	2-1	10-7
Moyer, Jamie	3-1	1-0	1-1	0-0	2-0	0-0	0-0	2-0	2-0	1-1	2-0	4-1	2-0	0-2	20-6
Nelson, Jeff	0-0	0-0	1-0	0-0	0-1	0-0	1-0	0-0	0-0	0-0	0-0	1-1	0-0	0-1	4-3
Paniagua, Jose	1-0	0-0	1-0	0-0	0-1	0-0	0-0	0-0	0-0	1-0	0-0	1-1	0-0	0-1	4-3
Pineiro, Joel	0-0	2-0	0-0	1-0	0-0	2-0	0-0	0-0	0-1	0-1	1-0	0-0	0-0	0-0	6-2
Rhodes, Arthur	0-0	0-0	0-0	1-0	0-0	0-0	1-0	0-0	2-0	0-0	1-0	1-0	1-0	0-0	8-0
Sasaki, Kazuhiro	0-1	0-0	0-0	0-1	0-0	0-0	0-0	0-1	0-1	0-1	0-0	0-0	0-0	0-0	0-4
Sele, Aaron	1-1	1-1	1-1	1-0	0-0	1-1	1-1	1-0	0-0	3-0	0-0	2-0	0-0	2-0	15-5
Stark, Denny	1-0	0-0	0-0	0-0	0-0	0-0	0-0	0-0	0-0	0-0	0-0	0-0	0-0	0-1	1-1
Tomko, Brett	0-0	0-0	0-0	1-0	0-0	0-0	0-0	0-0	0-0	0-0	0-0	1-1	1-0	0-0	3-1
Totals	15-4	8-1	6-3	7-2	5-2	5-2	6-3	8-1	6-3	10-9	7-2	15-5	6-3	12-6	116-46

INTERLEAGUE: Sele 1-0, Abbott 1-0, Halama 0-1 vs. Diamondbacks; Fuentes 1-0, Abbott 1-0, Moyer 0-1 vs. Rockies; Garcia 1-0, Sele 1-0, Paniagua 0-1 vs. Dodgers; Halama 2-0, Garcia 1-1, Abbott 1-0, Nelson 0-1 vs. Padres; Rhodes 1-0, Garcia 1-0, Moyer 0-1 vs. Giants. Total: 12-6.

TAMPA BAY—62-100

Pitcher	Ana. W-L	Bal. W-L	Bos. W-L	Chi. W-L	Cle. W-L	Det. W-L	K.C. W-L	Min. W-L	N.Y. W-L	Oak. W-L	Sea. W-L	Tex. W-L	Tor. W-L	N.L. W-L	Total W-L
Bierbrodt, Nick	0-0	0-0	0-0	0-1	0-0	0-0	0-0	1-1	1-1	0-1	0-0	0-0	1-0	0-0	3-4
Callaway, Mickey	0-0	0-0	0-0	0-0	0-0	0-0	0-0	0-0	0-0	0-0	0-0	0-0	0-0	0-0	0-0
Colome, Jesus	0-0	0-0	1-0	0-0	0-0	0-0	0-0	0-0	0-1	0-0	0-0	0-0	1-1	0-0	2-3
Creek, Doug	0-0	1-0	1-1	0-0	0-1	0-0	0-0	0-0	0-1	0-1	0-0	0-0	0-1	0-0	2-5
Fiore, Tony	0-0	0-0	0-0	0-0	0-0	0-0	0-0	0-0	0-0	0-0	0-0	0-0	0-0	0-0	0-0
Harper, Travis	0-0	0-0	0-2	0-0	0-0	0-0	0-0	0-0	0-0	0-0	0-0	0-0	0-0	0-0	0-2
Hill, Ken	0-0	0-0	0-0	0-0	0-0	0-0	0-0	0-0	0-0	0-0	0-0	0-0	0-1	0-0	0-1
Judd, Mike	0-0	0-0	0-0	0-0	0-0	0-0	1-0	0-0	0-0	0-0	0-0	0-0	0-0	0-0	1-0
Kennedy, Joe	0-2	0-0	0-0	1-1	0-0	0-0	0-0	1-0	1-1	0-0	0-0	0-1	1-3	3-1	7-8
Lopez, Albie	0-1	1-0	0-1	0-1	0-0	0-2	1-0	0-2	0-1	0-2	0-1	0-0	1-1	2-2	5-12
Meacham, Rusty	0-1	1-2	0-0	0-0	0-0	0-0	0-0	0-0	0-0	0-0	0-0	0-0	0-0	0-0	1-3
Phelps, Travis	0-0	1-0	0-0	0-0	0-0	0-0	0-0	1-0	0-0	0-0	0-1	0-0	0-1	0-0	2-2

Pitcher	Ana. W-L	Bal. W-L	Bos. W-L	Chi. W-L	Cle. W-L	Det. W-L	K.C. W-L	Min. W-L	N.Y. W-L	Oak. W-L	Sea. W-L	Tex. W-L	Tor. W-L	N.L. W-L	Total W-L
Prieto, Ariel	0-0	0-0	0-0	0-0	0-0	0-0	0-0	0-0	0-0	0-0	0-0	0-0	0-0	0-0	0-0
Rekar, Bryan	0-0	0-2	0-1	0-0	0-1	0-0	0-1	0-0	0-1	0-2	0-1	0-1	2-2	1-1	3-13
Rose, Brian	0-0	0-0	0-0	0-0	0-1	0-0	0-1	0-0	0-0	0-0	0-0	0-0	0-0	0-0	0-2
Rupe, Ryan	0-1	2-2	0-4	0-0	0-0	0-1	0-0	1-0	0-1	0-0	0-2	0-0	0-1	2-0	5-12
Seay, Bobby	0-0	0-0	0-0	0-1	0-0	0-0	0-0	0-0	0-0	1-0	0-0	0-0	0-0	0-0	1-1
Standridge, Jason	0-0	0-0	0-0	0-0	0-0	0-0	0-0	0-0	0-0	0-0	0-0	0-0	0-0	0-0	0-0
Sturtze, Tanyon	0-0	1-0	1-2	0-1	1-0	0-1	0-0	1-0	3-1	1-0	0-2	1-2	0-1	2-2	11-12
Wallace, Jeff	0-1	0-0	0-0	0-1	0-0	0-0	0-0	0-0	0-1	0-0	0-0	0-0	0-0	0-0	0-3
Wheeler, Dan	0-0	0-0	0-0	0-0	0-0	0-0	0-0	0-0	0-0	0-0	0-0	1-0	0-0	0-0	1-0
Wilson, Paul	1-1	1-1	2-1	0-0	0-1	1-0	1-1	1-0	0-2	0-1	1-0	0-0	0-1	0-0	8-9
Yan, Esteban	1-0	1-2	0-1	0-0	0-0	0-0	0-0	1-0	0-0	0-1	0-0	0-1	1-0	1-0	4-6
Zambrano, Victor	0-0	0-1	0-1	1-0	0-0	0-0	0-0	1-0	0-0	0-0	1-0	1-0	0-0	2-0	6-2
Totals	2-7	9-10	5-14	2-5	1-5	2-4	2-4	6-1	6-13	2-7	2-7	4-5	9-10	10-8	62-100

INTERLEAGUE: Lopez 1-0, Zambrano 1-0, Sturtze 0-1 vs. Braves; Lopez 1-1, Zambrano 1-0, Kennedy 0-2, Sturtze 0-1 vs. Marlins; Sturtze 1-0, Kennedy 0-1, Rekar 0-1 vs. Expos; Rupe 1-0, Sturtze 0-1, Lopez 0-1 vs. Mets; Kennedy 1-0, Rekar 1-0, Rupe 1-0 vs. Phillies. Total: 10-8.

TEXAS—73-89

Pitcher	Ana. W-L	Bal. W-L	Bos. W-L	Chi. W-L	Cle. W-L	Det. W-L	K.C. W-L	Min. W-L	N.Y. W-L	Oak. W-L	Sea. W-L	T.B. W-L	Tor. W-L	N.L. W-L	Total W-L
Bell, Rob	1-0	0-0	0-0	0-0	0-1	0-0	0-0	0-1	0-2	1-0	1-1	1-0	0-0	1-0	5-5
Benoit, Joaquin	0-0	0-0	0-0	0-0	0-0	0-0	0-0	0-0	0-0	0-0	0-0	0-0	0-0	0-0	0-0
Brantley, Jeff	0-0	0-0	0-0	0-0	0-0	0-0	0-0	0-0	0-0	0-0	0-0	0-0	0-1	0-0	0-1
Cordero, Francisco	0-0	0-0	0-0	0-0	0-0	0-0	0-0	0-0	0-1	0-0	0-0	0-0	0-0	0-0	0-1
Crabtree, Tim	0-0	0-0	0-0	0-0	0-1	0-1	0-0	0-0	0-0	0-0	0-1	0-0	0-0	0-2	0-5
Davis, Doug	1-1	0-0	1-1	0-0	1-2	0-1	1-1	0-0	1-0	3-0	1-3	1-0	0-0	1-1	11-10
Dickey, R.A.	0-0	0-0	0-0	0-1	0-0	0-0	0-0	0-0	0-0	0-0	0-0	0-0	0-0	0-0	0-1
Duchscherer, Justin	0-0	1-0	0-0	0-0	0-0	0-0	0-0	0-0	0-0	0-1	0-0	0-0	0-0	0-0	1-1
Foster, Kevin	0-0	0-0	0-0	0-0	0-0	0-0	0-0	0-0	0-0	0-0	0-1	0-0	0-0	0-0	0-1
Glynn, Ryan	0-2	0-1	0-0	1-0	0-0	0-0	0-0	0-1	0-0	0-0	0-1	0-0	0-0	0-0	1-5
Helling, Rick	2-2	1-0	0-1	0-1	0-1	1-1	2-0	1-1	0-0	1-0	0-2	2-0	0-1	2-1	12-11
Johnson, Jonathan	0-0	0-0	0-0	0-0	0-0	0-0	0-0	0-0	0-0	0-0	0-0	0-0	0-1	0-0	0-1
Judd, Mike	0-0	0-0	0-0	0-0	0-0	0-0	0-0	0-0	0-0	0-0	0-0	0-0	0-0	0-0	0-0
Kolb, Danny	0-0	0-0	0-0	0-0	0-0	0-0	0-0	0-0	0-0	0-0	0-0	0-0	0-0	0-0	0-0
Mahomes, Pat	1-0	0-1	0-0	1-1	1-0	0-0	0-2	0-0	1-1	1-0	0-0	1-1	1-0		7-6
Michalak, Chris	0-0	0-0	1-1	0-0	0-0	1-0	0-0	0-0	0-1	0-0	0-0	0-0	0-0		2-2
Moreno, Juan	1-0	0-0	0-1	0-0	0-0	0-0	0-0	0-0	0-0	0-0	0-1	1-0	0-0	0-1	3-3
Myette, Aaron	1-0	0-0	0-0	0-1	0-0	0-0	0-0	1-1	1-0	0-1	0-1	0-0	1-1	0-0	4-6
Oliver, Darren	3-0	1-0	0-1	0-0	0-0	0-1	0-1	1-0	2-0	2-2	0-2	0-1	0-1	2-2	11-11
Petkovsek, Mark	0-0	0-0	0-0	0-1	1-0	0-0	0-0	0-0	0-0	0-0	0-1	0-0	0-0	0-0	1-2
Rogers, Kenny	1-2	0-0	0-0	0-1	1-0	0-0	0-0	0-0	0-0	0-2	1-0	1-0	0-1	1-1	5-7
Smart, J.D.	0-0	1-0	0-0	0-0	0-0	0-0	0-0	0-0	0-0	0-0	0-1	0-0	0-0	0-1	1-2
Venafro, Mike	0-0	2-0	0-0	0-1	0-0	0-2	0-0	1-0	0-0	1-1	1-1	0-0	0-0	0-0	5-5
Villafuerte, Brandon	0-0	0-0	0-0	0-0	0-0	0-0	0-0	0-0	0-0	0-0	0-0	0-0	0-0	0-0	0-0
Zimmerman, Jeff	1-0	0-0	0-0	0-0	0-0	0-2	1-0	1-0	0-0	0-1	0-0	0-0	0-0	0-1	4-4
Totals	12-7	7-2	2-5	2-7	4-5	1-8	5-4	5-4	4-3	10-9	5-15	5-4	3-6	8-10	73-89

INTERLEAGUE: Rogers 1-0, Helling 1-0, Davis 0-1 vs. Rockies; Helling 1-0, Mahomes 1-0, Oliver 1-0, Crabtree 0-2, Zimmerman 0-1 vs. Astros; Oliver 1-0, Judd 0-1, Smart 0-1 vs. Dodgers; Davis 1-0, Helling 0-1, Oliver 0-1, Rogers 0-1 vs. Giants. Total: 8-10.

TORONTO—80-82

Pitcher	Ana. W-L	Bal. W-L	Bos. W-L	Chi. W-L	Cle. W-L	Det. W-L	K.C. W-L	Min. W-L	N.Y. W-L	Oak. W-L	Sea. W-L	T.B. W-L	Tex. W-L	N.L. W-L	Total W-L
Beirne, Kevin	0-0	0-0	0-0	0-0	0-0	0-0	0-0	0-0	0-0	0-0	0-0	0-0	0-0	0-0	0-0
Borbon, Pedro	0-0	0-1	1-0	0-0	0-0	0-1	0-0	0-0	0-0	0-1	0-1	1-0	0-0	0-0	2-4
Bowles, Brian	0-0	0-0	0-0	0-0	0-0	0-0	0-0	0-0	0-0	0-0	0-0	0-0	0-0	0-0	0-0
Carpenter, Chris	0-0	2-0	0-2	1-1	1-0	1-0	1-1	0-1	1-2	0-0	1-1	1-0	1-1	1-2	11-11
Coco, Pasqual	0-0	0-0	0-0	0-0	0-0	0-0	0-0	0-0	0-0	0-0	1-0	0-0	0-0	0-0	1-0
DeWitt, Matt	0-0	0-1	0-0	0-0	0-0	0-0	0-0	0-0	0-0	0-1	0-0	0-0	0-0	0-0	0-2
Escobar, Kelvim	0-1	2-0	1-1	0-1	0-0	0-0	0-0	1-0	0-2	1-0	0-1	0-2	0-0	1-0	6-8
Eyre, Scott	0-0	1-0	0-0	0-0	0-0	0-0	0-0	0-0	0-1	0-0	0-0	0-1	0-0	0-0	1-2
File, Bob	0-0	0-1	1-1	0-0	2-0	0-0	1-0	0-0	0-1	0-0	0-0	0-0	0-0	1-0	5-3
Frascatore, John	0-0	0-0	0-0	0-0	0-0	0-0	0-0	0-0	0-0	0-0	0-0	0-0	1-0	0-0	1-0
Halladay, Roy	0-0	1-0	0-0	0-0	1-0	0-1	0-0	2-0	1-0	0-0	0-1	0-0	0-0	0-0	5-3
Hamilton, Joey	0-0	0-2	0-2	1-1	0-0	0-0	0-0	0-1	0-0	0-1	2-0	0-0	0-0	2-0	5-8
Koch, Billy	0-0	0-0	0-2	1-0	0-0	0-0	0-0	0-0	0-1	1-0	0-0	0-1	0-1	1-0	2-5
Loaiza, Esteban	1-0	2-1	0-2	0-0	0-0	1-0	0-1	1-1	3-1	0-2	0-1	0-1	2-0	0-2	11-11
Lyon, Brandon	0-1	2-0	1-0	0-0	0-1	2-0	0-0	1-0	0-0	0-1	0-0	0-0	0-0	0-0	5-4
Michalak, Chris	1-1	0-1	1-0	0-0	0-0	0-0	0-0	1-0	2-0	0-1	0-0	0-2	0-1	1-1	6-7
Painter, Lance	0-0	0-0	0-0	0-0	0-0	0-0	0-0	0-0	0-0	0-0	0-0	0-0	0-0	0-1	0-1
Parris, Steve	1-1	0-0	0-1	1-0	0-0	0-0	0-0	0-0	0-2	0-0	1-0	1-1	0-0	0-1	4-6
Plesac, Dan	1-1	1-0	1-1	0-0	0-1	0-0	0-1	0-0	0-0	0-0	0-0	0-0	0-0	1-1	4-5
Quantrill, Paul	0-0	0-0	1-0	2-0	0-0	0-0	0-0	0-0	1-0	1-0	0-0	3-0	0-0	2-2	10-2
Totals	4-5	12-7	7-12	3-3	4-2	4-2	3-4	5-2	8-11	3-6	3-6	10-9	6-3	8-10	80-82

INTERLEAGUE: File 1-0, Hamilton 1-0, Parris 0-1 vs. Braves; Koch 1-0, Carpenter 0-1, Loaiza 0-1 vs. Marlins; Carpenter 1-0, Plesac 1-0, Michalak 1-0, Quantrill 0-2, Loaiza 0-1 vs. Expos; Michalak 0-1, Halladay 0-1, Carpenter 0-1 vs. Mets; Escobar 1-0, Hamilton 1-0, Plesac 0-1 vs. Phillies. Total: 8-10.

HOME RUNS BY PARKS

	At Ana.	At Bal.	At Bos.	At Chi.	At Cle.	At Det.	At K.C.	At Min.	At N.Y.	At Oak.	At Sea.	At T.B.	At Tex.	At Tor.	At N.L. Parks	Totals 2001	2000	HR Allow.
Anaheim	86	4	5	5	5	4	3	3	1	4	6	5	11	1	15	158	236	168
Baltimore	2	58	7	1	1	2	5	4	12	5	3	8	6	7	15	136	184	194
Boston	2	18	97	8	5	3	8	1	7	5	1	18	3	14	8	198	167	146
Chicago	8	7	2	114	12	7	18	16	1	1	6	3	2	5	12	214	216	181
Cleveland	5	4	2	14	116	11	14	11	10	2	1	2	6	4	10	212	221	148
Detroit	3	4	5	10	8	58	8	9	4	0	2	4	11	1	12	139	177	180
Kansas City	6	5	3	11	15	9	75	8	2	0	1	1	5	4	7	152	150	209
Minnesota	5	3	2	13	7	9	12	76	1	5	1	6	7	2	15	164	116	192
New York	4	15	8	6	3	4	5	2	116	5	2	12	6	9	6	203	205	158
Oakland	8	6	3	12	6	5	7	3	3	101	7	2	19	9	8	199	239	153
Seattle	7	2	7	3	3	0	4	5	4	14	79	4	17	3	17	169	198	160
Tampa Bay	4	9	10	1	4	1	1	1	2	4	6	60	4	7	7	121	162	207
Texas	11	4	3	14	5	5	7	6	8	18	11	9	124	10	11	246	173	222
Toronto	10	6	9	3	1	0	6	8	18	6	13	14	2	*94	5	195	244	165
N.L. clubs	11	7	11	5	9	11	14	12	9	6	8	10	10	8	....	148	158	
2001 Totals	172	152	174	220	200	129	187	165	198	176	147	158	233	178	148	2506	....	2483
2000 Totals	243	196	143	229	209	137	201	160	209	195	164	185	209	226	....	....	2688	....

*There were actually 176 home runs hit at Toronto in 2001. The total includes two home runs hit by the Blue Jays when they were the "home" team in a game against Texas at San Juan, Puerto Rico, April 1.

AT ANAHEIM (172):

Anaheim (86)—Glaus 22, Anderson 13, Salmon 11, Spiezio 8, Gil 6, B. Molina 6, Kennedy 4, Erstad 3, DaVanon 3, Wooten 3, Eckstein 3, Nieves 2, Hill 1, Barnes 1. **Arizona (3)**—Bell 1, Grace 1, Gonzalez 1. **Baltimore (2)**—Ripken 1, Bigbie 1. **Boston (2)**—Mirabelli 1, Hillenbrand 1. **Chicago (8)**—Ordonez 3, Lee 2, Alomar 1, Valentin 1, Rowand 1. **Cleveland (5)**—Burks 2, Thome 1, Cruz 1, Diaz 1. **Detroit (3)**—Palmer 1, Easley 1, T. Clark 1. **Kansas City (6)**—Beltran 2, McCarty 1, Zaun 1, Ibanez 1, Hinch 1. **Los Angeles (6)**—Lo Duca 2, Kreuter 1, Sheffield 1, Karros 1, Beltre 1. **Minnesota (5)**—Koskie 2, Hunter 1, Allen 1, LeCroy 1. **New York (4)**—O'Neill 1, Justice 1, B. Williams 1, Spencer 1. **Oakland (8)**—Chavez 2, Hernandez 2, Menechino 1, Ja. Giambi 1, Dye 1. **San Diego (2)**—Nevin 1, Trammell 1. **Seattle (7)**—Cameron 2, Javier 1, Martinez 1, Lampkin 1, Boone 1, Guillen 1. **Tampa Bay (4)**—Gomez 2, Vaughn 1, Huff 1. **Texas (11)**—A. Rodriguez 3, Sierra 2, Palmeiro 2, Curtis 1, Sheldon 1, Kapler 1, Pena 1. **Toronto (10)**—Delgado 4, Mondesi 2, Cruz 2, Stewart 1, Fullmer 1.

AT BALTIMORE (152):

Anaheim (4)—Glaus 4. **Baltimore (58)**—Gibbons 9, Mora 6, Richard 6, Segui 5, Conine 5, Batista 5, Hairston 5, Anderson 4, Ripken 3, Myers 3, Bordick 2, Kinkade 2, Raines Sr. 1, DeShields 1, Matos 1. **Boston (18)**—Nixon 4, Ramirez 2, Mirabelli 2, Daubach 2, Bichette 1, Offerman 1, Lansing 1, Everett 1, Stynes 1, Garciaparra 1, Pickering 1, Burkhart 1. **Chicago (2)**—Konerko 2, Liefer 2, Clayton 1, Graffanino 1, Lee 1. **Cleveland (4)**—Gonzalez 1, Diaz 1, Branyan 1. **Detroit (4)**—Encarnacion 2, Higginson 1, Fick 1. **Kansas City (5)**—Randa 1, Zaun 1, Ibanez 1, Febles 1, Beltran 1. **Minnesota (3)**—Hunter 1, Maxwell 1, J. Jones 1. **New York N.L. (4)**—Ventura 2, Zeile 1, Piazza 1. **New York A.L. (15)**—Brosius 5, Martinez 3, Knoblauch 2, O'Neill 1, B. Williams 1, Jeter 1, Soriano 1, Johnson 1. **Oakland (4)**—Chavez 3, Hernandez 2, Ja. Giambi 1. **Philadelphia (3)**—Lee 2, Rollins 1. **Seattle (2)**—Boone 1, Cameron 1. **Tampa Bay (9)**—Vaughn 3, McGriff 1, Flaherty 1, Johnson 1, Grieve 1, Winn 1, Huff 1. **Texas (4)**—Galarraga 1, Caminiti 1, Catalanotto 1, Kapler 1. **Toronto (6)**—Cruz 2, Fletcher 1, Gonzalez 1, Fullmer 1.

AT BOSTON (174):

Anaheim (5)—Anderson 2, Glaus 2, Salmon 1. **Atlanta (4)**—C. Jones 2, Jordan 1, A. Jones 1. **Baltimore (7)**—Matos 2, Segui 1, Fordyce 1, Batista 1, Blake 1, Richard 1. **Boston (97)**—Ramirez 21, Nixon 14, Daubach 11, O'Leary 9, Bichette 7, Everett 6, Lansing 5, Hillenbrand 5, Offerman 4, Mirabelli 4, Stynes 3, Garciaparra 3, Hatteberg 2, Varitek 2, Pickering 1. **Chicago (2)**—Clayton 1, Valentin 1. **Cleveland (2)**—Thome 2. **Detroit (5)**—T. Clark 1, Cruz 1, Halter 1, Encarnacion 1, Wakeland 1. **Florida (4)**—Lowell 2, Mabry 1, Lee 1. **Kansas City (3)**—Randa 1, Dye 1, Quinn 1. **Minnesota (2)**—Lawton 1, Rivas 1. **New York (8)**—O'Neill 2, B. Williams 2, Posada 2, Martinez 1, Soriano 1. **Oakland (3)**—Ja. Giambi 1, Valdez 1, Hernandez 1. **Philadelphia (3)**—Anderson 1, Burrell 1, Rollins 1. **Seattle (7)**—Martinez 3, Boone 2, Cameron 2. **Tampa Bay (10)**—Vaughn 3, Cox 2, DiFelice 1, Grieve 1, Winn 1, Huff 1, Abernathy 1. **Texas (3)**—A. Rodriguez 2, Monroe 1. **Toronto (9)**—Delgado 4, Mondesi 2, Gonzalez 1, Castillo 1, Fullmer 1, Izturis 1.

AT CHICAGO (220):

Anaheim (5)—Glaus 2, Anderson 1, Palmeiro 1, J. Molina 1. **Baltimore (1)**—Fordyce 1. **Boston (8)**—Ramirez 2, Bichette 1, Offerman 1, Lansing 1, O'Leary 1, Daubach 1, Hillenbrand 1. **Chicago N.L. (2)**—White 2. **Chicago A.L. (114)**—Konerko 19, Ordonez 17, Valentin 14, Lee 12, Liefer 10, Canseco 9, Durham 9, Clayton 6, Perry 5, Singleton 4, Rowand 3, Thomas 2, Johnson 2, Alomar 1, Graffanino 1. **Cincinnati (1)**—Clark 1. **Cleveland (14)**—Cordova 4, Thome 3, Gonzalez 2, Garcia 2, Burks 1, Alomar 1, Diaz 1. **Detroit (10)**—T. Clark 2, Fick 2, Palmer 1, Cedeno 1, Magee 1, Cruz 1, Simon 1, Macias 1. **Kansas City (11)**—Sweeney 3, Zaun 2, Randa 1, Ibanez 1, Febles 1, Beltran 1, Quinn 1, Berger 1. **Minnesota (13)**—Koskie 5, Ortiz 3, Lawton 2, Hunter 2, J. Jones 1. **New York (6)**—Jeter 2, Martinez 1, Posada 1, Spencer 1, Soriano 1. **Oakland (12)**—Chavez 3, Je. Giambi 2, Long 2, Myers 1, Ja. Giambi 1, Dye 1, Tejada 1, Hernandez 1. **Pittsburgh (2)**—Vander Wal 1, Ramirez 1. **Seattle (3)**—McLemore 1, Olerud 1, Boone 1. **Tampa Bay (1)**—Vaughn 1. **Texas (14)**—Palmeiro 3, Velarde 3, A. Rodriguez 3, Galarraga 1, Caminiti 1, Hubbard 1, Kapler 1, Mateo 1. **Toronto (3)**—Delgado 1, Batista 1, Cruz 1.

AT CLEVELAND (200):

Anaheim (5)—Salmon 2, Joyner 1, Spiezio 1, Glaus 1. **Baltimore (1)**—Conine 1. **Boston (5)**—Nixon 2, Bichette 1, Ramirez 1, Mirabelli 1. **Chicago (12)**—Canseco 3, Ordonez 3, Alomar 1, Durham 1, Konerko 1, Johnson 1, Liefer 1, Paul 1. **Cincinnati (2)**—Selby 1, Cromer 1. **Cleveland (116)**—Thome 30, Gonzalez 22, Burks 15, Branyan 11, Lofton 9, Cordova 9, Alomar 7, Fryman 3, Vizquel 2, Taubensee 2, Cordero 2, Cruz 2, Garcia 1, Cabrera 1. **Detroit (8)**—Palmer 2, Fick 2, Easley 1, Higginson 1, T. Clark 1, Encarnacion 1. **Kansas City (15)**—Sweeney 5, Beltran 5, Ibanez 3, Dye 1, Quinn 1. **Milwaukee (5)**—Houston 2, Jenkins 2, Sexson 1. **Minnesota (7)**—Hunter 2, Pierzynski 2, Mientkiewicz 1, Buchanan 1, LeCroy 1. **New York (3)**—B. Williams 1, Brosius 1, Posada 1. **Oakland (6)**—Saenz 1, Dye 1, Tejada 1, Je. Giambi 1, Chavez 1, Hernandez 1. **St. Louis (2)**—McGwire 1, Paquette 1. **Seattle (3)**—Boone 2, Wilson 1. **Tampa Bay (4)**—McGriff 1, Vaughn 1, Guillen 1, Cox 1. **Texas (5)**—Greer 2, A. Rodriguez 1, Catalanotto 1, Kapler 1, Toronto (1)—Mondesi 1.

AT DETROIT (129):

Anaheim (4)—Anderson 1, Erstad 1, Spiezio 1, J. Molina 1. **Baltimore (2)**—Ripken 1, Bordick 1. **Boston (3)**—Mirabelli 1, Nixon 1, Merloni 1. **Chicago N.L. (4)**—Sosa 2, Coomer 1, Brown 1. **Chicago A.L. (7)**—Valentin 2, Durham 2, Perry 1, Singleton 1, Paul 1. **Cleveland (11)**—Thome 4, Cordova 2, Burks 1, Alomar 1, Gonzalez 1, Cordero 1, Branyan 1. **Detroit (58)**—Fick 8, Higginson 7, T. Clark 7, Macias 7, Palmer 5, Easley 4, Halter 4, Encarnacion 4, Cedeno 3, Magee 3, Cruz 2, Simon 1, Jackson 1, Munson 1, J. Patterson 1. **Kansas City (9)**—Beltran 3, Alicea 1, Mayne 1, Randa 1, Ibanez 1, Perez 1, Brown 1. **Milwaukee (4)**—Burnitz 2, White 1, Houston 1. **Minnesota (9)**—Lawton 2, Hocking 1, Ortiz 1, Koskie 1, Mientkiewicz 1, Guzman 1, J. Jones 1, LeCroy 1. **New York (4)**—Martinez 2, B. Williams 1, Soriano 1. **Oakland (5)**—Myers 1, Ja. Giambi 1, Damon 1, Dye 1, Chavez 1. **Pittsburgh (3)**—Giles 1, J. Wilson 1, Mackowiak 1. **Tampa Bay (1)**—McGriff 1. **Texas (5)**—Palmeiro 2, Caminiti 2, Catalanotto 1.

AT KANSAS CITY (187):

Anaheim (3)—Glaus 2, Kennedy 1. **Arizona (6)**—Gonzalez 4, Finley 1, Durazo 1. **Baltimore (5)**—Ripken 1, Segui 1, Conine 1, Batista 1, Mora 1. **Boston (8)**—Varitek 4, Valentin 1, Everett 1, Ramirez 1, Nixon 1. **Chicago (18)**—Valentin 4, Durham 3, Lee 3, Ordonez 2, Konerko 2, Johnson 1, Singleton 1, Liefer 1, Paul 1. **Cleveland (14)**—Burks 4, Cordova 3, Gonzalez 2, Branyan 2, Alomar 1, Taubensee 1, Laker 1. **Detroit (8)**—Halter 3, Higginson 2, Simon 2, Cruz 1. **Houston (5)**—Bagwell 2, Berkman 2, Lopez 1. **Kansas City (75)**—Sweeney 10, Quinn 10, Randa 8, Dye 8, Beltran 7, Febles 6, McCarty 5, Ibanez 5, Hinch 4, Brown 4,

- 272 -

Alicea 1, Mayne 1, Zaun 1, Berger 1. **Minnesota (12)**—Prince 2, Ortiz 2, Koskie 2, Rivas 2, Lawton 1, Hunter 1, Buchanan 1, J. Jones 1. **New York (5)**—O'Neill 2, Posada 1, Coleman 1, Soriano 1. **Oakland (7)**—Myers 2, Chavez 2, Gant 1, Ja. Giambi 1, Je. Giambi 1. **St. Louis (3)**—McGwire 1, Renteria 1, Pujols 1. **Seattle (4)**—Martinez 1, Martin 1, Boone 1, Wilson 1. **Tampa Bay (1)**—Vaughn 1. **Texas (7)**—Sierra 2, Palmeiro 2, A. Rodriguez 1, Catalanotto 1, Lamb 1. **Toronto (6)**—Delgado 3, Mondesi 2, Fullmer 1.

AT MINNESOTA (165):

Anaheim (3)—Anderson 2, Glaus 1. **Baltimore (4)**—DeShields 2, Ripken 1, Fordyce 1. **Boston (1)**—Ramirez 1. **Chicago (16)**—Durham 3, Thomas 2, Valentin 2, Ordonez 2, Konerko 2, Canseco 1, Clayton 1, Perry 1, Lee 1, Liefer 1. **Cincinnati (3)**—Rivera 1, Young 1, LaRue 1. **Cleveland (11)**—Alomar 3, Gonzalez 3, Thome 3, Burks 2. **Detroit (9)**—Higginson 3, T. Clark 1, McMillon 1, Halter 1, Jackson 1, Fick 1, Wakeland 1. **Houston (4)**—Berkman 2, Bagwell 1, Castilla 1. **Kansas City (8)**—Sweeney 2, Quinn 2, McCarty 1, Zaun 1, Dye 1, Beltran 1. **Minnesota (76)**—Hunter 13, Koskie 11, Mientkiewicz 11, Buchanan 7, Guzman 7, Ortiz 6, J. Jones 5, Lawton 4, Prince 3, Pierzynski 3, Rivas 3, Hocking 1, Allen 1, Kielty 1. **New York (2)**—Justice 1, Martinez 1. **Oakland (3)**—Je. Giambi 1, Chavez 1, Menechino 1. **Pittsburgh (5)**—Giles 2, Hyzdu 2, Barkett 1. **Seattle (5)**—Cameron 2, Martinez 1, Martin 1, Bell 1. **Tampa Bay (1)**—Martinez 1. **Texas (6)**—Palmeiro 1, Velarde 1, Haselman 1, I. Rodriguez 1, A. Rodriguez 1, Catalanotto 1. **Toronto (8)**—Mondesi 2, Cruz 2, Delgado 2, Stewart 1, Fullmer 1, F. Lopez 1.

AT NEW YORK (198):

Anaheim (1)—Glaus 1. **Atlanta (4)**—C. Jones 2, Lopez 1, Helms 1. **Baltimore (12)**—Bordick 3, Richard 3, Myers 1, Anderson 1, Conine 1, Batista 1, Kinkade 1, Hairston 1. **Boston (4)**—Ramirez 4, O'Leary 1, Everett 1, Hillenbrand 1. **Chicago (10)**—Alomar 3, Thome 2, Lofton 2, Burks 1, Diaz 1, Branyan 1. **Detroit (4)**—Magee 1, Halter 1, Encarnacion 1, Fick 1. **Kansas City (2)**—Dye 1, Quinn 1. **Minnesota (1)**—Guzman 1. **Montreal (3)**—Smith 1, Vidro 1, Barrett 1. **New York N.L. (2)**—Zeile 1, Piazza 1. **New York A.L. (116)**—Martinez 22, B. Williams 14, Posada 14, O'Neill 13, Jeter 13, Justice 8, Soriano 6, Knoblauch 6, Brosius 6, Spencer 6, Bellinger 2, Oliver 1, Greene 1, Wilson 1, Johnson 1. **Oakland (3)**—Saenz 1, Tejada 1, Hernandez 1. **Seattle (4)**—Cameron 3, Lampkin 1. **Tampa Bay (2)**—Guillen 1, Cox 1. **Texas (8)**—A. Rodriguez 2, Palmeiro 1, I. Rodriguez 1, Ledee 1, Catalanotto 1, Kapler 1, Young 1. **Toronto (18)**—Cruz 6, Delgado 5, Gonzalez 3, Mondesi 1, Stewart 1, Latham 1, Fullmer 1.

AT OAKLAND (176):

Anaheim (4)—Glaus 2, Fabregas 1, Anderson 1. **Baltimore (5)**—Conine 1, Fordyce 1, Hairston 1, Matos 1, Richard 1. **Boston (5)**—Offerman 2, O'Leary 1, Everett 1, Stynes 1. **Chicago (1)**—Ordonez 1. **Cleveland (2)**—Gonzalez 1, Thome 1. **Colorado (2)**—L. Walker 1, Norton 1. **Los Angeles (2)**—Green 1, Lo Duca 1. **Minnesota (5)**—Prince 2, Hocking 1, Hunter 1, Koskie 1. **New York (5)**—Jeter 2, O'Neill 1, Soriano 1, Bellinger 1. **Oakland (101)**—Ja. Giambi 27, Tejada 17, Chavez 14, Dye 8, Saenz 6, Long 6, Je. Giambi 5, Hernandez 5, Menechino 4, Myers 2, Damon 2, Byrnes 2, Gant 1, Bellhorn 1, Wilson 1. **San Francisco (2)**—Kent 1, R. Davis 1. **Seattle (14)**—Martinez 4, Boone 3, Cameron 3, Bell 2, Olerud 1, Martin 1. **Tampa Bay (4)**—Vaughn 1, Guillen 1, Cox 1, Hall 1. **Texas (18)**—A. Rodriguez 4, Sierra 3, Velarde 2, I. Rodriguez 2, Greer 2, Galarraga 1, Palmeiro 1, Mirabelli 1, Sheldon 1, Young 1. **Toronto (6)**—Delgado 2, Mondesi 1, Gonzalez 1, Batista 1, Fullmer 1.

AT SEATTLE (147):

Anaheim (6)—Anderson 2, Wooten 2, Salmon 1, Eckstein 1. **Arizona (3)**—Finley 1, Sanders 1, Miller 1. **Baltimore (3)**—Ripken 1, Bordick 1, B. Roberts 1. **Boston (1)**—Hillenbrand 1. **Chicago (6)**—Valentin 2, Konerko 1, Lee 1, Singleton 1, Liefer 1. **Cleveland (1)**—Lofton 1. **Detroit (2)**—Halter 1, Encarnacion 1. **Kansas City (1)**—Quinn 1. **Minnesota (1)**—Pierzynski 1. **New York (2)**—Justice 1, Martinez 1. **Oakland (7)**—Tejada 2, Chavez 2, Damon 1, Long 1, Hernandez 1. **San Diego (1)**—Davis 1. **San Francisco (4)**—Aurilia 2, Bonds 1, Rios 1. **Seattle (79)**—Boone 19, Olerud 15, Martinez 10, Bell 7, Cameron 7, Suzuki 5, Wilson 4, Javier 2, McLemore 2, Buhner 2, Martin 2, Guillen 2, Lampkin 1, Sprague 1. **Tampa Bay (6)**—McGriff 1, Vaughn 1, Williams 1, DiFelice 1, Grieve 1, Cox 1. **Texas (11)**—Palmeiro 6, Caminiti 2, A. Rodriguez 2, Curtis 1. **Toronto (13)**—Mondesi 4, Fletcher 3, Fullmer 3, Delgado 1, Batista 1, Cruz 1.

AT TAMPA BAY (158):

Anaheim (5)—Joyner 1, Anderson 1, Erstad 1, Spiezio 1, Glaus 1. **Baltimore (8)**—Conine 2, Richard 2, Anderson 1, Segui 1, Batista 1, Bigbie 1. **Boston (18)**—Daubach 4, Everett 2, Ramirez 2, Nixon 2, Merloni 2, Hillenbrand 2, Bichette 1, Lewis 1, Stynes 1, Pickering 1. **Chicago (3)**—Canseco 1, Ordonez 1, Konerko 1. **Cleveland (2)**—Burks 1, Branyan 1. **Detroit (4)**—Easley 1, Palmer 1, Encarnacion 1. **Florida (2)**—Lee 1, Millar 1. **Kansas City (1)**—Brown 1. **Minnesota (6)**—Ortiz 3, Hunter 2, Koskie 1. **New York N.L. (5)**—Johnson 2, Ventura 1, Piazza 1, McEwing 1. **New York A.L. (12)**—B. Williams 3, Justice 2, Soriano 2, Bellinger 2, Brosius 1, Jeter 1, Spencer 1. **Oakland (2)**—Myers 1, Dye 1. **Philadelphia (3)**—Abreu 1, Lee 1, Burrell 1. **Seattle (4)**—Boone 1, Martinez 1, Bell 1. **Tampa Bay (60)**—Vaughn 12, McGriff 10, Gomez 5, Grieve 5, Huff 5, Flaherty 3, Williams 3, Winn 3, Cox 3, Abernathy 3, Castilla 2, Rolls 2, Sheets 1, Johnson 1, Hall 1, Sandberg 1. **Texas (9)**—A. Rodriguez 3, I. Rodriguez 2, Galarraga 1, Sierra 1, Greer 1, Kapler 1. **Toronto (14)**—Delgado 4, Cruz 3, Stewart 2, Mondesi 1, Gonzalez 1, Batista 1, F. Lopez 1, L. Lopez 1.

AT TEXAS (233):

Anaheim (11)—Glaus 3, Salmon 2, Joyner 1, Fabregas 1, Anderson 1, Palmeiro 1, Erstad 1, Kennedy 1. **Baltimore (6)**—Ripken 1, Anderson 1, Fordyce 1, Richard 1, Gibbons 1, B. Roberts 1. **Boston (3)**—Offerman 1, Everett 1, Nixon 1. **Chicago (2)**—Konerko 1, Lee 1. **Cleveland (6)**—Thome 2, Alomar 1, Gonzalez 1, Cordero 1, Branyan 1. **Colorado (2)**—Norton 1, T. Walker 1. **Detroit (11)**—Easley 3, Cruz 2, Palmer 1, Cedeno 1, Halter 1, Simon 1, Encarnacion 1, Fick 1. **Houston (5)**—Alou 2, Biggio 1, Merced 1, Eusebio 1. **Kansas City (5)**—Beltran 2, Alicea 1, Sweeney 1, Brown 1. **Minnesota (7)**—Ortiz 3, Hunter 1, Buchanan 1, Guzman 1, J. Jones 1. **New York (6)**—Justice 2, O'Neill 1, Martinez 1, Knoblauch 1, Jeter 1. **Oakland (19)**—Tejada 4, Ja. Giambi 3, Chavez 3, Menechino 3, Je. Giambi 2, Damon 1, Long 1, Hernandez 1, Byrnes 1. **San Francisco (3)**—E. Davis 1, Dunston 1, Aurilia 1. **Seattle (17)**—McLemore 2, Lampkin 2, Boone 2, Wilson 2, Bell 2, Suzuki 2, Martinez 1, Olerud 1, Martin 1, Cameron 1, Guillen 1. **Tampa Bay (4)**—Gomez 1, Grieve 1, Cox 1, Hall 1. **Texas (124)**—A. Rodriguez 26, Palmeiro 23, I. Rodriguez 16, Sierra 13, Kapler 11, Young 7, Galarraga 5, Catalanotto 4, Caminiti 3, Velarde 3, Haselman 2, Greer 2, Pena 2, Curtis 1, Mirabelli 1, Ledee 1, Sheldon 1, Porter 1, Lamb 1, Monroe 1. **Toronto (2)**—Gonzalez 1, Bush 1.

AT TORONTO (*178):

Anaheim (1)—Wooten 1. **Atlanta (2)**—Jordan 1, A. Jones 1. **Baltimore (7)**—Batista 3, Gibbons 2, Ripken 1, Conine 1, Hairston 1. **Boston (14)**—Ramirez 5, Daubach 3, Bichette 1, O'Leary 1, Everett 1, Nixon 1, Varitek 1, Hillenbrand 1. **Chicago (5)**—Durham 2, Valentin 1, Konerko 1, Liefer 1. **Cleveland (4)**—Garcia 2, Branyan 2. **Detroit (1)**—Simon 1. **Florida (1)**—Floyd 1. **Kansas City (4)**—Sweeney 4. **Minnesota (2)**—Mientkiewicz 1, Kielty 1. **Montreal (5)**—Stevens 1, Smith 1, Guerrero 1, Vidro 1, Cabrera 1. **New York (9)**—Justice 3, Martinez 2, Soriano 2, B. Williams 1, Posada 1. **Oakland (9)**—Tejada 4, Damon 2, Saenz 1, Ja. Giambi 1, Long 1. **Seattle (3)**—Cameron 2, Boone 1. **Tampa Bay (7)**—Johnson 2, Cox 2, McGriff 1, Grieve 1, Hall 1. **Texas (10)**—A. Rodriguez 3, Palmeiro 2, I. Rodriguez 2, Lamb 2, Galarraga 1. **Toronto (94)**—Cruz 15, Delgado 13, Mondesi 10, Gonzalez 9, *Batista 9, Fullmer 8, Fletcher 7, *Stewart 6, F. Lopez 3, Frye 2, Bush 2, Simmons 2, Woodward 2, L. Lopez 2, Fernandez 1, Latham 1, Wells 1, Izturis 1.

*Note: Totals for Batista and Stewart include one home run for each at Hiram Bithorn Stadium in San Juan, Puerto Rico.

2001 N.L. STATISTICS

Batting

Designated hitting

Pinch-hitting

Pitching

Fielding

Miscellaneous

BATTING

TEAM

Team	Avg.	G	TPA	AB	R	H	TB	2B	3B	HR	RBI	SH	SF	HP	BB	IBB	SO	SB	CS	GDP	LOB	ShO	Slg.	OBP
Colorado	.292	162	6393	5690	923	1663	2748	324	61	213	874	81	50	61	511	50	1027	132	54	116	1158	2	.483	.354
Houston	.271	162	6325	5528	847	1500	2495	313	29	208	805	71	56	89	581	52	1119	64	49	128	1151	3	.451	.347
St. Louis	.270	162	6177	5450	814	1469	2404	274	32	199	768	83	50	65	529	51	1089	91	35	125	1095	5	.441	.339
Arizona	.267	162	6346	5595	818	1494	2472	284	35	208	776	71	36	57	587	73	1052	71	38	105	1183	7	.442	.341
San Francisco	.266	162	6408	5612	799	1493	2582	304	40	235	775	67	54	50	625	79	1090	57	42	108	1242	4	.460	.342
Florida	.264	162	6184	5542	742	1461	2344	325	30	166	713	60	45	67	470	43	1145	89	40	118	1117	9	.423	.326
Cincinnati	.262	162	6222	5583	735	1464	2340	304	22	176	690	66	40	65	468	47	1172	103	54	130	1115	9	.419	.324
Chicago	.261	162	6219	5406	777	1409	2323	268	32	194	748	117	53	66	577	72	1077	67	36	132	1156	4	.430	.336
Atlanta	.260	162	6152	5498	729	1432	2265	263	24	174	696	64	52	45	493	51	1039	85	46	132	1095	8	.412	.324
Philadelphia	.260	162	6219	5497	746	1431	2276	295	29	164	708	67	61	43	551	52	1125	153	47	104	1157	5	.414	.329
Los Angeles	.255	162	6169	5493	758	1399	2335	264	27	206	714	57	44	56	519	45	1062	89	42	115	1075	8	.425	.323
Montreal	.253	162	6026	5379	670	1361	2130	320	28	131	622	64	45	60	478	59	1071	101	51	151	1024	15	.396	.319
San Diego	.252	162	6278	5482	789	1379	2187	273	26	161	753	29	48	41	678	37	1273	129	44	121	1160	4	.399	.336
Milwaukee	.251	162	6148	5488	740	1378	2308	273	30	209	712	65	35	72	488	44	1399	66	36	102	1067	15	.426	.319
New York	.249	162	6156	5459	642	1361	2111	273	18	147	608	52	35	65	545	59	1062	66	48	124	1181	12	.387	.323
Pittsburgh	.247	162	6027	5398	657	1333	2122	256	25	161	618	60	35	67	467	51	1106	93	73	114	1058	11	.393	.313
Totals	.261	1296	99449	88100	12186	23027	37472	4613	488	2952	11580	1074	739	969	8567	865	17908	1456	735	1925	18034	133	.425	.331

INDIVIDUAL

TOP QUALIFIERS FOR BATTING CHAMPIONSHIP

Minimum 502 plate appearances. *Lefthanded batter. †Switch-hitter.

Player, Team	Avg.	G	TPA	AB	R	H	TB	2B	3B	HR	RBI	SH	SF	HP	BB	IBB	SO	SB	CS	GDP	Slg.	OBP
Walker, Larry, Col.*	.350	142	601	497	107	174	329	35	3	38	123	0	8	14	82	6	103	14	5	9	.662	.449
Helton, Todd, Col.*	.336	159	697	587	132	197	402	54	2	49	146	1	5	5	98	15	104	7	5	14	.685	.432
Alou, Moises, Hou.	.331	136	581	513	79	170	284	31	1	27	108	0	8	3	57	14	57	5	1	18	.554	.396
Berkman, Lance, Hou.†	.331	156	688	577	110	191	358	55	5	34	126	0	6	13	92	5	121	7	9	8	.620	.430
Jones, Chipper, Atl.†	.330	159	677	572	113	189	346	33	5	38	102	0	5	2	98	20	82	9	10	13	.605	.427
Pujols, Albert, St.L.	.329	161	676	590	112	194	360	47	4	37	130	1	7	9	69	6	93	1	3	21	.610	.403
Bonds, Barry, S.F.*	.328	153	664	476	129	156	411	32	2	73	137	0	2	9	177	35	93	13	3	5	.863	.515
Sosa, Sammy, Chi.	.328	160	711	577	146	189	425	34	5	64	160	0	12	6	116	37	153	0	2	6	.737	.437
Pierre, Juan, Col.*	.327	156	683	617	108	202	256	26	11	2	55	14	1	10	41	1	29	46	17	6	.415	.378
Gonzalez, Luis, Ari.*	.325	162	728	609	128	198	419	36	7	57	142	0	5	14	100	24	83	1	1	14	.688	.429
Aurilia, Rich, S.F.	.324	156	689	636	114	206	364	37	5	37	97	3	3	0	47	2	83	1	3	14	.572	.369
Lo Duca, Paul, L.A.	.320	125	519	460	71	147	250	28	0	25	90	5	9	6	39	2	30	2	4	11	.543	.374
Vidro, Jose, Mon.†	.319	124	531	486	82	155	236	34	1	15	59	2	2	10	31	2	49	4	1	18	.486	.371
Floyd, Cliff, Fla.*	.317	149	629	555	123	176	321	44	4	31	103	0	5	10	59	19	101	18	3	9	.578	.390
Cirillo, Jeff, Col.	.313	138	586	528	72	165	250	26	4	17	83	1	9	5	43	6	63	12	2	15	.473	.364

DEPARTMENTAL LEADERS: G—Abreu, Phi., Cabrera, Mon., Gonzalez, Ari., 162; AB—Rollins, Phi., 656; R—Sosa, Chi., 146; H—Aurilia, S.F., 206; TB—Sosa, Chi., 425; 1B—Pierre, Col., 163; 2B—Berkman, Hou., 55; 3B—Rollins, Phi., 12; HR—Bonds, S.F., 73; RBI—Sosa, Chi., 160; SH—Glavine, Atl., Gutierrez, Chi., J. Wilson, Pit., 17; SF—Kent, S.F., 13; HP—Biggio, Hou., 28; BB—Bonds, S.F., 177; IBB—Sosa, Chi., 37; SO—Hernandez, Mil., 185; SB—Pierre, Col., Rollins, Phi., 46; CS—Pierre, Col., 17; GIDP—V. Guerrero, Mon., 24; Slg. Pct.—Bonds, S.F., .863; OB. Pct.—Bonds, S.F., .515.

ALL PLAYERS

*Lefthanded batter. †Switch-hitter.

Player, Team	Avg.	G	TPA	AB	R	H	TB	2B	3B	HR	RBI	SH	SF	HP	BB	IBB	SO	SB	CS	GDP	Slg.	OBP
Abbott, Jeff, Fla.	.262	28	46	42	5	11	14	3	0	0	5	0	0	1	3	0	7	0	0	1	.333	.326
Abbott, Kurt, Atl.	.222	6	9	9	0	2	2	0	0	0	0	0	0	0	0	0	3	1	0	0	.222	.222
Abreu, Bobby, Phi.*	.289	162	704	588	118	170	319	48	4	31	110	0	9	1	106	11	137	36	14	13	.543	.393
Acevedo, Jose, Cin.	.118	18	36	34	1	4	5	1	0	0	1	2	0	0	0	0	18	0	0	0	.147	.118
Acevedo, Juan, Col.-Fla.	.333	59	4	3	1	1	2	1	0	0	0	1	0	0	0	0	0	0	0	0	.667	.333
Adams, Terry, L.A.	.051	43	48	39	2	2	3	1	0	0	1	5	1	0	3	0	19	0	0	0	.077	.116
Agbayani, Benny, N.Y.	.277	91	339	296	28	82	118	14	2	6	27	1	1	5	36	0	73	4	5	11	.399	.364
Aldridge, Cory, Atl.*	.000	8	5	5	1	0	0	0	0	0	0	0	0	0	0	0	4	0	0	0	.000	.000
Alfonzo, Edgardo, N.Y.	.243	124	519	457	64	111	184	22	0	17	49	1	5	5	51	0	62	5	0	7	.403	.322
Alou, Moises, Hou.	.331	136	581	513	79	170	284	31	1	27	108	0	8	3	57	14	57	5	1	18	.554	.396
Anderson, Brian, Ari.	.135	33	37	37	1	5	8	1	1	0	2	0	0	0	0	0	9	0	0	2	.216	.135
Anderson, Jimmy, Pit.*	.119	34	69	59	2	7	8	1	0	0	3	6	0	0	4	0	15	0	0	1	.136	.175
Anderson, Marlon, Phi.*	.293	147	574	522	69	153	220	30	2	11	61	10	5	2	35	5	74	8	5	12	.421	.337
Ankiel, Rick, St.L*	.000	6	10	8	1	0	0	0	0	0	0	1	0	0	1	0	5	0	0	0	.000	.111
Appier, Kevin, N.Y.	.113	33	67	62	4	7	7	0	0	0	4	3	0	1	1	0	24	0	0	0	.113	.141
Arias, Alex, S.D.	.226	70	158	137	19	31	46	9	0	2	12	1	2	1	17	1	22	1	0	3	.336	.312
Armas, Tony J., Mon.	.151	34	59	53	2	8	9	1	0	0	4	6	0	0	0	0	17	0	0	0	.170	.151
Arroyo, Bronson, Pit.	.048	24	23	21	0	1	1	0	0	0	1	0	1	0	1	0	16	0	0	0	.048	.087
Ashby, Andy, L.A.	.500	3	5	2	1	1	1	0	0	0	1	2	0	0	1	0	0	0	0	0	.500	.667
Astacio, Pedro, Col.-Hou.	.094	26	64	53	2	5	5	0	0	0	3	11	0	0	0	0	17	0	0	0	.094	.094
Atchley, Justin, Cin.*	.000	15	1	1	0	0	0	0	0	0	0	0	0	0	0	0	1	0	0	0	.000	.000
Aurilia, Rich, S.F.	.324	156	689	636	114	206	364	37	5	37	97	3	3	0	47	2	83	1	3	14	.572	.369
Ausmus, Brad, Hou.	.232	128	461	422	45	98	144	23	4	5	34	6	2	1	30	6	64	4	1	13	.341	.284
Aven, Bruce, L.A.	.333	21	26	24	3	8	13	2	0	1	2	0	0	2	0	0	5	0	0	0	.542	.385
Aybar, Manny, Chi.	1.000	17	4	3	1	3	3	0	0	0	0	1	0	0	0	0	0	0	0	0	1.000	1.000
Baez, Benito, Fla.*	.000	8	1	1	0	0	0	0	0	0	0	0	0	0	0	0	0	0	0	0	.000	.000

Player, Team	Avg.	G	TPA	AB	R	H	TB	2B	3B	HR	RBI	SH	SF	HP	BB	IBB	SO	SB	CS	GDP	Slg.	OBP
Bagwell, Jeff, Hou.	.288	161	717	600	126	173	341	43	4	39	130	0	5	6	106	5	135	11	3	20	.568	.397
Bako, Paul, Atl.*	.212	61	157	137	19	29	47	10	1	2	15	0	0	0	20	2	34	1	0	3	.343	.312
Baldwin, James, L.A.	.077	12	27	26	0	2	3	1	0	0	1	1	0	0	0	0	12	0	0	1	.115	.077
Barajas, Rod, Ari.	.160	51	110	106	9	17	29	3	0	3	9	0	0	0	4	0	26	0	0	0	.274	.191
Barker, Glen, Hou.†	.083	70	30	24	12	2	2	0	0	0	1	0	1	2	3	0	6	4	6	0	.083	.233
Barkett, Andy, Pit.*	.304	17	51	46	5	14	19	2	0	1	3	0	0	1	4	1	7	1	0	2	.413	.373
Barrett, Michael, Mon.	.250	132	506	472	42	118	173	33	2	6	38	4	3	2	25	2	54	2	1	14	.367	.289
Bartee, Kimera, Col.	.000	12	19	15	0	0	0	0	0	0	1	0	1	1	2	1	5	0	0	0	.000	.158
Batista, Miguel, Ari.	.063	48	36	32	2	2	2	0	0	0	0	2	0	0	2	0	17	0	0	0	.063	.118
Bautista, Danny, Ari.	.302	100	239	222	26	67	97	11	2	5	26	2	0	1	14	1	31	3	2	7	.437	.346
Beckett, Josh, Fla.	.286	4	9	7	1	2	3	1	0	0	0	2	0	0	0	0	1	0	0	0	.429	.286
Beimel, Joe, Pit.*	.269	42	31	26	3	7	7	0	0	0	0	4	0	0	1	0	10	0	0	0	.269	.296
Belitz, Todd, Col.*	.000	8	1	1	0	0	0	0	0	0	0	0	0	0	0	0	1	0	0	0	.000	.000
Bell, Derek, Pit.	.173	46	183	156	14	27	45	3	0	5	13	2	0	0	25	5	38	0	2	4	.288	.287
Bell, Jay, Ari.	.248	129	509	428	59	106	171	24	1	13	46	8	4	4	65	3	79	0	1	9	.400	.349
Bell, Rob, Cin.	.143	9	10	7	0	1	1	0	0	0	0	2	0	0	1	0	4	0	0	0	.143	.250
Belliard, Ron, Mil.	.264	101	410	364	69	96	165	30	3	11	36	4	2	5	35	2	65	5	2	5	.453	.335
Beltre, Adrian, L.A.	.265	126	515	475	59	126	195	22	4	13	60	2	5	5	28	1	82	13	4	9	.411	.310
Benard, Marvin, S.F.*	.265	129	429	392	70	104	172	19	2	15	44	1	3	4	29	2	66	10	5	3	.439	.320
Benes, Alan, St.L	.500	9	2	2	1	1	1	0	0	0	0	0	0	0	0	0	0	0	0	0	.500	.500
Benes, Andy, St.L	.156	27	35	32	1	5	8	3	0	0	4	2	0	0	1	0	15	0	0	0	.250	.182
Benitez, Armando, N.Y.	.000	73	1	1	0	0	0	0	0	0	1	0	0	0	0	0	0	0	0	0	.000	.000
Bennett, Gary, Phi.-N.Y.-Col.	.244	46	148	131	15	32	46	6	1	2	10	2	2	1	12	4	24	0	0	1	.351	.308
Bere, Jason, Chi.	.194	32	69	62	2	12	16	4	0	0	2	7	0	0	0	0	18	0	0	2	.258	.194
Berg, Dave, Fla.	.242	82	235	215	26	52	78	12	1	4	16	2	2	2	14	0	39	0	1	3	.363	.292
Bergeron, Peter, Mon.*	.211	102	416	375	53	79	107	11	4	3	16	8	0	5	28	2	87	10	7	5	.285	.275
Berkman, Lance, Hou.†	.331	156	688	577	110	191	358	55	5	34	126	0	6	13	92	5	121	7	9	8	.620	.430
Betemit, Wilson, Atl.†	.000	8	5	3	1	0	0	0	0	0	0	0	0	0	2	0	3	1	0	0	.000	.400
Bierbrodt, Nick, Ari.*	.667	6	10	6	3	4	5	1	0	0	0	2	0	0	2	0	0	0	0	0	.833	.750
Biggio, Craig, Hou.	.292	155	717	617	118	180	281	35	3	20	70	0	6	28	66	4	100	7	4	11	.455	.382
Blanco, Henry, Mil.	.210	104	357	314	33	66	108	18	3	6	31	5	2	2	34	6	72	3	1	10	.344	.290
Blank, Matt, Mon.*	.500	5	8	8	0	4	5	1	0	0	1	0	0	0	0	0	2	0	0	0	.625	.500
Blum, Geoff, Mon.†	.236	148	514	453	57	107	159	25	0	9	50	3	5	10	43	8	94	9	5	12	.351	.313
Bocachica, Hiram, L.A.	.233	75	143	133	15	31	50	11	1	2	9	0	0	1	9	0	33	4	1	1	.376	.287
Boehringer, Brian, S.F.†	.000	29	3	3	0	0	0	0	0	0	0	0	0	0	0	0	2	0	0	0	.000	.000
Bogar, Tim, L.A.	.333	12	17	15	4	5	13	2	0	2	2	0	0	0	2	0	1	0	0	0	.867	.412
Bohanon, Brian, Col.*	.323	21	33	31	3	10	14	4	0	0	3	1	0	0	1	0	7	0	0	1	.452	.344
Bonds, Barry, S.F.*	.328	153	664	476	129	156	411	32	2	73	137	0	2	9	177	35	93	13	3	5	.863	.515
Bones, Ricky, Fla.	.500	61	3	2	0	1	1	0	0	0	1	0	1	0	0	0	1	0	0	0	.500	.333
Bonilla, Bobby, St.L†	.213	93	198	174	17	37	59	7	0	5	21	0	0	1	23	3	53	1	1	4	.339	.308
Boone, Aaron, Cin.	.294	103	427	381	54	112	184	26	2	14	62	3	6	8	29	1	71	6	3	9	.483	.351
Bottalico, Ricky, Phi.*	.333	66	3	3	1	1	2	1	0	0	1	0	0	0	0	0	0	0	0	0	.667	.333
Bottenfield, Kent, Hou.	.143	13	15	14	0	2	2	0	0	0	0	1	0	0	0	0	5	0	0	0	.143	.143
Bradley, Milton, Mon.†	.223	67	242	220	19	49	74	16	3	1	19	2	0	1	19	0	62	7	4	6	.336	.288
Bragg, Darren, N.Y.*	.263	18	63	57	4	15	21	6	0	0	5	1	0	1	4	0	23	3	2	0	.368	.323
Branson, Jeff, L.A.*	.286	13	21	21	3	6	6	0	0	0	0	0	0	0	0	0	4	0	0	0	.286	.286
Brock, Chris, Phi.	.333	24	3	3	0	1	1	0	0	0	0	0	0	0	0	0	0	0	0	0	.333	.333
Brogna, Rico, Atl.*	.248	72	223	206	15	51	69	9	0	3	21	1	1	1	14	1	46	3	1	9	.335	.297
Brohawn, Troy, Ari.*	.000	59	1	1	0	0	0	0	0	0	0	0	0	0	0	0	0	0	0	0	.000	.000
Brower, Jim, Cin.	.308	48	28	26	6	8	9	1	0	0	3	2	0	0	0	0	8	0	0	0	.346	.308
Brown, Adrian, Pit.†	.194	8	34	31	3	6	9	0	0	1	2	0	0	0	3	0	3	2	1	1	.290	.265
Brown, Emil, Pit.-S.D.	.190	74	155	137	21	26	41	4	1	3	13	0	0	2	16	1	49	12	4	2	.299	.284
Brown, Kevin, L.A.	.083	20	41	36	2	3	6	0	0	1	2	2	0	3	0	0	12	0	0	0	.167	.154
Brown, Kevin L., Mil.	.209	17	46	43	7	9	23	0	1	4	12	0	0	1	2	0	18	0	0	1	.535	.261
Brown, Roosevelt, Chi.*	.265	39	92	83	13	22	42	0	1	4	22	0	1	1	7	0	12	0	0	3	.506	.326
Brumbaugh, Cliff, Col.	.278	14	38	36	5	10	15	2	0	1	4	0	0	0	2	0	9	0	1	3	.417	.316
Buddie, Mike, Mil.	.250	31	4	4	1	1	1	0	0	0	0	0	0	0	0	0	3	0	0	0	.250	.250
Buford, Damon, Chi.	.176	35	89	85	11	15	26	2	0	3	8	0	0	0	4	0	23	0	0	3	.306	.213
Burkett, John, Atl.	.092	34	75	65	2	6	6	0	0	0	1	7	0	0	3	0	29	0	0	5	.092	.132
Burnett, A.J., Fla.	.080	27	59	50	0	4	5	1	0	0	0	7	0	1	1	0	27	0	0	0	.100	.115
Burnitz, Jeromy, Mil.*	.251	154	651	562	104	141	283	32	4	34	100	0	4	5	80	9	150	0	4	8	.504	.347
Burrell, Pat, Phi.	.258	155	618	539	70	139	253	29	2	27	89	0	4	5	70	7	162	2	1	12	.469	.346
Butler, Brent, Col.	.244	53	131	119	17	29	41	7	1	1	14	2	2	1	7	0	7	1	1	4	.345	.287
Byrd, Paul, Phi.	.500	4	3	2	0	1	1	0	0	0	0	1	0	0	0	0	0	0	0	0	.500	.500
Cabrera, Jose, Atl.	.000	55	1	1	0	0	0	0	0	0	0	0	0	0	0	0	1	0	0	0	.000	.000
Cabrera, Orlando, Mon.	.276	162	684	626	64	173	268	41	6	14	96	4	7	4	43	5	54	19	7	15	.428	.324
Cairo, Miguel, Chi.-St.L	.295	93	182	156	25	46	65	8	1	3	16	7	1	0	18	1	23	2	1	4	.417	.366
Caminiti, Ken, Atl.†	.222	64	193	171	12	38	65	9	0	6	16	0	1	0	21	1	44	0	1	2	.380	.306
Carrara, Giovanni, L.A.	.250	47	12	12	1	3	3	0	0	0	0	0	0	0	0	0	2	0	0	0	.250	.250
Casanova, Raul, Mil.†	.260	71	208	192	21	50	93	10	0	11	33	0	3	1	12	2	29	0	0	3	.484	.303
Casey, Sean, Cin.*	.310	145	588	533	69	165	244	40	0	13	89	0	3	9	43	8	63	3	1	16	.458	.369
Castilla, Vinny, Hou.	.270	122	484	445	62	120	219	28	1	23	82	0	4	3	32	3	86	1	4	19	.492	.320
Castillo, Luis, Fla.†	.263	134	612	537	76	141	183	16	10	2	45	4	3	1	67	0	90	33	16	6	.341	.344
Castro, Juan, Cin.	.223	96	261	242	27	54	73	10	0	3	13	4	2	0	13	2	50	0	0	9	.302	.261
Castro, Ramon, Fla.	.182	7	12	11	0	2	2	0	0	0	1	0	0	0	1	0	1	0	0	0	.182	.250
Chacon, Shawn, Col.	.043	27	55	47	2	2	2	0	0	0	1	7	0	1	0	0	22	0	0	1	.043	.063
Chen, Bruce, Phi.-N.Y.*	.128	27	52	47	1	6	6	0	0	0	0	5	0	0	0	0	19	0	0	1	.128	.128
Christensen, McKay, L.A.*	.327	28	55	49	7	16	21	2	0	1	7	0	0	3	3	0	10	3	2	0	.429	.400
Christenson, Ryan, Ari.	.250	19	5	4	3	1	2	1	0	0	1	0	0	0	1	0	1	1	0	0	.500	.400
Cintron, Alex, Ari.†	.286	8	7	7	0	2	4	0	1	0	0	0	0	0	0	0	0	0	0	0	.571	.286
Cirillo, Jeff, Col.	.313	138	586	528	72	165	250	26	4	17	83	1	9	5	43	6	63	12	2	15	.473	.364
Clapp, Stubby, St.L*	.200	23	26	25	0	5	7	2	0	0	1	0	0	0	1	0	7	0	0	0	.280	.231
Clark, Brady, Cin.	.264	89	157	129	22	34	55	3	0	6	18	4	1	1	22	1	16	4	1	6	.426	.373

Player, Team	Avg.	G	TPA	AB	R	H	TB	2B	3B	HR	RBI	SH	SF	HP	BB	IBB	SO	SB	CS	GDP	Slg.	OBP
Clement, Matt, Fla.	.080	32	61	50	2	4	4	0	0	0	0	8	0	0	3	0	18	0	0	0	.080	.132
Coggin, David, Phi.	.061	17	36	33	1	2	3	1	0	0	1	1	0	0	2	0	13	0	0	0	.091	.114
Colangelo, Mike, S.D.	.242	50	100	91	10	22	37	3	3	2	8	0	0	1	8	0	30	0	0	3	.407	.310
Colbrunn, Greg, Ari.	.289	59	110	97	12	28	48	8	0	4	18	0	0	4	9	0	14	0	0	5	.495	.373
Collier, Lou, Mil.	.252	50	148	127	19	32	48	8	1	2	14	1	2	1	17	0	30	5	1	0	.378	.340
Conti, Jason, Ari.*	.250	5	5	4	1	1	1	0	0	0	0	0	0	0	1	0	2	0	0	0	.250	.400
Cook, Dennis, N.Y.-Phi.*	.000	62	1	1	0	0	0	0	0	0	0	0	0	0	0	0	0	0	0	0	.000	.000
Coolbaugh, Mike, Mil.	.200	39	77	70	10	14	26	6	0	2	7	0	0	2	5	0	16	0	0	3	.371	.273
Coomer, Ron, Chi.	.261	111	386	349	25	91	136	19	1	8	53	0	6	2	29	1	70	0	0	23	.390	.316
Coppinger, Rocky, Mil.	.000	8	6	5	0	0	0	0	0	0	1	1	0	0	0	0	1	0	0	0	.000	.000
Cora, Alex, L.A.*	.217	134	449	405	38	88	124	18	3	4	29	3	2	8	31	6	58	0	2	16	.306	.285
Cormier, Rheal, Phi.*	.000	60	1	1	0	0	0	0	0	0	0	0	0	0	0	0	0	0	0	0	.000	.000
Cota, Humberto, Pit.	.222	7	9	9	0	2	2	0	0	0	1	0	0	0	0	0	5	0	0	0	.222	.222
Counsell, Craig, Ari.*	.275	141	533	458	76	126	166	22	3	4	38	6	6	2	61	3	76	6	8	9	.362	.359
Crespo, Cesar, S.D.†	.209	55	179	153	27	32	50	6	0	4	12	1	0	0	25	0	50	6	2	2	.327	.320
Crespo, Felipe, S.F.-Phi.†	.187	73	125	107	9	20	38	4	1	4	15	1	4	2	11	1	34	1	1	2	.355	.266
Cromer, D.T., Cin.*	.281	50	63	57	7	16	34	3	0	5	12	0	3	0	3	0	19	0	0	0	.596	.302
Cruz, Jacob, Col.*	.211	44	90	76	7	16	20	1	0	1	7	1	2	1	10	0	27	0	2	1	.263	.303
Cruz, Juan, Chi.	.125	11	18	16	0	2	2	0	0	0	1	2	0	0	0	0	5	0	0	1	.125	.125
Cruz, Nelson, Hou.	.167	66	6	6	0	1	1	0	0	0	0	0	0	0	0	0	2	0	0	0	.167	.167
Cummings, Midre, Ari.*	.300	20	21	20	1	6	7	1	0	0	1	0	1	0	0	0	4	0	0	2	.350	.286
Cunnane, Will, Mil.	.000	32	7	7	0	0	0	0	0	0	0	0	0	0	0	0	1	0	0	0	.000	.000
Cust, Jack, Ari.*	.500	3	3	2	0	1	1	0	0	0	0	0	0	0	1	0	0	0	0	0	.500	.667
Daal, Omar, Phi.*	.236	32	63	55	7	13	14	1	0	0	5	7	0	0	1	0	10	0	0	4	.255	.250
D'Amico, Jeff C., Mil.	.067	10	17	15	0	1	3	0	1	0	0	0	0	0	2	0	5	0	0	0	.200	.176
Darr, Mike, S.D.*	.277	105	331	289	36	80	101	13	1	2	34	0	2	1	39	3	72	6	2	8	.349	.363
Davenport, Joe, Col.	1.000	7	1	1	0	1	1	0	0	0	0	0	0	0	0	0	0	0	0	0	1.000	1.000
Davey, Tom, S.D.	.000	39	1	0	0	0	0	0	0	0	0	0	0	0	1	0	0	0	0	0	.000	1.000
Davis, Eric, S.F.	.205	74	171	156	17	32	57	7	3	4	22	0	1	1	13	0	38	1	1	4	.365	.269
Davis, Lance, Cin.	.121	21	37	33	3	4	5	1	0	0	2	4	0	0	0	0	15	0	0	0	.152	.121
Davis, Kane, Col.	.000	57	5	5	0	0	0	0	0	0	0	0	0	0	0	0	5	0	0	0	.000	.000
Davis, Ben, S.D.†	.239	138	526	448	56	107	160	20	0	11	57	1	7	4	66	5	112	4	4	13	.357	.337
Davis, Russ, S.F.	.257	53	189	167	16	43	79	13	1	7	17	2	2	1	17	2	49	1	0	5	.473	.326
DeJean, Mike, Mil.	.000	75	3	3	0	0	0	0	0	0	0	0	0	0	0	0	2	0	0	0	.000	.000
De La Rosa, Tomas, Mon.	.000	1	1	1	0	0	0	0	0	0	0	0	0	0	0	0	0	0	0	0	.000	.000
Dellucci, David, Ari.*	.276	115	241	217	28	60	104	10	2	10	40	0	0	2	22	4	52	2	1	2	.479	.349
Dempster, Ryan, Fla.	.049	34	78	61	1	3	4	1	0	0	0	16	0	0	1	0	29	0	0	0	.066	.065
DeRosa, Mark, Atl.	.287	66	184	164	27	47	64	8	0	3	20	1	2	5	12	6	19	2	1	3	.390	.350
DeShields, Delino, Chi.*	.276	68	195	163	26	45	66	9	3	2	16	3	1	0	28	0	35	12	1	5	.405	.380
Dessens, Elmer, Cin.	.193	35	70	57	3	11	12	1	0	0	2	10	0	0	3	0	12	0	0	0	.211	.233
DiFelice, Mike, Ari.	.048	12	23	21	1	1	1	0	0	0	1	1	0	1	0	0	10	0	0	0	.048	.091
Donnels, Chris, L.A.*	.170	66	101	88	8	15	26	2	0	3	8	0	0	1	12	2	25	0	0	2	.295	.277
Dotel, Octavio, Hou.	.091	61	12	11	0	1	1	0	0	0	0	1	0	0	0	0	5	0	0	0	.091	.091
Dreifort, Darren, L.A.	.152	16	37	33	4	5	10	2	0	1	2	3	0	0	1	0	20	1	0	0	.303	.176
Drew, J.D., St.L*	.323	109	443	375	80	121	230	18	5	27	73	3	4	4	57	4	75	13	3	6	.613	.414
Ducey, Rob, Phi.-Mon.*	.233	57	93	73	10	17	29	3	0	3	12	2	1	1	16	0	25	0	1	0	.397	.374
Duckworth, Brandon, Phi.	.227	11	26	22	1	5	6	1	0	0	1	2	0	0	2	0	4	0	0	1	.273	.292
Duncan, Courtney, Chi.*	.000	36	5	3	1	0	0	0	0	0	1	0	0	0	2	0	1	0	0	0	.000	.400
Dunn, Adam, Cin.*	.262	66	286	244	54	64	141	18	1	19	43	0	0	4	38	2	74	4	2	4	.578	.371
Dunston, Shawon, S.F.	.280	88	193	186	26	52	95	10	3	9	25	2	1	2	2	0	32	3	1	2	.511	.293
Dunwoody, Todd, Chi.*	.213	33	64	61	6	13	20	4	0	1	3	0	0	0	3	0	14	0	1	0	.328	.250
Durazo, Erubiel, Ari.*	.269	92	207	175	34	47	94	11	0	12	38	0	2	2	28	1	49	0	0	1	.537	.372
Eaton, Adam, S.D.	.105	23	44	38	3	4	5	1	0	0	2	2	0	0	4	0	12	1	0	0	.132	.190
Echevarria, Angel, Mil.	.256	75	145	133	12	34	60	11	0	5	13	0	1	3	8	0	29	0	1	2	.451	.310
Edmonds, Jim, St.L*	.304	150	608	500	95	152	282	38	1	30	110	1	10	4	93	12	136	5	5	8	.564	.410
Elarton, Scott, Hou.-Col.	.079	24	47	38	1	3	3	0	0	0	2	5	0	3	1	0	10	0	0	2	.079	.167
Ellis, Robert, Ari.	.154	19	28	26	2	4	4	0	0	0	1	1	0	0	1	0	12	0	0	0	.154	.185
Embree, Alan, S.F.*	.000	22	1	1	0	0	0	0	0	0	0	0	0	0	0	0	0	0	0	0	.000	.000
Encarnacion, Mario, Col.	.226	20	67	62	3	14	15	1	0	0	3	0	0	0	5	0	14	2	1	3	.242	.284
Escobar, Alex, N.Y.	.200	18	53	50	3	10	20	1	0	3	8	0	0	0	3	0	19	1	0	1	.400	.245
Estalella, Bobby, S.F.	.204	29	105	93	11	19	35	5	1	3	10	0	0	1	11	2	28	0	0	2	.376	.295
Estes, Shawn, S.F.	.071	27	52	42	2	3	3	0	0	0	1	6	1	0	3	0	11	0	0	1	.071	.130
Estrada, Johnny, Phi.†	.228	89	324	298	26	68	107	15	0	8	37	2	4	4	16	6	32	0	0	15	.359	.273
Eusebio, Tony, Hou.	.253	59	174	154	16	39	62	8	0	5	14	0	0	3	17	3	34	0	0	2	.403	.339
Everett, Adam, Hou.	.000	9	3	3	1	0	0	0	0	0	0	0	0	0	0	0	1	1	0	0	.000	.000
Farnsworth, Kyle, Chi.	.000	76	2	2	0	0	0	0	0	0	0	0	0	0	0	0	2	0	0	0	.000	.000
Fasano, Sal, Col.	.254	25	72	63	10	16	30	5	0	3	9	2	0	3	4	0	19	0	0	1	.476	.329
Fassero, Jeff, Chi.*	.000	82	2	2	0	0	0	0	0	0	0	0	0	0	0	0	2	0	0	0	.000	.000
Feliz, Pedro, S.F.	.227	94	238	220	23	50	82	9	1	7	22	3	3	2	10	2	50	2	1	5	.373	.264
Fernandez, Jared, Cin.	.000	5	2	2	0	0	0	0	0	0	0	0	0	0	0	0	0	0	0	0	.000	.000
Fernandez, Tony, Mil.†	.281	28	72	64	6	18	21	0	0	1	3	1	0	0	7	0	9	1	2	1	.328	.352
Fernandez, Osvaldo, Cin.	.053	20	23	19	1	1	1	0	0	0	0	3	0	0	1	0	8	0	0	0	.053	.100
Figueroa, Luis, Pit.†	.000	4	2	2	0	0	0	0	0	0	0	0	0	0	0	0	0	0	0	0	.000	.000
Figueroa, Nelson, Phi.	.250	19	26	24	4	6	7	1	0	0	1	1	0	0	1	0	11	0	0	0	.292	.280
Finley, Steve, Ari.*	.275	140	548	495	66	136	213	27	4	14	73	2	3	1	47	9	67	11	7	8	.430	.337
Floyd, Cliff, Fla.*	.317	149	629	555	123	176	321	44	4	31	103	0	5	10	59	19	101	18	3	9	.578	.390
Forbes, P.J., Phi.	.286	3	7	7	1	2	2	0	0	0	1	0	0	0	0	0	2	0	0	0	.286	.286
Fox, Andy, Fla.*	.185	54	98	81	8	15	26	0	1	3	7	0	0	2	15	1	17	1	0	2	.321	.327
Fox, Chad, Mil.	.000	65	3	3	0	0	0	0	0	0	0	0	0	0	0	0	1	0	0	0	.000	.000
Franco, Julio, Atl.	.300	25	101	90	13	27	40	4	0	3	11	0	0	1	10	1	20	0	0	3	.444	.376
Fultz, Aaron, S.F.*	.400	66	5	5	1	2	2	0	0	0	0	0	0	0	0	0	0	0	0	0	.400	.400
Furcal, Rafael, Atl.†	.275	79	359	324	39	89	120	19	0	4	30	4	6	1	24	1	56	22	6	5	.370	.321
Fyhrie, Mike, Chi.	.000	15	2	2	0	0	0	0	0	0	0	0	0	0	0	0	0	0	0	0	.000	.000

Player, Team	Avg.	G	TPA	AB	R	H	TB	2B	3B	HR	RBI	SH	SF	HP	BB	IBB	SO	SB	CS	GDP	Slg.	OBP
Gagne, Eric, L.A.	.136	33	51	44	3	6	13	2	1	1	2	6	0	0	1	0	13	0	1	2	.295	.156
Galarraga, Andres, S.F.	.288	49	174	156	17	45	80	12	1	7	35	0	2	3	13	1	49	0	3	3	.513	.351
Gant, Ron, Col.	.257	59	199	171	31	44	80	8	2	8	22	2	2	0	24	2	56	3	1	0	.468	.345
Garcia, Jesse, Atl.	.200	22	6	5	3	1	1	0	0	0	0	0	0	0	0	0	1	0	2	0	.200	.200
Gardner, Mark, S.F.	.000	23	26	21	1	0	0	0	0	0	1	4	0	0	1	0	8	0	0	0	.000	.045
Giles, Brian, Pit.*	.309	160	674	576	116	178	340	37	7	37	95	0	4	4	90	14	67	13	6	10	.590	.404
Giles, Marcus, Atl.	.262	68	273	244	36	64	105	10	2	9	31	1	0	0	28	0	37	2	5	8	.430	.338
Gilkey, Bernard, Atl.	.274	69	121	106	8	29	41	6	0	2	14	0	3	1	11	0	31	0	1	4	.387	.339
Ginter, Keith, Hou.	.000	1	1	1	0	0	0	0	0	0	0	0	0	0	0	0	0	0	0	0	.000	.000
Girardi, Joe, Chi.	.253	78	253	229	22	58	79	10	1	3	25	2	1	0	21	4	50	0	1	2	.345	.315
Glanville, Doug, Phi.	.262	153	674	634	74	166	238	24	3	14	55	10	7	4	19	1	91	28	6	7	.375	.285
Glavine, Tom, Atl.*	.140	35	78	57	4	8	10	2	0	0	2	17	0	0	4	0	21	0	0	1	.175	.197
Gomes, Wayne, Phi.-S.F.	1.000	55	2	1	0	1	1	0	0	0	1	0	0	0	0	0	0	0	0	1	1.000	1.000
Gomez, Chris, S.D.	.188	40	125	112	6	21	24	3	0	0	7	2	2	0	9	0	14	1	0	5	.214	.244
Gonzalez, Alex, Fla.	.250	145	561	515	57	129	194	36	1	9	48	3	3	10	30	6	107	2	2	13	.377	.303
Gonzalez, Dicky, N.Y.	.100	16	22	20	1	2	2	0	0	0	0	1	0	0	1	0	4	0	0	0	.100	.143
Gonzalez, Luis, Ari.*	.325	162	728	609	128	198	419	36	7	57	142	0	5	14	100	24	83	1	1	14	.688	.429
Gonzalez, Raul, Cin.	.214	11	15	14	0	3	3	0	0	0	0	0	0	0	1	0	3	0	0	1	.214	.267
Gonzalez, Wiki, S.D.	.275	64	176	160	16	44	74	6	0	8	27	0	1	4	11	1	28	2	0	3	.463	.335
Goodwin, Tom, L.A.*	.231	105	312	286	51	66	96	8	5	4	22	1	2	0	23	0	58	22	8	3	.336	.286
Grace, Mark, Ari.*	.298	145	553	476	66	142	222	31	2	15	78	1	5	4	67	6	36	1	0	7	.466	.386
Graves, Danny, Cin.	.250	66	4	4	1	1	4	0	0	1	2	0	0	0	0	0	2	0	0	1	1.000	.250
Green, Shawn, L.A.*	.297	161	701	619	121	184	370	31	4	49	125	0	5	5	72	10	107	20	4	10	.598	.372
Griffey, Ken Jr., Cin.*	.286	111	467	364	57	104	194	20	2	22	65	1	4	4	44	6	72	2	0	8	.533	.365
Grilli, Jason, Fla.	.286	6	9	7	1	2	5	0	0	1	2	2	0	0	0	0	2	0	0	0	.714	.286
Grissom, Marquis, L.A.	.221	135	468	448	56	99	181	17	1	21	60	0	2	2	16	0	107	7	5	12	.404	.250
Grudzielanek, Mark, L.A.	.271	133	586	539	83	146	212	21	3	13	55	3	5	11	28	0	83	4	4	9	.393	.317
Guerrero, Vladimir, Mon.	.307	159	671	599	107	184	339	45	4	34	108	0	3	9	60	24	88	37	16	24	.566	.377
Guerrero, Wilton, Cin.†	.338	60	147	142	16	48	58	5	1	1	8	2	0	0	3	0	17	5	2	1	.408	.352
Gulan, Mike, Fla.	.000	6	8	6	1	0	0	0	0	0	0	0	0	0	2	0	2	0	0	0	.000	.250
Gutierrez, Ricky, Chi.	.290	147	606	528	76	153	212	23	3	10	66	17	11	10	40	0	56	4	3	13	.402	.345
Guzman, Edwards, S.F.*	.243	61	121	115	8	28	43	6	0	3	7	0	1	0	5	2	16	0	0	2	.374	.273
Guzman, Geraldo, Ari.	.000	4	1	1	0	0	0	0	0	0	0	0	0	0	0	1	0	0	0	0	.000	.000
Gwynn, Tony, S.D.*	.324	71	112	102	5	33	47	9	1	1	17	0	0	0	10	1	9	1	0	1	.461	.384
Hackman, Luther, St.L	.000	35	3	1	0	0	0	0	0	0	0	2	0	0	0	0	0	0	0	0	.000	.000
Hamilton, Darryl, N.Y.*	.214	52	151	126	15	27	39	7	1	1	5	2	2	2	19	3	20	3	1	2	.310	.322
Hamilton, Joey, Cin.	.000	4	5	5	0	0	0	0	0	0	0	0	0	0	0	0	4	0	0	0	.000	.000
Hammonds, Jeffrey, Mil.	.247	49	194	174	20	43	74	11	1	6	21	0	2	4	14	1	42	5	3	2	.425	.314
Hampton, Mike, Col.	.291	43	86	70	20	23	46	2	0	7	16	5	0	0	2	0	21	0	1	1	.582	.309
Hansen, Dave, L.A.*	.236	92	175	140	13	33	49	10	0	2	20	0	3	0	32	5	29	0	1	3	.350	.371
Harnisch, Pete, Cin.	.273	8	12	11	2	3	4	1	0	0	0	1	0	0	0	0	5	0	0	0	.364	.273
Harris, Lenny, N.Y.*	.222	110	143	135	12	30	37	5	1	0	9	0	0	0	8	0	9	3	2	3	.274	.266
Hayes, Charlie, Hou.	.200	31	58	50	4	10	12	2	0	0	4	0	1	0	7	1	16	0	0	1	.240	.293
Haynes, Jimmy, Mil.	.154	32	59	52	5	8	10	2	0	0	5	0	0	0	2	0	16	0	0	0	.192	.185
Helms, Wes, Atl.	.222	100	239	216	28	48	94	10	3	10	36	0	1	1	21	2	56	1	1	3	.435	.293
Helton, Todd, Col.*	.336	159	696	587	132	197	402	54	2	49	146	1	5	5	98	15	104	7	5	14	.685	.432
Henderson, Rickey, S.D.	.227	123	465	379	70	86	133	17	3	8	42	0	2	3	81	0	84	25	7	8	.351	.366
Heredia, Felix, Chi.*	.000	48	1	1	0	0	0	0	0	0	0	0	0	0	0	0	1	0	0	0	.000	.000
Herges, Matt, L.A.*	.444	75	10	9	0	4	4	0	0	0	1	1	0	0	0	0	3	0	0	0	.444	.444
Hermansen, Chad, Pit.	.164	22	56	55	5	9	16	1	0	2	5	0	0	0	1	0	18	0	1	0	.291	.179
Hermanson, Dustin, St.L	.081	34	69	62	2	5	6	1	0	0	3	5	0	0	2	0	30	0	0	1	.097	.109
Hernandez, Alex, Pit.*	.091	7	11	11	0	1	1	0	0	0	0	0	0	0	0	0	2	0	0	1	.091	.091
Hernandez, Carlos E., Hou.†..	.200	3	6	5	0	1	1	0	0	0	0	0	1	0	0	0	2	0	0	0	.200	.200
Hernandez, Livan, S.F.	.296	35	85	81	7	24	31	4	0	1	8	4	0	0	0	0	4	0	0	4	.383	.296
Hernandez, Jose, Mil.	.249	152	592	542	67	135	240	26	2	25	78	5	4	2	39	8	185	5	4	9	.443	.300
Herndon, Junior, S.D.	.000	12	13	12	0	0	0	0	0	0	0	1	0	0	0	0	11	0	0	0	.000	.000
Hiatt, Phil, L.A.	.240	30	53	50	8	12	21	3	0	2	6	0	0	0	3	1	19	0	0	0	.420	.283
Hidalgo, Richard, Hou.	.275	146	593	512	70	141	233	29	3	19	80	0	11	16	54	3	107	3	5	15	.455	.356
Hinchliffe, Brett, N.Y.†	.000	1	1	1	0	0	0	0	0	0	0	0	0	0	0	0	1	0	0	0	.000	.000
Hitchcock, Sterling, S.D.*	.125	3	8	8	1	1	1	0	0	0	0	0	0	0	0	0	6	0	0	0	.125	.125
Hoffman, Trevor, S.D.	.000	62	4	4	0	0	0	0	0	0	0	0	0	0	0	0	1	0	0	0	.000	.000
Hollandsworth, Todd, Col.*	.368	33	125	117	21	43	78	15	1	6	19	0	0	0	8	2	20	5	0	1	.667	.408
Houston, Tyler, Mil.*	.289	75	256	235	36	68	111	7	0	12	38	2	0	1	18	1	62	0	0	3	.472	.343
Huckaby, Ken, Ari.	.000	1	1	1	0	0	0	0	0	0	0	0	0	0	0	0	1	0	0	0	.000	.000
Hundley, Todd, Chi.†	.187	79	276	246	23	46	92	10	0	12	31	0	2	3	25	0	89	0	0	7	.374	.268
Hunter, Brian L., Phi.	.276	83	166	145	22	40	52	6	0	2	16	3	2	0	16	0	25	14	3	3	.359	.344
Hutchinson, Chad, St.L	.000	3	1	1	0	0	0	0	0	0	0	0	0	0	0	0	0	0	0	0	.000	.000
Hyzdu, Adam, Pit.	.208	51	77	72	7	15	31	1	0	5	9	0	0	1	4	0	18	0	1	1	.431	.260
Irabu, Hideki, Mon.	.000	3	3	3	0	0	0	0	0	0	0	0	0	0	0	0	0	0	0	0	.000	.000
Jackson, Damian, S.D.	.241	122	495	440	67	106	151	21	6	4	38	2	3	6	44	2	128	23	6	6	.343	.316
Jackson, Mike, Hou.	.000	67	1	1	0	0	0	0	0	0	0	0	0	0	0	0	0	0	0	0	.000	.000
James, Mike, St.L	.000	40	1	1	0	0	0	0	0	0	0	0	0	0	0	0	0	0	0	0	.000	.000
Jarvis, Kevin, S.D.*	.180	34	74	61	8	11	17	3	0	1	10	5	2	1	5	0	20	0	1	2	.279	.246
Jenkins, Geoff, Mil.*	.264	105	446	397	60	105	188	21	1	20	63	0	5	8	36	7	120	4	2	11	.474	.334
Jennings, Jason, Col.*	.267	7	17	15	2	4	8	1	0	1	2	1	0	0	1	0	3	0	0	0	.533	.313
Jennings, Robin, Col.-Cin.* ..	.275	28	85	80	10	22	40	5	2	3	14	0	0	0	5	1	12	0	0	0	.500	.318
Jensen, Ryan, S.F.	.167	10	13	12	0	2	2	0	0	0	2	0	0	0	1	0	3	0	0	0	.167	.231
Jimenez, D'Angelo, S.D.†	.276	86	349	308	45	85	113	19	0	3	33	0	2	0	39	4	68	2	3	9	.367	.355
Jimenez, Jose, Col.	.000	56	1	1	0	0	0	0	0	0	0	0	0	0	0	0	1	0	0	0	.000	.000
Jodie, Brett, S.D.	.000	7	4	4	0	0	0	0	0	0	0	0	0	0	0	0	2	0	0	0	.000	.000
Johnson, J.J., L.A.	.250	3	4	4	0	1	1	0	0	0	1	0	0	0	0	0	1	0	0	0	.250	.250
Johnson, Charles, Fla.	.259	128	496	451	51	117	203	32	0	18	75	0	3	4	38	2	133	0	0	8	.450	.321
Johnson, Mark P., N.Y.*	.254	71	136	118	17	30	56	6	1	6	23	0	2	0	16	1	31	0	2	0	.475	.338

Player, Team	Avg.	G	TPA	AB	R	H	TB	2B	3B	HR	RBI	SH	SF	HP	BB	IBB	SO	SB	CS	GDP	Slg.	OBP
Johnson, Mike, Mon.*	.000	10	1	1	0	0	0	0	0	0	0	0	0	0	0	0	1	0	0	0	.000	.000
Johnson, Randy, Ari.	.100	35	91	80	2	8	8	0	0	0	2	7	0	1	3	0	38	0	0	3	.100	.143
Jones, Andruw, Atl.	.251	161	693	625	104	157	288	25	2	34	104	0	9	3	56	3	142	11	4	10	.461	.312
Jones, Chipper, Atl.†	.330	159	677	572	113	189	346	33	5	38	102	0	5	2	98	20	82	9	10	13	.605	.427
Jones, Bobby J., S.D.	.140	33	62	57	5	8	10	2	0	0	1	2	0	0	3	0	18	0	0	1	.175	.183
Jones, Terry, Mon.†	.260	30	79	77	8	20	25	5	0	0	2	0	0	0	2	0	11	3	0	2	.325	.278
Jordan, Brian, Atl.	.295	148	605	560	82	165	278	32	3	25	97	0	8	6	31	3	88	3	2	18	.496	.334
Jordan, Kevin, Phi.	.239	68	127	113	9	27	35	5	0	1	13	0	0	0	14	2	21	0	0	1	.310	.323
Karros, Eric, L.A.	.235	121	485	438	42	103	170	22	0	15	63	0	3	3	41	2	101	3	1	15	.388	.303
Karsay, Steve, Atl.	.000	43	2	2	0	0	0	0	0	0	0	0	0	0	0	0	1	0	0	0	.000	.000
Kendall, Jason, Pit.	.266	157	672	606	84	161	217	22	2	10	53	0	2	20	44	4	48	13	14	18	.358	.335
Kent, Jeff, S.F.	.298	159	696	607	84	181	308	49	6	22	106	0	13	11	65	4	96	7	6	11	.507	.369
Kieschnick, Brooks, Col.*	.238	35	45	42	5	10	23	2	1	3	9	0	0	0	3	0	13	0	0	1	.548	.289
Kile, Darryl, St.L	.127	34	81	71	5	9	16	4	0	1	4	5	0	0	5	0	33	0	0	0	.225	.184
Kim, Byung-Hyun, Ari.	.167	78	6	6	0	1	1	0	0	0	2	0	0	0	0	0	2	0	0	0	.167	.167
King, Ray, Mil.*	.000	82	2	2	0	0	0	0	0	0	0	0	0	0	0	0	1	0	0	0	.000	.000
Klesko, Ryan, S.D.*	.286	146	638	538	105	154	290	34	6	30	113	0	9	3	88	7	89	23	4	16	.539	.384
Kline, Steve, St.L†	.500	89	2	2	0	1	1	0	0	0	0	0	0	0	0	0	1	0	0	0	.500	.500
Knorr, Randy, Mon.	.220	34	103	91	13	20	31	2	0	3	10	2	1	1	8	0	22	0	0	4	.341	.287
Knott, Eric, Ari.*	.000	3	1	1	0	0	0	0	0	0	0	0	0	0	0	0	1	0	0	0	.000	.000
Knotts, Gary, Fla.	.500	2	2	2	0	1	1	0	0	0	0	0	0	0	0	0	0	0	0	0	.500	.500
Kolb, Brandon, Mil.	.000	10	1	1	0	0	0	0	0	0	0	0	0	0	0	0	0	0	0	0	.000	.000
Koplove, Mike, Ari.	.000	9	1	1	0	0	0	0	0	0	0	0	0	0	0	0	1	0	0	0	.000	.000
Kotsay, Mark, S.D.*	.291	119	460	406	67	118	179	29	1	10	58	1	3	2	48	1	58	13	5	11	.441	.366
Kreuter, Chad, L.A.†	.215	73	234	191	21	41	72	11	1	6	17	0	1	1	41	2	52	0	0	5	.377	.355
Lankford, Ray, St.L-S.D.*	.252	131	459	389	58	98	191	28	4	19	58	1	3	4	62	9	145	10	2	6	.491	.358
Larkin, Barry, Cin.	.256	45	185	156	29	40	58	12	0	2	17	0	0	2	27	2	25	3	2	2	.372	.373
Larson, Brandon, Cin.	.121	14	35	33	2	4	6	2	0	0	1	0	0	0	2	0	10	0	0	1	.182	.171
LaRue, Jason, Cin.	.236	121	403	364	39	86	147	21	2	12	43	1	2	9	27	4	106	3	3	11	.404	.303
Lawrence, Brian, S.D.	.115	27	29	26	0	3	5	2	0	0	3	2	1	0	0	0	7	0	0	1	.192	.111
Lawton, Matt, N.Y.*	.246	48	213	183	24	45	67	11	1	3	13	0	0	8	22	0	34	10	2	2	.366	.352
Leach, Jalal, S.F.*	.100	8	12	10	0	1	1	0	0	0	1	0	0	0	2	0	3	0	0	0	.100	.250
Lee, David, S.D.	.000	41	1	1	0	0	0	0	0	0	0	0	0	0	0	0	1	0	0	0	.000	.000
Lee, Derrek, Fla.	.282	158	625	561	83	158	266	37	4	21	75	0	6	8	50	1	126	4	2	18	.474	.346
Lee, Travis, Phi.*	.258	157	640	555	75	143	241	34	2	20	90	1	9	4	71	5	109	3	4	15	.434	.341
Leiter, Al, N.Y.*	.065	29	64	62	2	4	6	0	1	0	3	0	0	0	2	0	28	0	0	0	.097	.094
Leiter, Mark, Mil.	.143	20	7	7	0	1	1	0	0	0	0	0	0	0	0	0	4	0	0	1	.143	.143
Leskanic, Curtis, Mil.*	.000	70	1	1	0	0	0	0	0	0	0	0	0	0	0	0	0	0	0	0	.000	.000
Levis, Jesse, Mil.*	.242	12	36	33	6	8	10	2	0	0	3	0	0	0	3	0	7	0	0	1	.303	.306
Levrault, Allen, Mil.	.061	32	41	33	1	2	2	0	0	0	1	6	1	0	1	0	14	0	0	0	.061	.086
Lieber, Jon, Chi.*	.158	35	87	76	3	12	14	2	0	0	2	9	0	0	2	0	22	0	0	2	.184	.179
Lieberthal, Mike, Phi.	.231	34	136	121	21	28	42	8	0	2	11	0	0	3	12	2	21	0	0	2	.347	.316
Lima, Jose, Hou.	.000	14	17	16	0	0	0	0	0	0	0	1	0	0	0	0	5	0	0	0	.000	.000
Lincoln, Mike, Pit.	.250	31	5	4	0	1	1	0	0	0	0	1	0	0	0	0	0	0	0	0	.250	.250
Little, Mark, Col.	.341	51	90	85	18	29	44	6	0	3	13	0	0	4	1	1	20	5	2	0	.518	.378
Lloyd, Graeme, Mon.*	.000	84	3	2	0	0	0	0	0	0	0	0	0	0	1	0	0	0	0	0	.000	.333
Lockhart, Keith, Atl.*	.219	104	199	178	17	39	54	6	0	3	12	2	1	2	16	1	22	1	2	1	.303	.289
Lo Duca, Paul, L.A.	.320	125	519	460	71	147	250	28	0	25	90	5	9	6	39	2	30	2	4	11	.543	.374
Looper, Braden, Fla.	.000	71	2	2	0	0	0	0	0	0	0	0	0	0	2	0	0	0	0	0	.000	.000
Lopez, Albie, Ari.	.042	13	29	24	0	1	1	0	0	0	0	2	0	1	2	0	10	0	1	0	.042	.148
Lopez, Javy, Atl.	.267	128	482	438	45	117	186	16	1	17	66	1	5	10	28	3	82	1	0	12	.425	.322
Lopez, Luis, Mil.†	.270	92	247	222	22	60	86	8	3	4	18	5	1	5	14	2	44	0	1	6	.387	.326
Lopez, Mendy, Hou.-Pit.	.241	32	66	58	8	14	22	3	1	1	7	0	1	1	6	1	20	0	0	1	.379	.318
Loretta, Mark, Mil.	.289	102	429	384	40	111	135	14	2	2	29	7	3	7	28	0	46	1	2	6	.352	.346
Lowell, Mike, Fla.	.283	146	614	551	65	156	247	37	0	18	100	0	10	10	43	0	79	1	2	9	.448	.340
Lugo, Julio, Hou.	.263	140	586	513	93	135	191	20	3	10	37	15	7	5	46	0	116	12	11	7	.372	.326
Mabry, John, St.L-Fla.*	.208	87	174	154	14	32	57	7	0	6	20	0	2	5	13	1	46	1	0	6	.370	.287
Machado, Robert, Chi.	.222	52	146	135	13	30	46	10	0	2	13	3	0	1	7	3	26	0	0	4	.341	.266
Mackowiak, Rob, Pit.*	.266	83	237	214	30	57	88	15	2	4	21	2	3	3	15	5	52	4	3	3	.411	.319
MacRae, Scott, Cin.	.000	24	3	3	0	0	0	0	0	0	0	0	0	0	0	0	1	0	0	0	.000	.000
Maddux, Greg, Atl.	.188	35	81	64	3	12	12	0	0	0	3	13	0	2	2	0	19	0	0	1	.188	.235
Magadan, Dave, S.D.*	.250	91	142	128	12	32	42	7	0	1	12	0	1	1	12	0	20	0	0	1	.328	.317
Mahay, Ron, Chi.*	.000	17	2	2	0	0	0	0	0	0	0	0	0	0	0	0	1	0	0	0	.000	.000
Manzanillo, Josias, Pit.	.000	71	1	1	0	0	0	0	0	0	0	0	0	0	0	0	0	0	0	0	.000	.000
Marquis, Jason, Atl.*	.032	40	35	31	3	1	1	0	0	0	0	2	0	0	2	0	10	0	0	2	.032	.091
Marrero, Eli, St.L	.266	86	224	203	37	54	89	11	3	6	23	3	3	0	15	2	36	6	3	4	.438	.312
Marte, Damaso, Pit.*	.000	23	4	4	0	0	0	0	0	0	0	0	0	0	0	0	1	0	0	0	.000	.000
Martin, Tom, N.Y.*	.000	14	3	3	0	0	0	0	0	0	0	0	0	0	0	0	1	0	0	0	.000	.000
Martinez, Sandy, Mon.*	.000	1	1	1	0	0	0	0	0	0	0	0	0	0	0	0	0	0	0	1	.000	.000
Martinez, Dave, Atl.*	.287	120	259	237	33	68	91	11	3	2	20	0	0	1	21	0	44	3	3	10	.384	.347
Martinez, Ramon E., S.F.	.253	128	446	391	48	99	138	18	3	5	37	6	6	5	38	6	52	1	2	11	.353	.323
Martinez, Ramon J., Pit.*	.000	4	5	5	0	0	0	0	0	0	0	0	0	0	0	0	2	0	0	0	.000	.000
Mateo, Henry, Mon.†	.333	5	9	9	1	3	4	1	0	0	0	0	0	0	0	0	1	0	0	0	.444	.333
Matheny, Mike, St.L	.218	121	424	381	40	83	116	12	0	7	42	8	3	4	28	5	76	0	1	11	.304	.276
Mathews, T.J., Hou.	.000	10	3	3	0	0	0	0	0	0	0	0	0	0	0	0	0	0	0	0	.000	.000
Mattes, Troy, Mon.	.467	8	16	15	4	7	8	1	0	0	1	1	0	0	0	0	2	0	0	1	.533	.467
Matthews, Gary Jr., Chi.-Pit.†	.227	152	472	405	63	92	153	15	2	14	44	5	1	1	60	2	100	8	5	8	.378	.328
Matthews, Mike, St.L*	.118	52	18	17	2	2	5	0	0	1	1	1	0	0	0	0	6	0	0	0	.294	.118
Maurer, Dave, S.D.	.000	3	1	1	0	0	0	0	0	0	0	0	0	0	0	0	1	0	0	0	.000	.000
Mayne, Brent, Col.*	.331	49	179	160	15	53	60	7	0	0	20	0	3	0	16	3	24	0	0	4	.375	.385
McDonald, Keith, St.L	.000	2	2	2	0	0	0	0	0	0	0	0	0	0	0	0	1	0	0	1	.000	.000
McElroy, Chuck, S.D.*	.000	31	3	3	0	0	0	0	0	0	0	0	0	0	0	0	1	0	0	0	.000	.000
McEwing, Joe, N.Y.	.283	116	319	283	41	80	127	17	3	8	30	6	3	10	17	0	57	8	5	2	.449	.342

Player, Team	Avg.	G	TPA	AB	R	H	TB	2B	3B	HR	RBI	SH	SF	HP	BB	IBB	SO	SB	CS	GDP	Slg.	OBP
McGriff, Fred, Chi.*	.282	49	201	170	27	48	95	7	2	12	41	0	2	3	26	4	37	0	1	6	.559	.383
McGuire, Ryan, Fla.*	.185	48	63	54	8	10	15	2	0	1	8	0	2	0	7	0	15	1	0	0	.278	.270
McGwire, Mark, St.L	.187	97	364	299	48	56	147	4	0	29	64	0	6	3	56	3	118	0	0	7	.492	.316
McKnight, Tony, Hou.-Pit.*	.000	15	30	24	0	0	0	0	0	0	0	4	0	0	2	0	10	0	0	0	.000	.077
Meares, Pat, Pit.	.211	87	284	270	27	57	82	11	1	4	25	1	1	2	10	3	45	0	2	9	.304	.244
Melhuse, Adam, Col.†	.183	40	79	71	5	13	18	2	0	1	8	0	2	0	6	0	18	1	0	3	.254	.241
Mendez, Donaldo, S.D.	.153	46	127	118	11	18	25	2	1	1	5	1	0	3	5	2	37	1	2	2	.212	.206
Mercado, Hector, Cin.*	.000	56	2	2	0	0	0	0	0	0	0	0	0	0	0	0	1	0	0	0	.000	.000
Merced, Orlando, Hou.*	.263	94	153	137	19	36	62	6	1	6	29	0	1	1	14	1	32	5	1	3	.453	.333
Meyers, Chad, Chi.	.118	18	23	17	1	2	2	0	0	0	0	0	0	4	2	0	5	0	1	0	.118	.348
Michaels, Jason, Phi.	.167	6	6	6	0	1	1	0	0	0	1	0	0	0	0	0	2	0	0	0	.167	.167
Middlebrook, Jason, S.D.	.143	4	7	7	0	1	1	0	0	0	1	0	0	0	0	0	6	0	0	0	.143	.143
Millar, Kevin, Fla.	.314	144	495	449	62	141	250	39	5	20	85	0	2	5	39	2	70	0	0	8	.557	.374
Miller, Corky, Cin.	.184	17	57	49	5	9	20	2	0	3	7	0	2	2	4	0	16	1	0	1	.408	.263
Miller, Damian, Ari.	.271	123	425	380	45	103	161	19	0	13	47	4	2	4	35	9	80	0	1	9	.424	.337
Miller, Wade, Hou.	.167	32	78	66	6	11	13	2	0	0	1	10	0	0	2	0	20	0	0	0	.197	.191
Millwood, Kevin, Atl.	.093	21	45	43	3	4	4	0	0	0	2	1	0	0	1	0	16	0	0	1	.093	.114
Minor, Damon, S.F.*	.156	19	48	45	3	7	8	1	0	0	3	0	0	0	3	1	8	0	0	1	.178	.208
Minor, Ryan, Mon.	.158	55	107	95	10	15	23	2	0	2	13	0	2	1	9	0	31	0	1	3	.242	.234
Mlicki, Dave, Hou.	.115	19	30	26	2	3	3	0	0	0	0	4	0	0	0	0	10	0	0	0	.115	.115
Moeller, Chad, Ari.	.232	25	63	56	8	13	18	0	1	1	2	1	0	0	6	1	12	0	0	2	.321	.306
Moore, Trey, Atl.*	1.000	2	1	1	0	1	2	1	0	0	0	0	0	0	0	0	0	0	0	0	2.000	1.000
Mordecai, Mike, Mon.	.280	96	277	254	28	71	101	17	2	3	32	1	2	1	19	1	53	2	2	6	.398	.330
Morgan, Mike, Ari.	.000	31	1	0	0	0	0	0	0	0	0	0	0	0	1	0	0	0	0	0	.000	1.000
Morris, Matt, St.L	.139	34	85	72	5	10	12	2	0	0	5	11	0	0	2	0	33	0	0	0	.167	.162
Morris, Warren, Pit.*	.204	48	109	103	6	21	33	6	0	2	11	0	1	2	3	0	9	2	3	2	.320	.239
Moss, Damian, Atl.	.000	5	2	1	0	0	0	0	0	0	0	0	0	0	1	0	1	0	0	0	.000	.500
Mota, Guillermo, Mon.	.333	53	3	3	0	1	1	0	0	0	0	0	0	0	0	0	1	0	0	0	.333	.333
Mottola, Chad, Fla.	.000	5	10	7	1	0	0	0	0	0	0	1	0	1	2	0	2	0	0	0	.000	.200
Mouton, James, Mil.	.246	75	158	138	20	34	48	8	0	2	10	3	0	6	11	0	40	7	3	1	.348	.329
Mouton, Lyle, Fla.	.059	21	17	17	1	1	1	0	0	0	1	0	0	0	0	0	7	0	0	0	.059	.059
Mueller, Bill, Chi.†	.295	70	257	210	38	62	94	12	1	6	23	4	3	3	37	3	19	1	1	4	.448	.403
Mulholland, Terry, Pit.-L.A.	.000	41	9	9	0	0	0	0	0	0	0	0	0	0	0	0	5	0	0	0	.000	.000
Munoz, Bobby, Mon.	.000	15	11	11	0	0	0	0	0	0	0	0	0	0	0	0	6	0	0	0	.000	.000
Murray, Calvin, S.F.	.245	106	364	326	54	80	116	14	2	6	25	3	0	3	32	0	57	8	8	5	.356	.319
Myers, Rodney L., S.D.	.000	37	2	2	0	0	0	0	0	0	0	0	0	0	0	0	0	0	0	0	.000	.000
Neagle, Denny, Col.*	.196	30	68	56	6	11	21	4	0	2	9	8	1	1	2	0	12	0	0	0	.375	.233
Nen, Robb, S.F.	.000	79	1	1	0	0	0	0	0	0	0	0	0	0	0	0	0	0	0	0	.000	.000
Neugebauer, Nickolas, Mil.	.000	2	3	3	0	0	0	0	0	0	0	0	0	0	0	0	1	0	0	0	.000	.000
Nevin, Phil, S.D.	.306	149	624	546	97	167	321	31	0	41	126	0	3	4	71	7	147	4	4	13	.588	.380
Newhan, David, Phi.*	.333	7	8	6	2	2	3	1	0	0	1	0	1	0	1	0	0	0	0	0	.500	.375
Nichting, Chris, Cin.-Col.	.000	43	2	1	1	0	0	0	0	0	0	1	0	0	0	0	1	0	0	0	.000	.000
Norton, Greg, Col †	.267	117	246	225	30	60	116	13	2	13	40	0	2	0	19	2	65	1	0	6	.516	.321
Nunez, Abraham, Pit.†	.262	115	335	301	30	79	101	11	4	1	21	4	1	1	28	1	53	8	2	0	.336	.326
Nunez, Jose, L.A.-S.D.*	.000	62	3	3	0	0	0	0	0	0	0	0	0	0	0	0	2	0	0	0	.000	.000
Nunez, Vladimir, Fla.	.111	52	12	9	1	1	1	0	0	0	0	2	0	0	1	0	4	0	0	0	.111	.200
Ochoa, Alex, Cin.-Col.	.276	148	593	536	73	148	216	30	7	8	52	4	4	4	45	0	76	17	13	10	.403	.334
Ohka, Tomo, Mon.	.200	10	18	15	1	3	3	0	0	0	1	3	0	0	0	0	6	0	0	0	.200	.200
Ohman, Will, Chi.*	.000	11	2	2	0	0	0	0	0	0	0	0	0	0	0	0	1	0	0	0	.000	.000
Ojeda, Augie, Chi.†	.201	78	162	144	16	29	39	5	1	1	12	2	2	2	12	1	20	1	0	2	.271	.269
Olivares, Omar, Pit.	.222	47	27	27	3	6	11	2	0	1	6	0	0	0	0	0	10	0	0	0	.407	.222
Olsen, Kevin, Fla.	.000	4	4	3	0	0	0	0	0	0	0	1	0	0	0	0	3	0	0	0	.000	.000
Ordonez, Rey, N.Y.	.247	149	505	461	31	114	155	24	4	3	44	7	2	1	34	17	43	3	2	17	.336	.299
Ortega, Bill, St.L	.200	5	5	5	0	1	1	0	0	0	0	0	0	0	0	0	1	0	0	0	.200	.200
Ortiz, Jose, Col.	.255	53	224	204	38	52	101	8	1	13	35	1	1	4	14	0	36	3	1	5	.495	.314
Ortiz, Russ, S.F.	.194	33	81	67	6	13	19	6	0	0	6	8	1	0	5	0	19	0	0	1	.284	.247
Osik, Keith, Pit.	.208	50	137	120	9	25	35	4	0	2	13	0	1	3	13	0	24	1	0	1	.292	.299
Oswalt, Roy, Hou.	.191	28	51	47	3	9	10	1	0	0	3	3	0	0	1	0	12	0	0	0	.213	.208
Overbay, Lyle, Ari.*	.500	2	2	2	0	1	1	0	0	0	0	0	0	0	0	0	1	0	0	0	.500	.500
Owens, Eric, Fla.	.253	119	434	400	51	101	134	16	1	5	28	4	1	0	29	2	59	8	6	13	.335	.302
Padilla, Vicente, Phi.	.333	23	5	3	1	1	2	1	0	0	0	1	0	0	1	0	2	0	0	0	.667	.500
Paquette, Craig, St.L	.282	123	370	340	47	96	158	17	0	15	64	5	2	5	18	1	67	3	1	11	.465	.326
Park, Chan Ho, L.A.	.145	36	81	69	6	10	13	3	0	0	4	7	0	0	5	0	22	0	0	1	.188	.203
Patterson, Corey, Chi.*	.221	59	145	131	26	29	44	3	0	4	14	2	3	3	6	0	33	4	0	1	.336	.266
Pavano, Carl, Fla.	.077	8	14	13	0	1	1	0	0	0	0	1	0	0	0	0	5	0	0	0	.077	.077
Payton, Jay, N.Y.	.255	104	386	361	44	92	134	16	1	8	34	0	2	5	18	1	52	4	3	11	.371	.298
Pena, Angel, L.A.	.204	22	58	54	3	11	15	1	0	1	2	2	1	0	1	0	17	0	0	0	.278	.214
Pena, Elvis, Mil.†	.225	15	48	40	5	9	11	2	0	0	6	0	1	1	6	0	6	2	0	3	.275	.333
Penny, Brad, Fla.	.161	31	66	62	5	10	13	1	1	0	1	3	0	0	1	0	19	0	0	0	.210	.175
Perez, Eddie, Atl.	.300	5	10	10	0	3	3	0	0	0	0	0	0	0	0	0	2	0	0	0	.300	.300
Perez, Neifi, Col.†	.298	87	403	382	65	114	170	19	8	7	47	4	1	0	16	1	49	6	2	8	.445	.326
Perez, Odalis, Atl.*	.192	24	29	26	1	5	6	1	0	0	1	2	0	1	0	0	6	0	0	1	.231	.222
Perez, Robert, Mon.	.000	2	5	5	0	0	0	0	0	0	0	0	0	0	0	0	0	0	0	0	.000	.000
Perez, Santiago, S.D.†	.198	43	97	81	13	16	17	1	0	0	4	0	1	0	15	0	29	5	1	0	.210	.320
Perez, Timo, N.Y.*	.247	85	260	239	26	59	85	9	1	5	22	6	1	2	12	0	25	1	6	1	.356	.287
Perez, Tomas, Phi.†	.304	62	145	135	11	41	59	7	1	3	19	1	0	2	7	1	22	0	1	2	.437	.347
Person, Robert, Phi.	.119	33	75	67	4	8	15	1	0	2	6	5	0	0	3	0	36	0	0	0	.224	.157
Peters, Chris, Mon.*	.091	13	11	11	1	1	1	0	0	0	0	0	0	0	0	0	2	0	0	0	.091	.091
Peterson, Kyle, Mil.*	.200	3	5	5	1	1	2	1	0	0	1	0	0	0	0	0	1	0	0	0	.400	.200
Petrick, Ben, Col.	.238	85	282	244	41	58	112	15	3	11	39	1	3	3	31	3	67	3	3	5	.459	.327
Phillips, Jason, N.Y.	.143	6	7	7	2	1	2	1	0	0	0	0	0	0	0	0	1	0	0	0	.286	.143
Piazza, Mike, N.Y.	.300	141	573	503	81	151	288	29	0	36	94	0	1	2	67	19	87	0	2	20	.573	.384
Pickering, Calvin, Cin.*	.250	4	4	4	0	1	1	0	0	0	1	0	0	0	0	0	2	0	0	0	.250	.250

Player, Team	Avg.	G	TPA	AB	R	H	TB	2B	3B	HR	RBI	SH	SF	HP	BB	IBB	SO	SB	CS	GDP	Slg.	OBP
Pierre, Juan, Col.*	.327	156	683	617	108	202	256	26	11	2	55	14	1	10	41	1	29	46	17	6	.415	.378
Polanco, Placido, St.L	.307	144	610	564	87	173	216	26	4	3	38	14	1	6	25	0	43	12	3	22	.383	.342
Politte, Cliff, Phi.	.000	23	3	2	1	0	0	0	0	0	0	0	0	0	1	0	1	0	0	0	.000	.333
Powell, Jay, Hou.-Col.	.000	74	1	1	0	0	0	0	0	0	0	0	0	0	0	0	1	0	0	0	.000	.000
Powell, Dante, S.F.	.333	13	6	6	5	2	2	0	0	0	0	0	0	0	0	0	0	0	0	0	.333	.333
Powell, Brian, Hou.	.000	1	1	1	0	0	0	0	0	0	0	0	0	0	0	0	1	0	0	0	.000	.000
Pratt, Todd, N.Y.-Phi.	.185	80	212	173	18	32	52	8	0	4	11	1	1	3	34	3	61	1	0	6	.301	.327
Pride, Curtis, Mon.*	.250	36	87	76	8	19	27	3	1	1	9	0	0	2	9	0	22	3	2	4	.355	.345
Prokopec, Luke, L.A.*	.194	30	43	36	1	7	8	1	0	0	7	0	0	0	0	0	13	0	0	0	.222	.194
Pujols, Albert, St.L	.329	161	676	590	112	194	360	47	4	37	130	1	7	9	69	6	93	1	3	21	.610	.403
Punto, Nick, Phi.†	.400	4	5	5	0	2	2	0	0	0	0	0	0	0	0	0	0	0	0	0	.400	.400
Quevedo, Ruben, Mil.	.250	10	20	16	1	4	4	0	0	0	1	4	0	0	0	0	8	0	0	0	.250	.250
Raines, Tim Sr., Mon.†	.308	47	97	78	13	24	34	8	1	0	4	0	1	0	18	0	6	1	0	2	.436	.433
Ramirez, Aramis, Pit.	.300	158	655	603	83	181	323	40	0	34	112	0	4	8	40	4	100	5	4	9	.536	.350
Ransom, Cody, S.F.	.000	9	7	7	1	0	0	0	0	0	0	0	0	0	0	0	5	0	0	0	.000	.000
Reames, Britt, Mon.	.118	41	24	17	2	2	5	0	0	1	2	3	0	0	4	0	8	0	0	1	.294	.286
Reboulet, Jeff, L.A.	.266	94	253	214	35	57	85	15	2	3	22	5	0	1	33	1	48	0	1	3	.397	.367
Redding, Tim, Hou.	.214	13	16	14	0	3	3	0	0	0	1	2	0	0	0	0	11	0	0	0	.214	.214
Redman, Tike, Pit.*	.224	37	130	125	8	28	37	4	1	1	4	0	1	0	4	0	25	3	5	2	.296	.246
Redmond, Mike, Fla.	.312	48	158	141	19	44	60	4	0	4	14	1	1	2	13	4	13	0	0	6	.426	.376
Reed, Rick, N.Y.	.125	20	46	40	2	5	6	1	0	0	4	4	1	0	1	0	15	0	0	0	.150	.143
Reese, Pokey, Cin.	.224	133	474	428	50	96	147	20	2	9	40	5	4	3	34	4	82	25	4	7	.343	.284
Reith, Brian, Cin.	.250	9	12	12	0	3	3	0	0	0	2	0	0	0	0	0	4	1	0	0	.250	.250
Reitsma, Chris, Cin.	.104	38	58	48	3	5	6	1	0	0	1	7	0	1	2	0	24	0	0	1	.125	.157
Relaford, Desi, N.Y.†	.302	120	340	301	43	91	142	27	0	8	36	2	5	5	27	1	65	13	5	4	.472	.364
Remlinger, Mike, Atl.*	.000	75	2	2	0	0	0	0	0	0	0	0	0	0	0	0	1	0	0	0	.000	.000
Renteria, Edgar, St.L	.260	141	549	493	54	128	183	19	3	10	57	8	6	3	39	4	73	17	4	15	.371	.314
Reyes, Dennys, Cin.	.182	36	11	11	0	2	2	0	0	0	0	0	0	0	0	0	6	0	0	0	.182	.182
Reyes, Al, L.A.	.333	19	4	3	1	1	1	0	0	0	0	0	0	0	1	0	1	0	0	0	.333	.333
Reynolds, Shane, Hou.	.077	28	63	52	4	4	7	0	0	1	4	10	0	0	1	0	26	0	0	1	.135	.094
Reynoso, Armando, Ari.	.100	9	13	10	0	1	2	1	0	0	2	3	0	0	0	0	3	0	0	0	.200	.100
Riedling, John, Cin.	.000	29	1	1	0	0	0	0	0	0	0	0	0	0	0	0	0	0	0	0	.000	.000
Rigdon, Paul, Mil.	.200	15	25	20	1	4	4	0	0	0	1	5	0	0	0	0	3	0	0	0	.200	.200
Riggan, Jerrod, N.Y.	.000	35	2	2	0	0	0	0	0	0	0	0	0	0	0	0	2	0	0	0	.000	.000
Riggs, Adam, S.D.	.194	12	38	36	2	7	8	1	0	0	1	0	0	2	0	0	8	1	1	1	.222	.237
Rios, Armando, S.F.-Pit.*	.260	95	359	319	38	83	148	17	3	14	50	1	3	0	36	6	74	3	2	3	.464	.332
Ritchie, Todd, Pit.	.153	34	70	59	1	9	11	2	0	0	3	8	0	0	3	0	27	0	0	1	.186	.194
Rivera, Ruben, Cin.	.255	117	290	263	37	67	112	13	1	10	34	0	1	5	21	1	83	6	3	7	.426	.321
Roberts, Grant, N.Y.	.000	16	3	3	0	0	0	0	0	0	0	0	0	0	0	0	3	0	0	0	.000	.000
Robinson, Kerry, St.L*	.285	114	207	186	34	53	64	6	1	1	15	4	3	2	12	0	20	11	2	1	.344	.330
Rodriguez, Frankie, Cin.	.000	7	1	1	0	0	0	0	0	0	0	0	0	0	0	0	1	0	0	0	.000	.000
Rolen, Scott, Phi.	.289	151	653	554	96	160	276	39	1	25	107	0	12	13	74	6	127	16	5	6	.498	.378
Rollins, Jimmy, Phi.†	.274	158	720	656	97	180	275	29	12	14	54	9	5	2	48	2	108	46	8	5	.419	.323
Rose, Brian, N.Y.	.000	3	1	1	0	0	0	0	0	0	0	0	0	0	0	0	0	0	0	0	.000	.000
Rueter, Kirk, S.F.*	.172	36	74	58	5	10	10	0	0	0	5	10	1	0	5	0	5	0	0	1	.172	.234
Rusch, Glendon, N.Y.*	.056	33	61	54	0	3	3	0	0	0	5	6	0	0	1	0	23	0	0	1	.056	.073
Ryan, Rob, Ari.*	.000	1	1	1	0	0	0	0	0	0	0	0	0	0	0	0	1	0	0	0	.000	.000
Sadler, Donnie, Cin.	.202	39	95	84	9	17	23	3	0	1	3	2	0	0	9	0	20	3	3	3	.274	.280
Sanchez, Alex, Mil.*	.206	30	73	68	7	14	21	3	2	0	4	0	0	0	5	0	13	6	2	0	.309	.260
Sanchez, Jesus, Fla.*	.235	17	19	17	2	4	4	0	0	0	1	2	0	0	0	0	3	0	0	0	.235	.235
Sanchez, Rey, Atl.	.227	49	163	154	10	35	41	4	1	0	9	4	1	0	4	1	15	2	0	9	.266	.245
Sanders, Deion, Cin.*	.173	32	83	75	6	13	18	2	1	0	4	1	2	0	4	0	10	3	4	2	.240	.235
Sanders, Reggie, Ari.	.263	126	496	441	84	116	242	21	3	33	90	1	3	5	46	7	126	14	10	2	.549	.337
Santiago, Benito, S.F.	.262	133	515	477	39	125	176	25	4	6	45	7	6	2	23	0	78	5	4	19	.369	.295
Santiago, Jose, Phi.	.000	53	4	3	0	0	0	0	0	0	0	0	0	0	1	0	1	0	0	0	.000	.250
Saturria, Luis, St.L	.200	13	5	5	0	1	2	1	0	0	1	0	0	0	0	0	1	1	0	0	.400	.200
Sauerbeck, Scott, Pit.	.000	70	2	2	0	0	0	0	0	0	0	0	0	0	0	0	1	0	0	0	.000	.000
Schilling, Curt, Ari.	.133	35	98	83	4	11	12	1	0	0	1	14	0	0	1	0	28	0	0	0	.145	.143
Schmidt, Jason, Pit.-S.F.	.163	25	56	49	5	8	14	0	0	2	4	6	0	0	1	0	22	0	0	1	.286	.180
Schneider, Brian, Mon.*	.317	27	48	41	4	13	19	3	0	1	6	0	1	0	6	1	3	0	0	0	.463	.396
Sefcik, Kevin, Col.	.000	1	1	1	0	0	0	0	0	0	0	0	0	0	0	0	0	0	0	0	.000	.000
Seguignol, Fernando, Mon.†	.140	46	54	50	0	7	9	2	0	0	5	0	1	1	2	1	17	0	0	4	.180	.185
Selby, Bill, Cin.*	.228	36	100	92	7	21	36	7	1	2	12	1	1	1	5	1	13	0	0	1	.391	.273
Serrano, Wascar, S.D.	.111	20	11	9	0	1	1	0	0	0	0	2	0	0	0	0	4	0	0	0	.111	.111
Servais, Scott, Hou.	.375	11	18	16	1	6	6	0	0	0	2	0	0	0	2	0	3	0	0	0	.375	.444
Sexson, Richie, Mil.	.271	158	667	598	94	162	327	24	3	45	125	0	3	6	60	5	178	2	4	20	.547	.342
Sheets, Ben, Mil.	.071	25	48	42	4	3	3	0	0	0	1	2	0	0	4	0	29	0	0	0	.071	.152
Sheffield, Gary, L.A.	.311	143	618	515	98	160	300	28	2	36	100	0	5	4	94	13	67	10	4	12	.583	.417
Shinjo, Tsuyoshi, N.Y.	.268	123	438	400	46	107	162	23	1	10	56	4	2	7	25	3	70	4	5	8	.405	.320
Shumpert, Terry, Col.	.289	114	265	242	37	70	106	14	5	4	24	4	1	3	15	2	44	14	3	2	.438	.337
Silva, Jose, Pit.	.000	26	2	2	0	0	0	0	0	0	0	0	0	0	0	0	2	0	0	0	.000	.000
Smith, Chuck, Fla.	.192	15	29	26	1	5	5	0	0	0	3	2	0	0	1	0	8	0	0	0	.192	.222
Smith, Jason, Chi.*	.000	2	1	1	0	0	0	0	0	0	0	0	0	0	0	0	1	0	0	0	.000	.000
Smith, Mark, Mon.	.242	80	222	194	28	47	80	13	1	6	18	1	2	2	23	0	38	0	2	3	.412	.326
Smith, Bud, St.L*	.160	16	28	25	0	4	4	0	0	0	1	2	0	0	1	0	5	0	0	0	.160	.192
Smoltz, John, Atl.	.000	36	10	7	0	0	0	0	0	0	0	2	0	0	1	0	3	0	0	1	.000	.125
Snow, J.T., S.F.*	.246	101	348	285	43	70	108	12	1	8	34	0	4	4	55	10	81	0	0	7	.379	.371
Sosa, Juan, Ari.	.000	2	1	1	0	0	0	0	0	0	0	0	0	0	0	0	1	0	0	0	.000	.000
Sosa, Sammy, Chi.	.328	160	711	577	146	189	425	34	5	64	160	0	12	6	116	37	153	0	2	6	.737	.437
Speier, Justin, Col.	.000	42	7	7	0	0	0	0	0	0	0	0	0	0	0	0	2	0	0	0	.000	.000
Spiers, Bill, Hou.*	.333	4	4	3	0	1	1	0	0	0	0	0	0	1	0	0	0	0	0	0	.333	.500
Spivey, Junior, Ari.	.258	72	195	163	33	42	69	6	3	5	21	6	1	2	23	0	47	3	0	3	.423	.354
Springer, Dennis, L.A.	.000	4	7	6	0	0	0	0	0	0	0	0	0	0	0	0	3	0	0	0	.000	.000

Player, Team	Avg.	G	TPA	AB	R	H	TB	2B	3B	HR	RBI	SH	SF	HP	BB	IBB	SO	SB	CS	GDP	Slg.	OBP
Stairs, Matt, Chi.*	.250	128	403	340	48	85	157	21	0	17	61	1	3	7	52	7	76	2	3	4	.462	.358
Stechschulte, Gene, St.L	.667	69	4	3	1	2	5	0	0	1	3	0	0	0	1	0	1	0	0	0	1.667	.750
Stevens, Lee, Mon.*	.245	152	628	542	77	133	245	35	1	25	95	0	7	5	74	12	157	2	1	17	.452	.338
Stinnett, Kelly, Cin.	.257	63	211	187	27	48	86	11	0	9	25	1	1	5	17	3	61	2	2	5	.460	.333
Strickland, Scott, Mon.	.000	77	3	3	0	0	0	0	0	0	0	0	0	0	0	0	2	0	0	0	.000	.000
Strong, Joe, Fla.†	.000	5	1	1	0	0	0	0	0	0	0	0	0	0	0	0	1	0	0	0	.000	.000
Sullivan, Scott, Cin.	.000	79	3	3	0	0	0	0	0	0	0	0	0	0	0	0	3	0	0	0	.000	.000
Surhoff, B.J., Atl.*	.271	141	531	484	68	131	196	33	1	10	58	1	7	1	38	5	48	9	3	5	.405	.321
Sutton, Larry, St.L*	.119	33	44	42	3	5	9	1	0	1	3	1	0	0	1	0	10	0	0	1	.214	.140
Suzuki, Mac, Col.-Mil.	.000	18	22	18	0	0	0	0	0	0	0	3	0	0	1	0	10	0	0	1	.000	.053
Sweeney, Mark, Mil.*	.258	48	103	89	9	23	37	3	1	3	11	2	0	0	12	0	23	2	1	0	.416	.347
Tapani, Kevin, Chi.	.240	29	58	50	1	12	12	0	0	0	2	7	0	0	1	0	14	0	0	0	.240	.255
Tatis, Fernando, Mon.	.255	41	168	145	20	37	52	9	0	2	11	0	3	4	16	0	43	0	0	5	.359	.339
Tavarez, Julian, Chi.*	.122	34	55	41	4	5	5	0	0	0	4	11	0	0	3	0	17	0	0	1	.122	.182
Taylor, Reggie, Phi.*	.000	5	8	7	1	0	0	0	0	0	0	0	0	0	1	0	1	0	0	0	.000	.125
Telemaco, Amaury, Phi.	.095	24	25	21	2	2	2	0	0	0	0	2	0	0	2	0	8	0	0	1	.095	.174
Thompson, Ryan, Fla.	.290	18	32	31	6	9	14	5	0	0	2	0	0	0	1	0	8	0	0	2	.452	.313
Thomson, John, Col.	.241	14	36	29	3	7	9	0	1	0	1	6	0	0	1	0	15	0	0	0	.310	.267
Thurman, Mike, Mon.	.024	28	47	42	0	1	1	0	0	0	0	3	0	0	2	0	27	0	0	0	.024	.068
Timlin, Mike, St.L	.000	68	1	1	0	0	0	0	0	0	0	0	0	0	0	0	0	0	0	0	.000	.000
Toca, Jorge, N.Y.	.176	13	17	17	3	3	3	0	0	0	1	0	0	0	0	0	8	0	0	0	.176	.176
Tollberg, Brian, S.D.	.200	19	47	40	4	8	8	0	0	0	1	5	0	0	2	0	17	0	0	0	.200	.238
Torrealba, Steven, Atl.	.500	2	2	2	0	1	1	0	0	0	0	0	0	0	0	0	0	0	0	1	.500	.500
Torrealba, Yorvit, S.F.	.500	3	4	4	0	2	4	0	1	0	2	0	0	0	0	0	0	0	0	0	1.000	.500
Trachsel, Steve, N.Y.	.161	28	61	56	2	9	10	1	0	0	2	5	0	0	0	0	13	0	0	1	.179	.161
Tracy, Andy, Mon.*	.109	38	63	55	4	6	13	1	0	2	8	0	2	0	6	0	26	0	0	1	.236	.190
Trammell, Bubba, S.D.	.261	142	546	490	66	128	229	26	0	25	92	0	4	4	48	2	78	2	2	10	.467	.330
Truby, Chris, Hou.	.206	48	152	136	11	28	60	6	1	8	23	0	2	1	13	2	38	1	2	1	.441	.276
Tucker, Michael, Cin.-Chi.*	.252	149	500	436	62	110	181	19	8	12	61	10	6	2	46	4	102	16	8	8	.415	.322
Urbina, Ugueth, Mon.	.000	45	1	1	0	0	0	0	0	0	0	0	0	0	0	0	1	0	0	0	.000	.000
Uribe, Juan, Col.	.300	72	283	273	32	82	143	15	11	8	53	0	0	2	8	1	66	3	0	6	.524	.325
Valent, Eric, Phi.*	.098	22	46	41	3	4	6	2	0	0	1	0	0	1	4	0	11	0	0	1	.146	.196
Vander Wal, John, Pit.-S.F.*	.270	146	527	452	58	122	200	28	4	14	70	2	4	1	68	9	122	8	6	10	.442	.364
Van Poppel, Todd, Chi.	.286	59	7	7	1	2	2	0	0	0	0	0	0	0	0	0	3	0	0	0	.286	.286
Vazquez, Javier, Mon.	.258	32	82	62	5	16	18	2	0	0	1	16	1	1	2	0	11	0	0	1	.290	.288
Velandia, Jorge, N.Y.	.000	9	11	9	1	0	0	0	0	0	0	0	0	0	2	0	1	0	0	0	.000	.182
Ventura, Robin, N.Y.*	.237	142	549	456	70	108	191	20	0	21	61	0	4	1	88	10	101	2	5	13	.419	.359
Veras, Quilvio, Atl.†	.252	71	295	258	39	65	92	14	2	3	25	4	2	7	24	1	52	7	4	4	.357	.330
Veres, Dave, St.L	.000	71	4	3	0	0	0	0	0	0	0	1	0	0	0	0	1	0	0	0	.000	.000
Vidro, Jose, Mon.†	.319	124	531	486	82	155	236	34	1	15	59	2	2	10	31	2	49	4	1	18	.486	.371
Villone, Ron, Col.-Hou.*	.045	53	26	22	2	1	2	1	0	0	0	4	0	0	0	0	9	0	0	0	.091	.045
Vina, Fernando, St.L*	.303	154	690	631	95	191	264	30	8	9	56	3	2	22	32	3	35	17	7	7	.418	.357
Vizcaino, Jose, Hou.†	.277	107	282	256	38	71	88	8	3	1	14	9	0	2	15	0	33	3	2	6	.344	.322
Vogelsong, Ryan, S.F.-Pit.	.100	15	10	10	0	1	2	1	0	0	0	0	0	0	0	0	3	0	0	0	.200	.100
Walbeck, Matt, Phi.†	1.000	1	1	1	0	1	1	0	0	0	0	0	0	0	0	0	0	0	0	0	1.000	1.000
Walker, Larry, Col.*	.350	142	601	497	107	174	329	35	3	38	123	0	8	14	82	6	103	14	5	9	.662	.449
Walker, Pete, N.Y.	.000	2	2	2	0	0	0	0	0	0	0	0	0	0	0	1	0	0	0	0	.000	.000
Walker, Todd, Col.-Cin.*	.296	151	610	551	93	163	253	35	2	17	75	4	3	1	51	1	82	1	8	14	.459	.355
Wall, Donne, N.Y.	.000	0	33	33	0	1	0	0	0	0	0	0	0	0	0	0	0	0	0	0	.000	.000
Ward, Daryle, Hou.*	.263	95	235	213	21	56	98	15	0	9	39	0	2	1	19	4	48	0	0	3	.460	.323
Ward, Turner, Phi.†	.267	17	17	15	1	4	5	1	0	0	2	0	0	1	1	0	6	0	0	1	.333	.353
Wasdin, John, Col.	.333	18	3	3	1	1	2	1	0	0	1	0	0	0	0	0	0	0	0	0	.667	.333
Weathers, David, Mil.-Chi.	.000	80	2	1	0	0	0	0	0	0	0	0	0	0	1	0	1	0	0	0	.000	.500
Wehner, John, Pit.	.196	43	62	51	3	10	11	1	0	0	2	1	0	0	10	0	12	2	1	2	.216	.328
Wendell, Turk, N.Y.-Phi.*	.000	70	2	2	0	0	0	0	0	0	0	0	0	0	0	0	1	0	0	0	.000	.000
Wengert, Don, Pit.	.000	4	5	3	0	0	0	0	0	0	0	1	0	0	1	0	2	0	0	0	.000	.250
White, Devon, Mil.†	.277	126	432	390	52	108	179	25	2	14	47	1	1	12	28	1	95	18	3	6	.459	.343
White, Gabe, Col.*	.000	69	3	3	0	0	0	0	0	0	0	0	0	0	0	0	3	0	0	0	.000	.000
White, Rick, N.Y.	.000	55	3	3	0	0	0	0	0	0	0	0	0	0	0	0	0	0	0	0	.000	.000
White, Rondell, Chi.	.307	95	357	323	43	99	171	19	1	17	50	1	0	7	26	4	56	1	0	14	.529	.371
Wilkerson, Brad, Mon.*	.205	47	136	117	11	24	38	7	2	1	5	1	1	0	17	1	41	2	1	2	.325	.304
Wilkins, Rick, S.D.*	.182	12	24	22	3	4	8	1	0	1	8	0	0	0	2	0	8	0	0	1	.364	.250
Williams, David, Pit.*	.118	22	37	34	1	4	6	2	0	0	2	3	0	0	0	0	19	0	0	0	.176	.118
Williams, Woody, S.D.-St.L	.195	37	90	82	11	16	21	5	0	0	7	2	2	1	3	0	22	0	0	0	.256	.227
Williams, Jeff, L.A.	.000	15	4	4	0	0	0	0	0	0	0	0	0	0	0	0	0	0	0	0	.000	.000
Williams, Matt, Ari.	.275	106	430	400	58	112	190	30	4	16	65	0	3	3	22	3	70	1	0	15	.466	.314
Wilson, Craig, Pit.	.310	88	183	158	27	49	93	3	1	13	32	1	2	7	15	1	53	3	1	4	.589	.390
Wilson, Enrique, Pit.†	.186	46	133	129	7	24	30	3	0	1	8	0	1	0	3	0	23	0	3	7	.233	.203
Wilson, Jack, Pit.	.223	108	425	390	44	87	115	17	1	3	25	17	1	1	16	2	70	1	3	4	.295	.255
Wilson, Preston, Fla.	.274	123	513	468	70	128	231	30	2	23	71	0	3	6	36	2	107	20	8	14	.494	.331
Wilson, Vance, N.Y.	.298	32	62	57	3	17	20	3	0	0	6	0	1	2	2	0	16	0	1	1	.351	.339
Winchester, Scott, Cin.	.000	12	3	3	0	0	0	0	0	0	0	0	0	0	0	0	2	0	0	1	.000	.000
Witasick, Jay, S.D.	.000	31	1	1	0	0	0	0	0	0	0	0	0	0	0	0	1	0	0	0	.000	.000
Witt, Kevin, S.D.*	.185	14	30	27	5	5	11	0	0	2	5	0	1	0	2	0	7	0	0	0	.407	.233
Witt, Bobby, Ari.	.250	14	13	12	0	3	3	0	0	0	0	0	0	0	0	0	7	0	0	0	.250	.250
Wolf, Randy, Phi.*	.178	28	53	45	2	8	8	0	0	0	2	5	0	0	3	0	13	0	0	1	.178	.229
Womack, Tony, Ari.*	.266	125	518	481	66	128	166	19	5	3	30	7	1	6	23	2	54	28	7	4	.345	.307
Wood, Kerry, Chi.	.188	29	62	48	3	9	10	1	0	0	2	13	0	0	1	0	15	0	0	0	.208	.204
Worrell, Tim, S.F.	.000	73	3	2	0	0	0	0	0	0	0	1	0	0	0	0	2	0	0	0	.000	.000
Wright, Jamey, Mil.	.194	34	74	67	7	13	14	1	0	0	4	4	0	0	3	0	20	0	0	0	.209	.229
Yoshii, Masato, Mon.	.125	42	19	16	0	2	2	0	0	0	2	0	0	1	0	0	7	0	0	0	.125	.176
Young, Dmitri, Cin.†	.302	142	586	540	68	163	260	28	3	21	69	1	3	5	37	10	77	8	5	22	.481	.350
Young, Eric, Chi.	.279	149	672	603	98	168	237	43	4	6	42	15	3	9	42	1	45	31	14	15	.393	.333

Player, Team	Avg.	G	TPA	AB	R	H	TB	2B	3B	HR	RBI	SH	SF	HP	BB	IBB	SO	SB	CS	GDP	Slg.	OBP
Young, Kevin, Pit.	.232	142	507	449	53	104	179	33	0	14	65	0	5	11	42	3	119	15	11	17	.399	.310
Zambrano, Carlos, Chi.†	.000	6	2	2	0	0	0	0	0	0	0	0	0	0	0	0	0	0	0	0	.000	.000
Zeile, Todd, N.Y.	.266	151	612	531	66	141	198	25	1	10	62	0	2	6	73	3	102	1	0	15	.373	.359
Zerbe, Chad, S.F.*	.222	27	11	9	1	2	2	0	0	0	1	2	0	0	0	0	1	0	0	1	.222	.222
Zuleta, Julio, Chi.	.217	49	118	106	11	23	44	3	0	6	24	0	1	3	8	1	32	0	1	3	.415	.288

PLAYERS WITH TWO OR MORE TEAMS

Player, Team	Avg.	G	TPA	AB	R	H	TB	2B	3B	HR	RBI	SH	SF	HP	BB	IBB	SO	SB	CS	GDP	Slg.	OBP
Acevedo, Juan, Col.	.000	39	0	0	0	0	0	0	0	0	0	0	0	0	0	0	0	0	0	0	.000	.000
Acevedo, Juan, Fla.	.333	20	4	3	1	1	2	1	0	0	0	1	0	0	0	0	0	0	0	0	.667	.333
Astacio, Pedro, Col.	.095	22	52	42	2	4	4	0	0	0	3	10	0	0	0	0	12	0	0	0	.095	.095
Astacio, Pedro, Hou.	.091	4	12	11	0	1	1	0	0	0	0	1	0	0	0	0	5	0	0	0	.091	.091
Bennett, Gary, Phi.	.213	26	86	75	8	16	24	3	1	1	6	1	1	0	9	1	19	0	0	1	.320	.294
Bennett, Gary, N.Y.	1.000	1	1	1	0	1	1	0	0	0	0	0	0	0	0	0	0	0	0	0	1.000	1.000
Bennett, Gary, Col.	.273	19	61	55	7	15	21	3	0	1	4	1	1	1	3	3	5	0	0	0	.382	.317
Brown, Emil, Pit.	.203	61	140	123	18	25	40	4	1	3	13	0	0	2	15	1	42	10	4	2	.325	.300
Brown, Emil, S.D.	.071	13	15	14	3	1	1	0	0	0	0	0	0	0	1	0	7	2	0	0	.071	.133
Cairo, Miguel, Chi.	.285	66	147	123	20	35	46	3	1	2	9	7	1	0	16	1	21	2	1	3	.374	.364
Cairo, Miguel, St.L	.333	27	35	33	5	11	19	5	0	1	7	0	0	0	2	0	2	0	0	1	.576	.371
Chen, Bruce, Phi.*	.107	16	31	28	1	3	3	0	0	0	0	3	0	0	0	0	10	0	0	0	.107	.107
Chen, Bruce, N.Y.*	.158	11	21	19	0	3	3	0	0	0	0	2	0	0	0	0	9	0	0	1	.158	.158
Cook, Dennis, N.Y.*	.000	43	1	1	0	0	0	0	0	0	0	0	0	0	0	0	0	0	0	0	.000	.000
Cook, Dennis, Phi.*	.000	19	0	0	0	0	0	0	0	0	0	0	0	0	0	0	0	0	0	0	.000	.000
Crespo, Felipe, S.F.†	.197	40	78	66	8	13	26	1	0	4	10	1	2	2	7	1	26	1	1	2	.394	.286
Crespo, Felipe, Phi.†	.171	33	47	41	1	7	12	3	1	0	5	0	2	0	4	0	8	0	0	0	.293	.234
Ducey, Rob, Phi.*	.222	30	34	27	4	6	10	1	0	1	4	1	0	0	6	0	11	0	0	0	.370	.364
Ducey, Rob, Mon.*	.239	27	59	46	6	11	19	2	0	2	8	1	1	1	10	0	14	0	1	0	.413	.379
Elarton, Scott, Hou.	.067	20	39	30	1	2	2	0	0	0	2	5	0	3	1	0	8	0	0	1	.067	.176
Elarton, Scott, Col.	.125	4	8	8	0	1	1	0	0	0	0	0	0	0	0	0	2	0	0	1	.125	.125
Gomes, Wayne, Phi.	1.000	42	2	1	0	1	1	0	0	0	1	0	0	0	1	0	0	0	0	0	1.000	1.000
Gomes, Wayne, S.F.	.000	13	0	0	0	0	0	0	0	0	0	0	0	0	0	0	0	0	0	0	.000	.000
Jennings, Robin, Col.*	.000	1	3	3	0	0	0	0	0	0	0	0	0	0	0	0	1	0	0	0	.000	.000
Jennings, Robin, Cin.*	.286	27	82	77	10	22	40	5	2	3	14	0	0	0	5	1	11	0	0	0	.519	.329
Lankford, Ray, St.L*	.235	91	314	264	38	62	131	18	3	15	39	1	3	2	44	8	105	4	2	4	.496	.345
Lankford, Ray, S.D.*	.288	40	145	125	20	36	60	10	1	4	19	0	2	2	18	1	40	6	0	2	.480	.386
Lopez, Mendy, Hou.	.267	10	18	15	3	4	7	0	0	1	3	0	0	1	2	0	4	0	0	0	.467	.389
Lopez, Mendy, Pit.	.233	22	48	43	5	10	15	3	1	0	4	0	1	0	4	1	16	0	0	0	.349	.292
Mabry, John, St.L*	.000	5	7	7	0	0	0	0	0	0	0	0	0	0	0	0	2	0	0	0	.000	.000
Mabry, John, Fla.*	.218	82	167	147	14	32	57	7	0	6	20	0	2	5	13	1	44	1	0	6	.388	.299
Matthews, Gary Jr., Chi.†	.217	106	302	258	41	56	94	9	1	9	30	5	0	1	38	2	55	5	3	4	.364	.320
Matthews, Gary Jr., Pit.†	.245	46	170	147	22	36	59	6	1	5	14	0	1	0	22	0	45	3	2	4	.401	.341
McKnight, Tony, Hou.*	.000	3	7	7	0	0	0	0	0	0	0	0	0	0	0	0	1	0	0	0	.000	.000
McKnight, Tony, Pit.*	.000	12	23	17	0	0	0	0	0	0	0	0	4	0	0	0	2	9	0	0	.000	.105
Mulholland, Terry, Pit.	.000	22	3	3	0	0	0	0	0	0	0	0	0	0	0	0	2	0	0	0	.000	.000
Mulholland, Terry, L.A.	.000	19	6	6	0	0	0	0	0	0	0	0	0	0	0	0	3	0	0	0	.000	.000
Nichting, Chris, Cin.	.000	36	1	1	0	0	0	0	0	0	0	0	0	0	0	0	1	0	0	0	.000	.000
Nichting, Chris, Col.	.000	7	1	0	1	0	0	0	0	0	0	1	0	0	0	0	0	0	0	0	.000	.000
Nunez, Jose, L.A.*	.000	6	0	0	0	0	0	0	0	0	0	0	0	0	0	0	0	0	0	0	.000	.000
Nunez, Jose, S.D.*	.000	56	3	3	0	0	0	0	0	0	0	0	0	0	0	0	2	0	0	0	.000	.000
Ochoa, Alex, Cin.	.289	90	379	349	48	101	150	20	4	7	35	2	2	2	24	0	53	12	9	3	.430	.337
Ochoa, Alex, Col.	.251	58	214	187	25	47	66	10	3	1	17	2	2	2	21	0	23	5	4	7	.353	.330
Powell, Jay, Hou.	.000	35	1	1	0	0	0	0	0	0	0	0	0	0	0	0	1	0	0	0	.000	.000
Powell, Jay, Col.	.000	39	0	0	0	0	0	0	0	0	0	0	0	0	0	0	0	0	0	0	.000	.000
Pratt, Todd, N.Y.	.163	45	98	80	6	13	24	5	0	2	4	0	1	2	15	1	36	1	0	4	.300	.306
Pratt, Todd, Phi.	.204	35	114	93	12	19	28	3	0	2	7	1	0	1	19	2	25	0	0	2	.301	.345
Rios, Armando, S.F.*	.259	93	353	316	38	82	147	17	3	14	49	1	2	0	34	6	73	3	2	2	.465	.330
Rios, Armando, Pit.*	.333	2	6	3	0	1	1	0	0	0	1	0	1	0	2	0	1	0	0	1	.333	.500
Schmidt, Jason, Pit.	.174	14	28	23	2	4	7	0	0	1	1	5	0	0	0	0	10	0	0	1	.304	.174
Schmidt, Jason, S.F.	.154	11	28	26	3	4	7	0	0	1	3	1	0	0	1	0	12	0	0	0	.269	.185
Suzuki, Mac, Col.	.000	3	2	1	0	0	0	0	0	0	0	1	0	0	0	0	1	0	0	0	.000	.000
Suzuki, Mac, Mil.	.000	15	20	17	0	0	0	0	0	0	0	2	0	0	1	0	9	0	0	1	.000	.056
Tucker, Michael, Cin.*	.242	86	265	231	31	56	89	10	1	7	30	5	5	1	23	1	55	12	5	4	.385	.308
Tucker, Michael, Pit.*	.263	63	235	205	31	54	92	9	7	5	31	5	1	1	23	3	47	4	3	4	.449	.339
Vander Wal, John, Pit.*	.278	97	360	313	39	87	148	22	3	11	50	0	4	1	42	6	84	7	4	7	.473	.361
Vander Wal, John, S.F.*	.252	49	167	139	19	35	52	6	1	3	20	2	0	0	26	3	38	1	2	3	.374	.370
Villone, Ron, Col.*	.000	22	11	9	0	0	0	0	0	0	0	2	0	0	0	0	5	0	0	0	.000	.000
Villone, Ron, Hou.*	.077	31	15	13	2	1	2	1	0	0	0	2	0	0	0	0	4	0	0	0	.154	.077
Vogelsong, Ryan, S.F.	.125	13	8	8	0	1	2	1	0	0	0	0	0	0	0	0	2	0	0	0	.250	.125
Vogelsong, Ryan, Pit.	.000	2	2	2	0	0	0	0	0	0	0	0	0	0	0	0	1	0	0	0	.000	.000
Walker, Todd, Col.*	.297	85	321	290	52	86	144	18	2	12	43	3	3	0	25	1	40	1	3	8	.497	.349
Walker, Todd, Cin.*	.295	66	289	261	41	77	109	17	0	5	32	1	0	1	26	0	42	0	5	6	.418	.361
Weathers, David, Mil.	.000	52	2	1	0	0	0	0	0	0	0	0	0	0	1	0	1	0	0	0	.000	.500
Weathers, David, Chi.	.000	28	0	0	0	0	0	0	0	0	0	0	0	0	0	0	0	0	0	0	.000	.000
Wendell, Turk, N.Y.*	.000	49	2	2	0	0	0	0	0	0	0	0	0	0	0	0	1	0	0	0	.000	.000
Wendell, Turk, Phi.	.000	21	0	0	0	0	0	0	0	0	0	0	0	0	0	0	0	0	0	0	.000	.000
Williams, Woody, S.D.	.164	26	61	55	7	9	12	3	0	0	4	1	2	1	2	0	18	0	0	0	.218	.200
Williams, Woody, St.L	.259	11	29	27	4	7	9	2	0	0	3	1	0	0	1	0	4	0	0	0	.333	.286

AWARDED FIRST BASE ON OBSTRUCTION OR CATCHER'S INTERFERENCE—Counsell, Arizona 2 (Santiago 2); Barajas, Arizona (Pratt); Helton, Colorado (Lo Duca).

DESIGNATED HITTING

TEAM

Team	Avg.	G	TPA	AB	R	H	TB	2B	3B	HR	RBI	SH	SF	HP	BB	IBB	SO	SB	CS	GDP	Slg.	OBP
New York	.343	9	40	35	10	12	22	1	0	3	8	0	0	0	5	1	8	1	0	0	.629	.425
Chicago	.333	6	29	27	4	9	14	2	0	1	7	0	1	0	1	0	3	0	0	0	.519	.345
Pittsburgh	.333	9	39	33	6	11	14	0	0	1	4	0	0	0	6	0	10	3	0	0	.424	.436
Cincinnati	.323	9	38	31	5	10	14	1	0	1	4	2	0	1	4	0	5	1	2	1	.452	.417
Arizona	.303	9	39	33	7	10	18	2	0	2	7	0	1	0	5	0	5	0	0	1	.545	.385
St. Louis	.292	6	24	24	1	7	8	1	0	0	1	0	0	0	0	0	5	0	0	0	.333	.292
Atlanta	.286	9	39	35	4	10	15	2	0	1	4	0	1	1	2	2	6	0	0	0	.429	.333
Houston	.286	9	40	35	5	10	16	0	0	2	4	0	0	2	3	0	3	0	0	0	.457	.375
Los Angeles	.273	6	26	22	2	6	10	1	0	1	2	0	1	0	3	1	0	0	0	1	.455	.346
Florida	.257	9	41	35	6	9	17	2	0	2	7	0	0	0	6	3	6	2	0	2	.486	.366
Philadelphia	.219	9	37	32	4	7	9	2	0	0	0	0	0	0	5	0	8	0	0	0	.281	.324
Colorado	.217	6	25	23	3	5	11	3	0	1	2	0	0	0	2	0	4	0	0	0	.478	.280
Milwaukee	.179	6	29	28	2	5	7	2	0	0	3	1	0	0	0	0	4	0	0	3	.250	.179
Montreal	.176	9	38	34	5	6	10	1	0	1	4	0	0	0	4	0	11	0	0	0	.294	.263
San Diego	.174	6	26	23	3	4	4	0	0	0	2	0	0	0	3	0	5	0	0	1	.174	.269
San Francisco	.133	9	39	30	6	4	8	1	0	1	1	0	0	0	9	1	9	1	0	0	.267	.333
Totals	.260	154	549	480	73	125	197	21	0	17	60	3	4	4	58	8	92	8	2	9	.410	.342

TOP DESIGNATED HITTERS

Minimum 15 at-bats. *Lefthanded batter. †Switch-hitter.

Player, Team	Avg.	G	TPA	AB	R	H	TB	2B	3B	HR	RBI	SH	SF	HP	BB	IBB	SO	SB	CS	GDP	Slg.	OBP
Brown, Roosevelt, Chicago*	.533	3	15	15	4	8	13	2	0	1	5	0	0	0	0	0	2	0	0	0	.867	.533
Alou, Moises, Houston	.412	4	19	17	2	7	13	0	0	2	2	0	0	0	2	0	2	0	0	0	.765	.474
Piazza, Mike, New York	.400	5	22	20	3	8	15	1	0	2	5	0	0	0	2	1	5	0	0	0	.750	.455
Vander Wal, John, Pit.*	.320	7	30	25	5	8	11	0	0	1	4	0	0	0	5	0	6	3	0	0	.440	.433
Millar, Kevin, Florida	.292	6	26	24	3	7	12	2	0	1	3	0	0	0	2	0	4	0	0	1	.500	.346
Durazo, Erubiel, Arizona*	.286	7	26	21	6	6	11	2	0	1	5	0	0	0	5	0	4	0	0	0	.524	.423
Burrell, Pat, Philadelphia	.222	5	22	18	2	4	5	1	0	0	0	0	0	0	4	0	3	0	0	0	.278	.364
Walker, Larry, Colorado*	.211	5	21	19	3	4	10	3	0	1	2	0	0	0	2	0	3	0	0	0	.526	.286
Bonds, Barry, San Francisco*	.176	6	26	17	3	3	7	1	0	1	1	0	0	0	9	1	5	1	0	0	.412	.462
Loretta, Mark, Milwaukee	.167	4	19	18	1	3	3	0	0	0	1	1	0	0	0	0	3	0	0	1	.167	.167

ALL DESIGNATED HITTERS

*Lefthanded batter. †Switch-hitter.

Player, Team	Avg.	G	TPA	AB	R	H	TB	2B	3B	HR	RBI	SH	SF	HP	BB	IBB	SO	SB	CS	GDP	Slg.	OBP
Alou, Moises, Houston	.412	4	19	17	2	7	13	0	0	2	2	0	0	0	2	0	2	0	0	0	.765	.474
Barkett, Andy, Pittsburgh*	.000	1	2	1	1	0	0	0	0	0	0	0	0	0	1	0	0	0	0	0	.000	.500
Bell, Jay, Arizona	.333	3	13	12	1	4	7	0	0	1	2	0	1	0	0	0	1	0	0	1	.583	.308
Biggio, Craig, Houston	.250	1	6	4	2	1	1	0	0	0	0	0	0	2	0	0	0	0	0	0	.250	.500
Bonds, Barry, San Francisco*	.176	6	26	17	3	3	7	1	0	1	1	0	0	0	9	1	5	1	0	0	.412	.462
Bonilla, Bobby, St. Louis†	.222	2	9	9	0	2	2	0	0	0	1	0	0	0	0	0	3	0	0	0	.222	.222
Brown, Roosevelt, Chicago*	.533	3	15	15	4	8	13	2	0	1	5	0	0	0	0	0	2	0	0	0	.867	.533
Burrell, Pat, Philadelphia	.222	5	22	18	2	4	5	1	0	0	0	0	0	0	4	0	3	0	0	0	.278	.364
Cammill, Ken, Atlanta	.750	1	4	4	0	3	3	0	0	0	0	0	0	0	0	0	0	0	0	0	.750	.750
Casanova, Raul, Milwaukee†	.167	2	6	6	0	1	2	1	0	0	1	0	0	0	0	0	2	0	0	1	.333	.167
Casey, Sean, Cincinnati*	.300	3	11	10	1	3	3	0	0	0	2	0	0	0	1	0	1	0	0	1	.300	.364
Clark, Brady, Cincinnati	1.000	1	2	1	1	1	1	0	0	0	0	0	1	0	0	0	0	1	0	0	1.000	1.000
Collier, Lou, Milwaukee	.000	1	0	0	1	0	0	0	0	0	0	0	0	0	0	0	0	0	0	0	.000	.000
Coomer, Ron, Chicago	.200	1	5	5	0	1	1	0	0	0	1	0	0	0	0	0	0	0	0	0	.200	.200
Crespo, Felipe, S.F.†	.000	1	1	1	0	0	0	0	0	0	0	0	0	0	0	0	0	0	0	0	.000	.000
Cromer, D.T., Cincinnati*	.500	1	3	2	1	1	4	0	0	1	2	0	0	0	1	0	1	0	0	0	2.000	.667
Davis, Eric, San Francisco	.000	1	4	4	1	0	0	0	0	0	0	0	0	0	0	0	2	0	0	0	.000	.000
Davis, Russ, San Francisco	.000	1	3	3	0	0	0	0	0	0	0	0	0	0	0	0	0	0	0	0	.000	.000
DeRosa, Mark, Atlanta	.250	3	7	4	0	1	2	1	0	0	1	1	1	1	1	1	1	0	0	0	.500	.429
Ducey, Rob, Montreal*	.100	3	10	10	1	1	1	0	0	0	1	0	0	0	0	0	4	0	0	0	.100	.100
Dunston, Shawon, S.F.	.250	1	4	4	2	1	1	0	0	0	0	0	0	0	0	0	1	0	0	0	.250	.250
Durazo, Erubiel, Arizona*	.286	7	26	21	6	6	11	2	0	1	5	0	0	0	5	0	4	0	0	0	.524	.423
Echevarria, Angel, Milwaukee	.250	1	4	4	0	1	2	1	0	0	1	0	0	0	0	0	0	0	0	1	.500	.250
Feliz, Pedro, San Francisco	.000	1	1	1	0	0	0	0	0	0	0	0	0	0	0	0	1	0	0	0	.000	.000
Floyd, Cliff, Florida*	.182	3	14	11	2	2	5	0	0	1	4	0	0	0	3	3	2	1	0	1	.455	.357
Gilkey, Bernard, Atlanta	.000	1	3	3	0	0	0	0	0	0	0	0	0	0	0	0	0	0	0	0	.000	.000
Gonzalez, Wiki, San Diego	.250	1	5	4	1	1	1	0	0	0	1	0	0	0	1	0	0	0	0	0	.250	.400
Griffey, Ken Jr., Cincinnati*	.143	2	9	7	2	1	1	0	0	0	0	0	0	0	1	1	2	0	0	0	.143	.333
Grissom, Marquis, L.A.	.167	2	6	6	1	1	1	0	0	0	0	0	0	0	0	0	1	0	0	0	.167	.167
Guerrero, Wilton, Cincinnati†	.000	1	0	0	0	0	0	0	0	0	0	0	0	0	0	0	0	0	1	0	.000	.000
Gwynn, Tony, San Diego*	.000	1	3	2	0	0	0	0	0	0	0	0	0	0	1	0	1	0	0	0	.000	.333
Hansen, Dave, Los Angeles*	1.000	1	3	1	0	1	1	0	0	0	1	0	1	0	1	1	0	0	0	0	1.000	.667
Harris, Lenny, New York*	.400	2	6	5	4	2	2	0	0	0	0	0	0	0	1	0	0	1	0	0	.400	.500
Hayes, Charlie, Houston	.250	1	4	4	0	1	1	0	0	0	0	0	0	0	0	0	0	0	0	0	.250	.250
Henderson, Rickey, S.D.	.000	1	1	1	1	0	0	0	0	0	0	0	0	0	0	0	0	0	0	0	.000	.000
Hunter, Brian L., Philadelphia	.000	1	1	1	1	0	0	0	0	0	0	0	0	0	0	0	0	0	0	0	.000	.000
Johnson, Mark P., New York*	.111	3	11	9	3	1	4	0	0	1	3	0	0	0	2	0	3	0	0	0	.444	.273

Player, Team	Avg.	G	TPA	AB	R	H	TB	2B	3B	HR	RBI	SH	SF	HP	BB	IBB	SO	SB	CS	GDP	Slg.	OBP
Jones, Chipper, Atlanta†	.200	1	5	5	2	1	4	0	0	1	1	0	0	0	0	0	1	0	0	0	.800	.200
Jordan, Brian, Atlanta	.143	2	8	7	1	1	1	0	0	0	1	0	0	0	1	1	2	0	0	0	.143	.250
Kreuter, Chad, Los Angeles†	.333	1	3	3	1	1	4	0	0	1	1	0	0	0	0	0	0	0	0	0	1.333	.333
Lo Duca, Paul, Los Angeles	.250	1	4	4	0	1	1	0	0	0	0	0	0	0	0	0	0	0	0	0	.250	.250
Loretta, Mark, Milwaukee	.167	4	19	18	1	3	3	0	0	0	1	1	0	0	0	0	3	0	0	1	.167	.167
Mabry, John, Florida*	.000	1	1	0	0	0	0	0	0	0	0	0	0	0	1	0	0	0	0	0	.000	1.000
Magadan, Dave, San Diego*	.167	2	6	6	0	1	1	0	0	0	1	0	0	0	0	0	0	0	0	0	.167	.167
Martinez, Dave, Atlanta*	.500	1	2	2	1	1	1	0	0	0	0	0	0	0	0	0	1	0	0	0	.500	.500
McEwing, Joe, New York*	1.000	1	1	1	0	1	1	0	0	0	0	0	0	0	0	0	0	0	0	0	1.000	1.000
Millar, Kevin, Florida	.292	6	26	24	3	7	12	2	0	1	3	0	0	0	2	0	4	0	0	1	.500	.346
Minor, Ryan, Montreal	.333	3	5	3	2	1	1	0	0	0	0	0	0	0	2	0	2	0	0	0	.333	.600
Mordecai, Mike, Montreal	.000	1	1	1	0	0	0	0	0	0	0	0	0	0	0	0	0	0	0	0	.000	.000
Nevin, Phil, San Diego	.333	1	4	3	1	1	1	0	0	0	0	0	0	0	1	0	2	0	0	0	.333	.500
Norton, Greg, Colorado†	.250	1	4	4	0	1	1	0	0	0	0	0	0	0	0	0	1	0	0	0	.250	.250
Ochoa, Alex, Cincinnati	.750	1	4	4	0	3	4	1	0	0	0	0	0	0	0	0	0	0	0	0	1.000	.750
Owens, Eric, Florida	.000	1	0	0	1	0	0	0	0	0	0	0	0	0	0	0	0	1	0	0	.000	.000
Piazza, Mike, New York	.400	5	22	20	3	8	15	1	0	2	5	0	0	0	2	1	5	0	0	0	.750	.455
Polanco, Placido, St. Louis	.000	1	3	3	1	0	0	0	0	0	0	0	0	0	0	0	0	0	0	0	.000	.000
Pride, Curtis, Montreal*	.000	2	7	5	0	0	0	0	0	0	0	0	0	0	2	0	0	0	0	0	.000	.286
Pujols, Albert, St. Louis	.333	2	9	9	0	3	4	1	0	0	0	0	0	0	0	0	2	0	0	0	.444	.333
Renteria, Edgar, St. Louis	.667	1	3	3	0	2	2	0	0	0	0	0	0	0	0	0	0	0	0	0	.667	.667
Sadler, Donnie, Cincinnati	.000	1	1	1	0	0	0	0	0	0	0	0	0	0	0	0	0	0	0	0	.000	.000
Sanders, Deion, Cincinnati*	.200	2	7	5	0	1	1	0	0	0	0	1	0	0	1	0	1	0	1	0	.200	.333
Sheffield, Gary, Los Angeles	.250	2	10	8	0	2	3	1	0	0	0	0	0	0	2	1	0	0	0	0	.375	.400
Stairs, Matt, Chicago*	.000	2	9	7	0	0	0	0	0	0	0	1	0	1	0	1	1	0	0	0	.000	.111
Stinnett, Kelly, Cincinnati	.000	1	1	1	0	0	0	0	0	0	0	0	0	0	0	0	0	0	0	0	.000	.000
Surhoff, B.J., Atlanta*	.300	3	10	10	0	3	4	1	0	0	1	0	0	0	0	0	0	0	0	0	.400	.300
Tracy, Andy, Montreal*	.167	2	6	6	0	1	1	0	0	0	0	0	0	0	0	0	3	0	0	0	.167	.167
Trammell, Bubba, San Diego	.143	3	7	7	0	1	1	0	0	0	0	0	0	0	0	0	2	0	0	1	.143	.143
Valent, Eric, Philadelphia*	.231	4	14	13	1	3	4	1	0	0	0	0	0	0	1	0	5	0	0	0	.308	.286
Vander Wal, John, Pit.*	.320	7	30	25	5	8	11	0	0	1	4	0	0	0	5	0	6	3	0	0	.440	.433
Vidro, Jose, Montreal†	.333	2	9	9	2	3	7	1	0	1	3	0	0	0	0	0	2	0	0	0	.778	.333
Walker, Larry, Colorado*	.211	5	21	19	3	4	10	3	0	1	2	0	0	0	2	0	3	0	0	0	.526	.286
Ward, Daryle, Houston*	.100	3	11	10	1	1	1	0	0	0	2	0	0	0	1	0	1	0	0	0	.100	.182
Wilson, Craig A., Pittsburgh	.429	2	7	7	0	3	3	0	0	0	0	0	0	0	0	0	4	0	0	0	.429	.429

The following designated hitters, each of whom appeared in at least one game, had no plate appearances, runs scored or stolen base attempts: Burkett, John, Atlanta; Mouton, James, Milwaukee.

PINCH-HITTING

TEAM

Team	Avg.	G	TPA	AB	R	H	TB	2B	3B	HR	RBI	SH	SF	HP	BB	IBB	SO	SB	CS	GDP	Slg.	OBP
Arizona	.278	134	314	273	33	76	131	13	0	14	54	2	3	5	31	3	81	3	1	6	.480	.359
Atlanta	.253	138	269	233	26	59	82	17	0	2	28	2	0	0	34	2	64	5	2	4	.352	.348
San Francisco	.246	138	260	232	31	57	114	9	3	14	46	3	1	1	23	4	60	1	1	4	.491	.315
Philadelphia	.242	136	230	198	22	48	75	9	0	6	37	1	3	2	26	2	49	3	0	2	.379	.332
New York	.236	147	280	242	23	57	77	13	2	1	27	0	2	6	30	2	56	3	4	6	.318	.332
Cincinnati	.235	147	307	264	27	62	92	12	0	6	36	4	6	3	30	4	67	3	1	7	.348	.314
Chicago	.231	129	226	186	26	43	73	12	0	6	33	3	3	5	29	3	44	2	0	2	.392	.345
San Diego	.226	136	251	212	20	48	68	14	0	2	22	0	4	3	32	2	45	0	0	5	.321	.331
St. Louis	.222	135	252	230	16	51	84	15	0	6	27	3	1	1	17	1	54	1	0	4	.365	.277
Colorado	.214	139	310	276	22	59	90	12	2	5	31	2	3	2	27	2	82	2	2	5	.326	.286
Houston	.209	129	246	215	22	45	79	8	1	8	33	2	2	2	25	4	63	2	0	3	.367	.295
Los Angeles	.197	130	254	223	20	44	75	13	0	6	22	3	1	3	24	6	75	2	1	3	.336	.283
Milwaukee	.192	136	250	213	19	41	63	8	1	4	18	4	2	6	25	1	66	1	0	3	.296	.293
Montreal	.179	137	249	207	21	37	45	5	0	1	16	3	4	2	33	4	61	0	2	7	.217	.293
Pittsburgh	.174	129	248	218	27	38	76	8	0	10	36	1	3	0	26	2	56	1	1	3	.349	.271
Florida	.174	128	229	201	17	35	54	7	0	4	30	1	1	4	22	2	67	1	0	2	.269	.268
Totals	.221	2168	4175	3623	372	800	1278	175	9	95	496	34	36	48	434	44	990	30	15	66	.353	.310

INDIVIDUAL

TOP PINCH-HITTERS

Minimum 20 at-bats. *Lefthanded batter. †Switch-hitter.

Player, Team	Avg.	G	TPA	AB	R	H	TB	2B	3B	HR	RBI	SH	SF	HP	BB	IBB	SO	SB	CS	GDP	Slg.	OBP
Johnson, Mark P., New York*	.407	36	31	27	3	11	14	3	0	0	6	0	0	0	4	1	6	0	0	0	.519	.484
Hunter, Brian L., Philadelphia	.364	38	38	33	6	12	20	2	0	2	9	0	1	0	4	0	7	3	0	0	.606	.421
Bautista, Danny, Arizona	.350	46	44	40	2	14	21	4	0	1	7	0	0	1	3	1	5	0	0	0	.525	.409
Lockhart, Keith, Atlanta*	.326	59	54	46	8	15	22	4	0	1	6	0	0	0	8	1	5	0	0	0	.478	.426
Dellucci, David, Arizona*	.321	67	65	56	11	18	34	1	0	5	16	0	0	0	9	1	17	0	0	0	.607	.415
Zuleta, Julio, Chicago	.318	24	24	22	4	7	18	2	0	3	13	0	0	0	2	0	8	0	0	0	.818	.375
Guerrero, Wilton, Cincinnati†	.308	27	27	26	3	8	9	1	0	0	2	0	0	0	1	0	3	0	0	0	.346	.333
Paquette, Craig, St. Louis	.304	25	25	23	2	7	14	1	0	2	5	0	0	1	1	0	4	0	0	0	.609	.360
Gwynn, Tony, San Diego*	.298	53	53	47	0	14	20	6	0	0	10	0	0	0	6	0	6	0	0	1	.426	.377
Wilson, Craig A., Pittsburgh	.294	43	43	34	11	10	31	0	0	7	11	0	0	2	7	1	12	1	0	0	.912	.442
Dunston, Shawon, S.F.	.286	36	36	35	6	10	23	0	2	3	9	0	0	0	1	0	8	0	0	0	.657	.306
Benard, Marvin, S.F.*	.280	30	30	25	4	7	18	2	0	3	7	0	1	1	3	1	5	0	0	0	.720	.367
Little, Mark, Colorado	.280	25	25	25	2	7	9	2	0	0	3	0	0	0	0	0	6	0	1	0	.360	.280
Raines, Tim Sr., Montreal†	.273	27	27	22	3	6	8	2	0	0	3	0	1	0	4	0	3	0	0	0	.364	.370
McGuire, Ryan, Florida*	.273	39	38	33	5	9	13	1	0	1	6	0	0	0	5	0	11	1	0	0	.394	.368
McEwing, Joe, New York	.273	27	25	22	4	6	10	2	1	0	3	0	1	2	0	0	8	1	0	0	.455	.320

ALL PINCH-HITTERS

*Lefthanded batter. †Switch-hitter.

Player, Team	Avg.	G	TPA	AB	R	H	TB	2B	3B	HR	RBI	SH	SF	HP	BB	IBB	SO	SB	CS	GDP	Slg.	OBP
Abbott, Jeff, Florida	.250	9	9	8	1	2	2	0	0	0	1	0	0	0	1	0	2	0	0	0	.250	.333
Abbott, Kurt, Atlanta	.200	5	5	5	0	1	1	0	0	0	0	0	0	0	0	0	2	1	0	0	.200	.200
Abreu, Bobby, Philadelphia*	.000	3	3	1	1	0	0	0	0	0	0	0	0	0	2	1	1	0	0	0	.000	.667
Agbayani, Benny, New York	.286	8	8	7	0	2	2	0	0	0	0	0	0	0	1	0	2	0	0	1	.286	.375
Aldridge, Cory, Atlanta*	.000	1	1	1	0	0	0	0	0	0	0	0	0	0	0	0	1	0	0	0	.000	.000
Alfonzo, Edgardo, New York	.500	2	2	2	0	1	2	1	0	0	1	0	0	0	0	0	0	0	0	0	1.000	.500
Alou, Moises, Houston	.500	2	2	2	0	1	1	0	0	0	2	0	0	0	0	0	0	0	0	1	.500	.500
Anderson, Marlon, Phi.*	.250	8	8	8	2	2	5	0	0	1	2	0	0	0	0	0	1	0	0	0	.625	.250
Arias, Alex, San Diego	.333	16	16	12	3	4	6	2	0	0	2	0	2	1	1	0	1	0	0	0	.500	.375
Aurilia, Rich, San Francisco	.222	9	9	9	1	2	5	0	0	1	1	0	0	0	0	0	2	0	0	0	.556	.222
Aven, Bruce, Los Angeles	.250	13	13	12	2	3	3	0	0	0	0	0	0	1	0	0	4	0	0	0	.250	.308
Bagwell, Jeff, Houston	1.000	2	1	1	0	1	2	1	0	0	0	0	0	0	0	0	0	0	0	0	2.000	1.000
Bako, Paul, Atlanta*	.000	1	1	1	0	0	0	0	0	0	0	0	0	0	0	0	0	0	0	0	.000	.000
Barajas, Rod, Arizona	.333	3	3	3	1	1	1	0	0	0	1	0	0	0	0	0	2	0	0	0	.333	.333
Barker, Glen, Houston†	.000	5	5	5	0	0	0	0	0	0	0	0	0	0	0	0	1	0	0	0	.000	.000
Barkett, Andy, Pittsburgh*	.000	4	3	2	1	0	0	0	0	0	0	0	0	0	0	0	0	0	0	0	.000	.333
Barrett, Michael, Montreal	1.000	2	2	2	1	2	2	0	0	0	0	0	0	0	0	0	0	0	0	0	1.000	1.000
Bartee, Kimera, Colorado	.000	2	2	2	0	0	0	0	0	0	0	0	0	0	0	0	2	0	0	0	.000	.000
Batista, Miguel, Arizona	.000	2	2	2	0	0	0	0	0	0	0	0	0	0	0	0	2	0	0	0	.000	.000
Bautista, Danny, Arizona	.350	46	44	40	2	14	21	4	0	1	7	0	0	1	3	1	5	0	0	0	.525	.409
Bell, Derek, Pittsburgh	.000	1	1	1	0	0	0	0	0	0	0	0	0	0	0	0	0	0	0	0	.000	.000
Bell, Jay, Arizona	.182	13	13	11	1	2	3	1	0	0	0	0	0	1	0	0	4	0	0	0	.273	.250
Belliard, Ronnie, Milwaukee	.000	5	5	5	1	0	0	0	0	0	0	0	0	0	0	0	0	0	0	0	.000	.000
Beltre, Adrian, Los Angeles	.000	2	2	2	0	0	0	0	0	0	0	0	0	0	0	0	1	0	0	0	.000	.000
Benard, Marvin, S.F.*	.280	30	30	25	4	7	18	2	0	3	7	0	1	1	3	1	5	0	0	0	.720	.367
Bennett, Gary, Phi.-N.Y.	.333	3	3	3	0	1	1	0	0	0	0	0	0	0	0	0	1	0	0	0	.333	.333
Berg, Dave, Florida	.063	17	17	16	1	1	1	0	0	0	0	0	0	0	1	0	6	0	0	1	.063	.063
Bergeron, Peter, Montreal*	.000	1	1	1	0	0	0	0	0	0	0	0	0	0	0	0	0	0	0	0	.000	.000
Berkman, Lance, Houston†	.333	3	3	3	1	1	4	0	0	1	3	0	0	0	0	0	0	0	0	0	1.333	.333
Betemit, Wilson, Atlanta†	.000	5	5	3	0	0	0	0	0	0	0	0	0	0	2	0	3	1	0	0	.000	.400

Player, Team	Avg.	G	TPA	AB	R	H	TB	2B	3B	HR	RBI	SH	SF	HP	BB	IBB	SO	SB	CS	GDP	Slg.	OBP
Biggio, Craig, Houston	.000	1	1	1	0	0	0	0	0	0	0	0	0	0	0	0	0	0	0	0	.000	.000
Blanco, Henry, Milwaukee	.000	3	3	3	0	0	0	0	0	0	0	0	0	0	0	0	1	0	0	1	.000	.000
Blum, Geoff, Montreal†	.273	16	16	11	3	3	3	0	0	0	1	1	0	0	4	2	3	0	0	0	.273	.467
Bocachica, Hiram, L.A.	.121	36	36	33	1	4	7	3	0	0	1	0	0	0	3	0	9	2	1	0	.212	.194
Bogar, Tim, Los Angeles	.429	7	7	7	1	3	8	2	0	1	1	0	0	0	0	0	1	0	0	0	1.143	.429
Bohanon, Brian, Colorado*	.000	1	1	1	0	0	0	0	0	0	0	0	0	0	0	0	1	0	0	0	.000	.000
Bonds, Barry, San Francisco*	.400	5	5	5	1	2	5	0	0	1	1	0	0	0	0	0	2	0	0	0	1.000	.400
Bonilla, Bobby, St. Louis†	.167	54	54	48	2	8	13	2	0	1	6	0	0	0	6	0	15	0	0	0	.271	.259
Bradley, Milton, Montreal†	.000	2	2	2	0	0	0	0	0	0	0	0	0	0	0	0	2	0	0	0	.000	.000
Bragg, Darren, New York*	.333	4	4	3	0	1	1	0	0	0	1	0	0	0	1	0	0	0	0	0	.333	.500
Branson, Jeff, Los Angeles*	.000	5	5	5	0	0	0	0	0	0	0	0	0	0	0	0	3	0	0	0	.000	.000
Brogna, Rico, Atlanta*	.167	7	7	6	0	1	1	0	0	0	0	0	1	0	0	0	3	1	0	0	.167	.167
Brown, Adrian, Pittsburgh†	.000	1	1	1	0	0	0	0	0	0	0	0	0	0	0	0	0	0	0	0	.000	.000
Brown, Emil, Pit.-S.D	.231	16	16	13	4	3	4	1	0	0	2	0	0	0	3	0	5	0	1	0	.308	.375
Brown, Kevin L., Milwaukee	.000	1	1	1	0	0	0	0	0	0	0	0	0	0	0	0	1	0	0	0	.000	.000
Brown, Roosevelt, Chicago*	.091	15	14	11	1	1	2	1	0	0	2	0	0	1	2	0	1	0	0	0	.182	.286
Brumbaugh, Cliff, Colorado	.200	5	5	5	0	1	2	1	0	0	0	0	0	0	0	0	3	0	0	1	.400	.200
Buford, Damon, Chicago	.000	1	1	1	0	0	0	0	0	0	0	0	0	0	0	0	1	0	0	0	.000	.000
Burnitz, Jeromy, Milwaukee*	.000	1	1	1	0	0	0	0	0	0	0	0	0	0	0	0	1	0	0	0	.000	.000
Burrell, Pat, Philadelphia	.400	6	6	5	1	2	3	1	0	0	1	0	0	0	1	0	2	0	0	0	.600	.500
Butler, Brent, Colorado	.235	18	18	17	2	4	4	0	0	0	0	1	0	0	0	0	2	0	0	0	.235	.235
Cairo, Miguel, Chi.-St.L	.229	40	40	35	6	8	15	4	0	1	6	1	0	0	4	1	4	0	0	2	.429	.308
Caminiti, Ken, Atlanta†	.071	17	17	14	0	1	1	0	0	0	0	0	0	0	3	1	5	0	0	0	.071	.235
Casanova, Raul, Milwaukee†	.294	18	18	17	2	5	7	2	0	0	1	0	0	0	1	0	2	0	0	0	.412	.333
Casey, Sean, Cincinnati*	.600	8	8	5	1	3	3	0	0	0	3	0	0	0	3	0	0	0	0	0	.600	.750
Castilla, Vinny, Houston	.000	1	1	1	0	0	0	0	0	0	0	0	0	0	0	0	0	0	0	0	.000	.000
Castillo, Luis, Florida†	.000	1	1	1	0	0	0	0	0	0	0	0	0	0	0	0	0	0	0	0	.000	.000
Castro, Juan, Cincinnati	.100	12	12	10	0	1	1	0	0	0	0	1	0	0	1	0	4	0	0	1	.100	.182
Castro, Ramon, Florida	.500	4	4	4	0	2	2	0	0	0	1	0	0	0	0	0	0	0	0	0	.500	.500
Christensen, McKay, L.A.*	.167	7	7	6	1	1	1	0	0	0	0	0	0	1	0	0	1	0	0	0	.167	.286
Christenson, Ryan, Arizona	.500	3	3	2	0	1	2	1	0	0	1	0	0	0	1	0	1	0	0	0	1.000	.667
Cintron, Alex, Arizona†	.000	1	1	1	0	0	0	0	0	0	0	0	0	0	0	0	0	0	0	0	.000	.000
Cirillo, Jeff, Colorado	.000	1	1	1	0	0	0	0	0	0	0	0	0	0	0	0	0	0	0	0	.000	.000
Clapp, Stubby, St. Louis†	.267	17	16	15	0	4	6	2	0	0	1	0	0	0	1	0	4	0	0	0	.400	.313
Clark, Brady, Cincinnati	.271	61	61	48	7	13	17	1	0	1	8	3	1	0	9	1	5	2	0	3	.354	.379
Clement, Matt, Florida	.000	1	1	1	0	0	0	0	0	0	0	0	0	0	0	0	0	0	0	0	.000	.000
Colangelo, Mike, San Diego	.250	17	16	16	0	4	5	1	0	0	0	0	0	0	0	0	4	0	0	0	.313	.250
Colbrunn, Greg, Arizona	.188	37	36	32	3	6	16	1	0	3	7	0	0	3	1	0	5	0	0	3	.500	.278
Collier, Lou, Milwaukee	.429	12	12	7	2	3	6	0	0	1	2	0	0	1	4	0	3	0	0	0	.857	.667
Conti, Jason, Arizona*	.333	4	4	3	1	1	1	0	0	0	0	0	0	0	1	0	1	0	0	0	.333	.500
Coolbaugh, Mike, Milwaukee	.200	12	12	10	0	2	3	1	0	0	0	0	0	0	2	0	3	0	0	0	.300	.333
Coomer, Ron, Chicago	.200	17	17	15	2	3	6	0	0	1	3	0	1	0	1	0	1	0	0	0	.400	.235
Cora, Alex, Los Angeles*	.500	2	2	2	0	1	1	0	0	0	0	0	0	0	0	0	0	0	0	0	.500	.500
Cota, Humberto, Pittsburgh	.500	4	4	4	0	2	2	0	0	0	1	0	0	0	0	0	1	0	0	0	.500	.500
Counsell, Craig, Arizona*	.500	13	13	8	2	4	4	0	0	0	1	0	0	1	4	0	0	2	1	0	.500	.692
Crespo, Cesar, San Diego†	.500	2	2	2	1	1	4	0	0	1	2	0	0	0	0	0	1	0	0	0	2.000	.500
Crespo, Felipe, S.F.-Phi.†	.227	52	52	44	4	10	19	3	0	2	7	1	1	0	6	0	9	1	0	1	.432	.314
Cromer, D.T., Cincinnati*	.263	42	41	38	3	10	18	2	0	2	7	0	2	0	1	0	11	0	0	0	.474	.268
Cruz, Jacob, Colorado*	.188	23	22	16	1	3	3	0	0	0	2	0	1	0	5	0	6	0	0	0	.188	.364
Cummings, Midre, Arizona*	.313	17	17	16	1	5	6	1	0	0	1	0	1	0	0	0	4	0	0	2	.375	.294
Cust, Jack, Arizona*	.000	2	2	1	0	0	0	0	0	0	0	0	0	0	1	0	0	0	0	0	.000	.500
Darr, Mike, San Diego*	.286	10	9	7	3	2	6	1	0	1	1	0	0	0	2	0	3	0	0	0	.857	.444
Davis, Ben, San Diego†	.000	4	4	2	0	0	0	0	0	0	0	0	0	0	2	0	1	0	0	1	.000	.500
Davis, Eric, San Francisco	.241	31	31	29	6	7	12	2	0	1	7	0	0	0	2	0	9	0	1	1	.414	.290
Davis, Russ, San Francisco	.400	6	6	5	0	2	3	1	0	0	0	0	0	0	1	0	2	0	0	0	.600	.500
de la Rosa, Tomas, Montreal	.000	1	1	1	0	0	0	0	0	0	0	0	0	0	0	0	0	0	0	0	.000	.000
Dellucci, David, Arizona*	.321	67	65	56	11	18	34	1	0	5	16	0	0	0	9	1	17	0	0	0	.607	.415
DeRosa, Mark, Atlanta	.500	7	7	6	2	3	4	1	0	0	1	0	0	0	1	0	0	0	0	0	.667	.571
DeShields, Delino, Chicago*	.438	21	21	16	5	7	12	2	0	1	2	1	0	0	4	0	2	2	0	0	.750	.550
Dessens, Elmer, Cincinnati	.000	1	1	1	0	0	0	0	0	0	0	0	0	0	0	0	1	0	0	0	.000	.000
Donnels, Chris, Los Angeles*	.212	44	40	33	3	7	15	2	0	2	6	0	0	1	6	1	10	0	0	0	.455	.350
Drew, J.D., St. Louis*	.000	3	3	2	0	0	0	0	0	0	0	1	0	1	0	0	1	0	0	0	.000	.000
Ducey, Rob, Phi.-Mon.*	.269	38	37	26	3	7	11	1	0	1	4	2	0	0	9	0	8	0	1	0	.423	.457
Dunn, Adam, Cincinnati*	.000	3	3	3	0	0	0	0	0	0	0	0	0	0	0	0	0	0	0	0	.000	.000
Dunston, Shawon, S.F.	.286	36	36	35	6	10	23	0	2	3	9	0	0	0	1	0	8	0	0	0	.657	.306
Dunwoody, Todd, Chicago*	.286	7	7	7	1	2	3	1	0	0	0	0	0	0	0	0	3	0	0	0	.429	.286
Durazo, Erubiel, Arizona*	.244	49	48	45	7	11	28	2	0	5	13	0	1	0	2	0	22	0	0	1	.622	.271
Eaton, Adam, San Diego	.000	1	1	1	0	0	0	0	0	0	0	0	0	0	0	0	0	0	0	0	.000	.000
Echevarria, Angel, Milwaukee	.139	42	41	36	1	5	11	3	0	1	5	0	1	2	2	0	9	0	0	1	.306	.220
Edmonds, Jim, St. Louis*	.000	5	5	5	0	0	0	0	0	0	0	0	0	0	0	0	1	0	0	0	.000	.000
Escobar, Alex, New York	.000	2	2	2	0	0	0	0	0	0	0	0	0	0	0	0	1	0	0	0	.000	.000
Estalella, Bobby, S.F.	.000	1	1	1	0	0	0	0	0	0	0	0	0	0	0	0	0	0	0	0	.000	.000
Estrada, Johnny, Phi.†	.500	5	5	4	1	2	5	0	0	1	3	0	0	0	1	0	0	0	0	1	1.250	.600
Eusebio, Tony, Houston	.167	13	13	12	1	2	5	0	0	1	2	0	0	0	1	0	2	0	0	0	.417	.231
Everett, Adam, Houston	.000	3	3	3	0	0	0	0	0	0	0	0	0	0	0	0	0	0	0	0	.000	.000
Feliz, Pedro, San Francisco	.308	14	14	13	3	4	8	2	1	0	2	0	0	0	1	0	3	0	0	0	.615	.357
Fernandez, Tony, Milwaukee†	.182	15	15	11	2	2	2	0	0	0	1	0	0	0	4	0	4	1	0	0	.182	.400
Figueroa, Luis, Pittsburgh†	.000	1	1	1	0	0	0	0	0	0	0	0	0	0	0	0	0	0	0	0	.000	.000
Finley, Steve, Arizona*	.273	13	13	11	2	3	3	0	0	0	1	0	0	0	2	0	2	0	0	0	.273	.385
Floyd, Cliff, Florida*	.000	4	4	3	1	0	0	0	0	0	0	0	0	0	1	0	3	0	0	0	.000	.250
Forbes, P.J., Philadelphia	.000	2	2	2	0	0	0	0	0	0	0	0	0	0	0	0	1	0	0	0	.000	.000
Fox, Andy, Florida*	.087	30	30	23	0	2	2	0	0	0	0	0	0	1	6	1	6	0	0	0	.087	.300

Player, Team	Avg.	G	TPA	AB	R	H	TB	2B	3B	HR	RBI	SH	SF	HP	BB	IBB	SO	SB	CS	GDP	Slg.	OBP
Franco, Julio, Atlanta	.333	3	3	3	0	1	1	0	0	0	0	0	0	0	0	0	2	0	0	0	.333	.333
Galarraga, Andres, S.F.	.222	10	10	9	1	2	2	0	0	0	0	0	0	0	1	0	4	0	0	0	.222	.300
Gant, Ron, Colorado	.000	11	9	8	1	0	0	0	0	0	0	0	0	0	1	0	4	0	0	0	.000	.111
García, Jesse, Atlanta.............	.000	2	2	1	0	0	0	0	0	0	0	1	0	0	0	0	1	0	0	0	.000	.000
Giles, Marcus, Atlanta	.167	7	7	6	1	1	2	1	0	0	0	0	0	0	1	0	2	0	0	0	.333	.286
Gilkey, Bernard, Atlanta..........	.219	36	35	32	0	7	11	4	0	0	2	0	0	0	3	0	11	0	1	1	.344	.286
Ginter, Keith, Houston	.000	1	1	1	0	0	0	0	0	0	0	0	0	0	0	0	0	0	0	0	.000	.000
Girardi, Joe, Chicago.............	.333	10	9	9	0	3	3	0	0	0	0	0	0	0	0	0	0	0	0	1	.333	.333
Glanville, Doug, Philadelphia..	.000	4	4	4	0	0	0	0	0	0	0	0	0	0	0	0	1	0	0	0	.000	.000
Gomez, Chris, San Diego	.000	2	2	2	0	0	0	0	0	0	0	0	0	0	0	0	0	0	0	1	.000	.000
Gonzalez, Alex, Florida	.000	2	2	2	0	0	0	0	0	0	0	0	0	0	0	0	0	0	0	0	.000	.000
Gonzalez, Luis, Arizona*	.000	1	1	1	0	0	0	0	0	0	0	0	0	0	0	0	1	0	0	0	.000	.000
Gonzalez, Raul, Cincinnati......	.143	8	8	7	0	1	1	0	0	0	0	0	0	0	1	0	2	0	0	0	.143	.250
Gonzalez, Wiki, San Diego	.133	19	19	15	0	2	2	0	0	0	0	0	0	0	4	1	2	0	0	1	.133	.316
Goodwin, Tom, Los Angeles* ..	.067	17	17	15	2	1	1	0	0	0	0	0	0	0	2	0	8	0	0	0	.067	.176
Grace, Mark, Arizona*...........	.500	10	10	8	0	4	4	0	0	0	4	0	1	0	1	0	1	0	0	0	.500	.500
Green, Shawn, Los Angeles* .	.000	1	1	1	0	0	0	0	0	0	0	0	0	0	0	0	1	0	0	0	.000	.000
Griffey, Ken Jr., Cincinnati* ...	.071	19	19	14	0	1	2	1	0	0	0	0	0	1	4	2	5	0	0	0	.143	.316
Grissom, Marquis, L.A.	.190	21	21	21	4	4	10	0	0	2	4	0	0	0	0	0	7	0	0	0	.476	.190
Guerrero, Wilton, Cincinnati†..	.308	27	27	26	3	8	9	1	0	0	2	0	0	0	1	0	3	0	0	0	.346	.333
Gulan, Mike, Florida	.000	5	5	3	1	0	0	0	0	0	0	0	0	0	2	0	0	0	0	0	.000	.400
Gutierrez, Ricky, Chicago	.333	5	5	3	0	1	1	0	0	0	1	0	1	1	0	0	0	0	0	0	.333	.400
Guzman, Edwards, S.F.*	.217	23	23	23	1	5	8	0	0	1	2	0	0	0	0	0	3	0	0	1	.348	.217
Gwynn, Tony, San Diego*	.298	53	53	47	0	14	20	6	0	0	10	0	0	0	6	0	6	0	0	1	.426	.377
Hamilton, Darryl, New York*..	.154	18	16	13	3	2	3	1	0	0	0	0	0	0	3	1	2	0	0	0	.231	.313
Hammonds, Jeffrey, Mil.	.000	1	1	1	0	0	0	0	0	0	0	0	0	0	0	0	0	0	0	0	.000	.000
Hampton, Mike, Colorado	.000	3	3	2	1	0	0	0	0	0	0	0	0	0	1	0	1	0	0	0	.000	.333
Hansen, Dave, Los Angeles*..	.225	55	50	40	3	9	14	5	0	0	4	0	1	0	9	4	13	0	0	0	.350	.360
Harris, Lenny, New York*	.253	95	89	83	8	21	27	4	1	0	8	0	0	0	6	0	5	1	2	2	.325	.303
Hayes, Charlie, Houston.........	.200	19	19	15	1	3	4	1	0	0	1	0	0	0	4	1	6	0	0	0	.267	.368
Helms, Wes, Atlanta	.222	20	20	18	4	4	9	2	0	1	6	0	0	0	2	0	8	0	0	0	.500	.300
Helton, Todd, Colorado*........	.000	2	2	2	0	0	0	0	0	0	0	0	0	0	0	0	2	0	0	0	.000	.000
Henderson, Rickey, S.D.	.182	14	14	11	2	2	2	0	0	0	0	0	0	0	3	0	3	0	0	0	.182	.357
Hermansen, Chad, Pit.	.000	2	2	2	0	0	0	0	0	0	0	0	0	0	0	0	2	0	0	0	.000	.000
Hernandez, Alex, Pittsburgh*.	.000	2	2	2	0	0	0	0	0	0	0	0	0	0	0	0	1	0	0	0	.000	.000
Hernandez, Jose, Milwaukee..	.000	1	1	1	0	0	0	0	0	0	0	0	0	0	0	0	0	0	0	0	.000	.000
Hernandez, Livan, S.F.	.000	1	1	1	0	0	0	0	0	0	0	0	0	0	0	0	1	0	0	0	.000	.000
Hiatt, Phil, Los Angeles..........	.300	11	11	10	0	3	4	1	0	0	1	0	0	0	1	1	6	0	0	0	.400	.364
Hidalgo, Richard, Houston......	.000	4	4	3	0	0	0	0	0	0	0	0	0	0	1	1	1	0	0	0	.000	.250
Hollandsworth, Todd, Col.* ...	.000	3	3	3	0	0	0	0	0	0	0	0	0	0	0	0	1	0	0	0	.000	.000
Houston, Tyler, Milwaukee* ...	.111	13	12	9	1	1	4	0	0	1	2	0	0	0	3	0	3	0	0	0	.444	.333
Hundley, Todd, Chicago†........	.273	12	12	11	1	3	6	0	0	1	1	0	0	0	1	0	6	0	0	0	.545	.333
Hunter, Brian L., Philadelphia.	.364	38	38	33	6	12	20	2	0	2	9	0	1	0	4	0	7	3	0	0	.606	.421
Hyzdu, Adam, Pittsburgh	.222	22	21	18	1	4	5	1	0	0	1	0	0	1	2	0	6	0	0	0	.278	.333
Jackson, Damian, San Diego ..	.000	1	1	1	0	0	0	0	0	0	0	0	0	0	0	0	0	0	0	0	.000	.000
Jarvis, Kevin, San Diego*	.000	2	2	1	0	0	0	0	0	0	0	0	0	0	1	0	1	0	0	0	.000	.500
Jenkins, Geoff, Milwaukee* ...	1.000	1	1	1	0	1	1	0	0	0	1	0	0	0	0	0	0	0	0	0	1.000	1.000
Jennings, Robin, Cincinnati*..	.333	6	6	6	1	2	2	0	0	0	0	0	0	0	0	0	0	0	0	0	.333	.333
Jimenez, D'Angelo, S.D.†.......	.000	1	1	1	0	0	0	0	0	0	0	0	0	0	0	0	1	0	0	0	.000	.000
Johnson, Brian, Los Angeles .	.000	1	1	1	0	0	0	0	0	0	0	0	0	0	0	0	0	0	0	0	.000	.000
Johnson, Charles, Florida	.250	8	8	8	2	2	8	0	0	2	6	0	0	0	0	0	5	0	0	0	1.000	.250
Johnson, Mark P., New York*..	.407	36	31	27	3	11	14	3	0	0	6	0	0	0	4	1	6	0	0	0	.519	.484
Jones, Chipper, Atlanta†........	.000	2	2	2	0	0	0	0	0	0	0	0	0	0	0	0	0	0	0	0	.000	.000
Jones, Terry, Montreal†	.222	10	10	9	1	2	2	0	0	0	1	0	0	0	1	0	3	0	0	0	.222	.300
Jordan, Brian, Atlanta	.333	3	3	3	0	1	1	0	0	0	1	0	0	0	0	0	2	0	0	0	.333	.333
Jordan, Kevin, Philadelphia....	.184	43	43	38	2	7	10	0	0	1	5	0	0	0	5	0	9	0	0	0	.263	.279
Karros, Eric, Los Angeles.......	.000	2	2	2	0	0	0	0	0	0	0	0	0	0	0	0	2	0	0	0	.000	.000
Kendall, Jason, Pittsburgh	.000	3	3	3	0	0	0	0	0	0	0	0	0	0	0	0	0	0	0	0	.000	.000
Kent, Jeff, San Francisco	.000	1	1	1	0	0	0	0	0	0	0	0	0	0	0	0	1	0	0	0	.000	.000
Kieschnick, Brooks, Col.*	.269	28	27	26	2	7	13	1	1	1	6	0	0	0	1	0	7	0	0	1	.500	.296
Klesko, Ryan, San Diego*	.000	2	2	2	0	0	0	0	0	0	0	0	0	0	0	0	2	0	0	0	.000	.000
Knorr, Randy, Montreal	.143	7	7	7	1	1	1	0	0	0	0	0	0	0	0	0	2	0	0	0	.143	.143
Kotsay, Mark, San Diego*	.000	6	6	4	1	0	0	0	0	0	0	0	0	0	2	1	1	0	0	0	.000	.333
Kreuter, Chad, Los Angeles†..	.000	2	2	2	0	0	0	0	0	0	0	0	0	0	0	0	0	0	0	0	.000	.000
Lankford, Ray, St.L.-S.D.* ..	.182	14	13	11	1	2	3	1	0	0	0	0	0	1	1	1	4	0	0	0	.273	.308
Larkin, Barry, Cincinnati.........	.000	1	1	1	0	0	0	0	0	0	0	0	0	0	0	0	0	0	0	0	.000	.000
Larson, Brandon, Cincinnati..	.333	4	3	3	1	1	2	1	0	0	0	0	0	0	1	0	1	0	0	0	.667	.333
LaRue, Jason, Cincinnati.......	.400	11	11	10	2	4	6	2	0	0	1	0	0	1	0	0	1	0	0	0	.600	.455
Leach, Jalal, San Francisco*..	.000	7	7	7	0	0	0	0	0	0	0	0	0	0	0	0	2	0	0	0	.000	.000
Lee, Derrek, Florida..............	.333	5	5	3	1	1	4	0	0	1	2	0	0	1	1	0	1	0	0	0	1.333	.600
Lee, Travis, Philadelphia*.......	.500	4	4	2	1	1	1	0	0	0	3	0	0	0	2	0	0	0	0	0	.500	.750
Levis, Jesse, Milwaukee*.......	1.000	1	1	1	1	1	2	1	0	0	0	0	0	0	0	0	0	0	0	0	2.000	1.000
Lieber, Jon, Chicago*............	.000	1	1	1	0	0	0	0	0	0	0	0	0	0	0	0	1	0	0	0	.000	.000
Lieberthal, Mike, Philadelphia..	1.000	1	1	1	0	1	2	1	0	0	2	0	0	0	0	0	0	0	0	0	2.000	1.000
Little, Mark, Colorado	.280	25	25	25	2	7	9	2	0	0	3	0	0	0	0	0	6	0	1	0	.360	.280
Lockhart, Keith, Atlanta*........	.326	59	54	46	8	15	22	4	0	1	6	0	0	0	8	1	5	0	0	0	.478	.426
Lo Duca, Paul, Los Angeles ...	.000	6	5	5	0	0	0	0	0	0	0	0	0	0	0	0	2	0	0	2	.000	.000
Lopez, Javy, Atlanta...............	.375	10	10	8	1	3	3	0	0	0	3	0	0	0	2	0	1	0	0	1	.375	.500
Lopez, Luis, Milwaukee†	.095	26	26	21	2	2	2	0	0	0	0	2	0	1	2	1	5	0	0	0	.095	.208
Lopez, Mendy, Hou.-Pit.	.200	11	11	10	0	2	2	0	0	0	0	0	0	0	1	0	0	0	0	0	.200	.273
Loretta, Mark, Milwaukee.......	.000	2	2	2	0	0	0	0	0	0	0	0	0	0	0	0	0	0	0	0	.000	.000
Lowell, Mike, Florida..............	.000	2	2	2	0	0	0	0	0	0	0	0	0	0	0	0	1	0	0	0	.000	.000

Player, Team	Avg.	G	TPA	AB	R	H	TB	2B	3B	HR	RBI	SH	SF	HP	BB	IBB	SO	SB	CS	GDP	Slg.	OBP
Lugo, Julio, Houston............	.286	8	8	7	0	2	2	0	0	0	0	0	0	1	0	0	2	0	0	0	.286	.375
Mabry, John, Florida*	.171	49	47	41	1	7	8	1	0	0	5	0	1	1	4	1	16	0	0	0	.195	.255
Machado, Robert, Chicago.....	.286	8	7	7	0	2	3	1	0	0	2	0	0	0	0	0	1	0	0	0	.429	.286
Mackowiak, Rob, Pittsburgh*..	.111	23	21	18	2	2	3	1	0	0	1	0	0	0	3	1	6	0	0	0	.167	.238
Maddux, Greg, Atlanta	.000	1	1	1	0	0	0	0	0	0	0	0	0	0	0	0	0	0	0	0	.000	.000
Magadan, Dave, San Diego* ..	.226	64	62	53	6	12	15	3	0	0	2	0	1	1	7	0	9	0	0	1	.283	.323
Marrero, Eli, St. Louis	.083	14	13	12	0	1	2	1	0	0	0	0	0	0	1	0	6	0	0	0	.167	.154
Martinez, Dave, Atlanta*	.232	68	65	56	9	13	17	4	0	0	3	0	0	0	9	0	13	2	1	2	.304	.338
Martinez, Ramon E., S.F.	.000	8	8	6	0	0	0	0	0	0	0	1	0	0	1	0	1	0	0	0	.000	.143
Mateo, Henry, Montreal†........	.000	2	2	2	0	0	0	0	0	0	0	0	0	0	0	0	0	0	0	0	.000	.000
Matthews, Gary Jr., Chi.-Pit.†..	.412	20	20	17	5	7	10	0	0	1	6	0	0	0	3	0	5	0	0	0	.588	.500
Mayne, Brent, Colorado*	.286	7	7	7	0	2	2	0	0	0	0	0	0	0	0	0	2	0	0	0	.286	.286
McDonald, Keith, St. Louis	.000	1	1	1	0	0	0	0	0	0	0	0	0	0	0	0	0	0	0	1	.000	.000
McEwing, Joe, New York	.273	27	25	22	4	6	10	2	1	0	3	0	1	2	0	0	8	1	0	0	.455	.320
McGuire, Ryan, Florida*	.273	39	38	33	5	9	13	1	0	1	6	0	0	0	5	0	11	1	0	0	.394	.368
McGwire, Mark, St. Louis	.143	8	8	7	0	1	1	0	0	0	0	0	0	0	1	0	2	0	0	0	.143	.250
Meares, Pat, Pittsburgh	.333	3	3	3	0	1	1	0	0	0	1	0	0	0	0	0	1	0	0	0	.333	.333
Melhuse, Adam, Colorado†......	.125	18	18	16	1	2	2	0	0	0	0	0	0	0	2	0	4	0	0	1	.125	.222
Merced, Orlando, Houston* ...	.259	65	65	58	12	15	32	3	1	4	17	0	1	0	6	0	18	2	0	1	.552	.323
Meyers, Chad, Chicago	.000	8	8	3	0	0	0	0	0	0	0	0	0	3	2	0	1	0	0	0	.000	.625
Michaels, Jason, Philadelphia .	.200	5	5	5	0	1	1	0	0	0	1	0	0	0	0	0	2	0	0	0	.200	.200
Millar, Kevin, Florida..............	.222	28	28	27	2	6	10	4	0	0	9	0	0	1	0	0	6	0	0	1	.370	.250
Miller, Damian, Arizona	.000	4	4	3	0	0	0	0	0	0	0	0	0	0	1	1	2	0	0	0	.000	.250
Minor, Damon, S.F.*..............	.000	8	7	7	0	0	0	0	0	0	0	0	0	0	0	0	3	0	0	1	.000	.000
Minor, Ryan, Montreal	.154	31	31	26	4	4	4	0	0	0	3	0	1	0	4	0	7	0	0	1	.154	.258
Moeller, Chad, Arizona	.000	2	2	2	0	0	0	0	0	0	0	0	0	0	0	0	0	0	0	0	.000	.000
Mordecai, Mike, Montreal	.095	22	22	21	0	2	2	0	0	0	1	0	0	0	1	0	5	0	0	2	.095	.136
Morris, Warren, Pittsburgh* ..	.105	20	19	19	0	2	4	2	0	0	2	0	0	0	0	0	3	0	0	1	.211	.105
Mottola, Chad, Florida............	.000	1	1	1	0	0	0	0	0	0	0	0	0	0	0	0	0	0	0	0	.000	.000
Mouton, James, Milwaukee ...	.357	19	19	14	4	5	8	0	0	1	2	2	0	2	1	0	4	0	0	0	.571	.471
Mouton, Lyle, Florida	.000	8	8	8	0	0	0	0	0	0	0	0	0	0	0	0	1	0	0	0	.000	.000
Mueller, Bill, Chicago†	.200	8	8	5	1	1	1	0	0	0	0	0	0	0	3	0	0	0	0	0	.200	.500
Murray, Calvin, San Francisco .	.500	4	4	4	1	2	5	0	0	1	4	0	0	0	0	0	1	0	0	0	1.250	.500
Nevin, Phil, San Diego	.500	3	3	2	0	1	1	0	0	0	2	0	0	0	1	0	0	0	0	0	.500	.667
Newhan, David, Philadelphia*.	.500	6	5	4	1	2	3	1	0	0	1	0	1	0	0	0	1	0	0	0	.750	.400
Norton, Greg, Colorado†.........	.270	69	69	63	7	17	33	5	1	3	11	0	1	0	5	0	19	0	0	2	.524	.319
Nunez, Abraham, Pittsburgh†..	.143	35	35	35	2	5	10	2	0	1	5	0	0	0	0	0	5	0	0	0	.286	.143
Ochoa, Alex, Cin.-Col	.375	11	11	8	1	3	4	1	0	0	2	0	0	0	3	0	2	0	0	0	.500	.545
Ojeda, Augie, Chicago†	.000	12	12	11	0	0	0	0	0	0	0	0	0	0	1	0	5	0	0	0	.000	.083
Olivares, Omar, Pittsburgh	.000	2	2	2	0	0	0	0	0	0	0	0	0	0	0	0	1	0	0	0	.000	.000
Ordonez, Rey, New York	1.000	1	1	1	1	1	1	0	0	0	0	0	0	0	0	0	0	0	0	0	1.000	1.000
Ortega, Bill, St. Louis	.200	5	5	5	0	1	1	0	0	0	0	0	0	0	0	0	1	0	0	0	.200	.200
Ortiz, Jose, Colorado..............	.000	3	3	2	0	0	0	0	0	0	0	0	0	0	1	0	2	0	0	0	.000	.333
Osik, Keith, Pittsburgh	.111	9	9	9	0	1	2	1	0	0	2	0	0	0	0	0	2	0	0	0	.222	.111
Overbay, Lyle, Arizona*	.500	2	2	2	0	1	1	0	0	0	0	0	0	0	0	0	1	0	0	0	.500	.500
Owens, Eric, Florida	.167	13	13	12	1	2	3	1	0	0	0	0	0	0	1	0	3	0	0	0	.250	.231
Paquette, Craig, St. Louis	.304	25	25	23	2	7	14	1	0	2	5	0	0	1	1	0	4	0	0	0	.609	.360
Patterson, Corey, Chicago*....	.200	13	13	10	3	2	3	1	0	0	2	1	1	0	1	0	5	0	0	0	.300	.250
Payton, Jay, New York	.000	3	3	2	0	0	0	0	0	0	0	0	0	0	1	0	1	0	0	0	.000	.333
Pena, Angel, Los Angeles	.143	7	7	7	1	1	1	0	0	0	0	0	0	0	0	0	4	0	0	0	.143	.143
Pena, Elvis, Milwaukee†.........	.250	4	4	4	1	1	1	0	0	0	0	0	0	0	0	0	2	0	0	0	.250	.250
Perez, Eddie, Atlanta	.000	2	2	2	0	0	0	0	0	0	0	0	0	0	0	0	1	0	0	0	.000	.000
Perez, Robert, Milwaukee	.000	1	1	1	0	0	0	0	0	0	0	0	0	0	0	0	0	0	0	0	.000	.000
Perez, Santiago, San Diego†..	.111	9	9	9	0	1	1	0	0	0	0	0	0	0	0	0	2	0	0	0	.111	.111
Perez, Timo, New York*	.250	13	13	12	1	3	6	0	0	1	1	0	0	0	1	0	1	0	0	0	.500	.308
Perez, Tomas, Philadelphia†..	.250	17	17	16	1	4	4	0	0	0	1	0	0	0	1	0	3	0	0	0	.250	.294
Petrick, Ben, Colorado	.143	7	7	7	0	1	1	0	0	0	1	0	0	0	0	0	5	0	0	0	.143	.143
Phillips, Jason, New York	.000	1	1	1	0	0	0	0	0	0	0	0	0	0	0	0	0	0	0	0	.000	.000
Piazza, Mike, New York	.200	7	7	5	0	1	2	1	0	0	4	0	0	0	2	0	1	0	0	0	.400	.429
Pickering, Calvin, Cincinnati*.	.250	4	4	4	0	1	1	0	0	0	1	0	0	0	0	0	2	0	0	0	.250	.250
Pierre, Juan, Colorado*	.000	6	6	5	1	0	0	0	0	0	0	0	0	1	0	0	1	0	0	0	.000	.167
Polanco, Placido, St. Louis	.286	7	7	7	0	2	4	2	0	0	1	0	0	0	0	0	1	0	0	0	.571	.286
Powell, Dante, San Francisco.	.000	1	1	1	0	0	0	0	0	0	0	0	0	0	0	0	1	0	0	0	.000	.000
Pratt, Todd, New York	.000	16	15	11	0	0	0	0	0	0	0	0	0	0	4	0	9	0	0	0	.000	.267
Pride, Curtis, Montreal*	.167	15	15	12	1	2	2	0	0	0	0	0	0	1	2	0	7	0	0	2	.167	.333
Pujols, Albert, St. Louis	.000	2	2	2	0	0	0	0	0	0	0	0	0	0	0	0	1	0	0	0	.000	.000
Punto, Nick, Philadelphia†.....	1.000	1	1	1	0	1	1	0	0	0	0	0	0	0	0	0	0	0	0	0	1.000	1.000
Raines, Tim, Montreal†	.273	27	27	22	3	6	8	2	0	0	3	0	1	0	4	0	3	0	0	0	.364	.370
Ramirez, Aramis, Pittsburgh..	.500	2	2	2	0	1	1	0	0	0	2	0	0	0	0	0	0	0	0	0	.500	.500
Ransom, Cody, S.F.	.000	4	4	4	0	0	0	0	0	0	0	0	0	0	0	0	2	0	0	0	.000	.000
Reboulet, Jeff, Los Angeles ...	.368	25	25	19	2	7	10	0	0	1	5	3	0	0	3	0	3	0	0	1	.526	.455
Redman, Tike, Pittsburgh*......	.000	2	2	2	0	0	0	0	0	0	0	0	0	0	0	0	1	0	0	0	.000	.000
Redmond, Mike, Florida	1.000	1	1	1	0	1	1	0	0	0	0	0	0	0	0	0	0	0	0	0	1.000	1.000
Reese, Pokey, Cincinnati........	.200	5	5	5	0	1	2	1	0	0	0	0	0	0	0	0	2	1	0	0	.400	.200
Relaford, Desi, New York†.......	.160	31	31	25	1	4	5	1	0	0	0	0	0	3	3	0	9	1	1	1	.200	.323
Renteria, Edgar, St. Louis	.333	3	3	3	1	1	1	0	0	0	2	0	0	0	0	0	0	0	0	0	.333	.333
Reyes, Dennys, Cincinnati......	.000	1	1	1	0	0	0	0	0	0	0	0	0	0	0	0	0	0	0	0	.000	.000
Rios, Armando, S.F.*	.125	11	11	8	1	1	2	1	0	0	1	0	0	0	3	1	2	0	0	0	.250	.364
Rivera, Ruben, Cincinnati........	.261	27	27	23	5	6	14	2	0	2	6	0	0	1	3	0	12	0	0	1	.609	.346
Robinson, Kerry, St. Louis*	.256	50	49	43	4	11	12	1	0	0	1	2	0	0	4	0	6	1	0	1	.279	.319
Rollins, Jimmy, Philadelphia†.	.000	1	1	1	0	0	0	0	0	0	0	0	0	0	0	0	0	0	0	0	.000	.000
Rueter, Kirk, San Francisco* ..	.000	1	1	1	0	0	0	0	0	0	0	0	0	0	0	0	0	0	0	0	.000	.000

Player, Team	Avg.	G	TPA	AB	R	H	TB	2B	3B	HR	RBI	SH	SF	HP	BB	IBB	SO	SB	CS	GDP	Slg.	OBP
Ryan, Rob, Arizona*	.000	1	1	1	0	0	0	0	0	0	0	0	0	0	0	0	1	0	0	0	.000	.000
Sadler, Donnie, Cincinnati	.286	7	7	7	0	2	3	1	0	0	0	0	0	0	0	0	1	0	0	0	.429	.286
Sanchez, Alex, Milwaukee*	.143	15	15	14	0	2	4	0	1	0	0	0	0	0	1	0	5	0	0	0	.286	.200
Sanchez, Rey, Atlanta	.000	1	1	1	0	0	0	0	0	0	0	0	0	0	0	0	0	0	0	0	.000	.000
Sanders, Deion, Cincinnati*	.091	14	12	11	0	1	1	0	0	0	0	0	0	0	1	0	5	0	1	0	.091	.167
Sanders, Reggie, Arizona	.125	9	9	8	0	1	2	1	0	0	1	0	0	0	1	0	5	0	0	0	.250	.222
Santiago, Benito, S.F.	.667	3	3	3	0	2	2	0	0	0	3	0	0	0	0	0	0	0	0	0	.667	.667
Saturria, Luis, St. Louis	.250	4	4	4	0	1	2	1	0	0	1	0	0	0	0	0	1	0	0	0	.500	.250
Schneider, Brian, Montreal*	.273	13	13	11	1	3	4	1	0	0	1	0	0	0	2	0	1	0	0	0	.364	.385
Sefcik, Kevin, Colorado	.000	1	1	1	0	0	0	0	0	0	0	0	0	0	0	0	0	0	0	0	.000	.000
Seguignol, Fernando, Mon.†	.120	29	29	25	0	3	4	1	0	0	3	0	1	1	2	1	10	0	0	0	.160	.207
Selby, Bill, Cincinnati*	.222	9	9	9	1	2	5	0	0	1	1	0	0	0	0	1	0	0	0	0	.556	.222
Servais, Scott, Houston	.000	2	2	2	0	0	0	0	0	0	0	0	0	0	0	0	0	0	0	0	.000	.000
Shinjo, Tsuyoshi, New York	.000	9	9	7	0	0	0	0	0	0	0	0	0	0	1	1	0	0	1	0	.000	.222
Shumpert, Terry, Colorado	.227	49	49	44	3	10	14	1	0	1	3	1	1	1	2	0	8	1	1	0	.318	.271
Smith, Jason, Chicago*	.000	1	1	1	0	0	0	0	0	0	0	0	0	0	0	0	1	0	0	0	.000	.000
Smith, Mark, Montreal	.150	27	26	20	2	3	3	0	0	0	0	0	0	0	6	0	1	0	1	1	.150	.346
Snow, J.T., San Francisco*	.444	15	15	9	2	4	4	0	0	0	4	0	0	0	6	2	0	0	0	0	.444	.667
Spiers, Bill, Houston*	.333	4	4	3	0	1	1	0	0	0	0	0	0	0	1	1	0	0	0	0	.333	.500
Spivey, Junior, Arizona	.286	8	8	7	0	2	3	1	0	0	1	0	0	0	1	0	3	0	0	0	.429	.375
Stairs, Matt, Chicago*	.231	19	18	13	1	3	4	1	0	0	1	0	0	0	5	1	3	0	0	0	.308	.444
Stechschulte, Gene, St.L.	1.000	2	2	1	1	1	4	0	0	1	2	0	0	0	1	0	0	0	0	0	4.000	1.000
Stevens, Lee, Montreal*	.000	1	1	1	0	0	0	0	0	0	0	0	0	0	0	0	0	0	0	0	.000	.000
Stinnett, Kelly, Cincinnati	.333	5	4	3	0	1	1	0	0	0	0	0	0	0	1	0	1	0	0	0	.333	.500
Surhoff, B.J., Atlanta*	.455	13	13	11	1	5	6	1	0	0	6	0	0	0	2	0	3	0	0	1	.545	.538
Sutton, Larry, St. Louis*	.200	25	25	25	2	5	9	1	0	1	3	0	0	0	0	0	7	0	0	1	.360	.200
Sweeney, Mark, Milwaukee*	.240	27	27	25	1	6	7	1	0	0	2	0	0	0	2	0	10	0	0	0	.280	.296
Tatis, Fernando, Montreal	.000	1	1	1	0	0	0	0	0	0	0	0	0	0	0	0	0	0	0	0	.000	.000
Taylor, Reggie, Philadelphia*	.000	1	1	1	0	0	0	0	0	0	0	0	0	0	0	0	1	0	0	0	.000	.000
Thompson, Ryan, Florida	.000	3	3	3	1	0	0	0	0	0	0	0	0	0	0	0	2	0	0	0	.000	.000
Toca, Jorge, New York	.000	8	8	8	0	0	0	0	0	0	0	0	0	0	0	0	5	0	0	0	.000	.000
Torrealba, Steve, Atlanta	1.000	1	1	1	0	1	1	0	0	0	0	0	0	0	0	0	0	0	0	0	1.000	1.000
Tracy, Andy, Montreal*	.056	22	21	18	2	1	4	0	0	1	2	0	1	0	2	0	10	0	0	1	.222	.143
Trammell, Bubba, San Diego	.333	15	15	12	2	4	5	1	0	0	2	0	1	0	2	0	3	0	0	1	.417	.400
Truby, Chris, Houston	.182	12	12	11	1	2	6	1	0	1	1	0	0	0	1	0	5	0	0	0	.545	.250
Tucker, Michael, Cin.-Chi.*	.053	27	26	19	2	1	1	0	0	0	4	0	3	0	4	0	6	0	0	1	.053	.192
Uribe, Juan, Colorado	.333	3	3	3	0	1	1	0	0	0	1	0	0	0	0	0	1	0	0	0	.333	.333
Valent, Eric, Philadelphia*	.000	11	11	9	1	0	0	0	0	0	0	0	0	0	1	0	3	0	0	0	.000	.182
Vander Wal, John, Pit.-S.F.*	.071	10	18	14	2	1	4	0	0	1	3	1	0	0	3	0	6	0	0	1	.286	.235
Ventura, Robin, New York*	1.000	6	4	2	2	2	2	0	0	0	1	0	0	0	2	0	0	0	0	0	1.000	1.000
Veras, Quilvio, Atlanta†	.333	7	7	6	0	2	2	0	0	0	0	0	0	0	1	0	1	0	0	0	.333	.429
Vidro, Jose, Montreal†	.000	1	1	0	0	0	0	0	0	0	0	0	0	0	1	1	0	0	0	0	.000	1.000
Vina, Fernando, St. Louis*	.000	2	2	1	0	0	0	0	0	0	0	0	1	0	0	0	0	0	0	0	.000	.000
Vizcaino, Jose, Houston†	.156	51	51	45	3	7	7	0	0	0	2	0	0	4	0	0	14	0	0	1	.156	.224
Walbeck, Matt, Philadelphia†	1.000	1	1	1	0	1	1	0	0	0	0	0	0	0	0	0	0	0	0	0	1.000	1.000
Walker, Larry, Colorado*	.400	9	9	5	0	2	3	1	0	0	3	0	0	0	4	2	2	0	0	0	.600	.667
Walker, Todd, Col.-Cin.*	.143	17	17	14	1	2	2	0	0	0	2	0	0	0	3	0	4	0	0	0	.143	.294
Ward, Daryle, Houston*	.216	46	45	37	3	8	13	2	0	1	7	0	1	0	7	1	13	0	0	1	.351	.333
Ward, Turner, Philadelphia†	.267	17	17	15	1	4	5	1	0	0	2	0	0	1	1	1	6	0	0	1	.333	.353
Wehner, John, Pittsburgh	.100	20	18	10	0	1	1	0	0	0	1	1	0	0	7	0	2	0	0	0	.100	.471
White, Devon, Milwaukee†	.185	31	31	27	1	5	5	0	0	0	2	0	1	0	3	0	11	0	0	1	.185	.258
White, Rondell, Chicago	.250	5	5	4	0	1	2	1	0	0	1	0	0	0	1	1	1	0	0	0	.500	.400
Wilkerson, Brad, Montreal*	.222	10	10	9	2	2	3	1	0	0	0	1	0	0	0	0	6	0	0	0	.333	.222
Wilkins, Rick, San Diego*	.000	4	4	4	0	0	0	0	0	0	0	0	0	0	0	0	2	0	0	0	.000	.000
Williams, Matt, Arizona	.250	5	5	4	0	1	1	0	0	0	1	0	0	0	1	0	1	0	0	0	.250	.400
Williams, Woody, San Diego	.000	1	1	1	0	0	0	0	0	0	0	0	0	0	0	0	1	0	0	0	.000	.000
Wilson, Craig A., Pittsburgh	.294	43	43	34	11	10	31	0	0	7	11	0	0	2	7	1	12	1	0	0	.912	.442
Wilson, Enrique, Pittsburgh†	.077	13	13	13	1	1	1	0	0	0	1	0	0	0	0	0	2	0	0	1	.077	.077
Wilson, Jack, Pittsburgh	1.000	1	1	1	0	1	1	0	0	0	0	0	0	0	0	0	0	0	0	0	1.000	1.000
Wilson, Preston, Florida	.000	2	2	1	0	0	0	0	0	0	0	0	0	0	1	0	1	0	0	0	.000	.500
Wilson, Vance, New York	.000	5	5	4	0	0	0	0	0	0	0	0	0	0	0	0	0	0	0	1	.000	.200
Witt, Kevin, San Diego*	.000	3	3	2	1	0	0	0	0	0	0	0	0	0	0	0	0	0	0	0	.000	.333
Womack, Tony, Arizona*	.167	8	8	6	2	1	1	0	0	0	0	0	1	0	1	0	1	1	0	0	.167	.286
Wright, Jamey, Milwaukee	.000	1	1	1	0	0	0	0	0	0	0	0	0	0	0	0	1	0	0	0	.000	.000
Young, Dmitri, Cincinnati†	.000	7	7	6	1	0	0	0	0	0	0	0	0	0	1	1	1	0	0	1	.000	.143
Young, Eric, Chicago	.333	3	3	3	1	1	2	1	0	0	0	0	0	0	0	0	0	0	0	0	.667	.333
Young, Kevin, Pittsburgh	.222	9	9	9	2	2	5	0	0	1	1	0	0	0	0	0	3	0	0	0	.556	.222
Zeile, Todd, New York	.250	5	5	4	0	1	1	0	0	0	2	0	1	0	0	0	1	0	0	1	.250	.200
Zuleta, Julio, Chicago	.318	24	24	22	4	7	18	2	0	3	13	0	0	0	2	0	8	0	0	0	.818	.375

PINCH-HITTERS WITH TWO OR MORE TEAMS

Player, Team	Avg.	G	TPA	AB	R	H	TB	2B	3B	HR	RBI	SH	SF	HP	BB	IBB	SO	SB	CS	GDP	Slg.	OBP
Bennett, Gary, Philadelphia	.000	2	2	2	0	0	0	0	0	0	0	0	0	0	0	0	1	0	0	0	.000	.000
Bennett, Gary, New York	1.000	1	1	1	0	1	1	0	0	0	0	0	0	0	0	0	0	0	0	0	1.000	1.000
Brown, Emil, Pittsburgh	.250	15	15	12	4	3	4	1	0	0	2	0	0	0	3	0	5	0	1	0	.333	.400
Brown, Emil, San Diego	.000	1	1	1	0	0	0	0	0	0	0	0	0	0	0	0	0	0	0	0	.000	.000
Cairo, Miguel, Chicago	.063	20	20	16	2	1	2	1	0	0	2	1	0	0	3	1	3	0	0	1	.125	.211
Cairo, Miguel, St. Louis	.368	20	20	19	4	7	13	3	0	1	4	0	0	0	1	0	1	0	0	1	.684	.400
Crespo, Felipe, S.F.†	.316	23	23	19	3	6	13	1	0	2	4	1	0	0	3	0	5	1	0	1	.684	.409
Crespo, Felipe, Philadelphia†	.160	29	29	25	1	4	6	2	0	0	3	0	1	0	3	0	4	0	0	0	.240	.241
Ducey, Rob, Philadelphia*	.200	27	26	20	3	4	8	1	0	1	3	1	0	0	5	0	7	0	0	0	.400	.360
Ducey, Rob, Montreal*	.500	11	11	6	0	3	3	0	0	0	1	1	0	0	4	0	1	0	1	0	.500	.700

Player, Team	Avg.	G	TPA	AB	R	H	TB	2B	3B	HR	RBI	SH	SF	HP	BB	IBB	SO	SB	CS	GDP	Slg.	OBP
Lankford, Ray, St. Louis*.......	.143	9	8	7	0	1	2	1	0	0	0	0	0	0	1	1	1	0	0	0	.286	.250
Lankford, Ray, San Diego*	.250	5	5	4	1	1	1	0	0	0	0	0	0	1	0	0	3	0	0	0	.250	.400
Lopez, Mendy, Houston	.400	6	6	5	0	2	2	0	0	0	0	0	0	1	0	0	0	0	0	0	.400	.500
Lopez, Mendy, Pittsburgh	.000	5	5	5	0	0	0	0	0	0	0	0	0	0	0	0	1	0	0	0	.000	.000
Matthews, Gary Jr., Chicago†	.357	16	16	14	3	5	5	0	0	0	3	0	0	0	2	0	4	0	0	0	.357	.438
Matthews, Gary Jr., Pit.†.......	.667	4	4	3	2	2	5	0	0	1	3	0	0	0	1	0	1	0	0	0	1.667	.750
Ochoa, Alex, Cincinnati	.250	5	5	4	1	1	1	0	0	0	1	0	0	0	1	0	2	0	0	0	.250	.400
Ochoa, Alex, Colorado...........	.500	6	6	4	0	2	3	1	0	0	1	0	0	0	2	0	0	0	0	0	.750	.667
Tucker, Michael, Cincinnati*...	.063	23	22	16	1	1	1	0	0	0	4	0	3	0	3	0	6	0	0	1	.063	.182
Tucker, Michael, Chicago*......	.000	4	4	3	1	0	0	0	0	0	0	0	0	0	1	0	0	0	0	0	.000	.250
Vander Wal, John, Pit.*	.000	9	9	7	1	0	0	0	0	0	2	0	0	0	2	0	1	0	0	1	.000	.222
Vander Wal, John, S.F.*	.143	9	9	7	1	1	4	0	0	1	1	1	0	0	1	0	5	0	0	0	.571	.250
Walker, Todd, Colorado*	.000	14	14	11	1	0	0	0	0	0	0	0	0	0	3	0	4	0	0	0	.000	.214
Walker, Todd, Cincinnati*.......	.667	3	3	3	0	2	2	0	0	0	2	0	0	0	0	0	0	0	0	0	.667	.667

PITCHING

TEAM

Team	W	L	Pct.	ERA	G	ShO	Rel.	Sv.	IP	H	TBF	R	ER	HR	SH	SF	HB	BB	IBB	SO	WP	Bk.
Atlanta	88	74	.543	3.59	162	13	411	41	1447.1	1363	6089	643	578	153	53	54	33	499	77	1133	41	8
Arizona	92	70	.568	3.87	162	13	421	34	1459.2	1352	6090	677	627	195	64	41	59	461	30	1297	45	6
St. Louis	93	69	.574	3.93	162	11	484	38	1435.1	1389	6121	684	627	196	72	35	72	526	36	1083	45	6
Chicago	88	74	.543	4.03	162	6	452	41	1437.0	1357	6159	701	643	164	60	41	50	550	43	1344	48	5
New York	82	80	.506	4.07	162	14	397	48	1445.2	1418	6107	713	654	186	63	50	43	438	60	1191	53	7
Philadelphia	86	76	.531	4.15	162	7	473	47	1445.1	1417	6198	719	667	170	73	49	70	527	60	1086	40	6
San Francisco	90	72	.556	4.18	162	8	439	47	1463.1	1437	6294	748	680	145	58	61	33	579	49	1080	50	3
Los Angeles	86	76	.531	4.25	162	5	408	46	1450.2	1387	6201	744	685	184	69	39	72	524	37	1212	44	11
Florida	76	86	.469	4.32	162	11	430	32	1438.0	1397	6227	744	691	151	63	44	70	617	53	1119	40	3
Houston	93	69	.574	4.37	162	6	405	48	1454.2	1453	6236	769	707	221	62	44	70	486	22	1228	42	3
San Diego	79	83	.488	4.52	162	6	422	46	1440.2	1519	6278	812	724	219	58	47	56	476	54	1088	46	5
Milwaukee	68	94	.420	4.64	162	8	489	28	1436.1	1452	6338	806	740	197	81	40	72	667	107	1057	58	3
Montreal	68	94	.420	4.68	162	11	491	28	1431.1	1509	6250	812	745	190	74	43	61	525	40	1103	55	4
Cincinnati	66	96	.407	4.77	162	2	461	35	1442.2	1572	6324	850	765	198	69	50	48	515	46	943	53	4
Pittsburgh	62	100	.383	5.05	162	9	410	36	1416.1	1493	6222	858	794	167	58	50	80	549	74	908	49	4
Colorado	73	89	.451	5.29	162	8	476	26	1430.0	1522	6306	906	841	239	60	43	64	598	71	1058	38	1
Totals	1290	1302	.498	4.36	1296	138	7069	621	23074.1	23037	99440	12186	11168	2975	1037	731	953	8537	859	17930	747	79

NOTE—Totals for earned runs for several clubs do not agree with composite total for all pitchers of each respective club due to instances in which provisions of Section 10.18(i) of the Scoring Rules were applied. The following differences are to be noted: Arizona pitchers add to 629; St. Louis pitchers add to 631; New York pitchers add to 655; Philadelphia pitchers add to 668; San Francisco pitchers add to 682; Houston pitchers add to 709; Milwaukee pitchers add to 742; Montreal pitchers add to 746; Cincinnati pitchers add to 766.

INDIVIDUAL

TOP QUALIFIERS FOR EARNED-RUN AVERAGE TITLE

Minimum 162 innings. *Throws lefthanded.

Pitcher, Team	W	L	Pct.	ERA	G	GS	CG	ShO	GF	Sv.	IP	H	TBF	R	ER	HR	SH	SF	HB	BB	IBB	SO	WP	Bk.
Johnson, Randy, Arizona*	21	6	.778	2.49	35	34	3	2	1	0	249.2	181	994	74	69	19	10	5	18	71	2	372	8	1
Schilling, Curt, Arizona	22	6	.786	2.98	35	35	6	1	0	0	256.2	237	1021	86	85	37	8	5	1	39	0	293	4	0
Burkett, John, Atlanta	12	12	.500	3.04	34	34	1	1	0	0	219.1	187	902	83	74	17	6	7	0	70	13	187	5	1
Maddux, Greg, Atlanta	17	11	.607	3.05	34	34	3	3	0	0	233.0	220	927	86	79	20	12	11	7	27	10	173	2	0
Kile, Darryl, St. Louis	16	11	.593	3.09	34	34	2	1	0	0	227.1	228	956	83	78	22	13	5	11	65	3	179	6	1
Morris, Matt, St. Louis	22	8	.733	3.16	34	34	2	1	0	0	216.1	218	909	86	76	13	14	5	13	54	3	185	5	1
Ortiz, Russ, San Francisco	17	9	.654	3.29	33	33	1	1	0	0	218.2	187	911	90	80	13	10	4	0	91	3	169	8	1
Leiter, Al, New York*	11	11	.500	3.31	29	29	0	0	0	0	187.1	178	772	81	69	18	9	6	4	46	3	142	5	2
Wood, Kerry, Chicago	12	6	.667	3.36	28	28	1	1	0	0	174.1	127	740	70	65	16	4	5	10	92	3	217	9	0
Miller, Wade, Houston	16	8	.667	3.40	32	32	1	0	0	0	212.0	183	873	91	80	31	7	5	4	76	3	183	8	0
Vazquez, Javier, Montreal	16	11	.593	3.42	32	32	5	3	0	0	223.2	197	898	92	85	24	9	2	3	44	4	208	3	1
Park, Chan Ho, Los Angeles	15	11	.577	3.50	36	35	2	1	0	0	234.0	183	981	98	91	23	16	7	20	91	1	218	3	3
Glavine, Tom, Atlanta*	16	7	.696	3.57	35	35	1	1	0	0	219.1	213	929	92	87	24	5	8	2	97	10	116	2	0
Appier, Kevin, New York	11	10	.524	3.57	33	33	1	1	0	0	206.2	181	856	90	82	22	6	7	15	64	4	172	12	0
Penny, Brad, Florida	10	10	.500	3.69	31	31	1	1	0	0	205.0	183	833	92	84	15	8	2	7	54	3	154	2	0

DEPARTMENTAL LEADERS. W—Morris, St.L., Schilling, Ari., 22; L—Jones, S.D., 19; G—Kline, St.L., 89; GS—Glavine, Atl., Park, L.A., Schilling, Ari., 35; CG—Schilling Ari., 6; ShO—Maddux, Atl., Vazquez, Mon., 3; GF—Nen, S.F., 71; Sv—Nen, S.F., 45; IP—Schilling, Ari., 256.2; H—Hernandez, S.F., 266; TBF—Schilling, Ari., 1021; R—Hernandez, S.F., 143; ER—Hernandez, S.F., 132; HR—Jarvis, S.D., Jones, S.D., Schilling, Ari., 37; SH—Park, L.A., 16; SF—Hernandez, S.F., 12; HB—Park, L.A., Wright, Mil., 20; TBB—Dempster, Fla., 112; IBB—Haynes, Mil., 17; SO—Johnson, Ari., 372; WP—Clement, Fla., 15; BK—Daal, Phi., Park, L.A., O. Perez, Atl., 3.

ALL PITCHERS

*Throws lefthanded.

Pitcher, Team	W	L	Pct.	ERA	G	GS	CG	ShO	GF	Sv.	IP	H	TBF	R	ER	HR	SH	SF	HB	BB	IBB	SO	WP	Bk.
Acevedo, Jose, Cin.	5	7	.417	5.44	18	18	0	0	0	0	96.0	101	417	61	58	17	6	3	3	34	2	68	4	0
Acevedo, Juan, Col.-Fla.	2	5	.286	4.18	59	0	0	0	20	0	60.1	68	282	35	28	6	3	3	2	35	9	47	1	0
Adams, Terry, L.A.	12	8	.600	4.33	43	22	0	0	10	0	166.1	172	708	84	80	9	6	0	3	54	1	141	7	2
Ainsworth, Kurt, S.F.	0	0	.000	13.50	2	0	0	0	2	0	2.0	3	12	3	3	1	0	0	1	2	0	3	0	0
Alfonseca, Antonio, Fla.	4	5	.444	3.00	50	0	0	0	52	28	61.2	68	268	24	21	6	5	1	5	15	3	40	2	0
Almanza, Armando, Fla.*	2	2	.500	4.83	52	0	0	0	8	0	41.0	34	178	24	22	8	1	3	0	26	1	45	2	0
Anderson, Brian, Ari.*	4	9	.308	5.20	29	22	1	0	1	0	133.1	156	571	93	77	25	7	4	1	30	2	55	2	1
Anderson, Jimmy, Pit.*	9	11	.346	5.10	34	34	1	0	0	0	206.1	232	922	123	117	15	11	9	11	83	14	89	6	1
Ankiel, Rick, St.L*	1	2	.333	7.13	6	6	0	0	0	0	24.0	25	124	21	19	7	2	3	3	25	0	27	5	0
Appier, Kevin, N.Y.	11	10	.524	3.57	33	33	1	1	0	0	206.2	181	856	90	82	22	6	7	15	64	4	172	12	0
Armas, Tony, Mon.	9	14	.391	4.03	34	34	0	0	0	0	196.2	180	851	101	88	18	15	6	10	91	6	176	9	1
Arroyo, Bronson, Pit.	5	7	.417	5.09	24	13	1	0	1	0	88.1	99	390	54	50	12	4	6	4	34	6	39	4	1
Ashby, Andy, L.A.	2	0	1.000	3.86	2	2	0	0	0	0	11.2	14	49	5	5	2	0	0	0	1	0	7	0	0
Astacio, Pedro, Col.-Hou.	8	14	.364	5.09	26	26	4	1	0	0	169.2	181	733	101	96	22	6	5	13	54	3	144	2	0
Atchley, Justin, Cin.*	0	0	.000	6.10	15	0	0	0	4	0	10.1	12	48	7	7	4	0	0	1	5	2	8	1	0
Aybar, Manny, Chi.	2	1	.667	6.35	17	1	0	0	1	0	22.2	28	113	19	16	5	1	1	2	17	0	16	2	0
Baez, Benito, Fla.*	0	0	.000	13.50	8	0	0	0	3	0	9.1	22	55	14	14	3	0	0	0	6	0	14	0	0
Baldwin, James, L.A.	3	6	.333	4.20	12	12	0	0	0	0	79.1	82	333	39	37	10	4	2	3	25	1	53	3	0
Batista, Miguel, Ari.	11	8	.579	3.36	48	18	0	0	6	0	139.1	113	581	57	52	13	0	3	10	60	2	90	6	0
Beckett, Josh, Fla.	2	2	.500	1.50	4	4	0	0	0	0	24.0	14	99	9	4	3	0	0	1	11	0	24	1	0
Beimel, Joe, Pit.*	7	11	.389	5.23	42	15	0	0	9	0	115.1	131	511	72	67	12	3	1	6	49	4	58	3	0
Belitz, Todd, Col.*	1	1	.500	7.71	8	0	0	0	3	0	9.1	9	40	8	8	2	1	0	0	3	0	5	0	0

Pitcher, Team	W	L	Pct.	ERA	G	GS	CG	ShO	GF	Sv.	IP	H	TBF	R	ER	HR	SH	SF	HB	BB	IBB	SO	WP	Bk.
Bell, Rob, Cin.	0	5	.000	5.48	9	9	0	0	0	0	44.1	46	188	28	27	9	0	1	3	17	1	33	1	0
Benes, Alan, St.L	2	0	1.000	7.36	9	1	0	0	4	0	14.2	14	68	12	12	5	0	0	0	12	0	10	0	0
Benes, Andy, St.L	7	7	.500	7.38	27	19	0	0	3	0	107.1	122	500	92	88	30	3	4	6	61	0	78	1	0
Benitez, Armando, N.Y.	6	4	.600	3.77	73	0	0	0	64	43	76.1	59	320	32	32	12	2	1	1	40	6	93	5	0
Bere, Jason, Chi.	11	11	.500	4.31	32	32	2	0	0	0	188.0	171	801	99	90	24	7	6	1	77	7	175	6	0
Bierbrodt, Nick, Ari.*	2	2	.500	8.22	5	5	0	0	0	0	23.0	29	108	21	21	6	0	1	0	12	0	17	0	0
Blank, Matt, Mon.*	2	2	.500	5.16	5	4	0	0	0	0	22.2	23	104	14	13	5	1	2	2	13	1	11	0	0
Boehringer, Brian, S.F.	0	3	.000	4.19	29	0	0	0	9	1	34.1	32	156	20	16	4	1	2	2	17	5	27	0	0
Bohanon, Brian, Col.*	5	8	.385	7.14	20	19	0	0	0	0	97.0	127	456	79	77	20	8	1	7	47	3	47	2	0
Bones, Ricky, Fla.	4	4	.500	5.06	61	0	0	0	19	0	64.0	71	288	39	36	7	2	2	3	33	9	41	0	0
Bonilla, Bobby, St.L	0	0	.000	18.00	1	0	0	0	1	0	1.0	3	6	2	2	1	0	0	0	1	0	0	1	0
Borowski, Joe, Chi.	0	1	.000	32.40	1	1	0	0	0	0	1.2	6	13	6	6	1	1	0	0	3	0	1	0	0
Bottalico, Ricky, Phi.	3	4	.429	3.90	66	0	0	0	18	3	67.0	58	281	31	29	11	7	4	4	25	2	57	5	0
Bottenfield, Kent, Hou.	2	5	.286	6.40	13	9	0	0	1	1	52.0	61	235	44	37	16	1	4	2	16	0	39	1	0
Brock, Chris, Phi.	3	0	1.000	4.13	24	0	0	0	6	0	32.2	35	147	16	15	6	2	1	2	15	2	26	2	0
Brohawn, Troy, Ari.*	2	3	.400	4.93	59	0	0	0	10	1	49.1	55	220	27	27	5	2	4	1	23	2	30	2	0
Brower, Jim, Cin.	7	10	.412	3.97	46	10	0	0	13	1	129.1	119	559	65	57	17	9	3	5	60	5	94	5	1
Brown, Kevin, L.A.	10	4	.714	2.65	20	19	1	0	0	0	115.2	94	465	41	34	8	5	0	2	38	2	104	3	1
Buddie, Mike, Mil.	0	1	.000	3.89	31	0	0	0	7	2	41.2	34	174	20	18	2	0	2	4	17	2	22	3	0
Burkett, John, Atl.	12	12	.500	3.04	34	34	1	1	0	0	219.1	187	902	83	74	17	6	7	6	70	13	187	5	1
Burnett, A.J., Fla.	11	12	.478	4.05	27	27	2	1	0	0	173.1	145	733	82	78	20	6	8	7	83	3	128	7	1
Byrd, Paul, Phi.	0	1	.000	8.10	3	1	0	0	1	0	10.0	10	45	9	9	1	2	2	1	4	0	3	1	0
Cabrera, Jose, Atl.	7	4	.636	2.88	55	0	0	0	23	2	59.1	52	253	24	19	5	2	6	2	25	4	43	3	1
Carrara, Giovanni, L.A.	6	1	.857	3.16	47	3	0	0	2	0	85.1	73	348	30	30	12	6	1	1	24	3	70	0	0
Chacon, Shawn, Col.	6	10	.375	5.06	27	27	0	0	0	0	160.0	157	711	96	90	26	6	3	10	87	10	134	6	0
Chen, Bruce, Phi.-N.Y.*	7	7	.500	4.87	27	27	0	0	0	0	146.0	146	634	90	79	29	4	7	1	59	4	126	5	0
Chiasson, Scott, Chi.	1	1	.500	2.70	6	0	0	0	3	0	6.2	5	28	2	2	2	0	0	1	2	0	6	1	0
Chouinard, Bobby, Col.	0	0	.000	8.22	8	0	0	0	5	0	7.2	10	34	7	7	4	0	0	0	1	1	5	0	0
Christiansen, Jason, St.L-S.F.*	2	1	.667	3.22	55	0	0	0	11	3	36.1	29	149	13	13	5	1	3	1	15	1	31	4	0
Christman, Tim, Col.*	0	0	.000	4.50	1	0	0	0	1	0	2.0	1	7	1	1	0	1	0	0	0	0	2	0	0
Clement, Matt, Fla.	9	10	.474	5.05	31	31	0	0	0	0	169.1	172	760	102	95	15	14	3	15	85	2	134	15	0
Coggin, David, Phi.	6	7	.462	4.17	17	17	0	0	0	0	95.0	99	415	46	44	7	4	3	5	39	6	62	3	0
Cook, Dennis, N.Y.-Phi.*	1	1	.500	4.53	62	0	0	0	14	0	45.2	43	194	23	23	8	3	1	2	14	3	38	3	1
Coppinger, Rocky, Mil.	1	0	1.000	6.75	8	3	0	0	2	0	22.2	24	104	17	17	5	2	1	1	15	0	15	2	0
Corey, Mark, N.Y.	0	0	.000	16.20	2	0	0	0	0	0	1.2	5	13	3	3	0	0	0	0	3	1	3	0	0
Cormier, Rheal, Phi.*	5	6	.455	4.21	60	0	0	0	16	1	51.1	49	222	26	24	5	3	0	4	17	4	37	1	0
Cruz, Juan, Chi.	3	1	.750	3.22	8	8	0	0	0	0	44.2	40	185	16	16	4	2	2	17	1	39	0	0	
Cruz, Nelson, Hou.	3	3	.500	4.15	66	0	0	0	16	2	82.1	72	342	41	38	11	3	2	9	24	4	75	0	1
Cubillan, Darwin, Mon.	0	3	.000	4.10	29	0	0	0	11	0	26.1	31	121	13	12	1	1	3	0	12	1	19	1	0
Cunnane, Will, Mil.	0	3	.000	5.40	31	1	0	0	6	0	51.2	66	238	34	31	6	7	1	2	22	6	37	0	0
Daal, Omar, Phi.*	13	7	.650	4.46	32	32	0	0	0	0	185.2	199	801	100	92	26	7	5	5	56	3	107	5	0
D'Amico, Jeff C., Mil.	2	4	.333	6.08	10	10	0	0	0	0	47.1	60	216	42	32	11	2	1	1	16	4	32	2	0
Darensbourg, Vic, Fla.*	1	2	.333	4.25	58	0	0	0	19	1	48.2	52	202	24	23	4	1	2	1	10	6	33	0	0
Davenport, Joe, Col.	0	0	.000	3.48	7	0	0	0	3	0	10.1	8	44	7	4	1	1	0	0	7	0	8	0	0
Davey, Tom, S.D.	2	4	.333	4.50	39	0	0	0	8	0	38.0	41	169	22	19	3	0	1	1	17	3	37	3	1
Davis, Lance, Cin.*	8	4	.667	4.74	20	20	1	0	0	0	106.1	124	461	60	56	12	4	0	1	34	0	53	2	0
Davis, Kane, Col.	2	4	.333	4.35	57	0	0	0	6	0	68.1	66	301	36	33	11	2	4	1	32	4	47	4	0
DeJean, Mike, Mil.	4	2	.667	2.77	75	0	0	0	19	2	84.1	75	371	31	26	4	1	4	9	39	7	68	8	0
De Los Santos, Valerio, Mil.*	0	0	.000	9.00	1	0	0	0	1	0	1.0	1	5	1	1	0	0	0	0	1	0	1	0	0
Dempster, Ryan, Fla.	15	12	.556	4.94	34	34	2	1	0	0	211.1	218	954	123	116	21	15	7	10	112	5	171	5	0
Dessens, Elmer, Cin.	10	14	.417	4.48	34	34	1	1	0	0	205.0	221	862	103	102	32	7	7	1	56	1	128	4	1
Dingman, Craig, Col.	0	0	.000	13.50	7	0	0	0	4	1	7.1	11	37	11	11	4	1	0	2	3	2	2	0	0
Donnels, Chris, L.A.	0	0	.000	0.00	1	0	0	0	1	0	0.1	1	1	0	0	0	0	0	0	0	0	0	0	0
Dotel, Octavio, Hou.	7	5	.583	2.66	61	4	0	0	20	2	105.0	79	438	35	31	5	2	2	2	47	2	145	4	0
Dreifort, Darren, L.A.	4	7	.364	5.13	16	16	0	0	0	0	94.2	89	416	62	54	11	7	1	6	47	0	91	10	0
Duckworth, Brandon, Phi.	3	2	.600	3.52	11	11	0	0	0	0	69.0	57	289	29	27	2	7	3	6	29	5	40	2	0
Duncan, Courtney, Chi.	3	3	.500	5.06	36	0	0	0	15	0	42.2	42	193	24	24	5	1	3	2	25	3	49	2	0
Eaton, Adam, S.D.	8	6	.615	4.32	17	17	2	0	0	0	116.2	108	499	61	56	20	3	2	5	40	3	109	3	0
Eischen, Joey, Mon.*	0	1	.000	4.85	24	0	0	0	7	0	29.2	29	131	17	16	4	1	0	1	16	1	19	1	0
Elarton, Scott, Hou.-Col.	4	10	.286	7.06	24	24	0	0	0	0	132.2	146	595	105	104	34	7	6	4	59	2	87	5	0
Ellis, Robert, Ari.	6	5	.545	5.77	19	17	0	0	1	0	92.0	106	413	61	59	12	6	7	4	34	2	41	3	2
Embree, Alan, S.F.*	0	2	.000	11.25	22	0	0	0	7	0	20.0	34	106	26	25	7	0	3	2	10	2	25	1	0
Estes, Shawn, S.F.*	9	8	.529	4.02	27	27	0	0	0	0	159.0	151	693	78	71	11	5	9	5	77	7	109	10	1
Estrada, Horacio, Col.*	1	1	.500	14.54	4	0	0	0	2	0	4.1	8	22	7	7	1	0	0	1	1	0	4	0	0
Farnsworth, Kyle, Chi.	4	6	.400	2.74	76	0	0	0	24	2	82.0	65	339	26	25	8	2	1	2	29	2	107	2	2
Fassero, Jeff, Chi.*	4	4	.500	3.42	82	0	0	0	30	12	73.2	66	308	31	28	6	1	2	1	23	5	79	3	0
Fernandez, Jared, Cin.	0	1	.000	4.38	5	2	0	0	2	0	12.1	13	57	9	6	1	0	0	2	6	0	5	1	0
Fernandez, Osvaldo, Cin.	5	6	.455	6.92	20	14	0	0	2	0	79.1	103	366	62	61	8	4	3	0	33	3	35	0	0
Fetters, Mike, L.A.-Pit.	3	2	.600	5.51	54	0	0	0	21	9	47.1	49	223	32	29	7	1	3	4	26	1	37	7	0
Figueroa, Nelson, Phi.	4	5	.444	3.94	19	13	0	0	1	0	89.0	95	393	40	39	8	4	0	7	37	3	61	2	0
Fikac, Jeremy, S.D.	2	0	1.000	1.37	23	0	0	0	5	0	26.1	15	99	6	4	2	2	0	1	5	1	19	0	0
Finley, Steve, Ari.*	0	0	.000	0.00	1	0	0	0	1	0	1.0	0	4	0	0	0	0	0	0	1	0	0	0	0
Fox, Chad, Mil.	5	2	.714	1.89	65	0	0	0	9	2	66.2	44	287	16	14	6	2	1	5	36	7	80	5	1
Franco, John, N.Y.*	6	2	.750	4.05	58	0	0	0	16	2	53.1	55	232	25	24	8	2	1	2	19	2	50	4	1
Franklin, Wayne, Hou.*	0	0	.000	6.75	11	0	0	0	3	0	12.0	17	60	9	9	4	0	0	9	0	9	0	0	
Fultz, Aaron, S.F.*	3	1	.750	4.56	66	0	0	0	17	1	71.0	70	300	40	36	9	3	4	1	21	3	67	1	0
Fyhrie, Mike, Chi.	0	2	.000	4.20	15	0	0	0	4	0	15.0	16	64	7	7	1	0	0	0	7	0	6	0	0
Gagne, Eric, L.A.	6	7	.462	4.75	33	24	0	0	3	0	151.2	144	649	90	80	24	6	8	16	46	1	130	3	1
Gandarillas, Gus, Mil.	0	0	.000	5.49	16	0	0	0	5	0	19.2	25	91	13	12	3	0	0	13	3	7	1	0	
Gardner, Mark, S.F.	5	5	.500	5.40	23	15	0	0	2	0	91.2	93	398	57	55	17	4	3	4	34	3	53	0	0
Glavine, Tom, Atl.*	16	7	.696	3.57	35	35	1	1	0	0	219.1	213	929	92	87	24	5	8	2	97	10	116	2	0
Gomes, Wayne, Phi.-S.F.	6	3	.667	5.29	55	0	0	0	16	1	63.0	72	285	37	37	7	6	4	1	29	6	52	4	0

Pitcher, Team	W	L	Pct.	ERA	G	GS	CG	ShO	GF	Sv.	IP	H	TBF	R	ER	HR	SH	SF	HB	BB	IBB	SO	WP	Bk.
Gonzalez, Dicky, N.Y.	3	2	.600	4.88	16	7	0	0	2	0	59.0	72	261	33	32	4	2	6	1	17	3	31	5	0
Gordon, Tom, Chi.	1	2	.333	3.38	47	0	0	0	40	27	45.1	32	187	18	17	4	0	0	1	16	1	67	2	0
Graves, Danny, Cin.	6	5	.545	4.15	66	0	0	0	54	32	80.1	83	337	41	37	7	3	2	4	18	6	49	2	1
Grilli, Jason, Fla.	2	2	.500	6.08	6	5	0	0	1	0	26.2	30	115	18	18	6	1	0	2	11	0	17	0	0
Guzman, Geraldo, Ari.	0	0	.000	2.89	4	0	0	0	0	0	9.1	7	37	4	3	2	0	0	0	3	1	4	0	0
Hackman, Luther, St.L	1	2	.333	4.29	35	0	0	0	8	1	35.2	28	149	18	17	7	1	0	2	14	0	24	1	1
Hamilton, Joey, Cin.	1	2	.333	6.23	4	4	0	0	0	0	17.1	23	79	12	12	3	2	0	1	6	0	10	0	0
Hampton, Mike, Col.*	14	13	.519	5.41	32	32	2	1	0	0	203.0	236	904	138	122	31	8	6	8	85	7	122	6	0
Harnisch, Pete, Cin.	1	3	.250	6.37	7	7	0	0	0	0	35.1	48	172	29	25	9	0	3	1	17	0	17	2	0
Haynes, Jimmy, Mil.	8	17	.320	4.85	31	29	0	0	0	0	172.2	182	756	98	93	20	14	7	4	78	17	112	8	0
Heredia, Felix, Chi.*	2	2	.500	6.17	48	0	0	0	9	0	35.0	45	165	27	24	6	1	3	2	16	1	28	3	0
Herges, Matt, L.A.	9	8	.529	3.44	75	0	0	0	22	1	99.1	97	435	39	38	8	4	3	8	46	12	76	2	0
Hermanson, Dustin, St.L	14	13	.519	4.45	33	33	0	0	0	0	192.1	195	830	100	95	34	7	2	8	73	3	123	6	0
Hernandez, Carlos E., Hou.*	1	0	1.000	1.02	3	3	0	0	0	0	17.2	11	70	2	2	1	1	0	0	7	0	17	2	0
Hernandez, Livan, S.F.	13	15	.464	5.24	34	34	2	0	0	0	226.2	266	1008	143	132	24	12	12	3	85	7	138	7	0
Herndon, Junior, S.D.	2	6	.250	6.33	12	8	0	0	2	0	42.2	55	201	34	30	5	2	0	3	25	5	14	1	0
Hinchliffe, Brett, N.Y.	0	1	.000	36.00	1	1	0	0	0	0	2.0	9	17	8	8	2	1	0	1	1	0	2	0	0
Hitchcock, Sterling, S.D.*	1	2	.667	3.32	3	3	0	0	0	0	19.0	22	85	9	7	1	1	0	1	3	0	15	1	0
Hoffman, Trevor, S.D.	3	4	.429	3.43	62	0	0	0	55	43	60.1	48	248	25	23	10	2	2	1	21	2	63	3	0
Hutchinson, Chad, St.L	0	0	.000	24.75	3	0	0	0	0	0	4.0	9	27	11	11	3	0	0	1	6	0	2	1	0
Irabu, Hideki, Mon.	0	2	.000	4.86	3	3	0	0	0	0	16.2	22	74	9	9	3	0	1	0	3	0	18	0	0
Jackson, Mike, Hou.	5	3	.625	4.70	67	0	0	0	16	4	69.0	68	292	36	36	14	4	2	2	22	3	46	2	0
James, Mike, St.L	1	2	.333	5.21	40	0	0	0	11	0	38.0	43	173	24	22	5	3	1	5	17	2	26	3	0
Jarvis, Kevin, S.D.	12	11	.522	4.79	32	32	1	1	0	0	193.1	189	809	107	103	37	7	4	5	49	4	133	1	0
Jennings, Jason, Col.	4	1	.800	4.58	7	7	1	1	0	0	39.1	42	174	21	20	2	1	1	1	19	0	26	1	0
Jensen, Ryan, S.F.	1	2	.333	4.25	10	7	0	0	2	0	42.1	44	193	21	20	5	0	4	0	25	0	26	2	0
Jimenez, Jose, Col.	6	1	.857	4.09	56	0	0	0	49	17	55.0	56	237	27	25	6	2	1	0	22	4	37	3	0
Jodie, Brett, S.D.	0	1	.000	4.63	7	2	0	0	0	0	23.1	19	96	12	12	7	1	0	0	12	1	13	1	0
Johnson, Mike, Mon.	0	0	.000	4.76	10	0	0	0	0	0	11.1	13	50	6	6	3	0	0	2	4	0	10	2	0
Johnson, Randy, Ari.*	21	6	.778	2.49	35	34	3	2	1	0	249.2	181	994	74	69	19	10	5	18	71	2	372	8	1
Jones, Bobby J., S.D.	8	19	.296	5.12	33	33	1	0	0	0	195.0	250	880	137	111	37	9	9	4	38	6	113	3	0
Karnuth, Jason, St.L	0	0	.000	1.80	4	0	0	0	1	0	5.0	6	24	1	1	0	0	1	0	4	0	1	0	0
Karsay, Steve, Atl.	3	4	.429	3.43	43	0	0	0	21	7	44.2	44	190	21	17	4	3	3	1	17	8	39	1	0
Kile, Darryl, St.L	16	11	.593	3.09	34	34	2	1	0	0	227.1	228	950	80	78	22	13	5	11	65	3	179	6	1
Kim, Byung-Hyun, Ari.	5	6	.455	2.94	78	0	0	0	44	19	98.0	58	392	32	32	10	5	0	8	44	3	113	5	1
King, Ray, Mil.*	0	4	.000	3.60	82	0	0	0	19	1	55.0	49	234	22	22	5	3	2	1	25	7	40	2	0
Kline, Steve, St.L*	3	3	.500	1.80	89	0	0	0	26	9	75.0	53	303	16	15	3	4	5	4	29	7	54	1	0
Knott, Eric, Ari.*	0	1	.000	1.93	3	1	0	0	0	0	4.2	8	25	9	1	0	0	2	0	4	0	4	0	0
Knotts, Gary, Fla.	0	1	.000	6.00	2	1	0	0	0	0	6.0	7	28	4	4	1	0	0	2	1	0	9	0	0
Kolb, Brandon, Mil.	0	0	.000	13.03	10	0	0	0	3	0	9.2	16	53	16	14	6	0	2	0	8	0	8	1	0
Koplove, Mike, Ari.	0	1	.000	3.60	9	0	0	0	1	0	10.0	8	50	7	4	1	1	0	2	9	1	14	1	0
Lawrence, Brian, S.D.	5	5	.500	3.45	27	15	1	0	5	0	114.2	107	484	53	44	10	4	3	5	34	5	84	1	0
Lee, David, S.D.	1	0	1.000	3.70	41	0	0	0	11	0	48.2	52	222	20	20	6	1	1	6	27	1	42	1	1
Leiter, Al, N.Y.*	11	11	.500	3.31	29	29	0	0	0	0	187.1	178	772	81	69	18	9	6	4	46	3	142	5	2
Leiter, Mark, Mil.	2	1	.667	3.75	20	3	0	0	3	0	36.0	32	149	16	15	6	1	0	2	8	2	26	3	0
Leskanic, Curtis, Mil.	2	6	.250	3.63	70	0	0	0	58	17	69.1	63	297	30	28	11	3	0	2	31	5	64	2	0
Levrault, Allen, Mil.	6	10	.375	6.06	32	20	1	0	0	0	130.2	146	593	93	88	27	3	4	7	59	7	80	2	1
Lieber, Jon, Chi.	20	6	.769	3.80	34	34	5	1	0	0	232.1	226	948	104	98	25	13	9	7	41	4	148	4	1
Ligtenberg, Kerry, Atl.	3	3	.500	3.02	53	0	0	0	24	1	59.2	50	254	22	20	4	1	2	0	30	8	56	3	0
Lima, Jose, Hou.	1	2	.333	7.30	14	9	0	0	3	0	53.0	77	249	48	43	12	4	4	5	16	1	41	3	0
Lincoln, Mike, Pit.	2	1	.667	2.68	31	0	0	0	5	0	40.1	34	168	16	12	3	1	1	4	11	0	24	2	0
Linebrink, Scott, Hou.	0	0	.000	2.61	9	0	0	0	2	0	10.1	6	44	4	3	0	1	2	6	0	9	1	0
Lira, Felipe, Mon.	0	0	.000	12.60	4	0	0	0	1	0	5.0	11	28	7	7	1	1	0	0	2	0	3	0	0
Lloyd, Graeme, Mon.*	9	5	.643	4.35	84	0	0	0	28	1	70.1	74	303	38	34	6	2	2	6	21	2	44	1	0
Loewer, Carlton, S.D.	0	2	.000	24.92	2	2	0	0	0	0	4.1	13	29	12	12	2	1	0	0	3	0	1	0	0
Loiselle, Rich, Pit.	0	0	.000	11.50	18	0	0	0	9	1	18.0	28	101	24	23	3	2	0	4	17	4	9	3	0
Looper, Braden, Fla.	3	3	.500	3.55	71	0	0	0	21	3	71.0	63	295	28	28	8	0	3	2	30	3	52	0	0
Lopez, Albie, Ari.	4	7	.364	4.00	13	13	2	2	0	0	81.0	74	329	36	36	10	3	2	0	24	2	69	1	0
Loretta, Mark, Mil.	0	0	.000	0.00	1	0	0	0	1	0	1.0	1	5	0	0	0	0	0	0	1	0	2	0	0
Lundquist, David, S.D.	0	1	.000	5.95	17	0	0	0	9	0	19.2	20	86	13	13	1	0	1	1	7	1	19	2	1
Mabry, John, Fla.	0	0	.000	135.00	1	0	0	0	0	0	0.1	3	7	5	5	0	0	0	0	3	0	0	0	0
MacRae, Scott, Cin.	0	1	.000	4.02	24	0	0	0	7	0	31.1	33	136	15	14	0	0	2	2	8	0	18	1	0
Maddux, Greg, Atl.	17	11	.607	3.05	34	34	3	3	0	0	233.0	220	927	86	79	20	12	11	7	27	10	173	2	0
Mahay, Ron, Chi.*	0	0	.000	2.61	17	0	0	0	4	0	20.2	14	86	6	6	4	0	0	0	15	1	24	1	0
Mann, Jim, Hou.	0	0	.000	3.38	4	0	0	0	1	0	5.1	3	23	2	2	0	0	0	2	4	0	5	0	0
Mantei, Matt, Ari.	0	0	.000	2.57	8	0	0	0	7	2	7.0	6	31	2	2	2	0	0	0	4	0	12	2	0
Manzanillo, Josias, Pit.	3	2	.600	3.39	71	0	0	0	25	2	79.2	60	329	32	30	4	5	8	5	26	3	80	4	0
Marquis, Jason, Atl.	5	6	.455	3.48	38	16	0	0	9	0	129.1	113	556	62	50	14	6	5	4	59	4	98	1	2
Marte, Damaso, Pit.*	0	1	.000	4.71	23	0	0	0	4	0	36.1	34	154	21	19	5	1	2	3	12	3	39	1	0
Martin, Tom, N.Y.*	1	0	1.000	10.06	14	0	0	0	2	0	17.0	23	85	22	19	4	1	1	1	10	2	12	0	0
Martinez, Ramon J., Pit.	0	2	.000	8.62	4	4	0	0	0	0	15.2	16	77	15	15	4	0	1	2	16	0	9	1	0
Mathews, T.J., St.L	1	1	.500	3.07	10	0	0	0	3	0	14.2	11	56	6	5	2	0	1	0	10	0	10	0	0
Mattes, Troy, Mon.	3	3	.500	6.00	8	8	0	0	0	0	45.0	51	207	33	30	9	2	1	4	21	2	26	6	0
Matthews, Mike, St.L*	3	4	.429	3.24	51	10	0	0	7	1	89.0	74	368	32	32	11	4	1	4	33	4	72	4	1
Maurer, Dave, S.D.*	0	0	.000	10.80	3	0	0	0	1	0	5.0	8	27	6	6	1	0	0	0	4	0	4	1	0
McElroy, Chuck, S.D.*	1	1	.500	5.16	31	0	0	0	6	0	29.2	38	144	24	17	6	1	1	0	18	4	25	3	0
McKnight, Tony, Hou.-Pit.	3	6	.333	4.95	15	15	0	0	0	0	87.1	109	396	52	48	19	4	3	5	24	4	46	5	0
Mercado, Hector, Cin.*	3	2	.600	4.08	56	0	0	0	10	0	53.0	55	240	27	24	6	1	2	0	30	1	59	4	0
Mesa, Jose, Phi.	3	3	.500	2.34	71	0	0	0	59	42	69.1	65	291	26	18	4	3	2	2	20	2	59	2	1
Miceli, Dan, Fla.-Col.	5	2	.286	4.80	51	0	0	0	15	1	45.0	47	199	29	24	7	2	2	0	16	2	48	4	0
Middlebrook, Jason, S.D.	2	1	.667	5.12	4	3	0	0	0	0	19.1	18	85	11	11	6	1	0	1	10	1	10	0	0
Miller, Wade, Hou.	16	8	.667	3.40	32	32	1	0	0	0	212.0	183	873	91	80	31	7	5	4	76	3	183	8	0

Pitcher, Team	W	L	Pct.	ERA	G	GS	CG	ShO	GF	Sv.	IP	H	TBF	R	ER	HR	SH	SF	HB	BB	IBB	SO	WP	Bk.
Millwood, Kevin, Atl.	7	7	.500	4.31	21	21	0	0	0	0	121.0	121	515	66	58	20	7	2	1	40	6	84	5	1
Mlicki, Dave, Hou.	7	3	.700	5.09	19	14	0	0	1	0	86.2	85	381	53	49	18	6	6	9	33	1	49	5	0
Mohler, Mike, Ari.*	0	0	.000	7.24	13	0	0	0	5	0	13.2	14	61	11	11	3	2	1	0	9	0	7	1	0
Moore, Trey, Atl.*	0	0	.000	11.25	2	0	0	0	0	0	4.0	7	21	5	5	0	0	0	0	2	0	1	1	0
Morgan, Mike, Ari.	1	0	1.000	4.26	31	1	0	0	9	0	38.0	45	168	20	18	2	2	2	0	17	4	24	2	0
Morris, Matt, St.L	22	8	.733	3.16	34	34	2	1	0	0	216.1	218	909	86	76	13	14	5	13	54	3	185	5	1
Moss, Damian, Atl.*	0	0	.000	3.00	5	1	0	0	2	0	9.0	3	41	3	3	1	1	0	0	9	0	8	1	0
Mota, Guillermo, Mon.	1	3	.250	5.26	53	0	0	0	12	0	49.2	51	212	30	29	9	3	2	1	18	1	31	1	0
Mulholland, Terry, Pit.-L.A.*	1	1	.500	4.66	41	4	0	0	8	0	65.2	78	285	35	34	12	1	1	2	17	1	42	1	0
Munoz, Bobby, Mon.	0	4	.000	5.14	15	7	0	0	4	0	42.0	53	193	25	24	6	5	0	2	21	1	21	2	0
Myers, Mike, Col.*	2	3	.400	3.60	73	0	0	0	14	0	40.0	32	169	17	16	2	1	1	1	24	7	36	0	0
Myers, Rodney L., S.D.	1	2	.333	5.32	37	0	0	0	16	1	47.1	53	211	31	28	6	1	4	4	20	0	29	2	0
Neagle, Denny, Col.*	9	8	.529	5.38	30	30	0	0	0	0	170.2	192	760	107	102	29	8	9	7	60	3	139	2	0
Neal, Blaine, Fla.	0	0	.000	6.75	4	0	0	0	0	0	5.1	7	28	4	4	0	0	0	0	5	0	3	1	0
Nelson, Joe, Atl.	0	0	.000	36.00	2	0	0	0	0	0	2.0	7	16	9	8	1	0	1	1	2	0	0	0	0
Nen, Robb, S.F.	4	5	.444	3.01	79	0	0	0	71	45	77.2	58	312	28	26	6	0	3	1	22	6	93	2	0
Neugebauer, Nickolas, Mil.	1	1	.500	7.50	2	2	0	0	0	0	6.0	6	30	5	5	1	0	0	0	6	0	11	0	0
Nichting, Chris, Cin.-Col.	0	3	.000	4.46	43	0	0	0	11	1	42.1	55	189	27	21	8	3	2	0	8	1	40	2	0
Nickle, Doug, Phi.	0	0	.000	0.00	2	0	0	0	2	0	2.0	1	7	0	0	0	0	0	0	0	0	1	0	0
Nitkowski, C.J., N.Y.*	1	0	1.000	0.00	5	0	0	0	2	0	5.2	3	21	0	0	0	0	0	0	3	1	4	0	0
Nunez, Jose, L.A.-S.D.*	4	2	.667	4.58	62	0	0	0	10	0	59.0	62	265	35	30	7	2	2	4	25	3	60	5	0
Nunez, Vladimir, Fla.	4	5	.444	2.74	52	3	0	0	13	0	92.0	79	380	33	28	9	2	5	5	30	5	64	1	1
Ohka, Tomo, Mon.	1	4	.200	4.77	10	10	0	0	0	0	54.2	65	228	30	29	8	1	1	1	10	0	31	1	0
Ohman, Will, Chi.*	0	1	.000	7.71	11	0	0	0	0	0	11.2	14	54	10	10	2	0	0	0	6	0	12	2	0
Olivares, Omar, Pit.	6	9	.400	6.55	45	12	1	0	15	1	110.0	123	494	87	80	17	3	4	10	42	8	69	3	1
Olsen, Kevin, Fla.	0	0	.000	1.20	4	2	0	0	0	0	15.0	11	56	2	2	0	0	0	0	2	1	13	0	0
Olson, Gregg, L.A.	0	1	.000	8.03	28	0	0	0	10	0	24.2	26	120	24	22	4	0	3	0	20	1	24	1	0
Oropesa, Eddie, Phi.*	1	0	1.000	4.74	30	0	0	0	4	0	19.0	16	87	10	10	1	1	0	0	17	6	15	1	0
Orosco, Jesse, L.A.*	0	1	.000	3.94	35	0	0	0	7	0	16.0	17	69	7	7	3	0	1	0	7	1	21	0	0
Ortiz, Russ, S.F.	17	9	.654	3.29	33	33	1	1	0	0	218.2	187	911	90	80	13	10	4	0	91	3	169	8	1
Osting, Jimmy, S.D.*	0	0	.000	0.00	3	0	0	0	1	0	2.0	1	9	0	0	0	0	0	0	2	1	3	0	0
Oswalt, Roy, Hou.	14	3	.824	2.73	28	20	3	1	4	0	141.2	126	575	48	43	13	4	4	6	24	2	144	0	0
Padilla, Vicente, Phi.	3	1	.750	4.24	23	0	0	0	5	0	34.0	36	144	18	16	1	0	0	0	12	0	29	1	0
Painter, Lance, Mil.*	1	0	1.000	4.22	13	0	0	0	4	0	10.2	11	48	5	5	3	0	0	0	7	2	6	0	0
Park, Chan Ho, L.A.	15	11	.577	3.50	36	35	2	1	0	0	234.0	183	981	98	91	23	16	7	20	91	1	218	3	3
Pavano, Carl, Mon.	1	6	.143	6.33	8	8	0	0	0	0	42.2	59	199	33	30	7	2	1	2	16	1	36	0	1
Penny, Brad, Fla.	10	10	.500	3.69	31	31	1	1	0	0	205.0	183	833	92	84	15	8	2	7	54	3	154	2	0
Perez, Odalis, Atl.*	7	8	.467	4.91	24	16	0	0	1	0	95.1	108	418	55	52	7	3	3	1	39	0	71	2	3
Person, Robert, Phi.	15	7	.682	4.19	33	33	3	1	0	0	208.1	179	867	103	97	34	8	6	8	80	3	183	10	1
Peters, Chris, Mon.*	2	4	.333	7.55	13	6	0	0	1	0	31.0	47	149	26	26	7	2	2	2	15	1	14	4	0
Peterson, Kyle, Mil.	1	2	.333	5.52	3	2	0	0	0	0	14.2	19	68	10	9	3	1	0	0	4	2	12	0	0
Piersoll, Chris, Cin.	0	0	.000	2.38	11	0	0	0	3	0	11.1	12	52	4	3	0	0	0	1	6	0	7	0	0
Politte, Cliff, Phi.	2	3	.400	2.42	23	0	0	0	7	0	26.0	24	109	8	7	2	1	3	1	8	3	23	1	0
Powell, Jay, Hou.-Col.	5	3	.625	3.24	74	0	0	0	20	7	75.0	75	327	36	27	9	5	1	2	31	3	54	0	1
Powell, Brian, Hou.	0	1	.000	18.00	1	1	0	0	0	0	3.0	5	17	6	6	1	0	0	0	3	0	3	0	0
Prinz, Bret, Ari.	4	1	.800	2.63	46	0	0	0	26	9	41.0	33	174	13	12	4	3	1	1	19	1	27	1	1
Prokopec, Luke, L.A.	8	7	.533	4.88	29	22	0	0	2	0	138.1	146	596	80	75	27	4	3	4	40	1	91	3	2
Quevedo, Ruben, Mil.	4	5	.444	4.61	10	10	0	0	0	0	56.2	56	253	30	29	9	3	2	0	30	4	60	1	0
Reames, Britt, Mon.	4	8	.333	5.59	41	13	0	0	3	0	95.0	101	432	68	59	16	7	2	5	48	3	86	2	0
Redding, Tim, Hou.	3	1	.750	5.50	13	9	0	0	1	0	55.2	62	249	38	34	11	2	3	3	24	0	55	2	0
Reed, Rick, N.Y.	8	6	.571	3.48	20	20	3	1	0	0	134.2	119	531	53	52	16	8	1	1	17	3	99	2	0
Reed, Steve, Atl.	2	2	.500	3.48	39	0	0	0	6	1	31.0	30	134	14	12	3	3	1	1	13	3	25	0	0
Reith, Brian, Cin.	0	7	.000	7.81	9	8	0	0	0	0	40.1	56	192	37	35	13	4	2	2	16	0	22	1	0
Reitsma, Chris, Cin.	7	15	.318	5.29	36	29	0	0	1	0	182.0	209	800	121	107	23	13	8	5	49	6	96	5	0
Relaford, Desi, N.Y.	0	0	.000	0.00	1	0	0	0	1	0	1.0	0	3	0	0	0	0	0	0	0	0	1	0	0
Remlinger, Mike, Atl.*	3	3	.500	2.76	74	0	0	0	6	1	75.0	67	313	25	23	9	2	0	2	23	4	93	4	0
Reyes, Dennys, Cin.*	2	6	.250	4.92	35	6	0	0	2	0	53.0	51	246	35	29	5	2	2	1	35	1	52	5	0
Reyes, Al, L.A.	2	1	.667	3.86	19	0	0	0	9	1	25.2	28	120	13	11	3	0	2	1	13	1	23	0	1
Reynolds, Shane, Hou.	14	11	.560	4.34	28	28	3	0	0	0	182.2	208	772	95	88	24	13	2	4	36	2	102	2	0
Reynoso, Armando, Ari.	1	6	.143	5.98	9	9	0	0	0	0	46.2	58	207	32	31	13	2	2	4	13	2	15	1	0
Riedling, John, Cin.	1	1	.500	2.41	29	0	0	0	14	1	33.2	22	136	9	9	1	2	0	2	14	0	23	5	0
Rigdon, Paul, Mil.	3	5	.375	5.79	15	15	0	0	0	0	79.1	86	360	52	51	13	9	2	3	46	6	49	1	0
Riggan, Jerrod, N.Y.	3	3	.500	3.40	35	0	0	0	12	0	47.2	42	202	19	18	5	2	3	0	24	7	41	4	0
Rijo, Jose, Cin.	0	0	.000	2.12	13	0	0	0	4	0	17.0	19	80	6	4	2	1	0	0	9	2	12	1	1
Ritchie, Todd, Pit.	11	15	.423	4.47	33	33	4	2	0	0	207.1	211	887	118	103	23	9	5	7	52	7	124	7	0
Roberts, Grant, N.Y.	1	0	1.000	3.81	16	0	0	0	2	0	26.0	24	110	11	11	2	1	1	0	8	1	29	0	1
Rocker, John, Atl.*	2	2	.500	3.09	30	0	0	0	28	19	32.0	25	135	13	11	2	0	1	2	16	1	36	5	0
Rodriguez, Felix, S.F.	9	1	.900	1.68	80	0	0	0	13	0	80.1	53	314	16	15	5	1	3	1	27	2	91	1	0
Rodriguez, Frankie, Cin.	0	0	.000	11.42	7	0	0	0	2	0	8.2	16	47	12	11	1	1	1	0	5	2	9	2	0
Rodriguez, Wilfredo, Hou.*	0	0	.000	15.00	2	0	0	0	1	0	3.0	6	16	5	5	2	0	1	0	1	0	3	0	0
Rose, Brian, N.Y.	0	1	.000	4.15	3	0	0	0	0	0	8.2	10	37	4	4	3	0	0	0	2	1	4	0	0
Rueter, Kirk, S.F.*	14	12	.538	4.42	34	34	0	0	0	0	195.1	213	840	105	96	25	11	6	4	66	4	83	1	0
Ruffin, Johnny, Fla.	0	0	.000	4.91	3	0	0	0	1	0	3.2	5	21	4	2	0	0	0	1	4	1	4	0	0
Rusch, Glendon, N.Y.*	8	12	.400	4.63	33	33	1	0	0	0	179.0	216	785	101	92	23	11	5	7	43	2	156	3	2
Sabel, Erik, Ari.	3	2	.600	4.38	42	0	0	0	11	0	51.1	57	218	26	25	8	1	0	3	12	3	25	1	0
Sanchez, Jesus, Fla.*	2	4	.333	4.74	16	9	0	0	3	0	62.2	61	274	33	33	7	2	1	2	31	2	46	0	0
Santiago, Jose, Phi.	2	4	.333	3.61	53	0	0	0	5	0	62.1	66	261	25	25	3	1	2	2	13	1	28	0	0
Sauerbeck, Scott, Pit.*	2	2	.500	5.60	70	0	0	0	14	2	62.2	61	281	41	39	4	2	0	2	40	6	79	3	0
Scanlan, Bob, Mon.	0	0	.000	7.86	18	0	0	0	6	0	26.1	37	127	23	23	0	3	0	1	14	0	5	1	0
Schilling, Curt, Ari.	22	6	.786	2.98	35	35	6	1	0	0	256.2	237	1021	86	85	37	8	5	1	39	0	293	4	0
Schmidt, Jason, Pit.-S.F.	13	7	.650	4.07	25	25	1	0	0	0	150.1	138	641	75	68	13	5	3	7	61	3	142	8	1
Seanez, Rudy, S.D.-Atl.	0	2	.000	2.75	38	0	0	0	8	1	36.0	23	150	12	11	4	0	1	1	19	0	41	4	0

Pitcher, Team	W	L	Pct.	ERA	G	GS	CG	ShO	GF	Sv.	IP	H	TBF	R	ER	HR	SH	SF	HB	BB	IBB	SO	WP	Bk.
Seelbach, Chris, Atl.	0	0	.000	7.88	5	0	0	0	1	0	8.0	9	38	7	7	3	0	0	5	1	8	1	0
Serrano, Wascar, S.D.	3	3	.500	6.56	20	5	0	0	8	0	46.2	60	222	37	34	7	5	2	21	1	39	6	1
Shaw, Jeff, L.A.	3	5	.375	3.62	77	0	0	0	66	43	74.2	63	303	32	30	10	3	2	18	8	58	0	1
Sheets, Ben, Mil.	11	10	.524	4.76	26	25	1	1	0	0	151.1	166	653	89	80	23	8	5	5	48	6	94	3	0
Silva, Jose, Pit.	3	3	.500	6.75	26	0	0	0	10	0	32.0	35	140	24	24	6	2	0	0	9	1	23	0	0
Slusarski, Joe, Mil.-Hou.	0	1	.000	9.00	12	0	0	0	5	0	16.0	25	76	16	16	4	1	1	0	4	0	11	0	0
Smith, Chuck, Fla.	5	5	.500	4.70	15	15	0	0	0	0	88.0	89	385	47	46	10	4	4	6	35	4	71	0	1
Smith, Bud, St.L*	6	3	.667	3.83	16	14	1	1	1	0	84.2	79	351	40	36	12	9	1	1	24	5	59	0	0
Smoltz, John, Atl.	3	3	.500	3.36	36	5	0	0	20	10	59.0	53	238	24	22	7	1	2	2	10	2	57	0	0
Sobkowiak, Scott, Atl.	0	0	.000	9.00	1	0	0	0	1	0	1.0	2	5	1	1	0	0	0	0	0	0	0	0	0
Speier, Justin, Col.	4	3	.571	3.70	42	0	0	0	8	0	56.0	47	228	24	23	8	2	4	5	12	3	47	4	1
Spooneybarger, Tim, Atl.	0	0	.000	2.25	4	0	0	0	3	0	4.0	5	19	1	1	0	0	1	0	2	1	3	0	0
Springer, Dennis, L.A.	1	1	.500	3.32	4	3	0	0	1	0	19.0	19	75	7	7	3	1	0	3	2	0	7	2	0
Springer, Russ, Ari.	0	0	.000	7.13	18	0	0	0	9	1	17.2	20	79	16	14	5	1	1	0	4	0	12	2	0
Stechschulte, Gene, St.L	1	5	.167	3.86	67	0	0	0	18	6	70.0	71	301	35	30	10	4	3	4	30	2	51	2	0
Stewart, Scott, Mon.*	3	1	.750	3.78	62	0	0	0	9	3	47.2	43	199	20	20	5	2	4	3	13	0	39	2	0
Stone, Ricky, Hou.	0	0	.000	2.35	6	0	0	0	3	0	7.2	8	33	3	2	1	0	0	0	2	1	4	0	0
Strickland, Scott, Mon.	2	6	.250	3.21	77	0	0	0	31	9	81.1	67	351	36	29	9	3	1	4	41	5	85	4	0
Strong, Joe, Fla.	0	0	.000	1.35	5	0	0	0	2	0	6.2	3	25	1	1	1	0	0	0	3	0	4	0	0
Sullivan, Scott, Cin.	7	1	.875	3.31	79	0	0	0	16	0	103.1	94	437	44	38	10	1	5	8	36	8	82	0	0
Suzuki, Mac, Col.-Mil.	3	7	.300	6.35	18	10	0	0	1	0	62.1	61	291	49	44	8	4	0	5	48	3	52	10	0
Swindell, Greg, Ari.*	2	6	.250	4.53	64	0	0	0	18	2	53.2	51	214	27	27	12	1	1	0	8	2	42	1	0
Tabaka, Jeff, St.L*	0	0	.000	7.36	8	0	0	0	0	0	3.2	6	17	3	3	1	0	0	1	0	3	0	0
Tapani, Kevin, Chi.	9	14	.391	4.49	29	29	0	0	0	0	168.1	186	729	93	84	24	12	3	7	40	6	149	3	0
Tavarez, Julian, Chi.	10	9	.526	4.52	34	28	0	0	1	0	161.1	172	712	98	81	13	8	4	11	69	4	107	2	1
Taylor, Billy, Pit.	0	0	.000	4.50	1	0	0	0	0	0	2.0	2	8	1	1	1	0	0	0	0	0	3	0	0
Telemaco, Amaury, Phi.	5	5	.500	5.54	24	14	1	0	2	0	89.1	93	388	59	55	15	5	2	9	32	3	59	3	0
Telford, Anthony, Mon.	0	1	.000	10.29	8	0	0	0	0	0	7.0	14	41	12	8	2	1	0	1	5	1	5	1	0
Thomson, John, Col.	4	5	.444	4.04	14	14	1	1	0	0	93.2	84	386	46	42	15	3	3	4	25	3	68	1	0
Thurman, Mike, Mon.	9	11	.450	5.33	28	26	0	0	0	0	147.0	172	658	90	87	21	8	9	6	50	7	96	8	0
Timlin, Mike, St.L	4	5	.444	4.09	67	0	0	0	19	3	72.2	78	307	35	33	6	1	2	3	19	4	47	3	1
Tollberg, Brian, S.D.	10	4	.714	4.30	19	19	0	0	0	0	117.1	133	503	58	56	15	5	7	2	25	3	71	1	0
Trachsel, Steve, N.Y.	11	13	.458	4.46	28	28	1	1	0	0	173.2	168	726	90	86	28	8	7	3	47	7	144	4	0
Trombley, Mike, L.A.	0	4	.000	6.56	19	0	0	0	10	0	23.1	27	108	17	17	5	4	1	0	13	3	27	0	0
Urbina, Ugueth, Mon.	2	1	.667	4.24	45	0	0	0	40	15	46.2	42	201	24	22	8	1	1	0	21	1	57	2	1
Valdes, Marc, Atl.	1	0	1.000	7.71	9	0	0	0	3	0	7.0	7	28	6	6	4	0	0	0	1	0	3	0	0
Van Poppel, Todd, Chi.	4	1	.800	2.52	59	0	0	0	18	0	75.0	63	324	22	21	9	4	0	0	38	4	90	5	1
Vazquez, Javier, Mon.	16	11	.593	3.42	32	32	5	3	0	0	223.2	197	890	92	85	24	0	2	3	44	4	208	3	1
Veres, Dave, St.L	3	2	.600	3.70	71	0	0	0	44	15	65.2	57	279	29	27	12	2	1	2	28	1	61	6	0
Villone, Ron, Col.-Hou.*	6	10	.375	5.89	53	12	0	0	12	0	114.2	133	523	81	75	18	1	1	5	53	5	113	4	1
Vogelsong, Ryan, S.F.-Pit.	0	5	.000	6.75	15	2	0	0	8	0	34.2	39	164	31	26	6	0	1	2	20	1	24	2	0
Vosberg, Ed, Phi.*	0	0	.000	2.84	18	0	0	0	4	0	12.2	8	46	4	4	0	0	0	0	3	0	11	0	1
Wagner, Billy, Hou.*	2	5	.286	2.73	64	0	0	0	50	39	62.2	44	261	19	19	5	3	1	5	20	0	79	3	0
Walker, Kevin, S.D.*	0	0	.000	3.00	16	0	0	0	5	0	12.0	5	49	4	4	0	0	0	8	2	17	0	1
Walker, Pete, N.Y.	0	0	.000	2.70	2	0	0	0	1	0	6.2	6	25	2	2	0	0	0	0	0	0	4	0	0
Wall, Donne, N.Y.	0	4	.000	4.85	32	0	0	0	14	0	42.2	51	193	24	23	8	3	2	1	17	6	31	1	0
Wasdin, John, Col.	2	1	.667	7.03	18	0	0	0	2	0	24.1	32	110	19	19	7	0	1	1	8	2	17	1	0
Weathers, David, Mil.-Chi.	4	5	.444	2.41	80	0	0	0	25	4	86.0	65	351	24	23	6	10	3	3	34	8	66	0	0
Wendell, Turk, N.Y.-Phi.	4	5	.444	4.43	70	0	0	0	22	1	67.0	63	297	36	33	12	2	4	4	34	9	56	2	0
Wengert, Don, Pit.	0	2	.000	12.38	4	4	0	0	0	0	16.0	33	84	22	22	2	1	0	0	6	2	4	0	0
White, Gabe, Col.*	1	7	.125	6.25	69	0	0	0	16	0	67.2	70	290	47	47	18	2	2	1	26	5	47	1	0
White, Rick, N.Y.	4	5	.444	3.80	55	0	0	0	15	2	69.2	71	299	38	30	7	2	2	17	4	51	1	0
Whiteside, Matt, Atl.	0	1	.000	7.16	13	0	0	0	8	0	16.1	23	81	14	13	5	0	1	1	7	1	10	2	0
Wilkins, Marc, Pit	0	1	.000	6.75	14	0	0	0	6	0	17.1	22	80	13	13	2	2	0	1	8	1	11	2	0
Williams, David, Pit.*	3	7	.300	3.71	22	18	0	0	1	0	114.0	100	472	53	47	15	3	8	7	45	4	57	0	0
Williams, Woody, S.D.-St.L	15	9	.625	4.05	34	34	3	1	0	0	220.0	224	922	110	99	35	13	8	8	56	5	154	5	0
Williams, Jeff, L.A.*	1	1	.667	6.29	15	1	0	0	2	0	24.1	26	109	18	17	5	1	2	1	17	1	9	1	0
Williams, Mike, Pit.-Hou.	6	4	.600	3.80	65	0	0	0	48	22	64.0	60	285	28	27	9	3	1	0	35	3	59	2	0
Williamson, Scott, Cin.	0	0	.000	0.00	2	0	0	0	1	0	0.2	1	6	0	0	0	0	0	1	2	0	1	0	0
Winchester, Scott, Cin.	0	2	.000	4.50	12	1	0	0	6	0	24.0	29	105	19	12	7	3	3	3	4	3	9	0	0
Witasick, Jay, S.D.	5	2	.714	1.86	31	0	0	0	9	1	38.2	31	164	14	8	3	3	0	4	15	3	53	1	0
Witt, Bobby, Ari.	4	1	.800	4.78	14	7	0	0	0	0	43.1	36	193	23	23	6	1	2	3	25	1	31	2	0
Wohlers, Mark, Cin.	3	1	.750	3.94	30	0	0	0	11	0	32.0	36	139	20	14	5	4	1	1	7	2	21	4	0
Wolf, Randy, Phi.*	10	11	.476	3.70	28	25	4	2	1	0	163.0	150	684	74	67	15	11	7	10	51	4	152	1	0
Wood, Kerry, Chi.	12	6	.667	3.36	28	20	1	1	0	0	174.1	127	740	70	65	16	4	5	10	92	3	217	9	0
Worrell, Tim, S.F.	2	5	.286	3.45	73	0	0	0	12	0	78.1	71	339	33	30	4	3	4	3	33	4	63	2	0
Wright, Jamey, Mil.	11	12	.478	4.90	33	33	1	1	0	0	194.2	201	868	115	106	26	7	5	20	98	10	129	6	1
Yoshii, Masato, Mon.	4	7	.364	4.78	42	11	0	0	4	0	113.0	127	493	65	60	18	4	3	5	26	2	63	4	0
Zambrano, Carlos, Chi.	1	2	.333	15.26	6	1	0	0	1	0	7.2	11	42	13	13	2	1	1	1	8	0	4	1	0
Zerbe, Chad, S.F.*	3	0	1.000	3.92	27	1	0	0	9	0	39.0	41	162	21	17	3	3	2	1	10	0	22	0	0

PITCHERS WITH TWO OR MORE TEAMS

Pitcher, Team	W	L	Pct.	ERA	G	GS	CG	ShO	GF	Sv.	IP	H	TBF	R	ER	HR	SH	SF	HB	BB	IBB	SO	WP	Bk.
Acevedo, Juan, Col.	0	2	.000	5.63	39	0	0	0	14	0	32.0	37	153	24	20	4	2	1	1	19	6	26	0	0
Acevedo, Juan, Fla.	2	3	.400	2.54	20	0	0	0	6	0	28.1	31	129	11	8	2	1	2	1	16	3	21	1	0
Astacio, Pedro, Col.	6	13	.316	5.49	22	22	4	1	0	0	141.0	151	617	91	86	21	5	4	10	50	3	125	2	0
Astacio, Pedro, Hou.	2	1	.667	3.14	4	4	0	0	0	0	28.2	30	116	10	10	1	1	1	3	4	0	19	0	0
Chen, Bruce, Phi.*	4	5	.444	5.00	16	16	0	0	0	0	86.1	90	381	53	48	19	2	4	1	31	4	79	2	0
Chen, Bruce, N.Y.*	3	2	.600	4.68	11	11	0	0	0	0	59.2	56	253	37	31	10	2	3	0	28	0	47	3	0
Christiansen, Jason, St.L*	1	1	.500	4.66	30	0	0	0	8	3	19.1	15	83	10	10	4	0	1	1	10	1	19	0	0

Pitcher, Team	W	L	Pct.	ERA	G	GS	CG	ShO	GF	Sv.	IP	H	TBF	R	ER	HR	SH	SF	HB	BB	IBB	SO	WP	Bk.
Christiansen, Jason, S.F.*	1	0	1.000	1.59	25	0	0	0	3	0	17.0	14	66	3	3	1	1	2	0	5	0	12	4	0
Cook, Dennis, N.Y.*	1	1	.500	4.25	43	0	0	0	11	0	36.0	28	148	18	17	6	1	1	1	10	1	34	3	1
Cook, Dennis, Phi.*	0	0	.000	5.59	19	0	0	0	3	0	9.2	15	46	6	6	2	2	0	1	4	2	4	0	0
Elarton, Scott, Hou.	4	8	.333	7.14	20	20	0	0	0	0	109.2	126	499	88	87	26	7	2	6	49	1	76	5	0
Elarton, Scott, Col.	0	2	.000	6.65	4	4	0	0	0	0	23.0	20	96	17	17	8	0	0	0	10	1	11	0	0
Fetters, Mike, L.A.	2	1	.667	6.07	34	0	0	0	7	1	29.2	33	139	23	20	6	1	3	1	13	0	26	6	0
Fetters, Mike, Pit.	1	1	.500	4.58	20	0	0	0	14	8	17.2	16	84	9	9	1	0	3	3	13	1	11	1	0
Gomes, Wayne, Phi.	4	3	.571	4.31	42	0	0	0	12	1	48.0	51	215	23	23	4	4	3	1	22	4	35	2	0
Gomes, Wayne, S.F.	2	0	1.000	8.40	13	0	0	0	4	0	15.0	21	70	14	14	3	2	1	0	7	2	17	2	0
McKnight, Tony, Hou.	1	0	1.000	4.00	3	3	0	0	0	0	18.0	21	80	8	8	4	1	1	2	3	0	10	1	0
McKnight, Tony, Pit.	2	6	.250	5.19	12	12	0	0	0	0	69.1	88	316	44	40	15	3	2	3	21	4	36	4	0
Miceli, Dan, Fla.	0	5	.000	6.93	29	0	0	0	9	0	24.2	29	114	21	19	5	1	1	0	11	2	31	3	0
Miceli, Dan, Col.	2	0	1.000	2.21	22	0	0	0	6	1	20.1	18	85	8	5	2	1	1	0	5	0	17	1	0
Mulholland, Terry, Pit.*	0	0	.000	3.72	22	1	0	0	3	0	36.1	38	150	15	15	5	1	1	1	10	1	17	1	0
Mulholland, Terry, L.A.*	1	1	.500	5.83	19	3	0	0	5	0	29.1	40	135	20	19	7	0	0	1	7	0	25	0	0
Nichting, Chris, Cin.	0	3	.000	4.46	36	0	0	0	11	1	36.1	46	162	24	18	6	2	2	0	8	1	33	2	0
Nichting, Chris, Col.	0	0	.000	4.50	7	0	0	0	0	0	6.0	9	27	3	3	2	1	0	0	0	0	7	0	0
Nunez, Jose, L.A.*	0	1	.000	13.50	6	0	0	0	2	0	7.1	14	42	15	11	4	1	0	0	5	0	11	0	0
Nunez, Jose, S.D.*	4	1	.800	3.31	56	0	0	0	8	0	51.2	48	223	20	19	3	1	2	4	20	3	49	5	0
Powell, Jay, Hou.	2	2	.500	3.72	35	0	0	0	5	0	36.1	41	170	18	15	4	1	1	0	19	0	28	0	1
Powell, Jay, Col.	3	1	.750	2.79	39	0	0	0	15	7	38.2	34	157	18	12	5	4	0	2	12	3	26	0	0
Schmidt, Jason, Pit.	6	6	.500	4.61	14	14	1	0	0	0	84.0	81	357	46	43	11	3	2	7	28	2	77	3	1
Schmidt, Jason, S.F.	7	1	.875	3.39	11	11	0	0	0	0	66.1	57	284	29	25	2	2	1	0	33	1	65	5	0
Seanez, Rudy, S.D.	0	2	.000	2.63	26	0	0	0	8	1	24.0	15	102	8	7	3	0	1	1	15	0	24	1	0
Seanez, Rudy, Atl.	0	0	.000	3.00	12	0	0	0	4	0	12.0	8	48	4	4	1	0	0	0	4	0	17	3	0
Slusarski, Joe, Atl.	0	0	.000	9.00	4	0	0	0	1	0	6.0	9	28	6	6	2	1	0	0	1	0	5	0	0
Slusarski, Joe, Hou.	0	1	.000	9.00	8	0	0	0	4	0	10.0	16	48	10	10	2	0	1	0	3	0	6	0	0
Suzuki, Mac, Col.	0	2	.000	15.63	3	1	0	0	0	0	6.1	9	39	12	11	3	0	0	1	11	0	5	2	0
Suzuki, Mac, Mil.	3	5	.375	5.30	15	9	0	0	1	0	56.0	52	252	37	33	5	4	0	4	37	3	47	8	0
Villone, Ron, Col.*	1	3	.250	6.36	22	6	0	0	6	0	46.2	56	222	35	33	6	1	1	1	29	4	48	2	0
Villone, Ron, Hou.*	5	7	.417	5.56	31	6	0	0	6	0	68.0	77	301	46	42	12	0	0	4	24	1	65	2	1
Vogelsong, Ryan, S.F.	0	3	.000	5.65	13	0	0	0	8	0	28.2	29	130	21	18	5	0	1	2	14	0	17	2	0
Vogelsong, Ryan, Pit.	0	2	.000	12.00	2	2	0	0	0	0	6.0	10	34	10	8	1	0	0	0	6	1	7	0	0
Weathers, David, Mil.	3	4	.429	2.03	52	0	0	0	21	4	57.2	37	233	14	13	3	8	1	2	25	7	46	0	0
Weathers, David, Chi.	1	1	.500	3.18	28	0	0	0	4	0	28.1	28	118	10	10	3	2	2	1	9	1	20	0	0
Wendell, Turk, N.Y.	4	3	.571	3.51	49	0	0	0	14	1	51.1	42	218	23	20	8	2	3	2	22	6	41	1	0
Wendell, Turk, Phi.	0	0	.000	7.47	21	0	0	0	8	0	15.2	21	79	13	13	4	0	1	1	12	3	15	1	0
Williams, Woody, S.D.	8	8	.500	4.97	23	23	0	0	0	0	145.0	170	632	88	80	28	8	8	5	37	4	102	4	0
Williams, Woody, St.L	7	1	.875	2.28	11	11	3	1	0	0	75.0	54	290	22	19	7	5	0	3	19	1	52	1	0
Williams, Mike, Pit.	2	4	.333	3.67	40	0	0	0	38	22	41.2	39	183	18	17	6	2	0	0	21	2	43	1	0
Williams, Mike, Hou.	4	0	1.000	4.03	25	0	0	0	10	0	22.1	21	102	10	10	3	1	1	0	14	1	16	1	0

COMBINATION SHUTOUTS: **Arizona (8)**—Johnson, Kim and Prinz; Reynoso, Guzman, Sabel, Brohawn, Kim, Batista and Swindell; Schilling and Johnson; Johnson, Brohawn and Sabel; Johnson and Brohawn; Schilling, Brohawn and Morgan; Witt, Swindell, Prinz and Kim; Batista, Knott and Brohawn. **Atlanta (8)**—Maddux, Remlinger and Rocker; O. Perez, Remlinger and Rocker; Glavine, Remlinger and Rocker; Burkett, Remlinger and Rocker; Burkett, Remlinger and Rocker; O. Perez and Rocker; Burkett and Marquis; Glavine, Remlinger and Reed. **Chicago (4)**—Tapani, Farnsworth and Fassero; Wood, Farnsworth and Gordon; Wood, Zambrano and Chiasson; Wood, Van Poppel and Farnsworth. **Cincinnati (1)**—Reitsma and Graves. **Colorado (4)**—Hampton and Jimenez; Hampton and Davis; Neagle, Wasdin, White and Jimenez; J. Jennings, Speier, Powell and Jimenez. **Florida (8)**—Dempster, Bones and Nunez; Penny, Almanza and Alfonseca; Burnett and Alfonseca; Burnett and Alfonseca; Penny and Bones; Penny and Alfonseca; Sanchez, Bones, Darensbourg and Looper; Penny, Darensbourg and Alfonseca. **Houston (5)**—Lima and Wagner; Miller, J. Powell and Jackson; Reynolds, Dotel and Wagner; Hernandez and Dotel; Miller and Wagner. **Los Angeles (4)**—Park, Fetters and Shaw; Brown and Shaw; Brown and Shaw; Brown and Reyes. **Milwaukee (6)**—Sheets, Fox, Weathers and DeJean; Haynes, King and Leskanic; Wright and Leskanic; Wright, Leskanic, King and Weathers; Haynes, Painter and DeJean; Suzuki, Buddie and DeJean. **Montreal (8)**—Vazquez, Stewart and Urbina; Vazquez, Mota and Strickland; Armas Jr., Mota and Urbina; Vazquez and Stewart; Vazquez, Strickland and Lloyd; Vazquez and Strickland; Ohka, Munoz, Mota, Stewart and Strickland; Reames, Stewart and Strickland. **New York (11)**—Rusch and Wendell; Rusch, Franco and Benitez; Reed and Benitez; Leiter and Wendell; Appier, Cook and Benitez; Appier, Franco and Benitez; Rusch and Benitez; Trachsel and Benitez; Leiter, Wendell, Cook and Benitez; Chen, Franco and Benitez; Appier and Riggan. **Philadelphia (4)**—Wolf and Bottalico; Chen, Santiago and Gomes; Person, Bottalico and Mesa; Daal, Bottalico and Mesa. **Pittsburgh (7)**—Anderson, Sauerbeck and M. Williams; Anderson, Manzanillo, Sauerbeck, Silva and M. Williams; Schmidt, Manzanillo and M. Williams; Ritchie, Lincoln and M. Williams; Anderson and M. Williams; Anderson and M. Williams; D. Williams, Sauerbeck, Manzanillo and Olivares. **St. Louis (7)**—Morris, Karnuth and Kline; Kile, Christiansen, Stechschulte, Kline and Veres; Kile and Veres; Williams, Hackman and Stechschulte; Morris, Kline and Timlin; Kile and Matthews; Morris, Kline and Stechschulte. **San Diego (5)**—Jones, Seanez and Myers; Tollberg and Hoffman; Herndon, McElroy and Lundquist; Jarvis, McElroy and Fikac; Lawrence, Hoffman, Nunez, Fikac, McElroy and Serrano. **San Francisco (7)**—Estes, Rodriguez and Nen; Rueter and Zerbe; Ortiz and Nen; Rueter, Worrell, Rodriguez and Nen; Hernandez, Rodriguez, Fultz and Nen; Rueter, Worrell and Nen; Schmidt, Worrell, Rodriguez and Nen.

FIELDING

TEAM

Team	Pct.	G	PO	A	E	TC	DP	TP	PB
Arizona	.986	162	4379	1559	84	6022	148	0	12
Philadelphia	.985	162	4336	1603	91	6030	145	0	9
Colorado	.984	162	4290	1694	96	6080	167	0	14
Milwaukee	.983	162	4309	1729	103	6141	156	0	11
New York	.983	162	4337	1576	101	6014	132	0	11
Florida	.983	162	4314	1667	103	6084	174	0	10
Atlanta	.983	162	4342	1636	103	6081	133	0	9
Chicago	.982	162	4311	1493	109	5913	113	0	13
Montreal	.982	162	4294	1621	108	6023	139	0	12
St. Louis	.982	162	4306	1664	110	6080	156	0	7
Houston	.982	162	4364	1662	110	6136	138	0	4
Los Angeles	.981	162	4352	1586	116	6054	138	0	9
San Francisco	.981	162	4390	1650	118	6158	170	0	8
Cincinnati	.978	162	4328	1733	138	6199	136	0	21
Pittsburgh	.978	162	4249	1799	133	6181	168	0	9
San Diego	.976	162	4322	1607	145	6074	127	0	15
Totals	.982	1296	69223	26279	1768	97270	2340	0	174

INDIVIDUAL

FIRST BASEMEN

NOTE: All caps denotes fielding-percentage leader based on 81 games for catchers, 108 for all other non-pitchers and 162 innings for pitchers. *Throws lefthanded.

Player, Team	Pct.	G	PO	A	E	TC	DP
Arias, Alex, S.D.	.980	17	91	9	2	102	6
Bagwell, Jeff, Hou.	.992	160	1291	143	12	1446	123
Barkett, Andy, Pit.*	1.000	4	30	0	0	30	2
Blum, Geoff, Mon.	.988	14	74	9	1	84	9
Bogar, Tim, L.A.	1.000	3	9	0	0	9	1
Bonilla, Bobby, St.L.	.992	33	228	10	2	240	27
Brogna, Rico, Atl.*	.994	67	431	42	3	476	30
Cairo, Miguel, St.L.	.000	1	0	0	0	0	0
Caminiti, Ken, Atl.	.977	33	240	14	6	260	19
Casey, Sean, Cin.	.994	136	1146	62	7	1215	89
Castro, Juan, Cin.	1.000	1	10	3	0	13	0
Colbrunn, Greg, Ari.	.987	14	67	9	1	77	7
Coomer, Ron, Cin.	1.000	36	136	13	0	149	10
Counsell, Craig, Ari.	1.000	2	1	1	0	2	0
Crespo, Felipe, S.F.-Phi.	.977	18	122	3	3	128	13
Cromer, D.T., Cin.*	.973	8	32	4	1	37	3
Davis, Ben, S.D.	1.000	2	9	1	0	10	0
DeShields, Delino, Chi.	1.000	1	1	0	0	1	0
Donnels, Chris, L.A.	1.000	7	40	2	0	42	4
Dunston, Shawon, S.F.	.000	1	0	0	0	0	0
Durazo, Erubiel, Ari.*	.993	38	248	17	2	267	22
Echevarria, Angel, Mil.	1.000	10	47	2	0	49	5
Edmonds, Jim, St.L.*	1.000	2	14	2	0	16	2
Franco, Julio, Atl.	.995	23	181	16	1	198	20
Galarraga, Andres, S.F.	.984	41	288	13	5	306	38
Grace, Mark, Ari.*	.995	135	995	62	5	1062	99
Green, Shawn, L.A.*	1.000	1	5	0	0	5	1
Guzman, Edwards, S.F.	.973	7	34	2	1	37	2
Hansen, Dave, L.A.	.984	25	169	12	3	184	11
Harris, Lenny, N.Y.	.949	7	33	4	2	39	1
Hayes, Charlie, Hou.	1.000	2	7	0	0	7	0
Helms, Wes, Atl.	.991	77	433	31	4	468	41
HELTON, Todd, Col.*	.999	157	1302	120	2	1424	139
Hernandez, Alex, Pit.*	1.000	2	4	0	0	4	1
Hiatt, Phil, L.A.	.952	6	20	0	1	21	3
Houston, Tyler, Mil.	1.000	3	12	0	0	12	0
Hyzdu, Adam, Pit.	1.000	4	15	2	0	17	0
Jennings, Robin, Cin.*	1.000	8	51	6	0	57	9
Johnson, Mark P., N.Y.*	.991	21	101	7	1	109	10
Jordan, Kevin, Phi.	.948	10	53	2	3	58	4
Karros, Eric, L.A.	.996	119	963	71	4	1038	82
Kent, Jeff, S.F.	.990	30	193	14	2	209	19
Kieschnick, Brooks, Col.	1.000	1	1	0	0	1	0
Klesko, Ryan, S.D.*	.991	145	1135	84	11	1230	92
LaRue, Jason, Cin.	1.000	1	5	0	0	5	0
Lee, Derrek, Fla.	.994	156	1271	115	8	1394	142
Lee, Travis, Phi.*	.996	156	1332	75	6	1413	121
Lo Duca, Paul, L.A.	.990	33	185	17	2	204	17
Mabry, John, St.L.-Fla.	1.000	3	10	1	0	11	1
Mackowiak, Rob, Pit.	.000	1	0	0	0	0	0
Magadan, Dave, S.D.	.963	9	24	2	1	27	2
Marrero, Eli, St.L.	1.000	6	19	1	0	20	4
Martinez, Dave, Atl.*	1.000	10	51	6	0	57	6
Matheny, Mike, St.L.	1.000	2	7	0	0	7	2
Mayne, Brent, Col.	.000	1	0	0	0	0	0
McEwing, Joe, N.Y.	.750	3	2	1	1	4	1
McGriff, Fred, Chi.*	.990	49	366	23	4	393	29
McGuire, Ryan, Fla.*	1.000	4	7	0	0	7	0
McGwire, Mark, St.L.	.994	90	686	33	4	723	60
Melhuse, Adam, Col.	1.000	1	1	0	0	1	0
Merced, Orlando, Hou.	1.000	1	1	0	0	1	0
Millar, Kevin, Fla.	1.000	15	117	6	0	123	10
Minor, Damon, S.F.*	.989	11	86	4	1	91	4
Minor, Ryan, Mon.	.750	1	3	0	1	4	0
Mordecai, Mike, Mon.	1.000	1	1	0	0	1	0
Norton, Greg, Col.	1.000	13	66	4	0	70	6
Osik, Keith, Pit.	1.000	5	21	0	0	21	3
Paquette, Craig, St.L.	.978	23	125	10	3	138	17
Petrick, Ben, Col.	1.000	2	3	0	0	3	1
Pratt, Todd, Phi.	1.000	1	6	1	0	7	0
Pujols, Albert, St.L.	.984	42	283	19	5	307	27
Renteria, Edgar, St.L.	1.000	1	2	0	0	2	1
Santiago, Benito, S.F.	1.000	2	7	0	0	7	0
Seguignol, Fernando, Mon.	.920	7	20	3	2	25	3
Selby, Bill, Cin.	1.000	2	5	0	0	5	0
Sexson, Richie, Mil.	.995	158	1356	129	8	1493	126
Smith, Mark, Mon.	1.000	1	1	0	0	1	0
Snow, J.T., S.F.*	.999	92	658	47	1	706	76
Stairs, Matt, Chi.	.993	89	516	51	4	571	38
Stevens, Lee, Mon.*	.986	152	1287	92	19	1398	113
Sutton, Larry, St.L.*	1.000	11	38	5	0	43	3
Sweeney, Mark, Mil.*	1.000	2	3	0	0	3	2
Toca, Jorge, N.Y.	1.000	3	14	1	0	15	1
Tracy, Andy, Mon.	1.000	3	11	0	0	11	1
Truby, Chris, Hou.	1.000	1	1	0	0	1	0
Tucker, Michael, Chi.	.909	4	14	6	2	22	2
Vander Wal, John, Pit.-S.F.*	.992	14	113	4	1	118	13
Ward, Daryle, Hou.*	1.000	9	19	0	0	19	2
Wehner, John, Pit.	1.000	11	51	1	0	52	2
Wilkins, Rick, S.D.	1.000	1	1	0	0	1	0
Wilson, Craig A., Pit.	.994	26	166	12	1	179	16
Witt, Kevin, S.D.	1.000	9	69	3	0	72	4
Young, Dmitri, Cin.	1.000	38	219	19	0	238	16
Young, Kevin, Pit.	.994	137	1154	70	7	1231	118
Zeile, Todd, N.Y.	.992	149	1184	112	11	1307	105
Zuleta, Julio, Chi.	.991	35	213	7	2	222	11

FIRST BASEMEN WITH TWO OR MORE TEAMS

Player, Team	Pct.	G	PO	A	E	TC	DP
Crespo, Felipe, S.F.	.972	16	101	3	3	107	10
Crespo, Felipe, Phi.	1.000	2	21	0	0	21	3
Mabry, John, St.L.	1.000	2	3	0	0	3	1
Mabry, John, Fla.	1.000	1	7	1	0	8	0
Vander Wal, John, Pit.*	.991	13	111	4	1	116	13
Vander Wal, John, S.F.*	1.000	1	2	0	0	2	0

SECOND BASEMEN

Player, Team	Pct.	G	PO	A	E	TC	DP
Abbott, Kurt, Atl.	1.000	1	1	6	0	7	0
Alfonzo, Edgardo, N.Y.	.987	122	211	301	7	519	61
Anderson, Marlon, Phi.	.982	140	270	387	12	669	86
Arias, Alex, S.D.	.974	13	19	19	1	39	3
Bell, Jay, Ari.	.994	80	153	168	2	323	43
Belliard, Ronnie, Mil.	.990	96	213	290	5	508	66
Berg, Dave, Fla.	.965	34	54	85	5	144	21
Biggio, Craig, Hou.	.984	154	280	389	11	680	86

– 299 –

Player, Team	Pct.	G	PO	A	E	TC	DP
Blum, Geoff, Mon.	.989	25	39	47	1	87	5
Bocachica, Hiram, L.A.	.941	19	23	41	4	68	8
Branson, Jeff, L.A.	1.000	6	7	10	0	17	2
Butler, Brent, Col.	.959	23	44	49	4	97	14
Cairo, Miguel, Chi.-St.L.	.947	16	13	23	2	38	4
Castillo, Luis, Fla.	.980	133	260	387	13	660	99
Castro, Juan, Cin.	1.000	37	45	59	0	104	10
Clapp, Stubby, St.L.	1.000	4	1	6	0	7	0
Cora, Alex, L.A.	1.000	1	1	1	0	2	0
Counsell, Craig, Ari.	.996	55	95	133	1	229	34
Crespo, Cesar, S.D.	.970	34	62	67	4	133	12
Crespo, Felipe, S.F.-Phi.	.875	3	4	3	1	8	1
DeRosa, Mark, Atl.	1.000	5	7	20	0	27	3
DeShields, Delino, Chi.	1.000	16	28	21	0	49	1
Figueroa, Luis, Pit.	1.000	3	1	4	0	5	1
Forbes, P.J., Phi.	1.000	1	2	2	0	4	0
Fox, Andy, Fla.	1.000	2	4	4	0	8	0
Garcia, Jesse, Atl.	1.000	4	3	2	0	5	1
Giles, Marcus, Atl.	.978	62	104	166	6	276	31
Gomez, Chris, S.D.	1.000	8	9	11	0	20	5
Grudzielanek, Mark, L.A.	.984	133	245	359	10	614	75
Guerrero, Wilton, Cin.	1.000	11	21	23	0	44	4
Guzman, Edwards, S.F.	.750	3	3	0	1	4	0
Harris, Lenny, N.Y.	1.000	1	1	0	0	1	0
Jackson, Damian, S.D.	.986	118	241	323	8	572	68
Jordan, Kevin, Phi.	.953	10	13	28	2	43	4
Kent, Jeff, S.F.	.987	140	269	390	9	668	91
Lockhart, Keith, Atl.	1.000	47	65	85	0	150	20
Lopez, Luis, Mil.	1.000	15	24	34	0	58	7
Lopez, Mendy, Hou.-Pit.	.975	12	19	20	1	40	4
Loretta, Mark, Mil.	.992	52	115	144	2	261	31
Lugo, Julio, Hou.	.000	2	0	0	0	0	0
Mackowiak, Rob, Pit.	.947	21	34	55	5	94	8
Magadan, Dave, S.D.	.000	1	0	0	0	0	0
Martinez, Ramon E., S.F.	.993	42	54	98	1	153	21
Mateo, Henry, Mon.	.818	2	3	6	2	11	0
McEwing, Joe, N.Y.	1.000	5	5	6	0	11	2
Meares, Pat, Pit.	.973	85	149	213	10	372	53
Meyers, Chad, Chi.	1.000	4	3	10	0	13	1
Mordecai, Mike, Mon.	.990	32	46	58	1	105	13
Morris, Warren, Pit.	.965	29	41	69	4	114	15
Mueller, Bill, Chi.	1.000	1	0	1	0	1	0
Newhan, David, Phi.	1.000	1	2	0	0	2	0
Nunez, Abraham, Pit.	.990	48	93	103	2	198	27
Ojeda, Augie, Chi.	1.000	10	8	13	0	21	3
Ortiz, Jose, Col.	.965	51	86	137	8	231	30
Osik, Keith, Pit.	1.000	2	1	2	0	3	0
Paquette, Craig, St.L.	1.000	4	3	5	0	8	0
Pena, Elvis, Mil.	.980	11	14	36	1	51	7
Perez, Santiago, S.D.	1.000	2	4	2	0	6	0
Perez, Tomas, Phi.	1.000	29	36	49	0	85	11
Polanco, Placido, St.L.	1.000	15	22	36	0	58	10
Reboulet, Jeff, L.A.	.984	22	25	35	1	61	8
Reese, Pokey, Cin.	.980	51	100	142	5	247	28
Relaford, Desi, N.Y.	.969	54	85	105	6	196	24
Riggs, Adam, S.D.	1.000	11	12	20	0	32	5
Sadler, Donnie, Cin.	.947	15	15	21	2	38	5
Selby, Bill, Cin.	1.000	21	34	49	0	83	13
Shumpert, Terry, Col.	.968	41	51	71	4	126	20
Spivey, Junior, Ari.	.985	66	96	104	3	203	27
Stairs, Matt, Chi.	.000	1	0	0	0	0	0
Veras, Quilvio, Atl.	.991	67	132	181	3	316	37
Vidro, Jose, Mon.	.983	121	204	315	9	528	63
VINA, Fernando, St.L.	.987	151	313	383	9	705	100
Vizcaino, Jose, Hou.	.980	18	22	26	1	49	6
Walker, Todd, Col.-Cin.	.984	142	293	366	11	670	82
Wehner, John, Pit.	1.000	1	3	1	0	4	1
Wilson, Enrique, Pit.	.972	10	16	19	1	36	9
Young, Eric, Chi.	.981	147	263	366	12	641	67

SECOND BASEMEN WITH TWO OR MORE TEAMS

Player, Team	Pct.	G	PO	A	E	TC	DP
Cairo, Miguel, Chi.	.938	11	11	19	2	32	2
Cairo, Miguel, St.L.	1.000	5	2	4	0	6	2
Crespo, Felipe, S.F.	.833	2	2	3	1	6	1
Crespo, Felipe, Phi.	1.000	1	2	0	0	2	0
Lopez, Mendy, Hou.	1.000	3	5	2	0	7	0
Lopez, Mendy, Pit.	.970	9	14	18	1	33	4
Walker, Todd, Col.	.981	77	155	198	7	360	49
Walker, Todd, Cin.	.987	65	138	168	4	310	33

THIRD BASEMEN

Player, Team	Pct.	G	PO	A	E	TC	DP
Arias, Alex, S.D.	.957	18	5	17	1	23	1
Bell, Jay, Ari.	.940	40	22	56	5	83	3
Beltre, Adrian, L.A.	.952	124	99	215	16	330	18
Berg, Dave, Fla.	.895	16	1	16	2	19	2
Blum, Geoff, Mon.	.966	72	49	120	6	175	12
Bocachica, Hiram, L.A.	.778	8	1	6	2	9	0
Bogar, Tim, L.A.	.000	1	0	0	0	0	0
Boone, Aaron, Cin.	.936	103	72	207	19	298	17
Branson, Jeff, L.A.	.000	1	0	0	0	0	0
Butler, Brent, Col.	1.000	6	0	10	0	10	1
Cairo, Miguel, Chi.-St.L.	.882	43	13	32	6	51	6
Caminiti, Ken, Atl.	.933	13	9	19	2	30	3
Castilla, Vinny, Hou.	.963	121	82	230	12	324	18
Castro, Juan, Cin.	.958	19	3	20	1	24	3
CIRILLO, Jeff, Col.	.982	137	78	308	7	393	25
Colbrunn, Greg, Ari.	.875	10	6	8	2	16	1
Collier, Lou, Mil.	.914	16	8	24	3	35	2
Coolbaugh, Mike, Mil.	.971	27	11	23	1	35	5
Coomer, Ron, Chi.	.954	76	43	101	7	151	11
Counsell, Craig, Ari.	.977	38	27	58	2	87	4
Crespo, Cesar, S.D.	1.000	2	1	0	0	1	0
Davis, Russ, S.F.	.890	46	20	61	10	91	9
DeRosa, Mark, Atl.	.000	1	0	0	0	0	0
DeShields, Delino, Chi.	.667	5	0	4	2	6	0
Donnels, Chris, L.A.	.897	14	6	20	3	29	2
Feliz, Pedro, S.F.	.908	86	40	79	12	131	6
Fernandez, Tony, Mil.	.966	13	3	25	1	29	4
Fox, Andy, Fla.	1.000	9	6	6	0	12	1
Guerrero, Wilton, Cin.	.889	4	3	5	1	9	1
Gulan, Mike, Fla.	1.000	1	2	2	0	4	0
Guzman, Edwards, S.F.	1.000	7	4	7	0	11	1
Hansen, Dave, L.A.	.927	21	4	34	3	41	5
Harris, Lenny, N.Y.	.875	11	3	4	1	8	0
Hayes, Charlie, Hou.	1.000	11	7	12	0	19	2
Helms, Wes, Atl.	1.000	17	4	10	0	14	1
Hiatt, Phil, L.A.	1.000	17	9	8	0	17	1
Houston, Tyler, Mil.	.928	62	30	99	10	139	11
Jones, Chipper, Atl.	.945	149	75	233	18	326	12
Jordan, Kevin, Phi.	1.000	10	4	7	0	11	0
Larson, Brandon, Cin.	.939	9	10	21	2	33	2
LaRue, Jason, Cin.	.909	3	4	6	1	11	0
Lockhart, Keith, Atl.	1.000	4	1	0	0	1	0
Lopez, Luis, Mil.	.922	46	30	53	7	90	9
Lopez, Mendy, Hou.-Pit.	1.000	6	2	6	0	8	1
Loretta, Mark, Mil.	.933	39	16	54	5	75	0
Lowell, Mike, Fla.	.976	144	107	261	9	377	35
Mackowiak, Rob, Pit.	1.000	2	0	2	0	2	1
Magadan, Dave, S.D.	.950	22	5	23	2	40	2
Martinez, Ramon E., S.F.	.974	70	44	105	4	153	7
McEwing, Joe, N.Y.	.977	25	15	28	1	44	5
Merced, Orlando, Hou.	.000	2	0	0	0	0	0
Meyers, Chad, Chi.	.000	1	0	0	0	0	0
Millar, Kevin, Fla.	1.000	10	5	11	0	16	1
Minor, Ryan, Mon.	.970	24	12	20	1	33	0
Mordecai, Mike, Mon.	.974	42	21	53	2	76	2
Morris, Warren, Pit.	1.000	1	0	1	0	1	0
Mueller, Bill, Chi.	.942	64	33	96	8	137	6
Nevin, Phil, S.D.	.930	145	96	265	27	388	26
Norton, Greg, Col.	.895	24	8	26	4	38	2
Nunez, Abraham, Pit.	.000	1	0	0	0	0	0
Ojeda, Augie, Chi.	.913	35	8	34	4	46	4
Osik, Keith, Pit.	1.000	3	1	3	0	4	0
Paquette, Craig, St.L.	.965	33	20	35	2	57	5
Perez, Tomas, Phi.	.969	9	13	18	1	32	2
Polanco, Placido, St.L.	.985	103	60	199	4	263	16
Pujols, Albert, St.L.	.938	55	40	111	10	161	17
Ramirez, Aramis, Pit.	.945	157	92	335	25	452	33
Reboulet, Jeff, L.A.	.714	7	1	4	2	7	0
Relaford, Desi, N.Y.	.939	20	10	21	2	33	0
Riggs, Adam, S.D.	1.000	1	1	4	0	5	0
Rolen, Scott, Phi.	.973	151	104	325	12	441	22
Selby, Bill, Cin.	.882	8	7	8	2	17	2
Shumpert, Terry, Col.	.870	12	2	18	3	23	1
Sosa, Juan, Ari.	1.000	1	0	1	0	1	0
Tatis, Fernando, Mon.	.889	41	18	54	9	81	2
Tracy, Andy, Mon.	1.000	11	5	12	0	17	0
Truby, Chris, Hou.	.923	35	17	55	6	78	4
Velandia, Jorge, N.Y.	.000	1	0	0	0	0	0
Ventura, Robin, N.Y.	.957	139	91	264	16	371	24

Player, Team	Pct.	G	PO	A	E	TC	DP
Vizcaino, Jose, Hou.	.500	7	0	2	2	4	0
Wehner, John, Pit.	.857	6	0	6	1	7	2
Williams, Matt, Ari.	.963	102	57	177	9	243	17
Wilson, Enrique, Pit.	1.000	2	0	1	0	1	1
Young, Dmitri, Cin.	.890	36	16	57	9	82	9

THIRD BASEMEN WITH TWO OR MORE TEAMS

Player, Team	Pct.	G	PO	A	E	TC	DP
Cairo, Miguel, Chi.	.900	40	13	32	5	50	6
Cairo, Miguel, St.L.	.000	3	0	0	1	1	0
Lopez, Mendy, Hou.	1.000	2	0	1	0	1	1
Lopez, Mendy, Pit.	1.000	4	2	5	0	7	0

SHORTSTOPS

Player, Team	Pct.	G	PO	A	E	TC	DP
Abbott, Kurt, Atl.	1.000	1	1	2	0	3	0
Arias, Alex, S.D.	.971	13	17	16	1	34	3
Aurilia, Rich, S.F.	.975	149	246	423	17	686	108
Beltre, Adrian, L.A.	1.000	2	4	3	0	7	0
Berg, Dave, Fla.	.976	19	11	29	1	41	3
Betemit, Wilson, Atl.	.000	1	0	0	0	0	0
Blum, Geoff, Mon.	1.000	4	2	3	0	5	1
Bogar, Tim, L.A.	1.000	2	1	2	0	3	0
Branson, Jeff, L.A.	.000	2	0	0	1	1	0
Butler, Brent, Col.	.947	10	5	13	1	19	3
CABRERA, Orlando, Mon.	.986	162	246	514	11	771	106
Cairo, Miguel, Chi.-St.L.	1.000	2	1	1	0	2	0
Castilla, Vinny, Hou.	1.000	3	1	1	0	2	0
Castro, Juan, Cin.	.944	46	38	81	7	126	14
Cintron, Alex, Ari.	1.000	7	2	6	0	8	0
Coolbaugh, Mike, Mil.	1.000	3	2	5	0	7	1
Cora, Alex, L.A.	.962	132	178	328	20	526	63
Counsell, Craig, Ari.	.975	58	70	124	5	199	31
Crespo, Cesar, S.D.	1.000	1	1	1	0	2	0
DeRosa, Mark, Atl.	.960	48	52	117	7	176	21
Everett, Adam, Hou.	.667	6	2	2	2	6	1
Fox, Andy, Fla.	.938	12	14	31	3	48	9
Furcal, Rafael, Atl.	.970	70	126	224	11	361	49
Garcia, Jesse, Atl.	1.000	2	0	1	0	1	0
Gomez, Chris, S.D.	.937	36	31	58	6	95	14
Gonzalez, Alex, Fla.	.960	142	220	396	26	642	101
Guerrero, Wilton, Cin.	.927	16	20	31	4	55	9
Gutierrez, Ricky, Cin.	.971	144	173	360	16	549	67
Hansen, Dave, L.A.	.000	1	0	1	0	0	0
Hernandez, Jose, Mil.	.972	150	204	427	18	649	90
Jackson, Damian, S.D.	1.000	3	2	6	0	8	0
Jimenez, D'Angelo, S.D.	.948	85	130	255	21	406	47
Larkin, Barry, Cin.	.951	44	65	108	9	182	23
Lopez, Luis, Mil.	.978	17	16	29	1	46	5
Lopez, Mendy, Pit.	1.000	6	6	12	0	18	4
Loretta, Mark, Mil.	.969	9	11	20	1	32	4
Lugo, Julio, Hou.	.964	133	211	373	22	606	74
Magadan, Dave, S.D.	.000	1	0	0	0	0	0
Martinez, Ramon E., S.F.	.965	24	25	58	3	86	16
McEwing, Joe, N.Y.	.966	12	7	21	1	29	1
Mendez, Donaldo, S.D.	.920	46	47	91	12	150	15
Mordecai, Mike, Mon.	1.000	4	3	6	0	9	2
Nunez, Abraham, Pit.	.989	48	51	131	2	184	24
Ojeda, Augie, Chi.	.978	31	34	56	2	92	10
Ordonez, Rey, N.Y.	.980	148	213	383	12	608	79
Perez, Neifi, Col.	.976	87	145	264	10	419	64
Perez, Santiago, S.D.	.900	8	8	10	2	20	1
Perez, Tomas, Phi.	1.000	8	8	20	0	28	4
Polanco, Placido, St.L.	1.000	42	51	109	0	160	16
Punto, Nick, Phi.	1.000	1	1	2	0	3	0
Ransom, Cody, S.F.	1.000	6	0	4	0	4	0
Reboulet, Jeff, L.A.	.961	56	77	96	7	180	33
Reese, Pokey, Cin.	.972	78	117	224	10	351	34
Relaford, Desi, N.Y.	.958	25	20	48	3	71	7
Renteria, Edgar, St.L.	.961	137	207	390	24	621	85
Rollins, Jimmy, Phi.	.979	157	216	426	14	656	99
Sadler, Donnie, Col.	1.000	12	10	31	0	41	4
Sanchez, Rey, Atl.	.986	48	62	146	3	211	31
Shumpert, Terry, Col.	1.000	4	5	1	0	6	1
Smith, Jason, Chi.	1.000	1	2	0	0	2	0
Spivey, Junior, Ari.	.000	1	0	0	0	0	0
Uribe, Juan, Col.	.983	69	108	184	5	297	45
Velandia, Jorge, N.Y.	1.000	8	2	8	0	10	2
Vizcaino, Jose, Hou.	.937	53	50	114	11	175	21
Walker, Todd, Cin.	1.000	1	0	1	0	1	0
Williams, Matt, Ari.	1.000	2	3	5	0	8	1

Player, Team	Pct.	G	PO	A	E	TC	DP
Wilson, Enrique, Pit.	.974	28	40	72	3	115	15
Wilson, Jack, Pit.	.968	107	136	342	16	494	67
Womack, Tony, Ari.	.955	118	152	311	22	485	74

SHORTSTOPS WITH TWO OR MORE TEAMS

Player, Team	Pct.	G	PO	A	E	TC	DP
Cairo, Miguel, Chi.	1.000	1	1	1	0	2	0
Cairo, Miguel, St.L.	.000	1	0	0	0	0	0

OUTFIELDERS

Player, Team	Pct.	G	PO	A	E	TC	DP
Abbott, Jeff, Fla.*	.963	17	26	0	1	27	0
Abreu, Bobby, Phi.	.976	162	308	11	8	327	4
Agbayani, Benny, N.Y.	.954	84	123	1	6	130	0
Aldridge, Cory, Atl.	1.000	4	2	0	0	2	0
Alou, Moises, Hou.	.991	130	205	10	2	217	3
Aven, Bruce, L.A.	1.000	9	5	0	0	5	0
Barker, Glen, Hou.	1.000	60	36	0	0	36	0
Barkett, Andy, Pit.*	1.000	10	14	1	0	15	0
Bartee, Kimera, Col.	.889	10	8	0	1	9	0
Bautista, Danny, Ari.	1.000	61	102	4	0	106	2
Bell, Derek, Pit.	.988	46	78	3	1	82	1
Benard, Marvin, S.F.*	.965	109	213	5	8	226	2
Bergeron, Peter, Mon.	.996	101	220	6	1	227	1
Berkman, Lance, Hou.*	.981	155	306	6	6	318	1
Blum, Geoff, Mon.	1.000	35	51	1	0	52	0
Bocachica, Hiram, L.A.	.889	13	8	0	1	9	0
Bonds, Barry, S.F.*	.977	143	246	8	6	260	1
Bonilla, Bobby, St.L.	1.000	10	11	1	0	12	0
Bradley, Milton, Mon.	.988	65	155	5	2	162	1
Bragg, Darren, N.Y.	1.000	16	21	1	0	22	0
Brown, Adrian, Pit.	1.000	7	18	0	0	18	0
Brown, Emil, Pit.-S.D.	.989	85	88	4	1	93	1
Brown, Roosevelt, Chi.	.952	22	20	0	1	21	0
Brumbaugh, Cliff, Col.	1.000	11	15	0	0	15	0
Buford, Damon, Chi.	1.000	34	53	0	0	53	0
Burnitz, Jeromy, Mil.	.981	153	295	13	6	314	4
Burrell, Pat, Phi.	.972	146	226	18	7	251	2
Cairo, Miguel, St.L.	1.000	6	7	0	0	7	0
Christensen, McKay, L.A.*	.917	14	22	0	2	24	0
Christensen, Ryan, Ari.	1.000	5	1	0	0	1	0
Clapp, Stubby, St.L.	1.000	4	3	0	0	3	0
Clark, Brady, Cin.	.981	43	52	0	1	53	0
Colangelo, Mike, S.D.	.979	40	45	1	1	47	0
Collier, Lou, Mil.	.976	23	40	1	1	42	0
Conti, Jason, Ari.	.000	1	0	0	0	0	0
Crespo, Cesar, S.D.	1.000	18	29	1	0	30	0
Crespo, Felipe, S.F.-Phi.	1.000	5	8	1	0	9	0
Cruz, Jacob, Col.*	.931	24	26	1	2	29	0
Cummings, Midre, Ari.	1.000	4	4	0	0	4	0
Cust, Jack, Ari.	.000	1	0	0	0	0	0
Darr, Mike, S.D.	.990	93	183	6	2	191	2
Davis, Eric, S.F.	.962	48	74	1	3	78	0
Dellucci, David, Ari.*	.989	58	90	0	1	91	0
DeRosa, Mark, Atl.	.000	1	0	0	0	0	0
DeShields, Delino, Chi.	.976	33	40	1	1	42	0
Drew, J.D., St.L.	.973	107	209	7	6	222	1
Ducey, Rob, Phi.-Mon.	1.000	17	28	1	0	29	0
Dunn, Adam, Cin.	.986	63	136	3	2	141	1
Dunston, Shawon, S.F.	.966	60	80	4	3	87	2
Dunwoody, Todd, Chi.*	.973	26	35	1	1	37	0
Durazo, Erubiel, Ari.*	1.000	2	4	1	0	5	0
Echevarria, Angel, Mil.	.931	23	27	0	2	29	0
Edmonds, Jim, St.L.*	.982	147	311	12	6	329	1
Encarnacion, Mario, Col.	1.000	20	35	1	0	36	2
Escobar, Alex, N.Y.	.935	15	26	3	2	31	1
Finley, Steve, Ari.*	.994	131	300	6	2	308	3
Floyd, Cliff, Fla.	.972	142	269	8	8	285	2
Fox, Andy, Fla.	1.000	2	1	0	0	1	0
Gant, Ron, Col.	.965	51	81	2	3	86	0
Giles, Brian, Pit.*	.969	159	307	7	10	324	2
Gilkey, Bernard, Atl.	1.000	36	40	0	0	40	0
Glanville, Doug, Phi.	.991	150	413	9	4	425	3
GONZALEZ, Luis, Ari.	1.000	161	280	8	0	288	1
Gonzalez, Raul, Cin.	1.000	2	4	0	0	4	0
Goodwin, Tom, L.A.	.994	78	153	1	1	155	0
Green, Shawn, L.A.*	.982	159	312	8	6	326	0
Griffey, Ken Jr., Cin.*	.985	90	195	1	3	199	0
GRISSOM, Marquis, L.A.	1.000	123	227	6	0	233	2
Guerrero, Vladimir, Mon.	.965	158	320	14	12	346	5
Guerrero, Wilton, Cin.	1.000	6	6	0	0	6	0

Player, Team	Pct.	G	PO	A	E	TC	DP
Guzman, Edwards, S.F.	.000	2	0	0	0	0	0
Gwynn, Tony, S.D.*	1.000	17	17	2	0	19	0
Hamilton, Darryl, N.Y.	1.000	37	66	2	0	68	0
Hammonds, Jeffrey, Mil.	.982	46	106	2	2	110	0
Harris, Lenny, N.Y.	1.000	8	5	0	0	5	0
Helms, Wes, Atl.	1.000	1	2	0	0	2	0
Henderson, Rickey, S.D.*	.982	104	158	5	3	166	2
Hermansen, Chad, Pit.	1.000	20	30	1	0	31	1
Hernandez, Alex, Pit.*	1.000	4	3	1	0	4	0
Hernandez, Jose, Mil.	1.000	2	2	0	0	2	0
Hidalgo, Richard, Hou.	.991	144	332	11	3	346	4
Hollandsworth, Todd, Col.*	.981	31	51	2	1	54	0
Hunter, Brian L., Phi.	1.000	41	69	3	0	72	2
Hyzdu, Adam, Pit.	1.000	27	27	0	0	27	0
Jackson, Damian, S.D.	1.000	2	2	0	0	2	0
Jenkins, Geoff, Mil.	.986	104	210	8	3	221	2
Jennings, Robin, Col.-Cin.*	.862	16	23	2	4	29	1
Johnson, Mark P., N.Y.*	1.000	19	10	0	0	10	0
Jones, Andruw, Atl.	.987	161	461	10	6	477	6
Jones, Chipper, Atl.	1.000	8	16	0	0	16	0
Jones, Terry, Mon.	.977	22	41	2	1	44	1
Jordan, Brian, Atl.	.991	144	321	11	3	335	2
Kendall, Jason, Pit.	.906	27	47	1	5	53	0
Kieschnick, Brooks, Col.	.818	12	9	0	2	11	0
Kotsay, Mark, S.D.*	.986	111	277	4	4	285	1
Lankford, Ray, St.L.-S.D.*	.971	123	198	6	6	210	1
LaRue, Jason, Cin.	1.000	2	1	0	0	1	0
Lawton, Matt, N.Y.	1.000	48	96	1	0	97	0
Leach, Jalal, S.F.*	1.000	3	1	0	0	1	0
Little, Mark, Col.	1.000	29	36	3	0	39	3
Lo Duca, Paul, L.A.	.900	5	9	0	1	10	0
Lugo, Julio, Hou.	1.000	8	2	0	0	2	0
Mabry, John, St.L.-Fla.	.958	41	44	2	2	48	0
Mackowiak, Rob, Pit.	.986	46	70	3	1	74	1
Marrero, Eli, St.L.	.923	15	11	1	1	13	0
Martinez, Dave, Atl.*	1.000	52	69	2	0	71	1
Matthews Jr., Gary, Chi.-Pit.	.974	144	259	4	7	270	0
McEwing, Joe, N.Y.	1.000	62	72	2	0	74	1
McGuire, Ryan, Fla.*	1.000	9	16	0	0	16	0
Merced, Orlando, Hou.	.975	31	38	1	1	40	0
Meyers, Chad, Chi.	1.000	4	3	0	0	3	0
Michaels, Jason, Phi.	.000	1	0	0	0	0	0
Millar, Kevin, Fla.	.986	86	144	2	2	148	0
Minor, Ryan, Mon.	.000	2	0	0	0	0	0
Mordecai, Mike, Mon.	1.000	1	2	0	0	2	0
Mottola, Chad, Fla.	1.000	5	8	1	0	9	0
Mouton, James, Mil.	.965	53	81	2	3	86	1
Mouton, Lyle, Fla.	1.000	11	4	0	0	4	0
Murray, Calvin, S.F.	.979	104	232	4	5	241	1
Norton, Greg, Col.	1.000	25	16	1	0	17	0
Nunez, Abraham, Pit.	.000	1	0	0	0	0	0
Ochoa, Alex, Cin.-Col.	.989	137	266	12	3	281	5
Osik, Keith, Pit.	1.000	1	2	0	0	2	0
Owens, Eric, Fla.	.984	106	180	6	3	189	1
Paquette, Craig, St.L.	1.000	56	70	2	0	72	1
Patterson, Corey, Chi.	.976	54	82	0	2	84	0
Payton, Jay, N.Y.	.984	103	237	6	4	247	1
Perez, Robert, Mil.	1.000	1	3	0	0	3	0
Perez, Santiago, S.D.	.947	26	35	1	2	38	0
Perez, Timo, N.Y.*	1.000	73	128	5	0	133	1
Perez, Tomas, Phi.	.000	1	0	0	0	0	0
Pierre, Juan, Col.*	.979	154	362	3	8	373	1
Powell, Dante, S.F.	1.000	9	8	0	0	8	0
Pride, Curtis, Mon.	1.000	23	32	1	0	33	0
Pujols, Albert, St.L.	.964	78	128	6	5	139	0
Raines, Tim, Mon.	1.000	20	23	0	0	23	0
Reboulet, Jeff, L.A.	.000	2	0	0	0	0	0
Redman, Tike, Pit.*	.980	35	92	5	2	99	2
Rios, Armando, S.F.-Pit.*	.971	89	196	7	6	209	2
Rivera, Ruben, S.F.	.983	99	171	4	3	178	2
Robinson, Kerry, St.L.*	.981	74	101	2	2	105	0
Sadler, Donnie, Cin.	.857	8	5	1	1	7	0
Sanchez, Alex, Mil.*	.963	19	24	2	1	27	0
Sanders, Deion, Cin.*	1.000	16	34	4	0	38	1
Sanders, Reggie, Ari.	.996	119	231	5	1	237	3
Saturria, Luis, St.L.	1.000	9	2	0	0	2	0
Seguignol, Fernando, Mon.	1.000	13	8	1	0	9	0
Sheffield, Gary, L.A.	.972	141	195	17	6	218	0
Shinjo, Tsuyoshi, N.Y.	.989	119	256	12	3	271	3
Shumpert, Terry, Col.	.976	24	38	2	1	41	0
Smith, Mark, Mon.	1.000	60	99	2	0	101	1
Sosa, Sammy, Chi.	.982	160	326	8	6	340	1

Player, Team	Pct.	G	PO	A	E	TC	DP
Stairs, Matt, Chi.	1.000	22	31	1	0	32	0
Surhoff, B.J., Atl.	.986	129	200	8	3	211	0
Sutton, Larry, St.L.*	1.000	3	1	0	0	1	0
Sweeney, Mark, Mil.*	.968	20	30	0	1	31	0
Taylor, Reggie, Phi.	1.000	2	4	0	0	4	0
Thompson, Ryan, Fla.	.923	16	11	1	1	13	0
Toca, Jorge, N.Y.	1.000	2	2	0	0	2	0
Trammell, Bubba, S.D.	.985	132	261	5	4	270	0
Tucker, Michael, Cin.-Chi.	.984	127	237	9	4	250	1
Valent, Eric, Phi.*	1.000	8	20	2	0	22	0
Vander Wal, John, Pit.-S.F.*	.985	114	188	3	3	194	0
Walker, Larry, Col.	.984	129	243	8	4	255	4
Ward, Daryle, Hou.*	.985	42	62	2	1	65	1
Wehner, John, Pit.	1.000	8	7	0	0	7	0
White, Devon, Mil.	1.000	100	190	3	0	193	1
White, Rondell, Chi.	.979	90	133	4	3	140	0
Wilkerson, Brad, Mon.*	.970	38	62	2	2	66	0
Wilson, Craig A., Pit.	.947	14	17	1	1	19	0
Wilson, Preston, Fla.	.993	121	287	12	2	301	4
Womack, Tony, Ari.	.000	1	0	0	0	0	0
Young, Dmitri, Cin.	.957	87	146	8	7	161	1

OUTFIELDERS WITH TWO OR MORE TEAMS

Player, Team	Pct.	G	PO	A	E	TC	DP
Brown, Emil, Pit.	.988	54	79	4	1	84	1
Brown, Emil, S.D.	1.000	11	9	0	0	9	0
Crespo, Felipe, S.F.	1.000	1	2	0	0	2	0
Crespo, Felipe, Phi.	1.000	4	6	1	0	7	0
Ducey, Rob, Phi.	1.000	3	5	0	0	5	0
Ducey, Rob, Mon.	1.000	14	23	1	0	24	0
Jennings, Robin, Col.*	.000	1	0	0	1	1	0
Jennings, Robin, Cin.*	.893	15	23	2	3	28	1
Lankford, Ray, St.L.*	.966	85	135	5	5	145	1
Lankford, Ray, S.D.*	.985	38	63	1	1	65	0
Mabry, John, St.L.	.000	2	0	0	0	0	0
Mabry, John, Fla.	.958	39	44	2	2	48	0
Matthews, Gary Jr., Chi.	.976	100	159	3	4	166	0
Matthews, Gary Jr., Pit.	.971	44	100	1	3	104	0
Ochoa, Alex, Cin.	.989	85	176	6	2	184	2
Ochoa, Alex, Col.	.990	52	90	6	1	97	3
Rios, Armando, S.F.*	.971	87	196	7	6	209	2
Rios, Armando, Pit.*	.000	2	0	0	0	0	0
Tucker, Michael, Cin.	.978	70	126	7	3	136	1
Tucker, Michael, Chi.	.991	57	111	2	1	114	0
Vander Wal, John, Pit.*	.973	73	106	2	3	111	0
Vander Wal, John, S.F.*	1.000	41	82	1	0	83	0

CATCHERS

Player, Team	Pct.	G	PO	A	E	TC	DP	PB
AUSMUS, Brad, Hou.	.997	127	948	62	3	1013	9	1
Bako, Paul, Atl.	.991	60	319	29	3	351	1	4
Barajas, Rod, Ari.	.995	50	179	11	1	191	3	0
Barrett, Michael, Mon.	.993	131	880	50	7	937	6	8
Bennett, Gary, Phi.-Col.	.992	43	247	9	2	258	3	3
Blanco, Henry, Mil.	.992	102	645	68	6	719	9	6
Brown, Kevin L., Mil.	1.000	16	68	6	0	74	0	2
Casanova, Raul, Mil.	.991	56	305	25	3	333	6	2
Castro, Ramon, Fla.	1.000	3	10	1	0	11	0	0
Cota, Humberto, Pit.	1.000	3	11	0	0	11	0	0
Davis, Ben, S.D.	.990	135	845	60	9	914	14	8
DiFelice, Mike, Ari.	.982	12	53	3	1	57	1	1
Estalella, Bobby, S.F.	1.000	28	185	14	0	199	5	0
Estrada, Johnny, Phi.	.993	89	543	30	4	577	4	3
Eusebio, Tony, Hou.	.991	48	300	22	3	325	4	2
Fasano, Sal, Col.	.982	25	153	14	3	170	5	0
Girardi, Joe, Chi.	1.000	71	504	33	0	537	2	6
Gonzalez, Wiki, S.D.	.989	47	246	21	3	270	3	6
Guzman, Edwards, S.F.	.990	26	86	10	1	97	1	0
Huckaby, Ken, Ari.	1.000	1	5	0	0	5	0	0
Hundley, Todd, Chi.	.993	70	547	25	4	576	3	6
Johnson, Brian, L.A.	1.000	2	3	0	0	3	0	0
Johnson, Charles, Fla.	.996	125	846	62	4	912	15	8
Kendall, Jason, Pit.	.985	133	739	52	12	803	7	7
Knorr, Randy, Mon.	.989	27	168	5	2	175	0	2
Kreuter, Chad, L.A.	1.000	70	486	29	0	515	4	5
LaRue, Jason, Cin.	.991	107	569	75	6	650	8	15
Levis, Jesse, Mil.	.984	11	59	3	1	63	1	1
Lieberthal, Mike, Phi.	.992	33	243	9	2	254	3	0
Lo Duca, Paul, L.A.	.991	99	643	53	6	702	8	4
Lopez, Javy, Atl.	.989	127	826	50	10	886	7	5
Machado, Robert, Chi.	.997	47	317	20	1	338	3	1

Player, Team	Pct.	G	PO	A	E	TC	DP	PB
Marrero, Eli, St.L.	.984	65	352	21	6	379	2	1
Martinez, Sandy, Mon.	1.000	1	2	0	0	2	0	0
Matheny, Mike, St.L.	.995	121	772	69	4	845	9	6
Mayne, Brent, Col.	.997	44	317	19	1	337	4	1
McDonald, Keith, St.L.	1.000	2	1	1	0	2	0	0
Melhuse, Adam, Col.	.991	23	104	4	1	109	0	2
Miller, Corky, Cin.	.991	17	104	12	1	117	2	2
Miller, Damian, Ari.	.993	121	966	81	7	1054	6	10
Moeller, Chad, Ari.	1.000	25	111	7	0	118	0	1
Mordecai, Mike, Mon.	1.000	1	1	0	0	1	0	0
Osik, Keith, Pit.	.995	39	188	12	1	201	1	1
Pena, Angel, L.A.	1.000	15	125	11	0	136	0	0
Perez, Eddie, Atl.	1.000	5	10	1	0	11	0	0
Petrick, Ben, Col.	.984	77	456	29	8	493	8	11
Phillips, Jason, N.Y.	1.000	5	15	0	0	15	0	0
Piazza, Mike, N.Y.	.991	131	919	58	9	986	5	7
Pratt, Todd, N.Y.-Phi.	.989	65	342	11	4	357	1	5
Redmond, Mike, Fla.	.994	47	291	23	2	316	5	2
Santiago, Benito, S.F.	.994	130	830	62	5	897	12	8
Schneider, Brian, Mon.	1.000	14	77	7	0	84	1	2
Servais, Scott, Hou.	1.000	9	38	1	0	39	0	1
Stinnett, Kelly, Cin.	.966	59	322	21	12	355	3	4
Torrealba, Steve, Atl.	1.000	2	2	0	0	2	0	0
Torrealba, Yorvit, S.F.	1.000	3	8	0	0	8	0	0
Wehner, John, Pit.	1.000	1	1	0	0	1	0	0
Wilkins, Rick, S.D.	1.000	7	38	0	0	38	0	1
Wilson, Craig A., Pit.	.960	10	22	2	1	25	0	1
Wilson, Vance, N.Y.	.993	27	130	9	1	140	1	2

CATCHERS WITH TWO OR MORE TEAMS

Player, Team	Pct.	G	PO	A	E	TC	DP	PB
Bennett, Gary, Phi.	.987	24	151	5	2	158	2	3
Bennett, Gary, Col.	1.000	10	96	4	0	100	1	0
Pratt, Todd, N.Y.	.994	31	152	4	1	157	0	2
Pratt, Todd, Phi.	.985	34	190	7	3	200	1	3

PITCHERS

Player, Team	Pct.	G	PO	A	E	TC	DP
Acevedo, Jose, Cin.	1.000	18	4	10	0	14	1
Acevedo, Juan, Col.-Fla.	.909	59	4	6	1	11	1
Adams, Terry, L.A.	.978	43	13	31	1	45	2
Ainsworth, Kurt, S.F.	.000	2	0	0	0	0	0
Alfonseca, Antonio, Fla.	1.000	58	6	8	0	14	1
Almanza, Armando, Fla.*	1.000	52	0	3	0	3	0
Anderson, Brian, Ari.*	.953	29	9	32	2	43	2
Anderson, Jimmy, Pit.*	.938	34	8	37	3	48	0
Ankiel, Rick, St.L.*	1.000	6	0	3	0	3	0
Appier, Kevin, N.Y.	.941	33	11	21	2	34	2
Armas, Tony Jr., Mon.	.919	34	14	20	3	37	1
Arroyo, Bronson, Pit.	.900	24	3	15	2	20	1
Ashby, Andy, L.A.	1.000	2	0	1	0	1	0
Astacio, Pedro, Col.-Hou.	.972	26	10	25	1	36	1
Atchley, Justin, Cin.*	.000	15	0	0	0	0	0
Aybar, Manny, Chi.*	.800	17	2	2	1	5	0
Baez, Benito, Fla.*	1.000	8	0	1	0	1	0
Baldwin, James, L.A.	.929	12	5	8	1	14	1
Batista, Miguel, Ari.	.960	48	7	17	1	25	1
Beckett, Josh, Fla.	1.000	4	0	6	0	6	0
Beimel, Joe, Pit.*	.909	42	3	17	2	22	0
Belitz, Todd, Col.*	1.000	8	0	1	0	1	0
Bell, Rob, Cin.	1.000	9	1	6	0	7	1
Benes, Alan, St.L.	1.000	9	1	0	0	1	0
Benes, Andy, St.L.	1.000	27	7	9	0	16	1
Benitez, Armando, N.Y.	1.000	73	4	4	0	8	0
Bere, Jason, Chi.	.964	32	12	15	1	28	0
Bierbrodt, Nick, Ari.*	1.000	5	1	8	0	9	1
Blank, Matt, Mon.*	1.000	5	1	7	0	8	0
Boehringer, Brian, S.F.	1.000	29	1	0	0	1	0
Bohanon, Brian, Col.*	1.000	20	5	12	0	17	0
Bones, Ricky, Fla.	.952	61	4	16	1	21	3
Bonilla, Bobby, St.L.	.000	1	0	0	0	0	0
Borowski, Joe, Chi.	.000	1	0	0	0	0	0
Bottalico, Ricky, Phi.	.929	66	3	10	1	14	0
Bottenfield, Kent, Hou.	1.000	13	0	5	0	5	0
Brock, Chris, Phi.	.857	24	3	3	1	7	0
Brohawn, Troy, Ari.*	1.000	59	2	8	0	10	1
Brower, Jim, Cin.	.951	46	10	29	2	41	2
Brown, Kevin, L.A.	.941	20	10	22	2	34	1
Buddie, Mike, Mil.	1.000	31	4	13	0	17	1
Burkett, John, Atl.	1.000	34	15	26	0	41	1
Burnett, A.J., Fla.	.950	27	11	27	2	40	1

Player, Team	Pct.	G	PO	A	E	TC	DP
Byrd, Paul, Phi.	1.000	3	3	1	0	4	0
Cabrera, Jose, Atl.	.900	55	2	7	1	10	1
Carrara, Giovanni, L.A.	1.000	47	5	10	0	15	1
Chacon, Shawn, Col.	1.000	27	8	16	0	24	0
Chen, Bruce, Phi.-N.Y.*	.962	27	4	21	1	26	1
Chiasson, Scott, Chi.	1.000	6	1	2	0	3	0
Chouinard, Bobby, Col.	1.000	8	1	1	0	2	0
Christiansen, Jason, St.L.-S.F.	1.000	55	1	5	0	6	0
Christman, Tim, Col.*	.000	1	0	0	0	0	0
Clement, Matt, Fla.	.971	31	14	20	1	35	1
Coggin, Dave, Phi.	1.000	17	9	12	0	21	0
Cook, Dennis, N.Y.-Phi.*	.833	62	2	3	1	6	0
Coppinger, Rocky, Mil.	.667	8	1	1	1	3	1
Corey, Mark, N.Y.	.000	2	0	0	0	0	0
Cormier, Rheal, Phi.*	.941	60	6	10	1	17	2
Cruz, Juan, Chi.	1.000	8	3	5	0	8	1
Cruz, Nelson, Hou.	.957	66	8	14	1	23	0
Cubillan, Darwin, Mon.	.500	29	0	1	1	2	0
Cunnane, Will, Mil.	1.000	31	4	10	0	14	0
Daal, Omar, Phi.*	.974	32	7	31	1	39	4
D'Amico, Jeff, Mil.	1.000	10	1	5	0	6	0
Darensbourg, Vic, Fla.*	.917	58	1	10	1	12	1
Davenport, Joe, Col.	1.000	7	0	2	0	2	0
Davey, Tom, S.D.	1.000	39	2	6	0	8	0
Davis, Kane, Col.	1.000	57	1	12	0	13	1
Davis, Lance, Cin.*	.967	20	6	23	1	30	2
DeJean, Mike, Mil.	1.000	75	7	17	0	24	1
de los Santos, Valerio, Mil.*	.000	1	0	0	0	0	0
Dempster, Ryan, Fla.	.946	34	16	36	3	55	7
Dessens, Elmer, Cin.	1.000	34	6	26	0	32	3
Dingman, Craig, Col.	1.000	7	0	2	0	2	0
Donnels, Chris, L.A.	.000	1	0	0	0	0	0
Dotel, Octavio, Hou.	.929	61	4	22	2	28	3
Dreifort, Darren, L.A.	.938	16	4	11	1	16	2
Duckworth, Brandon, Phi.	.846	11	4	7	2	13	0
Duncan, Courtney, Chi.	.571	30	2	2	3	7	0
Eaton, Adam, S.D.	.939	17	13	18	2	33	2
Eischen, Joey, Mon.*	1.000	24	3	4	0	7	0
Elarton, Scott, Hou.-Col.	.938	24	9	21	2	32	2
Ellis, Robert, Ari.	1.000	19	8	12	0	20	0
Embree, Alan, S.F.*	1.000	22	0	1	0	1	0
Estes, Shawn, S.F.*	.923	27	3	33	3	39	2
Estrada, Horacio, Col.*	1.000	4	0	1	0	1	0
Farnsworth, Kyle, Chi.	1.000	76	3	4	0	7	0
Fassero, Jeff, Chi.*	1.000	82	3	9	0	12	2
Fernandez, Jared, Cin.	1.000	5	1	4	0	5	0
Fernandez, Osvaldo, Cin.	.957	20	2	20	1	23	2
Fetters, Mike, L.A.-Pit.	.900	54	1	8	1	10	0
Figueroa, Nelson, Phi.	1.000	19	2	6	0	8	1
Fikac, Jeremy, S.D.	1.000	23	0	4	0	4	0
Finley, Steve, Ari.*	.000	1	0	0	0	0	0
Fox, Chad, Mil.	.909	65	4	6	1	11	0
Franco, John, N.Y.*	.889	58	1	7	1	9	0
Franklin, Wayne, Hou.*	1.000	11	0	2	0	2	0
Fultz, Aaron, S.F.*	1.000	66	4	14	0	18	1
Fyhrie, Mike, Chi.	1.000	15	2	4	0	6	1
Gagne, Eric, L.A.	.955	33	10	11	1	22	0
Gandarillas, Gus, Mil.	1.000	16	2	3	0	5	1
Gardner, Mark, S.F.	1.000	23	2	10	0	12	0
Glavine, Tom, Atl.*	1.000	35	12	40	0	52	2
Gomes, Wayne, Phi.-S.F.	1.000	55	2	5	0	7	0
Gonzalez, Dicky, N.Y.	1.000	16	4	8	0	12	0
Gordon, Flash, Chi.	1.000	47	1	1	0	2	0
Graves, Danny, Cin.	1.000	66	6	21	0	27	0
Grilli, Jason, Fla.	1.000	6	1	3	0	4	0
Guzman, Geraldo, Ari.	.000	4	0	0	0	0	0
Hackman, Luther, St.L.	1.000	35	1	5	0	6	0
Hamilton, Joey, Cin.	1.000	4	2	5	0	7	1
Hampton, Mike, Col.*	1.000	32	12	46	0	58	5
Harnisch, Pete, Cin.	1.000	7	3	1	0	4	0
Haynes, Jimmy, Mil.	1.000	31	12	24	0	36	1
Heredia, Felix, Chi.*	1.000	48	3	1	0	4	0
Herges, Matt, L.A.	.952	75	5	15	1	21	1
Hermanson, Dustin, St.L.	.955	33	4	17	1	22	0
Hernandez, Carlos, Hou.*	1.000	3	1	2	0	3	1
Hernandez, Livan, S.F.	1.000	34	13	44	0	57	2
Herndon, Junior, S.D.	1.000	12	2	10	0	12	2
Hinchliffe, Brett, N.Y.	.000	1	0	0	0	0	0
Hitchcock, Sterling, S.D.*	1.000	3	0	2	0	2	0
Hoffman, Trevor, S.D.	1.000	62	5	4	0	9	0
Hutchinson, Chad, St.L.	.000	3	0	0	0	0	0
Irabu, Hideki, Mon.	1.000	3	0	5	0	5	0

Player, Team	Pct.	G	PO	A	E	TC	DP
Jackson, Mike, Hou.	1.000	67	7	4	0	11	0
James, Mike, St.L.	1.000	40	3	4	0	7	1
Jarvis, Kevin, S.D.	.981	32	20	33	1	54	0
Jennings, Jason, Col.	1.000	7	4	7	0	11	3
Jensen, Ryan, S.F.	.900	10	5	4	1	10	1
Jimenez, Jose, Col.	1.000	56	2	12	0	14	0
Jodie, Brett, S.D.	1.000	7	0	1	0	1	0
Johnson, Mike, Mon.	.000	10	0	0	0	0	0
Johnson, Randy, Ari.*	.879	35	2	27	4	33	1
Jones, Bobby J., S.D.	1.000	33	7	28	0	35	0
Karnuth, Jason, St.L.	.000	4	0	0	0	0	0
Karsay, Steve, Atl.	.909	43	4	6	1	11	0
Kile, Darryl, St.L.	.952	34	11	29	2	42	2
Kim, Byung-Hyun, Ari.	.958	78	4	19	1	24	0
King, Ray, Mil.*	.933	82	5	9	1	15	0
Kline, Steve, St.L.*	1.000	89	3	10	0	13	0
Knott, Eric, Ari.*	.000	3	0	0	0	0	0
Knotts, Gary, Fla.	1.000	2	1	0	0	1	0
Kolb, Brandon, Mil.	1.000	10	0	1	0	1	0
Koplove, Mike, Ari.	1.000	9	0	1	0	1	0
Lawrence, Brian, S.D.	.875	27	2	26	4	32	0
Lee, David, S.D.	1.000	41	2	2	0	4	0
Leiter, Al, N.Y.*	.933	29	6	22	2	30	2
Leiter, Mark, Mil.	1.000	20	4	7	0	11	0
Leskanic, Curtis, Mil.	.846	70	7	4	2	13	0
Levrault, Allen, Mil.	.905	32	8	11	2	21	1
Lieber, Jon, Chi.	1.000	34	16	35	0	51	4
Ligtenberg, Kerry, Atl.	.500	53	2	1	3	6	0
Lima, Jose, Hou.	.900	14	0	9	1	10	2
Lincoln, Mike, Pit.	.923	31	1	11	1	13	1
Linebrink, Scott, Hou.	.000	9	0	0	0	0	0
Lira, Felipe, Mon.	1.000	4	1	0	0	1	0
Lloyd, Graeme, Mon.*	.952	84	7	13	1	21	3
Loewer, Carlton, S.D.	.000	2	0	0	0	0	0
Loiselle, Rich, Pit.	1.000	18	1	4	0	5	0
Looper, Braden, Fla.	1.000	71	4	8	0	12	1
Lopez, Albie, Ari.	1.000	13	1	12	0	13	0
Loretta, Mark, Mil.	.000	1	0	0	0	0	0
Lundquist, David, S.D.	1.000	17	1	3	0	4	0
Mabry, John, Fla.	.000	1	0	0	0	0	0
MacRae, Scott, Cin.	1.000	24	2	1	0	3	0
Maddux, Greg, Atl.	.986	34	19	54	1	74	3
Mahay, Ron, Chi.*	1.000	17	2	3	0	5	1
Mann, Jim, Hou.	1.000	4	0	1	0	1	0
Mantei, Matt, Ari.	.000	8	0	0	0	0	0
Manzanillo, Josias, Pit.	.900	71	3	6	1	10	0
Marquis, Jason, Atl.	.909	38	9	21	3	33	2
Marte, Damaso, Pit.*	1.000	23	1	2	0	3	0
Martin, Tom, N.Y.*	1.000	14	1	1	0	2	0
Martinez, Ramon, Pit.	1.000	4	2	2	0	4	2
Mathews, T.J., St.L.	1.000	10	3	0	0	3	0
Mattes, Troy, Mon.	.875	8	2	5	1	8	0
Matthews, Mike, St.L.*	.917	51	4	7	1	12	0
Maurer, Dave, S.D.*	1.000	3	1	1	0	2	0
McElroy, Chuck, S.D.*	1.000	31	3	6	0	9	0
McKnight, Tony, Hou.-Pit.	.944	15	4	13	1	18	2
Mercado, Hector, Cin.*	.833	56	0	5	1	6	0
Mesa, Jose, Phi.	1.000	71	4	9	0	13	0
Miceli, Dan, Fla.-Col.	.833	51	2	3	1	6	0
Middlebrook, Jason, S.D.	1.000	4	0	2	0	2	0
Miller, Wade, Hou.	.963	32	16	36	2	54	3
Millwood, Kevin, Atl.	1.000	21	10	12	0	22	1
Mlicki, Dave, Hou.	1.000	19	6	9	0	15	1
Mohler, Mike, Ari.*	1.000	13	0	2	0	2	0
Moore, Trey, Atl.*	.000	2	0	0	0	0	0
Morgan, Mike, Ari.	.000	31	0	0	1	1	0
Morris, Matt, St.L.	.951	34	8	31	2	41	0
Moss, Damian, Atl.*	.500	5	0	1	1	2	0
Mota, Guillermo, Mon.	.917	53	1	10	1	12	3
Mulholland, Terry, Pit.-L.A.*	1.000	41	2	14	0	16	1
Munoz, Bobby, Mon.	.923	15	3	9	1	13	3
Myers, Mike, Col.*	1.000	73	2	12	0	14	1
Myers, Rodney, S.D.	.846	37	4	7	2	13	0
Neagle, Denny, Col.*	.963	30	9	17	1	27	1
Neal, Blaine, Fla.	.000	4	0	0	0	0	0
Nelson, Joe, Atl.	.000	2	0	0	0	0	0
Nen, Robb, S.F.	1.000	79	5	3	0	8	0
Neugebauer, Nick, Mil.	.000	2	0	0	0	0	0
Nichting, Chris, Cin.-Col.	1.000	43	3	9	0	12	0
Nickle, Doug, Phi.	.000	2	0	0	0	0	0
Nitkowski, C.J., N.Y.*	1.000	5	0	1	0	1	0
Nunez, Jose Antonio, L.A.-S.D.	.750	62	0	6	2	8	0
Nunez, Vladimir, Fla.	1.000	52	7	11	0	18	1
Ohka, Tomokazu, Mon.	1.000	10	4	8	0	12	0
Ohman, Will, Chi.*	1.000	11	1	0	0	1	0
Olivares, Omar, Pit.	1.000	45	4	19	0	23	1
Olsen, Kevin, Fla.	1.000	4	3	2	0	5	1
Olson, Gregg, L.A.	.750	28	0	3	1	4	0
Oropesa, Eddie, Phi.*	1.000	30	0	2	0	2	0
Orosco, Jesse, L.A.*	1.000	35	1	1	0	2	0
Ortiz, Russ, S.F.	.979	33	12	34	1	47	4
Osting, Jimmy, S.D.*	.000	3	0	0	0	0	0
Oswalt, Roy, Hou.	.971	28	19	15	1	35	1
Padilla, Vicente, Phi.	1.000	23	4	2	0	6	1
Painter, Lance, Mil.*	1.000	13	3	3	0	6	0
Park, Chan Ho, L.A.	.963	36	12	40	2	54	2
Pavano, Carl, Mon.	1.000	8	1	3	0	4	0
Penny, Brad, Fla.	1.000	31	10	27	0	37	1
Perez, Odalis, Atl.*	1.000	24	5	11	0	16	0
Person, Robert, Phi.	1.000	33	5	19	0	24	1
Peters, Chris, Mon.*	1.000	13	0	6	0	6	0
Peterson, Kyle, Mil.	1.000	3	1	2	0	3	0
Piersoll, Chris, Cin.	1.000	11	1	0	0	1	0
Politte, Cliff, Phi.	.800	23	4	4	2	10	0
Powell, Brian, Hou.	.000	1	0	0	0	0	0
Powell, Jay, Hou.-Col.	.947	74	10	8	1	19	2
Prinz, Bret, Ari.	1.000	46	3	6	0	9	1
Prokopec, Luke, L.A.	.920	29	8	15	2	25	2
Quevedo, Ruben, Mil.	1.000	10	6	4	0	10	0
Reames, Britt, Mon.	1.000	41	1	23	0	24	1
Redding, Tim, Hou.	1.000	13	4	5	0	9	1
Reed, Rick, N.Y.	1.000	20	11	25	0	36	0
Reed, Steve, Atl.	1.000	39	3	6	0	9	0
Reith, Brian, Cin.	1.000	9	1	3	0	4	0
Reitsma, Chris, Cin.	1.000	36	13	39	0	52	1
Relaford, Desi, N.Y.	.000	1	0	0	0	0	0
Remlinger, Mike, Atl.*	1.000	74	1	6	0	7	0
Reyes, Al, L.A.	1.000	19	3	3	0	6	0
Reyes, Dennys, Cin.*	.750	35	0	6	2	8	0
Reynolds, Shane, Hou.	1.000	28	9	30	0	39	2
Reynoso, Armando, Ari.	.923	9	1	11	1	13	2
Riedling, John, Cin.	1.000	29	3	6	0	9	0
Rigdon, Paul, Mil.	1.000	15	10	11	0	21	1
Riggan, Jerrod, N.Y.	1.000	35	2	5	0	7	1
Rijo, Jose, Cin.	.500	13	0	1	1	2	0
Ritchie, Todd, Pit.	.955	33	11	31	2	44	3
Roberts, Grant, N.Y.	1.000	16	2	1	0	3	0
Rocker, John, Atl.*	.833	30	1	4	1	6	0
Rodriguez, Felix, S.F.	.750	80	1	2	1	4	0
Rodriguez, Frank, Cin.	1.000	7	0	3	0	3	0
Rodriguez, Wilfredo, Hou.*	.000	2	0	0	0	0	0
Rose, Brian, N.Y.	1.000	3	0	1	0	1	0
RUETER, Kirk, S.F.*	1.000	34	11	50	0	61	11
Ruffin, Johnny, Fla.	.000	3	0	0	0	0	0
Rusch, Glendon, N.Y.*	.875	33	5	9	2	16	2
Sabel, Erik, Ari.	1.000	42	3	5	0	8	1
Sanchez, Jesus, Fla.*	.875	16	2	5	1	8	0
Santiago, Jose, Phi.	.889	53	4	4	1	9	1
Sauerbeck, Scott, Pit.*	.857	70	1	5	1	7	0
Scanlan, Bob, Mon.	.889	18	4	4	1	9	0
Schilling, Curt, Ari.	.973	35	15	21	1	37	4
Schmidt, Jason, Pit.-S.F.	1.000	25	6	9	0	15	0
Seanez, Rudy, S.D.-Atl.	1.000	38	4	3	0	7	0
Seelbach, Chris, Atl.	.000	5	0	0	0	0	0
Serrano, Wascar, S.D.	1.000	20	2	11	0	13	0
Shaw, Jeff, L.A.	1.000	77	8	14	0	22	0
Sheets, Ben, Mil.	.944	25	10	24	2	36	2
Silva, Jose, Pit.	1.000	26	1	4	0	5	0
Slusarski, Joe, Atl.-Hou.	1.000	12	2	1	0	3	0
Smith, Bud, St.L.*	1.000	16	3	18	0	21	0
Smith, Chuck, Fla.	.947	15	10	8	1	19	1
Smoltz, John, Atl.	.938	36	8	7	1	16	0
Sobkowiak, Scott, Atl.	.000	1	0	0	0	0	0
Speier, Justin, Col.	1.000	42	2	3	0	5	0
Spooneybarger, Tim, Atl.	.000	4	0	0	0	0	0
Springer, Dennis, L.A.	1.000	4	1	1	0	2	0
Springer, Russ, Ari.	.800	18	1	3	1	5	0
Stechschulte, Gene, St.L.	.944	67	7	10	1	18	1
Stewart, Scott, Mon.*	.917	62	0	11	1	12	1
Stone, Ricky, Hou.	.000	6	0	0	0	0	0
Strickland, Scott, Mon.	.857	77	3	9	2	14	2
Strong, Joe, Fla.	1.000	5	0	4	0	4	0
Sullivan, Scott, Cin.	1.000	79	6	10	0	16	0
Suzuki, Mac, Col.-Mil.	1.000	18	0	6	0	6	0

Player, Team	Pct.	G	PO	A	E	TC	DP
Swindell, Greg, Ari.*	1.000	64	1	3	0	4	1
Tabaka, Jeff, St.L.*	1.000	8	0	2	0	2	0
Tapani, Kevin, Chi.	.972	29	5	30	1	36	1
Tavaroz, Julian, Chi.	.938	34	14	31	3	48	6
Taylor, Billy, Pit.	.000	1	0	0	0	0	0
Telemaco, Amaury, Phi.	.944	24	6	11	1	18	2
Telford, Anthony, Mon.	1.000	8	1	1	0	2	0
Thomson, John, Col.	.962	14	17	8	1	26	3
Thurman, Mike, Mon.	.966	28	10	18	1	29	1
Timlin, Mike, St.L.	.952	67	6	14	1	21	2
Tollberg, Brian, S.D.	.929	19	6	20	2	28	1
Trachsel, Steve, N.Y.	.972	28	15	20	1	36	3
Trombley, Mike, L.A.	1.000	19	0	1	0	1	0
Urbina, Ugueth, Mon.	1.000	45	0	5	0	5	0
Valdes, Marc, Atl.	1.000	9	1	0	0	1	1
Van Poppel, Todd, Chi.	.714	59	2	8	4	14	2
Vazquez, Javier, Mon.	1.000	32	24	32	0	56	10
Veres, Dave, St.L.	.833	71	3	7	2	12	0
Villone, Ron, Col.-Hou.*	1.000	53	4	13	0	17	1
Vogelsong, Ryan, S.F.-Pit.	.909	15	4	6	1	11	2
Vosberg, Ed, Phi.*	1.000	18	1	1	0	2	0
Wagner, Billy, Hou.*	.857	64	1	5	1	7	0
Walker, Kevin, S.D.*	1.000	16	0	1	0	1	0
Walker, Pete, N.Y.	1.000	2	1	0	0	1	0
Wall, Donne, N.Y.	1.000	32	4	7	0	11	0
Wasdin, John, Col.	1.000	18	1	2	0	3	0
Weathers, Dave, Mil.-Chi.	.900	80	4	14	2	20	1
Wendell, Turk, N.Y.-Phi.	1.000	70	11	7	0	18	1
Wengert, Don, Pit.	1.000	4	0	4	0	4	0
White, Gabe, Col.*	1.000	69	3	6	0	9	1
White, Rick, N.Y.	.909	55	3	7	1	11	1
Whiteside, Matt, Atl.	.600	13	2	1	2	5	0
Wilkins, Marc, Pit.	1.000	14	1	3	0	4	0
Williams, Dave, Pit.*	1.000	22	6	19	0	25	1
Williams, Jeff, L.A.*	1.000	15	4	5	0	9	1
Williams, Mike, Pit.-Hou.	.923	65	5	7	1	13	1
Williams, Woody, S.D.-St.L.	.907	34	16	23	4	43	3
Williamson, Scott, Cin.	.000	2	0	0	0	0	0
Winchester, Scott, Cin.	1.000	12	3	4	0	7	0
Witasick, Jay, S.D.	.750	31	1	5	2	8	1
Witt, Bobby, Ari.	1.000	14	1	6	0	7	0
Wohlers, Mark, Cin.	.667	30	0	4	2	6	0
Wolf, Randy, Phi.*	.950	20	4	19	1	24	2
Wood, Kerry, Chi.	.971	28	11	22	1	34	1
Worrell, Tim, S.F.	.875	73	4	10	2	16	1
Wright, Jamey, Mil.	.980	33	17	31	1	49	4
Yoshii, Masato, Mon.	.885	42	5	18	3	26	1
Zambrano, Carlos, Chi.	1.000	6	0	2	0	2	1
Zerbe, Chad, S.F.*	.875	27	1	6	1	8	2

PITCHERS WITH TWO OR MORE TEAMS

Player, Team	Pct.	G	PO	A	E	TC	DP
Acevedo, Juan, Col.	1.000	39	4	3	0	7	1
Acevedo, Juan, Fla.	.750	20	0	3	1	4	0
Astacio, Pedro, Col.	.963	22	8	18	1	27	1
Astacio, Pedro, Hou.	1.000	4	2	7	0	9	0
Chen, Bruce, Phi.*	1.000	16	2	10	0	12	1
Chen, Bruce, N.Y.*	.929	11	2	11	1	14	0
Christiansen, Jason, St.L.*	1.000	30	0	2	0	2	0
Christiansen, Jason, S.F.*	1.000	25	1	3	0	4	0
Cook, Dennis, N.Y.*	.833	43	2	3	1	6	0
Cook, Dennis, Phi.*	.000	19	0	0	0	0	0
Elarton, Scott, Hou.	.931	20	9	18	2	29	2
Elarton, Scott, Col.	1.000	4	0	3	0	3	0
Fetters, Mike, L.A.	.800	34	1	3	1	5	0
Fetters, Mike, Pit.	1.000	20	0	5	0	5	0
Gomes, Wayne, Phi.	1.000	42	1	4	0	5	0
Gomes, Wayne, S.F.	1.000	13	1	1	0	2	0
McKnight, Tony, Hou.	.833	3	1	4	1	6	1
McKnight, Tony, Pit.	1.000	12	3	9	0	12	1
Miceli, Dan, Fla.	1.000	29	1	1	0	2	0
Miceli, Dan, Col.	.750	22	1	2	1	4	0
Mulholland, Terry, Pit.*	1.000	22	0	12	0	12	1
Mulholland, Terry, L.A.*	1.000	19	2	2	0	4	0
Nichting, Chris, Cin.	1.000	36	2	6	0	8	0
Nichting, Chris, Col.	1.000	7	1	3	0	4	0
Nunez, Jose Antonio, L.A.*	.000	6	0	0	1	1	0
Nunez, Jose Antonio, S.D.*	.857	56	0	6	1	7	0
Powell, Jay, Hou.	.875	35	3	4	1	8	1
Powell, Jay, Col.	1.000	39	7	4	0	11	1
Schmidt, Jason, Pit.	1.000	14	3	7	0	10	0
Schmidt, Jason, S.F.	1.000	11	3	2	0	5	0
Seanez, Rudy, S.D.	1.000	26	4	2	0	6	0
Seanez, Rudy, Atl.	1.000	12	0	1	0	1	0
Slusarski, Joe, Atl.	1.000	4	2	0	0	2	0
Slusarski, Joe, Hou.	1.000	8	0	1	0	1	0
Suzuki, Mac, Col.	.000	3	0	0	0	0	0
Suzuki, Mac, Mil.	1.000	15	0	6	0	6	0
Villone, Ron, Col.*	1.000	22	2	3	0	5	0
Villone, Ron, Hou.*	1.000	31	2	10	0	12	1
Vogelsong, Ryan, S.F.	.909	13	4	6	1	11	2
Vogelsong, Ryan, Pit.	.000	2	0	0	0	0	0
Weathers, Dave, Mil.	.923	52	3	9	1	13	0
Weathers, Dave, Chi.	.857	28	1	5	1	7	1
Wendell, Turk, N.Y.	1.000	49	8	5	0	13	1
Wendell, Turk, Phi.	1.000	21	3	2	0	5	0
Williams, Mike, Pit.	.857	40	1	5	1	7	1
Williams, Mike, Hou.	1.000	25	4	2	0	6	0
Williams, Woody, S.D.	.889	23	9	15	3	27	2
Williams, Woody, St.L.	.938	11	7	8	1	16	1

MISCELLANEOUS

SHUTOUT GAMES

Read across for wins, down for losses.

Team	Col.	St.L.	S.F.	Hou.	Ari.	Atl.	Chi.	Phi.	Fla.	N.Y.	Pit.	Mon.	L.A.	Mil.	S.D.	Cin.	A.L.	W	L	Pct.
Colorado..........	..	1	0	0	0	0	0	0	0	2	0	0	0	1	4	0	0	8	2	.800
St. Louis..........	0	..	0	0	0	1	0	1	1	1	3	0	0	1	2	1	0	11	5	.688
San Francisco...	1	0	..	0	1	0	1	0	0	0	1	1	0	0	1	0	2	8	4	.667
Houston..........	0	0	0	..	1	0	1	0	0	0	1	0	0	3	0	0	0	6	3	.667
Arizona	0	0	2	0	..	1	1	0	1	1	2	0	2	1	2	0	0	13	7	.650
Atlanta	0	0	0	0	1	..	0	1	1	1	1	2	0	1	1	0	4	13	8	.619
Chicago	0	0	0	0	0	0	..	0	0	1	0	0	1	1	0	3	0	6	4	.600
Philadelphia......	0	0	0	1	0	0	0	..	2	0	1	2	0	0	0	1	0	7	5	.583
Florida	1	0	0	0	0	2	0	0	..	0	1	1	3	0	1	0	2	11	9	.550
New York.........	0	0	0	0	0	1	0	1	0	..	1	3	1	1	1	0	5	14	12	.538
Pittsburgh........	0	1	0	1	0	0	0	0	0	0	..	0	0	2	1	1	3	9	11	.450
Montreal	0	0	1	0	1	1	0	1	1	3	0	..	1	1	0	0	0	11	15	.423
Los Angeles......	0	0	0	0	0	0	0	1	0	0	0	0	..	2	1	0	0	5	8	.385
Milwaukee	0	3	0	0	0	1	1	0	0	0	0	2	0	..	1	0	0	8	15	.348
San Diego	0	0	0	0	1	0	0	1	1	1	0	0	0	1	..	1	0	6	16	.273
Cincinnati	0	0	0	0	0	0	0	1	1	0	0	0	0	0	0	..	0	2	9	.182
A.L. Clubs........	0	0	1	1	2	0	0	0	0	0	0	2	3	0	0	2	..	..	..	..
Lost	2	5	4	3	7	8	4	5	9	12	11	15	8	15	16	9	..	138	133	.509

N.L. shutouts vs. A.L. clubs (16): New York vs. Toronto 2, New York vs. Boston, New York vs. New York, New York vs. Tampa Bay, Atlanta vs. Boston 2, Atlanta vs. Tampa Bay, Atlanta vs. Toronto, Pittsburgh vs. Kansas City 2, Pittsburgh vs. Cleveland, Florida vs. Baltimore, Florida vs. Tampa Bay, San Francisco vs. Anaheim, San Francisco vs. Oakland.

HOME RECORD

Read across for home wins, down for road losses.

Team	St.L.	S.F.	Chi.	Ari.	Phi.	Fla.	Hou.	L.A.	N.Y.	Col.	Atl.	Pit.	Mil.	S.D.	Mon.	Cin.	A.L.	W	L	Pct.
St. Louis..........	..	2	5	1	3	2	3	2	2	2	2	8	4	2	2	7	7	54	28	.659
San Francisco...	3	..	1	3	2	3	0	4	3	6	1	3	3	8	3	0	6	49	32	.605
Chicago..........	7	1	..	2	2	2	3	3	2	2	0	6	4	1	1	6	6	48	33	.593
Arizona	0	4	5	..	1	3	1	5	2	8	2	3	2	7	1	2	2	48	33	.593
Philadelphia......	2	2	1	2	..	9	1	3	3	2	6	3	1	2	5	1	4	47	34	.580
Florida	1	2	2	2	4	..	1	1	4	2	5	2	1	7	2	8	4	46	34	.575
Houston..........	4	0	5	2	1	1	..	2	2	3	1	5	5	1	3	6	3	44	37	.543
Los Angeles......	2	6	2	4	3	3	3	..	1	6	2	2	3	2	1	0	4	44	37	.543
New York.........	0	3	1	2	5	6	2	2	..	2	4	1	3	1	6	0	6	44	37	.543
Colorado..........	5	5	2	5	1	3	2	4	3	..	1	1	3	3	1	1	1	41	40	.506
Atlanta	2	2	1	0	6	5	1	1	5	2	..	2	1	2	5	1	4	40	41	.494
Pittsburgh........	1	1	4	2	1	1	6	1	0	2	0	..	9	1	1	3	5	38	43	.469
Milwaukee	4	2	3	2	1	3	1	3	1	1	1	5	..	1	2	4	2	36	45	.444
San Diego	0	3	2	5	1	1	1	3	3	3	2	2	3	..	1	1	4	35	46	.432
Montreal	1	1	1	1	5	4	0	2	4	2	2	3	1	1	..	1	5	34	47	.420
Cincinnati	4	1	3	0	0	3	2	1	1	1	0	5	2	0	2	..	2	27	54	.333
A.L. Clubs........	5	5	3	4	6	5	3	4	5	5	4	6	3	4	6	7	..	..	..	..
Lost on Road	41	40	41	37	42	52	32	39	43	49	33	57	49	37	47	42	..	675	621	.521

HOME RECORDS IN INTERLEAGUE GAMES

Team	Bal.	Bos.	N.Y.	T.B.	Tor.
Atlanta..........	2-1	1-2	..	1-2	..
Florida..........	3-0	..	2-1	3-0	..
Montreal..........	..	1-2	..	2-1	2-1
New York	..	2-1	1-2	..	3-0
Philadelphia ..	2-1	..	1-2	..	1-2

Team	Chi.	Cle.	Det.	K.C.	Min.	Tex.
Chicago.........	1-2	..	..	2-1	3-0	..
Cincinnati......	..	1-2	1-2	..	..	..
Houston..........	..	2-1	..	..	..	1-2
Milwaukee	0-3	..	..	1-2	1-2	..
Pittsburgh.....	..	3-0	..	2-1	..	..
St. Louis	3-0	..	1-2	..	3-0	..

Team	Ana.	Oak.	Sea.	Tex.	Det.	K.C.
Arizona..........	..	0-3	..	..	2-1	..
Colorado......	0-3	..	1-2	..	..	..
Los Angeles ..	1-2	..	1-2	2-1	..	..
San Diego	..	1-2	1-2	2-1	..	..
San Francisco	3-0	3-0	..	..	..	..

ROAD RECORD

Read across for road wins, down for home losses.

Team	Hou.	Atl.	S.D.	Ari.	L.A.	S.F.	Chi.	St.L.	Cin.	Phi.	N.Y.	Mon.	Mil.	Col.	Fla.	Pit.	A.L.	W	L	Pct.
Houston..........	..	2	2	2	0	3	4	5	5	2	1	3	7	1	2	4	6	49	32	.605
Atlanta..........	2	..	1	2	1	2	3	1	3	4	5	8	2	2	4	3	5	48	33	.593
San Diego	5	1	..	2	7	2	2	1	3	1	2	2	7	3	2	2	4	44	37	.543
Arizona	1	3	5	..	5	6	1	2	3	2	1	2	1	5	1	1	5	44	37	.543
Los Angeles.....	1	3	7	5	..	5	0	1	2	0	1	1	2	5	2	5	2	42	39	.519
San Francisco...	3	1	6	6	4	..	2	1	2	1	1	2	1	4	1	2	4	41	40	.506
Chicago	5	2	1	1	1	2	..	2	7	2	2	4	1	1	4	3	3	40	41	.494
St. Louis	4	1	3	3	1	0	3	..	3	1	3	2	6	1	1	6	1	39	41	.488
Cincinnati	4	2	2	1	3	3	1	3	..	2	3	2	4	2	1	4	2	39	42	.481
Philadelphia......	2	3	3	2	0	1	1	0	3	..	5	5	2	2	5	2	3	39	42	.481
New York.........	1	5	0	1	2	0	1	1	2	6	..	5	0	1	6	3	4	38	43	.469
Montreal	0	4	2	2	2	1	2	1	1	4	4	..	1	2	3	2	5	34	47	.420
Milwaukee	2	2	0	1	0	3	6	3	6	2	0	2	..	0	1	1	3	32	49	.395
Colorado..........	0	1	6	1	4	4	1	1	5	1	1	2	2	..	1	1	1	32	49	.395

Team	Hou.	Atl.	S.D.	Ari.	L.A.	S.F.	Chi.	St.L.	Cin.	Phi.	N.Y.	Mon.	Mil.	Col.	Fla.	Pit.	A.L.	W	L	Pct.
Florida	2	5	2	0	1	0	1	2	0	1	3	5	2	0	..	2	4	30	52	.366
Pittsburgh........	2	1	1	0	1	0	2	2	5	0	2	0	2	2	1	..	3	24	57	.296
A.L. Clubs........	3	5	5	4	5	0	3	2	4	5	3	4	7	5	1	1	..	..	..	..
Lost at Home	37	41	46	33	37	32	33	28	54	34	37	47	45	40	34	43	..	615	681	.475

PITCHING AGAINST EACH CLUB

ARIZONA—92-70

	Atl.	Chi.	Cin.	Col.	Fla.	Hou.	L.A.	Mil.	Mon.	N.Y.	Phi.	Pit.	S.D.	S.F.	St.L.	A.L.	Total
Pitcher	W-L	W-L	W-L	W-L	W-L	W-L	W-L	W-L	W-L	W-L	W-L	W-L	W-L	W-L	W-L	W-L	W-L
Anderson, Brian.....	0-0	0-0	1-0	1-0	0-0	0-0	0-2	0-0	0-2	0-0	0-1	0-0	0-0	2-1	0-0	0-3	4-9
Batista, Miguel.......	1-0	0-1	1-0	0-0	0-0	0-1	3-0	0-0	0-0	0-2	1-1	1-0	1-0	2-2	0-0	1-1	11-8
Bierbrodt, Nick	0-0	1-0	0-0	1-0	0-0	0-1	0-0	0-0	0-0	0-0	0-0	0-0	0-1	0-0	0-0	0-0	2-2
Brohawn, Troy	0-0	0-0	1-0	1-1	0-0	0-0	0-0	0-0	0-0	0-0	0-0	0-1	0-0	0-0	0-0	0-1	2-3
Ellis, Robert..........	1-0	0-1	0-0	0-0	0-0	0-1	0-0	0-0	0-0	0-1	0-0	0-0	0-1	1-0	1-0	2-1	6-5
Finley, Steve	0-0	0-0	0-0	0-0	0-0	0-0	0-0	0-0	0-0	0-0	0-0	0-0	0-0	0-0	0-0	0-0	0-0
Guzman, Geraldo....	0-0	0-0	0-0	0-0	0-0	0-0	0-0	0-0	0-0	0-0	0-0	0-0	0-0	0-0	0-0	0-0	0-0
Johnson, Randy	0-1	3-0	0-0	4-1	2-0	1-0	2-0	1-0	0-0	1-0	1-0	1-1	3-0	1-1	0-2	1-0	21-6
Kim, Byung-Hyun ..	0-0	0-0	0-0	2-2	0-0	0-0	0-1	0-0	1-0	0-0	1-0	0-0	0-1	0-1	0-0	0-0	5-6
Knott, Eric	0-0	0-0	0-0	0-0	0-0	0-0	0-0	0-1	0-0	0-0	0-0	0-0	0-0	0-0	0-0	0-0	0-1
Koplove, Mike	0-0	0-0	0-0	0-0	0-0	0-0	0-1	0-0	0-0	0-0	0-0	0-0	0-0	0-0	0-0	0-0	0-1
Lopez, Albie..........	1-0	1-0	0-0	0-1	0-1	0-0	0-0	1-1	0-1	0-0	0-1	1-0	0-0	0-2	0-0	0-0	4-7
Mantei, Matt..........	0-0	0-0	0-0	0-0	0-0	0-0	0-0	0-0	0-0	0-0	0-0	0-0	0-0	0-0	0-0	0-0	0-0
Mohler, Mike..........	0-0	0-0	0-0	0-0	0-0	0-0	0-0	0-0	0-0	0-0	0-0	0-0	0-0	0-0	0-0	0-0	0-0
Morgan, Mike	0-0	0-0	0-0	0-0	0-0	0-0	1-0	0-0	0-0	0-0	0-0	0-0	0-0	0-0	0-0	0-0	1-0
Prinz, Bret	0-0	0-0	0-0	1-0	1-0	0-0	0-0	0-0	0-0	0-0	0-0	0-0	1-1	0-0	0-0	1-0	4-1
Reynoso, Armando	0-1	0-0	0-0	0-1	0-0	0-0	0-2	0-0	0-0	0-0	0-0	0-0	0-0	1-1	0-1	0-1	1-6
Sabel, Erik	1-0	0-0	1-0	0-0	0-0	0-0	0-1	0-1	0-0	0-0	0-0	0-0	1-0	0-0	0-0	0-0	3-2
Schilling, Curt........	1-0	0-1	1-0	1-0	1-0	1-1	4-0	0-0	2-0	2-0	0-1	1-1	3-0	3-1	0-0	2-1	22-6
Springer, Russ	0-0	0-0	0-0	0-0	0-0	0-0	0-0	0-0	0-0	0-0	0-0	0-0	0-0	0-0	0-0	0-0	0-0
Swindell, Greg	0-0	0-0	0-1	1-0	0-1	0-0	0-2	0-0	0-0	0-0	0-0	0-0	1-1	0-1	0-0	0-0	2-6
Witt, Bobby	0-0	1-0	0-0	0-0	0-0	0-0	0-0	0-0	0-0	0-0	0-0	0-0	1-0	0-0	1-0	0-1	4-1
Totals	5-2	6-3	5-1	13-6	4-2	2-4	10-9	3-3	3-3	3-3	3-4	4-2	12-7	10-9	2-4	7-8	92-70

INTERLEAGUE: Schilling 1-0, Prinz 1-0, Anderson 0-1 vs. Angels; Ellis 1-0, Schilling 1-0, Brohawn 0-1 vs. Tigers; Johnson 1-0, Ellis 1-0, Reynoso 0-1 vs. Royals; Anderson 0-1, Batista 0-1, Schilling 0-1 vs. Athletics; Batista 1-0, Ellis 0-1, Anderson 0-1 vs. Mariners. Total: 7-8.

ATLANTA—88-74

	Ari.	Chi.	Cin.	Col.	Fla.	Hou.	L.A.	Mil.	Mon.	N.Y.	Phi.	Pit.	S.D.	S.F.	St.L.	A.L.	Total
Pitcher	W-L	W-L	W-L	W-L	W-L	W-L	W-L	W-L	W-L	W-L	W-L	W-L	W-L	W-L	W-L	W-L	W-L
Burkett, John	1-0	0-1	1-1	1-0	0-3	0-0	1-0	1-1	2-1	0-1	1-2	2-0	1-0	0-0	0-0	1-2	12-12
Cabrera, Jose	0-0	0-0	0-0	1-0	0-0	0-1	0-0	1-1	1-0	0-0	1-0	0-0	0-0	1-1	1-0	1-1	7-4
Glavine, Tom.........	1-0	1-0	1-0	0-0	2-1	1-0	0-1	0-0	3-0	1-0	2-0	1-1	0-0	0-1	1-1	2-2	16-7
Karsay, Steve	0-0	1-0	0-0	0-1	0-0	0-0	0-0	0-0	1-0	0-1	0-0	0-0	0-1	0-0	0-0	1-1	3-4
Ligtenberg, Kerry ..	0-0	1-0	0-0	0-0	1-0	0-1	0-0	0-0	0-0	0-2	0-0	0-0	0-0	1-0	0-0	0-0	3-3
Maddux, Greg........	0-2	0-1	0-0	0-0	2-1	1-0	0-1	1-0	3-1	2-0	2-3	1-0	1-1	1-0	0-1	3-0	17-11
Marquis, Jason	0-1	0-0	0-0	0-0	2-1	0-0	0-0	0-0	1-1	1-1	0-0	0-0	1-0	0-0	0-1	0-0	5-6
Millwood, Kevin.....	0-1	1-0	1-0	1-0	1-0	1-0	0-0	0-1	0-2	0-2	1-1	0-0	1-0	0-0	0-0	0-0	7-7
Moore, Trey	0-0	0-0	0-0	0-0	0-0	0-0	0-0	0-0	0-0	0-0	0-0	0-0	0-0	0-0	0-0	0-0	0-0
Moss, Damian	0-0	0-0	0-0	0-0	0-0	0-0	0-0	0-0	0-0	0-0	0-0	0-0	0-0	0-0	0-0	0-0	0-0
Nelson, Joe	0-0	0-0	0-0	0-0	0-0	0-0	0-0	0-0	0-0	0-0	0-0	0-0	0-0	0-0	0-0	0-0	0-0
Perez, Odalis	0-1	0-0	0-0	0-0	0-0	0-1	1-0	0-0	1-0	2-2	2-2	0-0	0-0	0-0	0-1	1-2	7-8
Reed, Steve	0-0	0-0	0-0	0-0	0-0	0-0	0-0	0-0	0-1	2-0	0-0	0-0	0-0	0-1	0-0	0-0	2-2
Remlinger, Mike	0-0	0-0	0-1	1-0	0-0	0-0	0-1	0-0	0-0	1-0	0-0	0-1	0-0	1-0	0-0	0-0	3-3
Rocker, John	0-0	0-0	0-0	0-0	1-2	0-0	0-0	0-0	0-0	0-0	1-0	0-0	0-0	0-0	0-0	0-0	2-2
Seanez, Rudy	0-0	0-0	0-0	0-0	0-0	0-0	0-0	0-0	0-0	0-0	0-0	0-0	0-0	0-0	0-0	0-0	0-0
Seelbach, Chris	0-0	0-0	0-0	0-0	0-0	0-0	0-0	0-0	0-0	0-0	0-0	0-0	0-0	0-0	0-0	0-0	0-0
Slusarski, Joe	0-0	0-0	0-0	0-0	0-0	0-0	0-0	0-0	0-0	0-0	0-0	0-0	0-0	0-0	0-0	0-0	0-0
Smoltz, John	0-0	0-0	0-0	0-1	0-1	0-0	0-0	0-0	1-0	1-0	0-1	1-0	0-0	0-0	0-0	0-0	3-3
Sobkowiak, Scott...	0-0	0-0	0-0	0-0	0-0	0-0	0-0	0-0	0-0	0-0	0-0	0-0	0-0	0-0	0-0	0-0	0-0
Spooneybarger, T. .	0-0	0-0	0-0	0-0	0-1	0-0	0-0	0-0	0-0	0-0	0-0	0-0	0-0	0-0	0-0	0-0	0-1
Valdes, Marc..........	0-0	0-0	1-0	0-0	0-0	0-0	0-0	0-0	0-0	0-0	0-0	0-0	0-0	0-0	0-0	0-0	1-0
Whiteside, Matt	0-0	0-0	0-0	0-0	0-0	0-0	0-1	0-0	0-0	0-0	0-0	0-0	0-0	0-0	0-0	0-0	0-1
Totals	2-5	4-2	4-2	4-2	9-10	3-3	2-5	3-3	13-6	10-9	10-9	5-1	3-3	4-2	3-3	9-9	88-74

INTERLEAGUE: Maddux 1-0, Glavine 1-0, Burkett 0-1 vs. Orioles; Burkett 1-0, Karsay 1-0, Glavine 1-0, Cabrera 0-1, Marquis 0-1, Perez 0-1 vs. Red Sox; Cabrera 1-0, Maddux 1-0, Glavine 0-1 vs. Yankees; Maddux 1-0, Perez 0-1, Karsay 0-1 vs. Devil Rays; Perez 1-0, Burkett 0-1, Glavine 0-1 vs. Blue Jays. Total: 9-9.

CHICAGO—88-74

	Ari.	Atl.	Cin.	Col.	Fla.	Hou.	L.A.	Mil.	Mon.	N.Y.	Phi.	Pit.	S.D.	S.F.	St.L.	A.L.	Total
Pitcher	W-L	W-L	W-L	W-L	W-L	W-L	W-L	W-L	W-L	W-L	W-L	W-L	W-L	W-L	W-L	W-L	W-L
Aybar, Manny	0-0	0-0	0-0	0-0	0-0	0-0	0-0	0-0	0-1	0-0	0-0	1-0	0-0	1-0	0-0	0-0	2-1
Bere, Jason	0-2	0-1	3-0	1-0	2-0	0-2	0-0	0-1	0-0	1-0	2-0	1-2	0-1	0-0	0-2	1-0	11-11
Borowski, Joe........	0-0	0-0	0-0	0-0	0-0	0-0	0-0	0-0	0-0	0-0	0-0	0-0	0-1	0-0	0-0	0-0	0-1
Chiasson, Scott	0-0	0-0	0-0	0-0	0-0	1-0	0-0	0-0	0-0	0-0	0-1	0-0	0-0	0-0	0-0	0-0	1-1
Cruz, Juan	0-0	1-0	0-0	0-0	0-0	0-0	0-1	0-0	0-0	0-0	1-0	0-0	0-0	1-0	0-0	0-0	3-1
Duncan, Courtney..	0-0	0-0	2-0	0-1	0-0	0-0	0-0	0-0	0-0	0-0	1-1	0-0	0-0	0-0	0-0	0-1	3-3
Farnsworth, Kyle ...	0-0	0-1	0-2	1-0	1-0	1-1	0-0	1-0	0-0	0-1	0-0	0-0	0-0	0-0	0-1	0-0	4-6
Fassero, Jeff..........	0-0	0-0	0-0	0-0	0-1	0-0	0-0	0-0	0-0	0-0	0-1	1-1	0-1	0-0	2-0	1-0	4-4
Fyhrie, Mike..........	0-0	0-0	0-0	0-0	0-0	0-0	0-0	0-0	0-1	0-0	0-0	0-0	0-0	0-0	0-1	0-0	0-2
Gordon, Tom	0-0	0-0	0-0	0-0	0-1	0-0	1-1	0-0	0-0	0-0	0-0	0-0	0-0	0-0	0-0	0-0	1-2

– 307 –

Pitcher	Ari. W-L	Atl. W-L	Cin. W-L	Col. W-L	Fla. W-L	Hou. W-L	L.A. W-L	Mil. W-L	Mon. W-L	N.Y. W-L	Phi. W-L	Pit. W-L	S.D. W-L	S.F. W-L	St.L. W-L	A.L. W-L	Total W-L
Heredia, Felix	0-0	0-0	0-0	0-0	0-0	0-0	0-0	0-0	0-0	0-0	0-0	1-0	0-1	0-0	0-0	1-1	2-2
Lieber, Jon	0-1	0-0	5-0	1-0	0-1	2-1	0-0	0-0	1-0	0-1	2-0	2-0	1-0	1-0	3-1	2-1	20-6
Mahay, Ron	0-0	0-0	0-0	0-0	0-0	0-0	0-0	0-0	0-0	0-0	0-0	0-0	0-0	0-0	0-0	0-0	0-0
Ohman, Will	0-1	0-0	0-0	0-0	0-0	0-0	0-0	0-0	0-0	0-0	0-0	0-0	0-0	0-0	0-0	0-0	0-1
Tapani, Kevin	1-2	0-2	0-1	0-1	0-0	0-2	1-0	4-1	2-0	0-1	1-0	0-0	0-1	0-2	0-1	0-1	9-14
Tavarez, Julian	0-0	1-0	0-1	0-1	0-0	0-1	1-1	0-3	1-0	1-0	1-0	2-0	0-1	2-0	0-0	1-1	10-9
Van Poppel, Todd	0-0	0-0	2-0	0-0	0-0	0-1	0-0	1-0	0-0	0-0	0-0	0-0	0-0	0-0	0-0	1-0	4-1
Weathers, Dave	0-0	0-0	0-0	0-0	0-0	1-1	0-0	0-0	0-0	0-0	0-0	0-0	0-0	0-0	0-0	0-0	1-1
Wood, Kerry	2-0	0-0	1-0	0-0	0-0	2-0	1-0	2-2	0-1	1-0	0-0	0-0	0-1	1-0	1-1	1-1	12-6
Zambrano, Carlos	0-0	0-0	0-0	0-0	0-0	1-0	0-0	0-1	0-0	0-0	0-0	0-1	0-0	0-0	0-0	0-0	1-2
Totals	3-6	2-4	13-4	3-3	3-3	8-9	4-2	8-9	3-3	4-2	4-2	10-6	2-4	3-3	9-8	9-6	88-74

INTERLEAGUE: Van Poppel 1-0, Fassero 1-0, Duncan 0-1, Tavarez 0-1, Lieber 0-1, Wood 0-1 vs. White Sox; Heredia 1-1, Lieber 1-0 vs. Tigers; Lieber 1-0, Bere 1-0, Tapani 0-1 vs. Royals; Tavarez 1-0, Lieber 1-0, Wood 1-0 vs. Twins. Total: 9-6.

CINCINNATI—66-96

Pitcher	Ari. W-L	Atl. W-L	Chi. W-L	Col. W-L	Fla. W-L	Hou. W-L	L.A. W-L	Mil. W-L	Mon. W-L	N.Y. W-L	Phi. W-L	Pit. W-L	S.D. W-L	S.F. W-L	St.L. W-L	A.L. W-L	Total W-L
Acevedo, Jose	0-0	0-1	1-1	1-0	0-1	0-0	0-0	1-1	1-0	0-0	0-0	1-1	0-0	0-0	0-2	0-0	5-7
Atchley, Justin	0-0	0-0	0-0	0-0	0-0	0-0	0-0	0-0	0-0	0-0	0-0	0-0	0-0	0-0	0-0	0-0	0-0
Bell, Rob	0-0	0-0	0-1	0-0	0-0	0-1	0-0	0-0	0-0	0-0	0-0	0-0	0-1	0-0	0-1	0-1	0-5
Brower, Jim	0-1	1-1	0-2	0-1	0-0	1-2	0-0	0-0	0-1	1-0	1-0	1-0	1-0	0-0	0-0	1-2	7-10
Davis, Lance	0-0	0-0	0-0	0-0	2-0	0-0	1-0	1-1	0-0	0-0	1-1	0-2	0-0	0-0	2-0	1-0	8-4
Dessens, Elmer	0-0	0-1	1-0	1-1	1-0	1-1	1-0	1-2	1-0	0-1	0-1	1-2	0-1	0-0	2-1	0-3	10-14
Fernandez, Jared	0-0	0-0	0-0	0-0	0-0	0-0	0-0	0-0	0-0	0-1	0-0	0-0	0-0	0-0	0-0	0-0	0-1
Fernandez, Osvaldo	0-0	0-0	0-2	0-0	0-0	1-0	0-0	0-1	0-0	2-0	1-0	0-1	1-0	0-1	0-1	0-0	5-6
Graves, Danny	1-1	0-0	1-0	0-1	0-0	1-0	0-0	0-0	0-1	0-0	0-0	1-0	0-1	0-1	1-0	1-0	6-5
Hamilton, Joey	0-0	0-0	0-1	0-0	0-0	0-0	0-0	0-0	0-0	0-0	1-1	0-0	0-0	0-0	0-0	0-0	1-2
Harnisch, Pete	0-0	0-0	0-0	0-0	0-0	0-1	0-0	0-2	0-0	0-0	1-0	0-0	0-0	0-0	0-0	0-0	1-3
MacRae, Scott	0-0	0-0	0-1	0-0	0-0	0-0	0-0	0-0	0-0	0-0	0-0	0-0	0-0	0-0	0-0	0-0	0-1
Mercado, Hector	0-1	0-0	0-0	1-1	0-0	0-0	0-0	0-0	0-0	0-0	0-0	0-0	0-0	1-0	1-0	0-0	3-2
Nichting, Chris	0-0	0-0	0-0	0-0	0-0	0-1	0-0	0-0	0-0	0-0	0-0	0-0	0-0	0-0	0-2	0-0	0-3
Piersoll, Chris	0-0	0-0	0-0	0-0	0-0	0-0	0-0	0-0	0-0	0-0	0-0	0-0	0-0	0-0	0-0	0-0	0-0
Reith, Brian	0-1	0-0	0-1	0-0	0-0	0-1	0-0	0-1	0-0	0-0	0-0	0-1	0-0	0-0	0-2	0-0	0-7
Reitsma, Chris	0-0	0-0	0-3	0-2	1-1	0-3	0-1	1-0	1-0	1-1	0-0	2-0	0-1	0-0	0-1	1-2	7-15
Reyes, Dennys	0-0	0-1	0-0	0-0	0-0	0-2	0-0	0-2	0-0	0-0	0-0	1-0	0-0	1-0	0-1	0-0	2-6
Riedling, John	0-0	0-0	0-0	0-0	0-0	0-0	0-0	0-0	0-0	0-0	0-0	0-1	0-0	1-0	0-0	0-0	1-1
Rijo, Jose	0-0	0-0	0-0	0-0	0-0	0-0	0-0	0-0	0-0	0-0	0-0	0-0	0-0	0-0	0-0	0-0	0-0
Rodriguez, Frank	0-0	0-0	0-0	0-0	0-0	0-0	0-0	0-0	0-0	0-0	0-0	0-0	0-0	0-0	0-0	0-0	0-0
Sullivan, Scott	0-0	1-0	1-0	0-0	0-0	1-0	0-0	1-0	1-0	0-0	0-0	1-1	0-0	0-0	1-0	0-0	7-1
Williamson, Scott	0-0	0-0	0-0	0-0	0-0	0-0	0-0	0-0	0-0	0-0	0-0	0-0	0-0	0-0	0-0	0-0	0-0
Winchester, Scott	0-0	0-0	0-1	0-0	0-0	0-0	0-0	0-0	0-0	0-0	0-0	0-0	0-0	0-1	0-0	0-0	0-2
Wohlers, Mark	0-1	0-0	0-0	0-0	0-0	1-0	1-0	1-0	0-0	0-0	0-0	0-0	0-0	0-0	0-0	0-0	3-1
Totals	1-5	2-4	4-13	3-6	4-2	6-11	4-2	6-10	4-2	4-2	2-4	9-8	2-4	4-2	7-10	4-11	66-96

INTERLEAGUE: Dessens 0-1, Bell 0-1, Brower 0-1 vs. White Sox; Reitsma 1-1, Brower 1-0, Graves 1-0, Fernandez 0-1, Dessens 0-1 vs. Indians; Davis 1-0, Nichting 0-1, Reitsma 0-1 vs. Tigers; Nichting 0-1, Brower 0-1, Dessens 0-1 vs. Twins. Total: 4-11.

COLORADO—73-89

Pitcher	Ari. W-L	Atl. W-L	Chi. W-L	Cin. W-L	Fla. W-L	Hou. W-L	L.A. W-L	Mil. W-L	Mon. W-L	N.Y. W-L	Phi. W-L	Pit. W-L	S.D. W-L	S.F. W-L	St.L. W-L	A.L. W-L	Total W-L
Acevedo, Juan	0-0	0-0	0-0	0-0	0-0	0-0	0-0	0-0	0-0	0-0	0-0	0-0	0-0	0-1	0-0	0-1	0-2
Astacio, Pedro	1-1	0-0	0-0	0-0	0-1	0-1	0-3	0-0	0-1	1-0	0-1	0-0	2-0	1-0	1-2	0-3	6-13
Belitz, Todd	0-0	0-0	0-0	0-0	0-0	0-0	0-0	0-0	0-0	0-0	0-0	1-0	0-1	0-0	0-0	0-0	1-1
Bohanon, Brian	0-1	0-0	0-1	1-1	0-0	1-0	2-0	0-0	0-0	0-1	1-0	0-1	0-1	0-1	0-0	0-1	5-8
Chacon, Shawn	0-1	0-1	0-0	0-0	0-0	0-2	1-0	0-0	0-0	1-1	0-0	0-2	0-0	2-2	0-0	2-1	6-10
Chouinard, Bobby	0-0	0-0	0-0	0-0	0-0	0-0	0-0	0-0	0-0	0-0	0-0	0-0	0-0	0-0	0-0	0-0	0-0
Christman, Tim	0-0	0-0	0-0	0-0	0-0	0-0	0-0	0-0	0-0	0-0	0-0	0-0	0-0	0-0	0-0	0-0	0-0
Davenport, Joe	0-0	0-0	0-0	0-0	0-0	0-0	0-0	0-0	0-0	0-0	0-0	0-0	0-0	0-0	0-0	0-0	0-0
Davis, Kane	0-2	0-0	0-0	0-1	0-0	0-0	1-0	0-0	1-0	0-0	0-0	0-0	0-1	0-0	0-0	0-0	2-4
Dingman, Craig	0-0	0-0	0-0	0-0	0-0	0-0	0-0	0-0	0-0	0-0	0-0	0-0	0-0	0-0	0-0	0-0	0-0
Elarton, Scott	0-0	0-0	0-0	0-0	0-0	0-0	0-0	0-0	0-0	0-0	0-0	0-0	0-1	0-0	0-1	0-0	0-2
Estrada, Horacio	1-0	0-0	0-0	0-0	0-0	0-0	0-0	0-0	0-0	0-0	0-0	0-0	0-0	0-0	0-1	0-0	1-1
Hampton, Mike	1-2	0-2	2-0	0-0	1-0	1-0	0-3	1-0	0-0	1-1	0-0	2-0	1-2	2-1	2-0	0-2	14-13
Jennings, Jason	0-0	0-0	0-0	0-0	0-0	1-0	0-0	0-0	1-0	0-0	0-0	1-0	1-1	0-0	0-0	0-0	4-1
Jimenez, Jose	0-1	1-0	1-0	0-0	0-0	0-0	1-0	1-0	0-0	1-0	0-0	0-0	1-0	0-0	0-0	0-0	6-1
Miceli, Dan	0-0	0-0	0-0	1-0	0-0	0-0	0-0	0-0	0-0	0-0	0-0	0-0	1-0	0-0	0-0	0-0	2-0
Myers, Mike	2-0	0-0	0-0	0-1	0-0	0-0	0-1	0-0	0-0	0-0	0-0	0-1	0-0	0-0	0-0	0-0	2-3
Neagle, Denny	1-1	1-0	0-0	0-0	1-0	0-0	1-3	1-0	1-0	0-0	0-2	1-0	0-0	1-0	2-0	0-1	9-8
Nichting, Chris	0-0	0-0	0-0	0-0	0-0	0-0	0-0	0-0	0-0	0-0	0-0	0-0	0-0	0-0	0-0	0-0	0-0
Powell, Jay	0-0	0-0	0-0	1-0	0-0	0-0	1-0	1-0	0-1	0-0	0-0	0-0	0-0	0-0	0-0	0-0	3-1
Speier, Justin	0-0	0-0	0-1	0-0	0-0	0-0	1-0	1-0	0-0	1-0	0-0	0-0	1-1	0-1	0-0	0-0	4-3
Suzuki, Mac	0-0	0-0	0-0	1-0	0-0	0-0	0-0	0-0	0-0	0-0	0-0	0-0	1-1	0-0	0-0	0-1	2-2
Thomson, John	0-0	0-0	0-1	0-0	1-1	0-0	0-0	1-0	0-1	0-0	0-1	0-0	1-0	1-1	0-0	0-0	4-5
Villone, Ron	0-1	0-0	0-0	0-0	0-0	1-0	0-1	0-0	0-0	0-0	0-1	0-0	0-0	0-0	0-0	0-0	1-3
Wasdin, John	0-0	0-1	0-0	1-0	0-0	0-0	0-0	0-0	0-0	0-0	0-0	0-0	0-0	0-0	1-0	0-0	2-1
White, Gabe	0-3	0-0	0-0	0-0	0-0	0-0	0-1	0-0	0-0	0-0	0-0	0-1	0-1	0-0	0-1	0-0	1-7
Totals	6-13	2-4	3-3	6-3	4-2	2-4	8-11	5-1	3-4	4-3	2-4	2-4	9-10	9-10	6-3	2-10	73-89

INTERLEAGUE: Hampton 0-1, Suzuki 0-1, Chacon 0-1 vs. Angels; Bohanon 0-1, Neagle 0-1, Astacio 0-1 vs. Athletics; Chacon 1-0, Acevedo 0-1, Astacio 0-1 vs. Mariners; Chacon 1-0, Astacio 0-1, Hampton 0-1 vs. Rangers. Total: 2-10.

FLORIDA—76-86

Pitcher	Ari. W-L	Atl. W-L	Chi. W-L	Cin. W-L	Col. W-L	Hou. W-L	L.A. W-L	Mil. W-L	Mon. W-L	N.Y. W-L	Phi. W-L	Pit. W-L	S.D. W-L	S.F. W-L	St.L. W-L	A.L. W-L	Total W-L
Acevedo, Juan	0-0	1-0	0-0	0-0	0-0	0-0	0-0	0-0	0-1	1-1	0-1	0-0	0-0	0-0	0-0	0-0	2-3
Alfonseca, Antonio	0-0	0-0	0-0	0-0	0-0	1-0	0-0	0-0	0-0	1-1	1-1	1-0	0-0	0-0	0-1	0-1	4-4
Almanza, Armando	0-1	0-0	1-0	0-0	0-1	0-0	0-0	1-0	0-0	0-0	0-0	0-0	0-0	0-0	0-0	0-0	2-2
Baez, Benito	0-0	0-0	0-0	0-0	0-0	0-0	0-0	0-0	0-0	0-0	0-0	0-0	0-0	0-0	0-0	0-0	0-0
Beckett, Josh	0-0	0-1	1-0	0-0	0-0	0-0	0-0	0-0	0-1	0-0	1-0	0-0	0-0	0-0	0-0	0-0	2-2
Bones, Ricky	0-0	0-0	0-1	0-0	0-0	1-0	0-0	0-0	1-0	1-0	0-1	1-0	0-0	0-0	0-0	0-2	4-4
Burnett, A.J.	0-0	1-2	0-0	1-1	1-0	0-1	1-1	0-0	1-1	0-2	0-1	1-0	1-1	0-1	0-1	4-0	11-12
Clement, Matt	1-0	1-1	0-2	1-1	0-0	0-1	0-1	0-1	0-2	0-1	2-0	0-0	1-0	1-0	0-0	2-0	9-10
Darensbourg, Vic	1-0	0-1	0-0	0-0	0-0	0-0	0-0	0-0	0-0	0-0	0-0	0-0	0-1	0-0	0-0	0-0	1-2
Dempster, Ryan	0-1	1-2	0-0	0-0	0-2	1-1	0-2	2-0	2-0	4-1	1-1	1-0	0-0	0-1	1-0	2-1	15-12
Grilli, Jason	0-1	0-0	0-0	0-0	0-0	0-0	0-0	0-0	2-0	0-0	0-0	0-0	0-0	0-0	0-0	0-0	2-2
Knotts, Gary	0-0	0-0	0-0	0-0	0-0	0-0	0-0	0-1	0-0	0-0	0-0	0-0	0-0	0-0	0-0	0-0	0-1
Looper, Braden	0-0	2-0	0-0	0-0	0-0	0-0	0-0	0-0	1-0	0-0	0-2	0-0	0-1	0-0	0-0	0-0	3-3
Mabry, John	0-0	0-0	0-0	0-0	0-0	0-0	0-0	0-0	0-0	0-0	0-0	0-0	0-0	0-0	0-0	0-0	0-0
Miceli, Dan	0-0	0-1	0-0	0-0	0-0	0-0	0-0	0-0	0-2	0-1	0-1	0-0	0-0	0-0	0-0	0-0	0-5
Neal, Blaine	0-0	0-0	0-0	0-0	0-0	0-0	0-0	0-0	0-0	0-0	0-0	0-0	0-0	0-0	0-0	0-0	0-0
Nunez, Vladimir	0-0	1-0	1-0	0-0	0-0	0-0	0-1	0-0	0-1	0-1	0-2	0-0	0-0	2-0	0-0	0-0	4-5
Olsen, Kevin	0-0	0-0	0-0	0-0	0-0	0-0	0-0	0-0	0-0	0-0	0-0	0-0	0-0	0-0	0-0	0-0	0-0
Penny, Brad	0-0	1-0	0-0	0-2	1-0	0-0	1-0	0-0	4-0	0-2	0-0	0-1	1-1	0-0	0-1	2-1	10-10
Ruffin, Johnny	0-0	0-0	0-0	0-0	0-0	0-0	0-0	0-0	0-0	0-0	0-0	0-0	0-0	0-0	0-0	0-0	0-0
Sanchez, Jesus	0-1	0-0	0-0	0-0	0-1	0-0	0-0	1-0	0-0	0-0	0-0	0-1	0-1	0-0	1-0	0-0	2-4
Smith, Chuck	0-0	2-0	0-0	0-0	0-0	0-0	0-0	0-0	0-1	0-1	0-2	0-0	0-0	1-0	0-0	1-1	5-5
Strong, Joe	0-0	0-0	0-0	0-0	0-0	0-0	0-0	0-0	0-0	0-0	0-0	0-0	0-0	0-0	0-0	0-0	0-0
Totals	2-4	10-9	3-3	2-4	2-4	3-3	2-5	4-2	12-7	7-12	5-14	4-2	3-4	2-4	3-3	12-6	76-86

INTERLEAGUE: Clement 1-0, Sanchez 1-0, Burnett 1-0 vs. Orioles; Clement 1-0, Dempster 0-1, Smith 0-1 vs. Red Sox; Burnett 1-0, Smith 1-0, Alfonseca 0-1 vs. Yankees; Dempster 2-0, Penny 1-1, Burnett 1-0, Bones 0-1 vs. Devil Rays; Burnett 1-0, Penny 1-0, Bones 0-1 vs. Blue Jays. Total: 12-6.

HOUSTON—93-69

Pitcher	Ari. W-L	Atl. W-L	Chi. W-L	Cin. W-L	Col. W-L	Fla. W-L	L.A. W-L	Mil. W-L	Mon. W-L	N.Y. W-L	Phi. W-L	Pit. W-L	S.D. W-L	S.F. W-L	St.L. W-L	A.L. W-L	Total W-L
Astacio, Pedro	0-0	0-0	0-1	0-0	0-0	1-0	0-0	0-0	0-0	0-0	1-0	0-0	0-0	0-0	0-0	0-0	2-1
Bottenfield, Kent	0-0	0-0	0-0	1-1	0-0	0-0	0-0	0-0	0-0	0-1	0-1	0-1	0-0	1-0	0-1	0-0	2-5
Cruz, Nelson	0-0	0-1	0-0	1-0	0-0	0-0	0-0	0-0	0-0	1-1	0-0	0-0	0-0	0-0	1-0	0-0	3-3
Dotel, Octavio	1-0	1-1	0-0	1-2	0-0	0-0	1-1	0-1	0-0	0-0	0-0	1-0	0-0	1-0	0-0	1-0	7-5
Elarton, Scott	0-1	0-1	0-0	0-0	0-1	0-0	0-0	1-0	1-0	0-1	0-0	0-1	0-1	0-0	2-0	0-2	4-8
Franklin, Wayne	0-0	0-0	0-0	0-0	0-0	0-0	0-0	0-0	0-0	0-0	0-0	0-0	0-0	0-0	0-0	0-0	0-0
Hernandez, Carlos	0-0	0-0	0-0	0-0	0-0	0-0	0-0	0-0	0-0	0-0	1-0	0-0	0-0	0-0	0-0	0-0	1-0
Jackson, Mike	0-0	1-0	1-0	0-0	0-0	0-0	0-0	0-1	0-0	0-1	1-1	0-0	0-0	0-0	1-0	1-0	5-3
Lima, Jose	0-0	0-0	0-0	0-1	0-0	1-0	0-0	0-0	0-0	0-0	0-0	0-0	0-0	0-1	0-0	0-0	1-2
Linebrink, Scott	0-0	0-0	0-0	0-0	0-0	0-0	0-0	0-0	0-0	0-0	0-0	0-0	0-0	0-0	0-0	0-0	0-0
Mann, Jim	0-0	0-0	0-0	0-0	0-0	0-0	0-0	0-0	0-0	0-0	0-0	0-0	0-0	0-0	0-0	0-0	0-0
McKnight, Tony	0-0	0-0	0-0	0-0	0-0	0-0	0-0	0-0	0-0	0-0	0-0	1-0	0-0	0-0	0-0	0-0	1-0
Miller, Wade	1-0	0-0	0-0	2-0	1-1	1-0	0-1	5-0	1-0	0-0	0-1	1-2	1-1	0-0	2-2	1-0	16-8
Milicki, Dave	1-0	0-0	0-1	1-0	0-0	1-0	0-0	0-0	0-0	0-0	0-0	2-1	0-0	1-1	1-0	0-0	7-3
Oswalt, Roy	1-0	0-0	1-2	3-0	1-0	0-0	1-1	2-0	1-0	0-0	0-0	2-0	1-0	0-0	1-0	0-0	14-3
Powell, Brian	0-0	0-0	0-0	0-0	0-0	0-1	0-0	0-0	0-0	0-0	0-0	0-0	0-0	0-0	0-0	0-0	0-1
Powell, Jay	0-0	0-0	0-0	0-0	0-0	0-0	0-0	0-0	0-0	0-0	0-0	0-0	0-0	0-1	1-1	0-0	2-2
Redding, Tim	0-0	0-0	1-0	0-0	0-0	1-0	0-0	0-0	0-0	0-0	0-0	0-0	0-0	0-1	1-0	0-0	3-1
Reynolds, Shane	0-1	1-0	5-0	2-0	2-0	0-1	0-1	2-0	0-2	1-2	0-1	1-0	0-2	0-0	0-0	0-0	14-11
Rodriguez, Wilf.	0-0	0-0	0-0	0-0	0-0	0-0	0-0	0-0	0-0	0-0	0-0	0-0	0-0	0-0	0-0	0-0	0-0
Slusarski, Joe	0-0	0-0	0-0	0-1	0-0	0-0	0-0	0-0	0-0	0-0	0-0	0-0	0-0	0-0	0-0	0-0	0-1
Stone, Ricky	0-0	0-0	0-0	0-0	0-0	0-0	0-0	0-0	0-0	0-0	0-0	0-0	0-0	0-0	0-0	0-0	0-0
Villone, Ron	0-0	0-0	0-4	0-0	0-0	0-0	0-0	0-1	1-0	0-0	0-0	0-0	1-0	0-0	1-2	2-0	5-7
Wagner, Billy	0-0	0-0	0-0	0-1	0-0	0-1	0-0	0-1	0-0	1-0	1-0	0-1	0-1	0-0	0-0	0-0	2-6
Williams, Mike	0-0	0-0	1-0	0-0	0-0	0-0	0-0	1-0	0-0	0-0	1-0	0-0	0-0	1-0	0-0	0-0	4-0
Totals	4-2	3-3	9-8	11-6	4-2	3-3	2-4	12-5	6-0	3-3	3-3	9-8	3-6	3-3	9-7	9-6	93-69

INTERLEAGUE: Redding 1-0, Villone 1-0, Reynolds 0-1 vs. Indians; Miller 1-0, Villone 1-0, Jackson 1-0 vs. Royals; Oswalt 1-0, Elarton 0-1, Reynolds 0-1 vs. Twins; Powell 1-1, Cruz 1-0, Dotel 1-0, Bottenfield 0-1, Elarton 0-1 vs. Rangers. Total: 9-6.

LOS ANGELES—86-76

Pitcher	Ari. W-L	Atl. W-L	Chi. W-L	Cin. W-L	Col. W-L	Fla. W-L	Hou. W-L	Mil. W-L	Mon. W-L	N.Y. W-L	Phi. W-L	Pit. W-L	S.D. W-L	S.F. W-L	St.L. W-L	A.L. W-L	Total W-L
Adams, Terry	0-1	1-0	0-0	0-1	3-0	0-1	0-0	0-0	0-0	1-1	1-1	3-0	0-1	2-1	1-0	0-1	12-8
Ashby, Andy	2-0	0-0	0-0	0-0	0-0	0-0	0-0	0-0	0-0	0-0	0-0	0-0	0-0	0-0	0-0	0-0	2-0
Baldwin, James	1-0	0-0	1-0	0-0	0-2	1-0	0-0	0-0	0-0	0-0	0-1	0-0	0-0	1-1	0-1	0-0	3-6
Brown, Kevin	0-1	0-0	0-0	1-0	1-1	0-0	0-0	0-0	0-0	0-1	0-0	2-0	3-0	0-0	2-0	0-1	10-4
Carrara, Giovanni	0-0	0-0	0-0	0-0	0-0	1-0	0-0	0-0	1-0	0-0	0-0	1-0	2-0	1-0	0-0	0-1	6-1
Donnels, Chris	0-0	0-0	0-0	0-0	0-0	0-0	0-0	0-0	0-0	0-0	0-0	0-0	0-0	0-0	0-0	0-0	0-0
Dreifort, Darren	1-3	0-0	0-1	0-0	0-1	1-0	0-1	0-0	1-0	0-0	0-0	0-1	0-0	0-0	1-0	0-0	4-7
Fetters, Mike	0-0	0-0	0-0	0-0	0-0	0-0	2-1	0-0	0-0	0-0	0-0	0-0	0-0	0-0	0-0	0-0	2-1
Gagne, Eric	1-0	0-2	0-0	0-0	2-0	0-0	0-0	0-1	0-0	0-1	1-0	1-0	1-0	1-1	0-1	0-1	6-7
Herges, Matt	1-0	0-0	0-1	0-1	2-2	0-0	0-0	1-1	0-0	0-0	1-0	1-2	1-0	0-0	2-1	0-0	9-8
Mulholland, Terry	0-1	0-0	1-0	0-0	0-0	0-0	0-0	0-0	0-0	0-0	0-0	0-0	0-0	0-0	0-0	0-0	1-1
Nunez, Jose A.	0-0	0-0	0-0	0-0	0-0	0-0	0-0	0-0	0-0	0-0	0-0	0-0	0-0	0-0	0-0	0-0	0-0
Olson, Gregg	0-0	0-0	0-0	0-0	0-0	0-0	0-0	0-0	0-0	0-0	0-0	0-0	0-1	0-0	0-0	0-0	0-1
Orosco, Jesse	0-0	0-0	0-0	0-1	0-0	0-0	0-0	0-0	0-0	0-0	0-0	0-0	0-0	0-0	0-0	0-0	0-1
Park, Chan Ho	2-0	1-0	0-2	0-0	3-0	1-0	1-0	3-0	0-1	0-1	1-0	0-2	0-1	2-2	0-1	1-1	15-11
Prokopec, Luke	1-1	2-0	0-0	1-1	0-1	0-1	1-0	0-0	0-0	1-0	0-0	0-0	1-2	1-0	0-0	0-1	8-7

Pitcher	Ari. W-L	Atl. W-L	Chi. W-L	Cin. W-L	Col. W-L	Fla. W-L	Hou. W-L	Mil. W-L	Mon. W-L	N.Y. W-L	Phi. W-L	Pit. W-L	S.D. W-L	S.F. W-L	St.L. W-L	A.L. W-L	Total W-L
Reyes, Al	0-0	0-0	0-0	0-0	0-0	0-0	0-0	0-0	0-0	0-0	0-0	0-0	0-0	1-1	0-0	1-0	2-1
Shaw, Jeff	1-0	1-0	0-0	0-0	0-1	0-0	0-0	0-0	0-1	0-0	0-0	0-0	0-1	0-1	0-0	1-1	3-5
Springer, Dennis	0-0	0-0	0-0	0-0	0-0	0-0	0-0	1-0	0-0	0-0	0-0	0-0	0-0	0-1	0-0	0-0	1-1
Trombley, Mike	0-1	0-0	0-0	0-0	0-0	0-0	0-0	0-0	0-1	0-1	0-0	0-0	0-1	0-0	0-0	0-0	0-4
Williams, Jeff	0-0	0-0	0-0	0-0	0-0	0-0	0-0	0-0	0-0	0-0	0-0	0-0	1-0	1-0	0-0	0-1	2-1
Totals	9-10	5-2	2-4	2-4	11-8	5-2	4-2	5-1	2-4	2-4	3-3	7-2	9-10	11-8	3-3	6-9	86-76

INTERLEAGUE: Shaw 1-1, Park 1-0, Carrara 0-1, Herges 0-1, Gagne 0-1 vs. Angels; Reyes 1-0, Adams 0-1, Park 0-1 vs. Athletics; Herges 1-0, Brown 0-1, Williams 0-1 vs. Mariners; Dreifort 1-0, Herges 1-0, Prokopec 0-1 vs. Rangers. Total: 6-9.

MILWAUKEE—68-94

Pitcher	Ari. W-L	Atl. W-L	Chi. W-L	Cin. W-L	Col. W-L	Fla. W-L	Hou. W-L	L.A. W-L	Mon. W-L	N.Y. W-L	Phi. W-L	Pit. W-L	S.D. W-L	S.F. W-L	St.L. W-L	A.L. W-L	Total W-L
Buddie, Mike	0-1	0-0	0-0	0-0	0-0	0-0	0-0	0-0	0-0	0-0	0-0	0-0	0-0	0-0	0-0	0-0	0-1
Coppinger, Rocky	0-0	0-0	0-0	0-0	0-0	0-0	0-0	0-0	0-0	0-0	0-0	1-0	0-0	0-0	0-0	0-0	1-0
Cunnane, Will	0-0	0-0	0-0	0-3	0-0	0-0	0-0	0-0	0-0	0-0	0-0	0-0	0-0	0-0	0-0	0-0	0-3
D'Amico, Jeff	1-0	0-0	0-0	0-0	0-1	0-0	1-1	0-0	0-0	0-0	0-0	0-0	0-0	0-1	0-1	0-0	2-4
de los Santos, Val	0-0	0-0	0-0	0-0	0-0	0-0	0-0	0-0	0-0	0-0	0-0	0-0	0-0	0-0	0-0	0-0	0-0
DeJean, Mike	0-0	0-0	0-0	0-0	1-0	0-0	0-0	0-0	0-0	1-1	0-1	0-0	2-0	0-0	0-0	0-0	4-2
Fox, Chad	1-0	0-0	0-0	0-0	0-0	0-0	2-0	0-0	0-0	1-0	0-0	0-1	0-0	0-0	0-0	1-1	5-2
Gandarillas, Gus	0-0	0-0	0-0	0-0	0-0	0-0	0-0	0-0	0-0	0-0	0-0	0-0	0-0	0-0	0-0	0-0	0-0
Haynes, Jimmy	0-0	1-0	0-2	2-1	0-1	0-1	0-2	0-0	0-1	1-1	1-0	0-2	1-1	1-1	1-1	0-3	8-17
King, Ray	0-0	0-0	0-1	0-0	0-0	0-1	0-0	0-0	0-0	0-0	0-0	0-1	0-0	0-0	0-0	0-1	0-4
Kolb, Brandon	0-0	0-0	0-0	0-0	0-0	0-0	0-0	0-0	0-0	0-0	0-0	0-0	0-0	0-0	0-0	0-0	0-0
Leiter, Mark	0-0	0-0	0-0	0-0	1-0	0-0	0-0	0-0	0-1	0-0	0-0	0-0	0-0	0-0	0-0	0-0	2-1
Leskanic, Curtis	0-0	0-0	0-0	0-0	0-1	0-0	0-2	0-0	0-0	1-0	1-1	0-0	0-1	0-0	0-0	0-1	2-6
Levrault, Allen	0-1	0-0	1-1	1-0	0-0	1-0	0-1	0-2	0-0	0-1	0-1	1-2	0-1	0-0	1-0	1-0	6-10
Loretta, Mark	0-0	0-0	0-0	0-0	0-0	0-0	0-0	0-0	0-0	0-0	0-0	0-0	0-0	0-0	0-0	0-0	0-0
Neugebauer, Nick	0-0	0-0	0-0	1-0	0-1	0-0	0-0	0-0	0-0	0-0	0-0	0-0	0-0	0-0	0-0	0-0	1-1
Painter, Lance	0-0	1-0	0-0	0-0	0-0	0-0	0-0	0-0	0-0	0-0	0-0	0-0	0-0	0-0	0-0	0-0	1-0
Peterson, Kyle	0-0	0-0	0-0	0-0	0-0	0-0	0-0	0-0	0-0	0-0	0-0	0-0	0-0	1-1	0-1	0-0	1-2
Quevedo, Ruben	0-1	0-1	1-0	0-1	0-1	0-0	1-0	0-0	1-0	0-0	1-0	0-0	0-0	0-0	0-1	0-0	4-5
Rigdon, Paul	0-0	0-1	0-1	0-0	0-0	0-0	0-0	0-0	0-1	0-0	0-0	0-0	0-0	2-0	1-1	0-1	3-5
Sheets, Ben	1-0	1-1	3-0	1-0	0-0	0-1	1-2	1-0	0-0	0-0	0-0	1-1	0-1	0-0	1-3	1-1	11-10
Suzuki, Mac	0-0	0-0	1-1	1-1	0-0	0-0	0-2	0-0	0-0	0-0	0-0	0-1	0-0	0-0	0-0	0-0	3-5
Weathers, Dave	0-0	0-0	1-1	0-0	0-0	0-0	1-1	0-0	0-0	0-0	0-0	0-1	0-0	0-0	0-0	0-1	3-4
Wright, Jamey	0-0	0-0	0-0	2-1	3-0	0-1	0-1	0-2	0-1	1-0	0-1	0-0	1-2	0-1	2-2	2-0	11-12
Totals	3-3	3-3	9-8	10-6	1-5	2-4	5-12	1-5	4-2	3-3	3-3	6-11	1-5	5-4	7-10	5-10	68-94

INTERLEAGUE: Sheets 0-1, King 0-1, Haynes 0-1 vs. White Sox; Fox 1-1, Sheets 1-0 vs. Indians; Wright 1-0, Rigdon 0-1, Leskanic 0-1 vs. Tigers; Wright 1-0, Peterson 0-1, Haynes 0-1 vs. Royals; Levrault 1-0, Haynes 0-1, Weathers 0-1 vs. Twins. Total: 5-10.

MONTREAL—68-94

Pitcher	Ari. W-L	Atl. W-L	Chi. W-L	Cin. W-L	Col. W-L	Fla. W-L	Hou. W-L	L.A. W-L	Mil. W-L	N.Y. W-L	Phi. W-L	Pit. W-L	S.D. W-L	S.F. W-L	St.L. W-L	A.L. W-L	Total W-L
Armas, Tony Jr.	1-0	0-2	0-2	0-0	1-0	0-5	0-1	1-0	0-0	1-1	2-1	1-0	1-0	0-1	0-0	1-1	9-14
Blank, Matt	0-0	0-1	0-0	0-0	0-0	0-0	0-0	0-0	1-0	0-0	0-0	0-0	0-0	0-0	0-0	1-1	2-2
Cubillan, Darwin	0-0	0-0	0-0	0-0	0-0	0-0	0-0	0-0	0-0	0-0	0-0	0-0	0-0	0-0	0-0	0-0	0-0
Eischen, Joey	0-0	0-0	0-0	0-1	0-0	0-0	0-0	0-0	0-0	0-0	0-0	0-0	0-0	0-0	0-0	0-0	0-1
Irabu, Hideki	0-0	0-1	0-0	0-0	0-0	0-0	0-0	0-0	0-0	0-0	0-0	0-0	0-0	0-0	0-0	0-1	0-2
Johnson, Mike	0-0	0-0	0-0	0-0	0-0	0-0	0-0	0-0	0-0	0-0	0-0	0-0	0-0	0-0	0-0	0-0	0-0
Lira, Felipe	0-0	0-0	0-0	0-0	0-0	0-0	0-0	0-0	0-0	0-0	0-0	0-0	0-0	0-0	0-0	0-0	0-0
Lloyd, Graeme	0-1	0-1	2-0	0-0	2-0	1-0	0-0	1-0	0-0	0-1	1-0	0-0	0-0	0-0	0-0	2-1	9-5
Mattes, Troy	0-0	0-2	0-0	0-0	0-0	0-0	0-0	0-0	0-0	0-0	0-0	2-0	0-0	0-0	0-0	1-1	3-3
Mota, Guillermo	0-0	0-0	0-0	0-0	0-1	0-1	0-0	0-0	0-0	0-1	0-0	0-0	0-0	0-0	0-0	1-0	1-3
Munoz, Bobby	0-1	0-0	0-0	0-1	0-0	0-0	0-1	0-1	0-0	0-0	0-0	0-0	0-0	0-0	0-0	0-0	0-4
Ohka, Tomokazu	0-0	1-1	0-0	0-0	0-0	0-0	0-0	0-0	0-0	0-0	0-0	0-1	0-0	0-1	0-0	0-1	1-4
Pavano, Carl	0-0	0-0	0-0	0-0	0-0	0-0	1-0	0-1	0-0	0-2	0-2	0-0	0-0	0-1	0-0	0-0	1-6
Peters, Chris	0-0	0-0	0-0	0-0	0-1	1-0	0-0	0-1	0-0	1-2	0-0	0-0	0-0	0-0	0-0	0-0	2-4
Reames, Britt	0-1	1-0	0-0	0-0	0-0	1-0	1-1	1-1	0-0	0-2	0-0	0-0	0-1	0-0	0-0	0-1	4-8
Scanlan, Bob	0-0	0-0	0-0	0-0	0-0	0-0	0-0	0-0	0-0	0-0	0-0	0-0	0-0	0-0	0-0	0-0	0-0
Stewart, Scott	0-0	0-0	0-0	2-0	0-1	1-0	0-0	0-0	0-0	0-0	0-0	0-0	0-0	0-0	0-0	0-0	3-1
Strickland, Scott	0-0	0-2	0-0	0-0	0-0	0-1	0-0	0-0	0-0	0-1	1-1	1-1	0-0	0-0	0-0	1-1	2-6
Telford, Anthony	0-0	0-0	0-0	0-0	0-0	0-0	0-1	0-0	0-0	0-0	0-0	0-0	0-0	0-0	0-0	0-0	0-1
Thurman, Mike	1-0	2-0	0-1	0-1	0-0	0-3	0-0	1-1	0-0	2-1	1-0	1-1	0-1	0-1	0-0	0-1	9-11
Urbina, Ugueth	0-0	0-0	0-0	0-0	0-0	0-0	0-1	0-0	0-0	0-0	0-0	1-1	0-0	0-0	0-0	0-0	2-1
Vazquez, Javier	1-0	2-2	0-0	0-0	0-0	2-1	0-1	1-1	1-1	2-1	3-0	0-0	1-1	2-0	0-2	1-2	16-11
Yoshii, Masato	0-0	0-1	0-0	0-1	1-0	0-1	0-0	0-0	0-0	0-1	1-0	0-1	0-1	0-0	2-0	0-1	4-7
Totals	3-3	6-13	3-3	2-4	4-3	7-12	0-6	4-2	2-4	8-11	9-10	5-1	3-3	2-5	2-4	8-10	68-94

INTERLEAGUE: Lloyd 1-0, Blank 0-1, Vazquez 0-1 vs. Orioles; Mattes 1-0, Thurman 0-1, Lloyd 0-1 vs. Red Sox; Strickland 1-0, Irabu 0-1, Yoshii 0-1 vs. Yankees; Vazquez 1-0, Armas Jr. 1-0, Mattes 0-1 vs. Devil Rays; Blank 1-0, Mota 1-0, Lloyd 1-0, Vazquez 0-1, Strickland 0-1, Armas Jr. 0-1 vs. Blue Jays. Total: 8-10.

NEW YORK—82-80

Pitcher	Ari. W-L	Atl. W-L	Chi. W-L	Cin. W-L	Col. W-L	Fla. W-L	Hou. W-L	L.A. W-L	Mil. W-L	Mon. W-L	Phi. W-L	Pit. W-L	S.D. W-L	S.F. W-L	St.L. W-L	A.L. W-L	Total W-L
Appier, Kevin	1-0	3-0	0-1	1-1	1-1	2-1	0-0	0-1	0-0	2-1	0-0	0-0	0-0	0-1	0-1	1-2	11-10
Benitez, Armando	0-0	2-2	0-0	0-0	0-0	0-0	0-1	1-0	0-0	2-1	0-0	0-0	0-0	0-0	1-0	0-0	6-4
Chen, Bruce	0-0	0-0	0-0	0-0	0-0	0-0	0-0	0-0	1-0	1-0	0-1	0-0	1-0	0-1	0-0	0-0	3-2
Cook, Dennis	0-0	1-0	0-0	0-0	0-0	0-0	0-0	0-0	0-0	0-0	0-0	0-0	0-0	0-0	0-0	0-1	1-1
Corey, Mark	0-0	0-0	0-0	0-0	0-0	0-0	0-0	0-0	0-0	0-0	0-0	0-0	0-0	0-0	0-0	0-0	0-0
Franco, John	0-0	0-0	0-0	0-0	0-0	2-0	0-0	0-0	0-0	1-2	1-0	0-0	0-0	0-0	0-0	2-0	6-2

Pitcher	Ari. W-L	Atl. W-L	Chi. W-L	Cin. W-L	Col. W-L	Fla. W-L	Hou. W-L	L.A. W-L	Mil. W-L	Mon. W-L	Phi. W-L	Pit. W-L	S.D. W-L	S.F. W-L	St.L. W-L	A.L. W-L	Total W-L
Gonzalez, Dicky	0-0	0-0	0-0	0-0	1-0	1-0	0-0	0-0	0-0	0-1	0-0	1-0	0-0	0-1	0-0	0-0	3-2
Hinchliffe, Brett	0-0	0-0	0-0	0-0	0-0	0-0	0-0	0-0	0-1	0-0	0-0	0-0	0-0	0-0	0-0	0-0	0-1
Leiter, Al	0-1	0-1	0-1	0-2	1-0	2-0	0-0	1-0	1-0	2-2	1-0	0-0	0-1	1-0	0-0	2-3	11-11
Martin, Tom	0-0	0-0	0-0	0-0	0-0	0-0	1-0	0-0	0-0	0-0	0-0	0-0	0-0	0-0	0-0	0-0	1-0
Nitkowski, C.J.	0-0	0-0	0-0	0-0	0-0	0-0	0-0	0-0	0-0	0-0	1-0	0-0	0-0	0-0	0-0	0-0	1-0
Reed, Rick	1-0	1-2	0-1	1-0	0-1	0-0	0-0	0-0	0-0	1-0	1-2	0-0	1-0	0-0	0-0	2-0	8-6
Relaford, Desi	0-0	0-0	0-0	0-0	0-0	0-0	0-0	0-0	0-0	0-0	0-0	0-0	0-0	0-0	0-0	0-0	0-0
Riggan, Jerrod	0-0	0-1	0-0	0-0	0-0	0-0	0-2	1-0	0-0	0-0	0-0	1-0	0-0	1-0	0-0	0-0	3-3
Roberts, Grant	0-0	0-0	0-0	0-0	0-0	1-0	0-0	0-0	0-0	0-0	0-0	0-0	0-0	0-0	0-0	0-0	1-0
Rose, Brian	0-0	0-0	0-0	0-0	0-0	0-0	0-0	0-0	0-0	0-1	0-0	0-0	0-0	0-0	0-0	0-0	0-1
Rusch, Glendon	1-0	0-0	1-0	0-0	0-2	2-3	0-0	0-1	0-0	3-1	0-1	0-1	0-1	0-0	0-2	1-0	8-12
Trachsel, Steve	0-1	2-2	0-1	0-1	0-0	0-1	1-0	1-0	1-1	0-2	4-0	1-0	0-2	0-0	0-0	1-2	11-13
Walker, Pete	0-0	0-0	0-0	0-0	0-0	0-0	0-0	0-0	0-0	0-0	0-0	0-0	0-0	0-0	0-0	0-0	0-0
Wall, Donne	0-0	0-1	0-0	0-0	0-0	0-0	0-0	0-0	0-1	0-0	0-1	0-0	0-0	0-1	0-0	0-0	0-4
Wendell, Turk	0-0	0-0	0-0	0-0	0-0	2-2	0-0	0-0	0-0	1-0	0-0	0-0	0-0	0-0	0-0	1-1	4-3
White, Rick	0-1	0-1	1-0	0-0	0-0	0-0	1-0	0-0	0-0	2-0	0-0	0-0	0-1	0-1	0-1	0-0	4-5
Totals	3-3	9-10	2-4	2-4	3-4	12-7	3-3	4-2	3-3	11-8	11-8	4-2	1-5	3-4	1-5	10-8	82-80

INTERLEAGUE: Reed 1-0, Franco 1-0, Trachsel 0-1 vs. Orioles; Leiter 1-0, Rusch 1-0, Appier 0-1 vs. Red Sox; Wendell 1-1, Franco 1-0, Leiter 0-2, Appier 0-1 vs. Yankees; Appier 1-0, Trachsel 0-1, Leiter 0-1 vs. Devil Rays; Reed 1-0, Trachsel 1-0, Leiter 1-0 vs. Blue Jays. Total: 10-8.

PHILADELPHIA—86-76

Pitcher	Ari. W-L	Atl. W-L	Chi. W-L	Cin. W-L	Col. W-L	Fla. W-L	Hou. W-L	L.A. W-L	Mil. W-L	Mon. W-L	N.Y. W-L	Pit. W-L	S.D. W-L	S.F. W-L	St.L. W-L	A.L. W-L	Total W-L
Bottalico, Ricky	1-0	1-0	0-0	0-0	0-0	1-0	0-1	0-1	0-1	0-0	0-0	0-0	0-0	0-0	0-0	0-1	3-4
Brock, Chris	0-0	0-0	0-0	0-0	0-0	1-0	0-0	0-0	0-0	1-0	0-0	0-0	0-0	0-0	1-0	0-0	3-0
Byrd, Paul	0-0	0-0	0-0	0-0	0-0	0-0	0-0	0-0	0-0	0-1	0-0	0-0	0-0	0-0	0-0	0-0	0-1
Chen, Bruce	0-0	0-1	0-1	0-0	0-0	2-0	0-0	0-0	0-1	1-0	0-0	0-1	1-0	0-1	0-0	0-0	4-5
Coggin, Dave	0-1	2-0	0-0	1-1	1-0	0-1	0-0	0-0	1-0	0-3	0-0	1-0	0-0	0-0	0-1	0-0	6-7
Cook, Dennis	0-0	0-0	0-0	0-0	0-0	0-0	0-0	0-0	0-0	0-0	0-0	0-0	0-0	0-0	0-0	0-0	0-0
Cormier, Rheal	0-0	0-0	0-0	0-0	0-1	2-0	0-0	0-0	0-0	1-2	0-1	1-0	0-0	0-1	0-0	1-1	5-6
Daal, Omar	1-0	1-1	0-0	1-1	1-0	1-0	0-0	0-0	1-0	0-2	0-2	2-1	1-0	1-0	1-0	2-0	13-7
Duckworth, Dran.	0-0	0-1	0-0	0-0	0-0	1-0	0-0	1-0	0-0	0-1	0-0	0-0	1-0	0-0	0-0	0-0	3-2
Figueroa, Nelson	0-0	0-0	0-0	0-0	0-0	1-0	0-0	0-1	1-0	0-1	1-1	0-0	0-0	0-1	0-0	0-2	4-6
Gomes, Wayne	0-0	1-1	0-0	0-0	0-0	1-0	0-0	0-1	1-0	0-0	1-0	0-0	0-0	0-0	0-1	0-0	4-3
Mesa, Jose	0-0	0-0	0-0	0-0	0-0	2-0	0-0	0-0	0-0	0-1	1-2	0-0	0-0	0-0	0-1	0-0	3-3
Nickle, Doug	0-0	0-0	0-0	0-0	0-0	0-0	0-0	0-0	0-0	0-0	0-0	0-0	0-0	0-0	0-0	0-0	0-0
Oropesa, Eddie	0-0	0-0	0-0	0-0	0-0	0-0	0-0	0-0	0-0	1-0	0-0	0-0	0-0	0-0	0-0	0-0	1-0
Padilla, Vicente	0-0	0-0	1-1	0-0	0-0	0-0	0-0	0-0	0-0	0-0	0-0	0-0	0-0	0-0	0-0	1-0	3-1
Person, Robert	1-1	2-2	1-0	0-0	0-1	1-0	2-0	1-0	0-0	3-0	1-1	1-0	0-1	0-1	1-0	1-0	15-7
Politte, Cliff	0-1	0-0	0-0	0-0	0-0	0-1	0-0	0-0	1-0	0-0	0-0	0-0	0-0	0-1	0-0	2-3
Santiago, Jose	0-0	0-1	0-0	0-0	0-0	0-1	0-1	0-0	0-0	2-0	0-0	0-0	0-0	0-0	0-1	2-4
Telemaco, Amaury	0-0	1-0	0-0	0-0	1-0	1-1	1-0	0-0	0-0	0-0	1-0	0-0	0-0	0-0	0-1	0-3	5-5
Vosberg, Ed	0-0	0-0	0-0	0-0	0-0	0-0	0-0	0-0	0-0	0-0	0-0	0-0	0-0	0-0	0-0	0-0	0-0
Wendell, Turk	0-0	0-0	0-0	0-0	0-0	0-0	0-0	0-0	0-0	0-1	0-0	0-0	0-0	0-0	0-1	0-0	0-2
Wolf, Randy	1-0	1-3	0-2	2-0	1-0	0-1	0-0	0-1	0-0	1-1	0-1	1-0	1-0	1-0	0-0	1-2	10-11
Totals	4-3	9-10	2-4	4-2	4-2	14-5	3-3	3-3	3-3	10-9	8-11	5-1	5-2	3-3	2-4	7-11	86-76

INTERLEAGUE: Padilla 1-0, Cormier 1-0, Brock 1-0, Wolf 1-0, Telemaco 0-1, Figueroa 0-1 vs. Orioles; Daal 1-0, Wolf 0-1, Cormier 0-1 vs. Red Sox; Person 1-0, Gomes 0-1, Telemaco 0-1 vs. Yankees; Telemaco 0-1, Bottalico 0-1, Wolf 0-1 vs. Devil Rays; Daal 1-0, Santiago 0-1, Figueroa 0-1 vs. Blue Jays. Total: 7-11.

PITTSBURGH—62-100

Pitcher	Ari. W-L	Atl. W-L	Chi. W-L	Cin. W-L	Col. W-L	Fla. W-L	Hou. W-L	L.A. W-L	Mil. W-L	Mon. W-L	N.Y. W-L	Phi. W-L	S.D. W-L	S.F. W-L	St.L. W-L	A.L. W-L	Total W-L
Anderson, Jimmy	0-1	0-1	1-0	1-1	0-1	0-1	1-3	0-2	1-2	0-1	1-0	0-1	1-0	0-0	1-2	2-1	9-17
Arroyo, Bronson	0-0	1-0	0-2	0-0	0-1	0-0	2-0	0-0	1-0	0-0	1-0	0-1	0-1	0-0	0-1	0-1	5-7
Beimel, Joe	0-1	0-0	2-0	1-0	1-0	0-0	2-1	0-1	0-2	0-2	0-0	1-0	0-1	0-1	0-1	0-1	7-11
Fetters, Mike	0-0	0-0	0-0	0-0	0-0	0-0	0-0	0-0	1-0	0-0	0-1	0-0	0-0	0-0	0-0	0-0	1-1
Lincoln, Mike	0-0	0-0	1-0	0-1	1-0	0-0	0-0	0-0	0-0	0-0	0-0	0-0	0-0	0-0	0-0	0-0	2-1
Loiselle, Rich	0-0	0-0	0-0	0-1	0-0	0-0	0-0	0-0	0-0	0-0	0-0	0-0	0-0	0-0	0-0	0-0	0-1
Manzanillo, Josias	0-0	0-0	0-0	0-0	0-0	0-1	0-0	0-1	1-0	0-0	0-0	1-0	0-0	0-0	1-0	3-2
Marte, Damaso	0-1	0-0	0-0	0-0	0-0	0-0	0-0	0-0	0-0	0-0	0-0	0-0	0-0	0-0	0-0	0-1
Martinez, Ramon	0-0	0-0	0-1	0-0	0-0	0-0	0-0	0-0	0-0	0-0	0-0	0-0	0-0	0-1	0-0	0-2
McKnight, Tony	1-0	0-0	0-1	1-0	0-0	0-0	0-1	0-1	0-0	0-0	0-1	0-0	0-1	0-1	2-6
Mulholland, Terry	0-0	0-0	0-0	0-0	0-0	0-0	0-0	0-0	0-0	0-0	0-0	0-0	0-0	0-0	0-0	0-0	0-0
Olivares, Omar	1-0	0-1	1-0	0-1	0-0	1-1	1-0	1-0	0-0	0-1	0-1	0-1	0-0	0-2	0-1	6-9
Ritchie, Todd	0-0	0-2	0-1	1-3	1-0	0-1	2-1	1-1	2-0	1-0	0-1	0-0	0-0	0-4	3-1	11-15
Sauerbeck, Scott	0-0	0-0	0-1	0-0	0-0	0-0	0-0	0-0	1-0	0-0	0-0	0-0	0-0	0-0	1-0	2-2
Schmidt, Jason	0-0	0-0	0-0	1-0	0-0	1-0	0-1	0-1	2-0	0-1	0-0	0-0	0-0	1-1	1-1	6-6
Silva, Jose	0-0	0-0	0-1	0-0	0-0	1-0	0-0	0-0	0-0	0-0	0-0	1-1	0-1	0-0	3-3
Taylor, Billy	0-0	0-0	0-0	0-0	0-0	0-0	0-0	0-0	0-0	0-0	0-0	0-0	0-0	0-0	0-0	0-0
Vogelsong, Ryan	0-0	0-0	0-0	0-1	0-0	0-0	0-0	0-0	0-1	0-0	0-0	0-0	0-0	0-0	0-0	0-2
Wengert, Don	0-0	0-1	0-0	0-0	0-0	0-0	0-0	0-0	0-0	0-0	0-0	0-0	0-0	0-0	0-0	0-2
Wilkins, Marc	0-0	0-0	0-0	0-0	0-0	0-0	0-0	0-0	0-0	0-0	0-0	0-1	0-0	0-0	0-1
Williams, Dave	0-1	0-0	0-1	1-1	0-0	0-0	0-1	0-0	1-0	0-0	0-0	0-1	0-0	1-1	0-1	3-7
Williams, Mike	0-0	0-0	1-2	0-0	0-0	0-1	1-0	0-0	0-0	0-1	0-0	0-0	0-0	0-0	0-0	2-4
Totals	2-4	1-5	6-10	8-9	4-2	2-4	8-9	2-7	11-6	1-5	2-4	1-5	2-4	1-5	3-14	8-7	62-100

INTERLEAGUE: Manzanillo 1-0, Schmidt 0-1, Ritchie 0-1 vs. White Sox; Anderson 1-0, Schmidt 1-0, Ritchie 1-0 vs. Indians; Ritchie 1-0, Beimel 0-1, Arroyo 0-1 vs. Tigers; Anderson 1-0, Ritchie 1-0, Williams 0-1 vs. Royals; Sauerbeck 1-0, Olivares 0-1, Anderson 0-1 vs. Twins. Total: 8-7.

ST. LOUIS—93-69

Pitcher	Ari. W-L	Atl. W-L	Chi. W-L	Cin. W-L	Col. W-L	Fla. W-L	Hou. W-L	L.A. W-L	Mil. W-L	Mon. W-L	N.Y. W-L	Phi. W-L	Pit. W-L	S.D. W-L	S.F. W-L	A.L. W-L	Total W-L
Ankiel, Rick	1-0	0-0	0-0	0-0	0-0	0-0	0-0	0-2	0-0	0-0	0-0	0-0	0-0	0-0	0-0	0-0	1-2
Benes, Alan	0-0	0-0	0-0	1-0	0-0	0-0	0-0	1-0	0-0	0-0	0-0	0-0	0-0	0-0	0-0	0-0	2-0
Benes, Andy	0-0	0-0	1-1	2-1	1-1	0-1	0-0	0-0	0-1	1-0	0-0	0-1	1-0	0-0	0-1	1-0	7-7
Bonilla, Bobby	0-0	0-0	0-0	0-0	0-0	0-0	0-0	0-0	0-0	0-0	0-0	0-0	0-0	0-0	0-0	0-0	0-0
Christiansen, Jason	0-0	0-0	0-1	0-0	0-0	0-0	0-0	0-0	0-0	0-0	0-0	0-0	0-0	0-0	1-0	0-0	1-1
Hackman, Luther	0-0	0-0	0-0	0-0	0-0	0-0	0-1	0-0	0-0	0-1	0-0	0-0	0-0	0-0	1-0	0-0	1-2
Hermanson, Dustin	1-1	2-0	0-2	2-2	0-1	0-1	1-0	0-2	1-1	0-0	1-0	1-0	3-2	0-0	0-1	2-0	14-13
Hutchinson, Chad	0-0	0-0	0-0	0-0	0-0	0-0	0-0	0-0	0-0	0-0	0-0	0-0	0-0	0-0	0-0	0-0	0-0
James, Mike	0-0	0-0	0-0	0-0	0-0	0-0	0-0	0-0	0-1	0-1	0-0	0-0	0-0	0-0	0-0	0-0	1-2
Karnuth, Jason	0-0	0-0	0-0	0-0	0-0	0-0	0-0	0-0	0-0	0-0	0-0	0-0	0-0	0-0	0-0	0-0	0-0
Kile, Darryl	2-0	1-0	2-1	1-2	0-1	0-0	1-2	0-1	3-1	2-0	2-0	0-0	1-0	0-1	0-0	1-2	16-11
Kline, Steve	0-0	0-0	0-0	0-0	0-1	1-0	0-0	0-0	0-1	0-0	0-0	1-0	0-0	0-0	0-1	1-0	3-3
Mathews, T.J.	0-0	0-0	0-0	0-0	0-0	0-0	0-0	1-0	0-0	0-0	0-0	0-0	0-0	0-0	0-0	0-0	1-0
Matthews, Mike	0-0	0-0	0-1	0-0	0-1	0-0	0-0	0-0	2-1	0-0	0-0	1-0	0-0	0-0	0-0	0-1	3-4
Morris, Matt	0-1	0-0	3-1	2-0	1-1	1-0	2-2	0-0	3-1	1-0	1-0	1-0	3-0	2-0	1-0	1-2	22-8
Smith, Bud	0-0	0-1	1-0	0-1	0-0	0-0	0-0	0-0	1-1	0-0	0-0	0-0	2-0	1-0	0-0	1-0	6-3
Stechschulte, Gene	0-0	0-1	0-0	0-1	0-0	0-0	0-2	0-0	0-0	0-0	0-0	0-0	1-0	0-0	0-1	0-0	1-5
Tabaka, Jeff	0-0	0-0	0-0	0-0	0-0	0-0	0-0	0-0	0-0	0-0	0-0	0-0	0-0	0-0	0-0	0-0	0-0
Timlin, Mike	0-0	0-1	0-1	1-0	1-0	0-0	1-0	0-0	0-0	0-0	0-0	0-1	0-1	0-0	0-1	1-0	4-5
Veres, Dave	0-0	0-0	1-0	0-0	0-0	0-0	0-1	0-0	0-0	0-0	1-0	0-0	0-0	0-0	0-0	0-1	3-2
Williams, Woody	0-0	0-0	0-1	1-0	0-0	1-0	1-0	1-0	0-0	0-0	0-0	0-0	2-0	1-0	0-0	0-0	7-1
Totals	4-2	3-3	8-9	10-7	3-6	3-3	7-9	3-3	10-7	4-2	5-1	4-2	14-3	5-1	2-4	8-7	93-69

INTERLEAGUE: Benes 1-0, Hermanson 1-0, Smith 1-0 vs. White Sox; Timlin 1-0, Morris 0-1, Veres 0-1 vs. Indians; Morris 1-0, Kile 0-1, Matthews 0-1 vs. Tigers; Kile 0-1, Morris 0-1, Stechschulte 0-1 vs. Royals; Hermanson 1-0, Kline 1-0, Kile 1-0 vs. Twins. Total: 8-7.

SAN DIEGO—79-83

Pitcher	Ari. W-L	Atl. W-L	Chi. W-L	Cin. W-L	Col. W-L	Fla. W-L	Hou. W-L	L.A. W-L	Mil. W-L	Mon. W-L	N.Y. W-L	Phi. W-L	Pit. W-L	S.F. W-L	St.L. W-L	A.L. W-L	Total W-L
Davey, Tom	0-1	0-0	0-0	0-0	0-1	0-0	0-0	0-0	0-0	0-0	0-0	0-0	0-0	0-1	0-0	2-1	2-4
Eaton, Adam	0-1	0-0	0-0	1-0	1-2	0-0	1-0	1-1	0-0	0-0	1-0	0-1	1-0	2-0	0-0	0-0	8-5
Fikac, Jeremy	1-0	0-0	0-0	0-0	0-0	0-0	0-0	0-0	0-0	0-0	1-0	0-0	0-0	0-0	0-0	0-0	2-0
Herndon, Junior	0-0	0-0	0-0	0-0	0-1	1-0	0-0	0-0	0-0	0-1	1-0	0-1	0-0	0-1	0-2	0-0	2-6
Hitchcock, Sterling	0-1	0-0	0-0	0-0	1-0	0-0	0-0	0-0	1-0	0-0	0-0	0-0	0-0	0-0	0-0	0-0	2-1
Hoffman, Trevor	0-0	0-0	0-0	0-0	0-0	0-0	0-0	2-2	0-0	0-0	0-0	0-0	0-0	1-1	0-0	0-0	3-4
Jarvis, Kevin	1-2	1-0	0-1	0-1	1-1	1-0	2-0	1-1	1-0	0-1	1-0	2-0	0-0	0-2	0-1	1-1	12-11
Jodie, Brett	0-1	0-0	0-0	0-0	0-0	0-0	0-0	0-0	0-0	0-0	0-0	0-0	0-0	0-0	0-0	0-0	0-1
Jones, Bobby J.	0-2	0-1	2-0	0-0	1-1	0-1	1-1	0-2	1-1	2-0	0-1	0-1	0-1	0-3	0-2	1-2	8-19
Lawrence, Brian	0-0	0-1	0-1	0-0	1-1	0-0	0-0	1-0	0-0	0-1	0-0	0-0	1-0	0-1	1-0	1-0	5-5
Lee, David	1-0	0-0	0-0	0-0	0-0	0-0	0-0	0-0	0-0	0-0	0-0	0-0	0-0	0-0	0-0	0-0	1-0
Loewer, Carlton	0-0	0-0	0-0	0-0	0-0	0-0	0-0	0-0	0-0	0-0	0-0	0-0	0-0	0-0	0-2	0-0	0-2
Lundquist, David	0-0	0-0	0-0	0-0	0-1	0-0	0-0	0-0	0-0	0-0	0-0	0-0	0-0	0-0	0-0	0-0	0-1
Maurer, Dave	0-0	0-0	0-0	0-0	0-0	0-0	0-0	0-0	0-0	0-0	0-0	0-0	0-0	0-0	0-0	0-0	0-0
McElroy, Chuck	0-0	0-0	1-0	0-0	0-0	0-0	0-0	0-0	0-0	0-0	0-0	0-0	0-1	0-0	0-0	0-0	1-1
Middlebrook, Jason	0-0	0-0	0-0	0-0	0-0	0-0	0-0	2-0	0-0	0-0	0-0	0-0	0-1	0-0	0-0	0-0	2-1
Myers, Rodney	0-0	1-0	0-0	0-0	0-0	0-0	0-1	0-0	0-0	0-0	0-1	0-0	0-0	0-0	0-0	0-0	1-2
Nunez, Jose A.	1-0	1-0	0-0	0-0	1-0	0-0	0-0	1-0	0-0	0-0	0-0	0-0	0-0	0-0	0-0	0-1	4-1
Osting, Jimmy	0-0	0-0	0-0	0-0	0-0	0-0	0-0	0-0	0-0	0-0	0-0	0-0	0-0	0-0	0-0	0-0	0-0
Seanez, Rudy	0-0	0-0	0-0	0-1	0-0	0-0	0-0	0-1	0-0	0-0	0-0	0-0	0-0	0-0	0-0	0-0	0-2
Serrano, Wascar	2-1	0-0	0-0	0-0	0-0	0-1	0-1	0-0	0-0	1-0	0-0	0-0	0-0	0-0	0-0	0-0	3-3
Tollberg, Brian	0-0	0-1	1-0	2-0	3-0	1-0	0-0	0-1	1-0	0-0	0-0	0-1	1-0	1-0	0-0	0-1	10-4
Walker, Kevin	0-0	0-0	0-0	0-0	0-0	0-0	0-0	0-0	0-0	0-0	0-0	0-0	0-0	0-0	0-0	0-0	0-0
Williams, Woody	1-2	0-0	0-0	1-0	1-1	0-0	1-1	0-0	1-0	0-0	1-0	0-0	1-0	0-2	0-0	1-1	8-8
Witasick, Jay	0-0	0-0	0-0	0-0	0-0	1-1	1-0	2-0	0-0	0-0	0-0	0-0	1-1	0-0	0-0	0-0	5-2
Totals	7-12	3-3	4-2	4-2	10-9	4-3	6-3	10-9	5-1	3-3	5-1	2-5	4-2	5-14	1-5	6-9	79-83

INTERLEAGUE: Lawrence 1-0, Tollberg 0-1, Davey 0-1 vs. Angels; Davey 1-0, Williams 0-1, Nunez 0-1 vs. Athletics; Jones 1-1, Davey 1-0, Loewer 0-2, Jarvis 0-1 vs. Mariners; Jarvis 1-0, Williams 1-0, Jones 0-1 vs. Rangers. Total: 6-9.

SAN FRANCISCO—90-72

Pitcher	Ari. W-L	Atl. W-L	Chi. W-L	Cin. W-L	Col. W-L	Fla. W-L	Hou. W-L	L.A. W-L	Mil. W-L	Mon. W-L	N.Y. W-L	Phi. W-L	Pit. W-L	S.D. W-L	St.L. W-L	A.L. W-L	Total W-L
Ainsworth, Kurt	0-0	0-0	0-0	0-0	0-0	0-0	0-0	0-0	0-0	0-0	0-0	0-0	0-0	0-0	0-0	0-0	0-0
Boehringer, Brian	0-0	0-0	0-0	0-0	0-0	0-0	0-0	0-1	0-0	0-0	0-0	0-0	0-0	0-1	0-0	0-1	0-3
Christiansen, Jason	0-0	0-0	0-0	1-0	0-0	0-0	0-0	0-0	0-0	0-0	0-0	0-0	0-0	0-0	0-0	0-0	1-0
Embree, Alan	0-0	0-0	0-0	0-1	0-0	0-0	0-0	0-0	0-0	0-0	0-0	0-0	0-0	0-0	0-1	0-0	0-2
Estes, Shawn	1-0	0-0	1-1	0-0	1-1	0-0	0-0	0-1	1-1	1-1	0-0	0-1	0-1	3-0	0-0	1-1	9-8
Fultz, Aaron	1-0	0-0	0-0	0-0	0-0	0-0	0-0	1-0	0-0	0-0	0-1	0-0	1-0	0-0	0-0	0-1	3-1
Gardner, Mark	1-0	0-0	0-1	0-0	0-1	0-0	0-0	2-0	0-2	0-0	0-0	0-0	1-0	0-0	0-0	1-1	5-5
Gomes, Wayne	0-0	0-0	0-0	0-0	1-0	0-0	0-0	0-0	0-0	0-0	0-0	1-0	0-0	0-0	0-0	0-0	2-0
Hernandez, Livan	2-2	0-2	1-1	0-1	1-1	1-0	0-1	1-4	0-0	0-1	0-0	2-0	0-0	2-1	1-0	2-1	13-15
Jensen, Ryan	0-1	0-0	0-0	0-0	1-0	0-0	0-0	0-0	0-0	0-0	0-0	0-0	0-0	0-0	0-1	0-1	1-2
Nen, Robb	0-0	0-1	0-0	0-0	1-1	1-0	0-2	0-0	0-0	0-0	1-1	0-0	0-0	1-0	0-0	0-0	4-5
Ortiz, Russ	1-2	0-0	0-0	1-0	2-2	0-1	1-0	1-0	1-1	2-0	1-1	0-0	1-0	4-1	0-1	2-0	17-9
Rodriguez, Felix	0-0	0-0	0-0	0-0	1-0	0-0	0-0	2-1	0-0	1-0	1-0	0-0	1-0	0-0	2-0	1-0	9-1
Rueter, Kirk	1-3	0-1	1-0	0-1	2-2	0-1	1-0	1-2	1-0	1-0	0-1	0-1	2-0	1-0	0-0	3-0	14-12
Schmidt, Jason	2-0	1-0	0-0	0-1	0-0	1-0	1-0	0-0	0-0	0-0	0-0	0-0	1-0	1-0	0-0	0-0	7-1

Pitcher	Ari. W-L	Atl. W-L	Chi. W-L	Cin. W-L	Col. W-L	Fla. W-L	Hou. W-L	L.A. W-L	Mil. W-L	Mon. W-L	N.Y. W-L	Phi. W-L	Pit. W-L	S.D. W-L	St.L. W-L	A.L. W-L	Total W-L
Vogelsong, Ryan ...	0-1	0-0	0-0	0-0	0-0	0-0	0-0	0-1	0-0	0-0	0-0	0-0	0-0	0-1	0-0	0-0	0-3
Worrell, Tim	0-1	1-0	0-0	0-0	0-1	1-0	0-0	0-2	0-0	0-0	0-0	0-0	0-0	0-1	0-0	0-0	2-5
Zerbe, Chad	0-0	0-0	0-0	0-0	0-0	0-0	0-0	0-0	1-0	0-0	1-0	0 0	0-0	0-0	1-0	0-0	3-0
Totals	9-10	2-4	3-3	2-4	10-9	4-2	3-3	8-11	4-5	5-2	4-3	3-3	5-1	14-5	4-2	10-5	90-72

INTERLEAGUE: Rueter 1-0, Ortiz 1-0, Gardner 1-0 vs. Angels; Hernandez 1-1, Estes 1-0, Rodriguez 1-0, Rueter 1-0, Gardner 0-1 vs. Athletics; Ortiz 1-0, Boehringer 0-1, Estes 0-1 vs. Mariners; Hernandez 1-0, Rueter 1-0, Jensen 0-1 vs. Rangers. Total: 10-5.

HOME RUNS BY PARKS

	At Ari.	At Atl.	At Chi.	At Cin.	At Col.	At Fla.	At Hou.	At L.A.	At Mil.	At Mon.	At N.Y.	At Phi.	At Pit.	At St.L.	At S.D.	At S.F.	At A.L. Parks	Totals 2001	Totals 2000	HR Allow.
Arizona	107	2	2	6	14	3	3	11	6	3	2	7	1	6	14	9	12	208	179	195
Atlanta	7	87	5	5	6	6	5	1	3	12	12	8	4	1	2	0	10	174	179	153
Chicago	4	4	95	12	1	2	18	2	9	4	5	4	8	10	5	5	6	194	183	164
Cincinnati	1	1	10	83	2	3	18	8	11	7	1	1	3	14	5	2	6	176	200	198
Colorado	11	4	3	9	124	3	5	12	5	5	2	2	2	3	17	2	4	213	161	239
Florida	5	9	4	1	4	84	6	2	1	10	10	12	4	3	4	0	7	166	160	151
Houston	11	0	6	6	4	9	108	3	10	6	8	0	8	11	2	2	14	208	249	221
Los Angeles	15	6	1	5	19	4	7	94	7	2	3	1	7	5	15	7	8	206	211	184
Milwaukee	11	4	9	13	6	3	7	1	107	4	4	5	11	6	3	6	9	209	177	197
Montreal	3	6	2	2	9	6	2	1	3	68	5	9	1	3	1	2	8	131	178	190
New York	2	10	4	2	4	7	1	5	6	8	65	9	7	3	1	2	11	147	198	186
Philadelphia	4	6	1	2	5	10	3	4	3	10	14	83	1	2	5	2	9	164	144	170
Pittsburgh	3	3	5	13	6	1	11	3	8	6	2	2	75	9	2	2	10	161	168	167
St. Louis	6	2	10	11	11	4	13	1	11	3	6	3	7	100	5	1	5	199	235	196
San Diego	8	2	4	14	4	11	9	5	5	5	3	3	6		69	6	3	161	157	219
San Francisco	22	9	0	7	20	3	5	12	6	7	6	3	6	4	17	97	9	235	226	145
A.L. clubs	8	9	6	9	19	2	7	14	21	12	6	12	2	9	11	1	....	148	140	....
2001 Totals	228	164	170	190	268	153	230	183	222	172	156	164	150	195	178	146	131	2952		2975
2000 Totals	173	166	*188	206	245	152	266	193	151	190	165	158	172	229	162	171	....		3005	....

*There were actually 187 home runs hit at Chicago and 162 hit at New York in 2000. The totals include two homers hit by the Cubs and one by the Mets when the Mets were the "home" team at Tokyo Stadium on March 29, and one homer hit by the Mets when the Cubs were the "home" team at Tokyo Stadium on March 30.

AT ARIZONA (228):

Arizona (107)—Gonzalez 26, Sanders 19, Miller 8, Finley 8, Williams 7, Bell 6, Grace 6, Dellucci 5, Colbrunn 4, Counsell 4, Durazo 4, Spivey 4, Womack 2, Barajas 2, Moeller 1. **Atlanta (7)**—Veras 2, A. Jones 2, Surhoff 1, Jordan 1, C. Jones 1. **Chicago (1)**—Sosa 1, White 1, Matthews 1, Patterson 1. **Cincinnati (1)**—Casey 1. **Colorado (11)**—Helton 3, L. Walker 2, Hampton 1, Hollandsworth 1, Norton 1, Petrick 1, Melhuse 1, Brumbaugh 1. **Detroit (5)**—T. Clark 2, Higginson 1, Fick 1, J. Patterson 1. **Florida (5)**—Johnson 2, Floyd 1, Lee 1, Wilson 1. **Houston (11)**—Alou 4, Berkman 3, Biggio 1, Bagwell 1, Castilla 1, Ward 1. **Los Angeles (15)**—Green 5, Grissom 3, Sheffield 2, Goodwin 1, Karros 1, Hiatt 1, Lo Duca 1, Beltre 1. **Milwaukee (11)**—Burnitz 5, Sexson 3, Lopez 1, Echevarria 1, Blanco 1. **Montreal (3)**—Cabrera 2, Stevens 1. **New York (2)**—Johnson 1, Lawton 1. **Oakland (2)**—Damon 1, Tejada 1. **Philadelphia (4)**—Glanville 2, Lee 2. **Pittsburgh (3)**—Giles 2, Kendall 1. **St. Louis (6)**—Paquette 1, Matheny 1, Renteria 1, Marrero 1, Drew 1, Pujols 1. **San Diego (0)**—Nevin 4, Trammell 1, Davis 1, Colangelo 1, Gonzalez 1. **San Francisco (22)**—Aurilia 6, Bonds 5, Kent 2, Feliz 2, Galarraga 1, Vander Wal 1, R. Davis 1, Schmidt 1, Benard 1, Rios 1, Guzman 1.

AT ATLANTA (164):

Arizona (2)—Williams 1, Finley 1. **Atlanta (87)**—C. Jones 19, A. Jones 16, Jordan 14, Lopez 10, Helms 6, Surhoff 5, Giles 5, DeRosa 3, Furcal 3, Franco 2, Caminiti 2, Gilkey 1, Brogna 1. **Baltimore (4)**—Ripken 2, Batista 1, Gibbons 1. **Chicago (4)**—Hundley 2, Sosa 1, Stairs 1. **Cincinnati (1)**—Young 1. **Colorado (4)**—L. Walker 2, Cirillo 1, Helton 1. **Florida (9)**—Lee 2, Wilson 2, Floyd 1, Mabry 1, Johnson 1, Millar 1, Gonzalez 1. **Los Angeles (6)**—Green 3, Sheffield 2, Grissom 1. **Milwaukee (6)**—Burnitz 1, Houston 1, Casanova 1, Sexson 1. **Montreal (6)**—Stevens 3, Guerrero 1, Vidro 1, Blum 1. **New York (10)**—Ventura 3, Piazza 2, Alfonzo 2, Zeile 1, McEwing 1, Perez 1. **Philadelphia (6)**—Burrell 3, Abreu 2, Rolen 1. **Pittsburgh (3)**—Kendall 1, Osik 1, Ramirez 1. **St. Louis (2)**—Renteria 1, Pujols 1. **San Diego (2)**—Klesko 1, Kotsay 1. **San Francisco (9)**—Bonds 6, Snow 1, Benard 1, Martinez 1. **Tampa Bay (5)**—McGriff 3, Grieve 1, Winn 1.

AT CHICAGO (170):

Arizona (2)—Bautista 1, Durazo 1. **Atlanta (5)**—A. Jones 2, Surhoff 1, C. Jones 1, Giles 1. **Chicago A.L. (3)**—Valentin 1, Konerko 1, Lee 1. **Chicago N.L. (95)**—Sosa 34, McGriff 7, Gutierrez 7, White 7, Stairs 5, Zuleta 5, Hundley 4, Young 4, Tucker 3, Coomer 3, Mueller 3, Brown 3, DeShields 2, Machado 2, Matthews 2, Girardi 1, Cairo 1, Patterson 1, Ojeda 1. **Cincinnati (10)**—Dunn 2, Miller 2, Griffey 1, Rivera 1, Castro 1, Jennings 1, Young 1, Cromer 1. **Colorado (3)**—Hampton 1, Helton 1, Butler 1. **Florida (4)**—Wilson 2, Millar 1, Lowell 1. **Houston (6)**—Castilla 2, Merced 1, Euseblo 1, Hidalgo 1, Truby 1. **Kansas City (1)**—Ibanez 1. **Los Angeles (1)**—Grissom 1. **Milwaukee (9)**—Sexson 2, Hernandez 1, Burnitz 1, Lopez 1, Sweeney 1, Loretta 1, Houston 1, Brown 1. **Minnesota (2)**—Hunter 1, J. Jones 1. **Montreal (2)**—Vidro 1, Tracy 1. **New York (4)**—Zeile 1, Ventura 1, Piazza 1, McEwing 1. **Philadelphia (1)**—Burrell 1. **Pittsburgh (5)**—Vander Wal 1, Young 1, Giles 1, Ramirez 1, Hermansen 1. **St. Louis (10)**—McGwire 3, Edmonds 3, Paquette 1, Renteria 1, Polanco 1, Pujols 1. **San Diego (4)**—Davis 2, Henderson 1, Nevin 1. **San Francisco (3)**—Bonds 1, Aurilia 1, Hernandez 1.

AT CINCINNATI (190):

Arizona (6)—Gonzalez 3, Williams 1, Grace 1, Sanders 1. **Atlanta (5)**—Lockhart 2, Martinez 1, A. Jones 1, Furcal 1. **Chicago (12)**—Stairs 3, White 3, Sosa 2, Matthews 2, McGriff 1, Gutierrez 1. **Cincinnati (83)**—Griffey 12, Boone 10, Young 8, Dunn 8, Stinnett 6, Rivera 6, Ochoa 5, Casey 5, Reese 4, Clark 4, Walker 3, LaRue 3, Jennings 2, Larkin 1, Sanders 1, Tucker 1, Selby 1, Guerrero 1, Cromer 1, Miller 1. **Cleveland (5)**—Gonzalez 2, Burks 1, Alomar 1, Thome 1. **Colorado (9)**—L. Walker 3, Helton 2, Gant 1, Neagle 1, Petrick 1, Ortiz 1. **Detroit (4)**—Fick 2, Higginson 1, Cedeno 1. **Florida (1)**—Lee 1. **Houston (6)**—Lugo 2, Biggio 1, Bagwell 1, Castilla 1, Berkman 1. **Los Angeles (5)**—Grissom 2, Brown 1, Sheffield 1, Karros 1. **Milwaukee (13)**—Hernandez 3, Burnitz 2, Brown 2, Belliard 2, Sexson 2, White 1, Jenkins 1. **Montreal (2)**—Stevens 1, Cabrera 1. **New York (2)**—Alfonzo 1, Shinjo 1. **Philadelphia (2)**—Burrell 1, Rollins 1. **Pittsburgh (13)**—Giles 5, Ramirez 2, Hyzdu 2, Vander Wal 1, Young 1, A. Brown 1, J. Wilson 1. **St. Louis (11)**—Paquette 1, Edmonds 2, Drew 2, Pujols 2, McGwire 1, Marrero 1, Matthews 1. **San Diego (4)**—Klesko 2, Trammell 1, Gonzalez 1. **San Francisco (7)**—Bonds 2, Galarraga 1, Vander Wal 1, Kent 1, Benard 1, Guzman 1.

AT COLORADO (268):

Anaheim (11)—Gil 2, Anderson 2, Erstad 2, Spiezio 2, DaVanon 2, Wooten 1. **Arizona (14)**—Gonzalez 5, Sanders 3, Bell 1, Williams 1, Dellucci 1, Miller 1, Durazo 1, Barajas 1. **Atlanta (6)**—Surhoff 1, Jordan 1, Lopez 1, C. Jones 1, A. Jones 1, Giles 1. **Chicago (1)**—Hundley 1. **Cincinnati (2)**—Boone 1, Sadler

1. **Colorado (124)**—Helton 27, L. Walker 20, T. Walker 10, Cirillo 9, Ortiz 9, Norton 7, Perez 7, Petrick 7, Gant 6, Hampton 4, Shumpert 3, Hollandsworth 3, Fasano 3, Little 3, Uribe 3, Neagle 1, Bennett 1, Kieschnick 1. **Florida (4)**—Millar 2, Floyd 1, Lee 1. **Houston (4)**—Biggio 1, Alou 1, Bagwell 1, Hidalgo 1. **Los Angeles (19)**—Lo Duca 4, Sheffield 3, Green 3, Grudzielanek 2, Beltre 2, Kreuter 1, Grissom 1, Hansen 1, Karros 1, Hiatt 1. **Milwaukee (6)**—Hernandez 1, Burnitz 1, Echevarria 1, Blanco 1, Sexson 1, Jenkins 1. **Montreal (9)**—Guerrero 2, Vidro 2, Blum 2, Mordecai 1, Barrett 1, Bradley 1. **New York (4)**—Relaford 2, Piazza 1, Alfonzo 1. **Philadelphia (5)**—Burrell 3, Pratt 1, Glanville 1. **Pittsburgh (6)**—Ramirez 3, Young 1, Kendall 1, Hyzdu 1. **St. Louis (11)**—Lankford 3, Pujols 3, Edmonds 2, Matheny 1, Renteria 1, Drew 1. **San Diego (14)**—Nevin 5, Kotsay 2, Davis 2, Crespo 2, Trammell 1, Witt 1, Mendez 1. **San Francisco (20)**—Bonds 4, Dunston 3, Aurilia 3, Benard 3, Feliz 2, Kent 1, Snow 1, R. Davis 1, Rios 1, Murray 1. **Seattle (8)**—Boone 2, Javier 1, Martinez 1, Sprague 1, Wilson 1, Bell 1, Cameron 1.

AT FLORIDA (153):

Arizona (3)—Williams 1, Sanders 1, Miller 1. **Atlanta (6)**—A. Jones 3, C. Jones 2, Jordan 1. **Baltimore (2)**—Ripken 1, Gibbons 1. **Chicago (2)**—Tucker 1, Coomer 1. **Cincinnati (3)**—Walker 1, Boone 1, Cromer 1. **Colorado (3)**—L. Walker 1, Hampton 1, Helton 1. **Florida (84)**—Floyd 16, Millar 13, Lowell 12, Wilson 9, Lee 8, Johnson 5, Gonzalez 5, Owens 4, Fox 3, Redmond 3, Mabry 2, Berg 2, Castillo 1, McGuire 1. **Houston (9)**—Bagwell 3, Castilla 2, Berkman 2, Biggio 1, Ward 1. **Los Angeles (4)**—Green 2, Sheffield 1, Grudzielanek 1. **Milwaukee (3)**—Hernandez 1, Hammonds 1, Mouton 1. **Montreal (6)**—Stevens 2, Ducey 1, Guerrero 1, Tatis 1, Cabrera 1. **New York (7)**—Piazza 2, Ventura 1, Ordonez 1, Payton 1, Perez 1, Shinjo 1. **Philadelphia (10)**—Abreu 4, Rolen 2, Lieberthal 1, Glanville 1, Lee 1, Burrell 1. **Pittsburgh (1)**—Young 1. **St. Louis (4)**—Lankford 2, Marrero 1, Drew 1. **San Diego (4)**—Nevin 1, Jackson 1, Trammell 1, Davis 1. **San Francisco (2)**—Bonds 1, Estalella 1.

AT HOUSTON (230):

Arizona (3)—Gonzalez 3. **Atlanta (5)**—C. Jones 3, A. Jones 1, Helms 1. **Chicago (18)**—Sosa 8, McGriff 3, Hundley 2, Girardi 2, Stairs 1, Coomer 1, Cairo 1, Patterson 1. **Cincinnati (18)**—Tucker 4, Casey 3, Young 2, Dunn 2, Griffey 1, Stinnett 1, Rivera 1, Graves 1, Reese 1, Boone 1, LaRue 1. **Cleveland (4)**—Alomar 2, Lofton 2. **Colorado (5)**—Gant 1, Cirillo 1, Norton 1, Helton 1, Pierre 1. **Florida (6)**—Johnson 2, Floyd 1, Owens 1, Wilson 1, Lowell 1. **Houston (108)**—Bagwell 21, Alou 15, Hidalgo 13, Berkman 13, Biggio 10, Castilla 10, Lugo 6, Ward 5, Ausmus 4, Truby 4, Merced 3, Eusebio 3, Vizcaino 1. **Los Angeles (7)**—Green 2, Bogar 1, Grudzielanek 1, Cora 1, Beltre 1, Gagne 1. **Milwaukee (7)**—Burnitz 2, Jenkins 2, Hernandez 1, Collier 1, Sexson 1. **Montreal (2)**—Stevens 1, Bergeron 1. **New York (1)**—Alfonzo 1. **Philadelphia (3)**—Lieberthal 1, Rolen 1, Abreu 1. **Pittsburgh (11)**—Kendall 3, Ramirez 3, Matthews 2, Meares 1, Giles 1, J. Wilson 1. **St. Louis (13)**—McGwire 4, Pujols 3, Drew 2, Vina 1, Paquette 1, Edmonds 1, Polanco 1. **San Diego (11)**—Klesko 4, Nevin 2, Kotsay 2, Magadan 1, Jarvis 1, Jackson 1. **San Francisco (5)**—Bonds 1, Santiago 1, Kent 1, Benard 1, Martinez 1. **Texas (3)**—Palmeiro 1, A. Rodriguez 1, Catalanotto 1.

AT LOS ANGELES (183):

Anaheim (3)—Anderson 2, Erstad 1. **Arizona (11)**—Gonzalez 6, Williams 1, Grace 1, Finley 1, Bautista 1, Durazo 1. **Atlanta (1)**—Jordan 1. **Chicago (2)**—Sosa 2. **Cincinnati (8)**—Griffey 2, Young 2, LaRue 2, Boone 1, Casey 1. **Colorado (12)**—Helton 7, Cirillo 3, Kieschnick 2. **Florida (2)**—Floyd 1, Lee 1. **Houston (3)**—Berkman 3. **Los Angeles (94)**—Green 19, Sheffield 16, Lo Duca 11, Grissom 9, Grudzielanek 8, Karros 7, Kreuter 4, Beltre 4, Reboulet 3, Donnels 2, Cora 2, Bocachica 2, Hansen 1, Goodwin 1, Bogar 1, Dreifort 1, Aven 1, Pena 1, Christensen 1. **Milwaukee (1)**—Sexson 1. **Montreal (1)**—Bergeron 1. **New York (1)**—Piazza 2, Alfonzo 1, Ordonez 1, Shinjo 1. **Philadelphia (4)**—Anderson 2, Abreu 1, Burrell 1. **Pittsburgh (3)**—Vander Wal 1, Young 1, E. Brown 1. **St. Louis (1)**—Edmonds 1. **San Diego (9)**—Klesko 3, Trammell 2, Lankford 1, Nevin 1, Gonzalez 1, Jimenez 1. **San Francisco (12)**—R. Davis 2, Benard 2, Rios 2, Dunston 1, Bonds 1, Santiago 1, Kent 1, Aurilia 1, Martinez 1. **Seattle (5)**—Olerud 1, Martin 1, Wilson 1, Bell 1, Suzuki 1. **Texas (6)**—Sierra 2, Palmeiro 2, I. Rodriguez 1, Young 1.

AT MILWAUKEE (222):

Arizona (6)—Grace 1, Finley 1, Gonzalez 1, Bautista 1, Womack 1, Durazo 1. **Atlanta (3)**—Helms 2, Martinez 1. **Chicago A.L. (6)**—Lee 2, Canseco 1, Alomar 1, Johnson 1, Liefer 1. **Chicago N.L. (9)**—Sosa 3, Stairs 3, White 2, Buford 1. **Cincinnati (11)**—Young 2, LaRue 2, Dunn 2, Griffey 1, Tucker 1, Ochoa 1, Walker 1, Reese 1. **Colorado (5)**—L. Walker 2, Helton 1, Ortiz 1, Uribe 1. **Florida (1)**—Johnson 1. **Houston (10)**—Bagwell 3, Berkman 2, Biggio 1, Castilla 1, Hidalgo 1, Lugo 1, Truby 1. **Kansas City (5)**—Alicea 1, Randa 1, Dye 1, Hinch 1, Beltran 1. **Los Angeles (7)**—Green 3, Sheffield 2, Karros 1, Beltre 1. **Milwaukee (107)**—Sexson 28, Burnitz 16, Jenkins 11, Hernandez 9, Casanova 7, Belliard 7, White 6, Houston 6, Blanco 4, Hammonds 3, Echevarria 3, Lopez 2, Coolbaugh 2, Mouton 1, Sweeney 1, Collier 1. **Minnesota (10)**—Koskie 3, J. Jones 3, Hunter 2, Pierzynski 1, Mientkiewicz 1. **Montreal (3)**—Guerrero 1, Cabrera 1, Tracy 1. **New York (6)**—Alfonzo 3, Piazza 2, Relaford 1. **Philadelphia (3)**—Rolen 2, Abreu 1. **Pittsburgh (8)**—Ramirez 3, Vander Wal 2, Giles 1, E. Wilson 1, C. Wilson 1. **St. Louis (11)**—Drew 3, McGwire 2, Vina 2, Edmonds 2, Bonilla 1, Marrero 1. **San Diego (5)**—Nevin 2, Trammell 2, Klesko 1. **San Francisco (6)**—Bonds 3, Snow 1, R. Davis 1, Aurilia 1.

AT MONTREAL (172):

Arizona (3)—Bell 1, Williams 1, Gonzalez 1. **Atlanta (12)**—Caminiti 4, A. Jones 2, Franco 1, Jordan 1, Brogna 1, Lopez 1, C. Jones 1, Giles 1. **Boston (6)**—Stynes 2, Ramirez 1, Hatteberg 1, Nixon 1, Daubach 1. **Chicago (4)**—Sosa 3, White 1. **Cincinnati (7)**—Dunn 2, Griffey 1, Castro 1, Casey 1, LaRue 1, Cromer 1. **Colorado (5)**—Ortiz 2, L. Walker 1, Cirillo 1, Ochoa 1. **Florida (10)**—Johnson 2, Wilson 2, Floyd 1, Lee 1, Berg 1, Gonzalez 1, Lowell 1, Grilli 1. **Houston (6)**—Bagwell 2, Alou 1, Hidalgo 1, Ward 1, Lugo 1. **Los Angeles (2)**—Goodwin 1, Green 1. **Milwaukee (4)**—Burnitz 2, Loretta 1, Sexson 1. **Montreal (68)**—Guerrero 21, Stevens 12, Cabrera 7, Vidro 6, Blum 6, Knorr 3, Smith 3, Barrett 3, Ducey 1, Mordecai 1, Minor 1, Bergeron 1, Schneider 1, Reames 1, Wilkerson 1. **New York (8)**—Piazza 2, Ventura 1, Alfonzo 1, Relaford 1, Agbayani 1, Perez 1, Shinjo 1. **Philadelphia (10)**—Abreu 4, Rolen 2, Rollins 2, Glanville 1, Estrada 1. **Pittsburgh (6)**—C. Wilson 2, Olivares 1, Bell 1, Young 1, Giles 1. **St. Louis (3)**—Edmonds 1, Renteria 1, Pujols 1. **San Diego (5)**—Nevin 2, Henderson 1, Trammell 1, Kotsay 1. **San Francisco (7)**—Galarraga 2, Kent 2, Dunston 1, Bonds 1, Aurilia 1. **Tampa Bay (2)**—McGriff 1, Abernathy 1. **Toronto (4)**—Mondesi 1, Delgado 1, Stewart 1, Cruz 1.

AT NEW YORK (156):

Arizona (2)—Gonzalez 1, Dellucci 1. **Atlanta (12)**—Jordan 3, C. Jones 3, Surhoff 2, Lopez 2, Brogna 1, A. Jones 1. **Boston (2)**—Lansing 1, Ramirez 1. **Chicago (5)**—Coomer 2, Sosa 1, Gutierrez 1, Matthews 1. **Cincinnati (1)**—Reese 1. **Colorado (2)**—Helton 1, J. Jennings 1. **Florida (10)**—Wilson 5, Floyd 1, Mabry 1, Lee 1, Millar 1, Gonzalez 1. **Houston (8)**—Alou 2, Berkman 2, Biggio 1, Bagwell 1, Ausmus 1, Ward 1. **Los Angeles (3)**—Green 2, Grissom 1. **Milwaukee (4)**—Hernandez 1, Sweeney 1, Casanova 1, Sexson 1. **Montreal (5)**—Guerrero 2, Vidro 2, Smith 1. **New York A.L. (3)**—B. Williams 2, Spencer 1. **New York N.L. (65)**—Piazza 16, Ventura 9, Alfonzo 6, Payton 6, Zeile 4, Relaford 4, Agbayani 4, Shinjo 4, McEwing 3, Escobar 3, Johnson 2, Perez 2, Hamilton 1, Lawton 1. **Philadelphia (14)**—Glanville 3, Rolen 3, Burrell 3, Abreu 2, Pratt 1, Perez 1, Rollins 1. **Pittsburgh (2)**—Matthews 1, C. Wilson 1. **St. Louis (6)**—McGwire 2, Edmonds 1, Matheny 1, Renteria 1, Pujols 1. **San Diego (5)**—Henderson 2, Arias 1, Klesko 1, Trammell 1. **San Francisco (6)**—Snow 2, Aurilia 2, Bonds 1, Benard 1. **Toronto (1)**—Mondesi 1.

AT PHILADELPHIA (164):

Arizona (7)—Sanders 4, Gonzalez 2, Williams 1. **Atlanta (8)**—C. Jones 2, A. Jones 2, Jordan 1, Lopez 1, Lockhart 1, Giles 1. **Baltimore (9)**—Segui 2, Conine 2, Ripken 1, Anderson 1, Kinkade 1, Richard 1, Gibbons 1. **Chicago (4)**—Mueller 2, Sosa 1, Zuleta 1. **Cincinnati (1)**—Griffey 1. **Colorado (2)**—Hollandsworth 1, Norton 1. **Florida (12)**—Floyd 3, Johnson 3, Lee 2, Berg 1, Wilson 1, Redmond 1, Lowell 1. **Los Angeles (1)**—Green 1. **Milwaukee (5)**—Fernandez 1, White 1, Casanova 1, Belliard 1, Sexson 1. **Montreal (9)**—Stevens 2, Guerrero 2, Pride 1, Mordecai 1, Cabrera 1, Barrett 1, Minor 1. **New York A.L. (3)**—Posada 2, Jeter 1. **New York N.L. (9)**—Ventura 2, Piazza 2, Pratt 1, Alfonzo 1, Ordonez 1, Payton 1, Shinjo 1. **Philadelphia (83)**—Abreu 13, Rolen 12, Lee 11, Burrell 10, Rollins 8, Anderson 7, Estrada 7, Glanville 6, Hunter 2, Perez 2, Person 2, Ducey 1, Jordan 1, Bennett 1. **Pittsburgh (2)**—Giles 1, Osik 1. **St. Louis (3)**—Lankford 1, Vina 1, Drew 1. **San Diego (3)**—Jackson 1, Kotsay 1, Davis 1. **San Francisco (3)**—Aurilia 2, Bonds 1.

AT PITTSBURGH (150):

Arizona (1)—Grace 1. **Atlanta (4)**—Gilkey 1, C. Jones 1, A. Jones 1, Bako 1. **Chicago (8)**—Sosa 2, Hundley 2, Stairs 1, Gutierrez 1, Matthews 1, Patterson 1. **Cincinnati (3)**—Casey 2, Young 1. **Cleveland (1)**—Gonzalez 1. **Colorado (2)**—Norton 1, Helton 1. **Florida (4)**—Floyd 2, Johnson 1, Gonzalez 1. **Houston (8)**—Castilla 5, Alou 1, Hidalgo 1, Berkman 1. **Kansas City (1)**—Beltran 1. **Los Angeles (7)**—Karros 2, Beltre 2, Donnels 1, Green 1, Lo Duca 1. **Milwaukee (11)**—Hernandez 4, White 2, Burnitz 1, Houston 1, Brown 1, Sexson 1, Jenkins 1. **Montreal (1)**—Guerrero 1. **New York (7)**—Zeile 2, Piazza 2, Ventura 1, Lawton 1, McEwing 1. **Philadelphia (1)**—Lee 1. **Pittsburgh (75)**—Giles 18, Ramirez 16, C. Wilson 8, Young 7, Vander Wal 5, Bell 4, Kendall 3, Mackowiak 3, Meares 2, E. Brown 2, Morris 2, Matthews 2, Schmidt 1, Hermansen 1, Redman 1. **St. Louis (7)**—Pujols 2, Bonilla 1, McGwire 1, Lankford 1, Paquette 1, Drew 1. **San Diego (3)**—Henderson 1, Gwynn 1, Trammell 1. **San Francisco (6)**—Bonds 2, Rios 2, Kent 1, Benard 1.

AT ST. LOUIS (195):

Arizona (6)—Sanders 2, Bell 1, Gonzalez 1, Dellucci 1, Durazo 1. **Chicago A.L. (3)**—Ordonez 2, Konerko 1. **Chicago N.L. (10)**—Sosa 3, Stairs 2, Young 2, Buford 1, Dunwoody 1, Matthews 1. **Cincinnati (14)**—Griffey 2, Young 2, Dunn 2, Larkin 1, Stinnett 1, Tucker 1, Castro 1, Ochoa 1, Reese 1, LaRue 1, Clark 1. **Colorado (3)**—L. Walker 2, Helton 1. **Detroit (3)**—Higginson 1, T. Clark 1, Cardona 1. **Florida (3)**—Mabry 1, Castillo 1, Lee 1. **Houston (11)**—Berkman 3, Biggio 2, Bagwell 2, Truby 2, Merced 1, Hidalgo 1. **Los Angeles (5)**—Green 3, Goodwin 1, Grudzielanek 1. **Milwaukee (6)**—Hammonds 2, Jenkins 2, White 1, Hernandez 1. **Minnesota (3)**—Allen 2, Rivas 1. **Montreal (3)**—Stevens 1, Vidro 1, Tatis 1. **New York (3)**—Piazza 1, Agbayani 1, McEwing 1. **Philadelphia (2)**—Rolen 1, Burrell 1. **Pittsburgh (9)**—Giles 3, Ramirez 2, Young 1, Meares 1, Nunez 1, C. Wilson 1. **St. Louis (100)**—Pujols 18, Edmonds 16, Drew 15, McGwire 13, Paquette 8, Lankford 7, Vina 5, Matheny 4, Bonilla 3, Renteria 3, Marrero 2, Kile 1, Cairo 1, Sutton 1, Polanco 1, Robinson 1, Stechschulte 1. **San Diego (6)**—Klesko 3, Henderson 1, Nevin 1, Crespo 1. **San Francisco (4)**—Bonds 1, Santiago 1, Kent 1, Rios 1.

AT SAN DIEGO (178):

Arizona (14)—Grace 2, Gonzalez 2, Sanders 2, Bautista 2, Durazo 2, Bell 1, Finley 1, Dellucci 1, Spivey 1. **Atlanta (2)**—Veras 1, Bako 1. **Chicago (5)**—McGriff 1, Girardi 1, Hundley 1, Stairs 1, Tucker 1. **Cincinnati (5)**—Griffey 1, Young 1, Reese 1, LaRue 1, Dunn 1. **Colorado (17)**—L. Walker 4, Uribe 3, Cirillo 2, Helton 2, Shumpert 1, Hollandsworth 1, Cruz 1, T. Walker 1, Petrick 1, Pierre 1. **Florida (4)**—Floyd 2, Johnson 1, Millar 1. **Houston (2)**—Biggio 1, Reynolds 1. **Los Angeles (15)**—Sheffield 6, Lo Duca 3, Green 2, Grissom 1, Karros 1, Cora 1, Beltre 1. **Milwaukee (3)**—White 2, Belliard 1. **Montreal (1)**—Guerrero 1. **New York (1)**—Johnson 1. **Oakland (5)**—Menechino 2, Ja. Giambi 1, Wilson 1, Long 1. **Philadelphia (5)**—Lee 2, Rolen 1, Abreu 1, Anderson 1. **Pittsburgh (2)**—Giles 1, Ramirez 1. **St. Louis (5)**—Pujols 3, McGwire 1, Edmonds 1. **San Diego (69)**—Nevin 19, Klesko 15, Trammell 11, Gonzalez 5, Lankford 3, Kotsay 0, Davis 3, Henderson 2, Darr 2, Jimenez 2, Wilkins 1, Jackson 1, Witt 1, Colangelo 1. **San Francisco (17)**—Bonds 5, Kent 3, Rios 3, Aurilia 2, Murray 2, Benard 1, Martinez 1. **Seattle (4)**—Olerud 2, Cameron 1, Guillen 1. **Texas (2)**—Palmeiro 1, Young 1.

AT SAN FRANCISCO (146):

Anaheim (1)—Wooten 1. **Arizona (9)**—Bell 2, Williams 2, Grace 2, Gonzalez 1, Dellucci 1, Miller 1. **Chicago (5)**—Sosa 1, Buford 1, White 1, Mueller 1, Matthews 1. **Cincinnati (2)**—Stinnett 1, Rivera 1. **Colorado (2)**—Petrick 1, Uribe 1. **Houston (2)**—Alou 1, Bagwell 1. **Los Angeles (7)**—Sheffield 2, Grissom 2, Lo Duca 2, Green 1. **Milwaukee (6)**—Hernandez 3, Burnitz 1, Casanova 1, Sexson 1. **Montreal (2)**—Stevens 1, Guerrero 1. **New York (2)**—Pratt 1, Shinjo 1. **Philadelphia (2)**—Abreu 1, Burrell 1. **Pittsburgh (2)**—Kendall 1, Ramirez 1. **St. Louis (1)**—Lankford 1. **San Diego (6)**—Nevin 2, Trammell 2, Arias 1, Crespo 1. **San Francisco (97)**—Bonds 37, Aurilia 15, Kent 8, Crespo 4, E. Davis 3, Dunston 3, Galarraga 3, Santiago 3, Snow 3, Benard 3, Rios 3, Murray 3, Feliz 3, Estalella 2, Vander Wal 1, R. Davis 1, Martinez 1, Guzman 1.

HISTORY

All-time results

Award winners

Hall of Fame

Team by team

ALL-TIME RESULTS

AMERICAN LEAGUE CHAMPIONS

Year	Team	Manager
1901	Chicago	Clark Griffith
1902	Philadelphia	Connie Mack
1903	Boston	Jimmy Collins
1904	Boston	Jimmy Collins
1905	Philadelphia	Connie Mack
1906	Chicago	Fielder Jones
1907	Detroit	Hugh Jennings
1908	Detroit	Hugh Jennings
1909	Detroit	Hugh Jennings
1910	Philadelphia	Connie Mack
1911	Philadelphia	Connie Mack
1912	Boston	Jake Stahl
1913	Philadelphia	Connie Mack
1914	Philadelphia	Connie Mack
1915	Boston	Bill Carrigan
1916	Boston	Bill Carrigan
1917	Chicago	Pants Rowland
1918	Boston	Ed Barrow
1919	Chicago	Kid Gleason
1920	Cleveland	Tris Speaker
1921	New York	Miller Huggins
1922	New York	Miller Huggins
1923	New York	Miller Huggins
1924	Washington	Bucky Harris
1925	Washington	Bucky Harris
1926	New York	Miller Huggins
1927	New York	Miller Huggins
1928	New York	Miller Huggins
1929	Philadelphia	Connie Mack
1930	Philadelphia	Connie Mack
1931	Philadelphia	Connie Mack
1932	New York	Joe McCarthy
1933	Washington	Joe Cronin
1934	Detroit	Mickey Cochrane
1935	Detroit	Mickey Cochrane
1936	New York	Joe McCarthy
1937	New York	Joe McCarthy
1938	New York	Joe McCarthy
1939	New York	Joe McCarthy
1940	Detroit	Del Baker
1941	New York	Joe McCarthy
1942	New York	Joe McCarthy
1943	New York	Joe McCarthy
1944	St. Louis	Luke Sewell
1945	Detroit	Steve O'Neill
1946	Boston	Joe Cronin
1947	New York	Bucky Harris
1948	Cleveland*	Lou Boudreau
1949	New York	Casey Stengel
1950	New York	Casey Stengel
1951	New York	Casey Stengel
1952	New York	Casey Stengel
1953	New York	Casey Stengel
1954	Cleveland	Al Lopez
1955	New York	Casey Stengel
1956	New York	Casey Stengel
1957	New York	Casey Stengel
1958	New York	Casey Stengel
1959	Chicago	Al Lopez
1960	New York	Casey Stengel
1961	New York	Ralph Houk
1962	New York	Ralph Houk
1963	New York	Ralph Houk
1964	New York	Yogi Berra
1965	Minnesota	Sam Mele
1966	Baltimore	Hank Bauer
1967	Boston	Dick Williams
1968	Detroit	Mayo Smith
1969	Baltimore (East Division)	Earl Weaver
1970	Baltimore (East Division)	Earl Weaver
1971	Baltimore (East Division)	Earl Weaver
1972	Oakland (West Division)	Dick Williams
1973	Oakland (West Division)	Dick Williams
1974	Oakland (West Division)	Al Dark
1975	Boston (East Division)	Darrell Johnson
1976	New York (East Division)	Billy Martin
1977	New York (East Division)	Billy Martin
1978	New York (East Division)	Billy Martin, Bob Lemon
1979	Baltimore (East Division)	Earl Weaver
1980	Kansas City (West Division)	Jim Frey
1981	New York (East Division)	Gene Michael, Bob Lemon
1982	Milwaukee (East Division)	Buck Rodgers, Harvey Kuenn
1983	Baltimore (East Division)	Joe Altobelli
1984	Detroit (East Division)	Sparky Anderson
1985	Kansas City (West Division)	Dick Howser
1986	Boston (East Division)	John McNamara
1987	Minnesota (West Division)	Tom Kelly
1988	Oakland (West Division)	Tony La Russa
1989	Oakland (West Division)	Tony La Russa
1990	Oakland (West Division)	Tony La Russa
1991	Minnesota (West Division)	Tom Kelly
1992	Toronto (East Division)	Cito Gaston
1993	Toronto (East Division)	Cito Gaston
1994	None†	
1995	Cleveland (Central Division)	Mike Hargrove
1996	New York (East Division)	Joe Torre
1997	Cleveland (Central Division)	Mike Hargrove
1998	New York (East Division)	Joe Torre
1999	New York (East Division)	Joe Torre
2000	New York (East Division)	Joe Torre
2001	New York (East Division)	Joe Torre

*Defeated Boston in one-game playoff. †New York finished the strike-shortened season with the league's best record.

NATIONAL LEAGUE CHAMPIONS

Year	Team	Manager
1876	Chicago	Albert Spalding
1877	Boston	Harry Wright
1878	Boston	Harry Wright
1879	Providence	George Wright
1880	Chicago	Adrian Anson
1881	Chicago	Adrian Anson
1882	Chicago	Adrian Anson
1883	Boston	John Morrill
1884	Providence	Frank Bancroft
1885	Chicago	Adrian Anson
1886	Chicago	Adrian Anson
1887	Detroit	William Watkins
1888	New York	James Mutrie
1889	New York	James Mutrie
1890	Brooklyn	William McGunnigle
1891	Boston	Frank Selee
1892	Boston	Frank Selee
1893	Boston	Frank Selee
1894	Baltimore	Edward Hanlon
1895	Baltimore	Edward Hanlon
1896	Baltimore	Edward Hanlon
1897	Boston	Frank Selee
1898	Boston	Frank Selee
1899	Brooklyn	Edward Hanlon

Year	Team	Manager	Year	Team	Manager
1900—Brooklyn		Edward Hanlon	1955—Brooklyn		Walter Alston
1901—Pittsburgh		Fred Clarke	1956—Brooklyn		Walter Alston
1902—Pittsburgh		Fred Clarke	1957—Milwaukee		Fred Haney
1903—Pittsburgh		Fred Clarke	1958—Milwaukee		Fred Haney
1904—New York		John McGraw	1959—Los Angeles‡		Walter Alston
1905—New York		John McGraw	1960—Pittsburgh		Danny Murtaugh
1906—Chicago		Frank Chance	1961—Cincinnati		Fred Hutchinson
1907—Chicago		Frank Chance	1962—San Francisco§		Al Dark
1908—Chicago		Frank Chance	1963—Los Angeles		Walter Alston
1909—Pittsburgh		Fred Clarke	1964—St. Louis		Johnny Keane
1910—Chicago		Frank Chance	1965—Los Angeles		Walter Alston
1911—New York		John McGraw	1966—Los Angeles		Walter Alston
1912—New York		John McGraw	1967—St. Louis		Red Schoendienst
1913—New York		John McGraw	1968—St. Louis		Red Schoendienst
1914—Boston		George Stallings	1969—New York (East Division)		Gil Hodges
1915—Philadelphia		Pat Moran	1970—Cincinnati (West Division)		Sparky Anderson
1916—Brooklyn		Wilbert Robinson	1971—Pittsburgh (East Division)		Danny Murtaugh
1917—New York		John McGraw	1972—Cincinnati (West Division)		Sparky Anderson
1918—Chicago		Fred Mitchell	1973—New York (East Division)		Yogi Berra
1919—Cincinnati		Pat Moran	1974—Los Angeles (West Division)		Walter Alston
1920—Brooklyn		Wilbert Robinson	1975—Cincinnati (West Division)		Sparky Anderson
1921—New York		John McGraw	1976—Cincinnati (West Division)		Sparky Anderson
1922—New York		John McGraw	1977—Los Angeles (West Division)		Tommy Lasorda
1923—New York		John McGraw	1978—Los Angeles (West Division)		Tommy Lasorda
1924—New York		John McGraw	1979—Pittsburgh (East Division)		Chuck Tanner
1925—Pittsburgh		Bill McKechnie	1980—Philadelphia (East Division)		Dallas Green
1926—St. Louis		Rogers Hornsby	1981—Los Angeles (West Division)		Tommy Lasorda
1927—Pittsburgh		Donie Bush	1982—St. Louis (East Division)		Whitey Herzog
1928—St. Louis		Bill McKechnie	1983—Philadelphia (East Division)		Pat Corrales, Paul Owens
1929—Chicago		Joe McCarthy	1984—San Diego (West Division)		Dick Williams
1930—St. Louis		Gabby Street	1985—St. Louis (East Division)		Whitey Herzog
1931—St. Louis		Gabby Street	1986—New York (East Division)		Dave Johnson
1932—Chicago		Charlie Grimm	1987—St. Louis (East Division)		Whitey Herzog
1933—New York		Bill Terry	1988—Los Angeles (West Division)		Tommy Lasorda
1934—St. Louis		Frank Frisch	1989—San Francisco (West Division)		Roger Craig
1935—Chicago		Charlie Grimm	1990—Cincinnati (West Division)		Lou Piniella
1936—New York		Bill Terry	1991—Atlanta (West Division)		Bobby Cox
1937—New York		Bill Terry	1992—Atlanta (West Division)		Bobby Cox
1938—Chicago		Gabby Hartnett	1993—Philadelphia (East Division)		Jim Fregosi
1939—Cincinnati		Bill McKechnie	1994—None∞		
1940—Cincinnati		Bill McKechnie	1995—Atlanta (East Division)		Bobby Cox
1941—Brooklyn		Leo Durocher	1996—Atlanta (East Division)		Bobby Cox
1942—St. Louis		Billy Southworth	1997—Florida (East Division)		Jim Leyland
1943—St. Louis		Billy Southworth	1998—San Diego (West Division)		Bruce Bochy
1944—St. Louis		Billy Southworth	1999—Atlanta (East Division)		Bobby Cox
1945—Chicago		Charlie Grimm	2000—New York (East Division)		Bobby Valentine
1946—St. Louis*		Eddie Dyer	2001—Arizona (West Division)		Bob Brenly
1947—Brooklyn		Burt Shotton			
1948—Boston		Billy Southworth			
1949—Brooklyn		Burt Shotton			
1950—Philadelphia		Eddie Sawyer			
1951—New York†		Leo Durocher			
1952—Brooklyn		Charlie Dressen			
1953—Brooklyn		Charlie Dressen			
1954—New York		Leo Durocher			

*Defeated Brooklyn, two games to none, in playoff for pennant.

†Defeated Brooklyn, two games to one, in playoff for pennant.

‡Defeated Milwaukee, two games to none, in playoff for pennant.

§Defeated Los Angeles, two games to one, in playoff for pennant.

∞Montreal finished the strike-shortened season with the league's best record.

WORLD SERIES

Year	Winner	Loser	Games	Year	Winner	Loser	Games
1903—Boston A.L.	Pittsburgh N.L.		5-3	1918—Boston A.L.	Chicago N.L.		4-2
1904—No Series				1919—Cincinnati N.L.	Chicago A.L.		5-3
1905—New York N.L.	Philadelphia A.L.		4-1	1920—Cleveland A.L.	Brooklyn N.L.		5-2
1906—Chicago A.L.	Chicago N.L.		4-2	1921—New York N.L.	New York A.L.		5-3
1907—Chicago N.L.	Detroit A.L.		*4-0	1922—New York N.L.	New York A.L.		*4-0
1908—Chicago N.L.	Detroit A.L.		4-1	1923—New York A.L.	New York N.L.		4-2
1909—Pittsburgh N.L.	Detroit A.L.		4-3	1924—Washington A.L.	New York N.L.		4-3
1910—Philadelphia A.L.	Chicago N.L.		4-1	1925—Pittsburgh N.L.	Washington A.L.		4-3
1911—Philadelphia A.L.	New York N.L.		4-2	1926—St. Louis N.L.	New York A.L.		4-3
1912—Boston A.L.	New York N.L.		*4-3	1927—New York A.L.	Pittsburgh, N.L.		4-0
1913—Philadelphia A.L.	New York N.L.		4-1	1928—New York A.L.	St. Louis N.L.		4-0
1914—Boston N.L.	Philadelphia A.L.		4-0	1929—Philadelphia A.L.	Chicago N.L.		4-1
1915—Boston A.L.	Philadelphia N.L.		4-1	1930—Philadelphia A.L.	St. Louis N.L.		4-2
1916—Boston A.L.	Brooklyn N.L.		4-1	1931—St. Louis N.L.	Philadelphia A.L.		4-3
1917—Chicago A.L.	New York N.L.		4-2	1932—New York A.L.	Chicago N.L.		4-0

Year	Winner	Loser	Games	Year	Winner	Loser	Games
1933	New York N.L.	Washington A.L.	4-1	1968	Detroit A.L.	St. Louis N.L.	4-3
1934	St. Louis N.L.	Detroit A.L.	4-3	1969	New York N.L.	Baltimore A.L.	4-1
1935	Detroit A.L.	Chicago N.L.	4-2	1970	Baltimore A.L.	Cincinnati N.L.	4-1
1936	New York A.L.	New York N.L.	4-2	1971	Pittsburgh N.L.	Baltimore A.L.	4-3
1937	New York A.L.	New York N.L.	4-1	1972	Oakland A.L.	Cincinnati N.L.	4-3
1938	New York A.L.	Chicago N.L.	4-0	1973	Oakland A.L.	New York N.L.	4-3
1939	New York A.L.	Cincinnati N.L.	4-0	1974	Oakland A.L.	Los Angeles N.L.	4-1
1940	Cincinnati N.L.	Detroit A.L.	4-3	1975	Cincinnati N.L.	Boston A.L.	4-3
1941	New York A.L.	Brooklyn N.L.	4-1	1976	Cincinnati N.L.	New York A.L.	4-0
1942	St. Louis N.L.	New York A.L.	4-1	1977	New York A.L.	Los Angeles N.L.	4-2
1943	New York A.L.	St. Louis N.L.	4-1	1978	New York A.L.	Los Angeles N.L.	4-2
1944	St. Louis N.L.	St. Louis A.L.	4-2	1979	Pittsburgh N.L.	Baltimore A.L.	4-3
1945	Detroit A.L.	Chicago N.L.	4-3	1980	Philadelphia N.L.	Kansas City A.L.	4-2
1946	St. Louis N.L.	Boston A.L.	4-3	1981	Los Angeles N.L.	New York A.L.	4-2
1947	New York A.L.	Brooklyn, N.L.	4-3	1982	St. Louis N.L.	Milwaukee A.L.	4-3
1948	Cleveland A.L.	Boston N.L.	4-2	1983	Baltimore A.L.	Philadelphia N.L.	4-1
1949	New York A.L.	Brooklyn N.L.	4-1	1984	Detroit A.L.	San Diego N.L.	4-1
1950	New York A.L.	Philadelphia N.L.	4-0	1985	Kansas City A.L.	St. Louis N.L.	4-3
1951	New York A.L.	New York N.L.	4-2	1986	New York N.L.	Boston A.L.	4-3
1952	New York A.L.	Brooklyn N.L.	4-3	1987	Minnesota A.L.	St. Louis N.L.	4-3
1953	New York A.L.	Brooklyn N.L.	4-2	1988	Los Angeles N.L.	Oakland A.L.	4-1
1954	New York N.L.	Cleveland A.L.	4-0	1989	Oakland A.L.	San Francisco N.L.	4-0
1955	Brooklyn N.L.	New York A.L.	4-3	1990	Cincinnati N.L.	Oakland A.L.	4-0
1956	New York A.L.	Brooklyn N.L.	4-3	1991	Minnesota A.L.	Atlanta N.L.	4-3
1957	Milwaukee N.L.	New York A.L.	4-3	1992	Toronto A.L.	Atlanta N.L.	4-2
1958	New York A.L.	Milwaukee N.L.	4-3	1993	Toronto A.L.	Philadelphia N.L.	4-2
1959	Los Angeles N.L.	Chicago A.L.	4-2	1994	No Series		
1960	Pittsburgh N.L.	New York A.L.	4-3	1995	Atlanta N.L.	Cleveland A.L.	4-2
1961	New York A.L.	Cincinnati N.L.	4-1	1996	New York A.L.	Atlanta N.L.	4-2
1962	New York A.L.	San Francisco N.L.	4-3	1997	Florida N.L.	Cleveland A.L.	4-3
1963	Los Angeles N.L.	New York A.L.	4-0	1998	New York A.L.	San Diego N.L.	4-0
1964	St. Louis N.L.	New York A.L.	4-3	1999	New York A.L.	Atlanta N.L.	4-0
1965	Los Angeles N.L.	Minnesota A.L.	4-3	2000	New York A.L.	New York N.L.	4-1
1966	Baltimore A.L.	Los Angeles N.L.	4-0	2001	Arizona N.L.	New York A.L.	4-3
1967	St. Louis N.L.	Boston A.L.	4-3	*Includes tie game.			

DIVISION SERIES

AMERICAN LEAGUE

Year	Winner (Division)	Loser (Division)	Games
1981	New York (East)	Milwaukee (East)	3-2
	Oakland (West)	Kansas City (West)	3-0
1995	Cleveland (Central)	Boston (East)	3-0
	Seattle (West)	New York* (East)	3-2
1996	New York (East)	Texas (West)	3-1
	Baltimore (East)*	Cleveland (Central)	3-1
1997	Baltimore (East)	Seattle (West)	3-1
	Cleveland (Central)	New York (East)*	3-2
1998	New York (East)	Texas (West)	3-0
	Cleveland (Central)	Boston (East)*	3-1
1999	New York (East)	Texas (West)	3-0
	Boston (East)*	Cleveland (Central)	3-2
2000	New York (East)	Oakland (West)	3-2
	Seattle (West)*	Chicago (Central)	3-0
2001	New York (East)	Oakland (West)*	3-2
	Seattle (West)	Cleveland (Central)	3-2

NATIONAL LEAGUE

Year	Winner (Division)	Loser (Division)	Games
1981	Montreal (East)	Philadelphia (East)	3-2
	Los Angeles (West)	Houston (West)	3-2
1995	Atlanta (East)	Colorado* (West)	3-1
	Cincinnati (Central)	Los Angeles (West)	3-0
1996	Atlanta (East)	Los Angeles (West)*	3-0
	St. Louis (Central)	San Diego (West)	3-0
1997	Atlanta (East)	Houston (Central)	3-0
	Florida (East)*	San Francisco (West)	3-0
1998	Atlanta (East)	Chicago (Central)*	3-0
	San Diego (West)	Houston (Central)	3-1
1999	Atlanta (East)	Houston (Central)	3-1
	New York (East)*	Arizona (West)	3-1
2000	St. Louis (Central)	Atlanta (East)	3-0
	New York (East)*	San Francisco (West)	3-1
2001	Arizona (West)	St. Louis (Central)*	3-2
	Atlanta (East)	Houston (Central)	3-0

*Wild-card team.

CHAMPIONSHIP SERIES

AMERICAN LEAGUE

Year	Winner (Division)	Loser (Division)	Games
1969	Baltimore (East)	Minnesota (West)	3-0
1970	Baltimore (East)	Minnesota (West)	3-0
1971	Baltimore (East)	Oakland (West)	3-0
1972	Oakland (West)	Detroit (East)	3-2
1973	Oakland (West)	Baltimore (East)	3-2
1974	Oakland (West)	Baltimore (East)	3-1
1975	Boston (East)	Oakland (West)	3-0
1976	New York (East)	Kansas City (West)	3-2
1977	New York (East)	Kansas City (West)	3-2

Year	Winner (Division)	Loser (Division)	Games
1978	New York (East)	Kansas City (West)	3-1
1979	Baltimore (East)	California (West)	3-1
1980	Kansas City (West)	New York (East)	3-0
1981	New York (East)	Oakland (West)	3-0
1982	Milwaukee (East)	California (West)	3-2
1983	Baltimore (East)	Chicago (West)	3-1
1984	Detroit (East)	Kansas City (West)	3-0
1985	Kansas City (West)	Toronto (East)	4-3
1986	Boston (East)	California (West)	4-3
1987	Minnesota (West)	Detroit (East)	4-1
1988	Oakland (West)	Boston (East)	4-0

Year	Winner (Division)	Loser (Division)	Games
1989—Oakland (West)	Toronto (East)	4-1
1990—Oakland (West)	Boston (East)	4-0
1991—Minnesota (West)	Toronto (East)	4-1
1992—Toronto (East)	Oakland (West)	4-2
1993—Toronto (East)	Chicago (West)	4-2
1994—No series		
1995—Cleveland (Central)	Seattle (West)	4-2
1996—New York (East)	Baltimore (East)*	4-1
1997—Cleveland (Central)	Baltimore (East)	4-2
1998—New York (East)	Cleveland (Central)	4-2
1999—New York (East)	Boston (East)*	4-1
2000—New York (East)	Seattle (West)	4-2
2001—New York (East)	Seattle (West)	4-1

NATIONAL LEAGUE

Year	Winner (Division)	Loser (Division)	Games
1969—New York (East)	Atlanta (West)	3-0
1970—Cincinnati (West)	Pittsburgh (East)	3-0
1971—Pittsburgh (East)	San Francisco (West)	3-1
1972—Cincinnati (West)	Pittsburgh (East)	3-2
1973—New York (East)	Cincinnati (West)	3-2
1974—Los Angeles (West)	Pittsburgh (East)	3-1
1975—Cincinnati (West)	Pittsburgh (East)	3-0
1976—Cincinnati (West)	Philadelphia (East)	3-0
1977—Los Angeles (West)	Philadelphia (East)	3-1

Year	Winner (Division)	Loser (Division)	Games
1978—Los Angeles (West)	Philadelphia (East)	3-1
1979—Pittsburgh (East)	Cincinnati (West)	3-0
1980—Philadelphia (East)	Houston (West)	3-2
1981—Los Angeles (West)	Montreal (East)	3-2
1982—St. Louis (East)	Atlanta (West)	3-0
1983—Philadelphia (East)	Los Angeles (West)	3-1
1984—San Diego (West)	Chicago (East)	3-2
1985—St. Louis (East)	Los Angeles (West)	4-2
1986—New York (East)	Houston (West)	4-2
1987—St. Louis (East)	San Francisco (West)	4-3
1988—Los Angeles (West)	New York (East)	4-3
1989—San Francisco (West)	Chicago (East)	4-1
1990—Cincinnati (West)	Pittsburgh (East)	4-2
1991—Atlanta (West)	Pittsburgh (East)	4-3
1992—Atlanta (West)	Pittsburgh (East)	4-3
1993—Philadelphia (East)	Atlanta (West)	4-2
1994—No series		
1995—Atlanta (East)	Cincinnati (Central)	4-0
1996—Atlanta (East)	St. Louis (Central)	4-3
1997—Florida (East)*	Atlanta (East)	4-2
1998—San Diego (West)	Atlanta (East)	4-2
1999—Atlanta (East)	New York (East)*	4-2
2000—New York (East)*	St. Louis (Central)	4-1
2001—Arizona (West)	Atlanta (East)	4-1

*Wild-card team.

ALL-STAR GAME

Date	Site	Score (Winner)	Winning pitcher (Losing pitcher)	Winning manager (Losing manager)	Att.
7-6-33	Comiskey Park Chicago	4-2 (A.L.)	Lefty Gomez, Yankees (Bill Hallahan, Cardinals)	Connie Mack, Athletics (John McGraw, Giants)	47,595
7-10-34	Polo Grounds New York	9-7 (A.L.)	Mel Harder, Indians (Van Mungo, Dodgers)	Joe Cronin, Senators (Bill Terry, Giants)	48,363
7-8-35	Municipal Stadium Cleveland	4-1 (A.L.)	Lefty Gomez, Yankees (Bill Walker, Cardinals)	Mickey Cochrane, Tigers (Frankie Frisch, Cardinals)	69,831
7-7-36	Braves Field Boston	4-3 (N.L.)	Dizzy Dean, Cardinals (Lefty Grove, Red Sox)	Charlie Grimm, Cubs (Joe McCarthy, Yankees)	25,556
7-7-37	Griffith Stadium Washington	8-3 (A.L.)	Lefty Gomez, Yankees (Dizzy Dean, Cardinals)	Joe McCarthy, Yankees (Bill Terry, Giants)	31,391
7-6-38	Crosley Field Cincinnati	4-1 (N.L.)	Johnny Vander Meer, Reds (Lefty Gomez, Yankees)	Bill Terry, Giants (Joe McCarthy, Yankees)	27,067
7-11-39	Yankee Stadium New York	3-1 (A.L.)	Tommy Bridges, Tigers (Bill Lee, Cubs)	Joe McCarthy, Yankees (Gabby Hartnett, Cubs)	62,892
7-9-40	Sportsman's Park St. Louis	4-0 (N.L.)	Paul Derringer, Reds (Red Ruffing, Yankees)	Bill McKechnie, Reds (Joe Cronin, Red Sox)	32,373
7-8-41	Briggs Stadium Detroit	7-5 (A.L.)	Ed Smith, White Sox (Claude Passeau, Cubs)	Del Baker, Tigers (Bill McKechnie, Reds)	54,674
7-6-42	Polo Grounds New York	3-1 (A.L.)	Spud Chandler, Yankees (Mort Cooper, Cardinals)	Joe McCarthy, Yankees (Leo Durocher, Dodgers)	34,178
7-13-43	Shibe Park Philadelphia	5-3 (A.L.)	Dutch Leonard, Senators (Mort Cooper, Cardinals)	Joe McCarthy, Yankees (Billy Southworth, Cardinals)	31,938
7-11-44	Forbes Field Pittsburgh	7-1 (N.L.)	Ken Raffensberger, Phillies (Tex Hughson, Red Sox)	Billy Southworth, Cardinals (Joe McCarthy, Yankees)	29,589
1945	No game played.				
7-9-46	Fenway Park Boston	12-0 (A.L.)	Bob Feller, Indians (Claude Passeau, Cubs)	Steve O'Neill, Tigers (Charlie Grimm, Cubs)	34,906
7-8-47	Wrigley Field Chicago	2-1 (A.L.)	Frank Shea, Yankees (Johnny Sain, Braves)	Joe Cronin, Red Sox (Eddie Dyer, Cardinals)	41,123
7-13-48	Sportsman's Park St. Louis	5-2 (A.L.)	Vic Raschi, Yankees (Johnny Schmitz, Cubs)	Bucky Harris, Yankees (Leo Durocher, Dodgers)	34,009
7-12-49	Ebbets Field Brooklyn	11-7 (A.L.)	Virgil Trucks, Tigers (Don Newcombe, Dodgers)	Lou Boudreau, Indians (Billy Southworth, Braves)	32,577
7-11-50	Comiskey Park Chicago	4-3* (N.L.)	Ewell Blackwell, Reds (Ted Gray, Tigers)	Burt Shotton, Dodgers (Casey Stengel, Yankees)	46,127
7-10-51	Briggs Stadium Detroit	8-3 (N.L.)	Sal Maglie, Giants (Ed Lopat, Yankees)	Eddie Sawyer, Phillies (Casey Stengel, Yankees)	52,075
7-8-52	Shibe Park Philadelphia	3-2† (N.L.)	Bob Rush, Cubs (Bob Lemon, Indians)	Leo Durocher, Giants (Casey Stengel, Yankees)	32,785
7-14-53	Crosley Field Cincinnati	5-1 (N.L.)	Warren Spahn, Braves (Allie Reynolds, Yankees)	Chuck Dressen, Dodgers (Casey Stengel, Yankees)	30,846
7-13-54	Municipal Stadium Cleveland	11-9 (A.L.)	Dean Stone, Senators (Gene Conley, Braves)	Casey Stengel, Yankees (Walter Alston, Dodgers)	68,751

Date	Site	Score (Winner)	Winning pitcher (Losing pitcher)	Winning manager (Losing manager)	Att.
7-12-55	Milwaukee Co. Stadium Milwaukee	6-5‡ (N.L.)	Gene Conley, Braves (Frank Sullivan, Red Sox)	Leo Durocher, Giants (Al Lopez, Indians)	45,643
7-10-56	Griffith Stadium Washington	7-3 (N.L.)	Bob Friend, Pirates (Billy Pierce, White Sox)	Walter Alston, Dodgers (Casey Stengel, Yankees)	28,843
7-9-57	Busch Stadium St. Louis	6-5 (A.L.)	Jim Bunning, Tigers (Curt Simmons, Phillies)	Casey Stengel, Yankees (Walter Alston, Dodgers)	30,693
7-8-58	Memorial Stadium Baltimore	4-3 (A.L.)	Early Wynn, White Sox (Bob Friend, Pirates)	Casey Stengel, Yankees (Fred Haney, Braves)	48,829
7-7-59	Forbes Field Pittsburgh	5-4 (N.L.)	Johnny Antonelli, Giants (Whitey Ford, Yankees)	Fred Haney, Braves (Casey Stengel, Yankees)	35,277
8-3-59	Memorial Coliseum Los Angeles	5-3 (A.L.)	Jerry Walker, Orioles (Don Drysdale, Dodgers)	Casey Stengel, Yankees (Fred Haney, Braves)	55,105
7-11-60	Municipal Stadium Kansas City	5-3 (N.L.)	Bob Friend, Pirates (Bill Monbouquette, Red Sox)	Walter Alston, Dodgers (Al Lopez, White Sox)	30,619
7-13-60	Yankee Stadium New York	6-0 (N.L.)	Vernon Law, Pirates (Whitey Ford, Yankees)	Walter Alston, Dodgers (Al Lopez, White Sox)	38,362
7-11-61	Candlestick Park San Francisco	5-4§ (N.L.)	Stu Miller, Giants (Hoyt Wilhelm, Orioles)	Danny Murtaugh, Pirates (Paul Richards, Orioles)	44,115
7-31-61	Fenway Park Boston	1-1 (tie)		Paul Richards, Orioles (A.L.) Danny Murtaugh, Pirates (N.L.)	31,851
7-10-62	District of Col. Stad. Washington	3-1 (N.L.)	Juan Marichal, Giants (Camilo Pascual, Twins)	Fred Hutchinson, Reds (Ralph Houk, Yankees)	45,480
7-30-62	Wrigley Field Chicago	9-4 (A.L.)	Ray Herbert, White Sox (Art Mahaffey, Phillies)	Ralph Houk, Yankees (Fred Hutchinson, Reds)	38,359
7-9-63	Municipal Stadium Cleveland	5-3 (N.L.)	Larry Jackson, Cubs (Jim Bunning, Tigers)	Alvin Dark, Giants (Ralph Houk, Yankees)	44,160
7-7-64	Shea Stadium New York	7-4 (N.L.)	Juan Marichal, Giants (Dick Radatz, Red Sox)	Walter Alston, Dodgers (Al Lopez, White Sox)	50,850
7-13-65	Metropolitan Stadium Bloomington, Minn.	6-5 (N.L.)	Sandy Koufax, Dodgers (Sam McDowell, Indians)	Gene Mauch, Phillies (Al Lopez, White Sox)	46,706
7-12-66	Busch Stadium St. Louis	2-1§ (N.L.)	Gaylord Perry, Giants (Pete Richert, Senators)	Walter Alston, Dodgers (Sam Mele, Twins)	49,936
7-11-67	Anaheim Stadium Anaheim, Calif.	2-1∞ (N.L.)	Don Drysdale, Dodgers (Jim Hunter, Athletics)	Walter Alston, Dodgers (Hank Bauer, Orioles)	46,309
7-9-68	Astrodome Houston	1-0 (N.L.)	Don Drysdale, Dodgers (Luis Tiant, Indians)	Red Schoendienst, Cardinals (Dick Williams, Red Sox)	48,321
7-23-69	R.F.K. Stadium Washington	9-3 (N.L.)	Steve Carlton, Cardinals (Mel Stottlemyre, Yankees)	Red Schoendienst, Cardinals (Mayo Smith, Tigers)	45,259
7-14-70	Riverfront Stadium Cincinnati	5-4‡ (N.L.)	Claude Osteen, Dodgers (Clyde Wright, Angels)	Gil Hodges, Mets (Earl Weaver, Orioles)	51,838
7-13-71	Tiger Stadium Detroit	6-4 (A.L.)	Vida Blue, Athletics (Dock Ellis, Pirates)	Earl Weaver, Orioles (Sparky Anderson, Reds)	53,559
7-25-72	Atlanta Stadium Atlanta	4-3§ (N.L.)	Tug McGraw, Mets (Dave McNally, Orioles)	Danny Murtaugh, Pirates (Earl Weaver, Orioles)	53,107
7-24-73	Royals Stadium Kansas City	7-1 (N.L.)	Rick Wise, Cardinals (Bert Blyleven, Twins)	Sparky Anderson, Reds (Dick Williams, Athletics)	40,849
7-23-74	Three Rivers Stadium Pittsburgh	7-2 (N.L.)	Ken Brett, Pirates (Luis Tiant, Red Sox)	Yogi Berra, Mets (Dick Williams, Athletics)	50,706
7-15-75	Milwaukee Co. Stadium Milwaukee	6-3 (N.L.)	Jon Matlack, Mets (Jim Hunter, Yankees)	Walter Alston, Dodgers (Alvin Dark, Athletics)	51,480
7-13-76	Veterans Stadium Philadelphia	7-1 (N.L)	Randy Jones, Padres (Mark Fidrych, Tigers)	Sparky Anderson, Reds (Darrell Johnson, Red Sox)	63,974
7-19-77	Yankee Stadium New York	7-5 (N.L.)	Don Sutton, Dodgers (Jim Palmer, Orioles)	Sparky Anderson, Reds (Billy Martin, Yankees)	56,683
7-11-78	San Diego Stadium San Diego	7-3 (N.L.)	Bruce Sutter, Cubs (Rich Gossage, Yankees)	Tommy Lasorda, Dodgers (Billy Martin, Yankees)	51,549
7-17-79	Kingdome Seattle	7-6 (N.L.)	Bruce Sutter, Cubs (Jim Kern, Rangers)	Tommy Lasorda, Dodgers (Bob Lemon, Yankees)	58,905
7-8-80	Dodger Stadium Los Angeles	4-2 (N.L.)	Jerry Reuss, Dodgers (Tommy John, Yankees)	Chuck Tanner, Pirates (Earl Weaver, Orioles)	56,088
8-9-81	Municipal Stadium Cleveland	5-4 (N.L.)	Vida Blue, Giants (Rollie Fingers, Brewers)	Dallas Green, Phillies (Jim Frey, Royals)	72,086
7-13-82	Olympic Stadium Montreal	4-1 (N.L.)	Steve Rogers, Expos (Dennis Eckersley, Red Sox)	Tommy Lasorda, Dodgers (Billy Martin, Athletics)	59,057
7-6-83	Comiskey Park Chicago	13-3 (A.L.)	Dave Stieb, Blue Jays (Mario Soto, Reds)	Harvey Kuenn, Brewers (Whitey Herzog, Cardinals)	43,801
7-10-84	Candlestick Park San Francisco	3-1 (N.L.)	Charlie Lea, Expos (Dave Stieb, Blue Jays)	Paul Owens, Phillies (Joe Altobelli, Orioles)	57,756
7-16-85	Metrodome Minneapolis	6-1 (N.L.)	LaMarr Hoyt, Padres (Jack Morris, Tigers)	Dick Williams, Padres (Sparky Anderson, Tigers)	54,960
7-15-86	Astrodome Houston	3-2 (A.L.)	Roger Clemens, Red Sox (Dwight Gooden, Mets)	Dick Howser, Royals (Whitey Herzog, Cardinals)	45,774

Date	Site	Score (Winner)	Winning pitcher (Losing pitcher)	Winning manager (Losing manager)	Att.
7-14-87	Oak.-Alameda Co. Col. Oakland	2-0▲ (N.L.)	Lee Smith, Cubs (Jay Howell, Athletics)	Dave Johnson, Mets (John McNamara, Red Sox)	49,671
7-12-88	Riverfront Stadium Cincinnati	2-1 (A.L.)	Frank Viola, Twins (Dwight Gooden, Mets)	Tom Kelly, Twins (Whitey Herzog, Cardinals)	55,837
7-11-89	Anaheim Stadium Anaheim, Calif.	5-3 (A.L.)	Nolan Ryan, Rangers (John Smoltz, Braves)	Tony La Russa, Athletics (Tommy Lasorda, Dodgers)	64,036
7-10-90	Wrigley Field Chicago	2-0 (A.L.)	Bret Saberhagen, Royals (Jeff Brantley, Giants)	Tony La Russa, Athletics (Roger Craig, Giants)	39,071
7-9-91	SkyDome Toronto	4-2 (A.L.)	Jimmy Key, Blue Jays (Dennis Martinez, Expos)	Tony La Russa, Athletics (Lou Piniella, Reds)	52,383
7-14-92	Jack Murphy Stadium San Diego	13-6 (A.L.)	Kevin Brown, Rangers (Tom Glavine, Braves)	Tom Kelly, Twins (Bobby Cox, Braves)	59,372
7-13-93	Oriole Park at Camden Yards, Baltimore	9-3 (A.L.)	Jack McDowell, White Sox (John Burkett, Giants)	Cito Gaston, Blue Jays (Bobby Cox, Braves)	48,147
7-12-94	Three Rivers Stadium Pittsburgh	8-7§ (N.L.)	Doug Jones, Phillies (Jason Bere, White Sox)	Jim Fregosi, Phillies (Cito Gaston, Blue Jays)	59,568
7-11-95	Ballpark in Arlington Arlington, Texas	3-2 (N.L.)	Heathcliff Slocumb, Phillies (Steve Ontiveros, A's)	Felipe Alou, Expos (Buck Showalter, Yankees)	50,920
7-9-96	Veterans Stadium Philadelphia	6-0 (N.L.)	John Smoltz, Braves (Charles Nagy, Indians)	Bobby Cox, Braves (Mike Hargrove, Indians)	62,670
7-8-97	Jacobs Field Cleveland	3-1 (A.L.)	Jose Rosado, Royals (Shawn Estes, Giants)	Joe Torre, Yankees (Bobby Cox, Braves)	44,916
7-7-98	Coors Field Colorado	13-8 (A.L.)	Bartolo Colon, Indians (Ugueth Urbina, Expos)	Mike Hargrove, Indians (Jim Leyland, Marlins)	51,267
7-13-99	Fenway Park Boston	4-1 (A.L.)	Pedro Martinez, Red Sox (Curt Schilling, Phillies)	Joe Torre, Yankees (Bruce Bochy, Padres)	34,187
7-11-00	Turner Field Atlanta	6-3 (A.L.)	James Baldwin, White Sox (Al Leiter, Mets)	Joe Torre, Yankees (Bobby Cox, Braves)	51,323
7-10-01	Safeco Field Seattle	4-1 (A.L.)	Freddy Garcia, Mariners (Chan Ho Park, Dodgers)	Joe Torre, Yankees (Bobby Valentine, Mets)	47,364

*14 innings. †5 innings (rain). ‡12 innings. §10 innings. ∞15 innings. ▲13 innings.

AWARD WINNERS

THE SPORTING NEWS

MOST VALUABLE PLAYER

AMERICAN LEAGUE

Year	Player	Team	Pos.	Points
1929	Al Simmons	Philadelphia	OF	40
1930	Joe Cronin	Washington	SS	52
1931	Lou Gehrig	New York	1B	40
1932	Jimmie Foxx	Philadelphia	1B	46
1933	Jimmie Foxx	Philadelphia	1B	49
1934	Lou Gehrig	New York	1B	51
1935	Hank Greenberg	Detroit	1B	64
1936	Lou Gehrig	New York	1B	55
1937	Charley Gehringer	Detroit	2B	78
1938	Jimmie Foxx	Boston	1B	304
1939	Joe DiMaggio	New York	OF	280
1940	Hank Greenberg	Detroit	OF	292
1941	Joe DiMaggio	New York	OF	291
1942	Joe Gordon	New York	2B	270
1943	Spud Chandler	New York	P	246
1944	Bobby Doerr	Boston	2B	
1945	Eddie Mayo	Detroit	2B	

NATIONAL LEAGUE

Year	Player	Team	Pos.	Points
1929	No selection			
1930	Bill Terry	New York	1B	47
1931	Chuck Klein	Philadelphia	OF	40
1932	Chuck Klein	Philadelphia	OF	46
1933	Carl Hubbell	New York	P	64
1934	Dizzy Dean	St. Louis	P	57
1935	Arky Vaughan	Pittsburgh	SS	42
1936	Carl Hubbell	New York	P	61
1937	Joe Medwick	St. Louis	OF	70
1938	Ernie Lombardi	Cincinnati	C	229
1939	Bucky Walters	Cincinnati	P	303
1940	Frank McCormick	Cincinnati	1B	274
1941	Dolf Camilli	Brooklyn	1B	300
1942	Mort Cooper	St. Louis	P	263
1943	Stan Musial	St. Louis	OF	267
1944	Marty Marion	St. Louis	SS	
1945	Tommy Holmes	Boston	OF	

PLAYER AND PITCHER OF THE YEAR

AMERICAN LEAGUE

Year	Player	Team	Pos.
1944	Bobby Doerr	Boston	2B
	Hal Newhouser	Detroit	P
1945	Eddie Mayo	Detroit	2B
	Hal Newhouser	Detroit	P
1946	No selections		
1947	No selections		
1948	Lou Boudreau	Cleveland	SS
	Bob Lemon	Cleveland	P
1949	Ted Williams	Boston	OF
	Ellis Kinder	Boston	P
1950	Phil Rizzuto	New York	SS
	Bob Lemon	Cleveland	P
1951	Ferris Fain	Philadelphia	1B
	Bob Feller	Cleveland	P
1952	Luke Easter	Cleveland	1B
	Bobby Shantz	Philadelphia	P
1953	Al Rosen	Cleveland	3B
	Bob Porterfield	Washington	P
1954	Bobby Avila	Cleveland	2B
	Bob Lemon	Cleveland	P
1955	Al Kaline	Detroit	OF
	Whitey Ford	New York	P
1956	Mickey Mantle	New York	OF
	Billy Pierce	Chicago	P
1957	Ted Williams	Boston	OF
	Billy Pierce	Chicago	P
1958	Jackie Jensen	Boston	OF
	Bob Turley	New York	P
1959	Nellie Fox	Chicago	2B
	Early Wynn	Chicago	P
1960	Roger Maris	New York	OF
	Chuck Estrada	Baltimore	P
1961	Roger Maris	New York	OF
	Whitey Ford	New York	P
1962	Mickey Mantle	New York	OF
	Dick Donovan	Cleveland	P
1963	Al Kaline	Detroit	OF
	Whitey Ford	New York	P
1964	Brooks Robinson	Baltimore	3B
	Dean Chance	Los Angeles	P
1965	Tony Oliva	Minnesota	OF
	Jim Grant	Minnesota	P
1966	Frank Robinson	Baltimore	OF
	Jim Kaat	Minnesota	P

NATIONAL LEAGUE

Year	Player	Team	Pos.
1944	Marty Marion	St. Louis	SS
	Bill Voiselle	New York	P
1945	Tommy Holmes	Boston	OF
	Hank Borowy	Chicago	P
1946	No selections		
1947	No selections		
1948	Stan Musial	St. Louis	OF-1B
	Johnny Sain	Boston	P
1949	Enos Slaughter	St. Louis	OF
	Howard Pollet	St. Louis	P
1950	Ralph Kiner	Pittsburgh	OF
	Jim Konstanty	Philadelphia	P
1951	Stan Musial	St. Louis	OF
	Preacher Roe	Brooklyn	P
1952	Hank Sauer	Chicago	OF
	Robin Roberts	Philadelphia	P
1953	Roy Campanella	Brooklyn	C
	Warren Spahn	Milwaukee	P
1954	Willie Mays	New York	OF
	Johnny Antonelli	New York	P
1955	Duke Snider	Brooklyn	OF
	Robin Roberts	Philadelphia	P
1956	Hank Aaron	Milwaukee	OF
	Don Newcombe	Brooklyn	P
1957	Stan Musial	St. Louis	1B
	Warren Spahn	Milwaukee	P
1958	Ernie Banks	Chicago	SS
	Warren Spahn	Milwaukee	P
1959	Ernie Banks	Chicago	SS
	Sam Jones	San Francisco	P
1960	Dick Groat	Pittsburgh	SS
	Vern Law	Pittsburgh	P
1961	Frank Robinson	Cincinnati	OF
	Warren Spahn	Milwaukee	P
1962	Maury Wills	Los Angeles	SS
	Don Drysdale	Los Angeles	P
1963	Hank Aaron	Milwaukee	OF
	Sandy Koufax	Los Angeles	P
1964	Ken Boyer	St. Louis	3B
	Sandy Koufax	Los Angeles	P
1965	Willie Mays	San Francisco	OF
	Sandy Koufax	Los Angeles	P
1966	Roberto Clemente	Pittsburgh	OF
	Sandy Koufax	Los Angeles	P

HISTORY *Award winners*

Year	Player	Team	Pos.		Year	Player	Team	Pos.
1967—	Carl Yastrzemski	Boston	OF		1967—	Orlando Cepeda	St. Louis	1B
	Jim Lonborg	Boston	P			Mike McCormick	San Francisco	P
1968—	Ken Harrelson	Boston	OF		1968—	Pete Rose	Cincinnati	OF
	Denny McLain	Detroit	P			Bob Gibson	St. Louis	P
1969—	Harmon Killebrew	Minnesota	1B-3B		1969—	Willie McCovey	San Francisco	1B
	Denny McLain	Detroit	P			Tom Seaver	New York	P
1970—	Harmon Killebrew	Minnesota	3B		1970—	Johnny Bench	Cincinnati	C
	Sam McDowell	Cleveland	P			Bob Gibson	St. Louis	P
1971—	Tony Oliva	Minnesota	OF		1971—	Joe Torre	St. Louis	3B
	Vida Blue	Oakland	P			Ferguson Jenkins	Chicago	P
1972—	Dick Allen	Chicago	1B		1972—	Billy Williams	Chicago	OF
	Wilbur Wood	Chicago	P			Steve Carlton	Philadelphia	P
1973—	Reggie Jackson	Oakland	OF		1973—	Bobby Bonds	San Francisco	OF
	Jim Palmer	Baltimore	P			Ron Bryant	San Francisco	P
1974—	Jeff Burroughs	Texas	OF		1974—	Lou Brock	St. Louis	OF
	Jim Hunter	Oakland	P			Mike Marshall	Los Angeles	P
1975—	Fred Lynn	Boston	OF		1975—	Joe Morgan	Cincinnati	2B
	Jim Palmer	Baltimore	P			Tom Seaver	New York	P
1976—	Thurman Munson	New York	C		1976—	George Foster	Cincinnati	OF
	Jim Palmer	Baltimore	P			Randy Jones	San Diego	P
1977—	Rod Carew	Minnesota	1B		1977—	George Foster	Cincinnati	OF
	Nolan Ryan	California	P			Steve Carlton	Philadelphia	P
1978—	Jim Rice	Boston	OF		1978—	Dave Parker	Pittsburgh	OF
	Ron Guidry	New York	P			Vida Blue	San Francisco	P
1979—	Don Baylor	California	OF		1979—	Keith Hernandez	St. Louis	1B
	Mike Flanagan	Baltimore	P			Joe Niekro	Houston	P
1980—	George Brett	Kansas City	3B		1980—	Mike Schmidt	Philadelphia	3B
	Steve Stone	Baltimore	P			Steve Carlton	Philadelphia	P
1981—	Tony Armas	Oakland	OF		1981—	Andre Dawson	Montreal	OF
	Jack Morris	Detroit	P			Fernando Valenzuela	Los Angeles	P
1982—	Robin Yount	Milwaukee	SS		1982—	Dale Murphy	Atlanta	OF
	Dave Stieb	Toronto	P			Steve Carlton	Philadelphia	P
1983—	Cal Ripken Jr.	Baltimore	SS		1983—	Dale Murphy	Atlanta	OF
	LaMarr Hoyt	Chicago	P			John Denny	Philadelphia	P
1984—	Don Mattingly	New York	1B		1984—	Ryne Sandberg	Chicago	2B
	Willie Hernandez	Detroit	P			Rick Sutcliffe	Chicago	P
1985—	Don Mattingly	New York	1B		1985—	Willie McGee	St. Louis	OF
	Bret Saberhagen	Kansas City	P			Dwight Gooden	New York	P
1986—	Don Mattingly	New York	1B		1986—	Mike Schmidt	Philadelphia	3B
	Roger Clemens	Boston	P			Mike Scott	Houston	P
1987—	George Bell	Toronto	OF		1987—	Andre Dawson	Chicago	OF
	Jimmy Key	Toronto	P			Rick Sutcliffe	Chicago	P
1988—	Jose Canseco	Oakland	OF		1988—	Andy Van Slyke	Pittsburgh	OF
	Frank Viola	Minnesota	P			Orel Hershiser	Los Angeles	P
1989—	Ruben Sierra	Texas	OF		1989—	Kevin Mitchell	San Francisco	OF
	Bret Saberhagen	Kansas City	P			Mark Davis	San Diego	P
1990—	Cecil Fielder	Detroit	1B		1990—	Barry Bonds	Pittsburgh	OF
	Bob Welch	Oakland	P			Doug Drabek	Pittsburgh	P
1991—	Cal Ripken Jr.	Baltimore	SS		1991—	Barry Bonds	Pittsburgh	OF
	Roger Clemens	Boston	P			Tom Glavine	Atlanta	P

HISTORY Award winners

PITCHER OF THE YEAR

AMERICAN LEAGUE

Year	Pitcher	Team
1992—	Dennis Eckersley	Oakland
1993—	Jack McDowell	Chicago
1994—	Jimmy Key	New York
1995—	Randy Johnson	Seattle
1996—	Pat Hentgen	Toronto
1997—	Roger Clemens	Toronto
1998—	Roger Clemens	Toronto
1999—	Pedro Martinez	Boston
2000—	Pedro Martinez	Boston
2001—	Roger Clemens	New York

NATIONAL LEAGUE

Year	Pitcher	Team
1992—	Greg Maddux	Chicago
1993—	Greg Maddux	Atlanta
1994—	Greg Maddux	Atlanta
1995—	Greg Maddux	Atlanta
1996	John Smoltz	Atlanta
1997—	Pedro Martinez	Montreal
1998—	Kevin Brown	San Diego
1999—	Mike Hampton	Houston
2000—	Tom Glavine	Atlanta
2001—	Curt Schilling	Arizona

1946—Combined selection—Del Ennis, Philadelphia N.L., OF
1947—Combined selection—Jackie Robinson, Brooklyn N.L., 1B
1948—Combined selection—Richie Ashburn, Philadelphia N.L., OF

AMERICAN LEAGUE

Year	Player	Team	Pos.
1949—Roy Sievers	St. Louis	OF
1950—Whitey Ford	New York	P
1951—Minnie Minoso	Chicago	OF
1952—Clint Courtney	St. Louis	C
1953—Harvey Kuenn	Detroit	SS
1954—Bob Grim	New York	P
1955—Herb Score	Cleveland	P
1956—Luis Aparicio	Chicago	SS
1957—Tony Kubek	New York	IF-OF
(No pitcher named)		
1958—Albie Pearson	Washington	OF
Ryne Duren	New York	P
1959—Bob Allison	Washington	OF
1960—Ron Hansen	Baltimore	SS
1961—Dick Howser	Kansas City	SS
Don Schwall	Boston	P
1962—Tom Tresh	New York	OF-SS
1963—Pete Ward	Chicago	3B
Gary Peters	Chicago	P
1964—Tony Oliva	Minnesota	OF
Wally Bunker	Baltimore	P
1965—Curt Blefary	Baltimore	OF
Marcelino Lopez	California	P
1966—Tommie Agee	Chicago	OF
Jim Nash	Kansas City	P
1967—Rod Carew	Minnesota	2B
Tom Phoebus	Baltimore	P
1968—Del Unser	Washington	OF
Stan Bahnsen	New York	P
1969—Carlos May	Chicago	OF
Mike Nagy	Boston	P
1970—Roy Foster	Cleveland	OF
Bert Blyleven	Minnesota	P
1971—Chris Chambliss	Cleveland	1B
Bill Parsons	Milwaukee	P
1972—Carlton Fisk	Boston	C
Dick Tidrow	Cleveland	P
1973—Al Bumbry	Baltimore	OF
Steve Busby	Kansas City	P
1974—Mike Hargrove	Texas	1B
Frank Tanana	California	P
1975—Fred Lynn	Boston	OF
Dennis Eckersley	Cleveland	P
1976—Butch Wynegar	Minnesota	C
Mark Fidrych	Detroit	P
1977—Mitchell Page	Oakland	OF
Dave Rozema	Detroit	P
1978—Paul Molitor	Milwaukee	2B
Rich Gale	Kansas City	P
1979—Pat Putnam	Texas	1B
Mark Clear	California	P
1980—Joe Charboneau	Cleveland	OF
Britt Burns	Chicago	P
1981—Rich Gedman	Boston	C
Dave Righetti	New York	P
1982—Cal Ripken Jr.	Baltimore	SS-3B
Ed Vande Berg	Seattle	P
1983—Ron Kittle	Chicago	OF
Mike Boddicker	Baltimore	P
1984—Alvin Davis	Seattle	1B
Mark Langston	Seattle	P
1985 Ozzie Guillen	Chicago	SS
Teddy Higuera	Milwaukee	P
1986—Jose Canseco	Oakland	OF
Mark Eichhorn	Toronto	P
1987—Mark McGwire	Oakland	1B
Mike Henneman	Detroit	P
1988—Walt Weiss	Oakland	SS
Bryan Harvey	California	P

NATIONAL LEAGUE

Year	Player	Team	Pos.
1949—Don Newcombe	Brooklyn	P
1950—Combined A.L.-N.L. selection		
1951—Willie Mays	New York	OF
1952—Joe Black	Brooklyn	P
1953—Jim Gilliam	Brooklyn	2B
1954—Wally Moon	St. Louis	OF
1955—Bill Virdon	St. Louis	OF
1956—Frank Robinson	Cincinnati	OF
1957—Ed Bouchee	Philadelphia	1B
Jack Sanford	Philadelphia	P
1958—Orlando Cepeda	San Francisco	1B
Carlton Willey	Milwaukee	P
1959—Willie McCovey	San Francisco	1B
1960—Frank Howard	Los Angeles	OF
1961—Billy Williams	Chicago	OF
Ken Hunt	Cincinnati	P
1962—Ken Hubbs	Chicago	2B
1963—Pete Rose	Cincinnati	2B
Ray Culp	Philadelphia	P
1964—Dick Allen	Philadelphia	3B
Billy McCool	Cincinnati	P
1965—Joe Morgan	Houston	2B
Frank Linzy	San Francisco	P
1966—Tommy Helms	Cincinnati	3B
Don Sutton	Los Angeles	P
1967—Lee May	Cincinnati	1B
Dick Hughes	St. Louis	P
1968—Johnny Bench	Cincinnati	C
Jerry Koosman	New York	P
1969—Coco Laboy	Montreal	3B
Tom Griffin	Houston	P
1970—Bernie Carbo	Cincinnati	OF
Carl Morton	Montreal	P
1971—Earl Williams	Atlanta	C
Reggie Cleveland	St. Louis	P
1972—Dave Rader	San Francisco	C
Jon Matlack	New York	P
1973—Gary Matthews	San Francisco	OF
Steve Rogers	Montreal	P
1974—Greg Gross	Houston	OF
John D'Acquisto	San Francisco	P
1975—Gary Carter	Montreal	OF-C
John Montefusco	San Francisco	P
1976—Larry Herndon	San Francisco	OF
Butch Metzger	San Diego	P
1977—Andre Dawson	Montreal	OF
Bob Owchinko	San Diego	P
1978—Bob Horner	Atlanta	3B
Don Robinson	Pittsburgh	P
1979—Jeff Leonard	Houston	OF
Rick Sutcliffe	Los Angeles	P
1980—Lonnie Smith	Philadelphia	OF
Bill Gullickson	Montreal	P
1981—Tim Raines	Montreal	OF
Fernando Valenzuela	Los Angeles	P
1982—Johnny Ray	Pittsburgh	2B
Steve Bedrosian	Atlanta	P
1983—Darryl Strawberry	New York	OF
Craig McMurtry	Atlanta	P
1984—Juan Samuel	Philadelphia	2B
Dwight Gooden	New York	P
1985—Vince Coleman	St. Louis	OF
Tom Browning	Cincinnati	P
1986—Robby Thompson	San Francisco	2B
Todd Worrell	St. Louis	P
1987—Benito Santiago	San Diego	C
Mike Dunne	Pittsburgh	P
1988—Mark Grace	Chicago	1B
Tim Belcher	Los Angeles	P

Year	Player	Team	Pos.
1989	Craig Worthington	Baltimore	3B
	Tom Gordon	Kansas City	P
1990	Sandy Alomar Jr.	Cleveland	C
	Kevin Appier	Kansas City	P
1991	Chuck Knoblauch	Minnesota	2B
	Juan Guzman	Toronto	P
1992	Pat Listach	Milwaukee	SS
	Cal Eldred	Milwaukee	P
1993	Tim Salmon	California	OF
	Aaron Sele	Boston	P
1994	Bob Hamelin	Kansas City	DH
	Brian Anderson	California	P
1995	Garret Anderson	California	OF
	Julian Tavarez	Cleveland	P
1996	Derek Jeter	New York	SS
	James Baldwin	Chicago	P
1997	Nomar Garciaparra	Boston	SS
	Jason Dickson	Anaheim	P
1998	Ben Grieve	Oakland	OF
	Rolando Arrojo	Tampa Bay	P
1999	Carlos Beltran	Kansas City	OF
	Tim Hudson	Oakland	P
2000	Mark Quinn	Kansas City	OF-DH
	Kazuhiro Sasaki	Seattle	P
2001	Ichiro Suzuki	Seattle	OF
	C.C. Sabathia	Cleveland	P

Year	Player	Team	Pos.
1989	Jerome Walton	Chicago	OF
	Andy Benes	San Diego	P
1990	David Justice	Atlanta	OF
	Mike Harkey	Chicago	P
1991	Jeff Bagwell	Houston	1B
	Al Osuna	Houston	P
1992	Eric Karros	Los Angeles	1B
	Tim Wakefield	Pittsburgh	P
1993	Mike Piazza	Los Angeles	C
	Kirk Rueter	Montreal	P
1994	Raul Mondesi	Los Angeles	OF
	Steve Trachsel	Chicago	P
1995	Chipper Jones	Atlanta	3B
	Hideo Nomo	Los Angeles	P
1996	Jason Kendall	Pittsburgh	C
	Alan Benes	St. Louis	P
1997	Scott Rolen	Philadelphia	3B
	Matt Morris	St. Louis	P
1998	Todd Helton	Colorado	1B
	Kerry Wood	Chicago	P
1999	Preston Wilson	Florida	OF
	Scott Williamson	Cincinnati	P
2000	Rafael Furcal	Atlanta	2B-SS
	Rick Ankiel	St. Louis	P
2001	Albert Pujols	St. Louis	O-3-1B
	Roy Oswalt	Houston	P

FIREMAN OF THE YEAR

AMERICAN LEAGUE

Year	Pitcher	Team
1960	Mike Fornieles	Boston
1961	Luis Arroyo	New York
1962	Dick Radatz	Boston
1963	Stu Miller	Baltimore
1964	Dick Radatz	Boston
1965	Eddie Fisher	Chicago
1966	Jack Aker	Kansas City
1967	Minnie Rojas	California
1968	Wilbur Wood	Chicago
1969	Ron Perranoski	Minnesota
1970	Ron Perranoski	Minnesota
1971	Ken Sanders	Milwaukee
1972	Sparky Lyle	New York
1973	John Hiller	Detroit
1974	Terry Forster	Chicago
1975	Rich Gossage	Chicago
1976	Bill Campbell	Minnesota
1977	Bill Campbell	Boston
1978	Rich Gossage	New York
1979	Mike Marshall	Minnesota
	Jim Kern	Texas
1980	Dan Quisenberry	Kansas City
1981	Rollie Fingers	Milwaukee
1982	Dan Quisenberry	Kansas City
1983	Dan Quisenberry	Kansas City
1984	Dan Quisenberry	Kansas City
1985	Dan Quisenberry	Kansas City
1986	Dave Righetti	New York
1987	Dave Righetti	New York
	Jeff Reardon	Minnesota
1988	Dennis Eckersley	Oakland
1989	Jeff Russell	Texas
1990	Bobby Thigpen	Chicago
1991	Dennis Eckersley	Oakland
	Bryan Harvey	California
1992	Dennis Eckersley	Oakland
1993	Jeff Montgomery	Kansas City
1994	Lee Smith	Baltimore
1995	Jose Mesa	Cleveland
1996	John Wetteland	New York
1997	Mariano Rivera	New York
1998	Tom Gordon	Boston

NATIONAL LEAGUE

Year	Pitcher	Team
1960	Lindy McDaniel	St. Louis
1961	Stu Miller	San Francisco
1962	Roy Face	Pittsburgh
1963	Lindy McDaniel	Chicago
1964	Al McBean	Pittsburgh
1965	Ted Abernathy	Chicago
1966	Phil Regan	Los Angeles
1967	Ted Abernathy	Cincinnati
1968	Phil Regan	L.A.-Chicago
1969	Wayne Granger	Cincinnati
1970	Wayne Granger	Cincinnati
1971	Dave Giusti	Pittsburgh
1972	Clay Carroll	Cincinnati
1973	Mike Marshall	Montreal
1974	Mike Marshall	Los Angeles
1975	Al Hrabosky	St. Louis
1976	Rawly Eastwick	Cincinnati
1977	Rollie Fingers	San Diego
1978	Rollie Fingers	San Diego
1979	Bruce Sutter	Chicago
1980	Rollie Fingers	San Diego
	Tom Hume	Cincinnati
1981	Bruce Sutter	St. Louis
1982	Bruce Sutter	St. Louis
1983	Al Holland	Philadelphia
	Lee Smith	Chicago
1984	Bruce Sutter	St. Louis
1985	Jeff Reardon	Montreal
1986	Todd Worrell	St. Louis
1987	Steve Bedrosian	Philadelphia
1988	John Franco	Cincinnati
1989	Mark Davis	San Diego
1990	John Franco	New York
1991	Lee Smith	St. Louis
1992	Doug Jones	Houston
	Lee Smith	St. Louis
1993	Randy Myers	Chicago
1994	John Franco	New York
1995	Randy Myers	Chicago
1996	Trevor Hoffman	San Diego
1997	Jeff Shaw	Cincinnati
1998	Trevor Hoffman	San Diego

AMERICAN LEAGUE

Year	Pitcher	Team
1999—Mariano Rivera	New York
2000—Todd Jones	Detroit
2001—Mariano Rivera	New York

NATIONAL LEAGUE

Year	Pitcher	Team
1999— Ugueth Urbina	Montreal
2000— Antonio Alfonseca	Florida
2001— Armando Benitez	New York
Robb Nen	San Francisco

COMEBACK PLAYER OF THE YEAR

AMERICAN LEAGUE

Year	Pitcher	Team
1965—Norm Cash	Detroit
1966—Boog Powell	Baltimore
1967—Dean Chance	Minnesota
1968—Ken Harrelson	Boston
1969—Tony Conigliaro	Boston
1970—Clyde Wright	California
1971—Norm Cash	Detroit
1972—Luis Tiant	Boston
1973—John Hiller	Detroit
1974—Ferguson Jenkins	Texas
1975—Boog Powell	Cleveland
1976—Dock Ellis	New York
1977—Eric Soderholm	Chicago
1978—Mike Caldwell	Milwaukee
1979—Willie Horton	Seattle
1980—Matt Keough	Oakland
1981—Richie Zisk	Seattle
1982—Andre Thornton	Cleveland
1983—Alan Trammell	Detroit
1984—Dave Kingman	Oakland
1985—Gorman Thomas	Seattle
1986—John Candelaria	California
1987—Bret Saberhagen	Kansas City
1988—Storm Davis	Oakland
1989—Bert Blyleven	California
1990—Dave Winfield	California
1991—Jose Guzman	Texas
1992—Rick Sutcliffe	Baltimore
1993—Bo Jackson	Chicago
1994—Jose Canseco	Texas
1995—Tim Wakefield	Boston
1996—Kevin Elster	Texas
1997—David Justice	Cleveland
1998—Bret Saberhagen	Boston
1999—John Jaha	Oakland
2000—Frank Thomas	Chicago
2001—Ruben Sierra	Texas

NATIONAL LEAGUE

Year	Pitcher	Team
1965— Vernon Law	Pittsburgh
1966— Phil Regan	Los Angeles
1967— Mike McCormick	San Francisco
1968— Alex Johnson	Cincinnati
1969— Tommie Agee	New York
1970— Jim Hickman	Chicago
1971— Al Downing	Los Angeles
1972— Bobby Tolan	Cincinnati
1973— Dave Johnson	Atlanta
1974— Jim Wynn	Los Angeles
1975— Randy Jones	San Diego
1976— Tommy John	Los Angeles
1977— Willie McCovey	San Francisco
1978— Willie Stargell	Pittsburgh
1979— Lou Brock	St. Louis
1980— Jerry Reuss	Los Angeles
1981— Bob Knepper	Houston
1982— Joe Morgan	San Francisco
1983— John Denny	Philadelphia
1984— Joaquin Andujar	St. Louis
1985— Rick Reuschel	Pittsburgh
1986— Ray Knight	New York
1987— Rick Sutcliffe	Chicago
1988— Tim Leary	Los Angeles
1989— Lonnie Smith	Atlanta
1990— John Tudor	St. Louis
1991— Terry Pendleton	Atlanta
1992— Gary Sheffield	San Diego
1993— Andres Galarraga	Colorado
1994— Tim Wallach	Los Angeles
1995— Ron Gant	Cincinnati
1996— Eric Davis	Cincinnati
1997— Darren Daulton	Phi.-Fla.
1998— Greg Vaughn	San Diego
1999— Rickey Henderson	New York
2000— Andres Galarraga	Atlanta
2001— Matt Morris	St. Louis

MAJOR LEAGUE PLAYER OF THE YEAR

Year	Player	Team	Year	Player	Team	Year	Player	Team
1936—Carl Hubbell	New York N.L.	1959—Early Wynn	Chicago A.L.	1981—Fernando Valenzuela	Los Angeles N.L.
1937—Johnny Allen	Cleveland A.L.	1960—Bill Mazeroski	Pittsburgh N.L.	1982—Robin Yount	Milwaukee A.L.
1938—Johnny Vander Meer	Cincinnati N.L.	1961—Roger Maris	New York A.L.	1983—Cal Ripken Jr.	Baltimore A.L.
1939—Joe DiMaggio	New York A.L.	1962—Maury Wills	Los Angeles N.L.	1984—Ryne Sandberg	Chicago A.L.
1940—Bob Feller	Cleveland A.L.	Don Drysdale	Los Angeles N.L.	1985—Don Mattingly	New York A.L.
1941—Ted Williams	Boston A.L.	1963—Sandy Koufax	Los Angeles N.L.	1986—Roger Clemens	Boston A.L.
1942—Ted Williams	Boston A.L.	1964—Ken Boyer	St. Louis N.L.	1987—George Bell	Toronto A.L.
1943—Spud Chandler	New York A.L.	1965—Sandy Koufax	Los Angeles N.L.	1988—Orel Hershiser	Los Angeles N.L.
1944—Marty Marion	St. Louis N.L.	1966—Frank Robinson	Baltimore A.L.	1989—Kevin Mitchell	San Francisco N.L.
1945—Hal Newhouser	Detroit A.L.	1967—Carl Yastrzemski	Boston A.L.	1990—Barry Bonds	Pittsburgh N.L.
1946—Stan Musial	St. Louis N.L.	1968—Denny McLain	Detroit A.L.	1991—Cal Ripken Jr.	Baltimore A.L.
1947—Ted Williams	Boston A.L.	1969—Willie McCovey	San Francisco N.L.	1992—Gary Sheffield	San Diego N.L.
1948—Lou Boudreau	Cleveland A.L.	1970—Johnny Bench	Cincinnati N.L.	1993—Frank Thomas	Chicago A.L.
1949—Ted Williams	Boston A.L.	1971—Joe Torre	St. Louis N.L.	1994—Jeff Bagwell	Houston N.L.
1950—Phil Rizzuto	New York A.L.	1972—Billy Williams	Chicago N.L.	1995—Albert Belle	Cleveland A.L.
1951—Stan Musial	St. Louis N.L.	1973—Reggie Jackson	Oakland A.L.	1996—Alex Rodriguez	Seattle A.L.
1952—Robin Roberts	Philadelphia N.L.	1974—Lou Brock	St. Louis N.L.	1997—Ken Griffey Jr.	Seattle A.L.
1953—Al Rosen	Cleveland A.L.	1975—Joe Morgan	Cincinnati N.L.	1998—Sammy Sosa	Chicago N.L.
1954—Willie Mays	New York N.L.	1976—Joe Morgan	Cincinnati N.L.	1999—Rafael Palmeiro	Texas A.L.
1955—Duke Snider	Brooklyn N.L.	1977—Rod Carew	Minnesota A.L.	2000—Carlos Delgado	Toronto A.L.
1956—Mickey Mantle	New York A.L.	1978—Ron Guidry	New York A.L.	2001—Barry Bonds	San Francisco N.L.
1957—Ted Williams	Boston A.L.	1979—Willie Stargell	Pittsburgh N.L.		
1958—Bob Turley	New York A.L.	1980—George Brett	Kansas City A.L.		

MAJOR LEAGUE MANAGER OF THE YEAR

Year	Manager	Team	Year	Manager	Team	Year	Manager	Team
1936	Joe McCarthy	New York A.L.	1965	Sam Mele	Minnesota A.L.		Don Zimmer	Chicago N.L.
1937	Bill McKechnie	Boston N.L.	1966	Hank Bauer	Baltimore A.L.	1990	Jeff Torborg	Chicago A.L.
1938	Joe McCarthy	New York A.L.	1967	Dick Williams	Boston A.L.		Jim Leyland	Pittsburgh N.L.
1939	Leo Durocher	Brooklyn N.L.	1968	Mayo Smith	Detroit A.L.	1991	Tom Kelly	Minnesota A.L.
1940	Bill McKechnie	Cincinnati N.L.	1969	Gil Hodges	New York N.L.		Bobby Cox	Atlanta N.L.
1941	Billy Southworth	St. Louis N.L.	1970	Danny Murtaugh	Pittsburgh N.L.	1992	Tony La Russa	Oakland A.L.
1942	Billy Southworth	St. Louis N.L.	1971	Charlie Fox	San Francisco N.L.		Jim Leyland	Pittsburgh N.L.
1943	Joe McCarthy	New York A.L.	1972	Chuck Tanner	Chicago A.L.	1993	Johnny Oates	Baltimore A.L.
1944	Luke Sewell	St. Louis A.L.	1973	Gene Mauch	Montreal N.L.		Bobby Cox	Atlanta N.L.
1945	Ossie Bluege	Washington A.L.	1974	Bill Virdon	New York A.L.	1994	Buck Showalter	New York A.L.
1946	Eddie Dyer	St. Louis N.L.	1975	Darrell Johnson	Boston A.L.		Felipe Alou	Montreal N.L.
1947	Bucky Harris	New York A.L.	1976	Danny Ozark	Philadelphia N.L.	1995	Mike Hargrove	Cleveland A.L.
1948	Bill Meyer	Pittsburgh N.L.	1977	Earl Weaver	Baltimore A.L.		Don Baylor	Colorado N.L.
1949	Casey Stengel	New York A.L.	1978	George Bamberger	Milwaukee A.L.	1996	Johnny Oates	Texas A.L.
1950	Red Rolfe	Detroit A.L.	1979	Earl Weaver	Baltimore A.L.		Bruce Bochy	San Diego N.L.
1951	Leo Durocher	New York N.L.	1980	Bill Virdon	Houston N.L.	1997	Dave Johnson	Baltimore A.L.
1952	Eddie Stanky	St. Louis N.L.	1981	Billy Martin	Oakland A.L.		Dusty Baker	San Fran. N.L.
1953	Casey Stengel	New York A.L.	1982	Whitey Herzog	St. Louis N.L.	1998	Joe Torre	New York A.L.
1954	Leo Durocher	New York N.L.	1983	Tony La Russa	Chicago A.L.		Bruce Bochy	San Diego N.L.
1955	Walter Alston	Brooklyn N.L.	1984	Jim Frey	Chicago N.L.	1999	Jimy Williams	Boston A.L.
1956	Birdie Tebbetts	Cincinnati N.L.	1985	Bobby Cox	Toronto A.L.		Bobby Cox	Atlanta N.L.
1957	Fred Hutchinson	St. Louis N.L.	1986	John McNamara	Boston A.L.	2000	Jerry Manuel	Chicago A.L.
1958	Casey Stengel	New York A.L.		Hal Lanier	Houston N.L.		Dusty Baker	San Fran. N.L.
1959	Walter A.L.ston	Los Angeles N.L.	1987	Sparky Anderson	Detroit A.L.	2001	Lou Piniella	Seattle A.L.
1960	Danny Murtaugh	Pittsburgh N.L		Buck Rodgers	Montreal N.L.		Larry Bowa	Philadelphia N.L.
1961	Ralph Houk	New York A.L.	1988	Tony La Russa	Oakland A.L.			
1962	Bill Rigney	Los Angeles A.L.		Tom Lasorda	L.A. N.L. (tie)			
1963	Walter Alston	Los Angeles N.L.		Jim Leyland	Pit. N.L. (tie)			
1964	Johnny Keane	St. Louis N.L.	1989	Frank Robinson	Baltimore A.L.			

MAJOR LEAGUE EXECUTIVE OF THE YEAR

Year	Executive	Team	Year	Executive	Team	Year	Executive	Team
1936	Branch Rickey	St. Louis N.L.	1958	Joe Brown	Pittsburgh N.L.	1980	Tal Smith	Houston N.L.
1937	Ed Barrow	New York A.L.	1959	Buzzie Bavasi	L.A. N.L.	1981	John McHale	Montreal N.L.
1938	Warren Giles	Cincinnati N.L.	1960	George Weiss	New York A.L.	1982	Harry Dalton	Milwaukee A.L.
1939	Larry MacPhail	Brooklyn N.L.	1961	Dan Topping	New York A.L.	1983	Hank Peters	Baltimore A.L.
1940	Walter Briggs Sr.	Detroit A.L.	1962	Fred Haney	Los Angeles A.L.	1984	Dallas Green	Chicago N.L.
1941	Ed Barrow	New York A.L.	1963	Bing Devine	St. Louis N.L.	1985	John Schuerholz	Kansas City A.L.
1942	Branch Rickey	St. Louis N.L.	1964	Bing Devine	St. Louis N.L.	1986	Frank Cashen	New York N.L.
1943	Clark Griffith	Washington A.L.	1965	Cal Griffith	Minnesota A.L.	1987	Al Rosen	San Francisco N.L.
1944	Billy DeWitt	St. Louis A.L.	1966	Lee MacPhail	Commissioner's Office	1988	Fred Claire	Los Angeles N.L.
1945	Phil Wrigley	Chicago N.L.	1967	Dick O'Connell	Boston A.L.	1989	Roland Hemond	Baltimore A.L.
1946	Tom Yawkey	Boston A.L.	1968	Jim Campbell	Detroit A.L.	1990	Bob Quinn	Cincinnati N.L.
1947	Branch Rickey	Brooklyn N.L.	1969	John Murphy	New York N.L.	1991	Andy MacPhail	Minnesota A.L.
1948	Bill Veeck	Cleveland A.L.	1970	Harry Dalton	Baltimore A.L.	1992	Dan Duquette	Montreal N.L.
1949	Bob Carpenter	Philadelphia N.L.	1971	Cedric Tallis	Kansas City A.L.	1993	Lee Thomas	Philadelphia N.L.
1950	George Weiss	New York A.L.	1972	Roland Hemond	Chicago A.L.	1994	John Hart	Cleveland A.L.
1951	George Weiss	New York A.L.	1973	Bob Howsam	Cincinnati N.L.	1995	John Hart	Cleveland A.L.
1952	George Weiss	New York A.L.	1974	Gabe Paul	New York A.L.	1996	Doug Melvin	Texas A.L.
1953	Lou Perini	Milwaukee N.L.	1975	Dick O'Connell	Boston A.L.	1997	Cam Bonifay	Pittsburgh N.L.
1954	Horace Stoneham	New York N.L.	1976	Joe Burke	Kansas City A.L.	1998	Gerry Hunsicker	Houston N.L.
1955	Walter O'Malley	Brooklyn N.L.	1977	Bill Veeck	Chicago A.L.	1999	Billy Beane	Oakland A.L.
1956	Gabe Paul	Cincinnati N.L.	1978	Spec Richardson	San Francisco N.L.	2000	Walt Jocketty	St. Louis N.L.
1957	Frank Lane	St. Louis N.L.	1979	Hank Peters	Baltimore A.L.	2001	Pat Gillick	Seattle A.L.

MAJOR LEAGUE ALL-STAR TEAMS

1925
- 1B — Jim Bottomley, St. Louis N.L.
- 2B — Rogers Hornsby, St. Louis N.L.
- SS — Glenn Wright, Pittsburgh N.L.
- 3B — Pie Traynor, Pittsburgh N.L.
- OF — Kiki Cuyler, Pittsburgh N.L.
- OF — Max Carey, Pittsburgh N.L.
- OF — Goose Goslin, Washington A.L.
- C — Mickey Cochrane, Phil. A.L.
- P — Walter Johnson, Washington A.L.
- P — Ed Rommel, Philadelphia A.L.
- P — Dazzy Vance, Brooklyn N.L.

1926
- 1B — George Burns, Cleveland A.L.
- 2B — Rogers Hornsby, St. Louis N.L.
- SS — Joe Sewell, Cleveland A.L.
- 3B — Pie Traynor, Pittsburgh N.L.
- OF — Goose Goslin, Washington A.L.
- OF — John Mostil, Chicago A.L.
- OF — Babe Ruth, New York A.L.
- C — Bob O'Farrell, St. Louis N.L.
- P — Herb Pennock, New York A.L.
- P — George Uhle, Cleveland A.L.
- P — Grover Alexander, St. Louis N.L.

1927
- 1B — Lou Gehrig, New York A.L.
- 2B — Rogers Hornsby, New York N.L.
- SS — Travis Jackson, New York N.L.
- 3B — Pie Traynor, Pittsburgh N.L.
- OF — Babe Ruth, New York A.L.
- OF — Al Simmons, Philadelphia A.L.
- OF — Paul Waner, Pittsburgh N.L.
- C — Gabby Hartnett, Chicago N.L.
- P — Charley Root, Chicago N.L.
- P — Ted Lyons, Chicago A.L.

1928
1B— Lou Gehrig, New York A.L.
2B— Rogers Hornsby, Boston N.L.
SS— Travis Jackson, New York N.L.
3B— Fred Lindstrom, New York N.L.
OF— Babe Ruth, New York A.L.
OF— Heinie Manush, St. Louis A.L.
OF— Paul Waner, Pittsburgh N.L.
C— Mickey Cochrane, Phil. A.L.
P— Lefty Grove, Philadelphia A.L.
P— Waite Hoyt, New York A.L.

1929
1B— Jimmie Foxx, Philadelphia A.L.
2B— Rogers Hornsby, Chicago N.L.
SS— Travis Jackson, New York N.L.
3B— Pie Traynor, Pittsburgh, N.L.
OF— Al Simmons, Philadelphia A.L.
OF— Hack Wilson, Chicago N.L.
OF— Babe Ruth, New York A.L.
C— Mickey Cochrane, Phil. A.L.
P— Lefty Grove, Philadelphia A.L.
P— Burleigh Grimes, Pittsburgh N.L.

1930
1B— Bill Terry, New York N.L.
2B— Frank Frisch, St. Louis N.L.
SS— Joe Cronin, Washington A.L.
3B— Fred Lindstrom, New York N.L.
OF— Al Simmons, Philadelphia A.L.
OF— Hack Wilson, Chicago N.L.
OF— Babe Ruth, New York A.L.
C— Mickey Cochrane, Phil. A.L.
P— Lefty Grove, Philadelphia A.L.
P— Wes Ferrell, Cleveland A.L.

1931
1B— Lou Gehrig, New York A.L.
2B— Frank Frisch, St. Louis N.L.
SS— Joe Cronin, Washington A.L.
3B— Pie Traynor, Pittsburgh N.L.
OF— Al Simmons, Philadelphia A.L.
OF— Earl Averill, Cleveland A.L.
OF— Babe Ruth, New York A.L.
C— Mickey Cochrane, Phil. A.L.
P— Lefty Grove, Philadelphia A.L.
P— George Earnshaw, Phil. A.L.

1932
1B— Jimmie Foxx, Philadelphia A.L.
2B— Tony Lazzeri, New York A.L.
SS— Joe Cronin, Washington A.L.
3B— Pie Traynor, Pittsburgh N.L.
OF— Lefty O'Doul, Brooklyn N.L.
OF— Earl Averill, Cleveland A.L.
OF— Chuck Klein, Philadelphia N.L.
C— Bill Dickey, New York A.L.
P— Lefty Grove, Philadelphia A.L.
P— Lon Warneke, Chicago N.L.

1933
1B— Jimmie Foxx, Philadelphia A.L.
2B— Charley Gehringer, Detroit A.L.
SS— Joe Cronin, Washington A.L.
3B— Pie Traynor, Pittsburgh N.L.
OF— Al Simmons, Chicago A.L.
OF— Wally Berger, Boston N.L.
OF— Chuck Klein, Philadelphia N.L.
C— Bill Dickey, New York A.L.
P— Alvin Crowder, Washington A.L.
P— Carl Hubbell, New York N.L.

1934
1B— Lou Gehrig, New York A.L.
2B— Charley Gehringer, Detroit A.L.
SS— Joe Cronin, Washington A.L.
3B— Mike Higgins, Philadelphia A.L.
OF— Al Simmons, Chicago A.L.
OF— Earl Averill, Cleveland A.L.

OF— Mel Ott, New York N.L.
C— Mickey Cochrane, Detroit A.L.
P— Lefty Gomez, New York A.L.
P— Schoolboy Rowe, Detroit A.L.
P— Dizzy Dean, St. Louis N.L.

1935
1B— Hank Greenberg, Detroit A.L.
2B— Charley Gehringer, Detroit A.L.
SS— Arky Vaughan, Pittsburgh N.L.
3B— Pepper Martin, St. Louis N.L.
OF— Joe Medwick, St. Louis N.L.
OF— Doc Cramer, Philadelphia A.L.
OF— Mel Ott, New York N.L.
C— Mickey Cochrane, Detroit A.L.
P— Carl Hubbell, New York N.L.
P— Dizzy Dean, St. Louis N.L.

1936
1B— Lou Gehrig, New York A.L.
2B— Charley Gehringer, Detroit A.L.
SS— Luke Appling, Chicago A.L.
3B— Mike Higgins, Philadelphia A.L.
OF— Joe Medwick, St. Louis N.L.
OF— Earl Averill, Cleveland A.L.
OF— Mel Ott, New York N.L.
C— Bill Dickey, New York A.L.
P— Carl Hubbell, New York N.L.
P— Dizzy Dean, St. Louis N.L.

1937
1B— Lou Gehrig, New York A.L.
2B— Charley Gehringer, Detroit A.L.
SS— Dick Bartell, New York N.L.
3B— Red Rolfe, New York A.L.
OF— Joe Medwick, St. Louis N.L.
OF— Joe DiMaggio, New York A.L.
OF— Paul Waner, Pittsburgh N.L.
C— Gabby Hartnett, Chicago N.L.
P— Carl Hubbell, New York N.L.
P— Red Ruffing, New York A.L.

1938
1B— Jimmie Foxx, Boston A.L.
2B— Charley Gehringer, Detroit A.L.
SS— Joe Cronin, Boston A.L.
3B— Red Rolfe, New York A.L.
OF— Joe Medwick, St. Louis N.L.
OF— Joe DiMaggio, New York A.L.
OF— Mel Ott, New York N.L.
C— Bill Dickey, New York A.L.
P— Red Ruffing, New York A.L.
P— Lefty Gomez, New York A.L.
P— Johnny Vander Meer, Cin. N.L.

1939
1B— Jimmie Foxx, Boston A.L.
2B— Joe Gordon, New York A.L.
SS— Joe Cronin, Boston A.L.
3B— Red Rolfe, New York A.L.
OF— Joe Medwick, St. Louis N.L.
OF— Joe DiMaggio, New York A.L.
OF— Ted Williams, Boston A.L.
C— Bill Dickey, New York A.L.
P— Red Ruffing, New York A.L.
P— Bob Feller, Cleveland A.L.
P— Bucky Walters, Cincinnati N.L.

1940
1B— Frank McCormick, Cincinnati N.L.
2B— Joe Gordon, New York A.L.
SS— Luke Appling, Chicago A.L.
3B— Stan Hack, Chicago N.L.
OF— Hank Greenberg, Detroit A.L.
OF— Joe DiMaggio, New York A.L.
OF— Ted Williams, Boston A.L.
C— Harry Danning, New York N.L.
P— Bob Feller, Cleveland A.L.
P— Bucky Walters, Cincinnati N.L.
P— Paul Derringer, Cincinnati N.L.

1941
1B— Dolf Camilli, Brooklyn N.L.
2B— Joe Gordon, New York A.L.
SS— Cecil Travis, Washington A.L.
3B— Stan Hack, Chicago N.L.
OF— Ted Williams, Boston A.L.
OF— Joe DiMaggio, New York A.L.
OF— Pete Reiser, Brooklyn N.L.
C— Bill Dickey, New York A.L.
P— Bob Feller, Cleveland A.L.
P— Whitlow Wyatt, Brooklyn N.L.
P— Thornton Lee, Chicago A.L.

1942
1B— Johnny Mize, New York N.L.
2B— Joe Gordon, New York A.L.
SS— Johnny Pesky, Boston A.L.
3B— Stan Hack, Chicago N.L.
OF— Ted Williams, Boston A.L.
OF— Joe DiMaggio, New York A.L.
OF— Enos Slaughter, St. Louis N.L.
C— Mickey Owen, Brooklyn N.L.
P— Mort Cooper, St. Louis N.L.
P— Tiny Bonham, New York A.L.
P— Tex Hughson, Boston A.L.

1943
1B— Rudy York, Detroit A.L.
2B— Billy Herman, Brooklyn N.L.
SS— Luke Appling, Chicago A.L.
3B— Billy Johnson, New York A.L.
OF— Dick Wakefield, Detroit A.L.
OF— Stan Musial, St. Louis N.L.
OF— Bill Nicholson, Chicago N.L.
C— Walker Cooper, St. Louis N.L.
P— Spud Chandler, New York A.L.
P— Mort Cooper, St. Louis N.L.
P— Rip Sewell, Pittsburgh N.L.

1944
1B— Ray Sanders, St. Louis N.L.
2B— Bobby Doerr, Boston A.L.
SS— Marty Marion, St. Louis N.L.
3B— Bob Elliott, Pittsburgh N.L.
OF— Stan Musial, St. Louis N.L.
OF— Dick Wakefield, Detroit A.L.
OF— Dixie Walker, Brooklyn, N.L.
C— Walker Cooper, St. Louis N.L.
P— Hal Newhouser, Detroit A.L.
P— Mort Cooper, St. Louis N.L.
P— Dizzy Trout, Detroit A.L.

1945
1B— Phil Cavarretta, Chicago N.L.
2B— George Stirnweiss, N.Y. A.L.
SS— Marty Marion, St. Louis N.L.
3B— Whitey Kurowski, St. Louis N.L.
OF— Tommy Holmes, Boston N.L.
OF— Andy Pafko, Chicago N.L.
OF— Goody Rosen, Brooklyn N.L.
C— Paul Richards, Detroit A.L.
P— Hal Newhouser, Detroit A.L.
P— Boo Ferriss, Boston A.L.
P— Hank Borowy, Chicago N.L.

1946
1B— Stan Musial, St. Louis N.L.
2B— Bobby Doerr, Boston A.L.
SS— Johnny Pesky, Boston A.L.
3B— George Kell, Detroit A.L.
OF— Ted Williams, Boston A.L.
OF— Dom DiMaggio, Boston A.L.
OF— Enos Slaughter, St. Louis N.L.
C— Aaron Robinson, New York A.L.
P— Hal Newhouser, Detroit A.L.
P— Bob Feller, Cleveland A.L.
P— Boo Ferriss, Boston A.L.

1947
1B— Johnny Mize, New York N.L.
2B— Joe Gordon, Cleveland A.L.
SS— Lou Boudreau, Cleveland A.L.
3B— George Kell, Detroit A.L.
OF— Ted Williams, Boston A.L.
OF— Joe DiMaggio, New York A.L.
OF— Ralph Kiner, Pittsburgh N.L.
C— Walker Cooper, New York N.L.
P— Ewell Blackwell, Cincinnati N.L.
P— Bob Feller, Cleveland A.L.
P— Ralph Branca, Brooklyn N.L.

1948
1B— Johnny Mize, New York N.L.
2B— Joe Gordon, Cleveland A.L.
SS— Lou Boudreau, Cleveland A.L.
3B— Bob Elliott, Boston N.L.
OF— Ted Williams, Boston A.L.
OF— Joe DiMaggio, New York A.L.
OF— Stan Musial, St. Louis N.L.
C— Birdie Tebbetts, Boston A.L.
P— Johnny Sain, Boston N.L.
P— Bob Lemon, Cleveland A.L.
P— Harry Brecheen, St. Louis N.L.

1949
1B— Tommy Henrich, New York A.L.
2B— Jackie Robinson, Brooklyn N.L.
SS— Phil Rizzuto, New York A.L.
3B— George Kell, Detroit A.L.
OF— Ted Williams, Boston A.L.
OF— Stan Musial, St. Louis N.L.
OF— Ralph Kiner, Pittsburgh N.L.
C— Roy Campanella, Brooklyn N.L.
P— Mel Parnell, Boston A.L.
P— Ellis Kinder, Boston A.L.
P— Joe Page, New York A.L.

1950
1B— Walt Dropo, Boston A.L.
2B— Jackie Robinson, Brooklyn N.L.
SS— Phil Rizzuto, New York A.L.
3B— George Kell, Detroit A.L.
OF— Stan Musial, St. Louis N.L.
OF— Ralph Kiner, Pittsburgh N.L.
OF— Larry Doby, Cleveland A.L.
C— Yogi Berra, New York A.L.
P— Vic Raschi, New York A.L.
P— Bob Lemon, Cleveland A.L.
P— Jim Konstanty, Phil. N.L.

1951
1B— Ferris Fain, Philadelphia A.L.
2B— Jackie Robinson, Brooklyn N.L.
SS— Phil Rizzuto, New York A.L.
3B— George Kell, Detroit A.L.
OF— Stan Musial, St. Louis N.L.
OF— Ted Williams, Boston A.L.
OF— Ralph Kiner, Pittsburgh N.L.
C— Roy Campanella, Brooklyn N.L.
P— Sal Maglie, New York N.L.
P— Preacher Roe, Brooklyn N.L.
P— Allie Reynolds, New York A.L.

1952
1B— Ferris Fain, Philadelphia A.L.
2B— Jackie Robinson, Brooklyn N.L.
SS— Phil Rizzuto, New York A.L.
3B— George Kell, Boston A.L.
OF— Stan Musial, St. Louis N.L.
OF— Hank Sauer, Chicago N.L.
OF— Mickey Mantle, New York A.L.
C— Yogi Berra, New York A.L.
P— Robin Roberts, Philadelphia N.L.
P— Bobby Shantz, Philadelphia A.L.
P— Allie Reynolds, New York A.L.

1953
1B— Mickey Vernon, Washington A.L.
2B— Red Schoendienst, St. Louis N.L.
SS— Pee Wee Reese, Brooklyn N.L.
3B— Al Rosen, Cleveland A.L.
OF— Stan Musial, St. Louis N.L.
OF— Duke Snider, Brooklyn N.L.
OF— Carl Furillo, Brooklyn N.L.
C— Roy Campanella, Brooklyn N.L.
P— Robin Roberts, Philadelphia N.L.
P— Warren Spahn, Milwaukee N.L.
P— Bob Porterfield, Washington A.L.

1954
1B— Ted Kluszewski, Cincinnati N.L.
2B— Bobby Avila, Cleveland A.L.
SS— Alvin Dark, New York N.L.
3B— Al Rosen, Cleveland A.L.
OF— Willie Mays, New York N.L.
OF— Stan Musial, St. Louis N.L.
OF— Duke Snider, Brooklyn N.L.
C— Yogi Berra, New York A.L.
P— Bob Lemon, Cleveland A.L.
P— Johnny Antonelli, New York N.L.
P— Robin Roberts, Philadelphia N.L.

1955
1B— Ted Kluszewski, Cincinnati N.L.
2B— Nellie Fox, Chicago A.L.
SS— Ernie Banks, Chicago N.L.
3B— Ed Mathews, Milwaukee N.L.
OF— Duke Snider, Brooklyn N.L.
OF— Ted Williams, Boston A.L.
OF— Al Kaline, Detroit A.L.
C— Roy Campanella, Brooklyn N.L.
P— Robin Roberts, Philadelphia N.L.
P— Don Newcombe, Brooklyn N.L.
P— Whitey Ford, New York A.L.

1956
1B— Ted Kluszewski, Cincinnati N.L.
2B— Nellie Fox, Chicago A.L.
SS— Harvey Kuenn, Detroit A.L.
3B— Ken Boyer, St. Louis N.L.
OF— Mickey Mantle, New York A.L.
OF— Hank Aaron, Milwaukee N.L.
OF— Ted Williams, Boston A.L.
C— Yogi Berra, New York A.L.
P— Don Newcombe, Brooklyn N.L.
P— Whitey Ford, New York A.L.
P— Billy Pierce, Chicago A.L.

1957
1B— Stan Musial, St. Louis N.L.
2B— Red Schoendienst, N.Y.-Mil. N.L.
SS— Gil McDougald, New York A.L.
3B— Ed Mathews, Milwaukee N.L.
OF— Mickey Mantle, New York A.L.
OF— Ted Williams, Boston A.L.
OF— Willie Mays, New York N.L.
C— Yogi Berra, New York A.L.
P— Warren Spahn, Milwaukee N.L.
P— Billy Pierce, Chicago N.L.
P— Jim Bunning, Detroit A.L.

1958
1B— Stan Musial, St. Louis N.L.
2B— Nellie Fox, Chicago A.L.
SS— Ernie Banks, Chicago N.L.
3B— Frank Thomas, Pittsburgh N.L.
OF— Ted Williams, Boston A.L.
OF— Willie Mays, San Francisco N.L.
OF— Hank Aaron, Milwaukee N.L.
C— Del Crandall, Milwaukee N.L.
P— Bob Turley, New York A.L.
P— Warren Spahn, Milwaukee N.L.
P— Bob Friend, Pittsburgh N.L.

1959
1B— Orlando Cepeda, S.F. N.L.
2B— Nellie Fox, Chicago A.L.
SS— Ernie Banks, Chicago N.L.
3B— Ed Mathews, Milwaukee N.L.
OF— Minnie Minoso, Cleveland A.L.
OF— Willie Mays, San Francisco N.L.
OF— Hank Aaron, Milwaukee N.L.
C— Sherm Lollar, Chicago A.L.
P— Early Wynn, Chicago A.L.
P— Sam Jones, San Francisco N.L.
P— Johnny Antonelli, S.F. N.L.

1960
1B— Bill Skowron, New York A.L.
2B— Bill Mazeroski, Pittsburgh N.L.
SS— Ernie Banks, Chicago N.L.
3B— Ed Mathews, Milwaukee N.L.
OF— Minnie Minoso, Chicago A.L.
OF— Willie Mays, San Francisco N.L.
OF— Roger Maris, New York A.L.
C— Del Crandall, Milwaukee N.L.
P— Vernon Law, Pittsburgh N.L.
P— Warren Spahn, Milwaukee N.L.
P— Ernie Broglio, St. Louis N.L.

1961
AMERICAN LEAGUE
1B— Norm Cash, Detroit
2B— Bobby Richardson, New York
SS— Tony Kubek, New York
3B— Brooks Robinson, Baltimore
OF— Mickey Mantle, New York
OF— Roger Maris, New York
OF— Rocky Colavito, Detroit
C— Elston Howard, New York
P— Whitey Ford, New York
P— Frank Lary, Detroit

NATIONAL LEAGUE
1B— Orlando Cepeda, San Francisco
2B— Frank Bolling, Milwaukee
SS— Maury Wills, Los Angeles
3B— Ken Boyer, St. Louis
OF— Willie Mays, San Francisco
OF— Frank Robinson, Cincinnati
OF— Roberto Clemente, Pittsburgh
C— Smoky Burgess, Pittsburgh
P— Joey Jay, Cincinnati
P— Warren Spahn, Milwaukee

1962
AMERICAN LEAGUE
1B— Norm Siebern, Kansas City
2B— Bobby Richardson, New York
SS— Tom Tresh, New York
3B— Brooks Robinson, Baltimore
OF— Leon Wagner, Los Angeles
OF— Mickey Mantle, New York
OF— Al Kaline, Detroit
C— Earl Battey, Minnesota
P— Ralph Terry, New York
P— Dick Donovan, Cleveland

NATIONAL LEAGUE
1B— Orlando Cepeda, San Francisco
2B— Bill Mazeroski, Pittsburgh
SS— Maury Wills, Los Angeles
3B— Ken Boyer, St. Louis
OF— Tommy Davis, Los Angeles
OF— Willie Mays, San Francisco
OF— Frank Robinson, Cincinnati
C— Del Crandall, Milwaukee
P— Don Drysdale, Los Angeles
P— Bob Purkey, Cincinnati

HISTORY *Award winners*

1963
AMERICAN LEAGUE
1B— Joe Pepitone, New York
2B— Bobby Richardson, New York
SS— Luis Aparicio, Baltimore
3B— Frank Malzone, Boston
OF— Carl Yastrzemski, Boston
OF— Albie Pearson, Los Angeles
OF— Al Kaline, Detroit
C— Elston Howard, New York
P— Whitey Ford, New York
P— Gary Peters, Chicago

NATIONAL LEAGUE
1B— Bill White, St. Louis
2B— Jim Gilliam, Los Angeles
SS— Dick Groat, St. Louis
3B— Ken Boyer, St. Louis
OF— Tommy Davis, Los Angeles
OF— Willie Mays, San Francisco
OF— Hank Aaron, Milwaukee
C— John Edwards, Cincinnati
P— Sandy Koufax, Los Angeles
P— Juan Marichal, San Francisco

1964
AMERICAN LEAGUE
1B— Dick Stuart, Boston
2B— Bobby Richardson, New York
SS— Jim Fregosi, Los Angeles
3B— Brooks Robinson, Baltimore
OF— Harmon Killebrew, Minnesota
OF— Mickey Mantle, New York
OF— Tony Oliva, Minnesota
C— Elston Howard, New York
P— Dean Chance, Los Angeles
P— Gary Peters, Chicago

NATIONAL LEAGUE
1B— Bill White, St. Louis
2B— Ron Hunt, New York
SS— Dick Groat, St. Louis
3B— Ken Boyer, St. Louis
OF— Billy Williams, Chicago
OF— Willie Mays, San Francisco
OF— Roberto Clemente, Pittsburgh
C— Joe Torre, Milwaukee
P— Sandy Koufax, Los Angeles
P— Jim Bunning, Philadelphia

1965
AMERICAN LEAGUE
1B— Fred Whitfield, Cleveland
2B— Bobby Richardson, New York
SS— Zoilo Versalles, Minnesota
3B— Brooks Robinson, Baltimore
OF— Carl Yastrzemski, Boston
OF— Jimmie Hall, Minnesota
OF— Tony Oliva, Minnesota
C— Earl Battey, Minnesota
P— Jim Grant, Minnesota
P— Mel Stottlemyre, New York

NATIONAL LEAGUE
1B— Willie McCovey, San Francisco
2B— Pete Rose, Cincinnati
SS— Maury Wills, Los Angeles
3B— Deron Johnson, Cincinnati
OF— Willie Stargell, Pittsburgh
OF— Willie Mays, San Francisco
OF— Hank Aaron, Milwaukee
C— Joe Torre, Milwaukee
P— Sandy Koufax, Los Angeles
P— Juan Marichal, San Francisco

1966
AMERICAN LEAGUE
1B— Boog Powell, Baltimore
2B— Bobby Richardson, New York

SS— Luis Aparicio, Baltimore
3B— Brooks Robinson, Baltimore
OF— Frank Robinson, Baltimore
OF— Al Kaline, Detroit
OF— Tony Oliva, Minnesota
C— Paul Casanova, Washington
P— Jim Kaat, Minnesota
P— Earl Wilson, Detroit

NATIONAL LEAGUE
1B— Felipe Alou, Atlanta
2B— Pete Rose, Cincinnati
SS— Gene Alley, Pittsburgh
3B— Ron Santo, Chicago
OF— Willie Stargell, Pittsburgh
OF— Willie Mays, San Francisco
OF— Roberto Clemente, Pittsburgh
C— Joe Torre, Atlanta
P— Sandy Koufax, Los Angeles
P— Juan Marichal, San Francisco

1967
AMERICAN LEAGUE
1B— Harmon Killebrew, Minnesota
2B— Rod Carew, Minnesota
SS— Jim Fregosi, California
3B— Brooks Robinson, Baltimore
OF— Carl Yastrzemski, Boston
OF— Al Kaline, Detroit
OF— Frank Robinson, Baltimore
C— Bill Freehan, Detroit
P— Jim Lonborg, Boston
P— Earl Wilson, Detroit

NATIONAL LEAGUE
1B— Orlando Cepeda, St. Louis
2B— Bill Mazeroski, Pittsburgh
SS— Gene Alley, Pittsburgh
3B— Ron Santo, Chicago
OF— Hank Aaron, Atlanta
OF— Jim Wynn, Houston
OF— Roberto Clemente, Pittsburgh
C— Tim McCarver, St. Louis
P— Mike McCormick, San Francisco
P— Ferguson Jenkins, Chicago

1968
AMERICAN LEAGUE
1B— Boog Powell, Baltimore
2B— Rod Carew, Minnesota
SS— Luis Aparicio, Chicago
3B— Brooks Robinson, Baltimore
OF— Ken Harrelson, Boston
OF— Willie Horton, Detroit
OF— Frank Howard, Washington
C— Bill Freehan, Detroit
P— Dave McNally, Baltimore
P— Denny McLain, Detroit

NATIONAL LEAGUE
1B— Willie McCovey, San Francisco
2B— Tommy Helms, Cincinnati
SS— Don Kessinger, Chicago
3B— Ron Santo, Chicago
OF— Billy Williams, Chicago
OF— Curt Flood, St. Louis
OF— Pete Rose, Cincinnati
C— Johnny Bench, Cincinnati
P— Bob Gibson, St. Louis
P— Juan Marichal, San Francisco

1969
AMERICAN LEAGUE
1B— Boog Powell, Baltimore
2B— Rod Carew, Minnesota
SS— Rico Petrocelli, Boston
3B— Harmon Killebrew, Minnesota
OF— Frank Howard, Washington
OF— Paul Blair, Baltimore

OF— Reggie Jackson, Oakland
C— Bill Freehan, Detroit
RHP— Denny McLain, Detroit
LHP— Mike Cuellar, Baltimore

NATIONAL LEAGUE
1B— Willie McCovey, San Francisco
2B— Glenn Beckert, Chicago
SS— Don Kessinger, Chicago
3B— Ron Santo, Chicago
OF— Cleon Jones, New York
OF— Matty Alou, Pittsburgh
OF— Hank Aaron, Atlanta
C— Johnny Bench, Cincinnati
RHP— Tom Seaver, New York
LHP— Steve Carlton, St. Louis

1970
AMERICAN LEAGUE
1B— Boog Powell, Baltimore
2B— Dave Johnson, Baltimore
SS— Luis Aparicio, Chicago
3B— Harmon Killebrew, Minnesota
OF— Frank Howard, Washington
OF— Reggie Smith, Boston
OF— Tony Oliva, Minnesota
C— Ray Fosse, Cleveland
RHP— Jim Perry, Minnesota
LHP— Sam McDowell, Cleveland

NATIONAL LEAGUE
1B— Willie McCovey, San Francisco
2B— Glenn Beckert, Chicago
SS— Don Kessinger, Chicago
3B— Tony Perez, Cincinnati
OF— Billy Williams, Chicago
OF— Bobby Tolan, Cincinnati
OF— Hank Aaron, Atlanta
C— Johnny Bench, Cincinnati
RHP— Bob Gibson, St. Louis
LHP— Jim Merritt, Cincinnati

1971
AMERICAN LEAGUE
1B— Norm Cash, Detroit
2B— Cookie Rojas, Kansas City
SS— Leo Cardenas, Minnesota
3B— Brooks Robinson, Baltimore
OF— Merv Rettenmund, Baltimore
OF— Bobby Murcer, New York
OF— Tony Oliva, Minnesota
C— Bill Freehan, Detroit
RHP— Jim Palmer, Baltimore
LHP— Vida Blue, Oakland

NATIONAL LEAGUE
1B— Lee May, Cincinnati
2B— Glenn Beckert, Chicago
SS— Bud Harrelson, New York
3B— Joe Torre, St. Louis
OF— Willie Stargell, Pittsburgh
OF— Willie Davis, Los Angeles
OF— Hank Aaron, Atlanta
C— Manny Sanguillen, Pittsburgh
RHP— Ferguson Jenkins, Chicago
LHP— Steve Carlton, St. Louis

1972
AMERICAN LEAGUE
1B— Dick Allen, Chicago
2B— Rod Carew, Minnesota
SS— Luis Aparicio, Boston
3B— Brooks Robinson, Baltimore
OF— Joe Rudi, Oakland
OF— Bobby Murcer, New York
OF— Richie Scheinblum, Kansas City
C— Carlton Fisk, Boston
RHP— Gaylord Perry, Cleveland
LHP— Wilbur Wood, Chicago

NATIONAL LEAGUE
- 1B— Willie Stargell, Pittsburgh
- 2B— Joe Morgan, Cincinnati
- SS— Chris Speier, San Francisco
- 3B— Ron Santo, Chicago
- OF— Billy Williams, Chicago
- OF— Cesar Cedeno, Houston
- OF— Roberto Clemente, Pittsburgh
- C— Johnny Bench, Cincinnati
- RHP— Ferguson Jenkins, Chicago
- LHP— Steve Carlton, Philadelphia

1973
AMERICAN LEAGUE
- 1B— John Mayberry, Kansas City
- 2B— Rod Carew, Minnesota
- SS— Bert Campaneris, Oakland
- 3B— Sal Bando, Oakland
- OF— Reggie Jackson, Oakland
- OF— Amos Otis, Kansas City
- OF— Bobby Murcer, New York
- C— Thurman Munson, New York
- RHP— Jim Palmer, Baltimore
- LHP— Ken Holtzman, Oakland

NATIONAL LEAGUE
- 1B— Tony Perez, Cincinnati
- 2B— Dave Johnson, Atlanta
- SS— Bill Russell, Los Angeles
- 3B— Darrell Evans, Atlanta
- OF— Bobby Bonds, San Francisco
- OF— Cesar Cedeno, Houston
- OF— Pete Rose, Cincinnati
- C— Johnny Bench, Cincinnati
- RHP— Tom Seaver, New York
- LHP— Ron Bryant, San Francisco

1974
AMERICAN LEAGUE
- 1B— Dick Allen, Chicago
- 2B— Rod Carew, Minnesota
- SS— Bert Campaneris, Oakland
- 3B— Sal Bando, Oakland
- OF— Joe Rudi, Oakland
- OF— Paul Blair, Baltimore
- OF— Jeff Burroughs, Texas
- C— Thurman Munson, New York
- DH— Tommy Davis, Baltimore
- RHP— Jim Hunter, Oakland
- LHP— Mike Cuellar, Baltimore

NATIONAL LEAGUE
- 1B— Steve Garvey, Los Angeles
- 2B— Joe Morgan, Cincinnati
- SS— Dave Concepcion, Cincinnati
- 3B— Mike Schmidt, Philadelphia
- OF— Lou Brock, St. Louis
- OF— Jim Wynn, Los Angeles
- OF— Richie Zisk, Pittsburgh
- C— Johnny Bench, Cincinnati
- RHP— Andy Messersmith, Los Angeles
- LHP— Don Gullett, Cincinnati

1975
AMERICAN LEAGUE
- 1B— John Mayberry, Kansas City
- 2B— Rod Carew, Minnesota
- SS— Toby Harrah, Texas
- 3B— Graig Nettles, New York
- OF— Jim Rice, Boston
- OF— Fred Lynn, Boston
- OF— Reggie Jackson, Oakland
- C— Thurman Munson, New York
- DH— Willie Horton, Detroit
- RHP— Jim Palmer, Baltimore
- LHP— Jim Kaat, Chicago

NATIONAL LEAGUE
- 1B— Steve Garvey, Los Angeles
- 2B— Joe Morgan, Cincinnati
- SS— Larry Bowa, Philadelphia
- 3B— Bill Madlock, Chicago
- OF— Greg Luzinski, Philadelphia
- OF— Al Oliver, Pittsburgh
- OF— Dave Parker, Pittsburgh
- C— Johnny Bench, Cincinnati
- RHP— Tom Seaver, New York
- LHP— Randy Jones, San Diego

1976
AMERICAN LEAGUE
- 1B— Chris Chambliss, New York
- 2B— Bobby Grich, Baltimore
- 3B— George Brett, Kansas City
- SS— Mark Belanger, Baltimore
- OF— Joe Rudi, Oakland
- OF— Mickey Rivers, New York
- OF— Reggie Jackson, Baltimore
- C— Thurman Munson, New York
- DH— Hal McRae, Kansas City
- RHP— Jim Palmer, Baltimore
- LHP— Frank Tanana, California

NATIONAL LEAGUE
- 1B— Willie Montanez, S.F.-Atl.
- 2B— Joe Morgan, Cincinnati
- 3B— Mike Schmidt, Philadelphia
- SS— Dave Concepcion, Cincinnati
- OF— George Foster, Cincinnati
- OF— Cesar Cedeno, Houston
- OF— Ken Griffey, Cincinnati
- C— Bob Boone, Philadelphia
- RHP— Don Sutton, Los Angeles
- LHP— Randy Jones, San Diego

1977
AMERICAN LEAGUE
- 1B— Rod Carew, Minnesota
- 2B— Willie Randolph, New York
- 3B— Graig Nettles, New York
- SS— Rick Burleson, Boston
- OF— Jim Rice, Boston
- OF— Larry Hisle, Minnesota
- OF— Bobby Bonds, California
- C— Carlton Fisk, Boston
- DH— Hal McRae, Kansas City
- RHP— Nolan Ryan, California
- LHP— Frank Tanana, California

NATIONAL LEAGUE
- 1B— Steve Garvey, Los Angeles
- 2B— Joe Morgan, Cincinnati
- 3B— Mike Schmidt, Philadelphia
- SS— Garry Templeton, St. Louis
- OF— George Foster, Cincinnati
- OF— Dave Parker, Pittsburgh
- OF— Greg Luzinski, Philadelphia
- C— Ted Simmons, St. Louis
- RHP— Rick Reuschel, Chicago
- LHP— Steve Carlton, Philadelphia

1978
AMERICAN LEAGUE
- 1B— Rod Carew, Minnesota
- 2B— Frank White, Kansas City
- 3B— Graig Nettles, New York
- SS— Robin Yount, Milwaukee
- OF— Jim Rice, Boston
- OF— Larry Hisle, Milwaukee
- OF— Fred Lynn, Boston
- C— Jim Sundberg, Texas
- DH— Rusty Staub, Detroit
- RHP— Jim Palmer, Baltimore
- LHP— Ron Guidry, New York

NATIONAL LEAGUE
- 1B— Steve Garvey, Los Angeles
- 2B— Dave Lopes, Los Angeles
- 3B— Pete Rose, Cincinnati
- SS— Larry Bowa, Philadelphia
- OF— George Foster, Cincinnati
- OF— Dave Parker, Pittsburgh
- OF— Jack Clark, San Francisco
- C— Ted Simmons, St. Louis
- RHP— Gaylord Perry, San Diego
- LHP— Vida Blue, San Francisco

1979
AMERICAN LEAGUE
- 1B— Cecil Cooper, Milwaukee
- 2B— Bobby Grich, California
- 3B— George Brett, Kansas City
- SS— Roy Smalley, Minnesota
- OF— Jim Rice, Boston
- OF— Fred Lynn, Boston
- OF— Ken Singleton, Baltimore
- C— Darrell Porter, Kansas City
- DH— Don Baylor, California
- RHP— Jim Kern, Texas
- LHP— Mike Flanagan, Baltimore

NATIONAL LEAGUE
- 1B— Keith Hernandez, St. Louis
- 2B— Dave Lopes, Los Angeles
- 3B— Mike Schmidt, Philadelphia
- SS— Garry Templeton, St. Louis
- OF— Dave Kingman, Chicago
- OF— Omar Moreno, Pittsburgh
- OF— Dave Winfield, San Diego
- C— Ted Simmons, St. Louis
- RHP— Joe Niekro, Houston
- LHP— Steve Carlton, Philadelphia

1980
AMERICAN LEAGUE
- 1B— Cecil Cooper, Milwaukee
- 2B— Willie Randolph, New York
- 3B— George Brett, Kansas City
- SS— Robin Yount, Milwaukee
- OF— Ben Oglivie, Milwaukee
- OF— Al Bumbry, Baltimore
- OF— Reggie Jackson, New York
- DH— Reggie Jackson, New York
- C— Rick Cerone, New York
- RHP— Steve Stone, Baltimore
- LHP— Tommy John, New York

NATIONAL LEAGUE
- 1B— Keith Hernandez, St. Louis
- 2B— Manny Trillo, Philadelphia
- 3B— Mike Schmidt, Philadelphia
- SS— Garry Templeton, St. Louis
- OF— Dusty Baker, Los Angeles
- OF— Cesar Cedeno, Houston
- OF— George Hendrick, St. Louis
- C— Gary Carter, Montreal
- RHP— Jim Bibby, Pittsburgh
- LHP— Steve Carlton, Philadelphia

1981
AMERICAN LEAGUE
- 1B— Cecil Cooper, Milwaukee
- 2B— Bobby Grich, California
- 3B— Buddy Bell, Texas
- SS— Rick Burleson, California
- OF— Rickey Henderson, Oakland
- OF— Dwayne Murphy, Oakland
- OF— Tony Armas, Oakland
- C— Jim Sundberg, Texas
- DH— Richie Zisk, Seattle
- RHP— Jack Morris, Detroit
- LHP— Ron Guidry, New York

HISTORY *Award winners*

NATIONAL LEAGUE
1B— Pete Rose, Philadelphia
2B— Manny Trillo, Philadelphia
3B— Mike Schmidt, Philadelphia
SS— Dave Concepcion, Cincinnati
OF— George Foster, Cincinnati
OF— Andre Dawson, Montreal
OF— Pedro Guerrero, Los Angeles
C— Gary Carter, Montreal
RHP— Tom Seaver, Cincinnati
LHP— Fernando Valenzuela, Los Angeles

1982
AMERICAN LEAGUE
1B— Cecil Cooper, Milwaukee
2B— Damaso Garcia, Toronto
3B— Doug DeCinces, California
SS— Robin Yount, Milwaukee
OF— Dave Winfield, New York
OF— Gorman Thomas, Milwaukee
OF— Dwight Evans, Boston
C— Lance Parrish, Detroit
DH— Hal McRae, Kansas City
RHP— Dave Stieb, Toronto
LHP— Geoff Zahn, California

NATIONAL LEAGUE
1B— Al Oliver, Montreal
2B— Manny Trillo, Philadelphia
3B— Mike Schmidt, Philadelphia
SS— Ozzie Smith, St. Louis
OF— Lonnie Smith, St. Louis
OF— Dale Murphy, Atlanta
OF— Pedro Guerrero, Los Angeles
C— Gary Carter, Montreal
RHP— Steve Rogers, Montreal
LHP— Steve Carlton, Philadelphia

1983
AMERICAN LEAGUE
1B— Eddie Murray, Baltimore
2B— Lou Whitaker, Detroit
3B— Wade Boggs, Boston
SS— Cal Ripken, Baltimore
OF— Jim Rice, Boston
OF— Dave Winfield, New York
OF— Lloyd Moseby, Toronto
C— Carlton Fisk, Chicago
DH— Greg Luzinski, Chicago
RHP— LaMarr Hoyt, Chicago
LHP— Ron Guidry, New York

NATIONAL LEAGUE
1B— George Hendrick, St. Louis
2B— Glenn Hubbard, Atlanta
3B— Mike Schmidt, Philadelphia
SS— Dickie Thon, Houston
OF— Dale Murphy, Atlanta
OF— Andre Dawson, Montreal
OF— Tim Raines, Montreal
C— Tony Pena, Pittsburgh
RHP— John Denny, Philadelphia
LHP— Larry McWilliams, Pittsburgh

1984
AMERICAN LEAGUE
1B— Don Mattingly, New York
2B— Lou Whitaker, Detroit
3B— Buddy Bell, Texas
SS— Cal Ripken, Baltimore
OF— Tony Armas, Boston
OF— Dwight Evans, Boston
OF— Dave Winfield, New York
C— Lance Parrish, Detroit
DH— Dave Kingman, Oakland
RHP— Mike Boddicker, Baltimore
LHP— Willie Hernandez, Detroit

NATIONAL LEAGUE
1B— Keith Hernandez, New York
2B— Ryne Sandberg, Chicago
3B— Mike Schmidt, Philadelphia
SS— Ozzie Smith, St. Louis
OF— Dale Murphy, Atlanta
OF— Jose Cruz, Houston
OF— Tony Gwynn, San Diego
C— Gary Carter, Montreal
RHP— Rick Sutcliffe, Chicago
LHP— Mark Thurmond, San Diego

1985
AMERICAN LEAGUE
1B— Don Mattingly, New York
2B— Damaso Garcia, Toronto
3B— Wade Boggs, Boston
SS— Cal Ripken, Baltimore
OF— Rickey Henderson, New York
OF— Harold Baines, Chicago
OF— Phil Bradley, Seattle
C— Carlton Fisk, Chicago
DH— Don Baylor, New York
RHP— Bret Saberhagen, Kansas City
LHP— Ron Guidry, New York

NATIONAL LEAGUE
1B— Keith Hernandez, New York
2B— Tom Herr, St. Louis
3B— Tim Wallach, Montreal
SS— Ozzie Smith, St. Louis
OF— Dave Parker, Cincinnati
OF— Willie McGee, St. Louis
OF— Dale Murphy, Atlanta
C— Gary Carter, New York
RHP— Dwight Gooden, New York
LHP— John Tudor, St. Louis

1986
AMERICAN LEAGUE
1B— Don Mattingly, New York
2B— Tony Bernazard, Cleveland
3B— Wade Boggs, Boston
SS— Tony Fernandez, Toronto
OF— Jim Rice, Boston
OF— George Bell, Toronto
OF— Kirby Puckett, Minnesota
C— Rich Gedman, Boston
DH— Don Baylor, Boston
RHP— Roger Clemens, Boston
LHP— Teddy Higuera, Milwaukee

NATIONAL LEAGUE
1B— Keith Hernandez, New York
2B— Steve Sax, Los Angeles
3B— Mike Schmidt, Philadelphia
SS— Ozzie Smith, St. Louis
OF— Tim Raines, Montreal
OF— Tony Gwynn, San Diego
OF— Dave Parker, Cincinnati
C— Gary Carter, New York
RHP— Mike Scott, Houston
LHP— Fernando Valenzuela, Los Angeles

1987
AMERICAN LEAGUE
1B— Don Mattingly, New York
2B— Willie Randolph, New York
3B— Wade Boggs, Boston
SS— Alan Trammell, Detroit
OF— George Bell, Toronto
OF— Kirby Puckett, Minnesota
OF— Dwight Evans, Boston
C— Matt Nokes, Detroit
DH— Paul Molitor, Milwaukee
RHP— Roger Clemens, Boston
LHP— Jimmy Key, Toronto

NATIONAL LEAGUE
1B— Jack Clark, St. Louis
2B— Juan Samuel, Philadelphia
3B— Tim Wallach, Montreal
SS— Ozzie Smith, St. Louis
OF— Andre Dawson, Chicago
OF— Tony Gwynn, San Diego
OF— Eric Davis, Cincinnati
C— Benito Santiago, San Diego
RHP— Rick Sutcliffe, Chicago
LHP— Zane Smith, Atlanta

1988
AMERICAN LEAGUE
1B— George Brett, Kansas City
2B— Johnny Ray, California
3B— Wade Boggs, Boston
SS— Alan Trammell, Detroit
OF— Kirby Puckett, Minnesota
OF— Mike Greenwell, Boston
OF— Jose Canseco, Oakland
C— Ernie Whitt, Toronto
DH— Harold Baines, Chicago
RHP— Dave Stewart, Oakland
LHP— Frank Viola, Minnesota

NATIONAL LEAGUE
1B— Will Clark, San Francisco
2B— Ryne Sandberg, Chicago
3B— Bobby Bonilla, Pittsburgh
SS— Barry Larkin, Cincinnati
OF— Darryl Strawberry, New York
OF— Andy Van Slyke, Pittsburgh
OF— Kevin McReynolds, New York
C— Mike LaValliere, Pittsburgh
RHP— Orel Hershiser, Los Angeles
LHP— Danny Jackson, Cincinnati

1989
AMERICAN LEAGUE
1B— Fred McGriff, Toronto
2B— Julio Franco, Texas
3B— Carney Lansford, Oakland
SS— Cal Ripken, Baltimore
OF— Ruben Sierra, Texas
OF— Kirby Puckett, Minnesota
OF— Robin Yount, Milwaukee
C— Mickey Tettleton, Baltimore
DH— Harold Baines, Chi.-Tex.
RHP— Bret Saberhagen, Kansas City
LHP— Chuck Finley, California

NATIONAL LEAGUE
1B— Will Clark, San Francisco
2B— Ryne Sandberg, Chicago
3B— Howard Johnson, New York
SS— Shawon Dunston, Chicago
OF— Tony Gwynn, San Diego
OF— Kevin Mitchell, San Francisco
OF— Eric Davis, Cincinnati
C— Benito Santiago, San Diego
RHP— Mike Scott, Houston
LHP— Mark Davis, San Diego

1990
AMERICAN LEAGUE
1B— Cecil Fielder, Detroit
2B— Julio Franco, Texas
3B— Kelly Gruber, Toronto
SS— Alan Trammell, Detroit
OF— Rickey Henderson, Oakland
OF— Jose Canseco, Oakland
OF— Ellis Burks, Boston
C— Carlton Fisk, Chicago
DH— Dave Parker, Milwaukee
RHP— Bob Welch, Oakland
LHP— Chuck Finley, California

NATIONAL LEAGUE

1B— Eddie Murray, Los Angeles
2B— Ryne Sandberg, Chicago
3B— Matt Williams, San Francisco
SS— Barry Larkin, Cincinnati
OF— Barry Bonds, Pittsburgh
OF— Bobby Bonilla, Pittsburgh
OF— Darryl Strawberry, New York
C— Mike Scioscia, Los Angeles
RHP— Doug Drabek, Pittsburgh
LHP— Frank Viola, New York

1991
AMERICAN LEAGUE

1B— Cecil Fielder, Detroit
2B— Julio Franco, Texas
3B— Wade Boggs, Boston
SS— Cal Ripken, Baltimore
OF— Jose Canseco, Oakland
OF— Joe Carter, Toronto
OF— Ken Griffey Jr., Seattle
C— Mickey Tettleton, Detroit
RHP— Roger Clemens, Boston
LHP— Jim Abbott, California

NATIONAL LEAGUE

1B— Will Clark, San Francisco
2B— Ryne Sandberg, Chicago
3B— Terry Pendleton, Atlanta
SS— Barry Larkin, Cincinnati
OF— Barry Bonds, Pittsburgh
OF— Bobby Bonilla, Pittsburgh
OF— Ron Gant, Atlanta
C— Benito Santiago, San Diego
RHP— Jose Rijo, Cincinnati
LHP— Tom Glavine, Atlanta

1992
AMERICAN LEAGUE

1B— Mark McGwire, Oakland
2B— Roberto Alomar, Toronto
3B— Edgar Martinez, Seattle
SS— Travis Fryman, Detroit
OF— Joe Carter, Toronto
OF— Mike Devereaux, Baltimore
OF— Kirby Puckett, Minnesota
C— Mickey Tettleton, Detroit
RHP— Jack McDowell, Chicago
LHP— Dave Fleming, Seattle

NATIONAL LEAGUE

1B— Fred McGriff, San Diego
2B— Ryne Sandberg, Chicago
3B— Gary Sheffield, San Diego
SS— Barry Larkin, Cincinnati
OF— Barry Bonds, Pittsburgh
OF— Andy Van Slyke, Pittsburgh
OF— Larry Walker, Montreal
C— Darren Daulton, Philadelphia
RHP— Greg Maddux, Chicago
LHP— Tom Glavine, Atlanta

1993
AMERICAN LEAGUE

1B— Frank Thomas, Chicago
2B— Carlos Baerga, Cleveland
3B— Travis Fryman, Detroit
SS— Cal Ripken Jr., Baltimore
OF— Albert Belle, Cleveland
OF— Juan Gonzalez, Texas
OF— Ken Griffey Jr., Seattle
C— Mike Stanley, New York
DH— Paul Molitor, Toronto
RHP— Jack McDowell, Chicago
LHP— Jimmy Key, New York

NATIONAL LEAGUE

1B— Fred McGriff, S.D.-Atl.
2B— Robby Thompson, San Francisco

3B— Matt Williams, San Francisco
SS— Jay Bell, Pittsburgh
OF— Barry Bonds, San Francisco
OF— Lenny Dykstra, Philadelphia
OF David Justice, Atlanta
C— Mike Piazza, Los Angeles
RHP— Greg Maddux, Atlanta
LHP— Steve Avery, Atlanta

1994
AMERICAN LEAGUE

1B— Frank Thomas, Chicago
2B— Chuck Knoblauch, Minnesota
3B— Wade Boggs, New York
SS— Cal Ripken Jr., Baltimore
OF— Albert Belle, Cleveland
OF— Ken Griffey Jr., Seattle
OF— Kirby Puckett, Minnesota
C— Ivan Rodriguez, Texas
DH— Paul Molitor, Toronto
RHP— David Cone, Kansas City
LHP— Jimmy Key, New York

NATIONAL LEAGUE

1B— Jeff Bagwell, Houston
2B— Craig Biggio, Houston
3B— Matt Williams, San Francisco
SS— Barry Larkin, Cincinnati
OF— Moises Alou, Montreal
OF— Barry Bonds, San Francisco
OF— Tony Gwynn, San Diego
C— Mike Piazza, Los Angeles
RHP— Greg Maddux, Atlanta
LHP— Danny Jackson, Philadelphia

1995
AMERICAN LEAGUE

1B— Mo Vaughn, Boston
2B— Carlos Baerga, Cleveland
3B— Jim Thome, Cleveland
SS— Cal Ripken Jr., Baltimore
OF— Albert Belle, Cleveland
OF— Tim Salmon, California
OF— Jim Edmonds, California
        Manny Ramirez, Cleveland
C— Ivan Rodriguez, Texas
DH— Edgar Martinez, Seattle
RHP— Mike Mussina, Baltimore
LHP— Randy Johnson, Seattle

NATIONAL LEAGUE

1B— Eric Karros, Los Angeles
2B— Craig Biggio, Houston
3B— Vinny Castillo, Colorado
SS— Barry Larkin, Cincinnati
OF— Reggie Sanders, Cincinnati
OF— Dante Bichette, Colorado
OF— Sammy Sosa, Chicago
C— Mike Piazza, Los Angeles
RHP— Greg Maddux, Atlanta
LHP— Pete Schourek, Cincinnati

1996
AMERICAN LEAGUE

1B— Mark McGwire, Oakland
2B— Roberto Alomar, Baltimore
3B— Jim Thome, Cleveland
SS— Alex Rodriguez, Seattle
OF— Albert Belle, Cleveland
OF— Juan Gonzalez, Texas
OF— Ken Griffey Jr., Seattle
C— Ivan Rodriguez, Texas
DH— Paul Molitor, Minnesota
RHP— Pat Hentgen, Toronto
LHP— Andy Pettitte, New York

NATIONAL LEAGUE

1B— Jeff Bagwell, Houston
2B— Eric Young, Colorado

3B— Ken Caminiti, San Diego
SS— Barry Larkin, Cincinnati
OF— Barry Bonds, San Francisco
OF— Ellis Burks, Colorado
OF— Gary Sheffield, Florida
C— Mike Piazza, Los Angeles
RHP— John Smoltz, Atlanta
LHP— Al Leiter, Florida

1997
AMERICAN LEAGUE

1B— Tino Martinez, New York
2B— Chuck Knoblauch, Minnesota
3B— Matt Williams, Cleveland
SS— Nomar Garciaparra, Boston
OF— Ken Griffey Jr., Seattle
OF— David Justice, Cleveland
OF— Tim Salmon, Anaheim
C— Ivan Rodriguez, Texas
DH— Edgar Martinez, Seattle
RHP— Roger Clemens, Toronto
LHP— Randy Johnson, Seattle

NATIONAL LEAGUE

1B— Jeff Bagwell, Houston
2B— Craig Biggio, Houston
3B— Vinny Castillo, Colorado
SS— Jeff Blauser, Atlanta
OF— Barry Bonds, San Francisco
OF— Tony Gwynn, San Diego
OF— Larry Walker, Colorado
C— Mike Piazza, Los Angeles
RHP— Pedro Martinez, Montreal
LHP— Denny Neagle, Atlanta

1998
AMERICAN LEAGUE

1B— Rafael Palmeiro, Baltimore
2B— Roberto Alomar, Baltimore
3B— Scott Brosius, New York
SS— Alex Rodriguez, Seattle
OF— Ken Griffey Jr., Seattle
OF— Juan Gonzalez, Texas
OF— Albert Belle, Chicago
C— Ivan Rodriguez, Texas
DH— Jose Canseco, Toronto
RHP— Pedro Martinez, Boston
LHP— David Wells, New York

NATIONAL LEAGUE

1B— Mark McGwire, St. Louis
2B— Craig Biggio, Houston
3B— Vinny Castillo, Colorado
SS— Barry Larkin, Cincinnati
OF— Sammy Sosa, Chicago
OF— Moises Alou, Houston
OF— Greg Vaughn, San Diego
C— Mike Piazza, L.A.-Fla.-N.Y.
RHP— Kevin Brown, San Diego
LHP— Tom Glavine, Atlanta

1999
AMERICAN LEAGUE

1B— Rafael Palmeiro, Texas
2B— Roberto Alomar, Cleveland
3B— Dean Palmer, Detroit
SS— Nomar Garciaparra, Boston
OF— Shawn Green, Toronto
OF— Ken Griffey Jr., Seattle
OF— Manny Ramirez, Cleveland
C— Ivan Rodriguez, Texas
RHP— Pedro Martinez, Boston
LHP— Jamie Moyer, Seattle

NATIONAL LEAGUE

1B— Jeff Bagwell, Houston
2B— Edgardo Alfonzo, New York
3B— Chipper Jones, Atlanta
SS— Barry Larkin, Cincinnati

OF— Sammy Sosa, Chicago
OF— Vladimir Guerrero, Montreal
OF— Larry Walker, Colorado
C— Mike Piazza, New York
RHP— Jose Lima, Houston
LHP— Mike Hampton, Houston

2000
AMERICAN LEAGUE
1B— Carlos Delgado, Toronto
2B— Roberto Alomar, Cleveland
3B— Travis Fryman, Cleveland
SS— Alex Rodriguez, Seattle
OF— Darin Erstad, Anaheim
OF— Magglio Ordonez, Chicago
OF— Bernie Williams, New York
C— Jorge Posada, New York
RHP— Pedro Martinez, Boston
LHP— David Wells, Toronto

NATIONAL LEAGUE
1B— Todd Helton, Colorado
2B— Jeff Kent, San Francisco
3B— Chipper Jones, Atlanta
SS— Edgar Renteria, St. Louis
OF— Barry Bonds, San Francisco
OF— Vladimir Guerrero, Montreal
OF— Sammy Sosa, Chicago
C— Mike Piazza, New York
RHP— Greg Maddux, Atlanta
LHP— Tom Glavine, Atlanta

2001
AMERICAN LEAGUE
1B— Jim Thome, Cleveland
2B— Bret Boone, Seattle
3B— Troy Glaus, Anaheim
SS— Alex Rodriguez, Texas
OF— Juan Gonzalez, Cleveland

OF— Manny Ramirez, Boston
OF— Ichiro Suzuki, Seattle
C— Jorge Posada, New York
RHP— Roger Clemens, New York
LHP— Mark Mulder, Oakland
DH— Edgar Martinez, Seattle

NATIONAL LEAGUE
1B— Todd Helton, Colorado
2B— Craig Biggio, Houston
3B— Chipper Jones, Atlanta
SS— Rich Aurilia, San Francisco
OF— Barry Bonds, San Francisco
OF— Luis Gonzalez, Arizona
OF— Sammy Sosa, Chicago
C— Mike Piazza, New York
RHP— Curt Schilling, Arizona
LHP— Randy Johnson, Arizona

MINOR LEAGUE PLAYER OF THE YEAR

Year	Player, Team, League
1936	John Vander Meer, Durham, Piedmont
1937	Charlie Keller, Newark, International
1938	Fred Hutchinson, Seattle, Pacific Coast
1939	Lou Novikoff, Tulsa, Texas; Los Angeles, Pacific Coast
1940	Phil Rizzuto, Kansas City, American Association
1941	John Lindell, Newark, International
1942	Dick Barrett, Seattle, Pacific Coast
1943	Chet Covington, Scranton, Eastern
1944	Rip Collins, Albany, Eastern
1945	Gil Coan, Chattanooga, Southern
1946	Sibby Sisti, Indianapolis, American Association
1947	Hank Sauer, Syracuse, International
1948	Gene Woodling, San Francisco, Pacific Coast
1949	Orie Arntzen, Albany, Eastern
1950	Frank Saucier, San Antonio, Texas
1951	Gene Conley, Hartford, Eastern
1952	Bill Skowron, Kansas City, American Association
1953	Gene Conley, Toledo, American Association
1954	Herb Score, Indianapolis, American Association
1955	John Murff, Dallas, Texas
1956	Steve Bilko, Los Angeles, Pacific Coast
1957	Norm Siebern, Denver, American Association
1958	Jim O'Toole, Nashville, Southern
1959	Frank Howard, Victoria-Spokane
1960	Willie Davis, Spokane, Pacific Coast
1961	Howie Koplitz, Birmingham, Southern
1962	Bob Bailey, Columbus, International
1963	Don Buford, Indianapolis, International
1964	Mel Stottlemyre, Richmond, International
1965	Joe Foy, Toronto, International
1966	Mike Epstein, Rochester, International
1967	Johnny Bench, Buffalo, International
1968	Merv Rettenmund, Rochester, International
1969	Danny Walton, Oklahoma City, American Association
1970	Don Baylor, Rochester, International

Year	Player, Team, League
1971	Bobby Grich, Rochester, International
1972	Tom Paciorek, Albuquerque, Pacific Coast
1973	Steve Ontiveros, Phoenix, Pacific Coast
1974	Jim Rice, Pawtucket, International
1975	Hector Cruz, Tulsa, American Association
1976	Pat Putnam, Asheville, Western Carolina
1977	Ken Landreaux, S.L.C., Pacific Coast; El Paso, Texas
1978	Champ Summers, Indianapolis, American Association
1979	Mark Bomback, Vancouver, Pacific Coast
1980	Tim Raines, Denver, American Association
1981	Mike Marshall, Albuquerque, Pacific Coast
1982	Ron Kittle, Edmonton, Pacific Coast
1983	Kevin McReynolds, Las Vegas, Pacific Coast
1984	Alan Knicely, Wichita, American Association
1985	Jose Canseco, Hunt., Southern-Tac., Pacific Coast
1986	Tim Pyznarski, Las Vegas, Pacific Coast
1987	Randy Milligan, Tidewater, International
1988	Sandy Alomar Jr., Las Vegas, Pacific Coast Gary Sheffield, Denver, American Association (tie)
1989	Sandy Alomar Jr., Las Vegas, Pacific Coast
1990	Jose Offerman, Albuquerque, Pacific Coast
1991	Pedro Martinez, Albuquerque, Pacific Coast
1992	Tim Salmon, Edmonton, Pacific Coast
1993	Cliff Floyd, Harrisburg, Eastern
1994	Derek Jeter, Tampa, Florida State; Albany, Eastern; Columbus, International
1995	Karim Garcia, Albuquerque, Pacific Coast
1996	Vladimir Guerrero, West Palm Beach, Florida State; Harrisburg, Eastern
1997	Ben Grieve, Huntsville, Southern; Edmonton, Pacific Coast
1998	Gabe Kapler, Jacksonville, Southern
1999	Rick Ankiel, Arkansas, Texas; Memphis, Pacific Coast
2000	Jon Rauch, Win.-Salem, Carolina; Birmingham, Southern
2001	Josh Beckett, Brevard County, Fla. State; Portland, Eastern

MINOR LEAGUE MANAGER OF THE YEAR

Year	Manager, Team, League
1936	Al Sothoron, Milwaukee, American Association
1937	Jake Flowers, Salisbury, Eastern Shore
1938	Paul Richards, Atlanta, Southern
1939	Bill Meyer, Kansas City, American Association
1940	Larry Gilbert, Nashville, Southern
1941	Burt Shotton, Columbus, American Association
1942	Eddie Dyer, Columbus, American Association
1943	Nick Cullop, Columbus, American Association
1944	Al Thomas, Baltimore, International
1945	Lefty O'Doul, San Francisco, Pacific Coast
1946	Clay Hopper, Montreal, International
1947	Nick Cullop, Milwaukee, American Association
1948	Casey Stengel, Oakland, Pacific Coast

Year	Manager, Team, League
1949	Fred Haney, Hollywood, Pacific Coast
1950	Rollie Hemsley, Columbus, American Association
1951	Charlie Grimm, Milwaukee, American Association
1952	Luke Appling, Memphis, Southern
1953	Bobby Bragan, Hollywood, Pacific Coast
1954	Kerby Farrell, Indianapolis, American Association
1955	Bill Rigney, Minneapolis, American Association
1956	Kerby Farrell, Indianapolis, American Association
1957	Ben Geraghty, Wichita, American Association
1958	Cal Ermer, Birmingham, Southern
1959	Pete Reiser, Victoria, Texas
1960	Mel McGaha, Toronto, International
1961	Kerby Farrell, Buffalo, International

Year	Manager, Team, League	Year	Manager, Team, League
1962	Ben Geraghty, Jacksonville, International	1982	George Scherger, Indianapolis, American Association
1963	Rollie Hemsley, Indianapolis, International	1983	Bill Dancy, Reading, Eastern
1964	Harry Walker, Jacksonville, International	1984	Bob Rodgers, Indianapolis, American Association
1965	Grady Hatton, Oklahoma City, Pacific Coast	1985	Jim Fregosi, Louisville, American Association
1966	Bob Lemon, Seattle, Pacific Coast	1986	Joe Sparks, Indianapolis, American Association
1967	Bob Skinner, San Diego, Pacific Coast	1987	Terry Collins, Albuquerque, Pacific Coast
1968	Jack Tighe, Toledo, International	1988	Joe Sparks, Indianapolis, American Association
1969	Clyde McCullough, Tidewater, International	1989	Bob Bailor, Syracuse, International
1970	Tom Lasorda, Spokane, Pacific Coast	1990	Sal Rende, Omaha, American Association
1971	Del Rice, Salt Lake City, Pacific Coast	1991	Chris Chambliss, Greenville, Southern
1972	Hank Bauer, Tidewater, International	1992	Grady Little, Greenville, Southern
1973	Joe Morgan, Charleston, International	1993	Jim Tracy, Harrisburg, Eastern
1974	Joe Altobelli, Rochester, International	1994	Mike Jirschele, Wilmington, Carolina
1975	Joe Frazier, Tidewater, International	1995	Pete Mackanin, Ottawa, International
1976	Vern Rapp, Denver, American Association	1996	John Mizerock, Wilmington, Carolina
1977	Tommy Thompson, Arkan., Texas	1997	Marv Foley, Rochester, International
1978	Les Moss, Evansville, American Association	1998	Doug Davis, Columbia, South Atlantic
1979	Vern Benson, Syracuse, International	1999	DeMarlo Hale, Trenton, Eastern
1980	Hal Lanier, Springfield, American Association	2000	Joel Skinner, Buffalo, International
1981	Del Crandall, Albuquerque, Pacific Coast	2001	Tony Pena, New Orleans, Pacific Coast

MINOR LEAGUE EXECUTIVE OF THE YEAR (HIGHER CLASSIFICATIONS, 1936-1992)

(Restricted to Class AAA starting in 1963)

Year	Executive, Team, League	Year	Executive, Team, League
1936	Earl Mann, Atlanta, Southern	1965	Harold Cooper, Columbus, International
1937	Robert LaMotte, Savannah, Sally	1966	John Quinn Jr., Hawaii, Pacific Coast
1938	Louis McKenna, St. Paul, American Association	1967	Hillman Lyons, Richmond, International
1939	Bruce Dudley, Louisville, American Association	1968	Gabe Paul Jr., Tulsa, Pacific Coast
1940	Roy Hamey, Kansas City, American Association	1969	Bill Gardner, Louisville, International
1941	Emil Sick, Seattle, Pacific Coast	1970	Dick King, Wichita, American Association
1942	Bill Veeck, Milwaukee, American Association	1971	Carl Steinfeldt Jr., Rochester, International
1943	Clarence Rowland, Los Angeles, Pacific Coast	1972	Don Labbruzzo, Evansville, American Association
1944	William Mulligan, Seattle, Pacific Coast	1973	Merle Miller, Tucson, Pacific Coast
1945	Bruce Dudley, Louisville, American Association	1974	John Carbray, Sacramento, Pacific Coast
1946	Earl Mann, Atlanta, Southern	1975	Stan Naccarato, Tacoma, Pacific Coast
1947	William Purnhage, Waterloo, I.I.I.	1976	Art Teece, Salt Lake City, Pacific Coast
1948	Edward Glennon, Birmingham, Southern	1977	George Sisler Jr., Columbus, International
1949	Ted Sullivan, Indianapolis, American Association	1978	Willie Sanchez, Albuquerque, Pacific Coast
1950	Clearnce (Brick) Laws, Oakland, Pacific Coast	1979	George Sisler Jr., Columbus, International
1951	Robert Howsam, Denver, West	1980	Jim Burris, Denver, American Association
1952	Jack Cooke, Toronto, International	1981	Pat McKernan, Albuquerque, Pacific Coast
1953	Richard Burnett, Dallas, Texas	1982	A. Ray Smith, Louisville, American Association
1954	Edward Stumpf, Indianapolis, American Association	1983	A. Ray Smith, Louisville, American Association
1955	Dewey Soriano, Seattle, Pacific Coast	1984	Mike Tamburro, Pawtucket, International
1956	Robert Howsam, Denver American Association	1985	Patty Cox Hampton, Oklahoma City, American Association
1957	John Stiglmeier, Buffalo, International	1986	Bob Goughan, Rochester, International
1958	Edward Glennon, Birmingham, Southern	1987	Stu Kehoe, Vancouver, Pacific Coast
1959	Edward Leishman, Salt Lake City, Pacific Coast	1988	Bob Rich, Buffalo, American Association
1960	Ray Winder, Little Rock, Southern	1989	Larry Schmittou, Nashville, American Association
1961	Elten Schiller, Omaha, American Association	1990	Greg Corns, Phoenix, Pacific Coast
1962	George Sisler Jr., Rochester, International	1991	Tom Maloney, Denver, American Association
1963	Lewis Matlin, Hawaii, Pacific Coast	1992	Lou Schwechheimer, Pawtucket, International
1964	Edward Leishman, San Diego, Pacific Coast		

MINOR LEAGUE EXECUTIVE OF THE YEAR (LOWER CLASSIFICATIONS, 1950-1990)

(Separate awards for Class AA and Class A started in 1963; for Short Class A in 1988)

Year	Executive, Team, League	Year	Executive, Team, League
1950	H. Cooper, Hutchinson, Western Association	1963	Hugh Finnerty, Tulsa, Texas
1951	O. W. (Bill) Hayes, Triple, B.S.		Ben Jewell, M. Valley, Pioneer
1952	Hillman Lyons, Danville, MOV	1964	Glynn West, Birmingham, Southern
1953	Carl Roth, Peoria, I.I.I.		James Bayens, Rock Hill, W. Carolina
1954	James Meagham, Cedar Rapids, I.I.I.	1965	Dick Butler, Dallas-Ft. Worth, Texas
1955	John Petrakis, Dubuque, MOV		Ken. Blackman, Quad Cities, Midwest
1956	Marvin Milkes, Fresno, California	1966	Tom Fleming, Evansville, Southern
1957	Richard Wagner, Lincoln, West.		Cappy Harada, Lodi, California
1958	Gerald Waring, Macon, Sally	1967	Robert Quinn, Reading, Eastern
1959	Clay Dennis, Des Moines, I.I.I.		Pat Williams, Spar'burg, W.C.
1960	Hubert Kittle, Yakima, Northwest	1968	Phil Howser, Charlotte, Southern
1961	David Steele, Fresno, California		Merle Miller, Burlington, Midwest
1962	John Quinn Jr., San Jose, California	1969	Charlie Blaney, Albuquerque, Texas

Year	Executive, Team, League
	Bill Gorman, Visalia, California
1970	Carl Sawatski, Arkansas, Texas
	Bob Williams, Bakersfield, California
1971	Miles Wolff, Savannah, Dixie Association
	Ed Holtz, Appleton, Midwest
1972	John Begzos, S. Antonio, Texas
	Bob Piccinini, Modesto, California
1973	Dick Kravitz, Jacksonville, Southern
	Fritz Colschen, Clinton, Midwest
1974	Jim Paul, El Paso, Texas
	Bing Russell, Portland, Northwest
1975	Jim Paul, El Paso, Texas
	Cordy Jensen, Eugene, Northwest
1976	Woodrow Reid, Chattanooga, Southern
	Don Buchheister, Cedar Rapids, Midwest
1977	Jim Paul, El Paso, Texas
	Harry Pells, Quad Cities, Midwest
1978	Larry Schmittou, Nashville, Southern
	Dave Hersh, Appleton, Midwest
1979	Bill Rigney Jr., Midland, Texas
	Tom Romenesko, Greensboro, W.C.
1980	Frances Crockett, Charlotte, Southern
	Tom Romenesko, Greensboro, W.C.

Year	Executive, Team, League
1981	Allie Prescott, Memphis, Southern
	Dan Overstreet, Hagerstown, Caro.
1982	Art Clarkson, Birmingham, Southern
	Bob Carruesco, Stockton, California
1983	Edward Kenney, New Britain, Eastern
	Terry Reynolds, Vero Beach, Florida State
1984	Bruce Baldwin, Greenville, Southern
	Dave Tarrolly, Beloit, Midwest
1985	Ben Bernard, Albany-Colonie, Eastern
	Pete Vonachen, Peoria, Midwest
1986	Bill Davidson, Midland, Texas
	Rob Dlugozima, Durham, Carolina
1987	Joe Preseren, Tulsa, Texas
	Skip Weisman, Greensboro, South Atlantic
1988	Bill Valentine, Arkansas, Texas
	Dennis Bastien, Charleston (W.Va.), South Atlantic
	Bob Beban, Eugene, Northwest
1989	Chuck Domino, Reading, Eastern
	John Baxter, South Bend, Midwest
	Bill Pereira, Boise, Northwest
1990	Joe Preseren, Tulsa, Texas
	Dan Chapman, Stockton, California
	Dave Baggott, Salt Lake City, Pioneer

MINOR LEAGUE EXECUTIVE OF THE YEAR

Year	Executive, Team, League
1993	Todd Vander Woude, Harrisburg, Eastern (AA)
1994	Scott Lane, West Michigan, Midwest (A)
1995	Jack and Mary Cain, Portland, Northwest (A)
1996	Wayne Hodes, Trenton, Eastern (AA)
1997	Andy Milovich, Erie, New York-Pennsylvania (A)

Year	Executive, Team, League
1998	Chuck Domino, Reading, Eastern (AA)
1999	Ben Mondor, Pawtucket, International (AAA)
2000	Art Savage, Sacramento, Pacific Coast (AAA)
2001	Jay Miller, Round Rock, Texas (AA)

RAWLINGS GOLD GLOVE TEAMS

1957
MAJORS
P— Bobby Shantz, New York A.L.
C— Sherm Lollar, Chicago A.L.
1B— Gil Hodges, Brooklyn N.L.
2B— Nellie Fox, Chicago A.L.
3B— Frank Malzone, Boston A.L.
SS— Roy McMillan, Cincinnati N.L.
OF— Minnie Minoso, Chicago A.L.
OF— Willie Mays, New York N.L.
OF— Al Kaline, Detroit A.L.

1958
AMERICAN LEAGUE
P— Bobby Shantz, New York
C— Sherm Lollar, Chicago
1B— Vic Power, Cleveland
2B— Frank Bolling, Detroit
3B— Frank Malzone, Boston
SS— Luis Aparicio, Chicago
OF— Norm Siebern, New York
OF— Jimmy Piersall, Boston
OF— Al Kaline, Detroit

NATIONAL LEAGUE
P— Harvey Haddix, Cincinnati
C— Del Crandall, Milwaukee
1B— Gil Hodges, Los Angeles
2B— Bill Mazeroski, Pittsburgh
3B— Ken Boyer, St. Louis
SS— Roy McMillan, Cincinnati
OF— Frank Robinson, Cincinnati
OF— Willie Mays, San Francisco
OF— Hank Aaron, Milwaukee

1959
AMERICAN LEAGUE
P— Bobby Shantz, New York
C— Sherm Lollar, Chicago

1B— Vic Power, Cleveland
2B— Nellie Fox, Chicago
3B— Frank Malzone, Boston
SS— Luis Aparicio, Chicago
OF— Minnie Minoso, Cleveland
OF— Al Kaline, Detroit
OF— Jackie Jensen, Boston

NATIONAL LEAGUE
P— Harvey Haddix, Pittsburgh
C— Del Crandall, Milwaukee
1B— Gil Hodges, Los Angeles
2B— Charley Neal, Los Angeles
3B— Ken Boyer, St. Louis
SS— Roy McMillan, Cincinnati
OF— Jackie Brandt, San Francisco
OF— Willie Mays, San Francisco
OF— Hank Aaron, Milwaukee

1960
AMERICAN LEAGUE
P— Bobby Shantz, New York
C— Earl Battey, Washington
1B— Vic Power, Cleveland
2B— Nellie Fox, Chicago
3B— Brooks Robinson, Baltimore
SS— Luis Aparicio, Chicago
OF— Minnie Minoso, Chicago
OF— Jim Landis, Chicago
OF— Roger Maris, New York

NATIONAL LEAGUE
P— Harvey Haddix, Pittsburgh
C— Del Crandall, Milwaukee
1B— Bill White, St. Louis
2B— Bill Mazeroski, Pittsburgh
3B— Ken Boyer, St. Louis
SS— Ernie Banks, Chicago

OF— Wally Moon, Los Angeles
OF— Willie Mays, San Francisco
OF— Hank Aaron, Milwaukee

1961
AMERICAN LEAGUE
P— Frank Lary, Detroit
C— Earl Battey, Minnesota
1B— Vic Power, Cleveland
2B— Bobby Richardson, New York
3B— Brooks Robinson, Baltimore
SS— Luis Aparicio, Chicago
OF— Al Kaline, Detroit
OF— Jimmy Piersall, Cleveland
OF— Jim Landis, Chicago

NATIONAL LEAGUE
P— Bobby Shantz, Pittsburgh
C— John Roseboro, Los Angeles
1B— Bill White, St. Louis
2B— Bill Mazeroski, Pittsburgh
3B— Ken Boyer, St. Louis
SS— Maury Wills, Los Angeles
OF— Willie Mays, San Francisco
OF— Roberto Clemente, Pittsburgh
OF— Vada Pinson, Cincinnati

1962
AMERICAN LEAGUE
P— Jim Kaat, Minnesota
C— Earl Battey, Minnesota
1B— Vic Power, Minnesota
2B— Bobby Richardson, New York
3B— Brooks Robinson, Baltimore
SS— Luis Aparicio, Chicago
OF— Jim Landis, Chicago
OF— Mickey Mantle, New York
OF— Al Kaline, Detroit

NATIONAL LEAGUE
P— Bobby Shantz, St. Louis
C— Del Crandall, Milwaukee
1B— Bill White, St. Louis
2B— Ken Hubbs, Chicago
3B— Jim Davenport, San Francisco
SS— Maury Wills, Los Angeles
OF— Willie Mays, San Francisco
OF— Roberto Clemente, Pittsburgh
OF— Bill Virdon, Pittsburgh

1963
AMERICAN LEAGUE
P— Jim Kaat, Minnesota
C— Elston Howard, New York
1B— Vic Power, Minnesota
2B— Bobby Richardson, New York
3B— Brooks Robinson, Baltimore
SS— Zoilo Versalles, Minnesota
OF— Al Kaline, Detroit
OF— Carl Yastrzemski, Boston
OF— Jim Landis, Chicago

NATIONAL LEAGUE
P— Bobby Shantz, St. Louis
C— Johnny Edwards, Cincinnati
1B— Bill White, St. Louis
2B— Bill Mazeroski, Pittsburgh
3B— Ken Boyer, St. Louis
SS— Bobby Wine, Philadelphia
OF— Willie Mays, San Francisco
OF— Roberto Clemente, Pittsburgh
OF— Curt Flood, St. Louis

1964
AMERICAN LEAGUE
P— Jim Kaat, Minnesota
C— Elston Howard, New York
1B— Vic Power, Los Angeles
2B— Bobby Richardson, New York
3B— Brooks Robinson, Baltimore
SS— Luis Aparicio, Baltimore
OF— Al Kaline, Detroit
OF— Jim Landis, Chicago
OF— Vic Davalillo, Cleveland

NATIONAL LEAGUE
P— Bobby Shantz, Philadelphia
C— Johnny Edwards, Cincinnati
1B— Bill White, St. Louis
2B— Bill Mazeroski, Pittsburgh
3B— Ron Santo, Chicago
SS— Ruben Amaro, Philadelphia
OF— Willie Mays, San Francisco
OF— Roberto Clemente, Pittsburgh
OF— Curt Flood, St. Louis

1965
AMERICAN LEAGUE
P— Jim Kaat, Minnesota
C— Bill Freehan, Detroit
1B— Joe Pepitone, New York
2B— Bobby Richardson, New York
3B— Brooks Robinson, Baltimore
SS— Zoilo Versalles, Minnesota
OF— Al Kaline, Detroit
OF— Tom Tresh, New York
OF— Carl Yastrzemski, Boston

NATIONAL LEAGUE
P— Bob Gibson, St. Louis
C— Joe Torre, Atlanta
1B— Bill White, St. Louis
2B— Bill Mazeroski, Pittsburgh
3B— Ron Santo, Chicago
SS— Leo Cardenas, Cincinnati
OF— Willie Mays, San Francisco

OF— Roberto Clemente, Pittsburgh
OF— Curt Flood, St. Louis

1966
AMERICAN LEAGUE
P— Jim Kaat, Minnesota
C— Bill Freehan, Detroit
1B— Joe Pepitone, New York
2B— Bobby Knoop, California
3B— Brooks Robinson, Baltimore
SS— Luis Aparicio, Baltimore
OF— Al Kaline, Detroit
OF— Tommie Agee, Chicago
OF— Tony Oliva, Minnesota

NATIONAL LEAGUE
P— Bob Gibson, St. Louis
C— John Roseboro, Los Angeles
1B— Bill White, Philadelphia
2B— Bill Mazeroski, Pittsburgh
3B— Ron Santo, Chicago
SS— Gene Alley, Pittsburgh
OF— Willie Mays, San Francisco
OF— Curt Flood, St. Louis
OF— Roberto Clemente, Pittsburgh

1967
AMERICAN LEAGUE
P— Jim Kaat, Minnesota
C— Bill Freehan, Detroit
1B— George Scott, Boston
2B Bobby Knoop, California
3B— Brooks Robinson, Baltimore
SS— Jim Fregosi, California
OF— Carl Yastrzemski, Boston
OF— Paul Blair, Baltimore
OF— Al Kaline, Detroit

NATIONAL LEAGUE
P— Bob Gibson, St. Louis
C— Randy Hundley, Chicago
1B— Wes Parker, Los Angeles
2B— Bill Mazeroski, Pittsburgh
3B— Ron Santo, Chicago
SS— Gene Alley, Pittsburgh
OF— Roberto Clemente, Pittsburgh
OF— Curt Flood, St. Louis
OF— Willie Mays, San Francisco

1968
AMERICAN LEAGUE
P— Jim Kaat, Minnesota
C— Bill Freehan, Detroit
1B— George Scott, Boston
2B— Bobby Knoop, California
3B— Brooks Robinson, Baltimore
SS— Luis Aparicio, Chicago
OF— Mickey Stanley, Detroit
OF— Carl Yastrzemski, Boston
OF— Reggie Smith, Boston

NATIONAL LEAGUE
P— Bob Gibson, St. Louis
C— Johnny Bench, Cincinnati
1B— Wes Parker, Los Angeles
2B— Glenn Beckert, Chicago
3B— Ron Santo, Chicago
SS— Dal Maxvill, St. Louis
OF— Willie Mays, San Francisco
OF— Roberto Clemente, Pittsburgh
OF— Curt Flood, St. Louis

1969
AMERICAN LEAGUE
P— Jim Kaat, Minnesota
C— Bill Freehan, Detroit

1B— Joe Pepitone, New York
2B— Dave Johnson, Baltimore
3B— Brooks Robinson, Baltimore
SS— Mark Belanger, Baltimore
OF— Paul Blair, Baltimore
OF— Mickey Stanley, Detroit
OF— Carl Yastrzemski, Boston

NATIONAL LEAGUE
P— Bob Gibson, St. Louis
C— Johnny Bench, Cincinnati
1B— Wes Parker, Los Angeles
2B— Felix Millan, Atlanta
3B— Clete Boyer, Atlanta
SS— Don Kessinger, Chicago
OF— Roberto Clemente, Pittsburgh
OF— Curt Flood, St. Louis
OF— Pete Rose, Cincinnati

1970
AMERICAN LEAGUE
P— Jim Kaat, Minnesota
C— Ray Fosse, Cleveland
1B— Jim Spencer, California
2B— Dave Johnson, Baltimore
3B— Brooks Robinson, Baltimore
SS— Luis Aparicio, Chicago
OF— Mickey Stanley, Detroit
OF— Paul Blair, Baltimore
OF— Ken Berry, Chicago

NATIONAL LEAGUE
P— Bob Gibson, St. Louis
C— Johnny Bench, Cincinnati
1B— Wes Parker, Los Angeles
2B— Tommy Helms, Cincinnati
3B— Doug Rader, Houston
SS— Don Kessinger, Chicago
OF— Roberto Clemente, Pittsburgh
OF— Tommie Agee, New York
OF— Pete Rose, Cincinnati

1971
AMERICAN LEAGUE
P— Jim Kaat, Minnesota
C— Ray Fosse, Cleveland
1B— George Scott, Boston
2B— Dave Johnson, Baltimore
3B— Brooks Robinson, Baltimore
SS— Mark Belanger, Baltimore
OF— Paul Blair, Baltimore
OF— Amos Otis, Kansas City
OF— Carl Yastrzemski, Boston

NATIONAL LEAGUE
P— Bob Gibson, St. Louis
C— Johnny Bench, Cincinnati
1B— Wes Parker, Los Angeles
2B— Tommy Helms, Cincinnati
3B— Doug Rader, Houston
SS— Bud Harrelson, New York
OF— Roberto Clemente, Pittsburgh
OF— Bobby Bonds, San Francisco
OF— Willie Davis, Los Angeles

1972
AMERICAN LEAGUE
P— Jim Kaat, Minnesota
C— Carlton Fisk, Boston
1B— George Scott, Milwaukee
2B— Doug Griffin, Boston
3B— Brooks Robinson, Baltimore
SS— Ed Brinkman, Detroit
OF— Paul Blair, Baltimore
OF— Bobby Murcer, New York
OF— Ken Berry, California

NATIONAL LEAGUE
P— Bob Gibson, St. Louis
C— Johnny Bench, Cincinnati
1B— Wes Parker, Los Angeles
2B— Felix Millan, Atlanta
3B— Doug Rader, Houston
SS— Larry Bowa, Philadelphia
OF— Roberto Clemente, Pittsburgh
OF— Cesar Cedeno, Houston
OF— Willie Davis, Los Angeles

1973
AMERICAN LEAGUE
P— Jim Kaat, Chicago
C— Thurman Munson, New York
1B— George Scott, Milwaukee
2B— Bobby Grich, Baltimore
3B— Brooks Robinson, Baltimore
SS— Mark Belanger, Baltimore
OF— Paul Blair, Baltimore
OF— Amos Otis, Kansas City
OF— Mickey Stanley, Detroit

NATIONAL LEAGUE
P— Bob Gibson, St. Louis
C— Johnny Bench, Cincinnati
1B— Mike Jorgensen, Montreal
2B— Joe Morgan, Cincinnati
3B— Doug Rader, Houston
SS— Roger Metzger, Houston
OF— Bobby Bonds, San Francisco
OF— Cesar Cedeno, Houston
OF— Willie Davis, Los Angeles

1974
AMERICAN LEAGUE
P— Jim Kaat, Chicago
C— Thurman Munson, New York
1B— George Scott, Milwaukee
2B— Bobby Grich, Baltimore
3B— Brooks Robinson, Baltimore
SS— Mark Belanger, Baltimore
OF— Paul Blair, Baltimore
OF— Amos Otis, Kansas City
OF— Joe Rudi, Oakland

NATIONAL LEAGUE
P— Andy Messersmith, Los Angeles
C— Johnny Bench, Cincinnati
1B— Steve Garvey, Los Angeles
2B— Joe Morgan, Cincinnati
3B— Doug Rader, Houston
SS— Dave Concepcion, Cincinnati
OF— Cesar Cedeno, Houston
OF— Cesar Geronimo, Cincinnati
OF— Bobby Bonds, San Francisco

1975
AMERICAN LEAGUE
P— Jim Kaat, Chicago
C— Thurman Munson, New York
1B— George Scott, Milwaukee
2B— Bobby Grich, Baltimore
3B— Brooks Robinson, Baltimore
SS— Mark Belanger, Baltimore
OF— Paul Blair, Baltimore
OF— Joe Rudi, Oakland
OF— Fred Lynn, Boston

NATIONAL LEAGUE
P— Andy Messersmith, Los Angeles
C— Johnny Bench, Cincinnati
1B— Steve Garvey, Los Angeles
2B— Joe Morgan, Cincinnati
3B— Ken Reitz, St. Louis
SS— Dave Concepcion, Cincinnati
OF— Cesar Cedeno, Houston

OF— Cesar Geronimo, Cincinnati
OF— Garry Maddox, Philadelphia

1976
AMERICAN LEAGUE
P— Jim Palmer, Baltimore
C— Jim Sundberg, Texas
1B— George Scott, Milwaukee
2B— Bobby Grich, Baltimore
3B— Aurelio Rodriguez, Detroit
SS— Mark Belanger, Baltimore
OF— Joe Rudi, Oakland
OF— Dwight Evans, Boston
OF— Rick Manning, Cleveland

NATIONAL LEAGUE
P— Jim Kaat, Philadelphia
C— Johnny Bench, Cincinnati
1B— Steve Garvey, Los Angeles
2B— Joe Morgan, Cincinnati
3B— Mike Schmidt, Philadelphia
SS— Dave Concepcion, Cincinnati
OF— Cesar Cedeno, Houston
OF— Cesar Geronimo, Cincinnati
OF— Garry Maddox, Philadelphia

1977
AMERICAN LEAGUE
P— Jim Palmer, Baltimore
C— Jim Sundberg, Texas
1B— Jim Spencer, Chicago
2B— Frank White, Kansas City
3B— Graig Nettles, New York
SS— Mark Belanger, Baltimore
OF— Juan Beniquez, Texas
OF— Carl Yastrzemski, Boston
OF— Al Cowens, Kansas City

NATIONAL LEAGUE
P— Jim Kaat, Philadelphia
C— Johnny Bench, Cincinnati
1B— Steve Garvey, Los Angeles
2B— Joe Morgan, Cincinnati
3B— Mike Schmidt, Philadelphia
SS— Dave Concepcion, Cincinnati
OF— Cesar Geronimo, Cincinnati
OF— Garry Maddox, Philadelphia
OF— Dave Parker, Pittsburgh

1978
AMERICAN LEAGUE
P— Jim Palmer, Baltimore
C— Jim Sundberg, Texas
1B— Chris Chambliss, New York
2B— Frank White, Kansas City
3B— Graig Nettles, New York
SS— Mark Belanger, Baltimore
OF— Fred Lynn, Boston
OF— Dwight Evans, Boston
OF— Rick Miller, California

NATIONAL LEAGUE
P— Phil Niekro, Atlanta
C— Bob Boone, Philadelphia
1B— Keith Hernandez, St. Louis
2B— Dave Lopes, Los Angeles
3B— Mike Schmidt, Philadelphia
SS— Larry Bowa, Philadelphia
OF— Garry Maddox, Philadelphia
OF— Dave Parker, Pittsburgh
OF— Ellis Valentine, Montreal

1979
AMERICAN LEAGUE
P— Jim Palmer, Baltimore
C— Jim Sundberg, Texas

1B— Cecil Cooper, Milwaukee
2B— Frank White, Kansas City
3B— Buddy Bell, Texas
SS— Rick Burleson, Boston
OF— Dwight Evans, Boston
OF— Sixto Lezcano, Milwaukee
OF— Fred Lynn, Boston

NATIONAL LEAGUE
P— Phil Niekro, Atlanta
C— Bob Boone, Philadelphia
1B— Keith Hernandez, St. Louis
2B— Manny Trillo, Philadelphia
3B— Mike Schmidt, Philadelphia
SS— Dave Concepcion, Cincinnati
OF— Garry Maddox, Philadelphia
OF— Dave Parker, Pittsburgh
OF— Dave Winfield, San Diego

1980
AMERICAN LEAGUE
P— Mike Norris, Oakland
C— Jim Sundberg, Texas
1B— Cecil Cooper, Milwaukee
2B— Frank White, Kansas City
3B— Buddy Bell, Texas
SS— Alan Trammell, Detroit
OF— Fred Lynn, Boston
OF— Dwayne Murphy, Oakland
OF— Willie Wilson, Kansas City

NATIONAL LEAGUE
P— Phil Niekro, Atlanta
C— Gary Carter, Montreal
1B— Keith Hernandez, St. Louis
2B— Doug Flynn, New York
3B— Mike Schmidt, Philadelphia
SS— Ozzie Smith, San Diego
OF— Andre Dawson, Montreal
OF— Garry Maddox, Philadelphia
OF— Dave Winfield, San Diego

1981
AMERICAN LEAGUE
P— Mike Norris, Oakland
C— Jim Sundberg, Texas
1B— Mike Squires, Chicago
2B— Frank White, Kansas City
3B— Buddy Bell, Texas
SS— Alan Trammell, Detroit
OF— Dwayne Murphy, Oakland
OF— Dwight Evans, Boston
OF— Rickey Henderson, Oakland

NATIONAL LEAGUE
P— Steve Carlton, Philadelphia
C— Gary Carter, Montreal
1B— Keith Hernandez, St. Louis
2B— Manny Trillo, Philadelphia
3B— Mike Schmidt, Philadelphia
SS— Ozzie Smith, San Diego
OF— Andre Dawson, Montreal
OF— Garry Maddox, Philadelphia
OF— Dusty Baker, Los Angeles

1982
AMERICAN LEAGUE
P— Ron Guidry, New York
C— Bob Boone, California
1B— Eddie Murray, Baltimore
2B— Frank White, Kansas City
3B— Buddy Bell, Texas
SS— Robin Yount, Milwaukee
OF— Dwight Evans, Boston
OF— Dave Winfield, New York
OF— Dwayne Murphy, Oakland

OF— Cesar Geronimo, Cincinnati
OF— Garry Maddox, Philadelphia

NATIONAL LEAGUE
P— Phil Niekro, Atlanta
C— Gary Carter, Montreal
1B— Keith Hernandez, St. Louis
2B— Manny Trillo, Philadelphia
3B— Mike Schmidt, Philadelphia
SS— Ozzie Smith, St. Louis
OF— Andre Dawson, Montreal
OF— Dale Murphy, Atlanta
OF— Garry Maddox, Philadelphia

1983
AMERICAN LEAGUE
P— Ron Guidry, New York
C— Lance Parrish, Detroit
1B— Eddie Murray, Baltimore
2B— Lou Whitaker, Detroit
3B— Buddy Bell, Texas
SS— Alan Trammell, Detroit
OF— Dwight Evans, Boston
OF— Dave Winfield, New York
OF— Dwayne Murphy, Oakland

NATIONAL LEAGUE
P— Phil Niekro, Atlanta
C— Tony Pena, Pittsburgh
1B— Keith Hernandez, St.L.-N.Y
2B— Ryne Sandberg, Chicago
3B— Mike Schmidt, Philadelphia
SS— Ozzie Smith, St. Louis
OF— Andre Dawson, Montreal
OF— Dale Murphy, Atlanta
OF— Willie McGee, St. Louis

1984
AMERICAN LEAGUE
P— Ron Guidry, New York
C— Lance Parrish, Detroit
1B— Eddie Murray, Baltimore
2B— Lou Whitaker, Detroit
3B— Buddy Bell, Texas
SS— Alan Trammell, Detroit
OF— Dwight Evans, Boston
OF— Dave Winfield, New York
OF— Dwayne Murphy, Oakland

NATIONAL LEAGUE
P— Joaquin Andujar, St. Louis
C— Tony Pena, Pittsburgh
1B— Keith Hernandez, New York
2B— Ryne Sandberg, Chicago
3B— Mike Schmidt, Philadelphia
SS— Ozzie Smith, St. Louis
OF— Dale Murphy, Atlanta
OF— Bob Dernier, Chicago
OF— Andre Dawson, Montreal

1985
AMERICAN LEAGUE
P— Ron Guidry, New York
C— Lance Parrish, Detroit
1B— Don Mattingly, New York
2B— Lou Whitaker, Detroit
3B— George Brett, Kansas City
SS— Alfredo Griffin, Oakland
OF— Gary Pettis, California
OF— Dave Winfield, New York
OF— Dwight Evans, Boston (tie)
      Dwayne Murphy, Oakland (tie)

NATIONAL LEAGUE
P— Rick Reuschel, Pittsburgh
C— Tony Pena, Pittsburgh
1B— Keith Hernandez, New York
2B— Ryne Sandberg, Chicago
3B— Tim Wallach, Montreal
SS— Ozzie Smith, St. Louis

OF— Willie McGee, St. Louis
OF— Dale Murphy, Atlanta
OF— Andre Dawson, Montreal

1986
AMERICAN LEAGUE
P— Ron Guidry, New York
C— Bob Boone, California
1B— Don Mattingly, New York
2B— Frank White, Kansas City
3B— Gary Gaetti, Minnesota
SS— Tony Fernandez, Toronto
OF— Gary Pettis, California
OF— Jesse Barfield, Toronto
OF— Kirby Puckett, Minnesota

NATIONAL LEAGUE
P— Fernando Valenzuela, Los Angeles
C— Jody Davis, Chicago
1B— Keith Hernandez, New York
2B— Ryne Sandberg, Chicago
3B— Mike Schmidt, Philadelphia
SS— Ozzie Smith, St. Louis
OF— Tony Gwynn, San Diego
OF— Dale Murphy, Atlanta
OF— Willie McGee, St. Louis

1987
AMERICAN LEAGUE
P— Mark Langston, Seattle
C— Bob Boone, California
1B— Don Mattingly, New York
2B— Frank White, Kansas City
3B— Gary Gaetti, Minnesota
SS— Tony Fernandez, Toronto
OF— Jesse Barfield, Toronto
OF— Kirby Puckett, Minnesota
OF— Dave Winfield, New York

NATIONAL LEAGUE
P— Rick Reuschel, Pit.-S.F.
C— Mike LaValliere, Pittsburgh
1B— Keith Hernandez, New York
2B— Ryne Sandberg, Chicago
3B— Terry Pendleton, St. Louis
SS— Ozzie Smith, St. Louis
OF— Eric Davis, Cincinnati
OF— Tony Gwynn, San Diego
OF— Andre Dawson, Chicago

1988
AMERICAN LEAGUE
P— Mark Langston, Seattle
C— Bob Boone, California
1B— Don Mattingly, New York
2B— Harold Reynolds, Seattle
3B— Gary Gaetti, Minnesota
SS— Tony Fernandez, Toronto
OF— Kirby Puckett, Minnesota
OF— Devon White, California
OF— Gary Pettis, Detroit

NATIONAL LEAGUE
P— Orel Hershiser, Los Angeles
C— Benito Santiago, San Diego
1B— Keith Hernandez, New York
2B— Ryne Sandberg, Chicago
3B— Tim Wallach, Montreal
SS— Ozzie Smith, St. Louis
OF— Andy Van Slyke, Pittsburgh
OF— Eric Davis, Cincinnati
OF— Andre Dawson, Chicago

1989
AMERICAN LEAGUE
P— Bret Saberhagen, Kansas City
C— Bob Boone, Kansas City

1B— Don Mattingly, New York
2B— Harold Reynolds, Seattle
3B— Gary Gaetti, Minnesota
SS— Tony Fernandez, Toronto
OF— Kirby Puckett, Minnesota
OF— Devon White, California
OF— Gary Pettis, Detroit

NATIONAL LEAGUE
P— Ron Darling, New York
C— Benito Santiago, San Diego
1B— Andres Galarraga, Montreal
2B— Ryne Sandberg, Chicago
3B— Terry Pendleton, St. Louis
SS— Ozzie Smith, St. Louis
OF— Andy Van Slyke, Pittsburgh
OF— Tony Gwynn, San Diego
OF— Eric Davis, Cincinnati

1990
AMERICAN LEAGUE
P— Mike Boddicker, Boston
C— Sandy Alomar Jr., Cleveland
1B— Mark McGwire, Oakland
2B— Harold Reynolds, Seattle
3B— Kelly Gruber, Toronto
SS— Ozzie Guillen, Chicago
OF— Ken Griffey Jr., Seattle
OF— Ellis Burks, Boston
OF— Gary Pettis, Texas

NATIONAL LEAGUE
P— Greg Maddux, Chicago
C— Benito Santiago, San Diego
1B— Andres Galarraga, Montreal
2B— Ryne Sandberg, Chicago
3B— Tim Wallach, Montreal
SS— Ozzie Smith, St. Louis
OF— Barry Bonds, Pittsburgh
OF— Andy Van Slyke, Pittsburgh
OF— Tony Gwynn, San Diego

1991
AMERICAN LEAGUE
P— Mark Langston, California
C— Tony Pena, Boston
1B— Don Mattingly, New York
2B— Roberto Alomar, Toronto
3B— Robin Ventura, Chicago
SS— Cal Ripken, Baltimore
OF— Ken Griffey Jr., Seattle
OF— Kirby Puckett, Minnesota
OF— Devon White, Toronto

NATIONAL LEAGUE
P— Greg Maddux, Chicago
C— Tom Pagnozzi, St. Louis
1B— Will Clark, San Francisco
2B— Ryne Sandberg, Chicago
3B— Matt Williams, San Francisco
SS— Ozzie Smith, St. Louis
OF— Barry Bonds, Pittsburgh
OF— Andy Van Slyke, Pittsburgh
OF— Tony Gwynn, San Diego

1992
AMERICAN LEAGUE
P— Mark Langston, California
C— Ivan Rodriguez, Texas
1B— Don Mattingly, New York
2B— Roberto Alomar, Toronto
3B— Robin Ventura, Chicago
SS— Cal Ripken, Baltimore
OF— Ken Griffey Jr., Seattle
OF— Kirby Puckett, Minnesota
OF— Devon White, Toronto

NATIONAL LEAGUE
P— Greg Maddux, Chicago
C— Tom Pagnozzi, St. Louis
1B— Mark Grace, Chicago
2B— Jose Lind, Pittsburgh
3B— Terry Pendleton, Atlanta
SS— Ozzie Smith, St. Louis
OF— Barry Bonds, Pittsburgh
OF— Andy Van Slyke, Pittsburgh
OF— Larry Walker, Montreal

1993
AMERICAN LEAGUE
P— Mark Langston, California
C— Ivan Rodriguez, Texas
1B— Don Mattingly, New York
2B— Roberto Alomar, Toronto
3B— Robin Ventura, Chicago
SS— Omar Vizquel, Seattle
OF— Ken Griffey Jr., Seattle
OF— Kenny Lofton, Cleveland
OF— Devon White, Toronto

NATIONAL LEAGUE
P— Greg Maddux, Atlanta
C— Kirt Manwaring, San Francisco
1B— Mark Grace, Chicago
2B— Robby Thompson, San Fran.
3B— Matt Williams, San Francisco
SS— Jay Bell, Pittsburgh
OF— Barry Bonds, San Francisco
OF— Marquis Grissom, Montreal
OF— Larry Walker, Montreal

1994
AMERICAN LEAGUE
P— Mark Langston, California
C— Ivan Rodriguez, Texas
1B— Don Mattingly, New York
2B— Roberto Alomar, Toronto
3B— Wade Boggs, New York
SS— Omar Vizquel, Cleveland
OF— Ken Griffey Jr., Seattle
OF— Kenny Lofton, Cleveland
OF— Devon White, Toronto

NATIONAL LEAGUE
P— Greg Maddux, Atlanta
C— Tom Pagnozzi, St. Louis
1B— Jeff Bagwell, Houston
2B— Craig Biggio, Houston
3B— Matt Williams, San Francisco
SS— Barry Larkin, Cincinnati
OF— Barry Bonds, San Francisco
OF— Marquis Grissom, Montreal
OF— Darren Lewis, San Francisco

1995
AMERICAN LEAGUE
P— Mark Langston, California
C— Ivan Rodriguez, Texas
1B— J.T. Snow, California
2B— Roberto Alomar, Toronto
3B— Wade Boggs, New York
SS— Omar Vizquel, Cleveland
OF— Ken Griffey Jr., Seattle
OF— Kenny Lofton, Cleveland
OF— Devon White, Toronto

NATIONAL LEAGUE
P— Greg Maddux, Atlanta
C— Charles Johnson, Florida
1B— Mark Grace, Chicago
2B— Craig Biggio, Houston

3B— Ken Caminiti, San Diego
SS— Barry Larkin, Cincinnati
OF— Raul Mondesi, Los Angeles
OF— Marquis Grissom, Atlanta
OF— Steve Finley, San Diego

1996
AMERICAN LEAGUE
P— Mike Mussina, Baltimore
C— Ivan Rodriguez, Texas
1B— J.T. Snow, California
2B— Roberto Alomar, Baltimore
3B— Robin Ventura, Chicago
SS— Omar Vizquel, Cleveland
OF— Jay Buhner, Seattle
OF— Ken Griffey Jr., Seattle
OF— Kenny Lofton, Cleveland

NATIONAL LEAGUE
P— Greg Maddux, Atlanta
C— Charles Johnson, Florida
1B— Mark Grace, Chicago
2B— Craig Biggio, Houston
3B— Ken Caminiti, San Diego
SS— Barry Larkin, Cincinnati
OF— Barry Bonds, San Francisco
OF— Marquis Grissom, Atlanta
OF— Steve Finley, San Diego

1997
AMERICAN LEAGUE
P— Mike Mussina, Baltimore
C— Ivan Rodriguez, Texas
1B— Rafael Palmeiro, Baltimore
2B— Chuck Knoblauch, Minnesota
3B— Matt Williams, Cleveland
SS— Omar Vizquel, Cleveland
OF— Jim Edmonds, Anaheim
OF— Ken Griffey Jr., Seattle
OF— Bernie Williams, New York

NATIONAL LEAGUE
P— Greg Maddux, Atlanta
C— Charles Johnson, Florida
1B— J.T. Snow, San Francisco
2B— Craig Biggio, Houston
3B— Ken Caminiti, San Diego
SS— Rey Ordonez, New York
OF— Barry Bonds, San Francisco
OF— Raul Mondesi, Los Angeles
OF— Larry Walker, Colorado

1998
AMERICAN LEAGUE
P— Mike Mussina, Baltimore
C— Ivan Rodriguez, Texas
1B— Rafael Palmeiro, Baltimore
2B— Roberto Alomar, Baltimore
3B— Robin Ventura, White Sox
SS— Omar Vizquel, Cleveland
OF— Jim Edmonds, Anaheim
OF— Ken Griffey Jr., Seattle
OF— Bernie Williams, New York

NATIONAL LEAGUE
P— Greg Maddux, Atlanta
C— Charles Johnson, Fla.-L.A.
1B— J.T. Snow, San Francisco
2B— Bret Boone, Cincinnati
3B— Scott Rolen, Philadelphia
SS— Rey Ordonez, New York
OF— Barry Bonds, San Francisco
OF— Andruw Jones, Atlanta
OF— Larry Walker, Colorado

1999
AMERICAN LEAGUE
P— Mike Mussina, Baltimore
C— Ivan Rodriguez, Texas
1B— Rafael Palmeiro, Texas
2B— Roberto Alomar, Cleveland
3B— Scott Brosius, New York
SS— Omar Vizquel, Cleveland
OF— Shawn Green, Toronto
OF— Ken Griffey Jr., Seattle
OF— Bernie Williams, New York

NATIONAL LEAGUE
P— Greg Maddux, Atlanta
C— Mike Lieberthal, Philadelphia
1B— J.T. Snow, San Francisco
2B— Pokey Reese, Cincinnati
3B— Robin Ventura, New York
SS— Rey Ordonez, New York
OF— Steve Finley, Arizona
OF— Andruw Jones, Atlanta
OF— Larry Walker, Colorado

2000
AMERICAN LEAGUE
P— Kenny Rogers, Texas
C— Ivan Rodriguez, Texas
1B— John Olerud, Seattle
2B— Roberto Alomar, Cleveland
3B— Travis Fryman, Cleveland
SS— Omar Vizquel, Cleveland
OF— Jermaine Dye, Kansas City
OF— Darin Erstad, Anaheim
OF— Bernie Williams, New York

NATIONAL LEAGUE
P— Greg Maddux, Atlanta
C— Mike Matheny, St. Louis
1B— Todd Helton, Colorado
2B— Pokey Reese, Cincinnati
3B— Scott Rolen, Philadelphia
SS— Neifi Perez, Colorado
OF— Jim Edmonds, St. Louis
OF— Steve Finley, Arizona
OF— Andruw Jones, Atlanta

2001
AMERICAN LEAGUE
P— Mike Mussina, New York
C— Ivan Rodriguez, Texas
1B— Doug Mientkiewicz, Minnesota
2B— Roberto Alomar, Cleveland
3B— Eric Chavez, Oakland
SS— Omar Vizquel, Cleveland
OF— Mike Cameron, Seattle
OF— Torii Hunter, Minnesota
OF— Ichiro Suzuki, Seattle

NATIONAL LEAGUE
P— Greg Maddux, Atlanta
C— Brad Ausmus, Houston
1B— Todd Helton, Colorado
2B— Fernando Vina, St. Louis
3B— Scott Rolen, Philadelphia
SS— Orlando Cabrera, Montreal
OF— Jim Edmonds, St. Louis
OF— Andruw Jones, Atlanta
OF— Larry Walker, Colorado

1980

AMERICAN LEAGUE
1B— Cecil Cooper, Milwaukee
2B— Willie Randolph, New York
3B— George Brett, Kansas City
SS— Robin Yount, Milwaukee
OF— Ben Oglivie, Milwaukee
OF— Al Oliver, Texas
OF— Willie Wilson, Kansas City
C— Lance Parrish, Detroit
DH— Reggie Jackson, New York

NATIONAL LEAGUE
1B— Keith Hernandez, St. Louis
2B— Manny Trillo, Philadelphia
3B— Mike Schmidt, Philadelphia
SS— Garry Templeton, St. Louis
OF— Dusty Baker, Los Angeles
OF— Andre Dawson, Montreal
OF— George Hendrick, St. Louis
C— Ted Simmons, St. Louis
P— Bob Forsch, St. Louis

1981

AMERICAN LEAGUE
1B— Cecil Cooper, Milwaukee
2B— Bobby Grich, California
3B— Carney Lansford, Boston
SS— Rick Burleson, California
OF— Rickey Henderson, Oakland
OF— Dwight Evans, Boston
OF— Dave Winfield, New York
C— Carlton Fisk, Chicago
DH— Al Oliver, Texas

NATIONAL LEAGUE
1B— Pete Rose, Philadelphia
2B— Manny Trillo, Philadelphia
3B— Mike Schmidt, Philadelphia
SS— Dave Concepcion, Cincinnati
OF— Andre Dawson, Montreal
OF— George Foster, Cincinnati
OF— Dusty Baker, Los Angeles
C— Gary Carter, Montreal
P— Fernando Valenzuela, Los Angeles

1982

AMERICAN LEAGUE
1B— Cecil Cooper, Milwaukee
2B— Damaso Garcia, Toronto
3B— Doug DeCinces, California
SS— Robin Yount, Milwaukee
OF— Dave Winfield, New York
OF— Willie Wilson, Kansas City
OF— Reggie Jackson, California
C— Lance Parrish, Detroit
DH— Hal McRae, Kansas City

NATIONAL LEAGUE
1B— Al Oliver, Montreal
2B— Joe Morgan, San Francisco
3B— Mike Schmidt, Philadelphia
SS— Dave Concepcion, Cincinnati
OF— Dale Murphy, Atlanta
OF— Pedro Guerrero, Los Angeles
OF— Leon Durham, Chicago
C— Gary Carter, Montreal
P— Don Robinson, Pittsburgh

1983

AMERICAN LEAGUE
1B— Eddie Murray, Baltimore
2B— Lou Whitaker, Detroit
3B— Wade Boggs, Boston
SS— Cal Ripken Jr., Baltimore
OF— Jim Rice, Boston
OF— Dave Winfield, New York
OF— Lloyd Moseby, Toronto
C— Lance Parrish, Detroit
DH— Don Baylor, New York

NATIONAL LEAGUE
1B— George Hendrick, St. Louis
2B— Johnny Ray, Pittsburgh
3B— Mike Schmidt, Philadelphia
SS— Dickie Thon, Houston
OF— Andre Dawson, Montreal
OF— Dale Murphy, Atlanta
OF— Jose Cruz, Houston
C— Terry Kennedy, San Diego
P— Fernando Valenzuela, Los Angeles

1984

AMERICAN LEAGUE
1B— Eddie Murray, Baltimore
2B— Lou Whitaker, Detroit
3B— Buddy Bell, Texas
SS— Cal Ripken Jr., Baltimore
OF— Tony Armas, Boston
OF— Jim Rice, Boston
OF— Dave Winfield, New York
C— Lance Parrish, Detroit
DH— Andre Thornton, Cleveland

NATIONAL LEAGUE
1B— Keith Hernandez, New York
2B— Ryne Sandberg, Chicago
3B— Mike Schmidt, Philadelphia
SS— Garry Templeton, San Diego
OF— Dale Murphy, Atlanta
OF— Jose Cruz, Houston
OF— Tony Gwynn, San Diego
C— Gary Carter, Montreal
P— Rick Rhoden, Pittsburgh

1985

AMERICAN LEAGUE
1B— Don Mattingly, New York
2B— Lou Whitaker, Detroit
3B— George Brett, Kansas City
SS— Cal Ripken Jr., Baltimore
OF— Rickey Henderson, New York
OF— Dave Winfield, New York
OF— George Bell, Toronto
C— Carlton Fisk, Chicago
DH— Don Baylor, New York

NATIONAL LEAGUE
1B— Jack Clark, St. Louis
2B— Ryne Sandberg, Chicago
3B— Tim Wallach, Montreal
SS— Hubie Brooks, Montreal
OF— Willie McGee, St. Louis
OF— Dale Murphy, Atlanta
OF— Dave Parker, Cincinnati
C— Gary Carter, New York
P— Rick Rhoden, Pittsburgh

1986

AMERICAN LEAGUE
1B— Don Mattingly, New York
2B— Frank White, Kansas City
3B— Wade Boggs, Boston
SS— Cal Ripken Jr., Baltimore
OF— George Bell, Toronto
OF— Kirby Puckett, Minnesota
OF— Jesse Barfield, Toronto
C— Lance Parrish, Detroit
DH— Don Baylor, Boston

NATIONAL LEAGUE
1B— Glenn Davis, Houston
2B— Steve Sax, Los Angeles
3B— Mike Schmidt, Philadelphia
SS— Hubie Brooks, Montreal
OF— Tony Gwynn, San Diego
OF— Tim Raines, Montreal
OF— Dave Parker, Cincinnati
C— Gary Carter, New York
P— Rick Rhoden, Pittsburgh

1987

AMERICAN LEAGUE
1B— Don Mattingly, New York
2B— Lou Whitaker, Detroit
3B— Wade Boggs, Boston
SS— Alan Trammell, Detroit
OF— George Bell, Toronto
OF— Dwight Evans, Boston
OF— Kirby Puckett, Minnesota
C— Matt Nokes, Detroit
DH— Paul Molitor, Milwaukee

NATIONAL LEAGUE
1B— Jack Clark, St. Louis
2B— Juan Samuel, Philadelphia
3B— Tim Wallach, Montreal
SS— Ozzie Smith, St. Louis
OF— Andre Dawson, Chicago
OF— Eric Davis, Cincinnati
OF— Tony Gwynn, San Diego
C— Benito Santiago, San Diego
P— Bob Forsch, St. Louis

1988

AMERICAN LEAGUE
1B— George Brett, Kansas City
2B— Julio Franco, Cleveland
3B— Wade Boggs, Boston
SS— Alan Trammell, Detroit
OF— Kirby Puckett, Minnesota
OF— Jose Canseco, Oakland
OF— Mike Greenwell, Boston
C— Carlton Fisk, Chicago
DH— Paul Molitor, Milwaukee

NATIONAL LEAGUE
1B— Andres Galarraga, Montreal
2B— Ryne Sandberg, Chicago
3B— Bobby Bonilla, Pittsburgh
SS— Barry Larkin, Cincinnati
OF— Darryl Strawberry, New York
OF— Andy Van Slyke, Pittsburgh
OF— Kirk Gibson, Los Angeles
C— Benito Santiago, San Diego
P— Tim Leary, Los Angeles

1989

AMERICAN LEAGUE
1B— Fred McGriff, Toronto
2B— Julio Franco, Texas
3B— Wade Boggs, Boston
SS— Cal Ripken Jr., Baltimore
OF— Kirby Puckett, Minnesota
OF— Ruben Sierra, Texas
OF— Robin Yount, Milwaukee
C— Mickey Tettleton, Baltimore
DH— Harold Baines, Chi.-Tex.

NATIONAL LEAGUE
1B— Will Clark, San Francisco
2B— Ryne Sandberg, Chicago
3B— Howard Johnson, New York

HISTORY *Award Winners*

SS— Barry Larkin, Cincinnati
OF— Kevin Mitchell, San Francisco
OF— Tony Gwynn, San Diego
OF— Eric Davis, Cincinnati
 C— Craig Biggio, Houston
 P— Don Robinson, San Francisco

1990
AMERICAN LEAGUE
1B— Cecil Fielder, Detroit
2B— Julio Franco, Texas
3B— Kelly Gruber, Toronto
SS— Alan Trammell, Detroit
OF— Rickey Henderson, Oakland
OF— Jose Canseco, Oakland
OF— Ellis Burks, Boston
 C— Lance Parrish, California
DH— Dave Parker, Milwaukee

NATIONAL LEAGUE
1B— Eddie Murray, Los Angeles
2B— Ryne Sandberg, Chicago
3B— Matt Williams, San Francisco
SS— Barry Larkin, Cincinnati
OF— Barry Bonds, Pittsburgh
OF— Bobby Bonilla, Pittsburgh
OF— Darryl Strawberry, New York
 C— Benito Santiago, San Diego
 P— Don Robinson, San Francisco

1991
AMERICAN LEAGUE
1B— Cecil Fielder, Detroit
2B— Julio Franco, Texas
3B— Wade Boggs, Boston
SS— Cal Ripken Jr., Baltimore
OF— Jose Canseco, Oakland
OF— Joe Carter, Toronto
OF— Ken Griffey Jr., Seattle
 C— Mickey Tettleton, Detroit
DH— Frank Thomas, Chicago

NATIONAL LEAGUE
1B— Will Clark, San Francisco
2B— Ryne Sandberg, Chicago
3B— Howard Johnson, New York
SS— Barry Larkin, Cincinnati
OF— Barry Bonds, Pittsburgh
OF— Bobby Bonilla, Pittsburgh
OF— Ron Gant, Atlanta
 C— Benito Santiago, San Diego
 P— Tom Glavine, Atlanta

1992
AMERICAN LEAGUE
1B— Mark McGwire, Oakland
2B— Roberto Alomar, Toronto
3B— Edgar Martinez, Seattle
SS— Travis Fryman, Detroit
OF— Joe Carter, Toronto
OF— Juan Gonzalez, Texas
OF— Kirby Puckett, Minnesota
 C— Mickey Tettleton, Detroit
DH— Dave Winfield, Toronto

NATIONAL LEAGUE
1B— Fred McGriff, San Diego
2B— Ryne Sandberg, Chicago
3B— Gary Sheffield, San Diego
SS— Barry Larkin, Cincinnati
OF— Barry Bonds, Pittsburgh
OF— Andy Van Slyke, Pittsburgh
OF— Larry Walker, Montreal
 C— Darren Daulton, Philadelphia
 P— Dwight Gooden, New York

1993
AMERICAN LEAGUE
1B— Frank Thomas, Chicago
2B— Carlos Baerga, Cleveland
3B— Wade Boggs, New York
SS— Cal Ripken Jr., Baltimore
OF— Albert Belle, Cleveland
OF— Juan Gonzalez, Texas
OF— Ken Griffey Jr., Seattle
 C— Mike Stanley, New York
DH— Paul Molitor, Toronto

NATIONAL LEAGUE
1B— Fred McGriff, S.D.-Atl.
2B— Robby Thompson, San Fran.
3B— Matt Williams, San Francisco
SS— Jay Bell, Pittsburgh
OF— Barry Bonds, San Francisco
OF— Lenny Dykstra, Philadelphia
OF— David Justice, Atlanta
 C— Mike Piazza, Los Angeles
 P— Orel Hershiser, Los Angeles

1994
AMERICAN LEAGUE
1B— Frank Thomas, Chicago
2B— Carlos Baerga, Cleveland
3B— Wade Boggs, New York
SS— Cal Ripken Jr., Baltimore
OF— Albert Belle, Cleveland
OF— Ken Griffey Jr., Seattle
OF— Kirby Puckett, Minnesota
 C— Ivan Rodriguez, Texas
DH— Julio Franco, Chicago

NATIONAL LEAGUE
1B— Jeff Bagwell, Houston
2B— Craig Biggio, Houston
3B— Matt Williams, San Francisco
SS— Wil Cordero, Montreal
OF— Moises Alou, Montreal
OF— Barry Bonds, San Francisco
OF— Tony Gwynn, San Diego
 C— Mike Piazza, Los Angeles
 P— Mark Portugal, San Francisco

1995
AMERICAN LEAGUE
1B— Mo Vaughn, Boston
2B— Chuck Knoblauch, Minnesota
3B— Gary Gaetti, Kansas City
SS— John Valentin, Boston
OF— Albert Belle, Cleveland
OF— Tim Salmon, California
OF— Manny Ramirez, Cleveland
 C— Ivan Rodriguez, Texas
DH— Edgar Martinez, Seattle

NATIONAL LEAGUE
1B— Eric Karros, Los Angeles
2B— Craig Biggio, Houston
3B— Vinny Castilla, Colorado
SS— Barry Larkin, Cincinnati
OF— Dante Bichette, Colorado
OF— Tony Gwynn, San Diego
OF— Sammy Sosa, Chicago
 C— Mike Piazza, Los Angeles
 P— Tom Glavine, Atlanta

1996
AMERICAN LEAGUE
1B— Mark McGwire, Oakland
2B— Roberto Alomar, Baltimore
3B— Jim Thome, Cleveland

SS— Alex Rodriguez, Seattle
OF— Albert Belle, Cleveland
OF— Juan Gonzalez, Texas
OF— Ken Griffey Jr., Seattle
 C— Ivan Rodriguez, Texas
DH— Paul Molitor, Minnesota

NATIONAL LEAGUE
1B— Andres Galarraga, Colorado
2B— Eric Young, Colorado
3B— Ken Caminiti, San Diego
SS— Barry Larkin, Cincinnati
OF— Barry Bonds, San Francisco
OF— Ellis Burks, Colorado
OF— Gary Sheffield, Florida
 C— Mike Piazza, Los Angeles
 P— Tom Glavine, Atlanta

1997
AMERICAN LEAGUE
1B— Tino Martinez, New York
2B— Chuck Knoblauch, Minnesota
3B— Matt Williams, Cleveland
SS— Nomar Garciaparra, Boston
OF— Juan Gonzalez, Texas
OF— Ken Griffey Jr., Seattle
OF— David Justice, Cleveland
 C— Ivan Rodriguez, Texas
DH— Edgar Martinez, Seattle

NATIONAL LEAGUE
1B— Jeff Bagwell, Houston
2B— Craig Biggio, Houston
3B— Vinny Castilla, Colorado
SS— Jeff Blauser, Atlanta
OF— Barry Bonds, San Francisco
OF— Tony Gwynn, San Diego
OF— Larry Walker, Colorado
 C— Mike Piazza, Los Angeles
 P— John Smoltz, Atlanta

1998
AMERICAN LEAGUE
1B— Rafael Palmeiro, Baltimore
2B— Damion Easley, Detroit
3B— Dean Palmer, Kansas City
SS— Alex Rodriguez, Seattle
OF— Juan Gonzalez, Texas
OF— Ken Griffey Jr., Seattle
OF— Albert Belle, Chicago
 C— Ivan Rodriguez, Texas
DH— Jose Canseco, Toronto

NATIONAL LEAGUE
1B— Mark McGwire, St. Louis
2B— Craig Biggio, Houston
3B— Vinny Castilla, Colorado
SS— Barry Larkin, Cincinnati
OF— Sammy Sosa, Chicago
OF— Moises Alou, Houston
OF— Greg Vaughn, San Diego
 C— Mike Piazza, L.A.-Fla.-N.Y.
 P— Tom Glavine, Atlanta

1999
AMERICAN LEAGUE
1B— Carlos Delgado, Toronto
2B— Roberto Alomar, Cleveland
3B— Dean Palmer, Detroit
SS— Alex Rodriguez, Seattle
OF— Shawn Green, Toronto
OF— Ken Griffey Jr., Seattle
OF— Manny Ramirez, Cleveland
 C— Ivan Rodriguez, Texas
DH— Rafael Palmeiro, Texas

NATIONAL LEAGUE
1B— Jeff Bagwell, Houston
2B— Edgardo Alfonzo, New York
3B— Chipper Jones, Atlanta
SS— Barry Larkin, Cincinnati
OF— Sammy Sosa, Chicago
OF— Vladimir Guerrero, Montreal
OF— Larry Walker, Colorado
C— Mike Piazza, New York
P— Mike Hampton, Houston

2000
AMERICAN LEAGUE
1B— Carlos Delgado, Toronto
2B— Roberto Alomar, Cleveland
3B— Troy Glaus, Anaheim
SS— Alex Rodriguez, Seattle
OF— Darin Erstad, Anaheim
OF— Manny Ramirez, Cleveland

OF— Magglio Ordonez, Chicago
C— Jorge Posada, New York
DH— Frank Thomas, Chicago

NATIONAL LEAGUE
1B— Todd Helton, Colorado
2B— Jeff Kent, San Francisco
3B— Chipper Jones, Atlanta
SS— Edgar Renteria, St. Louis
OF— Sammy Sosa, Chicago
OF— Barry Bonds, San Francisco
OF— Vladimir Guerrero, Montreal
C— Mike Piazza, New York
P— Mike Hampton, New York

2001
AMERICAN LEAGUE
1B— Jason Giambi, Oakland
2B— Bret Boone, Seattle

3B— Troy Glaus, Anaheim
SS— Alex Rodriguez, Texas
OF— Juan Gonzalez, Cleveland
OF— Manny Ramirez, Boston
OF— Ichiro Suzuki, Seattle
C— Jorge Posada, New York
DH— Edgar Martinez, Seattle

NATIONAL LEAGUE
1B— Todd Helton, Colorado
2B— Jeff Kent, San Francisco
3B— Albert Pujols, St. Louis
SS— Rich Aurilia, San Francisco
OF— Barry Bonds, San Francisco
OF— Luis Gonzalez, Arizona
OF— Sammy Sosa, Chicago
C— Mike Piazza, New York
P— Mike Hampton, Colorado

BASEBALL WRITERS' ASSOCIATION OF AMERICA
MOST VALUABLE PLAYER

AMERICAN LEAGUE

Year	Player	Team	Pos.	Points
1931—Lefty Grove	Philadelphia	P	78
1932—Jimmie Foxx	Philadelphia	1B	75
1933—Jimmie Foxx	Philadelphia	1B	74
1934—Mickey Cochrane	Detroit	C	67
1935—Hank Greenberg	Detroit	1B	*80
1936—Lou Gehrig	New York	1B	73
1937—Charley Gehringer	Detroit	2B	78
1938—Jimmie Foxx	Boston	1B	305
1939—Joe DiMaggio	New York	OF	280
1940—Hank Greenberg	Detroit	OF	292
1941—Joe DiMaggio	New York	OF	291
1942—Joe Gordon	New York	2B	270
1943—Spud Chandler	New York	P	246
1944—Hal Newhouser	Detroit	P	236
1945—Hal Newhouser	Detroit	P	236
1946—Ted Williams	Boston	OF	224
1947—Joe DiMaggio	New York	OF	202
1948—Lou Boudreau	Cleveland	SS	324
1949—Ted Williams	Boston	OF	272
1950—Phil Rizzuto	New York	SS	284
1951—Yogi Berra	New York	C	184
1952—Bobby Shantz	Philadelphia	P	280
1953—Al Rosen	Cleveland	3B	*336
1954—Yogi Berra	New York	C	230
1955—Yogi Berra	New York	C	218
1956—Mickey Mantle	New York	OF	*336
1957—Mickey Mantle	New York	OF	233
1958—Jackie Jensen	Boston	OF	233
1959—Nellie Fox	Chicago	2B	295
1960—Roger Maris	New York	OF	225
1961—Roger Maris	New York	OF	202
1962—Mickey Mantle	New York	OF	234
1963—Elston Howard	New York	C	248
1964—Brooks Robinson	Baltimore	3B	269
1965—Zoilo Versalles	Minnesota	SS	275
1966—Frank Robinson	Baltimore	OF	*280
1967—Carl Yastrzemski	Boston	OF	275
1968—Denny McLain	Detroit	P	*280
1969—Harmon Killebrew	Minnesota	1B-3B	294
1970—Boog Powell	Baltimore	1B	234
1971—Vida Blue	Oakland	P	268
1972—Dick Allen	Chicago	1B	321
1973—Reggie Jackson	Oakland	OF	*336
1974—Jeff Burroughs	Texas	OF	248
1975—Fred Lynn	Boston	OF	326
1976—Thurman Munson	New York	C	304
1977—Rod Carew	Minnesota	1B	273
1978—Jim Rice	Boston	OF	352

NATIONAL LEAGUE

Year	Player	Team	Pos.	Points
1931—Frank Frisch	St. Louis	2B	65
1932—Chuck Klein	Philadelphia	OF	78
1933—Carl Hubbell	New York	P	77
1934—Dizzy Dean	St. Louis	P	78
1935—Gabby Hartnett	Chicago	C	75
1936—Carl Hubbell	New York	P	60
1937—Joe Medwick	St. Louis	OF	70
1938—Ernie Lombardi	Cincinnati	C	229
1939—Bucky Walters	Cincinnati	P	303
1940—Frank McCormick	Cincinnati	1B	274
1941—Dolf Camilli	Brooklyn	1B	300
1942—Mort Cooper	St. Louis	P	263
1943—Stan Musial	St. Louis	OF	267
1944—Marty Marion	St. Louis	SS	190
1945—Phil Cavarretta	Chicago	1B	279
1946—Stan Musial	St. Louis	1B	319
1947—Bob Elliott	Boston	3B	205
1948—Stan Musial	St. Louis	OF	303
1949—Jackie Robinson	Brooklyn	2B	264
1950—Jim Konstanty	Philadelphia	P	286
1951—Roy Campanella	Brooklyn	C	243
1952—Hank Sauer	Chicago	OF	226
1953—Roy Campanella	Brooklyn	C	297
1954—Willie Mays	New York	OF	283
1955—Roy Campanella	Brooklyn	C	226
1956—Don Newcombe	Brooklyn	P	223
1957—Hank Aaron	Milwaukee	OF	239
1958—Ernie Banks	Chicago	SS	283
1959—Ernie Banks	Chicago	SS	232½
1960—Dick Groat	Pittsburgh	SS	276
1961—Frank Robinson	Cincinnati	OF	219
1962—Maury Wills	Los Angeles	SS	209
1963—Sandy Koufax	Los Angeles	P	237
1964—Ken Boyer	St. Louis	3B	243
1965—Willie Mays	San Francisco	OF	224
1966—Roberto Clemente	Pittsburgh	OF	218
1967—Orlando Cepeda	St. Louis	1B	*280
1968—Bob Gibson	St. Louis	P	242
1969—Willie McCovey	San Francisco	1B	265
1970—Johnny Bench	Cincinnati	C	326
1971—Joe Torre	St. Louis	3B	318
1972—Johnny Bench	Cincinnati	C	263
1973—Pete Rose	Cincinnati	OF	274
1974—Steve Garvey	Los Angeles	1B	270
1975—Joe Morgan	Cincinnati	2B	321½
1976—Joe Morgan	Cincinnati	2B	311
1977—George Foster	Cincinnati	OF	291
1978—Dave Parker	Pittsburgh	OF	320

HISTORY *Award winners*

AMERICAN LEAGUE

Year	Player	Team	Pos.	Points
1979—Don Baylor	California	OF	347
1980—George Brett	Kansas City	3B	335
1981—Rollie Fingers	Milwaukee	P	319
1982—Robin Yount	Milwaukee	SS	385
1983—Cal Ripken Jr.	Baltimore	SS	322
1984—Willie Hernandez	Detroit	P	306
1985—Don Mattingly	New York	1B	367
1986—Roger Clemens	Boston	P	339
1987—George Bell	Toronto	OF	332
1988—Jose Canseco	Oakland	OF	*392
1989—Robin Yount	Milwaukee	OF	256
1990—Rickey Henderson	Oakland	OF	317
1991—Cal Ripken Jr.	Baltimore	SS	318
1992—Dennis Eckersley	Oakland	P	306
1993—Frank Thomas	Chicago	1B	*392
1994—Frank Thomas	Chicago	1B	372
1995—Mo Vaughn	Boston	1B	308
1996—Juan Gonzalez	Texas	OF	290
1997—Ken Griffey Jr.	Seattle	OF	*392
1998—Juan Gonzalez	Texas	OF	357
1999—Ivan Rodriguez	Texas	C	252
2000—Jason Giambi	Oakland	1B	317
2001—Ichiro Suzuki	Seattle	OF	289

NATIONAL LEAGUE

Year	Player	Team	Pos.	Points
1979—Willie Stargell	Pittsburgh	1B	216
Keith Hernandez	St. Louis	1B	216
1980—Mike Schmidt	Philadelphia	3B	*336
1981—Mike Schmidt	Philadelphia	3B	321
1982—Dale Murphy	Atlanta	OF	283
1983—Dale Murphy	Atlanta	OF	318
1984—Ryne Sandberg	Chicago	2B	326
1985—Willie McGee	St. Louis	OF	280
1986—Mike Schmidt	Philadelphia	3B	287
1987—Andre Dawson	Chicago	OF	269
1988—Kirk Gibson	Los Angeles	OF	272
1989—Kevin Mitchell	San Francisco	OF	314
1990—Barry Bonds	Pittsburgh	OF	331
1991—Terry Pendleton	Atlanta	3B	274
1992—Barry Bonds	Pittsburgh	OF	304
1993—Barry Bonds	San Francisco	OF	372
1994—Jeff Bagwell	Houston	1B	*392
1995—Barry Larkin	Cincinnati	SS	281
1996—Ken Caminiti	San Diego	3B	*392
1997—Larry Walker	Colorado	OF	359
1998—Sammy Sosa	Chicago	OF	438
1999—Chipper Jones	Atlanta	3B	432
2000—Jeff Kent	San Francisco	2B	392
2001—Barry Bonds	San Francisco	OF	438

*Unanimous selection.

CY YOUNG MEMORIAL AWARD

Year	Pitcher	Team	Votes
1956—Don Newcombe	Brooklyn	10
1957—Warren Spahn	Milwaukee	15
1958—Bob Turley	New York A.L.	5
1959—Early Wynn	Chicago A.L.	13
1960—Vernon Law	Pittsburgh	8
1961—Whitey Ford	New York A.L.	9
1962—Don Drysdale	Los Angeles N.L.	14
1963—Sandy Koufax	Los Angeles N.L.	*20
1964—Dean Chance	Los Angeles A.L.	17
1965—Sandy Koufax	Los Angeles N.L.	*20
1966—Sandy Koufax	Los Angeles N.L.	*20
1967—A.L.—Jim Lonborg	Boston	18
N.L.—Mike McCormick	San Francisco	18
1968—A.L.—Denny McLain	Detroit	*20
N.L.—Bob Gibson	St. Louis	*20
1969—A.L.—Denny McLain	Detroit	10
Mike Cuellar	Baltimore	10
N.L.—Tom Seaver	New York	23
1970—A.L.—Jim Perry	Minnesota	55
N.L.—Bob Gibson	St. Louis	118
1971—A.L.—Vida Blue	Oakland	98
N.L.—Fergie Jenkins	Chicago	97
1972—A.L.—Gaylord Perry	Cleveland	64
N.L.—Steve Carlton	Philadelphia	*120
1973—A.L.—Jim Palmer	Baltimore	88
N.L.—Tom Seaver	New York	71
1974—A.L.—Jim Hunter	Oakland	90
N.L.—Mike Marshall	Los Angeles	96
1975—A.L.—Jim Palmer	Baltimore	98
N.L.—Tom Seaver	New York	98
1976—A.L.—Jim Palmer	Baltimore	108
N.L.—Randy Jones	San Diego	96
1977—A.L.—Sparky Lyle	New York	56½
N.L.—Steve Carlton	Philadelphia	*104
1978—A.L.—Ron Guidry	New York	*140
N.L.—Gaylord Perry	San Diego	116
1979—A.L.—Mike Flanagan	Baltimore	136
N.L.—Bruce Sutter	Chicago	72
1980—A.L.—Steve Stone	Baltimore	100
N.L.—Steve Carlton	Philadelphia	118
1981—A.L.—Rollie Fingers	Milwaukee	126
N.L.—Fernando Valenzuela	Los Angeles	70

Year	Pitcher	Team	Votes
1982—A.L.—Pete Vuckovich	Milwaukee	87
N.L.—Steve Carlton	Philadelphia	112
1983—A.L.—LaMarr Hoyt	Chicago	116
N.L.—John Denny	Philadelphia	103
1984—A.L.—Willie Hernandez	Detroit	88
N.L.—Rick Sutcliffe	Chicago	*120
1985—A.L.—Bret Saberhagen	Kansas City	127
N.L.—Dwight Gooden	New York	*120
1986—A.L.—Roger Clemens	Boston	*140
N.L.—Mike Scott	Houston	98
1987—A.L.—Roger Clemens	Boston	124
N.L.—Steve Bedrosian	Philadelphia	57
1988—A.L.—Frank Viola	Minnesota	138
N.L.—Orel Hershiser	Los Angeles	*120
1989—A.L.—Bret Saberhagen	Kansas City	138
N.L.—Mark Davis	San Diego	107
1990—A.L.—Bob Welch	Oakland	107
N.L.—Doug Drabek	Pittsburgh	118
1991—A.L.—Roger Clemens	Boston	119
N.L.—Tom Glavine	Atlanta	110
1992—A.L.—Dennis Eckersley	Oakland	107
N.L.—Greg Maddux	Chicago	112
1993—A.L.—Jack McDowell	Chicago	124
N.L.—Greg Maddux	Atlanta	119
1994—A.L.—David Cone	Kansas City	108
N.L.—Greg Maddux	Atlanta	*140
1995—A.L.—Randy Johnson	Seattle	136
N.L.—Greg Maddux	Atlanta	*140
1996—A.L.—Pat Hentgen	Toronto	110
N.L.—John Smoltz	Atlanta	136
1997—A.L.—Roger Clemens	Toronto	134
N.L.—Pedro Martinez	Montreal	134
1998—A.L.—Roger Clemens	Toronto	*140
N.L.—Tom Glavine	Atlanta	99
1999—A.L.—Pedro Martinez	Boston	*140
N.L.—Randy Johnson	Arizona	134
2000—A.L.—Pedro Martinez	Boston	*140
N.L.—Randy Johnson	Arizona	133
2001—A.L.—Roger Clemens	New York	122
N.L.—Randy Johnson	Arizona	156

*Unanimous selection.

ROOKIE OF THE YEAR

1947—Combined selection—Jackie Robinson, Brooklyn N.L., 1B
1948—Combined selection—Alvin Dark, Boston N.L., SS

AMERICAN LEAGUE

Year	Player	Team	Pos.	Votes
1949	Roy Sievers	St. Louis	OF	10
1950	Walt Dropo	Boston	1B	15
1951	Gil McDougald	New York	3B	13
1952	Harry Byrd	Philadelphia	P	9
1953	Harvey Kuenn	Detroit	SS	23
1954	Bob Grim	New York	P	15
1955	Herb Score	Cleveland	P	18
1956	Luis Aparicio	Chicago	SS	22
1957	Tony Kubek	New York	IF-OF	23
1958	Albie Pearson	Washington	OF	14
1959	Bob Allison	Washington	OF	18
1960	Ron Hansen	Baltimore	SS	22
1961	Don Schwall	Boston	P	7
1962	Tom Tresh	New York	OF-SS	13
1963	Gary Peters	Chicago	P	10
1964	Tony Oliva	Minnesota	OF	19
1965	Curt Blefary	Baltimore	OF	12
1966	Tommie Agee	Chicago	OF	16
1967	Rod Carew	Minnesota	2B	19
1968	Stan Bahnsen	New York	P	17
1969	Lou Piniella	Kansas City	OF	9
1970	Thurman Munson	New York	C	23
1971	Chris Chambliss	Cleveland	1B	11
1972	Carlton Fisk	Boston	C	*24
1973	Al Bumbry	Baltimore	OF	13½
1974	Mike Hargrove	Texas	1B	16½
1975	Fred Lynn	Boston	OF	23
1976	Mark Fidrych	Detroit	P	22
1977	Eddie Murray	Baltimore	DH-1B	12½
1978	Lou Whitaker	Detroit	2B	21
1979	John Castino	Minnesota	3B	7
	Alfredo Griffin	Toronto	SS	7
1980	Joe Charboneau	Cleveland	OF	103
1981	Dave Righetti	New York	P	127
1982	Cal Ripken	Baltimore	SS-3B	132
1983	Ron Kittle	Chicago	OF	104
1984	Alvin Davis	Seattle	1B	134
1985	Ozzie Guillen	Chicago	SS	101
1986	Jose Canseco	Oakland	OF	110
1987	Mark McGwire	Oakland	1B	*140
1988	Walt Weiss	Oakland	SS	103
1989	Gregg Olson	Baltimore	P	136
1990	Sandy Alomar Jr.	Cleveland	C	*140
1991	Chuck Knoblauch	Minnesota	2B	136
1992	Pat Listach	Milwaukee	SS	122
1993	Tim Salmon	California	OF	*140
1994	Bob Hamelin	Kansas City	DH	134
1995	Marty Cordova	Minnesota	3B	105
1996	Derek Jeter	New York	SS	*140
1997	Nomar Garciaparra	Boston	SS	*140
1998	Ben Grieve	Oakland	OF	130
1999	Carlos Beltran	Kansas City	OF	133
2000	Kazuhiro Sasaki	Seattle	P	104
2001	Ichiro Suzuki	Seattle	OF	138

NATIONAL LEAGUE

Year	Player	Team	Pos.	Votes
1949	Don Newcombe	Brooklyn	P	21
1950	Sam Jethroe	Boston	OF	11
1951	Willie Mays	New York	OF	18
1952	Joe Black	Brooklyn	P	19
1953	Jim Gilliam	Brooklyn	2B	11
1954	Wally Moon	St. Louis	OF	17
1955	Bill Virdon	St. Louis	OF	15
1956	Frank Robinson	Cincinnati	OF	*24
1957	Jack Sanford	Philadelphia	P	16
1958	Orlando Cepeda	San Francisco	1B	*†21
1959	Willie McCovey	San Francisco	1B	*24
1960	Frank Howard	Los Angeles	OF	12
1961	Billy Williams	Chicago	OF	10
1962	Ken Hubbs	Chicago	2B	19
1963	Pete Rose	Cincinnati	2B	17
1964	Dick Allen	Philadelphia	3B	18
1965	Jim Lefebvre	Los Angeles	2B	13
1966	Tommy Helms	Cincinnati	3B	12
1967	Tom Seaver	New York	P	11
1968	Johnny Bench	Cincinnati	C	10½
1969	Ted Sizemore	Los Angeles	2B	14
1970	Carl Morton	Montreal	P	11
1971	Earl Williams	Atlanta	C	18
1972	Jon Matlack	New York	P	19
1973	Gary Matthews	San Francisco	OF	11
1974	Bake McBride	St. Louis	OF	16
1975	John Montefusco	San Francisco	P	12
1976	Butch Metzger	San Diego	P	11
	Pat Zachry	Cincinnati	P	11
1977	Andre Dawson	Montreal	OF	10
1978	Bob Horner	Atlanta	3B	12½
1979	Rick Sutcliffe	Los Angeles	P	20
1980	Steve Howe	Los Angeles	P	80
1981	Fernando Valenzuela	Los Angeles	P	107
1982	Steve Sax	Los Angeles	2B	63
1983	Darryl Strawberry	New York	OF	109
1984	Dwight Gooden	New York	P	118
1985	Vince Coleman	St. Louis	OF	*120
1986	Todd Worrell	St. Louis	P	118
1987	Benito Santiago	San Diego	C	*120
1988	Chris Sabo	Cincinnati	3B	79
1989	Jerome Walton	Chicago	OF	116
1990	Dave Justice	Atlanta	OF	118
1991	Jeff Bagwell	Houston	1B	118
1992	Eric Karros	Los Angeles	1B	116
1993	Mike Piazza	Los Angeles	C	*140
1994	Raul Mondesi	Los Angeles	OF	*140
1995	Hideo Nomo	Los Angeles	P	118
1996	Todd Hollandsworth	Los Angeles	OF	105
1997	Scott Rolen	Philadelphia	3B	*140
1998	Kerry Wood	Chicago	P	128
1999	Scott Williamson	Cincinnati	P	118
2000	Rafael Furcal	Atlanta	SS-2B	144
2001	Albert Pujols	St. Louis	OF-3B-1B	*160

*Unanimous selection. †Three writers did not vote.

MANAGER OF THE YEAR

AMERICAN LEAGUE

Year	Manager	Team	Points
1983	Tony La Russa	Chicago	17
1984	Sparky Anderson	Detroit	96
1985	Bobby Cox	Toronto	104
1986	John McNamara	Boston	95
1987	Sparky Anderson	Detroit	90
1988	Tony La Russa	Oakland	103
1989	Frank Robinson	Baltimore	125
1990	Jeff Torborg	Chicago	128

NATIONAL LEAGUE

Year	Manager	Team	Points
1983	Tommy Lasorda	Los Angeles	10
1984	Jim Frey	Chicago	101
1985	Whitey Herzog	St. Louis	86
1986	Hal Lanier	Houston	108
1987	Buck Rodgers	Montreal	92
1988	Tommy Lasorda	Los Angeles	101
1989	Don Zimmer	Chicago	118
1990	Jim Leyland	Pittsburgh	99

AMERICAN LEAGUE

Year	Manager	Team	Points
1991—Tom Kelly	Minnesota	138
1992—Tony La Russa	Oakland	132
1993—Gene Lamont	Chicago	72
1994—Buck Showalter	New York	132
1995—Lou Piniella	Seattle	86
1996—Johnny Oates	Texas	89
Joe Torre	New York	89
1997—Dave Johnson	Baltimore	88
1998—Joe Torre	New York	128
1999—Jimy Williams	Boston	115
2000—Jerry Manuel	Chicago	143
2001—Lou Piniella	Seattle	128

NATIONAL LEAGUE

Year	Manager	Team	Points
1991— Bobby Cox	Atlanta	96
1992— Jim Leyland	Pittsburgh	109
1993— Dusty Baker	San Francisco	105
1994— Felipe Alou	Montreal	138
1995— Don Baylor	Colorado	122
1996— Bruce Bochy	San Diego	76
1997— Dusty Baker	San Francisco	110
1998— Larry Dierker	Houston	102
1999— Jack McKeon	Cincinnati	115
2000— Dusty Baker	San Francisco	154
2001— Larry Bowa	Philadelphia	113

EARLY MOST VALUABLE PLAYER AWARDS
CHALMERS AWARD

AMERICAN LEAGUE

Year	Player	Team	Pos.	Points
1911—Ty Cobb	Detroit	OF	64
1912—Tris Speaker	Boston	OF	59
1913—Walter Johnson	Washington	P	54
1914—Eddie Collins	Philadelphia	2B	63

NATIONAL LEAGUE

Year	Player	Team	Pos.	Points
1911—Frank Schulte	Chicago	OF	29
1912—Larry Doyle	New York	2B	48
1913—Jake Daubert	Brooklyn	1B	50
1914—Johnny Evers	Boston	2B	50

LEAGUE AWARDS

AMERICAN LEAGUE

Year	Player	Team	Pos.	Points
1922—George Sisler	St. Louis	1B	59
1923—Babe Ruth	New York	OF	64
1924—Walter Johnson	Washington	P	55
1925—Roger Peckinpaugh	Washington	SS	45
1926—George Burns	Cleveland	1B	63
1927—Lou Gehrig	New York	1B	56
1928—Mickey Cochrane	Philadelphia	C	53
1929—No selection			

NATIONAL LEAGUE

Year	Player	Team	Pos.	Points
1922—No selection			
1923—No selection			
1924—Dazzy Vance	Brooklyn	P	74
1925—Rogers Hornsby	St. Louis	2B	73
1926—Bob O'Farrell	St. Louis	C	79
1927—Paul Waner	Pittsburgh	OF	72
1928—Jim Bottomley	St. Louis	1B	76
1929—Rogers Hornsby	Chicago	2B	60

HALL OF FAME

Name	Des.*	Elec. year	Votes rec.†	Votes cast‡	% of vote	Teams as player
Aaron, Hank	P	1982	406	415	97.8	Milwaukee NL, Atlanta NL, Milwaukee AL
Alexander, Grover C.	P	1938	212	262	80.9	Philadelphia NL, Chicago NL, St. Louis NL
Alston, Walter	M	1983	CV	—	—	St. Louis NL
Anderson, Sparky	M	2000	CV	—	—	Philadelphia NL
Anson, Cap	P	1939	C1	—	—	Chicago NL
Aparicio, Luis	P	1984	341	403	84.6	Chicago AL, Baltimore AL, Boston AL
Appling, Luke	P	1964	189	225	84.0	Chicago AL
Ashburn, Richie	P	1995	CV	—	—	Philadelphia NL, Chicago NL, New York NL
Averill, Earl	P	1975	CV	—	—	Cleveland AL, Detroit AL, Boston AL
Baker, Home Run	P	1955	CV	—	—	Philadelphia AL, New York AL
Bancroft, Dave	P	1971	CV	—	—	Philadelphia NL, New York NL, Boston NL, Brooklyn NL
Banks, Ernie	P	1977	321	383	83.8	Chicago NL
Barlick, Al	U	1989	CV	—	—	
Barrow, Ed	E	1953	CV	—	—	
Beckley, Jake	P	1971	CV	—	—	Pittsburgh NL, Pittsburgh PL, New York NL, Cincinnati NL, St. Louis NL
Bell, Cool Papa	P	1974	SCNL	—	—	Negro Leagues
Bench, Johnny	P	1989	431	447	96.4	Cincinnati NL
Bender, Chief	P	1953	CV	—	—	Philadelphia AL, Philadelphia NL, Chicago AL
Berra, Yogi	P	1972	339	396	85.6	New York AL, New York NL
Bottomley, Jim	P	1974	CV	—	—	St. Louis NL, Cincinnati NL, St. Louis AL
Boudreau, Lou	P	1970	232	300	77.3	Cleveland AL, Boston AL
Bresnahan, Roger	P	1945	C2	—	—	Washington NL, Chicago NL, Baltimore AL, New York NL, St. Louis NL
Brett, George	P	1999	488	497	98.2	Kansas City AL
Brock, Lou	P	1985	315	395	79.7	Chicago NL, St. Louis NL
Brouthers, Dan	P	1945	C2	—	—	Troy NL, Buffalo NL, Detroit NL, Boston NL, Boston PL, Boston AA, Brooklyn NL, Baltimore NL, Louisville NL, Philadelphia NL, New York NL
Brown, Three Finger	P	1949	C2	—	—	St. Louis NL, Chicago NL, Cincinnati NL
Bulkeley, Morgan	E	1937	CC	—	—	
Bunning, Jim	P	1996	CV	—	—	Detroit AL, Philadelphia NL, Pittsburgh NL, Los Angeles NL
Burkett, Jesse	P	1946	C2	—	—	New York NL, Cleveland NL, St. Louis NL, St. Louis AL, Boston AL
Campanella, Roy	P	1969	270	340	79.4	Brooklyn NL
Carew, Rod	P	1991	401	443	90.5	Minnesota AL, California AL
Carey, Max	P	1961	CV	—	—	Pittsburgh NL, Brooklyn NL
Carlton, Steve	P	1994	436	455	95.8	St. Louis NL, Philadelphia NL, San Francisco NL, Chicago AL, Cleveland AL, Minnesota AL
Cartwright, Alexander	O	1938	CC	—	—	
Cepeda, Orlando	P	1999	CV	—	—	San Francisco NL, St. Louis NL, Atlanta NL, Oakland AL, Boston AL, Kansas City AL
Chadwick, Henry	O	1938	CC	—	—	
Chance, Frank	P	1946	C2	—	—	Chicago NL, New York AL
Chandler, Happy	E	1982	CV	—	—	
Charleston, Oscar	P	1976	SCNL	—	—	Negro Leagues
Chesbro, Jack	P	1946	C2	—	—	Pittsburgh NL, New York AL, Boston AL
Chylak, Nestor	U	1999	CV	—	—	
Clarke, Fred	P	1945	C2	—	—	Louisville NL, Pittsburgh NL
Clarkson, John	P	1963	CV	—	—	Worcester NL, Chicago NL, Boston NL, Cleveland NL
Clemente, Roberto	P	1973	393	424	92.7	Pittsburgh NL
Cobb, Ty	P	1936	222	226	98.2	Detroit AL, Philadelphia AL
Cochrane, Mickey	P	1947	128	161	79.5	Philadelphia AL, Detroit AL
Collins, Eddie	P	1939	213	274	77.7	Philadelphia AL, Chicago AL
Collins, Jimmy	P	1945	C2	—	—	Boston NL, Louisville NL, Boston AL, Philadelphia AL
Combs, Earle	P	1970	CV	—	—	New York AL
Comiskey, Charley	F/P	1939	C1	—	—	St. Louis AA, Chicago PL, Cincinnati NL
Conlan, Jocko	U	1974	CV	—	—	Chicago AL
Connolly, Tommy	U	1953	CV	—	—	
Connor, Roger	P	1976	CV	—	—	Troy NL, New York NL, New York PL, Philadelphia NL, St. Louis NL
Coveleski, Stan	P	1969	CV	—	—	Philadelphia AL, Cleveland AL, Washington AL, New York AL
Crawford, Sam	P	1957	CV	—	—	Cincinnati NL, Detroit AL
Cronin, Joe	P	1956	152	193	78.8	Pittsburgh NL, Washington AL, Boston AL
Cummings, Candy	P	1939	C1	—	—	Hartford NL, Cincinnati NL
Cuyler, Kiki	P	1968	CV	—	—	Pittsburgh NL, Chicago NL, Cincinnati NL, Brooklyn NL

Name	Des.*	Elec. year	Votes rec.†	Votes cast‡	% of vote	Teams as player
Dandridge, Ray	P	1987	CV	—	—	Negro Leagues
Davis, George S.	P	1998	CV	—	—	Cleveland NL, New York NL, Chicago AL
Day, Leon	P	1995	CV	—	—	Negro Leagues
Dean, Dizzy	P	1953	209	264	79.2	St. Louis NL, Chicago NL, St. Louis AL
Delahanty, Ed	P	1945	C2	—	—	Philadelphia NL, Cleveland PL, Washington AL
Dickey, Bill	P	1954	202	252	80.2	New York AL
Dihigo, Martin	P	1977	SCNL	—	—	Negro Leagues
DiMaggio, Joe	P	1955	223	251	88.8	New York AL
Doby, Larry	P	1998	CV	—	—	Cleveland AL, Chicago AL, Detroit AL
Doerr, Bobby	P	1986	CV	—	—	Boston AL
Drysdale, Don	P	1984	316	403	78.4	Brooklyn NL, Los Angeles NL
Duffy, Hugh	P	1945	C2	—	—	Chicago NL, Chicago PL, Boston AA, Boston NL, Milwaukee AL, Philadelphia NL
Durocher, Leo	M	1994	CV	—	—	New York AL, Cincinnati NL, St. Louis NL, Brooklyn NL
Evans, Billy	U	1973	CV	—	—	
Evers, Johnny	P	1946	C2	—	—	Chicago NL, Boston NL, Philadelphia NL, Chicago AL
Ewing, Buck	P	1939	C1	—	—	Troy NL, New York NL, New York PL, Cleveland NL, Cincinnati NL
Faber, Red	P	1964	CV	—	—	Chicago AL
Feller, Bob	P	1962	150	160	93.8	Cleveland AL
Ferrell, Rick	P	1984	CV	—	—	St. Louis AL, Boston AL, Washington AL
Fingers, Rollie	P	1992	349	430	81.2	Oakland AL, San Diego NL, Milwaukee AL
Fisk, Carlton	P	2000	397	499	79.6	Boston AL, Chicago AL
Flick, Elmer	P	1963	CV	—	—	Philadelphia NL, Philadelphia AL, Cleveland AL
Ford, Whitey	P	1974	284	365	77.8	New York AL
Foster, Bill	P	1996	CV	—	—	Negro Leagues
Foster, Rube	P	1981	CV	—	—	Negro Leagues
Fox, Nellie	P	1997	CV	—	—	Philadelphia AL, Chicago AL, Houston NL
Foxx, Jimmie	P	1951	179	226	79.2	Philadelphia AL, Boston AL, Chicago NL, Philadelphia NL
Frick, Ford	E	1970	CV	—	—	
Frisch, Frank	P	1947	136	161	84.5	New York NL, St. Louis NL
Galvin, Pud	P	1965	CV	—	—	Buffalo NL, Pittsburgh AA, Pittsburgh NL, Pittsburgh PL, St. Louis NL
Gehrig, Lou	P	1939	SE	—	—	New York AL
Gehringer, Charley	P	1949	159	187	85.0	Detroit AL
Gibson, Bob	P	1981	337	401	84.0	St. Louis NL
Gibson, Josh	P	1972	SCNL	—	—	Negro Leagues
Giles, Warren	E	1979	CV	—	—	
Gomez, Lefty	P	1972	CV	—	—	New York AL, Washington AL
Goslin, Goose	P	1968	CV	—	—	Washington AL, St. Louis AL, Detroit AL
Greenberg, Hank	P	1956	164	193	85.0	Detroit AL, Pittsburgh NL
Griffith, Clark	M	1946	C2	—	—	St. Louis AA, Boston AA, Chicago NL, Chicago AL, New York AL, Cincinnati NL, Washington AL
Grimes, Burleigh	P	1964	CV	—	—	Pittsburgh NL, Brooklyn NL, New York NL, Boston NL, St. Louis NL, Chicago NL, New York AL
Grove, Lefty	P	1947	123	161	76.4	Philadelphia AL, Boston AL
Hafey, Chick	P	1971	CV	—	—	St. Louis NL, Cincinnati NL
Haines, Jesse	P	1970	CV	—	—	Cincinnati NL, St. Louis NL
Hamilton, Billy	P	1961	CV	—	—	Kansas City AA, Philadelphia NL, Boston NL
Hanlon, Ned	M	1996	CV	—	—	Cleveland NL, Detroit NL, Pittsburgh NL, Pittsburgh PL, Baltimore NL
Harridge, Will	E	1972	CV	—	—	
Harris, Bucky	M	1975	CV	—	—	Washington AL, Detroit AL
Hartnett, Gabby	P	1955	195	251	77.7	Chicago NL, New York NL
Heilmann, Harry	P	1952	203	234	86.8	Detroit AL, Cincinnati NL
Herman, Billy	P	1975	CV	—	—	Chicago NL, Brooklyn NL, Boston NL, Pittsburgh NL
Hooper, Harry	P	1971	CV	—	—	Boston AL, Chicago AL
Hornsby, Rogers	P	1942	182	233	78.1	St. Louis NL, New York NL, Boston NL, Chicago NL, St. Louis AL
Hoyt, Waite	P	1969	CV	—	—	New York NL, Boston AL, New York AL, Detroit AL, Philadelphia AL, Brooklyn NL, Pittsburgh NL
Hubbard, Cal	U	1976	CV	—	—	
Hubbell, Carl	P	1947	140	161	87.0	New York NL
Huggins, Miller	M	1964	CV	—	—	Cincinnati NL, St. Louis NL
Hulbert, William	F	1995	CV	—	—	
Hunter, Catfish	P	1987	315	413	76.3	Kansas City AL, Oakland AL, New York AL
Irvin, Monte	P	1973	SCNL	—	—	New York NL, Chicago NL, Negro Leagues
Jackson, Reggie	P	1993	396	423	93.6	Kansas City AL, Oakland AL, Baltimore AL, New York AL, California AL
Jackson, Travis	P	1982	CV	—	—	New York NL
Jenkins, Ferguson	P	1991	334	443	75.4	Philadelphia NL, Chicago NL, Texas AL, Boston AL
Jennings, Hugh	P	1945	C2	—	—	Louisville AA, Louisville NL, Baltimore NL, Brooklyn NL, Philadelphia NL, Detroit AL
Johnson, Ban	E	1937	CC	—	—	

Name	Des.*	Elec. year	Votes rec.†	Votes cast‡	% of vote	Teams as player
Johnson, Judy	P	1975	SCNL	—	—	Negro Leagues
Johnson, Walter	P	1936	189	226	83.6	Washington AL
Joss, Addie	P	1978	CV	—	—	Cleveland AL
Kaline, Al	P	1980	340	385	88.3	Detroit AL
Keefe, Tim	P	1964	CV	—	—	Troy NL, New York AA, New York NL, New York PL, Philadelphia NL
Keeler, Willie	P	1939	207	274	75.5	New York NL, Brooklyn, NL, Baltimore NL, New York AL
Kell, George	P	1983	CV	—	—	Philadelphia AL, Detroit AL, Boston AL, Chicago AL, Baltimore AL
Kelley, Joe	P	1971	CV	—	—	Boston NL, Pittsburgh NL, Baltimore NL, Brooklyn NL, Baltimore AL, Cincinnati NL
Kelly, George	P	1973	CV	—	—	New York NL, Pittsburgh NL, Cincinnati NL, Chicago NL, Brooklyn NL
Kelly, Mike	P	1945	C2	—	—	Cincinnati NL, Chicago NL, Boston NL, Boston PL, Cincinnati AA, Boston AA, New York NL
Killebrew, Harmon	P	1984	335	403	83.1	Washington AL, Minnesota AL, Kansas City AL
Kiner, Ralph	P	1975	273	362	75.4	Pittsburgh NL, Chicago NL, Cleveland AL
Klein, Chuck	P	1980	CV	—	—	Philadelphia NL, Chicago NL, Pittsburgh NL
Klem, Bill	U	1953	CV	—	—	
Koufax, Sandy	P	1972	344	396	86.9	Brooklyn NL, Los Angeles NL
Lajoie, Nap	P	1937	168	201	83.6	Philadelphia NL, Philadelphia AL, Cleveland AL
Landis, Kenesaw M.	E	1944	C2	—	—	
Lasorda, Tom	M	1997	CV	—	—	Brooklyn NL, Kansas City AL
Lazzeri, Tony	P	1991	CV	—	—	New York AL, Chicago NL, Brooklyn NL, New York NL
Lemon, Bob	P	1976	305	388	78.6	Cleveland AL
Leonard, Buck	P	1972	SCNL	—	—	Negro Leagues
Lindstrom, Fred	P	1976	CV	—	—	New York NL, Pittsburgh NL, Chicago NL, Brooklyn NL
Lloyd, John Henry	P	1977	SCNL	—	—	Negro Leagues
Lombardi, Ernie	P	1986	CV	—	—	Brooklyn NL, Cincinnati NL, Boston NL, New York NL
Lopez, Al	M	1977	CV	—	—	Brooklyn NL, Boston NL, Pittsburgh NL, Cleveland AL
Lyons, Ted	P	1955	217	251	86.5	Chicago AL
Mack, Connie	M	1937	CC	—	—	Washington NL, Buffalo PL, Pittsburgh NL
MacPhail, Larry	E	1978	CV	—	—	
MacPhail, Lee	E	1998	CV	—	—	
Mantle, Mickey	P	1974	322	365	88.2	New York AL
Manush, Heinie	P	1964	CV	—	—	Detroit AL, St. Louis AL, Washington AL, Boston AL, Brooklyn NL, Pittsburgh NL
Maranville, Rabbit	P	1954	209	252	82.9	Boston NL, Pittsburgh NL, Chicago NL, Brooklyn NL, St. Louis NL
Marichal, Juan	P	1983	313	374	83.7	San Francisco NL, Boston AL, Los Angeles NL
Marquard, Rube	P	1971	CV	—	—	New York NL, Brooklyn NL, Cincinnati NL, Boston NL
Mathews, Eddie	P	1978	301	379	79.4	Boston NL, Milwaukee NL, Atlanta NL, Houston NL, Detroit AL
Mathewson, Christy	P	1936	205	226	90.7	New York NL, Cincinnati NL
Mays, Willie	P	1979	409	432	94.7	New York (Giants)NL, San Francisco NL, New York (Mets)NL
Mazeroski, Bill	P	2001	CV		—	Pittsburgh NL
McCarthy, Joe	M	1957	CV	—	—	
McCarthy, Tommy	P	1946	C2	—	—	Boston UA, Boston NL, Philadelphia NL, St. Louis AA, Brooklyn NL
McCovey, Willie	P	1986	346	425	81.4	San Francisco NL, San Diego NL, Oakland AL
McGinnity, Joe	P	1946	C2	—	—	Baltimore NL, Brooklyn NL, Baltimore AL, New York NL
McGowan, Bill	U	1992	CV	—	—	
McGraw, John	M	1937	CC	—	—	Baltimore AA, Baltimore NL, St. Louis NL, Baltimore AL, New York NL
McKechnie, Bill	M	1962	CV	—	—	Pittsburgh NL, Boston NL, New York AL, New York NL, Cincinnati
McPhee, Bid	P	2000	CV	—	—	Cincinnati AA, Cincinnati NL
Medwick, Joe	P	1968	240	283	84.8	St. Louis NL, Brooklyn NL, New York NL, Boston NL
Mize, Johnny	P	1981	CV	—	—	St. Louis NL, New York NL, New York AL
Morgan, Joe	P	1990	363	444	81.8	Houston NL, Cincinnati NL, San Francisco NL, Philadelphia NL, Oakland AL
Musial, Stan	P	1969	317	340	93.2	St. Louis NL
Newhouser, Hal	P	1992	CV	—	—	Detroit AL, Cleveland AL
Nichols, Kid	P	1949	C2	—	—	Boston NL, St. Louis NL, Philadelphia NL
Niekro, Phil	P	1997	380	473	80.3	Milwaukee NL, Atlanta NL, New York AL, Cleveland AL, Toronto AL
O'Rourke, Jim	P	1945	C2	—	—	Boston NL, Providence NL, Buffalo NL, New York NL, Washington NL, New York PL
Ott, Mel	P	1951	197	226	87.2	New York NL
Paige, Satchel	P	1971	SCNL	—	—	Cleveland AL, St. Louis AL, Kansas City AL, Negro Leagues
Palmer, Jim	P	1990	411	444	92.6	Baltimore AL

Name	Des.*	Elec. year	Votes rec.†	Votes cast‡	% of vote	Teams as player
Pennock, Herb	P	1948	94	121	77.7	Philadelphia AL, Boston AL, New York AL
Perez, Tony	P	2000	385	499	77.2	Cincinnati NL, Montreal NL, Boston AL, Philadelphia NL
Perry, Gaylord	P	1991	342	443	77.2	San Francisco NL, Cleveland AL, Texas AL, San Diego NL, New York AL, Atlanta NL, Seattle AL, Kansas City AL
Plank, Eddie	P	1946	C2	—	—	Philadelphia AL, St. Louis AL
Puckett, Kirby	P	2001	423	515	82.1	Minnesota AL
Radbourn, Hoss	P	1939	C1	—	—	Buffalo NL, Providence NL, Boston NL, Boston PL, Cincinnati NL
Reese, Pee Wee	P	1984	CV	—	—	Brooklyn NL, Los Angeles NL
Rice, Sam	P	1963	CV	—	—	Washington AL, Cleveland AL
Rickey, Branch	E	1967	CV	—	—	St. Louis AL, New York AL
Rixey, Eppa	P	1963	CV	—	—	Philadelphia NL, Cincinnati NL
Rizzuto, Phil	P	1994	CV	—	—	New York AL
Roberts, Robin	P	1976	337	388	86.9	Philadelphia NL, Baltimore AL, Houston NL, Chicago NL
Robinson, Brooks	P	1983	344	374	92.0	Baltimore AL
Robinson, Frank	P	1982	370	415	89.2	Cincinnati NL, Baltimore AL, Los Angeles NL, California AL, Cleveland AL
Robinson, Jackie	P	1962	124	160	77.5	Brooklyn NL
Robinson, Wilbert	M	1945	C2	—	—	Philadelphia AA, Baltimore AA, Baltimore NL, St. Louis NL, Baltimore AL
Rogan, Bullet Joe	P	1998	CV	—	—	
Roush, Edd	P	1962	CV	—	—	Chicago AL, New York NL, Cincinnati NL
Ruffing, Red	P	1967	266	306	86.9	Boston AL, New York AL, Chicago AL
Rusie, Amos	P	1977	CV	—	—	Indianapolis NL, New York NL, Cincinnati NL
Ruth, Babe	P	1936	215	226	95.1	Boston AL, New York AL, Boston NL
Ryan, Nolan	P	1999	491	497	98.8	New York NL, California AL, Houston NL, Texas AL
Schalk, Ray	P	1955	CV	—	—	Chicago AL, New York NL
Schmidt, Mike	P	1995	444	460	96.5	Philadelphia NL
Schoendienst, Red	P	1989	CV	—	—	St. Louis NL, New York (Giants) NL, Milwaukee NL
Seaver, Tom	P	1992	425	430	98.8	New York NL, Cincinnati NL, Chicago AL, Boston AL
Selee, Frank	M	1999	CV	—	—	
Sewell, Joe	P	1977	CV	—	—	Cleveland AL, New York AL
Simmons, Al	P	1953	199	264	75.4	Philadelphia AL, Chicago AL, Detroit AL, Washington AL, Boston NL, Cincinnati NL, Boston AL
Sisler, George	P	1939	235	274	85.8	St. Louis AL, Washington AL, Boston NL
Slaughter, Enos	P	1985	CV	—	—	St. Louis NL, New York AL, Kansas City AL, Milwaukee NL
Smith, Hilton	P	2001	CV	—	—	Negro Leagues
Smith, Ozzie	P	2002	433	472	91.7	San Diego NL, St. Louis NL
Snider, Duke	P	1980	333	385	86.5	Brooklyn NL, Los Angeles NL, New York NL, San Francisco NL
Spahn, Warren	P	1973	316	380	83.2	Boston NL, Milwaukee NL, New York NL, San Francisco NL
Spalding, Al	P	1939	C1	—	—	Chicago NL
Speaker, Tris	P	1937	165	201	82.1	Boston AL, Cleveland AL, Washington AL, Philadelphia AL
Stargell, Willie	P	1988	352	427	82.4	Pittsburgh NL
Stearnes, Turkey	P	2000	CV	—	—	Negro Leagues
Stengel, Casey	M	1966	CV	—	—	Brooklyn NL, Pittsburgh NL, Philadelphia NL, New York NL, Boston NL
Sutton, Don	P	1998	386	473	81.6	Los Angeles NL, Houston NL, Milwaukee AL, Oakland AL, California AL
Terry, Bill	P	1954	195	252	77.4	New York NL
Thompson, Sam	P	1974	CV	—	—	Detroit NL, Philadelphia NL, Detroit AL
Tinker, Joe	P	1946	C2	—	—	Chicago NL, Cincinnati NL
Traynor, Pie	P	1948	93	121	76.9	Pittsburgh NL
Vance, Dazzy	P	1955	205	251	81.7	Pittsburgh NL, New York AL, Brooklyn NL, St. Louis NL, Cincinnati NL
Vaughan, Arky	P	1985	CV	—	—	Pittsburgh NL, Brooklyn NL
Veeck, Bill	E	1991	CV	—	—	
Waddell, Rube	P	1946	C2	—	—	Louisville NL, Pittsburgh NL, Chicago NL, Philadelphia AL, St. Louis AL
Wagner, Honus	P	1936	215	226	95.1	Louisville NL, Pittsburgh NL
Wallace, Bobby	P	1953	CV	—	—	Cleveland NL, St. Louis NL, St. Louis AL
Walsh, Ed	P	1946	C2	—	—	Chicago AL, Boston NL
Waner, Lloyd	P	1967	CV	—	—	Pittsburgh NL, Boston NL, Cincinnati NL, Philadelphia NL, Brooklyn NL
Waner, Paul	P	1952	195	234	83.3	Pittsburgh NL, Brooklyn NL, Boston NL, New York AL
Ward, John Montgomery	P	1964	CV	—	—	Providence NL, New York NL, Brooklyn PL, Brooklyn NL
Weaver, Earl	M	1996	CV	—	—	

Name	Des.*	Elec. year	Votes rec.†	Votes cast‡	% of vote	Teams as player
Weiss, George	E	1971	CV	—	—	
Welch, Mickey	P	1973	CV	—	—	Troy NL, New York NL
Wells, Willie	P	1997	CV	—	—	
Wheat, Zack	P	1959	CV	—	—	Brooklyn NL, Philadelphia AL
Wilhelm, Hoyt	P	1985	331	395	83.8	New York NL, St. Louis NL, Cleveland AL, Baltimore AL, Chicago AL California AL, Atlanta NL, Chicago NL, Los Angeles NL
Williams, Billy	P	1987	354	413	85.7	Chicago NL, Oakland AL
Williams, Smokey Joe	P	1999	CV	—	—	Negro Leagues
Williams, Ted	P	1966	282	302	93.4	Boston AL
Willis, Vic	P	1995	CV	—	—	Boston NL, Pittsburgh NL, St. Louis NL
Wilson, Hack	P	1979	CV	—	—	New York NL, Chicago NL, Brooklyn NL, Philadelphia NL
Winfield, Dave	P	2001	435	515	84.5	San Diego NL, New York AL, California AL, Toronto AL, Minnesota AL, Cleveland AL
Wright, George	P	1937	CC	—	—	Boston NL, Providence NL
Wright, Harry	M	1953	CV	—	—	Boston NL
Wynn, Early	P	1972	301	396	76.0	Washington AL, Cleveland AL, Chicago AL
Yastrzemski, Carl	P	1989	423	447	94.6	Boston AL
Yawkey, Tom	E	1980	CV	—	—	
Young, Cy	P	1937	153	201	76.1	Cleveland NL, St. Louis NL, Boston AL, Cleveland AL, Boston NL
Youngs, Ross	P	1972	CV	—	—	New York NL
Yount, Robin	P	1999	385	497	77.5	Milwaukee AL

*Designation for which he was honored. Abbreviations: E—executive; F—founder; M—manager; O—organizer; P—player; U—umpire.

†Where an abbreviation is listed rather than a vote total, the enshrinee was selected by one of the following groups: Centennial Commission (CC), committee of old-time players and writers (C1), committee on old-timers (C2), Committee on Veterans (CV), special election by Baseball Writers' Association of America (SE) or Special Committee on Negro Leagues (SCNL).

‡Votes cast by eligible members of the Baseball Writers' Association of America.

League abbreviations: AA—American Association; AL—American League; NL—National League; PL—Players League; UA—Union Association.

TEAM BY TEAM
AMERICAN LEAGUE

ANAHEIM ANGELS
YEARLY FINISHES

(Known as Los Angeles Angels through September 1, 1965 and California Angels through 1996)

Year	Position	W	L	Pct.	*GB	Manager	Attendance
1961	8th	70	91	.435	38.5	Bill Rigney	603,510
1962	3rd	86	76	.531	10.0	Bill Rigney	1,144,063
1963	9th	70	91	.435	34.0	Bill Rigney	821,015
1964	5th	82	80	.506	17.0	Bill Rigney	760,439
1965	7th	75	87	.463	27.0	Bill Rigney	566,727
1966	6th	80	82	.494	18.0	Bill Rigney	1,400,321
1967	5th	84	77	.522	7.5	Bill Rigney	1,317,713
1968	8th	67	95	.414	36.0	Bill Rigney	1,025,956

WEST DIVISION

Year	Position	W	L	Pct.	*GB	Manager	Attendance
1969	3rd	71	91	.438	26.0	Bill Rigney, Lefty Phillips	758,388
1970	3rd	86	76	.531	12.0	Lefty Phillips	1,077,741
1971	4th	76	86	.469	25.5	Lefty Phillips	926,373
1972	5th	75	80	.484	18.0	Del Rice	744,190
1973	4th	79	83	.488	15.0	Bobby Winkles	1,058,206
1974	6th	68	94	.420	22.0	Bobby Winkles, Dick Williams	917,269
1975	6th	72	89	.447	25.5	Dick Williams	1,058,163
1976	4th (tied)	76	86	.469	14.0	Dick Williams, Norm Sherry	1,006,774
1977	5th	74	88	.457	28.0	Norm Sherry, Dave Garcia	1,432,633
1978	2nd (tied)	87	75	.537	5.0	Dave Garcia, Jim Fregosi	1,755,386
1979	1st†	88	74	.543	+3.0	Jim Fregosi	2,523,575
1980	6th	65	95	.406	31.0	Jim Fregosi	2,297,327
1981	4th/7th	51	59	.464	‡	Jim Fregosi, Gene Mauch	1,441,545
1982	1st†	93	69	.574	+3.0	Gene Mauch	2,807,360
1983	5th (tied)	70	92	.432	29.0	John McNamara	2,555,016
1984	2nd (tied)	81	81	.500	3.0	John McNamara	2,402,997
1985	2nd	90	72	.556	1.0	Gene Mauch	2,567,427
1986	1st†	92	70	.568	+5.0	Gene Mauch	2,655,872
1987	6th (tied)	75	87	.463	10.0	Gene Mauch	2,696,299
1988	4th	75	87	.463	29.0	Cookie Rojas	2,340,925
1989	3rd	91	71	.562	8.0	Doug Rader	2,647,291
1990	4th	80	82	.494	23.0	Doug Rader	2,555,688
1991	7th	81	81	.500	14.0	Doug Rader, Buck Rodgers	2,416,236
1992	5th (tied)	72	90	.444	24.0	Buck Rodgers	2,065,444
1993	5th (tied)	71	91	.438	23.0	Buck Rodgers	2,057,460
1994	4th	47	68	.409	5.5	Buck Rodgers, Marcel Lachemann	1,512,622
1995	2nd§	78	67	.538	1.0	Marcel Lachemann	1,748,680
1996	4th	70	91	.435	19.5	Marcel Lachemann, John McNamara, Joe Maddon	1,820,521
1997	2nd	84	78	.519	6.0	Terry Collins	1,767,330
1998	2nd	85	77	.525	3.0	Terry Collins	2,519,210
1999	4th	70	92	.432	25.0	Terry Collins, Joe Maddon	2,253,123
2000	3rd	82	80	.506	9.5	Mike Scioscia	2,066,977
2001	3rd	75	87	.463	41.0	Mike Scioscia	2,000,917

*Games behind winner. †Lost championship series. ‡First half 31-29; second 20-30. §Lost division playoff.

MANAGERIAL RECORDS

Terry Collins 220-237, Jim Fregosi 237-249, Dave Garcia 60-66, Marcel Lachemann 161-170, Joe Maddon 27-24, Gene Mauch 379-332, John McNamara 161-191, Lefty Phillips 222-225, Doug Rader 232-216, Del Rice 75-80, Bill Rigney 625-707, Buck Rodgers 179-223, Cookie Rojas 75-87, Mike Scioscia 157-167, Norm Sherry 76-71, Dick Williams 147-194, Bobby Winkles 109-127.

BALTIMORE ORIOLES
YEARLY FINISHES

(Known as Milwaukee Brewers in 1901 and St. Louis Browns through 1953)

Year	Position	W	L	Pct.	*GB	Manager	Attendance
1901	8th	48	89	.350	35.5	Hugh Duffy	139,034
1902	2nd	78	58	.574	5.0	Jimmy McAleer	272,283
1903	6th	65	74	.468	26.5	Jimmy McAleer	380,405
1904	6th	65	87	.428	29.0	Jimmy McAleer	318,108

Year	Position	W	L	Pct.	*GB	Manager	Attendance
1905	8th	54	99	.354	40.5	Jimmy McAleer	339,112
1906	5th	76	73	.510	16.0	Jimmy McAleer	389,157
1907	6th	69	83	.454	24.0	Jimmy McAleer	419,025
1908	4th	83	69	.546	6.5	Jimmy McAleer	618,947
1909	7th	61	89	.407	36.0	Jimmy McAleer	366,274
1910	8th	47	107	.305	57.0	John O'Connor	249,889
1911	8th	45	107	.296	56.5	Bobby Wallace	207,984
1912	7th	53	101	.344	53.0	Bobby Wallace, George Stovall	214,070
1913	8th	57	96	.373	39.0	George Stovall, Branch Rickey	250,330
1914	5th	71	82	.464	28.5	Branch Rickey	244,714
1915	6th	63	91	.409	39.5	Branch Rickey	150,358
1916	5th	79	75	.513	12.0	Fielder Jones	335,740
1917	7th	57	97	.370	43.0	Fielder Jones	210,486
1918	5th	58	64	.475	15.0	Fielder Jones, Jimmy Austin, Jimmy Burke	122,076
1919	5th	67	72	.482	20.5	Jimmy Burke	349,350
1920	4th	76	77	.497	21.5	Jimmy Burke	419,311
1921	3rd	81	73	.526	17.5	Lee Fohl	355,978
1922	2nd.	93	61	.604	1.0	Lee Fohl	712,918
1923	5th	74	78	.487	24.0	Lee Fohl, Jimmy Austin	430,296
1924	4th	74	78	.487	17.0	George Sisler	533,349
1925	3rd	82	71	.536	15.0	George Sisler	462,898
1926	7th	62	92	.403	29.0	George Sisler	283,986
1927	7th	59	94	.336	50.5	Dan Howley	247,879
1928	3rd	82	72	.532	19.0	Dan Howley	339,497
1929	4th	79	73	.520	26.0	Dan Howley	280,697
1930	6th	64	90	.416	38.0	Bill Killefer	152,088
1931	5th	63	91	.409	45.0	Bill Killefer	179,126
1932	6th	63	91	.409	44.0	Bill Killefer	112,558
1933	8th	55	96	.364	43.5	Bill Killefer, Allen Sothoron, Rogers Hornsby	88,113
1934	6th	67	85	.441	33.0	Rogers Hornsby	115,305
1935	7th	65	87	.428	28.5	Rogers Hornsby	80,922
1936	7th	57	95	.375	44.5	Rogers Hornsby	93,267
1937	8th	46	108	.299	56.0	Rogers Hornsby, Jim Bottomley	123,121
1938	7th	55	97	.362	44.0	Gabby Street	130,417
1939	8th	43	111	.279	64.5	Fred Haney	109,159
1940	6th	67	87	.435	23.0	Fred Haney	239,591
1941	6th (tied)	70	84	.455	31.0	Fred Haney, Luke Sewell	176,240
1942	3rd	82	69	.543	19.5	Luke Sewell	255,617
1943	6th	72	80	.474	25.0	Luke Sewell	214,392
1944	1st	89	65	.578	+1.0	Luke Sewell	508,644
1945	3rd	81	70	.536	6.0	Luke Sewell	482,986
1946	7th	66	88	.429	38.0	Luke Sewell, Zack Taylor	526,435
1947	8th	59	95	.383	38.0	Muddy Ruel	320,474
1948	6th	59	94	.386	37.0	Zack Taylor	335,546
1949	7th	53	101	.344	44.0	Zack Taylor	270,936
1950	7th	58	96	.377	40.0	Zack Taylor	247,131
1951	8th	52	102	.338	46.0	Zack Taylor	293,790
1952	7th	64	90	.416	31.0	Rogers Hornsby, Marty Marion	518,796
1953	8th	54	100	.351	46.5	Marty Marion	297,238
1954	7th	54	100	.351	57.0	Jimmie Dykes	1,060,910
1955	7th	57	97	.370	39.0	Paul Richards	852,039
1956	6th	69	85	.448	28.0	Paul Richards	901,201
1957	5th	76	76	.500	21.0	Paul Richards	1,029,581
1958	6th	74	79	.484	17.5	Paul Richards	829,991
1959	6th	74	80	.481	20.0	Paul Richards	891,926
1960	2nd	89	65	.578	8.0	Paul Richards	1,187,849
1961	3rd	95	67	.586	14.0	Paul Richards, Luman Harris	951,089
1962	7th	77	85	.475	19.0	Billy Hitchcock	790,254
1963	4th	86	76	.531	18.5	Billy Hitchcock	774,343
1964	3rd	97	65	.599	2.0	Hank Bauer	1,116,215
1965	3rd	94	68	.580	8.0	Hank Bauer	781,649
1966	1st	97	63	.606	+9.0	Hank Bauer	1,203,366
1967	6th (tied)	76	85	.472	15.5	Hank Bauer	955,053
1968	2nd.	91	71	.562	12.0	Hank Bauer, Earl Weaver	943,977

EAST DIVISION

Year	Position	W	L	Pct.	*GB	Manager	Attendance
1969	1st†	109	53	.673	+19.0	Earl Weaver	1,058,168
1970	1st†	108	54	.667	+15.0	Earl Weaver	1,057,069
1971	1st†	101	57	.639	+12.0	Earl Weaver	1,023,037
1972	3rd	80	74	.519	5.0	Earl Weaver	899,950
1973	1st‡	97	65	.599	+8.0	Earl Weaver	958,667
1974	1st‡	91	71	.562	+2.0	Earl Weaver	962,572
1975	2nd	90	69	.566	4.5	Earl Weaver	1,002,157
1976	2nd.	88	74	.543	10.5	Earl Weaver	1,058,609

Year	Position	W	L	Pct.	*GB	Manager	Attendance
1977	2nd (tied)	97	64	.602	2.5	Earl Weaver	1,195,769
1978	4th	90	71	.559	9.0	Earl Weaver	1,051,724
1979	1st†	102	57	.642	+8.0	Earl Weaver	1,681,009
1980	2nd	100	62	.617	3.0	Earl Weaver	1,797,438
1981	2nd/4th	59	46	.562	§	Earl Weaver	1,024,652
1982	2nd	94	68	.580	1.0	Earl Weaver	1,613,031
1983	1st†	98	64	.605	+6.0	Joe Altobelli	2,042,071
1984	5th	85	77	.525	19.0	Joe Altobelli	2,045,784
1985	4th	83	78	.516	16.0	Joe Altobelli, Earl Weaver	2,132,387
1986	7th	73	89	.451	22.5	Earl Weaver	1,973,176
1987	6th	67	95	.414	31.0	Cal Ripken Sr.	1,835,692
1988	7th	54	107	.335	34.5	Cal Ripken Sr., Frank Robinson	1,660,738
1989	2nd	87	75	.537	2.0	Frank Robinson	2,535,208
1990	5th	76	85	.472	11.5	Frank Robinson	2,415,189
1991	6th	67	95	.414	24.0	Frank Robinson, Johnny Oates	2,552,753
1992	3rd	89	73	.549	7.0	Johnny Oates	3,567,819
1993	3rd (tied)	85	77	.525	10.0	Johnny Oates	3,644,965
1994	2nd	63	49	.563	6.5	Johnny Oates	2,535,359
1995	3rd	71	73	.493	15.0	Phil Regan	3,098,475
1996	2nd∞‡	88	74	.543	4.0	Dave Johnson	3,646,950
1997	1st∞‡	98	64	.605	+2.0	Dave Johnson	3,711,132
1998	4th	79	83	.488	35.0	Ray Miller	3,685,194
1999	4th	78	84	.481	20.0	Ray Miller	3,433,150
2000	4th	74	88	.457	13.5	Mike Hargrove	3,295,128
2001	4th	63	98	.391	32.5	Mike Hargrove	3,094,841

*Games behind winner. †Won championship series. ‡Lost championship series. §First half 31-23; second 28-23. ∞Won division series.

MANAGERIAL RECORDS

Joe Altobelli 212-167, Jimmy Austin 29-38, Hank Bauer 407-318, Jim Bottomley 21-56, Jimmy Burke 172-180, Hugh Duffy 48-89, Jimmie Dykes 54-100, Lee Fohl 226-183, Fred Haney 125-227, Mike Hargrove 137-186, Lum Harris 17-10, Billy Hitchcock 163-161, Rogers Hornsby 255-381, Dan Howley 220-239, Dave Johnson 186-138, Fielder Jones 158-196, Bill Killefer 224-329, Marty Marion 96-161, Jimmy McAleer 551-632, Ray Miller 157-167, Johnny Oates 291-270, Jack O'Connor 47-107, Phil Regan 71-73, Paul Richards 517-539, Branch Rickey 139-179, Cal Ripken Sr. 67-101, Frank Robinson 230-285, Luke Sewell 432-410, George Sisler 218-241, Al Sothoron 2-6, George Stovall 91-158, Gabby Street 55-97, Zack Taylor 235-410, Bobby Wallace 57-134, Earl Weaver 1,481-1,060.

BOSTON RED SOX
YEARLY FINISHES

Year	Position	W	L	Pct.	*GB	Manager	Attendance
1901	2nd	79	57	.581	4.0	Jimmy Collins	289,448
1902	3rd	77	60	.562	6.5	Jimmy Collins	348,567
1903	1st	91	47	.659	+14.5	Jimmy Collins	379,338
1904	1st	95	59	.617	+1.5	Jimmy Collins	623,295
1905	4th	78	74	.513	16.0	Jimmy Collins	468,828
1906	8th	49	105	.318	45.5	Jimmy Collins, Chick Stahl	410,209
1907	7th	59	90	.396	32.5	George Huff, Bob Unglaub, Deacon McGuire	436,777
1908	5th	75	79	.487	15.5	Deacon McGuire, Fred Lake	473,048
1909	3rd	88	63	.583	9.5	Fred Lake	668,965
1910	4th	81	72	.529	22.5	Patsy Donovan	584,619
1911	5th	78	75	.510	24.0	Patsy Donovan	503,961
1912	1st	105	47	.691	+14.0	Jake Stahl	597,096
1913	4th	79	71	.527	15.5	Jake Stahl, Bill Carrigan	437,194
1914	2nd	91	62	.595	8.5	Bill Carrigan	481,359
1915	1st	101	50	.669	+2.5	Bill Carrigan	539,885
1916	1st	91	63	.591	+2.0	Bill Carrigan	496,397
1917	2nd	90	62	.592	9.0	Jack Barry	387,856
1918	1st	75	51	.595	+2.5	Ed Barrow	249,513
1919	6th	66	71	.482	20.5	Ed Barrow	417,291
1920	5th	72	81	.471	25.5	Ed Barrow	402,445
1921	5th	75	79	.487	23.5	Hugh Duffy	279,273
1922	8th	61	93	.396	33.0	Hugh Duffy	259,184
1923	8th	61	91	.401	37.0	Frank Chance	229,668
1924	7th	67	87	.435	25.0	Lee Fohl	448,556
1925	8th	47	105	.309	49.5	Lee Fohl	267,782
1926	8th	46	107	.301	44.5	Lee Fohl	285,155
1927	8th	51	103	.331	59.0	Bill Carrigan	305,275
1928	8th	57	96	.373	43.5	Bill Carrigan	396,920
1929	8th	58	96	.377	48.0	Bill Carrigan	394,620
1930	8th	52	102	.338	50.0	Heinie Wagner	444,045
1931	6th	62	90	.408	45.0	Shano Collins	350,975
1932	8th	43	111	.279	64.0	Shano Collins, Marty McManus	182,150
1933	7th	63	86	.423	34.5	Marty McManus	268,715

HISTORY Team by team

Year	Position	W	L	Pct.	*GB	Manager	Attendance
1934	4th	76	76	.500	24.0	Bucky Harris	610,640
1935	4th	78	75	.510	16.0	Joseph Cronin	558,568
1936	6th	74	80	.481	28.5	Joe Cronin	626,895
1937	5th	80	72	.526	21.0	Joe Cronin	559,659
1938	2nd	88	61	.591	9.5	Joe Cronin	646,459
1939	2nd	89	62	.589	17.0	Joe Cronin	573,070
1940	4th (tied)	82	72	.532	8.0	Joe Cronin	716,234
1941	2nd	84	70	.545	17.0	Joe Cronin	718,497
1942	2nd	93	59	.612	9.0	Joe Cronin	730,340
1943	7th	68	84	.447	29.0	Joe Cronin	358,275
1944	4th	77	77	.500	12.0	Joe Cronin	506,975
1945	7th	71	83	.461	17.5	Joe Cronin	603,794
1946	1st	104	50	.675	+12.0	Joe Cronin	1,416,944
1947	3rd	83	71	.539	14.0	Joe Cronin	1,427,315
1948	2nd†	96	59	.619	1.0	Joe McCarthy	1,558,798
1949	2nd	96	58	.623	1.0	Joe McCarthy	1,596,650
1950	3rd	94	60	.610	4.0	Joe McCarthy, Steve O'Neill	1,344,080
1951	3rd	87	67	.565	11.0	Steve O'Neill	1,312,282
1952	6th	76	78	.494	19.0	Lou Boudreau	1,115,750
1953	4th	84	69	.549	16.0	Lou Boudreau	1,026,133
1954	4th	69	85	.448	42.0	Lou Boudreau	931,127
1955	4th	84	70	.545	12.0	Pinky Higgins	1,203,200
1956	4th	84	70	.545	13.0	Pinky Higgins	1,137,158
1957	3rd	82	72	.532	16.0	Pinky Higgins	1,181,087
1958	3rd	79	75	.513	13.0	Pinky Higgins	1,077,047
1959	5th	75	79	.487	19.0	Pinky Higgins, Billy Jurges	984,102
1960	7th	65	89	.422	32.0	Billy Jurges, Pinky Higgins	1,129,866
1961	6th	76	86	.469	33.0	Pinky Higgins	850,589
1962	8th	76	84	.475	19.0	Pinky Higgins	733,080
1963	7th	76	85	.472	28.0	Johnny Pesky	942,642
1964	8th	72	90	.444	27.0	Johnny Pesky, Billy Herman	883,276
1965	9th	62	100	.383	40.0	Billy Herman	652,201
1966	9th	72	90	.444	26.0	Billy Herman, Pete Runnels	811,172
1967	1st	92	70	.568	+1.0	Dick Williams	1,727,832
1968	4th	86	76	.531	17.0	Dick Williams	1,940,788

EAST DIVISION

Year	Position	W	L	Pct.	*GB	Manager	Attendance
1969	3rd	87	75	.537	22.0	Dick Williams, Eddie Popowski	1,833,246
1970	3rd	87	75	.537	21.0	Eddie Kasko	1,595,278
1971	3rd	85	77	.525	18.0	Eddie Kasko	1,678,732
1972	2nd	85	70	.548	0.5	Eddie Kasko	1,441,718
1973	2nd	89	73	.549	8.0	Eddie Kasko	1,481,002
1974	3rd	84	78	.519	7.0	Darrell Johnson	1,556,411
1975	1st†	95	65	.594	+4.5	Darrell Johnson	1,748,587
1976	3rd	83	79	.512	15.5	Darrell Johnson, Don Zimmer	1,895,846
1977	2nd (tied)	97	64	.602	2.5	Don Zimmer	2,074,549
1978	2nd§	99	64	.607	1.0	Don Zimmer	2,320,643
1979	3rd	91	69	.569	11.5	Don Zimmer	2,353,114
1980	4th	83	77	.519	19.0	Don Zimmer, Johnny Pesky	1,956,092
1981	5th/2nd (tied)	59	49	.546	∞	Ralph Houk	1,060,379
1982	3rd	89	73	.549	6.0	Ralph Houk	1,950,124
1983	6th	78	84	.481	20.0	Ralph Houk	1,782,285
1984	4th	86	76	.531	18.0	Ralph Houk	1,661,618
1985	5th	81	81	.500	18.5	John McNamara	1,786,633
1986	1st‡	95	66	.590	+5.5	John McNamara	2,147,641
1987	5th	78	84	.481	20.0	John McNamara	2,231,551
1988	1st▲	89	73	.549	+1.0	John McNamara, Joe Morgan	2,464,851
1989	3rd	83	79	.512	6.0	Joe Morgan	2,510,012
1990	1st▲	88	74	.543	+2.0	Joe Morgan	2,528,986
1991	2nd (tied)	84	78	.519	7.0	Joe Morgan	2,562,435
1992	7th	73	89	.451	23.0	Butch Hobson	2,468,574
1993	5th	80	82	.494	15.0	Butch Hobson	2,422,021
1994	4th	54	61	.470	17.0	Butch Hobson	1,775,818
1995	1st◆	86	58	.597	+7.0	Kevin Kennedy	2,164,410
1996	3rd	85	77	.525	7.0	Kevin Kennedy	2,315,231
1997	4th	78	84	.481	20.0	Jimy Williams	2,226,136
1998	2nd◆	92	70	.568	22.0	Jimy Williams	2,343,947
1999	2nd■▲	94	68	.580	4.0	Jimy Williams	2,446,162
2000	2nd	85	77	.525	2.5	Jimy Williams	2,586,032
2001	2nd	82	79	.509	13.5	Jimy Williams, Joe Kerrigan	2,625,333

*Games behind winner. †Lost pennant playoff. ‡Won championship series. §Lost division playoff. ∞First half 30-26; second 29-23.
▲Lost championship series. ◆Lost division series. ■Won division series.

MANAGERIAL RECORDS

Ed Barrow 213-203, Jack Barry 90-62, Lou Boudreau 229-232, Bill Carrigan 489-500, Frank Chance 61-91, Jimmy Collins 455-376, Shano Collins 73-134, Joe Cronin 1,071-916, Patsy Donovan 159-147, Hugh Duffy 136-172, Lee Fohl 160-299, Bucky Harris 76-76, Billy Herman 128-182, Pinky Higgins 560-556, Butch Hobson 207-232, Ralph Houk 312-282, George Huff 2-6, Darrell Johnson 220-188, Billy Jurges 59-63, Eddie Kasko 346-295, Kevin Kennedy 171-135, Joe Kerrigan 17-26, Fred Lake 110-80, Joe McCarthy 223-145, Deacon McGuire 98-123, Marty McManus 95-153, John McNamara 297-273, Joe Morgan 301-262, Steve O'Neill 150-99, Johnny Pesky 147-179, Eddie Popowski 5-4, Pete Runnels 8-8, Chick Stahl 14-26, Jake Stahl 144-88, Bob Unglaub 9-20, Heinie Wagner 52-102, Dick Williams 260-217, Jimy Williams 414-352, Don Zimmer 411-304.

CHICAGO WHITE SOX
YEARLY FINISHES

Year	Position	W	L	Pct.	*GB	Manager	Attendance
1901	1st	83	53	.610	+4.0	Clark Griffith	354,350
1902	4th	74	60	.552	8.0	Clark Griffith	337,898
1903	7th	60	77	.438	30.5	Nixey Callahan	286,183
1904	3rd	89	65	.578	6.0	Nixey Callahan, Fielder Jones	557,123
1905	2nd	92	60	.605	2.0	Fielder Jones	687,419
1906	1st	93	58	.616	+3.0	Fielder Jones	585,202
1907	3rd	87	64	.576	5.5	Fielder Jones	666,307
1908	3rd	88	64	.579	1.5	Fielder Jones	636,096
1909	4th	78	74	.513	20.0	Billy Sullivan	478,400
1910	6th	68	85	.444	35.5	Hugh Duffy	552,084
1911	4th	77	74	.510	24.0	Hugh Duffy	583,208
1912	4th	78	76	.506	28.0	Nixey Callahan	602,241
1913	5th	78	74	.513	17.5	Nixey Callahan	644,501
1914	6th (tied)	70	84	.455	30.0	Nixey Callahan	469,290
1915	3rd	93	61	.604	9.5	Pants Rowland	539,461
1916	2nd	89	65	.578	2.0	Pants Rowland	679,923
1917	1st	100	54	.649	+9.0	Pants Rowland	684,521
1918	6th	57	67	.460	17.0	Pants Rowland	195,081
1919	1st	88	52	.629	+3.5	Kid Gleason	627,186
1920	2nd	96	58	.623	2.0	Kid Gleason	833,492
1921	7th	62	92	.403	36.5	Kid Gleason	543,650
1922	5th	77	77	.500	17.0	Kid Gleason	602,860
1923	7th	69	85	.448	30.0	Kid Gleason	573,778
1924	8th	66	87	.431	25.5	Johnny Evers	606,658
1925	5th	79	75	.513	18.5	Eddie Collins	832,231
1926	5th	81	72	.529	9.5	Eddie Collins	710,339
1927	5th	70	83	.458	29.5	Ray Schalk	614,423
1928	5th	72	82	.468	29.0	Ray Schalk, Lena Blackburne	494,152
1929	7th	59	93	.388	46.0	Lena Blackburne	426,795
1930	7th	62	92	.403	40.0	Donie Bush	406,123
1931	8th	56	97	.366	51.0	Donie Bush	403,550
1932	7th	49	102	.325	56.5	Lew Fonseca	233,198
1933	6th	67	83	.447	31.0	Lew Fonseca	397,789
1934	8th	53	99	.349	47.0	Lew Fonseca, Jimmie Dykes	236,559
1935	5th	74	78	.487	19.5	Jimmie Dykes	470,281
1936	3rd	81	70	.536	20.0	Jimmie Dykes	440,810
1937	3rd	86	68	.558	16.0	Jimmie Dykes	589,245
1938	6th	65	83	.439	32.0	Jimmie Dykes	338,278
1939	4th	85	69	.552	22.5	Jimmie Dykes	594,104
1940	4th (tied)	82	72	.532	8.0	Jimmie Dykes	660,336
1941	3rd	77	77	.500	24.0	Jimmie Dykes	677,077
1942	6th	66	82	.446	34.0	Jimmie Dykes	425,734
1943	4th	82	72	.532	16.0	Jimmie Dykes	508,962
1944	7th	71	83	.461	18.0	Jimmie Dykes	563,539
1945	6th	71	78	.477	15.0	Jimmie Dykes	657,981
1946	5th	74	80	.481	30.0	Jimmie Dykes, Ted Lyons	983,403
1947	6th	70	84	.455	27.0	Ted Lyons	876,948
1948	8th	51	101	.336	44.5	Ted Lyons	777,844
1949	6th	63	91	.409	34.0	Jack Onslow	937,151
1950	6th	60	94	.390	38.0	Jack Onslow, Red Corriden	781,330
1951	4th	81	73	.526	17.0	Paul Richards	1,328,234
1952	3rd	81	73	.526	14.0	Paul Richards	1,231,675
1953	3rd	89	65	.578	11.5	Paul Richards	1,191,353
1954	3rd	94	60	.610	17.0	Paul Richards, Marty Marion	1,231,629
1955	3rd	91	63	.591	5.0	Marty Marion	1,175,684
1956	3rd	85	69	.552	12.0	Marty Marion	1,000,090
1957	2nd	90	64	.584	8.0	Al Lopez	1,135,668
1958	2nd	82	72	.532	10.0	Al Lopez	797,451
1959	1st	94	60	.610	+5.0	Al Lopez	1,423,144
1960	3rd	87	67	.565	10.0	Al Lopez	1,644,460
1961	4th	86	76	.531	23.0	Al Lopez	1,146,019

Year	Position	W	L	Pct.	*GB	Manager	Attendance
1962	5th	85	77	.525	11.0	Al Lopez	1,131,562
1963	2nd	94	68	.580	10.5	Al Lopez	1,158,848
1964	2nd	98	64	.605	1.0	Al Lopez	1,250,053
1965	2nd	95	67	.586	7.0	Al Lopez	1,130,519
1966	4th	83	79	.512	15.0	Eddie Stanky	990,016
1967	4th	89	73	.549	3.0	Eddie Stanky	985,634
1968	8th (tied)	67	95	.414	36.0	Eddie Stanky, Al Lopez	803,775

WEST DIVISION

Year	Position	W	L	Pct.	*GB	Manager	Attendance
1969	5th	68	94	.420	29.0	Al Lopez, Don Gutteridge	589,546
1970	6th	56	106	.346	42.0	Don Gutteridge, Chuck Tanner	495,355
1971	3rd	79	83	.488	22.5	Chuck Tanner	833,891
1972	2nd	87	67	.565	5.5	Chuck Tanner	1,177,318
1973	5th	77	85	.475	17.0	Chuck Tanner	1,302,527
1974	4th	80	80	.500	9.0	Chuck Tanner	1,149,596
1975	5th	75	86	.466	22.5	Chuck Tanner	750,802
1976	6th	64	97	.398	25.5	Paul Richards	914,945
1977	3rd	90	72	.556	12.0	Bob Lemon	1,657,135
1978	5th	71	90	.441	20.5	Bob Lemon, Larry Doby	1,491,100
1979	5th	73	87	.456	14.0	Don Kessinger, Tony La Russa	1,280,702
1980	5th	70	90	.438	26.0	Tony La Russa	1,200,365
1981	3rd/6th	54	52	.509	†	Tony La Russa	946,651
1982	3rd	87	75	.537	6.0	Tony La Russa	1,567,787
1983	1st‡	99	63	.611	+20.0	Tony La Russa	2,132,821
1984	5th (tied)	74	88	.457	10.0	Tony La Russa	2,136,988
1985	3rd	85	77	.525	6.0	Tony La Russa	1,669,888
1986	5th	72	90	.444	20.0	Tony La Russa, Jim Fregosi	1,424,313
1987	5th	77	85	.475	8.0	Jim Fregosi	1,208,060
1988	5th	71	90	.441	32.5	Jim Fregosi	1,115,749
1989	7th	69	92	.429	29.5	Jeff Torborg	1,045,651
1990	2nd	94	68	.580	9.0	Jeff Torborg	2,002,357
1991	2nd	87	75	.537	8.0	Jeff Torborg	2,934,154
1992	3rd	86	76	.531	10.0	Gene Lamont	2,681,156
1993	1st‡	94	68	.580	+8.0	Gene Lamont	2,581,091

CENTRAL DIVISION

Year	Position	W	L	Pct.	*GB	Manager	Attendance
1994	1st	67	46	.593	+1.0	Gene Lamont	1,697,398
1995	3rd	68	76	.472	32.0	Gene Lamont, Terry Bevington	1,609,773
1996	2nd	85	77	.525	14.5	Terry Bevington	1,676,403
1997	2nd	80	81	.497	6.0	Terry Bevington	1,864,782
1998	2nd	80	82	.494	9.0	Jerry Manuel	1,391,146
1999	2nd	75	86	.466	21.5	Jerry Manuel	1,338,851
2000	1st§	95	67	.586	+5.0	Jerry Manuel	1,947,799
2001	3rd	83	79	.512	8.0	Jerry Manuel	1,766,172

*Games behind winner. †First half 31-22; second 23-30. ‡Lost championship series. §Lost division series.

MANAGERIAL RECORDS

Terry Bevington 222-214, Lena Blackburne 99-133, Donie Bush 118-189, Nixey Callahan 309-329, Eddie Collins 160-147, Red Corriden 52-72, Larry Doby 37-50, Hugh Duffy 145-159, Jimmie Dykes 899-940, Johnny Evers 66-87, Lew Fonseca 120-196, Jim Fregosi 193-226, Kid Gleason 392-364, Clark Griffith 157-113, Don Gutteridge 109-172, Fielder Jones 426-293, Don Kessinger 46-60, Tony La Russa 522-510, Gene Lamont 258-210, Bob Lemon 124-112, Al Lopez 840-650, Ted Lyons 185-245, Jerry Manuel 333-314, Marty Marion 179-138, Jack Onslow 71-133, Paul Richards 406-362, Pants Rowland 339-247, Ray Schalk 102-125, Eddie Stanky 206-197, Billy Sullivan 78-74, Chuck Tanner 401-414, Jeff Torborg 250-235.

CLEVELAND INDIANS
YEARLY FINISHES

Year	Position	W	L	Pct.	*GB	Manager	Attendance
1901	7th	54	82	.397	29.0	James McAleer	131,380
1902	5th	69	67	.507	14.0	Bill Armour	275,395
1903	3rd	77	63	.550	15.0	Bill Armour	311,280
1904	4th	86	65	.570	7.5	Bill Armour	264,749
1905	5th	76	78	.494	19.0	Nap Lajoie	316,306
1906	3rd	89	64	.582	5.0	Nap Lajoie	325,733
1907	4th	85	67	.559	8.0	Nap Lajoie	382,046
1908	2nd	90	64	.584	0.5	Nap Lajoie	422,242
1909	6th	71	82	.464	27.5	Nap Lajoie, Deacon McGuire	354,627
1910	5th	71	81	.467	32.0	Deacon McGuire	293,456
1911	3rd	80	73	.523	22.0	Deacon McGuire, George Stovall	406,296
1912	5th	75	78	.490	30.5	Harry Davis, J.L. Birmingham	336,844
1913	3rd	86	66	.566	9.5	J.L. Birmingham	541,000

Year	Position	W	L	Pct.	*GB	Manager	Attendance
1914	8th	51	102	.333	48.5	J.L. Birmingham	185,997
1915	7th	57	95	.375	44.5	J.L. Birmingham, Lee Fohl	159,285
1916	6th	77	77	.500	14.0	Lee Fohl	492,106
1917	3rd	88	66	.571	12.0	Lee Fohl	477,298
1918	2nd	73	54	.575	2.5	Lee Fohl	295,515
1919	2nd	84	55	.604	3.5	Lee Fohl, Tris Speaker	538,135
1920	1st	98	56	.636	+2.0	Tris Speaker	912,832
1921	2nd	94	60	.610	4.5	Tris Speaker	748,705
1922	4th	78	76	.507	16.0	Tris Speaker	528,145
1923	3rd	82	71	.536	16.5	Tris Speaker	558,856
1924	6th	67	86	.438	24.5	Tris Speaker	481,905
1925	6th	70	84	.455	27.5	Tris Speaker	419,005
1926	2nd	88	66	.571	3.0	Tris Speaker	627,426
1927	6th	66	87	.431	43.5	Jack McAllister	373,138
1928	7th	62	92	.403	39.0	Roger Peckinpaugh	375,907
1929	3rd	81	71	.533	24.0	Roger Peckinpaugh	536,210
1930	4th	81	73	.536	21.0	Roger Peckinpaugh	528,657
1931	4th	78	76	.506	30.0	Roger Peckinpaugh	483,027
1932	4th	87	65	.572	19.0	Roger Peckinpaugh	468,953
1933	4th	75	76	.497	23.5	Roger Peckinpaugh, Walter Johnson	387,936
1934	3rd	85	69	.552	16.0	Walter Johnson	391,338
1935	3rd	82	71	.536	12.0	Walter Johnson, Steve O'Neill	397,615
1936	5th	80	74	.519	22.5	Steve O'Neill	500,391
1937	4th	83	71	.539	19.0	Steve O'Neill	564,849
1938	3rd	86	66	.566	13.0	Ossie Vitt	652,006
1939	3rd	87	67	.565	20.5	Ossie Vitt	563,926
1940	2nd	89	65	.578	1.0	Ossie Vitt	902,576
1941	4th (tied)	75	79	.487	26.0	Roger Peckinpaugh	745,948
1942	4th	75	79	.487	28.0	Lou Boudreau	459,447
1943	3rd	82	71	.536	15.5	Lou Boudreau	438,894
1944	5th (tied)	72	82	.468	17.0	Lou Boudreau	475,272
1945	5th	73	72	.503	11.0	Lou Boudreau	558,182
1946	6th	68	86	.442	36.0	Lou Boudreau	1,057,289
1947	4th	80	74	.519	17.0	Lou Boudreau	1,521,978
1948	1st†	97	58	.626	+1.0	Lou Boudreau	2,620,627
1949	3rd	89	65	.578	8.0	Lou Boudreau	2,233,771
1950	4th	92	62	.597	6.0	Lou Boudreau	1,727,464
1951	2nd	93	61	.604	5.0	Al Lopez	1,704,984
1952	2nd	93	61	.604	2.0	Al Lopez	1,444,607
1953	2nd	92	62	.597	8.5	Al Lopez	1,069,176
1954	1st	111	43	.721	+8.0	Al Lopez	1,335,472
1955	2nd	93	61	.604	3.0	Al Lopez	1,221,780
1956	2nd	88	66	.571	9.0	Al Lopez	865,467
1957	6th	76	77	.497	21.5	Kerby Farrell	722,256
1958	4th	77	76	.503	14.5	Bobby Bragan, Joe Gordon	663,805
1959	2nd	89	65	.578	5.0	Joe Gordon	1,497,976
1960	4th	76	78	.494	21.0	Joe Gordon, Jimmie Dykes	950,985
1961	5th	78	83	.484	30.5	Jimmie Dykes	725,547
1962	6th	80	82	.494	16.0	Mel McGaha	716,076
1963	5th (tied)	79	83	.488	25.5	Birdie Tebbetts	562,507
1964	6th (tied)	79	83	.488	20.0	Birdie Tebbetts	653,293
1965	5th	87	75	.537	15.0	Birdie Tebbetts	934,786
1966	5th	81	81	.500	17.0	Birdie Tebbetts, George Strickland	903,359
1967	8th	75	87	.463	17.0	Joe Adcock	662,980
1968	3rd	86	75	.534	16.5	Alvin Dark	857,994

EAST DIVISION

Year	Position	W	L	Pct.	*GB	Manager	Attendance
1969	6th	62	99	.385	46.5	Alvin Dark	619,970
1970	5th	76	86	.469	32.0	Alvin Dark	729,752
1971	6th	60	102	.370	43.0	Alvin Dark, John Lipon	591,361
1972	5th	72	84	.462	14.0	Ken Aspromonte	626,354
1973	6th	71	91	.438	26.0	Ken Aspromonte	615,107
1974	4th	77	85	.475	14.0	Ken Aspromonte	1,114,262
1975	4th	79	80	.497	15.5	Frank Robinson	977,039
1976	4th	81	78	.509	16.0	Frank Robinson	948,776
1977	5th	71	90	.441	28.5	Frank Robinson, Jeff Torborg	900,365
1978	6th	69	90	.434	29.0	Jeff Torborg	800,584
1979	6th	81	80	.503	22.0	Jeff Torborg, Dave Garcia	1,011,644
1980	6th	79	81	.494	23.0	Dave Garcia	1,033,827
1981	6th/5th	52	51	.504	‡	Dave Garcia	661,395
1982	6th (tied)	78	84	.481	17.0	Dave Garcia	1,044,021
1983	7th	70	92	.432	28.0	Mike Ferraro, Pat Corrales	768,941
1984	6th	75	87	.463	29.0	Pat Corrales	734,079

Year	Position	W	L	Pct.	*GB	Manager	Attendance
1985	7th	60	102	.370	39.5	Pat Corrales	655,181
1986	5th	84	78	.519	11.5	Pat Corrales	1,471,805
1987	7th	61	101	.377	37.0	Pat Corrales, Doc Edwards	1,077,898
1988	6th	78	84	.481	11.0	Doc Edwards	1,411,610
1989	6th	73	89	.451	16.0	Doc Edwards, John Hart	1,285,542
1990	4th	77	85	.475	11.0	John McNamara	1,225,240
1991	7th	57	105	.352	34.0	John McNamara, Mike Hargrove	1,051,863
1992	4th (tied)	76	86	.469	20.0	Mike Hargrove	1,224,274
1993	6th	76	86	.469	19.0	Mike Hargrove	2,177,908

CENTRAL DIVISION

Year	Position	W	L	Pct.	*GB	Manager	Attendance
1994	2nd	66	47	.584	1.0	Mike Hargrove	1,995,174
1995	1st§∞	100	44	.694	+30.0	Mike Hargrove	2,842,745
1996	1st▲	99	62	.615	+14.5	Mike Hargrove	3,318,174
1997	1st§∞	86	75	.534	+6.0	Mike Hargrove	3,404,750
1998	1st§◆	89	73	.549	+9.0	Mike Hargrove	3,467,299
1999	1st▲	97	65	.599	+21.5	Mike Hargrove	3,468,456
2000	2nd	90	72	.556	5.0	Charlie Manuel	3,456,278
2001	1st▲	91	71	.562	+6.0	Charlie Manuel	3,175,523

*Games behind winner. †Won pennant playoff. ‡First half 26-24; second 26-27. §Won division series. ∞Won championship series. ▲Lost division series. ◆Lost championship series.

MANAGERIAL RECORDS

Joe Adcock 75-87, Bill Armour 232-195, Ken Aspromonte 220-260, Joe Birmingham 170-191, Lou Boudreau 728-649, Bobby Bragan 31-36, Pat Corrales 280-355, Alvin Dark 266-321, Harry Davis 54-71, Jimmie Dykes 103-115, Doc Edwards 173-207, Kerby Farrell 76-77, Mike Ferraro 40-60, Lee Fohl 327-310, Dave Garcia 247-244, Joe Gordon 184-151, Mike Hargrove 721-591, John Hart 8-11, Walter Johnson 179-168, Nap Lajoie 377-309, Johnny Lipon 18-41, Al Lopez 570-354, Charlie Manuel 181-143, Jimmy McAleer 54-82, Jack McCallister 66-87, Mel McGaha 80-82, Deacon McGuire 91-117, John McNamara 102-137, Steve O'Neill 199-168, Roger Peckinpaugh 490-481, Frank Robinson 186-189, Tris Speaker 617-520, George Stovall 74-62, George Strickland 15-24, Birdie Tebbetts 269-298, Jeff Torborg 157-201, Oscar Vitt 262-198.

DETROIT TIGERS

YEARLY FINISHES

Year	Position	W	L	Pct.	*GB	Manager	Attendance
1901	3rd	74	61	.548	8.5	George Stallings	259,430
1902	7th	52	83	.385	30.5	Frank Dwyer	189,469
1903	5th	65	71	.478	25.0	Ed Barrow	224,523
1904	7th	62	90	.408	32.0	Ed Barrow, Bobby Lowe	177,796
1905	3rd	79	74	.516	15.5	Bill Armour	193,384
1906	6th	71	78	.477	21.0	Bill Armour	174,043
1907	1st	92	58	.613	+1.5	Hughey Jennings	297,079
1908	1st	90	63	.588	+.5	Hughey Jennings	436,199
1909	1st	98	54	.645	+3.5	Hughey Jennings	490,490
1910	3rd	86	68	.558	18.0	Hughey Jennings	391,288
1911	2nd	89	65	.578	13.5	Hughey Jennings	484,988
1912	6th	69	84	.451	36.5	Hughey Jennings	402,870
1913	6th	66	87	.431	30.0	Hughey Jennings	398,502
1914	4th	80	73	.523	19.5	Hughey Jennings	416,225
1915	2nd	100	54	.649	2.5	Hughey Jennings	476,105
1916	3rd	87	67	.565	4.0	Hughey Jennings	616,772
1917	4th	78	75	.510	21.5	Hughey Jennings	457,289
1918	7th	55	71	.437	20.0	Hughey Jennings	203,719
1919	4th	80	60	.571	8.0	Hughey Jennings	643,805
1920	7th	61	93	.396	37.0	Hughey Jennings	579,650
1921	6th	71	82	.464	27.0	Ty Cobb	661,527
1922	3rd	79	75	.513	15.0	Ty Cobb	861,206
1923	2nd	83	71	.539	16.0	Ty Cobb	911,377
1924	3rd	86	68	.558	6.0	Ty Cobb	1,015,136
1925	4th	81	73	.526	16.5	Ty Cobb	820,766
1926	6th	79	75	.513	12.0	Ty Cobb	711,914
1927	4th	82	71	.536	27.5	George Moriarty	773,716
1928	6th	68	86	.442	33.0	George Moriarty	474,323
1929	6th	70	84	.455	36.0	Bucky Harris	869,318
1930	5th	75	79	.487	27.0	Bucky Harris	649,450
1931	7th	61	93	.396	47.0	Bucky Harris	434,056
1932	5th	76	75	.503	29.5	Bucky Harris	397,157
1933	5th	75	79	.487	25.0	Del Baker	320,972
1934	1st	101	53	.656	+7.0	Mickey Cochrane	919,161
1935	1st	93	58	.616	+3.0	Mickey Cochrane	1,034,929
1936	2nd	83	71	.539	19.5	Mickey Cochrane	875,948

Year	Position	W	L	Pct.	*GB	Manager	Attendance
1937	2nd	89	65	.578	13.0	Mickey Cochrane	1,072,276
1938	4th	84	70	.545	16.0	Mickey Cochrane, Del Baker	799,557
1939	5th	81	73	.526	26.5	Del Baker	836,279
1940	1st	90	64	.584	+1.0	Del Baker	1,112,693
1941	4th (tied)	75	79	.487	26.0	Del Baker	684,915
1942	5th	73	81	.474	30.0	Del Baker	580,087
1943	5th	78	76	.506	20.0	Steve O'Neill	606,287
1944	2nd	88	66	.571	1.0	Steve O'Neill	923,176
1945	1st	88	65	.575	+1.5	Steve O'Neill	1,280,341
1946	2nd	92	62	.597	12.0	Steve O'Neill	1,722,590
1947	2nd	85	69	.552	12.0	Steve O'Neill	1,398,093
1948	5th	78	76	.506	18.5	Steve O'Neill	1,743,035
1949	4th	87	67	.565	10.0	Red Rolfe	1,821,204
1950	2nd	95	59	.617	3.0	Red Rolfe	1,951,474
1951	5th	73	81	.474	25.0	Red Rolfe	1,132,641
1952	8th	50	104	.325	45.0	Red Rolfe, Fred Hutchinson	1,026,846
1953	6th	60	94	.390	40.5	Fred Hutchinson	884,658
1954	5th	68	86	.442	43.0	Fred Hutchinson	1,079,847
1955	5th	79	75	.513	17.0	Bucky Harris	1,181,838
1956	5th	82	72	.532	15.0	Bucky Harris	1,051,182
1957	4th	78	76	.506	20.0	Jack Tighe	1,272,346
1958	5th	77	77	.500	15.0	Jack Tighe, Bill Norman	1,098,924
1959	4th	76	78	.494	18.0	Bill Norman, Jimmie Dykes	1,221,221
1960	6th	71	83	.461	26.0	Jimmie Dykes, Billy Hitchcock, Joe Gordon	1,167,669
1961	2nd	101	61	.623	8.0	Bob Scheffing	1,600,710
1962	4th	85	76	.528	10.5	Bob Scheffing	1,207,881
1963	5th (tied)	79	83	.488	25.5	Bob Scheffing, Charlie Dressen	821,952
1964	4th	85	77	.525	14.0	Charlie Dressen	816,139
1965	4th	89	73	.549	13.0	Charlie Dressen, Bob Swift	1,029,645
1966	3rd§	88	74	.543	10.0	Charlie Dressen, Bob Swift, Frank Skaff	1,124,293
1967	2nd	91	71	.562	1.0	Mayo Smith	1,447,143
1968	1st	103	59	.636	+12.0	Mayo Smith	2,031,847

EAST DIVISION

Year	Position	W	L	Pct.	*GB	Manager	Attendance
1969	2nd	90	72	.556	19.0	Mayo Smith	1,577,481
1970	4th	79	83	.488	29.0	Mayo Smith	1,501,293
1971	2nd	91	71	.562	12.0	Billy Martin	1,591,073
1972	1st†	86	70	.551	+0.5	Billy Martin	1,892,386
1973	3rd	85	77	.525	12.0	Billy Martin, Joe Schultz	1,724,146
1974	6th	72	90	.444	19.0	Ralph Houk	1,243,080
1975	6th	57	102	.358	37.5	Ralph Houk	1,058,836
1976	5th	74	87	.460	24.0	Ralph Houk	1,467,020
1977	4th	74	88	.457	26.0	Ralph Houk	1,359,856
1978	5th	86	76	.531	13.5	Ralph Houk	1,714,893
1979	5th	85	76	.528	18.0	Les Moss, Dick Tracewski, Sparky Anderson	1,630,929
1980	5th	84	78	.519	19.0	Sparky Anderson	1,785,293
1981	4th/2nd (tied)	60	49	.550	‡	Sparky Anderson	1,149,144
1982	4th	83	79	.512	12.0	Sparky Anderson	1,636,058
1983	2nd	92	70	.568	6.0	Sparky Anderson	1,829,636
1984	1st§	104	58	.642	+15.0	Sparky Anderson	2,704,794
1985	3rd	84	77	.522	15.0	Sparky Anderson	2,286,609
1986	3rd	87	75	.537	8.5	Sparky Anderson	1,899,437
1987	1st†	98	64	.605	+2.0	Sparky Anderson	2,061,830
1988	2nd	88	74	.543	1.0	Sparky Anderson	2,081,162
1989	7th	59	103	.364	30.0	Sparky Anderson	1,543,656
1990	3rd	79	83	.488	9.0	Sparky Anderson	1,495,785
1991	2nd	84	78	.519	7.0	Sparky Anderson	1,641,661
1992	6th	75	87	.463	21.0	Sparky Anderson	1,423,963
1993	3rd (tied)	85	77	.525	10.0	Sparky Anderson	1,971,421
1994	5th	53	62	.461	18.0	Sparky Anderson	1,184,783
1995	4th	60	84	.417	26.0	Sparky Anderson	1,180,979
1996	5th	53	109	.327	39.0	Buddy Bell	1,168,610
1997	3rd	79	83	.488	19.0	Buddy Bell	1,365,157

CENTRAL DIVISION

Year	Position	W	L	Pct.	*GB	Manager	Attendance
1998	5th	65	97	.401	24.0	Buddy Bell, Larry Parrish	1,409,391
1999	3rd	69	92	.429	27.5	Larry Parrish	2,026,441
2000	3rd	79	83	.488	16.0	Phil Garner	2,533,752
2001	4th	66	96	.407	25.0	Phil Garner	1,921,305

*Games behind winner. †Lost championship series. ‡First half 31-26; second 29-23. §Won championship series.

MANAGERIAL RECORDS

Sparky Anderson 1,431-1,248, Bill Armour 150-152, Del Baker 392-336, Ed Barrow 97-117, Buddy Bell 184-277, Ty Cobb 479-444, Mickey Cochrane 379-278, Chuck Dressen 221-189, Frank Dwyer 52-83, Jimmie Dykes 118-115, Phil Garner 145-179, Joe Gordon 26-31, Bucky Harris 516-557, Ralph Houk 366-443, Fred Hutchinson 155-235, Hugh Jennings 1,131-972, Bobby Lowe 30-44, Billy Martin 248-204, George Moriarty 150-157, Les Moss 27-26, Bill Norman 58-64, Steve O'Neill 509-414, Larry Parrish 82-104, Red Rolfe 278-256, Bob Scheffing 210-173, Joe Schultz 14-14, Frank Skaff 40-39, Mayo Smith 363-285, George Stallings 74-61, Bob Swift 56-43, Jack Tighe 99-104.

KANSAS CITY ROYALS
YEARLY FINISHES
WEST DIVISION

Year	Position	W	L	Pct.	*GB	Manager	Attendance
1969	4th	69	93	.429	28	Joe Gordon	902,414
1970	4th (tied)	65	97	.401	33	Charlie Metro, Bob Lemon	693,047
1971	2nd	85	76	.528	16	Bob Lemon	910,784
1972	4th	76	78	.494	16.5	Bob Lemon	707,656
1973	2nd	88	74	.543	6	Jack McKeon	1,345,341
1974	5th	77	85	.475	13	Jack McKeon	1,173,292
1975	2nd	91	71	.562	7	Jack McKeon, Whitey Herzog	1,151,836
1976	1st†	90	72	.556	+2.5	Whitey Herzog	1,680,265
1977	1st†	102	60	.630	+8	Whitey Herzog	1,852,603
1978	1st†	92	70	.568	+5	Whitey Herzog	2,255,493
1979	2nd	85	77	.525	3	Whitey Herzog	2,261,845
1980	1st‡	97	65	.599	+14	Jim Frey	2,288,714
1981	5th/1st∞	50	53	.485	§	Jim Frey, Dick Howser	1,279,403
1982	2nd	90	72	.556	3	Dick Howser	2,284,464
1983	2nd	79	83	.488	20	Dick Howser	1,963,875
1984	1st†	84	78	.519	+3	Dick Howser	1,810,018
1985	1st‡	91	71	.562	+1	Dick Howser	2,162,717
1986	3rd (tied)	76	86	.469	16	Dick Howser, Mike Ferraro	2,320,794
1987	2nd	83	79	.512	2	Billy Gardner, John Wathan	2,392,471
1988	3rd	84	77	.522	19.5	John Wathan	2,350,181
1989	2nd	92	70	.568	7	John Wathan	2,477,700
1990	6th	75	86	.466	27.5	John Wathan	2,244,956
1991	6th	82	80	.506	13	John Wathan, Hal McRae	2,161,537
1992	5th (tied)	72	90	.444	24	Hal McRae	1,867,689
1993	3rd	84	78	.519	10	Hal McRae	1,934,578

CENTRAL DIVISION

Year	Position	W	L	Pct.	*GB	Manager	Attendance
1994	3rd	64	51	.557	4	Hal McRae	1,400,494
1995	2nd	70	74	.486	30	Bob Boone	1,233,530
1996	5th	75	86	.466	24	Bob Boone	1,435,997
1997	5th	67	94	.416	19	Bob Boone, Tony Muser	1,517,638
1998	3rd	72	89	.447	16.5	Tony Muser	1,494,875
1999	4th	64	97	.398	32.5	Tony Muser	1,506,068
2000	4th	77	85	.475	18.0	Tony Muser	1,677,915
2001	5th	65	97	.401	26.0	Tony Muser	1,536,371

*Games behind winner. †Lost championship series. ‡Won championship series. §First half 20-30; second 30-23. ∞Lost division series.

MANAGERIAL RECORDS

Bob Boone 181-206, Mike Ferraro 36-38, Jim Frey 127-105, Billy Gardner 62-64, Joe Gordon 69-93, Whitey Herzog 410-304, Dick Howser 404-365, Bob Lemon 207-218, Jack McKeon 215-205, Hal McRae 286-277, Charlie Metro 19-33, Tony Muser 309-416, John Wathan 288-270.

MINNESOTA TWINS
YEARLY FINISHES

(Known as original Washington Senators through 1960)

Year	Position	W	L	Pct.	*GB	Manager	Attendance
1901	6th	61	72	.459	20.5	Jimmy Manning	161,661
1902	6th	61	75	.449	22.0	Tom Loftus	188,158
1903	8th	43	94	.314	47.5	Tom Loftus	128,878
1904	8th	38	113	.251	55.5	Patsy Donovan	131,744
1905	7th	64	87	.421	29.5	Jake Stahl	252,027
1906	7th	55	95	.367	37.5	Jake Stahl	129,903
1907	8th	49	102	.325	43.5	Joe Cantillon	221,929
1908	7th	67	85	.441	22.5	Joe Cantillon	264,252
1909	8th	42	110	.276	56.0	Joe Cantillon	205,199

Year	Position	W	L	Pct.	*GB	Manager	Attendance
1910	7th	66	85	.437	36.5	Jimmy McAleer	254,591
1911	7th	64	90	.416	38.5	Jimmy McAleer	244,884
1912	2nd	91	61	.599	14.0	Clark Griffith	350,663
1913	2nd	90	64	.584	6.5	Clark Griffith	325,831
1914	3rd	81	73	.526	19.0	Clark Griffith	243,888
1915	4th	85	68	.556	17.0	Clark Griffith	167,332
1916	7th	76	77	.497	14.5	Clark Griffith	177,265
1917	5th	74	79	.484	25.5	Clark Griffith	89,682
1918	3rd	72	56	.563	4.0	Clark Griffith	182,122
1919	7th	56	84	.400	32.0	Clark Griffith	234,096
1920	6th	68	84	.447	29.0	Clark Griffith	359,260
1921	4th	80	73	.523	18.0	George McBride	456,069
1922	6th	69	85	.448	25.0	Clyde Milan	458,552
1923	4th	75	78	.490	23.5	Donie Bush	357,406
1924	1st	92	62	.597	+2.0	Bucky Harris	534,310
1925	1st	96	55	.636	+8.5	Bucky Harris	817,199
1926	4th	81	69	.540	8.0	Bucky Harris	551,580
1927	3rd	85	69	.552	25.0	Bucky Harris	528,976
1928	4th	75	79	.487	26.0	Bucky Harris	378,501
1929	5th	71	81	.467	34.0	Walter Johnson	355,506
1930	2nd	94	60	.610	8.0	Walter Johnson	614,474
1931	3rd	92	62	.597	16.0	Walter Johnson	492,657
1932	3rd	93	61	.604	14.0	Walter Johnson	371,396
1933	1st	99	53	.651	+7.0	Joe Cronin	437,533
1934	7th	66	86	.434	34.0	Joe Cronin	330,074
1935	6th	67	86	.438	27.0	Bucky Harris	255,011
1936	4th	82	71	.536	20.0	Bucky Harris	379,525
1937	6th	73	80	.477	28.5	Bucky Harris	397,799
1938	5th	75	76	.497	23.5	Bucky Harris	522,694
1939	6th	65	87	.428	41.5	Bucky Harris	339,257
1940	7th	64	90	.416	26.0	Bucky Harris	381,241
1941	6th (tied)	70	84	.455	31.0	Bucky Harris	415,663
1942	7th	62	89	.411	39.5	Bucky Harris	403,493
1943	2nd	84	69	.549	13.5	Ossie Bluege	574,694
1944	8th	64	90	.416	25.0	Ossie Bluege	525,235
1945	2nd	87	67	.565	1.5	Ossie Bluege	652,660
1946	4th	76	78	.494	28.0	Ossie Bluege	1,027,216
1947	7th	64	90	.416	33.0	Ossie Bluege	850,758
1948	7th	56	97	.366	40.0	Joe Kuhel	795,254
1949	8th	50	104	.325	47.0	Joe Kuhel	770,745
1950	5th	67	87	.435	31.0	Bucky Harris	699,697
1951	7th	62	92	.403	36.0	Bucky Harris	695,167
1952	5th	78	76	.506	17.0	Bucky Harris	699,457
1953	5th	76	76	.500	23.5	Bucky Harris	595,594
1954	6th	66	88	.429	45.0	Bucky Harris	503,542
1955	8th	53	101	.344	43.0	Chuck Dressen	425,238
1956	7th	59	95	.383	38.0	Chuck Dressen	431,647
1957	8th	55	99	.357	43.0	Chuck Dressen, Cookie Lavagetto	457,079
1958	8th	61	93	.396	31.0	Cookie Lavagetto	475,288
1959	8th	63	91	.409	31.0	Cookie Lavagetto	615,372
1960	5th	73	81	.474	24.0	Cookie Lavagetto	743,404
1961	7th	70	90	.438	38.0	Cookie Lavagetto, Sam Mele	1,256,723
1962	2nd	91	71	.562	5.0	Sam Mele	1,433,116
1963	3rd	91	70	.565	13.0	Sam Mele	1,406,652
1964	6th (tied)	79	83	.488	20.0	Sam Mele	1,207,514
1965	1st	102	60	.630	+7.0	Sam Mele	1,463,258
1966	2nd	89	73	.549	9.0	Sam Mele	1,259,374
1967	2nd (tied)	91	71	.562	1.0	Sam Mele, Cal Ermer	1,483,547
1968	7th	79	83	.488	24.0	Cal Ermer	1,143,257

WEST DIVISION

Year	Position	W	L	Pct.	*GB	Manager	Attendance
1969	1st†	97	65	.599	+9.0	Billy Martin	1,349,328
1970	1st†	98	64	.605	+9.0	Bill Rigney	1,261,887
1971	5th	74	86	.463	26.5	Bill Rigney	940,858
1972	3rd	77	77	.500	15.5	Bill Rigney, Frank Quilici	797,901
1973	3rd	81	81	.500	13.0	Frank Quilici	907,499
1974	3rd	82	80	.506	8.0	Frank Quilici	662,401
1975	4th	76	83	.478	20.5	Frank Quilici	737,156
1976	3rd	85	77	.525	5.0	Gene Mauch	715,394
1977	4th	84	77	.522	17.5	Gene Mauch	1,162,727
1978	4th	73	89	.451	19.0	Gene Mauch	787,878
1979	4th	82	80	.506	6.0	Gene Mauch	1,070,521
1980	3rd	77	84	.478	19.5	Gene Mauch, Johnny Goryl	769,206

Year	Position	W	L	Pct.	*GB	Manager	Attendance
1981	7th/4th	41	68	.376	‡	Johnny Goryl, Billy Gardner	469,090
1982	7th	60	102	.370	33.0	Billy Gardner	921,186
1983	5th (tied)	70	92	.432	29.0	Billy Gardner	858,939
1984	2nd (tied)	81	81	.500	3.0	Billy Gardner	1,598,422
1985	4th (tied)	77	85	.475	14.0	Billy Gardner, Ray Miller	1,651,814
1986	6th	71	91	.438	21.0	Ray Miller, Tom Kelly	1,255,453
1987	1st§	85	77	.525	+2.0	Tom Kelly	2,081,976
1988	2nd	91	71	.562	13.0	Tom Kelly	3,030,672
1989	5th	80	82	.494	19.0	Tom Kelly	2,277,438
1990	7th	74	88	.457	29.0	Tom Kelly	1,751,584
1991	1st§	95	67	.586	+8.0	Tom Kelly	2,293,842
1992	2nd	90	72	.556	6.0	Tom Kelly	2,482,428
1993	5th (tied)	71	91	.438	23.0	Tom Kelly	2,048,673

CENTRAL DIVISION

Year	Position	W	L	Pct.	*GB	Manager	Attendance
1994	4th	53	60	.469	14.0	Tom Kelly	1,398,565
1995	5th	56	88	.389	44.0	Tom Kelly	1,057,667
1996	4th	78	84	.481	21.5	Tom Kelly	1,437,352
1997	4th	68	94	.420	18.5	Tom Kelly	1,411,064
1998	4th	70	92	.432	19.0	Tom Kelly	1,165,980
1999	5th	63	97	.394	33.0	Tom Kelly	1,202,829
2000	5th	69	93	.426	26.0	Tom Kelly	1,059,715
2001	2nd	85	77	.525	6.0	Tom Kelly	1,782,926

*Games behind winner. †Lost championship series. ‡First half 17-39; second 24-29. §Won championship series.

MANAGERIAL RECORDS

Ossie Bluege 375-394, Donie Bush 75-78, Joe Cantillon 158-297, Joe Cronin 165-139, Patsy Donovan 38-113, Chuck Dressen 116-212, Cal Ermer 145-129, Billy Gardner 268-353, Johnny Goryl 34-38, Clark Griffith 693-646, Bucky Harris 1,336-1,416, Walter Johnson 350-264, Tom Kelly 1,140-1,244, Joe Kuhel 106-201, Cookie Lavagetto 271-384, Tom Loftus 104-169, Jimmy Manning 61-72, Billy Martin 97-65, Gene Mauch 378-394, Jimmy McAleer 130-175, George McBride 80-73, Sam Mele 524-436, Clyde Milan 69-85, Ray Miller 109-130, Frank Quilici 280-287, Bill Rigney 208-184, Jake Stahl 119-182.

NEW YORK YANKEES

YEARLY FINISHES

(Known as Baltimore Orioles through 1902)

Year	Position	W	L	Pct.	*GB	Manager	Attendance
1901	5th	68	65	.511	13.5	John McGraw	141,952
1902	8th	50	88	.362	34.0	John McGraw, Wilbert Robinson	174,606
1903	4th	72	62	.537	17.0	Clark Griffith	211,808
1904	2nd	92	59	.609	1.5	Clark Griffith	438,919
1905	6th	71	78	.477	21.5	Clark Griffith	309,100
1906	2nd	90	61	.596	3.0	Clark Griffith	434,709
1907	5th	70	78	.473	21.0	Clark Griffith	350,020
1908	8th	51	103	.331	39.5	Clark Griffith, Kid Elberfeld	305,500
1909	5th	74	77	.490	23.5	George Stallings	501,000
1910	2nd	88	63	.583	14.5	George Stallings, Hal Chase	355,857
1911	6th	76	76	.500	25.5	Hal Chase	302,444
1912	8th	50	102	.329	55.0	Harry Wolverton	242,194
1913	7th	57	94	.377	38.0	Frank Chance	357,551
1914	6th (tied)	70	84	.455	30.0	Frank Chance, Roger Peckinpaugh	359,477
1915	5th	69	83	.454	32.5	Bill Donovan	256,035
1916	4th	80	74	.519	11.0	Bill Donovan	469,211
1917	6th	71	82	.464	28.5	Bill Donovan	330,294
1918	4th	60	63	.488	13.5	Miller Huggins	282,047
1919	3rd	80	59	.576	7.5	Miller Huggins	619,164
1920	3rd	95	59	.617	3.0	Miller Huggins	1,289,422
1921	1st	98	55	.641	+4.5	Miller Huggins	1,230,696
1922	1st	94	60	.610	+1.0	Miller Huggins	1,026,134
1923	1st	98	54	.645	+16.0	Miller Huggins	1,007,066
1924	2nd	89	63	.586	2.0	Miller Huggins	1,053,533
1925	7th	69	85	.448	30.0	Miller Huggins	697,267
1926	1st	91	63	.591	+3.0	Miller Huggins	1,027,095
1927	1st	110	44	.714	+19.0	Miller Huggins	1,164,015
1928	1st	101	53	.656	+2.5	Miller Huggins	1,072,132
1929	2nd	88	66	.571	18.0	Miller Huggins, Art Fletcher	960,148
1930	3rd	86	68	.558	16.0	Bob Shawkey	1,169,230
1931	2nd	94	59	.614	13.5	Joe McCarthy	912,437
1932	1st	107	47	.695	+13.0	Joe McCarthy	962,320
1933	2nd	91	59	.607	7.0	Joe McCarthy	728,014

Year	Position	W	L	Pct.	*GB	Manager	Attendance
1934	2nd	94	60	.610	7.0	Joe McCarthy	854,682
1935	2nd	89	60	.597	3.0	Joe McCarthy	657,508
1936	1st	102	51	.667	+19.5	Joe McCarthy	976,913
1937	1st	102	52	.662	+13.0	Joe McCarthy	998,148
1938	1st	99	53	.651	+9.5	Joe McCarthy	970,916
1939	1st	106	45	.702	+17.0	Joe McCarthy	859,785
1940	3rd	88	66	.571	2.0	Joe McCarthy	988,975
1941	1st	101	53	.656	+17.0	Joe McCarthy	964,722
1942	1st	103	51	.669	+9.0	Joe McCarthy	988,251
1943	1st	98	56	.636	+13.5	Joe McCarthy	645,006
1944	3rd	83	71	.539	6.0	Joe McCarthy	822,864
1945	4th	81	71	.533	6.5	Joe McCarthy	881,846
1946	3rd	87	67	.565	17.0	Joe McCarthy, Bill Dickey, Johnny Neun	2,265,512
1947	1st	97	57	.630	+12.0	Bucky Harris	2,178,937
1948	3rd	94	60	.610	2.5	Bucky Harris	2,373,901
1949	1st	97	57	.630	+1.0	Casey Stengel	2,281,676
1950	1st	98	56	.636	+3.0	Casey Stengel	2,081,380
1951	1st	98	56	.636	+5.0	Casey Stengel	1,950,107
1952	1st	95	59	.617	+2.0	Casey Stengel	1,629,665
1953	1st	99	52	.656	+8.5	Casey Stengel	1,537,811
1954	2nd	103	51	.669	8.0	Casey Stengel	1,475,171
1955	1st	96	58	.623	+3.0	Casey Stengel	1,490,138
1956	1st	97	57	.630	+9.0	Casey Stengel	1,491,784
1957	1st	98	56	.636	+8.0	Casey Stengel	1,497,134
1958	1st	92	62	.597	+10.0	Casey Stengel	1,428,438
1959	3rd	79	75	.513	15.0	Casey Stengel	1,552,030
1960	1st	97	57	.630	+8.0	Casey Stengel	1,627,349
1961	1st	109	53	.673	+8.0	Ralph Houk	1,747,725
1962	1st	96	66	.593	+5.0	Ralph Houk	1,493,574
1963	1st	104	57	.646	+10.5	Ralph Houk	1,308,920
1964	1st	99	63	.611	+1.0	Yogi Berra	1,305,638
1965	6th	77	85	.475	25.0	Johnny Keane	1,213,552
1966	10th	70	89	.440	26.5	Johnny Keane, Ralph Houk	1,124,648
1967	9th	72	90	.444	20.0	Ralph Houk	1,259,514
1968	5th	83	79	.512	20.0	Ralph Houk	1,185,666

EAST DIVISION

Year	Position	W	L	Pct.	*GB	Manager	Attendance
1969	5th	80	81	.497	28.5	Ralph Houk	1,067,996
1970	2nd	93	69	.574	15.0	Ralph Houk	1,136,879
1971	4th	82	80	.506	21.0	Ralph Houk	1,070,771
1972	4th	79	76	.510	6.5	Ralph Houk	966,328
1973	4th	80	82	.494	17.0	Ralph Houk	1,262,103
1974	2nd	89	73	.549	2.0	Bill Virdon	1,273,075
1975	3rd	83	77	.519	12.0	Bill Virdon, Billy Martin	1,288,048
1976	1st†	97	62	.610	+10.5	Billy Martin	2,012,434
1977	1st†	100	62	.617	+2.5	Billy Martin	2,103,092
1978	1st‡†	100	63	.613	+1.0	Billy Martin, Bob Lemon	2,335,871
1979	4th	89	71	.556	13.5	Bob Lemon, Billy Martin	2,537,765
1980	1st§	103	59	.636	+3.0	Dick Howser	2,627,417
1981	1st/6th▲†	59	48	.551	∞	Gene Michael, Bob Lemon	1,614,533
1982	5th	79	83	.488	16.0	Bob Lemon, Gene Michael, Clyde King	2,041,219
1983	3rd	91	71	.562	7.0	Billy Martin	2,257,976
1984	3rd	87	75	.537	17.0	Yogi Berra	1,821,815
1985	2nd	97	64	.602	2.0	Yogi Berra, Billy Martin	2,214,587
1986	2nd	90	72	.556	5.5	Lou Piniella	2,268,030
1987	4th	89	73	.549	9.0	Lou Piniella	2,427,672
1988	5th	85	76	.528	3.5	Billy Martin, Lou Piniella	2,633,701
1989	5th	74	87	.460	14.5	Dallas Green, Bucky Dent	2,170,485
1990	7th	67	95	.414	21.0	Bucky Dent, Stump Merrill	2,006,436
1991	5th	71	91	.438	20.0	Stump Merrill	1,863,733
1992	4th (tied)	76	86	.469	20.0	Buck Showalter	1,748,733
1993	2nd	88	74	.543	7.0	Buck Showalter	2,416,965
1994	1st	70	43	.619	+6.5	Buck Showalter	1,675,556
1995	2nd◆	79	65	.549	7.0	Buck Showalter	1,705,263
1996	1st▲†	92	70	.568	+4.0	Joe Torre	2,250,877
1997	2nd◆	96	66	.593	2.0	Joe Torre	2,580,325
1998	1st▲†	114	48	.704	+22.0	Joe Torre	2,949,734
1999	1st▲†	98	64	.605	+4.0	Joe Torre	3,292,736
2000	1st▲†	87	74	.540	+2.5	Joe Torre	3,227,657
2001	1st▲†	95	65	.594	+13.5	Joe Torre	3,264,777

*Games behind winner. †Won championship series. ‡Won pennant playoff. §Lost championship series. ∞First half 34-22; second 25-26. ▲Won division series. ◆Lost division series.

MANAGERIAL RECORDS

Yogi Berra 192-148, Frank Chance 117-168, Hal Chase 86-80, Bucky Dent 36-53, Bill Dickey 57-48, Bill Donovan 220-239, Kid Elberfeld 27-71, Art Fletcher 6-5, Dallas Green 56-65, Clark Griffith 419-370, Bucky Harris 191-117, Ralph Houk 944-806, Dick Howser 103-59, Miller Huggins 1,067-719, Johnny Keane 81-101, Clyde King 29-33, Bob Lemon 99-73, Billy Martin 501-385, Joe McCarthy 1,460-867, John McGraw 94-96, Stump Merrill 120-155, Gene Michael 92-76, Johnny Neun 8-6, Roger Peckinpaugh 10-10, Lou Piniella 224-193, Wilbert Robinson 24-57, Bob Shawkey 86-68, Buck Showalter 311-268, George Stallings 152-136, Casey Stengel 1,149-696, Joe Torre 582-387, Bill Virdon 142-124, Harry Wolverton 50-102.

OAKLAND A'S
YEARLY FINISHES

(Known as Philadelphia A's through 1954 and Kansas City A's through 1967)

Year	Position	W	L	Pct.	*GB	Manager	Attendance
1901	4th	74	62	.544	9.0	Connie Mack	206,329
1902	1st	83	53	.610	+5.0	Connie Mack	442,473
1903	2nd	75	60	.556	14.5	Connie Mack	420,078
1904	5th	81	70	.536	12.5	Connie Mack	512,294
1905	1st	92	56	.622	+2.0	Connie Mack	554,576
1906	4th	78	67	.538	12.0	Connie Mack	489,129
1907	2nd	88	57	.607	1.5	Connie Mack	625,581
1908	6th	68	85	.444	22.0	Connie Mack	455,062
1909	2nd	95	58	.621	3.5	Connie Mack	674,915
1910	1st	102	48	.680	+14.5	Connie Mack	588,905
1911	1st	101	50	.669	+13.5	Connie Mack	605,749
1912	3rd	90	62	.592	15.0	Connie Mack	517,653
1913	1st	96	57	.627	+6.5	Connie Mack	571,896
1914	1st	99	53	.651	+8.5	Connie Mack	346,641
1915	8th	43	109	.283	58.5	Connie Mack	146,223
1916	8th	36	117	.235	54.5	Connie Mack	184,471
1917	8th	55	98	.359	44.5	Connie Mack	221,432
1918	8th	52	76	.406	24.0	Connie Mack	177,926
1919	8th	36	104	.257	52.0	Connie Mack	225,209
1920	8th	48	106	.312	50.0	Connie Mack	287,888
1921	8th	53	100	.346	45.0	Connie Mack	344,430
1922	7th	65	89	.422	29.0	Connie Mack	425,356
1923	6th	69	83	.454	29.0	Connie Mack	534,122
1924	5th	71	81	.467	20.0	Connie Mack	531,992
1925	2nd	88	64	.579	8.5	Connie Mack	869,703
1926	3rd	83	67	.553	6.0	Connie Mack	714,308
1927	2nd	91	63	.591	19.0	Connie Mack	605,529
1928	2nd	98	55	.641	2.5	Connie Mack	689,756
1929	1st	104	46	.693	+18.0	Connie Mack	839,176
1930	1st	102	52	.662	+8.0	Connie Mack	721,663
1931	1st	107	45	.704	+13.5	Connie Mack	627,464
1932	2nd	94	60	.610	13.0	Connie Mack	405,500
1933	3rd	79	72	.523	19.5	Connie Mack	297,138
1934	5th	68	82	.453	31.0	Connie Mack	305,847
1935	8th	58	91	.389	34.0	Connie Mack	233,173
1936	8th	53	100	.346	49.0	Connie Mack	285,173
1937	7th	54	97	.358	46.5	Connie Mack	430,733
1938	8th	53	99	.349	46.0	Connie Mack	385,357
1939	7th	55	97	.362	51.5	Connie Mack	395,022
1940	8th	54	100	.351	36.0	Connie Mack	432,145
1941	8th	64	90	.416	37.0	Connie Mack	528,894
1942	8th	55	99	.357	48.0	Connie Mack	423,487
1943	8th	49	105	.318	49.0	Connie Mack	376,735
1944	5th (tied)	72	82	.468	17.0	Connie Mack	505,322
1945	8th	52	98	.347	34.5	Connie Mack	462,631
1946	8th	49	105	.318	55.0	Connie Mack	621,793
1947	5th	78	76	.506	19.0	Connie Mack	911,566
1948	4th	84	70	.545	12.5	Connie Mack	945,076
1949	5th	81	73	.526	16.0	Connie Mack	816,514
1950	8th	52	102	.338	46.0	Connie Mack	309,805
1951	6th	70	84	.455	28.0	Jimmie Dykes	465,469
1952	4th	79	75	.513	16.0	Jimmie Dykes	627,100
1953	7th	59	95	.383	41.5	Jimmie Dykes	362,113
1954	8th	51	103	.331	60.0	Ed Joost	304,666
1955	6th	63	91	.409	33.0	Lou Boudreau	1,393,054
1956	8th	52	102	.338	45.0	Lou Boudreau	1,015,154
1957	7th	59	94	.386	38.5	Lou Boudreau, Harry Craft	901,067
1958	7th	73	81	.474	19.0	Harry Craft	925,090
1959	7th	66	88	.429	28.0	Harry Craft	963,683

Year	Position	W	L	Pct.	*GB	Manager	Attendance
1960	8th	58	96	.377	39.0	Bob Elliot	774,944
1961	9th (tied)	61	100	.379	47.5	Joe Gordon, Hank Bauer	683,817
1962	9th	72	90	.444	24.0	Hank Bauer	635,675
1963	8th	73	89	.451	31.5	Ed Lopat	762,364
1964	10th	57	105	.352	42.0	Ed Lopat, Mel McGaha	642,478
1965	10th	59	103	.364	43.0	Mel McGaha, Haywood Sullivan	528,344
1966	7th	74	86	.463	23.0	Alvin Dark	773,929
1967	10th	62	99	.385	29.5	Alvin Dark, Luke Appling	726,639
1968	6th	82	80	.506	21.0	Bob Kennedy	837,466

WEST DIVISION

Year	Position	W	L	Pct.	*GB	Manager	Attendance
1969	2nd	88	74	.543	9.0	Hank Bauer, John McNamara	778,232
1970	2nd	89	73	.549	9.0	John McNamara	778,355
1971	1st†	101	60	.627	+16.0	Dick Williams	914,993
1972	1st‡	93	62	.600	+5.5	Dick Williams	921,323
1973	1st‡	94	68	.580	+6.0	Dick Williams	1,000,763
1974	1st‡	90	72	.556	+5.0	Alvin Dark	845,693
1975	1st†	98	64	.605	+7.0	Alvin Dark	1,075,518
1976	2nd	87	74	.540	2.5	Chuck Tanner	780,593
1977	7th	63	98	.391	38.5	Jack McKeon, Bobby Winkles	495,599
1978	6th	69	93	.426	23.0	Bobby Winkles, Jack McKeon	526,999
1979	7th	54	108	.333	34.0	Jim Marshall	306,763
1980	2nd	83	79	.512	14.0	Billy Martin	842,259
1981	1st/2nd∞†	64	45	.587	§	Billy Martin	1,304,054
1982	5th	68	94	.420	25.0	Billy Martin	1,735,489
1983	4th	74	88	.457	25.0	Steve Boros	1,294,941
1984	4th	77	85	.475	7.0	Steve Boros, Jackie Moore	1,353,281
1985	4th (tied)	77	85	.475	14.0	Jackie Moore	1,334,599
1986	3rd (tied)	76	86	.469	16.0	Jackie Moore, Tony La Russa	1,314,646
1987	3rd	81	81	.500	4.0	Tony La Russa	1,678,921
1988	1st‡	104	58	.642	+13.0	Tony La Russa	2,287,335
1989	1st‡	99	63	.611	+7.0	Tony La Russa	2,667,225
1990	1st‡	103	59	.636	+9.0	Tony La Russa	2,900,217
1991	4th	84	78	.519	11.0	Tony La Russa	2,713,493
1992	1st†	96	66	.593	+6.0	Tony La Russa	2,494,160
1993	7th	68	94	.420	26.0	Tony La Russa	2,035,025
1994	2nd	51	63	.447	1.0	Tony La Russa	1,242,692
1995	4th	67	77	.465	11.5	Tony La Russa	1,174,310
1996	3rd	78	84	.481	12.0	Art Howe	1,148,380
1997	4th	65	97	.401	25.0	Art Howe	1,264,218
1998	4th	74	88	.457	14.0	Art Howe	1,232,339
1999	2nd	87	75	.537	8.0	Art Howe	1,434,610
2000	1st▲	91	70	.565	+0.5	Art Howe	1,728,888
2001	2nd▲	102	60	.630	14.0	Art Howe	2,133,277

*Games behind winner. †Lost championship series. ‡Won championship series. §First half 37-23; second 27-22. ∞Won division series. ▲Lost division series.

MANAGERIAL RECORDS

Luke Appling 10-30, Hank Bauer 187-226, Steve Boros 94-112, Lou Boudreau 151-260, Harry Craft 162-196, Alvin Dark 314-291, Jimmie Dykes 198-254, Bob Elliott 58-96, Joe Gordon 26-33, Art Howe 497-474, Eddie Joost 51-103, Bob Kennedy 82-80, Tony La Russa 695-614, Eddie Lopat 90-124, Connie Mack 3,582-3,814, Jim Marshall 54-108, Billy Martin 215-218, Mel McGaha 45-91, Jack McKeon 71-105, John McNamara 97-78, Jackie Moore 163-190, Haywood Sullivan 54-82, Chuck Tanner 87-74, Dick Williams 288-190, Bobby Winkles 61-86.

SEATTLE MARINERS
YEARLY FINISHES
WEST DIVISION

Year	Position	W	L	Pct.	*GB	Manager	Attendance
1977	6th	64	98	.395	38.0	Darrell Johnson	1,338,511
1978	7th	56	104	.350	35.0	Darrell Johnson	877,440
1979	6th	67	95	.414	21.0	Darrell Johnson	844,447
1980	7th	59	103	.364	38.0	Darrell Johnson, Maury Wills	836,204
1981	6th/5th	44	65	.404	†	Maury Wills, Rene Lachemann	636,276
1982	4th	76	86	.469	17.0	Rene Lachemann	1,070,404
1983	7th	60	102	.370	39.0	Rene Lachemann, Del Crandall	813,537
1984	5th (tied)	74	88	.457	10.0	Del Crandall, Chuck Cottier	870,372
1985	6th	74	88	.457	17.0	Chuck Cottier	1,128,696
1986	7th	67	95	.414	25.0	Chuck Cottier, Marty Martinez, Dick Williams	1,029,045
1987	4th	78	84	.481	7.0	Dick Williams	1,134,255
1988	7th	68	93	.422	35.5	Dick Williams, Jim Snyder	1,022,398
1989	6th	73	89	.451	26.0	Jim Lefebvre	1,298,443

Year	Position	W	L	Pct.	*GB	Manager	Attendance
1990	5th	77	85	.475	26.0	Jim Lefebvre	1,509,727
1991	5th	83	79	.512	12.0	Jim Lefebvre	2,147,905
1992	7th	64	98	.395	32.0	Bill Plummer	1,651,398
1993	4th	82	80	.506	12.0	Lou Piniella	2,051,853
1994	3rd	49	63	.438	2.0	Lou Piniella	1,104,206
1995	1st‡§∞	79	66	.545	+1.0	Lou Piniella	1,643,203
1996	2nd	85	76	.528	4.5	Lou Piniella	2,723,850
1997	1st▲	90	72	.556	+6.0	Lou Piniella	3,192,237
1998	3rd	76	85	.472	11.5	Lou Piniella	2,644,166
1999	3rd	79	83	.488	16.0	Lou Piniella	2,916,346
2000	2nd§∞	91	71	.562	0.5	Lou Piniella	3,148,317
2001	1st§∞	116	46	.716	+14.0	Lou Piniella	3,507,975

*Games behind winner. †First half 21-36; second 23-29. ‡Won division playoff. §Won division series. ∞Lost championship series. ▲Lost division series.

MANAGERIAL RECORDS

Chuck Cottier 98-120, Del Crandall 93-141, Darrell Johnson 226-362, Rene Lachemann 140-180, Jim Lefebvre 233-253, Lou Piniella 747-642, Bill Plummer 64-98, Jimmy Snyder 45-60, Dick Williams 159-192, Maury Wills 26-56.

TAMPA BAY DEVIL RAYS
YEARLY FINISHES
EAST DIVISION

Year	Position	W	L	Pct.	*GB	Manager	Attendance
1998	5th	63	99	.389	51.0	Larry Rothschild	2,506,023
1999	5th	69	93	.426	29.0	Larry Rothschild	1,562,827
2000	5th	69	92	.429	18.0	Larry Rothschild	1,549,052
2001	5th	62	100	.383	34.0	Larry Rothschild, Hal McRae	1,227,673

*Games behind winner.

MANAGERIAL RECORDS

Hal McRae 58-90, Larry Rothschild 205-294.

TEXAS RANGERS
YEARLY FINISHES

(Known as second Washington Senators through 1971)

Year	Position	W	L	Pct.	*GB	Manager	Attendance
1961	9th (tied)	61	100	.370	47.5	Mickey Vernon	597,287
1962	10th	60	101	.373	35.5	Mickey Vernon	729,775
1963	10th	56	106	.346	48.5	Mickey Vernon, Gil Hodges	535,604
1964	9th	62	100	.383	37.0	Gil Hodges	600,106
1965	8th	70	92	.432	32.0	Gil Hodges	560,083
1966	8th	71	88	.447	25.5	Gil Hodges	576,260
1967	6th (tied)	76	85	.472	15.5	Gil Hodges	770,863
1968	10th	65	96	.404	37.5	Jim Lemon	546,661

EAST DIVISION

Year	Position	W	L	Pct.	*GB	Manager	Attendance
1969	4th	86	76	.531	23.0	Ted Williams	918,106
1970	6th	70	92	.432	38.0	Ted Williams	824,789
1971	5th	63	96	.396	38.5	Ted Williams	655,156

WEST DIVISION

Year	Position	W	L	Pct.	*GB	Manager	Attendance
1972	6th	54	100	.351	38.5	Ted Williams	662,974
1973	6th	57	105	.352	37.0	Whitey Herzog, Del Wilber, Billy Martin	686,085
1974	2nd	84	76	.525	5.0	Billy Martin	1,193,902
1975	3rd	79	83	.488	19.0	Billy Martin, Frank Lucchesi	1,127,924
1976	4th (tied)	76	86	.469	14.0	Frank Lucchesi	1,164,982
1977	2nd	94	68	.580	8.0	Frank Lucchesi, Eddie Stanky, Connie Ryan, Billy Hunter	1,250,722
1978	2nd (tied)	87	75	.537	5.0	Billy Hunter, Pat Corrales	1,447,963
1979	3rd	83	79	.512	5.0	Pat Corrales	1,519,671
1980	4th	76	85	.472	20.5	Pat Corrales	1,198,175
1981	2nd/3rd	57	48	.543	†	Don Zimmer	850,076
1982	6th	64	98	.395	29.0	Don Zimmer, Darrell Johnson	1,154,432
1983	3rd	77	85	.475	22.0	Doug Rader	1,363,469
1984	7th	69	92	.429	14.5	Doug Rader	1,102,471
1985	7th	62	99	.385	28.5	Doug Rader, Bobby Valentine	1,112,497

HISTORY *Team by team*

Year	Position	W	L	Pct.	*GB	Manager	Attendance
1986	2nd	87	75	.537	5.0	Bobby Valentine	1,692,002
1987	6th (tied)	75	87	.463	10.0	Bobby Valentine	1,763,053
1988	6th	70	91	.435	33.5	Bobby Valentine	1,581,901
1989	4th	83	79	.512	16.0	Bobby Valentine	2,043,993
1990	3rd	83	79	.512	20.0	Bobby Valentine	2,057,911
1991	3rd	85	77	.525	10.0	Bobby Valentine	2,297,720
1992	4th	77	85	.475	19.0	Bobby Valentine, Toby Harrah	2,198,231
1993	2nd	86	76	.531	8.0	Kevin Kennedy	2,244,616
1994	1st	52	62	.456	+1.0	Kevin Kennedy	2,503,198
1995	3rd	74	70	.514	4.5	Johnny Oates	1,985,910
1996	1st‡	90	72	.556	+4.5	Johnny Oates	2,889,020
1997	3rd	77	85	.475	13.0	Johnny Oates	2,945,228
1998	1st‡	88	74	.543	+3.0	Johnny Oates	2,927,409
1999	1st‡	95	67	.586	+8.0	Johnny Oates	2,771,469
2000	4th	71	91	.438	20.5	Johnny Oates	2,800,147
2001	4th	73	89	.451	43.0	Johnny Oates, Jerry Narron	2,831,111

*Games behind winner. †First half 33-22; second 24-26. ‡Lost division series.

MANAGERIAL RECORDS

Pat Corrales 160-164, Toby Harrah 32-44, Whitey Herzog 47-91, Gil Hodges 321-444, Billy Hunter 146-108, Darrell Johnson 26-40, Kevin Kennedy 138-138, Jim Lemon 65-96, Frank Lucchesi 142-149, Billy Martin 137-141, Jerry Narron 62-72, Johnny Oates 506-476, Doug Rader 155-200, Connie Ryan 2-4, Eddie Stanky 1-0, Bobby Valentine 581-605, Mickey Vernon 135-227, Del Wilber 1-0, Ted Williams 273-364, Don Zimmer 95-106.

TORONTO BLUE JAYS
YEARLY FINISHES
EAST DIVISION

Year	Position	W	L	Pct.	*GB	Manager	Attendance
1977	7th	54	107	.335	45.5	Roy Hartsfield	1,701,052
1978	7th	59	102	.366	40.0	Roy Hartsfield	1,562,585
1979	7th	53	109	.327	50.5	Roy Hartsfield	1,431,651
1980	7th	67	95	.414	36.0	Bobby Mattick	1,400,327
1981	7th/7th	37	69	.349	†	Bobby Mattick	755,083
1982	6th (tied)	78	84	.481	17.0	Bobby Cox	1,275,978
1983	4th	89	73	.549	9.0	Bobby Cox	1,930,415
1984	2nd	89	73	.549	15.0	Bobby Cox	2,110,009
1985	1st‡	99	62	.615	+2.0	Bobby Cox	2,468,925
1986	4th	86	76	.531	9.5	Jimy Williams	2,455,477
1987	2nd	96	66	.593	2.0	Jimy Williams	2,778,429
1988	3rd (tied)	87	75	.537	2.0	Jimy Williams	2,595,175
1989	1st‡	89	73	.549	+2.0	Jimy Williams, Cito Gaston	3,375,883
1990	2nd	86	76	.531	2.0	Cito Gaston	3,885,284
1991	1st‡	91	71	.562	+7.0	Cito Gaston	4,001,527
1992	1st§	96	66	.593	+4.0	Cito Gaston	4,028,318
1993	1st§	95	67	.586	+7.0	Cito Gaston	4,057,947
1994	3rd	55	60	.478	16.0	Cito Gaston	2,907,933
1995	5th	56	88	.389	30.0	Cito Gaston	2,826,483
1996	4th	74	88	.457	18.0	Cito Gaston	2,559,573
1997	5th	76	86	.469	22.0	Cito Gaston, Mel Queen	2,589,297
1998	3rd	88	74	.543	26.0	Tim Johnson	2,454,183
1999	3rd	84	78	.519	14.0	Jim Fregosi	2,163,464
2000	3rd	83	79	.512	4.5	Jim Fregosi	1,819,886
2001	3rd	80	82	.494	16.0	Buck Martinez	1,915,438

*Games behind winner. †First half 16-42; second 21-27. ‡Lost championship series. §Won championship series.

MANAGERIAL RECORDS

Bobby Cox 355-292, Jim Fregosi 167-157, Cito Gaston 702-650, Roy Hartsfield 166-318, Tim Johnson 88-74, Buck Martinez 80-82, Bobby Mattick 104-164, Mel Queen 4-1, Jimy Williams 281-241.

NATIONAL LEAGUE

ARIZONA DIAMONDBACKS
YEARLY FINISHES
WEST DIVISION

Year	Position	W	L	Pct.	*GB	Manager	Attendance
1998	5th	65	97	.401	33.0	Buck Showalter	3,600,412
1999	1st†	100	62	.617	+14.0	Buck Showalter	3,019,654
2000	3rd	85	77	.525	12.0	Buck Showalter	2,942,516
2001	1st‡§	92	70	.556	+2.0	Bob Brenly	2,740,554

*Games behind winner. †Lost division series. ‡Won division series. §Won championship series.

MANAGERIAL RECORDS

Bob Brenly 92-70, Buck Showalter 250-236.

ATLANTA BRAVES
YEARLY FINISHES

(Known as Boston Braves through 1952 and Milwaukee Braves through 1965)

Year	Position	W	L	Pct.	*GB	Manager	Attendance
1901	5th	69	69	.500	20.5	Frank Selee	146,502
1902	3rd	73	64	.533	29.0	Al Buckenberger	116,960
1903	6th	58	80	.420	32.0	Al Buckenberger	143,155
1904	7th	55	98	.359	51.0	Al Buckenberger	140,694
1905	7th	51	103	.331	54.5	Fred Tenney	150,003
1906	8th	49	102	.325	66.5	Fred Tenney	143,280
1907	7th	58	90	.392	47.0	Fred Tenney	203,221
1908	6th	63	91	.409	36.0	Joe Kelley	253,750
1909	8th	45	108	.294	65.5	Frank Bowerman, Harry Smith	195,188
1910	8th	53	100	.346	50.5	Fred Lake	149,027
1911	8th	44	107	.291	54.0	Fred Tenney	116,000
1912	8th	52	101	.340	52.0	Johnny Kling	121,000
1913	5th	69	82	.457	31.5	George Stallings	208,000
1914	1st	94	59	.614	+10.5	George Stallings	382,913
1915	2nd	83	69	.546	7.0	George Stallings	376,283
1916	3rd	89	63	.586	4.0	George Stallings	313,495
1917	6th	72	81	.471	25.5	George Stallings	174,253
1918	7th	53	71	.427	28.5	George Stallings	84,938
1919	6th	57	82	.410	38.5	George Stallings	167,401
1920	7th	62	90	.408	30.0	George Stallings	162,483
1921	4th	79	74	.516	15.0	Fred Mitchell	318,627
1922	8th	53	100	.346	39.5	Fred Mitchell	167,965
1923	7th	54	100	.351	41.5	Fred Mitchell	227,802
1924	8th	53	100	.346	40.0	Dave Bancroft	117,478
1925	5th	70	83	.458	25.0	Dave Bancroft	313,528
1926	7th	66	86	.434	22.0	Dave Bancroft	303,598
1927	7th	60	94	.390	34.0	Dave Bancroft	288,685
1928	7th	50	103	.327	44.5	Jack Slattery, Rogers Hornsby	227,001
1929	8th	56	98	.364	43.0	Emil Fuchs	372,351
1930	6th	70	84	.455	22.0	Bill McKechnie	464,835
1931	7th	64	90	.416	37.0	Bill McKechnie	515,005
1932	5th	77	77	.500	13.0	Bill McKechnie	507,606
1933	4th	83	71	.539	9.0	Bill McKechnie	517,803
1934	4th	78	73	.517	16.0	Bill McKechnie	303,205
1935	8th	38	115	.248	61.5	Bill McKechnie	232,754
1936	6th	71	83	.461	21.0	Bill McKechnie	340,585
1937	5th	79	73	.520	16.0	Bill McKechnie	385,339
1938	5th	77	75	.507	12.0	Casey Stengel	341,149
1939	7th	63	88	.417	32.5	Casey Stengel	285,994
1940	7th	65	87	.428	34.5	Casey Stengel	241,616
1941	7th	62	92	.403	38.0	Casey Stengel	263,680
1942	7th	59	89	.399	44.0	Casey Stengel	285,332
1943	6th	68	85	.444	36.5	Casey Stengel	271,289
1944	6th	65	89	.422	40.0	Bob Coleman	208,691
1945	6th	67	85	.441	30.0	Bob Coleman, Del Bissonette	374,178
1946	4th	81	72	.529	15.5	Billy Southworth	969,673
1947	3rd	86	68	.558	8.0	Billy Southworth	1,277,361
1948	1st	91	62	.595	+6.5	Billy Southworth	1,455,439
1949	4th	75	79	.487	22.0	Billy Southworth	1,081,795
1950	4th	83	71	.539	8.0	Billy Southworth	944,391

Year	Position	W	L	Pct.	*GB	Manager	Attendance
1951	4th	76	78	.494	20.5	Billy Southworth, Tommy Holmes	487,475
1952	7th	64	89	.418	32.0	Tommy Holmes, Charlie Grimm	281,278
1953	2nd	92	62	.597	13.0	Charlie Grimm	1,826,397
1954	3rd	89	65	.578	8.0	Charlie Grimm	2,131,388
1955	2nd	85	69	.552	13.5	Charlie Grimm	2,005,836
1956	2nd	92	62	.597	1.0	Charlie Grimm, Fred Haney	2,046,331
1957	1st	95	59	.617	+8.0	Fred Haney	2,215,404
1958	1st	92	62	.597	+8.0	Fred Haney	1,971,101
1959	2nd▲	86	70	.551	2.0	Fred Haney	1,749,112
1960	2nd	88	66	.571	7.0	Chuck Dressen	1,497,799
1961	4th	83	71	.539	10.0	Chuck Dressen, Birdie Tebbetts	1,101,441
1962	5th	86	76	.531	15.5	Birdie Tebbetts	766,921
1963	6th	84	78	.519	15.0	Bobby Bragan	773,018
1964	5th	88	74	.543	5.0	Bobby Bragan	910,911
1965	5th	86	76	.531	11.0	Bobby Bragan	555,584
1966	5th	85	77	.525	10.0	Bobby Bragan, Billy Hitchcock	1,539,801
1967	7th	77	85	.475	24.5	Billy Hitchcock, Ken Silvestri	1,389,222
1968	5th	81	81	.500	16.0	Lum Harris	1,126,540

WEST DIVISION

Year	Position	W	L	Pct.	*GB	Manager	Attendance
1969	1st†	93	69	.574	+3.0	Lum Harris	1,458,320
1970	5th	76	86	.469	26.0	Lum Harris	1,078,848
1971	3rd	82	80	.506	8.0	Lum Harris	1,006,320
1972	4th	70	84	.455	25.0	Lum Harris, Eddie Mathews	752,973
1973	5th	76	85	.472	22.5	Eddie Mathews	800,655
1974	3rd	88	74	.543	14.0	Eddie Mathews, Clyde King	981,085
1975	5th	67	94	.416	40.5	Clyde King, Connie Ryan	534,672
1976	6th	70	92	.432	32.0	Dave Bristol	818,179
1977	6th	61	101	.377	37.0	Dave Bristol, Ted Turner	872,464
1978	6th	69	93	.426	26.0	Bobby Cox	904,494
1979	6th	66	94	.413	23.5	Bobby Cox	769,465
1980	4th	81	80	.503	11.0	Bobby Cox	1,048,411
1981	4th/5th	50	56	.472	‡	Bobby Cox	535,418
1982	1st†	89	73	.549	+1.0	Joe Torre	1,801,985
1983	2nd	88	74	.543	3.0	Joe Torre	2,119,935
1984	2nd (tied)	80	82	.494	12.0	Joe Torre	1,724,892
1985	5th	66	96	.407	29.0	Eddie Haas, Bobby Wine	1,350,137
1986	6th	72	89	.447	23.5	Chuck Tanner	1,387,181
1987	5th	69	92	.429	20.5	Chuck Tanner	1,217,402
1988	6th	54	106	.338	39.5	Chuck Tanner, Russ Nixon	848,089
1989	6th	63	97	.394	28.0	Russ Nixon	984,930
1990	6th	65	97	.401	26.0	Russ Nixon, Bobby Cox	980,129
1991	1st§	94	68	.580	+1.0	Bobby Cox	2,140,217
1992	1st§	98	64	.605	+8.0	Bobby Cox	3,077,400
1993	1st†	104	58	.642	+1.0	Bobby Cox	3,884,725

EAST DIVISION

Year	Position	W	L	Pct.	*GB	Manager	Attendance
1994	2nd	68	46	.596	6.0	Bobby Cox	2,539,240
1995	1st∞§	90	54	.625	+21.0	Bobby Cox	2,561,831
1996	1st∞§	96	66	.593	+8.0	Bobby Cox	2,901,242
1997	1st∞†	101	61	.623	+9.0	Bobby Cox	3,464,488
1998	1st∞†	106	56	.654	+18.0	Bobby Cox	3,361,350
1999	1st∞§	103	59	.636	+6.5	Bobby Cox	3,284,897
2000	1st◆	95	67	.586	+1.0	Bobby Cox	3,234,301
2001	1st◆	88	74	.543	+2.0	Bobby Cox	2,823,494

*Games behind winner. †Lost championship series. ‡First half 25-29; second 25-27. §Won championship series. ∞Won division series. ▲Lost pennant playoff. ◆Lost division series.

MANAGERIAL RECORDS

Dave Bancroft 249-363, Del Bissonette 25-34, Frank Bowerman 23-55, Bobby Bragan 310-287, Dave Bristol 131-192, Al Buckenberger 186-242, Bob Coleman 107-140, Bobby Cox 1,349-1,053, Chuck Dressen 159-124, Emil Fuchs 56-98, Charlie Grimm 341-285, Eddie Haas 50-71, Fred Haney 341-231, Billy Hitchcock 110-100, Tommy Holmes 61-69, Rogers Hornsby 39-83, Joe Kelley 63-91, Clyde King 96-101, Johnny Kling 52-101, Fred Lake 53-100, Eddie Mathews 149-161, Bill McKechnie 560-666, Fred Mitchell 186-274, Russ Nixon 130-216, Connie Ryan 9-18, Frank Selee 69-69, Ken Silvestri 0-3, Jack Slattery 11-20, Harry Smith 22-53, Billy Southworth 424-358, George Stallings 579-597, Casey Stengel 394-516, Chuck Tanner 153-208, Birdie Tebbetts 98-89, Fred Tenney 202-402, Joe Torre 257-229, Ted Turner 0-1, Bobby Wine 16-25.

Year	Position	W	L	Pct.	*GB	Manager	Attendance
1901	6th	53	86	.381	37.0	Tom Loftus	205,071
1902	5th	68	69	.496	34.0	Frank Selee	263,700
1903	3rd	82	56	.594	8.0	Frank Selee	386,205
1904	2nd	93	60	.608	13.0	Frank Selee	439,100
1905	3rd	92	61	.601	13.0	Frank Selee, Frank Chance	509,900
1906	1st	116	36	.763	+20.0	Frank Chance	654,300
1907	1st	107	45	.704	+17.0	Frank Chance	422,550
1908	1st	99	55	.643	+1.0	Frank Chance	665,325
1909	2nd	104	49	.680	6.5	Frank Chance	633,480
1910	1st	104	50	.675	+13.0	Frank Chance	526,152
1911	2nd	92	62	.597	7.5	Frank Chance	576,000
1912	3rd	91	59	.607	11.5	Frank Chance	514,000
1913	3rd	88	65	.575	13.5	Johnny Evers	419,000
1914	4th	78	76	.506	16.5	Hank O'Day	202,516
1915	4th	73	80	.477	17.5	Roger Bresnahan	217,058
1916	5th	67	86	.438	26.5	Joe Tinker	453,685
1917	5th	74	80	.481	24.0	Fred Mitchell	360,218
1918	1st	84	45	.651	+10.5	Fred Mitchell	337,256
1919	3rd	75	65	.536	21.0	Fred Mitchell	424,430
1950	5th (tied)	75	79	.487	18.0	Fred Mitchell	480,783
1921	7th	64	89	.418	30.0	Johnny Evers, Bill Killefer	410,107
1922	5th	80	74	.519	13.0	Bill Killefer	542,283
1923	4th	83	71	.539	12.5	Bill Killefer	703,705
1924	5th	81	72	.529	12.0	Bill Killefer	716,922
1925	8th	68	86	.442	27.5	Bill Killefer, Rabbit Maranville, George Gibson	622,610
1926	4th	82	72	.532	7.0	Joe McCarthy	885,063
1927	4th	85	68	.556	8.5	Joe McCarthy	1,159,168
1928	3rd	91	63	.591	4.0	Joe McCarthy	1,143,740
1929	1st	98	54	.645	+10.5	Joe McCarthy	1,485,166
1930	2nd	90	64	.584	2.0	Joe McCarthy, Rogers Hornsby	1,463,624
1931	3rd	84	70	.545	17.0	Rogers Hornsby	1,086,422
1932	1st	90	64	.584	+4.0	Rogers Hornsby, Charlie Grimm	974,688
1933	3rd	86	68	.558	6.0	Charlie Grimm	594,112
1934	3rd	86	65	.570	8.0	Charlie Grimm	707,525
1935	1st	100	54	.649	+4.0	Charlie Grimm	692,604
1936	2nd (tied)	87	67	.565	5.0	Charlie Grimm	699,370
1937	2nd	93	61	.604	3.0	Charlie Grimm	895,020
1938	1st	89	63	.586	+2.0	Charlie Grimm, Gabby Hartnett	951,640
1939	4th	84	70	.545	13.0	Gabby Hartnett	726,663
1940	5th	75	79	.487	25.5	Gabby Hartnett	534,878
1941	6th	70	84	.455	30.0	Jimmy Wilson	545,159
1942	6th	68	86	.442	38.0	Jimmy Wilson	590,872
1943	5th	74	79	.484	30.5	Jimmy Wilson	508,247
1944	4th	75	79	.487	30.0	Jimmy Wilson, Charlie Grimm	640,110
1945	1st	98	56	.636	+3.0	Charlie Grimm	1,036,386
1946	3rd	82	71	.536	14.5	Charlie Grimm	1,342,970
1947	6th	69	85	.448	25.0	Charlie Grimm	1,364,039
1948	8th	64	90	.416	27.5	Charlie Grimm	1,237,792
1949	8th	61	93	.396	36.0	Charlie Grimm, Frankie Frisch	1,143,139
1950	7th	64	89	.418	26.5	Frankie Frisch	1,165,944
1951	8th	62	92	.403	34.5	Frankie Frisch, Phil Cavarretta	894,415
1952	5th	77	77	.500	19.5	Phil Cavarretta	1,024,826
1953	7th	65	89	.422	40.0	Phil Cavarretta	763,658
1954	7th	64	90	.416	33.0	Stan Hack	748,183
1955	6th	72	81	.471	26.0	Stan Hack	875,800
1956	8th	60	94	.390	33.0	Stan Hack	720,118
1957	7th (tied)	62	92	.403	33.0	Bob Scheffing	670,629
1958	5th (tied)	72	82	.468	20.0	Bob Scheffing	979,904
1959	5th (tied)	74	80	.481	13.0	Bob Scheffing	858,255
1960	7th	60	94	.390	35.0	Charlie Grimm, Lou Boudreau	809,770
1961	7th	64	90	.416	29.0	Vedie Himsl, Harry Craft, Elvin Tappe, Lou Klein	673,057
1962	9th	59	103	.364	42.5	Charlie Metro, Elvin Tappe, Lou Klein	609,802
1963	7th	82	80	.506	17.0	Bob Kennedy	979,551
1964	8th	76	86	.469	17.0	Bob Kennedy	751,647
1965	8th	72	90	.444	25.0	Bob Kennedy, Lou Klein	641,361
1966	10th	59	103	.364	36.0	Leo Durocher	635,891
1967	3rd	87	74	.540	14.0	Leo Durocher	977,226
1968	3rd	84	78	.519	13.0	Leo Durocher	1,043,409

HISTORY *Team by team*

EAST DIVISION

Year	Position	W	L	Pct.	*GB	Manager	Attendance
1969	2nd	92	70	.568	8.0	Leo Durocher	1,674,993
1970	2nd	84	78	.519	5.0	Leo Durocher	1,642,705
1971	3rd (tied)	83	79	.512	14.0	Leo Durocher	1,653,007
1972	2nd	85	70	.548	11.0	Leo Durocher, Whitey Lockman	1,299,163
1973	5th	77	84	.478	5.0	Whitey Lockman	1,351,705
1974	6th	66	96	.407	22.0	Whitey Lockman, Jim Marshall	1,015,378
1975	5th (tied)	75	87	.463	17.5	Jim Marshall	1,034,819
1976	4th	75	87	.463	26.0	Jim Marshall	1,026,217
1977	4th	81	81	.500	20.0	Herman Franks	1,439,834
1978	3rd	79	83	.488	11.0	Herman Franks	1,525,311
1979	5th	80	82	.494	18.0	Herman Franks, Joe Amalfitano	1,648,587
1980	6th	64	98	.395	27.0	Preston Gomez, Joe Amalfitano	1,206,776
1981	6th/5th	38	65	.369	†	Joe Amalfitano	565,637
1982	5th	73	89	.451	19.0	Lee Elia	1,249,278
1983	5th	71	91	.438	19.0	Lee Elia, Charlie Fox	1,479,717
1984	1st‡	96	65	.596	+6.5	Jim Frey	2,104,219
1985	4th	77	84	.478	23.5	Jim Frey	2,161,534
1986	5th	70	90	.438	37.0	Jim Frey, John Vukovich, Gene Michael	1,859,102
1987	6th	76	85	.472	18.5	Gene Michael, Frank Lucchesi	2,035,130
1988	4th	77	85	.475	24.0	Don Zimmer	2,089,034
1989	1st‡	93	69	.574	+6.0	Don Zimmer	2,491,942
1990	4th	77	85	.475	18.0	Don Zimmer	2,243,791
1991	4th	77	83	.481	20.0	Don Zimmer, Joe Altobelli, Jim Essian	2,314,250
1992	4th	78	84	.481	18.0	Jim Lefebvre	2,126,720
1993	4th	84	78	.519	13.0	Jim Lefebvre	2,653,763

CENTRAL DIVISION

Year	Position	W	L	Pct.	*GB	Manager	Attendance
1994	5th	49	64	.434	16.5	Tom Trebelhorn	1,845,208
1995	3rd	73	71	.507	12.0	Jim Riggleman	1,918,265
1996	4th	76	86	.469	12.0	Jim Riggleman	2,219,110
1997	5th	68	94	.420	16.0	Jim Riggleman	2,190,308
1998	2nd§∞	90	73	.552	12.5	Jim Riggleman	2,623,000
1999	6th	67	95	.414	30.0	Jim Riggleman	2,813,854
2000	6th	65	97	.401	30.0	Don Baylor	2,789,511
2001	3rd	88	74	.543	5.0	Don Baylor	2,779,456

*Games behind winner. †First half 15-37; second 23-28. ‡Lost championship series. §Won wild-card playoff. ∞Lost division series.

MANAGERIAL RECORDS

Joe Amalfitano 66-116, Don Baylor 153-171, Lou Boudreau 54-83, Roger Bresnahan 73-80, Phil Cavarretta 169-213, Frank Chance 753-379, Harry Craft 7-9, Leo Durocher 535-526, Lee Elia 127-158, Jim Essian 59-63, Johnny Evers 130-121, Charlie Fox 17-22, Herman Franks 238-241, Jim Frey 196-182, Frank Frisch 141-196, George Gibson 12-14, Preston Gomez 38-52, Charlie Grimm 946-784, Stan Hack 196-265, Gabby Hartnett 203-176, Vedie Himsl 10-21, Rogers Hornsby 141-114, Roy Johnson 0-1, Bob Kennedy 182-198, Bill Killefer 299-292, Lou Klein 65-83, Jim Lefebvre 162-162, Whitey Lockman 157-162, Tom Loftus 53-86, Frank Lucchesi 8-17, Rabbit Maranville 23-30, Jim Marshall 175-218, Joe McCarthy 442-321, Charlie Metro 43-69, Gene Michael 114-124, Fred Mitchell 308-269, Hank O'Day 78-76, Jim Riggleman 374-419, Bob Scheffing 208-254, Frank Selee 295-223, Elvin Tappe 46-69, Joe Tinker 67-86, Tom Trebelhorn 49-64, John Vukovich 1-1, Jimmy Wilson 213-160, Don Zimmer 265-259.

CINCINNATI REDS
YEARLY FINISHES

Year	Position	W	L	Pct.	*GB	Manager	Attendance
1901	8th	52	87	.374	38.0	Bid McPhee	205,728
1902	4th	70	70	.500	33.5	Bid McPhee, Frank Bancroft, Joe Kelley	217,300
1903	4th	74	65	.532	16.5	Joe Kelley	351,680
1904	3rd	88	65	.575	18.0	Joe Kelley	391,915
1905	5th	79	74	.516	26.0	Joe Kelley	313,927
1906	6th	64	87	.424	51.5	Ned Hanlon	330,056
1907	6th	66	87	.431	41.5	Ned Hanlon	317,500
1908	5th	73	81	.474	26.0	John Ganzel	399,200
1909	4th	77	76	.503	33.5	Clark Griffith	424,643
1910	5th	75	79	.487	29.0	Clark Griffith	380,622
1911	6th	70	83	.458	29.0	Clark Griffith	300,000
1912	4th	75	78	.490	29.0	Hank O'Day	344,000
1913	7th	64	89	.418	37.5	Joe Tinker	258,000
1914	8th	60	94	.390	34.5	Buck Herzog	100,791
1915	7th	71	83	.461	20.0	Buck Herzog	218,878
1916	7th (tied)	60	93	.392	33.5	Buck Herzog, Christy Mathewson	255,846
1917	4th	78	76	.506	20.0	Christy Mathewson	269,056
1918	3rd	68	60	.531	15.5	Christy Mathewson, Heinie Groh	163,009
1919	1st	96	44	.686	+9.0	Pat Moran	532,501

Year	Position	W	L	Pct.	*GB	Manager	Attendance
1920	3rd	82	71	.536	10.5	Pat Moran	568,107
1921	6th	70	83	.458	24.0	Pat Moran	311,227
1922	2nd	86	68	.558	7.0	Pat Moran	493,754
1923	2nd	91	63	.591	4.5	Pat Moran	575,063
1924	4th	83	70	.542	10.0	Jack Hendricks	437,707
1925	3rd	80	73	.523	15.0	Jack Hendricks	464,920
1926	2nd	87	67	.565	2.0	Jack Hendricks	672,987
1927	5th	75	78	.490	18.5	Jack Hendricks	442,164
1928	5th	78	74	.513	16.0	Jack Hendricks	490,490
1929	7th	66	88	.429	33.0	Jack Hendricks	295,040
1930	7th	59	95	.383	33.0	Dan Howley	386,727
1931	8th	58	96	.377	43.0	Dan Howley	263,316
1932	8th	60	94	.390	30.0	Dan Howley	356,950
1933	8th	58	94	.382	33.0	Donie Bush	218,281
1934	8th	52	99	.344	42.0	Bob O'Farrell, Chuck Dressen	206,773
1935	6th	68	85	.444	31.5	Chuck Dressen	448,247
1936	5th	74	80	.481	18.0	Chuck Dressen	466,245
1937	8th	56	98	.364	40.0	Chuck Dressen, Bobby Wallace	411,221
1938	4th	82	68	.547	6.0	Bill McKechnie	706,756
1939	1st	97	57	.630	+4.5	Bill McKechnie	981,443
1940	1st	100	53	.654	+12.0	Bill McKechnie	850,180
1941	3rd	88	66	.571	12.0	Bill McKechnie	643,513
1942	4th	76	76	.500	29.0	Bill McKechnie	427,031
1943	2nd	87	67	.565	18.0	Bill McKechnie	379,122
1944	3rd	89	65	.578	16.0	Bill McKechnie	409,567
1945	7th	61	93	.396	37.0	Bill McKechnie	290,070
1946	6th	67	87	.435	30.0	Bill McKechnie	715,751
1947	5th	73	81	.474	21.0	Johnny Neun	899,975
1948	7th	64	89	.418	27.0	Johnny Neun, Bucky Walters	823,386
1949	7th	62	92	.403	35.0	Bucky Walters	707,782
1950	6th	66	87	.431	24.5	Luke Sewell	538,794
1951	6th	68	86	.442	28.5	Luke Sewell	588,268
1952	6th	69	85	.448	27.5	Luke Sewell, Rogers Hornsby	604,197
1953	6th	68	86	.442	37.0	Rogers Hornsby, Buster Mills	548,086
1954	5th	74	80	.481	23.0	Birdie Tebbetts	704,167
1955	5th	75	79	.407	23.5	Birdie Tebbetts	693,662
1956	3rd	91	63	.591	2.0	Birdie Tebbetts	1,125,928
1957	4th	80	74	.519	15.0	Birdie Tebbetts	1,070,850
1958	4th	76	78	.494	16.0	Birdie Tebbetts, Jimmie Dykes	788,582
1959	5th (tied)	74	80	.481	13.0	Mayo Smith, Fred Hutchinson	801,289
1960	6th	67	87	.435	28.0	Fred Hutchinson	663,486
1961	1st	93	61	.604	+4.0	Fred Hutchinson	1,117,603
1962	3rd	98	64	.605	3.5	Fred Hutchinson	982,085
1963	5th	86	76	.531	13.0	Fred Hutchinson	858,805
1964	2nd (tied)	92	70	.549	1.0	Fred Hutchinson, Dick Sisler	862,466
1965	4th	89	73	.549	8.0	Dick Sisler	1,047,824
1966	7th	76	84	.475	18.0	Don Heffner, Dave Bristol	742,958
1967	4th	87	75	.537	14.5	Dave Bristol	958,300
1968	4th	83	79	.512	14.0	Dave Bristol	733,354

WEST DIVISION

Year	Position	W	L	Pct.	*GB	Manager	Attendance
1969	3rd	89	73	.549	4.0	Dave Bristol	987,991
1970	1st†	102	60	.630	+14.5	Sparky Anderson	1,803,568
1971	4th (tied)	79	83	.488	11.0	Sparky Anderson	1,501,122
1972	1st†	95	59	.617	+10.5	Sparky Anderson	1,611,459
1973	1st‡	99	63	.611	+3.5	Sparky Anderson	2,017,601
1974	2nd	98	64	.605	4.0	Sparky Anderson	2,164,307
1975	1st†	108	54	.667	+20.0	Sparky Anderson	2,315,603
1976	1st†	102	60	.630	+10.0	Sparky Anderson	2,629,708
1977	2nd	88	74	.543	10.0	Sparky Anderson	2,519,670
1978	2nd	92	69	.571	2.5	Sparky Anderson	2,532,497
1979	1st‡	90	71	.559	+1.5	John McNamara	2,356,933
1980	3rd	89	73	.549	3.5	John McNamara	2,022,450
1981	2nd/2nd	66	42	.611	§	John McNamara	1,093,730
1982	6th	61	101	.377	28.0	John McNamara, Russ Nixon	1,326,528
1983	6th	74	88	.457	17.0	Russ Nixon	1,190,419
1984	5th	70	92	.432	22.0	Vern Rapp, Pete Rose	1,275,887
1985	2nd	89	72	.553	5.5	Pete Rose	1,834,619
1986	2nd	86	76	.531	10.0	Pete Rose	1,692,432
1987	2nd	84	78	.519	6.0	Pete Rose	2,185,205
1988	2nd	87	74	.540	7.0	Pete Rose	2,072,528
1989	5th	75	87	.463	17.0	Pete Rose, Tommy Helms	1,979,320
1990	1st†	91	71	.562	+5.0	Lou Piniella	2,400,892
1991	5th	74	88	.457	20.0	Lou Piniella	2,372,377

Year	Position	W	L	Pct.	*GB	Manager	Attendance
1992	2nd	90	72	.556	8.0	Lou Piniella	2,315,946
1993	5th	73	89	.451	31.0	Tony Perez, Dave Johnson	2,453,232

CENTRAL DIVISION

Year	Position	W	L	Pct.	*GB	Manager	Attendance
1994	1st	66	48	.579	+0.5	Dave Johnson	1,897,681
1995	1st∞‡	85	59	.590	+9.0	Dave Johnson	1,837,649
1996	3rd	81	81	.500	7.0	Ray Knight	1,861,428
1997	3rd	76	86	.469	8.0	Ray Knight, Jack McKeon	1,785,788
1998	4th	77	85	.475	25.0	Jack McKeon	1,793,679
1999	2nd▲	96	67	.589	1.5	Jack McKeon	2,061,222
2000	2nd	85	77	.525	10.0	Jack McKeon	2,577,351
2001	5th	66	96	.407	27.0	Bob Boone	1,882,732

*Games behind winner. †Won championship series. ‡Lost championship series. §First half 35-21; second 31-21. ∞Won division series. ▲Lost wild-card playoff.

MANAGERIAL RECORDS

Sparky Anderson 863-586, Frank Bancroft 9-7, Bob Boone 66-96, Dave Bristol 298-265, Donie Bush 58-94, Chuck Dressen 214-282, Jimmie Dykes 24-17, John Ganzel 73-81, Clark Griffith 222-238, Heinie Groh 7-3, Ned Hanlon 130-174, Don Heffner 37-46, Tommy Helms 14-21, Jack Hendricks 469-450, Buck Herzog 165-226, Rogers Hornsby 91-106, Dan Howley 177-285, Fred Hutchinson 443-372, Dave Johnson 204-172, Joe Kelley 275-230, Ray Knight 124-137, Christy Mathewson 164-176, Bill McKechnie 747-632, Jack McKeon 291-259, John McNamara 279-244, Bid McPhee 79-124, Buster Mills 4-4, Pat Moran 425-329, Johnny Neun 117-137, Russ Nixon 101-131, Hank O'Day 75-78, Bob O'Farrell 30-60, Tony Perez 20-24, Lou Piniella 255-231, Vern Rapp 51-70, Pete Rose 426-388, Luke Sewell 176-234, Dick Sisler 121-94, Mayo Smith 35-45, Birdie Tebbetts 372-357, Joe Tinker 64-89, Bobby Wallace 5-20, Bucky Walters 81-123.

COLORADO ROCKIES
YEARLY FINISHES
WEST DIVISION

Year	Position	W	L	Pct.	*GB	Manager	Attendance
1993	6th	67	95	.414	37.0	Don Baylor	4,483,350
1994	3rd	53	64	.453	6.5	Don Baylor	3,281,511
1995	2nd†	77	67	.535	1.0	Don Baylor	3,390,037
1996	3rd	83	79	.512	8.0	Don Baylor	3,891,014
1997	3rd	83	79	.512	7.0	Don Baylor	3,888,453
1998	4th	77	85	.475	21.0	Don Baylor	3,789,347
1999	5th	72	90	.444	28.0	Jim Leyland	3,481,065
2000	4th	82	80	.506	15.0	Buddy Bell	3,285,710
2001	5th	73	89	.451	19.0	Buddy Bell	3,159,385

*Games behind winner. †Lost division series.

MANAGERIAL RECORDS

Don Baylor 440-469, Buddy Bell 155-169, Jim Leyland 72-90.

FLORIDA MARLINS
YEARLY FINISHES
EAST DIVISION

Year	Position	W	L	Pct.	*GB	Manager	Attendance
1993	6th	64	98	.395	33.0	Rene Lachemann	3,064,847
1994	5th	51	64	.443	23.5	Rene Lachemann	1,937,467
1995	4th	67	76	.469	22.5	Rene Lachemann	1,700,466
1996	3rd	80	82	.494	16.0	Rene Lachemann, John Boles	1,746,767
1997	2nd†‡	92	70	.568	9.0	Jim Leyland	2,364,387
1998	5th	54	108	.333	52.0	Jim Leyland	1,750,395
1999	5th	64	98	.395	39.0	John Boles	1,369,421
2000	3rd	79	82	.491	15.5	John Boles	1,218,326
2001	4th	76	86	.469	12.0	John Boles, Tony Perez	1,261,220

*Games behind winner. †Won division series. ‡Won championship series.

MANAGERIAL RECORDS

John Boles 205-241, Rene Lachemann 222-285, Jim Leyland 146-178, Tony Perez 54-60.

HOUSTON ASTROS
YEARLY FINISHES

(Known as Houston Colt .45s through 1964)

Year	Position	W	L	Pct.	*GB	Manager	Attendance
1962	8th	64	96	.400	36.5	Harry Craft	924,456
1963	9th	66	96	.407	33.0	Harry Craft	719,502
1964	9th	66	96	.407	27.0	Harry Craft, Luman Harris	725,773
1965	9th	65	97	.401	32.0	Luman Harris	2,151,470
1966	8th	72	90	.444	23.0	Grady Hatton	1,872,108
1967	9th	69	93	.426	32.5	Grady Hatton	1,348,303
1968	10th	72	90	.444	25.0	Grady Hatton, Harry Walker	1,312,887

WEST DIVISION

Year	Position	W	L	Pct.	*GB	Manager	Attendance
1969	5th	81	81	.500	12.0	Harry Walker	1,442,995
1970	4th	79	83	.488	23.0	Harry Walker	1,253,444
1971	4th (tied)	79	83	.488	11.0	Harry Walker	1,261,589
1972	2nd	84	69	.549	10.5	Harry Walker, Salty Parker, Leo Durocher	1,469,247
1973	4th	82	80	.506	17.0	Leo Durocher, Preston Gomez	1,394,004
1974	4th	81	81	.500	21.0	Preston Gomez	1,090,728
1975	6th	64	97	.398	43.5	Preston Gomez, Bill Virdon	858,002
1976	3rd	80	82	.494	22.0	Bill Virdon	886,146
1977	3rd	81	81	.500	17.0	Bill Virdon	1,109,560
1978	5th	74	88	.457	21.0	Bill Virdon	1,126,145
1979	2nd	89	73	.549	1.5	Bill Virdon	1,900,312
1980	1st†‡	93	70	.571	+1.0	Bill Virdon	2,278,217
1981	3rd/1st∞	61	49	.555	§	Bill Virdon	1,321,282
1982	5th	77	85	.475	12.0	Bill Virdon, Bob Lillis	1,558,555
1983	3rd	85	77	.525	6.0	Bob Lillis	1,351,962
1984	2nd (tied)	80	82	.494	12.0	Bob Lillis	1,229,862
1985	3rd (tied)	83	79	.512	12.0	Bob Lillis	1,184,314
1986	1st‡	96	66	.593	+10.0	Hal Lanier	1,734,276
1987	3rd	76	86	.469	14.0	Hal Lanier	1,909,902
1988	5th	82	80	.506	12.5	Hal Lanier	1,933,505
1989	3rd	86	76	.531	6.0	Art Howe	1,834,908
1990	4th (tied)	75	87	.463	16.0	Art Howe	1,310,927
1991	6th	65	97	.401	29.0	Art Howe	1,196,152
1992	4th	81	81	.500	17.0	Art Howe	1,211,412
1993	3rd	85	77	.525	19.0	Art Howe	2,084,546

CENTRAL DIVISION

Year	Position	W	L	Pct.	*GB	Manager	Attendance
1994	2nd	66	49	.574	0.5	Terry Collins	1,561,136
1995	2nd	76	68	.528	9.0	Terry Collins	1,363,801
1996	2nd	82	80	.506	6.0	Terry Collins	1,975,888
1997	1st∞	84	78	.519	+5.0	Larry Dierker	2,046,781
1998	1st∞	102	60	.630	+12.5	Larry Dierker	2,450,451
1999	1st∞	97	65	.599	+1.5	Larry Dierker	2,706,017
2000	4th	72	90	.444	23.0	Larry Dierker	3,056,139
2001	1st (tied)∞	93	69	.574	0.0	Larry Dierker	2,904,280

*Games behind winner. †Won division playoff. ‡Lost championship series. §First half 28-29; second 33-20. ∞Lost division series.

MANAGERIAL RECORDS

Terry Collins 224-197, Harry Craft 191-280, Larry Dierker 448-362, Leo Durocher 98-95, Preston Gomez 128-161, Lum Harris 70-105, Grady Hatton 164-221, Art Howe 392-418, Hal Lanier 254-232, Bob Lillis 276-261, Bill Virdon 544-522, Harry Walker 355-353.

LOS ANGELES DODGERS
YEARLY FINISHES

(Known as Brooklyn Dodgers through 1957)

Year	Position	W	L	Pct.	*GB	Manager	Attendance
1901	3rd	79	57	.581	9.5	Ned Hanlon	189,200
1902	2nd	75	63	.543	27.5	Ned Hanlon	199,868
1903	5th	70	66	.515	19.0	Ned Hanlon	224,670
1904	6th	56	97	.366	50.0	Ned Hanlon	214,600
1905	8th	48	104	.316	56.5	Ned Hanlon	227,924
1906	5th	66	86	.434	50.0	Patsy Donovan	227,400
1907	5th	65	83	.439	40.0	Patsy Donovan	312,500
1908	7th	53	101	.344	46.0	Patsy Donovan	275,600
1909	6th	55	98	.359	55.5	Harry Lumley	321,300
1910	6th	64	90	.416	40.0	Bill Dahlen	279,321

Year	Position	W	L	Pct.	*GB	Manager	Attendance
1911	7th	64	86	.427	33.5	Bill Dahlen	269,000
1912	7th	58	95	.379	46.0	Bill Dahlen	243,000
1913	6th	65	84	.436	34.5	Bill Dahlen	347,000
1914	5th	75	79	.487	19.5	Wilbert Robinson	122,671
1915	3rd	80	72	.526	10.0	Wilbert Robinson	297,766
1916	1st	94	60	.610	+2.5	Wilbert Robinson	447,747
1917	7th	70	81	.464	26.5	Wilbert Robinson	221,619
1918	5th	57	69	.452	25.5	Wilbert Robinson	83,831
1919	5th	69	71	.493	27.0	Wilbert Robinson	360,721
1920	1st	93	61	.604	+7.0	Wilbert Robinson	808,722
1921	5th	77	75	.507	16.5	Wilbert Robinson	613,245
1922	6th	76	78	.494	17.0	Wilbert Robinson	498,856
1923	6th	76	78	.494	19.5	Wilbert Robinson	564,666
1924	2nd	92	62	.597	1.5	Wilbert Robinson	818,883
1925	6th (tied)	68	85	.444	27.0	Wilbert Robinson	659,435
1926	6th	71	82	.464	17.5	Wilbert Robinson	650,819
1927	6th	65	88	.425	28.5	Wilbert Robinson	637,230
1928	6th	77	76	.503	17.5	Wilbert Robinson	664,863
1929	6th	70	83	.458	28.5	Wilbert Robinson	731,886
1930	4th	86	68	.558	6.0	Wilbert Robinson	1,097,339
1931	4th	79	73	.520	21.0	Wilbert Robinson	753,133
1932	3rd	81	73	.526	9.0	Max Carey	681,827
1933	6th	65	88	.425	26.5	Max Carey	526,815
1934	6th	71	81	.467	23.5	Casey Stengel	434,188
1935	5th	70	83	.458	29.5	Casey Stengel	470,517
1936	7th	67	87	.435	25.0	Casey Stengel	489,618
1937	6th	62	91	.405	33.5	Burleigh Grimes	482,481
1938	7th	69	80	.463	18.5	Burleigh Grimes	663,087
1939	3rd	84	69	.549	12.5	Leo Durocher	955,668
1940	2nd	88	65	.575	12.0	Leo Durocher	975,978
1941	1st	100	54	.649	+2.5	Leo Durocher	1,214,910
1942	2nd	104	50	.675	2.0	Leo Durocher	1,037,765
1943	3rd	81	72	.529	23.5	Leo Durocher	661,723
1944	7th	63	91	.409	42.0	Leo Durocher	605,905
1945	3rd	87	67	.565	11.0	Leo Durocher	1,059,220
1946	2nd‡	96	60	.615	2.0	Leo Durocher	1,796,824
1947	1st	94	60	.610	+5.0	Clyde Sukeforth, Burt Shotton	1,807,526
1948	3rd	84	70	.545	7.5	Leo Durocher, Burt Shotton	1,398,967
1949	1st	97	57	.630	+1.0	Burt Shotton	1,633,747
1950	2nd	89	65	.578	2.0	Burt Shotton	1,185,896
1951	2nd‡	97	60	.618	1.0	Chuck Dressen	1,282,628
1952	1st	96	57	.627	+4.5	Chuck Dressen	1,088,704
1953	1st	105	49	.682	+13.0	Chuck Dressen	1,163,419
1954	2nd	92	62	.597	5.0	Walter Alston	1,020,531
1955	1st	98	55	.641	+13.5	Walter Alston	1,033,589
1956	1st	93	61	.604	+1.0	Walter Alston	1,213,562
1957	3rd	84	70	.545	11.0	Walter Alston	1,028,258
1958	7th	71	83	.461	21.0	Walter Alston	1,845,556
1959	1st†	88	68	.564	+2.0	Walter Alston	2,071,045
1960	4th	82	72	.532	13.0	Walter Alston	2,253,887
1961	2nd	89	65	.578	4.0	Walter Alston	1,804,250
1962	2nd‡	102	63	.618	1.0	Walter Alston	2,755,184
1963	1st	99	63	.611	+6.0	Walter Alston	2,538,602
1964	6th (tied)	80	82	.494	13.0	Walter Alston	2,228,751
1965	1st	97	65	.599	+2.0	Walter Alston	2,553,577
1966	1st	95	67	.586	+1.5	Walter Alston	2,617,056
1967	8th	73	89	.451	28.5	Walter Alston	1,664,362
1968	7th	76	86	.469	21.0	Walter Alston	1,581,093

WEST DIVISION

Year	Position	W	L	Pct.	*GB	Manager	Attendance
1969	4th	85	77	.525	8.0	Walter Alston	1,784,527
1970	2nd	87	74	.540	14.5	Walter Alston	1,697,142
1971	2nd	89	73	.549	1.0	Walter Alston	2,064,594
1972	3rd	85	70	.548	10.5	Walter Alston	1,860,858
1973	2nd	95	66	.590	3.5	Walter Alston	2,136,192
1974	1st§	102	60	.630	+4.0	Walter Alston	2,632,474
1975	2nd	88	74	.543	20.0	Walter Alston	2,539,349
1976	2nd§	92	70	.568	10.0	Walter Alston, Tommy Lasorda	2,386,301
1977	1st§	98	64	.605	+10.0	Tommy Lasorda	2,955,087
1978	1st§	95	67	.586	+2.5	Tommy Lasorda	3,347,845
1979	3rd	79	83	.488	11.5	Tommy Lasorda	2,860,954
1980	2nd∞	92	71	.564	1.0	Tommy Lasorda	3,249,287
1981	1st/4th◆§	63	47	.573	▲	Tommy Lasorda	2,381,292
1982	2nd	88	74	.543	1.0	Tommy Lasorda	3,608,881

– 378 –

Year	Position	W	L	Pct.	*GB	Manager	Attendance
1983	1st■	91	71	.652	+3.0	Tommy Lasorda	3,510,313
1984	4th	79	83	.488	13.0	Tommy Lasorda	3,134,824
1985	1st■	95	67	.506	ι5.5	Tommy Lasorda	3,264,593
1986	5th	73	89	.451	23.0	Tommy Lasorda	3,023,208
1987	4th	73	89	.451	17.0	Tommy Lasorda	2,797,409
1988	1st§	94	67	.584	+7.0	Tommy Lasorda	2,980,262
1989	4th	77	83	.481	14.0	Tommy Lasorda	2,944,653
1990	2nd	86	76	.531	5.0	Tommy Lasorda	3,002,396
1991	2nd	93	69	.574	1.0	Tommy Lasorda	3,348,170
1992	6th	63	99	.389	35.0	Tommy Lasorda	2,473,266
1993	4th	81	81	.500	23.0	Tommy Lasorda	3,170,392
1994	1st	58	56	.509	+3.5	Tommy Lasorda	2,279,355
1995	1st▼	78	66	.542	+1.0	Tommy Lasorda	2,766,251
1996	2nd▼	90	72	.556	1.0	Tommy Lasorda, Bill Russell	3,188,454
1997	2nd	88	74	.543	2.0	Bill Russell	3,319,504
1998	3rd	83	79	.512	15.0	Bill Russell, Glenn Hoffman	3,089,201
1999	3rd	77	85	.475	23.0	Dave Johnson	3,095,346
2000	2nd	86	76	.531	11.0	Dave Johnson	3,010,819
2001	3rd	86	76	.531	6.0	Jim Tracy	3,017,502

*Games behind winner. †Won pennant playoff. ‡Lost pennant playoff. §Won championship series. ∞Lost division playoff. ▲First half 36-21; second half 27-26. ◆Won division series. ■Lost championship series. ▼Lost division series.

MANAGERIAL RECORDS

Walter Alston 2,040-1,613, Max Carey 146-161, Bill Dahlen 251-355, Patsy Donovan 184-270, Chuck Dressen 298-166, Leo Durocher 738-565, Burleigh Grimes 131-171, Ned Hanlon 328-387, Glenn Hoffman 47-41, Dave Johnson 163-161, Tommy Lasorda 1,599-1,439, Harry Lumley 55-98, Wilbert Robinson 1,375-1,341, Bill Russell 173-149, Burt Shotton 326-215, Casey Stengel 208-251, Clyde Sukeforth 2-0, Jim Tracy 86-76.

MILWAUKEE BREWERS
YEARLY FINISHES

(Known as Seattle Pilots in 1969)

AMERICAN LEAGUE WEST DIVISION

Year	Position	W	L	Pct.	*GB	Manager	Attendance
1969	6th	64	98	.395	33	Joe Schultz	677,944
1970	4th	65	97	.401	33.0	Dave Bristol	933,690
1971	6th	69	92	.429	32.0	Dave Bristol	731,531

AMERICAN LEAGUE EAST DIVISION

Year	Position	W	L	Pct.	*GB	Manager	Attendance
1972	6th	65	91	.417	21.0	Dave Bristol, Del Crandall	600,440
1973	5th	74	88	.457	23.0	Del Crandall	1,092,158
1974	5th	76	86	.469	15.0	Del Crandall	955,741
1975	5th	68	94	.420	28.0	Del Crandall	1,213,357
1976	6th	66	95	.410	32.0	Alex Grammas	1,012,164
1977	6th	67	95	.414	33.0	Alex Grammas	1,114,938
1978	3rd	93	69	.574	6.5	George Bamberger	1,601,406
1979	2nd	95	66	.590	8.0	George Bamberger	1,918,343
1980	3rd	86	76	.531	17.0	George Bamberger, Buck Rodgers	1,857,408
1981	3rd/1st‡	62	47	.569	†	Buck Rodgers	878,432
1982	1st§	95	67	.586	+1.0	Buck Rodgers, Harvey Kuenn	1,978,896
1983	5th	87	75	.537	11.0	Harvey Kuenn	2,397,131
1984	7th	67	94	.416	36.5	Rene Lachemann	1,608,509
1985	6th	71	90	.441	28.0	George Bamberger	1,360,265
1986	6th	77	84	.478	18.0	George Bamberger, Tom Trebelhorn	1,265,041
1987	3rd	91	71	.562	7.0	Tom Trebelhorn	1,909,244
1988	3rd (tied)	87	75	.537	2.0	Tom Trebelhorn	1,923,238
1989	4th	81	81	.500	8.0	Tom Trebelhorn	1,970,735
1990	6th	74	88	.457	14.0	Tom Trebelhorn	1,752,900
1991	4th	83	79	.512	8.0	Tom Trebelhorn	1,478,729
1992	2nd	92	70	.568	4.0	Phil Garner	1,857,314
1993	7th	69	93	.426	26.0	Phil Garner	1,688,080

AMERICAN LEAGUE CENTRAL DIVISION

Year	Position	W	L	Pct.	*GB	Manager	Attendance
1994	5th	53	62	.461	15.0	Phil Garner	1,268,399
1995	4th	65	79	.451	35.0	Phil Garner	1,087,560
1996	3rd	80	82	.494	19.5	Phil Garner	1,327,155
1997	3rd	78	83	.484	8.0	Phil Garner	1,444,027

NATIONAL LEAGUE CENTRAL DIVISION

Year	Position	W	L	Pct.	*GB	Manager	Attendance
1998	5th	74	88	.457	28.0	Phil Garner	1,811,548
1999	5th	74	87	.460	22.5	Phil Garner, Jim Lefebvre	1,701,796
2000	3rd	73	89	.451	22.0	Davey Lopes	1,573,621
2001	4th	68	94	.420	25.0	Davey Lopes	2,811,041

*Games behind winner. †First half 31-25; second 31-22. ‡Lost division series. §Won championship series.

MANAGERIAL RECORDS

George Bamberger 377-351, Dave Bristol 144-209, Del Crandall 271-338, Phil Garner 563-617, Alex Grammas 133-190, Harvey Kuenn 160-118, Rene Lachemann 67-94, Jim Lefebvre 22-27, Davey Lopes 141-183, Buck Rodgers 124-102, Joe Schultz 64-98, Tom Trebelhorn 422-397.

MONTREAL EXPOS
YEARLY FINISHES
EAST DIVISION

Year	Position	W	L	Pct.	*GB	Manager	Attendance
1969	6th	52	110	.321	48.0	Gene Mauch	1,212,608
1970	6th	73	89	.451	16.0	Gene Mauch	1,424,683
1971	5th	71	90	.441	25.5	Gene Mauch	1,290,963
1972	5th	70	86	.449	26.5	Gene Mauch	1,142,145
1973	4th	79	83	.488	3.5	Gene Mauch	1,246,863
1974	4th	79	82	.491	8.5	Gene Mauch	1,019,134
1975	5th (tied)	75	87	.463	17.5	Gene Mauch	908,292
1976	6th	55	107	.340	46.0	Karl Kuehl, Charlie Fox	646,704
1977	5th	75	87	.463	26.0	Dick Williams	1,433,757
1978	4th	76	86	.469	14.0	Dick Williams	1,427,007
1979	2nd	95	65	.594	2.0	Dick Williams	2,102,173
1980	2nd	90	72	.556	1.0	Dick Williams	2,208,175
1981	3rd/1st‡§	60	48	.556	†	Dick Williams, Jim Fanning	1,534,564
1982	3rd	86	76	.531	6.0	Jim Fanning	2,318,292
1983	3rd	82	80	.506	8.0	Bill Virdon	2,320,651
1984	5th	78	83	.484	18.0	Bill Virdon, Jim Fanning	1,606,531
1985	3rd	84	77	.522	16.5	Buck Rodgers	1,502,494
1986	4th	78	83	.484	29.5	Buck Rodgers	1,128,981
1987	3rd	91	71	.562	4.0	Buck Rodgers	1,850,324
1988	3rd	81	81	.500	20.0	Buck Rodgers	1,478,659
1989	4th	81	81	.500	12.0	Buck Rodgers	1,783,533
1990	3rd	85	77	.525	10.0	Buck Rodgers	1,373,087
1991	6th	71	90	.441	26.5	Buck Rodgers, Tom Runnells	934,742
1992	2nd	87	75	.537	9.0	Tom Runnells, Felipe Alou	1,669,077
1993	2nd	94	68	.580	3.0	Felipe Alou	1,641,437
1994	1st	74	40	.649	+6.0	Felipe Alou	1,276,250
1995	5th	66	78	.458	24.0	Felipe Alou	1,309,618
1996	2nd	88	74	.543	8.0	Felipe Alou	1,616,709
1997	4th	78	84	.481	23.0	Felipe Alou	1,497,609
1998	4th	65	97	.401	41.0	Felipe Alou	914,717
1999	4th	68	94	.420	35.0	Felipe Alou	773,277
2000	4th	67	95	.414	28.0	Felipe Alou	926,263
2001	5th	68	94	.420	20.0	Felipe Alou, Jeff Torborg	609,473

*Games behind winner. †First half 30-25; second 30-23. ‡Won division series. §Lost championship series.

MANAGERIAL RECORDS

Felipe Alou 691-717, Jim Fanning 116-103, Charlie Fox 12-22, Karl Kuehl 43-85, Gene Mauch 499-627, Buck Rodgers 520-499, Tom Runnells 68-81, Jeff Torborg 47-62, Bill Virdon 146-147, Dick Williams 380-347.

NEW YORK METS
YEARLY FINISHES

Year	Position	W	L	Pct.	*GB	Manager	Attendance
1962	10th	40	120	.250	60.5	Casey Stengel	922,530
1963	10th	51	111	.315	48.0	Casey Stengel	1,080,108
1964	10th	53	109	.327	40.0	Casey Stengel	1,732,597
1965	10th	50	112	.309	47.0	Casey Stengel, Wes Westrum	1,768,389
1966	9th	66	95	.410	28.5	Wes Westrum	1,932,693
1967	10th	61	101	.377	40.5	Wes Westrum, Salty Parker	1,565,492
1968	9th	73	89	.451	24.0	Gil Hodges	1,781,657

EAST DIVISION

Year	Position	W	L	Pct.	*GB	Manager	Attendance
1969	1st†................	100	62	.617	+8.0	Gil Hodges....................	2,175,373
1970	3rd	83	79	.512	6.0	Gil Hodges....................	2,697,479
1971	3rd (tied)........	83	79	.512	14.0	Gil Hodges....................	2,266,680
1972	3rd	83	73	.532	13.5	Yogi Berra....................	2,134,185
1973	1st†................	82	79	.509	+1.5	Yogi Berra....................	1,912,390
1974	5th	71	91	.438	17.0	Yogi Berra....................	1,722,209
1975	3rd (tied)........	82	80	.506	10.5	Yogi Berra, Roy McMillan....	1,730,566
1976	3rd	86	76	.531	15.0	Joe Frazier....................	1,468,754
1977	6th	64	98	.395	37.0	Joe Frazier, Joe Torre........	1,066,825
1978	6th	66	96	.407	24.0	Joe Torre....................	1,007,328
1979	6th	63	99	.389	35.0	Joe Torre....................	788,905
1980	5th	67	95	.414	24.0	Joe Torre....................	1,192,073
1981	5th/4th	41	62	.398	‡	Joe Torre....................	704,244
1982	6th	65	97	.401	27.0	George Bamberger............	1,323,036
1983	6th	68	94	.420	22.0	George Bamberger, Frank Howard..	1,112,774
1984	2nd	90	72	.556	6.5	Dave Johnson................	1,842,695
1985	2nd	98	64	.605	3.0	Dave Johnson................	2,761,601
1986	1st†...............	108	54	.667	+21.5	Dave Johnson................	2,767,601
1987	2nd	92	70	.568	3.0	Dave Johnson................	3,034,129
1988	1st§..............	100	60	.625	+15.0	Dave Johnson................	3,055,445
1989	2nd	87	75	.537	6.0	Dave Johnson................	2,918,710
1990	2nd	91	71	.562	4.0	Dave Johnson, Bud Harrelson..	2,732,745
1991	5th	77	84	.478	20.5	Bud Harrelson, Mike Cubbage..	2,284,484
1992	5th	72	90	.444	24.0	Jeff Torborg....................	1,779,534
1993	7th	59	103	.364	38.0	Jeff Torborg, Dallas Green......	1,873,183
1994	3rd	55	58	.487	18.5	Dallas Green	1,151,471
1995	2nd (tied)........	69	75	.479	21.0	Dallas Green	1,273,183
1996	4th	71	91	.438	25.0	Dallas Green, Bobby Valentine..	1,588,323
1997	3rd	88	74	.543	13.0	Bobby Valentine..............	1,766,174
1998	2nd	88	74	.543	18.0	Bobby Valentine..............	2,287,942
1999	2nd∞§..........	97	66	.595	6.5	Bobby Valentine..............	2,725,668
2000	2nd▲†..........	94	68	.580	1.0	Bobby Valentine..............	2,800,221
2001	3rd	82	80	.506	6.0	Bobby Valentine..............	2,658,279

*Games behind winner. †Won championship series. ‡First half 17-34; second 24-28. §Lost championship series. ∞Won wild-card playoff. ▲Won division series.

MANAGERIAL RECORDS

George Bamberger 81-127, Yogi Berra 292-296, Mike Cubbage 3-4, Joe Frazier 101-106, Dallas Green 229-283, Bud Harrelson 145-129, Gil Hodges 339-309, Frank Howard 52-64, Davey Johnson 595-417, Roy McMillan 26-27, Salty Parker 4-7, Casey Stengel 175-404, Jeff Torborg 85-115, Joe Torre 286-420, Bobby Valentine 461-381, Wes Westrum 142-237.

PHILADELPHIA PHILLIES
YEARLY FINISHES

Year	Position	W	L	Pct.	*GB	Manager	Attendance
1901	2nd................	83	57	.593	7.5	Bill Shettsline................	234,937
1902	7th	56	81	.409	46.0	Bill Shettsline................	112,066
1903	7th	49	86	.363	39.5	Chief Zimmer................	151,729
1904	8th	52	100	.342	53.5	Hugh Duffy..................	140,771
1905	4th	83	69	.546	21.5	Hugh Duffy..................	317,932
1906	4th	71	82	.464	45.5	Hugh Duffy..................	294,680
1907	3rd	83	64	.565	21.5	Bill Murray..................	341,216
1908	4th	83	71	.539	16.0	Bill Murray..................	420,660
1909	5th	74	79	.484	36.5	Bill Murray..................	303,177
1910	4th	78	75	.510	25.5	Red Dooin..................	296,597
1911	4th	79	73	.520	19.5	Red Dooin..................	416,000
1912	5th	73	79	.480	30.5	Red Dooin..................	250,000
1913	2nd................	88	63	.583	12.5	Red Dooin..................	470,000
1914	6th	74	80	.481	20.5	Red Dooin..................	138,474
1915	1st	90	62	.592	+7.0	Pat Moran..................	449,898
1916	2nd................	91	62	.595	2.5	Pat Moran..................	515,365
1917	2nd................	87	65	.572	10.0	Pat Moran..................	354,428
1918	6th	55	68	.447	26.0	Pat Moran..................	122,266
1919	8th	47	90	.343	47.5	Jack Coombs, Gavvy Cravath..	240,424
1920	8th	62	91	.405	30.5	Gavvy Cravath..............	330,998
1921	8th	51	103	.331	43.5	Bill Donovan, Kaiser Wilhelm..	273,961
1922	7th	57	96	.373	35.5	Kaiser Wilhelm..............	232,471
1923	8th	50	104	.325	45.5	Art Fletcher................	228,168
1924	7th	55	96	.364	37.0	Art Fletcher................	299,818
1925	6th (tied)........	68	85	.444	27.0	Art Fletcher................	304,905
1926	8th	58	93	.384	29.5	Art Fletcher................	240,600
1927	8th	51	103	.331	43.0	Stuffy McInnis..............	305,420

Year	Position	W	L	Pct.	*GB	Manager	Attendance
1928	8th	43	109	.283	51.0	Burt Shotton	182,168
1929	5th	71	82	.464	27.5	Burt Shotton	281,200
1930	8th	52	102	.338	40.0	Burt Shotton	299,007
1931	6th	66	88	.429	35.0	Burt Shotton	284,849
1932	4th	78	76	.506	12.0	Burt Shotton	268,914
1933	7th	60	92	.395	31.0	Burt Shotton	156,421
1934	7th	56	93	.376	37.0	Jimmy Wilson	169,885
1935	7th	64	89	.418	35.5	Jimmy Wilson	205,470
1936	8th	54	100	.351	38.0	Jimmy Wilson	249,219
1937	7th	61	92	.399	34.5	Jimmy Wilson	212,790
1938	8th	45	105	.300	43.0	Jimmy Wilson, Hans Lobert	166,111
1939	8th	45	106	.298	50.5	Doc Prothro	277,973
1940	8th	50	103	.327	50.0	Doc Prothro	207,177
1941	8th	43	111	.279	57.0	Doc Prothro	231,401
1942	8th	42	109	.278	62.5	Hans Lobert	230,183
1943	7th	64	90	.416	41.0	Bucky Harris, Fred Fitzsimmons	466,975
1944	8th	61	92	.399	43.5	Fred Fitzsimmons	369,586
1945	8th	46	108	.299	52.0	Fred Fitzsimmons, Ben Chapman	285,057
1946	5th	69	85	.448	28.0	Ben Chapman	1,045,247
1947	7th (tied)	62	92	.403	32.0	Ben Chapman	907,332
1948	6th	66	88	.429	25.5	Ben Chapman, Dusty Cooke, Eddie Sawyer	767,429
1949	3rd	81	73	.526	16.0	Eddie Sawyer	819,698
1950	1st	91	63	.591	+2.0	Eddie Sawyer	1,217,035
1951	5th	73	81	.474	23.5	Eddie Sawyer	937,658
1952	4th	87	67	.565	9.5	Eddie Sawyer, Steve O'Neill	775,417
1953	3rd (tied)	83	71	.539	22.0	Steve O'Neill	853,644
1954	4th	75	79	.487	22.0	Steve O'Neill, Terry Moore	738,991
1955	4th	77	77	.500	21.5	Mayo Smith	922,886
1956	5th	71	83	.461	22.0	Mayo Smith	934,798
1957	5th	77	77	.500	19.0	Mayo Smith	1,146,230
1958	8th	69	85	.448	23.0	Mayo Smith, Eddie Sawyer	931,110
1959	8th	64	90	.416	23.0	Eddie Sawyer	802,815
1960	8th	59	95	.383	36.0	Eddie Sawyer, Andy Cohen, Gene Mauch	862,205
1961	8th	47	107	.305	46.0	Gene Mauch	590,039
1962	7th	81	80	.503	20.0	Gene Mauch	762,034
1963	4th	87	75	.537	12.0	Gene Mauch	907,141
1964	2nd (tied)	92	70	.568	1.0	Gene Mauch	1,425,891
1965	6th	85	76	.528	11.5	Gene Mauch	1,166,376
1966	4th	87	75	.537	8.0	Gene Mauch	1,108,201
1967	5th	82	80	.506	19.5	Gene Mauch	828,888
1968	7th (tied)	76	86	.469	21.0	Gene Mauch, George Myatt, Bob Skinner	664,546

EAST DIVISION

Year	Position	W	L	Pct.	*GB	Manager	Attendance
1969	5th	63	99	.389	37.0	Bob Skinner, George Myatt	519,414
1970	5th	73	88	.453	15.5	Frank Lucchesi	708,247
1971	6th	67	95	.414	30.0	Frank Lucchesi	1,511,223
1972	6th	59	97	.378	37.5	Frank Lucchesi, Paul Owens	1,343,329
1973	6th	71	91	.438	11.5	Danny Ozark	1,475,934
1974	3rd	80	82	.494	8.0	Danny Ozark	1,808,648
1975	2nd	86	76	.531	6.5	Danny Ozark	1,909,233
1976	1st†	101	61	.623	+9.0	Danny Ozark	2,480,150
1977	1st†	101	61	.623	+5.0	Danny Ozark	2,700,070
1978	1st†	90	72	.556	+1.5	Danny Ozark	2,583,389
1979	4th	84	78	.519	14.0	Danny Ozark, Dallas Green	2,775,011
1980	1st‡	91	71	.562	+1.0	Dallas Green	2,651,650
1981	1st/3rd∞	59	48	.551	§	Dallas Green	1,638,752
1982	2nd	89	73	.549	3.0	Pat Corrales	2,376,394
1983	1st‡	90	72	.556	+6.0	Pat Corrales, Paul Owens	2,128,339
1984	4th	81	81	.500	15.5	Paul Owens	2,062,693
1985	5th	75	87	.463	26.0	John Felske	1,830,350
1986	2nd	86	75	.534	21.5	John Felske	1,933,335
1987	4th (tied)	80	82	.494	15.0	John Felske, Lee Elia	2,100,110
1988	6th	65	96	.404	35.5	Lee Elia, John Vukovich	1,990,041
1989	6th	67	95	.414	26.0	Nick Leyva	1,861,985
1990	4th (tied)	77	85	.475	18.0	Nick Leyva	1,992,484
1991	3rd	78	84	.481	20.0	Nick Leyva, Jim Fregosi	2,050,012
1992	6th	70	92	.432	26.0	Jim Fregosi	1,927,448
1993	1st‡	97	65	.599	+3.0	Jim Fregosi	3,137,674
1994	4th	54	61	.470	20.5	Jim Fregosi	2,290,971
1995	2nd (tied)	69	75	.479	21.0	Jim Fregosi	2,043,598
1996	5th	67	95	.414	29.0	Jim Fregosi	1,801,677
1997	5th	68	94	.420	33.0	Terry Francona	1,490,638
1998	3rd	75	87	.463	31.0	Terry Francona	1,715,702

Year	Position	W	L	Pct.	*GB	Manager	Attendance
1999	3rd	77	85	.475	26.0	Terry Francona	1,825,337
2000	5th	65	97	.401	30.0	Terry Francona	1,612,769
2001	2nd	86	76	.531	2.0	Larry Bowa	1,782,460

*Games behind winner. †Lost championship series. ‡Won championship series. §First half 34-21; second 25-27. ∞Lost division series.

MANAGERIAL RECORDS

Larry Bowa 86-76, Ben Chapman 197-277, Andy Cohen 1-0, Dusty Cooke 6-6, Jack Coombs 18-44, Pat Corrales 132-115, Gavvy Cravath 91-137, Bill Donovan 31-71, Red Dooin 392-370, Hugh Duffy 206-251, Lee Elia 111-142, John Felske 190-194, Fred Fitzsimmons 102-179, Art Fletcher 231-378, Terry Francona 285-363, Jim Fregosi 431-463, Dallas Green 169-130, Bucky Harris 40-53, Nick Leyva 148-189, Hans Lobert 42-111, Frank Lucchesi 166-233, Gene Mauch 645-684, Stuffy McInnis 51-103, Terry Moore 35-42, Pat Moran 323-257, Bill Murray 240-214, George Myatt 21-35, Steve O'Neill 182-140, Paul Owens 161-158, Danny Ozark 594-510, Doc Prothro 138-320, Eddie Sawyer 390-424, Bill Shettsline 139-138, Burt Shotton 370-549, Bob Skinner 92-123, Mayo Smith 264-281, John Vukovich 5-4, Kaiser Wilhelm 77-128, Jimmy Wilson 280-477, Chief Zimmer 49-86.

PITTSBURGH PIRATES
YEARLY FINISHES

Year	Position	W	L	Pct.	*GB	Manager	Attendance
1901	1st	90	49	.647	+7.5	Fred Clarke	251,955
1902	1st	103	36	.741	+27.5	Fred Clarke	243,826
1903	1st	91	49	.650	+6.5	Fred Clarke	326,855
1904	4th	87	66	.569	19.0	Fred Clarke	340,615
1905	2nd	96	57	.627	9.0	Fred Clarke	369,124
1906	3rd	93	00	.608	23.5	Fred Clarke	394,877
1907	2nd	91	63	.591	17.0	Fred Clarke	010,506
1908	2nd	98	56	.636	1.0	Fred Clarke	382,444
1909	1st	110	42	.724	+6.5	Fred Clarke	534,950
1910	3rd	86	67	.562	17.5	Fred Clarke	436,586
1911	3rd	85	69	.552	14.5	Fred Clarke	432,000
1912	2nd	93	58	.616	10.0	Fred Clarke	384,000
1913	4th	78	71	.523	21.5	Fred Clarke	296,000
1914	7th	69	85	.448	25.5	Fred Clarke	139,620
1915	5th	73	81	.474	18.0	Fred Clarke	225,743
1916	6th	65	89	.422	29.0	Jimmy Callahan	289,132
1917	8th	51	103	.331	47.0	Jimmy Callahan, Honus Wagner, Hugo Bezdek	192,807
1918	4th	65	60	.520	17.0	Hugo Bezdek	213,610
1919	4th	71	68	.511	24.5	Hugo Bezdek	276,810
1920	4th	79	75	.513	14.0	George Gibson	429,037
1921	2nd	90	63	.588	4.0	George Gibson	701,567
1922	3rd (tied)	85	69	.552	8.0	George Gibson, Bill McKechnie	523,675
1923	3rd	87	67	.565	8.5	Bill McKechnie	611,082
1924	3rd	90	63	.588	3.0	Bill McKechnie	736,883
1925	1st	95	58	.621	+8.5	Bill McKechnie	804,354
1926	3rd	84	69	.549	4.5	Bill McKechnie	798,542
1927	1st	94	60	.610	+1.5	Donie Bush	869,720
1928	4th	85	67	.559	9.0	Donie Bush	495,070
1929	2nd	88	65	.575	10.5	Donie Bush, Jewel Ens	491,377
1930	5th	80	74	.519	12.0	Jewel Ens	357,795
1931	5th	75	79	.487	26.0	Jewel Ens	260,392
1932	2nd	86	68	.558	4.0	George Gibson	287,262
1933	2nd	87	67	.565	5.0	George Gibson	288,747
1934	5th	74	76	.493	19.5	George Gibson, Pie Traynor	322,622
1935	4th	86	67	.562	13.5	Pie Traynor	352,885
1936	4th	84	70	.545	8.0	Pie Traynor	372,524
1937	3rd	86	68	.558	10.0	Pie Traynor	459,679
1938	2nd	86	64	.573	2.0	Pie Traynor	641,033
1939	6th	68	85	.444	28.5	Pie Traynor	376,734
1940	4th	78	76	.506	22.5	Frankie Frisch	507,934
1941	4th	81	73	.526	19.0	Frankie Frisch	482,241
1942	5th	66	81	.449	36.5	Frankie Frisch	448,897
1943	4th	80	74	.519	25.0	Frankie Frisch	604,278
1944	2nd	90	63	.588	14.5	Frankie Frisch	498,740
1945	4th	82	72	.532	16.0	Frankie Frisch	604,694
1946	7th	63	91	.409	34.0	Frankie Frisch, Spud Davis	749,962
1947	7th (tied)	62	92	.403	32.0	Billy Herman, Bill Burwell	1,283,531
1948	4th	83	71	.539	8.5	Billy Meyer	1,517,021
1949	6th	71	83	.461	26.0	Billy Meyer	1,499,435
1950	8th	57	96	.373	33.5	Billy Meyer	1,166,267
1951	7th	64	90	.416	32.5	Billy Meyer	980,590
1952	8th	42	112	.273	54.5	Billy Meyer	686,673
1953	8th	50	104	.325	55.0	Fred Haney	572,757
1954	8th	53	101	.344	44.0	Fred Haney	475,494
1955	8th	60	94	.390	38.5	Fred Haney	469,397

HISTORY Team by team

Year	Position	W	L	Pct.	*GB	Manager	Attendance
1956	7th	66	88	.429	27.0	Bobby Bragan	949,878
1957	7th (tied)	62	92	.403	33.0	Bobby Bragan, Danny Murtaugh	850,732
1958	2nd	84	70	.545	8.0	Danny Murtaugh	1,311,988
1959	4th	78	76	.506	9.0	Danny Murtaugh	1,359,917
1960	1st	95	59	.617	+7.0	Danny Murtaugh	1,705,828
1961	6th	75	79	.487	18.0	Danny Murtaugh	1,199,128
1962	4th	93	68	.578	8.0	Danny Murtaugh	1,090,648
1963	8th	74	88	.457	25.0	Danny Murtaugh	783,648
1964	6th (tied)	80	82	.494	13.0	Danny Murtaugh	759,496
1965	3rd	90	72	.556	7.0	Harry Walker	909,279
1966	3rd	92	70	.568	3.0	Harry Walker	1,196,618
1967	6th	81	81	.500	20.5	Harry Walker, Danny Murtaugh	907,012
1968	6th	80	82	.494	17.0	Larry Shepard	693,485

EAST DIVISION

Year	Position	W	L	Pct.	*GB	Manager	Attendance
1969	3rd	88	74	.543	12.0	Larry Shepard, Alex Grammas	769,369
1970	1st†	89	73	.549	+5.0	Danny Murtaugh	1,341,947
1971	1st‡	97	65	.599	+7.0	Danny Murtaugh	1,501,132
1972	1st†	96	59	.619	+11.0	Bill Virdon	1,427,460
1973	3rd	80	82	.494	2.5	Bill Virdon, Danny Murtaugh	1,319,913
1974	1st†	88	74	.543	+1.5	Danny Murtaugh	1,110,552
1975	1st†	92	69	.571	+6.5	Danny Murtaugh	1,270,018
1976	2nd	92	70	.568	9.0	Danny Murtaugh	1,025,945
1977	2nd	96	66	.593	5.0	Chuck Tanner	1,237,349
1978	2nd	88	73	.547	1.5	Chuck Tanner	964,106
1979	1st‡	98	64	.605	+2.0	Chuck Tanner	1,435,454
1980	3rd	83	79	.512	8.0	Chuck Tanner	1,646,757
1981	4th/6th	46	56	.451	§	Chuck Tanner	541,789
1982	4th	84	78	.519	8.0	Chuck Tanner	1,024,106
1983	2nd	84	78	.519	6.0	Chuck Tanner	1,225,916
1984	6th	75	87	.463	21.5	Chuck Tanner	773,500
1985	6th	57	104	.354	43.5	Chuck Tanner	735,900
1986	6th	64	98	.395	44.0	Jim Leyland	1,000,917
1987	4th (tied)	80	82	.494	15.0	Jim Leyland	1,161,193
1988	2nd	85	75	.531	15.0	Jim Leyland	1,866,713
1989	5th	74	88	.457	19.0	Jim Leyland	1,374,141
1990	1st†	95	67	.586	+4.0	Jim Leyland	2,049,908
1991	1st†	98	64	.605	+14.0	Jim Leyland	2,065,302
1992	1st†	96	66	.593	+9.0	Jim Leyland	1,829,395
1993	5th	75	87	.463	22.0	Jim Leyland	1,650,593

CENTRAL DIVISION

Year	Position	W	L	Pct.	*GB	Manager	Attendance
1994	3rd (tied)	53	61	.465	13.0	Jim Leyland	1,222,520
1995	5th	58	86	.403	27.0	Jim Leyland	905,517
1996	5th	73	89	.451	15.0	Jim Leyland	1,332,150
1997	2nd	79	83	.488	5.0	Gene Lamont	1,657,022
1998	6th	69	93	.426	33.0	Gene Lamont	1,560,950
1999	3rd	78	83	.484	18.5	Gene Lamont	1,638,023
2000	5th	69	93	.426	26.0	Gene Lamont	1,748,908
2001	6th	62	100	.383	31.0	Lloyd McClendon	2,436,126

*Games behind winner. †Lost championship series. ‡Won championship series. §First half 25-23; second half 21-33.

MANAGERIAL RECORDS

Hugo Bezdek 166-187, Bobby Bragan 102-155, Bill Burwell 1-0, Donie Bush 246-178, Jimmy Callahan 85-129, Fred Clarke 1,343-909, Spud Davis 1-2, Jewel Ens 176-167, Frank Frisch 539-528, George Gibson 401-330, Alex Grammas 4-1, Fred Haney 163-299, Billy Herman 61-92, Gene Lamont 295-352, Jim Leyland 851-863, Lloyd McClendon 62-100, Bill McKechnie 409-293, Billy Meyer 317-452, Danny Murtaugh 1,115-950, Larry Shepard 164-155, Chuck Tanner 711-685, Pie Traynor 457-406, Bill Virdon 163-128, Honus Wagner 1-4, Harry Walker 224-184.

ST. LOUIS CARDINALS
YEARLY FINISHES

Year	Position	W	L	Pct.	*GB	Manager	Attendance
1901	4th	76	64	.543	14.5	Patsy Donovan	379,988
1902	6th	56	78	.418	44.5	Patsy Donovan	226,417
1903	8th	43	94	.314	46.5	Patsy Donovan	226,538
1904	5th	75	79	.487	31.5	Kid Nichols	386,750
1905	6th	58	96	.377	47.5	Kid Nichols, Jimmy Burke, Matt Robison	292,800
1906	7th	52	98	.347	63.0	John McCloskey	283,770
1907	8th	52	101	.340	55.5	John McCloskey	185,377
1908	8th	49	105	.318	50.0	John McCloskey	205,129

Year	Position	W	L	Pct.	*GB	Manager	Attendance
1909	7th	54	98	.355	56.0	Roger Bresnahan	299,982
1910	7th	63	90	.412	40.5	Roger Bresnahan	355,668
1911	5th	75	74	.503	22.0	Roger Bresnahan	447,768
1912	6th	63	90	.412	41.0	Roger Bresnahan	241,759
1913	8th	51	99	.340	49.0	Miller Huggins	203,531
1914	3rd	81	72	.529	13.0	Miller Huggins	256,099
1915	6th	72	81	.471	18.5	Miller Huggins	252,666
1916	7th (tied)	60	93	.392	33.5	Miller Huggins	224,308
1917	3rd	82	70	.539	15.0	Miller Huggins	288,491
1918	8th	51	78	.395	33.0	Jack Hendricks	110,599
1919	7th	54	83	.394	40.5	Branch Rickey	167,059
1920	5th (tied)	75	79	.487	18.0	Branch Rickey	326,836
1921	3rd	87	66	.569	7.0	Branch Rickey	384,773
1922	3rd (tied)	85	69	.552	8.0	Branch Rickey	536,998
1923	5th	79	74	.516	16.0	Branch Rickey	338,551
1924	6th	65	89	.422	28.5	Branch Rickey	272,885
1925	4th	77	76	.503	18.0	Branch Rickey, Rogers Hornsby	404,959
1926	1st	89	65	.578	+2.0	Rogers Hornsby	668,428
1927	2nd	92	61	.601	1.5	Bob O'Farrell	749,340
1928	1st	95	59	.617	+2.0	Bill McKechnie	761,574
1929	4th	78	74	.513	20.0	Bill McKechnie, Billy Southworth	399,887
1930	1st	92	62	.597	+2.0	Gabby Street	508,501
1931	1st	101	53	.656	+13.0	Gabby Street	608,535
1932	6th (tied)	72	82	.468	18.0	Gabby Street	279,219
1933	5th	82	71	.536	9.5	Gabby Street, Frankie Frisch	256,171
1934	1st	95	58	.621	+2.0	Frankie Frisch	325,056
1935	2nd	96	58	.623	4.0	Frankie Frisch	506,084
1936	2nd (tied)	87	67	.565	5.0	Frankie Frisch	448,078
1937	4th	81	73	.526	15.0	Frankie Frisch	430,811
1938	6th	71	80	.470	17.5	Frankie Frisch, Mike Gonzalez	291,418
1939	2nd	92	61	.601	4.5	Ray Blades	400,245
1940	3rd	84	69	.549	16.0	Ray Blades, Mike Gonzalez, Billy Southworth	324,078
1941	2nd	97	56	.634	2.5	Billy Southworth	633,645
1942	1st	106	48	.688	+2.0	Billy Southworth	553,552
1943	1st	105	49	.682	+18.0	Billy Southworth	517,135
1944	1st	105	49	.682	+14.5	Billy Southworth	461,968
1945	2nd	95	59	.617	3.0	Billy Southworth	594,630
1946	1st†	98	58	.628	+2.0	Eddie Dyer	1,061,807
1947	2nd	89	65	.578	5.0	Eddie Dyer	1,247,913
1948	2nd	85	69	.552	6.5	Eddie Dyer	1,111,440
1949	2nd	96	58	.623	1.0	Eddie Dyer	1,430,676
1950	5th	78	75	.510	12.5	Eddie Dyer	1,093,411
1951	3rd	81	73	.526	15.5	Marty Marion	1,013,429
1952	3rd	88	66	.571	8.5	Eddie Stanky	913,113
1953	3rd (tied)	83	71	.539	22.0	Eddie Stanky	880,242
1954	6th	72	82	.468	25.0	Eddie Stanky	1,039,698
1955	7th	68	86	.442	30.5	Eddie Stanky, Harry Walker	849,130
1956	4th	76	78	.494	17.0	Fred Hutchinson	1,029,773
1957	2nd	87	67	.565	8.0	Fred Hutchinson	1,183,575
1958	5th (tied)	72	82	.468	20.0	Fred Hutchinson, Stan Hack	1,063,730
1959	7th	71	83	.461	16.0	Solly Hemus	929,953
1960	3rd	86	68	.558	9.0	Solly Hemus	1,096,632
1961	5th	80	74	.519	13.0	Solly Hemus, Johnny Keane	855,305
1962	6th	84	78	.519	17.5	Johnny Keane	953,895
1963	2nd	93	69	.574	6.0	Johnny Keane	1,170,546
1964	1st	93	69	.574	+1.0	Johnny Keane	1,143,294
1965	7th	80	81	.497	16.5	Red Schoendienst	1,241,201
1966	6th	83	79	.512	12.0	Red Schoendienst	1,712,980
1967	1st	101	60	.627	+10.5	Red Schoendienst	2,090,145
1968	1st	97	65	.599	+9.0	Red Schoendienst	2,011,167

EAST DIVISION

Year	Position	W	L	Pct.	*GB	Manager	Attendance
1969	4th	87	75	.537	13.0	Red Schoendienst	1,682,783
1970	4th	76	86	.469	13.0	Red Schoendienst	1,629,736
1971	2nd	90	72	.556	7.0	Red Schoendienst	1,604,671
1972	4th	75	81	.481	21.5	Red Schoendienst	1,196,894
1973	2nd	81	81	.500	1.5	Red Schoendienst	1,574,046
1974	2nd	86	75	.534	1.5	Red Schoendienst	1,838,413
1975	3rd (tied)	82	80	.506	10.5	Red Schoendienst	1,695,270
1976	5th	72	90	.444	29.0	Red Schoendienst	1,207,079
1977	3rd	83	79	.512	18.0	Vern Rapp	1,659,287
1978	5th	69	93	.426	21.0	Vern Rapp, Jack Krol, Ken Boyer	1,278,215
1979	3rd	86	76	.531	12.0	Ken Boyer	1,627,256
1980	4th	74	88	.457	17.0	Ken Boyer, Jack Krol, Whitey Herzog, Red Schoendienst	1,385,147

Year	Position	W	L	Pct.	*GB	Manager	Attendance
1981	2nd/2nd	59	43	.578	‡	Whitey Herzog	1,010,247
1982	1st§	92	70	.568	+3.0	Whitey Herzog	2,111,906
1983	4th	79	83	.488	11.0	Whitey Herzog	2,317,914
1984	3rd	84	78	.519	12.5	Whitey Herzog	2,037,448
1985	1st§	101	61	.623	+3.0	Whitey Herzog	2,637,563
1986	3rd	79	82	.491	28.5	Whitey Herzog	2,471,974
1987	1st§	95	67	.586	+3.0	Whitey Herzog	3,072,122
1988	5th	76	86	.469	25.0	Whitey Herzog	2,892,799
1989	3rd	86	76	.531	7.0	Whitey Herzog	3,080,980
1990	6th	70	92	.432	25.0	Whitey Herzog, Red Schoendienst, Joe Torre	2,573,225
1991	2nd	84	78	.519	14.0	Joe Torre	2,448,699
1992	3rd	83	79	.512	13.0	Joe Torre	2,418,483
1993	3rd	87	75	.537	10.0	Joe Torre	2,844,328

CENTRAL DIVISION

Year	Position	W	L	Pct.	*GB	Manager	Attendance
1994	3rd (tied)	53	61	.465	13.0	Joe Torre	1,866,544
1995	4th	62	81	.434	22.5	Joe Torre, Mike Jorgensen	1,756,727
1996	1st∞▲	88	74	.543	+6.0	Tony La Russa	2,654,718
1997	4th	73	89	.451	11.0	Tony La Russa	2,634,014
1998	3rd	83	79	.512	19.0	Tony La Russa	3,194,092
1999	4th	75	86	.466	21.5	Tony La Russa	3,225,334
2000	1st∞▲	95	67	.586	+10.0	Tony La Russa	3,336,493
2001	1st (tied)◆	93	69	.574	0.0	Tony La Russa	3,113,091

*Games behind winner. †Won pennant playoff. ‡First half 30-20; second 29-23. §Won championship series. ∞Won division series. ▲Lost championship series. ◆Lost division series.

MANAGERIAL RECORDS

Ray Blades 106-85, Ken Boyer 166-190, Roger Bresnahan 255-352, Jimmy Burke 17-32, Patsy Donovan 175-236, Eddie Dyer 446-325, Frank Frisch 458-354, Mike Gonzalez 9-13, Stan Hack 3-7, Solly Hemus 190-192, Jack Hendricks 51-78, Whitey Herzog 835-739, Rogers Hornsby 153-116, Miller Huggins 346-415, Fred Hutchinson 232-220, Mike Jorgensen 42-54, Johnny Keane 317-249, Tony La Russa 507-464, Marty Marion 81-73, John McCloskey 153-304, Bill McKechnie 129-88, Kid Nichols 94-108, Bob O'Farrell 92-61, Vern Rapp 89-90, Branch Rickey 458-485, Stanley Robison 22-35, Red Schoendienst 1,028-944, Billy Southworth 620-346, Eddie Stanky 260-238, Gabby Street 312-242, Joe Torre 351-354, Harry Walker 51-67.

SAN DIEGO PADRES

YEARLY FINISHES

WEST DIVISION

Year	Position	W	L	Pct.	*GB	Manager	Attendance
1969	6th	52	110	.321	41.0	Preston Gomez	512,970
1970	6th	63	99	.389	39.0	Preston Gomez	643,679
1971	6th	61	100	.379	28.5	Preston Gomez	557,513
1972	6th	58	95	.379	36.5	Preston Gomez, Don Zimmer	644,273
1973	6th	60	102	.370	39.0	Don Zimmer	611,826
1974	6th	60	102	.370	42.0	John McNamara	1,075,399
1975	4th	71	91	.438	37.0	John McNamara	1,281,747
1976	5th	73	89	.451	29.0	John McNamara	1,458,478
1977	5th	69	93	.426	29.0	John McNamara, Bob Skinner, Alvin Dark	1,376,269
1978	4th	84	78	.519	11.0	Roger Craig	1,670,107
1979	5th	68	93	.422	22.0	Roger Craig	1,456,967
1980	6th	73	89	.451	19.5	Jerry Coleman	1,139,026
1981	6th/6th	41	69	.373	†	Frank Howard	519,161
1982	4th	81	81	.500	8.0	Dick Williams	1,607,516
1983	4th	81	81	.500	10.0	Dick Williams	1,539,815
1984	1st‡	92	70	.568	+12.0	Dick Williams	1,983,904
1985	3rd (tied)	83	79	.512	12.0	Dick Williams	2,210,352
1986	4th	74	88	.457	22.0	Steve Boros	1,805,716
1987	6th	65	97	.401	25.0	Larry Bowa	1,454,061
1988	3rd	83	78	.516	11.0	Larry Bowa, Jack McKeon	1,506,896
1989	2nd	89	73	.549	3.0	Jack McKeon	2,009,031
1990	4th (tied)	75	87	.463	16.0	Jack McKeon, Greg Riddoch	1,856,396
1991	3rd	84	78	.519	10.0	Greg Riddoch	1,804,289
1992	3rd	82	80	.506	16.0	Greg Riddoch, Jim Riggleman	1,722,102
1993	7th	61	101	.377	43.0	Jim Riggleman	1,375,432
1994	4th	47	70	.402	12.5	Jim Riggleman	953,857
1995	3rd	70	74	.486	8.0	Bruce Bochy	1,041,805
1996	1st§	91	71	.562	+1.0	Bruce Bochy	2,187,886
1997	4th	76	86	.469	14.0	Bruce Bochy	2,089,333
1998	1st∞	98	64	.605	+9.5	Bruce Bochy	2,555,901
1999	4th	74	88	.457	26.0	Bruce Bochy	2,523,538

Year	Position	W	L	Pct.	*GB	Manager	Attendance
2000	5th	76	86	.469	21.0	Bruce Bochy	2,423,149
2001	4th	79	83	.488	13.0	Bruce Bochy	2,377,969

*Games behind winner. †First half 23-33; second 18-36. ‡Won championship series. §Lost division series. ∞Won division series.

MANAGERIAL RECORDS

Bruce Bochy 564-552, Steve Boros 74-88, Larry Bowa 81-127, Jerry Coleman 73-89, Roger Craig 152-171, Alvin Dark 49-65, Preston Gomez 180-316, Frank Howard 41-69, Jack McKeon 193-164, John McNamara 224-310, Greg Riddoch 200-194, Jim Riggleman 112-179, Dick Williams 337-311, Don Zimmer 114-190.

SAN FRANCISCO GIANTS
YEARLY FINISHES

(Known as New York Giants through 1957)

Year	Position	W	L	Pct.	*GB	Manager	Attendance
1901	7th	52	85	.380	37.0	George Davis	297,650
1902	8th	48	88	.353	53.5	Horace Fogel, Heinie Smith, John McGraw	302,875
1903	2nd	84	55	.604	6.5	John McGraw	579,530
1904	1st	106	47	.693	+13.0	John McGraw	609,826
1905	1st	105	48	.686	+9.0	John McGraw	552,700
1906	2nd	96	56	.632	20.0	John McGraw	402,850
1907	4th	82	71	.536	25.5	John McGraw	538,350
1908	2nd (tied)	98	56	.636	1.0	John McGraw	910,000
1909	3rd	92	61	.001	18.5	John McGraw	783,700
1910	2nd	91	63	.591	13.0	John McGraw	511,785
1911	1st	99	54	.647	+7.5	John McGraw	675,000
1912	1st	103	48	.682	+10.0	John McGraw	638,000
1913	1st	101	51	.664	+12.5	John McGraw	630,000
1914	2nd	84	70	.545	10.5	John McGraw	364,313
1915	8th	69	83	.454	21.0	John McGraw	391,850
1916	4th	86	66	.566	7.0	John McGraw	552,056
1917	1st	98	56	.636	+10.0	John McGraw	500,264
1918	2nd	71	53	.573	10.5	John McGraw	256,618
1919	2nd	87	53	.621	9.0	John McGraw	708,857
1920	2nd	86	68	.558	7.0	John McGraw	929,609
1921	1st	94	59	.614	+4.0	John McGraw	773,477
1922	1st	93	61	.604	+7.0	John McGraw	945,809
1923	1st	95	58	.621	+4.5	John McGraw	820,780
1924	1st	93	60	.608	+1.5	John McGraw	844,068
1925	2nd	86	66	.566	8.5	John McGraw	778,993
1926	5th	74	77	.490	13.5	John McGraw	700,362
1927	3rd	92	62	.597	2.0	John McGraw	858,190
1928	2nd	93	61	.604	2.0	John McGraw	916,191
1929	3rd	84	67	.556	13.5	John McGraw	868,806
1930	3rd	87	67	.565	5.0	John McGraw	868,714
1931	2nd	87	65	.572	13.0	John McGraw	812,163
1932	6th (tied)	72	82	.468	18.0	John McGraw, Bill Terry	484,868
1933	1st	91	61	.599	+5.0	Bill Terry	604,471
1934	2nd	93	60	.608	2.0	Bill Terry	730,851
1935	3rd	91	62	.595	8.5	Bill Terry	748,748
1936	1st	92	62	.597	+5.0	Bill Terry	837,952
1937	1st	95	57	.625	+3.0	Bill Terry	926,887
1938	3rd	83	67	.553	5.0	Bill Terry	799,633
1939	5th	77	74	.510	18.5	Bill Terry	702,457
1940	6th	72	80	.474	27.5	Bill Terry	747,852
1941	5th	74	79	.484	25.5	Bill Terry	763,098
1942	3rd	85	67	.559	20.0	Mel Ott	779,621
1943	8th	55	98	.359	49.5	Mel Ott	466,095
1944	5th	67	87	.435	38.0	Mel Ott	674,083
1945	5th	78	74	.513	19.0	Mel Ott	1,016,468
1946	8th	61	93	.396	36.0	Mel Ott	1,219,873
1947	4th	81	73	.526	13.0	Mel Ott	1,600,793
1948	5th	78	76	.506	13.5	Mel Ott, Leo Durocher	1,459,269
1949	5th	73	81	.474	24.0	Leo Durocher	1,218,446
1950	3rd	86	68	.558	5.0	Leo Durocher	1,008,876
1951	1st (tied)†	98	59	.624	+1.0	Leo Durocher	1,059,539
1952	2nd	92	62	.597	4.5	Leo Durocher	984,940
1953	5th	70	84	.455	35.0	Leo Durocher	811,518
1954	1st	97	57	.630	+5.0	Leo Durocher	1,155,067
1955	3rd	80	74	.519	18.5	Leo Durocher	824,112
1956	6th	67	87	.435	26.0	Bill Rigney	629,179
1957	6th	69	85	.448	26.0	Bill Rigney	653,923
1958	3rd	80	74	.519	12.0	Bill Rigney	1,272,625

Year	Position	W	L	Pct.	*GB	Manager	Attendance
1959	3rd	83	71	.539	4.0	Bill Rigney	1,422,130
1960	5th	79	75	.513	16.0	Bill Rigney, Tom Sheehan	1,795,356
1961	3rd	85	69	.552	8.0	Alvin Dark	1,390,679
1962	1st†	103	62	.624	+1.0	Alvin Dark	1,592,594
1963	3rd	88	74	.543	11.0	Alvin Dark	1,571,306
1964	4th	90	72	.556	3.0	Alvin Dark	1,504,364
1965	2nd	95	67	.586	2.0	Herman Franks	1,546,075
1966	2nd	93	68	.578	1.5	Herman Franks	1,657,192
1967	2nd	91	71	.562	10.5	Herman Franks	1,242,480
1968	2nd	88	74	.543	9.0	Herman Franks	837,220

WEST DIVISION

Year	Position	W	L	Pct.	*GB	Manager	Attendance
1969	2nd	90	72	.556	3.0	Clyde King	873,603
1970	3rd	86	76	.531	16.0	Clyde King, Charlie Fox	740,720
1971	1st‡	90	72	.556	+1.0	Charlie Fox	1,106,043
1972	5th	69	86	.445	26.5	Charlie Fox	647,744
1973	3rd	88	74	.543	11.0	Charlie Fox	834,193
1974	5th	72	90	.444	30.0	Charlie Fox, Wes Westrum	519,987
1975	3rd	80	81	.497	27.5	Wes Westrum	522,919
1976	4th	74	88	.457	28.0	Bill Rigney	626,868
1977	4th	75	87	.463	23.0	Joe Altobelli	700,056
1978	3rd	89	73	.549	6.0	Joe Altobelli	1,740,477
1979	4th	71	91	.438	19.5	Joe Altobelli, Dave Bristol	1,456,402
1980	5th	75	86	.466	17.0	Dave Bristol	1,096,115
1981	5th/3rd	56	55	.505	§	Frank Robinson	632,274
1982	3rd	87	75	.537	2.0	Frank Robinson	1,200,948
1983	5th	79	83	.488	12.0	Frank Robinson	1,251,530
1984	6th	66	96	.407	26.0	Frank Robinson, Danny Ozark	1,001,545
1985	6th	62	100	.383	33.0	Jim Davenport, Roger Craig	818,697
1986	3rd	83	79	.512	13.0	Roger Craig	1,528,748
1987	1st‡	90	72	.556	+6.0	Roger Craig	1,917,168
1988	4th	83	79	.512	11.5	Roger Craig	1,785,297
1989	1st∞	92	70	.568	+3.0	Roger Craig	2,059,701
1990	3rd	85	77	.525	6.0	Roger Craig	1,975,528
1991	4th	75	87	.463	19.0	Roger Craig	1,737,478
1992	5th	72	90	.444	26.0	Roger Craig	1,561,987
1993	2nd	103	59	.636	1.0	Dusty Baker	2,606,354
1994	2nd	55	60	.478	3.5	Dusty Baker	1,704,608
1995	4th	67	77	.465	11.0	Dusty Baker	1,241,500
1996	4th	68	94	.420	23.0	Dusty Baker	1,413,922
1997	1st▲	90	72	.556	+2.0	Dusty Baker	1,690,869
1998	2nd♦	89	74	.546	9.5	Dusty Baker	1,925,634
1999	2nd	86	76	.531	14.0	Dusty Baker	2,078,399
2000	1st▲	97	65	.599	+11.0	Dusty Baker	3,315,330
2001	2nd	90	72	.556	2.0	Dusty Baker	3,277,244

*Games behind winner. †Won pennant playoff. ‡Lost championship series. §First half 27-32; second half 29-23. ∞Won championship series. ▲Lost division series. ♦Lost wild-card playoff.

MANAGERIAL RECORDS

Joe Altobelli 225-239, Dusty Baker 745-649, Dave Bristol 85-98, Roger Craig 586-566, Alvin Dark 366-277, Jim Davenport 56-88, George Davis 52-85, Leo Durocher 637-523, Horace Fogel 18-23, Charlie Fox 348-327, Herman Franks 367-280, Clyde King 109-95, John McGraw 2,604-1,801, Mel Ott 464-530, Danny Ozark 24-32, Bill Rigney 406-430, Frank Robinson 264-277, Tom Sheehan 46-50, Heinie Smith 5-27, Bill Terry 823-661, Wes Westrum 118-129.

MINOR LEAGUES

Farm systems

International League

Mexican League

Pacific Coast League

Eastern League

Southern League

Texas League

California League

Carolina League

Florida State League

Midwest League

New York-Pennsylvania League

Northwest League

South Atlantic League

Appalachian League

Arizona League

Gulf Coast League

Pioneer League

Minor league index

FARM SYSTEMS

AMERICAN LEAGUE

ANAHEIM (6): AAA—Salt Lake. AA—Arkansas. A—Cedar Rapids, Rancho Cucamonga. Rookie—Mesa Angels, Provo.
BALTIMORE (6): AAA—Rochester. AA—Bowie. A—Delmarva, Frederick. Rookie—Bluefield, Gulf Coast Orioles.
BOSTON (6): AAA—Pawtucket. AA—Trenton. A—Augusta, Lowell, Sarasota. Rookie—Gulf Coast Red Sox.
CHICAGO (6): AAA—Charlotte. AA—Birmingham. A—Kannapolis, Winston-Salem. Rookie—Bristol, Tucson White Sox.
CLEVELAND (6): AAA—Buffalo. AA—Akron. A—Columbus (GA), Kinston, Mahoning Valley. Rookie—Burlington.
DETROIT (6): AAA—Toledo. AA—Erie. A—Lakeland, Oneonta, West Michigan. Rookie—Gulf Coast Tigers.
KANSAS CITY (6): AAA—Omaha. AA—Wichita. A—Burlington, Spokane, Wilmington. Rookie—Gulf Coast Royals.
MINNESOTA (6): AAA—Edmonton. AA—New Britain. A—Fort Myers, Quad City. Rookie—Elizabethton, Gulf Coast Twins.
NEW YORK (6): AAA—Columbus (OH). AA—Norwich. A—Greensboro, Staten Island, Tampa. Rookie—Gulf Coast Yankees.
OAKLAND (6): AAA—Sacramento. AA—Midland. A—Modesto, Vancouver, Visalia. Rookie—Scottsdale A's.
SEATTLE (6): AAA—Tacoma. AA—San Antonio. A—Everett, San Bernardino, Wisconsin. Rookie—Peoria Mariners.
TAMPA BAY (6): AAA—Durham. AA—Orlando. A—Bakersfield, Charleston (SC), Hudson Valley. Rookie—Princeton.
TEXAS (6): AAA—Oklahoma. AA—Tulsa. A—Charlotte, Savannah. Rookie—Gulf Coast Rangers, Pulaski.
TORONTO (6): AAA—Syracuse. AA—Tennessee. A—Auburn, Charleston (WV), Dunedin. Rookie—Medicine Hat.

NATIONAL LEAGUE

ARIZONA (6): AAA—Tucson. AA—El Paso. A—Lancaster, South Bend, Yakima. Rookie—Missoula.
ATLANTA (7): AAA—Richmond. AA—Greenville. A—Jamestown, Macon, Myrtle Beach. Rookie—Danville, Gulf Coast Braves.
CHICAGO (6): AAA—Iowa. AA—West Tenn. A—Boise, Daytona, Lansing. Rookie—Mesa Cubs.
CINCINNATI (6): AAA—Louisville. AA—Chattanooga. A—Dayton, Stockton. Rookie—Billings, Gulf Coast Reds.
COLORADO (6): AAA—Colorado Springs. AA—Carolina. A—Asheville, Salem, Tri-City. Rookie—Casper.
FLORIDA (6): AAA—Calgary. AA—Portland (ME). A—Brevard County, Kane County, Utica. Rookie—Gulf Coast Marlins.
HOUSTON (6): AAA—New Orleans. AA—Round Rock. A—Lexington, Michigan, Tri-City. Rookie—Martinsville.
LOS ANGELES (6): AAA—Las Vegas. AA—Jacksonville. A—Vero Beach, Wilmington. Rookie—Great Falls, Gulf Coast Dodgers.
MILWAUKEE (6): AAA—Indianapolis. AA—Huntsville. A—Beloit, High Desert. Rookie—Maryvale, Ogden.
MONTREAL (6): AAA—Ottawa. AA—Harrisburg. A—Clinton, Jupiter, Vermont. Rookie—Gulf Coast Expos.
NEW YORK (6): AAA—Norfolk. AA—Binghamton. A—Brooklyn, Capital City, St. Lucie. Rookie—Kingsport.
PHILADELPHIA (6): AAA—Scranton/Wilkes-Barre. AA—Reading. A—Batavia, Clearwater, Lakewood. Rookie—Gulf Coast Phillies.
PITTSBURGH (6): AAA—Nashville. AA—Altoona. A—Hickory, Lynchburg, Williamsport. Rookie—Gulf Coast Pirates.
ST. LOUIS (6): AAA—Memphis. AA—New Haven. A—New Jersey, Peoria (IL), Potomac. Rookie—Johnson City.
SAN DIEGO (6): AAA—Portland (OR). AA—Mobile. A—Eugene, Fort Wayne, Lake Elsinore. Rookie—Idaho Falls.
SAN FRANCISCO (6): AAA—Fresno. AA—Shreveport. A—Hagerstown, Salem-Keizer, San Jose. Rookie—Arizona Giants.

INTERNATIONAL LEAGUE

LEAGUE OFFICE

President
Randy Mobley

Address
55 S. High St., Suite 202
Dublin, OH 43017

Phone
614-791-9300

TEAMS

BUFFALO BISONS

General manager
Mike Buczkowski

Manager
Eric Wedge

Ballpark (capacity, surface)
Dunn Tire Park (21,050, grass)

Affiliation
Indians

Address
P.O. Box 450
Buffalo, NY 14205

Phone
716-846-2000

CHARLOTTE KNIGHTS

General manager
Tim Newman

Manager
Nick Leyva

Ballpark (capacity, surface)
Knights Stadium (10,005, grass)

Affiliation
White Sox

Address
2280 Deerfield Drive
Fort Mill, SC 29715

Phone
704-357-8071

COLUMBUS CLIPPERS

General manager
Ken Schnacke

Manager
Brian Butterfield

Ballpark (capacity, surface)
Cooper Stadium (15,000, grass)

Affiliation
Yankees

Address
1155 W. Mound St.
Columbus, OH 43223

Phone
614-462-5250

DURHAM BULLS

General manager
George Habel

Manager
Bill Evers

Ballpark (capacity, surface)
Durham Bulls Athletic Park
(10,000, grass)

Affiliation
Devil Rays

Address
P.O. Box 507
Durham, NC 27702

Phone
919-687-6500

INDIANAPOLIS INDIANS

General manager
Cal Burleson

Manager
Ed Romero

Ballpark (capacity, surface)
Victory Field (15,000, grass)

Affiliation
Brewers

Address
501 W. Maryland St.
Indianapolis, IN 46225

Phone
317-269-3542

LOUISVILLE RIVERBATS

President
Gary Ulmer

Manager
Dave Miley

Ballpark (capacity, surface)
Louisville Slugger Field (13,131, grass)

Affiliation
Reds

Address
401 E. Main Street
Louisville, KY 40202

Phone
502-212-2287

NORFOLK TIDES

General manager
Dave Rosenfield

Manager
Bobby Floyd

Ballpark (capacity, surface)
Harbor Park (12,059, grass)

Affiliation
Mets

Address
150 Park Ave.
Norfolk, VA 23510

Phone
757-622-2222

OTTAWA LYNX

General manager
Kyle Bostwick

Manager
Tim Leiper

Ballpark (capacity, surface)
JetForm Park (10,332, grass)

Affiliation
Expos

Address
300 Coventry Rd.
Ottawa, Ontario K1K 4P5

Phone
613-747-5969

PAWTUCKET RED SOX

President
Mike Tamburro

Manager
Buddy Bailey

Ballpark (capacity, surface)
McCoy Stadium (10,000, grass)

Affiliation
Red Sox

Address
P.O. Box 2365
Pawtucket, RI 02861

Phone
401-724-7303

RICHMOND BRAVES

General manager
Bruce Baldwin

Manager
Fredi Gonzalez

Ballpark (capacity, surface)
The Diamond (12,156, grass)

Affiliation
Braves

Address
P.O. Box 6667
Richmond, VA 23230

Phone
804-359-4444

ROCHESTER RED WINGS

General manager
Dan Mason

Manager
Andy Etchebarren

Ballpark (capacity, surface)
Frontier Field (22,844, grass)

Affiliation
Orioles

Address
1 Morrie Silver Way
Rochester, NY 14608

Phone
716-454-1001

SCRANTON/WILKES-BARRE RED BARONS

General manager
Rick Muntean

Manager
Marc Bombard

Ballpark (capacity, surface)
Lackawanna County Multi-Purpose
Stadium (10,982, artificial)

Affiliation
Phillies

Address
P.O. Box 3449
Scranton, PA 18505

Phone
570-969-2255

CLASS AAA *International League*

SYRACUSE SKY CHIEFS

General manager
John Simone
Manager
Omar Malave
Ballpark (capacity, surface)
P&C Stadium (11,100, artificial)
Affiliation
Blue Jays

Address
One Tex Simone
Syracuse, NY 13208
Phone
315-474-7833

TOLEDO MUD HENS

General manager
Joe Napoli
Manager
Bruce Fields

Ballpark (capacity, surface)
Fifth Third Field (10,000, grass)
Affiliation
Tigers
Address
2901 Key Street
Maumee, OH 43537
Phone
419-893-9483

2001 FINAL STANDINGS

NORTH DIVISION

Team	W	L	T	Pct.	GB
Buffalo (Indians)	91	51	0	.641	...
Scranton/Wilkes-Barre (Phillies)	78	65	0	.545	13.5
Syracuse (Blue Jays)	71	73	0	.493	21.0
Ottawa (Expos)	68	76	0	.472	24.0
Pawtucket (Red Sox)	60	82	0	.423	31.0
Rochester (Orioles)	60	84	0	.417	32.0

SOUTH DIVISION

Team	W	L	T	Pct.	GB
Norfolk (Mets)	85	57	0	.599	...
Durham (Devil Rays)	74	70	0	.514	12.0
Richmond (Braves)	68	76	0	.472	18.0
Charlotte (White Sox)	67	77	0	.465	19.0

WEST DIVISION

Team	W	L	T	Pct.	GB
Louisville (Reds)	84	60	0	.583	...
Columbus (Yankees)	67	76	0	.469	16.5
Indianapolis (Brewers)	66	78	0	.458	18.0
Toledo (Tigers)	65	79	0	.451	19.0

COMPOSITE

Team	Buf.	Nor.	Lou.	SWB.	Dur.	Syr.	Rich.	Ott.	Col.	Char.	Ind.	Tol.	Paw.	Roch.	W	L	T	Pct.	GB
Buffalo (Indians)	...	4	4	8	6	11	7	10	5	5	3	6	11	11	91	51	0	.641	...
Norfolk (Mets)	2	...	7	4	7	6	10	6	7	11	6	8	4	7	85	57	0	.599	6.0
Louisville (Reds)	4	5	...	4	6	4	7	3	11	9	10	11	6	4	84	60	0	.583	8.0
Scranton/Wilkes-Barre (Phillies)	8	4	4	...	2	9	4	10	3	3	5	5	10	11	78	65	0	.545	13.5
Durham (Devil Rays)	2	9	6	6	...	3	10	2	6	9	5	8	2	6	74	70	0	.514	18.0
Syracuse (Blue Jays)	5	2	4	7	5	...	4	13	4	4	3	2	10	8	71	73	0	.493	21.0
Richmond (Braves)	1	6	5	4	6	4	...	2	7	9	8	6	4	6	68	76	0	.472	24.0
Ottawa (Expos)	6	2	5	6	3	6	...	...	5	4	4	5	8	8	68	76	0	.472	24.0
Columbus (Yankees)	3	5	5	5	6	4	5	3	...	6	8	7	5	5	67	76	0	.469	24.5
Charlotte (White Sox)	3	5	3	5	7	4	7	4	6	...	7	6	4	6	67	77	0	.465	25.0
Indianapolis (Brewers)	5	6	6	3	7	5	4	4	8	5	...	9	1	3	66	78	0	.458	26.0
Toledo (Tigers)	2	4	5	3	4	6	6	3	9	6	7	...	6	4	65	79	0	.451	27.0
Pawtucket (Red Sox)	5	4	2	5	6	6	4	8	2	4	7	2	...	5	60	82	0	.423	31.0
Rochester (Orioles)	5	1	4	5	2	2	8	3	2	5	4	11	...		60	84	0	.417	32.0

Major league affiliations in parentheses.

PLAYOFFS: Scranton/Wilkes-Barre defeated Buffalo three games to two; Louisville defeated Norfolk three games to two. Note: Louisville was leading final series one game to none and was declared International League champion due to stoppage of play in professional baseball.

REGULAR-SEASON ATTENDANCE: Buffalo, 652,245; Charlotte, 370,406; Columbus, 503,824; Durham, 505,314; Indianapolis, 604,407; Louisville, 649,232; Norfolk, 498,950; Ottawa, 205,916; Pawtucket, 647,928; Richmond, 447,020; Rochester, 455,123; Scranton/Wilkes-Barre, 452,004; Syracuse, 423,405; Toledo, 300,079. Total—6,715,853. Playoffs (11 games)—44,260; Class AAA All-Star Game at Indianapolis, Ind.—15,868.

MANAGERS: Buffalo, Eric Wedge; Charlotte, Nick Leyva; Columbus, Trey Hillman; Durham, Bill Evers; Indianapolis, Wendell Kim; Louisville, Dave Miley; Norfolk, John Gibbons; Ottawa, Stan Hough; Pawtucket, Gary Jones; Richmond, Carlos Tosca; Rochester, Andy Etchebarren; Scranton/Wilkes-Barre, Marc Bombard (through May 5 and July 14 through end of season), Jerry Martin (May 6 through May 7; June 1 through June 6 and June 10 through July 13), Don Long (May 11 through May 31), Bill Dancy (May 8 through 10), Milt Thompson (June 7), Ruben Amaro (June 8) and Mick Billmeyer (June 9); Syracuse, Omar Malave; Toledo, Bruce Fields.

ALL-STAR TEAM: 1B—Calvin Pickering, Rochester; 2B—P.J. Forbes, Scranton/Wilkes-Barre; 3B—Kevin Orie, Scranton/Wilkes-Barre; SS—Cesar Izturis, Syracuse; OF—Eric Valent, Scranton/Wilkes-Barre; OF—Chris Wakeland, Toledo; OF—Karim Garcia, Buffalo; C—Toby Hall, Durham; DH—Izzy Alcantara, Pawtucket; Starting pitcher—Brandon Duckworth, Scranton/Wilkes-Barre; Relief pitcher—Matt DeWitt, Syracuse; Most Valuable Player—Toby Hall, Durham; Rookie of the Year—Brandon Duckworth, Scranton/Wilkes-Barre; Manager of the Year—Eric Wedge, Buffalo.

2001 BATTING
TEAM

Team	Avg.	G	TPA	AB	R	H	TB	2B	3B	HR	RBI	SH	SF	HP	BB	IBB	SO	SB	CS	GDP	LOB	ShO	Slg.	OBP
Louisville	.277	144	5563	4978	728	1380	2115	296	29	127	673	39	42	72	432	25	957	75	49	125	1013	5	.425	.341
Durham	.273	144	5406	4861	677	1329	2040	256	28	133	616	44	34	61	406	13	896	110	52	113	966	7	.420	.335
Toledo	.268	144	5571	4967	686	1332	2143	277	39	152	632	62	41	52	449	20	996	95	48	112	1019	4	.431	.333
Syracuse	.267	144	5507	4905	690	1311	2067	270	51	128	633	39	53	52	458	26	938	148	83	93	970	5	.421	.333
Richmond	.267	144	5321	4861	559	1296	1823	261	31	68	516	62	41	46	311	26	866	87	71	124	924	11	.375	.314
Indianapolis	.262	144	5571	4941	666	1294	1992	264	31	124	629	51	43	74	462	25	1065	72	39	107	1038	10	.403	.332
Norfolk	.261	144	5335	4727	602	1232	1825	244	20	103	562	60	51	58	439	30	913	110	48	109	1003	6	.386	.328
Buffalo	.259	142	5359	4730	697	1225	1970	238	30	149	650	50	47	61	471	27	979	92	47	105	951	3	.416	.331
Scran./W.-B.	.259	143	5575	4947	642	1281	1921	276	32	100	594	42	29	62	495	32	989	131	64	113	1064	13	.388	.331
Columbus	.258	143	5381	4775	663	1234	1987	239	35	148	607	27	41	60	478	20	982	101	64	114	979	7	.416	.331
Pawtucket	.257	142	5346	4814	612	1235	2015	237	15	171	578	35	22	63	412	10	1098	59	28	113	999	8	.419	.322

Team	Avg.	G	TPA	AB	R	H	TB	2B	3B	HR	RBI	SH	SF	HP	BB	IBB	SO	SB	CS	GDP	LOB	ShO	Slg.	OBP
Charlotte	.256	144	5402	4882	611	1251	2007	253	19	155	567	48	32	52	388	12	922	72	32	95	977	9	.411	.316
Rochester	.251	144	5434	4903	576	1230	1812	243	27	95	544	48	33	52	398	14	1018	139	50	109	962	12	.370	.312
Ottawa	.248	144	5520	4919	573	1222	1856	242	37	106	533	60	26	64	451	34	1081	171	64	87	1060	9	.377	.318

INDIVIDUAL

TOP QUALIFIERS FOR BATTING CHAMPIONSHIP

Minimum 389 plate appearances. *Lefthanded batter. †Switch-hitter.

Player, Team	Avg.	G	TPA	AB	R	H	TB	2B	3B	HR	RBI	SH	SF	HP	BB	IBB	SO	SB	CS	GDP	Slg.	OBP
Hall, Toby, Dur	.335	94	408	373	59	125	212	28	1	19	72	0	3	3	29	7	22	1	3	15	.568	.385
Rios, Brian, Tol.	.325	104	402	372	47	121	202	29	5	14	62	2	2	4	22	2	66	2	4	17	.543	.368
Forbes, P.J., S./W.B.	.305	133	576	514	79	157	205	29	2	5	61	9	2	3	48	0	72	5	0	9	.399	.367
Malloy, Marty, Lou.	.303	126	510	468	69	142	204	36	4	6	49	7	6	2	27	0	51	8	7	8	.436	.340
Smith, Bobby, Dur.	.301	107	454	396	67	119	214	25	2	22	70	0	5	8	45	1	91	10	2	7	.540	.379
Gonzalez, Raul, Lou.	.299	142	609	539	90	161	235	39	1	11	66	0	5	1	64	2	70	6	8	20	.436	.371
Alcantara, Israel, Paw.	.297	119	516	451	80	134	270	26	1	36	90	0	3	5	57	3	107	9	2	9	.599	.380
Bridges, Kary, Col.*	.297	109	454	408	59	121	155	17	1	5	39	5	4	1	36	1	29	5	8	11	.380	.352
Scutaro, Marcos, Ind.	.295	132	575	495	87	146	214	29	3	11	50	5	3	10	62	2	83	11	11	9	.432	.382
Carter, Mike, Rich.	.294	104	420	388	55	114	142	16	3	2	20	15	3	4	10	1	45	10	10	5	.366	.316
Orie, Kevin, S./W.B.	.293	134	598	509	77	149	226	34	2	13	45	0	2	9	77	5	63	11	6	8	.444	.394
Caruso, Mike, Dur.*	.292	110	427	387	62	113	141	10	9	0	35	9	2	7	22	0	22	11	9	4	.364	.340
Tarasco, Tony, Nor.*	.292	105	418	366	53	107	167	31	4	7	57	0	4	0	48	8	43	14	8	5	.456	.371
Swann, Pedro, Rich.*	.291	139	559	488	68	142	209	33	5	8	72	1	10	8	52	3	95	12	6	14	.428	.362
Rodriguez, Liu, Char.†	.291	118	502	444	53	129	154	25	0	0	37	11	3	3	41	0	60	7	4	8	.347	.352

DEPARTMENTAL LEADERS: G—V. Gonzalez, 142; AB—Wakeland, 547; R—V. Gonzalez, 90; H—V. Gonzalez, 161; TB—Alcantara, 270; 2B—V. Gonzalez, 39; 3B—H. Mateo, 12; HR—Alcantara, 36; RBI—Pickering, 99; SH—J. Garcia, Allensworth, 21 each; SF—Swann, 10; HP—N. Johnson, 14; BB—N. Johnson, 81; IBB—Dave Hollins, Tarasco, 21 each; SO—Pickering, 151; SB—H. Mateo, 47; CS—R. Taylor, 15; GIDP—Veras, 24; Slg.—Alcantara, .599; OBP—N. Johnson, .407.

ALL PLAYERS

*Lefthanded batter. †Switch-hitter.

Player, Team	Avg.	G	TPA	AB	R	H	TB	2B	3B	HR	RBI	SH	SF	HP	BB	IBB	SO	SB	CS	GDP	Slg.	OBP
Abbott, Kurt, Rich.	.214	4	16	14	0	3	4	1	0	0	0	0	0	2	0	0	7	1	0	1	.206	.313
Abernathy, Brent, Dur.	.302	61	275	252	45	76	108	20	0	4	23	3	2	2	16	0	23	11	4	3	.429	.346
Agbayani, Benny, Nor.	.313	4	17	16	3	5	9	1	0	1	3	0	0	1	0	0	1	0	0	1	.563	.353
Airoso, Kurt, Tol	.200	10	34	30	2	6	13	0	2	1	1	0	0	0	4	0	7	0	1	1	.433	.294
Alcantara, Israel, Paw.	.297	119	516	451	80	134	270	26	1	36	90	0	3	5	57	3	107	9	2	9	.599	.380
Alfonzo, Edgardo, Nor.	.000	2	8	8	0	0	0	0	0	0	0	0	0	0	0	0	0	0	0	1	.000	.000
Allen, Dusty, Tol.	.218	29	108	87	18	19	32	1	0	4	11	0	2	0	19	1	31	0	0	0	.368	.352
Allensworth, Jermaine, Tol.	.272	133	566	485	57	132	198	22	7	10	52	21	3	8	49	3	74	13	9	4	.408	.347
Almonte, Erick, Col.	.287	97	400	345	55	99	160	19	3	12	55	7	2	2	44	1	90	4	5	7	.464	.369
Almonte, Wady, Roch.	.215	87	338	316	25	68	93	8	4	3	31	0	2	4	16	1	54	7	3	16	.294	.260
Anderson, Bryan, Lou.	.333	6	22	21	3	7	7	0	0	0	1	0	0	0	1	0	6	1	0	0	.333	.364
Andreopoulos, Alex, Buf.*	.216	37	118	102	14	22	36	5	0	3	9	2	0	1	13	0	16	1	0	3	.353	.310
Andrews, Clayton, Lou.	.000	8	7	5	1	0	0	0	0	0	0	2	0	0	0	0	2	0	0	0	.000	.000
Ashby, Chris, Char.	.228	62	215	197	21	45	61	8	1	2	12	2	0	0	16	0	39	2	2	8	.310	.286
Atchley, Justin, Lou.*	.000	16	2	2	0	0	0	0	0	0	0	0	0	0	0	0	2	0	0	0	.000	.000
Baez, Kevin, Nor.	.219	100	363	311	35	68	96	16	0	4	28	9	4	6	33	1	62	0	3	1	.309	.302
Baines, Harold, Char.*	.000	2	8	8	0	0	0	0	0	0	0	0	0	0	0	0	1	0	0	0	.000	.000
Balfe, Ryan, Syr.†	.253	51	210	190	22	48	75	10	1	5	24	0	1	1	18	2	55	1	2	3	.395	.319
Bard, Josh, Buf.†	.000	1	4	4	0	0	0	0	0	0	0	0	0	0	0	0	1	0	0	0	.000	.000
Barker, Kevin, Ind.*	.189	51	182	159	12	30	47	5	0	4	20	1	1	1	20	3	40	1	0	3	.296	.282
Barry, Jeff, Char.†	.122	13	49	41	6	5	6	1	0	0	2	0	2	1	5	0	7	0	1	0	.146	.224
Bates, Fletcher, S./W.D.†	.000	3	5	5	0	0	0	0	0	0	0	0	0	0	0	0	1	0	0	0	.000	.000
Battle, Howard, Rich.	.275	131	524	491	53	135	186	21	0	10	76	1	6	1	25	4	77	2	5	9	.379	.308
Beasley, Ray, Rich.	.000	65	7	6	0	0	0	0	0	0	0	0	0	0	1	0	3	0	0	0	.000	.143
Beattie, Andy, Lou.†	.222	7	9	9	0	2	2	0	0	0	0	0	0	0	0	0	5	0	0	0	.222	.222
Becker, Rich, Tol.*	.244	67	284	234	37	57	86	8	3	5	17	0	0	2	48	3	63	7	3	1	.368	.377
Bell, Rob, Lou.	.333	5	8	6	2	2	3	1	0	0	1	2	0	0	0	0	3	0	0	0	.500	.333
Bellinger, Clay, Col.	.214	26	104	98	13	21	34	10	0	1	9	0	0	1	5	1	22	3	0	0	.347	.260
Beltran, Rigo, S./W.B.*	.188	40	19	16	1	3	3	0	0	0	1	1	0	0	2	0	3	0	0	0	.188	.278
Bennett, Gary, Nor.	.299	20	73	67	7	20	31	5	0	2	14	0	1	1	4	1	12	0	0	1	.463	.342
Bennett, Ryan, Nor.	.143	12	26	21	2	3	3	0	0	0	1	0	0	0	4	0	7	0	0	1	.143	.280
Bergeron, Pete, Ott.*	.238	52	230	206	20	49	60	7	3	0	8	2	1	1	20	0	42	15	7	1	.291	.307
Berroa, Geronimo, Ott.	.286	16	66	56	8	16	25	3	0	2	2	0	0	1	9	2	8	0	0	3	.446	.394
Bierek, Kurt, Col.	.272	105	435	394	64	107	184	27	1	16	53	0	3	6	32	1	76	2	2	7	.467	.326
Bigbie, Larry, Roch.*	.310	10	45	42	5	13	20	4	0	1	2	0	0	0	3	0	8	1	1	0	.476	.356
Blank, Matt, Ott.*	.000	14	12	10	1	0	0	0	0	0	0	0	0	0	0	0	0	0	0	0	.000	.000
Boone, Aaron, Lou.	.250	1	4	4	0	1	1	0	0	0	1	0	0	0	0	0	1	0	0	0	.250	.250
Borders, Pat, Dur.	.236	87	332	313	26	74	97	15	1	2	28	1	0	2	16	0	61	3	2	14	.310	.278
Boyd, Jason, S./W.B.	.000	52	2	2	0	0	0	0	0	0	0	0	0	0	0	0	0	0	0	0	.000	.000
Bradley, Milton, Ott.-Buf.†.	.264	65	300	250	39	66	101	10	2	7	28	5	1	4	42	5	61	23	3	5	.404	.373
Bragg, Darren, Nor.-Col.*	.305	85	351	298	52	91	143	15	2	11	28	0	3	0	50	4	73	8	4	5	.480	.410
Bravo, Danny, Char.†	.190	39	135	126	11	24	35	2	0	3	13	2	0	0	7	0	16	1	1	4	.278	.233
Brazoban, Yhency, Col.	.200	1	5	5	2	1	2	1	0	0	2	0	0	0	0	0	0	0	0	0	.400	.400
Bridges, Donnie, Ott.	.500	13	9	8	1	4	5	1	0	0	2	1	0	0	0	0	2	0	0	0	.625	.500
Bridges, Kary, Col.*	.297	109	454	408	59	121	155	17	1	5	39	5	4	1	36	1	29	5	8	11	.380	.352
Brinkley, Darryl, Roch.	.306	9	39	36	4	11	20	3	0	2	7	0	2	1	0	0	5	1	0	0	.556	.308
Brittan, Corey, Nor.	.000	58	1	1	0	0	0	0	0	0	0	0	0	0	0	0	1	0	0	0	.000	.000
Brock, Chris, S./W.B.	.125	13	9	8	0	1	2	1	0	0	2	1	0	0	0	0	2	0	0	0	.250	.125
Brown, Brant, Ind.*	.201	50	172	154	20	31	56	8	1	5	21	0	0	3	12	1	47	1	2	1	.364	.272

Player, Team	Avg.	G	TPA	AB	R	H	TB	2B	3B	HR	RBI	SH	SF	HP	BB	IBB	SO	SB	CS	GDP	Slg.	OBP
Brown, Kevin, Ind.	.231	82	317	290	19	67	112	16	1	9	34	4	1	4	18	0	110	0	1	8	.386	.284
Bruce, Mo, Ott.	.133	6	17	15	1	2	2	0	0	0	0	0	0	0	2	0	7	0	0	0	.133	.235
Brunette, Justin, Nor.*	.000	24	1	1	0	0	0	0	0	0	0	0	0	0	0	0	0	0	0	0	.000	.000
Budzinski, Mark, Buf.*	.256	122	486	438	69	112	152	26	4	2	39	9	4	7	28	2	125	13	4	4	.347	.308
Buford, Damon, Roch.-Lou. ..	.286	52	241	203	34	58	96	15	1	7	26	0	3	3	32	0	43	3	2	4	.473	.386
Burkhart, Morgan, Paw.†	.269	120	490	412	64	111	207	19	1	25	62	0	2	8	68	4	113	1	0	4	.502	.382
Bush, Homer, Syr.	.250	9	38	32	11	8	10	2	0	0	3	0	1	2	3	0	6	0	0	1	.313	.342
Byrd, Paul, S./W.B.	.000	5	5	4	0	0	0	0	0	0	0	0	0	0	1	0	2	0	0	0	.000	.200
Calloway, Ron, Ott.*	.264	61	265	239	27	63	105	12	0	10	35	2	2	6	16	2	64	11	1	6	.439	.323
Cancel, Rob, Ind.	.215	51	186	172	16	37	45	5	0	1	18	1	3	1	9	2	38	0	0	5	.262	.254
Cardona, Javier, Tol.	.235	26	106	98	7	23	28	2	0	1	10	0	0	0	8	1	18	1	0	1	.286	.292
Carpenter, Bubba, Nor.*	.244	28	99	82	12	20	28	3	1	1	13	0	2	2	13	1	19	2	3	3	.341	.354
Carr, Dustin, Dur.	.242	73	264	227	25	55	75	6	1	4	26	6	1	5	25	0	47	5	2	5	.330	.329
Carroll, Jamey, Ott.	.240	83	290	267	26	64	76	8	2	0	16	2	1	2	18	1	41	5	5	8	.285	.292
Carter, Mike, Rich.	.294	104	420	388	55	114	142	16	3	2	20	15	3	4	10	1	45	10	10	5	.366	.316
Carter, Shannon, Syr.*	.111	4	11	9	1	1	2	1	0	0	1	0	0	1	1	0	2	0	0	0	.222	.273
Caruso, Mike, Dur.*	.292	110	427	387	62	113	141	10	9	0	35	9	2	7	22	0	22	11	9	4	.364	.340
Casimiro, Carlos, Roch.	.235	48	176	166	21	39	62	9	1	4	14	1	0	2	7	0	41	5	1	4	.373	.274
Castro, Ramon, Rich.	.222	36	146	135	14	30	45	8	2	1	15	3	0	1	7	0	30	1	2	5	.333	.266
Cedeno, Blas, S./W.B.	.500	35	4	4	3	2	5	0	0	1	3	0	0	0	0	0	2	0	0	0	1.250	.500
Cerda, Jaime, Nor.*	.500	3	2	2	0	1	1	0	0	0	0	0	0	0	0	0	0	0	0	0	.500	.500
Cerros, Juan, Nor.	.333	38	3	3	2	1	1	0	0	0	0	0	0	0	0	0	0	0	0	0	.333	.333
Cesar, Dionys, Ind.†	.310	35	145	129	12	40	56	11	1	1	17	1	2	3	10	1	23	1	0	3	.434	.368
Chamblee, Jim, Paw.	.241	103	421	378	40	91	143	22	0	10	32	5	1	6	31	4	104	8	5	4	.378	.308
Chantres, Carlos, Ind.	.200	29	23	20	2	4	5	1	0	0	3	2	1	0	0	0	7	0	0	0	.250	.190
Charles, Frank, Roch.	.242	68	260	240	15	58	73	12	0	1	24	2	4	3	11	0	56	1	1	6	.304	.279
Chen, Bruce, S./W.B.†	.000	3	3	3	0	0	0	0	0	0	0	0	0	0	0	0	1	0	1	0	.000	.000
Chevalier, Virgil, Paw.	.259	7	27	27	2	7	9	2	0	0	4	0	0	0	0	0	3	0	0	1	.333	.259
Christensen, McKay, Char.* ...	.275	69	312	273	53	75	123	15	6	7	25	4	3	2	30	0	52	17	3	3	.451	.347
Clark, Brady, Lou.*	.263	49	192	167	24	44	57	5	1	2	18	0	1	6	18	1	17	6	2	5	.341	.354
Clemente, Edgard, Paw.	.247	86	335	300	32	74	124	14	0	12	35	2	3	5	25	0	84	2	0	8	.413	.312
Coffie, Ivanon, Roch.*	.267	56	224	206	33	55	91	10	1	8	35	0	2	1	15	1	47	3	0	4	.442	.317
Coggin, Dave, S./W.B.	.000	15	11	7	0	0	0	0	0	0	0	3	0	0	1	0	6	0	0	0	.000	.125
Coleman, Michael, Col.	.238	29	116	101	16	24	45	3	3	4	17	0	0	2	13	0	35	3	3	4	.446	.336
Collier, Lou, Ind.	.288	86	349	312	48	90	153	17	2	14	36	3	3	7	24	1	64	9	3	6	.490	.350
Conti, Jason, Dur.*	.306	38	168	157	24	48	75	12	0	5	18	1	0	1	9	1	31	3	1	0	.478	.347
Coolbaugh, Mike, Ind.	.268	94	401	347	49	93	153	24	3	10	50	6	4	5	39	1	92	3	2	10	.441	.347
Coppinger, Rocky, Ind.	.600	15	12	10	1	6	6	0	0	0	2	2	0	0	0	0	2	0	0	0	.600	.600
Coquillette, Trace, Buf.-Tol. ...	.205	83	306	263	40	54	100	11	4	9	32	2	3	6	32	1	67	1	2	3	.380	.303
Coste, Chris, Buf.	.288	75	295	271	31	78	119	16	2	7	50	1	4	4	15	1	50	0	1	11	.439	.330
Cotton, John, Ott.*	.280	24	100	93	11	26	51	8	1	5	15	0	0	1	6	2	25	2	1	1	.548	.330
Crede, Joe, Char.	.276	124	521	463	67	128	215	34	1	17	65	1	3	7	46	3	88	2	1	5	.464	.349
Cromer, D.T., Lou.*	.285	62	261	242	35	69	118	12	2	11	49	0	2	2	15	3	48	4	2	7	.488	.330
Cubillan, Darwin, Ott.	.000	17	1	0	0	0	0	0	0	0	0	1	0	0	0	0	0	0	0	0	.000	.000
Cumberland, Chris, Rich.	.000	13	2	1	0	0	0	0	0	0	0	0	0	0	1	0	1	0	0	0	.000	.000
Cunnane, Will, Ind.	.000	7	2	2	0	0	0	0	0	0	0	0	0	0	0	0	0	0	0	0	.000	.000
Curry, Mike, Nor.*	.121	12	44	33	3	4	7	0	0	1	1	1	0	0	10	0	17	2	1	0	.212	.326
Dalesandro, Mark, Char.	.260	75	277	262	16	68	98	18	0	4	23	3	3	3	6	0	24	0	1	6	.374	.281
Darnell, Paul, Lou.	.000	21	1	1	0	0	0	0	0	0	0	0	0	0	1	0	1	0	0	0	.000	.000
Daubach, Brian, Paw.*	.250	1	4	4	0	1	1	0	0	0	0	0	0	0	0	0	2	0	0	0	.250	.250
Davis, Lance, Lou.	.200	13	5	5	1	1	1	0	0	0	0	0	0	0	0	0	1	0	0	0	.200	.200
Davis, Tommy, Lou.	.270	112	431	396	48	107	154	25	2	6	47	0	5	3	27	3	97	1	1	14	.389	.318
De La Rosa, Tomas, Ott.	.238	121	478	420	56	100	145	24	0	7	30	9	4	5	40	4	63	12	9	13	.345	.309
De Leon, Jorge, Paw.	.167	9	34	30	3	5	7	2	0	0	3	0	1	0	3	0	8	0	0	0	.233	.235
Dellaero, Jason, Char.†	.178	115	404	377	32	67	110	10	0	11	28	8	0	2	17	0	113	4	4	4	.292	.217
DeRosa, Mark, Rich.	.296	49	209	186	31	55	79	18	0	2	17	1	4	1	17	0	22	7	3	6	.425	.351
Diaz, Juan, Paw.	.269	74	303	279	45	75	154	17	1	20	51	0	1	6	17	2	85	0	0	10	.552	.323
Dina, Allen, Nor.	.000	7	14	12	0	0	0	0	0	0	2	0	2	0	0	0	2	0	0	0	.000	.000
Dominique, Andy, S./W.B.	.170	40	149	135	16	23	38	6	0	3	18	1	0	1	12	0	34	0	0	4	.281	.243
Ducey, Rob, S./W.B.*	.300	4	22	20	3	6	10	1	0	1	5	0	0	0	2	1	6	0	0	0	.500	.364
Duckworth, Brandon, S./W.B.†	.214	22	21	14	2	3	3	0	0	0	0	6	0	0	1	0	5	0	0	2	.214	.267
Dunn, Adam, Lou.*	.329	55	254	210	44	69	142	13	0	20	53	0	1	5	38	3	51	5	1	1	.676	.441
Edwards, Mike, Buf.	.222	3	10	9	1	2	2	0	0	0	1	0	0	0	1	0	3	0	0	1	.222	.300
Eischen, Joey, Ott.*	.000	34	5	4	1	0	0	0	0	0	0	0	0	0	1	0	0	0	0	0	.000	.200
Encarnacion, Angelo, Paw. ...	.265	47	166	155	16	41	51	5	1	1	11	2	0	1	8	0	17	1	0	6	.329	.305
Erickson, Corey, Buf.	.000	3	6	6	1	0	0	0	0	0	0	0	0	0	0	0	3	0	0	0	.000	.000
Escobar, Alex, Nor.	.267	111	441	397	55	106	171	21	4	12	52	1	5	3	35	2	146	18	3	10	.431	.327
Estalella, Bobby, Col.	.257	48	197	171	26	44	86	10	1	10	38	0	3	2	21	1	45	0	2	7	.503	.340
Estrada, Johnny, S./W.B.†	.290	32	138	131	13	38	51	13	0	0	16	0	1	1	5	0	6	0	0	5	.389	.319
Estrella, Leo, Nor.-Lou.	.250	43	6	4	1	1	1	0	0	0	0	2	0	0	0	0	2	0	0	0	.250	.250
Evans, Keith, Ott.	.000	45	7	6	0	0	0	0	0	0	0	1	0	0	0	0	2	0	0	0	.000	.000
Evans, Tom, Tol.	.266	50	199	169	26	45	76	12	2	5	19	0	0	4	26	0	33	1	3	4	.450	.377
Fernandez, Jared, Lou.*	.150	33	23	20	0	3	4	1	0	0	2	1	0	0	2	0	9	0	0	0	.200	.227
Fernandez, Ozzie, Lou.	.200	9	5	5	0	1	1	0	0	0	0	4	0	0	0	0	1	0	0	0	.200	.200
Figga, Mike, Col.-Nor.	.183	37	122	115	13	21	40	4	0	5	16	1	1	1	4	1	28	0	1	2	.348	.215
Figueroa, Luis, Nor.†	.259	17	64	58	7	15	23	3	1	1	5	1	0	0	5	0	6	0	0	1	.397	.317
Figueroa, Nelson, S./W.B.†	.000	13	10	7	0	0	0	0	0	0	0	3	0	0	0	0	2	0	0	0	.000	.000
Flanagan, Kevin, Col.	.000	3	7	5	1	0	0	0	0	0	0	0	0	0	2	0	0	0	0	0	.000	.286
Fonville, Chad, Col.†	.224	16	63	58	9	13	18	3	1	0	7	0	0	1	4	1	13	1	1	2	.310	.286
Forbes, P.J., S./W.B.	.305	133	576	514	79	157	205	29	2	5	61	9	2	3	48	0	72	5	0	9	.399	.367
Fordham, Tom, Ind.*	.000	18	2	1	0	0	0	0	0	0	0	0	0	0	1	0	0	0	0	0	.000	.000
Forster, Scott, Lou.	.000	9	1	1	0	0	0	0	0	0	0	0	0	0	0	0	1	0	0	0	.000	.000
Francia, Dave, S./W.B.*	.228	110	385	347	34	79	105	13	2	3	37	2	4	7	25	3	58	19	7	2	.303	.290

Player, Team	Avg.	G	TPA	AB	R	H	TB	2B	3B	HR	RBI	SH	SF	HP	BB	IBB	SO	SB	CS	GDP	Slg.	OBP
Franco, Matt, Nor.*	.245	124	492	433	49	106	157	25	1	8	47	0	5	2	52	7	72	5	2	16	.363	.325
Frank, Mike, Col.*	.253	106	413	356	45	90	144	20	2	10	53	4	7	5	41	3	52	11	3	10	.404	.333
Franklin, Micah, Ind †	.230	110	392	331	54	76	165	12	4	23	63	0	2	12	47	3	73	1	3	7	.498	.344
Freel, Ryan, Syr.	.260	85	376	319	60	83	125	21	3	5	33	6	2	7	42	0	42	22	9	8	.392	.357
Fryman, Travis, Buf.	.481	8	33	27	9	13	20	1	0	2	8	0	1	0	5	0	6	1	0	0	.741	.545
Gandarillas, Gus, Ind.	.000	28	3	3	0	0	0	0	0	0	0	0	0	0	0	0	0	0	0	0	.000	.000
Garabito, Eddy, Roch.†	.267	127	570	517	65	138	188	29	6	3	34	17	2	3	31	2	76	24	11	7	.364	.311
Garcia, Amaury, Char.	.237	34	130	118	9	28	34	4	1	0	7	4	0	1	7	0	26	4	0	2	.288	.286
Garcia, Carlos, Col.	.251	61	232	215	22	54	75	12	0	3	19	1	0	2	14	0	39	8	1	4	.349	.303
Garcia, Guillermo, Roch.	.053	5	21	19	1	1	1	0	0	0	0	0	0	0	2	0	5	0	0	1	.053	.143
Garcia, Jesse, Rich.	.267	105	423	375	50	100	134	22	3	2	22	21	1	4	22	1	54	18	6	9	.357	.313
Garcia, Karim, Buf.*	.264	125	514	462	73	122	239	16	4	31	85	1	6	1	44	6	106	4	4	9	.517	.326
Garciaparra, Nomar, Paw.	.438	4	18	16	3	7	12	2	0	1	4	0	1	0	1	0	2	0	0	0	.750	.500
Gazarek, Marty, Tol.	.214	17	61	56	10	12	19	4	0	1	3	0	0	0	5	0	5	2	0	1	.339	.279
Geary, Geoff, S./W.B.	.000	7	1	1	0	0	0	0	0	0	0	0	0	0	0	0	1	0	0	0	.000	.000
Gibralter, Dave, Ind.	.327	27	109	98	10	32	50	9	0	3	17	1	3	1	6	0	10	0	1	2	.510	.361
Gil, Geronimo, Roch.	.268	23	85	82	7	22	36	6	1	2	14	0	2	1	0	0	23	0	0	1	.439	.271
Giles, Marcus, Rich.	.333	67	279	252	48	84	123	19	1	6	44	0	3	2	22	1	48	13	5	4	.488	.387
Gilkey, Bernard, Rich.	.271	13	54	48	5	13	16	3	0	0	2	0	2	0	4	0	8	0	1	3	.333	.315
Glauber, Keith, Lou.	.000	23	2	2	0	0	0	0	0	0	0	0	0	0	0	0	1	0	0	0	.000	.000
Glavine, Mike, Rich.*	.136	23	51	44	1	6	8	2	0	0	4	0	1	0	6	2	11	0	0	1	.182	.235
Goelz, Jim, Buf.	.250	4	4	4	0	1	1	0	0	0	0	0	0	0	0	0	2	0	0	0	.250	.250
Gomez, Chris, Dur.	.301	23	104	93	16	28	47	5	1	4	17	0	0	0	11	0	5	1	1	5	.505	.375
Gonzalez, Dicky, Nor.	.300	17	13	10	1	3	3	0	0	0	1	1	0	0	2	0	2	0	0	0	.300	.417
Gonzalez, Jimmy, Ott.	.177	58	226	215	18	38	66	8	1	6	19	0	1	2	8	0	49	0	0	4	.307	.212
Gonzalez, Raul, Lou.	.299	142	609	539	90	161	235	39	1	11	66	0	5	1	64	2	70	6	8	20	.436	.371
Gooch, Arnie, Lou.	.143	28	19	14	2	2	2	0	0	0	1	0	0	1	0	0	4	0	0	1	.143	.333
Green, Nick, Rich.	.200	2	5	5	0	1	1	0	0	0	1	0	0	0	0	0	3	0	0	0	.200	.200
Greene, Charlie, Rich.	.167	23	70	66	4	11	12	1	0	0	4	1	0	0	3	1	17	0	0	4	.182	.203
Greene, Todd, Col.	.252	34	136	131	16	33	59	6	0	6	17	0	0	1	4	0	19	3	2	3	.450	.279
Gubanich, Creighton, Ind.-Char.	.218	62	217	197	25	43	78	8	0	9	23	0	2	1	17	2	51	0	0	4	.396	.281
Guerrero, Wilton, Lou.†	.304	54	243	227	23	69	87	14	2	0	28	3	0	1	12	0	30	12	5	4	.383	.342
Guevara, Giomar, Tol	.235	109	452	400	50	94	133	15	3	6	36	13	4	2	33	1	97	8	2	7	.333	.294
Guillen, Jose, Dur.	.294	33	124	119	18	35	65	9	0	7	29	0	2	0	3	0	28	0	0	3	.546	.306
Gunderson, Eric, Col.	.000	56	1	0	0	0	0	0	0	0	0	1	0	0	0	0	0	0	0	0	.000	.000
Hall, Noah, Lou.	.000	1	2	2	0	0	0	0	0	0	0	0	0	0	0	0	0	0	0	1	.000	.000
Hall, Toby, Dur.	.335	94	408	373	59	125	212	28	1	19	72	0	3	3	29	7	22	1	3	15	.568	.385
Haltiwanger, Garrick, Syr.	.233	23	87	73	8	17	26	1	1	2	12	0	1	2	11	0	21	2	2	0	.356	.345
Hamilton, Joey, Lou.	.500	1	2	2	1	1	1	0	0	0	0	0	0	0	0	0	0	0	0	0	.500	.500
Hamilton, Jon, Buf.*	.000	2	5	4	0	0	0	0	0	0	0	0	0	0	1	0	1	0	0	0	.000	.200
Hammond, Chris, Rich.*	.000	21	4	4	0	0	0	0	0	0	0	0	0	0	0	0	2	0	0	0	.000	.000
Hardtke, Jason, Buf.-Char.†	.259	96	379	336	52	87	144	21	3	10	39	4	0	5	34	1	43	2	2	2	.429	.336
Harikkala, Tim, Ind.	.050	31	22	20	0	1	1	0	0	0	0	1	0	0	1	0	7	0	0	1	.050	.095
Hatcher, Chris, Dur.	.267	69	277	251	31	67	112	12	0	11	30	0	4	3	19	0	63	4	2	3	.446	.321
Heintz, Chris, Char.	.100	5	11	10	1	1	2	1	0	0	1	0	1	0	0	0	3	0	0	0	.200	.091
Henriquez, Oscar, Nor.	1.000	39	1	1	0	1	1	0	0	0	1	0	0	0	0	0	0	0	0	0	1.000	1.000
Henry, Butch, Ind.*	.500	5	2	2	0	1	1	0	0	0	0	0	0	0	0	0	0	0	0	0	.500	.500
Henson, Drew, Col.	.222	71	281	270	29	60	99	6	0	11	38	0	1	0	10	1	85	2	1	8	.367	.249
Hernandez, Carlos, Nor.	.227	56	224	194	22	44	49	5	0	0	10	5	2	7	15	0	31	4	1	6	.253	.303
Hill, Ken, Lou.	.000	6	4	3	0	0	0	0	0	0	0	1	0	0	0	0	1	0	0	0	.000	.000
Hinchliffe, Brett, Nor.	.222	11	10	9	0	2	3	1	0	0	3	1	0	0	0	0	4	0	0	0	.333	.222
Holbert, Aaron, Syr.	.245	55	230	212	25	52	72	10	2	2	19	5	3	2	8	1	33	9	0	4	.340	.276
Hollins, Damon, Rich.	.263	43	176	160	27	42	71	10	2	5	24	0	2	0	14	2	34	2	2	7	.444	.318
Hollins, Dave, Buf.†	.272	89	370	316	50	86	163	25	2	16	67	0	2	7	45	8	79	0	0	7	.516	.373
Hoover, Paul, Dur.	.215	89	320	293	37	63	98	18	4	3	21	8	1	7	11	0	66	5	3	7	.334	.260
Howard, Dave, Nor.†	.125	4	8	8	0	1	2	1	0	0	0	0	0	0	0	0	4	0	0	0	.250	.125
Hudson, Orlando, Syr.†	.304	55	224	194	31	59	91	14	3	4	27	2	3	2	23	1	34	11	3	1	.469	.378
Huff, Aubrey, Dur.*	.288	17	71	66	14	19	34	6	0	3	10	0	0	0	5	0	7	0	0	3	.515	.338
Hughes, Bobby, Roch.	.000	1	3	3	0	0	0	0	0	0	0	0	0	0	0	0	0	0	0	0	.000	.000
Hunter, Brian, Syr.	.238	30	124	105	21	25	39	5	0	3	16	1	0	3	15	0	21	1	0	2	.371	.350
Hunter, Brian L., S./W.B.	.111	2	10	9	1	1	1	0	0	0	0	0	0	1	0	0	3	0	0	0	.111	.200
Hunter, Scott, Nor.	.280	65	262	239	23	67	93	12	4	2	31	10	3	2	8	1	40	6	3	6	.389	.306
Hutchins, Norm, Dur.†	.230	78	280	261	32	60	93	10	1	7	28	2	2	5	9	0	64	15	2	4	.356	.267
Inge, Brandon, Tol.	.289	27	102	90	11	26	45	11	1	2	15	1	3	1	7	0	24	1	0	2	.500	.337
Inglin, Jeff, Char.	.272	128	533	481	66	131	240	25	6	24	75	0	3	6	43	0	103	3	4	13	.499	.338
Izturis, Cesar, Syr.†	.292	87	362	342	32	100	128	16	3	2	35	4	5	1	10	0	22	24	9	4	.374	.310
Jackson, Ryan, Tol.*	.286	9	40	35	2	10	14	1	0	1	9	0	0	0	5	0	6	0	0	0	.400	.375
Jacobsen, Bucky, Ind.	.247	86	334	300	42	74	130	18	1	12	53	1	3	4	26	1	78	0	0	13	.433	.312
Jacquez, Tom, S./W.B.*	.000	33	7	6	0	0	0	0	0	0	0	0	0	0	1	0	4	0	0	1	.000	.143
Jennings, Robin, Lou.*	.301	28	123	113	18	34	64	6	0	8	15	1	0	0	9	5	22	2	2	1	.566	.352
Jensen, Marcus, Paw.†	.235	27	108	102	11	24	47	7	2	4	12	0	0	0	6	0	27	0	0	4	.461	.278
Jimenez, D'Angelo, Col.†	.262	56	245	214	33	56	84	11	1	5	19	2	4	1	24	0	31	5	6	2	.393	.333
Johannes, Todd, Ott.	.000	4	10	10	0	0	0	0	0	0	0	0	0	0	0	0	5	0	0	0	.000	.000
Johnson, Adam, Char.*	.444	7	20	18	1	8	10	2	0	0	4	1	0	1	0	0	2	0	0	0	.556	.474
Johnson, Mark, Char.*	.270	55	228	196	24	53	74	5	2	4	24	2	1	0	29	1	34	2	1	4	.378	.363
Johnson, Mark, Nor.*	.316	42	177	152	27	48	87	15	0	8	25	0	1	2	22	0	20	2	1	5	.572	.407
Johnson, Nick, Col.*	.256	110	459	359	68	92	166	20	0	18	49	0	5	14	81	3	105	9	2	6	.462	.407
Johnson, Rontrez, Paw.	.299	44	205	187	32	56	90	16	3	4	22	1	0	7	10	0	35	8	4	7	.481	.358
Jones, Chris, Syr-Rich.-Ind.	.248	100	359	315	44	78	122	8	3	10	40	3	5	3	32	3	86	7	5	4	.387	.318
Jones, Terry, Ott.†	.294	53	73	68	6	20	22	2	0	0	5	1	1	0	3	0	13	2	3	4	.324	.319
Keller, Kris, Tol.	.000	52	1	1	0	0	0	0	0	0	0	0	0	0	0	0	0	0	0	0	.000	.000
Kershner, Jason, S./W.B.*	.500	6	3	2	0	1	1	0	0	0	0	0	0	0	0	0	0	0	0	0	.500	.500
Kingsale, Eugene, Roch.†	.201	64	275	244	31	49	65	12	2	0	15	3	0	2	26	0	44	16	2	6	.266	.283

Player, Team	Avg.	G	TPA	AB	R	H	TB	2B	3B	HR	RBI	SH	SF	HP	BB	IBB	SO	SB	CS	GDP	Slg.	OBP
Klimek, Josh, Ind.*	.260	30	117	104	13	27	36	6	0	1	4	2	0	1	10	0	26	0	0	0	.346	.330
Knupfer, Jason, S./W.B.	.239	90	316	276	41	66	85	12	2	1	25	3	1	6	30	1	59	10	5	6	.308	.326
Kremblas, Mike, Syr.	.222	4	11	9	3	2	2	0	0	0	0	0	0	1	1	0	4	0	0	0	.222	.364
Laker, Tim, Buf.	.247	86	354	320	45	79	152	13	0	20	57	0	2	4	28	2	53	2	1	10	.475	.314
Langaigne, Selwyn, Syr.*	.239	62	223	201	31	48	66	7	1	3	23	2	2	1	17	0	53	4	2	8	.328	.299
LaRocca, Greg, Buf.	.310	61	237	216	39	67	117	12	1	12	37	2	1	6	12	0	35	2	1	4	.542	.362
Larson, Brandon, Lou.	.255	115	463	424	61	108	176	22	2	14	55	0	2	12	24	1	123	5	6	15	.415	.312
Latham, Chris, Syr.†	.278	79	346	288	57	80	157	20	9	13	54	0	6	1	51	5	90	14	11	6	.545	.382
Lawrence, Joe, Syr.	.220	93	362	318	27	70	92	11	4	1	26	1	1	6	36	0	62	6	9	6	.289	.310
Lennon, Pat, Col.	.136	14	54	44	6	6	12	1	1	1	2	0	0	1	9	0	14	0	0	0	.273	.296
Leon, Donny, Col.†	.163	12	47	43	4	7	8	1	0	0	3	0	1	0	3	1	14	1	0	1	.186	.213
Leon, Jose, Roch.	.279	109	448	416	54	116	180	20	4	12	53	2	1	4	25	0	96	7	3	14	.433	.325
Lesher, Brian, Ind.	.283	93	393	346	51	98	144	17	4	7	63	0	5	2	40	0	78	1	1	5	.416	.356
Levis, Jesse, Rich.-Ind.*	.272	79	264	232	22	63	79	7	0	3	34	3	0	3	26	2	21	2	0	9	.341	.352
Levrault, Allen, Ind.	.000	5	4	4	0	0	0	0	0	0	0	0	0	0	0	0	2	0	0	0	.000	.000
Lewis, Derrick, Rich.	.167	12	8	6	0	1	1	0	0	0	0	2	0	0	0	0	2	0	0	0	.167	.167
Lewis, Mark, Buf.	.299	48	208	184	22	55	79	10	1	4	29	1	1	4	18	2	26	0	1	9	.429	.372
Lewis, Richie, Nor.	.188	19	18	16	2	3	3	0	0	0	1	2	0	0	0	0	5	0	0	1	.188	.188
Liefer, Jeff, Char.*	.286	32	139	119	23	34	59	7	0	6	21	0	1	4	15	1	41	3	1	1	.496	.381
Lindstrom, Dave, Tol.	.256	61	226	203	21	52	73	16	1	1	22	9	1	3	10	0	24	1	1	8	.360	.300
Liniak, Cole, Syr.	.241	103	389	344	40	83	136	21	1	10	49	5	5	3	32	3	55	1	2	8	.395	.307
Linton, Doug, Nor.	.000	12	7	7	0	0	0	0	0	0	0	0	0	0	0	0	4	0	0	0	.000	.000
Lira, Felipe, Ott.-S./W.B.	.333	44	4	3	0	1	1	0	0	0	0	1	0	0	0	0	1	0	0	0	.333	.333
Lofton, James, Paw.†	.318	42	164	151	19	48	74	8	0	6	13	3	0	0	10	1	29	3	3	4	.490	.360
Lomasney, Steve, Paw.	.286	17	69	63	10	18	28	4	0	2	9	1	0	1	4	0	21	2	0	2	.444	.338
Lombard, George, Rich.*	.318	13	53	44	7	14	30	2	1	4	8	1	0	2	6	0	14	3	2	1	.682	.423
Lopez-Cao, Mike, Roch.*	.000	2	2	1	0	0	0	0	0	0	0	0	0	1	0	0	0	0	0	0	.000	.500
Lopez, Felipe, Syr.†	.279	89	397	358	65	100	181	19	7	16	44	2	4	3	30	4	94	13	5	5	.506	.337
Lopez, Luis, Syr.	.324	87	386	339	57	110	170	26	2	10	73	0	6	2	39	7	31	1	1	9	.501	.391
Loretta, Mark, Ind.	.097	8	33	31	4	3	3	0	0	0	1	0	0	0	2	0	4	0	0	1	.097	.152
Lowery, Terrell, Dur.	.261	71	287	253	28	66	89	14	3	1	18	3	2	1	28	0	69	6	3	6	.352	.335
Luebbers, Larry, Lou.	.333	22	22	21	2	7	9	2	0	0	2	0	0	0	1	0	3	0	0	1	.429	.364
MacRae, Scott, Lou.	.000	11	1	0	0	0	0	0	0	0	0	1	0	0	0	0	0	0	0	0	.000	.000
Maddox, Garry, Paw.*	.111	8	27	27	1	3	3	0	0	0	1	0	0	0	0	0	8	0	0	1	.111	.111
Magee, Wendell, Tol.	.444	2	9	9	0	4	4	0	0	0	1	0	0	0	0	0	0	0	0	1	.444	.444
Mallette, Brian, Ind.	.000	12	1	1	0	0	0	0	0	0	0	0	0	0	0	0	0	0	0	0	.000	.000
Malloy, Marty, Lou.	.303	126	510	468	69	142	204	36	4	6	49	7	6	2	27	0	51	8	7	5	.436	.340
Manon, Julio, Ott.*	.125	15	12	8	0	1	2	1	0	0	0	3	0	1	0	0	4	0	0	0	.250	.222
Marconi, Alex, Dur.	.000	1	4	4	0	0	0	0	0	0	0	0	0	0	0	0	1	0	0	0	.000	.000
Marquez, Rob, Ott.	.000	34	2	1	0	0	0	0	0	0	0	1	0	0	0	0	1	0	0	0	.000	.000
Martin, Tom, Nor.*	.000	23	1	1	0	0	0	0	0	0	0	0	0	0	0	0	0	0	0	0	.000	.000
Martinez, Casey, Syr.	.600	5	5	5	1	3	3	0	0	0	1	0	0	0	0	0	1	0	0	0	.600	.600
Martinez, Eddy, Roch.	.271	90	350	314	42	85	122	14	1	7	33	10	1	4	21	0	66	7	0	6	.389	.324
Martinez, Gabby, Nor.	.262	48	166	149	23	39	47	6	1	0	6	4	0	1	12	0	19	9	5	1	.315	.321
Martinez, Greg, Dur.†	.293	62	282	242	36	71	84	6	2	1	21	5	1	4	29	0	46	14	7	3	.347	.377
Martinez, Lou, Rich.	.042	9	26	24	1	1	1	0	0	0	2	1	1	0	0	0	3	0	1	1	.042	.040
Mateo, Henry, Ott.†	.268	118	552	500	71	134	187	14	12	5	43	11	1	7	33	3	89	47	14	2	.374	.322
Mateo, Ruben, Lou.	.251	65	274	251	35	63	93	16	4	2	25	0	2	8	13	0	45	2	0	7	.371	.292
Matos, Pascual, Col.	.219	77	274	256	23	56	82	12	1	4	26	3	1	2	12	0	60	1	3	6	.320	.258
Mattes, Troy, Ott.	.000	15	8	6	0	0	0	0	0	0	0	1	1	0	0	0	1	0	0	0	.000	.000
Maurer, Dave, Lou.	.000	18	1	1	0	0	0	0	0	0	0	0	0	0	0	0	1	0	0	0	.000	.000
McClendon, Matt, Rich.	.200	10	5	5	0	1	1	0	0	0	0	0	0	0	0	0	0	0	0	0	.200	.200
McDonald, Darnell, Roch.	.238	104	425	391	37	93	122	19	2	2	35	2	2	1	29	0	75	13	9	8	.312	.291
McDonald, Donzell, Col.†	.257	105	425	374	59	96	149	11	9	8	36	1	1	7	42	1	79	20	4	2	.398	.342
McDonald, John, Buf.	.244	116	464	410	52	100	125	17	1	2	33	9	6	6	33	0	72	17	10	11	.305	.305
McKinley, Dan, Ott.*	.281	105	389	360	31	101	146	18	6	5	39	4	1	4	20	0	85	12	6	7	.406	.325
McNally, Sean, Buf.	.225	51	206	178	24	40	76	10	1	8	29	0	2	2	24	1	71	0	1	3	.427	.320
McNamara, Rusty, S./W.B.*	.143	5	18	14	2	2	5	0	0	1	2	0	1	2	1	0	1	0	0	0	.357	.278
McNichol, Brian, Lou.*	1.000	26	2	2	0	2	2	0	0	0	0	0	0	0	0	0	0	0	0	0	1.000	1.000
Medrano, Tony, Buf.	.290	121	541	466	68	135	186	28	1	7	52	9	6	6	54	1	40	21	7	12	.399	.367
Mendez, Carlos, Tol.	.246	102	421	398	45	98	181	27	1	18	76	3	6	5	9	0	53	0	0	13	.455	.268
Meran, Jorge, Tol.	.190	7	25	21	0	4	4	0	0	0	2	1	1	0	2	0	7	1	0	1	.190	.250
Merloni, Lou, Paw.	.262	52	218	195	30	51	75	12	0	4	20	3	0	5	15	0	37	2	0	6	.385	.334
Metcalfe, Mike, Lou.†	.150	6	24	20	1	3	3	0	0	0	0	0	0	0	4	0	5	2	1	0	.150	.292
Michaels, Jason, S./W.B.	.261	109	464	418	58	109	185	19	3	17	69	0	1	8	37	2	126	11	3	7	.443	.332
Miller, Corky, Lou.	.347	44	167	144	30	50	82	11	0	7	28	0	1	12	10	0	19	2	0	2	.569	.431
Miller, Ryan, Nor.	.179	22	62	56	5	10	13	3	0	0	3	1	0	2	3	0	14	0	0	1	.232	.246
Milliard, Ralph, Buf.	.267	5	17	15	2	4	5	1	0	0	1	0	0	0	2	0	2	0	0	0	.333	.353
Minor, Ryan, Ott.	.245	42	166	143	20	35	60	6	2	5	19	0	1	6	16	0	41	0	0	1	.420	.343
Molina, Izzy, Syr.	.305	73	276	256	34	78	148	20	1	16	38	1	0	1	18	0	52	1	0	7	.578	.353
Montgomery, Ray, Nor.	.320	57	225	194	37	62	92	7	1	7	33	0	3	1	27	2	36	4	2	2	.474	.400
Moore, Trey, Rich.*	.231	29	26	26	1	6	9	1	1	0	3	0	0	0	0	0	2	0	0	0	.346	.346
Morales, Willie, Roch.	.232	52	175	164	18	38	48	7	0	1	11	3	2	1	5	0	32	2	1	2	.293	.256
Mosquera, Julio, Col.	.244	16	46	41	6	10	12	2	0	0	3	1	0	3	1	0	10	0	0	2	.293	.311
Moss, Damian, Rich.	.308	22	14	13	1	4	10	1	1	1	3	0	0	0	1	0	5	0	0	0	.769	.357
Mouton, James, Ind.	.444	2	9	9	0	4	6	2	0	0	2	0	0	0	0	0	0	0	0	0	.667	.444
Mouton, Lyle, Tol.	.317	67	297	262	59	83	159	18	2	18	49	0	1	5	29	3	66	4	1	12	.607	.394
Mulligan, Sean, Roch.	.333	7	28	27	5	9	14	2	0	1	4	0	0	0	1	0	5	0	1	0	.519	.357
Munoz, Bobby, Ott.	.273	19	14	11	0	3	4	1	0	0	3	0	0	0	0	0	6	0	0	0	.364	.273
Neill, Mike, Paw.*	.245	67	246	208	27	51	80	10	2	5	22	6	1	0	31	0	70	2	1	4	.385	.342
Nelson, Joe, Rich.	.000	29	2	2	0	0	0	0	0	0	0	0	0	0	0	0	2	0	0	0	.000	.000
Nettles, Jeff, Col.	.185	12	32	27	1	5	5	0	0	0	1	0	0	0	5	0	9	2	1	1	.185	.313
Neugebauer, Nick, Ind.	.500	4	11	8	2	4	7	0	0	1	3	2	1	0	0	0	1	0	0	0	.875	.444

Player, Team	Avg.	G	TPA	AB	R	H	TB	2B	3B	HR	RBI	SH	SF	HP	BB	IBB	SO	SB	CS	GDP	Slg.	OBP
Nevers, Tom, Lou.	.105	5	21	19	0	2	3	1	0	0	3	0	1	0	1	0	5	0	0	1	.158	.143
Newhan, David, S./W.B.*	.109	13	60	55	4	6	7	1	0	0	2	0	0	1	4	1	11	0	0	1	.127	.183
Nickle, Doug, S./W.B.	.222	47	9	9	0	2	2	0	0	0	0	0	0	0	0	0	4	0	0	0	.222	.222
Norris, Dax, Rich.	.281	95	341	317	26	80	123	25	0	3	38	1	2	5	16	0	44	2	2	5	.388	.324
Nunnari, Talmadge, Ott.*	.219	110	393	343	35	75	104	15	1	4	35	4	4	4	38	3	81	13	2	3	.303	.301
Ochoa, Pablo, Nor.	.000	19	9	9	0	0	0	0	0	0	0	0	0	0	0	0	6	0	0	0	.000	.000
Oliver, Joe, Paw.	.244	13	41	41	3	10	17	1	0	2	6	0	0	0	0	0	9	1	0	2	.415	.244
Ontiveros, Steve, Nor.	.000	7	4	2	0	0	0	0	0	0	0	2	0	0	0	0	1	0	0	0	.000	.000
Orie, Kevin, S./W.B.	.293	134	598	509	77	149	226	34	2	13	45	0	2	9	77	5	63	11	6	8	.444	.394
Ortiz, Luis, Ott.	.281	16	61	57	4	16	23	5	1	0	8	0	1	0	3	0	6	0	0	2	.404	.311
Ottavinia, Paul, Col.*	.272	42	165	147	20	40	65	11	4	2	14	0	1	3	14	0	16	3	4	6	.442	.345
Pacheco, Delvis, Rich.	.200	22	5	5	0	1	1	0	0	0	0	0	0	0	0	0	1	0	0	0	.200	.200
Padilla, Vicente, S./W.B.	.286	16	7	7	0	2	3	1	0	0	0	0	0	0	0	0	1	0	0	0	.429	.286
Palmer, Dean, Tol.	.500	1	4	2	0	1	1	0	0	0	0	0	0	0	2	0	0	0	0	0	.500	.750
Patterson, Jarrod, Tol.*	.296	69	247	213	41	63	103	15	2	7	25	0	3	1	30	1	47	2	1	9	.484	.381
Paul, Josh, Char.	.280	22	84	75	11	21	37	4	0	4	14	1	1	0	7	0	18	0	0	0	.493	.337
Pavano, Carl, Ott.	.333	4	3	3	0	1	1	0	0	0	0	0	0	0	0	0	2	0	0	0	.333	.333
Pena, Elvis, Ind.†	.240	127	484	437	56	105	129	15	3	1	28	7	2	8	30	0	76	12	5	8	.295	.300
Penney, Mike, Ind.	.250	22	4	4	0	1	1	0	0	0	0	0	0	0	0	0	1	0	0	0	.250	.250
Peoples, Danny, Buf.	.222	106	435	370	62	82	155	20	1	17	48	0	6	3	56	1	133	0	3	4	.419	.324
Perez, Jerson, Syr.	.125	5	18	16	1	2	3	1	0	0	0	1	0	0	1	0	7	0	0	0	.188	.176
Perez, Jhonny, Tol.	.250	32	134	120	19	30	44	7	2	1	14	3	1	1	9	0	24	7	2	2	.367	.305
Perez, Odaliz, Rich.*	.500	6	2	2	0	1	2	1	0	0	0	0	0	0	0	0	0	0	0	1	1.000	.500
Perez, Rob, Col.-Ind.	.326	56	244	230	33	75	127	16	3	10	43	0	1	5	8	2	34	6	6	11	.552	.361
Perez, Timo, Nor.*	.359	48	210	192	37	69	101	10	2	6	19	2	2	2	12	2	18	15	2	1	.526	.399
Perisho, Matt, Tol.*	.000	25	1	1	0	0	0	0	0	0	0	0	0	0	0	0	1	0	0	0	.000	.000
Perry, Chan, Rich.	.274	98	374	350	38	96	141	15	3	8	39	1	1	3	19	2	60	1	6	13	.403	.316
Peters, Chris, Lou.*	.500	8	4	2	0	1	1	0	0	0	1	2	0	0	0	0	0	0	0	0	.500	.500
Peterson, Kyle, Ind.	.154	22	20	13	0	2	2	0	0	0	1	4	0	1	2	0	3	0	0	0	.154	.313
Phelps, Tommy, Tol.*	.000	29	1	1	0	0	0	0	0	0	0	0	0	0	0	0	1	0	0	0	.000	.000
Phillips, Jason, Nor.	.303	19	74	66	8	20	28	2	0	2	14	0	1	0	7	0	8	0	0	2	.424	.365
Pickering, Calvin, Roch.-Lou.*	.282	132	543	465	63	131	222	25	0	22	99	0	3	10	65	7	151	0	1	16	.477	.379
Pride, Curt, Ott.*	.333	22	95	81	14	27	48	4	1	5	15	0	0	2	12	2	26	6	1	2	.593	.432
Prieto, Rick, Char.†	.231	11	33	26	4	6	6	0	0	0	1	1	0	0	6	0	6	0	0	2	.231	.375
Probst, Alan, Nor.	.150	23	66	60	4	9	14	2	0	1	5	0	2	0	4	0	19	0	0	3	.233	.197
Punto, Nick, S./W.B.†	.229	123	536	463	57	106	138	19	5	1	39	3	1	0	68	3	114	33	9	15	.298	.327
Rain, Steve, Ind.	.000	25	1	1	0	0	0	0	0	0	0	0	0	0	0	0	0	0	0	0	.000	.000
Raines, Tim, Roch.†	.256	40	146	133	19	34	47	5	1	2	12	2	0	0	11	0	30	11	3	2	.353	.313
Raines, Tim, Ott.†	.143	2	8	7	1	1	2	1	0	0	0	0	0	0	1	0	1	0	0	0	.286	.250
Ramirez, Julio, Char.	.216	88	344	319	36	69	106	11	1	8	25	2	1	2	20	0	80	15	6	1	.332	.266
Ramos, Kelly, Paw.†	.231	5	13	13	0	3	3	0	0	0	0	0	0	0	0	0	3	0	0	0	.231	.231
Reames, Britt, Ott.	.125	9	12	8	0	1	1	0	0	0	1	1	1	0	2	0	1	0	0	0	.125	.273
Reding, Josh, Ott.	.111	6	22	18	0	2	3	1	0	0	2	0	1	2	1	0	6	0	0	1	.167	.227
Reed, Jeff, S./W.B.*	.235	31	114	98	12	23	36	1	0	4	8	1	1	0	14	0	24	0	0	0	.367	.327
Reed, Keith, Roch.	.311	20	79	74	11	23	38	7	1	2	11	0	0	0	5	0	14	1	1	1	.514	.354
Reith, Brian, Lou.	.000	1	3	3	0	0	0	0	0	0	0	0	0	0	0	0	2	0	0	0	.000	.000
Reyes, Dennys, Lou.	.143	7	8	7	0	1	2	1	0	0	0	1	0	0	0	0	5	0	0	0	.286	.143
Rijo, Jose, Lou.	.000	6	1	1	0	0	0	0	0	0	0	0	0	0	0	0	0	0	0	0	.000	.000
Rios, Brian, Tol.	.325	104	402	372	47	121	202	29	5	14	62	2	2	4	22	2	66	2	4	17	.543	.368
Rivera, Juan, Col.	.327	55	218	199	39	65	120	11	1	14	40	0	3	1	15	1	31	4	5	7	.603	.372
Roach, Jason, Nor.	.000	4	5	5	0	0	0	0	0	0	0	0	0	0	0	0	2	0	0	0	.000	.000
Robbins, Jake, Rich.	.000	57	3	2	0	0	0	0	0	0	0	1	0	0	0	0	1	0	0	0	.000	.000
Roberge, J.P., S./W.B.	.271	26	108	96	10	26	34	8	0	0	10	1	1	1	9	1	18	0	1	5	.354	.336
Roberts, Brian, Roch.†	.267	44	190	161	16	43	52	4	1	1	12	1	0	0	28	0	22	23	3	0	.323	.376
Roberts, Dave, Buf.*	.303	62	272	241	34	73	93	12	4	0	22	8	3	2	18	0	44	17	6	2	.386	.352
Roberts, Grant, Nor.	.400	30	6	5	0	2	2	0	0	0	1	1	0	0	0	0	2	0	0	0	.400	.400
Robertson, Mike, Rich.*	.272	127	469	434	42	118	165	19	5	6	40	1	2	2	30	3	56	4	12	11	.380	.321
Rodriguez, Frank, Lou.	.250	45	9	8	1	2	5	0	0	1	1	0	0	0	1	0	1	0	0	0	.625	.333
Rodriguez, Henry, Col.*	.238	18	72	63	9	15	32	2	0	5	13	0	1	1	7	0	21	0	0	1	.508	.319
Rodriguez, Liu, Char.†	.291	118	502	444	53	129	154	25	0	0	37	11	3	3	41	0	60	7	4	8	.347	.352
Rodriguez, Luis, Paw.	.263	33	107	99	17	26	39	4	0	3	5	2	0	0	6	0	27	1	0	3	.394	.305
Rose, Ted, Ott.*	.250	38	9	8	0	2	2	0	0	0	1	0	0	0	1	0	2	0	0	0	.250	.333
Ross, Jason, Rich.	.208	49	136	125	15	26	48	5	1	5	7	0	1	3	7	0	45	3	2	3	.384	.265
Rowand, Aaron, Char.	.295	82	362	329	54	97	173	28	0	16	48	2	1	9	21	3	47	8	2	9	.526	.353
Royster, Aaron, S./W.B.	.316	8	19	19	3	6	7	1	0	0	1	0	0	0	0	0	5	0	0	0	.368	.316
Rumfield, Toby, Char.	.272	121	500	463	49	126	214	28	0	20	69	1	3	5	28	2	64	0	0	16	.462	.319
Rust, Brian, Roch.	.204	55	213	186	24	38	77	12	0	9	29	1	0	4	22	0	50	4	0	1	.414	.302
Salazar, Jeremy, S./W.B.	.231	47	173	160	16	37	53	13	0	1	16	2	1	0	10	0	35	0	0	6	.331	.275
Samuels, Scott, Paw.*	.256	38	140	125	14	32	55	9	1	4	14	1	0	0	14	0	21	5	2	2	.440	.331
Sanchez, Alex, Ind.*	.313	83	361	335	52	105	132	14	5	1	26	2	0	2	22	1	44	27	8	2	.394	.359
Sandberg, Jared, Dur.	.239	93	368	322	39	77	141	16	0	16	50	2	0	6	38	0	81	0	1	13	.438	.331
Sanders, Deion, Lou.-Syr.*	.337	44	198	181	27	61	90	11	6	2	15	4	0	4	9	0	16	11	7	2	.497	.381
Santana, Pedro, Tol.	.227	115	471	432	45	98	129	10	3	5	30	7	3	2	27	0	97	36	8	4	.299	.274
Santos, Angel, Paw.†	.200	4	17	15	1	3	4	1	0	0	2	0	1	0	1	0	4	1	0	0	.267	.235
Sasser, Rob, Ott.	.232	52	205	181	20	42	66	9	3	3	25	0	1	1	22	3	41	7	1	2	.365	.317
Saunders, Chris, Char.	.205	12	45	39	3	8	15	1	0	2	3	0	0	1	5	0	7	0	0	0	.385	.311
Schall, Gene, S./W.B.	.281	73	303	263	40	74	138	20	1	14	54	0	2	7	31	2	57	0	0	11	.525	.370
Schneider, Brian, Ott.*	.275	97	369	338	33	93	140	27	1	6	43	0	0	4	27	4	55	2	0	5	.414	.336
Scutaro, Marcos, Ind.	.295	132	575	495	87	146	214	29	3	11	50	5	3	10	62	2	83	11	11	9	.432	.382
Seabol, Scott, Col.	.266	78	304	282	32	75	126	19	1	10	42	2	2	4	14	1	56	3	4	6	.447	.308
Seelbach, Chris, Rich.	.000	22	8	6	0	0	0	0	0	0	0	2	0	0	0	0	3	0	0	0	.000	.000
Sefcik, Kevin, Buf.	.197	70	257	233	30	46	75	10	2	5	24	3	1	2	18	1	20	4	3	9	.322	.260
Seguignol, Fernando, Ott.†	.310	60	262	242	36	75	129	12	0	14	45	0	0	5	15	2	49	0	1	6	.533	.363

Player, Team	Avg.	G	TPA	AB	R	H	TB	2B	3B	HR	RBI	SH	SF	HP	BB	IBB	SO	SB	CS	GDP	Slg.	OBP
Selby, Bill, Lou.*	.258	88	362	330	47	85	148	19	1	14	56	1	4	2	25	3	47	1	0	6	.448	.310
Sell, Chip, Ind.*	.321	17	63	56	4	18	24	4	1	0	5	0	2	1	4	1	14	3	0	1	.429	.365
Seo, Jae, Nor.	.000	9	3	3	0	0	0	0	0	0	0	0	0	0	0	0	1	0	0	0	.000	.000
Serafini, Dan, Ind.†	.000	9	1	0	1	0	0	0	0	0	0	0	0	0	1	0	0	0	0	0	.000	1.000
Service, Scott, Lou.	.000	20	1	1	0	0	0	0	0	0	0	0	0	0	0	0	1	0	0	0	.000	.000
Sexton, Chris, Lou.	.279	105	463	409	59	114	151	25	3	2	47	4	8	1	40	2	57	5	5	13	.369	.338
Shave, Jon, Paw.	.256	84	344	308	35	79	107	10	0	6	27	5	1	8	22	0	49	3	3	6	.347	.322
Sheets, Andy, Dur.	.280	66	255	225	28	63	93	14	2	4	22	2	1	2	25	0	45	8	3	6	.413	.356
Sheets, Ben, Ind.	.333	2	3	3	0	1	1	0	0	0	2	0	0	0	0	0	2	0	0	0	.333	.333
Sheff, Chris, Lou.	.276	94	361	312	54	86	134	19	1	9	51	1	1	7	40	0	73	4	3	7	.429	.369
Shumaker, Tony, Roch.*	.000	53	1	0	0	0	0	0	0	0	0	1	0	0	0	0	0	0	0	0	.000	.000
Simmons, Brian, Syr.†	.264	52	225	201	24	53	71	10	1	2	20	2	1	2	19	0	36	4	5	6	.353	.332
Simon, Randy, Tol.*	.338	59	245	222	27	75	118	13	0	10	31	0	0	2	21	2	21	0	3	8	.532	.400
Sisco, Steve, Roch.-S./W.B. ..	.236	95	392	351	38	83	118	17	0	6	29	2	5	6	28	2	70	7	5	10	.336	.300
Small, Aaron, Rich.	.077	41	13	13	0	1	2	1	0	0	0	0	0	0	0	0	6	0	0	1	.154	.077
Smith, Bobby, Dur.	.301	107	454	396	67	119	214	25	2	22	70	0	5	8	45	1	91	10	2	7	.540	.379
Smith, Jason, Dur.*	.194	8	32	31	2	6	7	1	0	0	3	1	0	0	0	0	11	0	0	0	.226	.194
Smith, Mark, Ott.	.207	40	163	145	20	30	56	8	0	6	17	1	0	2	15	0	38	4	2	1	.386	.290
Snusz, Chris, Buf.	.000	1	1	1	0	0	0	0	0	0	0	0	0	0	0	0	0	0	0	0	.000	.000
Snyder, Earl, Nor.	.474	6	23	19	5	9	12	3	0	0	3	0	0	1	3	0	1	0	1	0	.632	.565
Snyder, John, Ind.	.067	33	18	15	1	1	1	0	0	0	1	0	1	1	1	0	5	0	0	0	.067	.167
Sorensen, Zach, Buf.†	.286	2	7	7	2	2	2	0	0	0	1	0	0	0	0	0	0	0	0	0	.286	.286
Spehr, Tim, Lou.	.163	68	211	184	22	30	52	7	0	5	25	0	2	7	18	0	73	2	1	3	.283	.261
Spencer, Sean, Ott.*	.000	52	1	1	0	0	0	0	0	0	0	0	0	0	0	0	0	0	0	0	.000	.000
Spencer, Shane, Col.	.231	49	201	173	17	40	61	10	1	3	14	0	3	2	23	0	21	4	1	9	.353	.323
Spooneybarger, Tim, Rich.	.500	42	2	2	1	1	1	0	0	0	0	0	0	0	0	0	1	0	0	0	.500	.500
Stenson, Dernell, Paw.*	.237	122	514	464	53	110	178	18	1	16	69	0	5	2	43	3	116	0	1	6	.384	.304
Stevens, Dave, Rich.	.000	39	1	1	0	0	0	0	0	0	0	0	0	0	0	0	0	0	0	0	.000	.000
Strange, Pat, Nor.	.333	1	3	3	0	1	1	0	0	0	1	0	0	0	0	0	2	0	0	0	.333	.333
Stratton, Rob, Nor.	.143	2	8	7	1	1	4	0	0	1	3	0	1	0	0	0	2	0	0	0	.571	.125
Stynes, Chris, Paw.	.333	4	17	15	1	5	6	1	0	0	1	0	0	1	1	0	2	0	0	0	.400	.412
Swann, Pedro, Rich.*	.291	139	559	488	68	142	209	33	5	8	72	1	10	8	52	3	95	12	6	14	.428	.362
Sweeney, Mark, Ind.*	.287	109	467	404	65	116	170	34	1	6	69	0	5	2	56	6	71	3	1	6	.421	.373
Tamargo, John, Nor.†	.288	40	129	111	11	32	38	3	0	1	11	3	2	1	12	0	16	0	0	2	.342	.357
Tarasco, Tony, Nor.*	.292	105	418	366	53	107	167	31	4	7	57	0	4	0	48	8	43	14	8	5	.456	.371
Taubensee, Eddie, Buf.*	.269	7	28	26	5	7	14	1	0	2	7	0	0	0	2	0	6	0	0	1	.538	.333
Taylor, Reggie, S./W.B.*	.263	111	464	464	56	122	181	20	9	7	50	1	4	3	24	4	94	31	15	10	.390	.301
Tebbs, Nate, Paw.-Rich.†	.183	74	237	219	17	40	47	7	0	0	8	4	0	0	14	0	59	6	2	2	.215	.232
Telemaco, Amaury, S./W.B.	.000	4	1	1	0	0	0	0	0	0	0	0	0	0	0	0	0	0	0	0	.000	.000
Telford, Anthony, Ott.	.143	28	8	7	0	1	2	1	0	0	1	1	0	0	0	0	3	0	0	0	.286	.143
Tessmer, Jay, Ind.	.000	35	5	4	0	0	0	0	0	0	0	1	0	0	0	0	1	0	0	0	.000	.000
Thomas, Evan, S./W.B.	.000	19	12	8	0	0	0	0	0	0	0	4	0	0	0	0	4	0	0	0	.000	.000
Thompson, Andy, Syr.	.230	48	201	178	15	41	69	5	1	7	28	0	5	4	14	1	42	2	4	3	.388	.294
Thompson, Rich, Syr.*	.245	17	61	53	5	13	15	0	1	0	3	3	1	0	4	0	12	5	1	1	.283	.293
Thompson, Ryan, Ott.	.165	21	89	85	6	14	24	4	0	2	9	0	1	0	3	0	22	0	2	3	.282	.202
Toca, Jorge, Nor.	.268	111	437	407	53	109	157	13	1	11	51	0	2	5	23	1	63	12	2	19	.386	.314
Traber, Billy, Nor.*	.000	1	2	2	0	0	0	0	0	0	0	0	0	0	0	0	1	0	0	0	.000	.000
Trachsel, Steve, Nor.	.000	3	2	2	0	0	0	0	0	0	0	0	0	0	0	0	0	0	0	0	.000	.000
Tracy, Andy, Ott.*	.205	53	217	190	17	39	64	11	1	4	19	0	1	2	24	1	72	4	2	2	.337	.300
Tucker, T.J., Ott.	.333	14	7	6	1	2	6	1	0	1	1	1	0	0	0	0	1	0	0	0	1.000	.333
Tyler, Brad, Lou.*	.278	13	38	36	7	10	18	5	0	1	2	0	0	0	2	0	16	0	1	0	.500	.316
Tyner, Jason, Dur.*	.312	39	179	157	25	49	53	2	1	0	12	1	4	2	15	1	10	11	5	1	.338	.371
Valdes, Marc, Rich.	.375	29	16	16	2	6	10	1	0	1	1	0	0	0	0	0	4	0	0	1	.625	.375
Valdez, Jerry, S./W.B.	.308	5	14	13	1	4	7	0	0	1	2	0	0	1	0	0	3	0	0	0	.538	.357
Valent, Eric, S./W.B.*	.272	117	508	448	65	122	219	30	2	21	78	0	3	8	49	4	105	0	1	13	.489	.352
Valentin, John, Paw.	.250	10	44	36	7	9	16	1	0	2	4	0	0	0	8	0	4	0	0	0	.444	.386
Valenzuela, Mario, Char.	.261	49	191	176	19	46	85	7	1	10	26	1	4	1	8	1	34	2	0	7	.483	.291
Velandia, Jorge, Nor.	.250	67	294	260	25	65	101	20	0	5	37	10	3	5	16	0	47	9	4	7	.388	.303
Veras, Quilvio, Paw.†	.300	3	10	10	1	3	4	1	0	0	0	0	0	0	0	0	3	0	0	0	.400	.300
Veras, Wilton, Paw.	.230	136	546	521	44	120	164	16	2	8	52	1	3	7	14	0	63	5	6	24	.315	.259
Villegas, Ismael, Rich.	.083	36	14	12	0	1	1	0	0	0	0	1	0	0	1	0	4	0	0	1	.083	.154
Vinas, Julio, Roch.	.218	38	159	142	17	31	47	5	1	3	21	0	3	1	13	1	23	0	0	5	.331	.283
Wakeland, Chris, Tol.*	.283	140	598	547	85	155	263	33	3	23	84	0	4	8	39	1	126	7	8	9	.481	.338
Walbeck, Matt, Lou.-S./W.B.†	.257	107	376	338	38	87	120	18	0	5	46	1	1	2	34	3	46	1	2	8	.355	.328
Walker, Pete, Nor.	.167	26	29	24	2	4	5	1	0	0	3	2	0	1	2	0	8	0	0	1	.208	.259
Walker, Tyler, Nor.	.000	8	5	5	0	0	0	0	0	0	0	0	0	0	0	0	2	0	0	0	.000	.000
Ward, Turner, S./W.B.†	.275	70	257	222	28	61	103	22	4	4	27	0	3	2	30	4	31	9	0	5	.464	.362
Ware, Jeremy, Ott.	.265	53	156	147	13	39	58	13	0	2	13	3	0	0	6	0	24	2	0	4	.395	.294
Wells, Vernon, Syr.	.281	107	448	413	57	116	187	27	4	12	52	0	2	4	29	0	68	15	11	3	.453	.333
Wigginton, Ty, Nor.	.250	78	292	260	29	65	98	12	0	7	24	1	2	2	27	0	45	3	3	4	.377	.323
Wilcox, Luke, Col.*	.150	11	44	40	3	6	13	1	0	2	6	0	1	0	3	0	6	1	0	1	.325	.205
Wilkerson, Brad, Ott.*	.270	69	300	233	43	63	109	10	0	12	48	2	2	3	60	0	68	12	5	2	.468	.423
Williams, George, Paw.†	.130	17	54	46	6	6	8	2	0	0	1	0	0	0	8	0	10	0	0	0	.174	.259
Williams, Matt, Ind.†	.000	51	2	1	0	0	0	0	0	0	0	0	0	0	0	0	0	0	0	0	.000	.000
Wilson, Travis, Rich.	.243	103	396	383	34	93	130	22	3	3	38	1	1	4	7	3	81	4	2	10	.339	.263
Wilson, Vance, Nor.	.246	65	253	228	24	56	88	14	0	6	31	1	3	9	12	2	34	0	1	7	.386	.306
Winchester, Scott, Lou.	.000	23	9	7	0	0	0	0	0	0	0	2	0	0	0	0	1	0	0	0	.000	.000
Wise, Dewayne, Syr.*	.231	3	13	13	1	3	3	0	0	0	0	0	0	0	0	0	8	0	1	0	.231	.231
Woods, Ken, Roc.-Ric.-S./W.B.	.248	50	167	149	16	37	46	7	1	0	11	1	0	1	16	0	14	6	3	4	.309	.325
Woodward, Chris, Syr.	.306	51	213	193	29	59	112	14	3	11	31	2	1	1	16	0	40	0	0	4	.580	.360
Wright, Ron, Dur.	.262	121	497	439	63	115	202	27	0	20	75	0	4	3	51	3	103	2	2	11	.460	.340
Zamora, Pete, S./W.B.*	.444	45	9	9	0	4	5	1	0	0	2	0	0	0	0	1	0	0	0	0	.556	.444
Zech, Scott, Ott.	.167	13	43	36	2	6	8	2	0	0	2	0	0	1	5	1	8	1	1	1	.222	.286

PLAYERS WITH TWO OR MORE TEAMS

Player, Team	Avg.	G	TPA	AB	R	H	TB	2B	3B	HR	RBI	SH	SF	HP	BB	IBB	SO	SB	CS	GDP	Slg.	OBP
Bradley, Milton, Ott.†	.272	35	164	136	21	37	54	7	2	2	13	2	1	2	23	4	30	14	1	3	.397	.383
Bradley, Milton, Buf.†	.254	30	136	114	18	29	47	3	0	5	15	3	0	0	19	1	31	9	2	0	.412	.361
Bragg, Darren, Nor.*	.333	32	124	99	22	33	49	4	0	4	7	0	0	2	23	1	22	5	2	1	.495	.468
Bragg, Darren, Col.*	.291	53	227	199	30	58	94	11	2	7	21	0	0	1	27	3	51	3	2	4	.472	.379
Buford, Damon, Roch.	.255	39	176	149	20	38	60	10	0	4	12	0	2	3	22	0	26	3	1	2	.403	.358
Buford, Damon, Lou.	.370	13	65	54	14	20	36	5	1	3	14	0	1	0	10	0	17	0	1	2	.667	.462
Coquillette, Trace, Buf.	.208	55	204	178	27	37	66	5	3	6	22	0	2	5	19	0	38	1	2	3	.371	.299
Coquillette, Trace, Tol.	.200	28	102	85	13	17	34	6	1	3	10	2	1	1	13	1	29	0	0	0	.400	.310
Estrella, Leo, Nor.	.000	8	1	1	0	0	0	0	0	0	0	0	0	0	0	0	0	0	0	0	.000	.000
Estrella, Leo, Lou.	.333	35	5	3	1	1	1	0	0	0	0	2	0	0	0	0	0	0	0	0	.333	.333
Figga, Mike, Col.	.000	1	5	5	0	0	0	0	0	0	0	0	0	0	0	0	2	0	0	0	.000	.000
Figga, Mike, Nor.	.191	36	117	110	13	21	40	4	0	5	16	1	1	1	4	1	26	0	1	2	.364	.224
Gubanich, Creighton, Ind.	.181	30	88	83	6	15	26	5	0	2	4	0	0	1	4	1	19	0	0	3	.313	.227
Gubanich, Creighton, Char.	.246	32	129	114	19	28	52	3	0	7	19	0	2	0	13	1	32	0	0	1	.456	.318
Hardtke, Jason, Buf.†	.258	39	147	128	19	33	46	7	3	0	14	2	0	1	16	1	16	0	1	2	.359	.345
Hardtke, Jason, Char.†	.260	57	232	208	33	54	98	14	0	10	25	2	0	4	18	0	27	2	1	0	.471	.330
Jones, Chris, Syr.	.219	37	154	137	17	30	45	2	2	3	15	0	3	1	13	2	35	7	2	2	.328	.286
Jones, Chris, Rich.	.246	32	79	65	7	16	20	4	0	0	4	2	1	1	10	1	26	0	3	0	.308	.351
Jones, Chris, Ind.	.283	31	126	113	20	32	57	2	1	7	21	1	1	1	9	0	25	0	0	2	.504	.339
Levis, Jesse, Rich.*	.297	67	221	192	18	57	66	6	0	1	27	3	0	2	24	2	15	2	0	6	.344	.381
Levis, Jesse, Ind.*	.150	12	43	40	4	6	13	1	0	2	7	0	0	1	2	0	6	0	0	3	.325	.209
Lira, Felipe, Ott.	.000	42	2	1	0	0	0	0	0	0	0	1	0	0	0	0	0	0	0	0	.000	.000
Lira, Felipe, S./W.B.	.500	2	2	2	0	1	1	0	0	0	0	0	0	0	0	0	1	0	0	0	.500	.500
Perez, Rob, Col.	.322	36	154	146	20	47	81	7	3	7	27	0	1	3	4	1	23	6	5	4	.555	.351
Perez, Rob, Ind.	.333	20	90	84	13	28	46	9	0	3	16	0	0	2	4	1	11	0	1	7	.548	.378
Pickering, Calvin, Roch.*	.282	131	538	461	62	130	218	25	0	21	98	0	3	10	64	7	149	0	1	16	.473	.379
Pickering, Calvin, Lou.*	.250	1	5	4	1	1	4	0	0	1	1	0	0	0	1	0	2	0	0	0	1.000	.400
Sanders, Deion, Lou.*	.459	19	81	74	12	34	51	4	5	1	9	2	0	3	2	0	4	6	3	0	.000	.404
Sanders, Deion, Syr.*	.252	25	117	107	15	27	39	7	1	1	6	2	0	1	7	0	12	5	4	2	.364	.304
Sisco, Steve, Roch.	.237	92	379	338	38	80	115	17	0	6	29	2	5	6	28	2	66	6	5	10	.340	.302
Sisco, Steve, S./W.B.	.231	3	13	13	0	3	3	0	0	0	0	0	0	0	0	0	4	1	0	0	.231	.231
Tebbs, Nate, Paw †	.235	46	148	136	15	32	39	7	0	0	6	3	0	0	9	0	35	5	2	1	.287	.283
Tebbs, Nate, Rich.†	.096	28	89	83	2	8	8	0	0	0	2	1	0	0	5	0	24	1	0	1	.096	.148
Walbeck, Matt, Lou.†	.228	67	221	197	20	45	61	7	0	3	25	1	0	0	23	2	26	1	0	6	.310	.309
Walbeck, Matt, S./W.B.†	.298	40	155	141	10	42	50	11	0	2	21	0	1	2	11	1	20	0	2	2	.418	.355
Woods, Ken, Roch.	.240	26	89	75	6	18	23	3	1	0	8	1	0	0	13	0	7	4	2	2	.307	.352
Woods, Ken, Rich.	.271	23	73	70	8	19	23	4	0	0	3	0	0	1	2	0	7	1	1	2	.329	.301
Woods, Ken, S./W.B.	.000	1	5	4	2	0	0	0	0	0	0	0	0	0	1	0	1	0	0	0	.000	.200

GRAND SLAMS: Burkhart, 3; McNally, 2; Alcantara, Battle, Bravo, Buford, Carpenter, Cromer, Diaz, Dunn, T. Evans, K. Garcia, Guevara, T. Hall, M. Lewis, Liefer, Liniak, Lomasney, L. Lopez, Michaels, Ottavinia, R. Perez, Pickering, Rivera, Schall, Tarasco, Velandia, Valenzuela, Walbeck, Wilkerson, R. Wright, 1 each.

AWARDED FIRST BASE ON CATCHER'S INTERFERENCE: Crede (Charles), C. Hernandez (Ramos), Hutchins (Andreopoulos), C. Jones (Greene), Larson (Coste), G. Martinez (Charles), Orie (Morales), Punto (Morales), Sexton (Charles), Valenzuela (Marconi), Zech (V. Wilson).

2001 PITCHING

TEAM

Team	W	L	Pct.	ERA	G	CG	ShO	Sv.	IP	H	TBF	R	ER	HR	SH	SF	HB	BB	IBB	SO	WP	Bk.
Scranton/W.-B.	78	65	.545	3.19	143	8	7	33	1300.1	1164	5365	507	461	116	52	26	47	395	34	1095	43	9
Norfolk	85	57	.599	3.55	142	4	10	52	1256.0	1246	5319	565	495	108	47	37	64	411	25	919	42	9
Buffalo	91	51	.641	3.59	142	8	11	53	1253.2	1212	5315	569	500	114	30	23	83	395	14	988	38	13
Durham	74	70	.514	3.76	144	4	10	37	1260.0	1228	5352	611	527	142	48	52	60	418	7	925	75	6
Ottawa	68	74	.479	3.89	144	5	11	40	1290.1	1241	5462	639	557	119	50	41	66	432	9	996	68	9
Louisville	84	60	.583	3.89	144	8	10	46	1287.0	1326	5479	632	556	136	52	27	60	382	18	912	66	2
Charlotte	67	77	.465	3.95	144	8	7	35	1268.0	1221	5406	623	557	133	47	41	51	464	40	1029	64	8
Syracuse	71	73	.493	4.08	144	5	9	37	1282.0	1293	5526	655	581	124	38	35	83	433	17	935	80	7
Rochester	60	84	.417	4.12	144	7	10	32	1287.2	1304	5643	709	589	131	53	42	50	474	29	1100	81	9
Richmond	68	76	.472	4.14	144	3	7	36	1275.0	1212	5443	634	587	113	57	40	45	506	52	1046	54	4
Columbus	67	76	.469	4.23	143	8	5	34	1240.0	1298	5417	690	583	121	44	39	50	456	17	1039	62	10
Indianapolis	66	78	.458	4.33	144	3	7	27	1279.1	1353	5600	716	616	127	54	43	60	465	20	898	49	9
Toledo	65	79	.451	4.36	144	5	3	32	1279.2	1402	5626	722	620	138	41	44	61	462	14	910	71	9
Pawtucket	60	82	.423	4.48	142	8	6	35	1237.0	1352	5349	710	616	137	45	45	49	357	25	908	43	17

INDIVIDUAL

TOP QUALIFIERS FOR EARNED-RUN AVERAGE TITLE

Minimum 115 innings. *Lefthanded pitcher.

Pitcher, Team	W	L	Pct.	ERA	G	GS	CG	ShO	GF	Sv.	IP	H	TBF	R	ER	HR	SH	SF	HB	BB	IBB	SO	WP	Bk.
Duckworth, Brandon, S./W.B.	13	2	.867	2.63	22	20	2	1	1	0	147.0	122	584	46	43	14	5	2	7	36	2	150	5	0
Beltran, Rigo, S./W.B.*	2	5	.286	2.96	37	11	0	0	6	2	115.2	87	460	40	38	10	2	3	1	41	6	113	5	0
Walker, Pete, Nor.	13	4	.765	2.99	26	26	0	0	0	0	168.1	145	681	64	56	12	5	5	46	5	106	2	1
Jodie, Brett, Col.	10	4	.714	3.01	19	19	2	1	0	0	119.2	123	498	46	40	9	3	3	25	0	59	3	1
Callaway, Mickey, Dur.	11	7	.611	3.07	29	21	2	1	3	0	129.0	131	532	50	44	9	5	3	5	24	0	81	7	1
Banks, Willie, Syr.-Paw.	10	5	.667	3.11	26	25	0	0	0	0	159.1	159	686	66	55	12	1	2	12	56	0	133	11	0
Bacsik, Mike, Buf.*	12	5	.706	3.26	21	20	2	0	0	0	121.1	115	501	47	44	13	2	0	3	25	0	81	0	0
Moore, Trey, Rich.*	9	8	.529	3.31	26	25	2	0	0	0	163.0	140	665	64	60	9	8	9	4	41	3	122	0	0
Castillo, Carlos, Paw.	9	11	.450	3.41	28	21	5	1	3	0	163.2	179	684	78	62	12	3	8	4	24	1	114	3	2
Douglass, Sean, Roch.	8	9	.471	3.49	27	27	0	0	0	0	162.1	160	710	79	63	13	5	4	5	61	0	156	6	0

Pitcher, Team	W	L	Pct.	ERA	G	GS	CG	ShO	GF	Sv.	IP	H	TBF	R	ER	HR	SH	SF	HB	BB	IBB	SO	WP	Bk.
Parrish, John, Roch.*	7	7	.500	3.52	26	19	1	0	1	0	133.0	115	565	68	52	11	6	5	6	51	4	126	13	0
Lewis, Richie, Buf.-Nor.	9	4	.692	3.55	24	21	0	0	1	1	121.2	102	516	54	48	11	2	0	6	60	2	77	7	0
Luebbers, Larry, Lou.	7	6	.538	3.57	21	18	2	1	1	0	121.0	129	494	54	48	8	5	2	6	24	1	60	3	0
Knight, Brandon, Col.	12	7	.632	3.66	25	25	3	0	0	0	162.1	174	681	77	66	16	4	1	2	45	0	173	9	1
Harper, Travis, Dur.	12	6	.667	3.70	25	25	1	1	0	0	155.2	140	642	70	64	25	11	2	12	38	0	115	7	2

DEPARTMENTAL LEADERS: W—Duckworth, 13; L—Thomas, 13; Pct.—Duckworth, .867; G—Bowles, 66; GS—Chantres, J. Fernandez, 28 each; CG—C. Castillo, 5; ShO—Gonzalez, 2; GF—DeWitt, 47; Sv.—DeWitt, 27; IP—J. Fernandez, 196.1; H—J. Fernandez, 218; TBF—J. Fernandez, 843; R—J. Snyder, 115; ER—Loux, 97; HR—Harper, 25; SH—T. Rose, 10; SF—Harikkala, Loux, 10 each; HB—Dillinger, Loux, 15 each; BB—Chantres, 93; IBB—Nickle, 7; SO—Knight, 173; WP—J. Fernandez, 20; BK—A. Hernandez, Bernero, 5 each.

ALL PITCHERS

*Lefthanded pitcher.

Pitcher, Team	W	L	Pct.	ERA	G	GS	CG	ShO	GF	Sv.	IP	H	TBF	R	ER	HR	SH	SF	HB	BB	IBB	SO	WP	Bk.
Adkins, Tim, Col.*	0	0	.000	0.00	1	0	0	0	1	0	0.1	2	3	0	0	0	0	0	0	0	0	1	0	0
Agamennone, Brandon, Ott.	1	0	1.000	2.38	8	0	0	0	2	0	11.1	6	46	5	3	0	1	0	1	3	0	7	0	0
Agosto, Stevenson, Dur.*	0	0	.000	10.13	3	0	0	0	0	0	5.1	5	27	6	6	2	0	0	0	5	0	5	1	0
Almanzar, Carlos, Col.	2	1	.667	2.43	35	0	0	0	27	18	33.1	36	137	10	9	2	2	0	0	6	2	26	1	0
Alvarez, Wilson, Dur.*	1	1	.500	3.00	4	4	0	0	0	0	18.0	20	79	8	6	2	0	2	0	6	0	16	1	0
Ambrose, John, Paw.	0	0	.000	10.80	2	0	0	0	0	0	3.1	7	21	4	4	0	0	0	0	3	0	0	1	0
Andrews, Clayton, Lou.*	2	2	.500	4.81	8	8	0	0	0	0	43.0	57	196	28	23	7	2	0	1	13	0	19	0	0
Aramboles, Ricardo, Col.	1	3	.250	3.04	4	4	0	0	0	0	23.2	26	102	11	8	2	3	3	0	4	0	14	0	0
Arias, Pablo, Tol.	0	0	.000	8.31	1	1	0	0	0	0	4.1	4	20	5	4	1	0	2	0	2	0	1	0	0
Atchley, Justin, Lou.*	1	0	1.000	0.64	15	0	0	0	3	2	14.0	14	57	1	1	0	1	0	0	3	0	15	0	0
Aybar, Manny, Dur.	1	3	.250	5.68	11	3	0	0	1	0	31.2	40	140	25	20	5	2	4	0	9	0	29	1	2
Bacsik, Mike, Buf.*	12	5	.706	3.26	21	20	2	0	0	0	121.1	115	501	47	44	13	2	0	3	25	0	81	0	0
Baez, Danny, Buf.	2	0	1.000	3.20	16	0	0	0	8	3	25.1	18	100	9	9	2	0	1	0	9	0	30	0	1
Baez, Kevin, Nor.	0	0	.000	10.80	2	0	0	0	2	0	1.2	2	7	2	2	1	0	0	0	3	0	0	0	0
Bailie, Matt, S./W.B.	0	0	.000	0.00	1	0	0	0	1	0	1.1	1	4	0	0	0	0	0	0	0	0	0	0	0
Baldwin, James, Char.	1	0	1.000	5.25	2	2	0	0	0	0	12.0	12	48	7	7	2	1	1	0	2	0	11	0	0
Bale, John, Roch.*	1	1	.500	2.05	9	7	0	0	0	0	30.2	31	125	8	7	1	0	2	0	5	0	41	1	0
Banks, Willie, Syr.-Paw.	10	5	.667	3.11	26	25	0	0	0	0	159.1	159	686	66	55	12	1	2	12	56	0	133	11	0
Baptist, Travis, Char.*	2	5	.286	5.14	33	9	0	0	5	3	61.1	74	279	38	35	8	1	1	2	19	2	43	2	4
Barcelo, Lorenzo, Char.	1	0	1.000	5.40	2	0	0	0	0	0	5.0	6	21	3	3	2	0	0	1	1	0	5	0	0
Bauer, Rick, Roch.	10	4	.714	3.89	19	18	1	1	0	0	113.1	119	493	63	49	10	5	3	4	28	0	89	4	0
Beasley, Ray, Rich.*	1	3	.250	3.76	65	0	0	0	13	0	55.0	58	241	26	23	4	1	2	3	22	5	37	2	0
Bechler, Steve, Roch.	1	1	.500	15.95	2	2	0	0	0	0	7.1	14	44	14	13	4	0	0	0	5	0	6	2	0
Beirne, Kevin, Syr.	1	1	.500	1.57	18	0	0	0	6	0	28.2	24	115	6	5	2	2	0	2	3	1	17	0	0
Bell, Jason, Syr.	1	0	1.000	10.38	8	0	0	0	1	0	8.2	10	44	10	10	4	0	0	1	7	0	7	1	0
Bell, Rob, Lou.	2	2	.500	3.33	5	4	0	0	0	0	27.0	32	118	10	10	4	1	1	1	4	0	26	1	0
Beltran, Rigo, S./W.B.*	2	5	.286	2.96	37	11	0	0	6	2	115.2	87	460	40	38	10	2	3	1	41	6	113	5	0
Bernero, Adam, Tol.	6	11	.353	5.13	26	25	1	0	1	0	140.1	172	641	90	80	13	7	3	10	54	0	99	1	5
Bertotti, Mike, Col.*	1	2	.333	3.70	19	4	0	0	6	0	41.1	37	189	21	17	4	4	1	1	28	0	43	2	0
Billingsley, Brent, Ott.*	0	0	.000	15.00	1	1	0	0	0	0	3.0	6	16	5	5	0	0	1	0	2	0	2	0	0
Blair, Willie, Buf.	4	3	.571	2.75	11	10	1	0	1	0	72.0	72	299	30	22	3	2	1	3	7	0	50	1	2
Blank, Matt, Ott.*	6	7	.462	5.18	14	14	1	0	0	0	81.2	89	367	52	47	13	3	5	8	30	0	58	3	2
Bleazard, Dave, Syr.	0	2	.000	9.88	5	2	0	0	2	0	13.2	15	66	15	15	2	0	0	1	11	0	7	0	0
Borkowski, Dave, Tol.	1	2	.333	3.54	18	0	0	0	4	1	28.0	22	118	14	11	1	3	0	3	9	1	22	2	0
Bowers, Cedrick, Dur.*	6	5	.545	3.06	42	11	0	0	14	0	94.0	83	412	38	32	10	4	4	3	56	1	67	3	0
Bowles, Brian, Syr.	3	5	.375	2.91	66	0	0	0	24	6	77.1	56	338	30	25	3	5	1	7	44	4	81	14	3
Boyd, Jason, S./W.B.*	2	7	.222	1.97	52	0	0	0	35	12	59.1	44	243	17	13	4	2	2	2	22	1	66	1	0
Brea, Lesli, Roch.	6	2	.250	3.83	63	0	0	0	22	1	82.1	80	367	44	35	6	4	2	2	35	3	98	6	1
Bridges, Donnie, Ott.	3	5	.375	7.48	13	13	0	0	0	0	55.1	60	269	50	46	11	2	2	9	43	0	49	8	0
Brittan, Corey, Nor.*	4	2	.667	1.98	58	0	0	0	15	4	81.2	86	347	22	18	4	1	1	3	26	2	45	0	1
Brock, Chris, S./W.B.*	6	2	.750	3.55	13	13	2	0	0	0	78.2	75	320	31	31	9	4	1	4	16	0	56	2	3
Brower, Jim, Lou.	1	0	1.000	4.09	2	2	0	0	0	0	11.0	12	47	5	5	1	0	0	1	2	0	11	0	0
Brown, Derek, Roch.	2	1	.667	8.68	9	0	0	0	5	1	18.2	25	87	18	18	4	1	0	1	6	2	14	1	1
Brunette, Justin, Nor.*	2	2	.500	9.69	24	0	0	0	6	0	26.0	42	132	32	28	5	3	0	0	15	3	23	1	0
Buddie, Mike, Ind.	4	1	.800	2.31	27	0	0	0	12	3	46.2	36	194	13	12	4	0	2	0	25	4	31	4	0
Buller, Sean, Tol.*	1	0	1.000	1.69	5	0	0	0	1	0	10.2	8	44	2	2	0	0	0	0	5	0	9	0	0
Bullinger, Kirk, Char.	0	3	.000	3.58	36	1	0	0	16	5	50.1	44	212	23	20	5	5	4	4	21	6	34	3	0
Burrows, Terry, Ott.*	0	1	.000	3.24	6	0	0	0	1	0	8.1	7	38	7	3	0	1	0	1	5	1	6	1	0
Byrd, Paul, S./W.B.	1	3	.250	3.65	5	5	0	0	0	0	37.0	34	155	18	15	4	2	0	4	7	0	35	0	0
Byrdak, Tim, Buf.*	2	0	1.000	4.67	4	3	0	0	0	0	17.1	18	75	10	9	1	1	0	1	5	0	17	1	0
Callaway, Mickey, Dur.	11	7	.611	3.07	29	21	2	1	3	0	129.0	131	532	50	44	9	5	3	5	24	0	81	7	1
Carter, Mike, Rich.	0	1	.000	13.50	1	0	0	0	1	0	0.2	0	6	1	1	0	1	0	0	4	1	0	0	0
Cassidy, Scott, Syr.	3	3	.500	2.71	11	11	0	0	0	0	63.0	60	276	24	19	6	0	1	6	26	0	48	1	0
Castillo, Carlos, Paw.	9	11	.450	3.41	28	21	5	1	3	0	163.2	179	684	78	62	12	3	8	4	24	1	114	3	2
Castillo, Frank, Paw.	0	0	.000	0.00	2	2	0	0	0	0	7.2	7	29	1	0	0	0	1	0	0	0	3	0	0
Cedeno, Blas, S./W.B.	3	4	.429	4.45	35	0	0	0	17	1	58.2	56	254	29	29	9	2	3	4	23	3	52	2	1
Cerda, Jaime, Nor.*	0	0	.000	3.86	3	0	0	0	1	0	4.2	2	18	2	2	0	0	0	0	2	0	4	1	0
Cerros, Juan, Nor.	1	3	.250	3.89	38	1	0	0	8	1	57.0	65	257	33	25	5	1	6	4	23	3	32	5	0
Chantres, Carlos, Ind.	7	11	.389	4.41	28	28	0	0	0	0	167.1	176	760	93	82	15	8	8	9	93	1	87	6	1
Chen, Bruce, S./W.B.*	1	0	1.000	3.86	3	3	0	0	0	0	18.2	14	74	8	8	2	2	0	1	5	0	14	2	0
Cho, Jin Ho, Paw.	3	10	.231	4.51	37	16	0	0	17	10	117.2	133	492	62	59	14	4	4	5	17	3	77	2	0
Choate, Randy, Col.*	0	1	.000	2.08	4	0	0	0	1	0	4.1	7	21	1	1	0	0	0	0	3	0	4	1	0
Chulk, Vinny, Syr.	1	0	1.000	1.50	5	0	0	0	2	0	6.0	5	25	1	1	0	0	0	0	4	0	3	3	0
Coco, Pasqual, Syr.	8	6	.571	4.66	22	22	0	0	0	0	121.2	128	529	67	63	11	1	7	8	50	0	82	9	3
Coggin, Dave, S./W.B.	5	5	.500	3.05	15	15	0	0	0	0	97.1	93	406	36	33	6	2	2	4	31	0	53	4	0
Colome, Jesus, Dur.	0	3	.000	6.23	13	0	0	0	3	0	17.1	22	79	13	12	1	1	1	2	6	0	18	3	0
Comolli, Mark, Syr.	0	0	.000	0.00	1	1	0	0	0	0	4.0	4	15	1	0	0	0	0	0	1	0	1	0	0
Cook, Dennis, S./W.B.*	0	0	.000	9.00	1	0	0	0	0	0	1.0	1	7	1	1	0	0	0	0	2	0	1	0	0

Pitcher, Team	W	L	Pct.	ERA	G	GS	CG	ShO	GF	Sv.	IP	H	TBF	R	ER	HR	SH	SF	HB	BB	IBB	SO	WP	Bk.
Coppinger, Rocky, Ind.	6	1	.857	1.88	15	5	0	0	3	0	48.0	25	182	10	10	2	2	1	1	20	1	42	2	0
Corbin, Archie, Char.	6	7	.462	3.14	58	0	0	0	20	4	77.1	58	336	29	27	3	4	1	6	54	6	64	13	0
Corey, Mark, Nor.	8	2	.800	1.47	28	0	0	0	20	10	36.2	24	147	7	6	1	3	0	0	22	0	42	0	0
Cornejo, Nate, Tol.	4	0	1.000	2.12	4	4	0	0	0	0	29.2	24	113	8	7	1	1	0	0	7	0	22	1	0
Cornett, Brad, Syr.-Dur.	5	2	.714	2.72	39	2	0	0	8	2	72.2	73	308	30	22	3	4	1	2	17	1	61	7	0
Crawford, Paxton, Paw.	1	3	.250	5.52	6	6	1	0	0	0	29.1	43	133	19	18	4	0	1	2	7	1	15	1	0
Croushore, Rich, Nor.	0	0	.000	3.38	10	1	0	0	3	0	13.1	8	55	5	5	1	0	2	4	5	0	10	2	0
Cubillan, Darwin, Ott.	2	2	.500	5.28	17	4	0	0	8	2	30.2	31	137	22	18	2	2	2	2	15	1	29	4	0
Cumberland, Chris, Rich.*	2	3	.400	4.86	13	1	0	0	3	1	16.2	23	76	11	9	1	0	1	0	7	1	10	1	1
Cunnane, Will, Ind.	0	1	.000	3.86	7	3	0	0	3	1	23.1	25	98	10	10	2	0	1	1	6	1	25	0	0
Curreri, Joe, Char.	1	0	1.000	0.00	1	0	0	0	0	0	3.0	4	12	0	0	0	0	0	0	0	0	3	0	0
Danaker, Pat, Syr.	2	5	.286	8.94	10	10	1	0	0	0	50.1	75	237	53	50	9	3	2	3	17	0	14	3	0
Darnell, Paul, Lou.*	2	0	1.000	2.57	21	0	0	0	5	0	21.0	15	90	6	6	3	2	0	0	11	1	32	1	0
Darwin, Dave, Buf.*	0	1	.000	3.06	4	3	0	0	0	0	17.2	20	73	12	6	1	0	0	4	8	0	13	0	0
Davis, Lance, Lou.*	7	2	.778	3.05	13	13	1	1	0	0	79.2	81	328	31	27	7	3	0	1	15	1	47	1	0
Davison, Scott, Dur.	0	0	.000	18.90	2	0	0	0	1	0	3.1	9	20	7	7	0	0	0	2	0	0	3	0	0
Dawley, Joey, Rich.	1	0	1.000	2.84	3	0	0	0	1	0	6.1	3	22	2	2	1	0	0	1	0	0	5	1	0
Day, Zach, Buf.-Ott.	3	2	.600	6.34	7	6	0	0	0	0	32.2	41	142	24	23	2	0	1	2	9	0	19	3	0
DeLucia, Rich, Tol.	1	1	.500	2.54	28	0	0	0	12	5	39.0	27	156	11	11	3	1	0	0	15	0	45	1	0
De Paula, Sean, Buf.	1	0	1.000	1.04	6	0	0	0	4	1	8.2	2	32	1	1	0	0	1	0	4	0	6	0	0
Deschenes, Marc, Buf.	2	2	.500	6.37	22	0	0	0	6	0	29.2	38	149	23	21	4	2	0	2	23	1	29	2	1
Dewitt, Matt, Syr.	3	2	.600	2.78	53	0	0	0	47	27	58.1	45	239	20	18	4	3	0	1	17	1	44	2	0
Dickson, Jason, Syr.	4	7	.364	7.18	11	11	0	0	0	0	57.2	75	267	52	46	11	5	3	6	19	0	40	0	0
Dillinger, John, Syr.	11	7	.611	3.99	26	26	1	1	0	0	155.2	150	669	79	69	10	4	5	15	58	1	108	15	0
Douglass, Sean, Roch.	8	9	.471	3.49	27	27	0	0	0	0	162.1	160	710	79	63	13	5	4	5	61	0	156	6	0
Drese, Ryan, Buf.	5	1	.833	4.01	11	10	0	0	0	0	60.2	60	255	28	27	7	2	1	6	17	0	52	1	1
Drew, Tim, Buf.	8	6	.571	3.92	18	18	1	1	0	0	108.0	115	467	54	47	13	2	0	8	27	1	75	6	1
Duckworth, Brandon, S./W.B.	13	2	.867	2.63	22	20	2	1	1	0	147.0	122	584	46	43	14	5	2	7	36	2	150	5	0
Ebert, Derrin, Paw.*	2	3	.400	4.53	10	7	1	0	0	0	43.2	50	192	29	22	4	1	1	1	10	0	34	2	0
Eischen, Joey, Ott.*	2	3	.400	2.24	34	1	0	0	17	7	52.1	42	205	16	13	6	1	0	2	11	0	54	1	0
Enders, Trevor, Dur.*	2	5	.286	4.98	32	1	0	0	10	0	47.0	51	201	26	26	8	4	5	3	14	2	26	1	0
Erdos, Todd, Paw.	5	1	.833	3.06	49	0	0	0	21	7	67.2	59	282	25	23	3	2	5	1	24	4	54	1	1
Eshelman, Vaughn, Nor.*	2	0	1.000	3.18	7	1	0	0	4	0	11.1	13	56	6	4	0	2	1	3	7	1	4	0	0
Espina, Rendy, Syr.*	6	1	.857	3.64	38	0	0	0	11	0	47.0	41	199	26	19	4	1	1	5	17	1	33	1	1
Estrella, Leo, Nor.-Lou.	3	1	.750	4.50	42	6	0	0	9	1	80.0	90	350	43	40	9	2	2	4	35	0	47	6	0
Evans, Keith, Ott.	7	3	.700	3.98	45	2	0	0	10	1	83.2	94	357	40	37	7	2	2	4	13	0	72	1	1
Eyre, Scott, Syr.*	4	6	.400	3.18	62	2	0	0	12	0	79.1	67	334	30	28	8	1	3	5	26	4	96	6	0
Farrell, Jim, Paw.	0	0	.000	0.00	1	0	0	0	0	0	1.0	1	4	0	0	0	0	0	0	0	0	1	0	0
Felix, Miguel, Roch.	0	1	.000	11.57	1	1	0	0	0	0	4.2	5	24	6	6	1	0	0	0	5	0	3	1	0
Fernandez, Jared, Lou.	10	9	.526	4.13	33	28	4	1	2	0	196.1	218	843	105	90	24	3	1	0	54	0	118	20	0
Fernandez, Ozzie, Lou.	3	2	.600	3.86	9	9	0	0	0	0	53.2	54	220	26	23	6	3	0	0	12	1	31	1	1
Fernandez, Sid, Col.*	0	0	.000	13.50	1	1	0	0	0	0	2.0	3	10	3	3	1	0	0	0	2	0	3	0	0
Figueroa, Nelson, S./W.B.	4	2	.667	2.47	13	12	3	0	0	0	87.1	74	359	33	24	6	4	1	5	18	2	74	3	0
File, Bob, Syr.	0	0	.000	0.00	2	0	0	0	1	0	4.0	1	14	0	0	0	0	0	2	0	0	3	0	0
Fiore, Tony, Dur.	1	0	1.000	0.00	15	0	0	0	9	3	20.1	7	76	0	0	0	0	1	8	0	11	0	0
Flores, Neomar, Syr.	0	0	.000	3.86	2	1	0	0	0	0	7.0	4	27	3	3	1	0	0	0	2	0	2	0	0
Flores, Randy, Col.*	0	1	.000	4.76	3	0	0	0	1	0	5.2	5	23	4	3	2	0	0	0	2	0	4	1	0
Florie, Bryce, Tol.	2	1	.667	6.17	10	0	0	0	5	0	11.2	14	59	8	8	1	0	0	13	0	10	3	0
Flury, Pat, Ott.-Col.	3	3	.500	2.90	44	0	0	0	24	3	59.0	39	242	19	19	5	3	3	2	27	1	75	2	0
Fogg, Josh, Char.	4	7	.364	4.79	40	16	0	0	19	4	114.2	129	497	68	61	19	6	1	4	30	1	89	4	0
Fordham, Tom, Ind.*	1	2	.333	2.58	18	5	1	0	5	0	38.1	25	152	15	11	6	1	1	0	13	0	35	2	1
Forster, Scott, Lou.*	1	0	1.000	1.74	9	0	0	0	2	0	10.1	7	46	3	2	0	1	0	0	9	1	9	2	0
Foster, Kris, Roch.	0	1	.000	5.40	9	0	0	0	9	6	10.0	11	47	8	6	1	2	0	1	6	1	11	1	0
Fox, Chad, Ind.	3	0	1.000	1.50	4	0	0	0	4	0	6.0	4	25	1	1	0	1	0	3	0	8	0	0
Frank, Mike, Col.*	0	0	.000	0.00	1	0	0	0	0	0	2.0	1	9	0	0	0	0	0	0	2	0	2	1	0
Frascatore, John, Syr.	1	4	.200	4.14	37	0	0	0	12	2	37.0	47	167	20	17	4	4	0	1	9	1	18	2	0
Gandarillas, Gus, Paw.-Ind.	4	3	.571	2.99	40	5	0	0	18	2	81.1	81	341	39	27	4	3	4	3	23	2	59	1	1
Garcia, Carlos, Col.	0	1	.000	27.00	1	0	0	0	1	0	0.2	1	4	2	2	0	0	1	0	1	0	0	0	0
Gardner, Lee, Dur.	5	2	.714	2.72	56	0	0	0	18	2	76.0	76	324	27	23	10	3	2	2	23	2	55	4	0
Garland, Jon, Char.	0	3	.000	2.73	5	5	1	0	0	0	33.0	31	134	10	10	1	2	1	1	11	1	26	0	0
Geary, Geoff, S./W.B.	0	3	.000	6.95	7	3	0	0	0	0	22.0	35	101	17	17	2	1	0	1	6	1	21	0	1
Ginter, Matt, Char.	2	3	.400	2.59	22	10	0	0	2	0	76.1	62	319	26	22	3	2	3	7	24	4	67	5	0
Glauber, Keith, Lou.	3	3	.500	5.65	23	0	0	0	6	0	36.2	45	167	30	23	8	2	1	5	10	1	24	4	0
Glover, Gary, Char.	2	1	.667	1.88	6	6	1	0	0	0	38.1	21	139	8	8	3	0	0	1	5	0	29	0	0
Gonzalez, Dicky, Nor.	6	5	.545	3.09	17	16	2	2	0	0	96.0	96	392	35	33	10	4	6	4	20	1	70	2	0
Gooch, Arnie, Lou.	7	10	.412	5.63	28	26	1	0	1	0	148.2	175	657	101	93	16	6	6	43	1	95	8	0
Guerrier, Matt, Char.	7	1	.875	3.54	12	12	3	0	0	0	81.1	75	328	33	32	7	4	2	4	10	0	43	2	0
Guevara, Giomar, Tol.	0	0	.000	0.00	1	0	0	0	1	0	1.0	1	4	0	0	0	0	0	0	0	0	1	0	0
Gunderson, Eric, Buf.-Col.*	2	4	.333	2.97	58	0	0	0	18	7	75.2	72	316	33	25	6	4	2	3	24	1	63	3	0
Guzman, Juan, Dur.	4	2	.667	4.77	10	10	0	0	0	0	60.1	50	259	35	32	7	5	4	5	30	0	42	4	0
Haines, Talley, Dur.	0	0	.000	0.00	1	0	0	0	1	0	2.0	0	6	0	0	0	0	0	0	0	0	1	0	0
Halladay, Roy, Syr.	1	0	1.000	3.21	2	2	0	0	0	0	14.0	12	55	5	5	2	1	0	0	0	0	13	2	0
Hamilton, Jimmy, Roch.*	0	3	.000	4.53	36	1	0	0	9	1	55.2	58	248	29	28	4	5	3	2	27	1	49	5	0
Hamilton, Joey, Lou.	1	0	1.000	5.40	1	1	0	0	0	0	5.0	4	20	3	3	1	0	1	0	1	0	1	0	0
Hammond, Chris, Buf.-Rich.*	10	4	.714	2.95	49	4	0	0	7	1	82.1	85	345	31	27	5	2	0	2	24	1	83	1	0
Hannah, Shawn, Tol.	0	0	.000	7.50	1	1	0	0	0	0	6.0	6	24	5	5	1	0	0	0	4	0	2	0	0
Harikkala, Tim, Ind.	11	10	.524	4.76	31	27	1	0	3	0	172.0	210	757	104	91	15	8	10	7	42	1	96	2	1
Harnisch, Pete, Lou.	0	1	.000	54.00	1	1	0	0	0	0	0.1	3	4	3	2	0	0	0	0	1	0	0	0	0
Harper, Travis, Dur.	12	6	.667	3.70	25	25	1	1	0	0	155.2	140	642	70	64	25	5	7	12	38	0	115	7	2
Hasselhoff, Derek, Char.	6	1	.857	2.03	34	0	0	0	17	6	44.1	29	173	14	10	4	2	1	0	12	2	41	0	1
Hazlett, Andy, Paw.*	2	0	1.000	1.59	9	1	0	0	3	1	22.2	14	83	4	4	3	0	0	3	0	18	0	0
Heams, Shane, Tol.	1	2	.333	9.00	14	0	0	0	5	0	18.0	20	100	19	18	4	0	0	1	27	0	21	9	0
Heiserman, Rick, Paw.	0	0	.000	6.23	3	0	0	0	2	0	4.1	4	20	3	3	1	0	0	0	4	0	2	0	0

Pitcher, Team	W	L	Pct.	ERA	G	GS	CG	ShO	GF	Sv.	IP	H	TBF	R	ER	HR	SH	SF	HB	BB	IBB	SO	WP	Bk.
Hendrickson, Mark, Syr.*	2	9	.182	4.66	38	6	0	0	7	0	73.1	80	315	43	38	13	2	0	3	18	1	33	2	0
Henriquez, Oscar, Nor.	2	4	.333	2.82	39	0	0	0	32	19	38.1	30	162	13	12	1	5	1	2	19	0	44	0	0
Henry, Butch, Syr.-Ind.-Col.* ..	8	8	.500	5.03	18	18	2	0	0	0	116.1	140	491	70	65	14	2	4	3	18	1	77	0	1
Hernandez, Adrian, Col.	8	7	.533	5.51	21	21	0	0	0	0	117.2	116	515	75	72	13	4	4	10	60	1	97	10	5
Hill, Ken, Lou.-Paw.	4	2	.667	5.57	14	14	0	0	0	0	63.0	75	289	46	39	9	5	2	2	23	0	33	6	0
Hinchliffe, Brett, Nor.	3	2	.600	3.02	11	10	0	0	1	0	59.2	67	257	30	20	7	0	0	0	17	1	46	0	0
Hooten, Dave, Buf.	1	0	1.000	1.80	1	1	0	0	0	0	5.0	5	20	1	1	0	0	0	0	1	0	2	0	0
Huisman, Rick, Roch.	0	1	.000	6.35	15	0	0	0	8	1	17.0	24	84	13	12	4	1	1	0	9	1	13	2	0
Irabu, Hideki, Ott.	1	2	.333	4.43	4	4	0	0	0	0	22.1	22	92	12	11	2	0	0	2	6	0	21	4	1
Jacquez, Tom, S./W.B.*	10	6	.625	3.13	33	9	1	0	6	0	109.1	100	443	43	38	8	3	2	3	29	1	86	0	0
James, Delvin, Dur.	3	7	.300	4.80	31	9	1	0	8	0	84.1	99	373	51	45	8	4	2	5	27	1	51	6	0
Jean, Domingo, Col.	2	4	.333	3.92	35	0	0	0	15	3	41.1	51	201	23	18	1	0	2	2	22	2	45	7	0
Jimenez, Jason, Dur.*	0	1	.000	4.70	15	0	0	0	8	1	23.0	23	102	12	12	4	0	0	0	14	0	25	0	0
Jodie, Brett, Col.	10	4	.714	3.01	19	19	2	1	0	0	119.2	123	498	46	40	9	3	3	3	25	0	59	3	1
Johnson, Barry, Col.	4	2	.667	4.12	38	1	0	0	16	1	63.1	64	268	32	29	7	2	4	2	19	2	37	0	0
Johnson, Mark, Tol.	7	11	.389	4.79	24	24	2	1	0	0	141.0	170	609	83	75	21	2	3	8	24	1	79	6	1
Johnson, Mike, Ott.	2	0	1.000	4.50	2	2	0	0	0	0	10.0	7	38	5	5	1	1	0	0	3	0	8	2	0
Jones, Bobby M., Nor.*	0	0	.000	0.00	1	1	0	0	0	0	2.0	0	6	0	0	0	0	0	0	0	0	0	0	0
Juden, Jeff, Char.	5	5	.500	3.32	12	11	1	0	0	0	65.0	44	281	34	24	5	0	0	2	46	0	63	2	1
Julio, Jorge, Roch.	1	2	.333	3.74	34	0	0	0	24	12	43.1	39	196	27	18	4	2	2	5	19	3	48	5	1
Kane, Kyle, Char.	0	0	.000	6.00	1	1	0	0	0	0	3.0	4	13	2	2	0	0	0	0	1	0	0	0	0
Keisler, Randy, Col.*	5	7	.417	5.18	18	18	3	1	0	0	97.1	111	444	67	56	10	3	3	3	39	0	88	0	0
Keller, Kris, Tol.	5	2	.714	4.48	52	0	0	0	23	4	68.1	64	302	42	34	10	0	4	3	38	3	60	10	0
Kennedy, Joe, Dur.*	2	0	1.000	2.42	4	4	0	0	0	0	26.0	22	109	8	7	2	1	0	2	9	0	23	7	0
Kershner, Jason, S./W.B.*	1	1	.500	3.60	6	1	0	0	1	0	15.0	12	63	8	6	3	0	2	0	3	0	7	0	0
Kim, Sun-Woo, Paw.	6	7	.462	5.36	19	14	0	0	3	0	89.0	93	384	55	53	10	7	2	6	27	1	79	4	1
Knight, Brandon, Col.	12	7	.632	3.66	25	25	3	0	0	0	162.1	174	681	77	66	16	4	1	2	45	0	173	9	1
Kohlmeier, Ryan, Roch.	1	4	.200	2.36	14	7	0	0	6	4	42.0	36	170	15	11	4	2	1	0	8	0	28	1	2
Kolb, Brandon, Ind.	3	5	.375	4.28	40	0	0	0	29	14	54.2	49	236	28	26	7	2	0	0	22	4	57	2	0
Kusiewicz, Mike, Paw.*	2	2	.500	4.66	8	7	0	0	0	0	36.2	42	162	23	19	3	1	0	2	12	0	31	1	0
Lail, Denny, Col.	6	6	.500	4.61	33	20	0	0	2	0	136.2	144	591	84	70	11	4	8	6	46	1	105	3	2
Lakman, Jason, Roch.	1	0	1.000	3.42	19	0	0	0	9	1	26.1	32	119	13	10	1	1	2	2	9	1	12	3	1
Lee, Sang, Paw.*	3	5	.375	5.43	43	0	0	0	21	4	53.0	52	227	33	32	11	2	2	1	16	3	44	3	2
Leek, Randy, Tol.*	0	0	.000	3.86	1	1	0	0	0	0	7.0	7	27	3	3	3	0	0	0	0	0	3	0	0
Levrault, Allen, Ind.	2	1	.667	2.64	5	5	0	0	0	0	30.2	22	120	9	9	1	1	0	1	8	1	30	0	0
Lewis, Derrick, Rich.	4	4	.500	4.45	12	12	0	0	0	0	60.2	50	256	34	30	2	1	1	1	37	2	50	5	0
Lewis, Richie, Buf.-Nor.	9	4	.692	3.55	24	21	0	0	1	1	121.2	102	516	54	48	11	2	0	6	60	1	77	7	0
Ligtenberg, Kerry, Rich.	0	0	.000	0.00	1	0	0	0	1	0	1.0	0	4	0	0	0	0	0	0	1	0	2	0	0
Lilly, Ted, Col.*	0	0	.000	2.84	5	5	0	0	0	0	25.1	16	101	10	8	2	0	1	1	8	0	30	1	0
Linton, Doug, Nor.	7	3	.700	3.21	12	12	0	0	0	0	75.2	74	302	28	27	8	4	3	2	10	0	67	2	1
Lira, Felipe, Ott.-S./W.B.	5	5	.500	2.47	44	2	0	0	19	6	69.1	73	285	22	19	4	8	0	0	10	2	53	1	0
Lohrman, Dave, Nor.	0	0	.000	6.00	2	0	0	0	1	0	3.0	4	12	2	2	1	0	0	0	0	0	3	0	0
Loux, Shane, Tol.	10	11	.476	5.78	28	27	2	0	1	0	151.0	203	727	111	97	22	4	10	15	73	0	72	14	1
Lovingier, Kevin, Col.*	0	2	.000	4.50	7	0	0	0	2	0	10.0	13	51	9	5	1	1	0	0	7	0	9	1	0
Lowe, Sean, Char.	1	1	.500	4.50	2	2	0	0	0	0	10.0	9	42	6	5	0	0	1	2	0	0	8	0	0
Luebbers, Larry, Lou.	7	6	.538	3.57	21	18	2	1	1	0	121.0	129	494	54	48	8	5	2	6	24	1	60	3	0
Lyon, Brandon, Syr.	5	3	.625	3.69	11	11	2	1	0	0	68.1	68	279	33	28	7	1	2	1	10	0	53	0	0
MacRae, Scott, Lou.	2	2	.500	1.23	11	0	0	0	3	2	22.0	14	83	5	3	1	1	0	1	6	2	15	0	0
Maduro, Calvin, Roch.	2	7	.222	4.03	12	11	1	1	0	0	67.0	61	286	37	30	9	2	2	4	22	0	48	4	0
Mallette, Brian, Ind.	0	1	.000	1.06	12	0	0	0	6	2	17.0	10	69	4	2	2	0	1	1	8	0	23	1	0
Manon, Julio, Ott.	1	4	.200	3.11	15	14	0	0	1	0	84.0	71	339	31	29	11	2	0	0	34	0	67	2	0
Maroth, Mike, Tol.*	7	10	.412	4.65	24	23	0	0	0	0	131.2	158	587	80	68	11	5	5	4	50	1	63	4	0
Marquez, Rob, Ott.	6	0	1.000	2.97	34	0	0	0	7	0	60.2	57	245	23	20	5	0	3	4	12	2	27	3	0
Martin, Tom, Nor.*	2	1	.667	6.26	23	0	0	0	8	1	23.0	31	108	17	16	4	0	2	2	10	0	24	1	0
Masaoka, Onan, Char.*	0	1	.000	4.30	14	0	0	0	8	5	14.2	11	59	8	7	2	1	0	1	5	0	22	0	0
Mattes, Troy, Ott.	5	5	.500	3.61	15	15	0	0	0	0	82.1	75	354	38	33	3	3	4	5	33	1	70	4	1
Maurer, Dave, Lou.*	0	1	.000	4.15	18	0	0	0	7	1	21.2	18	91	11	10	4	1	2	1	7	0	23	0	0
McClellan, Matt, Syr.	1	2	.333	3.27	29	1	0	0	12	2	52.1	49	228	21	19	4	1	3	2	20	1	44	6	0
McClendon, Matt, Rich.	0	6	.000	8.16	10	10	0	0	0	0	46.1	50	219	45	42	5	3	3	2	31	4	31	0	2
McDill, Allen, Paw.*	3	3	.500	3.42	47	0	0	0	12	5	71.0	62	295	27	27	7	6	2	5	19	1	72	4	2
McLeary, Marty, Paw.	1	2	.333	3.00	18	0	0	0	9	0	30.0	28	127	13	10	4	2	1	6	15	1	20	1	0
McNichol, Brian, Lou.*	4	1	.800	1.59	26	0	0	0	6	0	28.1	23	112	8	5	1	1	2	1	5	0	22	0	0
Meacham, Rusty, Dur.	2	1	.667	0.87	27	0	0	0	26	15	31.0	17	114	4	3	2	2	0	1	5	0	30	1	0
Mendoza, Geronimo, Char.	5	8	.385	4.95	17	15	0	0	1	0	96.1	103	407	57	53	16	2	5	1	31	2	68	6	0
Mercado, Hector, Lou.*	1	0	1.000	1.35	12	0	0	0	4	1	13.1	12	55	2	2	0	0	0	1	6	1	13	1	0
Mieses, Jose, Ind.	0	3	.000	6.08	3	3	0	0	0	0	13.1	23	72	12	9	4	1	0	0	7	0	13	2	0
Miller, Matt, Tol.*	1	2	.333	2.87	50	0	0	0	20	4	62.2	60	260	26	20	3	5	1	4	18	3	49	1	0
Miller, Ryan, Nor.	0	0	.000	108.00	1	0	0	0	1	0	0.1	2	5	4	4	0	0	0	0	1	0	0	1	0
Miller, Trever, Paw.*	3	11	.214	5.20	33	15	0	0	8	0	116.0	142	514	79	67	16	4	6	7	34	2	93	2	1
Mitchell, Scott, Ott.	0	1	.000	4.12	6	2	0	0	2	0	19.2	17	81	10	9	1	0	0	0	10	0	13	3	0
Mix, Greg, Paw.	0	0	.000	8.53	8	1	0	0	1	0	12.2	15	59	12	12	3	0	1	0	7	0	15	0	0
Moehler, Brian, Tol.	0	2	.000	4.35	2	2	0	0	0	0	10.1	12	45	6	5	2	0	0	2	0	0	6	2	0
Montane, Ivan, Nor.	1	4	.200	4.14	15	2	0	0	6	0	37.0	40	174	23	17	4	2	1	4	23	1	26	2	0
Moore, Trey, Rich.*	9	8	.529	3.31	26	25	2	0	0	0	163.0	140	665	64	60	9	8	9	4	41	3	122	6	0
Moss, Damian, Rich.*	5	4	.556	3.15	17	16	0	0	0	0	88.2	75	372	34	31	10	5	2	3	38	1	94	5	0
Mota, Guillermo, Ott.	0	0	.000	2.25	4	0	0	0	1	0	4.0	1	13	1	1	1	0	0	0	0	0	4	0	0
Munoz, Bobby, Ott.	4	6	.400	3.44	19	18	1	1	0	0	110.0	98	455	47	42	5	8	4	4	39	2	66	4	0
Murray, Heath, Tol.*	1	1	.500	2.00	11	3	0	0	1	1	36.0	22	131	9	8	5	0	0	2	0	0	44	0	0
Nagy, Charles, Buf.	5	1	.833	2.56	6	6	0	0	0	0	38.2	40	161	12	11	0	1	0	1	9	0	18	0	0
Nelson, Joe, Rich.	1	2	.333	1.13	29	0	0	0	12	8	39.2	23	152	5	5	1	4	0	0	14	2	40	3	0
Neugebauer, Nick, Ind.	2	1	.667	1.50	4	4	0	0	0	0	24.0	10	89	5	4	1	1	0	1	9	0	26	1	0
Nichting, Chris, Lou.	2	1	.667	2.97	27	0	0	0	23	17	33.1	24	135	11	11	5	2	1	2	10	0	45	0	0
Nickle, Doug, S./W.B.	9	3	.750	1.68	47	1	0	0	27	7	85.2	62	347	19	16	2	6	2	1	37	7	60	5	1

Pitcher, Team	W	L	Pct.	ERA	G	GS	CG	ShO	GF	Sv.	IP	H	TBF	R	ER	HR	SH	SF	HB	BB	IBB	SO	WP	Bk.
Nitkowski, C.J., Tol.*	0	0	.000	0.00	1	0	0	0	1	0	1.0	1	4	0	0	0	0	0	0	0	0	1	0	0
Ochoa, Pablo, Nor.	3	4	.429	3.67	19	13	0	0	0	0	73.2	71	315	38	30	7	1	1	4	27	0	49	1	2
Ogea, Chad, Col.	0	4	.000	7.81	6	6	0	0	0	0	27.2	34	127	24	24	6	1	0	0	15	1	21	0	0
Ohka, Tomo, Paw.	2	5	.286	5.57	8	8	1	0	0	0	42.0	55	188	35	26	5	4	3	1	9	0	33	3	0
Ontiveros, Steve, Nor.	2	2	.500	2.83	7	7	1	1	0	0	41.1	32	166	13	13	2	0	0	5	9	0	28	3	1
Oropesa, Eddie, S./W.B.*	1	1	.500	2.35	14	1	0	0	3	0	15.1	14	61	5	4	1	0	0	0	4	1	11	1	0
Pacheco, Delvis, Rich.	1	4	.200	5.28	22	9	1	0	5	0	58.0	78	269	36	34	4	2	2	1	24	2	51	2	1
Padilla, Vicente, S./W.B.	7	0	1.000	2.42	16	16	0	0	0	0	81.2	64	313	24	22	8	1	3	3	11	0	75	3	1
Painter, Lance, Ind.*	0	0	.000	5.00	8	0	0	0	3	0	9.0	10	43	5	5	3	2	1	0	6	0	7	0	0
Paronto, Chad, Roch.	3	3	.500	4.57	33	0	0	0	10	1	43.1	44	199	28	22	5	2	1	4	24	4	39	2	0
Parris, Steve, Syr.	0	0	.000	4.70	2	2	0	0	0	0	7.2	6	32	4	4	1	0	1	2	0	8	1	0
Parrish, John, Roch.*	7	7	.500	3.52	26	19	1	0	1	0	133.0	115	565	68	52	11	6	5	6	51	4	126	13	0
Pavano, Carl, Ott.	2	1	.667	3.58	4	4	0	0	0	0	27.2	27	118	13	11	4	1	0	3	5	0	19	1	0
Pena, Jesus, Paw.*	3	5	.375	6.59	26	8	0	0	4	0	72.1	92	341	59	53	10	2	5	4	38	3	42	3	3
Penney, Mike, Ind.	4	3	.571	5.37	22	5	0	0	5	1	57.0	70	254	38	34	8	2	2	1	23	0	35	0	0
Perez, Odaliz, Rich.*	1	0	1.000	2.74	5	5	0	0	0	0	23.0	23	92	7	7	1	0	0	0	2	0	22	0	0
Perisho, Matt, Tol.*	2	3	.400	1.71	25	2	0	0	19	9	42.0	42	173	10	8	3	0	1	0	11	0	28	0	0
Persails, Mark, Tol.	2	3	.400	5.77	12	5	0	0	4	0	48.1	53	218	37	31	5	2	3	2	21	0	24	1	0
Peters, Chris, Lou.-Col.*	5	5	.500	5.25	17	14	0	0	1	0	84.0	102	400	62	49	9	2	0	9	43	2	45	14	0
Peterson, Kyle, Ind.	2	10	.167	5.71	21	20	0	0	0	0	115.0	143	511	81	73	17	6	6	7	26	0	73	1	2
Pettyjohn, Adam, Tol.*	5	8	.385	3.44	17	17	0	0	0	0	107.1	107	449	51	41	9	3	6	4	26	0	78	5	1
Phelps, Tommy, Tol.*	3	2	.600	3.62	29	0	0	0	8	1	59.2	74	271	30	24	4	0	1	3	19	3	53	1	0
Phelps, Travis, Dur.	2	0	1.000	0.00	9	0	0	0	1	0	15.2	11	57	0	0	0	1	0	1	1	0	12	1	0
Phillips, Jason, Buf.	2	2	.500	3.34	8	6	1	0	1	0	35.0	27	138	15	13	3	0	1	2	8	0	25	0	0
Pichardo, Hipolito, Paw.	0	0	.000	5.40	3	3	0	0	0	0	5.0	3	21	3	3	0	0	0	0	4	0	2	0	0
Pina, Rafael, Roch.	1	3	.250	2.48	13	6	1	0	2	0	40.0	45	173	17	11	2	1	1	1	12	0	30	2	0
Pineda, Luis, Tol.	1	0	1.000	0.00	2	0	0	0	0	0	8.0	3	27	0	0	0	0	0	0	0	0	6	0	0
Porzio, Mike, Char.*	6	6	.500	4.35	31	23	0	0	2	0	134.1	138	592	76	65	14	6	6	8	55	2	107	9	1
Prieto, Ariel, Dur.	0	0	.000	1.35	3	0	0	0	0	0	6.2	3	25	2	1	0	0	0	2	0	0	10	0	0
Pujals, Denis, Dur.	0	0	.000	5.40	2	0	0	0	0	0	5.0	5	23	5	3	2	0	2	1	2	0	2	0	0
Pulsipher, Bill, Paw.*	1	1	.500	2.87	24	0	0	0	16	10	31.1	27	129	12	10	1	0	1	0	10	1	23	2	1
Radinsky, Scott, Buf.*	0	0	.000	4.11	16	0	0	0	5	1	15.1	13	56	7	7	0	1	2	0	1	0	7	0	1
Rain, Steve, Ind.	2	2	.500	7.39	25	0	0	0	11	1	35.1	35	180	34	29	4	2	0	5	34	2	34	5	0
Rauch, Jon, Char.	1	3	.250	5.79	6	6	0	0	0	0	28.0	28	121	20	18	8	0	0	1	7	0	27	1	0
Reames, Britt, Ott.	4	3	.571	3.50	8	8	1	0	0	0	54.0	47	212	24	21	4	3	1	1	13	0	38	1	0
Redman, Mark, Tol.*	0	1	.000	5.27	3	3	0	0	0	0	13.2	14	57	10	8	3	0	1	1	1	0	12	0	1
Reed, Brandon, Col.	1	2	.333	3.48	24	0	0	0	8	1	33.2	27	140	18	13	2	2	1	2	8	1	30	1	0
Reinike, Chris, Buf.	0	0	.000	9.00	1	0	0	0	0	0	1.0	0	6	1	1	0	0	0	3	0	1	2	0
Reith, Brian, Lou.	0	0	.000	3.60	1	1	0	0	0	0	5.0	7	21	2	2	0	1	0	1	0	6	0	0
Renwick, Tyler, Syr.	0	0	.000	3.18	2	0	0	0	0	0	5.2	7	20	2	2	1	0	1	4	0	2	0	0
Reyes, Dennys, Lou.*	4	2	.667	3.67	7	6	0	0	0	0	34.1	34	148	15	14	3	0	0	1	16	0	34	3	0
Riedling, John, Lou.	0	0	.000	0.00	1	0	0	0	0	0	1.0	0	4	0	0	0	0	0	0	1	0	1	0	0
Riggan, Jerrod, Nor.	2	0	1.000	1.95	28	0	0	0	16	13	32.1	26	122	7	7	4	1	0	0	4	1	37	5	1
Rijo, Jose, Lou.	0	0	.000	5.14	6	4	0	0	0	0	14.0	16	61	9	8	2	2	0	1	5	0	7	1	0
Rios, Brian, Tol.	0	0	.000	0.00	1	0	0	0	1	0	1.0	0	3	0	0	0	0	1	0	0	0	0	0	0
Riske, David, Buf.	1	2	.333	2.36	38	0	0	0	26	15	53.1	45	217	16	14	2	2	2	2	17	0	72	0	1
Roach, Jason, Nor.	1	2	.333	7.16	4	4	0	0	0	0	16.1	21	77	13	13	1	2	1	1	7	1	7	0	0
Robbins, Jake, Rich.	5	3	.625	5.51	57	0	0	0	17	1	78.1	73	352	51	48	1	4	1	6	51	3	53	9	0
Roberts, Chris, Ind.*	0	0	.000	6.48	5	0	0	0	1	0	8.1	12	43	6	6	0	2	0	3	5	1	5	1	0
Roberts, Grant, Nor.	3	5	.375	4.52	30	6	0	0	15	2	67.2	80	300	38	34	4	3	2	7	19	1	54	2	0
Rodriguez, Frank, Lou.	8	6	.571	2.46	43	0	0	0	18	5	80.1	67	330	25	22	5	6	1	5	24	2	56	3	0
Rodriguez, Nerio, Nor.-Buf.	2	3	.400	5.82	12	5	0	0	2	1	38.2	43	171	26	25	5	0	3	3	15	1	21	1	0
Roque, Rafael, Paw.*	8	5	.615	4.20	20	19	0	0	0	0	98.2	101	427	52	46	15	1	2	3	35	1	68	1	2
Rose, Brian, Dur.	9	2	.818	3.10	19	15	0	0	2	1	98.2	88	391	35	34	11	2	2	3	19	0	88	2	0
Rose, Ted, Ott.	7	9	.438	4.03	37	15	1	0	8	0	120.2	125	514	59	54	9	10	3	4	35	0	98	6	2
Ruffin, Johnny, Lou.	0	0	.000	0.00	9	0	0	0	8	5	8.1	6	33	1	0	0	1	0	3	0	11	0	0
Runyan, Sean, Tol.*	0	1	.000	8.44	11	0	0	0	0	0	10.2	15	61	17	10	3	2	2	0	11	0	6	1	0
Rupe, Ryan, Dur.	0	0	.000	0.82	2	2	0	0	0	0	11.0	3	36	1	1	0	1	0	1	0	17	0	0
Saberhagen, Bret, Paw.	0	0	.000	3.00	1	1	0	0	0	0	6.0	3	22	2	2	0	0	0	1	1	0	4	1	0
Santos, Victor, Tol.	2	1	.667	6.37	6	6	0	0	0	0	35.1	50	162	27	25	6	1	1	1	12	0	22	0	0
Scanlan, Bob, Ott.	0	5	.000	3.90	32	0	0	0	31	23	32.1	41	151	20	14	3	0	0	3	10	0	21	6	0
Schrenk, Steve, Char.	5	3	.625	3.00	30	0	0	0	14	2	39.0	38	166	13	13	4	1	2	1	13	2	43	1	0
Scott, Tim, Col.	2	3	.400	5.01	14	0	0	0	5	0	23.1	24	102	14	13	3	0	1	2	6	1	28	0	0
Secoda, Jason, Char.	3	9	.250	5.18	34	20	1	0	4	1	139.0	168	628	90	80	17	7	8	2	56	1	105	11	1
Seelbach, Chris, Rich.	7	7	.500	5.09	22	14	0	0	3	1	88.1	85	380	50	50	9	6	3	3	36	4	82	3	0
Sekany, Jason, Paw.	0	3	.000	8.62	7	2	0	0	2	0	15.2	22	76	16	15	4	1	0	1	7	0	8	0	2
Seo, Jae, Nor.	2	2	.500	3.42	9	9	0	0	0	0	47.1	53	191	18	18	4	4	0	2	6	1	25	0	1
Serafini, Dan, Nor.-Ind.*	7	4	.636	4.14	40	6	0	0	4	1	71.2	78	312	35	33	5	2	6	18	3	56	3	0
Serrano, Jim, Ott.	0	1	.000	4.50	9	0	0	0	5	0	8.0	11	42	5	4	0	0	0	1	6	0	11	1	0
Service, Scott, Lou.	2	0	1.000	4.74	20	0	0	0	11	5	24.2	22	106	13	13	6	1	1	3	10	1	27	1	0
Sheets, Ben, Ind.	1	1	.500	3.38	2	2	0	0	0	0	10.2	14	49	5	4	0	2	0	3	6	0	6	0	0
Shumaker, Tony, Roch.*	8	7	.533	3.96	53	0	0	0	20	4	72.2	70	311	35	32	7	4	1	1	31	2	53	3	0
Sinclair, Steve, Char.*	4	6	.400	4.69	53	0	0	0	19	1	63.1	66	274	35	33	5	1	2	4	23	5	57	3	0
Skrmetta, Matt, Lou.	2	4	.333	2.48	46	0	0	0	23	6	54.1	41	220	17	15	5	1	1	3	20	3	58	5	0
Slusarski, Joe, Rich.	0	0	.000	2.25	6	0	0	0	4	0	8.0	9	34	2	2	0	0	1	0	2	0	5	0	0
Small, Aaron, Rich.	10	7	.588	3.83	41	11	0	0	10	0	96.1	97	412	50	41	14	1	1	1	31	5	61	2	0
Smith, Dan, Buf.	6	4	.600	4.50	21	16	1	0	3	0	106.0	110	458	58	53	17	0	3	9	44	0	68	2	0
Smith, Roy, Buf.	0	5	.000	2.19	48	0	0	0	31	18	74.0	59	307	25	18	2	6	1	8	29	4	86	3	0
Snyder, John, Ind.	3	11	.214	5.56	32	23	0	0	4	0	147.1	202	683	115	91	15	4	12	37	0	84	8	1
Snyder, Matt, Rich.	0	0	.000	4.91	9	0	0	0	4	0	11.0	13	56	8	6	1	1	1	1	10	9	4	1
Sodowsky, Clint, S./W.B.	0	0	.000	3.86	7	0	0	0	4	3	7.0	8	33	4	3	0	0	0	2	3	1	8	0	0
Spencer, Sean, Ott.*	2	1	.667	2.94	52	0	0	0	12	0	64.1	53	271	23	21	4	3	3	2	27	0	59	5	0
Spoljaric, Paul, Buf.*	0	1	.000	17.36	4	0	0	0	2	0	4.2	11	31	11	9	1	2	0	1	4	0	3	1	0

Pitcher, Team	W	L	Pct.	ERA	G	GS	CG	ShO	GF	Sv.	IP	H	TBF	R	ER	HR	SH	SF	HB	BB	IBB	SO	WP	Bk.
Spooneybarger, Tim, Rich.	3	0	1.000	0.71	42	0	0	0	18	5	50.2	33	202	5	4	1	1	0	2	21	1	58	5	0
Spurgeon, Jay, Roch.	3	5	.375	4.55	15	15	1	0	0	0	87.0	85	373	48	44	12	3	3	5	27	0	61	1	1
Standridge, Jason, Dur.	5	10	.333	5.28	20	20	0	0	0	0	102.1	130	475	73	60	13	2	7	3	50	0	48	6	0
Stanford, Jason, Buf.*	1	0	1.000	0.00	1	1	1	1	0	0	9.0	3	29	0	0	0	0	0	0	0	0	10	0	0
Stephens, John, Roch.	2	5	.286	4.03	9	9	0	0	0	0	58.0	52	247	31	26	5	2	3	3	19	1	61	4	0
Stevens, Dave, Rich.	2	1	.667	6.90	39	0	0	0	10	1	58.2	67	270	49	45	14	4	4	4	31	6	47	3	0
Stewart, Scott, Ott.*	0	0	.000	1.80	4	0	0	0	3	0	5.0	5	20	1	1	0	1	0	0	1	0	4	0	0
Stoops, Jim, Col.	0	0	.000	2.25	5	0	0	0	2	0	12.0	8	50	4	3	2	0	0	0	5	0	10	3	0
Strange, Pat, Nor.	1	0	1.000	0.00	1	1	0	0	0	0	6.0	4	23	0	0	0	0	0	0	1	0	6	0	0
Sylvester, Billy, Rich.	0	4	.000	5.11	36	0	0	0	21	11	37.0	28	169	21	21	2	1	4	2	27	2	41	4	0
Telemaco, Amaury, S./W.B.	1	2	.333	4.01	4	4	0	0	0	0	24.2	31	108	11	11	4	1	0	0	6	0	25	0	0
Telford, Anthony, Ott.	3	5	.375	4.50	28	8	0	0	7	1	76.0	79	316	42	38	7	2	7	3	17	0	62	0	0
Tessmer, Jay, Ind.	7	5	.583	2.79	35	0	0	0	23	4	58.0	56	240	23	18	3	4	1	2	9	2	39	1	1
Thomas, Evan, S./W.B.	3	13	.188	5.28	19	18	0	0	0	0	104.0	123	464	68	61	14	5	0	2	36	1	74	3	0
Tolar, Kevin, Tol.*	3	4	.429	2.73	44	0	0	0	32	7	56.0	49	234	18	17	3	4	1	1	21	2	73	9	0
Towers, Josh, Roch.	3	1	.750	3.51	6	6	1	1	0	0	41.0	40	168	18	16	2	0	1	2	8	2	27	0	0
Traber, Billy, Nor.*	0	1	.000	1.29	1	1	0	0	0	0	7.0	5	26	3	1	0	0	0	0	0	0	0	1	1
Trachsel, Steve, Nor.	2	0	1.000	2.79	3	3	1	1	0	0	19.1	13	76	6	6	0	1	0	0	6	0	12	1	0
Tucker, T.J., Ott.	3	5	.375	3.11	14	14	1	0	0	0	84.0	68	354	42	29	11	6	2	4	33	0	63	3	2
Ulacia, Dennis, Char.*	1	0	1.000	2.57	1	1	1	0	0	0	7.0	6	27	2	2	1	0	0	0	1	0	3	0	0
Valdes, Marc, Rich.	9	11	.450	4.51	29	21	0	0	5	2	123.2	133	542	67	62	13	9	3	13	41	4	97	2	0
Valdez, Santo, Syr.	0	0	.000	1.80	1	1	0	0	0	0	5.0	5	18	1	1	0	1	0	0	1	0	2	0	0
Vargas, Martin, Buf.	0	3	.000	2.93	22	0	0	0	12	4	27.2	20	120	11	9	1	1	1	2	17	1	22	8	0
Veras, Dario, Buf.	5	1	.833	4.57	48	0	0	0	23	6	67.0	69	289	35	34	10	1	2	5	21	1	69	0	1
Villegas, Ismael, Rich.	4	7	.364	4.15	34	20	0	0	5	1	134.1	128	552	65	62	21	4	3	0	39	5	100	1	0
Vinas, Julio, Roch.	0	0	.000	0.00	1	0	0	0	1	0	1.0	0	3	0	0	0	0	0	0	0	0	2	0	0
Vining, Ken, Char.*	2	3	.400	1.96	41	0	0	0	9	4	46.0	35	188	10	10	2	1	2	1	19	5	47	0	0
Vosberg, Ed, S./W.B.*	1	0	1.000	3.00	27	0	0	0	12	5	27.0	24	113	9	9	1	2	0	0	13	3	22	2	0
Wagner, Paul, Nor.	1	1	.500	8.10	2	1	0	0	0	0	6.2	12	33	6	6	2	0	0	0	2	0	2	1	0
Walker, Jamie, Buf.*	7	2	.778	3.87	38	8	0	0	5	2	93.0	104	406	44	40	12	1	2	7	27	1	51	4	2
Walker, Pete, Nor.	13	4	.765	2.99	26	26	0	0	0	0	168.1	145	681	64	56	12	5	5	5	46	5	106	2	1
Walker, Tyler, Nor.	3	2	.600	4.02	8	8	0	0	0	0	40.1	34	160	19	18	7	2	1	1	8	0	35	1	0
Wall, Donne, Nor.	0	0	.000	10.38	4	0	0	0	1	1	4.1	8	26	6	5	1	0	1	0	5	0	1	0	0
Wallace, Jeff, Dur.*	0	0	.000	3.86	7	0	0	0	0	0	9.1	6	41	4	4	1	0	0	1	7	0	11	0	0
Walling, Dave, Col.	0	1	.000	6.00	1	1	0	0	0	0	6.0	5	25	5	4	1	0	2	1	0	0	7	0	0
Ward, Bryan, Paw.*	0	3	.000	4.28	19	1	0	0	7	0	33.2	47	155	23	16	2	2	0	2	6	2	18	1	0
Wasdin, John, Roch.	2	1	.667	3.98	5	3	0	0	2	0	20.1	27	91	9	9	3	0	2	0	5	0	20	1	0
Watson, Mark, Buf.*	0	1	.000	13.50	3	0	0	0	0	0	4.0	9	25	7	6	1	0	0	0	3	1	3	0	0
Wells, Kip, Char.	2	1	.667	3.55	4	4	0	0	0	0	25.1	26	110	11	10	2	1	1	0	8	0	24	2	0
Westbrook, Jake, Buf.	8	1	.889	3.20	12	12	0	0	0	0	64.2	60	273	27	23	2	1	0	8	23	0	45	0	2
Wheeler, Dan, Dur.	3	5	.375	5.23	18	10	0	0	2	0	65.1	72	284	51	38	11	1	2	3	11	0	39	1	1
White, Matt, Dur.	0	5	.000	7.80	7	7	0	0	0	0	30.0	33	144	28	26	4	1	4	4	25	0	16	9	0
Whiteside, Matt, Rich.	0	0	.000	0.00	9	0	0	0	8	4	10.0	4	36	0	0	0	0	0	0	1	1	9	0	0
Williams, Brian, Paw.-Col.	5	6	.455	5.08	19	9	0	0	5	0	62.0	74	281	43	35	5	3	0	4	27	1	36	3	0
Williams, Matt, Ind.*	2	2	.500	3.88	51	0	0	0	18	0	72.0	65	318	33	31	4	2	1	4	42	1	45	3	0
Williams, Todd, Col.	0	1	.000	7.11	17	0	0	0	9	2	19.0	31	100	19	15	5	0	0	3	9	3	14	2	0
Wilson, Jeff, Roch.*	2	11	.154	6.05	28	12	1	0	5	0	99.2	118	457	73	67	17	4	2	1	42	4	56	9	1
Winchester, Scott, Lou.	6	3	.667	3.54	23	6	0	0	3	0	53.1	50	221	26	21	5	1	3	3	10	0	37	0	1
Wolf, Randy, S./W.B.*	0	1	.000	5.00	2	2	0	0	0	0	9.0	10	42	6	5	2	1	1	0	5	0	7	0	0
Woodard, Steve, Buf.	4	2	.667	2.39	6	6	1	0	0	0	37.2	36	151	11	10	2	2	2	1	1	1	32	1	0
Wright, Jaret, Buf.	3	1	.750	4.71	7	7	0	0	0	0	28.2	25	124	18	15	3	1	0	3	13	0	28	1	0
Zambrano, Victor, Dur.	1	2	.333	2.08	29	0	0	0	27	12	30.1	26	126	10	7	2	0	1	1	12	1	29	4	0
Zamora, Pete, S./W.B.*	8	4	.667	2.93	45	6	0	0	22	3	89.0	64	369	29	29	7	6	2	3	41	6	79	5	2

PITCHERS WITH TWO OR MORE TEAMS

Pitcher, Team	W	L	Pct.	ERA	G	GS	CG	ShO	GF	Sv.	IP	H	TBF	R	ER	HR	SH	SF	HB	BB	IBB	SO	WP	Bk.
Banks, Willie, Syr.	8	5	.615	3.25	24	23	0	0	0	0	146.2	151	636	63	53	12	1	2	11	53	0	121	11	0
Banks, Willie, Paw.	2	0	1.000	1.42	2	2	0	0	0	0	12.2	8	50	3	2	0	0	0	1	3	0	12	0	0
Cornett, Brad, Syr.	1	0	1.000	6.35	6	0	0	0	2	0	11.1	17	53	8	8	0	0	1	0	5	1	6	1	0
Cornett, Brad, Dur.	4	2	.667	2.05	33	2	0	0	6	2	61.1	56	255	22	14	3	4	0	2	12	0	55	6	0
Day, Zach, Buf.	1	0	1.000	1.50	1	1	0	0	0	0	6.0	3	22	1	1	0	0	0	0	1	0	4	0	0
Day, Zach, Ott.	2	2	.500	7.43	6	5	0	0	0	0	26.2	38	120	23	22	2	0	1	2	8	0	15	3	0
Estrella, Leo, Nor.	2	0	1.000	3.12	8	1	0	0	0	0	17.1	23	77	7	6	1	0	1	3	8	0	10	3	0
Estrella, Leo, Lou.	1	1	.500	4.88	34	5	0	0	9	1	62.2	67	273	36	34	8	2	1	1	27	0	37	3	0
Flury, Pat, Ott.	0	1	.000	4.63	10	0	0	0	5	0	11.2	8	49	6	6	3	0	1	1	8	0	9	1	0
Flury, Pat, Col.	3	2	.600	2.47	34	0	0	0	19	3	47.1	31	193	13	13	2	3	2	1	19	1	66	1	0
Gandarillas, Gus, Paw.	2	1	.667	4.30	12	0	0	0	7	1	14.2	19	70	9	7	0	1	1	0	10	1	7	3	0
Gandarillas, Gus, Ind.	2	2	.500	2.70	28	5	0	0	11	1	66.2	62	271	30	20	4	2	3	3	13	1	52	6	1
Gunderson, Eric, Buf.*	0	0	.000	0.00	2	0	0	0	1	1	2.0	2	9	1	0	0	0	0	0	0	0	3	0	0
Gunderson, Eric, Col.*	2	4	.333	3.05	56	0	0	0	17	6	73.2	70	307	32	25	6	4	2	3	24	1	60	3	0
Hammond, Chris, Buf.*	7	3	.700	3.31	28	4	0	0	3	0	51.2	53	225	22	19	5	0	0	2	20	1	54	1	0
Hammond, Chris, Rich.*	3	1	.750	2.35	21	0	0	0	4	1	30.2	32	120	9	8	0	2	0	0	4	0	29	0	0
Henry, Butch, Syr.*	6	4	.600	4.02	12	12	1	0	0	0	78.1	91	323	38	35	5	2	3	2	9	1	49	0	0
Henry, Butch, Ind.*	2	3	.400	6.00	5	5	1	0	0	0	36.0	39	152	25	24	8	0	1	1	9	0	27	0	1
Henry, Butch, Col.*	0	1	.000	27.00	1	1	0	0	0	0	2.0	10	16	7	6	1	0	0	0	0	0	1	0	0
Hill, Ken, Lou.	2	1	.667	4.60	6	6	0	0	0	0	31.1	33	141	19	16	4	3	2	2	12	0	16	2	0
Hill, Ken, Paw.	2	1	.667	6.54	8	8	0	0	0	0	31.2	42	148	27	23	5	2	0	0	11	0	17	4	0
Lewis, Richie, Buf.	2	0	1.000	2.10	7	5	0	0	1	1	30.0	19	119	8	7	3	0	0	2	13	1	11	3	0
Lewis, Richie, Nor.	7	4	.636	4.03	17	16	0	0	0	0	91.2	83	397	46	41	8	2	0	4	47	1	66	4	0
Lira, Felipe, Ott.	5	4	.556	2.08	42	0	0	0	19	6	60.2	56	243	17	14	4	7	0	0	10	2	47	1	0
Lira, Felipe, S./W.B.	0	1	.000	5.19	2	2	0	0	0	0	8.2	17	42	5	5	0	1	0	0	0	0	6	0	0
Peters, Chris, Lou.*	3	1	.750	6.89	8	6	0	0	1	0	31.1	46	158	26	24	2	1	0	5	18	2	16	6	0

Pitcher, Team	W	L	Pct.	ERA	G	GS	CG	ShO	GF	Sv.	IP	H	TBF	R	ER	HR	SH	SF	HB	BB	IBB	SO	WP	Bk.
Peters, Chris, Col.*	2	4	.333	4.27	9	8	0	0	0	0	52.2	56	242	36	25	7	1	0	4	25	0	29	8	0
Rodriguez, Nerio, Nor.	0	0	.000	0.00	1	0	0	0	0	0	0.0	2	2	2	2	0	0	0	0	0	0	0	0	0
Rodriguez, Nerio, Buf.	2	3	.400	5.35	11	5	0	0	2	1	38.2	41	169	24	23	5	0	3	3	15	1	21	1	0
Serafini, Dan, Nor.*	5	2	.714	3.31	31	2	0	0	4	1	49.0	48	210	18	18	3	1	2	4	16	3	38	1	0
Serafini, Dan, Ind.*	2	2	.500	5.96	9	4	0	0	0	0	22.2	30	102	17	15	2	1	0	2	2	0	18	2	0
Williams, Brian, Paw.	0	0	.000	0.00	3	0	0	0	2	0	4.0	2	14	0	0	0	0	0	1	0	3	3	0	0
Williams, Brian, Col.	5	6	.455	5.43	16	9	0	0	0	3	58.0	72	267	43	35	5	3	0	4	26	1	33	3	0

COMBINATION SHUTOUTS: **Buffalo (9)**—Lewis-Baez-Riske, Woodward-Bacsik-Smith, Westbrook-Lewis, Nagy-Smith, Nagy-Smith-Smith, Walker-Rodriguez-Hammond-Riske, Woodard-Smith-Riske, Walker-Veras, Bacsik-Vargas-Radinsky. **Charlotte (6)**—Lowe-Secoda, Ginter-Vining-Fogg, Bullinger-Sinclair-Corbin-Baptist, Mendoza-Baptist-Bullinger, Mendoza-Bullinger, Secoda-Vining-Schrenk. **Columbus (3)**—Keisler-Gunderson-Jean, Lail-Jean-Almanzar, Aramboles-Johnson-Jean. **Durham (8)**—Callaway-Gardner-Zambrano, Callaway-Phelps-Enders, Standridge-Gardner-Phelps, Kennedy-Cornett-Bowers, Callaway-Rose, Rose-Wheeler-Bowers, Guzman-Gardner, Rose-James. **Indianapolis (6)**—Chantres-Rain, Fordham-Rain-Williams, Gandarillas-Rain-Tessmer-Williams, Coppinger-Williams-Tessmer, Neugebauer-Serafini-Snyder, Serafini-Mallette-Kolb. **Louisville (8)**—Bell-Nichting, Gooch-Nichting, Fernandez-McNichol, Winchester-Skrmetta-Service, Luebbers-Service, Fernandez-Skrmetta, Fernandez-Darnell-Service-Ruffin, Serafini-Mallette. **Norfolk (6)**—Gonzalez-Wagner-Cerros-Henriquez, Walker-Riggan, Linton-Henriquez, Hinchliffe-Roberts-Serafini-Riggan, Seo-Brittan-Corey, Walker-Cerros-Corey. **Ottawa (10)**—Mattes-Lira, Blank-Lira, Rose-Eischen-Scanlan, Munoz-Lira, Rose-Stewart-Cubillan, Munoz-Evans, Telford-Marquez-Spencer-Lira, Telford-Rose-Marquez, Manon-Cubillan, Day-Rose-Telford. **Pawtucket (5)**—Pichardo-Castillo, Kim-Pena-McDill-Lee-Pulsipher, Roque-Lee, Roque-Ward-Erdos, Hill-Ward-Lee-McDill-Cho. **Richmond (7)**—Moss-Nelson-Whiteside, Villegas-Small-Nelson, Valdes-Small-Spooneybarger, Small-Hammond-Robbins-Beasley-Spooneybarger, Seelbach-Spooneybarger-Sylvester, Seelbach-Hammond-Robbins, Moore-Robbins-Spooneybarger. **Rochester (7)**—Parrish-Shumaker-Paronto-Huisman, Spurgeon-Wilson, Maduro-Shumaker, Douglass-Parrish-Julio, Wasdin-Brown, Bauer-Pina, Douglass-Paronto-Shumaker. **Scranton/Wilkes-Barre (6)**—Thomas-Beltran-Boyd, Jacquez-Nickle-Boyd, Brook-Jacquez-Kershner, Telemaco-Nickle-Vosberg-Boyd, Padilla-Cedeno, Zamora-Geary-Boyd. **Syracuse (7)**—Dillinger-Beirne-DeWitt, Dillinger-File, Coco-Eyre-Bowles-DeWitt, Banks-DeWitt, Lyon-Frascatore, Cassidy-Espina, Eyre-Beirne. **Toledo (2)**—Johnson-Keller, Bernero-Keller-Perisho.

NO-HIT GAMES: Trachsel, Norfolk defeated Ottawa 3-0, May 29.

2001 FIELDING

TEAM

Team	Pct.	G	PO	A	E	TC	DP	TP	PB
Scranton/W.-B.	.982	143	3901	1546	100	5547	127	0	13
Richmond	.980	144	3825	1442	105	5372	115	1	9
Buffalo	.978	142	3761	1437	117	5315	147	0	6
Norfolk	.977	142	3768	1559	123	5450	151	0	12
Charlotte	.977	144	3804	1493	123	5420	121	0	12
Durham	.977	144	3780	1457	124	5361	136	0	12
Syracuse	.977	144	3846	1545	129	5520	147	0	16
Louisville	.975	144	3801	1632	138	5631	140	0	24
Ottawa	.975	144	3871	1592	139	5602	142	0	5
Indianapolis	.973	144	3838	1506	149	5493	133	0	9
Pawtucket	.972	142	3711	1412	149	5272	129	0	15
Columbus	.971	143	3727	1335	151	5213	127	0	13
Toledo	.970	144	3839	1630	172	5641	152	0	15
Rochester	.963	144	3863	1325	197	5385	109	0	19

INDIVIDUAL

FIRST BASEMEN

NOTE: All caps denotes fielding-percentage leader based on 72 games for catchers, 90 for all other non pitchers and 115 innings for pitchers. *Throws lefthanded.

Player, Team	Pct.	G	PO	A	E	TC	DP
Alcantara, Israel, Paw.	.978	6	43	1	1	45	3
Allen, Dusty, Tol.	.962	3	2	3	1	26	2
Balfe, Ryan, Syr.	.983	12	113	5	2	120	13
Barker, Kevin, Ind.*	1.000	16	150	12	0	162	13
Barry, Jeff, Char.	1.000	1	10	1	0	11	0
Battle, Howard, Rich.	1.000	4	28	5	0	33	3
Bellinger, Clay, Col.	1.000	1	5	0	0	5	1
Berroa, Geronimo, Ott.	1.000	3	26	0	0	26	4
Bierek, Kurt, Tol.	.991	35	302	30	3	335	42
Borders, Pat, Dur.	.987	9	72	4	1	77	9
Brown, Brant, Ind.*	.997	39	338	18	1	357	29
Burkhart, Morgan, Paw.*	.992	98	789	58	7	854	78
Carr, Dustin, Tol.	.984	8	55	5	1	61	5
Charles, Frank, Roch.	1.000	1	6	1	0	7	0
Chevalier, Virgil, Paw.	1.000	2	16	3	0	19	2
Coffie, Ivanon, Roch.	.934	12	91	8	7	106	11
Coste, Chris, Buf.	.994	19	162	14	1	177	20
Cromer, D.T., Lou.*	.989	42	398	34	5	437	33
Dalesandro, Mark, Char.	1.000	4	24	2	0	26	1
Davis, Tommy, Lou.	.997	73	704	51	2	757	63
Diaz, Juan, Paw.	.970	36	307	11	10	328	30
Dominique, Andy, S./W.B.	.985	37	318	17	5	340	22
Edwards, Mike, Buf.	1.000	3	28	4	0	32	3
Estalella, Bobby, Col.	1.000	2	8	1	0	9	1
Franco, Matt, Nor.	.997	40	282	26	1	309	37
Franklin, Micah, Ind.	1.000	3	18	0	0	18	1
Garcia, Carlos, Col.	.968	8	57	3	2	62	8
Garcia, Guillermo, Roch.	1.000	2	18	1	0	19	0
Garcia, Karim, Buf.*	.941	6	32	0	2	34	4

Player, Team	Pct.	G	PO	A	E	TC	DP
Gibralter, Dave, Ind.	1.000	1	8	2	0	10	0
Glavine, Mike, Rich.*	.950	3	17	2	1	20	2
Gubanich, Creighton, Char.	.941	2	15	1	1	17	1
Hardtke, Jason, Char.	1.000	1	2	0	0	2	0
Hollins, Dave, Buf.	.979	16	134	9	3	146	15
Hoover, Paul, Dur.	.992	13	117	11	1	129	8
Hunter, Brian, Syr.*	.990	23	199	8	2	209	19
Jackson, Ryan, Tol.*	1.000	1	12	0	0	12	2
Jacobsen, Bucky, Ind.	.986	81	661	45	10	716	56
Johnson, Mark, Char.	1.000	3	28	0	0	28	5
Johnson, Mark, Lou.*	.998	40	379	32	1	412	30
Johnson, Nick, Col.*	.989	109	856	63	10	929	87
Jones, Chris, Syr.	1.000	5	58	3	0	61	2
Knupfer, Jason, S./W.B.	.987	18	147	7	2	156	18
Laker, Tim, Buf.	1.000	3	32	1	0	33	2
Langalgne, Selwyn, Syr.*	.909	22	157	17	2	176	18
Larson, Brandon, Lou.	.923	3	11	1	1	13	0
Lawrence, Joe, Syr.	1.000	1	1	0	0	1	0
Lesher, Brian, Ind.*	.971	6	32	2	1	35	8
Liefer, Jeff, Char.	.996	28	250	21	1	272	17
Lopez, Luis, Syr.	1.000	80	728	45	0	773	78
Matos, Pascual, Col.	.963	5	26	0	1	27	4
McNally, Sean, Col.	.988	10	75	10	1	86	9
Mendez, Carlos, Tol.	.994	55	479	28	3	510	49
Morioni, Lou, Paw.	1.000	1	1	0	0	1	0
Minor, Ryan, Ott.	1.000	9	68	3	0	71	3
Montgomery, Ray, Nor.	.962	4	23	2	1	26	1
Nettles, Jeff, Col.	1.000	3	15	1	0	16	0
Norris, Dax, Rich.	1.000	4	26	1	0	27	5
Nunnari, Talmadge, Ott.*	.995	62	527	39	3	569	56
Oliver, Joe, Paw.	.000	1	0	0	0	0	0
Ortiz, Luis, Ott.	.992	13	119	6	1	126	10
Ottavinia, Paul, Col.*	1.000	11	78	9	0	87	7
Patterson, Jarrod, Tol.	.979	6	45	1	1	47	0
Peoples, Danny, Buf.	.988	87	713	50	9	772	82
Perry, Chan, Rich.	.991	68	536	41	5	582	47
Pickering, Calvin, Roch.-Lou.*	.986	70	520	31	8	559	53
Roberge, J.P., S./W.B.	1.000	16	128	13	0	141	18
Robertson, Mike, Rich.*	.995	71	562	29	3	594	45
Rumfield, Toby, Char.	.992	108	901	62	8	971	79
Rust, Brian, Roch.	.986	22	130	11	2	143	10
Saunders, Chris, Char.	1.000	3	19	1	0	20	3
Schall, Gene, S./W.B.	.994	54	484	38	3	525	37
Seabol, Scott, Col.	1.000	9	61	5	0	66	9
Seguignol, Fernando, Ott.	.992	54	452	37	4	493	47
Selby, Bill, Lou.	.984	24	171	11	3	185	17
Shave, Jon, Paw.	.944	3	17	0	1	18	1
Sheets, Andy, Dur.	1.000	1	4	0	0	4	0
Sheff, Chris, Lou.	1.000	2	18	1	0	19	3
Simon, Randy, Tol.*	.986	55	462	23	7	492	45
Sisco, Steve, Roch.	.995	27	180	16	1	197	11
Smith, Bobby, Dur.	1.000	2	22	1	0	23	2
Snyder, Earl, Nor.	.981	5	52	1	1	54	3
Spehr, Tim, Lou.	1.000	6	40	4	0	44	5
Sweeney, Mark, Ind.*	.985	7	59	7	1	67	10

CLASS AAA International League

Player, Team	Pct.	G	PO	A	E	TC	DP
Thompson, Ryan, Ott.	.964	3	26	1	1	28	1
Toca, Jorge, Nor.	.987	59	499	47	7	553	53
Tracy, Andy, Ott.	1.000	8	73	4	0	77	6
Tyler, Brad, Lou.	.968	4	29	1	1	31	4
Valent, Eric, S./W.B.*	.996	27	209	15	1	225	18
Vinas, Julio, Roch.	.988	23	158	9	2	169	15
Walbeck, Matt, S./W.B.	1.000	1	10	1	0	11	1
Ward, Turner, S./W.B.	1.000	1	1	0	0	1	0
Wigginton, Ty, Nor.	1.000	5	27	1	0	28	3
Wilson, Travis, Rich.	1.000	8	38	4	0	42	2
Woodward, Chris, Syr.	.971	4	33	1	1	35	3
WRIGHT, Ron, Dur.	.992	118	980	66	8	1054	102

TRIPLE PLAY: Robertson.

FIRST BASEMEN WITH TWO OR MORE TEAMS

Player, Team	Pct.	G	PO	A	E	TC	DP
Pickering, Calvin, Roch.*	.986	69	516	31	8	555	52
Pickering, Calvin, Lou.*	1.000	1	4	0	0	4	1

SECOND BASEMEN

Player, Team	Pct.	G	PO	A	E	TC	DP
Abbott, Kurt, Rich.	1.000	1	3	1	0	4	0
Abernathy, Brent, Dur.	.969	61	107	179	9	295	41
Alfonzo, Edgardo, Nor.	1.000	2	6	8	0	14	5
Anderson, Bryan, Lou.	1.000	5	10	13	0	23	5
Baez, Kevin, Nor.	.980	28	39	57	2	98	8
Beattie, Andy, Lou.	1.000	1	2	1	0	3	0
Bellinger, Clay, Col.	.000	1	0	0	0	0	0
Bravo, Danny, Char.	1.000	12	21	37	0	58	12
Bridges, Kary, Col.	.987	95	170	207	5	382	48
Bush, Homer, Syr.	1.000	9	13	23	0	36	3
Carr, Dustin, Dur.	.920	5	10	13	2	25	4
Carroll, Jamey, Ott.	.984	28	57	67	2	126	15
Caruso, Mike, Dur.	.975	59	102	173	7	282	36
Casimiro, Carlos, Roch.	1.000	1	2	1	0	3	1
Castro, Ramon, Rich.	1.000	6	14	10	0	24	3
Cesar, Dionys, Ind.	1.000	2	3	2	0	5	0
Chamblee, Jim, Paw.	.979	87	161	220	8	389	61
Collier, Lou, Ind.	.986	14	31	37	1	69	9
Coquillette, Trace, Buf.-Tol.	.959	23	40	53	4	97	17
Cotton, John, Ott.	1.000	1	2	5	0	7	0
Dalesandro, Mark, Char.	.750	1	2	1	1	4	1
DeRosa, Mark, Rich.	1.000	7	16	17	0	33	3
Erickson, Corey, Buf.	1.000	1	4	3	0	7	0
Figueroa, Luis, Nor.	1.000	2	6	11	0	17	1
Fonville, Chad, Col.	.964	13	25	29	2	56	4
Forbes, P.J., S./W.B.	.989	92	186	266	5	457	50
Freel, Ryan, Syr.	.953	10	18	23	2	43	2
Garabito, Eddy, Roch.	.956	106	209	247	21	477	58
Garcia, Amaury, Char.	.974	27	39	72	3	114	9
Garcia, Carlos, Col.	1.000	10	19	19	0	38	3
Garcia, Jesse, Rich.	.953	16	24	37	3	64	11
Giles, Marcus, Rich.	.974	63	130	166	8	304	32
Goelz, Jim, Buf.	.714	2	2	3	2	7	0
Green, Nick, Rich.	.833	1	4	1	1	6	0
Guerrero, Wilton, Lou.	.963	35	71	85	6	162	21
Hardtke, Jason, Buf.-Char.	.974	41	74	113	5	192	20
Hernandez, Carlos, Nor.	.964	44	71	118	7	196	30
Holbert, Aaron, Syr.	.982	29	67	93	3	163	27
Hoover, Paul, Dur.	1.000	1	1	1	0	2	0
Howard, Dave, Nor.	1.000	2	2	3	0	5	0
Hudson, Orlando, Syr.	.989	53	106	163	3	272	34
Izturis, Cesar, Syr.	.992	26	50	77	1	128	18
Jimenez, D'Angelo, Col.	.956	30	66	63	6	135	24
Knupfer, Jason, S./W.B.	.955	51	99	112	10	221	19
LaRocca, Greg, Buf.	1.000	1	1	2	0	3	1
Lewis, Mark, Buf.	.939	9	15	16	2	33	4
Lindstrom, Dave, Tol.	.944	6	8	9	1	18	5
Liniak, Cole, Syr.	.864	5	9	10	3	22	3
Lopez, Felipe, Syr.	.980	18	36	61	2	99	17
Loretta, Mark, Ind.	.714	1	1	4	2	7	2
Malloy, Marty, Lou.	.961	69	128	169	12	309	41
Martinez, Eddy, Roch.	.917	5	10	12	2	24	6
Martinez, Gabby, Nor.	.980	27	37	62	2	101	17
Martinez, Lou, Rich.	1.000	8	14	28	0	42	5
Mateo, Henry, Ott.	.963	116	251	328	22	601	76
McDonald, John, Buf.	.933	2	6	8	1	15	2
Medrano, Tony, Buf.	.984	48	105	135	4	244	41
Merloni, Lou, Paw.	.964	18	31	50	3	84	6
Metcalfe, Mike, Lou.	1.000	6	9	13	0	22	2
Miller, Ryan, Nor.	.974	9	17	21	1	39	7
Milliard, Ralph, Buf.	.913	5	7	14	2	23	3

Player, Team	Pct.	G	PO	A	E	TC	DP
Neill, Mike, Paw.*	1.000	1	1	3	0	4	1
Nettles, Jeff, Col.	1.000	1	1	0	0	1	0
Newhan, David, S./W.B.	.969	6	15	16	1	32	6
Patterson, Jarrod, Tol.	1.000	2	2	4	0	6	1
Pena, Elvis, Ind.	.929	14	25	27	4	56	6
Perez, Jhonny, Tol.	.913	6	10	11	2	23	3
Prieto, Rick, Char.	.889	3	7	1	1	9	2
Rios, Brian, Tol.	.918	9	23	33	5	61	6
Roberge, J.P., S./W.B.	1.000	2	2	5	0	7	0
Rodriguez, Liu, Char.	.979	94	179	245	9	433	54
Rodriguez, Luis, Paw.	1.000	1	1	0	0	1	0
Rust, Brian, Roch.	1.000	2	2	2	0	4	0
Santana, Pedro, Tol.	.948	112	234	328	31	593	87
Santos, Angel, Paw.	1.000	4	8	7	0	15	3
SCUTARO, Marcos, Ind.	.973	122	244	300	15	559	69
Sefcik, Kevin, Buf.	.981	45	79	130	4	213	33
Selby, Bill, Lou.	.977	36	60	113	4	177	24
Sexton, Chris, Lou.	1.000	4	10	9	0	19	2
Shave, Jon, Paw.	.962	30	55	71	5	131	19
Sheets, Andy, Dur.	1.000	1	3	5	0	8	1
Sisco, Steve, Roch.-S./W.B.	.979	42	86	99	4	189	21
Smith, Bobby, Nor.	.975	24	51	68	3	122	13
Sorensen, Zach, Buf.	1.000	2	3	4	0	7	1
Stynes, Chris, Paw.	1.000	1	2	3	0	5	1
Tamargo, John, Nor.	.983	30	49	66	2	117	22
Tebbs, Nate, Paw.-Rich.	.969	21	47	48	3	98	11
Velandia, Jorge, Nor.	1.000	3	6	10	0	16	2
Veras, Quilvio, Paw.	1.000	3	2	5	0	7	0
Wigginton, Ty, Nor.	.979	24	42	53	2	97	16
Wilson, Travis, Rich.	.952	38	72	86	8	166	19
Woodward, Chris, Syr.	1.000	4	7	13	0	20	2

SECOND BASEMEN WITH TWO OR MORE TEAMS

Player, Team	Pct.	G	PO	A	E	TC	DP
Coquillette, Trace, Buf.	.952	11	16	24	2	42	6
Coquillette, Trace, Tol.	.964	12	24	29	2	55	11
Hardtke, Jason, Buf.	.967	27	46	73	4	123	15
Hardtke, Jason, Char.	.986	14	28	40	1	69	5
Sisco, Steve, Roch.	.977	39	79	92	4	175	20
Sisco, Steve, S./W.B.	1.000	3	7	7	0	14	1
Tebbs, Nate, Paw.	.947	4	7	11	1	19	2
Tebbs, Nate, Rich.	.975	17	40	37	2	79	9

THIRD BASEMEN

Player, Team	Pct.	G	PO	A	E	TC	DP
Baez, Kevin, Nor.	.958	18	22	24	2	48	3
Balfe, Ryan, Syr.	.900	6	5	13	2	20	1
BATTLE, Howard, Rich.	.972	114	69	208	8	285	22
Bellinger, Clay, Col.	1.000	4	2	12	0	14	0
Bennett, Gary, Nor.	.000	1	0	0	0	0	0
Bierek, Kurt, Tol.	1.000	1	1	2	0	3	0
Boone, Aaron, Lou.	1.000	1	1	2	0	3	1
Bravo, Danny, Char.	1.000	5	2	0	0	2	0
Bridges, Kary, Col.	.857	2	1	5	1	7	1
Bruce, Mo, Ott.	.875	5	2	12	2	16	2
Cancel, Rob, Ind.	.857	2	0	6	1	7	0
Carr, Dustin, Dur.	.887	20	13	34	6	53	3
Carroll, Jamey, Ott.	.956	22	16	49	3	68	5
Castro, Ramon, Rich.	.000	1	0	0	0	0	0
Cesar, Dionys, Ind.	.870	9	6	14	3	23	2
Coffie, Ivanon, Roch.	.932	16	15	26	3	44	5
Collier, Lou, Ind.	.917	6	7	15	2	24	1
Coolbaugh, Mike, Ind.	.953	79	74	191	13	278	15
Coquillette, Trace, Tol.	.900	4	3	6	1	10	3
Coste, Chris, Buf.	1.000	1	1	1	0	2	1
Cotton, John, Ott.	.827	19	9	34	9	52	3
Crede, Joe, Char.	.946	123	93	258	20	371	25
Davis, Tommy, Lou.	.896	17	11	32	5	48	3
DeRosa, Mark, Rich.	.977	18	15	28	1	44	5
Dominique, Andy, S./W.B.	.000	1	0	0	0	0	0
Erickson, Corey, Buf.	1.000	2	0	2	0	2	0
Evans, Tom, Tol.	.936	49	33	99	9	141	12
Forbes, P.J., S./W.B.	.000	1	0	0	0	0	0
Franco, Matt, Nor.	.940	85	38	166	13	217	16
Franklin, Micah, Ind.	.863	30	21	42	10	73	1
Freel, Ryan, Syr.	.885	8	8	15	3	26	2
Fryman, Travis, Buf.	1.000	7	7	11	0	18	1
Garcia, Carlos, Col.	.958	18	14	32	2	48	2
Garcia, Jesse, Rich.	1.000	4	3	6	0	9	1
Giles, Marcus, Rich.	1.000	1	1	1	0	2	0
Hardtke, Jason, Buf.-Char.	1.000	15	16	26	0	42	1
Henson, Drew, Col.	.912	68	45	121	16	182	13

Player, Team	Pct.	G	PO	A	E	TC	DP
Hernandez, Carlos, Nor.	.950	6	6	13	1	20	0
Holbert, Aaron, Syr.	.857	13	6	24	5	35	0
Hollins, Dave, Buf.	1.000	1	1	3	0	4	0
Hoover, Paul, Dur.	.952	15	11	29	2	42	5
Hudson, Orlando, Syr.	.909	5	4	6	1	11	0
Huff, Aubrey, Dur.	.929	16	18	34	4	56	5
Jimenez, D'Angelo, Col.	.833	3	2	3	1	6	0
Klimek, Josh, Ind.	.939	18	10	21	2	33	4
Knupfer, Jason, S./W.B.	.964	14	1	26	1	28	0
LaRocca, Greg, Buf.	.955	49	24	103	6	133	8
Larson, Brandon, Lou.	.948	109	67	279	19	365	30
Lawrence, Joe, Syr.	.931	12	4	23	2	29	1
Leon, Donny, Col.	.769	11	7	13	6	26	1
Leon, Jose, Roch.	.933	108	74	219	21	314	18
Lewis, Mark, Buf.	.878	33	28	44	10	82	2
Liefer, Jeff, Char.	.800	2	2	6	2	10	1
Liniak, Cole, Syr.	.968	82	51	163	7	221	14
Lopez, Felipe, Syr.	.833	2	2	3	1	6	1
Lopez, Luis, Syr.	1.000	6	3	11	0	14	2
Loretta, Mark, Ind.	1.000	1	0	2	0	2	0
Malloy, Marty, Lou.	1.000	2	1	1	0	2	0
Martinez, Lou, Rich.	1.000	1	0	2	0	2	0
McDonald, John, Buf.	1.000	2	1	0	0	1	0
McNally, Sean, Buf.	.955	33	24	61	4	89	6
Medrano, Tony, Buf.	1.000	17	7	34	0	41	1
Merloni, Lou, Paw.	1.000	3	2	2	0	4	0
Miller, Ryan, Nor.	1.000	3	1	0	0	1	0
Minor, Ryan, Ott.	1.000	12	5	21	0	26	1
Nettles, Jeff, Col.	1.000	3	1	1	0	2	0
Orie, Kevin, S./W.B.	.965	133	91	267	13	371	14
Ortiz, Luis, Ott.	1.000	1	1	1	0	2	0
Patterson, Jarrod, Tol.	.946	41	16	89	6	111	4
Pena, Elvis, Ind.	.750	3	6	3	3	12	0
Perry, Chan, Rich.	.889	5	2	6	1	9	1
Reding, Josh, Ott.	.905	6	7	12	2	21	1
Rios, Brian, Tol.	.921	59	36	127	14	177	16
Ruet, Brian, Roch.	.933	4	3	11	1	15	1
Sandborg, Jared, Dur.	.948	92	56	181	13	250	17
Sasser, Rob, Ott.	.860	41	29	75	17	121	4
Saunders, Chris, Char.	.935	9	9	20	2	31	5
Scutaro, Marcos, Ind.	.857	5	3	9	2	14	1
Seabol, Scott, Col.	.885	40	25	75	13	113	5
Sefcik, Kevin, Buf.	.875	2	2	5	1	8	0
Selby, Bill, Lou.	.903	18	8	20	3	31	0
Sexton, Chris, Lou.	.944	7	3	14	1	18	0
Sheets, Andy, Dur.	1.000	4	4	3	0	7	0
Sisco, Steve, Roch.	.922	17	14	45	5	64	5
Smith, Bobby, Dur.	1.000	2	2	2	0	4	0
Stynes, Chris, Paw.	1.000	1	1	0	0	1	0
Tamargo, John, Nor.	1.000	8	0	12	0	12	0
Tebbs, Nate, Rich.	1.000	1	1	2	0	3	1
Tracy, Andy, Ott.	.932	37	25	85	8	118	15
Tyler, Brad, Lou.	.000	1	0	0	0	0	0
Valentin, John, Paw.	.850	8	5	12	3	20	4
Veras, Wilton, Syr.	.933	131	128	234	26	388	31
Wigginton, Ty, Nor.	.845	44	17	65	15	97	5
Wilson, Travis, Rich.	.880	11	6	16	3	25	2
Woodward, Chris, Syr.	.957	21	20	47	3	70	7
Zech, Scott, Ott.	.958	11	3	20	1	24	2

THIRD BASEMEN WITH TWO OR MORE TEAMS

Player, Team	Pct.	G	PO	A	E	TC	DP
Hardtke, Jason, Buf.	1.000	8	8	18	0	26	1
Hardtke, Jason, Char.	1.000	7	8	8	0	16	0

SHORTSTOPS

Player, Team	Pct.	G	PO	A	E	TC	DP
Abbott, Kurt, Rich.	1.000	1	1	2	0	3	0
Almonte, Erick, Col.	.936	96	134	258	27	419	53
Baez, Kevin, Nor.	.980	54	86	160	5	251	46
Battle, Howard, Rich.	1.000	1	4	3	0	7	0
Beattie, Andy, Lou.	1.000	2	3	0	0	3	0
Bellinger, Clay, Col.	.952	9	12	28	2	42	6
Bravo, Danny, Char.	.957	18	25	42	3	70	8
Bridges, Kary, Col.	.900	2	2	7	1	10	0
Carroll, Jamey, Ott.	.968	23	46	74	4	124	16
Caruso, Mike, Dur.	.956	52	82	133	10	225	29
Castro, Ramon, Rich.	.967	29	33	83	4	120	17
Cesar, Dionys, Ind.	.974	25	26	48	2	76	10
Coolbaugh, Mike, Ind.	.987	15	25	50	1	76	13
De La Rosa, Tomas, Ott.	.965	121	190	368	20	578	75
De Leon, Jorge, Paw.	.911	9	17	24	4	45	9

Player, Team	Pct.	G	PO	A	E	TC	DP
DELLAERO, Jason, Char.	.968	114	157	299	15	471	57
DeRosa, Mark, Rich.	.971	25	31	71	3	105	11
Evans, Tom, Tol.	1.000	1	2	1	0	3	0
Figueroa, Luis, Nor.	.968	16	20	41	2	63	7
Forbes, P.J., S./W.B.	.973	22	31	76	3	110	14
Freel, Ryan, Syr.	.974	8	16	22	1	39	7
Garabito, Eddy, Roch.	.927	24	29	60	7	96	15
Garcia, Amaury, Char.	1.000	1	2	4	0	6	2
Garcia, Carlos, Col.	.923	16	23	49	6	78	12
Garcia, Jesse, Rich.	.954	84	120	233	17	370	39
Garciaparra, Nomar, Paw.	.941	3	4	12	1	17	1
Giles, Marcus, Rich.	1.000	2	4	2	0	6	0
Goelz, Jim, Buf.	.000	1	0	0	0	0	0
Gomez, Chris, Dur.	.978	23	23	65	2	90	11
Guerrero, Wilton, Lou.	.956	12	17	26	2	45	5
Guevara, Giomar, Tol.	.954	108	163	354	25	542	73
Hernandez, Carlos, Nor.	.976	7	13	27	1	41	7
Holbert, Aaron, Syr.	1.000	2	2	3	0	5	1
Hoover, Paul, Dur.	.000	2	0	0	0	0	0
Izturis, Cesar, Syr.	.949	57	104	174	15	293	45
Jimenez, D'Angelo, Col.	1.000	15	16	43	0	59	8
Knupfer, Jason, S./W.B.	1.000	3	1	5	0	6	0
LaRocca, Greg, Buf.	1.000	8	16	28	0	44	7
Larson, Brandon, Lou.	1.000	6	7	7	0	14	2
Lawrence, Joe, Syr.	.000	1	0	0	0	0	0
Lofton, James, Paw.	.946	42	49	125	10	184	14
Lopez, Felipe, Syr.	.942	61	87	174	16	277	40
Loretta, Mark, Ind.	.909	3	2	8	1	11	2
Malloy, Marty, Lou.	.938	38	50	100	10	160	22
Martinez, Eddy, Roch.	.926	83	119	155	22	296	33
Martinez, Gabby, Nor.	1.000	2	3	3	0	6	1
McDonald, John, Buf.	.958	111	170	328	22	520	81
Medrano, Tony, Buf.	.981	26	40	65	2	107	19
Merloni, Lou, Paw.	.945	31	46	75	7	128	11
Miller, Ryan, Nor.	.923	11	14	22	3	39	6
Nettles, Jeff, Col.	.900	2	0	3	1	10	1
Nevers, Tom, Lou.	.850	5	5	12	3	20	2
Pena, Elvis, Ind.	.949	107	161	283	24	468	54
Perez, Jorgan, Syr.	.950	5	5	14	1	20	2
Perez, Jhonny, Tol.	.958	27	44	93	6	140	18
Punto, Nick, S./W.B.	.964	123	158	398	21	577	80
Rios, Brian, Tol.	.927	15	14	37	4	55	9
Roberts, Brian, Roch.	.927	44	62	104	13	179	16
Rodriguez, Liu, Char.	.942	19	30	51	5	86	11
Scutaro, Marcos, Ind.	.889	4	4	12	2	18	2
Seabol, Scott, Col.	1.000	7	11	16	0	27	5
Sexton, Chris, Lou.	.970	93	132	284	13	429	50
Shave, Jon, Paw.	.946	49	77	133	12	222	30
Sheets, Andy, Dur.	.958	61	103	145	11	259	38
Smith, Bobby, Dur.	.895	5	6	11	2	19	1
Smith, Jason, Dur.	.917	8	9	24	3	36	6
Tebbs, Nate, Paw.-Rich.	.948	27	35	56	5	96	11
Velandia, Jorge, Nor.	.977	63	91	205	7	303	41
Woodward, Chris, Syr.	.907	12	12	37	5	54	8

SHORTSTOPS WITH TWO OR MORE TEAMS

Player, Team	Pct.	G	PO	A	E	TC	DP
Tebbs, Nate, Paw.	.931	19	26	41	5	72	8
Tebbs, Nate, Rich.	1.000	8	9	15	0	24	3

OUTFIELDERS

Player, Team	Pct.	G	PO	A	E	TC	DP
Agbayani, Benny, Nor.	1.000	4	5	0	0	5	0
Airoso, Kurt, Tol.	1.000	7	18	1	0	19	0
Alcantara, Israel, Paw.	.975	61	145	8	4	157	2
Allen, Dusty, Tol.	.000	1	0	0	1	1	0
Allensworth, Jermaine, Tol.	.985	133	318	8	5	331	0
Almonte, Wady, Roch.	.984	80	169	11	3	183	0
Anderson, Bryan, Lou.	1.000	1	2	0	0	2	0
Ashby, Chris, Char.	.990	58	93	2	1	96	1
Balfe, Ryan, Syr.	1.000	10	18	1	0	19	0
Barker, Kevin, Ind.*	1.000	30	64	3	0	67	0
Barry, Jeff, Char.	1.000	8	9	1	0	10	1
Bates, Fletcher, S./W.B.	1.000	3	3	0	0	3	0
Becker, Rich, Tol.*	.974	46	72	3	2	77	0
Bellinger, Clay, Col.	.933	13	14	0	1	15	0
Bergeron, Pete, Ott.	.983	50	110	3	2	115	1
Berroa, Geronimo, Ott.	1.000	4	6	0	0	6	0
Bierek, Kurt, Tol.	.992	61	110	9	1	120	1
Bigbie, Larry, Roch.*	1.000	10	20	2	0	22	0
Bradley, Milton, Ott.-Buf.	.980	63	137	7	3	147	2
Bragg, Darren, Nor.-Col.	1.000	50	93	6	0	99	1

Player, Team	Pct.	G	PO	A	E	TC	DP
Brazoban, Yhency, Col.	1.000	1	3	0	0	3	0
Brinkley, Darryl, Roch.	1.000	7	11	0	0	11	0
Brown, Brant, Ind.*	1.000	7	15	1	0	16	1
BUDZINSKI, Mark, Buf.*	1.000	121	253	11	0	264	3
Buford, Damon, Roch.-Lou.	.991	45	108	1	1	110	0
Burkhart, Morgan, Paw.*	1.000	3	1	0	0	1	0
Calloway, Ron, Ott.*	.959	56	113	3	5	121	0
Carpenter, Bubba, Nor.*	.889	17	23	1	3	27	0
Carr, Dustin, Dur.	1.000	20	32	0	0	32	0
Carter, Mike, Rich.	.981	96	201	6	4	211	0
Carter, Shannon, Syr.*	1.000	4	10	0	0	10	0
Casimiro, Carlos, Roch.	.955	42	84	1	4	89	0
Cesar, Dionys, Ind.	.000	1	0	0	1	1	0
Chamblee, Jim, Paw.	1.000	13	23	3	0	26	1
Chevalier, Virgil, Paw.	1.000	3	9	0	0	9	0
Christensen, McKay, Char.*	.981	68	147	4	3	154	1
Clark, Brady, Lou.	.981	46	105	1	2	108	0
Clemente, Edgard, Paw.	.986	83	200	12	3	215	4
Coleman, Michael, Col.	.926	25	48	2	4	54	0
Collier, Lou, Ind.	.981	63	146	8	3	157	2
Conti, Jason, Dur.	.987	38	71	7	1	79	1
Coquillette, Trace, Buf.-Tol.	.988	46	77	4	1	82	1
Coste, Chris, Buf.	1.000	12	26	1	0	27	0
Curry, Mike, Nor.	1.000	9	14	2	0	16	0
Davis, Tommy, Lou.	1.000	6	7	0	0	7	0
Dina, Allen, Nor.	1.000	5	4	0	0	4	0
Ducey, Rob, S./W.B.	1.000	2	4	0	0	4	0
Dunn, Adam, Lou.	.954	54	93	10	5	108	3
Escobar, Alex, Nor.	.980	108	242	8	5	255	2
Fonville, Chad, Col.	1.000	3	4	0	0	4	0
Forbes, P.J., S./W.B.	1.000	21	33	1	0	34	0
Francia, Dave, S./W.B.*	.977	82	164	5	4	173	2
Franco, Matt, Nor.	1.000	1	2	0	0	2	0
Frank, Mike, Col.*	.988	91	165	6	2	173	2
Franklin, Micah, Ind.	.988	43	76	3	1	80	1
Freel, Ryan, Syr.	.974	58	103	8	3	114	0
Garcia, Karim, Buf.*	.978	112	208	11	5	224	1
Gazarek, Marty, Tol.	.964	16	26	1	1	28	0
Gibralter, Dave, Ind.	1.000	24	49	3	0	52	1
Giles, Marcus, Rich.	1.000	1	3	0	0	3	0
Gilkey, Bernard, Rich.	1.000	13	18	1	0	19	0
Gonzalez, Raul, Lou.	.973	137	313	7	9	329	2
Greene, Todd, Col.	1.000	2	3	0	0	3	0
Guerrero, Wilton, Lou.	1.000	4	10	0	0	10	0
Guillen, Jose, Dur.	.982	28	49	5	1	55	1
Hall, Noah, Lou.	1.000	1	1	0	0	1	0
Haltiwanger, Garrick, Syr.*	.981	21	51	0	1	52	0
Hamilton, Jon, Buf.*	1.000	1	3	0	0	3	0
Hardtke, Jason, Char.	1.000	24	36	2	0	38	0
Hatcher, Chris, Dur.	.978	27	44	1	1	46	0
Hernandez, Carlos, Nor.	.000	1	0	0	0	0	0
Holbert, Aaron, Syr.	.000	1	0	0	0	0	0
Hollins, Damon, Rich.*	.981	43	100	1	2	103	0
Hollins, Dave, Buf.	1.000	2	1	0	0	1	0
Hoover, Paul, Dur.	.950	14	18	1	1	20	0
Hunter, Brian, Syr.*	1.000	3	8	0	0	8	0
Hunter, Brian L., S./W.B.	.833	2	5	0	1	6	0
Hunter, Scott, Nor.	1.000	50	98	4	0	102	1
Hutchins, Norm, Dur.*	.975	77	193	5	5	203	0
Inglin, Jeff, Char.	.955	63	79	6	4	89	0
Jackson, Ryan, Tol.*	.900	7	9	0	1	10	0
Jennings, Robin, Lou.*	.952	27	36	4	2	42	2
Johnson, Adam, Char.*	1.000	5	8	0	0	8	0
Johnson, Mark, Nor.*	1.000	1	1	0	0	1	0
Johnson, Rontrez, Paw.	.989	43	91	1	1	93	0
Jones, Chris, Syr.-Rich.-Ind.	.953	79	151	10	8	169	2
Jones, Terry, Ott.	1.000	13	20	5	0	25	1
Kingsale, Eugene, Roch.	.965	57	134	2	5	141	1
Klimek, Josh, Ind.	.950	11	18	1	1	20	0
Knight, Brandon, Syr.	.000	1	0	0	0	0	0
Kremblas, Mike, Syr.	.000	2	0	0	0	0	0
Langaue, Selwyn, Syr.*	1.000	38	62	4	0	66	1
Latham, Chris, Syr.	.965	77	159	7	6	172	0
Lennon, Pat, Col.	1.000	2	5	0	0	5	0
Lesher, Brian, Ind.*	.979	78	137	4	3	144	0
Lindstrom, Dave, Tol.	.875	3	7	0	1	8	0
Lombard, George, Rich.	1.000	12	19	1	0	20	0
Lowery, Terrell, Dur.	.976	69	159	7	4	170	0
Maddox, Garry, Paw.	1.000	4	12	0	0	12	0
Magee, Wendell, Tol.	1.000	2	2	0	0	2	0
Martinez, Gabby, Nor.	.895	14	15	2	2	19	0
Martinez, Greg, Dur.	1.000	58	132	0	0	132	0
Mateo, Ruben, Lou.	.954	62	100	3	5	108	2

Player, Team	Pct.	G	PO	A	E	TC	DP
McDonald, Darnell, Roch.	.957	101	264	5	12	281	1
McDonald, Donzell, Col.	.979	101	232	4	5	241	1
McKinley, Dan, Ott.	1.000	91	161	0	0	161	0
Medrano, Tony, Buf.	.986	37	72	1	1	74	0
Michaels, Jason, S./W.B.	1.000	104	168	4	0	172	1
Minor, Ryan, Ott.	1.000	17	29	0	0	29	0
Montgomery, Ray, Nor.	.932	35	55	0	4	59	0
Mouton, James, Ind.	1.000	2	4	0	0	4	0
Mouton, Lyle, Tol.	.983	53	113	6	2	121	2
Neill, Mike, Paw.*	.992	54	110	7	1	118	2
Nettles, Jeff, Col.	1.000	2	4	0	0	4	0
Nunnari, Talmadge, Ott.*	1.000	14	28	2	0	30	1
Ottavinia, Paul, Col.*	.982	28	51	3	1	55	1
Patterson, Jarrod, Tol.	1.000	1	1	0	0	1	0
Peoples, Danny, Buf.	1.000	10	14	1	0	15	0
Perez, Rob, Col.-Ind.	.983	52	115	2	2	119	1
Perez, Timo, Nor.*	.951	46	90	8	5	103	2
Perry, Chan, Rich.	1.000	14	17	0	0	17	0
Pride, Curt, Ott.	.963	19	26	0	1	27	0
Prieto, Rick, Char.	1.000	6	10	0	0	10	0
Raines, Tim, Roch.	.986	37	70	1	1	72	0
Ramirez, Julio, Char.	.962	88	191	9	8	208	0
Reed, Keith, Roch.	.933	19	28	0	2	30	0
Rivera, Juan, Col.	.970	55	124	5	4	133	0
Roberge, J.P., S./W.B.	1.000	4	6	0	0	6	0
Roberts, Dave, Buf.*	.978	56	132	1	3	136	0
Robertson, Mike, Rich.*	1.000	21	28	1	0	29	0
Rodriguez, Henry, Col.*	1.000	3	3	0	0	3	0
Ross, Jason, Rich.	.957	47	84	4	4	92	0
Rowand, Aaron, Char.	.966	79	170	1	6	177	0
Royster, Aaron, S./W.B.	1.000	3	5	1	0	6	0
Rust, Brian, Roch.	1.000	22	37	0	0	37	0
Samuels, Scott, Paw.	.980	35	98	0	2	100	0
Sanchez, Alex, Ind.*	.968	79	178	2	6	186	0
Sanders, Deion, Lou.-Syr.*	.982	32	53	1	1	55	0
Seabol, Scott, Col.	1.000	12	28	2	0	30	0
Sefcik, Kevin, Buf.	1.000	16	27	0	0	27	0
Seguignol, Fernando, Ott.	1.000	3	5	0	0	5	0
Selby, Bill, Lou.	1.000	8	11	0	0	11	0
Sell, Chip, Ind.	.909	16	38	2	4	44	1
Sheets, Andy, Dur.	.000	2	0	0	0	0	0
Sheff, Chris, Lou.	.980	63	91	6	2	99	1
Simmons, Brian, Syr.	.970	48	91	5	3	99	2
Sisco, Steve, Roch.	1.000	12	11	0	0	11	0
Smith, Bobby, Dur.	.986	76	128	10	2	140	1
Smith, Mark, Ott.	.974	38	72	4	2	78	0
Snyder, John, Ind.	.000	1	0	0	0	0	0
Spencer, Shane, Col.	.985	32	64	2	1	67	0
Stenson, Dernell, Paw.*	.964	120	204	9	8	221	2
Stratton, Rob, Nor.	1.000	2	2	0	0	2	0
Swann, Pedro, Rich.	.985	124	245	10	4	259	1
Sweeney, Mark, Ind.*	1.000	49	105	0	0	105	0
Tarasco, Tony, Nor.	.991	98	204	13	2	219	4
Taylor, Reggie, S./W.B.	.980	108	243	6	5	254	0
Tebbs, Nate, Paw.	1.000	20	25	1	0	26	1
Thompson, Andy, Syr.	.983	29	58	1	1	60	1
Thompson, Rich, Syr.	1.000	17	43	1	0	44	0
Thompson, Ryan, Ott.	1.000	15	30	2	0	32	0
Toca, Jorge, Nor.	.963	41	75	2	3	80	1
Tyler, Brad, Lou.	.944	7	15	2	1	18	1
Tyner, Jason, Dur.*	1.000	39	88	2	0	90	2
Valent, Eric, S./W.B.*	.988	95	155	12	2	169	3
Valenzuela, Mario, Char.	.957	48	84	5	4	93	0
Villegas, Ismael, Rich.	.000	1	0	0	0	0	0
Wakeland, Chris, Tol.*	.966	113	213	13	8	234	2
Ward, Jeremy, S./W.B.	.946	23	34	1	2	37	0
Ware, Jeremy, Ott.	.986	33	64	4	1	69	1
Wells, Vernon, Syr.	.978	103	216	7	5	228	5
Wigginton, Ty, Nor.	1.000	1	3	0	0	3	0
Wilcox, Luke, Col.	1.000	10	21	1	0	22	0
Wilkerson, Brad, Ott.*	.973	55	101	6	3	110	1
Wilson, Travis, Rich.	.972	55	68	1	2	71	0
Wise, Dewayne, Syr.*	1.000	1	5	0	0	5	0
Woods, Ken, Roch.-Rich.-S./W.B.	.978	40	83	7	2	92	1

TRIPLE PLAY: Swann.

OUTFIELDERS WITH TWO OR MORE TEAMS

Player, Team	Pct.	G	PO	A	E	TC	DP
Bradley, Milton, Ott.	.966	34	80	4	3	87	1
Bradley, Milton, Buf.	1.000	29	57	3	0	60	1
Bragg, Darren, Nor.	1.000	23	41	2	0	43	0
Bragg, Darren, Col.	1.000	27	52	4	0	56	1
Buford, Damon, Roch.	1.000	32	86	0	0	86	0

Player, Team	Pct.	G	PO	A	E	TC	DP
Buford, Damon, Lou.	.958	13	22	1	1	24	0
Coquillette, Trace, Buf.	.987	42	72	4	1	77	1
Coquillette, Trace, Tol.	1.000	4	5	0	0	5	0
Jones, Chris, Syr.	.909	26	47	3	5	55	0
Jones, Chris, Rich.	1.000	23	42	3	0	45	1
Jones, Chris, Ind.	.957	30	62	4	3	69	1
Perez, Rob, Col.	1.000	32	68	2	0	70	1
Perez, Rob, Ind.	.959	20	47	0	2	49	0
Sanders, Deion, Lou.*	.973	19	36	0	1	37	0
Sanders, Deion, Syr.*	1.000	13	17	1	0	18	0
Woods, Ken, Roch.	.968	22	53	7	2	62	1
Woods, Ken, Rich.	1.000	17	28	0	0	28	0
Woods, Ken, S./W.B.	1.000	1	2	0	0	2	0

CATCHERS

Player, Team	Pct.	G	PO	A	E	TC	DP	PB
Andreopoulos, Alex, Buf.	.990	34	191	11	2	204	1	1
Bennett, Gary, Nor.	1.000	15	94	5	0	99	1	2
Bennett, Ryan, Nor.	1.000	10	46	2	0	48	0	0
Borders, Pat, Dur.	.989	40	253	27	3	283	3	3
Brown, Kevin, Ind.	.992	76	439	45	4	488	7	3
Cancel, Rob, Ind.	.993	45	262	43	2	307	6	4
Cardona, Javier, Tol.	.989	26	156	22	2	180	2	3
Charles, Frank, Roch.	.971	68	508	37	16	561	4	6
Coste, Chris, Buf.	.989	32	257	17	3	277	2	1
Dalesandro, Mark, Char.	.998	65	429	37	1	467	2	5
Davis, Tommy, Lou.	1.000	12	55	8	0	63	0	0
Dominique, Andy, S./W.B.	1.000	1	8	1	0	9	0	0
Encarnacion, Angelo, Paw.	.994	45	316	39	2	357	4	5
Estalella, Bobby, Col.	.993	36	259	18	2	279	1	0
Estrada, Johnny, S./W.B.	1.000	30	246	19	0	265	2	2
Figga, Mike, Col.-Nor.	.996	30	193	27	1	221	6	3
Gil, Geronimo, Roch.	.986	23	185	22	3	210	2	6
Gonzalez, Jimmy, Ott	.990	57	368	27	4	399	4	3
Greene, Charlie, Rich.	.987	22	136	11	2	149	1	1
Greene, Todd, Col.	.982	27	201	15	4	220	3	2
Gubanich, Creighton, Ind.-Char.	.988	35	227	22	3	252	6	5
Hall, Toby, Dur.	.987	64	400	43	6	457	3	2
Heintz, Chris, Char.	1.000	5	21	1	0	22	0	0
Hoover, Paul, Dur.	.993	43	263	19	2	284	3	7
Hughes, Bobby, Roch.	1.000	1	1	0	0	1	0	0
Inge, Brandon, Tol.	.989	27	160	20	2	182	1	6
Jensen, Marcus, Paw.	.994	25	146	11	1	158	3	2
Johannes, Todd, Ott.	.950	3	18	1	1	20	1	0
Johnson, Mark, Char.	.990	47	385	24	4	413	3	3
Kremblas, Mike, Syr.	.938	2	14	1	1	16	1	0
Laker, Tim, Buf.	.990	80	549	41	6	596	6	4
LAWRENCE, Joe, Syr.	.994	75	502	37	3	542	1	15
Levis, Jesse, Rich.-Ind.	.996	72	479	51	2	532	5	6
Lindstrom, Dave, Tol.	.981	54	349	22	7	378	4	4
Lomasney, Steve, Paw.	.969	17	121	2	4	127	0	2
Lopez-Cao, Mike, Roch.	1.000	2	8	0	0	8	0	0
Marconi, Alex, Dur.	.909	1	10	0	1	11	0	0
Martinez, Casey, Syr.	1.000	2	1	0	0	1	0	0
Matos, Pascual, Col.	.991	74	512	44	5	561	3	11
Mendez, Carlos, Ind.	.989	41	240	21	3	264	6	1
Meran, Jorge, Tol.	1.000	7	32	5	0	37	0	1
Miller, Corky, Lou.	.994	41	294	35	2	331	6	8
Molina, Izzy, Syr.	.987	70	451	19	6	476	6	1
Morales, Willie, Roch.	.990	52	359	25	4	388	2	6
Mosquera, Julio, Col.	.989	16	87	5	1	93	1	0
Mulligan, Sean, Roch.	.942	7	48	1	3	52	1	1
Neill, Mike, Paw.*	.000	2	0	0	0	0	0	0
Norris, Dax, Rich.	.993	74	531	38	4	573	4	2
Oliver, Joe, Paw.	.986	12	66	5	1	72	1	0
Paul, Josh, Char.	1.000	18	125	7	0	132	0	1
Phillips, Jason, Nor.	1.000	18	103	5	0	108	2	0
Probst, Alan, Nor.	.974	18	103	8	3	114	0	1
Ramos, Kelly, Paw.	.955	5	19	2	1	22	0	2
Reed, Jeff, S./W.B.	.995	29	187	15	1	203	2	2
Rodriguez, Luis, Paw.	.985	30	178	21	3	202	2	3
Salazar, Jeremy, S./W.B.	.987	47	360	19	5	384	2	4
Schneider, Brian, Ott.	.994	89	629	79	4	712	4	2
Snusz, Chris, Buf.	1.000	1	3	0	0	3	0	0
Spehr, Tim, Lou.	.982	48	303	33	6	342	3	8
Taubensee, Eddie, Buf.	.960	5	23	1	1	25	0	0
Valdez, Jerry, S./W.B.	1.000	5	21	3	0	24	0	1
Walbeck, Matt, Lou.-S./W.B.	1.000	95	588	53	0	641	8	13
Wigginton, Ty, Nor.	.000	1	0	0	0	0	0	0
Williams, George, Paw.	.990	16	94	5	1	100	0	1
Wilson, Vance, Nor.	.984	64	436	47	8	491	4	6

CATCHERS WITH TWO OR MORE TEAMS

Player, Team	Pct.	G	PO	A	E	TC	DP	PB
Figga, Mike, Col.	1.000	1	7	0	0	7	0	0
Figga, Mike, Nor.	.995	29	186	27	1	214	6	3
Gubanich, Creighton, Ind.	.993	22	135	12	1	148	3	2
Gubanich, Creighton, Char.	.981	13	92	10	2	104	3	3
Levis, Jesse, Rich.	.995	61	398	43	2	443	2	6
Levis, Jesse, Ind.	1.000	11	81	8	0	89	3	0
Walbeck, Matt, Lou.	1.000	56	300	34	0	334	5	8
Walbeck, Matt, S./W.B.	1.000	39	288	19	0	307	3	5

PITCHERS

Player, Team	Pct.	G	PO	A	E	TC	DP
Adkins, Tim, Col.*	.000	1	0	0	0	0	0
Agamennone, Brandon, Ott.	1.000	8	0	2	0	2	1
Agosto, Stevenson, Dur.*	1.000	3	0	1	0	1	0
Almanzar, Carlos, Col.	1.000	35	1	3	0	4	0
Alvarez, Wilson, Dur.*	1.000	4	0	2	0	2	1
Ambrose, John, Paw.	.000	2	0	0	0	0	0
Andrews, Clayton, Lou.*	.846	8	3	8	2	13	1
Aramboles, Ricardo, Col.	.900	4	3	6	1	10	0
Arias, Pablo, Tol.	1.000	1	0	4	0	4	0
Atchley, Justin, Lou.*	1.000	15	0	4	0	4	1
Aybar, Manny, Dur.	1.000	11	1	3	0	4	0
Bacsik, Mike, Buf.*	.895	21	5	12	2	19	0
Baez, Danny, Buf.	1.000	16	3	2	0	5	1
Baez, Kevin, Nor.	.000	2	0	0	0	0	0
Bailie, Matt, S./W.B.	.000	1	0	0	0	0	0
Baldwin, James, Char.	1.000	2	1	2	0	3	0
Bale, John, Roch.*	.800	9	3	1	1	5	0
Banks, Willie, Syr.-Paw.	.889	26	5	19	3	27	2
Baptist, Travis, Char.*	.941	33	5	11	1	17	0
Barcelo, Lorenzo, Char.	.000	2	0	0	0	0	0
Bauer, Rick, Roch.	.955	10	7	14	1	22	0
Beasley, Ray, Rich.*	1.000	65	7	4	0	11	0
Bechler, Steve, Roch.	.500	2	1	0	1	2	0
Beirne, Kevin, Syr.	1.000	18	1	4	0	5	0
Bell, Jason, Syr.	1.000	8	0	1	0	1	0
Bell, Rob, Lou.	1.000	5	2	2	0	4	0
Beltran, Rigo, S./W.B.*	.941	37	4	12	1	17	2
Bernero, Adam, Tol.	.944	26	12	22	2	36	0
Bertotti, Mike, Col.*	.889	19	3	5	1	9	1
Billingsley, Brent, Ott.*	1.000	1	1	0	0	1	0
Blair, Willie, Buf.	.889	11	5	3	1	9	1
Blank, Matt, Ott.*	.947	14	6	12	1	19	1
Bleazard, Dave, Syr.	1.000	5	1	1	0	2	0
Borkowski, Dave, Tol.	.889	18	2	6	1	9	1
Bowers, Cedrick, Dur.*	1.000	42	4	6	0	10	0
Bowles, Brian, Syr.	1.000	66	7	8	0	15	0
Boyd, Jason, S./W.B.	.875	52	7	7	2	16	2
Brea, Lesli, Roch.	.923	63	7	5	1	13	0
Bridges, Donnie, Ott.	.933	13	5	9	1	15	1
Brittan, Corey, Nor.	1.000	58	8	17	0	25	2
Brock, Chris, S./W.B.	.938	13	5	10	1	16	0
Brower, Jim, Lou.	1.000	2	1	2	0	3	0
Brown, Derek, Roch.	1.000	9	2	1	0	3	0
Brunette, Justin, Nor.*	.667	24	0	4	2	6	0
Buddie, Mike, Ind.	.900	27	3	6	1	10	1
Buller, Sean, Tol.*	1.000	5	1	1	0	2	0
Bullinger, Kirk, Char.	1.000	36	4	13	0	17	2
Burrows, Terry, Ott.*	1.000	6	0	2	0	2	0
Byrd, Paul, S./W.B.	.923	5	5	7	1	13	0
Byrdak, Tim, Buf.*	1.000	4	0	1	0	1	0
Callaway, Mickey, Dur.	.971	29	11	23	1	35	1
Carter, Mike, Rich.	1.000	1	0	1	0	1	0
Cassidy, Scott, Syr.	.833	11	2	8	2	12	0
Castillo, Carlos, Paw.	.906	28	7	22	3	32	0
Castillo, Frank, Paw.	1.000	2	0	1	0	1	0
Cedeno, Blas, S./W.B.	1.000	35	1	5	0	6	0
Cerda, Jaime, Nor.*	.000	3	0	0	0	0	0
Cerros, Juan, Nor.	1.000	38	9	8	0	17	2
CHANTRES, Carlos, Ind.	1.000	28	11	29	0	40	1
Chen, Bruce, S./W.B.*	1.000	3	0	3	0	3	0
Cho, Jin Ho, Paw.	1.000	37	8	18	0	26	2
Choate, Randy, Col.*	1.000	4	0	2	0	2	1
Chulk, Vinny, Syr.	.000	5	0	0	0	0	0
Coco, Pasqual, Syr.	.952	22	4	16	1	21	2
Coggin, Dave, S./W.B.	.933	15	9	19	2	30	4
Colome, Jesus, Dur.	1.000	13	3	1	0	4	0
Comolli, Mark, Syr.	1.000	1	0	1	0	1	0
Cook, Dennis, S./W.B.*	.000	1	0	0	0	0	0
Coppinger, Rocky, Ind.	.800	15	1	3	1	5	0

Player, Team	Pct.	G	PO	A	E	TC	DP
Corbin, Archie, Char.	.920	58	3	20	2	25	2
Corey, Mark, Nor.	1.000	28	2	6	0	8	0
Cornejo, Nate, Tol.	1.000	4	3	11	0	14	1
Cornett, Brad, Syr.-Dur.	.944	39	7	10	1	18	2
Crawford, Paxton, Paw.	1.000	6	3	1	0	4	0
Croushore, Rich, Nor.	1.000	10	0	1	0	1	0
Cubillan, Darwin, Ott.	.875	17	0	7	1	8	0
Cumberland, Chris, Rich.*	1.000	13	0	1	0	1	0
Cunnane, Will, Ind.	1.000	7	3	4	0	7	1
Curreri, Joe, Char.	.000	1	0	0	0	0	0
Daneker, Pat, Syr.	1.000	10	4	12	0	16	0
Darnell, Paul, Lou.*	.667	21	1	1	1	3	0
Darwin, Dave, Buf.*	1.000	4	0	1	0	1	0
Davis, Lance, Lou.*	1.000	13	1	14	0	15	1
Davison, Scott, Dur.	1.000	2	0	1	0	1	0
Dawley, Joey, Rich.	1.000	3	0	1	0	1	0
Day, Zach, Buf.-Ott.	1.000	7	0	6	0	6	0
DeLucia, Rich, Tol.	1.000	28	1	2	0	3	0
De Paula, Sean, Buf.	1.000	6	1	0	0	1	0
Deschenes, Marc, Buf.	1.000	22	3	1	0	4	0
Dewitt, Matt, Syr.	1.000	53	6	6	0	12	1
Dickson, Jason, Syr.	.929	11	5	8	1	14	0
Dillinger, John, Syr.	.952	26	10	10	1	21	3
Douglass, Sean, Roch.	.973	27	7	29	1	37	2
Drese, Ryan, Dur.*	.941	11	5	11	1	17	1
Drew, Tim, Buf.	.933	18	3	11	1	15	1
Duckworth, Brandon, S./W.B.	.963	22	6	20	1	27	3
Ebert, Derrin, Paw.*	1.000	10	2	7	0	9	0
Eischen, Joey, Ott.*	1.000	34	1	10	0	11	1
Enders, Trevor, Dur.*	.875	32	2	5	1	8	1
Erdos, Todd, Paw.	1.000	49	4	8	0	12	1
Eshelman, Vaughn, Nor.*	.000	7	0	0	0	0	0
Espina, Rendy, Syr.*	.917	36	2	9	1	12	3
Estrella, Leo, Nor.-Lou.	1.000	42	6	15	0	21	1
Evans, Keith, Ott.	.941	45	1	15	1	17	1
Eyre, Scott, Syr.*	.909	62	2	8	1	11	1
Farrell, Jim, Paw.	1.000	1	0	0	0	0	0
Felix, Miguel, Roch.	1.000	1	1	0	0	1	0
Fernandez, Jared, Lou.	.976	33	13	28	1	42	2
Fernandez, Ozzie, Lou.	1.000	9	5	5	0	10	0
Fernandez, Sid, Col.*	1.000	1	0	1	0	1	0
Figueroa, Nelson, S./W.B.	1.000	13	8	8	0	16	1
File, Bob, Syr.	1.000	2	1	1	0	2	1
Fiore, Tony, Dur.	1.000	15	2	2	0	4	0
Flores, Neomar, Syr.	.000	2	0	0	0	0	0
Flores, Randy, Col.*	1.000	3	1	2	0	3	2
Florie, Bryce, Tol.	1.000	10	1	3	0	4	1
Flury, Pat, Ott.-Col.	1.000	44	5	4	0	9	0
Fogg, Josh, Char.	.905	40	2	17	2	21	1
Fordham, Tom, Ind.*	1.000	18	0	8	0	8	0
Forster, Scott, Lou.*	1.000	9	0	1	0	1	0
Foster, Kris, Roch.	.500	9	1	0	1	2	0
Fox, Chad, Ind.	1.000	4	0	1	0	1	0
Frank, Mike, Col.*	.000	1	0	0	0	0	0
Frascatore, John, Syr.	.923	37	2	10	1	13	0
Gandarillas, Gus, Paw.-Ind.	.955	40	7	14	1	22	3
Garcia, Carlos, Col.	.000	1	0	0	0	0	0
Gardner, Lee, Dur.	.889	56	5	3	1	9	1
Garland, Jon, Char.	1.000	5	6	4	0	10	0
Geary, Geoff, S./W.B.	1.000	7	2	2	0	4	0
Ginter, Matt, Char.	.857	22	6	12	3	21	1
Glauber, Keith, Lou.	1.000	23	7	4	0	11	0
Glover, Gary, Char.	1.000	6	1	7	0	8	0
Gonzalez, Dicky, Nor.	1.000	17	7	11	0	18	1
Gooch, Arnie, Lou.	.958	28	17	29	2	48	2
Guerrier, Matt, Char.	1.000	12	0	26	0	26	1
Guevara, Giomar, Tol.	1.000	1	0	1	0	1	0
Gunderson, Eric, Buf.-Col.*	.955	58	8	13	1	22	3
Guzman, Juan, Dur.	1.000	10	6	10	0	16	0
Haines, Talley, Dur.	.000	1	0	0	0	0	0
Halladay, Roy, Syr.	1.000	2	1	2	0	3	0
Hamilton, Jimmy, Roch.*	.889	36	0	8	1	9	1
Hamilton, Joey, Lou.	1.000	1	0	3	0	3	0
Hammond, Chris, Buf.-Rich.*	.905	49	6	13	2	21	1
Hannah, Shawn, Tol.	1.000	1	1	0	0	1	0
Harikkala, Tim, Ind.	.978	31	9	35	1	45	2
Harnisch, Pete, Lou.	.000	1	0	0	0	0	0
Harper, Travis, Dur.	.933	25	10	4	1	15	1
Hasselhoff, Derek, Char.	.909	34	4	6	1	11	0
Hazlett, Andy, Paw.*	1.000	9	2	3	0	5	0
Heams, Shane, Tol.	.500	14	0	1	1	2	0
Heiserman, Rick, Paw.	1.000	3	0	1	0	1	0
Hendrickson, Mark, Syr.*	.950	38	3	16	1	20	1
Henriquez, Oscar, Nor.*	1.000	39	2	4	0	6	0
Henry, Butch, Col.-Syr.-Ind.*	.960	18	3	21	1	25	3
Hernandez, Adrian, Col.	.929	21	20	19	3	42	1
Hill, Ken, Lou.-Paw.	1.000	14	6	9	0	15	1
Hinchliffe, Brett, Nor.	.909	11	5	5	1	11	0
Hooten, Dave, Buf.	.000	1	0	0	0	0	0
Huisman, Rick, Roch.	1.000	15	1	1	0	2	0
Irabu, Hideki, Ott.	1.000	4	1	1	0	2	0
Jacquez, Tom, S./W.B.*	.905	33	9	10	2	21	3
James, Delvin, Dur.	.903	31	7	21	3	31	0
Jean, Domingo, Col.	.800	35	2	6	2	10	1
Jimenez, Jason, Dur.*	1.000	15	0	3	0	3	0
Jodie, Brett, Col.	.885	19	7	16	3	26	1
Johnson, Barry, Col.	1.000	38	3	6	0	9	1
Johnson, Mark, Tol.	1.000	24	15	22	0	37	1
Johnson, Mike, Ott.	1.000	2	0	2	0	2	0
Jones, Bobby M., Nor.*	.000	1	0	0	0	0	0
Juden, Jeff, Char.	.929	12	5	8	1	14	1
Julio, Jorge, Roch.	.750	34	1	5	2	8	2
Kane, Kyle, Char.	1.000	1	0	1	0	1	0
Keisler, Randy, Col.*	.882	18	7	8	2	17	0
Keller, Kris, Tol.	1.000	52	1	2	0	3	0
Kennedy, Joe, Dur.*	.833	4	2	3	1	6	1
Kershner, Jason, S./W.B.*	.667	6	0	4	2	6	0
Kim, Sun-Woo, Paw.	.870	19	4	16	3	23	1
Knight, Brandon, Col.	1.000	25	6	15	0	21	1
Kohlmeier, Ryan, Roch.	1.000	14	3	5	0	8	0
Kolb, Brandon, Ind.	.625	40	0	5	3	8	0
Kusiewicz, Mike, Paw.*	.833	8	0	5	1	6	0
Lail, Denny, Col.	.931	33	12	15	2	29	0
Lakman, Jason, Roch.	1.000	19	0	7	0	7	0
Lee, Sang, Paw.*	1.000	43	1	8	0	9	0
Leek, Randy, Tol.*	1.000	1	0	1	0	1	0
Levrault, Allen, Ind.	1.000	5	3	5	0	8	0
Lewis, Derrick, Rich.	1.000	12	4	12	0	16	0
Lewis, Richie, Buf.-Nor.	.957	24	8	14	1	23	0
Ligtenberg, Kerry, Rich.	.000	1	0	0	0	0	0
Lilly, Ted, Col.*	1.000	5	0	4	0	4	0
Linton, Doug, Nor.	1.000	12	6	10	0	16	0
Lira, Felipe, Ott.-S./W.B.	1.000	44	4	7	0	11	1
Lohrman, Dave, Nor.	1.000	2	0	1	0	1	0
Loux, Shane, Tol.	.923	28	5	31	3	39	3
Lovingier, Kevin, Col.*	.750	7	1	2	1	4	1
Lowe, Sean, Char.	.667	2	0	2	1	3	0
Luebbers, Larry, Lou.	1.000	21	10	25	0	35	2
Lyon, Brandon, Syr.	1.000	11	5	6	0	11	1
MacRae, Scott, Lou.	.750	11	0	3	1	4	0
Maduro, Calvin, Roch.	.900	12	3	6	1	10	1
Mallette, Brian, Ind.	.000	12	0	0	0	0	0
Manon, Julio, Ott.	.938	15	3	12	1	16	0
Maroth, Mike, Tol.*	.975	24	8	31	1	40	2
Marquez, Rob, Ott.	.917	34	2	9	1	12	1
Martin, Tom, Nor.*	1.000	23	0	3	0	3	0
Masaoka, Onan, Char.*	.750	14	1	2	1	4	0
Mattes, Troy, Ott.	1.000	15	10	7	0	17	1
Maurer, Dave, Lou.*	.750	18	1	2	1	4	0
McClellan, Matt, Syr.	1.000	29	2	13	0	15	1
McClendon, Matt, Rich.	.917	10	3	8	1	12	0
McDill, Allen, Paw.*	1.000	47	5	18	0	23	1
McLeary, Marty, Paw.	1.000	18	0	7	0	7	0
McNichol, Brian, Lou.*	1.000	26	0	3	0	3	1
Meacham, Rusty, Dur.	1.000	27	2	2	0	4	0
Mendoza, Geronimo, Char.	.950	17	5	14	1	20	1
Mercado, Hector, Lou.*	1.000	12	0	2	0	2	0
Mieses, Jose, Ind.	.667	3	1	1	1	3	0
Miller, Matt, Tol.*	1.000	50	2	9	0	11	0
Miller, Ryan, Nor.	.000	1	0	0	0	0	0
Miller, Trever, Paw.*	1.000	33	3	15	0	18	1
Mitchell, Scott, Ott.	1.000	6	1	3	0	4	0
Mix, Greg, Paw.	1.000	8	1	1	0	2	0
Moehler, Brian, Tol.	1.000	2	2	0	0	2	0
Montane, Ivan, Nor.	.909	15	4	6	1	11	0
Moore, Trey, Rich.*	.960	26	8	16	1	25	1
Moss, Damian, Rich.*	.952	17	6	14	1	21	1
Mota, Guillermo, Ott.	1.000	4	0	1	0	1	0
Munoz, Bobby, Ott.	.909	19	5	25	3	33	3
Murray, Heath, Tol.*	.875	11	1	6	1	8	0
Nagy, Charles, Buf.	1.000	6	1	8	0	9	0
Nelson, Joe, Rich.	.889	29	4	4	1	9	0
Neugebauer, Nick, Ind.	1.000	4	2	4	0	6	1
Nichting, Chris, Lou.	.857	27	2	4	1	7	0

Player, Team	Pct.	G	PO	A	E	TC	DP
Nickle, Doug, S./W.B.	1.000	47	5	18	0	23	3
Nitkowski, C.J., Tol.*	.000	1	0	0	0	0	0
Ochoa, Pablo, Nor.	1.000	19	3	2	0	5	0
Ogea, Chad, Col.	1.000	6	0	4	0	4	0
Ohka, Tomo, Paw.	.833	8	1	4	1	6	0
Ontiveros, Steve, Nor.	1.000	7	1	5	0	6	0
Oropesa, Eddie, S./W.B.*	1.000	14	2	1	0	3	1
Pacheco, Delvis, Rich.	1.000	22	2	12	0	14	2
Padilla, Vicente, S./W.B.	1.000	16	6	9	0	15	2
Painter, Lance, Ind.*	.750	8	0	3	1	4	1
Paronto, Chad, Roch.	.800	33	2	2	1	5	1
Parris, Steve, Syr.	1.000	2	1	0	0	1	0
Parrish, John, Roch.*	.809	26	11	27	9	47	1
Pavano, Carl, Ott.	.833	4	2	3	1	6	0
Pena, Jesus, Paw.*	1.000	26	3	12	0	15	1
Penney, Mike, Ind.	.957	22	8	14	1	23	3
Perez, Odaliz, Rich.*	1.000	5	1	4	0	5	1
Perisho, Matt, Tol.*	1.000	25	2	1	0	3	0
Persails, Mark, Tol.	.900	12	4	5	1	10	1
Peters, Chris, Lou.-Col.*	.941	17	4	12	1	17	0
Peterson, Kyle, Ind.	.905	21	8	11	2	21	1
Pettyjohn, Adam, Tol.*	1.000	17	5	11	0	16	0
Phelps, Tommy, Tol.*	.917	29	3	8	1	12	1
Phelps, Travis, Dur.	1.000	9	3	2	0	5	1
Phillips, Jason, Buf.	1.000	8	2	6	0	8	0
Pichardo, Hipolito, Paw.	1.000	3	0	2	0	2	0
Pina, Rafael, Roch.	.875	13	3	4	1	8	0
Pineda, Luis, Tol.	1.000	2	1	1	0	2	0
Porzio, Mike, Char.	.857	31	2	10	0	21	0
Prieto, Ariel, Dur.	.667	3	1	1	1	3	0
Pujals, Denis, Dur.	.000	2	0	0	0	0	0
Pulsipher, Bill, Paw.*	1.000	24	0	8	0	8	0
Radinsky, Scott, Buf.*	1.000	16	1	1	0	2	0
Rain, Steve, Ind.	.857	25	0	6	1	7	0
Rauch, Jon, Char.	.800	6	4	0	1	5	0
Reames, Britt, Ott.	1.000	8	10	10	0	20	1
Redman, Mark, Tol.*	.750	3	2	1	1	4	0
Reed, Brandon, Col.	.857	24	0	6	1	7	0
Reinike, Chris, Buf.	.000	1	0	0	0	0	0
Reith, Brian, Lou.	1.000	1	0	2	0	2	0
Renwick, Tyler, Syr.	1.000	2	1	0	0	1	1
Reyes, Dennys, Lou.*	1.000	7	2	6	0	8	1
Riedling, John, Lou.	.000	1	0	0	0	0	0
Riggan, Jerrod, Nor.	.857	28	1	5	1	7	1
Rijo, Jose, Lou.	1.000	6	2	3	0	5	0
Rios, Brian, Tol.	1.000	1	0	0	0	0	0
Riske, David, Buf.	1.000	38	1	5	0	6	1
Roach, Jason, Nor.	1.000	4	1	5	0	6	1
Robbins, Jake, Rich.	.958	57	6	17	1	24	2
Roberts, Chris, Ind.*	1.000	5	0	1	0	1	0
Roberts, Grant, Nor.	.737	30	4	10	5	19	2
Rodriguez, Frank, Lou.	.917	43	6	16	2	24	0
Rodriquez, Nerio, Nor.-Buf.	1.000	12	2	2	0	4	0
Roque, Rafael, Paw.*	.938	20	6	9	1	16	2
Rose, Brian, Dur.	1.000	19	2	17	0	19	0
Rose, Ted, Ott.	.931	37	6	21	2	29	1
Ruffin, Johnny, Lou.	1.000	9	0	1	0	1	0
Runyan, Sean, Tol.*	1.000	11	0	3	0	3	0
Rupe, Ryan, Dur.	1.000	2	3	0	0	3	0
Saberhagen, Bret, Paw.	1.000	1	0	1	0	1	0
Santos, Victor, Tol.	.400	6	0	2	3	5	0
Scanlan, Bob, Ott.	.833	32	5	5	2	12	0
Schrenk, Steve, Char.	1.000	30	5	3	0	8	0
Scott, Tim, Col.	1.000	14	2	2	0	4	0
Secoda, Jason, Char.	1.000	34	8	23	0	31	1
Seelbach, Chris, Rich.	1.000	22	4	11	0	15	0
Sekany, Jason, Paw.	.000	7	0	0	1	1	0
Seo, Jae, Nor.	1.000	9	1	11	0	12	1
Serafini, Dan, Nor.-Ind.*	1.000	40	1	8	0	9	0
Serrano, Jim, Ott.	1.000	9	0	1	0	1	0
Service, Scott, Lou.	1.000	20	1	5	0	6	0
Sheets, Ben, Ind.	.857	2	2	4	1	7	0
Shumaker, Tony, Roch.*	1.000	53	3	6	0	9	0
Sinclair, Steve, Char.*	1.000	53	2	12	0	14	1
Skrmetta, Matt, Lou.	1.000	46	3	2	0	5	0
Slusarski, Joe, Rich.	1.000	6	1	1	0	2	0
Small, Aaron, Rich.	1.000	41	6	5	0	11	0
Smith, Dan, Buf.	.947	21	10	8	1	19	1
Smith, Roy, Buf.	.909	48	8	12	2	22	1
Snyder, John, Ind.	.944	32	4	30	2	36	4
Snyder, Matt, Roch.	1.000	9	0	2	0	2	0
Sodowsky, Clint, S./W.B.	1.000	7	1	0	0	1	0
Spencer, Sean, Ott.*	1.000	52	1	15	0	16	0
Spoljaric, Paul, Buf.*	.000	4	0	0	1	1	0
Spooneybarger, Tim, Rich.	1.000	42	5	5	0	10	0
Spurgeon, Jay, Roch.	.933	15	3	11	1	15	1
Standridge, Jason, Dur.	1.000	20	3	9	0	12	2
Stanford, Jason, Buf.*	1.000	1	0	1	0	1	0
Stephens, John, Roch.	1.000	9	1	9	0	10	0
Stevens, Dave, Rich.	.667	39	2	6	4	12	0
Stewart, Scott, Ott.*	1.000	4	0	1	0	1	0
Stoops, Jim, Col.	.000	5	0	0	0	0	0
Strange, Pat, Nor.	.000	1	0	0	0	0	0
Sylvester, Billy, Rich.	1.000	36	0	4	0	4	0
Telemaco, Amaury, S./W.B.	1.000	4	2	2	0	4	0
Telford, Anthony, Ott.	1.000	28	5	15	0	20	0
Tessmer, Jay, Ind.	.933	35	5	9	1	15	1
Thomas, Evan, S./W.B.	.870	19	5	15	3	23	1
Tolar, Kevin, Tol.*	1.000	44	1	7	0	8	1
Towers, Josh, Roch.	1.000	6	5	5	0	10	0
Traber, Billy, Nor.*	.000	1	0	0	0	0	0
Trachsel, Steve, Nor.	1.000	3	0	4	0	4	0
Tucker, T.J., Ott.	1.000	14	8	13	0	21	2
Ulacia, Dennis, Char.*	1.000	1	0	1	0	1	0
Valdes, Marc, Rich.	.927	29	11	27	3	41	2
Valdez, Santo, Syr.	1.000	1	0	3	0	3	0
Vargas, Martin, Buf.	1.000	22	1	2	0	3	0
Veras, Dario, Buf.	1.000	48	8	6	0	14	2
Villegas, Ismael, Rich.	.966	34	10	18	1	29	3
Vinas, Julio, Roch.	.000	1	0	0	0	0	0
Vining, Ken, Char.*	.938	41	4	11	1	16	1
Vosberg, Ed, S./W.B.*	1.000	27	0	3	0	3	0
Wagner, Paul, Nor.	1.000	2	0	1	0	1	0
Walker, Jamie, Buf.*	.923	38	4	8	1	13	2
Walker, Pete, Nor.	1.000	26	12	21	0	33	1
Walker, Tyler, Nor.	1.000	8	4	4	0	8	1
Wall, Donne, Nor.	1.000	4	0	1	0	1	1
Wallace, Joff, Dur.*	1.000	7	1	0	0	1	0
Walling, Dave, Col.	.000	1	0	0	0	0	0
Ward, Bryan, Paw.*	.857	19	1	5	1	7	0
Wasdin, John, Roch.	.000	5	0	0	0	0	0
Watson, Mark, Buf.*	.000	0	0	0	0	0	0
Wells, Kip, Char.	1.000	4	4	1	0	5	0
Westbrook, Jake, Buf.	.941	12	5	11	1	17	1
Wheeler, Dan, Dur.	1.000	18	2	9	0	11	0
White, Matt, Dur.	.750	7	4	2	2	8	1
Whiteside, Matt, Rich.	1.000	9	1	2	0	3	0
Williams, Brian, Paw.-Col.	.833	19	1	9	2	12	2
Williams, Matt, Ind.*	.938	51	1	14	1	16	2
Williams, Todd, Col.	1.000	17	2	1	0	3	0
Wilson, Jeff, Roch.*	.944	28	5	12	1	18	0
Winchester, Scott, Lou.	1.000	23	7	9	0	16	0
Wolf, Randy, S./W.B.*	1.000	2	1	3	0	4	0
Woodard, Steve, Buf.	1.000	6	9	6	0	15	2
Wright, Jaret, Buf.	1.000	7	2	3	0	5	0
Zambrano, Victor, Dur.	1.000	29	1	5	0	6	0
Zamora, Pete, S./W.B.*	1.000	45	3	12	0	15	1

PITCHERS WITH TWO OR MORE TEAMS

Player, Team	Pct.	G	PO	A	E	TC	DP
Banks, Willie, Syr.	.913	24	3	18	2	23	2
Banks, Willie, Paw.	.750	2	2	1	1	4	0
Cornett, Brad, Syr.	1.000	6	1	2	0	3	0
Cornett, Brad, Dur.	.933	33	6	8	1	15	2
Day, Zach, Buf.	1.000	1	0	2	0	2	0
Day, Zach, Ind.	1.000	8	0	4	0	4	0
Estrella, Leo, Nor.	1.000	8	0	4	0	4	0
Estrella, Leo, Lou.	1.000	34	6	11	0	17	1
Flury, Pat, Ott.	.000	10	0	0	0	0	0
Flury, Pat, Col.	1.000	34	5	4	0	9	0
Gandarillas, Gus, Paw.	.900	12	2	7	1	10	2
Gandarillas, Gus, Ind.	1.000	28	5	7	0	12	1
Gunderson, Eric, Buf.*	1.000	2	1	0	0	1	0
Gunderson, Eric, Col.*	.952	56	7	13	1	21	3
Hammond, Chris, Buf.*	.833	28	3	7	2	12	1
Hammond, Chris, Rich.*	1.000	21	3	6	0	9	0
Henry, Butch, Col.*	1.000	1	0	1	0	1	1
Henry, Butch, Syr.*	.947	12	2	16	1	19	2
Henry, Butch, Ind.*	1.000	5	1	4	0	5	0
Hill, Ken, Lou.	1.000	6	4	5	0	9	0
Hill, Ken, Paw.	1.000	8	2	4	0	6	1
Lewis, Richie, Buf.	1.000	7	1	1	0	2	0
Lewis, Richie, Nor.	.952	17	7	13	1	21	0
Lira, Felipe, Ott.	1.000	42	4	6	0	10	1

Player, Team	Pct.	G	PO	A	E	TC	DP
Lira, Felipe, S./W.B.	1.000	2	0	1	0	1	0
Peters, Chris, Lou.*	.889	8	3	5	1	9	0
Peters, Chris, Col.*	1.000	9	1	7	0	8	0
Rodriguez, Nerio, Nor.	.000	1	0	0	0	0	0
Rodriguez, Nerio, Buf.	1.000	11	2	2	0	4	0
Serafini, Dan, Nor.*	1.000	31	1	5	0	6	0

Player, Team	Pct.	G	PO	A	E	TC	DP
Serafini, Dan, Ind.*	1.000	9	0	3	0	3	0
Williams, Brian, Paw.	1.000	3	0	1	0	1	0
Williams, Brian, Col.	.818	16	1	8	2	11	2

The following players appeared only as designated hitter, pinch-hitter or pinch runner: Baines, dh; Bard, dh; Daubach, dh; Flanagan, dh, ph; McNamara, dh, ph; Palmer, dh; Raines Sr., dh.

LEAGUE CHAMPIONS

Year	Team	Pct.
1884—	Trenton	.520
1885—	Syracuse	.584
1886—	Utica	.646
1887—	Toronto	.644
1888—	Syracuse	.723
1889—	Detroit	.649
1890—	Detroit	.617
1891—	Buffalo (reg. season)	.727
	Buffalo (supplemental)	.680
1892—	Providence	.615
	Binghamton*	.667
1893—	Erie	.606
1894—	Providence	.696
1895—	Springfield	.687
1896—	Providence	.602
1897—	Syracuse	.632
1898—	Montreal	.586
1899—	Rochester	.624
1900—	Providence	.616
1901—	Rochester	.642
1902—	Toronto	.669
1903—	Jersey City	.742
1904—	Buffalo	.657
1905—	Providence	.638
1906—	Buffalo	.607
1907—	Toronto	.619
1908—	Baltimore	.593
1909—	Rochester	.596
1910—	Rochester	.601
1911—	Rochester	.645
1912—	Toronto	.595
1913—	Newark	.625
1914—	Providence	.617
1915—	Buffalo	.632
1916—	Buffalo	.586
1917—	Toronto	.604
1918—	Toronto	.693
1919—	Baltimore	.671
1920—	Baltimore	.719
1921—	Baltimore	.717
1922—	Baltimore	.689
1923—	Baltimore	.677
1924—	Baltimore	.709
1925—	Baltimore	.633
1926—	Toronto	.657
1927—	Buffalo	.667
1928—	Rochester	.549
1929—	Rochester	.613
1930—	Rochester	.629
1931—	Rochester	.601
1932—	Newark	.649
1933—	Newark	.622
	Buffalo (4th)†	.494
1934—	Newark	.608
	Toronto (3rd)†	.559
1935—	Montreal	.597
	Syracuse (2nd)†	.565
1936—	Buffalo‡	.610

Year	Team	Pct.
1937—	Newark‡	.717
1938—	Newark‡	.684
1939—	Jersey City	.582
	Rochester (2nd)†	.556
1940—	Rochester	.611
	Newark (2nd)†	.594
1941—	Newark	.649
	Montreal (2nd)†	.584
1942—	Newark	.601
	Syracuse (3rd)†	.513
1943—	Toronto	.625
	Syracuse (3rd)†	.536
1944—	Baltimore‡	.553
1945—	Montreal	.621
	Newark (2nd)†	.582
1946—	Montreal‡	.649
1947—	Jersey City	.610
	Syracuse (3rd)†	.575
1948—	Montreal‡	.614
1949—	Buffalo	.584
	Montreal (3rd)†	.545
1950—	Rochester	.609
	Baltimore (3rd)†	.556
1951—	Montreal‡	.617
1952—	Montreal	.629
	Rochester (3rd)†	.619
1953—	Rochester	.630
	Montreal (2nd)†	.586
1954—	Toronto	.630
	Syracuse (4th)§	.510
1955—	Montreal	.617
	Rochester (4th)†	.497
1956—	Toronto	.566
	Rochester (2nd)†	.553
1957—	Toronto	.575
	Buffalo (2nd)†	.571
1958—	Montreal‡	.588
1959—	Buffalo	.582
	Havana (3rd)†	.523
1960—	Toronto‡	.649
1961—	Columbus	.597
	Buffalo (3rd)†	.559
1962—	Jacksonville	.610
	Atlanta (3rd)†	.539
1963—	Syracuse∞	.533
	Indianapolis‡	.562
1964—	Jacksonville	.589
	Rochester (4th)†	.532
1965—	Columbus	.582
	Toronto (3rd)†	.556
1966—	Rochester	.565
	Toronto (2nd-tied)†	.558
1967—	Richmond	.574
	Toledo (3rd)†	.525
1968—	Toledo	.565
	Jacksonville (4th)†	.514
1969—	Tidewater	.563
	Syracuse (3rd)†	.536

Year	Team	Pct.
1970—	Syracuse‡	.600
1971—	Rochester‡	.614
1972—	Louisville	.563
	Tidewater (3rd)†	.545
1973—	Charleston	.586
	Pawtucket†	.534
1974—	Memphis	.613
	Rochester ∞‡	.611
1975—	Tidewater‡	.610
1976—	Rochester	.638
	Syracuse (2nd)†	.590
1977—	Pawtucket	.571
	Charleston (2nd)‡	.557
1978—	Charleston	.607
	Richmond (4th)†	.511
1979—	Columbus‡	.612
1980—	Columbus‡	.593
1981—	Columbus‡	.633
1982—	Richmond	.590
	Tidewater (3rd)†	.540
1983—	Columbus	.593
	Tidewater (4th)†	.511
1984—	Columbus	.590
	Pawtucket (4th)†	.536
1985—	Syracuse	.564
	Tidewater (4th)†	.540
1986—	Richmond‡	.571
1987—	Tidewater	.579
	Columbus†	.550
1988—	Rochester◆	.546
	Tidewater	.546
1989—	Syracuse	.572
	Richmond◆	.555
1990—	Rochester◆	.614
	Columbus	.596
1991—	Columbus◆	.590
	Pawtucket	.552
1992—	Columbus◆	.660
	Scr. W.B.	.592
1993—	Charlotte◆	.610
	Rochester	.525
1994—	Richmond◆	.567
	Pawtucket	.549
1995—	Norfolk	.606
	Ottawa◆	.507
1996—	Columbus◆	.599
	Rochester	.511
1997—	Rochester◆	.589
	Columbus	.556
1998—	Buffalo■	.566
1999—	Columbus	.589
	Charlotte▲	.569
2000—	Buffalo	.593
	Indianapolis▲	.563
2001—	Buffalo	.641
	Louisville▼	.583

*Won split-season playoff. †Won four-team playoff. ‡Won championship and four-team playoff. §Defeated Havana in game to decide fourth place, then won four-team playoff. ∞League was divided into Northern, Southern divisions. ◆League divided into Eastern, Western divisions; won playoffs. ■League divided into Eastern, Northern and Southern divisions; won four-team playoff. ▲League divided into North, South and West divisions; won four-team playoff. ▼League divided into North, South and West divisions; was leading final series of four-team playoff and was declared champion when Professional Baseball declared a stoppage of play. (NOTE— Known as Eastern League in 1884, New York State League in 1885, International League in 1886-87, International Association in 1888, International League in 1889-90, Eastern Association in 1891 and Eastern League from 1892 until 1912.)

MEXICAN LEAGUE

2001 FINAL STANDINGS

FIRST HALF

EAST DIVISION

Team	W	L	T	Pct.	GB
Monclova	37	25	0	.607	...
Monterrey	33	28	0	.559	3.0
Reynosa	33	29	0	.532	4.5
Saltillo	30	30	0	.500	6.5
Torreon	28	33	0	.441	10.0
Dos Laredos	26	35	0	.417	11.5

CENTRAL DIVISION

Team	W	L	T	Pct.	GB
Mexico City Reds	41	21	0	.661	...
Mexico City Tigers	37	22	0	.627	2.5
Puebla	31	28	0	.525	8.5
Oaxaca	25	36	0	.410	15.5
Cordoba	22	37	0	.362	18.0

WEST DIVISION

Team	W	L	T	Pct.	GB
Campeche	32	29	0	.533	...
Yucatan	31	30	0	.508	1.5
Veracruz	28	33	0	.459	4.5
Tabasco	27	35	0	.435	6.0
Cancun	26	36	0	.419	7.0

SECOND HALF

EAST DIVISION

Team	W	L	T	Pct.	GB
Saltillo	38	22	0	.633	...
Reynosa	36	24	0	.600	2.0
Monterrey	35	25	0	.583	3.0
Torreon	33	26	0	.559	4.5
Monclova	30	27	1	.526	6.5
Dos Laredos	22	37	1	.373	15.5

CENTRAL DIVISION

Team	W	L	T	Pct.	GB
Mexico City Tigers	37	21	1	.638	...
Mexico City Reds	28	30	1	.483	9.0
Oaxaca	25	33	1	.431	12.0
Puebla	23	34	1	.404	13.5
Cordoba	16	41	0	.281	20.5

WEST DIVISION

Team	W	L	T	Pct.	GB
Yucatan	37	23	0	.617	...
Campeche	30	27	1	.526	5.5
Tabasco	29	31	0	.483	8.0
Veracruz	27	33	0	.450	10.0
Cancun	23	35	1	.397	13.0

COMPOSITE

Team	Tig.	Reds	Sal.	Rey.	Mono.	Yuc.	Mont.	Cam.	Tor.	Pue.	Tab.	Ver.	Oax.	Can.	D.L.	Cor.	W	L	T	Pct.	GB
Mexico City Tigers	...	7	3	4	0	9	3	2	4	4	3	6	8	4	5	9	74	43	1	.632	...
Mexico City Reds	7	...	5	2	3	4	2	1	3	7	5	10	7	5	2	6	69	51	1	.575	6.5
Saltillo	3	1	...	8	8	4	9	4	6	3	3	1	2	4	7	4	68	52	0	.567	7.5
Reynosa	2	4	4	...	8	3	6	1	7	5	4	3	3	5	10	3	69	53	0	.566	7.5
Monclova	2	3	4	4	...	1	7	4	8	2	2	6	5	4	11	4	67	52	1	.563	8.0
Yucatan	3	2	2	3	5	...	3	9	4	3	8	3	3	6	3	6	68	53	0	.562	8.0
Monterrey	3	4	5	6	5	3	...	4	6	4	3	5	4	3	8	5	68	53	0	.562	8.0
Campeche	3	5	2	5	2	3	2	...	2	4	8	7	2	8	2	7	62	56	1	.525	12.5
Torreon	2	3	6	5	6	2	6	4	...	4	4	3	4	3	5	4	61	59	0	.508	14.5
Puebla	6	3	2	1	4	3	1	2	2	...	4	3	8	5	3	7	54	62	1	.466	19.5
Tabasco	3	1	3	2	4	4	3	6	2	2	...	5	8	6	4	3	56	66	0	.459	20.5
Veracruz	0	2	5	2	0	3	1	5	3	3	7	...	4	8	4	8	55	66	0	.455	21.0
Oaxaca	4	5	4	3	0	3	2	4	2	5	4	2	...	4	2	6	50	69	1	.420	25.0
Cancun	2	1	2	1	2	8	3	2	3	7	6	4	2	...	3	3	49	71	1	.408	26.5
Dos Laredos	0	4	5	4	1	3	4	4	6	3	2	2	4	3	...	3	48	72	1	.400	27.5
Cordoba	3	6	0	3	1	0	1	4	1	5	3	0	5	3	3	...	38	78	0	.328	35.5

PLAYOFFS: Mexico City Reds defeated Yucatan four games to one; Monclova defeated Reynosa four games to two; Mexico City Tigers defeated Campeche four games to two; Monterrey defeated Saltillo four games to three; Mexico City Reds defeated Monclova four games to none; Mexico City Tigers defeated Monterrey four games to three; Mexico City Tigers defeated Mexico City Reds four games to two to win Mexican League championship.

2001 BATTING

TEAM

Team	Avg.	G	TPA	AB	R	H	TB	2B	3B	HR	RBI	SH	SF	HP	BB	IBB	SO	SB	CS	GDP	LOB	ShO	Slg.	OBP
M.C. Tigers	.310	118	4562	4036	695	1250	1940	231	33	131	646	35	38	60	393	40	627	87	41	107	852	2	.481	.376
Reynosa	.292	122	4710	4210	583	1228	1739	217	18	86	546	54	46	43	357	29	651	65	30	117	911	6	.413	.350
Monterrey	.286	121	4658	4100	553	1171	1652	177	11	94	516	61	32	81	384	39	687	112	46	110	930	8	.403	.356
Monclova	.283	120	4607	4024	632	1140	1717	203	10	118	600	34	39	49	461	30	675	100	43	78	878	7	.427	.361
M.C. Reds	.283	121	4743	4135	646	1171	1748	195	26	110	605	37	40	36	495	29	672	38	19	135	921	7	.423	.362
Torreon	.281	120	4730	4153	592	1166	1716	180	20	110	555	61	28	60	428	27	655	49	30	119	939	7	.413	.354
Oaxaca	.278	120	4642	4040	566	1122	1612	184	15	92	527	57	32	45	468	31	595	31	39	122	927	8	.399	.357
Puebla	.278	117	4418	3870	505	1074	1502	176	30	64	465	56	29	58	405	38	661	49	28	117	918	10	.388	.352
Saltillo	.276	120	4665	4033	613	1112	1688	168	21	122	573	46	36	54	496	23	747	102	46	119	899	8	.419	.360
Yucatan	.274	121	4699	4117	529	1126	1552	190	22	64	478	60	39	57	426	42	616	48	32	105	958	12	.377	.347
Tabasco	.271	122	4587	4080	487	1106	1512	161	14	71	448	64	25	75	343	39	593	71	46	113	891	4	.370	.337
Dos Laredos	.268	121	4694	4152	498	1113	1545	174	6	82	465	56	38	60	388	31	559	42	41	108	947	10	.372	.337
Campeche	.268	119	4461	3941	539	1055	1599	155	7	125	506	43	26	60	391	29	595	65	41	115	828	11	.406	.341
Cordoba	.262	116	4149	3720	421	976	1364	164	19	62	394	49	17	50	313	26	678	47	42	95	756	11	.367	.327
Cancun	.255	121	4495	4012	471	1024	1478	154	12	92	441	57	30	31	366	23	646	28	20	112	826	10	.368	.320
Veracruz	.250	121	4601	4053	484	1013	1473	144	8	100	457	50	32	43	423	27	695	81	25	107	863	13	.363	.325

CLASS AAA Mexican League

TOP QUALIFIERS FOR BATTING CHAMPIONSHIP

Minimum 329 plate appearances. *Lefthanded batter. †Switch-hitter.

Player, Team	Avg.	G	TPA	AB	R	H	TB	2B	3B	HR	RBI	SH	SF	HP	BB	IBB	SO	SB	CS	GDP	Slg.	OBP
Franco, Julio, Tig.	.437	110	469	407	90	178	276	34	5	18	90	0	7	5	50	11	56	15	6	15	.678	.497
Orantes, Ramon, Mont.	.363	102	382	355	46	129	174	15	0	10	50	2	0	7	18	3	31	0	3	15	.490	.405
Sherman, Darrell, Monc.*	.355	108	487	403	83	143	178	15	1	6	43	1	3	9	71	6	37	30	11	2	.442	.459
Castellano, Pedro, Mex.	.352	121	540	471	99	166	273	34	2	23	96	0	11	3	55	3	83	6	1	15	.580	.415
Bullet, Scott, Rey.*	.341	83	347	305	63	104	187	23	3	18	72	0	5	3	34	8	66	4	6	6	.613	.406
Chimelis, Joel, Lar.	.337	120	522	442	68	149	231	23	1	19	77	4	6	13	57	5	38	9	7	11	.523	.423
Iturbe, Pedro, Pue.*	.337	99	392	356	51	120	177	24	3	9	46	1	2	5	28	11	41	8	5	10	.497	.391
Clark, Howie, Yuc.†	.333	121	547	493	68	164	235	42	7	5	64	4	5	2	43	3	47	5	4	12	.477	.385
Garcia, Luis Carlos, Tig.†	.332	98	412	368	73	122	214	25	5	19	82	0	3	3	38	3	51	16	6	20	.582	.396
Tellez, Alonso, Rey.	.330	122	520	470	56	155	222	34	0	11	72	0	5	0	45	3	76	1	0	16	.472	.385
Zambrano, Roberto, Mont.	.329	97	411	340	43	112	157	19	1	8	49	0	6	23	42	2	60	1	1	6	.462	.431
Flores, Miguel, Mont.	.328	105	450	390	75	128	189	26	1	11	56	7	5	6	42	2	66	28	5	2	.485	.397
Cruz, Fausto, Tor.	.325	113	492	421	75	137	205	20	3	14	70	4	2	6	59	1	79	5	2	10	.487	.414
Espinoza, Ramon, Rey.	.321	120	554	523	83	168	227	30	1	9	44	3	2	6	20	0	41	15	6	14	.434	.352
Gastelum, Sergio, Tig.	.317	77	339	300	53	95	138	18	2	7	40	7	4	9	19	3	28	6	4	8	.460	.370

DEPARTMENTAL LEADERS: G—Tellez, 122; AB—R. Espinoza (Rey.), 523; R—B. Rodriguez, 103; H—Franco, 178; TB—Franco, 276; 2B—Clark, 42; 3B—D. Smith, Contreras, 9; HR—B. Rodriguez, Whiten, 33; RBI—B. Rodriguez, 100; SH—C. Rodriguez, 18; SF—Castellano, 11; HP—R. Zambrano, 23; BB—B. Rodriguez, 100; IBB—H. Castaneda, 13; SO—E. Jimenez, 111; SB—D. Smith, 36; CS—D. Smith, 18; GIDP—Colina, 22; Slg.—Franco, .678; OBP—Franco, .497.

ALL PLAYERS

*Lefthanded batter. †Switch-hitter.

Player, Team	Avg.	G	TPA	AB	R	H	TB	2B	3B	HR	RBI	SH	SF	HP	BB	IBB	SO	SB	CS	GDP	Slg.	OBP
Abrego, Jesus, Can.†	.238	78	274	240	26	57	90	6	0	9	27	4	2	2	26	3	31	1	3	3	.375	.315
Acosta, Jose Francisco, Tab.	.333	18	44	42	5	14	24	1	0	3	9	0	0	0	2	0	6	0	0	0	.571	.364
Acuna, Jose, Tor.†	.288	80	134	104	24	30	35	3	1	0	9	7	0	1	22	1	16	3	1	2	.337	.417
Adriana, Sharnol, Cam.	.313	118	509	425	89	133	247	28	1	28	84	1	3	12	68	5	80	21	14	10	.581	.419
Aganza, Ruben, Monc.	.228	86	310	289	24	66	91	10	0	5	21	2	3	2	14	1	31	0	0	3	.315	.266
Aguilera, Antonio, Cam.†	.229	24	57	48	7	11	18	4	0	1	4	1	0	0	8	0	13	0	0	0	.375	.339
Aguilera, Armando, Sal.	.500	10	7	6	2	3	6	0	0	1	3	0	0	0	1	0	0	0	0	1	1.000	.571
Aguilera, Raul, Cor.†	.265	26	82	68	5	18	20	2	0	0	5	2	0	1	11	0	14	1	2	0	.294	.375
Almeida, Shammar, Oax.*	.263	95	287	232	35	61	119	7	0	17	44	2	1	2	50	4	49	1	3	4	.513	.396
Alvarez, Hector, Oax.	.282	119	557	510	71	144	184	21	2	5	51	9	4	5	29	2	82	1	7	15	.361	.325
Alvarez, Rafael, Can.*	.240	8	32	25	4	6	7	1	0	0	2	0	0	1	6	0	3	0	0	2	.280	.406
Amador, Alonso, Ver.	.213	26	50	47	4	10	13	3	0	0	1	1	0	0	2	0	15	1	0	1	.277	.245
Amador, Jose, Tor.	.286	5	7	7	1	2	2	0	0	0	1	0	0	0	0	0	2	1	0	0	.286	.286
Amettler, Jesus, Tab.*	.264	12	55	53	8	14	16	2	0	0	3	0	0	0	2	2	2	1	0	1	.302	.291
Amezcua, Adan, Mont.	.238	44	164	147	9	35	46	8	0	1	12	2	2	4	9	2	33	3	1	3	.313	.296
Anthony, Eric, Mont.	.105	7	26	19	3	2	3	1	0	0	0	0	0	0	7	3	4	0	0	0	.158	.346
Arano, Eloy, Ver.*	.239	112	491	452	45	108	129	8	2	3	26	7	0	5	27	2	56	17	6	12	.285	.289
Arano, Marco Antonio, Tab.	.125	4	9	8	1	1	2	1	0	0	2	0	0	1	0	0	3	0	0	0	.250	.222
Arano, Wilfrido, Lar.*	.287	114	453	394	45	113	149	24	0	4	47	5	2	4	48	10	32	2	0	8	.378	.368
Arauz, Ignacio, Monc.	.111	6	10	9	1	1	1	0	0	0	0	1	0	0	0	0	3	0	0	0	.111	.111
Arauz, Leobardo, Yuc.†	.227	81	270	220	28	50	69	5	1	4	24	7	5	5	33	3	38	3	1	1	.314	.335
Arias, Francisco, Sal.	.253	54	112	99	12	25	32	2	1	1	10	5	0	2	6	1	22	3	0	0	.323	.308
Armenta, Guillermo, Cam.	.266	88	357	312	45	83	100	9	1	2	17	11	0	5	29	1	33	18	9	7	.321	.338
Arredondo, Eduardo, Ver.	.097	21	35	31	3	3	5	2	0	0	0	0	0	0	4	0	5	0	0	1	.161	.200
Arredondo, H'n'do, Cam.-Cor.	.276	95	329	312	25	86	111	13	0	4	32	3	3	2	9	0	58	6	2	6	.356	.298
Arredondo, Jesus, Pue.*	.258	77	326	279	37	72	90	9	0	3	17	5	1	5	36	1	30	5	2	8	.323	.352
Arredondo, Jesus, Yuc.*	.312	108	503	461	70	144	175	16	3	3	38	3	4	0	35	7	46	14	13	6	.380	.358
Avila, Carlos, Tab.-Lar.*	.238	54	92	84	12	20	23	3	0	0	1	2	0	2	4	0	18	3	2	2	.274	.289
Avila, Ignacio, Cor.	.372	15	52	43	11	16	21	0	1	1	5	0	0	2	7	0	9	0	0	1	.488	.481
Azocar, Oscar, Yuc.*	.232	23	100	95	10	22	24	2	0	0	5	0	0	2	3	0	3	2	0	3	.253	.270
Baez, Carlos, Tab.	.200	14	43	40	1	8	8	0	0	0	3	0	0	0	3	0	6	1	0	2	.200	.256
Ball, Jeff, Can.	.286	32	140	119	18	34	47	5	1	2	15	2	3	1	15	0	22	1	1	3	.395	.362
Barajas, Edison, Cor.*	.219	94	285	256	22	56	80	10	1	4	31	2	2	6	18	4	56	0	3	6	.313	.284
Barrera, Nelson, Oax.	.268	75	302	265	30	71	110	12	0	9	43	4	2	5	30	3	41	0	1	9	.415	.353
Barron, Tony, Can.-Cam.	.304	106	449	392	65	119	208	23	4	22	66	0	4	4	49	5	93	4	0	12	.531	.383
Beltran, Juan, Cam.	.194	34	71	62	5	12	13	1	0	0	2	0	0	2	5	0	18	0	0	0	.210	.275
Benitez, Yamil, Rey.	.347	29	128	121	21	42	65	6	1	5	28	1	0	0	6	0	21	6	1	6	.537	.378
Bernal, Cosme, Monc.	.200	6	12	10	0	2	2	0	0	0	0	0	0	0	1	0	2	0	0	0	.200	.273
Berroa, Geronimo, Cam.	.280	49	211	175	29	49	84	8	0	9	35	0	3	3	30	2	39	0	0	10	.480	.389
Bojorquez, Edson, Oax.*	.190	27	45	42	2	8	10	2	0	0	3	0	0	0	3	0	7	0	1	2	.238	.244
Bojorquez, Victor, Mex.	.195	100	326	307	20	60	80	8	3	2	17	8	3	1	7	2	42	2	1	11	.261	.214
Bolado, Carlos, Ver.*	.188	57	80	69	10	13	17	1	0	1	3	2	0	0	9	0	17	1	0	3	.246	.282
Borges, Luis, Can.*	.236	76	211	195	23	46	53	7	0	0	9	7	2	2	5	0	27	1	1	1	.272	.260
Boston, D.J., Cam.-Can.*	.244	89	367	311	44	76	110	7	0	9	37	0	2	1	53	7	55	8	3	9	.354	.354
Brena, Jaime, Oax.	.264	111	341	299	31	79	94	6	3	1	26	13	2	1	26	0	41	0	4	6	.314	.323
Brewer, Rod, Oax.-Ver.*	.282	117	495	404	58	114	213	21	0	26	86	0	5	4	82	10	80	3	1	6	.527	.404
Brinkley, Darryl, Cam.-Yuc.	.293	102	449	403	58	118	162	16	2	8	40	0	2	2	39	2	42	16	8	10	.402	.354
Buelna, Lorenzo, Pue.	.246	74	235	199	26	49	54	5	0	0	21	3	4	2	24	0	41	3	5	3	.271	.336
Bullet, Scott, Rey.*	.341	83	347	305	63	104	187	23	3	18	72	0	5	3	34	8	66	4	6	6	.613	.406
Bustamante, Omar, Sal.-Lar.	.162	33	77	74	4	12	16	1	0	1	5	2	0	0	1	0	17	0	1	3	.216	.173
Bustillos, Luis, Yuc.*	.248	75	128	113	16	28	42	8	0	2	9	3	0	3	9	0	16	1	1	2	.372	.320
Canizalez, Juan, Mont.	.306	108	443	386	53	118	164	17	1	9	60	3	3	5	46	8	44	7	3	18	.425	.384
Cansino, Jorge, Ver.*	.116	27	46	43	2	5	6	1	0	0	1	1	0	1	0	0	13	1	0	2	.140	.156
Cappuccio, Carmine, Yuc.*	.288	14	62	59	7	17	23	3	0	1	8	0	0	0	3	0	11	0	0	3	.390	.323

Player, Team	Avg.	G	TPA	AB	R	H	TB	2B	3B	HR	RBI	SH	SF	HP	BB	IBB	SO	SB	CS	GDP	Slg.	OBP
Carrasco, Ernesto, Pue.*	.252	97	358	317	35	80	106	7	2	5	29	5	2	5	29	3	43	2	2	12	.334	.323
Carrillo, Matias, Tig.*	.309	104	422	369	64	114	176	20	0	14	66	1	5	4	43	3	41	3	1	9	.477	.382
Castaneda, Hector, Yuc.*	.269	118	505	405	63	109	170	17	4	12	57	4	2	10	84	13	91	3	2	10	.420	.405
Castaneda, Rafael, Oax.-Rey.	.261	99	307	310	35	83	111	11	1	5	27	2	3	1	43	1	34	2	1	0	.349	.348
Castellano, Pedro, Mex.	.352	121	540	471	99	166	273	34	2	23	96	0	11	3	55	3	83	6	1	15	.580	.415
Castro, Arnoldo, Can.	.278	114	502	446	56	124	161	14	1	7	44	17	1	0	38	2	24	1	3	13	.361	.334
Castro, Carlos, Tab.	.091	15	35	33	0	3	4	1	0	0	2	2	0	0	0	0	10	0	1	0	.121	.091
Castro, Domingo, Monc.	.204	92	254	225	40	46	59	13	0	0	10	5	0	1	23	0	43	6	3	6	.262	.281
Castro, Gonzalo, Lar.	.256	44	93	90	9	23	31	5	0	1	6	0	0	0	3	0	33	0	0	3	.344	.280
Cazarin, Manuel, Cam.	.274	101	384	351	37	96	150	16	1	12	53	2	3	6	21	6	32	1	0	17	.427	.323
Cedeno, Domingo, Cor.†	.296	66	273	247	38	73	99	4	5	4	18	7	0	0	19	0	40	12	5	1	.401	.346
Cervantes, Ivan, Mex.	.234	49	122	111	15	26	40	7	2	1	9	2	1	0	8	0	13	1	0	3	.360	.283
Cervantes, Refugio, Sal.	.318	46	50	44	2	14	21	1	0	2	8	0	0	0	6	1	9	0	0	2	.477	.400
Cervera, Francisco, Yuc.	.240	108	408	338	43	81	130	13	3	10	50	5	4	13	48	2	78	2	3	6	.385	.352
Chimelis, Joel, Lar.	.337	120	522	442	68	149	231	23	1	19	77	4	6	13	57	5	38	9	7	11	.523	.423
Cisneros, Ventura, Rey.*	.300	14	13	10	0	3	4	1	0	0	1	0	1	0	2	0	2	0	0	0	.400	.385
Clark, Howie, Yuc.*	.333	121	547	493	68	164	235	42	7	5	64	4	5	2	43	3	47	5	4	12	.477	.385
Cobos, Rogelio, Ver.-Oax.-Mex.	.246	57	150	138	11	34	44	5	1	1	13	2	4	0	6	0	30	1	0	3	.319	.270
Colina, Roberto, Pue.*	.295	109	470	417	60	123	165	22	1	6	53	0	3	4	46	4	31	1	1	22	.396	.368
Connell, Lino, Ver.	.249	119	526	457	74	114	153	20	2	5	41	5	2	2	60	3	76	28	7	6	.335	.338
Contreras, Albino, Pue.	.313	86	338	294	45	92	144	16	9	6	52	4	4	9	27	0	66	7	2	8	.490	.383
Cruz, Fausto, Tor.	.325	113	492	421	75	137	205	20	3	14	70	4	2	6	59	1	79	5	2	10	.487	.414
Cruz, Marco, Tor.	.269	44	115	104	11	28	39	8	0	1	13	4	1	1	5	0	22	0	0	2	.375	.306
Dattola, Kevin, Cam.-Yuc.*	.212	14	63	52	8	11	15	1	0	1	8	1	0	0	10	0	8	1	1	2	.288	.339
De La Cruz, Lorenzo, Pue.	.291	99	399	344	48	100	161	16	3	13	67	0	2	6	47	9	85	9	3	8	.468	.383
De La Torre, Francisco, Oax.	.000	6	4	4	1	0	0	0	0	0	0	0	0	0	0	0	0	0	0	0	.000	.000
Delgado, Alex, Tab.	.150	11	45	40	3	6	7	1	0	0	4	0	0	2	3	0	3	0	1	0	.175	.244
Devarez, Cesar, Cor.	.317	85	314	287	30	91	124	19	1	4	38	3	0	7	17	3	31	3	3	9	.432	.370
Diaz, Alex, Tor.†	.295	77	338	315	53	93	152	18	1	13	60	0	1	1	21	6	54	9	4	7	.483	.340
Diaz, Luis, Can.*	.190	19	67	58	4	11	19	2	0	2	9	0	1	0	8	1	13	0	0	2	.328	.284
Diaz, Pedro, Pue.	.294	61	218	201	24	59	86	14	2	3	29	4	2	1	10	1	35	0	0	6	.428	.327
Diaz, Remigio, Mex.	.306	115	433	392	45	120	136	7	0	3	45	13	2	4	22	0	27	23	5	15	.347	.348
Dominguez, David, Ver.	.214	48	141	117	10	25	34	6	0	1	12	0	2	4	18	0	32	0	0	6	.291	.333
Duenas, Arnoldo, Yuc.-Can.	.149	44	112	101	10	15	19	1	0	1	4	4	0	1	6	0	34	1	0	5	.188	.204
Espino, Daniel, Tor.	.313	85	294	262	36	82	108	14	3	2	34	4	1	11	15	2	18	5	3	16	.412	.374
Espino, Omar, Lar.	.000	1	1	1	0	0	0	0	0	0	0	0	0	0	0	0	0	0	0	0	.000	.000
Espinoza, Jose, Lar.*	.286	103	465	416	51	119	163	23	0	7	32	4	3	9	33	1	43	6	6	9	.392	.349
Espinoza, Ramon, Rey.	.321	120	554	523	83	168	227	30	1	9	44	3	2	6	20	0	41	15	6	14	.434	.352
Espinoza, Ramon, Tor.	.200	4	5	5	0	1	1	0	0	0	0	0	0	0	0	0	2	0	0	0	.200	.200
Esquer, Ramon, Mex.*	.233	97	398	352	48	82	106	19	1	1	34	5	2	4	35	6	20	2	2	16	.301	.308
Estrada, Hector, Yuc.	.234	105	402	350	35	82	123	15	1	8	35	4	5	4	39	3	56	0	3	14	.351	.314
Estrada, Osmani, Sal.	.211	28	130	114	17	24	31	4	0	1	10	2	1	3	10	0	9	0	0	4	.272	.289
Estrella, Isaac, Lar.	.067	44	34	30	8	2	3	1	0	0	0	0	0	0	4	0	11	1	0	1	.100	.176
Felix, Junior, Yuc.	.305	75	315	256	44	78	118	17	1	7	42	0	2	8	49	7	51	5	1	3	.461	.429
Fentanes, Oscar, Tab.	.279	95	378	340	40	95	123	9	2	5	42	2	1	15	20	3	43	0	4	10	.362	.346
Fernandez, Daniel, Mex.*	.290	105	493	410	75	119	152	17	5	2	32	5	1	4	73	2	50	9	7	6	.371	.402
Flores, Miguel, Mont.	.328	105	450	390	75	128	189	26	1	11	56	7	5	6	42	2	66	28	5	2	.485	.397
Fornes, Daniel, Rey.*	.299	121	503	445	67	133	200	26	1	13	74	6	10	3	39	12	55	8	1	9	.449	.352
Franco, Julio, Tig.	.437	110	469	407	90	178	276	34	5	18	90	0	7	5	50	11	56	15	6	15	.678	.497
Freeman, Richard, Lar.*	.125	9	34	32	2	4	4	0	0	0	1	0	1	0	1	0	11	0	0	2	.125	.147
Gainer, Jonathan, Tab.-Cor.	.254	80	337	295	29	75	101	11	0	5	38	0	3	0	39	11	50	3	2	8	.342	.338
Garcia, Cornelio, Mex.*	.307	79	330	280	35	86	100	9	1	1	33	5	3	1	41	0	37	2	1	9	.357	.394
Garcia, Guillermo, Oax.	.288	34	150	132	22	38	69	7	0	8	24	0	2	2	14	0	26	0	1	11	.523	.360
Garcia, Hector, Mont.-Tab.	.261	94	333	307	32	80	87	7	0	0	16	9	0	4	13	0	21	5	5	6	.283	.299
Garcia, Heriberto, Oax.	.326	22	46	43	9	14	14	0	0	0	0	0	0	0	3	0	5	0	1	2	.326	.370
Garcia, Luis Carlos, Tig †	.332	98	412	368	73	122	214	25	5	19	82	0	3	3	38	3	51	16	6	20	.582	.392
Garcia, Omar, Ver.-Yuc.	.282	96	394	354	48	100	158	19	0	13	78	0	6	1	31	0	80	1	0	9	.446	.335
Garland, Tim, Tab.	.277	33	140	130	14	36	43	5	1	0	9	2	0	1	7	0	17	5	2	4	.331	.319
Garza, Gerardo, Tor.-Rey.	.267	66	162	150	14	40	52	6	0	2	15	5	2	0	5	0	25	0	0	3	.347	.287
Garzon, Eliseo, Lar.-Sal.	.225	87	315	275	20	62	85	11	0	4	31	7	2	5	26	1	47	0	2	7	.309	.302
Gastelum, Carlos, Pue.-Tig.	.279	60	152	136	12	38	44	6	0	0	9	6	1	1	8	0	19	1	0	6	.324	.324
Gastelum, Sergio, Tig.	.317	77	339	300	53	95	138	18	2	7	40	7	4	9	19	3	28	6	4	8	.460	.370
Gavia, Jesus, Ver.	.266	87	252	233	15	62	85	11	0	4	35	4	4	2	9	0	25	0	0	9	.365	.294
Gerardo, Benjamin, Monc.	.306	20	42	36	5	11	13	2	0	0	4	0	0	1	5	0	9	0	4	1	.361	.405
Gibson, Derrick, Pue.	.270	66	281	259	44	70	122	11	1	13	45	0	1	0	21	5	64	1	2	5	.471	.324
Gomez, Heber, Tab.	.301	111	479	425	62	128	180	26	1	8	44	8	3	9	34	4	48	12	6	5	.424	.363
Gonzalez, Fernando, Rey.	.214	79	217	206	16	44	61	8	0	3	20	6	0	1	4	0	57	2	0	9	.296	.232
Gonzalez, Manny, Lar.	.281	40	180	167	22	47	64	6	1	3	21	1	3	2	7	1	20	6	4	9	.383	.313
Gonzalez, Rolando, Monc.	.157	34	77	70	3	11	14	0	0	1	6	1	0	0	6	0	22	0	0	0	.200	.224
Gonzalez, Roman, Cor.	.173	88	251	243	18	42	61	11	1	2	17	3	0	2	3	0	61	0	0	3	.251	.190
Gordon, Keith, Sal.	.266	24	101	94	11	25	48	4	2	5	23	0	1	3	3	1	26	1	2	2	.511	.307
Gorr, Robert, Tab.	.265	27	108	98	15	26	39	4	0	3	11	2	0	1	7	1	21	1	1	3	.398	.321
Grijak, Kevin, Mex.*	.287	43	182	164	21	47	85	14	0	8	34	0	1	1	16	1	25	0	0	4	.518	.352
Grijalva, Lorenzo, Tab.	.071	8	17	14	1	1	2	1	0	0	0	0	0	0	3	0	4	1	0	0	.143	.235
Guerrero, Epifanio, Can.*	.288	88	373	326	45	94	138	12	1	10	54	1	3	2	41	3	36	1	2	5	.423	.368
Guerrero, Sergio, Lar.	.265	19	92	83	12	22	37	3	0	4	11	0	0	1	8	1	10	0	0	1	.446	.337
Guizar, Hector, Mex.	.291	105	397	371	35	108	131	15	1	2	50	4	6	0	16	0	30	5	5	12	.353	.316
Gutierrez, Andres, Pue.	.243	40	80	70	7	17	20	1	1	0	4	5	1	2	2	0	12	1	1	1	.286	.280
Hernandez, Esteban, Oax.	.000	6	0	0	1	0	0	0	0	0	0	0	0	0	0	0	0	0	0	0	.000	.000
Hernandez, Julio, Lar.	.287	119	549	450	62	131	169	18	2	4	41	8	5	8	72	2	48	3	7	11	.349	.390
Hernandez, Marlon, Mont.	.000	1	2	2	0	0	0	0	0	0	0	0	0	0	0	0	0	0	0	0	.000	.000
Herrera, Ramiro, Ver.	.048	11	31	21	5	1	1	0	0	0	0	0	0	0	10	0	7	1	1	0	.048	.355
Howard, Tom, Mont.*	.274	22	99	84	11	23	38	6	0	3	16	0	0	1	14	3	10	0	0	4	.452	.384

Player, Team	Avg.	G	TPA	AB	R	H	TB	2B	3B	HR	RBI	SH	SF	HP	BB	IBB	SO	SB	CS	GDP	Slg.	OBP
Hurtado, Hector, Mont.†	.247	62	176	162	14	40	60	5	0	5	13	7	0	5	2	1	46	0	2	3	.370	.278
Ibarra, Juvenal, Tor.*	.200	7	5	5	1	1	1	0	0	0	0	0	0	0	0	0	2	0	0	0	.200	.200
Ingram, Garey, Rey.	.179	11	44	39	7	7	10	0	0	1	3	0	0	2	3	0	4	0	0	2	.256	.273
Iturbe, Pedro, Pue.*	.337	99	392	356	51	120	177	24	3	9	46	1	2	5	28	11	41	8	5	10	.497	.391
Jimenez, Alfonso, Sal.	.250	2	8	8	1	2	2	0	0	0	0	0	0	0	0	0	1	0	0	0	.250	.250
Jimenez, Eduardo, Sal.*	.260	114	484	381	63	99	194	14	0	27	89	0	8	8	87	10	111	0	0	9	.509	.401
Lara, Jose Idelfonso, Ver.-Cor.	.274	79	283	263	30	72	110	11	0	9	30	2	1	3	14	1	60	0	2	9	.418	.317
Leday, Anthony, Rey.	.284	28	114	102	17	29	47	4	1	4	17	1	2	3	6	0	20	0	0	6	.461	.336
Lennon, Patrick, Yuc.	.240	7	32	25	5	6	6	0	0	0	2	0	0	1	6	0	8	0	0	1	.240	.406
Lewis, Anthony, Lar.*	.147	9	38	34	1	5	7	2	0	0	3	1	1	0	2	1	9	0	0	1	.206	.189
Leyva, German, Ver.*	.222	105	427	374	32	83	104	12	0	3	36	6	2	3	42	0	42	3	0	11	.278	.304
Leyva, Octavio, Ver.*	.185	11	28	27	2	5	5	0	0	0	4	0	0	0	1	0	8	1	0	1	.185	.214
Lopez, Fabian, Oax.*	.281	95	357	306	33	86	107	8	2	3	28	5	3	5	38	8	28	1	2	13	.350	.366
Lopez, Fortunato, Tab.	.000	4	4	4	0	0	0	0	0	0	0	0	0	0	0	0	2	0	0	0	.000	.000
Lopez, Gonzalo, Yuc.	.190	30	73	63	5	12	12	0	0	0	8	2	1	1	6	0	11	0	2	3	.190	.268
Lopez, Raul, Monc.	.313	22	77	67	14	21	40	4	0	5	11	0	1	0	9	1	11	0	2	0	.597	.390
Lugo, Roberto, Mont.	.140	23	45	43	3	6	7	1	0	0	4	0	1	1	0	0	16	0	0	1	.163	.156
Luna, Jose, Cor.	.119	41	108	101	6	12	14	2	0	0	4	3	0	2	2	0	25	1	2	2	.139	.152
Luque, Raul, Tab.*	.160	9	28	25	2	4	5	1	0	0	2	0	0	1	2	0	7	2	0	2	.200	.250
Machiria, Pablo, Cor.-Cam.	.206	57	185	170	22	35	48	4	0	3	13	0	0	5	10	0	18	0	0	2	.282	.270
Magallanes, Ever, Mont.*	.300	44	173	150	23	45	57	3	0	3	16	2	1	3	17	2	26	1	0	2	.380	.380
Magallanes, Roberto, Tig.-Pue.	.310	62	226	187	27	58	89	22	0	3	34	1	2	2	34	1	46	2	2	3	.476	.418
Malave, Jose, Ver.-Sal.	.304	18	79	69	9	21	31	4	0	2	10	0	2	1	7	0	9	0	0	4	.449	.367
Martinez, Abel, Can.	.217	67	217	203	20	44	52	5	0	1	11	1	1	4	8	0	31	1	0	8	.256	.259
Martinez, Augusto, Yuc.†	.000	3	2	2	0	0	0	0	0	0	0	0	0	0	0	0	0	0	0	0	.000	.000
Martinez, Enrique, Can.	.228	43	131	114	9	26	39	4	0	3	12	2	3	4	8	0	29	0	1	2	.342	.295
Martinez, Grimaldo, Tor.	.258	120	509	453	43	117	154	19	0	6	51	11	1	4	40	2	46	2	4	13	.340	.323
Martinez, Luis Carlos, Sal.	.292	118	423	390	48	114	141	16	1	3	36	10	1	3	19	1	48	9	7	13	.362	.329
Martinez, Raul, Tab.	.230	34	85	74	5	17	21	4	0	0	6	1	1	0	9	0	15	0	0	2	.284	.310
Martinez, Ray, Mex.	.275	108	451	382	63	105	167	15	1	15	75	0	5	6	58	4	94	7	1	14	.437	.375
Mata, Noe, Rey.	.314	54	96	86	14	27	38	6	1	1	12	1	1	2	6	0	23	1	1	1	.442	.368
Matos, Malvin, Tab.	.222	5	21	18	2	4	4	0	0	0	0	1	0	1	1	0	5	0	2	1	.222	.300
Medina, Jose, Sal.	.226	62	150	133	15	30	49	1	3	4	15	1	0	1	15	0	32	1	2	6	.368	.309
Mejia, Roberto, Tab.	.310	90	371	329	46	102	162	18	3	12	49	3	1	3	35	3	49	8	8	9	.492	.380
Mendez, Francisco, Mont.	.077	16	45	39	4	3	4	1	0	0	1	2	0	0	4	0	9	0	0	0	.103	.163
Mendez, Roberto, Oax.-Mex.	.314	105	445	366	67	115	189	27	1	15	70	4	8	1	66	3	51	12	6	15	.516	.413
Mendoza, Carlos, Sal.*	.319	18	84	72	9	23	26	3	0	0	6	1	1	2	8	0	5	4	1	5	.361	.398
Mendoza, Omar, Tab.	.262	85	305	271	36	71	103	12	1	6	24	9	1	2	22	1	52	2	0	12	.380	.321
Mere, Pedro, Ver.	.289	105	447	387	56	112	175	13	1	16	56	8	8	10	34	0	61	4	3	9	.452	.355
Meulens, Hensley, Sal.	.241	83	357	299	48	72	127	12	2	13	50	4	2	8	44	1	95	2	1	7	.425	.351
Meza, Alfredo, Ver.†	.245	107	394	367	16	90	119	11	0	6	32	11	3	2	11	2	55	0	0	14	.324	.269
Meza, Gonzalo, Mex.*	.275	68	193	171	21	47	84	7	0	10	32	1	0	2	19	1	34	0	0	8	.491	.354
Minjarez, Francisco, Pue.	.265	106	447	411	49	109	137	19	3	1	19	11	0	2	23	0	78	5	2	6	.333	.307
Montano, Angel, Cam.	.182	6	12	11	0	2	2	0	0	0	1	0	0	0	1	0	2	0	0	0	.182	.250
Morejon, Oswaldo, Yuc.	.279	119	517	477	51	133	167	20	1	4	44	13	1	4	22	1	52	2	0	16	.350	.315
Moreno, David, Cam.	.200	13	5	5	3	1	1	0	0	0	0	0	0	0	0	0	1	0	0	0	.200	.200
Munoz, Adan, Monc.*	.293	93	304	276	40	81	136	17	1	12	55	0	4	6	18	5	59	0	1	5	.493	.345
Munoz, Jose de Jesus, Sal.*	.283	119	545	459	78	130	168	14	3	6	42	1	5	3	77	0	84	31	17	12	.366	.386
Munoz, Jose Luis, Can.*	.193	26	99	83	6	16	20	1	0	1	10	1	2	0	13	0	11	0	1	6	.241	.296
Munoz, Noe, Sal.	.297	114	471	411	59	122	186	18	2	14	65	4	4	3	49	1	52	2	0	22	.453	.373
Murray, Glenn, Cam.	.261	63	258	222	39	58	127	13	1	18	50	0	1	5	30	2	65	1	1	3	.572	.360
Myers, Rod, Mont.*	.167	8	35	30	1	5	5	0	0	0	1	1	0	0	4	0	6	1	4	0	.167	.265
Nava, Lipso, Ver.-Tor.	.282	80	341	301	39	85	130	18	0	9	35	1	1	7	31	1	50	2	1	10	.432	.362
Newson, Warren, Tor.*	.302	110	491	404	90	122	216	19	3	23	71	0	1	2	84	7	100	7	4	4	.535	.424
Nunez, Jose Juan, Oax.	.000	19	0	0	1	0	0	0	0	0	0	0	0	0	0	0	0	0	0	0	.000	.000
Nunez, Raymond, Cor.-Tab.	.294	89	359	337	47	99	153	17	2	11	41	1	2	6	13	2	65	0	1	16	.454	.330
Ojeda, Miguel, Mex.	.310	114	489	422	78	131	202	17	3	16	65	2	5	4	55	4	74	4	2	9	.479	.391
Orantes, Ramon, Mont.	.363	102	382	355	46	129	174	15	0	10	50	2	0	7	18	3	31	0	3	15	.490	.405
Ortega, Antonio, Cam.	.225	34	80	71	7	16	21	2	0	1	5	0	0	1	8	0	12	0	0	4	.296	.313
Ortiz, Alejandro, Tor.	.292	101	437	380	51	111	165	18	0	12	56	2	3	6	46	3	69	1	0	15	.434	.375
Ortiz, Luis, Mont.-Tab.	.301	28	104	103	11	31	42	5	0	2	13	0	0	0	1	1	13	1	0	5	.408	.308
Osuna, Edgar, Tab.*	.273	20	37	33	3	9	10	1	0	0	5	0	0	0	4	0	8	0	1	0	.303	.351
Osuna, Hector, Can.	.273	8	14	11	3	3	3	0	0	0	1	1	0	0	2	0	1	0	0	0	.273	.385
Otanez, Willis, Mont.	.143	18	62	56	5	8	12	1	0	1	3	0	0	0	6	0	15	0	0	3	.214	.226
Otero, Ricky, Can.†	.301	106	460	402	60	121	181	22	7	8	35	7	0	2	49	3	46	8	5	6	.450	.380
Pacho, Carlos, Yuc.	.000	2	1	1	0	0	0	0	0	0	0	0	0	0	0	0	0	0	0	1	.000	.000
Pacho, Juan Jose, Yuc.	.238	83	286	265	21	63	70	5	1	0	23	8	2	1	10	0	27	0	0	3	.264	.266
Paez, Hector, Can.*	.193	65	207	197	12	38	50	6	0	2	15	1	1	1	7	2	13	2	0	7	.254	.223
Paez, Raul, Mex.†	.271	30	57	48	3	13	14	1	0	0	5	0	0	1	8	1	3	0	0	3	.292	.386
Palafox, Sergio, Sal.	.288	93	334	302	42	87	129	14	2	8	43	2	3	4	23	1	35	5	2	6	.427	.343
Payro, Edison, Cam.*	.224	73	231	196	30	44	50	6	0	0	11	3	0	2	30	2	31	1	2	8	.255	.333
Pearson, Eddie, Tab.*	.284	53	214	194	26	55	88	6	0	9	38	0	1	2	17	3	26	0	0	6	.454	.346
Pemberton, Rudy, Monc.	.306	108	457	396	63	121	199	34	1	14	84	0	4	14	43	4	50	9	3	12	.503	.389
Peraza, Rudy, Tab.	.174	16	28	23	7	4	4	0	0	0	0	0	0	0	5	0	3	2	1	1	.174	.321
Perez, Alfredo, Cam.	.303	50	120	109	14	33	39	3	0	1	9	7	0	0	4	1	12	0	2	0	.358	.327
Perez, Francisco, Rey.*	.298	39	52	47	3	14	15	1	0	0	4	1	0	0	4	0	8	1	1	1	.319	.353
Perez, Jorge, Pue.	.222	59	151	126	14	28	34	4	1	0	13	3	2	9	11	2	25	1	1	6	.270	.324
Perez, Jose, Mont.	.240	51	111	96	12	23	24	1	0	0	2	5	0	4	6	0	19	2	1	3	.250	.311
Peters, Anthony, Yuc.	.250	11	50	44	4	11	12	1	0	0	3	1	1	0	4	0	18	3	0	0	.273	.306
Peterson, Charles, Tor.	.000	3	10	10	0	0	0	0	0	0	1	0	0	0	0	0	3	0	0	1	.000	.000
Pinto, Placido, Cor.	.174	34	96	86	3	15	18	3	0	0	4	3	0	2	5	0	32	1	0	2	.209	.237
Poe, Charles, Lar.	.233	7	34	30	3	7	8	1	0	0	3	0	1	0	3	0	17	0	0	1	.267	.294
Polonia, Luis, Tig.*	.365	67	294	263	56	96	153	16	7	9	49	0	2	1	28	4	27	20	2	4	.582	.425

Player, Team	Avg.	G	TPA	AB	R	H	TB	2B	3B	HR	RBI	SH	SF	HP	BB	IBB	SO	SB	CS	GDP	Slg.	OBP
Powell, Corey, Rey.	.220	23	103	91	7	20	31	2	0	3	10	0	3	2	7	0	26	0	1	4	.341	.282
Presichi, Christian, Sal.	.278	88	239	205	43	57	87	9	3	5	22	5	1	4	24	0	52	12	3	5	.424	.363
Pulido, Raymundo, Cam.	.000	19	1	1	0	0	0	0	0	0	0	0	0	0	0	0	0	0	0	1	.000	.000
Pulliam, Harvey, Tab	.184	10	42	38	6	7	9	2	0	0	2	0	1	0	3	0	9	1	1	0	.237	.238
Quezada, Juan, Oax.	.063	11	19	16	0	1	2	1	0	0	1	1	0	1	1	0	4	0	0	0	.125	.167
Quinonez, Ruben, Monc.	.053	17	42	38	2	2	2	0	0	0	3	0	2	0	2	0	7	0	0	1	.053	.095
Quintero, Christian, Mex.	.250	75	165	144	27	36	55	4	6	1	21	3	1	1	16	1	23	1	0	5	.382	.327
Quintero, Edgar, Mont.*	.272	89	273	232	39	63	110	15	1	10	30	2	3	2	34	0	63	6	3	3	.474	.365
Quintero, Guillermo, Cor.-Ver.	.232	94	327	293	30	68	81	11	1	0	14	6	2	1	25	0	59	14	4	2	.276	.293
Ramirez, Efren, Cor.-Tor.	.212	69	195	170	12	36	49	4	0	3	14	1	1	11	12	0	32	0	0	9	.288	.304
Ramirez, Enrique, Can.-Mont.	.171	41	81	76	7	13	14	1	0	0	3	3	1	0	1	0	5	0	0	3	.184	.179
Ramirez, Hector, Oax.*	.200	12	5	5	0	1	1	0	0	0	0	0	0	0	0	0	0	0	0	0	.200	.200
Ramirez, Jesus, Oax.	.312	100	345	295	38	92	108	16	0	0	31	10	1	8	29	2	38	2	2	7	.366	.387
Ramirez, Oscar, Cam.	.222	14	30	27	3	6	6	0	0	0	3	0	1	0	2	0	6	0	1	1	.222	.267
Resendez, Carlos, Monc.	.250	56	164	144	19	36	58	4	0	6	20	2	1	4	13	0	40	1	1	4	.403	.327
Reyes, Jesus, Yuc.-Cor.	.192	42	81	73	4	14	14	0	0	0	6	3	0	0	5	0	14	2	1	1	.192	.244
Reyes, Jesus Eleazar, Oax.*	.280	75	170	161	23	45	52	3	2	0	5	2	1	1	5	0	14	3	3	3	.323	.304
Rincon, Isaias, Mex.-Ver.	.250	30	39	36	4	9	9	0	0	0	2	2	0	0	1	0	12	0	2	0	.250	.270
Rivera, Francisco, Ver.*	.224	52	127	116	7	26	31	5	0	0	9	0	0	1	10	1	23	0	0	3	.267	.291
Rivera, Jesus Manuel, Tab.*	.285	70	189	151	19	43	51	3	1	1	15	6	2	3	27	2	19	4	1	3	.338	.399
Rivera, Oscar, Ver.	.000	16	1	1	0	0	0	0	0	0	0	0	0	0	0	0	0	0	0	0	.000	.000
Roberson, Kevin, Cor.-Tor.†	.235	41	171	153	16	36	54	12	0	2	19	2	2	2	12	0	41	0	0	4	.353	.296
Robles, Javier, Tig.	.300	106	422	383	53	115	203	22	3	20	68	3	1	3	32	1	51	5	4	11	.530	.358
Robles, Juan, Mex.	.176	26	54	51	5	9	18	4	1	1	7	2	1	0	0	0	12	0	0	2	.353	.173
Robles, Oscar, Oax.*	.296	118	534	466	71	138	183	26	2	5	51	3	5	1	59	0	50	4	5	16	.393	.373
Robles, Trinidad, Tig.	.241	72	232	199	32	48	71	6	1	5	20	6	1	4	22	0	47	3	3	3	.357	.327
Rodarte, Raul, Rey.-Cor.	.293	114	455	389	62	114	181	27	2	12	65	1	5	5	55	3	61	20	3	12	.465	.383
Rodriguez, Armando, Tig.-Pue.	.205	75	243	205	24	42	56	7	2	1	21	5	3	3	27	0	51	2	1	9	.273	.303
Rodriguez, Boi, Monc.*	.303	116	512	402	103	122	249	24	2	33	100	1	5	4	100	9	97	11	2	8	.619	.442
Rodriguez, Carlos, Rey.†	.282	114	513	422	74	119	146	17	2	2	25	18	2	5	66	3	41	12	2	10	.346	.384
Rodriguez, Eric, Oax.	.294	28	72	68	7	20	25	5	0	0	4	0	0	1	3	0	5	0	0	1	.368	.333
Rodriguez, Fernando, Cam.	.272	118	477	430	49	117	194	17	0	20	73	2	4	7	34	2	49	1	0	17	.451	.333
Rodriguez, Jose, Tor	.000	9	4	4	2	0	0	0	0	0	0	0	0	0	0	0	1	0	0	0	.000	.000
Rojas, Homar, Oax	.240	79	294	258	27	62	97	14	0	7	41	4	0	5	24	1	26	0	0	8	.376	.314
Romero, Flavio, Sal.	.320	20	29	25	4	8	10	2	0	0	2	0	0	0	4	0	3	3	1	1	.400	.414
Romero, Marco, Sal.-Tor	.284	95	361	313	46	89	150	16	0	15	46	0	5	8	35	0	54	3	3	8	.479	.366
Romero, Oscar, Monc.	.301	59	227	196	25	59	74	6	0	3	17	3	0	1	27	1	25	5	2	3	.378	.388
Romero, Wilfredo, Sal.	.308	83	367	325	75	100	162	22	2	12	53	5	3	5	29	2	41	23	6	6	.498	.370
Romero, Yamil, Ver.*	.385	7	15	13	1	5	6	1	0	0	0	0	0	0	2	0	3	1	0	0	.462	.467
Rubio, Miguel, Mont.	.000	55	1	1	0	0	0	0	0	0	0	0	0	0	0	0	1	0	0	0	.000	.000
Rubio, Sergio, Tor.	.000	7	2	2	1	0	0	0	0	0	0	0	0	0	0	0	1	0	0	0	.000	.000
Ruiz, Juan, Mex.	.273	32	57	55	5	15	16	1	0	0	4	1	0	0	1	0	4	0	0	1	.291	.286
Saenz, Ricardo, Monc.	.304	117	494	424	80	129	218	30	1	19	92	0	7	4	59	3	91	8	0	5	.514	.389
Salas, H'berto, Cam. Cor. Yuc.	.285	85	279	249	36	71	99	17	1	3	19	2	1	6	21	1	25	4	2	5	.398	.354
Salazar, Carlos, Yuc.	.105	23	20	19	3	2	2	0	0	0	0	1	0	0	0	0	5	0	0	0	.105	.105
Samuels, Scott, Mont.	.210	20	90	81	12	17	22	5	0	0	8	0	0	1	8	1	20	4	2	2	.272	.289
Sanchez, Gerardo, Lar.-Tig.	.210	75	263	214	23	45	66	9	0	4	21	6	3	7	33	2	25	0	2	5	.308	.331
Sanchez, Jose, Lar.	.231	20	43	39	9	9	9	0	0	0	1	0	0	0	4	0	10	0	0	1	.231	.302
Sanchez, Orlando, Cor.	.253	89	314	281	20	71	86	11	2	0	21	7	0	1	25	1	64	0	4	8	.306	.316
Sanchez, Raul, Can.	.280	93	373	350	40	98	139	21	1	6	40	0	2	2	19	0	78	6	0	14	.397	.319
Sanchez, Roque, Cam.	.293	106	371	351	33	103	134	13	0	6	35	6	4	5	5	1	20	0	2	12	.382	.310
Sanchez, Wilfredo, Cor.	.216	69	202	185	19	40	46	4	1	0	13	4	1	3	9	0	39	0	0	2	.249	.263
Sandoval, Jose Luis, Mex.	.301	106	430	395	52	119	176	22	1	11	64	1	3	4	27	1	77	1	0	11	.446	.350
Sandoval, Octavio, Tig	.249	78	224	197	35	49	75	9	4	3	22	2	0	6	19	0	42	7	3	4	.381	.333
Santana, Mario, Mont.	.202	37	109	99	4	20	22	2	0	0	6	3	0	1	6	0	14	0	1	3	.222	.255
Santiago, Henry, Cam.	.175	18	68	63	4	11	19	0	1	2	7	1	0	1	3	0	17	0	0	2	.302	.224
Santos, Andres, Lar.	.198	55	125	116	10	23	41	3	0	5	17	1	0	1	7	1	30	0	0	2	.353	.250
Sauceda, Victor, Can.†	.152	50	118	105	9	16	20	2	1	0	4	3	1	1	8	0	21	0	0	3	.190	.217
Saucedo, Roberto, Can.	.263	104	399	365	37	96	168	15	0	19	56	2	2	3	27	0	78	0	0	9	.460	.317
Seitzer, Brad, Can.-Ver.	.306	89	372	327	33	100	136	19	1	5	51	1	2	4	38	4	60	0	2	16	.416	.383
Sherman, Darrell, Monc.*	.355	108	487	403	83	143	178	15	1	6	43	1	3	9	71	6	37	30	11	2	.442	.459
Sievers, Carlos, Tab.*	.234	83	290	239	34	56	86	9	0	7	27	4	3	10	34	3	39	1	1	9	.360	.350
Smith, Charles, Mont.	.277	69	304	267	47	74	140	15	0	17	62	0	4	1	32	6	55	2	0	10	.524	.352
Smith, Demond, Tab.-Mont.†	.313	86	383	326	68	102	171	21	9	10	39	5	1	8	43	4	73	36	18	0	.525	.405
Solano, Fausto, Pue.	.280	15	57	50	6	14	18	2	1	0	2	2	0	1	4	0	6	2	1	2	.360	.345
Soriano, Ricardo, Cor.*	.277	91	329	292	35	81	106	14	1	3	41	3	2	1	31	3	46	2	6	5	.363	.347
Soto, Saul, Mex.	.250	2	5	4	0	1	1	0	0	0	0	0	0	0	1	0	1	0	0	1	.250	.400
Sotomayor, Gilberto, Monc.*	.271	89	204	192	21	52	70	9	3	1	21	2	1	0	9	0	19	2	8	2	.365	.302
Suarez, Luis, Tig.*	.310	95	345	319	49	99	147	16	4	8	58	1	5	2	18	9	53	3	3	4	.461	.346
Sulu, Mario, Cam.-Can.	1.000	21	1	1	0	1	1	0	0	0	0	0	0	0	0	0	0	0	0	0	1.000	1.000
Tellez, Alonso, Rey.	.330	122	520	470	56	155	222	34	0	11	72	0	5	0	45	3	76	1	0	16	.472	.385
Tiquet, Lazaro, Tab.	.125	5	9	8	1	1	1	0	0	0	1	0	0	1	0	0	2	0	0	0	.125	.222
Torres, Paul, Tab.-Cor.	.377	40	168	146	27	55	95	10	0	10	31	0	1	2	19	3	30	1	1	6	.651	.452
Torres, Sebastian, Oax.	.261	10	24	23	4	6	10	1	0	1	5	0	0	1	0	0	8	0	0	0	.435	.292
Tovar, Jose, Rey.	.239	58	50	46	11	11	12	1	0	0	4	0	0	0	4	1	10	2	4	1	.261	.300
Trapaga, Julio, Tig.	.288	45	60	52	13	15	17	2	0	0	8	1	0	1	6	0	10	2	0	3	.327	.373
Tress, Irving, Cor.	.175	18	42	40	1	7	7	0	0	0	1	1	0	0	1	0	19	0	1	1	.175	.195
Tyler, Brad, Oax.*	.286	74	310	255	44	73	124	12	3	11	54	1	1	3	50	2	46	9	3	2	.486	.408
Valdez, Emmanuel, Tig.	.218	89	260	216	32	47	72	7	0	6	29	4	3	6	31	2	68	1	1	3	.333	.328
Valdez, Francisco, Tab.	.301	104	374	332	29	100	132	17	0	5	45	7	7	12	16	2	40	1	2	11	.398	.349
Valdez, Ramon, Cor.-Cam.*	.242	105	446	389	53	94	115	7	4	2	19	10	0	6	41	1	48	9	7	8	.296	.323
Valencia, Carlos, Lar.	.272	105	410	389	44	106	150	15	1	9	51	3	6	3	9	0	53	3	2	5	.386	.290
Valenzuela, Irving, Monc.	.224	50	121	107	14	24	29	5	0	0	8	2	0	1	11	0	26	0	0	2	.271	.303

Player, Team	Avg.	G	TPA	AB	R	H	TB	2B	3B	HR	RBI	SH	SF	HP	BB	IBB	SO	SB	CS	GDP	Slg.	OBP
Valle, Cosme, Rey.	.297	61	150	138	10	41	51	10	0	0	25	3	2	1	6	0	25	0	0	2	.370	.327
Valle, Jorge, Rey.	.278	119	481	439	45	122	155	14	5	3	55	6	5	9	22	0	72	0	3	12	.353	.322
Valle, Jose, Tor.	.238	68	175	160	23	38	48	2	4	0	16	4	1	4	6	0	18	1	0	5	.300	.281
Valle, Roberto, Tor.	.243	27	43	37	12	9	10	1	0	0	5	0	0	1	5	0	7	2	0	0	.270	.349
Vazquez, Felipe, Lar.	.185	53	131	119	12	22	24	2	0	0	6	4	1	0	7	0	21	0	2	5	.202	.228
Vazquez, Gregorio, Tab.	.242	112	400	364	27	88	100	8	2	0	30	12	0	4	20	1	31	13	4	11	.275	.289
Vazquez, Jorge Alberto, Tig. .	.284	91	254	232	35	66	92	11	0	5	24	1	1	6	14	1	55	0	1	4	.397	.340
Vega, Edgar, Pue.	.265	70	213	181	16	48	60	4	1	2	23	4	2	0	26	1	30	1	0	6	.331	.354
Vega, Jose, Oax.	.136	24	23	22	7	3	6	3	0	0	1	0	0	0	1	0	8	0	0	0	.273	.174
Velazquez, Guillermo, Sal.*....	.284	93	359	296	49	84	153	18	0	17	70	0	4	0	58	3	70	0	0	10	.517	.397
Velez, Manuel, Lar.-Sal.	.251	109	453	403	50	101	140	15	0	8	48	7	3	2	38	4	44	10	5	16	.347	.316
Verdugo, Vincente, Sal.	.252	37	126	119	8	30	33	3	0	0	5	4	1	0	2	0	10	1	1	3	.277	.262
Viera, Jose, Tor.	.202	29	124	114	13	23	42	4	0	5	15	0	2	0	8	1	29	0	1	3	.368	.250
Villanueva, Hector, Cor.-Pue. .	.266	90	362	289	35	77	120	16	0	9	46	0	5	1	67	8	45	0	1	12	.415	.401
Villarreal, Alejandro, Lar.	.305	79	259	236	21	72	95	9	1	4	25	3	1	5	14	1	21	1	1	4	.403	.355
Villegas, Fernando, Tor.	.226	65	177	146	21	33	48	4	1	3	17	2	2	2	25	2	24	0	2	5	.329	.343
Vizcarra, Roberto, Tig.	.310	117	516	458	79	142	214	26	2	14	58	3	4	7	44	2	32	4	3	12	.467	.376
White, Derrick, Mont.-Lar.	.295	114	498	430	59	127	183	17	0	13	67	0	3	6	59	6	73	6	4	15	.426	.386
Whiten, Mark, Ver.	.277	106	458	376	80	104	216	13	0	33	78	0	2	2	78	12	76	5	1	10	.574	.402
Williams, Eddie, Mex.	.295	69	297	241	51	71	118	11	0	12	54	0	0	4	52	3	49	0	1	14	.490	.428
Yuriar, Jesus, Can.	.221	54	166	145	17	32	38	3	0	1	14	5	1	3	12	0	32	1	0	5	.262	.292
Zambrano, Roberto, Mont. ...	.329	97	411	340	43	112	157	19	1	8	49	0	6	23	42	2	60	1	1	6	.462	.431
Zamudio, Rafael, Can.	.176	17	37	34	2	6	9	0	0	1	4	0	0	0	3	0	11	0	1	1	.265	.243
Zazueta, Juan, Tor.†	.271	103	439	391	44	106	138	9	4	5	29	16	2	5	25	1	37	11	5	5	.353	.322
Zazueta, Mauricio, Monc.*.....	.285	98	416	369	60	105	153	15	0	11	55	9	2	2	34	0	73	23	1	12	.415	.346

PLAYERS WITH TWO OR MORE TEAMS

Player, Team	Avg.	G	TPA	AB	R	H	TB	2B	3B	HR	RBI	SH	SF	HP	BB	IBB	SO	SB	CS	GDP	Slg.	OBP
Arredondo, Hernando, Cam. .	.275	66	214	204	19	56	76	8	0	4	26	3	2	2	3	0	43	1	0	2	.373	.289
Arredondo, Hernando, Cor. ...	.278	29	115	108	6	30	35	5	0	0	6	0	1	0	6	0	15	5	2	4	.324	.313
Avila, Carlos, Tab.*	.357	23	31	28	7	10	12	2	0	0	1	0	0	1	2	0	5	1	0	2	.429	.419
Avila, Carlos, Lar.*	.179	31	61	56	5	10	11	1	0	0	0	2	0	1	2	0	13	2	2	0	.196	.220
Barron, Tony, Can.	.310	82	348	303	49	94	164	19	0	17	54	0	4	3	38	4	72	3	0	10	.541	.388
Barron, Tony, Cam.	.281	24	101	89	16	25	44	4	0	5	12	0	0	1	11	1	21	1	0	2	.494	.366
Boston, D.J., Cam.*	.262	66	264	221	36	58	88	6	0	8	32	0	1	1	41	5	40	7	1	8	.398	.379
Boston, D.J., Can.*	.200	23	103	90	8	18	22	1	0	1	5	0	1	0	12	2	15	1	2	1	.244	.291
Brewer, Rod, Oax.*	.278	71	309	252	56	70	128	13	0	15	47	0	1	3	53	6	57	1	1	6	.508	.408
Brewer, Rod, Ver.*	.289	46	186	152	27	44	85	8	0	11	39	0	4	1	29	4	23	2	0	0	.559	.398
Brinkley, Darryl, Cam.	.283	75	333	300	42	85	115	11	2	5	26	0	4	1	28	1	31	12	6	7	.383	.342
Brinkley, Darryl, Yuc.	.320	27	116	103	16	33	47	5	0	3	14	0	1	1	11	1	11	4	2	3	.456	.388
Bustamante, Omar, Sal.	.176	15	18	17	1	3	3	0	0	0	0	0	0	0	1	0	6	0	1	0	.176	.222
Bustamante, Omar, Lar.	.158	18	59	57	3	9	13	1	0	1	5	2	0	0	0	0	11	0	0	3	.228	.158
Castaneda, Rafael, Oax.	.143	7	22	21	1	3	4	1	0	0	2	0	0	0	1	0	2	0	0	3	.190	.182
Castaneda, Rafael, Rey.	.269	92	345	297	34	80	107	10	1	5	25	2	3	1	42	1	32	2	1	7	.360	.359
Cobos, Rogelio, Ver.	.238	23	45	42	2	10	13	1	1	0	2	1	1	0	1	0	10	1	0	1	.310	.250
Cobos, Rogelio, Oax.	.256	27	94	86	9	22	29	4	0	1	10	1	2	0	5	0	17	0	0	1	.337	.290
Cobos, Rogelio, Mex.	.200	7	11	10	0	2	2	0	0	0	1	0	1	0	0	0	3	0	0	1	.200	.182
Dattola, Kevin, Cam.*............	.237	10	47	38	5	9	12	0	0	1	8	1	0	0	8	0	7	0	1	2	.316	.370
Dattola, Kevin, Yuc.*............	.143	4	16	14	3	2	3	1	0	0	0	0	0	0	2	0	1	1	0	0	.214	.250
Duenas, Arnoldo, Yuc.	.091	16	26	22	0	2	2	0	0	0	1	1	0	1	2	0	8	0	0	0	.091	.200
Duenas, Arnoldo, Can.	.165	28	86	79	10	13	17	1	0	1	3	3	0	0	4	0	26	1	0	5	.215	.205
Gainer, Jonathan, Tab.	.255	74	310	271	26	69	93	9	0	5	37	0	3	0	36	11	47	3	2	8	.343	.339
Gainer, Jonathan, Cor.	.250	6	27	24	3	6	8	2	0	0	1	0	0	0	3	0	3	0	0	0	.333	.333
Garcia, Hector, Mont.	.198	48	130	121	8	24	26	2	0	0	6	4	0	1	4	0	8	3	1	3	.215	.230
Garcia, Hector, Tab.	.301	46	203	186	24	56	61	5	0	0	10	5	0	3	9	0	13	2	4	3	.328	.343
Garcia, Omar, Ver.	.263	56	216	194	28	51	81	6	0	8	39	0	3	1	18	1	21	1	0	3	.418	.324
Garcia, Omar, Yuc.	.306	40	178	160	20	49	77	13	0	5	36	0	5	0	13	1	15	0	0	6	.481	.348
Garza, Gerardo, Tor.	.288	41	87	80	10	23	29	3	0	1	6	3	0	0	4	0	13	0	0	0	.363	.321
Garza, Gerardo, Rey.	.243	25	75	70	4	17	23	3	0	1	9	2	2	0	1	0	12	0	0	3	.329	.247
Garzon, Eliseo, Lar.	.234	81	298	261	19	61	81	11	0	3	30	7	2	5	23	1	42	0	2	7	.310	.306
Garzon, Eliseo, Sal.	.071	6	17	14	1	1	4	0	0	1	1	0	0	0	3	0	5	0	0	0	.286	.235
Gastelum, Carlos, Pue.	.326	20	52	46	3	15	16	1	0	0	5	3	1	1	1	0	3	0	0	3	.348	.347
Gastelum, Carlos, Tig.	.256	40	100	90	9	23	28	5	0	0	4	3	0	0	7	0	16	1	0	3	.311	.309
Lara, Jose Idelfonso, Ver.	.235	42	142	132	12	31	48	5	0	4	13	1	0	3	6	1	35	0	1	5	.364	.284
Lara, Jose Idelfonso, Cor.	.313	37	141	131	18	41	62	6	0	5	17	1	1	0	8	0	25	0	1	4	.473	.350
Machiria, Pablo, Cor.	.222	38	139	126	17	28	40	3	0	3	9	0	0	4	9	0	13	0	0	2	.317	.295
Machiria, Pablo, Cam.	.159	19	46	44	5	7	8	1	0	0	4	0	0	1	1	0	5	0	0	0	.182	.196
Magallanes, Roberto, Tig.	.248	30	113	101	12	25	40	9	0	2	17	1	0	1	10	1	29	1	2	1	.396	.321
Magallanes, Roberto, Pue.	.384	32	113	86	15	33	49	13	0	1	17	0	2	1	24	0	17	1	0	2	.570	.513
Malave, Jose, Ver.	.269	14	61	52	6	14	22	2	0	2	10	0	2	1	6	0	6	0	0	3	.423	.344
Malave, Jose, Sal.	.412	4	18	17	3	7	9	2	0	0	0	0	0	0	1	0	3	0	0	1	.529	.444
Mendez, Roberto, Oax.	.305	78	334	279	43	85	136	22	1	9	50	4	6	1	44	3	41	9	5	13	.487	.394
Mendez, Roberto, Mex.	.345	27	111	87	24	30	53	5	0	6	20	0	2	0	22	0	10	3	1	2	.609	.468
Nava, Lipso, Ver.	.220	23	92	82	11	18	31	4	0	3	11	0	0	2	8	0	19	1	0	3	.378	.304
Nava, Lipso, Tor.	.306	57	249	219	28	67	99	14	0	6	24	1	1	5	23	1	31	1	1	7	.452	.383
Nunez, Raymond, Cor.	.292	57	228	212	31	62	104	13	1	9	32	1	2	4	9	2	35	0	1	12	.491	.330
Nunez, Raymond, Tab.	.296	32	131	125	16	37	49	4	1	2	9	0	0	2	4	0	30	0	0	4	.392	.328
Ortiz, Luis, Mont.	.308	17	65	65	9	20	24	1	0	1	6	0	0	0	0	0	13	1	0	3	.369	.308
Ortiz, Luis, Tab.	.289	11	39	38	2	11	18	4	0	1	7	0	0	0	1	1	0	0	0	2	.474	.308
Quintero, Guillermo, Cor.	.105	9	21	19	1	2	3	1	0	0	4	0	1	0	1	0	5	1	0	0	.158	.143
Quintero, Guillermo, Ver.	.241	85	306	274	29	66	78	10	1	0	10	6	1	1	24	0	54	13	4	2	.285	.303
Ramirez, Efren, Cor.	.221	27	77	68	4	15	23	2	0	2	10	0	0	5	4	0	11	0	0	2	.338	.312
Ramirez, Efren, Tor.	.206	42	118	102	8	21	26	2	0	1	4	1	1	6	8	0	21	0	0	7	.255	.299

Player, Team	Avg.	G	TPA	AB	R	H	TB	2B	3B	HR	RBI	SH	SF	HP	BB	IBB	SO	SB	CS	GDP	Slg.	OBP
Ramirez, Enrique, Can.	.143	9	14	14	2	2	2	0	0	0	0	0	0	0	0	0	0	0	0	1	.143	.143
Ramirez, Enrique, Mont.	.177	32	67	62	5	11	12	1	0	0	3	3	1	0	1	0	5	0	0	2	.194	.188
Reyes, Jesus, Yuc.	.175	32	61	57	3	10	10	0	0	0	6	2	0	0	2	0	10	1	1	1	.175	.203
Reyes, Jesus, Cor.	.250	10	20	16	1	4	4	0	0	0	0	1	0	0	3	0	1	1	0	0	.250	.368
Rincon, Isaias, Mex.	.200	24	33	30	4	6	6	0	0	0	2	2	0	0	1	0	9	0	2	0	.200	.226
Rincon, Isaias, Ver.	.500	6	6	6	0	3	3	0	0	0	0	0	0	0	0	0	3	0	0	0	.500	.500
Roberson, Kevin, Cor.†	.200	17	67	60	9	12	20	5	0	1	5	0	0	1	6	0	20	0	0	1	.333	.284
Roberson, Kevin, Tor.†	.258	24	104	93	7	24	34	7	0	1	14	2	2	1	6	0	21	0	0	3	.366	.304
Rodarte, Raul, Rey.	.267	65	277	240	35	64	96	13	2	5	37	1	3	2	31	1	44	10	2	6	.400	.351
Rodarte, Raul, Cor.	.336	49	178	149	27	50	85	14	0	7	28	0	2	3	24	2	17	10	1	6	.570	.433
Rodriguez, Armando, Tig.	.188	25	82	69	7	13	19	3	0	1	9	2	2	1	8	0	17	0	1	3	.275	.275
Rodriguez, Armando, Pue.	.213	60	161	136	17	29	37	4	2	0	12	3	1	2	19	0	34	2	0	6	.272	.316
Romero, Marco Antonio, Sal.	.234	36	126	107	12	25	32	4	0	1	9	0	1	5	13	0	18	2	0	1	.299	.341
Romero, Marco Antonio, Tor.	.311	59	235	206	34	64	118	12	0	14	37	0	4	3	22	0	36	1	3	7	.573	.379
Salas, Heriberto, Cam.	.219	32	82	73	8	16	22	3	0	1	5	0	0	2	7	0	8	0	0	0	.301	.305
Salas, Heriberto, Yuc.	.293	27	103	92	9	27	39	7	1	1	9	1	1	1	8	0	10	1	2	2	.424	.353
Salas, Heriberto, Yuc.	.333	26	94	84	19	28	38	7	0	1	5	1	0	3	6	1	7	3	0	3	.452	.398
Sanchez, Gerardo, Lar.	.209	62	245	201	20	42	61	7	0	4	19	6	3	6	29	2	21	0	1	5	.303	.322
Sanchez, Gerardo, Tig.	.231	13	18	13	3	3	5	2	0	0	2	0	0	1	4	0	4	0	1	0	.385	.444
Seitzer, Brad, Can.	.264	29	122	106	11	28	38	7	0	1	17	0	0	0	16	3	25	0	0	5	.358	.361
Seitzer, Brad, Ver.	.326	60	250	221	22	72	98	12	1	4	34	1	2	4	22	1	35	0	2	11	.443	.394
Smith, Demond, Tab.†	.266	20	93	79	13	21	35	4	2	2	7	0	0	2	12	2	19	10	4	4	.443	.376
Smith, Demond, Mont.†	.328	66	290	247	55	81	136	17	7	8	32	5	1	6	31	2	54	26	14	0	.551	.414
Sulu, Mario, Cam.	.000	11	0	0	0	0	0	0	0	0	0	0	0	0	0	0	0	0	0	0	.000	.000
Sulu, Mario, Can.	1.000	10	1	1	0	1	1	0	0	0	0	0	0	0	0	0	0	0	0	0	1.000	1.000
Torres, Paul, Tab.	.333	7	30	27	6	9	16	1	0	2	4	0	1	0	2	0	9	0	0	2	.593	.367
Torres, Paul, Cor.	.387	33	138	119	21	46	79	9	0	8	27	0	0	2	17	3	21	1	1	4	.664	.471
Valdez, Ramon, Cor.*	.254	74	313	276	39	70	86	5	4	1	13	7	0	3	27	1	38	8	5	6	.312	.327
Valdez, Ramon, Cam.*	.212	31	133	113	14	24	29	2	0	1	6	3	0	3	14	0	10	1	2	2	.257	.315
Velez, Manuel, Lar.	.241	80	342	307	40	74	105	10	0	7	37	5	3	2	25	3	34	7	3	13	.342	.300
Velez, Manuel, Sal.	.281	29	111	96	10	27	35	5	0	1	11	2	0	0	13	1	10	3	2	3	.365	.367
Villanueva, Hector, Cor.	.319	59	235	191	27	61	94	12	0	7	35	0	4	0	40	7	25	0	0	9	.492	.430
Villanueva, Hector, Pue.	.163	31	127	98	8	16	26	4	0	2	11	0	1	1	27	1	20	0	1	3	.265	.346
White, Dorrick, Mont	.274	63	272	234	27	64	84	8	0	4	35	0	3	6	29	4	42	4	0	9	.359	.364
White, Derrick, Lar.	.321	51	226	196	32	63	99	9	0	9	32	0	0	0	30	2	31	2	4	6	.505	.412

GRAND SLAMS: N. Barrera, Mejia, Pemberton, F. Rodriguez, C. Smith, 2 each; Jo. Acosta, Boston, Bustillos, Canizalez, Carillo, H. Cervantes, Cervera, Chimelis, Contreras, P. Diaz, Esquer, O. Fontanes, Gu. Garcia, L. Garcia, O. Garcia, H. Gomez, Gorr, E. Jimenez, Ray Martinez, A. Munoz, Murray, Otero, Pearson, Ja. Robles, Rodarte, D. Rodriguez, Rojas, W. Romero, Santos, Resendo, Slevers, D. Smith, Tellez, S. Torres, Tyler, F. Valdez, J. Vazquez, Velez, Viera, Williams, 1 each

AWARDED FIRST BASE ON CATCHER'S INTERFERENCE: Jo. Ramirez 2 (Garzon, C. Gastelum), Galarin (Santana), H. Laplny (Ju. Robles), Ojeda (Rojas), G. Velozquez (F. Gonzalez).

2001 PITCHING

TEAM

Team	W	L	Pct.	ERA	G	CG	ShO	Sv.	IP	H	TBF	R	ER	HR	SH	SF	HB	BB	IBB	SO	WP	Bk.
Yucatan	68	53	.562	3.56	121	11	12	28	1075.2	1030	4555	472	425	76	47	36	39	367	17	831	60	1
Tabasco	56	66	.459	3.69	122	6	11	28	1066.2	1093	4620	501	437	77	62	34	56	386	45	595	35	6
Monterrey	68	53	.562	3.88	121	2	5	36	1063.0	1108	4620	518	458	80	68	38	41	426	30	793	54	4
Reynosa	69	53	.566	3.91	122	1	15	42	1080.1	1144	4776	527	469	106	45	22	46	472	25	677	62	4
Saltillo	68	52	.567	3.94	120	0	5	33	1060.1	1115	4620	534	464	77	45	28	49	404	19	729	47	7
Monclova	67	62	.563	4.03	120	19	14	26	1045.0	1093	4538	520	468	95	42	34	68	381	34	539	41	3
M.C. Reds	69	51	.575	4.08	121	10	11	30	1068.2	1100	4625	533	485	103	47	35	35	282	10	627	36	0
Puebla	54	62	.466	4.11	117	16	4	19	991.2	1066	4302	495	453	70	37	24	44	361	10	632	18	2
Veracruz	55	66	.455	4.18	121	13	10	35	1081.1	1115	4646	558	500	87	51	36	59	379	30	638	40	2
Campeche	62	56	.525	4.24	119	9	8	20	1030.2	1001	4471	504	485	119	53	28	74	427	48	622	49	2
M.C. Tigers	74	43	.632	4.30	118	3	5	44	1020.1	1046	4538	565	488	109	35	27	62	500	38	704	72	2
Dos Laredos	48	72	.400	4.50	121	10	13	23	1072.1	1087	4642	566	536	98	56	28	56	442	46	700	51	0
Torreon	61	59	.508	4.52	120	26	4	24	1067.1	1216	4688	596	536	111	53	42	55	374	23	624	36	2
Oaxaca	50	69	.420	4.79	120	6	6	23	1038.2	1229	4742	634	553	102	62	34	64	456	60	640	75	2
Cancun	49	71	.408	4.89	121	3	8	25	1055.1	1195	4744	661	573	113	59	39	43	480	30	548	72	2
Cordoba	38	78	.328	4.89	116	10	3	23	972.1	1121	4400	595	528	100	58	42	71	399	30	452	48	8

INDIVIDUAL

TOP QUALIFIERS FOR EARNED-RUN AVERAGE TITLE

Minimum 98 innings. *Lefthanded pitcher.

Pitcher, Team	W	L	Pct.	ERA	G	GS	CG	ShO	GF	Sv.	IP	H	TBF	R	ER	HR	SH	SF	HB	BB	IBB	SO	WP	Bk.
Manzanillo, Ravelo, Yuc.*	16	3	.842	1.52	24	24	8	2	0	0	183.2	100	694	35	31	6	9	2	4	56	0	202	2	0
Lopez, Jose, Rey.	5	4	.556	1.79	70	0	0	0	63	41	100.2	76	409	31	20	8	4	1	6	33	8	94	3	1
Ruiz, Cecilio, Tab.*	14	2	.875	1.94	19	19	1	0	0	0	120.2	114	498	37	26	8	7	4	2	20	1	67	1	0
Nunez, Jose, Lar.	6	5	.545	2.80	14	14	5	0	0	0	106.0	87	417	37	33	6	7	4	1	16	2	82	4	0
Keppen, Jeffrey, Lar.	11	7	.611	2.82	22	22	4	1	0	0	156.1	128	643	52	49	11	2	2	11	59	4	108	7	0
Romero, Alejandro, Monc.	9	3	.750	2.83	23	22	2	1	0	0	155.2	129	630	51	49	12	5	2	6	42	4	102	5	0
Moza, Leobardo, Ver.	7	4	.636	2.84	21	17	1	0	0	0	123.2	125	512	41	39	6	3	1	4	34	2	67	5	0
Leyva, Edgar, Mont.	10	5	.667	2.91	22	22	0	0	0	0	126.2	109	513	45	41	12	5	4	4	34	0	125	2	1
Rios, Daniel, Tor.	18	5	.783	2.98	26	26	19	2	0	0	208.2	207	877	83	69	17	7	4	10	70	3	126	4	0
Kelley, Richard, Pue.*	8	13	.381	3.08	25	25	9	1	0	0	166.1	161	698	67	57	9	6	3	10	57	1	124	4	0
Campos, Francisco, Cam.	10	7	.588	3.19	23	22	6	1	0	0	155.1	122	618	61	55	20	5	1	5	37	3	133	6	0
Quinonez, Enrique, Rey.	9	8	.529	3.24	25	25	0	0	0	0	147.1	148	623	60	53	11	8	5	8	38	2	76	1	0

CLASS AAA Mexican League

Pitcher, Team	W	L	Pct.	ERA	G	GS	CG	ShO	GF	Sv.	IP	H	TBF	R	ER	HR	SH	SF	HB	BB	IBB	SO	WP	Bk.
Armenta, Alejandro, Tig.*	15	4	.789	3.26	23	23	1	1	0	0	149.0	127	617	65	54	16	2	3	2	59	0	110	10	0
Patrick, Bronswell, Mex.	11	7	.611	3.27	23	23	4	4	0	0	156.2	149	617	67	57	16	4	1	3	23	1	92	3	0
Manrique, Alberto, Rey.	12	5	.706	3.28	24	24	1	1	0	0	142.2	141	600	58	52	17	3	3	10	42	0	101	6	1
Rivera, Oscar, Ver.	5	5	.500	3.28	16	15	1	0	0	0	98.2	89	425	52	36	6	5	3	8	40	0	72	6	0

DEPARTMENTAL LEADERS: W—D. Rios, 18; L—M. Gomez, Kelley, 13; Pct.—C. Ruiz, .875; G—E. Neri, Jo. Lopez, 70; GS—A. Moreno, D. Rios, 26; CG—D. Rios, 19; ShO—Palafox, Patrick, 4; GF—Jo. Lopez, 63; Sv.—Jo. Lopez, 41; IP—D. Rios, 208.2; H—A. Moreno, D. Rios, 207; TBF—D. Rios, 877; R—C. Leon, 86; ER—C. Leon, 80; HR—Campos, 20; SH—C. Leon, Rubio, 11; SF—A. Gonzalez, E, Lopez, Loya, Mora, L. Rivera, Salgado, Sinohui, 7; HB—Palafox, 17; BB—G. Garcia, 77; IBB—Barrios, Sinohui, 11; SO—Manzanillo, 202; WP—G. Garcia, 15; BK—C. Dominguez, Elvira, L. Perez, Quiroz, 2.

ALL PITCHERS

*Lefthanded pitcher.

Pitcher, Team	W	L	Pct.	ERA	G	GS	CG	ShO	GF	Sv.	IP	H	TBF	R	ER	HR	SH	SF	HB	BB	IBB	SO	WP	Bk.
Acosta, Aaron, Cor.-Cam.	6	4	.600	3.66	20	20	1	0	0	0	108.1	100	468	48	44	13	6	1	10	55	0	73	5	0
Acosta, Jaciel, Monc.*	2	4	.333	7.65	21	10	1	0	3	0	57.2	84	285	61	49	9	2	4	0	35	3	31	2	0
Aguilar, Hugo, Monc.	2	4	.333	4.46	21	9	1	0	4	0	66.2	69	301	34	33	5	1	2	3	38	2	28	5	0
Aguilar, Mario, Cam.*	1	0	1.000	21.60	7	1	0	0	0	0	3.1	7	26	10	8	0	0	1	0	9	0	2	2	0
Aguilar, Miguel, Pue.-Tor.*	1	0	1.000	5.17	40	0	0	0	9	2	15.2	22	73	9	9	2	2	0	0	8	0	9	2	0
Aguilera, Edgar, Yuc.-Can.	0	0	.000	8.10	8	0	0	0	1	0	10.0	12	51	9	9	1	0	1	1	10	0	10	3	0
Aguirre, Gaudencio, Tab.-Mont.	0	4	.000	4.23	15	5	0	0	2	1	38.1	38	169	21	18	7	3	1	5	12	1	27	0	1
Alberro, Jose, Sal.*	2	1	.667	3.54	12	7	0	0	4	1	40.2	29	168	17	16	4	1	4	3	14	0	38	1	0
Alejo, Nigel, Sal.	0	0	.000	7.71	3	3	0	0	0	0	14.0	22	69	12	12	0	1	0	0	6	0	10	1	0
Aleman, Paulo, Cor.	0	0	.000	3.18	6	0	0	0	4	0	5.2	5	29	2	2	1	0	0	1	5	1	1	2	0
Almeida, Rowsell, Lar.	2	2	.500	4.50	38	0	0	0	20	1	46.0	37	198	23	23	5	4	2	1	26	6	24	5	0
Alvarez, Antonio, Monc.	2	4	.333	6.97	8	4	0	0	0	0	20.2	31	99	19	16	1	2	0	3	3	1	7	2	0
Alvarez, Juan, Tab.*	4	8	.333	4.07	23	23	2	1	0	0	126.0	136	545	65	57	3	7	1	10	39	4	75	2	1
Alvarez, Octavio, Mex.	4	7	.364	4.91	16	15	1	1	0	0	91.2	114	401	54	50	12	6	5	3	19	2	54	2	0
Amador, Jesus, Cam.*	0	1	.000	2.79	10	0	0	0	0	0	9.2	10	47	5	3	1	1	1	0	7	1	3	0	0
Amarillas, Asdrubal, Mex.	1	1	.500	3.28	7	3	0	0	3	0	24.2	30	108	9	9	3	0	0	0	9	0	3	2	0
Andujar, Luis, Mont.	3	2	.600	4.67	13	0	0	0	9	3	17.1	20	79	9	9	2	2	0	0	10	0	12	1	0
Angulo, Victor, Tig.*	0	1	.000	6.10	20	2	0	0	7	0	20.2	25	107	16	14	1	0	1	2	18	0	13	1	1
Aragon, Angel, Rey.	2	4	.333	4.80	18	1	0	0	2	0	30.0	37	135	17	16	4	2	1	0	12	1	14	2	0
Arano, Ramon, Ver.	0	0	.000	2.70	1	1	0	0	0	0	3.1	4	15	1	1	1	0	0	0	1	0	0	0	0
Armenta, Alejandro, Tig.*	15	4	.789	3.26	23	23	1	1	0	0	149.0	127	617	65	54	16	2	3	2	59	0	110	10	0
Atondo, Sergio, Yuc.	4	6	.400	3.69	24	17	1	0	0	0	107.1	104	475	47	44	9	5	3	4	48	1	109	6	1
Ayala, Luis, Sal.	1	2	.333	2.03	33	0	0	0	33	21	40.0	34	164	11	9	2	3	2	0	11	4	34	0	0
Babineaux, Darrin, Lar.	1	5	.167	7.90	6	6	0	0	0	0	27.1	36	131	26	24	2	2	0	2	14	2	14	5	0
Baez, Sixto, Oax.	6	6	.500	3.33	47	0	0	0	37	9	51.1	47	221	22	19	3	5	3	6	17	7	36	4	0
Barradas, Roberto, Sal.	0	1	.000	7.52	15	0	0	0	2	0	20.1	30	100	20	17	3	1	0	0	9	1	11	4	0
Barrera, Sigfrido, Can.	0	6	.000	8.31	18	2	0	0	2	0	30.1	36	147	35	28	1	2	1	4	23	2	19	6	0
Barrios, Manuel, Oax.	5	8	.385	4.32	48	6	0	0	14	1	93.2	110	432	51	45	7	9	3	6	50	11	70	12	0
Beltran, Alonso, Tig.	9	5	.643	4.31	22	21	1	1	0	0	110.2	114	490	62	53	13	0	2	12	49	0	73	4	0
Bencomo, Juan, Ver.	1	0	1.000	6.75	5	0	0	0	1	0	10.2	15	55	12	8	0	0	1	3	7	0	4	0	0
Bernal, Manuel, Mex.	7	6	.538	4.32	22	20	1	1	1	0	127.0	173	564	68	61	12	5	6	4	30	0	65	1	0
Blancas, Rigoberto, Tab.*	0	7	.000	4.95	23	12	0	0	1	0	72.2	98	330	45	40	6	2	5	5	22	2	36	1	0
Bravo, Armando, Oax.	1	0	1.000	6.75	3	0	0	0	1	0	1.1	1	8	1	1	0	0	0	0	3	0	0	0	0
Burrows, Terry, Sal.	4	3	.571	3.36	10	10	1	0	0	0	59.0	57	257	27	22	3	1	4	1	31	0	35	4	1
Cabrales, Gabriel, Pue.	3	4	.429	6.06	20	8	0	0	2	0	65.1	90	295	48	44	7	1	1	1	15	1	27	2	0
Camara, Pedro, Cam.-Can.-Yuc.*	2	1	.667	12.00	21	0	0	0	4	0	12.0	16	62	16	16	2	0	0	0	12	1	12	1	0
Campillo, Jorge, Tig.	6	3	.667	3.53	30	9	0	0	4	2	86.2	95	386	43	34	12	5	3	2	37	4	64	7	1
Campos, Francisco, Cam.	10	7	.588	3.19	23	22	6	1	0	0	155.1	122	618	61	55	20	5	1	5	37	3	133	6	0
Cantu, Jacobo, Tab.	1	1	.500	5.14	24	1	0	0	7	1	42.0	60	194	26	24	6	1	3	3	16	2	15	3	0
Carrasco, Alejandro, Mex.-Ver.	6	5	.545	6.47	35	7	0	0	14	3	80.2	96	362	61	58	18	2	5	1	29	4	35	0	0
Castaneda, Aurelio, Pue.-Tor.	0	1	.000	8.85	15	0	0	0	3	1	20.1	41	108	21	20	4	0	1	2	7	3	10	0	0
Castillo, Felipe, Cor.	0	1	.000	3.18	5	0	0	0	4	2	5.2	9	28	3	2	0	0	0	1	2	1	2	0	0
Castro, Carlos, Tor.-Sal.	0	0	.000	13.50	4	0	0	0	3	0	4.0	7	25	6	6	2	0	1	2	4	0	5	0	0
Cazares, Rosario, Sal.	3	0	1.000	3.68	44	1	0	0	8	2	63.2	61	266	27	26	5	3	2	5	13	0	39	5	0
Cazarez, Tomas, Monc.*	0	2	.000	5.47	25	1	0	0	13	8	24.2	30	119	17	15	2	1	1	1	16	2	16	0	0
Cecena, Jose, Monc.	3	3	.500	3.78	36	0	0	0	9	2	50.0	57	215	24	21	5	1	6	1	17	4	32	3	1
Chavarria, Hector, Yuc.	4	2	.667	7.10	16	9	0	0	2	0	52.0	68	248	42	41	6	0	1	1	26	0	23	3	0
Chavez, Carlos, Yuc.	3	0	1.000	1.45	58	0	0	0	51	27	74.2	55	292	14	12	3	6	0	3	17	0	86	9	0
Cohuo, Enrique, Yuc.-Can.	2	4	.333	5.04	19	9	0	0	4	0	55.1	59	241	36	31	5	3	2	19	0	30	4	0
Conde, Argenis, Rey.	2	4	.333	4.77	11	11	0	0	0	0	60.1	75	269	33	32	6	2	1	25	1	41	3	0
Cortes, Martin, Cor.	2	2	.500	5.95	18	3	0	0	4	0	19.2	27	101	16	13	1	1	2	1	14	1	6	2	0
Crespo, Jorge, Oax.	0	0	.000	18.00	1	0	0	0	0	0	1.0	3	8	4	2	1	0	0	0	2	0	1	1	0
Cruz, Javier, Mex.	2	1	.667	3.71	43	0	0	0	15	1	51.0	51	209	23	21	6	7	3	1	15	1	45	1	0
Cruz, Juan, Tab.*	0	1	.000	9.53	10	1	0	0	2	0	5.2	6	27	6	6	0	0	1	5	0	2	0	1
Cruz, Luis, Pue.	1	3	.250	4.94	30	0	0	0	6	0	51.0	55	221	32	28	6	0	5	2	20	0	25	6	1
Cuervo, Bernardo, Yuc.	7	7	.500	3.82	23	21	0	0	1	0	117.2	142	514	61	50	7	4	6	2	37	0	51	5	0
Daniels, John, Tor.	0	2	.000	3.52	6	0	0	0	5	2	7.2	8	36	3	3	1	2	0	1	5	1	8	0	0
Davis, Ray, Ver.	0	3	.000	10.89	9	3	0	0	4	0	19.0	33	97	24	23	2	0	3	12	1	19	0	0
Delahoya, Javier, Sal.	7	4	.636	3.39	18	17	0	0	0	0	98.1	101	413	41	37	9	4	0	5	23	0	74	3	0
De Leon, Francisco, Can.	0	0	.000	6.14	7	1	0	0	3	0	7.1	13	41	8	5	0	0	0	9	0	3	0	0
Delfin, Adolfo, Lar.	5	5	.500	5.22	47	1	0	0	17	3	81.0	90	361	48	47	10	3	2	9	38	6	36	3	0
De Los Santos, Mariano, Monc.	0	1	.000	6.14	8	0	0	0	8	1	7.1	8	37	5	5	1	0	0	4	4	1	8	0	0
Diaz, Marco, Sal.	3	4	.429	5.11	41	5	0	0	17	5	74.0	75	323	50	42	6	2	1	4	26	2	60	1	1
Diaz, Rafael, Mont.	1	6	.143	3.76	13	10	0	0	0	0	52.2	55	236	33	22	6	4	1	1	27	0	48	2	0
Dishman, Glenn, Rey.*	3	3	.500	3.92	9	8	0	0	0	0	41.1	38	186	19	18	6	0	2	28	0	29	2	0
Dominguez, Carlos, Sal.*	3	4	.429	3.91	21	6	1	0	6	1	48.1	43	207	22	21	7	3	1	1	26	0	27	3	2
Dominguez, David, Mex.-Oax.	2	2	.500	2.05	16	4	0	0	7	0	44.0	35	177	13	10	2	1	2	11	1	28	5	0
Drahman, Brian, Lar.	7	9	.438	3.72	29	23	1	0	2	0	147.2	136	616	65	61	11	10	2	3	56	3	103	4	0
Duarte, Miguel, Sal.	1	2	.333	3.32	22	0	0	0	12	3	21.2	26	92	10	8	3	0	0	9	1	18	0	0

Pitcher, Team	W	L	Pct.	ERA	G	GS	CG	ShO	GF	Sv.	IP	H	TBF	R	ER	HR	SH	SF	HB	BB	IBB	SO	WP	Bk.
Duran, Roberto, Tig.*	2	1	.667	2.65	7	7	0	0	0	0	37.1	24	161	11	11	1	1	0	2	30	0	32	2	0
Elguezabal, Octavio, Cam.*	0	0	.000	27.00	1	1	0	0	0	0	0.2	2	5	2	2	0	0	0	0	2	0	0	2	0
Elizalde, Carlos, Oax.	4	5	.444	6.25	29	8	0	0	6	1	63.1	96	311	54	44	5	3	2	4	24	5	40	3	0
Elvira, Abraham, Cor.*	2	6	.250	5.13	22	17	0	0	1	0	94.2	95	425	59	54	6	6	2	10	57	2	37	6	2
Enriquez, Martin, Rey.	5	1	.833	2.45	30	1	0	0	9	0	47.2	48	203	18	13	2	3	2	1	17	3	37	2	1
Espejo, Humberto, Can.	0	1	.000	4.23	34	1	0	0	4	0	38.1	37	168	18	18	4	2	2	0	21	1	23	6	1
Esquer, Mercedes, Rey.*	10	5	.667	3.35	23	23	0	0	0	0	113.0	120	477	48	42	11	7	1	1	29	0	61	2	0
Federico, Gustavo, Mont.-Sal.	2	0	1.000	2.23	24	0	0	0	4	0	40.1	45	177	16	10	3	0	1	1	19	3	18	1	0
Felix, Jesus, Can.	1	0	1.000	5.85	13	0	0	0	4	0	20.0	34	101	15	13	2	1	1	2	7	0	6	4	0
Felix, Martin, Mex.*	0	1	.000	13.50	4	0	0	0	2	0	2.2	4	14	4	4	1	0	0	1	2	0	2	0	0
Felix, Miguel, Oax.*	0	1	.000	6.75	20	0	0	0	2	0	12.0	15	60	10	9	3	0	0	0	12	1	6	1	0
Fentanes, Ernesto, Ver.	0	1	.000	10.57	5	1	0	0	4	0	7.2	11	38	9	9	1	0	0	1	6	1	4	0	0
Ferrer, Jesus, Can.*	0	5	.000	7.07	31	4	0	0	4	0	42.0	53	217	44	33	5	4	2	3	40	2	19	13	0
Flores, Ignacio, Yuc.	4	4	.500	3.93	48	2	0	0	9	0	71.0	72	306	36	31	5	4	4	4	28	7	52	2	0
Flores, Jorge, Tor.*	3	3	.500	6.96	24	12	0	0	2	0	64.2	94	302	55	50	8	3	4	3	22	0	25	2	0
Flores, Pedro, Tor.	1	3	.250	8.02	25	0	0	0	6	1	33.2	44	162	30	30	11	1	1	2	21	0	7	2	0
Flynt, Will, Sal.	2	2	.500	5.40	5	5	0	0	0	0	30.0	45	141	20	18	1	0	1	0	7	0	17	0	0
Fontes, Agustin, Tab.	0	1	.000	9.82	3	0	0	0	1	0	3.2	8	20	4	4	0	0	0	0	1	0	1	0	0
Fregoso, Raul, Cam.-Cor.	0	1	.000	7.31	17	0	0	0	4	0	28.1	35	143	23	23	7	0	2	0	27	2	8	2	0
Galvez, Randy, Mex.	4	2	.667	3.31	8	8	2	0	0	0	54.1	54	217	23	20	3	3	1	1	14	0	22	3	0
Garcia, Adolfo, Cam.	0	0	.000	5.46	26	0	0	0	4	0	31.1	31	141	21	19	4	1	2	2	17	3	4	0	1
Garcia, Alfredo, Mex.	8	6	.571	4.26	26	20	2	1	2	1	137.1	158	590	70	65	10	5	4	4	44	2	56	3	0
Garcia, Gerardo, Tig.	7	7	.500	5.93	27	19	0	0	2	1	107.2	105	499	84	71	12	8	1	6	77	3	78	15	0
Garcia, Jose, Tig.-Pue.	9	2	.818	4.78	44	1	0	0	10	1	49.0	62	214	30	26	9	2	3	2	13	3	32	3	0
Garcia, Jose Luis, Pue.*	3	3	.500	2.62	38	4	1	0	27	13	75.2	70	308	26	22	6	6	0	2	17	2	64	1	0
Garcia, Mike, Mex.	0	2	.000	11.45	12	0	0	0	10	3	11.0	21	59	14	14	3	1	1	1	4	0	11	0	0
Garcia, Ramon, Mont.-Pue.	1	2	.333	4.26	29	1	0	0	9	0	44.1	51	204	26	21	2	1	1	0	28	0	26	3	0
Garduno, Daniel, Lar.,	1	5	.167	7.01	16	7	0	0	3	0	43.2	60	204	38	34	5	2	5	2	23	1	21	1	0
Garibay, Roberto, Rey.	5	1	.833	6.53	30	0	0	0	7	0	40.0	56	197	31	29	4	1	1	2	24	2	23	1	0
Garibay, Salvador, Lar.	4	3	.571	3.15	48	0	0	0	6	0	68.2	59	274	26	24	5	4	1	0	24	3	43	2	0
Garza, Conrado, Lar.*	0	0	.000	11.37	12	0	0	0	3	1	12.2	27	72	17	16	2	0	2	1	7	0	7	0	0
Gomez, Alejandro, Cor.	0	6	.000	5.49	30	3	0	0	16	1	60.2	72	261	37	37	13	5	4	2	13	1	25	1	0
Gomez, Martin, Can.	5	13	.278	4.76	22	22	3	0	0	0	124.2	167	579	86	66	15	8	3	8	39	3	58	3	1
Gonzalez, Arturo, Mont.	10	7	.588	3.68	22	22	2	0	0	0	120.0	117	508	54	49	10	8	7	5	35	3	49	4	0
Gonzalez, Erubiel, Ver.	6	6	.500	3.56	47	1	0	0	16	0	81.0	82	347	36	32	3	7	3	4	30	4	44	3	0
Grajales, Norberto, Tor	1	1	.500	1.80	1	1	0	0	0	0	5.0	6	18	1	1	0	0	0	0	0	0	4	0	0
Guerra, Pascual, Tab	3	5	.375	5.48	31	4	0	0	5	0	46.0	52	208	31	28	5	1	3	0	21	3	24	2	0
Gutierrez, Jorge, Tor.	3	8	.273	4.34	31	12	0	0	12	5	91.1	88	380	49	44	9	6	2	2	31	3	55	1	0
Gutierrez, Pablo, Cor.	3	3	.500	2.66	32	0	0	0	12	4	74.1	70	312	26	22	6	4	4	2	20	4	27	2	1
Harris, Reggie, Ver.	0	0	.000	2.65	19	0	0	0	17	13	17.0	10	64	5	5	1	0	0	0	8	0	17	2	0
Hartmann, Pete, Oax.*	2	0	1.000	2.33	3	3	0	0	0	0	19.1	16	82	7	5	1	1	1	0	6	0	17	2	0
Henry, Dwayne, Rey.	1	0	1.000	8.80	17	0	0	0	9	0	15.1	18	71	15	15	2	3	0	1	10	1	15	2	0
Henthorne, Kevin, Tig.	8	2	.800	3.82	21	16	1	1	1	0	108.1	124	463	48	46	12	1	3	8	31	0	49	0	0
Heredia, Hector, Tor.	2	3	.400	3.70	11	9	0	0	1	1	56.0	62	229	28	23	3	3	2	0	10	0	17	0	0
Hernandez, Esteban, Oax.	0	0	.000	5.23	5	0	0	0	2	0	10.1	13	47	6	6	2	1	0	0	4	1	2	0	0
Hernandez, Manuel, Monc.*	3	3	.500	3.97	39	1	0	0	5	1	65.2	82	284	30	29	6	2	1	2	15	2	29	2	0
Hernandez, Omar, Pue.	0	0	.000	5.40	3	0	0	0	3	0	5.0	4	24	3	3	1	0	0	0	5	0	2	2	0
Hernandez, Santos, Tig.	3	2	.600	2.30	53	0	0	0	49	38	62.2	55	271	19	16	4	5	0	3	28	7	66	6	0
Herrera, Calixto, Ver.	0	1	.000	8.74	14	0	0	0	7	3	11.1	16	58	12	11	2	0	1	0	5	0	4	0	0
Herrera, Enrique, Tor.	1	2	.333	4.50	38	0	0	0	11	1	54.0	67	231	27	27	6	3	1	4	13	2	34	4	1
Hidalgo, Romeo, Rey.-Oax.	0	0	.000	11.05	8	0	0	0	5	0	7.1	13	39	10	9	2	0	0	1	6	0	4	2	0
Huerta, Edgar, Tig.-Pue.*	1	0	1.000	3.04	20	1	0	0	6	0	26.2	21	113	10	9	1	1	0	1	15	2	26	7	0
Huerta, Francisco, Ver.-Cor.	0	0	.000	10.66	12	0	0	0	3	0	12.2	18	75	15	15	2	0	0	4	17	0	5	3	0
Huerta, Luis, Lar.	3	8	.273	4.88	22	22	0	0	0	0	103.1	118	458	59	56	12	8	1	6	37	3	56	1	0
Huisman, Rick, Mont.	0	0	.000	3.27	11	0	0	0	0	0	11.0	11	48	4	4	0	2	0	1	6	0	8	2	0
Huntsman, Scott, Pue.	0	0	.000	40.50	2	0	0	0	0	0	0.2	2	9	4	3	1	0	0	0	4	0	1	1	0
Izabal, Luis, Ver.	0	1	.000	5.28	8	1	1	0	4	0	15.1	16	68	10	9	2	2	0	1	7	1	2	2	0
Jimenez, German, Can.	1	4	.200	6.84	6	6	0	0	0	0	25.0	36	121	23	19	2	0	1	0	10	1	11	2	0
Jimenez, Isaac, Tab.*	1	1	.500	5.01	8	3	0	0	1	0	23.1	24	97	15	13	3	2	0	1	5	1	12	2	0
Jimenez, Jose, Can.	2	1	.667	3.30	14	8	0	0	1	0	46.1	51	212	19	17	2	3	2	2	23	2	27	2	1
Jimenez,Julio, Sal.-Tor.*	2	0	1.000	3.93	28	2	0	0	5	1	34.1	30	158	16	15	1	2	3	5	29	1	27	2	0
Kammar, Emil, Monc.	9	5	.643	3.44	18	16	3	2	1	0	102.0	97	433	45	39	10	3	2	8	36	4	34	10	0
Kelley, Richard, Pue.*	8	13	.381	3.08	25	25	9	1	0	0	166.1	161	698	67	57	9	6	3	10	57	1	124	4	0
Keppen, Jeffrey, Lar.	11	7	.611	2.82	22	22	4	1	0	0	156.1	128	643	52	49	11	2	2	11	59	4	108	7	0
Lara, Jorge, Sal.	1	2	.333	5.08	16	3	0	0	3	0	39.0	54	172	24	22	6	0	1	1	9	0	17	0	0
Larranaga, Miguel, Tab.	0	0	.000	27.00	1	0	0	0	0	0	0.1	3	4	1	1	1	0	0	0	0	0	0	0	0
Leal, Gerardo, Monc.	2	1	.667	3.92	11	2	0	0	5	0	20.2	24	93	9	9	2	0	2	1	13	0	6	0	0
Leon, Cupertino, Oax.	4	8	.333	5.82	30	20	1	1	2	0	123.2	169	575	86	80	18	11	6	11	51	7	50	3	1
Leon, Juan, Tab.	4	4	.500	4.50	36	5	0	0	10	0	58.0	51	259	33	29	3	3	2	4	31	4	50	4	1
Leyva, Edgar, Mont.	10	5	.667	2.91	22	22	0	0	0	0	126.2	109	513	45	41	12	5	4	4	34	0	125	2	1
Lezama, Rafael, Tor.*	0	0	.000	16.20	5	0	0	0	2	0	3.1	12	25	6	6	1	0	0	1	0	0	2	0	0
Loaiza, Sabino, Oax.	4	3	.308	4.93	18	18	0	0	0	0	98.2	99	436	59	54	6	6	4	4	44	2	34	3	0
Lomeli, Israel, Oax.	2	5	.286	4.91	23	7	0	0	6	1	58.2	65	278	38	32	6	1	2	5	38	1	42	5	0
Lomon, Kevin, Tor.	1	0	1.000	0.00	4	0	0	0	4	1	5.0	3	21	0	0	0	0	0	0	2	0	5	0	0
Lopez, Emigdio, Tor.	6	8	.429	4.49	24	24	0	0	0	0	146.1	170	645	82	73	17	7	7	12	46	3	83	2	0
Lopez, Gilberto, Ver.	1	3	.250	5.83	22	1	0	0	5	1	29.1	26	134	19	19	2	2	0	6	19	2	15	1	1
Lopez, Jesus, Ver.	2	2	.500	4.50	31	0	0	0	7	0	34.0	34	145	19	17	3	2	2	2	13	3	18	2	1
Lopez, Jose, Rey.	5	4	.556	1.79	70	0	0	0	63	41	100.2	76	409	31	20	8	4	1	6	33	8	94	3	1
Lopez, Mariano, Oax.	2	6	.250	6.22	27	12	0	0	1	0	76.2	101	372	55	53	6	3	2	3	52	1	37	5	0
Lopez, Miguel, Tig.	0	0	.000	4.50	30	0	0	0	10	0	30.0	32	147	15	15	4	2	0	4	22	6	24	2	0
Loya, Rigoberto, Mont.	6	6	.500	5.78	29	14	0	0	2	1	99.2	125	465	74	64	4	4	7	4	56	2	46	12	1
Luevano, Juan, Cam.	1	4	.200	6.22	31	2	0	0	8	0	46.1	64	223	39	32	9	8	2	9	13	4	19	0	0
Lugo, Aaron, Mont.*	0	1	.000	10.80	7	0	0	0	2	0	5.0	8	26	7	6	1	1	0	0	2	0	2	0	0

Pitcher, Team	W	L	Pct.	ERA	G	GS	CG	ShO	GF	Sv.	IP	H	TBF	R	ER	HR	SH	SF	HB	BB	IBB	SO	WP	Bk.
Macias, Luis, Monc.	1	1	.500	5.72	27	0	0	0	10	1	45.2	46	208	29	29	8	0	2	5	28	0	24	2	1
Madero, Francisco, Can.	4	6	.400	4.71	20	18	0	0	0	0	107.0	120	465	63	56	12	6	3	6	44	0	68	6	0
Magee, Danny, Monc.-Cam.*	7	6	.538	2.61	15	15	1	0	0	0	89.2	76	391	28	26	2	7	2	8	47	2	88	6	0
Manrique, Alberto, Rey.	12	5	.706	3.28	24	24	1	1	0	0	142.1	141	600	58	52	17	3	3	10	42	0	101	6	1
Manzanillo, Ravelo, Yuc.*	16	3	.842	1.52	24	24	8	2	0	0	183.2	100	694	35	31	6	9	2	4	56	0	202	2	0
Manzano, Adrian, Tig.	5	0	1.000	3.11	28	0	0	0	5	0	37.2	36	160	14	13	3	1	3	1	16	2	22	5	0
Marquez, Isidro, Cam.	9	2	.818	2.15	48	0	0	0	21	5	62.2	53	255	17	15	2	6	2	4	18	7	42	1	0
Martinez, Cesar, Can.*	0	0	.000	9.00	20	2	0	0	4	0	18.0	23	101	20	18	1	0	2	5	18	1	13	4	0
Martinez, Jesus, Ver.*	0	0	.000	4.26	3	0	0	0	1	0	6.1	10	29	3	3	0	0	0	0	1	0	1	1	0
Martinez, Jesus Jose, Cor.	0	2	.000	6.12	12	4	0	0	3	0	32.1	40	143	23	22	3	3	3	2	9	0	11	1	0
Martinez, Juan, Can.	0	0	.000	30.86	3	0	0	0	0	0	2.1	10	19	8	8	0	0	0	0	2	0	2	2	0
Martinez, Pedro, Cam.*	5	5	.500	3.81	14	13	0	0	1	0	75.2	71	326	36	32	5	3	2	1	37	2	44	1	0
Mathews, Delmer, Mont.*	0	1	.000	17.18	2	1	0	0	0	0	3.2	7	21	7	7	3	1	0	0	4	0	5	0	0
Mattson, Craig, Rey.	2	2	.500	5.79	22	2	0	0	2	0	32.2	34	158	21	21	2	0	1	4	29	0	17	5	0
Mattson, Rob, Tab.	4	6	.400	1.91	26	0	0	0	16	3	33.0	29	132	9	7	1	3	1	1	7	2	12	1	0
Medina, Alonso, Mont.	0	0	.000	7.36	3	0	0	0	2	0	3.2	6	20	3	3	1	0	0	0	3	0	2	0	0
Medina, Osvaldo, Pue.	0	0	.000	8.10	6	0	0	0	2	0	10.0	17	49	9	9	2	0	0	2	3	1	3	2	0
Melendez, Nestor, Rey.	1	0	1.000	5.40	47	0	0	0	12	0	51.2	53	250	33	31	3	3	2	2	44	1	53	13	0
Mendoza, Omar, Pue.	0	1	.000	5.63	4	1	0	0	1	0	8.0	10	36	5	5	0	0	0	0	4	0	7	0	0
Mere, Fernando, Can.	2	2	.500	4.99	34	6	0	0	13	1	70.1	63	305	43	39	9	4	3	3	34	5	23	4	1
Meza, Leobardo, Ver.	7	4	.636	2.84	21	17	1	0	0	0	123.2	125	512	41	39	6	3	1	4	34	2	67	5	0
Miranda, Angel, Mex.-Oax.*	4	4	.500	4.22	22	9	0	0	2	0	64.0	61	280	33	30	3	2	1	4	31	2	48	1	0
Molina, Primitivo, Tor.	1	0	1.000	9.69	10	1	0	0	3	0	13.0	21	67	14	14	3	0	2	1	8	0	4	3	0
Montemayor, Humberto, Mont.	6	6	.500	4.76	23	20	0	0	0	0	98.1	127	446	60	52	7	4	5	5	32	4	78	5	1
Mora, Eleazar, Ver.*	9	7	.563	3.51	24	24	2	1	0	0	153.2	163	645	67	60	6	8	7	5	32	2	90	3	0
Morales, Luis, Ver.*	7	9	.438	3.88	21	16	3	1	3	0	109.0	106	445	50	47	13	7	2	2	20	2	88	1	0
Moreno, Angel, Tor.*	9	11	.450	3.86	26	26	5	1	0	0	177.1	207	762	85	76	14	8	6	5	45	3	110	5	0
Moreno, Claudio, Mex.	10	2	.833	3.43	61	0	0	0	16	1	89.1	96	366	38	34	4	4	5	1	22	1	52	3	0
Moreno, Edgar, Oax.	1	2	.333	6.84	23	0	0	0	11	0	26.1	32	130	22	20	2	1	2	2	16	3	14	5	0
Munoz, Leonardo, Cam.*	4	10	.286	6.75	28	15	0	0	2	0	86.2	111	409	73	65	18	3	5	0	49	1	43	5	0
Munoz, Miguel, Can.	11	6	.647	3.30	22	22	0	0	0	0	136.1	138	569	58	50	14	5	3	4	26	1	56	5	0
Murillo, Felipe, Monc.	2	3	.400	4.60	37	0	0	0	28	6	31.1	41	139	18	16	2	2	1	2	5	3	17	1	0
Navarro, Hector, Sal.	0	0	.000	1.80	5	0	0	0	5	0	5.0	4	22	1	1	0	0	0	0	2	0	6	0	0
Navarro, Joel, Mex.-Oax.	6	0	1.000	3.80	21	14	0	0	0	0	97.0	113	415	45	41	9	4	2	4	28	0	44	9	0
Navarro, Jose, Tig.-Pue.	5	8	.385	5.04	24	16	0	0	0	0	84.0	104	383	50	47	6	1	5	5	36	2	52	4	0
Navarro, Luis, Yuc.	4	0	1.000	1.83	24	0	0	0	3	0	34.1	20	126	7	7	1	2	1	0	9	1	20	1	0
Neri, Braulio, Sal.*	1	1	.500	4.09	49	0	0	0	8	0	22.0	23	104	12	10	2	2	1	2	12	1	17	3	0
Neri, Eduardo, Oax.*	0	1	.000	6.27	70	0	0	0	9	1	37.1	45	168	29	26	9	4	1	0	19	4	23	3	0
Newman, Eric, Monc.	0	2	.000	5.06	13	0	0	0	11	6	10.2	12	53	7	6	1	1	1	2	8	1	8	2	0
Nieblas, Mauro, Mont.*	1	1	.500	3.03	51	0	0	0	7	0	38.2	38	180	16	13	2	6	1	1	30	3	37	1	0
Nieblas, Omar, Tab.	1	2	.333	6.59	19	0	0	0	5	2	27.1	31	136	21	20	1	2	1	5	21	2	15	2	0
Nunez, Javier, Cor.	7	4	.636	5.13	33	1	0	0	3	0	66.2	77	301	43	38	2	1	5	3	31	0	43	5	1
Nunez, Jose, Lar.	6	5	.545	2.80	14	14	5	0	0	0	106.0	87	417	37	33	6	7	4	1	16	2	82	4	0
Nunez, Jose Juan, Oax.	1	3	.250	4.19	17	4	0	0	4	0	38.2	45	180	25	18	4	4	3	1	17	2	26	3	0
Olague, Jesus, Pue.	9	7	.563	3.49	22	22	3	0	0	0	136.2	137	583	55	53	3	7	2	4	52	1	105	3	0
Orea, Flavio, Cor.	3	3	.500	2.37	38	0	0	0	33	13	49.1	43	199	14	13	3	3	3	1	12	0	28	2	1
Ortega, Pablo, Tig.	5	9	.357	5.21	26	20	0	0	3	1	114.0	128	517	79	66	9	6	2	11	49	3	71	8	0
Ortega, Roberto, Pue.*	2	1	.667	5.46	24	2	0	0	3	0	31.1	32	141	20	19	2	0	1	1	21	0	17	4	1
Ortega, Wilbert, Yuc.*	1	1	.500	3.18	24	0	0	0	4	0	17.0	18	70	7	6	4	0	0	0	5	3	15	1	0
Osuna, Adrian, Oax.	0	0	.000	13.50	5	0	0	0	1	0	4.0	8	23	6	6	0	1	0	1	5	1	2	2	0
Osuna, Ricardo, Tab.	8	6	.571	3.89	21	21	1	1	0	0	125.0	111	532	56	54	13	7	2	7	49	3	75	7	0
Palacios, Vicente, Sal.	0	0	.000	0.00	3	0	0	0	2	1	3.0	1	12	0	0	0	0	0	2	0	5	0	0
Palafox, Manuel, Monc.	13	4	.765	3.52	23	23	7	4	0	0	156.0	155	667	72	61	16	10	0	17	43	0	62	1	0
Parra, Jose, Mex.-Oax.	5	5	.500	2.70	57	0	0	0	48	33	63.1	50	272	24	19	3	2	1	9	30	2	63	7	0
Parra, Julio, Lar.-Mont.	2	6	.250	5.52	43	0	0	0	35	16	44.0	51	212	28	27	4	6	0	3	27	3	47	4	0
Patrick, Bronswell, Mex.	11	7	.611	3.27	23	23	4	4	0	0	156.2	149	617	67	57	16	4	1	3	23	1	92	3	0
Pena, Joel, Ver.*	5	6	.455	4.37	29	15	0	0	3	0	115.1	112	504	64	56	9	4	4	8	60	3	58	10	0
Pena, Juan, Tor.	1	0	1.000	0.00	5	0	0	0	0	0	1.2	2	8	0	0	0	0	1	0	2	0	0	0	0
Perez, Dario, Oax.	5	8	.385	4.06	16	13	2	0	1	1	88.2	100	370	45	40	11	1	3	1	12	2	32	0	0
Perez, Edgar, Cor.	5	11	.313	5.98	18	18	0	0	0	0	99.1	131	456	69	66	14	3	1	11	29	3	35	3	0
Perez, Jose, Monc.	0	0	.000	0.00	1	0	0	0	0	0	1.0	1	4	0	0	0	0	0	0	0	0	2	0	0
Perez, Juan, Lar.	0	2	.000	8.84	7	2	0	0	1	0	19.1	30	100	21	19	1	0	1	0	17	1	15	3	0
Perez, Leonardo, Cor.	7	7	.500	3.83	24	24	7	1	0	0	152.2	155	663	80	65	13	9	4	9	50	5	76	7	2
Perez, Sergio, Mont.	1	1	.500	5.40	33	0	0	0	13	0	31.2	35	155	22	19	3	1	3	4	23	2	29	6	0
Perez, Yorkis, Mex.*	2	4	.333	3.51	57	0	0	0	17	0	51.1	52	222	22	20	4	4	2	2	15	0	56	4	0
Pesqueira, Omar, Yuc.	1	4	.200	3.71	31	0	0	0	10	0	53.1	52	224	25	22	4	2	3	3	15	1	23	10	0
Pimentel, Roberto, Yuc.*	5	8	.385	5.08	29	19	1	0	4	0	102.2	125	460	64	58	11	6	3	4	36	0	74	1	0
Pina, Rafael, Oax.	1	2	.333	6.65	4	4	0	0	0	0	21.2	27	103	18	16	1	2	0	2	10	0	10	0	0
Pineda, Isauro, Mont.	5	2	.714	3.40	39	13	0	0	4	1	103.1	98	437	40	39	7	8	3	1	45	1	89	8	0
Pujals, Denis, Tig.	1	1	.500	6.27	16	0	0	0	6	1	18.2	21	86	13	13	4	0	0	1	12	3	10	1	0
Pulido, Raymundo, Cam.	0	4	.000	8.65	19	7	0	0	4	0	42.2	56	208	44	41	7	0	0	7	20	1	26	2	0
Purata, Julio, Rey.*	3	2	.600	4.38	32	2	0	0	3	0	37.0	37	167	19	18	5	4	0	1	20	2	19	2	0
Quimbar, Juan, Lar.*	0	0	.000	3.00	13	0	0	0	2	0	9.0	7	38	3	3	1	0	0	0	5	0	4	1	0
Quinonez, Enrique, Rey.	9	8	.529	3.24	25	25	0	0	0	0	147.1	148	623	60	53	11	8	5	8	38	2	76	1	0
Quintanilla, Juan, Lar.	1	6	.143	3.70	45	0	0	0	15	2	80.1	70	321	34	33	9	6	2	4	15	8	57	2	0
Quiroz, Aaron, Sal.	2	0	1.000	3.00	6	6	0	0	0	0	30.0	24	120	10	10	0	5	0	4	11	0	19	1	2
Ramirez, Carlos, Can.	1	0	1.000	6.91	8	0	0	0	1	0	14.1	23	79	17	11	1	0	1	1	13	0	3	0	0
Ramirez, Emilio, Ver.*	0	0	.000	0.84	15	0	0	0	4	0	10.2	7	45	1	1	1	1	2	1	3	0	5	1	0
Ramirez, Hector, Oax.*	1	2	.333	7.36	11	0	0	0	1	0	14.2	18	67	12	12	2	0	0	0	5	1	12	2	0
Ramirez, Jose, Monc.	0	0	.000	6.30	6	0	0	0	2	1	10.0	17	57	12	7	1	0	0	2	6	0	7	1	0
Ramirez, Roberto, Mex.*	9	3	.750	3.66	16	16	0	0	0	0	98.1	111	411	42	40	6	4	0	3	19	0	67	1	0
Ramon, Jose, Tab.	5	3	.625	2.09	43	1	1	1	15	0	81.2	72	325	21	19	6	5	1	2	19	1	35	3	0

Pitcher, Team	W	L	Pct.	ERA	G	GS	CG	ShO	GF	Sv.	IP	H	TBF	R	ER	HR	SH	SF	HB	BB	IBB	SO	WP	Bk.
Ramos, Edgar, Oax.	4	8	.333	3.88	17	17	3	1	0	0	106.2	116	465	55	46	9	6	2	9	28	6	91	10	0
Renovato, Nestor, Mont.	4	1	.800	3.66	25	0	0	0	4	0	32.0	27	136	14	13	1	0	0	2	15	3	21	0	0
Reyes, Nathanael, Sal.*	9	6	.600	3.41	29	18	0	0	4	0	105.2	107	444	45	40	5	3	1	3	30	2	63	3	0
Reynoso, Ignacio, Tab.	3	3	.500	2.35	33	1	0	0	23	10	46.0	41	206	13	12	1	6	5	2	28	7	35	2	1
Rios, Alejandro, Sal.	5	5	.500	3.95	47	1	0	0	7	0	73.0	90	334	38	32	4	6	3	3	35	5	52	10	0
Rios, Daniel, Tor.	18	5	.783	2.98	26	26	19	2	0	0	208.2	207	877	83	69	17	7	4	10	70	3	126	4	0
Rios, Jesus, Yuc.	10	10	.500	4.13	21	21	1	1	0	0	113.1	126	510	59	52	12	3	3	10	33	1	73	7	0
Rivas, Jesus, Tig.*	2	2	.500	5.65	47	1	0	0	6	0	28.2	31	134	21	18	3	0	1	2	18	1	12	1	0
Rivera, Francisco, Ver.	0	1	.000	189.00	1	1	0	0	0	0	0.1	5	8	7	7	0	0	0	0	2	0	0	0	0
Rivera, Lino, Monc.	14	6	.700	3.34	22	22	4	1	0	0	151.0	138	607	58	56	11	6	7	5	37	2	65	1	1
Rivera, Oscar, Ver.	5	5	.500	3.28	16	15	1	0	0	0	98.2	89	425	52	36	6	5	3	8	40	0	72	6	0
Rivera, Oscar, Yuc.*	2	1	.667	1.61	21	0	0	0	5	0	22.1	20	92	4	4	0	1	2	0	11	2	12	1	0
Rivera, Paul, Tab.*	0	2	.000	1.62	52	1	0	0	8	1	39.0	26	163	13	7	2	0	2	1	23	3	34	2	0
Robles, Jorge, Lar.	0	0	.000	6.00	3	0	0	0	0	0	3.0	4	18	2	2	0	0	0	2	3	0	3	0	0
Rodriguez, Eric, Oax.	0	0	.000	0.00	1	0	0	0	0	0	0.0	0	2	1	1	0	0	0	0	1	0	0	0	0
Rodriguez, Manuel, Cor.-Cam.	2	6	.250	7.65	16	10	0	0	3	0	40.0	50	204	38	34	7	1	3	0	38	0	16	1	0
Rodriguez, Raul, Rey.*	5	9	.357	4.65	23	19	0	0	0	0	100.2	121	461	58	52	12	4	2	4	42	0	38	8	1
Rodriguez, Rosario, Tor.*	1	1	.500	10.80	13	0	0	0	2	1	3.1	7	22	4	4	1	0	0	1	3	0	2	0	0
Rodriguez, Salvador, Yuc.	3	2	.600	3.40	15	4	0	0	6	1	47.2	48	194	18	18	3	1	0	2	6	0	36	4	0
Romano, Mike, Sal.	10	7	.588	3.97	21	20	2	1	0	0	133.2	140	587	71	59	9	2	2	9	55	1	103	4	1
Romero, Alejandro, Monc.	9	3	.750	2.83	23	22	2	1	0	0	155.2	129	630	51	49	12	5	2	6	42	4	102	5	0
Romero, Cesar, Lar.	0	0	.000	7.20	15	1	0	0	5	0	20.0	24	94	16	16	3	1	2	1	12	0	17	2	0
Romero, Juan, Cor.*	2	5	.286	4.12	37	1	0	0	15	2	59.0	62	264	32	27	4	8	3	7	24	8	35	7	0
Romo, Eduardo, Tab.	2	6	.250	6.90	20	13	0	0	0	0	61.1	73	288	47	47	7	1	2	4	36	1	29	5	0
Rossiter, Mike, Tab.	0	1	.000	3.18	16	0	0	0	14	10	17.0	16	78	7	6	0	4	0	0	12	2	14	1	0
Rubio, Miguel, Mont.	7	2	.778	1.07	55	0	0	0	36	18	67.0	55	268	11	8	1	11	1	0	20	3	71	2	0
Ruiz, Cecilio, Tab.*	14	2	.875	1.94	19	19	1	0	0	0	120.2	114	498	37	26	8	7	4	2	20	0	67	1	0
Ruiz, Juan, Tor.	0	1	.000	6.97	5	2	0	0	1	0	10.1	11	53	9	8	4	1	2	1	11	0	7	1	0
Ruiz, Omar, Tab.	0	0	.000	0.00	3	0	0	0	2	0	1.2	1	8	0	0	0	0	0	0	2	0	3	0	1
Sak, James, Cam.	0	0	.000	10.80	2	0	0	0	1	0	1.2	1	13	2	2	0	0	0	0	8	0	2	4	0
Saldana, Jose, Pue.	6	3	.667	3.61	19	18	3	1	1	0	97.1	100	413	45	39	4	3	2	3	28	0	47	3	0
Salgado, Eduardo, Sal.	8	11	.421	4.21	23	23	5	0	0	0	154.0	167	655	79	72	19	9	7	4	47	3	75	3	0
Sanchez, Alejandro, Can.	7	3	.700	2.91	53	0	0	0	31	11	77.1	68	318	26	25	6	6	4	3	32	5	34	1	0
Sanchez, Claudio, Oax.-Tor.	4	2	.667	4.50	17	1	0	0	3	1	26.0	34	115	19	13	0	2	1	0	8	0	14	0	0
Sanchez, Efrain, Cam.	3	1	.750	2.43	31	4	0	0	6	0	63.0	63	265	22	17	3	2	0	6	19	2	39	4	0
Sanchez, Hector, Pue.-Cam.	0	0	.000	4.63	6	1	0	0	0	0	11.2	14	51	6	6	3	0	2	0	4	0	5	0	0
Sandoval, Ricardo, Tor.*	1	1	.500	13.50	7	1	0	0	3	0	3.1	5	20	6	5	1	0	2	2	3	0	1	0	0
Sinohui, David, Cam.	9	5	.643	4.32	54	0	0	0	45	15	77.0	74	331	39	37	8	6	7	9	24	11	72	6	0
Solarte, Jose, Can.	7	6	.538	4.16	46	0	0	0	32	12	62.2	83	288	34	29	6	6	1	1	18	3	37	1	0
Sombra, Francisco, Cor.-Ver.*.	0	1	.000	8.18	18	0	0	0	1	0	11.0	13	57	11	10	3	0	0	1	11	1	6	0	0
Soto, Cruz, Mont.	2	1	.667	5.68	31	0	0	0	9	0	44.1	59	205	31	28	3	3	0	0	21	3	29	2	0
Soto, Daniel, Sal.	0	0	.000	18.00	2	0	0	0	1	0	2.0	5	12	4	4	1	0	0	0	1	0	2	0	0
Soto, Fernando, Can.	0	1	.000	5.54	4	1	0	0	0	0	13.0	17	57	8	8	3	0	1	2	0	0	6	0	0
Sulu, Mario, Cam.-Can.	1	5	.167	5.98	21	8	0	0	4	0	49.2	50	227	40	33	9	4	2	2	23	1	25	4	0
Tejeda, Felix, Cam.*	0	0	.000	2.70	28	1	0	0	7	0	30.0	21	116	9	9	4	0	0	1	10	2	15	0	0
Theodile, Robert, Sal.	6	6	.500	3.42	18	17	2	1	0	0	108.0	106	466	50	41	3	4	2	6	45	1	64	4	0
Tijerina, Carlos, Rey.	0	0	.000	1.50	3	0	0	0	2	0	6.0	6	30	1	1	0	1	0	2	6	1	2	0	0
Torres, Jorge, Cam.*	0	0	.000	0.96	14	0	0	0	4	0	9.1	12	51	6	1	2	0	0	3	6	0	5	1	0
Trevino, Jesus, Mex.*	0	0	.000	0.00	1	0	0	0	0	0	0.1	0	1	0	0	0	0	0	0	0	0	0	0	0
Trujillo, Jorge, Ver.	0	0	.000	5.59	2	2	0	0	0	0	9.2	8	42	6	6	1	0	1	1	6	0	7	0	0
Uribe, Juan, Tor.	0	3	.000	6.98	24	2	0	0	4	0	40.0	42	180	37	31	3	4	3	1	19	2	24	3	1
Uscanga, Alejandro, Vor.	0	0	.000	0.00	7	0	0	0	0	0	3.2	3	19	0	0	0	0	1	4	0	2	0	0
Valdez, Armando, Mont.	8	7	.533	4.03	26	19	0	0	1	0	109.1	119	467	51	49	11	5	2	8	29	2	69	1	1
Valdez, Carlos, Can.	1	4	.200	3.30	7	7	2	0	0	0	46.1	45	193	17	17	2	1	1	0	20	1	17	0	0
Valenzuela, Jesus, Oax.	0	0	.000	40.50	1	0	0	0	0	0	0.2	3	6	3	3	1	0	0	0	2	1	1	1	0
Valenzuela, Jose, Tig.	2	2	.500	3.64	24	0	0	0	4	1	29.2	29	134	15	12	2	0	3	3	18	0	18	3	0
Valenzuela, Saul, Cor.-Can.	0	9	.000	7.03	25	11	0	0	4	1	65.1	95	311	57	51	9	3	5	6	29	1	23	5	0
Valerio, Julio, Monc.*	0	2	.000	4.85	10	0	0	0	2	0	13.0	19	61	8	7	2	2	1	0	7	3	7	0	0
Vargas, Joel, Tab.	6	8	.429	3.70	24	24	1	1	0	0	138.2	150	601	67	57	10	9	2	7	53	8	57	1	0
Vazquez, Adrian, Cam.	10	8	.556	4.44	23	23	2	0	0	0	133.0	138	575	68	65	19	4	3	13	43	5	66	4	1
Vega, Mario, Cor.	0	1	.000	13.50	3	2	0	0	0	0	7.1	14	45	11	11	2	2	0	3	6	0	7	0	0
Vega, Obed, Can.	7	5	.583	3.44	21	17	1	1	3	1	99.1	96	419	43	38	8	8	1	0	36	0	84	3	0
Velazquez, Israel, Pue.	2	8	.200	4.41	27	11	0	0	4	0	85.2	101	379	44	42	8	3	3	6	18	1	54	2	0
Verdugo, Hugo, Lar.	3	3	.500	4.64	10	10	0	0	0	0	42.2	50	197	24	22	4	0	0	6	27	0	34	2	0
Verdugo, Orlando, Tor.	6	5	.545	4.26	51	2	0	0	21	8	67.2	66	298	33	32	5	4	3	4	30	3	63	6	0
Verdugo, Oswaldo, Yuc.	1	1	.500	4.03	21	0	0	0	7	0	20.0	28	120	13	13	2	1	2	0	9	0	24	3	0
Villalobos, Noe, Can.	1	4	.200	3.77	19	4	0	0	5	0	45.1	46	205	23	19	5	4	0	3	25	6	22	2	0
Villaluna, Juan, Mont.*	0	0	.000	3.10	26	0	0	0	7	0	20.1	23	83	8	7	2	0	1	1	5	0	11	2	0
Villarreal, Antonio, Tab.	2	1	.667	3.18	13	1	0	0	4	0	28.1	29	116	11	10	2	0	1	1	2	0	10	1	0
Villarreal, Salvador, Rey.*	0	0	.000	6.86	13	0	0	0	8	0	21.0	27	116	18	16	2	0	0	0	27	1	14	4	0
Villavicencio, Ismael, Tig.	0	0	.000	81.00	1	0	0	0	0	0	0.1	2	4	3	3	1	0	0	0	1	0	0	1	0
Villegas, Francisco, Can.	0	3	.000	3.20	16	0	0	0	5	0	19.2	19	88	9	7	1	2	3	0	12	1	16	2	0
Villegas, Jose, Pue.	7	8	.467	4.00	41	5	0	0	16	2	63.0	61	265	28	28	5	5	2	6	18	5	25	2	0
Wagner, Matt, Tig.-Pue.	1	1	.500	9.00	14	0	0	0	5	1	16.0	25	86	18	16	2	2	2	0	12	2	16	4	0
Wallace, Kent, Ver.	1	2	.333	3.68	19	0	0	0	18	13	22.0	20	88	9	9	3	0	1	0	4	1	22	0	0
Ward, Chad, Cam.*	0	2	.000	10.38	4	4	0	0	0	0	13.0	18	61	15	15	4	1	0	0	7	0	6	0	0
Warren, Brian, Mont.	0	2	.000	2.87	16	0	0	0	16	13	15.2	14	66	6	5	2	0	0	1	4	0	10	1	0
Weaver, Eric, Pue.	0	0	.000	2.93	13	1	0	0	10	1	15.1	15	67	6	5	1	1	0	0	10	1	15	1	0
Yepiz, Heriberto, Yuc.	0	0	.000	2.35	6	0	0	0	2	0	7.2	5	33	2	2	0	0	1	0	5	1	2	0	0
Zambrano, Baudel, Rey.	4	4	.500	3.92	31	6	0	0	4	1	78.0	93	358	39	34	9	0	1	0	40	2	33	5	0
Zamudio, Jeovani, Rey.	0	1	.000	4.26	11	0	0	0	6	0	12.2	15	58	8	6	2	0	0	1	5	0	9	1	0
Zavala, Marco, Tig.	3	2	.600	5.13	54	0	0	0	9	0	26.1	23	115	16	15	4	0	0	1	14	4	18	0	0

CLASS AAA Mexican League

PITCHERS WITH TWO OR MORE TEAMS

Pitcher, Team	W	L	Pct.	ERA	G	GS	CG	ShO	GF	Sv.	IP	H	TBF	R	ER	HR	SH	SF	HB	BB	IBB	SO	WP	Bk.
Acosta, Aaron, Cor.	0	1	.000	2.87	3	3	0	0	0	0	15.2	18	71	6	5	0	2	0	2	4	0	19	0	0
Acosta, Aaron, Cam...............	6	3	.667	3.79	17	17	1	0	0	0	92.2	82	397	42	39	13	4	1	8	51	0	54	5	0
Aguilar, Miguel, Pue.*	1	0	1.000	9.00	12	0	0	0	3	0	4.0	8	23	4	4	1	1	0	0	3	0	4	1	0
Aguilar, Miguel, Tor.*	0	0	.000	3.86	28	0	0	0	6	2	11.2	14	50	5	5	1	1	0	0	5	0	5	1	0
Aguilera, Edgar, Yuc.............	0	0	.000	6.75	7	0	0	0	1	0	9.1	8	45	7	7	1	0	1	1	10	0	9	2	0
Aguilera, Edgar, Can.............	0	0	.000	27.00	1	0	0	0	0	0	0.2	4	6	2	2	0	0	0	0	0	0	1	1	0
Aguirre, Gaudencio, Tab.........	0	4	.000	4.99	9	5	0	0	2	1	30.2	35	141	20	17	6	3	1	4	10	1	23	0	1
Aguirre, Gaudencio, Mont.	0	0	.000	1.17	6	0	0	0	0	0	7.2	3	28	1	1	0	1	0	1	2	0	4	0	0
Camara, Pedro, Cam.*	0	0	.000	5.40	2	0	0	0	1	0	1.2	2	7	1	1	0	0	0	1	1	1	1	1	0
Camara, Pedro, Can.*	0	1	.000	19.64	8	0	0	0	2	0	3.2	4	22	8	8	1	0	0	0	8	0	4	0	0
Camara, Pedro, Yuc.*...........	2	0	1.000	9.45	11	0	0	0	1	0	6.2	10	33	7	7	1	0	0	0	3	0	7	0	0
Carrasco, Alejandro, Mex.	3	1	.750	7.30	10	7	0	0	0	0	40.2	51	183	34	33	13	1	4	0	16	0	16	0	0
Carrasco, Alejandro, Ver........	3	4	.429	5.63	25	0	0	0	14	3	40.0	45	179	27	25	5	1	1	1	13	4	19	0	0
Castaneda, Aurelio, Pue.	0	0	.000	8.64	8	0	0	0	2	1	8.1	16	42	8	8	0	0	1	1	3	0	6	0	0
Castaneda, Aurelio, Tor..........	0	1	.000	9.00	7	0	0	0	1	0	12.0	25	66	13	12	4	0	1	1	3	2	7	0	0
Castro, Carlos, Tor.	0	0	.000	5.40	2	0	0	0	2	0	1.2	1	8	1	1	1	0	0	1	1	0	2	0	0
Castro, Carlos, Sal...............	0	0	.000	19.29	2	0	0	0	1	0	2.1	6	17	5	5	1	0	1	1	3	0	3	0	0
Cohuo, Enrique, Yuc..............	1	3	.250	6.92	14	4	0	0	4	0	26.0	29	119	24	20	1	3	1	1	12	0	13	3	0
Cohuo, Enrique, Can.	1	1	.500	3.38	5	5	0	0	0	0	29.1	30	122	12	11	4	2	2	1	7	0	17	1	0
Dominguez, David, Mex.	0	2	.000	3.68	9	1	0	0	6	0	14.2	13	63	8	6	1	0	0	1	4	0	8	2	0
Dominguez, David, Oax..........	2	0	1.000	1.23	7	3	0	0	1	0	29.1	22	114	5	4	1	0	1	1	7	1	20	3	0
Federico, Gustavo, Mont.	0	0	.000	1.57	10	0	0	0	2	0	23.0	21	91	6	4	0	0	1	1	6	2	10	1	0
Federico, Gustavo, Sal...........	2	0	1.000	3.12	14	0	0	0	4	0	17.1	24	86	10	6	3	0	0	0	13	1	8	0	0
Fregoso, Raul, Cam..............	0	1	.000	7.25	12	0	0	0	2	0	22.1	27	110	18	18	7	0	1	0	20	2	6	2	0
Fregoso, Raul, Cor..............	0	0	.000	7.50	5	0	0	0	2	0	6.0	8	33	5	5	0	0	1	0	7	0	2	0	0
Garcia, Jose, Tig................	6	2	.750	5.82	38	0	0	0	8	0	34.0	47	153	25	22	7	2	1	9	3	25	2	0
Garcia, Jose, Pue.	3	0	1.000	2.40	6	1	0	0	2	1	15.0	15	61	5	4	2	0	1	1	4	0	7	1	0
Garcia, Ramon, Mont.	0	0	.000	4.32	8	0	0	0	0	0	8.1	12	39	5	4	0	0	1	0	4	0	5	0	0
Garcia, Ramon, Pue.............	1	2	.333	4.25	21	1	0	0	9	0	36.0	39	165	21	17	2	1	0	0	24	0	21	3	0
Hidalgo, Romeo, Rey............	0	0	.000	0.00	2	0	0	0	2	0	2.1	1	8	0	0	0	0	0	0	1	0	1	0	0
Hidalgo, Romeo, Oax............	0	0	.000	16.20	6	0	0	0	3	0	5.0	12	31	10	9	2	0	0	1	5	0	3	2	0
Huerta, Edgar, Tig.*	0	0	.000	0.00	1	0	0	0	1	0	1.0	0	4	0	0	0	0	0	1	1	0	1	1	0
Huerta, Edgar, Pue.*	1	0	1.000	3.16	19	1	0	0	5	0	25.2	21	109	10	9	1	1	0	1	14	2	25	6	0
Huerta, Francisco, Ver..........	0	0	.000	0.00	1	0	0	0	0	0	0.0	0	2	1	1	0	0	0	0	2	0	0	0	0
Huerta, Francisco, Oax..........	0	0	.000	9.95	11	0	0	0	3	0	12.2	18	73	14	14	2	0	0	4	15	0	5	3	0
Jimenez, Julio, Sal.*	0	0	.000	5.79	5	1	0	0	1	0	9.1	8	44	7	6	0	1	2	1	11	0	7	0	0
Jimenez, Julio, Tor.*	2	0	1.000	3.24	23	1	0	0	5	0	25.0	22	114	9	9	1	1	1	4	18	1	20	2	0
Magee, Danny, Monc.*	5	4	.556	3.42	10	10	1	0	0	0	55.1	53	246	21	21	1	4	2	6	28	2	54	4	0
Magee, Danny, Cam.*	2	2	.500	1.31	5	5	0	0	0	0	34.1	23	145	7	5	1	3	0	2	19	0	34	2	0
Miranda, Angel, Mex.*	1	1	.500	6.75	12	0	0	0	0	0	8.0	5	34	7	6	0	0	1	0	6	1	7	0	0
Miranda, Angel, Oax.*	3	3	.500	3.86	10	9	0	0	0	0	56.0	56	246	26	24	3	1	1	4	25	1	41	1	0
Navarro, Joel, Mex.	3	0	1.000	4.12	15	8	0	0	0	0	59.0	62	248	30	27	6	1	2	3	17	0	24	5	0
Navarro, Joel, Oax.	3	0	1.000	3.32	6	6	0	0	0	0	38.0	51	167	15	14	3	3	0	1	11	0	24	0	0
Navarro, Jose, Tig.	0	0	.000	5.40	8	0	0	0	4	0	10.0	17	54	8	6	0	2	1	6	2	12	1	0
Navarro, Jose, Pue...............	5	8	.385	4.99	16	16	0	0	0	0	74.0	87	329	42	41	6	1	3	4	30	0	40	3	0
Parra, Jose, Mex.	4	5	.444	3.20	45	0	0	0	37	24	50.2	44	218	20	18	3	1	1	7	23	2	47	6	0
Parra, Jose, Oax.	1	0	1.000	0.71	12	0	0	0	11	9	12.2	6	54	1	1	0	1	0	2	7	0	16	1	0
Parra, Julio, Lar.	2	6	.250	5.52	43	0	0	0	35	16	44.0	51	212	28	27	4	6	0	3	27	3	47	4	0
Parra, Julio, Mont.	4	2	.667	4.18	20	0	0	0	7	0	23.2	19	103	11	11	1	3	0	1	13	2	35	0	0
Rodriguez, Manuel, Cor.........	2	6	.250	7.65	16	10	0	0	3	0	40.0	50	204	38	34	7	1	3	0	38	0	16	1	0
Rodriguez, Manuel, Cam.	2	0	1.000	0.00	6	0	0	0	3	0	8.2	3	33	0	0	0	0	0	6	1	6	1	0
Sanchez, Claudio, Oax...........	0	0	.000	0.00	2	0	0	0	1	0	1.1	2	10	5	0	0	1	0	3	0	1	0	0
Sanchez, Claudio, Tor.	4	2	.667	4.74	15	1	0	0	3	1	24.2	32	105	14	13	0	2	0	0	5	0	13	0	0
Sanchez, Hector, Pue.	0	0	.000	3.24	4	1	0	0	0	0	8.1	11	37	3	3	2	1	0	0	3	0	5	0	0
Sanchez, Hector, Cam.	0	0	.000	8.10	2	0	0	0	1	0	3.1	3	14	3	3	1	1	0	0	1	0	1	0	0
Sombra, Francisco, Cor.*	0	1	.000	10.13	12	0	0	0	1	0	5.1	5	28	7	6	2	0	0	1	6	0	1	0	0
Sombra, Francisco, Ver.*	0	0	.000	6.35	6	0	0	0	0	0	5.2	8	29	4	4	1	0	0	0	5	1	5	0	0
Sulu, Mario, Cam.	0	3	.000	7.53	11	0	0	0	3	0	14.1	19	68	13	12	3	2	1	0	8	1	9	2	0
Sulu, Mario, Can.	1	2	.333	5.35	10	7	0	0	1	0	35.1	40	159	27	21	6	2	1	2	15	0	16	2	0
Valenzuela, Saul, Cor...........	0	6	.000	5.75	11	8	0	0	2	1	40.2	49	184	30	26	6	2	4	3	18	1	18	3	0
Valenzuela, Saul, Can.	0	3	.000	9.12	14	3	0	0	2	0	24.2	46	127	27	25	3	1	3	11	0	5	2	0
Wagner, Matt, Tig...............	0	0	.000	7.71	7	0	0	0	3	0	7.0	11	38	8	6	1	2	1	0	5	0	5	3	0
Wagner, Matt, Pue..............	1	1	.500	10.00	7	0	0	0	5	1	9.0	14	48	10	10	1	0	1	0	7	2	11	1	0

COMBINATION SHUTOUTS: **Campeche (7)**—Acosta-Sinohui; Martinez-Marquez-Sinohui; Martinez-Sinohui; Pulido-Sinohui; Vazquez-Marquez-Sinohui; Vazquez-Sinohui; Vazquez-Tejeda-Sanchez-Rodriguez. **Cancun (7)**—Munoz-Villegas-Sanchez 2; Cohuo-Mere; Munoz-Martinez-Solarte; Munoz-Sanchez-Solarte; Vega-Villegas-Sanchez; Villalobos-Mere. **Cordoba (2)**—Elvira-Romero-Orea; Gomez-Orea. **Dos Laredos (12)**—Keppen-Parra 2; Babineaux-Garibay-Quintanilla; Drahman-Garibay; Drahman-Parra; Drahman-Quintanilla-Almeida-Parra; Huerta-Delfin-Drahman-Parra; Huerta-Garibay-Quintanilla-Parra; Nunez-Delfin; Parra-Keppen-Delfin-Garibay; Verdugo-Delfin-Parra; Verdugo-Garibay-Almeida-Parra. **Mexico City Reds (4)**—Bernal-Cruz-Perez-Parra; Bernal-Perez-Garcia; Galvez-Bernal-Moreno; Navarro-Perez-Parra. **Mexico City Tigers (2)**—Beltran-Campillo; Henthorne-Valenzuela. **Monclova (6)**—Aguilar-Cecena-Cazarez-Newman; Kammar-Cecena; Magee-Murillo; Romero-Cecena-Murillo; Romero-Hernandez-Murillo; Romero-Hernandez-Newman. **Monterrey (5)**—Gonzalez-Andujar; Gonzalez-Loya-Rubio; Leyva-Lugo-Nieblas-Perez; Leyva-Parra-Rubio; Pineda-Diaz-Rubio. **Oaxaca (4)**—Elizalde-Barrios-Baez; Jimenez-Baez-Parra; Miranda-Lopez-Neri-Barrios; Miranda-Ramirez-Baez. **Puebla (2)**—Kelley-Garcia; Navarro-Garcia. **Reynosa (14)**—Conde-Henry-Lopez; Dishman-Lopez; Dishman-Purata-Lopez; Esquer-Garibay-Purata-Lopez; Esquer-Mattson-Melendez-Lopez; Esquer-Melendez-Garibay; Esquer-Purata-Henry-Lopez; Manrique-Mattson-Melendez; Manrique-Melendez-Lopez; Manrique-Rodriguez-Melendez-Lopez; Quinonez-Lopez; Quinonez-Melendez; Rodriguez-Lopez; Zambrano-Mattson-Lopez. **Saltillo (3)**—Delahoya-Cazares-Lara; Reyes-Diaz-Ayala; Romano-Neri. **Tabasco (7)**—Alvarez-Leon; Alvarez-Mattson; Blancas-Villarreal-Rivera-Rossiter; Guerra-Leon-Reynoso; Jimenez-Nieblas; Osuna-Leon-Rossiter; Ruiz-Reynoso. **Torreon (1)**—Lopez-Aguilar-Roque. **Veracruz (8)**—Meza-Wallace 2; Mora-Carrasco; Mora-Gonzalez-Wallace; Mora-Harris; Morales-Pena-Gonzalez; Rivera-Wallace; Salgado-Harris. **Yucatan (9)**—Manzanillo-Chavez 2; Atondo-Chavez; Cuervo-Atondo-Verdugo-Chavez; Cuervo-Flores-Chavez; Manzanillo-Flores-Chavez; Pimentel-Rodriguez; Rios-Chavez; Rios-Flores-Chavez.

NO-HIT GAMES: Romano, Saltillo, defeated Monterrey, 6-0, May 20, first game; Manzanillo, Yucatan, defeated Campeche, 1-0, June 28, first game; Romero, Monclova, defeated Veracruz, 1-0, July 11.

TEAM

Team	Pct.	G	PO	A	E	TC	DP	TP	PB
Monterrey	.983	121	3189	1308	80	4577	142	0	8
Puebla	.981	117	2975	1369	83	4427	124	0	6
Mexico	.980	121	3206	1502	94	4802	165	0	8
Dos Laredos	.980	121	3217	1282	91	4590	139	0	7
Yucatan	.979	121	3226	1193	94	4513	96	0	12
Veracruz	.978	121	3244	1382	104	4730	132	0	10
Tigres	.977	118	3061	1301	101	4462	130	0	24
Campeche	.977	119	3092	1287	102	4481	106	0	19
Monclova	.977	120	3135	1323	105	4563	148	0	13
Saltillo	.976	120	3181	1415	112	4708	118	0	8
Torreon	.976	120	3202	1420	114	4736	133	0	8
Oaxaca	.976	120	3116	1450	113	4679	113	0	21
Reynosa	.976	122	3241	1279	112	4632	117	0	11
Cancun	.974	121	3169	1347	122	4638	144	0	24
Tabasco	.973	122	3200	1455	129	4784	130	0	13
Cordoba	.964	116	2917	1310	157	4384	141	0	23

INDIVIDUAL

FIRST BASEMEN

NOTE: All caps denotes fielding-percentage leader based on 60 games for catchers, 80 for all other non-pitchers and 98 innings for pitchers. *Throws lefthanded.

Player, Team	Pct.	G	PO	A	E	TC	DP
Acuna, Jose, Tor.	1.000	2	7	0	0	7	1
Adriana, Sharnol, Cam.	1.000	20	165	20	0	185	12
Aganza, Ruben, Monc.	.990	84	685	35	7	727	81
Aguilera, Armando, Sal.	1.000	2	4	0	0	4	0
Almeida, Shammar, Oax.*	.995	62	539	45	3	587	52
Amador, Alonso, Ver.	.929	1	11	2	1	14	1
Anthony, Eric, Mont.*	1.000	2	20	2	0	22	4
Arredondo, Hernando, Cam.-Cor.	1.000	10	86	14	0	100	8
Azocar, Oscar, Yuc.*	.979	12	85	10	2	97	7
Ball, Jeff, Can.	.923	1	9	3	1	13	1
Darajas, Edison, Cor.*	.975	42	325	24	9	358	47
Barrera, Nelson, Oax.	1.000	1	3	0	0	3	0
Barron, Tony, Can.-Cam.	.995	65	566	42	3	611	74
Bojorquez, Edson, Oax.	1.000	6	3	0	0	3	1
Bolado, Carlos, Ver.	.000	1	0	0	0	0	0
Boston, D.J., Cam.-Can.*	.988	88	740	90	10	840	84
BREWER, Rod, Oax.-Ver.*	.995	102	907	74	5	986	90
Bullet, Scott, Rey.*	1.000	6	47	2	0	49	8
Cappuccio, Carmine, Yuc.	1.000	1	1	0	0	1	0
Castaneda, Hector, Yuc.	.993	107	920	47	7	974	81
Castellano, Pedro, Mex.	.992	101	973	80	9	1062	124
Castro, Gonzalo, Lar.	1.000	8	10	1	0	11	5
Cervantes, Refugio, Sal.	1.000	3	17	1	0	18	3
Chimelis, Joel, Lar.	.994	114	1034	65	7	1106	114
Clark, Howie, Yuc.	1.000	3	8	2	0	10	0
Cobos, Rogelio, Ver.-Oax.	1.000	4	24	1	0	25	3
Colina, Roberto, Pue.*	.992	107	986	84	9	1079	108
Cruz, Fausto, Tor.	1.000	1	14	0	0	14	1
Dattola, Kevin, Tor.*	1.000	1	12	1	0	13	1
Diaz, Pedro, Pue.	.979	5	40	6	1	47	4
Espino, Daniel, Tor.	.997	38	322	28	1	351	37
Espinoza, Roman, Rey.	.985	9	61	3	1	65	5
Fornes, Daniel, Rey.*	.991	62	489	42	5	536	45
Franco, Julio, Tig.	.991	60	488	57	5	550	63
Gainer, Jonathan, Tab.-Cor.	.986	67	637	54	10	701	67
Garcia, Cornelio, Mex.*	1.000	14	154	11	0	165	20
Garcia, Guillermo, Oax.	1.000	1	3	1	0	4	0
Garcia, Omar, Ver.	1.000	14	118	6	0	124	21
Gavia, Jesus, Tor.	1.000	1	3	1	0	4	0
Gonzalez, Rolando, Monc.	.982	13	53	3	1	57	13
Gonzalez, Roman, Cor.	1.000	1	9	2	0	11	0
Gorr, Robert, Tab.	1.000	3	36	4	0	40	4
Grijak, Kevin, Mex.	1.000	2	15	1	0	16	1
Guerrero, Epifanio, Can.	.955	4	20	1	1	22	4
Hernandez, Marlon, Mont.	1.000	1	5	0	0	5	2
Ibarra, Juvenal, Tor.	1.000	1	1	0	0	1	0
Iturbe, Pedro, Pue.*	1.000	7	50	5	0	55	5
Lara, Jose, Ver.-Cor.	.990	23	181	8	2	191	23
Lewis, Anthony, Lar.*	.500	1	1	0	1	2	0
Lopez, Raul, Monc.	1.000	9	75	3	0	78	8
Luque, Raul, Lar.	.923	1	11	1	1	13	1
Machira, Pablo, Cor.-Cam.	.982	47	355	21	7	383	46

Player, Team	Pct.	G	PO	A	E	TC	DP
Malave, Jose, Ver.	1.000	2	16	2	0	18	0
Martinez, Abel, Can.	.988	17	151	10	2	163	19
Medina, Jose, Sal.	1.000	1	5	0	0	5	0
Mendez, Francisco, Mont.	1.000	6	25	3	0	28	5
Meulens, Hensley, Sal.	1.000	11	56	5	0	61	5
Munoz, Adan, Monc.	1.000	1	5	0	0	5	0
Munoz, Jose de Jesus, Sal.*	1.000	2	1	0	0	1	0
Nava, Lipso, Ver.-Tor.	1.000	22	155	13	0	168	14
Nunez, Raymond, Cor.-Tab.	.994	36	315	25	2	342	35
Ojeda, Miguel, Mex.	1.000	7	15	4	0	19	1
Orantes, Ramon, Mont.	1.000	14	107	10	0	117	17
Ortega, Antonio, Cam.	1.000	2	4	0	0	4	0
Ortiz, Alejandro, Tor.	1.000	2	15	1	0	16	3
Ortiz, Luis, Mont.	.964	8	51	2	2	55	7
Otanez, Willis, Mont.	1.000	9	64	10	0	74	4
Paez, Raul, Mex.*	.984	9	57	4	1	62	5
Payro, Edison, Cam.*	1.000	10	75	7	0	82	4
Pearson, Eddie, Tab.	.994	34	301	38	2	341	26
Perez, Francisco, Rey.*	1.000	15	62	4	0	66	7
Poe, Charles, Lar.	1.000	2	15	2	0	17	4
Presichi, Christian, Sal.	.000	1	0	0	0	0	0
Quintero, Edgar, Mont.*	1.000	1	8	0	0	8	0
Rivera, Francisco A., Ver.	1.000	6	42	7	0	49	5
Rivera, Jesus, Tab.	1.000	2	4	0	0	4	0
Rodriguez, Boi, Monc.	.993	41	252	13	2	267	28
Romero, Marco, Sal.-Tor.	.994	91	751	65	5	821	82
Romero, Oscar, Monc.	1.000	2	8	1	0	9	2
Sanchez, Gerardo, Lar.-Tig.	1.000	3	16	0	0	16	1
Sanchez, Roque, Lar.	1.000	7	32	2	0	34	1
Santos, Andres, Lar.	1.000	5	11	1	0	12	2
Saucedo, Roberto, Can.	1.000	22	169	16	0	185	16
Seitzer, Brad, Can.-Ver.	.997	31	268	27	1	296	23
Sievers, Carlos, Rey.	.967	12	79	10	3	92	10
Smith, Charles, Mont.	.989	43	336	32	4	372	45
Soriano, Ricardo, Cor.*	1.000	1	8	1	0	9	2
Suarez, Luis, Tig.*	1.000	2	13	1	0	14	2
Trapaga, Julio, Tig.	1.000	6	15	0	0	15	2
Tyler, Brad, Oax.	1.000	8	53	3	0	56	2
Valdez, Emmanuel, Tig.	.667	3	1	1	1	3	1
Velazquez, Guillermo, Sal.*	.989	87	790	56	9	855	76
Viera, Jose, Tor.	.993	27	271	27	2	300	30
Villanueva, Hector, Cor.	.989	9	84	2	1	87	11
Villarreal, Alejandro, Lar.	1.000	3	22	2	0	24	0
Vizcarra, Roberto, Tig.	.998	64	519	34	1	554	54
Zambrano, Roberto, Mont.	.989	50	419	27	5	451	45

FIRST BASEMEN WITH TWO OR MORE TEAMS

Player, Team	Pct.	G	PO	A	E	TC	DP
Arredondo, Hernando, Cam.	1.000	5	42	8	0	50	3
Arredondo, Hernando, Cor.	1.000	5	44	6	0	50	5
Barron, Tony, Can.	.995	57	515	33	3	551	68
Barron, Tony, Cam.	1.000	0	61	9	0	60	6
Boston, D.J., Cam.*	.990	66	534	72	6	612	60
Boston, D.J., Can.*	.982	22	206	18	4	228	24
Brewer, Rod, Oax.*	.995	59	546	42	3	591	50
Brewer, Rod, Ver.*	.995	43	361	32	2	395	40
Bustamante, Omar, Sal.	1.000	2	3	0	0	3	0
Castaneda, Rafael, Rey.	.985	33	244	12	4	260	29
Cobos, Rogelio, Ver.	1.000	2	11	0	0	11	3
Cobos, Rogelio, Oax.	1.000	2	13	1	0	14	0
Gainer, Jonathan, Tab.	.985	62	593	53	10	656	61
Gainer, Jonathan, Cor.	1.000	5	44	1	0	45	6
Lara, Jose, Ver.	.987	18	148	5	2	155	21
Lara, Jose, Cor.	1.000	5	33	3	0	36	2
Machiria, Pablo, Cor.	.978	32	251	14	6	271	39
Machiria, Pablo, Cam.	.991	15	104	7	1	112	7
Nava, Lipso, Ver.	1.000	16	132	10	0	142	11
Nava, Lipso, Tor.	1.000	6	23	3	0	26	3
Nunez, Raymond, Cor.	.990	20	192	8	2	202	17
Nunez, Raymond, Tab.	1.000	16	123	17	0	140	18
Ramirez, Efren, Cor.	1.000	6	41	5	0	46	2
Ramirez, Enrique, Mont.	1.000	1	1	0	0	1	0
Rodarte, Raul, Rey.	.986	23	128	11	2	141	14
Rodriguez, Armando, Pue.	.909	3	17	3	2	22	1
Romero, Marco, Sal.	.993	35	258	28	2	288	29
Romero, Marco, Tor.	.994	56	493	37	3	533	53
Sanchez, Gerardo, Lar.	1.000	2	13	0	0	13	1
Sanchez, Gerardo, Tig.	1.000	1	3	0	0	3	0
Seitzer, Brad, Can.	1.000	2	9	0	0	9	0
Seitzer, Brad, Ver.	.997	29	259	27	1	287	23

CLASS AAA Mexican League

CLASS AAA Mexican League

SECOND BASEMEN

Player, Team	Pct.	G	PO	A	E	TC	DP
Acosta, Jose Francisco, Tab.	.960	14	19	29	2	50	6
Adriana, Sharnol, Cam.	.960	75	186	174	15	375	38
Amador, Alonso, Ver.	1.000	5	9	16	0	25	5
Amador, Jose, Tor.	1.000	3	6	4	0	10	2
Arano, Marco Antonio, Tab.	1.000	1	1	1	0	2	0
Arias, Francisco, Sal.	.980	22	14	36	1	51	5
Armenta, Guillermo, Cam.	.975	42	96	97	5	198	26
Arredondo, Hernando, Cor.	1.000	5	13	11	0	24	4
Arredondo, Jesus, Pue.	.982	59	141	188	6	335	49
Avila, Ignacio, Cor.	.857	1	3	3	1	7	1
Barajas, Edison, Cor.*	1.000	1	2	0	0	2	0
Borges, Luis, Can.	1.000	1	3	2	0	5	2
Brena, Jaime, Oax.	1.000	5	1	3	0	4	0
Bustillos, Luis, Rey.*	1.000	5	11	15	0	26	3
Cansino, Jorge, Ver.	1.000	6	3	13	0	16	2
Carrasco, Ernesto, Pue.	.991	39	86	139	2	227	33
Castro, Arnoldo, Can.	.991	114	301	354	6	661	105
Castro, Domingo, Monc.	1.000	7	16	22	0	38	7
Cedeno, Domingo, Cor.	.968	66	180	208	13	401	63
Cervantes, Ivan, Mex.	1.000	18	27	43	0	70	13
Chimelis, Joel, Lar.	.000	1	0	0	0	0	0
Clark, Howie, Yuc.	1.000	6	7	9	0	16	2
Connell, Lino, Ver.	.973	14	24	48	2	74	6
Diaz, Remigio, Mont.	1.000	1	4	3	0	7	0
Duenas, Arnoldo, Yuc.	1.000	2	5	7	0	12	1
Esquer, Ramon, Mex.	.981	97	230	339	11	580	91
Flores, Miguel, Mont.	.979	93	230	284	11	525	83
Garcia, Heriberto, Oax.	.962	13	24	27	2	53	6
Gastelum, Carlos, Tig.	1.000	3	10	4	0	14	2
Gastelum, Sergio, Tig.	.971	74	178	224	12	414	65
Gorr, Robert, Tab.	.984	24	53	68	2	123	17
Grijalva, Lorenzo, Tab.	1.000	7	11	18	0	29	4
Guerrero, Epifanio, Can.	1.000	4	7	13	0	20	2
Guerrero, Sergio, Lar.	1.000	3	3	3	0	6	3
Gutierrez, Andres, Pue.	1.000	3	2	9	0	11	0
Leyva, Octavio, Ver.	1.000	1	1	0	0	1	0
Lopez, Fabian, Oax.	.974	63	148	188	9	345	42
Lopez, Gonzalo, Yuc.	1.000	4	1	5	0	6	2
Magallanes, Ever, Mont.	1.000	12	28	36	0	64	6
Martinez, Abel, Cam.	1.000	1	0	2	0	2	1
Martinez, Grimaldo, Tor.	.986	120	331	387	10	728	100
Mejia, Roberto, Tab.	.987	69	165	220	5	390	54
Mendoza, Omar, Tab.	.985	16	31	35	1	67	11
Mere, Pedro, Ver.	.984	105	271	293	9	573	92
Minjarez, Francisco, Pue.	.962	6	13	12	1	26	2
Morejon, Oswaldo, Yuc.	.980	117	224	361	12	597	65
Munoz, Jose Luis, Can.	1.000	1	2	1	0	3	1
Ojeda, Miguel, Mex.	1.000	1	2	5	0	7	1
Ortiz, Luis, Mont.	1.000	2	8	7	0	15	4
Palafox, Sergio, Sal.	.971	84	175	253	13	441	66
Peraza, Rudy, Tab.	1.000	1	1	0	0	1	0
Perez, Alfredo, Cam.	1.000	11	15	23	0	38	7
Perez, Jorge, Pue.	.965	23	49	62	4	115	16
Perez, Jose, Mont.	.966	21	40	46	3	89	10
Quintero, Guillermo, Cor.	1.000	7	14	18	0	32	5
Ramirez, Enrique, Mont.	.950	8	8	11	1	20	5
Ramirez, Jesus, Oax.	.983	54	104	127	4	235	24
Reyes, Jesus, Cor.	1.000	2	1	1	0	2	1
Reyes, Jesus Eleazar, Oax.	.500	1	0	1	1	2	0
Rivera, Jesus Manuel, Tab.	.978	15	21	24	1	46	5
Robles, Javier, Tig.	1.000	1	1	1	0	2	0
Robles, Oscar, Oax.	1.000	5	17	24	0	41	6
Robles, Trinidad, Tig.	.973	32	36	74	3	113	12
Rodriguez, Carlos, Rey.	.990	114	317	265	6	588	80
Rodriguez, Jose, Tor.	1.000	2	1	1	0	2	1
Romero, Flavio, Sal.	.000	1	0	0	0	0	0
Ruiz, Juan, Mex.	.987	20	34	41	1	76	11
Sanchez, Jose, Lar.	.963	13	20	32	2	54	8
Sanchez, Orlando, Cor.	.952	21	35	45	4	84	13
Sanchez, Wilfredo, Cor.	.972	33	68	105	5	178	26
Santos, Andres, Lar.	1.000	1	1	1	0	2	1
Sauceda, Victor, Can.	1.000	9	10	14	0	24	6
Tovar, Jose, Rey.	.971	19	13	20	1	34	4
Trapaga, Julio, Tig.	.962	27	24	27	2	53	5
Valencia, Carlos, Lar.	.965	36	73	93	6	172	23
Valenzuela, Irving, Monc.	.972	34	68	73	4	145	26
Valle, Roberto, Tor.	1.000	2	4	3	0	7	2
Vega, Jorge, Oax.	.714	4	0	5	2	7	0
Velez, Manuel, Lar.-Sal.	.984	84	183	237	7	427	64
Verdugo, Vincente, Sal.	.978	35	72	105	4	181	20
Villarreal, Alejandro, Lar.	.500	1	1	1	2	4	0
Vizcarra, Roberto, Tig.	.968	17	32	28	2	62	7
Zazueta, Juan, Tor.	1.000	1	0	1	0	1	0
ZAZUETA, Mauricio, Monc.	.994	97	224	313	3	540	80

SECOND BASEMEN WITH TWO OR MORE TEAMS

Player, Team	Pct.	G	PO	A	E	TC	DP
Velez, Manuel, Lar.	.983	80	180	235	7	422	64
Velez, Manuel, Sal.	1.000	4	3	2	0	5	0

THIRD BASEMEN

Player, Team	Pct.	G	PO	A	E	TC	DP
Adriana, Sharnol, Cam.	.887	16	16	39	7	62	4
Aganza, Ruben, Monc.	.000	1	0	0	0	0	0
Amador, Alonso, Ver.	.906	12	8	21	3	32	2
Amador, Jose, Tor.	.000	1	0	0	0	0	0
Amettler, Jesus, Tab.	.929	12	5	21	2	28	0
Arano, Marco Antonio, Tab.	1.000	3	1	8	0	9	1
Arias, Francisco, Sal.	.981	19	17	35	1	53	2
Arredondo, Hernando, Cor.	.500	5	0	4	4	8	0
Ball, Jeff, Can.	1.000	3	4	12	0	16	2
Beltran, Juan, Cam.	.000	3	0	0	0	0	0
Bustillos, Luis, Rey.*	1.000	1	0	1	0	1	1
Cansino, Jorge, Ver.	1.000	9	4	13	0	17	2
Carrasco, Ernesto, Pue.	.965	50	38	101	5	144	17
Castaneda, Rafael, Oax.-Rey.	.930	70	67	133	15	215	8
Castellano, Pedro, Mex.	.942	19	13	52	4	69	6
Castro, Gonzalo, Lar.	.000	2	0	0	0	0	0
Cervantes, Ivan, Mex.	.000	1	0	0	0	0	0
Cervera, Francisco, Yuc.	.927	108	86	157	19	262	8
Connell, Lino, Ver.	.750	4	5	4	3	12	1
Cruz, Fausto, Tor.	.937	50	36	97	9	142	13
De La Cruz, Lorenzo, Pue.	.000	2	0	0	0	0	0
Delgado, Alex, Tab.	.935	9	8	21	2	31	1
Diaz, Pedro, Pue.	.990	41	22	77	1	100	5
Duenas, Arnoldo, Yuc.-Can.	.913	34	21	52	7	80	9
Estrada, Osmani, Sal.	.963	28	20	58	3	81	3
Garcia, Guillermo, Oax.	.727	3	2	6	3	11	0
Gonzalez, Rolando, Monc.	.955	16	14	28	2	44	6
Gonzalez, Roman, Cor.	.750	1	2	1	1	4	0
Guerrero, Epifanio, Can.	.967	27	19	40	2	61	5
Guerrero, Sergio, Lar.	.914	18	20	33	5	58	3
Guizar, Hector, Monc.	.986	49	47	89	2	138	9
Gutierrez, Andres, Pue.	1.000	2	1	0	0	1	0
Ibarra, Juvenal, Tor.	.000	1	0	0	0	0	0
Jimenez, Alfonso, Sal.	.900	2	2	7	1	10	1
Lara, Jose, Cor.	1.000	3	0	3	0	3	0
Leyva, German, Ver.	.963	102	84	230	12	326	25
Lopez, Fabian, Oax.	.854	20	9	32	7	48	2
Lopez, Gonzalo, Yuc.	.973	20	8	28	1	37	0
Lopez, Raul, Monc.	.850	11	5	12	3	20	0
Magallanes, Ever, Mont.	.939	27	20	57	5	82	8
Magallanes, Roberto, Tig.-Pue.	.964	54	36	97	5	138	11
Martinez, Abel, Can.	.933	27	18	52	5	75	8
Martinez, Ray, Mex.	.929	103	63	172	18	253	16
Mejia, Roberto, Tab.	.906	19	10	48	6	64	5
Mendoza, Omar, Tab.	.872	44	33	90	18	141	12
Meulens, Hensley, Sal.	.922	46	29	90	10	129	5
Minjarez, Francisco, Pue.	.935	13	5	24	2	31	3
Morejon, Oswaldo, Yuc.	1.000	3	0	6	0	6	1
Munoz, Jose Luis, Can.	.891	24	19	38	7	64	3
Nava, Lipso, Ver.-Tor.	.967	61	46	99	5	150	7
Nunez, Raymond, Cor.-Tab.	.925	58	45	128	14	187	12
Orantes, Ramon, Mont.	.975	84	51	145	5	201	26
Ortiz, Luis, Mont.-Tab.	.825	17	6	27	7	40	1
Perez, Alfredo, Cam.	.815	11	7	15	5	27	1
Perez, Jose, Mont.	.800	8	2	2	1	5	0
Presichi, Christian, Sal.	.000	5	0	0	0	0	0
Ramirez, Enrique, Mont.	1.000	10	5	18	0	23	0
Ramirez, Jesus, Oax.	1.000	4	1	1	0	2	1
Ramirez, Oscar, Cam.	1.000	1	0	1	0	1	0
Reyes, Jesus, Cor.	1.000	1	0	3	0	3	0
Rivera, Jesus Manuel, Tab.	.944	8	7	10	1	18	0
Robles, Oscar, Oax.	.969	98	78	231	10	319	21
Robles, Trinidad, Tig.	.889	11	2	6	1	9	1
Rodarte, Raul, Rey.-Cor.	.938	90	82	159	16	257	20
Romero, Flavio, Sal.	.818	5	2	7	2	11	1
Romero, Oscar, Monc.	.959	57	35	107	6	148	11
Romero, Yamil, Ver.*	.000	1	0	0	0	0	0
Ruiz, Juan, Mex.	1.000	9	4	7	0	11	1
Ruiz, Ricardo, Ver.	.000	1	0	0	0	0	0
Salas, Heriberto, Yuc.	.000	1	0	0	0	0	0
Sanchez, Orlando, Cor.	.000	1	0	0	0	0	0

Player, Team	Pct.	G	PO	A	E	TC	DP
SANCHEZ, Roque, Cam.	.976	99	88	198	7	293	18
Sanchez, Wilfredo, Cor.	1.000	11	6	13	0	19	1
Santos, Andres, Lar.	.800	5	0	4	1	5	1
Sauceda, Victor, Can.	1.000	1	2	2	0	4	1
Seitzer, Brad, Can.-Ver.	.892	29	25	66	11	102	5
Smith, Charles, Mont.	.800	4	2	6	2	10	0
Torres, Paul, Tab.-Cor.*	.844	29	31	45	14	90	2
Torres, Sebastian, Oax.	.875	5	1	6	1	8	1
Tovar, Jose, Rey.	.000	2	0	0	0	0	0
Tyler, Brad, Oax.	.867	8	0	13	2	15	1
Valencia, Carlos, Lar.	.952	63	47	130	9	186	15
Valenzuela, Irving, Monc.	.889	7	1	7	1	9	0
Valle, Jorge, Rey.	.946	51	25	62	5	92	4
Valle, Roberto, Tor.	1.000	2	0	1	0	1	0
Vazquez, Jorge Alberto, Tig.	.914	58	34	115	14	163	12
Vega, Jose, Oax.	1.000	10	2	3	0	5	0
Velez, Manuel, Sal.	.961	29	15	59	3	77	6
Verdugo, Vincente, Sal.	.000	3	0	0	0	0	0
Viera, Jose, Tor.	.571	2	2	2	3	7	0
Villarreal, Alejandro, Lar.	.982	50	35	77	2	114	4
Vizcarra, Roberto, Tig.	.929	41	30	61	7	98	5
Zazueta, Juan, Tor.	.928	27	15	62	6	83	4

THIRD BASEMEN WITH TWO OR MORE TEAMS

Player, Team	Pct.	G	PO	A	E	TC	DP
Castaneda, Rafael, Oax.	.842	7	3	13	3	19	2
Castaneda, Rafael, Rey.	.939	63	64	120	12	196	6
Duenas, Arnoldo, Yuc.	.750	9	0	3	1	4	0
Duenas, Arnoldo, Can.	.921	25	21	49	6	76	9
Magallanes, Roberto, Tig.	.945	29	18	51	4	73	5
Magallanes, Roberto, Pue.	.985	25	18	46	1	65	6
Nava, Lipso, Ver.	1.000	6	3	10	0	13	0
Nava, Lipso, Tor.	.964	55	43	89	5	137	7
Nunez, Raymond, Cor.	.908	39	35	83	12	130	8
Nunez, Raymond, Tab.	.965	19	10	45	2	57	4
Ortiz, Luis, Mont.	.750	7	0	9	3	12	0
Ortiz, Luis, Tab.	.857	10	6	18	4	28	1
Rodarte, Raul, Rey.	.942	42	39	74	7	120	7
Rodarte, Raul, Cor.	.934	48	43	86	9	137	13
Seitzer, Brad, Can.	.892	28	25	66	11	102	5
Seitzer, Brad, Ver.	.000	1	0	0	0	0	0
Torres, Paul, Tab.*	.900	6	9	9	2	20	1
Torres, Paul, Cor.*	.020	23	22	36	12	70	1

SHORTSTOPS

Player, Team	Pct.	G	PO	A	E	TC	DP
Aguilera, Antonio, Cam.	.000	1	0	0	0	0	0
Amador, Jose, Tor.	.875	1	2	5	1	8	1
Arias, Francisco, Sal.	1.000	13	13	17	0	30	3
Armenta, Guillermo, Cam	.954	41	62	124	9	195	22
Beltran, Juan, Cam.	.962	27	37	65	4	106	12
Bolado, Carlos, Ver.	.000	1	0	0	0	0	0
Borges, Luis, Oan.	.969	74	115	163	9	287	43
Brena, Jaime, Oax.	.951	106	148	301	23	472	60
Bustillos, Luis, Rey.*	.918	65	50	85	12	147	23
Cansino, Jorge, Ver.	.909	10	2	8	1	11	2
Castro, Domingo, Monc.	.945	83	120	204	19	343	41
Cervantes, Ivan, Mex.	.935	28	37	78	8	123	15
Connell, Lino, Ver.	.940	29	40	70	7	117	17
Cruz, Fausto, Ver.	.963	72	130	205	13	348	42
Diaz, Remigio, Mont.	.981	114	186	323	10	519	80
Dominguez, David, Ver.	.000	2	0	0	0	0	0
Duenas, Arnoldo, Yuc.	1.000	2	0	1	0	1	0
Estrada, Osmani, Sal.	1.000	1	1	2	0	3	1
Garcia, Heriberto, Oax.	1.000	3	1	2	0	3	0
Garcia, Omar, Ver.	.000	1	0	0	0	0	0
Gomez, Heber, Tab.	.957	111	188	363	25	576	76
Guerrero, Epifanio, Can.	.961	18	26	47	3	76	9
Guizar, Hector, Monc.	.959	61	116	188	13	317	50
Gutierrez, Andres, Pue.	.962	26	33	67	4	104	16
Hernandez, Julio, Lar.	.964	119	224	343	21	588	94
Herrera, Ramiro, Ver.	.930	11	12	28	3	43	8
Leyva, Octavio, Ver.	.967	6	14	15	1	30	5
Lopez, Fabian, Oax.	1.000	1	1	0	0	1	0
Magallanes, Ever, Mont.	1.000	3	2	2	0	4	1
Magallanes, Roberto, Tig.	.000	1	0	0	0	0	0
Martinez, Abel, Can.	.907	23	25	53	8	86	15
Martinez, Augusto, Yuc.	.667	2	1	1	1	3	0
Martinez, Luis Carlos, Sal.	.959	117	203	424	27	654	86
Mendoza, Omar, Tab.	1.000	2	1	0	0	1	0
Minjarez, Francisco, Pue.	.978	89	136	264	9	409	52
Morejon, Oswaldo, Yuc.	.875	5	2	5	1	8	1

Player, Team	Pct.	G	PO	A	E	TC	DP
PACHO, Juan Jose, Yuc.	.982	82	128	207	6	341	49
Peraza, Rudy, Tab.	.875	8	12	23	5	40	5
Perez, Alfredo, Cam.	.960	13	26	22	2	50	6
Perez, Jorge, Pue.	1.000	3	0	2	0	2	0
Perez, Jose, Mont.	1.000	10	4	17	0	21	3
Quintero, Guillermo, Cor.-Ver.	.944	87	140	265	24	429	52
Ramirez, Enrique, Can.-Mont.	.909	19	14	36	5	55	6
Ramirez, Oscar, Cam.	.857	12	14	22	6	42	4
Reyes, Jesus, Yuc.-Cor.	.936	35	40	48	6	94	8
Rivera, Francisco Antonio, Ver.	.000	1	0	0	0	0	0
Rivera, Jesus Manuel, Tab.	.917	8	12	21	3	36	4
Robles, Javier, Tig.	.972	106	172	318	14	504	82
Robles, Oscar, Oax.	.967	42	36	80	4	120	14
Robles, Trinidad, Tig.	.923	20	21	51	6	78	11
Romero, Flavio, Sal.	1.000	7	3	7	0	10	2
Ruiz, Juan, Mex.	1.000	1	0	1	0	1	0
Salas, Heriberto, Cam.-Cor.-Yuc.	.975	82	130	217	9	356	49
Sanchez, Jose, Lar.	1.000	3	1	6	0	7	0
Sanchez, Orlando, Cor.	.924	66	100	204	25	329	46
Sanchez, Roque, Cam.	.000	2	0	0	0	0	0
Sanchez, Wilfredo, Cor.	.919	23	38	53	8	99	17
Sandoval, Jose Luis, Mex.	.976	106	178	420	15	613	106
Santiago, Henry, Cam.	.960	18	39	57	4	100	7
Santos, Andres, Lar.	1.000	1	0	1	0	1	0
Sauceda, Victor, Can.	.940	36	39	70	7	116	15
Solano, Fausto, Pue.	.912	12	24	28	5	57	5
Tovar, Jose, Rey.	1.000	10	7	12	0	19	1
Valencia, Carlos, Lar.	1.000	2	1	2	0	3	2
Valenzuela, Irving, Monc.	.905	7	8	11	2	21	2
Valle, Cosme, Rey.	1.000	1	0	4	0	4	0
Valle, Jorge, Rey.	.968	99	148	282	14	444	67
Valle, Jose, Tor.	.961	65	64	135	8	207	29
Valle, Roberto, Tor.	.945	17	14	38	3	55	10
Velez, Manuel, Lar.	.000	1	0	0	0	0	0
Zamudio, Rafael, Can.	.000	3	0	0	0	0	0
Zazueta, Juan, Tor.	1.000	1	0	1	0	1	0

SHORTSTOPS WITH TWO OR MORE TEAMS

Player, Team	Pct.	G	PO	A	E	TC	DP
Quintero, Guillermo, Cor.	.769	2	1	9	3	13	1
Quintero, Guillermo, Ver.	.950	85	139	256	21	416	51
Ramirez, Enrique, Can.	.935	9	7	22	2	31	2
Ramirez, Enrique, Mont.	.875	10	7	14	3	24	4
Reyes, Jesus, Yuc.	.932	28	32	37	5	74	6
Reyes, Jesus, Cor.	.950	7	8	11	1	20	2
Salas, Heriberto, Cam.	.981	30	43	61	2	106	16
Salas, Heriberto, Cor.	.960	27	49	95	6	150	20
Salas, Heriberto, Yuc.	.990	25	38	61	1	100	13

OUTFIELDERS

Player, Team	Pct.	G	PO	A	E	TC	DP
Abrego, Jesus, Can.	.977	24	38	5	1	44	1
Acuna, Jose, Tor.	1.000	57	65	7	0	72	0
Aguilera, Antonio, Cam.	1.000	12	16	1	0	17	0
Aguilera, Raul, Cor.	1.000	10	25	1	0	26	0
Almeida, Shammar, Oax.*	1.000	3	3	0	0	3	0
Alvarez, Hector, Oax.	.980	117	234	8	5	247	1
Alvarez, Rafael, Can.*	.813	8	12	1	3	16	0
Amador, Alonso, Ver.	.000	1	0	0	0	0	0
Amezcua, Adan, Mont.	.857	5	5	1	1	7	0
Anthony, Eric, Mont.*	.000	1	0	0	0	0	0
Arano, Eloy, Ver.	.988	111	245	11	3	259	3
ARANO, Wilfrido, Lar.	.995	112	189	15	1	205	3
Arauz, Leobardo, Yuc.	.980	55	96	4	2	102	1
Arredondo, Eduardo, Ver.	1.000	19	25	1	0	26	0
Arredondo, Hernando, Cam -Cor.	.991	67	107	7	1	115	3
Arredondo, Luis, Yuc.*	.965	107	247	4	9	260	0
Avila, Carlos, Tab.-Lar.*	.983	38	58	0	1	59	0
Avila, Ignacio, Can.	1.000	14	22	0	0	22	0
Azocar, Oscar, Yuc.*	.923	7	12	0	1	13	0
Baez, Carlos, Tab.	1.000	4	7	0	0	7	0
Ball, Jeff, Can.	1.000	7	9	0	0	9	0
Barajas, Edison, Cor.*	.982	34	54	2	1	57	2
Barron, Tony, Can.-Cam.	.983	32	58	1	1	60	0
Benitez, Yamil, Rey.	.985	29	61	4	1	66	0
Bernal, Cosme, Monc.	1.000	6	5	0	0	5	0
Berroa, Geronimo, Cam.	1.000	27	48	2	0	50	0
Bojorquez, Edson, Oax.	.750	8	6	0	2	8	0
Bojorquez, Victor, Mex.	.981	98	144	14	3	161	1
Bolado, Carlos, Ver.	1.000	49	46	0	0	46	0
Boston, D.J., Cam.*	.000	1	0	0	0	0	0
Brewer, Rod, Oax.*	1.000	10	12	2	0	14	0

Player, Team	Pct.	G	PO	A	E	TC	DP
Brinkley, Darryl, Cam.-Yuc.	.980	102	239	7	5	251	0
Buelna, Lorenzo, Pue.	.965	67	108	3	4	115	1
Bullet, Scott, Rey.*	.980	76	145	5	3	153	0
Canizalez, Juan, Mont.	.989	107	168	8	2	178	2
Cansino, Jorge, Ver.	.000	3	0	0	0	0	0
Cappuccio, Carmine, Yuc.	1.000	14	22	3	0	25	0
Carrillo, Matias, Tig.*	.980	100	141	6	3	150	0
Castro, Carlos, Tab.	1.000	13	10	0	0	10	0
Castro, Gonzalo, Lar.	.933	15	13	1	1	15	0
Cervantes, Ivan, Mex.	.000	2	0	0	0	0	0
Cisneros, Ventura, Rey.*	.000	2	0	0	0	0	0
Clark, Howie, Yuc.	.992	118	238	7	2	247	1
Cobos, Rogelio, Oax.	1.000	1	4	1	0	5	0
Connell, Lino, Ver.	.971	78	157	9	5	171	2
Contreras, Albino, Mont.	.987	70	147	4	2	153	0
Dattola, Kevin, Cam.-Yuc.*	1.000	13	34	1	0	35	1
De La Cruz, Lorenzo, Pue.	.994	94	168	4	1	173	0
De La Torre, Francisco, Oax.	1.000	4	1	0	0	1	0
Diaz, Alex, Tor.	.971	74	157	11	5	173	2
Diaz, Luis, Can.*	1.000	5	5	0	0	5	0
Diaz, Pedro, Pue.	.000	1	0	0	0	0	0
Dominguez, David, Ver.	.966	40	54	3	2	59	0
Espino, Daniel, Tor.	.955	24	40	2	2	44	0
Espino, Omar, Lar.	.000	1	0	0	0	0	0
Espinoza, Jose, Lar.	.994	96	170	8	1	179	1
Espinoza, Ramon, Rey.	.966	113	248	6	9	263	1
Estrella, Isaac, Lar.	1.000	30	17	0	0	17	0
Felix, Junior, Yuc.	.870	14	19	1	3	23	0
Fentanes, Oscar, Tab.	.968	93	173	9	6	188	0
Fernandez, Daniel, Mex.*	.986	105	204	5	3	212	1
Fornes, Daniel, Rey.*	.976	62	115	8	3	126	0
Franco, Julio, Tig.	1.000	3	1	0	0	1	0
Freeman, Richard, Lar.	1.000	9	10	0	0	10	0
Garcia, Cornelio, Mex.*	.941	27	30	2	2	34	1
Garcia, Guillermo, Oax.	1.000	9	8	0	0	8	0
Garcia, Hector, Mont.-Tab.	.987	84	146	4	2	152	0
Garcia, Luis Carlos, Tig.	.981	94	200	6	4	210	0
Garcia, Omar, Ver.-Yuc.	.987	36	72	3	1	76	0
Garland, Tim, Tab.	1.000	33	69	2	0	71	0
Gastelum, Sergio, Tig.	1.000	6	4	0	0	4	0
Gerardo, Benjamin, Monc.	1.000	13	16	1	0	17	0
Gibson, Derrick, Pue.	.947	42	72	0	4	76	0
Gonzalez, Manny, Lar.	.991	40	105	0	1	106	0
Gonzalez, Roman, Cor.	.980	82	139	9	3	151	0
Gordon, Keith, Sal.	.935	24	43	0	3	46	0
Grijak, Kevin, Mex.	.957	39	60	6	3	69	1
Guerrero, Epifanio, Can.	.968	35	58	2	2	62	0
Gutierrez, Andres, Pue.	1.000	2	4	0	0	4	0
Howard, Tom, Mont.*	1.000	19	22	0	0	22	0
Ingram, Garey, Rey.	1.000	11	19	0	0	19	0
Iturbe, Pedro, Pue.*	.984	91	121	5	2	128	0
Lara, Jose, Ver.-Cor.	.968	24	28	2	1	31	0
Leday, Anthony, Rey.	1.000	28	48	7	0	55	1
Lennon, Patrick, Yuc.	1.000	7	15	1	0	16	1
Lewis, Anthony, Lar.*	1.000	2	1	0	0	1	0
Lopez, Emigdio, Tor.	1.000	1	1	0	0	1	0
Lopez, Gonzalo, Yuc.	1.000	2	1	0	0	1	0
Lugo, Roberto, Mont.	1.000	1	2	0	0	2	0
Luna, Jose, Cor.	.975	34	75	2	2	79	0
Luque, Raul, Tab.	.933	7	14	0	1	15	0
Malave, Jose, Ver.-Sal.	1.000	13	19	1	0	20	0
Martinez, Enrique, Can.	.988	37	80	3	1	84	0
Martinez, Raul, Tab.	.000	1	0	0	0	0	0
Mata, Noe, Rey.	.987	43	72	2	1	75	0
Matos, Malvin, Tab.	1.000	5	19	0	0	19	0
Medina, Jose, Sal.	.917	42	51	4	5	60	0
Mejia, Roberto, Tab.	.000	1	0	0	0	0	0
Mendez, Francisco, Mont.	.923	6	12	0	1	13	0
Mendez, Roberto, Oax.-Mex.*	.977	103	154	13	4	171	1
Mendoza, Carlos, Sal.*	1.000	18	31	3	0	34	0
Meulens, Hensley, Cor.	.957	36	41	4	2	47	0
Meza, Gonzalo, Mex.	1.000	55	73	3	0	76	0
Moreno, David, Cam.	1.000	12	5	0	0	5	0
Munoz, Adan, Monc.	.000	1	0	0	0	0	0
Munoz, Jose de Jesus, Sal.*	.979	118	219	10	5	234	1
Murray, Glenn, Cam.	.983	63	113	2	2	117	0
Myers, Rod, Mont.*	1.000	8	18	0	0	18	0
Newson, Warren, Tor.*	.985	108	180	12	3	195	0
Ojeda, Miguel, Mex.	.900	7	9	0	1	10	0
Orantes, Ramon, Mont.	.000	1	0	0	0	0	0
Ortiz, Luis, Mont.	.000	1	0	0	1	1	0
Osuna, Edgar, Tab.	.923	18	24	0	2	26	0
Otero, Ricky, Can.*	.986	106	275	8	4	287	4
Paez, Hector, Can.	1.000	6	7	2	0	9	0
Palafox, Sergio, Sal.	1.000	2	2	0	0	2	0
Payro, Edison, Cam.*	.987	53	75	3	1	79	1
Pemberton, Rudy, Monc.	.931	17	26	1	2	29	0
Perez, Francisco, Rey.*	1.000	3	2	0	0	2	0
Perez, Jose, Mont.	1.000	1	1	0	0	1	0
Peters, Anthony, Yuc.	.958	11	20	3	1	24	0
Peterson, Charles, Tor.	.667	3	2	0	1	3	0
Pinto, Placido, Cor.	.000	1	0	0	0	0	0
Polonia, Luis, Tig.*	.970	18	30	2	1	33	0
Powell, Corey, Rey.	1.000	23	38	3	0	41	1
Presichi, Christian, Sal.	.966	67	78	6	3	87	0
Pulliam, Harvey, Tab.	1.000	9	14	1	0	15	0
Quintero, Christian Alan, Mex.	.976	68	79	3	2	84	0
Quintero, Edgar, Mont.*	.981	59	100	2	2	104	0
Ramirez, Efren, Cor.	.000	1	0	0	0	0	0
Ramirez, Enrique, Mont.	1.000	2	4	0	0	4	0
Ramirez, Hector, Oax.*	1.000	1	4	0	0	4	0
Ramirez, Jesus, Oax.	.986	46	68	4	1	73	0
Resendez, Carlos, Monc.	.000	1	0	0	0	0	0
Reyes, Jesus Eleazar, Oax.	1.000	54	87	5	0	92	0
Rincon, Isaias, Mex.-Ver.	1.000	17	15	1	0	16	0
Rivera, Jesus Manuel, Tab.	1.000	27	35	1	0	36	0
Roberson, Kevin, Cor.-Tor.	.967	32	54	4	2	60	2
Robles, Oscar, Oax.	.000	1	0	0	0	0	0
Robles, Trinidad, Tig.	.933	15	14	0	1	15	0
Rodarte, Raul, Rey.-Cor.	.955	16	21	0	1	22	0
Rodriguez, Boi, Monc.	.966	79	135	8	5	148	1
Rodriguez, Fernando, Cam.	.967	32	54	4	2	60	1
Romero, Marco Antonio, Sal.-Tor...	1.000	2	1	0	0	1	0
Romero, Wilfredo, Sal.	.977	82	167	6	4	177	0
Romero, Yamil, Ver.*	1.000	3	5	1	0	6	0
Rubio, Sergio, Tor.	.000	3	0	0	0	0	0
Saenz, Ricardo, Monc.	.959	108	203	7	9	219	1
Salazar, Carlos, Yuc.	1.000	14	4	0	0	4	0
Samuels, Scott, Mont.	1.000	18	39	5	0	44	2
Sanchez, Gerardo, Lar.-Tig.	1.000	31	48	0	0	48	0
Sanchez, Jose, Lar.	1.000	2	2	0	0	2	0
Sanchez, Raul, Can.	.968	93	198	15	7	220	2
Sandoval, Octavio, Tig.	.992	70	123	6	1	130	0
Santos, Andres, Lar.	1.000	3	7	0	0	7	0
Seitzer, Brad, Ver.	.900	21	24	3	3	30	1
Sherman, Darrell, Monc.*	.993	108	261	7	2	270	2
Sievers, Carlos, Tab.*	1.000	3	3	0	0	3	0
Smith, Charles, Mont.	1.000	6	5	0	0	5	0
Smith, Demond, Tab.-Mont.	.990	86	187	2	2	191	0
Soriano, Ricardo, Cor.*	.982	87	163	4	3	170	0
Sotomayor, Gilberto, Monc.*	.992	79	121	4	1	126	1
Suarez, Luis, Tig.*	.975	87	116	1	3	120	1
Tiquet, Lazaro, Tab.	.000	3	0	0	0	0	0
Torres, Paul, Tab.-Cor.*	.966	12	26	2	1	29	0
Trapaga, Julio, Tig.	1.000	6	4	0	0	4	0
Tress, Irving, Cor.	1.000	12	11	0	0	11	0
Tyler, Brad, Oax.	.967	67	103	15	4	122	3
Valdez, Francisco, Mont.	1.000	2	4	0	0	4	0
Valdez, Ramon, Cor.-Cam.*	.982	103	252	17	5	274	3
Valencia, Carlos, Lar.	.000	2	0	0	1	1	0
Valenzuela, Irving, Monc.	1.000	3	4	0	0	4	0
Valle, Cosme, Rey.	1.000	4	1	0	0	1	0
Vazquez, Gregorio, Tab.	.979	108	225	5	5	235	1
Vazquez, Jorge Alberto, Tig.	.917	6	10	1	1	12	0
Vega, Jose, Oax.	1.000	6	3	0	0	3	0
Velez, Manuel, Lar.	1.000	1	1	0	0	1	0
Villegas, Fernando, Tor.	.969	45	61	1	2	64	0
White, Derrick, Mont.-Lar.	.983	106	225	8	4	237	2
Whiten, Mark, Ver.	.991	48	96	9	1	106	2
Yuriar, Jesus, Can.	1.000	48	77	5	0	82	1
Zamudio, Rafael, Can.	1.000	5	4	0	0	4	0
Zavala, Marco, Tig.	.000	1	0	0	0	0	0
Zazueta, Juan, Tor.	.967	73	115	3	4	122	0

OUTFIELDERS WITH TWO OR MORE TEAMS

Player, Team	Pct.	G	PO	A	E	TC	DP
Arredondo, Hernando, Cam.	.990	55	91	7	1	99	3
Arredondo, Hernando, Cor.	1.000	12	16	0	0	16	0
Avila, Carlos, Tab.*	1.000	19	21	0	0	21	0
Avila, Carlos, Lar.*	.974	19	37	0	1	38	0
Barron, Tony, Can.	1.000	16	31	1	0	32	0
Barron, Tony, Can.	.964	16	27	0	1	28	0
Brinkley, Darryl, Cam.	.979	75	180	5	4	189	0
Brinkley, Darryl, Yuc.	.984	27	59	2	1	62	0
Dattola, Kevin, Cam.*	1.000	10	27	1	0	28	1
Dattola, Kevin, Yuc.*	1.000	3	7	0	0	7	0

Player, Team	Pct.	G	PO	A	E	TC	DP
Garcia, Hector, Mont.	.982	38	55	1	1	57	0
Garcia, Hector, Tab.	.989	46	91	3	1	95	0
Garcia, Omar, Ver.	1.000	27	55	2	0	57	0
Garcia, Omar, Yuc.	.947	9	17	1	1	19	0
Lara, Jose, Ver.	.963	20	25	1	1	27	0
Lara, Jose, Cor.	1.000	4	3	1	0	4	0
Malave, Jose, Ver.	1.000	9	14	1	0	15	0
Malave, Jose, Sal.	1.000	4	5	0	0	5	0
Mendez, Roberto, Oax.*	.969	77	114	9	4	127	0
Mendez, Roberto, Mex.*	1.000	26	40	4	0	44	1
Rincon, Isaias, Mex.	1.000	15	11	0	0	11	0
Rincon, Isaias, Ver	1.000	2	4	1	0	5	0
Roberson, Kevin, Cor.	1.000	8	11	2	0	13	2
Roberson, Kevin, Tor.	.957	24	43	2	2	47	0
Rodarte, Raul, Rey.	1.000	13	17	0	0	17	0
Rodarte, Raul, Cor.	.800	3	4	0	1	5	0
Romero, Marco Antonio, Sal.	1.000	1	1	0	0	1	0
Romero, Marco Antonio, Tor.	.000	1	0	0	0	0	0
Sanchez, Gerardo, Lar.	1.000	27	46	0	0	46	0
Sanchez, Gerardo, Tig.	1.000	4	2	0	0	2	0
Smith, Demond, Tab.	.980	20	49	1	1	51	0
Smith, Demond, Mont.	.993	66	138	1	1	140	0
Torres, Paul, Tab.*	1.000	1	2	0	0	2	0
Torres, Paul, Cor.*	.963	11	24	2	1	27	0
Valdez, Ramon, Cor.*	.980	72	189	9	4	202	2
Valdez, Ramon, Cam.*	.986	31	63	8	1	72	1
White, Derrick, Mont.	.991	59	105	2	1	108	0
White, Derrick, Lar.	.977	47	120	6	3	129	2

Player, Team	Pct.	G	PO	A	E	TC	DP	PB
Saucedo, Roberto, Can.	.987	31	140	15	2	157	2	3
Soto, Saul, Mex.	1.000	2	8	0	0	8	0	0
Valdez, Emmanuel, Tig.	.992	84	436	36	4	476	3	17
Valdez, Francisco, Tab.	.996	101	492	48	2	542	6	10
Valencia, Carlos, Lar.	.000	1	0	0	0	0	0	0
Valle, Cosme, Rey.	.977	54	237	13	6	256	2	8
Vazquez, Felipe, Lar.	.988	50	216	29	3	248	3	1
Vazquez, Jorge Alberto, Tig.	1.000	7	25	2	0	27	1	1
Vega, Edgar, Pue.	.984	69	343	31	6	380	0	5
Vega, Jose, Oax.	1.000	2	1	0	0	1	0	1
Villarreal, Alejandro, Lar.	.000	1	0	0	0	0	0	0

CATCHERS WITH TWO OR MORE TEAMS

Player, Team	Pct.	G	PO	A	E	TC	DP	PB
Bustamante, Omar, Sal.	1.000	9	25	2	0	27	0	0
Bustamante, Omar, Lar.	.980	17	90	8	2	100	1	2
Cobos, Rogelio, Ver.	.954	19	57	5	3	65	0	1
Cobos, Rogelio, Oax.	.975	24	103	14	3	120	2	2
Cobos, Rogelio, Mex.	.952	5	19	1	1	21	0	0
Garza, Gerardo, Tor.	.981	41	142	15	3	160	2	4
Garza, Gerardo, Rey.	1.000	25	127	11	0	138	1	1
Garzon, Eliseo, Lar.	.990	76	436	40	5	481	3	4
Garzon, Eliseo, Sal.	.960	6	23	1	1	25	0	0
Gastelum, Carlos, Pue.	.979	20	82	10	2	94	0	0
Gastelum, Carlos, Tig.	.978	34	123	13	3	139	0	5
Ramirez, Efren, Cor.	.987	18	69	9	1	79	0	3
Ramirez, Efren, Tor.	.979	42	163	21	4	188	3	1
Rodriguez, Armando, Tig.	.993	25	138	13	1	152	0	1
Rodriguez, Armando, Pue.	.988	46	222	23	3	248	1	1

CATCHERS

Player, Team	Pct.	G	PO	A	E	TC	DP	PB
Abrego, Jesus, Can.	.978	47	195	24	5	224	0	7
Aguilera, Armando, Sal.	1.000	3	3	0	0	3	0	0
Amador, Alonso, Ver.	.000	1	0	0	0	0	0	0
Amezcua, Adan, Mont.	.996	38	254	20	1	275	3	1
Arauz, Ignacio, Monc.	1.000	3	6	0	0	6	0	0
Baez, Carlos, Tab.	1.000	5	11	2	0	13	0	0
Bustamante, Omar, Sal.-Lar.	.984	26	115	10	2	127	1	2
Cazarin, Manuel, Cam.	.990	101	542	54	6	602	6	14
Cervantes, Refugio, Sal.	.000	1	0	0	0	0	0	0
Cisneros, Ventura, Rey.*	1.000	8	11	1	0	12	0	0
Cobos, Rogelio, Ver.-Oax.-Mex.	.966	48	179	20	7	206	2	3
Contreras, Albino, Pue.	.000	2	0	0	0	0	0	0
Cruz, Marco, Yuc.	.990	43	184	15	2	201	2	6
Delgado, Alex, Tab.	1.000	3	16	3	0	19	0	0
Devarez, Cesar, Cor.	.986	79	304	41	5	350	2	15
Espinoza, Ramon, Tor.	.000	2	0	0	0	0	0	0
Estrada, Hector, Yuc.	.993	98	680	42	5	727	3	6
Garcia, Guillermo, Oax.	.993	23	129	22	1	152	2	1
Garza, Gerardo, Tor.-Rey.	.990	66	269	26	3	298	3	5
Garzon, Eliseo, Lar.-Sal.	.988	82	459	41	6	506	3	4
Gastelum, Carlos, Pue.-Tig.	.979	54	205	23	5	233	0	5
Gaotolum, Sergin, Tig.	1.000	3	11	2	0	13	0	0
Gavia, Jesus, Tor.	.973	80	356	42	11	400	0	3
Gonzalez, Fernando, Rey.	.976	79	338	33	9	380	2	2
Hurtado, Hector, Mont.	.988	56	310	17	4	331	3	3
Lopez, Fortunato, Tab.	1.000	4	4	1	0	5	0	1
Lugo, Roberto, Mont.	.972	21	62	7	2	71	0	1
Martinez, Raul, Tab.	.992	31	108	11	1	120	2	2
MEZA, Alfredo, Ver.	.997	105	598	51	2	651	4	8
Montano, Angel, Cam.	.929	5	12	1	1	14	0	0
Munoz, Adan, Monc.	.987	83	342	27	5	374	6	7
Munoz, Noe, Sal.	.995	113	723	45	4	772	4	8
Ojeda, Miguel, Mex.	.990	104	563	54	6	623	9	6
Ortega, Antonio, Cam.	.991	28	101	4	1	106	1	6
Osuna, Jose, Can.	1.000	8	22	2	0	24	0	2
Pacho, Carlos, Yuc.	.667	2	2	0	1	3	0	0
Pacho, Juan Jose, Yuc.	1.000	1	1	0	0	1	0	0
Paez, Hector, Can.	.970	51	233	26	8	267	3	12
Perez, Jorge, Pue.	.000	2	0	0	0	0	0	0
Pinto, Placido, Cor.	1.000	31	110	11	0	121	0	5
Quezada, Juan, Mex.	1.000	11	29	1	0	30	0	0
Quinonez, Ruben, Monc.	1.000	17	47	4	0	51	0	1
Ramirez, Efren, Cor.-Tor.	.981	60	232	30	5	267	3	4
Resendez, Carlos, Monc.	.991	48	197	14	2	213	5	5
Rincon, Isaias, Ver.	.000	1	0	0	0	0	0	0
Rivera, Francisco Antonio, Ver.	1.000	16	45	4	0	49	0	1
Robles, Juan, Mex.	.989	25	79	8	1	88	0	2
Rodriguez, Armando, Tig.-Pue.	.990	71	360	36	4	400	1	2
Rodriguez, Eric, Oax.	.990	25	91	12	1	104	1	4
Rojas, Homar, Oax.	.983	57	317	32	6	355	1	13
Santana, Mario, Mont.	.995	36	197	20	1	218	2	3

PITCHERS

Player, Team	Pct.	G	PO	A	E	TC	DP
Acosta, Aaron, Cor.-Cam.	.912	20	12	19	3	34	1
Acosta, Jaciel, Monc.*	.909	21	1	9	1	11	0
Aguilar, Hugo, Monc.*	1.000	21	0	12	0	12	2
Aguilar, Mario, Cam.*	.000	7	0	0	0	0	0
Aguilar, Miguel, Pue.-Tor.*	.857	40	1	6	1	7	1
Aguilera, Edgar, Yuc.	1.000	8	0	1	0	1	1
Aguirre, Gaudencio, Tab.-Mont	1.000	15	1	8	0	9	0
Alberro, Jose, Sal.*	.917	12	4	7	1	12	1
Alejo, Nigel, Sal.	1.000	3	3	4	0	7	1
Aleman, Paulo, Cor.	1.000	6	0	1	0	1	0
Almeida, Rowsell, Lar.	1.000	38	2	8	0	10	0
Alvarez, Antonio, Monc.	.714	8	1	4	2	7	1
Alvarez, Juan Jesus, Tab.*	.921	23	12	23	3	38	4
Alvarez, Octavio, Mex.	1.000	16	8	17	0	25	3
Amador, Jesus, Cam.*	1.000	6	1	3	0	4	0
Amarillas, Asdrubal, Mex.	1.000	7	1	3	0	4	1
Andujar, Luis, Mont.	1.000	13	1	3	0	4	0
Angulo, Victor, Tig.*	1.000	20	0	4	0	4	0
Aragon, Angel, Rey.	.769	18	3	7	3	13	1
Arano, Ramon, Ver.	.000	1	0	0	0	0	0
Armenta, Alejandro, Tig.*	1.000	23	6	22	0	28	6
Atondo, Sergio, Yuc.	.909	24	1	9	1	11	0
Ayala, Luis Ignacio, Sal.	1.000	33	4	5	0	9	0
Babineaux, Darrin, Lar.	.667	6	2	2	2	6	0
Baez, Sixto, Oax.	1.000	47	6	14	0	20	0
Barradas, Roberto, Sal.	1.000	15	0	2	0	2	0
Barrera, Sigfrido, Can.	.917	18	4	7	1	12	1
Barrios, Manuel, Oax.	.955	48	5	16	1	22	1
Beltran, Alonso, Tig.	.963	22	11	15	1	27	2
Bencomo, Juan Carlos, Ver.	1.000	5	1	2	0	3	0
Bernal, Manuel, Mex.	1.000	22	13	20	0	33	4
Blancas, Rigoberto, Tab.*	1.000	23	4	13	0	17	1
Bravo, Armando, Oax.	.000	3	0	0	0	0	0
Burrows, Terry, Sal.	1.000	10	1	8	0	9	0
Cabrales, Gabriel, Pue.	1.000	20	2	9	0	11	0
Camara, Pedro, Cam.-Can.-Yuc.*	1.000	21	0	3	0	3	0
Campillo, Jorge, Tig.	1.000	30	6	6	0	12	0
CAMPOS, Francisco, Cam.	1.000	23	20	21	0	41	0
Cantu, Jacobo, Tab.	1.000	24	4	3	0	7	1
Carrasco, Alejandro, Mex.-Ver.	.947	35	5	13	1	19	1
Castaneda, Aurelio, Pue.-Tor.	1.000	15	2	1	0	3	1
Castillo, Felipe, Cor.	1.000	5	0	1	0	1	0
Castro, Carlos, Tor.-Sal.	1.000	4	0	1	0	1	0
Cazares, Rosario, Sal.	1.000	44	4	13	0	17	1
Cazares, Tomas, Monc.*	.875	25	2	5	1	8	0
Cecena, Jose Isabel, Monc.	.889	36	1	7	1	9	4
Chavarria, Hector, Yuc.	1.000	16	1	7	0	8	0
Chavez, Carlos, Yuc.	.875	58	3	11	2	16	1
Cohuo, Enrique, Yuc.-Can.	1.000	19	4	4	0	8	0
Conde, Argenis, Rey.	1.000	11	3	11	0	14	0

CLASS AAA Mexican League

Player, Team	Pct.	G	PO	A	E	TC	DP
Cortes, Martin Jonathan, Cor.*	1.000	18	0	5	0	5	0
Crespo, Jorge, Oax.	.000	1	0	0	0	0	0
Cruz, Javier, Mex.	1.000	43	2	6	0	8	2
Cruz, Juan Diego, Tab.*	1.000	10	0	1	0	1	0
Cruz, Luis Manuel, Pue.	1.000	30	3	12	0	15	1
Cuervo, Bernardo, Yuc.	.968	23	9	21	1	31	2
Daniels, John, Tor.	1.000	6	0	2	0	2	0
Davis, Ray, Ver.	1.000	9	0	2	0	2	0
Delahoya, Javier, Sal.	1.000	18	4	11	0	15	4
De Leon, Francisco, Can.	.000	7	0	0	0	0	0
Delfin, Adolfo, Lar.	1.000	47	2	18	0	20	1
De Los Santos, Mariano, Monc.	1.000	8	0	2	0	2	0
Diaz, Marco Antonio, Sal.	1.000	41	7	6	0	13	1
Diaz, Rafael, Mont.	.800	13	3	5	2	10	0
Dishman, Glenn, Mex.*	1.000	9	2	3	0	5	0
Dominguez, Carlos, Sal.*	.900	21	5	4	1	10	0
Dominguez, David, Mex.-Oax.	1.000	16	6	5	0	11	1
Drahman, Brian, Lar.	.935	29	5	24	2	31	0
Duarte, Miguel, Sal.	.833	22	2	3	1	6	0
Duran, Roberto, Tig.*	.750	7	1	2	1	4	0
Elguezabal, Octavio, Cam.*	.000	1	0	0	0	0	0
Elizalde, Carlos, Oax.	1.000	29	3	7	0	10	0
Elvira, Abraham, Cor.*	.970	22	5	27	1	33	3
Enriquez, Martin, Rey.	.889	30	3	5	1	9	1
Espejo, Humberto, Can.*	.900	34	3	6	1	10	0
Esquer, Mercedes, Rey.*	1.000	23	4	16	0	20	0
Federico, Gustavo, Mont.-Sal.	1.000	24	1	12	0	13	3
Felix, Jesus Arturo, Can.	1.000	13	0	5	0	5	0
Felix, Martin, Mex.*	.000	4	0	0	0	0	0
Felix, Miguel, Oax.*	.800	20	2	2	1	5	1
Fentanes, Ernesto, Ver.	1.000	5	0	1	0	1	0
Ferrer, Jesus, Can.*	.800	31	2	10	3	15	0
Flores, Ignacio, Yuc.	.905	48	5	14	2	21	1
Flores, Jorge Armando, Tor.*	.929	24	8	5	1	14	0
Flores, Pedro, Tor.	.889	25	2	6	1	9	1
Flynt, Will, Sal.*	1.000	5	1	2	0	3	0
Fontes, Agustin, Tab.	1.000	3	1	0	0	1	0
Fregoso, Raul, Cam.-Cor.	1.000	17	3	1	0	4	0
Galvez, Randy, Mex.	1.000	8	5	9	0	14	0
Garcia, Adolfo, Cam.	1.000	26	2	6	0	8	0
Garcia, Alfredo, Mex.	1.000	26	11	20	0	31	0
Garcia, Gerardo, Tig.	.952	27	21	19	2	42	2
Garcia, Jose, Tig.-Pue.	1.000	44	4	9	0	13	1
Garcia, Jose Luis, Pue.*	1.000	38	1	11	0	12	1
Garcia, Mike, Mex.	.000	12	0	0	0	0	0
Garcia, Ramon, Mont.-Pue.	.857	29	1	5	1	7	0
Garduno, Daniel, Lar.	1.000	16	3	5	0	8	1
Garibay, Roberto, Rey.	1.000	30	1	6	0	7	1
Garibay, Salvador, Lar.	1.000	48	3	8	0	11	2
Garza, Conrado, Lar.*	1.000	12	0	1	0	1	0
Gomez, Alejandro, Cor.	1.000	30	4	9	0	13	0
Gomez, Martin, Cor.	.875	22	6	22	4	32	2
Gonzalez, Arturo, Mont.	.952	22	1	19	1	21	0
Gonzalez, Erubiel, Ver.	.885	47	10	13	3	26	0
Grajales, Norberto, Tor.	1.000	1	0	1	0	1	0
Guerra, Pascual, Tab.	1.000	31	6	5	0	11	0
Gutierrez, Jorge, Tor.	1.000	31	6	23	0	29	2
Gutierrez, Pablo, Cor.	.963	32	6	20	1	27	2
Harris, Reggie, Ver.	1.000	19	1	0	0	1	0
Hartmann, Pete, Oax.*	1.000	3	4	4	0	8	1
Henry, Dwayne, Rey.	1.000	13	0	3	0	3	0
Henthorne, Kevin, Tig.	.968	21	10	20	1	31	3
Heredia, Hector, Tor.	1.000	11	7	16	0	23	2
Hernandez, Esteban, Oax.	1.000	5	3	2	0	5	0
Hernandez, Manuel, Monc.*	.952	39	5	15	1	21	2
Hernandez, Omar, Pue.	1.000	3	0	1	0	1	0
Hernandez, Santos, Tig.	1.000	53	7	11	0	18	1
Herrera, Calixto, Ver.	1.000	14	0	2	0	2	0
Herrera, Enrique, Tor.	1.000	38	4	12	0	16	0
Hidalgo, Romeo, Rey.-Oax.	.800	8	0	0	0	0	0
Huerta, Edgar, Tig.-Pue.*	1.000	20	1	3	0	4	0
Huerta, Francisco, Ver.-Cor.	.885	12	0	0	0	0	0
Huerta, Luis, Lar.	1.000	23	1	13	0	14	2
Huisman, Rick, Mont.	1.000	11	0	4	0	4	0
Huntsman, Scott, Pue.	.000	2	0	0	0	0	0
Izabal, Luis, Ver.	.750	8	0	3	1	4	0
Jimenez, German, Can.*	1.000	6	0	4	0	4	0
Jimenez, Isaac, Tab.*	.800	8	4	4	2	10	0
Jimenez, Jose DeJesus, Oax.*	1.000	14	2	6	0	8	0
Jimenez, Julio Cesar, Sal.-Tor.*	.857	28	2	4	1	7	1
Kammar, Emil, Monc.	.947	18	6	12	1	19	1
Kelley, Richard, Pue.*	.940	25	5	42	3	50	0
Keppen, Jeffrey, Lar.	.846	22	5	17	4	26	2
Lara, Jorge, Sal.	1.000	16	1	5	0	6	2
Larranaga, Miguel, Tab.	.000	1	0	0	0	0	0
Leal, Gerardo, Monc.	.500	11	0	1	1	2	0
Leon, Cupertino, Oax.	.974	30	6	31	1	38	2
Leon, Juan, Tab.	.875	36	1	6	1	8	0
Leyva, Edgar, Mont.	1.000	22	8	18	0	26	2
Lezama, Rafael, Tor.*	1.000	5	0	1	0	1	0
Loaiza, Sabino, Cam.	.971	18	14	19	1	34	2
Lomeli, Israel, Oax.	.889	23	5	3	1	9	0
Lomon, Kevin, Tor.	.000	4	0	0	0	0	0
Lopez, Emigdio, Tor.	1.000	24	12	18	0	30	1
Lopez, Gilberto, Ver.	1.000	22	1	4	0	5	1
Lopez, Jesus, Ver.	1.000	31	4	5	0	9	1
Lopez, Jose, Rey.	.875	70	10	11	3	24	0
Lopez, Mariano, Oax.	.929	27	3	10	1	14	1
Lopez, Miguel Angel, Tig.	1.000	30	5	4	0	9	1
Loya, Rigoberto, Mont.	.947	29	9	9	1	19	0
Luevano, Juan, Cam.	.857	31	1	5	1	7	0
Lugo, Aaron, Mont.*	1.000	7	0	2	0	2	0
Macias, Luis, Monc.	1.000	27	0	5	0	5	0
Madero, Francisco, Can.	.913	20	8	13	2	23	0
Magee, Danny, Monc.-Cam.*	.923	15	1	11	1	13	1
Manrique, Alberto, Rey.	.933	24	9	19	2	30	0
Manzanillo, Ravelo, Yuc.*	.929	24	8	31	3	42	1
Manzano, Adrian, Tig.	1.000	28	2	5	0	7	2
Marquez, Isidro, Cam.	.955	48	8	13	1	22	2
Martinez, Cesar, Can.*	1.000	20	0	4	0	4	0
Martinez, Jesus, Ver.*	1.000	3	2	2	0	4	1
Martinez, Jesus Jose, Cor.	1.000	12	2	6	0	8	1
Martinez, Juan, Can.	.000	3	0	0	0	0	0
Martinez, Pedro, Cam.*	1.000	14	4	12	0	16	1
Mathews, Delmer, Mont.*	.000	2	0	0	0	0	0
Mattson, Craig, Rey.	1.000	18	1	5	0	6	1
Mattson, Rob, Tab.	.800	26	2	6	2	10	1
Medina, Alonso, Mont.	.000	3	0	0	0	0	0
Medina, Osvaldo, Pue.	.800	6	0	4	1	5	0
Melendez, Nestor, Rey.*	.882	47	0	15	2	17	1
Mendoza, Omar, Pue.	1.000	4	0	1	0	1	1
Mere, Fernando, Can.	1.000	34	8	8	0	16	0
Meza, Leobardo, Ver.	.969	21	9	22	1	32	2
Miranda, Angel, Mex.-Oax.*	1.000	22	5	9	0	14	1
Molina, Primitivo, Tor.	1.000	10	0	1	0	1	1
Montemayor, Humberto, Mont.	.933	23	4	10	1	15	0
Mora, Eleazar, Ver.*	.914	24	15	38	5	58	3
Morales, Luis, Ver.*	.950	21	7	12	1	20	0
Moreno, Angel, Tor.*	.897	26	7	28	4	39	0
Moreno, Claudio, Mex.	.882	61	3	12	2	17	2
Moreno, Edgar, Oax.	1.000	23	0	1	0	1	0
Munoz, Leonardo, Can.*	.900	28	1	8	1	10	0
Munoz, Miguel, Can.	1.000	22	5	20	0	25	1
Murillo, Felipe, Monc.	1.000	37	0	2	0	2	0
Navarro, Hector, Sal.	.667	5	1	1	1	3	0
Navarro, Joel, Mex.-Oax.	1.000	21	14	10	0	24	3
Navarro, Jose, Tig.-Pue.	1.000	24	6	16	0	22	1
Navarro, Luis, Yuc.	1.000	24	0	5	0	5	0
Neri, Braulio, Sal.*	.667	49	2	2	2	6	0
Neri, Eduardo, Oax.*	1.000	70	1	8	0	9	0
Newman, Eric, Monc.	1.000	13	1	0	0	1	0
Nieblas, Mauro, Mont.*	1.000	51	0	6	0	6	0
Nieblas, Omar, Tab.*	1.000	19	1	6	0	7	0
Nunez, Javier, Cor.	1.000	33	3	9	0	12	2
Nunez, Jose, Lar.	1.000	14	8	6	0	14	0
Nunez, Jose Juan, Oax.	1.000	17	1	9	0	10	0
Olague, Jesus, Pue.	.968	22	13	17	1	31	3
Orea, Flavio, Cor.	1.000	38	3	4	0	7	0
Ortega, Pablo, Tig.	1.000	26	12	20	0	32	1
Ortega, Roberto, Pue.*	1.000	24	2	12	0	14	1
Ortega, Wilbert, Yuc.*	1.000	24	0	2	0	2	0
Osuna, Adrian, Oax.	.000	5	0	0	0	0	0
Osuna, Ricardo, Oax.	1.000	21	4	17	0	21	0
Palacios, Vicente, Sal.	1.000	3	1	0	0	1	0
Palafox, Manuel, Monc.	.967	23	5	24	1	30	3
Parra, Jose, Mex.-Oax.	.714	57	2	3	2	7	1
Parra, Julio Cesar, Lar.-Mont.	.857	63	3	9	2	14	0
Patrick, Bronswell, Mex.	1.000	23	17	18	0	35	4
Pena, Joel, Ver.*	.889	29	7	17	3	27	1
Pena, Juan Pablo, Tor.	.000	5	0	0	0	0	0
Perez, Dario, Oax.	.929	16	3	10	1	14	0
Perez, Edgar, Cor.	.882	18	7	8	2	17	1
Perez, Jose, Monc.	.000	1	0	0	0	0	0
Perez, Juan Rafael, Lar.	1.000	7	0	2	0	2	1
Perez, Leonardo, Cor.	.933	24	4	24	2	30	2
Perez, Sergio, Mont.	1.000	33	2	4	0	6	0

Player, Team	Pct.	G	PO	A	E	TC	DP
Perez, Yorkis, Mex.*	1.000	57	0	7	0	7	1
Pesqueira, Omar, Yuc.	1.000	31	4	8	0	12	1
Pimentel, Roberto, Yuc.*	1.000	29	6	25	0	31	1
Pina, Rafael, Oax.	1.000	4	1	7	0	8	0
Pineda, Isauro, Mont.	1.000	39	9	12	0	21	1
Pujals, Denis, Tig.	.833	16	1	4	1	6	0
Pulido, Raymundo, Cam.	1.000	19	3	2	0	5	0
Purata, Julio, Rey.*	1.000	32	3	12	0	15	1
Quimbar, Juan Antonio, Lar.*	1.000	13	0	2	0	2	0
Quinonez, Enrique, Rey.	1.000	25	8	21	0	29	1
Quintanilla, Juan Enrique, Lar.	1.000	45	5	10	0	15	4
Quiroz, Aaron, Sal.	1.000	6	2	5	0	7	0
Ramirez, Carlos, Can.	.667	8	2	0	1	3	0
Ramirez, Emilio, Ver.*	1.000	15	1	2	0	3	0
Ramirez, Hector, Oax.*	1.000	11	0	1	0	1	0
Ramirez, Jose, Monc.	1.000	6	0	1	0	1	0
Ramirez, Roberto, Mex.*	.955	16	7	14	1	22	2
Ramon, Jose, Tab.	.947	43	3	15	1	19	1
Ramos, Edgar, Oax.	.935	17	8	21	2	31	0
Renovato, Nestor, Mont.	1.000	25	3	4	0	7	3
Reyes, Nathanael, Sal.*	.923	29	4	8	1	13	0
Reynoso, Ignacio, Tab.	.944	33	0	17	1	18	1
Rios, Alejandro, Sal.	1.000	47	5	20	0	25	3
Rios, Daniel, Tor.	.947	26	16	38	3	57	5
Rios, Jesus, Yuc.	.933	21	4	10	1	15	1
Rivas, Jesus, Tig.*	1.000	47	1	8	0	9	1
Rivera, Francisco Javier, Ver.	.000	1	0	0	0	0	0
Rivera, Lino, Monc.	.963	22	9	17	1	27	1
Rivera, Oscar, Ver.	.952	16	4	16	1	21	0
Rivera, Oscar, Yuc.*	1.000	21	1	4	0	5	0
Rivera, Paul, Tab.*	.889	52	3	5	1	9	0
Robles, Jorge, Lar.	.000	3	0	0	0	0	0
Rodriguez, Eric, Oax.	.000	1	0	0	0	0	0
Rodriguez, Manuel, Cor.-Cam.	.900	22	1	8	1	10	0
Rodriguez, Raul, Rey.*	1.000	23	3	15	0	18	1
Rodriguez, Rosario, Tor.*	1.000	13	1	0	0	1	0
Rodriguez, Salvador, Yuc.	1.000	15	0	4	0	4	0
Romano, Mike, Sal.	.963	21	8	18	1	27	0
Romero, Alejandro, Mono.	.923	23	7	17	2	26	1
Romero, Cesar, Lar.	1.000	15	2	2	0	4	0
Romero, Juan Jose, Cor.*	.889	37	2	6	1	9	1
Romo, Eduardo, Lar.	1.000	20	3	11	0	14	2
Rossiter, Mike, Tab.	1.000	16	0	2	0	2	0
Rubio, Miguel, Mont.	1.000	55	1	6	0	7	0
Ruiz, Cecilio, Tab.*	.950	19	6	13	1	20	0
Ruiz, Juan, Tor.	1.000	5	1	0	0	1	0
Ruiz, Omar, Tab.	.000	3	0	0	0	0	0
Sak, James, Cam.	.000	2	0	0	0	0	0
Saldana, Jose, Pue.	.952	19	7	13	1	21	0
Salgado, Eduardo, Ver.	1.000	23	9	17	0	26	4
Sanchez, Alejandro, Can.	1.000	53	3	16	0	19	3
Sanchez, Claudio, Oax.-Tor.	1.000	17	1	3	0	4	0
Sanchez, Efrain, Cam.	1.000	31	5	18	0	23	4
Canohoz, Hector, Pue.-Cam	1.000	6	0	4	0	4	0
Sandoval, Ricardo, Tor.*	.000	7	0	0	0	0	0
Sinohui, David, Cam	1.000	54	10	13	0	23	4
Solarto, Jose, Can.	1.000	40	4	17	0	21	1
Sombra, Francisco, Cor.-Ver.*	1.000	18	0	1	0	1	0
Soto, Cruz Antonio, Mont.	1.000	31	2	10	0	12	0
Soto, Daniel, Sal.	1.000	2	0	1	0	1	0
Soto, Fernando, Can.	1.000	4	0	1	0	1	0
Sulu, Mario, Cam.-Can.	.750	21	3	6	3	12	0
Tejeda, Felix, Cam.*	1.000	28	0	3	0	3	1
Theodile, Robert, Sal.	1.000	18	7	12	0	19	1
Tijerina, Carlos, Rey.	1.000	3	2	1	0	3	1
Torres, Jorge, Cam.*	1.000	14	1	1	0	2	0
Trevino, Jesus, Mex.*	.000	1	0	0	0	0	0
Trujillo, Jorge, Ver.	.500	2	1	0	1	2	0
Uribe, Juan, Tor.	.857	24	1	5	1	7	1
Uscanga, Alejandro, Ver.*	.000	7	0	0	0	0	0
Valdez, Armando, Mont.	.974	26	12	26	1	39	1
Valdez, Carlos, Can.	1.000	7	5	7	0	12	0
Valenzuela, Jesus P., Oax.	.000	1	0	0	0	0	0
Valenzuela, Jose, Tig.	.667	24	0	2	1	3	0
Valenzuela, Saul, Cor.-Can.	.867	25	4	9	2	15	0
Valerio, Julio, Monc.*	1.000	10	1	1	0	2	0
Vargas, Joel, Tab.	1.000	24	5	28	0	33	2
Vazquez, Adrian, Cam.	.976	23	18	23	1	42	3
Vega, Mario Alberto, Cor.	1.000	3	0	2	0	2	0
Vega, Obed, Can.	.952	21	5	15	1	21	0
Velazquez, Israel, Pue.	1.000	27	2	14	0	16	0
Verdugo, Hugo, Can.	1.000	10	3	7	0	10	2
Verdugo, Orlando, Tor.	.905	51	9	10	2	21	1

Player, Team	Pct.	G	PO	A	E	TC	DP
Verdugo, Oswaldo, Yuc.	1.000	21	0	4	0	4	0
Villalobos, Noe, Can.	1.000	19	2	7	0	9	0
Villaluna, Juan, Mont.*	1.000	25	0	3	0	3	0
Villarreal, Antonio, Tab.	.800	13	1	3	1	5	0
Villarreal, Salvador, Rey.	1.000	13	0	3	0	3	0
Villavicencio, Ismael, Tig.	.000	1	0	0	0	0	0
Villegas, Francisco, Can.	1.000	16	2	2	0	4	0
Villegas, Jose, Pue.	1.000	41	1	8	0	9	1
Wagner, Matt, Tig.-Pue.	1.000	14	0	3	0	3	0
Wallace, Kent, Ver.	1.000	19	1	0	0	1	0
Ward, Chad, Cam.*	1.000	4	0	3	0	3	0
Warren, Brian, Mont.	1.000	16	1	4	0	5	0
Weaver, Eric, Pue.	1.000	13	2	2	0	4	0
Yepiz, Heriberto, Yuc.	.000	6	0	0	0	0	0
Zambrano, Baudel, Rey.	1.000	31	3	18	0	21	2
Zamudio, Jeovani, Rey.	1.000	11	2	0	0	2	0
Zavala, Marco, Tig.	1.000	54	0	4	0	4	1

PITCHERS WITH TWO OR MORE TEAMS

Player, Team	Pct.	G	PO	A	E	TC	DP
Acosta, Aaron, Cor.	1.000	3	1	3	0	4	0
Acosta, Aaron, Cam.	.900	17	11	16	3	30	1
Aguilar, Miguel, Pue.*	1.000	12	0	1	0	1	0
Aguilar, Miguel, Tor.*	.833	28	1	4	1	6	1
Aguilera, Edgar, Yuc.	1.000	7	0	1	0	1	1
Aguilera, Edgar, Can.	.000	1	0	0	0	0	0
Aguirre, Gaudencio, Tab.	1.000	9	1	6	0	7	0
Aguirre, Gaudencio, Mont.	1.000	6	0	2	0	2	0
Camara, Pedro, Cam.*	1.000	2	0	2	0	2	0
Camara, Pedro, Can.*	.000	8	0	0	0	0	0
Camara, Pedro, Yuc.*	1.000	11	0	1	0	1	0
Carrasco, Alejandro, Mex.	.900	10	1	8	1	10	1
Carrasco, Alejandro, Ver.	1.000	25	4	5	0	9	0
Castaneda, Aurelio, Pue.	1.000	8	0	1	0	1	1
Castaneda, Aurelio, Tor.	1.000	7	2	0	0	2	0
Castro, Carlos, Tor.	.000	2	0	0	0	0	0
Castro, Carlos, Sal.	1.000	2	0	1	0	1	0
Cohuo, Enrique, Yuc.	1.000	14	2	4	0	6	0
Cohuo, Enrique, Can.	1.000	5	2	0	0	2	0
Dominguez, David, Mex.	1.000	9	4	1	0	5	1
Dominguez, David, Oax.	1.000	7	2	4	0	6	0
Federico, Gustavo, Mont.	1.000	10	1	9	0	10	3
Federico, Gustavo, Sal.	1.000	14	0	3	0	3	0
Fregoso, Raul, Cam.	1.000	12	2	1	0	3	0
Fregoso, Raul, Cor.	1.000	5	1	0	0	1	0
Garcia, Jose, Tig.	1.000	38	3	8	0	11	1
Garcia, Jose, Pue.	1.000	6	1	1	0	2	0
Garcia, Ramon, Mont.	.000	8	0	0	0	0	0
Garcia, Ramon, Pue.	.857	21	1	5	1	7	0
Hidalgo, Romeo, Rey.	.000	2	0	0	0	0	0
Hidalgo, Romeo, Oax.	.000	6	0	0	0	0	0
Huerta, Edgar, Tig.*	.000	1	0	0	0	0	0
Huerta, Edgar, Pue.*	1.000	19	1	3	0	4	0
Huerta, Francisco, Ver.	.000	1	0	0	0	0	0
Huerta, Francisco, Cor.	.000	11	0	0	0	0	0
Jimenez, Julio Cesar, Sal.*	.500	5	0	1	1	2	0
Jimenez, Julio Cesar, Tor.*	1.000	23	2	3	0	5	1
Magee, Danny, Monc.*	.857	10	0	6	1	7	0
Magee, Danny, Cam.*	1.000	5	1	5	0	6	1
Miranda, Angel, Mex.*	.000	12	0	0	0	0	0
Miranda, Angel, Oax.*	1.000	10	5	9	0	14	1
Navarro, Joel, Mex.	1.000	15	12	7	0	19	2
Navarro, Joel, Can.	1.000	6	2	3	0	5	1
Navarro, Jose, Tig.	1.000	8	0	4	0	4	0
Navarro, Jose, Pue.	1.000	16	6	12	0	18	1
Parra, Jose, Mex.	.750	45	1	2	1	4	0
Parra, Jose, Oax.	.667	12	1	1	1	3	0
Parra, Julio Cesar, Lar.	.889	43	1	7	1	9	0
Parra, Julio Cesar, Mont.	.800	20	2	2	1	5	0
Rodriguez, Manuel, Cor.	.875	16	1	6	1	8	0
Rodriguez, Manuel, Cam.	1.000	6	0	2	0	2	0
Sanchez, Claudio, Oax.	.000	2	0	0	0	0	0
Sanchez, Claudio, Tor.	1.000	15	1	3	0	4	0
Sanchez, Hector, Pue.	1.000	4	0	2	0	2	0
Sanchez, Hector, Cam.	1.000	2	0	0	0	0	0
Sombra, Francisco, Cor.*	.000	12	0	0	0	0	0
Sombra, Francisco, Ver.*	1.000	6	0	1	0	1	0
Sulu, Mario, Cam.	.667	11	1	1	1	3	0
Sulu, Mario, Can.	.778	10	2	5	2	9	0
Valenzuela, Saul, Cor.	.818	11	2	7	2	11	0
Valenzuela, Saul, Cam.	1.000	14	2	2	0	4	0
Wagner, Matt, Tig.	1.000	7	0	2	0	2	0
Wagner, Matt, Pue.	1.000	7	0	1	0	1	0

CLASS AAA Mexican League

Year	Team	Pct.	Year	Team	Pct.	Year	Team	Pct.
1955—	Mexico City Tigers*	.539	1975—	Tampico∞	.541	1989—	Nuevo Laredo♦	.621
1956—	Mexico City Reds	.692		Cordoba	.649		Yucatan	.539
1957—	Yucatan	.567	1976—	Mexico City Reds∞	.543	1990—	Nuevo Laredo	.618
	Mex. C. Reds (2nd)†	.550		Union Laguna	.547		Leon♦	.565
1958—	Nuevo Laredo	.625	1977—	Mexico City Reds	.623	1991—	Monterrey♦	.683
1959—	Poza Rica	.575		Nuevo Laredo∞	.507		Mexico City Reds	.627
	Mex. C. Reds (3rd)†	.507	1978—	Aguascalientes∞	.589	1992—	Mexico City Tigers♦	.594
1960—	Mexico City Tigers	.538		Union Laguna	.523		Nuevo Laredo	.538
1961—	Veracruz	.575	1979—	Saltillo	.704	1993—	Nuevo Laredo	.589
1962—	Monterrey	.592		Puebla∞	.628		Tabasco♦	.528
1963—	Puebla	.606	1980—	No champion▲		1994—	Mexico City Red Devils♦	.646
1964—	Mexico City Reds	.586	1981—	Mexico City Reds	.615		Monterrey Sultans	.608
1965—	Mexico City Tigers	.590		Reynosa	.492	1995—	Mexico City Red Devils	.708
1966—	Mexico City Tigers‡	.614	1982—	Ciudad Juarez∞	.570		Monterrey Sultans♦	.570
	Mexico City Reds	.571		Mexico City Tigers	.508	1996—	Monterrey Sultans	.713
1967—	Jalisco	.607	1983—	Campeche♦	.614		Mexico City Reds♦	.619
1968—	Mexico City Reds	.586		Ciudad Juarez	.535	1997—	Mexico City Red Devils	.686
1969—	Reynosa	.591	1984—	Yucatan♦	.560		Mexico City Tigers■	.658
1970—	Aguila§	.580		Ciudad Juarez	.509	1998—	Monterrey	.672
	Mexico City Reds	.607	1985—	Mexico City Reds♦	.606		Oaxaca■	.576
1971—	Jalisco§	.558		Nuevo Laredo	.5275	1999—	Mexico City Tigers	.664
	Saltillo	.593	1986—	Puebla♦	.682		Mexico City Reds■	.632
1972—	Saltillo	.636		Monclova	.598	2000—	Saltillo	.647
	Cordoba§	.541	1987—	Mexico City Reds♦	.605		Mexico City Reds	.627
1973—	Saltillo	.656		Monterrey	.536	2001—	Mexico City Tigers■	.632
	Mexico City Reds∞	.590	1988—	Mexico City Reds♦	.646		Mexico City Reds	.575
1974—	Jalisco	.627		Nuevo Laredo	.602			
	Mexico City Reds∞	.551						

*Defeated Nuevo Laredo, two games to none, in playoff for pennant. †Won four-team playoff. ‡Won split-season playoff. §League divided into Northern, Southern divisions; won two-team playoff. ∞League divided into Northern, Southern zones; sub-divided into Eastern, Western divisions, won eight-team playoff. ▲ A players strike on July 1 forced the cancellation of the regular season and playoff schedule. ♦ League divided into Northern, Southern zones; four clubs from each zone qualified for postseason play. Won final series for league championship. ■ League divided into Northern, Central and Southern zones; played split season, with top eight teams qualifying for playoffs. Won final series for league championship.

CLASS AAA *Mexican League*

PACIFIC COAST LEAGUE

LEAGUE OFFICE

President
Branch Rickey

Address
1631 Mesa Ave.
Colorado Springs, CO 80906-2917

Phone
719-636-3399

TEAMS

CALGARY CANNONS
V.p, baseball operations/g.m.
John Traub
Manager
Rick Renteria
Ballpark (capacity, surface)
Burns Stadium (8,000, grass)
Affiliation
Marlins
Address
2255 Crowchild Trail N.W.
Calgary, Alberta T2M 4S7
Phone
403-284-1111

COLORADO SPRINGS SKY SOX
General manager/president
Robert Goughan
Manager
Chris Cron
Ballpark (capacity, surface)
Sky Sox Stadium (9,000, grass)
Affiliation
Rockies
Address
4385 Tutt Blvd.
Colorado Springs, CO 80922
Phone
719-597-1449

EDMONTON TRAPPERS
General manager
To be announced
Manager
John Russell
Ballpark (capacity, surface)
Telus Field (10,000; artificial infield, grass outfield)
Affiliation
Twins
Address
10233 96th Ave.
Edmonton, Alberta T5K 0A5
Phone
780-414-4450

FRESNO GRIZZLIES
General manager
Bill Gorman
Manager
Shane Turner
Ballpark (capacity, surface)
To be announced (12,500, grass)
Affiliation
Giants
Address
700 Van Ness Avenue
Fresno, CA 93721

Phone
559-442-1994

IOWA CUBS
General manager
Sam Bernabe
Manager
Bruce Kimm
Ballpark (capacity, surface)
Sec Taylor Stadium (10,500, grass)
Affiliation
Cubs
Address
350 SW First Street
Des Moines, IA 50309
Phone
515-243-6111

LAS VEGAS STARS
General manager/president
Don Logan
Manager
Brad Mills
Ballpark (capacity, surface)
Cashman Field (9,370, grass)
Affiliation
Dodgers
Address
850 Las Vegas Blvd. N
Las Vegas, NV 89101
Phone
702-386-7200

MEMPHIS REDBIRDS
General manager
Dan Maddon
Manager
Gaylen Pitts
Ballpark (capacity, surface)
Autozone Park (14,200; grass)
Affiliation
Cardinals
Address
175 Toyota Plaza, Suite 300
Memphis, TN 38103
Phone
901-721-6050

NASHVILLE SOUNDS
Chief operating officer
Glenn Yaeger
Manager
Marty Brown
Ballpark (capacity, surface)
Greer Stadium (11,500, grass)
Affiliation
Pirates
Address
534 Chestnut Street
Nashville, TN 37203

Phone
615-242-4371

NEW ORLEANS ZEPHYRS
Vice president/general manager
Dan Rajkowski
Manager
Chris Maloney
Ballpark (capacity, surface)
Zephyr Field (11,000, grass)
Affiliation
Astros
Address
6000 Airline Highway
Metairie, LA 70003
Phone
504-734-5155

OKLAHOMA REDHAWKS
President/general manager
Tim O'Toole
Manager
Bobby Jones
Ballpark (capacity, surface)
Southwestern Bell Bricktown Ball Park (13,066, grass)
Affiliation
Rangers
Address
2 South Mickey Mantle Drive
Oklahoma City, OK 73104
Phone
405-218-1000

OMAHA ROYALS
Vice president/general manager
Doug Stewart
Manager
Bucky Dent
Ballpark (capacity, surface)
Omaha's Rosenblatt Stadium (23,000, grass)
Affiliation
Royals
Address
1202 Bert Murphy Drive
Omaha, NE 68107
Phone
402-734-2550

PORTLAND BEAVERS
Interim general manager
Jennifer Gartz
Manager
Rick Sweet
Ballpark (capacity, surface)
PGE Park (20,000, artificial)
Affiliation
Padres
Address
920 SW Sixth Avenue, Mezzanine Level
Portland Ore. 97204

Phone
503-553-5400

SACRAMENTO RIVER CATS
General Manager
Gary Arthur
Manager
Bob Geren
Ballpark (capacity, surface)
Raley Field (10,500, grass)
Affiliation
Athletics
Address
400 Ballpark Drive
West Sacramento, CA 95691
Phone
916-376-4700

SALT LAKE STINGERS
Vice president/ asst. general manager
Dorsena Picknell

Manager
Mike Brumley
Ballpark (capacity, surface)
Franklin-Covey Field (15,500, grass)
Affiliation
Angels
Address
P.O. Box 4108
Salt Lake City, UT 84110
Phone
801-485-3800

TACOMA RAINIERS
General manager
Dave Lewis
Manager
Dan Rohn
Ballpark (capacity, surface)
Cheney Stadium (10,106, grass)
Affiliation
Mariners

Address
P.O. Box 11087
Tacoma, WA 98411
Phone
253-752-7707

TUCSON SIDEWINDERS
General manager
Rick Parr
Manager
Al Pedrique
Ballpark (capacity, surface)
Tucson Electric Park (11,000, grass)
Affiliation
Diamondbacks
Address
P.O. Box 27045
Tucson, AZ 85716
Phone
520-434-1021

2001 FINAL STANDINGS

EAST DIVISION

Team	W	L	T	Pct.	GB
New Orleans (Astros)	82	57	0	.590	...
Oklahoma (Rangers)	74	69	0	.517	10.0
Nashville (Pirates)	64	77	0	.454	19.0
Memphis (Cardinals)	62	81	0	.434	22.0

CENTRAL DIVISION

Team	W	L	T	Pct.	GB
Iowa (Cubs)	83	60	0	.580	...
Salt Lake (Angels)	79	64	0	.552	4.0
Omaha (Royals)	70	74	0	.486	13.5
Colorado Springs (Rockies)	62	79	0	.440	20.0

NORTH DIVISION

Team	W	L	T	Pct.	GB
Tacoma (Mariners)	85	59	0	.590	...
Calgary (Marlins)	72	71	0	.503	12.5
Portland (Padres)	71	73	0	.493	14.0
Edmonton (Twins)	60	83	0	.420	24.5

SOUTH DIVISION

Team	W	L	T	Pct.	GB
Sacramento (Athletics)	75	69	0	.521	...
Fresno (Giants)	68	71	0	.489	4.5
Las Vegas (Dodgers)	68	76	0	.472	7.0
Tucson (Diamondbacks)	65	77	0	.458	9.0

COMPOSITE

Team	Tac.	N.O.	Iowa	S.L.	Sac.	Okla.	Cal.	Port.	Fres.	Oma.	L.V.	Tuc.	Nash.	C.S.	Mem.	Edm.	W	L	T	Pct.	GB
Tacoma (Mariners)	...	2	3	3	5	7	10	9	6	4	5	7	3	4	6	11	85	59	0	.590	...
New Orleans (Astros)	6	...	4	3	5	8	4	4	3	4	4	3	13	5	10	6	82	57	0	.590	0.5
Iowa (Cubs)	5	3	...	10	4	3	5	4	6	8	4	3	7	11	5	5	83	60	0	.580	1.5
Salt Lake (Angels)	5	5	6	...	6	5	4	4	3	11	3	5	4	8	6	4	79	64	0	.552	5.5
Sacramento (Athletics)	3	3	4	2	...	2	5	3	7	6	11	9	7	3	6	4	75	69	0	.521	10.0
Oklahoma (Rangers)	1	7	5	3	6	...	5	3	4	5	4	5	8	5	8	5	74	69	0	.517	10.5
Calgary (Marlins)	6	4	3	4	3	3	...	9	2	5	5	5	4	6	3	10	72	71	0	.503	12.5
Portland (Padres)	7	4	4	4	5	5	7	...	5	5	6	3	4	4	2	6	71	73	0	.493	14.0
Fresno (Giants)	2	3	2	5	9	4	6	3	...	3	7	6	4	5	4	5	68	71	0	.489	14.5
Omaha (Royals)	4	4	8	5	2	3	3	3	5	...	4	5	3	11	5	5	70	74	0	.486	15.0
Las Vegas (Dodgers)	3	4	4	5	4	4	3	2	9	4	...	9	4	5	5	2	68	76	0	.472	17.0
Tucson (Diamondbacks)	1	5	5	3	7	3	3	5	8	3	7	...	2	5	4	4	65	77	0	.458	19.0
Nashville (Pirates)	5	3	1	3	1	8	3	4	4	5	4	6	...	3	10	4	64	77	0	.454	19.5
Colo. Springs (Rockies)	4	2	5	8	5	3	2	4	3	5	3	3	4	...	4	7	62	79	0	.440	21.5
Memphis (Cardinals)	2	6	3	2	2	8	5	6	4	3	3	4	6	3	...	5	62	81	0	.434	22.5
Edmonton (Twins)	5	2	4	4	3	6	10	2	3	6	4	4	1	3	...	...	60	83	0	.420	24.5

Major league affiliations in parentheses.

PLAYOFFS: New Orleans defeated Iowa three games to none; Tacoma defeated Sacramento three games to two. Note: Tacoma and New Orleans declared Pacific Coast League co-champions due to stoppage of play in professional baseball.

REGULAR-SEASON ATTENDANCE: Calgary, 246,991; Colorado Springs, 269,904; Edmonton, 372,244; Fresno, 292,886; Iowa, 475,342; Las Vegas, 332,742; Memphis, 887,976; Nashville, 305,385; New Orleans, 385,447; Oklahoma, 447,077; Omaha, 359,038; Portland, 439,686; Sacramento, 901,214; Salt Lake, 470,649; Tacoma, 320,329; Tucson, 244,761. Total—6,751,671. Playoffs (8 games)—40,052. Triple-A All-Star Game at Indianapolis, Ind.—15,868.

MANAGERS: Calgary, Chris Chambliss; Colorado Springs, Chris Cron; Edmonton, John Russell; Fresno, Shane Turner; Iowa, Bruce Kimm; Las Vegas, Rick Sofield; Memphis, Gaylen Pitts; Nashville, Marty Brown; New Orleans, Tony Pena; Oklahoma, Demarlo Hale; Omaha, John Mizerock; Portland, Rick Sweet; Sacramento, Bob Green; Salt Lake, Garry Templeton; Tacoma, Dan Rohn; Tucson, Tom Spencer.

ALL-STAR TEAM: 1B—Todd Betts, Tacoma; 2B—Chad Meyers, Iowa; 3B—Jose Fernandez, Salt Lake; SS—Ramon Vazquez, Tacoma; OF—Roosevelt Brown, Iowa; OF—Jason Conti, Tucson; OF—Jack Cust, Tucson; C—Ramon Castro, Calgary; DH—Phil Hiatt, Las Vegas; RHP—Dennis Stark, Tacoma; LHP—Bud Smith, Memphis; Relief pitcher—Jim Mann, New Orleans; Most Valuable Player—Phil Hiatt, Las Vegas; Rookie of the Year—Sean Burroughs, Portland; Manager of the Year—Dan Rohn, Tacoma.

CLASS AAA *Pacific Coast League*

TEAM

Team	Avg.	G	TPA	AB	R	H	TB	2B	3B	HR	RBI	SH	SF	HP	BB	IBB	SO	SB	CS	GDP	LOB	ShO	Slg.	OBP
Calgary	.292	143	5426	4887	810	1425	2343	315	21	187	758	43	33	55	408	17	1048	65	42	125	951	8	.479	.351
Colo. Springs	.290	141	5470	4908	774	1424	2225	293	35	146	734	35	50	53	424	20	1017	81	58	121	981	6	.453	.358
Salt Lake	.288	143	5540	5017	820	1444	2349	311	57	160	762	34	33	59	397	21	1016	114	55	90	960	3	.468	.345
Edmonton	.285	143	5498	4887	719	1395	2188	291	38	142	677	28	37	62	484	16	987	52	49	134	1058	8	.448	.355
Tacoma	.285	144	5474	4910	749	1399	2147	316	39	118	699	31	38	50	445	18	968	83	51	104	1015	5	.437	.348
Tucson	.277	142	5483	4910	682	1361	2058	269	37	118	630	57	38	50	428	26	968	74	49	115	1041	5	.419	.339
Fresno	.277	139	5163	4687	698	1297	2123	250	33	170	656	43	31	44	358	20	1041	86	37	93	890	8	.453	.332
Las Vegas	.276	144	5543	4932	740	1362	2277	291	36	184	684	61	34	58	458	23	1047	101	53	110	1004	3	.462	.343
Nashville	.276	141	5328	4811	669	1326	2024	244	32	130	617	52	30	55	372	22	987	85	50	89	977	8	.421	.332
Iowa	.276	143	5385	4830	698	1331	2122	302	36	139	659	57	39	64	395	19	1000	114	62	101	937	10	.439	.336
Oklahoma	.267	143	5487	4843	690	1291	2047	255	36	143	647	52	39	42	511	14	973	69	57	109	999	5	.423	.339
New Orleans	.266	139	5216	4573	683	1217	1927	256	32	130	635	57	38	87	461	15	1018	95	49	103	952	11	.421	.342
Sacramento	.266	144	5600	4892	750	1300	2128	269	20	173	695	28	49	70	561	22	1048	129	44	109	1060	2	.435	.347
Omaha	.265	144	5399	4795	687	1272	2015	243	22	152	637	41	52	71	440	10	975	95	57	116	955	11	.420	.333
Memphis	.262	143	5375	4868	643	1277	1931	254	29	114	601	34	30	59	384	20	1017	55	41	114	944	11	.397	.322
Portland	.256	144	5368	4840	623	1241	2020	255	31	154	585	43	36	52	397	17	1138	96	47	103	948	8	.417	.317

INDIVIDUAL

TOP QUALIFIERS FOR BATTING CHAMPIONSHIP

Minimum 389 plate appearances. *Lefthanded batter. †Switch-hitter.

Player, Team	Avg.	G	TPA	AB	R	H	TB	2B	3B	HR	RBI	SH	SF	HP	BB	IBB	SO	SB	CS	GDP	Slg.	OBP
Brown, Roosevelt, Iowa*	.346	88	388	364	68	126	228	34	1	22	77	0	2	8	14	1	67	3	5	8	.626	.381
Fernandez, Jose, S.L.	.338	122	522	452	99	153	282	37	1	30	114	0	3	12	55	2	91	9	7	9	.624	.421
McCracken, Quinton, Edm.†	.338	81	390	361	53	122	160	27	4	4	45	5	2	1	21	1	54	8	10	5	.468	.374
Castro, Ramon, Cal.	.336	108	433	390	81	131	245	33	0	27	90	0	4	1	38	3	74	1	1	11	.628	.393
Conti, Jason, Tuc.*	.331	92	413	362	68	120	182	23	6	9	52	3	3	12	33	1	54	2	5	2	.503	.402
Hiatt, Phil, L.V.	.330	113	495	436	107	144	315	29	5	44	99	0	2	5	52	6	109	6	4	9	.722	.406
LeCroy, Matthew, Edm.	.328	101	441	396	53	130	207	17	0	20	80	0	3	6	36	1	95	0	2	8	.523	.390
Gulan, Mike, Cal.	.324	124	533	485	78	157	271	44	2	22	92	0	5	8	35	1	145	2	6	12	.559	.375
Huskey, Butch, C.S.	.323	122	513	458	76	148	236	29	1	19	87	0	12	1	42	2	95	2	2	10	.515	.372
Burroughs, Sean, Port.*	.322	104	439	394	60	127	184	28	1	9	55	4	0	4	37	2	54	9	2	13	.467	.386
Brumbaugh, Cliff, Okla.-C.S.	.320	107	486	410	69	131	201	29	4	11	81	0	7	2	67	0	93	8	6	4	.490	.412
Melo, Juan, Fres.†	.312	100	405	375	48	117	174	22	4	9	55	1	5	5	19	1	64	0	9	8	.464	.349
Sears, Todd, Edm.	.311	118	456	408	61	127	195	25	2	13	50	1	3	3	41	2	71	2	1	16	.478	.376
Magruder, Chris, Fres.-Okla.†	.311	87	397	341	65	106	182	21	5	15	51	4	2	11	39	3	64	4	3	5	.534	.397
Erickson, Matt, Cal.*	.310	115	472	413	66	128	157	21	1	2	29	8	0	12	39	0	69	11	4	13	.380	.386

NOTE: Roosevelt Brown qualifies for the batting championship under section 10.23 of the Official Baseball Rules. He batted .346 in 388 plate appearances. By adding one at-bat to his actual total of 364, he would have an adjusted batting average of .344 and an adjusted total of 389 plate appearances, thereby making him the leading qualifier.

DEPARTMENTAL LEADERS: G—Dransfeldt, 143; AB—Dransfeldt, 551; R—Hiatt, 107; H—Gulan, 157; TB—Hiatt, 315; 2B—C. Alexander, 45; 3B—Gload, Redman, 10 each; HR—Hiatt, 44; RBI—Fernandez, 114; SH—Cintron, 20; SF—Huskey, 12; HP—C. Meyers, 26; BB—Cust, 102; IBB—Ryan, 9; SO—Cust, 160; SB—C. Meyers, 27; CS—McCracken, Hubbard, 10 each; GIDP—Craig F. Wilson, 21; Slg.—Hiatt, .722; OBP—Fernandez, .421.

ALL PLAYERS

*Lefthanded batter. †Switch-hitter.

Player, Team	Avg.	G	TPA	AB	R	H	TB	2B	3B	HR	RBI	SH	SF	HP	BB	IBB	SO	SB	CS	GDP	Slg.	OBP
Abad, Andy, Sac.*	.301	124	526	462	72	139	219	19	2	19	82	3	2	1	58	1	67	4	2	12	.474	.379
Abbott, Chuck, S.L.	.000	4	11	9	1	0	0	0	0	0	0	0	0	0	2	0	4	0	0	0	.000	.182
Abbott, Jeff, Cal.	.320	47	187	175	25	56	92	9	0	9	24	1	3	0	6	0	33	1	2	3	.526	.357
Abreu, Dennis, Iowa	.500	4	12	12	3	6	7	1	0	0	1	0	0	0	0	0	2	0	0	0	.583	.500
Ah Yat, Paul, Nash.	.000	8	1	1	0	0	0	0	0	0	0	0	0	0	0	0	1	0	0	0	.000	.000
Ahearne, Pat, Cal.	.143	28	31	28	2	4	4	0	0	0	1	2	0	0	1	0	12	0	0	1	.143	.172
Ainsworth, Kurt, Fres.	.125	27	35	32	1	4	4	0	0	0	4	2	0	0	1	0	13	0	0	0	.125	.152
Akers, Chad, Tac.	.297	86	334	316	44	94	125	16	3	3	32	1	1	3	13	0	36	6	5	7	.396	.330
Alexander, Chad, Tac.	.290	137	589	527	76	153	240	45	0	14	77	1	5	3	53	2	92	1	1	16	.455	.355
Alexander, Manny, Tac.	.282	97	366	344	46	97	151	26	2	8	51	3	3	2	14	0	55	5	9	6	.439	.311
Allen, Chad, Edm.	.364	6	27	22	4	8	13	2	0	1	1	0	0	1	4	0	1	2	0	0	.591	.481
Allen, Luke, L.V.*	.222	2	9	9	1	2	3	1	0	0	0	0	0	0	0	0	0	0	0	1	.333	.222
Alou, Felipe, Oma.	.219	11	35	32	1	7	8	1	0	0	2	0	1	1	1	0	15	1	0	0	.250	.257
Alvarez, Victor, L.V.*	.211	20	43	38	2	8	10	2	0	0	3	3	1	0	1	0	11	0	0	2	.263	.225
Alviso, Jerome, C.S.†	.241	111	294	266	30	64	79	12	0	1	18	7	3	4	14	1	43	3	1	5	.297	.286
Amezaga, Alfredo, S.L.†	.250	49	220	200	28	50	66	5	4	1	16	2	1	3	14	1	45	9	6	2	.330	.307
Anderson, Brian, Tuc.†	.500	2	4	2	1	1	1	0	0	0	0	0	0	0	1	0	0	0	0	0	.500	.500
Andra, Jeff, Fres.*	.000	9	10	7	0	0	0	0	0	0	0	2	0	0	1	0	5	0	0	0	.000	.125
Andrews, Shane, Mem.	.218	62	230	193	30	42	80	9	1	9	31	0	1	3	33	2	63	2	0	3	.415	.339
Ardoin, Danny, Edm.	.255	88	331	302	37	77	112	18	1	5	37	2	4	1	22	1	81	2	6	8	.371	.304
Arnold, Jamie, Fres.	.308	44	16	13	4	4	7	0	0	1	1	1	0	0	2	0	4	0	0	0	.538	.400
Arroyo, Bronson, Nash.	.235	11	20	17	1	4	7	1	1	0	1	2	1	0	0	0	11	0	0	0	.412	.222
Arteaga, J.D., N.O.*	.179	32	32	28	2	5	6	1	0	0	1	3	0	0	1	0	13	0	0	0	.214	.207
Ashby, Chris, Okla.	.231	33	136	121	11	28	41	7	0	2	16	0	2	1	12	2	24	0	2	4	.339	.301
Aven, Bruce, L.V.	.260	86	324	292	43	76	117	17	0	8	32	1	2	5	24	1	59	5	1	10	.401	.325
Averette, Rob, C.S.	.194	29	37	36	3	7	7	0	0	0	0	0	0	0	0	0	13	0	1	0	.194	.194
Aybar, Manny, Iowa	.083	8	13	12	0	1	1	0	0	0	0	2	1	0	0	0	5	0	0	0	.083	.083
Baez, Benito, Cal.*	.333	50	6	6	1	2	2	0	0	0	2	0	0	0	0	0	2	0	0	0	.333	.333

Player, Team	Avg.	G	TPA	AB	R	H	TB	2B	3B	HR	RBI	SH	SF	HP	BB	IBB	SO	SB	CS	GDP	Slg.	OBP
Balfe, Ryan, Mem.†	.319	67	258	232	35	74	122	20	2	8	37	0	1	2	23	0	59	1	1	8	.526	.384
Banks, Brian, Iowa-Cal.†	.280	118	438	396	72	111	220	29	4	24	67	0	3	3	36	3	108	5	4	7	.556	.342
Barajas, Rod, Tuc.	.321	45	176	162	23	52	92	13	0	9	32	1	1	3	9	2	23	3	1	2	.568	.366
Barker, Glen, N.O.†	.280	46	187	168	28	47	63	2	4	2	20	4	1	2	12	0	45	7	3	4	.375	.333
Barkett, Andy, Nash.*	.242	91	319	273	37	66	101	17	0	6	42	0	5	4	37	3	46	2	2	5	.370	.335
Barnes, John, Edm.	.293	81	351	311	42	91	140	21	2	8	42	0	2	11	27	2	28	3	2	8	.450	.368
Barnes, Larry, S.L.*	.290	100	436	404	78	117	208	21	8	18	73	0	2	1	29	1	90	6	1	6	.515	.337
Barry, Jeff, L.V.†	.290	89	353	314	49	91	151	20	2	12	42	0	3	3	33	0	66	11	5	6	.481	.360
Bartee, Kimera, S.L.-C.S.†	.249	64	276	245	37	61	104	15	2	8	42	3	2	1	25	2	57	8	1	1	.424	.319
Barthol, Blake, Tac.	.277	79	318	278	37	77	121	15	1	9	37	9	3	4	24	1	67	5	0	3	.435	.340
Bass, Jayson, Iowa*	.327	70	256	226	34	74	117	17	1	8	42	2	2	2	26	1	65	7	6	7	.518	.402
Baughman, Justin, S.L.	.302	77	317	288	52	87	121	15	5	3	32	2	2	5	20	0	54	21	6	7	.420	.356
Becker, Rich, Cal.*	.264	50	193	163	35	43	76	9	0	8	28	0	2	0	28	0	40	3	1	3	.466	.368
Belflower, Jay, Tuc.	.000	1	1	1	0	0	0	0	0	0	0	0	0	0	0	0	1	0	0	0	.000	.000
Belitz, Todd, C.S.*	.000	14	1	1	0	0	0	0	0	0	0	0	0	0	0	0	0	0	0	0	.000	.000
Bell, Derek, Nash.	.162	22	79	68	12	11	17	3	0	1	9	0	1	1	9	0	19	0	0	3	.250	.266
Bell, Mike, C.S.	.281	84	342	320	43	90	152	21	1	13	53	3	0	3	16	1	80	0	4	4	.475	.322
Bellhorn, Mark, Sac.†	.269	43	184	156	30	42	84	6	0	12	36	0	2	4	22	2	60	3	0	0	.538	.370
Beltre, Adrian, L.V.	.600	2	7	5	2	3	7	1	0	1	2	0	0	0	2	0	0	0	0	0	1.400	.714
Benes, Alan, Mem.	.185	25	29	27	2	5	6	1	0	0	0	0	2	0	0	0	7	0	0	0	.222	.185
Berblinger, Jeff, Oma.-Nash.	.222	79	316	288	39	64	101	13	3	6	24	4	0	1	23	1	58	9	5	6	.351	.282
Bergman, Sean, C.S.	.000	3	3	3	0	0	0	0	0	0	0	0	0	0	0	0	1	0	0	0	.000	.000
Berrios, Harry, Okla.	.255	61	250	231	33	59	96	8	4	7	33	0	2	3	14	0	47	3	0	7	.416	.304
Berroa, Cristian, N.O.†	.133	8	18	15	1	2	2	0	0	0	1	0	0	0	3	0	4	0	1	0	.133	.278
Betts, Todd, Tac.*	.308	135	565	506	87	156	248	40	5	14	65	1	4	3	51	4	55	3	4	11	.490	.372
Betzsold, James, Tac.	.159	48	181	157	20	25	57	4	2	8	25	0	0	3	21	0	71	0	0	3	.363	.254
Bevel, Bobby, L.V.*	.000	25	1	1	0	0	0	0	0	0	0	0	0	0	0	0	0	0	0	0	.000	.000
Bevins, Andy, Mem.	.253	43	163	146	24	37	66	8	0	7	20	0	1	4	12	1	47	0	2	2	.452	.325
Bierbrodt, Nick, Tuc.*	.125	7	17	16	2	2	2	0	0	0	0	0	0	0	1	0	6	0	0	0	.125	.176
Bieser, Steve, Mem.*	.000	7	10	8	1	0	0	0	0	0	0	0	0	1	1	0	5	0	0	1	.000	.200
Blake, Casey, Edm.	.309	94	417	375	64	116	182	24	6	10	49	2	0	6	34	0	66	14	3	11	.485	.376
Bogar, Tim, L.V.	.250	16	55	52	8	13	18	5	0	0	4	0	0	0	3	0	11	0	1	1	.346	.291
Bohanon, Brian, C.S.*	.000	1	2	2	0	0	0	0	0	0	0	0	0	0	0	0	1	0	0	0	.000	.000
Borders, Pat, Tac.	.273	3	13	11	2	3	6	0	0	1	2	0	0	1	1	0	1	0	0	1	.545	.333
Borowski, Joe, Iowa	.188	42	19	16	1	3	5	2	0	0	3	2	0	0	1	0	8	0	0	0	.313	.235
Boskie, Shawn, Tuc.	.200	12	17	15	1	3	3	0	0	0	0	1	0	0	1	0	3	0	0	0	.200	.250
Bost, Heath, C.S.	.000	45	4	4	0	0	0	0	0	0	0	0	0	0	0	0	1	0	0	0	.000	.000
Branson, Jeff, L.V.*	.273	96	323	289	28	79	109	18	0	4	20	3	3	2	26	2	71	3	2	4	.377	.334
Brohawn, Troy, Tuc.*	.000	2	1	1	0	0	0	0	0	0	0	0	0	0	0	0	0	0	0	0	.000	.000
Brown, Brant, Mem.*	.277	52	209	188	30	52	70	4	1	4	19	0	0	1	21	1	60	2	1	0	.372	.349
Brown, Dee, Oma.*	.297	10	42	37	5	11	17	0	0	2	6	0	1	1	3	0	5	0	0	3	.459	.357
Brown, Elliot, Fres.†	.333	8	10	9	2	3	3	0	0	0	0	0	1	0	0	0	2	0	0	1	.333	.333
Brown, Emil, Port.	.321	22	86	78	10	25	46	8	2	3	8	0	0	2	6	0	17	3	1	2	.590	.384
Brown, Jason, Cal.	.308	12	41	39	7	12	18	3	0	1	7	0	0	1	1	0	11	0	0	2	.462	.341
Brown, Roosevelt, Iowa*	.346	88	388	364	68	126	228	34	1	22	77	0	2	8	14	1	67	3	5	8	.626	.381
Brumbaugh, Cliff, Okla.-C.S.	.320	107	486	410	69	131	201	29	4	11	81	0	7	2	67	0	93	8	6	4	.490	.412
Bruntlett, Eric, N.O.	.125	5	19	16	3	2	2	0	0	0	1	1	0	0	2	0	1	0	0	1	.125	.222
Bruske, Jim, L.V.	.167	11	14	12	0	2	3	1	0	0	0	1	0	0	1	0	4	0	0	1	.250	.231
Buhner, Jay, Tac.	.235	11	40	34	5	8	17	0	0	3	9	0	0	1	5	0	13	0	0	1	.500	.333
Bullett, Scott, C.S.*	.256	21	79	78	7	20	32	4	1	2	11	0	1	0	0	0	17	1	0	1	.410	.253
Bullinger, Jim, Mem.	.000	10	8	7	0	0	0	0	0	0	0	1	0	0	0	0	1	0	0	0	.000	.000
Burke, Jamie, S.L.	.219	61	245	215	25	47	63	10	3	0	27	2	4	5	19	0	28	1	0	6	.293	.292
Burns, Kevin, N.O.*	.263	34	117	99	19	26	40	5	3	1	11	0	0	3	15	0	18	0	1	2	.404	.376
Burroughs, Sean, Port.*	.322	104	439	394	60	127	184	28	1	9	55	4	0	4	37	2	54	9	2	13	.467	.386
Butler, Brent, C.S.	.335	65	296	272	51	91	138	20	3	7	38	3	2	4	15	0	26	4	2	13	.507	.375
Byas, Mike, Fres.†	.190	17	31	21	4	4	5	1	0	0	1	3	0	0	7	0	5	0	0	2	.238	.393
Byrnes, Eric, Sac.	.289	100	462	415	81	120	207	23	2	20	51	2	7	5	33	1	66	25	3	10	.499	.343
Caceres, Wilmy, S.L.†	.249	87	346	325	38	81	94	5	4	0	21	4	2	3	12	1	45	12	6	8	.289	.281
Cadiente, Brett, Okla.*	.400	2	5	5	0	2	2	0	0	0	0	0	0	0	0	0	2	0	0	0	.400	.400
Cairo, Miguel, Iowa	.301	34	136	123	22	37	55	7	1	3	14	4	0	1	8	2	11	3	4	3	.447	.348
Camp, Shawn, Port.-Nash.	.000	15	2	2	0	0	0	0	0	0	0	0	0	0	0	0	1	0	0	0	.000	.000
Campusano, Carlos, Fres.	.136	13	22	22	1	3	4	1	0	0	3	0	0	0	0	0	5	0	0	1	.182	.136
Candelaria, Ben, Cal.*	.319	61	172	163	23	52	86	17	1	5	29	0	2	0	7	3	19	0	0	3	.528	.343
Carlson, Dan, Mem.	.000	7	3	3	0	0	0	0	0	0	0	0	0	0	0	0	0	0	0	0	.000	.000
Carpenter, Bubba, C.S.*	.264	49	146	125	22	33	53	14	0	2	10	0	0	3	18	2	23	3	2	2	.424	.370
Carrara, Giovanni, L.V.	.000	6	6	4	0	0	0	0	0	0	0	2	0	0	0	0	1	0	0	0	.000	.000
Castillo, Carlos, Sac.	.000	1	1	1	0	0	0	0	0	0	0	0	0	0	0	0	0	0	0	0	.000	.000
Castro, Nelson, Fres.	.130	6	24	23	3	3	4	1	0	0	1	0	0	0	1	0	5	0	0	1	.174	.167
Castro, Ramon, Cal.	.336	108	433	390	81	131	245	33	0	27	90	0	4	1	38	3	74	1	1	11	.628	.393
Chacon, Shawn, C.S.	.000	4	5	4	0	0	0	0	0	0	0	1	0	0	0	0	3	0	0	0	.000	.000
Chamblee, Jim, N.O.	.257	11	41	35	3	9	14	2	0	1	4	1	0	1	4	0	13	0	0	1	.400	.350
Charles, Frank, N.O.	.333	3	4	3	0	1	1	0	0	0	0	0	0	1	0	0	0	0	0	0	.333	.500
Chavez, Anthony, Tuc.	.000	51	7	7	0	0	0	0	0	0	1	0	0	0	0	0	3	0	0	0	.000	.000
Chavez, Endy, Oma.*	.337	23	108	104	18	35	41	6	0	0	4	3	1	0	0	0	13	4	3	1	.394	.333
Chavez, Raul, N.O.	.302	85	309	278	38	84	125	17	0	8	40	4	1	7	19	2	34	1	1	9	.450	.361
Chiaramonte, Giuseppe, Fres.	.210	37	109	100	11	21	33	6	0	2	12	0	1	4	4	0	19	0	1	2	.330	.246
Choi, Hee, Iowa*	.229	77	304	266	38	61	111	11	0	13	45	0	4	0	34	1	67	5	1	5	.417	.313
Christensen, McKay, L.V.*	.246	16	63	57	8	14	21	2	1	1	3	0	0	1	5	0	11	3	1	1	.368	.317
Christensen, Ryan, Sac.-Tuc.	.260	76	317	285	39	74	116	21	0	7	30	2	3	0	27	0	56	7	2	5	.407	.321
Christman, Tim, C.S.*	.000	38	2	2	0	0	0	0	0	0	0	0	0	0	0	0	1	0	0	0	.000	.000
Chrysler, Clint, Nash.*	.000	7	1	0	0	0	0	0	0	0	0	0	0	0	1	0	0	0	0	0	.000	1.000
Cintron, Alex, Tuc.†	.292	107	468	425	53	124	163	24	3	3	35	20	6	2	15	1	48	9	6	12	.384	.315
Cirillo, Jeff, C.S.	.750	1	5	4	2	3	4	1	0	0	3	0	0	0	1	0	0	0	0	0	1.000	.800

Player, Team	Avg.	G	TPA	AB	R	H	TB	2B	3B	HR	RBI	SH	SF	HP	BB	IBB	SO	SB	CS	GDP	Slg.	OBP
Clapinski, Chris, Cal.†	.251	58	218	199	31	50	83	10	1	7	20	0	0	2	17	0	43	1	2	2	.417	.317
Clapp, Stubby, Mem.*	.304	86	348	299	48	91	134	14	7	5	33	4	1	1	43	2	46	8	4	4	.448	.392
Clark, Jermaine, Tac.*	.250	74	250	216	35	54	70	7	3	1	26	3	1	3	27	0	39	13	2	6	.324	.340
Clontz, Brad, C.S.	.000	21	1	1	0	0	0	0	0	0	0	0	0	0	0	0	1	0	0	0	.000	.000
Colangelo, Mike, Port.	.261	61	219	180	27	47	69	11	1	3	22	I	I	6	31	1	44	5	3	2	.383	.385
Colbrunn, Greg, Tuc.	.385	5	15	13	1	5	6	1	0	0	4	0	0	0	2	0	0	0	0	1	.462	.467
Cole, Eric, N.O.	.264	121	447	397	47	105	143	25	2	3	41	5	0	7	38	1	94	1	4	18	.360	.339
Condrey, Clay, Port.	.167	39	6	6	0	1	1	0	0	0	0	0	0	0	0	0	3	0	0	0	.167	.167
Connelly, Steve, Fres.	.000	33	6	6	0	0	0	0	0	0	0	0	0	0	0	0	4	0	0	0	.000	.000
Conti, Jason, Tuc.*	.331	92	413	362	68	120	182	23	6	9	52	3	3	12	33	1	54	2	5	2	.503	.402
Cookson, Brent, L.V.	.284	59	219	190	30	54	107	13	2	12	48	0	2	5	22	0	34	1	1	7	.563	.370
Coomer, Ron, Iowa	.333	4	13	12	0	4	4	0	0	0	0	0	0	0	1	0	3	0	0	0	.333	.385
Corey, Bryan, Port.	.150	19	20	20	3	3	5	2	0	0	0	0	0	0	0	0	6	0	0	0	.250	.150
Cota, Humberto, Nash.	.297	111	414	377	61	112	180	22	2	14	72	1	3	8	25	1	74	7	2	8	.477	.351
Cotton, John, Nash.*	.200	30	86	80	7	16	23	4	0	1	9	1	0	0	5	1	22	0	2	3	.288	.247
Cotton, John, L.V.*	.205	42	140	127	15	26	52	2	0	8	17	0	0	2	11	3	44	1	1	2	.409	.279
Cox, Darron, C.S.	.278	76	241	209	33	58	79	10	1	3	25	2	1	5	24	1	42	3	1	8	.378	.364
Crabtree, Robbie, Fres.	.143	63	9	7	1	1	1	0	0	0	1	2	0	0	0	0	3	0	0	0	.143	.143
Crafton, Kevin, Mem.	.000	13	1	1	0	0	0	0	0	0	0	0	0	0	0	0	0	0	0	0	.000	.000
Crawford, Joe, Tuc.*	.083	10	12	12	2	1	2	1	0	0	0	0	0	0	0	0	1	0	0	0	.167	.083
Crespo, Cesar, Port.†	.260	78	319	273	46	71	119	18	3	8	29	5	1	1	39	1	66	23	3	4	.436	.354
Crespo, Felipe, Fres.†	.375	3	8	8	2	3	7	1	0	1	1	0	0	0	0	0	3	0	0	0	.875	.375
Crosby, Bubba, L.V.*	.214	13	43	42	5	9	13	2	1	0	5	0	0	0	1	0	8	1	1	0	.310	.233
Crowell, Jim, Port.	.000	11	3	2	0	0	0	0	0	0	0	0	1	0	0	0	1	0	0	0	.000	.000
Cruz, Jacob, C.S.*	.326	20	89	86	18	28	55	5	2	6	25	0	1	1	1	0	23	1	0	2	.640	.337
Cummings, Midre, Tuc.*	.331	77	290	263	38	87	143	23	9	5	38	0	3	0	24	1	49	2	3	4	.544	.383
Curtis, Chad, Okla.	.286	4	16	14	3	4	4	0	0	0	1	0	0	0	2	0	2	0	0	1	.286	.375
Cust, Jack, Tuc.*	.278	135	554	442	81	123	232	24	2	27	79	0	5	5	102	3	160	6	3	10	.525	.415
Dace, Derek, Tuc.*	.000	17	1	1	0	0	0	0	0	0	0	0	0	0	0	0	1	0	0	0	.000	.000
Daneker, Pat, Iowa	.000	16	3	3	1	0	0	0	0	0	0	0	0	0	0	0	0	0	0	0	.000	.000
DaVanon, Jeff, S.L.†	.313	69	296	256	46	80	145	19	8	10	48	1	4	3	32	2	57	8	3	4	.566	.390
Davenport, Joe, C.S.	1.000	31	2	2	0	2	2	0	0	0	0	0	0	0	0	0	0	0	0	0	1.000	1.000
DeCinces, Tim, Port.*	.056	7	19	18	1	1	1	0	0	0	0	0	0	0	1	0	8	0	0	0	.056	.105
DeHaan, Kory, Port.*	.253	87	328	304	35	77	117	9	5	7	28	1	1	2	20	1	71	12	9	4	.385	.303
De La Cruz, Jose, Sac.	.000	2	1	1	0	0	0	0	0	0	0	0	0	0	0	0	1	0	0	0	.000	.000
Delgado, Wilson, Oma †	.247	76	275	255	24	63	90	11	2	4	30	2	1	1	16	2	43	8	3	10	.353	.293
Demetral, Chris, Okla.*	.236	92	305	322	33	76	95	11	1	2	27	7	2	0	34	0	32	1	1	8	.295	.307
DeSilva, John, Cal.-L.V.	.000	40	8	7	0	0	0	0	0	0	0	1	0	0	0	0	4	0	0	0	.000	.000
Devey, Phil, L.V.*	.000	3	1	1	0	0	0	0	0	0	0	0	0	0	0	0	0	0	0	0	.000	.000
Diaz, Angel, S.L.	.231	7	27	26	5	6	8	2	0	0	4	0	0	1	0	0	7	0	0	0	.308	.259
Diaz, Edwin, Edm.	.273	113	419	381	59	104	169	26	3	11	56	5	3	5	25	0	65	3	6	5	.444	.324
Difelice, Mark, C.S.	.500	8	8	8	1	4	8	2	1	0	3	0	0	0	0	0	2	0	0	0	1.000	.500
Difelice, Mike, Tuc.	.346	7	29	26	6	9	12	0	0	1	2	0	0	0	3	0	6	0	0	2	.462	.414
Dingman, Craig, C.S.	.000	46	1	1	0	0	0	0	0	0	0	0	0	0	0	0	0	0	0	0	.000	.000
Donaldson, Bo, Port.	.000	8	3	2	0	0	0	0	0	0	0	1	0	0	0	0	1	0	0	0	.000	.000
Donnels, Chris, L.V.*	.234	39	159	137	17	32	58	5	0	7	25	0	1	0	21	0	24	0	1	7	.423	.333
Dougherty, Jim, L.V.	.250	59	4	4	0	1	1	0	0	0	0	0	0	0	0	0	2	0	0	0	.250	.250
Dransfeldt, Kelly, Okla.	.250	143	615	551	76	138	204	29	5	9	63	5	6	3	50	1	116	12	9	9	.370	.313
Driskill, Travis, N.O.	.121	28	37	33	1	4	4	0	0	0	1	3	0	0	1	0	12	0	0	0	.121	.147
Drumright, Mike, Cal.*	.333	19	3	3	0	1	1	0	0	0	0	0	0	0	0	0	2	0	0	0	.333	.333
Dunwoody, Todd, Iowa*	.283	75	272	251	31	71	119	18	3	8	32	0	2	2	17	3	75	6	4	1	.474	.331
Durazo, Erubiel, Tuc.*	.273	3	12	11	3	3	6	0	0	1	1	0	0	0	1	0	3	0	0	0	.545	.333
Durrington, Trent, L.V. S.L.	.294	61	203	177	30	52	89	15	5	4	23	2	2	3	19	0	43	10	5	3	.503	.368
Duvall, Mike, Edm	.000	55	1	1	0	0	0	0	0	0	0	0	0	0	0	0	1	0	0	0	.000	.000
Easterday, Matt, Cal.	.196	15	49	46	6	9	12	1	1	0	3	0	1	2	0	0	10	0	1	1	.261	.245
Eberwein, Kevin, Port.	.266	27	106	94	16	25	44	8	1	3	11	0	0	2	10	2	22	0	2	2	.468	.349
Edmondson, Brian, Cal.	.000	23	5	4	1	0	0	0	0	0	0	0	0	0	1	0	1	0	0	0	.000	.200
Ellis, Mark, Sac.	.273	132	541	472	71	129	197	38	0	10	53	5	5	5	54	4	78	21	7	13	.417	.351
Ellis, Robert, Cal.	.333	5	6	3	0	1	1	0	0	0	0	1	0	1	1	0	1	0	0	0	.333	.600
Embree, Alan, Fres.*	.000	7	1	1	0	0	0	0	0	0	0	0	0	0	0	0	0	0	0	0	.000	.000
Encarnacion, Bienvenido, S.L.	.304	6	25	23	6	7	7	0	0	0	3	0	0	0	2	0	6	0	0	0	.304	.360
Encarnacion, Mario, Sac.-C.S.	.303	67	259	231	37	70	129	13	2	14	43	0	1	5	21	2	69	4	4	6	.558	.372
Ensberg, Morgan, N.O.	.310	87	368	316	65	98	187	20	0	23	61	0	4	3	45	0	60	0	3	12	.592	.397
Epke, Brian, Tuc.	.000	2	5	3	1	0	0	0	0	0	0	0	0	1	1	0	2	0	0	0	.000	.400
Erickson, Matt, Cal.*	.310	115	472	413	66	128	157	21	1	2	29	8	0	12	39	0	69	11	4	13	.380	.386
Espada, Josue, Cal.-C.S.	.297	86	371	317	69	94	132	22	2	4	32	3	3	4	44	0	55	16	9	4	.416	.386
Estalella, Bobby, Fres.	.318	6	23	22	3	7	11	1	0	1	4	0	0	0	1	0	9	0	0	1	.500	.348
Estrada, Horacio, C.S.*	.286	16	15	14	0	4	4	0	0	0	1	1	0	0	0	0	1	0	0	0	.286	.286
Estrella, Luis, Fres.	.310	32	32	29	4	9	15	3	0	1	5	2	0	0	1	0	6	0	0	0	.517	.333
Evans, Dave, N.O.	.000	25	9	9	0	0	0	0	0	0	0	0	0	0	0	0	5	0	0	1	.000	.000
Everett, Adam, N.O.	.249	114	500	441	69	110	161	20	8	5	40	9	4	16	39	0	74	24	5	4	.365	.330
Fajardo, Al, Fres.	.281	27	37	32	5	9	10	1	0	0	3	1	0	0	4	0	14	0	0	0	.313	.361
Fasano, Sal, Oma.-C.S.	.281	141	546	473	74	119	171	21	8	5	43	10	4	16	43	0	88	24	5	4	.531	.384
Febles, Carlos, Oma.	.337	25	111	98	23	33	48	7	1	2	9	0	0	4	9	0	14	6	2	0	.490	.414
Feliciano, Pedro, L.V.*	1.000	6	1	1	0	1	2	1	0	0	0	0	0	0	0	0	0	0	0	0	2.000	1.000
Felix, Hersy, Oma.	.250	1	4	4	1	1	2	1	0	0	1	0	0	0	0	0	0	0	0	0	.500	.250
Fernandez, Jose, S.L.	.338	122	522	452	99	153	282	37	1	30	114	0	3	12	55	2	91	9	7	9	.624	.421
Figueroa, Luis, Tac.	.342	24	80	76	9	26	30	4	0	0	9	0	1	0	3	0	8	0	1	4	.395	.363
Figueroa, Luis, Nash.†	.300	92	387	347	45	104	129	11	1	4	29	6	2	1	31	1	26	8	5	8	.372	.357
Fikac, Jeremy, Port.	.000	1	1	1	0	0	0	0	0	0	0	0	0	0	0	0	0	0	0	0	.000	.000
Flores, Jose, C.S.	.294	100	372	316	61	93	130	21	5	2	36	4	1	3	48	1	57	8	2	1	.411	.391
Ford, Ben, Iowa	.000	5	4	3	0	0	0	0	0	0	0	0	0	0	1	0	3	0	0	0	.000	.250
Fox, Andy, Cal.*	.429	11	46	42	10	18	28	2	1	2	8	0	0	1	3	0	2	1	1	1	.667	.478

Player, Team	Avg.	G	TPA	AB	R	H	TB	2B	3B	HR	RBI	SH	SF	HP	BB	IBB	SO	SB	CS	GDP	Slg.	OBP
Franklin, Wayne, N.O.*	.167	41	7	6	0	1	1	0	0	0	0	1	0	0	0	0	0	0	0	0	.167	.167
Freeman, Corey, Tac.	.214	7	14	14	3	3	3	0	0	0	1	0	0	0	0	0	5	0	0	0	.214	.214
Frias, Hanley, Edm.-Mem.†	.220	107	412	382	42	84	108	14	2	2	26	1	1	2	26	0	72	8	7	6	.283	.273
Gagne, Eric, L.V.	.143	4	7	7	0	1	1	0	0	0	1	0	0	0	0	0	0	0	0	0	.143	.143
Gann, Jamie, Tuc.	.267	7	15	15	2	4	8	1	0	1	4	0	0	0	0	0	0	0	0	0	.533	.267
Garcia, Luis, Mem.	.256	118	439	422	42	108	151	20	1	7	44	1	3	4	8	0	71	2	1	20	.358	.275
Garcia, Osmani, Okla.	.237	47	184	173	15	41	55	11	0	1	21	4	3	1	3	0	19	1	2	6	.318	.250
Gautreau, Jake, Port.*	.286	2	9	7	2	2	5	0	0	1	2	0	0	0	2	1	2	0	0	0	.714	.444
German, Esteban, Sac.	.373	38	177	150	40	56	76	8	0	4	14	2	1	6	18	0	20	17	2	4	.507	.457
Giambi, Jeremy, Sac.*	.333	9	28	27	1	9	10	1	0	0	1	0	0	0	1	0	6	0	0	1	.370	.357
Gibson, Derrick, Tuc.	.247	32	106	97	8	24	40	8	1	2	15	0	0	4	5	0	19	5	0	2	.412	.311
Gil, Geronimo, L.V.	.295	82	302	281	40	83	125	15	0	9	40	0	3	2	16	1	56	0	1	9	.445	.334
Gilbert, Shawn, L.V.	.330	59	252	224	25	74	116	14	2	8	36	4	3	1	20	0	43	11	4	2	.518	.383
Ginter, Keith, N.O.	.269	132	547	457	76	123	212	31	5	16	70	2	4	23	61	1	147	8	6	6	.464	.380
Giron, Isabel, Port.	.250	45	8	8	0	2	3	1	0	0	0	0	0	0	0	0	4	0	0	0	.375	.250
Gload, Ross, Iowa*	.297	133	524	475	70	141	238	32	10	15	93	4	7	3	35	3	88	9	7	8	.501	.344
Gomez, Chris, Port.	.300	11	42	40	5	12	18	3	0	1	5	0	0	0	2	0	4	1	0	1	.450	.333
Gonzalez, Gabe, Port.*	.000	3	1	1	0	0	0	0	0	0	0	0	0	0	0	0	1	0	0	0	.000	.000
Goodwin, Curtis, Okla.*	.229	73	257	236	24	54	65	3	1	2	19	9	2	0	10	0	45	3	3	1	.275	.258
Grabowski, Jason, Tac.*	.297	114	463	394	60	117	182	32	3	9	58	0	5	2	61	5	94	7	4	8	.462	.390
Green, Chad, Port.†	.224	21	76	67	12	15	27	4	1	2	2	0	0	0	9	0	28	4	1	0	.403	.316
Green, Scarborough, Nash.†	.155	33	69	58	8	9	13	2	1	0	4	2	1	0	8	2	16	2	1	1	.224	.254
Greene, Charlie, Port.	.137	67	229	211	11	29	34	2	0	1	10	4	4	1	9	0	47	0	0	5	.161	.173
Grijak, Kevin, Cal.*	.246	45	161	142	17	35	57	7	0	5	27	0	3	4	12	0	13	1	0	6	.401	.317
Grilli, Jason, Cal.	.000	8	9	9	0	0	0	0	0	0	0	0	0	0	0	0	6	0	0	0	.000	.000
Gross, Kip, L.V.-C.S.	.000	28	14	13	0	0	0	0	0	0	0	1	0	0	0	0	6	0	0	0	.000	.000
Guerra, Mark, N.O.	.263	29	24	19	5	5	6	1	0	0	2	4	0	0	1	0	3	0	0	1	.316	.300
Guiel, Aaron, Oma.*	.267	121	513	442	78	118	214	27	3	21	73	1	6	13	51	3	92	6	4	12	.484	.355
Guiel, Jeff, S.L.*	.321	61	247	224	37	72	118	14	1	10	35	1	1	1	17	1	39	2	0	2	.527	.370
Gulan, Mike, Cal.	.324	124	533	485	78	157	271	44	2	22	92	0	5	8	35	1	145	2	6	12	.559	.375
Guy, Brad, Nash.	.000	22	6	6	0	0	0	0	0	0	0	0	0	0	0	0	2	0	0	0	.000	.000
Guzman, Ed, Fres.*	.361	18	78	72	13	26	33	3	2	0	11	2	0	0	4	1	3	0	1	1	.458	.395
Guzman, Geraldo, Tuc.	.000	20	17	15	1	0	0	0	0	0	0	1	0	0	1	0	7	0	0	0	.000	.063
Haad, Yamid, Nash.	.257	51	153	144	14	37	48	5	0	2	10	2	0	0	7	0	27	0	3	2	.333	.291
Hall, Justin, Fres.	.500	1	4	4	1	2	2	0	0	0	1	0	0	0	0	0	0	0	0	0	.500	.500
Hallmark, Pat, Oma.	.247	32	108	93	10	23	28	5	0	0	10	2	1	5	7	0	17	3	0	2	.301	.318
Hamilton, Darryl, C.S.*	.154	4	15	13	0	2	2	0	0	0	0	0	0	0	2	0	2	0	0	1	.154	.267
Hansen, Jed, Oma.	.253	80	333	288	37	73	119	14	1	10	22	5	3	3	34	0	86	10	6	3	.413	.335
Hart, Jason, Sac.	.247	134	563	494	71	122	207	26	1	19	75	0	8	4	57	0	102	3	3	11	.419	.325
Haselman, Bill, Okla.	.143	8	31	28	2	4	4	0	0	0	1	0	1	1	1	0	10	0	0	3	.143	.194
Hasselhoff, Derek, Fres.	.000	25	1	1	0	0	0	0	0	0	0	0	0	0	0	0	0	0	0	0	.000	.000
Haverbusch, Kevin, Nash.	.333	50	158	147	24	49	81	7	2	7	30	0	1	6	4	0	34	3	1	0	.551	.373
Heiserman, Rick, Mem.	.000	24	6	5	0	0	0	0	0	0	0	0	0	0	1	0	2	0	0	0	.000	.167
Hellman, Matthew, Port.	.000	1	3	3	0	0	0	0	0	0	0	0	0	0	0	0	1	0	0	0	.000	.000
Henderson, Rickey, Port.	.275	9	42	40	5	11	14	3	0	0	2	1	0	0	1	0	9	1	0	1	.350	.293
Hermansen, Chad, Nash.	.246	123	499	447	75	110	195	22	6	17	64	3	3	5	41	1	154	22	5	5	.436	.315
Hernandez, Alex, Nash.*	.295	88	365	342	45	101	143	16	1	8	36	1	4	4	13	2	65	3	4	10	.418	.325
Hernandez, Carlos, Mem.	.500	2	4	4	1	2	5	0	0	1	1	0	0	0	0	0	0	0	0	1	1.250	.500
Hernandez, John, L.V.	.067	5	15	15	1	1	2	1	0	0	1	0	0	0	0	0	3	1	0	0	.133	.067
Herndon, Junior, Port.	.042	22	28	24	2	1	1	0	0	0	0	2	0	0	2	0	15	0	0	0	.042	.115
Hiatt, Phil, L.V.	.330	113	495	436	107	144	315	29	5	44	99	0	2	5	52	6	109	6	4	9	.722	.406
Hill, Jason, S.L.	.370	8	29	27	3	10	13	1	1	0	3	0	0	0	2	0	4	0	0	1	.481	.414
Hinch, A.J., Oma.	.321	45	181	168	28	54	98	14	0	10	33	0	1	1	11	0	33	1	0	5	.583	.365
Hinske, Eric, Sac.*	.282	121	504	436	71	123	227	27	1	25	79	2	2	10	54	3	113	20	7	6	.521	.373
Hollins, Damon, Edm.	.276	69	259	232	29	64	94	8	2	6	30	2	1	2	22	0	44	3	3	8	.405	.342
Horgan, Joe, Fres.*	.500	4	2	2	0	1	1	0	0	0	2	0	0	0	0	0	0	0	0	0	.500	.500
Horner, Jim, Tac.	.284	65	262	236	45	67	101	16	0	6	29	2	2	12	10	1	41	1	0	7	.428	.342
House, Craig, C.S.	.333	55	3	3	1	1	4	0	0	1	1	0	0	0	0	0	2	0	0	0	1.333	.333
Howard, Tom, Nash.†	.200	13	33	30	2	6	8	2	0	0	1	0	0	1	2	0	7	0	0	0	.267	.273
Hubbard, Mike, Okla.	.310	35	144	129	22	40	68	8	1	6	23	2	0	2	11	0	20	0	1	3	.527	.373
Hubbard, Trenidad, Oma.-Iowa.	.301	98	421	346	73	104	180	20	4	16	59	0	4	4	67	1	61	25	10	5	.520	.416
Huckaby, Ken, Tuc.	.290	78	272	262	31	76	99	15	1	2	34	0	1	2	7	2	62	1	3	3	.378	.313
Huff, Larry, Edm.	.313	27	78	67	10	21	30	2	2	1	11	2	2	0	7	0	13	2	1	3	.448	.392
Huisman, Rick, Mem.	.000	8	1	1	0	0	0	0	0	0	0	0	0	0	0	0	1	0	0	0	.000	.000
Hundley, Todd, Iowa†	.196	15	57	51	7	10	20	1	0	3	8	0	1	1	4	0	23	0	0	1	.392	.263
Huskey, Butch, C.S.	.323	122	513	458	76	148	236	29	1	19	87	0	12	1	42	2	95	2	2	18	.515	.373
Husted, Brent, L.V.	.500	16	4	4	0	2	2	0	0	0	0	0	0	0	0	0	1	0	0	0	.500	.500
Hutchinson, Chad, Mem.	.364	28	26	22	2	8	10	2	0	0	4	0	0	0	0	0	8	0	0	1	.455	.364
Hyzdu, Adam, Nash.	.291	69	280	261	38	76	130	17	2	11	39	0	2	0	17	3	68	1	3	3	.498	.332
Ibanez, Raul, Oma.*	.148	8	29	27	3	4	11	1	0	2	5	1	0	0	1	0	10	0	0	0	.407	.179
Jackson, Damian, Port.	.300	3	13	10	4	3	6	3	0	0	0	0	0	3	0	0	1	0	1	0	.600	.462
Jacome, Jason, Tuc.*	.067	35	18	15	1	1	2	1	0	0	0	3	0	0	0	0	4	0	0	2	.133	.067
Jaha, John, Sac.	.190	23	95	84	9	16	33	5	0	4	11	0	0	0	11	1	32	0	0	2	.393	.284
James, Mike, Mem.	.000	10	1	1	0	0	0	0	0	0	0	0	0	0	0	0	0	0	0	0	.000	.000
Jennings, Jason, C.S.*	.286	25	36	35	3	10	17	1	0	2	7	0	1	0	0	0	10	0	0	1	.486	.278
Jennings, Robin, Sac.-C.S.*	.301	49	197	183	34	55	94	12	3	7	31	0	1	3	10	0	36	6	2	5	.514	.345
Jensen, Marcus, Okla.†	.298	53	235	188	42	56	92	10	1	8	25	0	0	1	46	1	46	0	0	7	.489	.438
Jensen, Ryan, Fres.	.125	20	22	16	1	2	2	0	0	0	1	5	0	0	1	0	4	0	0	0	.125	.176
Jodie, Brett, Port.	.000	5	7	6	1	0	0	0	0	0	0	1	0	0	0	0	3	0	0	0	.000	.143
Johnson, Brian, L.V.	.301	48	182	166	21	50	80	12	0	6	31	0	3	2	11	0	39	0	0	1	.482	.350
Johnson, Jonathan, Tuc.	.200	15	17	15	0	3	3	0	0	0	2	1	0	0	1	0	5	0	0	0	.200	.250
Johnson, Keith, L.V.	.251	125	475	435	55	109	185	32	4	12	50	14	2	7	17	0	87	4	5	11	.425	.289
Johnson, Lance, C.S.*	.341	35	142	135	26	46	64	8	2	2	16	1	2	0	14	0	14	9	4	2	.474	.355

Player, Team	Avg.	G	TPA	AB	R	H	TB	2B	3B	HR	RBI	SH	SF	HP	BB	IBB	SO	SB	CS	GDP	Slg.	OBP
Jones, Marcus, Sac.	.000	27	1	1	0	0	0	0	0	0	0	0	0	0	0	0	1	0	0	0	.000	.000
Kamioniocki, Scott, Iowa........	.000	8	5	4	0	0	0	0	0	0	0	1	0	0	0	0	1	0	0	0	.000	.000
Karl, Scott, Nash.*	.158	14	22	19	0	3	3	0	0	0	1	3	0	0	0	0	2	0	0	0	.158	.158
Karnuth, Jason, Mem.	.000	55	1	1	0	0	0	0	0	0	0	0	0	0	0	0	0	0	0	0	.000	.000
Kelly, Roberto, C.S.	.288	63	239	212	32	61	107	10	0	12	48	0	5	4	18	2	48	1	2	6	.505	.347
Kessel, Kyle, N.O.	.200	15	6	5	0	1	1	0	0	0	0	1	0	0	0	0	3	0	0	0	.200	.200
Kiefer, Mark, L.V.	.103	34	31	29	4	3	6	0	0	1	1	2	0	0	0	0	10	0	0	2	.207	.103
Kielty, Bobby, Edm.†	.287	94	404	341	58	98	163	25	2	12	50	2	2	6	53	1	76	5	0	11	.478	.391
Kieschnick, Brooks, C.S.*	.294	71	278	252	44	74	128	9	3	13	45	0	2	24	3	72	3	2	7	.508	.360
King, Cesar, Oma.	.286	19	59	56	5	16	28	6	0	2	12	0	2	0	1	0	5	1	0	2	.500	.288
Kingsale, Eugene, Tac.†	.293	51	228	215	30	63	94	14	4	3	24	2	0	3	8	0	25	12	4	1	.437	.327
Klassen, Danny, Tuc.	.222	7	21	18	5	4	7	0	0	1	3	0	0	1	2	0	3	0	0	0	.389	.333
Knoll, Brian, Fres.	.000	22	6	5	0	0	0	0	0	0	0	1	0	0	0	0	0	0	0	0	.000	.000
Knott, Eric, Tuc.*	.071	25	14	14	0	1	1	0	0	0	0	0	0	0	0	0	7	0	0	1	.071	.071
Knotts, Gary, Cal.	.111	21	33	27	1	3	3	0	0	0	3	4	0	0	2	0	11	0	0	0	.111	.172
Koonce, Graham, Port.*	.214	6	19	14	5	3	7	1	0	1	2	0	0	0	5	0	6	0	0	1	.500	.421
Kopitzke, Casey, Iowa	.200	4	5	5	1	1	1	0	0	0	2	0	0	0	0	0	1	0	0	0	.200	.200
Koplove, Mike, Tuc.	.000	17	1	1	0	0	0	0	0	0	0	0	0	0	0	0	0	0	0	0	.000	.000
Krivda, Rick, Mem.	.150	14	23	20	0	3	3	0	0	0	2	2	0	0	1	0	9	0	0	1	.150	.190
Lamb, Dave, C.S.-Cal.†	.289	28	93	76	16	22	31	6	0	1	6	4	0	2	11	0	15	0	0	3	.408	.393
Lamb, Mike, Okla.*	.297	69	295	273	35	81	130	19	3	8	40	2	4	3	13	0	31	0	2	8	.476	.331
Lambert, Jeremy, Mem.	.000	28	1	1	0	0	0	0	0	0	0	0	0	0	0	0	0	0	0	0	.000	.000
Lane, Ryan, Sac.	.210	56	210	186	17	39	59	8	0	4	14	1	1	1	21	0	39	6	1	3	.317	.292
Larkin, Andy, C.S.	.063	27	18	16	1	1	1	0	0	0	1	2	0	0	0	0	6	0	0	0	.063	.063
Lawrence, Brian, Port.	.333	9	10	9	1	3	4	1	0	0	0	1	0	0	0	0	3	0	0	0	.444	.333
Lawrence, Sean, Port.-Tuc.* ..	.000	43	2	2	0	0	0	0	0	0	0	0	0	0	0	0	2	0	0	0	.000	.000
Leach, Jalal, Fres.*	.285	130	502	467	68	133	217	30	3	16	70	0	3	1	31	3	94	13	6	11	.465	.329
LeCroy, Matthew, Edm.	.328	101	441	396	53	130	207	17	0	20	80	0	3	6	36	1	95	0	2	8	.523	.390
Ledee, Ricky, Okla.*	.500	4	17	16	4	8	12	1	0	1	3	0	0	0	1	0	1	0	0	1	.750	.529
Lee, Dave, Port.	.000	9	1	1	0	0	0	0	0	0	0	0	0	0	0	0	0	0	0	0	.000	.000
Leese, Brandon, Cal.	.286	9	12	7	1	2	2	0	0	0	0	0	5	0	0	0	0	0	0	0	.286	.200
Lemonic, Chris, Cal.-Tuc.*	.188	18	52	48	6	9	11	2	0	0	1	0	1	0	3	0	10	0	0	2	.229	.250
Leyritz, Jim, Port.	.261	16	53	46	8	12	28	1	0	5	10	0	1	1	5	0	13	1	0	0	.609	.340
Lidle, Kevin, S.L.-Mem †........	.228	43	141	123	11	28	39	8	0	1	12	2	1	3	11	0	41	2	1	0	.317	.304
Lincoln, Mike, Nash.	.150	18	22	20	3	3	4	1	0	0	2	0	0	0	0	0	4	0	0	0	.200	.150
Linebrink, Scott, N.O.	.167	50	8	6	0	1	1	0	0	0	0	2	0	0	0	0	2	0	0	0	.167	.167
Lipowicz, Nathan, L.V.	.125	2	8	8	0	1	2	1	0	0	0	0	0	0	0	0	3	0	0	0	.250	.125
Little, Mark, C.S.	.375	9	44	40	6	15	17	2	0	0	4	0	0	1	3	0	9	0	2	1	.425	.432
Lo Duca, Paul, L.V.	.333	3	10	9	3	3	5	2	0	0	3	0	0	0	1	0	0	0	0	0	.556	.400
Loewer, Carlton, Port.†	.214	14	14	14	2	3	3	0	0	0	0	0	0	0	0	0	4	0	0	0	.214	.214
Loiselle, Rich, Nash.	.000	26	1	1	0	0	0	0	0	0	0	0	0	0	0	0	1	0	0	0	.000	.000
Lopez, Mendy, N.O.	.279	63	230	208	37	58	113	11	1	14	36	0	1	3	18	0	49	2	2	5	.543	.343
Lopez, Norberto, S.L.	.000	2	5	5	0	0	0	0	0	0	0	0	0	0	0	0	1	0	0	0	.000	.000
Lopez, Rafael, Iowa...............	.167	24	57	54	6	9	12	3	0	0	2	0	0	0	3	0	12	0	0	4	.222	.211
Lopez, Rodrigo, Port.	.000	11	11	11	0	0	0	0	0	0	0	0	0	0	0	0	5	0	0	0	.000	.000
Lorenzana, Luis, Port.	.000	2	4	4	0	0	0	0	0	0	0	0	0	0	0	0	1	0	0	0	.000	.000
Lorraine, Andrew, Cal.*	.208	30	25	24	2	5	5	0	0	0	1	0	0	0	1	0	8	0	0	0	.208	.240
Loyd, Brian, Port.	.239	25	93	88	7	21	33	3	0	3	10	0	0	1	4	0	11	0	0	1	.375	.280
Lucca, Lou, Mem.	.265	135	520	479	58	127	188	32	1	9	64	2	2	10	27	4	67	2	3	12	.392	.317
Ludwick, Ryan, Sac.	.228	17	62	57	10	13	19	3	0	1	7	1	2	0	2	0	16	2	0	0	.333	.246
Lundquist, Dave, Nash.	.000	50	5	2	0	0	0	0	0	0	0	0	0	0	3	0	1	0	0	0	.000	.600
Luuloa, Keith, Port.-N.O.	.252	100	349	310	45	78	120	20	2	6	27	3	3	7	26	1	41	1	1	12	.387	.321
Lydy, Scott, N.O.	.265	95	336	283	37	75	118	20	1	7	43	2	2	2	47	1	62	8	5	3	.417	.371
Machado, Rob, Iowa	.283	53	195	180	20	51	86	11	0	8	30	2	0	2	11	2	36	0	0	5	.478	.332
Mackowiak, Rob, Nash.*	.263	32	128	118	14	31	48	5	0	4	14	2	1	0	7	0	39	1	1	0	.407	.302
Magruder, Chris, Fres.-Okla.† ..	.311	87	397	341	65	106	182	21	5	15	51	4	2	11	39	3	64	4	3	5	.534	.397
Mahay, Ron, Port.-Iowa*	.167	50	6	6	0	1	1	0	0	0	0	0	0	0	0	0	2	0	0	0	.167	.167
Mahoney, Mike, Iowa	.225	95	323	289	22	65	90	14	1	3	27	6	2	4	22	0	63	1	3	8	.311	.287
Maier, T.J., Mem.	.235	6	20	17	4	4	4	0	0	0	1	0	1	0	2	0	3	0	0	0	.235	.300
Mairena, Ozwaldo, Cal.*	.000	31	1	0	0	0	0	0	0	0	0	0	1	0	0	0	0	0	0	0	.000	.000
Mann, Jim, N.O.	.000	53	2	2	0	0	0	0	0	0	0	0	0	0	0	0	2	0	0	0	.000	.000
Martin, Norberto, Cal.	.306	93	351	333	45	102	145	20	4	5	38	1	2	1	14	3	41	8	3	13	.435	.334
Martines, Jason, Tuc.*	.000	12	1	1	0	0	0	0	0	0	0	0	0	0	0	0	0	0	0	0	.000	.000
Masaoka, Onan, L.V.	.231	31	14	13	3	3	3	0	0	0	1	1	0	0	0	0	5	0	0	0	.231	.231
Mashore, Damon, Mem.	.298	79	314	289	35	86	126	17	1	7	37	0	2	5	18	0	62	3	4	5	.436	.347
Mateo, Ruben, Okla.	.216	14	54	51	3	11	17	3	0	1	8	0	1	0	2	0	8	1	2	1	.333	.241
Matos, Julius, Port.	.279	106	410	383	40	107	144	12	2	7	34	3	6	15	2	48	6	8	6	.376	.314
Matranga, Dave, N.O.	.313	4	18	16	3	5	9	1	0	1	3	0	1	1	0	0	5	1	0	0	.563	.333
McConnell, Sam, Nash.*	.240	26	29	25	3	6	6	0	0	0	4	0	0	0	0	0	8	0	0	2	.240	.240
McCracken, Quinton, Edm.† ..	.338	81	390	361	53	122	169	27	4	4	45	5	2	1	21	1	54	8	10	5	.468	.374
McDade, Neal, Nash.	.000	8	2	2	0	0	0	0	0	0	0	0	0	0	0	0	1	0	0	0	.000	.000
McDonald, Keith, Mem.	.261	94	362	333	42	87	144	22	1	11	42	0	3	2	24	1	60	1	0	13	.432	.312
McGowan, Sean, Fres.	.286	104	418	391	59	112	188	30	2	14	65	0	2	23	0	95	1	0	10	.481	.328
McGuire, Ryan, Cal.*	.301	62	269	239	45	72	114	14	2	8	42	1	2	1	26	0	49	0	1	10	.477	.369
McKay, Cody, Sac.*	.263	99	385	350	36	92	129	19	0	6	41	2	1	5	27	1	64	1	0	12	.369	.324
McKeel, Walt, C.S.	.241	28	85	79	13	19	28	4	1	1	4	0	0	0	6	1	22	0	0	0	.354	.294
McKnight, Tony, N.O.*	.200	19	17	15	3	3	5	2	0	0	0	1	0	0	0	0	8	0	0	0	.333	.250
McNally, Sean, Tuc.	.241	74	277	249	24	60	87	5	2	6	28	0	1	3	24	2	77	4	1	1	.349	.314
McNaughton, Troy, Mem.*	.130	6	25	23	5	3	8	2	0	1	1	0	0	2	0	5	0	0	2	.348	.200
Medina, Rafael, Mem.	.000	27	2	2	0	0	0	0	0	0	0	0	0	0	0	0	2	0	0	0	.000	.000
Melhuse, Adam, C.S.†	.266	54	218	184	26	49	82	10	1	7	32	1	0	2	31	1	42	0	1	8	.446	.378
Meliah, Dave, Okla.*	.254	20	72	63	9	16	24	5	0	1	7	0	0	0	9	0	13	2	2	0	.381	.347
Melo, Juan, Fres.†	.312	100	405	375	46	117	174	22	4	9	55	1	5	5	19	1	64	9	9	8	.464	.349

– 439 –

Player, Team	Avg.	G	TPA	AB	R	H	TB	2B	3B	HR	RBI	SH	SF	HP	BB	IBB	SO	SB	CS	GDP	Slg.	OBP
Meyers, Chad, Iowa	.300	132	546	446	92	134	202	31	5	9	54	10	5	26	58	0	72	27	9	9	.453	.407
Meyers, Mike, Iowa	.136	25	24	22	3	3	3	0	0	0	0	0	0	0	2	0	6	0	0	0	.136	.208
Middlebrook, Jason, Port.	.150	15	23	20	1	3	3	0	0	0	2	1	0	1	1	0	5	0	0	0	.150	.227
Minor, Damon, Fres.*	.308	112	459	406	74	125	225	22	3	24	71	0	3	5	44	4	83	1	1	5	.554	.380
Moeller, Chad, Tuc.	.274	78	304	274	41	75	119	20	0	8	36	1	2	2	25	1	54	1	4	8	.434	.337
Mohler, Mike, Tuc.	.000	40	3	3	0	0	0	0	0	0	0	0	0	0	0	0	2	0	0	0	.000	.000
Molina, Bengie, S.L.	.278	5	20	18	2	5	6	1	0	0	3	0	0	0	2	0	3	0	0	2	.333	.350
Molina, Gabe, Cal.	.154	43	28	26	1	4	8	1	0	1	5	2	0	0	0	0	12	0	0	1	.308	.154
Molina, Jose, S.L.	.300	61	235	213	29	64	92	11	1	5	31	6	0	2	14	0	49	1	2	7	.432	.349
Monahan, Shane, Nash.*	.220	16	44	41	3	9	12	0	0	1	3	0	1	0	2	0	9	0	0	0	.293	.250
Monroe, Craig, Okla.	.280	114	465	410	60	115	210	25	5	20	75	1	3	5	46	2	85	10	8	11	.512	.358
Moody, Eric, Nash.	.278	42	20	18	1	5	5	0	0	0	2	2	0	0	0	0	0	0	1	0	.278	.278
Moraga, David, C.S.*	.500	2	2	2	0	1	1	0	0	0	0	0	0	0	0	0	1	0	0	0	.500	.500
Morales, Steve, Cal.†	.500	2	2	2	0	1	1	0	0	0	0	0	0	0	0	0	1	0	0	0	.500	.500
Morales, Willie, C.S.	.157	17	54	51	4	8	12	1	0	1	2	1	1	0	1	0	8	2	0	1	.235	.170
Moreta, Ramon, Tac.-S.L.	.224	25	87	76	8	17	25	3	1	1	14	0	3	2	6	0	31	3	4	3	.329	.287
Morgan, Scott, S.L.	.265	128	549	501	93	133	262	39	3	28	83	0	2	5	41	4	117	2	0	10	.523	.326
Moriarty, Mike, Edm.	.243	131	482	404	66	98	158	17	2	13	50	5	2	13	58	0	94	5	4	12	.391	.354
Morris, Warren, Nash.*	.305	57	241	223	26	68	103	16	2	5	40	1	3	2	12	0	21	3	4	5	.462	.342
Mota, Tony, L.V.†	.296	120	488	442	62	131	200	29	8	8	57	3	2	1	40	1	79	16	7	12	.452	.355
Mottola, Chad, Cal.	.295	119	492	457	66	135	207	23	2	15	66	0	1	4	30	0	85	11	5	5	.453	.343
Mouton, Lyle, N.O.	.333	2	9	9	1	3	7	1	0	1	1	0	0	0	0	0	3	0	0	0	.778	.333
Mueller, Bill, Iowa†	.423	8	27	26	3	11	14	3	0	0	4	0	0	0	1	0	2	0	0	0	.538	.444
Murphy, Nate, S.L.*	.249	53	197	177	28	44	69	8	1	5	21	2	0	2	16	1	53	1	3	2	.390	.318
Murray, Calvin, Fres.	.261	35	152	138	17	36	56	6	1	4	12	0	1	1	12	1	33	3	3	2	.406	.322
Myers, Adrian, Tac.	.254	71	281	260	30	66	92	10	8	0	33	1	1	1	18	0	59	4	4	5	.354	.304
Myers, Greg, Sac.*	.000	2	8	5	0	0	0	0	0	0	1	0	0	0	3	0	2	0	0	1	.000	.375
Myers, Rodney, Port.	.500	8	2	2	0	1	2	1	0	0	0	0	0	0	0	0	1	0	0	0	1.000	.500
Nathan, Joe, Fres.	.200	11	8	5	0	1	1	0	0	0	1	2	0	0	1	0	3	0	0	0	.200	.333
Nation, Joey, Iowa*	.286	14	8	7	0	2	2	0	0	0	0	1	0	0	0	0	1	0	0	0	.286	.286
Nelson, Bryant, Tuc.-Nash.†	.305	134	551	511	60	156	211	22	0	11	56	5	5	2	26	2	36	12	8	19	.413	.338
Nicholson, Kevin, Port.-C.S.†	.330	34	119	109	15	36	45	6	0	1	12	1	0	0	9	1	10	1	2	2	.413	.381
Nieves, Jose, S.L.	.329	61	273	258	50	85	141	15	4	11	37	2	2	3	8	0	36	8	7	3	.547	.354
Nieves, Melvin, C.S.†	.233	13	52	43	7	10	20	5	1	1	4	0	0	1	8	0	20	1	0	0	.465	.365
Norton, Phil, Iowa	.000	46	6	5	0	0	0	0	0	0	0	1	0	0	0	0	1	0	0	0	.000	.000
Nunnally, Jon, Oma.*	.209	97	374	316	50	66	129	9	0	18	53	0	1	3	54	2	109	11	3	3	.408	.329
O'Connor, Brian, Nash.*	.158	37	22	19	3	3	5	2	0	0	3	1	0	0	2	0	8	0	0	1	.263	.238
Ohman, Will, Iowa*	.000	40	3	3	0	0	0	0	0	0	0	0	0	0	0	0	2	0	0	0	.000	.000
Ordaz, Luis, Oma.	.308	14	59	52	5	16	20	1	0	1	4	2	0	3	2	0	10	3	0	2	.385	.368
Ortega, Bill, Mem.	.287	134	543	495	55	142	194	26	4	6	62	0	3	5	40	4	74	6	6	17	.392	.344
Ortiz, Hector, Oma.	.260	42	170	150	19	39	52	7	0	2	15	1	4	0	15	0	26	0	3	5	.347	.320
Ortiz, Jose, Sac.	.273	65	285	256	41	70	115	16	4	7	39	1	0	3	25	0	50	7	4	5	.449	.345
Ortiz, Nick, Oma.	.250	99	361	316	39	79	119	20	1	6	40	5	4	3	33	0	65	2	6	11	.377	.323
Osting, Jimmy, Port.	.000	5	6	3	0	0	0	0	0	0	0	3	0	0	0	0	1	0	0	0	.000	.000
Oswalt, Roy, N.O.	.222	5	10	9	1	2	2	0	0	0	0	1	0	0	0	0	1	0	0	0	.222	.222
Owens, Eric, Cal.	.267	3	15	15	2	4	6	2	0	0	2	0	0	0	0	0	2	1	0	1	.400	.267
Pachot, John, L.V.	.318	6	22	22	3	7	11	1	0	1	1	0	0	0	0	0	3	1	0	2	.500	.318
Patterson, Corey, Iowa*	.253	89	404	367	63	93	142	22	3	7	32	3	3	1	29	0	65	19	8	2	.387	.308
Patterson, John, Tuc.	.263	14	19	19	1	5	5	0	0	0	4	0	0	0	0	0	6	0	0	0	.263	.263
Pavlas, Dave, Nash.†	.000	41	1	1	0	0	0	0	0	0	0	0	0	0	0	0	1	0	0	0	.000	.000
Pearce, Josh, Mem.	.167	10	15	12	1	2	2	0	0	0	0	3	0	0	0	0	2	0	0	0	.167	.167
Peeples, Mike, C.S.	.300	115	462	424	71	127	215	23	4	19	69	0	5	6	27	0	63	9	9	11	.507	.346
Pellow, Kit, Oma.	.291	129	543	484	81	141	216	15	0	20	81	2	7	13	37	1	101	4	3	3	.446	.353
Pena, Angel, L.V.	.313	53	219	198	39	62	122	8	2	16	41	0	2	1	18	1	52	1	0	5	.616	.370
Pena, Carlos, Okla.*	.288	119	520	431	71	124	237	38	3	23	74	0	0	8	80	1	127	11	3	6	.550	.408
Perez, Carlos, L.V.*	.333	6	8	6	2	2	4	2	0	0	0	2	0	0	0	0	3	0	0	0	.667	.333
Perez, Santiago, Port.†	.272	46	203	184	31	50	77	12	0	5	10	2	0	2	15	0	59	18	3	2	.418	.333
Pernalete, Marco, Fres.†	.307	32	112	101	9	31	48	7	2	2	11	0	1	0	10	1	22	1	0	1	.475	.366
Petersen, Chris, Nash.-Tuc.	.264	64	203	178	25	47	66	7	0	4	26	6	2	6	11	1	33	2	2	6	.371	.325
Petrick, Ben, C.S.	.250	18	79	64	11	16	21	2	0	1	9	0	2	0	13	2	21	1	0	1	.328	.367
Piatt, Adam, Sac.	.257	35	124	109	14	28	40	9	0	1	15	0	1	3	11	0	27	2	0	5	.367	.339
Podsednik, Scott, Tac.*	.290	66	288	269	46	78	110	15	4	3	30	4	0	2	13	0	46	12	5	0	.409	.327
Polcovich, Kevin, Mem.	.295	72	205	183	35	54	77	10	2	3	20	1	1	8	12	2	39	4	0	1	.421	.363
Porter, Bo, Okla.	.246	58	259	224	40	55	107	9	2	13	40	4	2	3	26	0	60	10	4	3	.478	.329
Porter, Colin, N.O.*	.237	101	353	312	48	74	111	14	1	7	33	0	4	3	34	2	105	11	6	2	.356	.314
Pose, Scott, N.O.*	.271	17	63	59	5	16	18	2	0	0	3	0	0	0	4	0	6	6	2	2	.305	.317
Post, Dave, L.V.	.294	67	211	180	24	53	75	14	1	2	31	3	1	1	26	2	21	2	3	7	.417	.385
Powell, Brian, N.O.	.083	24	27	24	1	2	2	0	0	0	0	3	0	0	0	0	5	0	0	0	.083	.083
Powell, Dante, Fres.	.282	114	466	426	74	120	215	23	3	22	62	0	2	4	34	2	122	25	5	7	.505	.339
Powell, Jeremy, Port.	.091	11	11	11	0	1	2	1	0	0	0	0	0	0	0	0	5	0	0	0	.182	.091
Powers, Jeff, C.S.*	.125	7	18	16	1	2	5	0	0	1	3	1	0	0	1	0	3	0	0	2	.313	.176
Priest, Eddie, L.V.	.000	23	25	22	2	0	0	0	0	0	0	1	0	0	2	0	11	0	0	0	.000	.083
Prieto, Alejandro, Oma.	.282	105	421	376	45	106	157	21	3	8	44	4	3	1	36	0	59	9	2	12	.418	.344
Prieto, Chris, L.V.*	.291	118	529	446	98	130	226	27	6	19	58	2	1	13	67	3	79	25	7	6	.507	.398
Pritchett, Chris, S.L.*	.303	125	527	476	66	144	237	36	3	17	75	2	3	1	45	5	102	3	2	7	.498	.362
Prokopec, Luke, L.V.*	1.000	1	2	1	0	1	2	1	0	0	0	1	0	0	0	0	0	0	0	0	2.000	1.000
Pujols, Rafael, Sac.	.233	9	33	30	4	7	11	1	0	1	3	0	0	0	3	0	5	0	0	0	.367	.303
Quevedo, Ruben, Iowa	.179	23	31	28	4	5	7	2	0	0	1	2	0	1	0	0	11	0	0	1	.250	.207
Quinn, Mark, Oma.	.186	11	43	43	4	8	15	1	0	2	3	0	0	0	0	0	9	0	0	0	.349	.186
Radmanovich, Ryan, Por.-Nas.*	.269	123	467	390	61	105	189	25	1	19	66	2	5	0	70	3	108	3	4	6	.485	.376
Ramirez, Omar, N.O.	.251	118	403	363	40	91	117	20	0	2	39	2	6	3	29	1	42	9	4	4	.322	.307
Randall, Scott, C.S.	.100	19	10	10	0	1	1	0	0	0	1	0	0	0	0	0	6	0	0	0	.100	.100
Randolph, Steve, Tuc.*	.286	20	8	7	1	2	3	1	0	0	0	1	0	0	0	0	3	0	0	0	.429	.286

Player, Team	Avg.	G	TPA	AB	R	H	TB	2B	3B	HR	RBI	SH	SF	HP	BB	IBB	SO	SB	CS	GDP	Slg.	OBP
Ransom, Cody, Fres.	.241	134	521	469	77	113	215	21	6	23	78	3	5	0	44	1	137	17	2	10	.458	.303
Rath, Fred, Mem.	.000	27	14	13	0	0	0	0	0	0	1	0	1	0	0	0	5	0	0	0	.000	.071
Redding, Tim, N.O.	.000	6	6	4	0	0	0	0	0	0	0	2	0	0	0	0	2	0	0	0	.000	.000
Redman, Tike, Nash.* ,,,,,,,,,,	.304	95	432	398	53	121	168	18	10	3	42	3	3	4	24	2	37	21	7	6	.422	.347
Revenig, Todd, Tuc.	.000	46	5	4	1	0	0	0	0	0	0	0	0	0	1	0	2	0	0	0	.000	.200
Reyes, Al, L.V.	.250	19	6	4	1	1	1	0	0	0	0	0	2	0	0	0	3	0	0	0	.250	.250
Reyes, Carlos, Tuc.†	.000	8	1	1	0	0	0	0	0	0	0	0	0	0	0	0	0	0	0	0	.000	.000
Reynolds, Shane, N.O.	.000	1	2	2	0	0	0	0	0	0	0	0	0	0	0	0	1	0	0	0	.000	.000
Reynoso, Armando, Tuc.	.000	1	1	1	0	0	0	0	0	0	0	0	0	0	0	0	0	0	0	1	.000	.000
Ricketts, Chad, L.V.	.000	49	7	7	1	0	0	0	0	0	0	0	0	0	0	0	5	0	0	0	.000	.000
Riggins, Auntwan, Port.†	.000	1	1	1	0	0	0	0	0	0	0	0	0	0	0	0	1	0	0	0	.000	.000
Riggs, Adam, Port.	.261	110	413	394	42	103	188	18	2	21	65	5	2	0	12	1	78	8	3	9	.477	.282
Riley, Mike, Fres.*	.143	28	9	7	1	1	1	0	0	0	0	1	0	1	1	0	3	0	0	1	.143	.250
Rizzo, Todd, L.V.-Fres.	.000	49	3	3	0	0	0	0	0	0	0	0	0	0	0	0	2	0	0	0	.000	.000
Roa, Joe, Cal.	.000	19	19	15	0	0	0	0	0	0	0	3	0	0	1	0	7	0	0	0	.000	.063
Roberts, Mark, Cal.	.000	33	3	2	0	0	0	0	0	0	0	1	0	0	0	0	1	0	0	0	.000	.000
Robinson, Kerry, Mem.*	.325	10	44	40	4	13	14	1	0	0	3	0	0	0	4	0	10	4	1	1	.350	.386
Rodgers, Bobby, Cal.	.000	18	5	4	0	0	0	0	0	0	0	1	0	0	0	0	3	0	0	0	.000	.000
Rodriguez, Jose, Mem.*	.000	54	3	3	0	0	0	0	0	0	0	0	0	0	0	0	2	0	0	0	.000	.000
Rolison, Nate, Cal.*	.167	3	13	12	1	2	2	0	0	0	1	0	0	0	1	0	3	0	0	1	.167	.231
Romano, Jason, Okla.	.315	41	176	149	32	47	67	6	1	4	13	6	1	0	20	1	28	3	4	4	.450	.394
Romero, J.C., Edm.†	.000	12	1	1	0	0	0	0	0	0	0	0	0	0	0	0	1	0	0	0	.000	.000
Romero, Mandy, Cal.-Sac.† ...	.167	22	74	66	4	11	18	4	0	1	5	0	0	0	8	0	16	0	0	2	.273	.257
Romero, Willie, Tuc.	.231	9	28	26	2	6	7	1	0	0	1	0	0	0	2	0	7	0	1	0	.269	.286
Rosario, Mel, L.V.	.260	24	84	77	11	20	36	2	1	4	15	0	2	3	2	0	19	1	5	1	.468	.298
Rosario, Mel, Oma.-Tuc.†	.250	60	200	188	19	47	82	13	2	6	28	2	1	1	8	1	50	1	1	3	.436	.283
Rosario, Omar, Sac.*	.237	21	68	59	6	14	20	3	0	1	8	1	0	1	7	0	18	1	2	2	.339	.328
Rose, Mike, Tuc.†	.182	20	69	55	9	10	15	1	2	0	8	1	1	0	12	1	16	0	0	3	.273	.324
Roskos, John, Port.-Iowa	.246	80	252	224	25	55	86	14	1	5	34	0	4	1	23	2	51	0	0	6	.384	.313
Ryan, Jason, Nash.-L.V.†.......	.000	15	11	9	0	0	0	0	0	0	1	1	0	0	1	0	5	0	0	1	.000	.100
Ryan, Mike, Edm.*	.288	136	585	527	89	152	256	36	7	18	73	1	3	2	52	1	121	1	6	17	.486	.353
Ryan, Rob, Tuc.-Sac.*	.276	125	515	434	80	120	218	25	8	19	82	0	5	8	68	9	85	2	6	3	.502	.301
Sabel, Erik, Tuc.	.000	18	5	4	0	0	0	0	0	0	0	1	0	0	0	0	4	0	0	0	.000	.000
Sagmoen, Marc, Ed.-Mem.-Ok.*	.222	80	342	324	31	72	101	15	1	4	26	2	2	0	14	0	76	4	2	4	.312	.253
Salazar, Oscar, Sac.	.063	5	17	16	0	1	1	0	0	0	1	0	0	0	1	0	5	0	0	1	.063	.118
Sanchez, Jesus, Cal.*	.214	17	19	14	3	3	3	0	0	0	1	3	0	0	2	0	4	0	0	1	.214	.313
Sanders, Reggie, Tuc.	.333	2	8	6	0	2	3	1	0	0	1	0	0	0	2	0	1	0	2	0	.500	.500
Santana, Julio, Fres.	.214	25	34	28	2	6	7	1	0	0	2	6	0	0	0	0	10	0	0	1	.250	.214
Santangelo, F.P., Sac.|	.202	71	239	188	32	38	62	7	1	5	17	8	4	9	30	0	49	5	4	4	.330	.333
Saturria, Luis, Mem.	.225	110	467	413	63	93	158	16	5	13	40	3	4	6	31	0	115	6	8	5	.383	.280
Saylor, Jamie, Cal.*	.111	15	30	27	5	3	6	0	0	1	3	0	0	0	3	0	11	0	0	1	.222	.200
Schifano, Tony, N.O.	.222	11	10	9	2	2	2	0	0	0	1	0	0	0	0	0	3	0	0	0	.222	.300
Schmidt, Jason, Nash.	.000	1	2	2	0	0	0	0	0	0	0	0	0	0	0	0	1	0	0	0	.000	.000
Sears, Todd, Edm.	.311	118	456	408	61	127	195	25	2	13	50	1	3	3	41	2	71	2	1	16	.478	.376
Secrist, Reed, Nash.*	.305	104	393	338	61	103	191	20	1	22	61	1	1	5	48	3	81	4	0	3	.565	.398
Sefcik, Kevin, C.S.	.312	49	232	199	37	62	82	14	0	2	22	2	4	3	24	0	26	5	6	3	.412	.387
Sell, Chip, Tuc.*	.262	94	267	248	34	65	97	10	2	6	28	3	2	2	12	3	49	3	2	5	.391	.299
Serrano, Wascar, Port.	.190	28	21	21	2	4	4	0	0	0	0	0	0	0	0	0	11	0	0	0	.190	.190
Servais, Scott, N.O.	.338	44	167	148	22	50	80	10	1	6	31	1	3	3	12	1	21	0	0	1	.541	.392
Short, Rick, Iowa	.275	105	344	313	38	86	122	19	1	5	34	5	1	3	22	0	42	2	1	13	.390	.327
Shouse, Brian, N.O.*	.000	56	3	2	0	0	0	0	0	0	0	1	0	0	0	0	1	0	0	0	.000	.000
Sierra, Ruben, Okla.†	.266	24	104	94	14	25	38	2	1	3	12	0	0	0	10	2	14	2	0	5	.404	.337
Sikaras, Pete, Tuc.	.000	4	1	1	0	0	0	0	0	0	0	0	0	0	0	0	1	0	0	0	.000	.000
Simon, Ben, L.V.	.000	12	11	7	0	0	0	0	0	0	0	2	0	0	2	0	3	0	0	0	.000	.222
Simons, Mitch, Okla.	.240	34	134	121	14	29	36	7	0	0	7	1	0	1	11	0	23	0	2	1	.298	.308
Simontacchi, Jason, Edm.	.000	33	1	1	1	0	0	0	0	0	0	0	0	0	0	0	0	0	0	0	.000	.000
Skrehot, Shaun, Nash.	.224	18	68	58	8	13	19	3	0	1	7	1	0	1	8	0	12	1	2	1	.328	.328
Slusarski, Joe, N.O.	.000	31	2	2	0	0	0	0	0	0	0	0	0	0	0	0	1	0	0	0	.000	.000
Smith, Brian, Nash.	.000	36	1	1	0	0	0	0	0	0	0	0	0	0	0	0	0	0	0	0	.000	.000
Smith, Bud, Mem.*	.207	19	33	29	3	6	11	2	0	1	8	3	1	0	0	0	5	1	0	1	.379	.200
Smith, Cam, L.V.	.000	8	1	1	0	0	0	0	0	0	0	0	0	0	0	0	0	0	0	0	.000	.000
Smith, Chuck, Cal.	.000	2	6	5	0	0	0	0	0	0	0	1	0	0	1	0	2	0	0	0	.000	.167
Smith, Jason, Iowa*	.233	70	256	240	31	56	88	8	6	4	15	1	2	1	12	4	71	6	3	4	.367	.271
Snopek, Chris, Iowa.............	.277	130	513	470	65	130	205	33	0	14	57	4	5	2	32	0	67	6	5	10	.436	.322
Snow, J.T., Fres.*	.000	4	14	12	1	0	0	0	0	0	0	0	0	0	2	0	7	0	0	0	.000	.143
Sosa, Juan, C.S.-Tuc.	.198	78	245	222	19	44	53	7	1	0	14	5	3	1	14	1	29	6	2	16	.239	.246
Sparks, Steve, Nash.	.091	31	12	11	1	1	1	0	0	0	0	1	0	0	0	0	5	0	0	0	.091	.091
Spencer, Stan, Port.	.056	21	19	18	0	1	1	0	0	0	1	1	0	0	0	0	7	0	0	0	.056	.056
Spivey, Junior, Tuc.	.232	54	221	194	25	45	69	6	0	6	27	0	0	0	27	1	32	9	6	4	.356	.326
Sprague, Ed, Tac.	.316	5	23	19	6	6	14	2	0	2	4	0	1	2	1	0	5	0	0	0	.737	.391
Springer, Dennis, L.V.	.036	19	30	28	1	1	1	0	0	0	0	2	0	0	0	0	7	0	0	0	.036	.036
Springer, Russ, Tuc.	1.000	7	1	1	0	1	1	0	0	0	0	0	0	0	0	0	0	0	0	0	1.000	1.000
Stanifer, Rob, Iowa	.222	55	12	9	0	2	5	1	1	0	1	2	0	0	1	0	2	0	0	0	.556	.300
Stankiewicz, Andy, L.V.	.262	66	240	202	18	53	60	7	0	0	13	9	1	3	25	3	29	5	2	3	.297	.351
Steed, Dave, Okla.	.233	67	258	227	28	53	84	10	0	7	29	1	2	3	25	1	61	0	1	6	.370	.315
Steenstra, Kennie, Tuc.	.163	39	47	43	4	7	9	2	0	0	1	3	0	0	1	0	21	0	0	1	.209	.182
Stefanski, Mike, Mem.	.262	61	184	164	25	43	71	8	1	6	26	4	1	2	13	0	31	1	2	4	.433	.322
Stocker, Kevin, L.V.†	.000	1	0	0	1	0	0	0	0	0	0	0	0	0	0	0	0	0	0	0	.000	.000
Stone, Ricky, N.O.	.250	51	14	12	1	3	5	2	0	0	3	2	0	0	0	0	3	0	0	1	.417	.250
Strong, Joe, Cal.†	.000	46	1	1	0	0	0	0	0	0	0	0	0	0	0	0	0	0	0	0	.000	.000
Sutton, Larry, Mem.-Edm.*	.256	74	294	246	35	63	96	12	3	5	37	0	3	1	44	2	48	1	2	7	.390	.367
Tankersley, Dennis, Port.	.000	3	1	1	0	0	0	0	0	0	0	0	0	0	0	0	0	0	0	0	.000	.000
Taveras, Luis, Okla.	.182	12	38	33	3	6	6	0	0	0	3	2	0	0	3	0	12	0	1	1	.182	.250

Player, Team	Avg.	G	TPA	AB	R	H	TB	2B	3B	HR	RBI	SH	SF	HP	BB	IBB	SO	SB	CS	GDP	Slg.	OBP
Teut, Nate, Iowa	.097	29	36	31	2	3	3	0	0	0	1	4	0	0	1	0	10	0	0	0	.097	.125
Theodorou, Nick, L.V.†	.000	1	1	1	0	0	0	0	0	0	0	0	0	0	0	0	1	0	0	0	.000	.000
t'Hoen, E.J., S.L.	.219	18	67	64	8	14	25	5	0	2	7	0	0	2	1	0	18	0	1	3	.391	.254
Thomas, Juan, Tac.	.300	129	550	503	75	151	263	39	2	23	95	0	5	2	40	2	141	2	2	9	.523	.351
Thompson, Ryan, Cal.	.310	78	317	300	53	93	176	26	0	19	69	1	1	1	14	1	65	4	3	11	.587	.342
Thomson, John, C.S.	.077	12	15	13	1	1	1	0	0	0	0	0	0	0	2	0	6	0	0	0	.077	.200
Thrower, Jake, Port.†	.204	15	57	54	3	11	12	1	0	0	1	1	0	0	2	1	8	1	0	0	.222	.232
Tolentino, Juan, S.L.	.277	114	489	452	70	125	199	35	3	11	66	4	3	5	25	0	87	17	4	7	.440	.320
Tollberg, Brian, Port.	.000	4	3	2	0	0	0	0	0	0	0	1	0	0	0	0	1	0	0	0	.000	.000
Torcato, Tony, Fres.*	.320	35	152	150	20	48	64	8	1	2	8	0	0	0	2	0	20	0	1	5	.427	.329
Torrealba, Yorvit, Fres.	.274	115	422	394	56	108	161	23	3	8	36	3	2	4	19	0	65	2	3	11	.409	.313
Tremie, Chris, N.O.	.118	8	23	17	0	2	3	1	0	0	2	1	1	0	4	0	2	0	0	0	.176	.273
Truby, Chris, N.O.	.312	81	351	321	53	100	173	25	6	12	71	0	2	4	24	4	66	10	5	11	.539	.365
Tyler, Josh, Fres.	.287	77	256	230	21	66	92	15	1	0	20	0	2	3	18	4	40	5	3	4	.400	.344
Ullery, Dave, Oma.*	.157	17	58	51	4	8	11	1	1	0	1	1	0	1	5	0	20	1	0	0	.216	.246
Uribe, Juan, C.S.	.310	74	297	281	40	87	149	27	7	7	48	0	2	2	12	1	43	11	8	8	.530	.340
Valentin, Javier, Edm.†	.281	121	489	431	53	121	205	29	2	17	71	0	7	4	47	5	108	0	1	14	.476	.352
Vazquez, Ramon, Tac.*	.300	127	550	466	85	140	200	28	1	10	79	4	3	1	76	3	84	9	7	13	.429	.397
Ventura, Juan, C.S.	.167	2	7	6	1	1	1	0	0	0	1	0	0	1	0	0	2	0	1	1	.167	.286
Verplancke, Jeff, Fres.	.000	8	2	2	0	0	0	0	0	0	0	0	0	0	0	0	0	0	0	0	.000	.000
Vogelsong, Ryan, Fres.-Nash.	.222	17	19	18	1	4	6	2	0	0	0	1	0	0	0	0	4	0	0	1	.333	.222
Wainhouse, Dave, Iowa*	.200	49	5	5	0	1	1	0	0	0	0	0	0	0	0	0	3	0	0	0	.200	.200
Ward, Jeremy, Tuc.	.000	40	3	3	0	0	0	0	0	0	0	0	0	0	0	0	1	0	0	0	.000	.000
Waszgis, B.J., Cal.	.251	96	352	311	50	78	165	18	0	23	65	0	2	8	31	2	90	0	1	10	.531	.332
Watkins, Pat, Oma.	.253	67	269	245	29	62	97	12	1	7	29	4	3	4	13	0	41	2	7	10	.396	.298
Weibl, Clint, Mem.	.000	2	2	2	0	0	0	0	0	0	0	0	0	0	0	0	0	0	0	0	.000	.000
Wengert, Don, Nash.	.048	18	27	21	2	1	1	0	0	0	3	0	1	0	5	0	8	0	0	1	.048	.222
Whisenant, Matt, L.V.	.000	24	10	9	0	0	0	0	0	0	0	1	0	0	0	0	3	0	0	0	.000	.000
White, Walt, Tuc.	.215	35	89	79	11	17	23	4	1	0	8	2	0	0	8	0	23	1	0	1	.291	.287
Whitmore, Darrell, Mem.*	.277	112	356	328	47	91	146	22	0	11	52	0	3	3	22	3	61	2	3	6	.445	.326
Wilkins, Marc, Nash.	.000	32	1	1	0	0	0	0	0	0	0	0	0	0	0	0	1	0	0	0	.000	.000
Wilkins, Rick, Port.*	.212	68	246	222	18	47	84	15	2	6	33	1	7	1	15	0	77	0	1	3	.378	.257
Williams, Dave, Nash.*	.000	3	1	1	0	0	0	0	0	0	0	0	0	0	0	0	1	0	0	0	.000	.000
Williams, Jeff, L.V.	.286	16	17	14	0	4	4	0	0	0	0	0	2	0	1	0	5	0	0	0	.286	.333
Williams, Matt, Tuc.	.353	5	19	17	4	6	14	2	0	2	5	0	0	0	2	1	2	1	0	0	.824	.421
Wilson, Craig, Oma.	.296	125	534	473	78	140	206	27	3	11	69	3	9	4	45	0	58	6	4	21	.436	.360
Wilson, Craig, Nash.	.289	11	48	45	4	13	20	2	1	1	3	0	0	1	2	0	14	0	0	1	.444	.333
Wilson, Desi, Tuc.*	.328	83	337	320	45	105	136	20	1	3	38	0	1	2	14	0	48	4	2	8	.425	.359
Wilson, Jack, Nash.	.369	27	115	103	20	38	49	6	1	1	6	1	0	2	9	0	13	2	2	1	.476	.430
Wilson, Preston, Cal.	.500	4	15	10	3	5	7	2	0	0	1	0	0	0	5	0	1	2	0	0	.700	.667
Wilson, Tom, Sac.	.282	77	320	259	43	73	114	15	1	8	48	0	8	4	49	1	62	0	1	5	.440	.394
Wimberly, Larry, Nash.*	.333	4	5	3	0	1	1	0	0	0	0	0	2	0	0	0	2	0	0	0	.333	.333
Witt, Bobby, Tuc.	.000	5	2	1	0	0	0	0	0	0	0	0	0	0	1	0	0	0	0	0	.000	.500
Witt, Kevin, Port.*	.289	129	487	456	66	132	251	28	5	27	87	0	6	3	22	0	127	1	1	13	.550	.322
Wojciechowski, Steve, Cal.*	.000	8	1	0	0	0	0	0	0	0	0	0	1	0	0	0	0	0	0	0	.000	.000
Womack, Tony, Tuc.*	.385	4	13	13	1	5	7	0	1	0	2	0	0	0	0	0	1	0	1	0	.538	.385
Wood, Jason, Nash.	.243	113	447	379	46	92	137	19	1	8	38	4	1	6	27	3	73	0	0	12	.361	.303
Woods, Ken, Iowa	.250	11	37	36	3	9	10	1	0	0	2	0	0	1	0	0	9	0	0	2	.278	.270
Woolf, Jason, Mem.†	.188	5	19	16	3	3	6	0	0	1	4	0	1	0	2	0	2	2	0	0	.375	.263
Wright, Mike, Fres.	.375	2	8	8	2	3	6	0	0	1	3	0	0	0	0	0	2	0	0	0	.750	.375
Young, Ernie, Port.	.274	116	462	409	66	112	197	21	2	20	67	0	1	14	38	1	115	0	3	13	.482	.355
Young, Mike, Okla.	.291	47	214	189	28	55	87	8	0	8	28	2	2	1	20	0	34	3	3	6	.460	.358
Young, Travis, Fres.	.000	4	4	3	0	0	0	0	0	0	0	1	0	0	0	0	2	0	0	0	.000	.000
Zambrano, Carlos, Iowa*	.240	26	27	25	2	6	9	0	0	1	2	2	0	0	0	0	12	0	0	0	.360	.240
Zamora, Junior, S.L.	.300	6	22	20	3	6	15	1	1	2	4	0	0	0	2	0	3	0	0	0	.750	.364
Zancanaro, Dave, Mem.*	.100	27	25	20	1	2	2	0	0	0	1	4	0	0	1	0	6	0	0	0	.100	.143
Zaun, Greg, Oma.†	.279	11	48	43	5	12	19	4	0	1	8	0	1	1	3	0	3	0	0	2	.442	.333
Zerbe, Chad, Fres.*	.500	17	2	2	0	1	2	1	0	0	0	0	0	0	0	0	0	0	0	0	1.000	.500
Zinter, Alan, N.O.†	.265	104	371	332	58	88	161	16	0	19	65	0	3	3	33	1	85	1	1	13	.485	.334
Zuleta, Julio, Iowa	.308	37	158	146	18	45	79	13	0	7	29	0	2	3	7	0	33	3	1	4	.541	.348
Zuniga, Tony, Fres.	.271	123	477	413	77	112	208	16	1	26	74	0	3	6	55	2	83	6	1	7	.504	.363

PLAYERS WITH TWO OR MORE TEAMS

Player, Team	Avg.	G	TPA	AB	R	H	TB	2B	3B	HR	RBI	SH	SF	HP	BB	IBB	SO	SB	CS	GDP	Slg.	OBP
Banks, Brian, Iowa†	.179	17	43	39	2	7	12	2	0	1	4	0	0	0	4	0	11	0	0	2	.308	.256
Banks, Brian, Cal.†	.291	101	395	357	70	104	208	27	4	23	63	0	3	3	32	3	97	5	4	5	.583	.352
Bartee, Kimera, S.L.†	.275	40	189	167	23	46	72	13	2	3	27	2	1	0	19	2	26	5	1	1	.431	.348
Bartee, Kimera, C.S.†	.192	24	87	78	14	15	32	2	0	5	15	1	1	1	6	0	31	3	0	0	.410	.256
Berblinger, Jeff, Oma.	.215	73	297	270	36	58	91	12	3	5	23	4	0	1	22	1	54	8	5	6	.337	.276
Berblinger, Jeff, Nash.	.333	6	19	18	3	6	10	1	0	1	1	0	0	0	1	0	4	1	0	0	.556	.368
Brumbaugh, Cliff, Okla.	.307	54	240	202	38	62	103	11	3	8	42	0	3	2	33	0	41	3	3	3	.510	.404
Brumbaugh, Cliff, C.S.	.332	54	246	208	31	69	98	18	1	3	39	0	4	0	34	0	52	5	3	1	.471	.419
Camp, Shawn, Port.	.000	4	1	1	0	0	0	0	0	0	0	0	0	0	0	0	1	0	0	0	.000	.000
Camp, Shawn, Nash.	.000	11	1	1	0	0	0	0	0	0	0	0	0	0	0	0	0	0	0	0	.000	.000
Christenson, Ryan, Sac.	.171	19	74	70	7	12	19	4	0	1	3	0	0	0	4	0	13	2	0	1	.271	.216
Christenson, Ryan, Tuc.	.288	57	243	215	32	62	97	17	0	6	27	2	3	0	23	0	43	5	2	4	.451	.353
DeSilva, John, Cal.	.000	26	5	4	0	0	0	0	0	0	0	0	0	0	0	0	3	0	0	0	.000	.000
DeSilva, John, L.V.	.000	14	3	3	0	0	0	0	0	0	0	0	0	0	0	0	1	0	0	0	.000	.000
Durrington, Trent, L.V.	.218	22	64	55	10	12	21	4	1	1	2	0	0	1	8	0	19	3	1	0	.382	.324
Durrington, Trent, S.L.	.328	39	139	122	20	40	68	11	4	3	21	2	2	2	11	0	24	7	4	3	.557	.387
Encarnacion, Mario, Sac.	.285	51	209	186	29	53	101	8	2	12	33	0	1	4	17	2	61	4	3	5	.543	.356
Encarnacion, Mario, C.S.	.378	16	50	45	8	17	28	5	0	2	10	0	0	1	4	0	8	0	1	1	.622	.440

Player, Team	Avg.	G	TPA	AB	R	H	TB	2B	3B	HR	RBI	SH	SF	HP	BB	IBB	SO	SB	CS	GDP	Slg.	OBP
Espada, Josue, Cal.	.300	79	339	290	61	87	120	20	2	3	30	3	3	4	39	0	49	13	7	4	.414	.387
Espada, Josue, C.S.	.259	7	32	27	8	7	12	2	0	1	2	0	0	0	5	0	6	3	2	0	.444	.375
Fasano, Sal, Oma.	.230	13	55	46	6	11	18	1	0	2	7	0	0	5	4	0	11	0	0	1	.391	.364
Fasano, Sal, C.S.	.305	26	97	82	16	25	50	4	0	7	23	1	1	4	9	1	26	0	0	4	.610	.396
Frias, Hanley, Edm.†	.183	49	153	142	15	26	32	6	0	0	7	1	0	0	10	0	28	2	3	3	.225	.237
Frias, Hanley, Mem.†	.242	58	259	240	27	58	76	8	2	2	19	0	1	2	16	0	44	6	4	3	.317	.293
Gross, Kip, L.V.	.000	10	1	1	0	0	0	0	0	0	0	0	0	0	0	0	1	0	0	0	.000	.000
Gross, Kip, C.S.	.000	18	13	12	0	0	0	0	0	0	0	1	0	0	0	0	5	0	0	0	.000	.000
Hubbard, Trenidad, Oma.	.286	49	209	175	35	50	91	9	1	10	28	0	2	2	30	0	34	8	5	1	.520	.392
Hubbard, Trenidad, Iowa	.316	49	212	171	38	54	89	11	3	6	31	0	2	2	37	1	27	17	5	4	.520	.439
Jennings, Robin, Sac.*	.306	38	156	144	26	44	76	11	3	5	26	0	1	2	9	0	26	5	2	4	.528	.353
Jennings, Robin, C.S.*	.282	11	41	39	8	11	18	1	0	2	5	0	0	1	1	0	10	1	0	1	.462	.317
Lamb, Dave, C.S.†	.222	5	9	9	1	2	2	0	0	0	0	0	0	0	0	0	4	0	0	0	.222	.222
Lamb, Dave, Cal.†	.299	23	84	67	15	20	29	6	0	1	6	4	0	2	11	0	11	0	0	3	.433	.413
Lawrence, Sean, Port.*	.000	25	1	1	0	0	0	0	0	0	0	0	0	0	0	0	1	0	0	0	.000	.000
Lawrence, Sean, Tuc.*	.000	18	1	1	0	0	0	0	0	0	0	0	0	0	0	0	1	0	0	0	.000	.000
Lemonis, Chris, Cal.*	.160	9	28	25	3	4	4	0	0	0	1	0	0	1	2	0	7	0	0	1	.160	.250
Lemonis, Chris, Tuc.*	.217	9	24	23	3	5	7	2	0	0	0	0	0	0	1	0	3	0	0	1	.304	.250
Lidle, Kevin, S.L.†	.295	30	104	88	10	26	36	7	0	1	10	2	1	3	9	0	27	2	1	0	.409	.376
Lidle, Kevin, Mem.†	.057	13	37	35	1	2	3	1	0	0	2	0	0	0	2	0	14	0	0	0	.086	.108
Luuloa, Keith, Port.	.272	64	239	217	31	59	88	13	2	4	16	2	2	5	13	0	24	1	1	9	.406	.325
Luuloa, Keith, N.O.	.204	36	110	93	14	19	32	7	0	2	11	1	1	2	13	1	17	0	0	3	.344	.312
Magruder, Chris, Fres.†	.280	54	240	214	37	60	99	7	1	10	30	0	1	7	18	0	45	3	1	2	.463	.354
Magruder, Chris, Okla.†	.362	33	157	127	28	46	83	14	4	5	21	4	1	4	21	3	19	1	2	3	.654	.464
Mahay, Ron, Port.*	.000	14	1	1	0	0	0	0	0	0	0	0	0	0	0	0	0	0	0	0	.000	.000
Mahay, Ron, Iowa*	.200	36	5	5	0	1	1	0	0	0	0	0	0	0	0	0	2	0	0	0	.200	.200
Moreta, Ramon, Tac.	.217	23	80	69	8	15	23	3	1	1	13	0	3	2	6	0	31	3	3	3	.333	.288
Moreta, Ramon, S.L.	.286	2	7	7	0	2	2	0	0	0	1	0	0	0	0	0	0	0	1	0	.286	.286
Nelson, Bryant, Tuc.†	.301	85	349	326	37	98	131	15	0	6	41	1	3	1	16	2	20	9	5	12	.402	.332
Nelson, Bryant, Nash.†	.314	49	202	185	23	58	80	7	0	5	15	4	2	1	10	0	16	3	3	7	.432	.348
Nicholson, Kevin, Port.†	.194	11	35	31	1	6	7	1	0	0	1	0	0	0	4	0	3	0	1	0	.226	.286
Nicholson, Kevin, C.S.†	.385	23	84	78	14	30	38	5	0	1	11	1	0	0	5	1	7	1	1	2	.487	.422
Petersen, Chris, Nash.	.382	21	63	55	9	21	32	5	0	2	18	1	1	3	3	0	15	0	2	0	.582	.453
Petersen, Chris, Tuc.	.211	43	140	123	16	26	34	2	0	2	8	5	1	3	8	1	18	2	0	6	.276	.274
Radmanovich, Ryan, Port.* ...	.264	92	361	296	44	78	139	17	1	14	52	2	4	0	59	3	82	2	4	6	.470	.382
Radmanovich, Ryan, Nash.* ...	.287	31	106	94	17	27	50	8	0	5	14	0	1	0	11	0	26	1	0	0	.532	.358
Rizzo, Todd, L.V.	.000	13	1	1	0	0	0	0	0	0	0	0	0	0	0	0	0	0	0	0	.000	.000
Rizzo, Todd, Fres. ,,,,,,,,,,,,,,,,	.000	36	2	2	0	0	0	0	0	0	0	0	0	0	0	0	2	0	0	0	.000	.000
Romero, Mandy, Cal.†	.000	3	9	8	0	0	0	0	0	0	0	0	0	0	3	0	3	0	0	0	.000	.333
Romero, Mandy, Sac.†	.183	19	65	60	4	11	18	4	0	1	5	0	0	0	5	0	13	0	0	2	.300	.246
Rosario, Mel, Oma.†	.252	41	161	151	18	38	70	10	2	6	25	1	1	1	7	1	42	1	1	1	.464	.288
Rosario, Mel, Tuc.†	.243	19	39	37	1	9	12	3	0	0	3	1	0	0	1	0	8	0	0	2	.324	.263
Roskos, John, Port.	.239	40	148	134	15	32	52	9	1	3	20	0	3	0	11	1	31	0	0	6	.388	.291
Roskos, John, Iowa	.256	34	104	90	10	23	34	5	0	2	14	0	1	1	12	1	20	0	0	0	.378	.346
Ryan, Jason, Nash.†	.000	10	8	6	0	0	0	0	0	0	0	1	0	0	1	0	4	0	0	1	.000	.143
Ryan, Jason, L.V.†	.000	5	3	3	0	0	0	0	0	0	0	1	0	0	0	0	1	0	0	0	.000	.000
Ryan, Rob, Tuc.*	.329	63	252	216	45	71	134	17	5	12	50	0	2	5	29	3	34	1	3	3	.620	.417
Ryan, Rob, Sac.*	.225	62	263	218	35	49	84	8	3	7	32	0	3	3	39	6	51	1	3	0	.385	.346
Sagmoen, Marc, Edm.*	.081	9	39	37	2	3	4	1	0	0	1	0	0	0	2	0	8	0	0	1	.108	.128
Sagmoen, Marc, Mem.*	.250	12	56	52	7	13	17	4	0	0	9	0	0	0	4	0	15	1	0	2	.327	.304
Sagmoen, Marc, Okla.*	.238	59	247	235	22	56	80	10	1	4	16	2	2	0	8	0	53	3	2	1	.340	.261
Sosa, Juan, C.S.	.225	14	47	40	2	9	10	1	0	0	2	1	1	0	5	0	7	1	1	5	.250	.304
Sosa, Juan, Tuc.	.192	64	198	182	17	35	43	6	1	0	12	4	2	1	9	1	22	5	1	11	.236	.232
Sutton, Larry, Mem.*	.263	29	120	99	12	26	37	5	0	2	13	0	0	0	21	0	16	1	1	3	.374	.392
Sutton, Larry, Edm.*	.252	45	174	147	23	37	59	7	3	3	24	0	3	1	23	2	32	0	1	4	.401	.351
Vogelsong, Ryan, Fres.	.167	11	13	12	1	2	2	0	0	0	0	1	0	0	0	0	2	0	0	1	.167	.167
Vogelsong, Ryan, Nash.	.333	6	6	6	0	2	4	2	0	0	0	0	0	0	0	0	2	0	0	0	.667	.333

GRAND SLAMS: Hinske, 3; Brumbaugh, Melhuse, Moriarty, Nunnally, Truby, Valentin, Zuniga, 2 each; Abad, Akers, Andrews, Barker, Barkett, Bartee, Bass, M. Bell, Bellhorn, Berrios, Blake, Cota, C. Crespo, E. Diaz, Dunwoody, Durrington, Espada, Fasano, Fernandez, Ginter, Gload, Grabowski, Grijak, Guiel, Hiatt, Huckaby, Hyzdu, B. Johnson, K. Johnson, Kieschnick, McGuire, S. Morgan, Morris, Pellow, A. Pena, Pritchett, Riggs, Saturria, B. Smith, Steed, R. Vasquez, Waszgis, P. Watkins, Whitmore, K. Witt, Zinter.

AWARDED FIRST BASE ON CATCHER'S INTERFERENCE: Guiel 3 (Moeller, Petrick, Ortiz); Abbott 2 (Burke, McDonald), Nelson (Cota, Mottola), Encarnacion (Hernandez), L. Garcia (Hubbard), Grabowksi (Haselman), A. Hernandez (Gil), Lidle (Machado), C. Meyers (Wilkins), Minor (Huckaby), C. Patterson (Fasano), C. Pena (Zinter), Prieto (Barthol).

2001 PITCHING

TEAM

Team	W	L	Pct.	ERA	G	CG	ShO	Sv.	IP	H	TBF	R	ER	HR	SH	SF	HB	BB	IBB	SO	WP	Bk.
Tacoma...........	85	59	.590	3.74	144	11	11	38	1250.0	1210	5312	610	519	131	48	49	58	414	7	1079	41	4
New Orleans......	82	57	.590	3.75	139	8	8	41	1203.2	1211	5077	591	501	121	38	26	56	331	24	959	47	4
Iowa	83	60	.580	3.85	143	4	12	46	1263.1	1204	5399	599	540	133	58	39	55	475	36	1228	56	4
Portland	71	73	.493	4.18	144	0	11	36	1266.1	1300	5406	653	588	134	49	45	52	390	14	998	40	3
Oklahoma	74	69	.517	4.28	143	10	7	33	1266.1	1259	5470	677	602	133	41	32	61	495	6	1107	34	2
Nashville	64	77	.454	4.51	141	7	7	30	1222.0	1276	5304	702	613	147	46	37	45	426	25	840	57	4
Salt Lake	79	64	.552	4.55	143	9	4	34	1261.1	1320	5406	716	638	164	27	31	59	392	4	1036	59	9
Tucson	65	77	.458	4.58	142	4	6	33	1243.0	1405	5501	757	632	112	49	49	51	402	33	937	53	9
Sacramento.......	75	69	.521	4.70	144	7	4	27	1264.0	1359	5547	741	660	159	36	35	60	465	23	1075	52	2
Omaha	70	74	.486	4.80	144	2	2	34	1249.1	1359	5431	731	666	181	33	29	56	442	12	967	53	9
Memphis	62	81	.434	4.80	143	2	8	28	1252.1	1358	5574	761	668	156	55	47	66	505	11	962	52	2
Edmonton	60	83	.420	4.86	143	7	7	29	1229.0	1441	5441	755	664	149	32	39	49	439	10	968	60	2

Team	W	L	Pct.	ERA	G	CG	ShO	Sv.	IP	H	TBF	R	ER	HR	SH	SF	HB	BB	IBB	SO	WP	Bk.
Las Vegas	68	76	.472	4.98	144	5	10	33	1264.0	1412	5602	780	700	156	51	50	74	474	34	1090	55	9
Fresno	68	71	.489	5.03	139	1	4	40	1198.0	1297	5315	745	669	176	49	42	66	497	11	983	58	5
Colo. Springs	62	79	.440	5.25	141	5	6	21	1231.0	1459	5525	826	718	163	40	26	81	400	19	1042	69	7
Calgary	72	71	.503	5.34	143	3	5	34	1222.1	1492	5462	801	725	145	44	39	42	376	30	977	71	5

INDIVIDUAL

TOP QUALIFIERS FOR EARNED-RUN AVERAGE TITLE

Minimum 115 innings. *Lefthanded pitcher.

Pitcher, Team	W	L	Pct.	ERA	G	GS	CG	ShO	GF	Sv.	IP	H	TBF	R	ER	HR	SH	SF	HB	BB	IBB	SO	WP	Bk.
Stark, Dennis, Tac.	14	2	.875	2.37	24	24	0	0	0	0	151.2	124	613	52	40	12	8	5	7	41	0	130	5	1
Quevedo, Ruben, Iowa	9	5	.643	2.99	22	22	1	1	0	0	141.2	124	588	54	47	13	8	6	3	48	3	150	1	0
Arteaga, J.D., N.O.*	8	6	.571	3.07	32	21	1	0	4	1	138.0	143	578	60	47	11	5	1	9	27	2	90	4	0
Powell, Brian, N.O.	9	8	.529	3.17	24	23	3	2	0	0	144.2	142	599	65	51	13	4	2	6	39	1	96	3	1
Meyers, Mike, Iowa	7	4	.636	3.23	25	25	0	0	0	0	147.2	129	631	58	53	9	3	6	2	64	3	124	8	0
George, Chris, Oma.*	11	3	.786	3.53	20	20	0	0	0	0	117.1	103	489	54	46	14	2	1	1	51	0	84	0	1
D'Amico, Jeff, Oma.	5	7	.417	3.54	32	20	0	0	0	5	140.0	151	595	65	55	19	8	3	5	40	2	92	5	2
Benes, Alan, Mem.	7	6	.538	3.55	25	25	1	0	0	0	142.0	164	637	71	56	13	7	2	7	51	1	96	2	0
Dickey, R.A., Okla.	11	7	.611	3.75	24	24	3	0	0	0	163.0	164	687	77	68	14	7	2	7	45	1	120	3	0
Driskill, Travis, N.O.	11	5	.688	3.78	28	28	1	0	0	0	178.2	175	735	83	75	21	6	5	6	33	2	145	5	1
Zambrano, Carlos, Iowa	10	5	.667	3.88	26	25	1	0	1	0	150.2	124	639	73	65	9	5	3	14	68	1	155	10	1
Roa, Joe, Cal.	6	6	.500	3.92	19	19	1	0	0	0	124.0	134	508	58	54	16	5	1	4	12	2	81	1	1
Wooten, Greg, Tac.	11	8	.579	3.99	27	26	5	1	0	0	169.1	201	728	91	75	18	5	9	7	32	1	116	6	0
Tomko, Brett, Tac.	10	6	.625	4.04	19	18	3	2	0	0	127.0	124	528	64	57	12	7	5	3	25	1	117	2	0
Steenstra, Kennie, Tac.	9	6	.600	4.18	28	28	1	0	0	0	170.0	187	737	101	79	14	7	4	7	42	1	114	1	0

DEPARTMENTAL LEADERS: W—Stark, 14; L—Zancanaro, 14; Pct.—Stark, .875; G—Crabtree, 63; GS—Kinney, Teut, 29 each; CG—Wooten, 5; ShO—Tomko, B. Powell, Kiefer, 2 each; GF—Miadich, 54; Sv.—Miadich, Mann, 27 each; IP—Driskill, 178.2; H—Ireland, 696; TBF—Ireland, 771; R—Averette, 131; ER—Averette, 113; HR—Averette, 29; SH—Norton, 9; SF—Ramsay, 10; HB—J. Miller, 16; BB—Hutchinson, 104; IBB—Norton, Dougherty, Revinig, 7 each; SO—Kiefer, 174; WP—Hutchinson, 17; BK—V. Alvarez, 5.

ALL PITCHERS

*Lefthanded pitcher.

Pitcher, Team	W	L	Pct.	ERA	G	GS	CG	ShO	GF	Sv.	IP	H	TBF	R	ER	HR	SH	SF	HB	BB	IBB	SO	WP	Bk.
Abbott, Paul, Tac.	0	0	.000	0.00	1	1	0	0	0	0	4.0	1	18	0	0	0	0	1	4	0	4	0	0	
Acevedo, Juan, C.S.	0	0	.000	1.29	6	0	0	0	3	1	7.0	3	28	2	1	0	1	0	0	4	0	7	1	0
Adkins, Jon, Sac.	1	0	1.000	4.26	3	2	0	0	0	0	12.2	17	60	9	6	1	1	0	0	8	0	7	0	0
Ahearne, Pat, Cal.	6	10	.375	6.28	28	26	0	0	0	0	144.2	212	659	112	101	14	6	2	3	35	0	80	8	0
Ah Yat, Paul, Nash.*	1	4	.200	9.30	8	4	0	0	2	0	20.1	37	104	22	21	0	2	2	0	9	1	15	0	0
Ainsworth, Kurt, Fres.	10	9	.526	5.07	27	26	0	0	0	0	149.0	139	634	91	84	22	4	6	7	54	1	157	10	0
Akers, Chad, Tac.	0	0	.000	0.00	1	0	0	0	0	0	0.2	0	2	0	0	0	0	0	0	0	0	0	0	0
Almonte, Hector, Cal.	0	0	.000	8.39	18	0	0	0	11	0	24.2	36	123	29	23	6	0	2	0	15	0	21	2	0
Alvarez, Juan, S.L.*	2	2	.500	4.95	48	1	0	0	14	0	67.1	68	289	42	37	13	0	4	0	27	0	44	4	1
Alvarez, Victor, L.V.*	7	4	.636	4.27	20	20	0	0	0	0	118.0	115	502	63	56	12	4	2	6	41	0	94	4	5
Alviso, Jerome, C.S.	0	0	.000	0.00	1	0	0	0	0	0	1.0	0	3	0	0	0	0	0	1	0	0	0	0	0
Anderson, Brian, Tuc.*	1	0	1.000	1.50	2	2	0	0	0	0	12.0	7	44	2	2	0	0	0	0	2	0	8	0	0
Andra, Jeff, Fres.*	1	3	.250	6.38	9	6	0	0	0	0	36.2	50	169	32	26	8	2	3	1	14	0	22	4	0
Ankiel, Rick, Mem.*	0	2	.000	20.77	3	3	0	0	0	0	4.1	3	33	10	10	0	1	0	1	17	0	4	12	0
Arnold, Jamie, Fres.	1	4	.200	5.92	44	3	0	0	23	9	76.0	96	361	58	50	13	3	3	10	36	0	56	5	0
Arroyo, Bronson, Nash.	6	2	.750	3.93	9	9	2	1	0	0	66.1	63	276	32	29	6	2	1	2	15	1	49	4	0
Arteaga, J.D., N.O.*	8	6	.571	3.07	32	21	1	0	4	1	138.0	143	578	60	47	11	5	1	9	27	2	90	4	0
Austin, Jeff, Oma.	3	7	.300	6.88	28	8	0	0	9	2	70.2	89	319	56	54	14	3	2	4	27	1	55	5	2
Averette, Rob, C.S.	6	14	.300	6.11	27	27	0	0	0	0	166.1	204	741	131	113	29	4	2	5	48	2	125	11	1
Aybar, Manny, Iowa	1	2	.333	5.02	8	7	1	1	0	0	43.0	42	187	26	24	8	2	1	1	16	1	32	2	0
Ayers, Mike, Nash.*	0	0	.000	9.00	5	0	0	0	0	0	4.0	5	20	4	4	0	1	1	0	5	1	3	0	0
Baez, Benito, Cal.*	7	1	.875	3.03	49	0	0	0	15	1	59.1	53	232	22	20	5	3	0	1	7	1	56	4	0
Bailey, Cory, Oma.	1	0	1.000	0.00	5	0	0	0	4	1	10.0	2	37	0	0	1	0	0	0	5	0	7	0	0
Balfour, Grant, Edm.	2	2	.500	5.51	11	0	0	0	2	0	16.1	18	73	11	10	2	3	1	0	10	1	17	2	0
Barkett, Andy, Nash.*	0	0	.000	0.00	1	0	0	0	0	0	2.0	1	7	0	0	0	0	0	0	0	0	2	0	0
Beech, Matt, Okla.*	1	6	.143	5.88	10	10	0	0	0	0	59.2	83	284	49	39	10	2	1	4	24	0	44	2	0
Belflower, Jay, Tuc.	0	0	.000	0.00	1	0	0	0	0	0	1.2	2	8	0	0	0	0	0	0	1	0	2	1	0
Belitz, Todd, Sac.-C.S.*	4	4	.500	5.94	52	0	0	0	17	2	63.2	71	282	53	42	8	4	1	4	19	3	62	2	1
Benes, Alan, Mem.	7	6	.538	3.55	25	25	1	0	0	0	142.0	164	637	71	56	13	7	2	7	51	1	96	2	0
Benoit, Joaquin, Okla.	9	5	.643	4.19	24	24	1	0	0	0	131.0	113	566	63	61	14	2	4	4	73	0	142	7	0
Bergman, Sean, C.S.	2	1	.667	2.04	3	2	0	0	0	0	17.2	15	71	7	4	1	0	1	0	4	0	12	0	0
Bevel, Bobby, L.V.*	0	2	.000	4.58	25	1	0	0	4	0	35.1	36	153	19	18	5	2	4	1	16	3	29	1	0
Beverlin, Jason, S.L.	6	2	.750	4.23	19	12	1	0	0	0	83.0	82	350	41	39	9	0	2	4	29	0	74	2	2
Bierbrodt, Nick, Tuc.*	4	1	.800	2.18	7	6	0	0	0	0	45.1	48	185	15	11	0	3	1	1	9	1	56	1	0
Bochtler, Doug, Edm.	2	5	.286	2.76	34	1	0	0	20	3	45.2	41	192	16	14	5	1	0	0	19	0	65	0	0
Bohanon, Brian, C.S.*	0	0	.000	1.80	1	1	0	0	0	0	5.0	8	23	1	1	0	0	0	0	2	0	2	0	0
Borland, Toby, S.L.	7	3	.700	2.30	45	1	0	0	16	3	74.1	53	302	25	19	2	1	2	2	29	0	92	9	0
Borowski, Joe, Iowa	8	7	.533	2.62	39	12	1	1	7	0	110.0	87	433	35	32	10	2	0	2	26	3	131	1	0
Boskie, Shawn, Tuc.	4	6	.400	6.93	12	11	1	0	0	0	62.1	95	294	55	48	8	4	0	3	17	2	31	3	0
Bost, Heath, C.S.	2	2	.500	4.32	45	2	0	0	13	0	75.0	82	326	37	36	13	1	0	4	23	2	64	2	0
Bowie, Micah, Sac.*	6	8	.429	5.04	38	10	1	1	9	3	116.0	123	506	68	65	13	2	5		44	1	102	1	0
Bradford, Chad, Sac.	0	0	.000	0.38	12	0	0	0	3	2	23.2	15	87	2	1	0	0	0	0	2	0	24	0	0
Brewington, Jamie, Edm.	2	8	.200	5.91	35	4	0	0	9	0	67.0	87	313	48	44	11	3	2	3	31	1	53	7	0
Brink, Jim, Sac.	0	0	.000	3.00	1	0	0	0	0	0	3.0	2	12	1	1	1	0	0	0	0	0	5	0	0
Brocail, Doug, N.O.	0	0	.000	0.00	2	0	0	0	1	0	2.1	2	10	0	0	0	0	0	0	0	0	4	0	0
Brohawn, Troy, Tuc.*	0	0	.000	0.00	2	0	0	0	1	0	3.1	1	13	0	0	0	0	0	0	1	0	4	0	0

Pitcher, Team	W	L	Pct.	ERA	G	GS	CG	ShO	GF	Sv.	IP	H	TBF	R	ER	HR	SH	SF	HB	BB	IBB	SO	WP	Bk.
Brown, Elliot, Fres.	2	2	.500	7.86	8	7	0	0	0	0	34.1	61	180	32	30	4	3	3	4	18	0	21	1	0
Brunson, Will, S.L.*	2	2	.500	4.39	39	1	0	0	12	0	69.2	73	294	37	34	9	3	1	1	20	2	52	0	1
Bruske, Jim, S.L.-L.V.	5	3	.625	5.16	37	13	0	0	9	1	106.1	129	475	66	61	15	2	4	9	25	0	107	4	0
Bullinger, Jim, Mem.	1	8	.111	6.96	10	10	0	0	0	0	53.0	68	261	47	41	11	2	1	3	30	1	36	1	0
Camp, Shawn, Port.-Nash.	1	0	1.000	1.50	15	1	0	0	2	0	24.0	13	89	4	4	1	0	1	0	9	1	21	0	0
Carlson, Dan, Mem.	1	0	1.000	4.71	7	3	0	0	2	0	21.0	25	94	13	11	3	1	0	0	8	0	21	1	0
Carrara, Giovanni, L.V.	1	2	.333	3.10	6	6	0	0	0	0	29.0	27	122	10	10	5	1	0	3	9	0	35	0	1
Cather, Mike, Mem.	1	1	.500	5.82	15	0	0	0	4	0	21.2	27	102	14	14	3	0	1	1	9	1	21	0	0
Chacon, Shawn, C.S.	2	0	1.000	2.25	4	4	0	0	0	0	24.0	18	98	6	6	3	3	0	1	7	0	28	0	0
Charlton, Norm, Tac.*	0	1	.000	3.00	4	2	0	0	0	0	6.0	4	26	2	2	0	0	0	1	2	0	9	1	0
Chavez, Anthony, Tuc.	7	6	.538	4.57	51	8	1	0	9	1	86.2	109	406	59	44	5	7	2	6	37	2	76	4	0
Chiasson, Scott, Iowa	0	0	.000	2.25	11	0	0	0	10	10	12.0	11	49	3	3	1	0	0	2	0	0	14	0	0
Chouinard, Bobby, C.S.	3	1	.750	3.66	39	0	0	0	9	1	39.1	44	175	19	16	5	0	0	3	13	0	47	4	0
Christiansen, Jason, Mem.*	0	0	.000	2.25	7	1	0	0	0	0	8.0	9	33	2	2	0	1	0	0	0	0	8	0	0
Christman, Tim, C.S.*	2	5	.286	6.30	38	0	0	0	10	2	40.0	52	195	31	28	4	0	2	3	21	1	42	4	0
Chrysler, Clint, Nash.*	0	0	.000	2.70	7	0	0	0	2	0	10.0	14	48	4	3	2	0	1	4	0	6	0	0
Clontz, Brad, C.S.	2	1	.667	9.00	21	0	0	0	10	0	23.0	37	120	26	23	7	3	1	4	10	0	23	1	0
Cogan, Tony, Oma.*	1	1	.500	2.79	9	0	0	0	5	2	9.2	14	44	3	3	1	0	0	0	3	0	8	0	0
Cole, Victor, Mem.	0	1	.000	6.75	3	0	0	0	0	0	5.1	7	29	6	4	1	0	0	4	4	0	4	0	0
Condrey, Clay, Port.	1	3	.250	4.75	39	0	0	0	13	2	53.0	63	231	37	28	7	4	3	4	13	1	45	2	0
Connelly, Steve, Fres.	2	3	.400	3.68	33	0	0	0	12	4	58.2	47	244	26	24	2	4	2	5	23	0	40	1	0
Cooper, Brian, S.L.	12	8	.600	4.63	28	28	1	0	0	0	173.0	181	737	98	89	26	3	3	9	58	0	109	6	0
Cordero, Francisco, Okla.	0	1	.000	0.59	12	0	0	0	12	6	15.1	8	57	2	1	0	0	0	3	0	0	20	0	0
Cordova, Francisco, Nash.	0	0	.000	18.00	1	1	0	0	0	0	1.0	2	5	2	2	1	0	0	0	0	0	1	0	0
Corey, Bryan, Port.	8	7	.533	4.67	47	12	0	0	25	6	106.0	124	455	55	55	12	3	5	3	31	3	66	1	1
Cotton, Joe, Sac.	0	2	.000	8.53	6	0	0	0	1	0	6.1	7	31	6	6	1	1	1	0	5	0	7	0	0
Crabtree, Robbie, Fres.	8	10	.444	3.69	63	0	0	0	31	6	114.2	115	474	56	47	11	7	3	1	34	5	99	3	0
Crafton, Kevin, Mem	1	1	.500	8.05	13	0	0	0	2	0	19.0	34	100	20	17	2	1	1	1	6	0	13	1	0
Crawford, Joe, Tuc.*	2	4	.333	5.23	8	7	1	0	0	0	41.1	50	190	30	24	7	1	2	2	12	1	32	0	0
Cressend, Jack, Edm.	2	2	.500	3.50	12	0	0	0	3	1	18.0	19	78	12	7	2	3	0	1	7	2	9	0	0
Crowell, Jim, Port.*	0	0	.000	5.49	11	2	0	0	2	0	19.2	22	93	15	12	3	1	1	1	15	0	7	0	1
Cubillan, Darwin, Okla.	1	1	.500	10.38	9	0	0	0	4	2	13.0	20	72	16	15	4	1	0	2	12	0	8	0	0
Dace, Derek, Tuc.*	0	3	.000	5.40	17	0	0	0	6	0	21.2	29	104	19	13	2	0	2	2	7	0	14	0	0
D'Amico, Jeff, Oma.	5	7	.417	3.54	32	20	0	0	5	0	140.0	151	595	65	55	19	8	3	5	40	2	92	5	2
Daneker, Pat, Iowa	3	1	.750	9.14	16	0	0	0	10	0	21.2	41	115	26	22	2	2	3	2	9	2	9	3	1
Davenport, Joe, C.S.	2	2	.500	8.47	31	0	0	0	9	0	34.0	62	181	30	32	3	1	1	5	15	0	23	3	0
Davis, Doug, Okla.*	2	0	1.000	2.87	2	2	0	0	0	0	15.2	10	59	5	5	1	0	1	4	0	14	0	0
Davis, Kane, C.S.	0	0	.000	3.60	4	0	0	0	1	0	5.0	5	22	2	2	0	0	0	3	1	7	0	0
DeSilva, John, Cal.-L.V.	2	3	.400	4.06	10	3	0	0	14	1	63.2	82	287	40	35	7	1	1	4	13	3	56	2	0
Devey, Phil, L.V.*	0	2	.000	11.05	3	3	0	0	0	0	14.2	25	74	18	18	1	1	0	1	9	0	7	1	1
Dewey, Mark, Nash.	1	1	.500	1.74	11	0	0	0	2	0	10.1	9	43	3	2	0	1	1	0	3	0	3	1	0
Dickey, R.A., Okla.	11	7	.611	3.75	24	24	3	0	0	0	163.0	164	687	77	68	14	7	2	7	45	1	120	3	0
Difelice, Mark, C.S.	3	2	.600	5.28	8	8	0	0	0	0	46.0	56	207	29	27	11	2	1	8	8	3	43	1	0
Dingman, Craig, C.S.	3	5	.375	3.75	46	0	0	0	29	7	48.0	57	210	28	20	4	2	1	4	9	1	55	1	0
Donaldson, Bo, Nash.-Port.	3	1	.750	0.53	19	2	0	0	6	0	33.2	15	129	6	2	1	0	1	4	11	0	35	2	0
Donnelly, Brendan, S.L.	5	1	.833	2.40	29	0	0	0	12	1	41.1	38	165	11	11	4	1	1	0	8	0	50	2	0
Dougherty, Jim, L.V.	4	5	.444	4.22	59	0	0	0	45	14	81.0	82	344	39	38	8	2	2	0	34	7	85	2	0
Driskill, Travis, N.O.	11	5	.688	3.78	28	28	1	0	0	0	178.2	175	735	83	75	21	6	5	6	33	2	145	5	1
Drumright, Mike, Cal.	0	5	.000	3.73	19	0	0	0	10	1	31.1	30	143	15	13	1	4	3	0	24	2	39	4	0
Duchscherer, Justin, Okla.	3	3	.500	2.84	7	7	1	1	0	0	50.2	48	205	20	16	6	2	1	4	10	0	52	0	0
Duncan, Courtney, Iowa	1	0	1.000	3.24	7	0	0	0	1	0	8.1	7	36	3	3	1	0	0	5	1	15	0	0
Durbin, Chad, Oma.	2	2	.500	3.33	5	5	0	0	0	0	27.0	22	112	11	10	4	1	1	2	6	0	35	0	1
Durocher, Jayson, Okla.	4	1	.800	4.99	31	0	0	0	20	8	39.2	34	176	25	22	5	3	0	3	23	1	52	1	0
Durrington, Trent, L.V.	0	0	.000	18.00	1	0	0	0	1	0	1.0	2	5	2	2	1	0	0	0	1	0	1	0	0
Duvall, Mike, Edm.*	2	2	.500	4.45	55	0	0	0	19	3	62.2	73	277	32	31	7	1	3	1	21	1	63	4	0
Edmondson, Brian, Cal.	2	5	.286	8.49	23	0	0	0	12	0	29.2	43	148	33	28	7	2	2	1	15	2	20	4	0
Elarton, Scott, C.S.	0	1	.000	7.04	2	2	0	0	0	0	7.2	14	39	6	6	2	0	0	2	0	0	8	1	0
Elder, Dave, Okla.	5	4	.556	4.99	15	8	0	0	3	0	57.2	54	266	36	32	4	2	0	4	43	0	56	4	1
Ellis, Robert, Tuc.	1	1	.500	3.08	5	5	0	0	0	0	26.1	25	106	12	9	2	0	0	1	5	0	13	0	1
Embree, Alan, Fres.*	1	0	1.000	1.13	7	0	0	0	4	1	8.0	5	30	3	1	0	0	1	1	0	6	0	0
Eppolito, Vince, Tuc.	0	0	.000	4.50	2	0	0	0	2	0	2.0	1	10	1	1	0	0	0	3	0	3	0	0
Espina, Rendy, S.L.*	0	0	.000	3.86	2	0	0	0	2	0	2.1	1	7	1	1	1	0	0	0	0	1	0	0
Estrada, Horacio, C.S.*	8	4	.667	4.73	16	16	0	0	0	0	91.1	102	387	51	48	11	2	2	3	20	0	77	8	1
Estrella, Luis, Fres.	8	3	.727	4.51	30	17	0	0	2	0	115.2	123	501	60	58	19	3	1	2	52	2	73	3	1
Evans, Dave, N.O.	2	1	.667	6.38	25	7	1	1	7	1	42.1	50	201	37	30	11	1	1	2	27	1	40	4	0
Falkenborg, Brian, Tac.	2	4	.333	4.47	8	0	0	0	0	0	48.1	50	206	25	24	6	1	2	2	18	0	27	1	0
Feliciano, Pedro, L.V.*	0	1	.000	7.27	6	0	0	0	1	0	8.2	16	49	11	7	2	1	0	1	5	1	5	1	0
Fikac, Jeremy, Port.	0	0	.000	3.00	1	0	0	0	0	0	3.0	3	13	1	1	0	0	0	1	0	3	0	0
Fiore, Tony, Edm.	5	0	1.000	3.68	32	6	0	0	12	1	80.2	85	344	35	33	4	1	1	5	25	0	58	3	1
Fitzgerald, Brian, Tac.*	2	1	.667	3.89	20	1	0	0	9	0	34.2	40	153	19	15	5	0	0	0	11	0	26	2	0
Ford, Ben, Iowa	2	3	.400	5.79	5	5	0	0	0	0	23.1	31	108	15	15	3	1	0	3	9	0	16	0	0
Foster, Kevin, Okla.	3	1	.750	2.80	16	3	0	0	5	0	54.2	33	213	18	17	6	1	1	0	22	0	65	1	0
Foster, Kris, L.V.	0	1	.000	3.86	21	0	0	0	17	12	21.0	25	92	13	9	0	0	1	2	4	0	17	3	1
Franklin, Ryan, Tac.	0	0	.000	0.00	1	0	0	0	1	0	3.2	2	13	0	0	0	0	0	0	3	0	3	0	0
Franklin, Wayne, N.O.*	2	1	.667	3.81	41	0	0	0	8	0	49.2	47	216	28	21	6	2	0	3	18	2	51	2	0
Freeman, Corey, Tac.	0	0	.000	4.50	1	0	0	0	0	0	2.0	2	10	1	1	1	0	0	0	2	0	0	0	0
Fuentes, Brian, Tac.*	3	2	.600	2.94	35	0	0	0	13	6	52.0	35	205	19	17	4	1	6	25	0	70	5	1
Fussell, Chris, Oma.	2	6	.250	9.61	9	9	0	0	0	0	39.1	58	197	47	42	15	0	0	3	24	0	35	2	0
Fyhrie, Mike, Iowa	1	0	1.000	4.80	13	0	0	0	4	2	15.0	14	69	8	8	1	0	0	1	8	0	15	1	0
Gagne, Eric, L.V.	3	0	1.000	1.52	4	4	0	0	0	0	23.2	15	87	4	4	2	2	0	0	8	0	31	2	0
Galva, Claudio, Sac.*	1	0	1.000	3.60	4	0	0	0	1	0	5.0	7	26	2	2	1	0	0	5	2	6	0	0
Gardner, Mark, Fres.	0	1	.000	6.00	3	3	0	0	0	0	6.0	10	28	4	4	1	0	0	1	0	7	0	0
George, Chris, Oma.*	11	3	.786	3.53	20	20	0	0	0	0	117.1	103	489	54	46	14	2	1	1	51	0	84	0	1

Pitcher, Team	W	L	Pct.	ERA	G	GS	CG	ShO	GF	Sv.	IP	H	TBF	R	ER	HR	SH	SF	HB	BB	IBB	SO	WP	Bk.
Giron, Isabel, Port.	4	1	.800	4.87	44	0	0	0	14	0	64.2	74	293	36	35	14	0	2	4	27	0	69	1	0
Glynn, Ryan, Okla.	2	6	.250	6.49	13	13	1	0	0	0	79.0	87	357	62	57	10	1	2	5	41	0	52	2	0
Gonzalez, Gabe, Port.*	0	1	.000	12.46	3	0	0	0	0	0	4.1	9	25	6	6	1	0	2	0	3	0	1	0	0
Gordon, Tom, Iowa	0	0	.000	0.00	2	0	0	0	0	0	2.0	1	7	0	0	0	0	0	1	0	0	2	0	0
Green, Steve, S.L.	6	2	.750	3.66	10	10	1	0	0	0	59.0	59	247	30	24	3	0	1	3	13	0	40	3	1
Grilli, Jason, Cal.	1	2	.333	4.02	8	8	0	0	0	0	47.0	46	205	26	21	4	0	3	2	20	0	35	1	0
Gross, Kip, L.V.-C.S.	4	8	.333	5.87	28	12	1	1	8	0	99.2	138	441	76	65	15	0	4	4	16	1	56	3	0
Gryboski, Kevin, Tac.	2	5	.286	3.90	58	0	0	0	50	22	60.0	64	256	29	26	8	5	1	0	19	2	50	2	0
Guerra, Mark, N.O.	7	8	.467	3.90	28	15	1	1	4	0	108.1	129	466	56	47	9	1	3	2	21	1	56	4	0
Guttormson, Rick, Port.	0	1	.000	10.80	1	0	0	0	0	0	5.0	9	26	6	6	0	0	2	1	1	0	1	0	0
Guy, Brad, Nash.	2	2	.500	4.24	22	2	0	0	3	0	46.2	47	196	26	22	3	1	2	1	16	3	35	1	0
Guzman, Domingo, Port.	1	2	.333	6.75	11	0	0	0	4	1	17.1	20	78	13	13	0	2	1	2	5	1	16	1	0
Guzman, Geraldo, Tuc.	3	6	.333	4.85	20	14	0	0	1	0	94.2	92	403	56	51	9	4	4	4	30	1	85	3	3
Haad, Yamid, Nash.	0	0	.000	22.50	1	0	0	0	0	0	2.0	7	16	5	5	1	0	0	0	3	0	0	0	0
Hackman, Luther, Mem.	0	2	.000	2.78	16	0	0	0	5	0	22.2	21	86	7	7	2	1	0	1	1	0	12	0	0
Halama, John, Tac.*	2	0	1.000	0.47	3	3	1	1	0	0	19.0	9	65	2	1	1	0	0	0	0	0	22	0	0
Harville, Chad, Sac.	5	2	.714	3.98	33	0	0	0	23	8	40.2	35	169	20	18	5	1	2	2	12	0	55	5	0
Hasselhoff, Derek, Fres.	2	0	1.000	3.86	25	0	0	0	17	8	28.0	24	122	19	12	6	2	1	1	14	1	24	0	0
Head, Daniel, Tac.	1	0	1.000	0.00	2	0	0	0	2	0	2.0	1	7	0	0	0	0	0	0	1	0	1	0	0
Heiserman, Rick, Mem.	1	1	.500	4.59	24	4	0	0	1	0	49.0	61	213	26	25	9	0	0	5	11	0	33	1	0
Henderson, Rod, Sac.	4	1	.800	7.85	8	8	0	0	0	0	36.2	50	175	33	32	9	1	2	1	18	0	30	2	0
Herbert, John, Port.	0	0	.000	0.00	1	0	0	0	0	0	1.0	0	3	0	0	0	0	0	0	1	0	0	0	0
Hernandez, John, L.V.	0	0	.000	27.00	1	0	0	0	1	0	1.0	5	8	3	3	1	0	1	0	0	0	1	0	0
Herndon, Junior, Port.	9	5	.643	4.58	21	21	0	0	0	0	116.0	132	515	72	59	18	4	7	4	39	0	47	2	0
Hiljus, Erik, Sac.	8	5	.615	3.63	15	15	3	1	0	0	101.2	79	402	46	41	18	1	2	1	26	1	108	2	0
Hitchcock, Sterling, Port.*	2	0	1.000	3.71	3	3	0	0	0	0	17.0	20	70	7	7	1	2	0	1	2	0	11	0	0
Hodges, Kevin, Tac.	5	5	.500	4.15	14	14	2	1	0	0	86.2	97	374	50	40	8	0	2	6	25	0	55	1	1
Hooten, Dave, Edm.	1	1	.500	9.00	7	0	0	0	1	0	10.0	17	49	10	10	1	0	0	1	4	0	4	3	0
Horgan, Joe, Fres.*	0	0	.000	5.87	3	1	0	0	0	0	7.2	11	36	5	5	1	0	0	0	3	0	5	0	0
House, Craig, C.S.	2	2	.500	4.45	54	0	0	0	21	6	58.2	50	260	32	29	4	4	3	6	31	1	62	9	0
Huisman, Rick, Mem.	0	1	.000	7.20	8	0	0	0	3	0	15.0	18	71	17	12	4	1	0	0	9	0	16	1	0
Husted, Brent, L.V.	0	0	.000	3.66	14	0	0	0	8	0	19.2	25	89	9	8	1	0	0	2	7	0	11	2	0
Hutchinson, Chad, Mem.	4	9	.308	7.92	27	20	0	0	1	0	97.2	99	492	91	86	8	3	5	10	104	0	111	17	1
Ireland, Eric, Sac.	8	11	.421	5.24	29	28	0	0	0	0	168.1	215	771	120	98	24	5	4	10	56	3	102	6	0
Jacome, Jason, Tuc.*	1	8	.111	5.33	35	16	0	0	7	0	120.0	149	532	78	71	11	1	9	2	37	3	72	5	2
James, Mike, Mem.	0	0	.000	4.00	10	0	0	0	1	0	9.0	10	42	6	4	1	1	2	2	4	1	9	0	0
Janzen, Marty, S.L.	0	0	.000	12.27	2	0	0	0	0	0	3.2	5	20	5	5	0	1	1	3	0	3	1	0	
Jarvis, Matt, Tac.*	2	0	1.000	1.56	12	0	0	0	5	0	17.1	12	73	3	3	0	2	1	2	7	0	9	0	0
Jennings, Jason, C.S.	7	8	.467	4.72	22	22	4	0	0	0	131.2	145	572	80	69	9	6	2	7	41	0	110	3	2
Jensen, Ryan, Fres.	11	4	.846	3.48	20	17	1	1	2	0	106.0	97	445	43	41	11	4	1	5	34	0	95	2	0
Jodie, Brett, Port.	2	1	.667	4.75	5	5	0	0	0	0	30.1	33	128	16	16	7	1	0	0	8	1	19	1	0
Johnson, Adam, Edm.	1	1	.500	5.70	4	4	0	0	0	0	23.2	19	98	15	15	0	2	1	1	10	0	25	0	0
Johnson, Jonathan, Tuc.	4	4	.500	5.25	15	12	0	0	0	0	73.2	63	324	48	43	7	2	2	3	42	0	51	6	0
Johnson, Mike, Okla.	3	5	.375	4.58	23	8	1	0	6	2	88.1	101	382	48	45	12	2	3	3	22	0	67	3	0
Jones, Marcus, Sac.	2	3	.400	4.54	27	9	1	0	6	1	73.1	81	316	39	37	4	3	1	4	20	1	51	1	0
Joseph, Kevin, Fres.-Mem.	0	3	.000	7.08	17	0	0	0	8	0	20.1	17	92	16	16	2	2	2	1	15	2	8	2	0
Judd, Mike, Okla.	0	1	.000	10.13	2	0	0	0	1	0	2.2	6	16	3	3	0	1	0	0	2	0	3	0	0
Kamienjecki, Scott, Iowa	1	4	.200	3.65	8	4	0	0	1	0	37.0	34	150	16	15	3	4	1	2	10	0	38	6	0
Karl, Scott, Nash.*	4	3	.571	3.83	14	14	0	0	0	0	84.2	79	356	40	36	9	3	2	1	29	0	54	1	0
Karnuth, Jason, Mem.	4	4	.500	4.28	55	0	0	0	17	3	73.2	82	324	37	35	7	3	2	6	24	0	42	2	0
Kaye, Justin, Tac.	3	2	.600	2.92	56	0	0	0	15	4	77.0	51	332	27	25	5	6	1	6	46	2	107	3	1
Kessel, Kyle, N.O.*	1	3	.250	7.90	15	6	0	0	2	0	41.0	64	205	40	36	5	2	1	3	24	0	24	3	0
Kiefer, Mark, L.V.	11	7	.611	4.20	32	17	2	2	5	1	145.2	126	623	75	68	21	3	4	12	46	5	174	4	0
Kieschnick, Brooks, C.S.	0	0	.000	18.00	1	0	0	0	1	0	1.0	3	6	2	2	0	0	0	0	0	0	1	0	0
Kinney, Matt, Edm.	6	11	.353	5.07	29	29	2	0	0	0	161.2	178	727	101	91	25	2	8	7	74	0	146	11	0
Knoll, Brian, Fres.	0	3	.000	7.18	22	9	0	0	5	0	62.2	88	302	52	50	12	4	4	3	29	0	47	3	0
Knott, Eric, Tuc.*	6	2	.750	3.80	25	8	0	0	9	1	73.1	82	303	34	31	6	4	3	0	8	1	43	1	1
Knotts, Gary, Cal.	6	7	.462	5.46	21	21	1	1	0	0	118.2	136	528	77	72	16	3	3	2	43	0	104	5	0
Kolb, Dan, Okla.	0	1	.000	1.42	12	0	0	0	8	3	19.0	13	74	3	3	1	1	0	0	4	0	21	1	0
Koplove, Mike, Tuc.	4	1	.800	2.82	17	0	0	0	13	6	22.1	17	92	7	7	1	0	0	0	10	1	22	2	0
Krivda, Rick, Mem.*	4	6	.400	4.35	14	13	0	0	0	0	80.2	87	345	50	39	9	3	7	3	20	0	46	1	0
Lackey, John, S.L.	3	4	.429	6.71	10	10	1	0	0	0	57.2	75	253	44	43	5	2	1	1	16	0	42	3	1
Lambert, Jeremy, Mem.	5	1	.833	3.23	28	0	0	0	16	3	30.2	23	123	14	11	7	3	1	2	8	0	39	0	0
Lankford, Frank, Sac.	5	5	.500	4.80	40	0	0	0	16	2	69.1	87	308	44	37	8	3	2	1	23	3	37	5	0
Larkin, Andy, C.S.	4	8	.333	5.40	26	18	0	0	2	0	120.0	134	537	78	72	17	5	4	11	41	1	99	4	1
Lawrence, Brian, Port.	3	2	.600	3.80	9	8	0	0	1	0	45.0	42	196	22	19	3	1	0	2	17	2	42	2	0
Lawrence, Sean, Port.-Tuc.*	1	6	.143	3.55	43	0	0	0	15	0	58.1	52	255	31	23	3	3	1	3	22	3	76	3	0
Laxton, Brett, Oma.	3	7	.300	4.02	45	5	0	0	16	0	96.1	92	414	49	43	7	2	5	7	35	1	75	5	0
Lee, Corey, Okla.*	0	0	.000	18.00	2	0	0	0	1	0	3.0	5	19	7	6	1	0	0	0	4	0	1	0	0
Lee, Dave, Port.	1	0	1.000	0.75	9	0	0	0	2	1	12.0	5	45	1	1	0	1	1	0	5	1	14	1	0
Lee, Jon, Tuc.	0	0	.000	3.38	2	0	0	0	0	0	2.2	3	12	1	1	0	0	1	0	1	0	1	0	0
Leese, Brandon, Cal.	3	3	.500	6.95	9	9	0	0	0	0	44.0	68	203	36	34	8	1	3	1	7	1	30	2	0
Lidle, Cory, Sac.	1	0	1.000	3.00	1	1	0	0	0	0	6.0	6	26	2	2	0	0	0	0	3	0	2	2	0
Lidle, Kevin, S.L.-Mem.	0	0	.000	0.00	2	0	0	0	2	0	1.2	1	6	0	0	0	0	0	0	1	0	1	0	0
Lincoln, Mike, Nash.	5	4	.556	3.44	18	13	1	0	1	0	91.2	90	388	39	35	10	1	0	4	25	0	71	3	1
Linebrink, Scott, N.O.	7	6	.538	3.50	50	0	0	0	20	8	72.0	52	287	28	28	4	4	2	2	24	6	72	9	0
Loewer, Carlton, Port.	5	4	.556	3.87	14	12	0	0	0	0	81.1	97	341	42	35	7	2	1	4	15	0	64	1	0
Lohse, Kyle, Edm.	4	2	.667	3.12	8	8	1	1	0	0	49.0	50	208	21	17	3	0	0	4	13	0	48	3	0
Loiselle, Rich, Nash.	0	2	.000	6.15	26	1	0	0	12	0	33.2	33	157	24	23	2	3	0	6	23	3	18	3	0
Lopez, Johan, Okla.	0	0	.000	3.52	3	0	0	0	0	0	7.2	8	32	4	3	1	0	0	2	0	4	0	0	
Lopez, Rodrigo, Port.	2	2	.500	3.44	11	8	0	0	1	0	52.1	45	214	22	20	7	1	1	1	15	0	37	1	0
Lorraine, Andrew, Cal.*	9	5	.643	5.40	30	25	1	1	0	0	150.0	209	685	100	90	19	5	5	7	36	4	101	4	0
Lukasiewicz, Mark, S.L.*	3	0	1.000	1.48	20	0	0	0	8	2	30.1	12	105	5	5	4	0	0	0	2	0	41	0	0

Pitcher, Team	W	L	Pct.	ERA	G	GS	CG	ShO	GF	Sv.	IP	H	TBF	R	ER	HR	SH	SF	HB	BB	IBB	SO	WP	Bk.
Lundberg, Spike, Okla.	3	5	.375	6.71	13	8	0	0	2	0	55.0	72	257	51	41	8	2	3	3	15	1	31	1	0
Lundquist, Dave, Port.	4	7	.364	3.11	50	0	0	0	22	7	63.2	59	266	25	22	6	3	2	1	20	0	67	3	0
MacDougal, Mike, Oma.	8	8	.500	4.68	28	27	1	0	0	0	144.1	144	649	90	75	13	3	2	11	76	0	110	15	2
Mahay, Ron, Port.-Iowa*	4	3	.571	2.70	50	0	0	0	35	14	63.1	42	245	21	19	7	5	2	2	15	1	70	3	0
Mairena, Ozwaldo, Cal.*	3	2	.600	7.55	31	0	0	0	8	0	39.1	52	179	33	33	4	2	2	0	13	5	44	2	0
Mann, Jim, N.O.	6	3	.667	2.51	53	0	0	0	50	27	68.0	52	272	21	19	7	5	2	2	17	2	81	4	0
Marshall, Lee, Edm.	4	2	.667	2.35	39	0	0	0	30	11	53.2	50	229	18	14	2	2	0	2	20	1	37	1	0
Marte, Damaso, Nash.*	0	0	.000	3.38	4	0	0	0	1	0	5.1	3	19	2	2	2	1	0	0	0	0	4	0	0
Martines, Jason, Tuc.	0	3	.000	9.00	12	0	0	0	5	1	18.0	31	94	19	18	4	2	1	2	7	1	15	1	1
Martinez, Gustavo, Tac.	1	0	1.000	1.50	1	1	0	0	0	0	6.0	2	24	1	1	0	0	0	1	4	0	7	0	0
Martinez, Jose, Okla.	0	0	.000	0.00	1	1	0	0	0	0	6.2	1	22	0	0	0	0	0	0	1	0	3	0	0
Martinez, Willie, Edm.	7	8	.467	5.61	21	20	0	0	0	0	112.1	147	512	80	70	18	1	5	4	39	1	86	8	0
Masaoka, Onan, L.V.*	8	4	.667	5.55	31	5	0	0	4	1	73.0	87	331	49	45	9	3	6	3	28	4	61	5	0
Mathews, T.J., Mem.	1	1	.500	1.80	15	0	0	0	11	4	15.0	16	62	4	3	0	0	0	1	1	0	14	0	0
Maurer, Dave, Port.-Sac.*	0	0	.000	4.83	28	0	0	0	11	1	31.2	25	135	18	17	6	0	1	1	17	2	42	3	0
McConnell, Sam, Nash.*	7	10	.412	6.03	26	23	1	0	1	0	134.1	159	600	103	90	20	3	7	3	41	2	98	7	1
McDade, Neal, Nash.	1	1	.500	3.00	8	0	0	0	2	0	15.0	14	64	5	5	1	0	1	1	7	1	8	2	0
McKnight, Tony, N.O.	9	5	.643	4.76	18	18	1	0	0	0	92.2	104	396	56	49	10	2	4	3	24	0	61	0	0
McMullen, Mike, Edm.	0	0	.000	3.38	14	0	0	0	5	0	16.0	12	72	10	6	1	0	2	1	15	0	11	3	0
Meadows, Brian, Oma.	6	5	.545	6.17	18	18	0	0	0	0	105.0	143	460	73	72	21	1	3	5	20	1	74	1	0
Mecir, Jim, Sac.	0	0	.000	0.00	1	1	0	0	0	0	1.0	1	4	0	0	0	0	0	0	0	0	0	0	0
Medina, Rafael, Mem.	3	1	.750	3.72	27	0	0	0	9	0	38.2	30	165	17	16	6	1	1	3	16	0	36	2	0
Meyer, Jake, Tac.	0	0	.000	6.32	9	1	0	0	2	0	15.2	15	69	11	11	0	0	1	0	7	0	18	1	0
Meyers, Mike, Iowa	7	4	.636	3.23	25	25	0	0	0	0	147.2	129	631	58	53	9	3	6	2	64	3	124	8	0
Miadich, Bart, S.L.	4	4	.500	2.44	55	0	0	0	54	27	59.0	40	245	20	16	4	3	1	1	29	1	73	5	0
Miceli, Danny, C.S.	0	2	.000	6.00	4	0	0	0	2	0	3.0	2	12	2	2	0	1	0	0	1	1	4	3	0
Middlebrook, Jason, Port.	7	4	.636	3.29	15	15	0	0	0	0	90.1	86	374	34	33	5	2	3	2	23	1	66	3	0
Miller, Justin, Sac.	7	10	.412	4.75	29	28	1	0	0	0	165.0	174	718	94	87	26	4	4	16	64	1	134	11	0
Miller, Matt, Port.	1	7	.125	3.63	44	0	0	0	31	17	44.2	44	192	22	18	1	3	0	2	14	2	43	5	0
Mintz, Steve, S.L.	1	2	.333	5.79	13	3	0	0	6	0	37.1	50	175	20	24	6	2	2	3	11	0	21	0	1
Mitchell, Dean, Okla.	0	0	.000	7.11	4	0	0	0	4	0	6.1	9	27	6	5	1	0	0	1	1	0	2	1	0
Mix, Greg, Edm.	1	1	.500	2.45	7	0	0	0	1	1	11.0	12	44	6	3	2	1	1	0	0	0	5	1	0
Mohler, Mike, Tuc.*	5	0	1.000	3.18	40	0	0	0	14	3	45.1	52	207	28	16	4	2	3	2	14	0	48	4	0
Molina, Gabe, Cal.	5	9	.357	5.89	40	16	0	0	4	0	107.0	128	403	75	70	14	2	1	5	39	1	105	13	4
Montgomery, Matt, L.V.	0	0	.000	0.00	1	0	0	0	0	0	2.1	1	10	0	0	0	0	0	0	2	0	3	0	0
Moody, Eric, Nash.	5	6	.455	3.45	42	8	1	1	9	0	112.1	112	456	47	43	15	5	2	3	14	1	50	2	0
Moraga, David, C.S.*	0	1	.000	10.95	3	3	0	0	0	0	12.1	21	65	16	15	4	0	0	0	8	0	9	0	0
Moreno, Juan, Okla.*	0	0	.000	1.86	7	0	0	0	2	0	9.2	4	35	2	2	1	0	1	0	2	0	13	0	0
Moreno, Orber, Oma.	1	1	.500	4.71	17	0	0	0	11	3	21.0	19	90	11	11	4	0	0	0	8	0	25	1	0
Morgan, Mike, Tuc.	0	0	.000	3.00	2	2	0	0	0	0	3.0	5	14	1	1	0	0	0	0	0	0	4	0	0
Moriarty, Mike, Edm.	0	0	.000	18.00	1	0	0	0	1	0	1.0	2	7	2	2	1	0	0	1	0	0	0	0	0
Mota, Danny, Edm.-L.V.	4	5	.444	6.25	46	0	0	0	20	3	59.0	68	265	41	41	8	4	3	1	31	2	50	4	0
Mullen, Scott, Oma.*	5	4	.556	6.62	48	0	0	0	12	5	53.0	66	240	39	39	8	4	2	3	22	2	38	1	0
Munro, Pete, Okla.	8	6	.571	4.67	33	8	0	0	9	0	88.2	89	390	50	46	12	2	4	4	43	1	73	3	0
Murray, Dan, Oma.	3	3	.500	3.95	48	1	0	0	25	8	98.0	105	418	49	43	10	2	2	4	30	3	70	4	0
Myers, Randy, Tac.*	0	0	.000	0.00	1	0	0	0	0	0	0.0	3	4	4	4	1	0	0	0	1	0	0	0	0
Myers, Rodney, Port.	1	1	.500	3.00	8	1	0	0	1	0	15.0	13	63	5	5	1	2	1	2	5	0	14	2	0
Myette, Aaron, Okla.	4	3	.571	3.73	12	12	2	0	0	0	70.0	64	305	32	29	5	3	0	5	30	0	76	1	0
Nathan, Joe, Fres.	0	5	.000	7.77	10	10	0	0	0	0	46.1	63	236	47	40	13	4	5	5	33	0	21	6	0
Nation, Joey, Iowa*	3	2	.600	3.02	14	9	0	0	0	0	44.2	39	181	16	15	5	0	0	1	13	0	48	0	0
Nina, Elvin, S.L.	10	11	.476	5.47	29	28	1	0	0	0	158.0	195	730	112	96	19	3	5	7	79	1	101	10	0
Norton, Phil, Iowa*	6	3	.667	2.69	46	3	0	0	14	2	73.2	65	318	27	22	3	9	3	6	41	7	75	8	1
O'Connor, Brian, Nash.*	6	9	.400	6.21	37	16	0	0	7	1	111.2	124	512	87	77	15	5	2	3	58	3	74	12	1
Ohman, Will, Iowa*	5	2	.714	4.06	40	1	0	0	11	4	51.0	51	218	24	23	9	2	0	1	18	3	66	3	0
Oliver, Darren, Okla.*	0	0	.000	0.00	1	1	0	0	0	0	3.0	3	12	0	0	0	0	0	0	0	0	3	0	0
Ontiveros, Steve, Sac.	7	6	.538	4.55	16	15	0	0	0	0	85.0	94	375	50	43	11	2	6	4	20	1	64	3	1
Oquist, Mike, Edm.	5	8	.385	4.15	21	20	2	0	1	0	110.2	132	482	62	51	12	1	1	3	29	0	76	1	0
Orosco, Jesse, L.V.*	1	0	1.000	0.00	10	0	0	0	1	0	7.1	4	27	0	0	0	0	0	0	2	0	11	1	0
Osting, Jimmy, Port.*	1	4	.200	9.59	5	5	0	0	0	0	25.1	41	124	27	27	5	0	0	1	10	0	15	0	0
Oswalt, Roy, N.O.	2	3	.400	4.35	5	5	0	0	0	0	31.0	32	128	16	15	4	0	0	2	6	0	34	0	1
Patterson, John, Tuc.	2	7	.222	5.85	13	12	0	0	0	0	67.2	82	313	50	44	9	2	5	3	31	3	40	2	1
Pavlas, Dave, Nash.	1	4	.200	2.61	41	1	0	0	18	6	41.1	34	167	17	12	4	1	1	1	8	2	40	3	0
Pearce, Josh, Mem.	4	4	.500	4.26	10	10	0	0	0	0	69.2	72	291	43	33	11	2	5	1	12	1	36	3	0
Perez, Carlos, L.V.*	2	1	.667	6.53	6	6	0	0	0	0	30.1	42	142	24	22	3	0	0	0	11	0	20	1	0
Pineiro, Joel, Tac.	6	3	.667	3.62	18	10	0	0	2	0	77.0	68	316	31	31	8	0	1	1	33	0	64	4	0
Post, Dave, L.V.	0	0	.000	18.00	1	0	0	0	0	0	1.0	2	5	2	2	1	0	0	0	0	0	1	1	0
Powell, Brian, N.O.	9	8	.529	3.17	24	23	3	2	0	0	144.2	142	599	65	51	13	4	2	6	39	1	96	3	1
Powell, Jeremy, Port.	4	2	.667	1.59	11	11	0	0	0	0	73.2	43	273	14	13	2	2	1	2	14	0	63	2	0
Priest, Eddie, L.V.*	4	8	.333	6.17	23	15	0	0	1	0	93.1	132	431	75	64	14	5	2	6	31	1	67	7	0
Prinz, Bret, Tuc.	0	0	.000	0.00	5	0	0	0	5	3	5.2	1	18	0	0	0	0	0	0	0	0	6	0	0
Prokopec, Luke, L.V.	1	0	1.000	3.00	1	1	0	0	0	0	6.0	3	24	2	2	1	0	0	1	2	0	8	0	0
Pumphrey, Ken, Edm.	1	6	.143	7.22	7	7	0	0	0	0	38.2	55	186	39	31	3	1	0	4	18	1	17	1	0
Quevedo, Ruben, Iowa	9	5	.643	2.99	22	22	1	1	0	0	141.2	124	588	54	47	13	8	6	3	48	3	150	1	0
Rain, Steve, Iowa	0	0	.000	11.74	9	0	0	0	6	1	7.2	10	40	12	10	3	1	0	2	6	0	9	2	0
Rakers, Jason, Oma.	6	4	.600	4.45	44	5	0	0	24	5	97.0	100	401	50	48	16	1	3	3	16	0	99	2	0
Ramos, Mario, Sac.*	8	3	.727	3.14	13	13	1	1	0	0	80.1	74	340	32	28	5	2	2	2	27	0	82	4	0
Ramsay, Rob, Tac.*	10	11	.476	4.82	26	26	0	0	0	0	149.1	160	667	98	80	26	4	10	2	60	0	113	2	0
Randall, Scott, C.S.	6	5	.545	5.48	19	12	0	0	2	0	70.2	74	319	48	43	11	0	1	3	34	3	47	3	1
Randolph, Steve, Tuc.*	2	0	1.000	6.33	18	0	0	0	7	0	21.1	24	109	15	15	2	1	2	2	19	1	16	2	0
Rath, Fred, Mem.	4	5	.444	6.69	27	10	0	0	4	0	78.0	103	369	60	58	12	4	1	4	33	0	57	2	0
Ratliff, Jon, Sac.	1	7	.125	7.86	18	14	0	0	1	0	63.0	84	300	58	55	9	1	3	1	38	1	41	5	0
Redding, Tim, N.O.	4	1	.800	4.54	6	6	0	0	0	0	37.2	22	153	21	19	4	0	1	5	19	0	42	1	0
Redman, Mark, Edm.*	0	0	.000	13.50	1	1	0	0	0	0	1.1	3	8	2	2	0	0	1	0	1	0	0	0	0

Pitcher, Team	W	L	Pct.	ERA	G	GS	CG	ShO	GF	Sv.	IP	H	TBF	R	ER	HR	SH	SF	HB	BB	IBB	SO	WP	Bk.
Reichert, Dan, Oma.	1	5	.167	8.27	10	5	1	0	0	0	32.2	45	156	30	30	4	1	0	4	16	0	30	5	0
Revenig, Todd, Tuc.	4	5	.444	5.07	46	0	0	0	16	0	65.2	82	287	39	37	9	1	1	1	12	7	42	1	0
Reyes, Al, L.V.	0	1	.000	3.38	19	0	0	0	4	0	29.1	24	126	11	11	3	1	0	5	10	1	37	0	0
Reyes, Carlos, Sac.-Tuc.	2	1	.667	6.81	25	0	0	0	13	0	39.2	44	180	31	30	6	1	3	1	19	2	33	4	0
Reynolds, Shane, N.O.	1	0	1.000	0.00	1	1	0	0	0	0	7.0	8	29	0	0	0	0	0	0	0	0	7	0	0
Reynoso, Armando, Tuc.	0	0	.000	0.00	1	1	0	0	0	0	3.2	3	16	0	0	0	0	0	0	2	0	5	0	0
Ricketts, Chad, L.V.	1	3	.250	2.91	48	0	0	0	17	3	58.2	49	253	24	19	5	4	5	2	25	4	70	3	0
Riley, Mike, Fres.*	2	4	.333	6.08	28	5	0	0	7	0	53.1	59	255	41	36	9	1	0	4	33	0	52	3	1
Rizzo, Todd, L.V.-Fres.*	4	4	.500	4.26	49	0	0	0	17	6	63.1	66	290	35	30	6	1	5	5	36	1	58	6	1
Roa, Joe, Cal.	6	6	.500	3.92	19	19	1	0	0	0	124.0	134	508	58	54	16	5	1	4	12	2	81	1	1
Roberts, Mark, Cal.	6	3	.667	4.50	33	0	0	0	21	8	36.0	47	167	21	18	5	2	0	0	15	3	35	3	0
Rodgers, Bobby, Cal.	1	3	.250	6.03	18	2	0	0	3	0	37.1	35	166	25	25	7	3	3	2	20	0	28	4	0
Rodriguez, Jose, Mem.*	2	1	.667	3.56	54	0	0	0	17	1	60.2	52	262	25	24	7	2	2	2	31	0	54	0	0
Romero, J.C., Edm.*	3	3	.500	3.68	12	10	0	0	0	0	[illegible]	67	271	[illegible]	[illegible]	4	2	2	0	24	0	55	2	1
Ruffin, Johnny, Cal.	2	3	.400	4.36	37	0	0	0	32	22	33.0	37	148	17	16	1	1	2	2	10	3	47	3	0
Ryan, Jason, Nash.-L.V.	3	8	.273	6.42	14	14	1	0	0	0	67.1	80	313	59	48	10	7	4	5	26	0	31	3	0
Sabel, Erik, Tuc.	2	2	.500	2.95	18	2	0	0	7	2	39.2	35	162	14	13	3	4	1	4	7	1	32	2	0
Sanchez, Jesus, Cal.*	6	1	.857	3.21	16	11	0	0	0	0	75.2	61	322	32	27	4	1	2	3	33	0	58	2	0
Santana, Julio, Fres.	8	8	.500	5.83	25	25	0	0	0	0	132.2	160	601	94	86	28	4	2	9	50	0	125	9	1
Schmack, Brian, Okla.	2	2	.500	4.08	40	0	0	0	15	1	53.0	56	231	31	24	5	1	1	1	14	1	34	0	0
Schmidt, Jason, Nash.	1	0	1.000	0.00	1	1	0	0	0	0	7.0	4	25	0	0	0	0	0	0	0	0	6	0	0
Schrenk, Steve, Sac.	2	1	.667	2.49	16	0	0	0	10	3	21.2	21	91	9	6	1	0	1	1	6	1	22	0	0
Sedlacek, Shawn, Oma.	5	4	.556	5.00	14	13	0	0	1	0	81.0	98	348	49	45	13	4	2	3	22	2	44	3	1
Serafini, Dan, Fres.*	1	1	.500	10.32	7	0	0	0	2	0	11.1	17	59	14	13	2	1	2	1	9	1	9	0	0
Serrano, Wascar, Port.	6	5	.545	4.53	27	13	0	0	2	0	93.1	98	403	50	47	10	4	6	5	35	0	73	4	0
Shields, Scot, S.L.	6	11	.353	4.97	21	21	4	0	0	0	137.2	141	578	84	76	24	4	4	10	31	0	104	7	1
Shouse, Brian, N.O.*	2	2	.500	2.89	56	1	0	0	17	1	53.0	51	225	21	17	4	0	2	3	15	0	56	2	0
Sikaras, Pete, Tuc.	0	1	.000	12.00	4	0	0	0	1	0	6.0	11	34	10	8	2	0	1	1	4	0	4	4	0
Sikorski, Brian, Okla.	6	4	.600	3.61	14	14	1	0	0	0	87.1	89	354	37	35	8	2	4	2	23	0	73	0	1
Simon, Ben, L.V.	2	6	.250	7.35	12	9	0	0	2	0	52.2	61	243	48	43	8	8	2	7	23	1	43	1	0
Simontacchi, Jason, Edm.	7	13	.350	5.34	32	18	2	0	3	0	143.1	192	627	97	85	21	3	7	6	23	1	83	4	0
Slusarski, Joe, N.O.	5	2	.714	2.48	31	0	0	0	4	1	40.0	37	163	17	11	4	2	1	0	8	3	24	0	0
Small, Aaron, S.L.	0	1	.000	1.69	3	0	0	0	0	0	5.1	8	23	1	1	1	0	0	0	1	0	5	0	0
Smart, J.D., Okla.	2	2	.500	2.74	16	0	0	0	13	3	23.0	22	97	9	7	0	2	1	2	6	0	13	2	0
Smith, Brian, Nash.	1	2	.333	3.69	36	0	0	0	34	11	39.0	37	164	22	16	5	0	1	1	7	0	34	2	0
Smith, Bud, Mem.*	8	5	.615	2.75	17	17	0	0	0	0	108.0	114	462	38	33	6	6	5	4	28	2	78	1	1
Smith, Cam, L.V.	0	1	.000	8.74	8	0	0	0	1	0	11.1	12	68	14	11	2	0	2	1	19	0	9	3	0
Smith, Chuck, Cal.	2	0	1.000	2.84	2	2	0	0	0	0	12.2	12	49	4	4	0	0	0	0	2	0	9	0	0
Smith, Travis, N.O.	0	0	.000	0.00	1	0	0	0	0	0	2.0	3	10	0	0	0	0	0	0	1	0	0	0	0
Snyder, Matt, Iowa	0	0	.000	9.00	1	0	0	0	1	0	1.0	1	5	1	1	0	0	0	0	1	0	3	0	0
Sollecito, Gabe, Iowa	0	0	.000	4.82	7	0	0	0	5	0	9.1	9	36	5	5	2	0	0	0	1	0	9	0	0
Sonnier, Shawn, Oma.	5	5	.500	4.82	47	2	0	0	28	6	71.0	69	313	41	38	15	0	3	0	33	0	63	2	0
Sparks, Steve, Nash.	3	5	.375	5.06	31	10	1	0	9	3	74.2	77	358	50	42	10	5	0	3	64	2	63	6	0
Speier, Justin, C.S.	1	0	1.000	1.46	11	0	0	0	4	2	12.1	10	54	2	2	0	1	1	1	7	0	16	3	1
Spencer, Stan, Port.	5	6	.455	5.09	20	18	0	0	1	0	99.0	110	432	62	56	11	4	3	5	30	0	81	3	1
Spradlin, Jerry, Mem.	4	1	.800	2.20	29	0	0	0	26	14	32.2	17	118	8	8	2	1	1	1	7	1	28	1	0
Springer, Dennis, L.V.	7	7	.500	5.27	19	18	2	1	1	0	114.1	142	504	74	67	16	6	4	6	28	1	51	4	1
Springer, Russ, Tuc.	0	0	.000	4.91	7	3	0	0	0	0	7.1	7	32	4	4	1	0	0	1	3	0	6	0	0
Stanifer, Rob, Iowa	7	8	.467	4.24	54	0	0	0	19	6	74.1	85	330	38	35	9	7	5	2	28	6	79	4	0
Stark, Dennis, Tac.	14	2	.875	2.37	24	24	0	0	0	0	151.2	124	613	52	40	12	8	5	7	41	0	130	5	1
Steenstra, Kennie, Tuc.	9	6	.600	4.18	28	28	1	0	0	0	170.0	187	737	101	79	14	7	4	7	42	1	114	1	0
Stentz, Brent, Edm.	0	0	.000	5.65	17	0	0	0	14	7	14.1	19	66	9	9	2	0	0	0	5	0	12	0	0
Stephenson, Garrett, Mem.	0	0	.000	0.00	1	1	0	0	0	0	2.0	2	8	0	0	0	0	0	0	0	0	2	0	0
Stone, Ricky, N.O.	6	3	.667	3.59	51	8	0	0	15	2	95.1	98	404	42	38	8	4	1	8	27	4	78	6	1
Strong, Joe, Cal.	6	3	.667	6.25	46	0	0	0	13	1	59.0	80	275	45	41	9	3	4	5	18	4	48	6	0
Sturdy, Tim, Edm.	0	1	.000	16.71	2	2	0	0	0	0	7.0	15	40	14	13	2	0	0	1	6	0	3	2	0
Tabaka, Jeff, Mem.*	0	2	.000	2.60	32	0	0	0	14	2	27.2	24	116	10	8	2	3	3	0	10	2	23	1	0
Tankersley, Dennis, Port.	1	2	.333	6.91	3	3	0	0	0	0	14.1	16	68	13	11	2	2	2	0	8	0	16	0	0
Taylor, Bill, Nash.	0	3	.000	7.20	20	0	0	0	16	8	20.0	29	92	17	16	4	2	0	1	3	1	16	0	0
Tessmer, Jay, C.S.	1	0	1.000	6.59	10	0	0	0	8	0	13.2	23	71	14	10	4	2	1	1	6	2	10	1	0
Teut, Nate, Iowa*	13	8	.619	5.12	29	29	0	0	0	0	167.0	184	753	109	95	28	4	6	5	69	3	125	3	1
Thomas, Juan, Tac.	0	0	.000	3.38	2	0	0	0	2	0	2.2	4	13	1	1	1	0	0	1	0	0	0	0	0
Thompson, Travis, C.S.	0	2	.000	17.65	9	0	0	0	3	0	8.2	20	53	19	17	2	2	1	2	6	0	9	0	0
Thomson, John, C.S.	5	3	.625	3.31	12	12	0	0	0	0	68.0	74	285	29	25	6	0	1	1	13	0	52	2	0
Thurman, Corey, Oma.	0	0	.000	5.40	1	1	0	0	0	0	5.0	6	24	4	3	0	0	0	0	2	0	4	1	0
Tollberg, Brian, Port.	1	0	1.000	4.50	4	4	0	0	0	0	20.0	24	86	11	10	3	0	0	0	4	0	10	0	0
Tomko, Brett, Tac.	10	6	.625	4.04	19	18	3	2	0	0	127.0	124	528	64	57	12	7	5	3	25	1	117	2	0
Turman, Jason, Tac.	7	5	.583	2.26	29	5	0	0	4	1	75.2	54	311	26	19	6	2	4	8	26	1	85	3	1
Tyler, Josh, Fres.	0	0	.000	0.00	1	0	0	0	1	0	1.0	2	5	0	0	0	0	0	0	0	0	0	0	0
Vasquez, Leo, Sac.*	0	1	.000	5.28	36	0	0	0	22	0	44.1	52	213	28	26	4	1	0	3	31	0	36	2	0
Verplancke, Jeff, Fres.	2	1	.667	2.92	8	0	0	0	4	1	12.1	9	50	4	4	1	0	0	2	6	0	13	0	0
Villafuerte, Brandon, Okla.	5	5	.500	2.83	38	0	0	0	28	10	63.2	63	275	21	20	4	4	3	6	26	1	65	2	0
Vizcaino, Luis, Sac.	2	2	.500	2.14	27	0	0	0	19	7	42.0	35	171	10	10	5	1	0	1	10	4	56	1	0
Vogelsong, Ryan, Fres.-Nash.	5	6	.455	3.21	16	16	0	0	0	0	89.2	61	356	33	32	8	0	2	2	33	0	86	2	1
Wainhouse, Dave, Iowa	3	5	.375	4.16	49	1	0	0	19	6	75.2	86	330	38	35	9	5	3	4	24	2	61	1	0
Ward, Jeremy, Tuc.	3	4	.429	3.52	40	0	0	0	23	13	46.0	53	208	23	18	2	3	1	2	17	2	35	5	0
Washburn, Jarrod, S.L.*	0	1	.000	5.87	1	1	0	0	0	0	7.2	9	31	5	5	1	0	0	0	1	0	5	0	0
Watkins, Scott, C.S.*	0	1	.000	10.57	10	0	0	0	2	0	7.2	13	48	10	9	1	0	0	1	10	0	4	1	0
Watson, Mark, Tac.*	0	1	.000	2.25	3	0	0	0	2	1	4.0	4	20	2	1	1	0	0	0	2	0	1	0	0
Weibl, Clint, Mem.	1	0	1.000	2.25	2	2	0	0	0	0	12.0	10	48	3	3	0	0	1	2	2	0	9	0	0
Wengert, Don, Nash.	7	7	.500	4.10	18	18	0	0	0	0	112.0	135	483	60	51	16	3	7	5	20	2	67	3	0
Whisenant, Matt, L.V.*	1	7	.125	7.31	24	10	0	0	4	1	60.1	83	287	49	49	5	2	4	3	36	2	42	3	0
Wilkins, Marc, Nash.	4	1	.800	4.75	32	0	0	0	10	1	36.0	38	153	21	19	2	0	1	3	13	1	24	3	1

Pitcher, Team	W	L	Pct.	ERA	G	GS	CG	ShO	GF	Sv.	IP	H	TBF	R	ER	HR	SH	SF	HB	BB	IBB	SO	WP	Bk.
Williams, Dave, Nash.*	1	1	.500	3.38	2	2	0	0	0	0	10.2	9	45	5	4	3	0	1	0	5	0	6	0	0
Williams, Jeff, L.V.*	7	5	.583	3.97	16	16	1	1	0	0	90.2	102	388	49	40	12	4	2	3	24	0	61	0	0
Williams, Shad, S.L.	0	0	.000	8.78	8	1	0	0	1	0	13.1	26	69	13	13	6	0	1		7	0	9	0	0
Wilson, Craig, Oma.	0	0	.000	4.50	2	0	0	0	2	0	2.0	2	7	1	1	1	0	0	0	0	0	1	0	0
Wilson, Kris, Oma.	2	2	.500	2.79	6	5	0	0	0	0	29.0	31	118	9	9	2	0	0	1	0	0	10	1	0
Wimberly, Larry, Nash.*	2	1	.667	5.27	4	3	0	0	0	0	13.2	16	58	8	8	5	1	0	4	0	3	0	0	
Wise, Matt, S.L.	9	9	.500	5.04	21	21	0	0	0	0	123.1	134	527	79	69	19	3	1	12	17	0	111	4	1
Witt, Bobby, Tuc.	0	3	.000	3.63	5	5	0	0	0	0	22.1	18	92	11	9	1	1	2	0	8	1	18	1	0
Witt, Kevin, Port.	0	0	.000	13.50	2	0	0	0	2	0	1.1	4	10	3	2	1	0	0	0	1	0	0	0	0
Wojciechowski, Steve, Cal.*	0	1	.000	6.97	8	1	0	0	4	0	10.1	16	50	8	8	0	0	1	0	3	1	7	2	0
Wolff, Bryan, Edm.	2	4	.333	6.08	15	13	0	0	0	0	74.0	96	328	51	50	14	2	2	3	22	0	52	0	0
Wooten, Greg, Tac.	11	8	.579	3.99	27	26	5	1	0	0	169.1	201	728	91	75	18	5	9	7	32	1	116	6	0
Yates, Tyler, Sac.	1	0	1.000	0.00	4	0	0	0	2	1	5.1	3	20	0	0	0	0	0	1	1	0	3	0	0
Zambrano, Carlos, Iowa	10	5	.667	3.88	26	25	1	0	1	0	150.2	124	639	73	65	9	5	3	14	68	1	155	10	1
Zancanaro, Dave, Mem.*	6	14	.300	5.99	27	24	1	1	1	1	142.2	171	640	103	95	28	8	4	6	48	0	107	3	0
Zerbe, Chad, Fres.*	3	4	.429	3.55	17	0	0	0	12	5	25.1	28	114	13	10	2	1	0	1	9	0	17	0	0
Zimmerman, Jordan, Tac.*	4	3	.571	6.94	41	4	0	0	25	4	58.1	83	279	52	45	8	5	5	4	23	0	45	5	0

PITCHERS WITH TWO OR MORE TEAMS

Pitcher, Team	W	L	Pct.	ERA	G	GS	CG	ShO	GF	Sv.	IP	H	TBF	R	ER	HR	SH	SF	HB	BB	IBB	SO	WP	Bk.
Belitz, Todd, Sac.*	4	2	.667	5.13	38	0	0	0	12	0	52.2	52	225	38	30	6	4	1	3	16	3	54	1	1
Belitz, Todd, C.S.*	0	2	.000	9.82	14	0	0	0	5	2	11.0	19	57	15	12	2	0	0	1	3	0	8	1	0
Bruske, Jim, S.L.	3	1	.750	4.89	27	5	0	0	8	1	57.0	70	255	35	31	9	2	2	4	10	0	58	3	0
Bruske, Jim, L.V.	2	2	.500	5.47	10	8	0	0	1	0	49.1	59	220	31	30	6	0	2	5	15	0	49	1	0
Camp, Shawn, Port.	1	0	1.000	0.00	4	1	0	0	1	0	7.0	2	22	0	0	0	0	0	0	1	0	6	0	0
Camp, Shawn, Nash.	0	0	.000	2.12	11	0	0	0	1	0	17.0	11	67	4	4	1	0	1	0	8	1	15	0	0
DeSilva, John, Cal.	1	2	.333	6.75	26	3	0	0	7	1	38.2	59	189	33	29	5	1	0	4	9	1	29	1	0
DeSilva, John, L.V.	1	1	.500	2.16	14	0	0	0	7	0	25.0	23	98	7	6	2	0	1	0	6	2	27	1	0
Donaldson, Bo, Nash.	1	1	.500	0.64	11	0	0	0	3	0	14.0	9	60	4	1	1	0	1	2	9	0	17	2	0
Donaldson, Bo, Port.	2	0	1.000	0.46	8	2	0	0	3	0	19.2	6	69	2	1	0	0	2	2	0	18	0	0	
Gross, Kip, L.V.	3	1	.750	5.09	10	0	0	0	7	0	17.2	26	81	11	10	5	0	2	4	0	8	1	0	
Gross, Kip, C.S.	1	7	.125	6.04	18	12	1	1	1	0	82.0	112	360	65	55	10	0	2	4	12	1	48	2	0
Joseph, Kevin, Fres.	0	1	.000	7.56	5	0	0	0	2	0	8.1	9	36	7	7	0	1	1	0	4	1	2	2	0
Joseph, Kevin, Mem.	0	2	.000	6.75	12	0	0	0	6	0	12.0	8	56	9	9	2	1	1	1	11	1	6	0	0
Lawrence, Sean, Port.*	0	3	.000	3.53	25	0	0	0	7	0	35.2	32	154	16	14	1	3	0	1	13	0	44	2	0
Lawrence, Sean, Tuc.*	1	3	.250	3.57	18	0	0	0	8	0	22.2	20	101	15	9	2	0	1	2	9	3	32	1	0
Lidle, Kevin, S.L.	0	0	.000	0.00	1	0	0	0	1	0	1.0	0	4	0	0	0	0	0	0	1	0	1	0	0
Lidle, Kevin, Mem	0	0	.000	0.00	1	0	0	0	1	0	0.2	1	2	0	0	0	0	0	0	0	0	0	0	0
Mahay, Ron, Port.*	1	2	.333	3.78	14	0	0	0	5	0	16.2	13	69	9	7	2	2	0	0	5	0	10	0	0
Mahay, Ron, Iowa*	3	1	.750	2.31	36	0	0	0	30	14	46.2	29	176	12	12	5	3	2	2	10	1	52	3	0
Maurer, Dave, Port.*	0	0	.000	4.34	17	0	0	0	7	1	18.2	11	75	9	9	4	0	1	1	9	2	21	3	0
Maurer, Dave, Sac.*	0	0	.000	5.54	11	0	0	0	4	0	13.0	14	60	9	8	2	0	0	0	8	0	21	0	0
Mota, Danny, Edm.	3	3	.500	5.89	34	0	0	0	15	2	47.1	52	210	31	31	7	3	2	1	23	1	43	4	0
Mota, Danny, L.V.	1	2	.333	7.71	12	0	0	0	5	1	11.2	16	55	10	10	1	1	1	0	8	1	7	0	0
Reyes, Carlos, Sac.	2	0	1.000	6.23	17	0	0	0	9	0	30.1	31	135	21	21	5	1	2	1	14	1	26	1	0
Reyes, Carlos, Tuc.	0	1	.000	8.68	8	0	0	0	4	0	9.1	13	45	10	9	1	0	1	0	5	1	7	3	0
Rizzo, Todd, L.V.*	1	0	1.000	3.63	13	0	0	0	3	0	17.1	17	83	9	7	1	0	1	2	14	1	19	1	0
Rizzo, Todd, Fres.*	3	4	.429	4.50	36	0	0	0	14	6	46.0	49	207	26	23	5	1	4	3	22	0	39	5	1
Ryan, Jason, Nash.	3	5	.375	4.53	9	9	1	0	0	0	53.2	52	235	34	27	7	6	2	3	19	0	25	1	0
Ryan, Jason, Tuc.	0	3	.000	13.83	5	0	0	0	0	0	13.2	28	78	25	21	3	1	2	2	7	0	6	2	0
Vogelsong, Ryan, Fres.	3	3	.500	2.79	10	10	0	0	0	0	58.0	35	226	18	18	6	0	1	1	18	0	53	1	1
Vogelsong, Ryan, Nash.	2	3	.400	3.98	6	6	0	0	0	0	31.2	26	130	15	14	2	0	1	1	15	0	33	1	0

COMBINATION SHUTOUTS: **Calgary (3)**—Sanchez-Strong-Ruffin, Lorraine-Roberts, Grilli-Roberts. **Colorado Springs (5)**—Chacon-House-Christman, Thomson-Clontz-Dingman, Thomson-House-Christman, Randall Chouinard-Davenport, Larkin-Christman-House. **Edmonton (6)**—Kinney-Cressend-Duvall-McMullen-Stentz, Simontacchi-Duvall-Stentz, Brewington-Fiore, Romero-Balfour-Marshall-Duvall, Kinney-Duvall-Bochtler, Fiore-Brewington. **Fresno (3)** Vogelsong-Zerbe, Santana-Connelly Crabtree-Arnold, Estrella-Embree. **Iowa (9)**—Teut-Borowski, Meyers-Norton, Nation-Stanifer-Mahay, Zambrano-Ohman, Borowski-Wainhouse-Mahay, Zambrano-Norton, Meyers-Mahay, Zambrano-Mahay, Norton-Stanifer-Chiasson. **Las Vegas (6)**—Perez-Gross-Dougherty, Priest-Reyes-Foster, Alvarez-Masaoka-Dougherty, Alvarez-Reyes-Dougherty, Kiefer-Masaoka-Husted-Ricketts, Kiefer-Dougherty. **Memphis (7)**—Benes-Cather-Medina-Spradlin, Benes-Cather-Karnuth-Rodriguez-Spradlin, Rath-Karnuth-Spradlin, Smith-Hackman-Spradlin, Krivda-Spradlin, Smith-Huisman-Tabaka, Benes-James-Mathews. **Nashville (5)**—Lincoln-Ayers-Moody O'Connor-Pavlas, Schmidt-Pavlas-Taylor, Sparks-Moody, Wengert-Wilkins-Lincoln, Vogelsong-Wimberly-Loiselle. **New Orleans (4)**—Oswalt-Mann, Arteaga-Linebrink-Mann, Redding Shouse-Mann, Driskill-Linebrink-Mann. **Oklahoma (5)**—Sikorski-Cordero, Glynn-Johnson-Durocher, Johnson-Kolb-Villafuerte, Dickey-Kolb, Elder-Durocher. **Omaha (2)**—Fussell-Laxton-Sonnier, D'Amico-Austin. **Portland (11)**—Powell-Maurer, Serrano-Lundquist, Powell-Miller, Loewer-Lundquist-Maurer-Miller, Middlebrook-Miller, Herndon-Corey, Lawrence-Lundquist, Spencer-Serrano-Giron-Corey-Lundquist, Serrano-Donaldson-Condrey-Corey, Lopez-Giron, Middlebrook-Giron-Corey. **Sacramento (1)**—Miller-Belitz-Schrenk. **Salt Lake (4)**—Beverlin-Borland-Miadich, Wise-Alvarez, Beverlin-Borland-Miadich, Bruske-Alvarez-Donnelly. **Tacoma (6)**—Turman-Fuentes, Stark-Fuentes, Turman-Pineiro-Gryboski, Ramsay-Kaye-Jarvis, Stark-Fuentes-Gryboski, Ramsay-Kaye. **Tucson (6)**—Sabel-Mohler-Prinz, Bierbrodt-Ward, Bierbrodt-Ward, Steenstra-Koplove, Steenstra-Cabel, Ellis-Sabel-Koplove.

NO-HIT GAMES: Bowie, Sacramento defeated Tacoma 3-0, May 1. Powell, New Orleans defeated Omaha 5-0, May 6. Tomko, Tacoma defeated Oklahoma 7-0, July 3. Halama, Tacoma defeated Calgary 6-0, July 7.

2001 FIELDING

TEAM

Team	Pct.	G	PO	A	E	TC	DP	TP	PB
Portland	.980	144	3799	1466	110	5375	114	0	14
Fresno	.978	139	3594	1380	110	5084	129	0	14
Iowa	.978	143	3790	1325	114	5229	117	0	11
Tacoma	.978	144	3750	1403	116	5269	112	0	10
Edmonton	.978	143	3687	1449	117	5253	150	0	14
Omaha	.978	144	3748	1472	119	5339	159	0	18
Oklahoma	.977	143	3799	1428	125	5352	145	0	16
New Orleans	.977	139	3611	1459	122	5192	133	0	8
Calgary	.976	143	3667	1444	124	5235	121	0	14
Las Vegas	.976	144	3792	1425	127	5344	150	0	16
Sacramento	.976	144	3799	1409	127	5335	143	0	15
Memphis	.976	143	3757	1411	129	5297	115	0	8
Salt Lake	.975	143	3784	1456	136	5376	141	0	11
Colo. Springs	.972	141	3693	1468	146	5307	142	0	11
Tucson	.971	142	3729	1464	154	5347	106	0	12
Nashville	.969	141	3666	1533	165	5364	145	0	12

CLASS AAA Pacific Coast League

INDIVIDUAL

FIRST BASEMEN

NOTE: All caps denotes fielding-percentage leader based on 72 games for catchers, 96 for all other non-pitchers and 115 innings for pitchers. *Throws lefthanded.

Player, Team	Pct.	G	PO	A	E	TC	DP
Abad, Andy, Sac.*	.987	12	72	6	1	79	8
Alviso, Jerome, C.S.	1.000	20	77	3	0	80	13
Andrews, Shane, Mem.	.986	46	331	29	5	365	32
Balfe, Ryan, Mem.	1.000	12	83	8	0	91	4
Banks, Brian, Iowa-Cal.	.993	81	609	59	5	673	64
Barajas, Rod, Tuc.	.989	21	163	14	2	179	16
Barkett, Andy, Nash.*	.990	70	560	43	6	609	58
Barnes, Larry, S.L.*	.990	83	676	53	7	736	76
Barry, Jeff, L.V.	.985	20	125	10	2	137	19
Bell, Mike, C.S.	.971	11	29	4	1	34	3
Berblinger, Jeff, Oma.	1.000	2	16	2	0	18	4
Betts, Todd, Tac.	.992	105	817	56	7	880	70
Bevins, Andy, Mem.	.974	17	112	2	3	117	7
Blake, Casey, Edm.	.969	5	26	5	1	32	2
Brown, Brant, Mem.*	.998	48	384	33	1	418	35
Brumbaugh, Cliff, Okla.-C.S.	1.000	11	71	8	0	79	11
Burke, Jamie, S.L.	.980	6	44	5	1	50	6
Burns, Kevin, N.O.*	.972	28	224	18	7	249	23
Chamblee, Jim, N.O.	1.000	3	19	4	0	23	3
Chavez, Raul, N.O.	.000	1	0	0	0	0	0
Choi, Hee, Iowa*	.995	72	518	39	3	560	49
Colbrunn, Greg, Tuc.	1.000	5	24	3	0	27	4
Coomer, Ron, Iowa	1.000	2	9	0	0	9	2
Cotton, John, L.V.-Nash.	.995	25	185	7	1	193	20
Crespo, Felipe, Fres.	1.000	1	2	0	0	2	0
Cummings, Midre, Tuc.	1.000	5	39	1	0	40	1
Demetral, Chris, Okla.	1.000	1	3	0	0	3	0
Difelice, Mike, Tuc.	.875	1	7	0	1	8	1
Donnels, Chris, L.V.	.995	26	200	11	1	212	24
Durazo, Erubiel, Tuc.*	1.000	3	18	2	0	20	1
Eberwein, Kevin, Port.	.976	14	113	7	3	123	10
Estalella, Bobby, Fres.	1.000	1	9	1	0	10	1
Fasano, Sal, Oma.	.933	1	10	4	1	15	0
Fernandez, Jose, S.L.	1.000	1	6	0	0	6	0
Flores, Jose, C.S.	.939	4	27	4	2	33	1
Fox, Andy, Cal.	1.000	1	7	0	0	7	1
Gil, Geronimo, L.V.	.991	16	92	14	1	107	14
Gilbert, Shawn, L.V.	.000	1	0	0	0	0	0
Gload, Ross, Iowa*	.997	50	345	35	1	381	30
Grabowski, Jason, Tac.	1.000	20	148	9	0	157	16
Grijak, Kevin, Cal.	.977	23	165	7	4	176	14
Guzman, Ed, Fres.	.000	1	0	0	0	0	0
Haad, Yamid, Nash.	1.000	2	10	1	0	11	0
Hart, Jason, Sac.	.988	132	1130	62	15	1207	122
Hernandez, Alex, Nash.*	.984	48	415	18	7	440	42
Hiatt, Phil, L.V.	.984	19	116	8	2	126	16
Hubbard, Mike, Okla.	1.000	1	1	0	0	1	0
Huckaby, Ken, Tuc.	.990	28	188	11	2	201	11
Huskey, Butch, C.S.	.985	107	915	66	15	996	91
Hyzdu, Adam, Nash.	1.000	4	36	0	0	36	4
Jennings, Robin, Sac.-C.S.*	.917	3	21	1	2	24	1
Johnson, Brian, L.V.	.986	21	139	6	2	147	19
Johnson, Keith, L.V.	1.000	8	44	1	0	45	2
Kieschnick, Brooks, C.S.	.961	7	49	0	2	51	3
Koonce, Graham, Port.*	1.000	5	37	0	0	37	4
LeCroy, Matthew, Edm.	.969	10	92	3	3	98	11
Leyritz, Jim, Port.	.980	11	88	9	2	99	9
Lo Duca, Paul, L.V.	.750	1	2	1	1	4	0
Lopez, Mendy, N.O.	.981	5	48	3	1	52	3
Luuloa, Keith, Port.-N.O.	.989	26	167	12	2	181	13
Lydy, Scott, N.O.	.991	25	195	19	2	216	15
Mahoney, Mike, Iowa	1.000	1	1	0	0	1	0
McGowan, Sean, Fres.	.983	34	274	21	5	300	26
McGuire, Ryan, Cal.*	.992	29	228	28	2	258	22
McKeel, Walt, C.S.	1.000	6	31	2	0	33	4
McNally, Sean, Tuc.	1.000	7	29	1	0	30	4
Melhuse, Adam, C.S.	.985	7	59	7	1	67	7
Minor, Damon, Fres.*	.988	108	801	68	11	880	95
Morgan, Scott, S.L.	1.000	1	9	0	0	9	2
Nelson, Bryant, Tuc.	1.000	1	7	1	0	8	0
Pellow, Kit, Oma.	.993	121	1030	88	8	1126	130
Pena, Angel, L.V.	.967	15	113	3	4	120	9
Pena, Carlos, Okla.*	.989	117	925	89	11	1025	108
Petrick, Ben, C.S.	.947	2	17	1	1	19	1
Post, Dave, L.V.	.994	24	161	11	1	173	12

Player, Team	Pct.	G	PO	A	E	TC	DP
Pritchett, Chris, S.L.	.990	55	472	30	5	507	46
Rolison, Nate, Cal.	1.000	3	19	2	0	21	1
Rosario, Mel, Tuc.	1.000	1	3	0	0	3	0
Roskos, John, Port.-Iowa	.992	35	218	20	2	240	13
Sagmoen, Marc, Edm.-Okla.-Mem.*	.979	11	88	6	2	96	11
SEARS, Todd, Edm.	.993	107	842	69	6	917	107
Secrist, Reed, Nash.	.994	19	150	11	1	162	24
Sell, Chip, Tuc.	.985	34	240	23	4	267	25
Short, Rick, Iowa	1.000	4	10	0	0	10	0
Snow, J.T., Fres.*	1.000	4	26	0	0	26	1
Steed, Dave, Okla.	.992	13	116	10	1	127	12
Stefanski, Mike, Mem.	1.000	2	17	3	0	20	0
Sutton, Larry, Mem.-Edm.*	.993	30	204	19	2	285	27
Thomas, Juan, Tuc.	.995	27	191	16	1	208	13
Truby, Chris, N.O.	.992	30	231	11	2	244	26
Tyler, Josh, Fres.	.000	1	0	0	0	0	0
Valentin, Javier, Edm.	.994	20	137	19	1	157	11
Waszgis, B.J., Cal.	.969	22	178	10	6	194	15
Wilkins, Rick, Port.	1.000	6	40	3	0	43	2
Wilson, Craig, Oma.	.994	21	153	13	1	167	13
Wilson, Craig, Nash.	.963	6	50	2	2	54	3
Wilson, Desi, Tuc.*	.989	58	470	48	6	524	38
Wilson, Tom, Nash.	1.000	2	11	0	0	11	1
Witt, Kevin, Port.	.987	79	651	41	9	701	56
Wood, Jason, Nash.	1.000	1	10	0	0	10	0
Zinter, Alan, N.O.	.993	57	398	22	3	423	32
Zuleta, Julio, Iowa	.982	20	151	9	3	163	15
Zuniga, Tony, Fres.	1.000	2	4	1	0	5	0

FIRST BASEMEN WITH TWO OR MORE TEAMS

Player, Team	Pct.	G	PO	A	E	TC	DP
Banks, Brian, Iowa	1.000	2	6	1	0	7	2
Banks, Brian, Cal.	.992	79	603	58	5	666	62
Brumbaugh, Cliff, Okla.	1.000	5	39	4	0	43	4
Brumbaugh, Cliff, C.S.	1.000	6	32	4	0	36	7
Cotton, John, L.V.	1.000	21	148	5	0	153	17
Cotton, John, Nash.	.975	4	37	2	1	40	3
Jennings, Robin, Sac.*	.833	1	4	1	1	6	0
Jennings, Robin, C.S.*	.944	2	17	0	1	18	1
Luuloa, Keith, Port.	1.000	17	123	9	0	132	8
Luuloa, Keith, N.O.	.959	9	44	3	2	49	5
Roskos, John, Port.	.995	27	180	13	1	194	11
Roskos, John, Iowa	.978	8	38	7	1	46	2
Sagmoen, Marc, Edm.*	1.000	1	3	0	0	3	0
Sagmoen, Marc, Okla.*	.976	9	75	6	2	83	8
Sagmoen, Marc, Mem.*	1.000	1	10	0	0	10	3
Sutton, Larry, Mem.*	.995	27	202	14	1	217	23
Sutton, Larry, Edm.*	.985	9	62	5	1	68	4

SECOND BASEMEN

Player, Team	Pct.	G	PO	A	E	TC	DP
Abbott, Chuck, S.L.	1.000	3	3	3	0	6	1
Akers, Chad, Tac.	1.000	25	49	53	0	102	13
Alexander, Manny, Tac.	.974	60	87	136	6	229	31
Alviso, Jerome, C.S.	.974	46	67	84	4	155	24
Baughman, Justin, S.L.	.980	63	121	166	6	293	34
Bell, Mike, C.S.	.966	24	38	46	3	87	5
Bellhorn, Mark, Sac.	1.000	16	35	51	0	86	16
Berblinger, Jeff, Oma.-Nash.	.977	37	60	107	4	171	28
Berroa, Cristian, N.O.	1.000	3	1	11	0	12	2
Blake, Casey, Edm.	1.000	4	6	13	0	19	3
Branson, Jeff, L.V.	.973	43	78	103	5	186	33
Brumbaugh, Cliff, C.S.	1.000	1	0	0	0	0	0
Butler, Brent, C.S.	.979	54	103	134	5	242	33
Caceres, Wilmy, S.L.	.960	17	30	42	3	75	12
Cairo, Miguel, Iowa	.991	27	51	54	1	106	11
Castro, Nelson, Fres.	1.000	4	7	9	0	16	1
Chamblee, Jim, N.O.	.958	4	14	9	1	24	2
Cintron, Alex, Tuc.	.970	19	26	38	2	66	5
Clapinski, Chris, Cal.	.985	15	26	39	1	66	12
Clapp, Stubby, Mem.	.977	82	184	236	10	430	53
Clark, Jermaine, Tac.	.980	71	118	173	6	297	37
Cotton, John, L.V.	1.000	14	22	23	0	45	7
Crespo, Cesar, Port.	.982	34	66	94	3	163	15
Crespo, Felipe, Fres.	1.000	1	2	4	0	6	1
Delgado, Wilson, Oma.	.960	42	87	106	8	201	34
Demetral, Chris, Okla.	.970	50	83	141	7	231	36
Diaz, Edwin, Edm.	.991	75	115	203	3	321	54
Durrington, Trent, L.V.-S.L.	.974	33	62	85	4	151	24
Easterday, Matt, Cal.	.952	8	6	14	1	21	1
Erickson, Matt, Cal.	.978	56	107	159	6	272	35
Espada, Josue, Cal.	1.000	5	11	7	0	18	2

Player, Team	Pct.	G	PO	A	E	TC	DP
Fajardo, Al, Fres.	1.000	3	2	2	0	4	0
Febles, Carlos, Oma.	1.000	23	45	66	0	111	19
Figueroa, Luis, Nash.	.965	25	44	65	4	113	13
Flores, Jose, C.S.	.975	23	44	73	3	120	16
Fox, Andy, Cal.	1.000	3	9	7	0	16	1
Freeman, Corey, Mem.	1.000	5	10	8	0	18	1
Frias, Hanley, Edm.-Mem.	.994	47	76	97	1	174	23
Garcia, Luis, Mem.	1.000	1	1	1	0	2	0
German, Esteban, Sac.	.962	35	78	97	7	182	27
Gilbert, Shawn, L.V.	.984	25	51	73	2	126	19
Ginter, Keith, N.O.	.971	93	163	236	12	411	52
Gomez, Chris, Port.	1.000	1	3	1	0	4	0
Guzman, Ed, Fres.	1.000	1	1	1	0	2	0
Hall, Justin, Fres.	1.000	1	5	3	0	8	3
Hansen, Jed, Oma.	.889	4	2	6	1	9	1
Haverbusch, Kevin, Nash.	.813	7	12	14	6	32	2
Hinske, Eric, Sac.	.500	1	1	0	1	2	0
Huckaby, Ken, Tuc.	.000	1	0	0	0	0	0
Huff, Larry, Edm.	.983	12	22	35	1	58	4
Johnson, Keith, L.V.	1.000	4	4	12	0	16	2
Klassen, Danny, Tuc.	1.000	1	3	3	0	6	0
Lamb, Dave, C.S.-Cal.	.969	15	29	34	2	65	10
Lane, Ryan, Sac.	.970	16	25	39	2	66	11
Lemonis, Chris, Cal.-Tuc.	.929	12	24	41	5	70	6
Lopez, Mendy, N.O.	.995	33	75	109	1	185	28
Lucca, Lou, Mem.	.931	18	33	48	6	87	8
Luuloa, Keith, Port.-N.O.	.985	28	53	76	2	131	20
Mackowiak, Rob, Nash.	.981	10	27	25	1	53	9
Maier, T.J., Mem.	1.000	6	11	10	0	21	3
Martin, Norberto, Cal.	.995	39	73	121	1	195	21
Matos, Julius, Port.	1.000	10	20	22	0	42	3
Matranga, Dave, N.O.	1.000	2	4	4	0	8	2
Melo, Juan, Fres.	.980	94	200	235	9	444	71
MEYERS, Chad, Iowa	.965	106	188	227	15	430	52
Moriarty, Mike, Edm.	.000	1	0	0	0	0	0
Morris, Warren, Nash.	.967	47	103	131	8	242	32
Nelson, Bryant, Tuc.-Nash.	.977	57	131	170	7	308	37
Niuhuluun, Kevin, C.S.	1.000	6	4	15	0	19	7
Nieves, Jose, S.L.	.959	45	92	121	9	222	28
Ordaz, Luis, Oma.	1.000	3	4	8	0	12	1
Ortiz, Jose, Sac.	.961	60	112	134	10	256	42
Porez, Santiago, Port	.941	7	13	19	2	34	5
Pernalete, Marco, Fres.	.963	24	43	62	4	109	13
Petersen, Chris, Nash.-Tuc.	1.000	30	55	74	0	129	18
Polcovich, Kevin, Mem.	.962	26	42	58	4	104	12
Post, Dave, L.V.	.917	8	6	16	2	24	4
Powers, Jeff, C.S.	.964	4	14	13	1	28	3
Prieto, Alejandro, Oma.	1.000	39	68	116	0	184	33
Riggs, Adam, Port.	.964	82	150	221	14	385	41
Romano, Jason, Okla.	.975	18	26	52	2	80	13
Ryan, Mike, Edm.	.945	39	66	89	9	164	28
Salazar, Oscar, Sac.	1.000	5	7	6	0	13	2
Santangelo, F.P., Sac.	.991	26	46	61	1	108	14
Saylor, Jamie, Cal.	1.000	3	0	3	0	3	0
Schifano, Tony, N.O.	.857	2	3	3	1	7	0
Sefclk, Kevin, C.S.	.903	7	15	13	3	31	4
Short, Rick, Iowa	1.000	6	10	12	0	22	4
Simons, Mitch, Okla.	.988	33	67	104	2	173	25
Snopek, Chris, Iowa	.951	14	24	34	3	61	9
Sosa, Juan, Tuc.	.959	36	61	78	6	145	19
Spivey, Junior, Tuc.	.990	50	131	152	3	286	25
Stankiewicz, Andy, L.V.	.969	61	89	129	7	225	37
t'Hoen, E.J., S.L.	1.000	5	4	14	0	18	4
Thrower, Jake, Port.	1.000	6	10	16	0	26	3
Tyler, Josh, Fres.	.934	17	23	48	5	76	9
White, Walt, Tuc.	.932	24	35	61	7	103	10
Wilson, Craig, Oma.	1.000	6	11	22	0	33	3
Wood, Jason, Nash.	1.000	2	6	7	0	13	4
Young, Mike, Okla.	.972	46	60	114	5	179	26
Young, Travis, Fres.	1.000	2	4	1	0	5	1

SECOND BASEMEN WITH TWO OR MORE TEAMS

Player, Team	Pct.	G	PO	A	E	TC	DP
Berblinger, Jeff, Oma.	.976	36	58	104	4	166	27
Berblinger, Jeff, Nash.	1.000	1	2	3	0	5	1
Durrington, Trent, L.V.	.973	16	32	41	2	75	9
Durrington, Trent, S.L.	.974	17	30	44	2	76	15
Frias, Hanley, Edm.	1.000	28	34	55	0	89	15
Frias, Hanley, Mem.	.988	19	42	42	1	85	8
Lamb, Dave, C.S.	1.000	1	2	0	0	2	0
Lamb, Dave, Cal.	.968	14	27	34	2	63	10
Lemonis, Chris, Cal.	.909	7	17	23	4	44	4

Player, Team	Pct.	G	PO	A	E	TC	DP
Lemonis, Chris, Tuc.	.962	5	7	18	1	26	2
Luuloa, Keith, Port.	.988	18	32	47	1	80	14
Luuloa, Keith, N.O.	.980	10	21	29	1	51	6
Nelson, Bryant, Tuc.	.974	16	33	43	2	78	12
Nelson, Bryant, Nash.	.978	41	98	127	5	230	25
Petersen, Chris, Nash.	1.000	14	30	41	0	71	10
Petersen, Chris, Tuc.	1.000	16	25	33	0	58	8

THIRD BASEMEN

Player, Team	Pct.	G	PO	A	E	TC	DP
Abbott, Chuck, S.L.	.800	1	0	4	1	5	0
Abreu, Dennis, Iowa	1.000	2	2	4	0	6	2
Akers, Chad, Tac.	.893	30	23	44	8	75	5
Alexander, Manny, Tac.	.969	18	10	21	1	32	1
Alviso, Jerome, C.S.	.727	9	3	5	3	11	1
Andrews, Shane, Mem.	.935	16	5	24	2	31	3
Balfe, Ryan, Mem.	.925	17	11	26	3	40	3
Barajas, Rod, Tuc.	.000	1	0	0	0	0	0
Bell, Mike, C.S.	.938	65	41	124	11	176	14
Bellhorn, Mark, Sac.	.875	2	2	5	1	8	2
Beltre, Adrian, L.V.	.833	2	2	3	1	6	0
Berblinger, Jeff, Oma.-Nash.	.929	12	15	24	3	42	1
Betts, Todd, Tac.	.966	25	16	40	2	58	3
Blake, Casey, Edm.	.955	86	59	155	10	224	14
Bogar, Tim, L.V.	.800	3	2	2	1	5	0
Branson, Jeff, L.V.	1.000	17	6	22	0	28	2
Brumbaugh, Cliff, C.S.	.878	26	11	32	6	49	0
Burke, Jamie, S.L.	1.000	13	12	28	0	40	0
BURROUGHS, Sean, Port.	.964	96	79	192	10	281	18
Butler, Bront, C.S.	1.000	5	3	11	0	14	1
Cairo, Miguel, Iowa	.750	1	0	3	1	4	0
Chamblee, Jim, N.O.	1.000	3	0	3	0	3	0
Chavez, Raul, N.O.	1.000	1	0	3	0	3	0
Cirillo, Jeff, C.S.	1.000	1	1	2	0	3	1
Clapinski, Chris, Cal.	.963	12	8	18	1	27	2
Coomer, Ron, Iowa	1.000	2	1	4	0	5	0
Cotton, John, L.V.-Nash.	.875	10	5	16	3	24	2
Crespo, Cesar, Port.	.968	11	5	25	1	31	1
Delgado, Wilson, Oma.	.949	18	13	24	2	39	3
Demetral, Chris, Okla.	1.000	5	8	17	0	25	0
Diaz, Edwin, Edm.	.928	33	28	49	6	83	8
Donnels, Chris, L.V.	.929	4	4	9	1	14	3
Durrington, Trent, S.L.	.800	5	2	6	2	10	0
Eberwein, Kevin, Port.	1.000	13	8	19	0	27	1
Encarnacion, Bienvenido, S.L.	.889	2	1	7	1	9	0
Ensberg, Morgan, N.O.	.929	81	50	172	17	239	22
Erickson, Matt, Cal.	1.000	1	0	4	0	4	0
Espada, Josue, Cal.	.933	3	4	10	1	15	0
Fernandez, Jose, S.L.	.953	114	71	234	15	320	22
Figueroa, Luis, Tac.	.979	24	11	35	1	47	2
Figueroa, Luis, Nash.	1.000	1	0	3	0	3	1
Flores, Jose, C.S.	.947	26	7	47	3	57	8
Fox, Andy, Cal.	1.000	1	1	0	0	1	0
Frias, Hanley, Edm	.000	1	0	0	0	0	0
Garcia, Luis, Mem.	.879	15	4	25	4	33	2
Garcia, Osmani, Okla.	.963	44	25	79	4	108	3
Gautreau, Jake, Port.	1.000	2	0	5	0	5	0
Gilbert, Shawn, L.V.	1.000	2	0	1	0	1	0
Ginter, Keith, N.O.	1.000	3	3	6	0	9	1
Grabowski, Jason, Tac.	.903	58	38	111	16	165	8
Guiel, Jeff, S.L.	1.000	2	0	1	0	1	0
Gulan, Mike, Cal.	.935	118	62	196	18	276	17
Guzman, Ed, Fres.	1.000	8	4	23	0	27	1
Hansen, Jed, Oma.	.800	2	1	3	1	5	0
Hiatt, Phil, L.V.	.932	91	56	164	16	236	18
Hinske, Eric, Sac.	.944	120	72	197	16	285	14
Hubbard, Trenidad, Iowa	1.000	7	3	8	0	11	1
Huckaby, Ken, Tuc.	.879	11	7	22	4	33	1
Huff, Larry, Edm.	1.000	5	0	7	0	7	1
Hyzdu, Adam, Nash.	1.000	1	1	1	0	2	0
Johnson, Keith, L.V.	.919	32	27	41	6	74	2
Klassen, Danny, Tuc.	.909	5	2	8	1	11	1
Lamb, Dave, Cal.	.000	1	0	0	0	0	0
Lamb, Mike, Okla.	.908	69	39	109	15	163	9
Lane, Ryan, Sac.	.974	13	9	28	1	38	6
Lopez, Mendy, N.O.	1.000	1	1	0	0	1	0
Lucca, Lou, Mem.	.947	108	47	205	14	266	11
Luuloa, Keith, Port.-N.O.	.964	12	8	19	1	28	1
Lydy, Scott, N.O.	.000	2	0	0	0	0	0
Mackowiak, Rob, Nash.	.889	8	7	25	4	36	3
Mahoney, Mike, Iowa	.000	1	0	0	0	0	0
Martin, Norberto, Cal.	1.000	10	5	19	0	24	2

Player, Team	Pct.	G	PO	A	E	TC	DP
McKay, Cody, Sac.	1.000	8	4	15	0	19	2
McNally, Sean, Tuc.	.954	68	37	109	7	153	10
Meliah, Dave, Okla.	.905	16	9	29	4	42	3
Melo, Juan, Fres.	1.000	4	4	7	0	11	0
Meyers, Chad, Iowa	1.000	4	1	6	0	7	0
Morales, Willie, C.S.	1.000	1	0	1	0	1	0
Moriarty, Mike, Edm.	1.000	3	3	3	0	6	0
Morris, Warren, Nash.	.955	8	3	18	1	22	0
Mueller, Bill, Iowa	1.000	6	1	6	0	7	1
Nelson, Bryant, Tuc.-Nash.	.908	64	45	112	16	173	11
Nicholson, Kevin, C.S.	1.000	12	8	21	0	29	2
Nieves, Jose, S.L.	.889	5	3	5	1	9	0
Ordaz, Luis, Oma.	.800	2	1	3	1	5	0
Peeples, Mike, C.S.	.929	10	7	19	2	28	1
Polcovich, Kevin, Mem.	1.000	7	5	9	0	14	1
Post, Dave, L.V.	.969	12	13	18	1	32	2
Prieto, Alejandro, Oma.	.972	44	26	79	3	108	7
Pritchett, Chris, S.L.	1.000	1	0	4	0	4	0
Riggs, Adam, Port.	.923	12	7	17	2	26	3
Salazar, Oscar, Sac.	1.000	1	0	2	0	2	1
Santangelo, F.P., Sac.	1.000	1	0	4	0	4	0
Sears, Todd, Edm.	.000	1	0	0	0	0	0
Secrist, Reed, Nash.	.946	45	21	101	7	129	9
Sefcik, Kevin, C.S.	.909	6	2	18	2	22	1
Short, Rick, Iowa	.959	90	67	121	8	196	15
Snopek, Chris, Iowa	.966	45	31	54	3	88	4
Sosa, Juan, C.S.-Tuc.	.903	16	2	26	3	31	3
Sprague, Ed, Tac.	.000	1	0	0	0	0	0
Steed, Dave, Okla.	1.000	1	0	3	0	3	0
t'Hoen, E.J., S.L.	.941	5	3	13	1	17	2
Thrower, Jake, Port.	.833	7	3	7	2	12	1
Truby, Chris, N.O.	.946	57	48	109	9	166	6
Tyler, Josh, Fres.	.953	16	11	30	2	43	3
Valentin, Javier, Edm.	.887	25	19	44	8	71	6
White, Walt, Tuc.	1.000	2	1	0	0	1	0
Williams, Matt, Tuc.	.833	4	1	4	1	6	1
Wilson, Craig, Oma.	.974	73	53	136	5	194	14
Wilson, Tom, Sac.	.923	6	3	9	1	13	1
Witt, Kevin, Port.	1.000	1	0	1	0	1	0
Wood, Jason, Nash.	.944	78	52	151	12	215	12
Zamora, Junior, S.L.	.875	3	0	7	1	8	1
Zuleta, Julio, Iowa	.826	12	9	10	4	23	0
Zuniga, Tony, Fres.	.946	117	79	219	17	315	24

THIRD BASEMEN WITH TWO OR MORE TEAMS

Player, Team	Pct.	G	PO	A	E	TC	DP
Berblinger, Jeff, Oma.	.903	8	14	14	3	31	1
Berblinger, Jeff, Nash.	1.000	4	1	10	0	11	0
Cotton, John, L.V.	1.000	2	0	4	0	4	0
Cotton, John, Nash.	.850	8	5	12	3	20	2
Luuloa, Keith, Port.	.950	10	5	14	1	20	1
Luuloa, Keith, N.O.	1.000	2	3	5	0	8	0
Nelson, Bryant, Tuc.	.918	62	45	111	14	170	11
Nelson, Bryant, Nash.	.333	2	0	1	2	3	0
Sosa, Juan, C.S.	.909	8	2	18	2	22	3
Sosa, Juan, Tuc.	.889	8	0	8	1	9	0

SHORTSTOPS

Player, Team	Pct.	G	PO	A	E	TC	DP
Abreu, Dennis, Iowa	1.000	1	0	1	0	1	0
Akers, Chad, Tac.	1.000	1	1	0	0	1	0
Alexander, Manny, Tac.	.917	20	30	36	6	72	8
Alviso, Jerome, C.S.	.963	18	32	47	3	82	9
Amezaga, Alfredo, S.L.	.954	49	91	137	11	239	34
Baughman, Justin, S.L.	1.000	1	3	4	0	7	2
Bellhorn, Mark, Sac.	.929	4	3	10	1	14	3
Berroa, Cristian, N.O.	1.000	1	1	5	0	6	1
Blake, Casey, Edm.	1.000	3	2	2	0	4	1
Bogar, Tim, L.V.	.968	13	26	35	2	63	11
Branson, Jeff, L.V.	.975	42	61	93	4	158	27
Bruntlett, Eric, N.O.	1.000	4	5	11	0	16	2
Butler, Brent, C.S.	1.000	7	6	15	0	21	3
Caceres, Wilmy, S.L.	.963	70	128	206	13	347	47
Cairo, Miguel, Iowa	.960	7	7	17	1	25	1
Campusano, Carlos, Fres.	1.000	5	3	6	0	9	1
Castro, Nelson, Fres.	.938	2	3	12	1	16	4
Chamblee, Jim, N.O.	1.000	1	1	0	0	1	0
Cintron, Alex, Tuc.	.931	93	139	267	30	436	36
Clapinski, Chris, Cal.	.970	7	12	20	1	33	4
Crespo, Cesar, Port.	1.000	14	15	37	0	52	6

Player, Team	Pct.	G	PO	A	E	TC	DP
Delgado, Wilson, Oma.	.982	15	18	38	1	57	8
Demetral, Chris, Okla.	.000	1	0	0	0	0	0
Diaz, Edwin, Edm.	.947	5	6	12	1	19	3
Dransfeldt, Kelly, Okla.	.965	142	268	400	24	692	105
Durrington, Trent, S.L.	1.000	1	1	2	0	3	0
Ellis, Mark, Sac.	.968	131	199	382	19	600	87
Encarnacion, Bienvenido, S.L.	1.000	4	8	16	0	24	2
Ensberg, Morgan, N.O.	.000	1	0	0	0	0	0
Erickson, Matt, Cal.	.965	56	73	146	8	227	34
Espada, Josue, Cal.-C.S.	.976	75	112	210	8	330	41
Everett, Adam, N.O.	.956	113	189	329	24	542	70
Figueroa, Luis, Nash.	.959	67	113	235	15	363	47
Flores, Jose, C.S.	.930	35	53	79	10	142	14
Fox, Andy, Cal.	.900	3	1	8	1	10	1
Frias, Hanley, Edm.-Mem.	.937	58	92	130	15	237	36
Garcia, Luis, Mem.	.955	87	153	208	17	378	49
Gil, Geronimo, L.V.	.000	1	0	0	0	0	0
Gilbert, Shawn, L.V.	.974	23	21	55	2	78	14
Gomez, Chris, Port.	.956	10	10	33	2	45	5
Grabowski, Jason, Tac.	.600	1	1	2	2	5	1
Ibanez, Raul, Oma.	1.000	1	1	0	0	1	0
Jackson, Damian, Port.	1.000	3	3	11	0	14	2
Johnson, Keith, L.V.	.954	89	133	221	17	371	59
Klassen, Danny, Tuc.	1.000	1	1	3	0	4	0
Lamb, Dave, C.S.-Cal.	.941	9	16	16	2	34	7
Lane, Ryan, Sac.	1.000	10	12	17	0	29	5
Lopez, Mendy, N.O.	.983	16	22	36	1	59	9
Lorenzana, Luis, Port.	1.000	2	1	3	0	4	0
Lucca, Lou, Mem.	1.000	5	3	11	0	14	2
Luuloa, Keith, Port.-N.O.	.892	21	21	45	8	74	3
Martin, Norberto, Cal.	.930	10	20	33	4	57	8
Matos, Julius, Port.	.967	96	145	266	14	425	46
Matranga, Dave, N.O.	1.000	2	1	7	0	8	0
McNally, Sean, Tuc.	1.000	6	2	16	0	18	2
Melo, Juan, Fres.	1.000	2	2	2	0	4	0
Moriarty, Mike, Edm.	.965	125	198	359	20	577	89
Nicholson, Kevin, Port.-C.S.	.958	13	20	26	2	48	5
Nieves, Jose, S.L.	.945	14	17	35	3	55	6
Ordaz, Luis, Oma.	.952	5	8	12	1	21	6
Ortiz, Jose, Sac.	1.000	4	4	15	0	19	1
Ortiz, Nick, Oma.	.975	98	167	292	12	471	68
Perez, Santiago, Port.	1.000	3	2	6	0	8	1
Petersen, Chris, Nash.-Tuc.	.983	33	43	71	2	116	13
Polcovich, Kevin, Mem.	.947	21	24	47	4	75	7
Prieto, Alejandro, Oma.	.953	21	26	55	4	85	14
RANSOM, Cody, Fres.	.980	133	202	374	12	588	82
Santangelo, F.P., Sac.	1.000	1	1	3	0	4	0
Schifano, Tony, N.O.	.000	1	0	0	0	0	0
Skrehot, Shaun, Nash.	.898	18	24	55	9	88	17
Smith, Jason, Iowa	.942	67	108	199	19	326	47
Snopek, Chris, Iowa	.970	71	82	178	8	268	28
Sosa, Juan, C.S.-Tuc.	.947	21	23	49	4	76	7
Spivey, Junior, Tuc.	1.000	3	4	11	0	15	3
t'Hoen, E.J., S.L.	.929	7	5	21	2	28	4
Thrower, Jake, Port.	1.000	2	2	3	0	5	0
Uribe, Juan, C.S.	.960	73	156	230	16	402	58
Vazquez, Ramon, Tac.	.979	127	190	381	12	583	69
White, Walt, Tuc.	1.000	6	14	13	0	27	6
Wilson, Craig, Oma.	1.000	12	26	38	0	64	15
Wilson, Jack, Nash.	.974	27	30	81	3	114	19
Womack, Tony, Tuc.	.846	4	3	8	2	13	2
Wood, Jason, Nash.	.924	33	41	93	11	145	19
Woolf, Jason, Mem.	1.000	1	2	1	0	3	0
Young, Mike, Okla.	.909	2	2	8	1	11	2

SHORTSTOPS WITH TWO OR MORE TEAMS

Player, Team	Pct.	G	PO	A	E	TC	DP
Espada, Josue, Cal.	.973	68	101	188	8	297	38
Espada, Josue, C.S.	1.000	7	11	22	0	33	3
Frias, Hanley, Edm.	.958	17	29	40	3	72	11
Frias, Hanley, Mem.	.927	41	63	90	12	165	25
Lamb, Dave, C.S.	.857	3	3	3	1	7	2
Lamb, Dave, Cal.	.963	6	13	13	1	27	5
Luuloa, Keith, Port.	.957	16	14	30	2	46	3
Luuloa, Keith, N.O.	.786	5	7	15	6	28	0
Nicholson, Kevin, Port.	.950	9	18	20	2	40	4
Nicholson, Kevin, C.S.	1.000	4	2	6	0	8	1
Petersen, Chris, Nash.	.889	2	3	5	1	9	0
Petersen, Chris, Tuc.	.991	31	40	66	1	107	13
Sosa, Juan, C.S.	.864	5	5	14	3	22	3
Sosa, Juan, Tuc.	.981	16	18	35	1	54	4

OUTFIELDERS

Player, Team	Pct.	G	PO	A	E	TC	DP
Abad, Andy, Sac.*	.966	88	141	2	5	148	0
Abbott, Jeff, Cal.*	.974	44	72	2	2	76	0
Akers, Chad, Tac.	.979	35	42	4	1	47	0
Alexander, Chad, Tac.	.975	130	224	7	6	237	1
Alexander, Manny, Tac.	.000	2	0	0	0	0	0
Allen, Chad, Edm.	1.000	6	10	1	0	11	0
Allen, Luke, L.V.	.667	2	1	1	1	3	0
Alou, Felipe, Oma.	.889	11	16	0	2	18	0
Alviso, Jerome, C.S.	.944	14	17	0	1	18	0
Ardoin, Danny, Edm.	1.000	1	3	0	0	3	0
Ashby, Chris, Okla.	.977	27	43	0	1	44	0
Aven, Bruce, L.V.	.983	70	108	5	2	115	3
Balfe, Ryan, Mem.	.972	34	68	1	2	71	0
Banks, Brian, Iowa-Cal.	.920	20	22	1	2	25	0
Barker, Glen, N.O.	.980	42	91	6	2	99	2
Barkett, Andy, Nash.*	.857	12	11	1	2	14	0
Barnes, John, Edm.	1.000	78	132	8	0	140	1
Barnes, Larry, S.L.*	1.000	3	4	0	0	4	0
Barry, Jeff, L.V.	.984	69	122	2	2	126	1
Bartee, Kimera, S.L.-C.S.	.993	62	131	6	1	138	2
Bass, Jayson, Iowa*	.967	58	111	5	4	120	2
Baughman, Justin, S.L.	.920	13	22	1	2	25	0
Becker, Rich, Cal.*	.956	45	61	4	3	68	1
Bell, Derek, Nash.	.938	12	15	0	1	16	0
Bellhorn, Mark, Sac.	1.000	17	24	2	0	26	0
Berrios, Harry, Okla.	.972	31	34	1	1	36	0
Betzsold, James, Tac.	.966	42	52	5	2	59	2
Bevins, Andy, Mem.	1.000	19	28	2	0	30	0
Bieser, Steve, Mem.	1.000	1	2	0	0	2	0
Blake, Casey, Edm.	.000	1	0	0	0	0	0
Brown, Brant, Mem.*	1.000	1	1	0	0	1	0
Brown, Dee, Oma.	.950	8	16	3	1	20	2
Brown, Emil, Port.	1.000	21	39	2	0	41	0
Brown, Jason, Cal.	1.000	3	5	0	0	5	0
Brown, Roosevelt, Iowa	.971	79	127	7	4	138	1
Drumbaugh, Cliff, Okla.-C.S.	.965	84	160	7	6	173	4
Buhner, Jay, Tac.	1.000	6	10	0	0	10	0
Bullett, Scott, C.S.*	.964	20	25	2	1	28	1
Burke, Jamie, S.L.	1.000	2	4	0	0	4	0
Byas, Mike, Fres.	1.000	9	7	1	0	8	0
Byrnes, Eric, Sac.	.973	93	175	6	5	186	6
Candelaria, Ben, Cal.	.986	44	68	2	1	71	0
Carpenter, Bubba, C.S.*	.955	42	63	1	3	67	0
Chamblee, Jim, N.O.	1.000	1	1	0	0	1	0
Chavez, Endy, Oma.*	1.000	23	38	2	0	40	0
Christensen, McKay, L.V.*	.943	15	32	1	2	35	0
Christenson, Ryan, Sac.-Tuc.	.959	73	160	3	7	170	1
Clapinski, Chris, Cal.	.969	17	30	1	1	32	0
Clapp, Stubby, Mem.	1.000	2	2	1	0	3	0
Colangelo, Mike, Port.	.991	56	99	6	1	106	0
Cole, Eric, N.O.	.979	112	175	9	4	188	1
Conti, Jason, Tuc.	.991	89	205	5	2	212	1
Cookson, Brent, L.V.	.940	44	59	4	4	67	1
Cotton, John, L.V.-Nash.	1.000	4	3	0	0	3	0
Crespo, Cesar, Port.	1.000	23	43	2	0	45	1
Crespo, Felipe, Port.	1.000	1	2	0	0	2	0
Crosby, Bubba, L.V.*	1.000	12	38	0	0	38	0
Cruz, Jacob, C.S.*	1.000	19	39	5	0	44	2
Cummings, Midre, Tuc.	.978	46	84	5	2	91	1
Cust, Jack, Tuc.	.948	117	195	6	11	212	1
DaVanon, Jeff, S.L.	.992	66	123	5	1	129	1
DeHaan, Kory, Port.	.990	80	198	9	2	209	2
Demetral, Chris, Okla.	1.000	4	1	0	0	1	0
Dunwoody, Todd, Iowa*	.974	63	107	7	3	117	2
Durrington, Trent, S.L.	1.000	11	12	0	0	12	0
Easterday, Matt, Cal.	.889	6	7	1	1	9	0
Encarnacion, Mario, Sac.-C.S.	.959	55	88	6	4	98	2
Estrella, Luis, Fres.	1.000	1	4	0	0	4	0
Fajardo, Al, Fres.	1.000	6	2	0	0	2	0
Fernandez, Jose, S.L.	.000	1	0	0	0	0	0
Flores, Jose, C.S.	1.000	7	6	0	0	6	0
Fox, Andy, Cal.	1.000	2	1	0	0	1	0
Gann, Jamie, Tuc.	1.000	6	2	1	0	3	0
Garcia, Luis, Mem.	.000	1	0	0	0	0	0
Giambi, Jeremy, Sac.*	1.000	6	7	0	0	7	0
Gibson, Derrick, Tuc.	.962	28	49	2	2	53	0
Gilbert, Shawn, L.V.	.933	13	26	2	2	30	1
Ginter, Keith, N.O.	1.000	36	49	3	0	52	1
Gload, Ross, Iowa*	.983	72	112	6	2	120	0
Goodwin, Curtis, Okla.*	.969	71	120	7	4	131	4
Grabowski, Jason, Tac.	.912	23	28	3	3	34	2
Green, Chad, Port.	.950	17	38	0	2	40	0
Green, Scarborough, Nash.	.970	20	29	3	1	33	2
Greene, Charlie, Port.	.000	1	0	0	0	0	0
Grijak, Kevin, Cal.	1.000	18	35	1	0	36	0
Guiel, Aaron, Oma.	.973	113	202	13	6	221	3
Guiel, Jeff, S.L.	.977	44	84	2	2	88	0
Hallmark, Pat, Oma.	.976	24	38	3	1	42	0
Hamilton, Darryl, C.S.	1.000	3	7	1	0	8	0
Hansen, Jed, Oma.	.978	69	131	5	3	139	0
Haverbusch, Kevin, Nash.	.966	24	27	1	1	29	0
Hellman, Matthew, Port.	1.000	1	1	1	0	2	0
Henderson, Rickey, Port.*	.933	9	14	0	1	15	0
Hermansen, Chad, Nash.	.984	117	237	8	4	249	3
Hernandez, Alex, Nash.*	.969	36	59	4	2	65	1
Hinch, A.J., Oma.	.000	1	0	0	0	0	0
Hollins, Damon, Edm.*	.954	47	98	6	5	109	2
Horgan, Joe, Fres.*	.000	1	0	0	0	0	0
Howard, Tom, Nash.	.800	3	3	1	1	5	0
Hubbard, Trenidad, Oma.-Iowa	.995	88	175	5	1	181	2
Huff, Larry, Edm.	1.000	11	9	0	0	9	0
Huskey, Butch, C.S.	1.000	5	10	0	0	10	0
Hyzdu, Adam, Nash.	.993	58	132	3	1	136	0
Ibanez, Raul, Oma.	.833	5	5	0	1	6	0
Jennings, Robin, Sac.-C.S.*	.967	38	55	3	2	60	0
Johnson, Lance, C.S.*	.980	30	49	1	1	51	0
Kelly, Roberto, C.S.	1.000	39	44	5	0	49	1
Kielty, Bobby, Edm.	.991	94	221	11	2	234	1
Kieschnick, Brooks, C.S.	1.000	44	56	3	0	59	0
Kingsale, Eugene, Tac.	.976	51	115	5	3	123	0
Lane, Ryan, Sac.	.967	21	28	1	1	30	0
Leach, Jalal, Fres.*	.966	111	197	4	7	208	0
Ledee, Ricky, Okla.*	1.000	3	3	0	0	3	0
Leyritz, Jim, Port.	.000	1	0	0	0	0	0
Lipowicz, Nathan, L.V.	1.000	2	7	0	0	7	0
Little, Mark, C.S.	1.000	9	20	2	0	22	0
Lopez, Mendy, N.O.	1.000	3	3	0	0	3	0
Ludwick, Ryan, Sac.*	.981	17	51	1	1	53	1
Luuloa, Keith, Port.	1.000	4	7	0	0	7	0
Lydy, Scott, N.O.	.988	49	81	3	1	85	0
Mackowiak, Rob, Nash.	.926	14	23	2	2	27	0
Magruder, Chris, Fres.-Okla.	.990	84	187	4	2	193	0
Martin, Norberto, Cal.	1.000	25	53	2	0	55	0
Mashore, Damon, Mem.	1.000	72	151	7	0	158	4
Mateo, Ruben, Okla.	.957	14	22	0	1	23	0
McCracken, Quinton, Edm.	.971	72	164	3	5	172	1
McGowan, Sean, Fres.	.925	53	73	1	6	80	0
McGuire, Ryan, Cal.*	.985	34	61	3	1	65	0
McKay, Cody, Sac.	1.000	1	2	0	0	2	0
McNaughton, Troy, Mem.*	.889	5	8	0	1	9	0
Melhuse, Adam, C.S.	1.000	3	3	0	0	3	0
Mellah, Dave, Okla.	.000	1	0	0	0	0	0
Meyers, Chad, Iowa	.972	22	35	0	1	36	0
Minor, Damon, Fres.*	1.000	1	3	1	0	4	1
Monahan, Shane, Nash.	1.000	11	18	0	0	18	0
Monroe, Craig, Okla.	.975	97	185	9	5	199	3
Moreta, Ramon, Tac.-S.L.	1.000	25	53	3	0	56	0
Morgan, Scott, S.L.	.972	118	207	4	6	217	1
Mota, Tony, L.V.	.966	110	161	10	6	177	1
Mottola, Chad, Cal.	.968	119	235	9	8	252	2
Mouton, Lyle, N.O.	1.000	2	2	0	0	2	0
Murphy, Nate, S.L.*	1.000	38	55	2	0	57	1
Murray, Calvin, Fres.	.978	34	88	2	2	92	1
Myers, Adrian, Tac.	.981	71	153	4	3	160	1
Nelson, Bryant, Tuc.	1.000	5	7	0	0	7	0
Nieves, Melvin, C.S.	1.000	13	22	0	0	22	0
Nunnally, Jon, Oma.	.975	84	154	3	4	161	1
Ortega, Bill, Mem.	.970	124	219	8	7	234	0
Owens, Eric, Cal.	.667	3	2	0	1	3	0
Patterson, Corey, Iowa	.968	87	180	3	6	189	0
Peeples, Mike, C.S.	.990	84	99	2	1	102	0
Perez, Santiago, Port.	.987	36	73	4	1	78	0
Petrick, Ben, C.S.	.882	12	13	2	2	17	1
Piatt, Adam, Sac.	.933	32	40	2	3	45	0
Podsednik, Scott, Tac.*	.967	65	147	0	5	152	0
Porter, Bo, Okla.	1.000	54	110	3	0	113	2
Porter, Colin, N.O.*	1.000	89	174	3	0	177	1
Pose, Scott, N.O.	.968	16	30	0	1	31	0
Post, Dave, L.V.	.957	14	22	0	1	23	0
Powell, Dante, Fres.	.966	106	189	7	7	203	0
Prieto, Alejandro, Oma.	1.000	3	2	0	0	2	0
Prieto, Chris, L.V.*	.989	115	244	14	3	261	2

CLASS AAA *Pacific Coast League*

Player, Team	Pct.	G	PO	A	E	TC	DP
Quinn, Mark, Oma.	1.000	6	12	1	0	13	0
Radmanovich, Ryan, Port.-Nash.	.995	111	181	5	1	187	0
RAMIREZ, Omar, N.O.	.989	104	170	13	2	185	4
Redman, Tike, Nash.*	.970	94	216	12	7	235	3
Riggs, Adam, Port.	1.000	1	1	0	0	1	0
Robinson, Kerry, Mem.*	1.000	10	15	0	0	15	0
Romano, Jason, Okla.	1.000	13	26	0	0	26	0
Romero, Willie, Tuc.	.933	6	12	2	1	15	0
Rosario, Mel, L.V.	1.000	2	1	0	0	1	0
Rosario, Omar, Sac.*	.962	17	24	1	1	26	0
Roskos, John, Iowa	1.000	14	14	2	0	16	0
Ryan, Mike, Edm.	.988	94	152	7	2	161	3
Ryan, Rob, Tuc.-Sac.*	.984	103	175	4	3	182	1
Sagmoen, Marc, Edm.-Okla.-Mem.*	.993	64	140	6	1	147	2
Sanders, Reggie, Tuc.	1.000	2	2	0	0	2	0
Santangelo, F.P., Sac.	1.000	42	78	2	0	80	1
Saturria, Luis, Mem.	.972	115	344	7	10	361	1
Saylor, Jamie, Cal.	.667	3	2	0	1	3	0
Secrist, Reed, Nash.	.966	23	27	1	1	29	0
Sefcik, Kevin, C.S.	.972	40	69	0	2	71	0
Sell, Chip, Tuc.	.987	48	74	1	1	76	0
Short, Rick, Iowa	.000	1	0	0	0	0	0
Sierra, Ruben, Okla.	1.000	1	2	0	0	2	0
Sosa, Juan, Tuc.	.900	5	9	0	1	10	0
Sprague, Ed, Tac.	1.000	4	6	0	0	6	0
Sutton, Larry, Edm.*	.982	33	54	1	1	56	0
Thompson, Ryan, Cal.	.948	77	159	6	9	174	2
Tolentino, Juan, S.L.	.961	109	214	5	9	228	0
Torcato, Tony, Fres.	.985	34	64	3	1	68	0
Tyler, Josh, Fres.	1.000	29	35	1	0	36	0
Ventura, Juan, C.S.	1.000	2	2	1	0	3	0
Watkins, Pat, Oma.	.981	56	97	7	2	106	0
Whitmore, Darrell, Mem.	.958	45	67	1	3	71	0
Wilson, Desi, Tuc.*	.913	15	18	3	2	23	0
Wilson, Preston, Cal.	1.000	4	9	0	0	9	0
Wilson, Tom, Sac.	1.000	3	5	0	0	5	0
Witt, Kevin, Port.	.947	38	51	3	3	57	0
Woods, Ken, Iowa	1.000	10	13	0	0	13	0
Woolf, Jason, Mem.	1.000	3	4	0	0	4	0
Young, Ernie, Port.	.974	89	140	11	4	155	2
Zinter, Alan, N.O.	.000	1	0	0	0	0	0
Zuleta, Julio, Iowa	1.000	3	5	0	0	5	0

OUTFIELDERS WITH TWO OR MORE TEAMS

Player, Team	Pct.	G	PO	A	E	TC	DP
Banks, Brian, Iowa	1.000	10	12	0	0	12	0
Banks, Brian, Cal.	.846	10	10	1	2	13	0
Bartee, Kimera, S.L.	.989	39	88	4	1	93	1
Bartee, Kimera, C.S.	1.000	23	43	2	0	45	1
Brumbaugh, Cliff, Okla.	.976	50	115	5	3	123	3
Brumbaugh, Cliff, C.S.	.940	34	45	2	3	50	1
Christenson, Ryan, Sac.	1.000	16	30	1	0	31	1
Christenson, Ryan, Tuc.	.950	57	130	2	7	139	0
Cotton, John, L.V.	1.000	2	1	0	0	1	0
Cotton, John, Nash.	1.000	2	2	0	0	2	0
Encarnacion, Mario, Sac.	.947	41	66	5	4	75	2
Encarnacion, Mario, C.S.	1.000	14	22	1	0	23	0
Hubbard, Trenidad, Oma.	1.000	45	99	4	0	103	1
Hubbard, Trenidad, Iowa	.987	43	76	1	1	78	1
Jennings, Robin, Sac.*	.955	28	41	1	2	44	0
Jennings, Robin, C.S.*	1.000	10	14	2	0	16	0
Magruder, Chris, Fres.	.992	53	118	2	1	121	0
Magruder, Chris, Okla.	.986	31	69	2	1	72	0
Moreta, Ramon, Tac.	1.000	23	48	3	0	51	0
Moreta, Ramon, S.L.	1.000	2	5	0	0	5	0
Radmanovich, Ryan, Port.	1.000	84	140	5	0	145	0
Radmanovich, Ryan, Nash.	.976	27	41	0	1	42	0
Ryan, Rob, Tuc.*	.988	51	77	2	1	80	0
Ryan, Rob, Sac.*	.980	52	98	2	2	102	1
Sagmoen, Marc, Edm.*	1.000	9	16	1	0	17	0
Sagmoen, Marc, Okla.*	.989	44	90	4	1	95	1
Sagmoen, Marc, Mem.*	1.000	11	34	1	0	35	1

CATCHERS

Player, Team	Pct.	G	PO	A	E	TC	DP	PB
Ardoin, Danny, Edm.	.989	81	501	54	6	561	4	6
Banks, Brian, Cal.	.981	9	48	5	1	54	0	0
Barajas, Rod, Tuc.	.992	19	112	7	1	120	0	0
Barthol, Blake, Tac.	.997	77	596	28	2	626	4	6
Bell, Mike, C.S.	1.000	1	3	0	0	3	0	0
Borders, Pat, Tac.	1.000	3	20	4	0	24	0	0
Brown, Jason, Cal.	1.000	6	41	2	0	43	0	0

Player, Team	Pct.	G	PO	A	E	TC	DP	PB
Burke, Jamie, S.L.	.987	36	284	20	4	308	1	3
Castillo, Carlos, Sac.	1.000	1	3	0	0	3	0	0
Castro, Ramon, Cal.	.989	86	589	45	7	641	3	8
Charles, Frank, N.O.	1.000	1	4	0	0	4	0	0
Chavez, Raul, N.O.	.992	82	533	62	5	600	10	3
Chiaramonte, Giuseppe, Fres.	1.000	15	75	4	0	79	0	2
Cota, Humberto, Nash.	.986	91	523	27	8	558	0	5
Cox, Darron, C.S.	.998	56	380	32	1	413	3	2
DeCinces, Tim, Port.	1.000	6	32	2	0	34	0	1
De La Cruz, Jose, Sac.	1.000	2	1	0	0	1	0	0
Diaz, Angel, S.L.	1.000	7	59	4	0	63	0	0
Difelice, Mike, Tuc.	.952	5	40	0	2	42	0	0
Epke, Brian, Tuc.	1.000	1	1	0	0	1	0	0
Estalella, Bobby, Fres.	1.000	1	8	0	0	8	0	0
Fasano, Sal, Oma.-C.S.	.981	37	229	23	5	257	2	4
Felix, Hersy, Oma.	1.000	1	7	0	0	7	0	0
Gil, Geronimo, L.V.	.996	64	492	36	2	530	2	7
Greene, Charlie, Port.	.987	64	435	33	6	474	6	5
Guzman, Ed, Fres.	1.000	11	84	7	0	91	0	3
Haad, Yamid, Nash.	.988	37	222	22	3	247	4	6
Haselman, Bill, Okla.	.957	3	22	0	1	23	0	0
Hernandez, Carlos, Mem.	1.000	2	5	0	0	5	0	0
Hernandez, John, L.V.	.974	4	34	3	1	38	0	1
Hill, Jason, S.L.	.951	8	55	3	3	61	0	1
Hinch, A.J., Oma.	.995	24	188	6	1	195	0	0
Horner, Jim, Tac.	.991	65	493	42	5	540	5	4
Hubbard, Mike, Okla.	.987	34	278	16	4	298	2	3
Huckaby, Ken, Tuc.	.970	36	237	24	8	269	3	3
Hundley, Todd, Iowa	1.000	9	51	5	0	56	0	0
Jensen, Marcus, Okla.	1.000	47	375	18	0	393	3	4
Johnson, Brian, L.V.	.995	27	207	13	1	221	1	6
King, Cesar, Oma.	.983	19	107	12	2	121	1	5
Kopitzke, Casey, Iowa	1.000	1	3	0	0	3	0	0
LeCroy, Matthew, Edm.	.986	21	135	11	2	148	3	2
Lidle, Kevin, S.L.-Mem.	.973	40	214	34	7	255	2	4
Lo Duca, Paul, L.V.	1.000	2	15	1	0	16	0	0
Lopez, Norberto, S.L.	1.000	2	8	0	0	8	0	0
Lopez, Rafael, Iowa	.993	19	140	10	1	151	2	2
Loyd, Brian, Port.	.990	23	177	14	2	193	1	0
Machado, Rob, Iowa	.988	45	396	27	5	428	3	3
Mahoney, Mike, Iowa	.996	85	680	42	3	725	10	4
McDONALD, Keith, Mem.	.998	91	600	53	1	654	4	3
McKay, Cody, Sac.	.991	78	600	49	6	655	4	8
McKeel, Walt, C.S.	1.000	13	76	2	0	78	0	1
Melhuse, Adam, C.S.	.986	38	264	21	4	289	3	5
Moeller, Chad, Tuc.	.989	70	442	20	5	467	1	6
Molina, Bengie, S.L.	1.000	4	27	2	0	29	0	0
Molina, Jose, S.L.	.996	61	451	43	2	496	4	5
Morales, Willie, C.S.	1.000	15	119	8	0	127	1	0
Myers, Greg, Sac.	1.000	1	5	0	0	5	0	0
Ortiz, Hector, Oma.	.991	29	198	11	2	211	0	0
Pachot, John, L.V.	1.000	6	37	4	0	41	1	1
Pena, Angel, L.V.	.992	31	227	16	2	245	1	0
Petrick, Ben, C.S.	.982	8	51	5	1	57	0	0
Pujols, Rafael, Sac.	.889	1	8	0	1	9	0	0
Romero, Mandy, Cal.-Sac.	.989	21	163	9	2	174	1	3
Rosario, Mel, L.V.-Oma.-Tuc.	.969	61	438	37	15	490	4	10
Rose, Mike, Tuc.	1.000	15	101	13	0	114	1	2
Roskos, John, Port.	1.000	1	3	0	0	3	0	0
Saylor, Jamie, Cal.	1.000	1	2	0	0	2	0	0
Secrist, Reed, Nash.	.955	21	101	6	5	112	1	1
Servais, Scott, N.O.	.997	42	288	34	1	323	8	1
Steed, Dave, Okla.	.984	52	384	35	7	426	8	8
Stefanski, Mike, Mem.	.994	52	323	29	2	354	2	3
Taveras, Luis, Okla.	.989	12	84	7	1	92	0	1
Torrealba, Yorvit, Fres.	.989	114	779	62	9	850	5	6
Tremie, Chris, N.O.	1.000	5	43	3	0	46	1	0
Tyler, Josh, Fres.	.983	10	54	5	1	60	0	3
Ullery, Dave, Oma.	.964	17	98	9	4	111	0	3
Valentin, Javier, Edm.	.987	49	343	32	5	380	3	6
Waszgis, B.J., Cal.	.988	47	299	28	4	331	2	6
Wilkins, Rick, Port.	.989	57	401	29	5	435	1	8
Wilson, Craig, Nash.	1.000	4	27	3	0	30	0	0
Wilson, Tom, Sac.	.989	50	348	27	4	379	1	4
Wright, Mike, Fres.	1.000	2	10	0	0	10	0	0
Zaun, Greg, Oma.	.985	8	63	3	1	67	0	1
Zinter, Alan, N.O.	.992	21	117	5	1	123	0	4

CATCHERS WITH TWO OR MORE TEAMS

Player, Team	Pct.	G	PO	A	E	TC	DP	PB
Fasano, Sal, Oma.	.972	12	62	8	2	72	0	1
Fasano, Sal, C.S.	.984	25	167	15	3	185	2	3

Player, Team	Pct.	G	PO	A	E	TC	DP	PB
Lidle, Kevin, S.L.	.979	29	162	25	4	191	1	2
Lidle, Kevin, Mem.	.953	11	52	9	3	64	1	2
Romero, Mandy, Cal.	1.000	3	18	1	0	19	0	0
Romero, Mandy, Sac.	.987	18	145	8	2	155	1	3
Rosario, Mel, L.V.	.978	14	125	11	3	139	1	1
Rosario, Mel, Oma.	.961	40	279	20	12	311	3	8
Rosario, Mel, Tuc.	1.000	7	34	6	0	40	0	1

PITCHERS

Player, Team	Pct.	G	PO	A	E	TC	DP
Abbott, Paul, Tac.	1.000	1	0	1	0	1	0
Acevedo, Juan, C.S.	1.000	6	0	2	0	2	0
Adkins, Jon, Sac.	1.000	3	2	1	0	3	0
Ahearne, Pat, Cal.	.935	28	12	17	2	31	4
Ah Yat, Paul, Nash.*	1.000	8	1	5	0	6	0
Ainsworth, Kurt, Fres.	1.000	27	10	14	0	24	0
Akers, Chad, Tac.	1.000	1	0	1	0	1	0
Almonte, Hector, Cal.	1.000	18	0	1	0	1	0
Alvarez, Juan, S.L.*	1.000	48	3	8	0	11	1
Alvarez, Victor, L.V.*	.938	20	2	13	1	16	0
Alviso, Jerome, S.L.	.000	1	0	0	0	0	0
Anderson, Brian, Tuc.*	1.000	2	2	2	0	4	0
Andra, Jeff, Fres.*	.929	9	4	9	1	14	0
Ankiel, Rick, Mem.*	1.000	3	0	2	0	2	0
Arnold, Jamie, Fres.	.875	44	2	12	2	16	2
Arroyo, Bronson, Nash.	.750	9	2	7	3	12	2
Arteaga, J.D., N.O.*	.967	32	9	20	1	30	1
Austin, Jeff, Oma.	.944	28	8	9	1	18	2
Averette, Rob, C.S.	.972	27	10	25	1	36	3
Aybar, Manny, Iowa	1.000	8	3	4	0	7	0
Ayers, Mike, Nash.*	1.000	5	0	2	0	2	0
Baez, Benito, Cal.*	.941	49	5	11	1	17	0
Bailey, Cory, Nash.	1.000	5	3	1	0	4	0
Balfour, Grant, Edm.	1.000	11	2	3	0	5	0
Barkott, Andy, Nash.*	.000	1	0	0	0	0	0
Beech, Matt, Okla.*	1.000	10	4	7	0	11	1
Belflower, Jay, Tuc.	.000	1	0	0	0	0	0
Belitz, Todd, Sac.-C.S.*	.917	52	1	10	1	12	0
Benes, Alan, Mem.	.920	25	10	7	2	26	2
Benoit, Joaquin, Okla.	.933	24	8	6	1	15	0
Bergman, Sean, C.S.	1.000	3	1	5	0	6	0
Bevel, Bobby, L.V.*	1.000	25	1	3	0	4	0
Beverlin, Jason, S.L.	.750	19	2	4	2	8	0
Bierbrodt, Nick, Tuc.*	1.000	7	0	13	0	13	0
Bochtler, Doug, Edm.	1.000	34	1	2	0	3	1
Bohanon, Brian, C.S.*	1.000	1	0	1	0	1	1
Borland, Toby, S.L.	1.000	45	2	7	0	9	1
Borowski, Joe, Iowa	.933	39	6	8	1	15	1
Boskie, Shawn, Tuc.	1.000	12	4	8	0	12	0
Bost, Heath, C.S.	.857	45	5	7	2	14	1
Bowie, Micah, Sac.*	1.000	38	6	11	0	17	1
Bradford, Chad, Sac.	1.000	12	1	6	0	7	0
Brewington, Jamie, Edm.	.917	35	5	6	1	12	0
Brink, Jim, Sac.	1.000	1	1	0	0	1	0
Brocail, Doug, N.O.	.000	2	0	0	0	0	0
Brohawn, Troy, Tuc.*	.000	2	0	0	0	0	0
Brown, Elliot, Fres.	.833	8	2	3	1	6	1
Brunson, Will, S.L.*	1.000	39	4	12	0	16	1
Bruske, Jim, S.L.-L.V.	.950	37	3	16	1	20	1
Bullinger, Jim, Mem.	1.000	10	4	7	0	11	0
Camp, Shawn, Port.-Nash.	1.000	15	3	4	0	7	1
Carlson, Dan, Mem.	.750	7	0	3	1	4	0
Carrara, Giovanni, L.V.	1.000	6	3	7	0	10	0
Cather, Mike, Mem.	1.000	15	0	6	0	6	0
Chacon, Shawn, C.S.	1.000	4	0	4	0	4	0
Charlton, Norm, Tac.*	.000	4	0	0	1	1	0
Chavez, Anthony, Tuc.	.944	51	5	12	1	18	0
Chiasson, Scott, Iowa	1.000	11	1	2	0	3	0
Chouinard, Bobby, C.S.	1.000	39	0	6	0	6	0
Christiansen, Jason, Mem.*	1.000	7	1	5	0	6	0
Christman, Tim, C.S.*	.889	38	4	4	1	9	1
Chrysler, Clint, Nash.*	.000	7	0	0	1	1	0
Clontz, Brad, C.S.	1.000	21	2	4	0	6	0
Cogan, Tony, Oma.*	1.000	9	2	3	0	5	1
Cole, Victor, Mem.	1.000	3	1	1	0	2	0
Condrey, Clay, Port.	1.000	39	2	9	0	11	2
Connelly, Steve, Fres.	1.000	33	1	9	0	10	1
Cooper, Brian, S.L.	.927	28	20	18	3	41	5
Cordero, Francisco, Okla.	1.000	12	2	0	0	2	0
Cordova, Francisco, Nash.	.000	1	0	0	0	0	0
Corey, Bryan, Port.	1.000	47	5	13	0	18	2
Cotton, Joe, Sac.	1.000	6	0	1	0	1	0
Crabtree, Robbie, Fres.	.968	63	5	25	1	31	3
Crafton, Kevin, Mem.	1.000	13	0	2	0	2	0
Crawford, Joe, Tuc.*	1.000	8	3	4	0	7	0
Cressend, Jack, Edm.	.800	12	1	3	1	5	0
Crowell, Jim, Port.*	1.000	11	1	4	0	5	1
Cubillan, Darwin, Okla.	1.000	9	0	2	0	2	0
Dace, Derek, Tuc.*	1.000	17	2	1	0	3	0
D'Amico, Jeff, Oma.	.964	32	16	11	1	28	0
Daneker, Pat, Iowa	1.000	16	1	5	0	6	1
Davenport, Joe, C.S.	.800	31	2	2	1	5	0
Davis, Doug, Okla.*	1.000	2	0	6	0	6	0
Davis, Kane, C.S.	.000	4	0	0	0	0	0
DeSilva, John, Cal.-L.V.	.900	40	3	6	1	10	0
Devey, Phil, L.V.*	1.000	3	1	0	0	1	0
Dewey, Mark, Nash.	1.000	11	1	4	0	5	0
Dickey, R.A., Okla.	.909	24	10	20	3	33	0
Difelice, Mark, C.S.	.900	8	2	7	1	10	0
Dingman, Craig, C.S.	1.000	46	1	3	0	4	0
Donaldson, Bo, Nash.-Port.	1.000	19	0	4	0	4	1
Donnelly, Brendan, S.L.	1.000	29	1	2	0	3	0
Dougherty, Jim, L.V.	1.000	59	5	11	0	16	1
Driskill, Travis, N.O.	.897	28	10	16	3	29	1
Drumright, Mike, Cal.	1.000	19	0	4	0	4	0
Duchscherer, Justin, Okla.	.800	7	4	4	2	10	2
Duncan, Courtney, Iowa	1.000	7	0	1	0	1	0
Durbin, Chad, Oma.	1.000	5	2	3	0	5	0
Durocher, Jayson, Okla.	1.000	31	2	5	0	7	0
Durrington, Trent, L.V.	.000	1	0	0	0	0	0
Duvall, Mike, Edm.*	1.000	55	4	8	0	12	0
Edmondson, Brian, Cal.	.857	23	2	4	1	7	0
Elarton, Scott, C.S.	1.000	2	0	1	0	1	0
Elder, Dave, Okla.	.917	15	5	6	1	12	0
Ellis, Robert, Tuc.	.750	5	1	2	1	4	0
Embree, Alan, Fres.*	.000	7	0	0	0	0	0
Eppolito, Vince, Tuc.	.000	2	0	0	0	0	0
Espina, Rendy, S.L.*	.000	2	0	0	0	0	0
Estrada, Horacio, C.S.*	.905	16	3	16	2	21	0
Estrella, Luis, Fres.	.977	30	22	21	1	44	3
Evans, Dave, N.O.	.800	25	0	3	2	5	1
Falkenborg, Brian, Tac.	1.000	8	4	4	0	8	0
Feliciano, Pedro, L.V.*	1.000	6	2	0	0	2	0
Fikac, Jeremy, Port.	1.000	1	1	0	0	1	0
Fiore, Tony, Edm.	.857	32	9	9	3	21	2
Fitzgerald, Brian, Tac.*	.875	20	1	6	1	8	1
Ford, Ben, Iowa	1.000	5	0	6	0	6	0
Foster, Kevin, Okla.	1.000	16	1	8	0	9	0
Foster, Kris, L.V.	1.000	21	1	3	0	4	1
Franklin, Ryan, Tac.	1.000	1	1	0	0	1	0
Franklin, Wayne, N.O.*	.900	41	5	4	1	10	0
Freeman, Corey, Nash.	.000	1	0	0	0	0	0
Fuentes, Brian, Tac.*	.920	35	1	22	2	25	0
Fussell, Chris, Oma.	.800	9	1	3	1	5	0
Fyhrie, Mike, Iowa	1.000	13	1	3	0	4	0
Gagne, Eric, L.V.	1.000	4	2	6	0	8	2
Galva, Claudio, Sac.*	1.000	4	0	2	0	2	0
Gardner, Mark, Fres.	1.000	3	1	0	0	1	0
George, Chris, Oma.*	.917	20	2	9	1	12	3
Giron, Isabel, Port.	.923	44	3	9	1	13	1
Glynn, Ryan, Okla.	.933	13	6	8	1	15	2
Gonzalez, Gabe, Port.*	.000	3	0	0	0	0	0
Gordon, Tom, Iowa	.000	2	0	0	0	0	0
Green, Steve, S.L.	.800	10	2	6	2	10	1
Grilli, Jason, Cal.	1.000	8	7	6	0	13	1
Gross, Kip, L.V.-C.S.	.923	28	6	18	2	26	3
Gryboski, Kevin, Tac.	1.000	58	7	10	0	17	1
Guerra, Mark, N.O.	1.000	28	11	15	0	26	5
Guttormson, Rick, Port.	.000	1	0	0	0	0	0
Guy, Brad, Nash.	.923	22	5	7	1	13	2
Guzman, Domingo, Port.	1.000	11	0	1	0	1	0
Guzman, Geraldo, Tuc.	1.000	20	5	9	0	14	0
Haad, Yamid, Nash.	.000	1	0	0	0	0	0
Hackman, Luther, Mem.	1.000	16	1	2	0	3	0
Halama, John, Tac.*	.800	3	2	2	1	5	0
Harville, Chad, Sac.	1.000	33	0	1	0	1	0
Hasselhoff, Derek, Fres.	1.000	25	3	2	0	5	0
Head, Daniel, Tac.	.000	2	0	0	0	0	0
Heiserman, Rick, Mem.	1.000	24	1	3	0	4	0
Henderson, Rod, Sac.	.667	8	1	1	1	3	1
Herbert, John, Port.	.000	1	0	0	0	0	0
Hernandez, John, L.V.	.000	1	0	0	0	0	0
Herndon, Junior, Port.	.848	21	8	20	5	33	1
Hiljus, Erik, Sac.	1.000	15	1	4	0	5	0
Hitchcock, Sterling, Port.*	1.000	3	0	3	0	3	0

CLASS AAA Pacific Coast League

Player, Team	Pct.	G	PO	A	E	TC	DP
Hodges, Kevin, Tac.	.917	14	6	16	2	24	2
Hooten, Dave, Edm.	.857	7	3	3	1	7	1
Horgan, Joe, Fres.*	1.000	3	0	1	0	1	0
House, Craig, C.S.	.875	54	3	4	1	8	1
Huisman, Rick, Mem.	.667	8	1	1	1	3	0
Husted, Brent, L.V.	1.000	14	1	2	0	3	0
Hutchinson, Chad, Mem.	.769	27	4	6	3	13	1
Ireland, Eric, Sac.	.950	29	9	29	2	40	0
Jacome, Jason, Tuc.*	.913	35	8	13	2	23	2
James, Mike, Mem.	1.000	10	0	2	0	2	0
Janzen, Marty, S.L.	.000	2	0	0	0	0	0
Jarvis, Matt, Tac.*	1.000	12	3	3	0	6	1
Jennings, Jason, C.S.	.972	22	13	22	1	36	0
Jensen, Ryan, Fres.	1.000	20	6	13	0	19	1
Jodie, Brett, Port.	1.000	5	0	1	0	1	0
Johnson, Adam, Edm.	1.000	4	2	6	0	8	0
Johnson, Jonathan, Tuc.	1.000	15	4	6	0	10	2
Johnson, Mike, Okla.	.950	23	7	12	1	20	2
Jones, Marcus, Sac.	1.000	27	4	13	0	17	1
Joseph, Kevin, Fres.-Mem.	1.000	17	2	4	0	6	0
Judd, Mike, Okla.	.000	2	0	0	0	0	0
Kamieniecki, Scott, Iowa	.900	8	2	7	1	10	1
Karl, Scott, Nash.*	.867	14	2	11	2	15	0
Karnuth, Jason, Mem.	1.000	55	2	10	0	12	1
Kaye, Justin, Tac.	1.000	56	4	13	0	17	0
Kessel, Kyle, N.O.*	.778	15	1	6	2	9	0
Kiefer, Mark, L.V.	.938	32	14	16	2	32	2
Kieschnick, Brooks, C.S.	1.000	1	0	1	0	1	0
Kinney, Matt, Edm.	1.000	29	10	10	0	20	0
Knoll, Brian, Fres.	1.000	22	4	5	0	9	1
Knott, Eric, Tuc.*	.857	25	4	8	2	14	0
Knotts, Gary, Cal.	.957	21	7	15	1	23	0
Kolb, Dan, Okla.	.000	12	0	0	0	0	0
Koplove, Mike, Tuc.	1.000	17	2	3	0	5	0
Krivda, Rick, Mem.*	.857	14	1	11	2	14	0
Lackey, John, S.L.	.938	10	8	7	1	16	3
Lambert, Jeremy, Mem.	1.000	28	0	3	0	3	1
Lankford, Frank, Sac.	.947	40	3	15	1	19	1
Larkin, Andy, C.S.	.870	26	10	10	3	23	0
Lawrence, Brian, Port.	1.000	9	7	5	0	12	1
Lawrence, Sean, Port.-Tuc.*	.857	43	1	5	1	7	0
Laxton, Brett, Oma.	.842	45	9	7	3	19	2
Lee, Corey, Okla.*	1.000	2	0	1	0	1	0
Lee, Dave, Port.	1.000	9	1	0	0	1	0
Lee, Jon, Tuc.	.000	2	0	0	0	0	0
Leese, Brandon, Cal.	1.000	9	0	7	0	7	2
Lidle, Cory, Sac.	1.000	1	0	2	0	2	0
Lidle, Kevin, S.L.-Mem.	1.000	2	0	1	0	1	0
Lincoln, Mike, Nash.	.947	18	8	10	1	19	3
Linebrink, Scott, N.O.	.917	50	1	10	1	12	1
Loewer, Carlton, Port.	.900	14	2	7	1	10	0
Lohse, Kyle, Edm.	1.000	8	2	4	0	6	1
Loiselle, Rich, Nash.	1.000	26	2	4	0	6	0
Lopez, Johan, Okla.	1.000	3	0	1	0	1	0
Lopez, Rodrigo, Port.	1.000	11	1	10	0	11	1
Lorraine, Andrew, Cal.*	.964	30	12	15	1	28	1
Lukasiewicz, Mark, S.L.*	.833	20	1	4	1	6	0
Lundberg, Spike, Okla.	.846	13	3	8	2	13	0
Lundquist, Dave, Port.	1.000	50	6	6	0	12	0
MacDougal, Mike, Oma.	.886	28	10	21	4	35	2
Mahay, Ron, Port.-Iowa*	1.000	50	3	7	0	10	0
Mairena, Ozwaldo, Cal.*	1.000	31	1	6	0	7	0
Mann, Jim, N.O.	1.000	53	5	7	0	12	0
Marshall, Lee, Edm.	1.000	39	2	4	0	6	0
Marte, Damaso, Nash.*	.000	4	0	0	0	0	0
Martines, Jason, Tuc.	1.000	12	1	5	0	6	1
Martinez, Gustavo, Tac.	1.000	1	1	1	0	2	0
Martinez, Jose, Okla.	1.000	1	0	1	0	1	0
Martinez, Willie, Edm.	1.000	21	8	11	0	19	0
Masaoka, Onan, L.V.*	.941	31	4	12	1	17	0
Mathews, T.J., Mem.	1.000	15	1	2	0	3	0
Maurer, Dave, Port.-Sac.*	1.000	28	0	3	0	3	0
McConnell, Sam, Nash.*	.889	26	3	21	3	27	0
McDade, Neal, Nash.	1.000	8	0	3	0	3	1
McKnight, Tony, N.O.	.944	18	8	9	1	18	0
McMullen, Mike, Edm.	.727	14	3	5	3	11	0
Meadows, Brian, Oma.	.882	18	7	8	2	17	1
Mecir, Jim, Sac.	1.000	1	0	1	0	1	0
Medina, Rafael, Mem.	.857	27	4	2	1	7	1
Meyer, Jake, Tac.	1.000	9	1	2	0	3	0
Meyers, Mike, Iowa	.971	25	12	21	1	34	3
Miadich, Bart, S.L.	1.000	55	3	6	0	9	0
Miceli, Danny, C.S.	1.000	4	1	1	0	2	0
Middlebrook, Jason, Port.	1.000	15	3	11	0	14	0
Miller, Justin, Sac.	1.000	29	5	25	0	30	2
Miller, Matt, Port.	.889	44	3	5	1	9	0
Mintz, Steve, S.L.	.833	13	2	3	1	6	0
Mitchell, Dean, Okla.	1.000	4	0	4	0	4	1
Mix, Greg, Edm.	1.000	7	1	1	0	2	0
Mohler, Mike, Tuc.*	1.000	40	1	10	0	11	1
Molina, Gabe, Cal.	1.000	40	7	12	0	19	1
Montgomery, Matt, L.V.	.000	1	0	0	0	0	0
Moody, Eric, Nash.	1.000	42	8	10	0	18	2
Moraga, David, C.S.*	.667	3	0	2	1	3	0
Moreno, Juan, Okla.*	1.000	7	0	1	0	1	0
Moreno, Orber, Oma.	1.000	17	0	2	0	2	0
Morgan, Mike, Tuc.	.000	2	0	0	0	0	0
Moriarty, Mike, Edm.	.000	1	0	0	0	0	0
Mota, Danny, Edm.-L.V.	1.000	46	2	4	0	6	0
Mullen, Scott, Oma.*	.875	48	1	6	1	8	0
Munro, Pete, Okla.	1.000	33	11	9	0	20	2
Murray, Dan, Oma.	1.000	48	14	12	0	26	1
Myers, Randy, Tac.*	.000	1	0	0	0	0	0
Myers, Rodney, Port.	1.000	8	3	3	0	6	1
Myette, Aaron, Okla.	.938	12	9	6	1	16	2
Nathan, Joe, Fres.	.933	10	6	8	1	15	0
Nation, Joey, Iowa*	1.000	14	1	6	0	7	0
Nina, Elvin, S.L.	.840	29	10	11	4	25	0
Norton, Phil, Iowa*	.955	46	2	19	1	22	3
O'Connor, Brian, Nash.*	1.000	37	1	15	0	16	1
Ohman, Will, Iowa*	1.000	40	1	3	0	4	0
Oliver, Darren, Okla.*	.000	1	0	0	0	0	0
Ontiveros, Steve, Sac.	.875	16	7	7	2	16	0
Oquist, Mike, Edm.	.952	21	5	15	1	21	2
Orosco, Jesse, L.V.*	.000	10	0	0	0	0	0
Osting, Jimmy, Port.*	1.000	5	1	3	0	4	0
Oswalt, Roy, N.O.	1.000	5	2	5	0	7	0
Patterson, John, Tuc.	1.000	13	7	6	0	13	1
Pavlas, Dave, Nash.	.889	41	1	7	1	9	0
Pearce, Josh, Mem.	1.000	10	6	6	0	12	0
Perez, Carlos, L.V.*	.800	6	1	7	2	10	1
Pineiro, Joel, Tac.	1.000	18	6	5	0	11	1
Post, Dave, L.V.	.000	1	0	0	0	0	0
Powell, Brian, N.O.	.885	24	11	12	3	26	1
Powell, Jeremy, Port.	1.000	11	5	6	0	11	0
Priest, Eddie, L.V.*	1.000	23	2	14	0	16	1
Prinz, Bret, Tuc.	.000	5	0	0	0	0	0
Prokopec, Luke, L.V.	1.000	1	1	0	0	1	0
Pumphrey, Ken, Edm.	1.000	7	3	6	0	9	2
Quevedo, Ruben, Iowa	.958	22	6	17	1	24	3
Rain, Steve, Iowa	.500	9	0	1	1	2	1
Rakers, Jason, Oma.	1.000	44	4	5	0	9	0
Ramos, Mario, Sac.*	.917	13	2	9	1	12	0
Ramsay, Rob, Tac.*	.875	26	3	18	3	24	0
Randall, Scott, C.S.	.882	19	3	12	2	17	1
Randolph, Steve, Tuc.*	1.000	18	3	2	0	5	0
Rath, Fred, Mem.	1.000	27	4	7	0	11	0
Ratliff, Jon, Sac.	.833	18	2	8	2	12	0
Redding, Tim, N.O.	.900	6	4	5	1	10	1
Redman, Mark, Edm.*	1.000	1	0	0	0	0	0
Reichert, Dan, Oma.	.900	10	3	6	1	10	0
Revenig, Todd, Tuc.	1.000	46	7	6	0	13	1
Reyes, Al, L.V.	1.000	19	0	3	0	3	0
Reyes, Carlos, Sac.-Tuc.	.833	25	1	4	1	6	0
Reynolds, Shane, N.O.	1.000	1	1	0	0	1	0
Reynoso, Armando, Tuc.	1.000	1	0	1	0	1	0
Ricketts, Chad, L.V.	.714	48	3	2	2	7	1
Riley, Mike, Mem.*	1.000	28	4	5	0	9	0
Rizzo, Todd, L.V.-Fres.*	1.000	49	1	5	0	6	0
ROA, Joe, Cal.	1.000	19	11	31	0	42	5
Roberts, Mark, Cal.	1.000	33	1	2	0	3	0
Rodgers, Bobby, Cal.	1.000	18	1	6	0	7	1
Rodriguez, Jose, Mem.*	1.000	54	6	6	0	12	0
Romero, J.C., Edm.*	.950	12	10	9	1	20	1
Ruffin, Johnny, Cal.	1.000	37	4	2	0	6	0
Ryan, Jason, Nash.-L.V.	.923	14	2	10	1	13	0
Sabel, Erik, Tuc.	1.000	18	1	9	0	10	0
Sanchez, Jesus, Cal.*	1.000	16	6	14	0	20	0
Santana, Julio, Fres.	.917	25	14	8	2	24	4
Schmack, Brian, Okla.	.889	40	6	10	2	18	1
Schmidt, Jason, Nash.	1.000	1	0	1	0	1	0
Schrenk, Steve, Sac.	.667	16	1	1	1	3	0
Sedlacek, Shawn, Oma.	.929	14	10	16	2	28	0
Serafini, Dan, Fres.*	.000	7	0	0	0	0	0
Serrano, Wascar, Port.	.944	27	4	13	1	18	1
Shields, Scot, S.L.	.943	21	15	18	2	35	3

Player, Team	Pct.	G	PO	A	E	TC	DP
Shouse, Brian, N.O.*	1.000	56	1	7	0	8	0
Sikaras, Pete, Tuc.	.000	4	0	0	0	0	0
Sikorski, Brian, Okla.	.889	14	7	17	3	27	1
Simon, Ben, L.V.	1.000	12	0	8	0	8	0
Simontacchi, Jason, Edm.	.925	32	13	24	3	40	6
Slusarski, Joe, N.O.	1.000	31	2	2	0	4	2
Small, Aaron, S.L.	1.000	3	0	1	0	1	0
Smart, J.D., Okla.	1.000	16	1	5	0	6	0
Smith, Brian, Nash.	1.000	36	4	1	0	5	1
Smith, Bud, Mem.*	1.000	17	3	21	0	24	4
Smith, Cam, L.V.	1.000	8	0	1	0	1	0
Smith, Chuck, Cal.	1.000	2	1	0	0	1	0
Smith, Travis, N.O.	.000	1	0	0	0	0	0
Snyder, Matt, Iowa	.000	1	0	0	0	0	0
Sollecito, Gabe, Iowa	1.000	7	1	0	0	1	0
Sonnier, Shawn, Oma.	.846	47	3	8	2	13	0
Sparks, Steve, Nash.	.818	31	2	7	2	11	0
Speier, Justin, C.S.	1.000	11	0	1	0	1	0
Spencer, Stan, Port.	.905	20	3	16	2	21	0
Spradlin, Jerry, Mem.	1.000	29	1	3	0	4	0
Springer, Dennis, L.V.	.893	19	6	19	3	28	0
Springer, Russ, Tuc.	1.000	7	1	0	0	1	0
Stanifer, Rob, Iowa	1.000	54	4	17	0	21	2
Stark, Dennis, Tac.	.897	24	10	16	3	29	0
Steenstra, Kennie, Tuc.	.939	28	9	22	2	33	3
Stentz, Brent, Edm.	1.000	17	2	3	0	5	0
Stephenson, Garrett, Mem.	1.000	1	0	1	0	1	0
Stone, Ricky, N.O.	1.000	51	8	15	0	23	5
Strong, Joe, Cal.	1.000	46	4	5	0	9	0
Sturdy, Tim, Edm.	1.000	2	0	2	0	2	0
Tabaka, Jeff, Mem.*	1.000	32	1	7	0	8	0
Tankersley, Dennis, Port.	.667	3	2	0	1	3	0
Taylor, Bill, Nash.	1.000	20	0	1	0	1	0
Tessmer, Jay, C.S.	1.000	10	0	3	0	3	0
Teut, Nate, Iowa*	.875	29	4	17	3	24	1
Thomas, Juan, Tac.	1.000	2	1	2	0	3	0
Thompson, Travis, C.S.	1.000	9	0	2	0	2	0
Thomson, John, C.S.	1.000	12	6	7	0	13	1
Thurman, Corey, Oma.	.000	1	0	0	0	0	0
Tollberg, Brian, Port.	1.000	4	1	0	0	1	0
Tomko, Brett, Tac.	.952	19	6	14	1	21	1
Turman, Jason, Tac.	1.000	29	4	7	0	11	0
Tyler, Josh, Fres.	.000	1	0	0	0	0	0
Vasquez, Leo, Sac.*	1.000	36	1	2	0	3	0
Verplancke, Jeff, Fres.	.000	8	0	0	0	0	0
Villafuerte, Brandon, Okla.	1.000	38	4	9	0	13	0
Vizcaino, Luis, Sac.	1.000	27	1	3	0	4	0
Vogelsong, Ryan, Fres.-Nash.	.938	16	8	7	1	16	0
Wainhouse, Dave, Iowa	.875	49	3	11	2	16	2
Ward, Jeremy, Tuc.	1.000	40	4	6	0	10	0
Washburn, Jarrod, S.L.*	1.000	1	1	0	0	1	0
Watkins, Scott, C.S.*	.000	10	0	0	1	1	0
Watson, Mark, Tac.*	.000	3	0	0	1	1	0
Weibl, Clint, Mem.	1.000	2	0	2	0	2	0
Wengert, Don, Nash.	1.000	18	10	16	0	26	0
Whisenant, Matt, L.V.*	1.000	24	4	13	0	17	1
Wilkins, Marc, Nash.	1.000	32	0	5	0	5	0

Player, Team	Pct.	G	PO	A	E	TC	DP
Williams, Dave, Nash.*	.800	2	1	3	1	5	0
Williams, Jeff, L.V.*	1.000	16	6	15	0	21	0
Williams, Shad, S.L.	1.000	8	1	0	0	1	0
Wilson, Craig, Oma.	1.000	2	2	0	0	2	0
Wilson, Kris, Oma.	1.000	6	1	3	0	4	0
Wimberly, Larry, Nash.*	1.000	4	0	1	0	1	0
Wise, Matt, S.L.	.920	21	11	12	2	25	0
Witt, Bobby, Tuc.	.857	5	1	5	1	7	0
Witt, Kevin, Port.	.000	2	0	0	0	0	0
Wojciechowski, Steve, Cal.*	1.000	8	0	2	0	2	0
Wolff, Bryan, Edm.	.913	15	12	9	2	23	1
Wooten, Greg, Tac.	.944	27	9	25	2	36	0
Yates, Tyler, Sac.	.000	4	0	0	1	1	0
Zambrano, Carlos, Iowa	.953	26	15	26	2	43	3
Zancanaro, Dave, Mem.*	.929	27	6	33	3	42	2
Zerbe, Chad, Fres.*	1.000	17	2	4	0	6	1
Zimmerman, Jordan, Tac.*	.929	41	4	9	1	14	0

PITCHERS WITH TWO OR MORE TEAMS

Player, Team	Pct.	G	PO	A	E	TC	DP
Belitz, Todd, Sac.*	.909	38	1	9	1	11	0
Belitz, Todd, C.S.*	1.000	14	0	1	0	1	0
Bruske, Jim, S.L.	1.000	27	2	8	0	10	0
Bruske, Jim, L.V.	.900	10	1	8	1	10	1
Camp, Shawn, Port.	1.000	4	0	1	0	1	0
Camp, Shawn, Nash.	1.000	11	3	3	0	6	1
DeSilva, John, Cal.	.875	26	3	4	1	8	0
DeSilva, John, L.V.	1.000	14	0	2	0	2	0
Donaldson, Bo, Nash.	1.000	11	0	3	0	3	1
Donaldson, Bo, Port.	1.000	8	0	1	0	1	0
Gross, Kip, L.V.	1.000	10	0	1	0	1	0
Gross, Kip, C.S.	.920	18	6	17	2	25	3
Joseph, Kevin, Fres.	1.000	5	1	3	0	4	0
Joseph, Kevin, Mem.	1.000	12	1	1	0	2	0
Lawrence, Sean, Port.*	1.000	25	1	5	0	6	0
Lawrence, Sean, Tuc.*	.000	18	0	0	1	1	0
Lidle, Kevin, S.L.	1.000	1	0	1	0	1	0
Lidle, Kevin, Mem.	.000	1	0	0	0	0	0
Mahay, Ron, Port.*	1.000	14	1	0	0	1	0
Mahay, Ron, Iowa*	1.000	36	2	7	0	9	0
Maurer, Dave, Port.*	1.000	17	0	2	0	2	0
Maurer, Dave, Sac.*	1.000	11	0	1	0	1	0
Mota, Danny, Edm.	1.000	34	2	4	0	6	0
Mota, Danny, L.V.	.000	12	0	0	0	0	0
Reyes, Carlos, Sac.	.800	17	1	3	1	5	0
Reyes, Carlos, Tuc.	1.000	8	0	1	0	1	0
Rizzo, Todd, L.V.*	.000	13	0	0	0	0	0
Rizzo, Todd, Fres.*	1.000	36	1	5	0	6	0
Ryan, Jason, Nash.	.917	9	2	9	1	12	0
Ryan, Jason, L.V.	1.000	5	0	1	0	1	0
Vogelsong, Ryan, Fres.	.875	10	3	4	1	8	0
Vogelsong, Ryan, Nash.	1.000	6	5	3	0	8	0

The following players appeared only as designated hitter, pinch hitter or pinch runner: Cadiente, dh, ph; Curtis, dh; Jaha, dh; Morales, ph; Riggins, ph; Stocker, pr; Theodorou, ph.

LEAGUE CHAMPIONS

Year	Team	Pct.	Year	Team	Pct.	Year	Team	Pct.
1903—	Los Angeles	.630	1920—	Vernon	.556	1935—	Los Angeles	.648
1904—	Tacoma	.589	1921—	Los Angeles	.574		San Francisco*	.608
	Tacoma§	.571	1922—	San Francisco	.638	1936—	Portland‡	.549
	Los Angeles§	.571	1923—	San Francisco	.617	1937—	Sacramento	.573
1905—	Tacoma	.583	1924—	Seattle	.545		San Diego (3rd)†	.545
	Los Angeles*	.604	1925—	San Francisco	.643	1938—	Los Angeles	.590
1906—	Portland	.657	1926—	Los Angeles	.599		Sacramento (3rd)†	.537
1907—	Los Angeles	.608	1927—	Oakland	.615	1939—	Seattle	.589
1908—	Los Angeles	.585	1928—	San Francisco*	.630		Sacramento (4th)†	.500
1909—	San Francisco	.623		Sacramento∞	.626	1940—	Seattle‡	.629
1910—	Portland	.567		San Francisco∞	.626	1941—	Seattle‡	.598
1911—	Portland	.589	1929—	Mission	.643	1942—	Sacramento	.590
1912—	Oakland	.591		Hollywood*	.592		Seattle (3rd)†	.539
1913—	Portland	.559	1930—	Los Angeles	.576	1943—	Los Angeles	.710
1914—	Portland	.574		Hollywood*	.650		S. Francisco (2nd)†	.574
1915—	San Francisco	.570	1931—	Hollywood	.626	1944—	Los Angeles	.586
1916—	Los Angeles	.601		San Francisco*	.608		S. Francisco (3rd)†	.509
1917—	San Francisco	.561	1932—	Portland	.587	1945—	Portland	.622
1918—	Vernon	.569	1933—	Los Angeles	.610		S. Francisco (4th)†	.525
	Los Angeles (2nd)◆	.548	1934—	Los Angeles▼	.786	1946—	San Francisco‡	.628
1919—	Vernon	.613		Los Angeles▼	.689	1947—	Los Angeles▲	.567

Year	Team	Pct.	Year	Team	Pct.	Year	Team	Pct.
1948—	Oakland‡	.606	1971—	Salt Lake City	.534		Las Vegas*	.563
1949—	Hollywood‡	.583		Tacoma	.545	1987—	Calgary	.596
1950—	Oakland	.590	1972—	Albuquerque	.622		Albuquerque*	.542
1951—	Seattle‡	.593		Eugene	.534	1988—	Vancouver	.599
1952—	Hollywood	.606	1973—	Tucson	.583		Las Vegas*	.529
1953—	Hollywood	.589		Spokane•	.563	1989—	Albuquerque	.563
1954—	San Diego■	.604	1974—	Spokane•	.549		Vancouver*	.514
1955—	Seattle	.552		Albuquerque	.535	1990—	Albuquerque*	.641
1956—	Los Angeles	.637	1975—	Salt Lake City	.556		Edmonton	.553
1957—	San Francisco	.601		Hawaii•	.611	1991—	Albuquerque	.580
1958—	Phoenix	.578	1976—	Salt Lake City	.625		Tucson*	.564
1959—	Salt Lake City	.552		Hawaii•	.531	1992—	Colorado Springs*	.596
1960—	Spokane	.601	1977—	Phoenix•	.579		Portland	.576
1961—	Tacoma	.630		Hawaii	.541	1993—	Portland	.608
1962—	San Diego	.604	1978—	Tacoma††	.584		Tucson*	.580
1963—	Spokane	.620		Albuquerque††	.557	1994—	Albuquerque*	.597
	Oklahoma City•	.632	1979—	Albuquerque	.581		Vancouver	.542
1964—	Arkansas	.609		Salt Lake City‡‡	.541	1995—	Salt Lake	.549
	San Diego•	.576	1980—	Albuquerque	.578		Colorado Springs*	.538
1965—	Oklahoma City	.628		Hawaii	.539	1996—	Edmonton*	.592
	Portland	.547	1981—	Albuquerque*	.712		Phoenix	.479
1966—	Seattle•	.561		Tacoma	.561	1997—	Phoenix	.615
	Tulsa	.578	1982—	Albuquerque*	.594		Edmonton*	.556
1967—	San Diego•	.574		Spokane	.545	1998—	Iowa	.590
	Spokane	.541	1983—	Albuquerque	.594		New Orleans†	.535
1968—	Tulsa•	.642		Portland*	.528	1999—	Vancouver‡	.592
	Spokane	.586	1984—	Hawaii	.621	2000—	Salt Lake	.629
1969—	Tacoma•	.589		Edmonton*	.486		Memphis‡	.576
	Eugene	.603	1985—	Vancouver*	.522	2001—	Tacoma§§	.590
1970—	Spokane•	.644		Phoenix	.563		New Orleans§§	.590
	Hawaii	.671	1986—	Vancouver	.616			

*Won split-season playoff. †Won four-team playoff. ‡Won pennant and four-team playoff. §Tied for second-half title with Tacoma winning playoff. ∞Tied for second-half title, with Sacramento winning playoff. ▲Ended regular season in tie with San Francisco and won one-game playoff for pennant, then won four-club playoff. ◆Won playoff from first-place Vernon and awarded championship. ■Defeated Hollywood in one-game playoff for pennant. ▼Won both halves, no playoff. •League was divided into Northern, Southern divisions in 1963, 1969-70-71, and Eastern, Western divisions in 1964 through 1968 and 1972 through 1977, won two-team playoff. ††League divided into Eastern and Western divisions, Tacoma and Albuquerque declared co-champions following cancellation of four-team playoff due to continuing rain and wet grounds. ‡‡Won second-half title and defeated Hawaii in four-team playoff. §§Were entering finals of four-team playoff and were declared co-champions when Professional Baseball declared a stoppage of play.

EASTERN LEAGUE

LEAGUE OFFICE

President
Bill Troubh

Address
P.O. Box 9711
Portland, ME 04104

Phone
207-761-2700

TEAMS

AKRON AEROS
General manager/vice president
Jeff Auman
Manager
Brad Komminsk
Ballpark (capacity, surface)
Canal Park (9,097, grass)
Affiliation
Indians
Address
300 S. Main St.
Akron, OH 44308
Phone
330-253-5151

ALTOONA CURVE
General manager
Jeff Parker
Manager
Dale Sveum
Ballpark (capacity, surface)
Blair County Ballpark (6,120, grass)
Affiliation
Pirates
Address
P.O. Box 1029
Altoona, PA 16603
Phone
814-943-5400

BINGHAMTON METS
General manager
Bill Terlecky
Manager
Howie Freiling
Ballpark (capacity, surface)
NYSEG Stadium (6,012, grass)
Affiliation
Mets
Address
211 Henry Street
Binghamton, NY 13901
Phone
607-723-6387

BOWIE BAYSOX
General manager
Jon Danos
Manager
Dave Cash
Ballpark (capacity, surface)
Prince George's Stadium
(10,000, grass)
Affiliation
Orioles
Address
4101 NE Crain Highway
Bowie, MD 20716
Phone
301-805-6000

ERIE SEAWOLVES
General manager
John Frey
Manager
Kevin Bradshaw
Ballpark (capacity, surface)
Jerry Uht Park (6,000, grass)
Affiliation
Tigers
Address
110 E. 10th Street
Erie, PA 16501
Phone
814-456-1300

HARRISBURG SENATORS
General manager
Todd Vander Woude
Manager
Eric Fox
Ballpark (capacity, surface)
RiverSide Stadium (6,300, grass)
Affiliation
Expos
Address
RiverSide Stadium/City Island
Harrisburg, PA 17101
Phone
717-231-4444

NEW BRITAIN ROCK CATS
General manager
Bill Dowling
Manager
Stan Cliburn
Ballpark (capacity, surface)
New Britain Stadium (6,146, grass)
Affiliation
Twins
Address
South Main Street
New Britain, CT 06051
Phone
860-224-8383

NEW HAVEN RAVENS
General manager
To be announced
Manager
Mark DeJohn
Ballpark (capacity, surface)
Yale Field (6,200, grass)
Affiliation
Cardinals
Address
252 Derby Ave.
West Haven, CT 06516
Phone
203-782-1666

NORWICH NAVIGATORS
General manager
Brian Mahoney
Manager
Stump Merrill
Ballpark (capacity, surface)
Thomas J. Dodd Memorial Stadium
(6,000, grass)
Affiliation
Yankees
Address
14 Stott Ave.
Norwich, CT 06360
Phone
860-887-7962

PORTLAND SEA DOGS
General manager
Charles Eshbach
Manager
Dave Huppert
Ballpark (capacity, surface)
Hadlock Field (6,850, grass)
Affiliation
Marlins
Address
271 Park Avenue
Portland, ME 04102
Phone
207-874-9300

READING PHILLIES
General manager
Chuck Domino
Manager
Greg Legg
Ballpark (capacity, surface)
GPU Stadium (8,500, grass)
Affiliation
Phillies
Address
Route 61 South/1900 Centre Ave.
Reading, PA 19605
Phone
610-375-8469

TRENTON THUNDER
General manager
Rick Brenner
Manager
Ron Johnson
Ballpark (capacity, surface)
Samuel J. Plumeri, Sr. Field at Mercer
County Waterfront Park (6,300, grass)
Affiliation
Red Sox
Address
One Thunder Road
Trenton, NJ 08611
Phone
609-394-3300

CLASS AAA *Eastern League*

NORTH DIVISION

Team	W	L	T	Pct.	GB
New Britain (Twins)	87	55	0	.613	...
Norwich (Yankees)	83	59	0	.585	4.0
Portland (Marlins)	77	65	0	.542	10.0
Binghamton (Mets)	73	68	0	.518	13.5
Trenton (Red Sox)	67	75	0	.472	20.0
New Haven (Cardinals)	47	95	0	.331	40.0

SOUTH DIVISION

Team	W	L	T	Pct.	GB
Erie (Tigers)	84	58	0	.592	...
Reading (Phillies)	77	65	0	.542	7.0
Akron (Indians)	68	74	0	.479	16.0
Harrisburg (Expos)	66	76	0	.465	18.0
Altoona (Pirates)	63	79	0	.444	21.0
Bowie (Orioles)	59	82	0	.418	24.5

COMPOSITE

Team	N.B.	Erie	Nor.	Read.	Por.	Bing.	Akr.	Tren.	Har.	Alt.	Bow.	N.H.	W	L	T	Pct.	GB
New Britain (Twins)	...	4	13	5	15	10	5	7	6	5	3	14	87	55	0	.613	...
Erie (Tigers)	3	...	6	12	3	5	9	3	10	12	14	7	84	58	0	.592	3.0
Norwich (Yankees)	7	1	...	4	9	13	5	15	5	6	5	13	83	59	0	.585	4.0
Reading (Phillies)	2	8	3	...	5	6	11	1	10	12	14	5	77	65	0	.542	10.0
Portland (Marlins)	5	4	11	2	...	9	3	15	4	5	5	14	77	65	0	.542	10.0
Binghamton (Mets)	10	2	7	1	11	...	4	11	3	4	4	16	73	68	0	.518	13.5
Akron (Indians)	2	11	2	9	4	3	...	3	8	11	12	3	68	74	0	.479	19.0
Trenton (Red Sox)	13	4	5	6	5	9	4	...	4	4	4	9	67	75	0	.472	20.0
Harrisburg (Expos)	1	10	2	10	3	4	12	3	...	9	8	4	66	76	0	.465	21.0
Altoona (Pirates)	2	8	1	8	2	3	9	3	11	...	11	5	63	79	0	.444	24.0
Bowie (Orioles)	4	6	2	6	2	2	8	3	12	9	...	5	59	82	0	.418	27.5
New Haven (Cardinals)	6	0	7	2	6	4	4	11	3	2	2	...	47	95	0	.331	40.0

Major league affiliations in parentheses.

PLAYOFFS: New Britain defeated Norwich three games to one; Reading defeated Erie three games to one. Note: New Britain and Reading declared co-champions due to stoppage of play in professional baseball.

REGULAR-SEASON ATTENDANCE: Akron, 485,582; Atltoona, 348,316; Binghamton, 197,113; Bowie, 350,127; Erie, 246,404; Harrisburg, 279,691; New Britain, 261,331; New Haven, 186,301; Norwich, 231,481; Portland, 383,022; Reading, 458,585; Trenton, 411,322. Total—3,839,275. Playoffs (8 games)—30,047. Class AA All-Star Game at Round Rock—12,046.

MANAGERS: Akron, Chris Bando; Altoona, Dale Sveum; Binghamton, Howie Freiling; Bowie, Dave Machemer; Erie, Luis Pujols; Harrisburg, Luis Dorante; New Britain, Stan Cliburn; New Haven, Danny Sheaffer; Norwich, Stump Merrill; Portland, Rick Renteria; Reading, Gary Varsho; Trenton, Billy Gardner.

ALL-STAR TEAM: 1B—Eric Munson, Erie; 2B—Willie Harris, Bowie; 3B—Michael Cuddyer, New Britain; SS—Omar Infante, Erie; OF—Marcus Thames, Norwich; OF—Dustan Mohr, New Britain; OF—Marlon Byrd, Reading; C—Mike Rivera, Erie; Utility—J.P. Roberge, Reading; RHP—John Stephens, Bowie; LHP—Brad Thomas, New Britain; Relief pitcher—Alex Pacheco, Norwich; Most Valuable Player—Marlon Byrd, Reading; Rookie of the Year—Marlon Byrd, Reading; Manager of the Year—Stan Cliburn, New Britain.

2001 BATTING
TEAM

Team	Avg.	G	TPA	AB	R	H	TB	2B	3B	HR	RBI	SH	SF	HP	BB	IBB	SO	SB	CS	GDP	LOB	ShO	Slg.	OBP
Erie	.276	142	5393	4789	741	1320	2056	259	24	143	671	20	43	88	453	13	1014	120	58	97	983	7	.429	.346
Norwich	.269	142	5417	4862	703	1309	2063	287	22	141	646	25	40	77	413	27	1029	64	45	97	994	5	.424	.334
Trenton	.261	142	5296	4784	625	1250	1978	292	26	128	578	23	37	54	398	14	1029	87	55	93	964	8	.413	.323
New Britain	.261	142	5350	4823	620	1259	1955	250	34	126	575	54	34	60	379	22	892	60	49	98	962	8	.405	.321
Bowie	.261	141	5227	4678	597	1219	1778	238	24	91	529	34	34	55	426	14	1021	148	82	114	928	13	.380	.327
Reading	.260	142	5376	4782	691	1243	1950	237	34	134	634	48	45	80	421	26	872	123	52	99	966	10	.408	.327
Altoona	.258	142	5268	4760	557	1226	1842	267	38	91	514	45	29	58	376	21	1027	120	78	94	954	11	.387	.318
Binghamton	.255	141	5236	4688	618	1196	1917	252	20	143	572	40	24	57	427	23	1193	106	72	96	934	9	.409	.323
Akron	.255	142	5234	4749	606	1210	1935	260	30	135	560	40	46	48	351	16	996	108	73	70	915	10	.407	.310
Harrisburg	.252	142	5186	4635	587	1169	1744	203	39	98	527	63	34	56	398	23	950	161	77	86	909	14	.376	.317
Portland	.244	142	5366	4688	590	1142	1717	213	37	96	540	43	28	77	530	21	1097	131	89	105	1022	12	.366	.329
New Haven	.233	142	5130	4639	491	1079	1581	211	24	81	449	58	27	71	335	23	1028	151	89	94	868	16	.341	.293

INDIVIDUAL

TOP QUALIFIERS FOR BATTING CHAMPIONSHIP

Minimum 383 plate appearances. *Lefthanded batter. †Switch-hitter.

Player, Team	Avg.	G	TPA	AB	R	H	TB	2B	3B	HR	RBI	SH	SF	HP	BB	IBB	SO	SB	CS	GDP	Slg.	OBP
Mohr, Dustan, N.B.	.336	135	574	518	90	174	293	41	3	24	91	0	3	4	49	4	111	9	9	6	.566	.395
Thames, Marcus, Nor.	.321	139	603	520	114	167	311	43	4	31	97	0	3	7	73	8	101	10	4	6	.598	.410
Burnham, Gary, Read.*	.318	109	426	371	59	118	192	25	2	15	77	0	9	11	35	2	43	1	2	14	.518	.385
Byrd, Marlon, Read.	.316	137	582	510	108	161	283	22	8	28	89	2	7	11	52	3	93	32	5	7	.555	.386
Hooper, Kevin, Port.	.308	117	543	468	70	144	181	19	6	2	39	7	2	7	59	4	78	24	12	8	.387	.392
Harris, Willie, Bow.*	.305	133	590	525	83	160	222	27	4	9	49	10	4	5	46	3	71	54	16	6	.423	.364
Infante, Omar, Erie	.302	132	599	540	86	163	198	21	4	2	62	4	7	2	46	1	87	27	12	9	.367	.355
Cuddyer, Michael, N.B.	.301	141	593	509	95	153	285	36	3	30	87	0	3	6	75	3	106	5	9	6	.560	.395
Figueroa, Franky, Bow.	.300	137	562	534	61	160	234	32	0	14	72	1	4	2	21	2	138	0	4	23	.438	.326
Salazar, Ruben, N.B.	.298	137	582	530	70	158	221	29	2	10	66	2	6	7	37	4	77	6	1	17	.417	.348
Freire, Alejandro, Erie	.295	133	561	501	73	148	232	33	0	17	82	0	3	11	46	1	113	2	3	17	.463	.365
Curry, Mike, Bing.	.290	107	449	400	65	116	155	16	4	5	28	1	2	5	40	1	100	24	16	4	.388	.360
Brown, Tonayne, Tren.	.290	111	424	396	41	115	150	21	1	4	31	3	1	8	16	0	76	4	12	11	.379	.330
Rivera, Mike, Erie	.289	112	473	415	76	120	240	19	1	33	101	0	4	10	44	2	96	2	2	9	.578	.368
Rodriguez, John, Nor.*	.285	103	435	393	64	112	211	31	1	22	66	3	2	11	26	2	117	2	3	7	.537	.345

DEPARTMENTAL LEADERS: G—Munson, 142; AB—Infante, 540; R—Thames, 114; H—Mohr, 174; TB—Thames, 311; 2B—Thames, 43; 3B—A. Nunez, 9; HR—M. Rivera, 33; RBI—Munson, 102; SH—Stevens, 18; SF—Burnham, 9; HP—Wathan, 17; BB—Munson, 84; IBB—Restovich, Thames, 8 each; SO—Stratton, 201; SB—Snead, 64; CS—Snead, 23; GIDP—F. Figueroa, 23; Slg.—Thames, .598; OBP—Thames, .410.

CLASS AA Eastern League

ALL PLAYERS

*Lefthanded batter. †Switch-hitter.

Player, Team	Avg.	G	TPA	AB	R	H	TB	2B	3B	HR	RBI	SH	SF	HP	BB	IBB	SO	SB	CS	GDP	Slg.	OBP
Abbott, Chuck, Akr.	.195	17	44	41	6	8	20	1	1	3	8	1	0	0	2	0	17	1	1	0	.488	.233
Abbott, Jeff, Port.	.462	7	28	26	4	12	19	1	0	2	6	0	0	0	2	1	0	0	1	0	.731	.500
Agamennone, Brandon, Har.	.000	45	2	2	0	0	0	0	0	0	0	0	0	0	0	0	0	0	0	0	.000	.000
Aguila, Chris, Port.	.257	64	269	241	25	62	92	16	1	4	29	3	4	3	18	1	50	5	7	4	.382	.312
Ahumada, Alex, Tren.	.267	4	16	15	3	4	4	0	0	0	1	0	0	1	0	0	4	0	0	0	.267	.313
Airoso, Kurt, Erie.	.236	82	310	276	45	65	125	16	1	14	44	0	2	0	32	0	62	1	0	3	.453	.313
Alley, Chuck, Bow.†	.216	19	62	51	5	11	13	0	1	0	4	2	1	1	7	0	3	2	0	1	.255	.317
Almonte, Erick, Nor.	.250	3	13	12	2	3	3	0	0	0	0	0	0	0	1	0	6	1	0	0	.250	.308
Alvarado, Carlos, Alt.	.091	26	13	11	1	1	1	0	0	0	1	1	0	0	1	0	2	0	0	0	.091	.167
Alvarez, Tony, Alt.	.319	67	272	254	34	81	117	16	1	6	25	2	0	7	9	0	30	17	11	6	.461	.359
Ametller, Jesus, N.H.*	.000	3	3	3	0	0	0	0	0	0	0	0	0	0	0	0	1	0	0	0	.000	.000
Amezcua, Adan, Bow.	.215	38	149	135	19	29	52	7	2	4	21	0	1	4	9	1	25	0	0	6	.385	.282
Bailey, Jeff, Port.	.241	129	507	432	56	104	175	28	2	13	66	0	3	8	64	1	136	7	2	4	.405	.347
Bailey, Travis, N.H.	.273	27	95	88	9	24	41	3	1	4	10	0	1	2	4	1	35	2	2	2	.466	.316
Bailie, Matt, Read.	.333	38	9	9	1	3	3	0	0	0	1	0	0	0	0	0	3	0	0	0	.333	.333
Baisley, Brad, Read.	.000	12	10	9	1	0	0	0	0	0	0	0	0	0	1	0	4	0	0	0	.000	.100
Baker, Derek, Erie*	.278	6	22	18	2	5	5	0	0	0	3	0	0	1	3	0	4	0	0	1	.278	.409
Bard, Josh, Akr.†	.278	51	214	194	26	54	77	11	0	4	25	1	1	2	16	1	27	0	0	4	.397	.338
Barns, B.J., Alt.*	.220	30	119	109	12	24	52	6	2	6	15	0	3	7	7	0	37	3	1	1	.477	.286
Basak, Chris, Bing.	.372	13	49	43	11	16	27	6	1	1	7	0	1	2	3	0	10	2	0	1	.628	.429
Bass, Jayson, Alt.†	.235	67	185	170	18	40	63	14	3	1	13	2	1	2	10	1	47	9	5	1	.371	.284
Bates, Fletcher, Read.†	.135	15	45	37	5	5	10	2	0	1	4	1	0	0	7	0	5	0	2	1	.270	.273
Batson, Tom, Read.	.083	7	27	24	1	2	2	0	0	0	0	1	0	0	2	0	4	0	0	0	.083	.154
Beckett, Josh, Port.	.111	13	11	9	1	1	1	0	0	0	0	1	0	0	1	0	1	0	0	0	.111	.200
Bell, Heath, Bing.	.000	43	1	1	0	0	0	0	0	0	0	0	0	0	0	0	1	0	0	0	.000	.000
Benefield, Brian, Akr.	.204	63	171	157	16	32	45	7	0	2	9	2	2	0	10	0	28	5	4	3	.287	.249
Benham, Dave, N.H.	.242	46	141	132	8	32	40	5	0	1	15	2	1	2	4	1	31	2	0	2	.303	.273
Bennett, Jeff, Alt.	.000	1	2	2	0	0	0	0	0	0	0	0	0	0	0	0	0	0	0	0	.000	.000
Bennett, Ryan, Bing.	.167	2	6	6	0	1	1	0	0	0	1	0	0	0	0	0	3	0	0	0	.167	.167
Bevins, Andy, N.H.	.198	99	393	348	43	69	124	14	1	13	40	0	0	9	36	2	65	5	7	12	.356	.290
Bigbie, Larry, Bow.*	.294	71	303	262	41	77	120	13	3	8	33	0	1	0	40	1	54	10	7	5	.458	.386
Billingsley, Brent, Har.*	.133	19	19	15	1	2	2	0	0	0	2	2	0	0	2	0	4	0	0	0	.133	.235
Blakely, Darren, Nor.†	.300	10	24	20	2	6	6	0	0	0	2	0	0	2	2	0	4	3	2	0	.300	.417
Bolivar, Papo, N.B.	.268	43	161	142	15	38	51	7	0	2	20	5	1	4	9	0	25	1	1	2	.359	.327
Bordick, Mike, Bow.	.250	1	4	4	0	1	1	0	0	0	0	0	0	0	0	0	1	0	0	0	.250	.250
Borrego, Ramon, N.H.†	.184	60	159	136	17	25	30	6	2	1	3	8	0	1	14	0	30	5	0	2	.270	.265
Bost, Tom, Akr.*	.176	29	99	91	7	16	18	2	0	0	7	2	0	1	5	0	34	8	5	2	.198	.227
Bowers, Jason, N.H.	.239	137	503	460	35	110	146	19	4	3	33	11	4	3	25	0	111	10	10	10	.317	.280
Braswell, Bryan, Bing.*	.333	5	4	3	0	1	1	0	0	0	0	0	0	0	0	0	0	0	0	0	.333	.333
Bridges, Donnie, Har.	.000	3	1	1	0	0	0	0	0	0	0	0	0	0	0	0	0	0	0	1	.000	.000
Briggs, Stoney, Bow.	.244	55	193	164	25	40	71	5	1	8	22	1	1	3	24	0	40	2	2	8	.433	.349
Brown, Adrian, Alt.†	.333	7	32	30	7	10	13	1	1	0	1	0	1	0	1	0	7	1	2	0	.433	.344
Brown, Derek, Bow.	.500	36	2	2	1	1	2	1	0	0	0	0	0	0	0	0	0	0	0	0	1.000	.500
Brown, Jason, Port.	.333	17	56	51	6	17	23	3	0	1	10	0	0	0	5	1	12	0	0	0	.451	.393
Brown, Rich, Nor.*	.349	11	49	43	7	15	26	2	0	3	7	0	1	0	5	1	9	1	1	0	.605	.408
Brown, Tonayne, Tren.	.290	111	424	396	41	115	150	21	1	4	31	3	1	8	16	0	76	4	12	11	.379	.330
Bruce, Mo, Har.-Alt.	.206	55	186	170	23	35	51	7	0	3	17	2	1	1	12	0	47	14	4	3	.300	.261
Brunette, Justin, Bing.*	1.000	23	1	1	1	1	4	0	0	1	1	0	0	0	0	0	0	0	0	0	4.000	1.000
Bump, Nate, Port.	.125	11	9	8	0	1	1	0	0	0	0	0	0	0	1	0	3	0	0	0	.125	.222
Burnham, Gary, Read.*	.318	109	426	371	59	118	192	25	2	15	77	0	9	11	35	2	43	1	2	14	.518	.385
Burnside, Adrian, Alt.	.000	6	1	0	0	0	0	0	0	0	0	1	0	0	0	0	0	0	0	0	.000	.000
Burton, Darren, Alt.†	.288	85	329	299	36	86	126	15	2	7	32	1	1	5	23	2	62	5	1	3	.421	.348
Byrd, Marlon, Read.	.316	137	582	510	108	161	283	22	8	28	89	2	7	11	52	3	90	32	5	7	.555	.386
Calloway, Ron, Har.*	.330	74	314	279	48	92	149	22	4	9	47	5	3	3	24	2	46	25	7	2	.534	.385
Camilo, Juan, Erie*	.282	33	118	110	14	31	51	3	1	5	17	0	1	0	7	0	27	1	1	1	.464	.322
Camp, Shawn, Alt.	.400	8	8	5	2	2	3	1	0	0	1	1	0	0	2	0	1	0	0	0	.600	.571
Candelaria, Ben, Port.*	.305	29	114	95	11	29	43	6	1	2	15	1	1	1	16	1	13	0	1	4	.453	.407
Capista, Aaron, Tren.†	.213	117	436	404	48	86	125	25	4	2	40	3	6	3	20	2	48	2	1	8	.309	.252
Carrasco, Dan, Alt.	.000	27	3	3	0	0	0	0	0	0	0	0	0	0	0	0	2	0	0	0	.000	.000
Carreno, Jose, Har.	.158	40	135	120	3	19	20	1	0	0	8	0	2	1	12	2	24	0	2	2	.167	.237
Casillas, Uriel, Read.	.240	113	432	384	46	92	128	17	2	5	40	7	4	10	27	0	47	4	5	9	.333	.304
Casimiro, Carlos, Bow.	.222	80	322	302	22	67	96	15	1	4	24	1	0	1	18	2	81	2	5	6	.318	.268
Cedeno, Blas, Read.	.000	7	2	2	0	0	0	0	0	0	0	0	0	0	0	0	1	0	0	0	.000	.000
Cepicky, Matt, Har.*	.264	122	488	459	59	121	217	23	8	19	77	2	4	2	21	2	97	5	12	6	.473	.296
Cerda, Jaime, Bing.*	.000	12	4	4	0	0	0	0	0	0	0	0	0	0	0	0	1	0	0	0	.000	.000
Cerros, Juan, Bing.	.000	13	2	1	0	0	0	0	0	0	0	0	0	0	1	0	0	0	0	0	.000	.500
Cervenak, Mike, Nor.	.274	128	520	463	63	127	199	37	1	11	60	2	2	9	44	1	75	2	4	8	.430	.347
Chapman, Jake, Har.	.000	53	4	3	1	0	0	0	0	0	0	0	0	1	0	0	1	0	0	1	.000	.250
Chapman, Travis, Read.	.182	7	24	22	3	4	7	0	0	1	3	0	0	2	0	0	5	0	0	0	.318	.250
Chevalier, Virgil, Tren.	.261	121	509	456	59	119	194	25	1	16	67	0	7	3	43	2	58	3	3	12	.425	.324
Chiavacci, Ron, Har.	.105	25	20	19	1	2	2	0	0	0	0	1	0	0	0	0	7	0	0	0	.105	.150
Clapinski, Chris, Port.†	.222	5	24	18	6	4	7	0	0	1	2	2	0	0	4	2	1	0	1	1	.389	.364
Clark, Chris, Port.	.000	4	2	2	0	0	0	0	0	0	0	0	0	0	0	0	2	0	0	0	.000	.000
Clemente, Edgard, Tren.	.356	11	47	45	7	16	30	3	1	3	7	0	0	2	0	0	6	0	1	2	.667	.383
Coogan, Patrick, N.H.	.143	33	24	21	2	3	3	0	0	0	1	2	0	0	1	0	6	0	0	1	.143	.182
Cook, Andy, Bing.	.000	22	4	3	0	0	0	0	0	0	0	0	0	0	1	0	2	0	0	0	.000	.250
Cook, B.R., N.H.	.250	20	17	16	1	4	8	1	0	1	1	1	0	0	0	0	6	0	0	0	.500	.250
Corey, Mark, Bing.	.000	25	1	1	0	0	0	0	0	0	0	0	0	0	0	0	1	0	0	0	.000	.000
Cormier, Rheal, Read.*	.000	1	1	0	0	0	0	0	0	0	0	1	0	0	0	0	0	0	0	0	.000	.000
Coste, Chris, Akr.	.125	6	25	24	1	3	3	0	0	0	0	0	0	0	1	0	3	0	1	0	.125	.160

Player, Team	Avg.	G	TPA	AB	R	H	TB	2B	3B	HR	RBI	SH	SF	HP	BB	IBB	SO	SB	CS	GDP	Slg.	OBP
Cotton, John, Har.*	.294	5	18	17	5	5	14	0	0	3	8	0	0	0	1	0	5	0	0	0	.824	.333
Crudale, Mike, N.H.	.000	63	1	1	0	0	0	0	0	0	0	0	0	0	0	0	1	0	0	0	.000	.000
Crumpton, Chuck, Har.	.167	52	7	6	0	1	2	1	0	0	0	0	0	0	1	0	1	0	0	0	.333	.286
Cruz, Deivi, Erie	.417	4	12	12	2	5	9	1	0	1	3	0	0	0	0	0	1	0	0	0	.750	.417
Cuddyer, Michael, N.B.	.301	141	593	509	95	153	285	36	3	30	87	0	3	6	75	3	106	5	9	6	.560	.395
Curry, Mike, Bing.*	.290	107	449	400	65	116	155	16	4	5	28	1	2	5	40	1	100	24	16	4	.388	.360
Darrell, Tommy, Har.	.000	24	2	2	0	0	0	0	0	0	0	0	0	0	0	0	0	0	0	0	.000	.000
Davis, Allen, Har.*	.222	8	12	9	0	2	2	0	0	0	0	3	0	0	0	0	3	0	0	0	.222	.222
Davis, J.J., Alt.	.250	67	252	228	21	57	88	13	3	4	26	0	1	2	21	0	79	2	5	1	.386	.317
De Leon, Jorge, Tren.	.252	29	124	111	14	28	41	6	2	1	10	1	0	0	12	0	12	2	1	4	.369	.325
Del Rosario, Manny, Bow.†	.357	7	16	14	0	5	5	0	0	0	1	2	0	0	0	0	2	0	0	0	.357	.357
Della Ratta, Pete, Bing.	.500	22	4	4	0	2	2	0	0	0	1	0	0	0	0	0	1	0	0	0	.500	.500
Depippo, Jeff, Akr.	.263	82	275	240	32	63	95	10	2	6	28	3	4	14	14	0	51	5	8	9	.396	.335
Diaz, Miguel, N.H.	.274	58	123	117	7	32	38	4	1	0	6	0	0	0	1	1	20	2	5	1	.325	.309
Dina, Allen, Bing.	.275	85	297	269	33	74	102	17	1	3	35	6	3	2	17	1	53	9	6	4	.379	.320
Diorio, Mike, Alt.	.000	19	4	2	1	0	0	0	0	0	0	0	0	0	2	0	2	0	0	0	.000	.500
DiPace, Danny, Tren.*	.129	12	33	31	1	4	5	1	0	0	1	0	0	1	1	0	14	0	0	1	.161	.182
Dishington, Nate, N.H.*	.194	39	143	129	12	25	51	5	0	7	22	0	3	4	7	1	61	1	0	2	.395	.252
Dominique, Andy, Read.	.280	76	301	261	43	73	125	16	0	12	49	0	2	1	37	2	45	3	1	6	.479	.369
Doumit, Ryan, Alt.†	.250	2	5	4	0	1	1	0	0	0	2	0	0	0	1	0	1	0	0	0	.250	.400
Drumright, Mike, Port.*	.071	18	16	14	0	1	1	0	0	0	0	1	0	0	1	0	6	0	0	0	.071	.133
Eckelman, Alex, N.H.	.212	130	447	411	33	87	119	17	0	5	38	7	3	6	20	3	68	14	5	8	.290	.257
Edmondson, Brian, Port.	.000	14	2	2	0	0	0	0	0	0	0	0	0	0	0	0	0	0	0	0	.000	.000
Edwards, Mike, Akr.	.333	29	124	111	21	37	68	7	3	6	24	0	0	0	13	1	26	0	0	3	.613	.403
Emmons, Scott, Nor.	.133	10	16	15	2	2	3	1	0	0	0	0	0	0	1	0	4	1	0	0	.200	.188
Erickson, Corey, Akr.	.228	133	530	483	67	110	208	28	2	22	65	1	5	8	33	3	132	7	4	8	.431	.285
Evans, Lee, Alt.†	.248	118	476	428	53	106	176	21	8	11	48	4	2	5	37	3	116	12	5	4	.411	.301
Farnsworth, Troy, N.H.	.232	115	470	422	47	98	175	21	1	18	70	1	4	15	28	3	104	4	7	8	.415	.301
Figga, Mike, Bing.	.323	8	32	31	2	10	15	2	0	1	7	0	1	0	0	0	8	0	0	0	.484	.313
Figueroa, Franky, Bow.	.300	137	562	534	61	160	234	32	0	14	72	1	4	2	21	2	138	0	4	23	.438	.326
Fischer, Mark, Tren.	.222	127	493	463	48	103	162	22	2	11	55	1	4	0	25	1	148	3	1	9	.350	.260
Fitzgerald, Jason, Akr.*	.272	61	251	239	23	65	91	12	1	4	19	1	1	0	10	1	38	10	2	4	.381	.300
Ford, Lew, N.B.	.218	62	281	252	30	55	91	9	3	7	25	1	2	6	20	0	35	5	5	4	.361	.289
Foster, Quincy, Port.*	.215	68	231	200	34	43	57	2	3	2	14	4	0	2	25	0	31	23	9	4	.285	.308
France, Aaron, Alt.*	.250	7	5	4	0	1	1	0	0	0	1	1	0	0	0	0	0	0	0	0	.250	.250
Franks, Lance, N.H.	.000	28	5	5	0	0	0	0	0	0	0	0	0	0	0	0	1	0	0	0	.000	.000
Freire, Alejandro, Erie	.295	133	561	501	73	148	232	33	0	17	82	0	3	11	46	1	113	2	3	17	.463	.365
Fryman, Travis, Akr.	.360	6	27	25	3	9	14	2	0	1	3	0	0	2	0	0	5	0	0	0	.560	.407
Fuentes, Javier, Har.	.280	22	58	50	7	14	19	3	1	0	6	0	0	1	7	0	4	0	1	0	.380	.379
Galvez, Randy, Alt.	.188	15	17	16	2	3	6	0	0	1	1	1	0	0	0	0	2	0	0	0	.375	.188
Garcia, Guillermo, N.H.	.167	7	19	18	2	3	6	0	0	1	1	1	0	0	0	0	5	0	0	0	.333	.167
Garcia, Luis, Tren.	.310	63	258	229	35	71	135	20	1	14	45	0	1	0	28	0	68	0	1	3	.590	.384
Garrick, Matt, N.H.	.220	40	138	127	10	28	40	6	0	2	10	0	1	0	9	0	25	1	0	3	.315	.270
Gazarek, Marty, Erie	.267	31	115	101	13	27	31	4	0	0	6	1	1	4	8	0	16	1	1	1	.307	.342
Geary, Geoff, Read.	.188	29	20	16	1	3	3	0	0	0	3	2	0	0	2	0	4	0	0	0	.188	.278
Gibbs, Brian, Bow.	.228	32	84	79	7	18	20	2	0	0	6	0	1	0	4	0	23	0	1	1	.253	.262
Gillespie, Eric, Port.*	.225	82	273	240	28	54	86	16	2	4	35	1	2	1	29	3	45	3	1	6	.358	.309
Gingrich, Troy, Har.*	.000	13	37	34	0	0	0	0	0	0	0	0	0	0	3	0	10	0	0	0	.000	.081
Goelz, Jim, Akr.	.261	101	302	283	30	74	101	20	2	1	28	4	2	0	13	0	43	6	3	8	.357	.292
Gomez, Ramon, Read.	.190	38	114	105	7	20	33	7	3	0	10	0	1	3	5	0	42	2	2	1	.314	.224
Gomez, Rich, Erie	.269	93	390	346	60	93	160	21	2	14	44	1	2	16	25	0	75	26	7	4	.462	.344
Gonzalez, Luis, Akr.	.302	52	210	199	41	60	91	12	2	5	17	0	2	2	7	0	26	2	3	3	.457	.329
Gonzalez, Manny, Read.†	.294	64	261	238	32	70	98	19	0	3	24	5	2	3	13	0	37	2	3	4	.412	.336
Gonzalez, Mike, Alt.	.000	14	14	11	0	0	0	0	0	0	0	2	0	0	1	0	6	0	0	0	.000	.083
Goodell, Steve, Bow.	.244	41	166	135	27	33	59	6	1	6	26	0	2	5	24	0	36	1	3	5	.437	.373
Grabow, John, Alt.*	.200	10	6	5	0	1	1	0	0	0	0	0	0	0	1	0	3	0	0	0	.200	.333
Graham, Jess, Tren.*	.274	49	141	124	9	34	53	7	0	4	18	1	1	0	15	2	36	0	1	2	.427	.350
Green, Chad, Akr.†	.260	37	141	127	23	33	54	8	2	3	16	2	1	0	11	0	28	8	2	0	.425	.317
Green, Scarborough, Alt.-N.H.†	.251	74	286	251	24	63	73	8	1	0	16	3	3	2	27	1	57	22	4	3	.291	.326
Griffiths, Jeremy, Bing.	.000	2	2	2	0	0	0	0	0	0	0	0	0	0	0	0	2	0	0	0	.000	.000
Grilli, Jason, Port.	.000	1	1	1	0	0	0	0	0	0	0	0	0	0	0	0	0	0	0	0	.000	.000
Grindell, Nate, Akr.	.284	63	249	229	34	65	114	17	1	10	45	0	6	4	10	0	45	6	4	3	.498	.317
Guy, Brad, Alt.	.000	29	5	3	1	0	0	0	0	0	0	2	0	0	0	0	3	0	0	0	.000	.000
Haad, Yamid, Alt.	.000	1	3	3	0	0	0	0	0	0	0	0	0	0	0	0	0	0	0	0	.000	.000
Haas, Danny, Tren.*	.175	29	89	80	10	14	17	3	0	0	5	0	0	1	8	0	20	1	0	4	.213	.244
Hackett, Richard, Bow.	.125	3	9	8	0	1	1	0	0	0	0	0	0	1	0	0	5	0	1	0	.125	.222
Hamilton, Jon, Akr.*	.280	134	523	471	60	132	215	24	4	17	65	4	3	3	42	4	118	9	12	3	.456	.341
Hammond, Joey, Bow.	.278	102	394	342	49	95	115	13	2	1	26	2	2	6	42	1	59	2	3	8	.336	.355
Harper, Brandon, Port.	.239	76	283	247	21	59	81	13	0	3	24	1	3	5	27	1	52	0	0	7	.328	.323
Harris, Brian, Read.†	.245	135	573	511	71	125	201	27	5	13	58	7	3	7	45	2	62	20	9	7	.393	.313
Harris, Willie, Bow.*	.305	130	590	525	83	160	222	27	4	9	49	10	4	5	46	3	71	54	16	6	.423	.364
Haverbusch, Kevin, Alt.	.261	43	165	153	17	40	60	10	2	2	19	1	4	2	5	1	23	1	2	6	.392	.293
Hebson, Bryan, Har.	.000	26	5	5	0	0	0	0	0	0	0	0	0	0	0	0	2	0	0	0	.000	.000
Henderson, Scott, Port.	.000	39	5	5	0	0	0	0	0	0	0	0	0	0	0	0	1	0	0	0	.000	.000
Henson, Drew, Nor.	.368	5	21	19	2	7	8	1	0	0	2	0	1	1	1	0	4	0	1	1	.421	.429
Hernandez, Carlos, Bing.	.316	70	298	266	49	84	119	18	1	5	32	2	1	6	22	2	42	20	9	5	.447	.380
Hernandez, Jesus, Akr.*	.357	4	17	14	1	5	6	1	0	0	0	0	0	0	3	0	5	1	1	0	.429	.471
Hernandez, Michel, Nor.	.227	51	143	128	10	29	41	6	0	2	10	2	1	2	10	0	20	1	0	5	.320	.291
Hietpas, Joe, Bing.	.000	2	3	3	0	0	0	0	0	0	0	0	0	0	0	0	1	0	0	0	.000	.000
Hiles, Cary, Read.	.154	55	14	13	0	2	2	0	0	0	2	1	0	0	0	0	2	0	0	0	.154	.154
Hitchcox, Brian, Read.*	.120	9	25	25	1	3	3	0	0	0	1	0	0	0	0	0	5	1	0	1	.120	.120
Hodge, Kevin, N.B.	.173	44	155	139	16	24	33	4	1	1	6	0	0	2	14	0	39	1	2	3	.237	.258
Hodges, Scott, Har.*	.275	85	332	305	30	84	114	11	2	5	32	0	2	0	25	5	56	3	2	4	.374	.328

Player, Team	Avg.	G	TPA	AB	R	H	TB	2B	3B	HR	RBI	SH	SF	HP	BB	IBB	SO	SB	CS	GDP	Slg.	OBP
Honeycutt, Heath, Port.	.242	132	531	475	56	115	170	24	2	9	59	0	3	12	41	1	129	10	8	16	.358	.316
Hooper, Kevin, Port.	.308	117	543	468	70	144	181	19	6	2	39	7	2	7	59	4	78	24	12	8	.387	.392
House, J.R., Alt.	.258	112	470	426	51	110	170	25	1	11	56	0	2	5	37	2	103	1	1	12	.399	.323
Huff, B.J., Bing	.050	7	20	20	0	1	1	0	0	0	0	0	0	0	0	0	13	0	1	0	.050	.050
Hunter, Scott, Bing.	.269	65	268	253	44	68	122	9	0	15	41	3	2	3	7	0	47	13	6	5	.482	.294
Infante, Omar, Erie	.302	132	599	540	86	163	198	21	4	2	62	4	7	2	46	1	87	27	12	9	.367	.355
Izquierdo, Hansel, Port.	.300	10	12	10	0	3	3	0	0	0	0	1	0	0	1	0	2	0	0	0	.300	.364
Jackson, Brandon, Nor.	.316	11	41	38	5	12	16	1	0	1	5	1	0	0	2	0	7	0	2	0	.421	.350
James, Kenny, Har.†	.189	41	106	95	17	18	23	3	1	0	3	2	1	2	6	0	13	9	3	0	.242	.250
Janke, Cheyenne, N.H.	.000	17	4	3	0	0	0	0	0	0	0	1	0	0	0	0	3	0	0	0	.000	.000
Jenkins, Brian, Akr.	.217	6	25	23	4	5	9	4	0	0	3	0	1	1	0	0	5	0	0	0	.391	.240
Johnson, Jason, Read.	.264	65	217	197	26	52	62	10	0	0	10	4	2	5	9	2	41	9	4	4	.315	.310
Johnson, Rontrez, Tren.	.282	73	291	255	48	72	119	15	1	10	31	2	3	9	22	0	40	17	7	4	.467	.356
Jones, Jaime, Port.*	.202	31	107	94	9	19	26	4	0	1	10	0	0	1	12	0	29	2	1	2	.277	.299
Justice, Dave, Nor.*	.000	2	8	8	0	0	0	0	0	0	0	0	0	0	0	0	1	0	0	0	.000	.000
Kelly, Heath, Port.	.162	17	38	37	3	6	13	2	1	1	1	0	0	0	1	0	13	0	1	1	.351	.184
Kershner, Jason, Read.*	.000	28	19	16	2	0	0	0	0	0	0	1	0	0	2	0	4	0	0	0	.000	.111
Kessel, Kyle, Bing.	.000	3	1	0	0	0	0	0	0	0	0	0	0	0	1	0	0	0	0	0	.000	1.000
Keylor, Cory, Bow.*	.143	3	8	7	0	1	2	1	0	0	1	0	1	0	0	0	2	0	0	0	.286	.125
Kiil, Skip, Nor.	.188	10	23	16	5	3	8	2	0	1	5	0	1	1	5	0	8	1	0	0	.500	.391
Krause, Scott, Akr.	.254	87	339	303	47	77	140	16	1	15	52	1	5	4	26	1	84	0	3	4	.462	.317
Kropf, Andy, Erie†	.333	5	16	15	1	5	7	2	0	0	1	0	0	0	1	0	4	0	0	0	.467	.375
Kubes, Greg, Read.	.000	6	6	6	0	0	0	0	0	0	0	0	0	0	0	0	4	0	0	0	.000	.000
Lackey, Steve, Akr.	.222	13	33	27	4	6	7	1	0	0	0	2	0	0	4	0	7	2	0	0	.259	.323
Langston, James, Alt.†	.282	28	105	103	9	29	34	3	1	0	7	0	0	0	2	0	22	0	1	1	.330	.295
Lankford, Derrick, Alt.*	.158	6	20	19	2	3	6	1	1	0	2	0	0	0	1	0	6	0	0	0	.316	.200
LaRocca, Greg, Akr.	.317	31	126	104	16	33	51	9	0	3	19	0	2	2	18	1	11	0	2	1	.490	.421
Leach, Nick, Nor.*	.210	55	197	167	17	35	57	13	0	3	22	0	2	0	28	1	39	2	2	4	.341	.320
Leon, Carlos, Tren.†	.222	11	31	27	4	6	10	0	2	0	2	2	0	1	1	0	4	2	2	1	.370	.276
Leon, Donny, Nor.†	.255	116	466	436	45	111	186	26	2	15	74	0	6	5	19	2	115	0	2	10	.427	.290
Leon, Jose, Bow.	.358	26	104	95	18	34	57	9	1	4	20	0	0	1	8	0	21	1	1	2	.600	.413
LeBron, Juan, Bing.	.245	113	413	363	43	89	167	16	4	18	52	0	2	9	39	3	121	2	4	6	.460	.332
Lindsey, Rodney, Erie	.252	111	428	385	51	97	119	14	1	2	34	3	5	12	23	0	77	29	12	6	.309	.311
Lofton, James, Tren.†	.315	29	123	111	22	35	57	7	0	5	11	1	0	1	10	0	23	3	1	0	.514	.377
Loggins, Josh, Nor.	.267	52	197	176	24	47	65	12	0	2	27	1	2	2	16	0	52	2	2	3	.369	.332
Lohrman, Dave, Bing.	.000	13	3	3	0	0	0	0	0	0	0	0	0	0	0	0	2	0	0	0	.000	.000
Lomasney, Steve, Tren.	.249	58	235	209	24	52	100	14	2	10	29	0	0	3	23	1	76	0	1	8	.478	.332
Lopez-Cao, Mike, Bow.*	.201	61	200	174	18	35	58	11	0	4	20	1	1	5	17	1	34	0	2	4	.333	.289
Lopez, Jose, Alt.	.000	6	5	4	0	0	0	0	0	0	0	1	0	0	0	0	0	0	0	0	.000	.000
Lopez, Mickey, Read.†	.272	107	460	382	71	104	167	18	6	11	47	0	2	7	69	2	50	21	6	6	.437	.383
Lorenzo, Juan, N.B.†	.235	101	344	319	32	75	99	9	3	3	24	7	7	6	5	0	32	2	2	8	.310	.255
Machado, Albenis, Har.†	.261	99	404	341	57	89	117	13	3	3	33	15	0	4	44	2	56	10	7	5	.343	.352
Machado, Andy, Read.†	.149	31	117	101	13	15	20	2	0	1	8	3	1	0	12	0	25	5	2	1	.198	.237
Maddox, Garry, Tren.*	.300	84	334	287	47	86	154	25	5	11	48	0	4	3	40	1	76	4	5	2	.537	.386
Maier, T.J., N.H.	.282	74	302	255	46	72	108	20	2	4	35	1	2	6	38	2	58	9	4	2	.424	.385
Mairena, Ozwaldo, Port.*	.000	22	1	1	0	0	0	0	0	0	0	0	0	0	0	0	1	0	0	0	.000	.000
Malave, Dennis, Akr.*	.000	4	7	7	0	0	0	0	0	0	0	0	0	0	0	0	2	0	0	0	.000	.000
Malave, Jaime, Bing.	.105	7	21	19	2	2	3	1	0	0	1	0	0	1	1	0	4	0	0	0	.158	.190
Maness, Nick, Bing.	.273	28	25	22	1	6	7	1	0	0	1	2	0	0	1	0	9	0	0	0	.318	.304
Mangum, Mark, Har.	.278	26	21	18	2	5	5	0	0	0	0	3	0	0	0	0	1	0	0	0	.278	.278
Mann, Derek, Alt.*	.000	1	3	3	0	0	0	0	0	0	0	0	0	0	0	0	1	0	0	0	.000	.000
Manon, Julio, Har.*	.000	10	8	6	0	0	0	0	0	0	1	1	1	0	0	0	5	0	0	0	.000	.000
Marcinczyk, T.R., N.B.	.125	7	19	16	0	2	2	0	0	0	1	0	0	0	3	0	5	0	0	0	.125	.263
Marr, Jason, N.H.	.000	51	3	2	0	0	0	0	0	0	0	1	0	0	0	0	2	0	0	0	.000	.000
Marsters, Brandon, N.B.	.221	100	385	348	35	77	122	16	1	9	36	3	1	3	29	2	75	2	1	8	.350	.285
Martin, Justin, Alt.†	.329	63	179	161	20	53	60	7	0	0	13	1	1	2	14	1	21	16	6	2	.373	.388
Martine, Chris, N.H.	.211	62	197	180	21	38	44	6	0	0	5	2	1	2	12	0	46	2	2	3	.244	.267
Martinez, Eddy, Bow.	.287	32	140	122	21	35	39	1	0	1	10	1	2	1	14	0	31	5	3	2	.320	.360
Martinez, Gabby, Bing.	.264	25	93	87	6	23	36	6	2	1	10	1	0	2	3	0	14	8	2	0	.414	.304
Martinez, Jesus, Bing.*	.000	17	1	1	0	0	0	0	0	0	0	0	0	0	0	0	1	0	0	0	.000	.000
Matos, Luis, Bow.	.304	13	52	46	6	14	22	5	0	1	8	0	0	1	5	1	7	0	1	0	.478	.385
Matz, Brian, Har.*	.000	37	9	6	0	0	0	0	0	0	0	3	0	0	0	0	1	0	0	0	.000	.000
McClaskey, Tim, Port.	.000	37	1	1	0	0	0	0	0	0	0	0	0	0	0	0	1	0	0	0	.000	.000
McClure, Brian, Erie*	.251	75	282	255	29	64	85	14	2	1	22	1	1	2	23	0	45	0	0	13	.333	.317
McDade, Neal, Alt.	.000	19	11	7	0	0	0	0	0	0	0	4	0	0	0	0	3	0	0	0	.000	.000
McDonald, Darnell, Bow.	.282	30	128	117	16	33	51	7	1	3	21	0	1	1	9	0	28	3	3	1	.436	.336
McGee, Tom, Bow.	.160	48	173	156	15	25	37	6	0	2	14	2	0	3	12	0	32	0	1	5	.237	.234
McNamara, Rusty, Read.	.280	33	125	118	18	33	46	10	0	1	16	0	1	0	6	1	10	0	1	4	.390	.312
McNaughton, Troy, N.H.*	.235	115	429	387	57	91	150	29	3	8	39	2	0	3	37	3	108	6	10	8	.388	.307
McNeal, Aaron, Bing.	.201	70	276	264	26	53	93	7	0	11	25	0	0	0	12	0	77	1	3	13	.352	.236
Meier, Dan, Alt.*	.256	97	364	312	43	80	141	14	4	13	38	3	1	3	45	0	80	1	1	7	.452	.355
Melucci, Lou, Har.	.200	6	16	15	1	3	3	0	0	0	2	0	1	0	0	0	7	1	0	0	.200	.188
Meran, Jorge, Erie	.265	35	127	117	11	31	44	4	0	3	17	1	1	4	4	0	39	0	0	2	.376	.310
Merrill, Ronnie, Erie†	.293	37	163	147	22	43	69	14	0	4	18	2	2	0	12	1	27	0	1	3	.469	.342
Miller, Ryan, Bing.	.167	22	61	60	5	10	18	2	0	2	3	0	0	1	0	0	17	1	0	0	.300	.180
Mitchell, Scott, Har.	.000	10	6	5	0	0	0	0	0	0	0	0	0	0	1	0	1	0	0	0	.000	.167
Mohr, Dustan, N.B.	.336	135	574	518	90	174	293	41	3	24	91	0	3	4	49	4	111	9	9	6	.566	.395
Monahan, Shane, Alt.*	.296	21	76	71	9	21	35	6	1	2	10	1	0	0	4	1	12	1	2	1	.493	.333
Montane, Ivan, Bing.	.000	21	5	4	0	0	0	0	0	0	0	0	0	0	1	0	3	0	0	0	.000	.200
Morales, Andy, Nor.	.231	48	174	160	15	37	45	3	1	1	14	0	1	3	10	1	25	1	1	2	.281	.287
Moreno, Julio, Bing.	.000	12	1	1	0	0	0	0	0	0	0	0	0	0	0	0	0	0	0	0	.000	.000
Morneau, Justin, N.B.*	.158	10	42	38	3	6	7	1	0	0	4	0	1	0	3	0	8	0	0	1	.184	.214
Moskau, Ryan, Port.	.100	39	13	10	2	1	2	1	0	0	0	2	0	0	1	0	5	0	0	0	.200	.182

Player, Team	Avg.	G	TPA	AB	R	H	TB	2B	3B	HR	RBI	SH	SF	HP	BB	IBB	SO	SB	CS	GDP	Slg.	OBP
Mosquera, Julio, Nor.	.269	88	294	268	31	72	117	18	0	9	33	1	4	7	14	0	64	2	1	3	.437	.317
Mulligan, Sean, Bow.	.217	6	23	23	2	5	11	0	0	2	7	0	0	0	0	0	6	0	0	1	.478	.217
Munoz, Billy, Akr.*	.184	34	127	114	5	21	37	4	0	4	12	0	1	0	12	0	21	0	0	0	.325	.260
Munoz, Juan, N.H.*	.276	126	484	456	39	126	176	19	2	9	56	1	3	0	24	4	48	9	7	15	.386	.311
Munson, Eric, Erie*	.260	142	620	519	88	135	250	35	1	26	102	0	6	11	84	6	141	0	3	6	.482	.371
Myers, Brett, Read.	.143	26	22	21	1	3	5	0	1	0	2	0	1	0	0	0	11	0	0	1	.238	.136
Myers, Tootie, Har.	.263	123	442	396	49	104	165	15	8	10	49	4	2	6	34	1	118	17	7	7	.417	.329
Nadeau, Rick, Tren.	.167	6	18	18	1	3	4	1	0	0	1	0	0	0	0	0	5	0	0	1	.222	.167
Ndungidi, Ntema, Bow.*	.212	104	383	339	34	72	100	17	1	3	35	1	2	4	37	0	90	3	5	8	.295	.296
Nettles, Jeff, Nor.	.118	6	18	17	1	2	2	0	0	0	0	0	0	0	1	0	8	0	1	0	.118	.167
Nicholson, Derek, Erie*	.330	30	109	94	19	31	51	8	3	2	13	0	0	2	13	1	13	0	0	4	.543	.422
Niles, Drew, Port.†	.237	71	218	194	22	46	69	7	2	4	18	2	2	3	17	0	55	2	7	7	.356	.306
Nunez, Abraham, Port.†	.240	136	560	467	75	112	195	14	9	17	53	5	2	3	83	3	155	26	19	4	.418	.357
Nunoa, Franklin, Read.	.100	00	10	11	0	0	0	0	0	0	1	0	0	0	2	0	0	0	0	0	.273	.308
Nunez, Jose, N.H.	.159	39	88	82	7	13	15	2	0	0	1	0	0	1	5	0	20	5	1	1	.183	.216
Nunnari, Talmadge, Har.*	.156	9	35	32	4	5	10	2	0	1	4	0	1	1	1	0	6	0	0	1	.313	.200
Nye, Rodney, Bing.	.270	109	420	366	45	99	143	23	0	7	45	1	2	2	49	1	82	5	5	6	.391	.358
Olivares, Teuris, Nor.	.212	128	471	439	55	93	126	15	3	4	30	4	3	3	22	0	93	5	4	8	.287	.253
Olsen, Kevin, Port.	.000	26	16	14	1	0	0	0	0	0	0	1	1	0	0	1	9	0	0	1	.000	.067
Ortiz, David, N.B.*	.243	9	41	37	3	9	13	4	0	0	1	0	1	0	3	0	9	0	0	1	.351	.293
Ortiz, Matt, N.H.	.167	4	14	12	0	2	4	2	0	0	2	0	0	0	2	1	2	0	0	0	.333	.333
Ottavinia, Paul, Nor.*	.258	76	340	302	52	78	119	19	2	6	34	0	2	6	30	2	45	11	1	7	.394	.335
Outlaw, Mark, Read.*	.000	49	2	2	0	0	0	0	0	0	0	0	0	0	0	0	1	0	0	0	.000	.000
Padua, Geraldo, Alt.	.000	10	1	1	0	0	0	0	0	0	0	0	0	0	0	0	0	0	0	0	.000	.000
Pascucci, Val, Har.	.244	138	559	476	79	116	198	17	1	21	67	1	6	11	65	1	114	8	8	8	.416	.344
Patterson, Jarrod, Erie*	.400	20	82	70	17	28	56	5	1	7	18	0	1	0	11	0	11	0	0	0	.800	.476
Pavlovich, Tony, Alt.	.000	31	3	3	0	0	0	0	0	0	0	0	0	0	0	0	0	0	0	0	.000	.000
Paz, Rich, Alt.	.238	85	306	248	30	59	88	15	1	4	30	1	2	3	52	2	55	7	6	7	.355	.374
Pearce, Josh, N.H.	.133	18	20	15	1	2	2	0	0	0	0	5	0	0	0	0	3	0	0	1	.133	.133
Perez, Jhonny, Erie	.266	83	327	293	42	78	112	13	3	5	30	4	3	2	20	0	46	10	4	9	.382	.314
Perez, Josue, Read.†	.168	50	183	167	12	28	35	4	0	1	6	1	0	1	14	1	38	3	3	2	.210	.236
Peterman, Tommy, N.B.*	.238	88	328	302	35	72	99	16	1	3	34	2	1	2	21	1	40	1	1	11	.328	.291
Petersen, Chris, Alt.	.210	38	121	100	7	21	27	6	0	0	11	1	1	2	17	0	20	1	2	4	.270	.333
Phillips, Andy, Nor.	.268	51	206	183	23	49	80	9	2	6	25	0	2	0	21	2	54	1	0	6	.437	.340
Phillips, Brandon, Har.	.298	67	283	265	35	79	119	19	0	7	36	1	1	4	12	0	42	13	6	9	.449	.337
Phillips, Jason, Bing.	.293	93	357	317	42	93	147	21	0	11	55	1	3	5	31	3	25	0	1	9	.464	.362
Phoenix, Wynter, Port.-Bow.*	.229	105	363	327	41	75	120	19	4	6	26	0	4	3	29	2	77	11	6	7	.367	.295
Pierce, Kirk, Nor.	.286	12	37	28	5	8	13	2	0	1	4	0	0	5	4	0	8	0	0	0	.464	.459
Pogue, Jamie, N.H.	.200	5	18	15	3	3	5	0	1	0	1	0	0	1	2	0	1	0	0	0	.333	.294
Pond, Simon, Akr.*	.268	114	427	388	46	104	172	29	3	11	46	2	5	2	30	2	70	2	3	9	.443	.320
Prather, Scott, N.H.*	.000	23	5	2	0	0	0	0	0	0	0	1	0	1	1	0	2	0	0	0	.000	.500
Pratt, Scott, Akr.*	.280	68	294	264	33	74	107	13	4	4	24	2	0	2	26	0	48	16	11	6	.405	.349
Raines, Tim, Bow.†	.291	65	296	254	46	74	102	14	1	4	30	4	1	3	34	0	60	29	10	3	.402	.380
Ramos, Kelly, Tren.†	.209	56	192	182	14	38	67	6	1	7	27	1	2	1	6	0	49	0	0	4	.368	.236
Randolph, Jaisen, Bing.†	.179	11	45	39	7	7	8	1	0	0	0	0	0	0	6	0	5	0	4	0	.205	.289
Reding, Josh, Har.	.202	117	400	372	25	75	101	9	4	3	34	7	2	1	18	0	94	10	5	17	.272	.239
Reed, Keith, Bow.	.254	18	73	67	7	17	23	3	0	1	8	0	0	0	6	0	10	2	2	3	.343	.315
Reid, Justin, Alt.	.214	17	17	14	3	3	4	1	0	0	0	2	0	0	1	0	5	0	0	0	.286	.312
Restovich, Michael, N.B.	.269	140	565	501	69	135	245	33	4	23	84	0	4	6	54	8	125	15	7	8	.489	.345
Rickon, Jim, Akr.	.154	12	27	26	0	4	5	1	0	0	0	0	0	0	1	0	9	1	0	0	.192	.185
Rivera, Carlos, Alt.*	.234	111	408	389	44	91	151	30	0	10	50	1	4	1	13	2	71	0	2	11	.388	.258
Rivera, Juan, Nor.	.320	77	337	316	50	101	167	18	3	14	58	0	3	3	15	2	50	5	7	10	.528	.353
Rivera, Mike, Erie	.289	112	473	415	76	120	240	19	1	33	101	0	4	10	44	2	96	2	2	9	.578	.368
Roa, Joe, Port.	.000	7	9	9	0	0	0	0	0	0	0	0	0	0	0	0	5	0	0	0	.000	.000
Roach, Jason, Bing.	.214	22	16	14	2	3	3	0	0	0	1	0	0	1	1	0	4	0	0	1	.214	.313
Roberge, J.P., Read.	.321	87	376	343	61	110	182	13	1	19	71	1	3	4	25	6	40	12	4	14	.531	.371
Roberts, Brian, Bow.†	.296	22	96	81	12	24	34	7	0	1	7	2	2	1	9	0	12	10	0	2	.420	.366
Roberts, Dave, Akr.*	.203	17	77	64	9	13	18	5	0	0	2	2	1	1	9	0	8	4	0	1	.281	.307
Rodriguez, John, Nor.*	.285	103	435	393	64	112	211	31	1	22	66	3	2	11	26	2	117	2	3	7	.537	.345
Rodriguez, Luis, Tren.	.209	51	171	163	21	34	63	7	2	6	22	2	0	0	6	0	36	2	1	2	.387	.237
Rodriguez, Sammy, Bing.	.245	53	179	159	20	39	66	12	0	5	13	1	0	1	18	0	39	1	0	9	.415	.326
Rodriguez, Victor, Nor.	.294	57	241	218	33	64	84	9	1	3	17	7	0	1	15	0	18	2	3	7	.385	.342
Rogers, Ed, Bow.	.199	53	203	191	11	38	50	10	1	0	13	4	0	2	6	0	40	10	2	4	.262	.231
Rolison, Nate, Port.*	.211	5	20	19	1	4	5	1	0	0	2	0	0	1	0	0	7	0	0	2	.263	.250
Roneberg, Brett, Port.*	.262	49	182	164	17	43	69	11	0	5	19	0	1	0	17	0	25	1	0	6	.421	.333
Rose, Mike, Tren.†	.167	9	30	24	3	4	7	0	0	1	2	0	0	0	6	1	10	0	1	0	.292	.333
Rose, Pete, Read.*	.500	9	31	30	4	15	18	3	0	0	0	0	0	0	1	1	3	0	0	1	.600	.516
Royster, Aaron, Read.	.260	42	159	146	19	38	68	3	3	7	19	0	0	2	11	1	37	6	0	1	.466	.321
Ruan, Wilken, Har.	.248	30	123	117	14	29	36	7	0	0	6	1	0	2	3	0	18	6	0	1	.308	.279
Rust, Brian, Bow.	.302	38	139	129	16	39	60	6	0	5	19	0	2	2	6	0	33	1	5	4	.465	.338
Saenz, Jason, Bing.*	.059	28	18	17	0	1	1	0	0	0	0	1	0	0	0	0	9	0	0	0	.059	.059
Salazar, Ruben, N.B.	.298	137	582	530	70	158	221	29	2	10	66	2	6	7	37	4	77	6	1	17	.417	.348
Salzano, Jerry, Tren.	.283	125	518	453	65	128	182	31	1	7	54	1	2	12	50	1	90	15	6	6	.402	.368
Sanchez, Freddy, Tren.	.326	44	192	178	25	58	84	20	0	2	19	2	1	2	9	0	21	3	1	6	.472	.363
Sandusky, Scott, Har.	.248	114	433	387	36	96	124	20	1	2	23	3	1	7	35	5	76	7	2	9	.320	.321
Santana, Osmany, Akr.*	.125	11	46	40	1	5	5	0	0	0	1	4	0	0	2	0	10	1	0	0	.125	.167
Santos, Angel, Tren.†	.271	129	577	510	75	138	212	32	0	14	52	3	5	5	54	2	106	26	9	4	.416	.343
Saturrita, Luis, N.H.	.276	8	33	29	5	8	11	3	0	0	4	0	1	0	3	0	7	0	0	1	.379	.333
Saylor, Jamie, Bing.*	.224	56	178	156	18	35	55	6	1	4	21	2	2	2	16	0	42	2	4	3	.353	.301
Scheffer, Aaron, Port.*	.000	24	1	1	0	0	0	0	0	0	0	0	0	0	0	0	1	0	0	0	.000	.000
Schmidt, Jason, Alt.	1.000	3	2	1	0	1	2	1	0	0	1	0	0	0	1	0	0	0	0	0	2.000	1.000
Schumacher, Shawn, N.H.*	.221	41	129	122	8	27	38	5	0	2	11	3	0	1	3	1	10	3	1	6	.311	.246
Seabol, Scott, Nor.	.250	31	138	128	16	32	51	7	0	4	19	0	2	3	5	0	30	1	1	4	.398	.290

Player, Team	Avg.	G	TPA	AB	R	H	TB	2B	3B	HR	RBI	SH	SF	HP	BB	IBB	SO	SB	CS	GDP	Slg.	OBP
Secrist, Reed, Alt.*	.071	4	15	14	0	1	1	0	0	0	1	0	0	0	0	1	6	0	0	3	.071	.133
Seo, Jae, Bing.	.000	12	4	4	0	0	0	0	0	0	0	0	0	0	0	0	2	0	0	0	.000	.000
Serrano, Elio, Read.	.000	30	1	1	0	0	0	0	0	0	0	0	0	0	0	0	0	0	0	0	.000	.000
Sheredy, Kevin, N H	1.000	48	1	1	1	1	1	0	0	0	0	0	0	0	0	0	0	0	0	0	1.000	1.000
Shrum, Allen, N.B.	.000	7	12	12	0	0	0	0	0	0	0	0	0	0	0	0	4	0	0	1	.000	.000
Silva, Carlos, Read.	.161	29	34	31	2	5	5	0	0	0	1	2	1	0	0	0	10	0	0	0	.161	.156
Sismondo, Bobby, Read.*	.000	26	3	3	0	0	0	0	0	0	0	0	0	0	0	0	1	0	0	0	.000	.000
Skrehot, Shaun, Alt.	.267	117	514	468	61	125	185	30	6	6	45	6	5	5	30	2	63	24	15	10	.395	.315
Sledge, Terrmel, Har.*	.277	129	516	448	66	124	185	22	6	9	48	3	5	9	51	0	72	30	8	5	.413	.359
Smith, Brian, Alt.	.000	2	1	1	0	0	0	0	0	0	0	0	0	0	0	0	1	0	0	0	.000	.000
Smith, Bubba, Port.	.180	31	130	122	11	22	44	4	0	6	22	0	1	1	6	0	29	0	0	2	.361	.223
Smith, Casey, Akr.	.176	30	100	91	8	16	26	1	0	3	5	2	0	1	6	1	27	3	0	2	.286	.235
Smith, Jeff, N.B.*	.285	102	374	351	30	100	138	15	1	7	42	2	2	4	15	0	57	0	0	6	.393	.320
Smith, Nestor, N.B.†	.248	95	312	294	29	73	103	5	8	3	17	6	2	2	8	0	74	5	6	4	.350	.271
Snead, Esix, N.H.†	.233	133	583	520	71	121	157	21	6	1	33	5	1	12	44	0	115	64	23	4	.302	.307
Snusz, Chris, Akr.-Nor.	.326	44	148	132	17	43	57	4	2	2	22	3	2	2	9	0	24	1	0	3	.432	.372
Snyder, Earl, Bing.	.281	114	470	405	69	114	213	35	2	20	75	0	3	4	58	5	111	4	2	5	.526	.374
Sorensen, Zach, Akr.†	.232	46	208	194	24	45	68	6	1	5	16	3	0	0	11	1	30	10	8	3	.351	.273
Sparks, Steve, Alt.	.500	7	6	4	2	2	2	0	0	0	0	0	1	0	1	0	1	0	0	0	.500	.600
Sprague, Kevin, N.H.*	.000	1	2	1	0	0	0	0	0	0	0	0	0	0	1	0	1	0	0	0	.000	.000
Spurling, Chris, Alt.	.231	34	14	13	1	3	5	2	0	0	0	1	0	0	0	0	6	0	0	0	.385	.231
Stemle, Steve, N.H.	.188	26	19	16	0	3	3	0	0	0	0	0	0	2	0	1	5	0	0	1	.188	.235
Stevens, Tony, N.B.†	.171	72	275	245	19	42	54	7	1	1	21	18	0	2	10	0	29	3	3	1	.220	.210
Stocks, Nick, N.H.	.273	16	11	11	0	3	4	1	0	0	0	0	0	0	0	0	3	0	0	0	.364	.273
Stoner, Mike, Alt.	.252	42	142	135	15	34	52	7	1	3	21	0	1	4	2	0	21	0	3	6	.385	.282
Strange, Pat, Bing.	.227	26	27	22	3	5	5	0	0	0	2	5	0	0	0	0	12	0	0	0	.227	.227
Stratton, Rob, Bing.	.248	133	546	483	70	120	239	30	1	29	83	0	2	8	53	6	201	9	5	5	.495	.332
Tamargo, John, Bing.†	.252	49	171	151	13	38	51	8	1	1	10	7	0	0	13	0	19	3	3	7	.338	.311
Taubensee, Eddie, Akr.*	.143	2	8	7	1	1	1	0	0	0	1	0	0	0	1	0	1	0	0	0	.143	.250
Tejera, Mike, Port.*	.176	25	19	17	1	3	4	1	0	0	3	0	0	0	1	0	1	0	0	0	.235	.222
Terhune, Mike, Bing.†	.133	5	17	15	3	2	3	1	0	0	3	0	0	0	2	0	4	0	0	1	.200	.235
Thames, Damon, N.H.	.200	34	72	65	9	13	21	0	1	2	6	2	0	1	4	0	21	0	1	2	.323	.257
Thames, Marcus, Nor.	.321	139	603	520	114	167	311	43	4	31	97	0	3	7	73	8	101	10	4	6	.598	.410
Tillman, Kevin, Akr.*	.286	2	7	7	1	2	2	0	0	0	1	0	0	0	0	0	2	1	0	0	.286	.286
Torres, Andres, Erie†	.294	64	294	252	54	74	99	16	3	1	23	0	1	5	36	1	50	19	11	1	.393	.391
Torres, Gabby, N.B.	.308	41	148	133	24	41	61	12	1	2	13	0	0	5	10	0	11	0	2	7	.459	.378
Traber, Billy, Bing.*	.000	8	5	5	0	0	0	0	0	0	0	0	0	0	0	0	5	0	0	0	.000	.000
Treanor, Matt, Port.	.157	35	113	89	7	14	22	2	0	2	8	2	0	9	13	0	18	1	1	2	.247	.324
Tucker, T.J., Har.	.250	13	10	8	1	2	2	0	0	0	1	2	0	0	0	0	0	0	0	2	.250	.250
Tyson, Torre, Nor.†	.246	71	265	224	43	55	63	8	0	0	14	2	1	4	34	2	49	9	3	3	.281	.354
Ullery, Dave, Bow.*	.283	14	56	53	3	15	24	3	0	2	12	0	1	1	1	0	15	0	0	1	.453	.304
Ust, Brant, Erie	.238	87	350	323	36	77	115	16	1	6	31	3	3	6	15	0	81	1	1	8	.350	.282
Valdez, Jerry, Read.	.248	74	263	242	32	60	105	14	2	9	39	2	3	5	11	1	47	1	2	10	.434	.291
Valentin, John, Tren.	.154	3	14	13	1	2	3	1	0	0	0	0	0	0	1	0	3	0	0	0	.231	.214
Van Iten, Bobby, Read.*	.228	113	451	404	46	92	138	23	1	7	52	1	2	8	36	2	120	1	1	5	.342	.302
Vargas, Claudio, Port.	.045	27	25	22	0	1	1	0	0	0	1	2	0	0	1	0	10	0	0	1	.045	.087
Vega, Rene, Bing.*	.000	41	11	11	0	0	0	0	0	0	0	0	0	0	0	0	9	0	0	0	.000	.000
Velazquez, Gil, Bing.	.207	106	391	358	33	74	98	11	2	3	19	4	0	3	26	1	84	1	1	12	.274	.266
Walker, Adam, Read.*	.190	15	24	21	2	4	4	0	0	0	1	0	0	0	2	0	13	0	0	1	.190	.261
Walker, Tyler, Bing.	.333	4	4	3	0	1	1	0	0	0	0	1	0	0	0	0	0	0	0	0	.333	.333
Walrond, Les, N.H.*	.000	16	7	5	0	0	0	0	0	0	0	2	0	0	0	0	1	0	0	0	.000	.000
Ware, Jeremy, Har.	.287	27	94	87	12	25	40	6	0	3	16	0	0	7	1	0	14	1	1	0	.460	.340
Washington, Rico, Alt.*	.302	75	318	291	31	88	117	17	0	4	29	1	0	5	21	3	49	5	5	5	.402	.360
Wathan, Derek, Port.†	.252	127	526	469	65	118	158	12	8	4	35	5	5	2	45	0	83	25	16	12	.337	.317
Wathan, Dusty, Port.	.269	55	165	134	24	36	52	10	0	2	21	1	0	17	13	1	28	0	1	3	.388	.402
Wayne, Justin, Har.	.286	14	17	14	1	4	4	0	0	0	1	1	0	0	2	0	2	0	0	0	.286	.375
Wedel, Jeremy, Read.	.000	45	1	1	0	0	0	0	0	0	0	0	0	0	0	0	0	0	0	0	.000	.000
Wehner, John, Alt.	.228	25	97	92	10	21	24	3	0	0	8	0	1	1	3	0	11	4	0	1	.261	.258
Whitaker, Chad, Akr.*	.239	51	173	155	16	37	66	9	1	6	18	0	4	1	13	0	34	2	1	0	.426	.295
Wigginton, Ty, Bing.	.286	8	34	28	5	8	11	3	0	0	0	1	0	0	5	0	5	1	0	0	.393	.394
Wilcox, Luke, Port.*	.241	69	242	220	25	53	94	14	0	9	41	0	0	1	21	1	43	1	1	6	.427	.310
Williams, Dave, Alt.*	.000	9	10	10	0	0	0	0	0	0	0	0	0	0	0	0	7	0	0	0	.000	.000
Wimberly, Larry, Alt.*	.200	24	6	5	0	1	1	0	0	0	0	0	0	0	1	0	3	0	0	0	.200	.333
Wolf, Randy, Read.*	.500	1	3	2	1	1	2	1	0	0	0	0	0	0	1	0	0	0	0	0	1.000	.667
Zancanaro, Dave, N.H.*	.500	1	2	2	0	1	2	1	0	0	0	0	0	0	0	0	0	0	0	0	1.000	.500
Zech, Scott, Har.	.259	34	105	85	14	22	25	3	0	0	8	3	1	1	13	0	14	2	5	5	.294	.360

PLAYERS WITH TWO OR MORE TEAMS

Player, Team	Avg.	G	TPA	AB	R	H	TB	2B	3B	HR	RBI	SH	SF	HP	BB	IBB	SO	SB	CS	GDP	Slg.	OBP
Bruce, Mo, Har.	.228	45	147	136	19	31	46	6	0	3	15	1	1	1	8	0	36	14	2	2	.338	.274
Bruce, Mo, Alt.	.118	10	39	34	4	4	5	1	0	0	2	1	0	0	4	0	11	0	2	1	.147	.211
Green, Scarborough, Alt.†	.253	27	99	91	10	23	24	1	0	0	6	0	1	1	6	1	19	10	0	1	.264	.303
Green, Scarborough, N.H.†	.250	47	187	160	14	40	49	7	1	0	10	3	2	1	21	0	38	12	4	2	.306	.337
Phoenix, Wynter, Port.*	.250	24	63	60	9	15	23	2	0	2	6	0	0	3	0	0	15	0	1	2	.383	.286
Phoenix, Wynter, Bow.*	.225	81	300	267	32	60	97	17	4	4	20	0	4	3	26	2	62	11	5	5	.363	.297
Snusz, Chris, Akr.	.143	2	8	7	0	1	1	0	0	0	1	1	0	0	0	0	1	0	0	3	.143	.143
Snusz, Chris, Nor.	.336	42	140	125	17	42	56	4	2	2	21	2	2	2	9	0	23	1	0	0	.448	.384

GRAND SLAMS: Freire, 3; Wilcox, 2; C. Abbott, Airoso, Alvarez, Amezcua, Bolivar, Byrd, Calloway, Cepicky, Erickson, Evans, Farnsworth, Fischer, L. Garcia, M. Hernandez, Hunter, M. Lopez, Mohr, Mulligan, Munson, Ndungidi, Nye, B. Smith, J. Smith, Snyder, Thames, Van Iten, 1 each.

AWARDED FIRST BASE ON CATCHER'S INTERFERENCE: J. Perez 5 (Lomasney 2, Mosquera 2, Ramos); Lopez-Cao 2 (Garrick, M. Hernandez), Zech 2 (House, J. Valdez); Curry (Ramos), Garrick (Mosquera), C. Hernandez (Carreno), Roberts (M. Rivera), Snead (L. Rodriguez).

TEAM

Team	W	L	Pct.	ERA	G	CG	ShO	Sv.	IP	H	TBF	R	ER	HR	SH	SF	HB	BB	IBB	SO	WP	Bk.
New Britain	87	55	.613	3.02	142	5	11	44	1268.1	1136	5282	499	426	79	34	22	66	389	31	1148	56	3
Portland	77	65	.542	3.24	142	4	12	38	1257.0	1067	5118	517	452	143	55	19	55	356	15	1141	38	3
Norwich	83	59	.585	3.27	142	7	13	40	1253.1	1129	5328	578	455	95	37	39	49	463	11	1207	60	8
Altoona	63	79	.444	3.73	142	4	8	30	1245.2	1257	5345	613	516	83	43	31	59	430	19	872	50	10
Erie	84	58	.592	3.85	142	16	11	42	1235.2	1216	5274	612	529	129	36	42	80	395	16	1003	55	2
Akron	68	74	.479	3.93	142	8	12	31	1235.2	1203	5224	607	539	101	43	32	54	423	13	931	73	13
Reading	77	65	.542	4.02	142	8	12	35	1247.2	1233	5258	622	557	137	43	33	65	351	22	958	53	6
Harrisburg	66	76	.465	4.14	142	10	6	30	1224.0	1244	5303	666	563	148	43	43	75	440	23	958	58	5
Bowie	59	82	.418	4.16	141	13	11	28	1228.0	1263	5254	672	568	138	38	47	52	351	19	906	60	7
Trenton	67	75	.472	4.21	142	1	9	34	1232.2	1298	5326	683	577	114	34	24	90	380	23	1121	71	7
Binghamton	73	68	.518	4.23	141	4	9	40	1231.2	1328	5399	667	579	114	43	51	63	451	28	959	70	8
New Haven	47	95	.331	4.25	142	4	9	24	1229.2	1248	5382	690	580	126	44	38	73	478	23	944	69	4

INDIVIDUAL

TOP QUALIFIERS FOR EARNED-RUN AVERAGE TITLE

Minimum 114 innings. *Lefthanded pitcher.

Pitcher, Team	W	L	Pct.	ERA	G	GS	CG	ShO	GF	Sv.	IP	H	TBF	R	ER	HR	SH	SF	HB	BB	IBB	SO	WP	Bk.
Stephens, John, Bow.	11	4	.733	1.84	18	17	3	3	0	0	132.0	95	502	32	27	10	2	1	6	21	1	130	2	0
Thomas, Brad, N.B.*	10	3	.769	1.96	19	19	1	0	0	0	119.1	91	474	37	26	4	1	2	4	26	0	97	7	0
Claussen, Brandon, Nor.*	9	2	.818	2.13	21	21	1	1	0	0	131.0	101	554	42	31	6	7	6	5	55	0	151	5	3
Olsen, Kevin, Port.	10	3	.769	2.68	26	26	2	1	0	0	154.2	123	611	56	46	11	2	3	10	21	1	144	0	0
Cornejo, Nate, Erie	12	3	.800	2.68	19	19	3	1	0	0	124.1	107	519	47	37	12	3	0	7	41	0	105	4	0
Flores, Randy, Nor.*	14	6	.700	2.78	25	25	3	2	0	0	158.2	156	677	64	49	13	5	3	1	63	0	115	3	3
Fossum, Casey, Tren.*	3	7	.300	2.83	20	20	0	0	0	0	117.2	102	483	47	37	5	0	0	12	28	0	130	2	0
Rincon, Juan, N.B.	14	6	.700	2.88	29	23	2	1	0	0	153.1	130	645	60	49	9	3	3	8	57	5	133	9	1
Day, Zach, Akr.	9	10	.474	3.10	22	22	2	0	0	0	136.2	123	572	57	47	8	3	1	4	45	1	94	7	0
Spurling, Chris, Alt.	5	7	.417	3.11	34	15	0	0	11	1	121.2	133	512	48	42	9	1	3	4	28	1	63	2	0
Roach, Jason, Bing.	8	7	.533	3.26	22	21	0	0	0	0	116.0	129	500	54	42	7	6	4	4	28	1	70	1	2
Graman, Alex, Nor.*	12	9	.571	3.52	28	28	1	0	0	0	166.1	174	723	83	65	10	3	6	2	60	0	138	6	0
Tejera, Mike, Port.*	9	8	.529	3.57	25	25	0	0	0	0	141.0	143	595	61	56	17	7	1	8	41	0	131	6	0
Hancock, Josh, Tren.	8	6	.571	3.65	24	24	0	0	0	0	130.2	138	553	60	53	8	3	2	4	37	0	119	11	0
Pearce, Josh, N.H.	6	8	.429	3.75	18	18	0	0	0	0	115.1	111	484	55	48	11	4	2	6	34	1	96	5	0

DEPARTMENTAL LEADERS: W—C. Silva, Kalita, 15 each; L—Saenz, 15; Pct.—Claussen, .818; G—Crudale, 62; GS—Rogers, Kalita, 29 each; CG—Kalita, 5; ShO—Stephens, A. Walker, 3; GF—Pearson, 47; Sv.—Pacheco, 26; IP—Kalita, 200; H—C. Silva, 197; TBF—Kalita, 826; R—Kalita, Paradis, 98 each; ER—Saenz, 90; HR—Kalita, Vargas, 25 each; SH—Moskau, Vargas, 8 each; SF—J. Figueroa, 8; HB—Kirsten, 22; BB—Saenz, 80; IBB—Saenz, 16; SO—Chiavacci, 161; WP—Saenz, 16; BK—Radinsky, 6.

ALL PITCHERS

*Lefthanded pitcher.

Pitcher, Team	W	L	Pct.	ERA	G	GS	CG	ShO	GF	Sv.	IP	H	TBF	R	ER	HR	SH	SF	HB	BB	IBB	SO	WP	Bk.
Adkins, Tim, Nor.*	3	1	.750	3.38	40	5	0	0	13	0	80.0	70	344	36	30	7	1	2	5	30	1	83	4	0
Agamennone, Brandon, Har.	4	0	1.000	4.13	45	0	0	0	16	3	61.0	59	262	31	28	10	2	3	3	23	2	51	2	0
Albin, Scott, Har.	0	0	.000	4.91	4	0	0	0	0	0	3.2	4	17	2	2	1	0	0	0	2	1	4	0	0
Aldred, Scott, Nor.*	4	3	.571	3.65	11	7	0	0	2	0	37.0	36	154	19	15	3	1	0	2	7	0	43	1	0
Alvarado, Carlos, Alt.	5	7	.417	3.36	26	10	0	0	6	0	83.0	74	354	46	31	6	1	2	5	29	1	73	4	1
Ambrose, John, Tren.	0	0	.000	14.21	5	0	0	0	0	0	6.1	12	35	10	10	1	1	0	0	5	0	7	1	1
Andrews, Jeff, Har.	1	0	1.000	5.56	9	0	0	0	2	0	11.1	15	53	7	7	3	0	0	1	4	0	13	0	0
Arroyo, Luis, Tren.*	0	1	.000	9.22	7	0	0	0	2	0	13.2	28	81	17	14	1	1	0	1	10	1	10	2	0
Arthurs, Shane, Har.	0	0	.000	1.69	5	0	0	0	1	0	5.1	7	27	3	1	0	0	1	2	2	0	5	0	0
Ayers, Mike, Alt.*	1	1	.500	2.25	7	0	0	0	4	0	8.0	8	33	2	2	0	0	0	3	6	0	6	0	0
Babula, Shaun, Bow.*	2	4	.333	3.26	28	0	0	0	13	2	38.2	37	160	18	14	2	2	1	2	12	1	27	1	1
Bacsik, Mike, Akr.*	1	1	.500	1.98	4	4	1	1	0	0	27.1	21	104	7	6	2	0	0	0	3	0	19	0	0
Baez, Danny, Akr.	0	0	.000	0.00	1	0	0	0	0	0	2.0	1	7	0	0	0	0	0	0	0	0	2	0	0
Bailie, Matt, Read.	1	6	.143	6.85	35	6	0	0	7	0	67.0	76	303	52	51	13	3	7	2	30	1	72	3	0
Baisley, Brad, Read.	5	4	.556	6.50	12	10	0	0	0	0	62.1	82	285	50	45	14	1	3	6	14	0	37	5	0
Balfour, Grant, N.B.	2	1	.667	1.08	35	0	0	0	24	13	50.0	26	197	6	6	1	1	0	0	22	2	72	1	0
Barrios, Manny, Bing.	0	0	.000	9.00	4	0	0	0	1	0	6.0	6	28	6	6	1	0	0	1	5	0	3	1	0
Bauer, Rick, Bow.	2	6	.250	3.54	9	9	2	0	0	0	61.0	52	247	27	24	8	1	2	5	10	0	34	1	0
Baugh, Kenny, Erie	1	3	.250	2.97	5	5	1	0	0	0	30.1	23	122	16	10	5	1	0	4	6	0	30	2	0
Bean, Colter, Nor.	0	1	.000	9.00	1	0	0	0	1	0	1.0	1	5	1	1	1	0	0	0	0	0	0	0	0
Bechler, Steve, Bow.	3	5	.375	3.08	12	12	2	0	0	0	79.0	63	306	31	27	14	0	1	1	15	0	58	3	0
Beckett, Josh, Port.	8	1	.889	1.82	13	13	0	0	0	0	74.1	50	286	16	15	8	0	1	4	19	0	102	1	1
Bell, Heath, Bing.	3	1	.750	6.02	43	0	0	0	22	4	61.1	82	285	44	41	13	1	4	5	19	3	55	4	0
Benham, Dave, N.H.	0	0	.000	0.00	1	0	0	0	1	0	1.0	0	4	0	0	0	1	0	0	0	0	0	0	0
Bennett, Jeff, Alt.	0	0	.000	3.86	1	1	0	0	0	0	7.0	9	34	3	3	0	0	0	2	2	0	6	0	0
Bess, Steve, Erie	0	2	.000	2.89	10	1	0	0	2	0	18.2	15	73	6	6	1	0	1	2	4	0	8	0	0
Betancourt, Rafael, Tren.	0	1	.000	5.63	16	0	0	0	10	0	24.0	28	100	16	15	0	0	2	3	0	0	27	1	0
Billingsley, Brent, Har.*	7	9	.438	5.37	19	19	1	0	0	0	112.1	128	492	77	67	20	0	3	5	34	1	97	11	0
Blevins, Jeremy, Nor.	1	6	.143	2.98	50	0	0	0	22	6	63.1	46	265	30	21	2	4	2	1	26	3	63	3	0
Bottalico, Ricky, Read.	0	1	.000	1.80	3	3	0	0	0	0	5.0	3	19	2	1	1	0	0	0	1	0	5	0	0
Bowe, Brandon, Port.	0	2	.000	1.56	9	0	0	0	6	0	17.1	13	67	4	3	1	0	0	0	5	0	10	0	0
Bradley, Ryan, Nor.	4	5	.444	6.63	16	12	0	0	3	0	58.1	47	275	51	43	7	2	1	12	48	0	53	10	1
Braswell, Bryan, Bing.*	1	1	.500	4.42	5	3	0	0	1	0	18.1	26	84	9	9	0	0	1	0	7	0	14	0	0
Bridges, Donnie, Har.	1	2	.333	3.24	3	3	0	0	0	0	16.2	14	76	10	6	2	0	1	2	13	0	14	2	0

Pitcher, Team	W	L	Pct.	ERA	G	GS	CG	ShO	GF	Sv.	IP	H	TBF	R	ER	HR	SH	SF	HB	BB	IBB	SO	WP	Bk.
Brown, Derek, Bow.	4	4	.500	3.76	34	3	1	0	7	1	67.0	69	290	31	28	6	4	3	2	19	0	44	0	1
Brown, Jamie, Akr.	1	1	.500	5.03	4	4	0	0	0	0	19.2	22	88	11	11	2	0	0	2	7	0	12	0	0
Brunette, Justin, Bing.*	3	1	.750	5.46	23	0	0	0	12	4	29.2	43	132	20	18	4	1	0	0	7	0	33	0	1
Buller, Sean, Erie*	2	1	.667	5.82	16	0	0	0	8	2	21.2	27	96	15	14	2	1	0	0	4	1	11	0	0
Bullinger, Kirk, Akr.	0	1	.000	4.91	3	0	0	0	3	1	3.2	5	17	2	2	0	1	0	1	1	0	4	0	0
Bump, Nate, Port.	4	5	.444	5.27	11	8	0	0	2	0	54.2	55	228	41	32	10	2	1	3	10	0	41	0	0
Burnham, Gary, Read.*	0	0	.000	4.50	2	0	0	0	2	0	2.0	4	10	1	1	0	0	0	0	0	0	0	0	0
Burnside, Adrian, Alt.*	0	2	.000	3.62	6	6	0	0	0	0	32.1	28	138	15	13	3	2	1	2	14	0	32	2	2
Burton, Darren, Alt.	0	0	.000	18.00	1	0	0	0	1	0	1.0	3	7	2	2	0	0	0	0	1	0	2	0	0
Camp, Jared, Erie	1	1	.500	4.82	11	0	0	0	5	1	18.2	16	86	11	10	1	2	1	0	16	1	18	3	0
Camp, Shawn, Alt.	4	4	.500	4.24	8	3	0	0	1	0	23.1	25	103	14	11	3	0	2	3	8	1	19	1	1
Carnes, Matt, N.B.	4	5	.444	3.76	28	7	0	0	10	2	64.2	64	276	31	27	4	3	1	1	20	4	63	1	0
Carrasco, Dan, Alt.	2	2	.500	4.14	27	1	0	0	11	1	37.0	34	169	22	17	2	2	0	0	25	2	35	2	0
Cedeno, Blas, Read.	1	0	1.000	2.25	7	0	0	0	4	1	12.0	12	50	4	3	1	0	0	0	3	0	10	0	0
Cento, Tony, N.B.*	0	0	.000	9.00	9	0	0	0	6	0	10.0	19	50	10	10	1	0	0	0	3	0	8	0	0
Cerda, Jaime, Bing.*	1	0	1.000	3.10	12	0	0	0	9	3	20.1	17	82	7	7	1	1	1	1	6	0	22	2	0
Cerros, Juan, Bing.	1	2	.333	4.91	13	0	0	0	7	0	18.1	24	86	10	10	2	0	0	0	7	0	14	3	0
Chaney, Mike, Alt.*	0	0	.000	6.75	4	0	0	0	1	0	9.1	18	47	7	7	1	0	1	1	2	1	2	2	0
Chapman, Jake, Har.*	7	3	.700	2.39	53	0	0	0	10	2	67.2	55	286	26	18	5	3	1	3	27	4	69	1	0
Chen, Bruce, Read.*	1	0	1.000	0.00	1	1	0	0	0	0	6.0	3	22	0	0	0	0	0	0	0	0	7	1	0
Chiavacci, Ron, Har.	3	11	.214	3.97	25	25	2	1	0	0	147.1	137	648	77	65	12	7	5	7	76	2	161	9	1
Chrysler, Clint, Alt.*	4	3	.571	3.28	51	0	0	0	15	3	49.1	52	216	24	18	3	2	0	4	12	1	31	2	0
Cisar, Mark, Tren.	1	1	.500	4.31	21	0	0	0	12	3	31.1	30	123	15	15	2	1	0	1	7	0	21	2	0
Clark, Chris, Port.	1	0	1.000	3.18	4	0	0	0	1	0	5.2	3	25	2	2	1	0	0	0	5	0	6	0	0
Claussen, Brandon, Nor.*	9	2	.818	2.13	21	21	1	1	0	0	131.0	101	554	42	31	6	7	6	5	55	0	151	5	3
Coogan, Patrick, N.H.	8	8	.500	5.09	33	23	1	1	6	0	148.2	168	648	91	84	19	3	6	8	43	0	115	15	1
Cook, Andy, Bing.	2	2	.500	4.75	22	2	1	0	3	1	47.1	51	207	28	25	3	0	3	3	16	0	33	2	0
Cook, B.R., N.H.	5	8	.385	3.99	20	20	0	0	0	0	121.2	115	515	68	54	11	5	4	3	37	0	84	7	2
Cooper, Chris, Akr.*	0	0	.000	4.50	2	0	0	0	0	0	2.0	2	8	1	1	0	0	0	0	0	0	3	0	0
Corcoran, Tim, Bow.	1	0	1.000	0.77	7	0	0	0	4	0	11.2	4	41	1	1	0	0	0	3	0	13	1	0
Cordova, Francisco, Alt.	0	0	.000	4.15	1	1	0	0	0	0	4.1	6	19	2	2	0	0	0	1	0	4	0	0
Corey, Mark, Bing.	1	2	.333	1.80	25	0	0	0	23	17	35.0	23	137	10	7	1	2	0	1	12	0	50	2	0
Cormier, Rheal, Read.*	0	0	.000	0.00	1	1	0	0	0	0	2.0	7	0	0	0	0	0	0	1	0	2	0	0
Cornejo, Nate, Erie	12	3	.800	2.68	19	19	3	1	0	0	124.1	107	519	47	37	12	3	0	7	41	0	105	4	0
Crudale, Mike, N.H.	4	9	.308	3.25	62	0	0	0	30	9	80.1	76	334	42	29	7	2	2	0	22	4	85	7	0
Crumpton, Chuck, Har.	2	6	.250	4.32	52	0	0	0	24	4	66.2	73	292	39	32	6	3	4	5	25	5	44	3	1
Daniels, Dave, N.H.	1	1	.500	2.86	13	0	0	0	2	0	22.0	19	91	7	7	1	1	1	1	8	2	17	0	1
Darrell, Tommy, Har.	0	2	.000	7.79	24	1	0	0	9	0	34.2	45	173	37	30	4	1	1	3	19	0	15	5	0
Darwin, Dave, Akr.*	3	2	.600	4.15	19	7	0	0	3	0	56.1	62	245	34	26	6	2	2	3	18	3	43	3	0
Davis, Allen, Har.*	2	2	.500	2.89	8	8	1	0	0	0	53.0	48	216	20	17	4	2	1	4	9	0	36	1	0
Day, Zach, Akr.	9	10	.474	3.10	22	22	2	0	0	0	136.2	123	572	57	47	8	3	1	4	45	1	94	7	0
De La Rosa, Jorge, Tren.*	1	3	.250	5.84	29	0	0	0	4	0	37.0	56	187	35	24	4	1	1	4	20	1	27	6	0
De Leon, Jorge, Tren.	0	0	.000	6.75	1	0	0	0	1	0	1.1	2	5	1	1	1	0	0	0	0	0	0	1	0
Delgado, Ernie, Alt.	0	1	.000	3.24	6	0	0	0	3	1	8.1	5	31	3	3	1	1	1	0	1	0	9	1	0
Della Ratta, Pete, Bing.	4	2	.667	6.30	22	0	0	0	9	0	30.0	36	139	25	21	3	1	2	3	8	0	30	1	0
Deschenes, Marc, Akr.	2	2	.500	1.72	22	0	0	0	8	0	31.1	25	140	9	6	1	4	2	5	18	2	30	0	0
Diorio, Mike, Alt.	1	4	.200	7.91	18	0	0	0	2	0	33.0	40	155	34	29	5	0	2	2	19	0	14	0	0
Donaldson, Bo, Alt.	3	1	.750	3.10	17	0	0	0	12	5	20.1	12	81	7	7	2	0	3	7	0	22	0	0
Drese, Ryan, Akr.	5	7	.417	3.35	14	13	1	1	1	0	86.0	64	340	34	32	4	7	1	6	29	0	73	4	0
Drumright, Mike, Port.	5	8	.385	4.06	18	16	1	0	0	0	102.0	100	416	54	46	13	2	0	0	27	0	85	6	0
Duchscherer, Justin, Tren.	6	3	.667	2.44	12	12	1	1	0	0	73.2	49	293	25	20	6	0	0	5	14	1	69	0	0
Ebert, Derrin, Tren.*	7	9	.438	4.64	20	20	0	0	0	0	116.1	134	496	67	60	12	3	2	7	23	0	89	6	1
Eckelman, Alex, N.H.	0	0	.000	0.00	2	0	0	0	2	0	1.1	1	5	0	0	0	0	0	0	0	0	1	0	0
Eckenstahler, Eric, Erie*	4	2	.667	3.90	46	0	0	0	18	4	64.2	55	289	32	28	7	1	1	3	31	4	73	3	1
Edmondson, Brian, Port.	2	3	.400	1.73	14	0	0	0	6	1	26.0	16	97	7	5	3	3	1	1	5	1	16	1	0
Eibey, Scott, Bow.*	0	0	.000	6.13	38	0	0	0	21	0	69.0	84	318	53	47	9	4	5	2	22	4	48	2	0
Elmore, Chris, Tren.*	5	3	.625	2.29	14	13	0	0	0	0	78.2	76	328	34	20	4	2	1	8	19	0	56	9	0
Falteisek, Steve, Bow.	1	6	.143	7.87	11	5	0	0	4	0	42.1	59	198	45	37	11	2	4	0	15	1	25	7	0
Farmer, Tom, Erie	0	0	.000	2.53	2	2	0	0	0	0	10.2	12	45	3	3	1	1	0	0	4	0	8	1	0
Farroll, Jim, Tren.	0	0	.000	0.00	1	0	0	0	0	0	2.0	1	8	0	0	0	0	0	0	1	0	2	0	0
Felix, Miguel, Bow.	5	5	.500	4.39	15	14	1	1	0	0	80.0	73	337	44	39	7	1	1	7	32	1	58	6	2
Field, Luke, Akr.	0	1	.000	10.80	1	1	0	0	0	0	5.0	8	25	6	6	1	0	1	0	2	0	1	1	0
Figueroa, Juan, Bow.	3	10	.231	4.89	18	17	1	0	0	0	99.1	126	443	63	54	14	6	8	1	26	4	52	2	0
Finley, Chuck, Akr.*	1	1	.500	0.82	2	2	0	0	0	0	11.0	7	41	3	1	0	2	0	0	0	0	11	1	0
Fisher, Pete, N.H.	5	2	.714	1.89	9	8	0	0	0	0	52.1	52	219	20	11	3	1	0	4	11	0	39	1	0
Fitch, Steve, Akr.	0	0	.000	7.71	1	1	0	0	0	0	2.1	4	14	4	2	1	0	0	0	1	0	2	0	0
Fleming, Travis, Bow.	0	0	.000	9.00	3	0	0	0	2	0	4.0	15	30	11	4	2	0	0	2	0	0	2	0	0
Flohr, Adam, N.B.*	3	5	.375	4.86	18	12	0	0	1	0	74.0	94	321	43	40	8	3	0	3	15	0	49	4	0
Flores, Randy, Nor.*	14	6	.700	2.78	25	25	3	2	0	0	158.2	156	677	64	49	13	5	3	1	63	0	115	3	3
Florie, Bryce, Tren.	0	1	.000	1.64	6	1	0	0	2	2	11.0	5	47	4	2	0	1	0	3	6	0	17	2	0
Flury, Pat, Nor.	1	0	1.000	1.59	4	0	0	0	1	0	5.2	3	21	1	1	1	0	0	0	2	0	9	0	0
Fossum, Casey, Tren.*	3	7	.300	2.83	20	20	0	0	0	0	117.2	102	483	47	37	5	0	0	12	28	0	130	2	0
France, Aaron, Alt.	1	2	.333	5.68	7	5	0	0	0	0	25.1	36	120	19	16	4	3	2	3	10	0	17	1	0
Franks, Lance, N.H.	2	8	.200	4.08	28	11	0	0	4	0	90.1	86	409	60	41	11	3	3	9	48	0	72	5	0
Frederick, Kevin, N.B.	6	2	.750	1.63	44	0	0	0	18	7	82.2	56	331	17	15	5	6	2	8	28	7	109	4	0
Galvez, Randy, Alt.	5	6	.455	3.45	15	15	0	0	0	0	86.0	93	359	40	33	3	4	1	1	22	1	45	5	0
Garcia, Mike, Alt.	2	0	1.000	0.45	18	0	0	0	14	4	20.0	15	76	1	1	0	0	1	4	0	15	0	0
Garcia, Rosman, Nor.	1	0	1.000	0.00	1	1	0	0	0	0	6.0	5	28	4	0	0	0	1	2	0	6	2	0
Garcia, Sonny, Bow.	1	3	.250	5.72	5	5	1	0	0	0	28.1	33	130	22	18	4	0	0	9	22	1	21	3	0
Garrett, Hal, Nor.	4	4	.500	5.61	11	2	0	0	7	1	25.2	21	113	17	16	5	2	0	2	14	0	19	2	0
Garrett, Josh, Tren.	3	6	.333	5.64	46	4	0	0	13	0	81.1	84	379	61	51	10	2	3	14	44	2	60	11	0
Geary, Geoff, Read.	9	7	.563	3.61	29	13	0	0	10	2	112.1	101	449	48	45	14	7	5	3	21	3	88	4	3
Gibbs, Mark, Bow.	0	0	.000	0.00	1	0	0	0	0	0	1.0	0	3	0	0	0	0	0	0	0	0	1	0	0

Pitcher, Team	W	L	Pct.	ERA	G	GS	CG	ShO	GF	Sv.	IP	H	TBF	R	ER	HR	SH	SF	HB	BB	IBB	SO	WP	Bk.
Goetz, Geoff, Port.*	2	2	.500	1.53	25	0	0	0	6	0	29.1	22	120	10	5	2	0	1	0	12	0	24	3	0
Gonzalez, Mike, Alt.*	5	4	.556	3.71	14	14	1	1	0	0	87.1	81	367	38	36	5	6	2	0	36	0	66	2	1
Grabow, John, Alt.*	2	5	.286	3.38	10	10	0	0	0	0	50.2	30	214	23	19	1	2	0	2	39	0	42	5	3
Graman, Alex, Nor.*	12	9	.571	3.52	28	28	1	0	0	0	166.1	174	723	83	65	10	3	6	2	60	0	138	6	0
Griffiths, Jeremy, Bing.	2	0	1.000	0.69	2	2	1	0	0	0	13.0	8	51	3	1	0	1	0	0	4	0	12	1	0
Grilli, Jason, Port.	0	1	.000	2.25	1	1	0	0	0	0	4.0	3	15	1	1	1	0	0	0	0	0	3	0	0
Gronkiewicz, Lee, Akr.	0	0	.000	0.00	2	0	0	0	2	0	2.0	4	10	0	0	0	0	0	0	0	0	1	0	0
Guy, Brad, Alt.	3	4	.429	4.03	28	4	0	0	16	4	51.1	59	226	32	23	3	2	2	3	17	2	30	4	1
Hackman, Luther, N.H.	0	0	.000	2.25	3	1	0	0	0	0	4.0	2	15	2	1	0	0	1	0	1	0	5	0	0
Hale, Beau, Bow.	1	5	.167	5.11	12	12	0	0	0	0	61.2	74	268	39	35	8	3	5	3	15	1	40	4	2
Hamilton, Jimmy, Bow.*	3	1	.750	3.34	13	0	0	0	6	1	29.2	30	120	11	11	1	2	1	0	8	0	22	1	0
Hammond, Joey, Bow.	0	0	.000	32.40	2	0	0	0	1	0	1.2	6	12	6	6	3	0	0	0	1	0	0	0	0
Hancock, Josh, Tren.	8	6	.571	3.65	24	24	0	0	0	0	130.2	138	553	60	53	8	3	2	4	37	0	119	11	0
Hazlett, Andy, Tren.*	6	1	.857	3.81	14	7	0	0	4	1	52.0	51	213	24	22	4	0	1	4	13	0	39	1	0
Heams, Shane, Erie	5	3	.625	2.15	36	0	0	0	20	6	54.1	22	226	15	13	1	3	1	5	37	2	57	6	0
Hebson, Bryan, Har.	2	8	.200	4.44	26	8	2	0	6	0	75.0	78	320	40	37	12	3	4	7	19	0	54	2	0
Heiserman, Rick, N.H.	0	0	.000	3.52	5	0	0	0	2	0	7.2	7	33	4	3	1	1	0	0	3	0	5	1	0
Henderson, Scott, Port.	5	7	.417	4.76	39	0	0	0	15	4	56.2	52	238	31	30	9	6	1	0	23	2	55	5	0
Herrera, Alex, Akr.*	3	0	1.000	2.83	15	0	0	0	9	2	28.2	24	114	9	9	1	0	0	0	9	0	22	2	0
Hiles, Cary, Read.	2	3	.400	2.42	51	0	0	0	30	11	81.2	60	325	24	22	6	2	2	7	21	3	62	5	2
Hill, Terry, Tren.*	3	1	.750	3.79	22	0	0	0	7	0	38.0	38	167	25	16	3	0	0	5	10	2	42	3	0
Hoard, Brent, N.B.*	1	0	1.000	0.00	1	1	0	0	0	0	6.0	2	21	1	0	0	1	0	1	0	0	2	1	0
Hooten, Dave, Akr.	4	0	1.000	1.37	17	6	0	0	8	4	46.0	43	181	7	7	3	2	0	1	12	0	31	3	0
Howard, Tom, N.B.*	0	0	.000	9.00	4	0	0	0	2	0	4.0	6	21	4	4	0	0	1	4	0	0	2	0	0
Izquierdo, Hansel, Port.	7	2	.778	3.81	10	9	1	1	0	0	56.2	47	224	24	24	10	0	1	4	10	0	45	4	0
Janke, Cheyenne, N.H.	1	4	.200	5.52	17	5	0	0	5	0	44.0	65	201	31	27	5	1	1	0	14	0	20	2	0
Jean, Domingo, Nor.	3	2	.600	1.21	21	0	0	0	14	6	29.2	20	112	5	4	2	2	0	4	2	0	43	1	0
Jensen, Justin, Nor.*	0	0	.000	3.68	4	0	0	0	1	0	7.1	7	32	3	3	1	0	0	0	4	0	6	0	0
Jerzembeck, Mike, Nor.	1	2	.333	5.14	10	4	0	0	1	0	28.0	30	119	20	16	5	0	3	0	8	0	31	2	0
Jodie, Brett, Nor.	2	0	1.000	0.64	2	2	0	0	0	0	14.0	10	52	1	1	0	1	1	0	2	0	14	0	0
Johnson, Adam, N.B.	5	6	.455	3.82	18	18	0	0	0	0	113.0	105	481	53	48	10	4	5	9	39	2	110	5	0
Johnson, Barry, Nor.	1	1	.500	4.63	8	0	0	0	4	0	11.2	12	54	7	6	0	0	3	5	0	16	0	0	0
Johnson, James, Akr.*	4	0	1.000	2.91	31	0	0	0	6	0	46.1	35	193	15	15	2	1	1	2	19	0	55	9	0
Jones, Bobby M., Bing.*	0	0	.000	0.00	2	1	0	0	0	0	5.0	0	15	0	0	0	0	0	0	0	0	6	0	0
Journell, Jimmy, N.H.	1	0	1.000	0.00	1	1	1	1	0	0	7.0	2	21	0	0	0	0	0	0	3	0	6	0	0
Julio, Jorge, Bow.	0	0	.000	0.73	12	0	0	0	12	7	12.1	5	44	1	1	0	0	1	1	2	1	14	0	0
Kalita, Tim, Erie*	15	9	.625	3.83	30	29	5	0	0	0	200.0	190	826	98	85	25	3	7	11	49	0	147	5	0
Kershner, Jason, Read.*	5	9	.357	4.80	26	19	0	0	2	0	123.2	147	525	75	66	18	5	5	3	26	1	70	4	0
Kessel, Kyle, Bing.*	0	1	.000	8.00	3	2	0	0	1	0	9.0	12	41	10	8	2	0	0	2	7	0	7	0	0
Kirsten, Rick, Erie	14	8	.636	4.62	28	27	1	0	0	0	161.2	161	709	93	83	22	3	4	22	53	1	143	6	0
Krause, Scott, Akr.	0	0	.000	0.00	1	0	0	0	0	0	1.0	3	11	6	0	0	0	0	1	4	0	0	0	0
Kubes, Greg, Read.*	0	1	.000	3.67	6	5	0	0	1	0	27.0	32	110	12	11	1	0	2	0	7	0	12	0	0
Kusiewicz, Mike, Tren.*	4	5	.444	3.44	18	17	0	0	0	0	89.0	83	365	39	34	6	3	3	9	19	2	92	2	0
Lakman, Jason, Bow.	0	2	.000	8.13	18	1	0	0	7	0	34.1	48	161	34	31	6	0	4	2	12	0	26	2	0
Lambert, Jeremy, N.H.	2	2	.500	2.97	31	0	0	0	27	14	33.1	32	150	17	11	4	2	2	4	17	2	48	1	0
Lantz, Doug, Akr.	0	0	.000	0.00	1	1	0	0	0	0	6.0	1	18	0	0	0	0	0	0	0	0	3	0	0
Leach, Bryan, Tren.	2	2	.500	4.50	23	0	0	0	19	1	40.0	42	174	21	20	7	1	1	3	11	3	40	2	0
Leach, Nick, Nor.	0	0	.000	0.00	1	0	0	0	1	0	1.0	1	4	0	0	0	0	0	0	0	0	0	0	0
Leek, Randy, Erie*	11	7	.611	3.86	29	27	4	1	1	1	179.1	190	740	87	77	24	3	4	9	27	1	123	2	0
Levan, Matt, Port.*	0	0	.000	4.15	4	0	0	0	0	0	8.2	8	42	5	4	1	0	0	1	7	1	8	0	0
Lohrman, Dave, Bing.	2	1	.667	2.10	13	0	0	0	8	6	25.2	20	109	9	6	2	1	1	1	12	1	26	1	0
Lohse, Kyle, N.B.	3	1	.750	2.37	6	6	0	0	0	0	38.0	32	145	10	10	5	0	0	2	4	0	32	0	0
Looney, Brian, Nor.*	0	0	.000	8.44	11	0	0	0	5	0	16.0	23	84	18	15	2	0	3	1	10	0	16	0	0
Lopez, Jose, Alt.	1	2	.333	4.83	6	5	0	0	0	0	31.2	38	145	20	17	3	1	2	2	11	1	23	1	0
Lovingier, Kevin, Nor.*	3	5	.375	1.91	53	0	0	0	14	0	89.2	56	348	22	19	0	2	2	2	31	2	94	6	0
Mairena, Ozwaldo, Port.*	4	2	.667	1.57	22	0	0	0	7	3	34.1	27	134	12	6	3	5	0	0	8	2	27	2	0
Maness, Nick, Bing.	6	12	.333	4.97	28	26	1	0	1	0	143.0	168	654	94	79	13	5	7	6	65	4	107	5	0
Mangum, Mark, Har.	7	8	.467	4.62	26	26	2	1	0	0	140.1	161	613	88	72	14	6	5	14	36	1	59	3	0
Manon, Julio, Har.	4	3	.571	3.12	10	7	0	0	3	1	52.0	50	207	20	18	6	1	1	0	16	0	44	1	0
Manzueta, Roberto, Alt.	1	1	.500	5.40	12	0	0	0	4	0	20.0	19	88	13	12	0	0	1	2	11	2	14	0	0
Marr, Jason, N.H.	3	4	.429	4.96	51	0	0	0	23	0	61.2	68	275	36	34	5	3	1	3	25	3	27	1	0
Marshall, Lee, N.B.	1	3	.250	1.93	11	0	0	0	5	2	18.2	20	85	6	4	1	1	1	0	4	0	15	0	0
Marte, Damaso, Nor.*	3	1	.750	3.50	23	0	0	0	4	1	36.0	29	147	16	14	3	1	2	2	7	0	36	0	1
Martine, Chris, N.H.	0	0	.000	0.00	1	0	0	0	1	0	1.0	0	4	0	0	0	0	0	0	1	0	2	0	0
Martinez, Jesus, Bing.*	2	0	1.000	0.00	7	0	0	0	7	0	30.0	33	136	17	17	2	2	0	0	16	3	24	5	0
Matz, Brian, Har.*	1	8	.111	5.49	37	13	0	0	9	0	96.2	116	431	68	59	22	3	3	3	28	1	62	7	1
McClaskey, Tim, Port.	2	2	.500	2.86	37	0	0	0	13	2	50.1	38	201	17	16	5	4	1	3	10	2	52	1	0
McClure, Brian, Erie	0	0	.000	0.00	2	0	0	0	2	0	1.2	0	7	0	0	0	0	0	1	1	0	1	1	0
McCurtain, Paul, Port.	0	0	.000	5.02	10	0	0	0	2	0	14.1	17	71	9	8	2	0	0	0	13	0	14	1	1
McDade, Neal, Alt.	2	5	.286	4.05	19	9	0	0	3	0	73.1	85	323	38	33	3	2	0	3	24	0	55	3	1
McDonald, Jon, N.B.	8	3	.727	3.44	17	17	0	0	0	0	96.2	88	407	47	37	7	1	0	8	34	0	68	5	2
McLeary, Marty, Tren.	9	6	.600	3.46	35	0	0	0	14	2	54.2	58	252	30	21	2	4	1	5	30	5	42	2	0
Medina, Carlos, Bing.*	0	1	.000	3.55	24	0	0	0	5	1	33.0	36	151	15	13	2	3	2	1	13	2	17	4	0
Mills, Alan, Bow.	0	0	.000	2.25	7	0	0	0	2	0	8.0	5	31	2	2	0	0	0	3	0	10	1	0	0
Mills, Ryan, N.B.*	2	5	.286	6.42	8	8	0	0	0	0	40.2	45	182	31	29	3	1	1	5	14	0	29	2	0
Mitchell, Scott, Har.	1	2	.333	4.15	9	4	0	0	2	0	21.2	24	95	11	10	4	1	2	1	6	0	14	1	0
Montalbano, Greg, Tren.*	3	3	.500	4.50	10	10	0	0	0	0	48.0	50	199	25	24	8	1	0	1	14	0	45	0	3
Montane, Ivan, Bing.	2	2	.500	2.97	21	0	0	0	14	2	33.1	31	140	13	11	1	1	0	11	1	32	4	0	0
Moreno, Julio, Bing.	3	2	.600	4.87	12	0	0	0	3	0	20.1	21	91	13	11	3	0	0	9	0	17	1	0	0
Moskau, Ryan, Port.*	3	2	.600	3.48	39	10	0	0	9	2	103.1	103	430	45	40	12	8	4	5	29	3	78	2	0
Mulholland, Terry, Alt.*	0	2	.000	3.86	2	2	0	0	0	0	2.1	5	13	3	1	0	0	0	0	1	0	3	0	0
Munoz, Juan, N.H.*	0	0	.000	0.00	1	0	0	0	1	0	1.0	2	5	0	0	0	0	0	0	0	0	0	0	0
Myers, Brett, Read.	13	4	.765	3.87	26	23	1	1	0	0	156.0	156	661	71	67	21	3	1	10	43	1	130	5	0

Pitcher, Team	W	L	Pct.	ERA	G	GS	CG	ShO	GF	Sv.	IP	H	TBF	R	ER	HR	SH	SF	HB	BB	IBB	SO	WP	Bk.
Nakamura, Mike, N.B.	5	1	.833	1.77	48	1	0	0	19	5	86.1	75	357	20	17	3	3	1	2	24	5	109	3	0
Navarro, Jason, N.H.*	1	2	.333	5.25	52	0	0	0	17	0	61.2	64	291	47	36	11	2	1	11	37	2	48	3	0
Neal, Blaine, Port.	2	3	.400	2.36	54	0	0	0	44	21	53.1	43	225	17	14	1	4	1	2	21	3	45	2	0
Norton, Jason, Tren.	0	2	.000	12.12	6	4	0	0	0	0	16.1	24	81	25	22	5	2	1	1	8	0	17	1	0
Nunez, Franklin, Read.	8	7	.533	4.42	39	14	0	0	10	3	110.0	107	486	68	54	9	3	2	6	51	3	112	9	0
Olsen, Kevin, Port.	10	3	.769	2.68	26	26	2	1	0	0	154.2	123	611	56	46	11	2	3	10	21	1	144	0	0
Ormond, Rod, Bow.	0	0	.000	21.60	1	0	0	0	0	0	1.2	4	10	4	4	0	0	0	0	0	0	0	0	0
Outlaw, Mark, Read.*	4	6	.400	5.01	49	3	0	0	24	7	64.2	74	292	38	36	5	4	2	2	28	5	59	2	0
Pacheco, Alexander, Nor.	5	4	.556	1.26	43	0	0	0	41	26	50.0	25	192	9	7	2	0	1	0	16	2	65	5	0
Padua, Geraldo, Alt.-Nor.	1	1	.500	6.85	15	0	0	0	6	0	22.1	22	97	17	17	5	2	1	2	9	0	21	1	0
Palki, Jeromy, N.B.	3	1	.750	2.83	31	2	0	0	17	1	60.1	50	247	19	19	1	2	0	0	22	4	59	2	0
Paradis, Mike, Bow.	8	13	.381	4.71	27	26	1	0	0	0	137.2	157	634	98	72	13	4	2	4	62	1	108	14	1
Pautz, Brad, Read.	0	0	.000	1.93	5	0	0	0	3	0	4.2	3	20	2	1	0	0	0	0	4	1	4	1	0
Pavlovich, Tony, Alt.	0	3	.000	2.98	31	0	0	0	26	12	42.1	38	174	15	14	0	2	1	3	13	5	26	1	0
Paz, Rich, Alt.	1	0	1.000	0.00	1	0	0	0	1	0	1.0	0	4	0	0	0	1	0	0	1	0	0	0	0
Pearce, Josh, N.H.	6	8	.429	3.75	18	18	0	0	0	0	115.1	111	484	55	48	11	4	2	6	34	1	96	5	0
Pearson, Terry, Erie	4	4	.500	2.93	59	0	0	0	47	23	61.1	65	273	26	20	1	4	1	3	16	2	62	5	1
Pena, Jesus, Tren.*	2	4	.333	5.06	14	2	0	0	7	1	32.0	46	147	20	18	6	1	0	0	7	0	35	2	1
Perkins, Dan, Akr.	0	0	.000	15.00	1	1	0	0	0	0	3.0	7	16	5	5	1	0	0	0	0	0	4	0	0
Perkins, Mike, N.H.	0	1	.000	12.00	1	1	0	0	0	0	3.0	6	17	4	4	1	0	0	2	2	0	2	0	0
Persails, Mark, Erie	1	4	.200	7.28	9	7	0	0	1	0	38.1	62	188	37	31	5	1	5	1	18	0	15	3	0
Phelps, Tommy, Erie*	1	1	.500	3.58	15	2	0	0	5	2	32.2	33	139	14	13	1	3	2	3	8	2	31	2	0
Phillips, Jason, Alt.-Akr.	2	2	.500	5.73	16	4	0	0	3	0	33.0	36	150	22	21	2	0	2	2	19	0	24	4	0
Pina, Rafael, Bow.	0	1	.000	2.08	4	0	0	0	2	0	8.2	6	36	3	2	0	0	0	1	5	1	5	1	0
Pinales, Aquiles, Akr.	0	0	.000	9.00	5	0	0	0	2	0	8.0	13	40	9	8	1	0	0	4	6	1	1	1
Pineda, Luis, Erie	6	2	.750	3.05	16	12	2	1	2	0	85.2	68	340	33	29	8	3	5	2	28	0	92	3	0
Ponson, Sidney, Bow.	0	0	.000	0.00	1	1	0	0	0	0	4.0	3	14	0	0	0	0	0	0	1	0	2	0	0
Prather, Scott, N.H.*	1	3	.250	3.70	23	4	0	0	5	0	48.2	52	215	20	20	5	2	2	2	17	2	38	2	0
Pumphrey, Ken, N.B.	8	2	.800	2.88	22	14	2	1	3	1	103.0	89	415	38	33	5	1	2	7	26	0	52	4	0
Radinsky, Scott, Akr.*	2	2	.500	3.47	23	0	0	0	9	3	23.1	30	99	10	9	1	0	1	1	3	0	19	1	6
Rakers, Aaron, Bow.	4	4	.500	2.39	51	0	0	0	39	14	60.1	53	257	21	16	8	1	1	2	20	1	74	4	0
Rath, Fred, N.H.	0	0	.000	16.20	1	0	0	0	0	0	1.2	3	11	3	3	1	0	0	3	0	0	0	0
Reid, Justin, Alt.	5	5	.500	2.54	17	16	1	1	0	0	110.0	104	452	38	31	5	7	1	5	14	0	70	2	0
Reinike, Chris, Akr.	1	3	.250	5.33	27	0	0	0	13	5	52.1	55	226	34	31	5	0	0	2	18	0	40	6	1
Reynoso, Edison, Nor.	1	0	1.000	3.93	5	3	0	0	0	0	18.1	19	80	12	8	2	0	0	1	5	0	17	0	0
Rincon, Juan, N.B.	14	6	.700	2.88	29	23	2	1	0	0	153.1	130	645	60	49	9	3	3	8	57	5	133	9	1
Rivera, Homero, Erie*	1	2	.333	4.75	16	2	0	0	8	2	30.1	35	132	16	16	4	0	2	2	11	1	19	3	0
Rivera, Saul, N.B.	5	2	.714	3.16	33	0	0	0	27	13	42.2	35	181	16	15	3	2	1	1	18	1	55	1	0
Roa, Joe, Port.	0	2	.000	3.00	7	7	0	0	0	0	36.0	36	143	15	12	2	2	1	2	3	1	26	0	0
Roach, Jason, Bing.	0	7	.533	3.26	22	21	0	0	0	0	116.0	129	500	54	42	7	6	4	4	28	1	70	1	2
Rodgers, Bobby, Port.	3	2	.600	2.03	26	0	0	0	15	4	40.0	30	159	9	9	4	0	0	0	11	0	39	2	0
Rodney, Fernando, Erie	0	0	.000	4.26	4	0	0	0	2	1	6.1	7	30	3	3	1	0	1	2	3	0	8	0	0
Rodriguez, Eddy, Bow.	1	1	.500	2.08	5	0	0	0	3	2	8.2	7	37	2	2	0	1	1	0	6	1	10	0	0
Rodriguez, Frank, Alt.	0	0	.000	4.82	7	0	0	0	3	0	9.1	9	47	6	5	0	1	1	8	1	5	1	0
Rodriguez, Nerio, Akr.	6	2	.750	3.91	11	11	2	1	0	0	71.1	64	286	34	31	10	1	1	4	17	0	49	4	1
Rodriguez, Rich, Akr.*	0	0	.000	0.00	4	0	0	0	1	1	5.0	2	17	0	0	0	0	0	0	0	0	4	0	0
Rogers, Brian, Nor.	10	9	.526	3.96	29	29	1	0	0	0	177.1	187	775	97	78	21	7	4	8	63	1	150	10	0
Roller, Adam, Nor.	0	0	.000	0.00	2	0	0	0	1	0	3.0	3	11	0	0	0	1	0	0	0	0	2	0	0
Saberhagen, Bret, Tren.	0	0	.000	2.45	1	1	0	0	0	0	3.2	5	14	1	1	0	0	0	1	0	4	0	0
Sadler, Carl, Alt.*	2	3	.400	6.50	11	0	0	0	6	0	18.0	23	85	16	13	1	0	0	0	9	0	14	0	1
Saenz, Jason, Bing.*	8	15	.348	5.66	28	23	0	0	1	0	143.0	167	662	97	90	16	3	6	8	80	8	95	16	2
Salyers, Jeremy, Har.	4	2	.667	5.56	16	1	0	0	7	0	22.2	24	99	15	14	4	2	1	2	6	2	13	1	0
Sanders, Frankie, Akr.	0	0	.000	189.00	1	0	0	0	0	0	0.1	3	8	7	7	1	0	0	1	3	0	0	0	0
Sansom, Trevor, N.H.	0	0	.000	4.50	1	0	0	0	0	0	2.0	1	8	1	1	0	0	0	0	1	0	1	0	0
Scheffer, Aaron, Port.	2	1	.667	1.02	24	0	0	0	14	1	35.1	16	125	4	4	2	2	0	1	9	0	39	0	0
Schmidt, Jason, Alt.	0	1	.000	0.96	3	3	0	0	0	0	9.1	7	36	1	1	0	0	0	1	0	17	0	0
Schoening, Brent, N.B.	2	6	.250	4.73	12	6	0	0	3	0	45.2	48	195	25	24	6	1	1	1	16	1	37	2	0
Sekany, Jason, Tren.	1	5	.167	6.07	15	7	0	0	3	0	56.1	71	247	40	38	10	2	4	0	19	1	41	0	1
Seo, Jae, Bing.	5	1	.833	1.94	12	10	0	0	1	0	60.1	44	235	14	13	3	3	1	6	11	1	47	0	0
Serrano, Elio, Read.	1	1	.500	2.89	30	0	0	0	14	2	37.1	22	146	12	12	3	3	1	1	9	2	30	2	0
Serrano, Jim, Har.	6	3	.667	2.18	47	0	0	0	42	20	53.2	30	216	20	13	4	2	3	0	24	4	73	0	0
Sexton, Jeff, Akr.	0	1	.000	2.04	11	0	0	0	4	1	17.2	22	78	7	4	1	0	0	0	5	0	14	1	0
Sheredy, Kevin, N.H.	0	7	.000	2.95	48	0	0	0	12	1	64.0	46	267	29	21	6	5	2	2	34	3	58	6	0
Shuey, Paul, Akr.	0	0	.000	0.00	1	1	0	0	0	0	1.0	0	4	0	0	0	0	0	0	1	0	2	0	0
Sido, Wilson, Akr.	1	0	1.000	2.30	3	2	0	0	0	0	15.2	15	67	4	4	0	1	0	9	0	13	2	0
Silva, Carlos, Read.	15	8	.652	3.90	28	28	4	1	0	0	180.0	197	740	85	78	20	6	2	11	27	0	100	3	0
Silva, Jose, Alt.	0	0	.000	0.00	2	0	0	0	1	0	1.1	2	7	0	0	0	0	0	1	0	2	0	0
Sims, Ken, Bow.	8	4	.667	4.10	24	14	1	1	3	1	112.0	123	479	54	51	9	5	4	10	26	0	51	4	0
Sismondo, Bobby, Read.*	0	1	.000	4.24	26	0	0	0	9	2	34.0	32	152	20	16	5	2	1	1	19	0	27	2	0
Smith, Brian, Alt.	1	0	1.000	0.00	2	0	0	0	1	0	4.1	3	16	0	0	0	0	0	0	3	0	0
Sparks, Steve, Alt.	1	4	.200	3.76	7	6	1	0	0	0	38.1	31	166	19	16	2	0	2	1	25	0	32	5	0
Spencer, Corey, Tren.*	3	5	.375	4.52	55	0	0	0	43	20	77.2	85	349	41	39	9	5	4	1	31	5	82	5	0
Spiegel, Mike, Akr.*	0	0	.000	9.53	1	1	0	0	0	0	5.2	10	30	6	6	0	2	1	1	3	0	0	0	0
Spoljaric, Paul, Akr.*	0	0	.000	0.00	3	0	0	0	2	0	3.1	4	12	0	0	0	0	0	0	3	0	0	0	0
Sprague, Kevin, N.H.*	1	0	1.000	3.00	1	1	0	0	0	0	6.0	4	25	3	2	0	0	0	2	0	4	0	0
Spurling, Chris, Alt.	5	7	.417	3.11	34	15	0	0	11	1	121.2	133	512	48	42	9	1	3	4	28	1	63	2	0
Stanford, Jason, Akr.*	6	11	.353	4.07	24	24	1	0	0	0	141.2	152	602	71	64	11	3	7	10	32	4	108	2	1
Stemle, Steve, N.H.	7	10	.412	4.77	26	25	0	0	0	0	134.0	159	603	76	71	12	4	3	10	43	2	75	4	0
Stephens, John, Bow.	11	4	.733	1.84	18	17	3	3	0	0	132.0	95	502	32	27	10	2	1	6	21	1	130	2	0
Stocks, Nick, N.H.	2	12	.143	5.16	16	15	1	0	0	0	82.0	89	371	52	47	10	3	2	11	33	1	63	3	0
Stoops, Jim, Nor.	0	0	.000	6.00	6	0	0	0	1	0	9.0	14	48	10	6	3	0	0	6	0	9	0	0
Strange, Pat, Bing.	11	6	.647	4.87	26	24	1	0	1	0	153.1	171	669	94	83	18	5	6	12	52	1	106	7	0
Tejera, Mike, Port.*	9	8	.529	3.57	25	25	0	0	0	0	141.0	143	595	61	56	17	7	1	8	41	0	131	6	0

Pitcher, Team	W	L	Pct.	ERA	G	GS	CG	ShO	GF	Sv.	IP	H	TBF	R	ER	HR	SH	SF	HB	BB	IBB	SO	WP	Bk.
Tekavec, Nate, Erie	0	1	.000	6.75	1	1	0	0	0	0	1.1	3	7	1	1	1	0	0	0	0	0	2	0	0
Thomas, Brad, N.B.*	10	3	.769	1.96	19	19	1	0	0	0	119.1	91	474	37	26	4	1	2	4	26	0	97	7	0
Traber, Billy, Bing.*	4	3	.571	4.43	8	8	0	0	0	0	42.2	50	188	25	21	4	1	3	2	13	1	45	4	1
Tucker, Julien, Erie-Akr.	1	6	.143	5.67	28	1	0	0	8	0	54.0	62	256	39	34	2	3	4	3	35	2	27	7	0
Tucker, T.J., Har.	5	5	.500	3.73	13	13	0	0	0	0	82.0	77	348	38	34	10	4	2	3	37	0	57	4	2
Turnbow, Mark, Akr.	0	0	.000	3.00	1	0	0	0	0	0	3.0	1	11	1	1	0	0	1	0	2	0	1	0	0
Vanhekken, Andy, Erie*	5	0	1.000	4.69	8	8	0	0	0	0	48.0	63	210	29	25	5	1	3	1	8	0	29	1	0
Vargas, Claudio, Port.	8	9	.471	4.19	27	27	0	0	0	0	159.0	122	666	77	74	25	8	2	11	67	1	151	2	1
Vargas, Martin, Akr.	1	5	.167	5.63	32	0	0	0	24	9	40.0	52	189	29	25	1	3	2	1	23	0	35	8	0
Vega, Rene, Bing.*	3	6	.333	3.64	41	10	0	0	8	2	106.1	117	456	48	43	12	3	5	9	32	1	69	5	2
Walker, Adam, Read.-Bing.*	7	4	.636	1.80	17	17	3	3	0	0	95.0	53	368	22	19	2	1	0	6	30	0	88	6	0
Walker, Tyler, Bing.	1	0	1.000	0.40	4	3	0	0	0	0	22.1	9	88	2	1	1	3	1	0	13	1	13	1	0
Wall, Donne, Bing.	0	0	.000	0.00	4	4	0	0	0	0	5.0	1	16	0	0	0	0	0	0	1	0	5	0	0
Walling, Dave, Nor.	3	2	.600	5.40	5	5	1	0	0	0	31.2	44	140	22	19	1	0	1	1	9	0	21	0	0
Walrond, Les, N.H.*	2	8	.200	3.87	16	16	1	0	0	0	81.1	68	354	41	35	5	3	3	2	46	0	67	6	0
Wamback, Trevor, Har.	0	0	.000	10.57	3	0	0	0	1	0	7.2	12	34	9	9	1	0	1	0	3	0	3	0	0
Watson, Mark, Akr.*	3	1	.750	4.12	30	0	0	0	21	4	39.1	34	166	19	18	2	1	1	13	0	34	2	0
Wayne, Justin, Har.	9	2	.818	2.62	14	14	2	0	0	0	92.2	87	398	28	27	4	3	1	9	34	0	70	5	0
Wedel, Jeremy, Read.	5	3	.625	3.71	45	0	0	0	18	5	63.0	67	278	33	26	4	3	0	6	16	2	43	1	1
Wehner, John, Alt.	0	1	.000	11.57	2	0	0	0	1	0	2.1	5	14	3	3	0	0	1	1	0	2	0	0
Weis, Brad, N.B.*	0	0	.000	5.14	4	0	0	0	2	0	7.0	9	32	5	4	0	1	2	1	0	8	4	0
White, Matt, Akr.*	8	10	.444	4.81	25	25	0	0	0	0	144.0	151	618	84	77	18	6	3	3	60	1	72	7	2
Whiteley, Shad, Nor.	0	0	.000	4.50	1	0	0	0	1	0	2.0	2	8	1	1	1	0	0	0	0	0	2	0	0
Wiggins, Scott, Nor.*	0	0	.000	0.00	4	0	0	0	3	0	4.0	0	12	0	0	0	0	0	1	0	5	0	0
Williams, Dave, Alt.*	5	2	.714	2.61	9	8	1	0	1	0	58.2	45	228	17	17	8	1	1	1	12	0	39	0	0
Williams, Todd, Nor.	1	0	1.000	0.00	6	0	0	0	1	1	8.0	4	28	0	0	0	0	1	0	0	5	0	0
Wilson, Jeff, Bow.*	1	1	.500	3.97	5	5	0	0	0	0	34.0	32	146	19	15	3	0	2	2	9	0	31	1	0
Wimberly, Larry, Alt.*	3	2	.600	4.17	24	7	0	0	3	0	69.0	75	293	36	32	7	2	3	2	18	0	43	2	0
Wolf, Randy, Read.*	0	0	.000	4.50	1	1	0	0	0	0	6.0	5	27	3	3	0	0	1	2	0	7	0	0
Wolff, Bryan, Akr.	2	3	.400	4.05	8	8	1	1	0	0	53.1	52	222	24	24	8	2	2	15	1	47	1	0
Woodard, Steve, Akr.	0	0	.000	3.00	1	1	0	0	0	0	3.0	3	12	1	1	0	0	0	1	0	2	1	0
Wright, Jaret, Akr.	0	0	.000	1.29	1	1	0	0	0	0	7.0	2	23	1	1	1	0	0	0	4	0	4	0	0
Zancanaro, Dave, N.H.*	0	0	.000	1.80	1	1	0	0	0	0	5.0	4	22	1	1	0	0	0	4	1	5	1	0

PITCHERS WITH TWO OR MORE TEAMS

Pitcher, Team	W	L	Pct.	ERA	G	GS	CG	ShO	GF	Sv.	IP	H	TBF	R	ER	HR	SH	SF	HB	BB	IBB	SO	WP	Bk.
Padua, Geraldo, Alt.	0	1	.000	9.69	10	0	0	0	5	0	13.0	17	61	14	14	5	2	1	1	6	0	10	1	0
Padua, Geraldo, Nor.	1	0	1.000	2.89	5	0	0	0	1	0	9.1	5	36	3	3	0	0	0	1	3	0	11	0	0
Phillips, Jason, Alt.	0	1	.000	10.00	6	1	0	0	2	0	9.0	18	48	11	10	0	0	0	1	4	0	4	2	0
Phillips, Jason, Akr.	2	1	.667	4.13	10	3	0	0	1	0	24.0	18	102	11	11	2	0	2	1	15	0	20	2	0
Tucker, Julien, Erie	1	5	.167	4.93	23	0	0	0	5	0	45.2	52	217	30	25	2	3	4	2	30	2	21	5	0
Tucker, Julien, Akr.	0	1	.000	9.72	5	1	0	0	3	0	8.1	10	39	9	9	0	0	0	1	5	0	6	2	0
Walker, Adam, Read.*	7	4	.636	1.88	15	15	3	3	0	0	91.0	50	351	22	19	2	1	0	6	28	0	81	6	0
Walker, Adam, Bing.*	0	0	.000	0.00	2	2	0	0	0	0	4.0	3	17	0	0	0	0	0	0	2	0	7	0	0

COMBINATION SHUTOUTS: **Akron (8)**—Day-Bullinger, Drese-Baez-Rodriguez-Vargas, Drese-Johnson-Vargas, Phillips-Hooten-Radinsky-Vargas, Shuey-Sido-Johnson-Vargas, Finley-Sexton-Watson, Hooten-Reinike-Herrera, Stanford-Deschenes. **Altoona (5)**—Williams-Garcia-Guy, Reid-Donaldson-Carrasco-Chrysler-Paz, Camp-Diorio-Spurling-Pavlovich, Gonzalez-Carrasco-Pavlovich, Alvarado-Spurling, Grabow-Carrasco. **Binghamton (9)**—Saenz-Moreno-Vega, Maness-Corey, Saenz-Della Ratta-Corey, Wall-Roach-Montane, Jones-Walker-Vega, Traber-Cerda, Walker-Saenz, Maness-Braswell, Braswell-Lohrman. **Bowie (6)**—Stephens-Babula, Paradis-Eibey-Sims-Rakers, Felix-Brown-Julio, Paradis-Brown-Babula-Rakers, Stephens-Rakers, Stephens-Rakers. **Erie (8)**—Kalita-Tucker-Pearson, Leek-Tucker-Heams, Kalita-Buller, Cornejo-Pearson, Leek-Heams, Kirsten-Eckenstahler, Cornejo-Rivera-Pearson, Phelps-Kirsten-Eckenstahler-Rodney. **Harrisburg (4)**—Tucker-Agamennone-Serrano, Tucker-Serrano, Manon-Chapman-Albin-Andrews-Serrano, Davis-Chapman-Serrano. **New Britain (9)**—Thomas-Nakamura-Rivera, Lohse-Rincon-Rivera, Mills-Carnes-Nakamura, Pumphrey-Carnes-Frederick-Balfour, Carnes-Balfour, McDonald-Frederick-Balfour, Pumphrey-Frederick, McDonald-Balfour-Nakamura, Flohr-Frederick-Rivera. **New Haven (7)**—Pearce-Daniels-Lambert, Pearce-Lambert, Hackman-Stocks-Crudale, Pearce-Daniels-Lambert, Stemle-Crudale, Stemle-Crudale, Franks-Crudale. **Norwich (10)**—Jodie-Marte-Blevins, Flores-Lovingier-Pacheco, Bradley-Lovingier-Pacheco, Claussen-Lovingier-Pacheco, Flores-Lovingier, Aldred-Pacheco, Graman-Blevins, Rogers-Pacheco, Graman-Johnson, Claussen-Blevins-Jean. **Portland (10)**—Bump-Moskau-Henderson, Vargas-Moskau, Tejera-Rodgers-Henderson, Olsen-Henderson, Tejera-Henderson-Neal, Beckett-McClaskey-Edmondson, Beckett-Bowe-Scheffer, Beckett-Scheffer-Clark, Izquierdo-Bowe-Scheffer, Beckett-McClaskey-Moskau-Scheffer. **Reading (7)**—Kershner-Wedel-Outlaw, Silva-Serrano-Hiles-Outlaw, Geary-Bailie-Wedel, Chen-Geary-Wedel, Silva-Serrano-Geary, Myers-Serrano, Myers-Serrano-Wedel. **Trenton (8)**—Norton-McLeary-Betancourt, Kusiewicz-McLeary-Betancourt, Fossum-Spencer, Duchscherer-McLeary-Leach, Duchscherer-Florie, Florie-Kusiewicz-Spencer, Elmore-Hill-De la Rosa-Cisar, Ebert-De la Rosa.

NO-HIT GAMES: A. Walker, Reading defeated New Haven 4-0, June 13; Stephens, Bowie defeated Harrisburg 2-0, July 31; Walrond, New Haven defeated Portland 3-2, August 11; Journell, New Haven defeated Bowie 3-0, September 2.

2001 FIELDING

TEAM

Team	Pct.	G	PO	A	E	TC	DP	TP	PB
Portland	.980	142	3771	1317	105	5193	108	0	6
Akron	.978	142	3707	1518	120	5345	131	0	23
Reading	.974	142	3743	1504	139	5386	114	0	19
Harrisburg	.972	142	3672	1349	144	5165	120	0	16
New Britain	.972	142	3805	1523	153	5481	115	0	8
Altoona	.972	142	3737	1513	153	5403	126	1	18
Erie	.971	142	3707	1452	155	5314	114	0	12
Binghamton	.971	141	3695	1557	159	5411	150	0	11
New Haven	.970	142	3689	1434	157	5280	128	0	21
Trenton	.970	142	3698	1426	158	5282	121	0	24
Bowie	.968	141	3684	1422	167	5273	109	0	18
Norwich	.962	142	3760	1337	204	5301	107	0	26

INDIVIDUAL

FIRST BASEMEN

NOTE: All caps denotes fielding-percentage leader based on 71 games for catchers, 95 for all other non-pitchers and 114 innings for pitchers. *Throws lefthanded.

Player, Team	Pct.	G	PO	A	E	TC	DP
Abbott, Chuck, Akr.	1.000	1	11	1	0	12	0
Bailey, Jeff, Port.	.989	96	737	48	9	794	46
Bailey, Travis, N.H.	1.000	2	12	0	0	12	0
Baker, Derek, Erie	.964	3	25	2	1	28	0
Burnham, Gary, Read.*	.999	79	671	45	1	717	64
Casillas, Uriel, Read.	1.000	1	12	1	0	13	0
Cervenak, Mike, Nor.	.980	30	223	19	5	247	16
Chevalier, Virgil, Tren.	.989	79	582	55	7	644	52
Cotton, John, Har.	.857	3	10	2	2	14	0
Cuddyer, Michael, N.B.	.984	57	467	32	8	507	46

Player, Team	Pct.	G	PO	A	E	TC	DP
DiPace, Danny, Tren.	.800	3	12	0	3	15	1
Dominique, Andy, Read.	.972	10	97	6	3	106	7
Edwards, Mike, Akr.	.994	19	147	8	1	156	17
Emmons, Scott, Nor.	1.000	3	6	1	0	7	0
Erickson, Corey, Akr.	1.000	10	60	8	0	68	3
Evans, Lee, Alt.	.979	7	45	2	1	48	6
Farnsworth, Troy, N.H.	.990	27	184	10	2	196	22
FIGUEROA, Franky, Bow.	.992	120	969	84	8	1061	71
Freire, Alejandro, Erie	.980	10	92	6	2	100	6
Fuentes, Javier, Har.	1.000	1	1	0	0	1	0
Garcia, Guillermo, N.H.	1.000	1	8	0	0	8	1
Garcia, Luis, Tren.	.990	57	446	32	5	483	49
Gibbs, Mark, Bow.	.000	1	0	0	0	0	0
Gillespie, Eric, Port.	.993	21	125	13	1	139	19
Goelz, Jim, Akr.	1.000	1	1	0	0	1	0
Goodell, Steve, Bow.	1.000	11	101	6	0	107	7
Grindell, Nate, Akr.	1.000	15	128	9	0	137	10
Hammond, Joey, Bow.	1.000	1	1	0	0	1	0
Haverbusch, Kevin, Alt.	.966	6	28	0	1	29	5
House, J.R., Alt.	.990	12	100	3	1	104	8
Huff, B.J., Bing.	1.000	1	1	0	0	1	0
Kelly, Heath, Port.	.000	1	0	0	0	0	0
Leach, Nick, Nor.	.988	53	377	18	5	400	35
Leon, Donny, Nor.	.965	12	50	5	2	57	3
Marcinczyk, T.R., N.B.	1.000	3	23	0	0	23	3
Martinez, Gabby, Bing.	1.000	1	2	0	0	2	0
McNamara, Rusty, Read.	.000	1	0	0	0	0	0
McNeal, Aaron, Bing.	.987	59	484	47	7	538	60
Meier, Dan, Alt.*	.992	35	231	17	2	250	18
Morneau, Justin, N.B.	1.000	7	63	4	0	67	2
Mosquera, Julio, Nor.	1.000	1	1	0	0	1	1
Munoz, Billy, Akr.*	.997	32	278	22	1	301	16
Munoz, Juan, N.H.*	.988	123	1001	58	13	1072	92
Munson, Eric, Erie	.905	129	1031	93	17	1141	94
Nicholson, Derek, Erie	1.000	1	4	0	0	4	1
Nunnari, Talmadge, Har.*	1.000	3	24	2	0	26	3
Nye, Rodney, Bing.	1.000	5	24	2	0	26	4
Ortiz, David, N.B.*	1.000	9	78	4	0	82	9
Ottavinia, Paul, Nor.*	.993	48	364	39	3	406	33
Pascucci, Val, Har.	.992	19	110	8	1	119	5
Peterman, Tommy, N.B.*	.993	76	608	63	5	676	44
Pond, Simon, Akr.	.996	75	641	29	3	673	60
Restovich, Michael, N.B.	1.000	2	1	1	0	2	1
Rivera, Carlos, Alt.*	.989	100	863	48	10	921	80
Roberge, J.P., Read.	.994	21	157	10	1	168	9
Rodriguez, Luis, Tren.	1.000	3	22	2	0	24	3
Rolison, Nate, Port.	1.000	4	28	2	0	30	4
Roneberg, Brett, Port.*	1.000	1	10	1	0	11	1
Rose, Pete, Read.	1.000	1	2	0	0	2	0
Rust, Brian, Bow.	1.000	9	69	8	0	77	6
Salzano, Jerry, Tren.	.857	3	18	0	3	21	1
Sandusky, Scott, Har.	1.000	7	37	4	0	41	3
Seabol, Scott, Nor.	.893	4	23	2	3	28	1
Sledge, Terrmel, Har.*	.985	120	887	74	15	976	90
Smith, Bubba, Port.	.991	27	218	15	2	235	20
Smith, Casey, Akr.	1.000	1	2	1	0	3	0
Snusz, Chris, Nor.	.947	5	34	2	2	38	3
Snyder, Earl, Bing.	.989	83	733	52	9	794	67
Stoner, Mike, Alt.	1.000	3	17	2	0	19	1
Treanor, Matt, Port.	.000	1	0	0	0	0	0
Ullery, Dave, Bow.	.978	5	40	4	1	45	3
Van Iten, Bobby, Read.	.991	40	304	25	3	332	25
Wathan, Dusty, Port.	1.000	6	22	2	0	24	1

TRIPLE PLAYS: L. Garcia, Rivera.

SECOND BASEMEN

Player, Team	Pct.	G	PO	A	E	TC	DP
Abbott, Chuck, Akr.	.958	12	14	32	2	48	9
Ahumada, Alex, Tren.	.846	2	5	6	2	13	0
Alvarez, Tony, Alt.	1.000	1	1	0	0	1	0
Benefield, Brian, Akr.	.957	10	23	21	2	46	5
Borrego, Ramon, N.B.	.988	26	44	38	1	83	10
Bowers, Jason, N.H.	.000	1	0	0	0	0	0
Bruce, Mo, Har.-Alt.	.979	38	79	108	4	191	31
Capista, Aaron, Tren.	.962	6	14	11	1	26	6
Casillas, Uriel, Read.	.944	9	10	24	2	36	3
Cervenak, Mike, Nor.	.951	27	62	35	5	102	12
Clapinski, Chris, Port.	1.000	1	2	2	0	4	0
De Leon, Jorge, Tren.	1.000	2	2	3	0	5	1
Del Rosario, Manny, Bow.	.789	7	6	9	4	19	2
Eckelman, Alex, N.H.	.965	58	106	139	9	254	34
Erickson, Corey, Akr.	.975	12	21	18	1	40	4
Fuentes, Javier, Har.	.714	1	2	3	2	7	1

Player, Team	Pct.	G	PO	A	E	TC	DP
Gibbs, Mark, Bow.	.963	20	32	46	3	81	11
Goelz, Jim, Akr.	.911	17	24	27	5	56	10
Gonzalez, Luis, Akr.	.987	48	106	117	3	226	32
Goodell, Steve, Bow.	.714	2	1	4	2	7	0
Hammond, Joey, Bow.	1.000	2	3	2	0	5	1
Harris, Brian, Read.	.984	75	147	230	6	383	40
Harris, Willie, Bow.	.979	90	212	212	9	433	56
Haverbusch, Kevin, Alt.	.958	25	51	63	5	119	13
Hernandez, Carlos, Bing.	.978	65	128	184	7	319	57
Hitchcox, Brian, Read.	1.000	2	3	4	0	7	2
Hodge, Kevin, N.B.	1.000	14	16	21	0	37	5
HOOPER, Kevin, Port.	.986	117	231	257	7	495	63
Jackson, Brandon, Nor.	.957	11	23	22	2	47	7
Kelly, Heath, Port.	.947	10	8	10	1	19	2
LaRocca, Greg, Akr.	.900	2	5	4	1	10	1
Leon, Carlos, Tren.	.833	1	3	2	1	6	1
Lofton, James, Tren.	.960	7	12	12	1	25	3
Lopez-Cao, Mike, Bow.	1.000	1	0	2	0	2	0
Lopez, Mickey, Read.	.991	48	93	133	2	228	22
Lorenzo, Juan, N.B.	.919	6	11	23	3	37	4
Machado, Albenis, Har.	.966	81	150	162	11	323	48
Maier, T.J., N.H.	.986	72	139	213	5	357	52
Mann, Derek, Alt.	.800	1	3	1	1	5	0
Martin, Justin, Alt.	.978	30	59	73	3	135	9
Martinez, Eddy, Bow.	.976	8	16	25	1	42	3
Martinez, Gabby, Bing.	.982	12	21	33	1	55	6
McClure, Brian, Erie	.978	29	56	80	3	139	19
McNaughton, Troy, N.H.*	.000	1	0	0	0	0	0
Melucci, Lou, Har.	1.000	2	0	1	0	1	0
Merrill, Ronnie, Erie	.958	32	61	75	6	142	20
Miller, Ryan, Bing.	1.000	4	4	10	0	14	1
Myers, Tootie, Har.*	.938	32	40	65	7	112	14
Niles, Drew, Port.	.972	21	44	62	3	109	12
Nunez, Jose, N.H.	1.000	2	1	2	0	3	1
Paz, Rich, Alt.	.973	48	96	124	6	226	29
Perez, Jhonny, Erie	.972	83	156	219	11	386	48
Petersen, Chris, Alt.	.976	20	59	61	3	123	17
Phillips, Andy, Nor.	.915	47	92	91	17	200	20
Phillips, Brandon, Har.	1.000	1	2	2	0	4	0
Piatt, Scott, Akr.	.964	55	98	145	9	250	21
Reding, Josh, Har.	1.000	10	14	11	0	25	2
Roberge, J.P., Read.	.948	16	21	34	3	58	8
Roberts, Brian, Bow.	.966	21	30	54	3	87	9
Rodriguez, Victor, Nor.	.981	57	79	130	4	213	23
Salazar, Ruben, N.B.	.962	115	183	299	19	501	60
Santos, Angel, Tren.	.966	127	274	273	19	566	81
Saylor, Jamie, Bing.	.990	23	42	61	1	104	19
Tamargo, John, Bing.	.984	28	55	67	2	124	13
Terhune, Mike, Bing.	1.000	4	5	6	0	11	1
Thames, Damon, N.H.	.966	21	29	28	2	59	8
Tillman, Kevin, Akr.	1.000	2	3	3	0	6	1
Tyson, Torre, Nor.	.960	14	21	27	2	50	9
Velazquez, Gil, Bing.	1.000	11	23	37	0	60	9
Washington, Rico, Alt.	.936	23	54	48	7	109	13
Wehner, John, Alt.	1.000	1	5	5	0	10	2
Wigginton, Ty, Bing.	.813	5	5	8	3	16	1
Zech, Scott, Har.	.947	11	20	16	2	38	3

TRIPLE PLAY: Santos.

SECOND BASEMEN WITH TWO OR MORE TEAMS

Player, Team	Pct.	G	PO	A	E	TC	DP
Bruce, Mo, Har.	.978	30	56	79	3	138	24
Bruce, Mo, Alt.	.981	8	23	29	1	53	7

THIRD BASEMEN

Player, Team	Pct.	G	PO	A	E	TC	DP
Abbott, Chuck, Akr.	1.000	1	2	0	0	2	0
Ahumada, Alex, Tren.	1.000	2	3	11	0	14	2
Bailey, Travis, N.H.	.898	22	10	43	6	59	2
Batson, Tom, Read.	1.000	6	2	8	0	10	2
Benefield, Brian, Akr.	1.000	11	2	15	0	17	1
Borrego, Ramon, N.B.	.842	10	8	8	3	19	0
Brown, Derek, Bow.	1.000	1	2	2	0	4	0
Bruce, Mo, Har.-Alt.	.957	17	12	10	1	23	1
Capista, Aaron, Tren.	.894	39	20	81	12	113	5
Casillas, Uriel, Read.	.922	81	55	157	18	230	13
Casimiro, Carlos, Bow.	.931	65	46	130	13	189	11
Cervenak, Mike, Nor.	.942	40	21	77	6	104	2
Chapman, Travis, Read.	1.000	5	1	9	0	10	1
Clapinski, Chris, Port.	1.000	2	1	5	0	6	0
Cotton, John, Har.	1.000	2	0	3	0	3	0
Cruz, Deivi, Erie	1.000	2	1	6	0	7	0
Cuddyer, Michael, N.B.	.922	81	46	166	18	230	14

CLASS AA *Eastern League*

Player, Team	Pct.	G	PO	A	E	TC	DP
De Leon, Jorge, Tren.	.987	26	19	55	1	75	3
Dominique, Andy, Read.	.944	4	3	14	1	18	2
Eckelman, Alex, N.H.	.975	34	18	60	2	80	9
Edwards, Mike, Akr.	.885	9	7	16	3	26	1
ERICKSON, Corey, Akr.	.950	116	79	223	16	318	28
Evans, Lee, Alt.	.868	30	22	37	9	68	3
Farnsworth, Troy, N.H.	.937	93	68	185	17	270	13
Figueroa, Franky, Bow.	.857	5	1	5	1	7	0
Fuentes, Javier, Har.	.840	11	10	11	4	25	0
Gibbs, Mark, Bow.	.826	8	8	11	4	23	1
Gillespie, Eric, Port.	.944	18	6	28	2	36	0
Goelz, Jim, Akr.	.909	7	3	7	1	11	0
Gonzalez, Luis, Akr.	1.000	1	0	2	0	2	0
Grindell, Nate, Akr.	1.000	4	3	7	0	10	2
Hammond, Joey, Bow.	.951	16	8	31	2	41	3
Harris, Brian, Read.	1.000	5	4	14	0	18	0
Henson, Drew, Nor.	.842	5	8	8	3	19	0
Hodge, Kevin, N.B.	.889	17	9	31	5	45	0
Hodges, Scott, Har.	.918	76	54	137	17	208	11
Honeycutt, Heath, Port.	.945	125	77	217	17	311	20
Kelly, Heath, Port.	1.000	3	0	2	0	2	0
Langston, James, Alt.	.942	28	22	43	4	69	3
LaRocca, Greg, Akr.	.950	6	6	13	1	20	0
Leon, Donny, Nor.	.867	63	47	103	23	173	10
Leon, Jose, Bow.	.879	24	18	33	7	58	3
Lofton, James, Tren.	.913	10	5	16	2	23	2
Lopez-Cao, Mike, Bow.	.600	3	1	2	2	5	0
Lorenzo, Juan, N.B.	.938	46	17	103	8	128	10
Machado, Albenis, Har.	1.000	4	0	8	0	8	0
Martin, Justin, Alt.	.800	1	2	2	1	5	0
Martinez, Eddy, Bow.	.927	16	9	29	3	41	3
Martinez, Gabby, Bing.	1.000	3	3	10	0	13	2
McClure, Brian, Erie	.952	35	19	60	4	83	4
McGee, Tom, Bow.	1.000	2	1	0	0	1	0
Melucci, Lou, Har.	1.000	4	3	6	0	9	0
Miller, Ryan, Bing.	.846	4	3	8	2	13	2
Morales, Andy, Nor.	.960	25	20	28	2	50	3
Nettles, Jeff, Nor.	.833	4	0	5	1	6	0
Nicholson, Derek, Erie	.667	3	0	2	1	3	0
Niles, Drew, Port.	.889	7	6	10	2	18	2
Nunez, Jose, N.H.	.875	10	1	6	1	8	1
Nye, Rodney, Bing.	.927	107	61	230	23	314	26
Patterson, Jarrod, Erie.	.920	20	14	32	4	50	3
Paz, Rich, Alt.	.893	30	20	47	8	75	4
Petersen, Chris, Alt.	.955	8	9	12	1	22	1
Phillips, Brandon, Har.	1.000	1	0	1	0	1	0
Pond, Simon, Alt.	1.000	3	1	3	0	4	0
Reding, Josh, Har.	.940	35	28	51	5	84	9
Roberge, J.P., Read.	.888	40	25	62	11	98	1
Rodriguez, Luis, Tren.	.875	7	2	12	2	16	3
Rose, Pete, Read.	.714	7	6	9	6	21	1
Rust, Brian, Bow.	.880	10	5	17	3	25	1
Salazar, Ruben, N.B.	.867	6	4	9	2	15	0
Salzano, Jerry, Tren.	.905	68	46	135	19	200	16
Saylor, Jamie, Bing.	.880	11	4	18	3	25	0
Seabol, Scott, Nor.	.875	25	10	39	7	56	2
Smith, Bubba, Port.	.000	1	0	0	0	0	0
Snyder, Earl, Bing.	1.000	18	8	27	0	35	5
Tamargo, John, Bing.	1.000	9	4	7	0	11	0
Thames, Damon, N.H.	1.000	2	0	1	0	1	0
Ullery, Dave, Bow.	1.000	4	2	4	0	6	0
Ust, Brant, Erie	.949	87	47	158	11	216	15
Van Iten, Bobby, Read.	.875	4	0	7	1	8	0
Washington, Rico, Alt.	.953	49	39	102	7	148	6
Wathan, Dusty, Port.	1.000	1	1	0	0	1	0
Wehner, John, Alt.	1.000	1	1	0	0	1	0
Wigginton, Ty, Bing.	1.000	3	2	5	0	7	0
Zech, Scott, Har.	.956	17	12	31	2	45	3

THIRD BASEMEN WITH TWO OR MORE TEAMS

Player, Team	Pct.	G	PO	A	E	TC	DP
Bruce, Mo, Har.	1.000	15	11	9	0	20	1
Bruce, Mo, Alt.	.667	2	1	1	1	3	0

SHORTSTOPS

Player, Team	Pct.	G	PO	A	E	TC	DP
Abbott, Chuck, Akr.	1.000	3	3	3	0	6	0
Almonte, Erick, Nor.	.900	3	4	5	1	10	1
Basak, Chris, Bing.	1.000	12	12	40	0	52	9
Benefield, Brian, Akr.	1.000	8	11	18	0	29	2
Borrego, Ramon, N.B.	.920	23	27	42	6	75	12
Bowers, Jason, N.H.	.930	130	191	366	42	599	79
Bruce, Mo, Har.	1.000	1	2	1	0	3	1

Player, Team	Pct.	G	PO	A	E	TC	DP
Capista, Aaron, Tren.	.954	78	113	199	15	327	37
Casillas, Uriel, Read.	.943	18	37	46	5	88	15
Casimiro, Carlos, Bow.	.857	2	2	4	1	7	1
Cervenak, Mike, Nor.	.955	18	18	24	2	44	5
Clapinski, Chris, Port.	1.000	1	4	2	0	6	0
Cruz, Deivi, Erie	.857	3	3	3	1	7	0
De Leon, Jorge, Tren.	1.000	2	2	8	0	10	0
Eckelman, Alex, N.H.	1.000	13	10	24	0	34	7
Gibbs, Mark, Bow.	.857	3	3	3	1	7	1
Goelz, Jim, Akr.	.961	58	97	150	10	257	31
Gonzalez, Luis, Akr.	1.000	2	3	4	0	7	0
Hammond, Joey, Bow.	.957	78	106	204	14	324	36
Harris, Brian, Read.	.952	55	95	161	13	269	29
Hernandez, Carlos, Bing.	.778	2	3	4	2	9	1
Hitchcox, Brian, Read.	1.000	7	10	15	0	25	4
Hodge, Kevin, N.B.	.887	15	20	43	8	71	6
Infante, Omar, Erie	.955	132	206	370	27	603	71
Kelly, Heath, Port.	1.000	1	1	1	0	2	0
Lackey, Steve, Akr.	.925	10	17	32	4	53	5
LaRocca, Greg, Akr.	.944	25	32	69	6	107	10
Leon, Carlos, Tren.	.935	11	10	19	2	31	5
Lofton, James, Tren.	.964	12	22	31	2	55	9
Lopez, Mickey, Read.	.918	36	56	78	12	146	12
Lorenzo, Juan, N.B.	.948	53	64	117	10	191	18
Machado, Albenis, Har.	.931	16	19	35	4	58	8
Machado, Andy, Read.	.941	30	49	95	9	153	16
Martinez, Eddy, Bow.	.880	9	5	17	3	25	3
Martinez, Gabby, Bing.	.900	9	16	29	5	50	5
McClure, Brian, Erie	1.000	6	7	14	0	21	3
Merrill, Ronnie, Erie.	1.000	6	10	19	0	29	4
Miller, Ryan, Bing.	.939	8	9	22	2	33	7
Nettles, Jeff, Nor.	1.000	1	0	1	0	1	0
Niles, Drew, Port.	.981	26	37	64	2	103	15
Nunez, Jose, N.H.	.900	7	8	10	2	20	4
Olivares, Teuris, Nor.	.932	128	184	324	37	545	61
Paz, Rich, Alt.	1.000	6	8	12	0	20	2
Petersen, Chris, Alt.	.906	10	11	18	3	32	3
Phillips, Brandon, Har.	.957	66	105	165	12	282	31
Pratt, Scott, Akr.	.889	3	3	5	1	9	1
Reding, Josh, Har.	.961	71	123	173	12	308	37
Roberts, Brian, Bow.	1.000	1	1	5	0	6	1
Rogers, Ed, Bow.	.960	53	90	147	10	247	20
Sanchez, Freddy, Tren.	.948	44	55	110	9	174	26
Saylor, Jamie, Bing.	.923	11	8	28	3	39	2
Skrehot, Shaun, Alt.	.951	113	190	350	28	568	73
Sorensen, Zach, Akr.	.956	45	77	140	10	227	28
Stevens, Tony, N.B.	.952	72	94	203	15	312	35
Tamargo, John, Bing.	.960	10	16	32	2	50	4
Thames, Damon, N.H.	.917	5	3	8	1	12	2
Tyson, Torre, Nor.	.815	7	6	16	5	27	2
Valentin, John, Tren.	.917	3	3	8	1	12	0
Velazquez, Gil, Bing.	.942	94	150	273	26	449	65
Washington, Rico, Alt.	.000	1	0	0	0	0	0
WATHAN, Derek, Port.	.973	125	176	297	13	486	48
Wehner, John, Alt.	.962	18	26	50	3	79	8
Zech, Scott, Har.	1.000	3	2	5	0	7	1

TRIPLE PLAYS: Capista, Skrehot.

OUTFIELDERS

Player, Team	Pct.	G	PO	A	E	TC	DP
Abbott, Jeff, Port.*	1.000	7	9	0	0	9	0
Aguila, Chris, Port.	.969	64	93	2	3	98	2
Airoso, Kurt, Erie	.981	80	145	6	3	154	1
Alvarado, Carlos, Alt.	.000	1	0	0	0	0	0
Alvarez, Tony, Alt.	.968	65	112	8	4	124	0
Bailey, Jeff, Port.	.944	15	16	1	1	18	0
Bailey, Travis, N.H.	1.000	3	3	0	0	3	0
Barns, B.J., Alt.*	.948	30	71	2	4	77	1
Bass, Jayson, Alt.	.962	49	74	2	3	79	0
Bates, Fletcher, Read.	.923	14	10	2	1	13	0
Benefield, Brian, Akr.	.958	16	21	2	1	24	1
Bevins, Andy, N.H.	.978	82	132	4	3	139	1
Bigbie, Larry, Bow.*	.972	70	136	4	4	144	1
Blakely, Darren, Nor.	1.000	6	12	0	0	12	0
Bolivar, Papo, N.B.	1.000	20	23	0	0	23	0
Bost, Tom, Akr.	.982	28	54	2	1	57	0
Briggs, Stoney, Bow.	1.000	30	50	0	0	50	0
Brown, Tonayne, Tren.*	.985	109	191	10	3	204	1
Burton, Darren, Alt.	.980	74	142	5	3	150	0
BYRD, Marlon, Read.	.994	134	304	6	2	312	1
Calloway, Ron, Har.*	.969	63	121	6	4	131	0
Camilo, Juan, Erie	.955	32	62	1	3	66	0
Candelaria, Ben, Port.	.958	26	41	5	2	48	0

OUTFIELDERS

Player, Team	Pct.	G	PO	A	E	TC	DP
Casimiro, Carlos, Bow.	.941	15	16	0	1	17	0
Cepicky, Matt, Har.	.986	104	199	8	3	210	0
Chevalier, Virgil, Tren.	.982	26	50	5	1	56	1
Clemente, Edgard, Tren.	1.000	11	29	1	0	30	0
Cotton, John, Har.	.000	1	0	0	0	0	0
Cuddyer, Michael, N.B.	.920	19	22	1	2	25	0
Curry, Mike, Bing.	.991	98	221	4	2	227	2
Davis, J.J., Alt.	1.000	62	110	1	0	111	0
Depippo, Jeff, Akr.	.846	6	11	0	2	13	0
Diaz, Miguel, N.H.	.942	31	47	2	3	52	0
Dina, Allen, Bing.	.970	68	123	7	4	134	1
Dishington, Nate, N.H.	.978	28	44	1	1	46	0
Eckelman, Alex, N.H.	1.000	20	24	1	0	25	0
Evans, Lee, Alt.	1.000	26	32	4	0	36	0
Fischer, Mark, Tren.	.987	120	215	7	3	225	2
Fitzgerald, Jason, Akr.*	.991	55	112	0	1	113	0
Ford, Lew, N.B.	.974	60	108	5	3	116	0
Foster, Quincy, Port.	.975	60	76	3	2	81	1
Freire, Alejandro, Erie	.971	18	33	0	1	34	0
Gazarek, Marty, Erie	.938	28	45	0	3	48	0
Gillespie, Eric, Port.	.952	25	36	4	2	42	1
Gingrich, Troy, Har.*	.875	6	7	0	1	8	0
Goelz, Jim, Akr.	1.000	13	27	1	0	28	0
Gomez, Ramon, Read.	.966	29	55	1	2	58	0
Gomez, Rich, Erie	.966	92	163	6	6	175	0
Gonzalez, Manny, Read.	.973	61	99	8	3	110	0
Goodell, Steve, Bow.	1.000	3	1	0	0	1	0
Graham, Jess, Tren.*	.965	42	52	3	2	57	0
Green, Chad, Akr.	.975	36	71	6	2	79	2
Green, Scarborough, Alt.-N.H.	.994	71	160	8	1	169	0
Grindell, Nate, Akr.	.902	40	70	5	3	78	2
Haas, Danny, Tren.	1.000	12	15	2	0	17	0
Hackett, Richard, Bow.	1.000	3	9	0	0	9	0
Hamilton, Jon, Akr.*	.978	133	209	17	5	231	5
Hammond, Joey, Bow.	.000	1	0	0	0	0	0
Harris, Willie, Bow.	.950	41	101	8	5	114	0
Haverbusch, Kevin, Alt.	1.000	4	5	1	0	6	0
Hernandez, Jesus, Akr.*	1.000	1	2	0	0	2	0
Hiles, Cary, Read.	.000	1	0	0	0	0	0
Huff, B.J., Bing.	1.000	4	3	0	0	3	0
Hunter, Scott, Bing.	.933	53	81	3	6	90	1
James, Kenny, Har.	1.000	20	35	1	0	36	0
Jenkins, Brian, Akr.	1.000	6	6	0	0	6	0
Johnson, Jason, Read.	.972	63	98	8	3	109	1
Johnson, Rontrez, Tren.	.964	72	156	3	6	165	0
Jones, Jaime, Port.*	.959	23	45	2	2	49	0
Kelly, Heath, Port.	.000	1	0	0	0	0	0
Keylor, Cory, Bow.	1.000	3	2	0	0	2	0
Kill, Skip, Nor.	1.000	6	8	0	0	8	0
Krause, Scott, Akr.	.974	42	70	5	2	77	0
Lankford, Derrick, Alt.	1.000	4	3	1	0	4	1
Leon, Donny, Nor.	1.000	1	1	0	0	1	0
LeBron, Juan, Bing.	.962	95	173	5	7	185	1
Lindsey, Rodney, Erie	.982	111	258	11	5	274	4
Loggins, Josh, Nor.	.963	40	77	2	3	82	0
Lopez, Mickey, Read.	.962	20	24	1	1	26	1
Maddox, Garry, Tren.	.963	47	72	6	3	81	0
Malave, Dennis, Akr.*	1.000	4	7	1	0	8	0
Martin, Justin, Alt.	.976	29	40	1	1	42	0
Matos, Luis, Bow.	.955	9	20	1	1	22	1
McClure, Brian, Erie	1.000	2	1	0	0	1	0
McDonald, Darnell, Bow.	.968	30	59	1	2	62	0
McNaughton, Troy, N.H.*	.988	99	161	8	2	171	1
Meier, Dan, Alt.*	.985	52	78	4	2	84	0
Mohr, Dustan, N.B.	.978	133	261	9	6	276	1
Monahan, Shane, Alt.	.967	19	28	1	1	30	0
Munoz, Juan, N.H.*	.000	1	0	0	0	0	0
Myers, Tootie, Har.*	.983	77	168	8	3	179	2
Nadeau, Rick, Tren.	1.000	3	8	0	0	8	0
Ndungidi, Ntema, Bow.	.933	64	110	1	8	119	1
Nettles, Jeff, Nor.	1.000	2	3	0	0	3	0
Nicholson, Derek, Erie	.941	20	31	1	2	34	0
Niles, Drew, Port.	.000	1	0	0	0	0	0
Nunez, Abraham, Port.	.976	134	315	13	8	336	1
Nunnari, Talmadge, Har.*	.900	3	8	1	1	10	0
Ottavinia, Paul, Nor.*	1.000	30	48	1	0	49	1
Pascucci, Val, Har.	.978	119	220	7	5	232	2
Perez, Josue, Read.	.972	48	99	5	3	107	1
Phoenix, Wynter, Port.-Bow.*	.944	90	178	9	11	198	0
Pond, Simon, Akr.	.818	8	9	0	2	11	0
Pratt, Scott, Akr.	1.000	8	16	0	0	16	0
Raines, Tim, Bow.	.976	65	159	6	4	169	4
Randolph, Jaisen, Bing.	1.000	8	15	0	0	15	0
Reding, Josh, Har.	1.000	5	4	3	0	7	0
Reed, Keith, Bow.	1.000	18	40	3	0	43	0
Restovich, Michael, N.B.	.989	140	257	8	3	268	1
Rivera, Carlos, Alt.*	.000	1	0	0	0	0	0
Rivera, Juan, Nor.	.963	76	141	16	6	163	4
Roberge, J.P., Read.	.939	19	30	1	2	33	1
Roberts, Dave, Akr.*	.969	12	31	0	1	32	0
Rodriguez, John, Nor.*	.976	101	153	9	4	166	0
Rodriguez, Luis, Tren.	1.000	6	8	0	0	8	0
Roneberg, Brett, Port.*	1.000	46	51	2	0	53	1
Royster, Aaron, Read.	.984	35	59	4	1	64	0
Ruan, Wilken, Nor.	.976	28	81	2	2	85	0
Rust, Brian, Bow.	1.000	8	9	0	0	9	0
Santana, Osmany, Akr.*	.960	11	23	1	1	25	0
Saturria, Luis, N.H.	.846	8	11	0	2	13	0
Caylon, Jamie, Bing.	.000	2	0	0	0	0	0
Seabol, Scott, Nor.	.750	4	3	0	1	4	0
Secrist, Reed, Alt.	1.000	1	3	0	0	3	0
Skrehot, Shaun, Alt.	1.000	6	11	1	0	12	0
Sledge, Terrmel, Har.*	1.000	3	5	0	0	5	0
Smith, Jeff, N.B.	1.000	2	1	0	0	1	0
Smith, Nestor, N.B.	.991	72	102	4	1	107	0
Snead, Esix, N.H.	.983	132	347	10	6	363	4
Snyder, Earl, Bing.	1.000	8	8	0	0	8	0
Stoner, Mike, Alt.	1.000	21	29	0	0	29	0
Stratton, Rob, Bing.	.975	110	184	14	5	203	3
Thames, Marcus, Nor.	.973	137	277	7	8	292	0
Torres, Andres, Erie	.993	55	136	3	1	140	1
Tyson, Torre, Nor.	.968	42	86	4	3	93	0
Van Iten, Bobby, Read.	.923	32	36	0	3	39	0
Ware, Jeremy, Har.	1.000		45	3	0	48	2
Wehner, John, Alt.	1.000	4	8	0	0	8	0
Whitaker, Chad, Akr.	1.000	35	48	3	0	51	0
Wilcox, Luke, Port.	.963	42	74	3	3	80	1

OUTFIELDERS WITH TWO OR MORE TEAMS

Player, Team	Pct.	G	PO	A	E	TC	DP
Green, Scarborough, Alt.	.983	25	56	3	1	60	0
Green, Scarborough, N.H.	1.000	46	104	5	0	109	0
Phoenix, Wynter, Port.*	.920	14	22	1	2	25	0
Phoenix, Wynter, Bow.*	.948	76	156	8	9	173	0

CATCHERS

Player, Team	Pct.	G	PO	A	E	TC	DP	PB
Alley, Chuck, Bow.	.967	16	109	9	4	122	1	1
Amezcua, Adan, Bow.	.982	27	192	22	4	218	3	6
Bailey, Jeff, Port.	1.000	7	7	0	0	7	0	0
Bard, Josh, Akr.	.986	43	255	36	4	295	2	2
Benham, Dave, N.H.	.984	27	172	15	3	190	1	5
Bennett, Ryan, Bing.	1.000	2	11	0	0	11	0	0
Brown, Jason, Port.	.983	16	111	3	2	116	0	0
Carreno, Jose, Har.	.989	37	252	22	3	277	2	7
Chevalier, Virgil, Tren.	1.000	1	6	0	0	6	0	1
Coste, Chris, Akr.	.977	5	35	7	1	43	2	2
Depippo, Jeff, Akr.	.989	64	395	46	5	446	3	15
Dominique, Andy, Read.	.990	51	358	44	4	406	0	2
Doumit, Ryan, Alt.	1.000	1	3	1	0	4	0	0
Emmons, Scott, Nor.	1.000	7	23	2	0	25	0	1
Evans, Lee, Alt.	.988	49	276	48	4	328	4	4
Figga, Mike, Bing.	1.000	8	51	5	0	56	0	1
Garcia, Guillermo, N.H.	1.000	3	16	1	0	17	0	2
Garrick, Matt, N.H.	.976	34	263	19	7	289	1	2
Haad, Yamid, Alt.	1.000	1	8	1	0	9	0	0
Harper, Brandon, Port.	.997	69	556	47	2	605	6	4
Hernandez, Michel, Nor.	.981	47	338	31	7	376	4	6
Hietpas, Joe, Bing.	1.000	1	3	0	0	3	0	0
House, J.R., N.H.	.991	88	590	61	6	657	1	14
Kropf, Andy, Erie	1.000	5	28	2	0	30	1	0
Loggins, Josh, Nor.	.875	2	7	0	1	8	0	2
Lomasney, Steve, Tren.	.987	53	399	48	6	453	4	9
Lopez-Cao, Mike, Bow.	.990	46	263	34	3	300	5	3
Malave, Jaime, Bing.	.966	7	26	2	1	29	0	0
Marsters, Brandon, N.B.	.994	75	594	58	4	656	4	4
Martine, Chris, N.H.	.981	54	323	30	7	360	4	6
McGee, Tom, Bow.	.994	46	284	46	2	332	2	5
Meran, Jorge, Erie	.967	33	209	23	8	240	2	5
Mosquera, Julio, Nor.	.991	82	629	46	6	681	6	10
Mulligan, Sean, Bow.	1.000	6	34	3	0	37	0	1
PHILLIPS, Jason, Bing.	.995	83	561	54	3	618	6	4
Pierce, Kirk, Nor.	.962	11	69	6	3	78	1	1
Pogue, Jamie, N.H.	1.000	7	36	7	0	43	0	0
Ramos, Kelly, Tren.	.994	55	442	52	3	497	8	8
Rickon, Jim, Akr.	1.000	9	44	3	0	47	0	3
Rivera, Mike, Erie	.989	109	793	83	10	886	8	7

Player, Team	Pct.	G	PO	A	E	TC	DP	PB
Rodriguez, Luis, Tren.	.982	36	239	29	5	273	1	5
Rodriguez, Sammy, Bing.	.989	49	316	35	4	355	3	6
Rose, Mike, Tren.	1.000	9	51	8	0	59	0	1
Sandusky, Scott, Har.	.985	108	739	72	12	823	9	9
Schumacher, Shawn, N.H.	.994	29	160	18	1	179	0	6
Secrist, Reed, Alt.	1.000	2	6	1	0	7	0	0
Shrum, Allen, N.B.	1.000	2	4	0	0	4	0	0
Smith, Casey, Akr.	.991	28	197	30	2	229	3	1
Smith, Jeff, N.B.	.992	60	472	57	4	533	3	3
Snusz, Chris, Akr.-Nor.	.984	26	173	11	3	187	2	6
Taubensee, Eddie, Akr.	1.000	2	9	0	0	9	0	0
Torres, Gabby, N.B.	.976	9	76	5	2	83	1	1
Treanor, Matt, Port.	.996	32	235	12	1	248	1	2
Ullery, Dave, Bow.	.979	6	40	7	1	48	1	2
Valdez, Jerry, Read.	.993	58	391	47	3	441	3	10
Van Iten, Bobby, Read.	.993	41	249	22	2	273	1	7
Washington, Rico, Alt.	1.000	2	13	0	0	13	0	0
Wathan, Dusty, Port.	.990	45	278	22	3	303	1	0

TRIPLE PLAY: House.

CATCHERS WITH TWO OR MORE TEAMS

Player, Team	Pct.	G	PO	A	E	TC	DP	PB
Snusz, Chris, Akr.	1.000	1	10	0	0	10	0	0
Snusz, Chris, Nor.	.983	25	163	11	3	177	2	6

PITCHERS

Player, Team	Pct.	G	PO	A	E	TC	DP
Adkins, Tim, Nor.*	.938	40	4	11	1	16	0
Agamennone, Brandon, Har.	1.000	45	4	9	0	13	0
Albin, Scott, Har.	.000	4	0	0	0	0	0
Aldred, Scott, Nor.*	1.000	11	3	2	0	5	0
Alvarado, Carlos, Alt.	.857	26	1	11	2	14	1
Ambrose, John, Tren.	.333	5	0	1	2	3	0
Andrews, Jeff, Har.	1.000	9	1	3	0	4	0
Arroyo, Luis, Tren.*	1.000	7	1	3	0	4	0
Arthurs, Shane, Har.	1.000	5	1	0	0	1	1
Ayers, Mike, Alt.*	1.000	7	0	4	0	4	0
Babula, Shaun, Bow.*	.900	28	3	6	1	10	1
Bacsik, Mike, Akr.*	1.000	4	3	3	0	6	0
Baez, Danny, Akr.	1.000	1	0	1	0	1	0
Bailie, Matt, Read.	1.000	35	3	7	0	10	0
Baisley, Brad, Read.	1.000	12	6	5	0	11	1
Balfour, Grant, N.B.	1.000	35	1	6	0	7	0
Barrios, Manny, Bing.	.000	4	0	0	0	0	0
Bauer, Rick, Bow.	.955	9	10	11	1	22	1
Baugh, Kenny, Erie	.909	5	6	4	1	11	0
Bean, Colter, Nor.	.000	1	0	0	0	0	0
Bechler, Steve, Bow.	1.000	12	6	2	0	8	0
Beckett, Josh, Port.	1.000	13	2	5	0	7	1
Bell, Heath, Bing.	1.000	43	6	7	0	13	2
Benham, Dave, N.H.	.000	1	0	0	0	0	0
Bennett, Jeff, Alt.	1.000	1	1	1	0	2	1
Bess, Steve, Erie	1.000	10	1	0	0	1	0
Betancourt, Rafael, Tren.	1.000	16	2	4	0	6	0
Billingsley, Brent, Har.*	.952	19	8	12	1	21	1
Blevins, Jeremy, Nor.	.929	50	2	11	1	14	0
Bottalico, Ricky, Read.	.000	3	0	0	1	1	0
Bowe, Brandon, Port.	1.000	9	0	5	0	5	0
Bradley, Ryan, Nor.	.727	16	3	5	3	11	1
Braswell, Bryan, Bing.*	1.000	5	1	2	0	3	1
Bridges, Donnie, Har.	.750	3	2	1	1	4	0
Brown, Derek, Bow.	.955	34	6	15	1	22	1
Brown, Jamie, Akr.	1.000	4	3	4	0	7	0
Brunette, Justin, Bing.*	1.000	23	1	4	0	5	0
Buller, Sean, Erie*	1.000	16	2	7	0	9	0
Bullinger, Kirk, Akr.	.000	3	0	0	0	0	0
Bump, Nate, Port.	1.000	11	2	6	0	8	0
Burnham, Gary, Read.*	.000	2	0	0	0	0	0
Burnside, Adrian, Alt.*	1.000	6	0	3	0	3	0
Burton, Darren, Alt.	.000	1	0	0	0	0	0
Camp, Jared, Erie	1.000	11	1	4	0	5	1
Camp, Shawn, Alt.	.800	8	3	1	1	5	1
Carnes, Matt, N.B.	.944	28	6	11	1	18	2
Carrasco, Dan, Alt.	.909	27	2	8	1	11	0
Cedeno, Blas, Read.	1.000	7	0	2	0	2	0
Cento, Tony, N.B.*	1.000	9	1	0	0	1	0
Cerda, Jaime, Bing.*	1.000	12	1	2	0	3	1
Cerros, Juan, Bing.	1.000	13	3	2	0	5	1
Chaney, Mike, Alt.*	1.000	4	2	4	0	6	1
Chapman, Jake, Har.*	.950	53	4	15	1	20	1
Chen, Bruce, Read.*	1.000	1	0	1	0	1	0
Chiavacci, Ron, Har.	.900	25	3	6	1	10	1
Chrysler, Clint, Alt.*	.889	51	5	3	1	9	1

Player, Team	Pct.	G	PO	A	E	TC	DP
Cisar, Mark, Tren.	1.000	21	0	5	0	5	0
Clark, Chris, Port.	1.000	4	2	1	0	3	0
Claussen, Brandon, Nor.*	.933	21	6	22	2	30	1
Coogan, Patrick, N.H.	.938	33	12	18	2	32	0
Cook, Andy, Bing.	1.000	22	3	5	0	8	1
Cook, B.R., N.H.	.818	20	4	14	4	22	0
Cooper, Chris, Akr.*	1.000	2	0	1	0	1	0
Corcoran, Tim, Bow.	1.000	7	1	1	0	2	0
Cordova, Francisco, Alt.	.000	1	0	0	0	0	0
Corey, Mark, Bing.	.875	25	3	4	1	8	0
Cormier, Rheal, Read.*	1.000	1	1	0	0	1	0
Cornejo, Nate, Erie	.952	19	12	28	2	42	3
Crudale, Mike, N.H.	.941	62	5	11	1	17	1
Crumpton, Chuck, Har.	1.000	52	5	13	0	18	0
Daniels, Dave, N.H.	.500	13	1	0	1	2	0
Darrell, Tommy, Har.	1.000	24	2	1	0	3	0
Darwin, Dave, Akr.*	.944	19	1	16	1	18	1
Davis, Allen, Har.*	1.000	8	1	6	0	7	0
Day, Zach, Akr.	1.000	22	9	18	0	27	1
De La Rosa, Jorge, Tren.*	.900	29	3	6	1	10	0
De Leon, Jorge, Tren.	1.000	1	0	1	0	1	1
Delgado, Ernie, Bing.	1.000	6	0	1	0	1	0
Della Ratta, Pete, Bing.	.800	22	2	2	1	5	1
Deschenes, Marc, Akr.	1.000	22	0	9	0	9	1
Diorio, Mike, Alt.	1.000	18	1	4	0	5	1
Donaldson, Bo, Alt.	1.000	17	0	1	0	1	0
Drese, Ryan, Akr.	.968	14	6	24	1	31	1
Drumright, Mike, Port.	.917	18	5	6	1	12	0
DUCHSCHERER, Justin, Tren.	1.000	12	13	16	0	29	0
Ebert, Derrin, Tren.*	.955	20	6	15	1	22	0
Eckelman, Alex, N.H.	.000	2	0	0	0	0	0
Eckenstahler, Eric, Erie*	.875	46	3	11	2	16	0
Edmondson, Brian, Port.	1.000	14	1	7	0	8	0
Eibey, Scott, Bow.*	.800	38	5	11	4	20	0
Elmore, Chris, Tren.*	1.000	14	4	11	0	15	1
Falteisek, Steve, Bow.	.938	11	6	9	1	16	0
Farmer, Tom, Erie	.500	2	0	1	1	2	0
Farrell, Jim, Tren.	.000	1	0	0	0	0	0
Felix, Miguel, Bow.	1.000	15	8	9	0	17	0
Field, Luke, Akr.	1.000	1	0	2	0	2	0
Figueroa, Juan, Bow.	.889	18	5	11	2	18	0
Finley, Chuck, Akr.*	1.000	2	0	2	0	2	0
Fisher, Pete, N.B.	1.000	9	5	7	0	12	0
Fitch, Steve, Akr.	.000	1	0	0	0	0	0
Fleming, Travis, Bow.	1.000	3	1	0	0	1	0
Flohr, Adam, N.B.*	.941	18	3	13	1	17	1
Flores, Randy, Nor.*	.980	25	5	44	1	50	4
Florie, Bryce, Tren.	.000	6	0	0	0	0	0
Flury, Pat, Nor.	.000	4	0	0	0	0	0
Fossum, Casey, Tren.*	1.000	20	9	17	0	26	1
France, Aaron, Alt.	.833	7	2	3	1	6	1
Franks, Lance, N.H.	.938	28	5	10	1	16	1
Frederick, Kevin, N.B.	.938	44	8	7	1	16	0
Galvez, Randy, Alt.	.909	15	2	18	2	22	3
Garcia, Mike, Alt.	1.000	18	1	1	0	2	0
Garcia, Rosman, Nor.	1.000	1	0	1	0	1	0
Garcia, Sonny, Bow.	1.000	5	2	5	0	7	0
Garrett, Hal, Akr.	1.000	11	2	3	0	5	0
Garrett, Josh, Tren.	.778	46	3	11	4	18	0
Geary, Geoff, Read.	.867	29	4	9	2	15	1
Gibbs, Mark, Bow.	1.000	1	0	0	0	0	0
Goetz, Geoff, Port.*	1.000	25	2	8	0	10	0
Gonzalez, Mike, Alt.*	1.000	14	1	22	0	23	0
Grabow, John, Alt.*	.818	10	2	7	2	11	1
Graman, Alex, Nor.*	.962	28	4	21	1	26	1
Griffiths, Jeremy, Bing.	.333	2	0	1	2	3	0
Grilli, Jason, Port.	1.000	1	0	1	0	1	0
Gronkiewicz, Lee, Akr.	1.000	2	0	2	0	2	0
Guy, Brad, Alt.	.933	28	2	12	1	15	1
Hackman, Luther, N.H.	1.000	3	0	0	0	0	0
Hale, Beau, Bow.	.944	12	7	10	1	18	0
Hamilton, Jimmy, Bow.*	.923	13	2	10	1	13	0
Hammond, Joey, Bow.	1.000	2	0	1	0	1	0
Hancock, Josh, Tren.	1.000	24	6	10	0	16	1
Hazlett, Andy, Har.*	1.000	14	1	6	0	7	0
Heams, Shane, Erie	1.000	36	5	3	0	8	0
Hebson, Bryan, Har.	.923	26	5	7	1	13	0
Heiserman, Rick, N.H.	1.000	5	1	1	0	2	0
Henderson, Scott, Port.	.867	39	6	7	2	15	0
Herrera, Alex, Akr.*	1.000	15	2	4	0	6	1
Hiles, Cary, Read.	.950	51	4	15	1	20	0
Hill, Terry, Tren.*	.900	22	2	7	1	10	0
Hoard, Brent, N.B.*	.000	1	0	0	0	0	0
Hooten, Dave, Akr.	.929	17	4	9	1	14	1

Player, Team	Pct.	G	PO	A	E	TC	DP
Howard, Tom, N.B.*	1.000	4	0	1	0	1	0
Izquierdo, Hansel, Port.	.933	10	6	8	1	15	0
Janke, Cheyenne, N.H.	1.000	17	1	6	0	7	0
Jean, Domingo, Nor.	.750	21	0	3	1	4	1
Jensen, Justin, Nor.*	.000	4	0	0	0	0	0
Jerzembeck, Mike, Nor.	.667	10	0	2	1	3	1
Jodie, Brett, Nor.	1.000	2	1	3	0	4	2
Johnson, Adam, N.B.	.962	18	11	14	1	26	3
Johnson, Barry, Nor.	.500	8	0	1	1	2	0
Johnson, James, Akr.*	1.000	31	5	4	0	9	0
Jones, Bobby M., Bing.*	1.000	2	1	0	0	1	0
Journell, Jimmy, N.H.	1.000	1	0	2	0	2	1
Julio, Jorge, Bow.	1.000	12	2	1	0	3	0
Kalita, Tim, Erie*	.813	30	9	17	6	32	1
Kershner, Jason, Read.*	.944	26	12	22	2	36	2
Kessel, Kyle, Bing.*	.000	3	0	0	0	0	0
Kirsten, Rick, Erie	.906	28	8	21	3	32	0
Krause, Scott, Akr.	.000	1	0	0	0	0	0
Kubes, Greg, Read.*	1.000	6	0	3	0	3	0
Kusiewicz, Mike, Tren.*	.917	18	7	15	2	24	1
Lakman, Jason, Bow.	.909	18	6	4	1	11	0
Lambert, Jeremy, N.H.	1.000	31	1	4	0	5	0
Lantz, Doug, Akr.	1.000	1	1	2	0	3	0
Leach, Bryan, Tren.	.800	23	3	1	1	5	0
Leach, Nick, Nor.	.000	1	0	0	0	0	0
Leek, Randy, Erie*	.962	29	6	44	2	52	3
Levan, Matt, Port.*	1.000	4	0	1	0	1	0
Lohrman, Dave, Bing.	1.000	13	4	5	0	9	1
Lohse, Kyle, N.B.	.923	6	6	6	1	13	1
Looney, Brian, Nor.*	1.000	11	1	2	0	3	0
Lopez, Jose, Alt.	.889	6	2	6	1	9	0
Lovingier, Kevin, Nor.*	1.000	53	3	12	0	15	1
Mairena, Ozwaldo, Port.*	1.000	22	0	6	0	6	0
Maness, Nick, Bing.	.900	28	13	23	4	40	1
Mangum, Mark, Har.	.938	26	5	25	2	32	0
Manon, Julio, Bing.	.875	10	4	3	1	8	1
Manzueta, Roberto, Alt.	1.000	12	0	6	0	6	0
Marr, Jason, N.H.	.938	51	3	12	1	16	0
Marshall, Lee, N.B.	1.000	11	2	1	0	3	0
Marte, Damaso, Nor.*	1.000	23	0	4	0	4	0
Martine, Chris, N.H.	.000	1	0	0	0	0	0
Martinez, Jesus, Bing.*	.667	17	0	2	1	3	0
Matz, Brian, Har.*	1.000	37	6	14	0	20	0
McClaskey, Tim, Port.	1.000	37	1	8	0	9	1
McClure, Brian, Erie	1.000	2	0	1	0	1	0
McCurtain, Paul, Port.	1.000	10	1	0	0	1	0
McDade, Neal, N.H.	.933	19	3	11	1	15	0
McDonald, Jon, N.B.	.842	17	5	11	3	19	0
McLeary, Marty, Tren.	.826	35	5	14	4	23	2
Medina, Carlos, Bing.*	.800	24	0	4	1	5	0
Mills, Alan, Bow.	1.000	7	1	1	0	2	1
Mills, Ryan, N.B.*	1.000	8	2	4	0	6	0
Mitchell, Scott, Har.	1.000	9	1	2	0	3	0
Montalbano, Greg, Tren.*	1.000	10	1	6	0	7	1
Montane, Ivan, Bing.	.818	21	4	5	2	11	0
Moreno, Julio, Bing.	1.000	12	0	1	0	1	0
Moskau, Ryan, Port.*	.931	39	8	19	2	29	1
Mulholland, Terry, Alt.*	.000	2	0	0	0	0	0
Munoz, Juan, N.H.*	.000	1	0	0	0	0	0
Myers, Brett, Read.	.964	26	7	20	1	28	0
Nakamura, Mike, N.B.	1.000	48	4	10	0	14	0
Navarro, Jason, N.H.*	1.000	52	0	5	0	5	0
Neal, Blaine, Port.	.938	54	6	9	1	16	0
Norton, Jason, Tren.	.750	6	0	3	1	4	0
Nunez, Franklin, Read.	.909	39	2	8	1	11	0
Olsen, Kevin, Port.	.926	26	9	16	2	27	0
Ormond, Rod, Bow.	.000	1	0	0	0	0	0
Outlaw, Mark, Read.*	.941	49	5	11	1	17	2
Pacheco, Alexander, Nor.	.625	43	2	3	3	8	0
Padua, Geraldo, Alt.-Nor.	1.000	15	1	5	0	6	0
Palki, Jeromy, N.B.	1.000	31	4	10	0	14	0
Paradis, Mike, Bow.	.833	27	13	17	6	36	1
Pautz, Brad, Read.	1.000	5	0	1	0	1	1
Pavlovich, Tony, Alt.	.857	31	2	10	2	14	0
Paz, Rich, Alt.	1.000	1	0	1	0	1	0
Pearce, Josh, N.H.	1.000	18	5	14	0	19	1
Pearson, Terry, Erie	.647	59	6	5	6	17	0
Pena, Jesus, Tren.*	.714	14	1	4	2	7	0
Perkins, Dan, Akr.	1.000	1	0	1	0	1	0
Perkins, Mike, N.H.	.000	1	0	0	0	0	0
Persails, Mark, Erie	1.000	9	2	7	0	9	1
Phelps, Tommy, Erie*	1.000	15	2	4	0	6	0
Phillips, Jason, Alt.-Akr.	1.000	16	0	6	0	6	0
Pina, Rafael, Bow.	.000	4	0	0	0	0	0
Pinales, Aquiles, Akr.	1.000	5	2	3	0	5	0
Pineda, Luis, Erie	1.000	16	4	10	0	14	2
Ponson, Sidney, Bow.	1.000	1	1	0	0	1	0
Prather, Scott, N.H.*	1.000	23	2	4	0	6	0
Pumphrey, Ken, N.B.	.905	22	17	21	4	42	4
Radinsky, Scott, Akr.*	1.000	23	2	6	0	8	1
Rakers, Aaron, Bow.	.889	51	2	6	1	9	0
Rath, Fred, N.H.	.000	1	0	0	0	0	0
Reid, Justin, Alt.	1.000	17	7	20	0	27	0
Reinike, Chris, Akr.	.857	27	1	5	1	7	0
Reynoso, Edison, Nor.	.667	5	1	1	1	3	0
Rincon, Juan, N.B.	.919	29	14	20	3	37	0
Rivera, Homero, Erie*	.750	16	2	1	1	4	0
Rivera, Saul, N.B.	1.000	33	6	3	0	9	0
Roa, Joe, Port.	1.000	7	1	5	0	6	0
Roach, Jason, Bing.	.927	22	8	30	3	41	2
Rodgers, Bobby, Port.	1.000	26	5	3	0	8	0
Rodney, Fernando, Erie	.000	4	0	0	0	0	0
Rodriguez, Eddy, Bow.	.000	5	0	0	0	0	0
Rodriguez, Frank, Alt.	.000	7	0	0	0	0	0
Rodriguez, Nerio, Alt.	1.000	11	5	9	0	14	1
Rodriguez, Rich, Akr.*	1.000	4	0	0	0	0	0
Rogers, Brian, Nor.	.864	29	12	26	6	44	2
Roller, Adam, Nor.	1.000	2	0	1	0	1	0
Saberhagen, Bret, Tren.	1.000	1	0	1	0	1	0
Sadler, Carl, Akr.*	1.000	11	0	1	0	1	0
Saenz, Jason, Bing.*	.818	28	10	17	6	33	1
Salyers, Jeremy, Har.	.667	16	1	1	1	3	0
Sanders, Frankie, Akr.	.000	1	0	0	0	0	0
Sansom, Trevor, N.H.	1.000	1	0	2	0	2	0
Scheffer, Aaron, Port.	1.000	24	2	4	0	6	0
Schmidt, Jason, Alt.	1.000	3	0	2	0	2	0
Schoening, Brent, N.B.	1.000	12	2	8	0	10	0
Sekany, Jason, Tren.	1.000	15	5	4	0	9	0
Seo, Jae, Bing.	.933	12	2	12	1	15	0
Serrano, Elio, Read.	1.000	30	2	7	0	9	0
Serrano, Jim, Har.	.909	47	0	10	1	11	0
Sexton, Jeff, Akr.	.750	11	2	1	1	4	0
Sheredy, Kevin, N.H.	.917	48	4	7	1	12	1
Shuey, Paul, Akr.	.000	1	0	0	0	0	0
Sido, Wilson, Akr.	1.000	3	0	2	0	2	0
Silva, Carlos, Read.	.980	28	15	33	1	49	4
Silva, Jose, Alt.	.000	2	0	0	0	0	0
Sims, Ken, Bow.	.973	24	10	26	1	37	3
Sismondo, Bobby, Read.*	.857	26	1	5	1	7	0
Smith, Brian, Alt.	1.000	2	0	2	0	2	0
Sparks, Steve, Alt.	.867	7	6	7	2	15	0
Spencer, Corey, Tren.*	1.000	55	3	10	0	13	0
Spiegel, Mike, Akr.*	1.000	1	0	1	0	1	0
Spoljaric, Paul, Akr.*	1.000	3	0	0	0	0	0
Sprague, Kevin, N.H.*	1.000	1	1	0	0	1	0
Spurling, Chris, Alt.	1.000	34	4	24	0	28	2
Stanford, Jason, Akr.*	1.000	24	6	19	0	25	1
Stemle, Steve, N.H.	.880	26	8	14	3	25	1
Stephens, John, Bow.	.889	18	7	9	2	18	0
Stocks, Nick, N.H.	.818	16	4	14	4	22	1
Stoops, Jim, Nor.	1.000	6	0	1	0	1	1
Strange, Pat, Bing.	.911	26	18	23	4	45	3
Tejera, Mike, Port.*	.926	25	4	21	2	27	1
Tekavec, Nate, Erie.	1.000	1	1	0	0	1	0
Thomas, Brad, N.B.*	.955	19	5	16	1	22	3
Traber, Billy, Bing.*	1.000	8	4	9	0	13	1
Tucker, Julien, Erie-Akr.	.800	20	0	4	1	5	0
Tucker, T.J., Har.	1.000	13	7	11	0	18	0
Turnbow, Mark, Akr.	1.000	1	0	0	0	0	0
Vanhekken, Andy, Erie*	1.000	8	1	6	0	7	0
Vargas, Claudio, Port.	.958	27	9	14	1	24	0
Vargas, Martin, Akr.	1.000	32	3	10	0	13	2
Vega, Rene, Bing.*	.938	41	5	25	2	32	1
Walker, Adam, Read.-Bing.*	.833	17	2	3	1	6	0
Walker, Tyler, Bing.	.857	4	3	3	1	7	1
Wall, Donne, Bing.	1.000	4	1	0	0	1	0
Walling, Dave, Nor.	1.000	5	1	1	0	2	0
Walrond, Les, N.H.*	.909	16	0	20	2	22	0
Wamback, Trevor, Har.	1.000	3	1	1	0	2	0
Watson, Mark, Akr.*	.750	30	1	5	2	8	0
Wayne, Justin, Har.	.941	14	5	11	1	17	1
Wedel, Jeremy, Read.	1.000	45	6	15	0	21	2
Wehner, John, Alt.	.000	2	0	0	0	0	0
Weis, Brad, N.B.*	.000	1	0	0	1	1	0
White, Matt, Akr.*	1.000	25	5	18	0	23	1
Whiteley, Shad, Nor.	.000	1	0	0	0	0	0
Wiggins, Scott, Nor.*	1.000	4	0	2	0	2	0
Williams, Dave, All.*	.923	9	2	10	1	13	0

ayer, Team	Pct.	G	PO	A	E	TC	DP
Williams, Todd, Nor.	1.000	6	0	1	0	1	0
Wilson, Jeff, Bow.*	.875	5	2	5	1	8	0
Wimberly, Larry, Alt.*	1.000	24	2	10	0	12	0
Wolf, Randy, Read.*	1.000	1	1	1	0	2	0
Wolff, Bryan, Akr.	1.000	8	5	7	0	12	2
Woodard, Steve, Akr.	1.000	1	0	1	0	1	0
Wright, Jaret, Akr.	1.000	1	1	1	0	2	0
Zancanaro, Dave, N.H.*	1.000	1	0	2	0	2	0

PITCHERS WITH TWO OR MORE TEAMS

Player, Team	Pct.	G	PO	A	E	TC	DP
Padua, Geraldo, Alt.	1.000	10	0	4	0	4	0
Padua, Geraldo, Nor.	1.000	5	1	1	0	2	0
Phillips, Jason, Alt.	1.000	6	0	1	0	1	0
Phillips, Jason, Akr.	1.000	10	0	5	0	5	0
Tucker, Julien, Erie	.750	23	0	3	1	4	0
Tucker, Julien, Akr.	1.000	5	0	1	0	1	0
Walker, Adam, Read.*	.833	15	2	3	1	6	0
Walker, Adam, Bing.*	.000	2	0	0	0	0	0

The following players appeared only as designated hitter, pinch-hitter or pinch runner: Ametiller, ph; Bordick, dh; A. Brown, dh; R. Brown, dh; Fryman, dh; Justice, dh; Ortiz, dh.

LEAGUE CHAMPIONS

Year	Team	Pct.
1923—	Williamsport	.661
1924—	Williamsport	.654
1925—	York§	.583
	Williamsport§	.583
1926—	Scranton	.627
1927—	Harrisburg	.630
1928—	Harrisburg	.603
1929—	Binghamton	.597
1930—	Wilkes-Barre	.572
1931—	Harrisburg	.597
1932—	Wilkes-Barre	.561
1933—	Binghamton	.690
1934—	Binghamton	.694
	Williamsport*	.603
1935—	Scranton	.657
	Binghamton*	.580
1936—	Scranton*	.609
	Elmira	.629
1937—	Elmira†	.622
1938—	Binghamton	.622
	Elmira (3rd)‡	.522
1939—	Scranton†	.571
1940—	Scranton	.568
	Binghamton (2nd)‡	.554
1941—	Wilkes-Barre	.630
	Elmira (3rd)‡	.514
1942—	Albany	.600
	Scranton (2nd)‡	.593
1943—	Scranton	.630
	Elmira (2nd)‡	.568
1944—	Hartford	.723
	Binghamton (4th)‡	.474
1945—	Utica	.615
	Albany (3rd)‡	.564
1946—	Scranton†	.691
1947—	Utica†	.652
1948—	Scranton†	.636
1949—	Albany	.664
	Binghamton (4th)‡	.500
1950—	Wilkes-Barre‡	.652
1951—	Wilkes-Barre‡	.612
	Scranton (2nd)†	.562
1952—	Albany	.603
	Binghamton (2nd)‡	.562
1953—	Reading	.682

Year	Team	Pct.
	Binghamton (2nd)‡	.636
1954—	Wilkes-Barre	.576
	Albany (3rd)‡	.540
1955—	Reading	.613
	Allentown (2nd)‡	.565
1956—	Schenectady†	.609
1957—	Binghamton	.607
	Reading (3rd)‡	.529
1958—	Lancaster∞	.568
	Binghamton (6th)‡	.493
1959—	Springfield†	.607
1960—	Williamsport▲	.551
	Springfield (3rd)▲	.496
1961—	Springfield	.612
1962—	Williamsport	.593
	Elmira (2nd)‡	.514
1963—	Charleston	.593
1964—	Elmira	.586
1965—	Pittsfield	.607
1966—	Elmira	.633
1967—	Binghamton◆	.586
	Elmira	.532
1968—	Pittsfield	.604
	Reading (2nd)‡	.579
1969—	York	.640
1970—	Waterbury■	.560
	Reading■	.553
1971—	Three Rivers	.569
	Elmira▼	.561
1972—	West Haven▼	.600
	Three Rivers	.559
1973—	Reading▼	.551
	Pittsfield	.551
1974—	Thetford Miners (2nd)•	.536
	Pittsfield (2nd)	.496
1975—	Reading	.613
	Bristol*	.587
1976—	Three Rivers	.601
	West Haven††	.576
1977—	West Haven‡‡	.623
	Three Rivers	.551
1978—	Reading	.642
	Bristol*	.580
1979—	West Haven§§	.597
1980—	Holyoke*	.561

Year	Team	Pct.
	Waterbury	.540
1981—	Glens Falls	.615
	Bristol*	.577
1982—	West Haven*	.614
	Lynn	.590
1983—	Lynn	.554
	New Britain‡	.518
1984—	Waterbury	.543
	Vermont‡	.536
1985—	Albany	.540
	Vermont‡	.514
1986—	Reading	.566
	Vermont‡	.554
1987—	Pittsfield	.630
	Harrisburg‡	.550
1988—	Glens Falls	.584
	Albany‡	.522
1989—	Albany‡	.657
	Harrisburg	.522
1990—	Albany	.568
	London‡	.547
1991—	Harrisburg	.621
	Albany‡	.543
1992—	Canton/Akron	.580
	Binghamton‡	.572
1993—	Harrisburg‡	.681
	Canton/Akron	.543
1994—	Harrisburg	.633
	Binghamton‡	.582
1995—	New Haven	.556
	Reading‡	.514
1996—	Portland	.589
	Harrisburg‡	.521
1997—	Harrisburg‡	.606
	Portland	.556
1998—	New Britain	.585
	Harrisburg‡	.514
1999—	Trenton	.648
	Harrisburg‡	.535
2000—	Reading	.599
	New Haven‡	.577
2001—	New Britain∞∞	.613
	Reading∞∞	.542

*Won split-season playoff. †Won championship and four-team playoff. ‡Won four-team playoff. §Tied for pennant, York winning playoff. ∞League was divided into Northern, Southern divisions and played a split season; Lancaster was overall season leader. ▲Playoff finals canceled after one game because of rain with Williamsport and Springfield declared playoff co-champions. ◆League was divided into Eastern, Western divisions; Binghamton won playoff. ■Tied for pennant, Waterbury winning playoff. ▼League was divided into American, National divisions; won playoff. •League was divided into American and National divisions; won four-team playoff. ††League was divided into Northern, Southern divisions, won playoff. ‡‡League was divided into New England and Canadian-American divisions; won playoff. §§Won both halves of split season (no playoffs). ∞∞Were entering finals of four-team playoff and were declared co-champions when Professional Baseball declared a stoppage of play. (NOTE—Known as New York-Pennsylvania League prior to 1938.)

SOUTHERN LEAGUE

LEAGUE OFFICE

President/secretary-treasurer
Don Mincher

Address
1 Depot St., Suite 300
Marietta, GA 30060

Phone
770-428-4749

TEAMS

BIRMINGHAM BARONS

General manager
Tony Ensor
Manager
Nick Capra
Ballpark (capacity, surface)
Hoover Metropolitan Stadium
(10,800, grass)
Affiliation
White Sox
Address
P.O. Box 360007
Birmingham, AL 35236
Phone
205-988-3200

CAROLINA MUDCATS

General manager
Joe Kremer
Manager
To be announced
Ballpark (capacity, surface)
Five County Stadium (6,500, grass)
Affiliation
Rockies
Address
P.O. Drawer 1218
Zebulon, NC 27597
Phone
919-269-2287

CHATTANOOGA LOOKOUTS

President
J. Frank Burke
General manager
Rich Mozingo
Manager
Phil Wellman
Ballpark (capacity, surface)
BellSouth Park (6,100, grass)
Affiliation
Reds
Address
201 Power Alley
Chattanooga, TN 37402
Phone
423-267-2208

GREENVILLE BRAVES

General manager
Steve DeSalvo
Manager
Brian Snitker

Ballpark (capacity, surface)
Greenville Municipal Stadium (7,027,
grass)
Affiliation
Braves
Address
P.O. Box 16683
Greenville, SC 29606
Phone
864-299-3456

HUNTSVILLE STARS

President/general manager
Bryan Dingo
Manager
Frank Kremblas
Ballpark (capacity, surface)
Joe W. Davis Stadium (10,400, grass)
Affiliation
Brewers
Address
3125 Leeman Ferry Road
Huntsville, AL 35801
Phone
256-882-2562

JACKSONVILLE SUNS

Vice president/general manager
Peter Bragan Jr.
Manager
Dino Ebel
Ballpark (capacity, surface)
Wolfson Park (8,200, grass)
Affiliation
Dodgers
Address
P.O. Box 4756
Jacksonville, FL 32201
Phone
904-358-2846

MOBILE BAYBEARS

Vice president/general manager
Bill Shanahan
Manager
Craig Colbert
Ballpark (capacity, surface)
Hank Aaron Stadium (6,000, grass)
Affiliation
Padres
Address
755 Bolling Brothers Blvd.
Mobile, AL 36606

Phone
334-479-2327

ORLANDO RAYS

General manager
Mitch Lukevics
Manager
Mako Oliveras
Ballpark (capacity, surface)
Disney's Wide World of Sports
Complex (9,500, grass)
Affiliation
Devil Rays
Address
P.O. Box 10000
Lake Buena Vista, FL 32830
Phone
407-939-4263

TENNESSEE SMOKIES

General manager
Brian Cox
Manager
Rocket Wheeler
Ballpark (capacity, surface)
Smokies Park (6,000, grass)
Affiliation
Blue Jays
Address
3540 Line Drive
Kodak, TN 37764
Phone
865-637-9494

WEST TENN
DIAMOND JAXX

General manager/president
David Hersh
Manager
Bobby Dickerson
Ballpark (capacity, surface)
Pringles Park (6,000, grass)
Affiliation
Cubs
Address
4 Fun Place
Jackson, TN 38305
Phone
901-664-2020

CLASS AA *Southern League*

2001 FINAL STANDINGS

FIRST HALF

EAST DIVISION

Team	W	L	T	Pct.	GB
Jacksonville (Dodgers)	41	30	0	.577	...
Chattanooga (Reds)	39	32	0	.549	2.0
Carolina (Rockies)	31	39	0	.443	9.5
Orlando (Devil Rays)	31	40	0	.437	10.0
Greenville (Braves)	25	45	0	.357	15.5

WEST DIVISION

Team	W	L	T	Pct.	GB
Huntsville (Brewers)	42	29	0	.592	...
Tennessee (Blue Jays)	41	30	0	.577	1.0
Birmingham (White Sox)	37	34	0	.521	5.0
West Tenn (Cubs)	34	37	0	.479	8.0
Mobile (Padres)	33	38	0	.465	9.0

SECOND HALF

EAST DIVISION

Team	W	L	T	Pct.	GB
Jacksonville (Dodgers)	42	26	0	.618	...
Greenville (Braves)	35	34	0	.507	7.5
Chattanooga (Reds)	33	35	0	.485	9.0
Carolina (Rockies)	31	37	0	.456	11.0
Orlando (Devil Rays)	28	41	0	.406	14.5

WEST DIVISION

Team	W	L	T	Pct.	GB
Birmingham (White Sox)	43	26	0	.623	...
Tennessee (Blue Jays)	39	30	0	.565	4.0
Huntsville (Brewers)	33	34	0	.493	9.0
Mobile (Padres)	32	35	0	.478	10.0
West Tenn (Cubs)	25	43	0	.368	17.5

COMPOSITE

Team	Jax.	Tenn.	Birm.	Hunt.	Chat.	Mob.	Car.	Gre.	W.T.	Orl.	W	L	T	Pct.	GB
Jacksonville (Dodgers)	...	5	6	3	15	7	13	15	4	15	83	56	0	.597	...
Tennessee (Blue Jays)	3	...	10	11	9	10	15	5	13	4	80	60	0	.571	3.5
Birmingham (White Sox)	6	10	...	12	5	17	4	3	18	5	80	60	0	.571	3.5
Huntsville (Brewers)	5	14	5	...	7	11	7	7	16	3	75	63	0	.543	7.5
Chattanooga (Reds)	13	5	2	5	...	4	10	18	5	10	72	67	0	.518	11.0
Mobile (Padres)	1	6	12	6	4	...	6	3	16	11	65	73	0	.471	17.5
Carolina (Rockies)	8	6	8	1	10	2	...	12	4	11	62	76	0	.449	20.5
Greenville (Braves)	9	3	5	5	6	5	9	...	4	14	60	79	0	.432	23.0
West Tenn (Cubs)	4	7	9	11	4	8	4	4	...	8	59	80	0	.424	24.0
Orlando (Devil Rays)	7	4	3	9	7	9	8	12	0	...	59	81	0	.421	24.5

Carolina's home games played in Zebulon, N.C.; Tennessee's home games played in Knoxville, Tenn.; West Tenn's home games played in Jackson, Tenn.

Major league affiliations in parentheses.

PLAYOFFS: Jacksonville defeated Chattanooga three games to two; Huntsville defeated Birmingham three games to two. Note: Jacksonville and Huntsville declared Southern League co-champions due to stoppage of play in professional baseball.

REGULAR-SEASON ATTENDANCE: Birmingham, 311,362; Carolina, 257,558; Chattanooga, 288,047; Greenville, 243,900; Huntsville, 237,950; Jacksonville, 225,362; Mobile, 240,045; Orlando, 89,435; Tennessee, 266,037; West Tenn, 244,252. Total—2,403,948. Playoffs (10 games)—18,060. Class AA All-Star Game at Tennessee—5,086.

MANAGERS: Birmingham, Nick Capra; Carolina, Ron Gideon; Chattanooga, Phillip Wellman; Greenville, Paul Runge; Huntsville, Ed Romero; Jacksonville, John Shoemaker; Mobile, Tracy Woodson; Orlando, Mike Ramsey; Tennessee, Rocket Wheeler; West Tenn, Dave Bialas.

ALL-STAR TEAM: 1B—Ben Broussard, Chattanooga; 2B—Orlando Hudson, Tennessee; 3B—Josh Klimek, Huntsville; SS—Jorge Nunez, Jacksonville; OF—Joe Borchard, Birmingham; OF—Reed Johnson, Tennessee; OF—Bubba Crosby, Jacksonville; OF—Luke Allen, Jacksonville; C—Josh Phelps, Tennessee; DH—Josh Phelps, Tennessee; Utility—Brooks Badeaux, Orlando; RHP—Chris Baker, Tennessee; LHP—Steve Smyth, West Tenn; Relief pitcher—Ed Almonte, Birmingham; Most Valuable Player—Josh Phelps, Tennessee; Most Outstanding pitcher—Chris Baker, Tennessee; Manager of the Year—John Shoemaker, Jacksonville.

2001 BATTING

TEAM

Team	Avg.	G	TPA	AB	R	H	TB	2B	3B	HR	RBI	SH	SF	HP	BB	IBB	SO	SB	CS	GDP	LOB	ShO	Slg.	OBP
Tennessee	.271	140	5397	4732	717	1282	2018	257	37	135	664	43	42	76	504	24	1031	133	59	94	1025	6	.426	.348
Birmingham	.268	140	5409	4701	717	1262	1964	261	27	129	673	45	61	55	547	17	978	82	49	113	1035	4	.418	.348
Jacksonville	.260	139	5301	4638	623	1206	1837	248	37	103	556	84	42	58	479	20	993	165	72	77	1014	13	.396	.334
Chattanooga	.258	139	5276	4598	708	1187	1951	265	17	155	661	50	35	80	513	24	1013	122	63	99	931	6	.424	.341
Orlando	.256	140	5155	4657	514	1194	1649	223	29	58	469	54	35	73	336	12	886	98	62	104	955	13	.354	.314
Huntsville	.255	138	5167	4604	596	1174	1796	227	16	121	545	67	31	45	420	28	946	90	59	82	942	16	.390	.321
Carolina	.252	138	5228	4569	555	1152	1677	239	29	76	507	79	38	70	472	25	957	131	61	84	1029	10	.367	.329
Mobile	.249	138	5243	4651	528	1159	1714	234	30	87	500	45	47	41	459	17	1039	96	50	92	1020	11	.369	.324
Greenville	.247	139	5166	4596	541	1136	1756	224	18	120	495	48	28	67	427	11	1095	75	48	100	962	13	.382	.318
West Tenn	.244	139	5289	4620	590	1128	1706	200	30	106	553	46	40	82	501	16	1104	100	56	82	1013	10	.369	.326

INDIVIDUAL

TOP QUALIFIERS FOR BATTING CHAMPIONSHIP

Minimum 378 plate appearances. *Lefthanded batter. †Switch-hitter.

Player, Team	Avg.	G	TPA	AB	R	H	TB	2B	3B	HR	RBI	SH	SF	HP	BB	IBB	SO	SB	CS	GDP	Slg.	OBP
Broussard, Benjamin, Chat.*	.320	100	425	353	81	113	209	27	0	23	69	0	3	8	61	5	69	10	3	5	.592	.428
Johnson, Reed, Tenn.	.314	136	624	554	104	174	250	29	4	13	74	5	2	18	45	2	79	42	12	11	.451	.383
Crosby, Bubba, Jack.*	.302	107	443	384	68	116	166	22	5	6	47	7	7	8	37	2	60	22	6	7	.432	.369
Borchard, Joe, Birm.†	.295	133	597	515	95	152	262	27	1	27	98	0	5	10	67	1	158	5	4	13	.509	.384
Saunders, Chris, Birm.	.294	118	517	442	74	130	193	33	0	10	68	0	7	8	60	1	85	4	1	15	.437	.383
Phelps, Josh, Tenn.	.292	136	588	486	95	142	273	36	1	31	97	0	5	17	80	4	127	3	3	5	.562	.406
Hummel, Tim, Birm.	.290	134	610	524	83	152	218	33	6	7	63	8	10	5	62	2	69	14	3	12	.416	.364
Allen, Luke, Jack.*	.290	125	535	486	74	141	233	32	6	16	73	1	5	1	42	3	111	13	3	7	.479	.345
Metcalfe, Mike, Chat.†	.289	123	521	474	68	137	179	25	4	3	47	6	1	2	38	2	59	32	10	9	.378	.344

Player, Team	Avg.	G	TPA	AB	R	H	TB	2B	3B	HR	RBI	SH	SF	HP	BB	IBB	SO	SB	CS	GDP	Slg.	OBP
Burford, Kevin, Car.*	.289	101	419	363	51	105	152	21	4	6	35	0	3	8	45	2	79	4	1	5	.419	.377
Pickler, Jeff, Hun.*	.287	134	592	523	74	150	171	17	2	0	32	6	2	1	60	3	51	34	14	2	.327	.360
Werth, Jayson, Tenn.	.285	104	443	369	51	105	184	23	1	18	69	1	7	3	63	0	93	12	3	5	.499	.387
Perez, Jerson, Tenn.	.282	116	466	422	60	119	162	23	4	4	49	5	4	5	30	0	96	14	3	7	.384	.334
Pelaez, Alex, Mob.	.281	114	457	416	44	117	171	22	1	10	53	2	5	2	32	3	52	2	0	14	.411	.332
Dent, Darrell, Jack.*	.279	117	430	376	50	105	136	15	2	4	32	4	2	6	42	0	91	31	12	5	.362	.359

DEPARTMENTAL LEADERS: G—Ingram, Re. Johnson, Phelps, 136 each; AB—Re. Johnson, 554; R—Re. Johnson, 104; H—Re. Johnson, 174; TB—Phelps, 273; 2B—Phelps, 36; 3B—G. Davis, O. Hudson, 8 each; HR—Phelps, 31; RBI—Borchard, 98; SH—several tied, 11 each; SF—Hummel, 10; HP—Miller, 19; BB—Koonce, 89; IBB—Klimek, 8; SO—Ingram, 188; SB—Nunez, 44; CS—Crawford, 20; GIDP—Nevers, 17; Slg—Broussard, 592; OBP—Koonce, .429.

ALL PLAYERS

*Lefthanded batter. †Switch-hitter.

Player, Team	Avg.	G	TPA	AB	R	H	TB	2B	3B	HR	RBI	SH	SF	HP	BB	IBB	SO	SB	CS	GDP	Slg.	OBP
Abbott, Kurt, Gre.	.000	2	7	6	0	0	0	0	0	0	0	0	0	0	1	0	1	0	0	0	.000	.143
Abreu, Dennis, W.T.	.254	102	358	331	35	84	105	7	1	4	30	4	1	3	19	2	74	14	4	5	.317	.299
Abreu, Winston, Gre.	.250	34	8	8	2	2	3	1	0	0	1	0	0	0	0	0	1	0	0	0	.375	.250
Acevas, Jon, Birm.	.222	12	41	36	5	8	15	1	0	2	6	1	1	1	2	0	13	0	0	0	.417	.275
Acevedo, Jose, Chat.	.050	16	22	20	0	1	1	0	0	0	0	2	0	0	0	0	11	0	0	0	.050	.050
Achilles, Matt, W.T.	.167	9	6	6	0	1	1	0	0	0	0	0	0	0	0	0	3	0	0	0	.167	.167
Aldridge, Cory, Gre.*	.246	131	508	452	57	111	191	19	2	19	56	0	3	5	48	1	139	12	6	6	.423	.323
Allen, Luke, Jack.*	.290	125	535	486	74	141	233	32	6	16	73	1	5	1	42	3	111	13	3	7	.479	.345
Alvarez, Gabe, Chat.	.253	99	410	336	59	85	158	23	1	16	50	1	4	8	61	1	82	4	4	7	.470	.377
Alvarez, Jimmy, Tenn.†	.227	8	30	22	4	5	7	0	1	0	1	4	0	0	4	0	6	1	0	0	.318	.346
Alvarez, Victor, Jack.*	.200	8	13	10	1	2	2	0	0	0	0	2	0	0	1	0	1	0	0	0	.200	.273
Amrhein, Mike, W.T.	.241	96	349	311	30	75	101	14	0	4	33	1	4	10	23	0	45	0	1	11	.325	.310
Andrews, Clayton, Chat.	.286	6	9	7	1	2	2	0	0	0	1	1	1	0	0	0	3	0	0	0	.286	.250
Aramboles, Ricardo, Chat.	.000	2	3	3	0	0	0	0	0	0	0	0	0	0	0	0	1	0	0	0	.000	.000
Badeaux, Brooks, Orl.†	.249	127	521	470	48	117	143	11	6	1	27	11	2	5	33	2	50	14	7	10	.304	.304
Bair, Rod, Car.	.253	72	297	273	25	69	103	13	0	7	31	4	4	6	10	0	49	5	6	5	.377	.290
Bard, Josh, Car.†	.258	35	146	124	14	32	48	13	0	1	24	1	1	1	19	1	23	0	1	1	.307	.359
Barker, Kevin, Hun.*	.323	66	272	232	42	75	117	16	1	8	38	1	3	1	35	4	51	0	2	2	.504	.410
Bass, Jayson, W.T.*	.309	48	178	162	17	50	75	5	1	6	24	0	0	2	14	0	42	6	3	1	.463	.371
Battersby, Eric, Birm.	.253	133	534	438	69	111	174	19	1	14	67	4	9	3	80	1	87	6	4	12	.397	.366
Bauer, Greg, Jack.	.000	6	1	1	0	0	0	0	0	0	0	0	0	0	0	0	0	0	0	0	.000	.000
Beattie, Andy, Chat.†	.266	51	193	169	32	45	66	12	0	3	24	1	1	1	21	0	30	4	2	3	.391	.349
Becker, Brian, Orl.	.226	115	463	411	38	93	136	22	0	7	42	0	4	5	43	1	96	0	0	11	.331	.305
Beinbrink, Andy, Orl.	.273	126	513	443	51	121	170	22	6	5	49	2	7	6	55	1	69	4	2	16	.384	.356
Bell, Ricky, Jack.	.255	63	205	188	21	48	66	9	0	3	22	1	2	1	13	0	29	1	1	3	.351	.304
Benjamin, Al, Mob.	.273	110	403	374	50	102	165	23	2	12	50	0	8	3	18	2	73	8	0	9	.441	.305
Derry, Jon, Jack.	.000	3	3	3	0	0	0	0	0	0	0	0	0	0	0	0	0	0	0	0	.000	.000
Betemit, Wilson, Gre.†	.355	47	199	183	22	65	94	14	0	5	19	1	2	1	12	0	36	6	2	4	.514	.394
Bevel, Bobby, Jack.*	.333	31	3	3	1	1	1	0	0	0	0	0	0	0	0	0	2	0	0	0	.333	.333
Blakely, Darren, Mob.†	.217	28	131	115	19	25	51	4	2	6	15	1	1	3	11	0	41	4	4	0	.443	.300
Rooker, Chris, W.T.	.000	45	2	2	0	0	0	0	0	0	0	0	0	0	0	0	1	0	0	0	.000	.000
Borchard, Joe, Birm.†	.295	133	597	515	95	152	262	27	1	27	98	0	5	10	67	1	158	5	4	13	.509	.384
Brantley, Brian, Car.	.000	14	1	1	0	0	0	0	0	0	0	0	0	0	0	0	1	0	0	0	.000	.000
Bravo, Danny, Birm.†	.292	42	187	168	22	49	71	12	2	2	22	1	0	1	17	0	17	3	2	3	.423	.360
Brignac, Junior, Gre.	.202	62	232	203	21	41	55	9	1	1	12	3	0	4	22	0	70	4	2	3	.271	.293
Brooks, Antone, Gre.*	.000	11	2	2	0	0	0	0	0	0	0	0	0	0	0	0	2	0	0	0	.000	.000
Broussard, Benjamin, Chat.* .	.320	100	425	353	81	113	209	27	0	23	69	0	3	8	61	5	69	10	3	5	.592	.428
Brown, Jason, Orl.	.364	3	11	11	2	4	6	2	0	0	1	0	0	0	0	0	2	0	0	0	.545	.364
Brownson, Mark, Hun.*	.087	25	29	23	2	2	2	0	0	0	3	3	1	0	2	0	9	0	0	1	.087	.154
Bruback, Matt, W.T.	.000	9	12	9	1	0	0	0	0	0	0	1	0	0	2	0	9	0	0	0	.000	.182
Burford, Kevin, Car.*	.289	101	419	363	51	105	152	21	4	6	35	0	3	8	45	2	79	4	1	5	.410	.377
Burkhart, Lance, Hun.	.235	52	197	170	34	40	86	10	0	12	38	1	2	3	21	2	54	0	1	5	.506	.327
Burnside, Adrian, Jack.	.167	13	16	12	1	2	2	0	0	0	3	3	1	0	0	0	4	0	0	0	.167	.154
Bynum, Mike, Mob.*	.118	16	17	17	1	2	5	0	0	1	1	0	0	0	0	0	5	0	0	0	.294	.118
Cameron, Ryan, Car.	.000	18	18	13	1	0	0	0	0	0	0	3	0	0	2	0	6	0	0	0	.000	.133
Camp, Shawn, Mob.	.200	36	6	5	0	1	1	0	0	0	0	1	0	0	0	0	2	0	0	0	.200	.200
Cancel, Rob, Hun.	.174	29	96	86	8	15	17	2	0	0	5	2	1	1	6	0	17	0	5	7	.198	.234
Cantu, Jorge, Orl.	.256	130	549	512	58	131	175	26	3	4	45	5	7	8	17	0	93	4	9	13	.342	.287
Caraccioli, Lance, Jack.*	.042	28	30	24	1	1	1	0	0	0	0	0	0	0	0	0	12	0	1	0	.042	.080
Caradonna, Brett, Birm.*	.000	1	1	1	0	0	0	0	0	0	0	0	0	0	0	0	0	0	0	1	.000	.000
Carpenter, Bubba, Car.*	.230	32	117	100	12	23	33	7	0	1	12	0	0	1	16	0	17	3	1	0	.330	.342
Castro, Ramon, Gre.	.307	76	305	261	35	80	127	19	5	6	31	7	3	9	25	0	56	5	8	5	.487	.383
Cesar, Dionys, Hun.†	.282	60	258	227	38	64	102	12	1	8	31	4	2	0	25	0	50	4	3	6	.449	.350
Chen, Chin-Feng, Jack.	.313	66	269	224	47	70	141	16	2	17	50	1	1	2	41	4	65	5	4	7	.629	.422
Chiaffredo, Paul, Tenn.	.250	42	158	132	11	33	45	7	1	1	16	1	1	2	22	2	33	2	2	1	.341	.363
Childers, Jason, Hun.	.000	40	11	11	0	0	0	0	0	0	0	0	0	0	0	0	2	0	0	0	.000	.000
Childers, Matt, Hun.	.182	7	11	11	0	2	2	0	0	0	1	0	0	0	0	0	3	0	0	0	.182	.182
Christensen, Ben, W.T.	.000	3	6	6	0	0	0	0	0	0	0	0	0	0	0	0	3	0	0	0	.000	.000
Colangelo, Mike, Mob.	.265	9	38	34	5	9	14	5	0	0	4	0	0	0	4	0	8	0	0	0	.412	.342
Colina, Javier, Car.	.042	7	25	24	0	1	1	0	0	0	0	0	0	1	0	0	9	0	1	1	.042	.042
Collins, Mike, Jack.	.128	17	46	39	1	5	5	0	0	0	3	3	0	2	5	0	9	2	1	2	.128	.217
Coppinger, Rocky, Hun.	.000	16	3	3	0	0	0	0	0	0	0	0	0	0	0	0	2	0	0	0	.000	.000
Cortes, David, Gre.	1.000	14	1	1	1	1	1	0	0	0	0	0	0	0	0	0	0	0	0	0	1.000	1.000
Cosentino, Tony, Mob.	.000	5	12	10	0	0	0	0	0	0	0	0	0	0	2	0	2	0	0	1	.000	.167
Cox, Steve, Orl.*	.214	4	16	14	2	3	7	1	0	1	3	0	0	0	2	1	1	0	0	0	.500	.313
Crawford, Carl, Orl.*	.274	132	587	537	64	147	189	24	3	4	51	6	2	4	36	2	90	36	20	3	.352	.323
Cridland, Mark, Hun.*	.231	70	248	234	26	54	85	8	1	7	31	1	0	1	12	1	56	3	4	1	.363	.271
Crosby, Bubba, Jack.*	.302	107	443	384	68	116	166	22	5	6	47	7	7	8	37	2	60	22	6	7	.432	.369
Crowder, Chuck, Car.*	.053	33	24	19	3	1	1	0	0	0	1	2	0	0	3	0	12	0	0	0	.053	.182

CLASS AA Southern League

er, Team	Avg.	G	TPA	AB	R	H	TB	2B	3B	HR	RBI	SH	SF	HP	BB	IBB	SO	SB	CS	GDP	Slg.	OBP
Juan, W.T.	.226	23	34	31	3	7	12	2	0	1	5	2	0	0	1	0	8	0	0	1	.387	.250
umberland, Chris, Gre.	.077	20	29	26	1	2	3	1	0	0	2	1	1	0	1	0	11	0	0	0	.115	.107
Curry, Chris, W.T.	.213	42	125	108	9	23	29	3	0	1	11	4	1	0	12	0	34	0	0	3	.269	.289
D'Amico, Jeff, Hun.	.000	1	2	2	1	0	0	0	0	0	0	0	0	0	0	0	0	0	0	0	.000	.000
Darnell, Paul, Chat.	.111	21	9	9	0	1	1	0	0	0	0	0	0	0	0	0	5	0	0	0	.111	.111
Darr, Mike, Mob.*	.200	2	7	5	1	1	1	0	0	0	0	0	0	0	2	0	4	0	0	0	.200	.429
Darula, Bobby, Hun.*	.277	22	71	65	6	18	28	2	1	2	7	1	0	1	4	0	7	1	1	0	.431	.329
Davidson, Cleatus, Mob.†	.218	125	501	467	39	102	134	18	4	2	34	9	2	0	23	0	101	13	8	4	.287	.254
Davis, Glenn, Jack.†	.243	134	556	478	62	116	221	29	8	20	89	0	8	3	67	2	142	14	5	11	.462	.335
Davis, Tim, Hun.*	.000	28	3	3	0	0	0	0	0	0	0	0	0	0	0	0	0	0	0	0	.000	.000
Dawkins, Travis, Chat.	.226	104	435	394	59	89	135	16	3	8	40	4	3	2	32	1	88	14	4	9	.343	.285
Dawley, Joey, Gre.	.133	22	35	30	4	4	6	2	0	0	3	4	1	0	0	0	13	0	0	0	.200	.129
Deardorff, Jeff, Hun.	.279	58	219	201	30	56	111	11	1	14	43	2	1	2	13	0	66	1	1	4	.552	.327
DeCinces, Tim, Mob.*	.206	56	202	180	11	37	55	4	1	4	25	0	3	0	19	0	29	0	0	8	.306	.277
DeHaan, Kory, Mob.*	.296	42	188	159	29	47	71	8	2	4	23	2	3	2	22	1	27	12	4	2	.447	.382
De La Rosa, Maximo, Chat.	.500	39	4	4	0	2	2	0	0	0	2	0	0	0	0	0	2	0	1	0	.500	.500
De Los Santos, Eddy, Orl.	.258	114	454	415	33	107	128	13	1	2	38	10	2	5	22	0	60	14	11	10	.308	.302
Dent, Darrell, Jack.*	.279	117	430	376	50	105	136	15	2	4	32	4	2	6	42	0	91	31	12	5	.362	.359
Dent, Doug, Mob.	1.000	3	1	1	0	1	1	0	0	0	0	0	0	0	0	0	0	0	0	0	1.000	1.000
De Renne, Keoni, Gre.	.238	130	511	453	42	108	136	15	2	3	42	6	3	5	44	3	57	4	2	8	.300	.311
Derosso, Tony, Hun.-Mob.	.234	93	352	312	29	73	122	22	0	9	43	2	5	5	28	1	56	0	1	14	.391	.303
Devey, Phil, Jack.*	.167	24	23	18	1	3	4	1	0	0	1	3	0	0	2	0	4	0	0	0	.222	.250
Dewey, Jason, Car.	.239	71	271	243	24	58	94	21	0	5	27	1	2	2	23	1	78	1	0	4	.387	.307
DeWitt, Scott, Car.	.375	43	9	8	1	3	3	0	0	0	1	0	0	0	0	0	2	0	0	0	.375	.375
Diaz, Alejandro, Chat.	.299	25	91	87	13	26	37	2	0	3	10	0	1	1	2	0	12	0	1	2	.425	.319
Difelice, Mark, Car.	.400	19	19	10	2	4	5	1	0	0	1	5	1	0	3	0	2	0	0	0	.500	.500
Dorame, Randey, Car.*	.000	5	6	5	0	0	0	0	0	0	0	1	0	0	0	0	3	0	0	0	.000	.000
Dunn, Adam, Chat.*	.343	39	168	140	30	48	93	9	0	12	31	1	0	3	24	3	31	6	3	1	.664	.449
Dunn, Scott, Chat.	.056	17	21	18	3	1	1	0	0	0	3	1	0	0	2	0	7	0	0	1	.056	.150
Duplissea, Bill, Jack.	.150	17	49	40	1	6	8	2	0	0	4	1	0	3	5	1	14	0	0	1	.200	.292
Emiliano, Jamie, Car.	.000	50	5	3	1	0	0	0	0	0	0	0	0	0	1	0	3	0	0	0	.000	.250
Ernster, Mark, Hun.	.148	28	90	81	6	12	19	4	0	1	4	1	0	3	4	1	23	0	1	2	.235	.216
Estrella, Leo, Chat.	.000	3	4	3	0	0	0	0	0	0	0	0	0	0	1	0	2	0	0	0	.000	.250
Feliciano, Pedro, Jack.*	.250	56	12	12	3	3	4	1	0	0	0	0	0	0	0	0	5	0	0	1	.333	.333
Figgins, Chone, Car.†	.220	86	382	332	41	73	103	14	5	2	25	6	2	2	40	2	73	27	8	0	.310	.306
Fikac, Jeremy, Mob.	.000	53	4	3	0	0	0	0	0	0	0	0	0	0	1	0	3	0	0	0	.000	.250
Fiore, Curtis, Gre.	.154	13	42	39	2	6	8	2	0	0	3	0	0	0	0	0	13	0	0	1	.205	.195
Fischer, Mike, Jack.	.000	12	6	5	0	0	0	0	0	0	0	0	0	0	1	0	0	0	0	0	.000	.167
Fleming, Ryan, Tenn.*	.278	106	398	349	57	97	154	19	4	10	35	4	5	2	38	5	49	6	6	6	.441	.348
Foster, John, Gre.*	.000	50	4	4	0	0	0	0	0	0	0	0	0	0	0	0	2	0	0	0	.000	.000
Foster, Kris, Jack.	.000	17	1	0	0	0	0	0	0	0	0	1	0	0	0	0	0	0	0	0	.000	.000
Fox, Jason, Hun.†	.246	90	318	289	32	71	94	10	2	3	28	8	2	1	18	0	74	19	7	3	.325	.290
Frese, Nate, W.T.	.180	72	280	233	25	42	61	5	1	4	19	2	2	5	38	1	62	0	1	7	.262	.306
Gagliano, Steve, W.T.	.000	35	5	4	1	0	0	0	0	0	0	0	0	0	1	0	3	0	0	0	.000	.200
Garcia, Jose, Hun.	.208	22	24	24	3	5	7	2	0	0	0	0	0	0	0	0	6	0	0	1	.292	.208
Garcia, Tony, Birm.	.143	2	7	7	1	1	4	0	0	1	1	0	0	0	0	0	3	0	0	0	.571	.143
Gibralter, Dave, Hun.	.271	95	405	354	54	96	154	19	0	13	48	0	3	10	36	4	48	1	2	5	.435	.352
Gibralter, Steve, Chat.	.275	82	343	306	51	84	155	21	1	16	53	2	4	6	25	1	66	10	2	7	.507	.337
Gil, Dave, Chat.	.231	11	15	13	2	3	4	1	0	0	2	2	0	0	0	0	2	0	0	0	.308	.231
Giron, Isabel, Mob.	.000	14	2	2	0	0	0	0	0	0	0	0	0	0	0	0	0	0	0	0	.000	.000
Gissell, Chris, W.T.	.194	28	32	31	2	6	7	1	0	0	1	0	0	0	1	0	11	0	0	0	.226	.219
Glauber, Keith, Chat.	.000	22	9	6	1	0	0	0	0	0	0	2	0	0	1	0	1	0	0	0	.000	.143
Goldbach, Jeff, W.T.	.204	32	109	98	11	20	35	4	1	3	6	1	0	1	9	1	17	1	0	1	.357	.278
Gomes, Tony, Jack.	.000	17	3	3	0	0	0	0	0	0	0	0	0	0	0	0	1	0	0	0	.000	.000
Gomez, Heber, Chat.	.189	10	40	37	2	7	9	2	0	0	1	0	0	2	1	1	7	1	0	1	.243	.225
Gonzalez, Gabe, Mob.*	.000	8	1	1	0	0	0	0	0	0	0	0	0	0	0	0	1	0	0	0	.000	.000
Goudie, Jaime, Tenn.	.253	45	168	154	19	39	53	7	2	1	15	5	2	0	7	0	22	3	1	3	.344	.282
Grace, Mike, Chat.	.000	21	1	1	0	0	0	0	0	0	0	0	0	0	0	0	1	0	0	0	.000	.000
Gray, Mike, Gre.*	.500	25	3	2	0	1	1	0	0	0	0	1	0	0	0	0	1	0	0	0	.500	.500
Green, Chad, Mob.†	.226	42	150	137	14	31	48	8	3	1	15	1	1	0	11	1	42	3	2	0	.350	.282
Grice, Daniel, W.T.	.143	7	18	14	1	2	3	1	0	0	1	1	1	1	1	0	3	0	0	0	.214	.235
Gripp, Ryan, W.T.	.227	68	288	255	31	58	101	19	0	8	45	0	1	7	25	0	60	2	0	2	.396	.313
Gross, Gabe, Tenn.*	.244	11	51	41	8	10	20	1	0	3	11	0	1	3	6	1	12	0	1	1	.488	.373
Grummitt, Dan, Orl.	.238	71	278	244	37	58	104	11	1	11	41	0	0	11	23	1	74	2	2	7	.426	.331
Gulin, Lindsay, Jack.*	.115	26	29	26	0	3	3	0	0	0	0	3	0	0	0	0	8	0	0	1	.115	.115
Guttormson, Rick, Mob.	.208	30	26	24	1	5	8	3	0	0	2	1	0	1	0	0	9	0	0	1	.333	.240
Haas, Chris, W.T.*	.245	126	490	417	64	102	201	16	4	25	72	1	4	3	65	5	151	2	2	6	.482	.348
Hall, Bill, Hun.	.256	41	168	160	14	41	60	8	1	3	14	3	0	5	0	0	46	5	3	5	.375	.279
Haltiwanger, Garrick, Tenn.	.263	46	156	133	23	35	55	9	1	3	15	3	1	1	18	0	33	8	4	5	.414	.353
Hamilton, Josh, Orl.*	.180	23	95	89	5	16	21	5	0	0	4	0	1	0	5	2	22	2	0	1	.236	.221
Harrell, Tim, Jack.	.000	47	6	4	0	0	0	0	0	0	0	0	0	0	1	1	3	0	0	0	.000	.333
Heintz, Chris, Birm.	.235	37	134	119	14	28	42	8	0	2	8	2	1	2	10	0	23	0	2	3	.353	.303
Hessman, Mike, Gre.	.230	129	524	478	66	110	215	23	2	26	80	0	0	7	39	2	124	2	4	5	.450	.290
High, Andy, Hun.*	.167	6	7	6	0	1	1	0	0	0	0	0	0	1	0	0	2	0	0	1	.167	.286
Hill, Bobby, W.T.†	.301	57	246	209	30	63	82	8	1	3	21	1	2	2	32	1	39	20	8	7	.392	.396
Hopper, Shane, Mob.	.257	69	214	191	27	49	65	10	0	2	23	2	1	4	16	2	52	5	4	4	.340	.325
Horn, Jeff, Gre.	.257	72	216	187	18	48	64	10	0	2	16	0	2	1	26	0	42	1	0	8	.342	.347
Howard, Ben, Mob.	.250	7	5	4	0	1	1	0	0	0	0	1	0	0	0	0	3	0	0	0	.250	.250
Howington, Ty, Chat.†	.000	7	7	5	0	0	0	0	0	0	0	0	1	0	1	0	3	0	0	0	.000	.167
Hudson, Luke, Car.	.143	29	32	28	2	4	8	1	0	1	4	3	0	0	1	0	8	0	0	0	.286	.172
Hudson, Orlando, Tenn.†	.307	84	349	306	51	94	144	22	8	4	52	1	2	3	37	3	42	8	3	12	.471	.385
Hummel, Tim, Birm.	.290	134	610	524	83	152	218	33	6	7	63	8	10	5	62	2	69	14	3	12	.416	.364
Hundley, Todd, W.T.†	.333	4	13	12	1	4	6	2	0	0	1	0	0	0	1	0	3	0	0	0	.500	.385

Player, Team	Avg.	G	TPA	AB	R	H	TB	2B	3B	HR	RBI	SH	SF	HP	BB	IBB	SO	SB	CS	GDP	Slg.	OBP
Hunter, Johnny, Mob.	.308	20	17	13	1	4	5	1	0	0	1	0	1	0	3	0	5	1	0	0	.385	.438
Husted, Brent, Jack.	.000	24	3	2	0	0	0	0	0	0	0	1	0	0	0	0	0	0	0	0	.000	.000
Hutchins, Norm, Orl.†	.219	30	115	105	14	23	32	1	1	2	9	1	0	3	6	0	30	4	2	0	.305	.281
Ingram, Darron, Birm.	.263	136	578	514	77	135	243	34	4	22	91	0	8	4	52	3	188	6	6	7	.473	.330
Isenia, Chairon, Orl.	.163	15	47	43	2	7	8	1	0	0	4	1	0	0	3	0	7	0	0	0	.186	.217
Jacobs, Ryan, Hun.	.000	10	1	1	0	0	0	0	0	0	0	0	0	0	0	0	1	0	0	0	.000	.000
Jacobsen, Bucky, Hun.	.441	27	110	93	21	41	80	9	0	10	28	0	1	1	15	2	14	1	2	3	.860	.518
Jennings, Jason, Car.*	.222	4	9	9	1	2	3	1	0	0	0	0	0	0	0	0	1	0	0	0	.333	.222
Johnson, Adam, Birm.*	.257	43	158	148	13	38	53	9	0	2	11	0	0	1	9	1	28	0	0	7	.358	.304
Johnson, Gary, W.T.	.261	135	544	463	87	121	183	28	5	8	64	0	8	15	58	1	105	15	5	6	.395	.357
Johnson, Reed, Tenn.	.314	136	624	554	104	174	250	29	4	13	74	5	2	18	45	2	79	42	12	11	.451	.383
Johnson, Russ, Orl.	.667	1	4	3	0	2	2	0	0	0	0	0	0	0	1	0	0	0	0	1	.667	.750
Jorgensen, Ryan, W.T.	.119	32	123	109	8	13	23	4	0	2	7	0	3	0	11	0	38	0	0	5	.211	.195
Junge, Eric, Jack.	.216	27	41	37	1	8	9	1	0	0	3	4	0	0	0	0	10	0	0	0	.243	.216
Kalinowski, Josh, Car.*	.222	25	30	27	2	6	8	2	0	0	2	1	0	1	1	0	10	0	0	0	.296	.276
Kearns, Austin, Chat.	.268	59	241	205	30	55	88	11	2	6	36	2	2	6	26	0	43	7	5	4	.429	.364
Keck, Brian, Car.	.263	100	362	327	35	86	115	15	1	4	41	7	5	1	22	1	46	12	5	6	.352	.307
Kellner, Ryan, Jack.	.297	25	95	91	5	27	34	4	0	1	9	1	0	0	3	0	20	0	0	1	.374	.319
Kelton, Dave, W.T.	.313	58	251	224	33	70	123	9	4	12	45	0	2	1	24	0	55	1	3	1	.549	.378
Kent, Nathan, Gre.	.139	26	40	36	2	5	6	1	0	0	4	0	0	0	0	0	13	0	0	0	.167	.139
Kibler, Ryan, Car.	.250	8	16	12	1	3	6	0	0	1	3	1	1	0	2	0	5	0	0	0	.500	.333
Kimball, Andy, Hun.	.000	48	2	2	0	0	0	0	0	0	0	0	0	0	0	0	2	0	0	0	.000	.000
Kirby, Scott, Hun.	.228	68	212	184	27	42	73	13	0	6	23	1	1	4	22	1	63	3	0	0	.397	.322
Klimek, Josh, Hun.*	.284	96	363	310	48	88	158	12	2	18	51	3	4	1	45	8	65	2	1	4	.510	.372
Knox, Ryan, Hun.	.188	28	103	96	11	18	20	2	0	0	4	1	0	1	5	0	15	8	2	1	.208	.235
Koonce, Graham, Mob.*	.266	109	416	320	52	85	142	18	0	13	48	1	2	4	89	1	83	0	0	3	.444	.429
Koronka, John, Chat.*	.063	9	18	16	1	1	1	0	0	0	0	0	0	1	0	0	8	0	0	0	.063	.118
Kramer, Aaron, Mob.†	.000	23	5	4	0	0	0	0	0	0	0	0	0	0	1	0	1	0	0	0	.000	.200
Krawczyk, Jack, Hun.	.250	47	5	4	0	1	1	0	0	0	2	1	0	0	0	0	2	0	0	0	.250	.250
Kuilan, Hector, Oar.	.100	10	40	40	3	0	10	2	0	1	0	0	0	0	0	0	0	0	1	0	.002	.200
Lamb, Dave, Car.†	.272	82	341	287	32	78	109	16	0	5	32	11	2	4	37	4	39	2	3	7	.380	.361
Landaeta, Luis, Car.*	.202	66	262	241	27	68	90	11	4	1	23	2	2	1	16	1	27	8	6	2	.373	.327
Langaigne, Selwyn, Tenn.*	.274	19	66	62	6	17	21	4	0	0	7	0	0	1	3	0	11	1	2	2	.339	.318
LaForest, Pete, Orl.*	.005	7	00	01	0	0	0	0	0	0	1	1	0	0	0	0	0	0	0	0	.000	.000
Lee, Derek, Hun.*	.250	30	28	1	7	9	2	0	0	3	1	0	0	1	0	4	0	0	0	.321	.276
Lee, Garrett, Gre.	.063	32	17	16	0	1	1	0	0	0	2	0	0	0	1	0	6	0	0	1	.063	.118
Logan, Matt, Tenn.*	.206	90	313	277	32	57	90	12	1	9	34	1	2	5	20	1	82	3	1	10	.354	.200
Loggins, Josh, Mob.	.191	34	97	89	10	17	26	3	0	2	6	0	1	1	6	1	27	0	0	4	.292	.247
Lontayo, Alejandro, Gre.*	.111	9	11	9	1	1	2	1	0	0	0	1	0	0	1	0	3	0	0	0	.222	.200
Lopez, Felipe, Tenn.†	.222	19	81	72	12	16	26	2	1	2	4	0	0	0	9	0	23	4	4	1	.361	.309
Lopez, Rafael, W.T.	.333	22	75	69	8	23	32	4	1	1	12	1	0	0	5	0	9	0	0	2	.464	.378
Lorenzana, Luis, Mob.	.182	5	13	11	1	2	2	0	0	0	0	0	1	0	1	0	5	0	0	0	.182	.250
Lowe, Benny, Chat.*	.000	26	2	1	0	0	0	0	0	0	0	0	0	0	1	0	1	0	0	0	.000	.500
Loyd, Brian, Tenn.	.220	15	54	50	4	11	14	3	0	0	2	0	0	2	2	0	11	2	0	2	.280	.278
Luebbers, Larry, Chat.	.077	8	15	13	0	1	1	0	0	0	0	0	2	0	0	0	6	0	0	0	.077	.077
MacRae, Scott, Chat.	.231	19	13	13	0	3	3	0	0	0	0	0	0	0	0	0	5	0	0	0	.231	.231
Mallard, Randi, W.T.	.000	8	1	1	0	0	0	0	0	0	0	0	0	0	0	0	0	0	0	0	.000	.000
Mallette, Brian, Hun.	.000	44	5	5	0	0	0	0	0	0	0	0	0	0	0	0	3	0	0	0	.000	.000
Martinez, Belvani, Car.	.260	115	461	430	46	112	162	21	7	5	37	11	3	10	7	1	59	29	13	9	.377	.287
Martinez, Felix, Orl.†	.100	3	10	10	1	1	2	1	0	0	0	0	0	0	0	0	2	1	0	2	.200	.100
Martinez, Lou, Gre.	.182	46	107	99	11	18	21	3	0	0	2	2	0	2	4	0	14	1	0	4	.212	.229
Martinez, Luis, Hun.*	.000	7	1	1	0	0	0	0	0	0	0	0	0	0	0	0	1	0	0	0	.000	.000
Mashore, Justin, Car.	.250	57	187	172	21	43	67	12	0	4	23	1	2	1	11	1	42	4	3	3	.390	.296
Mathis, Jared, Hun.	.245	87	223	204	15	50	69	11	1	2	17	8	0	5	6	1	25	1	1	4	.338	.284
Matos, Julius, Mob.	.320	19	72	67	13	22	28	6	0	0	2	2	1	1	1	0	5	1	2	2	.418	.343
Matthews, Lamont, Jack.†	.145	18	68	55	4	8	12	4	0	0	7	0	1	0	12	0	25	0	1	2	.218	.294
McBride, Chris, Jack.*	.200	4	6	5	0	1	2	1	0	0	1	0	0	0	1	0	2	0	0	0	.400	.333
McClendon, Matt, Gre.	.000	2	3	3	0	0	0	0	0	0	0	0	0	0	0	0	1	0	0	0	.000	.000
McKeel, Walt, Car.	.221	24	89	68	11	15	26	2	0	3	9	3	0	4	14	1	14	0	0	2	.382	.384
McNeal, Aaron, Mob.	.291	59	239	220	27	64	97	13	1	6	29	0	1	2	16	1	53	0	1	14	.441	.343
McNichol, Brian, Chat.*	.200	22	5	5	1	1	1	0	0	0	0	0	0	0	0	0	3	0	0	0	.200	.200
Meadows, Randy, W.T.	.257	64	156	140	16	36	45	7	1	0	15	6	1	3	6	0	35	1	3	0	.321	.300
Meadows, Tydus, W.T.	.269	67	245	197	42	53	99	10	3	10	29	0	0	8	40	2	57	0	2	5	.503	.412
Melian, Jackson, Chat.†	.237	120	473	426	64	101	171	22	0	16	52	0	1	10	36	1	95	10	7	11	.401	.311
Metcalfe, Mike, Chat.†	.289	123	521	474	68	137	179	25	4	3	47	6	1	2	38	2	59	32	10	9	.378	.344
Middlebrook, Jason, Mob.	.000	10	15	13	0	0	0	0	0	0	0	0	0	0	2	0	8	0	0	0	.000	.133
Mieses, Jose, Hun.	.000	5	4	3	0	0	0	0	0	0	0	0	1	0	0	0	0	0	0	0	.000	.250
Miles, Aaron, Birm.†	.259	84	377	343	53	89	135	16	3	8	42	3	3	2	26	0	35	3	5	10	.394	.313
Miller, Corky, Chat.	.276	59	215	170	25	47	86	12	0	9	42	1	0	19	25	1	32	1	2	1	.506	.425
Millwood, Kevin, Gre.	.000	2	3	2	0	0	0	0	0	0	0	0	1	0	0	0	0	0	0	0	.000	.000
Mitchell, Derek, Birm.	.211	82	286	237	37	50	66	8	1	2	21	8	4	3	34	1	68	5	4	5	.278	.313
Montgomery, Matt, Jack.	.000	14	2	2	0	0	0	0	0	0	0	0	0	0	0	0	1	0	0	0	.000	.000
Moon, Brian, Hun.†	.157	97	320	287	17	45	60	11	2	0	16	10	1	2	20	0	50	0	2	7	.209	.216
Moore, Mike, Gre.	.159	27	69	63	8	10	18	2	0	2	6	0	0	2	4	0	33	0	0	0	.286	.232
Moraga, David, W.T.*	.000	23	13	9	0	0	0	0	0	0	0	2	0	0	2	0	7	0	0	0	.000	.182
Morris, Bobby, Chat.*	.281	85	272	224	35	63	110	18	1	9	44	0	4	3	41	2	41	4	4	2	.491	.393
Mortimer, Mark, Gre.	.253	33	95	87	9	22	35	2	1	3	8	0	0	2	6	0	13	0	0	1	.402	.316
Moss, Damian, Gre.	.000	3	3	3	0	0	0	0	0	0	0	0	0	0	0	0	1	0	0	0	.000	.000
Murphy, Mike, Car.	.263	114	485	410	57	108	150	19	1	7	43	1	4	8	62	3	114	21	5	13	.366	.368
Myers, Aaron, Hun.	.308	34	13	13	1	4	5	1	0	0	2	0	0	0	0	0	5	0	0	0	.385	.308
Nanco, Shane, Jack.*	.000	28	5	3	0	0	0	0	0	0	0	1	0	0	1	0	2	0	0	0	.000	.250
Neuberger, Scott, Orl.	.265	120	463	419	49	111	150	25	1	4	43	3	1	4	36	1	83	5	3	9	.358	.328
Neugebauer, Nick, Hun.	.259	21	30	27	1	7	9	2	0	0	5	0	0	0	0	0	6	0	1	0	.333	.259

CLASS AA Southern League

Player, Team	Avg.	G	TPA	AB	R	H	TB	2B	3B	HR	RBI	SH	SF	HP	BB	IBB	SO	SB	CS	GDP	Slg.	OBP
Nevers, Tom, Chat.	.251	120	453	402	63	101	187	33	1	17	67	0	4	4	43	2	101	4	5	17	.465	.327
Nieves, Wil, Mob.	.300	95	356	330	28	99	132	24	0	3	41	2	4	2	18	2	40	1	0	8	.400	.336
Noyce, Dave, W.T.*	.200	51	15	15	1	3	3	0	0	0	2	0	0	0	0	0	5	0	0	0	.200	.200
Nunez, Jorge, Jack.	.260	123	520	473	63	123	154	15	2	4	28	10	1	2	33	3	88	44	11	6	.326	.310
Olivo, Miguel, Birm.	.259	93	368	316	45	82	149	23	1	14	55	5	3	7	37	4	62	6	3	4	.472	.347
Osting, Jimmy, Car.-Mob.	.091	19	28	22	3	2	2	0	0	0	1	2	0	0	4	0	6	0	0	0	.091	.231
Otanez, Willis, Gre.	.266	93	359	308	39	82	136	14	2	12	43	0	5	4	42	3	60	2	2	14	.442	.357
Owens, Jeremy, Mob.	.215	107	462	395	46	85	138	20	6	7	26	5	5	2	55	1	149	33	12	2	.349	.311
Owens, Ryan, Car.	.268	111	466	392	66	105	153	20	2	8	47	1	2	8	63	1	107	12	4	7	.390	.378
Pachot, John, Jack.	.243	46	158	152	12	37	66	15	1	4	22	0	2	0	4	0	20	0	2	4	.434	.259
Paciorek, Pete, Jack.*	.213	65	169	150	17	32	54	8	1	4	20	2	0	1	15	0	42	3	1	6	.360	.289
Palma, Rick, W.T.*	.000	57	6	6	0	0	0	0	0	0	0	0	0	0	0	0	2	0	0	1	.000	.000
Parra, Christian, Gre.	.250	18	23	20	2	5	11	0	0	2	4	2	0	0	1	0	8	0	0	0	.550	.286
Parrish, Wade, Jack.*	.000	4	1	1	0	0	0	0	0	0	0	0	0	0	0	0	0	0	0	0	.000	.000
Pearson, Jason, Mob.*	.250	55	9	8	1	2	2	0	0	0	0	0	0	0	1	0	3	0	0	0	.250	.333
Peavy, Jake, Mob.	.000	5	1	1	0	0	0	0	0	0	0	0	0	0	0	0	1	0	0	0	.000	.000
Pelaez, Alex, Mob.	.281	114	457	416	44	117	171	22	1	10	53	2	5	2	32	3	52	2	0	14	.411	.332
Penney, Mike, Hun.	.143	21	7	7	0	1	1	0	0	0	0	0	0	0	0	0	4	0	0	0	.143	.143
Peralta, Juan, Tenn.†	.500	3	2	2	1	1	1	0	0	0	2	0	0	0	0	0	0	0	0	0	.500	.500
Perez, Eddie, Gre.	.342	10	39	38	7	13	27	2	0	4	5	0	0	1	0	0	9	0	0	0	.711	.359
Perez, Jerson, Tenn.	.282	116	466	422	60	119	162	23	4	4	49	5	4	5	30	0	96	14	3	7	.384	.334
Peters, Tony, Tenn.	.246	91	292	256	46	63	107	9	1	11	33	4	1	4	25	0	83	8	1	5	.418	.322
Phelps, Josh, Tenn.	.292	136	588	486	95	142	273	36	1	31	97	0	5	17	80	4	127	3	3	5	.562	.406
Phillips, J.R., Car.*	.294	31	132	119	18	35	67	8	0	8	23	0	0	1	12	3	33	0	1	1	.563	.364
Pickler, Jeff, Hun.*	.287	134	592	523	74	150	171	17	2	0	32	6	2	1	60	3	51	34	14	2	.327	.360
Piedra, Jorge, W.T.*	.245	124	495	441	55	108	170	26	6	8	54	2	7	8	37	2	80	12	5	8	.385	.310
Piersoll, Chris, Chat.	.000	50	2	2	0	0	0	0	0	0	0	0	0	0	0	0	1	0	0	0	.000	.000
Pigott, Anthony, Orl.	.240	82	272	250	29	60	78	10	1	2	28	11	2	2	7	1	39	8	3	8	.312	.264
Poe, Ryan, Hun.	.250	7	8	8	1	2	2	0	0	0	1	0	0	0	0	0	3	0	0	0	.250	.250
Post, Dave, Jack.	.286	5	15	14	3	4	7	1	1	0	3	0	0	0	1	0	3	0	0	0	.500	.333
Powers, Jeff, Car.*	.190	30	94	84	5	16	20	2	1	0	5	3	0	1	6	0	12	0	1	2	.238	.253
Powers, John, Mob.*	.276	96	365	315	41	87	126	15	6	4	35	4	6	3	37	1	58	7	5	4	.400	.352
Pressley, Josh, Orl.*	.279	30	117	111	10	31	38	2	1	1	12	0	0	0	6	0	22	0	0	4	.342	.316
Prieto, Rick, Birm.†	.240	92	373	313	51	75	107	12	4	4	34	4	1	3	52	0	47	9	6	8	.342	.342
Proctor, Scott, Jack.	.091	10	14	11	1	1	2	1	0	0	0	3	0	0	0	0	8	0	0	0	.182	.091
Quataro, Matt, Orl.	.325	81	300	271	38	88	134	24	2	6	35	1	4	7	17	0	60	4	1	2	.494	.375
Quintero, Humberto, Birm. ...	.211	5	20	19	0	4	4	0	0	0	2	0	1	0	0	0	2	0	0	1	.211	.250
Ramirez, Horacio, Gre.*	.000	3	4	4	0	0	0	0	0	0	0	0	0	0	0	0	1	0	0	0	.000	.000
Ramsey, Brad, W.T.	.250	9	24	20	5	5	12	1	0	2	4	0	0	1	3	0	6	0	0	1	.600	.375
Randall, Scott, Car.	.000	1	2	2	0	0	0	0	0	0	0	0	0	0	0	0	0	0	0	0	.000	.000
Randolph, Jaisen, W.T.†	.230	102	425	365	43	84	97	11	1	0	17	6	1	3	50	1	61	23	15	4	.266	.327
Regalado, Maximo, Jack.	.000	18	1	1	0	0	0	0	0	0	0	0	0	0	0	0	1	0	0	0	.000	.000
Reith, Brian, Chat.	.118	18	23	17	0	2	2	0	0	0	1	3	0	1	2	0	9	0	0	1	.118	.250
Riggins, Auntwan, Mob.†	.147	14	37	34	0	5	5	0	0	0	1	0	0	1	2	0	8	1	1	1	.147	.216
Riggs, Eric, Jack.†	.256	118	455	394	52	101	149	28	1	6	36	11	3	5	42	3	49	7	4	2	.378	.333
Rijo, Jose, Chat.	.000	1	1	0	0	0	0	0	0	0	0	1	0	0	0	0	0	0	0	0	.000	.000
Rivera, Roberto, Gre.†	.237	121	433	392	49	93	132	19	1	6	27	3	2	6	30	0	78	9	4	11	.337	.300
Robinson, Dustin, W.T.	.000	17	1	1	0	0	0	0	0	0	0	0	0	0	0	0	1	0	0	0	.000	.000
Rodriguez, Mike, Tenn.	.300	12	44	40	5	12	24	6	0	2	13	0	1	0	3	0	3	1	0	0	.600	.341
Rodriguez, Tony, W.T.	.282	33	145	131	13	37	45	5	0	1	15	3	2	5	4	0	23	3	3	2	.344	.324
Rose, Pete, Chat.*	.264	35	99	91	8	24	33	6	0	1	14	0	1	0	7	0	16	0	0	5	.363	.313
Ross, Dave, Jack.	.264	74	293	246	35	65	113	13	1	11	45	0	3	10	34	0	72	1	1	5	.459	.372
Ross, Jason, Gre.	.257	63	232	187	27	48	90	7	1	11	30	2	2	8	33	0	55	15	6	5	.481	.387
Rushford, Jim, Hun.*	.342	57	218	187	35	64	103	16	1	7	30	0	3	5	23	0	22	3	2	3	.551	.422
Saipe, Mike, Gre.	.111	7	10	9	1	1	1	0	0	0	0	1	0	0	0	0	4	0	0	0	.111	.111
Sanchez, Wellington, Hun.	.226	89	237	212	28	48	61	10	0	1	14	3	0	0	22	0	56	4	3	3	.288	.299
Sandberg, Jared, Orl.	.286	8	34	28	4	8	13	2	0	1	4	0	0	6	0	0	10	0	0	1	.464	.412
Sandoval, Danny, Birm.	.281	58	230	203	24	57	66	7	1	0	29	6	3	1	17	1	26	17	4	5	.325	.335
Saunders, Chris, Birm.	.294	118	517	442	74	130	193	33	0	10	68	0	7	8	60	1	85	4	1	15	.437	.383
Scheschuk, John, Mob.*	.181	21	90	83	8	15	22	4	0	1	9	0	2	2	5	0	14	1	0	1	.265	.244
Schrager, Tony, W.T.	.244	26	86	78	9	19	26	4	0	1	10	0	0	1	7	0	16	0	0	1	.333	.314
Seal, Scott, Car.*	.204	70	230	186	24	38	59	7	1	4	26	4	3	4	33	2	34	2	2	8	.317	.332
Seifert, Ryan, Car.	.250	34	21	20	0	5	6	1	0	0	0	0	1	0	0	0	4	0	0	0	.300	.250
Shiell, Jason, Mob.	.000	45	11	10	0	0	0	0	0	0	0	1	0	0	0	0	4	0	0	0	.000	.000
Short, Rick, W.T.	.263	8	25	19	5	5	5	0	0	0	0	0	1	0	5	0	1	0	1	0	.263	.440
Shumate, Jacob, Hun.	.000	8	1	1	0	0	0	0	0	0	0	0	0	0	0	0	1	0	0	0	.000	.000
Simon, Ben, Jack.	.067	15	21	15	2	1	1	0	0	0	1	3	0	0	3	0	9	0	0	0	.067	.222
Singleton, Justin, Tenn.*	.278	15	42	36	5	10	10	0	0	0	3	1	1	0	4	0	13	1	1	1	.278	.341
Sismondo, Bobby, Hun.*	1.000	8	1	1	0	1	1	0	0	0	0	0	0	0	0	0	0	0	0	0	1.000	1.000
Smith, Cam, Chat.	.000	29	5	4	0	0	0	0	0	0	0	0	0	0	1	0	1	0	0	0	.000	.200
Smothers, Stewart, Gre.	.233	19	134	120	10	28	35	7	0	0	5	0	0	0	14	1	34	1	2	0	.292	.313
Smyth, Steve, W.T.*	.200	18	34	30	0	6	8	2	0	0	4	2	0	0	2	0	13	0	0	0	.267	.250
Sobkowiak, Scott, Gre.	.000	12	13	9	0	0	0	0	0	0	0	1	2	1	1	0	6	0	0	0	.000	.091
Sollmann, Scott, Chat.*	.314	47	143	121	22	38	43	3	1	0	8	3	0	0	19	2	17	12	6	1	.355	.407
Soto, Saul, Jack.	.333	3	3	3	1	1	1	0	0	0	0	0	0	0	0	0	0	0	0	0	.333	.333
Spooneybarger, Tim, Gre.	1.000	15	1	1	0	1	1	0	0	0	0	0	0	0	0	0	0	0	0	0	1.000	1.000
Stephenson, Brian, Jack.	.000	7	1	0	0	0	0	0	0	0	0	1	0	0	0	0	0	0	0	0	.000	.000
Stevenson, Jason, Mob.	.000	10	1	0	0	0	0	0	0	0	0	0	0	1	0	0	0	0	0	0	.000	1.000
Stoner, Mike, Car.	.265	45	177	155	25	41	60	7	3	2	27	2	1	5	14	1	19	0	0	6	.387	.343
Stull, Everett, Hun.	.286	6	7	7	0	2	2	0	0	0	0	0	0	0	0	0	4	0	0	0	.286	.286
Suarez, Luis, Birm.	.118	6	19	17	4	2	4	2	0	0	2	0	0	1	1	0	6	0	0	1	.235	.211
Sylvester, Billy, Gre.	.000	26	1	1	0	0	0	0	0	0	0	0	0	0	0	0	0	0	0	0	.000	.000
Taglienti, Jeff, Chat.	.000	51	2	2	0	0	0	0	0	0	0	0	0	0	0	0	2	0	0	0	.000	.000

Player, Team	Avg.	G	TPA	AB	R	H	TB	2B	3B	HR	RBI	SH	SF	HP	BB	IBB	SO	SB	CS	GDP	Slg.	OBP
Takeoka, Kazuhiro, Gre.	.167	45	8	6	0	1	1	0	0	0	1	2	0	0	0	0	4	0	0	0	.167	.167
Tankersley, Dennis, Mob.	.167	13	14	12	1	2	5	0	0	1	1	2	0	0	0	0	1	0	0	0	.417	.167
Theodorou, Nick, Jack.†	.294	55	136	102	15	30	35	5	0	0	11	6	1	2	25	2	15	2	1	2	.343	.438
Thompson, Doug, Car.	.333	26	3	3	0	1	1	0	0	0	0	0	0	0	0	0	2	0	0	0	.333	.333
Thompson, Mark, Car.	.200	10	17	15	0	3	4	1	0	0	0	1	0	1	0	0	6	0	0	0	.267	.250
Thompson, Travis, Chat.	.170	31	56	47	5	8	15	4	0	1	1	7	0	0	2	0	13	0	1	1	.319	.204
Thompson, Travis, Car.	.250	28	4	4	0	1	1	0	0	0	0	0	0	0	0	0	0	0	0	0	.250	.250
Thrower, Jake, Mob.†	.272	103	441	386	46	105	144	25	1	4	31	4	1	5	45	1	66	3	3	8	.373	.355
Thurston, Jerrey, Chat.	.160	28	88	81	11	13	21	2	0	2	3	2	0	1	4	0	29	0	0	1	.259	.209
Thurston, Joe, Jack.*	.267	134	616	544	80	145	205	25	7	7	46	9	3	12	48	0	65	20	18	5	.377	.338
Torrealba, Steve, Gre.	.271	90	333	295	37	80	125	21	0	8	34	4	0	1	33	0	54	0	0	8	.424	.347
Trujillo, J.J., Mob.	.000	43	1	1	0	0	0	0	0	0	0	0	0	0	0	0	0	0	0	0	.000	.000
Tucci, Pete, Mob.	.185	18	69	65	3	12	12	0	0	0	7	0	1	0	3	0	22	1	1	0	.185	.217
Tyler, Brad, Chat.*	.255	14	52	47	7	12	21	4	1	1	11	0	0	0	5	0	13	1	1	0	.447	.327
Uribe, Juan, Car.	.231	3	13	13	1	3	4	1	0	0	1	0	0	0	0	0	4	1	0	1	.308	.231
Urquiola, Carlos, Gre.*	.303	40	150	132	18	40	45	5	0	0	10	0	2	1	15	0	15	6	4	1	.341	.373
Valencia, Vic, Chat.	.230	76	266	230	24	53	83	8	2	6	33	3	3	3	27	2	59	2	0	8	.361	.316
Valenzuela, Mario, Birm.	.290	88	373	341	50	99	158	17	3	12	53	3	6	2	21	2	61	4	5	8	.463	.330
Valera, Yohanny, Orl.	.256	75	282	250	26	64	108	20	3	6	32	3	3	13	13	0	67	0	2	6	.432	.323
Van Rossum, Chris, Chat.*	.222	18	28	27	5	6	8	2	0	0	3	0	0	0	1	0	12	0	0	0	.296	.250
Voyles, Brad, Gre.	.000	15	2	2	0	0	0	0	0	0	0	0	0	0	0	0	2	0	0	0	.000	.000
Watkins, Steve, Mob.	.000	23	14	14	0	0	0	0	0	0	0	0	0	0	0	0	6	0	0	0	.000	.000
Weekly, Chris, Tenn.*	.260	45	152	131	16	34	52	4	1	4	23	2	0	4	14	1	35	0	2	3	.397	.349
Welsh, Eric, Chat.*	.203	25	74	69	5	14	25	2	0	3	11	0	2	0	3	0	24	0	2	2	.362	.230
Werth, Jayson, Tenn.	.285	104	443	369	51	105	184	23	1	18	69	1	7	3	63	0	93	12	3	5	.499	.387
White, Rondell, W.T.	.143	9	31	28	2	4	11	1	0	2	4	0	0	2	1	0	7	0	0	1	.393	.226
Williams, Glenn, Tenn.†	.255	130	544	487	63	124	185	28	0	11	65	2	5	5	45	4	120	1	5	8	.380	.321
Wilson, Travis, Gre.	.325	31	128	123	13	40	56	8	1	2	21	0	1	1	3	1	24	2	5	4	.455	.344
Winkelsas, Joe, Gre.	.000	20	4	4	0	0	0	0	0	0	0	0	0	0	0	0	2	0	0	0	.000	.000
Wise, Dewayne, Tenn.*	.239	87	379	351	44	84	133	13	6	8	44	4	2	1	21	1	58	13	5	6	.379	.283
Wright, Nato, Jack.	.000	1	1	1	0	0	0	0	0	0	0	0	0	0	0	0	0	0	0	0	.000	.000
Wrigley, Jase, Car.	.333	47	8	3	1	1	1	0	0	0	0	0	0	0	5	0	2	0	0	0	.333	.750
Wuertz, Mike, W.T.	.114	27	43	35	2	4	5	1	0	0	1	6	0	0	2	0	15	0	0	1	.143	.162
Zapp, A.J., Gre.*	.233	75	318	292	36	68	109	17	0	8	34	0	0	5	21	0	87	5	1	11	.373	.296

PLAYERS WITH TWO OR MORE TEAMS

Player, Team	Avg.	G	TPA	AB	R	H	TB	2B	3B	HR	RBI	SH	SF	HP	BB	IBB	SO	SB	CS	GDP	Slg.	OBP
Derosso, Tony, Hun.	.234	65	245	218	21	51	86	17	0	6	25	2	4	2	19	1	36	0	1	12	.394	.296
Derosso, Tony, Mob.	.234	28	107	94	8	22	36	5	0	3	18	0	1	3	9	0	20	0	0	2	.303	.318
Osting, Jimmy, Car.	1.000	1	2	1	2	1	1	0	0	0	0	0	0	0	1	0	0	0	0	0	1.000	1.000
Osting, Jimmy, Mob.	.048	18	26	21	1	1	1	0	0	0	1	2	0	0	3	0	6	0	0	0	.048	.167

GRAND SLAMS: Gibralter, Nevers, Peters, 2; D. Abreu, Allen, Battersby, Beattie, Broussard, Crawford, Darula, Dewey, Hessman, Hill, Re. Johnson, Mashore, Miles, Morris, Nieves, J. Perez, Prieto, Rivera, D. Ross, Joe Thurston, Valenzuela, Welsh, Werth, 1 each.

AWARDED FIRST BASE ON CATCHER'S INTERFERENCE: Crawford (Ross 2), Gibralter (Heintz, Quatraro), Peters (Mortimer, Ross), 2 each; Ernster (Miller), Hummel (Torrealba), Nunez (McKeel), Paciorek (LaForest), Weekly (Acevas), 1 each.

2001 PITCHING

TEAM

Team	W	L	Pct.	ERA	G	CG	ShO	Sv.	IP	H	TBF	R	ER	HR	SH	SF	HB	BB	IBB	SO	WP	Bk.
Jacksonville	83	56	.597	3.29	139	2	8	42	1232.1	1109	5164	530	451	119	58	28	70	417	11	1031	43	8
Huntsville	75	63	.543	3.46	138	2	12	39	1215.2	1149	5191	540	467	103	50	37	57	429	25	1085	63	3
Tennessee	80	60	.571	3.75	140	14	14	38	1229.0	1155	5199	576	512	134	48	33	82	386	14	874	51	1
Mobile	65	73	.471	3.94	138	1	8	39	1225.2	1171	5252	613	536	110	59	49	63	473	26	975	45	2
Greenville	60	79	.432	3.96	139	4	7	33	1212.2	1181	5237	614	534	106	76	41	47	484	32	1012	69	13
Birmingham	80	60	.571	4.01	140	3	12	43	1230.1	1215	5311	642	548	86	40	44	72	488	19	935	78	9
Chattanooga	72	67	.518	4.04	139	6	14	30	1216.2	1206	5293	625	546	92	67	36	45	497	16	1084	45	4
Orlando	59	81	.421	4.04	140	3	13	30	1220.1	1242	5298	640	548	116	50	44	66	457	11	956	73	9
Carolina	62	76	.449	4.18	138	6	11	28	1210.0	1256	5367	655	562	105	54	43	73	508	14	976	67	6
West Tenn	59	80	.424	4.26	139	5	9	28	1216.1	1196	5330	654	576	119	59	44	72	519	26	1114	73	5

INDIVIDUAL

TOP QUALIFIERS FOR EARNED-RUN AVERAGE TITLE

Minimum 112 innings.*Lefthanded pitcher.

Pitcher, Team	W	L	Pct.	ERA	G	GS	CG	ShO	GF	Sv.	IP	H	TBF	R	ER	HR	SH	SF	HB	BB	IBB	SO	WP	Bk.
Smyth, Steve, W.T.*	9	3	.750	2.54	18	18	3	1	0	0	120.1	110	497	38	34	9	4	1	5	40	1	93	6	0
Gulin, Lindsay, Jack.*	7	5	.583	2.64	26	21	1	1	0	0	126.1	128	541	46	37	10	5	3	6	46	0	111	0	2
Wright, Danny, Birm.	7	7	.500	2.82	20	20	0	0	0	0	134.0	112	548	54	42	6	3	7	6	41	0	128	6	2
Magrane, Jim, Orl.	8	12	.400	2.97	29	28	1	0	0	0	182.0	166	755	87	60	15	6	7	4	56	1	126	13	1
Dawley, Joey, Gre.	7	5	.583	3.04	22	21	1	0	0	0	127.1	95	518	50	43	15	6	4	4	46	0	130	3	1
Difelice, Mark, Car.	6	4	.600	3.15	19	18	2	1	0	0	123.0	108	498	47	43	13	3	5	3	23	0	98	1	0
Baker, Chris, Tenn.	15	6	.714	3.37	28	26	4	1	2	1	179.0	162	729	73	67	22	8	7	8	42	0	121	8	0
Lee, Derek, Hun.*	7	11	.389	3.38	28	28	0	0	0	0	162.1	173	695	76	61	10	5	8	2	39	2	109	4	0
Junge, Eric, Jack.	10	11	.476	3.46	27	27	1	1	0	0	164.0	143	686	72	63	19	11	3	13	56	2	116	6	0
Cumberland, Chris, Gre.*	3	7	.300	3.46	20	20	2	1	0	0	125.0	126	529	51	48	5	9	4	3	40	0	85	2	1
Devey, Phil, Jack.*	8	2	.800	3.77	24	17	0	0	2	1	112.1	121	482	56	47	12	3	4	8	21	0	76	4	2
Thompson, Travis, Chat.	12	10	.545	3.88	28	28	3	1	0	0	167.0	170	708	82	72	10	10	2	6	46	3	118	3	0
Agosto, Stevenson, Orl.*	8	10	.444	3.90	30	18	2	2	4	0	129.1	114	545	62	56	12	10	5	3	57	1	113	4	4

Pitcher, Team	W	L	Pct.	ERA	G	GS	CG	ShO	GF	Sv.	IP	H	TBF	R	ER	HR	SH	SF	HB	BB	IBB	SO	WP	Bk.
Chacin, Gustavo, Tenn.*	11	8	.579	3.98	25	23	1	1	0	0	140.1	138	588	66	62	17	2	3	7	39	0	86	5	0
Wuertz, Mike, W.T.	4	9	.308	3.99	27	27	1	1	0	0	160.0	160	694	80	71	20	9	6	6	58	2	135	10	0

DEPARTMENTAL LEADERS: W—Baker, Wylie, 15 each; L—Guttormson, 16; Pct.—Devey, .800; G—Booker, 61; GS—Hudson, De. Lee, Magrane, Travis R. Thompson, 28 each; CG—Baker, Cassidy, 4 each; ShO—Cassidy, 3; GF—Almonte, 48; Sv.—Almonte, 36; IP—Magrane, 182; H—Kent, 186; TBF—Magrane, 755; R—Purvis, 96; ER—Purvis, 82; HR—Baker, 22; SH—John Foster, Kimball, 7 each; SF—Gissell, De. Lee, Shiell, 8 each; HB—Cruz, 16; BB—Dunn, 71; IBB—John Foster, Kimball, 7 each; SO—Neugebauer, 149; WP—Hudson, 18; BK—Agosto, 4.

ALL PITCHERS

*Lefthanded pitcher.

Pitcher, Team	W	L	Pct.	ERA	G	GS	CG	ShO	GF	Sv.	IP	H	TBF	R	ER	HR	SH	SF	HB	BB	IBB	SO	WP	Bk.
Abreu, Winston, Gre.	3	5	.375	4.64	34	7	0	0	4	0	73.2	56	319	40	38	9	5	2	5	45	2	93	2	1
Acevedo, Jose, Chat.	4	4	.500	3.69	16	11	0	0	1	0	78.0	68	319	34	32	6	5	1	3	25	1	82	2	0
Achilles, Matt, W.T.	3	4	.429	4.10	9	9	0	0	0	0	52.2	56	223	26	24	2	3	0	2	22	1	39	2	1
Agosto, Stevenson, Orl.*	8	10	.444	3.90	30	18	2	2	4	0	129.1	114	545	62	56	12	10	5	3	57	1	113	4	4
Almonte, Ed, Birm.	1	4	.200	1.49	54	0	0	0	48	36	66.1	58	272	16	11	4	2	0	0	16	4	62	2	0
Alvarez, Victor, Jack.*	2	0	1.000	1.20	8	8	0	0	0	0	45.0	27	163	6	6	1	1	0	1	7	0	40	2	0
Alvarez, Wilson, Orl.*	1	3	.250	4.43	5	5	0	0	0	0	20.1	24	92	10	10	2	0	1	1	6	0	18	1	0
Andrews, Clayton, Chat.*	1	3	.250	6.00	6	6	0	0	0	0	36.0	41	163	27	24	4	1	3	0	16	0	19	0	0
Aramboles, Ricardo, Chat.	0	2	.000	8.00	2	1	0	0	1	0	9.0	12	42	8	8	1	1	1	3	0	0	5	0	0
Backe, Brandon, Orl.	1	0	1.000	5.73	14	0	0	0	3	0	22.0	20	94	14	14	1	0	0	4	11	0	20	2	0
Bajenaru, Jeff, Birm.	0	0	.000	0.00	2	0	0	0	1	0	4.1	4	21	0	0	0	0	0	0	3	0	5	1	0
Baker, Chris, Tenn.	15	6	.714	3.37	28	26	4	1	2	1	179.0	162	729	73	67	22	8	7	8	42	0	121	8	0
Baptist, Travis, Birm.*	1	4	.200	1.93	10	3	0	0	5	2	37.1	37	156	16	8	0	4	4	9	3	42	3	0
Bartosh, Cliff, Mob.*	1	2	.333	3.97	20	0	0	0	9	2	22.2	20	103	12	10	5	2	1	1	13	1	20	2	0
Bauer, Greg, Jack.	0	1	.000	6.28	6	0	0	0	2	0	14.1	17	69	13	10	4	1	0	0	10	0	8	0	0
Bauer, Pete, Tenn.	6	8	.429	5.11	21	21	0	0	0	0	128.2	147	574	84	73	12	5	3	10	37	1	71	8	1
Bausher, Andy, Mob.*	0	1	.000	12.00	4	0	0	0	1	0	6.0	9	36	8	8	1	1	0	0	4	1	0	0	0
Beaumont, Matt, Birm.*	1	0	1.000	18.00	4	0	0	0	1	0	4.0	8	23	8	8	1	0	1	1	2	0	3	2	0
Berry, Jon, Jack.	0	1	.000	3.00	3	1	0	0	0	0	9.0	6	35	3	3	0	1	0	0	4	0	5	0	0
Bevel, Bobby, Jack.*	2	2	.500	1.96	31	0	0	0	16	6	46.0	42	189	14	10	3	2	2	2	11	0	33	1	0
Bleazard, Dave, Tenn.	0	0	.000	1.35	3	3	0	0	0	0	20.0	15	75	3	3	1	0	0	0	5	0	11	0	0
Bohannan, Brad, Birm.	3	5	.375	5.65	29	0	0	0	12	0	51.0	61	234	36	32	9	4	5	3	21	2	25	2	0
Booker, Chris, W.T.-Chat.	4	6	.400	4.24	61	0	0	0	17	2	68.0	52	307	36	32	8	6	3	1	47	2	101	7	0
Brantley, Brian, Car.	0	2	.000	7.36	14	0	0	0	11	0	22.0	31	108	19	18	1	2	2	0	16	2	23	3	0
Brooks, Antone, Gre.*	0	1	.000	6.62	11	0	0	0	3	0	17.2	18	77	13	13	2	1	2	1	9	0	10	1	0
Brownson, Mark, Hun.	10	5	.667	4.47	24	23	0	0	0	0	131.0	143	571	67	65	18	3	2	8	35	0	115	3	0
Bruback, Matt, W.T.	2	5	.286	9.00	9	9	0	0	0	0	38.0	58	197	44	38	3	1	2	6	20	1	43	2	2
Burnside, Adrian, Jack.*	4	3	.571	2.66	13	12	0	0	0	0	67.2	44	280	21	20	6	2	0	5	30	0	67	4	2
Bynum, Mike, Mob.*	2	7	.222	5.02	16	15	0	0	0	0	84.1	90	368	53	47	14	4	3	3	35	0	69	0	0
Cameron, Ryan, Car.	7	6	.538	5.22	18	13	0	0	1	0	89.2	112	427	64	52	10	3	3	4	45	0	74	4	0
Camp, Shawn, Mob.	6	2	.750	4.44	35	1	0	0	6	0	48.2	46	204	24	24	2	5	2	6	15	1	55	2	0
Caraballo, Angel, Tenn.	3	3	.500	5.47	26	5	1	0	4	1	52.2	51	227	36	32	7	0	2	2	21	1	36	1	0
Caraccioli, Lance, Jack.*	8	4	.667	4.64	28	18	0	0	4	1	130.0	139	561	76	67	7	8	5	8	45	0	87	7	0
Casey, Joe, Tenn.	4	3	.571	4.72	42	0	0	0	12	1	61.0	74	275	36	32	8	7	1	5	16	1	42	6	0
Cassidy, Scott, Tenn.	6	6	.500	3.44	16	15	4	3	0	0	96.2	78	394	45	37	10	3	0	7	27	0	81	1	0
Chacin, Gustavo, Tenn.*	11	8	.579	3.98	25	23	1	1	0	0	140.1	138	588	66	62	17	2	3	7	39	0	86	5	0
Chiasson, Scott, W.T.	3	4	.429	1.76	52	0	0	0	45	24	61.1	43	247	15	12	2	4	1	4	20	4	62	7	0
Childers, Jason, Hun.	7	6	.538	2.87	40	2	0	0	10	2	87.2	76	364	32	28	7	2	2	2	30	3	85	2	0
Childers, Matt, Hun.	2	2	.500	3.43	7	7	0	0	0	0	39.1	41	172	19	15	3	1	1	5	12	0	21	3	0
Christensen, Ben, W.T.	2	1	.667	6.48	3	3	0	0	0	0	16.2	20	74	12	12	2	1	0	0	9	0	9	1	0
Chulk, Vinny, Tenn.	2	5	.286	3.14	24	1	0	0	7	0	43.0	34	169	15	15	5	5	4	2	8	1	43	1	0
Coco, Pasqual, Tenn.	0	1	.000	3.94	3	3	0	0	0	0	16.0	13	65	7	7	3	0	0	5	5	0	13	1	0
Condrey, Clay, Mob.	2	2	.500	4.54	27	0	0	0	23	12	33.2	33	144	23	17	1	4	2	0	15	4	21	0	0
Cook, Derrick, W.T.	0	2	.000	8.10	4	0	0	0	2	0	6.2	9	33	6	6	2	2	0	0	5	1	3	0	0
Coppinger, Rocky, Hun.	2	0	1.000	2.12	16	0	0	0	7	4	29.2	28	125	9	7	1	2	0	2	11	0	24	1	0
Cortes, David, Gre.	0	3	.000	8.15	14	0	0	0	6	0	17.2	19	85	18	16	2	1	0	1	11	2	10	3	1
Crowder, Chuck, Car.*	6	6	.500	5.35	32	14	0	0	3	0	101.0	126	482	64	60	7	1	4	7	63	1	71	8	2
Crowell, Jim, Mob.*	1	0	1.000	2.08	5	0	0	0	1	0	4.1	2	18	1	1	0	1	0	0	4	0	0	0	0
Cruz, Juan, W.T.	9	6	.600	4.01	23	23	0	0	0	0	121.1	107	534	56	54	6	6	2	16	60	1	137	4	0
Cueto, Jose, W.T.	0	1	.000	8.68	2	2	0	0	0	0	9.1	10	44	9	9	5	1	0	2	6	0	10	1	0
Cumberland, Chris, Gre.*	3	7	.300	3.46	20	20	2	1	0	0	125.0	126	529	51	48	5	9	4	3	40	0	85	2	1
D'Amico, Jeff, Hun.	1	0	1.000	2.57	1	1	0	0	0	0	7.0	3	25	2	2	2	0	0	0	2	0	5	0	0
Daneker, Pat, W.T.	0	0	.000	13.50	2	0	0	0	0	0	1.1	3	9	2	2	0	0	0	0	2	0	1	0	0
Darnell, Paul, Chat.*	3	1	.750	2.58	21	4	0	0	1	0	38.1	39	169	13	11	1	4	1	2	13	0	43	0	1
Davis, Tim, Hun.*	1	2	.333	2.87	28	0	0	0	11	2	37.2	36	167	15	12	1	2	1	5	18	3	32	1	0
Dawley, Joey, Gre.	7	5	.583	3.04	22	21	1	0	0	0	127.1	95	518	50	43	15	6	4	4	46	0	130	3	1
DeCinces, Tim, Mob.	0	0	.000	0.00	1	0	0	0	1	0	3.0	3	21	3	0	0	1	0	2	5	0	3	0	0
De La Rosa, Maximo, Chat.	2	6	.250	5.21	38	0	0	0	17	2	46.2	57	213	31	27	4	1	4	2	13	1	52	1	0
Dent, Doug, Mob.	0	1	.000	10.13	3	1	0	0	0	0	5.1	10	31	6	6	0	0	1	5	0	0	2	0	0
Devey, Phil, Jack.*	8	2	.800	3.77	24	17	0	0	2	1	112.1	121	482	56	47	12	3	4	8	21	0	76	4	2
DeWitt, Scott, Car.*	2	6	.250	3.57	43	1	0	0	17	1	63.0	66	286	36	25	5	3	7	28	0	52	1	0
Dickson, Jason, Tenn.	2	1	.667	3.31	5	5	0	0	0	0	32.2	30	138	12	12	1	1	0	2	11	0	21	0	0
Difelice, Mark, Car.	6	4	.600	3.15	19	18	2	1	0	0	123.0	108	498	47	43	13	3	5	3	23	0	98	1	0
Dimma, Doug, Tenn.*	0	2	.000	5.40	19	0	0	0	4	1	13.1	16	61	8	8	2	1	1	2	9	1	5	0	0
Dorame, Randey, Car.*	0	4	.000	4.82	5	5	0	0	0	0	28.0	33	120	17	15	3	0	3	0	6	0	17	1	0
Dunn, Scott, Chat.	7	2	.778	4.12	17	17	0	0	0	0	98.1	96	450	51	45	10	8	2	2	71	0	87	8	0
Emiliano, Jamie, Car.	3	6	.333	3.34	50	0	0	0	25	2	64.2	56	281	29	24	4	5	0	6	30	3	38	1	0
Enders, Trevor, Orl.*	3	3	.500	4.94	13	6	0	0	1	0	47.1	51	196	26	26	9	1	0	3	5	0	38	2	0
Esslinger, Cam, Car.	1	1	.500	4.93	40	0	0	0	29	16	42.0	32	192	26	23	0	4	2	2	31	1	51	8	0
Estrella, Leo, Chat.	0	1	.000	3.68	3	3	0	0	0	0	14.2	13	59	6	6	0	0	0	1	4	0	14	0	0
Feliciano, Pedro, Jack.*	5	4	.556	1.94	54	0	0	0	38	17	60.1	41	229	14	13	3	4	0	3	11	1	55	2	0

Pitcher, Team	W	L	Pct.	ERA	G	GS	CG	ShO	GF	Sv.	IP	H	TBF	R	ER	HR	SH	SF	HB	BB	IBB	SO	WP	Bk.
Fikac, Jeremy, Mob.	6	0	1.000	1.97	53	0	0	0	33	18	68.2	54	276	16	15	3	4	2	3	20	4	75	3	0
File, Bob, Tenn.	0	0	.000	3.00	3	0	0	0	3	1	3.0	3	10	1	1	1	0	0	0	0	0	2	0	0
Fiore, Curtis, Gre.	0	0	.000	0.00	1	0	0	0	1	0	1.0	2	5	0	0	0	0	0	0	0	0	0	0	0
Fischer, Mike, Jack.	1	0	1.000	5.14	12	4	0	0	1	0	28.0	30	124	18	16	7	2	0	4	8	1	28	1	0
Forster, Scott, Hun.*	1	1	.500	6.23	6	1	0	0	1	0	8.2	10	43	8	6	1	1	2	0	7	0	6	1	0
Foster, John, Gre.*	8	7	.533	3.01	50	0	0	0	21	7	68.2	71	303	30	23	6	11	3	2	33	7	63	5	0
Foster, Kris, Jack.	3	0	1.000	1.00	17	0	0	0	17	7	18.0	6	64	2	2	1	0	0	1	3	0	29	0	0
Freeman, Kai, Birm.	5	3	.625	5.08	28	10	0	0	6	0	83.1	100	375	53	47	4	2	3	9	33	2	38	4	0
Gagliano, Steve, W.T.	1	2	.333	4.25	35	1	0	0	3	0	48.2	49	217	24	23	5	3	2	1	23	3	44	2	1
Garcia, Jose, Hun.	6	5	.545	3.73	21	21	1	0	0	0	111.0	99	481	52	46	6	4	7	8	49	1	84	6	0
Gardner, Lee, Orl.	0	0	.000	0.00	1	0	0	0	0	0	1.2	0	4	0	0	0	0	0	0	0	0	0	0	0
Garibaldi, Cecilio, Orl.	5	6	.455	4.49	35	12	0	0	5	1	104.1	111	448	57	52	16	2	2	6	37	0	66	6	0
Gil, Dave, Chat.	6	1	.857	3.10	11	10	0	0	1	1	61.0	65	269	23	21	4	1	2	2	30	0	55	4	1
Giron, Isabel, Mob.	0	0	.000	1.96	14	0	0	0	2	0	18.1	15	74	5	4	2	1	0	1	4	0	20	0	0
Gissell, Chris, W.T.	5	11	.313	4.51	28	27	0	0	0	0	159.2	159	695	91	80	13	5	8	9	63	0	136	7	0
Glauber, Keith, Chat.	2	1	.667	4.26	22	4	0	0	5	0	44.1	53	188	21	21	9	3	2	1	8	0	30	0	0
Gomes, Tony, Jack.	1	1	.500	2.86	17	0	0	0	5	2	28.1	30	129	13	9	1	1	1	0	15	2	31	1	1
Gonzalez, Gabe, Mob.*	1	0	1.000	1.32	8	0	0	0	1	0	13.2	18	57	6	2	0	2	0	0	1	0	8	0	0
Gonzalez, Lariel, W.T.	1	1	.500	4.63	11	0	0	0	3	0	11.2	15	59	11	6	1	2	0	0	7	0	8	0	0
Grace, Mike, Chat.	3	2	.600	5.67	21	1	0	0	7	0	33.1	44	161	26	21	2	1	1	4	15	3	27	3	0
Gray, Mike, Gre.*	3	1	.750	3.79	25	0	0	0	10	0	40.1	41	177	23	17	4	2	2	13	2	22	0	0
Guerrier, Matt, Birm.	11	3	.786	3.10	15	15	1	1	0	0	98.2	85	402	42	34	8	5	0	5	32	1	75	5	0
Gulin, Lindsay, Jack.*	7	5	.583	2.64	26	21	1	0	0	0	126.1	128	541	46	37	10	5	3	6	46	0	111	0	2
Guttormson, Rick, Mob.	5	16	.238	4.71	27	24	0	0	2	0	143.1	146	624	84	75	18	4	4	13	51	0	78	5	0
Guzman, Juan, Orl.	2	0	1.000	0.75	2	2	0	0	0	0	12.0	8	45	1	1	0	0	0	4	0	9	0	0
Haines, Talley, Orl.	6	6	.500	3.64	58	0	0	0	38	8	71.2	73	316	32	29	7	8	1	2	29	3	73	6	0
Halladay, Roy, Tenn.	2	1	.667	2.12	5	5	3	0	0	0	34.0	25	132	9	8	2	0	0	2	6	0	29	2	0
Harrell, Tim, Jack.	5	4	.556	3.00	47	1	0	0	23	5	81.0	70	338	32	27	11	3	1	3	29	2	71	4	0
Hessman, Mike, Gre.	0	0	.000	0.00	1	0	0	0	1	0	1.0	1	4	0	0	0	0	0	0	0	0	2	0	0
High, Andy, Hun.*	2	1	.667	2.12	6	5	0	0	0	0	29.2	22	117	9	7	4	3	2	0	6	0	28	1	0
Howard, Ben, Mob.	2	0	1.000	2.40	7	5	0	0	1	0	30.0	17	117	9	8	3	0	0	0	15	0	29	3	0
Howington, Ty, Chat.*	1	3	.250	3.27	7	7	0	0	0	0	41.1	36	181	18	15	3	3	2	2	24	1	38	4	1
Hubbel, Travis, Tenn.	1	0	1.000	3.38	6	5	0	0	0	0	26.2	20	114	11	10	3	1	1	3	18	0	12	2	0
Hudson, Luke, Car.	7	12	.368	4.20	29	28	1	0	0	0	165.0	159	729	90	77	19	5	4	15	68	0	145	18	1
Hunter, Johnny, Mob.	3	6	.333	4.85	19	16	1	0	1	0	98.1	105	428	57	53	7	5	2	6	37	1	61	1	0
Husted, Brent, Jack.	3	3	.500	5.50	23	0	0	0	6	1	37.2	52	171	25	23	6	1	1	3	13	0	21	1	0
Jacobs, Ryan, Hun.*	0	1	.000	2.77	10	0	0	0	2	0	13.0	10	58	6	4	0	1	0	1	5	1	15	0	0
James, Delvin, Orl.	2	0	1.000	1.65	7	7	0	0	0	0	43.2	25	163	8	8	1	2	1	2	9	0	31	2	1
Jennings, Jason, Car.	2	0	1.000	2.88	4	4	0	0	0	0	25.0	25	106	9	8	1	0	0	1	8	0	24	0	0
Jimenez, Jason, Orl.*	3	3	.500	3.18	35	4	0	0	22	10	51.0	46	218	20	18	2	2	1	3	24	1	40	2	0
Johnson, Adam, Birm.*	0	0	.000	0.00	1	0	0	0	1	0	1.0	1	4	0	0	0	0	0	0	0	0	1	0	0
Junge, Eric, Jack.	10	11	.476	3.46	27	27	1	1	0	0	164.0	143	686	72	63	19	11	3	13	56	2	116	6	0
Kalinowski, Josh, Car.*	7	8	.467	4.06	25	25	0	0	0	0	137.1	151	616	76	62	15	8	5	5	65	0	116	5	1
Kane, Kyle, Birm.	2	1	.667	1.85	26	0	0	0	12	3	34.0	20	127	9	7	1	2	0	3	6	1	43	6	0
Kennedy, Joe, Orl.*	4	0	1.000	0.19	7	7	0	0	0	0	47.0	29	170	3	1	0	1	1	2	3	0	52	2	0
Kent, Nathan, Gre.	8	10	.444	4.07	26	26	0	0	0	0	154.2	186	679	89	70	12	4	5	3	38	2	111	2	1
Kibler, Ryan, Car.	4	1	.800	2.11	8	8	1	0	0	0	47.0	38	198	17	11	0	1	1	1	19	0	41	6	0
Kimball, Andy, Hun.	8	6	.571	3.03	48	0	0	0	16	2	71.1	73	314	32	24	7	7	2	3	28	7	39	5	0
Kingrey, Jarrod, Tenn.	5	3	.625	2.47	51	0	0	0	45	27	54.2	41	236	17	15	6	2	1	7	32	2	52	1	0
Kofler, Ed, Orl.	2	7	.222	7.84	13	13	0	0	0	0	59.2	81	290	57	52	7	0	4	5	26	0	39	3	0
Koronka, John, Chat.*	1	5	.167	5.73	9	9	0	0	0	0	55.0	62	251	37	35	7	4	1	1	28	0	44	1	1
Kramer, Aaron, Mob.-W.T.	2	7	.222	5.65	25	4	0	0	5	0	51.0	56	225	35	32	12	4	3	2	12	1	43	3	0
Krawczyk, Jack, Hun.	6	2	.750	3.43	47	0	0	0	19	1	81.1	67	321	33	31	9	3	0	4	16	3	66	6	1
Krug, Dustin, W.T.	0	0	.000	9.90	7	0	0	0	3	0	10.0	16	53	12	11	1	0	1	3	5	0	9	0	0
Langone, Steve, Jack.	0	0	.000	1.50	1	1	0	0	0	0	6.0	2	20	1	1	0	0	1	0	0	0	8	0	0
Lantigua, Eduardo, Birm.	4	0	1.000	3.71	7	7	2	1	0	0	43.2	40	183	19	18	2	0	4	0	18	0	34	2	0
Lee, Dave, Mob.	0	0	.000	0.00	2	0	0	0	0	0	2.0	2	7	0	0	0	0	0	0	0	0	3	1	0
Lee, Derek, Hun.*	7	11	.389	3.38	28	28	0	0	0	0	162.1	173	695	76	61	10	5	8	2	39	2	109	4	0
Lee, Garrett, Gre.	4	9	.308	4.60	32	9	1	1	11	0	92.0	103	393	55	47	12	5	4	4	17	2	63	2	1
Lontayo, Alejandro, Gre.*	3	5	.375	5.19	9	9	0	0	0	0	50.1	59	232	34	29	3	3	1	0	26	2	43	1	2
Lowe, Benny, Chat.*	3	2	.600	4.19	26	1	0	0	8	0	38.2	29	168	21	18	1	3	2	1	24	0	35	1	0
Luebbers, Larry, Chat.	2	3	.400	2.98	8	8	1	0	0	0	54.1	48	222	23	18	2	1	2	2	12	0	48	1	0
Lyon, Brandon, Tenn.	5	0	1.000	3.68	9	9	0	0	0	0	58.2	57	241	25	24	7	2	1	3	9	0	45	1	0
MacRae, Scott, Chat.	5	2	.714	3.68	19	8	1	0	3	0	58.2	60	248	29	24	4	3	1	0	14	0	42	2	0
Magrane, Jim, Orl.	8	12	.400	2.97	29	28	1	0	0	0	182.0	166	755	87	60	15	6	7	4	56	1	126	13	1
Mallard, Randi, W.T.	0	1	.000	9.90	8	0	0	0	1	0	10.0	13	54	12	11	1	2	0	3	9	2	7	0	0
Mallette, Brian, Hun.	7	2	.778	1.96	44	0	0	0	39	17	55.0	43	232	13	12	4	4	1	3	23	4	71	4	0
Malone, Corwin, Birm.*	2	0	1.000	2.33	4	4	0	0	0	0	19.1	8	76	5	5	2	0	0	1	12	0	20	1	0
Manias, Jim, Chat.*	1	1	.500	3.12	24	0	0	0	9	0	26.0	13	101	9	9	3	2	4	6	23	1	41	2	0
Martinez, Javier, Chat.	0	0	.000	135.00	1	0	0	0	0	0	0.1	2	7	6	5	1	1	0	0	3	0	0	0	0
Martinez, Luis, Hun.*	0	0	.000	6.75	7	0	0	0	0	0	9.1	13	48	7	7	0	0	0	0	9	0	13	0	0
Mathis, Jared, Hun.	0	0	.000	0.00	1	0	0	0	1	0	1.0	1	3	0	0	0	0	0	0	0	0	0	0	0
McBride, Chris, Jack.	2	1	.667	4.74	4	4	0	0	0	0	19.0	24	81	12	10	2	0	0	0	3	0	19	1	0
McClellan, Matt, Tenn.	2	2	.500	2.41	19	0	0	0	9	1	18.2	17	83	10	5	3	0	2	0	8	0	20	1	0
McClendon, Matt, Gre.	0	0	.000	5.91	2	2	0	0	0	0	10.2	10	48	7	7	1	1	0	7	0	9	2	0
McDaniel, Denny, Birm.*	1	2	.333	7.71	18	0	0	0	7	0	21.0	30	101	18	18	2	1	1	2	9	0	13	1	0
McNichol, Brian, Chat.*	4	0	1.000	1.04	21	1	0	0	5	0	26.0	19	106	4	3	0	4	1	1	9	1	32	1	0
Meadows, Randy, W.T.	0	0	.000	7.71	2	0	0	0	0	0	2.1	3	10	2	2	1	0	0	0	1	0	1	0	0
Mendoza, Geronimo, Birm.	5	4	.556	5.06	12	12	0	0	0	0	69.1	84	312	51	39	7	2	3	2	28	0	38	3	0
Middlebrook, Jason, Mob.	3	0	1.000	1.20	10	9	0	0	0	0	52.2	36	200	10	7	1	0	2	1	9	0	51	0	0
Mieses, Jose, Hun.	0	0	.000	2.22	5	4	0	0	1	0	24.1	21	97	7	6	2	0	1	2	3	0	35	2	0
Millwood, Kevin, Gre.	0	1	.000	4.50	2	2	0	0	0	0	10.0	9	42	6	5	2	0	2	0	3	0	10	1	0
Montgomery, Matt, Jack.	0	1	.000	3.20	14	0	0	0	3	0	25.1	20	103	9	9	1	2	1	1	8	0	17	4	1

Pitcher, Team	W	L	Pct.	ERA	G	GS	CG	ShO	GF	Sv.	IP	H	TBF	R	ER	HR	SH	SF	HB	BB	IBB	SO	WP	Bk.
Moraga, David, W.T.*	4	5	.444	4.10	23	12	1	0	2	0	83.1	82	349	44	38	11	2	5	0	21	2	58	8	0
Moss, Damian, Gre.*	0	1	.000	3.00	3	2	0	0	1	0	9.0	7	34	3	3	3	0	0	0	0	0	10	0	0
Myers, Aaron, Hun.	3	4	.429	3.60	34	7	0	0	9	2	70.0	53	304	31	28	4	2	1	3	40	0	68	3	1
Nance, Shane, Jack.*	7	0	1.000	1.59	28	0	0	0	11	5	45.1	31	179	11	8	4	2	1	0	17	1	44	1	0
Neugebauer, Nick, Hun.	5	6	.455	3.46	21	21	1	1	0	0	106.2	94	453	46	41	6	5	3	2	52	0	149	13	0
Nevers, Tom, Chat.	0	0	.000	0.00	1	0	0	0	1	0	1.1	1	7	0	0	0	0	0	0	2	0	1	0	0
Noyce, Dave, W.T.*	3	8	.273	4.03	50	8	0	0	12	1	96.0	98	437	53	43	9	4	6	7	48	3	87	5	1
Osting, Jimmy, Car.-Mob.*	10	4	.714	3.51	19	19	0	0	0	0	102.2	88	436	42	40	7	4	3	5	45	1	72	7	0
Ozuna, Francisco, Tenn.*	1	0	1.000	1.50	12	0	0	0	5	0	12.0	11	51	3	2	0	0	1	2	4	0	7	0	0
Palma, Rick, W.T.*	4	9	.308	3.06	57	0	0	0	21	0	70.2	61	292	29	24	6	4	4	0	25	1	70	2	0
Parra, Christian, Gre.	3	8	.273	5.44	18	18	0	0	0	0	89.1	87	404	58	54	9	3	4	3	56	2	82	8	1
Parris, Steve, Tenn.	0	0	.000	0.00	1	1	0	0	0	0	3.0	2	12	0	0	0	0	0	0	1	0	2	1	0
Parrish, Wade, Jack.-Birm.*	5	1	.833	2.18	20	1	0	0	7	0	33.0	26	132	8	8	1	2	1	3	10	1	20	3	0
Payne, Jerrod, Tenn	2	3	.400	6.14	22	0	0	0	6	1	30.1	37	155	22	20	4	2	1	0	9	1	18	1	0
Pearson, Jason, Mob.*	5	5	.500	4.17	54	5	0	0	16	1	86.1	91	371	40	40	5	4	6	3	30	3	67	3	0
Peavy, Jake, Mob.	2	1	.667	2.57	5	5	0	0	0	0	28.0	19	114	8	3	0	0	3	12	1	44	1	0
Pelaez, Alex, Mob.	1	1	.500	3.48	8	0	0	0	8	0	10.1	13	46	4	4	2	1	1	0	3	2	1	0	0
Penney, Mike, Hun.	4	3	.571	3.31	21	5	0	0	13	7	49.0	50	222	24	18	4	4	1	22	0	30	1	0
Piersoll, Chris, Chat.	1	4	.200	3.38	50	0	0	0	41	19	56.0	48	245	24	21	2	1	0	1	30	2	78	3	0
Poe, Ryan, Hun.	1	2	.333	3.86	7	7	0	0	0	0	35.0	30	137	15	15	5	0	0	1	7	0	40	0	0
Porzio, Mike, Birm.*	1	0	1.000	1.38	2	2	0	0	0	0	13.0	3	49	2	2	1	0	1	5	0	10	2	0
Powalski, Rick, Orl.*	0	0	.000	5.40	3	0	0	0	0	0	3.1	6	20	2	2	0	0	2	3	0	5	0	0
Proctor, Scott, Jack.	4	3	.571	4.17	10	9	0	0	0	0	49.2	39	215	26	23	6	3	2	2	31	1	48	2	0
Pruett, Jason, Orl.*	2	5	.286	5.12	38	0	0	0	13	1	51.0	59	236	38	29	5	3	5	2	19	0	29	3	0
Pujals, Denis, Orl.	0	0	.000	7.36	7	0	0	0	2	0	11.0	19	56	9	9	3	0	1	1	4	0	3	0	0
Purvis, Rob, Birm.	5	9	.357	5.27	24	23	0	0	1	0	140.0	165	629	96	82	9	2	6	4	70	0	53	14	2
Ramirez, Horacio, Gre.*	1	1	.500	4.91	3	3	0	0	0	0	14.2	17	66	8	8	2	2	0	1	8	0	17	0	0
Randall, Scott, Car.	0	0	.000	0.00	1	1	0	0	0	0	6.0	5	21	0	0	0	0	0	0	3	0	0	0
Regalado, Maximo, Jack.	2	3	.400	6.35	18	0	0	0	5	1	22.2	20	110	18	16	3	0	2	22	0	33	1	0
Reimers, Cameron, Tenn.	1	2	.333	6.60	5	4	0	0	0	0	30.0	32	126	22	22	8	0	1	3	5	0	19	1	0
Reith, Brian, Chat.	6	4	.600	3.97	18	18	1	1	0	0	104.1	103	448	63	46	10	2	5	4	42	1	89	1	0
Rekar, Bryan, Orl.	0	1	1.000	2.25	3	3	0	0	0	0	12.0	8	47	3	3	0	0	1	1	0	11	2	0
Reyes, Eddy, Orl.	2	3	.400	5.44	31	0	0	0	7	1	43.0	45	202	30	26	2	3	1	4	27	1	28	0	0
Rijo, Jose, Chat.	0	0	.000	0.00	1	1	0	0	0	0	3.0	1	11	0	0	0	0	0	1	0	3	1	0
Robinson, Dustin, W.T.	1	1	.500	4.35	17	0	0	0	10	1	20.2	24	94	10	10	3	1	1	2	9	3	18	3	0
Rosario, Juan, Orl.	1	3	.250	3.56	44	0	0	0	16	3	68.1	69	310	36	27	3	6	4	14	27	1	55	5	2
Ruhl, Nathan, Orl.	3	3	.500	3.88	31	0	0	0	20	6	51.0	54	227	25	22	7	3	1	2	23	2	54	4	0
Saipe, Mike, Orl.	4	2	.667	2.39	7	7	0	0	0	0	49.0	43	193	13	13	2	2	0	13	1	36	2	0
Sanders, Dave, Birm.*	3	0	1.000	2.65	36	0	0	0	12	0	34.0	27	150	12	10	1	1	2	3	25	1	25	2	0
Seay, Bobby, Orl.*	2	5	.286	5.98	15	13	0	0	0	0	64.2	81	296	48	43	9	2	4	3	26	0	49	2	0
Seifert, Ryan, Car.	4	6	.400	3.14	33	12	1	1	9	1	103.1	103	433	42	36	10	4	4	3	28	0	88	2	0
Severino, Ronni, Orl.*	3	8	.273	5.00	38	11	0	0	9	0	90.0	116	419	58	50	12	1	5	2	47	0	63	12	1
Shelby, Anthony, Orl.*	0	0	.000	4.15	4	0	0	0	0	0	4.1	4	20	2	2	1	0	0	2	0	2	1	0
Shiell, Jason, Mob.	2	3	.400	4.44	45	2	0	0	8	0	81.0	91	353	46	40	5	4	8	1	32	2	60	4	0
Shumate, Jacob, Hun.	0	1	.000	15.43	8	0	0	0	9	0	9.1	18	52	17	16	3	1	0	1	16	2	10	2	0
Simon, Ben, Jack.	7	6	.538	3.32	15	15	0	0	0	0	81.1	64	328	34	30	12	5	2	7	21	0	76	1	0
Sismondo, Bobby, Hun.*	1	2	.333	2.18	8	2	0	0	3	1	20.2	24	88	9	5	3	0	2	4	1	16	1	1
Smith, Cam, Chat.	1	5	.167	5.03	29	1	0	0	11	0	53.2	49	250	32	30	5	3	1	5	36	2	49	7	0
Smith, Mike, Tenn.	6	2	.750	2.42	14	14	1	0	0	0	93.0	80	393	32	25	7	4	1	8	26	2	77	6	0
Smoltz, John, Gre.	0	0	.000	0.00	1	1	0	0	0	0	3.0	2	10	0	0	0	0	0	0	0	6	0	0
Smyth, Steve, W.T.*	9	3	.750	2.54	18	18	3	1	0	0	120.1	110	497	38	34	9	4	1	5	40	1	93	6	0
Snyder, Matt, W.T.	2	1	.667	8.90	25	0	0	0	9	1	31.1	36	147	33	31	6	0	2	3	17	1	31	3	0
Sobkowiak, Scott, Gre.	2	5	.286	5.54	12	12	0	0	0	0	65.0	71	305	45	40	10	4	2	5	40	0	48	6	1
Spooneybarger, Tim, Gre.	1	1	.500	5.14	15	0	0	0	6	0	21.0	20	86	12	12	1	1	0	4	0	24	5	0
Standridge, Jason, Orl.	0	2	.000	5.59	2	2	0	0	0	0	9.2	12	44	6	6	0	0	4	0	7	0	0
Stephenson, Brian, Jack.	1	0	1.000	1.13	7	1	0	0	1	0	8.0	6	33	4	1	0	0	1	0	2	0	3	0	0
Stevens, Dave, Gre.	0	1	.000	3.09	9	0	0	0	6	2	11.2	4	45	5	4	1	1	2	0	6	1	8	2	0
Stevenson, Jason, Mob.	1	2	.333	3.57	10	1	0	0	2	0	17.2	20	82	8	7	3	0	0	10	0	9	0	0
Stewart, Josh, Birm.*	3	4	.429	6.67	16	16	0	0	0	0	82.1	110	388	68	61	7	3	8	42	0	47	2	2
Stull, Everett, Hun.	1	1	.500	3.86	6	4	0	0	1	1	25.2	21	102	11	11	3	0	2	5	0	23	4	0
Sylvester, Billy, Gre.	1	0	1.000	2.37	26	0	0	0	24	12	30.1	18	129	8	8	3	1	0	2	24	0	41	4	0
Taglienti, Jeff, Chat.	5	5	.500	4.72	51	0	0	0	22	7	55.1	64	235	30	29	3	3	1	1	14	1	45	1	0
Takeoka, Kazuhiro, Gre.	5	3	.625	2.68	45	0	0	0	21	3	74.0	76	326	31	22	2	10	1	10	21	6	46	9	1
Tankersley, Dennis, Mob.	4	1	.800	2.07	13	13	0	0	0	0	69.2	44	282	23	16	6	1	4	24	1	89	2	1
Thompson, Doug, Car.	2	5	.286	3.76	26	0	0	0	8	1	38.1	33	167	16	16	2	4	3	5	19	1	33	2	1
Thompson, Mark, Car.	3	2	.600	5.06	8	8	1	1	0	0	48.0	43	206	29	27	4	0	1	8	15	1	38	0	0
Thompson, Travis, Chat.	12	10	.545	3.88	28	28	3	1	0	0	167.0	170	708	82	72	10	10	2	6	46	3	118	3	0
Thompson, Travis, Car.	1	1	.500	4.58	28	0	0	0	13	5	37.1	39	165	20	19	6	3	1	4	13	1	28	5	1
Tokarse, Brian, Birm.	2	6	.250	3.97	39	0	0	0	14	0	65.2	56	293	33	29	4	4	2	4	39	1	81	7	0
Trujillo, J.J., Mob.	3	3	.500	2.65	43	0	0	0	21	6	51.0	44	217	20	15	1	3	4	20	2	44	4	1
Ulacia, Dennis, Birm.*	1	1	.500	2.25	3	3	0	0	0	0	20.0	11	78	7	5	1	0	0	2	5	0	18	2	0
Veronie, Shanin, Gre.	0	0	.000	0.00	2	0	0	0	1	0	3.0	4	13	0	0	0	0	0	0	1	0	4	0	0
Voyles, Brad, Gre.	0	0	.000	1.08	15	0	0	0	8	6	16.2	11	72	3	2	0	2	2	1	10	1	25	6	0
Waligora, Tom, W.T.	4	1	.800	3.48	22	0	0	0	8	0	31.0	22	129	13	12	3	0	2	13	0	36	3	0
Wallace, Jeff, Orl.*	0	0	.000	0.00	1	0	0	0	1	0	1.0	0	5	0	0	0	0	1	0	3	0	0
Watkins, Steve, Mob.	4	8	.333	5.73	23	19	0	0	2	0	97.1	108	447	74	62	14	6	4	53	2	55	3	0
Weaver, Eric, Birm.	3	3	.500	3.45	24	0	0	0	10	2	31.1	25	133	14	12	3	0	0	16	2	31	2	0
Weymouth, Marty, Birm.	0	0	.000	7.45	10	0	0	0	4	0	9.2	13	47	9	8	0	0	0	1	5	2	0
Wheeler, Dan, Orl.	0	2	.000	2.81	3	3	0	0	0	0	16.0	15	68	5	5	2	0	0	6	1	12	0	0
Winkelsas, Joe, Gre.	4	2	.667	3.27	20	0	0	0	11	3	33.0	24	133	12	12	0	2	0	14	2	14	3	2
Woodards, Orlando, Tenn.	1	2	.333	7.00	15	0	0	0	5	0	18.0	19	89	15	14	1	1	1	15	0	16	4	0
Wright, Danny, Birm.	7	7	.500	2.82	20	20	0	0	0	0	134.0	112	548	54	42	6	3	7	6	41	0	128	6	2
Wrigley, Jase, Car.	6	6	.500	6.30	47	0	0	0	16	2	64.1	93	310	53	45	4	6	2	2	28	4	33	2	0

Pitcher, Team	W	L	Pct.	ERA	G	GS	CG	ShO	GF	Sv.	IP	H	TBF	R	ER	HR	SH	SF	HB	BB	IBB	SO	WP	Bk.
Wuertz, Mike, W.T.	4	9	.308	3.99	27	27	1	1	0	0	160.0	160	694	80	71	20	9	6	6	58	2	135	10	0
Wylie, Mitch, Birm.	15	4	.789	4.21	24	24	0	0	0	0	141.0	138	612	70	66	13	2	6	12	46	1	123	4	3
Yan, Esteban, Orl.	0	0	.000	3.00	2	2	0	0	0	0	3.0	3	12	1	1	0	0	0	0	0	0	4	1	0

PITCHERS WITH TWO OR MORE TEAMS

Pitcher, Team	W	L	Pct.	ERA	G	GS	CG	ShO	GF	Sv.	IP	H	TBF	R	ER	HR	SH	SF	HB	BB	IBB	SO	WP	Bk.
Booker, Chris, W.T.	2	6	.250	4.33	45	0	0	0	13	1	52.0	39	235	29	25	7	5	3	1	36	2	76	7	0
Booker, Chris, Chat.	2	0	1.000	3.94	16	0	0	0	4	1	16.0	13	72	7	7	1	1	0	0	11	0	25	0	0
Kramer, Aaron, Mob.	2	7	.222	5.26	23	4	0	0	5	0	49.2	53	218	32	29	11	4	2	3	12	1	41	3	0
Kramer, Aaron, W.T.	0	0	.000	20.25	2	0	0	0	0	0	1.1	3	7	3	3	1	0	0	0	0	0	2	0	0
Osting, Jimmy, Car.*	1	0	1.000	1.80	1	1	0	0	0	0	5.0	3	22	1	1	1	0	0	0	3	0	3	0	0
Osting, Jimmy, Mob.*	9	4	.692	3.59	18	18	0	0	0	0	97.2	85	414	41	39	6	4	3	5	42	1	69	7	0
Parrish, Wade, Jack.*	1	1	.500	5.14	4	0	0	0	3	0	7.0	7	34	4	4	0	1	1	5	1	5	0	0
Parrish, Wade, Birm.*	4	0	1.000	1.38	16	1	0	0	4	0	26.0	19	98	4	4	1	1	1	2	5	0	15	3	0

COMBINATION SHUTOUTS: **Birmingham (10)**—Porzio-Beaumont-Tokarse, Wylie-Weymouth-Sanders, Wright-Almonte, Wright-Weaver, Wright-Weaver, Wylie-Tokarse, Wylie-Weaver-Almonte, Parrish-Weaver-Almonte, Purvis-Bohannan-Weaver, Malone-Purvis. **Carolina (7)**—Hudson-Esslinger, Cameron-Seifert, Dorame-Esslinger-Wrigley, Cameron-Emiliano-Thompson-Esslinger, Kibler-Wrigley-Emiliano, M. Thompson-T. Thompson, Kibler-Thompson-Emiliano. **Chattanooga (11)**—Thompson-Gil, Reith-Piersoll-Manias-De la Rosa, Gil-De la Rosa, Reith-De la Rosa, Acevedo-Darnall, Acevedo-McNichol-Piersoll, Darnell-De la Rosa-McNichol-Taglienti, Thompson-McNichol-Piersoll, Reith-Glauber, Howington-Glauber, Gil-Taglienti. **Greenville (5)**—Ramirez-Foster-Takeoka-Sylvester, Parra-Abreu-Foster-Spooneybarger, Dawley-Takeoka, Cumberland-Lee, Saipe-Foster. **Huntsville (11)**—Mieses-Childers-Jacobs-Krawczyk-Mallette, Poe-Krawczyk-Jacobs, Garcia-Jacobs-Mallette, Neugebauer-Childers-Mallette, Neugebauer-Childers-Mallette, Myers-Martinez-Krawczyk, Lee-Childers-Davis, Lee-Mallette, Brownson-Davis, Lee-Myers, Stull-Childers. **Jacksonville (6)**—Alvarez-Devey-Regalado-Foster, Simon-Gulin-Montgomery-Nance-Harrell, Gulin-Nance-Feliciano, Burnside-Husted, Gulin-Nance-Feliciano, Gulin-Feliciano. **Mobile (8)**—Watkins-Pearson-Camp-Condrey, Bynum-Camp-Fikac-Pearson, Guttormson-Giron-Condrey, Osting-Condrey-Fikac, Osting-Trujillo-Fikac, Howard-Shiell-Trujillo-Bartosh, Pearson-Stevenson-Bartosh-Fikac, Peavy-Shiell-Trujillo. **Orlando (11)**—Kennedy-Rosario, Kennedy-Jimenez, Magrane-Pruett, Kennedy-Rosario-Jimenez, Magrane-Pujals-Severino, Guzman-Garibaldi-Reyes, Magrane-Pruett, Seay-Garibaldi-Backe-Ruhl, Enders-Haines, Magrane-Backe. **Tennessee (9)**—Baker-Woodards-Kingrey-File, Cassidy-Kingrey, Chacin-Woodards, Lyon-Kingrey, Chacin-Dimma-Castellanos, Dickson-Baker, Smith-Chulk-Kingrey, Hubbel-Payne-Kingrey, Smith-Chulk. **West Tenn (7)**—Cruz-Palma-Waligora-Gonzalez, Cruz-Palma-Chiasson, Smyth-Noyce, Moraga-Booker-Waligora, Cruz-Booker-Chiasson, Gissell-Palma-Snyder-Chiasson, Cruz-Snyder-Chiasson.

NO-HIT GAMES: Cassidy, Tennessee defeated Carolina, 5-0, May 27.

2001 FIELDING

TEAM

Team	Pct.	G	PO	A	E	TC	DP	TP	PB
Mobile	.977	138	3677	1416	122	5215	114	0	15
Jacksonville	.976	139	3697	1381	126	5204	109	0	14
West Tenn	.975	139	3649	1248	127	5022	100	0	19
Greenville	.972	139	3638	1483	146	5267	112	0	12
Orlando	.972	140	3661	1475	147	5283	131	0	35
Birmingham	.972	140	3691	1550	151	5392	137	0	30
Tennessee	.972	140	3687	1522	151	5360	138	1	8
Carolina..........	.972	138	3630	1471	149	5250	115	0	19
Huntsville	.971	138	3647	1381	151	5179	86	0	18
Chattanooga	.971	139	3650	1372	152	5174	105	0	6

INDIVIDUAL

FIRST BASEMEN

NOTE: All caps denotes fielding-percentage leader based on 70 games for catchers, 93 for all other non-pitchers and 112 innings for pitchers. * Throws lefthanded.

Player, Team	Pct.	G	PO	A	E	TC	DP
Abreu, Dennis, W.T.	.000	1	0	0	0	0	0
Alvarez, Gabe, Chat.	.984	17	121	5	2	128	12
Amrhein, Mike, W.T.	1.000	40	274	14	0	288	31
Barker, Kevin, Hun.*	.992	57	471	33	4	508	35
BATTERSBY, Eric, Birm.*	.995	133	1183	93	7	1283	119
Becker, Brian, Orl.	.996	51	449	28	2	479	42
Beinbrink, Andy, Orl.	1.000	1	1	0	0	1	0
Broussard, Benjamin, Chat.*	.990	93	737	55	8	800	58
Burford, Kevin, Car.*	.971	77	621	70	21	712	55
Burkhart, Lance, Hun.	1.000	2	13	0	0	13	3
Chiaffredo, Paul, Tenn.	1.000	2	15	0	0	15	1
Cox, Steve, Orl.*	.962	4	24	1	1	26	4
Davis, Glenn, Jack.*	.991	132	1064	96	10	1170	91
Deardorff, Jeff, Hun.	.968	7	55	5	2	62	5
DeCinces, Tim, Mob.	1.000	1	3	0	0	3	0
Derosso, Tony, Hun.-Mob.	1.000	3	12	0	0	12	0
Fiore, Curtis, Gre.	1.000	1	9	0	0	9	0
Gibralter, Dave, Hun.	.998	51	381	30	1	412	22
Grummitt, Dan, Orl.	.993	51	409	31	3	443	40
Haas, Chris, W.T.	.991	100	708	39	7	754	51
Hessman, Mike, Gre.	1.000	5	25	1	0	26	0
Hopper, Shane, Mob.	1.000	1	1	0	0	1	0
Horn, Jeff, Gre.	.984	7	55	6	1	62	10
Jacobsen, Bucky, Hun.	.984	23	174	11	3	188	8
Johnson, Adam, Birm.*	.984	7	58	3	1	62	6
Keck, Brian, Car.	.992	16	122	7	1	130	13
Klimek, Josh, Hun.	1.000	4	20	2	0	22	3
Koonce, Graham, Mob.*	.998	56	409	27	1	437	32

Player, Team	Pct.	G	PO	A	E	TC	DP
Langaigne, Selwyn, Tenn.*	1.000	9	64	6	0	70	5
Logan, Matt, Tenn.	.987	93	716	50	10	776	59
McKeel, Walt, Car.	1.000	1	5	1	0	6	0
McNeal, Aaron, Mob.	.978	49	400	46	10	456	35
Morris, Bobby, Chat.	.986	9	65	4	1	70	4
Mortimer, Mark, Gre.	1.000	2	12	1	0	13	2
Murphy, Mike, Car.	1.000	4	44	0	0	44	4
Nevers, Tom, Chat.	1.000	2	26	1	0	27	3
Otanez, Willis, Gre.	.994	53	450	30	3	483	34
Paciorek, Pete, Jack.*	1.000	6	48	6	0	54	6
Pelaez, Alex, Mob.	1.000	17	153	7	0	160	13
Perez, Eddie, Gre.	.955	5	21	0	1	22	1
Peters, Tony, Tenn.	.978	19	81	7	2	90	8
Phillips, J.R., Car.*	.993	29	245	26	2	273	18
Pressley, Josh, Car.	.981	18	140	13	3	156	11
Quatraro, Matt, Orl.	.995	22	165	17	1	183	17
Ramsey, Brad, W.T.	1.000	4	22	2	0	24	3
Rodriguez, Mike, Tenn.	.963	7	51	1	2	54	5
Rose, Pete, Chat.	1.000	2	23	0	0	23	0
Sandberg, Jared, Orl.	1.000	1	4	0	0	4	1
Saunders, Chris, Birm.	.978	5	42	2	1	45	6
Scheschuk, John, Mob.*	.995	21	179	9	1	189	20
Schrager, Tony, W.T.	1.000	1	2	0	0	2	0
Seal, Scott, Car.*	1.000	2	10	0	0	10	1
Short, Rick, W.T.	1.000	2	18	2	0	20	3
Stoner, Mike, Car.	.976	15	116	6	3	125	11
Theodorou, Nick, Jack.	1.000	1	3	0	0	3	1
Thurston, Jerrey, Chat.	1.000	1	6	0	0	6	2
Valencia, Vic, Chat.	1.000	3	4	0	0	4	0
Weekly, Chris, Tenn.	.988	8	75	4	1	80	6
Welsh, Eric, Chat.*	.980	20	142	8	3	153	16
Werth, Jayson, Tenn.	.992	28	227	14	2	243	22
Williams, Glenn, Tenn.	.982	8	50	4	1	55	8
Wilson, Travis, Gre.	1.000	1	10	0	0	10	0
Zapp, A.J., Gre.	.992	74	592	66	5	663	59

TRIPLE PLAY: Logan.

FIRST BASEMEN WITH TWO OR MORE TEAMS

Player, Team	Pct.	G	PO	A	E	TC	DP
Derosso, Tony, Hun.	1.000	2	2	0	0	2	0
Derosso, Tony, Mob.	1.000	1	10	0	0	10	0

SECOND BASEMEN

Player, Team	Pct.	G	PO	A	E	TC	DP
Abbott, Kurt, Gre.	1.000	1	6	7	0	13	3
Abreu, Dennis, W.T.	.979	49	81	102	4	187	19
Badeaux, Brooks, Orl.	.956	53	123	138	12	273	37
Beattie, Andy, Chat.	.978	29	53	79	3	135	8
Bravo, Danny, Birm.	.967	16	25	62	3	90	13

Player, Team	Pct.	G	PO	A	E	TC	DP
Castro, Ramon, Gre.	.957	9	18	27	2	47	4
Cesar, Dionys, Hun.	1.000	4	8	9	0	17	1
Colina, Javier, Car.	1.000	1	0	2	0	2	0
Collins, Mike, Jack.	1.000	3	6	11	0	17	3
Davidson, Cleatus, Mob.	1.000	7	12	15	0	27	7
De Los Santos, Eddy, Orl.	.953	91	193	232	21	446	63
De RENNE, Keoni, Gre.	.986	94	183	232	6	421	48
Figgins, Chone, Car.	.974	77	155	221	10	386	45
Gomez, Heber, Chat.	.909	2	6	4	1	11	1
Goudie, Jaime, Tenn.	.960	45	101	141	10	252	28
Grice, Daniel, W.T.	1.000	1	3	4	0	7	0
Haas, Chris, W.T.	1.000	1	1	2	0	3	1
Hill, Bobby, W.T.	.973	54	98	118	6	222	28
Hudson, Orlando, Tenn.	.979	72	131	203	7	341	46
Hummel, Tim, Birm.	.973	93	178	254	12	444	70
Johnson, Russ, Orl.	.818	1	3	6	2	11	2
Keck, Brian, Car.	1.000	2	1	5	0	6	1
Lamb, Dave, Car.	.946	8	14	21	2	37	5
Lopez, Felipe, Tenn.	.923	6	16	20	3	39	6
Lorenzana, Luis, Mob.	.889	4	6	10	2	18	1
Martinez, Belvani, Car.	.969	35	66	92	5	163	19
Martinez, Lou, Gre.	.955	24	31	54	4	89	11
Mathis, Jared, Hun.	1.000	8	9	9	0	18	0
Matos, Julius, Mob.	1.000	7	12	18	0	30	5
Meadows, Randy, W.T.	.990	32	50	48	1	99	10
Metcalfe, Mike, Chat.	.982	84	149	223	7	379	45
Miles, Aaron, Birm.	.970	16	24	41	2	67	5
Mitchell, Derek, Birm.	.941	6	7	9	1	17	3
Morris, Bobby, Chat.	.978	21	38	50	2	90	15
Nevers, Tom, Chat.	.967	7	8	21	1	30	4
Nunez, Jorge, Jack.	.926	9	11	14	2	27	3
Pelaez, Alex, Mob.	1.000	4	6	3	0	9	1
Peralta, Juan, Tenn.	1.000	2	1	1	0	2	1
Perez, Jerson, Tenn.	.964	7	16	11	1	28	5
Pickler, Jeff, Hun.	.979	132	269	326	13	608	56
Powers, Jeff, Car.	.968	23	35	55	3	93	14
Powers, John, Mob.	.966	43	79	119	7	205	21
Prieto, Rick, Birm.	.982	10	21	35	1	57	7
Riggs, Eric, Jack.	1.000	5	8	15	0	23	3
Rodriguez, Tony, W.T.	1.000	2	3	6	0	9	2
Sanchez, Wellington, Hun.	1.000	1	2	3	0	5	1
Schrager, Tony, W.T.	.968	22	45	46	3	94	13
Short, Rick, W.T.	1.000	1	0	1	0	1	0
Suarez, Luis, Birm.	1.000	4	7	11	0	18	3
Theodorou, Nick, Jack.	.905	3	12	7	2	21	4
Thrower, Jake, Mob.	.981	85	152	208	7	367	38
Thurston, Joe, Jack.	.976	121	287	275	14	576	64
Williams, Glenn, Tenn.	.964	22	32	48	3	83	11
Wilson, Travis, Gre.	.973	24	48	59	3	110	15

THIRD BASEMEN

Player, Team	Pct.	G	PO	A	E	TC	DP
Abreu, Dennis, W.T.	.882	7	4	11	2	17	1
Alvarez, Gabe, Chat.	.838	67	31	109	27	167	6
Badeaux, Brooks, Orl.	.972	31	20	85	3	108	11
Bair, Rod, Car.	1.000	7	7	9	0	16	1
Bausher, Andy, Mob.*	.000	1	0	0	0	0	0
Beattie, Andy, Chat.	.944	6	10	7	1	18	1
BEINBRINK, Andy, Orl.	.948	103	68	221	16	305	23
Bell, Ricky, Jack.	.942	52	27	102	8	137	8
Bravo, Danny, Birm.	1.000	1	0	1	0	1	0
Burkhart, Lance, Hun.	.750	5	1	5	2	8	0
Castro, Ramon, Gre.	1.000	5	2	7	0	9	1
Cesar, Dionys, Hun.	1.000	1	0	1	0	1	0
Colina, Javier, Car.	.929	7	3	10	1	14	1
Collins, Mike, Jack.	.944	8	3	14	1	18	1
Crowell, Jim, Mob.*	1.000	1	1	0	0	1	0
Deardorff, Jeff, Hun.	1.000	3	1	1	0	2	0
Derosso, Tony, Hun.-Mob.	.917	78	40	147	17	204	9
Fiore, Curtis, Gre.	.840	9	9	12	4	25	1
Gomez, Heber, Chat.	1.000	5	3	7	0	10	0
Gripp, Ryan, W.T.	.892	62	50	99	18	167	16
Haas, Chris, W.T.	.892	13	12	21	4	37	2
Heintz, Chris, Birm.	.500	1	0	2	2	4	0
Hessman, Mike, Gre.	.918	113	74	217	26	317	20
Hopper, Shane, Mob.	.813	7	4	9	3	16	2
Horn, Jeff, Gre.	.000	2	0	0	0	0	0
Hudson, Orlando, Tenn.	.971	13	7	27	1	35	4
Hummel, Tim, Birm.	.857	5	3	3	1	7	1
Keck, Brian, Car.	.952	25	20	39	3	62	5
Kelton, Dave, W.T.	.883	54	26	87	15	128	5
Klimek, Josh, Hun.	.924	51	35	74	9	118	7

Player, Team	Pct.	G	PO	A	E	TC	DP
Lamb, Dave, Car.	1.000	6	2	4	0	6	1
Martinez, Lou, Gre.	1.000	6	1	9	0	10	1
Mathis, Jared, Hun.	.973	15	7	29	1	37	1
Meadows, Randy, W.T.	1.000	7	3	15	0	18	0
Miles, Aaron, Birm.	.917	23	16	28	4	48	1
Mitchell, Derek, Birm.	.875	4	3	4	1	8	0
Mortimer, Mark, Gre.	1.000	1	1	0	0	1	0
Nevers, Tom, Chat.	.946	62	33	89	7	129	11
Otanez, Willis, Gre.	.900	19	9	27	4	40	2
Owens, Ryan, Car.	.922	103	65	171	20	256	21
Pelaez, Alex, Mob.	.964	89	57	156	8	221	23
Peters, Tony, Car.	.818	7	2	7	2	11	1
Post, Dave, Jack.	1.000	2	1	4	0	5	1
Powers, John, Mob.	.938	37	16	60	5	81	3
Prieto, Rick, Birm.	.750	2	2	1	1	4	0
Riggs, Eric, Jack.	.941	85	51	157	13	221	17
Rodriguez, Mike, Tenn.	.857	4	1	5	1	7	1
Rose, Pete, Chat.	.818	4	1	8	2	11	1
Sanchez, Wellington, Hun.	.918	16	8	37	4	49	5
Sandberg, Jared, Orl.	1.000	8	6	20	0	26	3
Sandoval, Danny, Birm.	.925	16	9	28	3	40	3
Saunders, Chris, Birm.	.941	88	50	173	14	237	13
Short, Rick, W.T.	.000	0	0	0	0	0	0
Suarez, Luis, Birm.	.800	2	0	4	1	5	0
Theodorou, Nick, Jack.	1.000	5	3	5	0	8	3
Thrower, Jake, Mob.	.667	3	3	1	2	6	0
Valencia, Vic, Chat.	.000	1	0	0	0	0	0
Weekly, Chris, Tenn.	.958	33	25	67	4	96	5
Williams, Glenn, Tenn.	.934	98	62	223	20	305	27
Wright, Nate, Jack.	1.000	1	0	1	0	1	0

THIRD BASEMEN WITH TWO OR MORE TEAMS

Player, Team	Pct.	G	PO	A	E	TC	DP
Derosso, Tony, Hun.	.898	61	29	120	17	166	8
Derosso, Tony, Mob.	1.000	17	11	27	0	38	1

SHORTSTOPS

Player, Team	Pct.	G	PO	A	E	TC	DP
Abreu, Dennis, W.T.	.956	37	44	87	6	137	20
Alvarez, Jimmy, Tenn.	.971	8	12	22	1	35	7
Beattie, Andy, Chat.	.968	6	8	22	1	31	4
Betemit, Wilson, Gre.	.954	47	56	132	9	197	24
Bravo, Danny, Birm.	.973	15	31	42	2	75	12
Cantu, Jorge, Orl.	.948	121	177	296	26	499	59
Castro, Ramon, Gre.	.972	62	80	164	7	251	27
Cesar, Dionys, Hun.	.947	55	63	151	12	226	18
Collins, Mike, Jack.	1.000	2	4	5	0	9	1
Davidson, Cleatus, Mob.	.947	117	178	343	29	550	54
DAWKINS, Travis, Chat.	.964	98	166	261	16	443	47
De Los Santos, Eddy, Orl.	.931	19	26	55	6	87	15
De Renne, Keoni, Gre.	.970	31	39	89	4	132	22
Ernster, Mark, Hun.	.903	26	35	49	9	93	9
Figgins, Chone, Car.	.872	10	15	26	6	47	5
Frese, Nate, W.T.	.996	70	97	178	1	276	35
Gomez, Heber, Chat.	.929	2	5	8	1	14	2
Grice, Daniel, W.T.	1.000	5	5	5	0	10	2
Hall, Bill, Hun.	.925	41	60	125	15	200	18
Hill, Bobby, W.T.	1.000	1	3	0	0	3	0
Hummel, Tim, Birm.	.926	36	62	100	13	175	21
Keck, Brian, Car.	.972	54	73	137	6	216	24
Lamb, Dave, Car.	.967	70	106	212	11	329	40
Lopez, Felipe, Tenn.	.886	12	10	29	5	44	9
Martinez, Felix, Orl.	.800	3	0	4	1	5	1
Martinez, Lou, Gre.	.857	6	5	13	3	21	3
Mathis, Jared, Hun.	1.000	3	1	3	0	4	1
Matos, Julius, Mob.	.909	13	18	32	5	55	8
Meadows, Randy, W.T.	.786	4	3	8	3	14	3
Mitchell, Derek, Birm.	.958	72	113	231	15	359	55
Nevers, Tom, Chat.	.952	36	56	104	8	168	22
Nunez, Jorge, Jack.	.940	111	148	287	28	463	48
Owens, Ryan, Car.	.953	7	19	22	2	43	4
Perez, Jerson, Tenn.	.939	108	159	304	30	493	54
Powers, Jeff, Car.	1.000	2	2	6	0	8	0
Riggs, Eric, Jack.	.952	19	21	39	3	63	9
Rodriguez, Tony, W.T.	.964	31	37	71	4	112	9
Sanchez, Wellington, Hun.	.931	27	31	50	6	87	9
Sandoval, Danny, Birm.	.960	21	33	62	4	99	16
Thrower, Jake, Mob.	.967	16	24	35	2	61	5
Thurston, Joe, Jack.	.943	12	20	30	3	53	7
Uribe, Juan, Car.	.833	3	4	6	2	12	1
Williams, Glenn, Tenn.	.932	15	22	33	4	59	6
TRIPLE PLAY: Perez.							

OUTFIELDERS

Player, Team	Pct.	G	PO	A	E	TC	DP
Abreu, Dennis, W.T.	1.000	2	1	1	0	2	0
Aldridge, Cory, Gre.	.964	117	208	7	8	223	0
Allen, Luke, Jack.	.972	120	225	15	7	247	3
Alvarez, Gabe, Chat.	.958	16	22	1	1	24	0
Amrhein, Mike, W.T.	1.000	2	1	0	0	1	0
Badeaux, Brooks, Orl.	.979	47	87	6	2	95	0
Bair, Rod, Car.	.978	51	89	2	2	93	1
Barker, Kevin, Hun.*	1.000	7	11	1	0	12	0
Bass, Jayson, W.T.*	.971	35	63	3	2	68	0
Beattie, Andy, Chat.	1.000	2	1	0	0	1	0
Benjamin, Al, Mob.	.966	98	162	6	6	174	1
Blakely, Darren, Mob.	.988	28	82	0	1	83	0
Borchard, Joe, Birm.	.964	133	318	10	12	330	3
Bravo, Danny, Birm.	.944	12	17	0	1	18	0
Brignac, Junior, Gre.	.970	61	123	7	4	134	0
Broussard, Benjamin, Chat.*	1.000	3	3	0	0	3	0
Carpenter, Bubba, Car.*	1.000	26	60	0	0	60	0
Chen, Chin-Feng, Jack.	.966	50	80	5	3	88	1
Colangelo, Mike, Mob.	.909	9	7	3	1	11	1
Crawford, Carl, Orl.*	.981	130	309	5	6	320	0
Cridland, Mark, Hun.	.982	65	101	9	2	112	2
Crosby, Bubba, Jack.*	.985	100	197	5	3	205	0
Darr, Mike, Mob.	1.000	2	2	0	0	2	0
Darula, Bobby, Hun.	.952	10	20	0	1	21	0
Deardorff, Jeff, Hun.	.973	42	70	1	2	73	0
DeHaan, Kory, Mob.	.988	42	80	3	1	84	0
DENT, Darrell, Jack.*	1.000	105	235	6	0	241	1
Diaz, Alejandro, Chat.	.964	23	51	3	2	56	0
Dunn, Adam, Chat.	.961	39	65	8	3	76	1
Fleming, Ryan, Tenn.*	.981	97	153	6	3	162	0
Fox, Jason, Hun.	.982	86	165	3	3	171	0
Gibralter, Dave, Hun.	.987	40	70	4	1	75	0
Gibralter, Steve, Chat.	.970	81	155	6	5	166	1
Green, Chad, Mob.	.971	39	68	0	2	70	0
Gross, Gabe, Tenn.	1.000	9	25	3	0	28	1
Haas, Chris, W.T.	1.000	2	4	0	0	4	0
Halliwanger, Garrick, Tenn.*	.917	31	51	4	5	60	1
Hamilton, Josh, Orl.*	.957	23	40	5	2	47	2
Hessman, Mike, Gre.	.964	18	24	3	1	28	0
Hopper, Shane, Mob.	.984	38	60	0	1	61	0
Hunter, Johnny, Mob.	.000	1	0	0	0	0	0
Hutchins, Norm, Orl.*	.920	28	44	2	4	50	0
Ingram, Darron, Birm.	.985	77	128	3	2	133	0
Johnson, Adam, Birm.*	.939	19	30	1	2	33	0
Johnson, Gary, W.T.	.980	127	286	11	6	303	2
Johnson, Reed, Tenn.	.983	133	222	12	4	238	2
Kearns, Austin, Chat.	.979	55	92	2	2	96	0
Kirby, Scott, Hun.	.971	62	97	2	3	102	1
Klimek, Josh, Hun.	.889	29	39	1	5	45	1
Knox, Ryan, Hun.	.981	28	51	1	1	53	0
Koonce, Graham, Mob.*	.941	27	31	1	2	34	0
Landaeta, Luis, Car.	.947	54	84	6	5	94	1
Langaigne, Selwyn, Tenn.*	1.000	12	19	0	0	19	0
Loggins, Josh, Mob.	.979	27	44	3	1	48	0
Lopez, Rafael, W.T.	.000	1	0	0	0	0	0
Martinez, Belvani, Car.	.951	76	123	12	7	142	2
Mashore, Justin, Car.	.942	43	61	4	4	69	0
Mathis, Jared, Hun.	1.000	37	54	2	0	56	0
Matthews, Lamont, Jack.*	.970	15	28	4	1	33	0
Meadows, Randy, W.T.	1.000	2	1	0	0	1	0
Meadows, Tydus, W.T.	.971	54	93	7	3	103	3
Melian, Jackson, Chat.	.948	114	184	15	11	210	1
Metcalfe, Mike, Chat.	.962	32	75	0	3	78	0
Moore, Mike, Gre.	.929	13	11	2	1	14	0
Morris, Bobby, Chat.	.960	20	22	2	1	25	0
Mortimer, Mark, Gre.	.833	4	5	0	1	6	0
Murphy, Mike, Car.	.992	102	235	3	2	240	0
Neuberger, Scott, Orl.	.990	120	202	5	2	209	1
Otanez, Willis, Gre.	1.000	8	9	0	0	9	0
Owens, Jeremy, Mob.	.985	106	251	15	4	270	5
Paciorek, Pete, Jack.*	1.000	12	20	0	0	20	0
Peters, Tony, Tenn.	.984	66	118	8	2	128	2
Phillips, J.R., Car.*	1.000	1	1	0	0	1	0
Piedra, Jorge, W.T.*	.980	118	231	9	5	245	1
Pigott, Anthony, Orl.	.969	74	117	7	4	128	0
Post, Dave, Jack.	1.000	2	4	0	0	4	0
Prieto, Rick, Birm.	.959	80	111	7	5	123	0
Quatraro, Matt, Orl.	1.000	11	13	2	0	15	0
Randolph, Jaisen, W.T.	1.000	96	181	9	0	190	3
Riggins, Auntwan, Mob.	1.000	10	17	0	0	17	0
Riggs, Eric, Jack.	1.000	1	0	1	0	1	0
Rivera, Roberto, Gre.	.965	99	158	6	6	170	0
Ross, Jason, Gre.	.991	58	108	4	1	113	1
Rushford, Jim, Hun.*	.989	46	83	3	1	87	0
Sanchez, Wellington, Hun.	.943	21	32	1	2	35	0
Sandoval, Danny, Hun.	.941	21	30	2	2	34	2
Saunders, Chris, Birm.	1.000	2	3	0	0	3	0
Seal, Scott, Car.*	.991	53	100	5	1	106	0
Short, Rick, W.T.	1.000	2	4	0	0	4	0
Singleton, Justin, Tenn.	1.000	12	19	0	0	19	0
Smothers, Stewart, Gre.	.977	38	82	4	2	88	0
Sollmann, Scott, Car.*	1.000	32	70	1	0	71	0
Stoner, Mike, Car.	1.000	21	34	1	0	35	0
Theodorou, Nick, Jack.	1.000	24	51	0	0	51	0
Tucci, Pete, Mob.	1.000	17	34	5	0	39	1
Tyler, Brad, Chat.	.968	11	29	1	1	31	1
Urquiola, Carlos, Gre.	.980	28	48	0	1	49	0
Valenzuela, Mario, Birm.	.963	88	169	11	7	187	0
Van Rossum, Chris, Chat.*	1.000	6	11	1	0	12	0
White, Rondell, W.T.	1.000	3	2	0	0	2	0
Wilson, Travis, Gre.	1.000	7	9	0	0	9	0
Wise, Dewayne, Tenn.*	.976	86	198	9	5	212	5

CATCHERS

Player, Team	Pct.	G	PO	A	E	TC	DP	PB
Acevas, Jon, Birm.	.967	12	76	13	3	92	0	3
Amrhein, Mike, W.T.	.985	45	351	35	6	392	5	6
Bard, Josh, Car.	.993	35	258	26	2	286	1	4
Brown, Jason, Orl.	1.000	3	9	1	0	10	0	0
Burkhart, Lance, Hun.	.995	30	217	4	1	222	0	5
Cancel, Rob, Hun.	.991	22	193	25	2	220	1	2
Chiaffredo, Paul, Tenn.	.984	19	113	13	2	128	1	0
Cosentino, Tony, Mob.	1.000	4	21	0	0	21	0	1
Curry, Chris, W.T.	.992	34	219	18	2	239	2	5
DeCinces, Tim, Mob.	.997	49	308	18	1	327	3	2
Dewey, Jason, Car.	.987	69	504	42	7	553	2	8
Duplissea, Bill, Jack.	.990	13	88	14	1	103	1	1
Garcia, Tony, Birm.	1.000	2	10	1	0	11	0	1
Goldbach, Jeff, W.T.	.992	27	224	13	2	239	1	6
Heintz, Chris, Birm.	.991	30	191	26	2	219	0	7
Horn, Jeff, Gre.	.988	48	325	24	5	354	1	1
Hundley, Todd, W.T.	1.000	2	7	1	0	8	0	0
Isenia, Chairon, Orl.	.981	15	99	7	2	108	0	2
Jorgensen, Ryan, W.T.	.981	32	240	23	5	268	0	0
Kellner, Ryan, Jack.	.989	25	168	18	2	188	1	1
Kuilan, Hector, Car.	.990	12	90	9	1	100	0	5
LaForest, Pete, Orl.	.968	7	55	5	2	62	0	6
Lopez, Rafael, W.T.	1.000	16	98	12	0	110	1	2
Loyd, Brian, Tenn.	.982	11	51	4	1	56	0	0
Mathis, Jared, Hun.	1.000	8	42	3	0	45	0	0
McKeel, Walt, Car.	.971	23	148	20	5	173	4	2
Miller, Corky, Chat.	.985	54	432	39	7	478	8	1
Moon, Brian, Hun.	.985	94	651	74	11	736	9	11
Mortimer, Mark, Gre.	.965	11	74	8	3	85	0	1
NIEVES, Wil, Mob.	.996	91	696	63	3	762	9	12
Olivo, Miguel, Birm	.988	90	633	78	9	720	4	19
Pachot, John, Jack.	1.000	39	264	31	0	295	1	6
Perez, Eddie, Gre.	1.000	6	35	4	0	39	0	0
Peters, Tony, Tenn.	1.000	3	10	0	0	10	0	0
Phelps, Josh, Tenn.	.996	69	447	29	2	478	4	5
Quataro, Matt, Orl.	.991	48	296	27	3	326	2	10
Quintero, Humberto, Birm.	.971	5	26	7	1	34	2	0
Rodriguez, Mike, Tenn.	1.000	1	1	0	0	1	0	0
Ross, Dave, Jack.	.985	70	530	51	9	590	1	6
Theodorou, Nick, Jack.	1.000	2	11	1	0	12	0	0
Thurston, Jerrey, Chat.	.988	21	163	7	2	172	2	2
Torrealba, Steve, Gre.	.979	85	596	64	14	674	3	10
Valencia, Vic, Chat.	.904	66	522	43	9	574	2	3
Valera, Yohanny, Orl.	.995	75	509	62	3	574	5	17
Werth, Jayson, Tenn.	.985	46	294	36	5	335	8	3

PITCHERS

Player, Team	Pct.	G	PO	A	E	TC	DP
Abreu, Winston, Gre.	1.000	34	4	9	0	13	2
Acevedo, Jose, Chat.	1.000	16	4	7	0	11	1
Achilles, Matt, W.T.	.786	9	5	6	3	14	0
Agosto, Stevenson, Orl.*	.926	30	1	24	2	27	3
Almonte, Ed, Birm.	.933	54	7	7	1	15	0
Alvarez, Victor, Jack.*	1.000	8	5	6	0	11	1
Alvarez, Wilson, Orl.*	1.000	5	1	2	0	3	0
Andrews, Clayton, Chat.*	1.000	6	5	7	0	12	0
Aramboles, Ricardo, Chat.	1.000	2	2	1	0	3	0
Backe, Brandon, Orl.	1.000	14	2	5	0	7	0

Player, Team	Pct.	G	PO	A	E	TC	DP
Bajenaru, Jeff, Birm.	1.000	2	0	2	0	2	0
BAKER, Chris, Tenn.	1.000	28	17	18	0	35	1
Baptist, Travis, Birm.*	1.000	10	2	13	0	15	0
Bartosh, Cliff, Mob.*	1.000	20	0	3	0	3	0
Bauer, Greg, Jack.	1.000	6	1	2	0	3	0
Bauer, Pete, Tenn.	.882	21	12	18	4	34	0
Bausher, Andy, Mob.*	.800	4	3	1	1	5	0
Beaumont, Matt, Birm.*	.000	4	0	0	0	0	0
Berry, Jon, Jack.	1.000	3	0	1	0	1	0
Bevel, Bobby, Jack.*	.667	31	3	1	2	6	0
Bleazard, Dave, Tenn.	1.000	3	3	3	0	6	2
Bohannan, Brad, Birm.	.933	29	5	9	1	15	0
Booker, Chris, W.T.-Chat.	.667	61	2	2	2	6	0
Brantley, Brian, Car.	1.000	14	2	4	0	6	0
Brooks, Antone, Gre.*	1.000	11	1	6	0	7	0
Brownson, Mark, Hun.	.852	24	8	15	4	27	2
Bruback, Matt, W.T.	.714	9	3	2	2	7	0
Burnside, Adrian, Jack.*	.800	13	1	3	1	5	0
Bynum, Mike, Mob.*	.880	16	5	17	3	25	1
Cameron, Ryan, Car.	.957	18	13	9	1	23	0
Camp, Shawn, Mob.	.909	35	3	7	1	11	1
Caraballo, Angel, Tenn.	1.000	26	4	5	0	9	0
Caraccioli, Lance, Jack.*	.930	28	13	27	3	43	0
Casey, Joe, Tenn.	.900	42	8	10	2	20	0
Cassidy, Scott, Tenn.	.917	16	6	16	2	24	0
Castellanos, Hugo, Tenn.	1.000	43	1	20	0	21	0
Chacin, Gustavo, Tenn.*	.963	25	7	19	1	27	4
Chiasson, Scott, W.T.	.875	52	3	4	1	8	0
Childers, Jason, Hun.	.960	40	5	19	1	25	1
Childers, Matt, Hun.	.900	7	4	5	1	10	1
Christensen, Ben, W.T.	1.000	3	2	4	0	6	0
Chulk, Vinny, Tenn.	1.000	24	0	4	0	4	0
Coco, Pasqual, Tenn.	1.000	3	1	1	0	2	0
Condrey, Clay, Mob.	1.000	27	5	4	0	9	0
Cook, Derrick, W.T.	1.000	4	0	1	0	1	0
Coppinger, Rocky, Hun.	.800	16	2	2	1	5	0
Cortes, David, Gre.	1.000	14	1	3	0	4	0
Crowder, Chuck, Car.*	.941	32	3	13	1	17	1
Crowell, Jim, Mob.*	1.000	5	0	1	0	1	0
Cruz, Juan, W.T.	1.000	23	4	7	0	11	0
Cueto, Jose, W.T.	1.000	2	1	1	0	2	0
Cumberland, Chris, Gre.*	.925	20	12	25	3	40	3
D'Amico, Jeff, Hun.	.000	1	0	0	1	1	0
Daneker, Pat, W.T.	.000	2	0	0	0	0	0
Darnell, Paul, Chat.*	1.000	21	1	8	0	9	0
Davis, Tim, Hun.*	1.000	28	1	6	0	7	0
Dawley, Joey, Gre.	1.000	22	8	15	0	23	1
DeCinces, Tim, Mob.	1.000	1	0	1	0	1	0
De La Rosa, Maximo, Chat.	.917	38	3	8	1	12	1
Dent, Doug, Mob.	.000	3	0	0	0	0	0
Devey, Phil, Jack.*	.886	24	6	25	4	35	2
DeWitt, Scott, Car.*	.955	43	3	18	1	22	2
Dickson, Jason, Tenn.	1.000	5	2	4	0	6	0
Difelice, Mark, Car.	.952	19	7	13	1	21	1
Dimma, Randey, Tenn.*	1.000	19	0	1	0	1	1
Dorame, Randey, Car.*	1.000	5	0	4	0	4	1
Dunn, Scott, Chat.	.813	17	2	11	3	16	1
Emiliano, Jamie, Car.	1.000	50	8	16	0	24	1
Enders, Trevor, Orl.*	1.000	13	0	6	0	6	0
Esslinger, Cam, Car.	.867	40	4	9	2	15	1
Estrella, Leo, Chat.	.500	3	1	0	1	2	0
Feliciano, Pedro, Jack.*	.929	54	2	11	1	14	1
Fikac, Jeremy, Mob.	1.000	53	2	10	0	12	0
File, Bob, Tenn.	1.000	3	1	1	0	2	1
Fiore, Curtis, Gre.	.000	1	0	0	0	0	0
Fischer, Mike, Jack.	1.000	12	1	5	0	6	0
Forster, Scott, Hun.*	.667	6	1	1	1	3	0
Foster, John, Gre.*	1.000	50	1	16	0	17	1
Foster, Kris, Jack.	1.000	17	0	1	0	1	0
Freeman, Kai, Birm.	.933	28	5	9	1	15	0
Gagliano, Steve, W.T.	1.000	35	2	7	0	9	0
Garcia, Jose, Hun.	.966	21	8	20	1	29	0
Gardner, Lee, Orl.	.000	1	0	0	0	0	0
Garibaldi, Cecilio, Orl.	.857	35	5	19	4	28	3
Gil, Dave, Chat.	1.000	11	1	8	0	9	1
Giron, Isabel, Mob.	1.000	14	4	3	0	7	0
Gissell, Chris, W.T.	.867	28	5	21	4	30	1
Glauber, Keith, Chat.	.800	22	0	4	1	5	0
Gomes, Tony, Jack.	1.000	17	1	1	0	2	0
Gonzalez, Gabe, Mob.*	1.000	8	0	4	0	4	1
Gonzalez, Lariel, W.T.	1.000	11	2	4	0	6	0
Grace, Mike, Chat.	1.000	21	2	4	0	6	0
Gray, Mike, Gre.*	.900	25	3	6	1	10	2
Guerrier, Matt, Birm.	.971	15	9	24	1	34	1
Gulin, Lindsay, Jack.*	1.000	26	3	16	0	19	0
Guttormson, Rick, Mob.	.868	27	12	21	5	38	1
Guzman, Juan, Orl.	1.000	2	3	1	0	4	0
Haines, Talley, Orl.	1.000	58	8	12	0	20	2
Halladay, Roy, Tenn.	1.000	5	7	5	0	12	2
Harrell, Tim, Jack.	.800	47	6	6	3	15	0
Hessman, Mike, Gre.	.000	1	0	0	0	0	0
High, Andy, Hun.*	1.000	6	2	2	0	4	0
Howard, Ben, Mob.	1.000	7	2	3	0	5	0
Howington, Ty, Chat.*	1.000	7	2	10	0	12	0
Hubbel, Travis, Tenn.	1.000	6	3	1	0	4	0
Hudson, Luke, Car.	.950	29	18	20	2	40	1
Hunter, Johnny, Mob.	.889	19	5	11	2	18	1
Husted, Brent, Jack.	1.000	23	7	8	0	15	1
Jacobs, Ryan, Hun.*	1.000	10	1	4	0	5	0
James, Delvin, Orl.	1.000	7	4	9	0	13	0
Jennings, Jason, Car.	1.000	4	1	9	0	10	1
Jimenez, Jason, Orl.*	.909	35	1	9	1	11	0
Johnson, Adam, Birm.*	.000	1	0	0	0	0	0
JUNGE, Eric, Jack.	1.000	27	15	20	0	35	1
Kalinowski, Josh, Car.*	.921	25	8	27	3	38	0
Kane, Kyle, Birm.	1.000	26	1	2	0	3	0
Kennedy, Joe, Orl.*	1.000	7	4	7	0	11	0
Kent, Nathan, Gre.	.969	26	13	18	1	32	0
Kibler, Andy, Car.	.857	8	4	14	3	21	0
Kimball, Andy, Hun.	1.000	48	6	9	0	15	0
Kingrey, Jarrod, Tenn.	.833	51	0	5	1	6	1
Kofler, Ed, Orl.	.833	13	4	6	2	12	1
Koronka, John, Chat.*	1.000	9	2	8	0	10	0
Kramer, Aaron, Mob.-W.T.	.875	25	2	5	1	8	0
Krawczyk, Jack, Hun.	1.000	47	4	13	0	17	1
Krug, Dustin, W.T.	1.000	7	1	0	0	1	0
Langone, Steve, Jack.	1.000	1	0	2	0	2	1
Lantigua, Eduardo, Birm.	1.000	7	2	7	0	9	1
Lee, Dave, Mob.	.000	2	0	0	0	0	0
Lee, Derek, Hun.*	.911	28	9	32	4	45	0
Lee, Garrett, Gre.	.875	32	5	9	2	16	1
Lontayo, Alejandro, Gre.*	.900	9	4	5	1	10	0
Lowe, Benny, Chat.*	1.000	26	1	8	0	9	0
Luebbers, Larry, Chat.	.958	8	7	16	1	24	0
Lyon, Brandon, Tenn.	1.000	9	5	13	0	18	0
MacRae, Scott, Chat.	.933	19	7	7	1	15	0
Magrane, Jim, Orl.	.936	29	12	32	3	47	3
Mallard, Randi, W.T.	1.000	8	1	1	0	2	0
Mallette, Brian, Hun.	.900	44	3	6	1	10	1
Malone, Corwin, Birm.*	1.000	4	0	4	0	4	1
Manias, Jim, Chat.*	1.000	24	1	4	0	5	0
Martinez, Javier, Chat.	.000	1	0	1	1	1	0
Martinez, Luis, Hun.*	1.000	7	0	1	0	1	0
Mathis, Jared, Hun.	1.000	1	0	1	0	1	0
McBride, Chris, Jack.	1.000	4	3	1	0	4	0
McClellan, Matt, Tenn.	.000	19	0	0	0	0	0
McClendon, Matt, Gre.	1.000	2	1	0	0	1	0
McDaniel, Denny, Birm.*	1.000	18	1	9	0	10	0
McNichol, Brian, Chat.*	1.000	21	1	2	0	3	0
Meadows, Randy, W.T.	.000	2	0	0	0	0	0
Mendoza, Geronimo, Birm.	.786	12	5	6	3	14	1
Middlebrook, Jason, Mob.	.909	10	4	6	1	11	1
Mieses, Jose, Hun.	1.000	5	2	3	0	5	0
Millwood, Kevin, Gre.	1.000	2	1	0	0	1	1
Montgomery, Matt, Jack.	1.000	14	2	2	0	4	0
Moraga, David, W.T.*	.929	23	4	9	1	14	1
Moss, Damian, Gre.*	1.000	3	0	3	0	3	0
Myers, Aaron, Hun.	.947	34	7	11	1	19	0
Nance, Shane, Jack.*	1.000	28	1	7	0	8	0
Neugebauer, Nick, Hun.	.938	21	5	10	1	16	0
Nevers, Tom, Chat.	.000	1	0	0	0	0	0
Noyce, Dave, W.T.*	.900	50	3	6	1	10	0
Osting, Jimmy, Car.-Mob.*	1.000	19	3	15	0	18	1
Ozuna, Francisco, Tenn.*	.667	12	0	2	1	3	0
Palma, Rick, W.T.*	1.000	57	2	12	0	14	1
Parra, Christian, Gre.	.895	18	7	10	2	19	0
Parris, Steve, Tenn.	.000	1	0	0	0	0	0
Parrish, Wade, Jack.-Birm.*	1.000	20	4	9	0	13	2
Payne, Jerrod, Tenn.	1.000	22	0	7	0	7	1
Pearson, Jason, Mob.*	1.000	54	7	22	0	29	0
Peavy, Jake, Mob.	1.000	5	1	0	0	1	0
Pelaez, Alex, Mob.	1.000	8	0	3	0	3	0
Penney, Mike, Hun.	.900	21	4	5	1	10	0
Piersoll, Chris, Chat.	.818	50	3	6	2	11	1
Poe, Ryan, Hun.	1.000	7	1	5	0	6	0
Porzio, Mike, Birm.*	1.000	2	0	1	0	1	0

Player, Team	Pct.	G	PO	A	E	TC	DP
Powalski, Rick, Orl.*	1.000	3	0	1	0	1	0
Proctor, Scott, Jack.	.900	10	2	7	1	10	0
Pruett, Jason, Orl.*	.917	38	5	6	1	12	0
Pujals, Denis, Orl.	.000	7	0	0	0	0	0
Purvis, Rob, Birm.	.947	24	20	34	3	57	6
Ramirez, Horacio, Gre.*	1.000	3	1	3	0	4	0
Randall, Scott, Car.	1.000	1	1	2	0	3	0
Regalado, Maximo, Jack.	1.000	18	2	2	0	4	0
Reimers, Cameron, Tenn.	1.000	5	2	1	0	3	0
Reith, Brian, Chat.	.929	18	3	10	1	14	2
Rekar, Bryan, Orl.	1.000	3	2	2	0	4	0
Reyes, Eddy, Orl.	1.000	31	5	7	0	12	0
Rijo, Jose, Chat.	.000	1	0	0	0	0	0
Robinson, Dustin, W.T.	1.000	17	2	3	0	5	0
Rosario, Juan, Orl.	1.000	44	6	8	0	14	0
Ruhl, Nathan, Orl.	.778	31	1	6	2	9	0
Saipe, Mike, Gre.	1.000	7	2	12	0	14	0
Sanders, Dave, Birm.*	1.000	36	4	6	0	10	0
Seay, Bobby, Orl.*	.900	15	6	12	2	20	0
Seifert, Ryan, Car.	1.000	33	5	11	0	16	2
Severino, Ronni, Orl.*	.857	38	1	17	3	21	1
Shelby, Anthony, Orl.*	1.000	4	0	1	0	1	0
Shiell, Jason, Mob.	.944	45	4	13	1	18	1
Shumate, Jacob, Hun.	1.000	8	1	1	0	2	0
Simon, Ben, Jack.	1.000	15	5	7	0	12	0
Sismondo, Bobby, Hun.*	1.000	8	0	2	0	2	0
Smith, Cam, Chat.	.917	29	2	9	1	12	0
Smith, Mike, Tenn.	.960	14	9	15	1	25	1
Smoltz, John, Gre.	1.000	3	1	0	0	1	0
Smyth, Steve, W.T.*	.939	18	8	23	2	33	3
Snyder, Matt, W.T.	1.000	25	0	1	0	1	0
Sobkowiak, Scott, Gre.	.833	12	5	5	2	12	0
Spooneybarger, Tim, Gre.	1.000	15	3	4	0	7	0
Standridge, Jason, Orl.	1.000	2	1	1	0	2	1
Stephenson, Brian, Jack.	.500	7	0	1	1	2	0
Stevens, Dave, Gre.	.333	9	0	1	2	3	0
Stevenson, Jason, Mob.	1.000	10	1	2	0	3	1
Stewart, Josh, Birm.*	1.000	16	2	19	0	21	1
Stull, Everell, Hun.	1.000	6	2	1	0	3	0
Sylvester, Billy, Gre.	.800	26	0	4	1	5	0

Player, Team	Pct.	G	PO	A	E	TC	DP
Taglienti, Jeff, Chat.	1.000	51	3	11	0	14	1
Takeoka, Kazuhiro, Gre.	.978	45	10	35	1	46	2
Tankersley, Dennis, Mob.	1.000	13	5	6	0	11	0
Thompson, Doug, Car.	.900	26	4	5	1	10	0
Thompson, Mark, Car.	1.000	8	1	3	0	4	0
Thompson, Travis, Chat.	.973	28	7	29	1	37	2
Thompson, Travis, Car.	1.000	28	3	6	0	9	0
Tokarse, Brian, Birm.	.900	39	2	7	1	10	0
Trujillo, J.J., Mob.	1.000	43	5	11	0	16	2
Ulacia, Dennis, Birm.*	1.000	3	0	3	0	3	0
Veronie, Shanin, Gre.	1.000	2	0	1	0	1	0
Voyles, Brad, Gre.	1.000	15	1	2	0	3	0
Waligora, Tom, W.T.	.833	22	2	3	1	6	0
Wallace, Jeff, Orl *	.000	1	0	0	0	0	0
Watkins, Steve, Mob.	.867	23	7	6	2	15	1
Weaver, Eric, Birm.	1.000	24	0	1	0	1	0
Weymouth, Marty, Birm.	.750	10	0	3	1	4	0
Wheeler, Dan, Orl.	1.000	3	0	1	0	1	0
Winkelsas, Joe, Gre.	.889	20	3	5	1	9	0
Woodards, Orlando, Tenn.	1.000	15	2	2	0	4	0
Wright, Danny, Birm.	.833	20	5	10	3	18	0
Wrigley, Jase, Car.	1.000	47	8	10	0	18	0
Wuertz, Mike, W.T.	.833	27	5	20	5	30	0
Wylie, Mitch, Birm.	.964	24	10	17	1	28	2
Yan, Esteban, Orl.	1.000	2	1	0	0	1	0

PITCHERS WITH TWO OR MORE TEAMS

Player, Team	Pct.	G	PO	A	E	TC	DP
Booker, Chris, W.T.	.500	45	0	2	2	4	0
Booker, Chris, Chat.	1.000	16	2	0	0	2	0
Kramer, Aaron, Mob.	.875	23	2	5	1	8	0
Kramer, Aaron, W.I.	.000	2	0	0	0	0	0
Osting, Jimmy, Car.*	1.000	1	0	1	0	1	0
Osting, Jimmy, Mob.*	1.000	18	3	14	0	17	1
Parrish, Wade, Jack.*	.000	4	0	0	0	0	0
Parrish, Wade, Birm.*	1.000	16	4	9	0	13	2

The following players appeared only as designated hitter, pinch-hitter or pinch runner: Cardonna, ph; Soto, ph.

LEAGUE CHAMPIONS

Year	Team	Pct.
1904—	Macon	.598
1905—	Macon	.625
1906—	Savannah	.637
1907—	Charleston	.620
1908—	Jacksonville	.694
1909—	Chattanooga*	.738
	Augusta	.702
1910—	Columbus	.588
1911—	Columbus*	.681
	Columbia	.710
1912—	Jacksonville*	.679
	Columbus	.632
1913—	Savannah	.754
	Savannah	.593
1914—	Savannah*	.667
	Albany	.650
1915—	Macon	.588
	Columbus*	.686
1916—	Augusta*	.617
	Columbia	.631
1917—	Charleston	.741
	Columbia*	.667
1918—	Did not operate.	
1919—	Columbia	.585
1920—	Columbia	.633
1921—	Columbia	.642
1922—	Charleston	.625
1923—	Charlotte*	.653
	Macon	.580
1924—	Augusta	.612
1925—	Spartanburg	.620
1926—	Greenville	.662
1927—	Greenville	.622
1928—	Asheville	.664
1929—	Greenville	.605
	Knoxville*	.634
1930—	Greenville*	.620
	Macon	.643

Year	Team	Pct.
1931-35—Did not operate.		
1936—	Jacksonville	.652
	Columbus*	.650
1937—	Columbus	.572
	Savannah (3rd)†	.565
1938—	Savannah	.574
	Macon (2nd)†	.570
1939—	Columbus	.601
	Augusta (2nd)†	.597
1940—	Savannah	.627
	Columbus (2nd)‖	.693
1941—	Macon	.643
	Columbia (2nd)†	.636
1942—	Charleston	.620
	Macon (2nd)†	.585
1943-45—Did not operate.		
1946—	Columbus	.568
	Augusta (4th)†	.547
1947—	Columbus	.575
	Savannah (2nd)†	.563
1948—	Charleston	.572
	Greenville (3rd)†	.549
1949—	Macon‡	.623
1950—	Macon‡	.588
1951—	Montgomery	.607
1952—	Columbia	.649
	Montgomery (3rd)†	.558
1953—	Jacksonville	.679
	Savannah (2nd)†	.571
1954—	Jacksonville	.593
	Savannah (2nd)†	.571
1955—	Columbia	.636
	Augusta (3rd)†	.543
1956—	Jacksonville‡	.621
1957—	Augusta	.636
	Charlotte (2nd)†	.562
1958—	Augusta	.550
	Macon (3rd)†	.500

Year	Team	Pct.
1959—	Knoxville	.557
	Gastonia (4th)†	.504
1960—	Columbia	.597
	Savannah (3rd)†	.561
1961—	Asheville	.635
1962—	Savannah	.662
	Macon (2nd)†	.576
1963—	Augusta*	.661
	Lynchburg	.662
1964—	Lynchburg	.579
1965—	Columbus	.572
1966—	Mobile	.629
1967—	Birmingham	.604
1968—	Asheville	.614
1969—	Charlotte	.579
1970—	Columbus	.569
1971—	Did not operate as league—clubs were members of Dixie Association.	
1972—	Asheville	.583
	Montgomery§	.561
1973—	Montgomery§	.580
	Jacksonville	.559
1974—	Jacksonville	.565
	Knoxville§	.533
1975—	Orlando	.587
	Montgomery§	.545
1976—	Montgomery∞	.591
	Orlando	.540
1977—	Montgomery∞	.628
	Jacksonville	.522
1978—	Knoxville∞	.611
	Savannah	.500
1979—	Columbus	.587
	Nashville∞	.576
1980—	Memphis	.576
	Charlotte∞	.500
1981—	Nashville	.566
	Orlando∞	.556

CLASS AA Southern League

Year	Team	Pct.	Year	Team	Pct.	Year	Team	Pct.
1982—	Jacksonville	.576	1989—	Birmingham∞	.615	1996—	Chattanooga	.579
	Nashville∞	.535		Greenville	.504		Jacksonville∞	.543
1983—	Birmingham∞	.628	1990—	Orlando	.590	1997—	Huntsville	.554
	Jacksonville	.531		Memphis∞	.507		Greenville∞	.529
1984—	Charlotte∞	.510	1991—	Greenville	.611	1998—	Mobile∞	.614
	Knoxville	.483		Orlando∞	.535		Jacksonville	.614
1985—	Charlotte	.545	1992—	Greenville∞	.699	1999—	West Tenn	.596
	Huntsville∞	.542		Chattanooga	.629		Orlando∞	.507
1986—	Huntsville	.553	1993—	Birmingham∞	.549	2000—	West Tenn∞	.580
	Columbus∞	.500		Knoxville	.500		Jacksonville	.493
1987—	Charlotte	.586	1994—	Huntsville∞	.587	2001—	Jacksonville▲	.597
	Birmingham∞	.476		Carolina	.529		Huntsville▲	.543
1988—	Greenville	.604	1995—	Carolina∞	.618			
	Chattanooga∞	.566		Chattanooga	.580			

*Won split season playoff. †Won four-club playoff. ‡Won championship and four-club playoff. §League was divided into Eastern and Western divisions; won play-off. ∞League was divided into Eastern and Western divisions and played split season; won playoff. ▲Were entering finals of four-team playoff and were declared co-champions when Professional Baseball declared a stoppage of play.

CLASS AA Southern League

TEXAS LEAGUE

LEAGUE OFFICE

President/treasurer
Tom Kayser

Address
2442 Facet Oak
San Antonio, TX 78232

Phone
210-545-5297

TEAMS

ARKANSAS TRAVELERS

Vice president/general manager
Bill Valentine
Manager
Doug Sisson
Ballpark (capacity, surface)
Ray Winder Field (6,083, grass)
Affiliation
Angels
Address
P.O. Box 55066
Little Rock, AR 72215
Phone
501-664-1555

EL PASO DIABLOS

General manager
Andrew Wheeler
Manager
Chip Hale
Ballpark (capacity, surface)
Cohen Stadium (9,765, grass)
Affiliation
Diamondbacks
Address
9700 Gateway Blvd. N.
El Paso, TX 79924
Phone
915-755-2000

MIDLAND ROCKHOUNDS

General manager
Monty Hoppel
Manager
Tony DeFrancesco
Ballpark (capacity, surface)
Scharbauer Sports Complex (5,000, grass)
Affiliation
Athletics
Address
P.O. Box 51187
Midland, TX 79710

Phone
915-000-4051

ROUND ROCK EXPRESS

General manager
Jay Miller
Manager
Jackie Moore
Ballpark (capacity, surface)
The Dell Diamond (7,500, grass)
Affiliation
Astros
Address
P.O. Box 5309
Round Rock, TX 78683
Phone
512-255-2255

SAN ANTONIO MISSIONS

President
Burl Yarbrough
Manager
Dave Brundage
Ballpark (capacity, surface)
Nelson Wolff Stadium (6,300, grass)
Affiliation
Mariners
Address
5757 Highway 90 West
San Antonio, TX 78227
Phone
210-675-7275

SHREVEPORT SWAMP DRAGONS

General manager
Roxy Dancy
Manager
Mario Mondoza
Ballpark (capacity, surface)
Fair Grounds Field (6,200, grass)
Affiliation
Giants

Address
2901 Pershing Blvd.
Shreveport, LA 71109
Phone
318-636-5555

TULSA DRILLERS

Executive v.p./general manager
Chuck Lamson
Manager
Tim Ireland
Ballpark (capacity, surface)
Drillers Stadium (10,842, grass)
Affiliation
Rangers
Address
4802 E. 15th
Tulsa, OK 74112
Phone
918-744-5998

WICHITA WRANGLERS

General manager
Steve Shaad
Manager
Keith Bodie
Ballpark (capacity, surface)
Lawrence-Dumont Stadium (6,111, artificial infield, grass outfield)
Affiliation
Royals
Address
P.O. Box 1420
Wichita, KS 67201
Phone
316-267-3372

2001 FINAL STANDINGS

FIRST HALF

EAST DIVISION

Team	W	L	T	Pct.	GB
Arkansas (Angels)	38	32	0	.543	...
Wichita (Royals)	36	31	0	.537	0.5
Tulsa (Rangers)	28	41	0	.406	9.5
Shreveport (Giants)	27	42	0	.391	10.5

WEST DIVISION

Team	W	L	T	Pct.	GB
Round Rock (Astros)	50	20	0	.714	...
Midland (Athletics)	43	27	0	.614	7.0
San Antonio (Mariners)	29	38	0	.433	19.5
El Paso (Diamondbacks)	25	45	0	.357	25.0

SECOND HALF

EAST DIVISION

Team	W	L	T	Pct.	GB
Wichita (Royals)	43	27	0	.614	...
Tulsa (Rangers)	41	29	0	.586	2.0
Arkansas (Angels)	28	38	0	.424	13.0
Shreveport (Giants)	27	39	0	.409	14.0

WEST DIVISION

Team	W	L	T	Pct.	GB
San Antonio (Mariners)	41	29	0	.586	...
Round Rock (Astros)	36	34	0	.514	5.0
El Paso (Diamondbacks)	32	38	0	.457	9.0
Midland (Athletics)	28	42	0	.400	13.0

CLASS AA *Texas League*

COMPOSITE

Team	R.R.	Wich.	S.A.	Mid.	Tul.	Ark.	E.P.	Shre.	W	L	T	Pct.	GB
Round Rock (Astros)	...	6	13	18	11	13	17	8	86	54	0	.614	...
Wichita (Royals)	10	...	5	6	14	15	11	18	79	58	0	.577	5.5
San Antonio (Mariners)	11	8	...	7	9	6	19	10	70	67	0	.511	14.5
Midland (Athletics)	10	10	17	...	6	7	11	10	71	69	0	.507	15.0
Tulsa (Rangers)	5	10	7	10	...	12	9	16	69	70	0	.496	16.5
Arkansas (Angels)	3	11	10	9	14	...	7	12	66	70	0	.485	18.0
El Paso (Diamondbacks)	7	5	9	13	7	9	...	7	57	83	0	.407	29.0
Shreveport (Giants)	8	8	6	6	9	8	9	...	54	81	0	.400	29.5

Arkansas' home games played in Little Rock, Ark.

Major league affiliations in parentheses.

PLAYOFFS: Arkansas defeated Wichita three games to one; Round Rock defeated San Antonio three games to two; Arkansas led final series two games to none over Round Rock. Note: Arkansas declared Texas League champions due to stoppage of play in professional baseball.

REGULAR-SEASON ATTENDANCE: Arkansas, 185,905; El Paso, 253,994; Midland, 148,292; Round Rock, 668,792; San Antonio, 309,113; Shreveport, 59,316; Tulsa, 314,973; Wichita, 130,438. Total—2,070,823. Playoffs (11 games)—50,632. Class AA All-Star Game at Round Rock, Texas—12,046.

MANAGERS: Arkansas, Mike Brumley; El Paso, Al Pedrique; Midland, Tony Defrancesco; Round Rock, Jackie Moore; San Antonio, Dave Brundage; Shreveport, Bill Russell; Tulsa, Paul Carey; Wichita, Keith Bodie.

ALL-STAR TEAM: 1B—Lyle Overbay, El Paso; 2B—David Matranga, Round Rock; 3B—Hank Blalock, Tulsa; SS—Alfredo Amezaga, Arkansas; OF—Brandon Berger, Wichita; OF—Jason Lane, Round Rock; OF—Ryan Ludwick, Midland; C—Brad Cresse, El Paso; DH—Jacques Landry, Midland; Utility—Brian Dallimore, El Paso; RHP—Keff Heaverlo, San Antonio; RHP—Tim Redding, Round Rock; RHP—Travis Smith, Round Rock; RHP—Corey Thurman, Wichita; LHP—Jeremy Affeldt, Wichita; LHP—Carlos Hernandez, Round Rock; Most Valuable Player—Jason Lane, Round Rock; Pitcher of the Year—Tim Redding, Round Rock; Manager of the Year—Jackie Moore, Round Rock.

2001 BATTING

TEAM

Team	Avg.	G	TPA	AB	R	H	TB	2B	3B	HR	RBI	SH	SF	HP	BB	IBB	SO	SB	CS	GDP	LOB	ShO	Slg.	OBP
El Paso	.281	140	5439	4862	650	1368	1979	311	33	78	608	39	40	69	429	25	1054	95	61	100	1089	16	.407	.346
Wichita	.280	137	5195	4678	776	1308	2076	252	39	146	733	44	47	6	420	19	842	116	76	110	949	10	.444	.337
Round Rock	.274	140	5420	4812	713	1317	2073	273	33	139	645	45	37	84	442	30	962	117	57	85	1028	8	.431	.343
Arkansas	.266	136	5112	4578	654	1217	1888	255	43	110	596	20	43	53	418	23	948	146	86	68	939	7	.412	.332
Midland	.260	140	5486	4764	742	1241	2010	280	36	139	677	38	40	96	548	12	1031	123	54	92	1044	7	.422	.346
Shreveport	.260	135	5151	4589	564	1192	1658	224	28	62	513	56	44	65	397	15	982	141	66	90	968	11	.361	.325
Tulsa	.257	139	5389	4747	650	1218	1896	260	35	116	606	69	39	61	473	17	965	87	55	85	1025	10	.399	.329
San Antonio	.255	137	5310	4729	615	1205	1731	227	28	81	567	36	43	43	459	12	925	109	52	98	996	8	.366	.324

INDIVIDUAL

TOP QUALIFIERS FOR BATTING CHAMPIONSHIP

Minimum 378 plate appearances. *Lefthanded batter. †Switch-hitter.

Player, Team	Avg.	G	TPA	AB	R	H	TB	2B	3B	HR	RBI	SH	SF	HP	BB	IBB	SO	SB	CS	GDP	Slg.	OBP
Overbay, Lyle, E.P.*	.352	138	612	532	82	187	281	49	3	13	100	0	8	5	67	11	92	5	4	6	.528	.423
Dallimore, Brian, E.P.	.327	127	573	517	74	169	243	38	6	8	67	12	1	13	30	1	56	11	13	9	.470	.378
Lane, Jason, R.R.	.316	137	610	526	103	166	320	36	2	38	124	1	1	21	61	11	98	14	2	6	.608	.407
Huffman, Royce, R.R.	.309	137	581	511	75	158	207	35	1	4	49	3	4	12	51	0	90	13	8	6	.405	.382
Berger, Brandon, Wich.	.308	120	515	454	98	140	294	28	3	40	118	1	3	14	43	2	91	14	6	9	.648	.383
Matranga, Dave, R.R.	.302	103	457	387	78	117	185	34	2	10	60	7	4	14	45	1	91	17	7	2	.478	.391
Castro, Nelson, Shre.	.296	122	540	479	76	142	214	27	6	11	60	8	4	7	42	0	122	38	11	7	.447	.359
Quinlan, Robb, Ark.	.295	129	559	492	82	145	234	33	7	14	79	0	7	6	53	9	84	0	4	12	.476	.366
Devore, Doug, E.P.*	.294	128	532	476	67	140	239	32	11	15	74	1	4	4	46	7	118	11	3	7	.502	.358
Robinson, Bo, S.A.	.293	133	566	474	75	139	203	31	1	13	74	1	7	3	81	4	56	3	0	7	.428	.395
Weber, Jake, S.A.*	.293	126	506	451	66	132	180	28	4	4	58	3	4	8	40	1	53	11	6	4	.399	.358
Cresse, Brad, E.P.	.289	118	498	429	55	124	207	39	1	14	81	0	7	18	44	0	116	0	1	11	.483	.373
Dillon, Joe, Wich.	.287	101	417	369	62	106	176	19	3	15	59	1	3	8	36	1	60	4	3	10	.477	.361
German, Esteban, Mid.	.284	92	414	335	79	95	139	20	3	6	30	4	0	12	63	0	66	31	11	6	.415	.415
Mensik, Todd, Mid.*	.283	132	571	502	69	142	242	35	1	21	79	0	5	4	60	2	104	0	1	16	.482	.361
Metzler, Rod, Wich.†	.283	110	439	381	62	108	146	20	3	4	62	4	3	5	46	3	81	13	11	10	.383	.366

DEPARTMENTAL LEADERS: G—Overbay, 138; AB—Overbay, 532; R—Lane, 103; H—Overbay, 187; TB—Lane, 320; 2B—Overbay, 49; 3B—Devore, 11; HR—Berger, 40; RBI—Lane, 124; SH—Solano, 18; SF—Harvey, Overbay, 8 each; HP—Pecci, 26; BB—Robinson, 81; IBB—Lane, Overbay, 11 each; SO—Landry, 184; SB—Castro, 38; CS—Amezaga, Haynes, C. Wright, 15 each; GIDP—Connors, 19; Slg.—Berger, .648; OBP—Overbay, .423.

ALL PLAYERS

*Lefthanded batter. †Switch-hitter.

Player, Team	Avg.	G	TPA	AB	R	H	TB	2B	3B	HR	RBI	SH	SF	HP	BB	IBB	SO	SB	CS	GDP	Slg.	OBP
Alfaro, Jason, R.R.	.243	87	298	284	26	69	95	16	2	2	29	3	2	2	7	1	40	2	1	13	.335	.264
Allen, Jeff, Shre.	.217	20	71	60	5	13	15	2	0	0	8	0	1	0	10	0	16	0	1	1	.250	.324
Amezaga, Alfredo, Ark.†	.312	70	314	285	50	89	121	10	5	4	21	3	0	4	22	1	55	24	15	0	.425	.370
Andra, Jeff, Shre.*	.000	18	10	8	2	0	0	0	0	0	0	1	1	0	1	0	6	0	0	0	.000	.111
Asche, Kirk, Mid.	.214	16	66	56	9	12	23	2	0	3	5	0	0	1	9	0	16	0	0	0	.411	.333
Beamon, Trey, S.A.*	.256	64	260	238	33	61	82	14	2	1	19	1	1	2	18	0	32	7	3	2	.345	.313
Benefield, Brian, Wich.	.150	9	23	20	2	3	11	0	1	2	4	0	0	1	2	0	6	0	0	1	.550	.261
Berger, Brandon, Wich.	.308	120	515	454	98	140	294	28	3	40	118	1	3	14	43	2	91	14	6	9	.648	.383
Berrios, Harry, Tul.	.262	37	159	149	20	39	70	10	0	7	23	0	0	0	10	1	33	4	1	2	.470	.308
Berroa, Angel, Wich.	.296	80	352	304	63	90	142	20	4	8	42	6	3	22	17	0	55	15	6	6	.467	.373
Berroa, Cristian, R.R.†	.204	38	123	113	12	23	28	3	1	0	2	1	2	0	7	1	15	6	4	1	.248	.246
Bierbrodt, Nick, E.P.*	.000	4	3	2	0	0	0	0	0	0	0	0	0	0	0	0	0	0	0	0	.000	.000

Player, Team	Avg.	G	TPA	AB	R	H	TB	2B	3B	HR	RBI	SH	SF	HP	BB	IBB	SO	SB	CS	GDP	Slg.	OBP
Blalock, Hank, Tul.*	.327	68	315	272	50	89	148	18	4	11	61	0	2	2	39	1	38	3	3	5	.544	.413
Bloomquist, Willie, S.A.	.255	123	531	491	59	125	152	23	2	0	28	7	4	1	28	0	55	34	9	11	.310	.294
Brito, Juan, Wich.	.267	70	261	236	22	63	85	10	0	4	28	1	0	0	17	0	29	3	3	9	.360	.315
Brown, Elliot, Shre.†	.333	14	3	3	1	1	2	1	0	0	0	0	0	0	0	0	0	0	0	0	.667	.333
Brummett, Sean, Ark.*	.000	26	4	4	0	0	0	0	0	0	0	0	0	0	0	0	0	0	0	0	.000	.000
Bruntlett, Eric, R.R.	.266	123	569	503	84	134	172	23	3	3	40	5	3	8	50	1	76	23	7	7	.342	.340
Burns, Kevin, R.R.*	.272	89	361	305	57	83	167	20	2	20	56	0	4	7	45	6	79	2	0	6	.548	.374
Byas, Mike, Shre.†	.266	83	376	316	55	84	101	13	2	0	25	5	3	3	49	0	57	21	10	4	.320	.367
Cadiente, Brett, Tul.*	.279	67	283	262	32	73	108	16	5	3	24	3	2	1	15	1	66	8	5	3	.412	.318
Calderon, Henry, Wich.	.263	97	362	327	50	86	132	21	5	5	49	3	4	10	18	0	51	4	8	11	.404	.318
Camilli, Jason, E.P.-Tul.	.258	68	257	213	28	55	75	9	1	3	27	4	2	4	34	1	44	4	3	5	.352	.368
Campusano, Carlos, Shre.	.143	27	70	63	6	9	12	3	0	0	1	1	0	1	5	0	18	0	1	1	.190	.217
Cannon, Jon, Shre.	.500	17	2	2	0	1	1	0	0	0	1	0	0	0	0	0	0	0	0	0	.500	.500
Capuano, Chris, E.P.*	.154	28	17	13	1	2	4	2	0	0	2	2	1	1	0	0	6	0	0	0	.308	.250
Carlson, Dan, E.P.	.000	32	1	1	0	0	0	0	0	0	0	0	0	0	0	0	0	0	0	0	.000	.000
Carter, Charley, R.R.	.263	133	567	525	65	138	241	26	1	25	97	0	5	2	35	3	106	1	1	11	.459	.309
Caruso, Joe, Wich.	.264	120	507	424	75	112	164	26	1	8	59	5	5	23	50	1	65	12	6	8	.387	.369
Casper, Brett, Shre.	.077	10	34	26	1	2	2	0	0	0	1	1	1	1	5	0	15	0	0	0	.077	.242
Castillo, Ruben, S.A.	.198	40	137	126	12	25	29	4	0	0	7	2	1	1	7	0	27	1	0	1	.230	.244
Castro, Nelson, Shre.	.296	122	540	479	76	142	214	27	6	11	60	8	4	7	42	0	122	38	11	7	.447	.359
Cervantes, Chris, E.P.*	.167	45	6	6	0	1	1	0	0	0	0	0	0	0	0	0	3	0	0	0	.167	.167
Chapman, Scott, R.R.	.300	3	10	10	2	3	4	1	0	0	1	0	0	0	0	0	4	0	0	0	.400	.300
Chavez, Endy, Wich.*	.298	43	190	168	27	50	61	6	1	1	13	3	3	0	16	0	13	11	6	1	.363	.353
Chiaramonte, Giuseppe, Shre.	.205	13	49	44	3	9	11	2	0	0	3	0	1	0	4	0	6	0	1	2	.250	.265
Christensen, Mike, Ark.	.235	86	320	298	32	70	115	23	2	6	33	0	2	1	19	0	76	4	2	2	.386	.281
Clark, Doug, Shre.*	.275	123	472	414	53	114	156	16	4	6	51	6	4	3	45	4	83	20	5	8	.377	.348
Connors, Greg, S.A.	.240	121	498	455	68	109	168	14	6	11	69	1	5	5	32	0	94	5	5	19	.369	.294
Cordido, Julio, Shre.	.217	121	472	433	45	94	115	14	2	1	47	1	4	3	31	1	68	11	3	15	.266	.272
Cosme, Caonabo, Mid.	.192	34	108	99	9	19	25	2	2	0	4	5	0	0	4	0	32	1	2	0	.253	.223
Cox, Ryan, Shre.	.250	24	13	12	0	3	3	0	0	0	0	0	0	0	0	0	5	0	0	0	.250	.250
Crawford, Joe, F.P.*	.000	7	2	2	0	0	0	0	0	0	0	0	0	0	0	0	1	0	0	0	.000	.000
Cresse, Brad, E.P.	.289	118	498	429	55	124	207	39	1	14	81	0	7	18	44	0	110	0	1	11	.483	.373
Curl, John, S.A.*	.259	52	200	174	23	45	70	7	0	6	20	0	1	2	23	2	47	3	1	0	.402	.350
Curtis, Chad, Tul.	.182	6	29	22	3	4	7	0	0	1	2	1	0	2	5	0	6	1	0	0	.318	.379
Dallimore, Brian, E.P.*	.327	127	573	517	74	169	243	38	6	8	67	12	1	13	30	1	56	11	13	9	.470	.378
Devore, Doug, E.P.*	.294	128	532	476	67	140	239	32	11	15	74	1	4	4	46	7	118	11	3	7	.502	.358
Diaz, Angel, Ark.	.265	35	129	117	17	31	52	9	0	4	15	1	0	3	8	0	23	0	1	1	.444	.328
Dillon, Joe, Wich.	.287	101	417	369	62	106	176	19	3	15	59	1	3	8	36	1	60	4	3	10	.477	.361
Dodson, Jeremy, Wich.*	.204	35	127	113	13	23	29	1	1	1	7	1	0	2	11	1	31	3	0	4	.257	.286
Durrington, Trent, Ark	.291	51	217	182	37	53	95	12	0	10	35	1	1	7	26	0	47	22	2	2	.522	.398
Fatheree, Danny, R.R.	.130	8	25	23	3	3	6	0	0	1	2	0	0	0	2	0	2	0	0	0	.261	.200
Felix, Hersy, Wich.	.222	3	10	9	1	2	5	0	0	1	1	1	0	0	0	0	5	0	0	0	.556	.222
Figgins, Chone, Ark.†	.268	39	158	138	21	37	53	12	2	0	12	3	3	0	14	0	26	7	2	0	.384	.329
Figueroa, Luis, S.A.	.141	18	66	64	5	9	11	2	0	0	4	0	0	1	1	0	6	1	0	2	.172	.167
Flores, Javier, Tul.	.241	32	128	116	8	28	34	4	1	0	11	0	1	2	9	0	10	2	2	6	.293	.305
Foley, Steve, S.A.	.230	30	98	87	9	20	27	5	1	0	10	2	1	2	6	1	14	4	1	1	.310	.292
Freeman, Corey, Wich.	.176	26	83	74	6	13	19	3	0	1	3	4	0	0	5	0	18	1	0	3	.257	.228
Furniss, Eddy, Mid.*	.250	38	152	132	11	33	50	10	2	1	13	0	0	1	19	0	43	0	0	2	.379	.349
Gallagher, Shawn, Wich.	.264	96	377	345	44	91	154	19	4	12	48	2	3	2	25	1	62	5	7	7	.446	.315
Gann, Jamie, E.P.	.216	55	203	190	20	41	52	5	0	2	18	2	0	4	7	0	44	5	3	9	.274	.259
Garcia, Osmani, Tul.	.258	71	277	260	29	67	107	14	4	6	35	2	4	1	10	1	27	0	2	4	.412	.284
German, Esteban, Mid.	.284	92	414	335	79	95	139	20	3	6	30	4	0	12	63	0	66	31	11	6	.415	.415
Gibson, Derrick, E.P.	.347	18	81	72	13	25	35	4	0	2	16	0	1	2	6	1	18	3	1	2	.486	.407
Glassey, Josh, E.P.*	.167	8	21	18	1	3	3	0	0	0	0	0	0	0	3	0	5	0	0	1	.167	.286
Glendenning, Mike, Shre.-E.P.	.205	100	393	347	37	71	113	12	0	10	36	1	2	4	39	1	117	1	0	10	.326	.291
Gomez, Alexis, Wich.*	.281	83	378	342	55	96	135	15	6	4	34	1	4	4	27	1	70	16	10	4	.395	.337
Gonzalez, Manny, E.P.†	.192	9	27	26	3	5	6	1	0	0	1	0	0	0	1	0	4	0	1	0	.231	.222
Good, Andrew, E.P.	.250	10	4	4	1	1	1	0	0	0	0	0	0	0	0	0	1	0	0	0	.250	.250
Gray, Mike, E.P.*	.000	29	1	1	0	0	0	0	0	0	0	0	0	0	0	0	1	0	0	0	.000	.000
Greer, Rusty, Tul.*	.000	1	4	3	0	0	0	0	0	0	0	0	0	0	1	0	1	0	0	0	.000	.250
Gregorio, Tom, Ark.	.191	45	171	157	15	30	43	10	0	1	23	2	1	4	7	0	37	0	0	3	.274	.243
Guerra, Mark, R.R.	.250	9	4	4	0	1	1	0	0	0	0	0	0	0	0	0	1	0	0	0	.250	.250
Guiel, Jeff, Ark.*	.313	55	205	176	33	55	110	12	2	13	36	0	4	4	21	2	52	3	2	2	.625	.390
Guzman, Elpidio, Ark.*	.244	117	483	459	58	112	170	21	8	7	46	2	3	2	17	1	89	18	14	6	.370	.272
Guzman, Leiby, Shre.	.000	11	1	0	0	0	0	0	0	0	0	0	0	0	1	0	0	0	0	0	.000	1.000
Hafner, Travis, Tul.*	.282	88	389	323	59	91	176	25	0	20	74	0	3	4	59	5	82	3	1	10	.545	.396
Halloran, Matt, Tul.	.214	27	79	70	7	15	23	5	0	1	4	3	0	2	4	0	15	1	0	3	.329	.276
Hammock, Rob, E.P.	.162	26	82	74	6	12	17	5	0	0	4	0	1	0	7	0	18	2	2	1	.230	.235
Hansen, Jed, Wich.	.368	17	68	57	17	21	38	8	0	3	6	1	0	1	9	0	10	5	2	1	.667	.463
Harris, Cedrick, E.P.	.204	16	52	49	4	10	14	1	0	1	4	0	1	0	2	0	15	1	0	0	.286	.231
Hart, Corey, Wich.†	.220	17	52	41	8	9	11	2	0	0	1	1	0	0	10	0	5	0	1	0	.268	.373
Hartman, Pete, E.P.*	.000	19	1	1	0	0	0	0	0	0	0	0	0	0	0	0	1	0	0	0	.000	.000
Harvey, Ken, Wich.	.338	79	344	314	54	106	159	20	3	9	63	0	8	4	18	0	60	3	0	12	.506	.372
Haynes, Nathan, Ark.*	.310	79	353	316	49	98	134	11	5	5	23	2	0	3	32	2	65	33	15	4	.424	.379
Hernandez, Carlos, R.R.*	.211	24	21	19	3	4	4	0	0	0	1	1	1	0	0	0	6	0	0	1	.211	.200
Hernandez, John, E.P.	.143	8	21	21	1	3	4	1	0	0	0	0	0	0	0	0	6	0	0	1	.190	.143
Hill, Jason, Ark.	.258	85	326	298	42	77	128	18	0	11	45	1	4	4	18	1	58	1	1	9	.430	.306
Hochgesang, Josh, Mid.	.231	83	345	303	48	70	112	18	3	6	33	1	1	10	30	1	84	8	3	2	.370	.320
Hodges, Kerry, R.R.	.000	1	3	3	0	0	0	0	0	0	0	0	0	0	0	0	2	0	0	0	.000	.000
Hood, Jay, Ark.	.291	17	58	55	8	16	21	2	0	1	9	0	0	0	3	1	15	0	1	2	.382	.328
Horgan, Joe, Shre.*	.667	31	3	3	0	2	2	0	0	0	2	0	0	0	0	0	0	0	0	0	.667	.667
Huckaby, Ken, E.P.	.346	30	116	104	14	36	46	4	0	2	14	1	4	3	3	0	16	0	0	3	.442	.368
Huffman, Royce, R.R.	.309	137	581	511	75	158	207	35	1	4	49	3	4	12	51	0	90	13	8	6	.405	.382

Player, Team	Avg.	G	TPA	AB	R	H	TB	2B	3B	HR	RBI	SH	SF	HP	BB	IBB	SO	SB	CS	GDP	Slg.	OBP
Huisman, Jason, Ark.	.278	109	419	371	55	103	155	22	0	10	51	1	4	4	39	0	63	4	9	5	.418	.349
Jamison, Ryan, R.R.	.500	10	5	2	1	1	1	0	0	0	0	3	0	0	0	0	0	0	0	0	.500	.500
Jester, Joe, Shre.	.320	40	167	150	26	48	84	14	2	6	27	1	1	3	12	0	33	4	1	2	.560	.380
Johnson, Gary, Ark.*	.245	128	538	466	63	114	175	24	2	11	72	0	5	7	60	4	93	8	7	8	.376	.336
Jones, Jason, Tul.†	.215	30	111	107	8	23	35	6	0	2	8	0	0	1	3	1	17	0	0	4	.327	.243
Jones, Jeremy, Tul.	.232	93	355	311	34	72	97	13	0	4	29	8	2	4	30	1	61	1	3	9	.312	.305
Joseph, Kevin, Shre.	.000	24	2	1	0	0	0	0	0	0	0	0	0	0	0	0	0	1	0	0	.000	.000
Kapler, Gabe, Tul.	.333	5	21	15	2	5	6	1	0	0	0	0	0	0	6	0	1	0	1	0	.400	.524
Kata, Matt, E.P.†	.438	4	18	16	4	7	9	2	0	0	4	0	0	0	2	0	2	0	1	0	.563	.500
Keith, Rusty, Mid.	.261	89	343	291	39	76	107	20	1	3	31	4	2	0	46	0	43	1	4	9	.368	.360
Kelly, Kenny, S.A.	.262	121	536	478	72	125	188	20	5	11	46	5	5	3	45	0	111	18	12	9	.393	.326
Kessel, Kyle, R.R.	.154	14	14	13	0	2	3	1	0	0	0	1	0	0	0	1	2	0	0	0	.231	.214
King, Brad, S.A.	.313	80	303	262	34	82	128	16	0	10	56	1	2	5	33	1	33	4	4	13	.489	.397
Knoll, Brian, Shre.	.000	2	2	1	0	0	0	0	0	0	0	0	1	0	0	0	1	0	0	0	.000	.000
Knoll, Eric, E.P.	.000	17	1	1	0	0	0	0	0	0	0	0	0	0	0	0	1	0	0	0	.000	.000
Koplove, Mike, E.P.	.000	35	6	6	0	0	0	0	0	0	0	0	0	0	0	0	2	0	0	0	.000	.000
Kuzmic, Craig, S.A.†	.282	131	558	479	79	135	221	31	5	15	91	1	5	6	67	2	133	7	4	11	.461	.373
Landry, Jacques, Mid.	.241	134	589	506	102	122	252	14	4	36	95	0	4	15	64	2	184	37	7	4	.498	.341
Lane, Jason, R.R.	.316	137	610	526	103	166	320	36	2	38	124	1	1	21	61	11	98	14	2	6	.608	.407
Leday, A.J., Ark.	.125	4	19	16	1	2	2	0	0	0	2	0	1	0	2	0	8	0	0	0	.125	.211
Lemonis, Chris, E.P.*	.309	87	366	333	45	103	132	19	2	2	52	2	4	4	23	1	51	8	3	13	.396	.396
Lidge, Brad, R.R.	.000	5	4	2	0	0	0	0	0	0	0	0	0	0	1	0	1	0	0	0	.000	.333
Lira, James, R.R.	.000	27	1	1	0	0	0	0	0	0	0	0	0	0	0	0	0	0	0	0	.000	.000
Lockwood, Mike, Mid.*	.260	131	559	493	71	128	188	36	3	6	69	4	5	8	49	1	80	9	4	8	.381	.333
Logan, Kyle, R.R.*	.314	73	283	258	36	81	127	22	3	6	32	1	1	4	19	3	44	12	3	4	.492	.369
Lopez, Javier, E.P.*	1.000	22	1	1	0	1	1	0	0	0	0	0	0	0	0	0	0	0	0	0	1.000	1.000
Lopez, Norberto, Ark.	.167	2	7	6	0	1	2	1	0	0	0	0	0	0	0	0	3	0	0	0	.333	.286
Luderer, Brian, Mid.	.257	86	344	307	30	79	116	20	1	5	34	6	4	4	23	1	49	1	1	10	.378	.314
Ludwick, Ryan, Mid.	.269	119	513	443	82	119	223	23	3	25	96	1	5	7	56	1	113	9	10	6	.503	.356
Luster, Jeremy, Shre.†	.273	130	551	506	54	138	187	33	2	4	76	0	5	7	33	3	94	6	3	11	.370	.323
Luther, Ryan, Shre.	.280	127	510	453	54	127	169	26	2	4	42	8	2	15	32	0	78	6	8	9	.373	.347
Madonna, Chris, Mid.*	.236	40	130	106	21	25	41	2	1	4	16	2	3	2	17	1	31	0	1	3	.387	.344
Magruder, Chris, Shre.†	.255	40	171	149	22	38	56	6	3	2	11	4	0	3	15	2	27	5	3	2	.376	.335
Maldonado, Carlos, R.R.	.286	76	295	262	29	75	101	14	0	4	33	0	3	3	27	0	55	1	2	11	.385	.356
Martin, Billy, E.P.	.176	4	18	17	3	3	5	0	1	0	1	0	0	0	1	0	4	0	0	0	.294	.222
Martines, Jason, E.P.*	.500	51	2	2	1	1	2	1	0	0	1	0	0	0	0	0	0	0	0	0	1.000	.500
Matranga, Dave, R.R.	.302	103	457	387	78	117	185	34	2	10	60	7	4	14	45	1	91	17	7	2	.478	.391
Maynard, Scott, S.A.	.183	70	257	229	17	42	53	11	0	0	19	6	0	1	21	0	59	3	0	3	.231	.255
McGowan, Sean, Shre.	.304	31	132	125	11	38	53	6	0	3	17	0	2	0	5	0	19	0	1	3	.424	.326
Medrano, Steve, Wich.†	.243	46	157	140	16	34	39	5	0	0	15	3	0	0	14	0	22	3	2	5	.279	.312
Meliah, Dave, Tul.*	.290	90	334	307	40	89	150	17	4	12	47	1	1	1	24	2	47	4	4	4	.489	.342
Melton, John, E.P.	.500	2	5	4	0	2	3	1	0	0	2	0	0	0	1	0	2	0	0	0	.750	.600
Mench, Kevin, Tul.	.265	120	521	475	78	126	242	34	2	26	83	0	6	6	34	0	76	4	6	7	.509	.319
Mendoza, Hatuey, E.P.	.000	8	5	3	0	0	0	0	0	0	0	0	0	1	0	1	0	2	0	0	.000	.250
Mensik, Todd, Mid.*	.283	132	571	502	69	142	242	35	1	21	79	0	5	4	60	2	104	0	1	16	.482	.361
Metzler, Rod, Wich.†	.283	110	439	381	62	108	146	20	3	4	62	4	3	5	46	3	81	13	11	10	.383	.366
Miller, Benji, Shre.	.000	37	2	0	0	0	0	0	0	0	0	0	0	0	2	0	0	0	0	0	.000	1.000
Montas, Ricardo, E.P.	.250	28	107	96	5	24	32	5	0	1	9	1	0	0	10	0	17	0	1	3	.333	.321
Moreta, Ramon, Shre.	.284	30	118	109	14	31	41	4	0	2	14	0	1	2	6	1	15	9	6	3	.376	.331
Morillo, Cesar, R.R.†	.183	33	102	93	11	17	25	1	2	1	8	3	0	0	6	1	12	2	0	3	.269	.232
Mott, Bill, Ark.*	.319	25	103	94	9	30	43	5	4	0	9	0	0	0	9	1	21	10	4	0	.457	.379
Murphy, Nate, E.P.*	.262	38	142	122	22	32	58	8	3	4	18	0	1	0	19	0	29	6	1	1	.475	.359
Myers, Adrian, S.A.	.233	33	152	129	14	30	38	4	2	0	15	2	3	1	17	0	30	6	4	4	.295	.320
Nathan, Joe, Shre.	.000	21	2	0	0	0	0	0	0	0	0	0	1	0	0	0	1	0	0	0	.000	1.000
Neal, Steve, E.P.*	.172	7	30	29	0	5	8	3	0	0	1	0	0	0	1	0	10	0	0	0	.276	.200
Nieckula, Aaron, Mid.	.385	12	45	39	8	15	23	5	0	1	10	1	1	2	2	0	7	0	0	0	.590	.432
Norris, Ben, E.P.*	.400	16	6	5	0	2	2	0	0	0	1	1	0	0	0	0	1	0	0	0	.400	.400
Oliver, Brian, Tul.	.225	12	50	40	5	9	12	1	1	0	5	1	2	1	6	0	8	0	0	0	.300	.327
Olson, Tim, E.P.	.317	46	185	167	29	53	72	13	0	2	24	0	1	6	11	0	36	4	4	4	.431	.378
Overbay, Lyle, E.P.*	.352	138	612	532	82	187	281	49	3	13	100	0	8	5	67	11	92	5	4	6	.528	.423
Owens, Ryan, E.P.	.232	16	61	56	4	13	15	2	0	0	1	0	0	0	5	0	18	0	1	2	.268	.295
Ozias, Todd, Shre.	.000	30	1	1	0	0	0	0	0	0	0	0	0	0	0	0	1	0	0	0	.000	.000
Pearsall, J.J., Tul.*	.000	43	1	1	0	0	0	0	0	0	0	0	0	0	0	0	0	0	0	0	.000	.000
Pecci, Jay, Mid.†	.260	125	548	469	72	122	176	31	7	3	49	8	2	26	42	1	56	16	7	11	.375	.353
Perez, Antonio, S.A.	.143	5	21	21	3	3	3	0	0	0	0	0	0	0	0	0	7	0	0	0	.143	.143
Pernalete, Marco, Shre.†	.280	29	110	93	9	26	39	5	1	2	12	1	5	2	9	0	17	0	1	1	.419	.339
Piniella, Juan, S.A.	.260	110	430	373	51	97	134	24	2	3	34	10	4	5	38	1	98	13	3	0	.359	.333
Porter, Colin, R.R.*	.320	25	106	100	14	32	53	5	5	2	12	0	0	1	5	2	25	1	3	0	.530	.358
Puffer, Brandon, R.R.	.000	56	4	3	0	0	0	0	0	0	0	0	0	0	1	0	0	0	0	0	.000	.000
Pujols, Rafael, Mid.	.220	19	66	59	5	13	18	3	1	0	6	0	1	0	4	0	13	0	0	3	.305	.277
Quinlan, Robb, Ark.	.295	129	559	492	82	145	234	33	7	14	79	0	7	6	53	9	84	0	4	12	.476	.366
Ramirez, Erasmo, Shre.*	.000	22	1	1	0	0	0	0	0	0	0	0	0	0	1	0	0	0	0	0	.000	.000
Ramirez, Joslin, E.P.	1.000	4	1	1	0	1	1	0	0	0	0	0	0	0	0	0	0	0	0	0	1.000	1.000
Randolph, Steve, E.P.*	.200	21	11	10	0	2	2	0	0	0	0	0	0	0	1	0	7	0	0	0	.200	.273
Redding, Tim, R.R.	.333	14	7	6	0	2	2	0	0	0	0	0	1	0	0	0	2	0	0	0	.333	.286
Reynolds, Shane, R.R.	.000	1	3	1	1	0	0	0	0	0	0	0	0	2	0	0	0	1	0	0	.000	.500
Riley, Mike, Shre.*	.400	7	5	5	1	2	3	1	0	0	2	0	0	0	0	0	2	0	0	0	.600	.400
Roberts, Nick, R.R.	.000	8	2	2	0	0	0	0	0	0	0	0	0	0	0	0	2	0	0	0	.000	.000
Robertson, Jeriome, R.R.*	.000	58	7	6	0	0	0	0	0	0	0	0	0	0	1	0	3	0	0	0	.000	.143
Robinson, Bo, S.A.	.293	133	566	474	75	139	203	23	1	13	74	1	7	3	81	4	56	3	0	7	.428	.395
Rodriguez, Guillermo, Shre.	.204	65	238	216	21	44	66	7	0	5	25	5	3	6	8	0	40	3	0	5	.306	.249
Rodriguez, Wil, R.R.*	.000	42	4	3	0	0	0	0	0	0	0	0	0	0	1	0	3	0	0	0	.000	.250

CLASS AA Texas League

Player, Team	Avg.	G	TPA	AB	R	H	TB	2B	3B	HR	RBI	SH	SF	HP	BB	IBB	SO	SB	CS	GDP	Slg.	OBP
Romano, Jason, Tul.	.242	46	207	186	19	45	59	9	1	1	19	3	1	1	16	0	31	8	3	8	.317	.304
Romero, Mandy, Mid.†	.311	29	117	103	12	32	43	8	0	1	12	1	1	1	11	0	10	0	0	1	.417	.379
Rosamond, Mike, R.R.	.290	31	124	107	14	31	43	5	2	1	12	4	1	0	12	0	27	3	5	2	.402	.358
Rose, Mike, E.P.†	.259	62	243	205	28	53	77	13	1	3	23	0	1	0	37	1	40	4	4	8	.376	.370
Salazar, Oscar, Mid.	.267	130	579	521	75	139	232	31	4	18	95	1	6	2	49	2	100	10	3	11	.445	.329
Sanchez, Duaner, E.P.	.167	13	6	6	0	1	1	0	0	0	1	0	0	0	0	0	2	0	0	0	.167	.167
Santora, Jack, E.P.†	.234	86	310	265	35	62	76	14	0	0	13	7	1	2	35	1	48	4	5	2	.287	.327
Sell, Chip, E.P.*	.194	17	65	62	8	12	17	5	0	0	11	0	1	0	2	0	15	0	0	0	.274	.215
Sessions, Doug, R.R.	.375	41	8	8	1	3	4	1	0	0	1	0	0	0	0	0	1	0	0	0	.500	.375
Shabala, Adam, Shre.*	.343	12	43	35	9	12	15	0	0	1	4	1	0	0	7	0	10	2	0	0	.429	.452
Shackelford, Brian, Wich.*	.260	110	415	366	62	95	179	18	3	20	72	4	6	6	33	3	79	4	4	4	.489	.326
Shearn, Tom, R.R.	.000	43	7	6	0	0	0	0	0	0	0	0	0	0	1	0	2	0	0	0	.000	.143
Silva, Doug, Tul.	.000	14	1	1	0	0	0	0	0	0	0	0	0	0	0	0	0	0	0	0	.000	.000
Silvestre, Juan, S.A.	.228	101	397	372	29	85	122	13	0	8	39	0	3	1	21	0	113	0	2	4	.328	.270
Smith, Travis, R.R.	.056	30	20	18	2	1	1	0	0	0	0	0	0	0	2	0	6	0	0	0	.056	.150
Snyder, Matt, Tul.	.000	5	1	1	0	0	0	0	0	0	0	0	0	0	0	0	0	0	0	0	.000	.000
Socarras, Tony, Ark.*	.167	3	6	6	0	1	1	0	0	0	0	0	0	0	0	0	1	0	0	0	.167	.167
Solano, Danny, Tul.	.246	120	497	423	58	104	148	16	5	6	45	18	4	6	46	0	77	3	4	6	.350	.326
Sosa, Juan, E.P.	.257	29	122	113	14	29	36	5	1	0	8	1	1	0	7	0	20	5	2	5	.319	.298
Specht, Brian, Ark.†	.265	45	170	155	14	41	60	9	2	2	15	1	0	1	13	0	32	2	2	2	.387	.325
Strankman, Elliott, Shre.	.077	9	15	13	1	1	1	0	0	0	0	0	0	1	1	0	9	0	0	0	.077	.200
Sykes, Jamie, E.P.	.250	64	233	216	22	54	70	7	0	3	16	0	1	3	13	0	75	9	2	3	.324	.300
Taveras, Luis, Tul.	.206	55	205	180	31	37	60	4	2	5	22	4	2	1	18	0	35	5	0	5	.333	.279
Terrero, Luis, E.P.	.299	34	156	147	29	44	72	13	3	3	8	2	0	3	4	0	45	9	2	2	.490	.331
t'Hoen, E.J., Ark.	.172	30	109	93	11	16	29	5	1	2	7	1	1	2	12	1	31	5	3	1	.312	.278
Thurman, Corey, Wich.	.000	26	0	0	1	0	0	0	0	0	0	0	0	0	0	0	0	0	0	0	.000	.000
Tonis, Mike, Wich.	.270	63	253	226	36	61	101	11	1	9	43	0	1	4	22	2	41	1	1	7	.447	.344
Torcato, Tony, Shre.*	.293	36	163	147	13	43	57	9	1	1	23	0	3	4	9	3	15	0	1	6	.388	.344
Tremie, Chris, R.R.	.227	66	248	220	28	50	72	7	0	5	28	3	1	2	22	0	33	0	4	8	.327	.302
Tyler, Josh, Shre.	.273	17	49	44	3	12	15	3	0	0	3	1	0	0	4	0	8	3	2	1	.341	.333
Ullery, Dave, Wich.*	.286	12	48	42	8	12	15	3	0	0	9	0	0	0	6	1	6	0	0	0	.357	.375
Urban, Jeff, Shre.	.091	27	14	11	1	1	1	0	0	0	0	2	0	0	1	0	5	0	0	0	.091	.167
Urquhart, Derick, Ark.*	.264	81	289	250	42	66	96	11	2	5	45	1	5	0	33	0	37	4	1	4	.384	.344
Urquiola, Carlos, E.P.*	.281	41	165	153	26	43	52	7	1	0	9	2	0	0	10	0	16	7	3	2	.340	.325
Valderrama, Carlos, Shre.	.308	41	179	159	29	49	68	12	2	1	8	2	0	0	18	0	29	11	5	1	.428	.379
Valverde, Jose, E.P.	.000	39	1	1	0	0	0	0	0	0	0	0	0	0	0	0	1	0	0	0	.000	.000
Velarde, Randy, Tul.	.381	6	24	21	5	8	10	2	0	0	5	0	2	0	1	0	5	0	0	0	.476	.375
Verplancke, Jeff, Shre.	.000	43	1	1	0	0	0	0	0	0	0	0	0	0	0	0	1	0	0	0	.000	.000
Villano, Miko, Shre.	.000	7	1	0	0	0	0	0	0	0	0	0	0	1	0	0	0	0	0	0	.000	1.000
Villarreal, Oscar, E.P.*	.200	27	17	15	2	3	3	0	0	0	1	0	0	1	0	0	7	0	1	1	.200	.250
Walker, Mark, Shre.	.233	43	99	90	14	21	38	6	1	3	9	0	1	0	8	0	36	2	1	0	.422	.293
Ward, Jeremy, E.P.	.000	7	1	1	0	0	0	0	0	0	0	0	0	0	0	0	1	0	0	0	.000	.000
Warriax, Brandon, Tul.	.135	23	82	74	4	10	15	5	0	0	3	5	0	0	3	0	31	0	0	0	.203	.169
Weber, Jake, S.A.*	.293	126	506	451	66	132	180	28	4	4	58	3	4	8	40	1	53	11	6	4	.399	.358
Wesson, Barry, R.R.	.252	133	530	472	67	119	204	23	7	16	54	7	4	6	41	0	135	20	10	4	.432	.317
White, Bill, E.P.*	.000	7	6	6	0	0	0	0	0	0	0	0	0	0	0	0	2	0	0	0	.000	.000
White, Walt, E.P.	.151	27	94	86	7	13	15	2	0	0	3	1	0	0	7	1	25	0	1	1	.174	.215
Whiteman, Tom, R.R.	.250	4	17	16	1	4	7	0	0	1	1	0	0	1	0	0	5	0	0	0	.438	.294
Williams, Jerome, Shre.	.000	23	13	13	0	0	0	0	0	0	0	0	0	0	0	0	8	0	0	0	.000	.000
Williams, Peanut, S.A.	.200	38	141	125	11	25	37	9	0	1	9	0	1	1	14	1	37	1	1	4	.296	.284
Wright, Corey, Tul.*	.254	117	496	418	62	106	131	19	3	0	26	7	1	12	58	2	103	23	15	4	.313	.360
Wright, Mike, Shre.	.242	62	201	182	13	44	63	10	0	3	19	4	2	1	12	1	62	0	2	1	.346	.289
Young, Travis, Shre.	.357	6	14	14	2	5	6	1	0	0	1	0	0	0	0	0	3	0	0	0	.429	.357
Zamora, Junior, Ark.	.208	42	157	144	15	30	49	5	1	4	18	1	2	1	9	0	32	1	1	5	.340	.256
Zywica, Mike, Tul.	.239	47	175	163	23	39	63	9	0	5	22	0	1	5	6	0	60	0	1	0	.387	.286

PLAYERS WITH TWO OR MORE TEAMS

Player, Team	Avg.	G	TPA	AB	R	H	TB	2B	3B	HR	RBI	SH	SF	HP	BB	IBB	SO	SB	CS	GDP	Slg.	OBP
Camilli, Jason, E.P.	.333	13	42	39	7	13	14	1	0	0	3	0	1	0	2	0	8	0	2	0	.359	.357
Camilli, Jason, R.R.	.241	55	215	174	21	42	61	8	1	3	24	4	1	4	32	1	36	4	1	5	.351	.370
Glendenning, Mike, Shre.	.184	60	231	207	20	38	62	3	0	7	18	0	1	2	21	0	71	0	0	7	.300	.264
Glendenning, Mike, E.P.	.236	40	162	140	17	33	51	9	0	3	18	1	1	2	18	1	46	1	0	3	.364	.329

GRAND SLAMS: Cresse, 2; Berger, A. Berroa, Blalock, Brito, Christensen, Durrington, Gibson, Glendenning, E. Guzman, Harvey, Johnson, King, Meliah, Mensik, Morillo, Overbay, Robinson, G. Rodriguez, Salazar, Shabala, Shackelford, Solano, Thoen, Tonis, Weber, 1 each.

AWARDED FIRST BASE ON CATCHER'S INTERFERENCE: Devore (M. Wright), Hill (Luther), Huckaby (M. Wright), Ludwick (Taveras), Pecci (Tremie), Pujols (Chapman), Quinlan (Huckaby).

2001 PITCHING
TEAM

Team	W	L	Pct.	ERA	G	CG	ShO	Sv.	IP	H	TBF	R	ER	HR	SH	SF	HB	BB	IBB	SO	WP	Bk.
Round Rock	86	54	.614	3.62	140	3	17	39	1241.1	1136	5265	569	499	105	43	45	56	461	5	1138	56	4
San Antonio	70	67	.511	3.85	137	7	16	36	1236.0	1277	5348	622	529	92	54	35	78	387	25	1062	66	6
Wichita	79	58	.577	4.06	137	3	13	39	1200.0	1181	5211	619	541	116	34	34	73	472	24	965	68	9
Shreveport	54	81	.400	4.07	135	5	7	33	1193.1	1232	5182	647	540	116	60	46	71	378	24	774	56	6
Tulsa	69	70	.496	4.28	139	8	8	28	1237.1	1222	5355	666	588	115	44	43	74	474	12	1063	73	6
Midland	71	69	.507	4.40	140	1	8	41	1237.2	1379	5494	709	605	117	37	26	60	433	37	926	44	8
Arkansas	66	70	.485	4.78	136	9	3	27	1170.0	1246	5191	722	621	113	35	46	91	434	4	757	80	9
El Paso	57	83	.407	4.90	140	3	5	35	1220.0	1393	5563	810	664	97	40	58	74	547	22	1024	81	19

TOP QUALIFIERS FOR EARNED-RUN AVERAGE TITLE

Minimum 112 innings.*Lefthanded pitcher.

Pitcher, Team	W	L	Pct.	ERA	G	GS	CG	ShO	GF	Sv.	IP	H	TBF	R	ER	HR	SH	SF	HB	BB	IBB	SO	WP	Bk.
Smith, Travis, R.R.	15	8	.652	3.09	29	22	1	0	1	1	160.1	154	653	66	55	7	5	4	5	26	0	85	2	0
Heaverlo, Jeff, S.A.	11	6	.647	3.12	27	27	4	4	0	0	178.2	164	744	75	62	12	8	2	9	40	0	173	8	0
Calero, Kiko, Wich.	14	5	.737	3.33	27	19	0	0	1	0	124.1	110	531	57	46	10	3	6	7	51	1	94	7	1
Thurman, Corey, Wich.	13	5	.722	3.37	25	25	0	0	0	0	155.0	117	636	66	58	16	2	2	1	65	1	148	4	1
Lackey, John, Ark.	9	7	.563	3.46	18	18	3	2	0	0	127.1	106	509	55	49	11	6	5	3	29	0	94	8	0
Hernandez, Carlos, R.R.*	12	3	.800	3.69	24	23	0	0	0	0	139.0	115	591	60	57	11	7	4	7	69	0	167	3	0
Cox, Ryan, Shre.	8	8	.500	3.69	24	24	1	0	0	0	136.2	145	575	70	56	8	3	6	6	24	0	61	2	0
Putz, Joe, S.A.	7	9	.438	3.83	27	26	0	0	0	0	148.0	145	642	80	63	11	10	5	9	59	2	125	12	0
Affeldt, Jeremy, Wich.*	10	6	.625	3.90	25	25	0	0	0	0	145.1	153	621	74	63	9	6	5	10	46	0	128	3	1
Urban, Jeff, Shre.*	7	11	.389	3.91	27	27	0	0	0	0	156.2	178	675	85	68	16	9	6	9	32	0	117	7	0
Stephens, Jason, Ark.	6	7	.462	3.92	19	19	2	0	0	0	119.1	117	502	64	52	12	2	5	8	26	2	75	7	0
Williams, Jerome, Shre.	9	7	.563	3.95	23	23	2	1	0	0	130.0	116	542	69	57	14	2	3	9	34	0	84	6	1
Baerlocher, Ryan, Wich.	13	8	.619	3.99	28	28	2	1	0	0	180.2	180	777	94	80	26	2	6	12	55	2	124	6	2
Pena, Juan, Mid.	11	9	.550	4.07	27	27	0	0	0	0	148.1	164	645	88	67	13	4	2	5	46	0	106	4	1
Harang, Aaron, Mid.	10	8	.556	4.14	27	27	0	0	0	0	150.0	173	654	81	69	9	0	3	6	37	1	112	3	0

DEPARTMENTAL LEADERS: W—Smith, 15; L—Bergman, 13; Pct.—Redding, .833; G—Wade, 60; GS—Capuano, Baerlocher, 28 each; CG—Heaverlo, 4; ShO—Heaverlo, 4; GF—Wade, 54; Sv.—Wade, 23; IP—Baerlocher, 180.2; H—Lehr, 206; TBF—Baerlocher, 702; R—Capuano, 109; ER—; HR—Baerlocher, 26; SH—Putz, 10; SF—Bergman, Capuano, 8 each; HB—Lewis, 16; BB—Capuano, 75; IBB—Yates, 8; SO—Heaverlo, 173; WP—Lewis, 16; BK—Villarreal, 11.

ALL PITCHERS

*Lefthanded pitcher.

Pitcher, Team	W	L	Pct.	ERA	G	GS	CG	ShO	GF	Sv.	IP	H	TBF	R	ER	HR	SH	SF	HB	BB	IBB	SO	WP	Bk.
Adkins, Jon, Mid.	8	8	.500	4.46	24	24	1	1	0	0	137.1	147	590	71	68	9	5	2	9	36	1	74	0	0
Affeldt, Jeremy, Wich.*	10	6	.625	3.90	25	25	0	0	0	0	145.1	153	621	74	63	9	6	5	10	46	0	128	3	1
Alfano, Jeff, Shre.	0	0	.000	0.00	1	0	0	0	1	0	1.0	0	4	0	0	0	0	0	0	1	0	0	0	0
Alfaro, Jason, R.R.	0	0	.000	36.00	1	0	0	0	1	0	1.0	4	8	4	4	1	0	0	0	2	0	0	0	0
Andra, Jeff, Shre.*	3	9	.250	4.68	18	18	0	0	0	0	98.0	116	437	59	51	11	4	3	1	32	0	57	5	0
Atchison, Scott, S.A.	9	10	.474	4.24	24	24	1	0	0	0	136.0	171	596	84	64	11	8	5	12	28	0	83	6	0
Ayala, Julio, S.A.*	0	0	.000	6.35	3	0	0	0	2	0	5.2	7	29	4	4	2	0	0	1	2	0	4	0	0
Baerlocher, Ryan, Wich.	13	8	.619	3.99	28	28	2	1	0	0	180.2	180	777	94	80	26	2	6	12	55	2	124	6	2
Bazzell, Shane, Mid.	0	2	.000	19.64	2	2	0	0	0	0	7.1	20	45	17	16	2	0	1	0	2	1	4	1	0
Beech, Matt, Tul.*	3	1	.750	3.13	8	7	1	1	0	0	46.0	41	182	17	16	7	0	0	2	10	0	39	2	0
Benoit, Joaquin, Tul.	1	0	1.000	3.32	4	4	0	0	0	0	21.2	23	94	8	8	1	0	0	1	6	0	23	2	0
Bergman, Dusty, Ark.*	7	13	.350	5.11	27	25	1	0	0	0	153.1	196	704	100	87	10	4	8	14	53	0	83	15	2
Bermudez, Manny, Shre.	2	3	.400	3.71	12	0	0	0	3	0	26.2	25	115	11	11	0	3	1	7	7	2	13	1	0
Beverlin, Jason, Ark.	4	2	.667	2.75	6	6	0	0	0	0	39.1	36	164	15	12	4	0	1	3	11	0	30	4	0
Bevis, P.J., E.P.	0	0	.000	2.16	14	0	0	0	9	6	16.2	11	67	4	4	2	0	1	6	0	19	0	0
Bierbrodt, Nick, E.P.*	2	1	.667	1.87	4	4	0	0	0	0	19.2	13	76	3	3	1	0	0	0	6	0	18	0	0
Bochtler, Doug, Wich.	0	0	.000	2.90	15	2	0	0	7	4	31.0	26	123	10	10	1	1	1	9	1	38	0	0
Bootcheck, Chris, Ark.	3	3	.500	5.45	6	6	1	0	0	0	36.1	39	161	25	22	3	0	0	3	11	0	22	1	1
Bottenfield, Kent, R.R.	0	1	.000	20.25	1	1	0	0	0	0	2.2	4	15	6	6	1	0	2	0	3	0	3	0	0
Brink, Jim, Mid.	0	1	.000	4.02	20	0	0	0	11	2	31.1	34	144	15	14	5	3	2	20	1	24	2	0
Brocail, Doug, R.R.	0	0	.000	0.00	1	1	0	0	0	0	1.0	0	3	0	0	0	0	0	0	0	1	0	0
Brown, Elliot, Shre.	0	8	.000	5.04	14	10	0	0	0	0	62.0	77	280	50	31	6	5	2	2	17	2	28	2	1
Brummett, Sean, Ark.*	2	4	.333	5.62	25	5	2	0	7	0	65.2	65	302	46	41	8	4	2	12	28	0	45	4	0
Bukvich, Ryan, Wich.	0	0	.000	3.75	7	0	0	0	3	0	12.0	9	47	6	5	2	0	0	2	0	14	2	0
Calero, Kiko, Wich.	14	5	.737	3.33	27	19	0	0	1	0	124.1	110	531	57	46	10	3	6	7	51	1	94	7	1
Callier, Jeremy, Ark.	2	0	1.000	7.13	16	0	0	0	7	1	24.0	31	114	19	19	3	1	4	1	10	0	6	2	1
Camp, Jared, Wich.	1	2	.333	5.05	33	0	0	0	21	4	46.1	44	214	28	26	7	1	0	1	35	2	44	6	0
Cannon, Jon, Shre.*	2	0	1.000	3.19	17	2	0	0	4	1	36.2	23	155	15	13	4	3	1	2	19	1	39	1	1
Capuano, Chris, E.P.*	10	11	.476	5.31	28	28	2	2	0	0	159.1	184	733	109	94	13	4	8	11	75	0	167	9	2
Carlson, Dan, E.P.	4	2	.667	3.68	32	0	0	0	12	5	51.1	53	214	22	21	4	0	3	1	12	3	55	3	1
Caruso, Joe, R.R.	0	0	.000	0.00	1	0	0	0	0	0	0.1	0	1	0	0	0	0	0	0	0	0	0	0	0
Cervantes, Chris, E.P.*	3	7	.300	5.44	45	7	0	0	9	1	96.0	110	436	68	58	14	3	4	7	36	2	87	10	0
Clark, Chris, Ark.	3	3	.500	6.78	28	6	0	0	9	0	66.1	74	303	53	50	8	2	1	9	35	1	34	12	0
Cogan, Tony, Wich.*	1	1	.500	2.08	8	0	0	0	4	1	17.1	13	68	6	4	2	1	1	1	4	0	12	1	1
Connors, Greg, S.A.	0	0	.000	0.00	1	0	0	0	1	0	1.0	0	3	0	0	0	0	0	0	0	0	0	0	0
Cook, Derrick, Tul.	0	1	.000	9.00	7	0	0	0	4	1	10.0	15	50	12	10	2	2	0	0	6	0	4	1	0
Cotton, Joe, Mid.	6	1	.857	2.77	47	0	0	0	19	7	65.0	50	272	21	20	4	2	3	2	28	2	63	1	1
Cox, Ryan, Shre.	8	8	.500	3.69	24	24	1	0	0	0	136.2	145	575	70	56	8	3	6	6	24	0	61	2	0
Crabtree, Tim, Tul.	0	1	.000	3.00	2	2	0	0	0	0	3.0	3	13	1	1	0	0	0	1	0	0	1	0	0
Crawford, Joe, E.P.*	0	4	.000	5.31	7	7	0	0	0	0	40.2	49	181	30	24	1	6	1	2	12	0	30	1	0
Cummings, Ryan, Ark.	6	3	.667	3.56	42	0	0	0	18	6	65.2	61	286	34	26	3	2	2	6	21	0	42	4	0
DeHart, Rick, Wich.*	2	2	.500	6.56	13	0	0	0	3	0	23.1	30	107	20	17	3	0	0	1	7	0	16	0	0
Demouy, Chris, Ark.*	2	1	.667	6.11	24	0	0	0	10	0	35.1	42	167	25	24	4	1	3	2	22	0	16	2	0
Donnelly, Brendan, Ark.	4	1	.800	2.48	27	0	0	0	24	12	29.0	21	120	8	8	2	0	1	1	13	1	37	1	0
Duchscherer, Justin, Tul.	4	0	1.000	2.08	6	6	1	0	0	0	43.1	39	176	14	10	3	1	2	2	10	0	55	0	0
Durocher, Jayson, Tul.	0	0	.000	0.00	3	0	0	0	0	0	3.2	0	15	0	0	0	0	1	3	0	4	2	0
Dykhoff, Radhames, Ark.*	2	3	.400	4.57	27	14	0	0	7	0	80.2	85	357	46	41	4	1	5	5	35	0	37	1	0
Elder, Dave, Tul.	4	6	.400	3.00	13	13	0	0	0	0	72.0	64	308	28	24	1	0	3	2	43	0	78	3	0
Ellison, Jason, S.A.	2	8	.200	3.74	46	1	0	0	26	9	65.0	76	296	30	27	3	6	2	4	28	7	57	5	0
Enochs, Chris, Mid.	5	4	.556	4.33	39	10	0	0	9	1	99.2	102	440	57	48	9	3	2	4	39	3	67	6	0
Estrella, Luis, Shre.	1	0	1.000	3.12	7	0	0	0	1	0	8.2	10	41	6	3	1	1	0	0	5	0	8	1	0
Evans, Dave, R.R.	0	0	.000	9.64	1	1	0	0	0	0	4.2	6	20	5	5	2	0	0	0	0	0	4	0	0
Falkenborg, Brian, S.A.	5	6	.455	5.45	12	12	2	1	0	0	66.0	80	296	47	40	9	2	3	5	24	0	56	5	0

Pitcher, Team	W	L	Pct.	ERA	G	GS	CG	ShO	GF	Sv.	IP	H	TBF	R	ER	HR	SH	SF	HB	BB	IBB	SO	WP	Bk.
Farnsworth, Jeff, S.A.	11	10	.524	4.35	27	27	0	0	0	0	155.1	182	688	92	75	10	4	3	8	47	0	113	3	3
Field, Nathan, Wich.	4	2	.667	1.48	52	0	0	0	44	19	73.0	61	300	16	12	3	3	2	2	18	3	67	5	0
Figueroa, Carlos, Tul.*	0	1	.000	2.08	3	0	0	0	2	0	4.1	3	19	1	1	0	0	0	1	3	0	2	2	0
Fitzgerald, Brian, S.A.*	4	1	.800	1.96	30	0	0	0	10	1	41.1	33	174	10	9	0	3	0	3	16	4	26	1	0
Freeman, Corey, S.A.	0	0	.000	0.00	1	0	0	0	1	0	1.0	0	3	0	0	0	0	0	0	0	0	1	0	0
Fuller, Jody, E.P.	0	2	.000	5.59	12	0	0	0	3	0	19.1	23	90	13	12	1	0	0	1	12	1	12	1	0
Galva, Claudio, Mid.*	1	2	.333	2.82	55	0	0	0	24	11	60.2	56	268	24	19	5	5	2	1	27	6	44	2	1
Garza, Chris, Tul.*	0	1	.000	3.09	16	0	0	0	4	0	23.1	15	100	11	8	1	0	1	1	16	0	23	1	0
Gilfillan, Jason, Wich.	0	0	.000	6.23	11	0	0	0	3	0	17.1	23	89	13	12	0	0	1	1	13	2	13	4	0
Good, Andrew, E.P.	2	3	.400	5.88	10	9	0	0	0	0	56.2	79	270	44	37	2	1	2	3	20	0	46	3	0
Goodrich, Randy, Shre.	1	1	.500	7.56	19	0	0	0	7	0	33.1	46	155	28	28	7	1	0	1	12	0	19	1	0
Gray, Mike, E.P.*	3	1	.750	1.72	29	0	0	0	18	4	31.1	32	132	11	6	1	1	1	1	8	0	13	0	0
Gregg, Kevin, Mid.	5	5	.500	4.54	44	1	0	0	10	1	81.1	88	366	48	41	5	1	0	4	40	4	72	8	1
Guerra, Mark, R.R.	2	0	1.000	1.75	9	4	1	0	0	0	36.0	21	133	8	7	3	1	2	1	5	0	27	0	0
Guerrero, Junior, Wich.	1	2	.333	8.62	15	0	0	0	7	1	15.2	30	92	10	15	1	0	2	0	14	1	11	1	0
Guzman, Leiby, Tul.-Shre.	4	1	.800	4.88	36	0	0	0	18	1	62.2	65	276	39	34	7	3	4	1	17	0	45	3	0
Harang, Aaron, Mid.	10	8	.556	4.14	27	27	0	0	0	0	150.0	173	654	81	69	9	0	3	6	37	1	112	3	0
Harriger, Mark, Ark.	2	3	.400	4.65	10	9	0	0	0	0	50.1	52	223	33	26	7	0	2	3	23	0	31	3	1
Hartmann, Pete, E.P.*	0	4	.000	7.76	19	3	0	0	6	0	31.1	46	174	32	27	3	1	1	1	31	3	27	2	0
Heaverlo, Jeff, S.A.	11	6	.647	3.12	27	27	4	4	0	0	178.2	164	744	75	62	12	8	2	9	40	0	173	8	0
Hernandez, Carlos, R.R.*	12	3	.800	3.69	24	23	0	0	0	0	139.0	115	591	60	57	11	7	4	7	69	0	167	3	0
Horgan, Joe, Shre.*	3	5	.375	3.65	31	14	0	0	3	1	103.2	97	438	51	42	10	6	7	4	27	1	61	2	0
Hughes, Travis, Tul.	5	7	.417	4.64	47	5	0	0	29	8	87.1	91	393	52	45	8	3	4	4	45	2	86	2	1
Hundley, Jeff, Ark.*	2	6	.250	6.17	10	9	0	0	1	0	54.0	63	254	48	37	7	4	2	6	25	0	31	2	0
Jamison, Ryan, R.R.	5	2	.714	3.50	10	9	0	0	0	0	46.1	49	211	25	18	5	0	3	2	23	0	32	5	0
Jarvis, Matt, S.A.*	1	1	.500	5.09	23	0	0	0	15	8	23.0	23	103	14	13	1	0	1	3	11	1	18	3	0
Jenks, Bobby, Ark.	1	0	1.000	3.60	2	2	0	0	0	0	10.0	8	47	5	4	0	0	0	2	5	0	10	3	0
Joseph, Kevin, Shre.	2	1	.667	2.43	24	0	0	0	11	1	33.1	31	145	9	9	1	0	2	2	13	3	27	4	0
Keith, Rusty, Mid.	0	0	.000	0.00	1	0	0	0	1	0	1.0	1	4	0	0	0	0	0	0	0	0	1	0	0
Kelley, Rich, Ark.*	1	1	.500	3.72	5	3	0	0	0	0	19.1	19	85	13	8	0	1	0	0	8	0	14	2	0
Kessel, Kyle, R.R.*	3	6	.333	5.97	13	10	0	0	1	0	57.1	75	271	43	38	7	2	3	4	26	0	39	5	0
Kirkreit, Daron, Ark.	2	1	.667	6.92	17	0	0	0	9	0	26.0	38	124	23	20	4	1	1	1	9	0	9	3	0
Knoll, Brian, Shre.	0	0	.000	2.25	2	1	0	0	1	0	4.0	5	20	1	1	0	0	0	0	3	0	2	1	0
Knott, Eric, E.P.*	4	1	.800	3.12	17	0	0	0	2	0	26.0	29	116	13	9	2	2	0	1	8	2	20	1	0
Kolb, Dan, Tul.	1	0	1.000	0.00	1	0	0	0	0	0	2.0	0	7	0	0	0	0	0	0	0	0	0	0	0
Koplove, Mike, E.P.	3	2	.600	2.66	34	0	0	0	14	4	44.0	44	193	18	13	3	3	3	2	19	3	43	0	0
Lackey, John, Ark.	9	7	.563	3.46	18	18	3	2	0	0	127.1	106	509	55	49	11	6	5	3	29	0	94	8	0
Lamber, Justin, Wich.*	0	2	.000	5.50	19	0	0	0	5	1	36.0	42	169	22	22	6	2	1	1	24	1	21	1	0
Lee, Corey, Tul.*	5	12	.294	5.31	25	17	1	0	4	0	125.1	117	532	78	74	14	2	5	7	51	2	103	2	2
Loo, Jon, E.P.	0	0	.000	6.75	3	0	0	0	1	0	2.2	3	15	3	2	0	1	0	0	6	0	1	3	0
Lehr, Chuck, Mid.	11	12	.478	5.45	29	27	0	0	2	0	155.1	206	709	107	94	20	6	2	11	43	1	103	4	2
Lewis, Colby, Tul.	10	10	.500	4.50	25	25	1	0	0	0	156.0	150	686	85	78	15	8	6	10	62	2	162	16	0
Lidge, Brad, R.R.	2	0	1.000	1.73	5	5	0	0	0	0	26.0	21	107	5	5	1	1	1	2	7	0	42	1	0
Lira, James, R.R.	0	1	.000	3.00	27	0	0	0	13	2	39.0	32	158	16	13	2	1	3	2	10	0	27	2	1
Lopez, Aquilino, S.A.	4	3	.571	3.02	42	0	0	0	13	2	62.2	40	205	24	21	4	2	2	6	26	2	79	5	0
Lopez, Javier, E.P.*	1	0	1.000	7.43	22	1	0	0	4	0	40.0	64	191	39	33	6	2	1	0	14	2	21	1	0
Lundberg, Spike, Tul.	5	3	.625	3.48	18	8	1	1	8	6	67.1	75	282	27	26	4	2	2	6	9	0	41	2	0
Luster, Jeremy, Shre.	0	1	.000	18.00	1	0	0	0	1	0	1.0	2	7	2	2	0	0	0	0	2	0	0	0	0
Martines, Jason, E.P.	4	3	.571	3.00	51	0	0	0	15	1	69.0	62	290	32	23	3	4	5	8	20	3	49	0	0
Martinez, Gustavo, S.A.	0	0	.000	1.93	3	0	0	0	2	0	9.1	5	34	2	2	2	0	0	1	2	0	6	0	0
Martinez, Jose, Tul.	6	6	.500	4.73	24	13	0	0	3	0	93.1	98	419	61	49	12	2	4	5	39	0	58	11	1
Matzenbacher, Brian, E.P.	1	0	1.000	1.80	4	0	0	0	1	0	5.0	5	22	1	1	0	1	0	0	2	0	4	0	0
Mazur, Bryan, Mid.*	0	0	.000	1.93	6	0	0	0	3	0	4.2	10	23	1	1	1	0	0	0	1	0	2	0	0
McMullen, Mike, Wich.	0	0	.000	11.42	6	1	0	0	2	0	8.2	13	53	11	11	3	1	0	2	12	1	5	1	1
Mendoza, Hatuey, E.P.	1	5	.167	6.28	8	5	0	0	0	0	28.2	29	135	25	20	3	1	1	3	17	0	20	1	1
Messman, Joe, Shre.	1	1	.500	4.10	12	1	0	0	3	0	26.1	24	119	15	12	3	4	3	2	14	0	13	1	1
Meyer, Jake, S.A.	1	4	.200	5.94	25	1	0	0	9	1	36.1	43	167	26	24	7	2	1	0	17	1	35	3	1
Miller, Benji, Shre.	1	6	.143	4.23	37	0	0	0	20	2	66.0	63	296	33	31	7	2	3	3	35	2	39	5	1
Miller, Greg, R.R.*	5	3	.625	3.25	14	14	0	0	0	0	55.1	38	236	22	20	3	1	4	3	35	0	37	1	0
Milo, Tony, Ark.*	1	2	.333	5.34	19	2	0	0	6	1	30.1	29	136	18	18	5	1	0	2	17	0	35	1	0
Mobley, Kevin, Tul.	3	0	1.000	3.96	36	1	0	0	10	0	75.0	71	325	40	33	6	4	3	9	32	2	58	6	0
Moreno, Juan, Tul.*	1	1	.500	0.00	6	0	0	0	6	1	8.2	6	34	1	0	0	3	1	0	3	0	10	1	0
Moreno, Orber, Wich.	0	0	.000	0.00	5	0	0	0	2	1	8.2	3	31	0	0	0	0	0	1	2	0	10	0	1
Morrison, Cody, S.A.	0	0	.000	13.03	8	0	0	0	4	1	9.2	15	48	14	14	2	1	0	1	4	0	8	0	0
Myette, Aaron, Tul.	1	0	1.000	0.00	1	1	0	0	0	0	6.0	3	22	0	0	0	0	0	0	2	0	5	0	0
Nathan, Joe, Shre.	3	6	.333	6.93	21	7	0	0	6	0	62.1	73	294	49	48	11	7	2	4	37	5	33	7	1
Newman, Eric, E.P.	0	1	.000	8.84	13	0	0	0	5	1	18.1	26	93	19	18	5	0	4	1	13	0	20	5	0
Nix, Wayne, Mid.	0	0	.000	8.71	2	2	0	0	0	0	10.1	24	54	15	10	1	0	1	0	1	0	12	0	0
Noriega, Ray, Mid.*	0	1	.000	9.41	17	0	0	0	3	0	22.0	34	119	24	23	5	1	0	4	16	3	20	0	0
Norris, Ben, E.P.*	1	6	.143	7.25	16	10	0	0	1	0	58.1	104	299	61	47	1	1	5	5	30	0	25	2	0
Oliver, Darren, Tul.*	0	1	.000	5.40	1	1	0	0	0	0	5.0	4	21	3	3	1	1	0	1	2	0	5	0	0
Ozias, Todd, Shre.-Tul.	3	3	.500	3.56	39	0	0	0	14	0	68.1	62	297	31	27	8	2	1	7	30	5	42	5	0
Patterson, John, E.P.	1	2	.333	4.26	5	5	0	0	0	0	25.1	30	112	15	12	2	0	0	2	9	0	19	1	0
Pearsall, J.J., Tul.*	6	4	.600	3.26	43	0	0	0	27	10	58.0	54	248	27	21	7	3	1	4	18	3	58	2	0
Pena, Juan, Mid.*	11	9	.550	4.07	27	27	0	0	0	0	148.1	164	645	88	67	13	4	2	5	46	0	106	4	1
Peralta, Joel, Ark.	0	1	.000	6.30	9	0	0	0	9	2	10.0	15	53	10	7	2	0	1	2	5	0	14	0	1
Persails, Mark, R.R.	0	1	.000	13.50	1	0	0	0	1	0	1.1	2	6	2	2	0	0	0	0	0	0	0	0	0
Pine, Chris, Ark.	1	0	1.000	4.15	4	0	0	0	1	1	4.1	6	25	3	2	0	0	0	2	6	0	4	0	0
Pratt, Andy, Tul.*	8	10	.444	4.61	27	26	3	1	0	0	168.0	175	730	99	86	18	8	5	6	57	0	132	9	1
Puffer, Brandon, R.R.	6	1	.857	2.07	56	0	0	0	33	8	82.2	52	331	19	19	4	1	1	7	35	2	91	3	0
Putz, Joe, S.A.	7	9	.430	3.03	27	26	0	0	0	0	148.0	145	642	80	63	11	10	5	9	59	2	135	12	0
Ramirez, Erasmo, Shre.-Tul.*.	4	1	.800	2.90	34	1	0	0	12	1	49.2	42	198	18	16	4	0	0	3	10	0	57	2	0
Ramirez, Joslin, E.P.	1	0	1.000	1.42	4	0	0	0	1	0	6.1	5	27	2	1	0	0	1	0	2	0	9	0	1

Pitcher, Team	W	L	Pct.	ERA	G	GS	CG	ShO	GF	Sv.	IP	H	TBF	R	ER	HR	SH	SF	HB	BB	IBB	SO	WP	Bk.
Ramos, Mario, Mid.*	8	1	.889	3.07	15	15	0	0	0	0	93.2	71	384	37	32	7	3	1	4	28	0	68	1	2
Randolph, Steve, E.P.*	5	6	.455	5.16	18	14	1	1	0	0	75.0	69	342	50	43	11	1	2	3	53	1	66	7	1
Rayborn, Kenny, S.A.	1	0	1.000	6.86	14	0	0	0	8	0	19.2	26	93	15	15	1	0	1	5	8	1	11	1	0
Redding, Tim, R.R.	10	2	.833	2.18	14	14	1	1	0	0	90.2	64	364	26	22	5	1	0	3	25	0	113	1	0
Regilio, Nick, Tul.	1	3	.250	5.54	10	10	0	0	0	0	52.0	62	236	34	32	2	2	1	4	20	0	40	2	0
Reynolds, Shane, R.R.	1	0	1.000	1.29	1	1	0	0	0	0	7.0	5	27	1	1	0	0	0	0	2	0	5	0	0
Riley, Mike, Shre.*	3	2	.600	4.81	7	7	2	0	0	0	43.0	55	189	26	23	6	3	2	4	12	0	34	1	0
Roberts, Nick, R.R.	2	4	.333	5.16	8	7	0	0	0	0	45.1	52	198	27	26	6	3	5	3	10	0	26	0	0
Robertson, Jeriome, R.R.*	5	1	.833	3.91	57	0	0	0	11	3	73.2	89	326	33	32	10	2	1	1	21	0	72	6	0
Rodriguez, Guillermo, Shre.	0	0	.000	0.00	1	0	0	0	0	0	3.0	1	11	0	0	0	0	1	2	0	1	0	0
Rodriguez, Wil, R.R.*	5	9	.357	4.78	42	10	0	0	12	0	92.1	94	415	61	49	10	6	1	1	56	0	94	13	1
Rose, Mike, E.P.	0	0	.000	0.00	1	0	0	0	1	0	1.0	1	4	0	0	0	0	0	0	0	0	0	0	0
Sanches, Brian, Wich.	7	9	.438	5.98	29	21	0	0	3	0	134.0	152	610	96	89	12	7	3	13	61	4	95	12	1
Sanchez, Duaner, E.P.	3	7	.300	6.78	13	13	0	0	0	0	70.1	92	323	56	53	5	1	7	6	25	1	41	5	0
Sedlacek, Shawn, Wich.	6	7	.462	3.63	14	14	1	1	0	0	86.2	85	360	37	35	7	1	2	8	14	1	66	3	0
Sessions, Doug, R.R.	6	4	.600	4.37	41	9	0	0	4	1	103.0	98	433	53	50	13	3	6	3	33	0	78	0	0
Shackelford, Brian, Wich.*	0	0	.000	18.00	1	0	0	0	1	0	1.0	3	7	2	2	0	0	0	1	0	0	0	0	0
Shearn, Tom, R.R.	5	6	.455	3.85	43	8	0	0	7	1	110.0	94	470	54	47	7	5	5	7	51	0	136	10	0
Silva, Doug, Tul.	0	1	.000	3.32	14	0	0	0	8	1	19.0	19	82	10	7	1	0	2	0	5	0	15	1	0
Simpson, Allan, S.A.	2	1	.667	1.86	22	0	0	0	16	9	38.2	25	157	8	8	1	1	3	2	15	1	37	2	0
Smith, Travis, R.R.	15	8	.652	3.09	29	22	1	0	1	1	160.1	154	653	66	55	7	5	4	5	26	0	85	2	0
Snyder, Bill, Mid.	1	3	.250	5.53	31	0	0	0	14	0	42.1	59	203	32	26	9	0	1	2	21	2	24	2	0
Snyder, Matt, Tul.	1	0	1.000	8.10	4	0	0	0	2	0	10.0	14	47	9	9	0	1	0	3	6	0	2	0	0
Soriano, Rafael, S.A.	2	2	.500	3.35	8	8	0	0	0	0	48.1	34	193	18	18	5	0	0	2	14	0	53	2	1
Stark, Dennis, S.A.	1	0	1.000	0.00	1	1	0	0	0	0	6.0	2	24	0	0	0	0	0	3	0	7	0	0
Stephens, Jason, Ark.	6	7	.462	3.92	19	19	2	0	0	0	119.1	117	502	64	52	12	2	5	8	26	2	75	7	0
Suarez, Felipe, Ark.	2	5	.286	4.46	34	1	0	0	15	3	66.2	77	294	37	33	12	3	3	4	18	0	46	3	0
Sweeney, Brian, S.A.	7	4	.636	3.80	37	9	0	0	8	1	104.1	117	448	47	44	8	3	3	5	23	1	96	7	0
Thompson, Eric, Mid.	1	4	.200	4.31	35	5	0	0	8	2	64.2	74	292	32	31	9	3	4	5	21	3	69	3	0
Thurman, Corey, Wich.	13	5	.722	3.37	25	25	0	0	0	0	155.0	117	636	66	58	16	2	2	1	65	1	148	8	0
Turnbow, Derrick, Ark.	0	0	.000	2.57	3	3	0	0	0	0	14.0	12	56	4	4	0	1	0	0	5	0	11	0	1
Ulloa, Enmanuel, S.A.	2	2	.500	3.04	45	1	0	0	15	4	80.0	81	345	32	27	3	4	4	2	21	5	64	3	1
Urban, Jeff, Shre.*	7	11	.389	3.91	27	27	0	0	0	0	156.2	178	675	85	68	16	9	6	9	32	0	117	7	0
Urquhart, Derick, Ark.*	0	0	.000	0.00	1	0	0	0	1	0	1.0	2	5	0	0	0	0	0	0	0	0	0	0	0
Valverde, Jose, E.P.	2	2	.500	3.92	39	0	0	0	28	13	41.1	36	193	19	18	1	1	1	4	27	0	72	6	1
Verplancke, Jeff, Shre.	1	8	.111	4.44	43	0	0	0	40	22	48.2	50	217	27	24	3	4	3	5	20	3	46	3	0
Villano, Mike, Wich.-Shre.	6	7	.462	4.11	44	2	0	0	27	9	76.2	85	342	44	35	9	2	1	10	30	4	47	7	1
Villarreal, Oscar, E.P.*	6	9	.400	4.41	27	27	0	0	0	0	140.2	154	644	96	69	10	4	7	8	63	1	108	14	11
Voyles, Brad, Wich.	1	0	1.000	0.00	11	0	0	0	8	4	15.1	8	63	0	0	0	2	1	1	10	1	19	1	0
Wade, Travis, R.R.	2	3	.400	3.15	60	0	0	0	54	23	65.2	67	286	33	23	7	4	0	5	22	3	56	2	2
Wagner, Billy, R.R.*	0	0	.000	0.00	1	1	0	0	0	0	1.0	0	3	0	0	0	0	0	0	0	0	2	0	0
Ward, Jeremy, E.P.	0	0	.000	1.13	6	0	0	0	6	0	8.0	2	26	2	1	1	0	0	0	1	0	6	0	0
White, Bill, E.P.*	0	4	.000	4.54	7	7	0	0	0	0	37.2	38	165	23	19	2	2	2	3	20	0	26	6	1
Williams, Jerome, Shre.	9	7	.563	3.95	23	23	2	1	0	0	130.0	116	542	69	57	14	2	3	9	34	0	84	6	1
Williams, Shad, Ark.	3	4	.429	5.86	11	6	0	0	3	1	35.1	42	162	26	23	3	1	0	0	13	0	22	2	1
Wilson, Phil, Ark.	1	1	.500	11.37	2	2	0	0	0	0	6.1	10	38	12	8	1	0	0	2	6	0	5	0	1
Yates, Tyler, Mid.	4	6	.400	4.31	56	0	0	0	35	17	62.2	66	282	39	30	4	1	0	1	27	8	61	7	0

PITCHERS WITH TWO OR MORE TEAMS

Pitcher, Team	W	L	Pct.	ERA	G	GS	CG	ShO	GF	Sv.	IP	H	TBF	R	ER	HR	SH	SF	HB	BB	IBB	SO	WP	Bk.
Guzman, Leiby, Tul.	2	0	1.000	5.40	25	0	0	0	13	1	48.1	48	209	30	29	7	2	3	1	15	0	31	1	0
Guzman, Leiby, Shre.	2	1	.667	3.14	11	0	0	0	5	0	14.1	17	67	9	5	0	1	1	0	2	0	14	2	0
Ozias, Todd, Shre.	3	3	.500	2.73	30	0	0	0	11	0	56.0	47	240	21	17	6	2	1	6	22	4	32	2	0
Ozias, Todd, Tul.	0	0	.000	7.30	9	0	0	0	3	0	12.1	15	57	10	10	2	0	0	1	8	1	10	3	0
Ramirez, Erasmo, Shre.*	2	0	1.000	2.16	22	1	0	0	6	1	33.1	25	130	10	8	1	0	0	3	5	0	39	2	0
Ramirez, Erasmo, Tul.*	2	1	.667	4.41	12	0	0	0	6	0	16.1	17	68	8	8	3	0	0	5	0	0	18	0	0
Villano, Mike, Wich.	6	7	.462	4.50	37	2	0	0	20	4	68.0	79	312	43	34	8	2	1	10	29	3	40	7	1
Villano, Mike, Shre.	0	0	.000	1.04	7	0	0	0	7	5	8.2	6	30	1	1	1	0	0	0	1	1	7	0	0

COMBINATION SHUTOUTS: **Arkansas (1)**—Lacky-Kirkett. **El Paso (2)**—Villarreal-Martines-Koplove, Good-Bevis. **Midland (7)**—Harang-Thompson-Cotton, Sedlacek-Calero-Camp, Ramos-Yates, Ramos-Galva, Pena-Enochs-Thompson, Ramos-Yates-Galva, Harang-Noriega, Pena-Thompson-Cotton. **Round Rock (16)**—Redding-Rodriguez, Lidge-Shearn-Wade, Hernandez-Robertson, Hernandez-Robertson, Miller-Smith, Sessions-Robertson-Wade, Redding-Robertston-Wade, Miller-Smith-Robertson, Kessel-Guerra-Robertson-Wade, Smith-Rodriguez, Kessel-Sessions-Wade, Jamison-Lira-Rodriguez, Rodriguez-Puffer-Lira, Smith-Robertson, Miller-Sessions-Wade, Miller-Roberts-Shearn. **San Antonio (11)**—Atchison-Morrison-Fitzgerald, Atchison-Fitzgerald-Ulloa, Atchison-Lopez-Sweeney, Soriano-Sweeney-Meyer-Ellison, Stark-Ulloa-Fitzgerald-Simpson, Putz-Ellison, Heaverlo-Meyer-Sweeney, Putz-Lopez-Sweeney-Rayborn, Atchison-Lopez, Putz-Meyer, Sweeney-Meyer. **Shreveport (6)**—Urban-Bermudez-Estrella-Joseph-Verplancke, Urban-Miller, Williams-Miller-Ozias, Horgan-Ramirez, Horgan-Cannon, Cox-Guzman. **Tulsa (5)**—Elder-Pearsall-Moreno, Benoit-Silva-Hughes, Beech-Hughes, Martinez-Kolb-Pearsall-Lundberg, Lewis-Ozias. **Wichita (11)**—Baerlocher-Camp, Thurman-Villano-Camp, Villano-Camp, Sanches-Field, Baerlocher-Moreno-Field, Thurman-Villano-Field, Baerlocher-Camp, Calero-Camp, Sedlacek-Gilfillan-DeHart-Voyles, Thurman-Field.

NO-HIT GAMES: Pratt, Tulsa defeated Arkansas, 1-0, April 13; Randolph, El Paso defeated Arkansas, 2-0, August 14.

2001 FIELDING

TEAM

Team	Pct.	G	PO	A	E	TC	DP	TP	PB
Round Rock	.976	140	3724	1390	127	5241	115	0	11
Wichita	.975	137	3600	1356	125	5081	89	0	12
Tulsa	.974	139	3712	1410	135	5257	103	0	20
San Antonio	.972	137	3708	1429	148	5285	108	0	19
Shreveport	.971	135	3580	1444	152	5176	99	0	16
Arkansas	.970	136	3510	1442	151	5103	114	0	19
Midland	.968	140	3713	1574	176	5463	116	0	18
El Paso	.966	140	3660	1492	183	5335	124	0	21

FIRST BASEMEN

NOTE: All caps denotes fielding-percentage leader based on 70 games for catchers, 93 for all other non-pitchers and 112 innings for pitchers. *Throws lefthanded.

Player, Team	Pct.	G	PO	A	E	TC	DP
Beamon, Trey, S.A.	1.000	1	2	1	0	3	0
Berrios, Harry, Tul.	1.000	1	9	2	0	11	0
Burns, Kevin, R.R.*	.984	42	340	25	6	371	30
CARTER, Charley, R.R.	.993	100	790	40	6	836	81
Caruso, Joe, Wich.	1.000	1	2	0	0	2	0
Christensen, Mike, Ark.	1.000	1	10	0	0	10	1
Connors, Greg, S.A.	.992	85	738	42	6	786	57
Curl, John, S.A.	.981	18	145	12	3	160	8
Diaz, Angel, Ark.	1.000	1	10	0	0	10	1
Dillon, Joe, Wich.	.987	54	410	46	6	462	32
Flores, Javier, Tul.*	.956	5	42	1	2	45	3
Furniss, Eddy, Mid.*	1.000	5	35	3	0	38	0
Gallagher, Shawn, Wich.	.987	36	297	10	4	311	18
Garcia, Osmani, Tul.	1.000	4	37	3	0	40	0
Glendenning, Mike, Shre.	1.000	1	2	0	0	2	1
Guiel, Jeff, Ark.	1.000	7	67	1	0	68	6
Hafner, Travis, Tul.	.993	78	672	40	5	717	54
Halloran, Matt, Tul.	1.000	3	26	1	0	27	3
Hammock, Rob, E.P.	.960	7	38	10	2	50	4
Harvey, Ken, Wich.	.990	55	442	34	5	481	28
Hill, Jason, Ark.	1.000	2	21	1	0	22	1
Huckaby, Ken, E.P.	.986	16	129	12	2	143	13
Huffman, Royce, R.R.	.000	1	0	0	0	0	0
Huisman, Jason, Ark.	1.000	5	29	3	0	32	3
Jones, Jason, Tul.	.988	29	235	10	3	248	14
Jones, Jeremy, Tul.	.974	9	70	4	2	76	12
King, Brad, S.A.	1.000	1	9	1	0	10	0
Landry, Jacques, Mid.	.880	3	21	1	3	25	2
Lemonis, Chris, E.P.	1.000	1	6	0	0	6	0
Luster, Jeremy, Wich.	.990	119	1046	78	11	1135	78
Madonna, Chris, Mid.	.982	8	50	5	1	56	4
Martin, Billy, E.P.	1.000	2	14	2	0	16	2
McGowan, Sean, Shre.	.992	13	112	6	1	119	7
Meliah, Dave, Tul.	1.000	13	83	6	0	89	0
Mensik, Todd, Mid.*	.985	130	1178	87	19	1284	100
Montas, Ricardo, E.P.	1.000	3	15	2	0	17	2
Neal, Steve, E.P.*	1.000	7	61	5	0	66	8
Overbay, Lyle, E.P.*	.990	106	874	75	10	959	83
Pernalete, Marco, Shre.	1.000	4	30	0	0	30	2
Pujols, Rafael, Mid.	1.000	2	2	0	0	2	0
Quinlan, Robb, Ark.	.993	113	963	97	8	1068	86
Robinson, Bo, S.A.	.985	20	129	4	2	135	12
Rodriguez, Guillermo, Shre.	.941	3	15	1	1	17	1
Sell, Chip, E.P.	1.000	1	7	0	0	7	0
Shackelford, Brian, Wich.*	1.000	1	9	2	0	11	0
Tremie, Chris, R.R.	1.000	4	21	0	0	21	0
Williams, Peanut, S.A.	.975	26	212	26	6	244	17
Zamora, Junior, Ark.	1.000	9	84	12	0	96	6

SECOND BASEMEN

Player, Team	Pct.	G	PO	A	E	TC	DP
Alfaro, Jason, R.R.	.976	28	56	68	3	127	19
Benefield, Brian, Wich.	.947	4	10	8	1	19	2
Berroa, Cristian, R.R.	.950	15	26	31	3	60	10
Bloomquist, Willie, S.A.	.979	57	82	146	5	233	33
Camilli, Jason, E.P.-Tul.	.971	52	107	130	7	244	22
Campusano, Carlos, Shre.	1.000	2	5	6	0	11	0
Caruso, Joe, Wich.	.968	20	23	37	2	62	5
Connors, Greg, S.A.	1.000	1	0	1	0	1	0
Cordido, Julio, Shre.	1.000	2	3	2	0	5	0
Dallimore, Brian, E.P.	.945	19	44	42	5	91	14
Dillon, Joe, Wich.	.965	11	30	25	2	57	2
Durrington, Trent, Ark.	.966	38	68	75	5	148	17
Figgins, Chone, Ark.	.950	34	72	80	8	160	23
Figueroa, Luis, S.A.	1.000	7	11	11	0	22	2
Garcia, Osmani, Tul.	1.000	1	1	2	0	3	0
German, Esteban, Mid.	.963	78	170	242	16	428	48
Halloran, Matt, Tul.	.969	15	28	35	2	65	7
Hansen, Jed, Wich.	1.000	1	0	6	0	6	1
Hood, Jay, Ark.	.833	1	1	4	1	6	1
Huisman, Jason, Ark.	.975	57	105	131	6	242	27
Jester, Joe, Shre.	.970	40	82	115	6	203	17
Kata, Matt, E.P.	1.000	4	8	9	0	17	2
Kuzmic, Craig, S.A.	.969	89	151	221	12	384	35
Lemonis, Chris, E.P.	.972	80	168	184	10	362	59
Luther, Ryan, Shre.	.951	93	181	210	20	411	50
MATRANGA, Dave, R.R.	.987	100	178	268	6	452	57

Player, Team	Pct.	G	PO	A	E	TC	DP
Medrano, Steve, Wich.	.975	14	18	21	1	40	6
Meliah, Dave, Tul.	.970	30	58	73	4	135	20
Metzler, Rod, Wich.	.971	102	197	231	13	441	44
Montas, Ricardo, E.P.	.983	13	24	33	1	58	2
Morillo, Cesar, R.R.	.941	3	8	8	1	17	0
Oliver, Brian, Tul.	.921	9	15	20	3	38	3
Pecci, Jay, Mid.	.976	52	92	154	6	252	22
Pernalete, Marco, Shre.	1.000	1	0	1	0	1	0
Romano, Jason, R.R.	.962	45	105	97	8	210	17
Salazar, Oscar, Mid.	.962	12	32	44	3	79	14
Santora, Jack, E.P.	.990	24	45	53	1	99	10
Strankman, Elliott, Shre.	.867	5	6	7	2	15	1
t'Hoen, E.J., Ark.	.983	13	23	36	1	60	10
Velarde, Randy, Tul.	1.000	3	4	9	0	13	0
Weber, Duke, S.A.	.000	1	0	0	0	0	0
White, Walt, E.P.	1.000	11	16	24	0	40	2
Young, Travis, Shre.	1.000	2	0	3	0	3	0
Zamora, Junior, Ark.	1.000	4	5	7	0	12	2

SECOND BASEMEN WITH TWO OR MORE TEAMS

Player, Team	Pct.	G	PO	A	E	TC	DP
Camilli, Jason, E.P.	.933	4	4	10	1	15	1
Camilli, Jason, Tul.	.974	48	103	120	6	229	21

THIRD BASEMEN

Player, Team	Pct.	G	PO	A	E	TC	DP
Alfaro, Jason, R.R.	.900	14	4	23	3	30	3
Blalock, Hank, Tul.	.953	67	37	125	8	170	9
CALDERON, Henry, Wich.	.949	94	57	185	13	255	11
Camilli, Jason, E.P.-Tul.	.833	5	3	7	2	12	1
Campusano, Carlos, Shre.	.500	1	0	1	1	2	0
Caruso, Joe, Wich.	.950	16	11	27	2	40	0
Christensen, Mike, Ark.	.925	81	51	158	17	226	16
Connors, Greg, S.A.	.500	2	1	2	3	6	0
Cordido, Julio, Shre.	.940	110	86	245	21	362	10
Cosme, Caonabo, Mid.	.944	14	8	26	2	36	1
Curl, John, S.A.	.000	1	0	0	1	1	0
Dallimore, Brian, E.P.	.938	106	85	216	20	321	17
Dillon, Joe, Wich.	.938	31	21	69	6	96	2
Durrington, Trent, Ark.	.917	4	3	8	1	12	1
Figgins, Chone, Ark.	.750	1	0	3	1	4	0
Figueroa, Luis, S.A.	1.000	4	2	4	0	6	0
Garcia, Osmani, Tul.	.934	62	42	114	11	167	7
Guiel, Jeff, Ark.	.839	10	6	20	5	31	1
Hammock, Rob, E.P.	.900	7	5	13	2	20	1
Hansen, Jed, Wich.	1.000	2	2	4	0	6	0
Hill, Jason, Ark.	1.000	1	0	2	0	2	1
Hochgesang, Josh, Mid.	.907	74	44	170	22	236	13
Hood, Jay, Ark.	.957	12	4	18	1	23	1
Huffman, Royce, R.R.	.918	134	72	229	27	328	14
Huisman, Jason, Ark.	.750	9	7	14	7	28	1
Kuzmic, Craig, S.A.	.926	46	20	68	7	95	6
Landry, Jacques, Mid.	1.000	10	3	12	0	15	1
Meliah, Dave, Tul.	.750	5	1	5	2	8	2
Montas, Ricardo, E.P.	.842	9	3	13	3	19	2
Morillo, Cesar, R.R.	.800	2	2	2	1	5	0
Owens, Ryan, E.P.	.839	16	8	18	5	31	3
Pecci, Jay, Mid.	.962	12	3	22	1	26	3
Pernalete, Marco, Shre.	.905	16	10	20	4	42	3
Robinson, Bo, S.A.	.931	99	60	155	16	231	13
Rose, Mike, E.P.	.000	1	0	0	1	1	0
Salazar, Oscar, Mid.	.880	34	16	79	13	108	6
Santora, Jack, E.P.	1.000	5	2	13	0	15	1
Sell, Chip, E.P.	.000	1	0	0	0	0	0
Solano, Danny, Tul.	.909	7	2	8	1	11	0
Strankman, Elliott, Shre.	1.000	1	0	2	0	2	1
t'Hoen, E.J., Ark.	1.000	6	3	6	0	9	0
Tyler, Josh, Shre.	1.000	2	3	5	0	8	1
Velarde, Randy, Tul.	1.000	2	1	3	0	4	0
White, Walt, E.P.	1.000	1	1	2	0	3	0
Young, Travis, Shre.	1.000	2	0	7	0	7	1
Zamora, Junior, Ark.	.930	25	20	46	5	71	4

THIRD BASEMEN WITH TWO OR MORE TEAMS

Player, Team	Pct.	G	PO	A	E	TC	DP
Camilli, Jason, E.P.	.800	3	3	5	2	10	1
Camilli, Jason, Tul.	1.000	2	0	2	0	2	0

SHORTSTOPS

Player, Team	Pct.	G	PO	A	E	TC	DP
Alfaro, Jason, R.R.	.948	16	19	36	3	58	8
Amezaga, Alfredo, Ark.	.964	70	132	214	13	359	43
Benefield, Brian, Wich.	1.000	1	0	2	0	2	0

Player, Team	Pct.	G	PO	A	E	TC	DP
Berroa, Angel, Wich.	.965	78	148	213	13	374	44
Berroa, Cristian, R.R.	.938	13	16	29	3	48	7
Bloomquist, Willie, S.A.	.945	76	103	226	19	348	32
Bruntlett, Eric, R.R.	.956	111	174	329	23	526	67
Camilli, Jason, E.P.	.867	4	4	9	2	15	0
Campusano, Carlos, Shre.	1.000	3	5	6	0	11	1
Caruso, Joe, Wich.	.933	16	29	27	4	60	6
Castillo, Ruben, S.A.	.949	40	73	115	10	198	24
Castro, Nelson, Shre.	.948	122	207	373	32	612	61
Cosme, Caonabo, Mid.	.943	17	30	52	5	87	13
Dillon, Joe, Wich.	.714	1	1	4	2	7	0
Durrington, Trent, Ark.	.892	8	12	21	4	37	2
Figgins, Chone, Ark.	.947	3	6	12	1	19	1
Figueroa, Luis, S.A.	1.000	5	5	7	0	12	2
Freeman, Corey, S.A.	.958	25	35	57	4	96	11
Garcia, Osmani, Tul.	.000	1	0	0	0	0	0
Hansen, Jed, Wich.	1.000	3	0	3	0	3	0
Hart, Corey, Wich.	.923	16	12	36	4	52	9
Hood, Jay, Ark.	1.000	3	6	7	0	13	2
Huisman, Jason, Ark.	1.000	2	2	8	0	10	0
Jester, Joe, Shre.	.000	1	0	0	0	0	0
Kuzmic, Craig, S.A.	.000	1	0	0	0	0	0
Landry, Jacques, Mid.	.800	1	2	2	1	5	0
Medrano, Steve, Wich.	.975	33	49	70	3	122	9
Meliah, Dave, Tul.	.773	5	4	13	5	22	1
Montas, Ricardo, E.P.	.923	4	1	11	1	13	2
Olson, Tim, E.P.	.914	46	74	138	20	232	26
Pecci, Jay, Mid.	.958	47	67	136	9	212	29
Perez, Antonio, S.A.	.818	5	9	18	6	33	4
Pernalete, Marco, Shre.	1.000	1	0	1	0	1	0
Salazar, Oscar, Mid.	.947	77	125	253	21	399	36
Santora, Jack, E.P.	.930	52	75	151	17	243	27
SOLANO, Danny, Tul.	.971	113	181	358	16	555	65
Sosa, Juan, E.P.	.947	29	48	78	7	133	17
Specht, Brian, Ark.	.906	44	73	140	22	235	24
Strankman, Elliott, Shre.	.667	2	0	2	1	3	0
t'Hoen, E.J., Ark.	.909	10	13	27	4	44	5
Tyler, Josh, Shre.	.911	10	15	36	5	56	4
Warriax, Brandon, Tul.	.959	23	28	65	4	97	6
White, Walt, E.P.	.935	16	18	40	4	62	12
Whiteman, Tom, R.R.	1.000	4	4	10	0	14	2
Young, Travis, Shre.	1.000	2	4	5	0	9	2

OUTFIELDERS

Player, Team	Pct.	G	PO	A	E	TC	DP
Alfaro, Jason, R.R.	1.000	19	28	1	0	29	0
Allen, Jeff, Shre.	.963	16	26	0	1	27	0
Asche, Kirk, Mid.	1.000	15	26	2	0	28	1
Beamon, Trey, S.A.	.958	44	67	1	3	71	0
Benefield, Brian, Wich.	1.000	2	2	0	0	2	0
Berger, Brandon, Wich.	.971	88	131	4	4	139	0
Berrios, Harry, Tul.	.950	23	38	0	2	40	0
Brito, Juan, Wich.	1.000	1	1	0	0	1	0
Byas, Mike, Shre.	.987	83	216	7	3	226	1
Cadiente, Brett, Tul.*	.976	56	78	5	2	85	0
Calderon, Henry, Wich.	.000	1	0	0	0	0	0
Carter, Charley, R.R.	1.000	20	20	0	0	20	0
Caruso, Joe, Wich.	.992	68	119	3	1	123	1
Casper, Brett, Shre.	1.000	8	13	0	0	13	0
Chapman, Scott, R.R.	1.000	1	1	0	0	1	0
Chavez, Endy, Wich.*	.990	42	95	4	1	100	1
Clark, Doug, Shre.	.982	110	219	5	4	228	1
Connors, Greg, S.A.	.917	9	9	2	1	12	1
Curl, John, S.A.	.962	13	25	0	1	26	0
Curtis, Chad, Tul.	.917	5	11	0	1	12	0
Devore, Doug, E.P.*	.953	120	231	11	12	254	3
Diaz, Angel, Ark.	1.000	1	2	1	0	3	1
Dodson, Jeremy, Wich.	1.000	34	55	4	0	59	0
Durrington, Trent, Ark.	1.000	1	1	0	0	1	0
Foley, Steve, S.A.	.979	29	45	2	1	48	1
Gallagher, Shawn, Wich.	1.000	9	12	1	0	13	0
Gann, Jamie, E.P.	.992	53	124	6	1	131	1
Gibson, Derrick, E.P.	.960	18	47	1	2	50	0
Glendenning, Mike, Shre.-E.P.	.965	39	52	3	2	57	0
Gomez, Alexis, Wich.*	.971	83	203	1	6	210	0
Gonzalez, Manny, E.P.	1.000	3	4	0	0	4	0
Guiel, Jeff, Ark.	1.000	16	28	1	0	29	0
Guzman, Elpidio, Ark.*	.984	110	231	10	4	245	1
Hammock, Rob, E.P.	1.000	7	13	0	0	13	0
Hansen, Jed, Wich.	1.000	8	7	0	0	7	0
Harris, Cedrick, E.P.	1.000	14	29	1	0	30	0
Harvey, Ken, Wich.	.000	1	0	0	0	0	0
Haynes, Nathan, Ark.*	.985	71	190	3	3	196	0

Player, Team	Pct.	G	PO	A	E	TC	DP
Hill, Jason, Ark.	1.000	3	1	0	0	1	0
Hodges, Kerry, R.R.	1.000	1	1	0	0	1	0
Huisman, Jason, Ark.	1.000	26	35	3	0	38	0
Johnson, Gary, Ark.*	.989	105	178	8	2	188	2
Kapler, Gabe, Tul.	1.000	3	2	0	0	2	0
Keith, Rusty, Mid.	.991	61	103	3	1	107	0
Kelly, Kenny, S.A.	.981	121	252	6	5	263	3
Kuzmic, Craig, S.A.	1.000	9	6	0	0	6	0
Landry, Jacques, Mid.	.965	107	159	7	6	172	1
Lane, Jason, R.R.*	.992	134	226	8	2	236	1
Leday, A.J., Ark.	.000	1	0	0	0	0	0
LOCKWOOD, Mike, Mid.*	.992	127	252	9	2	263	0
Logan, Kyle, R.R.	.964	68	104	4	4	112	0
Ludwick, Ryan, Mid.*	.977	116	250	4	6	260	1
Luster, Jeremy, Shre.	1.000	2	5	0	0	5	0
Luther, Ryan, Shre.	1.000	1	1	0	0	1	0
Magruder, Chris, Shre.	.979	39	93	0	2	95	0
McGowan, Sean, Shre.	1.000	2	3	0	0	3	0
Meliah, Dave, Tul.	1.000	10	16	2	0	18	1
Mench, Kevin, Tul.	.983	117	228	10	4	242	3
Mensik, Todd, Mid.*	.000	3	0	0	0	0	0
Metzler, Rob, Wich.	.909	10	9	1	1	11	0
Moreta, Ramon, Shre.	.965	30	52	3	2	57	0
Mott, Bill, Ark.	.971	15	32	2	1	35	0
Murphy, Nate, E.P.*	.967	34	55	3	2	60	0
Myers, Adrian, S.A.	1.000	27	46	0	0	46	0
Overbay, Lyle, E.P.*	.897	25	25	1	3	29	0
Piniella, Juan, Tul.	.977	98	167	4	4	175	0
Porter, Colin, R.R.*	.983	25	58	1	1	60	0
Quinlan, Robb, Ark.	1.000	8	17	0	0	17	0
Rosamond, Mike, R.R.	.989	31	83	3	1	87	1
Rose, Mike, E.P.	1.000	11	6	1	0	7	0
Salazar, Oscar, Mid.	1.000	1	3	0	0	3	0
Sell, Chip, E.P.	1.000	14	16	1	0	17	0
Shabala, Adam, Shre.	1.000	12	26	2	0	28	1
Shackelford, Brian, Wich.*	.959	95	155	7	7	169	2
Silvestre, Juan, S.A.	.981	65	98	4	2	104	0
Sykes, Jamie, E.P.	.977	54	83	2	2	87	0
Terrero, Luis, E.P.	.943	34	78	4	5	87	0
Torcato, Tony, Shre.	.975	36	76	3	2	81	0
Tyler, Josh, Shre.	1.000	2	2	0	0	2	0
Urquhart, Derick, Ark.*	.992	63	126	5	1	132	0
Urquiola, Carlos, E.P.	.972	26	35	0	1	36	0
Valderrama, Carlos, Shre.	1.000	41	85	3	0	88	1
Walker, Mark, Shre.	.943	37	48	2	3	53	0
Weber, Jake, S.A.	.962	122	220	6	9	235	1
Wesson, Barry, R.R.	.990	133	288	10	3	301	2
Wright, Corey, Tul.*	.984	110	240	4	4	248	1
Zywica, Mike, Tul.	.923	20	22	2	2	26	0

OUTFIELDERS WITH TWO OR MORE TEAMS

Player, Team	Pct.	G	PO	A	E	TC	DP
Glendenning, Mike, Shre.	.917	14	19	3	2	24	0
Glendenning, Mike, E.P.	1.000	25	33	0	0	33	0

CATCHERS

Player, Team	Pct.	G	PO	A	E	TC	DP	PB
Brito, Juan, Wich.	.996	66	451	47	2	500	2	7
Caruso, Joe, Wich.	.000	1	0	0	0	0	0	0
Chapman, Scott, R.R.	.966	2	25	3	1	29	0	1
Connors, Greg, S.A.	1.000	5	34	3	0	37	0	0
Cresse, Brad, E.P.	.991	96	665	83	7	755	3	17
Diaz, Angel, Ark.	1.000	18	94	8	0	102	0	4
Fatheree, Danny, R.R.	.964	7	50	3	2	55	0	1
Felix, Hersy, Wich.	1.000	3	25	2	0	27	0	1
Flores, Javier, Tul.	.990	14	86	15	1	102	2	2
Glassey, Josh, E.P.	.955	4	20	1	1	22	0	0
Gregorio, Tom, Ark.	.989	43	245	33	3	281	3	4
Hammock, Rob, E.P.	.929	2	11	2	1	14	0	1
Hansen, Jed, Wich.	1.000	1	3	1	0	4	0	0
Hernandez, John, E.P.	1.000	7	40	2	0	42	0	0
Hill, Jason, Ark.	.989	76	415	36	5	456	3	10
Huckaby, Ken, E.P.	.978	12	77	11	2	90	0	0
Jones, Jeremy, Tul.	.989	77	594	56	7	657	0	9
King, Brad, S.A.	.991	72	508	61	5	574	6	14
Lopez, Norberto, Ark.	1.000	2	10	2	0	12	0	0
Luderer, Brian, Mid.	.978	73	470	56	12	538	4	6
Luther, Ryan, Shre.	.975	31	138	18	4	160	1	3
Madonna, Chris, Mid.	.979	24	131	10	3	144	0	6
Maldonado, Carlos, R.R.	.992	74	590	50	5	645	2	8
MAYNARD, Scott, S.A.	.993	70	526	73	4	603	8	5
Melton, John, E.P.	1.000	1	1	0	0	1	0	0
Nieckula, Aaron, Mid.	.970	12	82	15	3	100	0	1

Player, Team	Pct.	G	PO	A	E	TC	DP	PB
Pujols, Rafael, Mid.	1.000	12	75	8	0	83	1	3
Rodriguez, Guillermo, Shre.	.983	61	362	35	7	404	3	7
Romero, Mandy, Mid.	.991	27	199	12	2	213	2	3
Rose, Mike, E.P.	.987	27	209	23	3	235	0	3
Socarras, Tony, Ark.	1.000	3	8	2	0	10	0	1
Taveras, Luis, Tul.	.988	55	390	37	5	432	1	9
Tonis, Mike, Wich.	.985	59	412	43	7	462	1	2
Tremie, Chris, R.R.	.992	63	472	47	4	523	1	1
Ullery, Dave, Wich.	1.000	12	82	8	0	90	0	2
Wright, Mike, Shre.	.989	59	306	40	4	350	6	6

PITCHERS

Player, Team	Pct.	G	PO	A	E	TC	DP
Adkins, Jon, Mid.	1.000	24	13	17	0	30	0
Affeldt, Jeremy, Wich.*	.973	25	7	29	1	37	1
Alfano, Jeff, Shre.	.000	1	0	0	0	0	0
Alfaro, Jason, R.R.	1.000	1	0	1	0	1	0
Andra, Jeff, Shre.*	1.000	18	1	13	0	14	0
Atchison, Scott, S.A.	.929	24	8	18	2	28	2
Ayala, Julio, S.A.*	1.000	3	2	1	0	3	0
Baerlocher, Ryan, Wich.	.927	28	11	27	3	41	2
Bazzell, Shane, Mid.	.667	2	2	0	1	3	0
Beech, Matt, Tul.*	1.000	8	2	4	0	6	0
Benoit, Joaquin, Tul.	.667	4	0	2	1	3	0
Bergman, Dusty, Ark.*	.958	27	18	28	2	48	1
Bermudez, Manny, Shre.	.889	12	2	6	1	9	0
Beverlin, Jason, Ark.	.857	6	1	5	1	7	1
Bevis, P.J., E.P.	1.000	14	1	1	0	2	1
Bierbrodt, Nick, E.P.*	1.000	4	1	2	0	3	0
Bochtler, Doug, Wich.	.800	15	0	4	1	5	0
Bootcheck, Chris, Ark.	1.000	6	3	4	0	7	1
Bottenfield, Kent, R.R.	.000	1	0	0	0	0	0
Brink, Jim, Mid.	1.000	20	5	10	0	15	1
Brocail, Doug, R.R.	.000	1	0	0	0	0	0
Brown, Elliot, Shre.	.900	14	3	6	1	10	1
Brummett, Sean, Ark.*	.667	25	1	7	4	12	1
Bukvich, Ryan, Wich.	.000	7	0	0	0	0	0
Calero, Kiko, Wich.	.906	27	6	23	3	32	1
Callier, Jeremy, Ark.	1.000	16	2	4	0	6	0
Camp, Jared, Wich.	1.000	33	1	3	0	4	0
Cannon, Jon, Shre.*	1.000	17	2	9	0	11	0
Capuano, Chris, E.P.*	.923	28	8	28	3	39	0
Carlson, Dan, E.P.	.800	32	1	3	1	5	0
Caruso, Joe, Wich.	.000	1	0	0	0	0	0
Cervantes, Chris, E.P.*	.900	45	1	17	2	20	0
Clark, Chris, Ark.	.867	28	5	8	2	15	0
Cogan, Tony, Wich.*	.833	8	2	3	1	6	0
Connors, Greg, S.A.	1.000	1	1	0	0	1	0
Cook, Derrick, Tul.	.667	7	1	3	2	6	1
Cotton, Joe, Mid.	1.000	47	5	9	0	14	2
Cox, Ryan, Shre.	1.000	24	11	17	0	28	1
Crabtree, Tim, Tul.	1.000	2	1	0	0	1	0
Crawford, Joe, E.P.*	.846	7	0	11	2	13	0
Cummings, Ryan, Ark.	1.000	42	3	9	0	12	0
DeHart, Rick, Wich.*	1.000	13	0	2	0	2	0
Demouy, Chris, Ark.*	.889	24	2	6	1	9	0
Donnelly, Brendan, Ark.	1.000	27	0	2	0	2	0
Duchscherer, Justin, Tul.	.857	6	1	5	1	7	1
Durocher, Jayson, Tul.	1.000	3	0	1	0	1	0
Dykhoff, Radhames, Ark.*	1.000	27	3	8	0	11	2
Elder, Dave, Tul.	.789	13	7	8	4	19	0
Ellison, Jason, S.A.	.929	46	3	10	1	14	1
Enochs, Chris, Mid.	.905	39	6	13	2	21	0
Estrella, Luis, Shre.	1.000	7	1	1	0	2	0
Evans, Dave, R.R.	.000	1	0	0	0	0	0
Falkenborg, Brian, S.A.	.778	12	2	5	2	9	0
Farnsworth, Jeff, S.A.	.882	27	7	23	4	34	4
Field, Nathan, Wich.	.875	52	1	13	2	16	0
Figueroa, Carlos, Tul.*	1.000	3	0	1	0	1	0
Fitzgerald, Brian, S.A.*	.900	30	3	6	1	10	0
Freeman, Corey, S.A.	.000	1	0	0	0	0	0
Fuller, Jody, E.P.	1.000	2	1	0	0	1	0
Galva, Claudio, Mid.*	1.000	55	1	8	0	9	0
Garza, Chris, Tul.*	1.000	16	0	4	0	4	1
Gilfillan, Jason, Wich.	1.000	11	0	1	0	1	0
Good, Andrew, E.P.	.750	10	3	3	2	8	0
Goodrich, Randy, Shre.	1.000	19	5	3	0	8	0
Gray, Mike, E.P.*	1.000	29	3	1	0	4	0
Gregg, Kevin, Mid.	1.000	44	9	5	0	14	2
Guerra, Mark, R.R.	1.000	9	4	8	0	12	1
Guerrero, Junior, Wich.	.000	15	0	0	1	1	0
Guzman, Leiby, Tul.-Shre.	1.000	36	2	7	0	9	0
Harang, Aaron, Mid.	.933	27	15	13	2	30	3

Player, Team	Pct.	G	PO	A	E	TC	DP
Harriger, Mark, Ark.	.952	10	7	13	1	21	0
Hartmann, Pete, E.P.*	.857	19	2	4	1	7	0
Heaverlo, Jeff, S.A.	.971	27	15	19	1	35	0
Hernandez, Carlos, R.R.*	.920	24	4	19	2	25	1
Horgan, Joe, Shre.*	.963	31	8	18	1	27	0
Hughes, Travis, Tul.	1.000	47	2	8	0	10	0
Hundley, Jeff, Ark.*	.895	10	3	14	2	19	0
Jamison, Ryan, R.R.	.800	10	4	4	2	10	0
Jarvis, Matt, S.A.*	1.000	23	1	5	0	6	1
Jenks, Bobby, Ark.	.500	2	1	0	1	2	0
Joseph, Kevin, Shre.	1.000	24	5	8	0	13	0
Keith, Rusty, Mid.	1.000	1	0	1	0	1	0
Kelley, Rich, Ark.*	.500	5	1	1	2	4	0
Kessel, Kyle, R.R.*	.923	13	3	9	1	13	0
Kirkreit, Daron, Ark.	1.000	17	3	2	0	5	0
Knoll, Brian, Shre.	1.000	2	1	0	0	1	0
Knott, Eric, E.P.*	1.000	17	2	5	0	7	0
Kolb, Dan, Tul.	1.000	1	0	1	0	1	0
Koplove, Mike, E.P.	.882	34	7	8	2	17	0
Lackey, John, Ark.	.951	18	15	24	2	41	1
Lamber, Justin, Wich.*	1.000	19	4	4	0	8	0
Lee, Corey, Tul.*	1.000	25	9	19	0	28	0
Lee, Jon, E.P.	.000	3	0	0	0	0	0
Lehr, Chuck, Mid.	.956	29	13	30	2	45	2
Lewis, Colby, Tul.	.917	25	3	19	2	24	1
Lidge, Brad, R.R.	.750	5	1	2	1	4	0
Lira, James, R.R.	1.000	27	4	6	0	10	1
Lopez, Aquilino, S.A.	1.000	42	4	4	0	8	0
Lopez, Javier, E.P.*	1.000	22	4	10	0	14	0
Lundberg, Spike, Tul.	.958	18	8	15	1	24	3
Luster, Jeremy, Shre.	.000	1	0	0	0	0	0
Martinez, Jason, E.P.	1.000	51	4	11	0	15	0
Martinez, Gustavo, S.A.	1.000	3	2	0	0	2	0
Martinez, Jose, Tul.	.786	24	5	6	3	14	1
Matzenbacher, Brian, E.P.	1.000	1	0	2	0	2	0
Mazur, Bryan, Mid.*	.000	6	0	0	0	0	0
McMullen, Mike, Wich.	1.000	6	1	2	0	3	0
Mendoza, Hatuey, E.P.	.833	8	4	6	2	12	0
Messman, Joe, Shre.	1.000	12	2	4	0	6	0
Meyer, Jake, S.A.	1.000	25	1	1	0	2	0
Miller, Benji, Shre.	.826	37	7	12	4	23	0
Miller, Greg, R.R.*	1.000	14	1	6	0	7	0
Milo, Tony, Ark.*	1.000	19	1	4	0	5	0
Mobley, Kevin, Tul.	.867	36	3	10	2	15	0
Moreno, Juan, Tul.*	1.000	6	1	3	0	4	0
Moreno, Orber, Wich.	1.000	5	0	2	0	2	0
Morrison, Cody, S.A.	.833	8	2	3	1	6	0
Myette, Aaron, Tul.	.000	1	0	0	0	0	0
Nathan, Joe, Shre.	.867	21	5	8	2	15	0
Newman, Eric, E.P.	.667	13	1	1	1	3	1
Nix, Wayne, Mid.	1.000	2	1	0	0	1	0
Norlega, Ray, Mid.*	.600	17	0	3	2	5	0
Norris, Ben, E.P.*	.909	16	2	8	1	11	0
Oliver, Darren, Tul.*	1.000	1	0	2	0	2	0
Ozias, Todd, Shre.-Tul.	1.000	39	3	11	0	14	1
Patterson, John, E.P.	.750	5	0	3	1	4	0
Pearsall, J.J., Tul.*	.889	43	2	6	1	9	1
Pena, Juan, Mid.*	.778	27	1	20	6	27	1
Peralta, Joel, Ark.	.000	9	0	0	0	0	0
Persails, Mark, R.R.	1.000	1	0	1	0	1	0
Pine, Chris, Ark.	.000	4	0	0	0	0	0
Pratt, Andy, Tul.*	.892	27	5	28	4	37	2
Puffer, Brandon, R.R.	1.000	56	5	12	0	17	1
Putz, Joe, S.A.	.943	27	13	20	2	35	0
Ramirez, Erasmo, Shre.-Tul.*	1.000	34	2	5	0	7	0
Ramirez, Joslin, E.P.	1.000	4	1	0	0	1	0
Ramos, Mario, Mid.*	.909	15	2	8	1	11	1
Randolph, Steve, C.P.*	1.000	18	2	14	0	16	0
Rayborn, Kenny, S.A.	1.000	14	3	1	0	4	1
Redding, Tim, R.R.	1.000	14	0	8	0	8	0
Regilio, Nick, Tul.	1.000	10	2	6	0	8	0
Reynolds, Shane, R.R.	1.000	1	1	1	0	2	0
Riley, Mike, Shre.*	.923	7	1	11	1	13	2
Roberts, Nick, R.R.	1.000	8	3	4	0	7	0
Robertson, Jeriome, R.R.*	1.000	57	4	9	0	13	1
Rodriguez, Guillermo, Shre.	.000	1	0	0	0	0	0
Rodriguez, Wil, R.R.*	.800	42	5	11	4	20	0
Rose, Mike, E.P.	1.000	1	0	1	0	1	0
Sanches, Brian, Wich.	.967	29	10	19	1	30	0
Sanchez, Duaner, E.P.	.958	13	11	12	1	24	2
Sedlacek, Shawn, Wich.	1.000	14	9	10	0	19	2
Sessions, Doug, R.R.	.846	41	3	8	2	13	0
Shackelford, Brian, Wich.*	.000	1	0	0	0	0	0
Shearn, Tom, R.R.	.875	43	8	13	3	24	0

Player, Team	Pct.	G	PO	A	E	TC	DP
Silva, Doug, Tul.	1.000	14	1	0	0	1	0
Simpson, Allan, S.A.	1.000	22	1	7	0	8	0
SMITH, Travis, R.R.	1.000	29	15	27	0	42	0
Snyder, Bill, Mid.	.889	31	3	5	1	9	0
Snyder, Matt, Tul.	.000	4	0	0	0	0	0
Soriano, Rafael, S.A.	1.000	8	1	5	0	6	0
Stark, Dennis, S.A.	1.000	1	0	1	0	1	0
Stephens, Jason, Ark.	.875	19	16	12	4	32	2
Suarez, Felipe, Ark.	1.000	34	6	15	0	21	4
Sweeney, Brian, S.A.	1.000	37	10	15	0	25	1
Thompson, Eric, Mid.	.900	35	0	9	1	10	0
Thurman, Corey, Wich.	1.000	25	11	18	0	29	0
Turnbow, Derrick, Ark.	1.000	3	3	7	0	10	0
Ulloa, Emmanuel, S.A.	.842	45	6	10	3	19	1
Urban, Jeff, Shre.*	.946	27	9	26	2	37	1
Urquhart, Derick, Ark.*	.000	1	0	0	0	0	0
Valverde, Jose, E.P.	1.000	39	2	3	0	5	0
Verplancke, Jeff, Shre.	1.000	43	2	7	0	9	0
Villano, Mike, Wich.-Shre.	.882	44	4	11	2	17	0
Villarreal, Oscar, E.P.	.879	27	17	12	4	33	3
Voyles, Brad, Wich.	1.000	11	2	1	0	3	1
Wade, Travis, R.R.	.800	60	3	13	4	20	2

Player, Team	Pct.	G	PO	A	E	TC	DP
Wagner, Billy, R.R.*	.000	1	0	0	0	0	0
Ward, Jeremy, E.P.	.000	6	0	0	0	0	0
White, Bill, E.P.*	.714	7	0	5	2	7	1
Williams, Jerome, Shre.	.963	23	9	17	1	27	1
Williams, Shad, Ark.	1.000	11	5	4	0	9	1
Wilson, Phil, Ark.	1.000	2	2	0	0	2	1
Yates, Tyler, Mid.	.947	56	9	9	1	19	0

PITCHERS WITH TWO OR MORE TEAMS

Player, Team	Pct.	G	PO	A	E	TC	DP
Guzman, Leiby, Tul.	1.000	25	2	6	0	8	0
Guzman, Leiby, Shre.	1.000	11	0	1	0	1	0
Ozias, Todd, Shre.	1.000	30	2	10	0	12	1
Ozias, Todd, Tul.	1.000	9	1	1	0	2	0
Ramirez, Erasmo, Shre.*	1.000	22	2	4	0	6	0
Ramirez, Erasmo, Tul.*	1.000	12	0	1	0	1	0
Villano, Mike, Wich.	.867	37	4	9	2	15	0
Villano, Mike, Shre.	1.000	7	0	2	0	2	0

The following players appeared only as designated hitter, pinch-hitter or pinch runner: Chiaramonte, dh, ph; Greer, dh.

LEAGUE CHAMPIONS

Year	Team	Pct.
1888—	Dallas	.671
1889—	Houston	.551
1890—	Galveston	.705
1892—	Houston	.741
	Houston	.613
1895—	Dallas	.754
	Fort Worth*	.750
1896—	Fort Worth	.757
	Houston*	.679
	Galveston†	.548
1897—	San Antonio†	.657
	Galveston†	.717
1898—League disbanded.		
1899—	Galveston	.632
	Galveston	.762
1900-01—Did not operate.		
1902—	Corsicana	.866
	Corsicana	.682
1903—	Paris-Waco	.615
	Dallas*	.648
1904—	Corsicana*	.615
	Fort Worth	.800
1905—	Fort Worth	.545
1906—	Fort Worth	.677
	Cleburne∞	.609
1907—	Austin	.629
1908—	San Antonio	.664
1909—	Houston	.601
1910—	Dallas†	.586
	Houston†	.586
1911—	Austin	.575
1912—	Houston	.626
1913—	Houston	.620
1914—	Houston†	.671
	Waco†	.671
1915—	Waco	.592
1916—	Waco	.587
1917—	Dallas	.600
1918—	Dallas	.584
1919—	Shreveport*	.677
	Fort Worth	.651
1920—	Fort Worth	.703
	Fort Worth	.750
1921—	Fort Worth	.691
	Fort Worth	.662
1922—	Fort Worth	.694
	Fort Worth	.711
1923—	Fort Worth	.632
1924—	Fort Worth	.689
	Fort Worth	.763
1925—	Fort Worth	.711
	Fort Worth▲	.653
1926—	Dallas	.574
1927—	Wichita Falls	.654
1928—	Houston*	.679

Year	Team	Pct.
	Wichita Falls	.731
1929—	Dallas*	.588
	Wichita Falls	.620
1930—	Wichita Falls	.697
	Fort Worth*	.632
1931—	Houston♦	.625
	Houston	.734
1932—	Beaumont*	.640
	Dallas	.727
1933—	Houston	.623
	San Antonio (4th)§	.523
1934—	Galveston‡	.579
1935—	Oklahoma City‡	.590
1936—	Dallas	.604
	Tulsa (3rd)§	.519
1937—	Oklahoma City	.635
	Fort Worth (3rd)§	.535
1938—	Beaumont	.635
1939—	Houston	.606
	Fort Worth (4th)§	.540
1940—	Houston‡	.652
1941—	Houston	.673
	Dallas (4th)§	.519
1942—	Beaumont	.605
	Shreveport (2nd)§	.576
1943-44-45—Did not operate.		
1946—	Fort Worth	.656
	Dallas (2nd)§	.591
1947—	Houston‡	.623
1948—	Fort Worth‡	.601
1949—	Fort Worth	.649
	Tulsa (2nd)§	.584
1950—	Beaumont	.595
	San Antonio (4th)§	.513
1951—	Houston‡	.619
1952—	Dallas	.571
	Shreveport (3rd)§	.522
1953—	Dallas‡	.571
1954—	Shreveport	.559
	Houston (2nd)§	.553
1955—	Dallas	.581
	Shreveport (3rd)§	.540
1956—	Houston‡	.623
1957—	Dallas	.662
	Houston (2nd)§	.630
1958—	Fort Worth	.582
	Cor. Christi (3rd)§	.507
1959—	Victoria	.589
	Austin (2nd)§	.548
1960—	Rio Grande Valley	.590
	Tulsa (3rd)	.528
1961—	Amarillo	.643
	San Antonio (3rd)§	.532
1962—	El Paso	.571
	Tulsa (2nd)§	.550

Year	Team	Pct.
1963—	San Antonio	.564
	Tulsa (3rd)§	.529
1964—	San Antonio‡	.607
1965—	Tulsa	.574
	Albuquerque■	.550
1966—	Arkansas	.579
1967—	Albuquerque	.557
1968—	Arkansas	.586
	El Paso■	.562
1969—	Amarillo	.593
	Memphis■	.504
1970—	Albuquerque♦	.615
	Memphis	.507
1971—	Did not operate as league—clubs were members of Dixie Association.	
1972—	Alexandria	.600
	El Paso■	.557
1973—	San Antonio	.590
	Memphis■	.558
1974—	Victoria■	.581
	El Paso	.555
1975—	Lafayette▼	.558
	Midland▼	.604
1976—	Amarillo■	.600
	Shreveport	.515
1977—	El Paso	.600
	Arkansas•	.485
1978—	El Paso•	.593
	Jackson	.567
1979—	Arkansas•	.571
	Midland	.563
1980—	Arkansas•	.596
	San Antonio	.544
1981—	San Antonio	.571
	Jackson•	.507
1982—	El Paso	.559
	Tulsa•	.515
1983—	Jackson	.507
	Beaumont•	.500
1984—	Beaumont	.654
	Jackson•	.610
1985—	El Paso	.632
	Jackson•	.537
1986—	El Paso•	.630
	Jackson	.533
1987—	Wichita•	.515
	Jackson	.515
1988—	El Paso	.552
	Tulsa•	.522
1989—	Arkansas•	.585
	Wichita	.537
1990—	San Antonio	.582
	Shreveport•	.489
1991—	Shreveport•	.632
	El Paso	.596

Year	Team	Pct.	Year	Team	Pct.	Year	Team	Pct.
1992—	Shreveport	.566	1995—	Shreveport•	.652	1998—	Arkansas	.571
	Wichita•	.515		Midland	.485		Tulsa•	.557
1993—	El Paso	.563	1996—	Jackson•	.547	1999—	Wichita•	.593
	Jackson•	.541		Wichita	.500	2000—	Round Rock*	.593
1994—	El Paso•	.647	1997—	San Antonio•	.604	2001—	Round Rock	.614
	Jackson	.548		Shreveport	.551		Arkansas††	.485

*Won split-season playoff. †Won playoff for title. ‡Finished first and won four-club playoff. §Won four-club playoff. ∞Title to Cleburne by default. ▲Tied with Dallas in second half and won playoff for championship. ◆Tied with Beaumont at end of first half and won title in best-of-five series played as part of second-half schedule. ■League divided into Eastern, Western divisions; won two-team playoff. ▼League divided into Eastern, Western divisions; declared co-champions when playoffs were not completed. •League divided into Eastern and Western divisions and played split-season; won playoffs. NOTE—Championship awarded to winner of four-team playoff, 1933-51; first-place team and playoff winner co-champions, 1952-64. ††Was leading final round of split-season playoff, two games to none, and was declared champion when Professional Baseball declared a stoppage of play.

CALIFORNIA LEAGUE

LEAGUE OFFICE

President
Joe Gagliardi
Address
2380 S. Bascom Ave., Suite 200
Campbell, CA 95008
Phone
408-369-8038

Teams (affiliation)
Bakersfield Blaze (Devil Rays)
High Desert Mavericks (Brewers)
Lake Elsinore Storm (Padres)
Lancaster Jethawks (Diamondbacks)
Modesto A's (A's)
Rancho Cucamonga Quakes (Angels)

San Bernardino Stampede (Mariners)
San Jose Giants (Giants)
Stockton Ports (Reds)
Visalia Oaks (A's)

2001 FINAL STANDINGS

FIRST HALF

NORTHERN DIVISION

Team	W	L	T	Pct.	GB
San Jose (Giants)	37	33	0	.529	...
Bakersfield (Devil Rays)	37	33	0	.529	...
Mudville (Reds)	36	34	0	.514	1.0
Visalia (Athletics)	33	37	0	.471	4.0
Modesto (Athletics)	23	47	0	.329	14.0

SOUTHERN DIVISION

Team	W	L	T	Pct.	GB
Lake Elsinore (Padres)	50	20	0	.714	...
High Desert (Brewers)	37	33	0	.529	13.0
Rancho Cucamonga (Angels)	35	35	0	.500	15.0
San Bernardino (Mariners)	33	37	0	.471	17.0
Lancaster (Diamondbacks)	29	41	0	.414	21.0

SECOND HALF

NORTHERN DIVISION

Team	W	L	T	Pct.	GB
San Jose (Giants)	40	30	0	.571	...
Mudville (Reds)	38	32	0	.543	2.0
Bakersfield (Devil Rays)	34	36	0	.486	6.0
Modesto (Athletics)	32	38	0	.457	8.0
Visalia (Athletics)	28	42	0	.400	12.0

SOUTHERN DIVISION

Team	W	L	T	Pct.	GB
San Bernardino (Mariners)	43	27	0	.614	...
Lake Elsinore (Padres)	41	29	0	.586	2.0
High Desert (Brewers)	34	36	0	.486	9.0
Lancaster (Diamondbacks)	32	38	0	.457	11.0
Rancho Cucamonga (Angels)	28	42	0	.400	15.0

COMPOSITE

Team	L.E.	S.J.	S.B.	Mud.	H.D.	Bak.	R.C.	Vis.	Lan.	Mod.	W	L	T	Pct.	GB
Lake Elsinore (Padres)	...	9	13	9	15	9	9	8	11	8	91	49	0	.650	...
San Jose (Giants)	3	...	7	9	3	13	10	13	7	12	77	63	0	.550	14.0
San Bernardino (Mariners)	7	5	...	5	9	5	11	8	16	10	76	64	0	.543	15.0
Mudville (Reds)	3	11	7	...	7	7	7	13	7	12	74	66	0	.529	17.0
High Desert (Brewers)	5	9	11	5	...	7	13	3	11	7	71	69	0	.507	20.0
Bakersfield (Devil Rays)	3	7	7	13	5	...	6	13	7	10	71	69	0	.507	20.0
Rancho Cucamonga (Angels)	11	2	9	5	7	6	...	5	10	8	63	77	0	.450	28.0
Visalia (Athletics)	4	7	4	7	9	7	7	...	6	10	61	79	0	.436	30.0
Lancaster (Diamondbacks)	9	5	4	5	9	5	10	6	...	8	61	79	0	.436	30.0
Modesto (Athletics)	4	8	2	8	5	10	4	10	4	...	55	85	0	.393	36.0

Major league affiliations in parentheses.

High Desert plays home games in Adelanto, Calif.; Mudville plays home games in Stockton, Calif.

PLAYOFFS: Bakersfield defeated Mudville two games to one; High Desert defeated San Bernardino two games to one; Lake Elsinore defeated High Desert three games to none; San Jose led Bakersfield two games to one. Note: Lake Elsinore and San Jose declared California League co-champions due to stoppage of play in professional baseball.

REGULAR-SEASON ATTENDANCE: Bakersfield, 88,878; High Desert, 143,361; Lake Elsinore, 223,712; Lancaster, 173,621; Modesto, 141,337; Mudville, 71,869; Rancho Cucamonga, 292,107; San Bernardino, 151,832; San Jose, 145,225; Visalia, 55,232. Total—1,487,174. Playoffs (12 games)—25,008. California-Carolina League All-Star Game at Lancaster—3,737.

MANAGERS: Bakersfield, Charlie Montoyo; High Desert, Frank Kremblas; Lake Elsinore, Craig Colbert; Lancaster, Scott Coolbaugh; Modesto, Greg Sparks; Mudville, Dave Oliver; Rancho Cucamonga, Tim Wallach; San Bernardino, Daren Brown; San Jose, Lenn Sakata; Visalia, Juan Navarrete.

ALL-STAR TEAM: 1B—Xavier Nady, Lake Elsinore; 2B—Matt Kata, Lancater; 3B—Billy Martin, Lancater; SS—Bill Hall, High Desert; OF—Matt Diaz, Bakersfield; OF—Chris Snelling, San Bernardino; OF—Jamal Strong, San Bernardino; C—Lance Burkhart, High Desert; DH—Nate Kaup, Bakersfield; RHP—Luke Anderson, San Jose; RHP—Rafael Soriano, San Bernardino; RHP— Dennis Tankersley; LHP—Matt Thornton, San Bernardino; LHP—Craig Anderson, San Bernardino; Pitcher of the Year—Matt Thornton, San Bernardino; Most Valuable Player—Xavier Nady, Lake Elsinore; Rookie of the Year—Xavier Nady, Lake Elsinore; Manager of the Year—Craig Colbert, Lake Elsinore.

2001 BATTING

TEAM

Team	Avg.	G	TPA	AB	R	H	TB	2B	3B	HR	RBI	SH	SF	HP	BB	IBB	SO	SB	CS	GDP	LOB	ShO	Slg.	OBP
Lancaster	.281	140	5560	4927	801	1385	2191	269	51	145	737	36	34	52	511	16	1127	132	81	74	1040	3	.445	.353
High Desert	.279	140	5567	4887	837	1364	2215	291	43	158	753	33	46	95	506	15	1267	211	96	90	989	4	.453	.355
Bakersfield	.273	140	5441	4932	677	1344	1986	292	31	96	603	51	34	76	348	17	1048	82	39	95	1035	8	.403	.328
Lake Elsinore	.264	140	5444	4806	683	1268	1935	270	35	109	634	22	41	79	496	16	1167	124	56	111	1047	9	.403	.340
San Jose	.262	140	5378	4744	667	1245	1846	258	38	89	598	51	45	76	462	15	1165	147	69	92	1045	9	.389	.335
Visalia	.258	140	5542	4813	763	1242	1958	262	32	130	677	31	42	80	576	18	1215	160	74	92	1053	7	.407	.354
R. Cucamonga	.257	140	5292	4767	629	1226	1840	256	47	88	562	54	28	64	379	20	1157	167	62	94	929	8	.386	.319
S. Bernardino	.257	140	5543	4895	689	1257	1810	235	45	76	619	63	38	80	467	21	1112	137	56	98	1035	7	.370	.325
Modesto	.254	140	5545	4818	665	1225	1804	233	38	90	594	45	44	87	554	15	1200	177	61	87	1124	9	.374	.329
Mudville	.251	140	5360	4755	623	1195	1783	238	25	100	572	42	44	63	456	25	1066	102	46	116	994	10	.375	.322

TOP QUALIFIERS FOR BATTING CHAMPIONSHIP

Minimum 378 plate appearances. *Lefthanded batter. †Switch-hitter.

Player, Team	Avg.	G	TPA	AB	R	H	TB	2B	3B	HR	RBI	SH	SF	HP	BB	IBB	SO	SB	CS	GDP	Slg.	OBP
Snelling, Chris, S.B.*	.336	114	521	450	90	151	221	29	10	7	73	2	3	21	45	4	63	12	5	7	.491	.418
O'Keefe, Mike, R.C.*	.330	115	459	409	75	135	215	25	5	15	91	1	6	1	42	2	81	20	1	9	.526	.389
Diaz, Matt, Bak.	.328	131	571	524	79	172	267	40	2	17	81	4	5	14	24	3	73	11	5	11	.510	.370
Kaup, Nathan, Bak.	.323	113	474	427	65	138	217	34	3	13	68	0	7	5	35	2	81	3	2	9	.508	.376
Strong, Jamal, S.B.	.311	81	393	331	74	103	118	11	2	0	32	6	0	5	51	2	60	47	8	4	.356	.411
Moore, Frank, Bak.*	.307	129	544	505	75	155	217	29	6	7	60	6	2	6	25	3	106	9	3	9	.430	.346
Allen, Jeff, S.J.	.305	99	429	371	60	113	182	19	4	14	61	1	2	12	43	2	103	12	5	7	.491	.393
Gordon, Brian, Lan.*	.304	103	428	392	74	119	208	21	10	16	70	4	4	1	28	1	100	13	7	3	.531	.345
Hall, Bill, H.D.	.303	89	378	346	61	105	183	21	6	15	51	4	3	3	22	0	78	18	9	3	.529	.348
Nady, Xavier, L.E.	.302	137	604	524	96	158	276	38	1	26	100	0	8	10	62	7	109	6	0	14	.527	.381
Martin, Billy, Lan.	.299	130	578	472	98	141	260	33	4	26	106	0	4	7	95	2	130	0	4	1	.551	.420
Bikowski, Scott, R.C.*	.297	128	555	482	81	143	211	28	5	10	53	3	2	5	63	2	94	24	9	8	.438	.382
Kata, Matt, Lan.†	.296	119	545	494	80	146	207	19	6	10	54	1	1	5	41	3	79	30	8	4	.419	.355
Raymundo, Gregg, R.C.	.293	109	439	389	49	114	175	30	2	9	58	3	3	19	25	3	75	4	4	15	.450	.362
Closser, J.D., Lan.†	.291	128	540	468	85	136	237	26	6	21	87	1	4	2	65	4	106	6	7	9	.506	.377
Wagner, Jeff, R.C.	.291	113	452	402	51	117	180	37	1	8	56	1	2	9	38	2	82	4	3	2	.448	.364

DEPARTMENTAL LEADERS: G—Scarborough, 138; AB—Scarborough, 546; R—Scarborough, 101; H—M. Diaz, 172; TB—Nady, 276; 2B—McDougall, 43; 3B—McDowell, 11; HR—Nady, Martin, Flaherty, 26 each; RBI—Martin, 106; SH—Gastelum, 23; SF—Scott, 9; HP—Basabe, 27; BB—Martin, 95; IBB—Welsh, 8; SO—Flaherty, 162; SB—C. Rosario, 54; CS—C. Rosario, 24; GIDP—Christianson, 17; Slg.—Martin, .551; OBP—Martin, .420.

ALL PLAYERS

*Lefthanded batter. †Switch-hitter.

Player, Team	Avg.	G	TPA	AB	R	H	TB	2B	3B	HR	RBI	SH	SF	HP	BB	IBB	SO	SB	CS	GDP	Slg.	OBP
Abruzzo, Jared, R.C.†	.208	28	111	101	13	21	28	1	0	2	13	0	1	0	9	0	30	1	0	1	.277	.270
Alcala, Juan, S.B.	.254	72	254	232	23	59	70	9	1	0	24	4	3	6	9	2	55	1	1	8	.302	.296
Alfano, Jeff, S.J.	.213	56	182	164	15	35	60	7	0	6	22	2	1	5	10	0	57	0	3	2	.366	.278
Allegra, Matt, Mod.	.209	51	183	153	19	32	45	3	2	2	17	2	3	4	21	0	61	3	1	3	.294	.315
Allen, Jeff, S.J.	.305	99	429	371	60	113	182	19	4	14	61	1	2	12	43	2	103	12	5	7	.491	.393
Alvarado, Damien, S.B.*	.000	3	9	9	0	0	0	0	0	0	0	0	0	0	0	0	2	0	0	1	.000	.000
Alvarado, Joel, H.D.	.141	22	76	64	9	9	13	1	0	1	5	1	2	1	8	0	12	2	2	2	.203	.240
Amado, Jose, Mud.	.241	52	199	174	17	42	55	7	0	2	17	1	1	4	19	0	15	2	0	9	.316	.328
Asche, Kirk, Vis.	.267	105	457	405	64	108	199	24	2	21	89	0	7	12	33	2	111	10	6	8	.491	.335
Barski, Chris, R.C.*	.213	30	100	89	9	19	29	3	2	1	10	1	0	1	9	1	23	0	1	4	.326	.293
Bartee, Kimera, R.C.†	.267	7	31	30	3	8	10	2	0	0	1	0	0	1	0	0	11	3	0	0	.333	.290
Basabe, Jesus, Mud.	.258	119	505	426	74	110	208	21	7	21	93	1	4	27	47	1	130	12	5	6	.488	.365
Beattie, Andy, Mud.†	.313	60	260	227	37	71	109	17	0	7	31	1	1	3	28	0	50	11	2	3	.480	.394
Beinbrink, Andy, Bak.	.250	7	25	24	4	6	8	2	0	0	3	1	0	0	0	0	4	0	0	3	.333	.250
Benjamin, Al, L.E.	.215	16	67	65	6	14	19	3	1	0	5	0	1	0	1	0	15	1	1	1	.292	.224
Bikowski, Scott, R.C.*	.297	128	555	482	81	143	211	28	5	10	53	3	2	5	63	2	94	24	9	8	.438	.382
Bitter, Jarrod, L.E.	.218	35	126	119	13	26	41	9	0	2	16	0	1	1	5	0	37	0	0	3	.345	.254
Bowser, Matt, Vis.*	.273	131	566	479	92	131	240	32	7	21	83	0	8	9	70	3	92	10	5	6	.501	.371
Brooks, Conor, Vis.*	.000	47	3	3	0	0	0	0	0	0	0	0	0	0	0	0	2	0	0	0	.000	.000
Broussard, Benjamin, Mud.*	.245	30	125	102	14	25	45	5	0	5	21	0	3	4	16	0	31	0	0	2	.441	.360
Burkhart, Lance, H.D.	.313	65	280	233	57	73	158	23	1	20	55	1	3	0	44	2	50	4	2	0	.678	.434
Burnett, Mark, Mud.*	.224	123	529	434	67	97	138	16	5	5	43	3	7	1	84	4	88	11	4	3	.318	.346
Burns, Kevan, Lan.*	.361	74	280	255	48	92	160	21	7	11	45	0	1	1	23	2	42	11	4	1	.627	.414
Burress, Andy, Mud.	.270	33	132	122	13	33	50	6	1	3	16	0	0	0	10	0	40	8	2	2	.410	.326
Bynum, Freddie, Mod.*	.261	120	487	440	59	115	154	19	7	2	46	4	1	1	41	0	95	28	11	8	.350	.325
Calitri, Mike, Mud.	.176	22	86	74	0	13	21	2	0	2	10	0	0	1	11	0	28	0	0	2	.284	.291
Campana, Wandel, Mud.	.228	43	180	167	14	38	50	9	0	1	15	3	0	3	7	0	34	2	2	4	.299	.271
Campusano, Carlos, S.J.	.200	11	40	40	2	8	14	3	0	1	7	0	0	0	0	0	9	0	1	4	.350	.200
Carvajal, Jhonny, S.J.	.261	113	498	448	57	117	151	20	1	4	50	8	3	3	31	0	70	14	7	11	.337	.308
Castillo, Alberto, Bak.*	.274	94	378	347	45	95	144	12	2	11	54	1	1	1	28	4	120	1	3	4	.415	.329
Castillo, Carlos, Mod.	.143	3	9	7	3	1	1	0	0	0	0	0	0	0	2	0	3	0	0	1	.143	.333
Castillo, Ruben, S.B.	.222	76	287	270	31	60	74	7	2	1	26	7	2	3	5	0	53	10	2	5	.274	.243
Cerda, Jose, S.J.	.218	30	96	87	10	19	27	4	2	0	9	2	0	3	4	0	25	0	0	0	.310	.277
Ceriani, Matt, H.D.	.190	25	88	84	5	16	22	3	0	1	8	0	0	0	4	0	22	0	0	2	.262	.227
Chavez, Angel, S.J.	.244	84	341	316	37	77	112	22	2	3	28	5	3	1	16	0	60	10	4	9	.354	.280
Chirinos, Germain, Vis.	.267	94	295	251	49	67	93	11	0	5	27	3	0	3	38	0	78	12	7	7	.371	.370
Christianson, Ryan, S.B.	.248	134	590	528	65	131	210	42	5	12	85	0	4	5	53	6	112	3	2	17	.415	.320
Closser, J.D., Lan.†	.291	128	540	468	85	136	237	26	6	21	87	1	4	2	65	4	106	6	7	9	.506	.377
Contreras, Sergio, R.C.*	.271	104	391	351	47	95	129	15	5	3	37	3	2	5	29	2	68	15	9	4	.368	.333
Cook, Josh, S.J.	.421	8	21	19	2	8	11	3	0	0	5	0	0	0	2	1	2	0	0	1	.579	.476
Cosentino, Tony, L.E.	.213	53	199	174	21	37	60	9	1	4	21	1	3	1	20	0	32	1	1	6	.345	.293
Cosme, Caonabo, Mod.	.292	58	266	233	43	69	90	16	1	1	21	6	2	2	20	1	54	22	6	2	.381	.350
Craig, Beau, Vis.†	.195	96	375	344	34	67	88	16	1	1	32	4	2	2	23	0	77	1	1	9	.256	.248
Crespo, Manny, S.B.	.500	2	6	6	0	3	3	0	0	0	0	0	0	0	0	0	0	0	0	0	.500	.500
Cridland, Mark, H.D.*	.326	12	52	46	13	15	31	5	1	3	8	0	0	0	6	0	15	4	1	0	.674	.404
Crosby, Bobby, Mod.	.395	11	41	38	7	15	23	5	0	1	3	0	0	0	3	0	8	0	1	1	.605	.439
Cruz, Israel, S.B.	.179	31	72	67	6	12	14	2	0	0	3	2	0	1	2	0	22	3	1	2	.209	.214
Cullen, Ryan, Mod.*	.000	40	1	1	0	0	0	0	0	0	0	0	0	0	0	0	0	0	0	0	.000	.000
Daeley, Scott, S.J.	.226	114	492	411	77	93	118	14	1	3	29	9	2	6	64	0	76	30	5	4	.287	.337
Darula, Bobby, H.D.*	.303	74	310	254	42	77	105	10	6	2	39	3	2	9	42	2	26	15	4	8	.413	.417
Deardorff, Jeff, H.D.	.304	69	289	260	40	79	144	18	1	15	57	0	4	3	22	1	70	5	4	4	.554	.360
De La Cruz, Eric, H.D.	.304	9	24	23	4	7	7	0	0	0	3	0	0	0	0	0	4	1	1	0	.304	.333
De La Cruz, Jose, Vis.	.177	45	147	130	10	23	33	7	0	1	23	0	1	1	15	0	32	4	1	0	.254	.265

CLASS A California League

Player, Team	Avg.	G	TPA	AB	R	H	TB	2B	3B	HR	RBI	SH	SF	HP	BB	IBB	SO	SB	CS	GDP	Slg.	OBP
Dement, Dan, Bak.	.059	5	19	17	0	1	1	0	0	0	1	1	0	0	1	0	3	0	0	0	.059	.111
Diaz, Angel, R.C.	.167	26	93	84	9	14	20	4	1	0	5	0	0	2	7	1	27	1	0	3	.238	.247
Diaz, Matt, Bak.	.328	131	571	524	79	172	267	40	2	17	81	4	5	14	24	3	73	11	5	11	.510	.370
Dobbs, Greg, S.B.*	.385	3	14	13	2	5	9	1	0	1	3	0	1	0	0	0	4	0	0	0	.692	.357
Donovan, Todd, L.E.	.304	41	190	168	37	51	61	7	0	1	12	2	0	1	19	0	25	23	2	5	.363	.378
Durango, Ariel, S.B.†	.184	27	101	87	8	16	17	1	0	0	6	3	0	1	10	0	18	7	4	2	.195	.276
Eberwein, Kevin, L.E.	.333	9	37	30	6	10	20	4	0	2	4	0	0	1	6	1	6	0	0	1	.667	.459
Eddlemon, Kelly, Bak.	.229	104	412	367	46	84	138	25	4	7	49	1	5	3	36	3	85	7	4	8	.376	.299
Edge, Dwight, Lan.	.194	20	69	62	5	12	13	1	0	0	6	0	1	0	6	0	23	3	3	0	.210	.261
Encarnacion, Bienvenido, R.C.	.202	35	116	104	13	21	27	4	1	0	4	2	0	2	8	1	31	0	1	3	.260	.272
Faison, Vince, L.E.*	.233	73	304	275	27	64	102	11	3	7	36	1	2	2	24	1	94	12	7	2	.371	.297
Fajardo, Al, S.J.	.243	40	155	136	22	33	49	9	2	1	12	3	0	0	16	0	30	9	4	1	.360	.322
Fernandez, Alex, S.B.*	.286	111	459	416	51	119	176	21	6	8	52	5	1	2	35	3	67	17	6	9	.423	.344
Figueroa, Luis, S.B.	.323	32	144	124	24	40	52	10	1	0	16	0	1	2	17	0	15	2	0	1	.419	.410
Flaherty, Tim, S.J.	.255	135	544	466	69	119	233	26	5	26	83	0	4	8	66	2	162	2	5	12	.500	.355
Foley, Steve, S.B.	.252	34	150	127	20	32	41	4	1	1	9	3	3	7	10	0	25	2	0	0	.323	.333
Foster, Brian, H.D.	.250	9	34	28	6	7	18	3	1	2	5	1	0	0	5	0	14	1	0	1	.643	.364
Fulse, Sheldon, S.B.†	.164	34	141	122	14	20	30	2	1	2	11	1	1	3	14	0	43	7	6	3	.246	.264
Furniss, Eddy, Vis.*	.347	80	350	294	54	102	174	20	2	16	49	0	4	3	49	7	72	4	0	5	.592	.440
Gandolfo, Rob, S.B.*	.205	94	343	312	33	64	76	6	3	0	26	3	2	3	23	1	47	4	6	3	.244	.265
Gann, Jamie, Lan.	.200	31	99	90	14	18	23	2	0	1	10	0	2	2	5	0	21	1	2	2	.256	.253
Garcia, Isaac, Mod.	.250	53	180	168	11	42	57	7	1	2	16	0	3	1	8	0	40	5	1	3	.339	.283
Garrett, Shawn, L.E.†	.313	77	310	275	41	86	139	16	8	7	44	2	4	5	24	1	57	16	7	5	.505	.373
Gastelum, Carlos, R.C.	.204	118	408	363	39	74	97	11	6	0	28	23	3	4	15	0	57	20	6	11	.267	.242
Glassey, Josh, Lan.*	.150	8	29	20	6	3	3	0	0	0	1	0	1	0	8	0	2	1	1	0	.150	.414
Glendenning, Mike, Lan.	.242	9	37	33	2	8	18	4	0	2	6	0	0	0	4	0	13	0	0	1	.545	.324
Goldfield, Josh, Lan.*	.176	5	18	17	2	3	3	0	0	0	1	0	0	1	0	0	2	0	0	2	.176	.222
Gomez, Andre, L.E.	.229	21	74	70	7	16	22	3	0	1	11	0	1	0	3	0	24	0	0	2	.314	.257
Gomez, Frank, Vis.	.234	120	426	384	43	90	124	15	2	5	45	7	3	4	28	0	100	9	7	9	.323	.291
Gonzalez, Wiklenman, L.E.	.154	4	16	13	1	2	2	0	0	0	1	0	1	0	2	0	6	0	0	0	.154	.250
Gordon, Brian, Lan.*	.304	103	428	392	74	119	208	21	10	16	70	4	4	1	26	1	100	13	7	3	.531	.345
Gregg, Mitch, Vis.*	.247	121	471	401	66	99	174	22	1	17	68	0	3	9	58	3	154	10	2	8	.434	.352
Grummitt, Dan, Bak.	.321	46	192	165	31	53	102	22	0	9	28	0	0	9	18	0	50	3	2	1	.618	.417
Guerrero, Cristian, H.D.	.312	85	347	327	50	102	145	18	2	7	41	0	1	1	18	1	79	22	11	9	.443	.349
Hall, Bill, H.D.	.303	89	378	346	61	105	183	21	6	15	51	4	3	3	22	0	78	18	9	3	.529	.348
Hall, Justin, Mod.-S.J.	.261	74	277	238	32	62	87	14	1	3	22	2	0	4	33	0	59	3	2	4	.366	.360
Hammock, Rob, Lan.	.311	45	217	190	33	59	88	11	3	4	36	0	4	7	16	1	42	3	2	6	.463	.378
Harris, Cedrick, Lan.	.276	84	355	319	63	88	121	13	1	6	34	4	3	3	26	0	77	21	8	2	.379	.333
Hernandez, Orlando, S.B.	.167	18	52	48	4	8	8	0	0	0	3	1	0	0	3	0	15	0	0	1	.167	.216
Hill, Glenallen, R.C.	.167	3	12	12	1	2	6	1	0	1	3	0	0	0	0	0	5	0	0	1	.500	.167
Hoffpauir, Josh, Mod.*	.237	71	256	228	27	54	73	13	3	0	21	2	4	3	19	0	26	10	2	5	.320	.299
Holt, Daylan, Mod.	.179	101	390	341	31	61	84	15	1	2	39	3	4	2	40	0	90	5	2	2	.246	.266
Hopper, Shane, L.E.	.270	31	138	126	24	34	55	7	1	4	21	0	1	0	11	2	33	5	3	5	.437	.336
Howe, Matt, Mod.	.254	134	592	507	81	129	231	28	4	22	73	4	6	8	67	0	123	13	3	8	.456	.347
Huguet, J.C., Mud.	.400	3	6	5	2	2	5	0	0	1	1	0	0	1	0	0	2	0	0	0	1.000	.500
Hurtado, Omar, Mud.	.104	17	59	48	8	5	7	2	0	0	1	0	1	0	10	0	16	3	0	3	.146	.254
Isenia, Chairon, Bak.	.290	76	312	290	42	84	124	16	0	8	50	1	1	4	16	1	41	2	3	4	.428	.334
Jackson, Steve, Vis.	.253	121	449	435	72	110	191	27	3	16	64	1	1	6	46	1	123	5	5	5	.439	.332
Jacobs, Greg, Lan.*	1.000	21	1	1	0	1	1	0	0	0	0	0	0	0	0	0	0	0	0	1	1.000	1.000
Jester, Joe, S.J.	.254	81	346	295	51	75	117	17	2	7	41	3	1	12	35	1	77	20	5	4	.397	.356
Johnson, Ben, L.E.	.276	136	571	503	79	139	222	35	6	12	63	1	2	11	54	1	141	22	7	15	.441	.358
Johnson, Kade, H.D.	.254	101	425	370	57	94	180	21	1	21	67	0	6	14	35	1	118	9	2	12	.486	.336
Jones, Ryan, Lan.	.271	125	507	446	74	121	218	25	3	22	77	2	6	8	44	0	100	2	3	13	.489	.343
Kata, Matt, Lan.†	.296	119	545	494	80	146	207	19	6	10	54	4	1	5	41	3	79	30	8	4	.419	.355
Kaup, Nathan, S.B.	.323	113	474	427	65	138	217	34	3	13	68	0	7	5	35	2	81	3	2	9	.508	.376
Keller, G.W., Vis.	.094	11	37	32	3	3	3	0	0	0	3	1	0	2	2	0	9	0	0	2	.094	.194
Kennedy, Adam, R.C.*	.375	3	11	8	3	3	5	2	0	0	1	0	0	1	2	0	1	3	0	0	.625	.545
Kenney, Jeff, H.D.	.290	49	206	169	32	49	72	12	1	3	21	5	1	6	25	0	46	8	2	6	.426	.398
Kiil, Skip, Mud.	.300	5	22	20	1	6	9	0	0	1	3	0	0	2	0	0	4	1	1	0	.450	.364
Kison, Robbie, Mud.	.250	67	236	204	31	51	68	11	0	2	23	3	2	3	24	0	38	4	4	8	.333	.330
Knox, Ryan, H.D.	.319	75	357	304	65	97	136	17	5	4	29	0	1	7	45	0	57	37	13	3	.447	.417
Krynzel, Dave, H.D.*	.277	89	419	383	65	106	150	19	5	5	33	3	2	4	27	1	122	34	17	0	.392	.329
Laird, Gerald, Mod.	.255	119	511	443	71	113	151	13	5	5	46	4	6	10	48	1	101	10	9	9	.341	.337
Lehr, Ryan, R.C.	.269	54	216	197	28	53	85	14	3	4	25	0	2	4	13	0	40	1	1	9	.431	.324
Leone, Justin, S.B.	.233	130	556	485	70	113	214	27	4	22	69	6	3	5	57	2	158	4	3	8	.441	.318
Lopez, Chuck, S.B.*	.294	24	110	102	14	30	49	1	3	4	24	0	1	1	6	1	23	2	1	2	.480	.336
Lopez, Norberto, R.C.	.150	9	20	20	0	3	3	0	0	0	0	0	0	0	0	0	8	0	0	0	.150	.150
Lorenzana, Luis, L.E.	.269	70	270	234	32	63	72	7	1	0	17	4	0	8	24	0	48	5	1	6	.308	.357
Loyd, Brian, L.E.	.304	14	52	46	8	14	17	3	0	0	10	1	1	1	3	0	6	0	0	4	.370	.353
Lundquist, Ryan, Mud.	.273	122	505	436	66	119	192	31	4	14	72	3	6	6	54	2	117	9	2	12	.440	.354
Maldonado, Edwin, S.J.	.325	44	172	160	23	52	84	9	1	7	24	3	3	3	3	0	34	0	2	4	.525	.343
Marconi, Alex, Bak.	.239	34	115	109	11	26	32	3	0	1	11	0	0	0	6	0	27	0	0	5	.294	.278
Martin, Billy, Lan.	.299	130	578	472	98	141	260	33	4	26	106	0	4	7	95	2	130	0	4	1	.551	.420
Martinez, Guillermo, S.B.†	.253	44	189	166	26	42	55	8	1	1	16	7	1	2	13	1	43	1	2	4	.331	.313
Massiatte, Danny, Bak.	.212	96	372	330	37	70	106	20	2	4	29	6	4	6	26	0	84	1	2	9	.321	.279
McCallum, Geoff, S.B.	.245	32	117	98	13	24	30	6	0	0	12	1	0	0	18	1	34	2	1	1	.306	.362
McCorkle, Shawn, S.B.*	.275	136	603	520	81	143	226	36	4	13	81	5	6	3	69	2	151	2	2	10	.435	.360
McDougall, Marshall, Vis.	.257	134	598	534	79	137	230	43	7	12	84	7	4	7	46	2	110	14	2	9	.431	.321
McDowell, Arturo, S.J.*	.242	118	479	425	57	103	140	12	11	1	31	3	1	4	46	3	132	25	14	4	.329	.321
Melton, John, Lan.	.200	31	102	85	10	17	25	3	1	1	8	2	0	2	13	0	36	0	1	1	.294	.320
Messner, Jake, S.J.*	.244	83	319	279	36	68	90	14	1	2	39	0	3	3	34	1	83	1	2	11	.323	.339
Molina, Bengie, R.C.	.545	3	11	11	1	6	7	1	0	0	2	0	0	0	0	0	1	0	0	0	.636	.545
Montas, Ricardo, Lan.	.293	70	234	205	28	60	71	8	0	1	16	2	1	2	24	1	46	3	4	2	.346	.371

Player, Team	Avg.	G	TPA	AB	R	H	TB	2B	3B	HR	RBI	SH	SF	HP	BB	IBB	SO	SB	CS	GDP	Slg.	OBP
Moore, Darin, Vis.	.000	38	1	1	0	0	0	0	0	0	0	0	0	0	0	0	0	0	0	0	.000	.000
Moore, Frank, Bak.*	.307	129	544	505	75	155	217	29	6	7	60	6	2	6	25	3	106	9	3	9	.430	.346
Moore, Jason, L.E.†	.253	132	587	509	79	129	202	30	2	13	67	5	8	4	61	0	110	1	3	8	.397	.333
Moreta, Ramon, R.C.-S.J.	.294	45	193	177	28	52	70	13	1	1	15	3	0	1	12	0	41	22	10	5	.395	.342
Mott, Bill, R.C.*	.304	17	80	69	14	21	37	5	1	3	16	1	2	0	8	0	11	5	1	0	.536	.367
Mounts, J.R., R.C.	.220	106	400	378	49	83	133	15	4	9	38	3	2	2	15	2	145	13	6	6	.352	.252
Murch, Jeremy, Bak.*	.235	72	242	221	27	52	99	12	4	9	32	1	1	1	18	1	63	1	1	4	.448	.295
Murphy, Tommy, R.C.	.190	50	207	200	16	38	46	8	0	0	11	1	0	1	5	0	69	7	3	4	.230	.214
Myers, Corey, Lan.	.284	53	198	183	20	52	82	13	1	5	33	0	0	0	15	0	49	0	0	0	.448	.338
Nady, Xavier, L.E.	.302	137	604	524	96	158	276	38	1	26	100	0	8	10	62	7	109	6	0	14	.527	.381
Napoli, Michael, R.C.	.200	7	28	20	3	4	7	0	0	1	4	0	0	0	8	0	11	0	0	0	.350	.429
Nieckula, Aaron, Mod.-Vis.	.292	69	251	212	38	62	92	7	1	7	26	2	3	15	19	0	53	2	2	3	.434	.386
Niekro, Lance, S.J.	.288	42	171	163	18	47	67	11	0	3	34	0	4	0	4	0	14	4	2	2	.411	.298
Nix, Wayne, Vis.	.000	28	1	0	0	0	0	0	0	0	0	0	0	0	1	0	0	0	0	0	.000	1.000
O'Donnell, Ryan, L.E.	.255	15	57	51	7	13	15	2	0	0	1	0	0	1	5	0	10	0	1	0	.294	.333
O'Keefe, Mike, R.C.*	.330	115	459	409	75	135	215	25	5	15	91	1	6	1	42	2	81	20	1	9	.526	.389
Olmedo, Ranier, Mud.	.244	139	585	536	57	131	162	23	4	0	28	13	4	8	24	0	121	38	17	15	.302	.285
Olson, Tim, Lan.	.289	61	258	239	36	69	107	12	4	6	32	2	0	3	14	0	49	13	9	4	.448	.336
Owens, Jeremy, L.E.	.198	24	101	91	8	18	30	1	1	3	9	0	1	1	7	0	39	4	2	0	.330	.260
Patten, Chris, H.D.	.226	103	396	345	42	78	91	5	1	2	34	2	2	12	35	0	123	11	5	10	.264	.317
Perez, Nestor, Bak.	.241	118	448	407	44	98	120	16	3	0	37	9	3	2	27	0	57	11	4	8	.295	.289
Pernalete, Marco, S.J.†	.351	48	192	171	25	60	79	11	1	2	22	0	2	2	17	1	45	3	1	0	.462	.411
Piatt, Adam, Mod.	.467	4	17	15	4	7	12	2	0	1	2	0	0	1	1	0	5	0	0	0	.800	.529
Pichardo, Maximo, R.C.	.300	3	10	10	1	3	5	0	1	0	0	0	0	0	0	0	2	0	1	1	.500	.300
Pines, Gregory, S.B.	.200	18	39	35	1	7	7	0	0	0	4	2	0	0	2	0	8	0	0	1	.200	.243
Pujols, Rafael, Mod.	.269	64	273	223	33	60	78	13	1	1	23	3	1	1	45	3	34	4	1	6	.350	.393
Quintana, Wil, S.B.	.223	48	193	175	21	39	57	7	1	3	27	1	2	5	10	2	50	1	1	4	.326	.281
Rainey, Jason, S.B.*	.214	15	48	42	2	9	12	3	0	0	5	2	1	3	0	0	17	0	1	0	.286	.261
Raymundo, Gregg, R.C.	.293	109	439	389	49	114	175	30	2	9	58	3	3	19	25	3	75	4	4	15	.450	.362
Royoo, Christian, Mod.†	.100	01	100	91	13	18	25	4	0	1	4	1	0	1	15	0	32	1	1	2	.275	.319
Riggins, Auntwan, L.E.†	.227	17	72	66	7	15	15	0	0	0	5	1	0	1	4	0	22	2	2	1	.227	.282
Rios, Fernando, Mud.	.277	114	466	426	57	118	154	16	4	4	49	2	1	3	34	1	45	6	5	14	.362	.334
Risinger, Ben, L.E.	.251	105	402	351	32	88	107	16	0	1	46	2	4	13	32	0	86	2	5	9	.305	.333
Rodriguez, Guillermo, S.J.	.270	35	148	126	18	34	50	10	0	2	21	4	1	8	9	0	26	2	2	4	.397	.354
Rodriguez, Sorafin, Mud.	.240	50	217	200	22	40	65	9	1	2	25	5	2	2	8	0	27	0	0	6	.325	.274
Rogers, Brandon, R.C.	.211	24	84	76	4	16	23	4	0	1	11	0	1	1	6	0	20	0	1	1	.303	.274
Rosario, Carlos, Vis.†	.261	110	525	441	91	115	154	15	3	6	42	6	3	2	73	0	98	54	24	6	.349	.366
Rosario, Omar, Vis.-Mod.*	.219	90	377	301	41	66	90	13	1	3	29	1	0	9	66	3	88	19	4	8	.299	.375
Rowan, Chris, H.D.	.222	90	342	320	45	71	135	16	5	13	44	2	0	0	12	0	124	7	3	2	.422	.268
Rushford, Jim, H.D.*	.363	65	305	259	68	94	162	22	2	14	61	0	3	5	38	4	35	3	3	5	.625	.449
Ryan, Kelvin, Bak.	.264	103	392	363	46	96	142	26	1	6	36	3	1	16	9	0	83	4	2	7	.391	.311
Salmon, Tim, R.C.	.143	2	8	7	1	1	1	0	0	0	0	0	0	0	1	0	4	0	0	0	.143	.250
Santana, Henry, S.J.†	.333	7	26	24	1	8	14	1	1	1	5	2	0	0	0	0	7	1	0	0	.583	.333
Santos, Luis, Lan.	.189	14	38	37	4	7	7	0	0	0	1	0	0	0	1	0	2	0	0	2	.189	.211
Sardinha, Dane, Mud.	.235	109	445	422	45	99	154	24	2	9	55	4	4	3	12	2	97	0	1	12	.365	.259
Scales, Bobby, L.E.†	.271	98	417	362	46	98	145	24	4	5	42	1	0	10	44	1	78	20	7	7	.401	.365
Scarborough, Steve, H.D.	.255	138	632	546	101	139	225	36	4	14	91	9	7	5	65	1	126	21	6	8	.412	.335
Schader, Troy, S.J.	.242	94	398	363	55	88	155	17	4	14	55	0	1	6	28	1	111	1	4	6	.427	.307
Scheschuk, John, L.E.*	.283	96	405	346	48	98	151	28	2	7	46	1	2	1	55	1	60	3	3	10	.436	.381
Schmidt, J.P., Vis.*	.270	18	67	63	5	17	20	3	0	0	7	0	0	0	4	0	13	3	2	4	.317	.313
Schneidmiller, Gary, Vis.	.278	113	439	374	60	104	138	17	4	3	34	2	3	7	53	0	83	12	8	9	.369	.375
Schrock, Chris, Bak.	.244	94	351	320	38	78	94	16	0	0	24	9	1	3	18	0	51	3	3	10	.294	.289
Scott, Bill, H.D.	.283	132	581	513	73	145	237	42	1	16	102	1	9	8	50	2	135	9	11	15	.462	.350
Senjem, Guye, Mud.*	.355	42	166	141	25	50	91	9	1	10	32	1	1	1	22	1	31	0	1	0	.645	.442
Serrano, Sammy, S.J.	.209	39	150	139	14	29	46	12	1	1	12	1	2	1	7	1	38	0	0	3	.331	.248
Shabala, Adam, S.J.*	.143	3	9	7	1	1	1	0	0	0	0	0	0	0	2	0	4	0	0	0	.143	.333
Shaffer, Josh, R.C.*	.280	58	209	193	17	54	71	7	2	2	20	4	0	1	11	2	34	2	4	0	.368	.322
Sledd, Aaron, Mud.*	.000	1	3	3	0	0	0	0	0	0	0	0	0	0	0	0	2	0	0	1	.000	.000
Snelling, Chris, S.B.*	.336	114	521	450	90	151	221	29	10	7	73	2	3	21	45	1	63	12	5	7	.491	.418
Socarras, Tony, R.C.*	.131	56	193	176	10	23	42	4	0	5	9	3	0	0	14	1	68	1	1	2	.239	.195
Soler, Ramon, Bak.†	.263	103	478	418	72	110	138	14	4	2	27	8	3	0	46	0	75	25	5	2	.330	.338
Sollmann, Scott, Mud.*	.333	4	18	18	2	6	10	2	1	0	1	0	0	0	0	0	5	1	0	0	.556	.333
Sosa, Nick, Mod.	.277	125	534	462	54	128	198	31	0	13	63	1	3	3	65	3	157	1	2	10	.429	.368
Soto, Jorge, Mod.	.200	19	68	55	5	11	24	2	1	3	12	1	0	0	12	0	31	0	0	0	.436	.343
Specht, Brian, R.C.†	.242	65	295	264	45	64	110	13	6	7	31	3	1	3	24	1	78	17	3	1	.417	.312
Spoerl, Josh, Mud.	.257	116	479	420	56	108	179	23	6	12	60	0	4	8	47	6	124	1	2	7	.426	.340
Strong, Jamal, S.B.	.311	81	393	331	74	103	118	11	2	0	32	6	0	5	51	2	60	47	9	3	.356	.411
Sykes, Jamie, Lan.	.245	43	168	155	21	38	61	11	0	4	19	2	0	1	10	0	42	4	5	3	.394	.295
Terrero, Luis, Lan.	.451	19	73	71	16	32	55	9	1	4	11	0	0	1	1	1	14	5	0	1	.775	.466
Thompson, Zachary, H.D.*	.077	5	17	13	2	1	1	0	0	0	1	1	0	0	3	0	3	0	0	0	.077	.250
Thurston, Jerrey, L.E.-Mud.	.167	21	72	66	5	11	11	0	0	0	2	0	0	1	5	0	27	0	0	3	.167	.236
Torcato, Tony, S.J.*	.341	67	286	258	38	88	119	21	2	2	47	0	7	4	17	3	40	9	3	5	.461	.381
Urquhart, Derick, R.C.*	.244	25	49	41	8	10	16	3	0	1	2	1	0	1	6	0	6	4	0	0	.390	.354
Urquiola, Carlos, Lan.*	.328	14	68	61	9	20	25	5	0	0	12	0	0	1	6	0	3	5	2	2	.410	.397
Valdez, Mario, Mod.*	.421	6	22	19	3	8	15	1	0	2	5	0	0	1	2	0	1	0	1	2	.789	.500
Van Rossum, Chris, Mud.*	.167	47	164	156	14	26	28	2	0	0	5	2	0	1	5	1	37	5	3	0	.179	.198
Vaz, Roberto, Mod.*	.294	48	207	180	24	53	69	13	0	1	25	0	2	2	23	3	35	19	2	8	.383	.377
Wagner, Jeff, R.C.	.291	113	452	402	51	117	180	37	1	8	56	1	2	9	38	2	82	4	3	2	.448	.364
Waldron, Jeff, Lan.*	.291	54	171	151	13	44	64	12	1	2	35	3	2	2	13	1	22	0	0	3	.424	.351
Welsh, Eric, Mud.*	.258	105	454	399	65	103	187	24	0	20	64	1	6	10	38	8	107	0	0	11	.469	.333
Wenner, Mike, Mod.	.270	114	402	427	57	118	153	14	3	5	48	9	2	6	18	0	73	33	10	5	.358	.313
Wilder, Paul, Bak.*	.265	30	116	98	15	26	37	5	0	2	13	0	0	3	15	0	45	1	0	1	.378	.379
Wilfong, Nick, S.J.*	.208	17	60	48	7	10	15	2	0	1	7	2	1	0	9	0	23	1	1	1	.313	.328

CLASS A *California League*

Player, Team	Avg.	G	TPA	AB	R	H	TB	2B	3B	HR	RBI	SH	SF	HP	BB	IBB	SO	SB	CS	GDP	Slg.	OBP
Williams, Jason, Lan.	.210	95	339	295	38	62	89	14	2	3	29	7	1	1	35	0	78	6	5	9	.302	.295
Williams, P.J., S.B.	.231	30	125	108	13	25	27	2	0	0	8	2	3	1	11	0	20	7	4	0	.250	.301
Woods, Blake, S.B.	.091	10	27	22	3	2	5	0	0	1	4	0	0	1	4	0	7	3	0	5	.227	.259
Woodward, Steve, Lan.†	.201	47	164	144	19	29	37	6	1	0	6	2	0	1	17	0	40	5	5	1	.257	.290
Yakopich, Joseph, Lan.*	.190	14	46	42	3	8	8	0	0	0	2	1	0	1	2	0	9	0	0	0	.190	.244
Zamora, Junior, R.C.	.288	12	53	52	9	15	28	2	1	3	8	0	0	0	1	0	14	3	0	2	.538	.302
Zeber, Ryan, R.C.	.239	31	104	92	11	22	32	4	0	2	12	0	1	1	10	0	29	0	0	2	.348	.317

PLAYERS WITH TWO OR MORE TEAMS

Player, Team	Avg.	G	TPA	AB	R	H	TB	2B	3B	HR	RBI	SH	SF	HP	BB	IBB	SO	SB	CS	GDP	Slg.	OBP
Hall, Justin, Mod.	.253	32	100	87	10	22	28	3	0	1	9	1	0	3	9	0	20	2	2	1	.322	.343
Hall, Justin, S.J.	.265	42	177	151	22	40	59	11	1	2	13	1	0	1	24	0	39	1	0	3	.391	.369
Moreta, Ramon, R.C.	.321	34	148	137	23	44	62	13	1	1	13	1	0	1	9	0	32	19	7	5	.453	.367
Moreta, Ramon, S.J.	.200	11	45	40	5	8	8	0	0	0	0	0	0	0	3	0	7	2	2	0	.200	.256
Nieckula, Aaron, Mod.	.289	26	98	83	12	24	36	1	1	3	11	2	0	5	8	0	19	0	1	2	.434	.385
Nieckula, Aaron, Vis.	.295	43	153	129	26	38	56	6	0	4	15	0	3	10	11	0	34	2	1	1	.434	.386
Rosario, Omar, Vis.*	.274	30	142	113	17	31	41	4	0	2	12	0	0	3	26	0	27	10	3	4	.363	.423
Rosario, Omar, Mod.*	.186	60	235	188	24	35	49	9	1	1	17	1	0	6	40	3	61	9	1	4	.261	.346
Thurston, Jerrey, L.E.	.156	14	48	45	3	7	7	0	0	0	2	0	0	1	2	0	20	0	0	1	.156	.208
Thurston, Jerrey, Mud.	.190	7	24	21	2	4	4	0	0	0	0	0	0	0	3	0	7	0	0	2	.190	.292

GRAND SLAMS: Martin, 3; Asche, Basabe, F. Gomez, Olson, Scarborough, 2 each; Burkhart, Burnett, Burns, Carvajal, Cosentino, M. Diaz, Eddleman, Faison, Gregg, Howe, R. Jones, Kata, Knox, McCorkle, Mounts, O'Keefe, Quintana, C. Rosario, Rushford, Senjam, Sosa, Soto, Spoerl, 1 each.

AWARDED FIRST BASE ON CATCHER'S INTERFERENCE: Contreras (K. Johnson), Gordon (K. Johnson), R. Jones (Napoli), Owens (Hammock).

2001 PITCHING
TEAM

Team	W	L	Pct.	ERA	G	CG	ShO	Sv.	IP	H	TBF	R	ER	HR	SH	SF	HB	BB	IBB	SO	WP	Bk.
Lake Elsinore	91	49	.650	3.03	140	1	13	44	1255.2	1069	5248	534	423	76	42	27	43	427	25	1343	72	11
San Bernardino	76	64	.543	3.45	140	2	12	36	1283.0	1133	5457	598	492	83	45	39	0	487	15	1262	67	9
Mudville	74	66	.529	3.60	140	3	9	38	1248.2	1204	5448	618	500	93	40	34	58	548	7	1209	80	9
Bakersfield	71	69	.507	4.04	140	1	9	41	1244.1	1268	5448	668	559	101	39	36	72	471	16	1206	77	9
Modesto	55	85	.393	4.24	140	1	5	23	1239.1	1313	5453	721	584	93	57	37	65	447	49	1006	64	4
San Jose	77	63	.550	4.32	140	1	7	40	1225.2	1233	5349	686	588	110	34	48	81	460	6	954	92	10
R. Cucamonga	63	77	.450	4.61	140	5	7	36	1238.2	1318	5511	742	637	116	44	39	88	484	20	1110	109	11
Visalia	61	79	.436	4.80	140	1	2	31	1232.2	1398	5545	796	657	125	47	44	76	451	18	1133	97	8
Lancaster	61	79	.436	4.95	140	3	6	26	1233.0	1423	5573	827	678	128	50	47	88	463	19	1118	100	18
High Desert	71	69	.507	5.27	140	1	4	30	1249.1	1392	5644	844	731	156	30	42	81	517	9	1183	103	3

INDIVIDUAL

TOP QUALIFIERS FOR EARNED-RUN AVERAGE TITLE

Minimum 112 innings.*Lefthanded pitcher.

Pitcher, Team	W	L	Pct.	ERA	G	GS	CG	ShO	GF	Sv.	IP	H	TBF	R	ER	HR	SH	SF	HB	BB	IBB	SO	WP	Bk.
Anderson, Craig, S.B.*	11	4	.733	2.26	28	28	0	0	0	0	179.0	142	718	65	45	16	3	7	7	39	0	178	4	1
Gray, Brett, Mud.	10	4	.714	2.42	29	18	0	0	2	0	141.1	133	585	48	38	6	2	2	4	37	0	110	8	1
Thornton, Matt, S.B.*	14	7	.667	2.52	27	27	0	0	0	0	157.0	126	650	56	44	9	2	5	11	60	0	192	12	0
Bazzell, Shane, Mod.	10	4	.714	2.73	28	20	0	0	1	0	135.0	116	549	51	41	9	1	4	3	38	1	129	6	3
Rojas, Chris, L.E.	10	5	.667	3.43	28	28	0	0	0	0	160.0	135	681	72	61	14	3	2	12	71	0	149	16	2
Walk, Mitch, S.J.*	9	6	.600	3.54	27	19	0	0	0	0	117.0	115	499	57	46	13	4	6	7	39	0	59	3	0
Cozier, Vance, S.J.	15	7	.682	3.61	30	29	1	0	0	0	169.2	158	698	71	68	17	5	4	6	45	1	98	9	0
Cordova, Jorge, Mud.	9	8	.529	3.72	30	25	0	0	1	0	154.2	157	671	81	64	11	6	8	3	67	0	132	13	1
Stokes, Brian, Bak.	8	6	.571	3.92	32	20	1	0	5	1	128.2	118	565	65	56	11	4	5	8	64	0	92	9	0
Wagner, Denny, Mod.	7	9	.438	3.99	30	30	1	0	0	0	169.0	181	744	101	75	14	6	6	12	59	3	127	8	0
Webb, Brandon, Lan.	6	10	.375	3.99	29	28	0	0	0	0	162.1	174	711	90	72	9	3	6	27	44	0	158	11	1
Nix, Wayne, Vis.	9	7	.563	4.01	26	25	1	0	1	0	148.0	149	628	81	66	18	3	2	6	36	0	167	12	1
Salmon, Brad, Mud.	5	8	.385	4.06	33	18	1	0	3	0	135.1	132	587	75	61	10	5	3	6	51	0	110	11	0
Torres, Melqui, S.B.	7	7	.500	4.15	26	26	0	0	0	0	154.0	159	666	79	71	4	10	4	23	56	0	113	8	1
Santos, Alex, Bak.	11	9	.550	4.15	24	24	0	0	0	0	134.1	149	603	75	62	10	2	5	6	49	0	150	4	1

DEPARTMENTAL LEADERS: W—Cozier, 15; L—Gwyn, 13; Pct.—Shibilo, .833; G—Shibilo, 60; GS—Wagner, 30; CG—Soriano, 2; ShO—Several tied at 1; GF—L. Anderson, 56; Sv.—L. Anderson, 30; IP—C. Anderson, 179; H—Slaten, 207; TBF—Wagner, 744; R—Stewart, 106; ER—Wilson, 93; HR—Stewart, 23; SH—Torres, 10; SF—Cordova, Stewart, Wilson, 8 each; HB—Webb, 27; BB—Rojas, 71; IBB—C. Sanchez, 9; SO—Thornton, 192; WP—Wilson, 19; BK—Slaten, 5.

ALL PITCHERS

*Lefthanded pitcher.

Pitcher, Team	W	L	Pct.	ERA	G	GS	CG	ShO	GF	Sv.	IP	H	TBF	R	ER	HR	SH	SF	HB	BB	IBB	SO	WP	Bk.
Ah Yat, Paul, S.J.*	2	1	.667	4.50	5	4	0	0	0	0	18.0	14	79	13	9	4	1	1	0	17		4	1	
Alfano, Jeff, S.J.	0	0	.000	5.63	8	0	0	0	8	0	8.0	8	39	8	5	1	0	3	1	5	0	5	2	0
Allen, Rod, H.D.	4	6	.400	4.37	43	0	0	0	13	1	78.1	72	329	44	38	9	6	3	2	28	1	95	5	0
Altman, Gene, H.D.	2	2	.500	7.85	38	0	0	0	29	12	39.0	46	207	36	34	2	3	2	1	39	0	46	13	0
Ammons, Cary, Mud.*	1	4	.200	2.94	14	9	0	0	2	0	64.1	53	277	28	21	6	0	1	3	31	0	81	2	1
Andersen, Derek, Bak.*	2	1	.667	3.38	18	0	0	0	0	0	24.0	19	93	9	9	1	1	0	1	6	0	26	1	1
Anderson, Craig, S.B.*	11	4	.733	2.26	28	28	0	0	0	0	179.0	142	718	65	45	16	3	7	7	39	0	178	4	1
Anderson, Luke, S.J.	2	2	.500	2.59	59	0	0	0	56	30	66.0	56	268	22	19	4	0	1	0	13	0	76	4	0
Backe, Brandon, Bak.	1	0	1.000	1.09	17	0	0	0	12	3	24.2	13	97	7	3	1	0	2	0	8	0	33	2	0
Baek, Cha, S.B.	1	0	1.000	3.43	5	4	0	0	0	0	21.0	17	81	10	8	0	0	2	0	5	0	14	0	0
Balbuena, Caleb, S.B.	0	5	.000	6.86	36	5	0	0	4	1	63.0	78	321	57	48	4	1	2	13	44	0	56	5	0
Barber, Scott, Lan.	7	7	.500	7.20	29	12	0	0	8	2	85.0	121	405	76	68	16	0	1	5	27	2	83	5	0

Pitcher, Team	W	L	Pct.	ERA	G	GS	CG	ShO	GF	Sv.	IP	H	TBF	R	ER	HR	SH	SF	HB	BB	IBB	SO	WP	Bk.
Bartosh, Cliff, L.E.*	6	2	.750	1.58	38	0	0	0	25	10	45.2	42	194	17	8	2	2	1	2	12	5	66	7	2
Bausher, Andy, L.E.*	2	2	.500	2.76	37	2	0	0	12	1	65.1	55	269	28	20	3	2	0	1	16	2	53	1	1
Bazzell, Shane, Mod.	10	4	.714	2.73	28	20	0	0	1	0	135.0	116	549	51	41	9	1	4	3	38	1	129	6	3
Belflower, Jay, Lan.	2	2	.500	0.62	27	0	0	0	22	11	29.0	15	115	5	2	1	2	1	3	6	3	24	1	0
Bermudez, Manny, S.J.	8	2	.800	3.56	43	0	0	0	11	1	81.0	87	346	36	32	3	6	1	8	23	0	40	2	0
Birdsong, Tim, Mud.	3	4	.429	5.02	23	0	0	0	20	5	28.2	39	143	21	16	3	1	1	2	15	2	31	2	1
Bootcheck, Chris, R.C.	8	4	.667	3.93	15	14	1	0	0	0	87.0	84	359	45	38	11	0	1	0	23	0	86	4	0
Bowser, Matt, Vis.*	0	0	.000	0.00	1	0	0	0	1	0	1.0	1	1	0	0	0	0	0	0	0	0	0	0	0
Bradley, Dave, Mud.	1	1	.500	6.32	15	1	0	0	5	1	31.1	36	153	25	22	2	2	3	3	24	0	31	1	0
Brink, Jim, Mod.	0	3	.000	3.03	24	0	0	0	18	4	32.2	33	137	17	11	2	3	0	3	10	4	26	1	0
Brooks, Conor, Vis.	5	5	.500	4.48	45	4	0	0	12	0	84.1	98	376	55	42	11	3	5	8	22	1	64	2	1
Brous, Dave, S.J.*	2	4	.333	6.19	11	9	0	0	2	0	32.0	28	160	25	22	2	2	1	4	36	0	18	4	0
Brown, Elliot, S.J.	4	0	1.000	0.93	5	5	0	0	0	0	29.0	15	107	3	3	1	0	0	0	7	0	26	1	0
Brummett, Sean, R.C.*	2	4	.333	4.93	7	6	1	0	0	0	38.1	40	109	24	21	4	1	1	3	10	0	28	4	0
Burnstead, Mike, L.E.	1	2	.333	6.68	19	0	0	0	6	0	32.1	05	140	25	24	5	1	1	0	18	5	33	1	0
Callier, Jeremy, R.C.	0	0	.000	0.00	2	1	0	0	0	0	4.0	1	13	0	0	0	0	0	0	0	0	3	0	0
Cannon, Jon, S.J.	3	1	.750	3.24	22	0	0	0	6	2	41.2	36	174	17	15	2	1	1	3	18	0	48	4	0
Carbajal, Alex, Bak.*	2	1	.667	7.11	24	0	0	0	13	0	31.2	43	150	26	25	7	1	1	1	11	0	34	1	0
Carter, Justin, Mud.*	3	5	.375	4.35	10	10	1	1	0	0	49.2	42	225	32	24	1	2	2	3	38	0	43	7	0
Cash, David, S.J.	4	0	1.000	2.08	20	0	0	0	6	1	39.0	23	157	9	9	4	1	1	3	17	0	46	3	0
Castillo, Dan, Lan.	1	3	.250	5.30	23	7	0	0	12	4	52.2	56	235	33	31	6	1	1	3	21	0	64	12	0
Ceriani, Matt, H.D.	0	0	.000	0.00	1	0	0	0	1	0	1.0	0	4	0	0	0	0	0	1	0	0	0	0	0
Childers, Matt, H.D.	6	11	.353	6.44	20	20	0	0	0	0	117.1	155	529	95	84	19	3	7	6	29	0	76	5	0
Coleman, Jeff, Vis.	0	4	.000	6.45	16	4	0	0	0	0	37.2	57	186	32	27	3	1	1	3	16	0	38	2	0
Cook, Josh, S.J.	0	0	.000	27.00	1	0	0	0	1	0	1.0	6	9	4	3	1	0	0	0	0	0	0	0	0
Cordova, Jorge, Mud.	9	8	.529	3.72	30	25	0	0	1	0	154.2	157	671	81	64	11	6	8	3	67	0	132	13	1
Corey, Mike, H.D.	3	3	.500	4.14	47	0	0	0	19	2	76.0	83	338	45	35	7	3	1	5	35	2	70	6	0
Cornejo, Jesse, Bak.*	0	1	.000	4.05	9	0	0	0	1	0	13.1	17	69	12	6	3	1	0	1	8	1	16	0	0
Cotts, Neal, Vis.*	3	2	.600	2.32	7	7	0	0	0	0	31.0	27	139	14	8	0	0	1	3	15	0	34	0	0
Coward, Tim, Bak.	2	2	.500	2.00	32	4	0	0	10	3	67.1	59	279	20	15	1	2	0	1	22	2	65	2	0
Cozler, Vance, S.J.	15	7	.682	3.61	30	29	1	0	0	0	169.2	158	698	71	68	17	5	4	6	45	1	98	9	0
Crawford, Wesley, R.C.*	6	7	.462	5.21	21	13	0	0	1	0	93.1	109	418	60	54	9	2	2	5	28	0	56	2	0
Crowell, Kyle, Mod.	3	10	.231	5.37	37	10	0	0	8	2	112.1	135	502	70	67	6	8	4	10	33	4	97	3	0
Cullen, Ryan, Mod.*	2	4	.333	4.23	40	3	0	0	12	1	83.0	112	380	58	39	5	3	1	4	24	3	53	2	0
Culp, Brandon, Mud.	1	0	1.000	4.07	9	3	0	0	1	0	24.1	24	110	15	11	2	0	2	2	14	0	25	0	0
Cyr, Eric, L.E.*	7	4	.636	1.61	21	16	0	0	0	0	100.2	68	399	28	18	1	3	0	3	24	0	131	1	0
Darnell, Paul, Mud.*	2	1	.667	3.38	5	5	0	0	0	0	32.0	27	131	13	12	4	0	0	2	8	0	33	0	0
Dehart, Casey, Mud.*	4	3	.571	2.23	49	0	0	0	20	4	68.2	54	292	20	17	3	5	2	3	36	1	64	7	0
De La Cruz, Jose, Vis.	0	0	.000	9.00	1	0	0	0	1	0	1.0	3	7	1	1	0	0	1	0	0	0	0	0	0
Delgado, Danny, S.B.	4	7	.364	5.40	36	10	0	0	7	1	103.1	130	464	68	62	13	3	7	6	24	1	90	4	0
Domouy, Chris, R.C.*	0	1	.000	2.70	7	0	0	0	2	0	10.0	7	39	3	3	1	0	0	3	0	6	1	0
Dent, Doug, Mud.	6	3	.667	3.92	24	3	0	0	6	2	64.1	69	286	34	28	6	2	3	7	24	0	63	5	1
DePaula, Freddy, Vis.*	2	1	.667	5.63	15	5	0	0	5	0	32.0	31	141	20	20	3	1	0	1	19	0	30	0	1
Diaz, Alex, Vis.	3	1	.750	5.55	32	0	0	0	7	0	48.2	62	219	33	30	10	3	2	3	12	2	33	1	0
Dunn, Scott, Mud.	5	3	.625	2.11	10	10	1	1	0	0	59.2	45	248	17	14	2	0	1	1	31	0	73	4	0
Eriksen, Tanner, Lan.	3	6	.333	6.46	19	13	0	0	1	0	71.0	95	351	66	51	3	4	5	2	49	1	52	11	0
Espina, Rendy, R.C.*	0	0	.000	21.60	2	1	0	0	0	0	1.2	4	11	4	4	1	0	1	2	0	0	2	0	0
Esteves, Jake, S.J.	0	3	.000	7.36	9	9	0	0	0	0	14.2	13	65	12	12	3	0	1	9	10	0	19	0	0
Farley, Joe, S.J.*	1	0	1.000	7.09	18	0	0	0	4	0	26.2	28	126	22	21	3	0	2	1	20	0	15	4	1
Farmer, Jason, S.J.	6	1	.857	4.62	14	13	0	0	0	0	62.1	77	281	37	32	4	2	0	5	20	0	52	0	0
Fischer, Steve, Vis.	7	7	.500	4.61	34	20	0	0	6	1	121.0	140	540	77	62	12	5	6	7	41	2	88	5	0
Flores, Ron, Mod.*	5	2	.714	2.86	47	0	0	0	23	6	66.0	53	282	24	21	4	6	2	1	29	7	71	3	0
Frendling, Neal, Bak.	6	8	.429	4.58	20	20	0	0	0	0	112.0	105	486	62	57	8	5	4	10	38	0	107	12	0
Frias, Juan, S.J.	0	0	.000	10.50	4	0	0	0	1	0	6.0	9	37	8	7	0	0	1	1	9	0	5	4	0
Fuller, Jody, Lan.	2	3	.400	4.50	23	1	0	0	8	0	36.0	43	168	23	18	4	3	0	1	19	0	27	4	0
Gaal, Bryan, L.E.	3	3	.500	3.64	35	0	0	0	11	3	47.0	37	195	23	19	3	1	4	2	17	1	50	4	1
Gann, Jamie, Lan.	0	1	.000	6.10	9	0	0	0	4	0	10.1	5	43	7	7	1	0	0	0	7	0	10	2	0
Garber, Mike, Lan.*	0	2	.000	6.38	25	0	0	0	3	0	24.0	41	126	22	17	4	1	3	0	14	1	21	4	0
German, Frank, Vis.	2	4	.333	3.98	53	0	0	0	45	19	63.1	67	294	34	28	7	3	2	2	31	1	93	11	0
Giron, Roberto, H.D.	3	2	.600	3.27	45	0	0	0	30	12	63.1	64	283	35	23	4	4	4	3	20	1	86	6	0
Gomez, Andre, L.E.	1	0	1.000	0.00	1	0	0	0	1	0	2.0	0	8	0	0	0	1	0	0	2	1	1	0	0
Good, Andrew, Lan.	8	6	.571	4.80	19	18	0	0	0	0	101.1	108	454	63	54	12	6	4	13	27	0	104	5	0
Goodrich, Randy, S.J.	0	9	.000	8.63	15	13	0	0	1	0	56.1	89	282	58	54	7	1	3	6	23	0	34	1	0
Gray, Brett, Mud.	10	4	.714	2.42	29	18	0	0	2	0	141.1	133	585	48	38	6	2	2	4	37	0	110	8	1
Grezlovski, Ben, R.C.	2	4	.333	4.20	48	0	0	0	21	8	64.1	60	285	37	30	6	3	7	2	29	1	74	8	1
Gwyn, Mark, Mod.	3	13	.188	4.63	28	25	0	0	1	0	140.0	137	617	85	72	9	6	4	9	59	3	101	6	0
Harris, Julian, R.C.*	0	1	.000	3.28	25	0	0	0	10	0	35.2	36	160	22	13	3	1	2	0	17	1	31	3	0
Harville, Chad, Mod. Vis.	0	0	.000	1.50	3	2	0	0	0	0	6.0	5	24	2	1	0	1	0	0	4	0	6	0	0
Hasegawa, Shigetoshi, R.C.	0	0	.000	0.00	2	2	0	0	0	0	2.0	3	10	1	0	0	2	0	0	1	0	1	0	0
Haworth, Brent, R.C.	0	0	.000	13.50	5	0	0	0	2	0	8.0	15	43	13	12	2	0	0	4	2	0	4	0	0
Hensley, Matt, R.C.	2	7	.222	5.93	14	12	0	0	0	0	68.1	85	319	57	45	4	2	7	8	24	0	58	4	1
Hitchcock, Sterling, L.E.*	0	0	.000	4.10	6	6	0	0	0	0	26.1	33	116	18	12	3	1	1	0	1	0	31	1	0
Hoerman, Jared, S.B.	0	0	.000	3.86	11	0	0	0	5	0	18.2	16	84	11	8	1	1	0	4	7	0	18	0	0
Holtz, Mike, R.C.*	0	0	.000	9.00	2	0	0	0	2	0	2.0	3	9	2	2	1	0	0	0	1	0	3	0	0
Howard, Ben, L.E.	8	2	.800	2.83	18	18	0	0	0	0	101.2	86	414	37	32	4	3	1	32	0	107	3	0
Howington, Ty, Mud.*	3	2	.600	2.43	7	7	0	0	0	0	37.0	33	168	18	10	2	2	1	4	20	0	44	2	0
Huggins, Dave, H.D.	2	1	.667	6.92	14	9	0	0	2	0	53.1	68	259	51	41	10	3	0	5	24	0	35	3	0
Hundley, Jeff, R.C.*	2	1	.667	4.19	13	7	0	0	0	0	53.2	48	222	25	25	10	3	2	3	17	1	38	1	0
Hunter, Johnny, L.E.	3	0	1.000	3.82	7	5	0	0	0	0	33.0	27	134	19	14	1	0	1	0	11	0	29	1	0
Jacobs, Greg, R.C.-Lan.*	3	5	.375	6.82	51	0	0	0	9	0	64.2	79	308	59	49	10	4	1	8	30	1	71	3	1
Johnson, Rett, S.B.	6	2	.750	4.09	12	12	0	0	0	0	66.0	56	283	36	30	5	1	2	4	33	0	70	5	2
Jones, Greg, R.C.	1	3	.250	4.23	6	6	0	0	0	0	27.2	25	118	15	13	2	1	1	4	11	0	27	3	0
Joseph, Kevin, S.J.	0	0	.000	3.38	9	0	0	0	4	1	13.1	12	53	6	5	0	0	3	2	1	0	15	2	0

Pitcher, Team	W	L	Pct.	ERA	G	GS	CG	ShO	GF	Sv.	IP	H	TBF	R	ER	HR	SH	SF	HB	BB	IBB	SO	WP	Bk.
Kenney, Jeff, H.D.	0	0	.000	0.00	1	0	0	0	1	0	1.1	0	4	0	0	0	0	0	0	0	0	0	0	0
Kent, Steve, S.B.*	0	3	.000	2.20	51	0	0	0	12	1	65.1	50	285	21	16	2	3	2	2	34	0	73	4	1
Kison, Robbie, Mud.	0	0	.000	0.00	2	0	0	0	2	0	2.0	1	10	0	0	0	0	0	0	3	0	1	0	0
Kofler, Ed, Bak.	5	6	.455	4.23	15	14	0	0	0	0	78.2	88	344	43	37	11	1	1	1	25	0	74	0	1
Koronka, John, Mud.*	5	2	.714	4.94	12	12	0	0	0	0	71.0	78	321	44	39	10	1	1	2	39	0	66	3	3
Lara, Nelson, Mud.	0	0	.000	16.88	2	0	0	0	0	0	2.2	4	20	5	5	0	0	0	1	7	0	0	0	0
Lee, Jon, Lan.	0	1	.000	11.37	5	0	0	0	1	0	6.1	14	35	12	8	0	1	1	1	1	1	4	1	1
Leyva, Julian, Mod.	0	0	.000	7.71	5	0	0	0	0	0	14.0	21	67	16	12	4	0	0	1	2	0	7	0	0
Loewer, Carlton, L.E.	0	1	.000	1.59	4	4	0	0	0	0	11.1	6	47	7	2	0	0	1	4	0	14	0	0
Looper, Aaron, S.B.	6	11	.353	2.79	56	0	0	0	24	5	71.0	59	295	34	22	1	5	2	3	22	5	77	7	0
Lopez, Javier, Lan.*	1	3	.250	2.63	17	0	0	0	10	1	24.0	30	103	9	7	2	2	0	0	5	0	18	1	1
Lopez, Rodrigo, L.E.	0	1	.000	0.69	9	0	0	0	2	0	13.0	15	60	7	1	1	1	0	4	0	9	0	0
Lowe, Benny, Mud.*	1	1	.500	4.05	4	0	0	0	3	0	6.2	4	27	3	3	0	0	1	1	3	0	7	1	0
Luque, Roger, L.E.*	0	0	.000	27.00	1	0	0	0	0	0	1.0	3	7	3	3	1	0	0	1	1	0	1	0	0
Lynch, Jim, H.D.	2	5	.286	6.64	37	8	0	0	8	0	66.1	99	401	71	63	15	0	7	40	1	114	10	0
Malaska, Mark, Bak.*	2	1	.667	4.08	3	3	0	0	0	0	17.2	14	70	8	8	1	1	0	0	5	0	13	1	0
Manias, Jim, Mud.*	3	2	.600	2.78	24	0	0	0	7	2	45.1	38	187	16	14	5	2	0	2	12	0	45	2	0
Martinez, Javier, Mud.	3	0	1.000	2.16	16	0	0	0	8	0	16.2	14	68	4	4	2	0	0	1	6	0	21	1	0
Martinez, Luis, H.D.*	8	9	.471	5.19	22	22	0	0	0	0	112.2	112	498	67	65	9	2	2	4	64	0	121	9	1
Martinez, Renan, R.C.*	4	3	.571	4.33	43	1	0	0	16	0	54.0	65	261	34	26	5	3	2	7	28	0	49	3	1
Mateo, Julio, S.B.	5	4	.556	2.86	56	0	0	0	47	26	66.0	58	273	28	21	5	2	1	2	16	5	79	1	1
Mathews, Dan, H.D.	4	3	.571	6.14	36	0	0	0	15	1	51.1	61	238	38	35	6	1	0	4	25	0	59	3	1
Matzenbacher, Brian, Lan.	5	4	.556	3.55	48	0	0	0	16	3	78.2	85	340	39	31	4	6	2	5	23	1	85	7	0
Mazur, Bryan, Vis.*	3	7	.300	5.95	48	0	0	0	19	5	62.0	81	292	48	41	4	8	2	5	27	2	45	3	0
McCall, Derell, Mod.	1	6	.143	4.15	39	4	0	0	23	3	86.2	105	378	50	40	8	6	1	1	20	2	55	10	1
McClain, Kevin, R.C.	2	0	1.000	4.25	23	0	0	0	2	0	36.0	33	155	17	17	3	2	3	4	12	0	40	2	1
McCutcheon, Mike, Lan.*	1	2	.333	10.38	12	0	0	0	4	1	8.2	9	41	10	10	1	1	1	0	7	2	8	1	0
McDougall, Marshall, Vis.	1	0	1.000	0.00	1	0	0	0	1	0	1.0	1	3	0	0	0	0	0	0	0	0	0	0	0
McGerry, Kevin, Mod.	1	7	.125	8.49	15	9	0	0	4	0	35.0	39	194	45	33	4	0	2	5	45	0	30	3	0
Mears, Chris, S.B.	7	6	.538	4.46	38	12	0	0	4	0	107.0	104	470	59	53	10	7	3	11	49	1	74	6	1
Medders, Brandon, Lan.	1	2	.333	1.32	31	0	0	0	15	3	41.0	26	163	8	6	1	2	1	2	15	3	53	2	1
Mendoza, Hatuey, Lan.	8	5	.615	4.70	24	16	1	1	1	0	105.1	114	455	69	55	17	2	5	4	43	0	72	7	3
Mendoza, Mario, R.C.	2	4	.333	5.44	8	8	0	0	0	0	43.0	56	200	37	26	5	2	4	12	0	22	4	1
Messman, Joe, S.J.	3	1	.750	3.86	23	0	0	0	8	2	42.0	47	186	28	18	3	2	2	2	15	0	24	7	2
Miller, Benji, S.J.	0	0	.000	0.00	1	0	0	0	0	0	1.0	0	3	0	0	0	0	0	0	0	0	2	0	0
Miller, Corey, Mod.	5	4	.556	3.45	43	0	0	0	17	2	70.1	70	297	29	27	9	3	2	0	25	7	65	1	0
Milo, Tony, R.C.*	3	1	.750	0.97	24	0	0	0	8	2	37.0	24	150	5	4	0	4	1	0	17	4	45	3	0
Minaya, Edwin, Vis.	0	3	.000	5.34	13	3	0	0	2	2	28.2	31	145	33	17	1	0	5	0	16	0	22	9	1
Minix, Travis, S.B.	5	1	.833	3.34	44	0	0	0	25	10	67.1	67	287	27	25	3	2	1	1	19	3	70	4	1
Montgomery, Matt, Bak.	2	3	.400	4.76	14	0	0	0	3	1	22.2	20	94	13	12	3	1	2	0	7	1	29	3	0
Montgomery, Steve, L.E.	0	0	.000	21.60	2	1	0	0	0	0	1.2	4	9	4	4	2	0	1	0	0	0	2	1	0
Montoya, Saul, Lan.	0	1	.000	5.65	9	0	0	0	4	0	14.1	20	68	11	9	3	0	0	2	7	0	8	1	1
Moore, Darin, Vis.	1	4	.200	8.74	38	3	0	0	8	0	58.2	66	307	69	57	7	0	5	12	51	3	56	15	1
Navarro, Scott, Vis.*	0	1	.000	5.06	14	0	0	0	5	1	21.1	20	91	12	12	2	1	0	2	7	0	22	0	0
Neu, Mike, Mud.	3	2	.600	2.37	53	0	0	0	44	21	64.2	50	277	21	17	3	4	1	3	30	4	102	5	1
Nicolas, Mike, L.E.	0	1	.000	5.25	8	0	0	0	2	0	12.0	11	51	7	7	2	1	0	1	5	0	15	1	0
Nix, Wayne, Vis.	9	7	.563	4.01	26	25	1	0	1	0	148.0	149	628	81	66	18	3	2	6	36	0	167	12	1
Noriega, Ray, Mod.*	3	1	.750	1.69	13	0	0	0	8	2	21.1	13	83	4	4	1	1	0	3	7	2	19	1	0
Norris, Ben, Lan.*	1	0	1.000	5.68	2	2	0	0	0	0	12.2	16	55	9	8	2	0	0	1	2	1	18	0	0
O'Brien, Matt, Vis.*	9	9	.500	4.70	27	24	0	0	2	0	145.2	161	637	86	76	12	4	4	6	39	0	148	12	0
O'Neal, Brandon, R.C.	0	3	.000	5.63	10	6	0	0	0	0	32.0	37	157	24	20	1	2	1	5	25	0	20	7	0
Ortiz, Jose, Bak.	3	3	.500	3.79	35	0	0	0	16	0	71.1	77	321	34	30	5	4	3	8	29	3	57	7	2
Oxspring, Chris, L.E.	0	0	.000	0.64	7	0	0	0	2	0	14.0	10	56	2	1	1	0	0	0	6	2	17	0	0
Pace, Adam, R.C.*	1	1	.500	4.15	3	3	1	0	0	0	21.2	30	98	11	10	2	0	0	0	6	2	13	0	0
Parker, Brandon, S.B.	4	0	1.000	4.30	15	0	0	0	5	0	23.0	18	102	13	11	5	1	0	1	18	0	28	0	0
Parker, Matt, H.D.	13	6	.684	4.30	28	28	1	0	0	0	161.0	167	704	88	77	17	2	6	8	67	1	134	9	0
Patterson, John, Lan.	0	0	.000	5.79	2	2	0	0	0	0	9.1	9	40	6	6	3	0	0	0	3	0	9	0	0
Pavon, Julio, S.J.	1	0	1.000	8.74	6	0	0	0	3	0	11.1	14	50	12	11	2	0	1	2	2	1	14	0	0
Peavy, Jake, L.E.	7	5	.583	3.08	19	19	0	0	0	0	105.1	76	422	41	36	6	2	1	6	33	1	144	5	0
Pember, Dave, H.D.	9	6	.600	4.82	20	20	0	0	0	0	121.1	135	533	73	65	12	2	7	7	35	1	96	14	0
Perez, Oliver, L.E.*	2	4	.333	2.72	9	9	0	0	0	0	53.0	45	231	22	16	4	3	2	1	25	0	62	6	0
Phillips, Mark, L.E.*	2	1	.667	2.57	5	5	0	0	0	0	28.0	19	116	8	8	0	1	1	0	14	0	34	2	0
Pines, Gregory, S.B.	0	1	.000	6.75	1	0	0	0	1	0	1.1	4	9	1	1	0	0	1	1	1	0	0	0	0
Polanco, Elvis, H.D.	3	3	.500	4.50	42	0	0	0	13	2	84.0	98	371	47	42	16	0	2	8	19	1	77	6	1
Pugmire, Rob, Mud.	0	2	.000	7.79	4	4	0	0	0	0	17.1	25	85	16	15	4	1	0	0	10	0	19	1	0
Ramirez, Erasmo, S.J.*	3	2	.600	3.41	17	0	0	0	6	1	31.2	23	126	14	12	2	2	0	5	0	33	2	0
Ramos, Juan, S.B.	4	3	.571	2.63	39	0	0	0	10	2	65.0	45	275	23	19	1	3	0	6	30	1	57	7	2
Ratliff, Jon, Mod.	0	0	.000	1.29	4	0	0	0	2	0	7.0	4	28	1	1	0	0	0	3	0	6	1	0
Renteria, Juan, Bak.	0	0	.000	0.00	1	0	0	0	1	0	1.1	0	4	0	0	0	0	0	0	1	0	1	0	0
Rheinecker, John, Mod.*	0	1	.000	6.30	2	2	0	0	0	0	10.0	10	45	7	7	1	0	0	5	1	5	1	0
Robinson, Dustin, Mud.	2	4	.333	3.98	30	0	0	0	8	3	54.1	53	234	28	24	3	4	1	2	19	0	43	2	0
Robinson, Jeff, H.D.	2	1	.667	5.56	5	5	0	0	0	0	22.2	20	105	16	14	2	0	0	5	15	0	24	0	0
Robinson, Jeremy, Bak.*	0	1	.000	11.05	5	0	0	0	2	0	7.1	12	43	11	9	0	0	1	0	12	0	3	1	0
Rodarmel, Rich, Vis.	0	0	.000	11.57	2	0	0	0	2	1	2.1	3	13	3	3	0	0	0	0	3	0	0	0	0
Rodriguez, Francisco, R.C.	5	7	.417	5.38	20	20	1	1	0	0	113.2	127	523	72	68	13	2	1	6	55	1	147	17	4
Rojas, Chris, L.E.*	10	5	.667	3.43	28	28	0	0	0	0	160.1	135	681	72	61	14	3	2	12	71	0	149	16	2
Ruhl, Nathan, Bak.*	1	2	.333	4.94	12	4	0	0	2	1	31.0	37	149	17	17	3	0	2	1	13	2	31	2	1
Salmon, Brad, Mud.	5	8	.385	4.06	33	18	1	0	8	0	135.1	132	587	75	61	10	5	3	6	51	0	110	11	0
Sanchez, Cade, Mod.	3	6	.333	3.93	39	0	0	0	21	3	55.0	57	260	30	24	1	6	3	9	34	9	54	8	0
Sanchez, Duaner, Lan.	2	4	.333	4.58	10	10	1	0	0	0	53.0	65	270	44	30	7	4	4	7	18	0	49	3	4
Santos, Alex, Bak.	11	9	.550	4.15	24	24	0	0	0	0	134.1	149	603	75	62	10	2	5	6	49	0	150	4	1
Schneider, Scott, R.C.	4	6	.400	4.23	53	0	0	0	17	3	78.2	81	358	37	37	4	5	0	5	42	5	79	12	2
Schneidmiller, Gary, Vis.	0	0	.000	9.00	1	0	0	0	0	0	1.0	3	8	2	1	1	0	0	0	1	0	0	0	0

Pitcher, Team	W	L	Pct.	ERA	G	GS	CG	ShO	GF	Sv.	IP	H	TBF	R	ER	HR	SH	SF	HB	BB	IBB	SO	WP	Bk.
Schultz, Jeff, Vis.	3	6	.333	3.45	56	0	0	0	20	2	73.0	75	328	34	28	4	4	1	6	33	5	60	6	2
Seabury, Jaron, H.D.	0	1	.000	19.89	3	0	0	0	1	0	6.1	18	45	17	14	2	0	0	0	6	0	5	4	0
Seanez, Rudy, L.E.	2	0	1.000	2.08	7	0	0	0	0	0	8.2	7	34	3	2	1	0	0	0	2	0	8	0	0
Shabansky, Rob, Lan.*	0	2	.000	7.42	29	0	0	0	9	0	30.1	41	150	31	25	3	2	0	3	17	0	35	6	0
Shaffar, Ben, Mud.	3	2	.600	3.52	6	6	0	0	0	0	30.2	29	130	15	12	3	0	1	3	12	0	24	3	0
Shibilo, Andy, L.E.	10	2	.833	1.96	60	0	0	0	30	15	82.2	66	343	24	18	4	2	2	6	27	1	105	8	2
Shiyuk, Todd, L.E.*	6	3	.667	3.98	50	0	0	0	18	2	72.1	66	305	35	32	4	4	3	1	28	4	75	5	0
Sikaras, Pete, Lan.	1	1	.500	6.20	18	0	0	0	7	1	24.2	25	112	22	17	2	0	1	1	18	1	20	4	0
Simpson, Allan, S.B.	1	0	1.000	1.80	16	0	0	0	5	1	30.0	19	121	7	6	1	1	1	0	12	1	40	2	0
Slaten, Doug, Lan.*	9	8	.529	4.79	28	27	1	0	0	0	157.2	207	723	105	84	16	5	5	4	45	3	110	6	5
Smith, Hans, Bak.*	1	0	1.000	1.45	31	0	0	0	23	17	37.1	36	165	10	6	2	1	2	0	15	1	42	1	0
Soriano, Rafael, S.B.	6	3	.667	2.53	15	15	2	1	0	0	89.0	49	346	28	25	4	2	2	4	39	0	98	2	0
Stafford, Mike, H.D.*	1	1	.500	4.35	24	0	0	0	6	0	20.2	20	88	10	10	2	0	0	0	6	0	17	0	0
Stephens, Jason, R.C.	3	2	.600	2.20	8	5	0	0	0	0	32.2	35	135	11	8	1	1	1	2	4	0	19	0	1
Stevenson, Jason, L.E.	1	1	.500	5.65	11	9	0	0	0	0	14.1	26	71	12	9	2	1	1	0	9	0	19	0	1
Stewart, Paul, R.C.	9	8	.529	5.16	28	27	1	0	1	0	151.2	169	693	106	87	23	3	8	15	64	1	127	12	0
Stockman, Phil, Lan.	0	0	.000	5.09	8	0	0	0	1	0	17.2	11	70	11	10	2	1	4	1	9	0	18	1	0
Stokes, Brian, Bak.	8	6	.571	3.92	32	20	1	0	5	1	128.2	118	565	65	56	11	4	5	8	64	0	92	9	0
Stokley, Billy, R.C.	2	0	1.000	4.18	27	0	0	0	24	10	28.0	27	126	15	13	2	0	0	1	18	3	24	2	0
Stull, Everett, H.D.	0	1	.000	16.88	1	1	0	0	0	0	2.2	6	15	5	5	1	0	0	0	1	0	1	0	0
Surkont, Keith, Mod.	8	9	.471	5.31	24	24	0	0	0	0	123.2	152	564	90	73	7	3	7	1	42	0	93	8	0
Tankersley, Dennis, L.E.	5	1	.833	0.52	9	8	0	0	0	0	52.1	29	196	5	3	1	1	0	0	12	0	68	0	0
Taschner, Jack, S.J.*	4	4	.500	4.11	14	14	0	0	0	0	65.2	62	292	33	30	7	1	3	5	29	0	72	8	2
Thames, Charlie, R.C.	4	2	.667	1.52	29	0	0	0	26	13	29.2	21	118	9	5	1	1	0	0	9	1	26	2	0
Therneau, Dave, Mud.	1	5	.167	6.07	10	9	0	0	0	0	46.0	64	213	39	31	5	1	1	0	11	0	41	0	0
Thompson, Mike, L.E.	5	4	.556	5.35	19	12	0	0	1	0	74.0	82	318	46	44	7	5	2	3	25	0	39	5	2
Thornton, Matt, S.B.*	14	7	.667	2.52	27	27	0	0	0	0	157.0	126	650	56	44	9	2	5	11	60	0	192	12	0
Threets, Erick, S.J.*	0	10	.000	4.25	14	14	0	0	0	0	59.1	49	270	34	28	2	1	3	7	40	0	60	14	3
Tollberg, Brian, L.E.	0	2	.000	6.30	2	2	0	0	0	0	10.0	18	49	11	7	1	2	0	1	0	0	9	0	0
Torres, Melqui, S.B.	7	7	.500	4.15	26	26	0	0	0	0	154.0	159	666	79	71	4	10	4	23	56	1	113	8	1
Trejo, Francisco, Lan.*	0	0	.000	4.00	5	0	0	0	1	0	9.0	14	43	4	4	0	1	0	0	4	0	7	0	0
Trosper, Tanner, Mod.	0	0	.000	18.00	2	0	0	0	1	0	2.0	5	12	6	4	1	0	0	0	1	0	3	0	0
Trujillo, J.J., L.E.	4	1	.800	1.86	23	0	0	0	21	13	29.0	20	119	7	6	1	0	0	2	13	2	31	1	0
Uzzell, Todd, S.J.	1	1	.500	4.36	15	0	0	0	7	0	33.0	30	148	18	16	1	2	1	4	18	0	25	2	0
Valera, Greg, Lan.	2	5	.286	8.14	25	4	0	0	6	0	42.0	59	208	40	38	7	3	1	2	24	0	39	6	0
Van Duson, Dorriok, C.D.*	0	1	.000	5.40	1	1	0	0	0	0	3.1	3	14	2	2	0	0	0	1	0	0	3	0	0
Vent, Kevin, S.J.	5	6	.455	4.69	41	10	0	0	7	0	103.2	105	456	70	54	14	0	4	8	34	2	74	7	0
Voras, Enger, Dak.	9	8	.529	4.53	27	27	0	0	0	0	153.0	163	678	104	77	13	5	4	20	55	0	138	14	2
Villalon, Julio, Bak.	4	9	.308	4.87	25	24	0	0	0	0	133.0	148	582	83	72	12	2	3	8	45	0	146	8	0
Wagner, Denny, Mod.	7	9	.438	3.99	30	30	1	0	0	0	169.0	181	744	101	75	14	6	6	12	59	3	127	8	0
Walk, Mitch, S.J.*	9	6	.600	3.64	27	19	0	0	0	0	117.0	115	499	57	46	13	4	6	7	39	0	60	3	0
Watkins, Steve, L.E.	2	0	1.000	1.84	5	5	1	1	0	0	29.1	23	120	6	6	0	1	1	0	7	0	23	2	0
Webb, Brandon, Lan.	6	10	.375	3.99	29	28	0	0	0	0	162.1	174	711	90	72	9	3	6	27	44	0	158	11	1
Wilson, Phil, R.C.	8	10	.444	5.23	26	26	1	0	0	0	160.0	173	704	102	93	15	2	8	13	55	0	134	19	0
Withers, Darvin, Vis.	4	7	.364	5.00	28	17	0	0	2	0	117.0	128	513	75	65	17	3	6	3	43	1	85	10	1
Wolcott, Bob, Mud.	0	3	.000	7.20	3	3	0	0	0	0	15.0	22	69	13	12	2	0	1	1	0	0	10	0	0
Wolensky, Dave, R.C.	2	0	1.000	3.34	8	7	0	0	1	0	32.1	24	132	13	12	2	2	1	2	14	0	26	5	0
Wood, Mike, Mod.	4	3	.571	3.09	10	9	0	0	0	0	58.1	46	233	22	20	6	3	0	2	10	3	52	2	0
Wright, Chris, Bak.	7	7	.500	3.49	49	0	0	0	24	5	87.2	83	369	42	34	6	2	3	4	32	4	79	5	0
Yacco, Anthony, S.J.	1	0	1.000	3.38	7	0	0	0	1	0	13.1	10	61	7	5	2	1	0	1	12	0	15	1	0
Young, Doug, L.E.	4	0	1.000	3.03	20	0	0	0	5	0	29.2	26	136	17	10	2	1	0	1	12	1	23	1	0
Ziegler, Mike, Vis.	9	11	.450	4.32	29	27	0	0	0	0	152.0	181	665	87	73	13	8	2	8	39	1	142	8	0
Zirelli, Mike, S.J.	3	3	.500	5.75	38	1	0	0	7	0	83.0	119	377	62	53	8	2	7	3	13	2	62	4	1

PITCHERS WITH TWO OR MORE TEAMS

Pitcher, Team	W	L	Pct.	ERA	G	GS	CG	ShO	GF	Sv.	IP	H	TBF	R	ER	HR	SH	SF	HB	BB	IBB	SO	WP	Bk.
Harville, Chad, Mod.	0	0	.000	3.00	2	1	0	0	0	0	3.0	2	12	2	1	0	1	0	0	0	0	3	0	0
Harville, Chad, Vis.	0	0	.000	0.00	1	1	0	0	0	0	3.0	3	12	0	0	0	0	0	0	0	0	3	0	0
Jacobs, Greg, R.C.*	2	4	.333	7.57	31	0	0	0	5	0	44.0	59	219	47	37	8	3	1	7	22	1	49	3	0
Jacobs, Greg, Lan.*	1	1	.500	5.23	20	0	0	0	4	0	20.2	20	89	12	12	2	1	0	1	8	0	22	0	1

COMBINATION SHUTOUTS: **Bakersfield (9)**—Kofler-Robinson-Ortiz-Smith, Ruhl-Minix-Smith, Veras-Wright, Villalon-Smith, Veras-Wright, Frendling-Backe, Stokes-Anderson-Minix, Santos-Wright, Kofler-Montgomery. **High Desert (4)**—Parker-Corey-Giron, Stewart-Corey, Parker-Lynch, Pember-Allen-Giron. **Lake Elsinore (12)**—Hitchcock-Cyr-Trujillo-Bartosh, Tankersley-Shiyuk-Bartosh, Howard-Shibilo-Bartosh-Trujillo, Tankersley-Cyr-Trujillo, Tankersley-Shiyuk-Bartosh, Howard-Bausher, Hunter-Young-Shibilo-Bartosh, Loewer-Tankersley-Shibilo-Trujillo, Rojas-Seanez-Bartosh, Howard-Shibilo-Bartosh, Bausher-Bumstead-Gaal, Cyr-Gaal-Shibilo. **Lancaster (5)**—Good-Sikaras, Eriksen-Matzenbacher-McCutcheon-Sikaras, Good-Bellflower, Slaten-Matzenbacher-Jacobs-Bellflower, Webb-Medders. **Modesto (5)**—Surkont-McGerry-Miller-Sanchez, Bazzell-Cullen-Noriega, Gwyn-Sanchez, Bazzell-Flores, Bazzell-Crowell-Flores. **Mudville (7)**—Cordova-Dent-Neu, Gray-Martinez, Howington-Dent, Cordova-Manias-Martinez, Cordova-Dehart-Neu-Martinez, Howington-Dehart-Neu, Gray-Dehart. **Rancho Cucamonga (6)**—Bootcheck-Martinez-Grozlovski-Thames, Mendoza-Milo-Thames, Rodriguez-Schneider-Milo-Thames, Holtz-Crawford-O'Neal-Schneider-Milo-Martinez, Wilson-Martinez-Grezlovski, Bootcheck-Schneider. **San Bernardino (11)**—Thornton-Ramos-Kent-Mateo, Anderson-Looper-Mateo, Torres-Simpson-Mateo, Soriano-Ramos, Thornton-Kent-Simpson, Anderson-Mears-Ramos-Looper, Thornton-Mateo, Thornton-Looper-Balbuena, Johnson-Kent-Looper-Mateo, Johnson-Looper-Kent, Anderson-Balbuena. **San Jose (7)**—Brous-Pavon-Ramirez-Anderson, Cozier-Farley-Anderson, Brous-Anderson, Vent-Ramirez-Anderson, Walk-Cannon, Brown-Bermudez-Cannon-Anderson, Brown-Anderson. **Visalia (2)**—Harville-Nix, Cotts-Navarro.

NO-HIT GAMES: None.

2001 FIELDING

TEAM

Team	Pct.	G	PO	A	E	TC	DP	TP	PB
San Jose	.971	140	3677	1459	153	5289	117	0	28
San Bernardino .	.970	140	3849	1416	165	5430	116	0	16
Bakersfield	.968	140	3733	1406	168	5307	116	0	18
Lake Elsinore.....	.967	140	3767	1297	171	5235	88	0	22
Mudville	.966	140	3746	1353	178	5277	106	0	17
R. Cucamonga ..	.965	140	3716	1504	188	5408	113	0	22
Visalia	.964	140	3698	1414	189	5301	115	0	30

Team	Pct.	G	PO	A	E	TC	DP	TP	PB
High Desert	.964	140	3748	1471	195	5414	114	0	24
Lancaster	.960	140	3699	1429	213	5341	130	0	26
Modesto	.960	140	3718	1488	218	5424	97	0	30

INDIVIDUAL

FIRST BASEMEN

NOTE: All caps denotes fielding-percentage leader based on 70 games for catchers, 93 for all other non-pitchers and 112 innings for pitchers. *Throws lefthanded.

Player, Team	Pct.	G	PO	A	E	TC	DP
Alcala, Juan, S.B.	.958	3	21	2	1	24	1
Amado, Jose, Mud.	1.000	1	9	0	0	9	1
Barski, Chris, R.C.	1.000	9	74	6	0	80	7
Broussard, Benjamin, Mud.*	.992	30	238	18	2	258	22
Burkhart, Lance, H.D.	.977	11	80	6	2	88	8
Calitri, Mike, Mud.	1.000	2	4	0	0	4	0
Castillo, Alberto, Bak.*	.981	82	601	53	13	667	63
Ceriani, Matt, H.D.	.963	3	23	3	1	27	1
Contreras, Sergio, R.C.*	.984	52	329	31	6	366	27
Darula, Bobby, H.D.	.972	5	30	5	1	36	2
Deardorff, Jeff, H.D.	.985	30	244	17	4	265	20
De La Cruz, Jose, Vis.	1.000	2	19	0	0	19	0
Flaherty, Tim, S.J.	.988	130	1087	66	14	1167	97
Foster, Brian, H.D.	1.000	1	7	3	0	10	1
Furniss, Eddy, Vis.*	1.000	2	18	0	0	18	1
Gregg, Mitch, Vis.	.969	22	170	18	6	194	17
Grummitt, Dan, Bak.	.988	39	320	21	4	345	24
Hammock, Rob, Lan.	1.000	3	17	1	0	18	2
Howe, Matt, Mod.	.972	26	163	12	5	180	11
Isenia, Chairon, Bak.	.950	3	16	3	1	20	2
Jackson, Steve, Vis.	.988	117	943	65	12	1020	81
Jones, Ryan, Lan.	.993	90	666	49	5	720	85
Kaup, Nathan, Bak.	.964	18	125	8	5	138	6
Kenney, Jeff, H.D.	1.000	4	24	1	0	25	2
Laird, Gerald, Mod.	1.000	7	36	1	0	37	4
Lehr, Ryan, R.C.	.972	4	34	1	1	36	4
Marconi, Alex, Bak.	.978	7	41	3	1	45	1
Martin, Billy, Lan.	.992	58	457	38	4	499	38
McCorkle, Shawn, S.B.	.986	136	1168	66	17	1251	105
McDougall, Marshall, Vis.	1.000	2	4	0	0	4	0
Messner, Jake, S.J.*	.986	11	68	3	1	72	7
Montas, Ricardo, Lan.	1.000	1	12	0	0	12	0
Moore, Frank, Bak.	1.000	1	10	0	0	10	0
Myers, Corey, Lan.	1.000	1	3	0	0	3	1
NADY, Xavier, L.E.	.989	110	852	61	10	923	59
Nieckula, Aaron, Mod.-Vis.	1.000	7	34	1	0	35	4
O'Keefe, Mike, R.C.*	1.000	1	1	0	0	1	1
Patten, Chris, H.D.	1.000	11	99	3	0	102	8
Pernalete, Marco, S.J.	1.000	7	46	4	0	50	3
Pines, Gregory, S.B.	.909	2	10	0	1	11	2
Pujols, Rafael, Mod.	.974	28	180	9	5	194	13
Risinger, Ben, L.E.	1.000	3	30	2	0	32	6
Rodriguez, Guillermo, S.J.	1.000	4	30	2	0	32	2
Rosario, Omar, Mod.*	1.000	3	9	0	0	9	0
Rushford, Jim, H.D.*	.996	26	248	21	1	270	23
Scheschuk, John, L.E.*	.985	28	241	21	4	266	19
Schrock, Chris, Bak.	1.000	3	12	1	0	13	0
Scott, Bill, H.D.	.982	53	417	27	8	452	41
Sosa, Nick, Mod.	.982	85	721	52	14	787	48
Soto, Jorge, Mod.	.969	14	90	5	3	98	9
Spoerl, Josh, Mud.	.966	12	80	5	3	88	9
Wagner, Jeff, R.C.	.982	90	729	70	15	814	64
Waldron, Jeff, Lan.	1.000	1	1	0	0	2	0
Welsh, Eric, Mud.*	.984	100	760	62	13	835	69
Zamora, Junior, R.C.	1.000	4	34	1	0	35	4

FIRST BASEMEN WITH TWO OR MORE TEAMS

Player, Team	Pct.	G	PO	A	E	TC	DP
Nieckula, Aaron, Mod.	1.000	1	7	0	0	7	1
Nieckula, Aaron, Vis.	1.000	6	27	1	0	28	3

SECOND BASEMEN

Player, Team	Pct.	G	PO	A	E	TC	DP
Beattie, Andy, Mud.	.936	11	20	24	3	47	4
Burnett, Mark, Mud.	.962	67	115	136	10	261	29
Bynum, Freddie, Mod.	.922	53	125	124	21	270	25
Campana, Wandel, Mud.	.959	43	87	125	9	221	31
Campusano, Carlos, S.J.	.857	1	2	4	1	7	1
Cruz, Israel, S.B.	.961	18	14	35	2	51	9
Durango, Ariel, S.B.	.940	26	51	75	8	134	18
Eddlemon, Kelly, Bak.	.966	45	65	107	6	178	25

Player, Team	Pct.	G	PO	A	E	TC	DP
Encarnacion, Bienvenido, R.C.	.963	19	35	43	3	81	8
Figueroa, Luis, S.B.	.977	12	16	27	1	44	5
Gandolfo, Rob, S.B.	.982	78	140	185	6	331	46
Garcia, Isaac, Mod.	.958	28	35	56	4	95	10
GASTELUM, Carlos, R.C.	.982	108	216	330	10	556	67
Hall, Justin, Mod.-S.J.	.971	50	99	137	7	243	25
Hammock, Rob, Lan.	.500	1	1	0	1	2	0
Hoffpauir, Josh, Mod.	.953	56	107	135	12	254	23
Howe, Matt, Mod.	.889	4	8	8	2	18	3
Jester, Joe, S.J.	.969	74	143	206	11	360	45
Kata, Matt, Lan.	.956	113	245	301	25	571	75
Keller, G.W., Vis.	.800	2	2	2	1	5	0
Kennedy, Adam, R.C.	1.000	3	2	7	0	9	1
Kenney, Jeff, H.D.	.949	13	22	34	3	59	11
Kison, Robbie, Mud.	.962	21	51	49	4	104	9
Laird, Gerald, Mod.	1.000	1	0	1	0	1	0
Lorenzana, Luis, L.E.	1.000	4	12	7	0	19	1
Maldonado, Edwin, S.J.	.976	33	73	87	4	164	9
McCallum, Geoff, S.B.	.974	17	24	50	2	76	9
McDougall, Marshall, Vis.	.985	38	58	76	2	136	24
Montas, Ricardo, Lan.	.950	18	30	27	3	60	4
Moore, Frank, Bak.	.940	26	48	62	7	117	19
Moore, Jason, L.E.	.968	56	85	156	8	249	26
Patten, Chris, H.D.	.967	41	76	102	6	184	18
Pernalete, Marco, S.J.	1.000	7	10	19	0	29	3
Pichardo, Maximo, R.C.	1.000	3	6	8	0	14	4
Raymundo, Gregg, R.C.	.000	1	0	0	0	0	0
Risinger, Ben, L.E.	.980	26	35	62	2	99	14
Rosario, Carlos, Vis.	.964	104	196	265	17	478	49
Scales, Bobby, L.E.	.972	59	95	144	7	246	19
Scarborough, Steve, H.D.	.973	90	206	261	13	480	54
Schmidt, J.P., Vis.	.923	14	22	26	4	52	8
Schrock, Chris, Bak.	.965	13	25	30	2	57	6
Shaffer, Josh, R.C.	.929	20	33	46	6	85	8
Soler, Ramon, Bak.	.959	75	120	206	14	340	33
Williams, Jason, Lan.	.963	14	22	30	2	54	7
Woods, Blake, S.B.	1.000	7	5	9	0	14	1
Yakopich, Joseph, Lan.	.909	7	12	18	3	33	8

SECOND BASEMEN WITH TWO OR MORE TEAMS

Player, Team	Pct.	G	PO	A	E	TC	DP
Hall, Justin, Mod.	.980	24	39	57	2	98	6
Hall, Justin, S.J.	.966	26	60	80	5	145	19

THIRD BASEMEN

Player, Team	Pct.	G	PO	A	E	TC	DP
Amado, Jose, Mud.	.938	29	19	56	5	80	6
Beattie, Andy, Mud.	1.000	5	3	9	0	12	2
Beinbrink, Andy, Bak.	1.000	7	3	11	0	14	1
Burkhart, Lance, H.D.	.857	3	1	5	1	7	1
Bynum, Freddie, Mod.	1.000	5	2	8	0	10	0
Calitri, Mike, Mud.	.833	21	13	37	10	60	5
Campusano, Carlos, S.J.	1.000	4	1	9	0	10	0
Chavez, Angel, S.J.	.937	82	63	174	16	253	16
Cook, Josh, S.J.	1.000	4	1	9	0	10	0
Cosme, Caonabo, Mod.	.833	10	5	15	4	24	1
Cruz, Israel, S.B.	1.000	3	1	1	0	2	0
De La Cruz, Jose, Vis.	1.000	3	0	3	0	3	0
Dement, Dan, Bak.	.842	5	6	10	3	19	2
Eberwein, Kevin, L.E.	.857	6	5	7	2	14	0
Eddlemon, Kelly, Bak.	.906	72	48	107	16	171	9
Encarnacion, Bienvenido, R.C.	.714	7	5	10	6	21	0
Figueroa, Luis, S.B.	.909	11	5	25	3	33	0
Flaherty, Tim, S.J.	1.000	1	1	1	0	2	0
Gastelum, Carlos, R.C.	.889	5	2	6	1	9	2
Hall, Justin, S.J.	.929	5	3	10	1	14	1
Hammock, Rob, Lan.	.500	4	0	1	1	2	0
Hoffpauir, Josh, Mod.	.923	9	2	10	1	13	1
Howe, Matt, Mod.	.914	105	75	224	28	327	13
Jester, Joe, S.J.	.667	3	2	4	3	9	0
Kaup, Nathan, Bak.	.829	19	11	23	7	41	1
Kenney, Jeff, H.D.	.968	20	15	46	2	63	5
Kison, Robbie, Mud.	.883	34	17	51	9	77	7
Laird, Gerald, Mod.	.000	1	0	0	0	0	0
Lehr, Ryan, R.C.	.878	36	7	72	11	90	4
LEONE, Justin, S.B.	.928	127	97	240	26	363	25
Lundquist, Ryan, Mud.	.930	62	37	109	11	157	8
Marconi, Alex, Bak.	1.000	2	0	4	0	4	1
Martin, Billy, Lan.	.870	47	18	96	17	131	12
Martinez, Guillermo, S.B.	.000	1	0	0	0	0	0
McCallum, Geoff, S.B.	1.000	2	3	3	0	6	0
McDougall, Marshall, Vis.	.936	83	39	152	13	204	15
Montas, Ricardo, Lan.	.920	25	7	16	2	25	2

Player, Team	Pct.	G	PO	A	E	TC	DP
Moore, Jason, L.E.	.964	15	6	21	1	28	1
Myers, Corey, Lan.	.880	50	13	82	13	108	10
Nieckula, Aaron, Vis.	.000	1	0	0	0	0	0
Niekro, Lance, S.J.	.927	32	31	71	8	110	6
Olson, Tim, Lan.	.913	28	18	55	7	80	5
Patten, Chris, H.D.	.933	38	20	77	7	104	5
Pernalete, Marco, S.J.	.931	15	5	22	2	29	3
Raymundo, Gregg, R.C.	.910	77	41	160	20	221	10
Reyes, Christian, Mod.	.908	26	15	54	7	76	3
Risinger, Ben, L.E.	.960	41	35	61	4	100	8
Rowan, Chris, H.D.	.914	85	50	173	21	244	18
Santos, Luis, Lan.	.818	10	3	15	4	22	3
Schader, Troy, L.E.	.890	87	69	126	24	219	11
Schneidmiller, Gary, Vis.	.871	75	45	104	22	171	8
Schrock, Chris, Bak.	.937	55	30	74	7	111	5
Shaffer, Josh, R.C.	.900	16	9	27	4	40	2
Sosa, Nick, Mod.	.000	1	0	0	0	0	0
Yakopich, Joseph, Lan.	.875	3	0	7	1	8	0
Zamora, Junior, R.C.	.800	8	2	10	3	15	1

SHORTSTOPS

Player, Team	Pct.	G	PO	A	E	TC	DP
Beattie, Andy, Mud.	.958	6	9	14	1	24	0
Bynum, Freddie, Mod.	.919	68	83	144	20	247	25
Campusano, Carlos, S.J.	.960	6	13	11	1	25	4
Carvajal, Jhonny, S.J.	.955	112	156	350	24	530	60
Castillo, Ruben, S.B.	.925	76	140	195	27	362	45
Chavez, Angel, S.J.	1.000	2	2	3	0	5	0
Cosme, Caonabo, Mod.	.947	49	77	139	12	228	19
Crosby, Bobby, Mod.	.889	10	13	19	4	36	2
Cruz, Israel, S.B.	.929	8	10	16	2	28	2
Encarnacion, Bienvonido, R.C.	1.000	6	5	8	0	13	2
Gandolfo, Rob, S.B.	.962	16	22	29	2	53	7
Garcia, Isaac, Mod.	.940	25	30	49	5	84	7
Gastelum, Carlos, R.C.	.882	4	6	9	2	17	1
Gomez, Frank, Vis.	.924	117	160	299	38	497	59
Hall, Bill, H.D.	.929	89	134	256	30	420	49
Hall, Justin, H.D.	1.000	1	0	2	0	2	0
Hoffpauir, Josh, Mod.	1.000	1	1	0	0	1	1
Kata, Matt, Lan.	.867	6	12	14	4	30	2
Keller, G.W., Vis.	1.000	1	1	0	0	1	0
Kenney, Jeff, H.D.	.917	3	6	5	1	12	2
Kison, Robbie, Mud.	.974	12	15	23	1	39	5
Laird, Gerald, Mod.	.000	1	0	0	0	0	0
Lorenzana, Luis, L.E.	.977	65	91	164	6	261	29
Martinez, Guillermo, S.B.	.952	44	62	138	10	210	26
McCallum, Geoff, S.B.	.933	8	5	9	1	15	2
McDougall, Marshall, Vis.	.928	27	26	51	6	83	5
Montas, Ricardo, Lan.	.985	32	41	89	2	132	14
Moore, Frank, Bak.	1.000	8	9	21	0	30	5
Moore, Jason, L.E.	.926	65	72	167	19	258	28
Murphy, Tommy, R.C.	.936	49	50	141	13	204	25
Olmedo, Ranier, Mud.	.930	129	186	346	40	572	65
Olson, Tim, Lan.	.903	33	58	101	17	176	27
PEREZ, Neslor, Bak.	.967	118	150	325	16	491	65
Pernalete, Marco, S.J.	.945	15	25	44	4	73	9
Reyes, Christian, Mod.	.929	4	6	7	1	14	1
Riggins, Auntwan, L.E.	.870	15	15	32	7	54	5
Rosario, Carlos, Vis.	.091	13	14	27	5	46	6
Santana, Henry, S.J.	.880	7	12	10	3	25	2
Scarborough, Steve, H.D.	.931	51	57	131	14	202	27
Schrock, Chris, Bak.	.922	24	36	47	7	90	8
Shaffer, Josh, R.C.	.069	22	30	63	3	96	11
Specht, Brian, R.C.	.946	63	95	170	15	280	32
Williams, Jason, Lan.	.911	77	115	212	32	359	41

OUTFIELDERS

Player, Team	Pct.	G	PO	A	E	TC	DP
Allegra, Matt, Mod.	.965	51	78	5	3	86	2
Allen, Jeff, S.J.	.963	91	170	10	7	187	2
Amado, Jose, Mud.	1.000	17	29	0	0	29	0
Asche, Kirk, Vis.	.979	104	221	7	5	233	0
Bartee, Kimera, R.C.	1.000	7	13	0	0	13	0
Basabe, Jesus, Mod.	.970	114	183	10	6	199	0
Beattie, Andy, Mud.	.938	39	74	1	5	80	0
Benjamin, Al, L.E.	1.000	15	16	2	0	18	0
Bikowski, Scott, R.C.*	.959	124	196	12	9	217	1
Bowser, Matt, Vis.*	.958	126	202	5	9	216	1
Burnett, Mark, Mud.	.978	52	84	3	2	89	0
Burns, Kevan, Lan.*	1.000	50	76	1	0	77	0
Burress, Andy, Mud.	.960	32	46	2	2	50	0
Castillo, Alberto, Bak.*	.750	4	3	0	1	4	0
Chirinos, Germain, Vis.	.980	86	136	8	3	147	1

Player, Team	Pct.	G	PO	A	E	TC	DP
Closser, J.D., Lan.	.000	1	0	0	0	0	0
Contreras, Sergio, R.C.*	.987	51	75	2	1	78	0
Cook, Josh, S.J.	.750	2	3	0	1	4	0
Craig, Beau, Vis.	.000	1	0	0	0	0	0
Cridland, Mark, H.D.	1.000	8	11	2	0	13	0
Cruz, Israel, S.B.	.000	1	0	0	0	0	0
Daeley, Scott, S.J.	.984	112	230	13	4	247	4
Darula, Bobby, H.D.	.929	24	26	0	2	28	0
Deardorff, Jeff, H.D.	.937	39	58	1	4	63	0
De La Cruz, Eric, H.D.	1.000	9	12	3	0	15	1
Diaz, Matt, Bak.	.961	130	228	17	10	255	5
Dobbs, Greg, S.B.	1.000	3	2	0	0	2	0
Donovan, Todd, L.E.	.962	37	73	2	3	78	1
Edge, Dwight, Lan.	.955	20	41	1	2	44	0
Encarnacion, Bienvonido, R.C.	.000	1	0	0	0	0	0
Faison, Vince, L.E.	.905	71	113	1	12	126	0
Fajardo, Al, S.J.	1.000	30	51	0	0	51	0
Fernandez, Alex, S.B.*	.957	64	106	4	5	115	0
Flaherty, Tim, S.J.	.750	6	3	0	1	4	0
Foley, Steve, S.B.	.982	34	53	1	1	55	0
Fulse, Sheldon, S.B.	.966	34	57	0	2	59	0
Gann, Jamie, Lan.	1.000	21	40	3	0	43	1
Garrett, Shawn, L.E.	.966	72	110	5	4	119	0
Glendenning, Mike, Lan.	.900	8	9	0	1	10	0
Gomez, Andre, L.E.	1.000	13	16	0	0	16	0
Gordon, Brian, Lan.	.973	95	136	8	4	148	2
Gregg, Mitch, Vis.	.944	71	82	3	5	90	0
Guerrero, Cristian, H.D.	.949	84	124	5	7	136	0
Hammock, Rob, Lan.	1.000	31	54	4	0	58	0
Harris, Cedrick, Lan.	.987	81	152	4	2	158	0
Hernandez, Orlando, S.B.	1.000	16	16	0	0	16	0
Holt, Daylan, Mod	.975	99	185	7	5	197	3
Hopper, Shane, L.E.	1.000	30	43	1	0	44	1
Hurtado, Omar, Mud.	1.000	17	31	3	0	34	0
Johnson, Ben, L.E.	.948	133	211	8	12	231	2
Johnson, Kade, H.D.	.917	16	18	4	2	24	0
Jones, Ryan, Lan.	.951	28	39	0	2	41	0
Kaup, Nathan, Bak	.976	56	75	5	2	82	1
Keller, G.W., Vis.	1.000	4	5	0	0	5	0
Kenney, Jeff, H.D.	.920	9	23	0	2	25	0
Kiil, Skip, Mud.	1.000	5	6	0	0	6	0
Knox, Ryan, H.D.	.986	75	138	4	2	144	0
Krynzel, Dave, H.D.*	.977	89	201	8	5	214	0
Laird, Gerald, Mod.	.875	9	12	2	2	16	0
Lehr, Ryan, R.C.	.900	6	9	0	1	10	0
Leone, Justin, S.B.	.875	5	6	1	1	8	0
Lopez, Chuck, S.B.*	1.000	12	13	1	0	14	0
Lundquist, Ryan, Bak.	.963	61	101	3	4	108	0
McDowell, Arturo, S.J.*	.957	114	218	7	10	235	0
Messner, Jake, S.J.*	1.000	37	44	2	0	46	0
Moore, Frank, Bak.	.963	97	174	7	7	188	1
Moreta, Ramon, R.C.-S.J.	.981	44	99	3	2	104	1
Mott, Bill, R.C.	.974	17	37	0	1	38	0
Mounts, J.R., R.C.	.968	104	208	7	7	222	1
Murch, Jeromy, Bak.*	.961	59	73	1	3	77	0
Nieckula, Aaron, Vis.	1.000	2	4	0	0	4	0
Nix, Wayne, Vis.	.000	1	0	0	0	0	0
O'Donnell, Ryan, L.E.	1.000	15	28	4	0	32	0
O'Keefe, Mike, R.C.*	.971	92	131	5	4	140	0
Olson, Tim, Lan.	.000	1	0	0	0	0	0
Owens, Jeremy, L.E.	1.000	13	44	2	0	46	0
Patten, Chris, H.D.	1.000	10	10	1	0	11	0
Piatt, Adam, Mod.	1.000	4	7	0	0	7	0
Pujols, Rafael, Mod.	1.000	1	1	0	0	1	0
Quintana, Wil, S.B.	.915	47	85	1	8	94	0
Rainey, Jason, S.B.*	.929	7	12	1	1	14	0
Riggins, Auntwan, L.E.	.000	2	0	0	0	0	0
RIOS, Fernando, Mud.	.984	113	239	14	4	257	3
Rodriguez, Serafin, Mud.	.946	55	83	5	5	93	0
Rosario, Carlos, Vis.	.000	2	0	0	0	0	0
Rosario, Omar, Vis.-Mod.*	.972	88	132	7	4	143	0
Rowan, Chris, H.D.	1.000	1	1	0	0	1	0
Rushford, Jim, H.D.*	.938	38	71	5	5	81	0
Ryan, Kelvin, Bak.	.983	98	167	6	3	176	0
Salmon, Tim, R.C.	.667	2	2	0	1	3	0
Santos, Luis, Lan.	1.000	4	5	0	0	5	0
Scales, Bobby, L.E.	.975	22	39	0	1	40	0
Schader, Troy, L.E.	1.000	8	7	2	0	9	1
Schmidt, J.P., Vis.	.800	3	4	0	1	5	0
Schneidmiller, Gary, Vis.	.982	34	53	1	1	55	0
Schrock, Chris, Bak.	1.000	5	13	0	0	13	0
Scott, Bill, H.D.	.953	32	41	0	2	43	0
Shabala, Adam, S.J.	.000	2	0	0	0	0	0
Snelling, Chris, S.B.*	.978	106	166	12	4	182	1

CLASS A California League

Player, Team	Pct.	G	PO	A	E	TC	DP
Sollmann, Scott, Mud.*	.857	4	6	0	1	7	0
Strong, Jamal, S.B.	.977	81	164	5	4	173	0
Sykes, Jamie, Lan.	.961	39	73	0	3	76	0
Terrero, Luis, Lan.	.971	18	33	1	1	35	0
Thompson, Zachary, H.D.*	1.000	4	7	0	0	7	0
Torcato, Tony, S.J.	.952	15	20	0	1	21	0
Urquhart, Derick, R.C.*	1.000	21	19	1	0	20	0
Urquiola, Carlos, Lan.	1.000	12	17	0	0	17	0
Valdez, Mario, Mod.	1.000	4	2	0	0	2	0
Van Rossum, Chris, Mud.*	.989	47	88	6	1	95	0
Welsh, Eric, Mud.*	.333	2	1	0	2	3	0
Wenner, Mike, Mod.	.963	112	222	9	9	240	3
Wilfong, Nick, S.J.	1.000	17	31	1	0	32	0
Williams, Jason, Lan.	.000	1	0	0	0	0	0
Williams, P.J., O.D.	.000	00	10	1	2	11	0
Withers, Darvin, Vis.	.000	1	0	0	0	0	0
Woodward, Steve, Lan.*	.960	44	66	6	3	75	1

OUTFIELDERS WITH TWO OR MORE TEAMS

Player, Team	Pct.	G	PO	A	E	TC	DP
Moreta, Ramon, R.C.	.974	34	75	1	2	78	0
Moreta, Ramon, S.J.	1.000	10	24	2	0	26	1
Rosario, Omar, Vis.*	.960	30	46	2	2	50	0
Rosario, Omar, Mod.*	.978	58	86	5	2	93	0

CATCHERS

Player, Team	Pct.	G	PO	A	E	TC	DP	PB
Abruzzo, Jared, R.C.	.984	22	166	13	3	182	1	4
Alcala, Juan, S.B.	.987	33	277	22	4	303	1	3
Alfano, Jeff, S.J.	.983	49	316	26	6	348	1	16
Alvarado, Damien, S.B.	1.000	2	8	1	0	9	0	0
Alvarado, Joel, H.D.	.990	22	183	19	2	204	1	3
Barski, Chris, R.C.	.892	8	29	4	4	37	0	0
Bitter, Jarrod, L.E.	.992	31	250	11	2	263	1	5
Burkhart, Lance, H.D.	.998	49	374	40	1	415	0	10
Castillo, Carlos, Mod.	1.000	3	21	3	0	24	0	0
Cerda, Jose, S.J.	.990	30	191	15	2	208	0	6
Ceriani, Matt, H.D.	.983	19	159	14	3	176	1	4
CHRISTIANSON, Ryan, S.B.	.993	109	993	88	8	1089	2	13
Closser, J.D., Lan.	.981	95	745	74	16	835	0	18
Cosentino, Tony, L.E.	.996	47	419	31	2	452	1	7
Craig, Beau, Vis.	.985	84	652	67	11	730	4	10
De La Cruz, Jose, Vis.	.988	34	225	30	3	258	5	16
Diaz, Angel, R.C.	1.000	18	111	6	0	117	0	2
Foster, Brian, H.D.	.930	8	61	5	5	71	0	2
Glassey, Josh, Lan.	.985	8	63	3	1	67	1	1
Goldfield, Josh, Lan.	1.000	4	23	4	0	27	0	2
Gomez, Andre, L.E.	.985	9	61	6	1	68	0	2
Gonzalez, Wiklenman, L.E.	.973	4	32	4	1	37	0	0
Hammock, Rob, Lan.	.961	14	114	9	5	128	0	1
Huguet, J.C., Mud.	1.000	2	3	0	0	3	0	0
Isenia, Chairon, Bak.	.983	39	322	26	6	354	3	6
Johnson, Kade, H.D.	.962	52	393	39	17	449	3	5
Kaup, Nathan, Bak.	1.000	1	4	0	0	4	0	0
Laird, Gerald, Mod.	.977	85	583	82	16	681	6	17
Lopez, Norberto, R.C.	.981	9	48	5	1	54	1	0
Loyd, Brian, L.E.	.970	12	90	6	3	99	0	1
Marconi, Alex, Bak.	.992	18	113	7	1	121	1	4
Massiatte, Danny, Bak.	.990	93	793	76	9	878	10	8
Melton, John, Lan.	.971	6	32	2	1	35	0	0
Molina, Bengie, R.C.	1.000	3	15	4	0	19	0	1
Napoli, Michael, R.C.	.981	7	49	3	1	53	1	1
Nieckula, Aaron, Mod.-Vis.	.984	54	393	42	7	442	2	5
Pines, Gregory, S.B.	1.000	1	0	1	0	1	0	0
Pujols, Rafael, Mod.	.987	40	276	23	4	303	2	12
Risinger, Ben, L.E.	.995	39	366	24	2	392	0	4
Rodriguez, Guillermo, S.J.	.991	32	199	21	2	222	1	1
Rogers, Brandon, R.C.	.984	23	167	15	3	185	1	5
Sardinha, Dane, Mud.	.991	109	962	89	10	1061	4	12
Senjem, Guye, Mud.	.991	26	204	24	2	230	3	4
Serrano, Sammy, S.J.	.987	39	273	21	4	298	2	5
Socarras, Tony, R.C.	.982	53	438	45	9	492	1	4
Sykes, Jamie, Lan.	1.000	1	1	0	0	1	0	0
Thurston, Jerrey, L.E.-Mud.	.972	21	193	13	6	212	1	4
Waldron, Jeff, Lan.	.987	27	149	6	2	157	0	4
Zeber, Ryan, R.C.	.977	13	84	1	2	87	0	5

CATCHERS WITH TWO OR MORE TEAMS

Player, Team	Pct.	G	PO	A	E	TC	DP	PB
Nieckula, Aaron, Mod.	.988	23	151	14	2	167	0	1
Nieckula, Aaron, Vis.	.982	31	242	28	5	275	2	4
Thurston, Jerrey, L.E.	.973	14	137	8	4	149	1	3
Thurston, Jerrey, Mud.	.968	7	56	5	2	63	0	1

PITCHERS

Player, Team	Pct.	G	PO	A	E	TC	DP
Ah Yat, Paul, S.J.*	.500	5	0	1	1	2	0
Alfano, Jeff, S.J.	.000	8	0	0	0	0	0
Allen, Rod, H.D.	.824	43	6	8	3	17	2
Altman, Gene, H.D.	1.000	38	0	6	0	6	0
Ammons, Cary, Mud.*	.917	14	2	9	1	12	0
Andersen, Derek, Bak.*	1.000	18	4	1	0	5	1
Anderson, Craig, S.B.*	.912	28	9	22	3	34	0
Anderson, Luke, S.J.	1.000	59	7	7	0	14	1
Backe, Brandon, Bak.	.714	17	1	4	2	7	0
Baek, Cha, S.B.	1.000	5	1	5	0	6	0
Balbuena, Caleb, S.B.	.875	36	3	4	1	8	0
Barber, Scott, Lan.	.923	29	4	8	1	13	1
Bartosh, Cliff, L.E.*	.600	38	1	2	2	5	0
Bausher, Andy, L.E.*	.750	37	1	11	4	16	0
Bazzell, Shane, Mod.	.944	28	5	12	1	18	1
Belflower, Jay, Lan.	1.000	27	2	3	0	5	0
BERMUDEZ, Manny, S.J.	1.000	43	2	27	0	29	0
Birdsong, Tim, Mud.	1.000	23	2	4	0	6	1
Bootcheck, Chris, R.C.	1.000	15	10	6	0	16	0
Bowser, Matt, Vis.*	.000	1	0	0	0	0	0
Bradley, Dave, Mud.	.667	15	1	3	2	6	1
Brink, Jim, Mod.	1.000	24	4	8	0	12	0
Brooks, Conor, Vis.	.963	45	9	17	1	27	1
Brous, Dave, S.J.*	.778	11	3	4	2	9	1
Brown, Elliot, S.J.	.833	5	2	3	1	6	1
Brummett, Sean, R.C.*	1.000	7	4	7	0	11	0
Bumstead, Mike, L.E.	1.000	19	5	0	0	5	0
Callier, Jeremy, R.C.	.000	2	0	0	0	0	0
Cannon, Jon, S.J.*	1.000	22	3	5	0	8	0
Carbajal, Alex, Bak.*	1.000	24	2	4	0	6	1
Carter, Justin, Mud.*	1.000	10	2	5	0	7	1
Cash, David, S.J.	1.000	20	1	2	0	3	0
Castillo, Dan, Lan.	1.000	23	5	5	0	10	0
Ceriani, Matt, H.D.	.000	1	0	0	0	0	0
Childers, Matt, H.D.	.964	20	12	15	1	28	1
Coleman, Jeff, Vis.	1.000	16	1	2	0	3	0
Cook, Josh, S.J.	.000	1	0	0	0	0	0
Cordova, Jorge, Mud.	.885	30	10	13	3	26	0
Corey, Mike, H.D.	.895	47	2	15	2	19	5
Cornejo, Jesse, Bak.*	1.000	9	2	2	0	4	0
Cotts, Neal, Vis.*	.833	7	0	5	1	6	0
Coward, Tim, Bak.	1.000	32	2	10	0	12	0
Cozier, Vance, S.J.	1.000	30	7	17	0	24	0
Crawford, Wesley, R.C.*	.889	21	5	11	2	18	0
Crowell, Kyle, Mod.	.917	37	4	18	2	24	1
Cullen, Ryan, Mod.*	.889	40	4	12	2	18	0
Culp, Brandon, Mud.	.750	9	0	3	1	4	1
Cyr, Eric, L.E.*	1.000	21	4	9	0	13	0
Darnell, Paul, Mud.*	1.000	5	2	1	0	3	0
Dehart, Casey, Mud.*	.900	49	1	8	1	10	0
De La Cruz, Jose, Vis.	.000	1	0	0	0	0	0
Delgado, Danny, S.B.	1.000	36	6	6	0	12	1
Demouy, Chris, R.C.*	1.000	7	2	2	0	4	0
Dent, Doug, Mud.	.857	24	2	10	2	14	2
DePaula, Freddy, Vis.*	1.000	15	3	7	0	10	0
Diaz, Alex, Vis.	1.000	32	3	9	0	12	0
Dunn, Scott, Mud.	.800	10	4	4	2	10	0
Eriksen, Tanner, Lan.	.667	19	1	7	4	12	0
Espina, Rendy, R.C.*	.000	2	0	0	0	0	0
Esteves, Jake, S.J.	1.000	9	1	0	0	1	0
Farley, Joe, S.J.*	1.000	18	1	3	0	4	0
Farmer, Jason, S.J.	.833	14	6	9	3	18	1
Fischer, Steve, Vis.	.905	34	14	24	4	42	3
Flores, Ron, Mod.*	1.000	47	4	7	0	11	0
Frendling, Neal, Bak.	1.000	20	6	14	0	20	0
Frias, Juan, S.J.	.000	4	0	0	0	0	0
Fuller, Jody, Lan.	1.000	23	7	6	0	13	1
Gaal, Bryan, L.E.	.667	35	1	3	2	6	0
Gann, Jamie, Lan.	1.000	9	1	2	0	3	0
Garber, Mike, Lan.*	.500	25	0	1	1	2	0
German, Frank, Vis.	.917	53	6	5	1	12	2
Giron, Roberto, H.D.	1.000	45	5	11	0	16	1
Gomez, Andre, L.E.	1.000	1	1	2	0	3	0
Good, Andrew, Lan.	.909	19	10	10	2	22	0
Goodrich, Randy, S.J.	1.000	15	7	9	0	16	0
Gray, Brett, Mud.	.974	29	15	23	1	39	2
Grezlovski, Ben, R.C.	.909	48	1	9	1	11	0
Gwyn, Mark, Mod.	.897	28	12	23	4	39	1
Harris, Julian, R.C.*	.833	25	2	3	1	6	0
Harville, Chad, Mod.-Vis.	1.000	3	1	2	0	3	0
Hasegawa, Shigetoshi, R.C.	1.000	2	0	1	0	1	0
Haworth, Brent, R.C.	1.000	5	0	1	0	1	0

Player, Team	Pct.	G	PO	A	E	TC	DP
Hensley, Matt, R.C.	.833	14	5	5	2	12	1
Hitchcock, Sterling, L.E.*	.875	6	1	6	1	8	1
Hoerman, Jared, S.B.	1.000	11	0	3	0	3	0
Holtz, Mike, R.C.*	.000	2	0	0	0	0	0
Howard, Ben, L.E.	.889	18	6	2	1	9	0
Howington, Ty, Mud.*	1.000	7	2	3	0	5	0
Huggins, Dave, H.D.	1.000	14	1	3	0	4	0
Hundley, Jeff, R.C.*	.938	13	7	8	1	16	0
Hunter, Johnny, L.E.	1.000	7	3	5	0	8	1
Jacobs, Greg, R.C. -Lan.*	1.000	51	7	6	0	13	0
Johnson, Rett, S.B.	1.000	12	3	11	0	14	2
Jones, Greg, R.C.	1.000	6	2	2	0	4	1
Joseph, Kevin, S.J.	1.000	9	1	2	0	3	0
Kenney, Jeff, H.D.	1.000	1	0	1	0	1	0
Kent, Steve, S.B.*	.938	51	0	15	1	16	1
Kison, Robbie, Mud.	.000	2	0	0	0	0	0
Kofler, Ed, S.B.	.875	15	6	8	2	16	1
Koronka, John, Mud.*	1.000	12	1	12	0	13	0
Lara, Nelson, Mud.	1.000	2	0	1	0	1	0
Lee, Jon, Lan.	.000	5	0	0	0	0	0
Leyva, Julian, Mod.	.500	5	0	1	1	2	1
Loewer, Carlton, L.E.	1.000	4	0	1	0	1	0
Looper, Aaron, S.B.	1.000	56	2	14	0	16	1
Lopez, Javier, Lan.*	1.000	17	2	6	0	8	0
Lopez, Rodrigo, L.E.	1.000	9	0	2	0	2	0
Lowe, Benny, Mud.*	1.000	4	2	1	0	3	0
Luque, Roger, L.E.*	1.000	1	1	0	0	1	0
Lynch, Jim, H.D.	.688	37	6	5	5	16	1
Malaska, Mark, Bak.*	1.000	3	2	3	0	5	0
Manias, Jim, Mud.*	1.000	24	1	3	0	4	1
Martinez, Javier, Mud.	1.000	16	1	1	0	2	0
Martinez, Luis, H.D.*	.786	22	1	10	3	14	0
Martinez, Renan, R.C.*	1.000	43	5	15	0	20	1
Mateo, Julio, S.B.	1.000	56	0	6	0	6	0
Mathews, Dan, H.D.	.786	36	5	6	3	14	0
Matzenbacher, Brian, Lan.	.917	48	4	7	1	12	1
Mazur, Bryan, Vis.*	.960	48	3	21	1	25	1
McCall, Derell, Mod.	.957	39	6	16	1	23	3
McClain, Kevin, R.C.	1.000	23	0	3	0	3	0
McCutcheon, Miko, Lan.*	.667	12	0	2	1	3	0
McDougall, Marshall, Vis.	.000	1	0	0	0	0	0
McGerry, Kevin, Mod.	.750	15	1	2	1	4	0
Mears, Chris, S.B.	1.000	38	8	14	0	22	0
Medders, Brandon, Lan.	1.000	31	3	2	0	5	0
Mendoza, Hatuey, Lan.	.913	24	5	16	2	23	4
Mendoza, Mario, R.C.	.846	8	4	7	2	13	2
Messman, Joe, S.J.	.857	23	5	7	2	14	0
Miller, Benji, S.J.	.000	1	0	0	0	0	0
Miller, Corey, Mod.	1.000	43	4	14	0	18	0
Milo, Tony, R.C.*	1.000	24	2	6	0	8	1
Minaya, Edwin, Vis.	.750	13	1	2	1	4	0
Minix, Travis, Bak.	1.000	44	2	13	0	15	0
Montgomery, Matt, Bak.	1.000	14	1	1	0	2	0
Montgomery, Steve, L.E.	.000	2	0	0	0	0	0
Montoya, Saul, Lan.	1.000	9	1	0	0	1	0
Moore, Darin, Vis.	.846	38	4	7	2	13	0
Navarro, Scott, Vis.*	1.000	14	3	4	0	7	0
Neu, Mike, Mud.	1.000	53	4	5	0	9	0
Nicolas, Mike, l F	.750	8	1	2	1	4	0
Nix, Wayne, Vis.	.850	26	7	10	3	20	0
Noriega, Ray, Mod.*	1.000	13	3	4	0	7	0
Norris, Ben, Lan.*	1.000	2	1	1	0	2	0
O'Brien, Matt, Vis.*	.967	27	3	26	1	30	0
O'Neal, Brandon, R.C.	.750	10	7	2	3	12	0
Ortiz, Jose, Bak.	.895	35	8	9	2	19	0
Oxspring, Chris, L.E.	1.000	7	0	1	0	1	0
Pace, Adam, R.C.*	1.000	3	0	2	0	2	0
Parker, Brandon, S.B.	1.000	15	1	3	0	4	0
Parker, Matt, H.D.	1.000	28	8	18	0	26	0
Patterson, John, Lan.	.000	2	0	0	1	1	0
Pavon, Julio, S.J.	1.000	6	4	0	0	4	0
Peavy, Jake, L.E.	.889	19	4	12	2	18	2
Pember, Dave, H.D.	.931	20	9	18	2	29	0
Perez, Oliver, L.E.*	.900	9	1	8	1	10	0
Phillips, Mark, L.E.*	1.000	5	1	6	0	7	0
Pines, Gregory, S.B.	.000	1	0	0	0	0	0
Polanco, Elvis, H.D.	.944	42	8	9	1	18	0
Pugmire, Rob, Mud.	.800	4	1	3	1	5	0
Ramirez, Erasmo, S.J.*	1.000	17	4	8	0	12	0
Ramos, Juan, S.B.	.950	39	2	17	1	20	1
Ratliff, Jon, Mod.	.000	4	0	0	0	0	0
Renteria, Juan, Bak.	.000	1	0	0	0	0	0
Rheinecker, John, Mod.*	1.000	2	0	2	0	2	0
Robinson, Dustin, Mud.	1.000	30	5	3	0	8	0
Robinson, Jeff, H.D.	1.000	5	2	3	0	5	0
Robinson, Jeremy, Bak.*	.000	5	0	0	0	0	0
Rodarmel, Rich, Vis.	1.000	2	0	1	0	1	0
Rodriguez, Francisco, R.C.	.826	20	7	12	4	23	0
Rojas, Chris, L.E.	.857	28	19	29	8	56	3
Ruhl, Nathan, Bak.	.833	12	3	7	2	12	1
Salmon, Brad, Mud.	.923	33	9	15	2	26	0
Sanchez, Cade, Mod.	1.000	39	2	5	0	7	0
Sanchez, Duaner, Lan.	.882	10	9	6	2	17	0
Santos, Alex, Bak.	.955	24	8	13	1	22	1
Schneider, Scott, R.C.	1.000	62	1	00	0	00	0
Schneidmiller, Gary, Vis.	.000	1	0	0	0	0	0
Schultz, Jeff, Vis.	1.000	56	4	10	0	14	2
Seabury, Jaron, H.D.	1.000	3	1	0	0	1	0
Seanez, Rudy, L.E.	1.000	7	0	1	0	1	0
Shabansky, Rob, Lan.*	1.000	29	2	3	0	5	0
Shaffar, Ben, Mud.	.833	6	2	3	1	6	0
Shibilo, Andy, L.E.	.870	60	5	15	3	23	0
Shiyuk, Todd, L.E.*	.818	50	2	7	2	11	0
Sikaras, Pete, Lan.	.800	18	3	1	1	5	0
Simpson, Allan, S.B.	.667	16	0	2	1	3	0
Slaten, Doug, Lan.*	.861	28	6	25	5	36	2
Smith, Hans, Bak.*	.800	31	2	2	1	5	0
Soriano, Rafael, S.B.	.933	15	3	11	1	15	2
Stafford, Mike, H.D.*	1.000	24	1	3	0	4	0
Stephens, Jason, R.C.	.833	8	3	2	1	6	0
Stevenson, Jason, L.E.	.500	11	0	1	1	2	0
Stewart, Paul, H.D.	.060	28	11	13	1	25	3
Stockman, Phil, Lan.	1.000	8	1	4	0	5	1
Stokes, Brian, Bak.	.926	32	10	15	2	27	1
Stokley, Billy, R.C.	.857	27	4	2	1	7	0
Stull, Everett, H.D.	1.000	1	0	1	0	1	0
Surkont, Keith, Mod.	.938	24	10	20	2	32	1
Tankersley, Dennis, L.E.	1.000	9	3	3	0	6	0
Taschner, Jack, S.J.*	.818	14	4	5	2	11	0
Thames, Charlie, R.C.	.917	20	4	7	1	12	1
Therneau, Dave, Mud.	1.000	10	1	1	0	2	0
Thompson, Mike, L.E.	1.000	19	5	9	0	14	0
Thornton, Matt, S.B.*	.821	27	5	18	5	28	2
Threets, Erick, S.J.*	.800	14	4	4	2	10	0
Tollberg, Brian, L.E.	1.000	2	0	1	0	1	0
Torres, Melqui, S.B.	.909	26	12	18	3	33	0
Trejo, Francisco, Lan.*	1.000	5	0	1	0	1	1
Trosper, Tanner, Mod.	1.000	2	0	1	0	1	0
Trujillo, J.J., L.E.	1.000	23	3	4	0	7	1
Uzzell, Todd, S.J.	.800	15	1	3	1	5	0
Valera, Greg, Lan.	.778	25	1	6	2	9	0
Van Dusen, Derrick, S.B.*	.000	1	0	0	0	0	0
Vent, Kevin, S.J.	1.000	41	0	9	0	9	2
Veras, Enger, Bak.	.885	27	9	14	3	26	3
Villalon, Julio, Bak.	.931	25	16	11	2	29	2
Wagner, Denny, Mod.	.947	30	17	37	3	57	2
Walk, Mitch, S.J.*	1.000	27	5	15	0	20	2
Watkins, Steve, L.E.	.800	5	0	4	1	5	0
Webb, Brandon, Lan.	.900	29	10	26	4	40	0
Wilson, Phil, R.C.	.970	26	15	17	1	33	2
Withers, Darvin, Vis.	.905	28	12	7	2	21	1
Wolcott, Bob, Mod.	1.000	3	1	4	0	5	0
Wolensky, Dave, R.C.	1.000	8	1	5	0	6	1
Wood, Mike, Mod.	.875	10	5	9	2	16	0
Wright, Chris, Bak.	1.000	49	9	13	0	22	1
Yacco, Anthony, S.J.	.500	7	0	1	1	2	0
Young, Doug, L.E.	.800	20	1	3	1	5	1
Ziegler, Mike, Vis.	.062	20	8	17	1	20	2
Zirelli, Mike, S.J.	.867	38	2	11	2	15	1

PITCHERS WITH TWO OR MORE TEAMS

Player, Team	Pct.	G	PO	A	E	TC	DP
Harville, Chad, Mod.	1.000	2	0	2	0	2	0
Harville, Chad, Vis.	1.000	1	1	0	0	1	0
Jacobs, Greg, R.C.*	1.000	31	5	4	0	9	0
Jacobs, Greg, Lan.*	1.000	20	2	2	0	4	0

The following players appeared only as designated hitter, pinch-hitter or pinch runner: Crespo, dh, ph; Hill, dh; Sledd, dh; Vaz, dh, ph; Wilder, dh, ph.

CLASS A California League

LEAGUE CHAMPIONS

Year	Team	Pct.
1914—	Fresno	.571
1915—	Modesto	.857
1916-40—	Did not operate.	
1941—	Fresno	.643
	Santa Barbara (2nd)*	.597
1942—	Santa Barbara†	.642
1943-44-45—	Did not operate.	
1946—	Stockton‡	.600
1947—	Stockton‡	.679
1948—	Fresno	.607
	Santa Barbara (3rd)*	.529
1949—	Bakersfield	.612
	San Jose (4th)*	.543
1950—	Ventura	.607
	Modesto (2nd)*	.586
1951—	Santa Barbara‡	.599
1952—	Fresno‡	.629
1953—	San Jose‡	.664
1954—	Modesto‡	.623
1955—	Stockton	.733
	Fresno§	.718
1956—	Fresno§	.650
1957—	Visalia∞	.622
	Salinas (4th)*	.504
1958—	Fresno*	.639
	Bakersfield	.672
1959—	Bakersfield	.592
	Modesto§	.643
1960—	Reno	.614
	Reno	.657
1961—	Reno	.743
	Reno	.643
1962—	San Jose§	.686
	Reno	.587
1963—	Modesto	.589
	Stockton§	.687
1964—	Fresno	.638
	Fresno	.600

Year	Team	Pct.
1965—	San Jose	.586
	Stockton§	.614
1966—	Modesto	.577
	Modesto	.671
1967—	San Jose§	.676
	Modesto	.586
1968—	San Jose	.629
	Fresno§	.623
1969—	Stockton§	.600
	Visalia	.614
1970—	Bakersfield	.667
	Bakersfield	.671
1971—	Visalia§	.583
	Fresno	.500
1972—	Modesto§	.547
	Bakersfield	.629
1973—	Lodi§	.657
	Bakersfield	.571
1974—	Fresno§	.607
	San Jose	.579
1975—	Reno	.614
	Reno	.614
1976—	Salinas	.650
	Reno§	.547
1977—	Salinas	.564
	Lodi§	.579
1978—	Visalia§	.698
	Lodi	.607
1979—	San Jose§	.636
	Reno	.525
1980—	Stockton§	.638
	Visalia	.507
1981—	Visalia	.621
	Lodi§	.521
1982—	Modesto§	.671
	Visalia	.586
1983—	Visalia	.621
	Redwood§	.529

Year	Team	Pct.
1984—	Modesto§	.597
	Bakersfield	.486
1985—	Fresno§	.575
	Stockton	.566
1986—	Palm Springs	.613
	Stockton§	.585
1987—	Fresno§	.559
	Reno	.535
1988—	Stockton	.657
	Riverside§	.599
1989—	Stockton	.627
	Bakersfield§	.577
1990—	Visalia	.638
	Stockton§	.582
1991—	San Jose	.676
	High Desert§	.537
1992—	Stockton§	.610
	Visalia	.551
1993—	High Desert§	.620
	Modesto	.529
1994—	Modesto	.706
	Rancho Cucamonga§	.566
1995—	San Bernardino§	.612
	San Jose	.550
1996—	San Jose	.636
	Lake Elsinore‡	.550
1997—	High Desert▲	.593
	San Bernardino	.486
1998—	San Jose▲	.593
	Rancho Cucamonga	.550
1999—	Modesto	.629
	San Bernardino▲	.567
2000—	Lancaster	.636
	San Bernardino▲	.550
2001—	Lake Elsinore◆	.650
	San Jose◆	.550

*Won four-club playoff. †League disbanded June 28. ‡Won championship and four-club playoff. §Won split-season playoff. ∞Won both halves of split season. ▲Played split season and won six-club playoff. ◆Played split season and were in midst of six-club playoff and declared co-champions when Professional Baseball declared a stoppage of play.

CLASS A *California League*

CAROLINA LEAGUE

LEAGUE OFFICE

President/treasurer
John Hopkins
Address
P.O. Box 9503
Greensboro, NC 27429
Phone
336-691-9030

Teams (affiliation)
Frederick Keys (Orioles)
Kinston Indians (Indians)
Lynchburg Hillcats (Pirates)
Myrtle Beach Pelicans (Braves)
Potomac Cannons (Cardinals)
Salem Avalanche (Rockies)

Wilmington (Del.) Blue Rocks (Royals)
Winston-Salem Warthogs (White Sox)

2001 FINAL STANDINGS

FIRST HALF

NORTHERN DIVISION

Team	W	L	T	Pct.	GB
Wilmington (Royals)	39	31	0	.557	...
Frederick (Orioles)	36	34	0	.514	3.0
Potomac (Cardinals)	35	35	0	.500	4.0
Lynchburg (Pirates)	27	40	0	.403	10.5

SOUTHERN DIVISION

Team	W	l	T	Prt	GB
Kinston (Indians)	44	26	0	.629	...
Myrtle Beach (Braves)	39	30	0	.565	4.5
Salem (Rockies)	33	35	0	.485	10.0
Winston-Salem (White Sox)	24	46	0	.343	20.0

SECOND HALF

NORTHERN DIVISION

Team	W	L	T	Pct.	GB
Wilmington (Royals)	39	31	0	.557	...
Frederick (Orioles)	34	35	0	.493	4.5
Potomac (Cardinals)	31	39	0	.443	8.0
Lynchburg (Pirates)	31	39	0	.443	8.0

SOUTHERN DIVISION

Team	W	L	T	Pct.	GB
Kinston (Indians)	45	25	0	.643	...
Salem (Rockies)	37	33	0	.529	8.0
Myrtle Beach (Braves)	32	37	0	.464	12.5
Winston-Salem (White Sox)	30	40	0	.429	15.0

COMPOSITE

Team	Kin.	Wil.	M.B.	Sal.	Fred.	Pot.	Lyn.	W.S.	W	L	T	Pct.	GB
Kinston (Indians)	...	10	16	14	14	15	9	11	89	51	0	.636	...
Wilmington (Royals)	10	...	11	10	10	13	15	9	78	62	0	.557	11.0
Myrtle Beach (Braves)	4	9	...	13	10	10	12	13	71	67	0	.514	17.0
Salem (Rockies)	6	10	7	...	11	11	12	13	70	68	0	.507	18.0
Frederick (Orioles)	6	10	9	9	...	9	13	14	70	69	0	.504	18.5
Potomac (Cardinals)	5	7	10	9	11	...	11	13	66	74	0	.471	23.0
Lynchburg (Pirates)	11	5	7	6	7	9	...	13	58	79	0	.423	29.5
Winston-Salem (White Sox)	9	11	7	7	6	7	7	...	54	86	0	.386	35.0

Major league affiliations in parentheses.

PLAYOFFS: Wilmington defeated Frederick two games to none; Salem defeated Kinston two games to one; Salem defeated Wilmington three games to two to win Carolina League Championship.

REGULAR-SEASON ATTENDANCE: Frederick, 320,262; Lynchburg, 112,310; Myrtle Beach, 214,160; Potomac, 181,758; Salem, 203,375; Wilmington, 336,074; Winston-Salem, 141,164 Total—1,642,272. Playoffs (10 games)—23,079. Carolina-California All-Star Game at Lancaster, Calif.—3,737.

MANAGERS: Frederick, Dave Cash; Kinston, Brad Komminsk; Lynchburg, Curtis Wilkerson; Myrtle Beach, Brian Skinner; Potomac, Joe Cunningham; Salem, Dave Collins; Wilmington, Jeff Garber; Winston-Salem, Wally Backman.

ALL-STAR TEAM: 1B—Garret Atkins, Salem; 2B—Javier Colina, Salem; 3B—Troy Cameron, Myrtle Beach-Kinston; SS—Wilson Betemit, Myrtle Beach; Utility INF—Napoelan Calzado, Frederick; OF—Covelli Crisp, Potomac; OF—Ryan Langerhans, Myrtle Beach; OF—Dan Phillips, Salem; Utility OF—Dee Haynes, Potomac; C—Victor Martinez, Kinston; DH—Ryan Hankins, Winston-Salem; SP—Jimmy Journell, Potomac; RP—Scotty Layfield, Potomac; Most Valuable Player—Victor Martinez, Kinston; Pitcher of the Year (tie)—Trey Hodges, Myrtle Beach and Jimmy Journell, Potomac; Manager of the Year—Brad Komminsk, Kinston.

2001 BATTING

TEAM

Team	Avg.	G	TPA	AB	R	H	TB	2B	3B	HR	RBI	SH	SF	HP	BB	IBB	SO	SB	CS	GDP	LOB	ShO	Slg.	OBP
Kinston	.252	140	5310	4694	629	1182	1759	233	34	92	564	34	34	88	460	14	1066	131	79	91	986	10	.375	.328
Potomac	.251	140	5086	4619	532	1160	1655	229	22	74	469	43	24	74	326	19	1003	127	84	92	927	5	.358	.309
Wilmington	.251	140	5229	4583	610	1149	1595	204	25	64	534	85	22	18	521	28	1091	110	62	117	1039	15	.348	.328
Frederick	.249	139	5078	4597	538	1146	1639	209	16	84	480	41	23	69	348	16	964	134	79	110	890	10	.357	.310
Salem	.248	138	5126	4540	558	1124	1717	257	24	95	509	53	45	83	405	24	961	88	58	77	972	13	.378	.318
Lynchburg	.244	137	5049	4542	538	1110	1569	208	25	67	478	30	29	66	382	12	1144	123	67	96	907	20	.345	.310
Win.-Salem	.241	140	5225	4658	507	1122	1569	226	19	61	459	66	36	76	389	20	987	147	91	97	937	12	.337	.308
Myrtle Beach	.241	138	4986	4499	553	1083	1617	221	14	95	512	23	36	6	422	16	1147	97	72	102	922	11	.359	.304

INDIVIDUAL

TOP QUALIFIERS FOR BATTING CHAMPIONSHIP

Minimum 378 plate appearances. *Lefthanded batter. †Switch-hitter.

Player, Team	Avg.	G	TPA	AB	R	H	TB	2B	3B	HR	RBI	SH	SF	HP	BB	IBB	SO	SB	CS	GDP	Slg.	OBP
Martinez, Victor, Kin.†	.329	114	470	420	59	138	205	33	2	10	57	0	3	8	39	1	60	3	3	12	.488	.394
Atkins, Garrett, Sal.	.325	135	555	465	70	151	219	43	5	5	67	2	6	8	74	10	98	6	4	8	.471	.421

Player, Team	Avg.	G	TPA	AB	R	H	TB	2B	3B	HR	RBI	SH	SF	HP	BB	IBB	SO	SB	CS	GDP	Slg.	OBP
Crisp, Covelli, Pot.†	.306	139	591	530	80	162	224	23	3	11	47	7	1	1	52	6	64	39	21	8	.423	.368
Haynes, Dee, Pot.	.290	114	448	417	45	121	190	24	3	13	72	4	2	11	14	1	82	5	1	12	.456	.329
Paulino, Ron, Lyn.	.290	103	400	352	30	102	138	16	1	6	51	3	7	2	36	0	76	4	1	11	.392	.353
Langerhans, Ryan, M.B.*	.287	125	516	450	66	129	186	30	3	7	48	2	0	8	55	3	104	22	13	6	.413	.374
Calzado, Napolean, Fred.	.287	121	495	464	50	133	172	20	2	5	41	5	4	6	16	2	52	34	14	9	.371	.316
Colina, Javier, Sal.	.285	113	487	439	67	125	199	33	7	9	58	5	12	9	22	1	61	9	4	8	.453	.324
Cunningham, Marco, Wil.	.284	138	621	497	82	141	183	22	4	4	61	9	1	19	95	7	119	17	8	14	.368	.417
Fiore, Curtis, M.B.	.283	100	405	329	56	93	135	20	2	6	42	3	5	19	47	2	69	5	1	13	.410	.398
Cabrera, Ray, Fred.	.274	123	497	460	62	126	197	21	4	14	65	1	1	12	23	1	73	16	7	15	.428	.325
Oborn, Spencer, W.S.	.274	120	438	402	54	110	148	25	2	3	37	11	3	2	20	0	64	13	3	11	.368	.309
Nelson, Eric, Wil.†	.271	113	476	421	44	114	159	27	6	2	41	16	2	7	30	2	99	6	6	6	.378	.328
Hankins, Ryan, W.S.	.267	108	454	389	54	104	175	26	0	15	58	0	1	7	57	5	76	4	5	6	.450	.370
Jones, Damien, M.B.*	.265	129	509	460	57	122	151	20	3	1	41	4	4	3	38	3	114	9	12	10	.328	.323
Langston, James, Lyn.†	.265	101	401	381	29	101	137	30	0	2	45	0	3	2	15	2	83	0	4	7	.360	.294

DEPARTMENTAL LEADERS: G—Crisp, 139; AB—Crisp, 530; R—Cunningham, 82; H—Crisp, 162; TB—Crisp, 224; 2B—Atkins, 43; 3B—Colina, Castillo, 7 each; HR—Gredvig, 20; RBI—Cameron, 76; SH—Nelson, 16; SF—Colina, 12; HP—Fiore, Cunningham, 19 each; BB—Cunningham, 95; IBB—Atkins, 10; SO—Ross, 159; SB—Durham, 50; CS—Durham, 22; GIDP—Cabrera, 15; Slg.—V. Martinez, .488; OBP—Atkins, .421.

ALL PLAYERS

*Lefthanded batter. †Switch-hitter.

Player, Team	Avg.	G	TPA	AB	R	H	TB	2B	3B	HR	RBI	SH	SF	HP	BB	IBB	SO	SB	CS	GDP	Slg.	OBP
Acevas, Jon, W.S.	.214	70	256	220	33	47	77	8	2	6	27	4	3	5	24	1	65	2	0	6	.350	.302
Alley, Chuck, Fred.†	.183	43	159	126	13	23	31	5	0	1	10	1	0	3	27	0	25	2	1	6	.246	.340
Alvarez, Tony, Lyn.	.344	25	100	93	10	32	42	4	0	2	11	0	0	0	7	0	11	7	3	2	.452	.390
Ascencion, Quincy, Fred.	.182	18	60	55	7	10	18	2	0	2	9	0	0	2	3	0	13	1	0	3	.327	.250
Aspito, Jason, W.S.*	.254	127	445	402	46	102	156	30	3	6	35	10	2	10	21	4	113	7	10	8	.388	.306
Atkins, Garrett, Sal.	.325	135	555	465	70	151	219	43	5	5	67	2	6	8	74	10	98	6	4	8	.471	.421
Bailey, Travis, Pot.	.216	73	248	227	25	49	88	13	4	6	24	0	2	4	15	2	75	3	6	1	.388	.274
Barmes, Clint, Sal.	.248	38	142	121	17	30	39	3	3	0	9	2	0	4	15	0	20	4	1	5	.322	.350
Barns, B.J., Lyn.*	.246	103	433	386	60	95	139	18	4	6	57	0	3	13	31	0	87	5	2	7	.360	.321
Bass, Chris, Lyn.	.150	7	25	20	4	3	4	1	0	0	3	0	0	0	5	0	8	1	1	1	.200	.320
Becker, Jeff, Kin.	.246	24	81	69	7	17	25	5	0	1	11	0	0	3	9	0	16	0	0	2	.362	.358
Bell, Mike, Sal.	.385	4	18	13	1	5	6	1	0	0	0	0	0	0	5	0	1	1	0	0	.462	.556
Benefield, Brian, Kin.	.333	17	72	57	14	19	29	5	1	1	8	1	1	5	8	1	9	5	0	2	.509	.451
Berger, Matt, W.S.	.259	70	269	239	20	62	97	18	1	5	24	2	3	5	20	1	74	0	3	5	.406	.356
Berroa, Angel, Wil.	.317	51	228	199	43	63	107	18	4	6	25	3	3	14	9	1	41	10	6	7	.538	.382
Betemit, Wilson, M.B.†	.277	84	346	318	38	88	131	20	1	7	43	0	4	1	23	1	71	8	5	8	.412	.324
Bonifay, Josh, Lyn.	.297	85	355	323	42	96	151	14	1	13	41	0	2	4	26	0	87	5	4	6	.467	.355
Boscan, Jean, M.B.	.167	18	60	54	3	9	11	2	0	0	6	1	1	1	3	0	25	0	1	1	.204	.220
Bost, Tom, Kin.*	.254	50	152	130	18	33	60	7	1	6	21	0	1	5	16	0	31	3	1	1	.462	.355
Brandes, Landon, Pot.	.220	27	88	82	6	18	31	4	0	3	13	2	1	0	3	0	23	1	2	0	.378	.244
Brignac, Junior, M.B.†	.193	66	264	233	28	45	71	8	0	6	19	4	1	2	24	0	68	6	9	6	.305	.273
Brown, Adrian, Lyn.†	.333	4	20	18	2	6	6	0	0	0	1	0	0	1	1	0	3	2	0	0	.333	.400
Brueggemann, Dean, Sal.*	.000	49	1	1	0	0	0	0	0	0	0	0	0	0	0	0	1	0	0	0	.000	.000
Cabrera, Ray, Fred.	.274	123	497	460	62	126	197	21	4	14	65	1	1	12	23	1	73	16	7	15	.428	.325
Calahan, Larry, W.S.*	.250	13	52	44	5	11	16	2	0	1	11	2	1	1	4	0	8	0	2	0	.364	.320
Calzado, Napolean, Fred.	.287	121	495	464	50	133	172	20	2	5	41	5	4	6	16	2	52	34	14	9	.371	.316
Cameron, Troy, M.B.-Kin.†...	.251	126	518	447	66	112	188	27	2	15	76	1	2	9	59	2	115	2	6	13	.421	.348
Caradonna, Brett, W.S.*	.235	104	388	345	34	81	103	14	1	2	25	3	4	5	29	2	66	7	7	12	.299	.300
Carvajal, Ramon, Pot.†	.217	125	495	456	59	99	147	16	4	8	39	10	2	5	22	0	115	17	4	5	.322	.256
Castillo, Jose, Lyn.	.245	125	521	485	57	119	174	20	7	7	49	4	2	9	21	2	94	23	10	9	.359	.288
Catalanotte, Greg, Sal.†	.217	119	457	401	45	87	144	24	0	11	40	5	2	5	44	1	125	8	5	6	.359	.301
Cates, Gary, Fred.	.242	28	98	91	8	22	26	4	0	0	4	3	0	0	4	0	16	0	1	0	.286	.274
Cercy, Rick, Sal.	.000	40	1	1	0	0	0	0	0	0	0	0	0	0	0	0	0	0	0	0	.000	.000
Church, Ryan, Kin.*	.241	24	103	83	16	20	42	7	0	5	15	0	1	1	18	2	23	1	0	1	.506	.379
Clark, Greg, Pot.	.200	8	15	15	0	3	5	2	0	0	2	0	0	0	0	0	4	0	1	0	.333	.200
Cleto, Ambioris, Lyn.	.166	71	211	193	22	32	47	12	0	1	14	5	1	3	9	0	53	7	1	3	.244	.214
Coates, Brad, Kin.	.113	18	60	53	4	6	7	1	0	0	3	0	1	1	5	0	20	0	0	1	.132	.200
Colina, Javier, Sal.	.285	113	487	439	67	125	199	33	7	9	58	5	12	9	22	1	61	9	4	8	.453	.324
Combs, Chris, Lyn.*	.227	133	536	463	68	105	167	18	4	12	53	0	2	5	66	4	153	2	1	11	.361	.328
Crisp, Covelli, Pot.†	.306	139	591	530	80	162	224	23	3	11	47	7	1	1	52	6	64	39	21	8	.423	.368
Crocker, Nick, M.B.*	.215	81	271	246	27	53	83	10	1	6	27	1	0	4	20	1	91	6	5	2	.337	.284
Cruz, Edgar, Kin.	.128	15	50	47	5	6	7	1	0	0	3	0	0	0	3	0	10	0	0	1	.149	.180
Cunningham, Marco, Wil.	.284	138	621	497	82	141	183	22	4	4	61	9	1	19	95	7	119	17	8	14	.368	.417
De Caster, Yurendell, Lyn.	.104	13	51	48	1	5	7	2	0	0	4	0	0	0	3	0	16	0	0	3	.146	.157
Diaz, Maikell, Fred.	.248	95	333	310	34	77	99	14	1	2	18	7	1	4	11	0	75	9	9	4	.319	.282
Dodson, Jeremy, Wil.*	.214	70	256	215	27	46	73	8	2	5	30	0	1	7	32	3	78	7	0	4	.340	.333
Duncan, Chris, Pot.*	.179	49	180	168	12	30	45	6	0	3	16	1	0	1	10	0	47	4	4	5	.268	.229
Durham, Chad, W.S.	.254	133	589	528	56	134	164	16	4	2	38	9	6	3	43	1	92	50	22	9	.311	.310
Escobar, Gustavo, Pot.	.375	4	9	8	0	3	3	0	0	0	0	0	0	1	0	0	1	0	0	0	.375	.444
Espinoza, Efren, Lyn.	.145	19	65	62	4	9	11	2	0	0	4	0	0	1	2	0	19	1	1	0	.177	.185
Ewing, Byron, Kin.	.243	90	344	301	41	73	110	14	1	7	38	0	0	8	35	0	67	7	7	6	.365	.337
Fatur, Brian, Pot.	.235	60	244	226	20	53	72	13	0	2	20	4	2	6	6	1	38	3	1	5	.319	.271
Felix, Hersy, Wil.	.071	4	16	14	1	1	1	0	0	0	1	0	1	0	1	0	1	0	0	0	.071	.125
Fennell, Jason, W.S.†	.189	63	196	175	17	33	38	5	0	0	14	0	0	3	18	1	33	1	1	3	.217	.276
Fiore, Curtis, M.B.	.283	100	405	329	56	93	135	20	2	6	42	3	5	19	47	2	69	5	1	13	.410	.398
Flores, Ralphs, W.S.	.200	25	84	80	5	16	16	0	0	0	6	0	0	0	4	0	14	1	1	2	.200	.238
Freeman, Choo, Sal.	.240	132	570	517	63	124	174	16	5	8	42	8	5	9	31	1	108	19	7	8	.337	.292
Friar, Roddy, W.S.	.220	18	48	41	4	9	11	2	0	0	3	0	0	1	6	0	20	1	1	0	.268	.333
Galante, Matt, Pot.	.167	4	7	6	0	1	1	0	0	0	0	0	0	0	1	0	2	0	0	0	.167	.286
Gall, John, Pot.	.317	84	349	319	44	101	138	25	0	4	33	0	1	3	24	4	40	5	6	9	.433	.369
Garcia, Tony, W.S.	.223	63	223	206	12	46	61	6	3	1	18	1	2	7	0	0	45	4	4	4	.296	.270

Player, Team	Avg.	G	TPA	AB	R	H	TB	2B	3B	HR	RBI	SH	SF	HP	BB	IBB	SO	SB	CS	GDP	Slg.	OBP
Garrett, Shawn, Lyn.†	.294	52	214	194	28	57	97	13	0	9	28	0	0	3	17	0	64	6	4	3	.500	.360
Gettis, Byron, Wil.	.251	82	339	303	34	76	119	21	2	6	51	3	1	12	20	1	70	4	5	7	.393	.321
Gibbs, Mark, Fred.	.207	42	135	121	12	25	38	4	0	3	12	3	0	3	8	0	42	2	1	1	.314	.273
Gomez, Alexis, Wil.*	.302	48	183	169	29	51	66	8	2	1	9	2	0	1	11	2	43	7	3	4	.391	.348
Gonzalez, Luis, Kin.	.322	52	208	183	31	59	88	14	0	5	19	1	2	8	14	0	36	3	5	1	.481	.391
Gordon, Alex, Fred.*	.275	27	87	80	4	22	30	3	1	1	15	0	1	2	4	0	31	2	0	3	.375	.322
Gredvig, Doug, Fred.	.254	129	531	484	71	123	222	35	2	20	62	0	2	5	37	1	125	2	3	8	.459	.313
Green, Nick, M.B.	.266	80	341	297	49	79	129	18	1	10	42	1	3	7	32	0	70	9	2	2	.434	.348
Green, Steve, Pot.*	.000	2	6	5	0	0	0	0	0	0	0	0	0	0	1	0	3	0	0	0	.000	.167
Grindell, Nate, Kin.	.276	69	296	272	41	75	112	17	1	6	41	0	5	3	16	3	42	1	3	6	.412	.318
Haad, Yamid, Lyn.	.182	3	11	11	0	2	3	1	0	0	1	0	0	0	0	0	3	1	0	0	.273	.182
Haase, Jeff, Kin.	.200	19	66	60	4	12	22	2	1	2	9	0	0	2	4	0	20	0	0	1	.367	.273
Hammond, Joey, Fred.	.319	25	112	94	12	30	37	5	1	0	8	1	1	0	16	0	18	1	3	1	.394	.414
Hankins, Ryan, W.S.	.267	108	454	389	54	104	175	26	0	15	58	0	1	7	57	5	76	4	5	6	.450	.370
Hansen, Jed, Wil.	.328	17	76	64	8	21	41	3	1	5	20	1	1	0	10	1	18	2	2	1	.641	.413
Hart, Bo, Pot.	.305	81	316	279	48	85	129	23	3	5	34	4	1	15	17	1	69	16	7	3	.462	.375
Hart, Corey, Wil.†	.287	75	345	282	53	81	107	14	0	4	26	4	1	3	55	4	62	1	6	9	.379	.408
Harts, Jeremy, Lyn.†	.210	125	469	410	50	86	114	17	1	3	34	5	2	6	46	0	151	10	11	10	.278	.297
Harvey, Ken, Wil.	.380	35	156	137	22	52	81	9	1	6	27	0	0	6	13	0	21	3	1	5	.591	.455
Hattenburg, Ray, Wil.†	.209	83	294	244	28	51	60	9	0	0	25	5	0	6	39	0	67	4	4	7	.246	.342
Haynes, Dee, Pot.	.290	114	448	417	45	121	190	24	3	13	72	4	2	11	14	1	82	5	1	12	.456	.329
Hernandez, Jesus, Kin.*	.159	23	96	82	15	13	29	3	2	3	7	1	1	2	10	0	20	1	1	0	.354	.263
Hernandez, Johnny, Pot.†	.231	131	502	464	42	107	138	20	4	1	28	1	3	2	32	2	108	7	12	9	.297	.281
Hernandez, Jose, Lyn.	.163	24	89	80	7	13	16	3	0	0	6	3	0	2	4	1	13	1	0	2	.200	.221
Holliday, Matt, Sal.	.275	72	296	255	36	70	121	16	1	11	52	0	5	3	33	3	42	11	3	10	.475	.358
Hopper, Norris, Wil.	.247	110	437	389	38	96	109	6	2	1	38	11	0	5	32	2	60	16	4	15	.280	.312
Izturis, Maicer, Kin.†	.240	114	486	433	47	104	135	16	6	1	39	10	4	8	31	1	81	32	9	8	.312	.300
Janowicz, Nate, Kin.*	.253	46	178	154	21	39	48	7	1	0	23	1	3	2	18	0	30	4	1	3	.312	.333
Jenkins, Brian, Kin.	.349	23	92	83	10	29	41	5	2	1	14	0	1	1	7	0	13	2	3	1	.494	.402
Johnson, Eric, Kin.	.230	127	556	492	77	111	160	17	5	7	45	4	3	10	57	1	124	22	14	8	.330	.322
Johnson, Gabe, Pot.	.189	86	309	281	24	53	79	14	0	4	22	1	3	3	21	0	113	2	3	8	.281	.250
Johnston, Clint, Lyn.*	1.000	12	1	1	0	1	1	0	0	0	0	0	0	0	0	0	0	0	0	0	1.000	1.000
Jones, Damien, M.B.*	.265	129	509	460	57	122	151	20	3	1	41	4	4	3	38	3	114	9	12	10	.328	.323
Kane, Kyle, W.S.*	.000	14	1	1	0	0	0	0	0	0	0	0	0	0	0	0	1	0	0	0	.000	.000
Katz, Damon, Kin.	.161	13	37	31	0	5	6	1	0	0	0	0	0	3	3	0	9	0	0	3	.194	.297
Langerhans, Ryan, M.B.*	.287	125	516	450	66	129	186	30	3	7	48	2	0	8	55	3	104	22	13	6	.413	.374
Langston, James, Lyn.†	.265	101	401	381	20	101	137	30	0	2	45	0	3	2	15	2	83	0	4	7	.360	.294
LaRoche, Adam, M.B.*	.251	126	514	471	49	118	170	31	0	7	47	0	4	9	30	3	108	10	8	13	.361	.305
Leal, Jaeme, M.B.	.214	63	252	215	32	46	100	7	1	15	39	0	3	14	20	1	88	0	0	6	.465	.317
Leon, Alfredo, Fred.	.188	10	35	32	2	6	7	1	0	0	0	0	0	1	2	0	7	0	1	1	.219	.257
Lincoln, Justin, Cal.	.107	50	172	150	15	20	41	6	0	3	10	2	1	4	9	0	63	1	1	0	.263	.229
Lindsey, John, Sal.	.280	51	186	168	19	47	81	13	0	7	32	0	0	5	13	2	51	1	1	2	.482	.349
Lopez-Cao, Mike, Fred.*	.372	15	48	43	4	16	26	1	0	3	8	0	0	1	4	1	10	0	1	0	.605	.438
Mack, Tony, Fred.	.199	110	360	332	33	66	93	12	0	5	33	6	2	2	18	0	102	9	8	9	.280	.243
Mann, Dorok, Lyn.*	.275	30	113	102	14	28	35	3	2	0	11	2	0	0	9	0	25	4	2	3	.343	.333
Manning, Pat, M.B.	.223	62	256	220	23	49	91	12	0	10	30	2	1	5	28	0	41	2	3	4	.414	.323
Martin, Justin, Lyn.†	.287	50	203	181	25	52	62	8	1	0	7	2	1	2	17	1	34	4	9	1	.343	.353
Martinez, Lou, Sal.	.143	2	8	7	0	1	1	0	0	0	0	1	0	0	0	0	0	0	0	0	.143	.143
Martinez, Octavio, Fred.	.217	98	362	336	23	73	90	14	0	1	29	4	1	11	10	0	47	3	2	15	.268	.263
Martinez, Victor, Kin.†	.329	114	470	420	59	138	205	33	2	10	57	0	3	8	39	1	60	3	3	12	.488	.394
Matcuk, Steve, Sal.	.000	25	1	1	0	0	0	0	0	0	0	0	0	0	0	0	0	0	0	0	.000	.000
Matos, Luis, Fred.	.429	2	8	7	3	3	6	0	0	1	2	0	0	1	1	0	3	0	0	0	.857	.500
McAuley, Jim, Wil.	.209	54	190	163	17	34	39	5	0	0	15	5	1	2	19	1	46	1	0	4	.239	.297
McQueen, Eric, Sal.	.000	2	7	5	0	0	0	0	0	0	0	1	0	0	1	0	5	0	0	0	.000	.167
Medrano, Steve, Wil.†	.205	42	168	146	22	30	33	3	0	0	7	4	0	4	14	0	37	2	2	1	.226	.293
Meier, Dan, Lyn.*	.288	20	84	73	11	21	37	7	0	3	12	0	1	0	10	0	21	1	1	2	.507	.369
Mercado, Wilkins, Wil.	.145	60	182	165	10	24	34	7	0	1	13	5	0	1	11	0	43	0	0	3	.206	.203
Morriman, Terrell, W.S.*	.104	17	57	48	4	5	5	0	0	0	1	0	0	0	9	0	17	4	0	0	.104	.246
Minges, Tyler, Kin.	.252	66	271	250	30	63	94	12	2	5	35	2	3	4	12	1	48	3	2	6	.376	.294
Moore, Chris, Sal.*	.159	19	54	44	3	7	9	2	0	0	1	0	1	0	9	0	11	0	0	0	.205	.296
Moraga, Omar, Kin.*	.233	13	44	43	4	10	14	1	0	1	2	0	0	0	1	0	6	0	1	1	.326	.250
Moreno, Christopher, Fred.	.063	19	37	32	7	2	4	2	0	0	2	1	0	0	4	0	15	0	0	0	.125	.167
Moreno, Jorge, Kin.	.204	101	406	368	31	75	99	7	1	5	35	8	1	3	26	2	94	7	8	6	.269	.261
Mortimer, Mark, M.B.	.193	50	206	181	18	35	45	4	0	2	17	0	3	5	17	0	31	0	0	7	.249	.277
Muro, Robert, W.S.	.246	96	411	354	39	87	148	25	0	12	54	0	1	9	47	2	71	4	4	6	.418	.348
Nelson, Eric, Wil.†	.271	113	476	421	44	114	159	27	6	2	41	16	2	7	30	2	99	6	6	6	.378	.328
Neubart, Adam, Wil.	.182	26	67	55	13	10	13	3	0	0	5	1	1	4	6	0	13	0	2	0	.236	.303
Nicholson, Tommy, W.S.*	.245	138	537	477	46	117	147	22	1	2	40	10	3	5	42	2	97	10	14	7	.308	.311
Oborn, Spencer, W.S.	.274	120	438	402	54	110	148	25	2	3	37	11	3	2	20	0	64	13	3	11	.368	.309
Orr, Pete, M.B.*	.233	92	351	317	38	74	98	10	1	4	23	3	1	11	19	0	70	17	6	3	.309	.299
Paulino, Ron, Lyn.	.290	103	400	352	30	102	138	16	1	6	51	3	7	2	36	0	76	4	1	11	.392	.353
Pena, Amaury, W.S.	.181	62	144	127	9	23	33	5	1	1	12	1	1	4	11	0	45	4	6	4	.260	.266
Peralta, John, Kin.	.240	125	505	441	57	106	155	24	2	7	47	2	3	1	58	0	148	4	8	9	.351	.328
Phillips, Dan, Sal.	.262	132	545	493	65	129	212	35	0	16	68	5	6	14	27	2	106	11	12	9	.430	.315
Pichardo, Henry, Kin.	.289	14	50	45	6	13	19	3	0	1	7	0	0	1	4	0	11	0	1	3	.422	.340
Pogue, Jamie, Pot.	.240	108	419	354	48	85	124	15	0	8	42	1	1	7	55	1	61	11	7	6	.350	.353
Pollaro, Dallas, Pot.	.253	50	173	162	15	41	48	7	0	0	15	1	0	0	10	0	26	4	0	6	.296	.297
Pond, Simon, Kin.*	.340	25	110	97	13	33	55	8	1	4	24	0	2	1	10	0	12	1	1	0	.567	.400
Powers, Jeff, Sal.*	.186	44	132	118	9	22	28	4	1	0	6	6	0	1	7	0	15	0	2	3	.237	.238
Price, Ryan, Sal.	.000	29	1	1	0	0	0	0	0	0	0	0	0	0	0	0	1	0	0	0	.000	.000
Prieto, Jon, Lyn.†	.210	127	444	395	41	83	102	12	2	1	32	2	4	8	37	1	76	21	7	6	.258	.285
Quintero, Humberto, W.S.	.240	43	166	154	15	37	43	6	0	0	12	2	3	2	5	0	19	9	3	3	.279	.268
Rachels, Wes, Fred.	.261	108	426	357	43	93	105	12	0	0	26	3	2	6	58	4	52	4	5	8	.294	.371

Player, Team	Avg.	G	TPA	AB	R	H	TB	2B	3B	HR	RBI	SH	SF	HP	BB	IBB	SO	SB	CS	GDP	Slg.	OBP
Raines, Tim Jr., Fred.†	.250	23	98	84	15	21	35	3	1	3	13	1	0	0	13	0	23	14	4	2	.417	.351
Ravelo, Manny, Lyn.	.250	20	95	80	17	20	24	0	2	0	2	2	0	4	9	1	15	16	3	2	.300	.355
Reed, Keith, Fred.	.270	72	283	267	28	72	107	14	0	7	29	1	1	1	13	1	57	8	6	7	.401	.305
Requena, Alex, Kin.†	.212	62	285	259	30	55	76	7	4	2	13	3	0	4	19	1	80	32	10	1	.293	.277
Reyes, Guillermo, W.S.†	.208	59	240	216	24	45	51	4	1	0	24	4	1	5	14	0	33	16	4	7	.236	.271
Reyes, Milver, Lyn.	.103	9	32	29	2	3	3	0	0	0	1	0	0	1	2	0	7	0	0	1	.103	.188
Rickon, Jim, Kin.	.225	29	88	80	13	18	33	3	0	4	13	0	0	2	6	0	23	0	1	3	.413	.295
Rodgers, Albert, Pot.	.271	36	139	129	19	35	50	9	0	2	10	1	0	3	6	0	39	0	2	4	.388	.319
Rodriguez, Jeff, M.B.	.206	76	278	248	22	51	73	10	0	4	27	0	1	5	24	1	57	0	1	6	.294	.288
Rogers, Ed, Fred.	.260	73	318	292	39	76	126	20	3	8	41	2	2	8	14	0	47	18	6	8	.432	.310
Ross, Don, Wil.*	.209	134	547	459	60	96	155	18	1	13	59	5	5	16	62	4	159	3	0	10	.338	.321
Ruiz, Willy, Wil.	.240	105	376	337	45	81	87	6	0	0	30	7	3	0	29	0	44	26	13	8	.258	.298
Sanchez, Tino, Sal.†	.233	91	322	283	32	66	84	9	0	3	26	2	2	3	32	2	30	4	4	6	.297	.316
Sandoval, Danny, W.S.	.273	48	198	176	25	48	68	11	0	3	14	6	2	3	11	1	31	11	2	3	.386	.323
Santamarina, Juan, W.S.*	.200	17	64	60	9	12	20	2	0	2	0	1	0	0	3	0	18	0	0	0	.333	.230
Schumacher, Shawn, Pot.*	.285	68	274	249	15	71	87	8	1	2	38	2	4	6	13	1	20	2	1	8	.349	.331
Seal, Scott, Sal.*	.181	34	106	94	9	17	27	4	0	2	9	2	0	2	8	2	20	1	1	1	.287	.260
Shier, Peter, Fred.	.200	13	42	40	5	8	9	1	0	0	3	0	0	0	2	0	7	1	1	0	.225	.238
Sickles, Jeremy, Lyn.	.239	29	101	92	4	22	34	6	0	2	6	1	0	2	6	0	23	1	2	3	.370	.300
Sosa, Jovanny, Fred.	.179	64	243	207	27	37	62	4	0	7	25	0	1	1	34	2	72	1	1	6	.300	.296
Stepka, Tom, Sal.	1.000	33	1	1	0	1	1	0	0	0	0	0	0	0	0	0	0	0	0	0	1.000	1.000
Suarez, Luis, W.S.	.133	6	15	15	0	2	3	1	0	0	1	0	0	0	0	0	7	0	0	1	.200	.133
Taylor, Seth, Sal.	.263	131	520	480	52	126	178	26	1	8	45	8	2	4	26	0	66	6	8	7	.371	.305
Terveen, Bryce, M.B.*	.180	20	69	61	7	11	20	3	0	2	7	0	1	3	4	0	17	0	0	3	.328	.261
Thames, Damon, Pot.	.190	44	125	116	16	22	29	4	0	1	6	2	1	3	3	0	28	6	1	3	.250	.221
Thomas, Chuck, M.B.*	.159	12	48	44	4	7	8	1	0	0	6	0	1	0	3	1	8	1	0	3	.182	.208
Thompson, Doug, Sal.	.000	18	1	1	0	0	0	0	0	0	0	0	0	0	0	0	1	0	0	0	.000	.000
Tonis, Mike, Wil.	.252	33	142	123	15	31	48	8	0	3	18	2	0	2	15	0	34	0	0	6	.390	.344
Tucker, Mamon, Fred.	.285	69	287	256	33	73	87	9	1	1	23	2	4	0	25	3	46	7	5	4	.340	.344
Um, Jong, M.B.	.153	24	82	72	5	11	15	1	0	1	7	1	0	2	7	0	33	0	0	1	.208	.247
Vilorio, Miguel, Sal.	.356	12	45	45	6	16	18	2	0	0	0	0	0	0	0	0	9	1	0	0	.400	.356
Walter, Scott, Wil.	.249	60	231	201	19	50	80	9	0	7	33	2	1	9	18	1	36	1	0	6	.398	.336
Warren, Chris, Sal.†	.197	74	164	132	20	26	53	7	1	6	18	1	1	4	26	0	51	3	4	1	.402	.344
Webster, Robert, Fred.	.438	5	18	16	3	7	9	2	0	0	2	0	0	1	1	0	2	0	0	0	.563	.500
Weichard, Paul, Lyn.†	.243	19	75	70	10	17	18	1	0	0	5	1	1	0	3	0	22	1	1	0	.257	.270
White, Kenneth, Fred.†	.182	3	11	11	0	2	3	1	0	0	0	0	0	0	0	0	4	0	0	0	.273	.182
Williams, Charles, Pot.†	.141	42	104	85	10	12	16	1	0	1	6	2	0	1	16	0	25	1	4	0	.188	.284
Winchester, Jeff, Sal.	.161	95	341	304	29	49	83	13	0	7	26	4	2	8	23	0	75	2	2	3	.273	.237
Young, Colin, Sal.*	.000	48	1	1	0	0	0	0	0	0	0	0	0	0	0	0	1	0	0	0	.000	.000

PLAYERS WITH TWO OR MORE TEAMS

Player, Team	Avg.	G	TPA	AB	R	H	TB	2B	3B	HR	RBI	SH	SF	HP	BB	IBB	SO	SB	CS	GDP	Slg.	OBP
Cameron, Troy, M.B.†	.251	65	254	223	27	56	92	13	1	7	38	0	2	6	23	0	62	2	6	7	.413	.335
Cameron, Troy, Kin.†	.250	61	264	224	39	56	96	14	1	8	38	1	0	3	36	2	53	0	4	5	.429	.361

GRAND SLAMS: Cameron, Cunningham, Rodriguez, 2 each; Aspito, Bailey, Betemit, Bost, Carvajal, Ewing, Gordon, Langston, LaRoche, Leal, Mortimer, 1 each.

AWARDED FIRST BASE ON CATCHER'S INTERFERENCE: Gredvig 3 (Winchester, Quintero, Haase); Alley 2 (Winchester, Paulino); Caradonna 2 (Leon, Pogue), Fiore 2 (Sanchez, Pogue); Gall 2 (V. Martinez, Mortimer); Dodson (V. Martinez), Green (Pogue), Langerhans (V. Martinez), Pogue (Winchester).

2001 PITCHING

TEAM

Team	W	L	Pct.	ERA	G	CG	ShO	Sv.	IP	H	TBF	R	ER	HR	SH	SF	HB	BB	IBB	SO	WP	Bk.
Kinston	89	51	.636	2.73	140	6	17	46	1251.1	1073	5186	461	380	65	34	24	65	390	19	1260	39	5
Frederick	70	69	.504	3.21	139	8	10	40	1220.0	1127	5112	526	435	82	47	35	85	372	16	1137	63	6
Potomac	66	74	.471	3.26	140	8	12	38	1207.0	1128	5093	566	437	92	43	33	90	348	26	909	67	7
Wilmington	78	62	.557	3.27	140	2	13	35	1235.1	1115	5171	537	449	62	48	39	8	379	15	1052	81	5
Myrtle Beach	71	67	.514	3.36	138	4	16	39	1205.2	1086	5018	526	450	88	51	27	53	347	14	1102	54	8
Winston-Salem	54	86	.386	3.66	140	10	7	27	1243.2	1191	5382	611	506	83	63	35	89	532	30	1022	61	5
Salem	70	68	.507	3.77	138	3	12	44	1198.0	1165	5178	607	502	73	38	21	3	458	13	985	98	13
Lynchburg	58	79	.423	3.87	137	8	9	37	1192.0	1191	5164	631	513	88	51	35	87	427	16	896	55	8

INDIVIDUAL

TOP QUALIFIERS FOR EARNED-RUN AVERAGE TITLE

Minimum 112 innings. *Lefthanded pitcher.

Pitcher, Team	W	L	Pct.	ERA	G	GS	CG	ShO	GF	Sv.	IP	H	TBF	R	ER	HR	SH	SF	HB	BB	IBB	SO	WP	Bk.
Journell, Jimmy, Pot.	14	6	.700	2.50	26	26	0	0	0	0	151.0	121	620	54	42	8	6	5	18	42	0	156	7	0
Gobble, Jimmy, Wil.*	10	6	.625	2.55	27	27	0	0	0	0	162.1	134	649	58	46	8	9	4	9	33	3	154	7	0
Hodges, Trey, M.B.	15	8	.652	2.76	26	26	1	0	0	0	173.0	156	686	64	53	13	4	2	5	18	0	139	7	0
Bong, Jung, M.B.*	13	9	.591	3.00	28	28	0	0	0	0	168.0	151	677	67	56	7	6	3	4	47	0	145	7	1
Tallet, Brian, Kin.*	9	7	.563	3.04	27	27	2	0	0	0	160.0	134	644	62	54	12	3	2	4	38	0	164	2	0
Lantigua, Eduardo, W.S.	8	6	.571	3.06	22	19	1	1	1	0	120.2	92	499	46	41	7	5	2	7	58	1	113	8	0
Cook, Aaron, Sal.	11	11	.500	3.08	27	27	0	0	0	0	155.0	157	649	73	53	4	5	1	7	38	0	122	6	1
Vance, Cory, Sal.*	10	8	.556	3.10	26	26	1	0	0	0	154.0	129	641	65	53	9	3	2	14	65	0	142	4	4
Garcia, Sonny, Fred.	8	9	.471	3.27	25	20	2	0	3	1	143.0	132	593	67	52	9	8	2	10	33	3	139	4	1
Natale, Mike, Wil.	9	8	.529	3.28	28	27	0	0	0	0	159.1	152	662	75	58	8	2	6	13	33	0	134	13	1
Sprague, Kevin, Pot.*	9	8	.529	3.40	26	26	2	0	0	0	164.1	155	674	64	62	9	3	4	11	43	3	113	9	1
Bennett, Jeff, Lyn.	11	10	.524	3.42	25	25	1	0	0	0	166.0	171	691	78	63	14	6	2	13	30	1	98	2	0
West, Brian, W.S.	7	12	.368	3.46	28	28	3	1	0	0	169.0	179	735	75	65	11	8	10	9	70	2	130	8	0

CLASS A Carolina League

Pitcher, Team	W	L	Pct.	ERA	G	GS	CG	ShO	GF	Sv.	IP	H	TBF	R	ER	HR	SH	SF	HB	BB	IBB	SO	WP	Bk.
Ennis, John, M.B.	6	8	.429	3.58	25	25	1	0	0	0	138.1	111	569	63	55	12	4	5	7	45	0	144	2	3
Burch, Matt, Wil.	11	10	.524	3.70	28	22	0	0	1	0	148.1	145	639	73	61	6	9	7	21	50	2	92	8	0

DEPARTMENTAL LEADERS: W—Hodges, 15; L—Tejeda, 14; Pct.—Wallace, .833; G—Jackson, 53; GS—Bong, West, 28 each; CG—Ulacia, 4; ShO—Several tied at 1; GF—Jackson, 47; Sv.—Layfield, 31; IP—Hodges, 173; H—Ledden, 184; TBF—West, 735; R—Ledden, 112; ER—Ledden, 92; HR—Ledden, 18; SH—Butler, Burch, Gobble, 9 each; SF—West, 10; HB—Burch, 21; BB—Price, 85; IBB—Kohl, 8; SO—Tallet, 164; WP—Price, 45; BK—Bent, Vance, 4 each.

ALL PITCHERS

*Lefthanded pitcher.

Pitcher, Team	W	L	Pct.	ERA	G	GS	CG	ShO	GF	Sv.	IP	H	TBF	R	ER	HR	SH	SF	HB	BB	IBB	SO	WP	Bk.
Alcala, Jason, Lyn.	0	2	.000	2.36	18	0	0	0	17	7	26.2	21	105	7	7	2	1	1	1	5	1	27	2	0
Alvarado, Carlos, Lyn.	0	0	.000	3.27	4	1	0	0	1	0	11.0	8	42	5	4	0	0	0	7	0	8	2	0
Ammons, Cary, Wil.*	2	6	.250	3.88	12	12	1	0	0	0	58.0	50	240	26	25	5	5	3	4	21	0	64	1	1
Andrade, Jancy, Fred.	5	5	.500	4.44	20	13	0	0	2	0	75.0	80	326	47	37	6	4	6	6	28	1	57	6	1
Ayelson, Josh, Pot.	2	5	.286	5.66	10	10	1	0	0	0	56.2	61	251	41	35	10	2	1	7	19	0	38	2	0
Ayala, Luis, Sal.	0	1	.000	4.05	13	0	0	0	12	7	13.1	19	61	10	6	0	1	0	2	5	0	10	2	1
Bajenaru, Jeff, W.S.	2	4	.333	3.35	35	0	0	0	28	10	40.1	32	174	16	15	3	4	0	1	21	2	51	3	1
Baker, Jason, Kin.	4	1	.800	3.44	13	8	1	1	1	0	49.2	44	212	21	19	5	0	1	1	22	0	44	3	0
Bechler, Steve, Fred.	5	2	.714	2.27	13	13	1	1	0	0	83.1	73	330	24	21	3	3	4	2	22	0	71	3	0
Bedard, Erik, Fred.*	9	2	.818	2.15	17	17	0	0	0	0	96.1	68	382	27	23	4	3	1	9	26	0	130	3	0
Bennett, Jeff, Lyn.	11	10	.524	3.42	25	25	2	1	0	0	166.0	171	691	78	63	14	6	2	13	30	1	98	2	0
Bent, Andy, M.B.	1	5	.167	3.38	29	0	0	0	9	1	56.0	44	237	29	21	5	5	2	3	25	3	53	3	4
Bohannon, Brad, W.S.	2	1	.667	1.73	23	0	0	0	12	5	36.1	33	152	10	7	0	4	0	1	10	1	33	2	0
Bong, Jung, M.B.*	13	9	.591	3.00	28	28	0	0	0	0	168.0	151	677	67	56	7	6	3	4	47	0	145	7	1
Bradley, Bobby, Lyn.	1	2	.333	3.12	9	9	0	0	0	0	49.0	44	209	23	17	3	3	0	1	20	0	46	5	0
Brantley, Brian, Sal.	5	3	.625	2.78	28	1	0	0	11	2	58.1	43	253	23	18	3	3	2	12	21	2	55	11	2
Brueggemann, Dean, Sal.*	2	0	1.000	4.78	48	0	0	0	18	2	64.0	66	294	40	34	0	1	3	14	37	1	36	2	1
Bukvich, Ryan, Lyn.	1	0	1.000	1.72	37	0	0	0	29	13	57.2	41	248	16	11	1	0	2	4	31	0	80	5	1
Bumatay, Mike, Lyn.*	1	7	.125	7.27	23	1	0	0	13	2	43.1	55	214	39	35	4	1	1	4	26	3	40	3	0
Burch, Matt, Wil	11	10	.524	3.70	28	22	0	0	1	0	148.1	145	639	73	61	6	9	7	21	50	2	92	8	0
Butler, Matt, M.B.	7	8	.467	5.89	22	22	1	0	0	0	114.2	127	514	81	75	12	9	5	5	48	0	78	1	0
Cali, Carmen, Pot.*	1	0	1.000	2.19	12	0	0	0	4	0	12.1	12	52	4	3	1	2	0	1	6	1	9	3	0
Cameron, Ryan, Sal.	0	1	.000	2.25	2	2	0	0	0	0	8.0	5	36	4	2	1	0	1	0	5	0	12	0	0
Carrasco, Dan, Lyn.	4	0	1.000	1.50	22	0	0	0	11	7	36.0	18	141	7	6	0	1	0	2	14	1	40	1	2
Cercy, Rick, Sal	4	1	.800	3.16	30	0	0	0	12	5	57.0	47	240	22	20	5	4	2	3	24	6	51	2	0
Chaney, Mike, Lyn.*	3	3	.500	3.71	28	3	0	0	9	2	68.0	69	289	31	28	5	2	0	3	22	0	44	2	2
Clark, Greg, Pot.	0	0	.000	0.00	1	0	0	0	1	0	0.1	1	3	0	0	0	0	0	1	0	0	0	0	0
Clontz, Brad, M.B.	0	1	.000	1.59	9	0	0	0	6	0	11.1	8	51	4	2	1	0	0	3	5	1	12	0	0
Cook, Aaron, Sal.	11	11	.500	3.08	27	27	0	0	0	0	155.0	157	649	73	53	6	5	1	7	38	0	122	6	1
Cook, B.R., Pot.	4	2	.667	2.86	8	8	0	0	0	0	50.1	35	198	20	16	2	1	3	12	0	36	1	1
Corcoran, Tim, Fred.	6	5	.545	2.68	33	0	0	0	25	6	50.1	37	205	16	15	4	5	1	2	19	3	42	5	0
Cortes, David, M.B.	2	2	.500	5.91	9	0	0	0	2	2	10.2	11	49	7	7	2	1	0	0	5	0	9	2	0
Cowie, Steve, Kin.-Sal.	0	1	.000	4.82	3	1	0	0	1	0	9.1	11	38	5	5	0	1	0	3	0	5	0	0
Cummings, Jeremy, Pot.	0	3	.000	8.53	4	4	0	0	0	0	19.0	25	87	18	18	2	1	2	5	2	1	15	2	0
Curreri, Joe, W.S.	3	3	.500	4.81	33	0	0	0	7	1	48.2	46	209	27	26	5	4	2	3	19	0	44	1	0
Curtiss, Tom, M.B.*	0	1	.000	4.26	12	0	0	0	9	0	12.2	11	57	7	6	3	1	0	0	8	0	10	1	0
Dawley, Joey, M.B.	1	0	1.000	1.80	5	0	0	0	2	0	10.0	4	34	2	2	0	0	0	0	1	0	16	0	0
DeHart, Rick, Wil.*	0	1	.000	1.59	5	0	0	0	1	0	5.2	5	23	2	1	0	0	0	3	1	2	0	0
Denney, Kyle, Kin.	5	3	.625	2.05	11	10	0	0	0	0	57.0	32	219	14	13	2	1	1	3	13	1	80	0	1
Dorame, Randey, Sal.*	2	5	.286	5.26	17	14	0	0	2	0	78.2	95	353	50	46	10	4	3	4	28	0	57	4	1
Douglass, Ryan, Wil.	1	0	1.000	0.00	1	1	0	0	0	0	5.1	1	18	0	0	0	0	0	3	0	7	0	0
Dukeman, Greg, Lyn.	6	6	.500	4.01	27	12	0	0	5	0	107.2	108	462	66	48	9	3	2	10	36	1	70	2	0
Ennis, John, M.B.	6	8	.429	3.58	25	25	1	0	0	0	138.1	111	569	63	55	12	4	5	7	45	0	144	2	3
Evans, Kyle, Kln.	2	1	.667	2.70	7	7	0	0	0	0	30.0	35	123	9	9	0	0	1	1	9	0	16	1	0
Evert, Brett, M.B.	7	2	.778	2.24	13	13	1	1	0	0	72.1	63	300	25	18	4	2	0	4	15	0	75	2	0
Ferguson, Ian, Wil	10	3	.769	3.83	18	18	0	0	0	0	98.1	85	403	47	41	5	1	2	11	27	0	72	5	0
Figueroa, Juan, Fred	5	0	1.000	1.59	7	7	0	0	0	0	39.2	37	158	8	7	0	0	2	0	3	0	26	0	0
Fischer, Eric, W.S.*	3	13	.188	5.31	25	22	0	0	1	0	123.2	144	554	87	73	9	4	3	10	47	1	84	3	0
Fitch, Steve, Kin.	4	4	.500	4.15	13	11	0	0	1	0	65.0	77	290	36	30	3	2	2	2	22	0	45	2	1
Fleming, Travis, Fred.	1	3	.250	2.51	44	0	0	0	40	23	57.1	53	249	18	16	2	1	2	6	20	1	59	2	0
Ford, Tom, Fred.*	1	1	.500	3.21	33	0	0	0	18	5	47.2	45	203	18	17	3	0	1	4	16	0	55	2	0
Forystek, Brian, Fred.*	1	3	.250	2.88	41	1	0	0	8	0	59.1	61	264	27	19	3	2	1	4	30	1	68	9	0
Fullor, Jody, Wil.	1	1	.500	4.08	15	0	0	0	9	1	17.2	20	80	8	8	1	2	0	1	10	3	11	2	0
Garcia, Sonny, Fred.	8	9	.471	3.27	25	20	2	0	3	1	143.0	132	593	67	52	9	8	2	10	33	3	139	4	1
Garza, Alberto, Kin.	5	3	.625	3.17	41	0	0	0	14	2	76.2	60	336	29	27	3	2	5	48	3	123	2	0
Gawer, Matt, M.B.*	2	0	1.000	2.51	42	0	0	0	37	14	43.0	41	193	18	12	1	1	1	4	16	1	46	2	0
Gehrke, Jay, Wil.	5	7	.417	5.65	42	0	0	0	21	3	71.2	82	325	51	45	3	5	2	5	32	0	65	11	0
Gilfillan, Jason, Wil.	4	1	.800	0.98	33	0	0	0	23	5	55.0	35	219	8	6	0	3	0	4	17	1	68	3	0
Gobble, Jimmy, Wil.*	10	6	.625	2.55	27	27	0	0	0	0	162.1	134	649	58	46	8	9	4	9	33	3	154	7	0
Gonzalez, Mike, Lyn.*	2	2	.500	2.93	14	2	0	0	7	0	30.2	28	127	14	10	3	3	1	0	7	1	32	5	1
Grabow, John, Lyn.*	1	3	.250	6.38	7	7	0	0	0	0	36.2	42	174	30	26	3	3	0	2	26	0	35	2	0
Grassing, Bryan, Pot.	5	1	.833	4.91	48	0	0	0	14	0	62.1	80	289	51	34	8	5	2	7	22	1	25	7	0
Grippo, Mike, Pot.*	0	0	.000	18.00	6	0	0	0	1	0	4.0	9	29	8	8	2	0	0	2	5	0	2	0	0
Guerrero, Junior, Wil.	5	4	.556	3.66	14	14	0	0	0	0	83.2	78	345	35	34	7	3	2	12	24	0	59	4	1
Guillory, Dan, Kin.	2	1	.667	1.24	23	0	0	0	19	7	29.0	19	113	5	4	0	0	1	1	6	1	36	3	0
Hale, Beau, Fred.	1	2	.333	1.32	5	5	1	0	0	0	34.0	30	133	8	5	1	0	1	4	0	35	0	0
Hart, Corey, Wil.	0	0	.000	0.00	3	0	0	0	3	0	3.0	0	9	0	0	0	1	0	0	0	0	6	0	0
Hernandez, Buddy, M.B.	1	1	.500	1.17	34	0	0	0	22	6	53.2	28	211	7	7	1	1	0	1	18	2	77	5	0
Herndon, Eric, M.B.	2	2	.500	2.42	24	2	0	0	6	2	44.2	39	179	13	12	5	4	1	0	18	0	38	4	0
Herrera, Alex, Kin.*	4	0	1.000	0.60	28	0	0	0	8	3	59.2	36	231	6	4	1	0	0	2	18	0	83	2	0
Hill, Jeremy, Wil.	4	0	1.000	0.73	9	0	0	0	7	2	12.1	10	52	2	1	0	1	0	0	8	1	13	2	0
Hodges, Trey, M.B.	15	8	.652	2.76	26	26	1	0	0	0	173.0	156	686	64	53	13	4	5	18	0	139	7	0

Pitcher, Team	W	L	Pct.	ERA	G	GS	CG	ShO	GF	Sv.	IP	H	TBF	R	ER	HR	SH	SF	HB	BB	IBB	SO	WP	Bk.
Hollifield, Alec, W.S.	0	8	.000	4.97	9	9	0	0	0	0	41.2	53	196	29	23	3	1	1	3	21	1	28	0	1
Hughes, Rocky, W.S.*	1	0	1.000	1.93	16	0	0	0	7	1	28.0	20	119	8	6	1	2	0	0	16	3	19	0	0
Hurley, Derek, Lyn.*	0	3	.000	3.52	17	1	0	0	13	1	38.1	39	171	23	15	0	8	5	2	19	2	20	2	0
Jackson, Brian, Kin.	2	6	.250	2.65	53	0	0	0	47	25	68.0	66	296	25	20	2	4	1	6	28	6	53	1	0
Jacobsen, Landon, Lyn.	5	7	.417	3.34	17	17	1	1	0	0	105.0	101	450	50	39	7	3	2	11	38	1	83	4	0
Janke, Cheyenne, Pot.	0	0	.000	2.48	15	5	0	0	1	0	36.1	44	159	16	10	2	1	0	2	9	0	17	2	0
Johnson, James, Kin.*	0	0	.000	0.73	4	1	0	0	0	0	12.1	8	45	2	1	1	0	1	0	2	0	13	1	0
Johnston, Clint, Lyn.*	1	1	.500	5.29	11	0	0	0	4	0	17.0	15	82	11	10	1	2	4	2	14	1	23	1	0
Johnston, Mike, Lyn.*	4	4	.500	3.34	11	10	1	0	0	0	62.0	66	276	27	23	2	4	2	3	24	0	44	4	2
Jones, Sean, Fred.	5	4	.556	3.24	39	0	0	0	15	1	83.1	86	358	35	30	3	5	2	7	21	3	57	10	0
Journell, Jimmy, Pot.	14	6	.700	2.50	26	26	0	0	0	0	151.0	121	620	54	42	8	6	5	18	42	0	156	7	0
Kane, Kyle, W.S.	1	0	1.000	2.08	14	0	0	0	5	1	21.2	10	81	5	5	1	0	0	3	8	0	32	0	0
Katz, Damon, Kin.	0	0	.000	0.00	1	0	0	0	1	1	1.0	3	5	0	0	0	0	0	0	0	0	0	0	0
Kelly, Dan, M.B.*	2	1	.667	2.03	18	1	0	0	5	1	40.0	31	154	10	9	4	3	0	0	7	2	22	1	0
Kibler, Ryan, Sal.	7	0	1.000	1.55	11	11	0	0	0	0	[illegible]	[illegible]	[illegible]	10	13	0	1	0	9	16	0	61	2	0
King, Jay, Wil.*	4	3	.571	2.92	11	9	1	0	0	0	52.1	41	202	20	17	5	1	1	2	11	0	46	2	0
Kohl, Doug, Pot.	3	5	.375	2.08	51	0	0	0	30	6	56.1	40	236	21	13	2	3	0	3	21	8	44	2	1
Kozlowski, Ben, M.B.*	0	2	.000	3.77	2	2	0	0	0	0	14.1	15	61	7	6	1	1	2	1	3	1	13	2	0
Lakman, Jason, Fred.	1	0	1.000	1.69	3	0	0	0	1	0	5.1	4	22	1	1	0	0	0	1	0	0	8	0	0
Lamber, Justin, Wil.*	4	4	.500	1.71	20	1	0	0	9	2	47.1	32	189	11	9	2	0	0	3	13	0	39	1	1
Langen, Brian, Pot.*	2	2	.500	2.77	43	0	0	0	8	0	48.2	48	220	28	15	4	1	2	2	27	2	32	9	0
Lantigua, Eduardo, W.S.	8	6	.571	3.06	22	19	1	1	1	0	120.2	92	499	46	41	7	5	2	7	58	1	113	8	0
LaRoche, Adam, M.B.*	1	0	1.000	0.00	1	0	0	0	1	0	1.0	1	4	0	0	0	1	0	0	0	0	1	0	0
Larson, Ryan, Kin.	3	1	.750	1.55	12	0	0	0	6	2	29.0	20	115	7	5	0	1	0	1	6	0	30	3	0
Layfield, Scotty, Pot.	1	2	.333	1.84	47	0	0	0	44	31	53.2	36	214	13	11	1	0	2	2	18	3	66	1	0
Ledden, Ryan, Lyn.	9	13	.409	5.42	27	25	3	0	0	0	152.2	184	695	112	92	18	3	6	16	53	2	73	6	1
Lewis, Richard, Fred.	0	1	.000	9.00	1	0	0	0	0	0	4.0	8	22	7	4	1	1	0	0	1	0	2	0	0
Lontayo, Alejandro, M.B.*	5	2	.714	4.29	20	4	0	0	3	0	50.1	56	232	26	24	3	3	1	3	27	1	42	4	0
Lopez, Jose, Lyn.	5	4	.556	2.37	13	13	0	0	0	0	76.0	63	316	28	20	5	3	4	4	23	0	70	2	0
Lopez, Juan, W.S.*	0	1	.000	3.93	26	0	0	0	9	0	36.2	34	166	23	16	3	0	1	7	21	1	37	6	0
Majewski, Gary, W.S.	4	2	.667	2.93	9	6	1	0	3	0	43.0	42	176	15	14	3	2	0	6	10	0	31	1	0
Malone, Corwin, W.S.*	0	1	.000	1.72	5	5	0	0	0	0	36.2	25	143	10	7	1	3	0	0	10	1	38	0	0
Mangrum, Micah, Wil.	4	2	.667	3.07	29	0	0	0	19	3	58.2	52	245	27	20	3	3	2	5	11	2	55	5	0
Manzueta, Roberto, Lyn.	0	3	.000	2.66	15	0	0	0	11	1	23.2	18	103	11	7	2	1	1	1	12	0	30	0	0
Martin, Chandler, Sal.	3	5	.375	4.74	9	9	0	0	0	0	57.0	68	250	35	30	5	0	0	5	14	0	32	2	1
Matcuk, Steve, Sal.	4	1	.800	2.98	24	0	0	0	9	3	42.1	47	189	19	14	0	2	1	9	13	2	33	4	0
Matsko, Rick, Kin.	0	0	.000	5.63	10	0	0	0	6	0	16.0	14	72	15	10	2	1	1	3	9	1	19	2	0
McClendon, Matt, M.B.	1	2	.333	8.68	8	0	0	0	1	0	9.1	7	48	10	9	0	1	1	4	9	0	10	8	0
McDaniel, Denny, W.S.*	1	3	.250	2.93	32	0	0	0	5	0	46.0	43	198	18	15	1	2	1	1	21	3	25	6	0
McWhirter, Kris, W.S.	2	3	.400	5.34	13	10	0	0	1	0	57.1	60	254	39	34	7	5	1	5	25	1	49	1	0
Medlock, Chet, Pot.	1	1	.500	0.55	12	0	0	0	4	0	16.1	17	70	5	1	0	1	1	1	5	0	14	0	0
Mills, Alan, Fred.	0	0	.000	1.80	5	0	0	0	1	1	5.0	3	20	4	1	0	0	0	1	0	0	10	0	0
Montilla, Felix, Lyn.	0	1	.000	9.00	7	0	0	0	5	1	7.0	11	34	7	7	2	0	0	1	2	0	3	1	0
Moreno, Orber, Wil.	1	1	.500	2.53	8	1	0	0	2	0	10.2	12	48	5	3	1	0	0	1	1	0	16	1	0
Morris, Cory, Fred.	3	5	.375	3.38	13	12	0	0	0	0	69.1	50	282	30	26	7	1	3	6	24	1	81	2	0
Mortimer, Mark, M.B.	0	0	.000	0.00	1	0	0	0	1	0	1.0	0	4	0	0	0	0	0	0	2	0	0	0	0
Mozingo, Dan, W.S.*	0	3	.000	11.91	3	3	0	0	0	0	11.1	21	63	19	15	3	0	0	2	6	0	17	2	0
Murray, Brad, W.S.*	3	2	.600	1.98	32	0	0	0	9	0	50.0	42	218	13	11	1	2	0	3	30	5	30	2	0
Narveson, Chris, Pot.*	4	3	.571	2.57	11	11	1	0	0	0	66.2	52	263	22	19	4	2	3	0	13	1	53	3	0
Natale, Mike, Wil.	9	8	.529	3.28	28	27	0	0	0	0	159.1	152	662	75	58	8	2	6	13	33	0	134	13	1
Neil, Dan, Kin.*	3	0	1.000	0.82	16	0	0	0	2	0	33.0	26	130	6	3	1	3	1	1	3	0	27	3	0
Newell, Mark, Wil.	2	0	1.000	5.96	18	0	0	0	6	0	25.2	34	132	22	17	1	2	4	7	15	0	7	2	0
Obermueller, Wes, Wil.	0	2	.000	3.08	20	6	0	0	1	0	38.0	38	163	15	13	3	2	1	1	16	1	28	2	0
Olivo, Rigal, W.S.	0	0	.000	4.73	8	0	0	0	3	1	13.1	16	57	9	7	2	0	0	0	3	0	9	3	0
Ortega, Carlos, W.S.*	0	3	.000	4.73	10	6	0	0	3	0	40.0	43	173	23	21	5	0	4	7	10	0	33	2	0
Pacheco, Delvis, M.B.	1	0	1.000	0.00	2	2	0	0	0	0	10.0	4	36	0	0	0	0	0	0	2	0	7	0	0
Pacheco, Enemencio, Sal.	4	2	.667	4.68	27	3	0	0	14	1	42.1	55	198	27	22	4	2	2	0	18	0	29	1	0
Patten, Scott, W.S.	0	1	.000	27.00	2	1	0	0	0	0	1.0	2	9	3	3	0	0	0	2	3	0	0	0	0
Pavlovich, Tony, Lyn.	1	0	1.000	0.39	20	0	0	0	20	13	23.0	13	86	1	1	0	1	1	0	5	0	27	0	0
Pena, Alex, Lyn.	2	4	.333	6.11	25	3	0	0	13	3	53.0	61	257	39	36	3	3	2	9	35	2	31	3	0
Pena, Ed, W.S.*	1	6	.143	4.18	31	5	0	0	7	0	47.1	52	225	30	22	6	7	2	7	24	3	35	4	1
Perez, Randy, Fred.*	8	7	.533	3.96	20	20	3	0	0	0	122.2	145	520	56	54	8	6	3	5	23	0	101	3	0
Perkins, Mike, Pot.	1	3	.250	3.94	11	5	0	0	1	0	29.2	32	130	15	13	2	1	0	1	13	0	25	3	0
Pichardo, Carlos, Wil.	1	2	.333	4.52	31	2	0	0	7	2	65.2	67	275	36	33	3	0	2	4	19	1	38	6	0
Pinales, Aquiles, Kin.	4	5	.444	4.47	36	0	0	0	15	3	58.1	65	268	34	29	2	3	1	5	25	3	55	4	1
Plank, Terry, Fred.	2	8	.200	5.32	38	4	0	0	12	1	71.0	71	328	51	42	8	2	1	9	43	2	58	5	1
Ponce Deleon, Damon, Pot.	1	4	.200	2.85	23	3	0	0	5	0	41.0	30	171	19	13	6	0	1	5	12	2	30	3	1
Prather, Scott, Pot.*	2	1	.667	3.60	20	0	0	0	7	0	25.0	24	112	15	10	1	1	1	1	7	0	27	1	0
Price, Ryan, Sal.	4	11	.267	7.34	28	21	0	0	2	0	103.0	101	497	93	84	12	4	1	12	85	0	79	45	1
Ramirez, Enrique, Fred.	2	1	.667	1.54	7	0	0	0	6	1	11.2	5	43	2	2	1	0	0	1	4	0	9	2	0
Randall, Scott, Sal.	0	0	.000	4.50	2	0	0	0	0	0	6.0	9	27	3	3	0	0	0	0	1	0	7	0	0
Reid, Justin, Lyn.	2	4	.333	2.25	8	8	1	0	0	0	56.0	50	221	15	14	4	0	1	2	6	0	48	2	0
Rupp, Mike, W.S.	2	3	.400	3.38	27	3	0	0	11	0	53.1	56	227	29	20	3	2	2	2	17	0	45	3	2
Sadler, Carl, Kin.*	6	0	1.000	1.88	27	2	0	0	10	2	62.1	51	258	19	13	2	0	0	3	18	1	78	1	0
Sansom, Trevor, Pot.	6	4	.600	2.71	50	0	0	0	12	0	69.2	72	307	33	21	2	5	3	4	22	3	45	0	0
Schwager, Matt, Fred.	0	1	.000	3.62	7	3	0	0	2	1	27.1	28	114	13	11	2	0	2	2	3	0	30	0	0
Sequea, Jacobo, Fred.	6	9	.400	3.97	18	18	0	0	0	0	102.0	85	426	54	45	16	2	2	7	37	1	80	4	1
Sido, Wilson, Kin.	9	2	.818	2.33	17	17	1	1	0	0	92.2	69	367	29	24	7	1	3	5	20	0	96	3	3
Smalley, Mike, M.B.*	0	6	.000	6.67	9	5	0	0	0	0	29.2	42	139	25	22	5	2	2	1	10	0	25	0	0
Spiegel, Mike, Kin.*	7	7	.500	2.82	21	17	0	0	1	0	108.2	83	448	37	34	9	5	3	11	38	2	90	1	0
Sprague, Kevin, Pot.*	9	8	.529	3.40	26	26	2	0	0	0	164.1	155	674	64	62	9	3	4	11	43	3	113	9	1
Stahl, Rich, Fred.*	1	1	.500	1.95	6	6	1	1	0	0	32.1	26	134	13	7	1	3	2	2	15	0	24	3	1
Stepka, Tom, Sal.	2	2	.500	3.72	32	2	0	0	13	2	67.2	72	299	36	28	5	4	2	1	25	1	42	2	0

CLASS A Carolina League

Pitcher, Team	W	L	Pct.	ERA	G	GS	CG	ShO	GF	Sv.	IP	H	TBF	R	ER	HR	SH	SF	HB	BB	IBB	SO	WP	Bk.
Stewart, Josh, W.S.*	4	6	.400	3.82	12	12	1	0	0	0	63.2	64	287	41	27	6	3	4	4	28	1	38	3	0
Stiles, Brad, Wil.*	0	0	.000	0.00	1	0	0	0	0	0	0.2	1	5	0	0	0	0	0	1	1	0	2	1	0
Tallet, Brian, Kin.*	9	7	.563	3.04	27	27	2	0	0	0	160.0	134	644	62	54	12	3	2	4	38	0	164	2	0
Tejeda, Frank, Pot.	6	14	.300	4.43	25	25	2	0	0	0	136.0	152	574	76	67	14	3	3	7	19	0	70	2	2
Thompson, Doug, Sal.	2	2	.500	4.02	17	0	0	0	5	1	31.1	30	135	15	14	1	2	0	0	16	1	35	4	0
Thoms, Hank, Kin.	7	2	.778	2.26	14	14	1	0	0	0	79.2	70	321	26	20	2	1	1	3	20	0	74	3	0
Torres, Luis, Lyn.	0	0	.000	13.50	4	0	0	0	1	0	3.1	6	19	7	5	1	0	0	0	3	0	4	4	0
Truitt, Derrick, M.B.	2	2	.500	8.39	16	0	0	0	3	0	24.2	37	117	24	23	3	1	0	2	10	0	25	1	0
Tsao, Chin-hui, Sal.	0	4	.000	4.67	4	4	0	0	0	0	17.1	23	78	11	9	1	2	1	1	5	0	18	1	1
Ulacia, Dennis, W.S.*	5	3	.625	3.64	10	10	4	0	0	0	64.1	57	265	27	26	2	2	2	5	26	1	47	1	0
Valentine, Joe, W.S.	5	1	.833	1.01	27	0	0	0	18	8	44.2	18	179	7	5	0	3	0	1	27	3	50	2	0
Vance, Cory, Sal.*	10	8	.556	3.10	26	26	1	0	0	0	154.0	129	641	65	53	9	3	2	14	65	0	142	4	4
Vargas, Jose, Kin.	0	1	.000	1.35	8	0	0	0	2	1	13.1	6	54	2	2	0	1	0	2	7	1	22	0	0
Veronie, Shanin, M.B.	1	2	.333	2.48	35	0	0	0	21	9	54.1	47	224	17	15	2	1	2	2	10	3	57	2	0
Voyles, Brad, W.S.	0	0	.000	0.00	2	0	0	0	2	1	1.1	0	0	0	0	0	0	0	1	0	1	3	0	0
Wallace, Shane, Kin.*	10	2	.833	1.61	13	13	1	1	0	0	84.0	65	328	22	15	3	0	1	5	16	0	60	1	0
Warren, Chris, Sal.	0	0	.000	0.00	2	0	0	0	2	0	2.0	1	7	0	0	0	0	0	0	0	0	5	0	0
West, Brian, W.S.	7	12	.368	3.46	28	28	3	1	0	0	169.0	179	735	75	65	11	8	10	9	70	2	130	8	0
Williams, Blake, Pot.	4	10	.286	2.43	17	17	2	1	0	0	107.1	82	434	43	29	12	5	2	8	30	1	92	10	1
Winkelsas, Joe, M.B.	1	0	1.000	0.00	4	0	0	0	4	3	5.2	2	20	0	0	0	0	0	0	1	0	5	0	0
Wylie, Mitch, W.S.	0	1	.000	3.60	1	1	0	0	0	0	5.0	7	23	2	2	0	0	0	1	4	0	4	0	0
Yankosky, L.J., M.B.	2	3	.400	2.60	9	8	0	0	0	0	55.1	50	216	20	16	4	0	2	4	0	50	0	0
Young, Colin, Sal.*	4	3	.571	1.42	47	0	0	0	35	21	57.0	35	215	11	9	5	0	0	12	0	72	1	0
Young, Jason, Sal.	6	7	.462	3.44	17	17	2	1	0	0	104.2	104	439	47	40	8	0	0	10	28	0	91	5	0
Young, Simon, Kin.*	3	5	.375	6.75	15	13	0	0	0	0	60.0	85	290	54	45	9	4	1	1	21	0	48	1	0

PITCHERS WITH TWO OR MORE TEAMS

Pitcher, Team	W	L	Pct.	ERA	G	GS	CG	ShO	GF	Sv.	IP	H	TBF	R	ER	HR	SH	SF	HB	BB	IBB	SO	WP	Bk.
Cowie, Steve, Kin.	0	0	.000	1.50	2	0	0	0	1	0	6.0	5	21	1	1	0	1	0	0	1	0	4	0	0
Cowie, Steve, Sal.	0	1	.000	10.80	1	0	0	0	1	0	3.1	6	17	4	4	0	0	0	0	2	0	4	0	0

COMBINATION SHUTOUTS: **Frederick (8)**—Bechler-Garcia, Bedard-Jones Fleming, Dedard-Forystek, Bedard-Corcoran, Bedard-Jones-Mills Corcoran, Morris-Schwager-Fleming, Morris-Fleming, Morris-Ford-Ramirez. **Kinston (14)**—Evans-Denney-Sadler, Wallace-Vargas, Tallet-Vargas, Tallet-Pinales-Jackson-Sadler, Denney-Sadler, Spiegel-Pinales, Tallet-Guillory-Jackson, Tallet-Herrera, Thoms-Garza-Pinales, Thoms-Pinales-Jackson, Spiegel-Neil-Guillory, Tallet-Larson-Pinales, Sido-Neil-Guillory, Sido-Neil. **Lynchburg (7)**—Reid-Carrasco, Lopez-Chaney-Johnston-Pavlovich, Bennett-Carrasco-Pavlovich, Bennett-Dukeman-Gonzalez, Lopez Dukeman Carrasco, Jacobsen-Pena-Carrasco, Bennett-Bumatay. **Myrtle Beach (15)**—Bong Kelly-Veronie, Butler-Truitt-Gawer, Kelly-Dawley-Veronie-Curtiss, Hodges-Hernandez, Ennis-Lontayo-Veronie-Gawer, Evert-Herndon-Hernandez, Evert-Winkelsas, Bong-Hernandez-Gawer, Hodges-Gawer, Bong-Winkelsas, Hodges-Gawer, Hodges-Hernandez, Bong-Bent-Veronie, Ennis-Clontz-Veronie. **Potomac (11)**—Williams-Kohl, Journell-Layfield, Journell-Langen-Kohl-Layfield, Journell-Grassing, Sprague-Kohl, Journell-Perkins-Sansom-Langen, Journell-Ponce Deleon-Grassing, Sprague-Medlock-Kohl, Journell-Medlock-Layfield, Sprague-Layfield. **Salem (11)**—Cook-Thompson-Young-Ayala, Vance-Thompson, Vance-Cercy-Young, Kibler-Brueggemann, Cook-Young, Cook-Cercy, Vance-Matcuk-Young, Vance-Matcuk-Young, Martin-Matcuk-Young, Cook Corey, Cook-Matcuk. **Wilmington (13)**—Gobble-Pichardo-Newell-Bukvich, Ammons-Obermueller-Gilfillan, Natale-Obermueller-Bukvich, Natale-Lamber, Natale-Gehrke, Gobble-Newell-Bukvich, Burch-Moreno-Gilfillan, Ferguson-Gehrke, Burch-Dehart-Mangrum, Ferguson-Fuller-Bukvich, Natale-Obermueller-Fuller, Gobble-Fuller-Lamber, Natale-Mangrum. **Winston-Salem (5)**—Lantigua-Bohannon-Kane-Bajenaru, Fischer-Bohannon, Lantigua-Rupp-McDaniel-Bajenaru, Lantigua-Murray, Pena-McDaniel-Valentine.

NO-HIT GAMES: None.

2001 FIELDING

TEAM

Team	Pct.	G	PO	A	E	TC	DP	TP	PB
Myrtle Beach	.972	138	3617	1381	144	5142	102	0	29
Wilmington	.971	140	3706	1408	154	5268	109	0	15
Frederick	.970	140	3660	1385	157	5202	99	0	15
Kinston	.968	140	3754	1480	175	5409	103	0	19
Winston-Salem	.967	140	3731	1590	180	5501	141	0	13
Salem	.967	140	3594	1631	177	5402	154	0	26
Lynchburg	.965	137	3576	1494	183	5253	130	0	29
Potomac	.965	140	3621	1580	190	5391	151	0	22

INDIVIDUAL

FIRST BASEMEN

NOTE: All caps denotes fielding-percentage leader based on 70 games for catchers, 93 for all other non-pitchers and 112 innings for pitchers. *Throws lefthanded.

Player, Team	Pct.	G	PO	A	E	TC	DP
Acevas, Jon, W.S.	.972	13	101	2	3	106	10
ATKINS, Garrett, Sal.	.995	130	1200	73	7	1280	125
Bailey, Travis, Pot.	.974	18	139	9	4	152	16
Becker, Jeff, Kin.	.988	10	76	3	1	80	5
Bell, Mike, Sal.	.950	2	16	3	1	20	2
Berger, Matt, W.S.	.983	67	577	48	11	636	65
Bonifay, Josh, Lyn.	.982	6	47	8	1	56	3
Combs, Chris, Lyn.	.988	111	943	70	12	1025	100
Duncan, Chris, Pot.	.982	47	478	21	9	508	48
Ewing, Byron, Kin.	.989	85	731	52	9	792	51
Fennell, Jason, W.S.	.983	38	278	20	5	303	23
Fiore, Curtis, M.B.	1.000	1	3	0	0	3	0
Gall, John, Pot.	.991	47	391	29	4	424	43

Player, Team	Pct.	G	PO	A	E	TC	DP
Garcia, Tony, W.S.	1.000	3	28	3	0	31	5
Gredvig, Doug, Fred.	.991	125	999	65	10	1074	76
Grindell, Nate, Kin.	1.000	17	149	6	0	155	15
Haase, Jeff, Kin.	.976	5	39	1	1	41	3
Hankins, Ryan, W.S.	.990	22	188	10	2	200	22
Harvey, Ken, Wil.	.984	20	166	18	3	187	15
Hattenburg, Ray, Wil.	.950	6	38	2	0	40	4
Johnson, Gabe, Pot.	1.000	1	3	0	0	3	0
Langston, James, Lyn.	1.000	11	110	11	0	121	8
LaRoche, Adam, M.B.*	.993	120	1042	52	8	1102	81
Leal, Jaeme, M.B.	.991	15	105	9	1	115	9
Meier, Dan, Lyn.*	1.000	5	49	5	0	54	2
Mercado, Wilkins, Wil.	1.000	7	52	4	0	56	4
Moore, Chris, Sal.	.969	9	59	3	2	64	8
Mortimer, Mark, M.B.	.976	5	36	5	1	42	3
Nelson, Eric, Wil.	1.000	2	8	0	0	8	1
Oborn, Spencer, W.S.	1.000	1	8	1	0	9	0
Pena, Amaury, W.S.	.000	1	0	0	0	0	0
Pichardo, Henry, Kin.	1.000	1	1	1	0	2	1
Pond, Simon, Kin.	.989	22	173	12	2	187	9
Powers, Jeff, Sal.	1.000	1	4	0	0	4	2
Rachels, Wes, Fred.	.982	14	102	6	2	110	8
Rickon, Jim, Kin.	.980	8	40	8	1	49	4
Rodgers, Albert, Pot.	.997	34	294	20	1	315	34
Rodriguez, Jeff, M.B.	1.000	1	0	1	0	1	0
Ross, Don, Wil.	.987	114	884	79	13	976	70
Sanchez, Tino, Sal.	.000	1	0	0	0	0	0
Santamarina, Juan, W.S.	1.000	7	54	1	0	55	4
Seal, Scott, Sal.*	.920	3	22	1	2	25	1
Sickles, Jeremy, Lyn.	1.000	6	50	0	0	50	4
Terveen, Bryce, M.B.	1.000	2	10	1	0	11	0
Warren, Chris, Sal.	.846	2	11	0	2	13	1

CLASS A *Carolina League*

SECOND BASEMEN

Player, Team	Pct.	G	PO	A	E	TC	DP
Bailey, Travis, Pot.	1.000	1	1	2	0	3	0
Becker, Jeff, Kin.	1.000	6	7	19	0	26	4
Benefield, Brian, Kin.	.923	7	12	12	2	26	3
Bonifay, Josh, Lyn.	.893	12	15	35	6	56	7
Calahan, Larry, W.S.	.917	5	11	11	2	24	2
Cates, Gary, Fred.	.956	25	45	64	5	114	10
Cleto, Ambioris, Lyn.	.958	18	34	35	3	72	9
Coates, Brad, M.B.	.000	1	0	0	0	0	0
Colina, Javier, Sal.	.962	113	224	366	23	613	94
Diaz, Maikell, Fred.	.985	47	92	102	3	197	22
Escobar, Gustavo, Pot.	.875	2	1	6	1	8	1
Fatur, Brian, Pot.	1.000	10	25	18	0	43	6
Fiore, Curtis, M.B.	.926	7	15	10	2	27	3
Flores, Ralphs, W.S.	1.000	1	1	1	0	2	1
Galante, Matt, Pot.	1.000	4	4	4	0	8	2
Gibbs, Mark, Fred.	.957	31	64	91	7	162	22
Gonzalez, Luis, Kin.	1.000	13	29	30	0	59	6
Green, Nick, M.B.	.963	74	105	184	11	300	36
Hammond, Joey, Fred.	1.000	15	30	28	0	58	6
Hart, Bo, Pot.	.986	72	144	219	5	368	57
Hattenburg, Ray, Wil.	.000	1	0	0	0	0	0
Hopper, Norris, Wil.	1.000	1	1	3	0	4	0
Izturis, Maicer, Kin.	.959	102	162	233	17	412	61
Katz, Damon, Kin.	.964	8	12	15	1	28	1
Mann, Derek, Lyn.	.932	15	22	33	4	59	9
Manning, Pat, M.B.	.979	46	79	105	4	188	19
Martin, Justin, Lyn.	1.000	14	19	35	0	54	6
Moraga, Omar, Kin.	1.000	7	14	15	0	29	3
Moreno, Christopher, Fred.	1.000	3	7	6	0	13	0
Nelson, Eric, Wil.	.975	103	189	244	11	444	45
NICHOLSON, Tommy, W.S.	.978	131	275	345	14	634	84
Orr, Pete, M.B.	.975	21	33	46	2	81	8
Pena, Amaury, W.S.	.982	14	23	32	1	56	8
Pichardo, Henry, Kin.	1.000	2	5	7	0	12	1
Pollaro, Dallas, Pot.	.948	43	78	123	11	212	33
Powers, Jeff, Sal.	1.000	5	5	10	0	15	3
Prieto, Jon, Lyn.	.966	83	142	228	13	383	57
Rachels, Wes, Fred.	.990	27	50	46	1	97	9
Ruiz, Willy, Wil.	.978	40	86	88	4	178	27
Suarez, Luis, W.S.	1.000	2	3	9	0	12	3
Taylor, Seth, Sal.	.885	5	7	16	3	26	4
Thames, Damon, Pot.	.961	20	33	40	3	76	12
Vilorio, Miguel, Sal.	.936	12	17	27	3	47	6
Warren, Chris, Sal.	.980	15	14	34	1	49	4
White, Kenneth, Fred.	.875	2	2	5	1	8	0

THIRD BASEMEN

Player, Team	Pct.	G	PO	A	E	TC	DP
Atkins, Garrett, Sal.	1.000	6	2	8	0	10	1
Bailey, Travis, Pot.	1.000	9	2	16	0	18	3
Becker, Jeff, Kin.	.929	6	3	10	1	14	1
Bell, Mike, Sal.	.857	3	1	5	1	7	0
Benefield, Brian, Kin.	.824	7	4	10	3	17	2
Bonifay, Josh, Lyn.	.769	5	4	6	3	13	3
Brandes, Landon, Pot.	1.000	1	0	1	0	1	0
Calahan, Larry, W.S.	.870	9	4	16	3	23	0
CALZADO, Napolean, Fred.	.923	118	97	202	25	324	16
Cameron, Troy, M.B.-Kin.	.938	122	74	258	22	354	21
Cleto, Ambioris, Lyn.	.932	34	19	50	5	74	6
De Caster, Yurendell, Lyn.	.913	9	3	18	2	23	1
Diaz, Maikell, Fred.	1.000	3	1	4	0	5	1
Espinoza, Efren, Lyn.	.897	15	7	28	4	39	5
Fatur, Brian, Pot.	.806	14	7	22	7	36	4
Fiore, Curtis, M.B.	.918	60	32	103	12	147	6
Gall, John, Pot.	.907	32	15	53	7	75	4
Gonzalez, Luis, Kin.	.904	22	13	53	7	73	2
Grindell, Nate, Kin.	.876	47	24	117	20	161	7
Hammond, Joey, Fred.	.929	13	9	17	2	28	0
Hankins, Ryan, W.S.	.907	45	22	75	10	107	9
Hansen, Jed, Wil.	.913	17	13	29	4	46	3
Hart, Bo, Pot.	.950	6	6	13	1	20	2
Hart, Corey, Wil.	.929	21	15	37	4	56	2
Hattenburg, Ray, Wil.	.846	7	3	8	2	13	1
Johnson, Gabe, Pot.	.900	83	54	172	25	251	12
Katz, Damon, Kin.	.000	1	0	0	0	0	0
Langston, James, Lyn.	.880	87	42	142	25	209	12
Leon, Alfredo, Fred.	1.000	2	1	8	0	9	0
Lincoln, Justin, Sal.	.920	49	27	77	9	113	9
Manning, Pat, M.B.	.915	18	7	36	4	47	2
Martinez, Lou, M.B.	1.000	2	2	2	0	4	0
Mercado, Wilkins, Wil.	.950	50	20	94	6	120	7

SECOND BASEMEN (continued — right column top)

Player, Team	Pct.	G	PO	A	E	TC	DP
Moreno, Christopher, Fred.	.778	9	6	15	6	27	2
Muro, Robert, W.S.	.919	59	44	127	15	186	16
Nelson, Eric, Wil.	1.000	1	0	1	0	1	0
Orr, Pete, M.B.	1.000	4	1	3	0	4	0
Pena, Amaury, W.S.	.952	26	12	48	3	63	4
Pichardo, Henry, Kin.	1.000	1	1	0	0	1	0
Powers, Jeff, Sal.	.960	16	5	19	1	25	1
Rodgers, Albert, Sal.	.750	2	1	8	3	12	0
Ruiz, Willy, Wil.	.953	60	44	98	7	149	5
Sanchez, Tino, Sal.	.914	23	13	51	6	70	2
Santamarina, Juan, W.S.	.821	11	8	24	7	39	2
Suarez, Luis, W.S.	.000	1	0	0	0	0	0
Taylor, Seth, Sal.	.918	40	14	75	8	97	9
Thames, Damon, Pot.	.000	1	0	0	0	0	0
Warren, Chris, Sal.	.875	17	3	25	4	32	1

THIRD BASEMEN WITH TWO OR MORE TEAMS

Player, Team	Pct.	G	PO	A	E	TC	DP
Cameron, Troy, M.B.	.931	62	40	122	12	174	9
Cameron, Troy, Kin.	.944	60	34	136	10	180	12

SHORTSTOPS

Player, Team	Pct.	G	PO	A	E	TC	DP
Barnes, Clint, Sal.	.934	38	55	130	13	198	25
Becker, Jeff, Kin.	1.000	2	4	5	0	9	1
Berroa, Angel, Wil.	.933	51	89	149	17	255	21
Betemit, Wilson, M.B.	.944	83	130	257	23	410	45
Calzado, Napolean, Fred.	1.000	2	2	6	0	8	1
Carvajal, Ramon, Pot.	.925	125	166	428	48	642	83
Castillo, Jose, Lyn.	.939	121	220	354	37	611	85
Cates, Gary, Fred.	.750	4	4	2	2	8	0
Cleto, Ambioris, Lyn.	.947	19	30	41	4	75	7
Coates, Brad, M.B.	.908	18	26	43	7	76	9
Diaz, Maikell, Fred.	.933	45	61	107	12	180	18
Escobar, Gustavo, Pot.	.000	2	0	0	0	0	0
Espinoza, Efren, Lyn.	1.000	2	0	6	0	6	1
Fatur, Brian, Pot.	.900	2	4	5	1	10	1
Flores, Ralphs, W.S.	.963	25	30	73	4	107	15
Gibbs, Mark, Fred.	.893	8	9	16	3	28	2
Gonzalez, Luis, Kin.	.935	8	8	21	2	31	2
Green, Nick, M.B.	.833	3	2	8	2	12	1
Hart, Corey, Wil.	.926	47	63	111	14	188	21
Johnson, Gabe, Pot.	.500	1	0	1	1	2	0
Katz, Damon, Kin.	.929	5	5	8	1	14	1
Mann, Derek, Lyn.	.773	7	3	14	5	22	1
Medrano, Steve, Wil.	.961	40	67	107	7	181	26
Nicholson, Tommy, W.S.	1.000	4	5	17	0	22	2
Orr, Pete, M.B.	.966	39	60	113	6	179	20
Pena, Amaury, W.S.	1.000	15	14	26	0	40	8
PERALTA, John, Kin.	.952	125	172	358	27	557	60
Pichardo, Henry, Kin.	.950	4	5	14	1	20	0
Powers, Jeff, Sal.	.962	21	28	74	4	106	17
Reyes, Guillermo, W.S.	.935	59	89	171	18	278	34
Rogers, Ed, Fred.	.956	73	109	193	14	316	32
Ruiz, Willy, Wil.	1.000	7	5	8	0	13	2
Sandoval, Danny, W.S.	.929	48	70	139	16	225	30
Shier, Peter, Fred.	.968	13	22	39	2	63	8
Taylor, Seth, Sal.	.934	76	118	247	26	391	55
Thames, Damon, Pot.	.931	17	31	50	6	87	13
Warren, Chris, Sal.	.929	12	20	32	4	56	6

OUTFIELDERS

Player, Team	Pct.	G	PO	A	E	TC	DP
Alvarez, Tony, Lyn.	.893	21	25	0	3	28	0
Ascencion, Quincy, Fred.	1.000	15	11	0	0	11	0
Aspito, Jason, W.S.	.956	121	208	8	10	226	3
Bailey, Travis, Pot.	.969	20	31	0	1	32	0
BARNS, B.J., Lyn.*	.990	101	190	6	2	198	2
Bass, Chris, Lyn.	1.000	4	9	0	0	9	0
Becker, Jeff, Kin.	.000	1	0	0	1	1	0
Bonifay, Josh, Lyn.	.946	51	84	4	5	93	1
Bost, Tom, Kin.	.936	26	40	4	3	47	1
Brandes, Landon, Pot.	.000	3	0	0	0	0	0
Brignac, Junior, M.B.	.961	66	114	10	5	129	1
Cabrera, Ray, Fred.	.961	116	211	8	9	228	3
Caradonna, Brett, W.S.	.922	58	81	2	7	90	0
Catalanotte, Greg, Sal.	.977	103	157	14	4	175	4
Church, Ryan, Kin.*	.947	21	36	0	2	38	0
Cleto, Ambioris, Lyn.	1.000	2	3	0	0	3	0
Crisp, Covelli, Pot.	.975	137	222	11	6	239	2
Crocker, Nick, M.B.*	.976	59	77	6	2	85	0
Cunningham, Marco, Wil.	.978	109	215	7	5	227	4

Player, Team	Pct.	G	PO	A	E	TC	DP
Dodson, Jeremy, Wil.	.948	66	103	7	6	116	4
Durham, Chad, W.S.	.973	132	277	16	8	301	5
Espinoza, Efren, Lyn.	1.000	3	3	0	0	3	0
Fatur, Brian, Pot.	1.000	40	58	5	0	63	0
Fennell, Jason, W.S.	1.000	5	1	0	0	1	0
Fiore, Curtis, M.B.	.929	26	38	1	3	42	0
Freeman, Choo, Sal.	.979	123	228	9	5	242	2
Garrett, Shawn, Lyn.	.989	42	90	0	1	91	0
Gettis, Byron, Wil.	.967	78	139	7	5	151	2
Gomez, Alexis, Wil.*	.957	48	108	3	5	116	1
Gordon, Alex, Fred.*	.970	17	30	2	1	33	0
Green, Steve, Pot.	.000	2	0	0	0	0	0
Haase, Jeff, Kin.	1.000	1	3	0	0	3	0
Hankins, Ryan, W.S.	.000	1	0	0	0	0	0
Hart, Bo, Pot.	1.000	1	3	0	0	3	0
Harts, Jeremy, Lyn.*	.952	124	260	16	14	290	4
Hattenburg, Ray, Wil.	.889	10	8	0	1	9	0
Haynes, Dee, Pot.	.975	77	148	6	4	158	0
Hernandez, Jesus, Kin.*	.963	20	24	2	1	27	0
Hernandez, Johnny, Pot.*	.981	131	255	6	5	266	1
Holliday, Matt, Sal.	1.000	30	33	2	0	35	1
Hopper, Norris, Wil.	.975	108	226	9	6	241	2
Janowicz, Nate, Kin.*	.941	30	46	2	3	51	0
Jenkins, Brian, Kin.	.919	21	31	3	3	37	0
Johnson, Eric, Kin.	.969	117	207	9	7	223	1
Johnston, Clint, Lyn.*	.000	1	0	0	0	0	0
Jones, Damien, M.B.*	.963	110	178	4	7	189	0
Langerhans, Ryan, M.B.*	.972	121	230	12	7	249	4
Langston, James, Lyn.	.000	1	0	0	0	0	0
LaRoche, Adam, M.B.*	1.000	3	2	0	0	2	0
Mack, Tony, Fred.	.967	98	172	3	6	181	0
Martin, Justin, Lyn.	.972	33	68	2	2	72	1
Meier, Dan, Lyn.*	.938	7	15	0	1	16	0
Merriman, Terrell, W.S.*	.967	15	29	0	1	30	0
Minges, Tyler, Kin.	.967	47	85	4	3	92	1
Moreno, Jorge, Kin.	.972	86	131	8	4	143	1
Neubart, Adam, Wil.	1.000	19	32	1	0	33	0
Oborn, Spencer, W.S.	.963	114	170	12	7	189	1
Orr, Pete, M.B.	.935	26	42	1	3	46	0
Pena, Amaury, W.S.	.000	1	0	0	0	0	0
Phillips, Dan, Sal.	.955	121	179	14	9	202	2
Pichardo, Henry, Kin.	1.000	4	6	1	0	7	0
Pollaro, Dallas, Pot.	.000	1	0	0	0	0	0
Rachels, Wes, Fred.	.955	19	21	0	1	22	0
Raines, Tim, Fred.	.976	19	40	1	1	42	0
Ravelo, Manny, Lyn.	.974	20	36	1	1	38	0
Reed, Keith, Fred.	.948	67	118	9	7	134	1
Requena, Alex, Kin.	.979	55	90	2	2	94	0
Ross, Don, Wil.	.000	2	0	0	0	0	0
Sanchez, Tino, Sal.	.947	17	17	1	1	19	0
Seal, Scott, Sal.*	.909	25	28	2	3	33	0
Sosa, Jovanny, Fred.	.879	22	29	0	4	33	0
Thomas, Chuck, M.B.*	1.000	11	29	0	0	29	0
Tucker, Mamon, Fred.	.964	67	103	3	4	110	0
Warren, Chris, Sal.	1.000	20	15	1	0	16	0
Weichard, Paul, Lyn.*	.969	13	28	3	1	32	0
White, Kenneth, Fred.	.000	1	0	0	0	0	0
Williams, Charles, Pot.*	.981	41	50	2	1	53	1

CATCHERS

Player, Team	Pct.	G	PO	A	E	TC	DP	PB
Acevas, Jon, W.S.	.981	48	329	35	7	371	1	7
Alley, Chuck, Fred.	.992	39	309	42	3	354	3	4
Boscan, Jean, M.B.	.994	18	147	9	1	157	1	7
Clark, Greg, Pot.	1.000	7	24	2	0	26	0	1
Cruz, Edgar, Kin.	.983	14	100	16	2	118	2	5
Felix, Hersy, Wil.	1.000	2	11	2	0	13	0	0
Fennell, Jason, W.S.	.947	4	13	5	1	19	0	0
Friar, Roddy, Pot.	.982	18	100	11	2	113	2	4
Garcia, Tony, W.S.	.993	52	388	52	3	443	5	6
Haad, Yamid, Lyn.	.943	3	27	6	2	35	0	1
Haase, Jeff, Kin.	.955	10	77	8	4	89	1	4
Hernandez, Jose, Lyn.	.994	22	156	22	1	179	0	5
Leon, Alfredo, Fred.	.976	4	38	3	1	42	0	1
Lopez-Cao, Mike, Fred.	1.000	3	27	4	0	31	0	0
Martinez, Octavio, Fred.	.986	91	740	106	12	858	9	10
Martinez, Victor, Kin.	.985	106	967	78	16	1061	8	8
McAuley, Jim, Wil.	.975	54	388	45	11	444	2	6
McQueen, Eric, Sal.	1.000	2	19	1	0	20	0	2
Mortimer, Mark, M.B.	.995	22	196	9	1	206	0	5
PAULINO, Ron, Lyn.	.994	87	574	74	4	652	4	20
Pogue, Jamie, Pot.	.985	86	524	55	9	588	2	10

Player, Team	Pct.	G	PO	A	E	TC	DP	PB
Quintero, Humberto, W.S.	.992	43	325	46	3	374	2	0
Reyes, Milver, Lyn.	1.000	9	50	10	0	60	2	1
Rickon, Jim, Kin.	.993	17	117	20	1	138	2	2
Rodriguez, Jeff, M.B.	.994	64	468	35	3	506	2	11
Sanchez, Tino, Sal.	.986	51	330	26	5	361	3	8
Schumacher, Shawn, Pot.	.997	43	272	33	1	306	3	7
Sickles, Jeremy, Lyn.	.984	20	113	10	2	125	3	2
Terveen, Bryce, M.B.	.993	17	130	10	1	141	1	2
Tonis, Mike, Wil.	.992	33	223	35	2	260	0	3
Um, Jong, M.B.	.995	24	183	9	1	193	1	4
Walter, Scott, Wil.	.987	60	421	52	6	479	4	6
Webster, Robert, Fred.	.979	5	38	8	1	47	0	0
Winchester, Jeff, Sal.	.981	95	666	73	14	753	11	16

PITCHERS

Player, Team	Pct.	G	PO	A	E	TC	DP
Alcala, Jason, Lyn.	1.000	18	4	2	0	6	1
Alvarado, Carlos, Lyn.	.000	4	0	0	0	0	0
Ammons, Cary, Wil.*	1.000	12	5	10	0	15	0
Andrade, Jancy, Fred.	1.000	20	1	3	0	4	0
Axelson, Josh, Pot.	1.000	10	1	12	0	13	1
Ayala, Luis, Sal.	1.000	13	1	3	0	4	0
Bajenaru, Jeff, W.S.	1.000	35	3	6	0	9	3
Baker, Jason, Kin.	.727	13	1	7	3	11	1
Bechler, Steve, Fred.	1.000	13	3	10	0	13	0
Bedard, Erik, Fred.*	1.000	17	2	19	0	21	2
Bennett, Jeff, Lyn.	.980	25	13	37	1	51	3
Bent, Andy, M.B.	1.000	29	1	13	0	14	1
Bohannon, Brad, W.S.	1.000	23	2	12	0	14	0
Bong, Jung, M.B.*	.872	28	8	33	6	47	1
Bradley, Bobby, Lyn	.929	9	4	9	1	14	0
Brantley, Brian, Sal.	.909	28	5	5	1	11	0
Brueggemann, Dean, Sal.*	1.000	48	0	16	0	16	1
Bukvich, Ryan, Wil.	1.000	37	0	6	0	6	0
Bumatay, Mike, Lyn.*	.750	23	0	6	2	8	1
Burch, Matt, Wil	.918	28	19	26	4	49	1
Butler, Matt, M.B.	1.000	22	2	10	0	12	0
Cali, Carmen, Pot.*	.667	12	1	1	1	3	0
Cameron, Ryan, Sal.	.500	2	1	0	1	2	0
Carrasco, Dan, Lyn.	1.000	22	6	7	0	13	1
Cercy, Rick, Sal.	1.000	39	3	6	0	9	0
Chaney, Mike, Lyn.*	.947	28	4	14	1	19	1
Clark, Greg, Pot.	.000	1	0	0	0	0	0
Clontz, Brad, M.B.	1.000	9	0	1	0	1	0
COOK, Aaron, Sal.	1.000	27	6	32	0	38	3
Cook, B.R., Pot.	.867	8	4	9	2	15	2
Corcoran, Tim, Fred.	.929	33	4	9	1	14	0
Cortes, David, M.B.	1.000	9	2	1	0	3	0
Cowie, Steve, Kin.-Sal.	.800	3	0	0	0	0	0
Cummings, Jeremy, Pot.	.800	4	1	3	1	5	0
Curreri, Joe, W.S.	.900	33	2	7	1	10	0
Curtiss, Tom, M.B.*	1.000	12	0	5	0	5	1
Dawley, Joey, M.B.	1.000	5	1	1	0	2	0
Denney, Kyle, Kin.	1.000	11	2	7	0	9	0
DeHart, Rick, Wil.	.500	5	0	1	1	2	0
Dorame, Randey, Sal.*	1.000	17	4	20	0	24	1
Douglass, Ryan, Wil.	.000	1	0	0	0	0	0
Dukeman, Greg, Lyn.	.800	27	8	16	6	30	4
Ennis, John, M.B.	.958	25	7	16	1	24	2
Evans, Kyle, Kin.	1.000	7	4	2	0	6	0
Evert, Brett, M.B.	.900	13	3	6	1	10	0
Ferguson, Ian, Wil.	.929	18	9	4	1	14	0
Figueroa, Juan, Fred.	1.000	7	3	4	0	7	0
Fischer, Eric, W.S.*	1.000	25	8	25	0	33	1
Fitch, Steve, Kin.	1.000	13	4	11	0	15	1
Fleming, Travis, Fred.	1.000	44	4	1	0	5	0
Ford, Tom, Fred.*	1.000	33	1	5	0	6	0
Forystek, Brian, Fred.*	.895	41	3	14	2	19	2
Fuller, Jody, Wil.	1.000	15	0	3	0	3	0
Garcia, Sonny, Fred.	.925	25	14	23	3	40	4
Garza, Alberto, Kin.	.933	41	1	13	1	15	1
Gawer, Matt, M.B.*	.667	42	0	4	2	6	0
Gehrke, Jay, Wil.	.870	42	7	13	3	23	1
Gilfillan, Jason, Wil.	1.000	33	5	3	0	8	0
Gobble, Jimmy, Wil.*	1.000	27	11	18	0	29	0
Gonzalez, Mike, Lyn.*	.833	14	0	5	1	6	0
Grabow, John, Lyn.*	1.000	7	1	4	0	5	0
Grassing, Bryan, Pot.	.857	48	4	14	3	21	0
Grippo, Mike, Pot.*	.000	6	0	0	0	0	0
Guerrero, Junior, Wil.	1.000	14	4	16	0	20	3
Guillory, Dan, Kin.	.714	23	5	0	2	7	0
Hale, Beau, Fred.	.875	5	2	5	1	8	1

Player, Team	Pct.	G	PO	A	E	TC	DP	Player, Team	Pct.	G	PO	A	E	TC	DP
Hart, Corey, Wil.	1.000	3	0	1	0	1	0	Pacheco, Delvis, M.B.	1.000	2	2	1	0	3	0
Hernandez, Buddy, M.B.	1.000	34	1	8	0	9	0	Pacheco, Enemencio, Sal.	1.000	27	1	6	0	7	1
Herndon, Eric, M.B.	1.000	24	2	6	0	8	1	Patten, Scott, W.S.	.000	2	0	0	0	0	0
Herrera, Alex, Kin.*	.857	28	3	3	1	7	0	Pavlovich, Tony, Lyn.	1.000	20	1	4	0	5	1
Hill, Jeremy, Wil.	1.000	9	1	2	0	3	1	Pena, Alex, Lyn.	1.000	25	2	7	0	9	0
Hodges, Trey, M.B.	.972	26	10	25	1	36	2	Pena, Ed, W.S.*	.941	31	2	14	1	17	0
Hollifield, Alec, W.S.	.765	9	6	7	4	17	0	Perez, Randy, Fred.*	.920	20	5	18	2	25	0
Hughes, Rocky, W.S.*	.833	16	1	4	1	6	0	Perkins, Mike, Pot.	1.000	11	1	1	0	2	0
Hurley, Derek, Lyn.*	.933	17	7	7	1	15	1	Pichardo, Carlos, Wil.	1.000	31	6	4	0	10	0
Jackson, Brian, Kin.	1.000	53	5	11	0	16	1	Pinales, Aquiles, Kin.	.900	36	6	3	1	10	0
Jacobsen, Landon, Lyn.	.962	17	2	23	1	26	1	Plank, Terry, Fred.	1.000	38	2	13	0	15	0
Janke, Cheyenne, Pot.	1.000	15	0	8	0	8	1	Ponce Deleon, Damon, Pot.	1.000	23	5	1	0	6	0
Johnson, James, Kin.*	1.000	4	0	2	0	2	0	Prather, Scott, Pot.*	.500	20	1	0	1	2	0
Johnston, Clint, Lyn.*	1.000	11	0	2	0	2	0	Price, Ryan, Sal.	.939	28	10	21	2	33	2
Johnston, Mike, Lyn.*	.938	11	3	12	1	16	1	Ramirez, Enrique, Fred.	1.000	7	1	2	0	3	0
Jones, Sean, Fred.	1.000	39	4	9	0	13	1	Randall, Scott, Sal.	1.000	2	1	0	0	1	0
Journell, Jimmy, Pot.	.867	26	8	18	4	30	0	Reid, Justin, Lyn.	.950	8	8	11	1	20	1
Kane, Kyle, W.S.	1.000	14	1	0	0	1	0	Rupp, Mike, W.S.	.947	27	4	14	1	19	2
Katz, Damon, Kin.	.000	1	0	0	0	0	0	Sadler, Carl, Kin.*	.824	27	4	10	3	17	0
Kelly, Dan, M.B.*	1.000	18	0	6	0	6	0	Sansom, Trevor, Pot.	.929	50	4	9	1	14	2
Kibler, Ryan, Sal.	.857	11	5	13	3	21	0	Schwager, Matt, Fred.	1.000	7	3	5	0	8	0
King, Jay, Wil.*	1.000	11	4	16	0	20	0	Sequea, Jacobo, Fred.	1.000	18	5	18	0	23	0
Kohl, Doug, Pot.	1.000	51	3	11	0	14	3	Sido, Wilson, Kin.	1.000	17	6	13	0	19	0
Kozlowski, Ben, M.B.*	1.000	2	1	2	0	3	0	Smalley, Mike, M.B.*	1.000	9	2	6	0	8	0
Lakman, Jason, Fred.	.000	3	0	0	0	0	0	Spiegel, Mike, Kin.*	.962	21	3	22	1	26	1
Lamber, Justin, Wil.*	.900	20	3	6	1	10	0	Sprague, Kevin, Pot.*	.950	26	3	35	2	40	2
Langen, Brian, Pot.*	.895	43	4	13	2	19	0	Stahl, Rich, Fred.*	.846	6	2	9	2	13	0
Lantigua, Eduardo, W.S.	.882	22	2	13	2	17	2	Stepka, Tom, Sal.	.900	32	4	14	2	20	1
LaRoche, Adam, M.B.*	.000	1	0	0	0	0	0	Stewart, Josh, W.S.*	1.000	12	3	12	0	15	0
Larson, Ryan, Kin.	.889	12	1	7	1	9	1	Stiles, Brad, Wil.*	.000	1	0	0	1	1	0
Layfield, Scotty, Pot.	.818	47	2	7	2	11	0	Tallet, Brian, Kin.*	.970	27	10	22	1	33	0
Ledden, Ryan, Lyn.	.964	27	15	39	2	56	2	Tejeda, Frank, Pot.	.957	25	4	18	1	23	1
Lewis, Richard, Fred.	1.000	1	1	1	0	2	1	Thompson, Doug, Sal.	.714	17	0	5	2	7	0
Lontayo, Alejandro, M.B.*	.750	20	1	5	2	8	0	Thoms, Hank, Kin.	.941	14	3	13	1	17	1
Lopez, Jose, Lyn.	.917	13	7	15	2	24	0	Torres, Luis, Lyn.	.000	4	0	0	0	0	0
Lopez, Juan, W.S.*	.700	26	1	6	3	10	0	Truitt, Derrick, M.B.	1.000	16	1	6	0	7	0
Majewski, Gary, W.S.	1.000	9	2	10	0	12	0	Tsao, Chin-hui, Sal.	.800	4	0	4	1	5	0
Malone, Corwin, W.S.*	1.000	5	1	7	0	8	0	Ulacia, Dennis, W.S.*	1.000	10	2	5	0	7	0
Mangrum, Micah, Wil.	.813	29	3	10	3	16	2	Valentine, Joe, W.S.	1.000	27	2	3	0	5	0
Manzueta, Roberto, Lyn.	1.000	15	0	1	0	1	0	Vance, Cory, Sal.*	.973	26	6	30	1	37	1
Martin, Chandler, Sal.	1.000	9	0	11	0	11	2	Vargas, Jose, Kin.	.800	8	1	3	1	5	0
Matcuk, Steve, Sal.	.900	24	2	7	1	10	0	Veronie, Shanin, M.B.	.909	35	3	7	1	11	0
Matsko, Rick, Kin.	1.000	10	0	4	0	4	0	Voyles, Brad, M.B.	.000	2	0	0	0	0	0
McClendon, Matt, M.B.	1.000	8	1	2	0	3	0	Wallace, Shane, Kin.*	1.000	13	4	8	0	12	0
McDaniel, Denny, W.S.*	1.000	32	1	13	0	14	1	Warren, Chris, Sal.	1.000	2	1	0	0	1	0
McWhirter, Kris, W.S.	.857	13	2	4	1	7	1	West, Brian, W.S.	.935	28	17	26	3	46	2
Medlock, Chet, Pot.	.750	12	0	3	1	4	0	Williams, Blake, Pot.	.966	17	10	18	1	29	0
Mills, Alan, Fred.	.000	5	0	0	1	1	0	Winkelsas, Joe, M.B.	1.000	4	0	1	0	1	0
Montilla, Felix, Lyn.	1.000	7	1	0	0	1	0	Wylie, Mitch, W.S.	1.000	1	0	1	0	1	0
Moreno, Orber, Wil.	1.000	8	0	1	0	1	0	Yankosky, L.J., M.B.	.944	9	7	10	1	18	0
Morris, Cory, Fred.	1.000	13	1	6	0	7	0	Young, Colin, Sal.*	1.000	47	1	6	0	7	0
Mortimer, Mark, M.B.	.000	1	0	0	0	0	0	Young, Jason, Sal.	.905	17	6	13	2	21	1
Mozingo, Dan, W.S.*	1.000	3	0	3	0	3	0	Young, Simon, Kin.*	.938	15	4	11	1	16	0
Murray, Brad, W.S.*	.889	32	3	13	2	18	2								
Narveson, Chris, Pot.*	.818	11	1	8	2	11	0								
Natale, Mike, Wil.	.944	28	4	13	1	18	0								
Neil, Dan, Kin.*	1.000	16	4	5	0	9	0								
Newell, Mark, Wil.	1.000	18	3	3	0	6	1								
Obermueller, Wes, Wil.	1.000	20	5	4	0	9	0								
Olivo, Rigal, W.S.	1.000	8	0	3	0	3	0								
Ortega, Carlos, W.S.*	1.000	10	0	7	0	7	2								

PITCHERS WITH TWO OR MORE TEAMS

Player, Team	Pct.	G	PO	A	E	TC	DP
Cowie, Steve, Kin.	.000	2	0	0	0	0	0
Cowie, Steve, Sal.	.000	1	0	0	0	0	0

The following players appeared only as designated hitter, pinch-hitter or pinch runner: Brown, dh; Lindsey, dh, ph; Matos, dh.

CLASS A Carolina League

LEAGUE CHAMPIONS

Year	Team	Pct.	Year	Team	Pct.	Year	Team	Pct.
1945—	Danville	.681	1955—	HP-Thomasville	.580		Greensboro§	.590
1946—	Greensboro	.599		Danville (2nd)†	.533		Wilson (2nd)†	.535
	Raleigh (2nd)†	.563	1956—	HP-Thomasville	.591	1964—	Kinston§	.572
1947—	Burlington	.613		Fayetteville (4th)§	.523		Winston-Salem§†	.590
	Raleigh (3rd)†	.574	1957—	Durham	.632	1965—	Peninsula§	.597
1948—	Raleigh	.592		HP-Thomasville	.622		Durham§	.580
	Martinsville (2nd)†	.570	1958—	Danville	.576		Tidewater†	.528
1949—	Danville	.601		Burlington (4th)†	.511	1966—	Kinston§	.547
	Burlington (4th)†	.500	1959—	Raleigh	.600		Winston-Salem§	.586
1950—	Winston-Salem*	.693		Wilson (2nd)†	.550		Rocky Mount†	.533
1951—	Durham	.600	1960—	Greensboro‡	.636	1967—	Durham∞(West.)	.536
	Winston-Salem (2nd)†	.583		Burlington	.586		Raleigh (East.)	.542
1952—	Raleigh	.581	1961—	Wilson	.594	1968—	Salem (West.)	.607
	Reidsville (4th)†	.536	1962—	Durham	.636		Ral-Dur (East.)	.597
1953—	Raleigh	.593		Wilson	.600		HP-Thom.▲(W.)	.493
	Danville (2nd)†	.572		Kinston (2nd)†	.593	1969—	Rocky M (East.)	.569
1954—	Fayetteville*	.628	1963—	Kinston§	.538		Salem (West.)	.542

Year	Team	Pct.	Year	Team	Pct.	Year	Team	Pct.
	Ral-Dur◆(East.)	.560	1981—	Peninsula	.522	1992—	Lynchburg	.570
1970—	Winston-Salem‡	.586		Hagerstown‡	.507		Peninsula‡	.536
	Burlington	.597	1982—	Alexandria‡	.597	1993—	Wilmington	.532
1971—	Peninsula‡	.647		Durham	.588		Winston-Salem‡	.514
	Kinston	.623	1983—	Lynchburg‡	.691	1994—	Wilmington‡	.681
1972—	Salem‡	.657		Winston-Salem	.529		Winston-Salem	.555
	Burlington	.632	1984—	Lynchburg‡	.645	1995—	Wilmington	.601
1973—	Lynchburg	.588		Durham	.486		Kinston‡	.591
	Winston-Salem‡	.557	1985—	Lynchburg	.679	1996—	Wilmington▼	.571
1974—	Salem	.671		Winston-Salem‡	.417		Kinston	.551
	Salem	.582	1986—	Hagerstown	.655	1997—	Kinston	.621
1975—	Rocky Mount	.667		Winston-Salem‡	.594		Lynchburg†	.586
	Rocky Mount	.614	1987—	Salem‡	.576	1998—	Wilmington▼	.614
1976—	Winston-Salem	.618		Kinston	.536		Winston-Salem	.568
	Winston-Salem	.551	1988—	Kinston§	.620	1999—	Kinston	.577
1977—	Lynchburg	.591		Lynchburg	.486		Myrtle Beach•	.568
	Peninsula‡	.556	1989—	Durham	.609		Wilmington•	.568
1978—	Peninsula	.696		Prince William‡	.522	2000—	Myrtle Beach▼	.629
	Lynchburg‡	.614	1990—	Kinston	.652	2001—	Kinston	.636
1979—	Winston-Salem■	.607		Frederick‡	.544		Salem▼	.507
1980—	Peninsula‡	.714	1991—	Kinston‡	.645			
	Durham	.600		Lynchburg	.482			

*Won championship and four-club playoff. †Won four-club playoff. ‡Won split-season playoff. §League was divided into Eastern, Western divisions. ∞Won eight-club, two-division playoff. ▲Won eight-club, two-division playoff against Raleigh-Durham. ◆Won eight-club, two-division playoff against Burlington. ■Won both halves of split season (no playoffs). ▼League divided into Northern and Southern divisions and played a split-season, won playoffs. •Declared co-champions after final series cancelled due to hurricane.

CLASS A *Carolina League*

FLORIDA STATE LEAGUE

LEAGUE OFFICE

President
Chuck Murphy
Address
P.O. Box 349
Daytona Beach, FL 32115
Phone
386-252-7479

Teams (affiliation)
Brevard County Manatees (Marlins)
Charlotte Rangers (Rangers)
Clearwater Phillies (Phillies)
Daytona Cubs (Cubs)
Dunedin Blue Jays (Blue Jays)
Fort Myers Miracle (Twins)

Jupiter Hammerheads (Expos)
Lakeland Tigers (Tigers)
St. Lucie Mets (Mets)
Sarasota Red Sox (Red Sox)
Tampa Yankees (Yankees)
Vero Beach Dodgers (Dodgers)

2001 FINAL STANDINGS

FIRST HALF

EAST DIVISION

Team	W	L	T	Pct.	GB
Vero Beach (Dodgers)	40	28	0	.588	...
Brevard County (Marlins)	39	29	0	.574	1.0
Lakeland (Tigers)	38	29	0	.567	1.5
Daytona (Cubs)	37	30	0	.552	2.5
St. Lucie (Mets)	32	36	0	.471	8.0
Jupiter (Expos)	29	38	0	.433	10.5

WEST DIVISION

Team	W	L	T	Pct.	GB
Charlotte (Rangers)	35	33	0	.515	...
Dunedin (Blue Jays)	33	34	0	.493	1.5
Clearwater (Phillies)	32	35	0	.478	2.5
Fort Myers (Twins)	32	36	0	.471	3.0
Tampa (Yankees)	29	38	0	.433	5.5
Sarasota (Red Sox)	29	39	0	.426	6.0

SECOND HALF

EAST DIVISION

Team	W	L	T	Pct.	GB
Brevard County (Marlins)	41	26	0	.612	...
Jupiter (Expos)	41	31	0	.569	2.5
Daytona (Cubs)	31	38	0	.449	11.0
St. Lucie (Mets)	31	40	0	.437	12.0
Lakeland (Tigers)	29	40	0	.420	13.0
Vero Beach (Dodgers)	27	38	0	.415	13.0

WEST DIVISION

Team	W	L	T	Pct.	GB
Tampa (Yankees)	48	24	0	.667	...
Dunedin (Blue Jays)	38	30	0	.559	8.0
Fort Myers (Twins)	36	33	0	.522	10.5
Clearwater (Phillies)	36	34	0	.514	11.0
Charlotte (Rangers)	32	37	0	.464	14.5
Sarasota (Red Sox)	25	44	0	.362	21.5

COMPOSITE

Team	B.C.	Tam	Dun.	V.B.	Jup.	Day.	F.M.	Cle.	Lak.	Char.	St.L.	Sar.	W	L	T	Pct.	GB
Brevard County (Marlins)	...	5	6	14	9	10	4	4	11	6	6	5	80	55	0	.593	...
Tampa (Yankees)	3	...	8	3	3	5	6	12	8	11	3	15	77	62	0	.554	5.0
Dunedin (Blue Jays)	2	8	...	1	6	9	8	12	2	9	5	9	71	64	0	.526	9.0
Vero Beach (Dodgers)	11	5	4	...	7	8	1	6	6	3	12	4	67	66	0	.504	12.0
Jupiter (Expos)	7	5	2	9	...	6	6	3	6	3	16	7	70	69	0	.504	12.0
Daytona (Cubs)	6	2	5	8	10	...	4	9	8	3	11	2	68	68	0	.500	12.5
Fort Myers (Twins)	4	10	7	7	2	3	...	7	3	13	6	6	68	69	0	.496	13.0
Clearwater (Phillies)	2	4	10	2	4	5	9	...	5	9	5	13	68	69	0	.496	13.0
Lakeland (Tigers)	5	6	5	10	10	8	4	3	...	3	5	8	67	69	0	.493	13.5
Charlotte (Rangers)	2	5	7	5	5	5	15	7	3	...	5	8	67	70	0	.489	14.0
St. Lucie (Mets)	10	5	3	3	12	5	2	3	11	3	...	6	63	76	0	.453	19.0
Sarasota (Red Sox)	3	7	7	4	1	4	10	3	6	7	2	...	54	83	0	.394	27.0

Brevard County played home games in Melbourne, Fla.; Charlotte played home games in Port Charlotte, Fla.

Major league affiliations in parentheses.

PLAYOFFS: Tampa defeated Charlotte two games to none; Brevard County defeated Vero Beach two games to none. Note: Brevard County and Tampa declared Florida State League Co-Champions due to stoppage of play in professional baseball.

REGULAR-SEASON ATTENDANCE: Brevard County, 118,307; Charlotte, 31,312; Clearwater, 76,406; Daytona, 105,606; Dunedin, 47,514; Fort Myers, 98,514; Jupiter, 114,301; Lakeland, 21,280; St. Lucie, 67,141; Sarasota, 51,125; Tampa, 102,998; Vero Beach, 49,177. Total—883,681. Playoff (7 games)—6,646. Florida State League All-Star Game at Jupiter—4,126.

MANAGERS: Brevard County, Dave Huppert; Charlotte, Darryl Kennedy; Clearwater, Ramon Aviles; Daytona, Dave Trembley; Dunedin, Marty Pevey; Fort Myers, Jose Marzan; Jupiter, Tim Leiper; Lakeland, Kevin Bradshaw; St. Lucie, Tony Tijerina; Sarasota, Ron Johnson; Tampa, Brian Butterfield; Vero Beach, Bob Mariano.

ALL-STAR TEAM: 1B—Jason Jones, Charlotte; 2B—Chase Utley, Clearwater; 3B—Jim Deschaine, Daytona; SS—Travis Chapman, Clearwater; Utility INF—Nick Alvarez, Vero Beach; OF—Matt Watson, Jupiter; OF—Nic Jackson, Daytona; OF—Michael Vento, Tampa; Utility OF—Rich Thompson, Dunedin; C (tie)—Kevin Cash, Dunedin and Max St. Pierre, Lakeland; DH—Dave Huppert, Brevard County; RHP—Josh Beckett, Brevard County; RHP—Ricardo Rodriguez, Vero Beach; RHP—Miguel Asencio, Clearwater; RHP—Greg Runser, Charlotte; LHP—Andy Vanhekken, Lakeland; LHP—Anthony Ferrari, Jupiter; Most Valuable Player—Michael Vento, Tampa; Most Valuable Pitcher—Ricardo Rodriguez, Vero Beach; Manager of the Year—Dave Huppert, Brevard County.

2001 BATTING
TEAM

Team	Avg.	G	TPA	AB	R	H	TB	2B	3B	HR	RBI	SH	SF	HP	BB	IBB	SO	SB	CS	GDP	LOB	ShO	Sig.	OBP
Brev. County	.265	135	5141	4469	677	1186	1707	213	25	86	595	34	42	76	520	19	899	158	52	90	1011	4	.382	.349
Dunedin	.265	135	5257	4613	701	1224	1735	232	33	71	625	42	39	69	494	12	1030	136	54	91	1023	8	.376	.343
Clearwater	.256	137	5125	4506	618	1152	1691	230	33	81	563	37	50	85	447	21	923	189	73	92	948	14	.375	.331

CLASS A *Florida State League*

Team	Avg.	G	TPA	AB	R	H	TB	2B	3B	HR	RBI	SH	SF	HP	BB	IBB	SO	SB	CS	GDP	LOB	ShO	Slg.	OBP
Lakeland	.255	136	5171	4506	625	1150	1665	233	36	70	567	50	54	62	499	15	935	154	53	86	1002	5	.370	.334
Daytona	.255	136	5073	4455	604	1134	1678	211	21	97	553	36	40	71	471	13	915	112	80	86	955	9	.377	.333
Vero Beach	.254	133	4947	4336	517	1101	1524	192	21	63	461	50	34	77	450	14	804	94	55	113	983	12	.351	.332
Fort Myers	.250	137	5301	4602	614	1151	1563	193	24	57	546	45	44	81	529	19	890	111	49	110	1064	12	.340	.335
St. Lucie	.249	139	5068	4473	590	1116	1643	222	28	83	528	46	47	59	443	13	1016	191	90	77	911	6	.367	.322
Jupiter	.249	139	5150	4535	578	1129	1539	201	40	43	498	45	24	74	472	16	952	162	83	93	954	9	.339	.328
Charlotte	.247	137	5060	4544	529	1123	1604	219	38	62	476	44	27	44	401	27	910	97	67	87	929	6	.353	.313
Sarasota	.245	137	5172	4576	550	1121	1668	222	26	91	499	28	37	68	463	16	1039	101	67	98	968	11	.365	.321
Tampa	.244	139	5155	4439	634	1083	1732	233	40	112	574	26	50	85	555	17	1038	95	73	88	964	5	.390	.336

INDIVIDUAL

TOP QUALIFIERS FOR BATTING CHAMPIONSHIP

Minimum 378 plate appearances. *Lefthanded batter. †Switch-hitter.

Player, Team	Avg.	G	TPA	AB	R	H	TB	2B	3B	HR	RBI	SH	SF	HP	BB	IBB	SO	SB	CS	GDP	Slg.	OBP
Watson, Matt, Jup.*	.330	124	518	446	70	147	203	33	4	5	74	0	3	6	63	4	45	17	9	11	.455	.417
Thompson, Rich, Dun.*	.311	112	514	454	90	141	170	14	6	1	60	3	4	9	44	1	72	39	11	3	.374	.380
Chapman, Travis, Cle.	.307	96	392	329	39	101	135	22	0	4	50	2	6	11	44	3	39	3	1	12	.410	.400
Matthews, Lamont, V.B.*	.307	107	453	349	61	107	169	26	3	10	57	0	2	4	95	4	106	1	3	5	.484	.458
Fagan, Shawn, Dun.	.301	132	567	475	68	143	201	18	5	10	71	0	4	2	86	1	114	7	2	11	.423	.407
Vento, Mike, Tam.	.300	130	514	457	71	137	237	20	10	20	87	0	3	9	45	1	88	13	10	9	.519	.372
Roneberg, Brett, B.C.*	.299	88	395	331	49	99	160	20	4	11	63	1	9	4	50	2	54	5	3	6	.483	.388
Jackson, Nick, Day.*	.296	131	557	503	87	149	248	30	6	19	85	0	5	10	39	5	96	24	10	7	.493	.355
Padgett, Matt, B.C.*	.293	125	515	440	68	129	194	37	2	8	81	0	3	8	64	4	101	10	1	9	.441	.390
Deschaine, James, Day.	.289	134	555	485	68	140	233	26	2	21	82	1	3	4	62	2	103	6	10	10	.480	.372
Dzurilla, Mike, Day.	.288	123	486	434	60	125	174	21	2	8	45	4	5	5	38	0	77	9	6	8	.401	.349
Alvarez, Nick, V.B.	.286	118	472	420	63	120	202	15	2	21	71	2	4	17	29	1	80	14	7	11	.481	.353
Espy, Nate, Cle.	.285	133	571	470	75	134	202	31	2	11	68	0	7	6	88	3	90	6	2	10	.430	.399
Cash, Kevin, Dun.	.283	105	427	371	55	105	168	27	0	12	66	4	1	8	43	2	80	4	3	11	.453	.369
Jones, Jason, Char.*	.283	102	436	375	50	106	181	26	2	15	81	0	4	1	56	5	48	1	3	12	.483	.374
Alvaroz, Jimmy, Dun.†	.283	123	529	467	88	132	183	19	4	8	56	7	4	2	49	0	87	29	7	7	.392	.351

DEPARTMENTAL LEADERS: G—M. Jones, 137; AB—R. Martinez, 515; R—Medrano, 93; H—N. Jackson, 149; TB—N. Jackson, 248; 2B—Padgett, 37; 3B—Vento, 10; HR—N. Alvarez, Deschaine, M. Jones, 21 each; RBI—Vento, 87; SH—L. Rodriguez, Santiago, Shipp, 14 each; SF—Phillips, 10; HP—N. Alvarez, 17; BB—Matthews, 95; IBB—Blalock, 7; SO—C. Rodriguez, 144; SB—Medrano, 61; CS—R. Martinez, 18; GIDP—C. Rodriguez, 21; Slg.—Vento, .519; OBP—Matthews, .458.

ALL PLAYERS

*Lefthanded batter. †Switch-hitter.

Player, Team	Avg.	G	TPA	AB	R	H	TB	2B	3B	HR	RBI	SH	SF	HP	BB	IBB	SO	SB	CS	GDP	Slg.	OBP
Abbott, Jeff, B.C.	.250	3	10	8	2	2	2	0	0	0	2	0	1	0	1	0	1	0	0	0	.250	.300
Abreu, Dave, St.L.†	.250	20	45	40	6	10	13	0	0	1	2	1	0	0	4	0	5	2	4	1	.325	.318
Ackerman, Scott, Jup.	.250	90	356	324	31	81	104	12	1	3	44	4	3	0	25	1	52	1	4	7	.321	.301
Acuna, Ron, St.L.	.244	33	129	119	13	29	44	9	0	2	13	2	1	1	6	0	22	7	1	3	.370	.283
Agramonte, Marcos, Char.†	.324	10	37	37	2	12	21	3	3	0	3	0	0	0	0	0	7	1	2	0	.568	.324
Aguila, Chris, B.C.	.276	73	299	292	44	75	126	15	3	10	34	0	4	2	21	1	54	8	4	7	.463	.328
Ahumada, Alex, Sar.	.243	112	434	379	48	92	133	23	0	6	42	6	4	11	34	2	73	22	9	7	.351	.320
Alvarez, Jimmy, Dun.†	.283	123	529	467	88	132	183	19	4	8	56	7	4	2	49	2	87	29	7	7	.392	.351
Alvarez, Nick, V.B.	.286	118	472	420	63	120	202	15	2	21	71	2	4	17	29	1	80	14	7	11	.481	.353
Anderson, Jon, Sar.†	.000	4	8	7	0	0	0	0	0	0	0	1	0	0	1	0	1	0	1	0	.000	.125
Angell, Rick, Char.	.217	46	179	161	12	35	40	5	0	0	10	4	1	3	10	0	30	4	5	5	.248	.274
Aracena, Sandy, V.B.	.333	2	7	6	0	2	2	0	0	0	0	0	1	0	0	0	1	0	0	0	.333	.429
Arias, Leandro, St.L.	.200	5	15	15	1	3	4	1	0	0	1	0	0	0	0	0	5	1	0	0	.267	.200
Arroyo, William, B.C.†	.231	6	15	13	3	3	3	0	0	0	1	0	0	0	2	0	2	0	0	0	.231	.333
Aybar, Willy, V.B.†	.286	2	8	7	0	2	2	0	0	0	0	0	0	0	1	0	2	0	0	0	.286	.375
Baker, Derek, Lak.*	.268	77	279	213	31	57	73	16	0	0	34	1	2	3	60	5	43	1	2	3	.343	.432
Barningham, Steve, Char.*	.279	70	271	219	50	61	87	15	4	1	24	2	3	5	42	2	30	17	0	6	.397	.401
Baron, Brian, F.M.*	.306	69	289	265	38	81	100	10	3	1	37	2	3	1	18	1	40	0	0	8	.377	.348
Basak, Chris, St.L.	.233	126	536	472	71	110	149	19	4	4	46	4	8	5	47	0	125	30	9	8	.316	.305
Bass, Kevin, Day.†	.188	87	304	276	32	52	84	11	0	7	20	0	0	4	28	0	106	4	2	9	.304	.263
Bates, Fletcher, St.L.†	.247	82	329	300	45	74	129	18	2	11	46	0	2	0	27	2	48	13	5	3	.430	.307
Batson, Tom, Cle.	.216	9	39	37	3	8	8	0	0	0	1	0	0	0	2	0	6	3	0	0	.216	.256
Bautista, Rayner, Lak.	.260	101	389	354	43	92	142	18	4	8	43	6	7	2	20	0	89	8	4	3	.401	.298
Bay, Jason, Jup.	.195	38	145	123	12	24	33	4	1	1	10	1	1	2	18	1	26	10	3	4	.268	.306
Bell, Ricky, V.B.	.250	6	25	24	3	6	6	0	0	0	0	0	0	0	0	0	5	0	0	0	.250	.280
Beltre, Adrian, V.B.	.444	3	12	9	0	4	5	1	0	0	1	0	0	1	2	0	1	0	0	0	.556	.583
Bennett, Ryan, St.L.	.293	26	97	82	12	24	29	2	0	1	5	0	1	2	12	0	13	1	0	1	.354	.392
Bernhardt, Joe, Dun.	.255	120	450	420	50	107	155	25	1	7	52	1	3	4	28	0	100	2	3	9	.369	.305
Berry, Sean, Dun.	.190	12	53	42	9	8	16	2	0	2	7	0	1	2	8	1	10	0	0	2	.381	.340
Blakely, Darren, Tam.*	.256	98	372	313	47	80	140	14	5	12	39	3	2	13	41	0	94	24	11	3	.447	.363
Blalock, Hank, Char.*	.380	63	268	237	46	90	132	19	1	7	47	0	4	1	26	7	31	7	4	6	.557	.437
Blasi, Blake, Day.†	.243	46	174	144	17	35	38	1	1	0	14	2	2	1	25	0	14	3	4	2	.264	.355
Bledsoe, Hunter, V.B.	.323	65	259	232	28	75	95	8	0	4	25	0	1	2	24	0	27	5	2	15	.409	.390
Blum, Greg, Jup.	.194	64	239	201	22	39	61	10	0	3	22	1	1	15	21	0	53	2	2	5	.303	.315
Bolivar, Papo, F.M.	.291	57	253	227	42	66	85	6	2	3	25	0	2	2	25	0	33	15	3	6	.374	.356
Boone, Matt, Lak.	.256	104	411	375	47	96	134	16	5	4	33	3	3	1	29	0	95	8	3	11	.357	.309
Botts, Jason, Char.†	.167	4	16	12	1	2	3	1	0	0	0	0	0	0	4	0	4	0	0	0	.250	.375
Bozanich, Sam, Tam.	.182	14	53	44	6	8	8	0	0	0	0	0	0	1	8	0	10	1	3	1	.182	.321
Brown, Andy, Tam.*	.193	93	362	306	45	59	111	13	3	11	45	0	2	9	52	3	129	7	5	2	.363	.315
Brown, Jason, B.C.	.276	34	146	127	14	35	49	6	1	2	20	2	0	7	10	0	29	0	0	4	.386	.361
Brown, Rich, Tam.*	.600	1	5	5	0	3	4	1	0	0	2	0	0	0	0	0	0	0	0	0	.800	.600
Burns, Pat, St.L.†	.238	131	522	466	54	111	159	22	1	8	68	1	4	3	40	5	131	1	4	0	.341	.311
Bush, Brian, Cle.	.100	4	12	10	0	1	1	0	0	0	0	2	0	1	0	2	0	1	0	.100	.167
Bush, Darren, Cle.*	.175	46	162	137	15	24	37	5	1	2	18	1	2	4	18	0	33	1	1	2	.270	.286

Player, Team	Avg.	G	TPA	AB	R	H	TB	2B	3B	HR	RBI	SH	SF	HP	BB	IBB	SO	SB	CS	GDP	Slg.	OBP
Bush, Homer, Dun.	.353	4	19	17	4	6	6	0	0	0	2	0	0	0	2	0	3	1	0	0	.353	.421
Cadiente, Brett, Char.*	.279	68	301	272	39	76	103	14	5	1	21	1	1	1	26	4	44	10	8	2	.379	.343
Calabrese, Tony, Tam.	.233	20	71	60	8	14	16	2	0	0	3	1	0	2	8	0	9	3	1	1	.267	.343
Callahan, Dave, B.C.*	.254	123	539	476	68	121	166	14	2	9	68	3	3	3	54	2	89	10	7	13	.349	.332
Camilo, Juan, Lak.*	.301	55	224	193	34	58	102	10	5	8	37	0	1	4	26	3	52	7	2	1	.528	.393
Campos, Julio, Cle.	.208	9	25	24	1	5	6	1	0	0	1	1	0	0	0	0	4	1	0	0	.250	.208
Carroll, Wes, Cle.	.200	7	19	15	2	3	3	0	0	0	1	0	0	1	3	0	2	0	0	0	.200	.368
Carter, Shannon, Dun.*	.273	48	170	161	25	44	53	7	1	0	17	0	1	3	5	0	44	6	6	4	.329	.306
Cash, Kevin, Dun.	.283	105	427	371	55	105	168	27	0	12	66	4	1	8	43	2	80	4	3	11	.453	.369
Chapman, Scott, Day.	.061	18	71	66	3	4	4	0	0	0	2	0	0	0	5	0	15	0	0	2	.061	.127
Chapman, Travis, Cle.	.307	96	392	329	39	101	135	22	0	4	50	2	6	11	44	3	39	3	1	12	.410	.400
Chen, Chin-Feng, V.B.	.268	62	270	235	38	63	99	15	3	5	41	0	1	6	28	2	56	2	0	3	.421	.359
Chiaffredo, Paul, Dun.	.213	28	107	94	13	20	37	6	1	3	20	0	2	5	5	0	26	0	0	2	.394	.283
Clapinski, Chris, B.C.†	.345	10	44	29	10	10	13	0	0	1	6	0	0	1	14	2	5	0	0	4	.448	.568
Coleman, Andy, Tam.	.059	7	23	17	3	1	2	1	0	0	1	1	0	2	3	0	7	0	0	0	.118	.273
Collins, Mike, V.B.	.276	74	315	268	29	74	91	11	0	2	24	6	2	2	37	0	26	5	3	6	.340	.366
Cooper, Sam, Day.†	.108	13	45	37	6	4	5	1	0	0	0	1	0	3	4	0	8	1	0	4	.135	.250
Curry, Chris, Day.	.263	12	42	38	2	10	14	4	0	0	5	0	0	0	4	0	12	0	0	0	.368	.333
Daigle, Leo, Lak.	.252	95	347	313	42	79	133	19	1	11	58	0	5	5	24	3	77	4	1	5	.425	.311
Deitrick, Jeremy, Cle.	.205	55	207	195	12	40	70	11	2	5	28	1	0	3	8	0	62	3	3	1	.359	.248
Deschaine, James, Day.	.289	134	555	485	68	140	233	26	2	21	82	1	3	4	62	2	103	6	10	10	.480	.372
Deschenes, Pat, St.L.*	.258	65	244	213	26	55	68	8	1	1	24	0	2	2	27	5	32	1	1	7	.319	.344
Dina, Allen, St.L.	.361	16	63	61	13	22	39	6	1	3	12	0	0	0	2	0	10	4	0	0	.639	.381
Downing, Brad, Lak.*	.255	34	117	94	15	24	46	7	0	5	27	2	4	1	16	0	19	0	0	2	.489	.357
Downing, Phil, Jup.*	.238	67	259	227	28	54	84	15	3	3	30	0	2	1	29	0	69	8	4	2	.370	.324
Duarte, Justin, Cle.	.236	48	171	157	17	37	50	10	0	1	22	0	2	4	8	0	42	0	0	5	.318	.287
Duplissea, Bill, V.B.	.187	39	128	107	8	20	28	4	2	0	6	3	0	7	11	0	37	1	0	2	.262	.304
Duran, Deudis, Cle.†	.190	5	21	21	1	4	5	1	0	0	2	0	0	0	0	0	7	0	0	1	.238	.190
Dzurilla, Mike, Day.	.288	123	486	434	60	125	174	21	2	8	45	4	5	5	38	0	77	9	6	8	.401	.349
Edwards, John, F.M.	.209	87	306	278	24	58	88	14	2	4	33	0	2	4	22	0	77	4	2	12	.317	.275
Elwood, Brad, Tam.	.212	45	129	118	11	25	31	6	0	0	10	1	0	2	8	0	21	1	1	3	.263	.273
Espy, Nate, Cle.	.285	133	571	470	75	134	202	31	2	11	68	0	7	6	88	3	90	6	2	10	.430	.399
Everett, Carl, Sar.†	.429	2	9	7	0	3	3	0	0	0	0	0	0	0	2	0	0	0	0	0	.429	.556
Fagan, Shawn, Dun.	.301	132	567	475	68	143	201	18	5	10	71	0	4	2	86	1	114	7	2	11	.423	.407
Feliciano, Jesus, V.B.*	.262	116	442	401	48	105	131	11	3	3	29	4	2	4	31	2	35	22	10	15	.327	.320
Ferrand, Frank, B.C.*	.195	31	117	113	14	22	33	0	1	3	13	0	0	0	4	0	28	0	0	2	.292	.222
Figga, Mike, St.L.	.278	25	95	90	10	25	42	3	1	4	11	0	1	0	4	0	22	0	1	2	.467	.305
Flores, Javier, Char.	.173	19	62	52	3	9	12	3	0	0	2	1	0	2	7	0	3	0	0	2	.231	.295
Ford, Lew, F.M.	.298	67	301	265	42	79	104	15	2	2	24	1	2	12	21	3	30	19	9	3	.392	.373
Foster, Quincy, B.C.*	.299	41	176	154	29	46	54	6	1	0	12	0	1	2	19	0	25	16	5	2	.351	.381
Frick, Matt, B.C.	.226	42	148	133	19	30	48	12	0	2	12	0	1	4	10	0	30	1	0	2	.361	.292
Frye, Jeff, Dun.	.500	4	14	12	4	6	6	0	0	0	1	0	0	0	2	0	1	1	0	1	.500	.571
Fuentes, Omar, Tam.	.833	2	8	6	4	5	9	1	0	1	3	0	0	0	2	0	0	0	0	0	1.500	.875
Gajewski, Matt, Char.†	.139	26	91	79	4	11	20	4	1	1	4	0	0	0	12	1	26	0	0	0	.253	.253
Gallo, Ismael, V.B.*	.253	64	271	237	26	60	81	9	3	2	22	7	3	0	24	0	15	2	1	5	.342	.318
Garbe, B.J., F.M.	.242	127	529	463	55	112	152	14	4	6	61	0	3	12	51	2	86	13	7	8	.328	.331
Garcia, Douglas, Char.*	.243	127	512	473	40	115	158	17	7	4	51	4	3	5	27	4	78	11	4	7	.334	.283
Garcia, Luis, Sar.	.303	65	287	267	38	81	133	14	1	12	44	0	1	1	18	2	61	2	2	8	.498	.348
Garland, Ross, Lak.	.250	1	4	4	0	1	1	0	0	0	0	0	0	0	0	0	2	0	0	0	.250	.250
German, Franklin, Day.	.184	71	230	196	29	36	46	6	2	0	12	6	0	3	25	0	63	13	7	4	.235	.286
Gingrich, Troy, Jup.*	.241	70	247	199	30	48	63	9	3	0	15	2	1	8	37	1	37	6	7	7	.317	.380
Giron, Alejandro, Cle.	.261	113	445	418	59	109	159	26	3	6	41	2	2	4	19	1	84	9	9	10	.380	.298
Goldbach, Jeff, Day.	.193	46	164	145	14	28	47	5	1	4	17	1	1	2	15	0	28	0	0	1	.324	.276
Gomez, Ramon, Cle.	.338	21	91	77	16	26	36	3	2	1	8	1	0	0	13	0	21	13	3	1	.468	.433
Gomon, Dusty, F.M.	.278	6	18	18	2	5	8	0	0	1	3	0	0	0	0	0	6	0	0	0	.444	.278
Goodman, Scott, B.C.*	.242	34	115	99	12	24	39	12	0	1	13	3	0	1	12	1	23	0	0	0	.394	.330
Goudie, Jaime, Dun.	.270	47	185	174	23	47	64	9	1	2	23	1	1	2	7	0	30	3	2	3	.368	.304
Graham, Jess, Sar.*	.255	17	53	47	6	12	17	2	0	1	2	0	0	0	6	0	11	0	1	0	.362	.340
Grice, Daniel, Day.	.128	28	103	94	7	12	14	2	0	0	7	2	1	0	6	0	16	2	0	2	.149	.178
Gripp, Ryan, Day.	.295	67	280	241	35	71	105	19	0	5	49	0	5	7	27	1	57	6	5	5	.436	.375
Gross, Gabe, Dun.*	.302	35	155	126	23	38	63	9	2	4	15	0	1	2	26	1	29	4	2	2	.500	.426
Grove, Jason, Tam.*	.400	1	5	5	1	2	4	2	0	0	2	0	0	0	0	0	2	0	0	0	.800	.400
Guerrero, Hector, V.B.*	.257	39	154	148	16	38	51	11	1	0	10	1	0	1	4	0	35	2	3	2	.345	.281
Gulledge, Kelley, F.M.	.268	58	242	213	33	57	103	16	1	10	45	0	1	7	20	1	60	1	1	5	.484	.349
Guyton, Eric, St.L.	.182	5	13	11	0	2	3	1	0	0	0	0	0	0	2	0	6	0	0	0	.273	.308
Halloran, Matt, Char.	.227	26	95	88	12	20	32	9	0	1	8	2	0	2	3	0	20	1	1	0	.364	.269
Hannahan, Buzz, Cle.	.261	82	319	268	43	70	85	10	1	1	27	3	3	6	39	2	44	17	7	6	.317	.364
Hansen, Dave, V.B.*	.000	3	10	9	1	0	0	0	0	0	0	0	0	0	1	0	2	0	0	0	.000	.100
Harper, Brandon, B.C.	.238	29	116	101	14	24	36	6	0	2	16	1	0	2	12	0	14	0	1	4	.356	.330
Hawthorne, Kyle, F.M.	.218	47	181	165	16	36	53	5	0	4	21	0	4	5	7	0	29	3	2	4	.321	.265
Headley, Justin, Sar.*	.254	114	476	409	54	104	152	28	1	6	53	4	5	4	54	2	60	13	6	4	.372	.343
Hensley, Anthony, Cle.†	.158	12	44	38	4	6	11	3	1	0	3	1	2	0	3	0	9	2	0	1	.289	.209
Henson, Drew, Tam.	.143	5	19	14	2	2	5	0	0	1	3	0	1	2	2	0	7	1	0	0	.357	.316
Hernandez, Anderson, Lak.†	.190	7	23	21	2	4	6	0	1	0	1	2	0	0	0	0	8	0	0	0	.286	.190
Hernandez, John, V.B.	.202	38	125	114	8	23	32	9	0	0	22	0	3	3	5	0	19	1	1	2	.281	.248
Hicks, Scott, B.C.*	.286	2	7	7	0	2	2	0	0	0	0	0	0	0	0	0	0	0	0	0	.286	.286
Hill, Bobby, St.L.*	.249	63	194	173	22	43	59	6	2	2	18	4	1	1	15	0	34	6	9	3	.341	.311
Hill, Willy, B.C.*	.297	10	44	37	6	11	11	0	0	0	2	4	0	1	2	0	7	1	2	0	.297	.350
Hitchcox, Brian, Cle.*	.195	32	100	87	9	17	24	2	1	1	6	3	1	1	8	0	6	2	3	3	.276	.268
Hodge, Kevin, F.M.	.235	61	262	221	35	52	86	13	0	7	27	0	1	4	36	1	51	3	1	2	.389	.351
Hooper, Clay, Tam.	.216	93	315	268	43	58	75	10	2	1	20	3	6	3	35	0	44	3	9	5	.280	.317
Huber, Justin, St.L.	.000	2	6	6	0	0	0	0	0	0	0	0	0	0	0	0	2	0	0	0	.000	.000
Huff, B.J., St.L.	.226	31	116	106	12	24	34	7	0	1	13	0	1	1	7	0	35	5	4	3	.321	.278

Player, Team	Avg.	G	TPA	AB	R	H	TB	2B	3B	HR	RBI	SH	SF	HP	BB	IBB	SO	SB	CS	GDP	Slg.	OBP
Jackson, Brandon, Tam.	.231	69	257	225	23	52	69	8	0	3	26	0	4	3	25	0	45	3	7	7	.307	.311
Jackson, Nick, Day.*	.296	131	557	503	87	149	248	30	6	19	85	0	5	10	39	5	96	24	10	7	.493	.355
Jacobson, Russ, Cle.	.208	102	396	351	35	73	110	21	2	4	40	2	5	10	27	0	99	1	0	11	.313	.280
Jaile, Chris, Char.	.219	42	168	151	17	33	44	5	0	2	10	2	2	1	12	1	31	0	0	3	.291	.277
James, Kenny, Jup.†	.273	74	314	282	49	77	101	8	5	2	19	9	0	5	17	2	40	22	8	1	.358	.326
Jaramillo, Milko, V.B.†	.183	50	163	153	15	28	37	2	2	1	5	5	0	1	4	0	25	1	0	5	.242	.209
Jenkins, Brian, St.L.	.270	35	137	126	15	34	53	5	1	4	15	0	2	4	5	0	26	4	3	2	.421	.314
Jenkins, Neil, Lak.	.302	23	89	86	14	26	39	8	1	1	6	0	1	0	2	0	25	0	1	5	.453	.315
Jimenez, Carlos, Lak.	.193	54	155	135	17	26	35	7	1	0	11	2	0	1	17	0	47	6	2	3	.259	.288
Johannes, Todd, Jup.	.086	22	66	58	5	5	8	0	0	1	2	0	0	1	7	0	23	0	0	1	.138	.197
Johnson, Jason, Cle.	.289	46	207	187	26	54	72	12	0	2	32	2	4	1	12	0	32	22	3	0	.385	.328
Johnstone, Ben, Day.	.266	82	338	308	39	82	91	6	0	1	30	7	3	10	10	0	32	20	13	1	.295	.308
Jones, Jack, Day.	.238	9	22	21	3	5	6	1	0	0	2	0	0	1	0	0	4	0	0	0	.286	.273
Jones, Jason, Char.†	.283	102	436	375	50	106	181	26	2	15	81	0	4	1	56	5	48	1	3	12	.483	.374
Jones, Mitch, Tam.	.224	137	581	487	85	109	214	36	3	21	71	1	5	7	81	3	135	9	2	12	.439	.340
Jones, Terry, Jup.†	.160	7	26	25	4	4	5	1	0	0	1	0	0	0	1	0	3	0	0	0	.200	.192
Jorgensen, Ryan, Day.	.282	54	213	188	24	53	91	12	1	8	29	0	0	2	23	0	39	1	3	6	.484	.366
Keene, Kurt, Dun.	.182	53	150	132	16	24	28	4	0	0	8	4	2	3	9	0	23	0	2	5	.212	.247
Kellner, Ryan, V.B.	.208	66	262	236	15	49	71	8	1	4	21	2	1	6	17	0	52	0	2	6	.301	.277
Kerner, Craig, Jup.*	.200	8	20	15	2	3	3	0	0	0	1	0	0	2	3	0	6	0	0	0	.200	.400
Kerrigan, Joe, Sar.*	.248	103	428	367	43	91	124	14	2	5	31	4	3	5	49	3	51	5	3	7	.338	.342
King, Brennan, V.B.	.243	73	274	255	24	62	75	10	0	1	28	1	2	3	13	0	48	0	0	6	.294	.286
Koone, Chuck, Char.†	.333	7	20	18	1	6	6	0	0	0	0	1	0	0	1	0	4	0	2	0	.333	.368
Kopitzke, Casey, Day.	.240	38	117	96	15	23	24	1	0	0	8	3	1	6	11	0	17	0	2	2	.250	.351
Kremblas, Mike, Dun.	.191	49	168	141	17	27	35	6	1	0	15	1	2	6	18	0	34	0	3	5	.248	.305
Kropf, Andy, Lak.†	.231	48	187	169	16	39	56	8	0	3	15	0	1	0	16	0	27	1	0	5	.331	.296
Lane, Rich, Jup.*	.235	125	485	447	41	105	143	20	3	4	49	0	0	5	33	1	118	2	5	10	.320	.295
Langs, Ronte, V.B.	.273	5	13	11	1	3	3	0	0	0	1	0	0	0	2	0	1	1	1	0	.273	.385
Lara, David, Lak.	.238	16	45	42	4	10	17	5	1	0	4	0	0	1	2	0	11	2	0	3	.405	.289
Larned, Drew, Sar.	.182	69	231	192	23	35	48	10	0	1	18	2	3	2	32	0	53	3	5	5	.250	.301
Leach, Nick, Tam.*	.269	59	232	201	24	54	88	6	2	8	33	1	6	5	19	2	42	0	6	5	.438	.338
Leaumont, Jeff, Tam.*	.241	76	275	249	28	60	95	11	3	6	22	0	3	2	21	4	50	1	1	5	.382	.302
Leer, David, Lak.	.209	50	139	129	17	27	39	6	3	0	5	2	0	5	3	0	36	8	1	2	.302	.255
Lipowicz, Nathan, V.B.	.238	33	112	101	8	24	28	4	0	0	9	1	1	2	7	0	22	0	0	2	.277	.297
Lugo, Felix, Jup.†	.245	77	293	269	31	66	105	12	6	5	36	0	4	6	14	1	89	7	3	4	.390	.294
Lush, Zach, B.C.	.150	10	23	20	2	3	4	1	0	0	0	0	0	1	2	0	7	0	0	0	.200	.261
Mabry, John, B.C.*	.154	4	16	13	0	2	2	0	0	0	4	0	1	0	2	0	1	0	0	0	.154	.250
Machado, Andy, Cle.†	.261	82	320	272	49	71	107	5	8	5	36	10	3	4	31	2	66	23	9	3	.393	.342
Magness, Pat, B.C.*	.274	35	135	117	11	32	42	7	0	1	16	0	1	1	16	1	28	0	0	0	.359	.363
Malave, Jaime, St.L.	.444	2	10	9	2	4	4	0	0	0	0	1	0	0	0	0	5	0	1	0	.444	.444
Martin, Tyler, Char.†	.218	47	171	147	24	32	54	6	2	4	15	1	3	0	20	1	30	0	1	2	.367	.306
Martinez, Casey, Dun.	.176	7	18	17	1	3	4	1	0	0	3	1	0	0	0	0	2	0	0	0	.235	.176
Martinez, Dionnar, Day.†	.267	26	71	60	10	16	19	3	0	0	0	3	0	1	7	0	11	1	0	1	.317	.353
Martinez, Ramon, Char.†	.241	128	557	515	69	124	152	20	1	2	32	8	1	5	28	0	65	28	18	7	.295	.286
Matthews, Lamont, V.B.*	.307	107	453	349	61	107	169	26	3	10	57	0	2	4	95	4	106	1	3	5	.484	.458
Maxwell, Jason, F.M.	.444	2	9	9	1	4	5	1	0	0	2	0	0	0	0	0	0	0	0	1	.556	.444
Mayorson, Manuel, Dun.	.189	18	39	37	6	7	7	0	0	0	2	0	0	0	2	0	2	0	0	0	.189	.231
McAffee, Josh, St.L.	.067	5	17	15	0	1	1	0	0	0	0	0	0	0	2	0	6	0	0	0	.067	.176
McKinley, Josh, Jup.†	.252	128	542	464	63	117	146	19	2	2	54	0	5	3	70	2	83	28	10	11	.315	.351
McKinney, Tony, Dun.	.267	128	513	450	68	120	164	25	5	3	48	6	3	6	48	0	106	23	6	8	.364	.343
McMillin, Brian, F.M.	.180	93	288	250	31	45	61	10	0	2	15	7	1	1	29	0	76	15	3	5	.244	.267
McNamara, Rusty, Cle.	.429	9	36	28	5	12	18	6	0	0	11	0	0	2	6	0	2	2	0	2	.643	.556
Meadows, Randy, Jup.-Day.	.088	10	36	34	1	3	3	0	0	0	0	1	0	0	1	0	11	1	0	0	.088	.114
Meadows, Tydus, Day.	.350	5	25	20	5	7	11	1	0	1	4	0	0	2	3	0	4	0	0	1	.550	.480
Medrano, Jesus, B.C.	.251	124	521	454	93	114	136	15	2	1	32	7	4	5	51	0	81	61	8	9	.300	.331
Melucci, Lou, Jup.	.219	65	233	201	20	44	55	6	1	1	16	6	0	1	25	0	61	3	4	4	.274	.308
Miller, Eric, Jup.	.270	19	70	63	4	17	22	3	1	0	7	2	1	1	3	0	8	2	1	1	.349	.309
Minus, Steve, Sar.	.227	112	454	387	41	88	130	10	4	8	40	1	4	3	59	0	102	6	2	7	.336	.331
Morales, Steve, B.C.†	.248	48	176	157	19	39	58	7	0	4	15	3	1	5	10	0	15	0	0	4	.369	.312
Morneau, Justin, F.M.*	.294	53	234	197	25	58	86	10	3	4	40	0	5	8	24	1	41	0	0	4	.437	.385
Morrow, Alvin, Dun.	.213	52	201	174	20	37	53	8	1	2	30	2	1	1	23	0	65	1	1	5	.305	.307
Myrow, Brian, Tam.*	.255	48	192	149	30	38	60	11	1	3	28	4	2	5	32	0	29	5	1	4	.403	.399
Nadeau, Rick, Sar.	.261	96	388	348	32	91	127	17	2	5	45	1	3	3	33	0	55	6	5	13	.365	.328
Navarro, Mandy, Day.†	.333	3	8	6	2	2	2	0	0	0	0	0	0	0	2	0	3	0	0	0	.333	.500
Nelson, Reggie, V.B.	.227	102	421	348	51	79	91	12	0	0	23	10	5	12	46	1	54	22	13	7	.261	.333
Nettles, Jeff, Tam.	.202	77	282	253	28	51	77	14	0	4	31	1	3	1	24	1	53	0	2	6	.304	.270
Nettles, Tim, Tam.	.056	10	19	18	2	1	1	0	0	0	1	0	0	0	1	0	5	1	0	0	.056	.105
Nicholson, Derek, Lak.*	.267	39	137	116	12	31	37	4	1	0	18	0	3	2	16	2	16	2	0	5	.319	.358
Nina, Amuarys, Char.	.232	99	355	323	27	75	99	9	3	3	18	3	0	4	25	0	99	8	3	6	.307	.295
Nix, Laynce, Char.*	.297	9	38	37	4	11	16	3	1	0	2	0	0	0	1	0	13	0	0	2	.432	.316
Nowlin, Cody, Char.*	.250	53	206	188	16	47	69	10	3	2	25	0	0	1	17	2	48	0	0	6	.367	.316
Nunez, Manuel, V.B.	.136	16	50	44	5	6	10	1	0	1	5	3	0	0	3	0	21	0	1	0	.227	.191
Olivares, Teuris, Tam.	.267	4	17	15	2	4	6	2	0	0	0	0	0	0	2	0	3	1	0	1	.400	.353
Oliver, Brian, Char.	.238	8	21	21	2	5	5	0	0	0	1	0	0	0	0	0	0	0	0	0	.238	.238
Ortiz, David, F.M.*	.000	1	4	3	0	0	0	0	0	0	0	0	0	0	1	0	0	0	0	0	.000	.250
Osborne, Mark, F.M.*	.219	47	160	137	14	30	43	4	0	3	8	0	1	1	21	2	36	1	1	3	.314	.325
Osborne, Steve, Tam.	.200	6	16	15	2	3	4	1	0	0	1	0	0	1	0	0	5	0	0	2	.267	.250
Paciorek, Pete, V.B.*	.196	46	160	143	13	28	47	5	1	4	17	2	1	0	13	1	33	0	0	5	.329	.261
Padgett, Matt, B.C.*	.293	125	515	440	68	129	194	37	2	8	81	0	3	8	64	4	101	10	1	9	.441	.390
Padilla, Jorge, Cle.	.260	100	408	358	62	93	158	13	2	16	66	0	3	7	40	4	73	23	6	11	.441	.343
Parrish, Dave, Tam.	.253	115	432	367	43	93	136	25	0	6	49	4	2	5	54	1	88	2	1	7	.371	.355
Payton, Jay, St.L.	.375	4	20	16	7	6	9	3	0	0	0	0	0	0	4	0	1	0	0	0	.563	.500
Pearson, Shawn, Dun.	.183	30	72	60	13	11	12	1	0	0	1	2	0	0	10	0	14	3	1	0	.200	.300

Player, Team	Avg.	G	TPA	AB	R	H	TB	2B	3B	HR	RBI	SH	SF	HP	BB	IBB	SO	SB	CS	GDP	Slg.	OBP
Pena, Rodolfo, Sar.	.237	64	215	198	13	47	57	4	0	2	11	2	1	6	8	0	40	0	2	4	.288	.286
Perkins, Kevin, B.C.	.236	56	218	195	25	46	69	3	1	6	18	0	0	8	15	1	45	0	4	4	.354	.317
Phillips, Andy, Tam.	.302	75	327	288	43	87	145	17	4	11	50	1	10	3	25	1	55	3	3	6	.503	.353
Phillips, Brandon, Jup.	.284	55	239	194	36	55	83	12	2	4	23	0	1	6	38	0	45	17	3	3	.428	.414
Piercy, Mike, St.L.*	.286	7	17	14	4	4	5	1	0	0	2	1	0	1	1	0	1	2	0	0	.357	.375
Pittman, Tom, Jup.	.214	78	310	281	31	60	85	7	3	4	37	0	0	6	23	1	83	2	2	11	.302	.287
Pride, Curt, Jup.*	.190	6	24	21	3	4	5	1	0	0	0	0	0	0	3	0	3	0	1	0	.238	.292
Probst, Alan, St.L.	.152	37	129	112	6	17	26	6	0	1	9	2	0	3	12	0	38	0	1	6	.232	.252
Raines, Tim, Jup.†	.348	8	29	23	7	8	14	1	1	1	5	0	1	0	5	0	4	1	0	0	.609	.448
Ramos, Kelly, Sar.†	.167	17	68	66	4	11	13	2	0	0	3	0	0	1	1	0	15	0	0	1	.197	.191
Ramsey, Brad, Day.	.226	96	365	332	28	75	112	16	0	7	41	1	2	7	23	3	75	2	3	9	.337	.288
Rapp, Travis, Char.	.154	5	14	13	0	2	2	0	0	0	0	0	0	0	1	0	7	0	0	0	.154	.214
Redman, Prentice, St.L.	.261	132	553	495	70	129	176	18	1	9	65	4	6	6	42	0	91	29	8	7	.356	.322
Renick, Josh, F.M.	.268	49	171	142	17	38	45	7	0	0	17	1	3	0	25	0	17	3	1	5	.317	.371
Reyes, Ambiorix, Cle.	.305	27	101	95	17	29	31	2	0	0	7	0	0	1	5	0	12	7	1	2	.326	.347
Reyes, Deurys, F.M.*	.240	95	318	263	47	63	75	10	1	0	20	7	4	1	41	0	80	12	3	6	.285	.340
Reyes, Ivan, Tam.	.500	3	7	4	2	2	5	0	0	1	1	0	0	0	3	0	1	0	0	0	1.250	.714
Richardson, Corey, Lak.†	.263	131	581	498	76	131	166	23	3	2	38	2	2	8	71	0	93	31	11	5	.333	.363
Riepe, Andy, Sar.	.182	5	12	11	2	2	2	0	0	0	1	0	0	0	1	0	2	0	0	1	.182	.250
Rigsby, Randy, B.C.*	.272	95	354	320	41	87	117	15	3	3	38	1	4	7	22	1	62	14	5	1	.366	.329
Rodriguez, Carlos, Sar.	.213	128	541	502	56	107	168	21	2	12	54	0	4	8	27	2	144	15	15	21	.335	.262
Rodriguez, Luis, F.M.†	.274	125	571	463	71	127	166	21	3	4	64	14	5	6	82	2	42	11	8	14	.359	.387
Rodriguez, Mike, Dun.	.184	13	39	38	4	7	7	0	0	0	6	0	1	0	0	0	5	0	0	0	.184	.179
Rodriguez, Sammy, St.L.	.159	21	69	63	2	10	17	4	0	1	6	0	1	0	5	0	14	0	0	2	.270	.217
Rodriguez, Victor, Tam.	.272	41	180	151	22	41	58	10	2	1	15	1	2	5	21	0	15	5	3	3	.384	.374
Rolison, Nate, B.C.*	.378	14	57	45	7	17	23	3	0	1	6	0	1	1	10	1	7	0	0	4	.511	.491
Romano, Jason, Char.	.400	3	14	10	3	4	6	2	0	0	1	0	0	0	4	0	1	1	0	0	.600	.571
Roneberg, Brett, B.C.*	.299	88	395	331	49	99	160	20	4	11	63	1	9	4	50	2	54	5	3	6	.483	.388
Roper, Chad, Char.	.210	42	157	143	13	30	45	9	0	2	14	0	0	0	14	0	31	0	0	5	.315	.280
Ross, Cody, Lak.	.276	127	546	482	84	133	222	34	5	15	80	6	9	5	44	0	96	28	5	9	.461	.337
Rouse, Michael, Dun.*	.272	48	202	180	27	49	85	17	2	5	24	6	1	2	13	0	45	3	1	2	.472	.327
Ruan, Wilken, Jup.	.283	72	314	293	41	83	101	8	2	2	26	7	1	3	10	2	35	25	14	3	.345	.313
St. Pierre, Maxim, Lak.	.248	99	382	330	42	82	109	15	0	4	43	0	5	4	43	1	50	2	5	11	.330	.338
Sanchez, Freddy, Sar.	.339	69	310	280	40	95	125	19	4	1	24	3	3	2	22	1	30	5	3	3	.446	.388
Sandberg, Eric, F.M.*	.234	81	315	274	37	64	83	11	1	2	33	1	0	5	35	2	50	0	1	9	.303	.331
Santana, Pedro, Tam.	.241	17	59	54	4	13	19	3	0	1	6	0	0	3	2	0	17	1	1	1	.352	.305
Santiago, Ramon, Lak.†	.268	120	512	429	64	115	142	15	3	2	46	14	4	11	54	0	60	34	8	7	.331	.361
Santoro, Pat, Sar.	.206	106	375	335	44	69	111	10	1	10	35	5	1	4	30	1	112	3	4	6	.331	.278
Santos, Jose, B.C.	.265	121	507	411	73	109	185	22	0	18	81	0	7	11	78	3	93	10	5	12	.450	.391
Santos, Juan, Lak.†	.161	23	66	62	7	10	17	2	1	1	4	0	1	0	3	1	18	0	0	2	.274	.197
Scanlon, Matt, F.M.*	.253	107	397	348	39	88	113	12	2	3	35	3	0	3	43	4	67	2	1	6	.325	.340
Schifano, Tony, V.B.	.281	62	222	199	23	56	80	12	0	4	23	2	2	4	15	1	39	6	1	8	.402	.341
Schrager, Tony, Day.	.314	89	362	299	55	94	162	22	2	14	56	0	4	5	54	1	49	10	6	5	.542	.423
Seale, Marvin, St.L.†	.238	129	557	479	72	114	176	24	4	10	38	5	2	10	61	0	127	37	18	3	.367	.335
Sequea, Jorge, Lak.†	.247	104	379	328	39	81	117	16	1	6	54	8	6	5	32	0	47	9	7	1	.357	.318
Sherrod, Justin, Sar.	.305	37	157	141	20	43	78	8	3	7	23	0	3	2	11	0	37	5	1	2	.553	.357
Shipp, Brian, St.L.	.277	114	426	372	47	103	160	21	6	8	48	14	4	11	25	0	107	25	6	3	.430	.337
Sisk, Aaron, Dun.	.114	15	40	35	2	4	10	1	1	1	4	2	0	1	2	0	14	1	1	0	.286	.184
Sitzman, Jay, Cle.*	.247	118	518	465	63	115	166	21	6	6	34	7	3	8	35	2	100	31	17	5	.357	.309
Sledd, Aaron, Day.*	.118	7	21	17	1	2	2	0	0	0	1	0	1	0	3	0	6	0	0	1	.118	.238
Smith, Ryan, St.L.	.286	31	88	70	9	20	23	3	0	0	5	2	1	4	11	0	18	2	1	1	.329	.407
Soto, Jose, B.C.†	.200	2	6	5	1	1	1	0	0	0	0	0	0	0	1	0	2	0	0	0	.200	.333
Soto, Saul, V.B.	.000	1	4	2	0	0	0	0	0	0	0	0	0	0	2	0	0	0	0	0	.000	.500
Stafford, Mike, Tam.†	.250	5	4	4	0	1	1	0	0	0	0	0	0	0	0	0	0	0	0	0	.250	.250
Stevens, Tony, F.M.†	.178	65	229	197	23	35	42	5	1	0	12	8	3	4	17	0	35	7	5	4	.213	.253
Swenson, Leland, Char.	.175	47	146	120	16	21	24	3	0	0	12	3	1	1	21	0	30	0	2	5	.200	.301
Tarasco, Tony, St.L.*	.231	3	13	13	1	3	5	2	0	0	2	0	0	0	0	0	4	0	0	1	.385	.231
Terhune, Mike, St.L.†	.260	80	303	262	26	68	96	15	2	3	31	5	5	2	28	1	30	6	5	7	.366	.330
Theodorou, Nick, V.B.†	.000	8	26	17	3	0	0	0	0	0	1	0	1	0	8	0	4	0	0	1	.000	.308
Theriot, Ryan, Day.	.204	30	129	103	20	21	26	5	0	0	9	3	1	1	21	0	17	2	4	2	.252	.341
Thomas, Chuck, V.B.	.261	66	281	253	28	66	87	18	0	1	20	1	3	1	23	2	58	9	6	6	.344	.321
Thompson, Andy, Dun.	.529	9	41	34	5	18	27	6	0	1	6	0	0	2	5	3	7	0	0	0	.794	.610
Thompson, Rich, Dun.*	.311	112	514	454	90	141	170	14	6	1	60	3	4	9	44	1	72	39	11	3	.374	.380
Torres, Frederick, Char.	.248	111	436	407	37	101	148	18	1	9	52	3	2	3	20	0	103	1	0	5	.364	.287
Torres, Gabby, F.M.	.261	49	173	157	17	41	52	8	0	1	18	1	3	5	7	0	28	2	0	3	.331	.308
Tousa, Scott, Lak.*	.216	39	134	111	18	24	28	4	0	0	8	2	0	3	18	0	21	3	1	1	.252	.341
Tucci, Pete, St.L.	.258	77	313	264	43	68	116	17	2	9	49	0	5	2	42	0	56	15	9	5	.439	.358
Tyson, Torre, Tam.†	.254	31	144	114	28	29	39	6	2	0	10	1	1	2	24	1	19	6	4	3	.342	.390
Ugueto, Luis, B.C.†	.263	121	442	392	53	103	134	12	5	3	43	9	1	2	38	0	96	22	7	7	.342	.330
Utley, Chase, Cle.*	.257	122	523	467	65	120	197	25	2	16	59	1	6	12	37	4	88	19	8	6	.422	.324
Valdez, Angel, Tam.	.236	46	161	148	22	35	51	9	2	1	7	2	2	2	7	0	43	5	1	1	.345	.277
Valdez, Wilson, Jup.	.249	64	255	233	34	58	81	13	2	2	19	10	0	2	10	0	33	7	3	4	.348	.286
Vargas, Inakel, Lak.	.182	7	26	22	1	4	4	0	0	0	2	0	0	1	3	0	3	0	0	2	.182	.308
Vento, Mike, Tam.	.300	130	514	457	71	137	237	20	10	20	87	0	3	9	45	1	88	13	10	9	.519	.372
Victorino, Shane, V.B.	.167	2	9	6	2	1	1	0	0	0	0	0	0	0	3	0	1	0	0	0	.167	.444
Villegas, Ernest, Char.	.270	34	137	126	7	34	45	5	0	2	15	2	1	6	2	0	35	3	0	2	.357	.311
Wallis, Jacob, Jup.	.143	2	7	7	0	1	1	0	0	0	0	0	0	0	0	0	4	0	0	0	.143	.143
Ward, Brian, F.M.	.255	15	55	47	5	12	13	1	0	0	6	0	1	0	7	0	6	0	1	2	.277	.345
Warren, Chris, Sar.	.264	106	430	382	49	101	157	20	3	10	51	0	2	14	32	0	112	11	5	4	.411	.342
Warriax, Brandon, Char.	.191	97	353	320	34	61	100	13	4	6	28	7	1	3	22	0	84	4	6	4	.313	.249
Washington, Dion, Tam.	.190	29	96	84	5	16	22	4	1	0	8	1	0	1	10	0	22	0	1	1	.262	.284
Watson, Matt, Jup.*	.330	124	518	446	70	147	203	33	4	5	74	0	3	6	63	4	45	17	9	11	.455	.417
Weekly, Chris, Dun.*	.254	67	275	240	33	61	87	12	1	4	47	2	3	4	26	1	68	2	2	5	.363	.333

Player, Team	Avg.	G	TPA	AB	R	H	TB	2B	3B	HR	RBI	SH	SF	HP	BB	IBB	SO	SB	CS	GDP	Slg.	OBP
Werth, Jayson, Dun.	.200	21	87	70	9	14	23	3	0	2	14	0	0	0	17	0	19	1	1	2	.329	.356
Wigginton, Ty, St.L.	.333	3	14	9	1	3	4	1	0	0	1	0	0	1	4	0	2	0	0	0	.444	.571
Wilkerson, Brad, Jup.*	.231	6	29	26	3	6	9	3	0	0	1	0	0	0	3	0	10	0	0	0	.346	.310
Williams, Brady, Sar.	.195	79	296	251	37	49	90	20	3	5	21	0	0	2	43	1	80	5	3	5	.359	.318
Wise, Dewayne, Dun.*	.223	25	111	103	9	23	34	3	1	2	16	0	3	0	5	0	13	5	0	1	.330	.252
Wright, Nate, V.B.	.000	2	3	2	0	0	0	0	0	0	0	0	0	0	1	0	1	0	0	1	.000	.333
Yepez, Jose, Dun.	.000	4	4	3	0	0	0	0	0	0	0	0	0	1	0	1	0	0	0		.000	.250
Zech, Scott, Jup.	.222	32	116	99	10	22	23	1	0	0	7	2	0	1	14	0	17	2	0	4	.232	.325
Zieour, Neesan, Dun.	.256	29	102	86	19	22	37	9	0	2	11	0	1	4	11	2	16	1	0	3	.430	.363
Zoccolillo, Peter, Day.*	.264	96	370	326	42	86	118	18	4	2	35	2	6	1	35	1	57	7	5	4	.362	.332

PLAYERS WITH TWO OR MORE TEAMS

Player, Team	Avg.	G	TPA	AB	R	H	TB	2B	3B	HR	RBI	SH	SF	HP	BB	IBB	SO	SB	CS	GDP	Slg.	OBP
Meadows, Randy, Jup.	.071	5	15	14	1	1	1	0	0	0	0	1	0	0	0	5	0	0	0	.071	.071
Meadows, Randy, Day.	.100	5	21	20	0	2	2	0	0	0	0	0	0	0	1	0	6	1	0	0	.100	.143

GRAND SLAMS: Padilla, Santos, 2 each; Ahumada, Blakely, Burns, J. Brown, Callahan, Cash, Daigle, Garbe, Headley, Hodge, N. Jackson, M. Jones, Ramsey, Santoro, Schrager, Sequea, Tucci, Vento, Weekly, 1 each.

AWARDED FIRST BASE ON CATCHER'S INTERFERENCE: Matthews 3 (Pena, Edwards, Torres); Reyes 2 (Torres, Flores); Chiaffredo (Larned), Gulledge (Jacobson), Huff (Fagan), Jacobson (McAffee), James (R. Pena), Jason Johnson (Jaile), Kropf (Edwards), L. Rodriguez (Torres), Terhune (Edwards), Torres (Gulledge), Tyson (Gulledge).

2001 PITCHING

TEAM

Team	W	L	Pct.	ERA	G	CG	ShO	Sv.	IP	H	TBF	R	ER	HR	SH	SF	HB	BB	IBB	SO	WP	Bk.
Tampa	77	62	.554	3.17	139	7	11	44	1193.2	1097	5095	539	421	52	32	36	66	431	23	1132	82	15
Jupiter	70	60	.604	3.21	139	4	13	37	1206.2	1131	5155	551	431	79	54	41	60	406	7	875	55	10
Charlotte	67	70	.489	3.37	137	5	9	41	1203.1	1050	5104	566	451	64	48	46	77	491	21	986	74	15
Brevard County	80	55	.593	3.43	135	4	14	38	1163.0	1119	4989	579	443	64	45	36	65	438	15	828	37	5
Fort Myers	68	69	.496	3.60	137	1	6	31	1211.2	1151	5224	605	484	58	35	52	58	529	26	951	86	11
Vero Beach	67	66	.504	3.69	133	5	9	42	1160.1	1070	4992	557	476	111	39	32	72	504	9	1060	80	15
St. Lucie	63	76	.453	3.75	139	5	5	27	1182.2	1132	5127	594	493	52	55	34	76	468	9	895	68	10
Clearwater	68	69	.496	3.81	137	9	6	38	1184.2	1160	5139	601	502	77	30	37	63	513	17	931	69	9
Daytona	68	68	.500	3.82	136	4	10	33	1167.0	1120	5070	601	495	67	35	38	64	471	30	1020	60	9
Lakeland	67	69	.493	3.93	136	6	9	41	1178.1	1158	5161	607	514	88	41	41	85	521	16	847	81	8
Sarasota	54	83	.394	4.13	137	2	5	26	1201.0	1242	5313	701	551	95	40	38	80	443	16	990	59	15
Dunedin	71	64	.526	4.66	135	5	4	35	1177.1	1240	5209	736	610	100	28	67	95	529	13	836	95	8

INDIVIDUAL

TOP QUALIFIERS FOR EARNED-RUN AVERAGE TITLE

Minimum 112 innings. *Lefthanded pitcher.

Pitcher, Team	W	L	Pct.	ERA	G	GS	CG	ShO	GF	Sv.	IP	H	TBF	R	ER	HR	SH	SF	HB	BB	IBB	SO	WP	Bk.
Asencio, Miguel, Cle.	12	5	.706	2.84	28	21	2	1	1	0	155.1	124	649	62	49	7	3	6	2	70	1	123	9	2
Freed, Mark, Day.*	6	8	.429	3.12	23	22	1	1	0	0	130.0	120	541	54	45	7	4	3	2	51	4	90	6	1
Rodriguez, Ricardo, V.B.	14	6	.700	3.21	26	26	2	0	0	0	154.1	133	645	67	55	13	7	2	3	60	0	154	18	1
Sneed, John, F.M.	8	3	.727	3.24	25	19	0	0	3	0	114.0	95	480	51	41	5	1	1	4	49	0	88	5	0
Sergent, Joe, B.C.*	12	6	.667	3.33	27	25	0	0	1	0	143.1	154	607	70	53	11	1	4	5	32	1	89	1	1
Martinez, Anastasio, Sar.	9	12	.429	3.35	25	24	1	0	0	0	145.0	130	606	69	54	12	4	1	9	39	0	123	6	0
Hannah, Shawn, Lak.	7	5	.583	3.35	34	17	0	0	7	0	129.0	123	558	63	48	9	5	10	54	1		55	4	1
Dittfurth, Ryan, Char.	9	6	.600	3.48	27	24	2	2	2	0	147.1	123	632	66	57	9	6	1	17	66	1	134	15	0
Kiepacki, Ed, Jup.	9	9	.500	3.50	26	26	1	0	0	0	136.1	135	582	69	53	10	9	6	5	49	0	74	3	0
Marsonek, Sam, Tam.	8	8	.500	3.51	24	23	5	2	0	0	138.1	128	590	67	54	6	5	2	21	39	2	120	12	1
Garcia, Reynaldo, Char.	5	10	.333	3.56	35	16	0	0	9	4	116.1	107	499	62	46	7	6	4	8	45	3	111	8	1
An, Byeong, B.C.*	2	8	.200	3.62	23	21	1	0	1	0	119.1	122	523	68	48	10	4	3	11	42	0	84	8	5
Griffiths, Jeremy, St.L.	7	8	.467	3.75	23	20	2	0	0	0	132.0	126	551	63	55	9	5	3	5	35	1	95	11	3
Sturdy, Tim, F.M.	8	10	.444	3.82	28	19	1	0	2	0	129.2	122	552	74	55	2	8	4	10	53	2	54	9	2
Madson, Ryan, Cle.	9	9	.500	3.90	22	21	1	0	0	0	117.2	137	530	68	51	4	0	5	49	1		101	5	1

DEPARTMENTAL LEADERS: W—R. Rodriguez, 14; L—Collins, Joseph, A. Martinez, Dean, 12 each; Pct.—Montalbano, Langone, .750 each; G—Watson, 57; GS—Moreno, 28; CG—Marsonek, 5; ShO—Shaffar, Marsonek, Dittfurth, 2 each; GF—Padilla, 49; Sv.—Runser, 30; IP—Franco, 161.1; H—Franco, 178; TBF—Dean, 720; R—Dean, 113; ER—Dean, 97; HR—Brooks, 18; SH—Figueroa, 11; SF—Dean, 10; HB—Marsonek, 21; BB—Chipperfield, 81; IBB—Several tied with 6; SO—R. Rodriguez, 154; WP—R. Rodriguez, 18; BK—An, 5.

ALL PITCHERS

*Lefthanded pitcher.

Pitcher, Team	W	L	Pct.	ERA	G	GS	CG	ShO	GF	Sv.	IP	H	TBF	R	ER	HR	SH	SF	HB	BB	IBB	SO	WP	Bk.
Abbott, David, Dun.	5	4	.556	5.96	10	10	0	0	0	0	51.1	61	229	35	34	9	1	4	3	20	0	35	3	0
Achilles, Matt, Day.	4	8	.333	2.59	16	15	1	1	0	0	93.2	84	381	37	27	1	4	5	22	1		60	1	0
Acosta, Manuel, Tam.	0	1	.000	7.71	2	2	0	0	0	0	7.0	7	31	7	6	1	0	0	0	6	0	8	4	0
Alston, Travis, Cle.	1	2	.333	5.40	12	1	0	0	5	2	18.1	19	91	13	11	1	0	1	1	16	0	7	0	0
Ambrose, John, Sar.	0	1	.000	2.87	10	1	0	0	2	1	15.2	13	67	8	5	0	1	0	3	5	0	18	1	0
An, Byeong, Sar.*	2	8	.200	3.62	23	21	1	0	1	0	119.1	122	523	68	48	10	4	3	11	42	0	84	8	5
Anderson, Wes, B.C.	1	6	.143	5.63	8	8	0	0	0	0	32.0	48	164	26	20	3	1	2	4	21	0	17	1	0
Aramboles, Ricardo, Tam.	7	2	.778	4.06	12	11	0	0	0	0	68.2	72	289	37	31	5	1	1	2	19	0	59	3	0
Arias, Pablo, Lak.	3	1	.750	4.89	8	7	0	0	0	0	42.1	48	188	26	23	5	0	1	1	16	0	28	3	0
Arrojo, Rolando, Sar.	0	1	.000	6.00	2	2	0	0	0	0	3.0	4	14	2	2	2	0	0	0	1	0	5	0	0
Arthurs, Shane, Jup.	2	0	1.000	3.54	28	3	0	0	7	1	56.0	69	261	29	22	1	2	2	6	19	0	33	6	2
Artiles, Carlos, Tam.*	0	1	.000	5.00	5	0	0	0	1	0	9.0	7	38	5	5	2	1	0	0	5	1	9	0	0

Pitcher, Team	W	L	Pct.	ERA	G	GS	CG	ShO	GF	Sv.	IP	H	TBF	R	ER	HR	SH	SF	HB	BB	IBB	SO	WP	Bk.
Asencio, Miguel, Cle.	12	5	.706	2.84	28	21	2	1	1	0	155.1	124	649	62	49	7	3	6	2	70	1	123	9	2
Backsmeyer, Justin, Char.	1	2	.333	3.75	33	0	0	0	10	0	60.0	56	276	32	25	3	1	5	5	42	2	47	6	1
Bailey, Dave, Day.	0	2	.000	4.99	34	0	0	0	25	8	39.2	45	177	25	22	5	1	4	1	15	2	39	2	1
Baisley, Brad, Cle.	2	4	.333	3.78	11	9	0	0	1	0	64.1	59	267	31	27	4	1	1	7	18	0	43	1	0
Baker, Brad, Sar.	7	9	.438	4.73	24	23	0	0	0	0	120.0	132	563	77	63	8	2	3	9	64	0	103	12	0
Bauer, Greg, V.B.	2	3	.400	3.91	12	0	0	0	5	1	23.0	28	112	13	10	3	3	0	1	13	2	15	1	0
Beal, Andy, Tam.*	5	5	.500	3.00	17	17	0	0	0	0	99.0	101	431	57	33	6	2	4	1	30	1	72	7	0
Bean, Colter, Tam.	7	1	.875	1.46	32	0	0	0	10	2	49.1	27	195	9	8	0	0	0	3	18	2	77	2	0
Beckett, Josh, B.C.	6	0	1.000	1.23	13	12	0	0	0	0	65.2	32	238	13	9	0	2	1	0	15	0	101	1	1
Beech, Matt, Char.*	0	0	.000	0.00	1	1	0	0	0	0	4.2	3	18	1	0	0	0	0	0	2	0	7	0	0
Beltran, Frank, Day.	6	9	.400	5.00	21	18	0	0	0	0	95.1	93	424	62	53	10	1	4	9	40	1	72	4	0
Bennett, Steve, St.L.	0	1	.000	7.86	7	6	0	0	0	0	26.1	31	122	26	23	1	0	1	2	12	0	20	1	1
Berry, Jon, V.B.	2	4	.333	3.78	33	5	0	0	13	8	69.0	58	300	34	29	4	0	2	4	37	0	71	8	0
Bess, Steve, Lak.	2	3	.400	2.65	33	0	0	0	20	10	37.1	25	151	12	11	1	1	2	4	12	1	39	2	0
Blanton, Jason, Day.	3	0	1.000	0.44	6	2	0	0	3	0	20.2	10	83	3	1	0	0	1	0	15	2	21	1	0
Bohannon, Gary, St.L.	1	0	1.000	3.64	15	0	0	0	7	1	29.2	35	126	15	12	2	3	1	1	10	1	11	2	0
Borrell, Danny, Tam.*	7	9	.438	3.97	22	20	0	0	0	0	111.0	109	474	58	49	6	4	6	5	38	2	84	8	2
Bowe, Brandon, B.C.	6	4	.600	1.55	42	0	0	0	27	11	58.0	52	237	21	10	1	7	3	2	11	1	45	2	0
Bradley, Ryan, Tam.	3	1	.750	3.08	7	7	0	0	0	0	38.0	27	167	15	13	2	1	1	4	22	0	32	5	0
Braswell, Bryan, St.L.*	1	1	.500	3.63	4	2	0	0	2	0	17.1	15	74	8	7	0	1	1	2	5	0	12	1	0
Bridges, Donnie, Jup.	0	1	.000	6.75	1	1	0	0	0	0	4.0	7	23	6	3	0	0	0	1	3	0	2	0	0
Brooks, Frank, Cle.*	5	10	.333	4.71	37	15	0	0	5	1	112.2	113	504	70	59	18	1	5	9	58	2	92	9	0
Bruback, Matt, Day.	6	3	.667	3.00	14	14	0	0	0	0	84.0	70	346	33	28	3	1	3	7	21	0	87	3	0
Burnett, A.J., B.C.	0	0	.000	1.93	2	2	0	0	0	0	9.1	4	35	2	2	0	0	0	0	4	0	10	0	0
Bye, Chris, Jup.	1	0	1.000	3.04	19	0	0	0	13	0	23.2	24	103	8	8	3	2	0	1	9	0	15	4	0
Byrd, Paul, Cle.	0	3	.000	3.42	4	4	0	0	0	0	23.2	24	98	10	9	1	1	1	1	5	0	17	1	0
Byron, Terry, B.C.	0	0	.000	10.29	4	0	0	0	1	0	7.0	7	35	9	8	1	0	0	2	5	1	7	0	0
Caraballo, Angel, Dun.	3	1	.750	4.80	12	2	0	0	2	0	30.0	30	135	19	16	3	1	1	2	18	2	21	2	1
Caraccioli, Lance, V.B.*	2	1	.667	1.82	5	5	0	0	0	0	29.2	23	114	6	6	2	0	0	2	7	0	22	0	0
Carter, Ryan, Cle.*	3	4	.429	5.55	11	11	1	0	0	0	58.1	67	270	39	36	9	1	1	3	36	0	56	3	0
Cedeno, Jovanny, Char.	0	0	.000	1.86	3	3	0	0	0	0	9.2	3	38	2	2	0	0	0	1	5	0	12	0	0
Cento, Tony, F.M.*	3	2	.600	3.43	39	1	0	0	7	0	57.2	49	238	27	22	3	1	4	3	21	0	47	2	0
Cerda, Jaime, St.L.*	2	1	.667	0.97	28	0	0	0	15	6	55.2	40	213	8	6	3	3	1	1	12	0	56	0	0
Charron, Eric, Jup.	0	1	.000	6.00	2	0	0	0	2	0	3.0	4	13	3	2	1	0	0	0	1	0	1	0	0
Chavez, Wilton, Day.	3	4	.429	4.12	17	16	0	0	0	0	89.2	96	401	46	41	8	4	3	7	30	1	59	3	0
Chenard, Ken, St.L.	0	2	.000	37.80	2	2	0	0	0	0	1.2	3	12	7	7	1	0	0	1	4	0	2	0	0
Chipperfield, Calvin, Lak.	7	8	.467	4.79	24	24	1	0	0	0	124.0	132	574	73	66	5	4	4	8	81	1	109	5	0
Chulk, Vinny, Dun.	1	2	.333	3.12	16	1	0	0	4	1	34.2	38	157	16	12	2	2	2	0	13	1	50	4	0
Cisar, Mark, Sar.	1	1	.500	4.50	27	0	0	0	14	6	38.0	41	170	21	19	4	3	1	3	15	1	39	0	0
Clark, Chris, B.C.	0	1	.000	5.68	4	0	0	0	3	1	6.1	6	34	5	4	0	1	0	0	9	0	7	1	0
Claussen, Brandon, Tam.*	5	2	.714	2.73	8	8	0	0	0	0	56.0	47	227	21	17	2	2	2	0	13	0	69	1	2
Cole, Joey, St.L.	1	0	1.000	6.00	1	1	0	0	0	0	6.0	3	26	4	4	1	0	0	0	6	0	2	0	0
Collins, Pat, Jup.	9	12	.429	4.31	33	12	0	0	7	1	110.2	101	513	71	53	6	2	6	12	71	0	90	12	0
Colson, Jason, Dun.	0	0	.000	0.00	1	1	0	0	0	0	1.1	0	7	1	0	0	0	1	0	3	0	1	0	0
Colyer, Steve, V.B.*	4	8	.333	3.96	24	24	0	0	0	0	120.1	101	524	62	53	16	4	4	7	77	0	118	3	1
Cone, David, Sar.	0	0	.000	0.00	1	1	0	0	0	0	4.0	2	14	0	0	0	0	0	0	0	0	6	0	0
Contreras, Jean, F.M.*	0	0	.000	3.38	6	0	0	0	4	1	8.0	6	33	3	3	0	0	0	0	6	0	4	0	1
Cook, Andy, St.L.	5	2	.714	2.29	16	6	0	0	4	0	51.0	39	218	16	13	2	3	1	4	22	2	50	1	0
Cook, Derrick, Char.	0	0	.000	0.00	2	2	0	0	0	0	8.0	7	32	2	0	0	0	0	0	1	0	5	0	0
Corbin, John, Day.	2	0	1.000	3.74	10	0	0	0	9	2	21.2	26	94	9	9	2	0	1	0	4	2	12	0	0
Corcoran, Roy, Jup.	0	0	.000	0.00	1	0	0	0	0	0	2.0	0	8	0	0	0	0	0	0	2	0	0	0	0
Cordero, Jesus, V.B.	0	1	.000	4.32	4	1	0	0	1	0	8.1	7	36	5	4	0	1	1	0	3	0	10	1	1
Corona, Ronnie, F.M.	3	1	.750	2.19	16	7	0	0	3	0	49.1	45	206	15	12	3	1	2	1	16	0	47	2	1
Corrado, Matthew, Lak.	3	7	.300	5.68	16	12	1	0	0	0	63.1	62	280	45	40	9	2	1	7	31	0	48	7	1
Croushore, Rich, St.L.	0	0	.000	0.00	2	2	0	0	0	0	3.0	1	10	0	0	0	0	0	0	0	0	5	0	0
Crumpton, Chuck, Jup.	0	1	.000	1.50	3	0	0	0	2	0	6.0	4	24	2	1	0	1	0	0	3	1	3	0	0
Cueto, Jose, Day.	1	2	.333	3.03	6	6	0	0	0	0	38.2	31	165	19	13	6	1	2	2	13	0	41	3	1
Darrell, Tommy, Jup.	1	1	.500	2.57	11	0	0	0	4	0	21.0	14	91	6	6	0	1	0	0	16	0	16	2	0
Dean, Aaron, Dun.	11	12	.478	5.46	27	27	2	1	0	0	160.0	172	720	113	97	16	4	10	10	75	1	121	14	4
De La Rosa, Jorge, Sar.*	0	1	.000	1.21	12	0	0	0	10	2	29.2	13	114	7	4	0	0	0	0	12	0	27	2	0
De Paula, Julio, Tam.	9	5	.643	3.58	16	13	0	0	1	0	83.0	65	365	43	33	3	1	2	3	53	2	77	3	1
Devey, Phil, V.B.*	0	0	.000	2.57	3	0	0	0	1	1	7.0	8	29	2	2	1	0	0	0	0	0	6	0	0
Dickinson, Rodney, Sar.	3	5	.375	6.75	29	0	0	0	25	11	29.1	46	149	29	22	5	2	1	1	13	2	27	1	0
Dickson, Jason, Dun.	1	1	.500	1.50	4	4	0	0	0	0	18.0	14	73	3	3	1	0	0	1	1	0	20	1	0
Dimma, Doug, Dun.*	1	2	.333	4.88	24	2	0	0	12	0	48.0	58	231	31	26	4	1	1	3	30	2	27	6	0
Dittfurth, Ryan, Char.	9	6	.600	3.48	27	24	2	2	2	0	147.1	123	632	66	57	9	6	1	17	66	1	134	15	0
Dominguez, Jose, Char.	1	0	1.000	3.60	2	0	0	0	0	0	5.0	4	19	2	2	1	0	1	0	1	0	5	0	0
Dunn, Gerald, Lak.	1	1	.500	4.50	2	1	0	0	1	0	6.0	11	28	3	3	0	0	0	0	1	0	2	0	0
Dunning, Justin, St.L.	5	4	.556	3.43	39	0	0	0	21	1	65.2	46	305	31	25	4	5	2	7	62	1	64	8	0
Duplissea, Bill, V.B.	1	0	1.000	0.00	1	0	0	0	0	0	1.0	1	4	0	0	0	0	0	0	0	0	1	0	0
Dzurilla, Mike, Day.	0	0	.000	0.00	1	0	0	0	1	0	1.0	2	5	0	0	0	0	0	0	0	0	2	0	0
Eckenstahler, Eric, Lak.*	1	0	1.000	1.50	4	0	0	0	2	1	6.0	3	22	1	1	0	0	0	1	2	0	7	2	0
Edmondson, Brian, B.C.	5	2	.714	1.73	16	0	0	0	7	3	26.0	23	104	8	5	0	1	2	2	4	1	21	0	0
Elmore, Chris, Sar.*	6	2	.750	2.41	17	5	0	0	5	1	59.2	58	247	25	16	1	3	1	3	12	1	40	0	0
Eppeneder, James, Day.*	4	2	.667	3.48	42	0	0	0	17	5	67.1	54	296	37	26	3	0	1	5	34	0	56	3	1
Eyre, Willie, F.M.	2	5	.286	2.52	32	0	0	0	10	1	64.1	54	280	27	18	2	2	7	4	33	2	51	5	0
Farizo, Brad, B.C.	4	2	.667	2.15	9	7	0	0	1	0	46.0	39	179	13	11	2	1	2	0	5	0	31	1	0
Feliciano, Jesus, V.B.*	0	1	.000	6.75	2	0	0	0	1	0	4.0	4	18	3	3	1	0	1	0	3	0	4	0	0
Ferrari, Anthony, Jup.*	2	3	.400	0.79	51	0	0	0	40	21	56.2	36	226	11	5	1	4	1	4	17	0	45	1	0
Figueroa, Carlos, Char.*	2	4	.333	2.48	44	0	0	0	17	3	69.0	50	296	27	19	1	11	7	3	39	6	51	7	2
Fischer, Mike, V.B.	1	0	1.000	1.59	26	0	0	0	10	2	45.1	31	183	8	8	2	0	0	2	18	0	44	10	0
Fisher, Marc, Day.	0	0	.000	2.25	2	1	0	0	1	0	4.0	5	17	1	1	0	0	0	0	1	0	4	0	1
Fisher, Pete, F.M.	4	5	.444	3.34	31	9	0	0	8	2	91.2	91	402	48	34	5	4	2	5	32	5	77	7	0

CLASS A *Florida State League*

Pitcher, Team	W	L	Pct.	ERA	G	GS	CG	ShO	GF	Sv.	IP	H	TBF	R	ER	HR	SH	SF	HB	BB	IBB	SO	WP	Bk.
Flohr, Adam, F.M.*	1	2	.333	5.09	21	2	0	0	5	1	40.2	47	177	31	23	5	1	4	2	9	1	40	0	2
Florie, Bryce, Sar.	0	0	.000	0.00	2	0	0	0	0	0	4.2	3	21	0	0	0	0	0	0	5	0	7	0	0
Fontana, Tony, Sar.	2	3	.400	3.51	9	7	0	0	2	0	48.2	57	208	25	19	3	0	3	4	8	0	32	1	0
Foote, Joe, F.M.	2	8	.200	3.87	17	14	0	0	1	0	86.0	101	373	45	37	5	3	5	4	25	2	57	6	1
Ford, Matt, Dun.*	2	7	.222	5.85	13	12	0	0	0	0	60.0	67	270	41	39	8	0	3	2	37	0	48	7	0
Frachiseur, Zach, Day.	1	3	.250	5.10	22	0	0	0	11	4	30.0	34	130	19	17	3	3	0	0	10	1	34	2	1
Franco, Martire, Cle.	11	8	.579	4.13	26	24	4	0	1	0	161.1	178	694	84	74	12	6	5	8	41	1	97	7	2
Frederick, Kevin, F.M.	2	0	1.000	1.00	9	0	0	0	4	1	18.0	9	65	2	2	1	0	0	0	3	1	19	0	0
Freed, Mark, Day.*	6	8	.429	3.12	23	22	1	1	0	0	130.0	120	541	54	45	7	4	3	2	51	4	90	6	1
Fry, Justin, Cle.	2	2	.500	4.67	30	0	0	0	12	1	54.0	54	251	34	28	3	4	3	4	34	0	43	3	0
Gagliano, Steve, Day.	1	2	.333	4.22	17	0	0	0	11	7	21.1	23	98	11	10	0	1	0	0	14	2	16	2	0
Gamble, Jerome, Sar.	0	0	.000	7.88	3	2	0	0	1	0	8.0	11	37	8	7	0	0	0	0	4	0	7	1	0
Garcia, Reynaldo, Char.	5	10	.333	3.56	35	16	0	0	9	4	116.1	107	499	62	46	7	6	4	8	45	3	111	8	1
Garcia, Rosman, Iam.	2	6	.250	3.47	26	7	0	0	4	1	59.2	56	263	30	23	2	4	2	5	22	6	42	4	0
Gardner, Hayden, Char.	1	0	1.000	1.59	1	1	0	0	0	0	5.2	5	23	1	1	0	0	0	1	0	0	1	0	0
George, Todd, Jup.	1	0	1.000	0.00	1	0	0	0	0	0	3.0	4	13	0	0	0	0	0	0	2	0	2	0	0
German, Yon, St.L.*	1	0	1.000	3.86	2	0	0	0	1	0	4.2	5	21	2	2	0	1	0	0	4	0	0	0	0
Glaser, Eric, Sar.	4	3	.571	2.54	37	5	0	0	12	1	88.2	74	364	28	25	6	2	2	5	27	1	82	2	0
Gomer, Jeramy, Day.*	3	1	.750	6.24	24	2	0	0	7	1	49.0	51	223	36	34	4	1	2	5	29	0	44	3	0
Gomes, Tony, V.B.	1	1	.500	2.31	11	0	0	0	7	4	23.1	13	94	6	6	0	3	0	2	11	1	26	2	0
Gonzalez, Gilberto, St.L.*	0	1	.000	5.25	7	0	0	0	3	0	12.0	11	57	9	7	1	0	1	7	0	0	6	0	0
Good, Eric, Jup.*	5	5	.500	2.82	21	20	1	0	0	0	108.1	104	456	42	34	4	3	4	4	26	0	70	4	1
Gordon, Tom, Day.	0	0	.000	0.00	2	2	0	0	0	0	2.0	0	6	0	0	0	0	0	0	0	0	3	0	0
Grace, Bryan, Tam.	0	0	.000	13.50	3	0	0	0	0	0	2.0	5	13	4	3	0	0	1	0	1	0	5	0	0
Gracesqui, Frank, Dun.*	1	0	1.000	0.00	4	0	0	0	1	0	5.2	2	24	0	0	0	0	8	0	6	0	0	0	0
Graham, Frank, Sar.	2	10	.167	5.82	39	1	0	0	18	0	82.0	119	396	68	53	7	5	5	8	27	3	52	8	0
Graham, Tom, Char.	2	2	.500	2.66	9	0	0	0	4	1	23.2	13	87	7	7	1	1	0	0	9	2	20	1	0
Graves, Robert, Lak.*	0	1	.000	2.73	15	0	0	0	2	0	26.1	21	114	12	8	1	1	2	2	14	0	14	1	0
Griffiths, Jeremy, St.L.	7	8	.467	3.75	23	20	2	0	0	0	132.0	126	551	63	55	9	9	3	5	35	1	95	11	3
Grilli, Jason, B.C.	2	0	1.000	1.98	3	3	0	0	0	0	13.2	12	57	4	3	0	0	0	5	0	0	14	0	0
Hadden, Randy, V.B.	4	4	.500	5.10	34	1	0	0	12	2	67.0	75	305	44	38	9	3	1	7	29	1	58	4	0
Halladay, Roy, Dun.*	0	1	.000	3.97	13	0	0	0	5	2	22.2	28	99	12	10	1	1	1	2	3	0	15	3	0
Halvorson, Greg, St.L.	5	6	.455	4.32	22	13	2	0	4	2	100.0	109	430	55	48	7	5	3	3	24	1	47	3	0
Hamann, Rob, Dun.	4	0	1.000	4.41	39	0	0	0	20	5	65.1	69	279	40	32	9	1	1	6	17	0	44	6	0
Hammons, Marc, St.L.	1	1	.500	3.70	7	0	0	0	0	0	24.1	26	114	16	10	0	1	0	3	13	0	27	2	0
Hamulack, Tim, B.C.*	2	4	.333	3.15	40	0	0	0	13	1	71.1	83	319	42	25	3	3	3	3	21	1	39	1	0
Hannah, Shawn, Lak.	7	5	.583	3.35	34	17	0	0	7	0	129.0	128	558	63	48	9	5	5	10	54	1	55	4	1
Harber, Ryan, B.C.*	6	4	.600	3.49	29	5	0	0	8	1	90.1	94	393	44	35	8	3	1	1	30	1	48	1	0
Haring, Brett, Char.*	1	1	.500	2.36	17	2	0	0	7	1	45.2	41	187	17	12	3	1	0	3	13	1	22	2	0
Harrell, Tim, V.B.	0	0	.000	0.00	2	0	0	0	0	0	4.0	1	14	0	0	0	0	0	0	1	0	3	0	0
Hawkins, Chad, Char.	2	1	.667	3.71	4	4	0	0	0	0	17.0	18	71	7	7	0	1	1	2	3	0	8	2	1
Hee, Aaron, St.L.*	0	0	.000	6.00	2	0	0	0	2	1	3.0	4	16	2	2	0	0	0	0	3	0	3	1	0
Heilman, Aaron, St.L.	0	1	.000	2.35	7	7	0	0	0	0	38.1	26	153	11	10	0	1	1	1	13	0	39	1	0
Henriquez, Hector, B.C.*	0	1	.000	6.18	25	0	0	0	10	0	39.1	36	186	28	27	2	0	3	5	33	1	28	4	2
Herauf, Jeremy, Lak.	0	0	.000	10.80	6	0	0	0	0	0	6.2	13	30	8	8	0	0	1	5	0	3	0	0	0
Hernandez, Orlando, Tam.	0	0	.000	0.00	2	2	0	0	0	0	7.0	6	29	2	0	0	0	0	1	0	8	0	0	0
Hoard, Brent, F.M.*	7	4	.636	3.36	17	15	0	0	1	0	80.1	78	336	31	30	5	4	4	3	28	0	70	7	0
Hodge, Kevin, F.M.	0	0	.000	0.00	2	0	0	0	2	1	1.1	0	4	0	0	0	0	0	0	0	0	2	0	0
Houston, Ryan, Dun.	7	5	.583	4.19	26	23	0	0	3	1	133.1	147	583	77	62	10	4	7	12	46	0	85	5	0
Howard, Tom, F.M.*	6	3	.667	6.02	33	1	0	0	12	0	58.1	58	286	45	39	6	3	4	1	64	1	57	14	1
Hubbel, Travis, Dun.	1	3	.250	6.14	12	4	0	0	2	0	29.1	26	146	31	20	3	2	6	25	0	20	11	0
Huffaker, Mike, Char.	4	3	.571	1.88	43	0	0	0	23	1	76.2	60	322	25	16	0	5	6	2	39	0	67	8	0
Irabu, Hideki, Jup.	0	0	.000	3.00	3	3	0	0	0	0	9.0	5	39	3	3	1	0	1	1	4	0	9	0	0
Izquierdo, Hansel, B.C.	2	0	1.000	2.70	4	4	0	0	0	0	26.2	15	105	8	8	3	1	0	4	6	0	22	0	0
Jacob, Russell, Sar.	0	0	.000	6.75	3	0	0	0	1	0	4.0	4	19	4	3	0	0	2	2	0	0	2	1
Jensen, Justin, Tam.*	3	3	.500	2.32	37	2	0	0	13	0	69.0	52	275	22	18	1	4	1	3	30	0	07	7	0
Johnson, Jeremy, Lak.	1	1	.500	5.25	4	2	0	0	1	0	12.0	15	55	8	7	2	0	0	2	6	1	6	0	0
Jones, Bobby M., St.L.*	0	1	.000	0.93	4	4	0	0	0	0	9.2	6	40	2	1	0	1	0	4	0	9	0	0
Jones, Jack, Day.	0	0	.000	0.00	1	0	0	0	0	0	1.0	0	5	0	0	0	0	0	0	0	0	0	0	0
Jones, Kiki, Char.	0	1	.000	18.69	3	0	0	0	0	0	4.1	9	26	9	9	0	0	1	0	4	0	2	0	0
Joseph, Jake, St.L.	4	12	.250	5.34	25	24	0	0	1	0	128.0	162	586	93	76	6	5	6	9	52	0	69	9	0
Keelin, Chris, Clc.	2	4	.333	2.00	46	0	0	0	36	14	72.0	44	294	22	16	3	2	1	7	40	6	87	10	0
Kegley, Chuck, Dun.	6	9	.400	6.03	26	20	0	0	2	0	112.0	120	533	94	75	13	5	4	12	76	0	76	9	0
Klepacki, Ed, Jup.	9	9	.500	3.50	26	26	1	0	0	0	136.1	135	582	69	53	10	9	6	5	49	0	74	3	0
Knowles, Mike, Tam.	0	0	.000	10.13	8	0	0	0	5	2	8.0	15	45	10	9	0	0	2	0	8	0	9	1	1
Kolb, Dan, Char.	1	2	.333	3.86	7	3	0	0	2	0	18.2	21	78	8	8	1	0	0	2	6	0	16	0	0
Kosdorka, Matt, Char.	1	1	.500	6.75	7	0	0	0	1	0	12.0	16	56	11	9	1	0	0	6	0	10	1	0
Kremer, John, Tam.	0	0	.000	6.00	6	0	0	0	2	0	9.0	15	47	7	6	0	0	1	1	3	0	8	3	0
Kropf, Andy, Lak.	0	0	.000	72.00	1	0	0	0	1	0	1.0	6	11	8	8	3	0	0	0	2	0	0	0	0
Krug, Dustin, Day.	3	2	.600	5.23	20	0	0	0	6	1	31.0	46	149	21	18	1	1	1	0	12	2	22	2	0
Kubes, Greg, Cle.*	10	6	.625	3.79	20	19	0	0	0	0	111.2	124	495	59	47	7	3	2	3	50	1	89	0	0
Langone, Steve, V.B.	9	3	.750	2.46	23	13	1	1	5	0	98.2	94	400	32	27	8	1	2	3	18	0	89	3	2
Lara, Nelson, Sar.	1	3	.250	10.50	27	0	0	0	16	1	30.0	40	165	40	35	2	4	3	8	28	2	29	6	3
Lavigne, Tim, St.L.	1	0	1.000	0.00	4	0	0	0	3	0	5.1	4	22	2	0	0	1	0	2	0	2	1	0
Lee, Clifton, Jup.*	6	7	.462	2.79	21	20	0	0	1	0	109.2	78	451	43	34	13	5	4	4	46	0	129	2	3
Levan, Matt, B.C.*	1	0	1.000	3.48	15	0	0	0	6	1	20.2	21	94	10	8	2	0	1	0	10	0	18	2	0
Lewis, Colby, Char.	1	0	1.000	0.00	1	0	0	0	0	0	4.1	0	13	0	0	0	0	0	0	8	0	0	0
Lewis, Craig, Jup.	2	1	.667	1.05	17	0	0	0	2	0	25.2	20	107	10	3	1	1	0	2	5	2	9	2	0
Lima, Juan, Jup.	0	0	.000	0.00	1	0	0	0	1	0	2.0	0	6	0	0	0	0	0	0	1	0	0	0
Lohrman, Dave, St.L.	3	1	.750	1.67	20	0	0	0	6	2	37.2	18	151	8	7	4	1	2	4	20	0	53	5	0
Lopez, Gustavo, B.C.	3	1	.750	3.21	8	8	2	0	0	0	33.2	32	139	18	12	4	1	1	0	6	0	19	0	0
Maberry, Mark, St.L.*	1	0	1.000	0.00	3	0	0	0	1	0	5.2	2	20	0	0	0	0	0	0	2	1	2	1	0
Madson, Ryan, Cle.	9	9	.500	3.90	22	21	1	0	0	0	117.2	137	530	68	51	4	0	5	5	49	1	101	5	1

Pitcher, Team	W	L	Pct.	ERA	G	GS	CG	ShO	GF	Sv.	IP	H	TBF	R	ER	HR	SH	SF	HB	BB	IBB	SO	WP	Bk.
Majewski, Gary, V.B.	4	5	.444	6.24	23	13	0	0	5	1	75.0	103	351	57	52	9	3	4	5	36	0	41	3	1
Markwell, Diegomar, Dun.*	3	1	.750	3.21	5	5	0	0	0	0	33.2	27	136	12	12	4	1	1	1	13	0	26	1	0
Marrero, Darwin, Jup.	5	8	.385	3.67	21	17	1	0	0	0	103.0	103	426	47	42	10	3	1	1	25	0	62	1	0
Marsonek, Sam, Tam.	8	8	.500	3.51	24	23	5	2	0	0	138.1	128	590	67	54	6	5	2	21	39	2	120	12	1
Martinez, Anastacio, Sar.	9	12	.429	3.35	25	24	1	0	0	0	145.0	130	606	69	54	12	4	1	9	39	0	123	6	0
Martinez, Dave, Tam.*	0	3	.000	6.05	4	3	1	0	1	0	19.1	20	85	15	13	3	0	1	0	9	0	19	1	0
Martinez, Oscar, Tam.	2	3	.400	3.07	29	0	0	0	23	14	29.1	26	129	12	10	2	0	1	3	10	0	40	1	0
Marx, Tommy, Lak.*	8	11	.421	4.91	28	27	1	0	0	0	150.1	160	674	92	82	14	4	8	8	78	0	97	11	3
Matthews, Barry, Lak.*	2	2	.500	4.04	22	7	1	1	3	0	62.1	70	278	31	28	6	2	1	2	23	1	42	8	1
Matthews, Lamont, V.B.*	1	0	1.000	0.00	1	0	0	0	0	0	1.0	1	4	0	0	0	0	0	0	0	0	0	0	0
Maust, David, Jup.*	0	1	.000	15.00	1	1	0	0	0	0	3.0	7	15	5	5	2	0	0	0	1	0	0	0	0
McAvoy, Jeff, Jup.	2	2	.500	2.70	46	1	0	0	12	3	76.2	70	321	31	23	8	6	2	2	20	1	52	1	3
McCasland, Ralph, Jup.*	0	1	.000	4.50	17	0	0	0	3	0	28.0	32	119	15	14	3	1	0	0	6	0	10	2	0
McClaskey, Tim, B.C.	3	1	.750	0.88	26	0	0	0	24	14	30.2	21	124	3	3	0	1	0	3	8	3	41	0	0
McCrotty, Will, V.B.	0	2	.000	4.37	20	0	0	0	14	5	22.2	22	105	11	11	3	1	1	2	14	1	17	2	0
McCurtain, Paul, B.C.	0	1	.000	6.97	7	0	0	0	2	1	10.1	11	47	10	8	0	0	0	0	6	0	10	0	0
McDonald, Jon, F.M.	4	2	.667	1.98	9	9	0	0	0	0	50.0	44	206	15	11	0	0	0	1	15	1	44	8	1
Meldahl, Todd, Cle.*	0	0	.000	1.59	7	0	0	0	3	0	11.1	8	46	2	2	1	0	0	1	5	0	10	2	0
Messenger, Randall, B.C.	7	4	.636	4.08	18	18	0	0	0	0	92.2	99	401	55	42	3	1	3	5	35	0	42	3	0
Meyer, Dave, V.B.	0	1	.000	6.28	12	0	0	0	8	3	14.1	20	70	11	10	0	3	1	3	6	1	13	1	2
Miller, Trever, Sar.*	0	0	.000	2.25	3	2	0	0	0	0	8.0	3	29	2	2	0	1	0	1	1	0	6	0	0
Montalbano, Greg, Sar.*	9	3	.750	2.96	17	15	0	0	0	0	91.1	66	367	36	30	11	4	5	4	25	1	77	3	3
Montero, Agustin, V.B.	1	0	1.000	3.45	16	0	0	0	7	1	31.1	29	134	14	12	7	1	1	3	13	0	23	1	0
Montero, Jose, Char.	0	4	.000	10.57	6	0	0	0	2	0	7.2	9	41	10	9	2	1	0	3	7	0	5	1	1
Montero, Oscar, Day.	2	0	1.000	3.38	11	1	0	0	0	0	16.0	7	68	6	6	1	0	0	0	14	0	13	3	0
Moreno, Edwin, Char.	8	9	.471	4.03	28	28	1	1	0	0	152.0	142	645	83	68	10	2	5	11	51	0	92	4	0
Moreno, Julio, St.L.	5	4	.556	3.09	20	5	1	0	7	2	55.1	52	230	22	19	3	1	1	3	9	0	43	0	0
Morse, Bryan, B.C.*	3	2	.600	4.06	37	0	0	0	12	3	62.0	57	270	32	28	2	6	2	1	36	3	33	4	0
Moser, Todd, B.C.*	0	0	.000	1.69	2	2	0	0	0	0	5.1	3	22	3	1	0	2	1	0	1	0	2	0	0
Mosley, Eric, Tam.	0	1	.000	4.50	1	1	1	0	0	0	6.0	6	25	3	3	0	0	0	0	3	0	0	3	0
Murphy, Matt, Day.*	4	6	.400	3.96	53	0	0	0	18	3	75.0	82	332	44	33	0	7	1	5	25	4	77	4	1
Musser, Neal, St.L.*	3	4	.429	3.55	9	9	0	0	0	0	45.2	45	201	24	18	2	0	2	5	19	0	40	2	0
Nance, Shane, V.B.*	6	3	.667	2.63	21	0	0	0	13	4	48.0	28	196	15	14	3	1	0	3	21	1	63	2	0
Negrette, Richard, Day.	0	1	.000	33.00	4	0	0	0	1	0	3.0	11	29	12	11	1	0	0	1	7	1	1	2	0
Nettles, Tim, Tam.	0	0	.000	54.00	1	0	0	0	0	0	0.1	1	3	2	2	0	0	0	0	2	0	0	0	0
Ogea, Chad, Tam.	0	0	.000	3.00	2	2	0	0	0	0	9.0	10	42	3	3	0	2	1	1	3	0	6	1	0
Orloski, Joe, Dun.	4	2	.667	2.84	46	0	0	0	28	10	66.2	55	283	28	21	4	0	3	3	29	2	52	2	0
Oropesa, Eddie, Cle.*	0	0	.000	0.00	2	0	0	0	0	0	2.0	2	10	0	0	0	0	0	1	1	0	3	0	0
Orr, Ben, Day.*	0	1	.000	5.40	5	0	0	0	4	1	5.0	6	27	4	3	0	2	2	0	6	2	6	2	0
Ortiz, Omar, B.C.	4	10	.286	5.38	28	21	0	0	2	0	112.0	120	509	78	67	12	4	3	8	65	0	78	9	0
Padilla, Juan, F.M.	6	4	.600	2.99	56	0	0	0	49	23	69.1	72	306	35	23	2	1	1	3	25	6	77	1	0
Padilla, Roy, B.C.*	0	0	.000	5.68	6	0	0	0	3	0	6.1	6	33	4	4	1	0	0	0	12	0	3	0	0
Padua, Geraldo, Tam.	0	0	.000	0.00	1	0	0	0	1	0	1.0	0	3	0	0	0	0	0	0	1	0	1	0	0
Painter, Lance, Dun.*	1	1	.500	0.96	5	1	0	0	0	0	9.1	10	37	1	1	0	2	0	0	1	0	10	1	0
Palki, Jeromy, F.M.	1	1	.500	1.80	12	0	0	0	6	1	20.0	13	82	5	4	1	0	1	0	10	0	24	2	0
Parrish, Wade, V.B.*	4	1	.800	1.85	23	0	0	0	15	6	39.0	34	153	9	8	3	0	0	1	7	0	42	4	0
Pautz, Brad, Cle.	3	2	.600	3.38	44	0	0	0	37	16	64.0	62	273	29	24	1	4	4	1	24	3	51	6	0
Pavano, Carl, Jup.	1	1	.500	2.19	3	3	0	0	0	0	12.1	10	51	7	3	1	1	0	1	2	0	11	0	0
Payne, Jerrod, Dun.	2	2	.500	2.30	21	0	0	0	16	8	27.1	25	118	13	7	2	0	1	0	8	1	22	0	0
Pena, Juan, Sar.	0	3	.000	5.19	8	8	0	0	0	0	26.0	29	118	15	15	3	0	0	1	11	0	31	1	1
Perez, Frank, Cle.	4	2	.667	3.52	31	0	0	0	17	3	64.0	58	272	29	25	2	1	1	7	26	2	45	8	2
Perez, George, Dun.	4	3	.571	3.12	41	0	0	0	23	8	86.2	81	380	39	30	3	1	7	6	42	1	48	7	1
Perez, Julio, Jup.	6	3	.667	3.61	34	0	0	0	20	4	47.1	58	218	26	19	1	1	3	4	16	1	46	1	0
Persails, Mark, Lak.	0	0	.000	2.84	3	0	0	0	2	1	6.1	6	26	2	2	1	0	0	1	1	0	6	0	0
Persby, Andy, F.M.	1	3	.250	6.92	18	0	0	0	6	0	26.0	25	128	22	20	0	2	0	4	23	1	14	3	0
Pichardo, Hipolito, Sar.	0	0	.000	4.50	3	3	0	0	0	0	6.0	8	29	3	3	1	0	0	0	2	0	8	0	0
Politte, Cliff, Cle.	0	1	.000	2.45	7	7	0	0	0	0	11.0	8	43	4	3	0	0	0	0	3	0	15	0	0
Polk, Scott, St.L.	1	0	1.000	7.04	6	0	0	0	4	0	7.2	9	39	6	6	1	1	0	1	10	0	4	1	0
Porter, Scott, Dun.	0	1	.000	21.00	3	0	0	0	0	0	3.0	8	19	7	7	1	0	1	1	2	0	2	2	0
Pridie, Jon, F.M.	1	3	.250	4.58	14	9	0	0	2	0	57.0	54	257	31	29	3	2	0	3	37	2	42	6	1
Proctor, Scott, V.B.	6	4	.600	2.48	15	15	0	0	0	0	90.2	73	366	30	25	8	2	2	9	30	1	79	3	0
Queen, Mike, St.L.*	4	3	.571	3.47	31	0	0	0	13	1	62.1	60	276	32	24	3	5	4	9	23	1	39	1	1
Ramirez, Victor, Char.	0	3	.000	11.00	3	3	0	0	0	0	9.0	11	51	16	11	1	0	1	0	13	0	11	2	0
Reames, Jay, Jup.	0	0	.000	1.46	12	0	0	0	2	0	12.1	11	56	5	2	0	2	1	0	8	1	4	1	0
Regilio, Nick, Char.	6	2	.750	1.55	11	11	1	1	0	0	64.0	47	254	16	11	5	1	1	1	16	0	60	0	1
Reimers, Cameron, Dun.	10	6	.625	4.40	22	22	3	0	0	0	141.0	150	604	81	69	13	4	5	20	24	1	88	2	2
Reyes, Eddy, B.C.	2	0	1.000	3.60	13	0	0	0	9	2	15.0	13	71	13	6	1	0	1	3	10	1	9	1	0
Reynolds, Josh, St.L.	3	6	.333	4.95	17	11	0	0	1	0	60.0	83	279	39	33	1	4	2	4	20	0	48	0	1
Reynoso, Edison, Tam.	0	0	.000	0.00	1	1	0	0	0	0	3.2	1	12	0	0	0	0	0	0	0	0	5	0	0
Riccobono, Rick, Sar.	1	3	.250	5.81	35	6	0	0	14	0	79.0	100	382	62	51	9	3	5	5	38	4	50	2	0
Richardson, Jason, F.M.	1	0	1.000	2.19	8	1	0	0	3	0	12.1	10	53	5	3	0	0	3	1	7	0	6	3	0
Riepe, Andy, Sar.	0	1	.000	9.00	1	0	0	0	1	0	2.0	1	10	2	2	1	0	0	0	3	0	2	0	0
Rijo, Fernando, V.B.	0	1	.000	5.73	2	2	0	0	0	0	11.0	7	49	7	7	2	2	0	0	10	0	11	1	0
Rivas, Gabriel, Lak.	0	0	.000	0.00	1	0	0	0	0	0	2.0	0	6	0	0	0	0	0	0	1	0	2	0	0
Rivera, Homero, Lak.*	3	4	.429	2.19	35	0	0	0	13	3	49.1	30	193	13	12	1	4	0	2	18	2	31	3	0
Roberts, Rick, V.B.*	4	5	.444	2.72	29	14	0	0	8	4	86.0	70	379	42	26	6	2	3	7	47	0	92	7	2
Robertson, Nathan, B.C.*	11	4	.733	2.88	19	19	2	0	0	0	106.1	95	445	44	34	3	6	2	5	43	1	67	5	1
Robinson, Dustin, Day.	0	0	.000	2.08	2	0	0	0	1	0	4.1	2	16	1	1	1	0	0	0	1	0	7	0	0
Rodney, Fernando, Lak.	4	2	.667	3.42	16	9	0	0	4	0	55.1	53	235	26	21	2	2	0	1	19	1	44	1	1
Rodriguez, Cristobal, Jup.	1	0	1.000	3.29	14	0	0	0	12	7	13.2	11	59	5	5	0	2	0	0	7	0	19	1	0
Rodriguez, George, Cle.	0	2	.000	10.22	8	0	0	0	2	0	12.1	14	61	14	14	1	0	1	0	13	0	7	3	0
Rodriguez, Luis, Char.	0	3	.000	7.58	5	5	0	0	0	0	19.0	20	94	17	16	1	0	3	1	20	0	15	4	0
Rodriguez, Ricardo, V.B.	14	6	.700	3.21	26	26	2	0	0	0	154.1	133	645	67	55	13	7	2	3	60	0	154	18	1

Pitcher, Team	W	L	Pct.	ERA	G	GS	CG	ShO	GF	Sv.	IP	H	TBF	R	ER	HR	SH	SF	HB	BB	IBB	SO	WP	Bk.
Rojas, Jose, V.B.	0	0	.000	6.00	1	0	0	0	1	0	3.0	3	14	2	2	0	0	1	1	0	3	0	0
Roller, Adam, Tam.	2	3	.400	1.20	51	0	0	0	36	23	67.2	42	264	14	9	0	2	2	3	15	3	76	3	2
Runser, Greg, Char.	3	4	.429	2.93	50	0	0	0	47	30	67.2	66	289	26	22	3	5	3	0	28	4	66	2	0
Russ, Christopher, Char.*	5	2	.714	3.47	13	12	0	0	0	0	70.0	87	293	36	27	5	1	2	4	19	0	56	0	4
Russo, Scott, Jup.*	0	0	.000	0.00	5	0	0	0	1	0	6.0	3	22	0	0	0	0	0	1	0	0	8	1	0
Saberhagen, Bret, Sar.	0	0	.000	6.75	1	1	0	0	0	0	4.0	5	17	3	3	0	0	0	0	0	0	3	0	0
Salyers, Jeremy, Jup.	3	1	.750	3.57	9	1	0	0	2	0	22.2	22	98	10	9	0	3	1	2	6	1	10	0	1
Sampson, Benj, F.M.*	2	3	.400	3.20	15	15	0	0	0	0	70.1	61	293	30	25	4	0	4	2	31	0	36	2	0
Sams, Aaron, Sar.*	0	0	.000	0.00	2	0	0	0	2	1	3.0	1	13	2	0	0	0	0	0	2	0	2	0	0
Sandoval, Marcos, Dun.	1	0	1.000	11.57	5	1	0	0	0	0	7.0	6	41	10	9	0	1	0	1	12	0	2	3	0
Scheffer, Aaron, B.C.	0	0	.000	0.00	3	0	0	0	1	0	5.0	1	17	0	0	0	0	0	0	1	0	4	0	0
Schoening, Brent, F.M.	5	9	.357	4.88	17	16	0	0	0	0	86.2	97	373	54	47	5	0	3	5	32	0	69	3	1
Schroder, Chris, Jup.	1	0	1.000	2.30	10	0	0	0	2	0	15.2	12	64	5	4	1	0	0	4	0	0	20	4	0
Seibel, Phil, Jup.*	10	7	.588	3.95	29	21	0	1	0	0	134.1	144	572	70	59	12	5	6	8	28	0	88	5	1
Seo, Jae, St.L.	2	3	.400	3.55	6	5	0	0	0	0	25.1	21	104	10	10	2	0	1	0	0	0	19	0	0
Sergent, Joe, B.C.*	12	6	.667	3.33	27	25	0	0	0	0	143.1	154	607	70	53	11	1	4	5	32	1	89	1	1
Serrano, Elio, Cle.	2	2	.500	3.31	17	1	0	0	5	1	35.1	34	140	14	13	0	3	0	2	7	0	22	0	1
Serrano, Willy, Lak.	3	8	.273	3.17	50	0	0	0	14	4	82.1	91	366	41	29	7	3	5	4	28	4	56	10	0
Shaffar, Ben, Day.	6	4	.600	3.12	19	19	2	2	0	0	106.2	83	448	42	37	3	1	2	6	45	3	118	4	1
Sheffield, Christopher, Dun.	1	0	1.000	22.85	6	0	0	0	4	0	4.1	9	33	11	11	1	0	1	1	11	1	2	4	0
Silva, Doug, Char.	3	1	.750	2.29	23	1	0	0	6	1	55.0	45	211	16	14	3	1	0	10	0	50	2	0
Simpson, Andre, V.B.	1	3	.250	8.69	5	5	0	0	0	0	19.2	23	99	24	19	1	0	2	1	20	1	17	0	0
Sismondo, Bobby, Cle.*	2	2	.500	3.00	6	4	1	0	0	0	30.0	26	123	13	10	2	0	0	1	10	0	15	1	1
Smith, Chuck, B.C.	0	0	.000	3.38	2	2	0	0	0	0	8.0	7	31	3	3	1	0	0	1	0	6	0	0
Smith, Clint, Lak.	0	2	.000	4.60	20	0	0	0	2	0	29.1	25	140	18	15	2	0	1	2	24	0	37	6	0
Smith, Jason, Tam.	1	0	1.000	0.00	1	0	0	0	0	0	3.0	1	12	0	0	0	0	0	2	1	1	0	0
Smith, Matt, Tam.*	6	2	.750	2.24	11	11	0	0	0	0	68.1	54	276	21	17	2	1	1	22	0	71	4	4
Sneed, John, F.M.	8	3	.727	3.24	25	19	0	0	3	0	114.0	95	480	51	41	5	1	4	49	0	88	5	0
Snyder, Matt, Char.	0	1	.000	32.40	1	1	0	0	0	0	1.2	7	13	6	6	1	0	1	0	1	0	2	0	0
Solano, Alex, Sar.	2	9	.182	4.78	39	2	0	0	11	1	90.1	113	413	71	48	5	2	5	2	32	1	61	1	0
Song, Seung, Sar.	5	2	.714	1.68	8	8	0	0	0	0	48.1	28	190	11	9	1	0	0	18	0	56	1	1
Spear, Russ, Lak.	1	1	.500	5.11	8	0	0	0	1	0	12.1	5	58	8	7	2	0	1	5	13	0	18	4	0
Squires, Matt, Cle.*	0	1	.000	6.75	4	0	0	0	3	0	5.1	5	28	4	4	1	0	0	0	7	0	4	0	0
Stafford, Mike, Tam.*	0	1	.000	7.71	4	0	0	0	2	0	2.1	8	15	2	2	0	0	0	0	1	0	4	0	0
Stamler, Keith, Char.	8	4	.667	2.48	23	11	1	0	2	0	87.0	64	351	35	24	3	3	2	7	28	2	61	4	0
Stanton, Timothy, Tam.*	1	0	1.000	1.89	26	0	0	0	11	1	47.2	46	192	15	10	2	0	1	0	13	2	39	1	1
Steele, Mike, Lak.	0	1	.000	3.86	15	0	0	0	13	4	18.2	17	83	12	8	0	2	1	4	7	1	10	0	0
Sturdy, Tim, F.M.	8	10	.444	3.82	28	19	1	0	2	0	129.2	122	552	74	55	2	8	4	10	53	2	54	9	2
Tejada, Frailyn, B.C.*	0	2	.000	6.35	2	1	0	0	0	0	5.2	13	30	8	4	0	2	0	0	1	0	4	0	0
Tekavec, Nate, Lak.	8	1	.889	2.84	18	11	0	0	3	0	79.1	77	325	27	25	5	3	4	3	17	1	56	4	0
Telford, Anthony, Jup.	0	1	.000	7.20	4	2	0	0	0	0	5.0	9	25	5	4	0	0	0	0	1	0	5	0	0
Tetz, Kris, Jup.	0	0	.000	3.00	2	0	0	0	1	0	3.0	1	12	1	1	0	0	0	1	1	0	3	0	0
Thurman, Mike, Jup.	1	0	1.000	0.00	1	1	1	1	0	0	5.0	2	15	0	0	0	0	0	0	0	0	3	0	0
Totten, Heath, V.B.	0	8	.000	7.07	9	9	2	0	0	0	49.2	64	218	40	39	9	1	3	1	10	0	25	1	1
Traber, Billy, St.L.*	6	5	.545	2.66	18	18	0	0	0	0	101.2	85	415	36	30	2	3	2	5	23	0	79	4	1
Tranchina, Scott, Day.	11	8	.579	3.59	42	8	0	0	17	1	92.2	91	404	50	37	8	2	3	4	42	1	89	6	0
Valdez, Domingo, Char.	3	4	.429	4.89	9	9	0	0	0	0	42.1	36	189	26	23	3	0	1	8	19	0	40	4	4
Vanhekken, Andy, Lak.*	10	4	.714	3.17	19	19	2	0	0	0	110.2	105	460	43	39	8	3	2	5	33	0	82	1	0
Viera, Rolando, Sar.*	0	2	.000	6.00	6	0	0	0	1	0	12.0	12	55	8	8	2	0	1	6	0	12	1	1
Viole, Paul, St.L.	1	5	.167	3.47	46	0	0	0	37	11	59.2	47	278	32	23	1	2	0	7	50	0	55	11	0
Walker, Tyler, St.L.	0	2	.000	8.04	4	4	0	0	0	0	15.2	19	69	14	14	0	0	0	3	0	11	3	0
Walling, Dave, Tam.	1	1	.500	5.19	4	4	0	0	0	0	17.1	23	79	12	10	2	1	0	2	0	9	0	0
Ward, Bryan, Tam.*	0	0	.000	33.75	1	0	0	0	0	0	1.1	7	13	7	5	2	0	0	1	1	0	0	0
Watson, Greg, Lak.	3	6	.333	3.14	57	0	0	0	32	9	66.0	59	298	35	23	5	3	12	35	2	53	9	0
Wayno, Justin, Jup.	2	3	.400	3.02	8	7	0	0	0	0	41.2	31	166	16	14	0	0	2	3	9	0	35	2	0
Webb, John, Day.	1	1	.500	5.40	5	4	0	0	0	0	20.0	23	91	13	12	0	0	2	7	1	20	2	1
Weis, Brad, F.M.*	1	1	.500	2.61	17	0	0	0	8	0	20.2	20	94	9	6	1	2	3	2	10	2	26	1	0
Weslowski, Rob, St.L.	1	3	.250	5.94	9	0	0	0	2	0	16.2	25	83	16	11	0	0	0	6	1	10	1	0
Whiteley, Shad, Tam.	1	0	1.000	2.79	9	0	0	0	2	0	9.2	9	43	4	3	0	0	0	6	0	9	0	0
Wiggins, Scott, Tam.*	4	3	.571	3.03	36	5	0	0	9	1	68.1	72	302	29	23	5	1	2	10	23	1	77	8	0
Williams, Adam, V.B.*	0	1	.000	6.43	10	0	0	0	1	0	14.0	16	76	13	10	1	1	2	5	12	0	13	5	4
Witte, Lou, Tam.	3	1	.750	2.67	29	0	0	0	11	0	33.2	39	134	13	10	0	0	2	0	5	0	29	0	1
Woodards, Orlando, Dun.-B.C.	2	1	.667	4.39	26	0	0	0	11	0	41.0	52	195	26	20	3	1	2	5	17	1	28	2	0

PITCHERS WITH TWO OR MORE TEAMS

Pitcher, Team	W	L	Pct.	ERA	G	GS	CG	ShO	GF	Sv.	IP	H	TBF	R	ER	HR	SH	SF	HB	BB	IBB	SO	WP	Bk.
Woodards, Orlando, Dun.	2	1	.667	5.74	17	0	0	0	9	0	26.2	37	132	21	17	2	0	1	3	15	1	15	2	0
Woodards, Orlando, B.C.	0	0	.000	1.88	9	0	0	0	2	0	14.1	15	63	5	3	1	1	1	2	2	0	13	0	0

COMBINATION SHUTOUTS: **Brevard County (14)**—Anderson-Bowe-Hamulack, Ortiz-Hamulack-McClaskey-Bowe, Beckett-Edmondson-Morse-Bowe, Burnett-Morse-Farizo-Edmondson-McClaskey, Beckett-Morse-Bowe, Beckett-Hamulack-McClaskey, Beckett-Edmondson, Ortiz-Bowe, Beckett-McCurtain, Sergent-Henriquez-Levan, Sergent-Scheffer, Ortiz-Hamulack-Bowe, Robertson-Bowe, Sergent-Bowe. **Charlotte (4)**—Russ-Runser, Regilio-Silva, Moreno-Huffaker, Garcia-Graham-Huffaker-Haring. **Clearwater (5)**—Brooks-Keelin, Asencio-Pautz, Asencio-Alston, Baisley-Franco, Madson-Meldahl-Perez. **Daytona (6)**—Freed-Tranchina-Eppender-Bailey, Shaffar-Eppeneder, Chavez-Eppeneder-Gagliano, Freed-Achilles-Bailey-Eppeneder, Bruback-Eppeneder, Freed-Corbin. **Dunedin (3)**—Kegley-Halladay, Reimers-Halladay-Perez, Markwell-Orloski. **Fort Myers (6)**—McDonald-Flohr-Padilla, McDonald-Sturdy-Padilla, Corona-Cento-Padilla, Sampson-Eyre-Weis, Sneed-Howard, Hoard-Padilla. **Jupiter (12)**—Good-Perez-Rodriguez, Lee-Salyers-Ferrari-Perez-Rodriguez, Marrero-McCasland-Perez, Lee-Arthurs-Perez, Klepacki-Darrell-Bye, Good-Collins-McAvoy-Ferrari, Marrero-Collins, Pavano-Collins, McAvoy-Lee, Seibel-Bye-Lewis-McAvoy, Klepacki-McAvoy-Ferrari, Lee-Ferrari. **Lakeland (9)**—Traber-Weslowski-Dunning, Vanhekken-Spear-Watson, Marx-Serrano-Bess, Vanhekken-Serrano-Rivera-Watson-Bess, Marx-Watson-Bess, Vanhekken-Spear-Serrano-Watson, Tekavec-Rivera, Tekavec-Bess, Marx-Graves. **St. Lucie (6)**—Martinez-Glaser-Lara, Baker-De La Rosa, Traber-Cerda-Viole, Moreno-Cerda, Musser-Viole, Heilman-Lavigne. **Sarasota (6)**—Proctor-Hadden, Colyer-Meyer, Rodriguez-Parrish, Martinez-Lara-De La Rosa, Montalbano-Glaser-De la rosa, Song-Solano-Dickinson. **Tampa (9)**—Aramboles-Jensen, Borrell-Wiggins, Reynoso-De Paula-Martinez, Jensen-Whiteley-Artiles-Martinez, Marsonek-Dean-Stanton, Smith-Garcia-Jensen, Bradley-Wiggins-Roller, Smith-Bean-Roller. **Vero Beach (5)**—Proctor-Gomes, Langone-Nance, Wiggins-Stanton, Langone-Fischer-Gomes, Roberts-Berry, Rodriguez-Williams.

NO-HIT GAMES: Regilio, Charlotte defeated Jupiter, 3-0, June 10.

TEAM

Team	Pct.	G	PO	A	E	TC	DP	TP	PB
Clearwater	.973	137	3554	1451	139	5144	133	0	32
Vero Beach	.972	133	3481	1260	136	4877	86	0	22
Fort Myers	.972	137	3635	1596	151	5382	150	0	34
Lakeland	.971	136	3535	1473	150	5158	119	0	30
Charlotte	.970	137	3610	1452	157	5219	130	0	25
St. Lucie	.970	139	3548	1548	159	5255	125	0	14
Brevard County	.967	135	3489	1423	167	5079	134	0	31
Daytona	.967	136	3501	1306	165	4972	86	0	14
Jupiter	.966	139	3620	1272	172	5064	99	0	17
Tampa	.965	139	3581	1440	180	5201	105	0	53
Dunedin	.965	135	3532	1466	180	5178	133	0	30
Sarasota	.958	137	3603	1350	216	5169	105	0	27

INDIVIDUAL

FIRST BASEMEN

NOTE: All caps denotes fielding-percentage leader based on 70 games for catchers, 93 for all other non-pitchers and 112 innings for pitchers. *Throws lefthanded.

Player, Team	Pct.	G	PO	A	E	TC	DP
Ahumada, Alex, Sar.	1.000	1	9	0	0	9	1
Alvarez, Nick, V.B.	.978	59	445	40	11	496	28
Baker, Derek, Lak.	.994	60	446	27	3	476	51
Bates, Fletcher, St.L.	1.000	4	22	6	0	28	1
Bernhardt, Joe, Dun.	.991	81	659	29	6	694	78
Bledsoe, Hunter, V.B.	.991	47	296	29	3	328	22
Brown, Jason, B.C.	1.000	2	15	0	0	15	1
Burns, Pat, St.L.*	.985	127	1148	67	19	1234	96
Callahan, Dave, B.C.*	.983	106	941	63	17	1021	94
Chiaffredo, Paul, Dun.	1.000	1	1	0	0	1	0
Curry, Chris, Day.	1.000	1	3	0	0	3	1
Daigle, Leo, Lak.	.986	84	646	58	10	714	49
Deschenes, Pat, St.L.	1.000	8	44	2	0	46	3
Downing, Brad, Lak.	1.000	1	5	0	0	5	0
Duarte, Justin, Cle.	.966	14	104	10	4	118	14
DZURILLA, Mike, Day.	.996	107	843	73	4	920	54
Espy, Nate, Cle.	.989	125	1016	90	12	1118	101
Gajewski, Matt, Char.	.990	11	93	5	1	99	12
Garcia, Luis, Sar.	.982	54	459	28	9	496	39
Gomon, Dusty, F.M.	1.000	5	31	1	0	32	5
Gripp, Ryan, Day.	1.000	1	1	0	0	1	0
Guyton, Eric, St.L.	1.000	1	9	0	0	9	1
Hawthorne, Kyle, F.M.	.975	4	35	4	1	40	3
Hernandez, John, V.B.	1.000	1	4	1	0	5	0
Huff, B.J., St.L.	.961	5	46	3	2	51	3
Jones, Jason, Char.	.988	98	905	56	12	973	82
Keene, Kurt, Dun.	.987	12	70	6	1	77	4
Kremblas, Mike, Dun.	1.000	2	10	0	0	10	1
Lane, Rich, Jup.*	.985	120	926	56	15	997	66
Leach, Nick, Tam.	.992	57	482	31	4	517	40
Leaumont, Jeff, Tam.*	.985	68	543	33	9	585	39
Lush, Zach, B.C.	.000	1	0	0	0	0	0
Magness, Pat, B.C.	1.000	6	51	4	0	55	6
Martinez, Casey, Dun.	1.000	2	7	1	0	8	1
Miller, Eric, Jup.	1.000	2	11	0	0	11	1
Minus, Steve, Sar.	.988	59	469	35	6	510	35
Morneau, Justin, F.M.	.994	48	449	25	3	477	49
Morrow, Alvin, Dun.	1.000	1	3	0	0	3	0
Nicholson, Derek, Lak.	1.000	12	77	9	0	86	12
Ortiz, David, F.M.*	1.000	1	10	1	0	11	2
Osborne, Mark, F.M.	.953	6	38	3	2	43	2
Paciorek, Pete, V.B.*	.993	32	245	25	2	272	26
Pittman, Tom, Jup.	.966	23	161	8	6	175	14
Ramsey, Brad, Day.	.964	23	155	7	6	168	13
Rapp, Travis, Char.	1.000	1	3	0	0	3	0
Renick, Josh, F.M.	1.000	7	47	3	0	50	0
Rodriguez, Mike, Dun.	1.000	1	1	1	0	2	1
Rolison, Nate, B.C.	.992	12	114	12	1	127	6
Roneberg, Brett, B.C.*	.989	12	91	3	1	95	13
Roper, Chad, Char.	1.000	1	5	3	0	8	1
Sandberg, Eric, F.M.*	.990	70	626	64	7	697	69
Scanlon, Matt, F.M.	.968	4	25	5	1	31	2
Schifano, Tony, V.B.	1.000	1	1	0	0	1	0
Swenson, Leland, Char.	1.000	1	1	0	0	1	0
Terhune, Mike, St.L.	1.000	1	1	0	0	1	0

Player, Team	Pct.	G	PO	A	E	TC	DP
Villegas, Ernest, Char.	.981	29	240	17	5	262	18
Washington, Dion, Tam.	.972	22	163	12	5	180	12
Weekly, Chris, Dun.	.992	57	431	39	4	474	35
Williams, Brady, Sar.	.991	25	208	9	2	219	20
Zieour, Neesan, Dun.	1.000	2	2	0	0	2	0
Zoccolillo, Peter, Day.	.969	13	84	10	3	97	6

SECOND BASEMEN

Player, Team	Pct.	G	PO	A	E	TC	DP
Abreu, Dave, St.L.	1.000	11	13	13	0	26	2
Agramonte, Marcos, Char.	1.000	10	10	15	0	35	8
Alvarez, Jimmy, Dun.	.971	16	24	43	2	69	10
Arias, Leandro, St.L.	1.000	4	4	15	0	19	2
Arroyo, William, B.C.	1.000	4	4	7	0	11	1
Bautista, Rayner, Lak.	1.000	1	0	3	0	3	0
Bay, Jason, Jup.	.000	1	0	0	0	0	0
Bernhardt, Joe, Dun.	.976	30	59	61	3	123	13
Blasi, Blake, Day.	.977	40	60	111	4	175	19
Bozanich, Sam, Tam.	.952	13	20	40	3	63	1
Bush, Homer, Dun.	1.000	4	3	9	0	12	4
Calabrese, Tony, Tam.	1.000	1	0	3	0	3	1
Carroll, Wes, Cle.	.882	5	4	11	2	17	2
Clapinski, Chris, B.C.	.929	4	6	7	1	14	2
Collins, Kevin, V.B.	1.000	15	27	33	0	60	9
Cooper, Sam, Day.	1.000	6	6	12	0	18	0
Duran, Deudis, Cle.	1.000	1	0	2	0	2	1
Dzurilla, Mike, Day.	.980	12	21	27	1	49	6
Frye, Jeff, Dun.	1.000	4	6	6	0	12	2
Gallo, Ismael, V.B.	.970	60	100	126	7	233	24
German, Franklin, Day.	.944	10	14	20	2	36	2
Goudie, Jaime, Dun.	.941	43	74	119	12	205	25
Halloran, Matt, Char.	.951	22	40	57	5	102	17
Hannahan, Buzz, Cle.	1.000	14	25	36	0	61	11
Hawthorne, Kyle, F.M.	.947	9	16	20	2	38	2
Hill, Bobby, St.L.	.956	9	21	22	2	45	6
Hitchcox, Brian, Cle.	1.000	6	12	18	0	30	6
Hodge, Kevin, F.M.	.983	38	73	96	3	172	21
Hooper, Clay, Tam.	.941	7	17	15	2	34	4
Jackson, Brandon, Tam.	1.000	4	7	13	0	20	3
Jaramillo, Milko, V.B.	1.000	1	1	3	0	4	1
Jimenez, Carlos, Lak.	.967	45	80	128	7	215	20
Jones, Jack, Day.	.923	4	6	6	1	13	2
Keene, Kurt, Dun.	.967	24	50	66	4	120	16
Kerrigan, Joe, Sar.	.941	48	93	131	14	238	31
Martin, Tyler, Char.	.800	2	3	5	2	10	0
Martinez, Dionnar, Day.	1.000	5	3	4	0	7	0
Martinez, Ramon, Char.	.967	94	206	260	16	482	69
Maxwell, Jason, F.M.	1.000	1	1	2	0	3	1
Mayorson, Manuel, Dun.	1.000	1	2	3	0	5	1
McKINLEY, Josh, Jup.	.975	128	255	287	14	556	56
Meadows, Randy, Day.	1.000	4	2	8	0	10	0
Medrano, Jesus, B.C.	.965	99	180	259	16	455	68
Melucci, Lou, Jup.	.963	14	29	23	2	54	6
Nelson, Reggie, V.B.	.933	51	75	105	13	193	19
Nunez, Manuel, V.B.	.667	1	1	1	1	3	1
Perkins, Kevin, B.C.	.987	24	32	45	1	78	9
Phillips, Andy, Tam.	.968	73	121	180	10	311	43
Renick, Josh, F.M.	.943	41	71	93	10	174	27
Reyes, Ambiorix, Cle.	1.000	1	0	3	0	3	1
Reyes, Ivan, Tam.	.917	2	4	7	1	12	1
Rodriguez, Luis, F.M.	.978	58	119	154	6	279	44
Rodriguez, Victor, Tam.	.971	40	65	105	5	175	21
Rouse, Michael, Dun.	.988	29	66	97	2	165	21
Santoro, Pat, Sar.	.944	74	120	185	18	323	37
Scanlon, Matt, F.M.	1.000	1	1	0	0	1	0
Schifano, Tony, V.B.	.974	8	21	16	1	38	2
Schrager, Tony, Day.	.990	70	120	169	3	292	26
Sequea, Jorge, Lak.	.983	63	120	166	5	291	34
Shipp, Brian, St.L.	.974	104	205	327	14	546	79
Sisk, Aaron, Dun.	1.000	1	1	1	0	2	1
Swenson, Leland, Char.	1.000	13	18	32	0	50	7
Terhune, Mike, St.L.	.988	15	24	55	1	80	9
Tousa, Scott, Lak.	.980	38	91	108	4	203	23
Ugueto, Luis, B.C.	.985	16	25	40	1	66	6
Utley, Chase, Cle.	.970	114	246	311	17	574	75
Ward, Brian, F.M.	.967	6	16	13	1	30	5
Wigginton, Ty, St.L.	1.000	3	5	9	0	14	1
Williams, Brady, Sar.	.951	16	28	30	3	61	6
Wright, Nate, V.B.	1.000	1	0	1	0	1	0

THIRD BASEMEN

Player, Team	Pct.	G	PO	A	E	TC	DP
Ahumada, Alex, Sar.	.922	51	44	97	12	153	7
Aybar, Willy, V.B.	1.000	2	1	4	0	5	0
Batson, Tom, Cle.	1.000	6	1	10	0	11	0
Bell, Ricky, V.B.	.909	6	4	6	1	11	0
Beltre, Adrian, V.B.	1.000	2	0	4	0	4	0
Bernhardt, Joe, Dun.	.909	11	6	14	2	22	1
Berry, Sean, Dun.	1.000	4	2	3	0	5	0
Blalock, Hank, Char.	.963	62	32	150	7	189	11
Blasi, Blake, Day.	1.000	4	1	4	0	5	0
Bledsoe, Hunter, V.B.	.500	1	0	1	1	2	0
Boone, Matt, Lak.	.901	104	68	222	32	322	24
Calabrese, Tony, Tam.	.833	14	10	30	8	48	1
Campos, Julio, Cle.	.333	1	0	1	2	3	0
Carroll, Wes, Cle.	.000	1	0	0	0	0	0
Chapman, Travis, Cle.	.953	89	72	174	12	258	12
Clapinski, Chris, B.C.	1.000	3	2	5	0	7	0
Collins, Mike, V.B.	1.000	2	1	1	0	2	0
Daigle, Leo, Lak.	1.000	4	0	3	0	3	0
Deschaine, James, Day.	.923	48	36	84	10	130	9
Deschenes, Pat, St.L.	.907	55	36	110	15	161	8
Duran, Deudis, Cle.	.917	4	4	7	1	12	0
Dzurilla, Mike, Day.	.889	4	0	8	1	9	1
Fagan, Shawn, Dun.	.902	115	65	257	35	357	25
Gajewski, Matt, Char.	1.000	5	0	11	0	11	1
Garcia, Luis, Sar.	1.000	1	1	1	0	2	0
German, Franklin, Day.	.714	2	1	4	2	7	0
Grice, Daniel, Day.	.950	9	7	12	1	20	0
Gripp, Ryan, Day.	.919	61	45	103	13	161	10
Guyton, Eric, St.L.	.000	1	0	0	0	0	0
Halloran, Matt, Char.	.909	5	1	9	1	11	0
Hannahan, Buzz, Cle.	.965	31	21	62	3	86	7
Hansen, Dave, V.B.	1.000	3	2	1	0	3	0
Hawthorne, Kyle, F.M.	.880	25	9	57	9	75	4
Henson, Drew, Tam.	.929	5	2	11	1	14	0
Hill, Bobby, St.L.	.909	20	14	46	6	66	2
Hitchcox, Brian, Cle.	.867	9	4	22	4	30	3
Hodge, Kevin, F.M.	.949	28	24	51	4	79	5
Hooper, Clay, Tam.	.500	1	0	1	1	2	0
Jackson, Brandon, Tam.	.880	10	6	16	3	25	2
Jaramillo, Milko, V.B.	1.000	3	0	2	0	2	0
Jimenez, Carlos, Lak.	1.000	2	0	2	0	2	0
Jones, Jack, Day.	.500	1	0	1	1	2	0
Jones, Mitch, Tam.	.910	20	15	46	6	67	1
Keene, Kurt, Dun.	.941	8	5	11	1	17	0
King, Brennan, V.B.	.962	72	49	104	6	159	8
Kropf, Andy, Lak.	.867	25	15	50	10	75	6
Lugo, Felix, Jup.	.883	76	51	146	26	223	11
Martin, Tyler, Char.	.940	36	21	73	6	100	9
Martinez, Dionnar, Day.	.933	11	2	12	1	15	0
Maxwell, Jason, F.M.	1.000	1	1	3	0	4	1
Mayorson, Manuel, Dun.	1.000	2	0	1	0	1	0
Meadows, Randy, Jup.	.714	4	3	7	4	14	1
Medrano, Jesus, B.C.	1.000	1	1	2	0	3	0
Melucci, Lou, Jup.	.875	28	15	41	8	64	2
Miller, Eric, Jup.	.862	11	8	17	4	29	0
Minus, Steve, Sar.	.898	36	24	73	11	108	6
Myrow, Brian, Tam.	.831	32	21	38	12	71	3
Nelson, Reggie, V.B.	.971	16	9	25	1	35	1
Nettles, Jeff, Tam.	.931	68	44	118	12	174	14
Nicholson, Derek, Lak.	.950	6	4	15	1	20	0
Perkins, Kevin, B.C.	.773	19	10	24	10	44	0
Rodriguez, Luis, F.M.	1.000	2	0	3	0	3	1
Roper, Chad, Char.	.926	24	15	35	4	54	2
Santos, Jose, B.C.	.916	115	78	258	31	367	23
SCANLON, Matt, F.M.	.925	97	52	181	19	252	17
Schifano, Tony, V.B.	.908	36	23	56	8	87	4
Schrager, Tony, Day.	.857	5	3	9	2	14	1
Sequea, Jorge, Lak.	1.000	2	2	6	0	8	0
Sherrod, Justin, Sar.	.854	36	23	59	14	96	3
Shipp, Brian, St.L.	.667	2	2	2	2	6	1
Sisk, Aaron, Dun.	.882	5	2	13	2	17	2
Swenson, Leland, Char.	.931	9	2	25	2	29	3
Terhune, Mike, St.L.	.932	62	42	122	12	176	10
Theodorou, Nick, V.B.	.857	3	1	5	1	7	0
Ward, Brian, F.M.	.857	6	4	8	2	14	2
Weekly, Chris, Dun.	1.000	1	1	4	0	5	1
Williams, Brady, Sar.	.864	18	10	41	8	59	1
Zech, Scott, Jup.	.897	26	21	40	7	68	5

SHORTSTOPS

Player, Team	Pct.	G	PO	A	E	TC	DP
Ahumada, Alex, Sar.	.940	54	87	162	16	265	34
Alvarez, Jimmy, Dun.	.925	106	149	294	36	479	57
Arroyo, William, B.C.	1.000	1	0	2	0	2	0
Basak, Chris, St.L.	.958	119	177	392	25	594	76
BAUTISTA, Rayner, Lak.	.959	99	148	277	18	443	45
Boone, Matt, Lak.	1.000	1	1	2	0	3	1
Calabrese, Tony, Tam.	.889	5	11	21	4	36	1
Campos, Julio, Cle.	.875	4	7	14	3	24	3
Carroll, Wes, Cle.	1.000	2	2	4	0	6	0
Clapinski, Chris, B.C.	1.000	3	5	7	0	12	0
Collins, Mike, V.B.	.967	57	95	143	8	246	27
Cooper, Sam, Day.	.929	6	6	7	1	14	1
Deschaine, James, Day.	.932	57	100	147	18	265	23
German, Franklin, Day.	.857	2	3	3	1	7	1
Grice, Daniel, Day.	.940	19	27	36	4	67	6
Hannahan, Buzz, Cle.	.922	27	31	63	8	102	8
Hawthorne, Kyle, F.M.	.897	9	7	19	3	29	4
Hernandez , Anderson, Lak.	.917	7	15	18	3	36	6
Hill, Bobby, St.L.	.947	19	24	65	5	94	14
Hitchcox, Brian, Cle.	1.000	1	0	3	0	3	1
Hodge, Kevin, F.M.	.923	3	5	7	1	13	1
Hooper, Clay, Tam.	.959	79	111	237	15	363	37
Jackson, Brandon, Tam.	.939	53	69	148	14	231	29
Jaramillo, Milko, V.B.	.960	44	73	121	8	202	17
Jimenez, Carlos, Lak.	.000	1	0	0	0	0	0
Jones, Jack, Day.	1.000	3	3	7	0	10	0
Keene, Kurt, Dun.	.789	3	4	11	4	19	4
Machado, Andy, Cle.	.962	82	152	251	16	419	58
Martinez, Dionnar, Day.	.915	9	19	24	4	47	6
Martinez, Ramon, Day.	.918	34	50	96	13	159	27
Mayorson, Manuel, Dun.	.930	10	13	27	3	43	6
Meadows, Randy, Day.	.909	2	3	7	1	11	0
Medrano, Jesus, B.C.	.988	21	27	55	1	83	5
Melucci, Lou, Jup.	.951	13	10	29	2	41	6
Miller, Eric, Jup.	.909	7	5	26	3	33	1
Navarro, Mandy, Day.	.667	3	1	1	1	3	0
Nelson, Reggie, V.B.	.935	24	42	74	8	124	12
Nottlos, Jeff, Tam.	.905	5	5	14	2	21	1
Nunez, Manuel, V.B.	.905	14	20	18	4	42	2
Olivares, Teuris, Tam.	1.000	4	3	6	0	9	2
Perkins, Kevin, B.C.	.939	9	15	16	2	33	8
Phillips, Brandon, Jup.	.930	55	88	152	18	258	28
Reyes, Ambiorix, Cle.	.969	26	46	78	4	128	26
Rodriguez, Luis, F.M.	.959	68	122	228	15	365	55
Rouse, Michael, Dun.	.975	23	51	64	3	118	16
Sanchez, Freddy, Sar.	.944	69	94	195	17	306	42
Schrager, Tony, Day.	.946	12	15	38	3	56	3
Sequea, Jorge, Lak.	.930	33	59	74	10	143	18
Shipp, Brian, St.L.	1.000	2	1	1	0	2	0
Stafford, Mike, Tam.*	1.000	1	1	0	0	1	0
Stevens, Tony, F.M.	.945	65	81	213	17	311	36
Swenson, Leland, Char.	.850	10	11	23	6	40	5
Terhune, Mike, St.L.	.909	2	3	7	1	11	0
Theriot, Ryan, Day.	.944	30	42	76	7	125	13
Ugueto, Luis, B.C.	.946	107	167	339	29	535	74
Valdez, Wilson, Jup.	.971	64	102	166	8	276	24
Warriax, Brandon, Char.	.953	97	135	294	21	450	46
Williams, Brady, Sar.	.875	17	21	42	9	72	7
Zech, Scott, Jup.	.778	6	3	4	2	9	0

OUTFIELDERS

Player, Team	Pct.	G	PO	A	E	TC	DP
Abbott, Jeff, B.C.*	1.000	3	3	0	0	3	0
Acuna, Ron, St.L.	.980	27	47	1	1	49	0
Aguila, Chris, B.C.	.984	73	175	4	3	182	1
Alvarez, Nick, V.B.	.986	47	67	2	1	70	1
Anderson, Jon, Sar.	1.000	3	4	0	0	4	0
Angell, Rick, Char.	1.000	45	70	0	0	70	0
Baker, Derek, Lak.	.000	1	0	0	0	0	0
Barningham, Steve, Char.	.982	67	102	8	2	112	1
Baron, Brian, F.M.	.986	49	68	1	1	70	0
Bass, Kevin, Day.	.944	53	82	2	5	89	0
Bates, Fletcher, St.L.	.991	57	102	5	1	108	0
Bay, Jason, Jup.	.963	36	75	4	3	82	1
Blakely, Darren, Tam.	.988	86	153	8	2	163	1
Bolivar, Papo, F.M.	.944	14	16	1	1	18	1
Botts, Jason, Char.	1.000	3	7	0	0	7	0
Burns, Pat, St.L.*	1.000	3	1	0	0	1	0
Bush, Brian, Cle.	1.000	4	7	0	0	7	0
Bush, Darren, Cle.	1.000	19	26	1	0	27	0

Player, Team	Pct.	G	PO	A	E	TC	DP
Cadiente, Brett, Char.*	.986	67	136	2	2	140	0
Callahan, Dave, B.C.*	.941	9	15	1	1	17	0
Camilo, Juan, Lak.	.982	52	104	6	2	112	1
Carter, Shannon, Dun.*	.944	46	81	3	5	89	0
Chapman, Scott, Day.	.952	11	20	0	1	21	0
Chen, Chin-Feng, V.B.	1.000	11	19	3	0	22	2
Deitrick, Jeremy, Cle.	.846	7	11	0	2	13	0
Deschaine, James, Day.	.926	18	23	2	2	27	1
Dina, Allen, St.L.	.957	13	22	0	1	23	0
Downing, Brad, Lak.	.977	34	41	1	1	43	0
Downing, Phil, Jup.*	.988	65	155	5	2	162	3
Edwards, John, F.M.	.926	21	23	2	2	27	1
Elwood, Brad, Tam.	1.000	1	1	0	0	1	0
Evre, Willie, F.M.	.000	1	0	0	0	0	0
FELICIANO, Jesus, V.B.*	1.000	111	276	8	0	284	1
Ferrand, Frank, B.C.*	.885	27	18	5	3	26	0
Ford, Lew, F.M.	.993	66	140	6	1	147	1
Foster, Quincy, B.C.	.959	40	84	9	4	97	0
Garbe, B.J., F.M.	.972	127	235	9	7	251	1
Garcia, Douglas, Char.*	.965	125	232	13	9	254	4
Garcia, Luis, Sar.	1.000	10	17	2	0	19	0
German, Franklin, Day.	.925	57	92	7	8	107	1
Gingrich, Troy, Jup.*	1.000	63	122	4	0	126	2
Giron, Alejandro, Cle.	.975	108	181	16	5	202	2
Gomez, Ramon, Cle.	1.000	16	42	1	0	43	0
Goodman, Scott, B.C.*	1.000	27	35	2	0	37	1
Graham, Jess, Sar.*	.971	15	27	6	1	34	0
Gross, Gabe, Dun.	.930	35	64	2	5	71	0
Grove, Jason, Tam.*	1.000	1	2	0	0	2	0
Guerrero, Hector, V.B.*	.960	26	48	0	2	50	0
Hawthorne, Kyle, F.M.	.000	1	0	0	0	0	0
Headley, Justin, Sar.*	.972	102	237	8	7	252	3
Hensley, Anthony, Cle.	.957	12	21	1	1	23	0
Hicks, Scott, B.C.	1.000	2	6	0	0	6	0
Hill, Bobby, St.L.	.000	1	0	0	0	0	0
Hill, Willy, B.C.*	1.000	8	9	0	0	9	0
Hitchcox, Brian, Cle.	.000	1	0	0	0	0	0
Hodge, Kevin, F.M.	1.000	5	3	1	0	4	1
Hooper, Clay, Tam.	1.000	3	3	2	0	5	0
Huff, B.J., St.L.	1.000	18	21	0	0	21	0
Jackson, Nick, Day.	.983	129	279	6	5	290	1
James, Kenny, Jup.	.985	74	196	5	3	204	1
Jaramillo, Milko, V.B.	1.000	1	1	0	0	1	0
Jenkins, Brian, St.L.	.939	23	30	1	2	33	0
Jenkins, Neil, Lak.	1.000	21	23	1	0	24	0
Johnson, Jason, Cle.	1.000	45	89	8	0	97	3
Johnstone, Ben, Day.	.994	79	159	4	1	164	3
Jones, Jason, Char.	.000	1	0	0	0	0	0
Jones, Mitch, Tam.	.974	115	141	6	4	151	2
Jones, Terry, Jup.	1.000	4	8	0	0	8	0
Keene, Kurt, Dun.	.000	1	0	0	0	0	0
Kerner, Craig, Jup.	1.000	6	9	0	0	9	0
Koone, Chuck, Char.	.923	6	11	1	1	13	0
Kopitzke, Casey, Day.	.000	1	0	0	0	0	0
Kremblas, Mike, Dun.	.944	15	16	1	1	18	0
Langs, Ronte, V.B.	1.000	4	6	0	0	6	0
Lara, David, Lak.	.952	15	19	1	1	21	1
Leaumont, Jeff, Tam.*	1.000	2	1	0	0	1	0
Leer, David, Lak.	.958	43	66	2	3	71	1
Lipowicz, Nathan, V.B.	.982	30	54	1	1	56	0
Mabry, John, B.C.	1.000	4	4	0	0	4	0
Matthews, Lamont, V.B.*	.964	107	176	10	7	193	1
McKinney, Tony, Dun.	.971	123	234	4	7	245	1
McMillin, Brian, F.M.	.991	80	111	3	1	115	1
Meadows, Randy, Jup.	.000	1	0	0	0	0	0
Meadows, Tydus, Day.	.923	5	11	1	1	13	0
Medrano, Jesus, B.C.	1.000	1	3	0	0	3	0
Melucci, Lou, Jup.	1.000	2	1	0	0	1	0
Morrow, Alvin, Dun.	.939	26	30	1	2	33	0
Nadeau, Rick, Sar.	.955	81	143	7	7	157	0
Nelson, Reggie, V.B.	1.000	5	4	0	0	4	0
Nettles, Jeff, Tam.	1.000	3	2	0	0	2	0
Nettles, Tim, Tam.	.889	8	7	1	1	9	0
Nicholson, Derek, Lak.	1.000	17	20	4	0	24	0
Nina, Amuarys, Char.	.978	93	132	2	3	137	0
Nix, Laynce, Char.*	1.000	9	16	0	0	16	0
Osborne, Steve, Tam.	1.000	6	6	1	0	7	0
Paciorek, Pete, V.B.*	.000	1	0	0	0	0	0
Padgett, Matt, B.C.*	.993	68	129	6	1	136	0
Padilla, Jorge, Cle.	.983	93	167	10	3	180	1
Payton, Jay, St.L.	1.000	2	5	1	0	6	0
Pearson, Shawn, Dun.	1.000	21	29	0	0	29	0
Perkins, Kevin, B.C.	1.000	7	15	0	0	15	0
Piercy, Mike, St.L.*	.889	5	8	0	1	9	0
Pride, Curt, Jup.	1.000	5	12	1	0	13	1
Raines, Tim, Jup.	1.000	3	2	0	0	2	0
Redman, Prentice, St.L.	.977	118	200	11	5	216	1
Reyes, Deurys, F.M.*	.993	87	140	4	1	145	2
Richardson, Corey, Lak.	.982	130	321	12	6	339	3
Rigsby, Randy, B.C.*	.949	90	165	2	9	176	0
Rodriguez, Carlos, Sar.	.958	127	267	8	12	287	0
Rodriguez, Mike, Dun.	1.000	4	5	0	0	5	0
Romano, Jason, Char.	1.000	3	10	0	0	10	0
Roneberg, Brett, B.C.*	.980	66	140	6	3	149	2
Ross, Cody, Lak.*	.984	126	227	23	4	254	3
Ruan, Wilken, Jup.	.931	72	170	8	7	101	1
Santana, Pedro, Tam.	.938	17	15	0	1	16	0
Schifano, Tony, V.B.	1.000	2	3	0	0	3	0
Seale, Marvin, St.L.	.995	103	197	3	1	201	0
Sisk, Aaron, Dun.	1.000	7	10	0	0	10	0
Sitzman, Jay, Cle.*	.974	117	222	4	6	232	1
Sledd, Aaron, Day.*	1.000	6	2	1	0	3	0
Soto, Jose, B.C.	1.000	2	7	0	0	7	0
Swenson, Leland, Char.	1.000	6	11	0	0	11	0
Tarasco, Tony, St.L.	1.000	2	2	0	0	2	0
Theodorou, Nick, V.B.	1.000	4	9	0	0	9	0
Thomas, Chuck, V.B.	.956	60	107	2	5	114	0
Thompson, Andy, Dun.	1.000	2	5	0	0	5	0
Thompson, Rich, Dun.	.989	108	247	11	3	261	3
Tucci, Pete, St.L.	.963	57	76	2	3	81	0
Tyson, Torre, Tam.	.984	31	60	0	1	61	0
Valdez, Angel, Tam.	.988	39	79	1	1	81	0
Vento, Mike, Tam.	.945	122	199	8	12	219	2
Victorino, Shane, V.B.	1.000	2	2	0	0	2	0
Villegas, Ernest, Char.	.500	1	1	0	1	2	0
Warren, Chris, Sar.	.981	83	151	5	3	159	0
Watson, Matt, Jup.	.982	107	204	11	4	219	3
Weekly, Chris, Dun.	1.000	3	6	1	0	7	1
Williams, Brady, Sar.	.000	1	0	0	0	0	0
Wise, Dewayne, Dun.*	1.000	25	66	3	0	69	1
Zieour, Neesan, Dun.	1.000	28	47	4	0	51	0
Zoccolillo, Peter, Day.	.957	76	105	6	5	116	0

CATCHERS

Player, Team	Pct.	G	PO	A	E	TC	DP	PB
Ackerman, Scott, Jup.	.985	68	423	35	7	465	4	6
Aracena, Sandy, V.B.	1.000	1	6	2	0	8	0	0
Bennett, Ryan, St.L.	.967	26	156	19	6	181	0	1
Blum, Greg, Jup.	.995	56	376	29	2	407	6	6
Brown, Jason, B.C.	.991	19	105	7	1	113	1	2
Cash, Kevin, Dun.	.979	80	481	88	12	581	5	18
Chiaffredo, Paul, Dun.	.993	20	124	14	1	139	3	5
Coleman, Andy, Tam.	.975	6	35	4	1	40	1	3
Curry, Chris, Day.	.972	4	30	5	1	36	0	0
Deitrick, Jeremy, Cle.	.978	27	203	22	5	230	1	5
Duarte, Justin, Cle.	.985	28	169	22	3	194	2	6
Duplissea, Bill, V.B.	.992	37	219	26	2	247	1	3
Edwards, John, F.M.	.976	60	340	60	10	410	3	13
Elwood, Brad, Tam.	.993	40	267	19	2	288	2	15
Fagan, Shawn, Dun.	.941	5	15	1	1	17	0	3
Figga, Mike, St.L.	.988	25	149	16	2	167	2	2
Flores, Javier, Char.	.985	19	116	13	2	131	1	2
Frick, Matt, B.C.	.988	41	237	20	3	260	5	12
Fuentes, Omar, Tam.	1.000	2	14	4	0	18	0	1
Gajewski, Matt, Char.	.923	2	11	1	1	13	0	0
Garland, Ross, Lak.	1.000	1	12	0	0	12	0	0
Goldbach, Jeff, Day.	.977	33	195	17	5	217	2	4
Gulledge, Kelley, F.M.	.990	53	350	41	4	395	7	9
Harper, Brandon, B.C.	.984	29	226	20	4	250	1	7
Hernandez, John, V.B.	.985	37	294	26	5	325	1	8
Huber, Justin, St.L.	1.000	2	23	0	0	23	0	1
Jacobson, Russ, Cle.	.992	85	572	67	5	644	7	21
Jaile, Chris, Char.	.980	30	228	23	5	256	4	4
Johannes, Todd, Jup.	.983	16	112	7	2	121	0	4
Jorgensen, Ryan, Day.	.986	40	302	47	5	354	6	0
Kellner, Ryan, V.B.	.984	66	550	73	10	633	6	11
Kopitzke, Casey, Day.	.983	36	259	22	5	286	3	0
Kremblas, Mike, Dun.	.981	25	137	16	3	156	2	2
Kropf, Andy, Lak.	1.000	23	124	14	0	138	2	5
Larned, Drew, Sar.	.978	66	424	30	10	464	2	16
Lush, Zach, B.C.	1.000	8	25	2	0	27	0	1
Malave, Jaime, St.L.	1.000	2	14	1	0	15	0	0
Martinez, Casey, Char.	1.000	3	14	0	0	14	0	0
McAffee, Josh, St.L.	.967	5	26	3	1	30	0	0

Player, Team	Pct.	G	PO	A	E	TC	DP	PB
Morales, Steve, B.C.	.983	45	267	28	5	300	2	9
Nelson, Reggie, V.B.	1.000	1	0	1	0	1	0	0
Osborne, Mark, F.M.	.989	12	87	7	1	95	0	3
PARRISH, Dave, Tam.	.992	104	812	89	7	908	7	34
Pena, Rodolfo, Sar.	.981	63	418	59	9	486	4	9
Probst, Alan, St.L.	.992	37	242	14	2	258	3	2
Ramos, Kelly, Sar.	.982	17	154	10	3	167	1	2
Ramsey, Brad, Day.	.988	33	228	21	3	252	0	10
Rapp, Travis, Char.	1.000	2	12	0	0	12	0	0
Riepe, Andy, Sar.	1.000	4	21	1	0	22	0	0
Rodriguez, Mike, Dun.	1.000	2	20	2	0	22	0	1
Rodriguez, Sammy, St.L.	.981	21	142	11	3	156	0	8
Rojas, Tom, Tam.	1.000	1	1	0	0	1	0	0
St. Pierre, Maxim, Lak.	.991	98	603	75	6	684	6	16
Santos, Juan, Lak.	.900	20	83	11	4	100	0	0
Smith, Ryan, St.L.	.984	31	168	15	3	186	4	1
Soto, Saul, V.B.	1.000	1	10	1	0	11	0	0
Torres, Frederick, Char.	.986	87	645	62	10	717	6	19
Torres, Gabby, F.M.	.995	26	170	23	1	194	3	9
Vargas, Inakel, Lak.	.979	7	45	2	1	48	1	1
Wallis, Jacob, Jup.	.714	2	5	0	2	7	0	1
Werth, Jayson, Dun.	1.000	9	66	7	0	73	1	1
Yepez, Jose, Dun.	1.000	2	1	0	0	1	0	0

PITCHERS

Player, Team	Pct.	G	PO	A	E	TC	DP
Abbott, David, Dun.	.929	10	3	10	1	14	0
Achilles, Matt, Day.	.824	16	6	8	3	17	0
Acosta, Manuel, Tam.	.857	2	1	5	1	7	0
Alston, Travis, Cle.	1.000	12	2	2	0	4	0
Ambrose, John, Sar.	.000	10	0	0	1	1	0
An, Byeong, Sar.*	.846	23	1	10	2	13	0
Anderson, Wes, B.C.	1.000	8	1	6	0	7	1
Aramboles, Ricardo, Tam.	.875	12	1	6	1	8	0
Arias, Pablo, Lak.	1.000	8	3	7	0	10	0
Arrojo, Rolando, Sar.	1.000	2	0	1	0	1	0
Arthurs, Shane, Jup.	.857	28	2	4	1	7	0
Artiles, Carlos, Tam.*	.500	5	0	1	1	2	0
Asencio, Miguel, Cle.	.917	20	16	17	3	36	0
Backsmeyer, Justin, Char.	.938	33	4	11	1	16	0
Bailey, Dave, Day.	1.000	34	2	7	0	9	0
Baisley, Brad, Cle.	.833	11	7	8	3	18	0
Baker, Brad, Sar.	.900	24	7	11	2	20	0
Bauer, Greg, V.B.	1.000	12	5	4	0	9	0
Beal, Andy, Tam.*	.882	17	5	25	4	34	1
Bean, Colter, Tam.	.875	32	3	4	1	8	1
Beckett, Josh, B.C.	.857	13	0	6	1	7	0
Beech, Matt, Char.*	1.000	1	0	1	0	1	0
Beltran, Frank, Day.	.875	21	8	13	3	24	0
Bennett, Steve, St.L.	1.000	7	1	6	0	7	0
Berry, Jon, V.B.	1.000	33	7	6	0	13	1
Dess, Steve, Lak.	1.000	33	3	5	0	8	0
Blanton, Jason, Day.	1.000	6	3	1	0	4	0
Bohannon, Gary, St.L.	1.000	15	1	8	0	9	1
Borrell, Danny, Tam.*	.977	22	12	31	1	44	0
Bowe, Brandon, B.C.	.833	42	2	8	2	12	1
Bradley, Ryan, Tam.	1.000	7	1	1	0	2	0
Braswell, Bryan, St.L.*	.750	4	1	2	1	4	0
Bridges, Donnie, Jup.	1.000	1	1	0	0	1	0
Brooks, Frank, Cle.*	1.000	37	5	13	0	18	1
Bruback, Matt, Day.	.800	14	5	7	3	15	0
Burnett, A.J., B.C.	1.000	2	0	1	0	1	0
Bye, Chris, Jup.	.750	19	1	2	1	4	0
Byrd, Paul, Cle.	1.000	4	6	3	0	9	0
Byron, Terry, B.C.	1.000	4	1	0	0	1	0
Caraballo, Angel, Dun.	1.000	12	0	2	0	2	0
Caraccioli, Lance, V.B.*	1.000	5	1	3	0	4	0
Carter, Ryan, Cle.*	.800	11	1	3	1	5	0
Cedeno, Jovanny, Char.	.000	3	0	0	0	0	0
Cento, Tony, F.M.*	1.000	39	4	7	0	11	2
Cerda, Jaime, St.L.*	.929	28	5	8	1	14	0
Charron, Eric, Jup.	1.000	2	0	1	0	1	0
Chavez, Wilton, Day.	1.000	17	9	12	0	21	0
Chenard, Ken, St.L.	.000	2	0	0	0	0	0
Chipperfield, Calvin, Lak.	.880	24	9	13	3	25	0
Chulk, Vinny, Dun.	1.000	16	2	5	0	7	1
Cisar, Mark, Sar.	1.000	27	1	9	0	10	0
Clark, Chris, B.C.	.500	4	0	1	1	2	0
Claussen, Brandon, Tam.*	.857	8	1	11	2	14	0
Cole, Joey, St.L.	1.000	1	2	1	0	3	0
Collins, Pat, Jup.	1.000	33	6	18	0	24	2
Colson, Jason, Dun.	.000	1	0	0	0	0	0
Colyer, Steve, V.B.*	.900	24	4	14	2	20	0
Cone, David, Sar.	.000	1	0	0	0	0	0
Contreras, Jean, F.M.*	1.000	6	1	1	0	2	1
Cook, Andy, St.L.	1.000	16	2	8	0	10	0
Cook, Derrick, Char.	1.000	2	0	2	0	2	0
Corbin, John, Day.	1.000	10	6	2	0	8	2
Corcoran, Roy, Jup.	1.000	1	1	0	0	1	0
Cordero, Jesus, V.B.	.000	4	0	0	0	0	0
Corona, Ronnie, F.M.	.900	16	1	8	1	10	0
Corrado, Matthew, Lak.	.900	16	5	4	1	10	0
Croushore, Rich, St.L.	.000	2	0	0	0	0	0
Crumpton, Chuck, Jup.	1.000	3	1	2	0	3	0
Cueto, Jose, Day.	.800	6	2	2	1	5	0
Darrell, Tommy, Jup.	.800	11	1	3	1	5	0
Dean, Aaron, Dun.	.770	97	1	10	4	19	1
De La Rosa, Jorge, Sar.*	1.000	12	0	3	0	3	0
De Paula, Julio, Tam.	.950	16	6	13	1	20	1
Devey, Phil, V.B.*	1.000	3	2	1	0	3	0
Dickinson, Rodney, Sar.	.500	29	0	3	3	6	0
Dickson, Jason, Dun.	1.000	4	0	1	0	1	0
Dimma, Doug, Dun.*	1.000	24	2	4	0	6	1
Dittfurth, Ryan, Char.	.811	27	7	23	7	37	0
Dominguez, Jose, Char.	.000	2	0	0	0	0	0
Dunn, Gerald, Lak.	.000	2	0	0	0	0	0
Dunning, Justin, St.L.	.765	39	3	10	4	17	1
Duplissea, Bill, V.B.	.000	1	0	0	0	0	0
Dzurilla, Mike, Day.	.000	1	0	0	0	0	0
Eckenstahler, Eric, Lak.*	1.000	4	0	2	0	2	0
Edmondson, Brian, B.C.	1.000	16	0	5	0	5	1
Elmore, Chris, Sar.*	.833	17	2	8	2	12	1
Eppeneder, James, Day.*	.909	42	3	7	1	11	0
Eyre, Willie, F.M.	.957	32	13	9	1	23	0
Farizo, Brad, B.C.	.909	9	1	9	1	11	0
Feliciano, Jesus, V.B.*	.000	2	0	0	0	0	0
Ferrari, Anthony, Jup.*	1.000	51	2	12	0	14	1
Figueroa, Carlos, Char.*	.824	44	2	12	3	17	1
Fischer, Mike, V.B.	1.000	26	1	1	0	2	0
Fisher, Marc, Day.	1.000	2	2	0	0	2	0
Fisher, Pete, F.M.	.957	31	9	13	1	23	1
Hohr, Adam, F.M.*	1.000	21	3	12	0	15	1
Horie, Bryce, Sar.	.000	2	0	0	0	0	0
Fontana, Tony, Sar.	.833	9	2	8	2	12	1
Foote, Joe, F.M.	1.000	17	8	6	0	14	0
Ford, Matt, Dun.*	.889	13	5	3	1	9	0
Frachiocur, Zach, Day.	.667	22	3	1	2	6	0
Franco, Martire, Cle.	.897	26	17	18	4	39	0
Frederick, Kevin, F.M.	1.000	9	1	2	0	3	0
Freed, Mark, Day.*	.926	23	4	21	2	27	1
Fry, Justin, Cle.	.909	30	5	5	1	11	0
Gagliano, Steve, Day.	.750	17	2	1	1	4	0
Gamble, Jerome, Sar.	.000	3	0	0	0	0	0
Garcia, Reynaldo, Char.	.952	35	4	16	1	21	1
Garcia, Rosman, Tam.	.750	26	2	10	4	16	0
Gardner, Hayden, Char.	.000	1	1	0	0	1	0
George, Todd, Jup.	.000	1	0	0	0	0	0
German, Yon, St.L.*	1.000	2	0	2	0	2	1
Glaser, Eric, Sar.	1.000	37	7	12	0	19	0
Gomer, Jeramy, Day.*	1.000	24	6	7	0	13	0
Gomes, Tony, V.B.	1.000	11	3	3	0	6	0
Gonzalez, Gilberto, St.L.*	1.000	7	2	4	0	6	0
Good, Eric, Jup.*	.824	21	1	13	3	17	0
Gordon, Tom, Day.	1.000	2	0	1	0	1	0
Grace, Bryan, Tam.	.000	3	0	0	0	0	0
Gracesqui, Frank, Dun.*	1.000	4	0	1	0	1	0
Graham, Frank, Sar.	.952	39	5	15	1	21	2
Graham, Tom, Char.	1.000	1	1	2	0	3	0
Graves, Robert, Lak.*	1.000	15	4	5	0	9	1
Griffiths, Jeremy, St.L.	.967	23	8	21	1	30	0
Grilli, Jason, B.C.	1.000	3	0	3	0	3	1
Hadden, Randy, V.B.	1.000	34	4	12	0	16	2
Halladay, Roy, Dun.	1.000	13	0	2	0	2	0
Halvorson, Greg, St.L.	1.000	22	2	13	0	15	1
Hamann, Rob, Dun.	1.000	39	1	8	0	9	0
Hammons, Matt, Day.	.875	7	3	4	1	8	1
Hamulack, Tim, B.C.*	1.000	40	3	14	0	17	2
Hannah, Shawn, Lak.	.875	34	7	21	4	32	2
Harber, Ryan, B.C.*	.857	29	2	16	3	21	0
Haring, Brett, Char.*	1.000	17	3	9	0	12	1
Harrell, Tim, V.B.	1.000	2	0	1	0	1	0
Hawkins, Chad, Char.	1.000	4	1	5	0	6	1
Hee, Aaron, St.L.*	1.000	2	2	0	0	2	0
Heilman, Aaron, St.L.	.900	7	1	8	1	10	1
Henriquez, Hector, B.C.*	1.000	25	2	6	0	8	1

Player, Team	Pct.	G	PO	A	E	TC	DP
Herauf, Jeremy, Lak.	1.000	6	1	0	0	1	0
Hernandez, Orlando, Tam.	.000	2	0	0	0	0	0
Hoard, Brent, F.M.*	1.000	17	5	11	0	16	0
Hodge, Kevin, F.M.	.000	2	0	0	0	0	0
Houston, Ryan, Dun.	.929	26	5	21	2	28	2
Howard, Tom, F.M.*	.769	33	3	7	3	13	1
Hubbel, Travis, Dun.	.857	12	3	3	1	7	0
Huffaker, Mike, Char.	.917	43	3	8	1	12	1
Irabu, Hideki, Jup.	.000	3	0	0	0	0	0
Izquierdo, Hansel, B.C.	1.000	4	3	3	0	6	1
Jacob, Russell, Sar.	1.000	3	0	1	0	1	0
Jensen, Justin, Tam.*	.750	37	4	5	3	12	1
Johnson, Jeremy, Lak.	1.000	4	1	0	0	1	0
Jones, Bobby M., St.L.*	1.000	4	1	1	0	2	0
Jones, Jack, Day.	1.000	1	0	1	0	1	0
Jones, Kiki, Char.	.000	3	0	0	0	0	0
Joseph, Jake, St.L.	.906	25	8	21	3	32	0
Keelin, Chris, Cle.	1.000	46	7	7	0	14	1
Kegley, Chuck, Dun.	.857	26	9	9	3	21	1
Klepacki, Ed, Jup.	.905	26	2	17	2	21	2
Knowles, Mike, Tam.	.000	8	0	0	0	0	0
Kolb, Dan, Char.	1.000	7	0	2	0	2	0
Kosderka, Matt, Char.	1.000	7	0	2	0	2	0
Kremer, John, Tam.	.000	6	0	0	0	0	0
Kropf, Andy, Lak.	1.000	1	0	1	0	1	0
Krug, Dustin, Day.	.833	20	1	9	2	12	0
Kubes, Greg, Cle.*	1.000	20	6	10	0	16	1
Langone, Steve, V.B.	.927	23	15	23	3	41	0
Lara, Nelson, Sar.	.750	27	3	3	2	8	0
Lavigne, Tim, St.L.	1.000	4	0	1	0	1	0
Lee, Clifton, Jup.*	.786	21	1	10	3	14	1
Levan, Matt, B.C.*	.000	15	0	0	0	0	0
Lewis, Colby, Char.	.000	1	0	0	0	0	0
Lewis, Craig, Jup.	.857	17	2	4	1	7	0
Lima, Juan, Jup.	1.000	1	0	1	0	1	0
Lohrman, Dave, St.L.	.750	20	1	2	1	4	0
Lopez, Gustavo, B.C.	.500	6	1	1	2	4	0
Maberry, Mark, St.L.	1.000	3	1	1	0	2	0
Madson, Ryan, Cle.	.792	22	7	12	5	24	1
Majewski, Gary, V.B.	.929	23	7	19	2	28	1
Markwell, Diegomar, Dun.*	1.000	5	2	10	0	12	1
Marrero, Darwin, Jup.	.875	21	5	9	2	16	1
Marsonek, Sam, Tam.	.758	24	10	15	8	33	2
Martinez, Anastacio, Sar.	.818	25	6	12	4	22	0
Martinez, Dave, Tam.*	1.000	4	1	2	0	3	0
Martinez, Oscar, Tam.	1.000	29	1	3	0	4	0
Marx, Tommy, Lak.*	.963	28	5	21	1	27	1
Matthews, Barry, Lak.*	.917	22	3	8	1	12	1
Matthews, Lamont, V.B.*	.000	1	0	0	0	0	0
Maust, David, Jup.*	1.000	1	0	1	0	1	0
McAvoy, Jeff, Jup.	.941	46	3	13	1	17	0
McCasland, Ralph, Jup.*	.500	17	0	1	1	2	0
McClaskey, Tim, B.C.	1.000	26	4	0	0	4	0
McCrotty, Will, V.B.	1.000	20	1	0	0	1	0
McCurtain, Paul, B.C.	1.000	7	2	0	0	2	0
McDonald, Jon, F.M.	1.000	9	4	5	0	9	0
Meldahl, Todd, Cle.*	1.000	7	0	1	0	1	0
Messenger, Randall, B.C.	.944	18	9	8	1	18	0
Meyer, Dave, V.B.	1.000	12	0	6	0	6	0
Miller, Trever, Sar.*	1.000	3	1	2	0	3	0
Montalbano, Greg, Sar.*	1.000	17	3	11	0	14	0
Montero, Agustin, V.B.	.875	16	1	6	1	8	0
Montero, Jose, Char.	1.000	6	2	1	0	3	0
Montero, Oscar, Day.	1.000	11	1	1	0	2	0
Moreno, Edwin, Char.	.931	28	17	10	2	29	0
Moreno, Julio, St.L.	.700	20	4	3	3	10	0
Morse, Bryan, B.C.*	.952	37	5	15	1	21	3
Moser, Todd, B.C.*	1.000	2	0	3	0	3	0
Mosley, Eric, Tam.	.000	1	0	0	1	1	0
Murphy, Matt, Day.*	1.000	53	4	9	0	13	0
Musser, Neal, St.L.*	1.000	9	2	2	0	4	0
Nance, Shane, V.B.*	.833	21	3	7	2	12	1
Negrette, Richard, Day.	.000	4	0	0	1	1	0
Nettles, Tim, Tam.	.000	1	0	0	0	0	0
Ogea, Chad, Tam.	.750	2	0	3	1	4	0
Orloski, Joe, Dun.	1.000	46	6	5	0	11	1
Oropesa, Eddie, Cle.*	.000	2	0	0	0	0	0
Orr, Ben, Day.*	.667	5	0	2	1	3	0
Ortiz, Omar, B.C.	.913	28	7	14	2	23	1
Padilla, Juan, F.M.	.929	56	3	10	1	14	1
Padilla, Roy, B.C.*	1.000	6	1	2	0	3	1
Padua, Geraldo, Tam.	.000	1	0	0	0	0	0
Painter, Lance, Dun.*	1.000	5	0	2	0	2	0
Palki, Jeromy, F.M.	1.000	12	0	3	0	3	0
Parrish, Wade, V.B.*	1.000	23	4	6	0	10	1
Pautz, Brad, Cle.	.938	44	8	7	1	16	0
Pavano, Carl, Jup.	1.000	3	2	1	0	3	0
Payne, Jerrod, Dun.	.875	21	5	2	1	8	0
Pena, Juan, Sar.	.667	8	2	2	2	6	0
Perez, Frank, Cle.	.950	31	6	13	1	20	1
Perez, George, Dun.	.923	41	6	6	1	13	1
Perez, Julio, Jup.	1.000	34	1	8	0	9	1
Persails, Mark, Lak.	1.000	3	2	0	0	2	0
Persby, Andy, F.M.	.833	18	2	3	1	6	0
Pichardo, Hipolito, Sar.	.000	3	0	0	0	0	0
Politte, Cliff, Cle.	.000	7	0	0	0	0	0
Polk, Scott, St.L.	1.000	6	0	1	0	1	0
Porter, Scott, Dun.	1.000	3	1	1	0	2	0
Pridie, Jon, F.M.	.929	14	4	9	1	14	1
Proctor, Scott, V.B.	.846	15	3	8	2	13	0
Queen, Mike, St.L.*	.923	31	2	10	1	13	2
Ramirez, Victor, Char.	.000	3	0	0	0	0	0
Reames, Jay, Jup.	.700	12	5	2	3	10	0
Regilio, Nick, Char.	.938	11	4	11	1	16	0
Reimers, Cameron, Dun.	.882	22	10	20	4	34	0
Reyes, Eddy, B.C.	1.000	13	4	1	0	5	0
Reynolds, Josh, St.L.	.929	17	3	10	1	14	1
Reynoso, Edison, Tam.	.000	1	0	0	0	0	0
Riccobono, Rick, Sar.	.923	35	5	7	1	13	1
Richardson, Jason, F.M.	1.000	8	1	0	0	1	0
Riepe, Andy, Sar.	.000	1	0	0	0	0	0
Rijo, Fernando, V.B.	1.000	2	1	2	0	3	0
Rivas, Gabriel, Lak.	.000	1	0	0	0	0	0
Rivera, Homero, Lak.*	1.000	35	1	7	0	8	0
Roberts, Rick, V.B.*	.857	29	6	12	3	21	2
Robertson, Nathan, B.C.*	.818	19	2	16	4	22	2
Robinson, Dustin, Day.	.000	2	0	0	0	0	0
Rodney, Fernando, Lak.	.733	16	3	8	4	15	1
Rodriguez, Cristobal, Jup.	1.000	14	1	2	0	3	0
Rodriguez, George, Cle.	1.000	8	1	3	0	4	0
Rodriguez, Luis, Char.	1.000	5	0	1	0	1	0
Rodriguez, Ricardo, V.B.	.971	26	16	17	1	34	0
Rojas, Jose, V.B.	.000	1	0	0	0	0	0
Roller, Adam, Tam.	.923	51	4	8	1	13	0
Runser, Greg, Char.	.900	50	3	6	1	10	0
Russ, Christopher, Char.*	.882	13	5	10	2	17	0
Russo, Scott, Jup.*	.000	5	0	0	0	0	0
Saberhagen, Bret, Sar.	.000	1	0	0	0	0	0
Salyers, Jeremy, Jup.	.875	9	2	5	1	8	0
Sampson, Benj, F.M.*	1.000	15	2	19	0	21	0
Sams, Aaron, Sar.*	.000	2	0	0	0	0	0
Sandoval, Marcos, Dun.	1.000	5	0	1	0	1	0
Scheffer, Aaron, B.C.	1.000	3	1	2	0	3	0
Schoening, Brent, F.M.	1.000	17	6	12	0	18	1
Schroder, Chris, Jup.	1.000	10	3	2	0	5	0
SEIBEL, Phil, Jup.*	1.000	29	9	22	0	31	1
Seo, Jae, St.L.	1.000	6	1	3	0	4	0
Sergent, Joe, B.C.*	.960	27	5	19	1	25	0
Serrano, Elio, Cle.	.875	17	2	5	1	8	2
Serrano, Willy, Lak.	1.000	50	5	8	0	13	1
Shaffar, Ben, Day.	.857	19	5	7	2	14	0
Sheffield, Christopher, Dun.	.000	6	0	0	0	0	0
Silva, Doug, Char.	1.000	23	5	11	0	16	0
Simpson, Andre, V.B.	.714	5	4	1	2	7	0
Sismondo, Bobby, Cle.*	.750	6	1	2	1	4	0
Smith, Chuck, B.C.	.000	2	0	0	0	0	0
Smith, Clint, Lak.	1.000	20	1	2	0	3	0
Smith, Jason, Tam.	.000	1	0	0	0	0	0
Smith, Matt, Tam.*	1.000	11	1	6	0	7	0
Sneed, John, F.M.	.950	25	6	13	1	20	1
Snyder, Matt, Char.	1.000	1	0	0	0	0	0
Solano, Alex, Sar.	.750	39	2	4	2	8	0
Song, Seung, Sar.	1.000	8	3	3	0	6	0
Spear, Russ, Lak.	1.000	8	1	2	0	3	1
Squires, Matt, Cle.*	.000	4	0	0	0	0	0
Stafford, Mike, Tam.*	.500	4	0	1	1	2	0
Stamler, Keith, Char.	.947	23	6	12	1	19	0
Stanton, Timothy, Tam.*	1.000	26	1	9	0	10	1
Steele, Mike, Lak.	.875	15	2	5	1	8	2
Sturdy, Tim, F.M.	.918	28	12	33	4	49	2
Tejada, Frailyn, B.C.*	1.000	2	0	2	0	2	0
Tekavec, Nate, Lak.	1.000	18	3	9	0	12	1
Telford, Anthony, Jup.	.000	4	0	0	0	0	0
Tetz, Kris, Jup.	1.000	2	0	1	0	1	0
Thurman, Mike, Jup.	.000	1	0	0	0	0	0
Totten, Heath, V.B.	1.000	9	4	7	0	11	0

Player, Team	Pct.	G	PO	A	E	TC	DP
Traber, Billy, St.L.*	.941	18	13	19	2	34	0
Tranchina, Scott, Day.	1.000	42	7	11	0	18	1
Valdez, Domingo, Char.	1.000	9	5	2	0	7	0
Vanhekken, Andy, Lak.*	.957	19	6	16	1	23	3
Viera, Rolando, Sar.*	.500	6	0	1	1	2	0
Viole, Paul, St.L.	.870	46	7	13	3	23	3
Walker, Tyler, St.L.	.667	4	1	1	1	3	0
Walling, Dave, Tam.	1.000	4	4	2	0	6	0
Ward, Bryan, Sar.*	.000	1	0	0	0	0	0
Watson, Greg, Lak.	.800	57	3	9	3	15	0
Wayne, Justin, Jup.	.900	8	1	8	1	10	1
Webb, John, Day.	1.000	5	0	1	0	1	0
Weis, Brad, F.M.*	.667	17	1	1	1	3	0
Weslowski, Rob, St.L.	1.000	9	2	2	0	4	0

Player, Team	Pct.	G	PO	A	E	TC	DP
Whiteley, Shad, Tam.	.000	9	0	0	0	0	0
Wiggins, Scott, Tam.*	1.000	36	5	8	0	13	0
Williams, Adam, V.B.*	.750	10	2	1	1	4	0
Witte, Lou, Tam.	1.000	29	0	3	0	3	0
Woodards, Orlando, Dun.-B.C.	.800	26	4	4	2	10	2

PITCHERS WITH TWO OR MORE TEAMS

Player, Team	Pct.	G	PO	A	E	TC	DP
Woodards, Orlando, Dun.	.714	17	3	2	2	7	2
Woodards, Orlando, B.C.	1.000	9	1	2	0	3	0

The following players appeared only as designated hitter, pinch-hitter or pinch runner: A. Brown, dh, ph, pr; R. Brown, dh; Everett, dh; McNamara, dh; Nowlin, dh, ph; Oliver, dh, ph, pr; Santiago, dh, ph, pr; Wilkerson, dh.

LEAGUE CHAMPIONS

Year	Team	Pct.
1919—	Sanford*	.605
	Orlando*	.703
1920—	Tampa	.654
	Tampa	.722
1921—	Orlando	.635
1922—	St. Petersburg	.503
	St. Petersburg	.618
1923—	Orlando	.667
	Orlando	.678
1924—	Lakeland	.695
	Lakeland	.683
1925—	St. Petersburg	.667
	Tampa†	.696
1926—	Sanford	.647
	Sanford	.623
1927—	Orlando†	.600
	Miami	.661
1928-35—Did not operate.		
1936—	Gainesville	.542
	St. Augustine (4th)†	.492
1937—	Gainesville§	.616
1938—	Leesburg	.626
	Gainesville (2nd)‡	.615
1939—	Sanford§	.787
1940—	Daytona Beach	.619
	Orlando (4th)‡	.507
1941—	St. Augustine	.659
	Leesburg (4th)‡	.488
1942-45—Did not operate.		
1946—	Orlando§	.681
1947—	St. Augustine	.625
	Gainesville (2nd)‡	.584
1948—	Orlando	.643
	Daytona Beach (2nd)‡	.616
1949—	Gainesville	.635
	St. Augustine (3rd)‡	.556
1950—	Orlando	.629
	DeLand (3rd)‡	.590
1951—	DeLand§	.643
1952—	DeLand∞	.704
	Palatka (3rd)‡	.569
1953—	Daytona Beach†	.657
	DeLand	.703
1954—	Jacksonville Beach	.629
	Lakeland†	.594
1955—	Orlando	.671
	Orlando	.643

Year	Team	Pct.
1956—	Cocoa	.614
	Cocoa	.671
1957—	Palatka	.629
	Tampa†	.681
1958—	St. Petersburg	.732
	St. Petersburg	.681
1959—	Tampa	.591
	St. Petersburg†	.612
1960—	Lakeland	.731
	Palatka†	.614
1961—	Tampa†	.710
	Sarasota	.696
1962—	Sarasota	.689
	Fort Lauderdale†	.623
1963—	Sarasota	.645
	Sarasota	.667
1964—	Fort Lauderdale†	.629
	St. Petersburg	.594
1965—	Fort Lauderdale	.627
	Fort Lauderdale	.634
1966—	Leesburg ǀ	.781
	St. Petersburg	.700
1967—	St. Petersburg▲	.691
	Orlando	.638
1968—	Miami	.613
	Orlando◆	.579
1969—	Miami■	.606
	Orlando	.606
1970—	Miami▼	.662
	St. Petersburg	.600
1971—	Miami▼	.667
	Daytona Beach	.588
1972—	Miami•	.562
	Daytona Beach	.606
1973—	St. Petersburg††	.575
	West Palm Beach	.580
1974—	West Palm Beach††	.598
	Fort Lauderdale	.626
1975—	St. Petersburg††	.652
	Miami	.581
1976—	Tampa	.559
	Lakeland††	.536
1977—	Lakeland††	.616
	West Palm Beach	.583
1978—	Lakeland	.565
	Miami§	.539
1979—	Fort Lauderdale	.643

Year	Team	Pct.
	Winter Haven‡‡	.577
1980—	Daytona Beach	.628
	Fort Lauderdale††	.606
1981—	Fort Myers	.554
	Daytona Beach§§	.504
1982—	Fort Lauderdale§§	.621
	Tampa	.546
1983—	Daytona Beach	.634
	Vero Beach§§	.515
1984—	Tampa	.532
	Fort Lauderdale§§	.521
1985—	Fort Myers∞∞	.590
	Fort Lauderdale	.550
1986—	St. Petersburg∞∞	.647
	West Palm Beach	.593
1987—	Fort Lauderdale∞∞	.616
	Osceola	.576
1988—	Osceola	.606
	St. Lucie▲▲	.532
1989—	Port Charlotte▲▲	.540
	St. Petersburg	.540
1990—	West Palm Beach	.697
	Vero Beach▲▲	.585
1991—	Clearwater	.623
	West Palm Beach▲▲	.550
1992—	Sarasota	.639
	Lakeland◆◆	.530
1993—	St. Lucie	.600
	Clearwater§§	.556
1994—	Tampa§§	.606
	Brevard County	.561
1995—	Daytona§§	.644
	Fort Myers	.577
1996—	Tampa	.627
	St. Lucie§§	.534
1997—	St. Petersburg■ ■	.591
	Vero Beach	.511
1998—	Charlotte	.594
	St. Lucie■ ■	.515
1999—	Dunedin	.628
	Kissimmee■ ■	.578
2000—	Dunedin	.609
	Daytona■ ■	.547
2001—	Brevard County▼▼	.593
	Tampa▼▼	.554

*Split-season playoff abandoned after each team won three games. †Won split-season playoff. ‡Won four-club playoff. §Won championship and four-club playoff. ∞Won both halves of split season. ▲League divided into Eastern and Western divisions in split season. St. Petersburg and Orlando won both halves of split season; St. Petersburg won playoff. ◆League divided into Eastern and Western divisions. Miami won regular-season pennant on basis of highest won-lost percentage. Orlando won four-club playoff involving first two teams in each division. ■ League divided into Southern and Central divisions. Miami won playoff between division leaders. (NOTE—Pennant awarded to playoff winner in 1936.) ▼League divided into Eastern and Western divisions. Miami won regular-season pennant on basis of highest won-loss percentage, and also won four-club playoff involving first two teams in each division. •League divided into Eastern and Western divisions. Won four-club playoff involving first two teams in each division. ††League divided into Northern and Southern divisions. Won four-club playoff involving first two teams in each division. ‡‡League divided into Northern and Southern divisions. Same two clubs won both halves; won playoffs. §§Won split-season playoff. ∞∞League divided into Western, Central and Southern divisions. Won four-club playoff. ▲▲League divided into Eastern, Western and Central divisions; played split-season. Won six-club playoff. ◆◆League divided into Eastern, Western and Central divisions; played split-season. Won eight-club playoff. ■ ■ League divided into East and West divisions and played split season; won four-club playoff. ▼▼League divided into East and West divisions and played split season; teams were about to start final round of playoffs, but were declared co-champions when Professional Baseball declared a stoppage of play.

CLASS A Florida State League

MIDWEST LEAGUE

LEAGUE OFFICE

President
George H. Spelius
Address
P.O. Box 936
Beloit, WI 53512
Phone
608-364-1188

Teams (affiliation)
Beloit Snappers (Brewers)
Burlington Bees (Royals)
Cedar Rapids Kernels (Angels)
Clinton Lumber Kings (Expos)
Dayton Dragons (Reds)
Fort Wayne Wizards (Padres)
Kane County Cougars (Marlins)

Lansing Lugnuts (Cubs)
Michigan Battle Cats (Astros)
Peoria Chiefs (Cardinals)
Quad City River Bandits (Twins)
South Bend Silver Hawks
  (Diamondbacks)
West Michigan Whitecaps (Tigers)
Wisconsin Timber Rattlers (Mariners)

2001 FINAL STANDINGS

FIRST HALF

EASTERN DIVISION

Team	W	L	T	Pct.	GB
Dayton (Reds)	41	29	0	.586	...
Michigan (Astros)	38	30	0	.559	2.0
West Michigan (Tigers)	33	34	1	.493	6.5
South Bend (Diamondbacks)	32	35	0	.478	7.5
Fort Wayne (Padres)	29	40	0	.420	11.5
Lansing (Cubs)	27	43	0	.386	14.0

WESTERN DIVISION

Team	W	L	T	Pct.	GB
Kane County (Marlins)	47	21	0	.691	...
Wisconsin (Mariners)	42	26	0	.618	5.0
Quad City (Twins)	42	26	0	.618	5.0
Burlington (Royals)	30	36	0	.455	16.0
Cedar Rapids (Angels)	30	37	0	.448	16.5
Beloit (Brewers)	30	39	0	.435	17.5
Clinton (Expos)	28	39	1	.418	18.5
Peoria (Cardinals)	28	42	0	.400	20.0

SECOND HALF

EASTERN DIVISION

Team	W	L	T	Pct.	GB
Michigan (Astros)	44	25	0	.638	...
Dayton (Reds)	41	28	0	.594	3.0
South Bend (Diamondbacks)	38	31	0	.551	6.0
Lansing (Cubs)	38	32	0	.543	6.5
West Michigan (Tigers)	32	38	0	.457	12.5
Fort Wayne (Padres)	25	43	0	.368	18.5

WESTERN DIVISION

Team	W	L	T	Pct.	GB
Wisconsin (Mariners)	42	26	0	.618	...
Kane County (Marlins)	41	29	0	.586	2.0
Quad City (Twins)	38	31	0	.551	4.5
Beloit (Brewers)	37	32	0	.536	5.5
Cedar Rapids (Angels)	30	40	0	.429	13.0
Peoria (Cardinals)	29	39	0	.426	13.0
Burlington (Royals)	25	43	0	.368	17.0
Clinton (Expos)	23	46	0	.333	19.5

COMPOSITE

Team	K.C.	Wis.	Mich.	Day.	Q.C.	S.B.	Bel.	W.M.	Lan.	C.R	Peo.	Burl.	F.W.	Clin.	W	L	T	Pct.	GB
Kane County (Marlins)	...	5	5	5	7	5	6	5	4	8	12	8	7	11	88	50	0	.638	...
Wisconsin (Mariners)	7	...	5	4	5	4	11	5	5	6	8	5	7	12	84	52	0	.618	3.0
Michigan (Astros)	3	2	...	8	4	11	6	9	9	5	4	4	12	5	82	55	0	.599	4.0
Dayton (Reds)	3	4	7	...	2	6	6	10	10	6	7	4	11	6	82	57	0	.590	6.5
Quad City (Twins)	5	6	4	6	...	2	9	3	4	10	5	11	5	10	80	57	0	.584	12.5
South Bend (Diamondbacks)	2	3	5	9	5	...	3	8	5	5	8	5	8	4	70	66	0	.515	13.0
Beloit (Brewers)	7	6	2	2	4	5	...	7	6	5	6	6	4	7	67	71	0	.486	14.0
West Michigan (Tigers)	3	3	6	5	4	7	1	...	10	5	5	7	6	3	65	72	1	.474	15.0
Lansing (Cubs)	4	3	6	5	4	10	2	6	...	4	5	4	9	3	65	75	0	.464	17.0
Cedar Rapids (Angels)	3	6	3	2	1	3	7	3	4	...	6	10	4	8	60	77	0	.438	19.0
Peoria (Cardinals)	5	7	4	1	7	0	4	3	3	7	...	5	5	6	57	81	0	.413	19.0
Burlington (Royals)	5	6	2	4	2	3	6	1	4	8	7	...	3	4	55	79	0	.410	23.5
Fort Wayne (Padres)	1	1	3	4	3	6	4	9	6	4	2	5	...	6	54	83	0	.394	24.0
Clinton (Expos)	2	0	3	2	9	4	6	3	5	4	6	5	2	...	51	85	1	.375	25.5

Quad City's home games played in Davenport, Iowa; Kane County's home games played in Geneva, Ill.; Michgan's home games played in Battle Creek, Mich.; West Michigan's home games played in Comstock Park, Mich.

Major league affiliations in parentheses.

PLAYOFFS: Dayton defeated Lansing two games to none; Kane County defeated Beloit two games to none; South Bend defeated Michigan two games to none; Wisconsin defeated Quad City two games to none; Kane County defeated Wisconsin two games to none; South Bend defeated Dayton two games to none. Note: Kane County led South Bend one game to none and was declared Midwest League Champion due to stoppage of play in professional baseball.

REGULAR-SEASON ATTENDANCE: Beloit, 69,682; Burlington, 54,564; Cedar Rapids, 132,722; Clinton, 70,106; Dayton, 578,578; Fort Wayne, 239,112; Kane County, 523,222; Lansing, 404,429; Michigan, 66,088; Peoria, 144,772; Quad City, 129,961; South Bend, 188,404; West Michigan, 422,892; Wisconsin, 207,823. Total—3,232,355. Playoff (13 games)—29,764. Midwest League All-Star Game—8,901.

MANAGERS: Beloit, Don Money; Burlington, Joe Szekely; Cedar Rapids, Tyrone Boykin; Clinton, Steve Phillips; Dayton, Donnie Scott; Fort Wayne, Tom Lawless (thru May 31) and Don Werner (June 1 thru end of season); Kane County, Russ Morman; Lansing, Julio Garcia; Michigan, John Massarelli; Peoria, Joe Hall; Quad City, Jeff Carter; South Bend, Steve Scarsone; West Michigan, Brent Gates; Wisconsin, Gary Thurman.

ALL-STAR TEAM: 1B—Adrian Gonzalez, Kane County; 2B—Pedro Liriano, Wisconsin; 3B—Blair Barbier, Lansing; SS—Miguel Cabrera, Kane County; OF—Wily Mo Pena, Dayton; OF—Jamal Strong, Wisconsin; OF—Will Smith, Kane County; C—Garett Gentry, Michigan; DH (tie)—Samone Peters, Dayton and Jim Kavourias, Kane County; RHP—Chad Qualls, Michigan; LHP—Luke Lockwood, Clinton; RH Relief pitcher—Henry Bonilla, Quad City; LH Relief pitcher—Feranc Jongejan, Lansing; Most Valuable Player—Adrian Gonzalez, Kane County; Prospect of the Year—Adrian Gonzalez, Kane County; Manager of the Year—Russ Morman, Kane County.

TEAM

Team	Avg.	G	TPA	AB	R	H	TB	2B	3B	HR	RBI	SH	SF	HP	BB	IBB	SO	SB	CS	GDP	LOB	ShO	Slg.	OBP
Michigan	.273	137	5251	4628	764	1264	2006	259	54	125	674	17	37	71	498	23	1033	222	67	91	938	4	.433	.350
Wisconsin	.271	136	5229	4622	688	1254	1804	248	40	74	610	40	52	84	431	12	946	245	98	72	973	5	.390	.341
Kane County	.271	138	5451	4779	767	1295	1961	268	37	108	690	20	51	86	515	14	899	120	59	106	1046	4	.410	.349
South Bend	.270	136	5124	4563	679	1232	1773	221	49	74	606	37	44	81	399	14	946	211	72	101	919	10	.389	.337
Lansing	.270	140	5316	4692	690	1266	1983	270	42	121	635	28	48	95	453	17	990	91	58	100	1000	9	.423	.343
Quad City	.262	137	5159	4641	666	1218	1779	239	32	85	589	42	50	13	413	12	880	114	49	105	1020	9	.383	.321
Clinton	.258	137	5210	4689	591	1208	1643	192	33	59	511	21	34	51	415	7	955	175	78	98	977	16	.350	.323
Beloit	.254	138	5246	4680	647	1191	1749	234	12	100	561	79	36	62	389	22	1012	93	40	80	952	9	.374	.318
Cedar Rapids	.251	137	5134	4608	639	1157	1685	227	20	87	552	56	34	14	422	8	1057	167	84	75	966	12	.366	.314
W. Michigan	.250	138	5271	4610	616	1152	1610	204	37	60	524	24	48	83	506	10	1009	205	78	95	1005	8	.349	.332
Burlington	.248	134	5066	4478	620	1109	1645	225	34	81	538	42	38	73	435	6	965	101	50	97	956	7	.367	.322
Dayton	.247	138	5221	4640	709	1145	1898	259	31	144	626	27	27	93	434	14	1241	119	63	73	901	3	.409	.322
Peoria	.247	138	5132	4566	599	1126	1692	253	32	83	514	46	42	51	427	8	1092	249	95	79	877	8	.371	.315
Fort Wayne	.244	137	5145	4556	560	1111	1583	224	19	70	496	36	40	59	454	10	1000	156	61	79	993	14	.347	.318

INDIVIDUAL

TOP QUALIFIERS FOR BATTING CHAMPIONSHIP

Minimum 378 plate appearances. *Lefthanded batter. †Switch-hitter.

Player, Team	Avg.	G	TPA	AB	R	H	TB	2B	3B	HR	RBI	SH	SF	HP	BB	IBB	SO	SB	CS	GDP	Slg.	OBP
Bay, Jason, Clin.	.362	87	373	318	67	115	182	20	4	13	61	1	2	4	48	0	62	15	2	4	.572	.449
Maule, Jason, Mich.*	.347	124	504	412	101	143	179	23	5	1	63	4	7	7	74	1	62	56	6	3	.434	.448
Sadler, Ray, Lan.	.341	94	408	378	74	129	192	27	3	10	50	1	4	3	22	3	58	18	7	3	.508	.378
Castellano, John, Wis.	.334	99	411	377	59	126	202	34	0	14	81	3	6	6	19	2	35	13	5	7	.536	.370
Ansman, Craig, S.B.	.330	97	396	345	73	114	215	30	4	21	82	0	6	16	29	2	85	4	1	5	.623	.402
Reese, Kevin, Ft.W.*	.329	125	524	459	84	151	232	30	6	13	73	2	4	5	54	3	62	30	10	5	.505	.402
Watson, Brandon, Clin.*	.327	117	525	489	74	160	200	16	9	2	38	3	3	1	29	0	65	33	20	6	.409	.364
Liriano, Pedro, Wis.	.326	113	487	442	76	144	190	28	3	4	47	2	6	7	30	2	50	65	20	5	.430	.373
Barbier, Blair, Lan.	.314	131	560	488	77	153	241	38	1	16	77	2	4	14	52	6	63	3	6	13	.494	.392
Campo, Mike, C.R.*	.313	100	435	358	69	112	159	20	3	7	46	3	5	26	43	0	65	21	11	1	.444	.419
Gonzalez, Adrian, K.C.*	.312	127	584	516	86	161	251	37	1	17	103	0	6	5	57	6	83	5	5	17	.486	.382
Roper, Zach, C.R.	.310	124	519	471	64	146	222	27	2	15	87	2	4	13	29	2	82	8	3	18	.471	.364
Tiffee, Terry, Q.C.†	.309	128	536	495	65	153	220	32	1	11	86	0	8	1	32	4	48	3	1	13	.444	.347
Morrissey, Adam, Lan.	.309	122	509	410	88	120	219	26	11	14	62	1	2	8	80	3	82	10	9	9	.524	.427
Bubela, Jaime, Wis.*	.304	132	578	530	90	161	230	27	12	6	68	1	2	1	44	4	116	34	13	5	.434	.357

NOTE: Jason Bay qualifies for the batting championship under section 10.23 of the Official Baseball Rules. He batted .362 in 373 plate appearances. By adding five at-bats to his actual total of 318, he would have an adjusted batting average of .356 and an adjusted total of 378 plate appearances, thereby making him the leading qualifier.

DEPARTMENTAL LEADERS: G—Pena, 135; AB—W. Smith, 535; R—Maule, 101; H—A. Gonzalez, 251; TB—A. Gonzalez, 251; 2B—Smitherman, 45; 3B—Bubela, Stanley, Guzman, Hall, 12 each; HR—Peters, 28; RBI—W. Pena, 113; SH—T. West, 26, SF—F. Johnson, 10; HP—K. West, 28; BB—Morris, 83; IBB—Gentry, 8; SO—Pena, 177; SB—Morris, 111; CS—C. Morris, 24; GIDP—Roper, 18; Slg.—Ansman, .623; OBP—Maule, .448.

ALL PLAYERS

*Lefthanded batter. †Switch-hitter.

Player, Team	Avg.	G	TPA	AB	R	H	TB	2B	3B	HR	RBI	SH	SF	HP	BB	IBB	SO	SB	CS	GDP	Slg.	OBP
Abruzzo, Jared, C.R.†	.241	87	373	323	41	78	128	20	0	10	53	0	1	5	44	2	104	1	1	3	.396	.340
Acevedo, Anthony, Mich.*	.259	120	508	429	74	111	190	35	4	12	70	0	3	7	69	3	130	21	5	3	.443	.368
Adames, Epidaro, C.R.	.238	53	223	202	16	48	61	11	1	0	17	4	1	7	9	0	46	2	3	5	.302	.292
Albright, Eric, Lan.	.000	35	0	0	1	0	0	0	0	0	0	0	0	0	0	0	0	0	0	0	.000	.000
Alfonzo, Eliezer, Bcl.	.277	106	424	397	52	110	184	28	2	14	48	3	8	13	13	0	65	0	1	10	.463	.311
Alvarez, Henrry, Bur.	.205	45	173	161	21	33	54	7	1	4	23	3	1	5	3	0	44	1	0	4	.335	.241
Amador, Jerry, W.M.	.221	81	311	289	24	64	85	7	1	4	31	1	1	5	15	0	47	4	3	8	.294	.271
Ambres, Chip, K.C.	.265	96	449	377	79	100	157	26	8	5	41	5	3	11	53	0	81	19	15	7	.416	.369
Ambrosini, Anthony, Clin.	.250	3	9	8	1	2	2	0	0	0	1	0	0	1	0	0	2	0	0	0	.250	.333
Ambrosini, Dominick, Clin.*	.194	67	272	252	19	49	59	8	1	0	21	0	2	1	17	1	58	3	4	7	.234	.246
Anderson, Bryan, Day.	.226	80	291	270	33	61	86	14	4	1	26	4	1	3	13	0	66	9	2	6	.319	.268
Anderson, Dennis, K.C.†	.236	78	298	242	43	57	93	14	2	6	35	2	3	14	37	0	45	2	3	6	.384	.365
Anderson, Syketo, Lan.*	.161	18	69	62	4	10	11	1	0	0	3	5	0	0	2	0	9	5	3	1	.177	.188
Anderson, Travis, Mich.	.000	32	1	0	1	0	0	0	0	0	0	0	0	0	1	0	1	0	0	0	.000	1.000
Andrianoff, Jon, Mich.	.184	14	47	38	5	7	8	1	0	0	1	0	0	1	8	0	12	3	1	1	.211	.340
Andujar, Elvin, Day	.188	5	17	16	2	3	3	0	0	0	1	0	0	0	1	0	6	1	0	1	.188	.235
Angel, Tony, Mich.	.260	65	236	219	35	57	88	16	0	5	26	0	3	6	8	1	30	3	1	5	.402	.301
Ansman, Craig, S.B.	.330	97	396	345	73	114	215	30	4	21	82	0	6	16	29	2	85	4	1	5	.623	.402
Arnerich, Tony, Mich.*	.162	11	41	37	0	6	8	2	0	0	3	0	1	0	3	0	9	0	0	1	.216	.220
Arroyo, Abner, Ft.W.*	.338	68	297	266	41	90	133	19	0	8	38	1	1	1	28	0	62	1	4	6	.500	.402
Ayala, Elio, Bel.	.265	101	453	400	65	106	129	19	2	0	25	9	3	7	34	2	61	11	2	7	.323	.331
Ayala, Odannys, Bur.	.211	53	200	180	16	38	60	6	5	2	16	2	1	0	17	0	25	2	1	7	.333	.278
Barbier, Blair, Lan.	.314	131	560	488	77	153	241	38	1	16	77	2	4	14	52	6	63	3	6	13	.494	.392
Bay, Jason, Clin.	.362	87	373	318	67	115	182	20	4	13	61	1	2	4	48	0	62	15	2	4	.572	.449
Belcher, Brian, Bel.*	.326	38	161	144	23	47	59	6	0	2	23	1	0	1	15	1	16	0	1	6	.410	.394
Berroa, Cristian, Mich.†	.325	36	137	123	19	40	50	4	0	2	23	1	1	5	7	0	13	5	7	4	.407	.382
Bitter, Jarrod, Ft.W.	.205	26	99	83	6	17	26	3	0	2	8	0	0	8	8	1	26	1	0	2	.313	.333
Blasi, Blake, Lan.†	.272	61	262	228	34	62	72	7	0	1	19	1	0	3	33	0	29	7	4	4	.316	.364
Boitel, Rafael, Q.C.†	.238	116	525	462	65	110	138	15	5	1	32	7	8	5	43	0	87	36	15	6	.299	.305
Bone, Blake, Wis.*	.218	78	302	257	40	56	98	19	1	7	36	3	3	2	37	0	50	6	2	7	.381	.318
Bowen, Rob, Q.C.†	.255	106	429	385	47	98	174	18	2	18	70	2	3	2	37	2	112	4	0	11	.452	.321
Boyd, Shaun, Peo.	.282	81	316	277	42	78	109	12	2	5	27	2	3	1	33	0	42	20	3	7	.394	.357
Boyer, Bret, Clin.†	.250	107	448	420	58	105	137	21	1	3	23	2	1	3	22	0	90	29	5	7	.326	.291

CLASS A Midwest League

Player, Team	Avg.	G	TPA	AB	R	H	TB	2B	3B	HR	RBI	SH	SF	HP	BB	IBB	SO	SB	CS	GDP	Slg.	OBP
Brand, Kevin, S.B.†	.243	14	42	37	3	9	12	1	1	0	3	2	0	1	2	0	5	2	0	1	.324	.300
Brandes, Landon, Peo.	.205	47	175	161	20	33	54	10	1	3	12	2	1	0	11	0	38	2	3	3	.335	.254
Brito, Obispo, Bel.	.224	21	81	76	5	17	22	5	0	0	5	1	1	2	1	0	16	1	0	2	.289	.250
Brooks, Jeff, S.B.	.169	18	70	65	2	11	15	2	1	0	8	0	0	2	3	0	24	0	0	0	.231	.229
Bubela, Jaime, Wis.*	.304	132	578	530	96	161	230	27	12	6	68	1	2	1	44	4	116	34	13	5	.434	.357
Buckley, Brandon, Mich.	.203	67	218	197	17	40	50	7	0	1	14	0	1	1	19	0	31	0	1	6	.254	.275
Burke, Chris, Mich.	.300	56	265	233	47	70	102	11	6	3	17	2	1	3	26	2	31	21	8	3	.438	.376
Cabrera, Miguel, K.C.	.268	110	465	422	61	113	161	19	4	7	66	1	3	2	37	2	76	3	0	10	.382	.328
Cahill, Jonathan, C.R.	.273	44	185	172	21	47	57	7	0	1	13	5	0	0	8	0	28	2	2	1	.331	.306
Calitri, Mike, Day.	.249	97	380	317	57	79	145	18	0	16	44	1	2	3	57	2	98	1	3	4	.457	.367
Cameron, Antoine, Lan.*	.265	94	388	343	47	91	142	20	2	9	47	2	3	3	37	3	87	2	2	4	.414	.339
Campana, Wandel, Day.	.264	79	321	295	46	78	103	19	3	0	23	10	2	4	10	0	41	8	5	4	.349	.296
Campo, Mike, C.R.*	.313	100	435	358	69	112	159	20	3	7	46	3	5	26	43	0	65	21	11	1	.444	.419
Candelaria, Scott, Bel.	.250	69	279	256	25	64	81	11	0	2	27	7	1	2	12	1	50	3	4	3	.316	.287
Carroll, Mark, Wis.	.230	84	317	257	34	59	72	10	0	1	27	2	3	10	45	0	63	2	4	5	.280	.362
Castellano, John, Wis.	.334	99	411	377	59	126	202	34	0	14	81	3	6	6	19	2	35	13	5	7	.536	.370
Castro, Renato, Ft.W.	.158	14	41	38	1	6	8	2	0	0	2	0	0	1	2	0	8	1	0	4	.211	.220
Cedeno, Ronny, Lan.	.196	17	59	56	9	11	20	4	1	1	2	0	0	1	2	0	18	0	2	1	.357	.237
Ceriani, Matt, Bel.	.266	22	90	79	8	21	27	3	0	1	6	1	1	1	8	1	16	2	0	1	.342	.337
Choo, Shin-soo, Wis.*	.462	3	15	13	1	6	6	0	0	0	3	0	0	1	1	0	3	2	0	0	.462	.533
Clark, Daryl, Bel.*	.283	133	579	501	76	142	233	24	2	21	92	2	8	7	61	3	135	4	5	8	.465	.364
Cleveland, Russ, W.M.	.244	61	221	205	18	50	65	9	0	2	13	0	0	3	13	0	51	0	3	3	.317	.299
Cooper, Sam, Lan.†	.273	3	11	11	0	3	3	0	0	0	1	0	0	0	0	0	1	0	1	0	.273	.273
Cordova, Ben, Bur.*	.294	108	426	384	58	113	161	30	0	6	44	0	2	2	38	0	55	7	2	8	.419	.359
Cotto, Luis, Bur.	.147	46	168	143	14	21	21	0	0	0	9	2	0	5	17	0	41	2	2	4	.147	.261
Coulie, Jason, C.R.	.242	117	473	434	49	105	160	22	3	9	50	4	2	10	23	0	105	9	7	7	.369	.294
Cowan, Justin, Bur.	.219	88	353	319	34	70	113	20	1	7	38	1	4	6	23	0	63	0	1	4	.354	.281
Curry, Chris, Lan.	.116	29	110	95	7	11	15	4	0	0	8	1	3	2	9	0	21	0	0	5	.158	.202
Daubert, Jake, Wis.*	.256	97	395	351	43	90	121	19	0	4	52	3	3	5	33	0	74	4	3	3	.345	.327
Davis, Michael, Ft.W.	.272	80	334	294	40	80	112	16	2	4	45	0	2	10	28	1	57	10	4	12	.381	.353
Day, Nick, Ft.W.	.000	5	13	12	0	0	0	0	0	0	0	0	1	0	0	0	3	0	0	0	.000	.000
Decola, Daniel, Q.C.	.218	34	118	101	6	22	29	4	0	1	13	2	1	8	6	1	23	0	0	1	.287	.310
De La Cruz, Eric, Bel.	.201	67	237	224	20	45	56	8	0	1	14	5	2	2	4	0	41	3	1	6	.250	.220
Delgado, Jorge, S.B.	.302	101	409	348	53	105	147	26	2	4	50	1	2	12	46	0	43	0	2	15	.422	.400
De Los Santos, Hector, Q.C.	.226	99	369	336	35	76	88	4	4	0	29	8	4	7	14	0	58	25	11	11	.262	.269
De Los Santos, Nelson, Bel.†	.196	28	113	107	9	21	27	3	0	1	10	3	1	0	2	0	22	0	2	0	.252	.209
Demarco, Matt, K.C.*	.252	77	256	222	25	56	66	6	2	0	22	4	6	4	20	0	31	9	2	5	.297	.317
Dempsey, Nick, Clin.	.304	34	126	115	16	35	44	6	0	1	18	0	0	3	8	0	29	0	0	1	.383	.365
Detillion, Jamie, W.M.*	.000	48	1	1	0	0	0	0	0	0	0	0	0	0	0	0	1	0	0	0	.000	.000
Diaz, Aneuris, Peo.	.239	120	442	418	43	100	141	22	5	3	43	3	3	2	16	0	122	10	8	4	.337	.269
Docen, Jose, Clin.†	.246	87	337	301	28	74	86	12	0	0	32	5	4	2	25	0	54	11	14	6	.286	.304
Dogero, Matt, Peo.	.235	17	38	34	3	8	12	1	0	1	3	0	0	0	3	0	6	2	1	0	.353	.297
Doudt, Anthony, C.R.	.186	39	140	129	13	24	40	7	0	3	15	6	0	2	3	0	32	1	1	3	.310	.216
Downing, Brad, W.M.*	.266	49	171	154	19	41	64	4	2	5	23	1	0	1	15	3	18	0	3	2	.416	.335
Downing, Phil, Clin.*	.252	37	147	123	18	31	59	4	6	4	20	1	1	0	22	1	35	2	0	2	.480	.363
Drew, J.D., Peo.*	.545	3	12	11	3	6	8	2	0	0	0	0	0	0	1	0	0	0	0	1	.727	.583
Dubois, Jason, Lan.	.296	118	508	443	76	131	249	28	9	24	92	2	3	14	46	2	120	1	2	8	.562	.377
Duncan, Chris, Peo.*	.306	80	337	297	44	91	157	23	2	13	59	0	1	3	36	2	55	13	3	10	.529	.386
Duran, Frank, C.R.	.171	50	212	170	26	29	39	4	0	2	16	4	2	6	30	1	40	12	3	1	.229	.313
Durango, Ariel, Wis.†	.287	87	340	307	48	88	118	10	4	4	31	4	0	4	25	1	71	32	11	6	.384	.348
Durham, Miles, W.M.*	.218	68	290	257	29	56	68	6	3	0	20	6	1	1	25	0	74	33	7	4	.265	.289
Dusan, Joe, Wis.*	.233	119	430	378	49	88	130	19	1	7	52	1	8	2	41	0	100	4	3	6	.344	.305
Easterday, Matt, K.C.	.262	72	236	195	42	51	68	7	2	2	16	1	3	4	33	0	37	10	3	6	.349	.374
Edge, Dwight, S.B.	.232	46	184	164	15	38	51	5	1	2	18	1	1	2	16	0	42	5	2	0	.311	.306
Edwards, Dytarious, Ft.W.*	.214	69	250	220	35	47	51	4	0	0	6	5	1	0	24	0	50	23	5	2	.232	.290
Encarnacion, Edwin, Day.	.162	9	38	37	2	6	11	2	0	1	6	0	0	0	1	0	5	0	1	1	.297	.184
Epke, Brian, S.B.	.250	18	61	56	5	14	15	1	0	0	5	0	0	2	3	0	11	1	0	1	.268	.311
Espinosa, David, Day.†	.262	122	555	493	88	129	195	29	8	7	37	2	1	4	55	1	120	15	10	3	.396	.340
Eylward, Thomas, C.R.	.233	23	99	90	12	21	35	6	1	2	12	1	1	2	5	0	21	0	0	2	.389	.286
Faison, Vince, Ft.W.*	.200	41	163	140	14	28	36	5	0	1	8	1	1	3	18	1	35	10	3	4	.257	.302
Fatheree, Danny, Mich.	.296	9	32	27	5	8	14	4	1	0	3	1	0	1	3	0	6	0	0	1	.519	.355
Fatur, Brian, Peo.	.207	56	227	193	27	40	62	7	0	5	24	4	2	3	25	0	35	9	10	1	.321	.305
Fears, Chris, Ft.W.†	.251	84	307	263	30	66	76	5	1	1	19	7	2	5	30	1	53	20	7	4	.289	.337
Felix, Hersy, Bur.	.211	35	127	114	9	24	31	4	0	1	8	1	0	0	12	0	23	0	0	3	.272	.286
Fenster, Darren, Bur.	.287	97	405	356	47	102	127	19	0	2	45	5	5	6	33	0	63	1	3	4	.357	.353
Fera, Aaron, Peo.	.169	16	63	59	5	10	20	4	0	2	9	0	0	0	4	0	32	1	1	0	.339	.222
Ferrand, Frank, K.C.*	.290	85	323	297	43	86	128	20	2	6	45	2	3	3	17	2	49	3	1	1	.431	.331
Figueroa, Eduardo, Wis.	.204	15	56	49	6	10	13	1	1	0	5	0	0	2	5	0	11	2	1	1	.265	.304
Flom, Dan, Peo.	.210	41	119	105	12	22	31	6	0	1	7	1	1	3	9	1	33	2	1	0	.295	.288
Floyd, Dan, Wis.	.260	90	378	338	47	88	124	19	1	5	38	5	5	10	20	1	61	6	6	6	.367	.316
Floyd, Mike, Peo.	.215	83	276	246	26	53	68	9	0	2	23	6	5	2	17	0	62	18	9	3	.276	.267
Foreman, Julius, S.B.*	.311	61	256	212	47	66	82	6	5	0	16	2	0	0	42	3	25	23	7	1	.387	.425
Foster, Brian, Bel.	.146	36	139	123	14	18	38	8	0	4	9	5	0	1	10	0	55	0	0	2	.309	.216
Freeman, Corey, Wis.	.151	37	125	106	14	16	23	4	0	1	10	4	2	5	8	0	24	3	6	2	.217	.240
Friar, Roddy, Peo.	.165	36	106	91	10	14	19	5	0	0	5	1	0	2	18	0	38	0	1	2	.224	.324
Fulse, Sheldon, Wis.†	.220	80	297	255	38	56	88	16	5	2	17	2	2	7	31	0	73	21	3	3	.345	.319
Furmaniak, Jason, Ft.W.	.220	123	505	436	57	96	141	24	3	5	35	3	7	4	55	0	117	11	6	10	.323	.309
Gall, John, Peo.	.302	57	232	205	27	62	97	23	0	4	44	0	7	4	16	1	18	0	3	3	.473	.353
Gallo, Mike, Mich.*	.000	45	1	0	0	0	0	0	0	0	0	0	0	0	1	0	0	0	0	0	.000	1.000
Garabito, Vianney, Day.	.087	10	25	23	4	2	6	1	0	1	2	0	0	1	1	0	4	0	0	1	.261	.160
Garcia, Hector, Bel.	.265	109	421	404	43	107	143	14	2	6	37	4	2	2	9	0	71	20	6	7	.354	.283
Gemoll, Justin, Bur.	.272	128	552	482	78	131	194	27	3	10	70	3	4	13	50	0	90	5	1	14	.402	.353
Gentry, Garett, Mich.*	.299	98	410	358	62	107	203	18	3	24	103	0	5	8	39	8	45	5	0	9	.567	.376

Player, Team	Avg.	G	TPA	AB	R	H	TB	2B	3B	HR	RBI	SH	SF	HP	BB	IBB	SO	SB	CS	GDP	Slg.	OBP
Gettis, Byron, Bur.	.314	37	162	140	26	44	72	9	2	5	26	1	3	4	14	1	25	4	3	3	.514	.385
Gil, Jerry, S.B.	.215	105	383	363	40	78	108	14	5	2	31	8	0	4	8	0	103	19	7	12	.298	.240
Gonzalez, Adrian, K.C.*	.312	127	584	516	86	161	251	37	1	17	103	0	6	5	57	6	83	5	5	17	.486	.382
Gonzalez, Reggie, Q.C.	.225	51	183	173	23	39	70	11	1	6	23	1	3	1	5	0	30	2	0	3	.405	.247
Green, Andy, S.B.	.300	128	562	477	76	143	188	18	6	5	59	11	8	7	59	1	50	51	15	7	.394	.379
Gulledge, Kelley, Q.C.	.275	39	145	131	15	36	54	9	0	3	16	0	3	3	8	0	37	0	2	4	.412	.324
Gutierrez, Derrick, Wis.	.265	10	40	34	5	9	14	2	0	1	6	0	0	2	4	0	8	1	1	0	.412	.375
Guzman, Jon, Bur.	.236	121	458	411	58	97	172	12	12	13	46	5	2	4	36	0	155	34	11	7	.418	.302
Guzman, Juan, Bur.†	.240	54	189	171	20	41	55	9	1	1	13	4	0	1	13	0	64	4	4	1	.322	.297
Guzman, Robert, Q.C.*	.234	21	88	77	12	18	21	1	1	0	5	4	0	3	4	1	14	4	0	1	.273	.298
Hake, Travis, Bel.	.200	6	19	15	2	3	6	3	0	0	0	1	0	0	3	0	3	0	0	1	.400	.333
Hall, Victor, S.B.*	.275	113	481	415	82	114	151	13	12	0	39	3	4	7	52	0	71	60	15	4	.364	.362
Hamill, Ryan, Peo.	.264	110	413	371	44	98	151	23	0	10	45	2	3	4	33	0	62	2	2	8	.407	.328
Hamilton, Mark, Mich.*	.251	107	413	371	59	93	163	23	4	13	50	0	0	5	37	2	98	15	7	9	.439	.327
Hammock, Rob, S.B.	.248	34	140	125	16	31	44	3	2	2	14	1	0	0	14	0	21	5	6	2	.352	.324
Hammond, Derry, Bel.	.269	96	401	360	57	97	177	23	0	19	73	1	5	3	32	3	109	2	1	7	.492	.330
Hannahan, John, W.M.*	.318	46	198	170	24	54	68	11	0	1	27	0	1	1	26	0	39	4	2	5	.400	.409
Hargreaves, Brad, Day.	.222	7	22	18	4	4	5	1	0	0	2	0	1	0	3	0	4	0	0	0	.278	.318
Harris, Brendan, Lan.	.274	32	136	113	25	31	50	5	1	4	22	1	3	2	17	0	26	5	1	4	.442	.370
Harris, Josh, Lan.	.303	22	84	76	10	23	30	5	1	0	9	1	2	3	2	0	6	0	1	4	.395	.337
Hawes, Bobby, Day.	.188	25	77	69	8	13	19	2	2	0	6	2	0	2	4	0	14	1	2	2	.275	.253
Helquist, Jon, Mich.	.241	112	461	415	55	100	169	17	5	14	47	0	1	8	37	0	107	10	3	11	.407	.315
Hicks, Scott, K.C.*	.667	1	3	3	1	2	3	1	0	0	0	0	0	0	0	0	0	0	1	0	1.000	.667
Hill, Willy, K.C.*	.333	6	21	21	3	7	8	1	0	0	1	0	0	0	0	0	2	0	1	1	.381	.333
Hooper, Kevin, K.C.	.292	17	77	65	11	19	21	2	0	0	4	0	1	0	11	0	13	3	1	0	.323	.390
Houston, Tyler, Bel.*	.000	1	3	3	0	0	0	0	0	0	0	0	0	0	0	0	1	0	0	0	.000	.000
Hudson, Ben, Wis.	.349	14	49	43	4	15	16	1	0	0	6	1	1	1	3	0	12	0	0	0	.372	.396
Huguet, J.C., Day.	.224	38	133	107	10	24	29	2	0	1	5	0	1	2	23	0	31	2	3	1	.271	.368
Hurtado, Omar, Day.	.234	63	228	205	23	48	74	7	2	5	20	1	1	2	19	0	59	3	3	4	.361	.304
Inge, Brandon, W.M.	.188	4	19	16	3	3	4	1	0	0	2	0	0	1	2	0	5	0	0	0	.250	.316
Jacobo, Kervin, S.D.†	.267	9	34	30	5	8	15	2	1	1	6	0	0	0	4	0	10	4	0	2	.500	.353
Jenkins, Geoff, Bel.*	.333	1	4	3	1	1	2	1	0	0	1	0	0	0	1	0	1	0	0	0	.667	.500
Johnson, Forrest, W.M.	.260	114	477	420	64	109	175	19	1	15	61	0	10	11	36	1	89	3	0	10	.417	.327
Johnson, Gabe, Peo.	.224	36	154	134	17	30	54	10	4	2	17	0	2	2	16	0	49	1	1	2	.403	.312
Jones, Brian, Day.*	.230	63	205	191	17	44	69	10	0	5	19	0	2	1	11	0	47	4	1	6	.361	.273
Kavourias, Jim, K.C.	.261	120	524	460	77	120	227	30	4	23	88	0	6	10	48	1	126	11	3	10	.493	.340
Kelly, Heath, K.C.	.176	11	35	34	1	6	6	0	0	0	3	0	0	1	0	0	10	0	1	0	.176	.200
Kennedy, Bryan, Q.C.*	.200	14	52	40	8	8	11	3	0	0	5	0	0	3	9	0	3	0	0	1	.275	.385
Kenney, Jeff, Bel.	.212	41	188	151	21	32	47	6	0	3	19	2	1	8	26	0	33	8	3	2	.311	.355
Keppinger, Billy, Bur.*	.244	70	300	279	42	68	89	13	1	2	26	1	5	5	43	1	45	9	3	5	.319	.349
Kerner, Craig, Clin.*	.189	53	217	190	21	36	52	7	0	3	17	0	3	3	21	0	49	10	4	4	.274	.276
Knight, Marcus, C.R.†	.250	27	102	92	13	23	42	4	0	5	17	1	3	1	5	0	14	0	1	2	.457	.287
Kroeger, Joshua, S.B.*	.274	79	315	292	36	80	106	15	1	3	37	0	1	4	18	0	49	4	4	10	.363	.324
Krynzel, Dave, Bel.*	.305	35	154	141	22	43	49	1	1	1	19	0	0	4	9	2	28	11	5	1	.348	.364
Kweon, Yoon-Min, Lan.	.270	48	356	326	33	88	123	15	1	6	51	1	9	5	15	0	44	0	0	10	.377	.304
Lagana, Shawn, S.B.	.239	43	140	134	13	32	42	7	0	1	16	2	2	0	2	0	25	5	2	3	.313	.246
Langill, Eric, Clin.	.201	47	154	134	14	27	38	8	0	1	9	1	0	3	16	0	31	1	2	5	.284	.301
Lee, Eric, Mich.	.262	69	236	210	27	55	70	8	2	1	26	1	1	3	21	1	58	6	5	4	.333	.336
Lehr, Ryan, C.R.	.259	22	91	81	12	21	38	8	0	3	16	0	2	1	7	0	7	0	0	2	.469	.319
Lemon, Tim, Peo.	.222	130	522	482	60	107	190	32	3	15	61	2	4	6	27	1	165	31	7	12	.394	.270
Lindsey, Cordell, C.R.	.250	65	267	248	31	62	99	14	1	7	32	0	3	2	14	0	46	4	4	11	.399	.292
Liriano, Pedro, Wis.	.326	113	487	442	76	144	190	28	3	4	47	2	6	7	30	2	50	65	20	5	.430	.373
Llamas, Juan, Bur.	.237	42	177	152	17	36	55	7	0	4	25	2	3	5	15	0	37	0	0	5	.362	.320
Loeb, Bryan, S.B.	.208	16	56	48	7	10	13	3	0	0	4	1	1	1	5	0	8	0	1	0	.271	.291
Logan, Nook, W.M.†	.262	128	584	522	82	137	175	19	8	1	27	3	4	2	53	2	129	67	19	3	.335	.330
Lopez, Chuck, Wis.*	.299	49	215	194	24	58	91	7	7	4	29	3	4	4	10	0	19	9	5	2	.469	.340
Lora, Tom, Bur.†	.249	112	501	442	80	110	141	11	7	2	28	9	0	5	45	0	84	27	15	4	.319	.325
Lutz, David, Clin.*	.240	7	27	25	4	6	7	1	0	0	2	0	0	2	0	0	2	1	0	0	.280	.296
Luuloa, Miles, W.M.†	.184	84	290	250	30	46	65	9	2	2	17	4	1	0	35	0	76	5	4	8	.260	.283
Lydic, Joe, Mich.	.245	94	346	330	38	81	120	22	1	5	38	1	3	4	8	0	95	2	4	6	.364	.278
Machado, Aleyandro, Bur.	.239	28	123	109	17	26	31	5	0	0	11	1	1	2	10	0	16	5	2	2	.284	.311
Magness, Pat, K.C.*	.256	68	285	227	25	58	90	14	0	6	39	0	2	3	53	1	41	2	1	6	.396	.400
Mallory, Mike, Lan.	.228	127	478	434	51	99	158	17	3	12	47	1	3	12	28	0	132	17	3	8	.364	.291
Martinez, Dionnar, Lan.†	.321	17	62	56	8	18	22	2	1	0	6	2	0	1	3	0	8	0	1	0	.393	.367
Martinez, Guillermo, Wis.†	.239	58	191	184	24	44	57	6	2	1	23	1	1	1	4	0	47	2	2	6	.310	.258
Martinez, Hipolito, Bel.	.200	7	25	25	3	5	11	1	1	1	2	0	0	0	0	0	13	0	0	1	.440	.200
Maule, Jason, Mich.*	.347	124	504	412	101	143	179	23	5	1	63	4	7	7	74	1	62	50	6	3	.434	.448
Maza, Luis, Q.C.	.280	116	488	429	74	120	173	24	1	9	46	2	2	23	30	0	66	12	4	9	.403	.357
McCasland, Ralph, Clin.*	.000	2	1	1	0	0	0	0	0	0	0	0	0	0	0	0	0	0	0	0	.000	.000
McCool, Lee, F.W.	.237	102	422	392	35	93	119	17	3	1	36	2	4	4	20	0	77	8	5	2	.304	.279
McMillan, Andrew, Clin.	.197	94	349	320	25	63	93	12	0	6	30	0	1	15	12	0	67	1	0	8	.291	.259
Mejia, Andy, Lan.	.135	12	38	37	3	5	7	2	0	0	3	0	0	0	1	0	9	0	0	0	.189	.158
Merrill, Ronnie, W.M.†	.317	83	360	309	58	98	139	11	3	8	53	2	6	7	36	2	47	15	7	5	.450	.394
Merritt, Timothy, Wis.	.308	3	14	13	1	4	4	0	0	0	1	0	0	0	0	0	2	0	1	0	.308	.286
Miller, Eric, Clin.	.286	69	293	276	28	79	102	11	3	2	35	0	1	0	16	0	42	8	1	8	.370	.324
Montanez, Luis, Lan.	.255	124	552	499	70	127	187	33	6	5	54	3	3	12	34	0	121	20	7	12	.375	.316
Morneau, Justin, Q.C.*	.356	64	269	236	50	84	141	17	2	12	53	0	4	3	26	1	38	0	0	4	.597	.420
Morris, Chris, Peo.†	.294	134	584	480	89	141	176	11	9	2	39	18	2	1	83	0	101	111	24	1	.367	.398
Morrissey, Adam, Lan.	.309	122	509	418	88	129	219	26	11	14	62	1	2	8	80	3	82	10	9	9	.524	.427
Murphy, Tommy, C.R.	.204	74	311	280	32	57	90	15	3	4	31	6	3	6	16	1	94	7	10	5	.321	.259
Myers, Corey, S.B.	.327	59	237	211	28	69	99	17	2	3	36	1	9	4	12	0	33	2	0	9	.469	.360
Napoli, Michael, C.R.	.232	43	183	155	23	36	63	10	1	5	18	1	1	2	24	0	54	3	2	1	.406	.341
Neal, Steve, S.B.*	.256	121	503	453	71	116	205	23	3	20	92	0	3	8	39	6	137	7	1	10	.453	.324

Player, Team	Avg.	G	TPA	AB	R	H	TB	2B	3B	HR	RBI	SH	SF	HP	BB	IBB	SO	SB	CS	GDP	Slg.	OBP
Neill, Ryan, W.M.	.239	130	512	419	68	100	156	23	6	7	61	1	2	19	71	1	122	35	8	4	.372	.372
Nunez, Argelis, S.B.	.215	82	312	284	36	61	87	13	2	3	25	3	2	7	16	0	108	11	5	6	.306	.272
Obradovich, Mark, Mich.†	.214	8	29	28	1	6	8	2	0	0	3	0	0	1	0	0	7	0	0	0	.286	.241
O'Connor, Brian, Mich.	.071	24	48	42	2	3	3	0	0	0	0	0	0	1	5	0	20	0	1	1	.071	.188
O'Donnell, Ryan, Ft.W.*	.269	29	121	108	16	29	33	4	0	0	7	3	1	0	9	0	20	4	0	0	.306	.322
Ortiz, Matt, Peo.	.245	65	241	216	23	53	68	13	1	0	23	1	3	2	19	0	31	4	3	5	.315	.308
Pagan, Andres, Ft.W.	.223	90	329	319	24	71	87	13	0	1	25	1	3	0	6	0	85	4	1	9	.273	.235
Parker, Chris, W.M.	.253	74	274	237	25	60	76	13	0	1	22	4	2	8	23	0	46	2	1	7	.321	.337
Patchett, Gary, Day.	.243	85	308	259	42	63	73	8	1	0	17	5	1	16	27	0	52	6	3	4	.282	.350
Peguero, Miguel, W.M.†	.226	109	398	368	31	83	103	15	1	1	30	1	5	2	22	0	73	5	6	10	.280	.270
Pena, Wily Mo, Day.	.264	135	565	511	87	135	248	25	5	26	113	0	4	17	33	1	177	26	10	6	.485	.327
Peters, Samone, Day.	.206	120	491	452	61	93	197	20	0	28	78	0	2	8	29	2	158	2	2	8	.436	.265
Peterson, Brian, Day.	.248	35	129	113	14	28	39	5	0	2	18	2	0	0	14	0	33	0	0	1	.345	.331
Pichardo, Maximo, C.R.	.208	44	192	178	21	37	46	4	1	1	12	3	0	2	9	0	30	11	7	3	.258	.254
Postell, Matthew, K.C.*	.284	34	107	95	16	27	42	6	0	3	6	0	0	1	11	0	36	2	2	1	.442	.364
Pregnalato, Bob, Bel.	.247	81	295	259	43	64	96	30	1	0	19	8	1	3	24	0	57	11	1	4	.371	.317
Puccinelli, John, Ft.W.	.190	64	206	179	14	34	48	8	0	2	13	2	0	0	25	0	49	1	2	2	.268	.289
Quattlebaum, Hugh, W.M.	.239	121	502	415	63	99	142	26	4	3	55	0	6	10	68	0	68	8	4	10	.342	.355
Quintana, Wil, Wis.	.229	35	145	131	21	30	64	6	2	8	29	2	2	2	8	0	43	1	1	4	.489	.280
Rabe, Josh, Q.C.	.282	119	444	397	58	112	161	25	3	6	44	4	3	8	32	0	64	9	7	9	.406	.345
Raburn, Johnny, C.R.†	.315	68	308	235	56	74	78	2	1	0	12	4	1	5	63	1	43	37	7	1	.332	.467
Reese, Kevin, Ft.W.*	.329	125	524	459	84	151	232	30	6	13	73	2	4	5	54	3	62	30	10	5	.505	.402
Richardson, Miguel, Wis.	.321	9	37	28	7	9	16	1	0	2	5	0	0	0	9	0	10	1	1	0	.571	.486
Ridley, Shayne, Bur.†	.050	7	25	20	0	1	1	0	0	0	1	0	1	0	4	0	8	0	1	0	.050	.200
Riggins, Auntwan, Ft.W.†	.239	32	136	117	15	28	32	4	0	0	5	2	0	1	16	0	29	12	3	2	.274	.336
Rivas, Norberto, Clin.	.148	7	27	27	2	4	7	0	0	1	2	0	0	0	0	0	9	0	1	0	.259	.148
Rodgers, Albert, Peo.	.215	77	288	261	31	56	99	14	1	9	33	2	1	6	18	2	83	8	5	4	.379	.280
Rodgers, Mackeel, Bur.†	.200	4	11	10	1	2	2	0	0	0	1	0	0	0	1	0	1	0	0	0	.200	.273
Rodriguez, Joe, Wis.	.229	39	130	109	9	25	40	6	0	3	22	2	2	6	11	0	33	2	2	2	.367	.328
Rogers, Brandon, C.R.	.343	19	81	70	13	24	31	7	0	0	10	0	0	3	8	0	16	0	1	1	.443	.432
Rombley, Danny, Clin.	.191	35	145	136	14	26	36	5	1	1	9	1	0	1	7	0	35	9	1	2	.265	.236
Rooi, Vince, Clin.	.254	120	493	422	53	107	156	22	0	9	60	0	6	4	61	1	94	5	4	12	.370	.349
Roper, Zach, C.R.	.310	124	519	471	64	146	222	27	2	15	87	2	4	13	29	2	82	8	3	18	.471	.364
Ruiz, Randy, Day.	.268	123	531	466	82	125	225	34	3	20	92	0	3	14	48	4	116	21	9	10	.483	.352
Saba, Cesar, Ft.W.†	.223	84	321	291	29	65	95	10	1	6	31	2	3	4	21	2	61	2	6	6	.326	.282
Sadler, Ray, Lan.	.341	94	408	378	74	129	192	27	3	10	50	1	4	3	22	3	58	18	7	3	.508	.378
Sandberg, Eric, Q.C.*	.319	42	188	166	28	53	77	8	2	4	23	1	1	4	16	1	25	1	1	2	.464	.390
Sandoval, Jhensy, S.B.	.200	9	40	35	6	7	14	1	0	2	5	0	1	0	4	0	13	0	0	1	.400	.275
Sandoval, Michael, Q.C.	.222	47	170	153	18	34	43	6	0	1	22	1	3	2	11	0	32	2	0	7	.281	.278
Santana, Sandy, Peo.	.203	65	215	197	19	40	52	7	1	1	17	2	3	6	7	0	36	5	5	5	.264	.249
Santos, Chad, Bur.*	.252	121	506	444	58	112	192	32	0	16	83	1	3	6	52	4	101	0	1	14	.432	.337
Schnabel, Nicholas, Clin.	.256	16	45	39	4	10	12	2	0	0	2	1	0	1	4	0	7	0	0	1	.308	.341
Seever, Brian, C.R.	.223	45	204	166	25	37	48	6	1	1	14	3	2	2	31	0	34	14	7	1	.289	.348
Segura, Rolando, Ft.W.	.196	12	50	46	3	9	9	0	0	0	2	0	1	1	2	0	9	0	0	2	.196	.240
Serafini, Matt, Bel.	.105	4	19	19	2	2	2	0	0	0	0	0	0	0	0	0	3	0	0	1	.105	.105
Silver, Travis, Lan.	.158	22	68	57	7	9	9	0	0	0	4	1	1	3	6	0	23	0	1	2	.158	.269
Sing, Brandon, Lan.	.245	121	478	417	54	102	181	27	2	16	50	2	5	8	46	0	109	3	5	6	.434	.328
Sizemore, Grady, Clin.*	.268	123	541	451	64	121	151	16	4	2	61	0	5	4	81	4	92	32	11	7	.335	.381
Sledd, Aaron, Day.*	.243	13	45	37	6	9	12	3	0	0	3	0	1	0	7	0	14	0	0	0	.324	.356
Smith, Will, K.C.*	.280	125	578	535	92	150	228	26	2	16	91	0	5	5	32	2	74	4	5	12	.426	.324
Smitherman, Steve, Day.	.280	134	552	497	89	139	248	45	2	20	73	0	2	10	43	1	113	16	7	9	.499	.348
Socarras, Tony, C.R.*	.216	16	62	51	10	11	18	1	0	2	11	0	1	3	7	0	20	0	0	1	.353	.339
Soto, T.J., Mich.	.287	110	448	404	73	116	219	27	5	22	62	1	4	4	35	1	128	19	5	12	.542	.347
Southward, Deshawn, Q.C.	.143	10	24	21	3	3	5	2	0	0	1	1	0	0	2	0	4	1	0	0	.238	.217
Sprowl, Jon-Mark, Lan.*	.219	54	181	155	12	34	52	9	0	3	28	1	3	4	18	0	24	0	3	6	.335	.311
Stanley, Henry, Mich.*	.300	114	478	400	75	120	210	24	12	14	76	2	1	1	73	4	84	30	5	7	.525	.408
Stockton, Jeff, C.R.	.120	7	25	25	3	3	4	1	0	0	0	0	0	0	0	0	7	0	0	0	.160	.120
Stockton, Rick, C.R.*	.273	8	26	22	2	6	8	2	0	0	3	0	1	1	2	0	5	1	0	0	.364	.346
Stone, Jon, Ft.W.†	.231	53	192	169	15	39	52	10	0	1	20	0	1	4	18	0	48	3	0	4	.308	.318
Strong, Jamal, Wis.	.353	51	231	184	41	65	79	12	1	0	19	1	1	5	40	2	27	35	4	2	.429	.478
Suarez, Marc, Day.	.253	47	169	150	18	38	65	9	0	6	23	0	2	4	13	0	44	4	0	1	.433	.325
Tamburrino, Brett, Q.C.†	.262	42	161	141	23	37	50	3	5	0	16	1	0	4	15	1	32	4	2	3	.355	.350
Terrero, Luis, S.B.	.157	24	91	89	4	14	19	2	0	1	8	0	0	2	0	0	29	3	0	2	.213	.176
Thompson, Craig, Ft.W.†	.261	87	364	310	53	81	142	27	2	10	59	4	7	2	41	1	35	8	1	2	.458	.344
Tiffee, Terry, Q.C.†	.309	128	536	495	65	153	220	32	1	11	86	0	8	1	32	4	48	3	1	13	.444	.347
Tolli, Barry, C.R.	.141	23	73	71	5	10	14	1	0	1	2	0	0	0	2	0	23	3	4	1	.197	.164
Tolzien, Edward, C.R.*	.183	20	80	71	9	13	15	2	0	0	8	0	0	3	6	1	20	0	0	2	.211	.275
Torres, Digno, Q.C.*	.193	88	305	264	31	51	79	15	2	3	27	1	1	6	33	0	72	1	2	9	.299	.296
Tracy, Chad, S.B.*	.340	54	239	215	43	73	96	11	0	4	36	0	3	2	19	2	19	3	0	4	.447	.393
Treanor, Matt, K.C.	1.000	1	4	1	2	1	1	0	0	0	0	0	0	0	3	0	0	0	0	0	1.000	1.000
Valdez, Angel, C.R.	.246	31	122	114	19	28	45	8	0	3	11	2	0	2	4	0	29	3	1	0	.395	.283
Valdez, Wilson, Clin.	.252	59	232	214	31	54	64	8	1	0	11	5	2	2	9	0	22	6	7	5	.299	.286
Vasquez, Geraldo, Peo.	.000	4	11	9	1	0	0	0	0	0	0	0	0	0	2	0	4	1	0	1	.000	.182
Villilo, Miguel, Wis.†	.167	14	46	42	1	7	8	1	0	0	3	0	0	1	3	0	14	0	4	0	.190	.239
Vizcaino, Maximo, S.B.	.236	52	173	165	18	39	49	8	1	0	16	1	1	0	6	0	35	2	5	5	.297	.262
Voltz, Robert, Bel.*	.236	126	522	462	68	109	183	18	1	18	69	0	2	3	55	6	135	3	2	4	.396	.320
Voshell, Chase, Peo.	.258	90	363	325	53	84	124	19	3	5	23	0	1	4	33	1	80	9	5	7	.382	.333
Walker, Matt, W.M.	.260	112	463	415	53	108	165	23	2	10	65	0	7	7	34	0	80	11	4	14	.398	.322
Wallis, Jacob, Clin.	.210	26	86	81	5	17	21	1	0	1	7	0	0	1	4	0	18	2	0	2	.259	.256
Walter, Scott, Bur.	.274	33	137	124	24	34	66	12	1	6	22	1	2	4	6	0	16	0	0	7	.532	.324
Warner, J.R., C.R.*	.189	14	58	53	9	10	14	2	1	0	4	0	0	1	4	0	11	1	0	1	.264	.259
Watkins, Tommy, Q.C.	.230	73	228	191	31	44	59	9	0	2	16	6	1	2	28	0	36	4	2	4	.309	.333
Watson, Brandon, Clin.*	.327	117	525	489	74	160	200	16	9	2	38	3	3	1	29	0	65	33	20	6	.409	.364

Player, Team	Avg.	G	TPA	AB	R	H	TB	2B	3B	HR	RBI	SH	SF	HP	BB	IBB	SO	SB	CS	GDP	Slg.	OBP
Webb, Ryan, C.R.	.310	44	158	145	14	45	52	5	1	0	14	5	0	1	7	0	28	7	4	1	.359	.346
West, Kevin, Q.C.	.271	126	539	443	74	120	183	33	3	8	62	1	5	28	62	1	99	6	2	7	.413	.390
West, Todd, Bel.	.235	132	504	408	62	96	110	14	0	0	40	26	3	7	60	0	62	16	4	5	.270	.341
Williams, Clyde, Clin.*	.251	88	364	347	45	87	135	12	3	10	52	1	3	2	11	0	92	7	2	6	.389	.275
Williamson, Chris, Day.*	.211	37	139	114	16	24	46	5	1	5	18	0	1	2	22	3	39	0	2	1	.404	.345
Willingham, Josh, K.C.	.259	97	390	320	57	83	128	20	2	7	36	4	4	13	53	0	85	24	2	7	.400	.382
Wilson, Josh, K.C.	.285	123	546	506	65	144	194	28	5	4	61	4	4	4	28	0	60	17	11	11	.383	.325
Withey, Ryan, C.R.	.248	62	232	202	31	50	79	11	0	6	28	2	1	7	20	0	53	20	5	1	.391	.335
Woods, Michael, W.M.	.270	44	203	163	30	44	60	8	4	0	17	1	2	5	32	1	44	13	7	2	.368	.401
Woodward, John, Ft.W.*	.196	116	471	414	48	81	151	23	1	15	64	0	2	6	49	0	114	7	4	1	.365	.289
Woody, Dominic, K.C.	.238	66	260	227	38	54	89	11	3	6	33	0	2	7	21	0	47	6	2	5	.392	.319
Wright, Gavin, Mich.	.273	100	434	392	68	107	160	17	6	8	52	4	5	5	28	0	76	26	6	6	.408	.326
Wyant, Hunter, K.C.	.000	7	14	13	0	0	0	0	0	0	0	1	0	0	0	0	3	0	0	0	.000	.000
Zapey, Winton, Q.C.	.000	1	1	1	0	0	0	0	0	0	0	0	0	0	0	0	0	0	0	1	.000	.000
Zoccolillo, Peter, Bel.*	.333	31	135	123	16	41	67	8	0	6	23	0	1	1	10	0	19	0	2	3	.545	.385

GRAND SLAMS: Dubois, 3; Acevedo, Bowen, Gentry, Kavourias, Pena, 2 each; Bay, Duncan, Durango, Gettis, Hamilton, Hammond, B. Harris, Kenney, Kerner, Lydic, Montanez, Morneau, Neill, Peters, Roper, Ruiz, Sadler, Santos, Sing, Sprowl, Tiffee, Voltz, Walker, Walter, Wilson, Woodward, 1 each.

AWARDED FIRST BASE ON CATCHER'S INTERFERENCE: Quatlebaum 3 (Alvarez, Alvarez, Stone), Woody 3 (Castellano, Parker, Alvarez); Maza 2 (Alvarez, Cleveland); Cotto (Castellano), Dogero (Castellano), Ferrand (Doudt), Lemon (Langill), McMillan (Abruzzo), Montanez (Langill), W. Smith (Castellano). Stanley (Foster).

2001 PITCHING

TEAM

Team	W	L	Pct.	ERA	G	CG	ShO	Sv.	IP	H	TBF	R	ER	HR	SH	SF	HB	BB	IBB	SO	WP	Bk.
Wisconsin	84	52	.618	2.96	136	4	16	34	1202.1	1049	5078	513	395	65	38	29	86	398	17	1225	71	13
Quad City	80	57	.584	3.60	137	7	14	42	1204.1	1112	5148	594	482	84	36	37	75	454	17	1010	89	13
Dayton	82	57	.590	3.68	139	6	13	40	1219.0	1226	5242	613	498	86	35	26	59	396	23	1049	94	13
West Michigan ..	65	72	.474	0.70	100	3	16	34	1214.2	1121	5275	609	502	69	21	46	76	545	30	1054	109	22
South Bend	70	66	.515	3.73	136	5	9	31	1176.2	1158	5074	609	488	75	43	47	68	420	14	960	75	16
Kane County	88	50	.638	3.86	130	1	4	39	1232.2	1223	5270	619	528	81	42	45	84	373	4	865	112	13
Michigan	82	55	.599	4.22	137	8	7	36	1189.0	1222	5228	661	558	93	34	36	24	380	7	948	75	13
Beloit.............	67	71	.486	4.23	138	2	5	35	1213.1	1156	5339	696	570	95	36	32	95	586	9	1153	113	15
Fort Wayne	54	83	.394	4.24	137	2	0	32	1184.2	1218	5172	695	558	100	31	45	68	433	24	1035	68	25
Clinton	51	85	.375	4.26	137	6	6	20	1197.1	1210	5277	704	567	118	42	55	80	487	3	853	84	18
Lansing	65	75	.464	4.32	140	8	0	35	1205.0	1203	5355	731	579	98	42	42	79	483	15	1132	88	17
Cedar Rapids.....	60	77	.438	4.38	137	7	3	33	1207.0	1218	5325	738	587	108	39	47	81	456	3	1054	111	12
Peoria	57	81	.413	4.38	138	3	4	30	1207.1	1286	5336	761	588	98	36	47	74	395	4	878	115	9
Burlington	55	79	.410	4.53	134	2	5	29	1151.0	1236	5052	692	579	101	40	47	67	385	7	809	84	13

INDIVIDUAL

TOP QUALIFIERS FOR EARNED-RUN AVERAGE TITLE
Minimum 112 innings. *Lefthanded pitcher.

Pitcher, Team	W	L	Pct.	ERA	G	GS	CG	ShO	GF	Sv.	IP	H	TBF	R	ER	HR	SH	SF	HB	BB	IBB	SO	WP	Bk.
Hall, Josh, Day.	11	5	.688	2.65	22	22	2	0	0	0	132.1	117	549	52	39	4	2	1	2	39	1	122	18	2
Lockwood, Luke, Clin.*	5	10	.333	2.70	26	26	3	1	0	0	163.1	152	688	78	49	8	6	6	14	49	0	114	8	1
Perez, Beltran, S.B.	12	4	.750	2.81	27	27	2	0	0	0	160.0	142	651	59	50	10	5	3	6	35	0	157	5	3
Wolfe, Brian, Q.C.	13	8	.619	2.81	28	23	2	2	2	0	160.0	128	641	64	50	11	2	4	5	32	2	128	8	0
Hendrickson, Benjamin, Bcl. ..	8	9	.471	2.84	25	25	1	0	0	0	133.1	122	576	56	42	3	1	1	6	72	0	133	9	1
Snare, Ryan, Day.*	9	5	.643	3.05	21	20	0	0	0	0	115.0	101	472	45	39	7	1	1	9	37	1	118	9	2
Nageotte, Clint, Wis.	11	8	.579	3.13	28	26	0	0	0	0	152.1	141	648	65	53	10	10	1	11	50	1	187	6	4
Holubec, Ken, Q.C.*	4	0	.000	0.22	27	22	1	0	3	1	134.0	107	568	57	48	7	4	3	9	63	0	129	9	1
Olore, Kevin, Wis.	13	4	.765	3.32	27	27	0	0	0	0	154.2	134	641	70	57	14	4	3	14	40	0	158	6	1
Grunwald, Erik, Wis.	8	6	.571	3.38	29	21	1	1	1	0	157.1	138	661	66	59	10	4	7	14	48	0	128	5	1
McAdoo, Duncan, Ft.W.	6	16	.273	3.54	28	28	0	0	0	0	157.2	173	683	87	62	15	1	6	11	36	0	121	4	3
Mottl, Ryan, Day.	15	6	.714	3.60	26	26	1	0	0	0	152.2	155	653	74	61	15	3	6	10	42	2	119	7	0
Qualls, Chad, Mich.	15	6	.714	3.72	26	26	3	2	0	0	162.0	149	673	77	67	8	2	6	11	31	0	125	10	2
Coughenour, Jory, Mich.	11	5	.688	3.78	35	14	0	0	4	3	126.1	152	554	68	53	4	4	3	4	22	1	65	5	1
Castillo, Ramon, K.C.	11	2	.846	3.80	28	28	0	0	0	0	158.2	178	688	79	67	19	1	3	12	31	1	108	11	1

DEPARTMENTAL LEADERS: W—Mottl, Qualls, 15 each; L—McAdoo, 16; Pct.—Castillo, .846; G—Sawyer, 55; GS—Castillo, McAdoo, Norderum, 28 each; CG—Qualls, Lockwood, 3 each; ShO—Cueto, E. Johnson, Wolfe, Qualls, 2 each; GF—Bonilla, 47; Sv.—Bonilla, 25; IP—Daigle, 164; H—Krawiec, 183; TBF—Daigle, 727; R—Leicester, 117; ER—Leicester, 90; HR—Baker, Castillo, Washburn, 19 each; SH—Nageotte, 10; SF—Gonzalez, 11; HB—Barrett, 24; BB—Gordon, 84; IBB—Oxspring, 6; SO—Nageotte, 187; WP—Diaz, 20; BK—Cassel, 5.

ALL PITCHERS
*Lefthanded pitcher.

Pitcher, Team	W	L	Pct.	ERA	G	GS	CG	ShO	GF	Sv.	IP	H	TBF	R	ER	HR	SH	SF	HB	BB	IBB	SO	WP	Bk.
Aguilar, Edwin, Mich.	2	1	.667	4.08	14	0	0	0	9	3	28.2	25	130	15	13	1	3	3	5	15	0	30	7	1
Albright, Eric, Lan.	1	5	.167	6.20	34	0	0	0	23	8	40.2	49	186	31	28	6	2	2	1	11	3	50	2	0
Alvarez, Larry, Lan.	1	2	.333	2.25	30	0	0	0	14	2	44.0	38	187	13	11	1	4	1	4	14	2	54	2	0
Anderson, Bryan, Day.	0	0	.000	0.00	1	0	0	0	1	0	0.2	0	4	0	0	0	0	0	0	2	0	0	0	0
Anderson, Travis, Mich.	6	8	.429	5.72	31	22	1	0	4	1	140.0	165	634	102	89	12	4	4	11	52	0	99	17	1
Andrade, Stephen, C.R.	2	1	.667	6.52	20	0	0	0	9	0	29.0	33	129	24	21	3	2	1	2	8	0	31	7	0
Andujar, Jesse, C.R.	0	0	.000	5.40	5	0	0	0	3	0	5.0	6	24	4	3	1	0	0	1	2	0	6	1	0
Aramboles, Ricardo, Day.	1	1	.333	3.66	4	4	0	0	0	0	19.2	23	81	8	8	2	0	0	0	4	0	9	1	0
Arias, Pablo, W.M.	9	4	.692	3.17	20	17	0	0	0	0	108.0	100	450	44	38	5	1	1	5	33	2	81	6	3
Arthur, Tony, C.R.*	3	1	.750	2.57	5	5	0	0	0	0	28.0	33	127	11	8	1	3	2	1	9	0	28	0	0
Artieta, Corey, Bel.*	2	1	.667	4.55	26	4	0	0	9	0	63.1	62	282	40	32	7	0	2	4	38	0	36	10	0

Pitcher, Team	W	L	Pct.	ERA	G	GS	CG	ShO	GF	Sv.	IP	H	TBF	R	ER	HR	SH	SF	HB	BB	IBB	SO	WP	Bk.
Axelson, Josh, Peo.	5	7	.417	4.61	18	18	1	0	0	0	109.1	112	467	62	56	12	2	6	7	28	0	77	19	0
Ayala, Julio, Wis.*	0	0	.000	4.50	1	0	0	0	1	0	2.0	1	7	1	1	0	0	0	0	0	0	0	0	0
Baker, Joey, Bur.	7	10	.412	5.34	27	23	0	0	2	0	140.0	155	613	97	83	19	4	6	8	45	1	71	9	0
Barnes, Pat, Wis.*	1	0	1.000	0.82	10	0	0	0	4	0	11.0	4	38	2	1	0	0	0	0	4	0	10	1	0
Barrett, Jimmy, Mich.	10	5	.667	4.48	27	25	1	0	2	0	130.2	122	594	76	65	12	0	4	24	62	0	98	8	1
Bass, Brian, Bur.	3	10	.231	4.65	26	26	1	1	0	0	139.1	138	613	82	72	16	3	5	15	53	0	75	14	1
Baugh, Kenny, W.M.	2	1	.667	1.59	6	6	0	0	0	0	34.0	31	146	14	6	0	0	1	5	10	2	39	2	0
Bautista, Denny, K.C.	3	1	.750	4.35	8	7	0	0	0	0	39.1	43	172	21	19	2	2	1	2	14	0	20	4	2
Belanger, Brandon, Ft.W.	1	3	.250	6.42	33	0	0	0	9	2	47.2	57	213	36	34	3	1	6	3	18	4	39	2	1
Belson, Greg, S.B.	6	4	.600	2.50	46	0	0	0	39	16	57.2	54	243	24	16	3	3	2	2	17	3	50	2	0
Blackwell, Scott, Q.C.	1	2	.333	5.12	13	0	0	0	3	0	19.1	17	87	17	11	1	2	0	2	9	2	19	0	1
Blanton, Jason, Lan.	0	0	.000	4.09	7	0	0	0	2	0	11.0	14	49	6	5	0	0	1	3	0	7	0	0
Bludau, Frank, Day.	6	3	.667	2.52	42	0	0	0	37	21	53.2	42	217	16	15	0	1	1	1	10	3	39	4	0
Bone, Blake, Wis.	0	1	.000	18.00	1	0	0	0	1	0	1.0	2	7	3	2	0	0	1	1	1	2	0	0
Bonilla, Henry, Q.C.	5	6	.455	3.22	53	0	0	0	47	25	58.2	61	259	22	21	3	2	1	2	23	2	55	4	0
Boutwell, Andy, Day.	4	4	.500	4.92	32	2	0	0	6	2	67.2	57	292	41	37	8	1	2	1	34	3	83	5	1
Bradley, Dave, Day.	0	2	.000	3.72	16	0	0	0	11	0	29.0	30	124	15	12	2	2	0	2	9	0	33	5	0
Brannon, Nick, Day.*	0	0	.000	12.46	2	0	0	0	0	0	4.1	8	22	6	6	2	0	0	0	2	0	4	1	0
Brown, Eric, Lan.	3	1	.750	2.61	16	0	0	0	7	1	20.2	18	85	6	6	0	1	1	0	5	1	23	1	0
Bruney, Brian, S.B.	1	4	.200	4.13	26	0	0	0	20	8	32.2	24	142	19	15	1	2	1	3	19	2	40	3	2
Bukowski, Stan, C.R.	2	4	.333	6.61	8	8	1	0	0	0	47.2	53	214	39	35	10	3	1	3	25	0	29	4	1
Bumstead, Mike, Ft.W.	4	2	.667	2.27	36	0	0	0	31	17	39.2	26	163	12	10	2	1	1	3	15	1	52	4	0
Burns, Casey, Ft.W.	5	8	.385	5.08	20	16	0	0	0	0	88.2	87	399	60	50	7	2	2	6	43	1	59	5	0
Burns, Mike, Mich.	7	7	.500	3.95	29	21	1	0	3	1	132.0	131	552	67	58	10	4	5	13	27	0	108	0	1
Burton, O.J., Wis.	4	3	.571	3.19	39	0	0	0	15	1	59.1	54	255	31	21	4	3	1	4	21	4	39	4	0
Butler, John, Wis.	5	3	.625	2.01	40	0	0	0	14	1	67.0	68	286	27	15	1	3	0	3	16	1	62	5	0
Bye, Chris, Clin.	1	1	.500	0.91	21	0	0	0	6	3	29.2	18	122	7	3	1	6	2	0	13	0	34	4	0
Byron, Terry, K.C.	1	2	.333	7.90	4	2	0	0	0	0	13.2	12	61	13	12	0	1	0	1	7	0	11	4	0
Cali, Carmen, Peo.*	7	3	.700	6.00	39	0	0	0	15	1	48.0	53	229	40	32	4	6	0	1	29	0	47	9	1
Campbell, Dayle, W.M.	1	7	.125	7.04	21	13	0	0	7	1	69.0	83	346	67	54	6	1	5	8	57	0	47	14	4
Campos, Juan, Mich.	5	4	.556	4.60	13	13	2	0	0	0	78.1	90	341	50	40	8	2	1	8	10	0	69	3	2
Candelaria, Scott, Bel.	0	0	.000	0.00	1	0	0	0	1	0	0.1	0	1	0	0	0	0	0	0	0	0	0	0	0
Caputo, Rob, Clin.	0	2	.000	0.00	4	0	0	0	4	0	5.0	4	27	4	0	0	0	1	0	5	0	8	2	1
Casadiego, Gerardo, Clin.	5	5	.500	3.98	42	1	0	0	28	6	72.1	67	311	37	32	8	5	6	4	28	1	43	8	3
Cassel, Jack, Ft.W.	4	14	.222	5.54	25	23	0	0	1	0	128.1	163	591	104	79	7	5	4	12	35	0	89	6	5
Castellanos, Jonathan, S.B.	1	3	.250	4.86	8	8	0	0	0	0	37.0	47	172	24	20	3	2	1	3	15	0	34	1	0
Castillo, Ramon, K.C.	11	2	.846	3.80	28	28	0	0	0	0	158.2	178	688	79	67	19	1	3	12	31	1	108	11	1
Charron, Eric, Clin.	1	0	1.000	1.77	14	0	0	0	7	0	20.1	19	89	11	4	0	0	0	5	0	21	0	0
Chavez, Wilton, Lan.	6	2	.750	4.02	8	8	2	1	0	0	47.0	38	207	24	21	4	2	2	3	27	0	60	2	1
Chisnall, Wes, Clin.	2	3	.400	4.76	24	1	0	0	6	0	51.0	67	222	31	27	4	2	3	4	7	0	18	5	3
Coa, Jesus, Bur.	2	3	.400	6.68	36	0	0	0	13	1	63.1	82	305	52	47	9	1	6	8	28	0	38	6	1
Collins, Clint, Day.	2	1	.667	4.63	6	1	0	0	2	0	11.2	20	56	7	6	1	0	0	3	0	7	3	0
Contreras, Jean, Q.C.*	2	0	1.000	2.67	26	0	0	0	11	2	33.2	28	139	14	10	0	2	2	1	11	1	38	3	0
Cook, Jeremy, Peo.	3	7	.300	3.71	52	0	0	0	34	14	68.0	78	310	37	28	7	3	0	5	20	2	61	2	0
Corbin, John, Lan.	1	3	.750	3.60	14	0	0	0	4	1	25.0	37	119	16	10	1	3	0	1	4	1	23	2	0
Cordero, Frangil, Lan.*	2	0	1.000	7.24	9	0	0	0	2	0	13.2	18	77	16	11	1	1	0	1	15	0	11	5	1
Cordero, Victor, Bel.	7	5	.583	4.56	46	0	0	0	24	5	81.0	61	354	45	41	10	3	2	7	45	2	98	9	2
Cotton, Nathan, Day.	0	1	.000	3.24	12	0	0	0	5	2	25.0	36	111	15	9	4	1	0	3	0	17	4	1
Coughenour, Jory, Mich.	11	5	.688	3.78	35	14	0	0	4	2	126.1	152	554	68	53	4	4	3	22	1	65	5	1
Cramblitt, Joey, S.B.	5	7	.417	3.36	35	8	0	0	14	2	104.1	104	426	54	39	9	4	3	4	19	2	91	1	0
Crowther, Jackson, Clin.	0	0	.000	6.39	8	0	0	0	1	0	12.2	19	57	10	9	0	0	1	1	0	9	2	0
Cuello, Manolin, W.M.	2	3	.400	5.40	23	3	0	0	9	1	55.0	47	266	44	33	7	0	4	5	47	0	61	13	2
Cueto, Jose, Lan.	4	4	.500	3.79	22	14	2	2	1	0	95.0	71	399	50	40	4	3	3	8	44	0	105	9	3
Cummings, Jeremy, Peo.	4	6	.400	3.22	18	18	0	0	0	0	95.0	93	388	45	34	5	1	3	3	10	0	75	1	1
Daigle, Casey, S.B.	10	10	.500	4.12	28	27	2	1	0	0	164.0	180	727	100	75	11	3	9	14	55	0	85	16	4
D'Amico, Jeff, Bel.	0	0	.000	5.40	2	2	0	0	0	0	8.1	11	37	6	5	1	0	0	1	0	6	0	0
Dequin, Benjamin, Clin.*	6	11	.353	5.30	26	24	0	0	0	0	129.0	125	576	81	76	18	5	4	7	70	0	129	7	0
Detillion, Jamie, W.M.*	2	3	.400	2.10	48	0	0	0	21	4	77.0	66	323	21	18	3	3	4	0	27	4	66	9	0
Devine, Travis, Ft.W.	3	3	.500	5.26	29	1	0	0	8	1	49.2	66	228	41	29	6	0	1	2	14	1	42	8	0
Diaz, Eddy, Lan.	0	2	.000	6.99	20	6	0	0	6	0	56.2	71	278	55	44	7	2	2	6	34	0	41	20	1
Dorn, Grant, Clin.	4	1	.800	5.59	31	0	0	0	19	4	48.1	56	215	33	30	7	1	3	0	21	0	33	1	0
Douglass, Ryan, Bur.	1	2	.333	5.87	7	1	0	0	3	0	15.1	18	68	10	10	1	0	0	0	5	0	7	0	0
Duran, Frank, C.R.	0	0	.000	0.00	1	0	0	0	1	0	2.0	0	8	0	0	0	0	0	1	0	1	0	0
Dusan, Joe, Wis.*	0	0	.000	6.75	1	0	0	0	0	0	1.1	2	8	1	1	0	0	0	1	1	0	2	0	0
Earey, Ryan, Ft.W.	1	4	.200	4.82	24	7	0	0	8	0	65.1	70	279	38	35	7	1	5	2	17	1	59	1	1
Edwards, Bryan, Day.	6	7	.462	4.68	29	14	1	0	6	0	107.2	127	496	75	56	8	4	0	7	40	0	58	14	1
Eppolito, Vince, S.B.	2	1	.667	5.40	25	0	0	0	11	1	36.2	34	173	24	22	2	3	1	2	28	0	31	8	0
Esquivia, Manuel, K.C.	8	7	.533	5.13	24	18	0	0	1	1	105.1	92	462	66	60	7	3	7	5	51	0	82	15	2
Eyre, Willie, Q.C.	3	0	1.000	2.42	17	0	0	0	6	4	22.1	19	87	6	6	1	0	0	1	2	0	21	1	0
Farmer, Tom, W.M.	3	2	.600	2.37	6	6	0	0	0	0	38.0	30	144	10	10	2	0	0	8	0	28	4	1
Ferguson, Ian, Day.	3	2	.600	5.28	10	10	0	0	0	0	58.0	62	240	39	34	9	3	3	4	10	0	30	2	1
Figueroa, Eduardo, Wis.	0	0	.000	27.00	1	0	0	0	0	0	0.1	0	5	2	1	0	0	0	0	4	0	0	1	0
Fingers, Jason, Bur.	1	6	.143	3.71	33	0	0	0	18	4	43.2	46	186	21	18	4	3	1	2	10	1	37	4	1
Fischer, Rich, C.R.	9	7	.563	4.20	20	20	2	0	0	0	130.2	131	550	73	61	8	5	6	5	33	0	97	6	1
Flading, Cameron, C.R.	0	0	.000	5.29	15	0	0	0	12	1	17.0	12	79	13	10	2	0	0	16	0	29	5	0
Flannery, Mike, K.C.	3	4	.429	4.79	53	0	0	0	33	16	56.1	58	260	35	30	5	2	3	3	31	0	47	5	1
Foote, Joe, Q.C.	3	2	.600	5.17	13	8	0	0	1	0	55.2	64	242	37	32	7	2	1	5	10	1	46	3	0
Fox, Ben, Ft.W.*	1	1	.500	7.48	11	5	0	0	1	0	27.2	43	132	25	23	2	0	0	13	1	22	3	1
Freeman, Corey, Wis.	0	0	.000	0.00	1	0	0	0	0	0	1.0	0	4	0	0	0	0	0	0	1	0	0	0	0
Fries, Scott, Lan.*	6	5	.545	3.27	43	0	0	0	19	5	71.2	65	291	35	26	4	1	2	2	11	1	64	1	1
Fuell, Jerrod, W.M.	0	1	.000	2.91	14	0	0	0	6	1	21.2	13	93	8	7	2	2	2	3	12	3	13	1	0
Gaal, Bryan, Ft.W.	1	1	.500	1.95	23	0	0	0	9	2	32.1	20	118	7	7	0	0	2	4	1	42	2	1
Gallo, Mike, Mich.*	9	2	.818	3.84	44	0	0	0	17	4	84.1	83	360	38	36	4	1	2	8	19	1	67	3	1

Pitcher, Team	W	L	Pct.	ERA	G	GS	CG	ShO	GF	Sv.	IP	H	TBF	R	ER	HR	SH	SF	HB	BB	IBB	SO	WP	Bk.
Garris, Antonio, Clin.	0	3	.000	5.29	15	0	0	0	10	1	17.0	16	84	14	10	3	1	1	1	18	0	11	1	0
Gates, Brian, Q.C.	2	1	.667	2.17	15	0	0	0	7	0	29.0	25	121	10	7	2	0	0	2	8	1	24	2	0
Geigel, Rolando, K.C.	3	3	.500	4.06	30	1	0	0	6	0	44.1	39	199	22	20	1	1	2	10	28	1	19	7	0
George, Brad, Day.	2	1	.667	5.97	8	8	0	0	0	0	34.2	44	155	26	23	3	1	5	4	13	2	13	0	0
George, Todd, Clin.	0	2	.000	7.36	2	2	0	0	0	0	11.0	12	51	9	9	2	0	1	2	4	0	8	1	0
Germano, Justin, Ft.W.	2	6	.250	4.98	13	13	0	0	0	0	65.0	80	293	47	36	7	2	3	7	16	1	55	6	0
Gil, Dave, Day.	1	0	1.000	0.77	2	2	0	0	0	0	11.2	11	47	1	1	0	1	0	0	3	0	15	0	0
Girdley, Josh, Clin.*	0	2	.000	3.68	6	6	0	0	0	0	29.1	28	133	15	12	2	0	0	1	18	0	21	1	0
Gomer, Jeramy, Lan.*	0	0	.000	2.45	10	1	0	0	4	0	22.0	22	96	8	6	1	1	1	0	12	2	22	3	0
Gonzalez, Cesar, S.B.	4	12	.250	4.01	26	26	1	0	0	0	146.0	142	630	81	65	9	3	11	10	53	0	92	10	0
Gordon, Justin, Bel.*	3	4	.429	4.42	27	24	0	0	1	0	124.1	112	563	83	61	13	2	4	14	84	0	103	16	2
Graves, Don, Peo.	2	6	.250	5.02	34	15	0	0	1	0	104.0	99	463	67	58	7	3	5	2	53	1	71	9	0
Gray, Rusty, Bel.	1	0	1.000	6.75	7	0	0	0	3	0	17.1	26	75	13	13	2	0	1	1	4	0	7	1	3
Gruban, Jarret, C.R.	0	2	.000	5.29	13	2	0	0	2	0	34.0	44	165	30	20	4	0	6	2	14	0	22	3	0
Grunwald, Erik, Wis.	8	6	.571	3.38	29	21	1	1	1	0	157.1	138	661	66	59	10	4	7	11	10	0	109	5	1
Gutierrez, Lazaro, Ft.W.*	1	1	.500	4.91	16	0	0	0	4	0	18.1	18	83	10	10	2	1	1	0	10	3	16	3	0
Halamicek, Kevin, K.C.	0	3	.000	4.70	20	0	0	0	9	0	30.2	31	137	17	16	3	3	1	4	13	0	17	5	0
Hall, Dan, Bel.	4	3	.571	4.10	38	0	0	0	30	13	52.2	47	235	30	24	5	1	1	3	27	0	53	7	0
Hall, Josh, Day.	11	5	.688	2.65	22	22	2	0	0	0	132.1	117	549	52	39	4	2	1	2	39	1	122	18	2
Hamilton, Mark, Mich.*	0	0	.000	4.22	10	0	0	0	6	0	10.2	16	52	7	5	2	1	0	2	3	0	13	2	1
Harris, Julian, C.R.*	2	2	.500	5.61	18	3	0	0	4	0	25.2	28	118	18	16	0	1	1	0	14	1	20	4	0
Harvey, Ian, Ft.W.	0	0	.000	2.84	8	0	0	0	6	3	12.2	6	49	4	4	0	1	0	0	5	1	15	0	0
Haynes, Brad, K.C.	7	3	.700	3.81	17	17	0	0	0	0	89.2	86	402	50	38	4	5	4	11	39	0	73	6	1
Head, Daniel, Wis.	3	1	.750	3.03	16	1	0	0	6	1	32.2	24	139	15	11	2	0	1	5	11	1	27	1	1
Heiberger, Heath, S.B.*	1	1	.500	3.86	12	0	0	0	1	0	18.2	15	77	10	8	0	1	0	0	7	0	21	1	0
Hendrickson, Benjamin, Bel.	8	9	.471	2.84	25	25	1	0	0	0	133.1	122	576	58	42	3	1	1	6	72	0	133	9	1
Henkel, Robert, K.C.*	0	0	.000	4.50	1	1	0	0	0	0	4.0	6	20	3	2	0	0	0	0	1	0	2	1	1
Hensley, Matt, C.R.	5	3	.625	3.64	11	11	1	0	0	0	71.2	80	321	42	29	10	0	2	4	19	0	63	6	3
Herbert, John, Ft.W.	1	0	1.000	7.20	2	0	0	0	0	0	5.0	6	28	5	4	0	0	0	0	4	0	2	1	0
Hernandez, Fausto, Wis.	1	1	.500	5.40	9	0	0	0	4	0	10.2	21	75	11	10	3	0	0	6	1	0	16	3	1
Hernandez, Runelvys, Bur.	7	5	.583	3.40	17	17	0	0	0	0	100.2	94	426	46	38	5	2	2	3	29	0	100	6	3
Herrera, Jose, Wis.	1	0	1.000	3.07	4	1	0	0	0	0	14.2	10	63	7	5	2	0	1	3	3	0	20	2	2
Hill, Jeremy, Bur.	0	2	.000	1.51	40	0	0	0	31	12	47.2	22	190	11	8	2	2	0	3	25	0	66	6	0
Hoerman, Jared, Wis.	9	2	.818	1.49	21	13	0	0	0	0	90.2	60	374	32	15	2	3	2	14	29	0	101	4	1
Holubec, Ken, Q.C.*	4	8	.333	3.22	27	22	1	0	3	1	134.0	107	568	67	48	7	4	3	9	63	0	129	9	1
Houlton, Dennis, Mich.	0	1	.000	5.40	1	1	0	0	0	0	5.0	7	24	5	3	0	0	0	1	4	0	4	0	0
Howell, Michael, W.M.	3	0	1.000	1.76	8	8	0	0	0	0	51.0	41	190	12	10	2	0	4	0	7	0	42	1	1
Howington, Ty, Day.*	4	0	1.000	1.15	6	6	1	0	0	0	39.0	15	141	7	5	0	0	2	1	9	0	47	0	0
Humrich, Chris, Clin.	2	6	.400	3.64	33	0	0	0	11	0	47.0	44	218	22	19	4	2	2	3	33	0	45	4	1
Izquierdo, Hansel, K.C.	7	1	.875	1.32	24	2	0	0	5	2	47.2	27	181	8	7	1	1	0	3	13	0	42	1	2
Jackson, Dan, C.R.	1	1	.500	2.40	8	5	0	0	0	0	30.0	24	127	9	8	1	0	0	3	14	0	28	4	1
Jenks, Bobby, C.R.	3	7	.300	5.27	21	21	0	0	0	0	99.0	90	450	74	58	10	2	4	12	64	0	98	13	1
Johnson, Jeremy, W.M.	1	1	.500	4.67	3	3	0	0	0	0	17.1	18	76	10	9	2	1	0	1	6	0	7	2	0
Johnson, Kelly, Peo.	1	0	1.000	5.03	13	0	0	0	4	0	19.2	20	83	13	11	3	1	2	1	5	0	11	3	0
Johnson, Rett, Wis.	5	5	.500	2.27	16	16	2	2	0	0	99.1	92	407	33	25	4	3	1	2	30	0	96	3	0
Johnson, Tyler, Peo.*	0	1	.000	3.95	3	3	0	0	0	0	13.2	14	65	9	6	1	0	0	0	10	0	15	2	1
Johnston, Rikki, W.M.*	2	8	.200	4.38	13	13	0	0	0	0	74.0	72	318	43	36	7	1	2	5	28	1	59	4	2
Jongejan, Ferenc, Lan.*	2	5	.286	1.99	48	0	0	0	41	16	58.2	64	257	21	13	4	3	1	2	31	4	52	1	1
Kemp, Beau, Q.C.	0	1	.000	2.51	31	0	0	0	15	4	43.0	29	175	17	12	4	3	3	2	15	2	46	1	0
Keppinger, Billy, Bur.*	0	0	.000	0.00	1	0	0	0	1	0	1.0	1	4	0	0	0	0	0	0	0	0	0	0	0
Key, Chris, K.C.*	7	1	1.000	2.35	54	1	0	0	13	3	92.0	89	369	30	24	6	6	2	2	10	1	71	7	0
Kinney, Josh, Peo.	1	4	.200	4.39	27	0	0	0	5	0	41.0	47	192	24	20	1	4	2	7	15	0	35	4	1
Koronka, John, Day.*	3	1	.750	0.75	5	5	0	0	0	0	24.0	23	100	12	2	0	0	2	8	0	25	0	0
Koziara, Matt, Day.	0	0	.000	4.34	14	0	0	0	9	2	18.2	27	86	10	9	1	0	2	4	2	0	14	2	0
Krawiec, Aaron, Lan.*	7	11	.389	4.58	27	26	1	0	1	0	153.1	183	695	100	78	15	6	8	13	51	0	170	7	3
Lacorte, Vince, C.R.	3	10	.231	4.37	36	10	0	0	11	2	105.0	119	461	61	51	9	5	3	3	19	0	87	8	1
Laesch, Michael, Day.	2	3	.400	3.91	29	0	0	0	14	3	50.2	41	221	25	22	3	3	2	3	25	2	62	7	1
Lajara, Fudy, K.C.*	5	2	.714	4.44	36	0	0	0	10	0	48.2	44	210	29	24	5	3	3	5	21	0	48	6	0
Landestoy, Gilbert, C.R.	3	2	.600	4.15	36	0	0	0	14	2	65.0	51	286	40	30	5	0	3	10	33	0	54	2	0
Lansford, Dustin, Bel.	1	1	.500	2.16	3	1	0	0	1	0	8.1	3	35	2	2	0	1	1	0	10	0	12	2	0
Lavery, Tim, Lan.*	2	1	.667	2.43	30	1	0	0	4	2	85.1	74	342	25	23	4	1	4	2	13	0	55	2	1
Leclair, Aric, S.B.*	3	1	.750	3.42	37	2	0	0	10	1	52.2	48	243	28	20	0	1	4	34	2	53	7	2
Leicester, Jon, Lan.	9	10	.474	5.29	28	27	1	0	1	0	153.0	182	693	117	90	16	2	4	16	58	0	109	12	1
Leiter, Mark, Bel.	0	0	.000	2.45	1	0	0	0	0	0	3.2	4	16	1	1	0	0	0	2	0	0	4	0	0
Leu, Trevor, W.M.*	1	3	.250	5.57	13	0	0	0	4	0	21.0	23	100	15	13	0	0	1	1	16	0	28	4	1
Leuenberger, Jeff, W.M.	3	2	.600	3.13	30	0	0	0	11	0	49.1	46	211	19	17	2	5	3	4	19	4	40	3	0
Lewis, Jeremy, W.M.*	3	4	.429	2.00	9	9	1	1	0	0	49.2	41	209	20	16	1	2	3	21	0	35	2	0
Lincoln, Jeff, Q.C.	7	4	.636	3.63	31	12	0	0	8	1	96.2	83	435	47	39	7	3	0	67	0	101	9	2
Lira, James, Mich.	2	2	.500	7.12	25	0	0	0	23	12	31.1	17	123	7	6	2	4	1	1	12	2	33	2	0
Lockwood, Luke, Clin.*	5	10	.333	2.70	26	26	3	1	0	0	163.1	152	688	78	49	8	6	6	14	49	0	114	8	1
Lopez, Gustavo, K.C.	6	4	.600	3.58	17	17	0	0	0	0	93.0	89	392	42	37	2	1	2	2	27	0	63	11	0
Lugo, Ruddy, Bel.	1	0	1.000	0.60	10	0	0	0	8	5	15.0	10	60	1	1	0	1	0	1	6	0	14	0	0
Luque, Roger, Ft.W.*	5	2	.714	2.40	42	0	0	0	14	0	60.0	47	243	24	16	6	2	0	2	17	0	61	2	3
Mangrum, Micah, Bur.	7	2	.778	1.95	23	0	0	0	9	2	37.0	33	149	10	8	3	3	1	1	6	1	34	3	0
Mansfield, Monte, Mich.	4	5	.444	5.60	40	3	0	0	15	2	72.1	72	340	52	45	12	2	2	11	42	1	81	3	0
Markray, Thad, Day.	2	3	.400	3.60	32	0	0	0	14	3	65.0	70	289	32	26	3	5	0	2	30	3	54	4	1
Martin, Lucas, Q.C.*	8	6	.571	3.99	33	19	1	1	5	1	137.2	146	580	74	61	12	2	6	1	32	0	117	6	3
Martin, Nick, Clin.*	0	1	.000	18.00	1	1	0	0	0	0	2.0	6	15	5	4	1	0	0	0	3	0	0	0	0
Martinez, Javier A., Day.	1	0	1.000	3.38	8	0	0	0	7	4	8.0	6	36	4	3	1	1	1	4	0	13	0	0
Martinez, Miguel, Peo.	5	8	.385	4.44	18	18	1	0	0	0	97.1	114	443	72	48	7	5	5	27	1	52	7	0
Maysonet, Roberto, Bel.	5	10	.333	4.42	28	17	0	0	4	0	111.0	99	495	64	52	0	5	3	11	61	0	109	12	1
McAdoo, Duncan, Ft.W.	6	16	.273	3.54	28	28	0	0	0	0	157.2	173	683	87	62	15	1	6	11	36	0	121	4	3
McCasland, Ralph, Clin.*	1	2	.333	3.07	26	0	0	0	19	4	41.0	31	164	15	14	2	2	0	0	13	0	22	1	1

Pitcher, Team	W	L	Pct.	ERA	G	GS	CG	ShO	GF	Sv.	IP	H	TBF	R	ER	HR	SH	SF	HB	BB	IBB	SO	WP	Bk.
McClain, Kevin, C.R.	2	1	.667	2.27	24	0	0	0	7	0	31.2	22	131	9	8	3	2	2	9	0	36	2	0
McClellan, Zach, Bur.	5	10	.333	4.54	24	22	0	0	0	0	127.0	142	554	79	64	5	2	3	6	36	0	87	7	0
McGee, Christopher, Bel.	4	2	.667	4.19	37	2	0	0	10	1	68.2	69	310	40	32	6	4	5	6	34	2	51	3	2
McGill, Trae, Bur.	0	2	.000	4.62	5	5	1	0	0	0	25.1	29	106	17	13	3	1	0	0	5	0	27	1	1
McMurray, Heath, Bel.	3	0	1.000	4.70	9	0	0	0	3	0	15.1	13	68	9	8	3	0	0	3	8	0	20	1	0
McNutt, Mike, K.C.	9	5	.643	3.94	28	25	1	0	1	1	146.1	152	602	72	64	14	2	5	6	20	0	107	13	3
Medlock, Chet, Peo.	2	2	.500	3.71	30	0	0	0	7	0	43.2	45	188	23	18	4	3	1	4	15	0	27	6	0
Mejia, Juan, Ft.W.	0	2	.000	5.14	9	0	0	0	3	0	14.0	18	65	8	8	1	1	1	0	7	0	6	2	0
Messenger, Randall, K.C.	2	1	.667	3.93	14	0	0	0	7	0	18.1	22	85	13	8	0	3	2	2	5	0	14	0	0
Meyer, Mike, Peo.	2	3	.400	3.00	17	0	0	0	5	1	24.0	29	112	19	8	0	1	2	1	5	0	17	3	0
Miller, Ryan, Bel.	10	6	.625	5.30	22	22	0	0	0	0	105.1	100	462	70	62	17	0	3	14	47	0	112	9	0
Miniel, Roberto, Bel.-Lan.	6	7	.462	4.25	33	21	1	1	4	0	135.2	130	577	75	64	10	4	3	8	38	0	140	6	1
Mitchell, Tom, Clin.	0	4	.000	6.45	5	5	0	0	0	0	22.1	29	105	20	16	5	0	1	0	9	0	5	4	1
Miyamoto, Eiji, Clin.	2	4	.333	4.08	20	0	0	0	6	1	28.2	22	130	21	13	3	2	2	3	19	1	23	5	2
Montoya, Saul, S.B.	0	0	.000	3.95	7	1	0	0	1	0	13.2	17	60	6	6	1	0	2	1	5	0	11	1	0
Morgan, Russ, Wis.*	2	1	.667	2.25	17	0	0	0	8	1	28.0	22	125	10	7	0	1	0	2	18	0	38	3	0
Morris, Will, C.R.	6	6	.500	4.44	40	0	0	0	12	6	81.0	99	373	51	40	11	6	3	4	23	0	88	4	1
Moseley, Dustin, Day.	10	8	.556	4.20	25	25	0	0	0	0	148.0	158	638	83	69	10	4	1	8	42	0	108	3	2
Moseley, Marcus, Q.C.	3	5	.375	6.28	20	8	0	0	5	0	57.1	52	278	44	40	4	3	4	14	46	2	35	13	1
Mottl, Ryan, Day.	15	6	.714	3.60	26	26	2	0	0	0	152.2	155	653	74	61	15	3	6	10	42	2	119	7	0
Nageotte, Clint, Wis.	11	8	.579	3.13	28	26	0	0	0	0	152.1	141	648	65	53	10	10	1	11	50	1	187	6	4
Narveson, Chris, Peo.*	3	3	.500	1.98	8	8	0	0	0	0	50.0	32	190	14	11	3	2	1	3	11	0	53	0	0
Nicolas, Mike, Ft.W.	1	5	.167	3.45	54	0	0	0	29	7	62.2	44	265	30	24	4	5	4	8	34	4	70	4	3
Norderum, Jason, Clin.*	7	7	.500	4.88	28	28	2	0	0	0	155.0	176	706	96	84	17	5	3	19	60	0	101	9	1
Novinsky, John, Peo.	9	11	.450	5.52	25	25	1	0	0	0	138.2	165	615	95	85	17	1	4	10	43	0	115	13	1
Nunez, Vladimir, K.C.	0	0	.000	9.00	1	1	0	0	0	0	1.0	3	5	1	1	0	0	0	0	0	0	0	0	0
Olore, Kevin, Wis.	13	4	.765	3.32	27	27	0	0	0	0	154.2	134	641	70	57	14	4	3	14	40	0	158	6	1
O'Neal, Brandon, C.R.	2	8	.200	5.88	16	15	0	0	0	0	82.2	95	385	67	54	6	1	3	11	40	0	51	9	2
Oxspring, Chris, Ft.W.	4	1	.800	4.15	41	2	0	0	8	0	56.1	66	256	29	26	5	3	3	25	5	54	2	2
Pace, Adam, C.R.*	5	6	.455	3.92	17	12	1	0	2	0	87.1	84	377	52	38	3	4	5	3	24	0	68	11	0
Pape, Stace, Day.	0	0	.000	8.18	7	0	0	0	3	0	11.0	20	57	13	10	3	0	0	0	7	0	13	0	0
Patchett, Gary, Day.	0	0	.000	7.71	3	0	0	0	3	0	4.2	3	20	4	4	1	0	0	0	3	0	2	1	0
Pember, Dave, Bel.	3	4	.429	3.27	8	8	0	0	0	0	44.0	49	185	20	16	3	0	2	1	10	0	39	5	0
Peralta, Joel, C.R.	0	0	.000	2.13	41	0	0	0	39	23	42.1	27	166	13	10	3	2	1	4	5	0	53	0	0
Percosky, Mark, Ft.W.	0	2	.000	5.65	8	6	0	0	1	0	28.2	33	130	20	18	5	0	0	2	12	0	30	2	1
Perez, Beltran, S.B.	12	4	.750	2.81	27	27	2	0	0	0	160.0	142	651	59	50	10	5	3	6	35	0	157	5	3
Perez, Frank, W.M.	7	2	.778	2.65	36	1	0	0	12	2	78.0	63	317	27	23	2	0	3	29	1	81	6	3
Perez, Oliver, Ft.W.*	8	5	.615	3.46	19	19	0	0	0	0	101.1	84	415	46	39	9	0	5	1	43	0	98	1	2
Perkins, Mike, Peo.	0	0	.000	0.79	7	0	0	0	4	0	11.1	3	43	2	1	0	0	1	0	2	0	8	1	0
Persby, Andy, Q.C.	3	0	1.000	1.00	20	0	0	0	5	1	27.0	18	108	6	3	1	0	1	2	13	0	17	3	0
Phillips, Mark, Ft.W.*	4	1	.800	2.64	5	5	0	0	0	0	30.2	19	127	11	9	1	1	0	3	14	0	27	1	0
Pike, Matthew, Day.	0	1	.000	5.40	2	1	0	0	0	0	6.2	7	30	4	4	3	0	0	1	3	0	8	0	0
Pine, Chris, C.R.	1	1	.500	1.76	12	0	0	0	7	2	15.1	6	59	3	3	1	1	0	0	7	0	24	2	0
Pinto, Renyel, Lan.*	4	8	.333	5.22	20	20	1	0	0	0	88.0	94	393	64	51	9	4	4	3	44	1	69	5	3
Pitney, James, W.M.	1	0	1.000	3.42	15	0	0	0	7	1	26.1	23	115	12	10	1	0	4	12	0	27	2	0
Polo, Bienvenido, Peo.	0	0	.000	4.50	18	1	0	0	2	0	28.0	25	134	22	14	4	1	4	19	0	19	10	1
Ponce Deleon, Damon, Peo.	1	1	.500	4.67	19	0	0	0	12	2	21.2	17	90	13	11	3	0	0	1	8	0	15	0	1
Prater, Andy, Ft.W.	0	0	.000	54.00	1	0	0	0	0	0	0.2	3	6	4	4	0	0	0	1	0	0	0	0	0
Pridie, Jon, Q.C.	6	3	.667	3.40	12	11	1	0	0	0	55.2	40	229	26	21	5	0	8	24	0	48	2	0
Puello, Ignacio, Clin.	3	3	.500	5.57	7	7	0	0	0	0	32.1	29	155	21	20	4	1	3	6	26	0	21	4	1
Qualls, Chad, Mich.	15	6	.714	3.72	26	26	3	2	0	0	162.0	149	673	77	67	8	2	6	11	30	0	125	10	2
Ramirez, Joslin, S.B.	6	5	.545	3.28	18	18	0	0	0	0	104.1	109	444	48	38	10	4	6	4	28	0	73	5	2
Ramos, Luis, Bel.	0	0	.000	4.50	2	0	0	0	2	1	4.0	4	18	2	2	0	0	0	2	0	8	1	0
Randazzo, Jeffrey, Q.C.*	9	3	.750	4.62	20	18	0	0	0	0	103.1	116	440	58	53	7	5	4	6	31	1	69	10	1
Ribaudo, Mike, Mich.	2	2	.500	3.59	30	0	0	0	19	0	47.2	50	223	26	19	5	2	1	5	30	1	37	5	1
Ricciardi, Joe, S.B.	5	4	.556	6.27	20	0	0	0	7	0	33.0	43	164	25	23	3	3	0	7	19	1	28	1	0
Rijo, Jose, Day.	0	0	.000	3.00	1	1	0	0	0	0	3.0	3	11	1	1	0	0	0	0	0	0	1	0	0
Rodney, Lee, W.M.	8	8	.500	3.87	27	27	0	0	0	0	158.0	149	684	85	68	14	3	4	7	70	4	149	9	1
Romero, Josmir, Q.C.	7	7	.500	4.44	30	14	2	0	5	1	121.2	134	531	72	60	11	3	7	9	40	1	61	9	4
Rundles, Rich, Clin.*	1	1	.500	2.33	4	4	0	0	0	0	27.0	26	112	10	7	0	0	3	3	1	20	1	0
Russelburg, Aaron, Peo.	4	3	.571	4.56	10	10	0	0	0	0	51.1	53	227	31	26	3	1	2	27	0	31	6	1
Russo, Scott, Clin.*	1	1	.500	1.80	15	0	0	0	9	1	20.0	13	88	9	4	1	0	2	0	12	0	21	1	0
Ryan, Jeremy, Mich.	0	3	.000	5.86	15	7	0	0	1	0	43.0	47	197	33	28	9	3	1	7	13	0	39	4	0
Saladin, Miguel, Mich.	7	3	.700	2.93	46	0	0	0	26	11	73.2	72	323	27	24	2	2	2	10	24	1	66	3	1
Samora, Santo, Peo.	1	7	.125	4.21	52	0	0	0	38	12	62.0	62	295	50	29	4	0	2	9	27	0	38	6	1
Sauer, Marc, K.C.	2	2	.500	4.20	9	5	0	0	0	0	30.0	30	123	15	14	2	0	0	5	1	0	13	1	0
Sawyer, Steve, K.C.	10	2	.833	4.20	55	0	0	0	25	7	70.2	78	316	39	33	5	3	4	4	27	0	37	10	2
Schaub, Greg, Bel.	0	2	.000	3.70	25	0	0	0	6	1	41.1	37	190	24	17	1	3	2	3	24	2	47	5	1
Service, Scott, Day.	0	0	.000	0.00	4	0	0	0	3	2	5.2	2	21	0	0	0	0	0	0	0	0	6	0	0
Sheefel, Adam, Day.*	3	4	.429	4.04	40	2	0	0	12	1	69.0	80	313	37	31	5	5	3	25	4	59	5	1
Shouse, Dan, Peo.*	1	0	1.000	5.14	11	0	0	0	3	0	14.0	17	61	9	8	0	0	4	11	1	9	1	0
Shrout, Kevin, Bel.	1	1	.500	8.31	6	0	0	0	3	0	13.0	22	63	13	12	1	0	0	0	4	0	11	1	0
Shwam, Mike, Bel.	9	3	.750	2.60	47	0	0	0	24	9	93.1	75	382	36	27	3	8	0	2	31	3	97	5	1
Sierra, Auvin, W.M.*	2	2	.500	5.09	17	1	0	0	3	0	23.0	24	105	15	13	2	1	0	3	16	0	20	2	0
Skinner, John, K.C.	1	4	.200	3.00	25	0	0	0	5	0	36.0	36	151	16	12	1	1	1	1	8	1	26	3	0
Sloan, Brandon, K.C.	3	4	.429	3.36	41	13	0	0	22	9	107.0	108	435	48	40	4	4	5	6	26	0	65	2	0
Smart, Pete, Mich.*	0	8	.000	3.07	11	11	0	0	0	0	70.1	64	294	30	24	2	4	2	4	24	0	47	5	0
Snare, Ryan, Day.*	9	5	.643	3.05	21	20	0	0	0	0	115.0	101	472	45	39	7	1	1	9	37	1	118	9	2
Sosa, Jorge, Wis.	0	0	.000	9.00	2	0	0	0	1	0	2.0	3	9	2	2	1	0	0	0	0	0	4	0	0
Sprowl, Jon-Mark, Lan.	0	0	.000	4.50	1	0	0	0	1	0	2.0	2	9	1	1	0	0	0	1	0	5	0	0
Stanford, Derek, Mich.	1	2	.333	2.74	5	5	0	0	0	0	23.0	24	108	11	7	2	1	4	17	0	14	3	0
Steele, Mike, W.M.	4	3	.571	1.16	38	0	0	0	36	19	46.2	23	194	13	6	2	0	0	4	26	4	78	2	0
Stiles, Brad, Bur.*	5	5	.500	5.04	30	6	0	0	7	0	60.2	81	290	45	34	3	2	6	1	33	1	49	5	3

Pitcher, Team	W	L	Pct.	ERA	G	GS	CG	ShO	GF	Sv.	IP	H	TBF	R	ER	HR	SH	SF	HB	BB	IBB	SO	WP	Bk.
Stockman, Landon, W.M.	2	2	.500	2.42	18	0	0	0	15	6	26.0	21	112	7	7	0	1	0	2	13	3	23	3	0
Stodolka, Michael, Bur.*	3	8	.273	4.67	20	20	0	0	0	0	94.1	105	420	67	49	9	5	5	7	30	0	49	6	0
Stokes, Shaun, Peo.	2	7	.222	7.14	13	13	0	0	0	0	58.0	87	278	57	46	8	1	4	2	22	0	42	1	0
Stokley, Billy, C.R.	5	3	.625	1.98	22	0	0	0	7	1	41.0	31	173	14	9	1	0	0	3	18	2	45	6	1
Stone, Jon, Ft.W.	0	1	.000	5.40	1	0	0	0	1	0	1.2	1	6	1	1	1	0	0	0	0	0	3	0	0
Sundbeck, Cody, S.B.	0	1	.000	3.77	11	0	0	0	3	0	14.1	8	62	6	6	1	0	0	2	10	2	16	2	0
Swindell, Jeremy, W.M.*	0	0	.000	16.20	4	0	0	0	0	0	1.2	1	12	3	3	0	0	0	0	6	0	1	0	0
Szuminski, Jason, Lan.	4	3	.571	6.44	14	4	0	0	2	0	36.1	56	177	27	26	2	1	1	2	17	0	22	2	0
Taylor, Aaron, Wis.	3	1	.750	2.45	28	0	0	0	26	9	29.1	19	119	9	8	1	2	1	2	11	2	50	4	2
Tejada, Sandy, Q.C.	0	1	.000	4.50	4	2	0	0	0	0	10.0	7	47	8	5	1	1	0	1	9	0	13	1	0
Thomas, Adam, C.R.	4	7	.364	5.14	19	16	2	1	0	0	96.1	109	409	63	55	13	1	1	6	23	0	61	4	0
Thompson, Mike, Ft.W.	0	1	.000	6.00	1	1	0	0	0	0	6.0	8	28	4	4	0	0	0	0	2	0	1	0	0
Torres, Joe, C.R.*	0	3	.000	5.82	4	4	0	0	0	0	17.0	16	80	12	11	0	1	1	2	14	0	14	4	0
Torres, Luis, Clin.	6	8	.429	5.18	18	18	0	0	0	0	104.1	116	461	76	60	10	1	7	5	42	0	56	9	0
Van Dusen, Derrick, Wis.*	5	4	.556	3.19	18	18	1	1	0	0	96.0	82	395	40	34	6	1	3	1	24	0	103	8	0
Vincent, Matt, Peo.*	0	1	.000	3.24	14	0	0	0	3	0	16.2	18	72	7	6	1	0	1	2	4	0	10	0	0
Vriesenga, Matt, Peo.	4	1	.800	4.01	35	0	0	0	6	0	92.0	103	391	50	41	4	1	2	5	11	0	48	10	0
Wagner, Frank, Bel.*	0	1	.000	21.60	8	0	0	0	2	0	8.1	18	59	20	20	1	0	0	4	13	0	8	2	1
Wallace, Ben, Bel.*	1	4	.200	9.55	8	6	0	0	1	0	27.1	44	135	32	29	3	0	1	3	14	0	15	5	0
Wallis, Jacob, Clin.	0	0	.000	0.00	1	0	0	0	1	0	1.0	0	3	0	0	0	0	0	0	1	0	1	0	0
Walton, Sam, Wis.*	0	1	.000	4.76	3	2	0	0	0	0	5.2	7	30	3	3	0	0	1	0	6	0	8	1	0
Warren, Andy, W.M.	1	1	.500	3.45	3	3	0	0	0	0	15.2	17	69	7	6	0	0	0	2	3	0	12	0	2
Washburn, Ben, Clin.	4	12	.250	4.79	30	15	1	1	4	0	129.2	141	560	84	69	19	3	6	7	30	0	89	6	3
Wawrzyniak, Alan, C.R.	2	2	.500	3.57	5	5	0	0	0	0	22.2	25	113	16	9	3	0	2	0	22	0	21	8	0
Wayne, Hawkeye, Wis.	4	2	.667	4.58	30	5	0	0	2	0	59.0	55	276	38	30	1	2	3	6	45	0	48	12	1
Webster, Jeremy, Ft.W.*	0	0	.000	2.96	16	0	0	0	2	0	27.1	19	119	15	9	3	4	1	0	22	0	31	4	0
Weis, Brad, Q.C.*	4	0	1.000	0.69	22	0	0	0	7	2	39.1	38	181	15	3	0	1	1	2	19	2	43	5	0
Wellemeyer, Todd, Lan.	13	9	.591	4.16	27	27	1	0	0	0	147.0	165	667	85	68	14	4	5	11	74	0	167	10	1
Wells, Carl, S.B.*	4	4	.500	2.89	40	0	0	0	15	2	71.2	74	303	31	23	2	4	4	2	13	0	52	7	2
Wells, Roy, Wis.	7	6	.538	3.23	30	6	0	0	15	3	92.0	82	389	37	33	4	2	2	3	27	3	97	3	0
Wheatland, Matt, W.M.	0	2	.000	10.93	3	3	0	0	0	0	14.0	21	71	18	17	1	0	2	2	4	0	17	4	1
White, Bill, S.B.*	9	3	.750	3.00	19	19	0	0	0	0	111.1	98	466	53	47	9	4	2	4	53	0	103	5	1
Wiedmeyer, Jason, Ft.W.*	1	1	.500	1.85	6	6	1	1	0	0	34.0	38	154	14	7	5	0	1	1	13	0	29	3	1
Wiles, Chad, Wis.	3	4	.429	2.17	39	0	0	0	36	17	45.2	49	192	19	11	2	0	2	0	8	4	45	2	0
Wilkerson, Wes, Bur.	1	4	.200	4.84	43	0	0	0	23	8	61.1	67	277	39	33	2	6	2	4	26	0	46	9	0
Wilkinson, Matthew, S.B.	1	2	.333	7.23	14	0	0	0	5	0	18.2	27	92	17	15	1	2	1	0	10	2	23	0	0
Wolfe, Brian, Q.C.	13	8	.619	2.01	20	23	2	2	2	0	160.0	128	641	64	50	11	2	4	5	32	2	128	8	0
Woodyard, Mark, W.M.	7	12	.368	4.51	25	25	2	1	0	0	143.2	147	636	81	72	5	1	6	9	69	2	84	13	0
Wrightman, Dusty, Bur.	5	6	.455	4.29	34	4	0	0	8	0	79.2	90	348	43	38	6	1	5	3	22	2	54	5	2
Yoshida, Nobuaki, Ft.W.*	1	2	.333	3.86	5	5	1	0	0	0	23.1	23	99	13	10	2	0	1	0	13	0	12	2	1
Zurita, Tom, Bur.	5	2	.714	4.76	35	0	0	0	17	2	56.2	71	263	34	30	5	2	2	2	22	1	39	1	0

PITCHERS WITH TWO OR MORE TEAMS

Pitcher, Team	W	L	Pct.	ERA	G	GS	CG	ShO	GF	Sv.	IP	H	TBF	R	ER	HR	SH	SF	HB	BB	IBB	SO	WP	Bk.
Miniel, Roberto, Bel.	4	6	.400	4.08	25	16	1	1	4	0	103.2	104	444	57	47	6	3	2	5	27	0	117	5	1
Miniel, Roberto, Lan.	2	1	.667	4.78	8	5	0	0	3	0	32.0	26	133	18	17	4	1	1	3	11	0	23	1	0

COMBINATION SHUTOUTS: **Beloit (4)**—Pember-Hall-Lugo, Hendrickson-Cordero-Hall, Hendrickson-Cordero-Artieta, Gordon-Hall. **Burlington (4)**—Stodolka-Fingers-Hill, McClellan-Coa, Hernandez-Hill, Hernandez-Wilkerson-Coa. **Cedar Rapids (2)**—Fischer-Stokley-Landestoy, O'Neal-Morris-Pine. **Clinton (4)**—Mitchell-Humrich, Dequin-Chisnall-Charron, Torres-Miyamoto-McCasland, Rundles-McCasland. **Dayton (13)**—Snare-Koziara-Markray, Koronka-Cotton-Bludau, Moseley-Sheefel-Bludau, Snare-Edwards-Sheefel-Boutwell, Hall-Markray, Howington-Laesch, Hall-Markray-Sheefel-Martinez, Edwards-Sheefel-Markray, Moseley-Laesch-Bradley-Service, Hall-Sheefel-Service, Mottl-Markray, Moseley-Bludau, Snare-Sheefel-Bludau. **Fort Wayne (8)**—Perez-Belanger-Gutierrez-Bumstead, Yoshida-Gutierrez-Bumstead, Perez-Nicolas-Gutierrez-Bumstead, McAdoo-Gaal, Perez Nicolas, McAdoo-Nicolas-Bumstead, Burns-Belanger-Oxspring-Bumstead, McAdoo-Luque-Nicolas. **Kane County (4)**—McNutt-Sawyer, Lopez-Key-Flannery, Sloan-Geigel-Lajara, Esquivia-Skinner-Sawyer. **Lansing (5)**—Pinto-Albright, Krawiec-Albright, Leicester-Albright, Wollemeyer-Jongejan, Wellemeyer-Blanton-Diaz. **Michigan (5)**—Anderson-Coughenour-Gallo, Barrett-Saladin, Coughenour-Mansfield, Barrett-Gallo, Qualls-Ribaudo. **Peoria (3)**—Martinez-Vincent-Cali-Ponce Deleon, Narveson-Ponce Deleon, Narveson-Ponce Deleon-Samora, Graves-Meyer-Cook. **Quad City (10)**—Randazzo-Martin-Eyre-Bonilla, Wolfe-Eyre-Bonilla, Randazzo-Blackwell, Randazzo-Weis-Bonilla, Randazzo-Persby-Weis-Bonilla, Pridie-Bonilla, Holubec-Kemp, Martin-Romero, Wolfe-Contreras-Kemp-Bonilla, Lincoln-Gates-Holubec, Wolfe-Kemp. **South Bend (7)**—White-Leclair Cramblitt, Gonzalez-Cramblitt, Castellanos-Leclair, Perez-Leclair-Bruney, White-Belson, Perez-Heiberger-Wilkinson-Belson, Ramirez-Heiberger, Daigle-Eppolito. **West Michigan (13)**—Warren-Pitney-Steele, Rodney-Pitney-Steele, Rodney-Detillion-Steele, Rodney-Detillion, Arias-Detillion-Pitney, Arias-Steele, Johnston-Steele, Arias-Steele, Arias-Fuell-Campbell, Arias-Perez-Steele, Campbell-Detillion, Howell-Leuenberger-Stockman, Farmer-Perez. **Wisconsin (11)**—Wayne-Grunwald-Wiles, Nageotte-Wiles, Hoerman-Wells, Van Dusen-Grunwald-Butler-Taylor, Nageotte-Hoerman-Wayne-Wells, Olore-Burton-Taylor, Olore-Walton-Grunwald-Taylor, Hoerman-Wayne, Van Dusen-Butler-Burton, Olore-Burton-Taylor, Hoerman-Burton-Taylor, Grunwald-Barnes-Taylor.

NO-HIT GAMES: Wolfe, Quad City defeated Dayton, 2-0, August 12; Van Dusen, Wisconsin defeated Cedar Rapids, 2-0, August 27.

2001 FIELDING

TEAM

Team	Pct.	G	PO	A	E	TC	DP	TP	PB
Quad City	.968	137	3613	1467	167	5247	103	0	22
Kane County......	.968	138	3698	1536	174	5408	124	1	28
Michigan	.967	137	3567	1380	170	5117	108	0	21
West Michigan ..	.966	138	3644	1404	178	5226	121	0	18
Beloit................	.965	138	3640	1410	183	5233	113	0	20
Burlington	.964	134	3453	1437	183	5073	94	0	19
Wisconsin	.963	136	3607	1398	194	5199	113	0	18
Dayton..............	.962	139	3657	1487	201	5345	100	0	19
South Bend	.961	136	3530	1458	200	5188	112	0	18
Fort Wayne	.961	137	3554	1362	199	5115	96	0	32
Lansing	.960	140	3615	1427	209	5251	111	0	20
Clinton..............	.960	137	3592	1560	216	5368	119	0	20

Team	Pct.	G	PO	A	E	TC	DP	TP	PB
Cedar Rapids.....	.956	137	3621	1369	228	5218	90	0	18
Peoria...............	.953	138	3622	1598	258	5478	125	0	17

INDIVIDUAL

FIRST BASEMEN

NOTE: All caps denotes fielding-percentage leader based on 70 games for catchers, 93 for all other non-pitchers and 112 innings for pitchers. *Throws lefthanded.

Player, Team	Pct.	G	PO	A	E	TC	DP
Acevedo, Anthony, Mich.*	1.000	1	4	1	0	5	0
Ambrosini, Dominick, Clin.*	.983	51	473	37	9	519	48
Angel, Tony, Mich.	.995	25	203	12	1	216	18
Ansman, Craig, S.B.	.978	5	45	0	1	46	8

Player, Team	Pct.	G	PO	A	E	TC	DP
Barbier, Blair, Lan.	.983	71	556	23	10	589	54
Bitter, Jarrod, Ft.W.	.941	3	15	1	1	17	0
Bone, Blake, Wis.	.988	9	77	5	1	83	8
Brandes, Landon, Peo.	1.000	2	4	0	0	4	0
Brooks, Jeff, S.B.	.950	9	87	8	5	100	4
Carroll, Mark, Wis.	1.000	1	5	0	0	5	0
Castellano, John, Wis.	.974	21	142	10	4	156	15
Cowan, Justin, Bur.	1.000	7	48	0	0	48	5
Daubert, Jake, Wis.	1.000	5	41	3	0	44	6
Demarco, Matt, K.C.	1.000	4	29	2	0	31	2
Dempsey, Nick, Clin.	1.000	20	162	10	0	172	15
Diaz, Aneuris, Peo.	1.000	3	14	2	0	16	2
Doudt, Anthony, C.R.	.983	21	164	10	3	177	13
Dubois, Jason, Lan.	.966	13	107	8	4	119	7
Duncan, Chris, Peo.	.972	70	733	16	21	790	50
DUSAN, Joe, Wis.*	.994	114	873	73	6	952	75
Eylward, Thomas, Lan.	.989	20	172	16	2	190	12
Gall, John, Peo.	.993	45	410	24	3	437	43
Garcia, Hector, Bel.	.964	14	100	8	4	112	6
Gonzalez, Adrian, K.C.*	.988	116	1091	85	14	1190	92
Hamilton, Mark, Mich.*	1.000	3	25	2	0	27	1
Johnson, Forrest, W.M.	.989	32	251	11	3	265	27
Kenney, Jeff, Bel.	1.000	4	29	1	0	30	1
Keppinger, Billy, Bur.*	.978	10	86	4	2	92	5
Lindsey, Cordell, C.R.	.989	33	256	24	3	283	16
Llamas, Juan, Bur.	1.000	1	13	1	0	14	1
Loeb, Bryan, S.B.	1.000	1	9	1	0	10	2
Lydic, Joe, Mich.	.982	15	106	3	2	111	4
Magness, Pat, K.C.	.992	14	124	7	1	132	10
Maule, Jason, Mich.	1.000	3	15	0	0	15	1
Miller, Eric, Clin.	.962	5	48	2	2	52	4
Morneau, Justin, Q.C.	.985	61	484	48	8	540	47
Myers, Corey, S.B.	.952	5	37	3	2	42	6
Napoli, Michael, C.R.	1.000	5	50	5	0	55	3
Neal, Steve, S.B.*	.984	119	1021	77	18	1116	81
Neill, Ryan, W.M.	.992	70	565	41	5	611	50
Peters, Samone, Day.	.963	71	617	41	25	683	45
Postell, Matthew, K.C.	1.000	7	44	2	0	46	3
Puccinelli, John, Ft.W.	.974	9	73	1	2	76	5
Quattlebaum, Hugh, W.M.	1.000	42	362	21	0	383	31
Rodgers, Albert, Peo.	.980	17	138	11	3	152	12
Roper, Zach, C.R.	.982	28	250	17	5	272	15
Ruiz, Randy, Day.	.981	67	590	29	12	631	43
Sandberg, Eric, Q.C.*	.992	40	367	22	3	392	27
Sandoval, Michael, Q.C.	1.000	2	9	2	0	11	0
Santos, Chad, Bur.*	.988	121	1072	84	14	1170	70
Segura, Rolando, Ft.W.	.962	3	24	1	1	26	2
Sing, Brandon, Lan.	.987	52	438	25	6	469	40
Soto, T.J., Mich.	.991	99	880	52	8	940	76
Sprowl, Jon-Mark, Lan.	.981	7	46	6	1	53	1
Thompson, Craig, Ft.W.	1.000	14	122	11	0	133	11
Tiffee, Terry, Q.C.	.986	27	195	14	3	212	15
Tolzien, Edward, C.R.*	.977	20	162	11	4	177	15
Torres, Digno, Q.C.*	.993	22	140	11	1	152	8
Tracy, Chad, S.B.	1.000	1	1	0	0	1	0
Voltz, Robert, Bel.*	.990	124	991	58	11	1060	90
Warner, J.R., C.R.*	.962	14	114	13	5	132	7
Williams, Clyde, Clin.*	.978	65	588	36	14	638	46
Williamson, Chris, Day.*	.957	4	19	3	1	23	1
Woodward, John, Ft.W.	.984	110	891	70	16	977	70
Woody, Dominic, K.C.	1.000	1	9	0	0	9	2

TRIPLE PLAY: Voltz.

Player, Team	Pct.	G	PO	A	E	TC	DP
Demarco, Matt, K.C.	1.000	27	34	66	0	100	15
Diaz, Aneuris, Peo.	.750	1	2	1	1	4	0
Docen, Jose, Clin.	.974	69	145	192	9	346	40
Duran, Frank, C.R.	.961	36	73	99	7	179	15
Durango, Ariel, Wis.	.983	12	23	34	1	58	7
Easterday, Matt, K.C.	.960	33	65	80	6	151	17
Edwards, Dytarious, Ft.W.	.968	22	38	53	3	94	8
Fatur, Brian, Peo.	.944	13	26	42	4	72	7
Fears, Chris, Ft.W.	.000	1	0	0	0	0	0
Fenster, Darren, Bur.	.956	33	49	80	6	135	11
Firlit, Dan, Peo.	.944	4	4	13	1	18	2
Floyd, Dan, Wis.	.982	13	19	35	1	55	7
Furmaniak, Jason, Ft.W.	1.000	3	4	9	0	13	1
Garabito, Vianney, Day.	.960	5	9	15	1	25	3
Gonzalez, Noggie, Q.C.	.944	30	43	39	6	108	13
GREEN, Andy, S.B.	.973	125	234	336	16	586	63
Gutierrez, Derrick, Wis.	1.000	1	0	2	0	2	0
Guzman, Juan, Bur.	.000	1	0	0	1	1	0
Hake, Travis, Bel.	.778	6	5	9	4	18	2
Harris, Brendan, Lan.	1.000	11	20	35	0	55	11
Harris, Josh, Lan.	.981	20	42	60	2	104	10
Helquist, Jon, Mich.	.956	64	112	191	14	317	43
Hooper, Kevin, K.C.	.957	17	38	52	4	94	7
Kelly, Heath, K.C.	1.000	5	12	21	0	33	4
Kenney, Jeff, Bel.	.981	34	65	88	3	156	15
Lagana, Stephen, S.B.	.500	1	1	0	1	2	0
Liriano, Pedro, Wis.	.955	106	189	281	22	492	62
Lora, Tom, Bur.	.961	105	213	255	19	487	59
Luuloa, Miles, W.M.	.947	66	132	171	17	320	45
Martinez, Dionnar, Lan.	.923	2	4	8	1	13	1
Martinez, Guillermo, Wis.	.963	9	10	16	1	27	2
Maule, Jason, Mich.	.944	48	80	140	13	233	22
Maza, Luis, Q.C.	1.000	1	1	0	0	1	0
McCool, Lee, Ft.W.	.935	95	170	232	28	430	42
Merritt, Timothy, Wis.	1.000	3	8	5	0	13	1
Miller, Eric, Clin.	.875	1	2	5	1	8	1
Morrissey, Adam, Lan.	.973	46	107	106	6	219	24
Patchett, Gary, Day.	.966	66	113	168	10	291	31
Peguero, Miguel, W.M.	.952	33	71	86	8	165	23
Pichardo, Maximo, C.R.	.955	43	84	108	9	201	20
Raburn, Johnny, C.R.	.933	52	87	121	15	223	17
Saba, Cesar, Ft.W.	.938	7	14	16	2	32	5
Sandoval, Michael, Q.C.	1.000	1	1	1	0	2	0
Santana, Sandy, Peo.	.947	48	89	143	13	245	35
Schnabel, Nicholas, Clin.	.930	14	32	34	5	71	12
Stockton, Jeff, C.R.	.957	5	11	11	1	23	1
Tamburrino, Brett, Q.C.	.968	16	23	37	2	62	7
Vizcaino, Maximo, S.B.	.947	12	14	22	2	38	5
Watkins, Tommy, Q.C.	.931	7	13	14	2	29	3
Willingham, Josh, K.C.	1.000	2	3	2	0	5	0
Wilson, Josh, K.C.	.975	67	143	173	8	324	42
Woods, Michael, W.M.	.952	44	80	120	10	210	19
Wyant, Hunter, K.C.	.889	3	4	4	1	9	1

TRIPLE PLAY: Candelaria.

SECOND BASEMEN

Player, Team	Pct.	G	PO	A	E	TC	DP
Anderson, Bryan, Day.	1.000	1	0	2	0	2	0
Angel, Tony, Mich.	.978	19	37	54	2	93	9
Ayala, Elio, Bel.	.962	80	173	210	15	398	46
Berroa, Cristian, Mich.	.975	10	11	28	1	40	3
Blasi, Blake, Lan.	.952	61	106	151	13	270	31
Bone, Blake, Wis.	.800	3	2	2	1	5	1
Boyd, Shaun, Peo.	.956	80	158	274	20	452	55
Boyer, Bret, Clin.	.918	56	117	130	22	269	34
Brand, Kevin, S.B.	.917	6	5	6	1	12	1
Cahill, Jonathan, C.R.	1.000	2	4	6	0	10	0
Campana, Wandel, Day.	.960	76	121	217	14	352	38
Candelaria, Scott, Bel.	.919	21	36	43	7	86	12
Cedeno, Ronny, Lan.	.968	6	10	20	1	31	6
Cooper, Sam, Lan.	1.000	1	3	2	0	5	0
Davis, Michael, Ft.W.	.911	12	20	31	5	56	6
Day, Nick, Ft.W.	1.000	1	0	1	0	1	0
De Los Santos, Hector, Q.C.	.946	92	177	226	23	426	49

THIRD BASEMEN

Player, Team	Pct.	G	PO	A	E	TC	DP
Adames, Epidaro, C.R.	.892	53	36	104	17	157	9
Anderson, Bryan, Day.	.966	27	15	41	2	58	5
Andrianoff, Jon, Mich.	.929	7	4	9	1	14	0
Angel, Tony, Mich.	1.000	8	2	13	0	15	0
Ayala, Elio, Bel.	.966	10	9	19	1	29	1
Barbier, Blair, Lan.	.949	48	38	92	7	137	6
Bone, Blake, Wis.	.886	35	17	53	9	79	6
Boyer, Bret, Clin.	.833	16	5	40	9	54	2
Brand, Kevin, S.B.	.857	2	1	5	1	7	0
Brandes, Landon, Peo.	.833	25	15	40	11	66	4
Cabrera, Miguel, K.C.	1.000	8	7	12	0	19	2
CALITRI, Mike, Day.	.932	96	62	199	19	280	17
Candelaria, Scott, Bel.	.895	7	6	11	2	19	0
Cedeno, Ronny, Lan.	1.000	5	7	9	0	16	0
Clark, Daryl, Bel.	.854	123	76	200	47	323	14
Daubert, Jake, Wis.	.860	57	30	87	19	136	9
Davis, Michael, Ft.W.	.873	27	22	33	8	63	3
De Los Santos, Hector, Q.C.	.600	4	0	6	4	10	0
Demarco, Matt, K.C.	.899	37	27	71	11	109	9
Diaz, Aneuris, Peo.	.883	74	46	143	25	214	10
Duran, Frank, C.R.	.846	3	4	7	2	13	0
Durango, Ariel, Wis.	1.000	2	0	4	0	4	0
Easterday, Matt, K.C.	1.000	1	1	3	0	4	0
Edwards, Dytarious, Ft.W.	.789	10	5	10	4	19	0
Encarnacion, Edwin, Day.	.962	9	8	17	1	26	4

Player, Team	Pct.	G	PO	A	E	TC	DP
Eylward, Thomas, C.R.	.750	3	2	7	3	12	0
Fatur, Brian, Peo.	.000	2	0	0	1	1	0
Fenster, Darren, Bur.	.962	7	3	22	1	26	1
Floyd, Dan, Wis.	.953	35	20	61	4	85	2
Freeman, Corey, Wis.	.889	4	4	4	1	9	0
Garabito, Vianney, Day.	1.000	1	0	1	0	1	0
Gemoll, Justin, Bur.	.901	83	54	191	27	272	12
Guzman, Juan, Bur.	.968	10	9	21	1	31	0
Hannahan, John, W.M.	.942	45	39	91	8	138	8
Harris, Brendan, Lan.	.900	9	3	15	2	20	0
Houston, Tyler, Bel.	.500	1	0	1	1	2	0
Hurtado, Omar, Day.	.750	3	3	3	2	8	0
Johnson, Gabe, Peo.	.846	35	20	68	16	104	8
Kolly, Heath, K.C.	1.000	4	8	5	0	13	1
Lagana, Shawn, S.B.	.921	22	11	24	3	38	0
Lehr, Ryan, C.R.	.857	14	7	29	6	42	1
Lindsey, Cordell, C.R.	.910	30	25	56	8	89	2
Llamas, Juan, Bur.	.866	27	20	38	9	67	5
Luuloa, Miles, W.M.	.000	2	0	0	0	0	0
Lydic, Joe, Mich.	.876	74	42	156	28	226	7
Martinez, Dionnar, Lan.	1.000	3	1	8	0	9	1
Martinez, Guillermo, Wis.	.893	9	8	17	3	28	2
Maule, Jason, Mich.	.943	49	34	98	8	140	10
McCool, Lee, Ft.W.	1.000	1	1	3	0	4	0
Miller, Eric, Clin.	.905	6	5	14	2	21	1
Morrissey, Adam, Lan.	.813	27	16	49	15	80	2
Myers, Corey, S.B.	.930	53	31	102	10	143	6
Patchett, Gary, Day.	.923	7	3	9	1	13	0
Peguero, Miguel, W.M.	.905	22	15	42	6	63	6
Postell, Matthew, K.C.	.667	2	0	2	1	3	0
Puccinelli, John, Ft.W.	.886	54	35	74	14	123	5
Quattlebaum, Hugh, W.M.	.910	74	52	129	18	199	11
Rabe, Josh, Q.C.	.667	1	0	2	1	3	0
Ridley, Shayne, Bur.	.833	7	3	12	3	18	1
Rodgers, Albert, Peo.	.891	15	14	27	5	46	4
Rooi, Vince, Clin.	.892	117	83	265	42	390	16
Roper, Zach, C.R.	.926	38	29	58	7	94	9
Saba, Cesar, Ft.W.	.922	60	32	98	11	141	7
Sandoval, Michael, Q.C.	.929	32	17	62	6	85	4
Santana, Sandy, Peo.	.833	3	3	2	1	6	1
Sing, Brandon, Lan.	.828	52	30	90	25	145	4
Soto, T.J., Mich.	.800	7	3	9	3	15	1
Sprowl, Jon-Mark, Lan.	.000	1	0	0	0	0	0
Stockton, Jeff, C.R.	.000	1	0	0	0	0	0
Stone, Jon, Ft.W.	.000	1	0	0	0	0	0
Tamburrino, Brett, Q.C.	.714	4	3	7	4	14	0
Tiffee, Terry, Q.C.	.912	98	72	209	27	308	18
Tracy, Chad, S.B.	.895	52	36	109	17	162	10
Villilo, Miguel, Wis.	.524	9	3	8	10	21	1
Vizcaino, Maximo, S.B.	.885	14	7	16	3	26	2
Watkins, Tommy, Q.C.	.889	13	9	15	3	27	2
Willingham, Josh, K.C.	.946	87	61	184	14	259	16
Wilson, Josh, K.C.	.886	11	7	24	4	35	1
Wyant, Hunter, K.C.	.833	3	0	5	1	6	0

TRIPLE PLAY: Clark.

SHORTSTOPS

Player, Team	Pct.	G	PO	A	E	TC	DP
Anderson, Bryan, Day.	.857	10	12	24	6	42	3
Andrianoff, Jon, Mich.	1.000	8	7	18	0	25	6
Berroa, Cristian, Mich.	.948	26	44	65	6	115	16
Boyer, Bret, Clin.	.947	24	33	56	5	94	13
Brand, Kevin, S.B.	.833	4	5	5	2	12	1
Brandes, Landon, Peo.	.000	1	0	0	0	0	0
Burke, Chris, Mich.	.931	55	81	150	17	248	27
Cabrera, Bryan, K.C.	.928	98	147	267	32	446	50
Cahill, Jonathan, C.R.	.928	42	40	120	13	101	21
Candelaria, Scott, Bel.	.960	6	13	11	1	25	4
Cedeno, Ronny, Lan.	.750	6	4	8	4	16	1
Cooper, Sam, Lan.	.750	2	1	2	1	4	0
Cotto, Luis, Bur.	.907	46	67	109	18	194	13
De Los Santos, Hector, Q.C.	.857	3	5	7	2	14	3
Demarco, Matt, K.C.	.833	2	1	4	1	6	0
Diaz, Aneuris, Peo.	.952	4	7	13	1	21	5
Docen, Jose, Clin.	1.000	11	18	48	0	66	6
Duran, Frank, C.R.	.921	11	11	24	3	38	3
Durango, Ariel, Wis.	.931	68	109	187	22	318	36
Edwards, Dytarious, Ft.W.	1.000	5	7	11	0	18	0
Espinosa, David, Day.	.909	121	161	319	48	528	49
Fatur, Brian, Peo.	.874	20	30	60	13	103	13
Fenster, Darren, Bur.	.952	20	31	48	4	83	10
Firlit, Dan, Peo.	.927	34	31	84	9	124	17

Player, Team	Pct.	G	PO	A	E	TC	DP
Freeman, Corey, Wis.	.931	28	51	84	10	145	15
Furmaniak, Jason, Ft.W.	.949	117	185	338	28	551	61
Gil, Jerry, S.B.	.937	103	170	334	34	538	70
Gutierrez, Derrick, Wis.	.806	8	8	17	6	31	2
Guzman, Jon, Bur.	1.000	1	4	4	0	8	2
Guzman, Juan, Bur.	.939	41	62	138	13	213	19
Harris, Brendan, Lan.	.952	8	10	30	2	42	9
Harris, Josh, Lan.	.933	2	5	9	1	15	0
Helquist, Jon, Mich.	.884	42	49	103	20	172	15
Jacobo, Kervin, S.B.	.854	9	17	18	6	41	3
Kelly, Heath, K.C.	1.000	1	3	1	0	4	0
Kenney, Jeff, Bel.	1.000	1	1	6	0	7	2
Lagana, Shawn, S.B.	.909	3	3	7	1	11	0
Luuloa, Miles, W.M.	.950	11	14	24	2	40	5
Machado, Aleyandro, Bur.	.978	28	36	95	3	134	15
Martinez, Dionnar, Lan.	.921	11	5	30	3	38	5
Martinez, Guillermo, Wis.	.941	40	55	105	10	170	27
Maule, Jason, Mich.	.903	10	11	17	3	31	3
Maza, Luis, Q.C.	.952	107	181	280	23	484	49
Merrill, Ronnie, W.M.	.964	82	138	241	14	393	52
Miller, Eric, Clin.	.918	47	69	144	19	232	30
Montanez, Luis, Lan.	.934	112	162	289	32	483	69
Morrissey, Adam, Lan.	1.000	2	3	5	0	8	0
Murphy, Tommy, C.R.	.908	71	108	177	29	314	23
Patchett, Gary, Day.	.932	11	15	26	3	44	5
Peguero, Miguel, W.M.	.936	53	82	151	16	249	22
Raburn, Johnny, C.R.	.897	13	14	38	6	58	5
Riggins, Auntwan, Ft.W.	.875	2	7	7	2	16	3
Saba, Cesar, Ft.W.	.896	16	20	40	7	67	3
Santana, Sandy, Peo.	1.000	1	2	4	0	6	0
Soto, T.J., Mich.	1.000	1	1	2	0	3	0
Valdez, Wilson, Clin.	.966	58	103	208	11	322	38
Vasquez, Geraldo, Peo.	.923	3	6	6	1	13	1
Villilo, Miguel, Wis.	1.000	1	0	3	0	3	0
Vizcaino, Maximo, S.B.	.961	21	22	51	3	76	7
Voshell, Chase, Peo.	.925	87	144	252	32	428	49
Watkins, Tommy, Q.C.	.949	36	62	104	9	175	15
WEST, Todd, Bel.	.983	132	214	374	10	598	72
Wilson, Josh, K.C.	.928	52	88	145	18	251	32

OUTFIELDERS

Player, Team	Pct.	G	PO	A	E	TC	DP
Acevedo, Anthony, Mich.*	.984	106	181	3	3	187	1
Amador, Jerry, W.M.	.967	66	85	2	3	90	1
Ambres, Chip, K.C.	.977	91	212	5	5	222	3
Ambrosini, Dominick, Clin.*	.909	6	9	1	1	11	0
Anderson, Bryan, Day.	.963	38	77	2	3	82	0
Anderson, Syketo, Lan.	.808	17	19	2	5	26	0
Andujar, Elvin, Day.	1.000	4	3	0	0	3	0
Angel, Tony, Mich.	1.000	1	2	0	0	2	0
Arroyo, Abner, Ft.W.*	.953	46	78	4	4	86	0
Ayala, Odannys, Bur.	.989	52	86	5	1	92	0
Barbier, Blair, Lan.	.889	6	8	0	1	9	0
Bay, Jason, Clin.	.984	78	172	14	3	189	1
Boitel, Rafael, Q.C.*	.977	113	204	12	5	221	2
Bono, Blake, Wis.	1.000	3	1	1	0	2	0
Bubela, Jaime, Wis.	.954	131	174	12	9	195	0
Calitri, Mike, Day.	.000	1	0	0	0	0	0
Cameron, Antoine, Lan.*	.981	73	99	5	2	106	1
Campo, Mike, C.R.	.968	87	145	6	5	156	1
Candelaria, Scott, Bel.	.955	16	21	0	1	22	0
Castro, Renato, Ft.W.	1.000	11	17	0	0	17	0
Choo, Shin-soo, Wis.*	.800	3	3	1	1	5	0
Clark, Daryl, Bel.	.000	1	0	0	0	0	0
Cleveland, Russ, W.M.	.000	1	0	0	0	0	0
Cordova, Ben, Bur.*	.971	108	199	2	6	207	1
Coulie, Jason, C.R.	.979	114	224	6	5	235	1
Cowan, Justin, Bur.	.978	29	42	2	1	45	0
Curry, Chris, Lan.	1.000	2	2	0	0	2	0
Daubert, Jake, Wis.	1.000	1	1	0	0	1	0
Davis, Michael, Ft.W.	.800	3	3	1	1	5	0
Day, Nick, Ft.W.	1.000	4	5	0	0	5	0
De La Cruz, Eric, Bel.	.946	65	103	3	6	112	2
De Los Santos, Nelson, Bel.	.917	15	20	2	2	24	0
Demarco, Matt, K.C.	1.000	2	5	0	0	5	0
Diaz, Aneuris, Peo.	.927	21	37	1	3	41	0
Downing, Brad, W.M.	1.000	11	12	0	0	12	0
Downing, Phil, Clin.*	1.000	23	42	3	0	45	0
Drew, J.D., Peo.	1.000	3	4	0	0	4	0
Dubois, Jason, Lan.	.979	87	136	3	3	142	0
Durham, Miles, W.M.	.982	65	105	5	2	112	1
Dusan, Joe, Wis.*	.000	1	0	0	0	0	0

Player, Team	Pct.	G	PO	A	E	TC	DP
Easterday, Matt, K.C.	.949	32	55	1	3	59	0
Edge, Dwight, S.B.	.979	46	88	4	2	94	2
Edwards, Dytarious, Ft.W.	.964	31	52	2	2	56	0
Faison, Vince, Ft.W.	.978	41	86	2	2	90	1
Fatur, Brian, Peo.	.972	23	32	3	1	36	0
Fears, Chris, Ft.W.	.982	73	103	5	2	110	0
Fera, Aaron, Peo.	1.000	7	15	0	0	15	0
Ferrand, Frank, K.C.*	.975	75	152	7	4	163	0
Figueroa, Eduardo, Wis.	1.000	14	13	0	0	13	0
Floyd, Dan, Wis.	.984	48	58	3	1	62	0
Floyd, Mike, Peo.	.959	66	111	6	5	122	0
Foreman, Julius, S.B.	.991	60	104	9	1	114	1
Foster, Brian, Bel.	1.000	5	4	0	0	4	0
Freeman, Corey, Wis.	1.000	4	6	1	0	7	0
Fulse, Sheldon, Wis.	.970	80	161	1	5	167	0
Garcia, Hector, Bel.	.971	97	161	9	5	175	0
Gemoll, Justin, Bur.	1.000	3	1	0	0	1	0
Gettis, Byron, Bur.	.990	37	92	10	1	103	1
Guzman, Jon, Bur.	.973	119	239	11	7	257	2
Guzman, Juan, Bur.	.000	2	0	0	0	0	0
Guzman, Robert, Q.C.*	.969	17	30	1	1	32	0
Hall, Victor, S.B.*	.956	111	232	5	11	248	1
Hamilton, Mark, Mich.*	.964	97	153	6	6	165	0
Hammock, Rob, S.B.	1.000	15	26	0	0	26	0
Hammond, Derry, Bel.	.962	95	142	10	6	158	2
Hawes, Bobby, Day.	.981	25	43	8	1	52	1
Helquist, Jon, Mich.	1.000	2	1	0	0	1	0
Hicks, Scott, K.C.	1.000	1	2	0	0	2	0
Hill, Willy, K.C.*	1.000	4	8	0	0	8	0
Huguet, J.C., Day.	.800	2	4	0	1	5	0
Hurtado, Omar, Day.	1.000	59	114	5	0	119	2
Jenkins, Geoff, Bel.	.000	1	0	0	0	0	0
Kavourias, Jim, K.C.	.985	106	193	10	3	206	1
Keppinger, Billy, Bur.*	.975	59	108	8	3	119	2
Kerner, Craig, Clin.	.951	40	55	3	3	61	0
Knight, Marcus, C.R.	1.000	15	33	1	0	34	0
Kroeger, Joshua, S.B.*	.926	71	109	3	9	121	0
Krynzel, Dave, Bel.*	.970	35	61	4	2	67	0
Lagana, Shawn, S.B.	.900	8	8	1	1	10	0
Lee, Eric, Mich.	1.000	61	94	8	0	102	1
Lemon, Tim, Peo.	.944	130	184	19	12	215	2
Loeb, Bryan, S.B.	.929	8	13	0	1	14	0
Logan, Nook, W.M.	.968	126	262	8	9	279	2
Lopez, Chuck, Wis.*	.983	47	56	3	1	60	0
Lora, Tom, Bur.	1.000	2	3	1	0	4	0
Magness, Pat, K.C.	.750	2	3	0	1	4	0
Mallory, Mike, Lan.	.981	123	254	9	5	268	1
Martinez, Hipolito, Bel.	1.000	4	3	1	0	4	0
Miller, Eric, Clin.	1.000	7	7	1	0	8	0
Morris, Chris, Peo.	.951	132	318	12	17	347	1
Morrissey, Adam, Lan.	.981	32	48	4	1	53	1
Neill, Ryan, W.M.	.960	57	95	2	4	101	0
Nunez, Argelis, S.B.	.961	76	117	7	5	129	2
O'Donnell, Ryan, Ft.W.	.983	28	52	7	1	60	1
Ortiz, Matt, Peo.	1.000	8	15	0	0	15	0
Pena, Wily Mo, Day.	.972	127	300	13	9	322	3
Pregnalato, Bob, Bel.	.938	75	130	7	9	146	1
Quintana, Wil, Wis.	.900	35	41	4	5	50	0
Rabe, Josh, Q.C.	.981	113	197	8	4	209	2
Reese, Kevin, Ft.W.*	.984	121	232	14	4	250	1
Richardson, Miguel, Wis.	.929	9	12	1	1	14	1
Riggins, Auntwan, Ft.W.	.943	30	46	4	3	53	1
Rivas, Norberto, Clin.	.923	6	12	0	1	13	0
Rodgers, Albert, Peo.	.988	45	80	0	1	81	0
Rodgers, Mackeel, Bur.	.000	3	0	0	1	1	0
Rombley, Danny, Clin.	.958	34	65	4	3	72	0
Roper, Zach, C.R.	.857	5	11	1	2	14	0
Sadler, Ray, Lan.	.942	90	140	6	9	155	0
Sandoval, Jhensy, S.B.	1.000	5	6	0	0	6	0
Santana, Sandy, Peo.	.000	1	0	0	0	0	0
Seever, Brian, C.R.	.956	43	86	1	4	91	0
Sizemore, Grady, Clin.*	.972	114	237	3	7	247	1
Sledd, Aaron, Day.*	1.000	12	15	0	0	15	0
SMITH, Will, K.C.	.990	117	182	10	2	194	0
Smitherman, Steve, Day.	.969	133	207	12	7	226	2
Soto, T.J., Mich.	.000	1	0	0	0	0	0
Southward, Deshawn, Q.C.	1.000	8	4	1	0	5	0
Stanley, Henry, Mich.*	1.000	72	149	3	0	152	1
Stockton, Rick, C.R.*	.889	7	8	0	1	9	0
Strong, Jamal, Wis.	.988	48	79	0	1	80	0
Tamburrino, Brett, Q.C.	1.000	12	16	1	0	17	0
Terrero, Luis, S.B.	1.000	24	37	3	0	40	0

Player, Team	Pct.	G	PO	A	E	TC	DP
Thompson, Craig, Ft.W.	1.000	45	77	5	0	82	0
Tolli, Barry, C.R.	.931	21	23	4	2	29	1
Torres, Digno, Q.C.*	.970	42	62	2	2	66	0
Valdez, Angel, C.R.	.951	28	58	0	3	61	0
Walker, Matt, W.M.	.949	101	144	6	8	158	2
Watkins, Tommy, Q.C.	1.000	12	3	0	0	3	0
Watson, Brandon, Clin.	.980	108	183	14	4	201	0
Webb, Ryan, C.R.	.957	41	62	5	3	70	0
West, Kevin, Q.C.	.976	121	196	5	5	206	0
Williamson, Chris, Day.*	1.000	33	60	3	0	63	1
Willingham, Josh, K.C.	.857	4	5	1	1	7	0
Withey, Ryan, C.R.	.976	57	120	4	3	127	1
Wright, Gavin, Mich.	.962	94	192	9	8	209	2
Zoccolillo, Peter, Bel.	.984	29	55	5	1	61	1

CATCHERS

Player, Team	Pct.	G	PO	A	E	TC	DP	PB
Abruzzo, Jared, C.R.	.977	66	506	53	13	572	0	6
Alfonzo, Eliezer, Bel.	.975	55	471	66	14	551	8	8
Alvarez, Henrry, Bur.	.973	42	256	37	8	301	2	17
Ambrosini, Anthony, Clin.	1.000	3	23	1	0	24	0	2
Anderson, Dennis, K.C.	.987	78	482	69	7	558	5	12
Ansman, Craig, S.B.	.985	67	456	72	8	536	1	7
Arnerich, Tony, Bur.	1.000	11	68	8	0	76	0	0
Barbier, Blair, Lan.	1.000	1	2	0	0	2	0	0
Belcher, Jason, Bel.	.994	17	145	16	1	162	0	0
Bitter, Jarrod, Ft.W.	.976	5	35	6	1	42	0	0
BOWEN, Rob, Q.C.	.993	98	751	72	6	829	1	14
Brito, Obispo, Bel.	.988	18	139	25	2	166	0	1
Buckley, Brandon, Mich.	.993	63	411	19	3	433	0	9
Carroll, Mark, Wis.	.992	75	656	65	6	727	3	4
Castellano, John, Wis.	.986	49	394	31	6	431	1	9
Ceriani, Matt, Bel.	.979	21	155	32	4	191	1	2
Cleveland, Russ, W.M.	.980	57	409	38	9	456	0	8
Cowan, Justin, Bur.	.971	20	95	6	3	104	0	4
Curry, Chris, Lan.	.989	23	170	17	2	189	1	2
Decola, Daniel, Q.C.	1.000	15	72	4	0	76	0	4
Delgado, Jorge, S.B.	.992	34	232	18	2	252	2	4
Docen, Jose, Clin.	.000	1	0	0	0	0	0	0
Dogero, Matt, Peo.	.980	15	48	1	1	50	0	2
Doudt, Anthony, C.R.	.983	16	103	11	2	116	1	4
Epke, Brian, S.B.	.960	16	110	11	5	126	2	5
Fatheree, Danny, Mich.	1.000	2	19	0	0	19	0	0
Felix, Hersy, Bur.	.984	35	228	20	4	252	2	9
Foster, Brian, Bel.	.979	29	211	24	5	240	3	8
Friar, Roddy, Peo.	.991	34	185	31	2	218	4	7
Gentry, Garett, Mich.	.992	71	458	30	4	492	1	10
Gulledge, Kelley, Q.C.	.972	16	93	12	3	108	0	3
Hamill, Ryan, Peo.	.985	100	567	80	10	657	0	8
Hammock, Rob, S.B.	.985	19	121	12	2	135	1	1
Hargreaves, Brad, Day.	.966	7	49	8	2	59	0	0
Hudson, Ben, Wis.	.987	10	71	5	1	77	0	4
Huguet, J.C., Day.	.980	32	214	35	5	254	1	3
Inge, Brandon, W.M.	1.000	2	12	0	0	12	0	0
Johnson, Forrest, W.M.	.989	19	164	10	2	176	1	4
Jones, Brian, Day.	.986	30	191	18	3	212	2	7
Kennedy, Bryan, Q.C.	.991	14	104	8	1	113	1	1
Kweon, Yoon-Min, Lan.	.989	83	671	79	8	758	4	9
Langill, Eric, Clin.	.971	41	210	24	7	241	0	6
Loeb, Bryan, S.B.	.959	6	44	3	2	49	1	1
Lutz, David, Clin.	1.000	5	21	4	0	25	0	0
McMillan, Andrew, Clin.	.979	84	500	67	12	579	1	10
Mejia, Andy, Lan.	.935	11	67	5	5	77	0	6
Napoli, Michael, C.R.	.996	35	258	26	1	285	2	5
Obradovich, Mark, Mich.	.977	8	40	3	1	44	0	0
O'Connor, Brian, Mich.	.982	16	49	5	1	55	0	2
Ortiz, Matt, Peo.	.960	16	65	7	3	75	0	0
Pagan, Andres, Ft.W.	.990	90	691	78	20	789	5	20
Parker, Chris, W.M.	.978	67	483	59	12	554	5	6
Peterson, Brian, Day.	.997	35	276	46	1	323	3	3
Postell, Matthew, K.C.	.966	18	97	17	4	118	1	2
Pregnalato, Bob, Bel.	1.000	2	3	0	0	3	0	1
Puccinelli, John, Ft.W.	1.000	1	1	0	0	1	0	0
Rodriguez, Joe, Wis.	.991	15	105	10	1	116	2	1
Rogers, Brandon, C.R.	.983	13	103	14	2	119	3	2
Serafini, Matt, Bel.	1.000	3	26	5	0	31	0	1
Silver, Travis, Lan.	.988	20	131	18	2	151	2	1
Socarras, Tony, C.R.	.971	12	90	12	3	105	1	1
Sprowl, Jon-Mark, Lan.	1.000	17	95	6	0	101	0	2
Stone, Jon, Ft.W.	.983	44	326	31	6	363	2	12
Suarez, Marc, Day.	.985	46	303	35	5	343	2	6
Treanor, Matt, K.C.	1.000	1	11	0	0	11	0	0

Player, Team	Pct.	G	PO	A	E	TC	DP	PB
Wallis, Jacob, Clin.	1.000	19	109	15	0	124	1	2
Walter, Scott, Bur.	.974	33	197	26	6	229	1	9
Woody, Dominic, K.C.	.988	51	288	41	4	333	1	14

PITCHERS

Player, Team	Pct.	G	PO	A	E	TC	DP
Aguilar, Edwin, Mich.	1.000	14	0	6	0	6	0
Albright, Eric, Lan.	.600	34	1	2	2	5	0
Alvarez, Larry, Lan.	1.000	30	1	4	0	5	0
Anderson, Bryan, Day.	.000	1	0	0	0	0	0
Anderson, Travis, Mich.	.919	31	11	23	3	37	0
Andrade, Stephen, C.R.	.875	20	4	3	1	8	1
Andujar, Jesse, C.R.	1.000	5	1	0	0	1	0
Aramboles, Ricardo, Day.	1.000	4	1	1	0	2	0
Arias, Pablo, W.M.	1.000	20	9	8	0	17	0
Arthur, Tony, C.R.*	.875	5	0	7	1	8	0
Artieta, Corey, Bel.*	1.000	26	1	4	0	5	0
Axelson, Josh, Peo.	1.000	18	7	18	0	25	2
Ayala, Julio, Wis.*	.000	1	0	0	0	0	0
Baker, Joey, Bur.	.944	27	11	23	2	36	2
Barnes, Pat, Wis.*	1.000	10	1	0	0	1	0
Barrett, Jimmy, Mich.	.955	27	5	16	1	22	1
Bass, Brian, Bur.	.909	26	13	37	5	55	2
Baugh, Kenny, W.M.	1.000	6	4	9	0	13	1
Bautista, Denny, K.C.	1.000	8	4	2	0	6	0
Belanger, Brandon, Ft.W.	1.000	33	6	6	0	12	2
Belson, Greg, S.B.	1.000	46	4	7	0	11	2
Blackwell, Scott, Q.C.	1.000	13	1	4	0	5	0
Blanton, Jason, Lan.	.000	7	0	0	1	1	0
Bludau, Frank, Day.	.933	42	4	10	1	15	0
Bone, Blake, Wis.	.000	1	0	0	0	0	0
Bonilla, Henry, Q.C.	1.000	53	5	11	0	16	0
Boutwell, Andy, Day.	.857	32	2	4	1	7	0
Bradley, Dave, Day.	1.000	16	0	4	0	4	0
Drannon, Nick, Day.*	1.000	2	0	3	0	3	0
Brown, Eric, Lan.	1.000	16	1	1	0	2	0
Bruney, Brian, S.B.	1.000	26	3	5	0	8	0
Bukowski, Stan, C.R.	.867	8	3	10	2	15	3
Burnstead, Mike, Ft.W.	.833	30	3	7	2	12	0
Burns, Casey, Ft.W.	.944	20	8	11	1	18	0
Burns, Mike, Mich.	1.000	29	9	15	0	24	1
Burton, O.J., Wis.	1.000	39	2	4	0	6	0
Butler, John, Wis.	.864	41	9	10	3	22	0
Byo, Chris, Clin.	.667	21	0	2	1	3	0
Byron, Terry, K.C.	.750	4	0	3	1	4	0
Cali, Carmen, Peo.*	.833	39	2	8	2	12	0
Campbell, Dayle, W.M.	.818	21	3	6	2	11	1
Campos, Juan, Mich.	1.000	13	6	6	0	12	1
Candelaria, Scott, Bel.	.000	1	0	0	0	0	0
Caputo, Rob, Clin.	.667	4	1	1	1	3	0
Casadiego, Gerardo, Clin.	.875	42	2	12	2	16	0
Cassel, Jack, Ft.W.	1.000	25	10	26	0	36	1
Castellanos, Jonathan, S.B.	1.000	8	4	9	0	13	0
Castillo, Ramon, K.C.	.917	28	5	17	2	24	0
Charron, Eric, Clin.	1.000	14	0	3	0	3	0
Chavez, Wilton, Lan.	.625	8	1	4	3	8	0
Chisnall, Wes, Clin.	.833	24	4	1	1	6	0
Coa, Jesus, Bur.	1.000	36	3	9	0	12	1
Collins, Clint, Day.	.667	6	0	2	1	3	0
Contreras, Jean, Q.C.*	.909	26	3	7	1	11	0
Cook, Jeremy, Peo.	.941	52	3	13	1	17	1
Corbin, John, Lan.	.800	14	2	2	1	5	0
Cordero, Frangil, Lan.*	1.000	9	1	4	0	5	0
Cordero, Victor, Bel.	.941	46	6	10	1	17	0
Cotton, Nathan, Day.	.667	12	0	2	1	3	0
Coughenour, Jory, Mich.	.970	35	8	24	1	33	2
Cramblitt, Joey, S.B.	.964	35	7	20	1	28	0
Crowther, Jackson, Clin.	.500	8	0	1	1	2	0
Cuello, Manolin, W.M.	.909	23	4	6	1	11	0
Cueto, Jose, Lan.	.889	22	6	10	2	18	0
Cummings, Jeremy, Peo.	.929	18	4	22	2	28	0
Daigle, Casey, S.B.	.829	28	10	24	7	41	2
D'Amico, Jeff, Bel.	1.000	2	0	1	0	1	0
Dequin, Benjamin, Clin.*	.815	26	6	16	5	27	0
Detillion, Jamie, W.M.*	.944	48	5	12	1	18	1
Devine, Travis, Ft.W.	1.000	29	4	4	0	8	0
Diaz, Eddy, Lan.	1.000	20	4	14	0	18	0
Dorn, Grant, Clin.	.941	31	7	9	1	17	1
Douglass, Ryan, Bur.	1.000	7	1	5	0	6	1
Duran, Frank, C.R.	1.000	1	0	1	0	1	0
Dusan, Joe, Wis.*	.000	1	0	0	0	0	0
Earey, Ryan, Ft.W.	.889	24	8	8	2	18	0

Player, Team	Pct.	G	PO	A	E	TC	DP
Edwards, Bryan, Day.	.939	29	7	24	2	33	0
Eppolito, Vince, S.B.	.857	25	1	5	1	7	1
Esquivia, Manuel, K.C.	.842	24	5	11	3	19	0
Eyre, Willie, Q.C.	1.000	17	3	5	0	8	1
Farmer, Tom, W.M.	1.000	6	2	4	0	6	0
Ferguson, Ian, Bur.	.917	10	2	9	1	12	0
Figueroa, Eduardo, Wis.	.000	1	0	0	0	0	0
Fingers, Jason, Bur.	.889	33	0	8	1	9	0
Fischer, Rich, C.R.	.923	20	9	15	2	26	1
Flading, Cameron, C.R.	1.000	15	0	2	0	-2	1
Flannery, Mike, K.C.	.889	53	2	6	1	9	0
Foote, Joe, Q.C.	.786	13	2	9	3	14	1
Fox, Ben, Ft.W.*	.750	11	1	2	1	4	0
Freeman, Corey, Wis.	.000	1	0	0	0	0	0
Fries, Scott, Lan.*	1.000	43	0	14	0	14	1
Fuell, Jerrod, W.M.	.500	14	0	2	2	4	1
Gaal, Bryan, Ft.W.	1.000	23	1	0	0	1	0
Gallo, Mike, Mich.*	.933	44	2	12	1	15	1
Garris, Antonio, Clin.	1.000	15	2	2	0	4	0
Gates, Brian, Q.C.	1.000	15	1	5	0	6	0
Geigel, Rolando, K.C.	.875	30	3	4	1	8	1
George, Brad, Day.	.700	8	0	7	3	10	1
George, Todd, Clin.	1.000	2	1	0	0	1	0
Germano, Justin, Ft.W.	.909	13	3	7	1	11	1
Gil, Dave, Day.	1.000	2	0	1	0	1	0
Girdley, Josh, Clin.*	.929	6	2	11	1	14	1
Gomer, Jeramy, Lan.*	1.000	10	0	2	0	2	0
Gonzalez, Cesar, S.B.	.971	26	8	25	1	34	2
Gordon, Justin, Bel.*	.750	27	5	7	4	16	1
Graves, Don, Peo.	1.000	34	5	17	0	22	0
Gray, Rusty, Bel.	.750	7	1	2	1	4	0
Gruban, Jarret, C.R.	.800	13	0	4	1	5	0
Grunwald, Erik, Wis.	.903	29	6	22	3	31	0
Gutierrez, Lazaro, Ft.W.*	1.000	16	1	2	0	3	0
Halamicek, Kevin, K.C.	1.000	20	3	6	0	9	0
Hall, Dan, Bel.	.900	38	2	7	1	10	0
Hall, Josh, Day.	.897	22	10	16	3	29	0
Hamilton, Mark, Mich.*	.750	10	0	3	1	4	0
Harris, Julian, C.R.*	.750	18	1	2	1	4	0
Harvey, Ian, Ft.W.	1.000	8	0	2	0	2	0
Haynes, Brad, K.C.	.789	17	5	10	4	19	0
Head, Daniel, Wis.	1.000	16	1	4	0	5	0
Heiberger, Heath, S.B.*	1.000	12	0	5	0	5	1
Hendrickson, Benjamin, Bel.	1.000	25	5	20	0	25	1
Henkel, Robert, K.C.*	1.000	1	0	1	0	1	0
Hensley, Matt, C.R.	1.000	11	5	6	0	11	0
Herbert, John, Ft.W.	.500	2	0	1	1	2	0
Hernandez, Fausto, W.M.	.500	9	0	1	1	2	0
Hernandez, Runelvys, Bur.	.929	17	9	17	2	28	0
Herrera, Jose, Wis.	1.000	4	1	1	0	2	0
Hill, Jeremy, Bur.	1.000	40	1	7	0	8	0
Hoerman, Jared, Wis.	.840	21	7	14	4	25	0
Holubec, Ken, Q.C.*	.902	27	8	29	4	41	0
Houlton, Dennis, Mich.	1.000	1	1	0	0	1	0
Howell, Michael, W.M.	1.000	8	3	5	0	8	0
Howington, Ty, Day.*	1.000	6	2	4	0	6	0
Humrich, Chris, Clin.	1.000	33	5	5	0	10	0
Izquierdo, Hansel, K.C.	.750	24	2	4	2	8	0
Jackson, Dan, C.R.	1.000	8	1	5	0	6	0
Jenks, Bobby, C.R.	.810	21	4	13	4	21	0
Johnson, Jeremy, W.M.	1.000	3	0	2	0	2	0
Johnson, Kelly, Peo.	1.000	13	1	5	0	6	1
Johnson, Rett, Wis.	.938	16	7	23	2	32	3
Johnson, Tyler, Peo.*	1.000	3	0	1	0	1	0
Johnston, Rikki, W.M.*	.833	13	2	18	4	24	1
Jongejan, Ferenc, Lan.*	.955	48	2	19	1	22	0
Kemp, Beau, Q.C.	.857	31	2	4	1	7	0
Keppinger, Billy, Bur.*	1.000	1	0	1	0	1	0
Key, Chris, K.C.*	.917	54	5	17	2	24	1
Kinney, Josh, Peo.	.917	27	4	7	1	12	0
Koronka, John, Day.*	1.000	5	1	2	0	3	0
Koziara, Matt, Day.	1.000	14	2	4	0	6	0
Krawiec, Aaron, Lan.*	.839	27	1	25	5	31	1
Lacorte, Vince, C.R.	1.000	36	11	10	0	21	0
Laesch, Michael, Day.	.889	29	1	7	1	9	0
Lajara, Eudy, K.C.*	1.000	36	1	5	0	6	0
Landestoy, Gilbert, C.R.	.929	36	2	11	1	14	0
Lansford, Dustin, Bel.	1.000	3	0	3	0	3	0
Lavery, Mark, Lan.*	1.000	30	2	23	0	25	0
Leclair, Aric, S.B.*	.625	37	1	4	3	8	1
Leicester, Jon, Lan.	.868	28	19	27	7	53	3
Leiter, Mark, Bel.	1.000	1	0	2	0	2	0

Player, Team	Pct.	G	PO	A	E	TC	DP
Leu, Trevor, W.M.*	1.000	13	0	3	0	3	0
Leuenberger, Jeff, W.M.	.900	30	5	4	1	10	0
Lewis, Jeremy, W.M.*	.800	9	1	3	1	5	2
Lincoln, Jeff, Q.C.	1.000	31	3	12	0	15	1
Lira, James, Mich.	.833	25	1	4	1	6	0
LOCKWOOD, Luke, Clin.*	1.000	26	7	41	0	48	6
Lopez, Gustavo, K.C.	.929	17	4	9	1	14	0
Lugo, Ruddy, Bel.	1.000	10	3	2	0	5	0
Luque, Roger, Ft.W.*	.917	42	0	11	1	12	0
Mangrum, Micah, Bur.	1.000	23	0	8	0	8	0
Mansfield, Monte, Mich.	.750	40	4	8	4	16	0
Markray, Thad, Day.	1.000	32	0	6	0	6	0
Martin, Lucas, Q.C.*	1.000	33	6	30	0	36	1
Martin, Nick, Lan.*	1.000	1	1	0	0	1	0
Martinez, Javier A., Day.	1.000	8	0	1	0	1	0
Martinez, Miguel, Peo.	.923	18	9	15	2	26	0
Maysonet, Roberto, Bel.*	.900	28	6	12	2	20	0
McAdoo, Duncan, Ft.W.	.917	28	7	15	2	24	0
McCasland, Ralph, Clin.*	1.000	26	1	5	0	6	0
McClain, Kevin, C.R.	.667	24	1	3	2	6	0
McClellan, Zach, Bur.	.871	24	11	16	4	31	1
McGee, Christopher, Bel.	.750	37	2	7	3	12	0
McGill, Trae, Bur.	1.000	5	2	4	0	6	0
McMurray, Heath, Bel.	1.000	9	0	3	0	3	0
McNutt, Mike, K.C.	.906	28	7	22	3	32	2
Medlock, Chet, Peo.	1.000	30	3	3	0	6	0
Mejia, Juan, Ft.W.	1.000	9	2	1	0	3	0
Messenger, Randall, K.C.	.833	14	1	9	2	12	0
Meyer, Mike, Peo.	1.000	17	1	5	0	6	0
Miller, Ryan, Bel.	.947	22	5	13	1	19	0
Miniel, Roberto, Bel.-Lan.	.964	33	13	14	1	28	0
Mitchell, Tom, Clin.	.778	5	1	6	2	9	0
Miyamoto, Eiji, Clin.	.833	20	1	4	1	6	0
Montoya, Saul, S.B.	.857	7	1	5	1	7	0
Morgan, Russ, Wis.*	1.000	17	3	3	0	6	0
Morris, Will, C.R.	.938	40	4	11	1	16	2
Moseley, Dustin, Day.	.919	25	10	24	3	37	1
Moseley, Marcus, Q.C.	.923	20	6	6	1	13	0
Mottl, Ryan, Day.	1.000	26	8	18	0	26	1
Nageotte, Clint, Wis.	.839	28	6	20	5	31	0
Narveson, Chris, Peo.*	.900	8	3	6	1	10	0
Nicolas, Mike, Ft.W.	.833	54	1	4	1	6	0
Norderum, Jason, Clin.*	.946	28	5	30	2	37	3
Novinsky, John, Peo.	.970	25	9	23	1	33	0
Nunez, Vladimir, K.C.	.000	1	0	0	0	0	0
Olore, Kevin, Wis.	.939	27	15	16	2	33	2
O'Neal, Brandon, C.R.	.880	16	7	15	3	25	1
Oxspring, Chris, Ft.W.	1.000	41	3	11	0	14	0
Pace, Adam, C.R.*	.731	17	6	13	7	26	0
Pape, Stace, Day.	1.000	7	1	0	0	1	0
Patchett, Gary, Day.	1.000	3	0	1	0	1	0
Pember, Dave, Bel.	.933	8	4	10	1	15	1
Peralta, Joel, C.R.	1.000	41	4	4	0	8	0
Percosky, Mark, Ft.W.	1.000	8	3	1	0	4	0
Perez, Beltran, S.B.	.886	27	13	18	4	35	1
Perez, Frank, W.M.	.929	36	3	10	1	14	1
Perez, Oliver, Ft.W.*	.767	19	2	21	7	30	1
Perkins, Mike, Peo.	1.000	7	0	1	0	1	0
Persby, Andy, Q.C.	1.000	20	2	5	0	7	0
Phillips, Mark, Ft.W.*	.833	5	1	4	1	6	0
Pike, Matthew, Day.	1.000	2	0	1	0	1	0
Pine, Chris, C.R.	1.000	12	0	2	0	2	0
Pinto, Renyel, Lan.*	.813	20	0	13	3	16	0
Pitney, James, W.M.	1.000	15	0	2	0	2	0
Polo, Bienvenido, Peo.	1.000	18	2	5	0	7	0
Ponce Deleon, Damon, Peo.	.833	19	4	1	1	6	0
Prater, Andy, Ft.W.	.000	1	0	0	0	0	0
Pridie, Jon, Q.C.	1.000	12	4	9	0	13	0
Puello, Ignacio, Clin.	.667	7	1	3	2	6	0
Qualls, Chad, Mich.	.967	26	8	21	1	30	2
Ramirez, Joslin, S.B.	.818	18	6	12	4	22	1
Ramos, Luis, Bel.	.000	2	0	0	0	0	0
Randazzo, Jeffrey, Q.C.*	1.000	20	9	25	0	34	0
Ribaudo, Mike, Mich.	.917	30	3	8	1	12	0
Ricciardi, Joe, S.B.	.833	20	0	5	1	6	0
Rijo, Jose, Day.	1.000	1	0	2	0	2	0
Rodney, Lee, W.M.	.897	27	7	19	3	29	1
Romero, Josmir, Q.C.	.944	30	11	23	2	36	2
Rundles, Rich, Clin.*	.750	4	1	2	1	4	0
Russelburg, Aaron, Peo.	.818	10	5	4	2	11	0
Russo, Scott, Clin.*	1.000	15	0	5	0	5	0
Ryan, Jeremy, Mich.	.846	15	2	9	2	13	0
Saladin, Miguel, Mich.	.941	46	4	12	1	17	0
Samora, Santo, Peo.	.563	52	1	8	7	16	0
Sauer, Marc, K.C.	.909	9	1	9	1	11	1
Sawyer, Steve, K.C.	1.000	55	3	8	0	11	0
Schaub, Greg, Bel.	1.000	25	1	5	0	6	0
Service, Scott, Day.	.000	4	0	0	2	2	0
Sheefel, Adam, Day.*	.938	40	1	14	1	16	0
Shouse, Dan, Peo.*	.857	11	3	3	1	7	1
Shrout, Kevin, Bel.	1.000	6	1	2	0	3	0
Shwam, Mike, Bel.	.968	47	9	21	1	31	1
Sierra, Auvin, W.M.*	1.000	17	2	4	0	6	0
Skinner, John, K.C.	1.000	25	1	5	0	6	0
Sloan, Brandon, K.C.	.938	41	5	10	1	16	1
Smart, Pete, Bel.	.893	11	8	17	3	28	1
Snare, Ryan, Day.*	1.000	21	3	30	0	33	1
Sosa, Jorge, Wis.	.000	2	0	0	0	0	0
Sprowl, Jon-Mark, Lan.	.000	1	0	0	0	0	0
Stanford, Derek, Mich.	1.000	5	3	4	0	7	1
Steele, Mike, W.M.	.938	38	6	9	1	16	2
Stiles, Brad, Bur.*	.824	30	1	13	3	17	0
Stockman, Landon, W.M.	1.000	18	3	2	0	5	0
Stodolka, Michael, Bur.*	.955	20	2	19	1	22	1
Stokes, Shaun, Peo.	1.000	13	2	8	0	10	1
Stokley, Billy, C.R.	.917	22	4	7	1	12	0
Stone, Jon, Ft.W.	.000	1	0	0	0	0	0
Sundbeck, Cody, S.B.	1.000	11	1	1	0	2	0
Swindell, Jeremy, W.M.*	1.000	4	1	0	0	1	0
Szuminski, Jason, Lan.	1.000	14	1	8	0	9	0
Taylor, Aaron, Wis.	.667	28	0	2	1	3	1
Tejada, Sandy, Q.C.	1.000	4	1	3	0	4	0
Thomas, Adam, C.R.	.875	19	11	17	4	32	0
Thompson, Mike, Ft.W.	1.000	1	0	3	0	3	0
Torres, Joe, C.R.*	1.000	4	1	2	0	3	0
Torres, Luis, Clin.	.913	18	8	13	2	23	1
Van Dusen, Derrick, Wis.*	.900	18	8	10	2	20	1
Vincent, Matt, Peo.*	1.000	14	3	1	0	4	0
Vriesenga, Matt, Peo.	.933	35	5	9	1	15	0
Wagner, Frank, Bel.*	.000	8	0	0	0	0	0
Wallace, Ben, Bel.*	.833	8	2	3	1	6	1
Wallis, Jacob, Clin.	.000	1	0	0	0	0	0
Walton, Sam, Wis.*	.000	3	0	0	0	0	0
Warren, Andy, W.M.	1.000	3	3	3	0	6	0
Washburn, Ben, Clin.	.917	30	9	13	2	24	0
Wawrzyniak, Alan, C.R.	1.000	5	1	1	0	2	0
Wayne, Hawkeye, Wis.	.929	30	5	8	1	14	3
Webster, Jeremy, Ft.W.*	1.000	16	0	7	0	7	0
Weis, Brad, Q.C.*	.909	22	0	10	1	11	1
Wellemeyer, Todd, Lan.	.846	27	4	18	4	26	0
Wells, Carl, S.B.*	.952	40	4	16	1	21	2
Wells, Roy, Wis.	.964	39	9	18	1	28	0
Wheatland, Matt, W.M.	1.000	3	2	1	0	3	0
White, Bill, S.B.*	.964	19	4	23	1	28	3
Wiedmeyer, Jason, Ft.W.*	1.000	6	1	4	0	5	0
Wiles, Chad, Wis.	.917	39	2	9	1	12	3
Wilkerson, Wes, Bur.	.938	43	5	10	1	16	0
Wilkinson, Matthew, S.B.	1.000	14	3	2	0	5	0
Wolfe, Brian, Q.C.	1.000	28	12	18	0	30	0
Woodyard, Mark, W.M.	.833	25	7	13	4	24	1
Wrightsman, Dusty, Bur.	.889	34	5	3	1	9	0
Yoshida, Nobuaki, Ft.W.*	.875	5	2	5	1	8	1
Zurita, Tom, Bur.	1.000	35	3	10	0	13	0

PITCHERS WITH TWO OR MORE TEAMS

Player, Team	Pct.	G	PO	A	E	TC	DP
Miniel, Roberto, Bel.	1.000	25	11	11	0	22	0
Miniel, Roberto, Lan.	.833	8	2	3	1	6	0

The following player appeared only as designated hitter, pinch-hitter or pinch runner: Zapey, ph.

LEAGUE CHAMPIONS

Year	Team	Pct.	Year	Team	Pct.	Year	Team	Pct.
1947—	Belleville	.667		Cedar Rapids	.762	1984—	Appleton•	.640
	Belleville	.672	1967—	Wisconsin Rapids	.685		Springfield	.504
1948—	West Frankfort*	.708		Appleton♦	.587	1985—	Kenosha▼	.568
1949—	Centralia	.627	1968—	Decatur	.656		Peoria	.536
	Paducah (4th)†	.454		Quad Cities♦	.648	1986—	Springfield	.621
1950—	Centralia‡	.675	1969—	Appleton	.648		Waterloo▼	.557
1951—	Paris§	.700		Appleton	.690	1987—	Springfield	.671
	Danville (4th)†	.432	1970—	Quincy♦	.691		Kenosha▼	.586
1952—	Danville∞	.685		Quad Cities	.581	1988—	Cedar Rapids■	.621
	Decatur (3rd)†	.584	1971—	Appleton	.642		Kenosha	.579
1953—	Decatur*	.576		Quad Cities■	.548	1989—	South Bend■	.644
1954—	Decatur	.587	1972—	Appleton	.598		Springfield	.541
	Danville (2nd)‡	.528		Danville■	.584	1990—	Cedar Rapids	.657
1955—	Dubuque*	.587	1973—	Wisconsin Rapids■	.562		Quad City■	.579
1956—	Paris▲	.656		Danville	.537	1991—	Clinton■	.583
	Dubuque	.603	1974—	Appleton	.593		Madison	.558
1957—	Decatur▲	.683		Danville■	.517	1992—	Quad City	.664
	Clinton	.623	1975—	Waterloo■	.727		Cedar Rapids■	.594
1958—	Michigan City	.623		Quad Cities	.624	1993—	Clinton	.597
	Waterloo♦	.613	1976—	Waterloo■	.600		South Bend■	.566
1959—	Waterloo	.613		Cedar Rapids	.595	1994—	Rockford	.640
	Waterloo	.613	1977—	Waterloo	.580		Cedar Rapids■	.554
1960—	Waterloo	.629		Burlington■	.511	1995—	Beloit††	.633
	Waterloo	.677	1978—	Appleton■	.708		Michigan	.543
1961—	Waterloo	.613		Burlington	.500	1996—	Wisconsin	.570
	Quincy♦	.594	1979—	Waterloo	.600		West Michigan††	.558
1962—	Dubuque♦	.667		Quad Cities■	.570	1997	Kane County	.507
	Waterloo	.625	1980—	Waterloo■	.610		Lansing**	.504
1963—	Clinton	.710		Quad Cities	.532	1998	West Michigan††	.593
	Clinton	.629	1981—	Wausau■	.636	1999—	Kane County	.569
1964—	Clinton	.667		Quad Cities	.570		Burlington**	.511
	Fox Cities♦	.667	1982—	Madison	.626	2000—	West Michigan■	.629
1965—	Burlington	.667		Appleton▼	.579		Michigan‡‡	.594
	Burlington	.677	1983—	Appleton•	.635	2001	Kane County▲▲	.638
1966—	Fox Cities♦	.689		Springfield	.576			

*Won championship and four-club playoff. †Won four-club playoff. ‡Playoff finals canceled because of bad weather. §Won both halves of split season. ∞Won first half of split season and tied Paris for second-half title. ▲Won first-half title and four-team playoff. ♦Won split season playoff. ■League divided into Northern and Southern divisions and played split season. Playoff winner. ▼League divided into Northern, Central and Southern divisions. Playoff winner. •League divided into Northern, Central and Southern divisions; regular season and playoff winner. ††League divided into Eastern, Central and Western divisions; regular season and playoff winner. **League divided into Eastern, Central and Western divisions, playoff winner. ‡‡League divided into Eastern and Western divisions and played split season. Playoff winner. (NOTE— Known as Illinois State League in 1947-48 and Mississippi-Ohio Valley League from 1949 through 1955.) ▲▲League divided into Eastern and Western divisions and played split season; was leading final series of four-team playoff and was declared champion when Professional Baseball declared a stoppage of play.

CLASS A *Midwest League*

NEW YORK-PENN LEAGUE

LEAGUE OFFICE

President
Ben Hayes
Address
9410 International Court North
St. Petersburg, FL 33716
Phone
727-576-6300

Teams (affiliation)
Auburn Doubledays (Blue Jays)
Batavia Muck Dogs (Phillies)
Brooklyn Cyclones (Mets)
Hudson Valley Renegades (Devil Rays)
Jamestown Jammers (Braves)
Lowell Spinners (Red Sox)
Mahoning Valley Scrappers (Indians)

New Jersey Cardinals (Cardinals)
Oneonta Tigers (Tigers)
Staten Island Yankees (Yankees)
Tri-City ValleyCats (Astros)
Utica Blue Sox (Marlins)
Vermont Expos (Expos)
Williamsport Crosscutters (Pirates)

2001 FINAL STANDINGS

McNAMARA DIVISION

Team	W	L	T	Pct.	GB
Williamsport (Pirates)	48	26	0	.649	...
Jamestown (Braves)	39	36	0	.520	9.5
Oneonta (Tigers)	37	37	0	.500	11.0
Batavia (Phillies)	37	39	0	.487	12.0
Auburn (Blue Jays)	32	42	0	.432	16.0
Utica (Marlins)	27	47	0	.365	21.0
Mahoning Valley (Indians)	26	49	0	.347	22.5

STEDLER DIVISION

Team	W	L	T	Pct.	GB
Brooklyn (Mets)	52	24	0	.684	...
Staten Island (Yankees)	48	28	0	.632	4.0
Pittsfield (Astros)	45	30	0	.600	6.5
Hudson Valley (Devil Rays)	39	37	0	.513	13.0
New Jersey (Cardinals)	35	41	0	.461	17.0
Lowell (Red Sox)	33	43	0	.434	19.0
Vermont (Expos)	28	47	0	.373	23.5

COMPOSITE

Team	Bkn.	Wpt.	S.I.	Pit.	Jam.	H.V.	One.	Bat.	N.J.	Low.	Aub.	Ver.	Uti.	M.V.	W	L	T	Pct.	GB
Brooklyn (Mets)	...	0	6	6	6	5	0	4	5	5	6	6	0	3	52	24	0	.684	...
Williamsport (Pirates)	0	...	0	1	4	0	2	6	4	5	6	7	5	8	48	26	0	.649	3.0
Staten Island (Yankees)	2	0	...	3	3	6	0	3	8	5	0	7	6	5	48	28	0	.632	4.0
Pittsfield (Astros)	2	6	5	...	0	7	6	0	5	3	4	2	5	0	45	30	0	.600	6.5
Jamestown (Braves)	1	4	4	0	...	3	4	5	3	0	4	0	5	6	39	36	0	.520	12.5
Hudson Valley (Devil Rays)	3	0	2	1	4	...	5	5	4	4	0	8	0	3	39	37	0	.513	13.0
Oneonta (Tigers)	0	4	0	1	4	2	...	4	0	4	6	3	5	4	37	37	0	.500	14.0
Batavia (Phillies)	3	2	4	0	3	2	4	...	4	0	4	0	4	7	37	39	0	.487	15.0
New Jersey (Cardinals)	3	3	0	3	4	0	4	3	...	6	0	5	0	4	35	41	0	.461	17.0
Lowell (Red Sox)	3	2	3	5	0	4	3	0	2	...	4	4	3	0	33	43	0	.434	19.0
Auburn (Blue Jays)	1	2	0	3	4	0	2	4	0	3	...	4	5	4	32	42	0	.432	19.0
Vermont (Expos)	2	0	1	5	0	0	4	0	3	4	3	...	6	0	28	47	0	.373	23.5
Utica (Marlins)	0	3	1	2	2	0	3	4	0	4	2	1	...	5	27	47	0	.365	24.0
Mahoning Valley (Indians)	4	0	2	0	2	4	4	1	3	0	3	0	3	...	26	49	0	.347	25.5

Major league affiliations in parentheses.

PLAYOFFS: Williamsport defeated Jamestown two games to one; Brooklyn defeated Staten Island two games to one; Brooklyn led final series one game to none over Williamsport. Note: Williamsport and Brooklyn declared New York-Penn League Co-Champions due to stoppage of play in professional baseball.

REGULAR-SEASON ATTENDANCE: Auburn, 54,994; Batavia, 43,257; Brooklyn, 289,381; Hudson Valley, 160,858; Jamestown, 63,069; Lowell, 185,000; Mahoning Valley, 181,617; New Jersey, 131,197; Oneonta, 52,825; Pittsfield, 56,747; Staten Island, 188,127; Utica, 47,135; Vermont, 115,560; Williamsport, 72,258. Total—1,642,025. Playoff (7 games)—24,933.

MANAGERS: Auburn, Paul Elliot; Batavia, Frank Klebe; Brooklyn, Edgar Alfonzo; Hudson Valley, Dave Howard; Jamestown, Jim Saul; Lowell, Arnie Beyeler; Mahoning Valley, Chris Bando; New Jersey, Brian Rupp; Oneonta, Gary Green; Pittsfield, Ivan DeJesus; Staten Island, David Jorn; Utica, Kevin Boles; Vermont, Steve Balboni; Williamsport, Tony Beasley.

ALL-STAR TEAM: 1B—Aaron Rifkin, Staten Island; 2B—Juan Francia, Oneota; 3B—Juan Camacho, Staten Isand; SS—Tony Pena, Jamestown; Utility INF—Edgar Gonzalez, Hudson Valley; OF—Chris Duffy, Williamsport; OF—Frank Corr, Brooklyn; OF—Todd Self, Pittsfield; OF—Angel Pagan, Brooklyn; C (tie)—Mike Rabelo, Oneota and Chris Shelton, Williamsport; DH—Walter Young, Williamsport; RHP—Jason Arnold, Staten Island; RHP—Ian Oquendo, Williamsport; LHP—Ross Peoples, Brooklyn; LHP—Brian Rodaway, Pittsfield; Most Valuable Player—Aaron Rifkin, Staten Island.

2001 BATTING

TEAM

Team	Avg.	G	TPA	AB	R	H	TB	2B	3B	HR	RBI	SH	SF	HP	BB	IBB	SO	SB	CS	GDP	LOB	ShO	Slg.	OBP
Brooklyn	.279	76	2839	2548	368	711	1056	143	14	58	321	12	21	59	199	6	524	97	67	53	499	5	.414	.343
Staten Island	.265	76	2916	2561	383	678	1004	138	25	46	346	15	26	49	265	6	498	71	30	63	574	1	.392	.342
Williamsport	.262	74	2777	2432	374	637	920	125	25	36	318	33	21	48	243	11	489	132	36	34	517	2	.378	.338
Oneonta	.258	74	2765	2450	327	631	874	98	35	25	282	19	19	33	244	4	597	73	48	52	531	2	.357	.331
Hudson Valley	.257	76	2978	2700	352	694	1008	143	24	41	315	12	27	29	210	12	599	91	43	53	571	6	.373	.315
New Jersey	.257	76	2954	2545	330	653	930	142	24	29	291	27	24	33	325	11	580	89	52	59	584	2	.365	.340
Lowell	.252	76	2993	2594	354	653	905	138	15	28	308	15	25	44	315	3	578	86	35	45	615	4	.349	.340
Pittsfield	.251	75	2883	2492	398	625	919	139	25	35	332	29	25	47	290	13	600	133	55	39	497	2	.369	.337
Jamestown	.247	75	2758	2452	292	606	839	115	20	26	250	19	22	48	217	2	511	68	35	54	523	9	.342	.318
Batavia	.241	76	2885	2565	323	617	876	129	23	28	295	27	23	41	229	11	581	58	41	46	522	3	.342	.310
Auburn	.239	74	2838	2547	306	610	854	107	19	33	261	21	22	42	206	5	507	94	40	52	491	1	.335	.305
Utica	.237	74	2782	2479	297	588	843	103	19	38	260	12	16	31	244	8	649	41	26	50	520	4	.340	.312
Mahoning Val.	.226	75	2801	2487	292	561	854	111	19	48	253	14	8	35	257	5	554	38	43	52	500	2	.343	.306
Vermont	.208	75	2729	2432	264	506	680	85	13	21	215	22	12	31	232	1	638	66	38	36	473	10	.280	.284

TOP QUALIFIERS FOR BATTING CHAMPIONSHIP

Minimum 205 plate appearances. *Lefthanded batter. †Switch-hitter.

Player, Team	Avg.	G	TPA	AB	R	H	TB	2B	3B	HR	RBI	SH	SF	HP	BB	IBB	SO	SB	CS	GDP	Slg.	OBP
Francia, Juan, One.†	.340	47	208	191	30	65	74	5	2	0	8	3	1	2	11	0	32	17	14	2	.387	.380
Gonzalez, Edgar, H.V.	.332	73	323	277	49	92	146	19	4	9	34	2	4	3	37	6	56	6	3	5	.527	.411
Caligiuri, Jay, Bkn.	.328	66	273	238	38	78	113	14	3	5	34	0	3	6	26	1	31	4	2	5	.475	.403
Rabelo, Mike, One.†	.325	53	222	194	27	63	71	4	2	0	32	0	1	4	23	0	45	1	2	4	.366	.405
Rifkin, Aaron, S.I.*	.318	69	285	245	41	78	137	19	5	10	49	2	5	2	31	0	47	3	2	6	.559	.392
Duffy, Chris, Wil.†	.317	64	277	221	50	70	93	12	4	1	24	4	2	17	33	1	33	30	5	0	.421	.440
Youkilis, Kevin, Low.	.317	59	260	183	52	58	85	14	2	3	28	0	2	5	70	0	28	4	3	0	.464	.512
Pagan, Angel, Bkn.†	.315	62	271	238	46	75	89	10	2	0	15	3	1	7	22	0	30	30	18	3	.374	.388
Griffin, John-ford, S.I.*	.311	66	284	238	46	74	108	17	1	5	43	1	2	3	40	0	41	10	4	5	.454	.413
Kent, Mailon, Jam.	.310	50	211	187	26	58	79	9	3	2	27	2	0	1	21	0	20	5	3	6	.422	.383
Hicks, Scott, Uti.*	.308	56	240	211	25	65	94	15	1	4	36	0	3	2	24	2	52	7	2	2	.445	.379
Harrison, Vince, H.V.	.305	57	216	197	21	60	75	10	1	1	30	0	1	2	16	1	34	4	4	6	.381	.361
Shelton, Chris, Wil.	.305	50	213	174	22	53	70	11	0	2	33	1	3	2	33	1	31	4	1	1	.402	.415
Self, Todd, Pit.*	.303	73	316	261	52	79	109	13	4	3	49	1	6	2	46	3	61	10	6	2	.418	.403
Corr, Frank, Bkn.	.302	61	234	212	38	64	126	21	1	13	46	1	0	7	14	2	32	6	6	5	.594	.365

DEPARTMENTAL LEADERS: G—McCarthy, 74; AB—DePaula, 303; R—Self, 52; H—E. Gonzalez, 92; TB—E. Gonzalez, 146; 2B—Durazo, 22; 3B—Raburn, 8; HR—Corr, Young, 13 each; RBI—Camacho, 51; SH—Cuello, 9; SF—A. Clark, Self, Conrad, 6 each; HP—Duffy, 17; BB—Youkilis, 70; IBB—; SO—Siriveaw, M. Davis, 88 each; SB—Duffy, Pagan, 30 each; CS—Pagan, 18; GIDP—Cannizaro, 15; Slg.—Corr, .594; OBP—Youkilis, .512.

ALL PLAYERS

*Lefthanded batter. †Switch-hitter.

Player, Team	Avg.	G	TPA	AB	R	H	TB	2B	3B	HR	RBI	SH	SF	HP	BB	IBB	SO	SB	CS	GDP	Slg.	OBP
Abreu, Dave, Bkn.†	.182	4	11	11	1	2	5	0	0	1	1	0	0	0	0	0	2	0	0	1	.455	.182
Alayon, Jean, M.V.†	.125	3	8	8	1	1	1	0	0	0	0	0	0	0	0	0	3	0	0	0	.125	.125
Aliondo, Humberto, Wil.	.211	45	165	152	17	32	49	9	1	2	15	0	0	1	11	0	45	1	0	2	.322	.268
Alvarado, Oscar, Pit.	.155	26	80	71	9	11	16	2	0	1	4	0	1	0	8	0	28	0	0	1	.225	.250
Alvarez, Aaron, Uti.	.208	20	55	48	7	10	14	1	0	1	2	0	1	0	6	0	13	0	0	0	.292	.291
Ambrosini, Dominick, Ver.*	.226	44	173	159	19	36	51	7	1	2	19	0	0	0	14	0	37	1	3	3	.321	.289
Anderson, Travis, Jam.	.246	37	150	130	16	32	46	11	0	1	17	2	0	7	11	0	19	1	0	4	.354	.338
Andrianoff, Jon, Pit.	.145	23	63	55	5	8	11	3	0	0	6	0	0	2	6	0	19	4	1	0	.200	.254
Arias, Leandro, Bkn.	.241	36	124	112	12	27	45	7	1	3	11	2	0	0	10	0	31	2	2	0	.402	.303
Arrieche, Gabriel, Aub.	.264	41	143	121	11	32	42	4	3	0	12	3	1	7	11	0	15	8	4	4	.347	.357
Aoghina, Jonathan, Uti.†	.217	30	67	60	6	13	14	1	0	0	4	0	0	1	6	0	14	0	0	0	.233	.299
Asprilla, Avelino, Wil.	.257	56	199	183	28	47	63	9	2	1	20	6	2	1	7	0	36	0	3	0	.344	.286
Ayala, Abraham, Pit.	.238	8	27	21	2	5	6	1	0	0	2	0	0	0	4	0	0	0	0	2	.286	.360
Bacani, David, Bkn.	.295	23	105	95	13	28	34	6	0	0	9	2	1	2	5	0	12	5	4	2	.358	.340
Bailie, Stefan, Low.	.233	23	99	90	9	21	31	4	0	2	15	0	0	3	6	0	21	0	0	0	.344	.303
Baker, Casey, S.I.	.071	6	15	14	0	1	1	0	0	0	0	0	0	0	1	0	3	0	0	0	.071	.133
Bard, Josh, S.I.	.273	13	51	44	7	12	22	4	0	2	8	0	0	1	6	0	2	0	1	1	.500	.373
Barnowski, Bryan, Low.	.157	14	59	51	7	8	16	5	0	1	2	0	0	2	6	0	22	0	0	0	.314	.271
Bastardo, Angel, M.V.	.262	36	138	130	12	34	51	8	0	3	13	0	0	2	6	0	19	1	1	4	.392	.304
Bautista, Jose, Wil.	.286	62	247	220	43	63	94	10	3	5	30	0	0	6	21	0	41	8	1	5	.427	.364
Bennett, Kris, Bat.	.242	44	177	157	13	38	44	4	1	0	14	1	0	5	14	0	22	5	5	4	.280	.324
Beuerlein, Tyler, Bkn.†	.253	21	85	75	10	19	24	5	0	0	6	0	0	2	8	0	26	0	1	1	.320	.341
Blackburn, Franco, Uti.*	.224	37	128	107	14	24	34	4	0	2	11	0	0	0	21	1	37	0	0	0	.318	.352
Brackley, Carlos, Low.	.360	6	27	25	6	9	17	3	1	1	6	0	0	1	1	0	8	0	1	0	.680	.407
Brosseau, Richard, Aub.*	.195	51	199	174	12	34	51	7	2	2	20	3	2	0	20	0	24	4	2	4	.293	.276
Brostrom, Jeremy, One.*	.333	2	7	3	2	1	2	1	0	0	0	0	0	0	0	0	0	0	0	0	.667	.714
Brown, Adrian, Wil.†	.333	4	19	18	4	6	8	0	1	0	4	0	0	0	1	0	2	2	0	0	.444	.368
Brown, Andrew, Jam.	.000	16	11	7	1	0	0	0	0	0	0	1	0	1	3	0	2	0	0	0	.000	.273
Brown, Kevin, Jam.	.158	49	199	158	17	25	51	8	0	6	20	0	2	6	33	0	70	0	1	6	.323	.322
Brown, Matthew, Ver.†	.218	53	213	197	22	43	71	14	1	4	22	0	0	1	15	0	61	4	3	5	.360	.277
Brunner, Ryan, Low.*	.241	69	307	261	35	63	84	16	1	1	34	0	1	3	41	0	57	1	0	4	.322	.350
Cabrera, Yoelmis, Wil.	.181	42	138	127	12	23	33	5	1	1	12	2	1	1	7	0	27	5	5	3	.260	.228
Caligiuri, Jay, Bkn.	.328	66	273	238	38	78	113	14	3	5	34	0	3	6	26	1	31	4	2	5	.475	.403
Camacho, Juan, S.I.†	.277	72	302	274	42	76	126	14	3	10	51	0	2	6	20	2	36	0	1	10	.460	.338
Campos, Mario, Low.	.231	60	242	225	22	52	83	16	0	5	31	1	3	2	11	0	80	2	3	5	.369	.270
Candelario, Luis, H.V.	.258	56	237	225	26	58	92	16	0	6	28	0	2	3	7	0	62	9	1	7	.409	.287
Cannizaro, Andy, S.I.	.283	67	288	254	38	72	85	9	2	0	20	3	3	6	22	1	21	5	3	15	.335	.351
Cano, Robinson, S.I.*	.250	2	8	8	0	2	2	0	0	0	2	0	0	0	0	0	2	0	0	0	.250	.250
Caracciolo, Tony, Ver.	.211	52	195	171	18	36	44	5	0	1	8	1	0	4	19	0	38	13	1	3	.257	.304
Carroll, Wes, Bat.	.286	12	47	42	7	12	14	2	0	0	3	1	0	0	4	0	2	2	1	0	.333	.348
Castro, Bernabel, S.I.†	.351	15	69	57	6	20	21	1	0	0	7	0	0	1	11	0	12	8	3	0	.368	.464
Chapman, Travis, Wil.	.291	17	59	55	6	16	21	3	1	0	4	0	1	2	1	0	9	0	1	0	.382	.322
Checksfield, Steven, Pit.	.190	60	226	200	32	38	74	7	4	7	23	2	3	3	18	1	49	5	3	3	.370	.263
Christensen, Jeff, S.I.*	.224	19	68	58	13	13	27	4	2	2	9	0	0	5	5	0	14	7	1	0	.466	.338
Ciofrone, Paul, Bat.*	.111	3	10	9	0	1	2	1	0	0	0	0	0	0	1	0	5	0	0	0	.222	.200
Clark, Aaron, H.V.*	.201	66	287	254	31	51	89	16	2	6	35	0	6	4	22	1	66	4	2	3	.350	.269
Clute, Kris, Uti.	.191	29	109	94	11	18	22	2	1	0	12	1	0	1	13	0	25	1	1	1	.234	.296
Coffey, Kris, Low.	.274	69	307	274	27	75	80	5	0	0	13	3	1	1	28	1	50	22	9	3	.292	.342
Colmenter, Jesus, M.V.†	.185	17	71	65	6	12	16	0	2	0	1	1	1	1	3	0	15	2	0	2	.246	.229
Conrad, Brooks, Plt.†	.280	65	281	232	41	65	103	16	5	4	39	4	6	13	26	3	52	14	2	1	.444	.375
Corr, Frank, Bkn.	.302	61	234	212	38	64	126	21	1	13	46	1	0	7	14	2	32	6	6	5	.594	.365
Cortes, Jorge, Wil.*	.254	51	210	189	23	48	73	17	1	2	31	0	1	2	20	2	25	2	2	5	.386	.329
Cortez, Fernando, H.V.*	.278	55	257	234	36	65	88	14	3	1	25	3	2	3	15	1	26	6	3	5	.376	.327
Coyne, Anthony, Bkn.	.000	1	2	2	0	0	0	0	0	0	0	0	0	0	0	0	1	0	0	0	.000	.000

CLASS A New York-Pennsylvania League

Player, Team	Avg.	G	TPA	AB	R	H	TB	2B	3B	HR	RBI	SH	SF	HP	BB	IBB	SO	SB	CS	GDP	Slg.	OBP
Cruz, Alex, Wil.	.181	26	91	83	9	15	18	1	1	0	11	2	2	0	4	0	14	1	0	1	.217	.213
Cuello, Domingo, Wil.	.278	62	256	230	35	64	95	9	2	6	30	9	0	1	16	1	40	28	6	3	.413	.328
Cummings, Frank, Jam.	.000	3	1	1	0	0	0	0	0	0	0	0	0	0	0	0	1	0	0	0	.000	.000
Dancy, Cliff, Bat.	.191	47	161	141	13	27	36	6	0	1	10	2	0	1	17	0	61	8	3	4	.255	.283
Daubach, Brian, Low.*	.000	1	3	2	0	0	0	0	0	0	0	0	0	0	1	0	1	0	0	0	.000	.333
Davidson, Seth, N.J.†	.276	63	252	217	18	60	69	7	1	0	15	5	3	4	23	1	13	5	13	3	.318	.352
Davis, Morrin, Aub.	.143	65	233	217	17	31	55	8	2	4	20	0	1	1	14	0	88	2	2	5	.253	.197
Davis, Rajai, Wil.†	.083	6	14	12	1	1	1	0	0	0	0	0	0	0	2	0	4	0	1	0	.083	.214
Dean, Herman, One.	.208	7	25	24	3	5	8	1	1	0	0	0	0	0	1	0	10	1	0	0	.333	.240
De Aza, Modesto, Pit.	.280	58	193	168	30	47	58	6	1	1	20	2	2	7	14	0	50	27	11	2	.345	.356
DeGroote, Casey, S.I.*	.182	14	26	22	0	4	7	3	0	0	4	0	0	0	4	0	10	0	0	0	.318	.308
De La Cruz, Miguel, Wil.	.206	42	153	131	19	27	40	9	2	0	15	1	2	1	18	0	33	1	2	2	.305	.303
Delfino, Lee, Aub.	.220	13	61	50	5	11	13	2	0	0	5	1	0	3	7	0	5	3	0	1	.260	.350
De Los Santos, Rene, N.J. ...	.226	66	291	252	34	57	68	9	1	0	17	6	2	2	29	0	57	18	4	1	.270	.305
Dempsey, Nick, Ver.	.300	15	64	60	4	18	27	3	0	2	10	1	0	0	2	1	10	0	0	0	.450	.322
De Paula, Luis, H.V.	.234	70	328	303	42	71	116	12	6	7	26	5	0	1	19	0	54	6	3	6	.383	.282
Devarez, Noel, Bkn.	.250	54	203	188	30	47	87	10	0	10	33	0	2	3	10	0	63	3	3	3	.463	.296
Dion, Nathanael, H.V.	.221	52	186	172	18	38	52	5	3	1	9	2	0	3	9	0	54	0	2	0	.302	.272
Dogero, Matt, N.J.	.000	4	5	5	0	0	0	0	0	0	0	0	0	0	0	0	1	0	0	0	.000	.000
Duffy, Chris, Wil.†	.317	64	277	221	50	70	93	12	4	1	24	4	2	17	33	1	33	30	5	0	.421	.440
Duncan, Shelly, S.I.	.245	70	302	273	43	67	112	17	2	8	39	0	2	6	21	1	62	5	3	5	.410	.311
Durazo, Ernie, Aub.*	.273	64	266	238	26	65	90	22	0	1	36	0	4	2	21	0	54	1	1	3	.378	.332
Edwards, Mike, M.V.	.366	20	84	71	19	26	49	5	0	6	24	0	0	1	12	0	7	0	1	0	.690	.464
Ellis, Ryan, Ver.	.234	42	158	137	15	32	44	3	3	1	13	5	1	2	13	0	24	4	2	3	.321	.307
Emmerick, Joshua, Ver.	.181	43	157	144	11	26	31	5	0	0	10	0	0	2	11	0	32	0	0	4	.215	.248
Espino, Jose, N.J.	.283	20	59	53	10	15	25	5	1	1	11	0	1	0	5	0	13	0	2	1	.472	.333
Evans, Mitch, S.I.	.122	26	58	49	1	6	8	2	0	0	3	0	0	1	8	0	16	0	0	3	.163	.259
Faulkner, Todd, S.I.	.218	24	61	55	4	12	15	1	1	0	3	0	1	1	4	0	13	1	0	0	.273	.279
Fernandez, Alejandro, S.I.	.190	29	98	84	7	16	21	2	0	1	5	3	0	3	8	0	26	0	0	1	.250	.261
Finnerty, Francis, M.V.†	.163	45	160	153	7	25	31	3	0	1	10	0	0	1	6	0	26	2	0	6	.203	.200
Fitzpatrick, Reggie, Ver.*	.125	4	16	16	2	2	2	0	0	0	1	0	0	0	0	0	2	1	1	1	.125	.125
Foster, Gregg, Bat.	.176	8	20	17	5	3	5	2	0	0	1	1	0	2	2	0	6	1	0	0	.294	.250
Fox, Mike, N.J.	.222	27	108	90	13	20	33	7	0	2	5	3	1	1	13	0	29	1	1	0	.367	.324
Francia, Juan, One.†	.340	47	208	191	30	65	74	5	2	0	8	3	1	2	11	0	32	17	14	2	.387	.380
Franco, Esterlin, Pit.	.246	42	155	134	20	33	40	5	1	0	10	4	2	0	15	0	22	5	1	6	.299	.318
Frazier, Charles, Uti.	.243	67	273	243	35	59	86	15	3	2	18	0	1	2	27	0	72	11	4	3	.354	.322
Freeman, Miguel, Ver.	.172	54	202	180	21	31	56	3	2	6	26	1	1	1	19	0	73	3	0	5	.311	.254
Gambino, Mike, Low.	.243	45	198	169	20	41	55	10	2	0	25	4	5	2	18	0	25	0	1	4	.325	.314
Garcia, Daniel, Bkn.	.321	15	62	56	10	18	23	2	0	1	6	0	0	2	4	0	10	3	2	0	.411	.387
Garcia, Kevys, Pit.	.182	20	55	44	3	8	13	0	1	1	9	3	2	0	6	0	13	1	0	0	.295	.269
Garland, Ross, One.	.151	32	114	106	8	16	24	3	1	1	10	0	0	3	5	0	31	0	1	2	.226	.211
Gay, Curt, M.V.*	.141	29	103	92	8	13	19	3	0	1	5	0	0	0	11	0	31	0	3	4	.207	.233
Godwin, Tyrell, Aub.*	.368	33	138	117	26	43	61	8	2	2	15	0	0	2	19	0	27	9	5	1	.521	.464
Gomersall, Richard, One.	.167	43	137	120	18	20	25	2	0	1	8	3	1	2	11	0	45	3	2	2	.208	.246
Gonzalez, Carlos, Low.	.222	3	10	9	1	2	2	0	0	0	0	0	0	0	1	0	3	0	0	0	.222	.300
Gonzalez, Daniel, Bat.†	.238	73	309	281	33	67	84	9	4	0	20	5	2	3	18	2	52	1	3	7	.299	.289
Gonzalez, Edgar, H.V.	.332	73	323	277	49	92	146	19	4	9	34	2	4	3	37	6	56	6	3	5	.527	.411
Gonzalez, Juan, One.†	.344	10	37	32	5	11	15	2	1	0	8	0	1	1	3	0	5	2	2	1	.469	.405
Green, Kevin, Jam.	.091	11	38	33	2	3	6	0	0	1	2	1	0	2	2	0	20	0	0	0	.182	.189
Griffin, Daniel, Ver.	.195	38	130	118	12	23	34	4	2	1	6	2	0	1	9	0	60	2	1	2	.288	.258
Griffin, John-ford, S.I.*	.311	66	284	238	46	74	108	17	1	5	43	1	2	3	40	0	41	10	4	5	.454	.413
Guglielmelli, Brad, M.V.	.141	20	71	64	4	9	18	3	0	2	5	0	0	2	5	0	15	0	2	2	.281	.225
Gutierrez, Said, Aub.	.214	41	144	131	10	28	43	6	0	3	13	1	1	4	7	0	28	1	1	3	.328	.273
Guzman, Carlos, Jam.	.000	6	6	6	2	0	0	0	0	0	0	0	0	0	0	0	3	0	0	0	.000	.000
Hambrick, Marcus, Jam.*	.144	36	107	97	8	14	23	7	1	0	1	1	0	1	8	0	32	1	3	1	.237	.217
Hannahan, John, One.*	.291	14	63	55	11	16	22	4	1	0	8	0	3	0	5	0	7	2	1	2	.400	.333
Harrison, Vince, H.V.	.305	57	216	197	21	60	75	10	1	1	30	0	1	2	16	1	34	4	4	6	.381	.361
Hartig, Philip, Uti.	.259	46	178	170	12	44	65	4	4	3	17	0	0	0	8	0	37	0	3	8	.382	.292
Hattig, John, Low.†	.111	11	49	45	4	5	10	0	1	1	5	0	0	1	3	0	7	1	0	6	.222	.184
Heath, Demetrius, One.	.313	6	18	16	0	5	5	0	0	0	1	1	0	0	1	0	2	0	1	0	.313	.353
Helps, Jason, Uti.†	.138	24	83	65	6	9	12	3	0	0	4	1	0	5	12	0	17	0	1	0	.185	.317
Hernandez, Vladimir, Bkn.	.245	15	52	49	2	12	15	1	1	0	4	0	1	0	2	0	7	2	2	2	.306	.269
Hicks, Scott, Uti.*	.308	56	240	211	25	65	94	15	1	4	36	0	3	2	24	2	52	7	2	2	.445	.379
Hoover, Clint, Pit.	.286	27	99	84	7	24	32	8	0	0	16	2	0	5	8	0	29	1	0	0	.381	.381
Howard, Ryan, Bat.*	.272	48	203	169	26	46	77	7	3	6	35	0	2	2	30	5	55	0	0	1	.456	.384
Huber, Justin, Bkn.	.000	3	9	9	0	0	0	0	0	0	0	0	0	0	0	0	4	0	0	1	.000	.000
Hudnall, Joshua, Wil.	.282	40	137	124	17	35	45	4	3	0	16	1	1	4	7	0	31	17	2	3	.363	.338
Jacobs, Mike, Bkn.*	.288	19	77	66	12	19	27	5	0	1	15	0	2	3	6	0	11	1	1	1	.409	.364
Jeffcoat, Bryon, Jam.	.238	36	139	122	15	29	44	3	3	2	16	0	1	4	12	0	24	1	1	2	.361	.324
Jiannetti, Joseph, Bkn.	.348	41	181	158	24	55	77	13	0	3	29	0	2	3	18	0	29	8	5	1	.487	.420
Jimenez, Rich, Aub.†	.281	35	126	114	12	32	37	3	1	0	6	1	1	3	7	1	25	14	2	3	.325	.336
Jimerson, Charlton, Pit.	.234	51	218	197	35	46	87	12	1	9	31	0	0	2	18	1	79	15	4	4	.442	.304
Johnson, Patrick, Low.*	.143	6	25	21	1	3	3	0	0	0	2	0	0	4	0	0	6	0	1	2	.143	.280
Johnson, Seth, Ver.	.178	57	231	208	15	37	47	7	0	1	19	3	4	2	13	0	37	2	2	2	.226	.229
Johnston, Ryan, Bat.	.200	13	46	40	3	8	9	1	0	0	6	2	1	0	3	0	10	0	0	0	.225	.289
Jones, Jeff, N.J.	.289	37	109	90	20	26	37	6	1	1	12	1	1	9	8	0	17	11	1	2	.411	.398
Jones, Kendall, Pit.	.177	36	133	113	11	20	29	6	0	1	14	1	0	0	19	0	20	1	0	4	.257	.295
Jova, Maikel, Aub.	.268	67	275	261	44	70	109	12	0	9	39	0	1	5	7	0	37	6	2	6	.418	.299
Kay, Brett, Bkn.	.311	49	201	180	28	56	84	13	0	5	18	1	0	4	16	0	28	2	1	9	.467	.380
Kelly, Donald, One.*	.286	67	292	262	41	75	89	8	3	0	25	2	3	0	25	1	16	8	5	6	.340	.345
Kelly, Heath, Uti.	.222	7	18	18	5	4	8	1	0	1	3	0	0	0	0	0	2	0	0	1	.444	.222
Kent, Bryan, Low.	.231	40	144	117	16	27	33	6	0	0	13	0	4	7	15	1	26	7	2	5	.282	.343
Kent, Mailon, Jam.	.310	50	211	187	26	58	79	3	3	2	27	2	0	1	21	0	20	5	3	6	.422	.383

Player, Team	Avg.	G	TPA	AB	R	H	TB	2B	3B	HR	RBI	SH	SF	HP	BB	IBB	SO	SB	CS	GDP	Slg.	OBP
Kirby, Brian, M.V.*	.202	37	144	124	12	25	44	11	1	2	14	1	0	0	19	0	45	1	1	1	.355	.308
Knoedler, Jason, One.†	.226	59	238	208	30	47	70	3	4	4	20	0	1	1	28	1	61	11	4	1	.337	.319
Kochen, Ryan, Pit.	.412	4	17	17	4	7	11	4	0	0	5	0	0	0	0	0	3	0	0	0	.647	.412
Kolodzey, Chris, One.	.249	65	266	237	29	59	88	13	5	2	25	2	3	4	20	0	37	4	5	5	.371	.314
Labandeira, John, Ver.	.333	1	3	3	2	1	1	0	0	0	0	0	0	0	0	0	0	0	0	0	.333	.333
Laidlaw, Jacob, Uti.	.229	65	262	223	27	51	82	12	2	5	25	1	4	5	29	1	59	2	1	10	.368	.326
Lawson, Forrest, Bkn.	.280	49	175	164	18	46	59	6	2	1	15	0	2	3	6	1	23	7	4	10	.360	.314
Lentini, Fehlandt, Pit.	.346	15	56	52	13	18	23	3	1	0	8	0	0	0	4	0	6	8	1	0	.442	.393
Lewis, Richard, Jam.	.242	71	315	285	37	69	90	7	1	4	27	3	3	4	20	2	50	16	4	7	.316	.298
Lewis, Russell, Low.*	.292	47	199	168	26	49	75	14	3	2	27	3	3	3	22	0	34	0	1	2	.446	.378
Likely, Cameron, Pit.	.291	40	89	79	20	23	29	1	1	1	11	0	0	2	8	0	10	6	3	0	.367	.371
Lillash, Keith, M.V.	.255	33	112	94	17	24	36	5	2	1	2	1	0	3	14	0	19	2	1	0	.383	.369
Louwsma, Chris, Uti.	.229	44	152	140	20	32	48	6	2	2	17	0	2	0	10	0	34	0	0	3	.343	.276
Lovelady, Greg, Uti.	.154	20	68	65	4	10	11	1	0	0	5	0	0	0	3	0	21	0	1	2	.169	.191
Lutz, David, Ver.*	.228	46	186	167	19	38	47	7	1	0	16	1	2	0	16	0	30	2	1	4	.281	.292
Lydon, Wayne, Bkn.†	.246	21	66	57	12	14	17	1	1	0	1	0	0	2	7	0	18	10	1	1	.298	.348
Lynam, Guy, Uti.	.351	22	64	57	10	20	28	5	0	1	10	0	1	2	4	0	10	1	0	2	.491	.406
Made, Maximo, M.V.*	.204	50	174	157	14	32	43	8	0	1	7	1	0	5	11	0	31	6	2	3	.274	.277
Maduro, Jorge, M.V.	.183	32	127	120	19	22	31	6	0	1	13	0	0	1	6	1	31	0	0	3	.258	.228
Malave, Dennis, M.V.*	.195	40	156	128	19	25	30	3	1	0	8	1	3	3	21	0	23	4	8	2	.234	.316
Malpica, Martin, Aub.	.235	40	151	136	17	32	38	3	0	1	7	2	2	2	9	0	24	3	0	7	.279	.289
Margalski, Ben, Bat.*	.223	40	146	130	16	29	44	6	3	1	18	2	1	0	12	0	41	0	0	2	.338	.287
Martin, Chris, S.I.	.200	27	80	75	8	15	20	2	0	1	5	0	0	1	4	0	18	0	0	1	.267	.250
Martinez, Edgar, Low.	.320	49	192	175	21	56	81	12	2	3	25	0	2	5	10	1	23	1	0	2	.463	.370
Mattle, David, One.*	.204	40	166	142	14	29	42	8	1	1	22	2	3	2	17	1	33	2	0	3	.296	.293
Mayorson, Manuel, Aub.	.263	62	282	247	28	65	70	5	0	0	18	5	5	4	21	0	19	25	13	3	.283	.325
McArthur, Kennon, Bat.†	.000	1	3	3	0	0	0	0	0	0	0	0	0	0	0	0	1	0	0	0	.000	.000
McCarthy, Bill, Jam.	.295	74	316	285	38	84	111	17	2	2	39	0	4	7	20	0	47	7	4	8	.389	.351
McIntyre, Robert, Bkn.	.197	67	256	233	35	46	82	10	1	8	35	1	1	3	18	1	67	7	5	1	.352	.263
McRoberts, Mark, Bat.	.350	7	22	20	2	7	9	2	0	0	3	0	0	2	0	0	3	0	0	1	.450	.409
Meath, Matt, Wil.†	.324	32	133	102	22	33	45	5	2	1	8	3	3	4	21	0	24	13	3	0	.441	.446
Medina, Rodney, Aub.†	.179	11	43	39	4	7	8	1	0	0	3	0	0	0	4	0	5	1	0	2	.205	.256
Mendez, Deivi, S.I.	.231	53	202	186	23	43	60	10	2	1	21	0	4	3	9	0	31	2	4	6	.323	.272
Merritt, Graig, H.V.	.259	35	128	116	13	30	37	4	0	1	12	0	3	0	9	0	14	1	1	1	.319	.305
Miller, Greg, Jam.	.279	61	271	240	24	67	81	10	2	0	17	2	3	5	20	0	28	9	5	2	.338	.343
Money, Freddie, Low.	.249	57	256	221	40	55	76	13	1	2	21	2	2	2	29	0	46	27	5	4	.344	.339
Monroy, Sam, H.V.*	.200	13	54	50	3	10	10	0	0	0	2	0	0	0	4	0	9	2	0	2	.200	.259
Morton, Rickie, M.V.	.282	69	276	238	34	67	124	15	3	12	40	1	0	0	37	2	55	3	3	5	.521	.378
Moylan, Dan, N.J.*	.292	59	239	192	23	56	70	9	1	1	22	1	1	0	45	0	31	6	7	11	.365	.424
Munoz, Billy, M.V.*	.302	12	46	43	3	13	18	3	1	0	0	0	0	0	3	0	6	0	0	3	.419	.348
Myers, Kenton, M.V.	.215	24	87	79	9	17	17	0	0	0	0	0	0	1	7	0	19	0	2	2	.215	.287
Myler, Jonathan, Wil.	.189	23	86	74	6	14	22	5	0	1	8	2	0	0	10	1	20	0	0	1	.297	.286
Nathans, John, Low.	.160	31	93	75	16	12	14	2	0	0	3	0	0	0	18	0	30	2	0	2	.187	.323
Negron, Miguel, Aub.*	.253	50	206	186	27	47	58	6	1	1	13	2	1	2	15	1	22	7	4	1	.312	.314
Nelson, Bruce, N.J.	.260	16	43	40	6	10	13	1	1	0	3	1	0	0	2	0	6	2	1	3	.325	.286
Nelson, John, N.J.	.238	66	299	252	43	60	106	16	3	8	26	4	5	3	35	3	76	14	3	3	.421	.332
Nelson, Nathan, Pit.	.231	38	145	134	9	31	42	8	0	1	14	2	0	2	7	0	22	7	5	7	.313	.280
Netwall, Chris, N.J.	.272	28	93	81	13	22	28	4	1	0	7	1	1	2	8	0	14	0	0	3	.346	.348
Noboa, Joel, Low.	.181	46	158	155	16	28	45	2	0	5	19	0	0	2	1	0	60	4	2	2	.290	.196
Norris, Shawn, Ver.*	.218	57	239	197	18	43	53	4	0	2	21	0	2	2	38	0	57	0	4	2	.269	.347
Obradovich, Mark, Pit.†	.248	42	166	141	21	35	53	10	1	2	23	0	3	1	21	4	36	7	5	2	.376	.343
O'Brien, Kevin, H.V.*	.276	55	221	203	24	56	68	10	1	0	17	0	4	1	13	0	44	1	2	4	.335	.317
Padilla, Juan, Ver.	.150	28	98	88	6	14	20	4	1	0	7	1	0	3	6	0	43	0	2	0	.227	.237
Pagan, Angel, Bkn.†	.315	62	271	238	46	75	89	10	2	0	15	3	1	7	22	0	30	30	18	3	.374	.388
Parrott, Tom, Jam.	.256	42	135	117	17	30	40	5	1	1	8	1	1	1	15	0	39	3	1	3	.342	.343
Peall, Matt, N.J.	.270	22	62	54	6	15	18	3	0	0	6	0	0	2	6	0	6	4	1	2	.333	.371
Pena, Tony, Jam.	.246	72	280	264	26	65	81	12	2	0	18	3	1	2	10	0	48	8	6	7	.307	.278
Perry, Rod, Bat.	.248	70	317	278	35	69	89	13	2	1	28	5	1	7	26	1	47	8	8	3	.320	.327
Peshke, Chad, M.V.	.250	52	192	168	23	42	60	10	1	2	14	2	0	3	19	0	21	2	5	6	.357	.337
Peterson, Ryan, Low.	.259	8	35	27	5	7	9	2	0	0	6	0	0	2	6	0	3	5	0	0	.333	.429
Phelps, Jeff, Bat.	.226	40	144	133	18	30	45	7	1	2	16	0	1	0	10	1	35	2	0	3	.338	.278
Piercy, Mike, Bkn.*	.000	3	2	1	0	0	0	0	0	0	1	0	0	0	1	0	1	0	0	0	.000	.500
Pimentel, Hector, Jam.	.271	53	195	181	22	49	78	8	3	5	24	2	2	3	7	0	39	6	2	4	.431	.306
Pitney, Jared, S.I.*	.000	3	8	7	0	0	0	0	0	0	0	0	0	0	1	0	6	1	0	0	.000	.125
Pittman, Richard, Bkn.†	.333	5	13	12	0	4	4	0	0	0	0	1	0	0	0	0	5	0	0	0	.333	.385
Pohle, Richard, Bat.*	.241	50	207	187	24	45	72	12	0	5	30	0	3	0	17	1	22	0	1	6	.385	.300
Porzel, Alec, Low.	.256	44	188	172	16	44	61	10	2	1	19	1	1	1	13	0	19	2	1	3	.355	.310
Quintana, Miguel, M.V.*	.222	69	297	279	29	62	102	17	4	5	33	0	1	4	10	0	65	6	3	6	.366	.266
Rabelo, Mike, One.†	.325	53	222	194	27	63	71	4	2	0	32	0	1	4	23	0	45	1	2	4	.366	.405
Raburn, Ryan, M.V.	.363	44	189	171	25	62	119	17	8	8	42	0	1	0	17	1	42	1	3	7	.696	.418
Reece, Eric, H.V.*	.273	68	307	271	35	74	105	20	1	3	48	0	4	3	29	2	56	0	1	5	.387	.345
Reed, Robert, Low.	.267	4	16	15	2	4	5	1	0	0	0	1	0	0	0	0	5	0	0	0	.333	.267
Resop, Chris, Uti.	.333	2	3	3	0	1	1	0	0	0	0	0	0	0	0	0	2	0	0	0	.333	.333
Rico, Matt, H.V.	.221	46	169	154	21	34	42	5	0	1	16	0	1	2	12	0	34	1	1	4	.273	.284
Riera, Zack, Wil.†	.500	2	8	4	3	2	2	0	0	0	1	0	0	0	4	0	0	1	1	0	.500	.750
Rifkin, Aaron, S.I.*	.318	69	285	245	41	78	137	19	5	10	49	2	5	2	31	0	47	3	2	6	.559	.392
Rittenhouse, Marc, Uti.	.234	40	148	128	21	30	45	6	0	3	12	1	0	3	16	1	43	0	1	4	.352	.333
Rivera, Erick, Bat.	.257	68	280	261	28	67	85	11	2	1	23	3	3	3	10	0	54	4	7	3	.326	.289
Roat, Kyle, Jam.	.215	33	119	107	10	23	28	5	0	0	4	1	0	1	10	0	32	2	0	2	.262	.288
Robison, Jordan, N.J.	.255	66	264	243	27	62	106	17	3	7	34	3	1	2	15	1	79	7	6	4	.436	.303
Rodriguez, Edgar, Bkn.	.239	27	101	92	8	22	42	5	0	5	13	0	2	3	4	0	23	0	0	3	.457	.287
Rodriguez, Ivan, Low.	.307	25	96	88	11	27	33	3	0	1	10	0	0	0	8	0	20	6	4	1	.375	.365
Rodriguez, Michael, Pit.*	.318	47	199	157	38	50	72	14	4	0	14	3	0	2	33	0	30	13	5	0	.459	.443

— 565 —

Player, Team	Avg.	G	TPA	AB	R	H	TB	2B	3B	HR	RBI	SH	SF	HP	BB	IBB	SO	SB	CS	GDP	Slg.	OBP
Roman, Jesse, N.J.*	.271	71	309	255	39	69	100	16	3	3	39	0	1	2	51	2	39	5	5	3	.392	.395
Rombley, Danny, Ver.	.210	70	294	267	42	56	64	4	2	0	12	3	1	6	19	0	70	19	12	1	.240	.276
Rueffert, Mark, One.	.221	24	81	68	6	15	16	1	0	0	3	0	0	0	13	0	26	1	1	2	.235	.346
Ruiz, Daniel, Jam.	.250	9	29	28	3	7	8	1	0	0	1	0	0	0	1	0	5	0	0	0	.286	.276
Rundgren, Rex, Uti.	.251	55	206	195	15	49	65	5	1	3	25	2	2	2	5	0	33	3	5	3	.333	.275
Ryan, Billy, One.	.182	11	41	33	2	6	6	0	0	0	4	3	0	4	1	0	7	1	0	0	.182	.289
Salas, Michael, Jam.†	.217	37	145	129	8	28	42	8	0	2	17	1	2	4	9	0	21	0	1	2	.326	.285
Salazar, Juan, Low.†	.269	7	32	26	1	7	7	0	0	0	4	0	1	2	3	0	4	2	2	0	.269	.375
Sandoval, Jjalil, Pit.†	.190	23	68	58	9	11	13	2	0	0	2	0	0	1	9	0	19	3	2	0	.224	.309
Santini, Travis, M.V.	.214	34	118	117	9	25	43	9	0	3	13	0	0	0	1	0	30	0	1	1	.368	.220
Santor, John, N.J.†	.227	54	208	185	17	42	64	12	2	2	26	0	1	0	22	0	64	3	2	4	.346	.308
Santos, Omir, S.I.	.274	44	127	117	11	32	39	5	1	0	8	1	2	1	6	0	25	0	1	2	.333	.310
Sato, G.G., Bat.	.261	37	147	138	22	36	64	10	3	4	21	2	0	1	6	1	33	2	1	2	.464	.297
Schmitt, Billy, N.J.	.244	62	252	238	14	58	79	9	3	2	37	0	4	1	9	2	59	1	2	9	.332	.270
Schnabel, Nicholas, Ver.	.205	27	106	83	11	17	19	2	0	0	6	3	0	3	17	0	13	6	2	1	.229	.359
Schumaker, Skip, N.J.*	.253	49	195	162	22	41	53	10	1	0	14	2	1	1	29	1	33	11	2	4	.327	.368
Scott, Charles, M.V.	.133	6	17	15	0	2	2	0	0	0	1	0	1	0	1	0	3	0	0	0	.133	.176
Scott, Mike, One.*	.000	2	3	3	0	0	0	0	0	0	0	1	0	0	0	0	2	0	0	0	.000	.000
Segar, Jeff, S.I.	.267	34	130	116	16	31	48	14	0	1	21	1	3	1	9	2	18	4	1	3	.414	.318
Self, Todd, Pit.*	.303	73	316	261	52	79	109	13	4	3	49	1	6	2	46	3	61	10	6	2	.418	.403
Shelton, Chris, Wil.	.305	50	213	174	22	53	70	11	0	2	33	1	3	2	33	1	31	4	1	1	.402	.415
Shinjo, Tsuyoshi, Bkn.	.286	2	8	7	0	2	2	0	0	0	1	0	0	0	1	0	2	0	1	0	.286	.375
Silvera, Andres, Bat.	.221	58	220	195	24	43	69	10	2	4	20	2	3	2	18	0	63	13	4	3	.354	.289
Siriveaw, Nom, Aub.†	.167	66	266	239	32	40	72	8	3	6	25	1	1	2	23	0	88	8	1	5	.301	.245
Small, Chris, M.V.	.500	2	3	2	0	1	1	0	0	0	0	0	0	0	1	0	1	0	0	0	.500	.667
Sorensen, Zach, M.V.†	.245	14	58	53	10	13	18	0	1	1	11	1	2	0	2	0	8	2	0	2	.340	.263
Sosa, Francisco, Bkn.	.389	24	76	72	12	28	36	3	1	1	8	0	0	2	2	0	7	2	4	3	.500	.421
Soto, Jose, Uti.†	.229	48	208	192	22	44	63	7	3	2	17	2	1	0	13	0	52	15	3	3	.328	.277
Stegall, Ryan, Pit.	.230	67	262	235	29	54	80	17	0	3	26	2	1	4	20	1	47	5	4	5	.340	.300
Stern, Adam, Jam.*	.307	21	92	75	20	23	31	4	2	0	11	0	2	0	15	0	11	9	4	0	.413	.413
Stokes, Jason, Uti.	.231	35	144	130	12	30	52	2	1	6	19	0	1	2	11	0	48	0	0	0	.400	.299
Stringham, Jed, One.	.187	44	144	134	10	25	33	5	0	1	11	1	0	1	8	0	38	1	1	6	.246	.238
Summerville, Kaazim, S.I.	.186	35	70	59	14	11	11	0	0	0	4	0	0	4	7	0	18	13	1	0	.186	.314
Thissen, Greg, Ver.	.235	59	246	221	27	52	68	13	0	1	19	1	1	3	20	0	43	9	4	0	.308	.306
Thompson, Eric, M.V.*	.212	26	71	66	5	14	14	0	0	0	3	2	0	0	3	0	28	2	2	0	.212	.246
Thompson, Kevin, S.I.	.262	68	304	260	46	68	105	11	4	6	33	1	2	5	36	0	48	11	5	5	.404	.360
Todd, Jeremy, Bkn.*	.182	17	55	44	4	8	9	1	0	0	3	0	3	1	7	0	13	0	1	0	.205	.291
Toner, John, Bkn.	.258	38	139	124	10	32	45	8	1	1	16	1	1	5	8	1	33	3	4	1	.363	.326
Tousa, Scott, One.*	.167	8	27	24	6	4	4	0	0	0	1	0	0	1	2	0	5	2	0	0	.167	.259
Trezza, Alex, One.*	.224	53	200	183	23	41	59	11	2	1	19	1	1	2	13	0	65	0	1	4	.322	.281
Truitt, Steve, Pit.	.308	11	39	39	8	12	18	1	1	1	6	0	0	0	0	0	5	1	2	0	.462	.308
Tucker, Michael, Uti.	.214	49	184	159	29	34	44	4	0	2	9	0	0	1	23	1	40	0	2	3	.277	.317
Turner, Jason, S.I.*	.336	33	132	110	24	37	51	7	2	1	19	3	0	0	18	0	31	1	1	1	.464	.430
Uegawachi, Bryce, M.V.†	.204	55	194	162	14	33	35	0	1	0	5	3	0	1	28	0	32	4	5	1	.216	.325
Van Benschoten, John, Wil. .	.227	32	86	75	9	17	22	5	0	0	8	0	2	2	7	0	23	3	2	2	.293	.302
Van Every, Jon, M.V.*	.252	41	170	135	30	34	60	4	2	6	17	0	0	7	28	1	50	1	2	1	.444	.406
Veleber, Troy, Wil.†	.154	14	29	26	8	4	8	1	0	1	2	2	0	0	1	0	8	6	0	0	.308	.185
Vukovich, Vince, Bat.*	.201	46	170	149	19	30	39	6	0	1	14	2	3	2	14	0	25	4	2	1	.262	.262
Wallis, Jacob, Ver.	.063	6	17	16	0	1	1	0	0	0	0	0	0	0	1	0	8	0	0	0	.063	.118
Walsh, Sean, Bat.	.274	63	257	215	35	59	89	20	2	2	24	1	3	11	27	0	44	8	6	6	.414	.379
Whittaker, Tim, Aub.	.299	42	146	127	23	38	55	7	2	2	16	1	1	4	13	2	20	1	3	2	.433	.379
Williams, Matt, N.J.	.294	41	166	136	25	40	61	11	2	2	17	0	1	4	25	1	43	1	2	6	.449	.416
Wolotka, Brian, H.V.*	.266	39	139	124	14	33	57	6	3	4	20	0	0	3	12	0	39	1	0	2	.460	.345
Wood, Stephen, Aub.	.209	33	137	129	9	27	40	5	1	2	11	0	1	0	7	1	25	0	0	1	.310	.248
Woods, Michael, One.	.270	9	42	37	6	10	12	2	0	0	3	0	0	1	4	0	5	5	1	0	.324	.357
Wyant, Hunter, Uti.	.277	30	106	94	11	26	32	6	0	0	6	3	0	3	6	0	14	1	2	1	.340	.340
Youkilis, Kevin, Low.	.317	59	260	183	52	58	85	14	2	3	28	0	2	5	70	0	28	4	3	0	.464	.512
Young, Walter, Wil.*	.289	66	258	232	40	67	118	10	1	13	47	0	2	5	19	5	43	1	1	6	.509	.353
Yount, Andy, One.	.271	63	245	207	31	56	90	8	4	6	31	1	0	5	32	0	83	11	4	5	.435	.381
Zapey, Winton, Uti.	.195	32	88	77	6	15	23	3	1	1	8	1	0	2	7	1	24	0	0	4	.299	.279
Zaragoza, Joel, Bkn.†	.170	28	58	53	5	9	11	2	0	1	1	0	1	3	0	16	1	1	1	.208	.228
Zieour, Neesan, Aub.	.381	5	23	21	3	8	12	0	2	0	2	0	0	1	0	1	1	0	1	.571	.435

GRAND SLAMS: Jimerson, 2; Aliendo, Campos, Checkersfield, Corr, Durazo, Edwards, K. Garcia, Hicks, Jacobs, Morton, Pohle, Turner, 1 each.

AWARDED FIRST BASE ON CATCHER'S INTERFERENCE: M. Rodriguez 4 (E. Martinez, K. Jones, Shelton, Sosa); Aliendo (Alvarado), Brunner (Zapey), A. Clark (Moylan), Durazo (Zapey), S. Johnson (E. Martinez), Kent (Lutz), Margalski (Sosa), Miller (Bastardo), M. Tucker (Bastardo), Turner (K. Jones), Zapey (Bastardo).

2001 PITCHING
TEAM

Team	W	L	Pct.	ERA	G	CG	ShO	Sv.	IP	H	TBF	R	ER	HR	SH	SF	HB	BB	IBB	SO	WP	Bk.
Brooklyn	52	24	.684	2.37	76	1	6	31	671.0	505	2769	223	177	20	14	17	38	261	3	644	43	3
Williamsport	48	26	.649	2.91	74	2	5	23	640.1	550	2651	275	207	34	27	15	30	229	3	567	41	3
Staten Island	48	28	.632	3.22	76	4	5	22	664.1	556	2787	284	238	34	14	14	46	240	4	633	42	8
New Jersey	35	41	.461	3.27	76	0	5	24	676.1	630	2861	317	246	44	16	13	49	234	6	621	44	1
Batavia	37	39	.487	3.44	76	4	3	17	679.1	686	2936	341	260	37	20	24	42	209	15	471	50	3
Pittsfield	45	30	.600	3.47	75	1	4	18	670.0	644	2899	349	258	23	20	19	34	260	6	564	60	9
Jamestown	39	36	.520	3.48	75	1	3	20	651.0	603	2752	297	252	43	14	15	25	242	6	556	46	2
Oneonta	37	37	.500	3.53	74	3	6	18	634.1	630	2779	357	249	27	21	31	45	223	8	529	54	9
Utica	27	47	.365	3.82	74	0	3	14	648.2	598	2783	356	275	35	22	25	40	231	6	458	50	4
Lowell	33	43	.434	3.90	76	1	2	16	673.1	666	2923	356	292	37	24	27	30	259	8	518	41	3
Hudson Valley	39	37	.513	3.91	76	2	1	20	683.2	669	2996	371	297	38	24	18	44	295	5	544	88	3

Team	W	L	Pct.	ERA	G	CG	ShO	Sv.	IP	H	TBF	R	ER	HR	SH	SF	HB	BB	IBB	SO	WP	Bk.
Auburn	32	42	.432	3.96	74	0	5	14	675.0	631	2940	349	297	39	21	17	45	306	2	685	61	2
Mahoning Val.	26	49	.347	4.25	75	0	4	18	660.2	722	2961	391	312	41	24	29	48	250	22	568	62	2
Vermont	28	47	.373	4.45	75	1	1	12	650.2	680	2876	394	322	40	16	27	54	237	2	527	50	6

INDIVIDUAL

TOP QUALIFIERS FOR EARNED-RUN AVERAGE TITLE

Minimum 61 innings. *Lefthanded pitcher.

Pitcher, Team	W	L	Pct.	ERA	G	GS	CG	ShO	GF	Sv.	IP	H	TBF	R	ER	HR	SH	SF	HB	BB	IBB	SO	WP	Bk.
Peeples, Ross, Bkn.*	9	3	.750	1.34	16	15	1	1	0	0	80.1	63	330	19	12	1	2	3	1	29	0	67	4	0
Oquendo, Ian, Wil.	7	0	1.000	1.39	10	9	1	0	0	0	64.2	55	255	16	10	2	3	2	1	10	0	56	2	0
Arnold, Jason, S.I.	7	2	.778	1.50	10	10	2	1	0	0	66.0	35	243	13	11	2	2	1	3	15	0	74	2	0
Ungs, Nick, Uti.	3	1	.750	1.62	12	11	0	0	0	0	61.0	57	236	14	11	3	1	2	0	0	0	40	1	1
Miner, Zach, Jam.	3	4	.429	1.89	15	15	0	0	0	0	90.2	76	358	26	19	6	2	0	4	16	0	68	4	1
Rodriguez, Juan, Wil.	8	2	.800	1.89	13	13	0	0	0	0	81.0	61	317	23	17	2	1	4	3	15	0	58	3	0
Portobanco, Luz, Bkn.	5	3	.625	2.04	13	12	0	0	0	0	70.2	51	293	20	16	1	4	4	13	29	0	52	3	2
Rodaway, Brian, Pit.*	7	3	.700	2.34	17	13	1	0	2	1	88.1	76	346	28	23	6	2	0	1	11	0	56	1	1
Flinn, Chris, H.V.	3	4	.429	2.36	15	10	0	0	4	2	68.2	54	284	33	18	3	2	0	3	21	0	72	12	1
Wilson, Mike, Bat.	4	4	.500	2.58	14	14	1	0	0	0	80.1	89	351	37	23	6	2	0	5	23	1	51	2	0
Asahina, Jonathan, Uti.	4	6	.400	2.58	15	13	0	0	1	0	69.2	56	283	27	20	3	2	2	5	19	0	55	3	0
Pope, Justin, N.J.	2	4	.333	2.60	15	15	0	0	0	0	69.1	64	286	32	20	6	0	0	5	14	0	66	0	0
Rhodes, Shane, Low.*	4	4	.500	2.89	15	14	1	0	0	0	71.2	62	302	28	23	2	2	2	6	25	0	58	2	0
Rudrude, Brett, Low.	5	3	.625	2.95	17	7	0	0	5	1	73.1	65	302	30	24	1	2	3	4	21	0	44	5	0
Delossantos, Carlos, Wil.	5	3	.625	2.98	14	13	0	0	0	0	81.2	73	338	34	27	7	3	0	7	29	0	80	3	0

DEPARTMENTAL LEADERS: W—Eckert, Peeples, 9 each; L—Dischiavo, Generelli, Kleine, Fulchino, 8 each; Pct.—Oquendo, 1.000; G—R. Clark, Barry, Merrigan, Khoury, Wood, 29 each; GS—Several players tied at 15; CG—Several players tied at 2; ShO—Kim, 2; GF—Bustillos, 24; Sv.—J. Miller, 15; IP—Miner, 90.2; H—Cromer, 94; TBF—Mayfield, 367; R—Dischiavo, 58; ER—Dischiavo, 53; HR—Colton, 9; SH—Crawford, Novoa, C. Clark, 5 each; SF—Mitchell, 6; HB—Portobanco, 13; DD—McGowan, 40; IDD—Ourtin, 7; CO—Manning, 07; WP—McGowan, 1C; DK—Fulchino, 0.

ALL PITCHERS

*Lefthanded pitcher.

Pitcher, Team	W	L	Pct.	ERA	G	GS	CG	ShO	GF	Sv.	IP	H	TBF	R	ER	HR	SH	SF	HB	BB	IBB	SO	WP	Bk.
Abrams, Grant, Jam.	3	3	.500	3.03	22	0	0	0	10	0	35.2	40	166	14	12	3	1	0	2	17	1	31	3	0
Aguilar, Edwin, Pit.	2	0	1.000	0.00	3	0	0	0	1	0	0.0	1	20	0	0	0	0	1	0	2	0	12	0	0
Aguilar, Ray, Jam.*	1	1	.500	1.50	2	2	0	0	0	0	12.0	7	46	4	2	1	0	0	0	3	0	16	0	0
Aiello, Nick, H.V.*	6	1	.857	2.48	22	0	0	0	7	0	40.0	36	163	17	11	0	4	2	1	8	1	24	4	0
Akens, Phil, Uti.	2	5	.286	3.24	9	9	0	0	0	0	50.0	40	208	24	18	3	2	3	1	22	0	34	1	0
Ally, Ben, Bat.	3	2	.600	1.05	21	0	0	0	5	1	43.0	42	183	15	5	1	1	5	0	14	2	26	5	0
Alvarado, Oscar, Pit.	0	0	.000	9.00	2	0	0	0	2	0	1.0	3	7	1	1	0	0	0	0	1	0	1	0	0
Anderson, Jason, S.I.	5	1	.833	1.70	7	7	0	0	0	0	47.2	32	184	9	9	2	0	0	4	12	0	56	1	1
Anderson, Julius, H.V.	0	0	.000	4.02	10	0	0	0	6	0	15.2	17	69	9	7	1	0	0	1	6	0	4	2	0
Arnold, Jason, S.I.	7	2	.778	1.50	10	10	2	1	0	0	66.0	35	243	13	11	2	2	1	3	15	0	74	2	0
Arteaga, Francisco, Jam.	0	0	.000	2.45	3	0	0	0	1	0	3.2	3	14	1	1	0	0	0	0	2	0	5	0	0
Artiles, Carlos, S.I.*	0	0	.000	0.00	1	1	0	0	0	0	5.0	1	18	0	0	0	0	0	0	3	0	4	0	0
Asahina, Jonathan, Uti.	4	6	.400	2.58	15	13	0	0	1	0	69.2	56	283	27	20	3	2	2	5	19	0	55	3	0
Barry, Kevin, Jam.	1	0	1.000	0.86	29	0	0	0	23	12	31.1	14	126	5	3	0	0	1	0	18	0	54	0	0
Barzilla, Philip, Pit.*	4	5	.444	4.71	16	14	0	0	0	0	78.1	87	352	52	41	1	1	2	1	34	0	56	9	0
Bautista, Denny, Uti.	3	1	.750	2.08	7	7	0	0	0	0	39.0	25	156	16	9	0	0	2	4	6	0	31	3	0
Baxter, Allen, Uti.	0	0	.000	3.60	1	1	0	0	0	0	5.0	3	21	2	2	0	0	0	1	3	0	5	2	0
Bayrer, Thomas, Pit.	0	0	.000	2.25	5	0	0	0	2	1	8.0	5	37	2	2	0	1	0	0	11	0	5	1	0
Beirne, Kevin, Aub.	0	0	.000	5.40	2	2	0	0	0	0	3.1	6	16	2	2	0	0	0	1	0	0	2	0	0
Bell, Tom, Uti.	0	1	.000	7.99	18	0	0	0	4	0	23.2	29	111	22	21	3	1	1	1	13	0	21	6	0
Benitez, Fabricio, Low.	0	3	.000	4.20	9	9	0	0	0	0	49.1	47	203	25	23	2	2	5	3	11	0	23	1	0
Bennett, Jamie, Bat.*	1	1	.500	3.60	18	0	0	0	4	1	30.0	26	128	14	12	0	1	0	1	2	0	31	3	0
Bentz, Chad, Ver.*	1	3	.250	4.91	8	8	0	0	0	0	36.2	39	163	23	20	2	2	2	0	11	0	38	4	0
Bernard, Jason, Bat.	2	6	.250	3.90	13	12	0	0	0	0	64.2	79	300	43	28	6	2	4	7	24	0	30	4	0
Biddlestone, Jason, Wil.	3	1	.750	1.44	16	1	0	0	7	1	31.1	28	135	11	5	1	1	3	0	17	0	25	2	0
Birtwell, John, One.	1	2	.333	3.76	23	0	0	0	18	7	26.1	25	114	12	11	1	1	0	4	6	0	43	1	0
Blankenship, John, S.I.*	4	0	1.000	3.09	5	5	0	0	0	0	35.0	29	143	16	12	2	0	1	0	8	0	22	1	0
Blasdell, Jared, N.J.	0	1	.000	1.26	26	0	0	0	19	11	28.2	18	114	6	4	2	1	0	4	7	1	36	2	0
Bobbitt, Seth, Pit.	0	0	.000	1.61	8	5	0	0	0	0	28.0	27	122	8	5	2	0	1	2	10	0	23	2	0
Borner, Brady, Wil.*	1	0	1.000	0.71	3	1	0	0	1	0	12.2	4	41	1	1	1	0	0	0	1	0	13	0	0
Bowen, Chad, Bkn.	1	2	.333	4.82	3	2	0	0	0	0	9.1	14	42	5	5	0	0	0	3	0	11	0
Braswell, Bryan, Bkn.*	1	0	1.000	2.08	5	2	0	0	0	0	13.0	12	53	3	3	1	0	0	0	6	0	13	0	0
Brown, Andrew, Jam.	3	4	.429	3.92	14	12	0	0	0	0	64.1	50	267	29	28	5	0	0	3	31	0	59	5	0
Burgess, Richie, N.J.	3	3	.500	4.02	16	6	0	0	4	1	62.2	66	282	31	28	4	2	2	5	28	1	44	5	0
Burruezo, Joseph, Wil.	1	2	.333	3.60	14	2	0	0	5	1	20.0	22	99	16	8	1	3	1	4	10	0	17	2	0
Bustillos, Oscar, H.V.	4	3	.571	2.70	26	0	0	0	24	13	33.1	25	145	21	10	2	0	1	16	1	44	3	0
Byard, David, Bkn.	3	1	.750	1.46	22	0	0	0	20	9	37.0	21	141	7	6	0	0	1	1	11	0	32	1	0
Cable, Taft, Bat.	1	3	.250	3.34	14	12	1	0	0	0	67.1	65	285	33	25	2	1	0	2	19	0	64	1	1
Cabrera, Yunior, Bkn.*	0	0	.000	3.00	1	0	0	0	0	0	3.0	4	15	1	1	0	0	0	2	0	4	1	0
Calvo, Jose, Pit.	0	0	.000	0.00	1	0	0	0	0	0	1.0	2	7	0	0	0	0	1	0	3	0	0
Caputo, Rob, Ver.	0	2	.000	4.75	20	1	0	0	6	3	30.1	32	144	20	16	5	1	1	5	16	0	28	3	0
Carlson, Steve, S.I.*	1	0	1.000	0.00	3	0	0	0	2	0	2.2	1	10	0	0	0	0	0	1	0	2	0	0
Carney, Jake, H.V.	1	0	1.000	0.64	8	0	0	0	2	1	14.0	8	57	2	1	0	1	0	0	6	2	16	0	0
Cataulin, Heath, Uti.	0	3	.000	7.41	25	0	0	0	11	4	37.2	44	179	37	31	5	2	5	4	19	1	32	2	0
Cave, Kevin, Uti.	1	2	.333	3.26	14	5	0	0	4	1	38.2	38	162	16	14	4	1	1	0	14	0	23	1	0
Cetani, Dryan, Jam.*	0	0	.000	18.20	1	0	0	0	0	0	1.2	1	10	5	3	0	0	0	0	1	0	0	0	0
Charron, Eric, Ver.	0	0	.000	3.72	7	0	0	0	2	0	9.2	9	39	4	4	0	0	0	2	0	12	0	0
Chisnall, Wes, Ver.	2	2	.500	2.65	18	0	0	0	2	1	37.1	37	158	16	11	2	2	1	1	7	0	30	0	0

Pitcher, Team	W	L	Pct.	ERA	G	GS	CG	ShO	GF	Sv.	IP	H	TBF	R	ER	HR	SH	SF	HB	BB	IBB	SO	WP	Bk.
Clark, Claudell, Wil.*	1	4	.200	3.86	18	0	0	0	7	1	30.1	17	130	19	13	2	5	1	1	24	1	26	3	0
Clark, Ryan, S.I.*	2	0	1.000	1.15	29	0	0	0	16	7	31.1	14	114	5	4	0	2	1	1	7	0	37	2	1
Clelland, James, Ver.	3	1	.750	4.73	18	0	0	0	8	0	32.1	40	151	22	17	2	0	3	5	6	0	24	4	0
Clifton, Derek, Pit.	2	0	1.000	5.56	9	0	0	0	3	0	11.1	11	52	9	7	0	1	0	3	6	0	6	0	0
Coenen, Matt, One.	2	2	.500	3.04	10	9	1	0	1	1	47.1	44	206	26	16	1	1	1	2	16	0	37	3	0
Collazo, William, Jam.*	3	1	.750	0.60	9	0	0	0	7	1	15.0	9	55	2	1	0	1	0	1	0	0	13	2	0
Colson, Jason, Aub.	1	2	.333	2.72	8	8	0	0	0	0	36.1	28	154	14	11	2	1	1	4	13	0	31	0	0
Colton, Kyle, Jam.	1	4	.200	7.11	11	8	0	0	0	0	38.0	45	180	32	30	9	1	1	1	23	0	26	4	0
Colvard, Ron, M.V.	0	1	.000	8.31	17	0	0	0	9	0	21.2	26	114	25	20	2	0	3	3	17	1	16	7	0
Comolli, Mark, Aub.	2	1	.667	4.74	10	0	0	0	6	1	19.0	21	81	11	10	1	2	0	6	6	0	21	6	0
Connolly, Jon, One.*	0	1	.000	18.00	1	1	0	0	0	0	3.0	8	17	6	6	1	1	0	0	1	0	1	1	0
Cooksey, Wes, S.I.	1	0	1.000	4.71	20	0	0	0	7	1	28.2	27	124	16	15	3	0	1	2	11	1	13	2	0
Cooper, Chris, M.V.*	0	5	.000	2.38	25	0	0	0	18	11	34.0	34	153	24	9	1	4	2	0	10	2	40	1	0
Corr, Frank, Bkn.	0	0	.000	4.50	1	0	0	0	0	0	2.0	3	9	1	1	0	0	0	1	1	0	1	0	0
Correa, Cristobal, N.J.	1	3	.250	5.40	15	1	0	0	4	3	40.0	48	189	34	24	3	0	2	7	17	0	32	2	0
Cox, Mike, Bkn.*	6	1	.857	2.91	13	7	0	0	0	0	52.2	40	234	25	17	2	1	1	2	41	0	73	6	0
Crawford, Chris, H.V.	1	1	.500	2.95	24	0	0	0	7	2	39.2	26	171	14	13	0	5	2	4	23	0	46	2	0
Cromer, Nathan, H.V.*	4	3	.571	3.99	15	15	0	0	0	0	79.0	94	344	38	35	6	2	3	0	24	0	39	8	0
Culp, Todd, M.V.	2	2	.500	3.63	22	0	0	0	5	2	44.2	36	191	21	18	3	0	2	4	21	0	60	3	0
Currier, Rik, S.I.	2	2	.500	3.77	7	7	0	0	0	0	31.0	37	149	20	13	2	0	1	3	13	0	27	1	1
Curtin, Brian, M.V.	1	3	.250	3.82	21	0	0	0	7	2	30.2	36	145	14	13	3	4	2	3	16	7	26	4	0
D'Amato, Dan, Wil.*	4	1	.800	2.17	20	0	0	0	14	2	29.0	21	117	10	7	1	1	0	0	13	0	32	5	0
David, Toby, Uti.*	0	3	.000	5.19	20	0	0	0	8	0	34.2	41	153	25	20	3	0	3	1	11	0	18	2	0
Davis, Tim, Bat.*	2	0	1.000	3.51	16	0	0	0	2	0	33.1	25	135	16	13	1	1	3	2	13	0	26	1	0
Delossantos, Carlos, Wil.	5	3	.625	2.98	14	13	0	0	0	0	81.2	73	338	34	27	7	3	0	7	29	0	80	3	0
Dinardo, Lenny, Bkn.*	1	2	.333	2.00	9	5	0	0	3	0	36.0	26	148	10	8	0	0	1	1	17	0	40	4	0
Dischiavo, John, H.V.	3	8	.273	6.50	15	15	1	0	0	0	73.1	91	342	58	53	7	1	5	8	31	0	51	13	0
Dorman, Rich, H.V.	3	0	1.000	2.58	17	3	0	0	3	0	45.1	37	189	14	13	2	3	0	2	20	1	34	6	0
Dumatrait, Phillip, Low.*	1	1	.500	3.48	2	2	0	0	0	0	10.1	9	44	4	4	0	0	0	0	4	0	15	1	0
Durham, Chad, Pit.	1	2	.333	2.30	8	0	0	0	5	0	15.2	13	61	4	4	1	0	1	2	0	0	23	0	0
Dutremble, Jeff, Wil.*	1	0	1.000	6.85	17	0	0	0	8	0	23.2	29	123	20	18	1	1	0	2	27	0	25	7	0
Eckert, Harold, Bkn.	9	1	.900	3.34	13	11	0	0	1	0	70.0	51	284	31	26	4	1	1	6	21	0	75	9	0
Ellis, Ryan, Ver.	0	0	.000	0.00	1	0	0	0	1	0	0.0	0	1	0	0	0	0	0	0	1	0	0	0	0
Esarey, Brad, Aub.*	2	0	1.000	3.86	17	0	0	0	4	0	35.0	33	152	18	15	2	1	1	3	12	0	34	1	0
Farman, Brian, M.V.	0	2	.000	2.81	10	0	0	0	6	1	16.0	16	67	5	5	0	2	0	1	2	1	12	1	0
Farmer, Tom, One.	1	1	.500	2.86	4	4	0	0	0	0	22.0	24	95	13	7	1	0	1	0	4	0	11	0	2
Fernley, Nathan, M.V.	0	2	.000	4.42	13	0	0	0	6	0	18.1	30	96	18	9	2	1	1	1	8	3	21	0	0
Field, Luke, M.V.	4	5	.444	3.89	14	14	0	0	0	0	69.1	80	310	48	30	5	3	2	3	25	1	53	6	0
Flinn, Chris, H.V.	3	4	.429	2.36	15	10	0	0	4	2	68.2	54	284	33	18	3	2	0	3	21	0	72	12	1
Flores, Neomar, Aub.	3	1	.750	4.80	12	4	0	0	2	0	54.1	45	232	33	29	6	0	3	5	19	0	51	3	0
Fortin, Michael, Wil.	1	0	1.000	6.00	4	0	0	0	0	0	6.0	5	26	4	4	2	0	0	0	6	0	5	0	0
Fortunato, Bartolome, H.V.	2	5	.286	5.13	16	9	0	0	2	0	59.2	70	266	35	34	3	1	0	2	29	0	53	11	0
Friedberg, Drew, Wil.*	0	0	.000	0.00	4	0	0	0	4	3	4.0	2	13	0	0	0	0	0	0	0	0	6	0	0
Friske, Parker, Low.*	3	2	.600	5.23	19	3	0	0	6	1	53.1	70	252	38	31	5	4	0	2	23	1	38	2	0
Fulchino, Jeff, Uti.	3	8	.273	3.56	14	13	0	0	1	0	60.2	48	267	34	24	2	1	0	8	31	0	33	3	3
Furnald, Donnie, Jam.	4	1	.800	6.64	11	5	0	0	2	0	39.1	37	181	30	29	3	1	2	0	34	0	34	8	0
Gahan, Matt, Bkn.	4	1	.800	1.99	10	3	0	0	5	4	40.2	29	164	16	9	1	1	0	1	7	0	42	2	0
Garces, Rich, Low.	0	0	.000	0.00	2	2	0	0	0	0	2.0	1	7	0	0	0	0	0	0	0	0	1	0	0
Garcia, Anderson, S.I.	0	1	.000	5.79	1	1	0	0	0	0	4.2	7	20	3	3	0	0	0	0	1	0	1	1	0
Garris, Antonio, Ver.	0	0	.000	1.62	15	0	0	0	14	5	16.2	12	74	7	3	1	0	3	9	0	20	1	0
Generelli, Daniel, Low.*	1	8	.111	4.71	16	14	0	0	0	0	70.2	69	318	49	37	4	3	5	4	38	0	51	6	1
George, Todd, Ver.	0	0	.000	4.24	5	2	0	0	0	0	17.0	20	70	8	8	1	0	1	4	0	15	0	0
Gerk, Jordan, One.*	1	0	1.000	2.25	4	0	0	0	1	0	8.0	10	37	3	2	0	0	0	2	1	10	0	0
Gilchrist, Ronald, Wil.*	4	0	1.000	3.18	16	0	0	0	5	0	22.2	21	98	8	8	0	0	1	3	8	0	27	0	0
Gill, Ryan, S.I.	2	2	.500	5.63	19	0	0	0	6	0	24.0	23	114	20	15	2	1	0	4	16	2	25	3	1
Glaser, Nick, Bat.	3	4	.429	2.51	24	0	0	0	21	6	28.2	27	126	13	8	0	1	2	0	7	2	21	6	0
Gomez, Mariano, M.V.*	1	0	1.000	5.40	1	1	0	0	0	0	5.0	5	22	3	3	1	0	0	2	0	6	1	0
Gomez, Ricardo, S.I.	1	1	.500	1.47	5	0	0	0	0	0	18.1	13	77	7	3	2	1	0	2	10	1	11	1	2
Gonzales, Jim, One.	3	3	.500	2.55	16	0	0	0	11	2	24.2	24	105	10	7	1	0	1	1	8	2	20	6	0
Goodrum, Kevin, S.I.*	1	1	.500	3.78	7	3	0	0	2	0	16.2	18	75	9	7	0	1	0	0	6	0	14	0	0
Goodwin, Ron, Uti.	3	3	.500	3.60	20	0	0	0	7	3	45.0	51	191	22	18	1	2	3	1	10	1	25	5	0
Grant, Michael, Low.	0	2	.000	6.10	5	0	0	0	2	1	10.1	14	51	7	7	0	0	0	1	6	0	7	0	0
Greco, Sam, N.J.	1	4	.200	4.50	21	0	0	0	1	0	30.0	30	134	19	15	1	1	3	5	11	0	29	3	0
Guerrero, Julio, Wil.	2	2	.500	4.50	7	0	0	0	1	0	16.0	18	69	14	8	1	1	0	1	4	1	13	0	0
Guerrero, Thomas, Ver.	0	0	.000	4.91	2	0	0	0	1	0	3.2	4	17	2	2	0	0	0	0	2	0	3	1	0
Halamicek, Kevin, Uti.	4	0	1.000	3.52	7	0	0	0	2	0	15.1	12	72	12	6	2	1	0	0	10	0	12	3	0
Hall, Chris, N.J.*	0	0	.000	3.68	18	0	0	0	7	0	22.0	26	103	11	9	1	0	1	4	11	0	13	0	0
Hall, Shane, Low.	0	3	.000	4.67	14	0	0	0	8	2	27.0	36	130	19	14	1	2	1	5	9	2	21	2	1
Hamilton, Ryan, Pit.	1	0	1.000	4.80	9	1	0	0	1	0	15.0	15	76	13	8	0	0	6	14	0	9	8	0
Haren, Danny, N.J.	3	3	.500	3.10	12	8	0	0	1	1	52.1	47	210	22	18	6	0	0	5	8	0	57	1	0
Harper, Jesse, Aub.	3	4	.429	4.79	14	14	0	0	0	0	67.2	79	304	40	36	3	1	2	8	20	0	58	0	0
Hashimoto, Kei, Ver.	0	1	.000	6.46	10	0	0	0	1	0	15.1	17	77	15	11	1	0	2	9	1	10	4	0
Hawk, David, Wil.*	0	0	.000	4.50	2	0	0	0	1	0	4.0	2	15	2	2	0	1	0	2	0	4	1	0
Hecker, Steven, Aub.	1	5	.167	3.06	17	1	0	0	12	0	35.1	34	160	18	12	1	3	1	3	19	0	37	4	0
Henkel, Robert, Uti.*	0	0	.000	4.32	3	0	0	0	1	0	8.1	7	39	4	4	0	0	0	6	0	11	2	0
Henn, Sean, S.I.*	3	1	.750	3.00	9	8	0	0	1	1	42.0	26	163	15	14	3	0	1	1	15	0	49	4	0
Herauf, Jeremy, One.	0	1	.000	2.31	5	0	0	0	1	0	11.2	10	49	5	3	0	1	0	1	3	0	13	3	0
Herbison, Brett, Bkn.	0	2	.000	6.75	5	0	0	0	0	0	12.0	15	59	11	9	0	0	1	6	0	9	1	0
Hernandez, Orlando, S.I.	1	0	1.000	0.00	1	1	0	0	0	0	6.0	2	21	0	0	0	0	0	1	0	11	0	0
Hill, Shawn, Ver.	2	2	.500	2.27	7	7	0	0	0	0	35.2	22	144	12	9	0	1	0	7	8	0	23	2	0
Hopper, Kevin, Jam.	1	0	1.000	5.00	7	0	0	0	4	0	9.0	15	41	6	5	0	0	0	1	0	8	0	0
Howell, Jason, Low.*	4	2	.667	5.64	20	0	0	0	6	2	52.2	55	227	38	33	6	1	1	0	16	1	38	3	0
Howell, Michael, One.	5	0	1.000	1.82	6	6	0	0	0	0	34.2	27	141	12	7	0	2	3	3	6	0	26	3	1

Pitcher, Team	W	L	Pct.	ERA	G	GS	CG	ShO	GF	Sv.	IP	H	TBF	R	ER	HR	SH	SF	HB	BB	IBB	SO	WP	Bk.
Huang, Jun-chung, Low.	5	2	.714	2.25	10	8	0	0	0	0	48.0	41	189	16	12	2	1	1	0	12	0	55	2	0
Hutchison, Ryan, Bat.	3	1	.750	0.55	26	0	0	0	23	9	33.0	21	132	3	2	0	3	0	3	10	5	31	1	0
Johnson, Jeremy, One.	7	1	.875	3.42	12	12	1	1	0	0	76.1	76	311	39	29	3	4	2	5	13	0	48	3	1
Johnson, Kelly, N.J.	0	0	.000	2.35	13	0	0	0	4	0	15.1	15	66	8	4	1	0	0	0	6	0	17	4	0
Julianel, Ben, N.J.*	6	6	.500	3.48	15	15	0	0	0	0	85.1	88	359	38	33	1	1	2	4	26	0	86	7	0
Kennedy, Jodie, Low.*	0	1	.000	3.06	9	0	0	0	7	1	17.2	17	74	6	6	1	1	0	0	6	0	6	0	0
Khoury, Josh, Uti.	2	4	.333	4.78	29	0	0	0	17	1	37.2	34	175	28	20	0	2	2	4	26	4	33	5	0
Kim, Il, Bat.	6	4	.600	3.08	13	13	2	2	0	0	76.0	72	306	28	26	5	2	1	1	9	0	48	3	2
Kinney, Josh, N.J.	2	0	1.000	0.00	3	0	0	0	0	0	5.2	2	18	0	0	0	0	0	0	0	0	5	0	0
Kleine, Victor, M.V.*	1	8	.111	5.25	14	14	0	0	0	0	70.1	88	320	42	41	5	1	3	5	25	1	50	7	0
Kobow, Mike, One.	1	0	1.000	6.55	7	0	0	0	2	0	11.0	16	49	8	8	3	1	0	0	1	0	13	0	0
Koenig, Ross, One.	4	2	.667	3.67	16	8	0	0	1	0	54.0	43	244	31	22	3	4	2	5	30	1	58	11	1
Kupper, Dustin, Uti.	0	1	.000	5.27	8	3	0	0	1	0	13.2	10	67	13	8	0	0	0	4	7	0	14	6	0
Landaeta, Argenis, S.I.	0	1	.000	6.00	1	1	0	0	0	0	6.0	8	27	4	4	0	0	0	1	2	0	6	2	0
Lane, Brian, Low.	2	1	.667	5.33	6	6	0	0	0	0	27.0	29	125	19	16	2	0	1	1	12	0	22	5	1
Lantz, Doug, M.V.	4	6	.400	3.44	11	11	0	0	0	0	55.0	65	235	28	21	2	2	1	6	11	1	33	2	0
Laplante, Reggie, S.I.	0	1	.000	5.26	19	0	0	0	8	0	25.2	28	128	15	15	0	1	0	5	17	0	32	4	1
Larrison, Preston, One.	1	3	.250	2.47	10	8	0	0	1	0	47.1	37	205	22	13	1	0	4	2	21	0	50	4	1
Lee, Seung, Bat.	0	3	.000	7.65	4	4	0	0	0	0	20.0	31	98	24	17	3	0	1	2	4	0	14	1	0
Leu, Trevor, One.*	3	0	1.000	1.02	8	0	0	0	2	0	17.2	13	73	5	2	0	1	1	3	7	1	18	3	0
Lewis, Craig, Ver.	1	1	.500	1.80	6	0	0	0	2	0	15.0	17	61	5	3	0	0	0	1	0	0	5	1	0
Lewis, Jeremy, One.*	2	5	.286	7.95	15	7	1	0	2	1	48.2	83	253	56	43	8	2	4	6	19	1	29	5	0
Lillash, Keith, M.V.	0	0	.000	0.00	1	0	0	0	1	0	0.1	0	1	0	0	0	0	0	0	0	0	0	0	0
Lima, Juan, Ver.	2	6	.250	4.68	12	9	0	0	1	0	50.0	55	217	34	26	4	1	1	4	17	0	34	2	2
Lissir, Alexander, Wil.	0	0	.000	1.80	2	0	0	0	0	0	5.0	4	19	1	1	0	0	0	0	2	0	6	0	0
Lockwood, Brian, H.V.	4	5	.444	3.24	12	10	0	0	1	0	58.1	50	237	28	21	5	1	3	2	20	0	48	5	0
Mackintosh, Jason, M.V.*	1	1	.500	7.43	6	1	0	0	4	0	13.1	20	64	13	11	0	1	1	0	2	1	14	4	0
Manning, Charlie, S.I.*	8	4	.667	3.49	14	14	0	0	0	0	80.0	73	326	33	31	4	0	2	5	21	0	87	5	0
Marceau, Pierre-Luc, Ver.*	1	7	.125	5.59	15	15	0	0	0	0	74.0	86	328	54	46	8	1	3	6	30	0	64	13	2
Marrero, Darwin, Ver.	1	0	1.000	3.00	1	1	0	0	0	0	6.0	7	27	4	2	0	0	0	0	0	0	5	0	0
Martin, Kevin, M.V.	0	2	.000	5.35	19	1	0	0	9	1	38.2	39	179	27	23	4	1	3	3	18	2	25	3	0
Martin, Tom, Bkn.*	0	0	.000	0.00	1	1	0	0	0	0	1.0	2	4	0	0	0	0	0	0	0	0	0	0	0
Martinez, Paul, M.V.*	0	0	.000	4.50	2	0	0	0	0	0	4.0	5	20	2	2	0	0	0	0	4	0	6	1	0
Mata, Gustavo, Ver.	0	3	.000	6.86	4	4	0	0	0	0	19.2	22	86	16	15	2	0	0	0	5	0	14	1	0
Mattison, Corey, N.J.	5	7	.417	3.86	15	15	0	0	0	0	79.1	70	331	44	34	8	4	0	2	26	0	59	5	0
Mattox, David, Bkn.	1	0	1.000	0.90	2	2	0	0	0	0	10.0	5	38	2	1	0	0	1	0	3	0	12	0	0
Maust, David, Ver.*	4	2	.667	0.72	18	3	1	0	7	1	40.2	30	188	10	4	0	2	3	4	6	0	45	1	0
Mayfield, James, Bat.	5	5	.500	4.24	15	14	0	0	0	0	85.0	88	367	47	40	6	4	5	7	27	0	42	5	0
McCrotty, Wes, Uti.*	1	7	.125	4.12	17	9	0	0	3	0	63.1	50	266	34	29	3	2	1	2	24	0	39	3	0
McDowell, Kevin, One.*	2	4	.333	2.74	14	7	0	0	1	0	46.0	40	204	25	14	3	1	3	4	27	0	35	4	1
McGinley, Blake, Bkn.*	5	0	1.000	1.94	18	0	0	0	14	4	46.1	30	179	12	10	3	0	1	3	11	0	59	3	1
McGowan, Dustin, Aub.	3	6	.333	3.76	15	14	0	0	0	0	67.0	57	300	33	28	1	1	2	4	49	0	80	16	0
Meldahl, Todd, Bat.*	0	0	.000	2.25	2	0	0	0	0	0	4.0	3	15	1	1	0	0	0	0	1	0	3	0	0
Mendoza, Marcos, M.V.*	4	3	.571	3.51	11	11	0	0	0	0	48.2	40	205	23	19	1	0	1	3	28	0	39	6	0
Merrigan, Josh, N.J.*	4	2	.667	2.14	29	0	0	0	9	0	33.2	33	136	13	8	2	2	1	0	8	2	30	4	0
Meyer, Mike, N.J.	1	2	.333	4.50	10	0	0	0	9	5	12.0	16	55	8	6	2	0	0	0	4	1	12	0	0
Mikels, Jason, Jam.	1	1	.500	3.48	7	3	0	0	1	0	20.2	18	82	8	8	1	0	1	0	5	0	13	0	0
Miller, Jeff, Wil.	0	0	.000	1.13	21	0	0	0	19	15	24.0	17	93	3	3	1	1	0	1	5	0	28	0	0
Miller, Josh, Bat.	2	1	.667	2.59	17	0	0	0	4	0	31.1	36	137	11	9	2	1	2	3	4	2	21	0	0
Miller, Matt, Jam.*	2	4	.333	3.15	28	0	0	0	10	1	40.0	40	173	14	14	0	2	1	3	12	2	36	2	0
Milner, Robert, Ver.	0	1	.000	5.40	19	0	0	0	8	0	33.1	42	157	23	20	2	1	2	3	14	0	37	1	0
Miner, Zach, Jam.	3	4	.429	1.89	15	15	0	0	0	0	90.2	76	358	26	19	6	2	0	4	16	0	68	4	1
Mitchell, Tom, Ver.	2	7	.222	6.93	14	14	0	0	0	0	61.0	84	303	55	47	3	2	6	6	39	0	33	8	1
Miyamoto, Eiji, Ver.	0	0	.000	0.00	1	0	0	0	0	0	1.0	0	3	0	0	0	0	0	0	0	0	1	0	0
Moates, Jason, One.	0	0	.000	0.00	1	0	0	0	0	0	2.0	1	7	0	0	0	0	0	0	0	0	4	0	0
Mora, Ramon, Aub.	2	2	.500	1.98	16	1	0	0	5	0	59.0	40	235	19	13	4	1	1	3	19	0	61	5	0
Moran, Nick, M.V.	5	2	.714	3.40	15	15	0	0	0	0	79.1	82	340	36	30	6	1	5	6	13	0	66	4	0
Mowday, Chris, Aub.	4	3	.571	3.89	17	2	0	0	4	0	37.0	28	156	17	16	2	2	0	5	21	1	50	5	1
Nall, Mike, Bat.	1	1	.500	8.67	16	0	0	0	7	0	27.0	34	132	27	26	1	1	0	0	20	1	26	11	0
Novoa, Roberto, Wil.	5	5	.500	3.39	14	13	1	0	1	0	79.2	76	331	40	30	4	5	1	7	20	0	55	4	1
Nunez, Mike, S.I.	0	0	.000	1.50	4	0	0	0	1	0	6.0	6	26	2	1	1	0	0	0	3	0	5	0	0
Ogle, Rylie, Bkn.*	0	1	.000	1.26	6	0	0	0	4	0	14.1	15	61	3	2	0	1	1	0	5	1	14	0	0
Olson, Ryan, Bkn.*	0	1	.000	2.16	7	1	0	0	4	2	25.0	15	99	6	6	0	1	0	0	9	0	22	3	0
Oquendo, Ian, Wil.	7	0	1.000	1.39	10	9	1	0	0	0	64.2	55	255	16	10	2	3	2	1	10	0	56	2	0
Ortiz, Javier, S.I.	1	1	.500	1.98	3	3	0	0	0	0	13.2	11	55	4	3	1	0	0	0	4	0	12	1	0
Ostlund, Ian, One.*	2	5	.286	3.15	14	10	0	0	2	0	65.2	63	276	29	23	1	1	4	0	20	1	44	0	0
Ough, Wayne, Bkn.	0	1	.000	6.48	7	3	0	0	0	0	16.2	11	80	12	12	1	1	0	1	17	1	19	2	0
Parrott, Rhett, N.J.	1	3	.250	4.93	11	11	0	0	0	0	45.2	45	202	27	25	3	1	0	1	28	0	58	4	0
Parrott, Tom, Jam.	0	0	.000	0.00	1	0	0	0	1	0	1.0	0	3	0	0	0	0	0	0	0	0	0	0	0
Patten, Lanny, Aub.	0	1	.000	27.00	3	0	0	0	1	0	2.2	7	21	9	8	1	0	0	0	5	0	2	3	0
Peeples, Jim, S.I.*	1	0	1.000	9.20	11	0	0	0	5	0	14.2	18	81	15	15	1	1	1	1	19	0	14	3	0
Peeples, Ross, Bkn.*	9	3	.750	1.34	16	15	1	1	0	0	80.1	63	330	19	12	1	2	3	1	29	0	67	4	0
Peguero, Radhame, H.V.	2	0	1.000	4.76	17	1	0	0	6	0	39.2	30	190	29	21	3	0	1	6	40	0	22	5	0
Pennington, Todd, M.V.	0	2	.000	3.52	13	0	0	0	1	0	30.2	27	135	12	12	0	1	2	1	18	1	32	3	0
Perkins, Vince, Aub.	1	4	.200	3.27	14	14	0	0	0	0	52.1	41	223	23	19	1	0	0	0	37	0	67	4	0
Perry, Andrew, Pit.	1	6	.143	5.79	23	1	0	0	7	0	42.0	50	205	37	27	2	3	3	0	23	1	39	7	1
Peterson, Matt, Bkn.	2	2	.500	1.62	6	6	0	0	0	0	33.1	26	139	7	6	0	1	1	3	14	0	19	2	0
Petty, Chad, One.*	0	1	.000	2.84	1	1	0	0	0	0	6.1	6	28	5	2	0	0	2	0	2	0	0	0	0
Pope, Justin, N.J.	2	4	.333	2.60	15	15	0	0	0	0	69.1	64	286	32	20	6	0	0	5	14	0	66	0	0
Portobanco, Luz, Bkn.	5	3	.625	2.04	13	12	0	0	0	0	70.2	51	293	20	16	1	4	4	13	29	0	52	3	2
Powell, Greg, Pit.	1	1	.500	0.48	8	1	0	0	3	0	18.2	13	74	7	1	1	0	2	1	2	0	9	0	0
Prendes, Alex, Low.*	1	2	.333	1.37	15	0	0	0	13	2	19.2	13	88	7	3	2	0	3	1	15	0	20	1	0
Rawson, Anthony, N.J.*	0	0	.000	3.00	3	0	0	0	3	0	3.0	3	14	1	1	0	0	0	0	2	0	3	0	0

Pitcher, Team	W	L	Pct.	ERA	G	GS	CG	ShO	GF	Sv.	IP	H	TBF	R	ER	HR	SH	SF	HB	BB	IBB	SO	WP	Bk.
Renwick, Tyler, Aub.	1	0	1.000	4.94	13	0	0	0	7	0	31.0	35	139	18	17	4	0	2	1	10	0	24	5	0
Reynolds, Eric, S.I.*	0	0	.000	6.75	2	0	0	0	1	0	2.2	3	13	2	2	0	0	0	0	2	0	3	0	0
Reynoso, Edison, S.I.	1	0	1.000	0.00	1	1	0	0	0	0	5.0	3	21	1	0	0	0	0	0	2	0	9	1	0
Rhodes, Shane, Low.*	4	4	.500	2.89	15	14	1	0	0	0	71.2	62	302	28	23	2	2	2	6	25	0	58	2	0
Roberson, Brandon, Pit.	5	4	.556	3.72	14	14	0	0	0	0	87.0	81	354	41	36	4	3	2	2	12	0	70	2	1
Rodaway, Brian, Pit.*	7	3	.700	2.34	17	13	1	0	2	1	88.1	76	346	28	23	6	2	0	1	11	0	56	1	1
Rodriguez, Jose, Jam.	5	5	.500	3.52	12	12	1	1	0	0	64.0	55	263	27	25	4	0	2	6	20	0	30	3	0
Rodriguez, Juan, Wil.	8	2	.800	1.89	13	13	0	0	0	0	81.0	61	317	23	17	2	1	4	3	15	0	58	3	0
Rogers, Devin, M.V.	0	1	.000	5.91	3	3	0	0	0	0	10.2	10	53	8	7	1	0	1	4	10	0	7	3	0
Rogers, Jed, Low.	2	2	.500	3.83	23	0	0	0	15	4	40.0	43	184	21	17	3	1	3	0	26	1	35	1	0
Rohlicek, Russel, Pit.*	4	1	.800	2.74	12	9	0	0	2	1	42.2	32	199	28	13	0	2	3	3	37	1	33	4	0
Roman, Orlando, Bkn.	1	1	.500	5.03	9	0	0	0	3	2	19.2	14	83	13	11	1	0	0	2	8	0	18	0	0
Romero, Felix, Aub.	2	2	.500	4.85	26	0	0	0	20	12	26.0	27	116	14	14	2	1	0	2	9	0	35	0	0
Rudrude, Brett, Low.	5	3	.625	2.95	17	7	0	0	5	1	73.1	65	302	30	24	1	2	3	6	14	0	44	5	0
Russ, Chris, S.I.	1	2	.333	1.88	20	0	0	0	18	12	24.0	15	91	7	5	1	1	0	0	4	0	21	0	0
Russelburg, Aaron, N.J.	3	0	1.000	1.40	5	5	0	0	0	0	25.2	19	101	6	4	0	1	1	1	10	0	17	4	0
Ryan, Jeremy, Pit.	1	0	1.000	3.60	2	2	0	0	0	0	10.0	8	43	4	4	1	0	0	1	6	0	12	2	0
Sams, Aaron, Low.*	2	1	.667	5.91	4	0	0	0	1	0	10.2	14	49	7	7	1	0	0	6	0	0	7	1	0
Sander, Richard, Low.	1	0	1.000	2.79	4	0	0	0	2	1	9.2	9	41	3	3	2	0	0	0	3	0	20	3	0
Santos, Bernaldo, Pit.	2	2	.500	3.50	24	0	0	0	14	5	36.0	39	158	25	14	0	2	1	3	15	1	19	5	1
Schroder, Chris, Ver.	0	0	.000	1.50	11	0	0	0	7	2	12.0	8	48	2	2	1	0	0	0	5	0	18	0	0
Sclafani, Anthony, Jam.	1	2	.333	3.00	8	0	0	0	3	1	21.0	17	87	7	7	3	2	2	1	7	1	15	2	0
Scobie, Jason, Bkn.	3	0	1.000	0.89	18	0	0	0	16	7	40.1	22	149	4	4	2	1	1	2	8	0	32	0	0
Scott, Josh, Bat.*	1	2	.333	3.27	14	0	0	0	5	0	22.0	17	92	10	8	1	0	1	0	11	0	12	2	0
Searles, Jonathan, Wil.	5	4	.556	3.82	14	11	0	0	0	0	73.0	63	299	38	31	8	0	1	0	23	0	65	4	2
Sherman, Chris, Bkn.	0	0	.000	3.72	3	0	0	0	2	1	9.2	10	40	4	4	1	0	0	5	6	0	6	1	0
Shields, James, H.V.	2	1	.667	2.30	5	5	0	0	0	0	27.1	27	113	8	7	1	1	0	1	5	0	25	1	1
Sierra, Auvin, One.*	1	2	.333	2.12	18	0	0	0	12	1	29.2	30	124	10	7	0	0	1	3	8	0	31	2	0
Silva, Jose, Wil.	0	0	.000	0.00	2	2	0	0	0	0	2.0	2	8	0	0	0	0	0	0	0	0	2	0	0
Silverio, Carlos, Bat.	3	2	.600	4.54	9	7	0	0	1	0	33.2	31	149	19	17	3	0	9	12	0	25	5	0	
Sinclair, Ernnie, Pit.	5	4	.556	4.15	16	15	0	0	0	0	80.1	86	346	46	37	3	0	3	1	29	0	70	7	2
Skaggs, Jon, S.I.	0	0	.000	1.93	1	1	0	0	0	0	4.2	4	19	1	1	1	0	0	0	1	0	4	1	1
Skinner, John, Uti.	0	0	.000	3.86	4	0	0	0	3	2	4.2	5	22	3	2	0	0	0	1	0	0	6	1	0
Smith, Dan, One.	1	2	.333	4.00	20	0	0	0	6	0	36.0	27	162	24	16	0	1	2	5	22	1	27	5	2
Smith, Jared, Pit.	1	0	1.000	1.50	8	0	0	0	2	1	12.0	4	52	2	2	0	0	2	12	0	22	0	1	
Smith, Jason, S.I.	0	1	.000	4.50	1	1	0	0	0	0	6.0	8	25	4	3	0	0	1	0	0	0	6	0	0
Smith, Toebius, Jam.	4	0	1.000	3.90	14	0	0	0	3	0	27.2	27	112	13	12	1	0	0	6	1	0	24	2	0
Staveland, Toby, Jam.	3	2	.600	4.14	15	11	0	0	0	0	54.1	62	240	33	25	2	1	1	3	21	0	42	7	0
Stephenson, Eric, Aub.*	3	6	.333	4.04	15	14	0	0	0	0	78.0	80	344	45	35	7	2	1	3	44	0	62	5	1
Stevenson, Jason, Ver.*	6	3	.667	5.83	25	1	0	0	10	0	41.2	49	184	31	27	3	2	2	1	17	1	33	1	1
Stockman, Landon, One.	0	1	1.000	2.53	11	0	0	0	11	6	10.2	9	44	4	3	0	0	1	1	0	7	0	0	
Story, Aaron, Wil.*	0	0	.000	9.00	3	0	0	0	0	0	4.0	7	21	4	4	0	1	0	3	0	5	0	0	
Strelitz, Brian, S.I.	3	3	.500	3.35	24	0	0	0	7	1	37.2	37	171	23	14	3	3	3	6	14	0	21	3	0
Sturkie, Scott, M.V.	2	1	.667	6.00	18	4	0	0	4	1	39.0	53	177	27	26	4	0	3	12	0	28	2	1	
Switzer, Jon, H.V.*	2	0	1.000	0.63	5	0	0	0	2	0	14.1	9	57	3	1	0	1	2	2	0	20	2	0	
Tacker, Trevor, S.I.	0	0	.000	6.30	3	0	0	0	0	0	10.0	8	46	7	7	1	0	0	3	4	0	8	2	0
Taylor, John, Aub.	1	2	.333	4.25	12	0	0	0	5	0	29.2	32	132	16	14	0	2	1	4	9	0	23	2	0
Teekel, Josh, N.J.	1	0	1.000	1.75	15	0	0	0	6	3	36.0	23	143	7	7	1	0	0	5	15	0	31	1	1
Thomas, Stephen, Uti.	1	2	.333	3.98	24	0	0	0	12	3	40.2	48	175	23	18	3	3	2	9	0	26	1	0	
Thompson, Tyson, H.V.	0	1	.000	6.75	12	0	0	0	7	1	20.0	21	108	18	15	1	0	0	4	21	0	15	12	0
Tillery, Josh, Jam.	2	0	1.000	2.33	21	1	0	0	5	2	38.2	43	162	14	10	2	1	1	0	12	1	39	2	1
Trevino, Chris, Jam.*	1	4	.200	3.77	15	6	0	0	3	0	43.0	44	186	27	18	3	2	2	0	11	0	43	0	0
Turnbow, Mark, M.V.	1	3	.250	3.77	21	0	0	0	5	0	31.0	30	134	15	13	1	2	0	2	8	1	34	4	1
Ungs, Nick, Uti.	3	1	.750	1.62	12	11	0	0	0	0	61.0	57	236	14	11	3	1	2	0	0	0	40	1	1
Valdez, Santo, Aub.	3	3	.500	3.92	14	0	0	0	8	1	41.1	38	175	19	18	2	4	2	0	13	1	47	2	0
Valles, Rolando, Pit.*	2	2	.500	5.50	22	0	0	0	7	0	34.1	48	169	29	21	1	2	0	4	20	1	35	9	2
Van Benschoten, John, Wil. ...	2	0	1.000	3.51	9	9	0	0	0	0	25.2	23	104	11	10	0	0	1	0	10	0	19	5	0
Vandermeer, Scott, H.V.	2	5	.286	6.02	12	8	1	0	3	1	55.1	74	261	44	37	4	3	1	7	23	0	31	2	1
Vargas, Javier, One.	0	1	1.000	13.50	2	1	0	0	0	0	5.1	14	35	12	8	0	0	0	0	6	0	4	0	0
Walker, Brian, Bkn.*	1	2	.333	2.57	13	1	0	0	6	2	28.0	26	125	11	8	2	0	1	1	12	1	24	1	0
Walker, Jason, Ver.*	3	6	.333	4.96	18	8	0	0	2	0	52.2	48	236	31	29	3	1	1	5	26	0	35	3	0
Weatherby iii, Charles, Low. ...	2	3	.400	3.02	13	10	0	0	0	0	50.2	45	208	21	17	0	1	2	2	15	0	41	1	0
Wilson, Mike, Bat.	4	4	.500	2.58	14	14	1	0	0	0	80.1	89	351	37	23	6	2	0	5	23	1	51	2	0
Wodnicki, Mike, N.J.	2	3	.400	2.43	22	0	0	0	9	0	29.2	17	118	10	8	3	3	1	1	13	1	26	2	0
Wood, Bobby, S.I.	3	4	.429	4.02	12	12	2	0	0	0	69.1	69	303	33	31	3	1	1	5	8	0	59	2	0
Wood, Brandon, Pit.	6	0	1.000	2.28	29	0	0	0	23	9	51.1	44	211	13	13	2	2	2	12	0	61	3	0	
Zervas, Paul, Low.	0	3	.000	4.60	17	0	0	0	10	1	29.1	27	129	18	15	3	4	0	1	11	3	16	5	0

COMBINATION SHUTOUTS: Auburn (5)—Colson-Romero-Renwick, Stephenson-Esarey-Romero-Comolli, Harper-Hecker-Romero, Harper-Comolli, Flores-Romero. **Batavia (1)**—Kim-Davis-Nall. **Brooklyn (5)**—Herbison-Portobanco-Byard, Peeples-McGinley, Peterson-Gahan, Portobanco-McGinley, Peeples-Gahan. **Hudson Valley (2)**—Searles-Dutremble, Flinn-Crawford-Bustillos. **Jamestown (2)**—Staveland-Miller-Barry, Rodriguez-Furnald-Barry. **Lowell (2)**—Rudrude-Kennedy, Rhodes-Rogers. **Mahoning Valley (4)**—Kleine-Farman, Mendoza-Culp-Cooper, Mendoza-Colvard-Turnbow-Cooper, Lantz-Turnbow. **New Jersey (5)**—Russelburg-Correa, Burgess-Johnson-Merrigan, Russelburg-Correa, Mattison-Teekel, Mattison-Teekel. **Oneota (5)**—Koenig-Birtwell-Sierra-Stockman, Ostlund-Leu, Coenen-Koenig-Smith, Ostlund-Gonzales, Johnson-Gonzales. **Pittsfield (4)**—Roberson-Durham-Valles, Rodaway-Wood, Roberson-Smith, Rodaway-Powell. **Staten Island (4)**—Henn-Clark-Laplante-Russ, Manning-Russ, Anderson-Peeples, Anderson-Cooksey. **Utica (3)**—Fulchino-Halamicek-Kupper, Ungs-Cataulin, Fulchino-Goodwin. **Vermont (1)**—Hill-Caputo-Stevenson-Garris. **Williamsport (4)**—Rodriguez-Hawk-Biddlestone, Searles-Miller, Oquendo-Gilchrist, Rodriguez-Clark.

NO-HIT GAMES: Arnold, Staten Island defeated Vermont, 8-0, July 27.

TEAM

Team	Pct.	G	PO	A	E	TC	DP	TP	PB
Jamestown	.972	75	1953	753	79	2785	65	0	15
Staten Island	.971	76	1993	781	84	2858	64	0	12
Williamsport	.967	74	1921	791	93	2805	67	0	25
New Jersey	.967	76	2029	861	100	2990	71	0	9
Lowell	.966	76	2020	849	102	2971	56	0	16
Auburn	.966	74	2025	774	100	2899	47	0	17
Brooklyn	.962	76	2013	869	113	2995	61	0	18
Hudson Valley	.961	76	2051	887	120	3058	76	0	19
Utica	.960	74	1946	893	119	2958	68	0	15
Mahoning Valley	.959	75	1982	842	121	2945	62	0	18
Batavia	.958	76	2038	782	124	2944	64	0	14
Pittsfield	.958	75	2010	910	129	3049	69	0	25
Oneonta	.956	74	1903	778	123	2804	68	0	22
Vermont	.955	75	1952	786	129	2867	70	0	29

INDIVIDUAL

FIRST BASEMEN

NOTE: All caps denotes fielding-percentage leader based on 38 games for catchers, 51 for all other non-pitchers and 61 innings for pitchers. *Throws lefthanded.

Player, Team	Pct.	G	PO	A	E	TC	DP
Aliendo, Humberto, Wil.	1.000	1	1	0	0	1	0
Ambrosini, Dominick, Ver.*	.067	10	81	7	3	91	6
Baille, Stefan, Low.	.982	21	199	16	4	219	10
Beuerlein, Tyler, Bkn.	.971	7	60	6	2	68	5
Brown, Andrew, Jam.	.960	2	23	1	1	25	0
Brown, Kevin, Jam.	.985	49	439	28	7	474	36
Brown, Matthew, Ver	.989	21	174	12	2	188	11
Brunner, Ryan, Low.*	.995	42	383	34	2	419	29
CALIGIURI, Jay, Bkn.	.996	55	455	38	2	495	28
Checksfield, Steven, Pit.	.987	34	272	21	4	297	29
Christensen, Jeff, S.I.*	1.000	4	35	1	0	36	1
Clark, Aaron, H.V.*	1.000	1	9	0	0	9	2
Daubach, Brian, Low.	1.000	1	4	0	0	4	0
DeGroote, Casey, S.I.*	1.000	2	11	0	0	11	1
De La Cruz, Miguel, Wil.	1.000	24	169	13	0	182	22
Dempsey, Nick, Ver.	.986	8	65	8	1	74	14
Durazo, Ernie, Aub.	.985	47	364	37	6	407	29
Ellis, Ryan, Ver.	1.000	1	5	0	0	5	0
Faulkner, Todd, S.I.	1.000	9	36	1	0	37	2
Finnerty, Francis, M.V.	1.000	5	19	2	0	21	0
Franco, Esterlin, Pit.	.923	1	10	2	1	13	0
Gay, Curt, M.V.*	.973	21	169	9	5	183	14
Gomersall, Richard, One.	1.000	7	25	1	0	26	2
Gonzalez, Juan, One.	1.000	7	45	1	0	46	7
Green, Kevin, Jam.	1.000	1	10	0	0	10	2
Gutierrez, Said, Aub.	.857	2	6	0	1	7	0
Hartig, Philip, Uti.	.986	40	401	33	6	440	23
Hattig, John, Low.	1.000	4	32	1	0	33	3
Hicks, Scott, Uti.	.992	26	245	16	2	263	23
Hoover, Clint, Pit.	.996	26	237	15	1	253	16
Howard, Ryan, Bat.*	.987	44	352	23	5	380	31
Jeffcoat, Bryon, Jam.	1.000	1	5	1	0	6	1
Jimenez, Rich, Aub.	.833	1	5	0	1	6	0
Johnson, Seth, Ver.	.981	35	294	16	6	316	28
Louwsma, Chris, Uti.	.976	14	115	6	3	124	16
Lutz, David, Ver.	.000	1	0	0	0	0	0
Malpica, Martin, Aub.	.985	18	125	6	2	133	8
Merritt, Graig, H.V.	.889	1	8	0	1	9	1
Morton, Rickie, M.V.	.988	49	443	44	6	493	39
Munoz, Billy, M.V.*	1.000	7	45	5	0	50	1
Nathans, John, Low.	.956	7	41	2	2	45	2
Nelson, Nathan, Pit.	.990	11	91	9	1	101	11
Noboa, Joel, Low.	1.000	5	37	2	0	39	3
Norris, Shawn, Ver.	1.000	1	14	2	0	16	1
Obradovich, Mark, Pit.	.984	13	117	7	2	126	8
O'Brien, Kevin, H.V.*	.987	46	423	18	6	447	35
Parrott, Tom, Jam.	.984	28	221	18	4	243	17
Phelps, Jeff, Bat.	.978	21	168	14	4	186	12
Pitney, Jared, S.I.*	.933	2	14	0	1	15	1
Reece, Eric, H.V.	.979	29	262	24	6	292	31
Rifkin, Aaron, S.I.*	.988	67	606	36	8	650	47
Roman, Jesse, N.J.*	.990	49	468	24	5	497	37

Player, Team	Pct.	G	PO	A	E	TC	DP
Rueffert, Mark, One.	.980	12	94	5	2	101	10
Santor, John, N.J.	1.000	22	185	8	0	193	18
Schmitt, Billy, N.J.	.985	8	62	5	1	68	6
Shelton, Chris, Wil.	.973	9	96	11	3	110	11
Stegall, Ryan, Pit.	1.000	1	6	1	0	7	2
Stringham, Jed, One.	.978	32	244	18	6	268	19
Thissen, Greg, Ver.	1.000	1	2	0	0	2	0
Todd, Jeremy, Bkn.	1.000	17	128	6	0	134	14
Trezza, Alex, One.	.971	26	217	21	7	245	22
Walsh, Sean, Bat.	.985	18	126	8	2	136	14
Wood, Stephen, Aub.	.980	12	88	8	2	98	4
Young, Walter, Wil.	.988	48	379	25	5	409	27
Zaragoza, Joel, Bkn.	.984	9	60	1	1	62	4

SECOND BASEMEN

Player, Team	Pct.	G	PO	A	E	TC	DP
Abreu, Dave, Bkn.	.900	2	5	4	1	10	1
Aliendo, Humberto, Wil.	.000	1	0	0	0	0	0
Arias, Leandro, Bkn.	.980	27	47	98	3	148	21
Arrieche, Gabriel, Aub.	.955	25	41	66	5	112	11
Asprilla, Avelino, Wil.	1.000	2	2	2	0	4	1
Bacani, David, Bkn.	.984	23	49	73	2	124	16
Baker, Casey, S.I.	.850	6	8	9	3	20	3
Bennett, Kris, Bat.	.963	24	54	51	4	109	12
Brosseau, Richard, Aub.	.967	33	53	66	4	123	11
Cannizaro, Andy, S.I.	.983	44	69	109	3	181	28
Carroll, Wes, Bat	1.000	1	2	3	0	5	0
Castro, Bernabel, S.I.	.984	15	26	34	1	61	8
Clute, Kris, Uti.	.963	28	58	72	5	135	15
Colmenter, Jesus, M.V.	.941	6	14	18	2	34	2
Conrad, Brooks, Pit.	.956	62	121	182	14	317	39
Cruz, Alex, Wil.	.982	12	23	32	1	56	4
Cuello, Domingo, Wil.	.965	62	124	178	11	313	40
Davidson, Seth, N.J.	.959	30	53	86	6	145	22
Davis, Rajai, Wil.	1.000	2	5	6	0	11	0
De Los Santos, Rene, N.J.	.938	36	46	60	7	113	12
Ellis, Ryan, Ver.	.973	24	55	55	3	113	15
Fox, Mike, N.J.	.894	23	37	56	11	104	17
Francia, Juan, One.	.951	40	78	117	10	205	24
Gambino, Mike, Low.	.949	27	43	88	7	138	10
Garcia, Daniel, Bkn.	.952	15	25	35	3	63	6
Garcia, Kevys, Pit.	.667	2	0	2	1	3	0
Gomersall, Richard, One.	.942	19	37	60	6	103	14
Gonzalez, Edgar, H.V.	.945	11	22	30	3	55	7
Gonzalez, Juan, One.	1.000	1	1	1	0	2	0
Harrison, Vince, H.V.	.972	56	127	155	8	290	38
Heath, Demetrius, One.	.950	5	9	10	1	20	4
Helps, Jason, Uti.	1.000	3	8	8	0	16	1
Hernandez, Vladimir, Bkn.	.977	10	13	29	1	43	5
Hudnall, Joshua, Wil.	.944	3	9	8	1	18	2
Jeffcoat, Bryon, Jam.	.955	6	11	10	1	22	3
Jimenez, Rich, Aub.	.969	7	12	19	1	32	2
Kelly, Heath, Uti.	.875	6	4	10	2	16	1
Kent, Bryan, Low.	1.000	2	2	4	0	6	2
LEWIS, Richard, Jam.	.975	69	100	170	7	277	35
Lewis, Russell, Low.	.960	37	66	104	7	177	19
Lillash, Keith, M.V.	.941	23	37	59	6	102	16
Made, Maximo, M.V.	.967	46	102	136	8	246	30
Martin, Chris, S.I.	.949	20	21	35	3	59	4
Mayorson, Manuel, Aub.	.979	10	22	25	1	48	7
Medina, Rodney, Aub.	.900	2	3	6	1	10	1
Monroy, Sam, H.V.	.983	12	28	29	1	58	10
Noboa, Joel, Low.	.972	6	16	19	1	36	4
Peshke, Chad, M.V.	1.000	8	9	7	0	16	1
Peterson, Ryan, Low.	.500	2	0	1	1	2	0
Raburn, Ryan, One.	1.000	1	0	1	0	1	0
Rittenhouse, Marc, Uti.	.960	33	63	105	7	175	25
Salazar, Juan, Low.	1.000	6	14	8	0	22	1
Sandoval, Jjallil, Pit.	.907	21	28	50	8	86	4
Schnabel, Nicholas, Ver.	.963	27	52	78	5	135	10
Silvera, Andres, Bat.	.951	56	108	143	13	264	28
Thissen, Greg, Ver	.960	28	43	76	5	124	20
Tousa, Scott, One.	.920	4	10	13	2	25	3
Williams, Matt, N.J.	1.000	1	1	0	0	1	0
Woods, Michael, One.	.966	7	16	12	1	29	6
Wyant, Hunter, Uti.	.873	12	15	40	8	63	3
Zaragoza, Joel, Bkn.	.833	1	3	2	1	6	0

THIRD BASEMEN

Player, Team	Pct.	G	PO	A	E	TC	DP
Andrianoff, Jon, Pit.	.867	14	9	30	6	45	2
Arias, Leandro, Bkn.	1.000	8	5	19	0	24	2
Arrieche, Gabriel, Aub.	1.000	3	0	7	0	7	0
Bautista, Jose, Wil.	.926	59	32	68	8	108	4
Bennett, Kris, Bat.	.811	16	8	22	7	37	2
Brown, Matthew, Ver.	.813	5	7	6	3	16	0
Caligiuri, Jay, Bkn.	.862	10	6	19	4	29	4
CAMACHO, Juan, S.I.	.974	70	42	142	5	189	10
Cano, Robinson, S.I.	.500	1	1	0	1	2	0
Carroll, Wes, Bat.	.875	8	10	18	4	32	1
Conrad, Brooks, Pit.	.714	2	1	4	2	7	0
Cortez, Fernando, H.V.	.888	54	40	134	22	196	16
Cruz, Alex, Wil.	1.000	2	0	2	0	2	0
Cummings, Frank, Jam.	1.000	2	0	1	0	1	1
DeGroote, Casey, S.I.*	1.000	4	3	6	0	9	1
De La Cruz, Miguel, Wil.	.949	15	8	29	2	39	2
Edwards, Mike, M.V.	.960	11	4	20	1	25	2
Ellis, Ryan, Ver.	.818	11	8	10	4	22	3
Faulkner, Todd, S.I.	.000	1	0	0	0	0	0
Finnerty, Francis, M.V.	.792	34	26	54	21	101	3
Fox, Mike, N.J.	.667	2	1	1	1	3	1
Francia, Juan, One.	.600	1	1	2	2	5	0
Franco, Esterlin, Pit.	.854	34	15	55	12	82	4
Gomersall, Richard, One.	.913	8	7	14	2	23	3
Gonzalez, Edgar, H.V.	.921	25	19	51	6	76	3
Gonzalez, Juan, One.	.000	1	0	0	1	1	0
Hannahan, John, One.	.943	12	9	24	2	35	2
Hattig, John, Low.	1.000	1	0	5	0	5	0
Hernandez, Vladimir, Bkn.	.000	1	0	0	0	0	0
Hudnall, Joshua, Wil.	.800	2	2	2	1	5	0
Jeffcoat, Bryon, Jam.	.935	21	15	43	4	62	9
Jiannetti, Joseph, Bkn.	.896	34	33	53	10	96	6
Johnson, Seth, Ver.	.786	5	3	8	3	14	1
Kelly, Heath, Uti.	.800	1	1	3	1	5	0
Kent, Bryan, Low.	.714	5	4	6	4	14	0
Kochen, Ryan, Pit.	.875	4	6	8	2	16	0
Lewis, Russell, Low.	.933	6	5	9	1	15	1
Lillash, Keith, M.V.	.000	1	0	0	1	1	0
Louwsma, Chris, Uti.	.891	21	10	39	6	55	3
Malpica, Martin, Aub.	.957	9	7	15	1	23	0
Martin, Chris, S.I.	.917	7	2	9	1	12	0
Nathans, John, Low.	1.000	2	1	0	0	1	0
Nelson, Nathan, Pit.	.886	26	11	59	9	79	1
Norris, Shawn, Ver.	.931	53	40	95	10	145	10
Parrott, Tom, Jam.	.857	6	2	4	1	7	0
Peshke, Chad, M.V.	.928	34	23	80	8	111	10
Peterson, Ryan, Low.	.909	8	2	18	2	22	0
Phelps, Jeff, Bat.	.905	13	13	25	4	42	4
Pimentel, Hector, Jam.	.930	49	28	104	10	142	8
Pohle, Richard, Bat.	.778	9	4	10	4	18	0
Raburn, Ryan, One.	.796	42	24	66	23	113	6
Rodriguez, Edgar, Bkn.	.929	24	7	45	4	56	7
Ryan, Billy, One.	.868	11	8	25	5	38	0
Santor, John, N.J.	.837	21	13	28	8	49	4
Schmitt, Billy, N.J.	.929	23	12	53	5	70	5
Scott, Charles, M.V.	.500	1	0	1	1	2	0
Siriveaw, Nom, Aub.	.888	63	48	134	23	205	7
Stegall, Ryan, Pit.	.875	4	2	5	1	8	0
Thissen, Greg, Ver.	.857	2	1	5	1	7	0
Tucker, Michael, Uti.	.936	47	40	107	10	157	9
Walsh, Sean, Bat.	.912	36	35	69	10	114	5
Williams, Matt, N.J.	.936	34	32	70	7	109	11
Wyant, Hunter, Uti.	.815	11	4	18	5	27	4
Youkilis, Kevin, Low.	.936	59	42	134	12	188	9
Zaragoza, Joel, Bkn.	.923	13	0	12	1	13	2

SHORTSTOPS

Player, Team	Pct.	G	PO	A	E	TC	DP
Alayon, Jean, M.V.	.900	3	5	4	1	10	1
Andrianoff, Jon, Pit.	.818	9	6	12	4	22	3
Asprilla, Avelino, Wil.	.930	54	67	159	17	243	32
Bennett, Kris, Bat.	.875	6	6	8	2	16	1
Brosseau, Richard, Aub.	.962	12	23	27	2	52	7
Camacho, Juan, S.I.	.875	2	1	6	1	8	1
Cannizaro, Andy, S.I.	.927	24	26	50	6	82	7
Cano, Robinson, S.I.	1.000	1	3	1	0	4	1
Caracciolo, Tony, Ver.	.896	48	71	153	26	250	34
Colmenter, Jesus, M.V.	.903	11	27	29	6	62	5
Cruz, Alex, Wil.	.957	13	19	25	2	46	5
Cuello, Domingo, Wil.	1.000	1	3	0	0	3	0
Davidson, Seth, N.J.	.934	34	53	103	11	167	14
Delfino, Lee, Aub.	.949	12	18	38	3	59	7
De Los Santos, Rene, N.J.	.958	40	75	131	9	215	25
De Paula, Luis, H.V.	.953	70	111	210	16	337	40
Ellis, Ryan, Ver.	1.000	1	0	1	0	1	0
Gambino, Mike, Low.	.947	3	7	11	1	19	2
Garcia, Kevys, Pit.	.902	18	18	56	8	82	8
Gomersall, Richard, One.	.933	9	16	26	3	45	6
Gonzalez, Daniel, Bat.	.929	73	129	198	25	352	42
Gonzalez, Edgar, H.V.	.806	6	10	15	6	31	4
Gonzalez, Juan, One.	1.000	1	0	1	0	1	1
Helps, Jason, Uti.	.930	21	26	67	7	100	18
Hernandez, Vladimir, Bkn.	1.000	5	1	8	0	9	0
Hoover, Clint, Pit.	1.000	1	2	1	0	3	1
Hudnall, Joshua, Wil.	.909	13	14	26	4	44	1
Jeffcoat, Bryon, Jam.	1.000	4	7	8	0	15	2
Kelly, Donald, One.	.933	67	98	196	21	315	39
Kent, Bryan, Low.	.930	31	46	74	9	129	12
Labandeira, John, Ver.	1.000	1	2	2	0	4	2
Lillash, Keith, M.V.	.857	3	3	3	1	7	0
Made, Maximo, M.V.	1.000	2	1	5	0	6	0
Martin, Chris, S.I.	1.000	1	1	1	0	2	1
Mayorson, Manuel, Aub.	.960	51	86	130	9	225	21
McIntyre, Robert, Bkn.	.917	67	76	189	24	289	30
MENDEZ, Deivi, S.I.	.966	53	57	141	7	205	27
Nelson, John, N.J.	1.000	6	5	17	0	22	5
Norris, Shawn, Ver.	1.000	1	3	3	0	6	1
Pena, Tony, Jam.	.928	71	113	184	23	320	42
Peshke, Chad, M.V.	1.000	1	0	2	0	2	0
Pittman, Richard, Bkn.	.889	4	3	13	2	18	2
Porzel, Alec, Low.	.927	44	70	121	15	206	22
Rundgren, Rex, Uti.	.934	55	77	192	19	288	24
Salazar, Juan, Low.	1.000	2	0	1	0	1	0
Sorensen, Zach, M.V.	.970	8	11	21	1	33	6
Stegall, Ryan, Pit.	.954	59	105	188	14	307	47
Thissen, Greg, Ver.	.957	26	52	81	6	139	18
Uegawachi, Bryce, M.V.	.958	55	64	142	9	215	26
Wyant, Hunter, Uti.	.941	5	7	9	1	17	2
Zaragoza, Joel, Bkn.	1.000	7	6	15	0	21	3

OUTFIELDERS

Player, Team	Pct.	G	PO	A	E	TC	DP
Aliendo, Humberto, Wil.	.926	17	20	5	2	27	1
Ambrosini, Dominick, Ver.*	.976	29	38	2	1	41	0
Arrieche, Gabriel, Aub.	1.000	7	10	0	0	10	0
Bautista, Jose, Wil.	1.000	3	1	0	0	1	0
Blackburn, Franco, Uti.	.972	25	32	3	1	36	1
Brackley, Carlos, Low.	1.000	6	2	1	0	3	0
Brostrom, Jeremy, One.*	1.000	1	1	0	0	1	0
Brown, Matthew, Ver.	.941	12	16	0	1	17	0
Brunner, Ryan, Low.*	.952	20	20	0	1	21	0
Cabrera, Yoelmis, Wil.	1.000	39	58	5	0	63	1
Campos, Mario, Low.	.963	56	96	9	4	109	5
Candelario, Luis, H.V.	.975	56	110	9	3	122	2
Checksfield, Steven, Pit.	.960	19	22	2	1	25	0
Christensen, Jeff, S.I.*	.895	15	16	1	2	19	1
Ciofrone, Paul, Bat.	1.000	3	5	1	0	6	0
Clark, Aaron, H.V.*	.973	64	98	9	3	110	1
Coffey, Kris, Low.	.974	62	143	4	4	151	2
Corr, Frank, Bkn.	.961	44	68	6	3	77	1
Cortes, Jorge, Wil.*	.975	49	73	4	2	79	0
Dancy, Cliff, Bat.	.979	45	90	3	2	95	0
Davis, Morrin, Aub.	.969	64	118	5	4	127	0
Davis, Rajai, Wil.	1.000	3	3	0	0	3	0
Dean, Herman, One.	.941	7	16	0	1	17	0
De Aza, Modesto, Pit.	.955	50	81	3	4	88	0
Devarez, Noel, Bkn.	.958	49	68	1	3	72	1
DeGroote, Casey, S.I.*	.000	1	0	0	0	0	0
Dion, Nathanael, H.V.	.956	49	103	5	5	113	0
Duffy, Chris, Wil.*	.992	60	115	8	1	124	1
Ellis, Ryan, Ver.	1.000	3	5	0	0	5	0
Espino, Jose, N.J.	1.000	12	15	3	0	18	1
Evans, Mitch, S.I.	.000	1	0	0	0	0	0
Faulkner, Todd, S.I.	.917	7	9	2	1	12	0
Fitzpatrick, Reggie, Ver.*	.750	4	3	0	1	4	0
Foster, Gregg, Bat.	1.000	6	7	0	0	7	0
Frazier, Charles, Uti.	.992	67	125	5	1	131	1
Freeman, Miguel, Ver.	.942	52	94	3	6	103	0
Godwin, Tyrell, Aub.	1.000	20	35	3	0	38	1

Player, Team	Pct.	G	PO	A	E	TC	DP
Gonzalez, Edgar, H.V.	.895	9	17	0	2	19	0
Griffin, Daniel, Ver.	.940	37	56	7	4	67	1
Griffin, John-ford, S.I.*	.943	66	80	2	5	87	1
Guzman, Carlos, Jam.	1.000	3	3	0	0	3	0
Hambrick, Marcus, Jam.*	.882	24	29	1	4	34	1
Hicks, Scott, Uti.	.935	29	39	4	3	46	0
Hudnall, Joshua, Wil.	.946	22	33	2	2	37	1
Jimenez, Rich, Aub.	1.000	23	21	0	0	21	0
Jimerson, Charlton, Pit.	.903	33	60	5	7	72	1
Johnson, Patrick, Low.*	1.000	6	9	1	0	10	0
Jones, Jeff, N.J.	1.000	23	33	1	0	34	1
Jova, Maikel, Aub.	.983	65	109	6	2	117	0
Kent, Mailon, Jam.	.973	50	100	10	3	113	1
Kirby, Brian, M.V.	.978	36	41	4	1	46	1
KNOEDLER, Jason, One.	1.000	58	133	6	0	139	1
Kolodzey, Chris, One.	.979	54	84	10	2	96	1
Laidlaw, Jacob, Uti.	.978	56	88	1	2	91	0
Lawson, Forrest, Bkn.	1.000	48	59	5	0	64	1
Lentini, Fehlandt, Pit.	1.000	14	8	1	0	9	0
Likely, Cameron, Pit.	1.000	29	30	0	0	30	0
Lydon, Wayne, Bkn.	.963	17	24	2	1	27	0
Malave, Dennis, M.V.*	1.000	44	60	0	0	60	0
Malpica, Martin, Aub.	1.000	2	1	1	0	2	0
Mattle, David, One.	.974	38	36	2	1	39	0
McCarthy, Bill, Jam.	.985	73	124	6	2	132	3
Meath, Matt, Wil.	.981	32	50	2	1	53	1
Medina, Rodney, Aub.	1.000	2	2	0	0	2	0
Miller, Greg, Jam.	.990	59	97	7	1	105	0
Money, Freddie, Low.	.958	56	110	3	5	118	0
Negron, Miguel, Aub.*	.971	50	97	4	3	104	3
Nelson, John, N.J.	.972	59	101	2	3	106	1
Noboa, Joel, Low.	.966	29	52	5	2	59	0
Padilla, Juan, Ver.	.962	27	49	2	2	53	0
Pagan, Angel, Bkn.	.962	54	98	3	4	105	0
Pearl, Matt, N.J.	.923	17	11	1	1	13	0
Perry, Rod, Bat.	.982	68	155	8	3	166	3
Peshke, Chad, M.V.	.500	2	1	0	1	2	0
Quintana, Miguel, M.V.	.978	69	130	4	3	137	0
Resop, Chris, Uti.	.000	2	0	0	0	0	0
Rico, Matt, H.V.	.894	34	40	2	5	47	0
Rittenhouse, Marc, Uti.	1.000	3	10	0	0	10	0
Rivera, Erick, Bat.	.969	68	149	5	5	159	0
Robison, Jordan, N.J.	.970	65	89	8	3	100	0
Rodriguez, Michael, Pit.*	.923	39	34	2	3	39	0
Roman, Jesse, N.J.*	.950	18	18	1	1	20	0
Rombley, Danny, Ver.	.955	67	141	8	7	156	1
Santini, Travis, M.V.	.881	32	30	7	5	42	0
Santor, John, N.J.	1.000	3	3	0	0	3	0
Schmitt, Billy, N.J.	.000	1	0	0	0	0	0
Schumaker, Skip, N.J.	.971	46	63	5	2	70	2
Scott, Mike, One.*	1.000	2	1	0	0	1	0
Segar, Jeff, S.I.	.978	33	43	1	1	45	0
Self, Todd, Pit.	.979	55	86	6	2	94	1
Shinjo, Tsuyoshi, Bkn.	1.000	2	2	0	0	2	0
Soto, Jose, Uti.	.880	46	66	7	10	83	1
Stern, Adam, Jam.	1.000	21	28	0	0	28	0
Stokes, Jason, Uti.	1.000	5	11	0	0	11	0
Stringham, Jed, One.	.889	8	15	1	2	18	1
Summerville, Kaazim, S.I.	.941	22	29	3	2	34	3
Thompson, Eric, M.V.*	.929	25	33	6	3	42	2
Thompson, Kevin, S.I.	.961	67	118	4	5	127	1
Toner, John, Bkn.	.943	28	31	2	2	35	0
Truitt, Steve, Pit.	1.000	10	14	1	0	15	0
Turner, Jason, S.I.*	.972	33	66	4	2	72	0
Van Every, Jon, M.V.^	.971	38	68	0	2	70	0
Veleber, Troy, Wil.	.889	9	8	0	1	9	0
Vukovich, Vince, Bat.	.966	46	85	1	3	89	1
Wolotka, Brian, H.V.*	.884	25	35	3	5	43	0
Yount, Andy, One.	.941	61	105	7	7	119	2
Zieour, Neesan, Aub.	1.000	2	2	1	0	3	0

CATCHERS

Player, Team	Pct.	G	PO	A	E	TC	DP	PB
Alvarado, Oscar, Pit.	.968	25	157	24	6	187	0	3
Alvarez, Aaron, Uti.	.957	20	81	9	4	94	0	1
Anderson, Travis, Jam.	1.000	31	220	23	0	243	1	5
Ayala, Abraham, Pit.	.984	8	55	5	1	61	1	1
Bard, Josh, M.V.	.769	3	8	2	3	13	0	0
Barnowski, Bryan, Low.	1.000	10	66	9	0	75	0	6
Bastardo, Angel, M.V.	.975	33	236	39	7	282	3	7

Player, Team	Pct.	G	PO	A	E	TC	DP	PB
Beuerlein, Tyler, Bkn.	.978	8	80	7	2	89	0	3
Chapman, Travis, Wil.	.977	12	75	11	2	88	0	4
Dogero, Matt, N.J.	1.000	1	3	0	0	3	0	0
Ellis, Ryan, Ver.	1.000	1	2	0	0	2	0	0
Emmerick, Joshua, Ver.	.976	43	306	25	8	339	3	15
Evans, Mitch, S.I.	.979	25	132	8	3	143	2	0
Fernandez, Alejandro, S.I.	.980	29	224	17	5	246	2	6
Garland, Ross, One.	.988	32	230	20	3	253	3	9
Gonzalez, Carlos, Low.	1.000	3	11	1	0	12	0	0
Green, Kevin, Jam.	1.000	1	1	0	0	1	0	0
Guglielmelli, Brad, M.V.	.972	18	128	10	4	142	0	5
Gutierrez, Said, Aub.	.979	40	341	41	8	390	2	12
Huber, Justin, Bkn.	1.000	3	22	1	0	23	0	0
Jacobs, Mike, Bkn.	.977	14	111	15	3	129	1	6
Johnston, Ryan, Bat.	.963	11	68	9	3	80	0	0
Jones, Kendall, Pit.	.989	34	251	20	3	274	1	13
Kay, Brett, Bkn.	.981	34	268	34	6	308	4	8
Kirby, Brian, M.V.	1.000	1	5	0	0	5	0	0
Lovelady, Greg, Uti.	.993	20	116	21	1	138	0	4
Lutz, David, Ver.	.972	28	190	21	6	217	2	11
Lynam, Guy, Uti.	.974	20	99	12	3	114	0	6
Maduro, Jorge, H.V.	.987	31	211	23	3	237	2	8
Malpica, Martin, Aub.	1.000	1	2	0	0	2	0	0
Margalski, Ben, Bat.	.970	33	193	34	7	234	1	6
Martinez, Edgar, Low.	.968	38	229	46	9	284	2	5
McRoberts, Mark, Bat.	.971	7	27	7	1	35	0	3
Merritt, Graig, H.V.	.977	33	242	49	7	298	3	5
Moylan, Dan, N.J.	.987	48	380	67	6	453	3	6
Myers, Kenton, M.V.	.988	22	149	9	2	160	0	6
Myler, Jonathan, Wil	.985	23	165	27	3	195	1	4
Nathans, John, Low.	1.000	12	67	7	0	74	0	1
Nelson, Bruce, N.J.	1.000	8	43	2	0	45	0	0
Netwall, Chris, N.J.	.991	28	195	34	2	231	3	3
Obradovich, Mark, Pit.	1.000	19	111	11	0	122	0	8
Rabelo, Mike, One.	.988	42	288	30	4	322	1	13
Reece, Eric, H.V.	.903	15	99	14	2	115	3	0
Reed, Robert, Low.	1.000	4	35	1	0	36	0	0
Riera, Zack, Wil.	1.000	2	15	0	0	15	0	2
Roal, Kyle, Jam.	.996	32	229	30	1	260	2	7
Rodriguez, Ivan, Low.	.992	18	117	14	1	132	1	4
Rueffert, Mark, One.	1.000	4	16	2	0	18	0	0
Salas, Michael, Jam.	.992	13	105	16	1	122	1	3
Santos, Omir, S.I.	.970	44	270	30	7	315	3	0
Sato, G.G., Bat.	.987	31	206	20	3	229	2	5
Scott, Charles, M.V.	1.000	4	38	1	0	39	0	0
Shelton, Chris, Wil.	.989	40	318	39	4	361	1	15
Small, Chris, M.V.	1.000	2	6	2	0	8	1	0
Sosa, Francisco, Bkn.	.966	23	155	14	6	175	0	1
Summerville, Kaazim, S.I.	.000	1	0	0	0	0	0	0
Wallis, Jacob, Ver.	.953	6	37	4	2	43	0	3
WHITTAKER, Tim, Aub.	.995	42	351	45	2	398	2	5
Zapey, Winton, Uti.	.968	32	161	22	6	189	1	4

PITCHERS

Player, Team	Pct.	G	PO	A	E	TC	DP
Abrams, Grant, Jam.	.889	22	4	4	1	9	0
Aguilar, Edwin, Pit.	1.000	3	0	1	0	1	0
Aguilar, Ray, Jam.*	1.000	2	0	3	0	3	0
Aiello, Nick, H.V.*	1.000	22	2	7	0	9	1
Akens, Phil, Uti.	.750	9	0	3	1	4	2
Ally, Ben, Bat.	.900	21	2	7	1	10	1
Alvarado, Oscar, Pit.	.000	2	0	0	0	0	0
Anderson, Jason, S.I.	1.000	7	3	9	0	12	0
Anderson, Julius, H.V.	1.000	10	1	1	0	2	0
Arnold, Jason, S.I.	1.000	10	1	9	0	10	0
Arteaga, Francisco, Jam.	1.000	1	0	1	0	1	0
Artiles, Carlos, S.I.*	1.000	1	0	1	0	1	0
Asahina, Jonathan, Uti.	1.000	15	4	14	0	18	0
Barry, Kevin, Jam.	1.000	29	3	4	0	7	0
Barzilla, Philip, Pit.*	.833	16	3	12	3	18	0
Bautista, Denny, Uti.	1.000	7	2	3	0	5	0
Baxter, Allen, Uti.	1.000	3	1	3	0	4	0
Bayrer, Thomas, Pit.	.000	5	0	0	0	0	0
Beirne, Kevin, Aub.	1.000	2	0	2	0	2	0
Bell, Tom, Uti.	1.000	18	2	2	0	4	0
Benitez, Fabricio, Low.	.909	9	4	6	1	11	0
Bennett, Jamie, Bat.*	1.000	18	2	5	0	7	1
Bentz, Chad, Ver.*	1.000	8	0	4	0	4	0
Bernard, Jason, Bat.	.920	13	4	19	2	25	2
Biddlestone, Jason, Wil.	.857	16	3	3	1	7	1

CLASS A *New York-Pennsylvania League*

Player, Team	Pct.	G	PO	A	E	TC	DP	Player, Team	Pct.	G	PO	A	E	TC	DP
Birtwell, John, One.	1.000	23	4	2	0	6	0	Gonzales, Jim, One.	1.000	16	2	6	0	8	1
Blankenship, John, S.I.*	1.000	5	3	6	0	9	0	Goodrum, Kevin, S.I.*	.667	7	0	2	1	3	0
Blasdell, Jared, N.J.	.750	26	1	2	1	4	0	Goodwin, Ron, Uti.	1.000	20	3	7	0	10	0
Bobbitt, Seth, Pit.	1.000	8	1	6	0	7	1	Grant, Michael, Low.	.000	5	0	0	0	0	0
Borner, Brady, Wil.*	1.000	3	0	3	0	3	1	Greco, Sam, N.J.	1.000	21	1	6	0	7	0
Bowen, Chad, Bkn.	1.000	3	1	0	0	1	0	Guerrero, Julio, Wil.	1.000	7	2	3	0	5	0
Braswell, Bryan, Bkn.*	.667	5	1	1	1	3	0	Guerrero, Thomas, Ver.	.000	2	0	0	1	1	0
Brown, Andrew, Jam.	.929	14	8	5	1	14	1	Halamicek, Kevin, Uti.	1.000	7	0	2	0	2	0
Burgess, Richie, N.J.	1.000	16	3	13	0	16	0	Hall, Chris, N.J.*	.875	18	1	6	1	8	0
Burruezo, Joseph, Wil.	.857	14	2	4	1	7	0	Hall, Shane, Low.	1.000	14	1	3	0	4	0
Bustillos, Oscar, H.V.	1.000	26	2	8	0	10	0	Hamilton, Ryan, Pit.	.833	9	2	3	1	6	0
Byard, David, Bkn.	1.000	22	2	7	0	9	0	Haren, Danny, N.J.	1.000	12	3	6	0	9	0
Cable, Taft, Bat.	.833	14	6	4	2	12	0	Harper, Jesse, Aub.	.889	14	3	5	1	9	0
Cabrera, Yunior, Bkn.*	.000	1	0	0	0	0	0	Hashimoto, Kai, Ver.	1.000	10	0	1	0	1	0
Calvo, Jose, Pit.	.000	1	0	0	0	0	0	Hawk, David, Wil.*	1.000	2	0	4	0	4	0
Caputo, Rob, Ver.	.750	20	2	4	2	8	1	Hecker, Steven, Aub.	.900	17	2	7	1	10	1
Carlson, Steve, S.I.*	.000	3	0	0	0	0	0	Henkel, Robert, Uti.*	1.000	3	0	1	0	1	0
Carney, Jake, H.V.	1.000	8	1	0	0	1	0	Henn, Sean, S.I.*	1.000	9	2	5	0	7	1
Cataulin, Heath, Uti.	.714	25	1	4	2	7	0	Herauf, Jeremy, One.	1.000	5	1	0	0	1	0
Cave, Kevin, Uti.	1.000	14	5	1	0	6	1	Herbison, Brett, Bkn.	.750	6	2	1	1	4	0
Cetani, Bryan, Jam.*	.000	3	0	0	0	0	0	Hernandez, Orlando, S.I.	1.000	1	2	0	0	2	0
Charron, Eric, Ver.	.000	7	0	0	0	0	0	Hill, Shawn, Ver.	.714	7	2	8	4	14	0
Chisnall, Wes, Ver.	1.000	18	1	6	0	7	0	Hopper, Kevin, Jam.	1.000	7	0	1	0	1	0
Clark, Claudell, Wil.*	.889	18	1	7	1	9	0	Howell, Jason, Low.*	1.000	20	4	7	0	11	1
Clark, Ryan, S.I.*	1.000	29	1	7	0	8	0	Howell, Michael, One.	.875	6	3	4	1	8	0
Clelland, James, Ver.	1.000	18	3	3	0	6	0	Huang, Jun-chung, Low.	1.000	10	3	4	0	7	1
Clifton, Derek, Pit.	1.000	9	0	1	0	1	0	Hutchison, Ryan, Bat.	.952	26	5	15	1	21	0
Coenen, Matt, One.*	.867	10	3	10	2	15	0	Johnson, Jeremy, One.	1.000	12	6	7	0	13	1
Collazo, William, Jam.*	1.000	9	1	3	0	4	0	Johnson, Kelly, N.J.	1.000	13	2	2	0	4	0
Colson, Jason, Aub.	.000	8	0	0	1	1	0	Julianel, Ben, N.J.*	.947	15	2	16	1	19	0
Colton, Kyle, Jam.	1.000	11	2	3	0	5	0	Kennedy, Jodie, Low.*	1.000	9	2	5	0	7	0
Colvard, Ron, M.V.	1.000	17	1	4	0	5	1	Khoury, Josh, Uti.	.900	29	3	6	1	10	0
Comolli, Mark, Aub.	.833	10	0	5	1	6	0	Kim, Il, Bat.	1.000	13	2	5	0	7	0
Connolly, Jon, One.*	1.000	1	0	1	0	1	0	Kinney, Josh, N.J.	.000	3	0	0	0	0	0
Cooksey, Wes, S.I.	1.000	20	6	6	0	12	1	KLEINE, Victor, M.V.*	1.000	14	7	23	0	30	2
Cooper, Chris, M.V.*	.857	25	2	4	1	7	0	Kobow, Mike, One.	1.000	7	2	2	0	4	0
Corr, Frank, Bkn.	.000	1	0	0	0	0	0	Koenig, Ross, One.	.778	16	1	6	2	9	0
Correa, Cristobal, N.J.	.778	15	1	6	2	9	1	Kupper, Dustin, Uti.	1.000	8	1	2	0	3	0
Cox, Mike, Bkn.*	.857	13	4	8	2	14	0	Landaeta, Argenis, S.I.	1.000	1	1	3	0	4	0
Crawford, Chris, H.V.	.857	24	0	6	1	7	1	Lane, Brian, Low.	1.000	6	3	0	0	3	0
Cromer, Nathan, H.V.*	.944	15	2	15	1	18	0	Lantz, Doug, M.V.	.955	11	9	12	1	22	0
Culp, Todd, M.V.	1.000	22	1	2	0	3	0	Laplante, Reggie, S.I.	1.000	19	1	5	0	6	0
Currier, Rik, S.I.	.875	7	4	3	1	8	0	Larrison, Preston, One.	1.000	10	3	7	0	10	0
Curtin, Brian, M.V.	1.000	21	1	1	0	2	0	Lee, Seung, Bat.	1.000	4	0	1	0	1	0
D'Amato, Dan, Wil.*	1.000	20	0	2	0	2	0	Leu, Trevor, One.*	.750	8	1	2	1	4	1
David, Toby, Uti.*	1.000	20	3	6	0	9	2	Lewis, Craig, Ver.	1.000	6	4	3	0	7	0
Davis, Tim, Bat.*	.833	16	2	3	1	6	1	Lewis, Jeremy, One.*	1.000	15	8	2	0	10	1
Delossantos, Carlos, Wil.	.636	14	1	6	4	11	2	Lillash, Keith, M.V.	.000	1	0	0	0	0	0
Dinardo, Lenny, Bkn.*	1.000	9	2	10	0	12	0	Lima, Juan, Ver.	.933	12	4	10	1	15	0
Dischiavo, John, H.V.	.909	15	2	8	1	11	0	Lissir, Alexander, Wil.	.000	2	0	0	0	0	0
Dorman, Rich, H.V.	.875	17	1	6	1	8	1	Lockwood, Brian, H.V.	.889	12	2	14	2	18	1
Dumatrait, Phillip, Low.*	1.000	2	1	2	0	3	0	Mackintosh, Jason, M.V.*	1.000	6	1	4	0	5	0
Durham, Chad, Pit.	1.000	8	1	2	0	3	0	Manning, Charlie, S.I.*	.917	14	0	22	2	24	1
Dutremble, Jeff, Wil.*	.714	17	0	5	2	7	0	Marceau, Pierre-Luc, Ver.*	.962	15	6	19	1	26	1
Eckert, Harold, Bkn.	.857	13	9	9	3	21	1	Marrero, Darwin, Ver.	1.000	1	1	1	0	2	0
Ellis, Ryan, Ver.	.000	1	0	0	0	0	0	Martin, Kevin, M.V.	.909	19	4	6	1	11	0
Esarey, Brad, Aub.*	.500	17	1	2	3	6	1	Martin, Tom, Bkn.*	1.000	1	0	0	0	0	0
Farman, Brian, M.V.	.800	10	0	4	1	5	1	Martinez, Paul, M.V.*	.000	2	0	0	0	0	0
Farmer, Tom, One.	1.000	4	2	3	0	5	0	Mata, Gustavo, Ver.	1.000	4	2	3	0	5	0
Fernley, Nathan, M.V.	.750	13	0	3	1	4	1	Mattison, Corey, N.J.	.857	15	6	6	2	14	0
Field, Luke, M.V.	.828	14	6	18	5	29	0	Mattox, David, Bkn.	.667	2	2	0	1	3	0
Flinn, Chris, H.V.	1.000	15	12	12	0	24	0	Maust, David, Ver.*	.933	18	5	9	1	15	1
Flores, Neomar, Aub.	1.000	12	2	4	0	6	0	Mayfield, James, Bat.	.941	15	3	13	1	17	0
Fortin, Michael, Wil.	1.000	4	1	1	0	2	0	McCrotty, Wes, Uti.*	.917	17	4	7	1	12	1
Fortunato, Bartolome, H.V.	.900	16	4	5	1	10	0	McDowell, Kevin, One.*	1.000	14	1	9	0	10	0
Friedberg, Drew, Wil.*	.000	4	0	0	0	0	0	McGinley, Blake, Bkn.*	1.000	18	1	2	0	3	0
Friske, Parker, Low.*	.941	19	6	10	1	17	0	McGowan, Dustin, Aub.	.882	15	8	7	2	17	1
Fulchino, Jeff, Uti.	.938	14	3	12	1	16	0	Meldahl, Todd, Bat.*	1.000	2	1	0	0	1	0
Furnald, Donnie, Jam.	1.000	11	3	6	0	9	0	Mendoza, Marcos, M.V.*	.923	11	4	8	1	13	1
Gahan, Matt, Bkn.	1.000	10	2	4	0	6	0	Merrigan, Josh, N.J.*	1.000	29	0	3	0	3	0
Garces, Rich, Low.	.000	2	0	0	0	0	0	Meyer, Mike, N.J.	1.000	10	0	2	0	2	0
Garcia, Anderson, S.I.	.000	1	0	0	0	0	0	Mikels, Jason, Jam.	1.000	7	1	2	0	3	0
Garris, Antonio, Ver.	1.000	15	1	1	0	2	0	Miller, Jeff, Wil.	1.000	21	3	3	0	6	0
Generelli, Daniel, Low.	.923	16	5	7	1	13	0	Miller, Josh, Bat.	.818	17	4	5	2	11	0
George, Todd, Ver.	.000	5	0	0	0	0	0	Miller, Matt, Jam.*	1.000	28	1	5	0	6	0
Gerk, Jordan, One.*	.833	4	1	4	1	6	0	Milner, Robert, Ver.	1.000	19	0	3	0	3	0
Gilchrist, Ronald, Wil.*	1.000	16	0	3	0	3	0	Miner, Zach, Jam.	.938	15	4	11	1	16	0
Gill, Ryan, S.I.	.889	19	3	5	1	9	3	Mitchell, Tom, Ver.	.867	14	5	8	2	15	0
Glaser, Nick, Bat.	.875	24	2	5	1	8	0	Miyamoto, Eiji, Ver.	.000	1	0	0	0	0	0
Gomez, Mariano, M.V.*	.000	1	0	0	0	0	0	Moates, Jason, One.	.000	1	0	0	0	0	0
Gomez, Ricardo, S.I.	1.000	8	0	3	0	3	0	Mora, Ramon, Aub.	.917	16	3	8	1	12	0

Player, Team	Pct.	G	PO	A	E	TC	DP	Player, Team	Pct.	G	PO	A	E	TC	DP
Moran, Nick, M.V.	.900	15	5	13	2	20	0	Scobie, Jason, Bkn.	.929	18	4	9	1	14	0
Mowday, Chris, Aub.	.800	17	0	4	1	5	0	Scott, Josh, Bat.*	1.000	14	2	5	0	7	0
Nall, Mike, Bat.	1.000	16	0	1	0	1	0	Searles, Jonathan, Wil.	.824	14	5	9	3	17	1
Novoa, Roberto, Wil.	1.000	14	3	19	0	22	0	Sherman, Chris, Bkn.	1.000	3	0	2	0	2	0
Nunez, Mike, S.I.	.000	4	0	0	0	0	0	Shields, James, H.V.	1.000	5	1	1	0	2	0
Ogle, Rylie, Bkn.*	1.000	6	0	5	0	5	1	Sierra, Auvin, One.*	.800	18	0	4	1	5	0
Olson, Ryan, Bkn.*	.875	7	2	5	1	8	0	Silva, Jose, Wil.	1.000	2	2	0	0	2	0
Oquendo, Ian, Wil.	.889	10	2	14	2	18	1	Silverio, Carlos, Bat.	1.000	9	0	7	0	7	0
Ortiz, Javier, S.I.	1.000	3	1	3	0	4	0	Sinclair, Ernnie, Pit.	.933	16	7	7	1	15	0
Ostlund, Ian, One.*	1.000	14	1	7	0	8	0	Skaggs, Jon, S.I.	.000	1	0	0	0	0	0
Ough, Wayne, Bkn.	.750	7	1	2	1	4	0	Skinner, John, Uti.	1.000	4	1	0	0	1	0
Parrott, Rhett, N.J.	.750	11	4	2	2	8	0	Smith, Dan, One.	.800	20	0	4	1	5	0
Parrott, Tom, Jam.	.000	1	0	0	0	0	0	Smith, Jared, Pit.	1.000	8	0	1	0	1	1
Patten, Lanny, Aub.	.000	3	0	0	0	0	0	Smith, Jason, S.I.	1.000	1	0	1	0	1	0
Peeples, Jim, S.I.*	1.000	11	0	1	0	1	0	Smith, Toebius, Jam.	.500	14	1	0	1	2	0
Peeples, Ross, Bkn.*	.829	16	6	23	6	35	1	Staveland, Toby, Jam.	.909	15	2	8	1	11	1
Peguero, Radhame, H.V.	1.000	17	1	9	0	10	0	Stephenson, Eric, Aub.*	.920	15	6	17	2	25	1
Pennington, Todd, M.V.	1.000	13	1	4	0	5	0	Stevenson, Jason, Ver.*	.889	25	1	7	1	9	0
Perkins, Vince, Aub.	.900	14	3	6	1	10	0	Stockman, Landon, One.	1.000	11	0	1	0	1	0
Perry, Andrew, Pit.	.900	23	2	7	1	10	0	Story, Aaron, Wil.*	.750	3	0	3	1	4	0
Peterson, Matt, Bkn.	.000	6	0	0	2	2	0	Strelitz, Brian, S.I.	.867	24	2	11	2	15	0
Petty, Chad, One.*	1.000	1	0	2	0	2	0	Sturkie, Scott, M.V.	1.000	18	3	8	0	11	0
Pope, Justin, N.J.	1.000	15	2	12	0	14	0	Switzer, Jon, H.V.*	1.000	5	0	1	0	1	0
Portobanco, Luz, Bkn.	1.000	13	2	19	0	21	0	Tacker, Trevor, S.I.	1.000	3	1	3	0	4	0
Powell, Greg, Pit.	.750	8	1	2	1	4	1	Taylor, John, Aub.	.818	12	3	6	2	11	0
Prendes, Alex, Low.*	1.000	15	3	2	0	5	1	Teekel, Josh, N.J.	.875	15	1	6	1	8	1
Rawson, Anthony, N.J.*	.000	3	0	0	0	0	0	Thomas, Stephen, Uti.	1.000	24	5	5	0	10	1
Renwick, Tyler, Aub.	.600	13	2	1	2	5	0	Thompson, Tyson, H.V.	.571	12	1	3	3	7	0
Reynolds, Eric, S.I.*	.000	2	0	0	0	0	0	Tillery, Josh, Jam.	.833	21	0	5	1	6	0
Reynoso, Edison, S.I.	1.000	1	0	2	0	2	0	Trevino, Chris, Jam.*	.923	15	1	11	1	13	0
Rhodes, Shane, Low.*	1.000	15	3	9	0	12	0	Turnbow, Mark, M.V.	1.000	21	2	2	0	4	0
Roberson, Brandon, Pit.	.962	14	6	19	1	26	2	Ungs, Nick, Uti.	1.000	12	4	8	0	12	0
Rodaway, Brian, Pit.*	.970	17	6	26	1	33	0	Valdez, Santo, Aub.	.875	14	1	6	1	8	0
Rodriguez, Jose, Jam.	.950	12	8	11	1	20	0	Valles, Rolando, Pit.*	1.000	22	4	6	0	10	1
Rodriguez, Juan, Wil.	.800	13	8	12	5	25	1	Van Benschoten, John, Wil.	1.000	9	1	1	0	2	0
Rogers, Devin, M.V.	1.000	3	0	1	0	1	0	Vandermeer, Scott, H.V.	1.000	12	5	11	0	16	2
Rogers, Jed, Low.	.750	23	1	2	1	4	0	Vargas, Javier, One.	1.000	2	0	3	0	3	1
Rohlicek, Russel, Pit.*	.944	12	2	15	1	18	0	Walker, Brian, Bkn.*	.818	13	3	6	2	11	0
Roman, Orlando, Bkn.	.667	9	1	1	1	3	0	Walker, Jason, Ver.*	1.000	18	6	6	0	12	0
Romero, Felix, Aub.	1.000	26	1	4	0	5	0	Weatherby Iii, Charles, Low.	1.000	13	3	7	0	10	1
Rudrude, Brett, Low.	.955	17	5	16	1	22	1	Wilson, Mike, Bat.	.833	14	3	7	2	12	0
Russ, Chris, S.I.	.813	20	4	9	3	16	0	Wodnicki, Mike, N.J.	1.000	22	4	6	0	10	0
Russelburg, Aaron, N.J.	.667	5	1	1	1	3	0	Wood, Bobby, S.I.	.923	12	0	12	1	13	0
Ryan, Jeremy, Pit.	1.000	2	0	1	0	1	0	Wood, Brandon, Pit.	.933	29	7	7	1	15	2
Sams, Aaron, Low.*	1.000	4	0	1	0	1	0	Zervas, Paul, Low.	.800	17	4	8	3	15	1
Sander, Richard, Low.	1.000	4	1	1	0	2	0								
Santos, Bernaldo, Pit.	.900	24	2	7	1	10	2								
Schroder, Chris, Ver.	.000	11	0	0	0	0	0								
Sclafani, Anthony, Jam.	.900	8	4	5	1	10	1								

The following players appeared only as designated hitter, pinch-hitter or pinch runner: A. Brown, dh; Coyne, dh; Duncan, dh; McArthur, dh; Piercy, ph; Ruiz, dh, ph.

LEAGUE CHAMPIONS

Year	Team	Pct.	Year	Team	Pct.	Year	Team	Pct.
1939—	Olean*	.631	1958—	Wellsville	.556	1976—	Elmira	727
1940—	Olean*	.625		Geneva (2nd)†	.548		Elmira	.703
1941—	Jamestown	.618	1959—	Wellsville†	.635	1977—	Oneonta▲	.671
	Bradford (2nd)†	.549	1960—	Erie	.643		Batavia	.600
1942—	Jamestown*	.672		Wellsville (2nd)†	.535	1978—	Oneonta	.729
1943—	Lockport	.591	1961—	Geneva	.616		Geneva♦	.718
	Wellsville (3rd)†	.532		Olean (4th)†	.512	1979—	Geneva	.725
1944—	Lockport	.608	1962—	Jamestown	.580		Oneonta♦	.818
	Jamestown (2nd)†	.565		Auburn (3rd)†	.521	1980—	Oneonta▲	.662
1945—	Batavia*	.677	1963—	Auburn	.585		Geneva	.649
1946—	Jamestown‡	.672		Batavia (3rd)†	.485	1981—	Oneonta▲	.658
	Batavia†	.672	1964—	Auburn§	.622		Jamestown	.649
1947—	Jamestown*	.690	1965—	Binghamton	.677	1982—	Oneonta	.566
1948—	Lockport*	.603		Binghamton	.607		Niagara Falls▲	.553
1949—	Bradford*	.635	1966—	Auburn∞	.620	1983—	Utica▲	.649
1950—	Hornell	.653		Binghamton	.646		Newark	.649
	Olean (2nd)†	.568	1967—	Auburn	.667	1984—	Newark	.622
1951—	Olean	.622	1968—	Auburn	.645		Little Falls▲	.587
	Hornell (3rd)†	.568		Oneonta (2nd)*	.558	1985—	Oneonta*	.705
1952—	Hamilton	.659	1969—	Oneonta	.662		Auburn	.603
	Jamestown (2nd)†	.643	1970—	Auburn	.623	1986—	Oneonta	.766
1953—	Jamestown*	.704	1971—	Oneonta	.662		St. Catharines♦	.632
1954—	Corning*	.621	1972—	Niagara Falls	.686	1987—	Geneva▲	.632
1955—	Hamilton*	.656	1973—	Auburn	.667		Watertown	.579
1956—	Wellsville*	.617	1974—	Oneonta	.768	1988—	Oneonta▲	.632
1957—	Wellsville	.632	1975—	Newark	.688		Jamestown	.618
	Erie (2nd)†	.598		Newark	.714	1989—	Pittsfield	.697

CLASS A New York-Pennsylvania League

Year	Team	Pct.	Year	Team	Pct.	Year	Team	Pct.
	Jamestown▲	.579	1994—	Auburn	.592		Oneonta††	.592
1990—	Oneonta■	.667		New Jersey▼	.573		Auburn††	.573
	Geneva	.662	1995—	Vermont	.645	1999—	Mahoning Valley	.566
1991—	Pittsfield	.662		Watertown▼	.630		Hudson Valley‡‡	.553
	Jamestown■	.654	1996—	Vermont▼	.649	2000—	Mahoning Valley	.632
1992—	Hamilton	.737		St. Catharines	.579		Staten Island§§	.622
	Geneva▼	.547	1997—	Batavia	.635	2001—	Brooklyn∞∞∞∞	.684
1993—	Niagara Falls▼	.603		Pittsfield▼	.568		Williamsport∞∞∞∞	.649
	Pittsfield	.533	1998—	Hudson Valley	.658			

*Won championship and four-club playoff. †Won four-club playoff. ‡Jamestown and Batavia declared co-champions; Batavia defeated Jamestown in final of four-club playoff. §Won championship and two-club playoff. ∞Won split-season playoff. ▲League divided into Eastern and Western divisions; won playoff. League divided into Wrigley and Yawkey divisions; won playoff. ■League divided into Eastern, Western and Stedler divisions; won playoff. ▼League divided into McNamara, Pinckney and Stedler divisions; won playoff. ††Named co-champions due to final series being rained out. ‡‡League divided into McNamara and Pinckney divisions; won playoff. §§League divided into McNamara and Stedler divisions; won playoff. ∞∞∞∞League divided into McNamara and Stedler divisions; Brooklyn was leading final series of four-team playoff over Williamsport, but both teams were declared co-champions when Professional Baseball declared a stoppage of play. (NOTE—Known as Pennsylvania-Ontario-New York League from 1939 through 1956.)

NORTHWEST LEAGUE

LEAGUE OFFICE

President/treasurer
Bob Richmond
Address
P.O. Box 1645
Boise, ID 83701
Phone
208-429-1511

Teams (affiliation)
Boise Hawks (Cubs)
Eugene Emeralds (Padres)
Everett AquaSox (Mariners)
Salem-Keizer Volcanoes (Giants)

Spokane Indians (Royals)
Tri-City Dust Devils (Rockies)
Vancouver Canadians (A's)
Yakima Bears (Diamondbacks)

2001 FINAL STANDINGS

NORTH DIVISION

Team	W	L	T	Pct.	GB
Boise (Cubs)	52	23	0	.693	...
Tri-City (Rockies)	39	36	0	.520	13.0
Yakima (Diamondbacks)	33	42	0	.440	19.0
Spokane (Royals)	22	54	0	.289	30.5

SOUTH DIVISION

Team	W	L	T	Pct.	GB
Salem-Keizer (Giants)	51	25	0	.671	...
Vancouver (Athletics)	37	39	0	.487	14.0
Everett (Mariners)	36	39	0	.480	14.5
Eugene (Padres)	32	44	0	.421	19.0

COMPOSITE

Team	Boi.	S.K.	T.C.	Van.	Ever.	Yak.	Eug.	Spo.	W	L	T	Pct.	GB
Boise (Cubs)	...	7	7	7	5	9	7	10	52	23	0	.693	...
Salem-Keizer (Giants)	3	...	7	9	8	8	9	7	51	25	0	.671	1.5
Tri-City (Rockies)	4	3	...	6	5	6	7	8	39	36	0	.520	13.0
Vancouver (Athletics)	3	3	4	...	10	4	5	0	37	39	0	.487	15.5
Everett (Mariners)	5	4	5	2	...	5	5	8	7	36	39	0	.480	16.0
Yakima (Diamondbacks)	3	2	6	6	4	...	5	7	33	42	0	.440	19.0
Eugene (Padres)	3	3	3	7	4	5	...	7	32	44	0	.421	20.5
Spokane (Royals)	2	3	4	2	3	5	5	...	22	54	0	.289	30.5

Major league affiliations in parentheses

PLAYOFFS: Salem-Keizer defeated Boise three games to none to win the Northwest League Championship.

REGULAR-SEASON ATTENDANCE: Boise, 99,840; Eugene, 126,592; Everett, 114,727; Salem-Keizer, 115,040; Spokane, 181,214; Tri-City, 55,613; Vancouver, 118,357; Yakima, 59,000. Total—870,683. Playoff (3 games)—6,689.

MANAGERS: Boise, Steve McFarland; Eugene, Jeff Gardner; Everett, Terry Pollreisz; Salem-Keizer, Fred Stanley; Spokane, Tom Poquette; Tri-City, Stu Cole; Vancouver, Webster Garrison; Yakima, Greg Lonigro.

ALL-STAR TEAM: 1B (tie)—Brad Bouras, Boise and Greg Dobbs, Everett; 2B (tie)—Tim Merritt, Everett and Dan Uggla, Yakima; 3B—Corey Slavik, Boise; SS—Jason Bartlett, Eugene; OF—J.J. Johnson, Boise, OF—Matt Allegra, Vancouver; OF—Syketo Anderson, Boise; C—Casey Myers, Vancouver; DH—Greg Sain, Eugene; RHP—Angel Guzman, Boise; LHP—Dontrelle Willis, Boise; RH Relief pitcher (tie)—Wes Hutchinson, Salem-Keizer and Jorge Sosa, Everett; LH Relief pitcher—Brett Price, Vancouver; Most Valuable Player—J.J. Johnson, Boise; Manager of the Year—Fred Stanley, Boise.

2001 BATTING

TEAM

Team	Avg.	G	TPA	AB	R	H	TB	2B	3B	HR	RBI	SH	SF	HP	BB	IBB	SO	SB	CS	GDP	LOB	ShO	Slg.	OBP
Boise	.291	75	2941	2637	441	768	1163	157	26	62	394	10	29	27	238	13	517	82	41	45	534	2	.441	.352
Everett	.265	75	2953	2636	376	698	1040	141	18	55	343	17	17	53	230	11	628	91	42	24	569	5	.395	.334
Salem-Keizer	.261	76	3017	2636	416	689	1026	141	17	54	372	27	25	50	279	6	483	59	21	50	582	3	.389	.340
Eugene	.252	76	2890	2540	361	641	960	116	16	57	320	8	27	45	270	4	681	80	37	38	567	5	.378	.332
Yakima	.248	75	2851	2556	327	633	899	138	10	36	287	17	19	49	210	2	631	45	30	49	530	5	.352	.315
Spokane	.244	76	2958	2608	327	637	850	94	22	25	277	35	22	40	253	13	615	82	35	42	574	7	.326	.318
Vancouver	.238	76	2872	2508	320	597	892	129	17	44	289	21	20	43	280	14	713	72	34	50	538	7	.356	.323
Tri-City	.224	75	2854	2513	322	563	833	126	30	28	279	15	21	69	236	12	669	84	34	41	515	3	.331	.306

INDIVIDUAL

TOP QUALIFIERS FOR BATTING CHAMPIONSHIP

Minimum 205 plate appearances. *Lefthanded batter. †Switch-hitter.

Player, Team	Avg.	G	TPA	AB	R	H	TB	2B	3B	HR	RBI	SH	SF	HP	BB	IBB	SO	SB	CS	GDP	Slg.	OBP
Anderson, Syketo, Boi.*	.376	70	307	290	70	109	152	13	6	6	41	0	2	3	12	2	34	24	7	1	.524	.404
Bouras, Brad, Boi.	.349	62	270	238	44	83	126	25	0	6	60	0	2	3	27	1	39	1	1	5	.529	.419
Cash, Condor, Boi.	.347	66	276	245	33	85	141	18	4	10	49	0	4	1	26	4	37	6	3	4	.576	.406
Dobbs, Greg, Ever.*	.321	65	284	249	37	80	119	17	2	6	41	1	2	2	30	3	39	5	3	2	.478	.396
Benavidez, Julian, S.K.	.319	50	215	188	36	60	101	12	1	9	39	0	2	1	24	0	54	2	1	2	.537	.395
Johnson, J.J., Boi.	.317	70	318	287	55	91	137	15	5	7	61	0	7	4	20	0	50	18	4	9	.477	.362
Figueroa, Eduardo, Ever.	.310	49	214	187	35	58	81	10	2	3	24	1	3	6	17	0	45	7	5	2	.433	.380
Gautreau, Jake, Eug.*	.309	48	208	178	28	55	92	19	0	6	36	0	4	4	22	0	47	1	1	2	.517	.389
Merritt, Timothy, Ever.	.306	51	209	196	30	60	94	13	3	5	30	1	.3	0	9	0	35	11	3	1	.480	.332
Bartlett, Jason, Eug.	.300	68	304	267	49	80	109	12	4	3	37	2	3	4	28	0	47	12	4	6	.408	.371
Nettles, Marcus, Eug.*	.300	55	251	213	37	64	67	3	0	0	10	5	1	3	27	0	54	35	17	2	.315	.385
Shanks, James, Spo.	.295	67	290	261	39	74	97	7	3	0	13	10	2	6	21	0	50	24	5	2	.347	.361
Sain, Greg, Eug.	.293	67	284	256	48	75	144	19	1	16	40	0	2	5	21	2	68	1	2	2	.563	.356

Player, Team	Avg.	G	TPA	AB	R	H	TB	2B	3B	HR	RBI	SH	SF	HP	BB	IBB	SO	SB	CS	GDP	Slg.	OBP
Meyer, Robert, S.K.	.292	70	307	274	47	80	116	19	1	5	35	1	2	5	25	0	53	0	0	11	.423	.359
Slavik, Corey, Boi.*	.286	63	268	227	43	65	112	15	1	10	31	0	2	0	39	3	47	5	3	5	.493	.388

DEPARTMENTAL LEADERS: G—Nichols, Von Schell, 75 each; AB—Von Schell, 293; R—S. Anderson, 70; H—S. Anderson, 109; TB—S. Anderson, 152; 2B—Bouras, 25; 3B—S. Anderson, 6; HR—Sain, 16; RBI—J. Johnson, 61; SH—Shanks, 10; SF—J. Johnson, 7; HP—Freeman, 13; BB—Slavik, 39; IBB—Fallon, 5; SO—Allegra, 104; SB—Nettles, 35; CS—Nettles, 17; GIDP—McMains, Meyer, 11 each; Slg.—Cash, .576; OBP—Bouras, .419.

ALL PLAYERS

*Lefthanded batter. †Switch-hitter.

Player, Team	Avg.	G	TPA	AB	R	H	TB	2B	3B	HR	RBI	SH	SF	HP	BB	IBB	SO	SB	CS	GDP	Slg.	OBP
Allegra, Matt, Van.	.220	71	310	273	36	60	113	16	2	11	39	1	1	5	30	1	104	5	6	2	.414	.307
Alleva, Joseph, Spo.*	.283	67	269	247	25	70	101	23	1	2	38	1	1	2	18	4	26	0	1	3	.409	.336
Anderson, Keith, S.K.	.206	57	180	155	18	32	53	9	0	4	21	3	1	3	18	1	34	1	0	4	.342	.299
Anderson, Syketo, Boi.*	.376	70	307	290	70	109	152	13	6	6	41	0	2	3	12	2	34	24	7	1	.524	.404
Artoaga, Joshua, Doi.	.319	49	171	157	31	50	72	13	0	3	27	1	2	1	10	0	28	3	4	2	.459	.359
Bacon, Dwaine, Boi.†	.193	57	172	150	22	29	34	5	0	0	3	2	0	3	17	0	51	8	5	1	.227	.288
Banks, Gary, Boi.*	.250	2	4	4	0	1	1	0	0	0	1	0	0	0	0	0	1	0	0	1	.250	.250
Barrera, Reinaldo, Yak.†	.207	45	152	140	12	29	33	4	0	0	5	2	0	0	10	0	22	1	2	5	.236	.260
Barrett, Rich, Yak.	.225	73	255	227	29	51	65	8	0	2	19	5	2	9	12	0	68	14	3	6	.286	.288
Bartlett, Jason, Eug.	.300	68	304	267	49	80	109	12	4	3	37	2	3	4	28	0	47	12	4	6	.408	.371
Basil, Jason, Van.	.260	50	205	177	23	46	71	8	1	5	30	0	2	3	23	2	42	1	0	6	.401	.351
Benavidez, Julian, S.K.	.319	50	215	188	36	60	101	12	1	9	39	0	2	1	24	0	54	2	1	2	.537	.393
Benick, Jon, Eug.†	.262	64	257	237	31	62	106	12	1	10	45	0	1	0	19	0	53	2	2	4	.447	.315
Bird, T.J., T.C.*	.244	52	183	164	20	40	64	10	1	4	22	1	2	3	13	1	37	0	0	4	.390	.308
Boll, Javier, Yak.	.323	17	68	62	10	20	33	7	0	2	8	1	1	0	4	0	13	2	1	2	.532	.358
Bouras, Brad, Boi.	.349	62	270	238	44	83	126	25	0	6	60	0	2	3	27	1	39	1	1	5	.529	.419
Brack, Josh, Van.	.221	42	162	136	16	30	39	7	1	0	12	0	0	1	25	1	41	2	1	4	.287	.346
Brooks, Doc, Eug.	.236	39	148	127	21	30	60	5	2	7	22	0	1	7	13	1	57	4	2	1	.472	.338
Brooks, Jeff, Yak.	.243	72	288	268	30	65	98	14	2	5	35	1	1	5	13	0	83	2	1	6	.366	.289
Brown, Trevor, Eug.	.280	31	97	75	11	21	32	5	0	2	17	0	2	5	15	1	17	0	0	6	.427	.423
Buhner, Jay, Ever.	.600	3	11	10	3	6	13	1	0	2	3	0	0	0	1	0	2	0	0	0	1.300	.636
Burkholder, David, T.C.*	.268	13	46	41	5	11	20	3	0	2	9	0	1	1	3	0	10	1	0	2	.488	.326
Cadena, Alejandro, Ever.	.100	3	10	10	0	1	2	1	0	0	1	0	0	0	0	0	4	0	0	0	.200	.100
Carter, Bryan, S.K.*	.223	67	269	238	36	53	85	12	1	6	31	2	1	6	22	1	46	13	5	4	.357	.303
Carter, Josh, Eug.	.186	23	91	86	6	16	24	3	1	1	9	0	1	1	3	0	14	2	0	0	.279	.220
Cash, Condor, Boi.	.347	66	276	245	33	85	141	18	4	10	49	0	4	1	26	4	37	6	3	4	.576	.406
Castillo, David, Eug.†	.195	36	99	82	8	16	21	0	1	1	5	0	1	2	14	0	26	4	1	1	.256	.323
Castro, Renato, Eug.	.194	9	33	31	2	6	7	1	0	0	3	0	1	0	1	0	9	0	0	0	.226	.212
Ceminaro, Michael, Boi.	.237	41	138	131	23	31	37	4	1	0	7	1	1	0	5	0	23	2	1	0	.282	.263
Chandler, Marcus, Spo.†	.244	41	130	119	15	29	37	4	2	0	10	1	2	0	8	0	29	4	2	1	.311	.287
Christy, Jeff, Van.*	.000	3	0	0	1	0	0	0	0	0	0	0	0	0	0	0	0	1	0	0	.000	.000
Cirone, Joseph, Van.	.226	37	141	133	13	30	35	5	0	0	10	0	1	0	7	1	43	3	2	6	.263	.262
Cleveland, Matt, Spo.†	.239	37	152	134	12	32	44	5	2	1	17	1	3	3	11	0	33	1	5	2	.328	.305
Cole, John, Ever.	.291	13	58	55	8	16	20	4	0	0	6	0	0	0	3	0	14	2	1	0	.364	.328
Colina, Alvin, T.C.	.213	47	182	164	12	35	60	10	0	5	17	2	0	4	12	0	50	0	2	2	.366	.283
Collins, Chris, Ever.	.083	4	13	12	0	1	1	0	0	0	0	2	0	0	1	0	8	0	0	1	.083	.154
Cotto, Luis, Spo.	.216	72	276	236	28	51	62	5	0	2	20	3	3	3	31	0	60	0	7	5	.263	.311
Dibetta, John, Eug.	.229	67	274	231	27	53	72	10	0	3	27	0	5	5	33	0	52	4	3	2	.312	.332
DiRosa, Michael, Yak.	.307	45	156	127	20	39	60	9	0	4	25	2	0	4	23	0	35	0	0	2	.472	.429
Dobbs, Greg, Ever.*	.321	65	284	249	37	80	119	17	2	6	41	1	2	2	30	3	39	5	3	2	.478	.394
Draper, John, Spo.	.261	58	258	222	34	58	83	7	0	6	31	3	1	10	22	1	37	7	2	4	.374	.353
Durand, Jose, Spo.	.130	16	51	46	4	6	10	2	1	0	0	0	0	2	3	0	19	0	0	0	.217	.216
Edge, Dwight, Yak.	.115	8	28	26	0	3	3	0	0	0	2	0	0	0	2	0	14	1	0	1	.115	.179
Ellis, Alvyn, Van.	.213	31	104	89	8	19	30	4	2	1	11	1	0	3	11	0	38	0	1	0	.337	.320
Encarnacion, Santos, Eug.	.186	33	109	102	11	19	24	3	1	0	3	1	0	1	5	0	35	4	0	4	.235	.231
Epke, Brian, Yak.	.083	5	14	12	2	1	1	0	0	0	4	0	1	0	1	0	3	0	0	0	.083	.143
Fallon, Chris, Spo.*	.253	64	236	198	28	50	64	8	0	2	26	2	4	0	32	5	57	2	0	1	.323	.350
Figueroa, Carlos, T.C.*	.156	42	145	128	10	20	21	1	0	0	11	1	2	1	13	0	23	1	3	1	.164	.236
Figueroa, Eduardo, Ever.	.310	49	214	187	35	58	81	10	2	3	24	1	3	6	17	0	45	7	5	2	.433	.380
Florence, Branden, S.K.	.274	32	142	124	20	34	45	6	1	1	15	0	2	4	12	1	8	2	0	3	.363	.352
Fox, Matt, Spo.	.274	58	245	226	25	62	75	6	2	1	29	4	3	5	6	0	39	5	2	3	.332	.304
Freeman, Ashley, T.C.	.203	66	272	236	39	48	70	13	3	1	28	1	4	13	18	0	52	6	1	2	.297	.292
Frome, Jason, T.C.*	.224	58	248	219	28	49	72	12	4	1	21	1	2	3	23	2	64	6	3	1	.329	.304
Gautreau, Jake, Eug.*	.309	48	208	178	28	55	92	19	0	6	36	0	4	4	22	0	47	1	1	2	.517	.389
Gearlds, Aaron, T.C.	.239	58	223	197	30	47	66	9	5	0	19	1	0	8	17	0	61	21	1	3	.335	.324
Gomez, Andre, Eug.	.143	6	15	14	1	2	5	0	0	1	3	0	0	1	0	0	4	1	0	0	.357	.200
Gretz, Nicholas, T.C.*	.348	29	105	92	5	32	42	6	2	0	21	0	1	1	11	4	18	0	1	3	.457	.419
Guance, Walkill, T.C.	.197	59	239	218	31	43	63	7	2	3	17	1	1	4	15	0	57	15	6	4	.289	.261
Gunny, Peter, Spo.	.182	29	84	77	7	14	18	1	0	1	7	1	1	1	4	0	26	3	1	0	.234	.229
Gutierrez, Derrick, Ever.	.259	10	31	27	5	7	10	0	0	1	3	2	0	2	0	0	10	3	0	0	.370	.310
Hairr, Kevin, Boi.*	.284	28	120	109	29	31	50	7	0	4	13	0	0	3	8	0	24	5	4	1	.459	.350
Hanna, Warren, Boi.*	.233	39	152	133	13	31	34	3	0	0	11	2	1	3	13	0	28	4	3	5	.256	.313
Hellman, Matthew, Eug.	.220	57	228	200	28	44	61	6	1	3	15	0	3	1	24	0	41	2	2	5	.305	.303
Hernandez, Orlando, Ever.	.304	32	129	115	16	35	45	5	1	1	17	0	2	2	10	0	21	3	4	2	.391	.364
Hilinski, Scott, Yak.	.250	6	15	12	1	3	5	2	0	0	5	0	0	0	3	0	4	0	0	0	.417	.400
Hoffpauir, Josh, Van.*	.312	28	108	93	18	29	32	3	0	0	5	2	1	1	11	1	7	15	4	1	.344	.387
Holm, Stephen, S.K.	.208	33	85	72	8	15	20	3	1	0	2	1	1	1	10	0	16	1	0	4	.278	.310
Holst, Micah, S.K.	.272	60	248	217	41	59	88	15	1	4	36	2	3	8	18	0	38	10	4	1	.406	.346
Huntingford, Matt, S.K.*	.227	62	248	220	35	50	74	5	5	3	37	2	2	11	13	1	37	8	3	4	.336	.301
Johnson, Dan, Van.*	.283	69	281	247	36	70	122	15	2	11	41	0	4	2	27	2	63	0	0	6	.494	.354
Johnson, J.J., Boi.	.317	70	318	287	55	91	137	15	5	7	61	0	7	4	20	0	50	18	4	0	.477	.362
Keating, Matt, S.K.*	.224	26	53	49	7	11	17	3	0	1	2	0	0	0	4	0	9	0	0	1	.347	.283

Player, Team	Avg.	G	TPA	AB	R	H	TB	2B	3B	HR	RBI	SH	SF	HP	BB	IBB	SO	SB	CS	GDP	Slg.	OBP
Lambert, Casey, T.C.	.227	55	207	172	20	39	49	5	1	1	16	0	2	5	28	1	31	3	4	3	.285	.348
Laureano, Wilfredo, Spo.	.158	6	19	19	1	3	3	0	0	0	1	0	0	0	0	0	7	0	0	1	.158	.158
Lawler, Daniel, Boi.*	.269	40	123	104	17	28	42	8	0	2	11	0	1	2	16	1	23	1	3	3	.404	.374
Lindsey, Cordell, Spo.	.095	6	22	21	2	2	5	0	0	1	4	0	0	0	1	0	4	1	0	1	.238	.136
Llamas, Juan, Spo.	.260	57	227	204	31	53	83	13	1	5	25	4	1	3	15	1	46	2	2	9	.407	.318
Loeb, Bryan, Yak.	.243	40	128	115	12	28	41	8	1	1	12	1	0	4	8	0	29	1	0	0	.357	.315
Lopez, Jose, Ever.	.256	70	315	289	42	74	95	15	0	2	20	1	2	10	13	0	44	13	6	3	.329	.309
Mace, Clark, Yak.*	.218	53	183	165	22	36	52	9	2	1	9	0	0	5	11	0	45	0	4	1	.315	.287
Macha, Erick, Yak.	.245	52	212	196	24	48	58	3	2	1	16	1	2	1	12	0	40	1	4	4	.296	.289
Madera, Sandy, Van.	.234	35	97	77	8	18	26	3	1	1	12	1	1	3	15	0	24	0	1	0	.338	.375
Maestrales, Peter, S.K.†	.258	19	71	66	6	17	27	5	1	1	11	1	0	1	3	0	19	0	0	0	.409	.300
Maldonado, Edwin, S.K.	.500	1	2	2	1	1	4	0	0	1	1	0	0	0	0	0	0	0	0	0	2.000	.500
McAuliff, James, S.K.	.242	20	79	66	10	16	21	2	0	1	4	1	0	2	10	0	18	3	1	1	.318	.359
McKnight, Lukas, Boi.*	.290	27	75	69	8	20	34	3	1	3	14	0	0	0	6	1	18	0	0	1	.493	.347
McMains, Derin, S.K.†	.271	69	299	258	40	70	104	18	2	4	40	5	3	1	32	0	26	6	1	11	.403	.350
Mejia, Andy, Boi.	.200	24	86	80	9	16	28	4	1	2	14	0	0	0	6	0	21	0	0	2	.350	.256
Menchaca, Eriberto, Ever.	.000	3	7	5	1	0	0	0	0	0	0	0	0	1	1	0	1	1	0	0	.000	.286
Merritt, Timothy, Ever.	.306	51	209	196	33	60	94	13	3	5	30	1	3	0	9	0	35	11	3	1	.480	.332
Meyer, Robert, S.K.	.292	70	307	274	47	80	116	19	1	5	35	1	2	5	25	0	53	0	0	11	.423	.359
Miranda, Miguel, S.K.†	.278	59	221	194	21	54	61	7	0	0	22	5	3	1	18	0	20	4	3	0	.314	.338
Montero, Esteban, T.C.	.194	57	186	165	23	32	56	10	4	2	16	2	2	5	12	0	63	1	1	2	.339	.266
Morency, Vernand, T.C.	.230	54	216	183	30	42	70	12	2	4	27	3	1	9	20	1	59	16	3	4	.383	.300
Morgan, Russ, Ever.	.000	2	1	0	0	0	0	0	0	0	0	0	1	0	0	0	0	0	0	0	.000	.000
Myers, Casey, Van.	.278	59	233	198	24	55	91	15	0	7	35	2	2	9	22	3	34	0	0	8	.460	.372
Navarro, Mandy, Boi.†	.229	30	110	96	10	22	33	5	0	2	11	1	2	1	10	0	17	1	1	1	.344	.303
Nettles, Marcus, Eug.*	.300	55	251	213	37	64	67	3	0	0	10	5	1	3	27	0	54	35	17	2	.315	.385
Neufeld, Andy, Van.*	.178	55	182	157	15	28	38	5	1	1	13	2	2	2	19	0	41	8	3	4	.242	.272
Nichols, Kyle, Yak.	.278	75	317	284	41	79	139	24	0	12	51	0	2	2	29	2	69	1	0	5	.489	.347
Oliveros, Luis, Ever.	.240	26	103	100	7	24	39	3	0	4	17	0	0	2	1	0	15	0	0	2	.390	.262
Olszta, Eddie, Ever.	.162	27	81	74	5	12	14	2	0	0	4	3	0	1	3	0	34	3	1	1	.189	.205
Ortega, Sixto, T.C.	.159	18	64	63	8	10	11	1	0	0	3	0	0	1	0	0	14	1	0	3	.175	.172
Peirce, Justin, Van.	.186	36	105	97	11	18	23	5	0	0	5	2	0	1	5	0	36	0	3	3	.237	.233
Pieper, William, Spo.	.142	37	122	106	8	15	21	1	1	1	8	0	0	2	14	1	43	0	1	3	.198	.254
Pinon, Alex, S.K.	.231	51	158	121	20	28	33	5	0	0	16	2	2	2	31	1	20	8	1	1	.273	.391
Pride, Joshua, T.C.	.260	42	145	127	12	33	52	10	0	3	22	0	2	1	15	0	43	1	1	2	.409	.338
Puccinelli, John, Eug.	.185	9	29	27	1	5	6	1	0	0	5	0	0	0	2	0	8	0	0	0	.222	.241
Rainey, Jason, Ever.*	.226	33	119	106	17	24	33	4	1	1	9	0	0	4	9	1	31	7	2	2	.311	.311
Reyes, Christian, Van.†	.221	59	226	195	30	43	57	12	1	0	20	3	2	0	26	1	55	3	0	1	.292	.309
Richardson, Miguel, Ever.	.276	23	82	76	8	21	33	4	1	2	11	0	0	1	5	0	25	2	0	1	.434	.329
Rivera, Rene, Ever.	.089	15	48	45	3	4	11	1	0	2	3	1	1	0	1	0	19	0	0	1	.244	.106
Roenicke, Jarett, Eug.*	.160	9	26	25	2	4	4	0	0	0	2	0	0	0	1	0	10	0	0	0	.160	.192
Romero, Nicholas, Eug.	.218	55	197	179	24	39	56	8	3	1	19	0	0	0	18	0	75	8	2	0	.313	.289
Rooke, Brian, Van.	.148	47	134	108	12	16	23	5	1	0	8	4	2	4	16	0	43	9	4	1	.213	.277
Rosario, Vicente, Ever.	.250	33	158	136	22	34	43	7	1	0	6	1	0	9	12	0	29	17	6	3	.316	.350
Rosario, Victor, Spo.*	.243	69	278	247	36	60	84	5	5	3	24	2	1	0	28	0	63	18	3	2	.340	.319
Sain, Greg, Eug.	.293	67	284	256	48	75	144	19	1	16	40	0	2	5	21	2	68	1	2	5	.563	.356
Santana, Emmanuel, Ever.* ...	.268	68	281	250	35	67	104	13	3	6	49	1	1	5	24	2	47	0	2	2	.416	.343
Santos, Sneideer, Yak.*	.173	31	88	81	11	14	26	2	2	2	10	0	0	0	7	0	32	1	1	0	.321	.239
Schmidt, J.P., Van.*	.295	32	131	122	18	36	49	9	2	0	10	0	0	0	9	1	24	7	4	0	.402	.344
Serrano, Eddie, Eug.	.294	7	20	17	2	5	9	1	0	1	1	0	0	1	2	0	5	0	0	0	.529	.400
Servais, Eric, Boi.*	.245	36	120	106	9	26	41	5	2	2	12	1	1	1	11	1	29	0	1	1	.387	.319
Shanks, James, Spo.	.295	67	290	251	39	74	87	7	3	0	13	10	2	6	21	0	50	24	5	2	.347	.361
Silver, Travis, Boi.	.167	3	8	6	1	1	4	0	0	1	2	0	0	0	2	0	0	0	0	0	.667	.167
Simpson, Bodie, Yak.	.236	56	216	195	25	46	60	11	0	1	19	0	2	3	16	0	39	4	2	4	.308	.301
Slavik, Corey, Boi.*	.286	63	268	227	43	65	112	15	1	10	31	0	2	0	39	3	47	5	3	5	.493	.388
Smiley, Jermaine, Spo.*	.225	61	212	182	22	41	50	5	2	0	17	2	0	3	25	1	56	4	4	7	.275	.329
Soto, Jorge, Van.	.206	44	178	165	16	34	69	12	1	7	21	0	0	5	8	0	84	0	0	2	.418	.264
Stocker, Myreon, Spo.†	.233	28	88	73	10	17	23	2	2	0	7	1	0	0	14	0	20	4	2	1	.315	.356
Stotts, J.T., Van.	.270	62	276	241	35	65	74	5	2	0	17	3	2	4	26	1	34	19	4	6	.307	.348
Terrero, Luis, Yak.	.317	11	43	41	7	13	17	2	1	0	0	0	0	0	2	0	8	0	3	0	.415	.349
Testa, Chris, T.C.*	.269	54	209	182	23	49	73	12	3	2	22	0	1	5	21	3	49	5	4	3	.401	.359
Thiessen, Mike, Yak.	.308	27	117	104	14	32	36	4	0	0	11	1	3	3	6	0	17	6	2	1	.346	.353
Thornton-Murray, Jandin, Boi.† .	.239	56	225	205	24	49	85	14	5	4	26	2	4	2	12	0	45	4	1	3	.415	.283
Tiesing, Tyler, Yak.	.186	30	95	86	6	16	22	6	0	0	5	0	0	2	7	0	30	0	1	1	.256	.263
Tracy, Chad, Yak.*	.278	10	40	36	2	10	11	1	0	0	5	0	0	1	3	0	5	1	0	1	.306	.350
Trzesniak, Nick, Eug.	.233	57	222	193	24	45	61	8	1	2	21	0	2	5	22	0	59	0	1	3	.316	.324
Turco, Anthony, S.K.*	.244	42	100	86	15	21	30	1	1	2	11	2	0	0	12	0	20	0	0	1	.349	.337
Uggla, Dan, Yak.	.277	72	312	278	39	77	113	21	0	5	40	1	4	9	20	0	52	8	4	9	.406	.341
Van Meetren, Jason, Ever.	.230	45	177	152	18	35	60	8	1	5	22	1	2	2	20	0	47	0	2	1	.395	.324
Ventura, Juan, T.C.	.204	47	184	162	26	33	44	5	3	0	8	2	0	5	15	0	38	7	4	2	.272	.291
Villilo, Miguel, Ever.†	.246	50	220	195	33	48	73	10	0	5	22	1	0	2	22	0	69	7	2	0	.374	.329
Von Schell, Tyler, S.K.	.273	75	326	293	50	80	132	18	2	10	45	0	3	4	26	1	63	1	2	2	.451	.337
Widger, Chris, Ever.	.077	5	19	13	2	1	1	0	0	0	0	0	0	0	6	1	1	0	0	0	.077	.368
Williams, Jon, S.K.*	.615	6	14	13	5	8	15	1	0	2	4	0	0	0	1	0	2	0	0	0	1.154	.643
Williamson, John, Ever.†	.277	53	216	188	26	52	87	16	2	5	34	1	1	4	22	2	52	2	1	0	.463	.363
Woods, Blake, Ever.	.260	43	167	146	20	38	62	7	1	5	19	1	0	2	18	0	36	8	4	0	.425	.349
Yakopich, Joseph, Yak.*	.228	45	126	101	16	23	26	3	0	0	6	2	1	1	21	0	23	2	2	1	.257	.363

GRAND SLAMS: Allegra, Denick, Cotto, Hairr, D. Johnson, Nichols, Romero, 1 each.

AWARDED FIRST BASE ON CATCHER'S INTERFERENCE: Mace 2 (Trzesniak, Durand), Nettles 2 (Durand, Oliveros); Fox (Mejia), D. Johnson (Draper).

TEAM

Team	W	L	Pct.	ERA	G	CG	ShO	Sv.	IP	H	TBF	R	ER	HR	SH	SF	HB	BB	IBB	SO	WP	Bk.
Boise	52	23	.693	3.19	75	1	8	24	667.2	626	2865	309	237	34	14	25	37	216	13	590	38	10
Vancouver	37	39	.487	3.54	76	0	4	17	670.1	602	2906	328	264	35	21	20	37	278	3	629	58	7
Tri-City	39	36	.520	3.61	75	2	8	20	676.0	638	2927	345	271	38	26	27	59	234	9	595	61	7
Salem-Keizer	51	25	.671	3.79	76	0	7	20	686.1	676	2938	338	289	55	18	23	49	223	15	660	52	11
Yakima	33	42	.440	4.10	75	0	4	22	663.1	706	2923	363	302	42	15	13	33	255	11	580	66	5
Everett	36	39	.480	4.22	75	0	2	20	668.0	625	2939	376	313	49	19	23	55	291	8	692	63	6
Eugene	32	44	.421	4.22	76	3	3	14	648.2	638	2831	373	304	42	21	29	37	240	4	593	44	9
Spokane	22	54	.289	5.12	76	1	1	10	670.1	715	3013	454	381	66	16	20	69	259	12	598	53	13

INDIVIDUAL

TOP QUALIFIERS FOR EARNED-RUN AVERAGE TITLE

Minimum 61 innings. *Lefthanded pitcher.

Pitcher, Team	W	L	Pct.	ERA	G	GS	CG	ShO	GF	Sv.	IP	H	TBF	R	ER	HR	SH	SF	HB	BB	IBB	SO	WP	Bk.
Foppert, Jesse, S.K.	8	1	.889	1.93	14	14	0	0	0	0	70.0	35	264	18	15	7	0	3	5	23	0	88	4	3
Guzman, Angel, Boi.	9	1	.900	2.23	14	14	0	0	0	0	76.2	68	318	27	19	2	2	5	0	19	0	63	2	1
Gonzalez, Christian, Van.	2	7	.222	2.67	16	16	0	0	0	0	87.2	90	368	36	26	4	1	3	5	15	1	59	5	2
Martinez, Gustavo, Ever.	5	3	.625	2.67	15	15	0	0	0	0	84.1	62	356	30	25	4	3	2	18	34	0	100	8	0
Bouknight, Kip, T.C.	3	5	.375	2.78	15	15	0	0	0	0	81.0	69	335	29	25	3	2	5	8	19	0	86	8	2
Wynegar, Adam, Boi.*	4	2	.667	2.92	14	12	0	0	1	0	71.0	77	306	34	23	7	1	3	3	19	0	63	2	0
Nicholson, Scott, T.C.*	4	3	.571	2.93	14	14	1	1	0	0	76.2	69	307	29	25	3	2	4	4	12	0	50	4	0
Willis, Dontrelle, Boi.*	8	2	.800	2.98	15	15	0	0	0	0	93.2	76	374	36	31	1	0	1	3	19	0	77	5	1
Pignatiello, Carmen, Boi.*	7	3	.700	3.00	16	12	0	0	3	1	78.0	70	337	37	26	2	4	1	6	22	0	83	6	0
Mitre, Sergio, Boi.	8	4	.667	3.07	15	15	1	1	0	0	91.0	85	371	37	31	2	0	0	3	18	1	71	3	3
Blackley, Travis, Ever.*	6	1	.857	3.32	14	14	0	0	0	0	78.2	60	319	34	29	7	2	2	1	29	0	90	3	0
Harden, James, Van.	2	4	.333	3.39	18	14	0	0	3	0	74.1	47	309	29	28	3	3	1	4	38	0	100	8	1
Germano, Justin, Eug.	6	5	.545	3.49	13	13	2	0	0	0	80.0	77	333	35	31	5	1	3	5	11	0	74	1	0
Castellanos, Jonathan, Yak.	2	3	.400	4.08	15	15	0	0	0	0	86.0	100	369	43	39	4	0	1	3	26	2	73	1	1
Pannone, Anthony, S.K.	7	1	.875	4.11	14	14	0	0	0	0	76.2	82	323	41	35	9	0	0	8	13	0	61	7	1

DEPARTMENTAL LEADERS: W—Guzman, 9; L—Anderegg, Armitage, Jones, Ch. Gonzalez, 7 each; Pct.—Guzman, .900; G—Soto, 30; GS—Ch. Gonzalez, 16; CG—Germano, 2; ShO—Nicholson, Mitre, 1 each; GF—Hutchison, 25; Sv.—Hutchison, 10; IP—Willis, 93.2; H—Castellanos, 100; TBF—Willis, 374; R—Armitage, Jones, 57 each; ER—Armitage, 49; HR—Merricks, Pannone, 9 each; SH—Merricks, 5; SF—Several players tied at 5; HB—Martinez, 18; BB—Cullen, 49; IBB—Several players tied at 4; SO—Harden, Martinez, 100 each; WP—Middleton, Valera, 10 each; BK—Vasquez, 10.

ALL PITCHERS

*Lefthanded pitcher.

Pitcher, Team	W	L	Pct.	ERA	G	GS	CG	ShO	GF	Sv.	IP	H	TBF	R	ER	HR	SH	SF	HB	BB	IBB	SO	WP	Bk.
Adinolfi, Timothy, Spo.*	2	3	.400	4.72	18	4	0	0	3	0	47.2	48	215	29	25	7	1	1	4	19	0	39	4	1
Allen, Travis, Ever.	0	0	.000	4.76	4	0	0	0	2	0	5.2	7	28	4	3	0	0	1	0	2	0	6	0	0
Almond, Casey, T.C.	0	0	.000	2.57	4	0	0	0	2	0	7.0	5	31	3	2	1	1	0	2	8	0	5	1	0
Anderegg, Jason, Eug.	3	7	.300	4.81	14	13	0	0	1	0	63.2	64	286	46	34	4	3	3	5	27	0	62	5	0
Arias, Miguel, Spo.	0	0	.000	10.57	5	0	0	0	1	0	7.2	12	49	13	9	2	0	3	3	10	1	6	1	0
Armitage, Barry, Spo.	1	7	.125	6.10	15	14	0	0	0	0	72.1	79	322	57	49	8	0	5	4	26	1	70	4	0
Ashlock, Chad, S.K.	4	3	.571	4.44	11	10	0	0	0	0	46.2	46	190	26	23	4	0	1	0	15	0	39	1	0
Barber, Scott, Yak.	2	0	1.000	2.25	2	2	0	0	0	0	12.0	11	48	3	3	1	0	0	1	3	0	11	0	0
Barnett, John, Spo.	0	3	.000	4.50	20	0	0	0	16	1	34.0	40	152	20	17	3	1	0	4	10	2	29	2	0
Bausher, Tim, Ever.	0	3	.000	8.62	11	1	0	0	3	1	15.2	25	80	15	15	2	1	0	0	8	0	18	2	1
Benick, Jon, Eug.	0	0	.000	0.00	1	0	0	0	1	0	1.0	1	4	0	0	0	0	0	0	0	0	1	0	0
Benik, Brett, Boi.	6	2	.750	3.82	20	0	0	0	10	2	33.0	34	153	30	14	3	3	2	3	9	4	29	6	1
Benjamin, Petersen, S.K.	3	1	.750	3.23	15	5	0	0	1	1	55.2	51	224	24	20	2	2	2	1	7	1	50	3	0
Bevis, P.J., Yak.	1	1	.500	0.64	12	0	0	0	11	8	14.0	9	57	1	1	0	0	0	0	7	2	22	1	0
Blackley, Travis, Ever.*	6	1	.857	3.32	14	14	0	0	0	0	78.2	60	319	34	29	7	2	2	1	29	0	90	3	0
Blanton, Jason, Boi.	0	3	.000	4.11	8	0	0	0	4	0	15.1	16	71	9	7	2	0	1	2	8	2	9	1	0
Blood, Justin, Ever.*	1	1	.500	10.03	10	0	0	0	5	0	11.2	15	57	15	13	1	0	1	0	9	0	14	2	0
Bott, Glenn, Ever.*	2	3	.400	2.30	19	0	0	0	11	4	43.0	32	189	17	11	4	1	1	1	23	0	57	8	0
Bouknight, Kip, T.C.	3	5	.375	2.78	15	15	0	0	0	0	81.0	69	335	29	25	3	2	5	8	19	0	86	8	2
Brandt, Jon, Eug.	3	2	.600	3.20	13	6	0	0	1	0	45.0	45	194	25	16	3	1	2	2	13	0	44	4	0
Bruney, Brian, Yak.	1	2	.333	5.14	14	0	0	0	11	2	21.0	19	102	14	12	2	3	2	11	0	28	7	0
Burres, Brian, S.K.*	3	1	.750	3.10	14	6	0	0	2	1	40.2	43	174	20	14	2	3	2	1	11	0	38	5	0
Carlsen, Jeff, Boi.	1	0	1.000	4.50	16	0	0	0	7	3	36.0	23	139	7	6	3	0	1	2	5	0	41	1	1
Carter, Mark, Boi.*	2	1	.667	4.62	16	0	0	0	7	1	25.1	30	122	15	13	3	0	0	1	17	1	31	3	0
Castellanos, Jonathan, Yak.	2	3	.400	4.08	15	15	0	0	0	0	86.0	100	369	43	39	4	0	1	3	26	2	73	1	1
Clark, Josh, Yak.	1	4	.200	5.80	17	7	0	0	2	0	49.2	58	223	38	32	4	0	2	6	17	0	42	5	0
Cotts, Neal, Van.*	0	1	.000	3.09	9	7	0	0	0	0	35.0	28	145	14	12	2	0	1	1	13	0	44	4	1
Cram, Josh, S.K.	5	2	.714	3.03	19	0	0	0	3	0	35.2	41	161	16	12	3	3	2	2	10	1	34	4	1
Crider, George, Van.	1	3	.250	3.27	22	0	0	0	14	3	33.0	20	145	15	12	3	2	0	3	26	0	29	5	1
Cruz, Jeffrey, T.C.	0	1	.000	8.49	12	0	0	0	3	0	11.2	21	67	15	11	3	0	0	8	0	6	4	0
Cullen, Phil, Ever.	1	4	.200	5.08	14	14	0	0	0	0	56.2	52	267	36	32	6	1	1	8	49	0	64	3	0
Dannemiller, Beau, T.C.	3	1	.750	2.15	23	1	0	0	14	6	46.0	33	189	13	11	2	1	1	2	17	0	53	5	0
DePaula, Freddy, Van.*	2	4	.333	3.52	7	7	0	0	0	0	30.2	27	141	16	12	2	1	4	0	20	0	37	1	0
Diaz, Alex, Van.	0	2	.000	2.55	10	0	0	0	3	1	17.2	20	82	6	5	1	0	1	2	5	0	12	0	0
Doble, Eric, Spo.	0	3	.000	4.46	18	0	0	0	10	3	34.1	41	160	22	17	4	4	0	2	11	2	31	4	0
Done, Juan, Ever.	0	0	.000	8.35	8	1	0	0	1	0	18.1	24	95	21	17	3	0	1	4	14	0	13	4	0
Dossett, William, Spo.	1	2	.333	5.91	12	0	0	0	3	0	21.1	34	105	20	14	1	2	0	3	7	2	13	1	0
Dulkowski, Marc, Eug.	1	1	.500	4.26	7	0	0	0	4	1	6.1	6	28	3	3	0	1	0	1	2	0	8	2	0

Pitcher, Team	W	L	Pct.	ERA	G	GS	CG	ShO	GF	Sv.	IP	H	TBF	R	ER	HR	SH	SF	HB	BB	IBB	SO	WP	Bk.
Earley, Andrew, Boi.	1	1	.500	3.56	14	3	0	0	4	0	30.1	32	148	16	12	1	1	3	7	20	1	15	1	1
Ellis, Steve, Boi.	2	1	.667	2.45	20	0	0	0	14	6	25.2	18	107	8	7	1	1	2	3	11	1	31	1	0
Eriksen, Tanner, Yak.	1	1	.500	3.45	3	3	0	0	0	0	15.2	17	67	9	6	3	0	0	0	4	0	14	2	1
Ferreras, Yorkin, Boi.*	1	0	1.000	3.16	18	0	0	0	12	6	25.2	27	114	12	9	2	1	3	0	13	2	23	1	1
Foppert, Jesse, S.K.	8	1	.889	1.93	14	14	0	0	0	0	70.0	35	264	18	15	7	0	3	5	23	0	88	4	3
Frary, Levi, T.C.	1	1	.500	5.40	22	0	0	0	14	9	21.2	27	95	17	13	0	2	0	3	5	1	11	1	1
Freeman, Eric, Spo.*	1	3	.250	4.82	21	0	0	0	7	1	37.1	40	169	23	20	3	1	1	1	18	0	24	2	0
Frias, Juan, S.K.	0	0	.000	9.00	4	0	0	0	1	0	5.0	7	25	5	5	0	0	0	1	3	0	2	3	0
Frick, Mike, Van.	7	2	.778	2.70	21	1	0	0	10	3	40.0	38	173	15	12	1	1	0	1	15	0	54	2	1
Gage, Matthew, Van.	1	1	.500	4.11	17	3	0	0	5	0	35.0	46	161	25	16	1	1	0	3	7	1	18	1	0
Gallagher, Shawn, T.C.*	0	3	.000	4.58	17	0	0	0	2	1	17.2	22	85	12	9	0	3	0	4	8	0	19	0	0
Garber, Mike, Yak.*	0	0	.000	3.38	3	0	0	0	0	0	2.2	3	11	2	1	0	0	1	0	0	0	2	1	0
Garcia, Rafael, Spo.	2	5	.286	7.13	10	10	0	0	0	0	41.2	51	198	41	33	7	0	2	5	17	0	33	4	0
Germano, Justin, Eug.	6	5	.545	3.49	13	13	0	0	0	0	80.0	77	333	35	31	5	1	3	5	11	0	74	1	0
Gilpatrick, Tyler, Van.	2	2	.500	3.83	19	1	0	0	7	1	42.1	42	179	23	18	3	1	3	3	14	0	34	1	0
Gonzalez, Carlos, Yak.	0	1	.000	3.38	13	0	0	0	5	3	24.0	19	105	12	9	1	1	0	1	15	1	21	5	0
Gonzalez, Christian, Van.	2	7	.222	2.67	16	16	0	0	0	0	87.2	90	368	36	26	4	1	3	5	15	1	59	5	2
Gonzalez, Giovanni, Spo.	0	3	.000	14.29	4	3	0	0	0	0	11.1	21	61	18	18	4	0	0	4	3	0	8	0	0
Griffin, Colt, Spo.	0	1	.000	27.00	3	2	0	0	0	0	2.1	4	18	7	7	0	0	0	7	0	0	2	1	1
Guzman, Angel, Boi.	9	1	.900	2.23	14	14	0	0	0	0	76.2	68	318	27	19	2	2	5	0	19	0	63	2	1
Haase, Frank, T.C.*	2	1	.667	1.45	19	0	0	0	8	0	31.0	22	133	11	5	2	2	1	1	19	0	25	5	0
Hampson, Justin, T.C.*	4	6	.400	4.52	15	15	0	0	0	0	81.2	84	354	55	41	5	1	5	9	23	0	63	4	0
Hannaman, Ryan, S.K.*	1	1	.500	2.08	3	3	0	0	0	0	13.0	8	58	5	3	1	0	0	0	8	0	19	0	1
Harden, James, Van.	2	4	.333	3.39	18	14	0	0	3	0	74.1	47	309	29	28	3	3	1	4	38	0	100	8	1
Head, Daniel, Ever.	4	4	.500	1.95	21	2	0	0	7	2	50.2	40	212	14	11	5	1	2	4	14	4	44	2	0
Hennessey, Brad, S.K.	1	0	1.000	2.38	9	9	0	0	0	0	34.0	28	140	9	9	1	0	0	4	11	0	22	2	0
Herbert, John, Eug.	3	1	.750	2.75	28	0	0	0	15	4	36.0	25	146	13	11	2	2	1	3	11	0	39	3	3
Hills, Mark, S.K.*	0	0	.000	9.22	10	0	0	0	1	0	13.2	20	78	17	14	4	0	2	4	12	0	11	1	0
Hintz, Beau, Ever.*	3	4	.429	6.00	16	11	0	0	2	1	56.1	63	250	50	40	5	0	3	2	15	1	43	1	2
Hixson, David, S.K.	3	1	.750	2.27	22	0	0	0	7	0	47.2	46	205	14	12	0	4	1	4	16	4	49	3	0
Hoyt, Michael, Eug.	1	1	.500	3.57	28	0	0	0	2	0	40.1	39	182	19	16	2	2	3	7	23	0	38	4	0
Hutchison, Wesley, S.K.	6	2	.750	1.64	25	0	0	0	25	10	33.0	21	132	8	6	2	1	1	3	14	3	45	2	0
Javier, Tony, Ever.	1	0	1.000	12.15	5	0	0	0	0	0	6.2	8	36	9	9	0	2	0	4	4	0	9	4	0
Jones, Geoffrey, Eug.^	3	7	.300	5.01	15	15	1	0	0	0	82.2	90	366	57	46	8	1	5	2	27	1	73	4	1
Kaanoi, Jason, Spo.	0	1	.000	9.00	2	2	0	0	0	0	6.0	9	31	7	6	1	1	0	0	4	0	4	0	0
Kelly, Scott, Eug.*	2	4	.333	5.06	14	14	0	0	0	0	64.0	73	294	42	36	5	1	3	3	26	0	66	5	2
Kesten, Michael, Ever.*	0	2	.000	10.80	5	0	0	0	2	0	6.2	9	35	8	8	0	1	0	1	8	1	5	2	0
Ketchner, Ryan, Ever.*	3	3	.500	2.92	20	5	0	0	6	2	52.1	38	215	19	17	3	2	0	3	18	0	58	4	0
King, Seth, Eug.	0	0	.000	0.00	1	0	0	0	0	0	1.0	1	4	0	0	0	0	0	0	1	0	1	0	0
Knoedler, Justin, S.K.	1	1	.500	1.26	13	0	0	0	2	1	28.2	22	116	4	4	0	2	1	0	9	1	38	1	0
Labitzke, Jesse, T.C.*	0	0	.000	3.22	17	0	0	0	2	0	22.1	16	104	12	8	0	0	3	15	0	15	5	1
Lee, Jon, Yak.	2	3	.400	4.40	18	0	0	0	9	1	30.2	32	132	17	15	4	1	0	1	10	1	23	8	0
Liriano, Francisco, S.K.*	0	1	.000	5.00	2	2	0	0	0	0	9.0	7	35	5	5	2	0	0	1	0	12	0	0
Loeb, Bryan, Yak.	0	0	.000	0.00	1	0	0	0	1	0	1.0	2	5	0	0	0	0	0	0	0	0	2	0	0
Lord, Justin, Spo.	0	0	.000	3.00	2	2	0	0	0	0	3.0	5	15	3	1	0	0	1	0	0	0	4	0	0
Lowry, Noah, S.K.*	1	1	.500	3.60	8	7	0	0	0	0	25.0	26	109	15	10	2	0	2	1	8	0	28	2	0
Lynch, Pat, T.C.	1	0	1.000	2.00	4	0	0	0	2	1	9.0	4	31	2	2	1	0	0	0	0	0	10	1	0
Mabeus, Christopher, Van.	2	5	.286	4.50	20	8	0	0	6	2	62.0	75	273	34	31	3	1	4	0	18	0	28	3	1
Martin, Chandler, T.C.	1	0	1.000	3.00	4	4	0	0	0	0	18.0	14	72	6	6	3	0	0	3	1	0	11	2	0
Martinez, Gustavo, Ever.	5	3	.625	2.67	15	15	0	0	0	0	84.1	62	356	30	25	4	3	2	18	34	1	100	8	0
Matos, Jesus, T.C.	2	1	.667	2.79	6	0	0	0	3	0	9.2	8	41	3	3	1	1	0	0	3	2	11	0	0
McGerry, Kevin, Van.	0	1	.000	19.50	8	0	0	0	1	0	6.0	4	43	15	13	0	0	1	4	17	0	7	6	0
McMachen, Clifford, Yak.*	2	3	.400	2.86	20	6	0	0	2	0	56.2	54	251	24	18	1	1	0	4	28	0	62	0	1
Meaux, Ryan, S.K.*	2	2	.500	5.59	17	3	0	0	6	0	29.0	39	137	20	18	4	0	2	4	11	0	27	4	3
Mejia, Juan, Eug.	0	1	.000	2.74	22	0	0	0	16	6	23.0	9	92	7	7	1	0	0	12	0	11	1	0
Melnyk, Brian, Spo.*	0	0	.000	0.00	4	1	0	0	1	1	8.2	4	35	1	0	0	0	0	1	2	0	11	1	0
Merricks, Charles, T.C.*	3	2	.600	5.69	13	13	0	0	0	0	55.1	71	258	48	35	9	5	3	6	24	0	35	6	2
Middleton, Kyle, Spo.	3	0	.000	4.00	16	14	0	0	0	0	79.1	92	345	48	41	5	0	0	15	23	0	68	10	1
Minaya, Edwin, Van.	1	0	1.000	1.74	13	0	0	0	10	5	20.2	13	83	7	4	3	1	0	0	7	0	19	2	0
Mitre, Sergio, Boi.	8	4	.667	3.07	15	15	1	1	0	0	91.0	85	371	37	31	2	0	0	3	18	1	71	3	3
Modica, Greg, Eug.	2	4	.333	6.20	17	1	0	0	5	0	24.2	37	114	21	17	1	2	1	0	8	2	15	2	0
Montes, Albert, S.K.	2	1	.667	3.57	17	0	0	0	13	7	22.2	21	96	10	9	1	1	0	2	6	2	19	3	1
Montoya, Saul, Yak.	1	2	.333	4.58	4	4	0	0	0	0	17.2	22	85	13	9	1	0	0	2	8	0	12	2	1
Moore, Greg, T.C.	4	2	.667	4.29	22	3	0	0	1	0	50.1	65	235	27	24	1	2	2	6	11	0	50	9	0
Morgan, Russ, Ever.*	2	5	.286	5.23	22	2	0	0	8	1	51.2	60	227	38	30	2	2	2	1	17	0	56	2	1
Munter, Scott, S.K.	1	2	.333	5.91	15	0	0	0	1	0	35.0	42	156	26	23	3	0	1	1	12	0	28	3	0
Nicholson, Scott, T.C.*	4	3	.571	2.93	14	14	1	1	0	0	76.2	69	307	29	25	3	2	4	4	12	0	50	4	0
Olszta, Eddie, Ever.	0	0	.000	0.00	1	0	0	0	1	0	0.1	1	2	0	0	0	0	0	0	0	0	1	1	0
Orr, Ben, Boi.*	0	3	.000	9.99	12	1	0	0	6	4	24.1	37	124	27	27	3	0	0	4	11	0	21	5	0
Ortega, Jose, Spo.*	2	2	.500	2.83	21	0	0	0	14	1	35.0	25	153	11	11	2	2	0	4	20	3	33	1	0
Ovalles, Juan, Yak.	2	5	.286	3.95	16	6	0	0	3	0	43.1	48	195	21	19	4	0	0	3	19	0	28	1	0
Padgett, Daniel, S.K.*	0	0	.000	21.60	4	0	0	0	1	0	3.1	11	22	8	8	1	0	0	1	2	0	1	1	0
Pannone, Anthony, S.K.	7	1	.875	4.11	14	14	0	0	0	0	76.2	82	323	41	35	9	0	0	8	13	0	61	7	1
Phillips, Mark, Eug.*	3	1	.750	3.74	4	4	0	0	0	0	21.2	16	87	10	9	1	0	0	1	9	0	19	1	0
Pignatiello, Carmen, Boi.*	3	1	.750	3.00	16	12	0	0	3	1	78.0	70	337	37	26	2	4	1	6	22	0	83	6	0
Price, Brett, Van.*	7	2	.778	2.34	20	4	0	0	3	0	50.0	32	211	18	13	2	4	0	3	31	0	59	3	0
Ransom, Troy, S.K.	0	2	.000	6.41	17	0	0	0	11	0	19.2	31	101	15	14	4	1	2	3	11	2	13	0	1
Reyes, Hipolito, Spo.	3	5	.375	5.19	19	0	0	0	7	0	43.1	31	190	26	25	5	1	2	4	27	0	49	2	0
Reyes, Junior, Boi.*	1	0	1.000	3.33	13	0	0	0	6	1	24.1	22	110	10	9	2	3	0	15	1	17	1	1
Rheinecker, John, Van.^	0	1	.000	1.59	6	6	0	0	0	0	22.2	13	86	5	4	0	1	0	0	4	0	17	1	0
Ricciardi, Joe, Van.*	1	3	.250	4.95	19	2	0	0	7	3	36.1	34	154	21	20	3	0	1	2	9	0	48	1	0
Rodriguez, Jose, Eug.	0	1	.000	8.64	9	0	0	0	5	0	8.1	11	49	9	8	2	0	0	13	0	9	2	2
Roenicke, Jarett, Eug.*	0	0	.000	0.00	1	0	0	0	1	0	1.0	0	5	0	0	0	0	0	1	0	3	0	0

Pitcher, Team	W	L	Pct.	ERA	G	GS	CG	ShO	GF	Sv.	IP	H	TBF	R	ER	HR	SH	SF	HB	BB	IBB	SO	WP	Bk.
Royce, Ramon, Ever.	3	5	.375	5.87	20	3	0	0	10	0	38.1	42	172	27	25	4	1	2	4	15	2	29	4	0
Sanchez, Felix, Boi.*	2	0	1.000	1.56	3	3	0	0	0	0	17.1	11	71	4	3	0	0	0	0	10	0	16	0	0
Scarcella, Christopher, Van. ...	1	1	.500	8.55	8	4	0	0	1	0	20.0	29	104	25	19	2	0	1	3	11	0	11	1	0
Shabansky, Rob, Yak.*	4	1	.800	5.12	19	2	0	0	3	0	38.2	45	175	24	22	1	3	1	0	18	2	32	3	0
Sikaras, Pete, Yak.	2	5	.286	3.56	16	0	0	0	13	3	30.1	31	137	16	12	2	0	0	0	15	2	24	4	1
Simpson, Gerrit, T.C.	2	1	.667	1.11	8	3	1	0	1	1	24.1	14	93	5	3	0	1	0	0	3	0	40	0	0
Sobscuk, Justin, Van.	2	2	.500	6.91	17	2	0	0	5	0	27.1	35	132	25	21	3	2	0	2	15	1	30	5	0
Songster, Judson, T.C.	2	1	.667	1.99	17	0	0	0	6	1	22.2	15	88	6	5	0	0	1	0	5	0	32	2	1
Sosa, Jorge, Ever.	3	1	.750	1.69	21	7	0	0	11	7	58.2	45	247	22	11	2	2	3	2	19	0	57	8	1
Soto, Darwin, Eug.	4	5	.444	3.80	30	1	0	0	7	0	42.2	35	179	23	18	1	2	1	1	15	0	39	3	0
Stockman, Phil, Yak.	3	4	.429	4.26	15	14	0	0	0	0	76.0	81	329	39	36	5	3	1	5	22	0	48	5	0
Sundbeck, Cody, Yak.	0	0	.000	3.00	4	0	0	0	1	0	6.0	7	29	2	2	0	1	0	0	4	0	3	0	0
Swanson, Erick, Ever.*	1	0	1.000	4.66	14	0	0	0	3	1	19.1	21	90	10	10	0	0	1	2	9	0	15	2	0
Tamayo, Ignacio, Spo.	3	2	.600	4.61	11	14	1	0	0	0	67.1	60	276	39	34	7	1	1	2	16	0	64	3	0
Thomas, Jebson, Spo.	2	0	1.000	2.97	15	2	0	0	6	3	39.1	36	172	18	13	3	0	1	3	15	0	33	7	0
Thompson, Mark, T.C.	1	1	.500	1.29	4	2	0	0	2	0	14.0	9	55	3	2	0	0	0	5	0	7	0	0
Trejo, Francisco, Yak.*	2	2	.500	5.90	13	6	0	0	5	1	39.2	61	193	38	26	4	1	2	0	17	0	23	8	0
Tricoglou, James, T.C.	1	1	.500	2.83	24	0	0	0	14	2	28.2	19	130	11	9	1	2	2	5	20	4	29	3	0
Trosper, Tanner, Van.	4	2	.667	3.05	18	2	0	0	6	2	44.1	26	185	16	15	2	2	0	3	18	0	47	8	0
Uzzell, Todd, S.K.	2	2	.500	8.16	6	2	0	0	1	0	14.1	19	70	13	13	1	0	0	3	9	0	6	0	0
Valera, Greg, Yak.	4	2	.667	3.30	8	8	0	0	0	0	46.1	39	187	18	17	2	1	0	2	14	1	39	10	0
Van Buren, Jermaine, T.C.	1	0	1.000	7.20	1	1	0	0	0	0	5.0	7	26	4	4	0	0	0	3	0	2	0	0
Vasquez, Jorge, Spo.	1	6	.143	5.01	10	8	0	0	0	0	50.1	50	214	33	28	3	1	2	5	13	0	67	3	10
Vazquez, Will, T.C.	0	5	.000	7.89	8	4	0	0	1	0	21.2	30	117	25	19	1	0	2	2	17	1	15	0	0
Velazquez, Ernesto, Eug.	0	0	.000	0.00	1	0	0	0	1	0	0.2	1	5	0	0	0	0	0	2	0	0	1	0
Villacis, Eduardo, T.C.	4	1	.800	4.26	11	0	0	0	6	0	19.0	14	81	9	9	2	1	1	1	8	1	20	1	0
Vitek, Josh, Eug.	0	0	.000	2.45	11	0	0	0	8	3	11.0	7	45	4	3	0	1	0	4	0	11	2	0
Waddell, Jason, S.K.*	1	1	.500	5.46	15	1	0	0	1	0	28.0	30	125	19	17	2	1	1	1	11	1	30	3	0
Watson, Tanner, Ever.	0	0	.000	0.00	1	0	0	0	0	0	2.0	1	8	0	0	0	0	0	0	1	0	2	1	0
Webster, Jeremy, Eug.*	0	0	.000	1.08	6	0	0	0	0	0	8.1	2	29	1	1	0	0	1	0	2	0	9	1	0
Wiedmeyer, Jason, Eug.*	1	3	.250	3.18	8	6	0	0	0	0	34.0	28	135	14	12	2	1	0	1	10	0	30	0	1
Wiley, Skip, Ever.	1	0	1.000	6.30	7	0	0	0	2	1	10.0	19	51	7	7	1	0	1	0	3	0	11	2	1
Wilkinson, Matthew, Yak.	2	0	1.000	1.72	9	0	0	0	2	1	15.2	14	69	8	3	0	2	1	8	0	23	2	0
Willis, Dontrelle, Boi.*	8	2	.800	2.98	15	15	0	0	0	0	93.2	76	374	36	31	1	0	1	3	19	0	77	5	1
Wood, Mike, Van.	2	0	1.000	1.25	5	2	0	0	2	0	21.2	17	86	4	3	0	0	1	0	4	0	24	2	0
Woods, Blake, Ever.	0	0	.000	0.00	1	0	0	0	0	0	1.0	1	3	0	0	0	0	0	0	0	0	0	0	0
Wykoff, Zach, Eug.	0	1	.000	9.68	25	0	0	0	6	0	30.2	48	161	37	33	4	2	4	4	19	1	24	3	0
Wynegar, Adam, Boi.*	4	2	.667	2.92	14	12	0	0	1	0	71.0	77	306	34	23	7	1	3	3	19	0	63	2	0
Yoshida, Nobuaki, Eug.*	0	0	.000	1.19	8	3	0	0	0	2	22.2	23	93	7	3	1	1	2	4	0	17	0	0
Zary, Richard, Spo.	1	1	.500	4.18	15	0	0	0	7	0	28.0	30	133	18	13	1	1	1	5	11	1	12	2	0

COMBINATION SHUTOUTS: **Boise (7)**—Mitre-Carter-Ellis, Guzman-Orr, Willis-Carlsen-Ferrera, Pignatiello-Carter, Willis-Benik-Reyes, Mitre-Carlsen, Sanchez-Benik-Reyes. **Eugene (3)**—Phillips-Mejia-Herbert, Kelly-Webster-Vitek-Rodriguez, Phillips-Rodriguez-Soto. **Everett (2)**—Blackley-Head, Martinez-Bott. **Salem-Keizer (7)**—Pannone-Waddell-Montes, Foppert-Waddell-Knoedler-Montes, Lowry-Benjamin-Cram, Lowry-Benjamin-Ransom, Hennessey-Hixson-Hutchison, Foppert-Cram-Ransom, Foppert-Benjamin-Meaux. **Spokane (1)**—Middleton-Freeman-Ortega. **Tri-City (7)**—Dannemiller-Labitzke-Moore-Tricoglou, Bouknight-Dannemiller, Nicholson-Thompson, Thompson-Simpson, Bouknight-Moore-Frary, Bouknight-Lynch, Nicholson-Dannemiller. **Vancouver (4)**—Mabeus-Rheinecker-Crider, Rheinecker-Price-Minaya, Depaula-Trosper-Frick, Harden-Frick. **Yakima (4)**—Ovalles-Wilkinson, Montoya-McMachen-Bevis, Casiellanos-Lee-Bevis, Valera-Clark-Ovalles.

NO-HIT GAMES: None.

2001 FIELDING

TEAM

Team	Pct.	G	PO	A	E	TC	DP	TP	PB
Salem-Keizer	.970	76	2059	826	90	2975	59	0	19
Yakima	.962	75	1990	797	110	2897	60	0	18
Tri-City	.962	75	2023	762	110	2895	55	0	20
Eugene	.961	76	1946	755	109	2810	44	0	14
Everett	.960	75	2004	718	114	2836	60	0	18
Vancouver	.959	75	2011	745	118	2874	42	0	16
Spokane	.959	76	2011	782	120	2913	61	0	23
Boise	.957	75	2003	843	128	2974	52	0	21

INDIVIDUAL

FIRST BASEMEN

NOTE: All caps denotes fielding-percentage leader based on 38 games for catchers, 51 for all other non-pitchers and 61 innings for pitchers. *Throws lefthanded.

Player, Team	Pct.	G	PO	A	E	TC	DP
Barrera, Reinaldo, Yak.	1.000	1	1	0	0	1	0
Benick, Jon, Eug.	.979	39	310	22	7	339	18
Bird, T.J., T.C.*	.973	25	204	12	6	222	16
Bouras, Brad, Boi.	.979	49	439	21	10	470	23
Brack, Josh, Van.	1.000	1	1	0	0	1	0
Brooks, Jeff, Van.	.987	16	139	12	2	153	13
Brown, Trevor, Eug.	1.000	1	12	0	0	12	3
Burkholder, David, T.C.*	.987	11	68	7	1	76	3
Cadena, Alejandro, Ever.	.963	3	25	1	1	27	2
Dobbs, Greg, Ever.	.971	50	379	23	12	414	31
Ellis, Alvyn, Van.	.974	23	175	10	5	190	10

Player, Team	Pct.	G	PO	A	E	TC	DP
Encarnacion, Santos, Eug.	1.000	11	66	4	0	70	4
Fallon, Chris, Spo.	.990	48	361	34	4	399	31
Freeman, Ashley, T.C.	.991	26	196	13	2	211	15
Gretz, Nicholas, T.C.	.983	22	212	16	4	232	15
Holm, Stephen, S.K.	1.000	2	12	1	0	13	2
Johnson, Dan, Van.	.975	59	435	37	12	484	29
Keating, Matt, S.K.	1.000	6	33	1	0	34	0
Lawler, Daniel, Boi.	.997	36	290	16	1	307	23
Lindsey, Cordell, Spo.	.926	3	25	0	2	27	2
Llamas, Juan, Spo.	1.000	14	98	7	0	105	9
Nichols, Kyle, Yak.	.988	60	531	38	7	576	43
Pieper, William, Spo.	.976	24	153	11	4	168	14
Puccinelli, John, Eug.	1.000	1	2	0	0	2	0
Roenicke, Jarett, Eug.*	.000	1	0	0	0	0	0
Romero, Nicholas, Eug.	1.000	1	2	0	0	2	0
Sain, Greg, Eug.	.996	29	231	15	1	247	15
Santana, Emmanuel, Ever.	.985	26	176	15	3	194	17
Soto, Jorge, Van.	1.000	1	2	0	0	2	0
Thiessen, Mike, Yak.	1.000	2	4	0	0	4	0
Trzesniak, Nick, Eug.	.000	1	0	0	0	0	0
Ventura, Juan, T.C.	1.000	1	3	0	0	3	0
VON SCHELL, Tyler, S.K.	.992	74	608	47	5	660	52
Widger, Chris, Ever.	1.000	2	7	0	0	7	2

SECOND BASEMEN

Player, Team	Pct.	G	PO	A	E	TC	DP
Barrera, Reinaldo, Yak.	.952	4	6	14	1	21	2
Brack, Josh, Van.	.945	19	33	36	4	73	5
Ceminaro, Michael, Boi.	.963	39	56	99	6	161	16
Cleveland, Matt, Spo.	.949	33	70	79	8	157	19

Player, Team	Pct.	G	PO	A	E	TC	DP
Cole, John, Ever.	.978	13	15	30	1	46	5
Dibetta, John, Eug.	.955	67	123	153	13	289	32
Encarnacion, Santos, Eug.	.000	1	0	0	0	0	0
Figueroa, Carlos, T.C.	.966	25	38	47	3	88	11
Fox, Matt, Spo.	.984	27	56	68	2	126	14
Guance, Walkill, T.C.	.944	54	104	115	13	232	18
Gutierrez, Derrick, Ever.	.931	8	15	12	2	29	5
Hoffpauir, Josh, Van.	.960	23	41	54	4	99	9
Lambert, Casey, T.C.	1.000	3	6	5	0	11	1
Lopez, Jose, Ever.	.919	7	18	16	3	37	2
Macha, Erick, Yak.	1.000	2	0	4	0	4	1
Maldonado, Edwin, S.K.	1.000	1	0	2	0	2	0
McMAINS, Derin, S.K.	.966	69	134	176	11	321	38
Menchaca, Eriberto, Ever.	1.000	3	4	3	0	7	1
Merritt, Timothy, Ever.	.960	33	54	65	5	124	17
Navarro, Mandy, Boi.	.935	21	31	55	6	92	10
Neufeld, Andy, Van.	.964	36	63	69	5	137	5
Pinon, Alex, S.K.	.929	11	20	19	3	42	5
Romero, Nicholas, Eug.	.912	10	16	15	3	34	6
Schmidt, J.P., Van.	1.000	5	13	9	0	22	0
Serrano, Eddie, Eug.	1.000	2	3	2	0	5	0
Servais, Eric, Boi.	.867	3	4	9	2	15	0
Stocker, Myreon, Spo.	.930	24	43	50	7	100	5
Thornton-Murray, Jandin, Boi.	.978	20	33	55	2	90	8
Uggla, Dan, Yak.	.960	71	133	175	13	321	41
Ventura, Juan, T.C.	1.000	1	1	2	0	3	0
Woods, Blake, Ever.	.945	20	28	41	4	73	11
Yakopich, Joseph, Yak.	1.000	1	2	1	0	3	1

THIRD BASEMEN

Player, Team	Pct.	G	PO	A	E	TC	DP
Barrera, Reinaldo, Yak.	.863	14	12	32	7	51	3
Benavidez, Julian, S.K.	.935	47	33	96	9	138	8
Brook, Josh, Van.	.863	18	10	34	7	51	1
Brooks, Jeff, Yak.	.908	54	29	79	11	119	6
Cleveland, Matt, Spo.	.667	1	0	2	1	3	0
Collins, Chris, Ever.	.750	4	1	8	3	12	2
Dobbs, Greg, Ever.	1.000	3	1	5	0	6	0
Encarnacion, Santos, Eug.	.765	8	3	10	4	17	0
Figueroa, Carlos, T.C.	.727	5	2	6	3	11	0
Fox, Matt, Spo.	.957	32	20	47	3	70	4
Freeman, Ashley, T.C.	.909	47	22	78	10	110	3
Gautreau, Jake, Eug.	.924	44	27	94	10	131	8
Guance, Walkill, T.C.	1.000	1	0	3	0	3	1
Holm, Stephen, S.K.	.935	15	6	23	2	31	2
Lambert, Casey, T.C.	.909	31	18	52	7	77	7
Lindsey, Cordell, Spo.	.833	2	1	4	1	6	0
Llamas, Juan, Spo.	.889	42	19	85	13	117	7
Maestrales, Peter, S.K.	.854	17	2	33	6	41	1
Merritt, Timothy, Ever.	.667	3	3	1	2	6	0
Navarro, Mandy, Boi.	.000	1	0	0	0	0	0
Neufeld, Andy, Van.	1.000	8	9	8	0	17	0
Pieper, William, Spo.	.857	11	6	18	4	28	1
Pinon, Alex, S.K.	1.000	2	0	3	0	3	2
Puccinelli, John, Eug.	.889	8	6	10	2	18	0
REYES, Christian, Van.	.930	58	37	110	11	158	4
Romero, Nicholas, Eug.	.778	2	2	5	2	9	0
Sain, Greg, Eug.	.865	14	10	22	5	37	1
Serrano, Eddie, Eug.	.933	5	5	9	1	15	1
Servais, Eric, Boi.	.706	16	7	17	10	34	1
Slavik, Corey, Boi.	.915	62	44	129	16	189	10
Thornton-Murray, Jandin, Boi.	.889	3	3	5	1	9	0
Tracy, Chad, Yak.	1.000	6	9	18	0	27	2
Villilo, Miguel, Ever.	.822	45	23	60	18	101	1
Woods, Blake, Ever.	.935	24	11	32	3	46	3
Yakopich, Joseph, Yak.	.933	11	3	11	1	15	0

SHORTSTOPS

Player, Team	Pct.	G	PO	A	E	TC	DP
Arteaga, Joshua, Boi.	.898	40	35	114	17	166	10
Barrera, Reinaldo, Yak.	.917	26	41	69	10	120	18
Bartlett, Jason, Eug.	.946	67	98	199	17	314	24
Ceminaro, Michael, Boi.	.000	1	0	0	0	0	0
Cleveland, Matt, Spo.	1.000	3	1	11	0	12	1
Cotto, Luis, Spo.	.901	71	98	175	30	303	37
Encarnacion, Santos, Eug.	.714	2	2	3	2	7	1
Figueroa, Carlos, T.C.	.500	1	0	1	1	2	0
Fox, Matt, Spo.	.903	6	10	18	3	31	5
Guance, Walkill, T.C.	.875	6	3	11	2	16	0
Hilinski, Scott, Yak.	.933	4	4	10	1	15	3
Lambert, Casey, T.C.	.969	25	32	61	3	96	11
LOPEZ, Jose, Ever.	.954	62	115	177	14	306	39
Macha, Erick, Yak.	.936	51	93	126	15	234	18
Merritt, Timothy, Ever.	.932	15	21	34	4	59	7
Meyer, Robert, S.K.	1.000	1	1	2	0	3	0
Miranda, Miguel, S.K.	.949	58	103	178	15	296	37
Montero, Esteban, T.C.	.932	57	63	158	16	237	20
Navarro, Mandy, Boi.	.904	9	9	38	5	52	6
Neufeld, Andy, Van.	.907	10	15	24	4	43	4
Pinon, Alex, S.K.	.898	25	26	53	9	88	6
Romero, Nicholas, Eug.	.857	11	13	17	5	35	5
Schmidt, J.P., Van.	.857	7	9	15	4	28	1
Stotts, J.T., Van.	.919	62	91	169	23	283	23
Thornton-Murray, Jandin, Boi.	.904	31	48	103	16	167	14
Villilo, Miguel, Ever.	1.000	1	4	5	0	9	1
Williams, Jon, S.K.	.000	1	0	0	0	0	0

OUTFIELDERS

Player, Team	Pct.	G	PO	A	E	TC	DP
Allegra, Matt, Van.	.975	70	145	9	4	158	3
Anderson, Syketo, Boi.	.967	31	28	1	1	30	0
Bacon, Dwaine, Boi.	.980	55	97	2	2	101	0
Banks, Gary, Boi.	1.000	2	1	0	0	1	0
Barrett, Rich, Yak.	.979	72	124	14	3	141	3
Basil, Jason, Van.	.946	40	47	6	3	56	1
Bird, T.J., T.C.*	1.000	11	15	0	0	15	0
Boll, Javier, Yak.	.977	16	39	3	1	43	1
Brooks, Doc, Eug.	.960	18	22	2	1	25	0
Buhner, Jay, Ever.	.000	3	0	0	0	0	0
Carter, Bryan, S.K.*	.967	60	113	3	4	120	0
Carter, Josh, Eug.	.970	22	31	1	1	33	0
Cash, Condor, Boi.	.910	62	73	8	8	89	0
Castillo, David, Eug.*	.981	35	51	2	1	54	0
Castro, Renato, Eug.	1.000	8	14	0	0	14	0
Chandler, Marcus, Spo.	.984	33	59	4	1	64	0
Cirone, Joseph, Van.	.978	34	42	3	1	46	0
Dobbs, Greg, Ever	1.000	6	12	1	0	13	0
Draper, John, Spo.	.938	20	28	2	2	32	1
Edge, Dwight, Yak.	1.000	8	14	0	0	14	0
Encarnacion, Santos, Eug.	.905	13	26	4	2	31	0
Figueroa, Eduardo, Ever.	.979	43	92	2	2	96	2
Florence, Branden, S.K.	1.000	2	3	1	0	4	0
Frome, Jason, T.C.*	.978	55	125	8	3	136	3
Gearlds, Aaron, T.C.	.967	46	57	1	2	60	0
Gunny, Peter, Spo.	.963	21	25	1	1	27	1
Hairr, Kevin, Boi.	.977	27	43	0	1	44	0
Hellman, Matthew, Eug.	.987	57	68	8	1	77	0
Hernandez, Orlando, Ever.	.960	29	46	2	2	50	0
Holst, Micah, S.K.	1.000	40	79	3	0	82	1
HUNTINGFORD, Matt, S.K.*	1.000	58	76	4	0	80	0
Johnson, J.J., Boi.	.985	65	130	3	2	135	0
Keating, Matt, S.K.	1.000	2	1	0	0	1	0
Loeb, Bryan, Yak.	1.000	5	4	1	0	5	0
Mace, Clark, Yak.*	.966	50	56	1	2	59	1
Madera, Sandy, Van.	1.000	3	5	0	0	5	0
McAuliff, James, S.K.	1.000	17	23	1	0	24	0
Meyer, Robert, S.K.	.976	64	80	3	2	85	0
Moronoy, Vernand, T.C.	.957	47	88	2	4	94	2
Nettles, Marcus, Eug.*	.968	55	117	3	4	124	0
Peirce, Justin, Van.	.966	32	55	2	2	59	0
Rainey, Jason, Ever.*	.971	24	32	2	1	35	1
Richardson, Miguel, Ever.	.900	12	9	0	1	10	0
Roenicke, Jarett, Eug.*	1.000	3	8	0	0	8	0
Romero, Nicholas, Eug.	.942	32	48	1	3	52	0
Rooke, Brian, Van.	.920	41	65	4	6	75	0
Rosario, Vicente, Ever.	.986	33	65	3	1	69	1
Rosario, Victor, Spo.	.935	63	91	9	7	107	2
Santos, Sneideer, Yak.	.885	16	23	0	3	26	0
Schmidt, J.P., Van.	1.000	20	32	1	0	33	0
Shanks, James, Spo.	.974	67	145	6	4	155	2
Simpson, Bodie, Yak.	.968	54	85	6	3	94	0
Smiley, Jermaine, Spo.*	1.000	50	59	2	0	61	2
Terrero, Luis, Yak.	1.000	11	17	0	0	17	0
Testa, Chris, T.C.*	.971	42	66	0	2	68	0
Thiessen, Mike, Yak.	.867	19	12	1	2	15	0
Tiesing, Tyler, Yak.	1.000	4	4	0	0	4	0
Trzesniak, Nick, Eug.	1.000	2	2	0	0	2	0
Van Meetren, Jason, Ever.	.900	33	52	2	6	60	0
Ventura, Juan, T.C.	.946	37	68	2	4	74	0
Williamson, John, Ever.	.967	52	81	6	3	90	1
Woods, Blake, Ever.	1.000	2	1	0	0	1	0
Yakopich, Joseph, Yak.	.000	1	0	0	0	0	0

CLASS A *Northwest League*

CATCHERS

Player, Team	Pct.	G	PO	A	E	TC	DP	PB
Alleva, Joseph, Spo.	.987	37	282	31	4	317	0	12
Anderson, Keith, S.K.	.987	57	416	48	6	470	3	11
Basil, Jason, Van.	1.000	4	40	7	0	47	0	1
Brown, Trevor, Eug.	.977	22	159	13	4	176	0	2
Colina, Alvin, T.C.	.982	46	347	44	7	398	0	8
DiROSA, Michael, Yak.	.993	40	259	34	2	295	0	11
Draper, John, Spo.	.987	31	219	17	3	239	1	7
Durand, Jose, Spo.	.982	16	97	15	2	114	0	4
Epke, Brian, Yak.	1.000	5	32	4	0	36	1	0
Gomez, Andre, Eug.	.972	5	30	5	1	36	0	0
Hanna, Warren, Boi.	.976	39	294	29	8	331	1	8
Holm, Stephen, S.K.	1.000	10	20	1	0	21	0	0
Loeb, Bryan, Yak.	.972	26	154	20	5	179	1	5
Madera, Sandy, Van.	.966	16	78	8	3	89	0	2
McKnight, Lukas, Boi.	.992	19	112	9	1	122	0	2
Mejia, Andy, Boi.	.990	24	179	13	2	194	0	11
Myers, Casey, Van.	.986	42	331	23	5	359	1	5
Oliveros, Luis, Ever.	.985	26	231	27	4	262	2	4
Olszta, Eddie, Ever.	.974	25	176	15	5	196	1	6
Ortega, Sixto, T.C.	.972	15	94	9	3	106	0	4
Pride, Joshua, T.C.	.987	16	152	5	2	159	0	8
Rivera, Rene, Ever.	.992	12	106	14	1	121	0	4
Sain, Greg, Eug.	.964	7	47	7	2	56	0	1
Santana, Emmanuel, Ever.	.995	21	170	11	1	182	2	4
Silver, Travis, Boi.	1.000	3	8	0	0	8	0	0
Soto, Jorge, Van.	.981	24	198	13	4	215	1	8
Tiesing, Tyler, Yak.	.993	17	121	18	1	140	0	2
Trzesniak, Nick, Eug.	.983	49	362	31	7	400	1	11
Turco, Anthony, S.K.	.992	42	209	30	2	241	0	8
Williams, Jon, S.K.	1.000	2	15	0	0	15	0	0

PITCHERS

Player, Team	Pct.	G	PO	A	E	TC	DP
Adinolfi, Timothy, Spo.*	.900	18	3	6	1	10	0
Allen, Travis, Ever.	.000	4	0	0	0	0	0
Almond, Casey, T.C.	1.000	4	1	0	0	1	0
Anderegg, Jason, Eug.	1.000	14	1	13	0	14	0
Arias, Miguel, Spo.	.000	5	0	0	1	1	0
Armitage, Barry, Spo.	.867	15	6	7	2	15	0
Ashlock, Chad, S.K.	1.000	11	7	10	0	17	2
Barber, Scott, Yak.	1.000	2	3	0	0	3	0
Barnett, John, Spo.	1.000	20	2	6	0	8	1
Bausher, Tim, Ever.	1.000	11	1	2	0	3	0
Benick, Jon, Eug.	.000	1	0	0	0	0	0
Benik, Brett, Boi.	.900	21	2	7	1	10	0
Benjamin, Petersen, S.K.	.941	15	7	9	1	17	0
Bevis, P.J., Van.	.833	12	3	2	1	6	0
Blackley, Travis, Ever.*	.882	14	5	10	2	17	0
Blanton, Jason, Boi.	1.000	8	1	4	0	5	1
Blood, Justin, Ever.*	.000	10	0	0	0	0	0
Bott, Glenn, Ever.*	.750	19	2	4	2	8	0
Bouknight, Kip, T.C.	1.000	15	5	4	0	9	0
Brandt, Jon, Eug.	.900	13	5	4	1	10	0
Bruney, Brian, Yak.	.833	15	1	4	1	6	0
Burres, Brian, S.K.*	.900	14	3	6	1	10	0
Carlsen, Jeff, Boi.	1.000	16	1	4	0	5	0
Carter, Mark, Boi.*	.667	16	0	2	1	3	1
Castellanos, Jonathan, Yak.	.875	15	4	10	2	16	1
Clark, Josh, Yak.	.875	17	2	5	1	8	0
Cotts, Neal, Van.*	.800	9	0	4	1	5	0
Cram, Josh, S.K.	.867	19	4	9	2	15	0
Crider, George, Van.	.800	22	3	5	2	10	0
Cruz, Jeffrey, T.C.*	1.000	12	0	1	0	1	0
Cullen, Phil, Ever.	.800	14	0	8	2	10	0
Dannemiller, Beau, T.C.	.909	23	6	4	1	11	1
DePaula, Freddy, Van.*	1.000	7	0	4	0	4	0
Diaz, Alex, Van.	1.000	10	1	2	0	3	0
Doble, Eric, Spo.	.917	18	3	8	1	12	2
Done, Juan, Ever.	.667	8	1	1	1	3	0
Dossett, William, Spo.	.000	12	0	0	2	2	0
Dulkowski, Marc, Eug.	1.000	7	0	2	0	2	0
Earley, Andrew, Boi.	.857	14	1	5	1	7	0
Ellis, Steve, Boi.	1.000	20	0	2	0	2	0
Eriksen, Tanner, Yak.	.500	3	0	3	3	6	0
Ferreras, Yorkin, Boi.*	.667	18	1	3	2	6	0
Foppert, Jesse, S.K.	.917	14	3	8	1	12	0
Frary, Levi, T.C.	.875	22	1	6	1	8	0
Freeman, Eric, Spo.*	1.000	21	5	8	0	13	0
Frias, Juan, S.K.	.000	4	0	0	0	0	0
Frick, Mike, Van.	.857	21	1	5	1	7	0
Gage, Matthew, Van.	1.000	17	6	3	0	9	0
Gallagher, Shawn, T.C.*	1.000	17	0	7	0	7	0
Garber, Mike, Yak.*	.000	3	0	0	0	0	0
Garcia, Rafael, Spo.	1.000	10	3	4	0	7	0
Germano, Justin, Eug.	1.000	13	5	7	0	12	0
Gilpatrick, Tyler, Van.	.917	19	5	6	1	12	1
Gonzalez, Carlos, Yak.	.571	13	1	3	3	7	0
Gonzalez, Christian, Van.	.900	16	2	16	2	20	2
Gonzalez, Giovanni, Spo.	1.000	4	1	1	0	2	1
Griffin, Colt, Spo.	1.000	3	0	1	0	1	0
Guzman, Angel, Boi.	.964	14	7	20	1	28	1
Haase, Frank, T.C.*	.800	19	1	3	1	5	0
Hampson, Justin, T.C.*	.905	15	6	13	2	21	1
Hannaman, Ryan, S.K.*	.000	3	0	0	1	1	0
Harden, James, Van.	.917	18	5	6	1	12	0
Head, Daniel, Ever.	.917	21	4	7	1	12	0
Hennessey, Brad, S.K.	.833	9	3	2	1	6	0
Herbert, John, Eug.	1.000	28	2	3	0	5	0
Hills, Mark, S.K.*	1.000	10	0	1	0	1	0
Hintz, Beau, Ever.*	.947	15	3	15	1	19	0
Hixson, David, S.K.	1.000	22	3	5	0	8	0
Hoyt, Michael, Eug.	1.000	28	0	5	0	5	0
Hutchison, Wesley, S.K.	.875	25	3	4	1	8	0
Javier, Tony, Ever.	.667	5	1	1	1	3	0
Jones, Geoffrey, Eug.*	.909	15	3	7	1	11	0
Kaanoi, Jason, Spo.	.000	2	0	0	0	0	0
Kelly, Scott, Eug.*	.750	14	2	10	4	16	1
Kesten, Michael, Ever.*	1.000	5	1	0	0	1	0
Ketchner, Ryan, Ever.*	1.000	20	0	8	0	8	1
King, Seth, Eug.	.000	1	0	0	0	0	0
Knoedler, Justin, S.K.	1.000	13	0	3	0	3	1
Labitzke, Jesse, T.C.*	1.000	17	0	2	0	2	0
Lee, Jon, Yak.	1.000	18	4	8	0	12	0
Liriano, Francisco, S.K.*	1.000	2	0	1	0	1	0
Loeb, Bryan, Yak.	1.000	1	0	0	0	0	0
Lord, Justin, Spo.	.000	2	0	0	0	0	0
Lowry, Noah, S.K.*	.750	8	1	2	1	4	0
Lynch, Pat, T.C.	1.000	4	0	2	0	2	0
Mabeus, Christopher, Van.	.938	20	5	10	1	16	0
Martin, Chandler, T.C.	.857	4	3	3	1	7	1
Martinez, Gustavo, Ever.	.929	15	5	21	2	28	2
Matos, Jesus, T.C.	1.000	6	0	3	0	3	0
McGerry, Kevin, Van.	.000	8	0	0	1	1	0
McMachen, Clifford, Yak.*	.833	20	4	11	3	18	0
Meaux, Ryan, S.K.*	.667	17	1	3	2	6	0
Mejia, Juan, Eug.	1.000	22	2	1	0	3	0
Melnyk, Brian, Spo.*	1.000	4	0	2	0	2	0
Merricks, Charles, T.C.*	.909	13	1	19	2	22	1
Middleton, Kyle, Spo.	1.000	16	5	19	0	24	2
Minaya, Edwin, Van.	1.000	13	0	3	0	3	0
MITRE, Sergio, Boi.	1.000	15	11	18	0	29	0
Modica, Greg, Eug.	1.000	17	1	8	0	9	0
Montes, Albert, S.K.	1.000	17	3	6	0	9	0
Montoya, Saul, Yak.	.857	4	1	5	1	7	0
Moore, Greg, T.C.	.923	22	4	8	1	13	4
Morgan, Russ, Ever.*	1.000	22	0	9	0	9	0
Munter, Scott, S.K.	.917	15	2	9	1	12	1
Nicholson, Scott, T.C.*	.900	14	5	13	2	20	1
Olszta, Eddie, Ever.	.000	1	0	0	0	0	0
Orr, Ben, Boi.*	1.000	12	3	4	0	7	0
Ortega, Jose, Spo.*	.857	21	0	6	1	7	0
Ovalles, Juan, Van.	1.000	16	2	9	0	11	1
Padgett, Daniel, S.K.*	.000	4	0	0	0	0	0
Pannone, Anthony, S.K.	.933	14	3	11	1	15	0
Phillips, Mark, Eug.*	.778	4	0	7	2	9	0
Pignatiello, Carmen, Boi.*	.789	16	2	13	4	19	2
Price, Brett, Van.*	.900	20	1	8	1	10	0
Ransom, Troy, S.K.	.833	17	1	4	1	6	0
Reyes, Hipolito, Spo.	.714	19	2	3	2	7	0
Reyes, Junior, Boi.*	.857	13	0	6	1	7	0
Rheinecker, John, Van.*	1.000	6	0	5	0	5	1
Ricciardi, Joe, Yak.	1.000	19	1	4	0	5	0
Rodriguez, Jose, Eug.	.000	9	0	0	0	0	0
Roenicke, Jarett, Eug.*	1.000	1	0	0	0	0	0
Royce, Ramon, Ever.	1.000	20	2	5	0	7	1
Sanchez, Felix, Boi.*	1.000	3	1	4	0	5	1
Scarcella, Christopher, Van.	1.000	8	4	5	0	9	1
Shabansky, Rob, Yak.*	.833	19	0	10	2	12	1
Sikaras, Pete, Yak.	.750	16	0	3	1	4	0
Simpson, Gerrit, T.C.	1.000	8	2	3	0	5	0
Sobscuk, Justin, S.K.	1.000	17	1	3	0	4	1
Songster, Judson, T.C.	1.000	17	0	2	0	2	0
Sosa, Jorge, Ever.	1.000	21	2	10	0	12	0
Soto, Darwin, Eug.	1.000	30	2	8	0	10	0

Player, Team	Pct.	G	PO	A	E	TC	DP		Player, Team	Pct.	G	PO	A	E	TC	DP
Stockman, Phil, Yak.	1.000	15	3	11	0	14	0		Waddell, Jason, S.K.*	.833	15	2	3	1	6	0
Sundbeck, Cody, Yak.	.667	4	1	1	1	3	0		Watson, Tanner, Ever.	.000	1	0	0	0	0	0
Swanson, Erick, Ever.*	1.000	14	4	3	0	7	0		Webster, Jeremy, Eug.*	1.000	6	1	4	0	5	0
Tamayo, Ignacio, Spo.	.900	14	3	6	1	10	1		Wiedmeyer, Jason, Eug.*	.929	8	2	11	1	14	0
Thomas, Jebson, Spo.	.923	15	6	6	1	13	0		Wiley, Skip, Ever.	1.000	7	0	1	0	1	0
Thompson, Mark, T.C.	1.000	4	1	1	0	2	0		Wilkinson, Matthew, Yak.	.667	9	1	1	1	3	1
Trejo, Francisco, Yak.*	1.000	13	6	10	0	16	0		Willis, Dontrelle, Boi.*	1.000	15	8	20	0	28	1
Tricoglou, James, T.C.	1.000	24	2	2	0	4	0		Wood, Mike, Van.	1.000	5	2	4	0	6	0
Trosper, Tanner, Van.	1.000	18	3	5	0	8	0		Woods, Blake, Ever.	.000	1	0	0	0	0	0
Uzzell, Todd, S.K.	.667	6	0	2	1	3	0		Wykoff, Zach, Eug.	.667	25	1	1	1	3	0
Valera, Greg, Yak.	1.000	8	2	6	0	8	0		Wynegar, Adam, Boi.*	1.000	14	1	5	0	6	2
Van Buren, Jermaine, T.C.	1.000	1	0	1	0	1	0		Yoshida, Nobuaki, Eug.*	1.000	8	3	2	0	5	0
Vasquez, Jorge, Spo.	.857	10	4	2	1	7	0		Zary, Richard, Spo.	.750	15	2	1	1	4	0
Vazquez, Will, T.C.	1.000	8	0	3	0	3	0									
Velazquez, Ernesto, Eug.	1.000	1	1	0	0	1	0									
Villacis, Eduardo, T.C.	.833	11	1	4	1	6	1									
Vitek, Josh, Eug.	1.000	11	0	5	0	5	0									

The following players appeared only as designated hitter, pinch-hitter or pinch runner: Laureano, dh, ph; Christy, pr.

LEAGUE CHAMPIONS

Year	Team	Pct.	Year	Team	Pct.	Year	Team	Pct.
1901—	Portland	.675	1954—	Vancouver*	.636	1979—	Central Oregon◆	.606
1902—	Butte	.608		Lewiston	.629		Walla Walla	.571
1903—	Butte	.578	1955—	Salem	.646	1980—	Bellingham•	.643
1904—	Boise	.625		Eugene*	.639		Eugene•	.529
1905—	Vancouver	.586	1956—	Yakima	.691	1981—	Medford◆	.600
	Everett*	.667		Yakima	.619		Bellingham	.557
1906—	Tacoma	.600	1957—	Eugene	.576	1982—	Medford	.757
1907—	Aberdeen	.625		Wenatchee*	.647		Salem◆	.486
1908—	Vancouver	.570	1958—	Lewiston	.621	1983—	Medford††	.735
1909—	Seattle	.653		Yakima*	.594		Bellingham	.588
1910—	Spokane	.596	1959—	Salem	.623	1984—	Tri-Cities††	.622
1911—	Vancouver	.628		Yakima*	.563		Medford	.608
1912—	Seattle	.600	1960—	Yakima	.638	1985—	Everett††	.541
1913—	Vancouver	.600		Yakima	.562		Eugene	.541
1914—	Vancouver	.632	1961—	Lewiston*	.621	1986—	Bellingham††	.608
1915—	Seattle	.564		Yakima	.600		Eugene	.608
1916—	Spokane	.622	1962—	Wenatchee*	.574	1987—	Spokane▲	.711
1917—	Great Falls	.602		Tri-City	.580		Everett	.653
1918—	Seattle	.588	1963—	Lewiston	.594	1988—	Southern Oregon	.605
1919—	Seattle	.590		Yakima*	.613		Spokane◆	.553
1920—	Victoria	.600	1964—	Eugene	.636	1989—	Southern Oregon	.600
1921—	Yakima	.710		Yakima*	.611		Spokane◆	.547
	Yakima	.660	1965—	Lewiston	.667	1990—	Boise	.697
1922—	Calgary‡	.600		Tri-City*	.681		Spokane◆	.645
1923-36—Did not operate.			1966—	Tri-City	.679	1991—	Boise◆	.658
1937—	Wenatchee	.603	1967—	Medford	.607		Yakima	.579
	Tacoma*	.627	1968—	Tri-City	.600	1992—	Bellingham◆	.566
1938—	Yakima	.583	1969—	Rogue Valley	.633		Bend	.566
	Bellingham (2nd)†	.511	1970—	Lewiston§	.538	1993—	Bellingham	.579
1939—	Wenatchee	.601		Coos Bay-No. Bend	.563		Boise◆	.539
	Tacoma (2nd)†	.533	1971—	Tri-City§	.625	1994—	Yakima	.645
1940—	Spokane	.587		Bend	.538		Boise◆	.579
	Tacoma (4th)†	.500	1972—	Lewiston§	.675	1995—	Boise◆	.640
1941—	Spokane	.669		Walla Walla	.513		Bellingham	.566
1942—	Vancouver	.594	1973—	Walla Walla∞	.638	1996—	Eugene	.645
1943-45—Did not operate.				Portland	.563		Yakima§	.526
1946—	Wenatchee	.622	1974—	Bellingham	.619	1997—	Boise	.671
1947—	Vancouver	.566		Eugene▲	.571		Portland◆	.579
1948—	Spokane	.614	1975—	Portland	.545	1998—	Spokane	.618
1949—	Yakima	.660		Eugene◆	.684		Boise	.618
	Vancouver (2nd)†	.615	1976—	Portland	.556		Salem-Keizer◆	.566
1950—	Yakima	.613		Walla Walla◆	.639	1999—	Spokane◆	.579
1951—	Spokane	.655	1977—	Bellingham■	.618	2000—	Yakima◆	.539
1952—	Victoria	.631		Portland	.667		Boise	.539
1953—	Salem	.635	1978—	Grays Harbor▼	.671	2001—	Boise	.693
	Spokane*	.590		Eugene	.514		Salem-Keizer◆	.071

*Won split-season playoff. †Won four-club playoff. ‡League disbanded June 18. §League divided into Northern and Southern divisions, declared champion under league rules. ∞League divided into Eastern and Western divisions, declared champion under league rules. ▲League divided into Eastern and Western divisions; won two-team playoff. ◆League divided into North and South divisions; won two-team playoff. ■League divided into Affiliate and Independent divisions; won two-team playoff. ▼Declared league champion after winning one-game playoff. Balance of playoff canceled due to rain and wet grounds. •Declared co-champion after winning one game. Balance of playoff canceled due to rain and wet grounds. ††League divided into Washington and Oregon divisions; won two-team playoff. (NOTE—Known as Pacific Northwest League 1901-02, Pacific National League 1903-04, Northwestern League 1905-18, Pacific Coast International League 1919-22 and Western International League 1937-54.)

SOUTH ATLANTIC LEAGUE

LEAGUE OFFICE

President/secretary-treasurer
John Moss

Address
P.O. Box 38
Kings Mountain, NC 28086

Phone
704-739-3466

Teams (affiliation)
Asheville Tourists (Rockies)
Augusta Greenjackets (Red Sox)
Capital City Bombers (Mets)
Charleston (S.C.) Riverdogs (Devil Rays)
Charleston (W.Va.) Alley Cats (Blue Jays)
Columbus Redstixx (Indians)
Delmarva Shorebirds (Orioles)
Greensboro Bats (Yankees)

Hagerstown Suns (Giants)
Hickory Crawdads (Pirates)
Kannapolis Intimidators (White Sox)
Lakewood BlueClaws (Phillies)
Lexington Legends (Astros)
Macon Braves (Braves)
Savannah Sand Gnats (Rangers)
Wilmington (N.C.) Waves (Dodgers)

2001 FINAL STANDINGS

FIRST HALF

NORTHERN DIVISION

Team	W	L	T	Pct.	GB
Lexington (Astros)	50	20	0	.714	...
Kannapolis (White Sox)	47	22	0	.681	2.5
Hagerstown (Giants)	38	32	0	.543	12.0
Greensboro (Yankees)	37	33	0	.529	13.0
Delmarva (Orioles)	30	40	0	.429	20.0
Hickory (Pirates)	29	41	0	.414	21.0
Lakewood (Phillies)	28	42	0	.400	22.0
Charleston, W.Va. (Blue Jays)	21	47	0	.309	28.0

SOUTHERN DIVISION

Team	W	L	T	Pct.	GB
Augusta (Red Sox)	42	28	0	.600	...
Columbus (Indians)	39	30	0	.565	2.5
Macon (Braves)	37	30	0	.552	3.5
Wilmington (Dodgers)	38	32	0	.543	4.0
Columbia (Mets)	30	36	0	.455	10.0
Charleston, S.C. (Devil Rays)	31	39	0	.443	11.0
Savannah (Rangers)	29	38	0	.433	11.5
Asheville (Rockies)	27	43	0	.386	15.0

SECOND HALF

NORTHERN DIVISION

Team	W	L	T	Pct.	GB
Hagerstown (Giants)	45	25	0	.643	...
Lexington (Astros)	42	28	0	.600	3.0
Hickory (Pirates)	38	32	0	.543	7.0
Greensboro (Yankees)	33	37	0	.471	12.0
Lakewood (Phillies)	32	37	0	.464	12.5
Delmarva (Orioles)	31	39	0	.443	14.0
Charleston, W.Va. (Blue Jays)	30	40	0	.429	15.0
Kannapolis (White Sox)	29	41	0	.414	16.0

SOUTHERN DIVISION

Team	W	L	T	Pct.	GB
Asheville (Rockies)	41	28	0	.594	...
Columbus (Indians)	38	29	0	.567	2.0
Wilmington (Dodgers)	37	31	0	.544	3.5
Macon (Braves)	35	31	0	.530	4.5
Charleston, S.C. (Devil Rays)	33	37	0	.471	8.5
Columbia (Mets)	32	37	0	.464	9.0
Augusta (Red Sox)	32	37	0	.464	9.0
Savannah (Rangers)	25	44	0	.362	16.0

COMPOSITE

Team	Lex.	Hag.	C'bus	Kan.	Wil.	Mac.	Aug.	Gbr.	Ash.	Hick.	C'bia	CSC	Del.	Lak.	Sav.	CWV	W	L	T	Pct.	GB
Lexington (Astros)	...	9	3	7	3	3	4	11	3	12	4	2	10	9	3	9	92	48	0	.657	...
Hagerstown (Giants)	7	...	3	10	3	1	2	7	4	8	0	3	10	11	4	10	83	57	0	.593	9.0
Columbus (Indians)	1	1	...	0	9	7	7	3	8	2	11	6	3	4	11	4	77	59	0	.566	13.0
Kannapolis (White Sox)	9	5	3	...	2	2	3	5	1	10	0	2	10	9	3	12	76	63	0	.547	15.5
Wilmington (Dodgers)	1	1	7	2	...	5	9	2	6	3	10	11	4	2	9	3	75	63	0	.543	16.0
Macon (Braves)	1	3	5	2	9	...	10	0	11	2	6	9	1	3	9	1	72	61	0	.541	16.5
Augusta (Red Sox)	0	2	7	5	7	6	...	4	9	3	9	11	2	0	6	3	74	65	0	.532	17.5
Greensboro (Yankees)	5	9	1	10	2	4	0	...	1	6	1	3	8	8	2	10	70	70	0	.500	22.0
Asheville (Rockies)	1	0	8	3	8	5	6	3	...	2	9	7	2	3	8	3	68	71	0	.489	23.5
Hickory (Pirates)	4	7	2	6	1	2	1	9	2	...	3	2	8	9	2	9	67	73	0	.479	25.0
Columbia (Mets)	0	4	5	0	4	8	7	3	7	1	...	5	2	5	9	2	62	73	0	.459	27.5
Charleston, S.C. (D. Rays)	2	1	10	2	5	7	5	1	7	2	9	...	1	2	9	1	64	76	0	.457	28.0
Delmarva (Orioles)	4	6	1	6	0	3	2	8	2	6	2	3	...	7	3	8	61	79	0	.436	31.0
Lakewood (Phillies)	5	5	0	5	2	1	0	8	1	7	2	2	9	...	2	11	60	79	0	.432	31.5
Savannah (Rangers)	1	0	4	1	7	5	8	2	8	2	5	7	1	2	...	1	54	82	0	.397	36.0
Charleston, W.Va. (B. Jays)	7	4	0	4	1	2	1	4	1	7	2	3	8	5	2	...	51	87	0	.370	40.0

Major league affiliations in parentheses.

PLAYOFFS: Lexington defeated Hagerstown two games to none; Asheville defeated Augusta two games to one. Note: Lexington led Asheville two games to none and declared South Atlantic League Champion due to stoppage of play in professional baseball.

REGULAR-SEASON ATTENDANCE: Asheville, 159,886; Augusta, 140,361; Columbia, 106,418; Charleston, S.C., 236,145; Charleston, W.V., 83,074; Columbus, 115,569; Delmarva, 268,143; Greensboro, 144,637; Hagerstown, 100,690; Hickory, 182,558; Kannapolis, 129,023; Lakewood, 482,206; Lexington, 451,076; Macon, 114,001; Savannah, 101,295; Wilmington, 135,548. Total—2,950,630. Playoff (7 games)—21,477. South Atlantic League All-Star Game at Hickory—4,498.

MANAGERS: Asheville, Joe Mikulik; Augusta, Mike Boulanger; Charleston, S.C., Rolando Pino; Charleston, W.V., Buddy Biancalana; Columbia, Ken Oberkfell; Columbus, Ted Kubiak; Delmarva, Joe Ferguson; Greensboro, Mitch Seoane; Hagerstown, Bill Hayes; Hickory, Pete Mackanin; Kannapolis, Razor Shines; Lakewood, Greg Legg; Lexington, J.J. Cannon; Macon, Randy Ingle; Savannah, Bill Slack (thru June 17) and Pedro Lopez (June 18 thru end of season); Wilmington, Dino Ebel.

ALL-STAR TEAM: 1B—Rene Reyes, Asheville; 2B—Felix Escalona, Lexington; 3B—Corey Smith, Columbus; SS—Kelly Johnson, Macon; Utility INF—Tom Whiteman, Lexington; OF—Jon Topolski, Lexington; OF—Ryan Church, Columbus; OF—Manny Ravelo, Hickory; Utility OF—Yhency Brazoban, Greensboro; C—Koyie Hill, Wilmington; DH—Jason Kinchen, Greensboro; RHP—Boof Bonser, Hagerstown; LHP—Corwin Malone, Kannapolis; Most Valuable Player—Rene Reyes, Asheville; Most Valuable Pitcher—Boof Bonser, Hagerstown; Rookie of the Year—Kelly Johnson, Macon; Manager of the Year—Joe Mikulik, Asheville.

2001 BATTING
TEAM

Team	Avg.	G	TPA	AB	R	H	TB	2B	3B	HR	RBI	SH	SF	HP	BB	IBB	SO	SB	CS	GDP	LOB	ShO	Slg.	OBP
Lexington	.275	140	5389	4799	781	1321	2163	297	43	153	706	18	35	90	447	19	1089	221	104	71	937	5	.451	.346
Greensboro	.253	140	5206	4625	637	1168	1811	216	38	117	574	30	59	57	435	20	1087	123	63	76	927	9	.392	.321
Asheville	.252	139	5176	4590	628	1157	1763	206	26	116	575	21	48	73	444	12	1152	183	83	78	951	5	.384	.325
Columbia	.251	135	5055	4473	615	1122	1643	211	47	72	549	46	38	74	424	9	1000	193	71	81	908	13	.367	.323
Columbus	.250	136	5095	4571	618	1143	1704	204	45	89	537	37	43	14	430	4	1127	149	73	70	982	9	.373	.314
Wilmington	.250	138	5072	4523	561	1130	1581	205	39	56	480	70	38	75	366	23	994	278	107	57	899	9	.350	.314
Hagerstown	.249	140	5274	4586	630	1143	1673	239	21	83	544	81	39	64	504	15	1091	137	67	104	979	5	.365	.329
Hickory	.247	140	5042	4585	570	1133	1664	183	36	92	505	50	36	8	363	11	1032	211	76	84	914	10	.363	.301
Macon	.246	133	5088	4479	614	1102	1670	198	23	108	557	38	28	77	466	22	1008	176	79	61	946	11	.373	.326
Kannapolis	.245	139	4891	4352	556	1067	1507	159	37	69	473	39	39	86	375	12	1003	181	99	84	815	12	.346	.315
Delmarva	.241	140	5107	4555	563	1090	1520	175	39	97	498	69	40	85	454	24	982	92	37	95	1004	10	.335	.319
Augusta	.238	139	5129	4530	556	1080	1531	196	21	71	486	44	37	90	428	16	1084	147	64	84	945	10	.338	.314
Lakewood	.236	139	5181	4669	508	1101	1576	240	26	61	449	36	33	72	371	16	1099	123	83	89	933	16	.338	.308
Savannah	.236	138	5005	4470	524	1053	1555	190	42	76	458	37	31	68	399	10	1146	149	84	81	899	10	.348	.306
Char'ton, W.Va.	.232	138	4949	4423	519	1028	1463	199	28	60	461	40	38	43	405	16	1052	131	77	83	835	14	.331	.301
Char'ton, S.C.	.225	140	5112	4584	530	1031	1538	198	36	79	473	46	40	78	364	20	1276	144	94	77	858	13	.336	.291

INDIVIDUAL

TOP QUALIFIERS FOR BATTING CHAMPIONSHIP

Minimum 378 plate appearances. *Lefthanded batter. †Switch-hitter.

Player, Team	Avg.	G	TPA	AB	R	H	TB	2B	3B	HR	RBI	SH	SF	HP	BB	IBB	SO	SB	CS	GDP	Slg.	OBP
Reyes, Rene, Ash.†	.322	128	528	484	71	156	220	27	2	11	61	0	4	12	28	2	80	53	12	9	.455	.371
Whiteman, Tom, Lex.	.319	114	438	389	58	124	220	26	8	18	57	4	4	7	34	1	106	17	13	4	.566	.380
Kinchen, Jason, Gre.*	.309	134	553	489	81	151	267	24	1	30	82	0	5	9	50	6	102	2	0	5	.546	.380
Botts, Jason, Sav.†	.309	114	466	392	63	121	176	24	2	9	50	0	1	20	53	4	88	13	7	10	.449	.416
Reyes, Jose, C'bia†	.307	108	435	407	71	125	192	22	15	5	48	5	3	2	18	0	71	30	10	4	.472	.337
Hill, Mike, Lex.	.305	119	528	465	82	142	221	31	6	12	65	0	4	11	48	3	102	27	9	12	.475	.381
Hill, Koyie, Wil.†	.301	134	562	498	65	150	198	20	2	8	79	2	6	7	49	14	82	21	12	7	.398	.368
Coleman, Alph, Mac.	.300	120	514	476	84	143	196	18	7	7	57	3	3	8	24	3	73	38	13	9	.412	.342
Ravelo, Manny, Hick.	.299	93	403	365	57	109	138	12	7	1	20	3	1	6	28	0	64	54	17	2	.378	.350
Grove, Jason, Gre.*	.296	115	494	446	68	132	214	21	8	15	68	1	5	6	36	2	108	0	2	10	.480	.353
Cates, Gary, Del.	.292	101	389	342	44	100	126	14	3	2	33	17	3	10	17	1	30	16	8	8	.368	.341
Ellison, Jason, Hag.	.291	130	593	494	95	144	212	38	3	8	55	13	5	10	71	3	68	19	15	6	.429	.388
Santos, Deivis, Hag.*	.290	131	554	520	64	151	220	27	3	12	80	0	5	4	25	6	91	16	10	15	.423	.325
De Caster, Yurendell, Hick.	.290	97	389	341	56	99	181	17	4	19	74	0	5	8	35	2	83	4	4	8	.531	.365
Escalona, Felix, Lex.	.289	130	592	536	92	155	249	42	2	16	64	5	5	16	30	2	85	46	12	8	.465	.342
Johnson, Kelly, Mac.*	.289	124	498	415	75	120	213	22	1	23	66	1	1	10	71	7	111	25	6	9	.513	.404

DEPARTMENTAL LEADERS: G—Richardson, 137; AB—Iopolski, 550; R—Topolski, 98; H—Topolski, 158; TB—Topolski, 271; 2B—Escalona, 42; 3B—Littleton, 18; HR—Kinchen, 30; RBI—Topolski, 96; SH—Gann, 20; SF—Rios, 14; HP—Sherrill, 27; BB—Topolski, 75; IBB—K. Hill, 14; SO—Schuda, 166; SB—B. Castro, 67; CS—Yan, 21; GIDP—Leon, 18; Slg.—Whiteman, .566; OBP—Botts, .416.

ALL PLAYERS

*Lefthanded batter. †Switch-hitter.

Player, Team	Avg.	G	TPA	AB	R	H	TB	2B	3B	HR	RBI	SH	SF	HP	BB	IBB	SO	SB	CS	GDP	Slg.	OBP
Abercrombie, Reggie, Wil.	.226	125	531	486	63	110	163	17	3	10	41	12	2	12	19	1	154	44	11	3	.335	.272
Abreu, Dave, C'bia†	.169	16	70	59	10	10	16	3	0	1	4	1	0	1	9	0	15	5	1	0	.271	.290
Acevedo, Carlos, Lak.	.252	109	447	409	33	103	133	18	3	2	47	3	4	3	28	1	74	10	10	8	.325	.302
Acevedo, Inocencio, Sav.	.232	109	434	302	52	91	123	14	6	2	20	11	2	6	23	1	79	34	11	3	.314	.284
Acuna, Ron, C'bia	.285	96	409	376	63	107	148	17	3	6	62	2	3	9	19	1	67	23	8	10	.394	.332
Agramonte, Marcos, Sav.†	.183	72	261	252	20	46	67	8	2	3	19	3	2	1	3	0	62	8	8	5	.266	.194
Alexander, Kevin, Hag.	.229	83	304	266	25	61	83	14	1	2	30	10	1	2	25	0	58	5	1	10	.312	.299
Aliendo, Humberto, Hick.	.130	19	74	69	3	9	10	1	0	0	5	0	1	2	2	0	21	1	0	1	.145	.176
Amador, Chris, Kan.	.196	102	356	322	42	63	92	8	3	3	28	8	2	8	15	2	127	29	12	1	.286	.248
Anderson, Jon, Aug.†	.211	47	139	128	12	27	29	2	0	0	6	1	1	1	8	0	30	5	4	0	.227	.261
Anderson, Melvin, Lak.	.103	21	48	39	8	4	5	1	0	0	1	2	1	2	4	0	17	1	1	0	.128	.217
Arias, Leandro, C'bia	.177	15	65	62	7	11	14	3	0	0	2	0	0	1	0	0	16	3	2	2	.226	.190
Asadoorian, Rick, Aug.	.212	116	460	406	50	86	129	13	6	6	40	2	1	4	47	2	139	13	4	6	.318	.299
Ascencion, Quincy, Del.	.211	48	171	152	11	32	42	3	2	1	13	2	1	4	12	0	38	5	1	1	.276	.284
Athas, Jamie, Hag.*	.274	65	276	234	44	64	86	10	3	2	20	6	0	5	31	0	55	17	5	3	.368	.370
Auterson, Jeff, Ash.	.206	28	106	97	9	20	32	4	1	2	9	0	0	2	7	0	32	4	1	1	.330	.274
Avila, Rob, Lak.	.272	91	345	305	31	83	106	21	1	0	32	2	1	8	24	1	50	1	3	9	.348	.340
Aybar, Willy, Wil.†	.237	120	485	431	45	102	143	25	2	4	48	3	5	3	43	3	64	7	9	4	.332	.307
Baker, Casey, Gre.-C'bus	.077	12	31	26	2	2	2	0	0	0	1	0	2	2	0	0	8	3	2	0	.077	.200
Baldelli, Rocco, C.S.C.	.249	113	451	406	58	101	160	23	6	8	55	5	6	11	23	0	89	25	9	7	.394	.334
Barmes, Clint, Ash.	.260	74	316	285	40	74	105	14	1	5	24	3	3	7	17	0	37	21	7	6	.368	.314
Barnette, Jason, Lak.*	.236	126	486	449	54	106	134	18	5	0	25	7	0	6	24	0	130	30	10	4	.298	.284
Barnowski, Bryan, Aug.	.189	42	163	143	17	27	42	6	0	3	15	0	1	6	13	0	50	0	1	2	.294	.282
Bass, Chris, Hick.	.247	106	388	352	34	87	116	18	1	3	34	3	5	6	22	0	80	6	3	10	.330	.299
Becker, Jeff, C'bus	.257	65	261	206	33	53	68	10	1	1	19	2	3	16	34	0	38	2	2	2	.330	.398
Bell, Derek, Hag.†	.252	111	454	381	50	96	136	30	2	2	49	3	6	2	62	2	76	1	3	8	.357	.355
Bernard, Dagoberto, Ash.	.275	38	112	109	9	30	37	7	0	0	11	1	0	1	0	0	24	3	7	4	.339	.288
Bernard, Miguel, Mac.	.189	47	173	159	19	30	40	1	0	3	17	1	3	2	8	1	41	5	2	6	.252	.233
Blanco, Tony, Aug.	.265	96	396	370	44	98	176	23	2	17	69	0	2	7	17	2	78	1	0	17	.476	.308
Bonifay, Josh, Hick.	.323	17	71	65	10	21	31	4	0	2	10	0	0	1	5	0	15	2	3	2	.477	.380

CLASS A   South Atlantic League

Player, Team	Avg.	G	TPA	AB	R	H	TB	2B	3B	HR	RBI	SH	SF	HP	BB	IBB	SO	SB	CS	GDP	Slg.	OBP
Bonner, Adam, C.S.C.*	.217	116	442	364	48	79	117	27	1	3	29	5	0	10	63	6	115	21	6	2	.321	.348
Bordick, Mike, Del.	.000	3	10	8	0	0	0	0	0	0	1	0	0	0	2	0	1	0	0	0	.000	.200
Boscan, Jean, Mac.	.282	35	142	124	16	35	54	7	0	4	22	2	1	1	14	0	27	2	0	1	.435	.357
Botts, Jason, Sav.†	.309	114	466	392	63	121	176	24	2	9	50	0	1	20	53	4	88	13	7	10	.449	.416
Bozanich, Sam, Gre.	.270	65	229	204	30	55	80	12	2	3	17	3	3	1	18	1	51	5	5	1	.392	.327
Brazell, Craig, C'bia*	.308	83	356	331	51	102	194	25	5	19	72	0	5	5	15	3	74	0	3	3	.586	.343
Brazoban, Yhency, Gre.	.273	124	504	469	51	128	175	23	3	6	52	2	5	9	19	4	98	6	3	12	.373	.311
Brewer, Jace, C.S.C.	.217	108	445	414	50	90	119	12	4	3	35	5	5	3	18	1	74	6	6	7	.287	.252
Brisson, Dustin, Aug.*	.295	90	369	319	49	94	139	13	1	10	53	1	4	4	40	7	76	3	0	0	.436	.376
Bryan, Jason, Sav.	.125	26	87	72	5	9	10	1	0	0	8	0	1	1	13	0	28	1	1	3	.139	.264
Buck, John, Lex.	.275	122	498	443	72	122	214	24	1	22	73	2	4	12	37	0	84	4	9	8	.483	.345
Burke, Erick, Sav.*	.000	34	1	0	0	0	0	0	0	0	0	1	0	0	0	0	0	0	0	0	.000	.000
Burrows, Angelo, Mac.*	.256	117	462	426	52	109	140	15	2	4	36	4	2	2	28	0	61	31	15	2	.329	.303
Bush, Brian, Lak.	.181	20	89	83	10	15	22	2	1	1	3	2	0	1	3	0	15	2	2	2	.265	.218
Buttler, Victor, Hick.*	.244	92	324	299	38	73	93	10	2	1	23	7	0	3	15	1	49	11	3	3	.311	.287
Cabrera, Leonel, Hag.	.300	10	32	30	8	9	10	1	0	0	1	1	0	0	1	0	7	3	3	0	.333	.323
Calabrese, Tony, Gre.	.291	43	159	134	25	39	64	8	1	5	20	1	2	0	22	0	29	1	1	3	.478	.386
Calahan, Larry, Kan.*	.154	6	14	13	1	2	2	0	0	0	2	0	0	0	1	0	2	0	0	1	.154	.214
Canales, Josh, Wil.	.227	52	190	163	14	37	44	2	1	1	12	10	1	2	14	0	28	10	5	2	.270	.294
Carroll, Wes, Lak.	.346	36	144	130	17	45	56	8	0	1	11	1	1	2	11	1	24	3	3	1	.431	.399
Carter, Bryan, Hag.*	.183	56	222	197	18	36	53	7	2	2	14	3	3	4	15	1	63	11	3	3	.269	.251
Castaneda, Jose, C'bia	.164	38	134	116	8	19	24	2	0	1	8	0	1	3	14	0	39	0	0	2	.207	.269
Castillo, Carlos, C'bia†	.242	83	344	310	42	75	101	8	3	4	30	10	2	1	21	2	63	9	4	4	.326	.290
Castro, Bernabel, Gre.†	.260	101	451	389	71	101	133	15	7	1	36	5	2	1	54	1	67	67	20	5	.342	.350
Castro, Julio, Kan.	.167	43	8	6	1	1	1	0	0	0	0	0	0	0	0	0	2	0	0	0	.167	.375
Castro, Vince, Hick.	.215	55	182	172	16	37	50	6	2	1	20	1	0	2	7	1	47	6	2	4	.291	.254
Cates, Gary, Del.	.292	101	389	342	44	100	126	14	3	2	33	17	3	10	17	1	30	16	8	8	.368	.318
Centeno, Irwin, C.S.C.	.231	102	432	372	61	86	103	8	3	1	22	6	1	12	41	1	91	48	12	5	.277	.326
Cerda, Jose, Hag.	.242	13	42	33	4	8	8	0	0	0	2	0	1	2	6	0	7	0	0	0	.242	.381
Chaves, Brandon, Hick.†	.199	110	403	356	29	71	97	12	4	2	32	4	5	10	28	0	89	8	4	11	.272	.273
Chavez, Angel, Hag.	.189	13	39	37	5	7	15	2	0	2	3	0	0	1	1	0	12	1	0	0	.405	.231
Choy Foo, Rodney, C'bus†	.250	12	45	40	2	10	10	0	0	0	5	0	1	0	4	0	9	1	0	2	.250	.311
Church, Ryan, C'bus*	.287	101	426	363	64	104	184	23	3	17	76	0	3	6	54	0	79	4	6	6	.507	.385
Ciarrachi, Kevin, Hick.	.000	2	8	7	1	0	0	0	0	0	0	0	0	0	1	0	3	0	0	1	.000	.125
Ciofrone, Paul, Lak.*	.000	7	14	12	0	0	0	0	0	0	0	0	0	0	2	0	5	0	0	0	.000	.143
Ciraco, Darren, Kan.	.253	111	423	388	43	98	142	15	7	5	52	1	6	3	25	1	92	14	11	11	.366	.299
Coleman, Alph, Mac.	.300	120	514	476	84	143	196	18	7	7	57	3	3	8	24	3	73	38	13	9	.412	.342
Coleman, Andy, Gre.	.125	3	8	8	0	1	1	0	0	0	0	0	0	0	0	0	4	0	0	0	.125	.125
Collazo, Julio, Lak.	.203	44	143	128	12	26	30	4	0	0	5	2	1	2	10	1	33	2	3	3	.234	.270
Colmenter, Jesus, C'bus†	.279	39	145	136	12	38	41	1	1	0	8	0	2	2	4	0	26	1	2	4	.301	.306
Conway, Dan, Ash.	.227	86	318	273	31	62	91	12	1	5	27	2	1	3	38	1	82	2	1	4	.333	.327
Cooper, Matt, Aug.	.177	37	147	124	9	22	35	4	0	3	12	0	2	7	14	0	46	1	1	3	.282	.293
Cordell, Brent, C.S.C.†	.143	2	9	7	2	1	1	0	0	0	1	0	0	0	2	0	2	0	0	0	.143	.333
Corporan, Elvis, Gre.*	.225	135	527	484	65	109	191	25	6	15	53	1	4	3	35	2	124	15	8	8	.395	.279
Cosby, Rob, C.W.Va.	.228	120	451	412	48	94	133	22	1	5	43	3	2	2	32	2	60	6	4	5	.323	.286
Cotten, Jeremy, Hick.	.253	125	502	443	58	112	211	20	2	25	78	0	2	15	42	1	132	12	5	9	.476	.337
Crespo, Manny, C.W.Va.	.220	61	224	186	21	41	59	9	0	3	12	7	1	3	27	2	45	0	2	2	.317	.327
Cronin, Shane, Gre.	.251	58	207	191	23	48	66	6	0	4	25	1	5	3	7	0	32	1	0	2	.346	.282
Crozier, Eric, C'bus*	.235	67	262	221	41	52	77	9	2	4	19	2	1	1	37	1	84	5	3	3	.348	.346
Cruz, Edgar, C'bus	.205	33	125	112	11	23	41	6	0	4	10	0	0	3	10	0	28	2	2	5	.366	.288
Cruz, Enrique, C'bia	.251	124	509	438	60	110	161	20	2	9	59	3	3	6	59	0	106	33	7	7	.368	.346
Cruz, Orlando, Sav.	.184	34	122	114	3	21	24	0	0	1	6	2	1	2	3	0	31	1	4	0	.211	.217
Cuello, Domingo, Hick.	.220	18	66	59	6	13	15	0	1	0	2	4	1	0	2	0	11	6	1	1	.254	.242
Dacey, Ryan, Wil.	.253	66	239	198	22	50	61	8	0	1	24	2	1	5	32	0	45	10	7	1	.308	.367
Dancy, Cliff, Lak.	.111	7	19	18	0	2	2	0	0	0	0	0	0	0	1	0	7	0	0	1	.111	.158
Daniel, Steve, Kan.	.194	57	210	180	25	35	49	5	3	1	13	0	1	5	23	0	39	4	3	3	.272	.301
Davenport, Ron, C.W.Va.*	.289	79	326	298	37	86	120	18	2	4	54	0	7	1	20	1	53	11	5	3	.403	.328
De Caster, Yurendell, Hick.	.290	97	389	341	56	99	181	17	4	19	74	0	5	8	35	2	83	4	4	8	.531	.365
Dees, Charlie, Sav.	.250	41	155	140	16	35	60	6	2	5	19	0	2	0	13	0	52	1	3	1	.429	.310
De La Cruz, Miguel, Hick.	.222	12	43	36	3	8	9	1	0	0	1	0	0	3	4	0	12	0	1	1	.250	.349
Delfino, Lee, C.W.Va.	.267	41	162	146	16	39	53	10	2	0	13	0	0	4	12	1	29	2	1	5	.363	.340
Delgado, Dario, Lak.	.192	84	303	281	19	54	76	11	1	3	27	2	1	8	11	1	53	0	0	8	.270	.243
Delgado, Mario, Lak.*	.268	60	242	224	27	60	102	11	2	9	36	0	3	3	12	3	58	3	2	4	.455	.310
Del Rosario, Manny, Del.†	.224	106	368	313	44	70	86	9	2	1	24	11	2	7	35	0	38	16	1	5	.275	.314
Dement, Dan, C.N.C.	.269	108	435	394	52	106	176	24	11	8	54	5	2	3	31	2	108	6	14	7	.447	.326
Deschenes, Pat, C'bia*	.272	53	222	195	26	53	65	10	1	0	36	0	2	0	24	0	33	2	2	3	.333	.348
Detienne, Dave, Wil.	.264	83	302	280	36	74	93	10	3	1	13	4	0	4	14	2	63	25	4	5	.332	.309
Devarez, Noel, C'bia	.156	9	36	32	4	5	10	2	0	1	3	0	0	1	3	0	12	0	0	0	.313	.250
Diaz, Jose, Wil.	.175	23	86	80	7	14	24	4	0	2	5	2	0	0	4	0	31	1	0	1	.300	.214
Dill, Jason, Sav.*	.121	43	154	132	8	16	23	4	0	1	7	0	0	0	22	0	35	1	0	3	.174	.247
Donato, Greg, Mac.	.250	3	14	12	1	3	3	0	0	0	1	0	0	0	2	0	1	0	0	0	.250	.357
Dorta, Melvin, Aug.	.267	36	148	135	19	36	42	4	1	0	18	1	1	3	8	0	16	6	5	2	.311	.320
Doumit, Ryan, Hick.†	.270	39	162	148	14	40	52	6	0	2	14	0	0	4	10	0	32	2	1	2	.351	.333
Duncan, Jeff, C'bia*	.217	88	373	318	49	69	110	16	8	3	23	4	2	3	46	0	97	41	3	2	.346	.320
Elder, Rick, Del.*	.251	112	449	382	66	96	174	20	5	16	64	0	2	2	63	10	130	7	1	4	.455	.359
Ellison, Jason, Hag.	.291	130	593	494	95	144	212	38	3	8	55	13	5	10	71	3	68	19	15	6	.429	.388
Encarnacion, Edwin, Sav.	.306	45	187	170	23	52	77	9	2	4	25	1	2	2	12	0	34	3	3	5	.453	.355
Escalera, Jose, Wil.	.147	9	35	34	4	5	5	0	0	0	5	0	1	0	0	0	7	0	0	1	.147	.143
Escalona, Felix, Lex.	.289	130	592	536	92	155	249	42	2	16	64	5	5	16	30	2	85	46	12	8	.465	.342
Espinoza, Efren, Hick.	.222	50	175	162	18	36	60	9	0	5	21	2	1	5	9	0	49	2	0	1	.370	.266
Esposito, Brian, Aug.	.190	90	333	311	21	59	81	13	0	3	30	2	5	2	13	0	81	0	0	5	.260	.234
Esquivel, Lale, Sav.	.237	51	193	177	13	42	67	10	0	5	20	0	3	2	11	0	43	0	1	5	.379	.285
Evans, Austin, Sav.*	.197	51	162	147	18	29	34	5	0	0	5	2	0	1	12	0	27	5	2	0	.231	.263

Player, Team	Avg.	G	TPA	AB	R	H	TB	2B	3B	HR	RBI	SH	SF	HP	BB	IBB	SO	SB	CS	GDP	Slg.	OBP
Fajardo, Al, Hag.	.162	12	49	37	4	6	6	0	0	0	3	1	0	1	10	0	14	3	0	0	.162	.354
Fatheree, Danny, Lex.	.230	21	69	61	8	14	20	3	0	1	9	0	0	1	7	0	13	0	0	1	.328	.319
Fennell, Jason, Kan.†	.136	10	25	22	1	3	3	0	0	0	0	0	0	0	3	0	2	0	0	1	.136	.240
Figueroa, Carlos, Ash.*	.250	12	45	40	6	10	12	2	0	0	5	1	0	0	4	0	8	4	1	0	.300	.318
Flannigan, Tim, C'bia	.208	15	59	53	3	11	12	1	0	0	3	1	0	2	3	0	10	2	1	2	.226	.276
Flores, Ralphs, Kan.	.285	61	207	186	18	53	63	7	0	1	19	2	3	3	13	0	39	3	3	6	.339	.337
Forbes, Mike, Mac.*	.257	117	458	378	53	97	150	23	0	10	64	2	3	3	72	2	106	10	8	4	.397	.377
Foster, Gregg, Lak.	.224	87	313	281	37	63	96	11	2	6	23	0	2	9	21	0	74	17	5	3	.342	.297
Fowler, David, Gre.	.199	110	329	291	30	58	94	15	3	5	26	4	2	5	27	0	125	8	12	6	.323	.277
Francisco, Ruben, Del.*	.214	39	111	103	14	22	34	4	4	0	13	2	0	0	6	0	17	1	3	2	.330	.257
Franco, Iker, C.S.C.	.200	87	292	265	15	53	76	10	2	3	21	4	3	1	19	0	81	1	2	7	.287	.253
Fuentes, Omar, Gre.	.266	100	405	342	59	91	141	24	1	8	62	2	7	9	45	2	57	0	2	9	.412	.360
Gajewski, Matt, Sav.†	.238	30	96	84	7	20	28	2	0	2	8	0	1	1	10	0	30	0	2	0	.333	.323
Gambino, Mike, Aug.	.077	7	28	26	2	2	3	1	0	0	0	0	0	0	2	0	4	0	1	0	.115	.143
Gann, Bryan, Hag.	.237	111	458	397	49	94	110	16	0	0	26	20	6	7	28	0	50	2	3	10	.277	.295
Garcia, Daniel, C'bia	.301	30	131	103	25	31	51	12	1	2	16	4	3	6	15	0	18	7	3	0	.495	.409
Garcia, Nick, Del.	.262	130	491	442	42	116	138	14	1	2	42	15	5	9	20	0	59	2	3	10	.312	.305
Garcia, Oscar, C'bus	.106	16	54	47	3	5	6	1	0	0	0	0	0	2	5	0	15	0	2	0	.128	.222
Garrido, Tomas, Hag.	.218	45	150	142	13	31	34	3	0	0	7	5	0	1	2	0	34	2	1	3	.239	.234
Gatti, William Jr., Wil.	.217	6	26	23	3	5	9	1	0	1	3	0	1	1	1	0	10	1	0	2	.391	.269
German, Ramon, Lex.†	.265	129	529	461	72	122	204	37	3	13	93	0	4	9	55	1	107	21	9	8	.443	.352
Gillikin, Joe, Kan.	.240	77	250	221	27	53	92	11	2	8	35	1	4	6	18	0	74	3	7	3	.416	.309
Goodwin, Tom, Wil.*	.400	2	7	5	2	2	4	0	1	0	1	0	1	0	1	0	0	0	0	0	.800	.429
Green, Kevin, Mac.	.147	17	40	34	5	5	10	2	0	1	3	0	1	2	3	0	18	0	0	1	.294	.250
Gretz, Nicholas, Ash.*	.556	3	9	9	1	5	5	0	0	0	3	0	0	0	0	0	1	0	0	0	.556	.556
Griggs, Reggie, Lak.*	.245	13	52	49	3	12	18	3	0	1	4	0	1	1	1	0	22	0	0	0	.367	.269
Grove, Jason, Gre.*	.296	115	494	446	68	132	214	21	8	15	68	1	5	6	36	2	108	0	2	10	.480	.353
Guerrero, Julio, Aug.	.197	94	341	314	27	62	76	9	1	1	25	3	2	1	21	0	56	14	6	7	.242	.249
Gutierrez, Said, C.W.Va.	.071	11	30	28	0	2	2	0	0	0	0	0	0	0	2	0	5	0	0	1	.071	.133
Haase, Jeff, C'bus	.237	41	157	135	15	32	44	9	0	1	12	1	2	6	13	0	26	2	5	3	.326	.327
Hamilton, Josh, C.S.C.*	.364	4	13	11	3	4	8	1	0	1	2	0	0	0	2	0	3	0	0	0	.727	.462
Harper, Brett, C'bia*	.182	10	36	33	1	6	7	1	0	0	4	0	0	0	3	0	14	0	0	0	.212	.250
Harris, Cory, C'bia	.258	102	424	357	52	92	141	23	1	8	49	3	6	15	43	0	57	13	9	8	.395	.356
Hattig, John, Aug.†	.285	50	205	179	25	51	65	9	1	1	23	0	1	3	22	1	42	4	1	3	.363	.371
Hawpe, Brad, Ash.*	.267	111	468	393	78	105	199	22	3	22	72	0	10	6	59	3	113	7	4	8	.506	.363
Heard, Scott, Sav.*	.228	77	304	268	25	61	91	13	1	5	36	2	2	2	30	0	71	1	2	4	.340	.308
Hensler, Brad, C'bia	.194	23	80	72	11	14	20	3	0	1	3	0	0	4	4	0	24	1	0	2	.278	.275
Hensley, Anthony, Lak.†	.220	64	264	214	38	47	71	10	4	2	13	1	1	2	46	1	57	19	12	3	.332	.361
Hernandez, Jose, Hick.	.161	53	182	161	19	26	33	4	0	1	13	2	2	5	12	0	35	3	0	7	.205	.239
Hernandez, Vladimir, C'bia	.143	5	23	21	2	3	4	1	0	0	1	1	0	0	1	0	2	1	0	0	.190	.102
Hewes, Robert, Sav.	.283	27	108	92	14	26	34	4	2	0	8	0	1	5	10	0	18	0	2	3	.370	.380
Hickman, Brian, Kan.	.263	7	25	19	1	5	5	0	0	0	2	1	0	1	4	0	4	0	0	0	.263	.417
Hill, Koyie, Wil.†	.301	134	562	498	65	150	198	20	2	8	79	2	6	7	49	14	82	21	12	7	.398	.368
Hill, Mike, Lex.	.305	119	528	465	82	142	221	31	6	12	65	0	4	11	48	3	102	27	9	12	.475	.381
Inglett, Joe, C'bus*	.300	62	263	237	34	71	90	9	2	2	33	0	2	0	24	0	22	5	3	7	.380	.361
Ison, Jeremy, Kan.	.154	21	59	52	7	8	12	1	0	1	2	1	0	0	6	0	21	0	0	2	.231	.241
Jackson, Brandon, Gre.	.250	5	23	20	3	5	5	0	0	0	2	0	1	0	2	1	5	2	0	0	.250	.304
Jacobs, John, C.S.C.	.187	79	225	198	18	37	49	5	2	1	11	5	3	4	15	0	69	6	2	1	.247	.255
Jacobs, Mike, C'bia*	.278	46	196	180	18	50	69	13	0	2	26	1	1	1	13	0	46	0	1	4	.383	.328
Janowicz, Nate, C'bus*	.294	51	215	201	29	59	85	10	5	2	26	2	2	1	9	0	38	4	1	5	.423	.324
Jeffcoat, Bryon, Mac.	.222	26	103	90	11	20	33	5	1	2	7	0	1	2	10	0	28	3	2	1	.367	.311
Jimenez, Rich, C.W.Va.†	.184	26	86	76	14	14	15	1	0	0	4	0	1	1	8	0	18	11	2	0	.197	.267
Johnson, Kelly, Mac.*	.289	124	498	415	75	120	213	22	1	23	66	1	1	10	71	7	111	25	6	0	.513	.404
Johnston, Ryan, Lak.	.167	4	7	6	1	1	2	1	0	0	0	0	0	0	1	0	2	0	0	0	.333	.286
Jova, Maikel, C.W.Va.	.173	46	165	162	12	28	43	6	0	3	14	1	1	0	1	0	33	1	1	4	.265	.177
Joyce, Jesse, Lex.	.113	18	70	53	12	6	13	1	0	2	4	0	0	2	15	0	16	3	1	1	.245	.329
Katz, Damon, C'bus	.119	14	46	42	3	5	8	0	0	1	3	0	0	3	1	0	9	1	0	4	.190	.196
Kaup, Nathan, C.S.C.	.267	4	16	15	0	4	6	2	0	0	2	0	1	0	0	0	3	0	0	2	.400	.250
Keono, Kurt, C.W.Va.	.172	16	58	58	7	10	15	2	0	1	4	0	0	0	0	0	10	0	0	2	.259	.172
Kessick, Jon, Del.	.278	34	135	115	14	32	56	9	0	5	21	1	2	2	15	1	40	0	2	0	.487	.366
Keylor, Cory, Del.*	.230	56	215	191	28	44	72	13	0	5	19	0	0	5	19	1	64	4	2	1	.377	.316
Kinchen, Jason, Gre.*	.309	134	553	489	81	151	267	24	1	30	82	0	5	9	50	6	102	2	0	5	.546	.380
Koonce, Chuck, Sav.†	.215	71	277	247	31	53	66	5	1	2	11	5	2	0	23	0	66	8	4	2	.267	.279
Lackaff, John, Kan.	.246	127	511	451	68	111	171	21	3	11	65	1	9	15	33	0	75	24	11	7	.379	.313
Langs, Ronte, Wil.	.269	105	437	376	49	101	134	14	8	1	29	9	2	7	43	2	88	18	7	5	.356	.353
Lankford, Derrick, Lak.*	.257	49	211	171	17	44	70	14	0	4	21	0	2	4	34	1	49	2	1	1	.409	.389
Lawson, Forrest, C'bia	.157	23	80	70	4	11	12	1	0	0	6	3	0	1	6	0	25	2	1	2	.171	.234
Lawson, Jarrod, Lak.	.000	25	0	0	1	0	0	0	0	0	0	0	0	0	0	0	0	0	0	0	.000	.000
Leaumont, Jeff, Gre.*	.245	27	104	94	9	23	28	5	0	0	5	0	2	0	8	0	25	0	1	2	.298	.298
Lebron, Francisco, Kan.	.286	35	130	112	13	32	55	8	0	5	14	0	2	0	16	0	31	0	1	1	.491	.369
Lentini, Fehlandt, Lex.	.295	29	134	122	27	36	54	11	2	1	21	0	1	1	10	0	16	10	4	2	.443	.351
Leon, Alfredo, Del.	.239	90	342	318	26	76	88	12	0	0	41	2	0	8	14	2	48	3	0	18	.277	.288
Lincoln, Justin, Ash.	.274	62	247	226	37	62	112	12	4	10	41	1	2	1	17	0	84	2	2	4	.496	.325
Littleton, Brandon, Del.†	.252	133	593	508	84	128	184	11	18	3	45	9	5	10	61	2	108	17	9	5	.362	.341
Lockhart, Paul, Lex.†	.247	99	360	320	48	79	122	17	4	6	40	3	3	5	29	0	73	3	2	5	.381	.317
Lopez, Raul, Mac.*	.207	45	161	150	14	31	54	9	1	4	25	2	1	0	8	1	26	0	1	2	.360	.245
Lucas, Matt, Lex.	.269	29	68	67	9	18	35	8	0	3	8	0	0	1	0	0	18	0	1	1	.522	.279
Luna, Hector, C'bus	.266	66	274	241	36	64	87	8	3	3	23	3	2	5	23	0	48	15	4	2	.361	.339
Lunsford, James, Hag.	.237	114	454	396	53	94	128	19	0	5	50	4	4	5	45	1	89	10	5	12	.323	.320
Machado, Aleyandro, Mac.	.271	82	358	306	43	83	98	6	3	1	24	5	0	13	34	1	56	20	13	1	.320	.368
Malpica, Martin, C.W.Va.	.183	15	62	60	4	11	12	1	0	0	6	1	0	0	1	0	14	0	0	0	.200	.197
Manley, Adam, Del.*	.152	23	74	66	1	10	18	3	1	1	9	0	0	1	7	0	26	1	1	1	.273	.243
Manning, Pat, Mac.	.284	62	263	211	40	60	114	13	1	13	29	5	4	6	37	0	46	6	2	5	.540	.399

Player, Team	Avg.	G	TPA	AB	R	H	TB	2B	3B	HR	RBI	SH	SF	HP	BB	IBB	SO	SB	CS	GDP	Slg.	OBP
Mapes, Jake, Hag.	.000	2	6	6	0	0	0	0	0	0	0	0	0	0	0	0	2	0	0	0	.000	.000
Marsh, Jason, C.S.C.	.245	66	227	216	24	53	74	9	0	4	24	2	1	4	4	1	41	3	2	4	.343	.271
Martel, Normand, Kan.*	.281	71	155	135	15	38	47	2	2	1	7	0	0	2	18	1	29	7	3	2	.348	.374
Martin, Brian, C.S.C.	.232	131	504	456	42	106	158	22	3	8	44	0	3	10	35	2	150	7	15	8	.346	.300
Martin, Tyler, Sav.†	.150	35	122	107	7	16	19	1	1	0	4	0	0	2	13	1	28	1	2	3	.178	.254
Martinez, Candido, Wil.	.260	120	485	443	69	115	171	27	4	7	66	1	6	6	29	0	138	54	18	3	.386	.310
Martinez, Casey, C.W.Va.	.145	27	86	83	7	12	17	2	0	1	4	0	0	1	2	0	23	1	0	1	.205	.174
Matos, Angel, Sav.	.200	26	71	65	6	13	15	2	0	0	4	1	0	1	4	0	27	0	0	0	.231	.257
Mayorson, Manuel, C.W.Va.	.000	1	2	2	0	0	0	0	0	0	0	0	0	0	0	0	1	0	0	0	.000	.000
McArthur, Kennon, Lak.†	.141	22	76	71	3	10	12	2	0	0	5	1	0	1	3	0	29	0	0	0	.169	.187
McKee, Mickey, Lex.	.269	73	264	238	35	64	103	16	4	5	35	0	2	3	21	1	61	4	3	5	.433	.333
McLouth, Nathan, Hick.*	.285	96	406	351	59	100	163	17	5	12	54	2	3	7	43	6	54	21	5	5	.464	.371
McNamara, Rusty, Lak.	.176	5	21	17	4	3	4	1	0	0	1	0	0	0	4	0	3	1	0	1	.235	.333
Mejia, Manuel, Hick.	.216	46	148	125	6	27	35	2	0	2	13	1	1	3	18	0	37	0	0	3	.280	.327
Mendoza, Deivi, Gro.	.215	49	195	172	25	37	49	6	0	2	15	5	2	2	14	0	35	5	2	4	.285	.279
Merritt, Graig, C.S.C.	.000	5	12	9	0	0	0	0	0	0	1	1	0	0	2	0	3	1	0	0	.000	.182
Michaelis, Derek, Wil.*	.197	33	130	117	10	23	29	4	1	0	17	1	3	3	6	0	36	6	0	4	.248	.248
Minges, Tyler, C'bus	.373	15	65	59	9	22	30	5	0	1	7	0	0	3	3	0	12	2	0	2	.508	.431
Money, Freddie, Aug.	.189	21	86	74	9	14	21	2	1	1	7	1	1	0	10	0	21	5	5	2	.284	.282
Mongeluzzo, Anthony, Sav.	.248	72	288	258	32	64	105	14	3	7	35	0	2	7	21	0	67	9	1	8	.407	.319
Monroy, Sam, C.S.C.*	.158	19	44	38	6	6	6	0	0	0	0	0	0	0	6	0	7	3	1	2	.158	.273
Mooney, Dan, Aug.	.239	27	97	88	11	21	38	8	0	3	14	0	1	6	2	0	23	1	0	3	.432	.299
Moore, Chris, Ash.*	.154	7	28	26	1	4	4	0	0	0	3	0	1	0	1	0	9	0	0	1	.154	.179
Morales, Michael, Mac.	.188	26	79	69	8	13	18	2	0	1	6	1	0	3	6	0	15	1	0	3	.261	.282
Morban, Jose, Sav.	.251	122	526	474	71	119	185	20	11	8	47	5	3	2	42	0	119	46	18	11	.390	.313
Moreno, Jorge, C'bus	.204	24	99	93	13	19	37	5	2	3	6	2	0	0	4	0	28	4	0	0	.398	.237
Morrow, Alvin, C.W.Va.	.250	54	209	172	22	43	71	8	1	6	23	0	0	1	36	0	73	0	4	4	.413	.383
Muth, Edmund, Ash.*	.261	117	462	398	53	104	185	21	3	18	70	3	4	10	44	2	105	13	3	6	.465	.346
Navarrete, Ray, Hick.	.268	92	391	354	53	95	152	23	2	10	49	3	5	8	21	0	70	9	4	4	.429	.320
Negron, Miguel, C.W.Va.*	.192	25	105	99	11	19	20	1	0	0	2	0	0	0	6	0	21	5	3	2	.202	.238
Nelson, Nathan, Lex.	.234	19	67	64	3	15	16	1	0	0	6	1	1	0	1	0	10	2	3	2	.250	.242
Nettles, Tim, Gre.	.364	3	11	11	0	4	4	0	0	0	1	0	0	0	0	0	3	0	0	0	.364	.364
Nicolas, Jose, Hick.	.206	31	114	102	13	21	39	7	1	3	10	0	1	2	9	0	41	3	0	0	.382	.281
Nieves, Raul, Aug.†	.246	114	437	390	49	96	112	13	0	1	37	11	4	6	26	1	75	12	2	12	.287	.300
Nix, Laynce, Sav.*	.278	104	452	407	50	113	179	26	8	8	59	1	5	2	37	2	94	9	6	7	.440	.337
Nunez, Felix, C.S.C.	.186	103	376	361	28	67	102	12	1	7	32	3	2	2	7	0	141	2	7	9	.283	.204
Ochoa, Javier, C'bus	.225	51	196	173	21	39	46	7	0	0	15	3	2	3	15	0	24	2	1	4	.266	.295
Oropeza, Asdrubal, Mac.	.207	109	408	362	37	75	117	18	0	8	40	3	1	4	38	0	105	4	5	4	.323	.289
Pack, Branden, Sav.†	.220	99	365	327	37	72	106	17	1	5	34	3	1	1	33	2	111	4	6	6	.324	.293
Pagan, Angel, C'bia†	.298	15	64	57	4	17	20	1	1	0	5	1	0	0	6	0	5	3	2	1	.351	.365
Peck, Bryan, Ash.	.271	72	271	214	48	58	86	13	0	5	26	0	4	6	47	0	51	7	2	6	.402	.410
Perez, Kenny, Aug.†	.248	120	463	407	44	101	144	21	2	6	37	3	2	3	48	0	62	11	6	9	.354	.330
Perich, Josh, C'bia	.242	89	324	297	32	72	110	11	3	7	38	2	0	2	23	0	78	6	2	13	.370	.301
Pichardo, Henry, C'bus	.241	84	347	299	49	72	134	12	1	16	44	2	3	7	36	0	67	11	6	4	.448	.333
Pierce, Sean, Wil.	.250	3	12	12	0	3	3	0	0	0	0	0	0	0	0	0	2	1	1	0	.250	.250
Powers, Jeff, Ash.*	.236	19	75	72	11	17	26	3	0	2	6	0	0	0	2	0	11	0	0	2	.361	.257
Quintero, Humberto, Kan.	.269	60	220	197	32	53	65	7	1	1	20	8	0	7	8	1	20	7	3	5	.330	.321
Quiroz, Guillermo, C.W.Va.	.199	82	303	261	25	52	85	12	0	7	25	7	0	6	29	0	67	5	1	5	.326	.294
Raffo, John, C'bia*	.167	17	69	60	6	10	14	1	0	1	4	0	1	0	8	0	17	1	1	2	.233	.261
Ramistella, John, Gre.	.286	2	7	7	0	2	2	0	0	0	0	0	0	0	0	0	5	0	0	0	.286	.286
Ravelo, Manny, Hick.	.299	93	403	365	57	109	138	12	7	1	20	3	1	6	28	0	64	54	17	2	.378	.358
Repko, Jason, Wil.	.220	88	364	337	36	74	111	17	4	4	32	6	3	3	15	0	68	17	8	2	.329	.257
Requena, Alex, C'bus†	.255	33	150	137	22	35	47	6	0	2	13	3	0	1	9	0	40	15	7	0	.343	.306
Reyes, Ambiorix, Lak.	.285	72	288	267	30	76	85	7	1	0	16	6	1	1	13	1	33	13	8	9	.318	.319
Reyes, Guillermo, Kan.†	.279	71	313	280	49	78	96	8	5	0	26	2	2	2	27	1	30	29	8	3	.343	.344
Reyes, Ivan, Gre.	.247	51	194	170	17	42	74	9	1	7	23	1	2	1	20	0	58	3	2	0	.435	.326
Reyes, Jose, C'bia†	.307	108	435	407	71	125	192	22	15	5	48	5	3	2	18	0	71	30	10	4	.472	.337
Reyes, Rene, Ash.†	.322	128	528	484	71	156	220	27	2	11	61	0	4	12	28	2	80	53	12	9	.455	.371
Rich, Dominic, C.W.Va.*	.278	91	391	327	67	91	121	16	1	4	32	4	3	10	47	1	54	20	8	3	.370	.382
Richardson, Juan, Lak.	.240	137	577	505	68	121	222	31	2	22	83	1	5	15	51	2	147	7	9	13	.440	.325
Ridley, Shayne, Del.†	.235	53	175	153	13	36	42	6	0	0	18	1	3	1	17	1	48	0	0	4	.275	.310
Riepe, Andy, Aug.	.234	33	123	107	11	25	27	2	0	0	17	1	1	1	13	0	23	0	0	2	.252	.320
Riera, Zack, Hick.†	.143	34	120	98	11	14	18	4	0	0	6	2	0	11	9	0	21	0	1	3	.184	.288
Riordan, Matt, Del.	.224	59	232	210	29	47	61	8	0	2	21	0	5	2	15	1	38	5	0	2	.290	.276
Rios, Alexis, C.W.Va.	.263	130	526	480	40	126	170	20	9	2	58	3	14	4	25	1	59	22	14	16	.354	.296
Rock, Jamie, Ash.	.198	30	114	106	8	21	30	6	0	1	17	2	2	1	3	0	25	1	1	3	.283	.223
Rodriguez, Mike, Del.*	.193	26	66	57	3	11	11	0	0	0	2	1	1	1	6	0	16	3	0	2	.193	.277
Rodriguez, Ricardo, Mac.	.188	5	20	16	2	3	3	0	0	0	2	1	0	2	1	0	5	1	0	0	.188	.316
Rogowski, Casey, Kan.*	.287	130	511	439	66	126	192	18	3	14	69	0	3	7	62	3	95	16	8	6	.437	.382
Rojas, Tom, Gre.	.333	1	3	3	0	1	1	0	0	0	0	0	0	0	0	0	2	0	0	0	.333	.333
Rosa, Wally, Kan.	.226	98	332	305	27	69	95	14	0	4	23	4	1	9	13	0	88	6	6	11	.311	.277
Rosamond, Mike, Lex.	.266	101	435	394	62	105	178	19	3	16	55	0	0	4	37	3	112	32	13	7	.452	.336
Rosario, Melvin, Ash.*	.228	102	330	276	44	63	67	4	0	0	18	2	2	6	44	0	89	23	13	6	.243	.345
Royer, Lissandro, C'bia	.265	35	114	102	15	27	30	3	0	0	7	1	0	1	10	0	15	4	4	1	.294	.336
Ruiz, Carlos, Lak.	.261	73	263	249	21	65	97	14	3	4	32	1	2	1	10	0	27	5	4	5	.390	.290
Ruiz, Reinaldo, Lex.	.200	3	5	5	0	1	1	0	0	0	1	0	0	0	0	0	0	0	0	0	.200	.200
Russell, Michael, Del.	.267	17	48	45	4	12	17	2	0	1	7	0	0	0	3	0	16	0	0	1	.378	.313
Salas, Jose, Mac.†	.158	12	40	38	0	6	8	2	0	0	3	0	1	1	0	0	11	1	0	2	.211	.175
Salas, Juan, C.S.C.	.228	135	530	500	53	114	166	25	3	7	62	1	8	4	17	1	93	9	15	11	.332	.255
Santa, Alexander, Gre.*	.000	3	9	9	0	0	0	0	0	0	0	0	0	0	0	0	1	0	0	2	.000	.000
Santamarina, Juan, Kan.*	.259	13	27	27	5	7	18	2	0	3	6	0	0	0	0	0	9	0	0	1	.667	.259
Santana, Pedro, Gre.	.105	6	21	19	2	2	3	1	0	0	0	0	0	2	0	0	2	0	0	0	.158	.190
Santos, Deivis, Hag.*	.290	131	554	520	64	151	220	27	3	12	80	0	5	4	25	6	91	16	10	15	.423	.325

Player, Team	Avg.	G	TPA	AB	R	H	TB	2B	3B	HR	RBI	SH	SF	HP	BB	IBB	SO	SB	CS	GDP	Slg.	OBP
Saucke, Casey, Del.	.200	20	53	45	4	9	11	2	0	0	5	1	0	0	7	0	20	0	1	1	.244	.308
Schmitt, Brian, Lex.*	.242	99	417	376	51	91	146	22	3	9	50	0	1	9	31	2	100	5	8	2	.388	.314
Schuda, Justin, C.S.C.*	.240	127	513	430	56	103	193	15	0	25	71	2	4	12	65	6	166	2	2	4	.449	.352
Schwager, Matt, Del.	.000	27	1	1	0	0	0	0	0	0	0	0	0	0	0	0	1	0	0	0	.000	.000
Scott, Ed, C.S.C.	.000	3	2	2	1	0	0	0	0	0	0	0	0	0	0	0	1	0	0	0	.000	.000
Seestedt, Mike, Del.	.221	90	284	231	28	51	63	9	0	1	18	4	1	9	39	0	37	0	0	7	.273	.354
Segar, Jeff, Gre.	.167	27	95	84	5	14	20	2	2	0	9	1	2	0	8	0	19	0	0	3	.238	.234
Seiber, Antron, Aug.	.223	120	529	462	59	103	140	16	3	5	27	7	2	8	50	1	113	36	12	5	.303	.308
Serrano, Ray, Mac.	.200	63	229	215	20	43	65	10	0	4	27	2	1	0	11	0	37	2	0	2	.302	.238
Shabala, Adam, Hag.*	.313	70	304	256	37	80	103	16	2	1	29	5	0	6	37	0	37	11	4	9	.402	.411
Sherrill, J.J., C'bus†	.251	111	480	407	62	102	155	19	11	4	50	10	4	27	32	0	123	29	9	1	.381	.343
Sherrod, Justin, Aug.	.290	87	365	307	53	89	152	24	3	11	43	1	2	21	34	1	102	16	7	4	.495	.396
Shrum, Allen, Hag.	.217	29	114	106	12	23	36	7	0	2	12	1	0	1	6	0	30	0	1	3	.340	.265
Singleton, Justin, C.W.Va.*	.232	100	385	345	51	80	111	15	5	2	25	6	0	0	33	0	138	24	7	1	.322	.299
Sisk, Aaron, C.W.Va.	.179	68	242	223	21	40	67	9	3	4	28	0	3	1	15	1	78	5	6	2	.300	.231
Smith, Corey, C'bus	.260	130	551	500	59	130	220	26	5	18	85	0	9	5	37	1	149	10	7	4	.440	.312
Smith, Ryan, C'bia	.094	20	62	53	5	5	5	0	0	0	1	0	1	2	6	0	20	0	1	2	.094	.210
Smith, Sam, Ash.	.152	30	117	105	5	16	20	4	0	0	7	0	0	4	8	1	37	1	1	0	.190	.239
Smith, Will, Aug.	.285	72	285	228	45	65	78	13	0	0	13	10	4	6	37	1	44	19	9	2	.342	.393
Snyder, Mike, C.W.Va.*	.220	119	459	414	47	91	137	18	2	8	45	1	2	2	40	6	101	12	5	14	.331	.290
Sosa, Jovanny, Del.	.274	34	137	117	17	32	52	5	0	5	18	0	2	2	16	0	37	1	0	2	.444	.365
Soto, Saul, Wil.	.262	75	296	252	32	66	101	17	0	6	34	1	1	9	33	0	34	4	4	7	.401	.366
Spidale, Mike, Kan.	.232	126	506	431	51	100	108	8	0	0	32	5	4	14	52	0	65	35	15	8	.251	.331
Stockton, Brad, Sav.*	.176	6	21	17	1	3	6	0	0	1	4	0	0	0	4	0	1	0	0	0	.353	.333
Storey, Eric, Ash.	.250	87	352	300	45	75	121	10	3	10	53	0	2	0	50	2	116	6	4	4	.403	.355
Story-Harden, Thomari, Wil.	.191	22	74	68	4	13	20	2	1	1	5	1	1	0	4	0	29	0	1	2	.294	.233
Strankman, Elliott, Hag.	.259	39	126	116	16	30	42	12	0	0	10	1	0	4	5	0	29	3	4	3	.362	.312
Sulbaran, Orlando, Sav.	.333	2	7	6	0	2	3	1	0	0	2	0	0	0	1	0	0	0	0	0	.500	.429
Sullivan, Cory, Ash.*	.275	67	285	258	36	71	100	12	1	5	22	0	0	2	25	0	56	13	9	2	.388	.344
Sutter, Tony, Gre.†	.163	16	54	43	7	7	10	0	0	1	6	1	1	1	8	0	9	0	1	3	.233	.302
Svihlik, D.J., Gre.*	.143	4	7	7	1	1	3	0	1	0	0	0	0	0	0	0	1	0	0	0	.429	.143
Swedlow, Sean, C'bus*	.200	106	438	401	30	80	114	18	2	4	35	1	3	5	28	1	146	1	2	5	.284	.259
Tablado, Raul, C.W.Va.	.253	122	445	388	49	98	152	23	2	9	44	4	3	5	45	1	127	5	10	6	.392	.336
Tapia, Roman, Kan.	.100	18	34	30	2	3	5	2	0	0	0	2	0	0	2	0	17	0	0	1	.167	.156
Taveras, Willy, C'bus	.271	97	431	395	55	107	145	15	7	3	32	4	3	6	22	0	73	29	9	7	.367	.317
Teilon, Nilson, Kan.	.190	67	177	163	20	31	48	6	1	3	8	1	1	1	11	0	47	2	2	4	.294	.244
Tejada, Mike, Ash.†	.204	107	389	363	35	74	136	17	0	15	49	0	3	1	22	1	102	3	0	3	.375	.249
Tena, Hector, Ash.	.146	32	114	103	5	15	22	1	0	2	19	0	6	0	5	0	32	0	0	4	.214	.175
Terveen, Bryce, Mac.*	.226	61	235	190	25	43	60	5	0	4	26	3	1	9	32	3	42	1	3	6	.316	.362
Thomas, Chuck, Mac.*	.250	108	446	408	59	102	164	19	6	11	69	0	3	3	32	3	87	17	7	6	.402	.307
Thompson, Alva, Mac.	.157	17	54	51	7	8	15	1	0	2	5	0	0	2	1	0	11	1	1	0	.294	.204
Todd, Jeremy, C'bia*	.164	19	76	67	5	11	16	2	0	1	7	0	2	0	7	0	35	0	0	2	.239	.237
Topolski, Jon, Lex.*	.287	136	633	550	98	158	271	27	7	24	96	1	3	4	75	6	128	28	11	3	.493	.375
Tosca, Daniel, Lak.*	.158	56	207	183	16	29	41	9	0	1	12	0	2	0	22	1	66	1	1	3	.224	.246
Toven, John, Lex.	.257	56	182	167	34	43	54	5	0	2	16	1	2	4	8	0	32	12	5	2	.323	.304
Truitt, Steve, Lex.	.295	28	100	88	18	26	42	7	0	3	13	1	1	1	9	0	26	7	1	0	.477	.364
Trumble, Dan, Hag.	.236	119	469	399	70	94	192	18	1	26	75	0	1	5	63	1	157	10	5	10	.481	.346
Tucker, Mamon, Del.	.246	59	260	224	37	55	70	7	1	2	24	2	4	2	28	1	44	10	3	3	.313	.329
Turner, Jason, Gre.*	.261	88	359	303	43	79	122	15	2	8	47	1	8	2	45	1	63	5	2	1	.403	.352
Umbria, Jose, C.W.Va.	.234	45	145	128	12	30	36	3	0	1	19	0	1	1	15	0	27	1	2	5	.281	.317
Van Buizen, Rodney, Wil.	.221	90	321	285	29	63	94	16	0	5	34	3	2	8	23	1	54	12	7	5	.330	.296
Victorino, Shane, Wil.	.283	112	490	435	71	123	174	21	9	4	32	13	1	5	36	0	61	47	13	3	.400	.344
Villegas, Ernest, Sav.	.223	39	146	130	22	29	57	4	0	8	21	0	0	10	6	0	35	4	1	2	.438	.308
Vilorio, Miguel, Ash.	.254	113	496	452	55	115	153	15	7	3	32	6	4	11	22	0	58	20	15	5	.338	.302
Volquez, Bolivar, C.S.C.	.167	38	145	126	13	21	24	3	0	0	7	2	1	2	14	0	39	4	1	1	.190	.259
Voshell, Key, Lak.	.270	36	122	111	18	30	38	8	0	0	12	2	1	2	6	0	27	2	3	4	.342	.317
Walker, Mark, Hag.	.160	58	205	169	19	27	47	4	2	4	12	2	2	0	32	0	74	8	2	5	.278	.291
Weston, Aron, Hick.*	.122	20	82	74	8	9	13	2	1	0	2	0	1	4	3	0	25	5	1	0	.176	.195
Whiteman, Tom, Lex.	.319	114	438	389	58	124	220	26	8	18	57	4	4	7	34	1	106	17	13	4	.566	.380
Whiteside, Dustin, Del.	.250	61	230	212	30	53	85	11	0	7	28	0	2	7	9	1	45	1	1	11	.401	.300
Wigginton, Derek, Kan.*	.263	114	402	373	42	98	146	16	4	8	50	2	1	3	23	3	95	2	6	8	.391	.310
Wilfong, Nick, Hag.*	.238	109	424	370	44	88	152	15	2	15	58	6	5	4	39	1	138	15	2	4	.411	.313
Wilken, Kris, Del.†	.211	93	353	304	26	64	90	13	2	3	30	1	2	3	43	3	81	0	1	8	.296	.313
Wilson, Heath, C'bus	.175	39	153	114	14	20	34	5	0	3	16	2	1	10	26	1	41	2	1	0	.298	.371
Wilson, John, C'bia	.250	88	365	304	41	76	97	10	1	3	32	2	3	9	47	3	41	7	6	5	.319	.364
Winrow, Gary, Gre.*	.167	63	241	222	21	37	63	5	0	7	24	0	1	3	15	0	56	2	1	0	.284	.228
Yan, Edwin, Hick.†	.283	128	509	440	58	126	148	8	4	2	26	4	2	3	42	0	62	56	21	6	.332	.347
Youkilis, Kevin, Aug.	.167	5	16	12	0	2	2	0	0	0	0	0	0	1	3	0	3	0	0	1	.167	.375
Youngbauer, Scott, Lak.†	.218	125	505	467	40	102	154	35	1	5	40	3	4	1	30	2	97	4	6	7	.330	.265
Zieour, Neesan, C.W.Va.	.280	22	88	75	8	21	24	3	0	0	6	3	0	1	9	0	16	0	2	2	.320	.365
Zumwalt, Sean, Mac.	.209	101	391	349	43	73	115	20	2	6	38	3	1	4	34	0	101	8	1	7	.330	.286

PLAYERS WITH TWO OR MORE TEAMS

Player, Team	Avg.	G	TPA	AB	R	H	TB	2B	3B	HR	RBI	SH	SF	HP	BB	IBB	SO	SB	CS	GDP	Slg.	OBP
Baker, Casey, Gre.	.071	8	17	14	1	1	1	0	0	0	1	1	0	0	2	0	6	1	1	0	.071	.188
Baker, Casey, C'bus	.083	4	14	12	1	1	1	0	0	0	0	0	0	2	2	0	2	1	0	0	.083	.214

GRAND SLAMS: En. Cruz, Grove, Perich, M. Tejada, 2 each; Blanco, Boscan, Brazell, Buck, Burrows, Carroll, Corporan, de Caster, Escalona, N. Garcia, Haase, Kessick, Lebron, Manley, Mongeluzzo, Muth, Oropeza, Pack, J. Reyes, Santos, Schuda, C. Smith, Storey, Tena, C. Thomas, Van Buizen, Whiteside, Wilfong, Wilken, H. Wilson, J. Wilson, Zumwalt, 1 each.

AWARDED FIRST BASE ON CATCHER'S INTERFERENCE: Avila 5 (C. Martinez, Lunsford, Marsh, J. Wilson, Quintero); Muth 3 (Fennell, Marsh, Heard); Lackaff 2 (Fuentes, Heard); Amador (Buck), Barmes (Ochoa), Brisson (Bernard), Colmenter (Franco), Conway (Boscan), Daniel (Quiroz), Deschenes (K. Hill), F. Nunez (Lunsford), Powers (Pack), Singleton (Ochoa), Taveras (Castaneda), Trumble (Marsh).

2001 PITCHING

TEAM

Team	W	L	Pct.	ERA	G	CG	ShO	Sv.	IP	H	TBF	R	ER	HR	SH	SF	HB	BB	IBB	SO	WP	Bk.
Augusta	74	65	.532	2.93	139	1	10	39	1213.2	1101	5029	539	395	66	36	41	53	314	9	1087	85	3
Wilmington	75	63	.543	3.03	138	2	12	44	1208.0	994	4997	496	407	89	44	34	81	449	11	1058	94	7
Kannapolis	76	63	.547	3.10	139	12	15	35	1179.2	1025	4925	499	406	61	44	45	70	441	37	1128	73	14
Lexington	92	48	.657	3.10	140	8	15	28	1245.1	1049	5141	505	429	93	49	33	66	424	7	1235	84	5
Columbus	77	59	.566	3.27	136	2	9	46	1207.0	1132	5105	568	439	96	37	33	65	381	11	979	97	10
Charleston, S.C.	64	76	.457	3.33	140	6	13	31	1233.2	1188	5279	599	457	75	55	37	68	369	28	1107	96	10
Lakewood	60	79	.432	3.37	139	12	11	31	1241.0	1130	5264	602	465	87	54	39	89	412	19	1001	48	9
Macon	72	61	.541	3.39	133	7	8	35	1180.2	1051	4962	568	445	82	48	40	53	387	11	1104	87	15
Greensboro	70	70	.500	3.49	140	7	11	37	1215.2	1116	5193	581	471	73	50	34	61	485	13	1106	71	12
Hagerstown	83	57	.593	3.69	140	1	12	52	1234.1	1154	5295	606	506	92	33	61	6	472	24	1120	87	12
Columbia	62	73	.459	3.73	135	2	6	33	1173.2	1120	5059	592	486	84	49	38	81	416	8	1115	106	9
Hickory	67	73	.479	3.73	140	8	4	34	1219.0	1215	5252	628	505	86	52	36	72	423	17	1063	76	8
Charleston, W.Va.	51	87	.370	3.84	138	10	6	23	1178.0	1137	5045	645	503	69	41	38	88	391	6	963	104	6
Asheville	68	71	.489	4.02	139	7	13	35	1199.2	1200	5199	674	536	112	42	30	6	385	25	1001	69	10
Delmarva	61	79	.436	4.02	140	5	8	34	1199.1	1175	5168	660	536	98	36	41	69	405	19	991	80	7
Savannah	54	82	.397	4.19	136	9	8	26	1181.0	1088	5160	650	550	96	32	42	26	521	4	1164	104	20

INDIVIDUAL

TOP QUALIFIERS FOR EARNED-RUN AVERAGE TITLE

Minimum 112 innings. *Lefthanded pitcher.

Pitcher, Team	W	L	Pct.	ERA	G	GS	CG	ShO	GF	Sv.	IP	H	TBF	R	ER	HR	SH	SF	HB	BB	IBB	SO	WP	Bk.
Malone, Corwin, Kan.*	11	4	.733	2.00	18	18	2	0	0	0	112.1	83	450	30	25	2	2	3	0	44	3	119	4	1
Rojas, Jose, Wil.	10	3	.769	2.12	24	23	1	0	0	0	135.2	107	540	42	32	7	7	2	7	42	0	116	9	0
Rosario, Rodrigo, Lex.	13	4	.765	2.14	30	21	1	0	5	2	147.0	105	584	46	35	8	7	2	10	36	1	131	3	0
Rundles, Rich, Aug.*	7	6	.538	2.43	19	19	0	0	0	0	115.0	109	468	46	31	5	5	7	10	0	94	4	0
Kozlowski, Ben, Mac.*	10	7	.588	2.48	26	23	1	1	1	0	145.1	134	588	60	40	8	8	2	10	27	0	147	7	1
Bonser, Boof, Hag.	16	4	.800	2.49	27	27	0	0	0	0	134.0	91	548	40	37	7	2	3	9	61	2	178	10	1
Burnett, Sean, Hick.*	11	8	.579	2.62	26	26	1	0	0	0	161.1	164	667	63	47	11	6	5	4	33	0	134	7	1
Nannini, Mike, Lex.	15	5	.750	2.70	28	27	4	1	0	0	190.1	176	771	70	57	17	10	5	6	36	0	151	7	0
Davis, Jason, C'bus	14	6	.700	2.70	27	27	1	1	0	0	160.0	147	677	72	48	9	2	2	14	51	1	115	5	2
Miniel, Rene, Aug.	8	4	.667	2.73	27	23	0	0	0	0	122.0	93	492	49	37	1	4	6	3	38	0	114	9	2
McClung, Mike, C.S.C.	10	11	.476	2.79	28	28	2	1	0	0	164.1	142	683	72	51	6	4	1	11	53	1	165	3	2
Malaska, Mark, C.S.C.*	7	12	.368	2.92	25	25	1	0	0	0	157.0	153	659	71	51	11	5	2	35	0	152	13	1
Roberts, Nick, Lex.	10	1	.909	2.95	20	20	3	1	0	0	137.1	118	540	49	45	10	3	4	4	21	0	128	3	0
Matheny, Brandon, C'bus*	7	8	.467	2.97	24	22	1	0	1	0	115.0	90	474	45	38	6	1	2	7	45	1	97	9	2
Rijo, Fernando, Wil.	11	7	.611	2.98	26	26	0	0	0	0	139.0	107	562	64	46	12	4	2	4	5	8	54	0	128	11	1

DEPARTMENTAL LEADERS: W—Bonser, 16; L—Buchholz, 14; Pct.—Roberts, .909; G—Faigin, Munoz, 60 each; GS—McClung, Wainwright, Dohmann, 28 each; CG—Buchholz, 5; ShO—Buchholz, 3; GF—Markert, 55; Sv.—Markert, 39; IP—Nannini, 190.1; H—Waechter, 179; TBF—Nannini, 771; R—Waechter, 97; ER—Dohmann, 83; HR—Dohmann, 27; SH—D. Gomez, Nannini, 10 each; SF—Nelson, 9; HB—Mead, 19; BB—Pluta, 86; IBB—D. Gomez, Castro, Ferrand, D. Adams, 6 each; SO—Wainwright, 184; WP—Echols, 21; BK—Munoz, R. Colon, 4 each.

ALL PITCHERS

*Lefthanded pitcher.

Pitcher, Team	W	L	Pct.	ERA	G	GS	CG	ShO	GF	Sv.	IP	H	TBF	R	ER	HR	SH	SF	HB	BB	IBB	SO	WP	Bk.
Abbott, David, C.W.Va.	2	3	.400	1.10	8	8	0	0	0	0	49.0	39	192	10	6	0	1	0	1	8	0	35	0	1
Abell, Joe, Ash.	2	2	.500	2.51	16	6	1	1	2	0	43.0	40	180	14	12	2	1	1	4	12	1	38	0	0
Acosta, Manuel, Gre.	5	2	.714	1.51	10	10	1	1	0	0	65.2	37	267	14	11	2	4	1	2	37	0	67	7	2
Adams, Brian, Aug.*	9	8	.529	3.52	34	2	0	0	7	1	79.1	81	345	45	31	2	8	3	4	36	2	60	6	0
Adams, Daniel, Lak.	4	6	.400	2.10	50	0	0	0	26	3	68.2	67	287	25	16	4	4	1	3	12	6	55	0	0
Advincola, Jose, Del.*	0	0	.000	9.26	11	0	0	0	3	0	11.2	20	64	14	12	2	0	0	2	5	0	7	1	0
Aguilera, Adrian, Wil.*	0	1	1.000	6.75	5	0	0	0	4	1	5.1	8	25	5	4	3	0	0	0	2	0	4	1	0
Alcala, Jason, Hick.	3	1	.750	1.76	34	0	0	0	18	7	41.0	35	173	12	8	0	1	0	2	13	1	56	4	1
Alexander, Kevin, Hag.	0	0	.000	0.00	1	0	0	0	0	0	1.0	1	5	0	0	0	0	0	0	1	1	2	1	0
Allen, Wyatt, Kan.	4	5	.444	3.16	12	11	2	0	0	0	62.2	60	263	29	22	4	2	3	5	16	1	45	4	1
Almonte, Henry, Hick.	2	2	.500	6.58	20	1	0	0	8	0	26.0	39	134	25	19	1	3	1	2	17	0	17	2	0
Altman, Heath, C'bus	1	0	1.000	15.75	3	0	0	0	0	0	4.0	6	25	7	7	0	0	2	5	0	6	5	0
Alvarez, Oscar, C'bus*	5	9	.357	4.17	17	17	0	0	0	0	95.0	94	409	54	44	11	2	3	8	37	1	69	10	2
Andersen, Derek, C.S.C.*	2	0	1.000	2.27	29	0	0	0	12	3	39.2	27	152	10	10	3	2	0	3	0	49	5	0
Anderson, Jason, Gre.	7	9	.438	3.76	23	19	1	0	3	1	124.1	127	530	68	52	9	3	4	3	40	1	101	8	0
Andrade, Jancy, Del.	2	4	.333	3.72	8	8	0	0	0	0	48.1	46	204	22	20	2	0	1	3	16	1	43	1	0
Andrews, Aron, Wil.	4	3	.571	2.05	15	1	0	0	7	2	44.0	40	176	14	10	3	1	3	3	7	0	26	2	0
Anez, Omar, Del.	0	0	.000	8.04	12	0	0	0	3	0	15.2	23	88	16	14	2	1	2	1	18	1	17	8	0
Backe, Brandon, C.S.C.	2	1	.667	2.92	16	0	0	0	15	7	24.2	17	98	8	8	2	2	0	4	7	1	20	2	0
Baker, Ryan, Mac.	2	3	.400	2.09	40	0	0	0	32	18	47.1	40	195	13	11	2	3	1	1	15	1	56	3	0
Barr, Adam, C'bus*	0	0	.000	12.91	6	0	0	0	1	0	7.2	9	44	14	11	2	0	1	1	11	0	10	0	0
Bartlett, Richard, Del.	5	9	.357	4.53	19	18	0	0	1	0	95.1	109	414	54	48	6	5	2	5	30	1	60	5	1
Bauer, Greg, Wil.	1	1	.500	1.78	25	0	0	0	22	17	30.1	22	115	6	6	3	1	1	0	8	0	32	1	0
Bauer, Pete, C.W.Va.	1	2	.333	2.39	6	6	0	0	0	0	37.2	26	151	15	10	0	1	0	5	10	0	47	0	0
Beal, Andy, Gre.*	1	0	1.000	0.89	2	2	0	0	0	0	10.1	10	40	1	0	0	0	0	3	0	6	2	0
Benedetti, John, C.S.C.	4	4	.333	3.28	44	0	0	0	22	4	68.2	74	312	35	25	4	8	6	21	4	63	4	0
Bennett, Steve, C'bia	0	4	.000	2.94	12	11	0	0	0	0	52.0	37	226	26	17	5	0	2	4	25	0	77	6	1
Berney, Scott, Ash.	2	2	.500	5.04	15	0	0	0	11	0	50.0	59	225	37	28	3	2	0	6	21	1	28	0	0
Bittner, Tim, Kan.*	0	3	.000	4.43	4	4	0	0	0	0	20.1	21	93	18	10	1	2	0	4	9	1	18	0	0
Blankenship, John, Gre.*	5	5	.500	2.38	27	9	0	0	3	0	75.2	53	305	21	20	5	3	1	4	28	0	85	5	0

Pitcher, Team	W	L	Pct.	ERA	G	GS	CG	ShO	GF	Sv.	IP	H	TBF	R	ER	HR	SH	SF	HB	BB	IBB	SO	WP	Bk.
Blethen, Matt, C'bus*	0	0	.000	13.50	1	0	0	0	0	0	2.0	7	16	5	3	1	0	0	0	3	0	1	0	1
Bonser, Boof, Hag.	16	4	.800	2.49	27	27	0	0	0	0	134.0	91	548	40	37	7	2	3	9	61	2	178	10	1
Borner, Brady, Hick.*	5	1	.833	2.43	9	8	3	1	1	0	59.1	43	226	18	16	5	1	0	0	12	0	58	0	1
Bowers, Rob, Sav.	0	0	.000	6.27	11	0	0	0	6	0	18.2	26	84	13	13	4	0	0	1	5	0	8	0	1
Bridenbaugh, Christian, Wil.*	3	6	.333	3.68	21	20	1	0	0	0	127.1	131	532	58	52	11	4	5	7	30	0	76	5	0
Brito, Eude, Lak.*	4	3	.571	2.73	44	0	0	0	20	6	69.1	53	273	28	21	7	5	0	2	14	2	58	3	2
Brous, Dave, Hag.*	2	1	.000	3.58	20	0	0	0	6	3	32.2	30	156	18	13	3	1	3	5	29	0	21	6	0
Buchanan, Brian, Gre.*	4	2	.667	4.08	37	4	0	0	4	0	79.1	82	348	42	36	9	4	3	6	34	0	82	1	2
Buchholz, Taylor, Lak.	9	14	.391	3.36	28	26	5	3	0	0	176.2	165	741	83	66	8	5	7	11	57	0	136	1	0
Bucktrot, Keith, Lak.	6	11	.353	5.28	24	24	3	0	0	0	134.2	139	604	93	79	16	8	7	15	58	0	97	11	0
Buglovsky, Chris, Ash.	8	10	.444	4.08	26	26	0	0	0	0	143.1	158	629	83	65	14	3	2	14	32	0	119	6	0
Bullard, Jim, Kan.*	3	2	.600	2.98	8	8	1	1	0	0	45.1	45	184	18	15	4	4	1	3	6	0	26	1	1
Bullock, Trevor, Lak.*	5	3	.625	1.13	48	0	0	0	35	16	72.0	53	280	14	9	5	4	3	2	17	3	62	3	0
Bumatay, Mike, Hick.*	1	0	1.000	2.73	15	1	0	0	2	0	26.1	20	107	10	8	0	1	1	1	8	1	31	2	0
Burke, Erick, Sav.*	2	6	.250	3.99	34	4	0	0	16	1	76.2	81	340	47	34	3	2	3	12	22	0	69	6	2
Burnett, Sean, Hick.*	11	8	.579	2.62	26	26	1	0	0	0	161.1	164	667	63	47	11	6	5	4	33	0	134	7	1
Cabell, Shannon, Hick.*	1	9	.100	3.45	42	0	0	0	13	2	62.2	73	281	35	24	3	5	3	1	26	2	58	5	1
Cabrera, Fernando, C'bus	5	6	.455	3.61	20	20	0	0	0	0	94.2	89	410	49	38	7	2	1	2	37	1	96	10	0
Campbell, Jarrett, C.S.C.	3	6	.333	3.95	39	5	0	0	4	0	84.1	90	372	51	37	6	4	5	7	18	4	71	10	3
Canale, Tom, C'bus.	3	1	.750	3.14	8	0	0	0	4	0	14.1	18	64	9	5	1	1	2	1	2	1	7	1	0
Cardwell, Brian, C.W.Va.	3	10	.231	5.18	19	19	2	0	0	0	92.0	101	410	70	53	9	2	4	9	33	1	60	10	0
Carney, Jake, C.S.C.	1	0	1.000	0.64	10	0	0	0	3	0	28.0	20	115	5	2	0	0	0	2	8	0	24	1	0
Carter, Ryan, Lak.*	3	7	.300	3.92	14	13	0	0	0	0	80.1	73	345	39	35	6	4	0	8	34	0	76	5	0
Castro, Julio, Sav.	3	1	.750	2.67	40	0	0	0	20	4	54.0	46	234	22	16	3	3	2	2	21	6	68	6	1
Cavazos, Andy, Sav.	6	10	.375	5.53	29	19	1	0	3	0	122.0	149	569	87	75	13	1	3	10	63	0	96	10	3
Chenard, Ken, C'bia	0	1	.000	4.50	4	4	0	0	0	0	16.0	14	68	8	8	1	1	0	1	8	0	12	2	0
Christ, John, C'bus.	0	0	.000	5.00	4	0	0	0	1	0	9.0	14	44	7	5	1	0	1	3	0	8	2	0
Clark, Jeff, Hag.	14	9	.609	3.65	27	27	0	0	0	0	148.0	152	608	72	60	18	2	8	10	15	1	131	4	0
Cole, Joey, C'bia	7	6	.538	3.87	25	25	0	0	0	0	137.1	125	593	69	59	7	3	6	11	67	0	123	17	0
Collazo, William, Mac.*	3	2	.600	2.70	12	0	0	0	6	1	23.1	13	88	9	7	3	3	3	2	4	0	23	2	0
Colon, Jose, C'bus	2	3	.400	1.92	44	0	0	0	42	22	51.2	38	210	19	11	5	1	1	4	6	0	47	2	0
Colon, Roman, Mac.	7	7	.500	3.59	23	21	0	0	1	0	128.0	136	543	69	51	9	5	7	3	26	0	91	16	4
Comolli, Mark, C.W.Va.	1	2	.333	3.90	8	5	0	0	0	0	32.1	28	132	16	14	2	0	1	5	6	0	27	2	0
Connolly, Mike, Hick.*	11	7	.611	3.94	33	15	2	0	0	0	121.0	116	509	59	53	10	5	3	6	41	1	107	9	0
Coose, Austin, C.S.C.	0	1	.000	4.61	10	0	0	0	7	2	13.2	13	61	8	7	0	1	0	1	7	0	21	0	0
Cordero, Jesus, Wil.	8	4	.667	2.47	33	1	0	0	22	9	69.1	49	278	20	19	1	4	4	6	25	0	56	13	1
Corroa, Dominic, Gre.	2	2	.500	4.42	16	0	0	0	12	3	18.1	12	77	9	9	1	3	0	1	9	1	17	1	0
Cortes, David, Mac.	1	0	1.000	7.11	10	0	0	0	4	0	12.2	14	61	11	10	1	0	1	1	5	0	8	2	0
Coward, Tim, C.S.C.	0	0	.000	0.00	6	0	0	0	0	0	10.0	11	43	3	1	0	0	0	0	4	2	13	1	0
Cox, Mike, C'bia*	2	3	.400	4.45	15	0	0	0	5	1	32.1	27	148	18	16	1	3	0	6	19	0	40	6	0
Cunningham, Jeremy, Hag.	1	1	.500	5.89	10	0	0	0	2	0	18.1	23	86	16	12	3	1	1	2	7	0	17	0	0
Currier, Rik, Gre.	0	4	.000	4.55	6	6	0	0	0	0	31.2	32	144	22	16	1	2	2	2	17	0	25	3	0
Davies, Kyle, Mac.	1	0	1.000	0.00	1	1	0	0	0	0	5.2	2	20	0	0	0	0	0	1	0	7	0	0
Davis, Jason, C'bus	14	6	.700	2.70	27	27	1	1	0	0	160.0	147	677	72	48	9	2	2	14	51	1	115	5	2
Deaton, Kevin, C'bia	0	0	.000	4.50	1	0	0	0	1	0	4.0	4	19	2	2	1	0	0	0	3	0	6	0	0
De La Cruz, Carlos, C'bus.	2	1	.667	4.30	6	6	0	0	0	0	29.1	29	124	17	14	4	2	1	0	13	0	31	0	1
Delossantos, Carlos, Hick.	2	5	.286	6.69	13	7	0	0	3	0	37.2	44	184	33	28	6	1	3	8	28	0	31	5	0
De Paula, Julio, Ash.-Gre.	7	2	.778	2.99	11	11	0	0	0	0	72.1	54	297	32	24	5	1	0	7	23	0	93	3	3
Deza, Fredy, Del.	0	2	.000	3.00	3	2	0	0	0	0	15.0	10	57	6	5	3	0	0	1	0	0	12	0	0
Diaz, Felix, Hag.	1	4	.200	3.66	15	12	0	0	0	0	51.2	49	222	27	21	4	0	2	4	16	0	56	3	0
Dickinson, Rodney, Aug.	2	0	1.000	1.86	23	0	0	0	21	11	29.0	28	114	7	6	0	1	1	0	0	0	30	1	0
Digby, Bryan, Mac.	1	0	1.000	1.13	3	1	0	0	0	0	8.0	3	33	1	1	0	0	0	1	7	0	6	1	0
Diggins, Ben, Wil.	7	6	.538	3.58	21	21	0	0	0	0	105.2	88	446	49	42	5	2	0	3	48	0	79	10	0
Dohmann, Christopher, Ash.	11	13	.458	4.32	28	28	3	1	0	0	173.0	165	717	88	83	27	5	3	18	33	5	154	3	0
Donaghey, Steve, C'bus	2	3	.400	4.17	23	0	0	0	11	4	49.2	58	211	28	23	8	0	4	0	7	0	23	3	0
Dorman, Rich, C.S.C.	1	5	.167	6.51	17	9	0	0	1	0	56.2	61	263	47	41	3	3	1	2	41	1	41	6	0
Dorn, Grant, Lex.	0	0	.000	2.05	10	0	0	0	5	1	22.0	23	89	6	5	2	2	0	1	2	0	17	2	0
Echols, Justin, Sav.	5	9	.357	3.80	36	13	1	0	8	3	123.0	88	524	58	52	4	5	3	11	67	1	156	21	1
Elliott, Chad, C'bia*	4	4	.500	3.32	35	3	0	0	19	5	84.0	78	358	44	31	4	5	0	3	26	1	91	4	0
Elskamp, Andy, Lak.	0	1	.000	2.27	23	0	0	0	10	1	39.2	28	168	15	10	4	2	1	2	19	1	41	3	0
Evert, Brett, Mac.	1	0	1.000	0.74	6	6	0	0	0	0	36.1	25	140	5	3	0	0	0	3	5	0	34	0	0
Faigin, Jason, Gre.	4	8	.333	3.41	60	1	0	0	33	8	66.0	63	291	32	25	0	2	0	2	26	3	67	3	1
Farren, Dave, Del.	4	7	.364	3.93	32	19	0	0	4	0	121.1	113	511	66	53	16	4	3	7	30	1	84	1	0
Faust, Wes, Hag.	7	5	.583	2.48	46	0	0	0	17	4	90.2	79	361	28	25	4	4	3	3	18	2	66	2	0
Feliciano, Ruben, Sav.	0	1	.000	7.98	6	0	0	0	2	0	14.2	16	74	14	13	3	0	0	7	7	0	6	0	0
Ferrand, Dario, Kan.	9	13	.409	3.06	27	27	3	1	0	0	162.0	156	672	67	55	9	2	4	11	36	6	111	7	1
Fitch, Steve, C'bus.	2	0	1.000	1.00	4	4	0	0	0	0	27.0	23	106	7	3	1	0	0	1	3	0	16	2	0
Fontana, Tony, Aug.	2	2	.500	1.94	24	4	0	0	11	6	69.2	66	289	21	15	2	0	1	9	0	62	7	0
Ford, Matt, C.W.Va.*	4	4	.500	2.42	11	11	1	0	0	0	70.2	62	287	28	19	2	2	1	0	22	0	69	8	1
Ford, Tom, Del.*	2	0	1.000	4.50	13	0	0	0	3	0	14.0	13	64	8	7	0	1	1	1	8	0	23	0	0
Francisco, Frank, Aug.	4	3	.571	2.91	37	0	0	0	8	2	68.0	40	280	25	22	3	5	1	6	30	0	90	6	1
Frias, Juan, Hag.	3	1	.750	3.19	24	0	0	0	5	1	31.0	36	139	17	11	3	5	4	2	10	2	27	1	1
Friedberg, Drew, Hick.*	0	1	.000	6.20	17	0	0	0	7	1	20.1	26	96	16	14	3	4	0	2	15	3	15	3	1
Gahan, Matt, C'bia	0	3	.000	5.79	5	4	0	0	0	0	14.0	20	67	14	9	2	0	0	4	0	11	1	0
Garcia, Nick, Del.	0	0	.000	0.00	1	0	0	0	1	0	1.0	0	5	0	0	0	0	0	0	3	1	1	0	0
Garza, Alberto, C'bus.	1	0	1.000	0.00	1	0	0	0	1	0	2.1	2	9	0	0	0	0	0	0	1	0	2	0	0
Garza, Rolando, Kan.	1	0	1.000	9.64	9	0	0	0	7	0	9.1	12	50	10	10	1	0	2	1	9	0	10	1	1
Gassner, Dave, C.W.Va.*	4	4	.500	3.03	13	11	1	0	1	0	74.1	72	307	30	25	3	0	2	2	11	0	51	4	0
George, Chris, Lex.	5	1	.833	3.88	40	0	0	0	27	2	51.0	43	232	26	22	7	0	1	2	30	0	65	9	0
Giese, Dan, Aug.	6	4	.600	2.19	46	0	0	0	39	9	74.0	65	297	27	18	2	0	0	8	8	3	95	2	0
Gilbert, Rich, Sav.*	6	11	.353	4.23	21	20	3	0	0	0	134.0	120	568	75	63	13	5	3	11	44	0	155	7	2
Glen, William, C.W.Va.	2	1	.667	3.40	23	0	0	0	9	1	45.0	46	204	27	17	5	0	1	0	26	0	50	4	0
Gomes, Wayne, Lak.	0	0	.000	3.00	2	2	0	0	0	0	3.0	2	13	1	1	0	0	0	0	3	0	1	0	0

Pitcher, Team	W	L	Pct.	ERA	G	GS	CG	ShO	GF	Sv.	IP	H	TBF	R	ER	HR	SH	SF	HB	BB	IBB	SO	WP	Bk.
Gomez, Benito, C.S.C.*	1	1	.500	3.86	39	0	0	0	22	5	58.1	59	257	32	25	9	2	1	19	4	46	7	0
Gomez, Diogenes, Ash.	12	4	.750	2.25	50	1	0	0	21	3	84.0	82	352	34	21	3	10	3	2	21	6	55	4	1
Gomez, Ricardo, Gre.	2	2	.500	8.80	9	2	0	0	1	1	15.1	20	79	19	15	0	3	0	2	12	0	10	1	0
Gonzales, Jose, Gre.	2	6	.250	5.14	35	0	0	0	11	0	49.0	52	210	30	28	5	2	4	1	19	3	36	2	1
Gonzalez, Alfredo, Wil.	1	0	1.000	3.00	2	1	0	0	1	0	9.0	10	42	4	3	0	1	1	0	3	0	12	1	0
Gonzalez, Gilberto, C'bia*	1	2	.333	2.37	5	4	0	0	1	0	19.0	15	80	6	5	1	1	0	2	5	0	24	2	1
Goodrum, Kevin, Gre.*	2	2	.500	4.19	7	7	0	0	0	0	38.2	45	169	21	18	4	2	0	3	12	0	25	0	0
Gracesqui, Frank, C.W.Va.*	2	8	.200	3.17	35	2	0	0	11	1	65.1	60	286	40	23	1	2	2	2	34	0	66	9	1
Graham, Elgin, Hag.	3	4	.429	5.91	32	9	0	0	6	1	67.0	75	317	56	44	9	3	8	4	43	3	37	12	0
Graham, Tom, Sav.	4	4	.200	2.50	40	0	0	0	32	17	54.0	46	217	19	15	0	3	2	5	10	0	71	2	1
Green, Sean, Ash.	3	4	.429	5.90	43	0	0	0	9	0	58.0	66	271	43	38	4	4	1	4	28	1	37	8	2
Gross, Kyle, Hag.	2	6	.250	6.45	22	12	0	0	1	0	53.0	43	262	45	38	2	2	3	18	51	1	46	12	0
Guerrero, Julio, Hick.	1	4	.200	4.45	11	9	0	0	1	0	54.2	65	251	37	27	4	4	2	4	17	1	24	0	1
Gutierrez, Fernando, Del.	1	1	.500	0.46	22	0	0	0	10	0	20.0	10	100	10	11	0	0	0	1	21	1	20	7	0
Guzman, Alex, C.W.Va.	2	7	.222	3.58	52	0	0	0	21	2	78.0	82	316	38	31	2	3	3	3	10	1	45	3	1
Hanrahan, Joel, Wil.	9	11	.450	3.38	27	26	0	0	1	0	144.0	136	615	71	54	13	5	1	11	55	0	116	8	1
Hawk, David, Hick.*	2	1	.667	4.01	17	3	0	0	3	0	24.2	25	117	15	11	0	1	1	1	17	0	18	4	0
Hawkins, Chad, Sav.	1	0	1.000	0.32	4	4	0	0	0	0	28.0	13	104	2	1	0	1	1	5	0	25	0	0
Hee, Aaron, C'bia*	4	6	.400	2.55	35	0	0	0	16	2	77.2	62	331	28	22	3	4	1	1	43	0	95	3	3
Henderson, Kenneth, Hick.*	0	3	.000	5.29	27	0	0	0	10	1	34.0	29	152	22	20	2	0	2	5	16	2	35	4	1
Herbison, Brett, C'bia	1	0	1.000	4.00	5	0	0	0	0	0	9.0	11	37	4	4	1	0	0	4	4	0	4	0	0
Hernandez, Buddy, Mac.	0	0	.000	3.21	7	0	0	0	3	0	14.0	13	58	8	5	1	0	1	0	1	0	29	0	0
Hernandez, Yoel, Lak.	6	9	.400	3.47	25	25	1	0	0	0	160.2	153	700	94	62	7	4	7	18	42	1	111	6	2
Herndon, Eric, Mac.	0	2	.000	1.93	10	0	0	0	5	2	18.2	13	73	5	4	0	1	1	1	6	1	15	1	1
Higgins, Joshua, Hick.	2	2	.500	2.07	55	0	0	0	49	23	61.0	40	239	15	14	3	3	2	4	11	1	71	2	0
Hills, Mark, Hag.*	0	3	.000	9.47	10	1	0	0	4	0	19.0	34	99	26	20	4	1	2	1	6	0	16	1	1
Hollifield, Alec, Kan.	0	2	.000	10.97	5	3	0	0	1	0	10.2	22	65	20	13	2	0	2	1	7	1	6	3	0
Hughes, Nial, Wil.*	1	4	.200	4.24	25	1	0	0	9	2	40.1	25	192	27	19	3	2	3	5	45	2	57	9	0
Hughes, Rocky, Kan.*	0	1	.000	5.08	19	0	0	0	8	1	28.1	30	129	16	16	2	1	2	0	19	1	21	4	0
Huisman, Justin, Ash.	0	3	.000	1.70	55	0	0	0	51	30	58.1	35	230	11	11	1	3	1	3	14	2	53	4	0
Hurley, Derek, Hick.*	4	7	.364	4.37	17	14	0	0	2	0	82.1	97	367	59	40	14	5	0	3	32	0	42	4	0
Jacobs, John, C.S.C.	0	0	.000	0.00	1	0	0	0	1	0	1.0	0	4	0	0	0	0	1	0	0	0	1	0	0
Jacobsen, Landon, Hick.	1	4	.000	3.38	9	0	0	0	0	0	53.1	45	213	24	20	3	2	1	3	9	0	50	0	0
Jamison, Ryan, Lex.	4	2	.667	2.28	9	8	0	0	1	0	55.1	40	215	17	14	3	1	2	6	9	0	63	6	0
Johnston, Mike, Hick.*	4	5	.444	3.38	16	16	0	0	0	0	93.1	88	404	47	35	5	0	4	5	42	1	80	7	1
Jones, Chris, Hag.*	6	3	.667	4.52	39	4	0	0	9	1	73.2	77	330	42	37	3	3	7	7	40	3	60	9	1
Jones, D.J., Del.*	1	4	.200	3.98	17	6	0	0	6	0	40.2	52	178	23	18	0	5	1	3	7	0	30	0	2
Jones, Quentin, Mac.	1	2	.333	5.59	35	0	0	0	25	0	37.0	32	172	26	23	3	1	3	4	33	1	51	6	1
Keirstead, Michael, Wil.	0	1	.000	4.82	7	1	0	0	5	0	9.1	9	42	7	5	0	0	0	5	0	12	1	0
Keppel, Bob, C'bia	6	7	.462	3.11	26	20	1	0	3	0	124.1	118	516	58	43	6	2	14	25	1	87	7	0
Kibler, Ryan, Ash.	3	5	.375	2.93	10	10	1	0	0	0	61.1	50	260	26	20	3	2	3	7	27	0	59	5	0
King, Jeremy, Gre.	0	1	.000	12.60	1	1	0	0	0	0	5.0	8	25	7	7	2	0	0	1	3	0	5	0	0
Kleine, Victor, C'bus*	0	0	.000	3.86	1	1	0	0	0	0	7.0	5	29	5	3	0	0	1	0	0	0	5	0	0
Knowles, Mike, Gre.	3	4	.429	3.22	38	7	0	0	29	21	64.1	63	287	26	23	4	2	3	2	35	3	62	5	2
Kozlowski, Ben, Mac.*	10	7	.588	2.48	26	23	1	1	1	0	145.1	134	588	60	40	8	8	2	10	27	0	147	7	1
Kremer, John, Gre.	4	1	.800	2.49	40	0	0	0	9	1	50.2	40	220	26	14	4	2	2	26	1	39	4	1
Krysa, Jonathan, Lex.	1	3	.250	3.68	16	0	0	0	4	1	29.1	24	120	13	12	3	1	2	3	8	1	25	5	0
Laplante, Reggie, Gre.	0	2	.000	8.10	7	0	0	0	4	2	6.2	9	34	7	6	0	2	1	4	0	5	0	0
Lara, Mauricio, Aug.*	7	6	.538	3.02	20	19	1	0	0	0	107.1	114	443	45	36	5	0	4	7	24	0	96	6	0
Laroche, Jeff, Ash.*	1	2	.333	4.82	26	0	0	0	8	0	37.1	45	183	37	20	6	2	3	3	24	1	21	3	0
Larson, Ryan, C'bus	5	1	.833	0.51	31	0	0	0	18	4	52.2	30	194	5	3	3	2	0	2	7	0	60	2	0
Lavigne, Tim, C'bia	5	3	.625	2.29	33	0	0	0	29	12	63.0	51	267	24	16	1	5	1	4	21	2	44	10	1
Lawson, Jarrod, Lak.	2	5	.286	4.35	23	11	0	0	3	0	72.1	76	318	42	35	7	6	0	8	22	0	62	0	0
Levesque, Ben, Hick.	1	2	.333	9.33	16	0	0	0	9	0	18.1	23	97	20	19	1	2	2	9	15	3	8	5	0
Lizarraga, Edgar, Wil.	0	0	.000	0.00	3	0	0	0	2	0	5.2	2	21	0	0	0	0	1	1	0	10	0	0
Lockhart, Paul, Lex.*	0	0	.000	0.00	1	0	0	0	1	0	2.0	2	8	0	0	0	0	0	1	0	1	0	0
Lopez, Rafael, C'bia	6	7	.462	4.13	25	24	0	0	0	0	122.0	127	522	66	56	10	4	8	7	36	0	87	7	0
Lorenzo, Javier, Ash.	0	0	.000	5.17	38	0	0	0	15	1	47.0	42	227	35	27	4	4	7	35	1	55	14	0
Lugo, Ruddy, Wil.	0	2	.000	3.77	16	0	0	0	7	2	31.0	29	133	14	13	2	2	4	2	13	0	23	2	0
Luna, Brandon, Sav.	2	1	.667	0.00	11	0	0	0	10	2	13.2	8	57	3	0	0	1	0	1	8	1	16	2	0
Madril, Steve, Kan.*	2	2	.500	2.89	42	2	0	0	7	2	65.1	68	285	28	21	3	4	3	21	3	59	7	1
Malaska, Mark, C.S.C.*	7	12	.368	2.92	25	25	1	0	0	0	157.0	153	659	71	51	11	8	2	2	35	0	152	13	1
Malerich, Will, Hag.*	0	0	.000	11.57	7	0	0	0	1	0	7.0	13	40	9	9	2	0	1	3	4	1	7	0	0
Malone, Corwin, Kan.*	11	4	.733	2.00	18	18	2	0	0	0	112.1	83	450	30	25	2	2	3	0	44	3	119	4	1
Marchetti, Dan, Del.	1	1	.500	2.45	10	0	0	0	2	1	18.1	10	76	5	5	0	0	3	1	8	0	17	4	0
Marietta, Ron, Gre.*	1	0	1.000	18.00	4	1	0	0	1	0	3.0	4	18	6	6	2	0	0	1	4	0	1	1	0
Markert, Jackson, Hag.	3	5	.500	2.82	58	0	0	0	55	39	60.2	57	259	26	19	4	1	2	4	18	2	45	4	0
Markwell, Diegomar, C.W.Va.*	5	7	.417	3.87	22	21	0	0	0	0	123.1	121	511	58	53	10	3	3	8	32	0	99	6	0
Martin, Chandler, Ash.	2	0	1.000	1.32	2	2	0	0	0	0	13.2	10	54	2	2	1	0	1	2	5	0	8	2	0
Martin, Larry, Gre.*	1	0	1.000	4.02	13	0	0	0	6	1	15.2	15	80	11	7	1	0	1	2	19	0	20	3	0
Martinez, Casey, C.W.Va.	0	0	.000	0.00	1	0	0	0	1	0	0.1	0	1	0	0	0	0	0	0	0	0	0	0	0
Martinez, Dave, Gre.*	6	0	1.000	1.13	11	11	3	2	0	0	79.1	54	312	17	10	1	0	0	4	28	0	67	6	0
Matheny, Brandon, C'bus*	7	8	.467	2.97	24	22	1	0	1	0	115.0	90	474	45	38	6	1	7	45	1	97	9	2
Mathiesen, Ryan, Mac.	0	0	.000	9.00	1	0	0	0	0	0	2.0	5	12	2	2	0	0	0	2	0	1	0	0
Matos, Jesus, Ash.	1	1	.500	5.06	21	0	0	0	3	0	32.0	36	139	19	18	6	1	0	2	8	3	25	2	0
Matsko, Rick, C'bia	3	2	.600	3.74	24	0	0	0	14	4	45.2	53	202	25	19	4	3	2	10	1	41	5	0
Mattioni, Nick, C'bia	8	4	.667	2.95	37	0	0	0	24	6	79.1	77	347	35	26	6	3	2	6	23	2	98	7	1
McClung, Mike, C.S.C.	10	11	.476	2.79	28	28	2	1	0	0	164.1	142	683	72	51	6	4	1	11	53	1	165	3	2
McCormick, Terry, C.S.C.*	3	0	1.000	1.40	14	0	0	0	12	2	19.1	14	80	3	3	0	4	2	1	8	2	12	0	0
McCrotty, Will, Wil.	2	1	.667	1.96	21	0	0	0	12	4	36.2	24	146	9	8	2	1	0	4	10	0	46	4	0
McCulloch, Andy, C.W.Va.*	5	2	.714	2.17	55	0	0	0	50	17	62.1	53	254	25	15	0	5	1	1	12	3	54	2	0
McMillan, Joshua, C.W.Va.*	1	1	.500	5.40	9	1	0	0	2	0	18.1	21	87	13	11	2	3	1	2	13	0	18	7	0
McWhirter, Kris, Kan.	7	6	.538	3.09	14	14	2	0	0	0	90.1	79	362	37	31	7	1	3	4	23	3	91	3	0

Pitcher, Team	W	L	Pct.	ERA	G	GS	CG	ShO	GF	Sv.	IP	H	TBF	R	ER	HR	SH	SF	HB	BB	IBB	SO	WP	Bk.
Mead, David, Sav.	2	10	.167	5.51	19	19	0	0	0	0	96.1	91	450	63	59	13	6	5	19	64	0	79	10	2
Meisenheimer, Matt, Sav.	0	1	.000	13.50	3	3	0	0	0	0	6.2	11	38	11	10	0	0	0	2	7	0	4	2	0
Meldahl, Todd, Lak.*	1	2	.333	2.66	11	0	0	0	3	0	20.1	16	90	12	6	2	1	0	1	11	0	14	0	0
Mendez, Dave, Mac.*	5	4	.556	4.08	35	1	0	0	12	2	68.1	55	291	34	31	7	3	1	4	29	1	55	12	1
Messer, Brian, Hick.	1	0	1.000	5.84	17	0	0	0	8	0	24.2	27	115	19	16	1	3	3	4	9	2	13	1	0
Middleton, Brian, Lex.	1	1	.500	5.30	11	1	0	0	3	0	18.2	18	85	13	11	2	2	0	0	11	1	19	1	0
Mikels, Jason, Mac.	1	4	.200	5.00	23	1	0	0	11	0	36.0	43	167	28	20	4	1	0	1	16	1	27	2	0
Millwood, Kevin, Mac.	0	0	.000	0.00	1	1	0	0	0	0	3.0	0	9	0	0	0	0	0	0	0	0	5	0	0
Miniel, Rene, Aug.	8	4	.667	2.73	27	23	0	0	0	0	122.0	93	492	49	37	1	4	6	3	38	0	114	9	2
Montano, Ignacio, C'bus*	1	1	.500	3.06	11	0	0	0	3	1	17.2	16	75	8	6	0	1	1	1	6	0	17	2	0
Montero, Agustin, Wil.	2	1	.667	3.29	18	0	0	0	9	1	27.1	13	113	11	10	1	0	1	5	19	1	30	5	1
Montilla, Elvis, Del.	7	6	.538	4.19	26	18	0	0	3	0	107.1	104	444	53	50	10	0	4	8	28	2	53	6	0
Mosley, Eric, Gre.	1	4	.200	4.93	11	10	0	0	0	0	45.2	48	214	31	25	5	3	3	6	22	1	32	2	0
Mowday, Chris, C.W.Va.	1	0	1.000	5.64	13	1	0	0	3	0	22.1	22	103	16	14	2	1	1	4	9	0	27	3	0
Mozingo, Dan, Kan.*	8	4	.667	2.39	37	9	1	0	5	1	94.0	59	378	30	25	6	5	3	4	43	1	114	8	0
Munoz, Arnaldo, Kan.*	6	3	.667	2.49	60	0	0	0	30	12	79.2	41	310	24	22	2	2	4	7	42	2	115	8	4
Munter, Scott, Hag.	1	0	1.000	3.38	1	1	0	0	0	0	5.1	5	23	3	2	0	1	0	1	0	0	2	0	0
Murray, Brad, Kan.*	0	0	.000	6.59	9	0	0	0	6	0	13.2	16	64	12	10	0	1	0	1	7	1	12	3	0
Musser, Neal, C'bia*	7	4	.636	2.84	17	17	1	0	0	0	95.0	86	387	38	30	3	4	3	3	18	0	98	8	1
Nannini, Mike, Lex.	15	5	.750	2.70	28	27	4	1	0	0	190.1	176	771	70	57	17	10	5	6	36	0	151	7	0
Neil, Dan, C'bus*	3	4	.429	1.69	24	0	0	0	13	2	48.0	33	189	14	9	3	5	1	1	8	1	35	2	0
Nelson, Kenny, Wil.	12	8	.600	3.93	25	24	2	0	1	0	151.0	144	649	76	66	16	5	9	6	57	1	154	9	1
Nunley, Derrek, C.W.Va.	1	2	.333	3.93	14	0	0	0	6	0	18.1	22	90	12	8	1	2	0	2	8	0	23	2	0
O'Brien, Patrick, Hick.	6	5	.545	3.16	11	11	0	0	0	0	74.0	73	303	30	26	5	2	1	3	14	0	67	4	0
Olson, Jason, Wil.	2	4	.333	3.68	15	0	0	0	11	1	29.1	23	125	12	12	2	1	1	2	15	3	28	4	1
Olson, Ryan, C'bia*	0	0	.000	2.45	1	0	0	0	0	0	3.2	5	16	1	1	0	1	0	0	1	0	4	1	0
Ormond, Rod, Del.	4	4	.500	4.18	24	8	0	0	3	0	56.0	59	250	37	26	6	2	1	4	14	1	59	3	0
Ozuna, Francisco, C.W.Va.*	2	1	.667	2.57	18	0	0	0	6	2	35.0	25	134	13	10	2	1	1	3	4	0	16	3	1
Pacheco, Enemencio, Ash.	1	2	.333	4.21	7	7	0	0	0	0	36.1	38	157	23	17	0	0	0	4	9	1	34	0	0
Padgett, Daniel, Hag.*	1	0	1.000	6.66	19	0	0	0	6	0	24.1	24	110	18	18	3	0	3	1	18	1	16	0	0
Padua, Geraldo, Gre.	1	1	.500	3.86	3	3	0	0	0	0	18.2	20	73	8	8	0	0	0	0	3	0	14	0	0
Parker, Josh, C.S.C.	2	1	.667	2.70	3	0	0	0	1	0	6.2	7	32	3	2	0	0	4	1	4	2	4	2	0
Patterson, Quenten, C'bia	3	4	.429	6.11	33	1	0	0	20	6	63.1	62	282	46	43	11	4	1	9	29	2	43	9	1
Pavon, Julio, Hag.	6	4	.600	3.12	29	15	1	1	4	2	112.2	109	455	45	39	6	1	2	3	21	0	107	4	3
Pearson, Brent, Hick.	2	0	1.000	0.00	3	0	0	0	3	0	4.2	3	17	0	0	0	0	0	0	2	0	4	1	0
Peeples, Jim, Gre.*	0	0	.000	0.00	1	0	0	0	0	0	1.0	0	3	0	0	0	0	0	0	0	0	0	0	0
Peguero, Darwin, Lex.*	8	10	.444	4.05	34	15	0	0	9	2	124.1	112	509	67	56	14	4	3	6	37	0	134	8	2
Percell, Brody, C'bus*	1	2	.333	3.81	26	0	0	0	6	2	54.1	55	235	34	23	5	3	4	2	22	2	41	11	0
Peres, Luis, Aug.*	8	8	.500	3.58	26	25	0	0	1	0	125.2	118	525	69	50	14	2	7	3	42	0	113	9	0
Perez, Elvis, Mac.	5	5	.500	2.98	27	0	0	0	8	0	51.1	35	215	22	17	3	2	3	10	2	40	1	1
Perich, Josh, C.S.C.	0	0	.000	36.00	1	0	0	0	1	0	1.0	4	9	4	4	0	0	0	2	0	1	0	0	0
Peterson, Matt, C'bia	2	6	.250	4.99	18	14	0	0	1	0	79.1	87	357	46	44	9	3	5	4	29	0	72	9	0
Phillips, Mike, Kan.*	2	7	.222	3.64	14	12	1	0	1	0	71.2	74	304	36	29	1	5	6	7	18	1	54	1	1
Pierce, Tony, Mac.	0	0	.000	13.50	2	0	0	0	2	0	4.0	7	22	6	6	2	0	0	3	0	4	3	0
Pluta, Tony, Lex.	12	4	.750	3.20	26	26	0	0	0	0	132.1	107	570	52	47	7	3	6	12	86	0	138	11	0
Portobanco, Luz, C'bia	0	1	.000	4.50	1	1	0	0	0	0	6.0	7	26	3	3	0	1	0	0	1	0	5	0	0
Prahm, Ryan, C'bus	7	2	.778	2.41	11	11	0	0	0	0	59.2	53	237	18	16	4	1	0	0	12	0	47	5	0
Prendes, Alex, Aug.*	1	0	1.000	2.57	8	0	0	0	4	2	21.0	22	88	7	6	3	2	0	1	5	1	14	2	0
Pruitt, Jason, Del.*	0	0	.000	5.29	12	0	0	0	1	1	17.0	14	76	10	10	2	0	1	2	9	0	13	4	0
Quick, Ben, C.W.Va.	3	1	.750	3.71	17	5	0	0	0	0	51.0	51	214	23	21	6	1	2	4	9	0	39	4	0
Ramirez, Enrique, Del.	6	4	.600	5.18	45	0	0	0	17	1	66.0	76	308	47	38	4	5	4	1	33	4	66	10	0
Ramirez, Santiago, Lex.	8	2	.800	3.63	45	0	0	0	23	4	79.1	69	328	35	32	2	4	2	3	28	1	85	8	1
Ramirez, Victor, Sav.	5	8	.385	5.08	19	16	0	0	2	0	88.2	93	418	60	50	12	0	6	15	57	0	94	12	2
Renteria, Juan, C.S.C.	4	4	.500	2.26	39	4	0	0	14	1	75.2	60	311	28	19	3	5	2	4	24	4	90	7	0
Renwick, Tyler, C.W.Va.	1	2	.333	11.57	7	0	0	0	2	0	11.2	17	63	16	15	1	2	2	0	13	1	8	5	0
Reynolds, Eric, Gre.*	0	0	.000	0.00	1	0	0	0	1	0	1.0	1	4	0	0	0	0	0	1	0	1	0	0	0
Ridgway, Jeff, C.S.C.*	7	8	.467	4.07	22	22	0	0	0	0	104.0	110	458	55	47	4	2	2	9	42	0	71	11	0
Riethmaier, Matthew, Lak.	4	4	.500	5.68	19	11	2	1	3	0	77.2	90	358	53	49	5	1	4	8	38	2	48	4	2
Rigueiro, Rafael, Hag.	5	3	.625	3.19	20	14	0	0	4	0	96.0	77	404	37	34	8	2	1	12	35	0	104	8	1
Rijo, Fernando, Wil.	11	7	.611	2.98	26	26	0	0	0	0	139.0	107	562	64	46	12	4	5	8	54	0	128	11	1
Rivard, Reggie, Sav.	5	4	.556	3.26	44	1	0	0	23	1	77.1	84	337	35	28	7	1	2	5	21	0	52	8	0
Rleal, Sendy, Del.	3	6	.333	3.57	20	20	1	0	0	0	103.1	99	420	50	41	9	0	5	7	27	0	83	6	2
Roberts, Nick, Lex.	10	1	.909	2.95	20	20	3	1	0	0	137.1	118	540	49	45	10	3	4	4	21	0	128	3	0
Roberts, Rick, Wil.*	3	1	.750	2.75	7	2	0	0	1	0	19.2	12	78	7	6	2	0	0	2	7	0	26	1	0
Rodriguez, Eddy, Del.	5	3	.625	3.39	41	0	0	0	6	1	61.0	58	261	27	23	4	0	1	2	23	0	64	4	0
Rodriguez, George, Lak.	4	3	.571	0.80	31	2	0	0	12	3	56.0	39	215	12	5	2	2	1	16	2	45	1	0
Rodriguez, Luis, Sav.	5	5	.500	3.71	16	16	1	0	0	0	77.2	60	327	38	32	9	1	3	9	30	0	88	1	0
Rodriguez, Mike, Del.	0	0	.000	9.64	5	0	0	0	2	0	4.2	6	25	5	5	1	0	1	6	0	5	0	0
Rogers, Brad, Del.	3	7	.300	4.58	34	14	0	0	6	1	92.1	106	410	63	47	8	2	2	5	36	2	79	5	0
Rogers, Devin, C'bus	2	3	.400	5.14	7	7	0	0	0	0	28.0	32	135	20	16	5	0	0	2	21	0	22	5	1
Rohling, Stuart, Kan.	0	0	.000	9.64	5	0	0	0	2	0	4.2	6	25	5	5	1	0	1	6	0	5	0	0
Rojas, Jose, Wil.	10	3	.769	2.12	24	23	1	0	0	0	135.2	107	540	42	32	7	7	2	7	42	0	116	9	0
Roman, Orlando, C'bia	1	2	.333	5.74	4	1	0	0	2	0	15.2	17	77	11	10	2	0	3	8	0	20	5	0
Roney, Matt, Ash.	8	10	.444	4.98	23	23	1	0	0	0	121.0	131	540	74	67	16	2	5	13	43	0	115	6	1
Rosario, Melvin, Ash.*	0	0	.000	20.25	1	0	0	0	0	0	1.1	3	10	4	3	0	0	1	0	2	0	1	2	0
Rosario, Rodrigo, Lex.	13	4	.765	2.14	30	21	1	0	5	2	147.0	105	584	46	35	8	7	2	10	36	1	131	3	0
Rundles, Rich, Aug.*	7	6	.538	2.43	19	19	0	0	0	0	115.0	109	468	46	31	5	5	7	10	0	94	4	0
Rust, Evan, C.S.C.	7	6	.538	3.06	35	11	0	0	20	12	97.0	88	411	47	33	3	6	2	6	27	2	88	5	0
Saarloos, Kirk, Lex.	1	1	.500	1.17	22	0	0	0	19	11	30.2	18	119	5	4	1	2	0	1	7	0	40	2	0
Sabens, Mike, Hick.	1	0	1.000	10.95	10	0	0	0	3	0	12.1	22	70	16	15	1	0	1	1	6	0	11	1	0
Sadowski, Chad, Lak.	4	2	.667	2.14	35	1	0	0	15	2	59.0	48	233	17	14	4	2	2	2	11	1	41	0	1
Sams, Aaron, Aug.*	1	1	.500	2.83	17	0	0	0	10	1	28.2	25	129	10	9	0	0	1	2	18	0	31	5	0
Sandoval, Marcos, C.W.Va.	1	6	.143	6.83	21	8	1	0	6	0	55.1	47	252	44	42	7	2	1	5	33	0	28	8	0

Pitcher, Team	W	L	Pct.	ERA	G	GS	CG	ShO	GF	Sv.	IP	H	TBF	R	ER	HR	SH	SF	HB	BB	IBB	SO	WP	Bk.
Santillan, Manny, Lex.	6	5	.545	3.54	38	7	0	0	8	1	96.2	83	408	43	38	4	5	3	6	43	1	90	7	0
Schmitt, Eric, Gre.	2	1	.667	3.38	7	7	0	0	0	0	37.1	32	152	15	14	4	0	1	3	9	0	35	1	0
Schwager, Matt, Del.	10	8	.556	2.26	27	14	4	1	8	1	103.1	85	411	41	26	7	2	3	6	14	1	80	2	0
Sclafani, Anthony, Mac.-Aug.	2	3	.400	3.90	13	0	0	0	11	1	30.0	31	128	14	13	3	2	0	0	10	0	22	3	0
Scuglik, Mike, Sav.*	0	1	.000	8.48	27	0	0	0	12	0	40.1	54	203	45	38	3	2	4	4	27	1	29	8	3
Seestedt, Mike, Del.	0	0	.000	9.00	4	0	0	0	3	0	6.0	9	29	6	6	1	0	0	0	2	0	5	0	0
Serrano, Alex, Ash.	0	0	.000	0.66	14	0	0	0	9	0	13.2	13	61	4	1	0	0	0	2	5	1	13	0	1
Shafer, Kurt, Hick.	0	0	.000	1.42	1	1	0	0	0	0	6.1	5	25	1	1	0	0	0	3	0	0	5	1	0
Sharber, Jeffery, Hick.	2	2	.500	1.99	7	7	0	0	0	0	45.1	34	185	13	10	2	1	0	1	19	0	57	4	0
Sheffield, Christopher, C.W.Va.	1	3	.250	10.32	6	3	0	0	0	0	11.1	7	60	13	13	0	0	1	2	20	0	12	4	0
Sherman, Chris, C'bia	0	0	.000	2.08	2	0	0	0	0	0	8.2	10	36	2	2	1	0	0	0	2	0	5	0	0
Shields, James, C.S.C.	4	5	.444	2.65	10	10	2	1	0	0	71.1	63	284	24	21	7	3	2	2	10	0	60	2	1
Simpson, Andre, Wil.	9	3	.750	2.30	24	9	0	0	6	1	97.1	75	386	27	25	8	4	1	3	20	0	96	2	0
Skyles, Matt, C'bus*	0	0	.000	2.90	11	1	0	0	6	2	31.0	30	135	13	10	2	1	1	1	8	1	23	3	1
Smalley, Mike, Mac.*	0	0	.000	12.46	5	0	0	0	4	0	4.1	12	28	10	6	0	1	0	0	0	1	2	0	0
Smith, Jason, Gre.	1	2	.333	5.73	5	4	0	0	0	0	22.0	34	105	19	14	3	3	0	3	7	0	13	0	0
Smith, Joe, Hag.-Gre.	10	8	.556	3.70	35	12	1	1	9	0	121.2	132	525	56	50	2	4	7	4	33	4	70	0	1
Smith, Matt, Gre.*	5	3	.625	2.59	16	16	1	1	0	0	97.1	69	389	37	28	1	3	1	3	32	0	116	8	0
Smith, Matthew, Kan.	2	3	.400	5.00	20	0	0	0	5	1	27.0	26	133	15	15	0	3	1	3	26	3	14	5	0
Smith, Mike, C.W.Va.	5	5	.500	2.10	14	14	2	1	0	0	94.1	78	378	32	22	2	1	2	6	21	0	85	6	0
Smoltz, John, Mac.	0	0	.000	1.80	1	1	0	0	0	0	5.0	4	17	1	1	0	0	0	0	0	0	5	0	0
Song, Seung, Aug.	3	2	.600	2.04	14	14	0	0	0	0	75.0	56	290	24	17	3	0	1	2	18	0	79	4	0
Sperring, Jayme, Del.	2	4	.333	2.97	53	0	0	0	46	26	63.2	50	268	25	21	6	3	0	3	30	3	75	5	1
Spillman, Jeromie, C.W.Va.*	1	2	.333	7.57	20	0	0	0	10	0	27.1	49	141	29	23	4	3	2	4	6	2	22	3	0
Stahl, Rich, Del.*	2	3	.400	2.67	6	6	0	0	0	0	33.2	24	135	15	10	3	1	0	2	15	0	31	3	0
Stamler, Keith, Sav.	2	1	.667	2.16	7	1	0	0	1	0	16.2	13	70	7	4	0	0	1	2	3	0	16	0	0
Stanford, Derek, Lex.	0	2	.000	6.94	3	3	0	0	0	0	11.2	9	48	9	9	2	1	0	1	7	0	5	0	0
Steffek, Brian, Wil.	0	1	.000	1.93	9	1	0	0	5	2	23.1	12	87	5	5	2	3	0	0	8	4	22	1	0
Stepka, Tom, Ash.	0	0	.000	3.18	2	0	0	0	0	0	5.2	5	24	4	2	0	0	0	1	0	0	4	0	0
Stevens, Josh, Gre.	1	0	1.000	2.95	19	2	0	0	3	0	36.2	29	145	12	12	3	0	0	2	9	0	42	0	0
Stiehl, Rob, Lex.	2	3	.400	1.98	14	12	0	0	0	0	50.0	28	207	17	11	2	0	2	34	0	59	5	2
Storey, Eric, Ash.	0	0	.000	0.00	1	0	0	0	1	0	2.0	0	6	0	0	0	0	0	0	1	0	0	0	0
Suttles, Donnie, C'bus	4	1	.800	3.50	21	0	0	0	5	4	43.2	36	180	19	17	2	2	1	6	15	0	29	4	0
Sweeney, James, Kan.*	8	4	.667	2.65	21	16	0	0	1	0	102.0	83	406	35	30	4	4	4	4	37	3	110	2	0
Tapia, Roman, Kan.	0	0	.000	0.00	1	0	0	0	0	0	0.0	0	1	0	0	0	0	0	0	1	0	0	0	0
Tate, Matt, Del.	2	3	.400	6.14	13	3	0	0	3	0	36.2	33	166	29	25	4	2	3	2	21	1	25	1	0
Tejeda, Rob, Lak.	8	9	.471	3.40	26	24	1	1	0	0	150.2	128	639	74	57	10	6	5	8	58	1	152	11	2
Templet, Eric, C'bia	0	2	.000	9.00	2	0	0	0	1	0	6.0	8	26	7	6	2	0	1	0	1	0	9	0	0
Tetz, Kris, C'bus	0	0	.000	0.00	1	0	0	0	0	0	2.0	0	6	0	0	0	0	0	0	1	0	3	0	0
Thomas, John, Hag.*	3	3	.500	4.16	15	15	0	0	0	0	71.1	70	302	40	33	5	1	3	6	22	0	65	3	2
Thompson, Derek, C'bus*	0	2	.000	9.75	2	2	0	0	0	0	12.0	16	54	13	13	2	0	1	0	3	0	5	1	0
Thompson, Matt, Aug.	9	10	.474	3.22	25	24	0	0	1	0	134.1	115	535	58	48	9	1	5	6	19	0	97	6	0
Thoms, Hank, C'bus	3	1	.750	2.98	19	1	0	0	8	1	45.1	40	194	20	15	3	5	0	1	15	1	51	2	0
Thorpe, Tracy, C.W.Va.	4	13	.235	5.08	24	23	0	0	0	0	102.2	108	472	77	58	8	6	6	10	51	0	81	11	1
Threets, Erick, Hag.*	2	0	1.000	0.75	12	0	0	0	3	1	24.0	13	94	3	2	1	0	1	9	0	32	2	1
Tomaszewski, Eliot, Del.	1	3	.250	4.43	18	4	0	0	4	2	40.2	59	187	25	20	3	1	3	1	7	0	32	3	0
Tremblay, Max, Lex.*	6	4	.600	4.14	48	0	0	0	27	4	67.1	74	308	37	31	9	4	3	3	29	2	84	7	0
Troilo, Joe, Aug.	4	3	.571	3.55	30	2	0	0	18	1	58.1	49	252	33	23	5	1	5	4	21	1	40	6	0
Ulacia, Dennis, Kan.*	8	1	.889	2.43	15	15	0	0	0	0	89.0	68	357	25	24	1	1	0	5	36	1	93	1	0
Urdaneta, Lino, Wil.	1	2	.333	7.61	10	4	0	0	3	0	23.2	31	110	23	20	7	0	2	3	11	0	16	2	0
Uzzell, Todd, Hag.	0	0	.000	3.60	1	1	0	0	0	0	5.0	5	20	2	2	1	0	0	0	3	0	3	0	0
Valdez, Domingo, Sav.	6	4	.600	3.24	15	15	1	0	0	0	86.0	50	346	33	31	7	1	3	8	38	1	107	7	1
Valentine, Joe, Kan.	2	2	.500	2.93	30	0	0	0	29	14	30.2	21	123	10	10	0	2	0	3	10	1	33	1	1
Vazquez, Will, Ash.	4	7	.364	5.67	16	14	0	0	1	0	85.2	92	383	62	54	9	3	2	5	35	2	64	4	2
Vigeland, Will, Sav.	5	4	.556	2.48	39	0	0	0	12	2	72.2	55	302	27	20	3	2	2	3	34	0	67	5	0
Villegas, Felix, Aug.	5	2	.286	3.59	34	7	0	0	11	6	90.1	100	409	63	36	9	5	2	6	30	2	62	10	0
Wade, Matt, C'bus	4	2	.667	3.36	10	10	0	0	0	0	59.0	61	249	23	22	4	2	0	5	16	0	33	4	0
Waechter, Doug, C.S.C.	8	11	.421	4.34	26	26	1	0	0	0	153.1	179	684	97	74	14	7	6	5	38	1	107	12	3
Wainwright, Adam, Mac.	10	10	.500	3.77	28	28	1	0	0	0	164.2	144	691	89	69	9	7	2	8	48	1	184	9	2
Waters, Chris, Mac.*	8	6	.571	3.35	25	24	3	1	0	0	147.2	131	616	75	55	14	4	4	7	52	0	78	8	1
Watkins, Dave, Mac.	3	1	.750	2.76	24	0	0	0	7	2	49.0	33	202	17	15	0	3	1	1	27	1	59	4	1
Webb, Nicholas, Ash.*	9	5	.643	3.33	19	18	1	0	1	1	116.1	111	475	52	43	10	2	1	7	27	0	92	5	3
Weslowski, Rob, C'bia	3	6	.333	4.28	23	5	0	0	11	1	61.0	68	264	32	29	7	2	6	3	16	0	59	2	0
Wilken, Kris, Del.	0	0	.000	0.00	2	0	0	0	2	0	1.1	3	7	0	0	0	0	0	0	1	0	0	0	0
Williams, Adam, Wil.*	1	1	.500	2.65	25	1	0	0	9	2	54.1	41	233	21	16	2	2	0	9	21	0	47	2	2
Wilson, C.J., Sav.*	1	2	.333	3.18	5	5	2	0	0	0	34.0	30	132	13	12	2	2	1	1	9	0	26	3	2
Wombacher, Mike, Gre.*	1	2	.333	3.62	38	0	0	0	14	0	49.2	54	214	26	20	4	2	3	0	13	0	41	6	0
Yacco, Anthony, Hag.	3	0	1.000	2.61	24	0	0	0	6	0	38.0	27	169	15	11	2	2	0	8	23	1	37	5	0
Yankosky, L.J., Mac.	0	0	.000	0.00	1	1	0	0	0	0	4.0	2	16	1	0	0	1	0	0	0	0	2	0	0
Young, Christopher, Hick.	5	3	.625	4.12	12	12	0	0	0	0	74.1	79	320	39	34	6	2	1	3	20	0	72	0	0
Young, Curtis, Kan.	0	0	.000	2.70	6	0	0	0	5	0	6.2	9	37	12	2	3	0	2	4	0	7	0	0
Young, Simon, C'bus*	0	2	.000	3.89	8	7	0	0	0	0	39.1	48	168	18	17	3	1	3	1	13	0	35	2	1

PITCHERS WITH TWO OR MORE TEAMS

Pitcher, Team	W	L	Pct.	ERA	G	GS	CG	ShO	GF	Sv.	IP	H	TBF	R	ER	HR	SH	SF	HB	BB	IBB	SO	WP	Bk.
De Paula, Julio, Ash.	1	1	.500	3.78	3	3	0	0	0	0	16.2	19	76	13	7	3	0	0	3	2	0	26	1	0
De Paula, Julio, Gre.	6	1	.857	2.75	8	8	0	0	0	0	55.2	35	221	19	17	2	1	0	4	21	0	67	2	3
Sclafani, Anthony, Mac.	1	0	1.000	1.93	5	0	0	0	4	1	14.0	11	55	4	3	0	0	0	4	0	12	1	0
Sclafani, Anthony, Aug.	1	3	.250	5.63	8	0	0	0	7	0	16.0	20	73	10	10	3	2	0	0	6	0	10	2	0
Smith, Joe, Hag.	7	2	.778	2.57	24	2	0	0	9	0	70.0	64	288	21	20	1	0	4	3	21	4	45	0	1
Smith, Joe, Gre.	3	6	.333	5.23	11	10	1	1	0	0	51.2	68	237	35	30	1	4	3	1	12	0	25	0	0

COMBINATION SHUTOUTS: **Asheville (11)**—Dohmann-Huisman, Abell-Berney-Gomez, Vazquez-Green-Huisman, Dohmann-Green-Huisman, Buglovsky-Lorenzo, Buglovsky-Huisman, Webb-Matos, Martin-Green-Lorenzo, Buglovsky-Serrano-Huisman, Berney-Green-Serrano-Huisman, Roney-Gomez. **Augusta (9)**—Song-Miniel-Dickinson, Rundles-Fontana, Thompson-Giese-Dickinson, Song-Dickinson, Thompson-Adams-Giese, Fontana-Adams-Giese, Miniel-Adams-Giese, Adams-Giese-Sams-Troilo, Perez-Francisco-Adams. **Columbia (6)**—Musser-Cox-Lavigne, Gonzalez-Elliott-Hee, Patterson-Peterson-Hee, Gonzalez-Mattinoni, Lopez-Herbison-Lavigne, Weslowski-Hee. **Charleston, S.C. (8)**—Ridgway-Anderson-Rust, McClung-Anderson-Backe, Rust-Benedetti, Ridgway-Benedetti-Anderson, McClung-Coose, Renteria-Benedetti, McClung-Carney-Coose, Waechter-Parker-Coose. **Charleston, W.V. (5)**—Bauer-Nunley-McCulloch, Malaska-Renteria, Smith-Ozuna-McCulloch, Gassner-Ozuna-McCulloch, Comolli-Gracesqui. **Columbus (7)**—Davis-Larson-Colon, Wade-Neil, Cabrera-Percell-Colon, Davis-Thoms-Canale, Alvarez-Suttles-Larson-Colon, Cabrera-Suttles-Colon, De la Cruz-Matsko-Donaghey. **Delmarva (6)**—Rogers-Schwager-Sperring, Rleal-Ramirez, Andrade-Rodriguez, Bartlett-Ramirez-Gutierrez-Ormond, Montilla-Farren-Sperring, Bartlett-Pruitt-Rogers-Sperring. **Greensboro (4)**—Smith-Anderson, De Paula-Blankenship-Faigin, Anderson-Faigin-Knowles, Blankenship-Faigin. **Hagerstown (10)**—Smith-Faust, Bonser-Smith-Markert, Smith-Faust, Thomas-Jones-Markert, Bonser-Smith-Jones-Faust, Bonser-Jones-Yacco-Markert, Bonser-Faust-Jones-Markert, Clark-Brous, Clark-Faust-Markert, Bonser-Brous, Bonser-Threets-Pavon. **Hickory (2)**—Hurley-Connolly-Higgins, Sharber-Higgins. **Kannapolis (11)**—McWhirter-Murray, Ulacia-Madrill, McWhirter-Munoz-Valentine, Ulacia-Munoz-Valentine, Ulacia-Munoz-Castro, Madrill-Mozingo-Munoz-Hughes, Ferrand-Castro, Ferrand-Munoz-Valentine, Malone-Munoz-Hughes, Ferrand-Munoz-Castro, Phillips-Castro. **Lakewood (6)**—Hernandez-Adams-Brito, Lawson-Rodriguez-Sadowski, Carter-Adams-Bullock-Sadowski-Elskamp, Lawson-Bullock, Buchholz-Rodriguez, Riethmaier-Adams. **Lexington (13)**—Nannini-Rosario, Stiehl-Peguero-George, Nannini-Peguero, Rosario-Ramirez, Stiehl-Santillan-George, Nannini-George, Roberts-Tremblay, Jamison-Peguero, Pluta-Georgo-Ramirez, Pluta-Krysa-Tremblay-George, Pluta-Saarloos-George-Tremblay, Stanford-George-Saarloos, Peguero-Middleton-Ramirez-Saarloos. **Macon (6)**—Waters-Jones, Kozlowski-Colon-Mendez-Baker, Colon-Baker, Mikels-Perez-Watkins, Kozlowski-Watkins-Mendez-Mikels, Davies-Collazo. **Savannah (7)**—Gilbert-Vigeland-Graham, Hawkins-Graham-Burke, Valdez-Burke-Rivard, Gilbert-Burke, Rodriguez-Rivard-Echols, Valdez-Echols, Echols-Rivard. **Wilmington (12)**—Rojas-Roberts-Bauer, Rijo-Montero-Keirstead, Rojas-Keirstead, Bridenbaugh-Montero-Keirstead, Hanrahan-McCrotty-Bauer, Rojas-Simpson-Bauer, Rijo-Bauer, Rijo-McCrotty, Rojas-Cordero-Lugo, Diggins-Hughes, Hanrahan-Cordero, Diggins-Lugo.

NO-HIT GAMES: Bucktrot, Lakewood defeated Hickory, 11-1 in seven innings, April 12.

2001 FIELDING

TEAM

Team	Pct.	G	PO	A	E	TC	DP	TP	PB
Lexington	.974	140	3736	1457	138	5331	105	0	27
Hagerstown	.972	140	3703	1487	152	5342	120	0	19
Kannapolis	.971	139	3539	1496	151	5186	80	0	18
Wilmington	.970	138	3624	1448	155	5227	102	0	25
Columbia	.965	135	3521	1469	180	5170	90	0	36
Greensboro	.965	140	3647	1480	188	5315	90	0	37
Macon	.964	133	3542	1374	182	5098	87	0	14
Savannah	.964	136	3543	1291	182	5016	102	0	17
Augusta	.963	139	3641	1456	194	5291	76	0	28
Lakewood	.963	139	3723	1411	196	5330	118	0	43
Asheville	.963	139	3599	1448	194	5241	122	0	19
Hickory	.962	140	3657	1550	206	5413	112	0	37
Delmarva	.961	140	3598	1399	203	5200	89	0	26
Charleston, S.C.	.960	140	3701	1510	216	5427	92	0	33
Columbus	.959	136	3621	1425	214	5260	115	0	22
Charleston, W.Va.	.958	138	3534	1471	219	5224	117	0	32

INDIVIDUAL

FIRST BASEMEN

NOTE: All caps denotes fielding-percentage leader based on 70 games for catchers, 93 for all other non-pitchers and 112 innings for pitchers. *Throws lefthanded.

Player, Team	Pct.	G	PO	A	E	TC	DP
Anderson, Melvin, Lak.	1.000	3	10	0	0	10	0
Avila, Rob, Kan.	.000	2	0	0	0	0	0
Bass, Chris, Hick.	.993	35	279	11	2	292	30
Becker, Jeff, C'bus	.986	14	132	10	2	144	14
Bell, Derek, Hag.	.990	11	88	8	1	97	7
Bernard, Dagoberto, Ash.	1.000	3	26	2	0	28	2
Botts, Jason, Sav.	.990	62	451	23	5	479	31
Brazell, Craig, C'bia	.989	58	509	24	6	539	39
Brisson, Dustin, Aug.	.982	82	722	63	14	799	46
Calabrese, Tony, Gre.	.923	3	11	1	1	13	1
Cooper, Matt, Aug.	.964	31	247	18	10	275	9
Cotten, Jeremy, Hick.	.984	110	901	78	16	995	70
Cronin, Shane, Gre.	.975	8	71	7	2	80	5
Crozier, Eric, C'bus*	.974	20	145	5	4	154	13
Dacey, Ryan, Wil.	.996	29	216	19	1	236	14
Delgado, Dario, Lak.	.977	68	518	38	13	569	39
Delgado, Mario, Lak.*	.973	50	405	26	12	443	40
Deschenes, Pat, C'bia	.983	42	369	25	7	401	27
Detienne, Dave, Wil.	.985	8	62	2	1	65	3
Dill, Jason, Sav.*	.987	20	141	10	2	153	13
Elder, Rick, Del.*	.970	49	401	19	13	433	24
Espinoza, Efren, Hick.	1.000	1	1	0	0	1	0
Esquivel, Lale, Sav.	.992	31	241	13	2	256	23
Fennell, Jason, Kan.	1.000	1	7	0	0	7	0
Forbes, Mike, Mac.	.983	76	597	42	11	650	46
Gajewski, Matt, Sav.	1.000	6	48	2	0	50	2
Gillikin, Joe, Kan.	1.000	2	22	2	0	24	0
Griggs, Reggie, Lak.*	.947	7	70	1	4	75	5
Gutierrez, Said, C.W.Va.	.978	6	44	1	1	46	4
Haase, Jeff, C'bus	.956	10	86	0	4	90	10

Player, Team	Pct.	G	PO	A	E	TC	DP
Harper, Brett, C'bia	.976	9	79	1	2	82	6
Hattig, John, Aug.	.983	27	220	13	4	237	15
Hawpe, Brad, Ash.*	.990	52	472	29	5	506	34
Hensler, Brad, C'bia	1.000	5	63	1	0	64	3
Hewes, Robert, Sav.	1.000	1	2	0	0	2	0
Jeffcoat, Bryon, Mac.	.960	4	22	2	1	25	1
Kaup, Nathan, C.S.C.	1.000	1	15	0	0	15	0
Keene, Kurt, C.W.Va.	.958	3	20	3	1	24	2
Kinchen, Jason, Gre.	.992	44	366	19	3	388	19
Lankford, Derrick, Lak.	.980	24	182	11	4	197	17
Leaumont, Jeff, Gre.*	.995	22	198	12	1	211	16
Lebron, Francisco, Kan.	.989	10	84	9	1	94	2
Leon, Alfredo, Del.	.967	12	112	6	4	122	11
Lopez, Raul, Mac.	.984	42	347	25	6	378	19
Lunsford, James, Hag.	1.000	1	3	0	0	3	2
Malpica, Martin, C.W.Va.	1.000	7	65	6	0	71	5
Manley, Adam, Del.*	1.000	2	6	1	0	7	0
Marsh, Jason, C.S.C.	.938	3	15	0	1	16	1
McKee, Mickey, Lex.	.990	36	286	26	3	315	23
Mejia, Manuel, Hick	1.000	4	14	3	0	17	1
Michaelis, Derek, Wil.*	.997	32	260	25	1	286	30
Monroy, Sam, C.S.C.	1.000	1	1	0	0	1	0
Moore, Chris, Ash.	.950	2	18	1	1	20	2
Morales, Michael, Mac.	1.000	1	1	0	0	1	0
Nelson, Nathan, Lex.	.991	12	109	4	1	114	7
Nunez, Felix, C.S.C.	.982	61	572	23	11	606	40
Pack, Branden, Sav.	.993	18	127	12	1	140	10
Perich, Josh, C'bia	1.000	3	19	3	0	22	1
Raffo, John, C'bia*	1.000	9	67	11	0	78	3
Reyes, Rene, Ash.	.989	60	505	36	6	547	44
Ridley, Shayne, Del.	.995	22	172	11	1	184	10
Riepe, Andy, Aug.	1.000	1	10	1	0	11	1
Rock, Jamie, Ash.	.990	10	89	7	1	97	10
ROGOWSKI, Casey, Kan.*	.995	128	1051	84	6	1141	69
Royer, Lissandro, C'bia	1.000	1	3	0	0	3	0
Santos, Deivis, Hag.*	.988	125	1048	83	14	1145	97
Saucke, Casey, Del.	1.000	1	2	0	0	2	1
Schmitt, Brian, Lex.*	.982	98	799	57	16	872	68
Schuda, Justin, C.S.C.	.978	79	661	53	16	730	38
Seestedt, Mike, Del.	.974	11	69	5	2	76	4
Sisk, Aaron, C.W.Va.	.932	7	52	3	4	59	7
Snyder, Mike, C.W.Va.	.989	118	989	85	12	1086	92
Soto, Saul, Wil.	.992	50	444	24	4	472	27
Storey, Eric, Ash.	.994	15	146	10	1	157	18
Story-Harden, Thomari, Wil.	.991	15	104	4	1	109	8
Sutter, Tony, Gre.	.976	7	41	0	1	42	0
Swedlow, Sean, C'bus	.974	96	794	60	23	877	64
Tapia, Roman, Kan.	.958	4	20	3	1	24	1
Terveen, Bryce, Mac.	.977	19	156	16	4	176	9
Thompson, Alva, Mac.	1.000	3	14	1	0	15	2
Todd, Jeremy, C'bia	.993	14	128	6	1	135	6
Trumble, Dan, Hag.	.957	9	62	5	3	70	2
Turner, Jason, Gre.*	.987	68	551	52	8	611	41
Umbria, Jose, C.W.Va.	1.000	2	14	4	0	18	2
Van Buizen, Rodney, Wil.	1.000	12	89	3	0	92	9
Villegas, Ernest, Sav.	.982	10	60	6	1	67	4
Volquez, Bolivar, C.S.C.	1.000	1	4	0	0	4	0
Wilken, Kris, Del.	.989	59	409	26	5	440	33

SECOND BASEMEN

Player, Team	Pct.	G	PO	A	E	TC	DP
Abreu, Dave, C'bia	.916	16	37	39	7	83	3
Acevedo, Inocencio, Sav.	.963	66	116	173	11	300	27
Agramonte, Marcos, Sav.	.957	66	116	150	12	278	35
Alexander, Kevin, Hag.	.984	28	52	72	2	126	18
Amador, Chris, Kan.	.976	101	179	231	10	420	42
Anderson, Jon, Aug.	.969	33	52	75	4	131	10
Arias, Leandro, C'bia	.985	15	23	42	1	66	8
Baker, Casey, Gre.-C'bus	1.000	5	6	6	0	12	1
Bass, Chris, Hick.	1.000	1	1	0	0	1	0
Becker, Jeff, C'bus	.974	17	38	36	2	76	9
Bernard, Dagoberto, Ash.	.962	10	21	29	2	52	4
Bonifay, Josh, Hick.	.958	8	21	25	2	48	4
Bozanich, Sam, Gre.	.944	42	71	96	10	177	16
Cabrera, Leonel, Hag.	1.000	9	17	12	0	29	1
Calahan, Larry, Kan.	1.000	1	0	1	0	1	0
Canales, Josh, Wil.	.965	12	17	38	2	57	7
Carroll, Wes, Lak.	.954	33	78	68	7	153	19
Castillo, Carlos, C'bia	.973	63	101	191	8	300	35
Castro, Bernabel, Gre.	.956	96	171	265	20	456	39
Castro, Julio, Kan.	1.000	1	1	4	0	5	0
Cates, Gary, Del.	.949	72	107	174	15	296	28
Centeno, Irwin, C.S.C.	.958	96	169	261	19	449	45
Choy Foo, Rodney, C'bus	.922	12	17	30	4	51	9
Collazo, Julio, Lak.	.958	42	88	96	8	192	22
Crespo, Manny, C.W.Va.	.910	18	30	41	7	78	6
Cuello, Domingo, Hick.	.955	17	36	49	4	89	11
Dacey, Ryan, Wil.	.985	16	26	38	1	65	7
Daniel, Steve, Kan.	1.000	2	2	1	0	3	1
Delfino, Lee, C.W.Va.	.980	12	18	31	1	50	9
Del Rosario, Manny, Del.	.978	69	114	156	6	276	28
Dement, Dan, C.S.C.	.943	41	77	121	12	210	16
Detienne, Dave, Wil.	.972	47	81	124	6	211	25
Dorta, Melvin, Aug.	.981	36	65	87	3	155	18
ESCALONA, Felix, Lex.	.979	109	203	298	11	512	60
Espinoza, Efren, Hick.	.957	33	78	99	8	185	21
Figueroa, Carlos, Ash.	.882	11	16	29	6	51	5
Flores, Ralphs, Kan.	.940	23	25	54	5	84	7
Gambino, Mike, Aug.	.939	7	12	19	2	33	2
Gann, Bryan, Hag.	.964	108	227	277	19	523	71
Garcia, Daniel, C'bia	.927	30	46	93	11	150	11
Garcia, Oscar, C'bus	1.000	9	18	27	0	45	5
Green, Kevin, Mac.	.882	8	12	18	4	34	5
Haase, Jeff, C'bus	1.000	1	1	2	0	3	0
Hattig, John, Aug.	.857	2	2	4	1	7	1
Hernandez, Jose, Hick.	1.000	1	2	1	0	3	1
Hernandez, Vladimir, C'bia	.966	5	14	14	1	29	2
Inglett, Joe, C'bus	.955	57	97	135	11	243	33
Ison, Jeremy, Kan.	.944	19	36	49	5	90	7
Jacobs, John, C.S.C.	.667	2	1	1	1	3	1
Jeffcoat, Bryon, Mac.	.968	16	24	36	2	62	7
Jimenez, Rich, C.W.Va.	.914	13	24	29	5	58	9
Keene, Kurt, C.W.Va.	.971	6	13	21	1	35	7
Lackaff, John, Kan.	1.000	1	0	1	0	1	0
Machado, Aleyandro, Mac.	.992	68	108	156	2	266	25
Manning, Pat, Mac.	.963	35	70	86	6	162	16
Martin, Tyler, Sav.	.972	10	14	21	1	36	4
McKee, Mickey, Lex.	.833	1	2	3	1	6	0
McLouth, Nathan, Hick.	.000	1	0	0	0	0	0
Monroy, Sam, C.S.C.	1.000	6	10	19	0	29	3
Morales, Michael, Mac.	.969	20	26	37	2	65	6
Navarrete, Ray, Hick.	.988	19	34	49	1	84	11
Nieves, Raul, Aug.	.961	68	106	188	12	306	23
Peck, Bryan, Ash.	1.000	2	5	4	0	9	2
Pichardo, Henry, C'bus	.991	48	90	127	2	219	25
Reyes, Ambiorix, Lak.	.973	46	92	128	6	226	25
Reyes, Ivan, Gre.	1.000	1	1	4	0	5	1
Rich, Dominic, C.W.Va.	.972	78	149	168	9	326	40
Ridley, Shayne, Del.	1.000	2	1	1	0	2	0
Rodriguez, Mike, Del.	.944	21	30	37	4	71	7
Rodriguez, Ricardo, Mac.	1.000	1	1	3	0	4	0
Royer, Lissandro, C'bia	.921	9	12	23	3	38	3
Saucke, Casey, Del.	.905	7	9	10	2	21	0
Sisk, Aaron, C.W.Va.	.953	16	21	40	3	64	8
Storey, Eric, Ash.	.867	6	13	13	4	30	6
Svihlik, D.J., Gre.	.875	3	3	4	1	8	2
Toven, John, Lex.	.963	34	43	87	5	135	12
Van Buizen, Rodney, Wil.	.984	67	130	187	5	322	35
Vilorio, Miguel, Ash.	.963	113	206	341	21	568	62
Voshell, Key, Lak.	.959	25	48	69	5	122	11
Wilken, Kris, Del.	.000	2	0	0	0	0	0
Yan, Edwin, Hick.	.944	68	146	173	19	338	32
Youngbauer, Scott, Lak.	.000	1	0	0	0	0	0

SECOND BASEMEN WITH TWO OR MORE TEAMS

Player, Team	Pct.	G	PO	A	E	TC	DP
Baker, Casey, Gre.	1.000	4	3	4	0	7	0
Baker, Casey, C'bus	1.000	1	3	2	0	5	1

THIRD BASEMEN

Player, Team	Pct.	G	PO	A	E	TC	DP
Acevedo, Inocencio, Sav.	.920	14	8	15	2	25	2
Agramonte, Marcos, Sav.	.818	3	0	9	2	11	2
Alexander, Kevin, Hag.	.955	38	17	68	4	89	4
Anderson, Jon, Aug.	.769	8	0	10	3	13	2
Anderson, Melvin, Lak.	.000	2	0	0	0	0	0
Avila, Rob, Lak.	1.000	1	1	0	0	1	0
Aybar, Willy, Wil.	.948	118	106	225	18	349	15
Bass, Chris, Hick.	.901	28	18	37	6	61	6
Becker, Jeff, C'bus	.913	16	14	28	4	46	0
Bell, Derek, Hag.	.943	95	68	162	14	244	19
Bernard, Dagoberto, Ash.	.000	3	0	0	0	0	0
Blanco, Tony, Aug.	.841	51	23	88	21	132	3
Bozanich, Sam, Gre.	.000	1	0	0	0	0	0
Calabrese, Tony, Gre.	.929	7	2	11	1	14	0
Calahan, Larry, Kan.	1.000	4	3	5	0	8	0
Carroll, Wes, Lak.	.857	4	1	5	1	7	0
Castillo, Carlos, C'bia	.889	5	4	12	2	18	1
Cates, Gary, Del.	.923	7	3	9	1	13	0
Chaves, Brandon, Hick.	.927	18	7	31	3	41	5
Chavez, Angel, Hag.	.667	8	1	9	5	15	0
Corporan, Elvis, Gre.	.933	135	81	211	21	313	13
Cosby, Rob, C.W.Va.	.905	116	99	252	37	388	21
Crespo, Manny, C.W.Va.	.767	11	3	20	7	30	1
Cruz, Enrique, C'bia	.924	102	70	196	22	288	17
Dacey, Ryan, Wil.	.875	8	4	10	2	16	1
Dancy, Cliff, Lak.	.600	2	1	2	2	5	0
De Caster, Yurendell, Hick.	.897	62	53	129	21	203	13
De La Cruz, Miguel, Hick.	.926	10	5	20	2	27	7
Del Rosario, Manny, Del.	.909	30	17	53	7	77	3
Dement, Dan, C.S.C.	.897	20	4	31	4	39	2
Deschenes, Pat, C'bia	1.000	1	0	4	0	4	1
Detienne, Dave, Wil.	.955	9	7	14	1	22	1
Encarnacion, Edwin, Sav.	.891	45	35	63	12	110	2
Espinoza, Efren, Hick.	.958	9	10	13	1	24	2
Flannigan, Tim, C'bia	.923	15	8	16	2	26	1
Flores, Ralphs, Kan.	.933	10	11	17	2	30	1
Forbes, Mike, Mac.	.778	12	3	18	6	27	1
Gajewski, Matt, Sav.	.750	1	1	2	1	4	0
Garcia, Oscar, C'bus	.833	3	2	3	1	6	0
German, Ramon, Lex.	.948	126	83	207	16	306	14
Green, Kevin, Mac.	.000	1	0	0	0	0	0
Hattig, John, Aug.	.871	11	2	25	4	31	3
Hensler, Brad, C'bia	1.000	1	1	0	0	1	0
Hewes, Robert, Sav.	.932	27	24	44	5	73	2
Jacobs, John, C.S.C.	.000	1	0	0	0	0	0
Jeffcoat, Bryon, Mac.	.870	5	4	16	3	23	1
Jimenez, Rich, C.W.Va.	1.000	1	0	2	0	2	0
Johnston, Ryan, Lak.	.000	1	0	0	0	0	0
LACKAFF, John, Kan.	.970	123	78	245	10	333	15
Leon, Alfredo, Del.	.903	74	59	127	20	206	9
Lincoln, Justin, Ash.	.858	62	35	104	23	162	13
Malpica, Martin, C.W.Va.	.667	2	0	2	1	3	0
Manning, Pat, Mac.	.933	21	14	28	3	45	1
Martin, Tyler, Sav.	.870	10	6	14	3	23	0
McKee, Mickey, Lex.	.885	13	10	13	3	26	0
Mongeluzzo, Anthony, Sav.	.895	41	32	53	10	95	6
Mooney, Dan, Aug.	.818	5	1	8	2	11	1
Navarrete, Ray, Hick.	.913	20	7	35	4	46	0
Nelson, Nathan, Lex.	.889	7	3	13	2	18	1
Nieves, Raul, Aug.	.923	23	15	40	5	60	2
Oropeza, Asdrubal, Mac.	.942	108	60	199	16	275	19
Pack, Branden, Sav.	.750	3	1	2	1	4	0
Peck, Bryan, Ash.	.887	16	12	35	6	53	2
Pichardo, Henry, C'bus	.933	4	4	10	1	15	1
Reyes, Ambiorix, Lak.	.909	3	1	9	1	11	0
Richardson, Juan, Lak.	.923	132	91	220	26	337	19
Ridley, Shayne, Del.	.933	17	10	18	2	30	2
Riepe, Andy, Aug.	.000	1	0	0	1	1	0
Royer, Lissandro, C'bia	.949	13	8	29	2	39	2
Salas, Juan, C.S.C.	.887	127	95	236	42	373	12
Santamarina, Juan, Kan.	.733	6	4	7	4	15	0
Saucke, Casey, Del.	1.000	2	1	7	0	8	0
Seestedt, Mike, Del.	1.000	1	0	1	0	1	0
Sherrod, Justin, Aug.	.897	49	29	84	13	126	5
Sisk, Aaron, C.W.Va.	.909	13	7	33	4	44	2
Smith, Corey, C'bus	.856	114	73	195	45	313	23

Player, Team	Pct.	G	PO	A	E	TC	DP
Smith, Sam, Ash.	.805	19	5	28	8	41	3
Storey, Eric, Ash.	.901	43	25	84	12	121	5
Strankman, Elliott, Hag.	.850	8	3	14	3	20	0
Sutter, Tony, Gre.	.692	4	1	8	4	13	0
Tapia, Roman, Kan.	.875	5	2	5	1	8	0
Van Buizen, Rodney, Wil.	1.000	7	6	14	0	20	1
Wilken, Kris, Del.	.925	29	18	44	5	67	4
Youkilis, Kevin, Aug.	1.000	5	6	11	0	17	1

SHORTSTOPS

Player, Team	Pct.	G	PO	A	E	TC	DP
Acevedo, Inocencio, Sav.	.934	23	27	58	6	91	11
Alexander, Kevin, Hag.	.929	5	6	7	1	14	1
Amador, Chris, Kan.	.000	1	0	0	0	0	0
Anderson, Jon, Aug.	1.000	4	5	12	0	17	2
Athas, Jamie, Hag.	.958	64	84	187	12	283	37
Baker, Casey, C'bus	.750	3	2	4	2	8	1
Barmes, Clint, Ash.	.943	74	128	237	22	387	49
Becker, Jeff, C'bus	.960	7	8	16	1	25	2
Bernard, Dagoberto, Ash.	.956	13	17	26	2	45	6
Bordick, Mike, Del.	.000	1	0	0	0	0	0
Brewer, Jace, C.S.C.	.937	101	142	286	29	457	35
Calabrese, Tony, Gre.	.949	32	42	87	7	136	15
Canales, Josh, Wil.	.959	40	56	108	7	171	18
Carroll, Wes, Lak.	1.000	1	0	1	0	1	0
Castillo, Carlos, C'bia	.957	8	9	13	1	23	2
Castro, Julio, Kan.	1.000	1	1	3	0	4	0
Cates, Gary, Del.	.855	20	24	35	10	69	5
Chaves, Brandon, Hick.	.952	90	127	273	20	420	45
Chavez, Angel, Hag.	1.000	5	10	12	0	22	5
Colmenter, Jesus, C'bus	.925	39	47	102	12	161	23
Cruz, Enrique, C'bia	.918	22	32	58	8	98	6
Dacey, Ryan, Wil.	.923	4	5	7	1	13	1
Daniel, Steve, Kan.	.913	54	72	137	20	229	14
Del Rosario, Manny, Del.	1.000	6	0	6	0	6	1
Delfino, Lee, C.W.Va.	.922	16	20	39	5	64	5
Dement, Dan, C.S.C.	.818	7	4	14	4	22	1
Detienne, Davo, Wil.	.929	19	25	40	5	70	8
Escalona, Felix, Lex.	.883	20	37	54	12	103	11
Espinoza, Efren, Hick.	1.000	1	2	3	0	5	0
Flores, Ralphs, Kan.	.881	17	18	34	7	59	5
Gann, Bryan, Hag.	.000	1	0	0	0	0	0
Garcia, Nick, Del.	.940	129	178	305	31	514	53
Garrido, Tomas, Hag.	.940	45	67	120	12	199	17
Ison, Jeremy, Kan.	1.000	2	0	2	0	2	0
Jackson, Brandon, Gre.	.913	5	4	17	2	23	3
Jeffcoat, Bryon, Mac.	1.000	5	5	15	0	20	1
Jimenez, Rich, C.W.Va.	.828	7	7	17	5	29	0
Johnson, Kelly, Mac.	.905	116	131	298	45	474	33
Katz, Damon, C'bus	.923	13	10	38	4	52	5
Keene, Kurt, C.W.Va.	.958	5	11	12	1	24	4
Luna, Hector, C'bus	.933	63	116	190	22	328	39
Machado, Aleyandro, Mac.	.943	14	14	36	3	53	7
Manning, Pat, Mac.	1.000	1	0	1	0	1	0
Martin, Tyler, Sav.	.000	1	0	0	0	0	0
Mayorson, Manuel, C.W.Va.	1.000	1	2	0	0	2	0
Mendez, Deivi, Sav.	.946	49	80	147	13	240	23
Mongeluzzo, Anthony, Sav.	.778	1	3	4	2	9	1
Morales, Michael, Mac.	.824	5	8	6	3	17	4
Morban, Jose, Sav.	.942	121	170	320	30	520	51
Nieves, Raul, Aug.	.911	21	33	49	8	90	8
Perez, Kenny, Aug.	.946	118	178	308	28	514	42
Pichardo, Henry, C'bus	.929	19	34	45	6	85	5
Powers, Jeff, Ash.	.986	19	25	45	1	71	10
Repko, Jason, Wil.	.921	77	109	195	26	330	40
Reyes, Ambiorix, Lak.	.968	23	31	61	3	95	13
Reyes, Guillermo, Gre.	.964	70	117	174	11	302	28
Reyes, Ivan, Gre.	.929	49	87	137	17	241	20
REYES, Jose, C'bia	.964	108	151	330	18	499	49
Rodriguez, Ricardo, Mac.	.909	3	2	8	1	11	1
Sherrod, Justin, Aug.	1.000	1	0	3	0	3	0
Sisk, Aaron, C.W.Va.	.800	2	5	3	2	10	2
Storey, Eric, Ash.	1.000	6	5	13	0	18	5
Strankman, Elliott, Hag.	.901	30	35	83	13	131	12
Sutter, Tony, Gre.	.958	5	9	14	1	24	2
Tablado, Raul, C.W.Va.	.924	107	154	310	38	502	60
Tena, Hector, Ash.	.936	32	51	81	9	141	9
Toven, John, Lex.	.977	10	19	24	1	44	2
Volquez, Bolivar, C.S.C.	.915	36	44	106	14	164	20
Whiteman, Tom, Lex.	.949	110	143	286	23	452	59
Yan, Edwin, Hick.	.918	53	73	141	19	233	22
Youngbauer, Scott, Lak.	.923	119	177	335	43	555	72

OUTFIELDERS

Player, Team	Pct.	G	PO	A	E	TC	DP
Abercrombie, Reggie, Wil.	.933	124	201	8	15	224	3
Acevedo, Carlos, Lak.	.983	109	221	16	4	241	1
Acuna, Ron, C'bia	.950	95	143	8	8	159	2
Aliendo, Humberto, Hick.	.976	19	39	2	1	42	0
Anderson, Jon, Aug.	1.000	1	1	0	0	1	0
Anderson, Melvin, Lak.	.966	12	28	0	1	29	0
Asadoorian, Rick, Aug.	.979	96	226	5	5	236	0
Ascencion, Quincy, Del.	.917	34	43	1	4	48	0
Auterson, Jeff, Ash.	.962	18	25	0	1	26	0
Avila, Rob, Lak.	.950	14	18	1	1	20	0
Baldelli, Rocco, C.S.C.	.964	112	229	11	9	249	1
BARNETTE, Jason, Lak.*	.996	121	254	3	1	258	0
Bonifay, Josh, Hick.	.875	8	6	1	1	8	0
Bonner, Adam, C.S.C.	.981	111	193	9	4	206	4
Botts, Jason, Sav.	.957	45	60	6	3	69	1
Brazoban, Yhency, Gre.	.959	122	193	19	9	221	4
Bryan, Jason, Sav.	.943	24	33	0	2	35	0
Burrows, Angelo, Mac.	.985	107	258	5	4	267	1
Bush, Brian, Lak.	.950	19	37	1	2	40	0
Buttler, Victor, Hick.*	.987	87	151	5	2	158	1
Carter, Bryan, Hag.*	.983	52	58	1	1	60	1
Castro, Vince, Hick.	.990	52	89	6	1	96	1
Cates, Gary, Del.	.960	14	22	2	1	25	0
Church, Ryan, C'bus*	.987	96	215	8	3	226	1
Ciofrone, Paul, Lak.	1.000	5	5	0	0	5	0
Ciraco, Darren, Kan.	.943	102	155	11	10	176	2
Coleman, Alph, Mac.	.982	105	159	7	3	169	2
Crespo, Manny, C.W.Va.	1.000	3	7	0	0	7	0
Crozier, Eric, C'bus*	.980	34	40	1	1	51	0
Cruz, Orlando, Sav.	.972	34	63	7	2	72	3
Dancy, Cliff, Lak.	.929	5	13	0	1	14	0
Davenport, Ron, C.W.Va.	.913	64	83	1	8	92	1
Dees, Charlie, Sav.	.983	35	54	3	1	58	2
Del Rosario, Manny, Del.	.000	1	0	0	0	0	0
Dement, Dan, C.S.C.	.974	28	35	3	1	39	1
Devarez, Noel, C'bia	1.000	9	15	0	0	15	0
Dill, Jason, Sav.*	1.000	26	33	2	0	35	0
Donato, Greg, Mac.	1.000	1	2	0	0	2	0
Duncan, Jeff, C'bia*	.959	87	136	6	6	148	0
Elder, Rick, Del.*	.973	43	69	2	2	73	0
Ellison, Jason, Hag.	.984	129	282	18	5	305	2
Escalera, Jose, Wil.	1.000	4	11	0	0	11	0
Espinoza, Efren, Hick.	.875	3	7	0	1	8	0
Evans, Austin, Sav.*	.986	46	70	0	1	71	0
Fajardo, Al, Hag.	.917	10	11	0	1	12	0
Farren, Dave, Del.	.000	1	0	0	0	0	0
Forbes, Mike, Mac.	1.000	12	11	2	0	13	0
Foster, Gregg, Lak.	.983	71	107	9	2	118	1
Fowler, David, Gre.	.961	109	192	6	8	206	0
Francisco, Ruben, Del.*	.894	23	41	1	5	47	0
Garcia, Daniel, C'bia	.000	1	0	0	0	0	0
Gatti, Jr., William, Wil.	.889	5	8	0	1	9	0
Gillikin, Joe, Kan.	.828	30	24	0	5	29	0
Goodwin, Tom, Wil.	1.000	2	3	0	0	3	0
Grove, Jason, Gre.*	.986	104	140	3	2	145	0
Guerrero, Julio, Aug.	.962	84	123	3	5	131	1
Hamilton, Josh, C.S.C.*	.000	1	0	0	1	1	0
Harris, Cory, C'bia	.960	101	159	10	7	176	0
Hattig, John, Aug.	1.000	1	2	0	0	2	0
Hawpe, Brad, Ash.*	.917	54	61	5	6	72	1
Hensler, Brad, C'bia	1.000	6	9	0	0	9	0
Hensley, Anthony, Lak.	.982	63	108	4	2	114	2
Hill, Mike, Lex.	.971	112	162	7	5	174	2
Jacobs, John, C.S.C.	.955	67	82	3	4	89	0
Janowicz, Nate, C'bus*	1.000	43	84	4	0	88	1
Jova, Maikel, C.W.Va.	.952	40	56	4	3	63	0
Joyce, Jesse, Lex.	1.000	1	2	0	0	2	0
Kaup, Nathan, C.S.C.	1.000	1	2	0	0	2	0
Keene, Kurt, C.W.Va.	.833	2	5	0	1	6	0
Keylor, Cory, Del.	.943	55	95	5	6	106	1
Koone, Chuck, Sav.	.970	66	125	4	4	133	0
Langs, Ronte, Wil.	.983	94	174	4	3	181	2
Lankford, Derrick, Lak.	1.000	16	24	1	0	25	0
Lawson, Forrest, C'bia	1.000	23	33	1	0	34	0
Leaumont, Jeff, Gre.*	.889	4	7	1	1	9	0
Lentini, Fehlandt, Lex.	1.000	29	54	4	0	58	0
Littleton, Brandon, Del.*	.993	128	283	8	2	293	1
Lockhart, Paul, Lex.*	.956	51	62	3	3	68	0
Manley, Adam, Del.*	.971	21	33	1	1	35	0
Marchetti, Dan, Del.	.000	1	0	0	0	0	0
Martel, Normand, Kan.	.968	58	59	2	2	63	0

Player, Team	Pct.	G	PO	A	E	TC	DP
Martin, Brian, C.S.C.	.955	123	164	7	8	179	2
Martinez, Candido, Wil.	.958	77	109	4	5	118	0
McKee, Mickey, Lex.	1.000	3	4	0	0	4	0
McLouth, Nathan, Hick.	.972	93	173	3	5	181	0
Minges, Tyler, C'bus	.968	15	28	2	1	31	1
Money, Freddie, Aug.	1.000	19	24	1	0	25	0
Mongeluzzo, Anthony, Sav.	.941	28	28	4	2	34	1
Moreno, Jorge, C'bus	.966	24	54	2	2	58	1
Morrow, Alvin, C.W.Va.	.968	19	28	2	1	31	0
Muth, Edmund, Ash.*	.988	96	155	10	2	167	3
Navarrete, Ray, Hick.	.955	43	56	8	3	67	0
Negron, Miguel, C.W.Va.*	.905	25	36	2	4	42	1
Nettles, Tim, Gre.	1.000	3	5	0	0	5	0
Nicolás, José, Hick.	.951	30	96	2	3	81	1
Nieves, Raul, Aug.	.889	5	7	1	1	9	0
Nix, Laynce, Sav.*	.976	103	192	12	5	209	1
Pagan, Angel, C'bia	.964	15	27	0	1	28	0
Peck, Bryan, Ash.	.934	32	51	6	4	61	1
Perich, Josh, C'bia.	.926	70	82	5	7	94	0
Pichardo, Henry, C'bus	.941	9	15	1	1	17	0
Pierce, Sean, Wil.	1.000	3	6	0	0	6	0
Ramistella, John, Gre.	1.000	2	4	0	0	4	0
Ravelo, Manny, Hick.	.915	90	114	4	11	129	0
Requena, Alex, C'bus	1.000	25	33	0	0	33	0
Reyes, Rene, Ash.	.948	63	82	9	5	96	2
Riepe, Andy, Aug.	1.000	9	10	0	0	10	0
Riordan, Matt, Del.	.954	53	80	3	4	87	0
Rios, Alexis, C.W.Va.	.944	127	206	13	13	232	0
Rock, Jamie, Ash.	.950	17	19	0	1	20	0
Rodriguez, Ricardo, Mac.	.000	1	0	0	0	0	0
Rosamond, Mike, Lex.	.965	101	191	3	7	201	2
Rosario, Melvin, Ash.*	.971	97	160	9	5	174	1
Royer, Lissandro, C'bia	1.000	8	11	1	0	12	0
Ruiz, Carlos, Lak.	1.000	2	1	0	0	1	0
Santa, Alexander, Gre.*	1.000	3	2	1	0	3	0
Santana, Pedro, Gre.	1.000	3	4	0	0	4	0
Santos, Deivis, Hag.*	1.000	1	1	0	0	1	0
Saucke, Casey, Del.	1.000	6	3	0	0	3	0
Scott, Ed, C.S.C.	1.000	2	2	0	0	2	0
Segar, Jeff, Gre.	.872	27	33	1	5	39	0
Seiber, Antron, Aug.	.972	117	229	13	7	249	0
Shabala, Adam, Hag.	.982	70	106	3	2	111	1
Sherrill, J.J., C'bus	.987	82	150	2	2	154	0
Sherrod, Justin, Aug.	.966	34	54	2	2	58	0
Singleton, Justin, C.W.Va.	.977	97	204	7	5	216	0
Sisk, Aaron, C.W.Va.	.966	30	54	3	2	59	0
Smith, Will, Aug.	.981	58	95	6	2	103	0
Sosa, Jovanny, Del.	.935	19	29	0	2	31	0
Spidale, Mike, Kan.	.979	120	230	3	5	238	1
Stockton, Brad, Sav.	1.000	6	9	0	0	9	0
Sullivan, Cory, Ash.*	.985	65	128	6	2	136	0
Taveras, Willy, C'bus	.952	91	203	17	11	231	2
Teilon, Nilson, Kan.	.976	56	76	6	2	84	0
Thomas, Chuck, Mac.*	.984	98	172	7	3	182	1
Topolski, Jon, Lex.	.994	106	151	16	1	168	2
Truitt, Steve, Lex.	.977	27	42	1	1	44	0
Trumble, Dan, Hag.	.933	19	27	1	2	30	0
Tucker, Mamon, Del.	.945	54	65	4	4	73	0
Turner, Jason, Gre.*	1.000	15	22	2	0	24	1
Van Buizen, Rodney, Wil.	.000	3	0	0	0	0	0
Victorino, Shane, Wil.	.976	109	232	12	6	250	2
Villegas, Ernest, Sav.	.966	15	27	1	1	29	0
Walker, Mark, Hag.	.986	52	67	3	1	71	1
Weston, Aron, Hick.*	.931	16	25	2	2	29	0
Wigginton, Derek, Kan.*	.969	97	121	4	4	129	1
Wilfong, Nick, Hag.	.994	100	150	3	1	154	0
Wilken, Kris, Del.	.000	1	0	0	0	0	0
Winrow, Gary, Gre.*	.991	60	101	4	1	106	1
Zieour, Neesan, C.W.Va.	.912	19	28	3	3	34	1
Zumwalt, Sean, Mac.	.983	91	165	7	3	175	4

CATCHERS

Player, Team	Pct.	G	PO	A	E	TC	DP	PB
Avila, Rob, Lak.	.984	42	281	27	5	313	3	15
Barnowski, Bryan, Aug.	.989	23	153	19	2	174	1	9
Bernard, Miguel, Mac.	.962	42	284	46	13	343	3	7
Boscan, Jean, Mac.	.972	31	253	29	8	290	6	4
BUCK, John, Lex.	.995	120	1006	118	6	1130	3	20
Castaneda, Jose, C'bia.	.977	34	224	29	6	259	2	9
Cerda, Jose, Hag.	1.000	13	101	14	0	115	0	1
Ciarrachi, Kevin, Hick.	.947	2	18	0	1	19	0	0
Coleman, Andy, Gre.	1.000	3	14	2	0	16	0	0

Player, Team	Pct.	G	PO	A	E	TC	DP	PB
Conway, Dan, Ash.	.984	84	610	56	11	677	4	9
Cordell, Brent, C.S.C.	.933	2	25	3	2	30	0	0
Cronin, Shane, Gre.	.981	48	328	38	7	373	1	17
Cruz, Edgar, C'bus	.992	32	210	34	2	246	2	6
Diaz, Jose, Wil.	.991	22	182	30	2	214	2	11
Doumit, Ryan, Hick.	.984	23	164	19	3	186	3	5
Esposito, Brian, Aug.	.982	89	675	80	14	769	5	16
Fatheree, Danny, Lex.	.990	13	97	4	1	102	0	1
Fennell, Jason, Kan.	.950	5	19	0	1	20	0	2
Franco, Iker, C.S.C.	.991	87	646	91	7	744	6	19
Fuentes, Omar, Gre.	.986	95	736	100	12	848	3	20
Gajewski, Matt, Sav.	.992	15	107	14	1	122	4	3
Gillikin, Joe, Kan.	.986	13	63	5	1	69	0	2
Gutierrez, Osld, O.W.Va.	.000	6	10	6	1	10	0	2
Haase, Jeff, C'bus	.974	25	169	22	5	196	0	6
Heard, Scott, Sav.	.983	69	571	65	11	647	7	8
Hensler, Brad, C'bia	1.000	2	17	0	0	17	0	1
Hernandez, Jose, Hick.	.978	50	328	36	8	372	3	16
Hickman, Brian, Kan.	.950	6	44	13	3	60	1	1
Hill, Koyie, Hick.	.977	93	669	102	18	789	8	13
Jacobs, Mike, C'bia	.988	37	294	24	4	322	2	10
Johnston, Ryan, Lak.	1.000	3	9	1	0	10	0	3
Kessick, Jon, Del.	.984	23	156	26	3	185	0	3
Lucas, Matt, Lex.	.994	25	140	14	1	155	0	5
Lunsford, James, Hag.	.986	109	876	101	14	991	6	13
Mapes, Jake, Hag.	1.000	1	5	1	0	6	1	0
Marsh, Jason, C.S.C.	.991	60	411	38	4	453	2	14
Martinez, Casey, C.W.Va.	.963	21	142	15	6	163	1	7
Matos, Angel, Sav.	.957	10	59	7	3	69	0	1
McArthur, Kennon, Lak.	.987	20	134	16	2	152	0	10
Mejia, Manuel, Hick.	.985	39	289	47	5	341	3	9
Merritt, Graig, C.S.C.	1.000	5	23	5	0	28	0	0
Mooney, Dan, Aug.	1.000	21	173	17	0	190	0	2
Ochoa, Javier, C'bus	.979	45	331	42	8	381	7	5
Pack, Branden, Sav.	.976	54	429	51	12	492	2	5
Peck, Bryan, Ash.	1.000	4	17	0	0	17	0	1
Quintero, Humberto, Sav.	.989	57	534	90	7	631	4	1
Quiroz, Guillermo, C.W.Va.	.986	82	562	73	9	644	2	17
Riepe, Andy, Aug.	1.000	13	83	14	0	97	0	1
Riera, Jason, Hick.	.993	33	255	32	2	289	2	7
Rojas, Tom, Gre.	1.000	1	1	1	0	2	0	0
Rosa, Wally, Kan.	.977	72	429	77	12	518	1	12
Ruiz, Carlos, Lak.	.990	41	267	23	3	293	3	9
Ruiz, Reinaldo, Lex.	1.000	3	14	0	0	14	0	0
Russell, Michael, Del.	.971	17	91	11	3	105	0	3
Salas, Jose, Mac.	.973	9	62	10	2	74	0	1
Seestedt, Mike, Del.	.981	63	385	33	8	426	3	10
Serrano, Ray, Mac.	.984	46	350	31	6	387	1	0
Shrum, Allen, Hag.	.983	21	145	26	3	174	0	5
Smith, Ryan, C'bia	1.000	12	75	6	0	81	0	1
Soto, Saul, Wil.	.992	25	210	27	2	239	1	1
Sulbaran, Orlando, Sav.	1.000	2	12	0	0	12	0	0
Tejada, Mike, Ash.	.982	60	401	30	8	439	2	9
Terveen, Bryce, Mac.	.994	20	140	13	1	154	0	2
Thompson, Alva, Mac.	1.000	2	2	0	0	2	0	0
Tosca, Daniel, Lak.	.980	49	355	35	8	398	6	6
Umbria, Jose, C.W.Va.	.996	38	238	32	1	271	1	6
Whiteside, Dustin, Del.	.991	54	390	58	4	452	0	10
Wilson, Heath, C'bus	.978	39	279	33	7	319	2	5
Wilson, John, C'bia	.978	55	479	56	12	547	3	15
Yan, Edwin, Hick.	1.000	1	4	1	0	5	0	0

PITCHERS

Player, Team	Pct.	G	PO	A	E	TC	DP
Abbott, David, C.W.Va.	1.000	8	1	1	0	2	0
Abell, Joe, Ash.	.667	16	1	3	2	6	1
Acosta, Manuel, Gre.	.882	10	3	12	2	17	1
Adams, Brian, Aug.*	.941	34	1	15	1	17	0
Adams, Daniel, Lak.	1.000	50	4	20	0	24	2
Advincola, Jose, Del.*	1.000	11	1	1	0	2	0
Aguilera, Adrian, Wil.*	.000	5	0	0	0	0	0
Alcala, Jason, Hick.	1.000	34	4	3	0	7	1
Alexander, Kevin, Hag.	1.000	1	1	0	0	1	0
Allen, Wyatt, Kan.	.813	12	4	9	3	16	0
Almonte, Henry, Hick.	1.000	20	2	5	0	7	0
Altman, Heath, C'bus	.000	3	0	0	0	0	0
Alvarez, Oscar, C'bus*	.826	17	3	16	4	23	1
Andersen, Derek, C.S.C.*	1.000	29	2	9	0	11	1
Anderson, Jason, Gre.	.886	23	7	24	4	35	0
Andrade, Jancy, Del.	1.000	8	2	7	0	9	0
Andrews, Aron, Wil.	.941	15	1	15	1	17	1
Anez, Omar, Del.	1.000	12	0	1	0	1	0

Player, Team	Pct.	G	PO	A	E	TC	DP
Backe, Brandon, C.S.C.	1.000	16	6	3	0	9	0
Baker, Ryan, Mac.	.889	40	3	5	1	9	0
Barr, Adam, C'bus*	.000	6	0	0	0	0	0
Bartlett, Richard, Del.	.889	19	10	22	4	36	0
Bauer, Greg, Wil.	1.000	25	2	2	0	4	0
Bauer, Pete, C.W.Va.	.667	6	1	3	2	6	0
Beal, Andy, Gre.*	1.000	2	1	3	0	4	1
Benedetti, John, C.S.C.	.840	44	2	19	4	25	2
Bennett, Steve, C'bia	.857	12	5	7	2	14	1
Berney, Scott, Ash.	1.000	33	3	7	0	10	2
Bittner, Tim, Kan.*	1.000	4	2	9	0	11	0
Blankenship, John, Gre.*	1.000	27	3	15	0	18	1
Blothon, Matt, C'bus*	.000	1	0	0	0	0	0
Bonser, Boof, Hag.	.880	27	10	12	3	25	I
Borner, Brady, Hick.*	1.000	9	4	14	0	18	1
Bowers, Rob, Sav.	.750	11	1	2	1	4	0
Bridenbaugh, Christian, Wil.*	.897	21	7	19	3	29	0
Brito, Eude, Lak.*	.846	44	4	18	4	26	3
Brous, Dave, Hag.*	1.000	20	2	1	0	3	1
Buchanan, Brian, Gre.*	1.000	37	2	10	0	12	0
Buchholz, Taylor, Lak.	.964	28	9	18	1	28	0
Bucktrot, Keith, Lak.	.929	24	3	23	2	28	1
Buglovsky, Chris, Ash.	.906	26	12	17	3	32	1
Bullard, Jim, Kan.*	1.000	8	1	14	0	15	0
Bullock, Trevor, Lak.*	.950	48	3	16	1	20	1
Bumatay, Mike, Hick.*	.857	15	1	5	1	7	0
Burke, Erick, Sav.*	1.000	34	1	12	0	13	0
BURNETT, Sean, Hick.*	1.000	26	14	33	0	47	3
Cabell, Shannon, Hick.*	.846	42	2	9	2	13	0
Cabrera, Fernando, C'bus	1.000	20	8	16	0	24	1
Campbell, Jarrett, C.S.C.	.966	39	7	21	1	29	1
Canale, Tom, C'bus	1.000	8	2	4	0	6	0
Cardwell, Brian, C.W.Va.	.813	19	4	9	3	16	0
Carney, Jake, C.S.C.	.000	10	0	0	0	0	0
Carter, Ryan, Lak.*	.857	14	3	15	3	21	0
Castro, Julio, Kan.	1.000	40	3	8	0	11	0
Cavazos, Andy, Sav.	.794	29	10	17	7	34	4
Chenard, Ken, C'bia	1.000	4	0	1	0	1	0
Christ, John, C'bus	.800	4	1	3	1	5	0
Clark, Jeff, Hag.	.929	27	8	20	2	28	1
Cole, Joey, C'bia	.893	25	3	22	3	28	2
Collazo, William, Mac.*	1.000	12	0	5	0	5	0
Colon, Jose, C'bus	1.000	44	3	4	0	7	0
Colon, Roman, Mac.	.914	23	14	18	3	35	1
Comolli, Mark, C.W.Va.	1.000	8	4	7	0	11	0
Connolly, Mike, Hick.*	.929	33	7	19	2	28	0
Coose, Austin, C.S.C.	1.000	10	1	2	0	3	0
Cordero, Jesus, Wil.	.818	33	2	7	2	11	0
Correa, Dominic, Gre.	1.000	16	1	4	0	5	0
Cortes, David, Mac.	.000	10	0	0	0	0	0
Coward, Tim, C.S.C.	1.000	5	1	1	0	2	0
Cox, Mike, C'bia*	.750	15	1	5	2	8	0
Cunningham, Jeremy, Hag.	.875	10	2	5	1	8	1
Currier, Rik, Gre.	.750	6	1	5	2	8	1
Davies, Kyle, Mac.	.000	1	0	0	0	0	0
Davis, Jason, C'bus	.905	27	12	26	4	42	1
Deaton, Kevin, C'bia	.000	1	0	0	0	0	0
De La Cruz, Carlos, C'bus	1.000	6	0	8	0	8	0
Delossantos, Carlos, Hick.	.286	13	0	2	5	7	0
De Paula, Julio, Ash.-Gre.	.917	11	5	6	1	12	0
Doza, Fredy, Del.	1.000	3	2	1	0	3	1
Diaz, Felix, Hag.	.900	15	5	4	1	10	0
Dickinson, Rodney, Aug.	1.000	23	1	5	0	6	0
Digby, Bryan, Mac.	1.000	3	2	0	0	2	0
Diggins, Ben, Wil.	.931	21	6	21	2	29	2
Dohmann, Christopher, Ash	1.000	28	4	10	0	14	0
Donaghey, Steve, C'bus	.900	23	3	6	1	10	1
Dorman, Rich, C.S.C.	.929	17	12	1	1	14	2
Dorn, Grant, Lex.	1.000	10	3	2	0	5	0
Echols, Justin, Sav.	.667	36	2	4	3	9	0
Elliott, Chad, C'bia*	.960	35	4	20	1	25	2
Elskamp, Andy, Lak.	1.000	23	3	3	0	6	0
Evert, Brett, Mac.	1.000	6	0	3	0	3	0
Faigin, Jason, Gre.	.714	60	8	7	6	21	0
Farren, Dave, Del.	.875	32	5	16	3	24	2
Faust, Wes, Hag.	.909	46	6	24	3	33	0
Feliciano, Ruben, Sav.	1.000	6	0	1	0	1	0
Ferrand, Dario, Kan.	.941	27	6	26	2	34	0
Fitch, Steve, C'bus	1.000	4	0	5	0	5	0
Fontana, Tony, Aug.	.850	24	6	11	3	20	1
Ford, Matt, C.W.Va.*	.941	11	6	10	1	17	2
Ford, Tom, Del.*	.667	13	0	2	1	3	0
Francisco, Frank, Aug.	.833	37	2	3	1	6	0
Frias, Juan, Hag.	.857	24	0	6	1	7	0
Friedberg, Drew, Hick.*	1.000	17	2	5	0	7	0
Gahan, Matt, C'bia	1.000	5	0	1	0	1	0
Garcia, Nick, Del.	.000	1	0	0	0	0	0
Garza, Alberto, C'bus	1.000	1	1	0	0	1	0
Garza, Rolando, Kan.	1.000	9	1	3	0	4	0
Gassner, Dave, C.W.Va.*	1.000	13	3	9	0	12	0
George, Chris, Lex.	1.000	40	2	10	0	12	0
Giese, Dan, Aug.	.929	46	5	8	1	14	1
Gilbert, Rich, Sav.*	.920	21	7	16	2	25	2
Glen, William, C.W.Va.	.909	23	5	5	1	11	0
Gomes, Wayne, Lak.	1.000	2	0	1	0	1	1
Gomez, Benito, C.S.C.*	1.000	39	2	11	0	13	1
Gomez, Diogenes, Ash.	.939	50	6	25	2	33	2
Gomez, Ricardo, Gre.	1.000	9	1	4	0	5	0
Gonzales, Jose, Gre.	1.000	35	5	7	0	12	1
Gonzalez, Alfredo, Wil.	1.000	2	0	3	0	3	0
Gonzalez, Gilberto, C'bia*	1.000	5	0	3	0	3	0
Goodrum, Kevin, Gre.*	.917	7	2	9	1	12	1
Gracesqui, Frank, C.W.Va.*	.926	35	7	18	2	27	0
Graham, Elgin, Hag.	1.000	32	4	18	0	22	1
Graham, Tom, Sav.	1.000	40	3	5	0	8	0
Green, Sean, Ash.	.882	43	7	8	2	17	0
Gross, Kyle, Hag.	.813	22	4	9	3	16	0
Guerrero, Julio, Hick.	.810	11	5	12	4	21	0
Gutierrez, Fernando, Del.	.800	22	1	3	1	5	0
Guzman, Alex, C.W.Va.	.964	52	7	20	1	28	2
Hanrahan, Joel, Wil.	.913	27	8	13	2	23	0
Hawk, David, Hick.	.875	17	1	6	1	8	0
Hawkins, Chad, Sav.	1.000	4	0	1	0	1	0
Hee, Aaron, C'bia*	.875	35	3	11	2	16	0
Henderson, Kenneth, Hick.*	1.000	27	1	3	0	4	0
Herbison, Brett, C'bia	1.000	5	1	0	0	1	0
Hernandez, Buddy, Mac.	.000	7	0	0	0	0	0
Hernandez, Yoel, Lak.	.936	25	17	27	3	47	2
Herndon, Eric, Mac.	1.000	10	1	3	0	4	0
Higgins, Joshua, Hick.	1.000	55	2	10	0	12	0
Hills, Mark, Hag.*	.000	10	0	0	0	0	0
Hollifield, Alec, Kan.	1.000	5	0	2	0	2	0
Hughes, Nial, Wil.*	.818	25	1	8	2	11	0
Hughes, Rocky, Kan.*	1.000	19	0	1	0	1	0
Huisman, Justin, Ash.	1.000	55	7	10	0	17	1
Hurley, Derek, Hick.*	.792	17	6	13	5	24	0
Jacobs, John, C.S.C.	.000	1	0	0	0	0	0
Jacobsen, Landon, Hick.	.818	9	1	8	2	11	1
Jamison, Ryan, Lex.	.944	9	3	14	1	18	0
Johnston, Mike, Hick.*	.905	16	4	15	2	21	1
Jones, Chris, Hag.*	1.000	39	6	9	0	15	0
Jones, D.J., Del.*	1.000	17	5	11	0	16	0
Jones, Quentin, Mac.	1.000	35	2	1	0	3	1
Keirstead, Michael, Wil.	1.000	7	1	1	0	2	1
Keppel, Bob, C'bia	.895	26	12	22	4	38	1
Kibler, Ryan, Ash.	.889	10	6	10	2	18	0
King, Jeremy, Gre.	1.000	1	1	0	0	1	0
Kleine, Victor, C'bus*	1.000	1	0	1	0	1	0
Knowles, Mike, Gre.	.714	38	2	3	2	7	0
Kozlowski, Ben, Mac.*	.825	26	9	24	7	40	0
Kremer, John, Gre.	.733	40	4	7	4	15	0
Krysa, Jonathan, Lex.	1.000	16	0	6	0	6	0
Laplante, Reggie, Gre.	.000	7	0	0	0	0	0
Lara, Mauricio, Aug.*	.968	20	10	20	1	31	0
Laroche, Jeff, Ash.*	.778	26	1	6	2	9	0
Larson, Ryan, C'bus	.929	31	2	11	1	14	2
Lavigne, Tim, C'bia	1.000	33	3	14	0	17	0
Lawson, Jarrod, Lak.	.750	23	4	8	4	16	1
Levesque, Ben, Hick.	.833	10	3	2	1	6	0
Lizarraga, Edgar, Wil.	.000	3	0	0	0	0	0
Lockhart, Paul, Lex.*	1.000	1	0	1	0	1	0
Lopez, Rafael, C'bia	.840	25	8	13	4	25	0
Lorenzo, Javier, Ash.	1.000	38	0	7	0	7	1
Lugo, Ruddy, Wil.	1.000	16	4	3	0	7	0
Luna, Brandon, Sav.	1.000	11	2	2	0	4	1
Madril, Steve, Kan.*	1.000	42	0	18	0	18	1
Malaska, Mark, C.S.C.*	.886	25	5	26	4	35	1
Malerich, Will, Hag.*	1.000	5	0	4	0	4	0
Malone, Corwin, Kan.*	.913	18	4	17	2	23	0
Marchetti, Dan, Mac.	1.000	10	1	2	0	3	0
Marietta, Ron, Gre.*	.000	4	0	0	1	1	0
Markert, Jackson, Hag	.842	58	7	9	3	19	0
Markwell, Diegomar, C.W.Va.*	.931	22	9	18	2	29	0
Martin, Chandler, Ash.	1.000	2	1	2	0	3	1

Player, Team	Pct.	G	PO	A	E	TC	DP
Martin, Larry, Gre.*	.800	13	2	2	1	5	1
Martinez, Casey, C.W.Va.	.000	1	0	0	0	0	0
Martinez, Dave, Gre.*	.875	11	4	24	4	32	0
Matheny, Brandon, C'bus*	.944	24	5	12	1	18	0
Mathiesen, Ryan, Mac.	.000	1	0	0	0	0	0
Matos, Jesus, Ash.	1.000	21	2	4	0	6	0
Matsko, Rick, C'bus	.923	24	6	6	1	13	0
Mattioni, Nick, C'bia	1.000	37	5	11	0	16	0
McClung, Mike, C.S.C.	.889	28	8	24	4	36	0
McCormick, Terry, C.S.C.*	1.000	14	1	4	0	5	0
McCrotty, Will, Wil.	.889	21	4	4	1	9	0
McCulloch, Andy, C.W.Va.	1.000	55	4	14	0	18	2
McMillan, Joshua, C.W.Va.*	1.000	9	0	2	0	2	0
McWhirter, Kris, Kan.	.867	14	6	7	2	15	0
Mead, David, Dav.	.733	19	5	6	4	15	0
Meisenheimer, Matt, Sav.	1.000	3	1	0	0	1	0
Meldahl, Todd, Lak.*	.889	11	1	7	1	9	0
Mendez, Dave, Mac.*	1.000	35	9	14	0	23	0
Messer, Brian, Hick.	1.000	17	1	6	0	7	0
Middleton, Brian, Lex.	1.000	11	2	4	0	6	0
Mikels, Jason, Mac.	1.000	23	0	3	0	3	0
Millwood, Kevin, Mac.	1.000	1	0	1	0	1	0
Miniel, Rene, Aug.	.962	27	4	21	1	26	0
Montano, Ignacio, C'bus*	1.000	11	1	1	0	2	0
Montero, Agustin, Wil.	.800	18	0	4	1	5	0
Montilla, Elvis, Del.	.909	26	4	16	2	22	2
Mosley, Eric, Gre.	.889	11	2	6	1	9	0
Mowday, Chris, C.W.Va.	.833	13	1	4	1	6	0
Mozingo, Dan, Kan.*	1.000	37	1	19	0	20	0
Munoz, Arnaldo, Kan.*	1.000	60	6	27	0	33	1
Munter, Scott, Hag.	.000	1	0	0	0	0	0
Murray, Brad, Kan.*	.667	9	1	1	1	3	0
Musser, Neal, C'bia*	.950	17	5	14	1	20	0
Nannini, Mike, Lex.	.872	28	13	28	6	47	4
Neil, Dan, C'bus*	.857	24	2	10	2	14	1
Nelson, Kenny, Mac.	.906	25	9	20	3	32	0
Nunley, Derrek, C.W.Va.	.857	14	2	4	1	7	0
O'Brien, Patrick, Hick.	.917	11	2	9	1	12	0
Olson, Jason, Wil.	1.000	15	0	6	0	6	0
Olson, Ryan, C'bia*	.000	1	0	0	0	0	0
Ormond, Rod, Del.	.938	24	4	11	1	16	0
Ozuna, Francisco, C.W.Va.*	1.000	18	1	1	0	2	1
Pacheco, Enemencio, Ash.	.923	7	4	8	1	13	0
Padgett, Daniel, Hag.*	.667	19	1	1	1	3	0
Padua, Geraldo, Gre.	1.000	3	1	1	0	2	1
Parker, Josh, C.S.C.	1.000	3	1	1	0	2	0
Patterson, Quenten, C'bia	.913	32	4	17	2	23	0
Pavon, Julio, Hag.	1.000	29	10	25	0	35	2
Pearson, Brent, Hick.	1.000	3	1	1	0	2	1
Peeples, Jim, Gre.*	.000	1	0	0	0	0	0
Peguero, Darwin, Lex.*	.917	34	4	18	2	24	0
Percell, Brody, C'bus*	1.000	26	3	7	0	10	0
Peres, Luis, Aug.*	.935	26	3	26	2	31	0
Perez, Elvis, Mac.	1.000	27	2	4	0	6	0
Perich, Josh, C'bia	.000	1	0	0	0	0	0
Peterson, Matt, C'bia	.778	18	4	10	4	18	0
Phillips, Mike, Kan.*	.941	14	3	13	1	17	0
Pierce, Tony, Mac.	.000	2	0	0	0	0	0
Pluta, Tony, Lex.	.960	26	6	18	1	25	1
Portobanco, Luz, C'bia	1.000	1	1	1	0	2	0
Prahm, Ryan, C'bus	1.000	11	2	12	0	14	1
Prendes, Alex, Aug.*	1.000	8	0	3	0	3	0
Pruitt, Jason, Del.*	1.000	12	0	2	0	2	0
Quick, Ben, C.W.Va.	1.000	17	7	6	0	13	1
Ramirez, Enrique, Del.	.833	45	4	11	3	18	0
Ramirez, Santiago, Lex.	1.000	45	3	10	0	13	1
Ramirez, Victor, Sav.	.857	19	6	6	2	14	1
Renteria, Juan, C.S.C.	1.000	39	7	13	0	20	1
Renwick, Tyler, C.W.Va.	1.000	7	2	2	0	4	0
Reynolds, Eric, Gre.*	.000	1	0	0	0	0	0
Ridgway, Jeff, C.S.C.*	.840	22	4	17	4	25	0
Riethmaier, Matthew, Lak.	.846	19	2	9	2	13	1
Rigueiro, Rafael, Hag.	.917	26	2	9	1	12	0
Rijo, Fernando, Wil.	.970	26	10	22	1	33	3
Rivard, Reggie, Sav.	1.000	44	2	12	0	14	0
Rleal, Sendy, Del.	.920	20	7	16	2	25	0
Roberts, Nick, Lex.	.944	20	16	18	2	36	0
Roberts, Rick, Wil.*	.667	7	1	1	1	3	0
Rodriguez, Eddy, Del.	1.000	41	2	7	0	9	0
Rodriguez, George, Lak.	.944	31	3	14	1	18	0
Rodriguez, Luis, Sav.	.900	16	4	5	1	10	2
Rodriguez, Mike, Del.	.000	1	0	0	0	0	0
Rogers, Brad, Del.	.938	34	4	11	1	16	1
Rogers, Devin, C'bus	.833	7	0	5	1	6	0
Rohling, Stuart, Kan.	1.000	5	1	0	0	1	0
Rojas, Jose, Wil.	.976	24	13	28	1	42	2
Roman, Orlando, C'bia	.875	4	2	5	1	8	0
Roney, Matt, Ash.	.773	23	4	13	5	22	1
Rosario, Melvin, Ash.*	.000	1	0	0	0	0	0
Rosario, Rodrigo, Lex.	.909	30	9	31	4	44	2
Rundles, Rich, Aug.*	.964	19	7	20	1	28	0
Rust, Evan, C.S.C.	.958	35	4	19	1	24	1
Saarloos, Kirk, Lex.	1.000	22	1	12	0	13	0
Sabens, Mike, Hick.	1.000	10	0	1	0	1	0
Sadowski, Chad, Lak.	.929	35	5	8	1	14	1
Sams, Aaron, Aug.*	.833	17	3	3	1	6	0
Sandoval, Marcos, C.W.Va.	1.000	21	6	8	0	14	1
Santillan, Manny, Lex.	.955	38	7	14	1	22	3
Schmitt, Eric, Gre.	1.000	7	5	4	0	9	0
Schwager, Matt, Del.	.921	27	8	27	3	38	1
Sclafani, Anthony, Mac.-Aug.	1.000	13	0	4	0	4	0
Scuglik, Mike, Sav.*	.842	27	6	10	3	19	1
Seestedt, Mike, Del.	1.000	4	0	1	0	1	0
Serrano, Alex, Ash.	1.000	14	1	2	0	3	0
Shafer, Kurt, Hick.	1.000	1	0	1	0	1	0
Sharber, Jeffery, Hick.	1.000	7	4	2	0	6	0
Sheffield, Christopher, C.W.Va.	1.000	6	2	2	0	4	0
Sherman, Chris, C'bia	1.000	2	0	2	0	2	0
Shields, James, C.S.C.	1.000	10	6	6	0	12	1
Simpson, Andre, Wil.	.857	24	4	8	2	14	1
Skyles, Matt, C'bus*	1.000	11	1	6	0	7	1
Smalley, Mike, Mac.*	.000	5	0	0	1	1	0
Smith, Jason, Gre.	1.000	5	2	4	0	6	1
Smith, Joe, Hag.-Gre.	1.000	35	16	27	0	43	3
Smith, Matt, Gre.*	1.000	16	2	18	0	20	0
Smith, Matthew, Kan.	.833	20	3	2	1	6	0
Smith, Mike, C.W.Va.	.897	14	10	25	4	39	3
Smoltz, John, Mac.	1.000	1	0	1	0	1	0
Song, Seung, Aug.	.933	14	5	9	1	15	0
Sperring, Jayme, Del.	.909	53	3	7	1	11	1
Spillman, Jeromie, C.W.Va.*	1.000	20	4	6	0	10	0
Stahl, Rich, Del.*	1.000	6	1	11	0	12	0
Stamler, Keith, Sav.	.714	7	0	5	2	7	0
Stanford, Derek, Lex.	1.000	3	1	6	0	7	0
Steffek, Brian, Wil.	1.000	9	3	5	0	8	1
Stepka, Tom, Ash.	1.000	2	0	2	0	2	0
Stevens, Josh, Gre.	1.000	19	1	6	0	7	0
Stiehl, Rob, Lex.	.875	14	3	11	2	16	0
Storey, Eric, Ash.	.000	1	0	0	0	0	0
Suttles, Donnie, C'bus	.923	21	6	6	1	13	0
Sweeney, James, Kan.*	.923	21	5	19	2	26	1
Tapia, Roman, Kan.	.000	1	0	0	0	0	0
Tate, Matt, Del.	.667	13	4	4	4	12	0
Tejeda, Rob, Lak.	.793	26	6	17	6	29	0
Templet, Eric, C'bia	.000	2	0	0	0	0	0
Tetz, Kris, C'bus	1.000	1	0	1	0	1	0
Thomas, John, Hag.*	1.000	15	6	19	0	25	0
Thompson, Derek, C'bus*	1.000	2	0	3	0	3	0
Thompson, Matt, Aug.	.880	25	3	19	3	25	0
Thoms, Hank, C'bus	.923	19	4	8	1	13	0
Thorpe, Tracy, C.W.Va.	1.000	24	9	15	0	24	2
Threets, Erick, Hag.*	1.000	12	2	1	0	3	0
Tomaszewski, Eliot, Del.	1.000	18	3	2	0	5	0
Tremblay, Max, Lex.*	1.000	48	1	12	0	13	1
Troilo, Joe, Aug.	.833	30	1	9	2	12	0
Ulacia, Dennis, Kan.*	.895	15	3	14	2	19	1
Urdaneta, Lino, Wil.	1.000	10	4	3	0	7	2
Uzzell, Todd, Hag.	1.000	1	1	0	0	1	0
Valdez, Domingo, Sav.	1.000	15	3	9	0	12	0
Valentine, Joe, Kan.	1.000	30	2	7	0	9	0
Vazquez, Will, Ash.	1.000	16	5	13	0	18	2
Vigeland, Will, Sav.	1.000	39	5	0	0	5	1
Villegas, Felix, Aug.	.885	34	7	16	3	26	1
Wade, Matt, C'bus	.833	10	1	9	2	12	0
Waechter, Doug, C.S.C.	.818	26	6	12	4	22	0
Wainwright, Adam, Mac.	.857	28	4	20	4	28	1
Waters, Chris, Mac.*	.961	25	8	41	2	51	0
Watkins, Dave, Mac.	1.000	24	2	4	0	6	0
Webb, Nicholas, Ash.*	1.000	19	4	16	0	20	1
Weslowski, Rob, C'bia	.941	23	3	13	1	17	1
Wilken, Kris, Del.	1.000	2	0	1	0	1	0
Williams, Adam, Wil.*	.857	25	1	11	2	14	1
Wilson, C.J., Sav.*	1.000	5	0	8	0	8	1
Wombacher, Mike, Gre.*	.941	38	2	14	1	17	0

Player, Team	Pct.	G	PO	A	E	TC	DP
Yacco, Anthony, Hag.	1.000	24	2	5	0	7	0
Yankosky, L.J., Mac.	1.000	1	0	1	0	1	0
Young, Christopher, Hick.	.917	12	3	8	1	12	0
Young, Curtis, Kan.	1.000	6	0	1	0	1	0
Young, Simon, C'bus*	.909	8	4	6	1	11	1

PITCHERS WITH TWO OR MORE TEAMS

Player, Team	Pct.	G	PO	A	E	TC	DP
De Paula, Julio, Ash.	1.000	3	2	0	0	2	0
De Paula, Julio, Gre.	.900	8	3	6	1	10	0
Sclafani, Anthony, Mac.	1.000	5	0	2	0	2	0
Sclafani, Anthony, Aug.	1.000	8	0	2	0	2	0
Smith, Joe, Hag.	1.000	24	9	16	0	25	3
Smith, Joe, Gre.	1.000	11	7	11	0	18	0

The following players appeared only as designated hitter, pinch-hitter or pinch runner: Gretz, dh, ph; McNamara, dh.

LEAGUE CHAMPIONS

Year	Team	Pct.	Year	Team	Pct.	Year	Team	Pct.
1948—	Lincolnton*	.627		Greenville	.619	1986—	Columbia‡	.682
1949—	Newton-Conover	.667	1971—	Greenwood	.631		Asheville	.643
	Rutherford Co. (2nd)†	.627		Greenwood	.759	1987—	Asheville	.655
1950—	Newton-Conover	.627	1972—	Spartanburg‡	.788		Myrtle Beach‡	.597
	Lenoir (2nd)†	.626		Greenville	.652	1988—	Charleston (S.C.)	.616
1951—	Morganton	.645	1973—	Spartanburg‡	.646		Spartanburg‡	.500
	Shelby (2nd)†	.604		Gastonia	.619	1989—	Gastonia	.657
1952—	Lincolnton	.649	1974—	Gastonia	.606		Augusta‡	.535
	Shelby (2nd)†	.645		Gastonia	.672	1990—	Columbia	.580
1953-59—	League inactive.		1975—	Spartanburg	.543		Charleston (W.Va.)‡	.538
1960—	Lexington	.707		Spartanburg	.614	1991—	Charleston (W.Va.)	.648
	Salisbury (2nd)†	.650	1976—	Asheville	.544		Columbia‡	.614
1961—	Salisbury	.627		Greenwood‡	.600	1992—	Columbia	.572
	Shelby (4th)†	.481	1977—	Greenwood	.557		Myrtle Beach‡	.522
1962—	Statesville	.563		Gastonia†	.600	1993	Savannah‡	.662
	Statesville	.700	1978—	Greenwood	.614		Greensboro	.603
1963—	Greenville†	.576		Greenwood	.565	1994—	Columbus	.630
	Salisbury	.631	1979—	Greenwood‡	.565		Savannah‡	.599
1964—	Rock Hill	.672		Spartanburg	.525	1995—	Piedmont	.586
	Salisbury‡	.631	1980—	Greensboro	.590		Augusta‡	.551
1965—	Salisbury	.641		Charleston	.561	1996—	Delmarva	.585
	Rock Hill‡	.603	1981—	Greensboro‡	.695		Savannah‡	.511
1966—	Spartanburg	.682		Greenwood	.549	1997—	Delmarva§	.543
	Spartanburg	.767	1982—	Greensboro‡	.681		Greensboro	.536
1967—	Spartanburg	.730		Florence	.546	1998—	Columbia§	.638
	Spartanburg	.567	1983—	Columbia	.620		Hagerstown	.574
1968—	Spartanburg	.597		Gastonia‡	.587	1999—	Hagerstown	.600
	Greenwood‡	.597	1984—	Charleston	.549		Augusta§	.496
1969—	Greenwood‡	.587		Asheville‡	.510	2000—	Piedmont	.657
	Shelby	.565	1985—	Florence‡	.599		Delmarva∞	.544
1970—	Greenville	.576		Greensboro	.540	2001—	Lexington††	.657

*Won championship and four-club playoff. †Won four-club playoff. ‡Won split-season playoff. §Won split season, eight-club playoff. ∞Won split season, four-club playoff. ††Was leading final series of split-season, four-club playoff and was declared champion when Professional Baseball declared a stoppage of play. (NOTE—Known as Western Carolina League from 1948 through 1962 and known as Western Carolinas League through 1979.)

APPALACHIAN LEAGUE

LEAGUE OFFICE

President
Lee Landers

Address
283 Deerchase Circle
Statesville, NC 28625

Phone
704-873-5300

Teams (affiliation)
Bluefield Orioles (Orioles)
Bristol White Sox (White Sox)
Burlington Indians (Indians)
Danville Braves (Braves)
Elizabethton Twins (Twins)
Johnson City Cardinals (Cardinals)

Kingsport Mets (Mets)
Martinsville Astros (Astros)
Princeton Devil Rays (Devil Rays)
Pulaski Rangers (Rangers)

2001 FINAL STANDINGS

NORTH DIVISION

Team	W	L	T	Pct.	GB
Bluefield (Orioles)	33	33	0	.500	...
Martinsville (Astros)	31	37	0	.456	3.0
Burlington (Indians)	31	37	0	.456	3.0
Danville (Braves)	30	38	0	.441	4.0
Princeton (Devil Rays)	28	39	0	.418	5.5

SOUTH DIVISION

Team	W	L	T	Pct.	GB
Elizabethton (Twins)	41	22	0	.651	...
Bristol (White Sox)	39	26	0	.600	3.0
Pulaski (Rangers)	38	30	0	.559	5.5
Johnson City (Cardinals)	31	35	0	.470	11.5
Kingsport (Mets)	31	36	0	.463	12.0

COMPOSITE

Team	Eliz.	Bris.	Pul.	Blue.	J.C.	King.	Mar.	Burl.	Dan.	Prin.	W	L	T	Pct.	GB
Elizabethton (Twins)	...	7	2	4	8	3	5	4	6	2	41	22	0	.651	...
Bristol (White Sox)	1	...	5	4	8	9	4	4	3	1	39	26	0	.600	3.0
Pulaski (Rangers)	4	1	...	5	2	3	7	5	3	8	38	30	0	.559	5.5
Bluefield (Orioles)	1	1	5	...	4	3	6	3	4	6	33	33	0	.500	9.5
Johnson City (Cardinals)	3	2	4	2	...	5	5	5	3	2	31	35	0	.470	11.5
Kingsport (Mets)	7	3	3	3	4	...	2	3	2	4	31	36	0	.463	12.0
Martinsville (Astros)	1	2	3	2	1	4	...	7	7	4	31	37	0	.456	12.5
Burlington (Indians)	2	2	3	3	1	3	3	...	6	8	31	37	0	.456	12.5
Danville (Braves)	0	3	3	6	3	4	3	4	...	4	30	38	0	.441	13.5
Princeton (Devil Rays)	3	5	2	4	4	2	2	2	4	...	28	39	0	.418	15.0

Major league affiliations in parentheses.

PLAYOFFS: Bluefield defeated Elizabethton two games to one to win the Appalachian League Championship.

REGULAR-SEASON ATTENDANCE: Bluefield, 26,160; Bristol, 19,300; Burlington, 36,371; Danville, 26,618; Elizabethton, 20,878; Johnson City, 42,816; Kingsport, 20,384; Martinsville, 35,392; Princeton, 35,404; Pulaski, 21,509. Total—284,832. Playoff (3 games)—1,580.

MANAGERS: Bluefield, Joe Almaraz; Bristol, John Orton; Burlington, David Turgeon; Danville, Ralph Henriquez; Elizabethton, Rudy Hernandez; Johnson City, Chris Maloney; Kingsport, Joey Cora; Martinsville, Jorge Orta; Princeton, Edwin Rodriguez; Pulaski, Bruce Crabbe.

ALL-STAR TEAM: 1B—Andy Baxter, Burlington; 2B—Omar Rogers, Bluefield; 3B—Randall Shelley, Pulaski; SS—Sean Pittman, Kingsport; Utility INF—Jason Bourgeois, Pulaski; OF—Jonny Gomes, Princeton; OF—James Tomlin, Elizabethton; OF—Justin Woodrow, Johnson City; Utility OF—Brad Stockton—Pulaski; C—Brayan Pena, Danville; DH—Rick Ankiel, Johnson City; RHP—D.J. Houlton, Martinsville; LHP—Rick Ankiel, Johnson City; Relief pitcher—Ryan Keefer, Bluefield; Most Valuable Player—Jonny Gomes, Princeton; Pitcher of the Year—Rick Ankiel; Manager of the Year—Rudy Hernandez, Elizabethton.

2001 BATTING

TEAM

Team	Avg.	G	TPA	AB	R	H	TB	2B	3B	HR	RBI	SH	SF	HP	BB	IBB	SO	SB	CS	GDP	LOB	ShO	Slg.	OBP
Bluefield	.264	66	2502	2162	357	570	858	109	19	47	304	14	15	50	261	3	557	109	40	47	477	2	.397	.354
Elizabethton	.260	63	2227	1972	271	512	733	109	14	28	225	12	16	43	184	2	456	58	27	42	429	3	.372	.334
Pulaski	.259	68	2562	2247	382	583	922	124	19	59	329	13	21	50	231	3	637	97	27	32	468	3	.410	.339
Bristol	.257	65	2299	2035	301	524	739	95	12	32	254	12	17	43	192	7	538	80	33	35	427	5	.363	.332
Kingsport	.257	67	2422	2123	315	545	800	111	21	34	255	10	19	43	227	2	602	120	53	36	414	5	.377	.338
Princeton	.256	67	2469	2175	338	557	888	99	17	66	292	16	16	61	201	0	596	54	31	32	455	2	.408	.334
Danville	.245	68	2496	2250	265	551	771	111	14	27	236	19	9	34	184	6	617	48	26	44	472	3	.343	.310
Johnson City	.241	66	2413	2105	286	508	773	95	13	48	255	19	16	41	232	3	558	38	25	38	453	2	.367	.319
Martinsville	.231	68	2375	2153	230	498	702	96	15	26	185	27	18	51	126	7	515	75	32	30	432	7	.326	.287
Burlington	.223	68	2524	2177	308	485	728	81	18	42	263	21	12	46	268	4	660	61	37	34	460	4	.334	.319

INDIVIDUAL

TOP QUALIFIERS FOR BATTING CHAMPIONSHIP

Minimum 184 plate appearances. *Lefthanded batter. †Switch-hitter.

Player, Team	Avg.	G	TPA	AB	R	H	TB	2B	3B	HR	RBI	SH	SF	HP	BB	IBB	SO	SB	CS	GDP	Slg.	OBP
Pena, Brayan, Dan.†	.370	64	269	235	39	87	110	16	2	1	33	1	2	0	31	2	30	3	1	5	.468	.440
Francisco, Ruben, Blue.*	.327	57	225	199	35	65	90	16	0	3	21	1	0	7	17	0	32	18	5	10	.452	.399
Rogers, Omar, Blue.	.323	60	248	226	41	73	93	12	1	2	32	1	2	10	29	1	41	22	10	4	.412	.419
Pittman, Richard, King.†	.320	47	208	181	24	58	78	11	3	1	26	3	0	21	0	36	17	7	3	.431	.385	
Cavin, Jonathan, Bris.*	.317	54	206	183	24	58	76	7	1	3	21	0	2	4	17	1	45	3	1	2	.415	.373
Huber, Justin, King.	.314	47	194	159	24	50	84	11	1	7	31	1	4	13	17	0	42	4	2	4	.528	.415
Woodrow, Justin, J.C.*	.313	60	252	211	32	66	89	11	3	2	21	1	1	1	38	0	27	4	4	4	.422	.418
Bourgeois, Jason, Pul.†	.311	62	284	251	60	78	115	12	2	7	34	0	1	6	26	0	47	21	7	3	.458	.387
Perea, Jean, Pul.	.305	68	291	256	40	78	102	15	0	3	39	2	4	5	24	1	53	13	1	6	.398	.370

SUMMER CLASS A Appalachian League

Player, Team	Avg.	G	TPA	AB	R	H	TB	2B	3B	HR	RBI	SH	SF	HP	BB	IBB	SO	SB	CS	GDP	Slg.	OBP
Tomlin, James, Eliz.	.300	63	271	237	38	71	96	14	4	1	23	3	2	8	21	0	33	15	7	2	.405	.373
Kochen, Ryan, Mar.	.300	56	199	180	29	54	87	12	3	5	23	6	2	1	10	1	37	5	1	3	.483	.337
Salvo, Andrew, Bris.*	.297	63	248	212	37	63	84	12	0	3	35	0	3	6	27	1	23	14	6	4	.396	.387
Thomas, Adam, Blue.*	.295	62	271	227	45	67	93	8	3	4	26	2	0	6	36	0	39	16	5	4	.410	.405
Gomes, Jonny, Prin.	.291	62	270	206	58	60	123	11	2	16	44	1	4	26	33	0	73	15	4	1	.597	.442
Monegan, Anthony, Bris.*	.286	55	219	192	37	55	68	6	2	1	19	1	3	1	22	1	59	22	8	1	.354	.358

DEPARTMENTAL LEADERS: G—Perea, 60; AB—Perea, 256; R—Bourgeois, 60; H—Pena, 87; TB—Gomes, 123; 2B—Stockton, 18; 3B—Eldridge, 6; HR—Gomes, 16; RBI—Baxter, 46; SH—Rojas, Martinsville; SF—Knox, Rojas, 5 each; HP—Gomes, 26; BB—Stockton, 40; IBB—Fagan, 3; SO—Shelley, Hileman, 81; SB—Rogers, Monegan, 22 each; CS—Rogers, 10; GIDP—Francisco, 10; Slg.—Gomes, .597; OBP—Gomes, .442.

ALL PLAYERS

*Lefthanded batter. †Switch-hitter.

Player, Team	Avg.	G	TPA	AB	R	H	TB	2B	3B	HR	RBI	SH	SF	HP	BB	IBB	SO	SB	CS	GDP	Slg.	OBP
Abram, Matt, Eliz.	.242	55	214	190	26	46	72	11	0	5	24	2	2	4	16	0	38	3	3	3	.379	.311
Acevedo, Freddy, Mar.	.173	56	187	173	16	30	43	3	2	2	10	2	0	8	4	0	66	7	1	2	.249	.227
Agar, Cory, Eliz.	.275	57	216	193	26	53	94	15	1	8	33	1	1	4	17	1	62	0	0	5	.487	.344
Alvarado, Oscar, Mar.	.190	5	22	21	1	4	6	2	0	0	2	0	0	0	1	0	5	0	0	0	.286	.227
Amaya, Pilar, J.C.†	.213	54	199	169	24	36	56	11	0	3	16	3	1	4	22	0	40	2	2	5	.331	.316
Ankiel, Rick, J.C.*	.286	41	118	105	21	30	67	7	0	10	35	0	0	2	11	1	26	0	0	1	.638	.364
Arko, Thomas, Blue.	.194	36	141	124	16	24	45	4	1	5	16	1	2	1	13	0	47	0	1	5	.363	.271
Avila, Esteban, Mar.*	.206	44	164	155	12	32	44	4	1	2	14	2	0	2	4	1	29	1	1	0	.284	.236
Ayala, Abraham, Mar.	.135	33	123	111	5	15	20	2	0	1	8	1	2	3	6	0	13	1	2	1	.180	.197
Bacani, David, King.	.352	19	85	71	19	25	41	8	1	2	13	0	0	1	13	0	12	5	2	0	.577	.459
Bass, Brian, Blue.†	.324	19	81	71	17	23	46	6	1	5	20	0	0	0	10	0	17	0	0	2	.648	.407
Baxter, Andy, Burl.*	.244	63	255	209	41	51	108	16	4	11	46	1	2	8	35	2	60	3	1	1	.517	.370
Bernard, Miguel, Dan.	.242	39	139	128	13	31	44	8	1	1	16	1	0	2	8	0	29	1	1	6	.344	.297
Bessa, Laumin, Dan.	.243	55	187	173	24	42	67	10	3	3	17	1	0	2	11	1	49	3	2	3	.387	.296
Blount, Pierre, Prin.	.260	41	162	127	33	33	65	2	3	8	18	1	0	5	29	0	58	8	1	1	.512	.416
Bourgeois, Jason, Pul.†	.311	62	284	251	60	78	115	12	2	7	34	0	1	6	26	0	47	21	7	3	.458	.387
Bryan, Jason, Pul.	.199	55	208	176	26	35	66	7	0	8	23	1	1	5	25	0	75	3	1	3	.375	.314
Calahan, Larry S., Bris.*	.255	18	64	51	10	13	22	2	2	1	7	0	1	1	11	0	9	1	1	3	.431	.391
Camacaro, Armando, Burl.	.205	40	145	122	11	25	31	3	0	1	8	4	0	7	12	0	27	3	4	3	.254	.313
Capellan, Jose, Dan.	.000	4	4	2	0	0	0	0	0	0	1	1	0	0	1	0	1	0	0	0	.000	.333
Caperton, Freddy, Pul.	.234	17	55	47	5	11	12	1	0	0	5	0	0	1	7	0	15	0	0	1	.255	.345
Castellanos, Jose, Dan.	.310	42	140	129	14	40	61	10	1	3	21	0	0	1	10	0	21	0	0	8	.473	.364
Cavin, Jonathan, Bris.*	.317	54	206	183	24	58	76	7	1	3	21	0	2	4	17	1	45	3	1	2	.415	.383
Choy Foo, Rodney, Burl.†	.333	7	25	24	2	8	13	2	0	1	3	0	0	0	1	0	5	0	2	0	.542	.360
Cliffords, Woody, Blue.*	.278	62	232	198	36	55	90	13	2	6	29	1	0	1	32	1	40	8	1	6	.455	.381
Cochrane, Mark, Bris.	.294	6	18	17	3	5	7	2	0	0	2	0	0	0	1	0	3	0	0	1	.412	.333
Conroy, Mike, Burl.	.244	43	172	156	19	38	53	7	1	2	23	3	0	0	13	1	49	5	5	3	.340	.302
Copeland, Nate, Dan.*	.272	43	97	81	13	22	25	3	0	0	8	1	1	1	13	0	24	2	1	1	.309	.375
Cordell, Brent, Prin.†	.307	48	183	163	23	50	84	13	0	7	26	0	3	5	12	0	32	0	3	0	.515	.366
Cruz, Orlando, Pul.	.247	47	199	178	25	44	62	9	3	1	18	6	2	1	12	0	59	9	2	3	.348	.295
Cuevas, Aneudi, Mar.	.283	57	192	173	23	49	63	9	1	1	16	1	0	6	12	0	57	8	7	3	.364	.351
Cust, Kevin, Dan.	.129	24	66	62	2	8	11	0	0	1	4	0	1	2	1	0	32	0	1	1	.177	.167
Davie, Andrew, J.C.*	.221	39	135	113	8	25	37	6	0	2	22	0	0	2	20	1	43	2	1	1	.327	.348
Davis, J.P., Prin.	.223	49	187	166	20	37	59	10	0	4	13	1	1	8	11	0	37	0	2	3	.355	.301
Dorner, Dwight, Prin.*	.202	27	94	84	13	17	22	2	0	1	4	2	0	0	8	0	18	0	0	5	.262	.272
Dorsey, Ryan, Pul.	.132	16	44	38	1	5	9	2	1	0	2	0	0	1	5	0	20	2	0	0	.237	.250
Eldridge, Nashad, Durl.†	.258	61	262	229	39	59	94	8	6	5	27	1	2	3	27	0	65	3	2	1	.410	.341
Encarnacion, Julio, Bris.	.211	26	78	76	11	16	25	3	0	2	12	1	0	1	0	0	31	2	0	2	.329	.221
Esprit, Jermaine, Burl.†	.241	35	119	112	13	27	28	1	0	0	2	1	0	2	4	0	29	8	4	1	.250	.280
Esquivel, Lale, Pul.	.259	7	30	27	2	7	15	2	0	2	8	1	0	0	2	0	5	0	0	0	.556	.310
Fagan, John, Mar.	.209	59	228	201	20	42	69	12	0	5	22	0	2	6	19	3	50	1	0	4	.343	.294
Farmer, John, Dan.	.250	12	19	16	1	4	5	1	0	0	1	0	0	2	1	0	4	0	0	1	.313	.368
Folsom, Mark, Burl.	.210	29	117	100	15	21	36	7	1	2	23	0	0	0	17	0	41	0	1	2	.360	.325
Francisco, Ruben, Blue.*	.327	57	225	199	35	65	90	16	0	3	21	1	0	7	17	0	32	18	5	10	.452	.399
Furbush, Mark, King.	.271	40	154	144	18	39	62	12	1	3	19	0	0	0	10	0	35	8	4	2	.431	.318
Garcia, Kenji, King.	.021	17	55	48	1	1	2	1	0	0	1	0	0	1	6	0	25	0	1	1	.042	.145
Garcia, Rafaelito, Burl.†	.256	51	221	195	28	50	61	6	1	1	12	5	0	1	20	0	37	12	5	5	.313	.329
German, Amado, Prin.†	.283	52	204	184	33	52	87	10	5	5	31	0	1	0	19	0	50	16	4	1	.473	.348
Gomes, Jonny, Prin.	.291	62	270	206	58	60	123	11	2	16	44	1	4	26	33	0	73	15	4	1	.597	.442
Gomez, Deibis, J.C.	.000	5	2	2	0	0	0	0	0	0	0	0	0	0	0	0	1	0	0	0	.000	.000
Gomez, Jose, J.C.	.143	16	43	35	4	5	8	1	1	0	2	0	0	6	0	0	13	1	0	1	.229	.268
Green, Steve, J.C.*	.296	44	142	125	21	37	51	4	2	2	9	0	0	7	10	0	28	4	1	1	.408	.380
Guante, Domingo, Eliz.	.131	40	101	84	16	11	12	1	0	0	5	0	0	1	16	0	27	4	1	2	.143	.277
Guilliams, Earl, Dan.	.167	18	50	48	3	8	8	0	0	0	2	0	0	1	1	0	12	0	0	2	.167	.200
Gunn, Cody, J.C.*	.197	25	81	71	4	14	19	5	0	0	5	1	0	3	6	0	30	1	1	1	.268	.288
Guzman, Robert, Eliz.*	.333	25	88	78	10	26	37	4	2	1	8	2	0	3	5	0	17	1	1	1	.474	.395
Habel, Jason, Prin.	.252	37	139	127	11	32	38	3	0	1	14	1	1	2	8	0	36	3	3	1	.299	.304
Hackett, Richard, Blue.	.247	39	121	97	19	24	43	4	0	5	20	0	2	4	18	0	32	1	4	0	.443	.380
Harper, Brett, King.*	.336	38	158	146	24	49	60	9	1	0	19	0	0	4	8	0	30	3	2	2	.411	.386
Heard, Scott, Pul.*	.298	32	128	114	24	34	57	6	1	5	20	0	2	0	12	0	31	3	1	4	.500	.359
Hensler, Brad, King.	.333	4	14	9	4	3	7	1	0	1	5	0	0	3	2	0	1	0	0	1	.778	.571
Herr, Aaron, Dan.	.243	64	273	239	31	58	78	12	1	2	21	3	1	6	24	0	64	6	4	7	.326	.326
Hietpas, Joe, King.	.185	11	34	27	3	5	6	1	0	0	1	0	0	1	6	0	11	0	0	0	.222	.353
Hilario, Enderson, Bris.	.292	26	93	89	9	26	37	11	0	0	11	0	0	2	2	0	14	0	0	4	.416	.323
Hileman, Jutt, J.C.	.255	61	251	220	36	56	95	8	2	9	35	1	3	2	25	0	81	4	4	4	.432	.332
Hodges, Kerry, Mar.	.246	49	200	179	19	44	62	15	0	1	16	3	2	8	8	0	40	5	5	2	.346	.305
Housel, David, King.†	.182	23	74	66	6	12	13	1	0	0	5	1	1	0	5	0	21	2	3	2	.197	.247
Huber, Justin, King.	.314	47	194	159	24	50	84	11	1	7	31	1	4	13	17	0	42	4	2	4	.528	.415

Player, Team	Avg.	G	TPA	AB	R	H	TB	2B	3B	HR	RBI	SH	SF	HP	BB	IBB	SO	SB	CS	GDP	Slg.	OBP
Huff, Ken, Eliz.*	.262	43	137	126	11	33	41	6	1	0	14	1	1	0	9	0	23	0	1	5	.325	.309
Humphries, Justin, Mar.	.225	19	43	40	3	9	11	2	0	0	5	0	0	0	3	0	20	0	0	0	.275	.279
Huson, Tim, Bris.*	.183	50	182	153	23	28	39	5	0	2	9	2	0	3	24	0	68	2	4	0	.255	.306
Ison, Jeremy, Bris.	.260	29	107	96	12	25	40	9	0	2	12	1	0	1	9	0	32	0	1	2	.417	.330
Ivy, Bjorn, Bris.	.199	56	187	156	30	31	39	4	2	0	11	3	0	3	25	0	47	18	3	1	.250	.321
Jacobson, Billy, Mar.	.458	26	27	24	6	11	12	1	0	0	2	0	0	2	1	0	6	0	0	1	.500	.519
Jaile, Chris, Pul.	.250	29	115	100	15	25	30	5	0	0	12	0	1	1	13	0	20	0	0	2	.300	.339
Jansen, Ardley, Dan.	.223	64	230	211	25	47	68	3	0	6	23	0	0	4	15	1	64	9	7	2	.322	.287
Jiannetti, Joseph, King.	.271	23	99	85	13	23	38	5	2	2	17	1	3	0	9	0	11	4	2	1	.447	.330
Johnson, Tripper, Blue.	.261	43	173	157	24	41	55	6	1	2	26	0	3	2	11	0	37	4	0	3	.350	.312
Jones, Garrett, Dan.*	.289	40	159	149	13	43	63	11	0	3	23	0	0	1	9	0	58	0	1	0	.423	.333
Kantrovitz, Dan, J.C.	.333	1	3	3	0	1	1	0	0	0	0	0	0	0	0	0	0	0	0	0	.333	.333
Kennedy, Bryan, Eliz.*	.250	10	32	28	2	7	8	1	0	0	1	0	0	0	4	0	6	0	0	0	.286	.344
Keylor, Cory, Blue.*	.538	3	15	13	5	7	13	1	1	1	4	0	0	0	2	0	4	0	0	0	1.000	.600
Kirby, Brian, Burl.*	.190	25	103	84	14	16	33	3	1	4	14	0	0	4	15	1	31	1	1	2	.393	.340
Knox, Matt, Burl.	.207	62	250	222	26	46	65	11	1	2	33	0	5	3	20	0	46	1	1	3	.293	.276
Kochen, Ryan, Mar.	.300	56	199	180	29	54	87	12	3	5	23	6	2	1	10	1	37	5	1	3	.483	.337
Krga, Mike, Prin.	.208	38	143	130	11	27	30	1	1	0	8	0	1	1	11	0	33	0	0	2	.231	.273
Kuhaulua, Kaulana, Eliz.	.246	20	73	69	8	17	23	4	1	0	6	2	0	1	1	0	19	4	1	1	.333	.268
Lebron, Edgardo, Eliz.†	.209	38	125	115	15	24	33	3	0	2	10	0	0	2	8	1	42	1	2	4	.287	.272
Lentini, Fehlandt, Mar.	.283	12	52	46	8	13	19	1	1	1	4	0	1	0	5	0	5	11	1	1	.413	.346
Levy, Mike, J.C.	.256	19	49	43	7	11	20	1	1	2	8	0	0	0	6	0	18	0	0	1	.465	.347
Lisk, Charles, Bris.	.289	13	47	38	8	11	12	1	0	0	6	0	1	1	7	0	14	3	0	1	.316	.404
Luna, Leonardo, Bris.	.196	17	51	46	6	9	9	0	0	1	3	1	1	0	5	0	15	3	2	1	.196	.288
Lydon, Wayne, King.†	.184	26	110	98	14	18	25	7	0	0	8	1	0	0	11	0	35	15	1	1	.255	.266
Macchi, Brandon, Mar.†	.106	42	123	113	12	12	16	4	0	0	5	0	1	0	9	0	30	5	2	3	.142	.171
Maddox, Jeremy, Prin.	.271	53	205	188	20	51	77	11	0	5	27	0	1	4	12	0	47	1	1	6	.410	.327
Madere, Ronnie, Prin.	1.000	20	1	1	1	1	2	1	0	0	0	0	0	0	0	0	0	0	0	0	2.000	1.000
Manley, Adam, Blue.*	.190	27	91	84	13	16	30	3	1	3	17	0	0	3	4	0	30	1	0	0	.357	.253
Manning, Ricky, Eliz.*	.253	22	88	75	15	19	25	4	1	0	4	0	0	4	9	0	15	4	3	1	.333	.364
Marte, Andy, Dan.	.200	37	148	125	12	25	34	6	0	1	12	1	2	0	20	0	45	3	0	3	.272	.306
Martin, Kyle, Blue.	.308	44	145	130	16	40	54	11	0	1	13	1	1	0	13	0	39	1	2	1	.415	.368
Martinez, Luis, King.	.122	29	91	82	14	10	16	3	0	1	4	0	0	2	7	0	26	2	1	0	.195	.209
Martinez, Peter, Eliz.†	.224	35	117	98	11	22	33	11	0	0	12	0	1	5	13	0	26	5	2	2	.337	.342
Mather, Joe, J.C.	.248	45	178	165	25	41	59	3	0	5	21	1	2	3	7	0	60	2	2	5	.358	.288
Matos, Bernie, Eliz.	.227	14	45	44	5	10	13	3	0	0	4	0	0	0	1	0	9	0	1	1	.295	.244
Mauer, Jake, Eliz.	.155	27	71	58	8	9	10	1	0	0	6	0	0	5	8	0	5	3	1	4	.172	.310
Mauer, Joe, Eliz.*	.400	32	130	110	14	44	54	6	2	0	14	0	0	1	19	0	10	4	0	5	.491	.492
Melo, Hanlet, Dan.	.225	55	190	178	22	40	56	7	3	1	12	1	1	1	9	0	47	7	3	1	.315	.263
Mercedes, Ramon, Prin.	.252	48	181	163	22	41	49	5	0	1	19	5	0	1	11	0	26	5	3	3	.301	.303
Merchan, Jesus, Eliz.	.271	47	144	133	19	36	51	10	1	1	14	0	3	2	6	0	18	4	2	1	.383	.306
Mojica, Robinson, J.C.	.220	36	125	118	7	26	33	5	1	0	8	1	2	1	3	0	25	0	3	1	.280	.242
Molina, Gustavo, Bris.	.283	46	184	166	18	47	62	9	0	2	24	1	3	5	9	1	26	3	1	2	.373	.333
Molina, Yadier, J.C.	.259	44	175	158	18	41	64	11	0	4	18	0	2	3	12	1	23	1	1	4	.405	.320
Monegan, Anthony, Bris.*	.286	55	219	192	37	55	68	6	2	1	19	1	3	1	22	1	59	22	8	1	.354	.358
Moore, Bryan, J.C.*	.229	54	212	179	20	41	57	7	0	3	26	1	2	9	21	0	37	4	1	6	.318	.336
Morse, Michael, Bris.†	.227	57	207	181	23	41	66	7	3	4	27	0	0	9	17	1	57	6	2	4	.365	.324
Mote, Trevor, Mar.†	.250	47	186	168	18	42	55	8	1	1	13	3	0	0	14	1	36	9	3	4	.327	.308
Nash, Toe, Prin.†	.240	47	192	171	23	41	77	10	1	8	29	0	1	1	19	0	69	0	1	1	.450	.318
Nichols, Thomas, Prin.	.205	43	160	151	14	31	40	4	1	1	18	1	0	2	6	0	51	1	0	4	.265	.245
Nixon, Jason, Burl.	.154	9	29	26	2	4	8	1	0	1	3	0	0	1	2	0	13	0	0	0	.308	.241
Nolasco, Jose, J.C.†	.204	55	219	191	25	39	55	7	0	3	22	5	0	1	22	0	48	8	3	1	.288	.290
Noviskey, Josh, Burl.†	.140	38	138	114	10	16	18	2	0	0	4	0	0	1	23	0	50	1	1	4	.158	.290
Nunez, Alexis, Eliz.*	.298	21	69	57	10	17	20	3	0	0	11	0	1	0	11	0	9	3	2	1	.351	.406
Ochoa, Ivan, Burl.	.216	51	216	176	30	38	40	2	0	0	14	5	0	11	24	0	57	14	5	1	.227	.346
Oeltjen, Trent, Eliz.*	.233	9	32	30	4	7	8	1	0	0	4	1	1	0	0	0	6	2	0	0	.267	.226
O'Kelly, Mike, Dan.	.200	52	181	165	14	33	56	12	1	3	22	4	1	2	9	1	60	0	0	3	.339	.249
Patty, Jason, Pul.*	.271	53	201	177	26	48	73	4	3	5	32	1	2	11	10	0	47	6	3	2	.412	.345
Paulk, Barry, King.*	.250	31	112	88	24	22	34	3	3	1	4	0	2	5	17	1	17	11	2	0	.386	.393
Pena, Brayan, Dan.†	.370	64	269	235	39	87	110	16	2	1	33	1	2	0	31	2	30	3	1	5	.468	.440
Perea, Jean, Pul.	.305	68	291	256	40	78	102	15	0	3	39	2	4	5	24	1	53	13	1	6	.398	.370
Perez, Felipe, Blue.	.212	55	205	189	27	40	74	9	2	7	32	1	2	4	9	1	66	9	3	1	.392	.260
Perez, Juan, King.	.293	42	153	140	18	41	62	4	4	3	15	2	0	3	8	0	35	14	7	0	.443	.344
Pickering, Kelvin, Blue.	.091	14	25	22	3	2	2	0	0	0	1	0	1	0	2	0	13	0	0	1	.091	.160
Pittman, Richard, King.†	.320	47	208	181	24	58	78	11	3	1	26	3	0	3	21	0	36	17	7	3	.431	.385
Quickstad, Barry, Eliz.*	.274	42	135	117	20	32	63	4	0	9	23	0	2	2	14	0	45	5	0	1	.538	.356
Ragsdale, Corey, King.	.141	23	82	71	9	10	20	3	2	1	5	0	0	1	10	0	38	4	5	2	.282	.256
Reyes, Eduardo, J.C.	.190	19	47	42	5	8	13	2	0	1	4	0	2	1	2	0	15	0	1	0	.310	.234
Reyes, Julio, Bris.*	.251	57	211	199	19	50	85	11	0	8	38	0	2	4	6	2	47	1	2	7	.427	.284
Reynoso, Danilo, King.	.167	12	30	30	0	5	6	1	0	0	0	0	0	0	0	0	13	0	0	0	.200	.167
Riggans, Shawn, Prin.	.345	15	67	58	15	20	48	4	0	8	17	0	0	0	9	0	18	1	0	0	.828	.433
Riley, Ryan, Prin.	.257	46	157	140	25	36	51	6	3	1	16	3	0	3	11	0	23	3	5	1	.364	.325
Rivas, Arturo, Blue.	.147	11	42	34	4	5	5	0	0	0	2	0	1	2	5	0	13	4	0	0	.147	.286
Rodriguez , Ricardo, Dan.	.190	58	258	231	30	44	59	5	2	2	14	3	0	7	17	0	62	12	5	1	.255	.267
Rodriguez, Andres, King.	.322	27	96	90	10	29	43	8	0	2	10	0	1	0	5	0	23	2	1	3	.478	.354
Rodriguez, Jose, Blue.†	.147	22	40	34	3	5	7	0	1	0	4	1	0	0	5	0	15	2	1	1	.206	.256
Rogers, Joe, J.C.*	.000	15	3	2	0	0	0	0	0	0	0	0	0	0	1	0	1	0	0	0	.000	.333
Rogers, Omar, Blue.	.323	63	268	226	41	73	93	12	1	2	32	1	2	10	29	1	41	22	10	4	.412	.419
Rojas, Randy, Mar.	.251	62	256	223	23	56	76	10	2	2	19	7	5	9	12	1	36	17	7	3	.341	.309
Rollins, Antwon, Pul.	.254	65	265	240	43	61	116	15	2	12	37	1	2	6	16	0	80	18	1	2	.483	.314
Ruiz, Daniel, Mar.	.244	23	86	78	9	19	26	7	0	0	6	2	2	0	4	0	15	2	0	0	.333	.298
Ruiz, Reinaldo, Mar.	.262	46	182	168	15	44	61	5	0	4	18	1	2	3	8	0	27	0	1	1	.363	.304
Russell, Michael, Blue.	.281	10	35	32	7	9	17	2	0	2	6	0	0	1	2	0	7	1	0	2	.531	.343

Player, Team	Avg.	G	TPA	AB	R	H	TB	2B	3B	HR	RBI	SH	SF	HP	BB	IBB	SO	SB	CS	GDP	Slg.	OBP
St. Clair, Jason, Prin.	.241	32	125	116	16	28	36	6	1	0	8	1	3	3	2	0	25	1	4	3	.310	.266
Salvesen, Matthew, Bris.*	.000	2	8	8	0	0	0	0	0	0	0	0	0	0	0	0	4	0	0	0	.000	.000
Salvo, Andrew, Bris.*	.297	63	248	212	37	63	84	12	0	3	35	0	3	6	27	1	23	14	6	4	.396	.387
Santamarina, Juan, Bris.*	.259	10	34	27	4	7	13	1	1	1	3	0	0	0	7	0	8	0	1	0	.481	.412
Santana, Hector, Burl.	.194	29	111	103	7	20	33	3	2	2	8	1	0	0	7	0	45	0	1	1	.320	.245
Santana, Mayobanex, Bris.	.269	42	155	145	27	39	55	5	1	3	16	0	1	1	8	0	36	2	1	1	.379	.310
Sassanella, Justin, King.*	.172	20	74	64	7	11	13	2	0	0	5	1	1	0	8	0	29	4	3	1	.203	.260
Scott, Charles, Burl.	.212	11	37	33	5	7	16	0	0	3	6	0	0	0	4	0	12	0	1	1	.485	.297
Shelley, Randall, Pul.	.249	67	278	233	47	58	105	18	1	9	43	0	2	8	35	0	81	8	2	1	.451	.363
Shier, Peter, Blue.	.238	65	245	202	30	48	65	10	2	1	19	3	1	3	36	0	51	17	4	6	.322	.360
Simoneaux, Neil, J.C.	.203	49	179	153	29	31	49	6	3	2	5	3	1	2	20	0	42	5	1	2	.320	.301
Soriano, Jairo, Blue.†	.206	41	121	102	14	21	31	4	3	0	15	2	0	5	12	0	30	4	4	1	.304	.319
Sosa, Francisco, King.	.000	1	4	4	0	0	0	0	0	0	0	1	0	0	0	0	1	0	0	0	.000	.000
Stockton, Brad, Pul.*	.259	64	279	232	43	60	107	18	4	7	41	1	4	2	40	2	67	3	3	2	.461	.367
Tavarez, Ydel, Burl.	.194	13	36	36	5	7	8	1	0	0	2	0	0	2	0	0	20	1	0	0	.222	.237
Thomas, Adam, Blue.*	.205	62	271	227	45	57	93	8	3	4	26	2	0	6	36	0	39	16	5	4	.410	.405
Threinen, Scott, Burl.	.200	37	141	110	19	22	29	2	1	1	12	0	1	3	25	0	34	6	3	1	.264	.360
Tillman, Kevin, Burl.*	.238	40	147	126	22	30	54	6	0	6	23	0	2	2	17	0	39	3	0	5	.429	.333
Tomlin, James, Eliz.	.300	63	271	237	38	71	96	14	4	1	23	3	2	8	21	0	33	15	7	2	.405	.373
Tope, Stephen, Eliz.	.215	40	139	130	13	28	40	7	1	1	9	0	2	1	6	0	46	0	0	3	.308	.252
Turay, Alhaji, King.	.245	43	176	163	21	40	60	8	3	2	20	1	2	1	9	0	46	8	3	5	.368	.286
Volquez, Julio, Pul.†	.219	48	185	178	25	39	53	10	2	0	15	0	0	3	4	0	37	11	6	3	.298	.249
Watts, Derran, King.	.245	17	63	53	10	13	13	0	0	0	3	0	0	1	9	0	21	5	0	0	.245	.365
Webster, Robert, Blue.	.238	10	27	21	2	5	5	0	0	0	1	0	0	1	5	0	4	1	0	0	.238	.407
Wendt, Justin, King.*	.275	30	112	91	16	25	31	3	0	1	17	0	1	4	16	1	21	0	6	4	.341	.402
Whitesides, Jake, Mar.*	.230	53	193	178	20	41	58	6	4	1	8	1	1	3	10	0	55	5	1	2	.326	.281
Wilson, Brandon, King.	.215	30	108	93	9	20	31	2	0	3	12	0	1	0	14	0	43	3	0	2	.333	.315
Woodrow, Justin, J.C.*	.313	60	252	211	32	66	89	11	3	2	21	1	1	1	38	0	27	4	4	4	.422	.418
Wright, David, King.	.300	36	138	120	27	36	55	7	0	4	17	0	0	2	16	0	30	9	1	3	.458	.391

GRAND SLAMS: Nash, 2; Agar, Ankiel, Baxter, Bourgeois, Conroy, German, Gomes, Morse, J. Reyes, H. Santana, Stockton, Tillman, 1 each.

AWARDED FIRST BASE ON CATCHER'S INTERFERENCE: Threinen 2 (Pickering, Dorner); Avila (Caperton), Francisco (H. Santana), Housel (Molina), Mercedes (Agar), Mote (Matos).

2001 PITCHING

TEAM

Team	W	L	Pct.	ERA	G	CG	ShO	Sv.	IP	H	TBF	R	ER	HR	SH	SF	HB	BB	IBB	SO	WP	Bk.
Martinsville	31	37	.456	3.05	68	3	6	14	573.0	494	2405	243	194	29	18	17	42	212	2	575	50	9
Elizabethton.......	41	22	.651	3.13	63	1	6	22	518.0	442	2208	229	180	34	16	17	43	192	4	500	47	0
Johnson City	31	35	.470	3.30	66	1	6	10	555.0	514	2307	285	201	31	19	10	49	189	4	629	61	12
Bristol	39	26	.600	3.58	65	5	4	15	530.2	514	2236	267	211	42	14	18	34	149	7	486	46	7
Pulaski	38	30	.559	3.71	68	4	2	19	575.0	546	2493	307	237	42	14	14	48	191	7	555	55	9
Danville	30	38	.441	3.80	68	2	4	17	583.0	529	2528	327	246	44	13	15	39	238	2	623	73	11
Kingsport	31	36	.463	4.11	67	1	1	11	564.2	588	2522	320	258	39	16	14	58	215	2	552	48	14
Burlington	31	37	.456	4.15	68	0	1	16	581.1	546	2562	341	268	55	18	16	49	256	1	606	58	12
Bluefield	33	33	.500	4.71	66	2	1	17	552.1	579	2486	360	289	52	19	21	54	222	7	562	61	10
Princeton..........	28	39	.418	5.13	67	2	3	11	552.1	581	2489	374	315	41	16	17	46	242	1	560	62	11

INDIVIDUAL

TOP QUALIFIERS FOR EARNED-RUN AVERAGE TITLE

Minimum 54 innings. *Lefthanded pitcher.

Pitcher, Team	W	L	Pct.	ERA	G	GS	CG	ShO	GF	Sv.	IP	H	TBF	R	ER	HR	SH	SF	HB	BB	IBB	SO	WP	Bk.
Ankiel, Rick, J.C.*	5	3	.625	1.33	14	14	1	0	0	0	87.2	42	327	20	13	1	1	0	6	18	0	158	8	0
Cabreja, Eny, Mar.*	4	3	.571	1.58	12	12	1	0	0	0	74.0	54	289	19	13	6	2	3	4	20	0	67	4	1
Albertus, Roberto, Dan.*	3	2	.600	2.39	16	5	0	0	3	2	60.1	46	239	20	16	3	0	0	1	13	0	56	4	0
Mattox, David, King.	5	1	.833	2.40	14	8	1	0	5	0	56.1	48	241	22	15	3	1	0	8	19	0	58	10	0
Gardner, Hayden, Pul.	4	4	.500	2.48	13	13	2	1	0	0	83.1	71	340	32	23	4	1	0	8	15	0	70	6	0
Houlton, Dennis, Mar.	5	4	.556	2.50	13	13	1	0	0	0	72.0	67	292	24	20	7	1	2	3	7	0	71	2	0
Merricks, Matt, Dan.*	4	5	.444	2.79	12	11	0	0	0	0	58.0	42	225	19	18	5	0	4	2	18	0	70	2	4
Lubisich, Nik, Bris.*	5	2	.714	2.83	11	11	2	1	0	0	70.0	65	274	26	22	2	2	3	2	12	0	49	0	2
Szado, Craig, Bris.*	2	3	.400	3.05	15	8	0	0	6	1	56.0	52	230	23	19	3	2	3	1	12	0	56	1	0
Mabry, Barry, Dan.	3	3	.500	3.20	20	2	0	0	3	0	56.1	60	245	26	20	3	2	1	1	18	2	55	2	1
Tejada, Sandy, Eliz.	5	3	.625	3.20	11	10	0	0	0	0	56.1	43	233	26	20	6	1	2	4	20	0	87	4	1
Beltre, Omar, Pul.	6	3	.667	3.38	13	12	0	0	0	0	69.1	56	290	28	26	4	3	3	9	23	0	83	12	1
Digby, Bryan, Dan.	3	5	.375	3.38	12	12	1	0	0	0	61.1	52	273	33	23	2	1	1	5	32	0	49	13	0
Doyne, Michael, Mar.	4	3	.571	3.54	13	13	0	0	0	0	61.0	57	264	31	24	2	2	2	3	30	0	56	5	1
Moravek, Rob, Pul.	4	2	.667	3.57	13	11	0	0	0	0	63.0	70	269	34	25	3	0	3	2	17	1	54	7	0

DEPARTMENTAL LEADERS: W—W. Martinez, Vorwald, Hemus, Bittner, Beltre, 6 each; L—Pinango, M. Gomez, 8 each; Pct.—Bittner, Hemus, Vorwald, .857; G—Keefer, 29; GS—Wright, Ankiel, 14 each; CG—Febles, Lubisich, Gardner, 2 each; ShO—Febles, 2; GF—Keefer, 27; Sv.—Keefer, 15; IP—Ankiel, 87.2; H—Tate, 80; TBF—Gardner, 340; R—M. Gomez, 47; ER—M. Gomez, 40; HR—Patten, 12; SH—Serafini, 5; SF—J. Sanchez, 6; HB—Anez, 10; BB—Kentner, 36; IBB—Mincey, Bowers, 3 each; SO—Ankiel, 158; WP—Digby, M. Wright, 13 each; BK—P. Martinez, T. Johnson, Pinango, 5 each.

ALL PITCHERS

*Lefthanded pitcher.

Pitcher, Team	W	L	Pct.	ERA	G	GS	CG	ShO	GF	Sv.	IP	H	TBF	R	ER	HR	SH	SF	HB	BB	IBB	SO	WP	Bk.
Abraham, Paul, Pul.	3	2	.600	4.94	15	0	0	0	9	2	31.0	26	140	22	17	2	1	1	5	16	0	28	6	1
Acosta, Domingo, King.	0	5	.000	5.54	17	5	0	0	6	0	39.0	49	181	31	24	2	2	2	4	11	0	39	3	0

Pitcher, Team	W	L	Pct.	ERA	G	GS	CG	ShO	GF	Sv.	IP	H	TBF	R	ER	HR	SH	SF	HB	BB	IBB	SO	WP	Bk.
Advincola, Jose, Blue.*	1	2	.333	5.26	22	0	0	0	5	0	39.1	37	177	28	23	6	2	3	4	22	0	50	9	2
Aguilar, Edwin, Mar.	0	0	.000	0.00	1	0	0	0	0	0	1.1	0	5	0	0	0	0	0	0	1	0	0	0	0
Albertus, Roberto, Dan.*	3	2	.600	2.39	16	5	0	0	3	2	60.1	46	239	20	16	3	0	0	1	13	0	56	4	0
Alvarado, Luis, Burl.*	1	0	1.000	4.60	16	0	0	0	4	0	31.1	34	141	18	16	1	0	0	4	12	0	31	3	2
Anez, Omar, Blue.	2	7	.222	7.62	15	6	0	0	3	0	41.1	51	206	46	35	5	0	4	10	17	0	46	8	0
Ankiel, Rick, J.C.*	5	3	.625	1.33	14	14	1	0	0	0	87.2	42	327	20	13	1	1	0	6	18	0	158	8	0
Aquino, Danny, Burl.	1	0	1.000	8.22	6	0	0	0	2	0	7.2	8	36	7	7	3	0	0	0	4	0	3	0	0
Asencio, Domingo, Bris.*	0	1	.000	4.91	6	3	0	0	2	0	18.1	24	78	10	10	3	2	0	2	4	1	6	2	1
Ayala, Roberto, Prin.*	0	0	.000	12.00	5	0	0	0	2	0	3.0	5	19	5	4	0	0	0	1	5	0	1	2	0
Barr, Adam, Burl.*	2	2	.500	3.91	8	3	0	0	0	0	23.0	17	111	15	10	2	0	1	2	25	0	29	1	1
Barrios, Angel, Mar.	3	5	.375	3.15	11	10	0	0	0	0	45.2	45	189	17	16	0	0	0	1	16	0	54	2	0
Basilio, Manuel, Prin.	2	4	.333	5.59	11	9	0	0	1	0	48.1	49	219	32	30	4	0	0	9	23	0	57	2	3
Batista, Roberto, J.C.	2	3	.400	3.38	20	3	0	0	3	0	42.2	54	190	23	16	3	1	0	5	9	0	30	6	3
Bayrer, Thomas, Mar.	0	3	.000	5.19	16	0	0	0	5	1	26.0	27	124	19	15	3	1	1	2	22	1	33	4	2
Belisle, Adam, Dan.*	0	2	.000	4.78	21	0	0	0	13	1	26.1	31	131	18	14	5	0	1	3	16	0	22	4	0
Beltre, Omar, Pul.	6	3	.667	3.38	13	12	0	0	0	0	69.1	56	290	28	26	4	3	3	9	23	0	83	12	1
Berry, Casey, Pul.	4	2	.667	3.92	14	1	0	0	9	2	41.1	40	183	20	18	6	1	0	3	15	1	38	2	0
Berube, Martin, Blue.	4	2	.667	6.11	11	11	0	0	0	0	53.0	78	247	42	36	6	2	4	2	10	0	49	4	0
Birkins, Kurt, Blue.*	4	1	.800	2.92	6	6	0	0	0	0	37.0	28	144	14	12	2	1	0	2	5	0	42	3	0
Bittner, Tim, Bris.*	6	1	.857	1.10	8	8	1	1	0	0	49.0	34	197	14	6	0	2	0	4	12	0	53	4	2
Blethen, Matt, Burl.*	4	1	.800	2.76	18	0	0	0	5	1	49.0	42	203	17	15	5	3	1	1	15	0	42	3	0
Bowers, Rob, Pul.	1	1	.500	4.00	4	0	0	0	0	0	9.0	13	46	7	4	0	1	0	0	4	3	7	0	0
Bowyer, Travis, Eliz.	2	5	.286	6.10	9	8	0	0	0	0	38.1	38	170	30	26	3	1	3	3	20	0	34	7	0
Boyer, Blaine, Dan.	4	5	.444	4.32	13	12	0	0	0	0	50.0	48	220	35	24	4	3	1	5	19	0	57	9	1
Bradshaw, Chris, Pul.	2	2	.500	3.97	14	3	0	0	3	1	47.2	42	206	28	21	2	0	0	7	14	0	52	2	3
Bravo, Edgar, J.C.	0	3	.000	5.06	18	0	0	0	11	1	21.1	17	95	15	12	1	1	2	3	16	2	15	3	1
Bright, Nathan, Pul.	1	3	.250	5.66	12	0	0	0	5	0	20.2	31	103	18	13	3	1	0	0	10	0	16	5	0
Brown, Jeremy, Eliz.	0	0	.000	3.27	3	2	0	0	0	0	11.0	10	46	4	4	1	0	0	0	3	0	9	0	0
Bullard, Jim, Bris.*	1	2	.333	3.05	4	4	1	0	0	0	20.2	20	84	12	7	4	0	1	0	1	0	31	3	0
Cabreja, Eny, Mar.*	4	3	.571	1.58	12	12	1	0	0	0	74.0	54	289	19	13	6	2	3	4	20	0	67	4	1
Cabrera, Yunior, Mar.*	3	3	.500	3.89	11	10	0	0	1	0	44.0	38	191	22	19	3	2	1	5	19	0	49	5	1
Camacaro, Armando, Burl.	0	0	.000	13.50	1	0	0	0	0	0	2.0	6	12	3	3	0	0	0	0	0	0	1	0	0
Camacho, Jose, Mar.	1	0	1.000	1.46	8	0	0	0	4	0	12.1	8	47	2	2	0	0	0	1	0	0	14	2	0
Cameron, Kevin, Eliz.	1	1	.500	1.57	22	0	0	0	22	13	23.0	16	94	4	4	0	0	0	3	5	0	30	3	0
Capellan, Jose, Dan.	0	0	.000	1.72	3	3	0	0	0	0	15.2	12	66	7	3	1	0	0	2	4	0	25	1	1
Cetani, Bryan, Dan.*	1	1	.500	6.11	15	0	0	0	7	2	17.2	29	103	20	12	1	2	1	2	17	0	13	2	0
Chourio, Jorge, Burl.	0	1	.000	23.63	3	0	0	0	1	0	2.2	8	17	7	7	2	0	0	1	1	0	1	1	0
Cislak, Chad, Burl.	0	0	.000	27.00	1	0	0	0	0	0	0.1	0	5	4	1	0	0	1	0	4	0	0	5	0
Coose, Austin, Prin.	0	0	.000	0.00	8	0	0	0	7	2	9.1	4	35	2	0	0	0	0	0	2	0	16	0	0
Cromer, Jason, Prin.*	2	0	1.000	1.59	5	2	0	0	0	0	22.2	14	85	5	4	2	0	1	0	8	0	18	2	0
Crouthers, Dave, Blue.	2	3	.400	4.43	10	10	1	0	0	0	44.2	41	194	28	22	7	1	2	4	18	0	45	3	0
Crump, Joel, Blue.*	0	0	.000	2.25	10	0	0	0	7	1	12.0	10	51	4	3	1	0	0	0	6	0	15	3	0
Danly, Ryan, King.*	1	2	.333	4.62	15	1	0	0	6	3	25.1	33	115	13	13	1	1	0	7	0	0	31	0	4
Daws, Josh, Eliz.	1	1	.500	1.39	20	1	0	0	6	2	45.1	34	172	8	7	2	1	4	3	5	1	56	2	1
Deaton, Kevin, King.	5	2	.714	2.09	17	4	0	0	4	1	47.1	40	193	17	11	2	0	0	7	10	0	43	0	0
De La Cruz, Carlos, Burl.	1	2	.333	2.83	6	4	0	0	0	0	28.2	17	118	11	9	2	0	1	3	12	0	33	1	0
Deleon, Joey, Mar.	1	2	.333	2.32	13	7	0	0	2	0	42.2	27	165	12	11	1	1	1	3	11	0	44	2	0
Denham, Dan, Burl.	0	4	.000	4.40	8	8	0	0	0	0	30.2	30	150	21	15	5	1	0	6	26	0	31	1	1
D'Frank, Carlos, Burl.	0	0	.000	3.86	5	0	0	0	1	0	7.0	5	28	3	3	2	0	0	2	1	0	6	1	0
Digby, Bryan, Dan.	3	5	.375	3.38	12	12	1	0	0	0	61.1	52	273	33	23	2	1	1	5	32	0	49	13	0
Dittler, Jake, Burl.	1	2	.333	3.68	6	5	0	0	0	0	22.0	25	101	14	9	0	1	0	1	12	0	20	4	0
Dobyns, Heath, Bris.	2	0	1.000	3.63	13	0	0	0	7	1	17.1	21	76	9	7	1	0	1	3	0	0	15	2	0
Doyne, Michael, Mar.	4	3	.571	3.54	13	13	0	0	0	0	61.0	57	264	31	24	2	2	3	3	30	0	56	5	1
Durbin, J.D., Eliz.	3	2	.600	1.87	8	7	0	0	0	0	33.2	23	145	13	7	2	1	1	4	17	0	39	5	1
Eckert, Harold, King.	1	0	1.000	2.25	2	2	0	0	0	0	12.0	8	44	3	3	1	0	0	0	1	0	17	0	0
Edwards, Michael, Blue.*	0	1	.000	5.60	16	1	0	0	3	0	35.1	25	159	23	22	3	1	2	3	28	0	37	9	0
Ewin, Ryan, Dan.	2	2	.500	4.54	10	9	0	0	0	0	37.2	36	160	20	19	4	0	0	4	13	0	39	3	0
Farrell, Sean, King.*	1	0	1.000	6.43	19	0	0	0	6	0	28.0	31	135	25	20	4	1	1	3	17	0	28	3	1
Febles, Hector, Prin.	3	5	.500	6.80	12	10	2	2	0	0	46.1	55	217	40	35	4	1	0	3	25	0	39	7	0
Feliciano, Ruben, Pul.	0	0	.000	0.00	4	0	0	0	2	1	7.2	1	27	0	0	0	0	0	1	4	0	6	0	1
Fields, Josh, Bris.	3	1	.750	3.67	18	0	0	0	10	2	34.1	34	144	22	14	3	1	1	2	8	1	37	2	0
Foley, Travis, Burl.	2	3	.400	2.80	10	10	0	0	0	0	45.0	26	175	16	14	4	2	3	3	15	0	59	1	0
Forbes, Derek, Blue.	1	1	.500	6.48	6	0	0	0	4	0	8.1	12	43	7	6	1	0	0	0	6	0	11	2	0
Frey, Jason, J.C.	1	0	1.000	4.15	3	3	0	0	0	0	13.0	11	51	6	6	2	1	0	2	4	0	13	1	0
Fries, Tim, Dan.	2	3	.400	4.91	24	0	0	0	13	5	36.2	39	172	22	20	1	1	2	3	20	0	54	7	1
Fryson, Andrew, Bris.	2	0	1.000	2.50	3	3	0	0	0	0	18.0	17	72	6	5	0	0	0	1	3	0	11	0	0
Gardner, Hayden, Pul.	4	4	.500	2.48	13	13	2	1	0	0	83.1	71	340	32	23	4	1	0	8	15	0	70	6	0
Garza, Rolando, Bris.	0	1	.000	7.04	5	0	0	0	3	0	7.2	9	40	6	6	2	0	0	0	10	0	4	5	0
Gomez, Deibis, J.C.	0	1	.000	3.00	4	0	0	0	1	1	3.0	6	17	2	1	0	0	0	0	2	0	2	2	0
Gomez, Jose, King.	0	0	.000	1.00	3	2	0	0	0	0	9.0	3	35	2	1	0	0	0	4	4	0	14	1	1
Gomez, Mariano, Burl.*	2	8	.200	6.07	13	12	0	0	0	0	59.1	69	265	47	40	4	2	3	0	21	0	57	5	1
Gonzalez, Kiwi, Prin.	3	2	.600	4.44	14	8	0	0	2	0	50.2	52	223	31	25	2	1	3	3	18	0	38	4	2
Gronkiewicz, Lee, Burl.	3	3	.500	2.56	25	0	0	0	23	11	31.2	28	124	11	9	1	1	1	2	8	0	47	2	0
Hamilton, Ryan, Mar.	0	0	.000	0.00	2	1	0	0	0	0	3.0	0	12	0	0	0	0	0	3	0	0	3	0	0
Hemus, Jared, Eliz.*	6	1	.857	1.48	16	6	0	0	4	3	48.2	33	193	9	8	3	2	0	6	16	0	49	1	0
Hines, Carlos, Prin.	2	3	.400	4.44	13	7	0	0	2	0	48.2	51	220	33	24	3	1	2	3	17	0	56	6	1
Hollifield, Alec, Bris.	2	1	.667	4.73	4	2	0	0	0	0	13.1	19	62	7	7	0	0	1	0	4	0	15	0	0
Honel, Kris, Bris.	2	3	.400	3.13	8	8	0	0	0	0	46.0	41	184	19	16	4	1	2	1	9	0	45	3	0
Hooker, Jon, Bris.	2	2	.500	5.46	17	0	0	0	6	0	29.2	27	131	24	18	3	1	1	14	2	0	35	7	1
Houlton, Dennis, Mar.	5	4	.556	2.50	13	13	1	0	0	0	72.0	67	292	24	20	7	1	2	3	12	0	71	2	0
Jacobson, Billy, Mar.	0	1	.000	1.06	18	0	0	0	7	3	34.0	20	135	7	4	0	2	0	9	8	0	25	4	1
Jimenez, Kelvin, Pul.	0	3	.000	6.28	4	4	0	0	0	0	14.1	24	73	14	10	2	0	0	1	4	0	10	1	0
Johnson, Tyler, J.C.*	1	1	.500	2.66	9	9	0	0	0	0	40.2	26	168	17	12	1	0	0	3	21	0	58	9	5

Pitcher, Team	W	L	Pct.	ERA	G	GS	CG	ShO	GF	Sv.	IP	H	TBF	R	ER	HR	SH	SF	HB	BB	IBB	SO	WP	Bk.
Jones, D.J., Blue.*	1	0	1.000	0.75	4	1	0	0	0	0	12.0	8	44	2	1	0	0	1	0	2	0	8	0	1
Keefer, Ryan, Blue.	1	0	1.000	0.59	29	0	0	0	27	15	30.2	20	125	4	2	1	2	0	3	8	2	46	1	0
Keiter, Ben, Pul.	4	2	.667	4.33	10	10	0	0	0	0	43.2	30	186	23	21	4	1	2	4	20	0	42	2	2
Kentner, Brandon, King.	1	0	1.000	4.30	21	0	0	0	11	1	29.1	26	152	18	14	1	0	2	1	36	0	37	5	1
Killalea, John, J.C.*	0	3	.000	6.39	7	7	0	0	0	0	25.1	32	120	19	18	1	2	0	2	16	0	29	4	1
King, Timothy, Prin.*	1	3	.250	4.54	11	7	0	0	3	0	35.2	40	163	20	18	1	2	1	2	15	0	26	1	0
Lawson, Brett, Eliz.	1	0	1.000	9.49	10	1	0	0	6	0	12.1	14	73	19	13	0	0	1	2	16	2	14	7	1
Ledbetter, Aaron, J.C.	1	7	.125	6.13	11	11	0	0	0	0	47.0	72	226	40	32	5	0	2	4	12	0	54	4	0
Little, Carmen, Mar.	2	6	.250	5.45	20	0	0	0	12	0	38.0	51	186	31	23	1	3	3	3	16	0	43	6	1
Lohse, Eric, Eliz.	1	1	.500	4.15	3	2	0	0	1	0	8.2	12	40	7	4	1	0	0	1	1	0	5	1	0
Lubisich, Nik, Bris.*	5	2	.714	2.83	11	11	2	1	0	0	70.0	65	274	26	22	2	2	3	2	12	0	49	0	2
Maberry, Mark, King.	0	0	.000	0.00	2	0	0	0	1	1	3.0	1	10	0	0	0	0	0	0	0	0	1	0	0
Mabry, Barry, Dan.	3	3	.500	3.20	20	2	0	0	3	0	56.1	60	245	26	20	3	2	1	1	18	2	55	2	1
Made, Luis, Prin.*	0	0	.000	8.10	8	0	0	0	3	0	16.2	18	80	16	15	2	0	0	2	13	0	14	6	0
Madere, Ronnie, Prin.	1	2	.333	10.71	19	0	0	0	7	0	21.0	32	113	31	25	2	0	4	14	0	22	4	1
Marcano, Luis, Pul.	3	2	.600	3.71	11	0	0	0	9	5	26.2	27	116	15	11	1	2	2	8	2	27	1	0
Martin, J.D., Burl.	5	1	.833	1.38	10	10	0	0	0	0	45.2	26	174	9	7	3	0	0	4	11	0	72	3	1
Martinez, Dan, Bris.*	3	1	.750	1.38	18	0	0	0	14	6	26.0	21	107	8	4	0	2	1	2	11	0	24	4	0
Martinez, Paul, Burl.*	2	2	.500	6.43	19	0	0	0	5	0	35.0	39	171	29	25	4	3	0	3	26	0	40	3	5
Martinez, Wilmer, J.C.	6	3	.667	2.10	23	0	0	0	11	0	34.1	32	150	18	8	0	2	1	5	11	1	25	6	1
Mattox, David, Blue.	5	1	.833	2.40	14	8	1	0	5	0	56.1	48	241	22	15	3	1	0	8	19	0	58	10	0
McNair, James, Mar.	1	2	.333	5.08	18	0	0	0	7	0	33.2	35	144	20	19	1	1	2	6	11	0	26	7	0
Merricks, Matt, Dan.*	4	5	.444	2.79	12	11	0	0	0	0	58.0	42	225	19	18	5	0	4	2	18	0	78	2	4
Middleton, Brian, Mar.	1	3	.250	3.10	10	0	0	0	4	0	20.1	13	90	9	7	2	2	0	16	0	22	2	1
Miller, Colby, Eliz.	5	1	.833	2.44	15	6	0	0	2	0	48.0	39	198	15	13	4	2	0	4	12	0	61	7	0
Miller, Eric, Prin.*	4	2	.667	5.05	16	1	0	0	3	0	35.2	32	164	23	20	5	4	0	3	18	0	40	8	0
Miller, Jason, Eliz.*	4	3	.571	4.05	12	11	1	0	0	0	53.1	46	228	26	24	4	1	3	4	19	0	66	3	1
Mincey, T.W., Blue.*	1	1	.500	6.75	15	1	0	0	4	1	30.2	38	155	31	23	2	2	1	4	21	3	29	2	0
Montani, Jeff, Blue.	0	0	.000	2.25	7	0	0	0	1	0	8.0	5	34	2	2	1	0	0	4	0	9	0	0
Montilla, Elvis, Blue.	2	2	.500	4.68	5	4	1	0	1	0	25.0	28	109	13	13	1	1	1	8	0	18	2	0
Morales, Juan, J.C.	0	0	.000	5.40	4	3	0	0	0	0	13.1	17	60	12	8	1	0	1	4	2	0	10	2	0
Moravek, Rob, Pul.	4	2	.667	3.57	13	11	0	0	0	0	63.0	70	269	34	25	3	0	3	2	17	1	54	7	0
Morban, Domingo, King.*	1	4	.200	7.77	16	0	0	0	9	1	22.0	29	118	20	19	2	2	0	8	16	1	26	6	0
Morris, Cory, Blue.	1	0	1.000	0.00	1	0	0	0	0	0	3.0	1	12	0	0	0	0	0	2	0	4	0	0
Nieve, Fernando, Mar.	4	2	.667	3.79	12	8	1	0	0	0	30.0	27	161	20	16	2	0	0	3	21	0	49	3	1
Ogle, Rylie, King.*	2	2	.500	3.42	6	5	0	0	0	0	23.2	31	108	15	9	2	0	0	7	0	18	1	0
Olivo, Rigal, Bris.	1	4	.200	3.95	11	6	0	0	2	0	41.0	41	185	22	18	4	1	1	7	11	0	40	1	1
Olson, Ryan, King.*	0	0	.000	2.45	2	1	0	0	0	0	7.1	9	33	4	2	1	1	0	1	1	0	6	0	0
Osberg, Tanner, King.	2	2	.500	4.28	13	13	0	0	0	0	67.1	72	290	34	32	4	0	5	9	22	0	36	6	1
Palmer, Travis, J.C.	1	2	.333	4.19	10	7	0	0	0	0	38.2	45	172	22	18	3	1	4	14	0	29	1	0
Parker, Josh, Prin.	2	1	.667	2.35	22	0	0	0	17	5	30.2	29	126	12	8	0	0	1	3	6	0	34	3	1
Patten, Scott, Bris.	3	4	.429	5.46	12	12	1	0	0	0	61.0	67	266	42	37	12	0	1	7	21	1	43	7	0
Patty, Jason, Pul.	0	0	.000	0.00	1	0	0	0	1	0	0.2	0	4	0	0	0	0	0	0	0	0	0	0	0
Paustian, Michael, Pul.	2	1	.667	3.38	14	2	0	0	9	5	29.1	25	130	16	11	2	3	1	1	16	0	27	5	0
Phillips, James, Blue.	3	5	.375	5.13	25	2	0	0	8	0	40.1	52	190	32	23	5	2	1	1	18	2	27	2	1
Pinango, Miguel, King.	3	8	.273	4.42	14	13	0	0	1	0	59.0	63	255	35	29	6	3	2	5	13	0	49	2	5
Plancich, Nick, J.C.	2	2	.500	1.18	9	9	0	0	0	0	38.0	32	154	12	5	0	0	1	1	10	0	19	3	0
Prahm, Ryan, Burl.	0	0	.000	10.38	1	1	0	0	0	0	4.1	8	22	5	5	0	0	0	0	1	0	4	1	0
Pruitt, Jason, Blue.*	0	0	.000	5.40	1	0	0	0	0	0	1.2	2	10	1	1	0	0	0	2	1	0	2	1	0
Ramos, Eddy, Pul.	2	1	.667	4.83	17	0	0	0	15	3	31.2	39	140	20	17	4	0	2	0	8	0	30	5	1
Rawson, Anthony, J.C.*	3	1	.750	0.60	23	0	0	0	20	10	30.0	19	115	3	2	0	3	0	2	7	0	45	2	0
Rice, Scott, Blue.*	4	3	.571	4.12	12	12	0	0	0	0	63.1	58	281	44	29	4	3	1	7	28	0	53	7	3
Roberts, Ralph, Dan.	0	1	.000	1.80	17	0	0	0	14	6	20.0	18	80	6	4	2	1	1	0	4	0	31	2	1
Rogers, Joe, J.C.*	1	1	.500	3.21	15	0	0	0	2	1	28.0	22	117	15	10	3	1	0	4	8	1	46	2	1
Rogers, Jon, Dan.	0	1	.000	2.16	6	0	0	0	4	1	8.1	5	37	7	2	1	1	1	1	2	0	11	0	0
Rojas, Yorlan, J.C.	2	0	1.000	3.96	19	0	0	0	5	0	25.0	23	110	15	11	3	1	2	2	12	0	25	4	0
Roman, Orlando, King.	1	0	1.000	1.00	4	1	0	0	2	1	9.0	4	34	2	1	0	0	0	1	2	0	13	0	0
Romero, Luis, Burl.	2	3	.400	3.82	16	0	0	0	11	3	33.0	37	152	25	14	3	1	1	8	16	0	24	6	0
Salazar, Richard, Blue.*	1	0	1.000	3.86	2	0	0	0	1	0	4.2	5	21	2	2	0	0	0	2	0	0	7	1	0
Sanchez, Juan, Prin.	2	6	.250	7.74	12	0	0	0	0	0	45.1	50	208	43	39	6	1	6	4	23	0	47	3	1
Santana, Leonardo, Mar.*	3	0	1.000	1.80	19	0	0	0	16	10	35.0	23	142	9	7	3	2	3	14	0	44	5	1
Seddon, Chris, Prin.*	1	2	.333	5.11	4	2	0	0	1	0	12.1	15	56	7	7	2	0	0	6	0	18	0	0
Serafini, Vince, Eliz.*	3	3	.500	3.81	14	9	0	0	1	0	52.0	54	217	24	22	4	5	2	3	8	0	40	2	1
Shaw, Elliott, Prin.	0	0	.000	5.93	6	0	0	0	0	0	13.2	15	63	10	9	0	0	1	11	0	17	3	0
Sherman, Chris, King.	3	3	.500	3.28	14	0	0	0	5	2	24.2	25	116	15	9	3	2	0	4	9	1	19	2	0
Shouse, Dan, J.C.*	2	2	.500	4.96	12	0	0	0	1	0	16.1	23	77	15	9	1	1	0	1	5	0	12	0	0
Skyles, Matt, Burl.*	0	2	.000	4.00	6	3	0	0	0	0	27.0	35	117	17	12	4	1	0	1	4	0	15	3	0
Smart, Richard, Eliz.*	3	0	1.000	3.31	17	0	0	0	6	0	32.2	32	158	22	12	3	1	1	1	25	1	31	1	0
Smith, Matthew, Bris.	1	0	1.000	4.50	4	0	0	0	3	2	8.0	4	35	4	4	0	0	0	2	5	1	6	2	0
Sokoll, Adam, Dan.	2	3	.400	6.21	22	0	0	0	8	0	29.0	21	131	28	20	2	0	5	19	0	19	5	0
Spaulding, Richard, Burl.*	0	0	.000	7.02	14	0	0	0	9	0	16.2	19	87	16	13	1	0	3	15	0	9	2	0
Szado, Craig, Bris.*	2	3	.400	3.05	15	8	0	0	6	1	56.0	52	230	23	19	3	2	3	1	12	0	56	1	0
Tarkington, Shawn, Eliz.	0	0	.000	11.25	6	0	0	0	3	0	8.0	17	41	10	10	1	0	0	3	0	7	0	0
Tate, Matt, Blue.	5	5	.500	4.94	12	12	0	0	0	0	62.0	80	284	37	34	7	2	1	9	18	0	64	4	3
Tejada, Sandy, Eliz.	5	3	.625	3.20	11	10	0	0	0	0	56.1	43	233	26	20	6	1	2	4	20	0	87	4	1
Templet, Eric, King.	1	2	.333	5.23	12	2	0	0	2	0	20.2	30	96	14	12	0	0	0	4	0	27	1	0
Thomas, Matt, J.C.	4	2	.667	4.68	20	0	0	0	8	0	25.0	23	107	17	13	4	3	0	0	7	0	22	1	0
Thomas, Scott, Burl.	0	0	.000	6.52	9	0	0	0	3	0	9.2	7	52	8	7	2	2	0	1	12	1	10	2	0
Thompson, Tyson, Prin.	0	1	.000	3.18	3	1	0	0	0	0	5.2	9	29	7	2	0	0	0	2	0	6	1	0
Tillman, Kevin, Burl.	0	0	.000	0.00	1	0	0	0	1	0	2.0	2	7	0	0	0	0	0	0	0	0	0	0	0
Truselo, Randy, Pul.	1	2	.333	8.00	4	4	0	0	0	0	18.0	27	91	24	16	3	0	1	7	0	16	1	0
Turner, Brad, J.C.	0	1	.000	2.81	15	0	0	0	3	0	25.2	18	111	14	8	2	1	1	15	0	37	3	0
Valdez, Fernando, Burl.	1	0	1.000	1.80	7	0	0	0	3	1	15.0	12	62	6	3	1	0	0	0	2	0	20	3	0

Pitcher, Team	W	L	Pct.	ERA	G	GS	CG	ShO	GF	Sv.	IP	H	TBF	R	ER	HR	SH	SF	HB	BB	IBB	SO	WP	Bk.
Victorino, Pedro, Prin.	2	3	.400	6.18	13	8	0	0	0	0	43.2	49	204	35	30	5	2	3	4	23	1	39	5	2
Vigue, John, Prin.	1	5	.167	3.24	20	0	0	0	14	4	33.1	34	139	13	12	1	1	2	1	6	0	35	4	0
Volquez, Bolivar, Prin.	2	2	.500	2.43	19	0	0	0	3	0	29.2	28	126	9	8	2	3	0	4	7	0	37	1	0
Vorwald, Matt, Eliz.	6	1	.857	1.16	23	0	0	0	11	4	46.2	31	200	12	6	0	1	0	5	22	0	60	4	0
Warden, Jim Ed, Burl.	4	5	.444	4.27	12	12	0	0	0	0	52.2	56	232	32	25	6	1	1	6	13	0	52	6	1
Weintraub, Jason, King.	1	2	.333	5.70	11	0	0	0	4	1	23.2	27	106	15	15	4	0	0	2	11	0	25	1	0
Weir, Jayson, King.*	0	0	.000	6.43	9	0	0	0	3	0	14.0	21	69	13	10	0	2	0	0	6	0	16	2	0
Williams, Ruddy, Mar.	2	3	.400	4.50	15	4	0	0	8	0	36.0	40	160	23	18	4	0	1	1	16	1	24	2	0
Wilson, C.J., Pul.*	1	0	1.000	0.96	8	8	0	0	0	0	37.2	24	149	6	4	2	0	0	4	9	0	49	0	0
Wing, Ryan, Bris.*	1	0	1.000	9.00	1	0	0	0	1	0	1.0	1	5	1	1	0	0	0	0	0	0	2	2	0
Wray, Fred, Dan.	3	0	1.000	6.00	17	0	0	0	1	0	33.0	30	145	26	22	6	0	2	3	17	0	25	6	0
Wright, Matt, Dan.	3	5	.375	3.72	14	14	1	0	0	0	72.2	60	301	40	30	4	2	0	2	26	0	89	13	2
Young, Curtis, Bris.	3	0	1.000	6.75	10	0	0	0	5	1	13.1	17	66	12	10	1	0	3	1	9	1	14	1	0

COMBINATION SHUTOUTS. **Bluefield (1)** **Daruba**-Advingola-Keefer. **Bristol (2)**—Szado-Martinez, Bittner-Szado. **Burlington (1)**—Martin-Alvarado-Gronkiewicz. **Danville (4)**—Merricks-Fries-Sokoll-Rogers, Boyer-Sokoll-Roberts, Merricks-Fries-Roberts, Albertus-Fries. **Elizabethton (6)**—Tejada-Vorwald-Helmus-Lawson-Cameron, Miller-Vorwald-Cameron, Brown-Miller-Lawson, Miller-Cameron, Daws-Lohse, Miller-Vorwald. **Johnson City (6)**—Johnson-Gomez-Bravo-Rawson, Batista-Shouse-Rawson, Palmer-Martinez-Rawson-Turner, Ledbetter-Rogers-Martinez-Bravo, Killalea-Martinez, Plancich-Turner-Shouse-Rojas. **Kingsport (1)**—Ogle-Farrell. **Martinsville (6)**—Cabreja-McNair-DeLeon, Hamilton-DeLeon-Little-Jacobson-Bayrer-McNair, Barrios-Bayrer-Santana, Houlton-Jacobson, Cabreja-Barrios-McNair, Williams-Santana. **Princeton (1)**—Basilio-Parker. **Pulaski (3)**—Beltre-Abraham, Wilson-Berry, Beltre-Marcano.

NO-HIT GAMES: None.

2001 FIELDING

TEAM

Team	Pct.	G	PO	A	E	TC	DP	TP	PB
Martinsville	.969	68	1719	651	76	2446	50	0	8
Elizabethton	.963	63	1554	564	82	2200	30	0	16
Bristol	.961	65	1592	695	92	2379	60	0	15
Burlington	.958	68	1744	663	106	2513	40	0	12
Danville	.956	68	1749	614	109	2472	43	0	25
Kingsport	.955	67	1694	682	113	2489	54	0	7
Pulaski	.955	68	1725	755	118	2598	51	0	18
Bluefield	.953	66	1657	642	114	2413	43	0	25
Princeton	.952	67	1657	622	114	2393	38	0	24
Johnson City	.951	66	1665	678	122	2465	53	0	24

INDIVIDUAL

FIRST BASEMEN

NOTE: All caps denotes fielding-percentage leader based on 34 games for catchers, 45 for all other non-pitchers and 54 innings for pitchers. *Throws lefthanded.

Player, Team	Pct.	G	PO	A	E	TC	DP
Amaya, Pilar, J.C.	1.000	1	3	0	0	3	0
Ayala, Abraham, Mar.	1.000	8	60	3	0	63	7
Baxter, Andy, Burl.	.992	62	479	36	4	519	32
Cliffords, Woody, Blue.	.977	15	78	8	2	88	6
Cust, Kevin, Dan.	.988	11	73	7	1	81	6
Davie, Andrew, J.C.	.971	10	65	3	2	70	7
Davis, J.P., Prin.	.991	38	284	29	3	316	22
Esquivel, Lale, Pul.	.929	1	13	0	1	14	2
FAGAN, John, Mar.	.994	55	433	28	3	464	29
Garcia, Kenji, King.	.956	14	105	3	5	113	6
Harper, Brett, King.	.971	26	229	8	7	244	30
Huff, Ken, Eliz.*	.980	22	134	11	3	148	4
Humphries, Justin, Mar.	1.000	4	18	2	0	20	4
Huson, Tim, Bris.	.989	24	166	12	2	180	12
Jones, Garrett, Dan.*	.974	39	276	19	8	303	26
Knox, Matt, Burl.	1.000	5	30	5	0	35	2
Kuhaulua, Kaulana, Eliz.	.977	5	41	1	1	43	2
Lebron, Edgardo, Eliz.	1.000	6	32	1	0	33	4
Manley, Adam, Blue.*	.980	17	137	7	3	147	13
Martin, Kyle, Blue.	.000	1	0	0	0	0	0
Molina, Gustavo, Bris.	1.000	4	37	2	0	39	4
Moore, Bryan, J.C.*	.988	53	479	16	6	501	37
Mote, Trevor, Mar.	1.000	4	33	1	0	34	2
Nichols Iv, Thomas, Prin.	.984	31	232	12	4	248	14
Nolasco, Jose, J.C.	1.000	4	28	3	0	31	4
Noviskey, Josh, Burl.	1.000	1	3	0	0	3	0
O'Kelly, Mike, Dan.	.967	22	129	17	5	151	10
Perea, Jean, Pul.	.988	67	628	46	8	682	45
Perez, Felipe, Blue.	.986	43	317	24	5	346	21
Rodriguez, Andres, King.	.991	24	199	13	2	214	12
Salvesen, Matthew, Bris.	1.000	2	14	2	0	16	0
Santana, Mayobanex, Bris.	.989	41	354	20	4	378	36
Scott, Charles, Burl.	.955	3	20	1	1	22	1
Shelley, Randall, Pul.	1.000	1	2	1	0	3	0
Tope, Stephen, Eliz.	.989	38	261	14	3	278	17
Wendt, Justin, King.	.985	9	60	6	1	67	5

SECOND BASEMEN

Player, Team	Pct.	G	PO	A	E	TC	DP
Abram, Matt, Eliz.	1.000	5	3	10	0	13	0
Amaya, Pilar, J.C.	.778	2	1	6	2	9	0
Bacani, David, King.	.961	19	39	60	4	103	15
Bourgeois, Jason, Pul.	.940	61	83	197	18	298	27
Calahan, Larry S., Bris.	.750	4	1	2	1	4	0
Choy Foo, Rodney, Burl.	.889	4	2	6	1	9	0
Dorsey, Ryan, Pul.	.947	6	3	15	1	19	2
Farmer, John, Dan.	.950	5	8	11	1	20	3
Garcia, Rafaelito, Burl.	.935	18	33	25	4	62	5
Herr, Aaron, Dan.	.939	64	101	146	16	263	26
Hileman, Jutt, J.C.	.783	6	10	8	5	23	3
Hodges, Kerry, Mar.	1.000	2	2	1	0	3	0
Housel, David, King.	.933	21	36	47	6	89	10
Ison, Jeremy, Bris.	1.000	1	1	2	0	3	0
Jacobson, Billy, Mar.	.750	1	2	1	1	4	0
Krga, Mike, Prin.	.972	38	49	90	4	143	9
Luna, Leonardo, Bris.	.952	6	7	13	1	21	3
Marte, Andy, Dan.	.000	1	0	0	0	0	0
Martinez, Luis, King.	.895	10	9	25	4	38	5
Martinez, Peter, Eliz.	.973	31	39	71	3	113	6
Mauer, Jake, Eliz.	1.000	9	16	15	0	31	6
Merchan, Jesus, Eliz.	1.000	6	4	9	0	13	0
Mote, Trevor, Mar.	.952	16	24	36	3	63	5
Nolasco, Jose, J.C.	.885	10	19	27	6	52	6
Nunez, Alexis, Eliz.	.937	21	29	30	4	63	6
Ochoa, Ivan, Burl.	.966	13	26	30	2	58	5
Patty, Jason, Pul.	1.000	2	4	6	0	10	1
Pittman, Richard, King.	.980	20	32	65	2	99	5
Reyes, Eduardo, J.C.	.891	13	21	28	6	55	6
Riley, Ryan, Prin.	.978	12	12	32	1	45	5
Rodriguez , Ricardo, Dan.	1.000	3	9	7	0	16	2
Rodriguez, Jose, Blue.	.939	15	20	26	3	49	10
Rogers, Omar, Blue.	.908	57	84	104	19	207	16
ROJAS, Randy, Mar.	.965	52	82	141	8	231	28
St. Clair, Jason, Prin.	.936	24	38	64	7	109	13
Salvo, Andrew, Bris.	.963	61	106	152	10	268	40
Simoneaux, Neil, J.C.	.966	40	49	95	5	149	17
Soriano, Jairo, Blue.	1.000	5	3	5	0	8	0
Tavarez, Ydel, Burl.	.000	1	0	0	0	0	0
Threinen, Scott, Burl.	.909	9	22	18	4	44	5
Tillman, Kevin, Burl.	.954	30	59	66	6	131	11

THIRD BASEMEN

Player, Team	Pct.	G	PO	A	E	TC	DP
Abram, Matt, Eliz.	.809	39	21	55	18	94	3
Amaya, Pilar, J.C.	1.000	2	2	2	0	4	0
Avila, Esteban, Mar.	.892	39	31	52	10	93	5
Baxter, Andy, Burl.	1.000	1	0	1	0	1	0
Bessa, Laumin, Dan.	.875	4	3	4	1	8	0
Calahan, Larry S., Bris.	.852	11	6	17	4	27	1
Davis, J.P., Prin.	.667	2	0	6	3	9	0
Dorner, Dwight, Prin.	.000	1	0	0	0	0	0
Dorsey, Ryan, Pul.	.000	1	0	0	0	0	0
Farmer, John, Dan.	.000	1	0	0	0	0	0
Harper, Brett, King.	.773	12	6	11	5	22	1
Hensler, Brad, King.	1.000	1	1	3	0	4	0

Player, Team	Pct.	G	PO	A	E	TC	DP
Huson, Tim, Bris.	.906	29	22	65	9	96	8
Ison, Jeremy, Bris.	.917	19	7	26	3	36	3
Jiannetti, Joseph, King.	.896	20	18	42	7	67	2
Johnson, Tripper, Blue.	.886	14	6	25	4	35	1
Knox, Matt, Burl.	.921	57	46	94	12	152	1
Kochen, Ryan, Mar.	.947	26	27	44	4	75	2
Lebron, Edgardo, Eliz.	.919	13	11	23	3	37	2
Luna, Leonardo, Bris.	.833	9	4	11	3	18	4
Maddox, Jeremy, Prin.	.868	49	36	56	14	106	1
Marte, Andy, Dan.	.936	37	32	56	6	94	7
Martinez, Luis, King.	1.000	1	0	1	0	1	0
Mather, Joe, J.C.	.901	41	23	50	8	81	8
Mauer, Jake, Eliz.	.966	16	7	21	1	29	1
Mercedes, Ramon, Prin.	.000	1	0	0	0	0	0
Morehan, Joseph, Clif.	1.000	0	1	2	0	3	0
Mote, Trevor, Mar.	.867	6	3	10	2	15	0
Nolasco, Jose, J.C.	.920	24	25	44	6	75	2
O'Kelly, Mike, Dan.	.897	28	24	37	7	68	11
Patty, Jason, Pul.	1.000	2	1	3	0	4	0
Reyes, Julio, Bris.	.000	1	0	0	0	0	0
Riley, Ryan, Prin.	.923	23	6	30	3	39	3
Rogers, Omar, Blue.	.800	10	4	8	3	15	2
Rojas, Randy, Mar.	.000	1	0	0	0	0	0
St. Clair, Jason, Prin.	.500	1	0	1	1	2	0
Santamarina, Juan, Bris.	.760	6	2	17	6	25	1
SHELLEY, Randall, Pul.	.924	67	48	134	15	197	8
Shier, Peter, Blue.	.925	24	10	39	4	53	2
Soriano, Jairo, Blue.	.898	28	13	31	5	49	0
Tavarez, Ydel, Burl.	.750	1	1	2	1	4	0
Threinen, Scott, Burl.	.944	11	6	11	1	18	1
Wendt, Justin, King.	1.000	1	0	1	0	1	0
Wright, David, King.	.939	36	20	57	5	82	5

SHORTSTOPS

Player, Team	Pct.	G	PO	A	E	TC	DP
Bass, Brian, Blue.	.851	19	19	44	11	74	4
Cuevas, Aneudl, Mar.	.930	57	55	143	15	213	20
Dorsey, Ryan, Pul.	.875	5	5	9	2	16	2
Farmer, John, Dan.	1.000	2	1	1	0	2	0
Garcia, Rafaelito, Burl.	.952	32	60	79	7	146	17
Hileman, Jutt, J.C.	.882	52	61	140	27	228	28
Ison, Jeremy, Bris.	.964	9	8	19	1	28	2
Knox, Matt, Burl.	1.000	1	0	1	0	1	0
Kochen, Ryan, Mar.	.933	13	15	27	3	45	6
Kuhaulua, Kaulana, Eliz.	.964	13	9	45	2	56	3
Lebron, Edgardo, Eliz.	.868	21	30	49	12	91	4
Luna, Leonardo, Bris.	.867	5	4	9	2	15	3
Martinez, Luis, King.	.930	18	13	53	5	71	10
Mather, Joe, J.C.	1.000	4	4	7	0	11	0
MERCEDES, Ramon, Prin.	.941	47	69	105	11	185	19
Merchan, Jesus, Bris.	.963	33	34	71	4	109	10
Morse, Michael, Bris.	.940	54	80	141	14	235	29
Nolasco, Jose, J.C.	.826	4	6	13	4	23	3
Ochoa, Ivan, Burl.	.923	38	54	113	14	181	18
Patty, Jason, Pul.	.867	18	28	50	12	90	12
Pittman, Richard, King.	.097	26	37	76	13	126	18
Ragsdale, Corey, King.	.894	23	32	52	10	94	9
Riley, Ryan, Prin.	.909	14	26	34	6	66	8
Rodriguez , Ricardo, Dan.	.918	53	74	106	16	196	15
Rojas, Randy, Mar.	1.000	2	4	3	0	7	0
Ruiz, Daniel, Dan.	.903	16	21	44	7	72	8
St. Clair, Jason, Prin.	.872	11	11	23	5	39	2
Shier, Peter, Blue.	.952	42	90	148	12	250	26
Simoneaux, Neil, J.C.	.926	7	7	18	2	27	4
Soriano, Jairo, Blue.	.867	8	7	19	4	30	1
Volquez, Julio, Pul.	.923	48	54	139	16	209	20

OUTFIELDERS

Player, Team	Pct.	G	PO	A	E	TC	DP
Abram, Matt, Eliz.	1.000	7	6	0	0	6	0
Acevedo, Freddy, Mar.	.936	56	96	7	7	110	1
Amaya, Pilar, J.C.	1.000	49	47	7	0	54	0
Bessa, Laumin, Dan.	.934	50	66	5	5	76	1
Blount, Pierre, Prin.	.900	35	51	3	6	60	0
Bryan, Jason, Pul.	.966	35	26	2	1	29	0
Castellanos, Jose, Dan.	.911	32	48	3	5	56	0
Cavin, Jonathan, Bris.	.938	43	59	2	4	65	0
CLIFFORDS, Woody, Blue.	1.000	48	56	3	0	59	1
Conroy, Mike, Burl.*	.955	40	62	2	3	67	0
Copeland, Nate, Dan.*	.971	32	33	1	1	35	0
Cruz, Orlando, Pul.	.946	45	82	5	5	92	0
Cust, Kevin, Dan.	.000	1	0	0	0	0	0

Player, Team	Pct.	G	PO	A	E	TC	DP
Davie, Andrew, J.C.	.750	3	2	1	1	4	0
Dorner, Dwight, Prin.	1.000	2	3	0	0	3	0
Eldridge, Rashad, Burl.	.970	58	93	3	3	99	3
Encarnacion, Julio, Bris.	.909	23	20	0	2	22	0
Esprit, Jermaine, Burl.	.961	31	48	1	2	51	0
Folsom, Mark, Burl.	.953	27	39	2	2	43	2
Francisco, Ruben, Blue.*	.940	55	85	9	6	100	1
Furbush, Mark, King.	1.000	40	51	2	0	53	1
German, Amado, Prin.	1.000	44	57	2	0	59	0
Gomes, Jonny, Prin.	.936	61	97	5	7	109	0
Gomez, Deibis, J.C.	1.000	1	1	0	0	1	0
Gomez, Jose, J.C.	1.000	15	16	1	0	17	0
Green, Steve, J.C.	.955	41	63	1	3	67	0
Guante, Domingo, Eliz.	.950	34	37	1	2	40	0
Guzman, Robert, Eliz.*	.968	23	28	2	1	31	0
Habel, Jason, Prin.	.957	32	42	2	2	46	0
Hackett, Richard, Blue.	.974	34	35	2	1	38	0
Hodges, Kerry, Mar.	.982	44	50	4	1	55	0
Huff, Ken, Eliz.*	1.000	21	22	0	0	22	0
Ivy, Bjorn, Bris.	.974	51	75	1	2	78	1
Jacobson, Billy, Mar.	1.000	6	8	2	0	10	1
Jansen, Ardley, Dan.	.954	64	140	6	7	153	0
Keylor, Cory, Blue.	1.000	2	4	0	0	4	0
Kirby, Brian, Burl.	1.000	14	10	1	0	11	0
Kochen, Ryan, Mar.	.000	1	0	0	1	1	0
Lentini, Fehlandt, Mar.	1.000	11	16	2	0	18	0
Lydon, Wayne, King.	.941	25	47	1	3	51	1
Macchi, Brandon, Mar.*	1.000	34	43	1	0	44	0
Manley, Adam, Blue.*	1.000	9	5	1	0	6	0
Manning, Ricky, Eliz.*	.966	21	28	0	1	29	0
Martinez, Peter, Eliz.	.750	4	3	0	1	4	0
Melo, Hanlet, Dan.	1.000	53	49	3	0	52	0
Merchan, Jesus, Eliz.	.000	1	0	0	0	0	0
Mojica, Robinson, J.C.	.946	35	51	2	3	56	1
Molina, Gustavo, Bris.	.000	1	0	0	0	0	0
Monegan, Anthony, Bris.	.962	55	97	4	4	105	0
Mote, Trevor, Mar.	.973	14	33	3	1	37	2
Nash, Toe, Prin.	.925	35	42	7	4	53	0
Nixon, Jason, Burl.	.875	9	6	1	1	8	0
Nolasco, Jose, J.C.	.923	11	11	1	1	13	0
Noviskey, Josh, Burl.	.938	26	29	1	2	32	1
Ochoa, Ivan, Burl.	1.000	1	2	0	0	2	0
Oeltjen, Trent, Eliz.*	1.000	9	13	0	0	13	0
Patty, Jason, Pul.	.920	17	23	0	2	25	0
Paulk, Barry, King.	.912	27	30	1	3	34	0
Perez, Felipe, Blue.	1.000	4	2	0	0	2	0
Perez, Juan, King.	.952	40	55	4	3	62	0
Pittman, Richard, King.	.000	1	0	0	2	2	0
Quickstad, Barry, Eliz.	.967	26	27	2	1	30	0
Reyes, Julio, Bris.	.951	28	35	4	2	41	2
Rivas, Arturo, Blue.	1.000	11	16	1	0	17	0
Rodriguez, Andres, King.	.000	1	0	0	0	0	0
Rollins, Antwon, Pul.	.895	62	75	10	10	95	4
Santana, Mayobanex, Bris.	.000	1	0	0	0	0	0
Sassanella, Justin, King.	.947	19	18	0	1	19	0
Stockton, Brad, Pul.	.917	48	51	4	5	60	0
Tavarez, Ydel, Burl.	.000	1	0	0	1	1	0
Thomas, Adam, Blue.*	.962	58	74	2	3	79	0
Threinen, Scott, Burl.	.875	8	7	0	1	8	0
Tomlin, James, Eliz.	.981	63	97	6	2	105	1
Turay, Alhaji, King.	.946	42	69	1	4	74	0
Watts, Derran, King.	.952	16	20	0	1	21	0
Whitesides, Jake, Mar.	.988	48	76	7	1	84	2
Woodrow, Justin, J.C.	.914	59	58	6	6	70	2

CATCHERS

Player, Team	Pct.	G	PO	A	E	TC	DP	PB
Agar, Cory, Eliz.	.987	23	202	21	3	226	0	4
Alvarado, Oscar, Mar.	1.000	5	42	6	0	48	0	2
Arko, Thomas, Blue.	.982	35	286	33	6	325	0	14
Ayala, Abraham, Mar.	1.000	20	144	13	0	157	0	1
Bernard, Miguel, Dan.	.996	28	228	26	1	255	0	11
Camacaro, Armando, Burl.	.988	39	358	40	5	403	0	5
Caperton, Freddy, Pul.	.983	16	106	12	2	120	0	4
Cochrane, Mark, Bris.	.875	5	13	1	2	16	0	0
Cordell, Brent, Prin.	.978	36	278	28	7	313	1	12
Dorner, Dwight, Prin	.975	23	179	17	5	201	1	9
Guante, Domingo, Eliz.	.000	1	0	0	0	0	0	0
Guilliams, Earl, Dan.	1.000	18	120	8	0	128	0	5
Gunn, Cudy, J.C.	.983	24	149	29	3	181	1	15
Heard, Scott, Pul.	.988	28	236	19	3	258	2	8
Hensler, Brad, King.	1.000	2	21	3	0	24	0	3

Player, Team	Pct.	G	PO	A	E	TC	DP	PB
Hietpas, Joe, King.	1.000	10	60	6	0	66	1	0
Hilario, Enderson, Bris.	.989	12	81	13	1	95	1	2
Huber, Justin, King.	.981	47	372	45	8	425	1	2
Humphries, Justin, Mar.	1.000	2	10	1	0	11	0	0
Ison, Jeremy, Bris.	.000	1	0	0	0	0	0	0
Jaile, Chris, Pul.	.991	28	208	24	2	234	1	4
Kennedy, Bryan, Eliz.	1.000	10	100	3	0	103	0	0
Kirby, Brian, Burl.	1.000	1	2	0	0	2	0	0
Levy, Mike, J.C.	.969	6	29	2	1	32	0	0
Lisk, Charles, Bris.	1.000	11	78	12	0	90	2	3
Martin, Kyle, Blue.	.976	21	154	11	4	169	0	6
Matos, Bernie, Eliz.	.968	13	113	8	4	125	0	1
Mauer, Joe, Eliz.	.980	19	178	14	4	196	1	11
Mullin, Gustavo, Dria.	.980	40	292	55	7	354	3	10
Molina, Yadier, J.C.	.986	42	409	81	7	497	2	9
Pena, Brayan, Dan.	.984	31	271	30	5	306	1	9
Perea, Jean, Pul.	1.000	1	4	1	0	5	0	2
Pickering, Kelvin, Blue.	.870	5	19	1	3	23	0	0
Reynoso, Danilo, King.	.978	12	76	12	2	90	0	2
Riggans, Shawn, Prin.	.975	12	106	13	3	122	0	3
RUIZ, Reinaldo, Mar.	.988	44	387	36	5	428	2	5
Russell, Michael, Blue.	.984	8	60	3	1	64	1	4
Santana, Hector, Burl.	.951	29	215	39	13	267	1	7
Scott, Charles, Burl.	.857	2	5	1	1	7	0	0
Sosa, Francisco, King.	1.000	1	8	1	0	9	0	0
Webster, Robert, Blue.	1.000	6	41	7	0	48	0	1

PITCHERS

Player, Team	Pct.	G	PO	A	E	TC	DP
Abraham, Paul, Pul.	1.000	15	2	6	0	8	0
Acosta, Domingo, King.	.800	17	1	3	1	5	0
Advincola, Jose, Blue.*	.857	22	1	5	1	7	0
Aguilar, Edwin, Mar.	.000	1	0	0	0	0	0
Albertus, Roberto, Dan.*	.818	16	1	8	2	11	0
Alvarado, Luis, Burl.*	1.000	16	0	6	0	6	0
Anez, Omar, Blue.	.727	15	4	4	3	11	0
Ankiel, Rick, J.C.*	.875	14	5	9	2	16	0
Aquino, Danny, Burl.	1.000	6	0	1	0	1	0
Asencio, Domingo, Bris.*	1.000	6	3	7	0	10	2
Ayala, Roberto, Prin.*	.000	5	0	0	0	0	0
Barr, Adam, Burl.*	.000	8	0	0	0	0	0
Barrios, Angel, Mar.	1.000	11	2	3	0	5	0
Basilio, Manuel, Prin.	.923	11	4	8	1	13	0
Batista, Roberto, J.C.	.750	20	0	6	2	8	0
Bayrer, Thomas, Mar.	1.000	16	2	6	0	8	0
Belicic, Adam, Dan.*	.900	21	5	4	1	10	0
Beltre, Omar, Pul.	.933	13	7	7	1	15	0
Berry, Casey, Pul.	.889	14	2	6	1	9	0
Berube, Martin, Blue.	.818	11	2	7	2	11	1
Birkins, Kurt, Blue.*	.818	6	0	9	2	11	1
Bittner, Tim, Bris.*	.818	8	1	8	2	11	1
Blethen, Matt, Burl.*	.846	18	3	8	2	13	0
Bowers, Rob, Pul.	.667	4	0	2	1	3	0
Bowyer, Travis, Eliz.	.889	9	3	5	1	9	0
Boyer, Blaine, Dan.	.750	13	1	5	2	8	0
Bradshaw, Chris, Pul.	.778	14	5	2	2	9	0
Bravo, Edgar, J.C.	1.000	18	3	4	0	7	1
Bright, Nathan, Pul.	.000	12	0	0	1	1	0
Brown, Jeremy, Eliz.	1.000	3	0	1	0	1	0
Bullard, Jim, Bris.*	1.000	4	0	1	0	1	0
Cabreja, Eny, Mar.*	.857	12	3	9	2	14	1
Cabrera, Yunior, King.*	.900	11	2	7	1	10	1
Camacaro, Armando, Burl.	.000	1	0	0	0	0	0
Camacho, Jose, Mar.	1.000	8	0	1	0	1	0
Cameron, Kevin, Eliz.	1.000	22	1	0	0	1	0
Capellan, Jose, Dan.	.000	3	0	0	0	0	0
Cetani, Bryan, Dan.*	.800	15	0	4	1	5	0
Chourio, Jorge, Burl.	.000	3	0	0	0	0	0
Cislak, Chad, Burl.	.000	1	0	0	0	0	0
Coose, Austin, Prin.	1.000	8	0	2	0	2	0
Cromer, Jason, Prin.*	1.000	5	2	2	0	4	0
Crouthers, Dave, Blue.	1.000	10	3	11	0	14	0
Crump, Joel, Blue.*	.667	10	1	1	1	3	0
Danly, Ryan, King.*	1.000	15	1	1	0	2	0
Daws, Josh, Eliz.	.917	20	1	10	1	12	0
Deaton, Kevin, King.	1.000	17	4	8	0	12	0
De La Cruz, Carlos, Burl.	.833	6	0	5	1	6	0
Deleon, Joey, Mar.	1.000	13	4	4	0	8	1
Denham, Dan, Burl.	.909	8	3	7	1	11	0
D'Frank, Carlos, Burl.	.000	5	0	0	0	0	0
Digby, Bryan, Dan.	.864	12	11	8	3	22	0
Dittler, Jake, Burl.	.667	6	1	1	1	3	0
Dobyns, Heath, Bris.	.000	13	0	0	0	0	0
Doyne, Michael, Mar.	.833	13	3	12	3	18	0
Durbin, J.D., Eliz.	1.000	8	0	8	0	8	1
Eckert, Harold, King.	1.000	2	0	3	0	3	0
Edwards, Michael, Blue.*	1.000	16	2	8	0	10	1
Ewin, Ryan, Dan.	1.000	10	5	1	0	6	0
Farrell, Sean, King.*	.875	19	2	5	1	8	0
Febles, Hector, Prin.	.923	12	2	10	1	13	0
Feliciano, Ruben, Pul.	1.000	4	1	4	0	5	1
Fields, Josh, Bris.	.750	18	0	6	2	8	0
Foley, Travis, Burl.	.900	10	6	3	1	10	0
Forbes, Derek, Blue.	.500	6	0	1	1	2	0
Frey, Jason, J.C.	1.000	3	0	1	0	1	0
Fries, Tim, Dan.	.833	24	2	3	1	6	0
Fryson, Andrew, Bris.	1.000	3	2	0	0	2	0
Gardner, Hayden, Pul.	.952	13	9	11	1	21	1
Garza, Rolando, Bris.	1.000	5	0	3	0	3	1
Gomez, Deibis, J.C.	.000	4	0	0	0	0	0
Gomez, Jose, King.	1.000	3	0	1	0	1	0
Gomez, Mariano, Burl.*	.857	13	1	5	1	7	1
Gonzalez, Kiwi, Prin.	1.000	14	5	6	0	11	1
Gronkiewicz, Lee, Burl.	1.000	25	0	3	0	3	0
Hamilton, Ryan, Mar.	.000	2	0	0	0	0	0
Hemus, Jared, Eliz.*	1.000	16	4	9	0	13	0
Hines, Carlos, Prin.	.875	13	4	3	1	8	0
Hollifield, Alec, Bris.	1.000	4	0	2	0	2	0
Honel, Kris, Bris.	.818	8	2	7	2	11	0
Hooker, Jon, Bris.	1.000	17	1	6	0	7	0
Houlton, Dennis, Mar.	1.000	13	1	8	0	9	1
Jacobson, Billy, Mar.	.667	18	5	3	4	12	0
Jimenez, Kelvin, Pul.	1.000	4	0	4	0	4	0
Johnson, Tyler, J.C.*	.833	9	1	4	1	6	1
Jones, D.J., Blue.*	1.000	4	1	4	0	5	0
Keefer, Ryan, Blue.	1.000	29	3	3	0	6	0
Keiter, Ben, Pul.	.824	10	8	6	3	17	0
Kentner, Brandon, King.	1.000	21	2	3	0	5	1
Killalea, John, J.C.*	.750	7	1	5	2	8	0
King, Timothy, Prin.*	.875	11	0	7	1	8	0
Lawson, Brett, Eliz.	1.000	10	2	1	0	3	0
Ledbetter, Aaron, J.C.	.615	11	6	2	5	13	0
Little, Carmen, Mar.	1.000	20	1	9	0	10	0
Lohse, Eric, Eliz.	1.000	3	0	4	0	4	0
LUBISICH, Nik, Bris.*	1.000	11	1	17	0	18	1
Maberry, Mark, King.	.000	2	0	0	0	0	0
Mabry, Barry, Dan.	.846	20	4	7	2	13	0
Made, Luis, Prin.*	1.000	8	1	1	0	2	0
Madere, Ronnie, Prin.	.600	19	2	1	2	5	0
Marcano, Luis, Pul.	1.000	11	1	5	0	6	0
Martin, J.D., Burl.	1.000	10	0	7	0	7	0
Martinez, Dan, Bris.*	1.000	18	4	7	0	11	1
Martinez, Paul, Burl.*	.833	19	1	9	2	12	0
Martinez, Wilmer, J.C.	.909	23	0	10	1	11	0
Mattox, David, King.	.857	14	6	6	2	14	0
McNair, James, Mar.	.833	18	1	4	1	6	0
Merricks, Matt, Dan.*	.846	12	3	8	2	13	1
Middleton, Brian, Mar.	1.000	10	0	4	0	4	0
Miller, Colby, Eliz.	1.000	15	2	7	0	9	0
Miller, Eric, Prin.*	.727	16	5	3	3	11	0
Miller, Jason, Eliz.*	.900	12	2	7	1	10	0
Mincey, T.W., Blue.*	1.000	15	0	4	0	4	0
Montani, Jeff, Blue.	1.000	7	2	1	0	3	0
Montilla, Elvis, Blue.	.833	5	2	3	1	6	0
Morales, Juan, J.C.	1.000	4	1	4	0	5	0
Moravek, Rob, Pul.	1.000	13	3	10	0	13	0
Morban, Domingo, King.*	.500	10	0	1	1	2	0
Morris, Cory, Dan.	.000	1	0	0	0	0	0
Nieve, Fernando, Mar.	1.000	12	2	3	0	5	0
Ogle, Rylie, King.*	1.000	6	3	10	0	13	0
Olivo, Rigal, Bris.	1.000	11	1	9	0	10	0
Olson, Ryan, King.*	1.000	2	0	1	0	1	0
Osberg, Tanner, King.	.941	13	3	13	1	17	2
Palmer, Travis, J.C.	.909	10	1	9	1	11	1
Parker, Josh, Prin.	.833	22	3	2	1	6	0
Patten, Scott, Bris.	.846	12	3	8	2	13	1
Patty, Jason, Pul.	1.000	1	1	0	0	1	0
Paustian, Michael, Pul.	1.000	14	1	6	0	7	0
Phillips, James, Blue.	.833	25	1	4	1	6	0
Pinango, Miguel, King.	1.000	14	5	7	0	12	0
Plancich, Nick, J.C.	.917	9	3	8	1	12	1
Prahm, Ryan, Burl.	1.000	1	2	0	0	2	0
Pruitt, Jason, Blue.*	.000	1	0	0	0	0	0
Ramos, Eddy, Pul.	.500	17	2	2	4	8	0

Player, Team	Pct.	G	PO	A	E	TC	DP
Rawson, Anthony, J.C.*	.909	23	1	9	1	11	0
Rice, Scott, Blue.*	1.000	12	3	8	0	11	0
Roberts, Ralph, Dan.	1.000	17	1	4	0	5	0
Rogers, Joe, J.C.*	1.000	15	1	3	0	4	0
Rogers, Jon, Dan.	.667	6	0	2	1	3	0
Rojas, Yorlan, J.C.	.833	19	0	5	1	6	0
Roman, Orlando, King.	.833	4	1	4	1	6	0
Romero, Luis, Burl.	.923	16	4	8	1	13	0
Salazar, Richard, Blue.*	1.000	2	1	0	0	1	0
Sanchez, Juan, Prin.	.750	12	2	4	2	8	1
Santana, Leonardo, Mar.*	1.000	19	0	4	0	4	0
Seddon, Chris, Prin.*	.000	4	0	0	2	2	0
Serafini, Vince, Eliz.*	1.000	14	2	7	0	9	0
Shaw, Elliott, Prin.	.667	6	1	1	1	3	1
Sherman, Chris, King.	1.000	14	0	5	0	5	0
Shouse, Dan, J.C.*	1.000	12	0	1	0	1	0
Skyles, Matt, Burl.*	.818	6	0	9	2	11	0
Smart, Richard, Eliz.*	.700	17	1	6	3	10	0
Smith, Matthew, Bris.	1.000	4	1	2	0	3	0
Sokoll, Adam, Dan.	1.000	22	4	6	0	10	0
Spaulding, Richard, Burl.*	.667	14	0	2	1	3	0
Szado, Craig, Bris.*	1.000	15	3	9	0	12	1
Tarkington, Shawn, Eliz.	1.000	6	0	2	0	2	0
Tate, Matt, Blue.	.824	12	6	8	3	17	0
Tejada, Sandy, Eliz.	.727	11	4	4	3	11	1

Player, Team	Pct.	G	PO	A	E	TC	DP
Templet, Eric, King.	.000	12	0	0	1	1	0
Thomas, Matt, J.C.	.889	20	2	6	1	9	1
Thomas, Scott, Burl.	1.000	9	1	2	0	3	1
Thompson, Tyson, Prin.	1.000	3	2	2	0	4	0
Tillman, Kevin, Burl.	.000	1	0	0	0	0	0
Truselo, Randy, Pul.	1.000	4	1	2	0	3	1
Turner, Brad, J.C.	1.000	15	1	1	0	2	0
Valdez, Fernando, Burl.	1.000	7	1	2	0	3	0
Victorino, Pedro, Prin.	.714	13	1	4	2	7	0
Vigue, John, Prin.	1.000	20	1	4	0	5	1
Volquez, Bolivar, Prin.	1.000	19	4	3	0	7	0
Vorwald, Matt, Eliz.	1.000	23	6	8	0	14	2
Warden, Jim Ed, Burl.	.833	12	4	6	2	12	0
Weintraub, Jason, King.	1.000	11	1	1	0	2	0
Weir, Jayson, King.*	.800	9	0	4	1	5	0
Williams, Ruddy, Mar.	.889	15	1	7	1	9	0
Wilson, C.J., Pul.*	.875	8	2	5	1	8	1
Wing, Ryan, Bris.*	.000	1	0	0	0	0	0
Wray, Fred, Dan.	1.000	17	2	2	0	4	0
Wright, Matt, Dan.	.905	14	4	15	2	21	1
Young, Curtis, Bris.	1.000	10	1	1	0	2	0

The following players appeared only as designated hitter, pinch-hitter or pinch runner: Kantrovitz, dh; B. Wilson, dh.

LEAGUE CHAMPIONS

Year	Team	Pct.	Year	Team	Pct.	Year	Team	Pct.
1921—	Greenville	.608	1954	Bluefield‡	.619		Johnson City	.478
	Johnson City*	.627	1955—	Salem■	.689	1983—	Paintsville	.653
1922—	Bristol	.557	1956—	Did not operate.		1984—	Elizabethton•	.580
1923—	Knoxville	.635	1957—	Bluefield	.701		Pulaski	.536
1924—	Knoxville*	.642	1958—	Johnson City	.662	1985—	Bristol††	.638
	Bristol	.607	1959—	Morristown	.603	1986—	Johnson City	.667
1925—	Greenville	.667	1960—	Wytheville	.614		Pulaski•	.621
1926-36—Did not operate.			1961—	Middlesboro	.591	1987—	Burlington•	.729
1937—	Elizabethton	.559	1962—	Bluefield	.671		Johnson City	.609
	Pennington Gap*	.500	1963—	Bluefield	.652	1988—	Kingsport•	.644
1938—	Elizabethton	.664	1964—	Johnson City	.662		Burlington	.529
	Greenville (3rd)†	.571	1965—	Salem	.614	1989—	Elizabethton•	.691
1939—	Elizabethton‡	.597	1966—	Marion	.623		Pulaski	.618
1940—	Johnson City§	.726	1967—	Bluefield	.627	1990—	Elizabethton	.761
	Elizabethton	.750	1968—	Marion	.583	1991—	Pulaski•	.662
1941—	Johnson City	.614	1969—	Pulaski▼	.576		Burlington	.597
	Elizabethton*	.661		Johnson City	.544	1992—	Elizabethton	.742
1942—	Bristol	.667	1970—	Bluefield	.638		Bluefield•	.597
	Bristol∞	.660	1971—	Bluefield▼	.609	1993—	Burlington∞	.647
1943—	Bristol	.755		Kingsport	.559		Elizabethton	.552
	Bristol▲	.617	1972—	Bristol▼	.588	1994—	Princeton•	.621
1944—	Kingsport‡	.575		Covington	.586		Johnson City	.818
1945—	Kingsport‡	.670	1973—	Kingsport	.757	1995—	Bluefield	.754
1946—	New River‡	.675	1974—	Bristol▼	.754		Kingsport•	.727
1947—	Pulaski	.648		Bluefield	.536	1996—	Kingsport	.716
	New River (3rd)†	.516	1975—	Marion	.515		Bluefield▼	.618
1948—	Pulaski‡	.680		Johnson City▼	.603	1997—	Pulaski	.632
1949—	Bluefield‡	.721	1976—	Johnson City▼	.714		Bluefield•	.580
1950—	Bluefield	.600		Bluefield	.600	1998—	Bristol•	.636
	Bluefield◆	.745	1977—	Kingsport	.623		Princeton	.559
1951—	Kingsport‡	.659	1978—	Elizabethton	.594	1999—	Bluefield	.696
1952—	Johnson City	.595	1979—	Paintsville	.800		Martinsville•	.586
	Welch (3rd)†	.509	1980—	Paintsville	.657	2000—	Elizabethton•	.719
1953—	Welch*	.705	1981—	Paintsville	.657	2001—	Elizabethton	.651
	Johnson City	.672	1982—	Bluefield▼	.681		Bluefield•	.500

*Won split-season playoff. †Won four-team playoff. ‡Won championship and four-team playoff. §Johnson City, first-half winner, won playoff involving six clubs. ∞Won both halves and defeated second-place Elizabethton in playoff. ▲Won both halves, but Erwin won four-team playoff. ◆Won both halves, but Bristol won two-club playoff. ■Salem and Johnson City declared playoff co-champions when weather forced cancellation of final series. ▼League was divided into Northern, Southern divisions; declared league champion based on highest won-lost percentage. •League was divided into North and South divisions; won playoff. ††Bristol declared league champion based on regular-season record.

ARIZONA LEAGUE

LEAGUE OFFICE

President/treasurer
Bob Richmond
Address
P.O. Box 1645
Boise, ID 83701
Phone
208-429-1511

Teams*
Angels
Athletics
Brewers
Cubs
Giants

Mariners
White Sox

*Teams play their games in Mesa, Peoria, Phoenix, Tucson and other Arizona sites to be announced.

2001 FINAL STANDINGS

FIRST HALF

Team	W	L	T	Pct.	GB
Mariners	18	10	0	.643	...
Brewers	16	12	0	.571	2.0
Athletics	15	13	0	.536	3.0
Giants	15	13	0	.536	3.0
Cubs	14	14	0	.500	4.0
White Sox	10	18	0	.357	8.0
Angels	10	18	0	.357	8.0

SECOND HALF

Team	W	L	T	Pct.	GB
Athletics	20	8	0	.714	...
Mariners	16	12	0	.571	4.0
Giants	14	14	0	.500	6.0
White Sox	13	15	0	.464	7.0
Angels	12	16	0	.429	8.0
Cubs	12	16	0	.429	8.0
Brewers	11	17	0	.393	9.0

COMPOSITE

Team	Ath.	Mar.	Gia.	Brew.	Cubs	W.S.	Ang.	W	L	T	Pct.	GB
Athletics	...	4	5	6	5	8	7	35	21	0	.625	...
Mariners	5	...	6	5	5	7	6	34	22	0	.607	1.0
Giants	4	3	...	5	4	6	7	29	27	0	.518	6.0
Brewers	3	5	5	...	5	5	3	6	27	29	0	.482	8.0
Cubs	5	4	5	4	...	4	4	26	30	0	.464	9.0
White Sox	2	3	3	6	5	...	4	23	33	0	.411	12.0
Angels	2	3	3	3	6	5	...	22	34	0	.393	13.0

Club names are major league affiliations.

Games played in Mesa, Peoria, Phoenix and Tucson.

PLAYOFFS: Athletics defeated Mariners one game to none to win Arizona League Championship.

REGULAR-SEASON ATTENDANCE: No total attendance figures reported.

MANAGERS: Angels, Brian Harper; Athletics, Ricky Nelson; Brewers, Carlos Lezcano; Cubs, Carmelo Martinez; Giants, Keith Comstock; Mariners, Omer Munoz; White Sox, Jerry Hairston.

ALL-STAR TEAM: 1B—Otis Kelly, Athletics; 2B—Leonel Cabrera, Giants; 3B—Christopher Collins, Mariners; SS—Andy Gonzalez, White Sox; OF—Chris Tritle, Athletics; OF—Anthony Webster, White Sox; OF—Shin-Soo Choo, Mariners; C—Pedro Esparragoza, Brewers; DH—Alejandro Cadena, Mariners; RHP—Johan Santana, Angels; LHP—Ryan Hannaman, Giants; RH Relief pitcher—Aaron Kirkland, White Sox; LH Relief pitcher—David Beck, Athletics; Most Valuable Player—Chris Tritle, Athletics; Manager of the Year—Jerry Hairston, White Sox.

2001 BATTING

TEAM

Team	Avg.	G	TPA	AB	R	H	TB	2B	3B	HR	RBI	SH	SF	HP	BB	IBB	SO	SB	CS	GDP	LOB	ShO	Slg.	OBP
Mariners	.300	56	2246	1974	360	592	832	110	26	26	301	13	16	55	188	5	391	34	24	38	447	1	.421	.374
Giants	.276	56	2199	1987	301	549	724	87	29	10	237	11	20	36	145	4	371	56	25	34	416	3	.364	.334
Cubs	.268	56	2132	1901	262	510	724	102	26	20	215	23	14	44	150	3	456	70	42	21	376	1	.381	.334
White Sox	.261	56	2154	1941	259	507	669	95	20	9	208	18	10	27	158	2	405	76	35	38	411	4	.345	.324
Brewers	.258	56	2152	1894	284	489	683	93	25	17	236	14	23	41	180	3	496	39	23	31	384	4	.361	.332
Athletics	.257	56	2239	1926	311	495	717	80	38	22	256	17	18	43	235	3	479	104	51	30	439	4	.372	.348
Angels	.250	56	2120	1869	258	467	613	63	25	11	215	13	20	50	168	4	435	81	40	21	375	2	.328	.325

INDIVIDUAL

TOP QUALIFIERS FOR BATTING CHAMPIONSHIP

Minimum 151 plate appearances. *Lefthanded batter. †Switch-hitter.

Player, Team	Avg.	G	TPA	AB	R	H	TB	2B	3B	HR	RBI	SH	SF	HP	BB	IBB	SO	SB	CS	GDP	Slg.	OBP
Cedeno, Ronny, Cubs	.350	52	229	206	36	72	96	13	4	1	17	3	2	5	13	0	32	17	10	3	.466	.398
Cordova, Roman, Mar.†	.343	42	160	140	25	48	60	6	3	0	14	3	0	8	9	0	23	4	4	8	.429	.414
Collins, Chris, Mar.	.342	42	184	161	25	55	75	14	0	2	29	1	1	1	20	0	26	0	1	2	.466	.415
McAuliff, James, Gia.	.337	43	197	172	41	58	81	14	3	1	18	0	0	2	23	0	35	6	3	0	.471	.421
Tritle, Chris, Ath.	.336	52	239	214	47	72	121	6	8	9	42	0	1	2	22	1	55	26	1	2	.565	.404
Cadena, Alejandro, Mar.	.333	56	250	222	41	74	123	23	1	8	60	1	4	9	14	0	23	0	1	5	.554	.390
Paulino, Robert, Cubs	.327	47	169	153	20	50	74	10	4	2	28	4	0	3	9	0	26	4	1	0	.484	.376
Williams, Jon, Gia.*	.324	39	161	136	24	44	66	7	3	3	26	0	3	5	16	1	14	1	1	2	.485	.406
Gonzalez, Andy, W.S.	.323	48	207	189	33	61	96	18	1	5	30	0	0	3	15	0	36	13	2	5	.508	.382
Cabrera, Leonel, Gia.	.322	46	216	205	45	66	87	14	2	1	31	1	2	2	6	0	22	12	1	3	.424	.344

Player, Team	Avg.	G	TPA	AB	R	H	TB	2B	3B	HR	RBI	SH	SF	HP	BB	IBB	SO	SB	CS	GDP	Slg.	OBP
Peless, Sean, Mar.*	.314	45	175	159	21	50	61	6	1	1	18	0	0	2	14	1	47	1	1	4	.384	.377
Lopez, Pedro, W.S.	.312	50	221	199	26	62	82	11	3	1	19	3	2	0	16	0	24	12	6	4	.412	.359
Kelly, Otis, Ath.	.311	45	201	164	34	51	83	13	2	5	26	0	1	4	32	0	36	5	2	2	.506	.433
Webster, Anthony, W.S.*	.307	55	243	225	38	69	92	9	7	0	30	5	3	1	9	0	33	18	7	4	.409	.332
Chavez, Ozzie, Brew.†	.305	52	228	210	38	64	88	12	6	0	27	0	3	2	13	0	36	9	8	8	.419	.346

DEPARTMENTAL LEADERS: G—Cadena, Gustafson, 56 each; AB—Webster, 225; R—Choo, 51; H—Cadena, 74; TB—Cadena, 123; 2B—Cadena, 23; 3B—Choo, 10; HR—Tritle, 9; RBI—Cadena, 60; SH—Chirinos, 6; SF—Suomi, Jimenez, Cadena, 4 each; HP—Banks, 11; BB—Choo, 34; IBB—Choo, Aybar, 2 each; SO—Banks, 80; SB—Tritle, 26; CS—Trinidad, Cedeno, 10 each; GIDP—Chavez, 8; Slg.—Tritle, .565; OBP—Kelly, .433.

ALL PLAYERS

*Lefthanded batter. †Switch-hitter.

Player, Team	Avg.	G	TPA	AB	R	H	TB	2B	3B	HR	RBI	SH	SF	HP	BB	IBB	SO	SB	CS	GDP	Slg.	OBP
Abad, Noel, Ang.	.293	19	65	58	9	17	23	1	1	1	7	1	1	2	3	0	14	6	1	1	.397	.344
Abreu, Lazaro, Mar.	.375	4	10	8	3	3	3	0	0	0	2	0	0	0	2	0	3	0	0	0	.375	.500
Aybar, Francisco, W.S.	.265	46	179	162	23	43	58	11	2	0	17	1	2	2	12	2	41	7	2	3	.358	.320
Banks, Gary, Cubs	.170	53	235	200	30	34	42	3	1	1	14	3	1	11	20	0	80	11	3	2	.210	.280
Batista, Christian, Ang.	.268	35	150	127	26	34	47	7	0	2	17	0	2	3	18	0	33	4	5	5	.370	.367
Batista, Juan, Ang.†	.125	36	83	72	8	9	15	2	2	0	7	0	1	1	9	0	34	6	0	0	.208	.229
Bell, Paul, Brew.	.292	18	71	65	13	19	21	2	0	0	9	0	0	3	3	1	12	1	0	2	.323	.352
Bounds, Brandon, W.S.*	.239	37	124	113	13	27	38	4	2	1	4	1	0	0	10	0	33	2	1	1	.336	.301
Brown, Larry, Mar.*	.279	34	126	111	23	31	45	3	1	3	13	0	1	1	13	1	19	3	0	2	.405	.357
Brown, Matthew, Ang.	.163	46	168	141	14	23	35	7	1	1	21	1	3	5	18	1	30	1	3	1	.248	.275
Cabrera, Andres, Gia.	.143	7	7	7	0	1	1	0	0	0	1	0	0	0	0	0	4	0	0	0	.143	.143
Cabrera, Leonel, Gia.	.322	46	216	205	45	66	87	14	2	1	31	1	2	2	6	0	22	12	1	3	.424	.344
Cadena, Alejandro, Mar.	.333	56	250	222	41	74	123	23	1	8	60	1	4	9	14	0	23	0	1	5	.554	.390
Castillo, Carlos, Ath.	.190	7	26	21	4	4	4	0	0	0	3	1	0	1	3	0	4	0	1	0	.190	.320
Castillo, Oscar, Ath.	.183	35	134	120	8	22	30	5	0	1	19	1	2	0	11	0	31	2	0	4	.250	.248
Cedeno, Ronny, Cubs.	.350	52	229	206	36	72	96	13	4	1	17	3	2	5	13	0	32	17	10	3	.466	.398
Chavez, Ozzie, Brew.†	.305	52	228	210	38	64	88	12	6	0	27	0	3	2	13	0	36	9	8	8	.419	.346
Chirinos, Robinson, Cubs	.234	47	177	154	15	36	54	12	0	2	15	6	3	4	10	0	42	4	3	0	.351	.292
Choo, Shin-soo, Mar.*	.302	51	245	199	51	60	102	10	10	4	35	0	3	9	34	2	49	12	4	1	.513	.420
Ciesluk, Chris, Gia.	.253	51	194	170	22	43	52	3	3	0	17	2	2	3	17	0	31	4	1	1	.306	.328
Cleto, Carlos, Gia.*	.262	54	236	214	38	56	77	10	4	1	35	0	2	2	18	0	55	6	1	5	.360	.322
Coats, Buck, Cubs*	.260	33	131	123	11	32	44	3	3	1	18	1	1	2	4	0	19	3	4	1	.358	.292
Cochrane, Mark, W.S.	.275	21	62	51	6	14	16	2	0	0	7	0	0	0	11	0	11	0	1	2	.314	.403
Cullins, Chris, Mar.	.342	42	184	161	25	55	75	14	0	2	29	1	1	1	20	0	26	0	1	2	.466	.415
Collins, Kevin, Cubs*	.280	39	156	132	25	37	64	6	6	3	16	0	1	1	22	1	55	2	2	1	.485	.385
Collins, Mike, Ang.	.179	20	43	39	2	7	7	0	0	0	1	0	0	1	3	0	11	1	0	1	.179	.256
Cordova, Roman, Mar.†	.343	42	180	140	25	48	60	6	3	0	14	3	0	8	9	0	23	4	4	8	.429	.414
Cosby, Quantwan, Ang.†	.243	41	162	148	21	36	42	4	1	0	8	3	1	1	9	1	40	8	7	1	.284	.289
Cruz, Nelson, Ath.	.250	23	93	88	11	22	36	3	1	3	16	1	0	0	4	0	29	6	3	1	.409	.283
Davis, Ryan, Gia.*	.285	54	219	193	23	55	70	11	2	0	20	0	3	4	19	0	34	6	2	3	.363	.356
Davis, Tyrel, W.S.	.243	43	155	140	11	34	40	4	1	0	11	2	1	2	10	0	37	1	3	5	.286	.301
Del Chiaro, Brent, Ang.	.259	20	68	58	9	15	21	1	1	1	4	0	0	3	7	0	18	0	0	0	.362	.368
DeLeon, Carlos, Ang.	.172	27	65	58	9	10	17	5	1	0	3	1	0	3	3	0	28	3	1	0	.293	.250
De Los Santos, Nelson, Brew.†	.253	26	110	95	15	24	39	6	3	1	15	0	3	1	11	0	15	1	0	1	.411	.327
Devinney, Rick, Cubs	.333	6	20	18	1	6	7	1	0	0	1	0	0	0	2	0	3	0	2	0	.389	.400
Diaz, Randor, Ang.	.286	16	25	21	3	6	7	1	0	0	2	1	0	0	3	0	6	1	0	0	.333	.375
D'Jesus, Francisco, Gia.	.250	45	169	160	16	40	55	4	1	3	20	0	2	3	4	0	32	0	2	3	.344	.278
Ellison, Josh, Mar.	.214	33	102	84	21	18	23	3	1	0	10	1	0	2	15	0	24	2	1	0	.274	.347
Esparragoza, Pedro, Brew.	.242	48	178	153	25	37	50	5	1	2	22	1	1	7	16	1	39	4	1	4	.327	.339
Esterlin, Ivan, Cubs*	.221	24	88	77	11	17	28	4	2	1	10	1	2	1	7	0	19	4	0	1	.364	.287
Felix, Kelvin, Ang.	.217	23	49	46	4	10	14	2	1	0	5	0	0	0	3	0	18	2	0	0	.304	.265
Francois, Francisco, Ath.	.168	42	182	155	22	26	35	5	2	0	7	4	0	8	16	0	37	10	0	1	.226	.275
Franke, Michael, Brew.†	.151	26	95	86	8	13	17	4	0	0	5	1	1	2	5	0	34	4	0	2	.198	.213
Garrido, Tomas, Gia.	.252	40	138	131	17	33	36	3	0	0	8	0	0	5	2	0	19	3	0	6	.275	.290
Gelotti, Matt, Brew.	.167	4	19	18	0	3	5	0	1	0	4	0	0	0	1	0	4	0	0	0	.278	.211
Gemoll, Brandon, Brew.*	.323	8	36	31	8	10	14	2	1	0	9	0	2	0	3	0	7	0	0	0	.452	.361
Golden, Bryan, Cubs	.140	22	69	57	11	8	15	1	0	2	4	0	0	1	11	0	15	0	3	3	.263	.290
Gomez, Raul, W.S.†	.229	39	151	131	8	30	41	7	2	0	16	0	1	0	19	0	42	1	2	3	.313	.325
Gonzalez, Andy, W.S.	.323	48	207	189	33	61	96	18	1	5	30	0	0	3	15	0	36	13	2	5	.508	.382
Gonzalez, Jose, Gia.	.200	6	18	15	1	3	3	0	0	0	2	0	1	0	2	0	7	0	0	0	.200	.278
Gregorio, Tom, Ang.	.273	4	14	11	1	3	3	0	0	0	1	0	0	0	3	0	2	0	0	0	.273	.429
Groff, Matt, Ath.	.333	24	90	72	14	24	32	4	2	0	9	1	1	4	12	0	9	6	6	2	.444	.449
Gustafson, Troy, Gia.	.279	56	237	222	28	62	78	10	3	0	22	0	2	5	8	0	28	10	6	7	.351	.316
Guzman, Junior, Ang	.307	28	111	101	12	31	37	4	1	0	13	0	1	4	5	0	10	2	2	2	.366	.360
Hammonds, Jeffrey, Brew.	.333	1	3	3	0	1	1	0	0	0	0	0	0	0	0	0	0	0	0	0	.333	.333
Hardy, J.J., Brew.	.250	5	22	20	6	5	9	2	1	0	1	1	0	0	1	0	2	0	0	0	.450	.286
Harris, Josh, Cubs	.250	2	8	8	3	2	2	0	0	0	2	0	0	0	0	0	2	1	0	0	.250	.250
Hickman, Brian, W.S.	.127	23	68	55	8	7	9	2	0	0	2	0	0	5	8	0	17	0	0	1	.164	.294
Hicks, Brian, Brew.*	.222	15	61	54	5	12	15	3	0	0	2	0	0	1	6	0	18	0	0	1	.278	.311
Hilario, Enderson, W.S.	.167	3	13	12	1	2	3	1	0	0	0	0	0	0	1	0	1	0	0	0	.250	.231
Hill, Bobby, Cubs†	.222	3	11	9	1	2	2	0	0	0	0	1	0	0	1	0	3	1	0	0	.222	.364
Hodges, Jarrod, Mar.*	.273	45	168	143	30	39	66	8	2	5	26	1	1	7	16	1	26	2	1	0	.462	.371
Hrynio, Mike, Mar.	.161	20	59	56	4	9	11	2	0	0	5	0	0	1	2	0	21	0	1	0	.196	.203
Hudson, Ben, Mar.	.167	5	21	18	3	3	4	1	0	0	1	0	0	2	1	0	1	0	0	1	.222	.286
Imperiali, Francesco, Mar.	.284	40	132	116	17	33	40	7	0	0	12	1	0	2	13	0	26	2	3	2	.345	.366
January, Javerro, Brew.	.284	38	157	134	27	38	46	6	1	0	10	3	1	6	13	0	42	6	3	3	.343	.370
Jenkins, Kevin, Ang.*	.174	42	132	115	15	20	28	3	1	1	11	0	5	5	12	0	39	5	5	0	.243	.280
Jimenez, Luis, Ath.*	.214	24	82	70	8	15	18	1	1	0	12	0	4	0	8	0	23	2	0	2	.257	.280
Jones, Jared, Mar.	.242	9	36	33	1	8	9	1	0	0	3	0	0	0	3	0	8	0	0	1	.273	.306
Keating, Matt, Gia.*	.270	16	70	63	9	17	25	1	2	1	16	0	1	0	6	1	10	0	0	0	.397	.329

Player, Team	Avg.	G	TPA	AB	R	H	TB	2B	3B	HR	RBI	SH	SF	HP	BB	IBB	SO	SB	CS	GDP	Slg.	OBP
Kelly, Otis, Ath.	.311	45	201	164	34	51	83	13	2	5	26	0	1	4	32	0	36	5	2	2	.506	.433
Kimpton, Nick, Ang.*	.269	49	212	186	30	50	58	4	2	0	23	0	1	4	21	0	39	9	5	3	.312	.354
Koslowski, Kasey, W.S.	.238	43	163	147	17	35	39	4	0	0	9	2	0	1	13	0	22	3	2	1	.265	.304
Kotchman, Casey, Ath.*	.600	4	19	15	5	9	13	1	0	1	5	0	1	0	3	1	2	0	0	0	.867	.632
Lachapel, Juan, Ath.	.256	10	46	43	7	11	14	1	1	0	3	0	0	2	1	0	11	3	0	0	.326	.304
Lebron, Freddie, W.S.†	.233	39	136	120	22	28	36	8	0	0	13	0	1	4	11	0	29	7	1	1	.300	.316
Lee, Carlos, W.S.	.278	23	96	90	14	25	34	3	0	2	18	0	0	3	3	0	4	2	0	3	.378	.323
Lopez, Pedro, W.S.	.312	50	221	199	26	62	82	11	3	1	19	3	2	0	16	0	24	12	6	4	.412	.359
Luna, Leonardo, W.S.	.243	28	112	103	12	25	33	4	2	0	14	4	0	0	5	0	14	1	4	5	.320	.278
Maestrales, Peter, Gia.†	.255	26	105	94	12	24	33	5	2	0	6	1	1	1	8	1	17	5	2	0	.351	.317
Marmol, Carlos, Cubs	.295	40	142	129	15	38	49	11	0	0	12	1	0	3	9	0	30	4	3	0	.380	.355
Martin, Craig, Brew.	.224	21	86	76	6	17	22	5	0	0	7	0	0	1	9	0	21	0	0	2	.289	.314
Mathis, Jeff, Ang.	.304	7	26	23	1	7	8	1	0	0	3	0	1	0	2	0	4	0	0	1	.348	.346
Mayo, Terry, Drew.	.213	19	70	61	4	13	21	1	2	1	6	1	2	3	3	0	31	0	1	0	.344	.275
McAuliff, James, Gia.	.337	43	197	172	41	58	81	14	3	1	18	0	0	2	23	0	35	6	3	0	.471	.421
McCormack, Taylor, Brew.	.198	36	148	131	15	26	32	4	1	0	18	1	1	2	13	0	48	1	0	2	.244	.273
Meadows, Tydus, Cubs	.000	1	2	2	0	0	0	0	0	0	0	0	0	0	0	0	1	0	0	0	.000	.000
Mejia, Andy, Cubs	.250	4	13	12	1	3	3	0	0	0	1	0	0	0	1	0	2	0	0	1	.250	.308
Melgarejo, Ransel, Ang.	.283	45	166	138	25	39	53	7	2	1	20	2	1	6	19	0	19	12	5	3	.384	.390
Menchaca, Eriberto, Mar.	.271	49	187	170	30	46	57	7	2	0	18	4	3	2	8	0	29	1	0	3	.335	.306
Miliano, Hector, Cubs	.260	52	209	196	22	51	76	10	3	3	25	1	1	4	7	0	52	6	6	4	.388	.298
Montero, Roberto, Gia.	.308	11	13	13	2	4	6	2	0	0	0	0	0	0	0	0	6	0	0	1	.462	.308
Morillo, Roberto, Gia.†	.250	4	5	4	1	1	1	0	0	0	0	0	0	1	0	0	2	0	0	0	.250	.400
Mott, Bill, Ang.*	.083	5	18	12	2	1	3	0	1	0	2	0	1	1	4	0	0	0	0	0	.250	.333
Mujica, Andres, Mar.	.283	45	177	159	27	45	57	6	3	0	24	1	0	2	15	0	36	5	3	6	.358	.342
Nagle, Austin, Ath.	.250	50	219	188	36	47	72	7	9	0	22	2	1	2	26	0	53	7	5	5	.383	.346
Navarro, Mandy, Cubs†	.318	8	23	22	3	7	11	0	2	0	1	0	0	0	1	0	4	1	0	0	.500	.348
Nelson, Brad, Brew.*	.302	17	75	63	10	19	27	6	1	0	13	1	1	2	8	0	18	0	0	1	.429	.392
Nevins, Ryan, Ang.*	.329	25	89	82	12	27	39	4	4	0	17	0	1	1	5	1	15	1	2	0	.476	.371
Nova, Willian, Brew.†	.213	25	93	80	7	17	24	2	1	1	8	4	2	0	7	0	22	2	0	0	.300	.270
Oliveros, Luis, Mar.	.374	25	100	91	21	34	45	6	1	1	15	0	0	3	5	0	10	2	2	2	.495	.424
Parnell, Sean, Mar.	.370	8	33	27	2	10	14	2	1	0	4	0	2	3	1	0	7	0	0	0	.519	.424
Parrott, Corry, Brew.	.250	4	15	12	1	3	3	0	0	0	0	0	0	0	3	0	3	0	0	0	.250	.400
Paulino, Robert, Cubs	.327	47	169	153	20	50	74	10	4	2	28	4	0	3	9	0	26	4	1	0	.484	.376
Peless, Sean, Mar.*	.314	45	175	159	21	50	61	6	1	1	18	0	0	2	14	1	47	1	1	4	.384	.377
Perez, Radhame, Ath.	.198	25	98	86	9	17	22	1	2	0	8	0	1	2	10	0	29	1	1	1	.256	.296
Pinango, Ever, Gia.†	.161	22	64	56	5	9	9	0	0	0	3	4	1	0	3	0	11	1	3	2	.161	.200
Plasencia, Francisco, Brew.*..	.270	49	231	200	38	54	63	7	1	0	19	0	0	0	31	1	46	10	4	2	.315	.368
Queroz, Pedro, Cubs	.287	49	184	164	24	47	64	9	1	2	21	2	2	3	13	1	18	8	3	1	.390	.346
Rafael, Alberto, W.S.	.138	17	30	29	2	4	5	1	0	0	2	0	0	0	1	0	16	1	0	0	.172	.167
Ramirez, Alexander, Gia.	.243	33	126	111	14	27	37	2	4	0	10	2	0	3	10	1	39	1	1	1	.333	.323
Ramirez, Manuel, Brew.	.303	46	194	175	27	53	93	17	4	5	30	0	3	4	12	0	20	0	2	3	.531	.356
Reyes, Jose, Ath.†	.272	42	183	158	25	43	51	4	2	0	9	2	1	7	15	0	40	13	9	2	.323	.359
Rivera, Rene, Mar.	.338	21	75	71	13	24	34	4	0	2	12	0	1	1	2	0	11	0	0	0	.479	.360
Salas, Francisco, Cubs	.353	15	56	51	12	18	23	2	0	1	4	0	0	3	2	0	8	3	1	0	.451	.411
Seever, Brian, Ang.	.412	5	17	17	5	7	9	0	1	0	1	0	0	0	0	0	2	1	1	0	.529	.412
Selmo, Wilson, Ang.†	.301	48	195	183	23	55	64	5	2	0	21	4	3	4	1	0	24	10	0	0	.350	.314
Serafini, Matt, Brew.	.351	20	82	74	16	26	53	6	0	7	24	0	0	2	6	0	19	0	0	1	.716	.390
Soto, Geovany, Cubs	.260	41	169	150	18	39	58	16	0	1	20	1	0	3	15	1	33	1	0	3	.387	.339
Stockton, Rick, Ang.*	.263	36	130	118	17	31	40	2	2	1	11	1	1	3	7	0	20	8	2	0	.339	.318
Suomi, Richard, Ath.*	.257	52	216	175	31	45	75	14	2	4	43	2	4	8	27	1	36	7	2	1	.429	.374
Terrero, Wandy, W.S.	.400	13	33	30	3	12	13	1	0	0	3	0	0	0	3	0	3	0	1	0	.433	.455
Thompson, Zachary, Brew.* ..	.194	22	83	67	7	13	14	1	0	0	3	1	0	5	10	0	32	1	1	0	.209	.341
Todd, Kelvin, Ath.	.235	5	18	17	2	4	5	1	0	0	4	0	0	0	1	0	5	0	0	0	.294	.278
Torres, Erik, Brew.	.000	1	4	3	0	0	0	0	0	0	0	0	0	1	0	0	0	0	0	0	.000	.250
Trinidad, Edgar, Ath.	.294	44	201	163	29	48	62	6	4	0	17	3	1	2	32	0	28	9	10	4	.380	.414
Tritle, Chris, Ath.	.336	52	239	214	47	72	121	6	8	9	42	0	1	2	22	1	55	26	1	2	.565	.402
Varitek, Justin, Mar.	.333	4	7	6	2	2	3	1	0	0	0	0	0	0	1	0	2	0	0	0	.500	.429
Vazquez, Rafael, Cubs	.467	6	16	15	2	7	8	1	0	0	3	0	0	0	0	0	2	0	0	0	.533	.438
Vega, Jesus, Ang.	.333	25	65	54	3	18	24	3	0	1	9	0	1	3	7	0	14	1	1	0	.444	.431
Viera, Orlando, Brew.*	.265	27	91	83	8	22	26	2	1	0	4	0	1	1	6	0	27	1	1	2	.313	.319
Wallace, Kellen, Ang.*	.119	27	73	67	5	8	13	0	1	1	5	0	0	0	6	0	19	1	0	3	.194	.192
Wayment, Kory, Ath.	.229	51	211	192	24	44	57	9	2	0	16	0	2	1	16	1	53	7	4	4	.297	.289
Webster, Anthony, W.S.*	.307	55	243	225	38	69	92	9	7	0	30	5	3	1	9	0	33	18	7	4	.409	.332
Williams, Jon, Gia.*	.324	39	161	136	24	44	66	7	3	3	26	0	3	5	16	1	14	1	1	2	.485	.406
Williamson, Chad, Cubs	.174	11	26	23	1	4	4	0	0	0	2	0	0	0	2	0	10	0	1	1	.174	.240
Young, Eddie, W.S.	.200	43	162	145	22	29	34	5	0	0	13	0	0	6	11	0	42	8	5	0	.234	.284

GRAND SLAMS: Cruz, Kotchman, Melgarejo, Millano, Suomi, Tritle.

AWARDED FIRST BASE ON CATCHER'S INTERFERENCE: P. Lopez (O. Castillo), Oliveros (O. Castillo), J. Williams (J. Guzman), Williamson (O. Castillo).

2001 PITCHING
TEAM

Team	W	L	Pct.	ERA	G	CG	ShO	Sv.	IP	H	TBF	R	ER	HR	SH	SF	HB	BB	IBB	SO	WP	Bk.
Athletics	35	21	.625	3.31	56	0	1	17	502.1	480	2123	244	185	20	19	14	39	127	1	469	34	13
White Sox	23	33	.411	3.35	56	1	4	16	491.0	473	2126	282	183	17	10	21	36	162	7	429	41	11
Giants..............	29	27	.518	3.79	56	0	6	9	496.2	463	2174	249	209	20	18	15	46	232	2	478	46	13
Angels..............	22	34	.393	4.33	56	2	5	8	488.0	566	2246	334	235	11	17	17	37	171	5	412	60	10
Brewers............	27	29	.482	4.36	56	0	0	9	493.0	546	2184	293	239	14	17	15	49	171	7	373	38	11
Cubs................	26	30	.464	4.51	56	1	1	17	497.1	532	2219	319	249	12	12	24	48	185	1	445	37	15
Mariners...........	34	22	.607	4.59	56	1	1	17	486.0	549	2174	314	248	21	16	15	41	176	1	427	40	8

TOP QUALIFIERS FOR EARNED-RUN AVERAGE TITLE

Minimum 45 innings.*Lefthanded pitcher.

Pitcher, Team	W	L	Pct.	ERA	G	GS	CG	ShO	GF	Sv.	IP	H	TBF	R	ER	HR	SH	SF	HB	BB	IBB	SO	WP	Bk.
Kirkland, Aaron, W.S.	0	2	.000	0.40	29	0	0	0	29	13	45.1	25	169	5	2	1	2	2	3	4	4	62	1	0
Hannaman, Ryan, Gia.*	4	1	.800	2.00	11	11	0	0	0	0	54.0	34	227	14	12	1	2	2	5	31	0	67	2	5
Steward, Edward, Ang.*	5	3	.625	2.02	19	4	1	1	5	1	49.0	47	205	19	11	1	1	0	2	11	1	40	1	0
Matos, Raymond, Gia.*	4	3	.571	2.34	14	12	0	0	0	0	61.2	64	284	35	16	0	2	1	6	29	0	66	12	0
Simmering, Bryan, Ath.	2	2	.500	2.40	13	6	0	0	3	0	48.2	41	186	16	13	1	0	1	3	5	0	57	0	0
Asencio, Domingo, W.S.*	2	1	.667	2.44	7	7	0	0	0	0	48.0	45	195	23	13	5	1	1	2	8	0	29	0	1
Oakes, Gerard, Brew.	2	4	.333	2.85	12	7	0	0	0	1	53.2	50	233	24	17	2	2	2	5	25	0	44	10	1
Garcia, Jairo, Ath.	4	2	.667	2.85	12	7	0	0	3	0	47.1	37	184	19	15	2	2	0	2	6	0	50	5	0
Perez, Armando, W.S.*	3	3	.500	2.98	15	5	1	1	1	0	63.1	56	265	27	21	1	2	0	2	23	2	44	6	1
Arias, Daniel, Ang.	1	2	.333	3.02	16	3	0	0	3	1	47.2	64	215	25	16	0	2	3	8	9	0	42	5	4
Reed, Rylan, W.S.	4	4	.500	3.10	13	13	0	0	0	0	58.0	56	277	46	20	2	1	6	10	34	0	53	6	3
Santana, Johan, Ang.	3	2	.600	3.22	10	9	1	1	0	0	58.2	40	256	27	21	0	2	0	2	35	0	69	8	1
Leon, Brigmer, Ath.	4	3	.571	3.28	14	7	0	0	3	0	46.2	46	196	26	17	2	3	1	3	7	0	40	4	4
Rojas, Ramon, Gia.	3	5	.375	3.40	27	0	0	0	5	0	45.0	43	202	21	17	2	3	1	6	14	0	27	1	1
Liriano, Francisco, Gia.*	5	4	.556	3.63	13	12	0	0	0	0	62.0	51	246	26	25	3	1	0	1	24	0	67	6	3

DEPARTMENTAL LEADERS: W—Watson, 8; L—D'Amico, Burnau, 6 each; Pct.—Watson, .800; G—Kirkland, 29; GS—Reed, 13; CG—Steward, Santana, Watson, A. Perez, 1 each; ShO—Steward, Santana, A. Perez, 1 each; GF—Kirkland, 29; Sv.—Kirkland, 13; IP—A. Perez, 63.1; H—Fruto, 73; TBF—Matos, 284; R—Reed, Reynoso, 46 each; ER—Fruto, 40; HR—Asencio, 5; SH—Johnson, Watson, 4 each; SF—Reed, 6; HB—Nascar, 11; BB—Santana, 35; IBB—Kirkland, 4; SO—Santana, 69; WP—A. Jones, 13; BK—Batista, Hannaman, 5 each.

ALL PITCHERS

*Lefthanded pitcher.

Pitcher, Team	W	L	Pct.	ERA	G	GS	CG	ShO	GF	Sv.	IP	H	TBF	R	ER	HR	SH	SF	HB	BB	IBB	SO	WP	Bk.
Abreu, Jonathan, Gia.*	2	2	.500	4.93	23	0	0	0	4	1	34.2	39	150	20	19	1	0	2	2	10	0	31	1	0
Allen, Travis, Mar.	2	2	.500	4.24	17	0	0	0	12	4	23.1	25	96	12	11	1	1	2	1	4	0	26	2	0
Amancio, Jose, Ath.	7	3	.700	3.71	14	8	0	0	2	0	53.1	51	225	23	22	3	1	2	8	16	0	33	1	0
Andujar, Jesse, Ang.	0	0	.000	5.06	3	0	0	0	0	0	5.1	6	20	3	3	0	0	0	2	4	0	6	1	0
Arias, Daniel, Ang.	1	2	.333	3.02	16	3	0	0	3	1	47.2	64	215	25	16	0	2	3	8	9	0	42	5	4
Artman, Dane, Brew.*	0	1	.000	5.84	5	5	0	0	0	0	12.1	15	58	8	8	0	0	1	0	5	0	14	0	0
Asencio, Domingo, W.S.*	2	1	.667	2.44	7	7	0	0	0	0	48.0	45	195	23	13	5	1	1	2	8	0	29	0	1
Astacio, Hector, Ang.	3	2	.600	3.07	22	4	0	0	7	1	44.0	46	186	21	15	1	1	2	5	6	0	36	0	1
Atencio, Donald, Ath.	0	2	.000	4.50	15	0	0	0	3	0	28.0	33	132	19	14	0	1	2	3	13	0	29	6	1
Daez, Hebel, Ath.	1	2	.333	3.57	12	4	0	0	3	0	35.1	41	166	24	14	2	2	2	3	7	0	22	1	2
Balser, Jeffrey, Ang.	2	3	.400	8.87	20	0	0	0	12	3	22.1	50	130	29	22	1	2	1	4	5	1	12	5	0
Bastardo, Jose, Gia.*	1	3	.250	5.19	18	0	0	0	6	0	17.1	16	88	14	10	3	0	0	0	20	0	24	1	0
Batista, Cristian, Brew.	0	1	.000	5.06	13	0	0	0	6	0	21.1	26	106	24	12	0	0	0	4	10	1	16	5	5
Beck, David, Ath.*	0	0	.000	1.00	18	0	0	0	17	9	18.0	13	76	3	2	0	0	3	7	1	0	32	0	0
Bott, Glenn, Mar.*	0	0	.000	6.00	2	0	0	0	2	1	3.0	5	14	2	2	0	0	0	0	0	0	4	0	0
Brown, Eric, Cubs	0	1	.000	1.04	11	0	0	0	8	4	17.1	15	77	4	2	0	1	1	2	4	0	14	1	0
Bukowski, Stan, Ang.	0	0	.000	4.09	4	4	0	0	0	0	11.0	11	52	6	5	0	0	1	0	5	0	8	0	0
Burnau, Ryan, Cubs	3	6	.333	4.89	14	9	0	0	1	0	49.2	58	229	43	27	0	1	2	3	20	0	46	4	1
Caminero, Concepcion, Cubs	1	1	.500	5.01	15	0	0	0	3	0	23.1	27	110	19	13	1	1	2	3	14	0	18	1	0
Carpenter, Calvin, Brew.	3	3	.500	4.06	11	10	0	0	0	0	37.2	39	169	24	17	0	2	2	1	22	0	29	3	1
Chirinos, Jesus, Brew.	5	3	.625	4.08	11	7	0	0	0	0	53.0	56	228	31	24	3	1	1	4	11	0	36	3	1
Cimorelli, Brett, Ang.	2	2	.500	7.08	11	2	0	0	3	0	20.1	25	104	22	16	2	1	1	0	13	0	14	5	1
Coleman, Jeff, Ath.	0	0	.000	1.54	8	0	0	0	7	6	11.2	7	43	2	2	0	2	0	1	3	0	8	0	0
Correa, Alexander, Brew.*	1	0	1.000	5.85	12	3	0	0	0	0	32.1	42	148	23	21	1	1	1	5	13	0	29	2	0
Cortez, Renee, Mar.	2	0	1.000	4.42	11	9	0	0	0	0	53.0	60	233	34	20	4	1	2	4	10	0	52	6	0
Cruz, Ramon, Mar.	1	2	.333	1.11	6	5	0	0	0	0	24.1	15	90	6	3	1	1	0	0	3	0	21	0	0
D'Amico, Leonardo, Ang.	0	6	.000	5.17	14	5	0	0	5	0	38.1	44	176	32	22	2	1	3	4	13	1	33	5	0
De La Rosa, Felix, Brew.	0	1	.000	5.17	6	0	0	0	1	0	15.2	20	71	10	9	0	1	1	3	7	0	5	1	0
Diaz, Randor, Gia.	0	0	.000	0.00	1	0	0	0	0	0	1.0	0	3	0	0	0	0	0	0	0	0	0	0	0
Done, Juan, Mar.	0	0	.000	1.00	5	0	0	0	2	2	9.0	5	40	3	1	0	0	0	6	0	12	1	0
Dowdy, Justin, W.S.*	5	3	.625	3.74	18	1	0	0	5	1	43.1	46	189	26	18	0	0	3	3	8	0	46	0	0
Featherstone, Deron, Gia.	2	1	.667	9.85	14	4	0	0	3	0	28.1	30	136	32	31	4	1	1	7	21	0	36	3	1
Fisher, Marc, Cubs	0	1	.000	1.20	15	1	0	0	10	7	30.0	19	111	5	4	0	1	1	2	3	0	35	1	0
Foli, Daniel, Cubs	2	5	.286	4.82	11	10	0	0	0	0	46.2	40	195	29	25	1	0	5	3	15	0	40	1	0
Ford, Ben, Cubs	0	1	.000	2.00	3	3	0	0	0	0	9.0	10	41	4	2	0	0	1	1	2	0	9	0	0
Fruto, Emiliano, Mar.	5	4	.556	5.84	12	12	0	0	0	0	61.2	73	302	45	40	3	2	4	3	22	0	51	1	2
Fryson, Andrew, W.S.	0	3	.000	3.09	8	6	0	0	1	0	23.1	29	100	14	8	0	1	0	3	0	0	23	2	0
Fyhrie, Mike, Cubs	0	0	.000	0.00	2	2	0	0	0	0	2.0	1	7	0	0	0	0	0	0	0	0	4	0	0
Garcia, Jairo, Ath.	4	2	.667	2.85	12	7	0	0	3	0	47.1	37	184	19	15	2	2	0	2	6	0	50	5	0
Garcia, Ruddy, Gia.	0	0	.000	3.18	5	0	0	0	2	0	5.2	7	28	3	2	0	0	0	5	0	5	3	1	0
Gelatka, Todd, Brew.	0	0	.000	6.75	1	0	0	0	0	0	1.1	2	6	1	1	0	0	0	0	0	0	1	0	0
Gill, Chris, Ath.	3	1	.750	6.00	13	1	0	0	2	0	24.0	23	105	20	16	1	0	2	1	9	0	21	1	0
Gittings, Christopher, Brew.	1	1	.500	7.71	6	3	0	0	2	0	11.2	15	49	10	10	1	0	1	1	1	0	12	1	0
Glascock, John-Paul, Cubs	0	1	.000	9.61	16	1	0	0	5	0	19.2	22	106	23	21	0	2	1	24	0	15	8	1
Gold, J.M., Brew.	0	1	.000	7.56	4	4	0	0	0	0	8.1	17	41	7	7	0	0	1	2	0	7	0	0
Haeger, Charles, W.S.	0	3	.000	6.39	13	4	0	0	1	0	31.0	44	153	29	22	2	1	3	1	17	0	17	4	1
Hannaman, Ryan, Gia.*	4	1	.800	2.00	11	11	0	0	0	0	54.0	34	227	14	12	1	2	2	5	31	0	67	2	5
Hannaway, Patrick, Gia.	1	1	.500	2.70	12	0	0	0	8	0	13.1	13	61	5	4	0	2	1	1	9	0	7	2	0
Hays, Sam, Mar.*	1	2	.333	6.83	7	7	0	0	0	0	29.0	36	137	25	22	0	1	1	6	14	0	22	2	2
Heflin, Theo, Mar.*	2	1	.667	6.55	18	0	0	0	9	1	23.1	34	118	21	17	1	3	1	2	13	0	21	2	0
Honel, Kris, W.S.	2	0	1.000	1.80	3	3	0	0	0	0	10.0	9	39	3	2	0	0	0	1	3	0	8	0	0
Javier, Tony, Mar.	3	1	.750	2.28	12	2	0	0	6	2	27.2	27	110	10	7	1	0	1	1	11	0	23	0	0

Pitcher, Team	W	L	Pct.	ERA	G	GS	CG	ShO	GF	Sv.	IP	H	TBF	R	ER	HR	SH	SF	HB	BB	IBB	SO	WP	Bk.
Jobe, John, Mar.*	1	1	.500	4.25	16	0	0	0	5	0	29.2	38	143	26	14	2	0	1	3	12	0	26	4	0
Johnson, Thad, Ath.	2	1	.667	3.72	13	8	0	0	1	0	46.0	45	194	25	19	4	4	0	2	10	0	44	3	1
Jones, Alvin, W.S.	0	3	.000	12.63	11	2	0	0	1	0	20.2	25	118	34	29	0	0	0	5	26	0	19	13	0
Jones, Greg, Ang.	0	0	.000	0.00	2	2	0	0	0	0	2.0	3	10	0	0	0	0	0	0	2	0	2	0	0
King, Robert, Gia.	2	0	1.000	5.29	12	1	0	0	2	0	17.0	21	78	11	10	1	0	0	2	7	0	19	4	0
Kirkland, Aaron, W.S.	0	2	.000	0.40	29	0	0	0	29	13	45.1	25	169	5	2	1	2	2	3	4	4	62	1	0
Korneev, Oleg, Mar.	0	0	.000	0.00	1	0	0	0	0	0	1.0	0	3	0	0	0	0	0	0	0	0	1	0	0
Landeros, Leonard, Ath.*	2	1	.667	2.82	11	4	0	0	1	1	38.1	35	164	16	12	1	1	1	2	13	0	31	2	0
Lebron, Obispo, Cubs	1	1	.500	5.11	12	0	0	0	12	3	12.1	16	67	7	7	1	0	1	2	5	0	14	0	1
Leon, Brigmer, Ath.	4	3	.571	3.28	14	7	0	0	3	0	46.2	46	196	26	17	2	3	1	3	7	0	40	4	4
Liriano, Francisco, Gia.*	5	4	.556	3.63	13	12	0	0	0	0	62.0	51	246	26	25	3	1	0	1	24	0	67	6	3
Luther, Heath, Ang.*	1	3	.250	4.66	13	6	0	0	3	0	38.2	52	185	26	20	2	3	2	3	15	1	34	2	0
Martin, Nick, Cubs*	3	1	.750	3.32	10	0	0	0	3	0	21.2	26	93	9	8	0	1	1	2	5	0	18	1	1
Martinez, Pedro, Atti.	1	1	.500	4.05	10	0	0	0	0	0	22.0	24	98	13	10	2	0	1	3	6	0	22	1	1
Matos, Raymond, Gia.*	4	3	.571	2.34	14	12	0	0	0	0	61.2	64	284	35	16	0	2	1	6	29	0	66	12	0
Mendoza, Edgardo, Mar.*	3	3	.500	4.29	13	4	0	0	1	0	42.0	38	187	25	20	0	1	1	3	21	0	34	6	2
Mendoza, Mario, Ang.	0	0	.000	2.25	3	0	0	0	1	0	4.0	2	15	1	1	0	0	0	1	0	0	2	1	0
Michaels, Carl, Brew.	2	1	.667	3.57	9	0	0	0	8	2	17.2	23	74	7	7	0	1	1	0	3	0	10	1	0
Mieses, Jose, Brew.	0	1	.000	0.00	2	2	0	0	0	0	4.1	3	19	1	0	0	0	0	0	1	0	5	1	0
Morales, Ruddy, W.S.	3	2	.600	2.48	6	5	0	0	0	0	29.0	31	126	15	8	2	1	1	6	0	26	0	2
Morban, Carlos, Ang.	0	1	.000	13.14	11	1	0	0	5	0	12.1	17	69	22	18	0	1	1	1	12	0	10	8	1
Moreira, Greg, Brew.	1	1	.500	4.91	4	4	0	0	0	0	14.2	17	65	10	8	0	1	2	1	0	1	11	1	0
Muessig, Jeff, Ath.	5	0	1.000	2.41	14	0	0	0	2	0	18.2	14	77	5	5	0	0	1	2	7	0	18	2	0
Nacar, Leslie, Gia.	0	3	.000	2.54	22	0	0	0	17	5	28.1	27	121	9	8	2	1	1	9	1	35	4	0
Nacar, Yimmy, Gia.	1	0	1.000	5.14	17	5	0	0	3	0	42.0	40	192	25	24	1	0	3	11	22	0	38	4	2
Nielsen, Brian, Brew.*	0	1	.000	3.70	7	6	0	0	0	0	24.1	21	101	12	10	0	1	1	5	0	21	1	0
Nolasco, Ricky, Cubs	1	0	1.000	1.50	5	4	0	0	0	0	18.0	11	69	3	3	0	0	1	5	0	23	1	0
Nova, Wanderliner, Brew.*	4	1	.800	5.64	16	0	0	0	9	0	22.1	32	105	15	14	1	1	1	4	9	1	10	2	0
Nunez, Severino, Brew.*	0	0	.000	4.70	9	0	0	0	1	0	15.1	11	65	8	8	1	0	0	0	4	0	19	1	0
Oakes, Gerard, Brew.	2	4	.333	2.85	12	7	0	0	1	0	53.2	50	233	24	17	2	2	2	5	25	0	44	10	1
O'Brien, Weston, Cubs	3	3	.500	3.27	13	3	0	0	3	0	41.1	49	175	18	15	0	1	2	5	8	0	34	0	3
Ockerman, Justin, Mar.	1	4	.200	4.91	10	10	0	0	0	0	40.1	49	186	30	22	1	0	5	16	0	27	4	1
Olivero, Pedro, Cubs	2	0	1.000	6.60	17	0	0	0	4	3	30.0	38	135	24	22	2	1	1	0	10	0	27	2	0
Ortega, Carlos, W.S.*	2	0	1.000	2.45	4	0	0	0	0	0	11.0	10	44	3	3	0	0	1	0	0	13	0	0
Parker, Brandon, Mar.	2	0	1.000	4.09	9	0	0	0	2	0	11.0	15	52	5	5	2	0	1	5	0	13	0	0
Paulino, Robert, Cubs	0	0	.000	0.00	1	0	0	0	1	0	1.0	1	4	0	0	0	0	0	0	0	0	0	0
Pena, Luismar, Brew.	3	4	.429	4.63	11	2	0	0	6	0	35.0	42	164	23	18	2	1	8	13	1	20	1	0
Perez, Armando, W.S.*	3	3	.500	2.98	15	5	1	1	1	0	63.1	56	265	27	21	1	2	0	2	23	2	44	6	1
Pine, Chris, Ang.	0	1	.000	4.50	3	0	0	0	0	0	4.0	5	18	3	2	0	0	0	0	2	0	2	0	0
Price, Matthew, Brew.	0	0	.000	12.00	2	0	0	0	1	0	3.0	4	14	4	4	0	0	0	0	1	0	1	0	0
Ramirez, Carlos, Brew.*	2	2	.500	4.66	11	2	0	0	0	0	36.2	43	158	22	19	2	1	0	3	9	0	25	0	1
Ramirez, Hector, Gia.	3	2	.600	2.82	25	0	0	0	12	3	38.1	31	157	12	12	1	3	2	1	14	1	20	2	1
Ramirez, Rafael, Gia.	1	0	1.000	3.55	9	9	0	0	0	0	38.0	35	157	17	15	1	0	0	15	0	32	2	0
Reed, Rylan, W.S.	4	4	.500	3.10	13	13	0	0	0	0	58.0	56	277	46	20	2	1	6	10	34	0	53	6	3
Reyes, Luis, Cubs	4	1	.800	6.23	15	0	0	0	6	0	26.0	38	130	21	18	0	2	4	15	1	12	3	2
Reynoso, Paulino, W.S.*	0	2	.000	3.66	15	3	0	0	2	1	39.1	41	175	27	16	1	0	2	4	13	1	31	5	1
Reynoso, Roberto, Ang.	1	4	.200	5.40	14	6	0	0	2	0	51.2	70	244	46	31	1	2	2	1	9	0	34	12	2
Rivera, Jimmy, Mar.	3	1	.750	4.10	16	0	0	0	6	2	37.1	44	167	21	17	2	2	1	17	0	18	3	1
Rodriguez, Kenneth, Brew.	0	1	.000	1.15	8	0	0	0	4	1	15.2	16	67	3	2	0	1	0	8	1	12	1	0
Rodriguez, Manuel, Ath.	2	2	.500	4.12	17	0	0	0	5	0	19.2	25	92	14	9	1	1	0	9	0	21	4	0
Rojas, Ramon, Gia.	3	5	.375	3.40	27	0	0	0	5	0	45.0	43	202	21	17	2	3	1	6	14	0	27	1	1
Rouwenhorst, Jonathon, Ang.*	1	0	1.000	0.00	7	0	0	0	2	0	8.2	2	35	1	0	0	1	5	1	14	0	0
Rowland-Smith, Ryan, Mar.*.	1	1	.500	2.97	17	0	0	0	10	5	33.1	25	128	11	11	1	1	0	2	9	1	39	0	0
Ryu, Jae-kuk, Cubs	1	0	1.000	0.61	4	3	0	0	0	0	14.2	11	61	2	1	0	0	0	5	0	20	2	0
Sabourin, Brian, Mar.	0	1	.000	18.00	1	1	0	0	0	0	2.0	5	10	4	4	0	0	1	0	1	0	3	0
Sanchez, Felix, Cubs*	2	5	.286	4.01	12	9	0	0	0	0	60.2	57	254	38	27	2	1	1	2	22	0	55	6	2
Sanchez, Jesus, Cubs	3	0	1.000	3.86	3	0	0	0	0	0	4.2	7	26	3	2	0	1	3	0	5	1	1
Santana, Johan, Ang.	3	2	.600	3.22	10	9	1	1	0	0	58.2	40	256	27	21	0	2	0	2	35	0	69	8	1
Sheffield, Aaron, Brew.	1	1	.500	7.82	8	0	0	0	4	0	12.2	14	59	12	11	0	1	0	6	7	0	11	2	0
Shell, Steven, Ang.	1	0	1.000	0.00	3	0	0	0	1	0	4.0	1	15	0	0	0	0	0	2	0	3	0	0
Shull, Johnathan, Ang.	2	3	.400	4.89	17	8	0	0	2	0	53.1	61	244	42	29	1	1	1	24	0	40	7	0
Sierra, Edwardo, Ath.	2	1	.667	3.02	12	6	0	0	1	1	44.2	45	185	19	15	2	3	9	0	41	4	4
Simmering, Bryan, Ath.	2	2	.500	2.40	13	6	0	0	3	0	48.2	41	186	16	13	1	1	5	3	0	57	0	0
Sisco, Andy, Cubs*	0	1	1.000	5.24	10	7	0	0	0	0	34.1	36	152	28	20	1	0	6	10	0	31	2	1
Stavros, Tony, Brew.	0	1	.000	0.61	5	0	0	0	0	0	14.2	13	57	2	1	0	0	3	1	11	0	0
Steward, Edward, Ang.*	5	3	.625	2.02	19	4	1	1	5	1	49.0	47	205	19	11	1	1	0	2	11	1	40	1	0
Stull, Everett, Brew.	0	0	.000	0.00	2	1	0	0	0	0	4.1	2	16	0	0	0	0	0	0	4	0	0
Stumm, Jason, W.S.	0	0	.000	2.25	4	4	0	0	0	0	12.0	6	45	4	3	0	1	0	5	0	12	0	1
Trytten, Ryan, Brew.	2	0	1.000	3.96	18	0	0	0	16	6	25.0	23	113	12	11	1	1	2	11	2	21	1	0
Valdez, Richard, Cubs	1	4	.200	8.23	12	4	0	0	1	0	35.0	50	177	39	32	4	1	1	10	15	0	25	3	2
Waddell, Jason, Gia.*	0	1	.000	3.00	1	1	0	0	0	0	6.0	8	26	3	2	0	0	1	0	0	3	0	0
Watson, Tanner, Mar.	8	2	.800	4.40	11	11	0	0	0	0	59.1	70	268	40	29	3	4	0	9	15	0	57	6	0
Wells, Matt, Gia.	0	1	.000	18.00	1	0	0	0	0	0	1.0	3	8	2	2	0	0	0	2	0	1	1	0
Worrell, Tim, Gia.	0	0	.000	0.00	1	0	0	0	1	0	3.0	1	10	0	0	0	0	0	2	0	1	0	0
Wright, Shayne, Ang.	0	1	.000	5.89	9	2	0	0	3	2	12.2	20	61	9	4	0	0	2	1	11	0	0
Zorrilla, Reinaldo, W.S.	1	3	.250	4.18	25	0	0	0	14	1	32.1	35	141	20	15	2	2	1	3	9	0	25	4	1

COMBINATION SHUTOUTS: **Angels (3)**—Shull-Andujar-Wright-Astacio, Steward-Wright, Luther-Wright-Mendoza-Rouwenhorst. **Athletics (1)**—Simmering-Rodriguez-Leon. **Brewers (0)**—None. **Cubs (2)**—Foli-Reyes-Sanchez-Lebron, Ryu-Nolasco-Burnau-Fisher. **Giants (6)**—Hannaman-Rojas-Nacar, Matos-Rojas-Nacar, Hannaman-Ramirez-Nacar, Hannaman-Hannaway-Featherstone, Liriano-King-Nacar, R. Ramirez-Diaz-Rojas-H. Ramirez. **Mariners (1)**—Fruto-Rivera. **White Sox (2)**—Reed-Reynoso-Kirkland, Morales-Reynoso.

NO-HIT GAMES: None.

TEAM

Team	Pct.	G	PO	A	E	TC	DP	TP	PB
Athletics	.965	56	1507	618	78	2203	31	0	27
Giants	.963	56	1490	569	79	2138	34	0	17
Brewers	.954	56	1479	612	101	2192	46	0	22
Cubs	.946	56	1492	558	117	2167	44	1	23
Mariners	.946	56	1458	571	116	2145	40	0	24
Angels	.937	56	1464	550	136	2150	38	0	23
White Sox	.937	56	1473	508	134	2115	31	0	8

INDIVIDUAL

FIRST BASEMEN

NOTE: All caps denotes fielding-percentage leader based on 28 games for catchers, 37 for all other non-pitchers and 45 innings for pitchers. *Throws lefthanded.

Player, Team	Pct.	G	PO	A	E	TC	DP
Batista, Christian, Ang.	.976	5	40	1	1	42	4
Bounds, Brandon, W.S.	.961	25	207	15	9	231	6
Cadena, Alejandro, Mar.	.980	18	137	12	3	152	5
Castillo, Carlos, Ath.	1.000	3	31	1	0	32	0
Collins, Chris, Mar.	.000	1	0	0	0	0	0
Collins, Kevin, Cubs*	.974	25	214	11	6	231	13
Davis, Ryan, Gia.*	.981	38	342	14	7	363	21
Davis, Tyrel, W.S.	1.000	1	1	0	0	1	0
DeLeon, Carlos, Ang.	.969	17	117	6	4	127	10
De Los Santos, Nelson, Brew.	1.000	13	104	6	0	110	8
Diaz, Randor, Gia.	1.000	8	32	2	0	34	1
D'Jesus, Francisco, Gia.	1.000	1	3	0	0	3	1
Esparragoza, Pedro, Brew.	1.000	2	4	0	0	4	0
Esterlin, Ivan, Cubs*	1.000	9	71	5	0	76	11
Franke, Michael, Brew.	1.000	3	17	1	0	18	1
Gemoll, Brandon, Brew.*	.969	6	58	4	2	64	3
Golden, Bryan, Cubs	1.000	6	33	1	0	34	0
Gomez, Raul, W.S.	.957	23	179	19	9	207	13
Gonzalez, Andy, W.U.	1.000	1	8	0	0	8	1
Guzman, Junior, Ang.	1.000	1	10	2	0	12	1
Imperiali, Francesco, Mar.	1.000	1	1	1	0	2	0
Jenkins, Kevin, Ang.*	.968	24	171	11	6	188	10
Jimenez, Luis, Ath.*	.957	5	63	3	3	69	3
Keating, Matt, Gia.	.983	16	148	21	3	172	8
KELLY, Otis, Ath.	.996	42	436	30	2	468	22
Kimpton, Nick, Ang.*	1.000	1	1	0	0	1	0
Koslowski, Kasey, W.S.	1.000	14	115	7	0	122	6
Kotchman, Casey, Ang.*	.974	4	36	2	1	39	2
Mejia, Andy, Cubs	1.000	1	0	1	0	1	1
Nelson, Brad, Brew.	.978	17	167	12	4	183	10
Peless, Sean, Mar.*	.976	44	381	26	10	417	33
Perez, Radhame, Ath.	1.000	1	14	0	0	14	0
Queroz, Pedro, Cubs	1.000	9	68	2	0	70	5
Ramirez, Manuel, Brew.	.973	9	71	1	2	74	7
Reyes, Jose, Ath.	.833	1	2	3	1	6	0
Scrafini, Matt, Brew.	1.000	11	94	6	0	100	11
Soto, Geovany, Cubs	.982	12	106	5	2	113	12
Stockton, Rick, Ang.*	.954	17	116	9	6	131	6
Suomi, Richard, Ath.	.857	2	5	1	1	7	0
Tritle, Chris, Ath.	.800	1	7	1	2	10	0
Wallace, Kellen, Ang.	1.000	2	6	0	0	6	0
Wayment, Kory, Ath.	1.000	3	17	3	0	20	0

TRIPLE PLAY: Collins.

SECOND BASEMEN

Player, Team	Pct.	G	PO	A	E	TC	DP
Aybar, Francisco, W.S.	.500	1	1	0	1	2	0
Batista, Christian, Ang.	1.000	1	1	2	0	3	0
Batista, Juan, Ang.	.851	14	17	23	7	47	2
Bell, Paul, Brew.	.944	3	11	6	1	18	3
Brown, Matthew, Ang.	.951	31	58	78	7	143	13
Cabrera, Leonel, Gia.	.983	35	75	99	3	177	17
Cedeno, Ronny, Cubs	1.000	1	2	0	0	2	0
Chavez, Ozzie, Brew.	1.000	4	10	20	0	30	1
Chirinos, Robinson, Cubs	.954	15	29	33	3	65	3
Collins, Mike, Ang.	1.000	1	0	1	0	1	0
Cordova, Roman, Mar.	.938	34	51	69	8	128	11
DeLeon, Carlos, Ang.	.000	1	0	0	0	0	0
De Los Santos, Nelson, Brew.	.909	3	5	5	1	11	2
D'Jesus, Francisco, Gia.	.000	1	0	0	0	0	0

THIRD BASEMEN

Player, Team	Pct.	G	PO	A	E	TC	DP
Batista, Christian, Ang.	.917	30	38	50	8	96	6
Batista, Juan, Ang.	.000	1	0	0	0	0	0
Bell, Paul, Brew.	.909	4	6	5	1	11	1
Brown, Matthew, Ang.	.805	17	8	26	8	41	2
Castillo, Carlos, Ath.	1.000	2	3	4	0	7	0
Chirinos, Robinson, Cubs	.830	33	21	57	16	94	10
CIESLUK, Chris, Gia.	.915	42	11	86	9	106	2
Collins, Chris, Mar.	.897	40	30	75	12	117	5
DeLeon, Carlos, Ang.	.000	1	0	0	0	0	0
Diaz, Randor, Gia.	1.000	2	0	1	0	1	0
Francois, Francisco, Ath.	.000	1	0	0	0	0	0
Franke, Michael, Brew.	.868	20	15	31	7	53	3
Garrido, Tomas, Gia.	1.000	5	1	9	0	10	0
Gomez, Raul, W.S.	.682	9	4	11	7	22	0
Groff, Matt, Ath.	.938	5	5	10	1	16	1
Hrynio, Mike, Mar.	.756	15	4	27	10	41	2
Imperiali, Francesco, Mar.	.880	10	2	20	3	25	1
Koslowski, Kasey, W.S.	1.000	6	2	15	0	17	1
Lebron, Freddie, W.S.	.667	1	1	1	1	3	0
Lee, Carlos, W.S.	.884	21	13	25	5	43	2
Lopez, Pedro, W.S.	.885	9	5	18	3	26	2
Luna, Leonardo, W.S.	.750	12	10	20	10	40	0
Maestrales, Peter, Gia.	1.000	5	2	5	0	7	1
McCormack, Taylor, Brew.	.828	33	25	57	17	99	7
Navarro, Mandy, Cubs	1.000	1	0	2	0	2	0
Nevins, Ryan, Ang.	.848	15	9	30	7	46	1
Oliveros, Luis, Mar.	.667	1	2	0	1	3	0
Paulino, Robert, Cubs	.667	2	0	2	1	3	1
Pinango, Ever, Gia.	1.000	7	6	2	0	8	0
Queroz, Pedro, Cubs	.911	22	12	39	5	56	1
Reyes, Jose, Ath.	.893	31	26	49	9	84	3
Soto, Geovany, Cubs	.500	2	1	0	1	2	0
Trinidad, Edgar, Ath.	.923	4	3	9	1	13	1
Vazquez, Rafael, Cubs	.769	4	2	8	3	13	0
Wayment, Kory, Ath.	.946	21	9	44	3	56	3
Webster, Anthony, W.S.	.000	1	0	0	0	0	0

SHORTSTOPS

Player, Team	Pct.	G	PO	A	E	TC	DP
Batista, Christian, Ang.	.875	3	2	5	1	8	0
Batista, Juan, Ang.	.839	19	15	37	10	62	2
Bell, Paul, Brew.	.941	4	8	8	1	17	1
Cabrera, Leonel, Gia.	.774	9	8	16	7	31	1
Cedeno, Ronny, Cubs	.901	51	84	116	22	222	19
CHAVEZ, Ozzie, Brew.	.933	48	83	152	17	252	24
Chirinos, Robinson, Cubs	.833	3	4	6	2	12	3
Ciesluk, Chris, Gia.	.000	1	0	0	0	0	0
Cordova, Roman, Mar.	.842	10	11	21	6	38	1
Francois, Francisco, Ath.	.923	32	44	88	11	143	5
Garrido, Tomas, Gia.	.955	32	49	98	7	154	10
Gomez, Raul, W.S.	1.000	1	0	3	0	3	0
Gonzalez, Andy, W.S.	.878	38	75	84	22	181	5

Player, Team	Pct.	G	PO	A	E	TC	DP
Esparragoza, Pedro, Brew.	1.000	3	6	10	0	16	2
Felix, Kelvin, Ang.	.920	18	24	22	4	50	3
Francois, Francisco, Ath.	.980	11	17	33	1	51	4
Hill, Bobby, Cubs	1.000	2	5	6	0	11	4
Imperiali, Francesco, Mar.	.912	33	41	52	9	102	11
Lebron, Freddie, W.S.	.958	25	38	54	4	96	6
Lopez, Pedro, W.S.	.947	20	37	52	5	94	4
Luna, Leonardo, W.S.	.865	11	22	23	7	52	2
Maestrales, Peter, Gia.	.967	8	16	13	1	30	1
Martin, Craig, Brew.	.938	21	33	58	6	97	8
Montero, Roberto, Gia.	.000	1	0	0	0	0	0
Mujica, Andres, Mar.	1.000	1	3	4	0	7	0
Nevins, Ryan, Ang.	.818	4	4	5	2	11	2
Nova, Willian, Brew.	.942	23	63	66	8	137	13
Paulino, Robert, Cubs	.918	35	49	85	12	146	13
Pinango, Ever, Gia.	.889	3	3	5	1	9	0
Ramirez, Alexander, Gia.	.900	13	16	20	4	40	1
Reyes, Jose, Ath.	1.000	9	4	17	0	21	1
Salas, Francisco, Cubs	.968	11	29	31	2	62	8
Selmo, Wilson, Ang.	.938	4	9	6	1	16	3
Torres, Erik, Brew.	1.000	1	4	0	0	4	0
TRINIDAD, Edgar, Ath.	.971	39	53	116	5	174	9
Wayment, Kory, Ath.	1.000	1	1	4	0	5	0

TRIPLE PLAY: Paulino.

Player, Team	Pct.	G	PO	A	E	TC	DP
Hardy, J.J., Brew.	.931	5	12	15	2	29	1
Harris, Josh, Cubs	.909	2	2	8	1	11	0
Lopez, Pedro, W.S.	.869	18	30	43	11	84	4
Luna, Leonardo, W.S.	1.000	1	0	4	0	4	1
Menchaca, Eriberto, Mar.	.930	49	74	151	17	242	20
Morillo, Roberto, Gia.	.000	1	0	0	0	0	0
Navarro, Mandy, Cubs	.750	1	2	1	1	4	0
Nova, Willian, Brew.	1.000	1	1	1	0	2	1
Paulino, Robert, Cubs	.667	2	1	1	1	3	0
Ramirez, Alexander, Gia.	.895	21	33	35	8	76	7
Salas, Francisco, Cubs	1.000	1	0	1	0	1	0
Selmo, Wilson, Ang.	.916	45	44	109	14	167	11
Vazquez, Rafael, Cubs	1.000	1	0	1	0	1	0
Wayment, Kory, Ath.	.951	26	39	78	6	123	11

OUTFIELDERS

Player, Team	Pct.	G	PO	A	E	TC	DP
Abad, Noel, Ang.	.962	14	24	1	1	26	0
Aybar, Francisco, W.S.	.925	44	47	2	4	53	0
Banks, Gary, Cubs	.939	53	86	6	6	98	0
Bounds, Brandon, W.S.	1.000	3	2	0	0	2	0
Brown, Larry, Mar.*	.907	27	36	3	4	43	0
Cabrera, Andres, Gia.	1.000	4	1	1	0	2	0
Choo, Shin-soo, Mar.*	.986	51	72	1	1	74	0
Ciesluk, Chris, Gia.	1.000	1	3	0	0	3	0
Cleto, Carlos, Gia.*	.892	51	63	3	8	74	1
Coats, Buck, Cubs	.981	27	50	3	1	54	1
Cosby, Quantwan, Ang.	.884	37	57	4	8	69	1
Cruz, Nelson, Ath.	1.000	21	30	1	0	31	0
Davis, Ryan, Gia.*	.800	8	4	0	1	5	0
Davis, Tyrel, W.S.	.958	32	42	4	2	48	1
De Los Santos, Nelson, Brew.	1.000	12	17	2	0	19	0
Ellison, Josh, Mar.	.870	24	18	2	3	23	0
Esparragoza, Pedro, Brew.	.000	1	0	0	0	0	0
Esterlin, Ivan, Cubs*	.923	9	12	0	1	13	0
Felix, Kelvin, Ang.	.000	1	0	0	0	0	0
Francois, Francisco, Ath.	1.000	1	1	0	0	1	0
Franke, Michael, Brew.	.000	1	0	0	0	0	0
Gelotti, Matt, Brew.	1.000	4	2	0	0	2	0
Gemoll, Brandon, Brew.*	1.000	1	1	0	0	1	0
Golden, Bryan, Cubs	1.000	1	2	0	0	2	0
Groff, Matt, Ath.	.923	13	10	2	1	13	0
Gustafson, Troy, Gia.	.989	56	85	6	1	92	0
Guzman, Junior, Ang.	1.000	4	5	0	0	5	0
Hammonds, Jeffrey, Brew.	.000	1	0	0	0	0	0
Hicks, Brian, Brew.	.867	10	13	0	2	15	0
Hodges, Jarrod, Mar.*	.944	39	62	5	4	71	0
January, Javerro, Brew.	.959	37	60	10	3	73	1
Jenkins, Kevin, Ang.*	.955	18	21	0	1	22	0
Jimenez, Luis, Ath.*	1.000	3	4	0	0	4	0
Jones, Jared, Mar.	.800	4	4	0	1	5	0
Kimpton, Nick, Ang.*	.955	45	84	1	4	89	0
Lachapel, Juan, Ath.	1.000	10	16	0	0	16	0
Luna, Leonardo, W.S.	1.000	1	1	0	0	1	0
Maestrales, Peter, Gia.	.917	8	10	1	1	12	1
Marmol, Carlos, Cubs	.840	19	19	2	4	25	0
Mathis, Jeff, Ang.	.000	1	0	0	0	0	0
Mayo, Terry, Brew.	.971	18	32	2	1	35	0
McAuliff, James, Gia.	.956	43	64	1	3	68	1
Melgarejo, Ransel, Ang.	.958	42	61	8	3	72	1
Miliano, Hector, Cubs	.960	52	87	8	4	99	2
Mott, Bill, Ang.	1.000	3	4	0	0	4	0
Mujica, Andres, Mar.	1.000	43	56	1	0	57	0
Nagle, Austin, Ath.	.980	47	49	0	1	50	0
Navarro, Mandy, Cubs	1.000	4	3	1	0	4	0
Nova, Willian, Brew.	.000	2	0	0	0	0	0
Parrott, Corry, Brew.	1.000	2	3	1	0	4	0
Perez, Radhame, Ath.	.955	15	21	0	1	22	0
Pinango, Ever, Gia.	1.000	12	8	0	0	8	0
Plasencia, Francisco, Brew.*	.990	49	92	6	1	99	0
Rafael, Alberto, W.S.	.818	9	8	1	2	11	0
Reyes, Jose, Ath.	.000	2	0	0	0	0	0
Salas, Francisco, Cubs	1.000	3	7	0	0	7	0
Seever, Brian, Ang.	1.000	4	2	0	0	2	0
Soto, Geovany, Cubs	.667	2	2	0	1	3	0
Stockton, Rick, Ang.*	.909	12	9	1	1	11	0
Suomi, Richard, Ath.	1.000	8	10	1	0	11	1
Thompson, Zachary, Brew.*	.950	16	18	1	1	20	0
Todd, Kelvin, Ath.	1.000	3	3	0	0	3	0
Trinidad, Edgar, Brew.	1.000	1	2	0	0	2	0
TRITLE, Chris, Ath.	1.000	51	84	2	0	86	0
Viera, Orlando, Brew.*	.925	25	34	3	3	40	0

Player, Team	Pct.	G	PO	A	E	TC	DP
Wallace, Kellen, Ang.	1.000	11	11	0	0	11	0
Wayment, Kory, Ath.	1.000	4	2	0	0	2	0
Webster, Anthony, W.S.	.957	54	86	2	4	92	0
Williamson, Chad, Cubs	1.000	4	4	0	0	4	0
Young, Eddie, W.S.	.937	38	67	7	5	79	1

CATCHERS

Player, Team	Pct.	G	PO	A	E	TC	DP	PB
Bell, Paul, Brew.	1.000	1	4	0	0	4	0	0
Cadena, Alejandro, Mar.	.978	12	79	9	2	90	1	3
Castillo, Carlos, Ath.	1.000	1	7	1	0	8	0	0
Castillo, Oscar, Ath.	.959	23	166	21	8	195	1	5
Cochrane, Mark, W.S.	1.000	13	93	8	0	101	1	1
Collins, Mike, Ang.	.973	15	63	9	2	74	0	6
Del Chiaro, Brent, Ang.	.971	15	93	7	3	103	0	4
Devinney, Rick, Cubs	1.000	4	28	0	0	32	0	3
D'JESUS, Francisco, Gia.	1.000	32	240	41	0	281	1	10
Esparragoza, Pedro, Brew.	.966	40	243	44	10	297	3	10
Golden, Bryan, Cubs	.986	10	62	9	1	72	0	7
Gonzalez, Jose, Gia.	.947	6	34	2	2	38	0	0
Gregorio, Tom, Ang.	.955	3	20	1	1	22	0	1
Guzman, Junior, Ang.	.973	17	101	9	3	113	1	6
Hickman, Brian, W.S.	.989	22	172	14	2	188	3	3
Hilario, Enderson, W.S.	.900	2	7	2	1	10	0	0
Hudson, Ben, Mar.	.962	5	48	2	2	52	0	2
Koslowski, Kasey, W.S.	.981	24	138	18	3	159	0	2
Marmol, Carlos, Cubs	.975	12	73	5	2	80	0	3
Mathis, Jeff, Ang.	1.000	3	19	2	0	21	0	1
Mejia, Andy, Cubs	.957	3	21	1	1	23	0	2
Montero, Roberto, Gia.	1.000	2	6	1	0	7	0	1
Morillo, Roberto, Gia.	1.000	1	1	0	0	1	0	1
Oliveros, Luis, Mar.	.978	21	165	12	4	181	0	10
Queroz, Pedro, Cubs	.993	19	140	12	1	153	2	4
Ramirez, Manuel, Brew.	.993	18	122	18	1	141	0	12
Rivera, Rene, Mar.	.977	20	145	24	4	173	3	8
Serafini, Matt, Brew.	1.000	4	14	2	0	16	0	0
Soto, Geovany, Cubs	.981	18	139	18	3	160	1	4
Suomi, Richard, Ath.	.976	35	295	34	8	337	0	22
Terrero, Wandy, W.S.	.976	7	35	6	1	42	0	2
Varitek, Justin, Mar.	1.000	4	7	0	0	7	0	1
Vega, Jesus, Ang.	.980	23	130	17	3	150	0	5
Williams, Jon, Gia.	.979	23	208	25	5	238	0	5

PITCHERS

Player, Team	Pct.	G	PO	A	E	TC	DP
Abreu, Jonathan, Gia.*	.800	23	1	3	1	5	0
Allen, Travis, Ang.	1.000	17	2	1	0	3	0
Amancio, Jose, Ath.	.889	14	3	5	1	9	0
Andujar, Jesse, Ang.	1.000	3	0	2	0	2	0
Arias, Daniel, Ang.	.800	16	3	5	2	10	0
Artman, Dane, Brew.*	.750	5	3	0	1	4	0
Asencio, Domingo, W.S.*	.700	7	4	3	3	10	0
Astacio, Hector, Ang.	.813	22	3	10	3	16	0
Atencio, Donald, Ath.	.500	15	0	1	1	2	0
Baez, Hebel, Ath.	.500	12	3	1	4	8	0
Balser, Jeffrey, Ang.	.857	20	1	5	1	7	0
Bastardo, Jose, Gia.*	1.000	18	1	1	0	2	0
Batista, Cristian, Brew.	.667	13	1	1	1	3	0
Beck, David, Ath.*	.500	18	1	1	2	4	0
Bott, Glenn, Mar.*	.000	2	0	0	0	0	0
Brown, Eric, Cubs	1.000	11	1	2	0	3	0
Bukowski, Stan, Ang.	1.000	4	1	0	0	1	0
Burnau, Ryan, Cubs	.842	14	3	13	3	19	0
Caminero, Concepcion, Cubs	.857	15	1	5	1	7	1
Carpenter, Calvin, Brew.	.800	11	1	7	2	10	1
Chirinos, Jesus, Brew.	.846	11	3	8	2	13	0
Cimorelli, Brett, Ang.	1.000	11	1	0	0	1	0
Coleman, Jeff, Ath.	1.000	8	0	2	0	2	0
Correa, Alexander, Brew.*	1.000	12	0	2	0	2	0
Cortez, Renee, Mar.	.833	11	2	3	1	6	0
Cruz, Ramon, W.S.	.833	6	1	4	1	6	0
D'Amico, Leonardo, Ang.	.875	14	3	4	1	8	1
De La Rosa, Felix, Brew.	.000	6	0	0	0	0	0
Diaz, Daniel, Gia.	1.000	1	0	1	0	1	0
Done, Juan, Mar.	1.000	5	1	0	0	1	0
Dowdy, Justin, W.S.*	1.000	18	1	5	0	6	1
Featherstone, Deron, Gia.	1.000	15	1	2	0	3	0
Fisher, Marc, Cubs	.889	15	1	7	1	9	0
Foli, Daniel, Cubs	.667	11	1	5	3	9	0
Ford, Ben, Cubs	1.000	3	0	1	0	1	0
Fruto, Emiliano, Mar.	.867	12	3	10	2	15	0
Fryson, Andrew, W.S.	.667	8	2	2	2	6	1

Player, Team	Pct.	G	PO	A	E	TC	DP
Fyhrie, Mike, Cubs	.000	2	0	0	0	0	0
Garcia, Jairo, Ath.	.700	12	1	6	3	10	0
Garcia, Ruddy, Gia.	1.000	5	0	1	0	1	0
Gelatka, Todd, Brew.	.000	1	0	0	0	0	0
Gill, Chris, Ath.	.857	13	3	3	1	7	0
Gittings, Christopher, Brew.	.000	6	0	0	0	0	0
Glascock, John-Paul, Cubs	1.000	16	1	5	0	6	0
Gold, J.M., Brew.	.750	4	0	3	1	4	0
Haeger, Charles, W.S.	.571	13	3	1	3	7	0
Hannaman, Ryan, Gia.*	.909	11	2	8	1	11	0
Hannaway, Patrick, Gia.	1.000	12	0	3	0	3	0
Hays, Sam, Mar.*	.750	7	2	1	1	4	0
Heflin, Theo, Mar.*	1.000	18	2	4	0	6	0
Honel, Kris, W.S.	.000	3	0	0	0	0	0
Javier, Tony, Mar.	1.000	12	2	3	0	5	2
Jobe, John, Mar.*	1.000	16	1	0	0	1	0
Johnson, Thad, Ath.	.923	13	2	10	1	13	0
Jones, Alvin, W.S.	.857	11	4	2	1	7	0
Jones, Greg, Ang.	.000	2	0	0	0	0	0
King, Robert, Gia.	1.000	12	0	3	0	3	2
Kirkland, Aaron, W.S.	1.000	29	2	3	0	5	0
Korneev, Oleg, Mar.	.000	1	0	0	0	0	0
Landeros, Leonard, Ath.*	1.000	11	3	3	0	6	0
Lebron, Obispo, Cubs	1.000	12	1	2	0	3	0
Leon, Brigmer, Ath.	1.000	14	4	7	0	11	0
Liriano, Francisco, Gia.*	.909	13	1	9	1	11	0
Luther, Heath, Ang.*	.923	13	5	7	1	13	0
Martin, Nick, Cubs*	1.000	10	1	2	0	3	1
Martinez, Pedro, Ath.*	1.000	16	1	2	0	3	0
Matos, Raymond, Gia.*	.818	14	2	7	2	11	0
Mendoza, Edgardo, Mar.*	.938	13	5	10	1	16	1
Mendoza, Mario, Ang.	1.000	3	1	0	0	1	0
Michaels, Carl, Brew.	1.000	9	0	4	0	4	0
Mieses, Jose, Brew.	1.000	2	0	2	0	2	0
Morales, Ruddy, W.S.	.714	6	1	4	2	7	0
Morban, Carlos, Ang.	.750	11	1	2	1	4	0
Moreira, Greg, Brew.	1.000	4	0	1	0	1	0
Muessig, Jeff, Ath.	1.000	14	1	3	0	4	0
Nacar, Leslie, Gia.	.833	23	2	3	1	6	0
Nacar, Yimmy, Gia.	1.000	16	1	3	0	4	1
Nielsen, Brian, Brew.*	1.000	7	0	1	0	1	0
Nolasco, Ricky, Cubs	.800	5	0	4	1	5	0
Nova, Wanderliner, Brew.*	.889	16	2	6	1	9	0
Nunez, Severino, Brew.*	1.000	9	2	0	0	2	0
Oakes, Gerard, Brew.	1.000	12	4	4	0	8	0
O'Brien, Weston, Cubs	.889	13	3	5	1	9	0
Ockerman, Justin, Mar.	.667	10	3	3	3	9	1
Olivero, Pedro, Cubs	1.000	17	1	2	0	3	0
Ortega, Carlos, W.S.*	1.000	4	0	2	0	2	0
Parker, Brandon, Mar.	.000	9	0	0	0	0	0
Paulino, Robert, Cubs	.000	1	0	0	0	0	0
Pena, Luismar, Brew.	.889	11	4	4	1	9	0
Perez, Armando, W.S.*	.933	15	2	12	1	15	0
Pine, Chris, Ang.	.000	3	0	0	0	0	0
Price, Matthew, Brew.	1.000	2	2	0	0	2	0
Ramirez, Carlos, Brew.*	.750	11	0	3	1	4	0
Ramirez, Hector, Gia.	1.000	25	4	6	0	10	1
Ramirez, Rafael, Gia.	.833	8	0	5	1	6	0
Reed, Rylan, W.S.	.818	13	7	2	2	11	0
Reyes, Luis, Cubs	1.000	15	6	1	0	7	1
Reynoso, Paulino, W.S.*	1.000	15	0	3	0	3	0
Reynoso, Roberto, Ang.	.727	14	4	4	3	11	1
Rivera, Jimmy, Mar.	.875	16	3	4	1	8	1
Rodriguez, Kenneth, Brew.	1.000	8	0	2	0	2	0
Rodriguez, Manuel, Ath.	1.000	17	0	3	0	3	0
Rojas, Ramon, Gia.	.889	27	3	5	1	9	0
Rouwenhorst, Jonathon, Ang.*	.800	7	2	2	1	5	0
Rowland-Smith, Ryan, Mar.*	.900	17	1	8	1	10	0
Ryu, Jae-kuk, Cubs	1.000	4	1	0	0	1	0
Sabourin, Brian, Mar.	.000	1	0	0	0	0	0
Sanchez, Felix, Cubs*	1.000	12	0	7	0	7	0
Sanchez, Jesus, Cubs	.000	3	0	0	0	0	0
Santana, Johan, Ang.	.818	10	5	13	4	22	0
Sheffield, Aaron, Brew.	1.000	8	0	2	0	2	0
Shell, Steven, Ang.	.000	3	0	0	0	0	0
Shull, Johnathan, Ang.	.857	17	0	6	1	7	0
SIERRA, Edwardo, Ath.	1.000	12	4	12	0	16	0
Simmering, Bryan, Ath.	1.000	13	2	3	0	5	0
Sisco, Andy, Cubs*	.714	10	1	4	2	7	0
Stavros, Tony, Brew.	1.000	5	3	6	0	9	1
Steward, Edward, Ang.*	.875	19	3	4	1	8	0
Stull, Everett, Brew.	1.000	2	1	1	0	2	1
Stumm, Jason, W.S.	1.000	4	0	2	0	2	0
Trytten, Ryan, Brew.	1.000	18	2	2	0	4	0
Valdez, Richard, Cubs	.500	12	0	2	2	4	0
Waddell, Jason, Gia.*	1.000	1	0	2	0	2	0
Watson, Tanner, Mar.	.818	11	2	7	2	11	0
Wells, Matt, Gia.	.000	1	0	0	0	0	0
Worrell, Tim, Gia.	.000	1	0	0	0	0	0
Wright, Shayne, Ang.	1.000	9	1	2	0	3	0
Zorrilla, Reinaldo, W.S.	.833	25	0	5	1	6	0

The following players appeared only as designated hitter, pinch-hitter or pinch runner: L. Abreu, ph, dh; Meadows, dh; Parnell, dh.

LEAGUE CHAMPIONS

Year	Team	Pct.	Year	Team	Pct.	Year	Team	Pct.
1988—	Peoria Brewers	.690	1993—	Scottsdale A's	.636	1998—	Rockies	.750
1989—	Peoria Brewers	.732	1994—	Chandler Cardinals	.607	1999—	Athletics	.696
1990—	Peoria Brewers	.679	1995—	Scottsdale A's	.661	2000—	Mariners	.709
1991—	Scottsdale A's	.650	1996—	Padres	.643	2001—	Athletics	.625
1992—	Scottsdale A's	.607	1997—	Cubs	.618			

SUMMER CLASS A Arizona League

GULF COAST LEAGUE

LEAGUE OFFICE

President
Tom Saffell

Address
1503 Clower Creek Dr., H-262
Sarasota, FL 34231

Phone
941-966-6407

Teams*
Braves
Dodgers
Expos
Marlins
Orioles
Phillies
Pirates
Rangers
Reds
Red Sox

Royals
Tigers
Twins
Yankees

*Teams play their games in Bradenton, Clearwater, Fort Myers, Haines City, Jupiter, Lakeland, Melbourne, Orlando, Port Charlotte, Sarasota, Tampa and Vero Beach.

2001 FINAL STANDINGS

EASTERN DIVISION

Team	W	L	T	Pct.	GB
Dodgers	41	19	0	.683	...
Braves	30	30	0	.500	11.0
Marlins	29	31	0	.483	12.0
Expos	20	40	0	.333	21.0

NORTHERN DIVISION

Team	W	L	T	Pct.	GB
Yankees	35	25	0	.583	...
Tigers	34	26	0	.567	1.0
Phillies	31	29	0	.517	4.0
Royals	20	40	0	.333	15.0

WESTERN DIVISION

Team	W	L	T	Pct.	GB
Red Sox	37	22	0	.627	...
Reds	36	22	0	.621	0.5
Twins	32	26	0	.552	4.5
Rangers	24	35	0	.407	13.0
Pirates	22	34	0	.393	13.5
Orioles	22	34	0	.393	13.5

COMPOSITE

Team	Dod.	R.S.	Reds	Yank.	Tig.	Twi.	Phi.	Brav.	Mar.	Rang.	Pir.	Ori.	Roy.	Exp.	W	L	T	Pct.	GB
Dodgers	...	0	0	0	0	0	0	15	11	0	0	0	0	15	41	19	0	.683	...
Red Sox	0	...	5	0	0	8	0	0	0	9	8	7	0	0	37	22	0	.627	3.5
Reds	0	6	...	0	0	6	0	0	0	8	9	7	0	0	36	22	0	.621	4.0
Yankees	0	0	0	...	12	0	8	0	0	0	0	0	15	0	35	25	0	.583	6.0
Tigers	0	0	0	8	...	0	13	0	0	0	0	0	13	0	34	26	0	.567	7.0
Twins	0	4	5	0	0	...	0	0	0	8	6	9	0	0	32	26	0	.552	8.0
Phillies	0	0	0	12	7	0	...	0	0	0	0	0	12	0	31	29	0	.517	10.0
Braves	5	0	0	0	0	0	0	...	11	0	0	0	0	14	30	30	0	.500	11.0
Marlins	9	0	0	0	0	0	0	9	...	0	0	0	0	11	29	31	0	.483	12.0
Rangers	0	3	4	0	0	4	0	0	0	...	8	5	0	0	24	35	0	.407	16.5
Pirates	0	4	3	0	0	5	0	0	4	...	6	0	0	22	34	0	.393	17.0
Orioles	0	5	5	0	0	3	0	0	0	6	3	...	0	0	22	34	0	.393	17.0
Royals	0	0	0	5	7	0	8	0	0	0	0	0	...	0	20	40	0	.333	21.0
Expos	5	0	0	0	0	0	0	6	9	0	0	0	0	...	20	40	0	.333	21.0

Games played in Bradenton, Dunedin, Fort Myers, Melbourne, Osceola, Port Charlotte, St. Lucie County, Sarasota, Tampa and West Palm Beach, Fla.

Club names are major league affiliations.

PLAYOFFS: Yankees defeated Red Sox one game to none; Yankees defeated Dodgers two games to one to win Gulf Coast League Championship.

REGULAR-SEASON ATTENDANCE: No total attendance figures reported.

MANAGERS: Braves, Rick Albert; Dodgers, Juan Bustabad; Expos, Dave Dangler; Marlins, Jon Deeble; Orioles, Jesus Alfaro; Phillies, Roly Dearmas; Pirates, Woody Huyke; Rangers, Carlos Subero; Red Sox, John Sanders; Reds, Edgar Caceres; Royals, Lino Diaz; Tigers, Howard Bushong; Twins, Al Newman; Yankees, Derek Shelton.

ALL-STAR TEAM: 1B—Adrian Mendoza, Dodgers; 2B—Victor Diaz, Dodgers; 3B—Juan Gonzalez, Tigers; SS—Bronson Sardinha, Yankees; OF—Carlos Brackley, Red Sox; OF—Carlos Duran, Red Sox; OF—Elvin Andujar, Reds; C—Dioneer Navarro, Yankees; SP—Chad Petty, Tigers; RP—Jannio Gutierrez, Twins; Manager of the Year—Derek Shelton, Yankees.

2001 BATTING

TEAM

Team	Avg.	G	TPA	AB	R	H	TB	2B	3B	HR	RBI	SH	SF	HP	BB	IBB	SO	SB	CS	GDP	LOB	ShO	Slg.	OBP
Twins	.262	58	2068	1819	237	477	667	100	24	14	201	19	16	32	182	12	376	77	30	24	405	4	.367	.337
Red Sox	.262	59	2164	1892	278	496	750	97	14	43	225	6	16	43	207	8	400	66	30	43	431	2	.396	.346
Dodgers	.260	60	2309	1983	315	516	686	84	13	20	252	31	28	79	188	2	461	70	20	27	469	3	.346	.344
Orioles	.257	56	1959	1739	214	447	640	92	19	21	189	20	15	24	161	11	445	55	26	31	372	4	.368	.326
Yankees	.256	60	2177	1905	298	487	691	87	18	27	257	9	22	32	209	9	434	69	22	37	407	4	.363	.336
Phillies	.251	60	2154	1911	261	480	676	88	13	24	222	15	9	30	189	3	449	39	24	38	410	4	.354	.327
Reds	.248	58	1981	1743	226	433	591	75	19	15	186	8	16	45	169	5	431	108	33	40	357	5	.339	.328
Tigers	.243	60	2123	1872	253	454	610	54	21	20	200	19	13	34	185	4	405	110	31	28	407	3	.326	.320
Rangers	.240	59	2086	1845	239	443	636	99	29	12	202	21	11	37	172	8	434	124	34	29	368	1	.345	.316
Royals	.236	60	2130	1884	210	444	577	86	7	11	173	22	10	36	178	5	446	63	27	33	425	8	.306	.312

Team	Avg.	G	TPA	AB	R	H	TB	2B	3B	HR	RBI	SH	SF	HP	BB	IBB	SO	SB	CS	GDP	LOB	ShO	Slg.	OBP
Braves	.227	60	2162	1939	227	441	607	76	9	24	194	12	16	48	147	0	446	64	23	20	389	6	.313	.296
Marlins	.221	60	2156	1923	209	425	549	80	7	10	168	16	10	41	166	2	490	100	43	27	384	7	.285	.295
Pirates	.221	56	1932	1686	185	372	501	65	11	14	141	11	14	31	190	3	398	81	21	38	375	11	.297	.309
Expos	.216	60	2137	1913	184	413	522	57	11	10	155	16	12	37	159	3	522	48	29	43	382	7	.273	.287

INDIVIDUAL

TOP QUALIFIERS FOR BATTING CHAMPIONSHIP

Minimum 162 plate appearances. *Lefthanded batter. †Switch-hitter.

Player, Team	Avg.	G	TPA	AB	R	H	TB	2B	3B	HR	RBI	SH	SF	HP	BB	IBB	SO	SB	CS	GDP	Slg.	OBP
Diaz, Victor, Dod.	.354	53	221	195	36	69	104	22	2	3	31	1	3	6	16	1	23	6	3	3	.533	.414
Gonzalez, Juan, Tig.†	.333	54	218	192	30	64	79	6	0	3	33	1	3	3	19	0	30	19	6	3	.411	.396
Brackley, Carlos, R.S.	.329	49	165	152	24	50	78	8	1	6	21	0	1	3	9	0	27	3	3	4	.513	.376
Legendre, Curtis, Roy.	.321	48	189	168	23	54	73	15	2	0	29	1	2	2	16	1	25	7	1	2	.435	.383
Herrera, Christian, Dod.	.320	46	178	153	24	49	52	3	0	0	20	6	3	4	12	0	23	9	2	3	.340	.378
Gotay, Ruben, Roy.†	.315	52	213	184	29	58	84	15	1	3	19	2	1	0	26	1	22	5	6	2	.457	.398
Duran, Carlos, Brav.*	.304	54	218	204	35	62	84	10	3	2	17	0	0	2	12	0	30	16	4	0	.412	.349
Sardinha, Bronson, Yan.*	.303	55	222	188	42	57	89	14	3	4	27	1	2	3	28	2	51	11	2	6	.473	.398
Heath, Demetrius, Tig.	.303	50	199	175	34	53	70	5	6	0	19	4	2	0	18	1	16	21	4	3	.400	.364
Mendoza, Adrian, Dod.*	.302	52	214	172	34	52	73	7	1	4	37	0	4	9	29	0	55	9	4	2	.424	.421
Tejeda, Juan, Tig.	.295	50	186	173	17	51	73	8	1	4	37	0	0	5	8	2	32	0	0	2	.422	.344
Andujar, Elvin, Reds	.294	58	220	197	32	58	94	9	9	3	34	0	2	5	16	1	43	21	4	6	.477	.359
White, Kenneth, Ori.†	.294	49	178	160	22	47	63	11	1	1	12	3	0	1	12	1	42	5	2	1	.394	.354
Guerrero, Jorge, Mar.	.293	46	163	140	18	41	58	9	1	2	13	2	1	2	18	0	27	11	6	4	.414	.379
Cancio, Antonio, Phi.	.292	49	190	171	22	50	69	13	0	2	29	0	0	3	16	0	51	0	0	6	.404	.363

DEPARTMENTAL LEADERS: G—E. Andujar, Brewer, Ezi, 58 each; AB—Ezi, 238; R—Sardinha, 42; H—V. Diaz, 69; TB—V. Diaz, 104; 2B—V. Diaz, 22; 3B—A. Hernandez, 11; HR—Cooper, 7; RBI—A. Mendoza, J. Tejeda, 37 each; SH—Herrera, Ezi, 6 each; SF—Nickerson, 7; HP—Porzo, 17; BB—Ciofrone, Ruiz, 33 each; IBB—R. Martinez, Buscher, Kubel, R. Smith, 3 each; SO—Ezi, 90; SB—A. Hernandez, 34; CS—Brewer, 10; GIDP—L. Cruz, 8; Slg.—V. Diaz, .533; OBP—U. Cabrera, .438.

ALL PLAYERS

*Lefthanded batter. †Switch-hitter.

Player, Team	Avg.	G	TPA	AB	R	H	TR	2B	3B	HR	RBI	SH	SF	HP	BB	IBB	SO	SB	CS	GDP	Slg.	OBP
Abreu, Nielsen, Phi.	.275	35	138	131	14	36	42	3	0	1	10	0	1	0	6	0	19	3	5	4	.321	.304
Acevedo, Juan, Reds†	.140	37	109	100	10	14	20	6	0	0	3	0	0	1	8	0	50	2	1	0	.200	.211
Acosta, Johe, Pir.	.212	20	78	66	7	14	20	2	2	0	10	0	0	4	8	0	17	2	0	1	.303	.333
Akens, Phil, Mar.	.500	7	2	2	0	1	1	0	0	0	0	0	0	0	0	0	0	0	0	0	.500	.500
Albert, Luke, Brav.†	.211	38	125	114	5	24	30	3	0	1	12	0	0	1	10	0	30	0	1	1	.263	.280
Alexander, Alexis, Roy.	.185	36	125	108	11	20	25	5	0	0	5	2	2	5	8	0	29	9	3	3	.231	.268
Alexander, Lawrence, Phi.	.276	39	146	127	21	35	38	3	0	0	10	1	0	2	16	0	26	3	4	0	.299	.366
Alou, Felipe, Roy.	.250	18	78	76	8	19	22	3	0	0	9	1	0	1	0	0	14	1	1	1	.289	.260
Ambrosini, Anthony, Exp.	.224	25	95	85	5	19	20	1	0	0	5	2	0	3	5	0	24	1	1	3	.235	.290
Anderson, Samuel, Tig.	.268	33	94	82	0	22	23	1	0	0	5	0	0	2	10	0	16	0	1	5	.280	.362
Andujar, Elvin, Reds	.294	58	220	197	32	58	94	9	9	3	34	0	2	5	16	1	43	21	4	6	.477	.359
Angell, Rick, Rang.	.364	3	11	11	1	4	6	0	1	0	0	0	0	0	0	0	2	0	0	0	.545	.364
Aristigueta, Darwin, Brav.†	.162	37	130	117	11	19	26	4	0	1	8	1	1	3	8	0	31	3	0	1	.222	.233
Arroyo, William, Mar.†	.257	42	161	144	15	37	40	1	1	0	14	2	1	2	12	1	28	5	1	2	.278	.321
Baez, Federico, Ori.	.259	28	95	81	9	21	24	3	0	0	6	0	0	0	14	0	29	2	3	0	.296	.368
Banks, Almonzo, Ori.	.150	38	116	100	8	15	24	4	1	1	8	1	1	2	12	0	39	3	0	4	.240	.252
Barrios, Rafael, Tig.	.000	24	1	1	0	0	0	0	0	0	0	0	0	0	0	0	1	0	0	0	.000	.000
Barthel, Cole, Brav.	.217	45	174	152	14	33	34	1	0	0	12	2	1	5	14	0	27	8	3	2	.224	.302
Bass, Brian, Ori.†	.297	21	81	74	12	22	37	3	6	0	7	0	2	0	5	0	25	4	0	1	.500	.333
Bastardo, Frederick, Mar.	.238	44	162	147	18	35	53	12	0	2	14	2	1	3	9	0	32	7	4	1	.361	.294
Batista, Jose, Roy.	.263	40	185	167	10	44	54	7	0	1	22	1	1	5	11	0	22	4	3	6	.323	.326
Bautista, Augusto, Reds	.190	20	47	42	7	8	11	0	0	1	7	1	1	2	1	0	16	0	3	2	.262	.239
Bellorin, Edwin, Dod.	.175	28	94	80	11	14	15	1	0	0	6	2	0	4	8	0	6	1	0	0	.188	.283
Birkell, Matthew, Tig.	.189	35	101	90	14	17	20	1	1	0	3	4	0	1	6	0	16	2	3	1	.222	.247
Blanco, Luis, Exp.	.199	45	163	151	11	30	42	6	0	2	13	0	2	4	6	0	54	1	0	5	.278	.245
Bledsoe, Hunter, Dod.	.385	4	14	13	2	5	6	1	0	0	1	0	0	0	1	0	1	1	0	0	.462	.429
Blue, Vincent, Tig.*	.248	42	140	113	16	28	34	2	2	0	4	3	0	0	24	0	24	8	4	0	.301	.380
Bonvechio, Brett, R.S.*	.217	19	79	69	4	15	25	5	1	1	5	0	1	0	9	0	12	0	2	3	.362	.304
Boscan, Jean, Brav.	.333	8	31	30	5	10	14	4	0	0	6	0	1	0	0	0	3	0	1	1	.467	.323
Brackley, Carlos, R.S.	.329	49	165	152	24	50	78	8	1	6	21	0	1	3	9	0	27	3	3	4	.513	.376
Brewer, Anthony, Mar.	.251	58	251	211	35	53	66	7	3	0	16	3	1	8	28	0	55	27	10	1	.313	.359
Brito, Anyelo, Phi.	.186	27	96	86	9	16	24	5	0	1	15	1	1	1	7	0	27	2	0	2	.279	.253
Brown, Dustin, R.S.	.254	36	135	126	15	32	45	5	4	0	14	0	2	0	7	0	24	1	2	3	.357	.289
Brown, Ira, Roy.	.444	15	9	9	1	4	8	1	0	1	2	0	0	0	0	0	2	0	0	0	.889	.444
Brown, Jason, Mar.	.333	1	3	3	0	1	1	0	0	0	1	0	0	0	0	0	2	0	0	0	.333	.333
Brown, Rich, Yan.*	.167	2	8	6	1	1	2	1	0	0	0	0	0	0	2	0	4	0	0	0	.333	.375
Brown, Tim, Pir.*	.211	46	177	142	11	30	42	4	1	2	18	0	2	4	29	1	32	1	0	2	.296	.356
Bunch, J.C., Rang.	.333	35	117	102	16	34	53	7	3	2	19	1	0	1	13	0	12	7	2	0	.520	.414
Burrus, Josh, Brav.	.193	52	223	197	24	38	59	8	2	3	19	2	3	8	14	0	40	10	2	6	.299	.271
Buscher, Gregory, Rang.	.240	40	134	121	14	29	45	9	2	1	10	0	0	2	11	3	35	1	0	1	.372	.313
Cabrerra, Ulises, Rang.	.286	42	162	126	26	36	47	9	1	0	8	2	0	11	23	1	32	15	2	3	.373	.438
Campos, Julio, Phi.	.150	13	43	40	2	6	8	2	0	0	1	0	1	1	1	0	9	0	1	1	.200	.186
Cancio, Antonio, Phi.	.292	49	190	171	22	50	69	13	0	2	29	0	0	3	16	0	51	0	0	6	.404	.363
Cano, Robinson, Yan.*	.230	57	233	200	37	46	73	14	2	3	34	0	2	3	28	0	27	11	2	4	.365	.330
Caraballo, Carlos, R.S.	.212	47	150	137	16	29	41	3	3	1	14	2	0	3	8	0	39	8	3	6	.299	.270
Cardona, David, Dod.	.232	47	185	168	20	39	46	6	1	0	21	5	0	2	10	0	42	2	1	3	.274	.283
Carolfiles, Bladimir, Mar.	.259	43	159	147	13	38	52	9	1	1	20	3	1	4	4	0	20	13	4	2	.354	.295
Carroll, Rich, Rang.	.259	48	174	158	22	41	61	15	1	1	18	0	2	1	13	0	37	2	0	3	.386	.316

Player, Team	Avg.	G	TPA	AB	R	H	TB	2B	3B	HR	RBI	SH	SF	HP	BB	IBB	SO	SB	CS	GDP	Slg.	OBP
Carter, Ryan, Dod.	.272	30	114	92	16	25	33	3	1	1	10	2	1	9	10	0	29	4	0	1	.359	.393
Charles, Julin, Rang.	.241	52	204	187	23	45	71	15	4	1	22	2	2	1	12	1	41	17	2	6	.380	.287
Chauncey, Clinton, Yan.	.111	10	20	18	1	2	2	0	0	0	0	0	0	1	1	0	8	0	0	0	.111	.200
Ciofrone, Paul, Phi.*	.269	42	169	134	23	36	57	7	1	4	21	0	1	1	33	0	42	2	0	3	.425	.414
Cisneros, Josh, Phi.	.288	24	85	73	8	21	24	3	0	0	7	0	0	5	6	1	9	1	0	5	.329	.381
Cockrell, Michael, Pir.	.280	48	190	168	32	47	56	7	1	0	11	1	1	1	19	0	17	31	5	7	.333	.354
Coffey, Josh, Mar.	.033	9	30	30	1	1	1	0	0	0	0	0	0	0	0	0	10	1	0	2	.033	.033
Coffie, Ivanon, Ori.*	.278	6	20	18	2	5	9	1	0	1	2	0	0	0	2	0	5	0	0	0	.500	.350
Collum, Michael, Pir.	.289	35	133	114	17	33	61	9	2	5	21	0	1	3	15	0	40	2	1	2	.535	.383
Cooper, Matt, R.S.	.267	56	229	187	33	50	87	14	1	7	34	0	1	9	32	1	57	2	0	2	.465	.397
Crosby, Kelly, Yan.	.290	22	68	62	9	18	21	3	0	0	5	0	0	2	4	0	8	1	1	2	.339	.353
Cruz, Alex, Pir.	.292	19	79	65	12	19	29	3	2	1	7	1	0	0	13	0	8	3	0	2	.446	.410
Cruz, Luis, R.S.	.259	53	207	197	18	51	69	9	0	3	18	0	2	1	7	0	17	1	4	8	.350	.285
Cust, Kevin, Brav.	.269	17	59	52	6	14	22	2	0	2	5	0	0	1	6	0	14	1	0	0	.423	.356
Davis, Daniel, Tig.*	.161	9	32	31	2	5	6	1	0	0	1	0	0	0	1	0	10	1	0	1	.194	.199
Davis, J.J., Pir.	.471	4	18	17	3	8	15	1	0	2	6	0	0	0	1	0	2	0	0	1	.882	.500
Davis, Rajai, Pir.†	.262	26	102	84	19	22	23	1	0	0	4	3	1	1	13	0	26	11	3	0	.274	.364
Dean, Herman, Tig.	.256	28	92	82	18	21	34	4	0	3	10	2	0	3	4	0	24	13	0	1	.415	.315
De Leon, Jorge, R.S.	.208	10	29	24	6	5	7	2	0	0	0	1	0	1	4	0	4	1	0	0	.292	.345
De Leon, Virgilio, Tig.	.243	9	39	37	2	9	14	2	0	1	5	0	0	1	1	0	5	1	1	2	.378	.282
Delgado, Mario, Phi.*	.500	2	8	8	1	4	7	0	0	1	4	0	0	0	0	0	1	0	0	0	.875	.500
DelosSantos, Esteban, Phi.†	.195	38	136	123	18	24	44	6	4	2	13	1	1	2	8	1	27	3	5	1	.358	.254
De Los Santos, Omar, Dod.	.303	9	38	33	7	10	14	4	0	0	3	1	1	0	3	0	4	1	1	0	.424	.351
Devries, Jonathan, R.S.	.316	21	67	57	8	18	23	5	0	0	6	0	0	4	6	1	19	0	0	0	.404	.418
Diaz, Frank, Exp.	.219	38	147	128	10	28	35	5	1	0	8	1	2	3	12	1	27	10	3	6	.273	.297
Diaz, Victor, Dod.	.354	53	221	195	36	69	104	22	2	3	31	1	3	6	16	1	23	6	3	3	.533	.414
Dorta, Melvin, R.S.	.408	21	88	76	19	31	43	6	0	2	8	0	0	1	11	0	5	7	3	0	.566	.489
Doumit, Ryan, Pir.†	.235	7	19	17	2	4	6	2	0	0	3	0	0	0	2	1	0	0	0	0	.353	.316
Duran, Carlos, Brav.*	.304	54	218	204	35	62	84	10	3	2	17	0	0	2	12	0	30	16	4	0	.412	.349
Duran, Deudis, Phi.†	.256	35	129	117	17	30	48	8	2	2	14	2	0	2	8	0	21	0	0	1	.410	.315
Encarnacion, Angelo, R.S.	.200	3	7	5	1	1	2	1	0	0	0	0	0	0	2	0	1	0	0	0	.400	.429
Encarnacion, Henry, Exp.†	.205	50	195	166	23	34	40	4	1	0	10	1	1	1	26	0	38	10	0	3	.241	.314
Engels, Jackson, Rang.*	.000	11	1	1	0	0	0	0	0	0	0	0	0	0	0	0	0	0	0	0	.000	.000
Escobar, Luis, Roy.*	.277	34	113	94	8	26	35	3	0	2	10	2	1	4	12	1	18	0	0	3	.372	.378
Espino, Damaso, Reds†	.250	39	114	104	8	26	31	2	0	1	11	1	2	2	5	0	26	6	2	4	.298	.293
Estilow, Chris, Mar.	.125	18	47	40	3	5	5	0	0	0	3	0	0	1	7	0	20	0	0	0	.125	.255
Everett, Carl, R.S.†	.200	3	11	10	2	2	8	0	0	2	2	0	0	0	1	0	3	0	0	0	.800	.273
Ezi, Travis, Dod.	.231	58	265	238	33	55	79	10	4	2	24	6	0	4	17	1	90	15	1	0	.332	.293
Fahey, Patrick, Dod.	.176	8	21	17	3	3	3	0	0	0	2	0	0	1	3	0	4	0	0	0	.176	.333
Farmer, John, Brav.	.000	2	6	6	0	0	0	0	0	0	0	0	0	0	0	0	2	0	0	0	.000	.000
Faulkner, Todd, Yan.	.105	7	21	19	2	2	3	1	0	0	0	0	0	0	2	0	6	0	0	0	.158	.190
Feliz, Henry, Yan.*	.203	25	70	64	7	13	20	2	1	1	9	2	1	1	2	0	22	0	1	2	.313	.245
Fermin, Angelo, Twi.†	.279	13	53	43	5	12	12	0	0	0	5	1	2	1	6	0	10	2	2	1	.279	.365
Figuereo, Anibal, Roy.	.227	51	199	176	18	40	57	7	2	2	18	2	0	3	18	0	47	8	2	3	.324	.310
Figueroa, Daniel, R.S.*	.256	27	113	86	16	22	46	4	1	6	24	0	5	1	21	1	28	3	0	0	.535	.389
Fitzpatrick, Reggie, Exp.*	.280	31	127	118	17	33	34	1	0	0	7	0	0	0	9	1	28	5	4	2	.288	.331
Fry, Ryan, Reds	.276	56	213	181	30	50	77	9	3	4	22	0	2	5	25	1	61	9	2	3	.425	.376
Gallo, Ismael, Dod.*	.167	4	8	6	2	1	1	0	0	0	0	0	0	1	1	0	1	0	0	0	.167	.375
Garcia, Juan-Carlos, Mar.†	.185	40	124	108	8	20	27	4	0	1	10	1	1	0	14	0	44	2	3	1	.250	.276
Garcia, Sandy, Yan.	.250	35	126	112	18	28	49	8	2	3	18	0	2	2	10	1	37	3	1	0	.438	.317
Gatti, William Jr., Dod.	.161	11	36	31	5	5	5	0	0	0	1	0	0	2	3	0	8	0	0	1	.161	.278
Gerlits, Gooby, Mar.	.163	16	45	43	1	7	8	1	0	0	2	0	0	1	1	0	12	0	0	0	.186	.200
Ghutzman, Phillip, Reds	.206	27	80	68	6	14	20	0	0	2	7	1	1	0	10	0	11	0	0	5	.294	.304
Gomon, Dusty, Twi.	.324	19	79	74	13	24	36	6	0	2	10	0	0	0	5	0	15	1	0	0	.486	.367
Gonzalez, Carlos, R.S.	.214	8	16	14	0	3	3	0	0	0	1	0	0	0	2	0	3	0	0	1	.214	.313
Gonzalez, Jose, Rang.†	.239	52	211	180	23	43	51	4	2	0	14	2	2	5	22	0	40	21	7	1	.283	.335
Gonzalez, Juan, Dod.	.269	26	75	67	9	18	18	0	0	0	7	3	2	0	3	0	8	3	0	1	.269	.292
Gonzalez, Juan, Tig.†	.333	54	218	192	30	64	79	6	0	3	33	1	3	3	19	0	30	19	6	3	.411	.396
Gordon, Alex, Ori.*	.333	9	29	24	7	8	19	2	0	3	10	0	0	1	4	1	14	1	0	0	.792	.448
Gotay, Ruben, Roy.†	.315	52	213	184	29	58	84	15	1	3	19	2	1	0	26	1	22	5	6	2	.457	.398
Graham, Tyson, Mar.	.172	35	104	93	12	16	22	1	1	1	6	1	0	2	8	0	32	1	0	1	.237	.252
Greene, Jason, Exp.*	.279	31	123	104	14	29	42	7	3	0	13	0	0	1	18	0	30	2	2	2	.404	.390
Guerrero, Jorge, Mar.	.293	46	163	140	18	41	58	9	1	2	13	2	1	2	18	0	27	11	6	4	.414	.379
Gutierrez, Franklin, Dod.	.269	56	258	234	38	63	91	16	0	4	30	2	2	4	16	0	39	9	3	1	.389	.324
Guy, Jason, Rang.*	.207	47	157	140	17	29	44	7	4	0	15	4	1	1	11	1	45	5	3	1	.314	.268
Guzman, Carlos, Brav.*	.266	40	159	139	20	37	53	7	0	3	23	0	1	4	15	0	44	3	2	1	.381	.352
Guzman, Cristian, Twi.†	.250	5	19	16	4	4	6	0	1	0	0	0	0	1	2	0	4	0	1	1	.375	.368
Guzman, Garrett, Twi.*	.355	39	153	138	22	49	79	14	5	2	22	0	2	3	9	1	16	4	2	1	.572	.401
Guzman, Jacob, Roy.	.184	29	88	76	4	14	16	2	0	0	4	1	0	1	10	0	19	0	1	2	.211	.287
Guzman, Wander, Mar.†	.226	51	207	199	16	45	52	7	0	0	13	1	0	4	3	0	34	14	2	1	.261	.252
Haas, Danny, R.S.*	.107	11	38	28	6	3	4	1	0	0	1	0	1	0	9	1	1	0	0	1	.143	.316
Hackett, Richard, Ori.	.238	7	23	21	2	5	6	1	0	0	1	0	0	0	2	0	4	0	1	1	.286	.304
Hadad, Jorge, Ori.	.234	15	51	47	4	11	15	4	0	0	5	0	0	1	3	0	11	0	0	1	.319	.294
Hansen, Bryan, Phi.*	.243	30	124	111	9	27	32	2	0	1	11	2	1	0	10	0	21	1	0	1	.288	.303
Heath, Demetrius, Tig.	.303	50	199	175	34	53	70	5	6	0	19	4	2	0	18	1	16	21	4	3	.400	.364
Hernandez , Anderson, Tig.†.	.264	55	234	216	37	57	84	5	11	0	18	3	2	0	13	0	38	34	8	0	.389	.303
Hernandez, Michel, Yan.	.000	2	6	5	0	0	0	0	0	0	0	0	0	1	0	0	1	0	0	1	.000	.167
Herrera, Christian, Dod.	.320	52	178	153	24	49	52	3	0	0	20	6	3	4	12	0	23	9	2	3	.340	.378
Hill, Joshua, Twi.	.000	15	7	6	0	0	0	0	0	0	0	0	0	1	0	0	3	0	0	0	.000	.143
Hiraldo, Inocencio, Twi.†	.282	49	182	163	26	46	72	12	4	2	18	2	2	2	13	1	31	12	3	2	.442	.339
Honeycutt, Shedrick, Exp.*	.198	38	140	131	9	26	29	3	0	0	8	1	2	1	5	0	38	4	3	1	.221	.230
Horsman, Stephen, Ori.*	.071	5	17	14	0	1	1	0	0	0	1	0	0	0	3	0	5	0	1	0	.071	.235
Infante, Franklin, Brav.	.242	43	136	128	10	31	42	7	2	0	16	3	2	2	1	0	38	3	0	1	.328	.256

Player, Team	Avg.	G	TPA	AB	R	H	TB	2B	3B	HR	RBI	SH	SF	HP	BB	IBB	SO	SB	CS	GDP	Slg.	OBP
Inge, Brandon, Tig.	.100	3	12	10	1	1	4	0	0	1	2	0	0	0	2	0	2	0	0	0	.400	.250
Jackson, Edwin, Dod.	.308	20	29	26	5	8	11	0	0	1	2	0	0	0	3	0	6	0	0	1	.423	.379
Jaramillo, Milko, Dod.†	.250	3	10	8	2	2	4	0	1	0	1	0	0	1	1	0	0	0	0	0	.500	.400
Jimenez, Luis, Yan.†	.200	10	32	30	2	6	7	1	0	0	2	0	0	1	1	0	10	0	0	1	.233	.250
Johnson, Brian, Dod.	.444	5	20	18	4	8	14	0	0	2	3	0	0	0	2	0	0	0	0	0	.778	.500
Johnson, Joshua, Twi.	.141	24	76	64	5	9	12	1	1	0	2	2	1	2	7	0	14	1	0	2	.188	.243
Johnson, Tristan, Pir.	.143	25	84	77	5	11	12	1	0	0	4	0	1	0	6	0	32	1	0	4	.156	.202
Jones, Terry, Phi.	.194	9	38	36	3	7	7	0	0	0	4	0	0	0	2	0	5	0	0	0	.194	.237
Jordan, Edward, Ori.	.276	50	183	156	32	43	72	9	1	6	22	5	1	4	17	1	35	16	2	2	.462	.360
Joyce, Thomas Jr., Ori.*	.217	49	177	152	18	33	43	8	1	0	12	3	2	0	20	1	45	2	4	1	.283	.305
Kahr, Danny, Exp.†	.169	16	64	59	5	10	17	2	1	1	6	0	0	1	4	0	24	0	0	0	.288	.234
Kearns, Austin, Reds..........	.176	6	22	17	2	3	5	2	0	0	4	0	3	0	2	0	7	0	0	0	.294	.227
Khairy, Masjid, Rang.†	.255	40	159	141	15	36	44	2	3	0	16	4	2	3	9	0	34	26	3	0	.312	.310
King, Brennan, Dod.	.556	3	11	9	3	5	10	2	0	1	4	0	1	1	0	0	0	0	0	0	1.111	.545
Kubel, Jason, Twi.*	.331	37	147	124	14	41	62	10	4	1	30	0	2	2	19	3	14	3	2	3	.500	.422
Lababera, Michael, Exp.	.231	34	110	104	9	24	26	2	0	0	4	0	0	2	3	0	11	3	2	3	.250	.266
Lambert, Shawn, Tig.	.131	36	119	107	5	14	20	3	0	1	5	0	2	1	9	0	49	0	0	0	.187	.202
Lanoix, Gilbert, Dod.*	.250	2	8	8	1	2	3	1	0	0	0	0	0	0	0	0	1	0	0	0	.375	.250
Legendre, Curtis, Roy.	.321	48	189	168	23	54	73	15	2	0	29	1	2	2	16	1	25	7	1	2	.435	.383
Lehmann, Thomas, Tig.*	.178	34	102	90	8	16	19	3	0	0	12	2	1	0	9	0	21	1	0	2	.211	.250
Lindberg, Russell, Mar.	.127	20	60	55	2	7	9	2	0	0	5	0	0	2	3	0	8	0	3	1	.164	.200
Lopez, Javier, Dod.*............	.000	14	1	1	0	0	0	0	0	0	0	0	0	0	0	0	0	0	0	0	.000	.000
Louisa, Lorvin, Exp.	.173	46	172	156	9	27	36	1	1	2	16	2	0	3	11	0	54	1	3	2	.231	.241
Lush, Zach, Mar.	.115	7	33	26	4	3	3	0	0	0	1	0	0	2	5	1	5	5	0	1	.115	.303
Mancebo, Deni, Exp.†	.193	46	197	166	21	32	36	2	1	0	7	4	2	8	17	0	44	6	3	0	.217	.295
Manley, Adam, Ori.*	.176	9	35	34	3	6	12	1	1	1	5	0	0	1	0	0	9	0	0	1	.353	.200
Manriquez, Salomon, Exp.	.217	34	131	120	8	26	35	9	0	0	8	0	0	3	7	1	30	0	0	4	.292	.277
Marin, Daniel, Twi.	.274	31	108	95	16	26	31	5	0	0	11	2	0	1	10	0	10	5	1	2	.326	.349
Mariot, Lino, Pir.	.165	31	91	85	6	14	14	0	0	0	2	0	0	2	4	0	22	4	1	3	.165	.220
Marshall, Andre, Phi.†	.287	36	129	115	22	33	45	9	0	1	13	0	0	3	11	0	32	5	1	1	.391	.364
Martin, Chris, Yan.	.000	2	6	5	1	0	0	0	0	0	1	0	0	0	1	0	1	0	0	0	.000	.167
Martinez, Raul, Ori.	.248	35	120	101	13	25	34	4	1	1	17	0	3	1	15	3	23	2	0	1	.337	.342
Masino, Adam, Twi.	.220	39	134	123	10	27	37	7	0	1	10	0	0	1	10	1	41	3	0	1	.301	.284
Mateo, Alejandro, Rang.	.153	32	90	72	6	11	14	1	1	0	7	1	0	1	16	0	30	6	3	2	.194	.315
Mateo, Daniel, Reds|	.244	53	202	180	29	44	53	6	0	1	14	1	0	6	15	0	48	27	6	2	.294	.323
Matos, Luis, Ori.	.286	3	14	14	1	4	6	2	0	0	2	0	0	0	0	0	3	0	0	0	.429	.286
Maxwell, Ray, Pir.	.500	3	11	10	2	5	7	2	0	0	0	0	0	0	1	0	2	0	0	0	.700	.545
McCuistion, Mike, Pir.*	.220	27	92	82	4	18	21	3	0	0	3	0	0	1	9	0	8	0	0	3	.256	.304
McDonald, Chamar, Roy.	.208	40	137	125	13	26	38	7	1	1	11	1	0	2	9	0	43	5	1	1	.304	.272
McMahon, Jamec, Ori.	.261	10	55	48	1	12	12	0	0	0	3	1	1	0	7	0	19	0	1	2	.261	.360
McNamara, Husty, Phi.	.000	1	4	4	0	0	0	0	0	0	0	0	0	0	0	0	3	0	0	0	.000	.000
McRoberts, Mark, Phi.	.200	27	90	80	14	16	33	3	1	4	6	0	0	0	10	0	25	0	0	1	.413	.289
Meath, Matt, Pir.†	.147	14	48	34	7	5	7	2	0	0	1	0	0	2	12	1	6	5	1	1	.206	.396
Medina, Ricardo, Exp.	.217	38	139	129	12	28	44	5	1	3	14	1	0	1	8	0	37	0	3	0	.341	.268
Mendoza, Adrian, Dod.*........	.302	52	214	172	34	52	73	7	1	4	37	0	4	9	29	0	55	9	4	2	.424	.421
Milauskas, Adam, Pir.	.217	31	105	92	8	20	20	0	0	0	3	0	1	2	10	0	18	0	0	3	.217	.305
Mitchell, Andy, Ori.	.300	19	21	20	1	6	7	1	0	0	1	0	0	0	1	0	6	0	0	0	.350	.333
Molina, Angel, Mar.	.255	36	120	110	9	28	38	7	0	1	13	0	0	0	10	0	26	0	2	2	.345	.317
Molina, Felix, Twi.	.286	51	209	189	27	54	78	12	3	2	21	3	1	0	16	1	25	8	6	0	.413	.340
Morales, Jose, Twi.†	.248	35	127	117	13	29	39	6	2	0	18	2	0	2	6	0	26	4	1	1	.333	.296
Morales, Michael, Brav.	.163	16	63	49	8	8	10	2	0	0	4	0	1	9	4	0	4	0	1	4	.204	.333
Morban, Dany, Reds*	.143	27	65	63	4	9	10	1	0	0	3	0	0	1	1	0	22	3	1	1	.159	.169
Moreno, Christopher, Ori.	.250	6	21	20	1	5	5	0	0	0	0	0	1	0	0	0	5	1	0	1	.250	.250
Motooka, Rafael, Reds..........	.250	26	87	80	5	20	25	2	0	1	10	1	0	0	6	0	8	1	0	1	.313	.302
Moye, Alan, Reds	.287	48	183	171	24	49	68	9	2	2	18	1	0	3	8	2	34	12	3	5	.398	.330
Mujica, Jean, Exp.	.258	41	143	128	16	33	42	4	1	1	12	2	0	2	11	0	34	1	0	5	.328	.326
Nathans, John, R.S.	.200	5	6	5	1	1	2	1	0	0	0	0	0	0	1	0	2	0	0	0	.400	.333
Navarrete, Ray, Pir.	.222	3	11	9	1	2	3	1	0	0	1	0	0	0	2	0	3	0	1	0	.333	.364
Navarro, Dioner, Yan.†	.280	43	166	143	27	40	58	10	1	2	22	1	5	0	17	0	23	6	0	4	.406	.345
Nickerson, Brian, Dod.	.252	36	124	103	9	26	30	4	0	0	14	1	7	8	5	0	14	4	1	6	.291	.317
Nowlin, Cody, Rang.*	.273	6	24	22	2	6	12	3	0	1	7	0	0	1	1	0	3	0	0	1	.545	.333
Nunez, Alexis, Twi.*	.182	4	11	11	1	2	2	0	0	0	0	0	0	0	0	0	1	0	0	0	.182	.182
Nunez, Andres, Yan.	.228	55	210	180	21	41	48	2	1	1	15	1	4	4	21	1	28	5	1	2	.267	.316
Oeltjen, Trent, Twi.*	.321	45	157	134	21	43	56	7	3	0	18	2	4	3	14	0	16	10	3	2	.418	.387
Oetting, Todd, Reds	.238	23	71	63	7	15	17	2	0	0	8	0	1	3	4	0	11	1	0	1	.270	.310
Oh, Chul, R.S.*	.192	42	152	130	16	25	32	4	0	1	9	2	2	1	17	0	41	1	0	2	.246	.287
Olivari, Reinaldo, Rang.	.232	54	220	203	24	47	75	14	4	2	27	2	0	3	12	2	45	8	5	5	.369	.284
Oliver, Joe, R.S.	1.000	2	5	5	2	5	8	0	0	1	1	0	0	0	0	0	0	0	0	0	1.600	1.000
Ortega, Felix, Phi.	.250	20	72	56	10	14	23	4	1	1	9	1	1	2	12	0	15	0	0	2	.411	.394
Ortiz, David, Twi.*	.400	4	13	10	3	4	4	0	0	0	1	0	0	0	3	1	1	1	0	0	.400	.538
Osborne, Steve, Yan.	.000	1	2	2	0	0	0	0	0	0	0	0	0	0	0	0	0	0	0	0	.000	.000
Pachot, John, Dod.	.200	1	5	5	1	1	4	1	0	1	1	0	0	0	0	0	1	0	0	0	.800	.200
Partridge, Dominique, Brav. ..	.205	26	93	83	13	17	25	2	0	2	9	1	1	2	6	0	26	3	1	1	.301	.272
Pearson, Brent, Pir.	.000	12	0	0	1	0	0	0	0	0	0	0	0	0	0	0	0	0	0	0	.000	.000
Pereyra, Joel, Roy.	.182	21	70	66	6	12	15	3	0	0	0	0	0	1	3	0	21	0	0	1	.227	.229
Perez, Josue, Phi.†	.308	10	44	39	9	12	17	3	1	0	3	0	0	0	5	0	4	3	1	2	.436	.386
Perozo, Hector, Dod.	.223	55	231	184	32	41	54	4	3	1	26	0	3	17	27	0	63	2	2	2	.293	.368
Petersen, Ryan, R.S.	.280	49	157	143	26	40	54	11	0	1	17	0	0	4	10	0	32	11	3	2	.378	.344
Pitney, Jared, Yan.*	.272	44	164	147	21	40	54	8	0	2	24	2	3	2	10	0	36	3	0	3	.367	.321
Polo, Fernando, Brav.	.203	38	128	118	13	24	36	3	0	3	13	0	0	0	10	0	33	5	2	1	.305	.266
Pospishil, Jason, Twi.†	.175	19	64	57	5	10	14	4	0	0	2	0	0	1	6	0	19	1	0	1	.246	.266
Post, Dave, Dod.	.000	1	2	2	0	0	0	0	0	0	0	0	0	0	0	0	1	0	0	0	.000	.000
Price, Jared, Dod.	.096	33	117	94	10	9	10	1	0	0	5	2	1	6	14	0	41	0	2	0	.106	.252

Player, Team	Avg.	G	TPA	AB	R	H	TB	2B	3B	HR	RBI	SH	SF	HP	BB	IBB	SO	SB	CS	GDP	Slg.	OBP
Quintin, Luis, Rang.	.042	10	28	24	0	1	2	1	0	0	2	0	0	1	3	0	11	2	1	0	.083	.179
Raburn, Ryan, Tig.	.155	19	70	58	4	9	14	2	0	1	5	0	0	3	9	1	19	2	1	0	.241	.300
Ramirez, Jordy, Reds†	.000	2	3	3	0	0	0	0	0	0	0	0	0	0	0	0	2	0	0	0	.000	.000
Ramistella, John, Yan.	.272	53	207	180	30	49	77	11	1	5	33	0	0	6	21	1	48	5	2	3	.428	.367
Ramos, Victor, Pir.*	.200	29	89	80	5	16	18	2	0	0	4	1	1	1	6	0	10	0	1	3	.225	.261
Recio, Bolivar, Pir.-Ori.	.274	35	127	113	18	31	50	9	2	2	9	4	1	3	6	1	25	1	1	5	.442	.325
Rengifo, Amado, Mar.	.308	3	14	13	4	4	4	0	0	0	0	0	0	0	1	0	2	2	2	0	.308	.357
Resop, Chris, Mar.	.116	26	96	86	5	10	12	2	0	0	5	1	1	1	7	0	34	0	3	4	.140	.189
Rethwisch, Justin, Pir.*	.193	39	142	135	11	26	34	8	0	0	11	0	1	1	5	0	41	4	1	1	.252	.225
Reyes, Milver, Pir.	.054	13	43	37	3	2	3	1	0	0	1	2	1	1	2	0	5	0	0	0	.081	.122
Rijo, Carlos, Ori.	.279	53	213	201	18	56	77	10	4	1	23	3	1	2	6	2	32	8	3	5	.383	.305
Rivas, Arturo, Ori.	.308	8	34	26	6	8	9	1	0	0	2	0	2	2	4	0	5	2	1	0	.346	.412
Rivas, Norberto, Exp.	.188	19	59	48	6	9	13	1	0	1	6	1	1	1	8	0	17	3	2	0	.271	.310
Rivera, Carlos, Phi.	.141	24	73	71	3	10	12	0	0	0	6	0	0	0	2	0	30	0	0	0	.169	.164
Rivero, Luis, Phi.	.250	38	141	128	17	32	44	7	1	1	11	2	0	2	9	0	27	4	1	4	.344	.309
Roberson, Chris, Phi.	.248	38	157	133	17	33	43	8	1	0	13	5	1	2	16	0	30	6	2	3	.323	.336
Roberts, Mike, Roy.	.000	1	4	3	0	0	0	0	0	0	0	0	0	0	1	0	1	0	0	0	.000	.250
Rodgers, Mackeel, Roy.†	.217	21	74	69	4	15	23	5	0	1	6	0	0	1	4	0	18	1	0	1	.333	.270
Rodriguez, Alexander, Roy.*	.235	50	193	166	24	39	43	4	0	0	13	2	3	3	19	0	43	8	2	1	.259	.319
Rodriguez, Carlos, Phi.†	.297	35	144	128	22	38	59	10	1	3	23	0	1	4	11	1	25	6	4	1	.461	.368
Rodriguez, Ivan, R.S.	.356	19	68	59	11	21	37	3	2	3	7	0	0	1	8	0	12	8	0	1	.627	.441
Rodriguez, John, Yan.*	.833	2	6	6	2	5	5	0	0	0	2	0	0	0	0	0	0	0	0	0	.833	.833
Rodriguez, Jose, Ori.†	.176	5	19	17	0	3	4	1	0	0	0	0	0	0	2	0	4	0	0	1	.235	.263
Rodriguez, Ronny, R.S.	.000	1	1	1	0	0	0	0	0	0	0	0	0	0	0	0	0	0	0	0	.000	.000
Rojas, Tom, Yan.	.348	25	74	66	12	23	29	6	0	0	8	0	0	1	7	1	10	2	1	1	.439	.419
Rolison, Nate, Mar.*	.500	2	7	4	1	2	2	0	0	0	1	0	0	0	3	0	1	0	0	0	.500	.714
Romano, Jason, Rang.	.143	5	22	21	2	3	3	0	0	0	0	0	0	0	1	0	8	1	0	0	.143	.182
Rosado, Francisco, Tig.	.184	34	114	98	9	18	28	4	0	2	4	0	0	3	13	0	26	2	0	2	.286	.298
Rudecindo, Carlos, Mar.	.000	3	10	9	0	0	0	0	0	0	1	0	0	0	1	0	7	0	0	0	.000	.100
Ruelas, Alonzo, Brav.	.276	47	150	134	16	37	53	10	0	2	12	0	1	3	12	0	16	6	0	3	.396	.347
Ruiz, Junior, Reds*	.289	45	184	149	31	43	53	4	3	0	12	0	0	2	33	1	17	13	3	2	.356	.424
Rush, Travis, Pir.	.244	33	98	82	4	20	30	5	1	1	5	1	0	3	12	0	16	5	2	0	.366	.361
Ryan, Billy, Tig.	.246	20	72	57	7	14	15	1	0	0	5	0	1	4	10	0	10	0	0	1	.263	.389
Salas, Jose, Brav.†	.250	3	4	4	0	1	1	0	0	0	0	0	0	0	0	0	0	0	0	0	.250	.250
Salazar, Juan, R.S.†	.248	46	181	161	23	40	42	2	0	0	12	1	1	3	15	1	12	16	7	1	.261	.322
Sanchez, Angel, Roy.	.242	30	103	95	10	23	27	4	0	0	6	2	0	0	6	0	28	3	1	2	.284	.287
Sanchez, Danilo, Tig.	.185	38	132	108	15	20	34	2	0	4	17	0	1	6	17	0	27	0	0	4	.315	.326
Sandoval, Abigail, Rang.	.207	36	117	111	14	23	33	3	2	1	9	1	1	1	3	0	20	3	2	2	.297	.233
Santa, Alexander, Yan.*	.263	52	207	179	32	47	62	1	4	2	16	2	0	3	23	1	52	10	5	0	.346	.356
Santana, Isidro, Tig.†	.357	7	31	28	6	10	12	2	0	0	1	0	0	0	2	0	6	1	0	1	.429	.400
Santana, Pedro, Yan.	.396	15	49	48	6	19	27	3	1	1	10	0	0	0	1	0	7	3	1	2	.563	.408
Santana, Roberto, Brav.*	.225	48	155	138	15	31	38	4	0	1	14	2	2	2	11	0	21	1	0	2	.275	.288
Sardinha, Bronson, Yan.*	.303	55	222	188	42	57	89	14	3	4	27	1	2	3	28	2	51	11	2	6	.473	.398
Searage, Ray, Mar.	.088	12	37	34	4	3	3	0	0	0	1	0	0	0	3	0	10	0	1	1	.088	.162
Severino, Wanell, Ori.	.304	34	134	125	21	38	43	5	0	0	16	1	1	1	6	0	17	8	5	1	.344	.338
Singer, Matt, Yan.*	.181	41	116	105	11	19	25	1	1	1	13	0	0	1	9	0	22	4	4	2	.238	.247
Smith, Brenton, Reds*	.261	47	171	138	16	36	43	7	0	0	10	2	1	8	22	0	35	11	6	4	.312	.391
Smith, Dustin, Rang.	.223	34	121	103	16	23	28	2	0	1	16	1	0	4	13	0	14	2	2	3	.272	.305
Smith, Ryan, Twi.†	.198	44	152	121	14	24	34	4	0	2	7	0	1	5	25	3	32	6	1	1	.281	.333
Smith, Sean, Pir.	.203	46	173	148	14	30	48	7	1	3	14	0	2	3	20	0	56	12	1	2	.324	.306
Spataro, Ryan, Twi.*	.208	16	53	48	4	10	10	0	0	0	2	1	1	0	3	0	16	1	1	1	.208	.250
Strong, Brian, Brav.*	.283	37	117	106	11	30	44	3	1	3	16	0	2	3	6	0	24	1	5	1	.415	.333
Suarez, Victor, Roy.†	.192	28	82	78	6	15	21	4	1	0	4	0	0	0	4	0	16	2	1	2	.269	.232
Sulbaran, Orlando, Rang.	.262	36	134	122	18	32	47	7	1	2	12	1	1	1	9	0	25	8	2	1	.385	.316
Tarbett, Brent, R.S.	.225	47	167	138	20	31	54	8	0	5	20	1	0	9	19	2	40	2	3	4	.391	.355
Taveras, Frank, Mar.	.213	28	104	89	12	19	21	2	0	0	4	0	1	2	12	0	29	6	2	0	.236	.317
Taylor, Mark, Pir.	.215	38	133	130	9	28	35	5	1	0	10	0	1	2	0	0	32	0	3	3	.269	.226
Taylor, Samuel, Twi.†	.261	35	109	92	14	24	30	1	1	1	8	1	0	3	13	0	10	8	2	3	.326	.370
Tejeda, Juan, Tig.	.295	50	186	173	17	51	73	8	1	4	37	0	0	5	8	2	32	0	0	2	.422	.344
Tejero, Armando, Brav.*	.098	20	62	51	2	5	7	2	0	0	0	0	0	0	11	0	19	1	0	0	.137	.258
Thede, Matthew, Exp.	.208	34	135	120	9	25	31	4	1	0	18	1	2	3	9	0	32	1	3	7	.258	.271
Thomas, Chuck, Dod.	.250	7	19	16	5	4	4	0	0	0	2	0	0	0	3	0	0	3	0	1	.250	.368
Thomman, John, Twi.	.203	36	89	79	7	16	24	5	0	1	10	0	0	4	6	1	30	0	2	1	.304	.292
Timaure, Jesus, Mar.	.224	44	176	156	18	35	50	12	0	1	21	0	2	8	10	0	45	3	0	2	.321	.301
Treanor, Matt, Mar.	.412	11	41	34	10	14	21	4	0	1	4	0	0	0	7	0	7	3	0	1	.618	.512
Ust, Brant, Tig.	.308	7	28	26	4	8	9	1	0	0	5	0	0	0	2	0	4	1	0	0	.346	.357
Valera, Luis, Reds	.500	14	15	12	2	6	10	1	0	1	4	0	0	0	3	0	2	0	0	0	.833	.600
Vasquez, Wuillians, Yan.†	.221	43	165	140	16	31	40	1	1	2	16	0	3	1	21	2	33	5	1	4	.286	.321
Vavao, Jason, Reds	.217	53	195	175	13	38	54	9	2	1	19	0	3	7	10	0	38	2	2	4	.309	.282
Watkins, Cedric, Roy.	.140	35	112	93	9	13	13	0	0	0	5	2	0	8	9	1	38	0	1	1	.140	.255
Webster, Robert, Ori.	.231	17	55	52	4	12	17	2	0	1	9	0	1	2	0	0	12	0	1	0	.327	.255
West, Eric, R.S.	.256	25	93	82	11	21	40	5	1	4	11	0	0	2	9	0	22	1	0	5	.488	.344
White, Dean, Brav.	.143	2	8	7	1	1	1	0	0	0	0	0	0	0	1	0	2	1	0	1	.143	.250
White, Kenneth, Ori.†	.294	49	178	160	22	47	63	11	1	1	12	3	0	3	12	1	42	5	2	1	.394	.354
Whitrock, Scott, Twi.	.171	36	116	105	11	18	22	4	0	0	6	3	0	1	7	0	40	7	2	1	.210	.230
Williams, Matt, Tig.†	.164	28	79	73	13	12	13	1	0	0	6	0	0	1	5	0	14	2	3	0	.178	.224
Williams, Mervin, Roy.*	.186	39	131	113	15	21	22	1	0	0	9	3	0	1	14	1	35	10	4	1	.195	.281
Wise, Bradley, Tig.*	.200	11	30	25	2	5	5	0	0	0	3	0	1	1	3	0	10	0	0	0	.200	.300
Woods, Ahmad, Brav.	.173	38	121	110	18	19	28	4	1	1	8	1	1	3	6	0	42	2	1	0	.255	.224
Wright, Nate, Dod.	.200	4	11	10	3	2	2	0	0	0	1	0	0	0	1	0	1	0	0	0	.200	.273
Yount, Dustin, Ori.*	.228	44	168	145	15	33	55	11	1	3	18	0	0	1	22	1	38	0	2	3	.379	.333
Zaun, Greg, Roy.†	.056	6	25	18	3	1	1	0	0	0	1	0	0	0	7	0	5	0	0	1	.056	.320

Player, Team	Avg.	G	TPA	AB	R	H	TB	2B	3B	HR	RBI	SH	SF	HP	BB	IBB	SO	SB	CS	GDP	Slg.	OBP
Recio, Bolivar, Pir.	.136	6	27	22	4	3	4	1	0	0	2	2	1	0	2	0	7	0	1	0	.182	.200
Recio, Bolivar, Ori.	.308	29	100	91	14	28	46	8	2	2	7	2	0	3	4	1	18	1	0	5	.505	.357

GRAND SLAMS: A. Bautista, Dean, V. Diaz, Gordon, Jordan, F. Molina, D. Sanchez, Sardinha, J. Tejada, Valera, 1 each.

AWARDED FIRST BASE ON CATCHER'S INTERFERENCE: Cisneros (Escobar), Dean (Pereyra), E. De los Santos (Legendre), F. Diaz (Ruelas), G. Guzman (Sulberan), Lababera (Ruelas), Manriquez (Strong), I. Santana (Legendre), Singer (Escobar).

2001 PITCHING
TEAM

Team	W	L	Pct.	ERA	G	CG	ShO	Sv.	IP	H	TBF	R	ER	HH	SH	SF	HB	BB	IBB	SO	WP	Bk.
Dodgers	41	19	.683	2.44	60	0	7	15	517.0	188	2073	171	140	14	11	11	38	149	0	442	26	4
Phillies	31	29	.517	2.77	60	0	6	9	494.0	449	2100	220	152	18	21	15	36	154	2	436	35	9
Marlins	29	31	.483	2.77	60	1	5	14	519.1	427	2181	226	160	17	25	22	66	148	3	460	46	5
Reds	36	22	.621	2.79	58	6	6	18	474.2	397	2010	185	147	6	14	13	33	176	4	477	22	6
Braves	30	30	.500	2.80	60	1	9	19	517.2	433	2185	221	161	17	18	12	35	163	3	562	43	7
Twins	32	26	.552	3.49	58	2	7	21	477.1	457	2029	224	185	17	6	8	28	176	4	434	51	4
Red Sox	37	22	.627	3.50	59	0	3	21	491.2	440	2067	217	191	18	17	20	28	176	11	440	30	5
Yankees	35	25	.583	3.66	60	3	7	16	497.0	473	2153	245	202	20	17	12	28	203	4	459	43	4
Orioles	22	34	.393	3.73	56	1	0	8	454.0	440	2022	251	188	30	19	13	49	196	17	354	36	10
Rangers...........	24	35	.407	3.77	59	3	6	9	487.1	490	2099	255	204	26	11	18	36	178	8	411	29	3
Tigers	34	26	.567	3.84	60	4	5	15	491.2	453	2155	257	210	24	16	11	33	218	4	468	44	19
Pirates	22	34	.393	3.88	56	3	5	12	449.2	444	1964	247	194	22	18	16	38	179	3	368	48	4
Royals	20	40	.333	3.99	60	1	1	10	490.0	490	2181	300	217	20	11	16	35	186	7	371	35	8
Expos	20	40	.333	4.12	60	0	9	9	515.1	535	2322	317	236	16	21	21	66	200	1	455	62	6

INDIVIDUAL
TOP QUALIFIERS FOR EARNED-RUN AVERAGE TITLE
Minimum 40 innings. *Lefthanded pitcher.

Pitcher, Team	W	L	Pct.	ERA	G	GS	CG	ShO	GF	Sv.	IP	H	TBF	R	ER	HR	SH	SF	HB	BB	IBB	SO	WP	Bk.
Petty, Chad, Tig.*	6	0	1.000	1.11	12	10	2	1	1	0	57.0	35	222	11	7	2	1	2	1	13	0	52	3	0
Ferreira, Emilo, Twi.	8	1	.889	1.20	12	10	0	0	0	0	60.0	52	233	10	8	2	0	2	0	10	0	47	3	0
Cuen, David, Dod.*	4	0	1.000	1.42	13	6	0	0	0	0	50.2	32	198	14	8	1	0	0	2	17	0	49	4	1
Rocado, Hooter, Roy.*	3	5	.375	1.73	14	6	1	0	7	2	52.0	44	222	19	10	1	1	1	1	15	2	48	3	0
Sanchez, Rafael, R.S.	5	1	.833	1.78	10	8	0	0	0	0	50.2	36	195	12	10	3	0	3	5	7	0	45	2	1
Murray, Arlington, Rang.*	3	3	.500	1.86	12	8	0	0	2	0	53.1	48	207	15	11	1	1	1	1	10	2	45	4	1
Smith, Jason, Yan.	5	2	.714	1.93	11	11	2	2	0	0	60.2	52	248	25	13	1	2	1	4	11	0	41	2	0
Acuna, Jose, Exp.	2	4	.333	1.93	14	6	0	0	3	0	51.1	41	201	13	11	2	3	0	6	11	0	45	4	0
Lopez, Javier, Dod.*	5	1	.833	2.04	14	7	0	0	3	1	61.2	40	230	20	14	2	0	2	0	12	0	45	2	0
Mata, Gustavo, Exp.	3	4	.429	2.05	10	9	0	0	0	0	48.1	44	212	27	11	0	2	1	4	13	0	38	5	0
Strayhorn, Kole, Dod.	5	3	.625	2.19	12	6	0	0	2	0	53.1	41	214	15	13	1	2	0	5	17	0	47	1	1
Davies, Kyle, Brav.	4	2	.667	2.25	12	9	1	1	1	0	56.0	47	220	17	14	2	1	0	1	8	0	53	2	0
Belizario, Ronald, Mar.	4	6	.400	2.34	13	10	1	1	0	0	73.0	62	309	29	19	4	4	3	11	20	0	54	8	1
Lopez, Gonzalo, Brav.	5	4	.556	2.45	12	11	0	0	0	0	58.2	44	230	17	16	2	3	2	3	10	0	69	3	2
Lohse, Eric, Twi.	4	3	.571	2.55	10	10	1	0	0	0	49.1	42	185	16	14	2	0	2	2	4	0	34	1	0

DEPARTMENTAL LEADERS: W—Ferreira, 8; L—E. Diaz, 7; Pct.—Ferreira, .889; G—Reina, 25; GS—Masset, 14; CG—G. Batista, Petty, J. Smith, 2 each; ShO—J. Smith, 2, GF—J. Gutierrez, 21; Sv.—J. Gutierrez, 16; IP—Belizario, 73; H—Belizario, L. Nunez, 62 each; TBF—Belizario, 309; R—E. Diaz, 42; ER—F. Diaz, 36; HR—L. Diaz, 6; SH—Squires, 5; SF—Several players tied at 4; HB—E. Diaz, 15; BB—Cabrera, 39; IBB—Sala, Huang, 4 each; SO—L. Diaz, 71; WP—J. Figueroa, 12; BK—J. Figueroa, 5.

ALL PITCHERS
*Lefthanded pitcher.

Pitcher, Team	W	L	Pct.	ERA	G	GS	CG	ShO	GF	Sv.	IP	H	TBF	R	ER	HR	SH	SF	HB	BB	IBB	SO	WP	Bk.
Abbott, Jim, Twi.	0	0	.000	5.40	2	0	0	0	1	0	1.2	1	8	1	1	0	0	0	2	0	1	0	0
Acuna, Jose, Exp.	2	4	.333	1.93	14	6	0	0	3	0	51.1	41	201	13	11	2	3	0	6	11	0	45	4	0
Aguilar, Ray, Brav.*	3	1	.750	1.50	7	5	0	0	1	0	30.0	18	115	5	5	1	1	0	0	6	0	42	2	0
Aguilera, Adrian, Dod.*	0	0	.000	7.71	4	0	0	0	0	0	4.2	2	22	4	4	1	1	1	0	3	0	6	0	0
Akens, Phil, Mar.	2	0	1.000	1.60	6	3	0	0	2	0	33.2	19	134	11	6	0	2	2	4	9	0	24	2	0
Albaladejo, Jonathan, Pir.	0	3	.000	4.74	10	2	0	0	5	1	19.0	22	85	13	10	1	2	3	1	2	0	24	2	0
Almeida, Brian, Brav.	0	0	.000	2.25	2	0	0	0	0	0	4.0	2	17	1	1	0	1	0	1	2	0	3	0	0
Almonte, Henry, Pir.	1	0	1.000	2.70	2	1	0	0	0	0	10.0	11	41	4	3	1	0	0	1	1	1	0	2	0
Alvarez, Juan, Brav.*	3	1	.750	1.73	11	6	0	0	1	0	41.2	36	177	15	8	0	1	0	1	13	0	39	5	0
Alvarez, Melvin, Pir.*	1	4	.200	4.00	7	3	0	0	1	0	27.0	34	118	16	12	0	2	4	0	7	0	16	1	0
Andara, Miguel, Pir.	0	4	.000	3.62	8	3	0	0	3	0	32.1	28	143	18	13	0	1	1	4	20	1	20	4	0
Anderson, Wes, Mar.	0	1	.000	27.00	1	1	0	0	0	0	0.1	3	6	2	1	1	0	0	0	1	0	0	0	0
Andrews, Aron, Dod.	0	0	.000	0.00	6	0	0	0	5	0	7.1	2	25	0	0	0	0	0	1	0	0	9	0	0
Arteaga, Erick, Phi.	4	1	.800	3.63	10	5	0	0	2	0	52.0	58	219	28	21	0	1	0	2	7	0	28	1	0
Arteaga, Francisco, Brav.	0	1	.000	2.41	18	0	0	0	14	5	33.2	20	140	13	9	1	0	1	3	13	0	30	0	2
Artiles, Carlos, Yan.*	1	3	.250	3.72	10	5	0	0	1	1	36.1	41	159	15	15	1	2	1	12	0	37	3	1
Astacio, Ezequiel, Phi.	4	2	.667	2.30	9	9	0	0	0	0	47.0	48	196	16	12	2	2	1	4	10	0	42	1	0
Baker, Bo, Roy.	0	0	.000	0.00	1	0	0	0	0	0	2.0	2	6	0	0	0	0	0	0	0	0	1	0	0
Bale, John, Ori.*	0	0	.000	2.25	2	2	0	0	0	0	4.0	1	14	1	1	0	1	0	0	2	0	7	1	0
Banks, Tyler, Mar.	0	2	.000	2.30	10	2	0	0	4	1	31.1	24	124	9	8	2	2	0	0	6	1	26	1	0
Barrios, Rafael, Tig.	3	3	.500	2.14	23	0	0	0	18	6	33.2	24	144	12	8	1	4	1	2	17	3	29	2	2
Bartel, Richard, Reds	0	0	.000	0.00	1	0	0	0	0	0	1.0	0	3	0	0	0	0	0	0	1	0	0	0	0
Bartsch, John, Ori.	2	1	.667	4.00	10	0	0	0	5	0	18.0	19	73	8	8	4	0	0	2	1	0	10	2	0

Pitcher, Team	W	L	Pct.	ERA	G	GS	CG	ShO	GF	Sv.	IP	H	TBF	R	ER	HR	SH	SF	HB	BB	IBB	SO	WP	Bk.
Batista, Gorky, Reds	5	3	.625	2.77	10	8	2	1	1	1	52.0	55	220	18	16	0	1	1	1	10	0	53	1	1
Baxter, Allen, Mar.	2	3	.400	2.38	9	7	0	0	0	0	34.0	25	138	13	9	0	1	3	5	8	0	40	4	0
Bedard, Erik, Ori.*	0	1	.000	3.00	2	2	0	0	0	0	6.0	4	25	2	2	0	0	0	2	3	0	7	0	0
Beigh, David, Pir.	0	5	.000	6.46	10	7	0	0	1	0	30.2	30	149	28	22	0	0	0	5	28	0	24	10	1
Belizario, Ronald, Mar.	4	6	.400	2.34	13	10	1	1	0	0	73.0	62	309	29	19	4	4	3	11	20	0	54	8	1
Birk, Ben, Mar.*	0	0	.000	0.00	3	0	0	0	1	0	6.0	3	22	0	0	0	0	0	0	1	0	4	0	0
Birkins, Kurt, Ori.*	2	1	.667	2.05	5	4	0	0	1	0	22.0	13	85	5	5	2	0	0	4	3	0	24	1	0
Blake, Peter, Twi.*	0	1	.000	3.52	6	0	0	0	1	0	7.2	5	26	3	3	0	0	0	1	1	0	7	0	0
Blaney, Matthew, Dod.	1	3	.250	9.56	11	0	0	0	8	1	16.0	21	75	17	17	2	0	0	8	5	0	8	2	0
Bostick, Adam, Mar.*	1	1	.500	4.26	7	1	0	0	0	0	12.2	16	57	8	6	0	0	1	0	3	0	13	2	0
Brandon, Keith, Tig.	2	0	1.000	5.67	19	0	0	0	5	0	33.1	44	162	28	21	1	1	0	0	20	0	35	2	2
Brannon, Nick, Reds*	1	2	.333	0.42	17	0	0	0	17	10	21.1	13	88	4	1	0	1	0	0	9	2	25	0	0
Brewington, Jamie, Twi.	0	0	.000	0.00	4	0	0	0	0	0	6.2	4	25	0	0	0	0	0	0	1	0	8	0	0
Bridges, Donnie, Exp.	0	1	.000	8.44	2	2	0	0	0	0	5.1	2	25	6	5	0	0	0	1	5	0	9	3	0
Britton, Chris, Ori.	2	3	.400	2.76	12	3	0	0	2	0	32.2	35	153	20	10	3	2	2	5	12	1	20	1	0
Brown, Ira, Roy.	2	5	.286	4.99	11	10	0	0	0	0	39.2	40	186	27	22	2	0	1	2	25	0	42	5	0
Bunch, J.C., Rang.	0	0	.000	0.00	1	0	0	0	1	0	1.0	0	3	0	0	0	0	0	0	0	0	0	0	0
Burnette, Weston, Reds	2	1	.667	8.49	10	0	0	0	3	0	11.2	13	54	13	11	0	0	0	1	5	0	17	1	0
Burzynski, Cole, Pir.	1	2	.333	6.46	7	5	0	0	0	0	23.2	26	119	19	17	5	1	1	1	23	0	28	3	0
Butto, Francisco, Phi.	2	3	.400	2.42	15	0	0	0	6	2	26.0	22	109	10	7	1	0	1	1	12	1	20	1	0
Cabrera, Carlos, Phi.	2	2	.500	2.91	10	8	0	0	0	0	43.1	35	194	23	14	2	2	3	7	23	0	40	6	3
Cabrera, Daniel, Ori.	2	3	.400	5.53	12	7	0	0	0	0	40.2	31	188	29	25	1	0	0	5	39	2	36	2	0
Campbell, Andrew, Rang.*	2	2	.500	4.56	14	0	0	0	13	5	23.2	25	105	15	12	2	1	0	3	9	1	11	3	0
Carlson, Steve, Yan.*	2	2	.500	1.15	21	0	0	0	12	3	31.1	19	122	7	4	0	1	1	0	12	0	41	1	0
Carrasco, Edelyn, Twi.	3	4	.429	3.51	14	9	1	1	1	0	51.1	49	215	26	20	3	0	0	3	15	0	45	2	1
Carter, Justin, Reds*	1	0	1.000	0.61	4	4	1	0	0	0	14.2	9	61	3	1	0	0	0	0	6	0	20	3	1
Carter, Ramsey, Roy.	2	0	1.000	1.69	9	0	0	0	5	2	16.0	13	65	5	3	0	2	1	1	5	0	15	0	0
Coffey, Todd, Reds	0	1	.000	4.26	3	2	0	0	0	0	12.2	11	55	11	6	1	1	1	1	5	0	15	0	0
Connolly, Jon, Tig.*	1	1	.500	3.82	8	6	0	0	0	0	35.1	30	147	16	15	0	2	2	1	10	1	23	2	0
Cooper, Dexter, Brav.	2	1	.667	4.66	12	1	0	0	3	0	19.1	18	97	19	10	1	0	1	2	18	0	21	5	0
Coppinger, Joe, Ori.	2	4	.333	5.85	11	8	0	0	1	0	40.0	53	205	37	26	3	2	0	7	17	1	28	5	1
Corcoran, Roy, Exp.	2	0	1.000	1.56	13	0	0	0	9	2	17.1	12	69	4	3	2	0	0	2	2	0	21	0	0
Crawford, Tristan, Twi.	0	0	.000	2.20	13	0	0	0	6	3	16.1	15	74	5	4	0	0	0	2	6	0	19	2	0
Cristobal, Luis, Rang.	0	1	.000	4.24	11	4	0	0	4	0	34.0	34	150	20	16	1	1	0	2	20	0	35	1	0
Crump, Joel, Ori.*	1	0	1.000	2.35	7	0	0	0	3	0	15.1	15	70	5	4	0	0	0	2	12	0	11	4	0
Cuello, Manolin, Tig.	0	0	.000	0.00	1	0	0	0	1	0	0.2	1	3	0	0	0	1	0	0	0	0	1	0	0
Cuen, David, Dod.*	4	0	1.000	1.42	13	6	0	0	0	0	50.2	32	198	14	8	1	0	0	2	17	0	49	4	1
Culp, Brandon, Reds	1	1	.500	1.59	6	4	0	0	1	0	28.1	23	117	6	5	0	1	0	1	13	0	33	0	1
Davies, Kyle, Brav.	4	2	.667	2.25	12	9	1	1	1	0	56.0	47	220	17	14	2	1	0	1	8	0	53	2	0
Davis, Lance, Mar.	2	1	.667	3.19	14	3	0	0	4	1	31.0	33	131	15	11	0	3	2	5	4	0	26	2	0
Dawson, Carl, Phi.	3	3	.500	2.08	10	8	0	0	1	1	47.2	42	196	20	11	2	0	0	1	5	0	51	4	1
DeChristofaro, Vinny, Phi.*	1	2	.333	2.17	9	9	0	0	0	0	37.1	32	156	12	9	0	1	0	0	14	0	33	3	0
Dejesus, Elvis, Mar.	0	4	.000	5.18	13	7	0	0	4	2	41.2	49	193	35	24	2	1	1	7	12	0	33	5	1
Delcarmen, Manny, R.S.	4	2	.667	2.54	11	8	0	0	2	1	46.0	35	195	16	13	0	2	1	7	19	0	62	2	0
Devenney, Nicholas, Rang.	0	1	.000	9.30	17	0	0	0	11	1	20.1	35	114	28	21	2	0	2	1	20	0	14	6	0
Deza, Fredy, Ori.	1	4	.200	3.14	9	7	1	0	0	0	48.2	49	210	26	17	3	2	4	2	15	2	42	2	1
Diaz, Eddie, Exp.	1	7	.125	10.34	13	6	0	0	0	0	31.1	33	167	42	36	0	1	1	15	27	0	30	5	0
Diaz, Luis, Tig.	2	4	.333	4.39	13	10	0	0	2	0	55.1	53	241	30	27	6	0	3	4	27	0	71	6	0
Dominguez, Jose, Rang.	4	2	.667	4.01	11	9	1	1	0	0	58.1	56	243	29	26	4	0	2	5	12	0	55	0	1
Dominguez, Raul, Yan.*	1	0	1.000	5.59	12	0	0	0	0	0	19.1	21	90	13	12	2	1	0	1	13	0	20	3	1
Dossett, William, Roy.	2	2	.500	2.20	8	0	0	0	6	0	16.1	11	59	5	4	0	0	1	1	0	0	11	0	0
Douglas, Rod, Brav.	0	2	.000	7.71	4	0	0	0	2	0	7.0	8	35	6	6	0	0	0	0	7	0	9	0	0
Douglass, Ryan, Roy.	0	0	.000	0.00	2	1	0	0	0	0	2.0	0	6	0	0	0	0	0	0	0	0	2	0	0
Dumatrait, Phillip, R.S.*	3	0	1.000	2.76	8	8	0	0	0	0	32.2	27	128	10	10	0	1	0	0	9	0	33	1	0
Dunn, Gerald, Tig.	2	4	.333	3.50	12	8	1	0	3	2	54.0	47	232	26	21	1	0	0	6	20	0	46	4	4
Engels, Jackson, Rang.*	2	2	.500	2.22	10	0	0	0	7	0	28.1	21	120	8	7	1	1	0	6	15	2	11	1	0
Escobedo, Edgar, Dod.	4	1	.800	1.66	17	4	0	0	0	0	43.1	42	175	9	8	1	0	0	3	9	0	24	3	0
Espaillat, Ezequiel, Mar.	0	0	.000	5.06	15	0	0	0	9	3	32.0	34	145	22	18	2	1	3	8	10	0	23	1	0
Evans, Louis, Mar.*	3	3	.500	2.16	14	0	0	0	8	0	25.0	18	109	10	6	0	4	1	4	12	2	26	3	1
Ewin, Ryan, Brav.	0	0	.000	9.00	1	0	0	0	0	0	2.0	4	11	2	2	0	0	0	0	1	0	4	0	0
Farley, Chris, R.S.	0	1	.000	16.62	3	2	0	0	0	0	4.1	8	28	8	8	0	1	0	0	8	0	3	0	0
Ferreira, Emilo, Twi.	8	1	.889	1.20	12	10	0	0	0	0	60.0	52	233	10	8	2	0	0	2	10	0	47	3	0
Figueroa, Juan, Tig.	1	4	.200	4.66	17	4	0	0	2	0	38.2	33	182	28	20	0	1	1	4	30	2	41	12	5
Figueroa, Williams, Exp.	1	2	.333	4.67	12	0	0	0	3	0	17.1	9	79	10	9	1	0	2	0	19	0	13	6	2
Frawley, Patrick, Mar.	0	1	.000	4.05	6	0	0	0	4	0	6.2	5	30	4	3	0	1	0	1	2	0	6	3	0
Frost, Clint, Roy.	0	1	.000	3.18	4	2	0	0	1	0	17.0	14	67	6	6	0	0	0	0	3	0	15	1	0
Furnald, Donnie, Brav.	0	0	.000	1.13	4	0	0	0	3	3	8.0	3	25	1	1	1	0	0	0	1	0	7	1	0
Gabbard, Kason, R.S.*	0	1	.000	5.65	6	6	0	0	0	0	14.1	11	65	11	9	1	0	2	1	9	0	17	3	0
Galarraga, Armando, Exp.	1	3	.250	3.12	14	1	0	0	5	2	34.2	37	157	21	12	2	2	2	3	15	1	24	3	1
Garcia, Angel, Twi.	0	3	.000	5.60	9	6	0	0	1	0	17.2	20	84	15	11	0	1	1	0	12	0	22	2	1
George, Brad, Reds	6	1	.857	1.29	7	7	0	0	0	0	42.0	33	174	7	6	0	1	2	2	14	0	33	0	2
George, Todd, Exp.	0	0	.000	2.70	8	0	0	0	5	1	10.0	8	44	3	3	1	0	0	3	3	0	13	0	0
Gil, Dave, Reds	0	2	.000	7.36	4	4	0	0	0	0	11.0	19	61	15	9	1	1	1	2	6	0	14	0	0
Gillman, Justin, Reds	4	2	.667	1.75	9	7	0	0	1	0	36.0	19	136	10	7	1	0	1	2	11	0	38	2	0
Gomez, Jose, Reds	0	1	.000	1.42	14	0	0	0	6	1	31.2	24	127	7	5	0	0	2	4	6	0	27	1	0
Gomez, Warmar, Exp.	0	1	.000	7.89	18	0	0	0	7	1	21.2	32	103	22	19	5	0	1	1	5	0	14	2	0
Gonzalez, Jose, R.S.	0	0	.000	0.00	1	0	0	0	0	0	2.0	0	7	0	0	0	1	0	0	2	0	0	0	0
Gonzalez, Luis, Dod.*	4	2	.667	3.55	13	2	0	0	0	0	25.1	25	117	15	10	0	0	1	1	14	0	25	2	0
Gooding, Jason, Roy.*	0	1	.000	18.00	1	1	0	0	0	0	1.0	3	6	2	2	0	0	0	0	0	0	0	0	0
Grabow, John, Pir.*	0	1	.000	3.75	6	6	0	0	0	0	12.0	11	50	6	5	1	0	0	1	4	0	9	2	0
Graves, Robert, Tig.*	2	0	1.000	0.83	9	1	0	0	2	0	21.2	13	81	5	2	1	0	0	2	6	0	31	0	0
Grilli, Jason, Mar.	0	0	.000	0.00	2	2	0	0	0	0	4.0	2	15	0	0	0	0	0	1	0	0	6	0	0
Griswold, Jordan, Exp.*	1	0	1.000	2.48	16	0	0	0	3	0	29.0	31	133	13	8	0	2	4	3	16	0	22	0	0

Pitcher, Team	W	L	Pct.	ERA	G	GS	CG	ShO	GF	Sv.	IP	H	TBF	R	ER	HR	SH	SF	HB	BB	IBB	SO	WP	Bk.
Guerrero, Jorge, Mar.	1	0	1.000	0.00	1	0	0	0	1	0	1.0	0	3	0	0	0	0	0	0	1	0	1	0	0
Guerrero, Julio, Pir.	0	0	.000	2.84	3	2	0	0	0	0	6.1	5	23	2	2	0	0	0	1	0	0	6	2	0
Guerrero, Thomas, Exp.	3	2	.600	5.46	19	0	0	0	14	3	28.0	31	126	21	17	1	1	0	2	7	0	37	4	0
Gutierrez, Jannio, Twi.	0	0	.000	0.31	23	0	0	0	21	16	28.2	11	110	2	1	0	1	1	0	13	2	48	0	0
Hall, Shane, R.S.	1	1	.500	2.89	4	0	0	0	1	1	9.1	6	48	3	3	0	2	0	3	10	2	10	3	1
Hampton, Royce, Rang.*	2	2	.500	4.19	12	4	0	0	3	1	43.0	38	182	23	20	3	2	3	0	15	1	29	2	0
Henkel, Robert, Mar.*	1	3	.250	1.52	9	8	0	0	0	0	29.2	17	121	9	5	0	0	0	1	11	0	38	4	0
Herrera, Junior, Tig.	0	0	.000	7.53	18	3	0	0	13	7	28.2	44	149	30	24	3	2	0	3	13	2	19	5	0
Hickman, Ben, Mar.	0	0	.000	1.42	5	0	0	0	2	0	6.1	6	25	1	1	0	2	1	0	1	0	6	0	0
Hill, Joshua, Twi.	2	2	.500	3.63	12	0	0	0	4	0	17.1	15	74	8	7	2	0	0	3	8	0	17	6	0
Hill, Terry, R.S.*	2	0	1.000	1.23	3	0	0	0	0	0	7.1	2	25	1	1	0	0	1	0	0	1	11	0	0
Hinckley, Michael, Exp.*	2	2	.500	5.24	8	5	0	0	0	0	34.1	46	158	23	20	1	1	2	3	12	0	28	6	1
Holdzkom, Lincoln, Mar.	1	3	.250	2.49	12	7	0	0	3	2	43.1	26	188	18	12	0	3	2	8	27	0	43	4	1
Hollis, Barton, R.S.	0	1	1.000	8.38	7	0	0	0	3	2	9.2	17	52	10	9	0	0	1	0	8	0	5	0	0
Huang, Jun-chung, R.S.	0	0	.000	3.65	10	0	0	0	10	3	12.1	14	60	5	5	0	2	0	0	10	4	15	2	0
Hughes, Nial, Dod.*	1	0	1.000	1.80	2	2	0	0	0	0	10.0	5	38	2	2	0	0	0	1	4	0	10	1	0
Imotichey, Tory, Exp.*	1	5	.167	3.12	10	8	0	0	0	0	40.1	39	184	23	14	0	1	4	7	16	0	32	4	0
Jackson, Edwin, Dod.	2	1	.667	2.45	12	2	0	0	1	0	22.0	14	106	12	6	1	3	0	3	19	0	23	2	0
Jacob, Russell, R.S.	1	1	.500	4.85	5	0	0	0	2	0	13.0	14	56	7	7	1	0	2	1	4	0	7	0	0
Jimenez, Kelvin, Rang.	3	3	.500	2.56	9	6	1	1	1	1	45.2	36	183	19	13	2	1	3	2	9	0	51	2	0
Johansen, Ryan, Dod.	6	2	.750	2.43	21	0	0	0	16	2	37.0	26	140	10	10	2	2	2	2	6	0	39	2	1
Johnson, James, Ori.	0	1	.000	3.86	7	4	0	0	0	0	18.2	17	81	10	8	3	1	0	2	7	1	19	1	0
Johnston, Clint, Pir.*	0	0	.000	0.00	2	2	0	0	0	0	3.0	1	10	0	0	0	0	0	0	1	0	4	0	0
Joyce, Thomas, Ori.*	0	0	.000	0.00	1	0	0	0	1	0	1.0	1	4	0	0	0	0	0	0	1	0	1	0	0
Kaanoi, Jason, Roy.	2	5	.286	5.87	14	3	0	0	3	1	38.1	40	172	29	25	3	1	3	6	8	0	24	2	1
Kennard, Jeff, Yan.	1	1	.500	1.52	19	0	0	0	16	9	23.2	17	100	4	4	0	0	1	3	10	1	30	3	0
Kennedy, Jodie, R.S.*	0	0	.000	1.80	3	0	0	0	3	2	5.0	3	17	2	1	0	0	0	0	0	0	6	0	0
Kiley, Jason, Pir.	1	2	.333	9.18	8	1	0	0	3	0	16.2	29	86	20	17	2	1	0	4	10	0	9	3	0
King, Jeremy, Yan.	5	2	.714	4.44	11	9	0	0	1	0	48.2	50	214	26	24	0	1	4	4	26	0	40	4	0
Kirkman, Tyler, Exp.*	0	0	.000	11.57	2	0	0	0	0	0	2.1	6	13	3	3	0	0	0	0	1	0	1	0	0
Kuo, Hong-chih, Dod.*	0	0	.000	2.33	7	6	0	0	0	0	19.1	13	78	5	5	0	0	0	2	4	0	21	0	0
Lababera, Michael, Exp.	0	0	.000	0.00	1	0	0	0	1	0	0.2	1	3	0	0	0	0	0	0	0	0	0	0	0
Lammers, Kris, Phi.*	0	1	.000	3.63	12	1	0	0	2	0	22.1	23	97	12	9	1	2	0	2	9	0	25	3	1
Landaeta, Argenis, Yan.	6	1	.857	2.40	10	7	0	0	3	0	45.0	35	186	17	12	2	0	1	4	15	0	42	1	0
Lara, Nelson, Reds	0	0	.000	2.16	4	1	0	0	0	0	8.1	2	32	2	2	0	0	0	1	4	0	9	0	0
Leach, Bryan, R.S.	2	0	1.000	2.16	5	0	0	0	4	2	8.1	6	31	2	2	0	0	0	1	0	0	10	1	0
Lee, Kevin, Pir.	2	2	.500	2.08	9	0	0	0	6	0	21.2	16	89	6	5	1	0	0	3	7	0	23	1	0
Lee, Seung, Phi.	1	0	1.000	3.00	3	3	0	0	0	0	9.0	12	42	7	3	1	1	0	0	4	0	4	0	0
Lerew, Anthony, Brav.	1	2	.333	2.92	12	7	0	0	1	0	49.1	43	205	25	16	3	0	1	0	14	0	40	4	2
Levinski, Donald, Exp.	0	0	.000	3.46	3	3	0	0	0	0	13.0	15	58	5	5	1	1	0	0	7	0	15	1	0
Lewis, Rommie, Ori.*	1	1	.500	2.14	10	7	0	0	1	0	33.2	37	144	16	8	3	1	1	2	6	0	27	2	1
Light, Scott, Reds	1	1	.500	3.41	8	7	0	0	0	0	29.0	23	128	12	11	0	2	1	3	15	0	30	3	1
Lissir, Alexander, Pir.	2	0	1.000	0.66	6	0	0	0	3	1	13.2	13	63	5	1	1	0	0	0	6	0	18	1	0
Lohse, Eric, Twi.	4	3	.571	2.55	10	10	1	0	0	0	49.1	42	195	16	14	2	0	2	2	4	0	34	1	0
Long, Nick, Exp.	1	1	.500	3.32	4	3	0	0	0	0	19.0	24	83	8	7	0	2	3	4	0	0	12	2	0
Lopez, Gonzalo, Brav.	5	4	.556	2.45	12	11	0	0	0	0	58.2	44	230	17	16	2	3	2	3	10	0	69	3	2
Lopez, Javier, Dod.*	5	1	.833	2.04	14	7	0	0	3	1	61.2	46	230	20	14	2	0	2	0	12	0	45	2	0
Lopez, Samuel, Roy.	0	0	.000	5.40	3	0	0	0	1	0	5.0	6	28	4	3	0	0	1	5	0	0	5	0	0
Lorenzen, Jonathan, Dod.	2	1	.667	1.77	7	1	0	0	2	0	20.1	18	84	5	4	0	0	1	3	5	0	19	1	0
Lowery, Devon, Roy.	2	3	.400	4.17	11	6	0	0	4	1	41.0	38	178	25	19	2	0	3	2	12	0	19	3	0
Lundgren, Wayne, R.S.	4	2	.667	5.31	13	1	0	0	7	2	42.1	48	184	26	25	3	3	0	1	15	2	20	2	0
Lutz, Kenneth, Reds	1	1	.500	4.96	6	3	0	0	0	0	16.1	20	82	10	9	0	0	3	13	0	0	10	1	0
Lyons, Thomas, Tig.	1	0	1.000	6.43	5	3	0	0	0	0	14.0	17	67	11	10	0	0	1	5	0	0	22	0	0
Machen, Mike, Brav.	2	2	.500	4.85	13	0	0	0	4	0	26.0	25	124	17	14	2	1	2	8	10	0	30	2	0
Marcano, Luis, Rang.	0	1	.000	9.00	3	2	0	0	0	0	10.0	16	50	10	10	1	0	1	2	5	0	10	2	0
Marietta, Ron, Yan.*	0	0	.000	2.70	2	0	0	0	1	0	3.1	1	12	1	1	0	0	0	1	0	0	5	2	0
Mason, Robert, Brav.*	3	3	.500	2.41	14	0	0	0	4	1	33.2	28	146	16	9	2	3	1	4	10	1	34	2	0
Masset, Nicholas, Rang.	0	6	.000	4.35	15	14	0	0	0	0	31.0	34	131	21	15	2	0	1	2	7	0	32	1	0
Mata, Gustavo, Exp.	3	4	.429	2.05	10	9	0	0	0	0	48.1	44	212	27	11	0	2	1	4	13	0	38	5	0
Mateo, Aneudis, R.S.	0	1	.000	0.00	3	2	0	0	0	0	7.2	6	30	4	0	0	0	0	0	6	1	1	1	0
Mathiesen, Ryan, Brav.	0	2	.000	3.00	22	0	0	0	19	10	27.0	25	114	9	9	1	0	4	5	0	0	38	4	0
Mau, Ryan, Mar.	1	0	1.000	0.90	4	0	0	0	3	0	10.0	6	38	1	1	0	0	1	3	0	0	6	1	0
McBride, Macay, Brav.*	4	4	.500	3.76	13	11	0	0	0	0	55.0	51	237	30	23	0	2	2	4	23	1	67	8	0
McCall, Dan, Phi.*	5	3	.625	2.43	16	0	0	0	7	2	33.1	23	135	13	9	2	1	1	0	11	1	34	3	0
McClendon, Matt, Brav.	0	0	.000	1.35	3	3	0	0	0	0	6.2	3	33	2	1	0	0	0	10	0	0	15	3	0
McGlinchy, Kevin, Brav.	0	0	.000	0.00	2	2	0	0	0	0	2.0	1	7	0	0	0	0	0	1	0	0	2	0	0
Meisenheimer, Matt, Rang.	3	3	.500	5.56	15	0	0	0	6	1	34.0	49	161	22	21	1	1	0	4	18	2	30	5	1
Mendoza, Cristian, Yan.	0	0	.000	5.06	3	0	0	0	2	0	5.1	5	25	3	3	0	2	0	2	2	0	8	0	0
Mendoza, Jorge, Rang.	5	5	.500	4.50	11	6	1	0	4	0	52.0	51	220	29	26	5	1	1	2	17	0	51	1	0
Metzger, Jon, Roy.*	0	0	.000	4.00	6	5	0	0	0	0	9.0	9	41	5	4	0	0	0	4	0	0	11	0	1
Meyer, Scott, Reds*	5	2	.714	1.78	14	0	0	0	8	3	30.1	24	129	7	6	0	3	0	1	13	2	34	0	0
Mims, Brandon, R.S.*	1	2	.333	4.09	11	6	0	0	3	1	50.2	56	215	25	23	3	2	4	0	14	0	34	3	0
Mitchell, Andy, Ori.	4	2	.667	2.55	12	0	0	0	11	2	24.2	18	103	10	7	1	2	0	3	10	3	21	1	1
Montero, Jose, Rang.	0	0	.000	1.29	5	1	0	0	4	0	7.0	4	29	1	1	1	1	1	0	6	0	6	0	0
Morel, Jhosandy, Pir.*	0	0	.000	1.93	6	0	0	0	4	0	9.1	7	41	2	2	1	0	0	1	5	0	12	1	0
Moreno, Victor, Phi.	4	2	.667	1.69	15	0	0	0	14	0	26.2	21	109	9	5	3	0	0	1	6	0	25	1	0
Morrison, Robbie, Roy.	0	0	.000	0.00	2	2	0	0	0	0	2.0	1	7	0	0	0	0	0	0	2	0	0	0	0
Moser, Todd, Mar.*	0	0	.000	9.00	1	1	0	0	0	0	2.0	2	8	2	2	0	0	0	0	0	0	3	0	0
Mosley, Eric, Yan.	4	1	.800	1.62	6	6	0	0	0	0	33.1	28	134	8	6	2	1	0	9	9	0	21	2	0
Murray, Arlington, Rang.*	3	3	.500	1.86	12	8	0	0	2	0	53.1	48	207	15	11	1	1	1	10	2	0	45	4	1
Mutch, Paul, Twi.	1	0	1.000	8.39	17	1	0	0	5	0	24.2	35	125	28	23	0	0	1	3	15	0	14	7	0
Nall, T.J., Dod.	0	0	.000	4.50	4	4	0	0	0	0	12.0	14	53	6	6	0	0	1	0	5	0	10	0	0
Nelson, Justin, Roy.*	1	6	.143	4.35	12	10	0	0	0	0	39.1	49	189	33	19	1	0	0	0	21	0	31	6	1

Pitcher, Team	W	L	Pct.	ERA	G	GS	CG	ShO	GF	Sv.	IP	H	TBF	R	ER	HR	SH	SF	HB	BB	IBB	SO	WP	Bk.
Nelson, Stephen, Dod.	1	2	.333	2.17	10	6	0	0	0	0	29.0	19	112	9	7	0	1	1	1	4	0	26	1	0
Nettles, Tim, Yan.	0	0	.000	5.40	3	0	0	0	2	0	3.1	6	20	3	2	0	0	0	0	2	0	2	0	1
Neuage, Leigh, Dod.	0	0	.000	1.59	3	2	0	0	0	0	5.2	2	21	1	1	0	0	0	0	3	0	3	0	0
Newell, Mark, Roy.	0	1	.000	12.27	5	0	0	0	1	0	7.1	12	52	18	10	0	0	1	5	13	0	4	5	0
Newton, Stan, Yan.	2	2	.500	3.24	19	0	0	0	8	1	33.1	38	154	14	12	0	4	0	0	13	1	34	5	0
Niedbalski, Nick, Twi.*	2	2	.500	4.24	14	8	0	0	1	0	46.2	44	196	25	22	1	1	0	1	16	0	41	5	0
Nunez, Kelvin, Roy.	3	1	.750	4.50	19	0	0	0	9	2	48.0	49	217	33	24	3	1	1	2	24	2	25	5	3
Nunez, Leo, Pir.	2	2	.500	4.39	10	7	1	1	0	0	53.1	62	236	28	26	4	3	3	3	9	0	34	4	0
Nunez, Renny, Reds	0	0	.000	4.67	8	0	0	0	4	0	17.1	18	79	11	9	2	0	1	1	6	0	12	3	0
Oquendo, Ian, Pir.	3	0	1.000	0.47	3	3	0	0	0	0	19.0	12	71	2	1	0	1	0	0	5	0	13	0	0
Ortiz, Javier, Yan.	0	0	.000	0.00	2	0	0	0	1	0	4.0	1	13	0	0	0	0	0	0	1	0	2	0	0
Owens, Henry, Pir.	1	0	1.000	1.29	6	0	0	0	5	1	7.0	5	28	1	1	0	0	0	0	2	0	8	0	0
Padilla, Roy, Mar.*	0	0	.000	0.00	4	0	0	0	1	1	6.0	1	20	1	0	0	1	0	1	0	0	6	0	1
Paz, Jackson, Brav.*	2	1	.667	3.58	12	0	0	0	4	0	32.2	40	148	19	13	1	2	1	1	7	1	31	1	0
Pearson, Brent, Pir.	0	2	.000	1.35	11	0	0	0	11	7	13.1	8	61	4	2	0	1	0	2	8	1	15	1	0
Pena, Geronimo, Exp.	1	3	.250	3.93	17	0	0	0	8	0	36.2	42	157	22	16	2	3	1	3	8	0	29	1	1
Perez, Carlos, Ori.*	1	1	.500	5.46	14	0	0	0	6	0	29.2	29	139	22	18	1	2	0	2	17	1	29	7	3
Petty, Chad, Tig.*	6	0	1.000	1.11	12	10	2	1	1	0	57.0	35	222	11	7	2	1	2	1	13	0	52	3	0
Puello, Ignacio, Exp.	1	3	.250	2.06	8	8	0	0	0	0	35.0	28	148	11	8	0	0	7	10	0	37	3	1
Purcell, Brian, Pir.*	2	0	1.000	4.41	9	0	0	0	3	1	16.1	17	74	10	8	1	0	1	1	6	0	15	2	0
Pylate, Chad, Twi.	1	1	.500	3.44	10	3	0	0	3	0	18.1	18	86	9	7	0	0	1	2	14	0	12	5	0
Rada, Gerald, Yan.	0	1	.000	8.27	8	1	0	0	2	0	16.1	20	71	16	15	4	0	0	0	5	0	21	0	0
Rahrer, Josh, Rang.	0	1	.000	3.00	5	0	0	0	4	0	6.0	9	29	4	2	0	0	2	0	1	0	8	0	0
Ramirez, Jordy, Reds	0	0	.000	0.00	1	0	0	0	1	0	0.2	2	4	0	0	0	0	0	0	0	0	0	0	0
Ramos, Victor, Pir.	0	0	.000	9.00	1	0	0	0	1	0	1.0	3	6	1	1	0	0	0	0	1	0	0	0	0
Reames, Jay, Exp.	0	0	.000	4.91	3	0	0	0	0	0	3.2	4	18	2	2	0	0	1	2	0	7	2	1
Reina, Dimas, Dod.	3	1	.750	1.30	25	0	0	0	20	8	41.2	34	167	6	6	0	2	0	5	6	0	35	1	0
Rengifo, Nohemar, Exp.	0	2	.000	5.87	14	0	0	0	4	0	30.2	38	148	30	20	0	3	1	3	13	0	28	4	0
Reyes, Maximo, Phi.	1	0	.000	2.42	17	0	0	0	13	2	26.0	16	105	9	7	2	0	2	7	0	33	2	2
Reynolds, Eric, Yan.*	1	3	.250	6.91	11	0	0	0	4	2	27.1	35	126	23	21	2	0	2	1	13	0	21	3	0
Richardson, Jason, Twi.	0	1	.000	1.35	4	1	0	0	0	0	6.2	4	29	1	1	0	0	1	5	0	7	0	0
Rivas, Gabriel, Tig.	5	3	.625	5.94	18	4	0	0	3	0	36.1	46	172	25	24	2	1	1	6	21	0	33	2	2
Rivera, Saul, Twi.	0	0	.000	0.00	3	0	0	0	0	0	3.0	2	13	0	0	0	0	0	0	1	0	4	0	0
Rodney, Fernando, Tig.	0	0	.000	0.00	1	1	0	0	0	0	1.0	0	3	0	0	0	0	0	0	1	0	1	0	0
Rodriguez, Enoc, Reds*	0	0	.000	4.50	2	0	0	0	1	0	4.0	5	17	2	2	0	0	0	1	0	2	0	0
Rodriguez, Miguel, R.S.	3	2	.600	2.59	11	7	0	0	4	0	55.2	52	228	18	16	2	2	0	1	12	1	53	2	1
Rollandini, David, Phi.	4	4	.400	3.43	9	8	0	0	0	0	39.1	37	173	23	15	0	2	1	5	14	0	38	3	0
Rosado, Hector, Roy.*	3	5	.375	1.73	14	6	1	0	7	2	52.0	44	222	19	10	1	1	1	15	2	48	3	0
Rose, Michael, Exp.	0	0	.000	2.35	3	3	0	0	0	0	7.2	9	34	3	2	0	2	1	1	0	5	2	0
Ross, Brian, Reds*	0	0	.000	60.75	2	2	0	0	0	0	1.1	10	14	9	9	1	0	0	0	1	0	2	0	0
Royal, Shannon, R.S.*	0	1	.000	3.38	10	0	0	0	9	2	10.2	7	41	4	4	0	1	0	1	3	1	5	1	0
Saberhagen, Bret, R.S.	0	1	.000	1.59	2	2	0	0	0	0	5.2	3	19	1	1	0	0	0	0	0	0	2	0	0
Sala, Marino, Ori.	1	5	.167	4.82	15	0	0	0	13	6	18.2	21	89	12	10	0	1	1	1	13	4	10	0	1
Salas, Jose, Brav.	0	1	.000	0.00	1	0	0	0	0	0	1.0	0	4	1	0	0	0	0	0	0	0	1	1	0
Salazar, Richard, Ori.*	0	0	.000	0.00	1	0	0	0	0	0	2.0	2	8	0	0	0	0	0	1	0	2	0	0
Sanchez, Elby, Roy.	2	3	.400	3.24	18	0	0	0	7	0	41.2	39	182	26	15	2	2	0	2	17	2	25	4	0
Sanchez, Rafael, R.S.	5	1	.833	1.78	10	8	0	0	0	0	50.2	36	195	12	10	3	0	3	5	7	0	45	2	1
Sanchez, Roberto, Roy.	0	1	.000	4.50	12	9	0	0	1	1	30.0	30	133	18	15	2	0	2	3	12	0	18	0	1
Santana, Eddy, Yan.	2	0	1.000	3.44	7	2	0	0	1	0	18.1	11	73	7	7	1	0	0	11	0	12	1	0
Schriner, Brian, Phi.	2	0	1.000	5.40	16	0	0	0	9	2	25.0	36	125	21	15	0	3	4	4	10	0	14	3	1
Selmo, Santo, Mar.	5	2	.714	2.97	17	0	0	0	13	4	36.1	28	148	16	12	2	1	0	5	7	0	22	6	0
Sexton, Joey, Brav.	0	0	.000	0.00	2	0	0	0	1	0	2.0	2	13	0	0	1	0	0	2	0	5	0	0
Shafer, Kurt, Pir.	3	4	.429	3.50	12	6	1	0	3	1	54.0	54	216	24	21	2	1	1	5	9	0	41	4	1
Sharber, Jeffery, Pir.	1	0	1.000	0.50	3	3	0	0	0	0	18.0	5	61	1	1	1	1	0	1	4	0	19	0	0
Shortslef, Josh, Pir.*	2	3	.400	3.63	10	4	1	0	2	0	34.2	39	148	23	14	1	4	1	1	9	0	14	0	2
Shroyer, Dustin, Pir.*	0	0	.000	17.36	5	0	0	0	2	0	4.2	3	32	11	9	0	1	4	11	0	4	3	0
Simon, Billy, R.S.	0	0	.000	1.00	3	3	0	0	0	0	9.0	6	32	2	1	0	0	2	1	0	7	1	0
Simon, Janewrys, Twi.	2	5	.286	4.74	13	7	0	0	0	0	43.2	51	200	29	23	2	2	2	4	22	1	33	6	1
Smiley, Gerald, Rang.	0	0	.000	1.59	3	0	0	0	0	0	5.2	4	25	1	1	0	0	1	4	0	2	0	0
Smith, Chris, Ori.*	0	0	.000	0.00	2	0	0	0	1	0	2.0	2	10	2	0	0	0	0	1	0	0	0	0
Smith, Jason, Yan.	5	2	.714	1.93	11	11	2	2	0	0	60.2	52	248	25	13	1	2	1	4	11	0	41	2	0
Sobkowiak, Scott, Brav.	0	0	.000	1.29	2	2	0	0	0	0	7.0	4	28	2	1	0	1	0	1	0	11	1	0
Spillers, Larry, Ori.*	3	3	.500	4.01	10	10	0	0	0	0	51.2	53	226	25	23	3	4	2	5	19	1	13	3	2
Squires, Matt, Phi.*	0	2	.000	1.21	17	0	0	0	5	0	29.2	16	117	5	4	0	5	1	3	11	0	33	2	0
Stahl, Rich, Ori.*	0	0	.000	0.00	1	1	0	0	0	0	2.0	1	7	0	0	0	0	0	1	0	1	0	0
Stentz, Brent, Twi.	2	1	.667	1.93	8	0	0	0	2	0	9.1	7	41	3	2	0	0	0	7	0	6	1	0
Sterrett, Adam, Mar.	0	0	.000	9.00	1	0	0	0	0	0	1.0	1	7	1	1	0	0	1	0	3	0	0	0	0
Stevens, Kris, Exp.*	1	0	1.000	0.00	4	4	0	0	0	0	11.1	7	45	0	0	0	0	5	0	7	2	0
Stewart, James, Dod.	1	1	.500	3.09	11	1	0	0	2	0	23.1	19	93	9	8	2	0	1	4	0	14	0	0
Strayhorn, Kole, Dod.	5	3	.625	2.19	12	6	0	0	2	0	53.1	41	214	15	13	1	2	0	5	17	0	47	1	1
Suarez, Pedro, R.S.	0	0	.000	5.65	8	0	0	0	2	1	14.1	17	74	9	9	1	0	2	1	13	1	14	1	0
Suarez, Victor, Roy.	0	0	.000	2.25	7	0	0	0	3	1	8.0	7	36	2	2	1	1	0	0	5	0	4	1	0
Sweeney, Matt, Phi.	2	2	.500	3.38	9	5	0	0	3	0	29.1	28	127	12	11	3	1	2	3	16	0	16	2	1
Tacker, Trevor, Yan.	1	3	.250	4.75	9	4	1	0	0	0	30.1	35	136	19	16	3	1	1	1	11	1	16	1	0
Tarkington, Shawn, Twi.	1	0	1.000	3.00	13	0	0	0	5	1	21.0	25	88	8	7	0	0	2	1	0	25	2	0
Taylor, David, Dod.	0	1	.000	3.00	3	3	0	0	0	0	6.0	5	24	3	2	0	1	0	0	6	4	0
Tejada, Frailyn, Mar.*	6	1	.857	2.58	10	8	0	0	0	0	52.1	47	210	19	15	2	0	1	4	7	0	54	0	0
Tejero, Armando, Brav.*	0	1	.000	0.00	1	0	0	0	1	0	1.0	1	5	1	0	0	0	0	0	1	0	0	0	0
Therneau, Dave, Reds	2	2	.500	2.40	5	5	0	0	0	0	30.0	26	113	12	8	0	1	0	0	0	0	35	0	0
Thigpen, Joshua, R.S.	4	2	.667	2.52	10	6	0	0	2	1	39.1	20	150	15	11	1	0	4	1	14	0	44	4	0
Tierney, Chris, Roy.*	0	2	.000	6.65	8	3	0	0	1	0	21.2	31	109	19	16	1	0	1	4	8	1	21	0	0
Tiller, James, Ori.	0	3	.000	3.68	16	1	0	0	6	0	36.2	30	160	18	15	3	1	2	5	15	1	44	4	0
Tingley, Pat, Twi.*	4	1	.800	8.86	15	0	0	0	7	1	21.1	35	101	22	21	5	0	0	0	8	0	18	2	1

– 630 –

Pitcher, Team	W	L	Pct.	ERA	G	GS	CG	ShO	GF	Sv.	IP	H	TBF	R	ER	HR	SH	SF	HB	BB	IBB	SO	WP	Bk.
Torres, Carlos, Reds	5	1	.833	2.97	11	4	0	0	4	0	39.1	27	164	13	13	0	2	2	5	18	0	29	1	0
Torres, Luis, Pir.	0	0	.000	3.00	3	1	0	0	0	0	3.0	3	14	3	1	0	0	0	0	1	0	2	2	0
Totten, Heath, Dod.	1	0	1.000	0.82	2	2	0	0	0	0	11.0	5	37	1	1	0	0	0	0	0	0	8	0	0
Truselo, Randy, Rang.	0	3	.000	0.53	7	5	0	0	0	0	34.0	30	147	10	2	0	1	2	4	15	0	21	1	0
Tyler, Scott, Twi.	0	1	.000	6.75	5	3	0	0	0	0	10.2	11	46	8	8	0	0	1	2	0	0	14	2	0
Valdez, Henry, R.S.*	5	2	.714	4.35	16	0	0	0	6	3	39.1	42	177	22	19	2	0	1	3	17	0	29	0	1
Valentin, Emmanuel, Tig.	7	1	.875	4.11	21	0	0	0	6	0	35.0	32	161	16	16	2	2	1	3	21	0	34	3	3
Valera, Luis, Reds	1	0	1.000	2.40	10	0	0	0	6	3	15.0	7	58	4	4	0	0	0	6	0	16	2	0
Vargas, Javier, Tig.	2	4	.333	3.55	9	7	1	0	0	0	38.0	31	156	19	15	5	1	0	0	11	0	25	3	1
Vasquez, Jorge, Roy.	0	1	.000	1.13	4	2	0	0	1	0	16.0	10	63	2	2	0	0	0	2	1	0	19	0	0
Vaughn, Josh, Exp.*	0	3	.000	8.22	11	2	0	0	6	0	23.0	38	114	27	21	0	2	1	1	6	0	17	4	0
Wagnon, Dwayne, Reds	1	1	.500	3.05	10	0	0	0	2	0	20.2	14	94	9	7	0	0	1	5	14	0	23	4	0
Ward, Bryan, R.S.*	0	0	.000	18.00	1	0	0	0	1	0	2.0	4	10	4	4	1	0	0	0	0	0	2	1	0
Wheatland, Matt, Tig.	0	0	.000	0.00	3	3	0	0	0	0	9.0	3	33	0	0	0	0	0	0	3	0	5	0	0
Wheeler, Adam, Yan.	3	2	.600	3.90	10	5	0	0	2	0	30.0	24	131	16	13	0	1	0	5	15	0	28	5	0
Wheldon, Rhys, Twi.	2	0	1.000	1.17	13	0	0	0	2	0	15.1	11	70	5	2	0	1	0	1	13	1	12	5	0
White, Kenneth, Ori.	0	1	.000	1.50	4	0	0	0	4	0	6.0	9	28	3	1	0	1	0	0	2	0	2	0	0
Williams, Todd, Yan.	0	0	.000	0.00	1	1	0	0	0	0	2.0	1	8	0	0	0	0	1	0	0	5	0	0
Witkelder, Gregory, Dod.*	1	0	1.000	4.15	6	6	0	0	0	0	17.1	15	72	8	8	1	0	1	0	11	0	15	0	1
Wright, Chase, Yan.*	2	3	.400	7.92	10	7	0	0	1	0	25.0	33	131	28	22	0	2	3	1	21	1	33	7	1
Yankosky, L.J., Brav.	1	1	.500	1.93	4	0	0	0	1	0	14.0	10	54	3	3	0	1	1	2	1	0	11	0	0

COMBINATION SHUTOUTS: **Braves (9)**—Davies-Furnald-Cooper, McClendon-Davies-Cooper, Lopez-Arteaga, Lopez-Mathiesen, Aguilar-Cooper-Arteaga, Davies-Lopez-Mathiesen, Aguilar-Mason-Arteaga, Aguilar-Machen-Mathiesen. **Dodgers (7)**—Totten-Reina-Andrews, Hughes-Reina-Andrews, Cuen-Johansen-Blaney, Escobedo-Cuen-Johansen, Lopez-Reina, Cuen-Stewart-Reina, Neuage-Cuen-Jackson. **Expos (2)**—Mata-Gomez-George, Acuna-Corcoran-Diaz-Griswold-Guerrero. **Marlins (4)**—Belizario-Henkel-Espaillat-Selmo, Belizario-Padilla, Akens-Holdzkom-Davis, Tejada-Mau-Frawley. **Orioles (0). Phillies (6)**—DeChristofaro-Dawson, Cabrera-Butto-Schriner, Rollandini-McCall, DeChristofaro-Moreno-Lammers, Sweeney-Schriner, Dawson-Squires-Butto-Moreno. **Pirates (4)**—Oquendo-Shafer, Oquendo-Shafer, Burzynski-Lee, Johnston-Shafer. **Rangers (4)**—Masset-Mendoza-Engles, Mendoza-Hampton, Masset-Dominguez-Campbell, Truselo-Hampton-Dominguez-Smiley-Cristobal. **Red Sox (3)**—Sanchez-Delcarmen, Gabbard-Lundgren-Huang, Mims-Valdez. **Reds (5)**—Culp-Gomez-Brannon, George-Brannon, Gillman-Brannon, George-Valera-Nunez, George-Wagnon-Burnette. **Royals (1)**—Brown-Carter-Lowery. **Tigers (4)**—Wheatland-Petty-Valentin, Petty-Dunn, Diaz-Connolly-Brandon-Herrera, Petty-Valentin-Barrios. **Twins (6)**—Ferreira-Carrasco-Tingley, Lohse-Carrasco-Simon-Garcia, Garcia-Stentz-Mutch, Lohse-Niedbalski-Gutierrez, Niedbalski-Crawford, Ferreira-Gutierrez. **Yankees (5)**—Santana-Wright-Carlson-Kennard, Tucker-Kennard, Mosley-Carlson-Kennard, Smith-Carlson-Kennard, Smith-Landaeta.

NO-HIT GAMES: None.

2001 FIELDING

TEAM

Team	Pct.	G	PO	A	E	TC	DP	TP	PB
Red Sox	.972	59	1475	595	60	2130	47	0	16
Dodgers	.970	60	1551	628	67	2246	44	0	16
Yankees	.966	60	1491	608	73	2172	45	0	9
Rangers	.966	59	1462	598	73	2133	64	0	21
Reds	.964	58	1424	484	71	1979	34	0	11
Tigers	.964	58	1475	570	77	2122	41	0	21
Twins	.963	58	1432	583	78	2093	63	0	7
Pirates	.961	56	1349	551	78	1978	45	0	21
Marlins	.960	60	1558	635	92	2285	45	0	18
Braves	.957	60	1553	549	95	2197	34	0	17
Phillies	.951	60	1482	573	105	2160	41	0	10
Royals	.951	60	1470	495	101	2066	46	0	31
Orioles	.951	56	1362	573	100	2035	38	0	7
Expos	.945	60	1546	627	126	2299	43	0	20

INDIVIDUAL

FIRST BASEMEN

NOTE: All caps denotes fielding-percentage leader based on 30 games for catchers, 40 for all other non-pitchers and 48 innings for pitchers. *Throws lefthanded.

Player, Team	Pct.	G	PO	A	E	TC	DP
Bastardo, Frederick, Mar.	1.000	7	72	2	0	74	3
Bellorin, Edwin, Dod.	.000	1	0	0	0	0	0
Blanco, Luis, Exp.	.981	43	339	22	7	368	25
Bledsoe, Hunter, Dod.	1.000	4	16	5	0	21	1
Brown, Tim, Pir.*	.988	36	301	25	4	330	24
Bunch, J.C., Rang.	.976	11	74	6	2	82	9
Cancio, Antonio, Phi.	.992	31	247	14	2	263	20
Carolfiles, Bladimir, Mar.	1.000	9	69	7	0	76	7
Carroll, Rich, Rang.	.987	41	339	28	5	372	32
Coffey, Josh, Mar.	1.000	1	7	1	0	8	1
Cooper, Matt, R.S.	.986	56	478	22	7	507	31
Cust, Kevin, Brav.	.963	8	47	5	2	54	4
Delgado, Mario, Phi.*	1.000	1	9	1	0	10	2
Faulkner, Todd, Yan.	1.000	3	23	0	0	23	2
Feliz, Henry, Yan.	.978	20	130	5	3	138	10
Figueroa, Anibal, Roy.	.906	51	410	26	6	442	34
Figueroa, Daniel, R.S.*	.000	1	0	0	0	0	0
Fry, Ryan, Reds	1.000	2	10	0	0	10	0

Player, Team	Pct.	G	PO	A	E	TC	DP
Garcia, Juan Carlos, Mar.	.975	17	145	14	4	163	11
Garcia, Sandy, Yan.	1.000	2	9	0	0	9	0
Gerlits, Gooby, Mar.	1.000	2	18	1	0	19	2
Ghutzman, Phillip, Reds	1.000	1	1	0	0	1	0
Gomon, Dusty, Twi.	.971	13	93	9	3	105	10
Gonzalez, Juan, Tig.	1.000	2	2	0	0	2	0
Guerrero, Jorge, Mar.	1.000	5	31	0	0	31	2
Guzman, Jacob, Roy.	.984	8	56	5	1	62	4
Hansen, Bryan, Phi.*	.976	19	151	9	4	164	9
Honeycutt, Shedrick, Exp.*	.958	9	67	2	3	72	4
Johnson, Tristan, Pir.*	.988	22	161	7	2	170	18
Joyce, Thomas, Ori.*	1.000	3	24	0	0	24	1
Lambert, Shawn, Tig.	.978	26	164	14	4	182	18
Lindberg, Russell, Mar.	.993	17	135	11	1	147	10
Lush, Zach, Mar.	1.000	2	17	0	0	17	0
Manley, Adam, Orl.*	1.000	5	39	4	0	43	4
Marin, Daniel, Twi.	.033	1	4	1	1	6	0
Martinez, Raul, Ori.	1.000	4	23	0	0	24	1
Masino, Adam, Twi.	.975	24	183	13	5	201	20
McDonald, Chamar, Roy.	1.000	5	41	1	0	42	1
Mendoza, Adrian, Dod.*	.992	42	353	21	3	377	28
Motoaka, Rafael, Reds	.750	1	3	0	1	4	0
Nickerson, Brian, Dod.	.980	20	138	8	3	149	9
Nunez, Andres, Yan.	1.000	1	10	0	0	10	1
Oh, Chul, R.S.	1.000	5	39	4	0	43	7
Olivari, Reinaldo, Rang.	.976	9	77	5	2	84	12
Pitney, Jared, Yan.*	.989	41	338	32	4	374	28
Price, Jared, Dod.	.750	1	3	0	1	4	1
Recio, Bolivar, Ori.	.951	4	36	3	2	41	3
Rijo, Carlos, Ori.	1.000	1	9	1	0	10	0
Rivera, Carlos, Phi.	.981	12	96	6	2	104	5
Rolison, Nate, Mar.	.938	2	15	0	1	16	0
SANTANA, Roberto, Brav.	.994	44	338	14	2	354	18
Smith, Brenton, Reds	1.000	4	30	2	0	32	2
Smith, Ryan, Twi.	.990	26	188	8	2	198	21
Sulbaran, Orlando, Rang.	1.000	1	2	0	0	2	0
Taveras, Frank, Mar.	.857	1	5	1	1	7	2
Tejeda, Juan, Tig	.985	40	312	22	5	339	20
Tejero, Armando, Brav.*	.981	18	148	6	3	157	9
Thede, Matthew, Exp.	.968	12	88	4	3	95	7
Timaure, Jesus, Mar.	.969	4	30	1	1	32	2
Vavao, Jason, Reds	.986	53	391	25	6	422	27
Yount, Dustin, Ori.	.992	40	346	22	3	371	25

SECOND BASEMEN

Player, Team	Pct.	G	PO	A	E	TC	DP
Abreu, Nielsen, Phi.	.943	34	61	88	9	158	18
Aristigueta, Darwin, Brav.	.980	13	24	24	1	49	1
Arroyo, William, Mar.	1.000	5	9	11	0	20	3
Baez, Federico, Ori.	.897	10	14	21	4	39	6
Bastardo, Frederick, Mar.	.951	21	39	39	4	82	11
Batista, Jose, Roy.	.952	11	19	21	2	42	6
Bautista, Augusto, Reds	.973	11	13	23	1	37	3
Campos, Julio, Phi.	1.000	2	2	4	0	6	1
Cano, Robinson, Yan.	.970	33	69	95	5	169	18
Cockrell, Michael, Pir.	.960	45	84	107	8	199	27
Collum, Michael, Pir.	1.000	1	2	6	0	8	2
Cruz, Alex, Pir.	.971	13	15	18	1	34	7
De Leon, Jorge, R.S.	.000	1	0	0	0	0	0
De Los Santos, Omar, Dod.	.968	7	10	20	1	31	3
Diaz, Victor, Dod.	.948	50	88	132	12	232	24
Dorta, Melvin, R.S.	.984	17	31	29	1	61	8
Duran, Deudis, Phi.	.910	30	31	60	9	100	6
Encarnacion, Henry, Exp.	.944	15	27	40	4	71	7
Espino, Damaso, Reds	1.000	1	0	2	0	2	0
Farmer, John, Brav.	1.000	2	6	5	0	11	0
Fermin, Angelo, Twi.	.973	9	18	18	1	37	4
Gallo, Ismael, Dod.	1.000	4	3	4	0	7	2
GONZALEZ, Jose, Rang.	.985	44	78	119	3	200	29
Gonzalez, Juan, Tig.	.947	9	15	21	2	38	6
Gonzalez, Juan, Dod.	.933	8	3	11	1	15	2
Gotay, Ruben, Roy.	.940	47	82	105	12	199	22
Greene, Jason, Exp.	.959	22	38	55	4	97	10
Guerrero, Jorge, Mar.	.978	12	14	30	1	45	5
Guzman, Wander, Mar.	.981	23	51	50	2	103	14
Heath, Demetrius, Tig.	.973	49	70	110	5	185	18
Infante, Franklin, Brav.	.935	30	55	60	8	123	10
Lababera, Michael, Exp.	.967	25	44	43	3	90	9
Mancebo, Deni, Exp.	1.000	1	5	2	0	7	0
Mateo, Daniel, Reds	.920	8	13	10	2	25	3
Meath, Matt, Pir.	.667	1	2	0	1	3	0
Molina, Felix, Twi.	.952	8	5	15	1	21	1
Morales, Jose, Twi.	.937	23	42	62	7	111	24
Morales, Michael, Brav.	.964	16	21	32	2	55	4
Moreno, Christopher, Ori.	1.000	1	0	4	0	4	0
Nickerson, Brian, Dod.	1.000	1	2	1	0	3	1
Nunez, Alexis, Twi.	1.000	2	1	2	0	3	0
Nunez, Andres, Yan.	1.000	3	3	4	0	7	0
Olivari, Reinaldo, Rang.	.945	15	19	33	3	55	12
Petersen, Ryan, R.S.	1.000	10	14	20	0	34	7
Pospishil, Jason, Twi.	.960	6	10	14	1	25	2
Recio, Bolivar, Ori.	.882	7	8	7	2	17	2
Rodriguez, Alexander, Roy.	.889	2	3	5	1	9	2
Romano, Jason, Rang.	.762	3	9	7	5	21	3
Rudecindo, Carlos, Mar.	.833	2	3	2	1	6	0
Ruiz, Junior, Reds	.954	41	70	76	7	153	17
Salazar, Juan, R.S.	.977	36	75	93	4	172	18
Sanchez, Angel, Roy.	.000	1	0	0	0	0	0
Santana, Isidro, Tig.	1.000	5	19	20	0	39	5
Santana, Roberto, Brav.	.000	1	0	0	0	0	0
Severino, Wanell, Ori.	.926	31	58	68	10	136	16
Strong, Brian, Brav.	.917	5	4	7	1	12	0
Taylor, Samuel, Twi.	.985	18	20	45	1	66	11
Vasquez, Wuillians, Yan.	.946	29	56	66	7	129	19
White, Kenneth, Ori.	.939	14	13	33	3	49	3

THIRD BASEMEN

Player, Team	Pct.	G	PO	A	E	TC	DP
Aristigueta, Darwin, Brav.	.896	19	7	36	5	48	1
Baez, Federico, Ori.	.833	4	1	4	1	6	0
Barthel, Cole, Brav.	.890	43	25	72	12	109	5
Bastardo, Frederick, Mar.	.820	12	8	33	9	50	2
Batista, Jose, Roy.	.941	13	12	20	2	34	1
Bonvechio, Brett, R.S.	.854	18	8	27	6	41	1
Brown, Dustin, R.S.	1.000	2	0	2	0	2	0
Bunch, J.C., Rang.	.857	5	3	3	1	7	1
Buscher, Gregory, Rang.	.988	30	22	57	1	80	9
Campos, Julio, Phi.	.944	10	6	11	1	18	0
Cano, Robinson, Yan.	1.000	10	9	19	0	28	5
Collum, Michael, Pir.	1.000	7	3	11	0	14	1
Cruz, Luis, R.S.	.933	15	8	34	3	45	3
De Leon, Jorge, R.S.	.917	10	4	7	1	12	1
De Los Santos, Omar, Dod.	1.000	2	2	2	0	4	0
DelosSantos, Esteban, Phi.	.889	38	26	62	11	99	2
Diaz, Victor, Dod.	1.000	3	1	1	0	2	0
Duran, Deudis, Phi.	.786	7	2	9	3	14	0
Encarnacion, Henry, Exp.	.833	18	10	40	10	60	1

(SECOND BASEMEN, continued)

Player, Team	Pct.	G	PO	A	E	TC	DP
Espino, Damaso, Reds	.900	25	12	24	4	40	1
Fermin, Angelo, Twi.	.857	2	2	4	1	7	0
Fry, Ryan, Reds	.908	39	29	50	8	87	3
Garcia, Juan-Carlos, Mar.	.860	19	14	35	8	57	2
Garcia, Sandy, Yan.	1.000	2	0	2	0	2	0
Gomon, Dusty, Twi.	1.000	3	2	3	0	5	0
Gonzalez, Juan, Tig.	.938	33	19	56	5	80	3
Gonzalez, Juan, Dod.	.000	1	0	0	0	0	0
Gotay, Ruben, Roy.	.857	2	2	4	1	7	1
Guerrero, Jorge, Mar.	.867	17	11	41	8	60	2
Hernandez , Anderson, Tig.	1.000	1	4	4	0	8	1
Hiraldo, Inocencio, Twi.	.923	13	8	16	2	26	4
Infante, Franklin, Brav.	.000	1	0	0	0	0	0
Jones, Terry, Phi.	.793	9	6	17	6	29	1
King, Brennan, Dod.	1.000	3	0	7	0	7	0
Lababera, Michael, Exp.	.929	5	6	7	1	14	0
Legendre, Curtis, Roy.	.818	19	7	29	8	44	2
Marin, Daniel, Twi.	1.000	2	0	2	0	2	0
Martin, Chris, Yan.	1.000	2	1	3	0	4	0
Maxwell, Jason, Twi.	1.000	1	0	4	0	4	0
Mitchell, Andy, Ori.	1.000	1	1	0	0	1	0
Molina, Felix, Twi.	.922	37	32	63	8	103	9
Morales, Jose, Twi.	1.000	3	0	2	0	2	0
Moreno, Christopher, Ori.	1.000	1	2	0	0	2	0
Mujica, Jean, Exp.	.890	41	22	83	13	118	4
Navarrete, Ray, Pir.	1.000	2	3	5	0	8	0
Nickerson, Brian, Dod.	.923	7	0	12	1	13	0
Nunez, Alexis, Twi.	1.000	1	1	1	0	2	1
Nunez, Andres, Yan.	.912	51	30	84	11	125	9
Olivari, Reinaldo, Rang.	.930	30	23	43	5	71	7
Perozo, Hector, Dod.	.906	51	35	90	13	138	5
Petersen, Ryan, R.S.	.942	24	17	48	4	69	2
Pospishil, Jason, Twi.	1.000	1	0	2	0	2	0
Post, Dave, Dod.	1.000	1	0	1	0	1	0
Raburn, Ryan, Tig.	.960	13	9	15	1	25	0
Recio, Bolivar, Pir.-Ori.	.765	8	4	9	4	17	1
RIJO, Carlos, Ori.	.916	49	51	102	14	167	4
Rush, Travis, Pir.	.889	9	10	14	3	27	1
Ryan, Billy, Tig.	.775	15	10	21	9	40	1
Salazar, Juan, R.S.	1.000	1	1	2	0	3	1
Sanchez, Angel, Roy.	.929	13	6	20	2	28	2
Santana, Roberto, Brav.	1.000	1	1	0	0	1	0
Strong, Brian, Brav.	.000	1	0	0	0	0	0
Suarez, Victor, Roy.	.833	15	14	11	5	30	2
Taveras, Frank, Mar.	.912	18	18	44	6	68	5
Taylor, Mark, Pir.	.870	38	25	55	12	92	5
Ust, Brant, Tig.	.833	3	1	4	1	6	1
Wise, Bradley, Tig.	.333	1	1	0	2	3	0
Yount, Dustin, Ori.	1.000	1	2	1	0	3	1

THIRD BASEMEN WITH TWO OR MORE TEAMS

Player, Team	Pct.	G	PO	A	E	TC	DP
Recio, Bolivar, Pir.	.750	5	4	5	3	12	1
Recio, Bolivar, Ori.	.800	3	0	4	1	5	0

SHORTSTOPS

Player, Team	Pct.	G	PO	A	E	TC	DP
Arroyo, William, Mar.	.969	36	40	117	5	162	14
Baez, Federico, Ori.	.948	16	17	38	3	58	5
Bass, Brian, Ori.	.958	18	38	54	4	96	8
Bautista, Augusto, Reds	.944	5	8	9	1	18	2
Brito, Anyelo, Phi.	.912	27	40	64	10	114	9
Burrus, Josh, Brav.	.896	48	52	129	21	202	17
Cabrerra, Ulises, Rang.	.941	38	60	100	10	170	19
Cano, Robinson, Yan.	.918	19	22	45	6	73	6
Collum, Michael, Pir.	.894	22	18	66	10	94	12
Cruz, Alex, Pir.	.946	8	11	24	2	37	1
Cruz, Luis, R.S.	.977	38	70	99	4	173	20
Dorta, Melvin, R.S.	1.000	2	0	5	0	5	0
Encarnacion, Henry, Exp.	.882	18	38	59	13	110	6
Espino, Damaso, Reds	.925	12	12	25	3	40	2
Fermin, Angelo, Twi.	1.000	2	4	7	0	11	1
Garcia, Juan-Carlos, Mar.	1.000	1	0	2	0	2	0
Gonzalez, Jose, Rang.	.935	8	10	19	2	31	8
Gonzalez, Juan, Tig.	.950	10	10	28	2	40	3
Gonzalez, Juan, Dod.	1.000	15	28	45	0	73	14
Guzman, Cristian, Twi.	1.000	2	4	3	0	7	2
Guzman, Wander, Mar.	.926	23	36	64	8	108	11
Hernandez , Anderson, Tig.	.911	54	90	126	21	237	25
HERRERA, Christian, Dod.	.955	46	62	130	9	201	19
Hiraldo, Inocencio, Twi.	.936	34	53	79	9	141	15
Infante, Franklin, Brav.	.895	12	19	32	6	57	1

Player, Team	Pct.	G	PO	A	E	TC	DP
Jaramillo, Milko, Dod.	.947	3	5	13	1	19	3
Jordan, Edward, Ori.	1.000	1	0	2	0	2	0
Lababera, Michael, Exp.	1.000	1	0	2	0	2	0
Mancebo, Deni, Exp.	.886	43	61	125	24	210	25
Mariot, Lino, Pir.	.888	31	38	57	12	107	13
Mateo, Daniel, Reds	.920	45	67	94	14	175	17
Maxwell, Jason, Twi.	1.000	2	0	3	0	3	0
Morales, Jose, Twi.	.935	9	13	16	2	31	3
Moreno, Christopher, Ori.	.733	3	3	8	4	15	2
Recio, Bolivar, Ori.	.880	7	12	10	3	25	4
Rijo, Carlos, Ori.	.500	1	0	1	1	2	0
Rodriguez, Alexander, Roy.	.914	48	76	115	18	209	23
Rodriguez, Carlos, Phi.	.922	34	53	88	12	153	20
Rodriguez, Jose, Ori.	.909	5	7	13	2	22	2
Salazar, Juan, R.S.	.938	6	3	12	1	16	1
Sanchez, Angel, Roy.	.930	16	17	36	4	57	8
Sandoval, Abigail, Rang.	.945	14	26	43	4	73	11
Sardinha, Bronson, Yan.	.907	46	43	103	15	161	11
Taylor, Samuel, Twi.	.963	16	17	35	2	54	10
Vasquez, Wuillians, Yan.	.800	1	0	4	1	5	0
West, Eric, R.S.	.969	18	14	49	2	65	9
White, Dean, Brav.	.818	2	1	8	2	11	0
White, Kenneth, Ori.	.891	13	15	26	5	46	5

OUTFIELDERS

Player, Team	Pct.	G	PO	A	E	TC	DP
Abreu, Nielsen, Phi.	.000	2	0	0	1	1	0
Acevedo, Juan, Reds	.971	23	33	1	1	35	0
Acosta, Johe, Pir.	.929	19	24	2	2	28	0
Alexander, Alexis, Roy.	.938	35	58	2	4	64	1
Alexander, Lawrence, Phi.	.960	35	46	2	2	50	1
Alou, Felipe, Roy.	1.000	18	40	1	0	41	0
Andujar, Elvin, Reds	.988	58	77	4	1	82	1
Angell, Rick, Rang.	1.000	3	3	0	0	3	0
Banks, Almonzo, Ori.	.938	36	75	0	5	80	0
Bastardo, Frederick, Mar.	1.000	2	1	0	0	1	0
Batista, Jose, Roy.	.909	8	9	1	1	11	1
Birkett, Matthew, Tig	.950	31	33	5	2	40	0
Blue, Vincent, Tig.	.981	34	51	0	1	52	0
Brackley, Carlos, R.S.	.969	47	55	8	2	65	2
Brewer, Anthony, Mar.	.984	58	120	4	2	126	2
Brown, Ira, Roy.	.000	1	0	0	1	1	0
Bunch, J.C., Rang.	1.000	8	6	0	0	6	0
Caraballo, Carlos, R.S.	.974	46	73	2	2	77	0
Cardona, David, Dod.	.959	47	68	3	3	74	0
Carolfiles, Bladimir, Mar.	.974	32	35	2	1	38	1
Carroll, Rich, Rang.	1.000	2	0	1	0	1	0
Carter, Ryan, Dod.	.889	11	8	0	1	9	0
Charles, Julin, Rang.	.978	49	85	4	2	91	0
Chauncey, Clinton, Yan.	.000	2	0	0	0	0	0
Ciofrone, Paul, Phi.	.951	30	37	2	2	41	0
Crosby, Kelly, Yan.	.935	20	25	4	2	31	0
Crump, Joel, Ori.*	.000	1	0	0	0	0	0
Davis, Daniel, Tig.*	.944	9	17	0	1	18	0
Davis, J.J., Pir.	.667	1	2	0	1	3	0
Davis, Rajai, Pir.	.980	26	45	4	1	50	1
De Leon, Virgilio, Tig.	.933	9	12	2	1	15	1
Dean, Herman, Tig.	.980	24	48	1	1	50	0
Diaz, Frank, Exp.	1.000	35	61	9	0	70	2
Duran, Carlos, Brav.*	.978	53	87	4	2	93	1
Everett, Carl, R.S.	1.000	3	5	0	0	5	0
Ezi, Travis, Dod.*	.975	57	116	1	3	120	0
Figueroa, Daniel, R.S.*	1.000	13	19	0	0	19	0
Fitzpatrick, Reggie, Exp.*	.959	31	68	2	3	73	0
Fry, Ryan, Reds	1.000	12	13	1	0	14	0
Garcia, Sandy, Yan.	1.000	25	26	0	0	26	0
Gatti, William, Dod.	.957	10	21	1	1	23	0
Gonzalez, Jose, Rang.	.000	1	0	0	0	0	0
Gonzalez, Juan, Tig.	1.000	2	2	0	0	2	0
Gordon, Alex, Ori.*	.833	8	5	0	1	6	0
Graham, Tyson, Mar.	.973	30	33	3	1	37	0
Gutierrez, Franklin, Dod.	.980	55	96	4	2	102	0
Guy, Jason, Rang.*	.971	46	61	5	2	68	1
Guzman, Carlos, Brav.	.981	40	50	2	1	53	1
Guzman, Garrett, Twi.*	.978	33	41	3	1	45	0
Haas, Danny, R.S.	1.000	10	16	1	0	17	0
Hackett, Richard, Ori.	1.000	6	10	0	0	10	0
Hill, Joshua, Twi.	1.000	2	3	0	0	3	0
Honeycutt, Shedrick, Exp.*	.977	29	39	3	1	43	1
Horsman, Stephen, Ori.	.667	3	2	0	1	3	0
Jimenez, Luis, Yan.	1.000	4	4	0	0	4	0
Jordan, Edward, Ori.	.966	48	80	5	3	88	0

Player, Team	Pct.	G	PO	A	E	TC	DP
Joyce, Thomas, Ori.*	1.000	45	62	0	0	62	0
Kearns, Austin, Reds	1.000	4	4	0	0	4	0
Khairy, Masjid, Rang.	.969	38	58	4	2	64	3
Kubel, Jason, Twi.	.980	34	46	4	1	51	2
Lababera, Michael, Exp.	1.000	1	2	0	0	2	0
Lehmann, Thomas, Tig.*	1.000	28	36	3	0	39	0
Louisa, Lorvin, Exp.	.987	45	73	4	1	78	1
Manley, Adam, Ori.*	.750	4	6	0	2	8	0
Marshall, Andre, Phi.	.984	36	58	2	1	61	1
Mateo, Alejandro, Rang.	1.000	31	48	4	0	52	1
McDonald, Chamar, Roy.	1.000	36	45	1	0	46	0
Meath, Matt, Pir.	1.000	13	12	1	0	13	0
Medina, Ricardo, Exp.	1.000	31	36	0	0	36	0
Milauskas, Adam, Pir.	1.000	31	47	4	0	51	0
Mitchell, Andy, Ori.	1.000	6	6	0	0	6	0
Molina, Felix, Twi.	1.000	9	11	0	0	11	0
Morban, Dany, Reds*	.914	24	31	1	3	35	0
Moye, Alan, Reds	.943	46	82	1	5	88	0
Navarrete, Ray, Pir.	1.000	1	2	0	0	2	0
Nunez, Andres, Yan.	.000	1	0	0	0	0	0
Oeltjen, Trent, Twi.*	.974	44	72	3	2	77	1
Oh, Chul, R.S.	.897	25	26	0	3	29	0
Olivari, Reinaldo, Rang.	1.000	1	2	0	0	2	0
Partridge, Dominique, Brav.	1.000	25	32	0	0	32	0
Perez, Carlos, Ori.*	.000	1	0	0	0	0	0
Perez, Josue, Phi.	.909	10	19	1	2	22	0
Petersen, Ryan, R.S.	.900	12	18	0	2	20	0
Polo, Fernando, Brav.	.909	35	49	1	5	55	0
Quintin, Luis, Rang.	1.000	7	11	1	0	12	0
Ramistella, John, Yan.	.969	48	60	2	2	64	1
Recio, Dolivar, Ori.	1.000	5	2	1	0	3	0
Rengifo, Amado, Mar.	1.000	3	6	0	0	6	0
Resop, Chris, Mar.	1.000	23	45	0	0	45	0
Rethwisch, Justin, Pir.*	.973	37	65	6	2	73	2
Rivas, Norberto, Exp.	1.000	19	26	6	0	32	1
Rivero, Luis, Phi.	.964	37	52	1	2	55	0
Roberson, Chris, Phi.	.976	38	73	8	2	83	2
Roberts, Mike, Roy.	1.000	1	1	0	0	1	0
Rodgers, Mackeel, Roy.	.970	21	32	0	1	33	0
Rodriguez, John, Yan.*	.000	2	0	0	0	0	0
Romano, Jason, Rang.	1.000	2	4	1	0	5	0
Rosado, Francisco, Tig.	1.000	31	33	2	0	35	0
Ruiz, Junior, Reds	.000	1	0	0	0	0	0
Rush, Travis, Pir.	1.000	8	4	1	0	5	0
Santa, Alexander, Yan.*	.963	52	75	3	3	81	0
Santana, Pedro, Yan.	.867	12	12	1	2	15	0
Santana, Roberto, Brav.	1.000	2	4	0	0	4	0
Searage, Ray, Mar.	.786	12	10	1	3	14	0
Severino, Wanell, Ori.	.000	1	0	0	0	0	0
Singer, Matt, Yan.*	.980	35	45	4	1	50	1
Smith, Brenton, Reds	1.000	19	26	0	0	26	0
Smith, Dustin, Rang.	1.000	1	1	0	0	1	0
SMITH, Sean, Pir.	1.000	41	65	4	0	69	0
Spataro, Ryan, Twi.	.870	14	18	2	3	23	1
Suarez, Victor, Roy.	.800	4	4	0	1	5	0
Sulbaran, Orlando, Rang.	.923	7	12	0	1	13	0
Tarbett, Brent, R.S.	1.000	41	43	2	0	45	0
Thomas, Chuck, Dod.	1.000	6	4	2	0	6	0
Thomman, John, Twi.	.978	32	42	3	1	46	1
Timaure, Jesus, Mar.	1.000	35	33	2	0	35	1
Watkins, Cedric, Roy.	.981	33	49	3	1	53	1
White, Kenneth, Ori.	1.000	21	20	2	0	22	1
Whitrock, Scott, Twi.	.930	30	36	4	3	43	3
Williams, Matt, Tig.	.952	24	37	3	2	42	0
Williams, Mervin, Roy.	.928	37	72	5	6	83	0
Woods, Ahmad, Brav.	.929	38	24	2	2	28	0
Wright, Nate, Dod.	1.000	4	6	0	0	6	0

CATCHERS

Player, Team	Pct.	G	PO	A	E	TC	DP	PB
Akens, Phil, Mar.	1.000	1	6	0	0	6	0	1
Albert, Luke, Brav.	.976	22	149	12	4	165	0	0
Ambrosini, Anthony, Exp.	.979	15	127	13	3	143	2	4
Anderson, Samuel, Tig.	.981	30	189	21	4	214	1	10
Bellorin, Edwin, Dod.	1.000	27	173	20	0	193	0	8
Boscan, Jean, Brav.	1.000	7	49	3	0	52	1	1
Brown, Dustin, R.S.	.996	29	203	27	1	231	2	8
Brown, Jason, Mar.	1.000	1	3	0	0	3	0	0
Bunch, J.C., Rang.	.973	6	32	4	1	37	1	5
Chauncey, Clinton, Yan.	1.000	6	21	1	0	22	1	0
Cisneros, Josh, Phi.	.973	24	162	21	5	188	2	3
Coffey, Josh, Mar.	1.000	1	10	0	0	10	0	2

Player, Team	Pct.	G	PO	A	E	TC	DP	PB
Cust, Kevin, Brav.	1.000	1	3	0	0	3	0	1
Devries, Jonathan, R.S.	.982	16	100	11	2	113	3	4
Doumit, Ryan, Pir.	.944	4	14	3	1	18	1	2
Encarnacion, Angelo, R.S.	.905	3	15	4	2	21	0	2
Encarnacion, Henry, Exp.	1.000	1	1	0	0	1	0	1
Escobar, Luis, Roy.	.986	32	207	9	3	219	1	4
Estilow, Chris, Mar.	.958	17	81	10	4	95	0	3
Fahey, Patrick, Dod.	1.000	8	50	2	0	52	0	1
Gerlits, Gooby, Mar.	.988	12	73	6	1	80	1	3
Ghutzman, Phillip, Reds	.982	21	152	15	3	170	0	4
Gonzalez, Carlos, R.S.	1.000	6	11	1	0	12	0	1
Guzman, Jacob, Roy.	.983	12	54	3	1	58	0	5
Hadad, Jorge, Ori.	1.000	5	18	5	0	23	0	0
Hernandez, Michel, Yan.	1.000	2	12	2	0	14	0	0
Inge, Brandon, Tig.	1.000	3	12	0	0	12	0	0
Johnson, Brian, Dod.	1.000	4	29	1	0	30	0	2
Johnson, Joshua, Twi.	.985	22	119	15	2	136	2	2
Kahr, Danny, Exp.	.955	8	58	5	3	66	0	5
Legendre, Curtis, Roy.	.889	8	36	4	5	45	1	10
Lush, Zach, Mar.	.968	3	26	4	1	31	0	1
Manriquez, Salomon, Exp.	.964	29	214	30	9	253	2	6
Marin, Daniel, Twi.	.984	30	222	25	4	251	2	4
Martinez, Raul, Ori.	.963	28	166	17	7	190	0	2
McCuistion, Mike, Pir.	.993	18	121	18	1	140	0	10
McMahon, James, Ori.	.949	16	82	12	5	99	1	2
McRoberts, Mark, Phi.	.993	22	134	18	1	153	0	5
Molina, Angel, Mar.	.989	34	233	27	3	263	2	5
Motooka, Rafael, Reds	.995	25	197	22	1	220	3	3
Nathans, John, R.S.	1.000	4	6	0	0	6	0	0
Navarro, Dioner, Yan.	.991	40	299	35	3	337	2	6
Oetting, Todd, Reds	1.000	15	91	9	0	100	2	1
Oliver, Joe, R.S.	1.000	2	6	1	0	7	0	0
Ortega, Felix, Phi.	.963	20	142	12	6	160	1	2
Pachot, John, Dod.	1.000	1	4	0	0	4	0	0
Pereyra, Joel, Roy.	.951	16	71	6	4	81	0	10
Price, Jared, Dod.	.991	32	206	25	2	233	1	5
Ramos, Victor, Pir.	.971	29	148	20	5	173	3	7
Reyes, Milver, Pir.	1.000	12	93	20	0	113	0	2
Rodriguez, Ivan, R.S.	.991	16	99	7	1	107	0	1
Rojas, Tom, Yan.	.986	22	125	15	2	142	1	3
Ruelas, Alonzo, Brav.	.977	39	300	34	8	342	2	10
Rush, Travis, Pir.	.000	1	0	0	0	0	0	1
Salas, Jose, Brav.	1.000	2	11	0	0	11	0	1
Sanchez, Danilo, Tig.	.993	37	256	33	2	291	0	11
SMITH, Dustin, Rang.	.996	31	209	31	1	241	2	7
Smith, Ryan, Twi.	.991	14	101	8	1	110	1	1
Strong, Brian, Brav.	.944	8	33	1	2	36	0	4
Sulbaran, Orlando, Rang.	.979	25	167	19	4	190	4	9
Thede, Matthew, Exp.	.987	11	75	2	1	78	1	5
Treanor, Matt, Mar.	.968	6	26	4	1	31	0	3
Valera, Luis, Reds	1.000	4	30	5	0	35	1	3
Webster, Robert, Ori.	.965	15	88	22	4	114	1	3
Zaun, Greg, Roy.	1.000	3	16	1	0	17	0	2

Player, Team	Pct.	G	PO	A	E	TC	DP
Beigh, David, Pir.	1.000	10	3	5	0	8	0
Belizario, Ronald, Mar.	.909	13	6	14	2	22	0
Birk, Ben, Mar.*	1.000	3	2	1	0	3	0
Birkins, Kurt, Ori.*	1.000	5	0	4	0	4	0
Blake, Peter, Twi.*	1.000	6	0	2	0	2	0
Blaney, Matthew, Dod.	1.000	11	1	3	0	4	1
Bostick, Adam, Mar.*	1.000	7	0	1	0	1	0
Brandon, Keith, Tig.	.600	19	0	3	2	5	0
Brannon, Nick, Reds*	.714	17	1	4	2	7	1
Brewington, Jamie, Twi.	1.000	4	0	2	0	2	0
Bridges, Donnie, Exp.	.000	2	0	0	0	0	0
Britton, Chris, Ori.	1.000	12	1	9	0	10	1
Brown, Ira, Roy.	.750	11	4	5	3	12	0
Burnette, Weston, Reds	1.000	10	1	3	0	4	0
Burzynski, Cole, Pir.	1.000	7	2	2	0	4	0
Butto, Francisco, Phi.	.750	15	0	3	1	4	0
Cabrera, Carlos, Phi.	1.000	10	6	7	0	13	0
Cabrera, Daniel, Ori.	.500	12	0	3	3	6	0
Campbell, Andrew, Rang.*	1.000	14	2	5	0	7	0
Carlson, Steve, Yan.*	1.000	21	3	6	0	9	1
Carrasco, Edelyn, Twi.	.813	14	4	9	3	16	1
Carter, Justin, Reds*	.667	4	0	2	1	3	0
Carter, Ramsey, Roy.	1.000	9	0	2	0	2	0
Coffey, Todd, Reds	.750	3	0	3	1	4	0
Connolly, Jon, Tig.*	1.000	8	0	2	0	2	0
Cooper, Dexter, Brav.	1.000	12	1	3	0	4	1
Coppinger, Joe, Ori.	.750	11	1	5	2	8	0
Corcoran, Roy, Exp.	1.000	13	3	1	0	4	0
Crawford, Tristan, Twi.	1.000	13	1	1	0	2	0
Cristobal, Luis, Rang.	.889	11	1	7	1	9	0
Crump, Joel, Ori.*	1.000	7	1	1	0	2	1
Cuello, Manolin, Tig.	1.000	1	1	0	0	1	0
Cuen, David, Dod.*	.769	13	2	8	3	13	0
Culp, Brandon, Reds	1.000	6	2	7	0	9	0
Davies, Kyle, Brav.	1.000	12	2	7	0	9	0
Davis, Lance, Mar.	1.000	14	1	5	0	6	0
Dawson, Carl, Phi.	.714	10	2	3	2	7	0
DeChristofaro, Vinny, Phi.*	1.000	9	2	5	0	7	0
Dejesus, Elvis, Mar.	1.000	13	0	6	0	6	0
Delcarmen, Manny, R.S.	.727	11	2	6	3	11	0
Devenney, Nicholas, Rang.	1.000	17	0	2	0	2	0
Deza, Fredy, Ori.	.889	9	1	7	1	9	0
Diaz, Eddie, Exp.	.818	13	3	6	2	11	2
Diaz, Luis, Tig.	.889	13	1	7	1	9	1
Dominguez, Jose, Rang.	1.000	11	1	9	0	10	0
Dominguez, Raul, Yan.*	.800	12	2	2	1	5	0
Dossett, William, Roy.	1.000	8	0	4	0	4	0
Douglas, Rod, Brav.	1.000	4	0	2	0	2	0
Douglass, Ryan, Roy.	1.000	2	0	1	0	1	0
Dumatrait, Phillip, R.S.*	1.000	8	0	5	0	5	0
Dunn, Gerald, Tig.	1.000	12	8	2	0	10	0
Engels, Jackson, Rang.*	.429	10	0	3	4	7	0
Escobedo, Edgar, Dod.	1.000	17	3	6	0	9	0
Espaillat, Ezequiel, Mar.	.000	15	0	0	0	0	0
Evans, Louis, Mar.*	.750	14	1	5	2	8	1
Ewin, Ryan, Brav.	.000	1	0	0	0	0	0
Farley, Chris, R.S.	1.000	3	0	1	0	1	0
Ferreira, Emilo, Twi.	.846	12	2	9	2	13	0
Figueroa, Juan, Tig.	.800	17	0	4	1	5	0
Figueroa, Williams, Exp.	1.000	12	1	0	0	1	0
Frawley, Patrick, Mar.	.000	6	0	0	2	2	0
Frost, Clint, Roy.	1.000	4	2	1	0	3	0
Furnald, Donnie, Brav.	.000	4	0	0	0	0	0
Gabbard, Kason, R.S.*	1.000	6	0	2	0	2	0
Galarraga, Armando, Exp.	.600	14	0	3	2	5	1
Garcia, Angel, Twi.	.800	9	3	1	1	5	0
George, Brad, Reds	.938	7	3	12	1	16	1
George, Todd, Exp.	.500	8	0	1	1	2	0
Gil, Dave, Reds	1.000	4	2	4	0	6	0
Gillman, Justin, Reds	1.000	9	3	4	0	7	1
Gomez, Jose, Reds	1.000	14	2	6	0	8	1
Gomez, Warmar, Exp.	1.000	18	1	5	0	6	0
Gonzalez, Jose, R.S.	1.000	1	0	1	0	1	0
Gonzalez, Luis, Dod.*	1.000	13	0	4	0	4	0
Gooding, Jason, Roy.*	.000	1	0	0	0	0	0
Grabow, John, Pir.*	.750	6	1	2	1	4	0
Graves, Robert, Tig.*	1.000	9	0	1	0	1	0
Grilli, Jason, Mar.	.000	2	0	0	0	0	0
Griswold, Jordan, Exp.*	.667	16	0	4	2	6	0
Guerrero, Jorge, Mar.	.000	1	0	0	0	0	0
Guerrero, Julio, Pir.	.750	3	0	3	1	4	0
Guerrero, Thomas, Exp.	1.000	19	1	2	0	3	0

PITCHERS

Player, Team	Pct.	G	PO	A	E	TC	DP
Abbott, Jim, Twi.	.000	2	0	0	0	0	0
Acuna, Jose, Exp.	.929	14	2	11	1	14	0
Aguilar, Ray, Brav.*	1.000	7	0	6	0	6	0
Aguilera, Adrian, Dod.*	.000	4	0	0	0	0	0
Akens, Phil, Mar.	1.000	6	1	5	0	6	0
Albaladejo, Jonathan, Pir.	1.000	10	0	6	0	6	0
Almeida, Brian, Brav.	.000	2	0	0	0	0	0
Almonte, Henry, Pir.	.000	2	0	0	0	0	0
Alvarez, Juan, Brav.*	1.000	11	0	4	0	4	0
Alvarez, Melvin, Pir.*	1.000	7	2	2	0	4	0
Andara, Miguel, Pir.	.875	8	2	5	1	8	0
Anderson, Wes, Mar.	.000	1	0	0	0	0	0
Andrews, Aron, Dod.	.000	6	0	0	0	0	0
Arteaga, Erick, Phi.	1.000	10	5	5	0	10	2
Arteaga, Francisco, Brav.	.889	18	4	4	1	9	1
Artiles, Carlos, Yan.*	.800	10	1	3	1	5	0
Astacio, Ezequiel, Phi.	.895	9	6	11	2	19	0
Baker, Bo, Roy.	.000	1	0	0	0	0	0
Bale, John, Ori.*	1.000	2	1	1	0	2	0
Banks, Tyler, Mar.	1.000	10	2	3	0	5	0
Barrios, Rafael, Tig.	1.000	23	4	3	0	7	0
Bartel, Richard, Reds	.000	1	0	0	0	0	0
Bartsch, John, Ori.	1.000	10	1	5	0	6	0
Batista, Gordy, Reds	1.000	10	2	8	0	10	0
Baxter, Allen, Mar.	.750	9	3	3	2	8	0
Bedard, Erik, Ori.*	1.000	2	0	2	0	2	1

Player, Team	Pct.	G	PO	A	E	TC	DP
Gutierrez, Jannio, Twi.	.875	23	1	6	1	8	0
Hall, Shane, R.S.	1.000	4	0	3	0	3	0
Hampton, Royce, Rang.*	.900	12	5	4	1	10	0
Henkel, Robert, Mar.*	1.000	9	0	2	0	2	0
Herrera, Junior, Tig.	1.000	18	3	5	0	8	0
Hickman, Ben, Mar.	1.000	5	0	1	0	1	0
Hill, Joshua, Twi.	.800	12	0	4	1	5	0
Hill, Terry, R.S.*	.000	3	0	0	0	0	0
Hinckley, Michael, Exp.*	.846	8	3	8	2	13	0
Holdzkom, Lincoln, Mar.	.714	12	4	6	4	14	0
Hollis, Barton, R.S.	1.000	7	0	2	0	2	0
Huang, Jun-chih, R.S.	1.000	10	2	1	0	3	0
Hughes, Nial, Dod.	1.000	2	0	3	0	3	0
Imotichey, Tory, Exp.*	.778	10	0	7	2	9	0
Jackson, Edwin, Dod.	.800	12	1	3	1	5	0
Jacob, Russell, R.S.	1.000	5	1	1	0	2	0
Jimenez, Kelvin, Rang.	.786	9	3	8	3	14	0
Johansen, Ryan, Dod.	1.000	21	0	5	0	5	0
Johnson, James, Ori.	.833	7	1	4	1	6	1
Johnston, Clint, Pir.*	1.000	2	0	1	0	1	0
Joyce, Thomas, Ori.*	.000	1	0	0	0	0	0
Kaanoi, Jason, Roy.	.833	14	2	3	1	6	0
Kennard, Jeff, Yan.	1.000	19	1	1	0	2	0
Kennedy, Jodie, R.S.*	1.000	3	0	2	0	2	1
Kiley, Jason, Pir.	1.000	8	2	5	0	7	0
King, Jeremy, Yan.	.900	11	5	4	1	10	0
Kirkman, Tyler, Exp.*	.000	2	0	0	0	0	0
Kuo, Hong-chih, Dod.*	1.000	7	0	1	0	1	0
Lababera, Michael, Exp.	1.000	1	1	0	0	1	0
Lammers, Kris, Phi.*	.875	12	1	6	1	8	0
Landaeta, Argenis, Yan.	1.000	10	6	11	0	17	0
Lara, Nelson, Reds	1.000	4	0	1	0	1	0
Leach, Bryan, R.S.	1.000	5	0	2	0	2	0
Lee, Kevin, Pir.	1.000	9	0	1	0	1	0
Lee, Seung, Phi.	.833	3	0	5	1	6	0
Lerew, Anthony, Brav.	.857	12	1	5	1	7	0
Levinski, Donald, Brav.	1.000	3	1	0	0	1	0
Lewis, Rommie, Ori.*	.857	10	1	5	1	7	0
Light, Scott, Reds	.833	8	1	4	1	6	0
Liscir, Aloxandor, Pir.	.400	8	0	2	3	5	0
Löhse, Eric, Twi.	.917	10	1	10	1	12	1
Long, Nick, Exp.	.750	4	1	2	1	4	0
Lopez, Gonzalo, Brav.	1.000	12	1	6	0	7	0
Lopez, Javier, Dod.*	.857	14	0	6	1	7	1
Lopez, Samuel, Roy.	1.000	3	0	1	0	1	0
Lorenzen, Jonathan, Dod.	.833	7	2	3	1	6	0
Lowery, Devon, Roy.	1.000	11	4	1	0	5	0
Lundgren, Wayne, R.S.	1.000	13	3	11	0	14	2
Lutz, Kenneth, Reds	.800	6	2	2	1	5	0
Lyons, Thomas, Tig.	1.000	5	1	2	0	3	2
Machen, Mike, Brav.	.800	13	1	3	1	5	0
Marcano, Luis, Rang.	.000	3	0	0	1	1	0
Marietta, Ron, Yan.*	1.000	2	0	1	0	1	0
Mason, Robert, Brav.*	.800	14	1	3	1	5	0
Masset, Nicholas, Rang.	.800	15	0	8	2	10	0
Mata, Gustavo, Exp.	1.000	10	1	9	0	10	0
Mateo, Aneudis, R.S.	1.000	3	1	0	0	1	0
Mathiesen, Ryan, Brav.	1.000	22	0	2	0	2	0
Mau, Ryan, Mar.	1.000	4	2	0	0	2	0
McBride, Macay, Brav.*	.875	13	1	6	1	8	0
McCall, Dan, Pir.	1.000	16	1	1	0	2	0
McClendon, Matt, Brav.	.000	3	0	0	0	0	0
McGlinchy, Kevin, Brav.	.000	2	0	0	0	0	0
Meisenheimer, Matt, Rang.	.667	15	1	3	2	6	0
Mendoza, Cristian, Yan.	.000	3	0	0	0	0	0
Mendoza, Jorge, Rang.	1.000	11	1	4	0	5	0
Metzger, Jon, Roy.*	1.000	6	0	4	0	4	0
Meyer, Scott, Reds*	1.000	14	2	7	0	9	2
Mims, Brandon, R.S.*	1.000	11	1	14	0	15	0
Mitchell, Andy, Ori.	1.000	12	5	6	0	11	0
Montero, Jose, Rang.	1.000	5	2	2	0	4	0
Morel, Jhosandy, Pir.*	.750	6	1	2	1	4	0
Moreno, Victor, Phi.	.714	15	3	2	2	7	0
Morrison, Robbie, Roy.	.000	2	0	0	0	0	0
Moser, Todd, Mar.*	1.000	1	0	1	0	1	0
Mosley, Eric, Yan.	1.000	6	4	3	0	7	0
Murray, Arlington, Rang.*	.900	12	4	5	1	10	1
Mutch, Paul, Twi.	1.000	17	1	7	0	8	0
Nall, T.J., Dod.	1.000	4	1	3	0	4	0
Nelson, Justin, Roy.*	.833	12	2	3	1	6	1
Nelson, Stephen, Dod.	1.000	10	0	4	0	4	1
Nettles, Tim, Yan.	.000	3	0	0	1	1	0

Player, Team	Pct.	G	PO	A	E	TC	DP
Neuage, Leigh, Dod.	.000	3	0	0	0	0	0
Newell, Mark, Roy.	.000	5	0	0	0	0	0
Newton, Stan, Yan.	1.000	19	1	7	0	8	0
Niedbalski, Nick, Twi.*	.857	14	0	6	1	7	0
Nunez, Kelvin, Roy.	.800	19	4	8	3	15	0
Nunez, Leo, Pir.	1.000	10	4	7	0	11	0
Nunez, Renny, Reds	.750	8	0	3	1	4	0
Oquendo, Ian, Pir.	1.000	3	2	2	0	4	0
Ortiz, Javier, Yan.	1.000	2	1	0	0	1	0
Owens, Henry, Pir.	.000	6	0	0	0	0	0
Padilla, Roy, Mar.*	1.000	4	1	0	0	1	0
Paz, Jackson, Brav.*	1.000	12	1	4	0	5	0
Pearson, Brent, Pir.	1.000	11	0	8	0	8	0
Peña, Geronimo, Roy.	.933	17	2	12	1	15	0
Perez, Carlos, Ori.*	.833	14	1	4	1	6	0
Petty, Chad, Tig.*	.778	12	0	7	2	9	0
Puello, Ignacio, Exp.	.800	8	0	4	1	5	0
Purcell, Brian, Pir.*	1.000	9	1	3	0	4	0
Pylate, Chad, Twi.	1.000	10	2	7	0	9	0
Rada, Gerald, Yan.	1.000	8	1	3	0	4	1
Rahrer, Josh, Rang.	.500	5	1	0	1	2	0
Ramirez, Jordy, Reds	.000	1	0	0	0	0	0
Ramos, Victor, Pir.	.000	1	0	0	0	0	0
Reames, Jay, Exp.	.000	3	0	0	1	1	0
Reina, Dimas, Dod.	1.000	25	4	2	0	6	1
Rengifo, Nohemar, Exp.	.250	14	0	1	3	4	0
Reyes, Maximo, Phi.	1.000	17	0	4	0	4	0
Reynolds, Eric, Yan.*	1.000	11	1	2	0	3	0
Richardson, Jason, Twi.	.000	4	0	0	0	0	0
Rivas, Gabriel, Tig.	1.000	18	1	4	0	5	0
Rivera, Saul, Twi.	1.000	3	0	1	0	1	0
Rodney, Fernando, Tig.	1.000	1	1	0	0	1	0
Rodriguez, Enoc, Reds*	1.000	2	0	1	0	1	0
Rodriguez, Miguel, R.S.	.800	11	1	7	2	10	1
Rollandini, David, Phi.	1.000	9	2	5	0	7	1
Rosado, Hector, Roy.*	1.000	14	2	5	0	7	0
Rose, Michael, Exp.	.500	3	1	0	1	2	0
Ross, Brian, Reds*	1.000	2	0	1	0	1	1
Royal, Shannon, R.S.*	1.000	10	1	4	0	5	0
Saborhagon, Brot, D.S.	.007	2	1	1	1	3	0
Sala, Marino, Ori.	1.000	15	0	3	0	3	0
Salas, Jose, Brav.	.500	1	0	1	1	2	0
Salazar, Richard, Ori.*	.000	1	0	0	0	0	0
Sanchez, Elby, Roy.	.900	18	4	5	1	10	0
Sanchez, Rafael, R.S.	.889	10	2	6	1	9	0
Sanchez, Roberto, Roy.	1.000	12	4	3	0	7	0
Santana, Eddy, Yan.	.833	7	3	2	1	6	0
Schriner, Brian, Phi.	1.000	16	0	4	0	4	0
Selmo, Santo, Mar.	.786	17	4	7	3	14	1
Sexton, Joey, Brav.	.000	2	0	0	0	0	0
Shafer, Kurt, Pir.	1.000	12	7	3	0	10	0
Sharber, Jeffery, Pir.	1.000	3	1	1	0	2	0
Shortslef, Josh, Pir.*	1.000	10	2	8	0	10	1
Shroyer, Dustin, Pir.*	.000	5	0	0	0	0	0
Simon, Billy, R.S.	.667	3	1	1	1	3	1
Simon, Janewrys, Twi.	.933	13	3	11	1	15	1
Smiley, Gerald, Rang.	.000	3	0	0	1	1	0
Smith, Chris, Ori.*	1.000	2	0	1	0	1	0
SMITH, Jason, Yan.	1.000	11	7	14	0	21	1
Sobkowiak, Scott, Brav.	1.000	2	0	1	0	1	0
Spillers, Larry, Ori.*	1.000	10	4	13	0	17	1
Squires, Matt, Phi.*	.700	17	0	7	3	10	1
Stahl, Rich, Ori.*	1.000	1	0	1	0	1	0
Stentz, Brent, Twi.	1.000	8	0	2	0	2	0
Sterrett, Adam, Mar.	.000	1	0	0	0	0	0
Stevens, Kris, Exp.*	1.000	4	1	3	0	4	0
Stewart, James, Dod.	1.000	11	1	0	0	1	0
Strayhorn, Kole, Dod.	.800	12	3	9	3	15	1
Suarez, Pedro, R.S.	.000	8	0	0	0	0	0
Suarez, Victor, Roy.	1.000	7	0	1	0	1	0
Sweeney, Matt, Phi.	1.000	9	1	5	0	6	1
Tacker, Trevor, Yan.	.900	9	2	7	1	10	1
Tarkington, Shawn, Twi.	.714	13	2	3	2	7	1
Taylor, David, Dod.	.667	3	2	0	1	3	0
Tejada, Frailyn, Mar.*	1.000	10	3	6	0	9	1
Tejero, Armando, Brav.*	.000	1	0	0	0	0	0
Therneau, Dave, Reds	1.000	5	0	2	0	2	0
Thigpen, Joshua, R.S.	.714	10	1	4	2	7	0
Tierney, Chris, Roy.*	.750	8	1	2	1	4	1
Tillor, Jameo, Ori.	.009	10	1	7	1	9	0
Tingley, Pat, Twi.*	.833	15	1	4	1	6	0
Torres, Carlos, Reds	.917	11	4	7	1	12	0

SUMMER CLASS A *Gulf Coast League*

Player, Team	Pct.	G	PO	A	E	TC	DP
Torres, Luis, Pir.	.000	3	0	0	0	0	0
Totten, Heath, Dod.	1.000	2	0	1	0	1	0
Truselo, Randy, Rang.	1.000	7	0	1	0	1	0
Tyler, Scott, Twi.	1.000	5	0	1	0	1	0
Valdez, Henry, R.S.*	.667	16	1	3	2	6	0
Valentin, Emmanuel, Tig.	1.000	22	1	6	0	7	0
Valera, Luis, Reds	1.000	10	1	0	0	1	0
Vargas, Javier, Tig.	1.000	9	1	11	0	12	1
Vasquez, Jorge, Roy.	.000	4	0	0	0	0	0
Vaughn, Josh, Exp.*	.750	11	1	2	1	4	0
Wagnon, Dwayne, Reds	.875	10	3	4	1	8	0
Ward, Bryan, R.S.*	1.000	1	0	1	0	1	0
Wheatland, Matt, Tig.	1.000	3	1	2	0	3	1
Wheeler, Adam, Yan.	1.000	10	5	5	0	10	1
Wheldon, Rhys, Twi.	1.000	13	0	3	0	3	0
White, Kenneth, Ori.	1.000	4	1	2	0	3	0
Williams, Todd, Yan.	1.000	1	1	0	0	1	0
Withelder, Gregory, Dod.*	1.000	6	1	5	0	6	0
Wright, Chase, Yan.*	1.000	10	0	8	0	8	0
Yankosky, L.J., Brav.	1.000	4	1	3	0	4	1

LEAGUE CHAMPIONS

Year	Team	Pct.	Year	Team	Pct.	Year	Team	Pct.
1964—	Sarasota Braves	.610	1982—	New York AL	.667	1992—	Royals∞	.695
1965—	Bradenton Astros	.632	1983—	Texas	.645		Expos	.593
1966—	New York AL	.667		Los Angeles†	.617	1993—	Rangers▲	.667
1967—	Kansas City	.614	1984—	White Sox	.651		Astros	.593
1968—	Oakland	.650		Rangers†	.571	1994—	Royals◆	.797
1969—	Montreal	.585	1985—	Yankees§	.705		Astros	.695
1970—	Chicago AL	.600		Rangers	.532	1995—	Royals■	.649
1971—	Kansas City	.755	1986—	Reds	.548		Tigers	.579
1972—	Chicago NL*	.651		Dodgers†	.541	1996—	Yankees◆	.638
	Kansas City*	.651	1987—	Dodgers†	.683		Rangers	.617
1973—	Texas	.732		Royals	.635	1997—	Mets▼	.700
1974—	Chicago NL	.702	1988—	Yankees†	.714		Rangers	.567
1975—	Texas	.774		Royals	.619	1998—	Marlins	.633
1976—	Texas	.704	1989—	Yankees‡	.651		Rangers◆	.567
1977—	Chicago AL	.731		Dodgers	.635	1999—	Mets◆	.650
1978—	Texas	.600	1990—	Expos	.635	2000—	Rangers◆	.679
1979—	Houston	.635		Dodgers‡	.603	2001—	Dodgers	.683
1980—	Kansas City-Blue	.635	1991—	Orioles	.593		Yankees◆	.583
1981—	Kansas City-Gold	.688		Expos∞	.533			

*Declared co-champions; no playoff. †League divided into Northern and Southern divisions; won one-game playoff for league championship. ‡League divided into Northern and Southern divisions; won best-of-three playoff for league championship. §Yankees declared champion based on winning percentage when one-game playoff against Rangers was rained out. ∞League divided into Northern, Southern and Central divisions; won best-of-three playoff for league championship. ▲League divided into Eastern, Central and Western divisions; won three-team playoff. ◆League divided into Eastern, Northern and Western divisions; won three-team playoff. ■League divided into Eastern, Northern, Northwest and Southwest divisions; won four-team playoff. ▼League divided into Eastern, Western and Northwest divisions; won four-club playoff. (Note—Known as Sarasota Rookie League in 1964 and Florida Rookie League in 1965.)

PIONEER LEAGUE

LEAGUE OFFICE

President
Jim McCurdy
Address
P.O. Box 2564
Spokane, WA 99220
Phone
509-456-7615

Teams (affiliation)
Billings Mustangs (Reds)
Casper Rockies (Rockies)
Great Falls Dodgers (Dodgers)
Idaho Falls Padres (Padres)

Medicine Hat Blue Jays (Blue Jays)
Missoula Osprey (Diamondbacks)
Ogden Raptors (Brewers)
Provo Angels (Angels)

2001 FINAL STANDINGS

FIRST HALF

NORTH DIVISION

Team	W	L	T	Pct.	GB
Billings (Reds)	25	12	0	.676	...
Missoula (Diamondbacks)	25	13	0	.658	1.0
Great Falls (Dodgers)	18	20	0	.474	5.0
Medicine Hat (Blue Jays)	9	29	0	.237	11.0

SOUTH DIVISION

Team	W	L	T	Pct.	GB
Provo (Angels)	29	9	0	.763	...
Casper (Rockies)	16	22	0	.421	13.0
Ogden (Brewers)	14	22	0	.389	14.0
Idaho Falls (Padres)	14	23	0	.378	14.5

SECOND HALF

NORTH DIVISION

Team	W	L	T	Pct.	GB
Missoula (Diamondbacks)	27	11	0	.711	...
Billings (Reds)	21	17	0	.553	6.0
Great Falls (Dodgers)	19	19	0	.500	8.0
Medicine Hat (Blue Jays)	11	27	0	.289	16.0

SOUTH DIVISION

Team	W	L	T	Pct.	GB
Provo (Angels)	24	14	0	.632	...
Ogden (Brewers)	22	16	0	.579	2.0
Casper (Rockies)	21	17	0	.553	4.0
Idaho Falls (Padres)	7	31	0	.184	17.0

COMPOSITE

Team	Pro.	Miss.	Bil.	G.F.	Cas.	Og.	I.F.	M.H.	W	L	T	Pct.	GB
Provo (Angels)	...	3	4	5	11	10	16	4	53	23	0	.697	...
Missoula (Diamondbacks)	3	...	10	9	5	5	5	15	52	24	0	.684	1.0
Billings (Reds)	2	11	...	10	3	5	4	11	46	29	0	.613	6.5
Great Falls (Dodgers)	1	6	6	...	3	2	4	15	37	39	0	.487	16.0
Casper (Rockies)	4	1	3	3	...	11	11	4	37	39	0	.487	16.0
Ogden (Brewers)	8	1	0	4	8	...	10	5	36	38	0	.486	16.0
Idaho Falls (Padres)	3	1	2	2	7	4	...	2	21	54	0	.280	31.5
Medicine Hat (Blue Jays)	2	1	4	6	2	1	4	...	20	56	0	.263	33.0

Club names are major league affiliations.

PLAYOFFS: Billings defeated Missoula two games to one; Provo defeated Casper two games to none; Billings defeated Provo two games to none to win Pioneer League championship.

REGULAR-SEASON ATTENDANCE: Billings, 104,524; Casper, 41,849; Great Falls, 88,198; Idaho Falls, 63,410; Medicine Hat, 25,930; Missoula, 54,868; Ogden, 100,360; Provo, 51,919. Total—540,058. Playoff (7 games)—14,472.

MANAGERS: Billings, Rick Burleson; Casper, P.J. Carey; Great Falls, Dave Silvestri; Idaho Falls, Jake Molina; Medicine Hat, Tom Bradley; Missoula, Chip Hale; Ogden, Ed Seder; Provo, Tom Kotchman.

ALL-STAR TEAM: 1B—Jesus Cota, Missoula; 2B—Scott Hairston, Missoula; 3B—Froilan Villanueava, Ogden; SS—Casey Smith, Provo; OF—Jose Garcia, Great Falls; OF—Tony Miller, Casper; OF—Sam Swenson, Provo; C—Al Corbeil, Provo; DH—Jesus Gutierrez, Billings; RHP—Pedro Liriano, Provo; LHP—Jason Dennis, Provo; Relief pitcher—Nathan Cotton, Billings; Most Valuable Player—Jesus Cota, Missoula; Pitcher of the Year—Pedro Liriano, Provo; Manager of the Year—Chip Hale, Missoula.

2001 BATTING

TEAM

Team	Avg.	G	TPA	AB	R	H	TB	2B	3B	HR	RBI	SH	SF	HP	BB	IBB	SO	SB	CS	GDP	LOB	ShO	Slg.	OBP
Provo	.304	76	3061	2631	557	801	1199	145	23	69	481	22	30	63	315	9	607	82	33	45	581	0	.456	.388
Missoula	.284	76	3091	2701	535	768	1183	146	31	69	472	11	19	70	290	12	596	47	26	36	587	3	.438	.366
Ogden	.284	74	2911	2575	460	731	1054	143	18	48	382	23	30	37	246	6	499	107	42	29	524	3	.409	.351
Billings	.278	75	2989	2637	452	734	1077	131	25	54	387	15	25	46	266	9	533	84	31	41	581	3	.408	.352
Casper	.277	76	2970	2614	448	724	1123	127	25	74	385	8	23	48	277	6	686	108	67	38	544	1	.430	.354
Idaho Falls	.260	75	2936	2619	405	680	979	130	20	43	341	6	21	43	247	5	722	60	31	49	528	5	.374	.331
Medicine Hat	.256	76	2958	2640	361	675	979	111	14	55	304	23	10	62	223	5	594	63	28	42	557	5	.371	.327
Great Falls	.254	76	2947	2590	400	657	936	109	22	42	346	18	18	48	273	13	496	137	47	57	512	6	.361	.334

TOP QUALIFIERS FOR BATTING CHAMPIONSHIP

Minimum 205 plate appearances. *Lefthanded batter. †Switch-hitter.

Player, Team	Avg.	G	TPA	AB	R	H	TB	2B	3B	HR	RBI	SH	SF	HP	BB	IBB	SO	SB	CS	GDP	Slg.	OBP
Cota, Jesus, Miss.*	.368	75	334	272	74	100	170	22	0	16	71	0	2	2	56	6	52	2	0	5	.625	.476
Corbeil, Alfred, Pro.*	.359	60	268	217	48	78	114	18	0	6	49	0	5	6	40	4	41	0	1	5	.525	.463
Varner, Gary, Bil.	.351	72	326	291	55	102	156	20	5	8	55	0	3	3	29	1	64	7	4	3	.536	.411
Swenson, Samuel, Pro.*	.351	63	267	225	61	79	142	16	4	13	55	0	4	14	24	0	64	7	1	5	.631	.438
Hairston, Scott, Miss.	.347	74	338	291	81	101	171	16	6	14	65	0	2	7	38	2	50	2	2	5	.588	.432
Chavez, Ender, Cas.*	.342	64	270	228	49	78	89	9	1	0	22	3	0	1	38	0	31	24	7	3	.390	.438
Hart, Jon, Og.	.340	69	296	262	53	89	142	18	1	11	62	0	6	2	26	1	47	14	1	4	.542	.395
Santana, Ralph, Og.*	.337	68	303	261	57	88	99	6	1	1	26	2	0	3	37	1	37	30	12	3	.379	.425
McEachran, Aaron, M.H.*	.336	69	297	256	34	86	113	12	1	5	41	1	0	0	0?	0	66	2	1	7	.449	.426
Tempesta, Nick, M.H.	.335	72	298	263	49	88	130	16	1	8	46	1	1	9	24	2	51	3	1	3	.494	.407
Bergolla, William, Bil.	.323	57	262	232	47	75	98	5	3	4	24	1	3	2	24	0	21	22	7	1	.422	.387
Smith, Casey, Pro.	.321	62	301	249	60	80	96	11	1	1	34	9	3	3	37	1	40	6	4	0	.386	.411
Lopez, Michael, Miss.	.313	73	339	284	70	89	142	21	4	8	37	2	1	16	36	0	52	6	2	2	.500	.418
Pierce, Sean, G.F.	.311	72	321	273	59	85	128	11	7	6	43	0	0	5	43	1	54	29	6	5	.469	.414
Barfield, Josh, I.F.	.310	66	300	277	51	86	121	15	4	4	53	0	4	3	16	1	54	12	4	7	.437	.350

DEPARTMENTAL LEADERS: G—Cota, 75; AB—J. Garcia, 306; R—Hairston, 81; H—Varner, 102; TB—Hairston, 171; 2B—J. Garcia, 23; 3B—Janz, 8; HR—Cota, Gutierrez, 16 each; RBI—Cota, 71; SH—S. Smith, 9; SF—Gutierrez, 7; HP—Lopez, 16; BB—Cota, 56; IBB—Cota, 6; SO—Vasquez, 96; SB—M. Nunez, 32; CS—R. Santana, 12; GIDP—J. Garcia, 9; Slg.—Swenson, .631; OBP—Cota, .476.

ALL PLAYERS

*Lefthanded batter. †Switch-hitter.

Player, Team	Avg.	G	TPA	AB	R	H	TB	2B	3B	HR	RBI	SH	SF	HP	BB	IBB	SO	SB	CS	GDP	Slg.	OBP
Adames, Epidaro, Pro.	.000	1	4	4	0	0	0	0	0	0	0	0	0	0	0	0	1	0	0	0	.000	.000
Alvarado, Joel, Og.	.192	18	57	52	5	10	10	0	0	0	3	1	0	1	3	0	5	0	1	1	.192	.250
Aquino, Jack, I.F.†	.250	56	224	196	30	49	70	5	5	2	23	2	3	0	23	0	35	6	5	2	.357	.324
Aracena, Sandy, G.F.	.256	44	180	164	26	42	65	9	1	4	25	1	1	2	12	0	20	2	0	4	.396	.313
Baez, Carlos, I.F.	.228	55	192	180	18	41	53	5	2	1	21	1	0	3	8	0	50	1	2	4	.294	.272
Ball, Jarred, Miss.†	.246	19	67	57	13	14	18	2	1	0	3	1	0	2	7	0	14	1	1	1	.316	.348
Bannon, Jeff, Bil.	.260	60	257	235	37	61	81	11	3	1	31	0	3	3	16	0	33	5	2	4	.345	.311
Barfield, Josh, I.F.	.310	66	300	277	51	86	121	15	4	4	53	0	4	3	16	1	54	12	4	7	.437	.350
Barnwell, Chris, Og.	.307	69	282	261	49	80	109	19	5	0	37	3	4	7	7	2	28	17	2	2	.418	.337
Batista, Christian, Pro.	.296	17	66	54	10	16	25	1	1	2	8	0	0	1	10	0	13	0	1	1	.463	.415
Bautista, Augusto, Bil.	.083	6	14	12	1	1	1	0	0	0	1	1	0	0	1	0	5	1	0	0	.083	.214
Bello, Vladimir, Cas.	.304	49	173	161	27	49	67	5	5	1	27	2	1	2	7	0	36	16	3	1	.416	.339
Bergolla, William, Bil.	.323	57	262	232	47	75	98	5	3	4	24	1	3	2	24	0	21	22	7	1	.422	.387
Blackburn, John, M.H.	.252	42	157	139	19	35	47	6	0	2	14	2	0	1	15	0	41	1	1	1	.338	.329
Boll, Javier, Miss.	.269	35	136	119	17	32	50	7	1	3	21	0	1	5	11	0	19	2	2	2	.420	.353
Boyd, Dan, Og.	.357	5	15	14	1	5	6	1	0	0	1	0	0	0	1	0	1	0	0	0	.429	.400
Brand, Kevin, Miss.†	.220	18	64	59	6	13	13	0	0	0	2	1	0	1	3	0	8	1	1	0	.220	.270
Cahill, Jonathan, Pro.	.419	8	34	31	7	13	16	3	0	0	5	0	0	1	2	0	2	4	1	0	.516	.471
Canales, Josh, G.F.	.500	3	34	30	4	15	17	2	0	0	6	0	0	2	2	1	3	0	0	0	.567	.559
Carrow, Tom, Og.	.331	45	194	157	37	52	74	7	0	5	20	0	1	3	33	1	34	7	3	1	.471	.454
Chavez, Ender, Cas.*	.342	64	270	228	49	78	89	9	1	0	22	3	0	1	38	0	31	24	7	3	.390	.438
Chilsom, Marques, Miss.	.194	21	44	36	6	7	8	1	0	0	2	1	0	0	7	0	14	0	1	0	.222	.326
Chourio, Jorjanis, Bil.	.233	45	147	133	24	31	46	6	3	1	12	2	0	2	10	0	37	5	5	0	.346	.297
Corbeil, Alfred, Pro.*	.359	60	268	217	48	78	114	18	0	6	49	0	5	6	40	4	41	0	1	5	.525	.463
Cordova, Ricardo, G.F.†	.198	34	132	116	17	23	28	3	1	0	11	1	3	0	12	0	22	0	1	3	.241	.267
Corporan, Roberto, Miss.†...	.000	3	7	5	1	0	0	0	0	0	0	0	0	0	2	0	3	0	0	0	.000	.286
Corrente, David, M.H.	.192	35	116	99	7	19	27	5	0	1	6	2	0	7	8	0	32	1	0	2	.273	.298
Cota, Jesus, Miss.*	.368	75	334	272	74	100	170	22	0	16	71	0	2	2	56	6	52	2	0	5	.625	.476
Davis, Justin, Bil.*	.295	25	102	88	18	26	35	7	1	0	18	0	0	1	13	1	11	3	0	1	.398	.392
Del Chiaro, Brent, Pro.	.158	22	67	57	2	9	10	1	0	0	5	1	2	0	7	0	20	1	0	0	.175	.242
De Los Santos, Omar, G.F.	.186	37	111	102	13	19	23	1	0	1	7	2	1	1	5	0	32	2	1	5	.225	.229
De Los Santos, Pedro, I.F.†...	.348	12	50	46	11	16	22	4	1	0	5	1	0	1	2	0	10	5	0	1	.478	.388
Diaz, Eduardo, Cas.	.279	71	305	269	44	75	125	17	6	7	51	1	4	0	31	0	63	13	10	3	.465	.349
Diaz, Jose, G.F.	.189	48	183	159	18	30	47	8	0	3	17	0	2	7	15	0	38	2	1	3	.296	.284
Diredo, Curtis, Miss.	.246	19	66	61	8	15	17	2	0	0	5	0	0	1	4	0	15	3	2	3	.279	.303
Encarnacion, Edwin, Bil.	.261	52	228	211	27	55	82	6	2	5	26	0	2	0	15	0	29	8	1	6	.389	.307
Escalera, Jose, G.F.	.167	9	46	42	4	7	7	0	0	0	2	0	1	0	3	1	5	0	0	1	.167	.217
Esparragoza, Pedro, Og.	.000	1	1	1	0	0	0	0	0	0	0	0	0	0	0	0	1	0	0	0	.000	.000
Essery, Frederick, Cas.	.150	24	63	60	4	9	9	0	0	0	9	1	0	1	0	0	12	0	0	2	.150	.161
Eure, Jeffrey, Og.	.215	50	159	144	16	31	47	7	0	3	24	1	1	6	7	0	41	6	2	3	.326	.278
Eylward, Thomas, Pro.	.300	7	25	20	7	6	9	3	0	0	5	0	0	3	2	0	5	0	0	0	.450	.440
Falcon, Omar, I.F.	.187	37	144	107	24	20	40	5	0	5	9	0	0	4	33	0	50	0	1	0	.374	.396
Fisher, Timothy, Miss.	.071	16	34	28	5	2	2	0	0	0	0	0	0	4	2	0	12	0	0	0	.071	.235
Fry, Ryan, Bil.	.222	3	9	9	1	2	2	0	0	0	2	0	0	0	0	0	4	0	0	1	.222	.222
Garabito, Vianney, Bil.	.179	10	43	39	9	7	11	4	0	0	4	0	1	0	3	0	5	0	0	0	.282	.233
Garcia, Jose, G.F.	.291	74	324	306	46	89	144	23	4	8	50	0	0	5	13	1	49	15	9	9	.471	.330
Garcia, Lino, Miss.	.243	46	161	140	34	34	56	6	2	4	22	2	0	5	14	0	32	8	2	1	.400	.333
Gates, James, Pro.	.294	48	205	170	31	50	72	13	0	3	33	0	6	29	0	43	4	3	6	.424	.415
Gemoll, Brandon, Og.*	.308	6	14	13	1	4	4	0	0	0	1	0	0	1	0	2	0	1	0	.308	.357
Gillitzer, Scott, G.F.	.261	66	284	253	34	66	80	11	0	1	41	3	3	4	21	2	23	10	1	5	.316	.324
Giorgis, David, I.F.†	.289	65	273	242	28	70	107	16	0	7	41	0	4	2	24	2	69	2	4	6	.442	.359
Gorneault, Nicholas, Pro.	.315	54	187	168	38	53	91	12	4	6	30	2	1	5	11	1	65	5	2	0	.542	.373
Gray, Josh, Pro.	.240	57	230	200	32	48	72	6	0	6	31	1	2	5	22	0	58	2	1	4	.360	.328
Guerrero, Armando, M.H.	.243	72	280	263	35	64	100	10	1	8	36	3	2	2	10	0	61	10	10	2	.380	.274

Player, Team	Avg.	G	TPA	AB	R	H	TB	2B	3B	HR	RBI	SH	SF	HP	BB	IBB	SO	SB	CS	GDP	Slg.	OBP
Guerrero, Hector, G.F.*	.210	31	133	124	18	26	44	5	2	3	12	1	0	2	6	1	15	6	2	1	.355	.258
Gutierrez, Jesse, Bil.	.294	72	312	269	45	79	148	21	0	16	61	0	7	7	29	2	43	1	0	7	.550	.369
Guzman, Junior, Pro.	.343	11	40	35	11	12	27	0	0	5	13	0	1	0	4	0	5	0	0	1	.771	.400
Haggard, Chris, Og.	.193	34	112	83	14	16	22	0	0	2	12	2	2	6	19	0	28	1	0	0	.265	.373
Hairston, Scott, Miss.	.347	74	338	291	81	101	171	16	6	14	65	0	2	7	38	2	50	2	2	5	.588	.432
Hardy, J.J., Og.	.248	35	144	125	20	31	42	5	0	2	15	3	1	0	15	0	12	1	2	2	.336	.326
Hart, Jon, Og.	.340	69	296	262	53	89	142	18	1	11	62	0	6	2	26	1	47	14	1	4	.542	.395
Hastings, Joseph, I.F.*	.339	34	141	124	24	42	73	16	0	5	34	0	1	0	15	1	32	1	1	0	.589	.407
Hawes, Bobby, Bil.	.269	47	198	182	30	49	54	5	0	0	19	1	1	3	11	0	26	5	4	2	.297	.320
Hetherington, Luke, M.H.	.207	51	198	174	22	36	53	3	4	2	14	1	0	5	18	0	54	6	1	4	.305	.299
Hicks, Brian, Og.*	.233	28	114	103	17	24	41	10	2	1	12	2	0	0	9	0	24	1	1	0	.398	.295
Hilinski, Scott, Miss.	.246	42	166	138	34	34	49	5	2	2	18	0	2	1	25	2	45	4	1	2	.355	.361
Hinton, Travis, Og.*	.277	69	269	235	44	65	106	17	0	8	41	0	5	0	29	1	58	3	4	3	.451	.349
Hyde, Nathan, M.H.	.232	57	209	190	27	44	66	7	3	3	18	1	1	4	12	0	47	5	0	4	.347	.290
Ingram, Bryan, Cas.	.237	22	87	76	7	18	28	3	2	1	10	0	1	4	6	0	25	0	2	1	.368	.322
Iorg, Isaac, M.H.	.250	24	82	80	8	20	29	3	0	2	10	0	0	1	1	0	16	0	1	2	.363	.268
Jacobo, Kervin, Miss.†	.269	59	245	219	36	59	90	10	3	5	36	1	2	1	22	2	72	4	3	1	.411	.336
January, Javerro, Og.	.263	11	22	19	6	5	8	1	1	0	3	0	0	1	2	0	6	0	0	0	.421	.364
Janz, Jeramy, Miss.*	.293	67	281	259	40	76	121	14	8	5	62	1	3	2	16	0	46	2	2	5	.467	.336
Johnson, Dale, Pro.	.277	27	95	83	12	23	26	3	0	0	12	4	1	3	4	0	17	0	1	0	.313	.330
Johnson, Michael, G.F.*	.247	45	188	154	32	38	47	3	3	0	13	1	0	2	31	2	32	14	4	2	.305	.380
Jung, Young-jin, I.F.	.158	23	66	57	9	9	11	2	0	0	3	0	0	2	7	0	23	0	0	0	.193	.273
Kimberley, Glynn, M.H.	.232	52	215	190	21	44	81	8	1	9	26	0	2	5	18	0	64	0	0	3	.426	.312
Klatt, Joel, I.F.	.208	45	140	125	13	26	39	7	0	2	10	0	0	1	14	0	47	3	0	4	.312	.293
Kotchman, Casey, Pro.*	.500	7	24	22	6	11	14	3	0	0	7	0	0	0	2	0	0	0	0	0	.636	.542
Kulbe, Eric, I.F.*	.125	15	21	16	4	2	3	1	0	0	0	0	0	1	4	0	5	0	0	1	.188	.333
Lagana, Shawn, Pro.	.266	38	159	143	27	38	49	6	1	1	17	3	1	2	10	0	22	5	2	4	.343	.321
Lanoix, Gilbert, G.F.*	.250	1	4	4	0	1	1	0	0	0	0	0	0	0	0	0	0	0	0	0	.250	.250
Lewis, Domonique, Bil.	.257	41	175	148	33	38	49	3	1	2	15	6	0	3	18	0	27	15	1	2	.331	.349
Lopez, Michael, Miss.	.313	73	339	284	70	89	142	21	4	8	37	2	1	16	36	0	52	6	2	2	.500	.418
Malone, Billy, G.F.	.210	55	209	176	23	37	44	5	1	0	18	0	3	5	25	1	49	15	6	6	.250	.321
Martin, Cesar, M.H.	.220	67	299	254	34	56	96	16	0	8	43	4	1	13	27	0	54	4	3	7	.378	.325
Martinez, Thomas, I.F.	.274	36	120	117	15	32	45	7	0	2	16	0	0	2	1	0	26	0	0	6	.385	.292
Mateo, Daniel, Bil.	.556	4	9	9	1	5	5	0	0	0	2	0	0	0	0	0	3	0	1	0	.556	.556
Materano, Oscar, Cas.	.251	69	289	271	34	68	97	11	0	6	38	0	2	7	9	0	59	5	5	5	.358	.291
Mathis, Jeff, Pro.	.299	22	93	77	14	23	35	6	3	0	18	0	3	2	11	0	13	1	0	1	.455	.387
Mayo, Terry, Og.	.235	8	21	17	3	4	6	2	0	0	1	0	1	0	3	0	8	0	1	0	.353	.333
McClanahan, Jonah, Og.	.296	26	106	98	17	29	40	5	3	0	8	5	0	1	2	0	13	2	0	0	.408	.317
McEachran, Aaron, M.H.*	.336	69	297	256	34	86	115	12	1	5	41	1	0	8	32	2	55	3	1	7	.449	.426
MoPherson, Dallas, Pro.*	.395	31	136	124	30	49	75	11	0	5	29	0	0	0	12	0	22	1	0	2	.605	.449
Medina, Frewing, M.H.	.000	19	1	1	0	0	0	0	0	0	0	0	0	0	0	0	0	0	0	0	.000	.000
Medina, Rodney, M.H.†	.308	50	218	195	37	60	88	7	0	7	21	2	0	2	19	0	29	6	2	2	.451	.375
Melton, John, Miss.	.281	13	39	32	5	9	16	1	0	2	6	0	0	0	7	0	11	1	0	1	.500	.410
Mercado, Onix, Bil.	.279	29	98	86	15	24	35	6	1	1	13	2	0	3	7	0	26	0	1	0	.407	.354
Michaelis, Derek, G.F.*	.276	37	153	134	21	37	60	9	1	4	28	1	0	1	17	1	31	2	1	2	.448	.362
Millan, Carlos, I.F.	.190	14	47	42	7	8	11	0	0	1	6	0	0	0	5	0	15	0	1	1	.262	.277
Miller, Tony, Cas.	.306	70	316	268	68	82	135	17	3	10	34	0	4	3	41	0	63	28	10	3	.504	.399
Molidor, David, Bil.	.246	53	232	191	28	47	66	10	0	3	30	1	2	7	31	2	55	5	1	7	.346	.368
Montilla, Samuel, Miss.	.264	46	164	159	21	42	54	8	2	0	20	0	1	1	2	0	20	2	1	1	.340	.276
Moore, Mewelde, I.F.	.236	24	99	89	19	21	25	1	0	1	5	0	0	4	6	0	29	4	2	1	.281	.313
Mora, Ruben, I.F.†	.201	54	209	184	33	37	51	6	4	0	17	2	2	3	18	0	55	12	3	3	.277	.280
Morel, Robinson, Cas.	.250	36	120	108	19	27	47	3	1	5	16	0	0	3	9	0	32	5	3	3	.435	.325
Mulqueen, Dave, Cas.†	.280	73	325	286	49	80	135	19	0	12	49	0	0	3	36	2	89	8	2	7	.472	.366
Nelson, Brad, Og.*	.262	13	47	42	5	11	15	4	0	0	10	0	2	0	3	0	9	0	0	2	.357	.298
Nelson, Chris, Bil.	.233	8	31	30	4	7	8	1	0	0	2	0	0	1	0	0	7	0	0	0	.267	.258
Nevels, Craig, Miss.	.230	48	164	135	21	31	42	8	0	1	20	0	0	9	10	0	32	1	0	1	.311	.325
Nevins, Ryan, Pro.*	.286	4	8	7	0	2	3	1	0	0	3	0	1	0	1	0	1	0	0	1	.429	.250
Nickerson, Brian, G.F.*	.158	8	30	38	3	6	6	0	0	0	3	0	0	1	0	0	5	0	0	1	.158	.179
Nix, Jayson, Cas.	.294	42	179	153	28	45	72	10	1	5	24	0	2	3	21	1	43	1	5	1	.471	.385
Nulton, Kevin, I.F.	.289	53	212	187	28	54	65	7	2	0	21	0	3	1	21	0	33	5	3	8	.348	.358
Nunez, Manuel, G.F.	.250	69	289	244	46	61	87	8	0	6	29	6	1	0	38	2	60	32	8	5	.357	.350
O'Connell, Bradley, G.F.	.310	23	93	84	12	26	39	3	2	2	11	1	0	5	3	0	16	3	3	1	.464	.370
Olson, David, I.F.	.245	48	112	98	21	24	25	1	0	0	9	0	1	3	10	0	45	4	5	0	.255	.330
Ortega, Sixto, Cas.	.324	10	40	37	4	12	16	1	0	1	5	0	0	1	2	0	7	0	1	1	.432	.375
Parrott, Corry, Og.	.197	31	74	71	9	14	17	1	1	0	3	0	0	0	3	0	17	1	1	1	.239	.230
Paula, Manuel, Bil.	.271	49	190	170	24	46	70	7	4	3	23	1	2	5	12	0	53	5	3	0	.412	.333
Peralta, Juan, M.H.†	.231	71	329	299	45	69	83	8	3	0	13	2	2	0	26	1	47	18	8	3	.278	.291
Perez, Jay, Cas.†	.354	35	147	127	22	45	72	7	1	6	27	0	1	2	16	1	28	3	0	4	.567	.432
Peterson, Brian, Bil.	.325	10	46	40	5	13	20	2	1	1	7	0	0	1	5	0	9	0	0	1	.500	.413
Pichardo, Maximo, Pro.	.364	22	100	88	16	32	47	7	1	2	16	0	1	5	6	0	8	12	5	2	.534	.430
Pickens, Jordan, I.F.	.235	52	212	183	29	43	82	13	1	8	26	0	1	9	19	1	57	0	0	2	.448	.335
Pierce, Sean, G.F.	.311	72	321	273	59	85	128	11	7	6	43	0	0	5	43	1	54	29	6	5	.469	.414
Pilkington, Ross, Cas.	.225	41	152	129	19	29	41	9	0	1	9	1	1	2	19	1	34	0	5	2	.318	.331
Porter, Gregory, Pro.	.331	39	148	127	34	42	77	3	1	10	34	0	2	1	18	1	21	3	1	2	.606	.412
Prince, Bryan, Bil.	.255	51	177	157	26	40	63	12	1	3	25	1	0	2	17	1	36	2	1	5	.401	.335
Rivera, William, M.H.*	.208	48	188	173	18	36	40	4	0	0	11	4	1	1	9	0	38	3	2	2	.231	.250
Robinson, Carlos, Miss.	.246	43	131	122	12	30	49	8	1	3	28	0	1	2	6	0	25	0	2	2	.402	.290
Roenicke, Jarett, I.F.*	.286	24	89	84	10	24	26	2	0	0	6	0	0	0	5	0	25	0	0	0	.310	.326
Ruiz, Junior, Bil.*	.000	5	15	9	1	0	0	0	0	0	0	0	0	0	4	0	0	0	0	1	.000	.400
Santana, Ralph, Og.*	.337	68	303	261	57	88	99	6	1	1	26	2	0	3	37	1	37	30	12	3	.379	.425
Selmo, Francisco, I.F.	.274	53	212	197	22	54	80	15	1	3	26	0	1	0	14	0	42	4	0	2	.406	.321
Serafini, Matt, Og.	.161	20	66	62	6	10	17	1	0	2	10	0	0	0	4	0	8	1	0	2	.274	.212
Serrano, Eddie, I.F.	.324	20	74	68	9	22	30	2	0	2	10	0	2	2	2	0	20	1	0	1	.441	.351

Player, Team	Avg.	G	TPA	AB	R	H	TB	2B	3B	HR	RBI	SH	SF	HP	BB	IBB	SO	SB	CS	GDP	Slg.	OBP
Sherlock, Jon, Miss.	.226	25	72	53	11	12	13	1	0	0	3	2	0	6	11	0	16	1	1	1	.245	.414
Smith, Casey, Pro.	.321	62	301	249	60	80	96	11	1	1	34	9	3	3	37	1	40	6	4	0	.386	.411
Soriano, Carlos, Og.	.308	60	252	224	39	69	109	15	2	7	43	2	4	2	20	0	77	18	6	1	.487	.364
Story-Harden, Thomari, G.F.	.263	24	99	80	11	21	34	4	0	3	14	0	1	6	12	0	25	2	2	1	.425	.394
Sweeney, James, Cas.	.278	26	103	90	19	25	40	4	1	3	12	0	1	4	8	0	32	1	1	1	.444	.359
Swenson, Samuel, Pro.*	.351	63	267	225	61	79	142	16	4	13	55	0	4	14	24	0	64	7	1	5	.631	.438
Tempesta, Nick, M.H.	.335	72	298	263	49	88	130	16	1	8	46	1	1	9	24	2	51	3	1	3	.494	.407
Tena, Hector, Cas.	.236	35	134	123	15	29	43	6	1	2	13	0	1	4	6	1	36	3	7	0	.350	.291
Tolzien, Edward, Pro.*	.265	39	154	132	27	35	52	9	1	2	23	0	0	1	18	1	22	4	1	4	.394	.370
Torres, Erik, Og.	.172	20	63	58	9	10	13	3	0	0	4	1	0	0	4	0	16	0	2	0	.224	.226
Turner, Justin, Pro.*	.216	52	205	176	36	38	59	3	0	6	27	0	0	1	28	1	65	9	4	3	.335	.327
Varner, Gary, Bil.	.351	72	326	291	55	102	156	20	5	8	55	0	3	3	29	1	64	7	4	3	.536	.411
Vasquez, Jose, Cas.*	.232	64	268	228	40	53	107	6	3	14	39	0	4	9	27	2	96	1	6	1	.469	.332
Villanueva, Florian, Og.	.308	68	300	273	52	84	127	21	2	6	53	1	3	5	18	0	27	5	3	4	.465	.358
Virgen, Constancio, G.F.	.262	31	125	107	13	28	35	4	0	1	16	1	2	0	15	0	17	3	2	1	.327	.347
Vugteveen, Dustin, Miss.	.293	60	252	232	40	68	102	14	1	6	51	0	4	5	11	0	58	7	3	3	.440	.333
Webb, Ryan, Pro.	.500	7	9	6	1	3	5	0	1	0	1	0	0	1	2	0	0	0	1	0	.833	.667
Welch, Ed, Pro.*	.282	59	237	216	47	61	83	9	5	1	26	2	3	0	16	0	59	18	4	1	.384	.328
Williamson, Chris, Bil.*	.271	29	118	96	21	26	47	3	0	6	18	0	1	1	20	2	39	0	0	0	.490	.398
Wood, Stephen, M.H.	.333	2	7	6	0	2	3	1	0	0	2	0	0	1	0	0	1	0	0	0	.500	.429
Yepez, Jose, M.H.	.276	18	65	58	5	16	21	5	0	0	3	0	0	3	4	0	4	3	0	0	.362	.354

GRAND SLAMS: Cota, Hastings, Lopez, 2 each; A. Guerrero, J. Guzman, Haggard, Jacobo, Janz, Pickens, Mulqueen, Tempesta, Vugteveen, 1 each.

AWARDED FIRST BASE ON CATCHER'S INTERFERENCE: Cota 2 (Aracena, Yepez); C. Batista (Villanueva), Hastings (Corbeil), Hyde (Montilla), J. Perez (Villanueva).

2001 PITCHING

TEAM

Team	W	L	Pct.	ERA	G	CG	ShO	Sv.	IP	H	TBF	R	ER	HR	SH	SF	HB	BB	IBB	SO	WP	Bk.
Missoula	52	24	.684	3.63	76	1	4	21	669.2	689	2952	375	270	43	14	19	43	222	4	532	64	10
Billings	46	29	.613	3.77	75	2	4	18	661.0	654	2834	350	277	42	14	15	46	196	6	608	42	5
Provo	53	23	.697	3.98	76	2	6	20	656.1	670	2881	365	290	43	14	19	40	226	10	688	57	7
Great Falls	37	39	.487	4.65	76	0	5	18	676.0	725	3055	454	349	53	19	16	62	247	7	668	75	10
Ogden	36	38	.486	5.15	74	0	1	18	643.1	702	2841	443	368	72	13	20	47	232	8	605	75	14
Casper	37	39	.487	5.32	76	2	1	21	657.2	777	3036	494	389	46	15	29	59	280	14	526	84	11
Medicine Hat	20	56	.263	5.67	76	0	3	12	662.1	740	3070	537	417	76	18	27	71	305	12	504	93	21
Idaho Falls	21	54	.280	6.66	75	0	2	10	653.0	813	3201	602	483	79	19	31	49	429	6	602	88	11

INDIVIDUAL

TOP QUALIFIERS FOR EARNED-RUN AVERAGE TITLE

Minimum 61 innings.*Lefthanded pitcher.

Pitcher, Team	W	L	Pct.	ERA	G	GS	CG	ShO	GF	Sv.	IP	H	TBF	R	ER	HR	SH	SF	HB	BB	IBB	SO	WP	Bk.
Dennis, Jason, Pro.*	5	0	1.000	2.05	14	13	0	0	1	0	74.2	53	299	20	17	3	1	1	2	21	0	79	2	0
Hosford, Clinton, G.F.	6	3	.667	2.50	15	12	0	0	3	0	79.1	72	322	28	22	3	2	1	4	16	0	69	3	1
Holsten, Ryan, Miss.	9	3	.750	2.53	17	12	0	0	1	0	89.0	84	361	33	25	5	0	2	1	12	0	60	4	0
Liriano, Pedro, Pro.	11	2	.846	2.78	15	14	0	0	1	0	77.2	80	342	39	24	3	1	3	5	31	0	76	4	3
Tisdale, Marlyn, Bil.	7	4	.636	3.05	14	14	1	1	0	0	82.2	88	336	31	28	1	2	2	6	13	0	76	8	0
Medina, Franklin, Miss.	8	2	.800	3.39	15	14	1	0	0	0	87.2	89	381	42	33	5	3	2	4	28	0	55	12	1
Childress, Daylan, Bil.	6	1	.857	3.55	14	8	0	0	1	0	63.1	59	263	32	25	4	1	1	4	17	0	54	3	0
Mercedes, Gabriel, Miss.	8	3	.727	3.71	15	14	0	0	0	0	80.0	81	357	47	33	1	1	3	5	30	0	66	10	2
McCracken, Vance, G.F.	4	5	.444	3.84	14	9	0	0	2	1	63.1	63	263	31	27	4	2	1	9	11	0	46	3	0
Severino, Cleris, Bil.*	3	3	.500	4.30	15	13	1	1	0	0	67.0	66	293	37	32	9	4	0	4	30	0	54	3	1
Castillo, Geraldo, Og.	6	4	.600	4.35	15	10	0	0	3	0	68.1	77	297	42	33	7	0	1	5	11	0	49	5	3
Chadwick, John, M.H.	1	1	.500	4.43	23	0	0	0	8	2	61.0	65	276	38	30	4	0	1	8	19	1	42	9	3
Astacio, Andres, G.F.	2	6	.250	5.01	17	12	0	0	3	0	73.2	87	332	52	41	6	3	2	6	13	0	62	2	3
Lizarraga, Sergio, Miss.	6	2	.750	5.09	15	15	0	0	0	0	81.1	104	372	57	46	10	1	1	8	23	0	57	7	3
Buret, Jorge, Cas.	4	6	.400	5.24	16	15	1	0	0	0	80.2	110	376	66	47	8	2	2	1	23	0	54	6	1

DEPARTMENTAL LEADERS: W—Liriano, 11; L—Huber, Pauley, 9 each; Pct.—Arthur, .875; G—Tucker, Villatoro, 30 each; GS—Several players tied at 15; CG—Several players tied at 1; ShO—Anthony, Severino, Tisdale, Woods, 1 each; GF—Cotton, 28; Sv.—Silva, 14; IP—Holsten, 89; H—Buret, 110; TBF—Medina, 381; R—Lawton, 69; ER—Lawton, 58; HR—Lawton, Ramirez, 12 each; SH—Several players tied at 4; SF—A. Martinez, Mordan, 6 each; HB—Fuller, 10; BB—Tucker, 50; IBB—Allen, Speier, 4 each; SO—Woods, 84; WP—Mitchell, 15; BK—Rosario, Steitz, 6 each.

ALL PITCHERS

*Lefthanded pitcher.

Pitcher, Team	W	L	Pct.	ERA	G	GS	CG	ShO	GF	Sv.	IP	H	TBF	R	ER	HR	SH	SF	HB	BB	IBB	SO	WP	Bk.
Adams, Jay, Bil.	1	1	.500	3.93	28	0	0	0	12	0	36.2	41	164	20	16	3	1	0	2	5	0	28	1	0
Adams, Jon, Og.	2	2	.500	2.81	23	0	0	0	21	12	32.0	26	129	10	10	4	1	1	3	6	1	44	0	0
Allen, Blakely, Pro.*	7	3	.700	2.13	28	0	0	0	18	8	50.2	35	193	13	12	0	1	0	1	8	4	55	2	0
Almond, Casey, Cas.	2	2	.500	7.39	19	0	0	0	2	0	31.2	37	149	30	26	3	0	3	6	15	1	20	2	0
Andrade, Stephen, Pro.	0	0	.000	0.00	1	0	0	0	0	0	2.0	3	9	0	0	0	0	0	0	0	0	5	0	0
Arellano, Salvador, I.F.	0	1	.000	3.65	3	3	0	0	0	0	12.1	17	65	13	5	0	0	0	3	5	0	8	2	0
Arthur, Tony, Pro.*	7	1	.875	3.76	10	10	1	1	0	0	55.0	48	222	32	23	5	0	3	2	11	0	49	4	0
Artman, Dane, Og.*	0	3	.000	15.88	6	6	0	0	0	0	11.1	21	62	22	20	4	0	0	1	8	0	10	3	0
Astacio, Andres, G.F.	2	6	.250	5.01	17	12	0	0	3	0	73.2	87	332	52	41	6	3	2	6	13	0	62	2	3
Bailey, Ryan, Pro.	4	1	.800	3.96	15	6	0	0	1	1	52.1	62	239	29	23	2	0	1	2	16	0	48	8	1
Barbarossa, Joshua, I.F.*	2	1	.667	3.90	7	1	0	0	0	0	27.2	33	136	22	12	2	1	0	2	17	0	25	3	0
Basham, Bobby, Bil.	1	2	.333	4.85	6	6	0	0	0	0	29.2	36	140	23	16	2	1	0	2	17	0	37	4	2
Beckstead, Jentry, Cas.	1	0	1.000	2.89	23	0	0	0	21	12	28.0	23	118	13	9	1	0	1	3	12	1	28	3	0

Pitcher, Team	W	L	Pct.	ERA	G	GS	CG	ShO	GF	Sv.	IP	H	TBF	R	ER	HR	SH	SF	HB	BB	IBB	SO	WP	Bk.
Bowles, Larry, Pro.*	4	1	.800	5.60	19	1	0	0	4	0	27.1	32	116	18	17	4	1	1	0	6	0	25	3	0
Bukowski, Stan, Pro.	0	0	.000	1.29	5	0	0	0	2	0	7.0	9	30	3	1	0	0	0	0	2	0	2	2	0
Buret, Jorge, Cas.	4	6	.400	5.24	16	15	1	0	0	0	80.2	110	376	66	47	8	2	2	1	23	0	54	6	1
Castillo, Geraldo, Og.	6	4	.600	4.35	15	10	0	0	3	0	68.1	77	297	42	33	7	0	1	5	11	0	49	5	3
Chadwick, John, M.H.	1	1	.500	4.43	23	0	0	0	8	2	61.0	65	276	38	30	4	0	1	8	19	1	42	9	3
Childress, Daylan, Bil.	6	1	.857	3.55	14	8	0	0	4	1	63.1	59	263	32	25	4	1	1	4	17	0	54	3	0
Clarke, Darren, Cas.	3	6	.333	6.02	14	14	0	0	0	0	55.1	76	271	47	37	3	1	3	8	33	0	42	5	0
Coffey, Todd, Bil.	2	2	.500	3.51	14	2	0	0	6	1	33.1	34	151	21	13	2	1	1	2	15	0	33	2	0
Collado, Jerry, Cas.	0	2	.000	5.59	21	0	0	0	3	1	29.0	36	141	24	18	1	1	0	4	15	1	18	5	1
Collins, Clint, Bil.	5	2	.714	2.75	10	10	0	0	0	0	55.2	46	220	19	17	2	1	2	2	14	0	45	2	1
Costello, Ryan, M.H.*	1	5	.167	3.83	14	8	0	0	1	1	51.2	38	217	33	22	5	3	2	1	21	1	56	4	1
Cotton, Nathan, Bil.	4	1	.800	2.79	28	0	0	0	28	13	29.0	30	127	10	9	2	0	1	4	3	1	37	1	0
D'Amico, Leonardo, Pro.	1	0	1.000	9.00	1	0	0	0	0	0	2.0	4	11	2	2	0	0	0	0	1	0	4	1	0
Davies, Michael, Cas.*	2	2	.500	4.50	10	7	0	0	0	0	36.0	40	161	23	18	2	2	2	4	10	1	37	3	1
Davis, Mikael, Miss.	4	1	.800	3.86	15	4	0	0	2	0	39.2	44	174	25	17	7	1	0	1	12	0	33	7	1
DeJesus, Henky, Miss.	0	1	.000	11.57	3	0	0	0	1	0	4.2	7	25	7	6	1	0	0	1	3	1	0	0	0
Dennis, Jason, Pro.*	5	0	1.000	2.05	14	13	0	0	1	0	74.2	53	299	20	17	3	1	1	2	21	0	79	2	0
Desalme, Gene, Og.*	0	0	.000	5.02	8	0	0	0	3	0	14.1	15	73	11	8	4	0	0	2	14	0	16	1	1
Diaz, Jose, G.F.	0	0	.000	0.00	1	0	0	0	1	0	1.0	0	4	0	0	0	0	0	1	0	0	2	0	1
Dotel, Melido, Cas.	0	0	.000	162.00	2	0	0	0	0	0	0.1	3	9	6	6	0	0	0	0	5	0	0	2	0
Dulkowski, Marc, I.F.	0	1	.000	5.33	22	0	0	0	15	2	25.1	25	118	17	15	1	3	2	1	16	0	25	3	0
Ferrand, Julian, Cas.	0	5	.000	6.59	17	0	0	0	5	0	28.2	40	141	27	21	3	1	2	3	11	0	26	4	0
Fisher, Timothy, Miss.	0	0	.000	0.00	1	0	0	0	1	0	0.2	2	2	0	0	0	0	0	0	0	0	0	0	0
Fox, Ben, I.F.*	1	1	.500	9.00	13	0	0	0	9	5	16.0	22	80	16	16	0	0	1	3	8	0	17	1	0
Fuller, Brendan, M.H.	0	1	.000	6.75	18	0	0	0	4	0	25.1	21	116	20	19	1	1	1	10	16	1	38	12	0
George, Brad, Bil.	0	2	.000	9.26	5	5	0	0	0	0	23.1	29	113	31	24	6	0	3	3	8	0	16	4	0
Gillman, Justin, Bil.	1	0	1.000	0.00	1	1	0	0	0	0	6.0	0	22	1	0	0	0	0	0	5	0	2	0	0
Gold, J.M., Og.	1	1	.500	2.17	7	7	0	0	0	0	29.0	20	116	12	7	1	0	1	1	9	0	42	2	0
Gonzalez, Alfredo, G.F.	3	4	.429	3.56	11	8	0	0	1	0	48.0	43	203	26	19	1	1	1	5	12	0	56	4	0
Gonzalez, Carlos, Miss.	0	2	.000	5.27	10	0	0	0	4	0	13.2	19	69	13	8	0	0	1	2	6	0	15	5	0
Gonzalez, Miguel, Cas.	2	2	.500	3.35	24	0	0	0	2	0	40.1	40	179	21	15	0	3	3	4	12	1	41	4	2
Granados, Bernie, Cas.	0	0	.000	6.84	21	0	0	0	1	0	25.0	33	126	24	19	5	0	1	5	13	1	23	6	1
Greenbush, Peter, Cas.	4	2	.667	5.10	14	6	0	0	2	1	42.1	55	193	32	24	1	0	1	3	15	2	26	6	3
Grimes, Sean, M.H.*	1	4	.200	4.97	12	7	0	0	0	0	38.0	48	182	26	21	3	2	1	3	20	1	21	11	1
Gruban, Jarret, Pro.	0	0	.000	0.00	1	0	0	0	0	0	1.0	2	5	1	0	0	0	0	0	0	0	0	0	1
Heal, Darren, M.H.	0	1	.000	19.29	9	0	0	0	2	0	9.1	21	69	29	20	5	0	1	4	13	1	7	8	0
Heiberger, Heath, Miss.*	0	0	.000	1.69	7	0	0	0	1	0	10.2	5	42	4	2	0	0	0	1	3	0	13	2	0
Hickman, Jason, G.F.*	1	2	.333	4.91	17	2	0	0	9	2	40.1	45	197	29	22	3	2	2	5	29	2	31	8	0
Holsten, Ryan, Miss.	9	3	.750	2.53	17	12	0	0	0	0	89.0	84	361	33	25	5	0	2	1	12	0	60	4	0
Horne, Travis, Og.*	0	0	.000	6.75	4	0	0	0	2	0	10.2	11	48	9	8	1	0	0	1	8	0	11	4	0
Hostord, Clinton, G.F.	6	3	.667	2.50	15	12	0	0	3	0	70.1	72	322	28	22	3	2	1	4	16	0	69	3	1
Howton, Jared, Bil.*	1	1	.500	4.71	18	1	0	0	3	0	36.1	39	156	25	19	1	0	0	1	7	0	35	1	0
Huber, Jon, I.F.	5	9	.357	6.04	15	15	0	0	0	0	73.0	77	344	61	49	7	4	4	7	48	0	75	10	0
Huggins, Rusty, Og.*	0	0	.000	3.55	10	0	0	0	3	0	12.2	18	54	6	5	2	0	0	0	2	0	6	3	0
Jackson, Dan, Pro.	0	0	.000	6.00	7	0	0	0	4	3	9.0	11	43	6	6	0	1	0	0	5	0	13	0	0
Jones, Mike, Og.	4	1	.800	3.74	9	7	0	0	0	0	33.2	29	137	17	14	1	0	1	3	10	0	32	6	0
Kauffman, Matt, G.F.*	0	0	.000	8.59	10	0	0	0	4	0	14.2	21	80	20	14	3	0	0	0	14	1	13	4	0
Keirstead, Michael, G.F.	1	1	.500	2.34	25	3	0	0	19	5	34.2	35	154	14	9	1	0	0	2	12	0	52	5	1
Kelly, Steve, Bil.	4	2	.667	2.30	12	7	0	0	0	0	54.2	50	227	16	14	3	2	1	1	11	1	54	2	0
Kolb, Dan, Og.	4	0	1.000	7.12	16	2	0	0	2	0	43.0	53	191	35	34	8	1	2	3	13	0	33	4	0
Lawton, Charles, I.F.	1	4	.200	8.51	23	7	0	0	5	0	61.1	99	314	69	58	12	1	2	5	32	0	34	3	1
League, Brandon, M.H.	2	2	.500	4.66	9	9	0	0	0	0	38.2	36	165	23	20	3	1	2	4	11	1	38	2	0
Linderbaum, Mason, I.F.*	1	0	1.000	7.80	23	0	0	0	6	0	30.0	45	160	28	26	3	0	0	5	20	0	27	3	2
Liriano, Pedro, M.H.	11	2	.846	2.78	15	14	0	0	1	0	77.2	80	342	39	24	3	1	3	5	31	0	76	4	3
Lizarraga, Edgar, G.F.	4	2	.667	3.54	14	4	0	0	7	2	48.1	43	203	25	19	4	3	0	4	11	0	56	4	1
Lizarraga, Sergio, Miss.	6	2	.750	5.09	15	15	0	0	0	0	81.1	104	372	57	46	10	1	1	8	23	0	57	7	3
Lorenzen, Jonathan, G.F.	0	0	.000	10.80	5	0	0	0	1	0	10.0	15	54	14	12	4	0	0	8	0	0	11	1	0
Luther, Heath, Pro.*	0	0	.000	0.00	3	0	0	0	0	0	3.1	4	15	0	0	0	0	0	0	1	0	2	0	0
Marquez, Jose, Miss.	1	0	1.000	6.52	15	0	0	0	5	0	19.1	22	104	23	14	3	0	1	3	19	1	10	4	0
Martinez, Angel, Pro.	4	3	.571	4.37	18	8	0	0	1	0	57.2	56	251	34	28	5	1	6	5	18	1	44	7	0
Martinez, Hancer, I.F.	1	0	1.000	4.15	11	1	0	0	0	0	21.2	25	97	11	10	2	0	2	0	10	1	21	2	0
Martinez, Javier A., I.F.	1	4	.200	6.43	10	8	0	0	0	0	42.0	42	195	35	30	6	2	2	4	26	0	38	4	0
McCracken, Vance, G.F.	4	5	.444	3.84	14	9	0	0	2	1	63.1	63	263	31	27	4	2	1	9	11	0	46	3	0
McMillan, Joshua, M.H.*	0	1	.000	10.52	15	0	0	0	5	1	25.2	41	144	35	30	7	0	2	1	27	1	15	8	0
McMurray, Heath, Og.	2	3	.400	3.28	10	0	0	0	3	1	24.2	24	101	14	9	0	1	0	2	7	1	24	2	1
McWilliams, Matt, Bil.*	2	2	.500	3.32	14	0	0	0	3	0	21.2	17	92	10	8	0	1	0	0	12	1	26	2	0
Medina, Franklin, Miss.	8	3	.800	3.39	15	14	1	0	0	0	87.2	89	381	42	33	5	3	2	4	28	0	55	12	1
Medina, Frewing, M.H.	3	5	.375	7.51	19	3	0	0	4	0	44.1	67	216	51	37	7	2	2	2	16	1	26	6	4
Medina, Roberto, Miss.*	3	2	.600	3.67	21	0	0	0	9	0	34.1	32	151	18	14	1	2	1	2	17	1	29	2	0
Medlin, Corbey, Miss.	2	1	.667	2.38	21	0	0	0	14	6	41.2	27	165	12	11	1	0	1	2	16	0	46	4	1
Mercedes, Gabriel, Miss.	8	3	.727	3.71	15	14	0	0	0	0	80.0	81	357	47	33	1	1	3	5	30	0	66	10	2
Mieses, Jose, Og.	0	1	.000	27.00	1	1	0	0	0	0	1.0	3	7	3	3	0	0	0	0	1	0	2	0	0
Mitchell, Jay, Cas.	4	5	.444	6.34	14	14	0	0	0	0	55.1	54	261	47	39	4	0	3	5	38	0	35	15	0
Moak, Curtus, Bil.*	3	1	.750	3.72	20	0	0	0	4	0	36.1	34	157	18	15	2	0	0	8	11	3	24	4	0
Mordan, Pedro, I.F.	1	7	.125	8.22	21	8	0	0	3	0	58.0	86	294	63	53	3	0	6	4	37	2	43	7	2
Morel, Eudy, I.F.	0	2	.000	4.95	14	0	0	0	6	0	20.0	24	92	15	11	3	1	1	6	0	25	3	0	
Nall, T.J., G.F.	2	2	.500	5.01	7	2	0	0	0	0	23.1	26	108	18	13	2	0	0	5	6	1	25	2	0
Neylan, Chris, M.H.*	0	2	.000	6.62	10	5	0	0	0	0	34.0	49	159	29	25	5	0	2	3	10	0	22	4	0
Nolasco, Dave, Og.	3	3	.500	4.43	20	2	0	0	7	2	42.2	38	184	27	21	3	0	3	3	14	3	35	6	0
Nunez, Severino, Og.*	0	0	.000	2.00	7	0	0	0	2	0	9.0	3	34	3	2	1	1	1	1	3	0	12	1	0
Ogiltree, John, M H	2	4	.333	3.38	28	0	0	0	23	6	32.0	33	138	17	12	1	4	1	4	10	2	25	3	0
Olson, Jason, G.F.	2	0	1.000	1.17	5	0	0	0	5	1	7.2	2	30	1	1	0	0	0	1	6	0	13	0	0
O'Sullivan, Mark, Pro.	1	2	.333	3.97	22	0	0	0	11	2	34.0	35	157	23	15	5	3	1	3	16	2	36	1	0

Pitcher, Team	W	L	Pct.	ERA	G	GS	CG	ShO	GF	Sv.	IP	H	TBF	R	ER	HR	SH	SF	HB	BB	IBB	SO	WP	Bk.
Ott, Thom, G.F.	2	1	.667	4.84	14	0	0	0	7	2	22.1	29	108	19	12	0	0	0	2	7	0	24	3	0
Parker, Zach, Cas.*	1	2	.333	7.52	8	8	0	0	0	0	26.1	42	122	26	22	2	0	1	1	12	0	19	3	1
Patten, Lanny, M.H.	1	4	.200	5.40	25	0	0	0	8	1	38.1	30	170	30	23	2	0	1	8	22	1	31	2	1
Pauley, David, I.F.	4	9	.308	6.03	15	15	0	0	0	0	68.2	88	315	57	46	8	1	3	1	24	0	53	6	0
Perez, Henry, I.F.	4	8	.333	6.28	15	15	0	0	0	0	71.2	79	328	60	50	10	2	2	5	39	0	82	4	1
Perkin, Greg, Miss.	1	2	.333	4.96	12	5	0	0	5	0	32.2	43	157	29	18	1	1	2	5	9	0	34	4	2
Pike, Matthew, Bil.	3	4	.429	5.20	13	8	0	0	2	0	55.1	60	242	39	32	5	0	1	6	15	0	57	3	1
Pilkington, Brian, G.F.	0	1	.000	5.63	5	2	0	0	0	0	16.0	19	69	11	10	2	1	1	1	2	0	17	2	0
Pinkerton, Bradley, Pro.*	0	2	.000	5.60	17	1	0	0	6	0	35.1	37	157	24	22	3	0	1	2	13	0	35	5	0
Powers, Joe, Bil.	3	1	.750	2.70	27	0	0	0	11	3	30.0	25	131	17	9	0	0	1	1	13	0	30	2	0
Ramirez, Ismael, M.H.	5	6	.455	5.35	14	14	0	0	0	0	74.0	77	319	48	44	12	2	2	6	21	0	35	2	1
Ramos, Luis, Og.	2	3	.400	8.87	15	0	0	0	5	0	23.1	31	114	26	23	4	0	2	4	7	0	25	1	0
Richards, John, I.F.*	0	0	.000	4.30	13	0	0	0	4	0	14.2	15	71	9	7	0	0	2	0	13	0	13	3	3
Richardson, Judd, Og.	0	1	.000	5.00	5	5	0	0	0	0	18.0	23	76	12	10	1	2	1	1	2	0	18	1	1
Rodriguez, Jose, I.F.	0	1	.000	7.29	18	0	0	0	2	0	21.0	27	112	23	17	5	0	0	2	21	0	28	4	0
Rodriguez, Orlando, G.F.*	3	3	.500	4.15	15	10	0	0	2	1	60.2	58	273	41	28	11	1	0	4	26	0	79	7	0
Rosario, Francisco, M.H.	3	7	.300	5.59	16	15	0	0	0	0	75.2	79	344	61	47	8	1	4	9	38	0	55	6	6
Saenz, Chris, Og.	3	1	.750	4.24	21	4	0	0	5	0	46.2	43	195	25	22	5	4	3	2	14	2	48	1	0
Santana, Johan, Pro.	2	1	.667	7.71	4	4	0	0	0	0	18.2	19	93	17	16	1	0	2	2	12	1	22	3	1
Sarfate, Dennis, Og.	1	2	.333	4.63	9	4	0	0	1	1	23.1	20	100	13	12	4	1	0	2	10	0	32	2	0
Scott, John, I.F.	0	1	.000	15.12	20	0	0	0	3	0	16.2	29	115	38	28	6	0	2	2	36	0	10	11	2
Serrano, Alex, Cas.	2	0	1.000	0.00	12	0	0	0	10	6	18.0	10	66	0	0	0	2	0	1	1	0	23	1	0
Severino, Cleris, Bil.*	3	3	.500	4.30	15	13	1	1	0	0	67.0	66	293	37	32	9	4	0	4	30	0	54	3	1
Shell, Steven, Pro.	0	3	.000	7.17	14	4	0	0	3	1	37.2	52	182	31	30	3	0	1	9	15	0	33	3	0
Shorey, Jeremy, Og.	3	2	.600	5.53	22	1	0	0	8	1	40.2	47	180	32	25	7	1	1	1	16	0	30	7	1
Silva, Jesus, Miss.	3	0	1.000	2.35	26	2	0	0	24	14	38.1	33	161	12	10	1	0	1	8	0	0	43	1	0
Simpson, Joe, Cas.	0	1	.000	8.24	19	0	0	0	14	0	19.2	30	100	19	18	2	0	0	1	12	0	17	5	0
Smart, Pete, Og.*	1	0	1.000	3.78	4	2	0	0	1	0	16.2	18	70	9	7	1	0	1	0	2	0	11	1	0
Smith, Cliff, Pro.	2	1	.667	3.34	21	0	0	0	7	1	35.0	29	151	20	13	5	2	0	2	15	1	47	7	0
Speier, Ryan, Cas.	1	2	.333	3.16	17	0	0	0	8	1	25.2	19	109	12	9	2	1	0	2	9	4	24	2	0
Spillman, Jeromie, M.H.*	3	0	1.000	4.12	28	0	0	0	10	1	39.1	41	183	23	18	5	0	1	1	18	0	42	6	0
Stefani, Jason, G.F.*	3	1	.750	5.03	19	2	0	0	2	1	39.1	48	187	30	22	2	1	3	2	19	2	35	7	1
Steffek, Brian, G.F.	0	2	.000	7.71	8	3	0	0	2	1	21.0	28	103	18	18	2	0	2	4	11	1	19	1	1
Steitz, Jon, Og.	2	4	.333	6.68	11	10	0	0	0	0	33.2	44	169	32	25	1	0	0	4	25	0	28	13	6
Steward, Edward, Pro.	1	0	1.000	5.40	1	0	0	0	0	0	6.2	7	29	4	4	1	0	1	1	0	0	9	0	0
Strayhorn, Kole, G.F.	0	0	.000	15.43	2	0	0	0	0	0	2.1	4	13	4	4	1	0	0	1	1	0	1	0	1
Sutton, Kris, Pro.	2	1	.667	3.96	23	0	0	0	15	4	25.0	43	130	20	11	0	1	1	1	8	2	20	4	0
Talanoa, Charles, M.H.	1	8	.111	5.73	15	15	0	0	0	0	55.0	65	268	53	35	3	2	1	6	33	1	30	8	4
Taulli, Sam, Miss.*	1	1	.500	6.27	15	0	0	0	2	0	18.2	26	93	16	13	0	1	1	0	12	0	18	1	0
Taylor, John, M.H.	0	0	.000	4.76	6	0	0	0	5	0	11.1	15	55	11	6	1	0	0	1	4	0	8	0	0
Tibbs, Jeff, G.F.	2	5	.286	10.02	15	7	0	0	0	0	41.1	62	217	57	46	2	2	3	3	30	0	25	10	0
Tisdale, Marlyn, Bil.	7	4	.636	3.05	14	14	1	1	0	0	82.2	88	336	31	28	1	2	2	6	13	0	76	8	0
Torres, Erik, Og.	0	0	.000	0.00	2	0	0	0	2	0	3.0	2	10	0	0	0	0	0	0	0	0	3	0	0
Torres, Joe, Pro.*	2	2	.500	4.02	9	8	0	0	0	0	31.1	32	145	20	14	2	1	1	5	15	0	39	5	0
Tucker, Rusty, I.F.*	0	2	.000	7.13	30	0	0	0	7	0	35.1	41	195	41	28	4	3	1	3	50	1	43	14	0
Turuda, Miyoki, G.F.	2	1	.667	3.14	17	0	0	0	8	2	28.2	25	135	16	10	2	1	0	3	18	0	32	9	0
Van Buren, Jermaine, Cas.	3	0	1.000	5.32	6	3	1	0	0	0	23.2	25	103	15	14	2	1	0	1	10	0	25	1	0
Vargas, Reynardo, Cas.	3	4	.429	6.11	21	0	0	0	5	0	28.0	43	135	25	19	2	0	0	3	14	1	21	4	1
Villacis, Eduardo, Cas.	1	0	1.000	0.00	1	1	0	0	0	0	6.0	5	25	1	0	0	0	0	2	0	3	0	0	0
Villatoro, Wilmer, I.F.	0	3	.000	5.26	30	0	0	0	15	3	37.2	39	170	24	22	7	1	1	1	21	2	35	5	0
Wallace, Ben, Og.*	0	3	.000	7.29	13	8	0	0	3	0	45.2	64	222	43	37	7	1	1	3	23	1	33	6	1
Waroff, Shane, Miss.	4	1	.800	2.48	26	0	0	0	6	1	40.0	38	169	16	11	4	1	3	1	9	0	24	1	0
Wassong, Michael, M.H.*	0	1	.000	8.31	11	0	0	0	6	0	8.2	14	49	10	8	4	0	3	0	6	0	13	2	0
Wechsler, Justin, Miss.	2	3	.400	2.89	10	10	0	0	0	0	37.1	35	169	21	12	3	3	1	6	15	1	29	0	0
Woods, Jake, Pro.	4	3	.571	5.29	15	14	1	1	1	0	64.2	70	291	41	38	6	2	3	2	29	0	84	2	2
Wright, Shayne, Pro.	0	0	.000	3.00	1	1	0	0	0	0	6.0	3	22	2	2	0	0	0	1	0	0	5	1	0
Yeatman, Matt, Og.	2	4	.333	4.95	13	8	0	0	3	1	60.0	72	272	40	33	6	0	1	5	27	0	61	6	0

COMBINATION SHUTOUTS: Billings (2)—Tisdale-Adams-Childress, Collins-Powers-Cotton. **Casper (1)**—Davies-Vargas-Serrano. **Great Falls (5)**—Gonzalez-Rodriguez-Kierstead, Astacio-Lizarraga, Astacio-Turuda-Lizarraga, Rodriguez-Pilkington-Kierstead, McCracken-Stefani. **Idaho Falls (2)**—Huber-Mordan-Villatoro, Huber-Villatoro-Dulkowski-Fox. **Medicine Hat (3)**—Ramirez-Ogiltree, Costello-Spillman, League-Costello. **Missoula (4)**—Medina-Silva, Wechsler-Medina-Medlin-Silva, Mercedes-Medina, Holsten-Silva. **Ogden (1)**—Sarfate-Nunez-Jones-Nolasco. **Provo (4)**—Dennis-Smith, Woods-Allen-Bowles, Liriano-Allen, Liriano-O'Sullivan-Allen.

NO-HIT GAMES: None.

2001 FIELDING

TEAM

Team	Pct.	G	PO	A	E	TC	DP	TP	PB
Ogden	.964	74	1930	837	103	2870	66	0	24
Casper	.959	76	1973	789	117	2879	68	0	33
Billings	.959	75	1983	818	121	2922	53	0	20
Provo	.955	76	1969	788	131	2888	54	0	13
Idaho Falls	.952	75	1959	736	137	2832	52	0	27
Great Falls	.947	76	2028	841	160	3029	59	0	20
Missoula	.946	76	2009	835	161	3005	65	0	19
Medicine Hat	.945	76	1987	860	167	3014	70	0	22

INDIVIDUAL

FIRST BASEMEN

NOTE: All caps denotes fielding-percentage leader based on 38 games for catchers, 51 for all other non-pitchers and 61 innings for pitchers. *Throws lefthanded.

Player, Team	Pct.	G	PO	A	E	TC	DP
Aracena, Sandy, G.F.	.941	5	44	4	3	51	3
Corbeil, Alfred, Pro.*	.967	21	170	6	6	182	9
Cota, Jesus, Miss.	.987	66	574	52	8	634	49
De Los Santos, Omar, G.F.	1.000	5	13	1	0	14	4
Diaz, Jose, G.F.	1.000	2	16	0	0	16	2
Eylward, Thomas, Pro.	1.000	6	34	2	0	36	4
Fry, Ryan, Bil.	.909	2	7	3	1	11	2
Garabito, Vianney, Bil.	.980	5	48	2	1	51	1

Player, Team	Pct.	G	PO	A	E	TC	DP
Gemoll, Brandon, Og.*	1.000	2	18	3	0	21	3
Gillitzer, Scott, G.F.	.991	11	110	3	1	114	8
GUTIERREZ, Jesse, Bil.	.992	52	470	25	4	499	30
Hart, Jon, Og.	.986	65	541	39	8	588	43
Hastings, Joseph, I.F.	.992	29	230	14	2	246	16
Hinton, Travis, Og.*	.989	10	87	7	1	95	9
Jung, Young-jin, I.F.	.963	11	75	3	3	81	5
Klatt, Joel, I.F.	.975	30	181	11	5	197	10
Kotchman, Casey, Pro.*	1.000	7	35	2	0	37	5
Martin, Cesar, M.H.	1.000	2	18	1	0	19	1
Martinez, Thomas, I.F.	.975	11	75	3	2	80	9
Materano, Oscar, Cas.	.959	6	44	3	2	49	5
McFachran, Aaron, M H	.980	55	503	27	11	541	44
McPherson, Dallas, Pro.	.978	6	44	0	1	45	5
Medina, Rodney, M.H.	.980	17	141	9	3	153	13
Mercado, Onix, Bil.	.833	2	5	0	1	6	0
Michaelis, Derek, G.F.*	.970	34	311	16	10	337	20
Molidor, David, Bil.	.995	18	175	6	1	182	12
Mulqueen, Dave, Cas.	.986	71	612	37	9	658	57
Nelson, Brad, Og.	.950	2	18	1	1	20	4
Nevels, Craig, Miss.	1.000	1	3	0	0	3	0
Robinson, Carlos, Miss.	.977	17	116	9	3	128	12
Roenicke, Jarett, I.F.*	.984	7	59	4	1	64	3
Story-Harden, Thomari, G.F.	.956	18	141	10	7	158	7
Tolzien, Edward, Pro.*	.989	38	322	27	4	353	26
Turner, Justin, Pro.	.979	6	44	2	1	47	4
Virgen, Constancio, G.F.	.986	8	65	3	1	69	5
Welch, Ed, Pro.	1.000	1	1	0	0	1	0
Wood, Stephen, M.H.	1.000	2	6	1	0	7	1
Yepez, Jose, M.H.	1.000	4	36	0	0	36	3

SECOND BASEMEN

Player, Team	Pct.	G	PO	A	E	TC	DP
Aquino, Jack, I.F.	1.000	2	1	1	0	2	1
Baez, Carlos, I.F.	1.000	1	1	1	0	2	0
Barfield, Josh, I.F.	.970	44	93	100	6	199	21
Barnwell, Chris, Og.	1.000	2	5	3	0	8	2
Batista, Christian, Pro.	1.000	3	6	4	0	10	0
Bautista, Augusto, Bil.	.929	5	6	7	1	14	0
Bergolla, William, Bil.	.946	42	72	121	11	204	22
Brand, Kevin, Miss.	1.000	5	9	7	0	16	0
Canales, Josh, G.F.	1.000	2	6	7	0	13	1
Cordova, Ricardo, G.F.	.893	5	10	15	3	28	2
De Los Santos, Omar, G.F.	.929	7	11	15	2	28	2
De Los Santos, Pedro, I.F.	.932	9	27	28	4	59	3
Diaz, Eduardo, Cas.	.953	69	108	176	14	298	42
Gillitzer, Scott, G.F.	.939	53	106	139	16	261	24
Hairston, Scott, Miss.	.935	62	123	178	21	322	33
Iorg, Isaac, M.H.	.900	5	9	18	3	30	0
Jacobo, Kervin, Miss.	1.000	9	17	26	0	43	5
Johnson, Dale, Pro.	.989	22	37	52	1	90	8
Lagana, Shawn, Pro.	.953	32	54	68	6	128	16
Lewis, Domonique, Bil.	.952	31	72	67	7	146	15
Lopez, Michael, Miss.	.750	2	2	7	3	12	1
Malone, Billy, G.F.	.958	11	24	22	2	48	5
Medina, Rodney, M.H.	1.000	2	2	0	0	2	0
Morel, Robinson, Cas.	.896	10	16	27	5	48	5
Nevins, Ryan, Pro.	.833	4	9	1	2	12	1
Nulton, Kevin, I.F.	.986	21	39	33	1	73	7
O'Connell, Bradley, G.F.	1.000	3	7	7	0	14	0
Pichardo, Maximo, Pro.	.923	22	52	44	8	104	15
Rivera, William, M.H.	.939	45	94	121	14	229	28
Ruiz, Junior, Bil.	1.000	2	5	1	0	6	0
SANTANA, Ralph, Og.	.961	60	132	139	11	282	37
Serrano, Eddie, I.F.	.913	10	18	24	4	46	3
Tempesta, Nick, M.H.	.964	31	61	73	5	139	19
Torres, Erik, Og.	.958	16	23	46	3	72	9
Turner, Justin, Pro.	1.000	1	1	3	0	4	1
Villanueva, Florian, Og.	1.000	1	1	1	0	2	0

THIRD BASEMEN

Player, Team	Pct.	G	PO	A	E	TC	DP
Adames, Epidaro, Pro.	1.000	1	2	4	0	6	0
Aracena, Sandy, G.F.	.875	3	0	7	1	8	0
Baez, Carlos, I.F.	.930	47	20	86	8	114	4
Barnwell, Chris, Og.	.919	32	21	81	9	111	10
Batista, Christian, Pro.	.788	14	3	23	7	33	0
Bautista, Augusto, Bil.	.000	1	0	0	0	0	0
Brand, Kevin, Miss.	1.000	1	3	2	0	5	0
Canales, Josh, G.F.	1.000	1	1	2	0	3	0
Cordova, Ricardo, G.F.	.805	12	7	26	8	41	2
De Los Santos, Omar, G.F.	.881	23	7	45	7	59	1

Player, Team	Pct.	G	PO	A	E	TC	DP
Diaz, Jose, G.F.	.000	1	0	0	0	0	0
Encarnacion, Edwin, Bil.	.863	51	35	110	23	168	12
Essery, Frederick, Cas.	.000	1	0	0	1	1	0
Eure, Jeffrey, Og.	.861	14	12	19	5	36	2
Fry, Ryan, Bil.	.667	1	0	2	1	3	2
Garabito, Vianney, Bil.	1.000	1	0	2	0	2	0
Iorg, Isaac, M.H.	.667	1	0	2	1	3	0
Jacobo, Kervin, Miss.	.650	8	3	10	7	20	2
Johnson, Dale, Pro.	1.000	2	1	3	0	4	0
Klatt, Joel, I.F.	.583	6	2	5	5	12	1
Lopez, Michael, Miss.	.934	65	39	130	12	181	14
Malone, Billy, G.F.	.852	23	18	34	9	61	2
Martin, Cesar, M.H.	.895	65	62	160	26	248	8
MATERANO, Oscar, Cas.	.942	58	48	130	11	189	9
McPherson, Dallas, Pro.	.848	21	11	45	10	66	3
Molidor, David, Bil.	.947	8	5	13	1	19	2
Morel, Robinson, Cas.	.868	22	12	47	9	68	6
Nevels, Craig, Miss.	.833	12	6	19	5	30	2
Nickerson, Brian, G.F.	.844	9	6	21	5	32	1
Nulton, Kevin, I.F.	.892	28	19	55	9	83	1
O'Connell, Bradley, G.F.	.920	11	4	19	2	25	1
Serrano, Eddie, I.F.	.818	5	3	6	2	11	2
Tempesta, Nick, M.H.	.857	12	10	26	6	42	2
Torres, Erik, Og.	.750	3	1	2	1	4	0
Turner, Justin, Pro.	.831	46	22	91	23	136	6
Varner, Gary, Bil.	.837	14	7	29	7	43	2
Villanueva, Florian, Og.	.885	30	11	66	10	87	6

SHORTSTOPS

Player, Team	Pct.	G	PO	A	E	TC	DP
Aquino, Jack, I.F.	.922	53	80	132	18	230	20
Baez, Carlos, I.F.	.917	6	4	7	1	12	2
BANNON, Jeff, Bil.	.943	58	83	184	16	283	22
Darfield, Josh, I.F.	.872	23	32	63	14	109	7
Barnwell, Chris, Og.	.940	35	42	114	10	166	19
Bergolla, William, Bil.	.881	15	19	43	10	72	5
Brand, Kevin, Miss.	.833	9	9	21	6	36	4
Cahill, Jonathan, Pro.	.848	8	10	18	5	33	3
Canales, Josh, G.F.	.846	2	2	9	2	13	1
Cordova, Ricardo, G.F.	.762	6	4	12	5	21	0
Corporan, Roberto, Miss.	.778	3	4	3	2	9	0
De Los Santos, Omar, G.F.	.000	1	0	0	2	2	0
Hardy, J.J., Og.	.948	35	45	118	9	172	16
Hillnski, Scott, Miss.	.895	41	47	124	20	191	20
Iorg, Isaac, M.H.	.667	4	4	6	5	15	1
Jacobo, Kervin, Miss.	.845	34	53	89	26	168	14
Johnson, Dale, Pro.	1.000	3	1	4	0	5	1
Klatt, Joel, I.F.	.000	1	0	0	0	0	0
Lagana, Shawn, Pro.	.929	5	4	9	1	14	1
Lewis, Domonique, Bil.	.000	1	0	0	0	0	0
Mateo, Daniel, Bil.	1.000	3	7	5	0	12	3
Morel, Robinson, Cas.	1.000	2	1	5	0	6	1
Nix, Jayson, Cas.	.913	50	59	108	16	183	26
Nunez, Manuel, G.F.	.922	68	87	232	27	346	41
Peralta, Juan, M.H.	.905	66	121	211	35	367	44
Santana, Ralph, Og.	.920	6	5	18	2	25	7
Smith, Casey, Pro.	.928	62	68	190	20	278	31
Tempesta, Nick, M.H.	.922	9	18	29	4	51	4
Tena, Hector, Cas.	.955	35	67	101	8	176	24

OUTFIELDERS

Player, Team	Pct.	G	PO	A	E	TC	DP
Ball, Jarred, Miss.	.944	17	33	1	2	36	0
Bello, Vladimir, Cas.	.973	47	69	4	2	75	0
Blackburn, John, M.H.	1.000	1	1	0	0	1	0
Boll, Javier, Miss.	.958	34	66	3	3	72	1
Boyd, Dan, Og.	1.000	4	4	1	0	5	0
Canales, Josh, G.F.	1.000	4	3	0	0	3	0
Carrow, Tom, Og.	1.000	35	69	4	0	73	0
Chavez, Ender, Cas.*	.974	63	137	11	4	152	5
Chilsom, Marques, Miss.	1.000	18	14	1	0	15	0
Chourio, Jorjanis, Bil.	.940	43	77	2	5	84	0
Davis, Justin, Bil.*	.967	19	29	0	1	30	0
De Los Santos, Omar, G.F.	.000	1	0	0	0	0	0
Diredo, Curtis, Miss.	1.000	14	17	0	0	17	0
Escalera, Jose, G.F.	1.000	9	5	0	0	5	0
Eure, Jeffrey, Og.	1.000	18	13	0	0	13	0
Garcia, Jose, G.F.	.919	74	118	7	11	136	2
Garcia, Lino, Miss.	.931	43	92	2	7	101	1
Gates, James, Pro.	.951	43	54	4	3	61	0
Giorgis, David, I.F.	.918	57	87	3	8	98	2
Gorneault, Nicholas, Pro.	.957	48	63	4	3	70	0

SUMMER CLASS A *Pioneer League*

Player, Team	Pct.	G	PO	A	E	TC	DP
Guerrero, Armando, M.H.	.936	70	127	5	9	141	0
Guerrero, Hector, G.F.*	.977	29	41	1	1	43	0
Hart, Jon, Og.	.800	3	3	1	1	5	0
Hawes, Bobby, Bil.	.967	38	56	3	2	61	1
Hetherington, Luke, M.H.	.943	43	78	4	5	87	0
Hicks, Brian, Og.	.967	28	57	1	2	60	0
Hinton, Travis, Og.*	.941	37	30	2	2	34	1
Hyde, Nathan, M.H.	.969	49	62	1	2	65	0
Jacobo, Kervin, Miss.	.000	1	0	0	0	0	0
January, Javerro, Og.	1.000	11	12	2	0	14	0
JANZ, Jeramy, Miss.	.989	63	89	5	1	95	0
Johnson, Michael, G.F.*	.976	29	38	2	1	41	0
Kimberley, Glynn, M.H.	.971	49	62	4	2	68	1
Kuide, Eric, I.F.	1.000	8	3	0	0	3	0
Lewis, Domonique, Bil.	.889	7	8	0	1	9	0
Malone, Billy, G.F.	.917	12	10	1	1	12	0
Martin, Cesar, M.H.	1.000	1	2	0	0	2	0
Materano, Oscar, Cas.	1.000	2	1	0	0	1	0
Mayo, Terry, Og.	.600	7	3	0	2	5	0
McClanahan, Jonah, Og.	.953	25	37	4	2	43	0
Medina, Rodney, M.H.	.897	24	23	3	3	29	1
Millan, Carlos, I.F.	.889	14	16	0	2	18	0
Miller, Tony, Cas.	.981	70	151	6	3	160	0
Moore, Mewelde, I.F.	.971	24	32	2	1	35	0
Mora, Ruben, I.F.	.949	53	89	4	5	98	1
Nelson, Chris, Bil.	1.000	8	14	0	0	14	0
O'Connell, Bradley, G.F.	1.000	6	7	0	0	7	0
Olson, David, I.F.	.925	43	57	5	5	67	0
Parrott, Corry, Og.	.962	25	24	1	1	26	0
Paula, Manuel, Bil.	.949	47	73	2	4	79	0
Pickens, Jordan, I.F.	.976	46	80	3	2	85	0
Pierce, Sean, G.F.	.969	72	119	5	4	128	1
Pilkington, Ross, Cas.	.930	36	52	1	4	57	0
Porter, Gregory, Pro.	1.000	35	44	1	0	45	0
Robinson, Carlos, Miss.	1.000	10	6	0	0	6	0
Roenicke, Jarett, I.F.*	1.000	11	12	0	0	12	0
Ruiz, Junior, Bil.	.750	3	3	0	1	4	0
Soriano, Carlos, Og.	.948	42	50	5	3	58	0
Swenson, Samuel, Pro.*	.974	59	71	5	2	78	2
Tolzien, Edward, Pro.*	1.000	1	1	0	0	1	0
Varner, Gary, Bil.	.974	48	73	2	2	77	0
Vasquez, Jose, Cas.*	.946	30	35	0	2	37	0
Villanueva, Florian, Og.	.962	15	25	0	1	26	0
Virgen, Constancio, G.F.	1.000	2	1	0	0	1	0
Vugteveen, Dustin, Miss.	.966	57	110	5	4	119	1
Webb, Ryan, Pro.	1.000	3	2	0	0	2	0
Welch, Ed, Pro.	.955	57	103	3	5	111	0
Williamson, Chris, Bil.*	.976	28	38	2	1	41	0

CATCHERS

Player, Team	Pct.	G	PO	A	E	TC	DP	PB
Alvarado, Joel, Og.	.975	16	103	16	3	122	0	3
Aracena, Sandy, G.F.	.984	26	212	29	4	245	3	7
Blackburn, John, M.H.	.977	40	265	32	7	304	2	13
Corbeil, Alfred, Pro.*	.984	33	275	38	5	318	2	1
Corrente, David, M.H.	.976	35	204	35	6	245	1	8
Del Chiaro, Brent+C11084, Pro.	.988	22	157	9	2	168	1	6
Diaz, Jose, G.F.	.979	43	359	52	9	420	2	11
Esparragoza, Pedro, Og.	.000	1	0	0	0	0	0	0
Essery, Frederick, Cas.	.946	23	107	16	7	130	1	6
Eure, Jeffrey, Og.	.971	9	32	1	1	34	0	2
Falcon, Omar, I.F.	.974	34	261	34	8	303	3	13
Fisher, Timothy, Miss.	.963	13	71	7	3	81	1	1
Guzman, Junior, Pro.	.987	10	66	10	1	77	0	2
Haggard, Chris, Og.	.993	34	251	28	2	281	2	9
Ingram, Bryan, Cas.	.978	14	78	12	2	92	0	2
Martinez, Thomas, I.F.	1.000	15	75	6	0	81	0	4
Mathis, Jeff, Pro.	.989	20	165	22	2	189	0	4
Melton, John, Miss.	.976	13	75	6	2	83	0	1
Mercado, Onix, Bil.	.971	26	176	25	6	207	0	8
Montilla, Samuel, Miss.	.979	46	255	25	6	286	0	11
Ortega, Sixto, Cas.	.975	10	71	6	2	79	1	4
Perez, Jay, Cas.	.974	21	138	13	4	155	1	10
Peterson, Brian, Bil.	.976	9	73	10	2	85	1	3
PRINCE, Bryan, Bil.	.995	50	316	52	2	370	3	9
Selmo, Francisco, I.F.	.981	34	263	43	6	312	3	10
Serafini, Matt, Og.	.992	17	113	12	1	126	1	4
Sherlock, Jon, Miss.	.986	23	123	18	2	143	1	6
Sweeney, James, Cas.	.993	19	132	8	1	141	0	11
Tempesta, Nick, M.H.	.000	1	0	0	0	0	0	0
Villanueva, Florian, Og.	.985	17	100	31	2	133	1	6
Virgen, Constancio, G.F.	.988	9	76	8	1	85	0	2
Yepez, Jose, M.H.	.965	9	47	8	2	57	0	1

PITCHERS

Player, Team	Pct.	G	PO	A	E	TC	DP
Adams, Jay, Bil.	.909	28	4	6	1	11	0
Adams, Jon, Og.	1.000	23	2	2	0	4	0
Allen, Blakely, Pro.*	1.000	28	2	8	0	10	1
Almond, Casey, Cas.	.875	19	5	2	1	8	0
Andrade, Stephen, Pro.	.000	1	0	0	0	0	0
Arellano, Salvador, I.F.	1.000	3	0	2	0	2	0
Arthur, Tony, Pro.*	1.000	10	3	14	0	17	0
Artman, Dane, Og.*	.667	6	0	2	1	3	0
Astacio, Andres, G.F.	.964	17	6	21	1	28	0
Bailey, Ryan, Pro.	.714	15	4	6	4	14	0
Barbarossa, Joshua, I.F.*	.667	7	3	1	2	6	0
Basham, Bobby, Bil.	1.000	6	0	2	0	2	0
Beckstead, Jentry, Cas.	1.000	23	2	1	0	3	0
Bowles, Larry, Pro.*	.889	19	1	7	1	9	0
Bukowski, Stan, Pro.	1.000	5	1	1	0	2	0
Buret, Jorge, Cas.	.857	16	3	9	2	14	0
Castillo, Geraldo, Og.	.947	15	6	12	1	19	0
Chadwick, John, M.H.	.875	23	1	6	1	8	0
Childress, Daylan, Bil.	1.000	14	4	8	0	12	1
Clarke, Darren, Cas.	.667	14	2	4	3	9	0
Coffey, Todd, Bil.	1.000	14	3	2	0	5	0
Collado, Jerry, Cas.	1.000	21	3	3	0	6	0
Collins, Clint, Bil.	.875	10	2	5	1	8	0
Costello, Ryan, M.H.*	1.000	14	2	4	0	6	0
Cotton, Nathan, Bil.	1.000	28	0	3	0	3	0
D'Amico, Leonardo, Pro.	.000	1	0	0	0	0	0
Davies, Michael, Cas.*	1.000	10	1	9	0	10	0
Davis, Mikael, Miss.	1.000	15	1	4	0	5	1
DeJesus, Henky, Miss.	1.000	3	1	1	0	2	0
DENNIS, Jason, Pro.*	1.000	14	7	16	0	23	2
Desalme, Gene, Og.*	.600	8	1	2	2	5	0
Diaz, Jose, G.F.	.000	1	0	0	0	0	0
Dotel, Melido, Cas.	.000	2	0	0	0	0	0
Dulkowski, Marc, I.F.	1.000	22	1	2	0	3	0
Ferrand, Julian, Cas.	1.000	17	1	3	0	4	0
Fisher, Timothy, Miss.	.000	1	0	0	0	0	0
Fox, Ben, I.F.*	1.000	13	2	3	0	5	0
Fuller, Brendan, M.H.	1.000	18	2	1	0	3	0
George, Brad, Bil.	1.000	5	0	4	0	4	0
Gillman, Justin, Bil.	1.000	1	1	0	0	1	0
Gold, J.M., Og.	1.000	7	2	1	0	3	1
Gonzalez, Alfredo, G.F.	.909	11	4	6	1	11	2
Gonzalez, Carlos, Miss.	1.000	10	1	1	0	2	0
Gonzalez, Miguel, Cas.	1.000	24	1	5	0	6	1
Granados, Bernie, Cas.	1.000	21	3	4	0	7	0
Greenbush, Peter, Cas.	.900	14	5	4	1	10	0
Grimes, Sean, M.H.*	.900	12	1	8	1	10	0
Gruban, Jarret, Pro.	.000	1	0	0	0	0	0
Heal, Darren, M.H.	.000	9	0	0	1	1	0
Heiberger, Heath, Miss.*	1.000	7	0	1	0	1	1
Hickman, Jason, G.F.*	1.000	17	1	3	0	4	0
Holsten, Ryan, Miss.	.920	17	10	13	2	25	0
Horne, Travis, Og.*	1.000	4	1	1	0	2	0
Hosford, Clinton, G.F.	.909	15	5	15	2	22	0
Howton, Jared, Bil.*	.857	18	0	6	1	7	0
Huber, Jon, I.F.	.846	15	1	10	2	13	0
Huggins, Rusty, Og.*	1.000	10	1	2	0	3	0
Jackson, Dan, Pro.	1.000	7	1	1	0	2	0
Jones, Mike, Og.	1.000	9	6	6	0	12	2
Kauffman, Matt, G.F.*	.667	10	0	2	1	3	1
Keirstead, Michael, G.F.	1.000	25	2	0	0	2	0
Kelly, Steve, Bil.	.875	12	2	5	1	8	0
Kolb, Dan, Og.	1.000	16	2	4	0	6	0
Lawton, Charles, I.F.	.667	23	2	2	2	6	0
League, Brandon, M.H.	1.000	9	3	7	0	10	0
Linderbaum, Mason, I.F.*	.800	23	0	4	1	5	0
Liriano, Pedro, Pro.	.833	15	3	12	3	18	0
Lizarraga, Edgar, G.F.	1.000	14	5	5	0	10	1
Lizarraga, Sergio, Miss.	.840	15	11	10	4	25	1
Lorenzen, Jonathan, G.F.	.000	5	0	0	0	0	0
Luther, Heath, Pro.*	1.000	3	0	2	0	2	0
Marquez, Jose, Miss.	1.000	15	2	1	0	3	0
Martinez, Angel, Cas.	.900	18	2	7	1	10	0
Martinez, Hancer, I.F.	.667	11	1	1	1	3	0
Martinez, Javier A., I.F.	1.000	10	2	4	0	6	0
McCracken, Vance, G.F.*	1.000	14	2	6	0	8	0
McMillan, Joshua, M.H.*	.333	15	0	1	2	3	0
McMurray, Heath, Og.	1.000	10	2	6	0	8	0
McWilliams, Matt, Bil.*	.833	14	1	4	1	6	0
Medina, Franklin, Miss.	.750	15	2	7	3	12	0
Medina, Frewing, M.H.	1.000	19	2	5	0	7	1
Medina, Roberto, Miss.*	1.000	21	3	10	0	13	1

Player, Team	Pct.	G	PO	A	E	TC	DP
Medlin, Corbey, Miss.	.857	21	4	2	1	7	0
Mercedes, Gabriel, Miss.	.833	15	5	15	4	24	0
Mieses, Jose, Og.	.000	1	0	0	0	0	0
Mitchell, Jay, Cas.	1.000	14	4	3	0	7	0
Moak, Curtus, Bil.*	.917	20	3	8	1	12	1
Mordan, Pedro, I.F.	.857	21	1	5	1	7	0
Morel, Eudy, I.F.	.667	14	0	2	1	3	0
Nall, T. J., G.F.	1.000	7	3	1	0	4	1
Neylan, Chris, M.H.*	1.000	10	0	4	0	4	0
Nolasco, Dave, Og.	.917	20	1	10	1	12	0
Nunez, Severino, Og.*	1.000	7	1	0	0	1	0
Ogiltree, John, M.H.	1.000	28	4	7	0	11	1
Olson, Jason, G.F.	1.000	5	0	2	0	2	0
O'Sullivan, Mark, Pro.	.750	22	1	2	1	4	0
Ott, Thom, G.F.	.857	14	2	4	1	7	0
Parker, Zach, Cas.*	.818	8	0	9	2	11	0
Patten, Lanny, M.H.	.778	25	4	3	2	9	0
Pauley, David, I.F.	.750	15	0	3	1	4	1
Perez, Henry, I.F.	.769	15	3	7	3	13	1
Perkin, Greg, Miss.	.429	12	2	1	4	7	0
Pike, Matthew, Bil.	.923	13	5	7	1	13	0
Pilkington, Brian, G.F.	1.000	5	1	2	0	3	0
Pinkerton, Bradley, Pro.*	.857	17	1	5	1	7	0
Powers, Joe, Bil.	1.000	27	2	2	0	4	0
Ramirez, Ismael, M.H.	.833	14	1	9	2	12	1
Ramos, Luis, Og.	1.000	15	1	2	0	3	0
Richards, John, I.F.*	1.000	13	0	2	0	2	0
Richardson, Judd, Og.	1.000	5	3	0	0	3	1
Rodriguez, Jose, I.F.	1.000	18	0	1	0	1	0
Rodriguez, Orlando, G.F.*	.545	15	1	5	5	11	0
Rocario, Francisco, M.H.	.818	16	5	13	4	22	1
Saenz, Chris, Og.	.833	21	2	3	1	6	0
Santana, Johan, Pro.	1.000	4	2	2	0	4	1
Sarfate, Dennis, Og.	1.000	9	0	3	0	3	0
Scott, John, I.F.	1.000	20	0	1	0	1	0
Serrano, Alex, Cas.	1.000	12	0	4	0	4	0
Severino, Cleris, Bil.*	.955	15	2	19	1	22	0
Shell, Steven, Pro.	1.000	14	1	2	0	3	0
Shorey, Jeremy, Og.	.750	22	1	2	1	4	1
Silva, Jesus, Miss.	1.000	26	3	2	0	5	0
Simpson, Joe, Cas.	1.000	19	1	1	0	2	0
Smart, Pete, Og.*	.667	4	2	0	1	3	0
Smith, Cliff, Pro.	.857	21	4	2	1	7	0
Speier, Ryan, Cas.	.750	17	0	3	1	4	0
Spillman, Jeromie, M.H.*	.714	28	2	3	2	7	0
Stefani, Jason, G.F.*	1.000	19	1	7	0	8	0
Steffek, Brian, G.F.	1.000	8	2	4	0	6	0
Steitz, Jon, Og.	.857	11	2	4	1	7	1
Steward, Edward, Pro.	1.000	1	1	1	0	2	0
Strayhorn, Kole, G.F.	.000	2	0	0	0	0	0
Sutton, Kris, Pro.	.857	23	0	6	1	7	0
Talanoa, Charles, M.H.	.833	15	4	11	3	18	1
Taulli, Sam, Miss.*	1.000	15	0	4	0	4	0
Taylor, John, M.H.	1.000	6	0	1	0	1	0
Tibbs, Jeff, G.F.	.625	15	3	2	3	8	0
Tisdale, Marlyn, Bil.	.955	14	2	19	1	22	1
Torres, Erik, Og.	.000	2	0	0	0	0	0
Torres, Joe, Pro.*	1.000	9	2	1	0	3	0
Tucker, Rusty, I.F.*	.909	30	5	5	1	11	1
Turuda, Miyoki, G.F.	.750	17	1	2	1	4	0
Van Buren, Jermaine, Cas.	1.000	6	1	2	0	3	0
Vargas, Reynardo, Cas.	1.000	21	1	4	0	5	0
Villacis, Eduardo, Cas.	1.000	1	0	1	0	1	0
Villatoro, Wilmer, I.F.	1.000	30	2	5	0	7	1
Wallace, Ben, Og.*	1.000	13	2	3	0	5	0
Waroff, Shane, Miss.	1.000	26	3	5	0	8	1
Wassong, Michael, M.H.*	1.000	11	0	1	0	1	0
Wechsler, Justin, Miss.	1.000	10	2	8	0	10	1
Woods, Jake, Pro.	.900	15	3	6	1	10	0
Wright, Shayne, Pro.	.000	1	0	0	0	0	0
Yeatman, Matt, Og.	.909	13	4	6	1	11	0

LEAGUE CHAMPIONS

Year	Team	Pct.	Year	Team	Pct.	Year	Team	Pct.
1939—	Twin Falls*	.581	1960—	Boise†	.686	1985—	Great Falls	.771
1940—	Salt Lake City	.608		Idaho Falls	.650		Salt Lake City▲	.657
	Ogden (4th)*	.492	1961—	Boise	.638	1986—	Salt Lake City◆	.643
1941—	Boise	.623		Great Falls*	.571		Great Falls	.571
	Ogden (2nd)*	.598	1962—	Boise§	.565	1987—	Salt Lake City◆	.700
1942—	Pocatello†	.690		Billings†	.706		Helena	.657
	Boise	.683	1963—	Idaho Falls	.702	1988—	Great Falls◆	.754
1943-44-45—Did not operate.				Magic Valley†	.643		Butte	.629
1946—	Twin Falls‡	.585	1964—	Treasure Valley	.615	1989—	Great Falls◆	.791
	Salt Lake City†	.585	1965—	Treasure Valley	.530		Butte	.621
1947—	Salt Lake City	.618	1966—	Ogden	.591	1990—	Great Falls◆	.706
	Twin Falls†	.600	1967—	Ogden	.621		Salt Lake	.618
1948—	Pocatello	.611	1968—	Ogden	.609	1991—	Salt Lake City◆	.700
	Twin Falls (2nd)*	.595	1969—	Ogden	.620		Great Falls	.657
1949—	Twin Falls	.624	1970—	Idaho Falls	.629	1992—	Salt Lake	.697
	Pocatello (3rd)*	.595	1971—	Great Falls	.643		Billings◆	.697
1950—	Pocatello	.635	1972—	Billings	.694	1993—	Billings◆	.653
	Billings (3rd)*	.571	1973—	Billings	.629		Helena	.589
1951—	Salt Lake City	.618	1974—	Idaho Falls	.569	1994—	Billings◆	.694
	Great Falls (3rd)*	.559	1975—	Great Falls	.577		Helena	.611
1952—	Pocatello	.595	1976—	Great Falls	.577	1995—	Billings	.710
	Idaho Falls (2nd)*	.573	1977—	Lethbridge	.629		Helena■	.690
1953—	Ogden	.679	1978—	Billings∞	.735	1996—	Helena■	.597
	Salt Lake City (4th)*	.527	1979—	Helena	.623		Ogden	.583
1954—	Salt Lake City	.595		Lethbridge▲	.559	1997—	Great Falls	.556
	Great Falls (4th)*	.530	1980—	Lethbridge▲	.743		Billings■	.549
1955—	Boise	.588		Billings	.629	1998—	Medicine Hat	.622
	Magic Valley (4th)*	.489	1981—	Calgary	.657		Idaho Falls■	.618
1956—	Boise	.561		Butte▲	.557	1999—	Idaho Falls	.640
1957—	Salt Lake City	.650	1982—	Medicine Hat▲	.629		Missoula■	.592
	Billings†	.582		Idaho Falls	.600	2000—	Idaho Falls■	.608
1958—	Great Falls	.582	1983—	Billings▲	.614	2001—	Provo	.697
	Boise†	.615		Calgary	.600		Billings■	.613
1959—	Boise	.633	1984—	Billings	.691			
	Billings (2nd)*	.523		Helena▲	.647			

*Won four-club playoff. †Won split-season playoff. ‡Ended first half in tie with Salt Lake City and won one-game playoff. §Ended first half in tie with Billings and Great Falls and won playoff. ∞Billings (first place) defeated Idaho Falls (second place) in first place-second place playoff. ▲League divided into Northern and Southern divisions; won two-club playoff. ◆Won two-club playoff. ■League divided into Northern and Southern divisions; won four-club playoff.

SUMMER CLASS A *Pioneer League*

MINOR LEAGUE INDEX

TEAMS AND CITIES